ARCHAEOLOGY

WIDENER LIBRARY SHELFLIST

Volumes in Print

5–6. LATIN AMERICA. 1966. 2 VOLS. ISBN 0–674–51247–2
9–13. AMERICAN HISTORY. 1967. 5 VOLS. ISBN 0–674–02400–1
15. PERIODICAL CLASSES. 1968. 758 PP. ISBN. 0–674–66300–4
16–17. EDUCATION. 1968. 2 VOLS. ISBN 0–674–23800–1
18. LITERATURE: GENERAL AND COMPARATIVE. 1968. 189 PP. ISBN 0–674–53650–9
19. SOUTHERN ASIA. 1968. 543 PP. ISBN 0–674–82500–4
20. CANADIAN HISTORY AND LITERATURE. 1968. 411 PP. ISBN 0–674–09351–8
21. LATIN AMERICAN LITERATURE. 1969. 498 PP. ISBN 0–674–51251–0
22. GOVERNMENT. 1969. 263 PP. ISBN 0–674–35786–8
23–24. ECONOMICS. 1970. 2 VOLS. ISBN 0–674–23125–2
25. CELTIC LITERATURES. 1970. 192 PP. ISBN 0–674–10480–3
26–27. AMERICAN LITERATURE. 1970. 2 VOLS. ISBN 0–674–02535–0
28–31. SLAVIC HISTORY AND LITERATURES. 1971. 4 VOLS. ISBN 0–674–81090–2
32. GENERAL EUROPEAN AND WORLD HISTORY. 1970. 959 PP. ISBN 0–674–34420–0
33. REFERENCE COLLECTIONS. 1971. 130 PP. ISBN 0–674–75201–5
34. AFRICAN HISTORY AND LITERATURES. 1971. 600 PP. ISBN 0–674–00780–8
35–38. ENGLISH LITERATURE. 1971. 4 VOLS. ISBN 0–674–25663–8
40. FINNISH AND BALTIC HISTORY AND LITERATURES. 1972. 250 PP. ISBN 0–674–30205–2
41. SPANISH HISTORY AND LITERATURE. 1972. 770 PP. ISBN 0–674–83095–4
42–43. PHILOSOPHY AND PSYCHOLOGY. 1973. 2 VOLS. ISBN 0–674–66486–8
44. HUNGARIAN HISTORY AND LITERATURE. 1974. 186 PP. ISBN 0–674–42700–9
45–46. SOCIOLOGY. 1973. 2 VOLS. ISBN 0–674–81625–0
47–48. FRENCH LITERATURE. 1973. 2 VOLS. ISBN 0–674–32215–0
49–50. GERMAN LITERATURE. 1974. 2 VOLS. ISBN 0–674–35070–7
51–52. ITALIAN HISTORY AND LITERATURE. 1974. 2 VOLS. ISBN 0–674–46955–0
53–54. BRITISH HISTORY. 1975. 2 VOLS. ISBN 0–674–08240–0
55. ANCIENT HISTORY. 1975. 363 PP. ISBN 0–674–03312–4
56. ARCHAEOLOGY. 1979. 442 PP. ISBN 0–674–04318–9
57. CLASSICAL STUDIES. 1979. 215 PP. ISBN 0–674–13461–3
58. ANCIENT GREEK LITERATURE. 1979. 638 PP. ISBN 0–674–03310–8
59. LATIN LITERATURE. 1979. 610 PP. ISBN 0–674–51295–2
60. GEOGRAPHY AND ANTHROPOLOGY. 1979. 270 PP. ISBN 0–674–34855–9

HARVARD UNIVERSITY LIBRARY

WIDENER LIBRARY SHELFLIST, 56

ARCHAEOLOGY

CLASSIFICATION SCHEDULES
CLASSIFIED LISTING BY CALL NUMBER
CHRONOLOGICAL LISTING
AUTHOR AND TITLE LISTING

Published by the Harvard University Library
Cambridge, Massachusetts
Distributed by the Harvard University Press
Cambridge, Massachusetts and London, England
1979

Library of Congress Cataloging in Publication Data

Harvard University. Library.
Archaeology : classification schedules, classified listing by call number, chronological listing, author and title listing.

(Widener Library shelflist ; 56)
1. Archaeology—Bibliography—Catalogs. 2. Harvard University. Library—Catalogs. I. Title. II. Series: Harvard University. Library. Widener Library shelflist ; 56.
Z5131.H37 1979 [CC165] 016.9301 79-555
ISBN 0-674-04318-9

INTERNATIONAL STANDARD BOOK NUMBER: 0-674-04318-9
PRINTED IN U.S.A.

Foreword

The shelflists of libraries not having classified catalogs have long been used by librarians and knowing readers as implements for systematically surveying holdings in a particular subject. Examining a shelflist, one can see all the titles that have been classified in a given area, and not merely those with legible spine lettering which happen to be on the shelves. However, the potential bibliographical usefulness of the shelflist has been difficult to exploit because it usually exists in only one copy kept in a relatively inaccessible location. Computer technology has made it possible to enlarge the concept of the shelflist and to expand its usefulness and accessibility while improving the techniques of maintaining it.

The Harvard University Library is converting to machine-readable form the shelflist and classification schedules of the Harry Elkins Widener Memorial Library, which houses Harvard's central research collections for the humanities and social sciences.* After each class or group of related classes is converted, it is published in the *Widener Library Shelflist* series.

Scope of this Volume

Each new volume in the series is comprehensive for materials housed in the Widener Library book stacks and cataloged before July 1976, when the Library's unique system of classifying materials was discontinued and the Library of Congress classification was adopted for new acquisitions. Works cataloged since that date are not included. Some books which were formerly shelved in Widener but subsequently moved to other locations are listed here, but complete coverage of this type of material has not been attempted. In particular, many rare or early books housed in the Houghton Library do not appear in this shelflist.

This volume, *Archaeology*, the fifty-sixth in the published series, lists 14,300 shelflist entries for the Widener *Arc* class. Detailed information on the scope and arrangement of this material and on its relation to other Harvard resources may be found in the Classification Schedule section of this book, beginning on page 3. Catalogs of the other Harvard library collections mentioned there are also available in book form. The holdings of the Tozzer Library are represented by the *Catalogue of the Library of the Peabody Museum of Archaeology and Ethnology, Harvard University. Authors.* (Boston: Hall, 1963) in two parts, *Authors* (26 v.) and *Subjects* (27 v.), each of which has three supplements. The *Catalogue of the Harvard University Fine Arts Library, the Fogg Art Museum,* (Boston: Hall 1971), in fifteen volumes, has been supplemented once. Among volumes in the Widener Library Shelflist, number 55, *Ancient History*, is particulary relevant.

Organization of this Volume

This catalog is arranged in four parts. The classification schedule is the first of these. It serves as an outline of the second part, which presents the entries in shelflist order; that is, in order by call number, as the books are arranged on the shelves. Together these two parts form a classified catalogue and browsing guide.

The third section lists the same items (excluding periodicals and other serials) in chronological order by date of publication. In addition to its obvious reference use, this list yields information on the quantity and rate of publication in the field. It can be helpful in determining patterns of collection development and in identifying existing strengths and weaknesses.

Access to the collection by author and by title is provided by the alphabetical list which constitutes the fourth part of the catalog. Computer-generated entries are included for titles of works listed elsewhere by author. This section equips the reader with a subject-oriented subset of the card catalog — a finding list which offers substantial advantages of conciseness and portability over the card catalog as a whole.

Bibliographic Limitations of the Shelflist

A shelflist has traditionally served as an inventory record of the books in the library and as an indispensable tool for assigning call numbers to books as they are added to the collection. Since the Widener Shelflist was designed and maintained to fulfill these two intramural functions, its bibliographic and syndetic standards are not equal to those that prevail in the public card catalogs. Shelflists entries are less complete than the public catalog entries and may contain errors and inconsistencies which have not been eliminated during the conversion process. Cross references and name added entries are not provided. Entries for serials rarely reflect changes in title, and serial holding statements are terse.

The reader must also bear in mind that the design of any classification schedule, or variations in its interpretation or application, may result in a book's not being classified in the first place one would expect to find it.

Interpreting the Entries

As a general rule, entries in the this catalog include call number, author, title, place and date of publication, and, if more than one, the number of physical volumes held by the Library. Title added entries generated for the Author and Title Listing have the author in parentheses following the title. For works of classical authors and certain other works, the "author" portion of the entry may include information about the edition; to wit, language, date, and editor.

For serials, a summary holdings statement giving the year or volume number of the first and last volumes in the Library replaces the publication date. Gaps are not

---

* For information on the relationship of the Widener Library to other units of the Harvard University Library, consult the Library's occasional publication, *The Research Services of the Harvard College Library*, or Edwin E. Williams, "Harvard University Library," *The Encyclopedia of Library and Information Science*, X (New York: Dekker, 1973), 317–373. A more extended description of the Widener Library Shelflist conversion project is provided by Richard De Gennaro, "Harvard University's Widener Library Shelflist Conversion and Publication Program," *College and Research Libraries*, XXXI (September 1970), 318–331.

specified. A plus sign following the beginning date or volume number indicates that the title is currently being received. The conventional serial records in the Widener Library should be consulted for detailed holdings information.

The letter *A* following a call number in the chronological or alphabetical lists indicates that the Library holds more than one copy of the book on this number. The Classified Listing shows all copies.

A book in the shelflist but not in the Widener stacks is identified either by a *V* preceding the call number or by one of the marginal notations listed below. In the latter case, the call number given in this volume may be obsolete. The current call number should be obtained from the card catalogs before requesting the book from the Widener Circulation Division.

Symbol	Location
Htn	Houghton Library (Rare books and special collections)
NEDL	New England Deposit Library
X Cg	Protective storage
RRC	Russian Research Collection (apply to Coolidge Hall Library for use)

Contents

Statistical Summaries of the *Arc* Class
August 1976

Analysis of Shelflist Entries by Language

Entries in the *Arc* Class 14,333

English	4,248	Portuguese	87	Hungarian	85
German	2,638	Rumanian	27	Turkish	71
Dutch	95	Catalan	10	Finnish	12
Swedish	85	Greek	107	Estonian	4
Danish	69	Russian	794	Latvian	3
Norwegian	22	Ukrainian	56	Lithuanian	9
Latin	456	Polish	299	Celtic languages	2
French	2,675	Yugoslav languages	105	Indic languages	1
Italian	1,744	Czech & Slovak	114	Other languages	2
Spanish	307	Bulgarian	55	Uncoded	182

Count of Titles

	Widener	Elsewhere	Total
Monographs	12,561	353	12,914
Serials	1,027	17	1,044
Pamphlets in Tract Volumes	1,639	29	1,688
Pamphlet Boxes	129	4	133
Total Titles	15,356	403	15,759

Count of Volumes

	Widener	Elsewhere	Total
Monograph	14,981	461	15,442
Serial	9,041	201	9,242
Tract	233	9	242
Total Volumes	24,255	671	24,926

WIDENER LIBRARY SHELFLIST, 56

ARCHAEOLOGY

CLASSIFICATION SCHEDULES

NOTE ON THE CLASSIFICATION

The Arc class provides for archaeology and the related disciplines of palaeography and diplomatics, sigillography, and numismatics. It should be noted that the Fine Arts Library at the Fogg Art Museum also contains many works on all these subjects and that the Tozzer Library of the Peabody Museum is Harvard's major research collection for prehistoric archaeology.

The accompanying Outline shows the overall arrangement of the class. The section for archaeology (Arc 1-1099) is the longest and most important. It is also the part which causes the most problems because of an apparent conflict with the various classes which provide for ancient history. The Arc class includes all material on prehistoric archaeology and prehistoric civilization, as well as reports of excavations which have uncovered prehistoric remains and books which describe the reconstruction of prehistoric buildings and objects. For the ancient historic period, the Arc class contains reports of excavations and books which describe the reconstruction of ancient buildings and objects, as well as books on archaeological methods and local history of archaeology. But books which recount historical events and those which describe the civilization and social life of the ancient historic period go in the appropriate history classes, such as AH. Many books on the primitive aspects of prehistoric culture are in the An class.

A few exceptions to the above should be noted. All books on Assyro-Babylonian archaeology go in AH. Books on the prehistoric archaeology and civilization of Scandinavia are in the Arc class, but books on the archaeology of the ancient historic period go in the Scan class. Many works on the aboriginal races of North America are in the US class. All books on the archaeology of Latin America are in the SA class. Those exceptions do not apply for Palaeography and Diplomatics, Sigillography, and Numismatics - except that Assyro-Babylonian cylinder seals are in AH 3017.

Originally, the Arc class had a section at the end for Ceramics. In 1963, all those books were transferred to the Fine Arts Library. Since then, some books on prehistoric and ancient pottery have been classed in the archaeology section (Arc 1-1099).

One other unusual feature of the Arc class should be noted. Nearly all periodicals and all bibliographies are kept together at the beginning of each major section.

During the present revision of the scheme, no major changes have been made. But many notes have been added to clarify the situation for the classifiers. It has not been possible as yet to reclassify all the books which had been wrongly classified.

Bartol Brinkler
Classification Specialist
March 1975

OUTLINE

	Archaeology
1-412	Periodicals; Bibliographies; Dictionaries; General works; etc.
	Local
415-543	Asia
545-609	Africa
610-938	Europe
940-983	North America
	Latin America. See SA
1005-1010	Oceania
1015-1099	Special topics
1125-1166	Palaeography
1175-1200	Diplomatics
	Sigillography
1202-1217	Periodicals; Bibliographies; Dictionaries; General works; etc.
1220-1296	Local
1297-1298	Special topics
	Numismatics
1300-1400	Periodicals; Bibliographies; Dictionaries; General works; etc.
1405-1655	Local
1660-1685	Special topics

Archaeology

	Periodicals and Societies
	[Include archaeological periodicals and the serial publications of archaeological societies. For a society, include its general serials and proceedings, annual reports, membership lists and histories of the society. Include also the proceedings of annual or continuing congresses. Except in a few cases where only one number is assigned, the works are arranged alphabetically, in blocks of 26 numbers. The alphabetization may be by the distinctive title of a serial, by the name of a society (sometimes by its original name), or by the place where a society is located.]
1-26	General and international (A-Z)
	Local
	[Include here periodicals and the serial publications of societies whose scope is limited to a particular area or country. Continuing reports of excavations at a special site generally class with the place in Arc 415-1010 rather than here.]
30-55	Asia and Africa (A-Z)
	[Include the continents in general and individual countries]
	Europe
	General. See Arc 1-26
65-90	Classical and Early Christian (A-Z)
	[Include ancient Greco-Roman, Byzantine, etc.]
93	Italy
94	Spain and Portugal
95-120	France (A-Z)
125-150	Great Britain (A-Z)
155-180	Switzerland (A-Z)
185-210	Germany (A-Z)
215-240	Austria and Hungary (A-Z)
	[Include also the Austro-Hungarian Empire as a whole]
245-270	Scandinavia (A-Z)
	[Prefer PScan]
273	Low Countries
	[Include Belgium and Holland]
275-300	Russia (A-Z)
302	Other Slavic
303	Other Europe
	America
305-330	General and North America (A-Z)
	Latin America, etc. See SA
332	Oceania
	Bibliographies
335	Indexes to periodicals
	[N.B. - Include here only indexes covering many periodicals. The index to an individual periodical goes with the periodical in Arc 1-332.]
340	General works
	[Include bibliographical periodicals]
	Local. See Arc 340
	Individual archaeologists. See Arc 385-410
[343-370]	Archaeological museums and collections
	[Discontinued. Material transferred to Fine Arts Library]
375	Dictionaries and encyclopedias
	Biographes of archaeologists
377	Collected
	Individual. See Arc 385-410
	Archaeology as a scholarly discipline, research methods. See Arc 380-412
	General works
	[Include works on archaeology which are worldwide in scope; also general histories of archaeology and general treatises on archaeological methods.]

Archaeology (cont.)

	General works (cont.)
[380]	Folios [Discontinued]
	Collected authors
382	Pamphlet volumes
383	Festschriften (99 scheme, A-Z by person or institution honored)
384	Other
	[Included collections of essays by several authors, reports of individual conferences, etc.]
385-410	Individual authors (A-Z)
	[Include here also biographies and memoirs of an individual archaeologist in the number where his general archaeological treatises would go.]
412	General special
	[Include underwater archaeology, industrial archaeology, use of models and aerial photography, other special techniques, etc. See also Arc 1015-1100 for special topics treated generally.]
	Local
	Asia in general
	[Include also western Asia in general. For Central Asia in general, prefer Arc 543.3]
[415]	Folios [Discontinued]
416	General works, Special topics
	China
419	Pamphlet volumes
[420]	Folios [Discontinued]
421	General works; Local; Special topics
	Japan
424	Pamphlet volumes
[425]	Folios [Discontinued]
426	General works; Local; Special topics
428	Korea
	India
	[Include also Pakistan, Burma, and Ceylon]
[430]	Folios [Discontinued]
432	General works
435	Archaeological Survey reports
	[N.B. - Class here only the publications of the Archaeological Survey of India, the Archaeological Survey of Ceylon, and reports of the Archaeology Dept. of India and the various states of India]
440-465	Local; Special topics (A-Z by place or topic)
	Mesopotamia, Iraq
	Assyria-Babylonia-Chaldea before 650 A.D. See AH
	Since 650 A.D., Islamic period
482	General works
483	Local; Special topics
	Persia, Iran
[485]	Folios [Discontinued]
487	Pamphlet volumes
488	General works
493	Local; Special topics
	[Include Azerbaijan]
	Palestine and Syria
	[Include also Jordan and Lebanon; also Biblical archaeology.]
[495]	Folios [Discontinued]
496	Pamphlet volumes
497	General works
	Palestine Exploration Fund publications
[500]	Folios [Discontinued]
501	General publications of the Fund
502	Publications of local Fund societies
503	Publications of other exploration societies
505	Local; Special topics

Archaeology (cont.)
Local (cont.)

Asia Minor
[N.B. - For works on the Turkish Empire as a whole and for works on European Turkey, see Arc 935.]
[510] Folios [Discontinued]
513 General works
518 Ephesus
520 Pergamon
522 Troy
530 Other Local; Special topics
[Include Armenia]

Cyprus
[535] Folios [Discontinued]
537 General works
540 Local; Special topics

Other Asia
[542] Folios [Discontinued]
543 General works; Local; Special topics
[Include Central Asia and Turkestan, Indonesia, and other countries and areas not specifically provided for above in Arc 415-540. For Siberia, see Arc 925.]
Africa in general. See Arc 603

Egypt
[545] Folios [Discontinued]
[547] Archaeological museums and collections
[Discontinued. Send material to Fine Arts Library]
[548] Bibliographies [Discontinued. See Arc 340.]
549 Pamphlet volumes
550-575 General works (A-Z)
[Include works on Egyptology as a science and biographies of Egyptologists. But works on historiography go in Eg.]
Institut Français d'Archéologie Orientale du Caire
580 General reports
582 Special reports
583 Bibliothèque de l'École des Hautes Études reports
584.1-.90 Egypt. Service des Antiquités reports
584.100 Société Archéologique d'Alexandrie reports
Egypt Exploration Society or Fund
585 Memoirs
586 Miscellaneous publications
587 Archaeological Survey reports
British School of Archaeology in Egypt
588 Research accounts
589 Other series
Special topics
590 Mummies and sarcophagi
[N.B. - Collected coffin texts go in Eg]
593 Obelisks
595 Pyramids
600 Local; Other Special topics
[N.B. - In addition to works on local archaeology, include here works on scarabs, temples, tombs, etc.]
603 Africa in general

North Africa except Egypt
[605] Folios [Discontinued]
606 Coxe Expedition to Nubia reports
607 Pamphlet volumes
608 General works; Local; Special topics
[Include the Barbary States, Libya, and Nubia; but Ethiopia goes in Arc 609]
609 Subsaharan Africa

Europe in general
[610] Folios [Discontinued]
611 Pamphlet volumes

Archaeology (cont.)
Local (cont.)
Europe in general (cont.)
612 General works; Special topics

Celtic in general
[615] Folios [Discontinued]
618 General works; Special topics

Greek and Roman together
[625] Folios [Discontinued]
626 Pamphlet volumes
628 General works
630 Special topics
[632] Miscellany [Discontinued]

Greece
[635] Folios [Discontinued]
638 Pamphlet volumes
640-665 General works (A-Z)
670-695 Local except Athens (A-Z by place)
[Include Crete and the Aegean and Ionian islands. Cyprus is in Arc 535-540]
700 Special topics
Athens
[705] Folios [Discontinued]
708 General works
710 Acropolis
712 Parthenon
716 Other special topics

Italy
[N.B. - See also Arc 730-815]
[720] Folios [Discontinued]
722 Pamphlet volumes
723 General works
726 Local; Special topics
[N.B. - Include here works relating to places in mainland Italy, except Rome, Herculaneum and Pompeii, and Etruscan material. Include also Malta, Sardinia and Corsica; but Sicily goes in Arc 730-736.]

Sicily
[730] Folios [Discontinued]
732 Pamphlet volumes
733 General works
736 Local; Special topics

Etruria
[740] Folios [Discontinued]
742 Pamphlet volumes
743 General works
746 Local; Special topics

Rome (City)
[N.B. - Include here primarily works on the city of Rome. Works relating to classical Roman remains throughout the entire Roman Empire may go here, but works on the Roman remains in a particular country or city go with that place elsewhere in Arc.]
[750] Folios [Discontinued]
754 Pamphlet volumes
755-780 General works (A-Z)
785 Special topics
[Include special buildings in Rome. See also the catacombs in Arc 1025.]

Herculaneum and Pompeii together
[790] Folios [Discontinued]
793 General works
796 Special topics

Herculaneum
800 General works
805 Special topics

Archaeology (cont.)
Local (cont.)

Pompeii
810 General works
815 Special topics

France
[820] Folios [Discontinued]
822 Pamphlet volumes
823 General works
825 Nîmes
830 Other Local; Special topics

Spain and Portugal
[835] Folios [Discontinued]
837 Pamphlet volumes
838 General works
843 Local; Special topics

Germany
[845] Folios [Discontinued]
847 Pamphlet volumes
848 General works
853 Local; Special topics

Great Britain
[855] Folios [Discontinued]
857 Pamphlet volumes
858 General works
England and neighboring islands
General works. See Arc 858
861 Local
865 Stonehenge
870 Special topics
875 Scotland
880 Ireland
885 Wales

Low Countries
[887] Folios [Discontinued]
888 General works
889 Local; Special topics

Scandinavia
[N.B. - Class here primarily works dealing with prehistoric times. Works on the archaeology of later periods go in Scan 3800-3899.]
[890] Folios [Discontinued]
891 Pamphlet volumes
893 General works
895 Local; Special topics

Austria and Hungary
[N.B. - Include also works dealing with the Austrian Empire as a whole]
[900] Folios [Discontinued]
902 Pamphlet volumes
903 General works
905 Local; Special topics
[N.B. - Some older books on the archaeology of Czechoslovakia and Yugoslavia have gone here. New books on those countries should go in Arc 936.]

Switzerland
[910] Folios [Discontinued]
912 Pamphlet volumes
913 General works
915 Local; Special topics

Russia
[Include also works on the Soviet Union as a whole; also works on Slavic archaeology in general.]
[920] Folios [Discontinued]
922 Pamphlet volumes
923 General works
925 Local; Special topics
[Include all parts of European Russia, except the Baltic States which go in Arc 938. Include also Siberia and the

in next column

Archaeology (cont.)
Local (cont.)
Russia (cont.)
Local; Special topics (cont.)
Soviet Far East. But Russian Central Asia goes in Arc 543. Use .13 for archaeology and art of Scythia and the Scythians; use .50 for Ukraine in general; use .150 for White Russia in general.]

Other Europe
[930] Folios [Discontinued]
932 Pamphlet volumes
933 General works
935 Turkey
[Include here works on the Turkish Empire as a whole and on European Turkey, especially Istanbul. For Asia Minor, see Arc 510-530.]
936 Other Local; Special topics
[Include Poland, Czechoslovakia, Rumania, Bulgaria, Yugoslavia, and Albania. For Greece, see Arc 635-716.]
938 Finland and Baltic States

Americas in general
[See also US 2201-2205 for general works on the aboriginal races.]
[940] Folios [Discontinued]
942 Pamphlet volumes
943 General works
945 Special topics

United States and Canada
[See also US 2201-2205 for general works on the aboriginal races.]
[950] Folios [Discontinued]
952 Pamphlet volumes
953 General works
955-980 Local (A-Z by state of the U.S. or province of Canada]
983 Special topics

Latin America. See SA

Pacific Islands
[1005] Folios [Discontinued]
1007 Pamphlet volumes
1008 General works
1010 Local; Special topics

Christian antiquities
[N.B. - Include here very general works on Christian archaeology, especially works relating to remains of the very early Christian period, e.g. catacombs, relics of saints, church treasures, early monuments, etc.]

Periodicals. See Arc 65-90
Bibliographies. See Arc 340

Folios
[1015] Catacombs [Discontinued]
[1016] Others [Discontinued]
1018 General works
1020 Local
[This number is used primarily for works on the relics and treasures of the churches of Europe and the Holy Lands. Reports on the excavation of early churches go in Arc 415-1010.]

Catacombs
1025 General works
[Include also works on the catacombs of Rome in general and on the underground cemeteries in general.]
1027 Special topics
[Include special topics relating to catacombs in general, works on individual catacombs of Rome and on catacombs elsewhere.]

Archaeology (cont.)
Christian antiquities (cont.)
1030 Christian inscriptions
1033 Other Special topics
[Include works on relics associated with individuals, etc.]

Islamic antiquities
Periodicals. See Arc 30-55
Bibliographies. See Arc 340
[1040] Folios [Discontinued]
1042 General works
1045 Local
1048 Special topics

Iconography
[N.B. - Include here primarily works on portraiture during the ancient and medieval periods.]
[1050] Folios [Discontinued]
1053 General works
Special topics, etc. See Arc 1053

Other special topics
[1070] Folios [Discontinued]
1075-1099 Monographs (A-Z by topic)
[Include local as well as general material on such subjects as bells, crosses, fibula, grave mounds, jade, masks, rings, stone (megalithic) monuments, swastika, etc.]

Palaeography
[Include here works on the study of ancient modes of writing and on the manuscripts produced - specimens of ancient writing, works on the characters and abbreviations used, works on the authentication, dating, forms of signatures, etc. Similar works limited to the study of legal and official documents go with Diplomatics in Arc 1172-1200.]
1125 Periodicals and Society publications
1130 Bibliographies
1133 Dictionaries
[1135] Folios [Discontinued]
[N.B. - Books of Portfolio size and many books of Folio size go in Room D.]
1137 Pamphlet volumes
1138 General works

Greek and Latin together
[1140] Folios [Discontinued. Prefer Room D.]
1143 General works

Greek
[1145] Folios [Discontinued. Prefer Room D.]
1148 General works

Latin
[1150] Folios [Discotninued. Prefer Room D.]
1153 General works

Other individual languages
[N.B. - Works dealing with more than one language, except Greek and Latin together, go in Arc 1137-1138 or 1166.]
[1160] Folios [Discontinued. Prefer Room D.]
1163 General works

Special topics
[1165] Folios [Discontinued. Prefer Room D.]
1166 Monographs

Diplomatics
[Include here works on the deciphering, authentication, dating, etc. of legal and official documents.]

Periodicals and Society publications. See Arc 1125
1172 Bibliographies
[1175] Folios [Discontinued]

Diplomatics (cont.)
1178 Pamphlet volumes
1180 Dictionaries
1185 General works
1190 Local
1200 Special topics

Sigillography
[Include here works on the study of seals - private, ecclesiastical, and governmental. The science is also known as sphragistics. Works dealing with both sigillography and numismatics go with Numismatics.]
1202 Periodicals and Society publications
1205 Bibliographies
[1207] Folios [Discontinued]
1208 Museums and Private collections
[Include catalogues, histories, etc. Catalogues of seals relating to a particular area or country go with the place in Arc 1220-1296.]
1209 Dictionaries
1210 Pamphlet volumes
1212 General works

Special periods
1213 Ancient
1215 Medieval
1217 Modern

Local
[N.B. - Works on the official seal of a country, state, or city go in the appropriate history class; so also do works on the seal of an individual or family.]

Asia in general
[1220] Folios [Discontinued]
1221 General works
1223 China
1225 Japan
1227 India
1229 Palestine and Syria
1232 Asia Minor
1234 Arabia
1237 Other Asia
[N.B. - For Assyro-Babylonian cylinder seals, see AH 3017.]

Africa in general
[1239] Folios [Discontinued]
1240 General works
1241 Egypt
1243 Other Africa

Europe in general
[1247] Folios [Discontinued]
1248 General works
1250 Greek and Roman together

Greek
1251 Ancient
1254 Byzantine and Modern Greece
1255 Roman

Italy
1258 General works
1259 Papal States
1260 Other
1261 Spain and Portugal

France
1263 Folios [Discontinued]
1264 General works
1266 Switzerland

Germany
[1268] Folios [Discontinued]
1269 General works
1271 Low Countries

Sigillography (cont.)
Local (cont.)

Great Britain
[1273] Folios [Discontinued]
1274 General works
1276 Scandinavian Countries
1279 Austria and Hungary

Russia
[1281] Folios [Discontinued]
1282 General works
1285 Other Europe

Americas in general
[1287] Folios [Discontinued]
1288 General works
1290 Canada
[1292] United States [Discontinued. See US]
1293 Mexico
1294 Central America
1295 South America
1296 Pacific Islands

Special topics
[1297] Folios [Discontinued]
1298 Monographs

Numismatics
[Include here works on the study of coins and medals - their history, artistic quality, description and classification. Works on coins as money go in Econ.]
1300-1325 Periodicals and Societies (A-Z)
[Include numismatical periodicals and the serial publications of numismatics societies. For a society, include its general serials and proceedings, annual reports, membership lists, and histories of the society. Include also annual congresses]

Bibliographies
[1329] Folios [Discontinued]
1330 General works
Local. See Arc 1330

Museums and Private collections
[Include catalogues, histories, etc. Catalogues of coins relating to a particular period, area or country go with the period or place in Arc 1350-1655.]
[1333] Folios [Discontinued]
1334 Pamphlet volumes
1335 General works
1340 Dictionaries
Numismatics as a scholarly discipline. See Arc 1345-1349

General works
[1345] Folios [Discontinued]
1347 Pamphlet volumes
1348 Monographs

Biographies of numismatists
1349.01-.099 Pamphlet volumes
1349.1-.19 Collected
1349.20-.299 Individual

General special. See Arc 1660-1685
Special periods
Ancient in general
[1350] Folios [Discontinued]
1353 Catalogues of collections
1355-1380 Monographs (A-Z)

Medieval in general
[1385] Folios [Discontinued]
1388 Catalogues of collections
1390 Monographs

Numismatics (cont.)
Special periods (cont.)

Modern in general
[1395] Folios [Discontinued]
1398 Catalogues of collections
1400 Monographs

Local
Asia in general
[1405] Folios [Discontinued]
1406 Pamphlet volumes
1408 General works

China
[1410] Folios [Discontinued]
1411 General works

Japan
[1412] Folios [Discontinued]
1413 General works

India
[1415] Folios [Discontinued]
1418 General works

Palestine and Syria
[1420] Folios [Discontinued]
1423 General works

Asia Minor
[N.B. - Include here general works on the coins of the Crusaders.]
[1425] Folios [Discontinued]
1428 General works

Other Asia
[N.B. - Include here general works on the coins of the Islamic countries.]
[1430] Folios [Discontinued]
1433 General works; Local

Africa in general
[1435] Folios [Discontinued]
1438 General works

Egypt
[1440] Folios [Discontinued]
1443 General works

Other Africa
[1445] Folios [Discontinued]
1448 General works; Local

Europe in general
[1450] Folios [Discontinued]
1453 General works
1454 Celtic

Greek and Roman together
[1455] Folios [Discontinued]
1456 Pamphlet volumes
1458 General works
1460 Special topics

Greek
Ancient
[1465] Folios [Discontinued]
1468 General works
1470 Local; Special topics
1473 Byzantine and Modern Greece
1474 Etruscan

Roman
[1475] Folios [Discontinued]
1476 Pamphlet volumes
1478 General works
1480 Special topics
[For Local material, see with the place in Arc 1405-1590.]

Numismatics (cont.)
Local (cont.)

Italy
[1485] Folios [Discontinued]
1486 Pamphlet volumes
1488 General works
1490 Local; Special topics
[See also Arc 1474-1480]

Spain and Portugal
[1492] Folios [Discontinued]
1493 General works
1494 Local; Special topics

France
[1495] Folios [Discontinued]
1496 Pamphlet volumes
1498 General works
1500 Local; Special topics

Switzerland
[1502] Folios [Discontinued]
1503 General works
1504 Local; Special topics

Germany
[1505] Folios [Discontinued]
1506 Pamphlet volumes
1508 General works
1510 Local; Special topics
1512 Low Countries in general

Belgium
[1515] Folios [Discontinued]
1518 General works
1520 Local; Special topics
1522 Luxemburg

Netherlands, Holland
[1525] Folios [Discontinued]
1528 General works
1530 Local; Special topics

Great Britain
[1535] Folios [Discontinued]
1536 Pamphlet volumes
1538 General works
1540 Local; Special topics
1542 Scandinavia in general

Denmark
[1545] Folios [Discontinued]
1548 General works
1550 Local; Special topics
1552 Iceland

Sweden
[1555] Folios [Discontinued]
1558 General works
1560 Local; Special topics

Norway
[1565] Folios [Discontinued]
1568 General works
1570 Local; Special topics

Austria
[1575] Folios [Discontinued]
1576 Pamphlet volumes
1578 General works
1580 Local; Special topics
[N.B. - Hungary is in Arc 1585-1590.]

Russia
[1582] Folios [Discontinued]
1583 General works
1584 Local; Special topics

Numismatics (cont.)
Local (cont.)

Other Europe
[1585] Folios [Discontinued]
1588 General works
1590 Local; Special topics

Americas in general
[1595] Folios [Discontinued]
1598 General works

Canada
[1600] Folios [Discontinued]
1601 Pamphlet volumes
1603 General works
1605 Local; Special topics

United States
[1610] Folios [Discontinued]
1611 Pamphlet volumes
1613 General works
1615 Local; Special topics

Mexico
[1620] Folios [Discontinued]
1623 General works
1625 Local; Special topics

Central America
[1630] Folios [Discontinued]
1631 Pamphlet volumes
1633 General works
1635 Local; Special topics

South America
[1640] Folios [Discontinued]
1643 General works
1645 Local; Special topics

Pacific Islands
[1650] Folios [Discontinued]
1653 General works
1655 Local; Special topics

Special topics
Historical coins and medals
[N.B. - Class here works relating to coins and medals which commemorate special historical events or personages. General works on the coins and medals of an area or country go in Arc 1405-1655.]
[1660] Folios [Discontinued]
1661 Pamphlet volumes
1663 Monographs

Special aspects
[N.B. - Class here works on such topics as abbreviations and symbols found on coins, alchemy and numismatics, etc.]
[1665] Folios [Discontinued]
1666 Pamphlet volumes
1668 Monographs

Medals, Tokens, and Jetons
[1670] Folios [Discontinued]
1671 Pamphlet volumes
1675 General works
[N.B. - Include here works dealing with medals, tokens, and jetons collectively; also general works limited to medals and works on non-historical medals. Works on medals depicting historical events and persons go in Arc 1660-1665. General works on the medals of a particular area or country go in Arc 1405-1655.]
1680 Tokens
1685 Jetons

[1700-1990] **Ceramics [Discontinued]**

[N.B. - All this material was transferred to the Fine Arts Library in 1963. Since then, some books on ceramics which were duplicated or not wanted at Fogg have been classed with Archaeology in Arc 1-1099.]

WIDENER LIBRARY SHELFLIST, 56

ARCHAEOLOGY

CLASSIFIED LISTING BY CALL NUMBER

Classified Listing

Arc 1 - 26 Archaeology - Periodicals and Societies - General and international (A-Z)

Arc 1.1 Archaeological Institute of America. Bulletin. Boston. 1,1883
Arc 1.1.2 Archaeological Institute of America. Annual report. Cambridge. 1-17,1879-1896 3v.
Arc 1.1.3 Ward, W.H. Report on the Wolfe Expedition to Babylonia, 1884-85. Boston, 1886.
Arc 1.1.4 Pamphlet box. Archaeological Institute of America.
Arc 1.1.5 Archaeological Institute of America. Index to publications, 1879-89. Cambridge, 1891.
Arc 1.1.6 Archaeological Institute of America. Report of the fellow in American archaeology. N.Y., 1907.
Arc 1.1.7 Archaeological Institute of America. Bulletin. Norwood, Mass. 1,1909+ 14v.
Arc 1.1.8 Art and archaeology. Baltimore. 1-35,1914-1934 20v.
Arc 1.1.10 Archeological Institute of America. School of American Archaeology. Bulletin. Washington.
Arc 1.1.11 Archaeological Institute of America. School of American Archaeology. Papers. Santa Fé. 1-43,1908-1919 3v.
Arc 1.1.12 Archaeological Institute of America. Schools of American Research. Annual report. Santa Fe? 1934-1947 2v.
Arc 1.1.13 Archaeological newsletter. N.Y. 1-25,1946-1956
Arc 1.1.15 American School of Prehistoric Research. Bulletin. Washington. 1-28 11v.
Arc 1.2 Archaeological Institute of America. Papers. Boston. 1-5,1881-1890 5v.
Arc 1.2.5 Archaeological Institute of America. Papers. 2nd ed. Boston. 1,1883
Arc 1.3 Archaeological Institute of America. Wisconsin Society. Reports of annual meeting. Madison.
Arc 1.3.9 Pamphlet box. Archaeological Institute of America. Boston Society.
Arc 1.4 Archaeological Institute of America. Papers. Boston. 1-3,1882-1890 4v.
Arc 1.5 American School of Classical Studies at Athens. Bulletin. Boston. 1-5,1883-1902 3v.
Arc 1.5F American School of Classical Studies at Athens. Bulletin. Boston. 3
Arc 1.5.2 American School of Classical Studies at Athens. Annual report. Cambridge, Mass. 1,1882+ 7v.
Arc 1.5.3 Pamphlet box. American School of Classical Studies at Athens. Washington.
Arc 1.5.4A American School of Classical Studies at Athens. Papers. Boston. 1-6,1882-1897 6v.
Arc 1.5.4B American School of Classical Studies at Athens. Papers. Boston. 1-5,1882-1890 5v.
Arc 1.5.4.5 American School of Classical Studies at Athens. Corinth excavations. Weekly report.
Arc 1.5.4.10 American School of Classical Studies at Athens. Excavations on the slopes of the Acropolis. Report. 7-20
Arc 1.5.4.15 American School of Classical Studies at Athens. Agora excavations. Weekly report.
Arc 1.5.4.20 American School of Classical Studies at Athens. Report of excavations at Gözlü Kule.
Arc 1.5.6 American School of Classical Studies at Athens. Annual report, 1-3. Reprint ed. Cambridge, 1886.
Arc 1.5.7 Hesperia. Cambridge. 1,1932+ 40v.
Arc 1.5.8 Pamphlet vol. The celebration of the seventy-fifth anniversary and dedication of the stoa of Attalus as the museum. 2 pam.
Arc 1.5.9 Hesperia. The American excavations in the Athenian Agora. Supplement. Athens. 1-13 6v.
Arc 1.5.10 Hesperia. Index 1-10, supplements 1-6. Baltimore, Md., 1946.
Arc 1.5.11 American School of Classical Studies at Athens. Alumni Association. Report. 1942
Arc 1.5.12 American School of Classical Studies at Athens. Directory of trustees, managing committee, faculty. 1882-1942
Arc 1.5.15A American School of Classical Studies in Rome. Supplementary papers. N.Y. 1-2,1905-1908 2v.
Arc 1.5.15B American School of Classical Studies in Rome. Supplementary papers. N.Y. 1,1905
Arc 1.5.17 American School of Classical Studies in Rome. Chairman of Managing Committee. Reports. Princeton, N.J.
Arc 1.5.19 Pamphlet vol. American School of Oriental Research, Jerusalem. Bagdad.
Arc 1.5.20 American School of Oriental Research, Jerusalem. Annual report of managing committee. Norwood, Mass.?
Arc 1.5.21 American School of Oriental Research, Jerusalem. Annual. New Haven. 1-40 27v.
Arc 1.5.22 American School of Oriental Research, Jerusalem. Bulletin. Philadelphia? 1,1919+ 11v.
Arc 1.5.23 American School of Oriental Research, Jerusalem. Handbook. Philadelphia?
Arc 1.5.24 American Schools of Oriental Research, Jerusalem. Catalogue. New Haven. 1935-1948 3v.
Arc 1.5.25 American School of Oriental Research, Jerusalem. Papers.
Arc 1.5.27 American School of Oriental Research, Jerusalem. Newsletter. Jerusalem. 1939-1958 5v.
Arc 1.5.28 Pamphlet vol. American School of Oriental Research, Jerusalem.
Arc 1.5.31F American School of Oriental Reserach, Bagdad. Publications. Excavations. Philadelphia. 1935-1950 2v.
Arc 1.5.50 Pamphlet vol. Archaeological Institute of America.
Arc 1.6 American journal of archaeology. Baltimore. 1-11 11v.
Arc 1.6.2 American journal of archaeology. 2nd series. 1897+ 74v.
Arc 1.6.15 American journal of archaeology. Index to I-X and appendix to XI. Princeton, n.d.
Arc 1.6.16 American journal of archaeology. Index to 2nd series. v.1-10, (1897-1906); v.11-70 (1907-66). N.Y., n.d. 2v.
Arc 1.7 Didron, A.N. Annales archéologiques. Paris, 1844-1870. 27v.
Arc 1.7.2 Barbier de Montault. Annales archéologiques. Index, v.28. Paris, 1881.
Arc 1.7.5 Annuaire de l'archéoloque du numismate et de l'antiquaire. Paris. 1,1862
Arc 1.8 Archeological review. London, 1888-90. 4v.
Arc 1.9 Archaeologist. London. 1-10
Arc 1.10 France. Ministre de l'Instruction Publique et des Beaux Arts. Archives des missions scientifiques. Paris. 1-31 30v.
Arc 1.10.2 France. Ministre de l'Instruction Publique et des Beaux Arts. Nouvelles archives des missions scientifiques. Paris. 1-18 31v.

Arc 1 - 26 Archaeology - Periodicals and Societies - General and international (A-Z) - cont.

Arc 1.11F France. Academie des Inscriptions. Monuments et memoirs. Paris. 1-55 45v.
Arc 1.12 Antiqua. Zürich. 1882-1891 2v.
Arc 1.13 American Academy, Rome. Annual report. Rome? 1913-1942 6v.
Arc 1.13.3 American Academy, Rome. Report of executive committee. Rome? 1913
Arc 1.13.5F American Academy, Rome. Memoirs. Bergamo. 1,1917+ 26v.
Arc 1.13.6F American Academy, Rome. The American Academy in Rome, 1894-1914. N.Y., 1914.
Arc 1.13.7F American Academy, Rome. Twenty fifth anniversary. N.Y.? 1920?
Arc 1.13.10 American Academy, Rome. Papers and monographs. Rome. 1,1919+ 25v.
Arc 1.13.10F American Academy, Rome. Papers and monographs. Rome.
Arc 1.13.15 La Farge, C.G. History of the American Academy in Rome. N.Y., 1915.
Arc 1.14F Accademia...Rome. Accademia Romana di Archeologia. Dissertazione. Roma. 1820-1921 32v.
Arc 1.14.2 Accademia...Rome. Accademia Romana di Archeologia. Indice delle dissertazioni e communicazioni. Roma, 1900.
Arc 1.14.10 Accademia...Rome. Accademia Romana di Archeologia. Rendiconti. 1,1921+ 31v.
Arc 1.14.15F Accademia...Rome. Accademia Romana di Archeologia. Memorie. 4,1934+ 6v.
Arc 1.14.20 Accademia...Rome. Accademia Romana di Archeologia. Annuario. 1,1951+ 2v.
Arc 1.14.30 Accademia...Rome. Accademia Romana di S. Tommaso di Aquina. Triplice omaggio a sua santita Pio XII. Città de Vaticano, 1958. 2v.
Arc 1.15 Archaeologische Studien zum Christlichen Altertum. Freiburg, 1895.
Arc 1.16 Antiquity. Gloucester, Eng. 1,1927+ 32v.
Arc 1.16.5 Antiquity. General index, v.1-25, 1927-1951. Gloucester, Eng., n.d.
Arc 1.18 Archaeology; a magazine dealing with the antiquity of the world. Cambridge, Mass. 1,1948+ 18v.
Arc 1.18.2 Archaeology. Index, v.11-26, 1958-1973. N.Y., 1974.
Arc 1.19 Archeologia classica. Roma. 1,1949+ 30v.
Arc 1.20F Archaeologia geographica. Hamburg. 1-5,1950-1956
Arc 1.21 Archeologia; rocznik Polskiego Towarzystwa Archeologicgnego. Warszawa. 1,1947+ 10v.
Arc 1.22 Archaeometry. Oxford. 4v.
Arc 1.23 Archéologie et civilisation. Paris. 1,1963
Arc 1.24 Annuaire des sciences historiques. Paris. 1877
VArc 1.25 Archeologia. Paris. 9,1966+ 5v.
VArc 1.25.5 Archeologia. Document Archéologie aérienne. Paris. 1,1973+
Arc 1.27 Archaeology abroad. London. 1,1972+
Arc 1.30 Archäologisches Korrespondenzblatt. Mainz am Rhein. 1,1971+
Arc 1.32 Antichnyi mir i arkheologiia. Saratov. 1,1972+
Arc 1.33 Archaeology into history. London. 1,1973+
Arc 1.37 Archäologische Informationen. Köln. 1,1972+
Arc 1.38 Archaeological news. Tallahassee. 1,1972+
Arc 1.39 Australian studies in archaeology. Sydney. 1,1973+
Arc 1.40 The archaeologists' year book. Christchurch. 1973+ 2v.
Arc 2.1 France. Ministère de l'Instruction. Bulletin de Comité des travaux historiques et scientifiques. Section historique et archéologique. Paris. 1882-1896 15v.
Arc 2.1.2 France. Comité des Travaux Historiques et Scientifiques. Bulletin archéologique. Paris. 1897+ 45v.
Arc 2.1.2.5 France. Comité des Travaux Historiques et Scientifiques. Bulletin archéologique. Paris. 1883-1915
Arc 2.1.3 France. Comité des Travaux Historiques et Scientifiques. Bulletin historique et philologique. Paris. 1897+ 44v.
Arc 2.1.3.5 France. Comité des Travaux Historiques et Scientifiques. Bulletin historique et philologique. Paris. 1882-1915
Arc 2.3F Beiträge zur ägyptischen Bauforschung und Altertumskunde. Kairo. 1-9 6v.
Arc 2.5 Berliner Jahrbuch für Vor- und Frühgeschichte. Berlin. 1,1961+ 8v.
Arc 2.6 Berliner Jahrbuch für Vor- und Frühgeschichte. Ergänzungsbände. Berlin. 1,1964+
Arc 2.8 Beitraege zur Archäologie. Würzburg. 1,1970+
Arc 2.10 Bonner Hefte zur Vorgeschichte. Bonn. 2,1974+
Arc 2.12 Bremer archäologische Blätter. Bremen. 2,1961+
Arc 3.1.5 Congrès International pour la Reproduction des Manuscrits. Actes. Bruxelles. 1905
Arc 3.1.21 Congrès International d'Archéologie Classique, 1st, Athens, 1905. Comptes rendus du Congrès International d'Archéologie Ire Session, Athènes, 1905. Athènes, 1905.
Arc 3.1.22 Congrès International d'Archéologie Classique, 2d, Cairo, 1909. Comptes rendus. Le Caire, 1909.
Arc 3.1.23 Congrès International d'Archéologie Classique, 3d, Rome, 1912. Bolletino riassuntivo. Roma, 1912.
Arc 3.1.24 Congrès International d'Archéologie Classique, 4th, Barcelona, 1929. IV Congresso internazionale d'archéologia; 23-29 settembre 1929. Barcelona? 1929.
Arc 3.1.25 Congrès International d'Archéologie Classique, 5th, Algiers, 1930. Cinquième Congrès international d'archéologie, Alger, 14-16 avril 1930. Alger, 1933.
Arc 3.1.26 Congrès International d'Archéologie Classique, 6th, Berlin, 1939. Vorläufiges Programm. Berlin? 1939?
Arc 3.1.26.5 Congrès International d'Archéologie Classique, 6th, Berlin, 1939. Bericht über den VI. Internationalen Kongress für Archäologie, Berlin, 21.-26. August, 1939. Berlin, 1940.
Arc 3.1.27 Congrès Internatonal d'Archéologie Classique, 7th, Rome and Naples, 1958. Atti del settimo Congresso internazionale di archeologia classica. Roma, 1961. 3v.
Arc 3.1.28 Congrès International d'Archéologie Classique, 8th, Paris, 1963. Le rayonnement des civilizations grecque et romaine sur les cultures périphériques. Paris, 1965. 2v.
Arc 3.2 Congrès International d'Archéologie Prehistorique et d'Anthropologie, 11th, Moscow, 1892. Congrès international d'archéologie préhistorique et d'anthropologie. v.1-2. Moscou, 1892-93.
Arc 3.3 Congresso Internazionale di Preistoria. Atti. Firenze, 1952.
Arc 3.4 Colloque International d'Archéologie Aérienne. Colloque international d'archéologie aérienne. Paris, 1964.
Arc 4.1 Demareteion. Paris. 1-2,1935-1936
Arc 4.6 Dissertationes archaeologicae gandenses. Brugge. 1-10 3v.

Classified Listing

Arc 1 - 26 Archaeology - Periodicals and Societies - General and international (A-Z) - cont.

Arc 5.5	Ethnographisch-archäologische Forschungen. Berlin. 1-6,1953-1959 2v.
Arc 5.10	Ethnographisch-archäologische Zeitschrift. Berlin. 1,1960+ 7v.
Arc 6.2	Fasti archaeologici. Firenze. 1,1946+ 20v.
Arc 7.1	Gazette archéologique. Paris, n.d. 14v.
Arc 7.1.2	Gazette archéologique. v.7. Paris, n.d.
Arc 8.2	Discovery; peoples, civilization. Philadelphia.
Arc 8.3	Hamburger Beiträge zur Archäologie. Hamburg. 1,1971+
Arc 8.3.3	Hamburger Beiträge zur Archäologie. Beiheft. Hamburg. 1,1974+
Arc 9.1	Institute Français d'Archeologie Orientale du Caire. Publications. Recherches d'archeologie. Le Caire. 1,1930+ 20v.
Arc 9.2.1	International Congress of Prehistoric and Protohistoric Sciences, 1st, London, 1932. Proceedings. London, 1934.
Arc 9.2.6	International Congress of Prehistoric and protohistoric Sciences, 6th, Rome, 1962. Atti del Congresso internazionale. Firenze, 1962.
Arc 9.2.7	International Congress of Prehistoric and Protohistoric Sciences. Actes du VIIe Congrès international des sciences préhistoriques et protohistoriques. Prague, 1970-71. 2v.
Arc 9.2.8	International Congress of Prehistoric and Protohistoric Sciences, 8th, Belgrad, 1971. Actes du VIIIe Congrès international des sciences préhistoriques et protohistoriques. Beograd, 1971- 3v.
Arc 9.5	Sources archeologiques de la civilisation européenne. International Association of South-East European Studies. Bucarest, 1970.
Arc 12.5	Long ago. London. 1,1873
Arc 13.5	Mainz. Römisch-Germanisches Zentralmuseum. Technische Beiträge Archäologie. 1,1959+ 2v.
Arc 13.10	Milan. Università Cattolica del Sacro Cuore. Istituto di Archeologia. Contributi. Milano. 1,1967+ 2v.
Arc 13.15	Moated Site Research Group. Report - Moated Site Research Group. Kirkleavington. 1,1973+
Arc 14.1	Neue Dokumente zur Menschheitsgeschichte. Weimar. 1,1928
Arc 14.3	La nouvelle clio. Bruxelles. 1-12,1949-1962 23v.
Arc 15.5	Office des Instituts d'Archéologie et d'Histoire de l'Art. Bulletin périodique. Paris. 2-3,1935-1937
Arc 16.1	Pennsylvania. University. University Museum. Transactions. Paris. 1-2,1904-1907
Arc 16.2	Préhistoire. Paris. 1-16 7v.
Arc 16.3	Phoenix. Leiden. 9,1963+ 3v.
Arc 16.4	Polska Akademiia Nauk Zakład Archeologei Antycznej. Prace. Warszawa. 1-25 6v.
Arc 16.5	Památky archeologické. Praha. 37,1953+ 41v.
Arc 18.1	Revue archéologique. Paris. 1844+ 185v.
Arc 18.1.2	Revue archéologique. Index, 1860-1869. Paris, n.d.
Arc 18.1.3	Revue archéologique. Index, v.23, 1870-1890. 3d series. Paris, 1893.
Arc 18.1.5	Revue archéologique. Tables des années, 1900-1955. Paris, 1949- 2v.
Arc 18.1.9	L'année épigraphique. Paris. 1964+ 2v.
Arc 18.1.10	Tables générales de l'année épigraphique. 1901-1950. Paris, 1912-1932.
Arc 18.2	Records of the past. N.Y. 1-13,1902-1914 12v.
Arc 19.1	Milani, L.A. Studi e materiali di archeologia e numismatica. v.1-3. Firenze, 1899. 4v.
Arc 19.3	Studien zur westeuropäischen Altertumskunde. Neuwied.
Arc 19.4	Société Française des Fouilles Archéologiques. Bulletin. Paris. 1-5,1904-1924 2v.
Arc 19.8	Studia archaeologica. Roma. 1-13 5v.
Arc 20.5	Teheraner Forschungen. Berlin. 1-2 3v.
Arc 22.3	Vorgeschichtliches Jahrbuch. Berlin. 1-4 4v.
Arc 22.5	Vorgeschichtliche Forschungen. Berlin. 1,1924+ 13v.
Arc 23.5	World archaeology. London. 1,1969+ 4v.
Arc 26.5	Z otchłani wieków. Wrocław. 24,1958+ 7v.
Arc 26.10	Zapiski archeologiczne. Warszawa. 3-12,1954-1959
Arc 26.15	Zeitschrift für Archäologie des Mittelalters. Köln. 1,1973+

Arc 30 - 55 Archaeology - Periodicals and Societies - Local - Asia and Africa (A-Z)

Arc 30.1	Der alte Orient. Leipzig. 1-43,1899-1945 24v.
Arc 30.1.2	Der alte Orient. Ergänzungsband. Leipzig, n.d. 2v.
Arc 30.1.10	Annales d'Ethiopie. Paris. 3-6 3v.
Arc 30.2	The ancient east. London. 2,1901
Arc 30.2.5	Ancient India; bulletin of the archaeological survey of India. Delhi. 1,1946+ 9v.
Arc 30.3	Annales du service des antiquités de l'Égypte. Le Caire. 1,1900+ 44v.
Arc 30.3.2	Annales du service des antiquités de l'Égypte. Index, 1-30. Le Caire, n.d. 3v.
Arc 30.3.3	Annales du service des antiquités de l'Égypte. Supplement. Le Caire. 1-22 10v.
Arc 30.9	Académie...Bona. Académie d'Hippone. Bulletin. Bona. 1-37,1865-1921 10v.
Arc 30.9F	Académie...Bona. Académie d'Hippone. Bulletin. Bona. 11,1873
Arc 30.9.10	Pamphlet vol. Académie d'Hippone. Bona, Algeria.
Arc 30.10	Algeria. Services des Monuments Historiques. Rapport sur les travaux de fouilles et consalidations. Algeria. 2v.
Arc 30.11	American Research Center in Egypt. Newsletter. Boston. 13,1954+ 23v.
Arc 30.12	American Institute for Persian Art and Archaeology. Bulletin. N.Y. 1-5,1931-1942 2v.
Arc 30.12.3F	American Institute for Iranian Art and Archaeology. Reprint [of the] American Institute. N.Y.
Arc 30.12.5	American Institute of Persian Art and Archaeology. What it is, etc. N.Y., 1932.
Arc 30.12.10	Iranian Institute of America. Announcement and outline of program. N.Y., 1930.
Arc 30.13	Anadolu. Séries 1: Prehistoire antiquité Byzance. Paris.
Arc 30.13.5	Anadolu. Séries 2: Turquie medievale et moderne. Paris.
Arc 30.15	Archaeologische Mitteilungen aus Iran. Berlin. 1,1929+ 10v.
Arc 30.15.5	Archaeologische Mitteilungen aus Iran. Ergänzungsband. Berlin. 1,1938
Arc 30.16	Atiqot; journal of the Israel Department of Antiquities. Jerusalem. 1+ 4v.
Arc 30.18	Archiv für ägyptische Archäologie. Wien. 1,1938
Arc 30.20	Athar-e-Iran. Paris. 1-4,1936-1949 4v.
Arc 30.21	Calcutta. University. Asutosh Museum of Indian Art and Archaeology. Asutosh Museum memoir.

Arc 30 - 55 Archaeology - Periodicals and Societies - Local - Asia and Africa (A-Z) - cont.

Arc 30.22	Anatolia; revue annuelle d'archéologie. Ankara. 1,1956+ 3v.
Arc 30.23F	Les annales archéologiques de Syrie. Damas. 1,1951+ 17v.
Arc 30.24	Anatolian studies. London. 15,1965+ 25v.
Arc 30.25	Azania. Nairobi. 1,1966+ 2v.
Arc 30.26	Anatolica; annuaire international pour les civilisations de l'Asie anterieure. Leiden. 1,1967+ 2v.
Arc 30.27	Ancient Pakistan. Peshawar. 1,1964+ 2v.
Arc 30.29	Antiquités africaines. Paris. 1,1967+
Arc 30.30	Africa. Tunis. 1,1966+
Arc 30.31	The Australian journal of Biblical archaeology. Sydney. 1,1968+
Arc 30.32	Ancient Ceylon. Colombo. 1,1971+ 2v.
Arc 31.1	Biblia. Meriden. 4-18,1891-1905 15v.
Arc 31.1.35	The Biblical archaeologist. New Haven. 1,1938+ 9v.
Arc 31.3	Paris. Musée Guimet. Bulletin archéologique. Paris. 1,1921
Arc 31.4	Berytus. Beirut. 1,1934+ 9v.
Arc 31.7F	British School of Archaeology in Jerusalem. Supplementary papers. London.
Arc 31.9	British Institute of Archaeology in Ankara. Occasional publications. London. 1,1949+ 10v.
Arc 31.11	Beirut. Musée National Libanais. Bulletin du musée de Beyrouth. Paris. 1,1937+ 9v.
Arc 31.12	British School of Archaeology in Jerusalem. Bulletin. 1-7,1922-1925 2v.
Arc 31.14	Buried history. Melbourne. 1,1964+
Arc 31.16	Beitraege zur Archäologie und Geologie des Zendan-I. Wiesbaden. 1,1968+
Arc 31.18	Boreas. Uppsala. 1,1970+
Arc 32.2F	Almstead, A.T. Travels and studies in...nearer East. Ithaca, N.Y., 1911.
Arc 32.5	Chicago. University. Oriental Institute. Communications. Chicago. 2-18 5v.
Arc 32.5.3	Chicago. University. Oriental Institute. Bulletin. Chicago.
Arc 32.8F	Centro Scavi e Ricerche Archeologiche in Asia dell'I.M.E.O. e di Torino. Reports and memoirs. Roma. 1,1962+ 13v.
Arc 32.10F	Colt Archaeological Institute. Monograph series. London. 1-5
Arc 33.2	Deutsches Institut für ägyptische Altertumskunde in Kairo. Mitteilungen. Augsburg. 1,1930+ 17v.
Arc 33.3F	Deutsches Archäologisches Institut. Abteilung Kairo. Abhandlungen. Hamburg. 5-6 2v.
Arc 33.4	Discoveries in the Judean Desert of Jordan. Oxford. 1,1955+ 7v.
Arc 33.5	Drevniaia istoriia iuga Vostochnoi Sibiri. Irkutsk. 1,1974+
Arc 34.2F	École Française d'Extreme Orient, Hanoi, Indo-China. Mémoires archéologiques. Paris. 1926-1932 10v.
Arc 34.2.5	Praehistorica Asiae Orientalis. Hanoi.
Arc 34.5	Epigrafika Vostoka. Moskva. 1-18 5v.
Arc 34.6	Epigrafika Kirgizii. Fruze.
Arc 34.10	Études sud-arabiques. Le Caire.
Arc 35.1	France. Commission Archéologique de l'Indochine. Bulletin. Paris. 1908-1934 3v.
Arc 35.4	Fouilles en Nubie. Le Caire. 1,1959+ 2v.
Arc 37.5	Hebrew Union College Biblical and Archaeological School in Jerusalem. Annual. Jerusalem. 1,1970+ 2v.
Arc 38.5F	Institut Français d'Archéologie de Stamboul. Mémoires. Paris. 2-7 6v.
Arc 38.5.5	Gabriel, Albert. İstanbul Türk kaleleri. İstanbul, 197-.
Arc 38.20	Indian archaeology; a review. Delhi. 1953+ 7v.
Arc 38.25	Iranica antiqua. Leiden. 1-6 5v.
Arc 38.25.5	Iranica antiqua. Supplements. Leiden. 1,1962
Arc 38.30	Institut Français d'Archéologie Orientale du Caire. Conférences. 3 2v.
Arc 38.35	Istanbuler Mitteilungen. Tübingen. 1,1933+ 8v.
Arc 38.36	Istanbuler Mitteilungen. Beiheft. Tübingen. 1,1966+ 3v.
Arc 38.40	Institut Ethiopien d'Archéologie. Cahiers. Addis-Ababa. 1,1965+
Arc 39.1	Journal of Egyptian archaeology. London. 17,1931+ 38v.
Arc 39.2	Jahrbuch für kleinasiatische Forschung. Heidelberg. 1-3 3v.
Arc 39.4	Anadolu araştirmalari. Istanbul. 1,1955+ 3v.
Arc 40.2	Karthago; revue trimestrielle l'archeologie africaine. Paris. 1-14 8v.
Arc 40.10	Kresh; journal of the Sudan Antiquities Service. Khartoum. 1,1953+ 9v.
Arc 41.1	Society of Biblical Archaeology. Proceedings. London. 1-40 37v.
Arc 41.1.5	Society of Biblical Archaeology. Proceedings. Index, v.11-30. London, n.d. 2v.
Arc 41.2	Society of Biblical Archaeology. Transactions. London. 1-9 9v.
Arc 41.2.2	Society of Biblical Archaeology. Transactions. Index, v.1-9. London, n.d.
Arc 41.4	Libyca; série archéologie-epigraphie. Alger. 1-7,1953-1959 9v.
Arc 41.5	Levant; journal of the British School of Archaeology in Jerusalem. London. 1,1969+ 2v.
Arc 42.1	Memnon, Zeitschrift für den Kunst...alten Orients. Leipzig. 1-7 3v.
Arc 42.5F	Mission Paul Pelliot. Documents archéologiques. Paris. 1-3 2v.
Arc 42.10	Misión Arqueológica Española en Nubia. Memorias. Madrid. 1,1963+ 9v.
Arc 42.15	Mesopotamia. Torino. 1,1966+ 5v.
Arc 42.20	Monumenta Aegyptiaca. Bruxelles. 1,1968+
Arc 42.25	Medelhavsmuseet. Bulletin. Stockholm. 2,1962+
Arc 42.30	Meroitica. Berlin. 1,1973+
Arc 45.1	Palästina Jährbuch. Berlin. 1-36,1905-1940 36v.
Arc 45.3	Pakistan archaeology. Karachi. 1,1964+ 3v.
Arc 45.5	Pahlari University. Asia Institute. Bulletin. Shiraz. 1,1969+
Arc 45.7	Pamiatniki Kirgizstana. Frunze. 1,1970+
Arc 46.5	Quaderni di archeologia della Libia. Roma. 1,1950+ 6v.
Arc 47.3	Recherches suisses d'archéologie copte. Genève. 1,1967+ 2v.
Arc 47.5	Ruinenstaedte Nordafrikas. Basel. 1-4 3v.
Arc 48.1	Sphinx. Revue critique. Upsala. 1-21 11v.
Arc 48.2	Syria; revue d'art oriental et d'archeologie. Paris. 1,1920+ 39v.

Classified Listing

Arc 30 - 55 Archaeology - Periodicals and Societies - Local - Asia and Africa (A-Z) - cont.

Arc 48.3 Sumer; a journal of archaeology in Iraq. Baghdad. 1,1945+ 24v.
Arc 48.3.2 Sumer; a journal of archaeology in Iraq. Index, v.1-21, 1945-1965. Baghdad, 1960-1968.
Arc 48.4 Sudan. Antiquities Service. Occasional papers. Khartoum. 1-5 3v.
Arc 48.6 Sudan. Antiquities Service. Museum pamphlet. Khartoum. 1,1953+
Arc 48.8 Studies in Mediterranean archaeology. Pocket-book. Göteborg. 1,1974+
Arc 48.10 Society for Libyan Studies. Annual report. London. 1,1969+
Arc 49.2 Travancore archaeological series. Madras. 1-7,1910-1931 4v.
Arc 49.6F Private tombs at Thebes. Oxford. 1-4 2v.
Arc 49.8 Taloha; publication hors série consacrée à l'archéologie des Annales de Université de Madagascar. Tananarive. 1,1965+
Arc 50.5 Uspekhii sredneaziatskoi arkheologii. Leningrad. 1,1972+
Arc 52.2 Vooraziatisch-Egyptische Gezelschap "Ex Oriente Lux". Mededeelingen en verhandelingen. Leiden. 1,1934+ 4v.
Arc 52.4 Vooraziatisch-Egyptische Gezelschap "Ex Oriente Lux". Jahresbericht. Leiden. 3,1935+ 10v.
Arc 55.1 Zeitschrift der Deutschen Palaestina-Vereins. Leipzig. 1+ 47v.
Arc 55.1.3 Zeitschrift der Deutschen Palaestina-Vereins. Index, v.6-25. Leipzig, n.d. 2v.
Arc 55.1.4 Deutschen Palästine Verein. Mitteilungen und Nachrichten-Register. Leipzig. 1895-1912 2v.

Arc 65 - 90 Archaeology - Periodicals and Societies - Local - Europe - Classical and Early Christian (A-Z)

Arc 65.1 Archaeologische Zeitung. Berlin. 1-43,1843-1885 28v.
Arc 65.1.2 Register zur archaeologische Zeitung. Berlin. 1-43,1843-1885
Arc 65.2 Archaeologische-Epigraphische Mittheilungen am Österreich. Vienna. 1-20,1877-1897 8v.
Arc 65.2.3 Archaeologische-Epigraphische Mittheilungen am Österreich. Vienna. 1-20,1877-1897
Arc 65.2.5 Oesterreich-Archäologisches Institut, Wien. Jahreshefte. Vienna. 1,1898+ 37v.
Arc 65.2.7F Oesterreichisches Archäologisches Institut, Vienna. Grabungen. Wien. 1965
Arc 65.3 Mittheilungen des deutsches archäologisches Institut in Athen. Athens. 1,1876+ 69v.
Arc 65.3.2 Register zu Mittheilungen. Athens. 1-5
Arc 65.3.3 Register zu Mittheilungen. Athens. 6-10
Arc 65.3.4 Register zu Mittheilungen. Athens. 11-15
Arc 65.3.5 Register zu Mittheilungen. Athens. 16-20
Arc 65.3.6 Deutsches Archäologisches Institut. Athenische Abteilung. Mitteilungen. Beiheft. Berlin. 1,1971+
Arc 65.3.10F Archäologisches Institut des Deutschen Reichs-Athenische Zweiganstalt. Argolis. Athens.
Arc 65.5 Die Antike. Berlin. 1-20,1925-1944 18v.
Arc 65.6F Associazione Internazionale degli Studi Mediterranei. Bolletino. Roma. 1-6,1930-1936 2v.
Arc 65.6.10 Association Internationale d'Archéologie Classique. Annuaire. Rome. 2,1956 3v.
Arc 65.7F Athens. R. Scuola Archeologica Italiana. Annuario. Bergamo. 1,1914+ 18v.
Arc 65.8 Archeion tōn Byzandinōn mnēmeiōn tēs Hellados. Athēnai. 1-9,1935-1961 5v.
Arc 65.9 Athens. École Française. Études péloponnésiennes. Paris. 1-5 5v.
Arc 65.10 Altino romana. Venezia. 1,1956
Arc 65.11 Archaeological reports. London. 1957-1964
Arc 65.12 Athens. École Française. Études chypriotes. Paris. 1-2,1961-1962 2v.
Arc 65.14 Archaiologika analekta ex Athenon. Athēnai. 1,1968+

Arc 66.1-66.1.220 Publications of the Bibliothèque des Ecôles Françaises d'Athènes et de Rome

Arc 66.1 Duchesne, L. Étude sur le liber pontificalis. Paris, 1877.
Arc 66.1.2 Collignon, M. Essai sur les monuments grecs et romains relatifs au mythe de psyché. Paris, 1877.
Arc 66.1.3 Collignon, M. Catalogue des vases peints du musée. Paris, 1878.
Arc 66.1.4 Muentz, E. Arts à la cour des papes. Paris, 1878-82. 3v.
Arc 66.1.5 Fernique, E. Inscriptions du pays des marses. Paris, 1879.
Arc 66.1.6 Berger, E. Notice sur des manuscrits de la Bibliothèque Vaticane. Paris, 1879.
Arc 66.1.7 Clédat, L. Role historique de Bertrand de Born. Paris, 1879.
Arc 66.1.8 Riemann, O. Les îles ioniennes. Paris, 1879-80. 3v.
Arc 66.1.10 Bayet, C. Peinture et sculpture chrétiennes en Orient. Paris, 1879.
Arc 66.1.11 Riemann, O. Études sur la langue de Yite-Live. Paris, 1879.
Arc 66.1.13 Duchesne, L. De codd. mss. graecis Pü II in Biblioteca Vaticana. Paris, 1880.
Arc 66.1.14 Chatelain, E. Manuscrits des poesies de S. Paulin de Nole. Paris, 1880.
Arc 66.1.15 Descemet, C. Inscriptions doliaires latines. Paris, 1880.
Arc 66.1.16 Martha, J. Catalogue des figurines en terre cuite. Paris, 1880.
Arc 66.1.17 Fernique, E. Étude sur préneste. Paris, 1880.
Arc 66.1.19 Delaborde, H.F. Chartes de terre sainte. Paris, 1880.
Arc 66.1.20 Cartault, A. La trière athénienne. Paris, 1881.
Arc 66.1.21 Cuq, E. Études d'epigraphie juridique. Paris, 1881.
Arc 66.1.22 Delaborde, H.F. Étude sur la chronique de Guillaume le Breton. Paris, 1881.
Arc 66.1.23 Girard, P. L'asclépicion d'Athènes. Paris, 1881.
Arc 66.1.24 Martin, A. Manuscrit d'Isocrate, Urbinas CXI. Paris, 1881.
Arc 66.1.25 Thomas, A. Recherches sur l'entrée de Spagne. Paris, 1882.
Arc 66.1.26 Martha, J. Sacerdoces anthéniens. Paris, 1882.
Arc 66.1.27 Martin, A. Scolies du ms. d'Aristophane à Ravenne. Paris, 1882.
Arc 66.1.29 Bloch, G. Origines du sénat romain. Paris, 1883.
Arc 66.1.30 Pottier, E. Étude sur les lécythes blancs attiques. Paris, 1883.

Arc 65 - 90 Archaeology - Periodicals and Societies - Local - Europe - Classical and Early Christian (A-Z) - cont.

Arc 66.1.31 Albert, M. Culte de castor et pollux en Italie. Paris, 1883.
Arc 66.1.32 Delaville Le Roulx, J. Les archives...à Malte. Paris, 1883.
Arc 66.1.33 Lafaye, G. Histoire du culte des divinités d'Alexandre. Photoreproduction. Paris, 1884.
X Cg Arc 66.1.33 Lafaye, G. Histoire du culte des divinités d'Alexandre. Paris, 1884. (Changed to XP 9785)
Arc 66.1.34 La Blanchere, M.R. de. Terracine. Paris, 1884.
Arc 66.1.35 Thomas, A. Francesco da Barberino. Paris, 1883.
Arc 66.1.36 Beaudoin, M. Étude du dialecte chypriote. Paris, 1884.
Arc 66.1.37 Jullian, C. Transformations politiques de l'Italie. Paris, 1884.
Arc 66.1.38 Haussoullier, B. La vie municipale en Attique. Paris, 1884.
Arc 66.1.40 Dubois, M. Les ligues étolienne et achéenne. Paris, 1885.
Arc 66.1.41 Hauvette-Besnault, A. Les stratèges athéniens. Paris, 1885.
Arc 66.1.42 Grousset, R. Étude sur l'histoire des sarcophages chrétiens. Paris, 1885.
Arc 66.1.43 Faucon, M. Libraire des papes d'Avignon. Paris, 1886. 2v.
Arc 66.1.44 Delaville Le Roulx, J. La France en Orient au XIVe siècle. Paris, 1886. 2v.
Arc 66.1.46 Durrieu, P. Archives angevines de Naples. Paris, 1886-1887. 2v.
Arc 66.1.47 Martin, A. Les cavaliers athéniens. Paris, 1886.
Arc 66.1.48 Muentz, E. Bibliothèque du Vatican au XVe siècle. Paris, 1887.
Arc 66.1.49 Homolle, T. Archives de l'intendance sacrée à Délos. Paris, 1887.
Arc 66.1.52 Lécrivain, C. Le Sénat Romain depuis Dioclétien. Paris, 1888.
X Cg Arc 66.1.53 Diehl, C. Études sur l'administration Byzantine. Paris, 1888.
Arc 66.1.54 Noiret, H. Lettres inedites de Michel Apostolis. Paris, 1889.
Arc 66.1.55 Diehl, C. L'église...du Couvent de Saint-Luc en Procide. Paris, 1889.
Arc 66.1.56 Auvray, L. Manuscrits de Dante des Bibliothèques de France. Paris, 1892.
Arc 66.1.57 Duerrbach, F. L'orateur Lycurgue. Paris, 1890.
Arc 66.1.58 Langlois, E. Origines et sources du Roman de la Rose. Paris, 1891.
Arc 66.1.59 Cadier, L. Essai sur l'administration du Royaume de Sicile. Paris, 1891.
Arc 66.1.60 Paris, P. Élatée. Paris, 1892.
Arc 66.1.62 Fabre, P. Étude sur le liber censuum. Paris, 1892.
Arc 66.1.63 Radet, Georges. La Lydie et le monde grec. Paris, 1893.
Arc 66.1.63.5 Radet, Georges. La Lydie et le monde grec au temps des Mesmnades, 687-546. Roma, 1967.
Arc 66.1.64 Clerc, M. Les meteques atheniens. Paris, 1893.
Arc 66.1.65 Gsell, S. Essai sur Domitien. Paris, 1894.
Arc 66.1.66 Enlart, C. Origines françaises de l'architecture gothique en Italie. Paris, 1894.
Arc 66.1.67 Bérard, V. Origine des cultes arcadiens. Paris, 1894.
Arc 66.1.68 Baudrillart, A. Divinités de la victoire en Grèce et en Italie. Paris, 1894.
Arc 66.1.69 Ridder, A. de. Catalogue des bronzes de la société archeologique d'Athènes. Paris, 1894.
Arc 66.1.70 Berger, E. Histoire de Blanche de Castile. Paris, 1895.
Arc 66.1.71 Rolland, R. Histoire de l'Opera en Europe. Paris, 1895.
Arc 66.1.73 Guiraud, J. L'état pontificale après le grand schisme. Paris, 1896.
Arc 66.1.74 Ridder, A. de. Catalogue des bronzes trouvés sur l'Acropole. Paris, 1896. 2v.
Arc 66.1.75 Pélissier, L.G. Louis XII et Ludovic Sforza. Paris, 1896. 3v.
Arc 66.1.78 Fougères, G. Mantinée et l'arcadie orientale. Paris, 1898.
Arc 66.1.79 Legrand, P.E. Étude sur Théocrite. Paris, 1898.
Arc 66.1.80 Loye, J. de. Les archives de la chambre apostolique XIVe siècle. Paris, 1899.
Arc 66.1.81 Courbaud, E. Le Bas-Relief Romain a représentations historiques. Paris, 1899.
Arc 66.1.82 Macé, A. Essai sur Suétone. Paris, 1900.
Arc 66.1.83 Dofourco, A. Etudes sur les gesta martyrum. Paris, 1900.
Arc 66.1.85 Collignon, M. Catalogue des vases peints. Paris, 1902. 4v.
Arc 66.1.86 Déprez, E. Les préliminaires de la guerre de cents ans. Paris, 1902.
X Cg Arc 66.1.87 Besiner, M. L'ile tiberine dans l'antiquité. Paris, 1902.
X Cg Arc 66.1.88 Yver, G. Le commerce et les marchands. Paris, 1903.
Arc 66.1.89 Homo, Leon. Essai sur le regne de l'empereur Aurélien. Paris, 1904.
Arc 66.1.91 Millet, J. Recueil des inscriptiosn chrétiennes du Mont Athos. Paris, 1904.
Arc 66.1.92 Lechat, Henri. La sculpture attique avant Phidias. Paris, 1904.
Arc 66.1.93 Colin, G. Le culte d'Apollon Pythien à Athènes. Paris, 1905.
Arc 66.1.94 Colin, G. Rome et la Grèce de 200 a 146 avant Jésus-Christ. Paris, 1905.
Arc 66.1.95 Bourquet, E. L'administration financiere du sanctuaire pythique. Paris, 1905.
Arc 66.1.96 Samarin, C.M.D. La fiscalité pontificale en France XIVe siècle. Paris, 1905.
Arc 66.1.97 Merlin, A. L'aventin dans l'antiquité. Paris, 1906.
Arc 66.1.98 Dubois, C. Pouzzoles antique. Paris, 1907.
Arc 66.1.99 Chapot, V. La frontière de l'Euphrate de Pompée à la Conquête Arabe. Paris, 1907.
Arc 66.1.100 Cavaignac, E. Études sur l'histoire financière d'Athènes au Ve siècle. Paris, 1908.
Arc 66.1.101 Perdrizet, P. La vierge de miséricorde. Paris, 1908.
Arc 66.1.102 Bourgin, G. La France et Rome de 1788 à 1797. Paris, 1909.
Arc 66.1.103 Celier, Léonce. Les dataires du XVe siècle et les origines de la daterie apostolique. Paris, 1910.
Arc 66.1.104 Jouguet, P. La vie municipale dans l'Égypte Romaine. Paris, 1911.
Arc 66.1.105 Hautecoeur, L. Rome et la Renaissance de l'antiquite. Photoreproduction. Paris, 1912.
Arc 66.1.106 Grenier, A. Bologne villanovienne et etrusque. Paris, 1912.
Arc 66.1.108 Leroux, Gabriel. Les origines de l'édifice hypostyle. Paris, 1913.

Classified Listing

Arc 65 - 90 **Archaeology - Periodicals and Societies - Local - Europe - Classical and Early Christian (A-Z) - cont.**

Arc 66.1.109 Millet, G. Recherches sur l'conographie de l'évangile aux XIV, XV et XVI siècles. Paris, 1916.
Arc 66.1.111 Roussel, Pierre. Délos; colonie athénienne. Paris, 1916.
Arc 66.1.112 Zeiller, Jacques. Les origines chrétiennes...provinces danubiennes. Paris, 1918.
Arc 66.1.113 Holleaux, Maurice. Stratēgos Ypatos. Paris, 1918.
Arc 66.1.117 Laurent, J. L'arménie entre Byzance et l'Islam. Paris, 1919.
Arc 66.1.118 De Boüard, A. Le régime politique et les institutions de Rome au Moyen-Age, 1252-1347. Paris, 1920.
Arc 66.1.119 Constans, L.A. Arles antique. Paris, 1921.
Arc 66.1.120 Hirschauer, C. La politique de St. Pie V en France. Paris, n.d.
Arc 66.1.121 Fawtier, Robert. Sainte Catherine de Sienne. Paris, 1921.
Arc 66.1.122 Roussel, Louis. Grammaire descriptive du Roméique littéraire. Paris, n.d.
Arc 66.1.123 Picard, Charles. Ephèse et Claros. Paris, 1922.
Arc 66.1.124 Holleaux, Maurice. Rome, la Grèce, et les monarchies hellénistiques. Paris, 1921.
Arc 66.1.125 Courby, Fernand. Les vases grecs à reliefs. n.p., n.d.
Arc 66.1.126 Boulanger, André. Relius Aristide. n.p., n.d.
Arc 66.1.127 Albertini, E. La composition dans les ouvrages philosophiques de Sévèque. n.p., n.d.
Arc 66.1.128 Constant, G. Confession a l'Allemagne. n.p., n.d. 2v.
Arc 66.1.129 Dugas, Charles. La céramique des cyclades. Paris, 1925.
Arc 66.1.130 Jardé, A. Les céréales dans l'antiquité grecque. Paris, 1925.
Arc 66.1.131 Bulard, M. La religion domestique. Paris, 1926.
Arc 66.1.132 Bayet, J. Les origines de l'Hercule Romain. Paris, 1926.
Arc 66.1.132.5 Bayet, J. Herclé, étude critique. Paris, 1926.
Arc 66.1.133 Pocquet, J. du Haut-Jusse. Les papes et les ducs de Bretagne. Paris, 1928. 2v.
Arc 66.1.134 Cahen, Emile. Callimaque. Paris, 1929.
Arc 66.1.134.5 Cahen, Emile. Les hymes de Callimaque. Paris, 1930.
Arc 66.1.135 Fawtier, Robert. Sainte Catherine de Sienne. Paris, 1930.
Arc 66.1.136 Demangel, R. La frise ionique. Paris, 1932.
Arc 66.1.137 Chapouthier, F. Les dioscures au service d'une déesse. Paris, 1935.
Arc 66.1.138 La Coste-Messelière, P. de. Au musée de Delphes. Paris, 1936.
Arc 66.1.139 Boüard, Michel de. La France et l'Italie au temps du Grand Schisme d'Occident. Paris, 1936.
Arc 66.1.140 Daux, Georges. Delphes au IIe et au Ier siècle. Paris, 1936.
Arc 66.1.141 Boyancé, Pierre. Le culte des muses. Paris, 1937.
Arc 66.1.142 Recueil Edmond Pottier. Paris, 1937.
Arc 66.1.143 Flacelière, Robert. Les Aitoliens a Dalphes. Paris, 1937.
Arc 66.1.144 Béquignon, Yves. La Vallée du spercheios. Paris, 1937.
Arc 66.1.145 Marrou, Henri-Irénée. Saint Augustin et la fin de la culture antique. v.1-2. Paris, 1958.
Arc 66.1.146 Durry, Marcel. Les cohortes prétoriennes. Paris, 1938.
Arc 66.1.147 Robert, Fernand. Thymélè. Paris, 1939.
Arc 66.1.148 Wirilleumier, Pierre. Tarente; des origines a la conquête romaine. Paris, 1939. 2v.
Arc 66.1.149 Thouvenot, R. Essai sur le province romaine de Béteque. Paris, 1940.
Arc 66.1.150 Bérard, Jean. La colonisation grecque de l'Italie meridionale et de la Sicilie. Paris, 1941.
Arc 66.1.151 Renouard, Yves. Les relations des papes d'Avignon. Paris, 1941.
Arc 66.1.152 Feyel, Michel. Palybe et l'histoire de Biotre. Paris, 1942.
Arc 66.1.153 Guillon, P. Les trépieds du Ptoion. Paris, 1943.
Arc 66.1.154 Heurgon, J. Recherches sur l'histoire, la religion et la civilisation. Paris, 1942.
Arc 66.1.155 Grimal, Pierre. Las jardins romains. Paris, 1943.
Arc 66.1.156 Boulet, Marquerite. Questiones Johannes Galli. Paris, 1944.
Arc 66.1.157 Vallois, René. L'architecture hellénique et hellenistique a Délos. Paris, 1944-53. 2v.
Arc 66.1.160 Chatelain, Louis. Le Maroc des romains. Paris, 1944. 2v.
Arc 66.1.161 Mahor, J.B. L'ordre cistercien et son gouvernement. Paris, 1945.
Arc 66.1.162 Seston, William. Dioclétien et la tétrarchie. Paris, 1946. 2v.
Arc 66.1.163 Effenterre, Henri van. La Crète et le monde grec. Paris, 1948.
Arc 66.1.164 Demargne, Pierre. La Crète dédalique. Paris, 1947. 2v.
Arc 66.1.165 Lapalus, Etienne. Le fronton sculpté en Grèce. Paris, 1947. 2v.
Arc 66.1.166 Simon, Marcel. Verus Israel. Paris, 1948.
Arc 66.1.167 Fabre, P. Saint Paulin de Nole. Paris, 1949.
Arc 66.1.168 Lesage, G. Marseille Angevine. Paris, 1950.
Arc 66.1.169 Launey, Marcel. Recherches sur les armées hellénistiques. Paris, 1949. 2v.
Arc 66.1.170 Amandry, P. La mantique Apollenienne a Delphes. Paris, 1950. 2v.
Arc 66.1.171 Aymard, Jacques. Essai sur les chasses romaines. Paris, 1951. 2v.
Arc 66.1.172 Metzger, H. Les représentations dans la céramique attique du IV siècle. Paris, 1951. 3v.
Arc 66.1.173 François, M. Le cardinal François de Tournon. Paris, 1951. 2v.
Arc 66.1.174 Martin, R. Recherches sur l'agora grecque. Paris, 1951.
Arc 66.1.175 Bruhl, A. Liber patér. Paris, 1953.
Arc 66.1.176 Lerat, Lucien. Les Locriens de l'ouest. v. 1-2. Paris, 1952.
Arc 66.1.177 Chamoux, F. Cyrène sous la monarchie des Battiades. Paris, 1953.
Arc 66.1.178 Schilling, R. La religion romaine de Venias depuis les origines jusqu'au temps d'Auguste. Paris, 1954.
Arc 66.1.179 Pouillaux, Jean. La Forteresse de Rhamnonte. Paris, 1954.
Arc 66.1.180 Lefèvre, Yves. L'elucidarium et les lucidaires. Paris, 1954.
Arc 66.1.181 Jannoray, Jean. Enserune. Paris, 1955.
Arc 66.1.182 Gagé, Jean. Apollon romain. Paris, 1955.
Arc 66.1.183 Will, Ernest. Le relief culturel greco-romain. Paris, 1955.
Arc 66.1.184 Delumeau, Jean. Vie economique et sociale de Rome. Paris, 1957. 2v.
Arc 66.1.185 Leveque, Pierre. Pyrrhos. Paris, 1957.
Arc 66.1.186 Dessenore, André. Le sphinx. Paris, 1957.
Arc 66.1.187 Picard, Gilbert. Les trophées romains. Paris, 1957.

Arc 65 - 90 **Archaeology - Periodicals and Societies - Local - Europe - Classical and Early Christian (A-Z) - cont.**

Arc 66.1.188 Laumonier, Alfred. Les cultes indigenes en Carie. Paris, 1958.
Arc 66.1.189 Vallet, Georges. Rhégion et Zanale. Paris, 1958.
Arc 66.1.190 Bompaire, J. Lucien écrivain. Paris, 1958.
Arc 66.1.191 Etienne, Robert. La culte imperial dans la peninsule iberique d'Auguste à Dioclétien. Paris, 1958.
Arc 66.1.192 Gallet de Santerre, Hubert. Délos primitive et archaique. Paris, 1958.
Arc 66.1.193 Thiriet, Freddy. La Romanie vénitienne au Moyen Age. Paris, 1959.
Arc 66.1.194 Festugière, Andre. Antioche paienne et chrétienne. Paris, 1959.
Arc 66.1.195 Villard, Francois. La ceramique grecque de Marseilles. Paris, 1960.
Arc 66.1.196 Delorme, Jean. Gymnasion; étude sur les monuments consacrés à l'éducation en Grèce des origines à l'Empire romain. Paris, 1960.
Arc 66.1.197 Grenade, P. Essai sur les origines du principat. Paris, 1961.
Arc 66.1.198 Hus, A. Recherches sur la statuaire en pierre étrusque archaique. Paris, 1961.
Arc 66.1.199 Roux, Georges. L'architecture de l'Argolide aux IV et IIIe siècles avant J.-C. Paris, 1961. 2v.
Arc 66.1.200 Ginouvès, René. Balaneutikè; recherches sur le bain dans l'antiquité grecque. Paris, 1962.
Arc 66.1.201 Guillemain, B. La cour pontificale d'Avignon, 1309-1376. Paris, 1962.
Arc 66.1.202 Fevrier, Paul Albert. Le developpement urbain en Provence. Paris, 1964.
Arc 66.1.203 Glenisson, Jean. Correspondance des légats et vicaires-généraux. Paris, 1964.
Arc 66.1.204 Boucher, Jean-Paul. Études sur Properce; problèmes d'inspiration et d'art. Paris, 1965.
Arc 66.1.205 Leglay, Marcel. Saturne africain; histoire. Paris, 1966.
Arc 66.1.206 Cèbe, Jean Pierre. La caricature et la parodie dans le monde romain, antique des origines a Juvenal. Paris, 1966.
Arc 66.1.207 Nicolet, Claude. L'ordre équestre. Paris, 1966-74. 2v.
Arc 66.1.208 Courbin, Paul. La céramique géométrique de l'Argolide. Paris, 1966. 2v.
Arc 66.1.209 Ducat, Jean. Les vases plastiques rhodiens. Paris, 1966.
Arc 66.1.210 Turcan, Robert. Les sarcophages romains à representations dionysiaques. Paris, 1966.
Arc 66.1.211 Favier, Jean. Les finances pontificales à l'époque du grand schisme d'Occident, 1378-1409. Paris, 1966.
Arc 66.1.212 Labrousse, Michel. Toulouse antique des origines à l'établissement des Wisigoths. Paris, 1968.
Arc 66.1.213 Bon, Antoine. La morée franque. Paris, 1969. 2v.
Arc 66.1.214 Callu, Jean Pierre. La politique monétaire des empereurs romains de 238 à 311. Paris, 1969.
Arc 66.1.215 Marcadé, Jean. Au musée de Délos. Paris, 1969.
Arc 66.1.217 Bruneau, Philippe. Recherches sur les cultes de Délos à l'époque hellénistique et à l'époque impériale. Paris, 1970.
Arc 66.1.218 Duval, Noël. Les églises africaines à deux absides. Paris, 1971- 2v.
Arc 66.1.219 Ducat, Jean. Les kouroi du Ptoion. Paris, 1971.
Arc 66.1.220 Bloch, Raymond. Recherches archéologique en territoire Volsinien. Paris, 1972.
Arc 66.2 France. Institutes. Rapports de la commission des écoles d'Athènes et de Rome. Paris. 1878-1889 2v.
Arc 66.2.80 Radet, G. L'histoire et l'oeuvre de l'école française d'Athènes. Paris, 1901.
Arc 66.2.85 Radet, G. Correspondance d'Emmanuel Roux. Bordeaux, 1898.
Arc 66.3 Athens. Bulletin de correspondance hellénique. Paris. 1,1877+ 92v.
Arc 66.3.2 Athens. Bulletin de correspondance hellénique. Table générale. Paris. 1877-1886
Arc 66.3.5 Athens. École française. Bulletin. Athènes. 1-12,1868-1871
Arc 66.4 Bulletino di archeologia cristiana. Roma. 1870-1894 11v.
Arc 66.4F Bulletino di archeologia cristiana. Roma. 1863-1869
Arc 66.4.1 Bulletino di archeologia cristiana. Indici generali, 1882-1889. 4. serie. Roma, n.d.
Arc 66.4.2 Nuovo bulletino de archeologia cristiana. Roma. 1-28,1895-1922 13v.
Arc 66.4.4 Rivista di archeologia cristiana. Milano. 1923
Arc 66.4.6 Rivista di archeologia cristiana. Roma. 1,1924+ 25v.
Arc 66.6 Bulletino archeologico napoletano. Naples. 1-8,1843-1863 14v.
Arc 66.6.2 Bulletino archeologico italiano. Naples. 1-2,1861-1862
Arc 66.7 Bulletino di commissione archeologico municipale. Roma. 1,1872+ 56v.
Arc 66.7.2 Bulletino di commissione archeologico municipale. Indici, 1872-1885. Roma, n.d. 3v.
Arc 66.7.3 Bulletino di commissione archeologico municipale. Indici generali dal 1922-1938. Roma, 1942.
Arc 66.8 British School at Athens. British School at Athens...annual. Rome. 1,1894+ 68v.
Arc 66.8.2 British School at Athens. British School at Athens...index, 1-32. London, n.d. 2v.
Arc 66.8.15 Pamphlet box. British School at Athens.
Arc 66.9 British School at Rome. Papers. London. 1,1902+ 41v.
NEDL Arc 66.10 British School at Rome. Annual reports. London.
Arc 66.11 British and American Archaeological Society of Rome. Journal. Rome.
Arc 66.11.5 British and American Archaeological Society of Rome. Proceedings. Rome.
Arc 67.1 Cronichetta mensuale. Rome. 1-26,1867-1894 11v.
Arc 67.3 Christianekē Archaiologikē Hetaireia, Athens. Katastatikon Psēphisthen yvo tēs Genikēs synelenseus. Athēnai. 1903
Arc 67.3.5 Christianekē Archaiologikē Hetaireia, Athens. Praktika. Athēnai. 1,1892+ 6v.
Arc 67.4 California. University. Publications in classical archaeology. Berkeley. 1-3,1929-1957 5v.
Arc 67.5 Congresso Nazionale di Archealogia Cristiana. Atti del 1 congresso nazionale di archealogia cristiana. Roma, 1952.
Arc 67.6 Durham, England. University. King's College, Newcastle upon Tyne. The congress of Roman frontier studies. Durham, 1952.
Arc 67.7 Collana di quaderni di antichità ravennati cristiane e bizantine. Ravenna. 1,1963+ 12v.
Arc 68.1 Greece. Genikē ephoreia tōn archaiotētōn kai mouseiōn. Deltion archaiologikon. Athēnai. 1888-1892 4v.

Classified Listing

Arc 65 - 90 Archaeology - Periodicals and Societies - Local - Europe - Classical and Early Christian (A-Z) - cont.

Arc 68.5F Greece. Hypourgeion tōn ekklesiasticon. Archailogikon deltion. Athēnai. 1,1915+ 29v.
Arc 68.10 Deutsches Archäologisches Institut. Bericht über die Ausgrabungen in Olympia. Berlin. 4,1940+ 5v.
Arc 68.15 Dialoghi di archeologia. Milano. 1,1967+ 4v.
Arc 69.1F Archaeological Society of Athens. Epheneriz Archaiologikē. Athēnai. 1837+ 54v.
Arc 69.2 Smyrna. Enaggelikēs Scholēs. Moyseion kai Bibliothēkē. Smyrna. 1873-1886 3v.
Arc 69.4 Athens. École Française. Études thasiennes. Paris. 1-8 8v.
Arc 70.5 Fouilles de Xanthos. Paris. 1,1958+ 7v.
Arc 71.1 Giornale degli Scavi di Pompei. Napoli. 1861-1865
Arc 71.1.2F Giornale degli Scavi di Pompei. Napoli. 1-4 2v.
Arc 72.5 Hellenic Travellers' Club. Proceedings. London? 1925-1930 7v.
Arc 72.6 Historia; studi storici per l'antichità classica. Milano. 1-9,1927-1935 9v.
Arc 72.7 Pamphlet vol. Hellenic Travellers' Club.
Arc 72.10 Hellenica. Limoges. 1-13 5v.
Arc 73.1 Rome. Istituto. Annali, bulletino, and tavole. Rome. 1829-1883 65v.
Arc 73.2 Rome. Istituto. Monumenti - annali - bulletini 1854-5 and Monumenti - annali 1856. Rome.
Arc 73.4 Rome. Istituto. Nuove memorie dell'instituto. Leipzig, 1865. 2v.
Arc 73.5 Rome. Istituto. Repertorio universale dell'opere dell'instituto. Rome. 1834-1885 5v.
Arc 73.6 Deutsches Archäologisches Institut. Römische Abteilung. Mittheilungen. Rom. 1,1886+ 60v.
Arc 73.6.2 Deutsches Archäologisches Institut. Römische Abteilung. Mittheilungen. Register, Bd. I-X. Rom, 1902.
Arc 73.6.10 Deutsches Archäologisches Institut. Römische Abteilung. Mittheilungen. Ergänzungsheft. München. 1,1931+ 19v.
Arc 73.6.15 Deutsches Archäologisches Institut. Römische Abteilung. Bilderhefte. Tübingen. 1,1962+ 4v.
Arc 73.7 Rome. Institut Archéologique. La Section Française. Nouvelles annales. Paris. 1-2,1836-1839 2v.
Arc 73.8F Archäologisches Institut des Deutschen Reichs. Denkmäler antiker Architektur. Berlin. 1-10 11v.
Arc 73.11 Archäologisches Institut des Deutschen Reichs. Jahrbuch. Berlin. 1,1886+ 23v.
Arc 73.11.2 Archäologisches Institut des Deutschen Reichs. Archäologischer Anzeiger. Berlin. 78,1963+ 9v.
Arc 73.11.3 Archäologisches Institut des Deutschen Reichs. Archäologische Bibliographie; Beilage zum Jahrbuch des Deutsches Archäologisches Institut. Berlin. 1942+ 13v.
Arc 73.11.10 Archäologisches Institut des Deutschen Reichs. Jahrbuch. Bibliographie, Register, 1-50. Berlin, 1904-21. 4v.
Arc 73.12 Archäologisches Institut des Deutschen Reichs. Jahrbuch. Ergänzungsheft. Berlin. 1,1888+ 22v.
Arc 73.15 Michaelis, A. Geschichte des deutschen archäologisches Institut. Berlin, 1879.
Arc 73.15.5 Michaelis, A. Storia dell'Instituto archeologico germanico, 1829-1879. Roma, 1879.
Arc 73.17 Pamphlet box. Archäologisches Institut des Deutschen Reichs.
Arc 73.20 Archäologisches Institut des Deutschen Reichs. Römisch-Germanische Kommission. Bericht. Frankfurt. 1904+ 27v.
Arc 73.20.5 Germania: Korrespondenzblatt der Römisch-germanische Kommission. Berlin. 1,1917+ 41v.
Arc 73.20.6 Germania. Gesamtinhaltsverzeichnis, v. 1-36 (1917-58). Berlin, 1960. 2v.
Arc 73.20.10F Römisch-germanische Forschungen. Berlin. 1,1928+ 24v.
Arc 73.20.15F Archäologisches Institut des Deutschen Reichs. Funfundzwanzig Jahre Römisch-Germanische Kommission. Römische-germanische Kommission. Berlin, 1930.
Arc 73.20.20 Archäologisches Institut des Deutschen Reichs. Mitteilungen. München. 1-6,1948-1953 3v.
Arc 73.100 International Congress of Christian Archaeology, 2nd, Rome, 1900. Commentarius authenticus. v.1-6. Rome, 1900.
Arc 73.100.5 International Congress of Christian Archaeology, 2nd, Rome, 1900. Atti del II Congresso internazionale...tenuto in Roma nell'aprile 1900. Roma, 1902.
Arc 74.4 Society for the Promotion of Hellenic Studies. Journal of Hellenic studies. London. 1,1880+ 60v.
Arc 74.4.1 Society for the Promotion of Hellenic Studies. Journal. Index. v.9-42. London, 1898-1923. 3v.
Arc 74.4.1.5 Society for the Promotion of Hellenic Studies. Journal. Numismatic index, 1880-1969. Cambridge, Eng., 1971.
Arc 74.4.2F Society for the Promotion of Hellenic Studies. Journal. Plates 1-83. v.1-8. London, 1888?
Arc 74.4.4 Society for the Promotion of Hellenic Studies. Supplementary papers. London. 3,1900+ 5v.
Arc 74.4.4F Society for the Promotion of Hellenic Studies. Supplementary papers. London. 1-2 2v.
Arc 74.4.12 Pamphlet box. Society for Promotion of Hellenic Studies.
Arc 74.4.14 Society for the Promotion of Hellenic Studies. Rules and list of members. London, 1891. 2 pam.
Arc 74.4.15 Society for the Promotion of Hellenic Studies. A classified catalogue of the books, pamphlets and maps in the library. London, 1924.
Arc 74.4.16 Society for the Promotion of Hellenic Studies. Supplement to subject catalogue of joint library. London. 1-19 15v.
Arc 74.4.17 Society for the Promotion of Hellenic Studies. First supplementary catalogue of lantern slides. London, 1914.
Arc 74.4.25 MacMillan, G.A. History of the Society for the promotion of Hellenic studies. n.p., n.d.
Arc 74.5 Journal of Roman studies. London. 1,1911+ 47v.
Arc 74.5.2 Journal of Roman studies. Consolidated index, v.21-60. London, 1955-75. 2v.
Arc 74.5.2.5 Journal of Roman studies. Numismatic index, 1911-65. Cambridge, Eng., 1970.
Arc 74.5.3 Journal of Roman studies. London. 13-28,1923-1938 16v.
Arc 76.2F Limesforschungen. Berlin. 1,1959+ 12v.
Arc 77.1 Museo Italiano di antichita classica. v.1-3 and atlas. Florence, 1884-90. 4v.
Arc 77.1.2 Monumenti antichi. Milan. 1-47 47v.
Arc 77.4 Marberger Winckelmann-Program. Marburg. 1956+ 4v.
Arc 77.5 Munz. Römisch-Germanisches Zentralmuseum. Jahrbuch. 1,1954+ 99v.

Arc 65 - 90 Archaeology - Periodicals and Societies - Local - Europe - Classical and Early Christian (A-Z) - cont.

Arc 77.8 Rome. Università. Centro di Studi Micenei. Incunabula Graeca. 1,1961+ 56v.
Arc 78.3 Rome. Accademia dei Lincei. Notizie degli Scavi. Rome. 1876+ 99v.
Arc 78.3.2 Rome. Accademia dei Lincei. Notizie degli Scavi. Indici epigrafici. 1876-85. Rome, 1886.
Arc 78.3.3 Rome. Accademia dei Lincei. Notizie degli Scavi. Indici generali, 1876-1955. Milano, 1904-1961. 3v.
Arc 79.2F Opuscula archaeologica; edidit Institutum Romanum regni Sueciae. Lund. 3-7,1944-1952 4v.
Arc 79.2.3F Opuscula Romana; edidit Institutum Romanum regni Sueciae. Lund. 1,1954+ 6v.
Arc 79.3F Opuscula Atheniensia. Lund. 1-6 4v.
Arc 80.1 Kastorkes, E. Historikē ekthesis tōn praxeon tēs Archaiologikēs Hetairias. Athēnai, 1879.
Arc 80.1.5 Kabbadias, P. Historia tēs Archaiologikēs Hetairias. Athēnai, 1900.
Arc 80.1.6 Archaiologikē Hetairia, Athens. To ergon tēs en Athēnais, Archaiologikēs Hetairias kata ten prōten autēs hekatontaetias. Athēnai, 1938.
Arc 80.1.7F Oikonomos, G.P. Ta hekaton etē tēs en Athēnais Archaiologikēs Hetaireias. Athēnai, 1938.
Arc 80.1.7.5F Archaiologikē Hetairia, Athens. Leukōma tēs hekatontaeteridos. Athēnai, 1952.
Arc 80.1.8 Archaiologikē Hetairia, Athens. To ergon tēs Archaiologikēs Hetaireias. Athēnai. 1954+ 9v.
Arc 80.8 Archaiologikē Hetairia, Athens. Organismos. Athēnai, 1876.
Arc 80.10 Archaeological Society, Athens. Praktika. Athēnai. 1,1837+ 40v.
Arc 80.15 Polemōn archaiologikon periodikon syggramma. Athēnai. 1-6,1929-1957 3v.
Arc 81.5 Quellen und Studien zur Geschichte und Kultur des Altertums, etc. Reihe A. Heidelberg.
Arc 81.6 Quellen und Studien zur Geschichte und Kultur des Altertums, etc. Reihe B. Heidelberg. 2 2v.
Arc 81.7 Quellen und Studien zur Geschichte und Kultur des Altertums, etc. Reihe C. Heidelberg.
Arc 81.7PF Quellen und Studien zur Geschichte und Kultur des Altertums, etc. Reihe C. Heidelberg. 1
Arc 81.8 Quellen und Studien zur Geschichte und Kultur des Altertums, etc. Reihe D. Heidelberg. 1-10,1934-1939
Arc 81.9 Quaderni per lo studeo dell'archeologia. Firenze. 1-6,1938-1943
Arc 81.10 Quaderni e guide di archeologia. Roma. 1,1958+ 3v.
Arc 81.11 Quaderni di studi romani; a cura della Sezione lombarda dell'Istituto di studi romani. Milano. 1-6,1948-1955 2v.
Arc 82.1 Rome, Italy. École Française. Mélanges d'archéologie et d'histoire. Paris. 1-82,1881-1970// 81v.
Arc 82.1.2 Rome, Italy. École Française. Mélanges d'archéologie et d'histoire. Tables des tomes 58-72, 1941-60. Paris, n.d.
Arc 82.1.3 Rome, Italy. École Française. Mélanges. Antiquité. Rome. 83,1971+
Arc 82.1.5 Geffroy, M.A. L'école française de Rome. Paris, 1884.
Arc 82.1.8 Carcopino, Jérome. Souvenirs romains. Paris, 1968.
Arc 82.1.10 Ravaisson-Mollien, F. Lettre à Mollien le directeur de la Revue archéologique. Paris, 1876.
Arc 82.2 Römische Quartalschrift für...Kirch. Rom. 1,1887+ 52v.
Arc 82.2.2 Römische Quartalschrift für...Kirch. Supplementheft. v.1-31. Rom, 1893. 14v.
Arc 82.3 Rome. Escuela Espagnola de Arqueologia é Historia. Cuadernos de trabajos. Madrid. 3-11 6v.
Arc 82.4 Romana tellus. Roma. 1-2,1912-1913
Arc 82.6 Rome. Università. Seminario di Archeologica e Storia dell'Arte Greca e Romana. Studi miscellanei. 1-16 6v.
Arc 83.1 Bulletino di commissione di antichita in Sicilia. Palermo, 1864.
Arc 83.2 Studi di antichita cristiana. Roma. 1,1929+ 30v.
Arc 83.2.10 Sussidi allo studio della antichita cristiane. Roma. 1-4,1936-1954 3v.
Arc 83.3.2 Studia Palmyreńskie. Warszawa. 1,1966+
Arc 83.3.5 Svenska Institutet i Rom. Skrifter. Lund. 2-10 6v.
Arc 83.4 Studies in classical archaeology. Stockholm. 3-5 3v.
Arc 83.5F Studies in Mediterranean archaeology. Lund. 1-20 4v.
Arc 84.5 Tuscia antiqua. Roma. 1,1963+
Arc 85.3 Thessalonikā archaiologikon periodikon dēmosieuma. Bolos. 1-3,1958-1960
Arc 86.1 Vienna. Abhandlungen des archaeologisches-epigrammisches Seminars. Wien. 1-15,1880-1913 5v.
Arc 86.2.2PF Benndorf, O. Vorlegeblätter für archaeologische Uebungen. Wien. 1888-1891 3v.

Arc 87.1-87.1.78 Berlin, Germany. Archäologische Gesellschaft. Programme zu den Winckelmannsfesten.

Arc 87.1 Gerhard, E. Kunstgeschichtliche Vasenbilder. Berlin, 1841.
Arc 87.1.2 Gerhard, E. Phrixos der Herold. Berlin, 1842.
Arc 87.1.3 Gerhard, E. Die Heilung des Telephos. Berlin, 1843-
Arc 87.1.5 Panofka, T.S. Antikenkranz. Berlin, 1845-
Arc 87.1.6 Gerhard, E. Das Orakel der Themis. Berlin, 1846.
Arc 87.1.12 Curtius, E. Herakles der Satyr und Dreifussränber. Berlin, 1852.
Arc 87.1.13 Panofka, T.S. Zur Erklärung der Plinius. Berlin, 1853.
Arc 87.1.14 Gerhard, E. Danae. Berlin, 1854.
Arc 87.1.17 Panofka, T.S. Poseidon Basileus und Athene Sthenias. Berlin, 1857.
Arc 87.1.18 Boetticher, C. Grab des Dionysos. Berlin, 1858.
Arc 87.1.19 Boetticher, C. Omphalos der Zeus zu Delphi. Berlin, 1859.
Arc 87.1.20 Lohde, L. Die Skene der Alten. Berlin, 1860.
Arc 87.1.21 Friederichs, K. Apollon mit den Lamm. Berlin, 1861.
Arc 87.1.24 Boetticher, C. Dirke. Berlin, 1864.
Arc 87.1.25 Jordan, Henri. Vesta und die Laren auf einem pompischen Wandgemälde. Berlin, 1865.
Arc 87.1.26 Huebner, E. Relief eines roemischen Kriegers. Berlin, 1866.
Arc 87.1.28 Huebner, E. Augustus. Berlin, 1868.
Arc 87.1.29 Curtius, E. Die knieenden Figuren der altgriechische Kunst. Berlin, 1870.
Arc 87.1.30 Heydemann, H. Humoristische Vasenbilder. Berlin, 1870.
Arc 87.1.31 Adler, F. Das Pantheon zu Rom. Berlin, 1871.
Arc 87.1.32 Hirschfeld, G. Athena und Marsyas. Berlin, 1872.
Arc 87.1.33 Huebner, E. Bildniss einer Roemerin. Berlin, 1873.
NEDL Arc 87.1.34 Adler, F. Stoa der Koenigs Attalos. Berlin, 1874.

Classified Listing

Arc 65 - 90 Archaeology - Periodicals and Societies - Local - Europe - Classical and Early Christian (A-Z) - cont.

Arc 87.1.35 Tren, G. Grosse Thongefaesse in Statuetten- und Buestenform. Berlin, 1875.
Arc 87.1.36 Trendelenburg, A. Der Musenchor. Berlin, 1876.
Arc 87.1.37 Schillbach, D. Beitrag zur griechischen Gewichtskunde. Berlin, 1877.
Arc 87.1.38 Conze, Alexander. Thesens und Minotauros. Berlin, 1878.
Arc 87.1.39 Robert, C. Thanatos. Berlin, 1879.
Arc 87.1.40 Furtwaengler, A. Der Satyr aus Pergamon. Berlin, 1880.
Arc 87.1.41 Doerpfeld, W. Die Verwendung von Terrakotten. Berlin, 1881.
Arc 87.1.42 Milchhoefer, A. Befreining des Prometheus. Berlin, 1882.
Arc 87.1.43 Furtwaengler, A. Goldfund von Vettersfelde. Berlin, 1883.
Arc 87.1.44 Weil, R. Kuenstlerinschriften der sicilienischen Muenzen. Berlin, 1884.
Arc 87.1.45 Richter, O. Antike Steinmetzzeichen. Berlin, 1885.
Arc 87.1.46 Huelsen, C. Septizonim des Septimius Severus. Berlin, 1886.
Arc 87.1.47 Puchstein, O. Das ionische Capitell. Berlin, 1887.
Arc 87.1.48 Herrmann, P. Graeberfeld von Marion. Berlin, 1888.
Arc 87.1.49 Kekule, R. Bronzestatue des sogenannten Idolino. Berlin, 1889.
Arc 87.1.50 Robert, C. Homerische Becher. Berlin, 1890.
Arc 87.1.51 Koldewery, R. Neandrid. Berlin, 1891.
Arc 87.1.52 Koepp, F. Das Bildnis Alexanders des Grossen. Berlin, 1892.
Arc 87.1.53 Kalkmann, A. Proportionen des Gesichts in der Grosse Kunst. Berlin, 1893.
Arc 87.1.54 Kekule, R. Ueber einen bisher Marcellus genannten Kopf. Berlin, 1894.
Arc 87.1.55 Winter, F. Eine attische Lekythos. Berlin, 1895.
Arc 87.1.56 Pernice, E. Griechisches Pferdegeschirr...Königlichen Museum. Berlin, 1896.
Arc 87.1.57 Kekule, R. Ueber Copien einer Frauenstatue. Berlin, 1897.
Arc 87.1.58 Pernice, E. Hellenistische Silbergefässe...Königlichen Museum. Berlin, 1898.
Arc 87.1.59 Winnefeld, H. Altgriechisches Bronzebecken aus Leontini. Berlin, 1899.
Arc 87.1.60 Schrader, H. Sechziges Program zum Winckelmannsfeste. Berlin, 1900.
Arc 87.1.61 Kekule, R. Über ein Bildnis des Perikles in den Königlichen Museum. Berlin, 1901.
Arc 87.1.62 Brueckner, A. Lebensregeln auf Athens. Hochzeitsgeschenken. Berlin, 1907.
Arc 87.1.63 Watzinger, C. Das Relief des Archelaos von Priene. Berlin, 1903.
Arc 87.1.64 Brueckner, A. Anakabypteria. Berlin, 1904.
Arc 87.1.65 Kekule, R. Echelos und Basile. Berlin, 1905.
Arc 87.1.67 Schröder, Bruno. Die Victoria von Calvatone. Berlin, 1907.
Arc 87.1.69 Kekule, R. Bronzes. Berlin, 1909.
Arc 87.1.70 Trendelenburg, A. Phantasiai. Berlin, 1910.
Arc 87.1.71 Gaertringen, F.H. Hira und Andania...zum Winckelmannsfeste. Berlin, 1911.
Arc 87.1.72 Frickenhaus, A. Lenäenvasen. Berlin, 1912.
Arc 87.1.73 Wiegand, Theodore. Bronzefigur einer Spinnerin. Berlin, 1913.
Arc 87.1.74 Schröder, Bruno. Griechische Bronzeeimer im berlinen Antiquarium. Berlin, 1914.
Arc 87.1.75 Scenika 75. Programm zum Winckelmannsfeste der Achäologischen Gesellschaft zu Berlin. Berlin, 1915.
Arc 87.1.76 Rodenwaldt, Gerhart. Griechische Porträts aus dem Ausgang der Antike. Berlin, 1919.
Arc 87.1.78 Archäologische Gesellschaft zu Berlin. Winckelmannsprogramm. Berlin. 77,1921+ 29v.

Arc 87.2.45-87.2.88 Rhine (Province). Verein von Alterthumsfreunden. Winckelmanns Programme.

Arc 87.2.45 Lersch, J.H.L. Das coelner Mosaik. Bonn, 1846.
Arc 87.2.46 Urlichs, K.L. Dreizehn Gemmen. Bonn, 1846.
Arc 87.2.48 Lersch, J.H.L. Schwert des Giberins. Bonn, 1849.
Arc 87.2.49 Braun, J.W.J. Die Kapitole. Bonn, 1849-
Arc 87.2.51 Overbeck, J.A. Roemische Villa bei Weingarten. Bonn, 1851.
Arc 87.2.61 Weerth, E. Bad der roemische Villa bei Allenz. Bonn, 1861-1870.
Arc 87.2.62 Frendenberg, J. Denkmal der Hercules Saxanus. Bonn, 1862.
Arc 87.2.63 Fiedler, F. Gripswalder Matronen- und Mereurius-Statuen. Bonn, 1863.
Arc 87.2.67 Urlichs, L. Die Gruppe des Pasquino. Bonn, 1867.
Arc 87.2.68 Wieseler, F. Hildesheimer Silberfund. Bonn, 1868.
Arc 87.2.69 Peters, F. Burg-Kapelle zu Iben. Bonn, 1869.
Arc 87.2.71 Keller, O. Vicus Aurelii. Bonn, 1871.
Arc 87.2.74 Gaedechens, R. Medusenhaupt von Blariacum. Bonn, 1874.
Arc 87.2.75 Aldenkirchen, J. Mittelalterliche Kunst in Soest. Bonn, 1875.
Arc 87.2.85 Veith, C. Das roemische Koeln. Bonn, 1885.
Arc 87.2.88 Roemische Lager in Bonn. Bonn, 1888.

Arc 87.3 Hallische Winckelmanns Programme

Arc 87.3 Hallisches Winckelmann's Program. Halle. 1-28 4v.
Arc 87.3F Hallisches Winckelmann's Program. Halle. 15,1891

Arc 93 Archaeology - Periodicals and Societies - Local - Europe - Italy

Arc 93.1 Ausonia; rivista della Società italiana di archeologia. Roma. 1-10 6v.
Arc 93.3 Societa Reale di Napoli. Memorie della Reale Academia. Napoli. 1-6,1911-1942 4v.
Arc 93.4 Macchioro, V. Neapolis, revista di archeologia, epigrafia e numio. Napoli. 1-2,1913-1915 2v.
Arc 93.5F Italy. Ministero delle Colonie. Notizie archeologico. Roma. 1-3,1916-1922 3v.
Arc 93.7 Società Piemontese di Archeologia e Belle Arti. Atti. Torino. 1875-1958 15v.
Arc 93.15 Accademia Etrusca, Cortona. Saggi di dissertazioni accademiche. Roma. 1-9,1742-1791 9v.
Arc 93.16 Neppi Modona, Aldo. I fasti dell'Accademia Etrusca di Cortona. Cortona, 1928.
Arc 93.18 Associazione Archeologica Romana. Bullettino. Roma. 1-7,1911-1917 3v.
Arc 93.21 L'Italia antichissima. Reggio. 1-12,1929-1938
Arc 93.24 Rivista archeologica della provincia e antica diocesi di Como. Como. 59,1910+ 19v.
Arc 93.24.3 Rivista archeologica della provincia e antica diocesi di Como. Indice generale, 85-139, 1923-1957. Como, 1934-1958. 2v.

Arc 93 Archaeology - Periodicals and Societies - Local - Europe - Italy - cont.

Arc 93.25 Italy. Ministero dell'Istruzione Pubblica. L'amministrazione delle antichità e belle arti in Italia. Roma, 1902.
Arc 93.25F Italy. Direzione generale della antichità e belle arti. Sull'ordinamento del servizio archeologico. Roma, 1885.
Arc 93.27 International Mediterranean Research Association. The International Mediterranean Research Association of Rome, Villa Celeniontana. Roma, 1930.
Arc 93.28F Istituto di Archeologia e Storia dell'Arte. Rivista. Roma. 1,1929+ 22v.
Arc 93.29 Collezione di monografie preistoriche ed archeologicho. Bordighera. 1-2,1946-1956 2v.
Arc 93.30 Accademia...Naples. Accademia dell'Archeologia, Lettere e Belle Arti. Memorie. Napoli. 1,1951+ 3v.
Arc 93.32F Scavi de ostia. Roma. 1,1953+ 8v.
Arc 93.35 Milan. Università. Istituto di Archeologia. Tesi dl laurear. Roma. 1-2
Arc 93.36F Studi d'archeologia e d'arte. Milano. 1,1939
Arc 93.37F Società di Storia Patria per la Sicilia Orientale, Catania. Monografie archeologiche della Sicilia. Series 3. 1,1956
Arc 93.38F Convegno Archeologico in Sardegna. Il Convegno archeologico en Sardegna. 2. ed. Reggio nell'Emilia, 1929.
Arc 93.40 Istituto di Studi Etruschi e Italici. Quaderni di studi etruschi. Serie 1: Ricerche preistoriche in Etruria. Firenze.
Arc 93.42 Sikelika. Palermo. 2-5 5v.
Arc 93.44F Monumenti etruschi. Firenze. 1,1967+ 3v.
Arc 93.46F Centro Studi e Documentazione sull'Italia Romana. Atti. Milano. 1,1967+ 6v.
Arc 93.46.3 Centro Studi e Documentazione sull'Italia Romana. Monografie a supplemento degli Atti. Milano. 1,1972+ 5v.
Arc 93.48 Dissertazioni di etruscologia e antichità italiche. Firenze. 1,1972+
Arc 93.50F Epigrafia e antichità. Faenza. 1,1969+
Arc 93.52 Topografia e storia delle ricerche archeologiche in Orvieto e nel suo contado. Roma. 1,1972+
Arc 93.54 Archeologia medievale. Firenze. 1,1974+

Arc 94 Archaeology - Periodicals and Societies - Local - Europe - Spain and Portugal

Arc 94.1 Institut d'Estudis Catalans. Anuari. Barcelona. 1907-1931 11v.
Arc 94.5 Spain. Junta Superior de Excavaciones y Antiguedades. Memoria. Madrid, 1915-1926. 7v.
Arc 94.7 Sociedad Arqueologica de Carmona. Memorias de la sociedad arqueologica de Carmona. Carmona, 1887. 9v.
Arc 94.10 Asociación Artistico-Arqueológica Barcelona. Revista. Barcelona. 1-5,1896-1908 5v.
Arc 94.11 Asociación Artistico-Arqueológica Barcelona. Boletin. Barcelona. 1-35,1891-1894
Arc 94.15 Sociedad Cordobesa de Arqueología y Excursiones. Boletín. Córdoba. 1928
Arc 94.17 Hispania antiqua epigraphica. Madrid. 1-5,1950-1954
Arc 94.18 Archivo español de arqueología. Madrid. 14,1940+ 18v.
Arc 94.20 Ampurias. Barcelona. 3,1941+ 14v.
Arc 94.25 Orense, Spain. Museo Arqueológico Provincial. Boletin. 1-4,1943-1948 2v.
Arc 94.30 Congreso Arqueológico del Sudeste Español. Cronica. Cartageno.
Arc 94.32 Estudios ibéricos. Valencia. 1-4,1953-1956
Arc 94.35 Institucione Fennando el Catolico Seminario de Arqueología y Numismatico Aragonesas. Publicaciones. Zaragoza. 1,1951+ 6v.
Arc 94.40F Acta arqueologica hispanica. Madrid. 1-5,1943-1950 3v.
Arc 94.43 Boletin arqueologico. Tarragona. 1,1921+ 12v.
Arc 94.45 Los monumentos arqueologicos y tesoro artistico de Tarragona y su provincia. 1936-1939
Arc 94.47 Zephyrus. Salamanca. 1,1950+ 15v.
Arc 94.50 Associação dos Arqueologos Portugueses. Trabalhos. Lisboa. 1-6,1934-1942 6v.
Arc 94.52 Sociedad Arqueológica Tarraconense. Premio "Cronista José Pujol". Tarragona. 2,1953
Arc 94.54F Bibliotheca praehistorica Hispana. Madrid. 1,1958+ 12v.
Arc 94.56 Madrider Mitteilungen. Heidelberg. 1,1960+ 14v.
Arc 94.58 Madrid, Spain. Casa de Velasquez. Publications de la Casa de Velasquez. Série archéologie. Paris. 1,1973+

Arc 95 - 120 Archaeology - Periodicals and Societies - Local - Europe - France (A-Z)

Arc 95.1 Mémoires de l'Académie Celtique. Paris. 1-5,1807-1810 5v.
Arc 95.2 Pro Alesia. Paris. 1-20,1906-1932 10v.
Arc 95.3 Arethuse. Paris. 1-8,1923-1931 5v.
Arc 95.3.10 Supplément commercial de la revue "Arethuse.". 2v.
Arc 95.4 Cahiers alsaciens d'archéologie, d'art et d'histoire. Strasbourg. 1,1957+
Arc 96.1 Bulletin archéologique. Paris. 1-4,1843-1848 4v.
Arc 96.1.2 Bulletin du Comité Historique-Archéologie. Paris. 1-4,1849-1853 2v.
Arc 97.3 La controverse de Glozel. Paris.
Arc 97.4 Cahien d'archéologie du Nord-Est. Laon. 1-8,1958-1965 3v.
Arc 97.5 Centre d'Études Gallo-Romaines. Publications. Villeurbanne. 1,1968+
Arc 97.6 Chantiers d'études médiévales. Strasbourg. 2,1966+
Arc 100.1 Société Nationale des Antiquaires de France. Mémoires. Paris. 1-9 86v.
Arc 100.1.6 Société Nationale des Antiquaires de France. Centenaire 1804-1904. Recueil de mémoires. Paris, 1904.
Arc 100.1.7 Société Nationale des Antiquaires de France. Centenaire (1804-1904). Compte-rendu de la journée du 11 avril 1904. Paris, 1904.
Arc 100.1.8 Société Nationale des Antiquaires de France. Bulletin. 1901+ 36v.
Arc 100.1.10 Société Nationale des Antiquaires de France. Annuaire. Paris. 1848-1855 4v.
Arc 100.1.12 Pamphlet box. Société Nationale des Antiquaires de France.
Arc 100.1.25 Prow, M. Table alphabétique...l'Académie Celtique...Antiquaires de France. Paris, 1894. 2v.
Arc 100.5 France. Comité des Travaux Historiques et Scientifiques. Section d'Archéologie. Actes du Congrès national des sociétés savantes. 85,1960+
Arc 100.10 Les fouilles de Mariana. Bastia. 1,1971+

Arc 95 - 120 Archaeology - Periodicals and Societies - Local - Europe - France (A-Z) - cont.

Arc 101.5 Société d'Histoire et d'Archéologie de Nimes et du Gard. Bulletin. Nimes. 1933-1939
Arc 101.10 Société d'Histoire, d'Archéologie et de Tradition Gauloises. Gaule. Paris. 2-24,1956-1963 2v.
Arc 101.11 Société d'Histoire, d'Archéologie et de Tradition Gauloises. Centre de documentation. Circulaire d'information. Paris. 1,1964+
Arc 101.13 Revue archéologique de Narbonnaise. Paris. 1,1968+ 2v.
Arc 103.1 Institut des Fouilles de Préhistoire et d'Archéologie des Alpes, Mautimes. Bulletin et memoires. Nice. 2-7 4v.
Arc 103.5 Journées Archéologiques d'Avignon, Avignon, 1956. Journées archéologiques d'Avignon. Avignon, 1957.
Arc 104.5 Journées Archéologiques Internationales. Communications. Paris. 1,1964+
Arc 110.1 Tro Nervia. Avesnes. 1-5,1923-1929
Arc 112.3 Revue des musées et collections archéologiques. Dijon. 1-6,1925-1931 2v.
Arc 112.5 Revue archéologique de l'est et du centre-est. Dijon. 1,1950+ 13v.
Arc 112.5.5 Revue archéologique de l'est et du centre-est. Tables décennales, v.1-10, 1950-1959. Dijon, 1960.
Arc 112.10 Etudes Roussillonnaises. Perpignan. 1-5,1951-1956 6v.
Arc 113.1 Société Française pour la Conservation des Monuments Historiques, Séances tennes en 1839. Caen, 1839.
Arc 113.2 France. Mémoires lus à la Sorbonne. Archéologie, 1861, 63-68. Paris, 1863-69. 7v.
Arc 113.2.5 Chabouillet. Discours et compte rendu des lectures...section d'archéologie. Réunion annuelle des délégués de société savantes à la Sorbonne. Paris, 1878-81. 3v.
Arc 113.3 France. Mémoires de la Société archéologique du midi de la France. Toulouse. 1-24 21v.
Arc 113.3.5 France. Mémoires de la Société archéologique du midi de la France. Tables générales. Toulouse. 1831-1871
Arc 113.3.7 France. Memoires de la Société archéologique du midi de la France. Tables générales. 1.-2. séries. Toulouse.
Arc 113.3.20 Société Archéologique du Midi de la France. Bulletin. Toulouse. 1869-1945 19v.
Arc 113.5 Société d'Archéologie de Saint-Jean-d'Angély et de sa Région. Bulletin. Saint-Jean-d'Angély. 2,1924+
Arc 113.10 Septentrion. Calais. 1,1969+
Arc 116.5 Bulletin archéologique du Vexin français. Guiry-en-Vexin. 2,1966+

Arc 125 - 150 Archaeology - Periodicals and Societies - Local - Europe - Great Britain (A-Z)

Arc 125.01 Pamphlet box. Archaeology. Great Britain.
NEDL Arc 125.1 The antiquary. London. 1-51 51v.
Arc 125.4 British Archaeological Association. Archaeological journal. London. 1+ 119v.
Arc 125.4.2 British Archaeological Association. Archaeological journal. General index, v.26-75 (1869-1918). London, 1955-73. 2v.
Arc 125.4.3 British Archaeological Association. Journal. London. 1+ 96v.
Arc 125.4.5 British Archaeological Association. Transactions at its 2nd Congress, 1845. London, 1846.
Arc 125.4.8 British Archaeological Association. Communications made to the association. London, 1862. 2v.
Arc 125.4.10 Pamphlet box. British Archaeological Association.
Arc 125.5 Archaeological Institute of Great Britain. Proceedings. London. 1845
Arc 125.5.2 Archaeological Institute of Great Britain. Proceedings. London. 1846
Arc 125.5.3 Archaeological Institute of Great Britain. Proceedings. London. 1847
NEDL Arc 125.5.4 Archaeological Institute of Great Britain. Proceedings. London. 1848
Arc 125.5.5 Archaeological Institute of Great Britain. Proceedings. London. 1849
X Cg Arc 125.5.6 Archaeological Institute of Great Britain. Proceedings. London. 1850
Arc 125.5.7 Archaeological Institute of Great Britain. Proceedings. London. 1851
Arc 125.5.8 Archaeological Institute of Great Britain. Proceedings. London. 1852 2v.
Arc 125.5.9 Archaeological Institute of Great Britain. Proceedings. London.
Arc 125.6 Liverpool. University. Institute of Archaeology. Annals of archaeology and anthropology. Liverpool. 1-28,1908-1948 21v.
Arc 125.8 Ancient Monuments Society. Year book. Manchester. 1926
Arc 125.8.5 Ancient Monuments Society. Transactions. London. 1,1953+ 20v.
Arc 125.9 Antiquarian Association of the British Isles. Journal. London. 1-3,1930-1932
Arc 125.10 The archaeological news letter. London. 1-7,1948-1965// 2v.
Arc 125.12 Architectural and Archaeological Society of Durham and Northumberland. Transactions. Gateshead on Tyne. 1-10,1862-1953 9v.
Arc 126.5 Bedfordshire archaeological journal. Luton, England.
Arc 127.3 Congress of Archaeological Societies in Union with the Society of Antiquaries. Report of the committee on ancient earthworks. London? 1905-1920
Arc 127.3.2 Congress of Archaeological Societies in Union with the Society of Antiquaries. Report of proceedings. London. 1901-1913
Arc 127.3.4 Congress of Archaeological Societies in Union with the Society of Antiquaries. Report of the earthworks committee. 1921-1939
Arc 127.3.10 Pamphlet box. Congress of Archaeological Societies.
Arc 127.5 Council for British Archaeology. London.
Arc 127.6 Archaeological bulletin for Great Britain and Ireland. 1940+ 7v.
Arc 127.7 Cornish archaeology. St. Austell. 1,1962+ 2v.
Arc 128.5 Derwent Archaeological Society. Research report. Matlock, Derbyshire, Eng. 1,1973+
Arc 128.10 Discovery and excavation in Scotland. Edinburgh. 1974+
Arc 131.1 Moore, William. The Gentlemen's Society at Spalding. Cambridge, 1909. 2 pam.
Arc 131.2 Group for the Study of Irish Historic Settlement. Bulletin. Belfast, Ire.? 1,1970+
Arc 131.3 Glasgow archaeological journal. Glasgow. 1,1969+

Arc 125 - 150 Archaeology - Periodicals and Societies - Local - Europe - Great Britain (A-Z) - cont.

Arc 131.4 Great Britain. Department of the Environment. Archaeological excavations. London. 1973+
Arc 132.5 Hastings area archaeological papers. Robertsbridge. 1,1973+
Arc 135.5 Kent Archaeological Research Groups' Council. Research report. Bromley. 1,1968+ 2v.
Arc 136.1 London Society of Antiquaries. Archaeologia. London. 1-104 123v.
X Cg Arc 136.1 London Society of Antiquaries. Archaeologia. London. 41-60
Arc 136.1.1 London Society of Antiquaries. Archaeologia. Table of contents. London. 1-88,1804-1938
Arc 136.1.2 London Society of Antiquaries. Index to Archaeologia. v.1-30. London, 1809-44. 2v.
Arc 136.1.3 London Society of Antiquaries. Index to Archaeologia. v.1-50. London, 1889.
Arc 136.1.4 London Society of Antiquaries. Index to Archaeologia. v.51-100 (1888-1966). London, 1970.
Arc 136.1.6 Society of Noviomagus. Momentores minutes of the meeting. London, 1845.
Arc 136.1.10 London Society of Antiquaries. Archaeologia. 2. ed., 3. ed. London. 1773-1809 2v.
Arc 136.1.11 London Society of Antiquaries. Review of Archaeologia. London, 1881.
Arc 136.1.50 London Society of Antiquaries. A copy of the royal charter and statutes. London, 1800.
Arc 136.1.60 Fenn, John. Three...tables...exhibiting a state of...Society of Antiquaries. London, 1784. 2 pam.
Arc 136.1.63 King, Edward. A speech...23rd April 1784. London, 1784.
Arc 136.1.75 Pamphlet box. London Society of Antiquaries.
Arc 136.1.80 Evans, Joan. A history of the Society of Antiquaries. Oxford, 1956.
NEDL Arc 136.2 London Society of Antiquaries. Proceedings. London. 1-32,1843-1920 34v.
NEDL Arc 136.2.3 Index Society. Index to engravings in proceedings of Society of Antiquaries. London, 1885.
Arc 136.2.5 The antiquaries journal. London. 1,1921+ 46v.
Arc 136.2.5.3 Antiquaries journal. General index. v.1-10. London, 1934.
NEDL Arc 136.2.15 London Society of Antiquaries. Index. v.1-20. 2d series. London, 1908.
Arc 136.4 London Society of Antiquaries. Report for 1909-1911. Old Sarum Excavation fund. Oxford, 1912.
Arc 136.4.5 Excavation Committee. Report for 1909. Oxford, 1910.
Arc 136.5 London Society of Antiquaries. Report of research committee. Oxford. 1-30 26v.
Arc 136.9 London and Middlesex Archaeological Society. Transactions. London. 1,1860+ 25v.
Arc 136.9.5 Pamphlet box. London and Middlesex Archaeological Society. 2 pam.
Arc 136.9.6 London and Middlesex Archaeological Society. Report of the council.
Arc 136.10 London. University. Institute of Archaeology. Annual report. London.
Arc 137.5 Mediaeval archaeology. London. 1,1957+ 9v.
Arc 137.6 Mediaeval archaeology. Index. v.1-5, (1957-61). London, n.d.
Arc 138.2 National ancient monuments yearbook. London. 1,1927
Arc 138.3F North Munster antiquarian journal. Limerick. 1-2,1936-1941
Arc 138.3 North Munster antiquarian journal. Limerick. 3,1942+ 3v.
Arc 138.10 North Munster Archaeologcial Society. Index to journal 1897-1919. Nenagh, 1958.
Arc 140.1 Prehistoric Society of East Anglia. Proceedings. London. 1,1908+ 40v.
Arc 140.1.10 Prehistoric Society of East Anglia. Minor publications. n.p., n.d.
Arc 140.1.20 Prehistoric Society of East Anglia. Occasional paper. Bayswater. 1,1929 2v.
Arc 140.5 Post-medieval archaeology. London. 1,1967+ 3v.
Arc 140.5.2 Post-medieval archaeology. Index. v.1-5 (1967-71). London, 1973.
NEDL Arc 142.2 Allen, J.R. The reliquary...archaeological journal. London. 1860-1909 49v.
Arc 142.10 Revue archeologique du centre. Vichy. 1,1962+ 6v.
NEDL Arc 143.1 Society of Antiquaries of Scotland. Proceedings. Edinburgh. 1-63,1851-1929
Arc 143.1 Society of Antiquaries of Scotland. Proceedings. Edinburgh. 64,1929+ 32v.
Arc 143.1.5 Society of Antiquaries of Scotland. Proceedings. Index. v.25-81. Edinburgh, 1897-1968. 2v.
Arc 143.1.10 Pamphlet box. Society of Antiquaries of Scotland.
Arc 143.2 Society of Antiquaries of Scotland. Archaeologia Scotica. Edinburgh, 1792- 5v.
Arc 143.2.5 Society of Antiquaries of Scotland. Account of the institution and progress of the society. Edinburgh. 2,1784
Arc 143.3 Scottish archaeological studies. Aberdeen. 1-2,1922-1936
Arc 143.6 Surrey Archaeological Society. Research papers. Guildford. 5
Arc 143.7 Somersetshire, England. Museum. Publication. 2v.
Arc 143.8 Surrey Archaeological Society. Research volume. Castle Arch. 1,1974+
Arc 147.5 Worcestershire archaeology newsletter. Worcester. 1,1967+
Arc 149.5 East Riding archaeologist. Hull, Eng. 1,1968+

Arc 155 - 180 Archaeology - Periodicals and Societies - Local - Europe - Switzerland (A-Z)

Arc 155.1 Anzeiger für Schweizerische Altertumskunde. Zürich. 1-40,1872-1938 28v.
Arc 155.5 Archaeologische Führer der Schweiz. Zürich. 1,1969+
Arc 155.10 Ausgrabungen in Augst. Basel. 2-4,1962-1974
Arc 155.11 Forschungen in Augst. Basel. 2,1975+
Arc 156.1.5 Gesellschaft für Vaterländische Alterthümer in Basel. Mittheilungen. Basel. 1-10,1843-1867
Arc 159.5 Eburodunum. Yverdon. 2,1975+
Arc 162.5 Helvetia archaeologica; Mittheilungsblatt der schweizerischen Gesellschaft für Ur- und Frühgeschichte. Basel. 1,1970+
Arc 173.1 Schweizerische Gesellschaft für Urgeschichte, Zürich. Jahresbericht. Zürich. 1,1909+ 23v.
Arc 173.5 Schweizer Beiträge zur Kulturgeschichte und Archäologie des Mittelalters. Olten. 1,1974+
Arc 175.1 Ur-Schweiz. Basil. 10-33,1946-1969 7v.
NEDL Arc 180.1 Zürich. Antiquarische Gesellschaft. Mittheilungen der Antiquarischen Gesellschaft. Zürich. 1-30,1841-1931

Classified Listing

Arc 155 - 180 Archaeology - Periodicals and Societies - Local - Europe - Switzerland (A-Z) - cont.

Arc 180.1 Zürich. Antiquarische Gesellschaft. Mittheilungen der Antiquarischen Gesellschaft. Zürich. 31-43 26v.
NEDL Arc 180.1.2 Zürich. Antiquarische Gesellschaft. Denkschrift zu fuenfzigjaehrigen Stiftungsfeier. Zürich, 1882?
Arc 180.1.25 Largiader, Anton. Hundert Jahre Antiquarische Gesellschaft in Zürich, 1832-1932. Zürich, 1932.
Arc 180.1.501 Antiquarische Gesellschaft in Zürich-Bibliothek. Liederchronik der Antiquarischen Gesellschaft in Zürich. Frauenfeld, 1880.
Arc 180.2F Zeitschrift für schweizerische Archaeologie und Kunstgeschichte. Basel. 1,1939+ 24v.

Arc 185 - 210 Archaeology - Periodicals and Societies - Local - Europe - Germany (A-Z)

Arc 185.1 Anzeiger für Kunde des deutschen Mittelalters. Nürnberg. 1-8,1832-1839 6v.
Arc 185.1.2 Anzeiger für Kunde des deutschen Mittelalters. Nürnberg. 1-30,1853-1883 15v.
Arc 185.2 Altschlesien. Breslau. 1-8,1922-1939 8v.
Arc 185.2.5 Slaskie sprawozdania archeologiczne. Wrocław. 6,1963+
Arc 185.3 Altpreussen. Königsburg. 1-8,1935-1943 3v.
Arc 185.4 Archaeologische für Pilzkunde. Frankfurt. 1-2
Arc 185.5 Ausgrabungen in Berlin; Forschungen und Funde zür Ur- und Frühgeschichte. Berlin. 1,1970+
Arc 186.1 Suchs, H. Schlesiens Vorzeit in Bild und Schrift. Breslau. 1-6,1870-1912 13v.
Arc 186.5 Berliner Blatter für Vor- und Frühgeschichte. Berlin. 1-12,1952-1972// 5v.
Arc 186.10 Beitraage zur Oberpfalzforschung. Kallmünz. 1,1965+
Arc 188.1F Die Denkmalpflegen. Berlin. 1899-1922
Arc 188.1 Die Denkmalpflegen. Berlin. 1923+ 37v.
Arc 188.1.5F Die Denkmalpflege. Inhattsverzeichnis der Jahrg, 1899-1913. Berlin, 1914.
Arc 188.2 Deutschen Orient Gesellschaft. Sendschriften. Leipzig. 1-6,1901-1938 7v.
Arc 188.5 Darmstadt, Germany. Amt für Badenlenkmalpflege im Regierungsbezirk. Inventar der Bodendenkmäler. 1,1959+
Arc 190.5 Fuehrer zu Vor- und Frühgeschichten Denkmälern. Mainz am Rhein. 2,1965+ 16v.
Arc 190.7 Fuehrer zu archäologischen Denkmalen in Bayern. Bayern. 1,1971+
Arc 190.10 Forschungen und Berichte zür Vor- und Frühgeschichte in Baden-Württemberg. Stuttgart. 1,1972+ 8v.
Arc 190.11 Forschungen und Berichte der Archäologie des Mittelalters in Baden-Württemberg. Stuttgart. 1,1972+ 4v.
Arc 191.2 Gesellschaft für Österreichische Frühmittelalterforschung. Veröffentlichungen. Linz.
Arc 193.1 Idunna und Hermode. Breslan. 1812-1816 2v.
Arc 194.1 Jahresschrift für die Vorgeschichte der sächsisch-thüringischen Länder. Halle. 1,1902+ 39v.
Arc 194.1.2 Jahresschrift für die Vorgeschichte der sächsisch-thüringischen Länder. Register. v.1-32, 1954. Halle, n.d.
Arc 195.3F Kiel. Universität. Schleswig-Holsteinisches Museum Vorgeschichtlicher Altertümer. Vor- und frühgeschichtliche Untersuchungen. Neumünster. 1,1933+ 27v.
Arc 195.5 Kurhessische Bodenaltertümer. Marburg. 1-4,1951-1964// 2v.
Arc 196.1 Limesblatt, 1892-1903. Trien, 1892.
Arc 196.2 Schoenenberg, J. Festschrift zum 50 Jährigen Jubiläum des Lahnsteiner Altertumsvereins. Oberlahnstein, 1930.
Arc 197.2F Münchner Beiträge zur Vor- und Frühgeschichte. München. 1,1950+ 18v.
Arc 197.2.5F Münchner Beiträge zur Vor- und Frühgeschichte. Ergänzungsband. München. 1,1974+ 2v.
Arc 198.5 Nachrichten zur Niedersachsens Urgeschichte. Hildesheim. 38,1969+ 8v.
Arc 201.5 Quellenschriften zür westdeutschen Vor- und Frühgeschichte. Bonn. 1,1939+ 3v.
Arc 202.5 Rheinische Ausgrabungen. Düsseldorf. 3,1968+ 14v.
Arc 203.5 Stendal, Germany. Altmarkisches Museum. Jahresgabe. 2v.
Arc 204.5 Treves. Rheinisches Landesmuseum. Führungsblätter.
Arc 205.2F Urkunden zur Vor- und Frühgeschichte aus Hohenzolleen. Stuttgart. 1-4 4v.
Arc 206.2 Vorzeit am Bodensee; Mitteilungen zur Vor- und Frühgeschichte und Heimatkunde des Bodenseeraumes. Überlingen. 1952-1963 2v.
Arc 206.4F Die vor- und frühgeschichtlichen Denkmäler und Funde im Gebiet der Deutschen Demokratischen Republik. Schwerin. 1-3 3v.
Arc 206.6 Verein für Geschichte und Altertumskunde Westfalens. Altertums-Kommission. Mitteilungen. Münster. 1-7,1899-1922// 4v.
Arc 207.5 Wegweiser zur Vor- und Frühgeschichte Niedersachsens. Hildesheim. 1,1971+
Arc 210.5 Zeitschrift zür Geschichte und Auslegung der alten Kunst. Göttingen. 1,1817

Arc 215 - 240 Archaeology - Periodicals and Societies - Local - Europe - Austria and Hungary (A-Z)

Arc 215.5 Archaeologische Forschungen in Tirol. Innsbruck. 1-2
Arc 215.10 Antiquitas hungarica. Budapest. 1947-1949
Arc 217.5 Carnuntum Jahrbuch. Wien. 1955-1960 2v.
Arc 220.5 Fundberichte aus Österreich. Wien. 1-5,1930-1952
Arc 220.10F Folia archaeologica. Budapest. 1-5,1939-1945// 10v.
Arc 220.10 Folia archaeologica. Budapest. 6,1954+ 15v.
Arc 224.5 Judenburger Museumsschriften. Judenburg.
Arc 225.1 Cluj, Rumania. Erdelye nemzeti. Dolgozatok. Erem-es régiségtárából. Kolozsvár. 2-7,1911-1916 3v.
Arc 225.1.5 Erdélyi Múzeum-Egyesület, Cluj. Emlékkünyv az Erdélyi Muzeum-Egyesületjélszázados ünnepére, 1859-1909. Kolozsvár, 1942.
Arc 225.3F Acta archeologica. Budapest. 1,1951+ 21v.
Arc 225.10 Budapest. Tudomany Egyetem-Régészeti Intézet. Régészeti dolgozatok. 3,1959+ 4v.
Arc 225.15 Studia archaeologica. Budapest. 1,1963+ 5v.
Arc 225.20 Szeged, Hungary. Móra Ferenc Múzeum. Kiadványok. 3v.
Arc 225.20F Szeged, Hungary. Móra Ferenc Múzeum. Kiadványok. 2
Arc 225.30 A Magyar régészet kézikönyve. Budapest. 1,1965+
Arc 225.35 Régészeti füzetek. Series 2. Budapest. 1-13,1958-1964 5v.
Arc 226.2 Orsjágos Magyar Régészeti Jársulat. Evkönyve. Budapest. 1-2,1920-1926

Arc 215 - 240 Archaeology - Periodicals and Societies - Local - Europe - Austria and Hungary (A-Z) - cont.

Arc 227.2 Archaeologiai értesito. 1882-1938 43v.
Arc 227.4 Magyarország régészeti topografiája. Budapest. 1,1966+ 4v.
Arc 227.10 Budapest régiségei; régészeti es történeti évkönyv. Budapest. 1-18,1889-1959 14v.
Arc 232.2 Römisches Österreich. Wien. 1,1973+
Arc 235.5 Linzer archäologische Forschungen. Linz. 1,1962+
Arc 235.6 Linzer archäologische Forschungen. Sonderheft. Linz. 1,1964+

Arc 245 - 270 Archaeology - Periodicals and Societies - Local - Europe - Scandinavia (A-Z)

Arc 245.2 Acta archaeologica. København. 1,1930+ 34v.
Arc 247.4 Nordiske Oldskrift-Selskab. Mémoires de la Société Royale des Antiquaires du Nord. Copenhagen. 1836-1933 15v.
Arc 247.4.2 Copenhagen. Mémoires de la Société Royale des Antiquaires du Nord (1840-44). Copenhagen, n.d.
Arc 247.4.3 Pamphlet box. Nordiske oldskrift selskab.
Arc 247.15 Pamphlet vol. Royal Society. Northern Antiquaries, Copenhagen.
Arc 248.3F Danske Oldsager. 1-4 2v.
Arc 265.1 Upsala. Universitet. Museum för Nordiska Fornsaker. Acta Musei antiquitatum septrionalium. Uppsala. 1-3,1942-1945 3v.

Arc 273 Archaeology - Periodicals and Societies - Local - Europe - Low Countries

Arc 273.1 Académie Royale d'Archéologie de Belgique. Bulletin. Anvers. 1863-1929 18v.
Arc 273.2 Académie Royale d'Archéologie de Belgique. Annales. Anvers. 1-77 69v.
Arc 273.2.3F Académie Royale d'Archéologie de Belgique. Annales. Anvers. 1-3,1843-1900 2v.
Arc 273.2.5 Académie Royale d'Archéologie de Belgique. Table des publications de l'Académie Royale d'Archéologie de Belgique, 1843 à 1900. Anvers? n.d.
Arc 273.2.10 Académie Royale d'Archéologie de Belgique. Minor publications.
Arc 273.2.15F Leyden. Rigksmuseum van Oudheden. Oudheidkundige mededeelingen. 29-50 17v.
Arc 273.2.25 Revue belge d'archéologie et d'histoire de l'art. Bruxelles. 1,1931+ 24v.
Arc 273.6 Belgium. Federation archéologique et historique. Annales. Anvers. 16-35 12v.
Arc 273.8 Vereeniging tot Bevordering der Kennis van de Antieke Beschaving. Bulletin. 's Gravenhage. 1,1926+
Arc 273.9 Vereeniging tot Bevordering der Kennis van de Antieke Beschaving. Bulletin. Index, v.1-40, 1926-1965. Leiden, n.d.
Arc 273.9.3 Bulletin antieke beschaving. Supplement. Leiden. 1,1975+
Arc 273.10 Société Royale d'Archéologie de Bruxelles. Annales. Bruxelles. 1-50,1887-1961 38v.
Arc 273.10.5 Société Royale d'Archéologie de Bruxelles. Annuaire. Bruxelles. 16-26,1905-1925 5v.
Arc 273.10.8 Société Royale d'Archéologie de Bruxelles. Tables des publications. Bruxelles. 1887-1911
Arc 273.10.12 Société Royale d'Archéologie de Bruxelles. Bulletin. Bruxelles.
Arc 273.12 Archaeolgica traiectina. Groningen. 1-6 3v.
Arc 273.14 Helinium. Wettern. 1,1961+ 8v.
Arc 273.16 Centre National de Recherches Archéologiques en Belgique. Série A: Répertoires archéologigues. Brussel. 1,1960+ 4v.
Arc 273.16.3 Centre National de Recherches Archéologiques en Belgique. Série B: Collections. Bruxelles. 1,1965+
Arc 273.16.5 Centre National de Recherches Archéologiques en Belgique. Série C: Répertoires divers. Brussel. 1,1964+ 2v.
Arc 273.18 Tongres, Belgium. Musée Provincial Gallo-Romains. Publicaties. 1,1964+
Arc 273.20 Archeologische monumenten in Nederland. Bussum. 1,1971+

Arc 275 - 300 Archaeology - Periodicals and Societies - Local - Europe - Russia (A-Z)

Arc 275.10F Arkheologicheskii s"ezd. Trud'y. 1869-1911 28v.
Arc 275.16 Arkheologicheskii s"ezd, 8th, Moscow, 1890. Katalog vystavki VIII Arkheologicheskago s"ezda v Moskve, 1890 g. Pt.1-10. Moskva, 1890.
Arc 275.17 Arkheologicheskii s"ezd, 16th, Pskov, 1915. Katalog vystaki. Pskov, 1915.
Arc 275.20 Pamphlet box. Arkheologicheskii s"ezd. Russian archeological congresses.
Arc 275.25F Archäologische Mitteilungen aus russischen Sammlungen. Berlin. 1-5,1928-1936 5v.
Arc 275.30 Arkheograficheskii ezhegodnik. Moskva. 1957+ 17v.
Arc 275.35 Arkheologicheskii sbornik. Leningrad. 4-8 2v.
Arc 275.40 Arkheologicheskii sbornik. Ulan-Ude.
Arc 275.45 Arkheologiia i ethnografiia Bashkirii. Ufa. 1,1962+ 5v.
Arc 275.50 Arkheologicheskie otkrytiia. Moskva. 1965+ 6v.
Arc 275.55 Arkheologo-ethnograficheskii sbornik. Groznyi. 3,1969+
Arc 275.60 Arkheolohiia. Kyiv. 1971+
Arc 275.65 Arkheologiia i etnografiia Tatarii. Kazan. 1,1971+
Arc 275.70 Azebardzhanskii Arkheologicheskii Komitet. Izvestiia. Baku. 2,1926
Arc 275.101 Miliukov, P.N. VIII Arkheologicheskii s"ezd v Moskve. Moskva, 1890.
Arc 279.2 Eurasia septentrionalis antiqua. Helsinki. 1-3
Arc 280.2 Mogil'niki Zapadnoi Fergany. Moskva. 1,1972+
Arc 282.1 Suomen Muinaimuistoyhdestys, Helsinki. Finska fornminnesföreningens tidskrift. 16,1896+ 24v.
Arc 285.5 Kemerovo. Pedagogicheskii Institut. Laboratoriia Arkheologicheskikh Issledovanii. Izvestiia. Kemerovo. 1,1967+ 2v.
Arc 287.2F Moskovskoe Arkheologicheskoe Obshchestvo. Slisok izdanii. Moskva, 1913.
Arc 287.3F Moskovskoe Arkheologicheskoe Obshchestvo. Drevnosti. Arkheologicheskii vestnike. Moskva. 1867-1868//
Arc 287.5 Moskovskoe Arkheologicheskoe Obshchestvo. Arkheologicheskiia izvestiia i zametki. Moskva. 2-7,1894-1900 7v.
Arc 287.6 Materialy po arkheologii i drevnei istoriia Severnoi Osetii. Ordzhonikidze. 1,1961+
Arc 287.7 Materialy po arkheologii Dagestana. Makhachkala. 1,1959+ 2v.
Arc 288.1 Nauchnoe Obshchestvo po Izucheniiu Votskogo Kraia. Trudy. Moskva. 4,1928

Classified Listing

Arc 275 - 300 Archaeology - Periodicals and Societies - Local - Europe - Russia (A-Z) - cont.

Arc 289.10 Odessa. Derzhavnyi Arkheolohichnye Muzei. Kratkie soobshcheniia o polevykh arkheologicheskikh issledovaniiskh. 1961-1963 3v.

Arc 289.10.5 Arkheologicheshie issledovaniia na Ukraine; informatsionnye soobshcheniia. Kiev. 1,1965+ 2v.

Arc 289.20 Otchety arkheologicheskikh ekspeditsii. Irkutsk. 1963+

Arc 290.1 Kruse, F. Russische Alterthümer 1844. Dorpat, 1844.

Arc 290.3 Problemy arkheologii. Leningrad. 1,1968+

NEDL Arc 292.10 Russia. Arkheologicheskaia Kommissiia. Izvestiia. Sankt Peterburg. 1-66,1901-1918 21v.

Arc 292.20F Russia. Arkheologicheskaia Kommissiia. Materialy po arkheologii Rossii. Petrograd. 3-37,1888-1918 24v.

Arc 292.30F Russia. Arkheologicheskaia Kommissiia. Otchet". Petrograd. 1889-1915 8v.

Arc 292.30.2F Russia. Arkheologicheskaia Kommissiia. Al'oom risunkov...v otchetakh. Sankt Peterburg. 1882-1906

Arc 292.30.5 Russia. Arkheologicheskaia Kommissiia. Ukazateli k otchetame za 1882-98. Sankt Peterburg, 1903.

Arc 292.40F Russia. Arkheologicheskaia Kommissiia. Compte rendu. St. Petersbourg. 1-21,1859-1888 9v.

Arc 292.40PF Russia. Arkheologicheskaia Kommissiia. Compte rendu. St. Petersbourg, n.d.

Arc 292.90 Russkoe Arkheologicheskoe Obshchestvo, Leningrad. Zapiski. Sankt Peterburg. 1-14,1847-1858 8v.

Arc 292.100 Russkoe Arkheologicheskoe Obshchestvo, Leningrad. Zapiski. Nouviia seriia. Sankt Peterburg. 1-12,1886-1902 10v.

Arc 292.110 Russkoe Arkheologicheskoe Obshchestvo, Leningrad. Zapiski. Sankt Peterburg. 1-13,1851-1918// 10v.

Arc 292.120F Russkoe Arkheologicheskoe Obshchestov, Leningrad. Izvestiia. Sankt Peterburg. 1-10,1859-1881// 6v.

Arc 292.125 Russkoe Arkheologicheskoe Obshchestvo, Leningrad. Protokoly obshchikhe sobraniia. Petrograd. 1899-1908

Arc 292.127 Russkoe Arkheologicheskoe Obshchestvo, Leningrad. Protokoly zasedaniia. Sankt Peterburg. 1897-1898

Arc 292.130 Russkoe Arkheologisheskoe Obshchestvo, Leningrad. Zapiski klassicheskago otdeleniia. Sankt Peterburg. 1-9 5v.

Arc 292.140 Russkoe Arkheologicheskoe Obshchestvo, Leningard. Zapiski Numizmaticheskago otdeleniia. Sankt Peterburg. 1-2,1906-1913

Arc 292.145 Russkoe Arkheologicheskoe Obshchestvo v Korolevstve S.Kh.S., Belgrade. Sbornik. Belgrad. 1,1927

Arc 292.150 Veselovskii, H.I. Istorii. Sankt Peterburg, 1900.

Arc 292.155 Polenov, D. Bibliografiia obozrenie trydov. Sankt Peterburg, 1871.

Arc 292.160 Russkoe Arkheologicheskoe Obshchestvo, Leningrad. Trudy vostochnago otdeleniia. v.1-11,13-14,16; photoreproductions. Sankt Peterburg. 1-22,1855-1898// 20v.

Arc 292.163 Russkoe Arkheologicheskoe Obshchestvo, Leningrad. Zapiski vostochnago otdeleniia. Sankt Peterburg. 1886-1921 12v.

Arc 293.1 Russkoe Arkheologicheskoe Obshchestvo, Leningrad. Mémoires. St. Pétersbourg. 1-6,1847-1852 6v.

Arc 293.2 Russkoe Arkheologicheskoe Obshchestvo, Leningrad. Bulletin. St. Pétersbourg. 21-25

Arc 293.3 Istanbul. Russkii Arkheologicheskii Institut. Izvestiia. Sofiia. 1-9 6v.

Arc 293.3F Istanbul. Russkii Arkheologicheskii Institut. Izvestiia. Sofiia. 10-16// 5v.

Arc 293.3PF Istanbul. Russkii Arkheologicheskii Institut. Izvestiia. Atlas. Sofiia, n.d.

Arc 293.5 Sovetskaia arkheologiia. Moskva. 1958+ 23v.

Arc 293.6 Materialy po arkheologii Sibiri i Dal'nego Vostoka. Novosibirsk. 1,1972+ 2v.

Arc 295.5 Voprosy istorii i arkheologii Mordovskoi ASSR. Saransk. 2,1973+

Arc 296.5 Voprosy arkheologii Urala. Sverdlovsk. 1,1961+ 10v.

Arc 300.5 Zadneprovskii, I.A. Arkheologicheskie pamiatniki iuzhnykh raionov osnskoi oblasti. Frunze, 1960.

Arc 302 Archaeology - Periodicals and Societies - Local - Europe - Other Slavic

Arc 302.2.4 Bulgarska Akademiia na Naukite, Sofia. Arkheologicheski institut. Trudove na sektsiata za slavianska arkheologiia. Sofiia. 1-2,1947-1948

Arc 302.2.5 Bulgarski ArkheologicheSki Institut, Sofia. Bulletin. Sophia. 1-7,1910-1920 7v.

Arc 302.2.6 Bulgarska Akademiia na Naukite, Sofia. Arkheologicheski Institut. Izvestiia. Sofiia. 1,1921+ 28v.

Arc 302.2.7 Gerasimov, T. Ukaz, kumuizv na bulgarekoto archeologichesko. Sofiia, 1934.

Arc 302.2.8 Materiali za arkheologicheska karta na Bulgariia. Sofiia. 1-8,1914-1956

Arc 302.2.9 Varnensko Arkheologichesko Druzhestvo, Stalin. Izvestiia. Stalin. 3-13 10v.

Arc 302.2.9.5 Varna, Bulgaria. Naroden Muzei. Izvestiia. 1,1965+ 4v.

Arc 302.2.14 Bulgarska Akademiia na Naukite, Sofia. Arkheolgicheski Institut. Serdika; arkheologicheski materiali. Sofiia, 1964.

Arc 302.7 Hrvatsko Arheološko Društvo u Zagrebu. Viestnik. Zagreb. 1-14 4v.

Arc 302.7.5 Hrvatsko Arheološko Društvo u Zagrebu. Viestnik. New series. Zagreb. 1-23,1895-1942 17v.

Arc 302.7.6 Zagreb. Arheološki Muzej. Vjesnik. Series III. Zagreb. 1,1958+

Arc 302.8.9 Hrvatsko arheološko društvo u Zagrebu. Izvješće. Zagreb. 1880-1886

Arc 302.8.10 Herakleja. Bitola. 2,1965+

Arc 302.9 Ochrona zakytków. Warszawa. 5+ 11v.

Arc 302.9.5 Polska Akademia Nauk. Zaktad Archeologii Śródziemnomorskiej. Travaux. Warsaw. 1968+ 2v.

Arc 302.9.10 Lubuskie Towarzystwo Naukowe. Komisja Archeologiczna. Materiały. Zielona Góra. 1,1965+

Arc 302.9.15 Kiss, Zsolt. Les publications du Centre d'archéologie méditerranéenne. Warszawa, 1974.

Arc 302.10F Monumenta archaeologica. Pragae. 1,1948+ 18v.

Arc 302.12 Archeologické studijné materiály. Praha. 1,1964+ 2v.

Arc 302.13 Výhledy do pravěku evropsk lidstva. Praha. 3,1948+

Arc 302.14 Československá Akademie Ved. Archeologický Ustav. Záchranné Oddělení. Bulletin. Praha. 2,1964+

Arc 302.15 Akademia nauk URSR, Kiev. Vseukrainha Akademia Nauk. Vseukrainshau Arkheologichnu Komitet, Kiev. Korotke zvidompennia. Kiev. 1926+

Arc 302.17 Koszalinskie zeszyty muzealne. Koszalin. 1,1971+

Arc 302.18F Starinar; organ Arkheoloshkog Instituta. Beograd. 1,1950+ 12v.

Arc 302 Archaeology - Periodicals and Societies - Local - Europe - Other Slavic - cont.

Arc 302.19 Starine Crne Gore. Cetinje. 2

Arc 302.20 Sofia. Naroden Arkheologicheski Muzei. Razkopki i prochzvani. Sofiia. 1+

Arc 302.20F Sofia. Naroden Arkheologicheski Muzei. Razkopki i prochzvani. Sofiia. 3+

Arc 302.21 Arkheologichesko Druzhestvo, Sofia. Izvestiia.

Arc 302.28 Argo; informativno glasilo za antiko. Ljubljana. 4,1965+

Arc 302.30 Arheološki vestnik. Ljubljana. 2+ 15v.

Arc 302.31 Balcanoslavica. Beograd. 1,1972+

Arc 302.32 Arheološki pregled. Beograd. 7,1965+ 4v.

Arc 302.33 Arheološko Društvo Jugoslaviji. Materijali. Beograd. 3,1966+ 2v.

Arc 302.34 Zagreb. Univerzitet. Filozofski Fakultet. Odsjek za Arheologiju. Opuscula archaeologia. 1-5,1956-1961

Arc 302.35 Archaeologia Iugoslavica. Beograd. 1-5,1954-1961 2v.

Arc 302.35.2 Monumenta archaeologica. Novi Sad. 1,1974+ 2v.

Arc 302.36 Skopje, Yugoslavia. Arheoloski muzej zbornik. 1955+ 2v.

Arc 302.37 Belgrade. Zavod za zoš title i naučno proučavanje e spomenika kulture NR Srbije. Saopštenja. 2+ 3v.

Arc 302.39 Varstvo spomenikov. Ljubljana. 10,1965+

Arc 302.45 Fontes archeologicae Moraviae. Brno. 1965+

Arc 302.45.5 Československá Akademie Věd. Archeologický Ústav. Pobočka v Brně. Studie. Praha. 1,1972+

Arc 302.46 Slovenská Akadémia Vied. Archeologický Ústav, Nitra. Studijné zvesti. Nitra. 2,1957+ 6v.

Arc 302.47 Materiały archeologiczne. Nowej huły. Kraków. 1,1968+

Arc 302.48 Informator archeologiczny; badania. Warszawa. 1967+ 2v.

Arc 302.49 Rzeszowski Ośrodek Archeologiczny. Materiały i sprawozdania. Rzeszów. 1964+

Arc 302.50 Starine Kosora i Metohije. Pristina. 4,1968+

Arc 302.51.6 Conference International d'Études Classiques des Pays Socialistes, 6th, Plovdiv, 1962. Acta antiqua Philippapolitana. Serdicae, 1963.

Arc 302.52 Informator konserwatora zabytków archeologicznych na Województwo Wrocławskie. Wrocław. 1964+

Arc 302.53 Muzeum Zup Krakowskich, Wieliczka. Badania archeologiczne. Wieliczka. 1968+

Arc 302.54 Materiały starożytne i wczesnośredniowieczne. Wrocław. 1,1971+ 2v.

Arc 302.55 Sprawozdania z badań archeologicznych prawadzonych na terenie Województwa Koszalińskiego. Koszalin. 1966+

Arc 303 Archaeology - Periodicals and Societies - Local - Europe - Other Europe

Arc 303.18.5 Rumania. Comisune Monumentelar Istoriće. Buletiuul. 1-38,1908-1945 13v.

Arc 303.18.10F Dacia. București. 1,1924+ 15v.

Arc 303.18.20F Arta si arheologia; revistă. București. 1-12,1927-1936

Arc 303.18.25 Bucharest. Muzeul de Istorie a Orasului. Cercetări arheologice ên București. București. 2,1965+

Arc 303.25 Kongress Baltischer Archäologen, 2d, Riga, 1930. Congressus secundus archaeologorum balticorum. Riga, 1931.

Arc 303.30 Fruehchristliche Türkei. Basel.

Arc 303.35 Academia...Bucharest. Academia Republicii Socialiste România. Muzeul National de Antichitati. Studii si cercetări de istorie veche. București. 5,1954+ 15v.

Arc 303.40F Academia...Bucharest. Academia Republicii Socialiste România. Institutul de Arheologie. Materiale si cercetări arheologice. București. 2,1956+ 9v.

Arc 303.45F Studies in North-European archaeology. Stockholm. 1-3

Arc 303.46 Studies in North-European archaeology. Series B. Stockholm. 3,1971+

Arc 303.50 Biblioteca de arheologie. București. 1,1957+ 16v.

Arc 303.50.5 Biblioteca de arheologie. Seria complementară. București. 1,1972+

Arc 303.60 Kulturno-povijesni spomenici Istre. Pula. 1,1963+ 2v.

Arc 303.60.5 Histria archaeologica. Pula. 1,1970+ 5v.

Arc 303.65 Arkheologicheskie pamiatniki Moldavii. Kishinev. 1,1967+

Arc 303.67 Academia...Bucharest. Academie Republicii Socialiste România. Arheologie Moldovei. București. 2,1964+ 4v.

Arc 303.70 Arkheologicheskie issledovaniia v Moldavii. Kishinev. 1968+

Arc 303.72 Antichità altoadriatiche. Trieste. 1,1972+ 4v.

Arc 305 - 330 Archaeology - Periodicals and Societies - Local - America - General and North America (A-Z)

NEDL Arc 305.1 American antiquarian. Cleveland. 1-36 35v.

Arc 305.3 Archaeological Institute of America. Southwest Society, Los Angeles. Bulletin. Los Angeles. 1-8 2v.

Arc 305.3.5 Archaeological Institute of America. Southwest Society, Los Angeles. Two great gifts. The Lummies Library and collections; the Munk Library. Los Angeles, 1910.

Arc 305.10 Alliance for the Preservation of Florida Antiquities. Papers. Jacksonville Beach.

Arc 307.2 California. University. Publications. Berkeley. 1-50,1904-1964 48v.

Arc 307.3 International Congress of Americanists. Compte-rendu. 1875+ 60v.

Arc 307.3.2 International Congress of Americanists, 4th, Madrid, 1881. Congreso international de Americanistas. Madrid, 1881.

Arc 307.3.4 International Congress of Americanists, 17th, Buenos Aires, 1910. Sumarios de la conferencias y memorias presentadas al congreso. Buenos Aires, 1910.

Arc 307.3.5F Pamphlet box. International Congress of Americanists. Miscellaneous pamphlets.

Arc 307.3.6 International Congress of Americanists, 9th, Madrid, 1892. Congreso internacional de Americanistas. Madrid, 1891.

Arc 307.3.7 International Congress of Americanists, 11th, Mexico, 1895. Congreso de Americanistas. Reunion en Mexico. México, 1895.

Arc 307.3.8 Currier, C.W. Seventeenth international congress of Americanists. Washington, 1910?

Arc 307.3.9 International Congress of Americanists, 17th, May 1910 (2d meeting, Mexico, Sept. 1910). Reseña de la segunda sesion del XVII Congresso...de Americanistes. México, 1912.

Arc 307.3.10 International Congress of Americanists, 24th, Hamburg, 1930. Internationale Amerikanisten Kongress. Vorläufiges Program. n.p., 1930.

Arc 307.3.12 Grairer, Gabriel. Allocution fait à la Société de Géographie...sur la 2e session des Congrés international de Americanistes. Rouen, 1877.

Arc 307.3.15 International Congress of Americanists, 26th, Seville, 1935. Programa. Madrid, 1935.

Arc 307.3.20 International Congress of Americanists, 27th, Mexico, 1939. Boletin. México.

Classified Listing

Arc 305 - 330 Archaeology - Periodicals and Societies - Local - America - General and North America (A-Z) - cont.

NEDL Arc 307.3.25F International Congress of Americanists, 27th, Mexico and Lima, 1939. Actas. México, 1942-47.
Arc 307.3.35 Comas, Juan. La congresos internacionales de Americanistas. Mexico, 1954.
Arc 307.3.50 Girard, Rafael. Guatemala en el XXXIII Congreso internacional de Americanistas. Guatemala, 1958.
Arc 309.10 Early Georgia. Athens, Ga.
Arc 309.15 Excavators' Club. Papers. Cambridge, Mass. 1-2,1940-1945
Arc 313.1 Indiana. Historical Society, Indianapolis. Prehistory research series. Indianapolis. 1-3,1937-1955 3v.
Arc 317.2 Missouri. Historical Society. Department of Archaeology. Bulletin. St. Louis. 1,1913
Arc 318.2 El palacio. 11,1921+ 8v.
Arc 318.5 New York State Archaeological Association. Occasional papers. Albany. 1-2,1958-1959
Arc 319.5 Ohio archaeologist. Columbus.
Arc 320.1 Numismatic and Antiquarian Society of Philadelphia. Reports of proceedings. Philadelphia. 1865-1935 5v.
Arc 320.1.2 Numismatic and Antiquarian Society of Philadelphia. Necrology. Philadelphia. 1882-1884
Arc 320.1.3 Pamphlet vol. Numismatic and Antiquarian Society of Philadelphia. Miscellaneous pamphlets. 4 pam.
Arc 320.1.4 Pamphlet vol. Numismatic and Antiquarian Society of Philadelphia. Miscellaneous pamphlets. 6 pam.
Arc 320.1.21 Pennsylvania. University. University Museum. Bulletin. Philadelphia. 1-3 2v.
Arc 320.1.27 Pennsylvania. University. Museum of American Archaeology. Annual report of the curator. Philadelphia. 1,1890
Arc 320.2 Harvard University. Peabody Museum. Reports. Cambridge. 1-3 3v.
Arc 320.2.5 Harvard University. Peabody Museum. Memoirs. Cambridge. 1-12 12v.
Arc 320.2.9 Harvard University. Peabody Museum. Papers. Cambridge. 1,1888+ 66v.
Arc 320.4 Point Loma, California. School of Antiquity. Papers. University extension series. Point Loma. 2-12,1915-1921
Arc 323.3 Southwestern lore. Gunnison, Colo. 1,1935+ 8v.
Arc 323.4 Society for American Archaeology. Seminars in archaeology: 1955. Salt Lake City, 1956.
Arc 324.5 Texas. University. Department of Anthropology. Archaeology series. Austin.
Arc 325.2 Utah. University. Archaeological number. 1,1910

Arc 332 Archaeology - Periodicals and Societies - Local - Oceania

Arc 332.5 Studies in historical archeology. Sydney. 1,1973+

Arc 335 Archaeology - Bibliographies - Indexes to periodicals

Arc 335.2 Gomme, G.L. Index of archaeological papers, 1665-1890. London, 1907.
Arc 335.3 Index of archaeological papers, 1891-1908. London, 1892- 2v.
Arc 335.5 British archaeological abstracts. London. 1967+ 4v.

Arc 340 Archaeology - Bibliographies - General works

Arc 340.1 Archaeological book lists. n.p., 1884-1891.
Arc 340.2 Deutsches Archäologisches Institut. Römische Abteilung. Bibliothek. Katalog der Bibliothek. Rom, 1900-02. 2v.
Arc 340.2.5 Deutsches Archäologisches Institut. Römische Abteilung. Bibliothek. Katalog der Bibliothek. v.1-2. Rom, 1913-32. 4v.
Arc 340.2.7 Deutsches Archäologisches Institut. Römische Abteilung. Bibliothek. Katalog der Bibliothek. Supplement. Berlin, 1930.
Arc 340.2.10 Istituto Nazionale d'Archeologia e Storia dell'Arte, Roma. Biblioteca. Annuario bibliografico di archeologia; opere e periodici. Modena. 1,1952+ 5v.
Arc 340.2.15 Archéologie de l'Afrique antique. Aix en Provence. 1970+
Arc 340.3F London. University. Library. Catalogue of books on archaeology and art. London, 1935-37. 2v.
Arc 340.3.2F London. University. Library. Catalogue of books on archaeology and art. Supplement. London, 1937.
Arc 340.3.5F London. University. Library. Catalogue of books on archaeology and art. Index. London, 1937.
Arc 340.4 Orlinsky, H.M. An indexed bibliography of the writings of W.F. Albright. New Haven, 1941.
Arc 340.5 American Academy in Rome. Library. A bibliographical guide to Latium and southern Eturia. Rome, 1916.
Arc 340.5.2 American Academy in Rome. Library. A bibliographical guide to Latium and southern Eturia. 2. ed. Rome, 1925.
Arc 340.5.3 American Academy in Rome. Library. A bibliographical guide to Latium and southern Eturia. 3. ed. Rome, 1933.
Arc 340.6 Svenska Arkeologiska Samfundet. Swedish archaeological bibliography. Uppsala. 1939+
Arc 340.7 French Bibliographical Digest. Archaeology, 1945-1955. N.Y., 1956- 2v.
Arc 340.8 Výběrova bibliografie československé archeologie. Praha. 1958+
Arc 340.8.5 Brünn. Universita. Knihovna. Minulost jižní Moravy. Brno, 1963.
Arc 340.8.10 Brünn. Universita. Knihovna. Přehled bibliografií a pokusů o soupisy moravské archeologické literatury. Brno, 1965.
Arc 340.9 Sviridova, I.N. Po sledam drevnikh kul'tur. Moskva, 1966.
Arc 340.10 Berlin. Universität. Institut für Ur- und Frühgeschichte. Bibliographie zur archäologischen Germanenforschung. Deutschsprachige Literatur 1941-1953. Berlin, 1966.
Arc 340.11 Georgieva, Sonia. Bibliografiia na bulgarskata arkheologiia, 1879-1955. Sofiia, 1957.
Arc 340.11.2 Georgieva, Sonia. Bibliografiia na bulgarskata arkheologiia, 1879-1966. 2. izd. Sofiia, 1974.
Arc 340.12 Phillipson, David W. An annotated bibliography of the archaeology of Zambia. Lusaka, 1968.
Arc 340.13 Holm, S.E. Bibliography of South African pre- and proto-historic archaeology. Pretoria, 1966.
Arc 340.15 Bibliografia d'archeologia classica. 1. ed. Roma, 1969.
Arc 340.16 Beilekchi, V.S. Bibliografiia po arkheologii Moldavii, 1946-1966. Kishinev, 1967.
Arc 340.17 Lyell, Arthur H. A bibliographical list descriptive of Romano-British architectural remains in Great Britain. Cambridge, 1912.
Arc 340.20.2 Lehmann, Herbert. Bibliographie zur Vor- und Frühgeschichte von Gross-Berlin. 2. Aufl. Berlin, 1968.
Arc 340.25 Sovetskaia arkheologicheskaia literatura; bibliografiia. Leningrad. 1918+ 4v.
Arc 340.25.5 Field, Henry. Bibliography of Soviet archaeology and physical anthropology, 1936-1964. Miami? 1964.

Arc 340 Archaeology - Bibliographies - General works - cont.

Arc 340.25.7 Field, Henry. Bibliography of Soviet archaeology and physical anthropology, 1936-1967. n.p., 1967.
Arc 340.25.9 Field, Henry. Bibliography of Soviet archaeology and physical anthropology, 1936-1972. no. 1-189. Coconut Grove, Fla., 1972.
Arc 340.30 Banner, János. A Közép-Dunamedence régészeti bibliográfiája a legrégibb időktöl a XI. századig. Budapest, 1954.
Arc 340.30.3 Banner, János. A Közép-Dunamedence régészeti bibliográfiája, 1954-1959. Budapest, 1961.
Arc 340.30.5 Banner, János. A Közép-Dunamedence régészeti bibliográfiája, 1960-1966. Budapest, 1968.
Arc 340.36 An anthropological bibliography of the eastern seaboard. New Haven, 1947-63. 2v.
Arc 340.37 Frontier Forts and Trails Survey. A partial bibliography of the archaeology of Pennsylvania and adjacent states. Harrisburg, 1941.
Arc 340.38 Ödekan, Ayla. Türkiyede 50 yılda yayımlanmış Arkeoloji, sanat tarihi...bibliyografyası. İstanbul, 1974.
Arc 340.39 Coulson, William D.E. An annotated bibliography of Greek and Roman art. N.Y., 1975.

Arc 343 - 370 Archaeology - Archaeological museums and collections [Discontinued]

Htn Arc 343.225F* Du Molinet, Claude. Le cabinet de la bibliothèque de Sainte Geneviève. Paris, 1692.
Htn Arc 362.1.20* Manilli, Jacomo. Villa Borghese. Roma, 1650.

Arc 375 Archaeology - Dictionaries and encyclopedias

Arc 375.1 Müller, H.A. Archäologisches Wörterbuch. Leipzig, 1877-78. 2v.
Arc 375.2 Fosbroke, T.D. Encyclopaedia of Antiquities. London, 1825. 2v.
Arc 375.2.2 Fosbroke, T.D. Foreign topography. Encyclopaedia of antiquites. v.3. London, 1828.
Arc 375.3F Gay, V. Glossaire archéologique. Paris, 1887-1928. 2v.
Arc 375.4 Otte, H. Archäologisches Wörterbuch. Leipzig, 1857.
Arc 375.4.2 Otte, H. Archäologisches Wörterbuch. Leipzig, 1883.
Arc 375.5 Schlemm, J. Wörterbuch zur Vorgeschichte. Berlin, 1908.
Arc 375.6 Forrer, R. Reallexikon der prähistorischen, klassischen...Altertümer. Berlin, 1907.
Arc 375.7 Deinard, S.N. Descriptive charts of ancient monuments. no.1-5. Minneapolis, 1912.
Arc 375.8 Ebert, Max. Reallexikon der Vorgeschichte. v.1-15. Berlin, 1924-32. 16v.
Arc 375.10 Bosc, E. Dictionnaire général de l'archéologie. Paris, 1881.
Arc 375.12 Archäologische Encyclopedie. Zeist, 1962.
Arc 375.13 Aken, Andreas Rudolphus Antonius van. Elseviers encyclopedie van de archeologie. Amsterdam, 1965.
Arc 375.14 Marois, Roger. English-French, French-English vocabulary of prehistoric archaeology. Montreal, 1972.
Arc 375.15 The concise encyclopedia of archaeology. 1. ed. N.Y., 1960.

Arc 380 Archaeology - General works - Folios [Discontinued]

Htn Arc 380.05PF* Pamphlet box. Archaeology. Miscellaneous plates.
Arc 380.199 Noris, Enrico. Lettere sopra vari punti di erudizione. n.p., 1720.
Arc 380.200 Montfaucon, B. de. L'antiquité expliquée. 2. éd. v.1-5. Paris, 1722. 10v.
Arc 380.200.2 Montfaucon, B. de. L'antiquité expliquée. Supplément. Paris, 1724. 5v.
Arc 380.201 Montfaucon, B. de. Antiquity explained. London, 1721. 7v.
Arc 380.202 Steinbüchel, A. von. Antiquarischer Atlas. Wien, 1833.
Arc 380.203 Rathgeber, D.G. Archäologische Schriften. Gotha, 1851-57.
Arc 380.204 Gaedechens, R. Unedirte antike Bildwerke. Jena, 1873.
Arc 380.205 Millingen, J. Ancient unedited monuments. London, 1822.
Arc 380.206 Allan, J.H. Pictorial tour in the Mediterranean. London, 1843.
Arc 380.207 Chevalier, N. Recherche curieuse d'antiquité. Utrecht, n.d.
Htn Arc 380.208* Beger, L. Spiciligium antiquitates. Coloniae Brandenburgicae, 1692.
Htn Arc 380.209* Winckelmann, J. Monumenti antichi inedite. v.1-2. Roma, 1767.
Arc 380.210 Quatremère de Quincy, A.C. Monuments et ouvrages d'art antiques. Paris, 1829.
Arc 380.212 Lubersac, M. Discours sur les monumens publics. Paris, 1775.
Arc 380.213 Leemans, C. Études archéologiques, linguistiques. Leide, 1885.
Arc 380.214 Wieland, C.A. Der Denkmal und Heimatschutz...der Gegenwart. Basel, 1905.

Arc 382 Archaeology - General works - Collected authors - Pamphlet volumes

Arc 382 Pamphlet box. Archaeology. Miscellaneous pamphlets. 38 pam.
Htn Arc 382.1* Pignoria, L. Vetustissimae tabulae aeneae. Venetiis, 1605.
Arc 382.2 Williams, John. On Carn Goch in Caermarthenshire. London, 1853. 17 pam.
Arc 382.3 Dümichen, J. Über die Tempel und Gräber im alten Ägypten. Strassburg, 1872. 7 pam.
Arc 382.4 Benndorf, O. De anthologiae Graecae epigrammatis. Bonn, 1862. 20 pam.
Arc 382.5 Michaelis, A. Anaglyphi vaticani explicatio. Tubingae, 1865. 15 pam.
Arc 382.6 Carus, K.G. Ueber die typisch gewordenen Abbildungen menschlichen Kopfformen. Jena, 1863. 15 pam.
Arc 382.7 Pamphlet vol. Prähistorie. 10 pam.
Arc 382.8 Pamphlet box. Archaeology. Miscellaneous pamphlets.
Arc 382.9 Birley, Eric. Archaeology in the north of England. Durham, Eng., 1958. 6 pam.

Arc 383 Archaeology - General works - Collected authors - Festschriften (99 scheme, A-Z by person or institution honored)

Arc 383.3 Anthemon. Firenze, 1955.
Arc 383.9 Mélanges d'archéologie, d'histoire, et d'histoire de l'art, offerts à Louis Bosset. Lausanne, 1950.
Arc 383.9.5 Drack, Walter. Beiträge zur Kulturgeschichte; Festschrfit Reinhold Bosch. Aarau, 1947.
Arc 383.9.10 Barcelona (Province). Instituto de Prehistoria y Arqueología. Miscelánea en homenaje al abate Hescri Breuil, 1877-1961. Barcelona, 1964-65. 2v.

Arc 383 Archaeology - General works - Collected authors - Festschriften (99 scheme, A-Z by person or institution honored) - cont.

Arc 383.9.25 Hiranyagarbha; a series of articles on the archaeological work and studies of Prof. Dr. F.D.K. Bosch. The Hague, 1964.

Arc 383.14 Grimes, W.F. Aspects of archaeology in Britain and beyond; essays presented to O.G.S. Crawford. London, 1951.

Arc 383.16 Academia...Bucharest. Academia Republicii Populare Romîne. Amagiu lui Constantin Daicoviciu cu prilejne. Bucureşti, 1960.

Arc 383.17 Hommages à Waldemar Deonna. Hommages à Waldemar Deonna. Bruxelles, 1957.

Arc 383.18 Plovdiv, Bulgaria. Durzhavna biblioteka "Ivan Vazov". Sbornik Boris Liabovich. Plovdiv, 1927.

Arc 383.20 Festschrfit Luitpold Dussler: 28 Studien zur Archäologie und Kunstgeschichte. München, 1972.

Arc 383.22A Festschrfit für Rudolf Egge. Klagenfurt, 1952-53. 3v.

Arc 383.22B Festschrift für Rudolf Egge. v.2. Klagenfurt, 1953.

Arc 383.29 Sen, D. Studies in prehistory; robert Bruce Foote memorial volume. Calcutta, 1966.

Arc 383.30F Analecta archaeologica. Köln, 1960.

Arc 383.31F Müller, Adrian von. Gandert-Festschrift zum sechzigsten Geburtstag. Berlin, 1959.

Arc 383.33 Amsterdam. Universiteit. Institut voor Prae- en Protohistorie. In het voetspoor van A.E. van Giffen. Groningen, 1961.

Arc 383.33.2 Amsterdam. Universiteit. Institut voor Prae- en Protohistorie. In het voetspoor van A.E. van Giffen. 2. druk. Groningen, 1966.

Arc 383.34 Tübingen. Universität. Vor- und Frühgeschichtliches Institut. Festschrift für Peter Goessler. Stuttgart, 1954.

Arc 383.34.5 Weinberg, S.S. The Aegean and the Near East. N.Y., 1956.

Arc 383.34.10 Renard, M. Hommages à Albert Grenier. Bruxelles, 1962. 3v.

Arc 383.34.15 Archaeological theory and practice. Festschrift: Wm. F. Grimes. London, 1973.

Arc 383.36 The European community in later prehistory: studies in honour of C.F.C. Hawkes. London, 1971.

Arc 383.39 Studia archaeologica Gerardo Van Hoorn Oblata. Leiden, 1951.

Arc 383.42 Schwarz, K. Strana praehistorica...Martin John. Halle, 1948.

Arc 383.42.5 Zylmann, Peter. Zur Ur- und Frühgeschichte Nordwestdeutschlands. Hildesheim, 1956.

Arc 383.42.10 Na granicach archeologii. Łódź, 1968.

Arc 383.43F Svenska arkeologiska samfundet. Arkeologiska forskningar och fynd. Stockholm, 1952.

Arc 383.43.5 Opuscula Iosepho Kastelíc sexagenario dicata. Ljubljana, 1974.

Arc 383.46 Przyjaciół Nauk. Poznańskie Tow. Munera archaeologica Iosepho Kostrzewski. Poznań, 1963.

Arc 383.46.5 Jażdżewski, Konrad. Liber Iosepho Kostrzewski octogenario a veneratoribus dicatur. Wrocław, 1968.

Arc 383.48F Kleemann, Otto. Documento archaeologica. Bonn, 1956.

Arc 383.49 Harden, D.B. Dark-age Britain. London, 1956.

Arc 383.50 Catania. Università. Scritti in onore di Guido Libertini. Firenze, 1958.

Arc 383.51 Homaxe a Florentino A.L. Cuevillas. Vigo, 1957.

Arc 383.53 Société Nationale des Antiquaires de France. Mélanges en hommage à la mémoire de Fr. Martroye. Paris, 1940.

Arc 383.53.5 Mainz. Römisch Germanisches Zentralmuseum. Festschrift des Römisch germanischen Zentralmuseums in Mainz. Mainz, 1952-53. 3v.

Arc 383.53.10F Mainz. Römisch Germanisches Zentralmuseum. Festschrift zur Feier des fünfundsiebzigjährigen Bestehens. Mainz, 1927.

Arc 383.53.15 Himmelmann-Wildschütz, N. Festschrift für Friedrich Matz. Mainz, 1962.

Arc 383.53.20 Homenaje a Pablo Martinez del Rio en el vigesimoquento aniversario. Mexico, 1961.

Arc 383.55.5 Mélanges offerts à Kazimierz Michałowski. Warszawa, 1966.

Arc 383.56 Morleyana. Santa Fe, New Mexico, 1950.

Arc 383.66 Miscellanea di studi sicelioti ed italioti in onore di Paolo Orsi. Catania, 1921.

Arc 383.67 Festschrift für August Oxé. Darmstadt, 1938.

Arc 383.69F Greifswalder Antiken. Berlin, 1961.

Arc 383.70 Chevallier, Raymond. Mélanges d'archéologie et d'histoire. Paris, 1966. 3v.

Arc 383.75 Behrens, Gustav. Reinecke Festschrift zum 75. Geburtstag von Paul Reinecke. Mainz, 1950.

Arc 383.77 Mylonas, G.C. Studies presented to David Moore Robinson. St. Louis, 1951-53. 2v.

Arc 383.79 Kleinasien und Byzanz. Berlin, 1950.

Arc 383.79.10 Kersten, Karl. Festschrift für Gustav Schwante. Neumünster, 1951.

Arc 383.79.12 Československá Adademie věd. Sekoe Jazyka a Literatury. Studie z antiky; Antonínu Salsčovi. Praha, 1955.

Arc 383.79.25 Lullies, R. Neue Beiträge zur klassischen Altertumswissenschaft. Stuttgart, 1954.

Arc 383.81 Bulgarska Akademiia na Naukite, Sofia. Arkheologicheski Institut. Izsledvaniia v pamet na Karel Shkorpil. Sofiia, 1961.

Arc 383.83 Corolla memoriae Erich Swoboda dedicata. Graz, 1966.

Arc 383.87 An address presented to Marcus N. Tod. Oxford, 1948.

Arc 383.89F Grimm, Paul. Varia archaeologica. Berlin, 1964.

Arc 383.90 Festschrift 50. Jahre Lehrkanzel für Urgeschichte. Wien, 1949.

Arc 383.90.10 Oviedo (Province). Diputacion Provincial. Servicio de Investigaciones Arqueologicas. Libro homenaje la Conde de la Vega del Sella. Oviedo, 1956.

Arc 383.92A Kirchner, H. Ur- und Frühgeschichte als historische Wissenschaft. Heidelberg, 1950.

Arc 383.92B Kirchner, H. Ur- und Frühgeschichte als historische Wissenschaft. Heidelberg, 1950.

Arc 383.93 Bruns, G. Festschrift für Carl Weickert. Berlin, 1955.

Arc 383.94F Mnemosynon Theodor Wiegand. München, 1938.

Arc 383.95 Società Archeologia Comense. Raccolta di scritti. Como, 1954.

Arc 384 Archaeology - General works - Collected authors - Other

Arc 384.2 Marek, Kurt W. The world of archaeology. London, 1966.

Arc 384.2.5 Marek, Kurt W. Hands on the past. 1. American ed. N.Y., 1966.

Arc 384.2.10 Marek, Kurt W. Götter, Gräber und Gelehrte in Dokumenten. Reinbek bei Hamburg, 1965.

Arc 384.3 Arkheologiia starogo i novogo sveta. Moskva, 1966.

Arc 384.5 Matson, Frederick R. Ceramics and man. Chicago, 1965.

Arc 384 Archaeology - General works - Collected authors - Other - cont.

Arc 384.10 Recherches d'archéologie et d'histoire de l'art (antiquité). Louvain, 1970.

Arc 384.12.3 Das Abenteuer Archäologie. 3. Aufl. München, 1967.

Arc 384.13 Z polskich badań nad epokş kamienia. Wrocław, 1971.

Arc 384.14 Anglo-Romanian Conference on Mathematics in the Archaeological and Historical Sciences. Mathematics in the archaeological and historical sciences; proceedings. Edinburgh, 1971.

Arc 384.15 Congrès International d'Archéologie Classique, 8th, Paris, 1963. VIIIe Congrès international d'archéologie classique. Photoreproduction. Paris, 1963.

Arc 384.16 Redman, Charles L. Research and theory in current archeology. N.Y., 1973.

Arc 384.17 Willey, Gordon Randolph. Archaeological researches in retrospect. Cambridge, Mass., 1974.

Arc 384.18 Deutsche Historiker Gesellschaft. Fachgruppe Ur- und Frühgeschichte. Evolution und Revolution in alten Orient und in Europa. Das Neolithikum als historische Erscheinung. Berlin, 1971.

Arc 385 - 410 Archaeology - General works - Individual authors (A-Z)

Arc 385.1 Aus der Anomia; archaeologische Beitraege. Berlin, 1890.

Arc 385.2 Astle, Thomas. Observations on stone pillars. London, 1800.

Arc 385.3.5 Artsikhovshii, A.V. Vvedenie v arkheologiiu. 3. izd. Moskva, 1947.

Arc 385.4 Akademiia Nauk SSR. Institut Arkheologii. Protiv vyl'garizatsii marksisma v arkheologii. Moskva, 1953.

Arc 385.5 Walker, John. John Allen. London, 1956?

Arc 385.6 Ardusin, D.A. Arkheologicheskie razvedki i rashopki. Moskva, 1959.

Arc 385.9 Amal'rikh, Aleksei S. V poiskakh ischeznuvshikh tsivilizatsii. Moskva, 1959.

Arc 385.9.2 Amal'rikh, Aleksei S. V poiskakh ischeznuvshikh tsivilizatsii. Izd. 2. Moskva, 1966.

Arc 385.9.5 Amal'rikh, Aleksei S. Chto tahoe arkheologiia. Izd. 3. Moskva, 1966.

Arc 385.10 Atkinson, R.J.C. Archaeology. Cardiff, 1960.

Arc 385.11 L'âge de pierre. Paris, 1960.

Arc 385.12 Andrae, Walter. Lebenserinnerungen eins Ausgräbers. Berlin, 1961.

Arc 385.14 Akademiia Nauk SSSR. Institut Arkheologii. Novye metody v arkheologicheskikh issledovaniiakh. Leningrad, 1963.

Arc 385.15 Kolchin, B.A. Arkheologiia i estestvennye nauki. Moskva, 1965.

Arc 385.16 Felgueiros, Francisco. Pequena história de uma vida gloriosa [Francisco M. Aloes]. Brâgança, 1965.

Arc 385.20 Arias, Paolo Enrico. Storia dell'archeologia. Milano, 1967.

Arc 385.21 Aston, Michael. Landscape archaeology. Newton Abbot, Eng., 1974.

Arc 385.22 Anti, Carlo. Propedeutica archeologica. Padova, 1966.

Arc 386.1 Bartlett, T.H. About monuments. Boston, 1878?

Arc 386.2 Baye, J. de. L'archéologie préhistorique. Paris, 1888.

Arc 386.3 Beulé, C.E. Fouilles et découvertes. Paris, 1873. 2v.

Arc 386.4 Borghesi, Bartolomeo. Oeuvres complètes. Paris, 1862-72. 10v.

Arc 386.4.25 Borghesi, Bartolomeo. Bartolomeo Borghesi. Firenze, 1905.

Arc 386.5 Böttiger, Carl August. Archäologie. Dresden, 1806.

Arc 386.5.2 Böttiger, Carl August. Archäologie und Kunst. Breslau, 1828.

Arc 386.5.3 Böttiger, Carl August. Kleine Schriften. 2. Aufl. Leipzig, 1850. 3v.

Arc 386.5.4A Böttiger, Carl August. Kleine Schriften. Dresden, 1837-38. 3v.

Arc 386.5.4B Böttiger, Carl August. Kleine Schriften. Dresden, 1837-38. 3v.

Arc 386.5.6 Böttiger, Carl August. Amalthea. v.1-3. Leipzig, 1820-25. 2v.

Arc 386.5.18 Böttiger, Carl Wilhelm. Karl August Böttiger. Leipzig, 1837.

Arc 386.6 Braun, J. Studien und Skizzen. Mannheim, 1854.

Arc 386.7 Bucke, C. Ruins of ancient cities. London, 1840. 2v.

Arc 386.8 Buckley, T.A. Great cities of the ancient world. London, 1852.

Arc 386.9 Burnouf, E. Mémoires sur l'antiquité. Paris, 1879.

Arc 386.10 Bertrand, A. Rapport sur les questions archéologiques...Congrès de Stockholm. Paris, 1875.

Arc 386.11 Bertrand, A. De la valeur historique des documents archéologiques. Chartres, 1879.

Arc 386.12 Blanchet, A. Guide pratique de l'antiquaire. Paris, 1899.

Arc 386.13 Brown, G.B. The care of ancient monuments. Cambridge, 1905.

Arc 386.14 Baudelot de Dairval, C.C. De l'utilité des voyages...la recherche des antiquitéz. Paris, 1686. 2v.

Arc 386.14.5 Baudelot de Dairval, C.C. De l'utilité des voyages...la recherche des antiquitéz. Rouen, 1727. 2v.

Arc 386.15.5 British Museum. How to observe in archaeology. 2. ed. London, 1929.

Arc 386.16 Beyermann, Erich. Das Recht an Denkmälern. Inaug. Diss. Halle, 1917.

Arc 386.17 Howard Crosby Butler, 1872-1922. Princeton, 1923.

Arc 386.17.5 Leach, H.S. A bibliography of Howard Crosby Butler, 1872-1922. Princeton, 1924.

Arc 386.18 Touzeskul, V. Otkrytyia XIX i nachala XX v. Sankt Peterburg, 1923.

Arc 386.19F Strena Buliciana; commentationes gratulatoriae F. Bulić. Zagrebiae, 1924.

Arc 386.20A Burkitt, M.C. Our early ancestors. Cambridge, 1926.

Arc 386.20B Burkitt, M.C. Our early ancestors. Cambridge, 1926.

Arc 386.20.10 Burkitt, M.C. The old stone age. Cambrige, 1933.

Arc 386.22 Tea, Eva. Giacomo Boni nella vita del suo tempo. Milano, 1932. 2v.

Arc 386.23 Brunn, H. von. Archäologie und Anschauung. München, 1885.

Arc 386.24 Baraldi, Giuseppe. Notizia biografica sul cardinale S. Borgia. Modena, 1830.

Arc 386.24.5 Millin, A.L. Notice sur la vie du Cardinal Borgia. n.p., n.d.

Arc 386.25 Burgess, Thomas. An essay on the study of antiquities. Oxford, 1781.

Arc 386.26 Breasted, C. Pioneer to the past. N.Y., 1943.

Arc 386.27 Vale, Giuseppe. Gian Domenico Bertoli. Aquileia, 1946.

Arc 386.28 A list of the published writings of John Davidson Beazley. Oxford, 1951.

Arc 386.29 Brion, Marcel. La résurrection des villes mortes. v.1-2. Paris, 1948-49.

Classified Listing

Arc 385 - 410 Archaeology - General works - Individual authors (A-Z) - cont.

Arc 386.29.10 Brion, Marcel. De Pompéi a l'île de Pâques. Paris, 1967.
Arc 386.30 Brayda, C. Norme per il restauro dei monumenti. Torino, 1954.
Arc 386.31 Schreiber, Hermann. Versunkene Städte. Wien, 1955.
Arc 386.31.5 Schreiber, Hermann. Vanished cities. N.Y., 1957.
Arc 386.32 Bradford, John. Ancient landscapes. London, 1957.
Arc 386.33 Mayes, Stanley. The great Belzoni. London, 1959.
Arc 386.35 Bacon, Edward. Digging for history. London, 1960.
Arc 386.40 Breccia, E. Uomini e libri. Pisa, 1959.
Arc 386.42 Behn, Friedrich. Ausgrabungen und Ausgräber. Stuttgart, 1961.
Arc 386.43 Blavatskii, V.D. Otkrytie zatonuvshezo mira. Moskva, 1963.
Arc 386.44 Binford, Lewis Roberts. An archaeological perspective. N.Y., 1972.
Arc 386.45 Kenawell, William W. The quest at Glastonbury, a biographical study of Frederick Bligh Bond. N.Y., 1965.
Arc 386.46 Berlitz, Charles F. Mysteries from forgotten worlds. Garden City, 1972.
Arc 387.1 Caylus, A.C.P. Recueil d'antiquités égyptiennes. Paris, 1752. 7v.
Arc 387.1.2 Caylus, A.C.P. Recueil d'antiquités. Paris, 1761.
Arc 387.1.25 Rocheblave, S. Essai sur le comte de Caylus. Paris, 1889.
Arc 387.2 Chabas, F. Études sur l'antiquité historique. Paris, 1873.
Arc 387.3 Curtius, E. Festrede. Göttingen, 1862.
Arc 387.4 Compendio completo di archeologia. Milano, 1834. 2v.
Arc 387.4.7 Catalogo di tutte le produzioni letterarie...dell'abate Francesco Girolamo Cancellieri. Roma, 1846. 2 pam.
Arc 387.4.8 Moroni, A. Nuovo catalogo delle opere...dell'abate Francesco Cancellieri. Roma, 1881.
Arc 387.5 Crawford, Osbert Guy S. Man and his past. London, 1921.
Arc 387.5.10 Crawford, Osbert Guy S. Archaeology in the field. London, 1953.
Arc 387.5.12 Crawford, Osbert Guy S. Archaeology in the field. N.Y., 1953.
Arc 387.6 Capitan, Louis. La préhistoire. Paris, 1922.
Arc 387.7 Champollion, J.F. Champollion inconnu. Paris, 1897.
Arc 387.8A Cleland, H.F. Our prehistoric ancestors. N.Y., 1928.
Arc 387.8B Cleland, H.F. Our prehistoric ancestors. N.Y., 1928.
Arc 387.9 Childe, Vere Gordon. Bronze age. Cambridge, Eng., 1930.
Arc 387.9.5A Childe, Vere Gordon. Progress and archaeology. London, 1944.
Arc 387.9.5B Childe, Vere Gordon. Progress and archaeology. London, 1944.
Arc 387.9.7.1 Childe, Vere Gordon. Piecing together the past. N.Y., 1969.
Arc 387.10 Gallo, Francesco. Biografia del generale americano e console in Cipro, Luigi Palma di Cesnola. Vercelli, 1869.
Arc 387.10.5 Vedova, Giuseppe. Il conte L. Palma di Cesnola e il Museo metropolitano di Nuova York. Roma, 1899.
Arc 387.10.10 Roversi, Luigi. Ricordi Canavesani. Luigi Palma di Cesnola. N.Y., 1901.
Arc 387.10.15 Toesca di Castellazzo, G. Commemoriazione del generale Luigi Palma di Cesnola. Torino, 1905.
Arc 387.11 Casson, Stanley. Progress of archaeology. London, 1934.
Arc 387.12.25 Brandoli, Placido. Monsignor Celestino Cavedoni. Modena, 1870.
Arc 387.12.30 Cappeli, A. Monsignor Celestino Cavedoni. Firenze, 1866.
Arc 387.12.31 Cappelli, A. Necrologia di Mons. Celestino Cavedoni. 2. ed. Modena, 1866.
Arc 387.13F Corolia Ludwig Curtius zum sechzigsten Geburtstag dargebracht. Stuttgart, 1937. 2v.
Arc 387.13.5 Curtius, Ludwig. Deutsche und antike Welt. Stuttgart, 1950.
Arc 387.13.7 Curtius, Ludwig. Humanistisches und Humanes. Basel, 1954.
Arc 387.13.10 Pasquali, G. Storia dello spirito tedesco. Firenze, 1953.
Arc 387.13.15 Curtius, Ludwig. Torso. Stuttgart, 1958.
Arc 387.13.30 Herbig, Reinhard. Ludwig Curtius, 1874-1954, zum Gedachtnis. Heidelberg, 1955.
Arc 387.14.5 Folkers, T. Liste des publications de Jean Capart. Leiden, 1938.
Arc 387.15 Sclopis de Salerano, F. Notizie degli studi conte Giancarlo Conestabile della Staffa. Torino, 1877.
Arc 387.16.5 Pamphlet box. Chase, G.H. Collected papers.
Arc 387.21A Clark, John Grahame Douglas. Archaeology and society. 2. ed. London, 1947.
Arc 387.21B Clark, John Grahame Douglas. Archaeology and society. 2. ed. London, 1947.
Arc 387.21.5A Clark, John Grahame Douglas. Archaeology and society. Cambridge, Mass., 1957.
Arc 387.21.5B Clark, John Grahame Douglas. Archaeology and society. Cambridge, Mass., 1957.
Arc 387.21.10 Clark, John Grahame Douglas. Archaeology and society. 3. ed. London, 1960.
Arc 387.23 Hagen, Victor Wolfgang von. Frederick Catherwood. N.Y., 1950.
Arc 387.23.6 Hagen, Victor Wolfgang von. F. Catherwood, architect-explorer of two worlds. Barre, Mass, 1968.
Arc 387.30A Cooper, Gordon. Dead cities and forgotten tribes. N.Y., 1952.
Arc 387.30B Cooper, Gordon. Dead cities and forgotten tribes. N.Y., 1952.
Arc 387.33 Cottrell, Leonard. Lost cities. N.Y., 1957.
Arc 387.35 Crawford, Osbert Guy S. Said and done. London, 1955.
Arc 387.40 Ashmole, Bernhard. Cyriac of Ancona. London, 1957.
Arc 387.45 Clarke, David Leonard. Analytical archaeology. London, 1968.
Arc 388.1 Demarsy, A. Le congrès international d'archéologie préhistorique de Copenhague en 1869. Arras, 1870.
Arc 388.2 Droop, J.P. Archaeological excavation. Cambridge, Eng., 1915.
Arc 388.3 Deonna, Waldemar. L'archéologie, son domaine, son but. Paris, 1922.
Arc 388.4 Dumont, A. Mélanges d'archéologie et d'épigraphie. Paris, 1892.
Arc 388.5.5 Daniel, G.E. A hundred years of archaeology. London, 1950.
Arc 388.6 Daux, Georges. Les étapes de l'archéologie. 2. éd. Paris, 1948.
Arc 388.7 Goessler, F.P. Wilhelm Dörpfeld. Stuttgart, 1951.
Arc 388.8 Diolé, P. Promenades d'archéologie sous-marine. Paris, 1952.
Arc 388.8.2 Diolé, P. 4,000 years under the sea. N.Y., 1954.
Arc 388.9 Dymond, David Percy. Archaeology and history. London8 1974.

Arc 385 - 410 Archaeology - General works - Individual authors (A-Z) - cont.

Arc 388.10 Paris. Université. Institut de Civilisation. Pierre Dupont. Paris, 1955.
Arc 388.12 Daniel, G.E. The idea of prehistory. London, 1962.
Arc 388.14 Deuel, Leo. Testaments of time. 1. ed. N.Y., 1965.
Arc 388.16 Driehaus, Jürgen. Archäologische Radiographie. Düsseldorf, 1968.
Arc 388.18 Donnell, Robert C. Systematics in prehistory. N.Y., 1971.
Arc 389.1 Camille, Enlart, 1862-1927. Paris, 1929.
Arc 389.2 Ely, Talfourd. Manual of archaeology. N.Y., 1890.
Arc 389.3 Evans, Joan. Time and chance; story of Arthur Evans and his forebears. London, 1943.
Arc 389.4.1 Eydoux, Henri Paul. In search of lost worlds. 1. American ed. N.Y., 1971.
Arc 389.5 Ehrich, R.W. Relative chronologies in old world archaeology. Chicago, 1954.
Arc 389.6.2 Eydoux, Henri Paul. Realités et énigmes de l'archéologie. 2. éd. Paris, 1964.
Arc 390.1 Falkener, E. Museum of classical antiquities. London, 1860.
Arc 390.2.8 Münchener archäologische Studien...A. Furtwängler. München, 1909.
Arc 390.2.12 Furtwängler, Adolf. Kleine Schriften. München, 1912. 2v.
Arc 390.3.25 Cenni biografici di Carlo Fea. Roma, n.d.
Arc 390.4 Swanton, J.R. Jesse Walter Fewkes. Washington, 1931.
Arc 390.5 Elliger, W. Forschungen zur Kirchengeschichte...Johannes Ficker als Festgabe. Leipzig, 1931.
Arc 390.5.5 Thulin, Oskar. Johannes Ficker. Halle, 1936.
Arc 390.6 Stephaniskos. Ernst Fabricius. Freiburg, 1927.
Arc 390.7F Notice sur Jules-Francois-Paul Fauris Saint-Vincens. Aix, 1807.
Arc 390.8 Feron, R. La préhistoire. Paris, 1928.
Arc 390.9 Fett, Harry. Pa kulturvernets veier. Oslo, 1949.
Arc 390.10 Fletcher y Valls, D. Nocines de prehistoria. Valencia, 1952.
Arc 390.11 Childe, Vere Gordon. Henri Frankfort, 1897-1954. London, 1955?
Arc 390.12 Mitchell, Charles. Felice Feliciano antiquarius. London, 1961?
Arc 390.13 Foster, I.L. Culture and environment. London, 1963.
Arc 390.14 Ford, J.A. Método cuantitativo para establecer cronologias culturas. Washington, 1962.
Arc 390.15 Furtwängler, Adolf. Briefe aus dem Bonner Privatdozentenjahr 1879/80. Stuttgart, 1965.
Arc 390.16 Frantov, Grigoriis. Geofizika v arkheologii. Leningrad, 1966.
Arc 391.1 Gurlitt, J. Archäologische Schriften. Altona, 1831.
Arc 391.2 Gerhard, Eduard. Über die Metallspiegel der Etrusker. Berlin, 1836. 11 pam.
Arc 391.2.5 Gerhard, Eduard. Über archäologische Sammlungen und Studien. Berlin, 1860.
Arc 391.2.15 Witte, J. Notice sur Edouard Gerhard. Bruxelles, 1871.
Arc 391.2.17 Jahn, Otto. Eduard Gerhard. Berlin, 1868.
Arc 391.3 Gori, A.F. Symbolia litterariae. Decas I. Florentiae, 1748-53. 10v.
Arc 391.3.5 Gori, A.F. Symbolia litterariae. Decas II. v.1-10. Romae, 1751-54. 5v.
Arc 391.4 Studien zur vorgeschichtlichen Archäologie Alfred Götze. Leipzig, 1925.
Arc 391.5 Simony, C. de. Un curieuse figure d'artiste, Girault de Prangey, 1802-1892. Dijon, 1937.
Arc 391.6 Hill, George. Percy Gardner, 1846-1937. London, 1937.
Arc 391.7 Garrod, Dorothy A.E. Environment, tools and man. Cambridge, 1946.
Arc 391.8 Giovannoni, G. Il restauro dei monumenti. Roma, 1941?
Arc 391.9 Garrood, J.R. Archaeological remains. London, 1949.
Arc 391.10 Gordon, C.H. Adventures in the Nearest East. Fair Lawn, N.J., 1957.
Arc 391.12 Gherardo Ghirardini nel centenario della nascità. Padova, 1958.
Arc 391.13 Gordon, William J. Nelson Glueck: a bibliography. Cincinnati? 1962.
Arc 391.15 Rome. Istituto di Studi Romani. Giulio Quirino Giglioli. Roma, 1958.
Arc 391.16 Gąsiorowski, Stanisław J. Pisma wybrane. Wrocław, 1969.
Arc 391.17 Niggl, Reto. Giacomo Grimaldi (1568-1623). Inaug. Diss. München, 1971.
Arc 391.18 Goodyear, Frank Haigh. Archaeological site science. N.Y., 1971.
Arc 392.1 Hunter-Duvar, J. Stone, bronze and iron ages. London, 1892.
Arc 392.2 Hutchinson, H.N. Prehistoric man and beast. N.Y., 1897.
Arc 392.3 Hogarth, David George. Authority and archaeology. N.Y., 1899.
Arc 392.3.25 Sayce, A.H. David George Hogarth, 1862-1927. London, 1928.
Arc 392.4 Hunter, R. Preservation of places of interest or beauty. Manchester, 1907.
Arc 392.5 Hammerton, J.A. Wonders of the past; the romance of antiquity and its splendours. N.Y., 1925-26. 4v.
Arc 392.5.7 Hammerton, J.A. Wonders of the past. N.Y., 1937. 2v.
Arc 392.6 Hanno, Georges. Les villes retrouvées. Paris, 1881.
Arc 392.7.80 MacDonald, G. F. Haverfield, 1860-1919. London, 1921.
Arc 392.8.80 Harrison, E.R. Harrison of Ightham. London, 1928.
Arc 392.9.80 Thompson, R.C. Harry R.H. Hall, 1873-1930. London, 1930.
Arc 392.10.5 Hewett, Edgar Lee. Campfire and trail. Albuquerque, 1943.
Arc 392.11 A tribute to Sir George Hill on his 80th birthday. Oxford, 1948.
Arc 392.12.80 Georg Habich zum 60. Geburtstag. München, 1928.
Arc 392.14 Hawkes, Jacquetta. The world of the past. 1. ed. N.Y., 1963. 2v.
Arc 392.15 Handbuch der Archäologie im Rahnen des Handbuchs der Altertumswissenschaft. München, 1969-
Arc 392.15F Haeberlin, Ernst Justus. Ernst Justus Haeberlin, sein Wirken. München, 1929. 2v.
Arc 392.16 Heizer, Robert F. The archaeologist at work. N.Y., 1959.
Arc 392.18 Brandt, Karl. Otto Hauser. Witten-Ruhr, 1970.
Arc 393.1 Vegni, V. de. Notizie biografiche del cavaliere Francesco Inghirami. Volterra, 1849.
Arc 393.5 International Institute of Intellectual Cooperation. Manuel de la technique des fouilles archéologiques. Paris, 1950.
Arc 393.10 Hensel, Witold. Archeologia żywa. Wyd. 1. Warszawa, 1973.
Arc 393.15 Libellus Richardo Indrelso sexagenario oblatuo. Stockholm, 1960.
Arc 394.1 Jahn, Otto. Aus der Alterthumswissenschaft. Bonn, 1868.

Arc 385 - 410 Archaeology - General works - Individual authors (A-Z) - cont.

Arc 394.1.5 Pamphlet vol. Jahn, Otto. Collection of articles on art and archaeology. 17 pam.
Arc 394.1.6 Pamphlet vol. Jahn, Otto. Collection of articles on art and archaeology. 16 pam.
Arc 394.1.20 Michaelis, A. Otto Jahn in seinen Briefen. Leipzig, 1913.
Arc 394.2 Cheynier, A. Jovannet, grand-père de la préhistoire. Brive, 1936.
Arc 395.1 Kenward, J. Place of archaeology in science. Birmingham, 1877.
Arc 395.1.2 Kulturhistorischer Bilder-Atlas. Leipzig, 1883-85. 2v.
Arc 395.1.5 Bernhardi, K. Textbuch zu Th. Schreibers Kulturhistorischem Bilderatlas des klassischen Altertums. Leipzig, 1888.
Arc 395.3 Körte, G. Archäologie und Geschichts Wissenschaft. Göttingen, 1911.
Arc 395.4 Koepp, Friedrich. Archäologie. 2. Aufl. v.2,4. Berlin, 1920. 2v.
Arc 395.5 Kabbadias, P. Proistorikē archaiologia. Athēnai, 1914.
Arc 395.6 Koldewey, Robert. Heitere und ernst Briefe aus einem deutschen Archäologenleben. Berlin, 1920.
Arc 395.6.10 Andrae, W. Babylon, die versunkene Weltstadt und ihr Ausgräber Robert Koldewey. Berlin, 1952.
Arc 395.7.2 Hauviller, E. Franz Xaver Kraus. München, 1905.
Arc 395.7.5 Kraus, Franz Xaver. Tagebücher. Köln, 1957.
Arc 395.7.10 Kraus, Franz Xaver. Liberal und integral: der Briefwechsel zwischen Franz Xaver Kraus und A. Stöck. Mainz, 1974.
Arc 395.8 Kondakov, N.P. Vospominaniia i dumy. Praga, 1927.
Arc 395.9 Nikodim Pavlovich Kondakov, 1844-1924. Praga, 1924.
Arc 395.10 Klotz, C.A. Ueber das Studium des Alterthums. Halle, 1766.
Arc 395.11.5 Stampfuss, Rudolf. Gustav Kossinna. Leipzig, 1935.
Arc 395.12 Kaufmann, C.M. Allah ist gross! Freiburg, 1950.
Arc 395.13 Kraft, G. Der Urmensch als Schöpfer. 2. Aufl. Tübingen, 1948.
Arc 395.15 Kenyon, Kathleen Mary. Beginning in archaeology. 2. ed. London, 1953.
Arc 395.15.2 Kenyon, Kathleen Mary. Beginning in archaeology. London, 1952.
Arc 395.15.5 Kenyon, Kathleen Mary. Beginning in archaeology. N.Y., 1961.
Arc 395.18 Kosidowski, Z. Gdy słońce było bogiem. Warszawa, 1958.
Arc 395.18.2 Kosidowski, Z. Gdy słońce było bogiem. Warszawa, 1962.
Arc 395.18.5.5 Kosidowski, Zenon. Rumaki Lizypa i inne opowiadania. 2. wyd. Warszawa, 1974.
Arc 395.20 Kühn, Herbert. Der Aufstieg der Menschheit. Frankfurt, 1957.
Arc 395.20.5 Kühn, Herbert. Der Aufstieg der Menschheit. Frankfurt, 1955.
Arc 395.22 Karo, Georg H. Fünfzig Jahre aus dem Leben. Baden-Baden, 1959.
Arc 395.24 Kir'ianov, A.V. Restavratsiia arkheologicheskikh predmetov. Moskva, 1960.
Arc 395.25 Kostrzewski, Józef. Z mego życia. Wrocław, 1970.
Arc 395.26 Kozłowski, Janusz K. Archeologia prahistoryczna. Wyd. 1. Kraków, 1972- 2v.
Arc 395.27 Kramarkowa, Irena. U źródeł archeologii. Wrocław, 1972.
Arc 395.28 Kahlke, Hans Dietrich. Ausgrabungen in aller Welt. 1. Aufl. Leipzig, 1972.
Arc 396.1 Longpérier, A. de. Oeuvres. Paris, 1883-87. 7v.
Arc 396.2 Lange, Konrad. Grundsätze der modernen Denkmalpflege. Tübingen, 1906.
Arc 396.3.18 Le duc de Loubat, 1831-1894. Paris, 1894.
Arc 396.3.20 Le duc de Loubat, 1894-1912. Paris, 1912.
Arc 396.4.20 Société des Antiquaires de l'Ouest, Poitiers. Monument érigé à la mémoire de R.P. de la Croix. Poitiers, 1912.
Arc 396.5 Leite de Vasconcellos, J. De Campolide a Melrose. Lisboa, 1915.
Arc 396.6 Linde, Richard. Alte Kulturstätten. 2. Aufl. Bielefeld, 1924.
Arc 396.7F Pamphlet box. Le Coq, A. von. Reprinted articles.
Arc 396.8 Aubert, M. Notice nécrologique sur le comte Robert de Lesteyrie du Saillant, 1849-1919. Paris, 1926.
Arc 396.9 Lucas, A. Antiques, their restoration and preservation. London, 1924.
Arc 396.9.5 Lucas, A. Antiques, their restoration and preservation. 2. ed. London, 1932.
Arc 396.10 Laet, Siegfried J. de. L'archélogie et ses problèmes. Berchem, 1954.
Arc 396.11 Sardi, Jorge. Obras completas. San Salvador, 1960.
Arc 396.12 Lemaire, Raymond. La restauration des monuments anciens. Anvers, 1935.
Arc 396.13 Leone, Mark P. Comptemporary archaeology. Carbondale, 1972.
Arc 396.15F Lugli, Giuseppe. Saggi di explorazione archeologica. Roma, 1939.
Arc 396.16 Conference on the Future of Archaeology, University of London, 1943. Conference on the future of archaeology held at the University of London. London, 1943?
Arc 396.20 Leopold, Hendrik M.R. Uit de school van de spade. Zutphen, 1928-34. 6v.
VArc 396.21 Lesicjewicz, Anna. 500 zagadek archeologicznych. Warszawa, 1966.
Arc 396.22 Laming, Annette. La découverte du passe. Paris, 1952.
Arc 397.1 Millin, A.L. Monumens antiques. Paris, 1802-06. 2v.
Arc 397.1.5 Pamphlet vol. Millin, A.L. Varia. 31 pam.
Arc 397.2 Mitchell, A. The past in the present. Edinburgh, 1880.
Arc 397.3 Müller, K.O. Kunstarchaeologische Werke. v.1-5. Berlin, 1873. 2v.
Arc 397.3.2 Müller, K.O. Nouveau manuel d'archéologie. v.1-2 and atlas. Paris, 1841. 3v.
Arc 397.4 Müntz, Eugène. Études iconographiques et archéologiques. Paris, 1887.
Arc 397.5 Müntz, Eugène. Richerche intorno...Grimaldi. Firenze, 1881. 8 pam.
Arc 397.6 March, H.C. An examination of the tithe. Rochdale, 1887. 5 pam.
Arc 397.7 Michaelis, A. Die archäologischen Entdeckungen des 19. Jahrhunderts. Leipzig, 1906.
Arc 397.8 Michaelis, A. A century of archaeological discoveries. London, 1908.
Arc 397.10 Mortel, Victor. Mélanges d'archéologie; antiquité romaine et moyen âge. Paris, 1914-15. 2v.
Arc 397.11 Marshall, John. Conservation manual. Calcutta, 1923.
Arc 397.12 Magoffin, Rolf V.D. Romance of archaeology. London, 1930.
Arc 397.13 Morin, Jean. Les artistes préhistoriques. Paris, 1933.
Arc 397.14 Marini, G. Lettere inedite. v.1-3. Roma, 1916-40. 2v.

Arc 397.15 Curle, Alexander O. Sir George Macdonald, 1862-1940. London, 1941?
Arc 397.16 Magoffin, Rolf V.D. Magic spades. N.Y., 1929.
Arc 397.17.3 Marek, Kurt W. Götter. Hamburg, 1950.
Arc 397.17.5A Marek, Kurt W. Gods, graves, and scholars. 1. American ed. N.Y., 1951.
Arc 397.17.5B Marek, Kurt W. Gods, graves, and scholars. 1. American ed. N.Y., 1951.
Arc 397.17.5C Marek, Kurt W. Gods, graves, and scholars. 1. American ed. N.Y., 1951.
Arc 397.17.6 Marek, Kurt W. Gods, graves, and scholars. 2. ed. N.Y., 1968.
Arc 397.17.7 Marek, Kurt W. Götter, Gräber und Gelehrt. Reinbeck, 1972.
Arc 397.17.10 Marek, Kurt W. The march of archaeology. 1. American ed. N.Y., 1958.
Arc 397.17.15 Marek, Kurt W. A picture history of archaeology. London, 1958.
Arc 397.18A Macaulay, Rose. Pleasure of ruins. London, 1953.
Arc 397.18B Macaulay, Rose. Pleasure of ruins. London, 1953.
Arc 397.18.2 Macaulay, Rose. Pleasure of ruins. London, 1966.
Arc 397.18.10F Macaulay, Rose. Roloff Beny interprets in photographs Pleasure of ruins. London, 1964.
Arc 397.20 Murray, M.A. My first hundred years. London, 1963.
Arc 397.22 Mongait, A.L. Arkheologiia i sovremennost'. Moskva, 1963.
Arc 397.24 Mellersh, Harold Edward Leslie. Archaeology: science and romance. Exeter, 1966.
Arc 397.25 McDaniel, Walton B. Riding a hobby in the classical lands. Cambridge, 1971.
Arc 397.26 Müller-Karpe, Hermann. Handbuch der Vorgeschichte. v.1-3. München, 1966- 6v.
Arc 398.1 Nadaillac, J.F.A. du Pouget de. Les premiers hommes. Paris, 1881. 2v.
Arc 398.1.2 Nadaillac, J.F.A. du Pouget de. Prehistoric peoples. N.Y., 1892.
Arc 398.2 Newton C.T. Essays on art and archaeology. London, 1880.
Arc 398.3 Nicole, J. Mélanges Nicole...recueil de mémoires. Genève, 1905.
Arc 398.4 Scritti in onore di Bartolomeo Nogara. Città del Vaticano, 1937.
Arc 398.5 Nau, Karl J. Urgeschichte der Kultur. Stuttgart, 1961.
Arc 398.6 Nylander, Carl. Den dijupa brunnen. Stockholm, 1964.
Arc 398.8 Noël Hume, Ivor. Historical archaeology. 1. ed. N.Y., 1969.
Arc 398.8.1 Noël Hume, Ivor. Historical archaeology. N.Y., 1975.
Arc 399.2 Zaratti-Bianco, Umberto. Paolo Orsi. n.p., n.d.
Arc 399.3 Larichev, Vitalii E. Bibliografiia nauchnykh trudov po arkheologii i istorii chlena-korrespondenta AN SSSR A.P. Okladnikova. Novosibirsk, 1968.
Arc 399.3.2 Vasilevskii, Ruslan S. Annotirovannaia bibliografiia nauchnykh trudov akademika A.P. Okladnikova (1968-1973 gg). Ulan-Ude, 1974.
Arc 399.3.5 Larichev, Vitalii E. Sorok let sredi sibirskikh drevnostei. Novosibirsk, 1970.
Arc 399.4 Odobescu, Alexandru Ionescu. Istoria archeologiei. București, 1961.
Arc 400.1 Perkins, F.B. Prehistoric man. San Francisco, 1883.
Arc 400.2 Perrot, G. Mémoires d'archéologie. Paris, 1875.
Arc 400.3 Porter, R.K. Travels in Georgia, Persia. London, 1821-22. 2v.
Arc 400.4 Pronti, D. Nuova raccolta representante i costumi. Roma, 1808.
Arc 400.5 Petersen, C. Ueber dea Verhaltniss des Broncealters. Hamburg, 1868.
Arc 400.6 Voss, Albert. Merkbuch. 2. Aufl. Berlin, 1894.
Arc 400.7 Parkyn, E.A. An introduction to the study of prehistoric art. London, 1915.
Arc 400.8 Pownall, T. Treatise on the study of antiquities. London, 1782.
Arc 400.9 Piper, Otto. Bedenken zur Vorgeschichts-Forschung. München, 1913.
Arc 400.11 Peake, Harold J.E. Hunters and artists. New Haven, 1927.
Arc 400.11.10 Peake, Harold J.E. Merchant venturers in bronze. New Haven, 1931.
Arc 400.11.20 Peake, Harold J.E. The horse and the sword. New Haven, 1933.
Arc 400.11.30 Peake, Harold J.E. Times and places. Oxford, 1956.
Arc 400.12.25 Herberger, T. Conrad Peutinger in seinem Verhältnisse zum Kaiser Maximilian I. Augsburg, 1851.
Arc 400.13 Pallu de Lessert, A.C. Julien Poinssot; souvenirs 1844-1900. Paris, 1905.
Arc 400.14.25 Porter, Lucy W. Kingsley. Writings of A. Kingsley Porter. Cambridge, 1934.
Arc 400.15 Paniagua, A. de. L'âge du renne. Paris, 1926.
Arc 400.16 Pietto, E. Études d'ethnographie préhistorique. Paris, 189-. 9 pam.
Arc 400.17 In onore di Luigi Pigorini, Roma, 11 gennaio 1914. Roma, 1914.
Arc 400.18 Passemard, L. (Mme). Les statuettes feminines paléolithiques dites venus stéatophyges. Thèse. Nimes, 1938.
Arc 400.19 Peyrony, D. Éléments de préhistoire. Ussel, 1923.
Arc 400.20 Powell, D. The traveller's journey is done. London, 1943.
Arc 400.21 Pick, Behrendt. Aufsätze zur Numismatik und Archäologie. Jena, 1931.
Arc 400.22F Poulik, Josef. Prehistoric art. London, 1956.
Arc 400.23 Paciaudi, Paolo M. Lettres au comte de Caylus. Paris, 1802.
Arc 400.24 Petrie, William M. Flinders. Methods and aims in archaeology. London, 1904.
Arc 400.25 Piggott, Stuart. Approach to archaeology. Cambridge, 1959.
Arc 400.25.5.2 Webster, Graham. Practical archaeology. 2. ed. London, 1974.
Arc 400.26 Pyddoke, E. The scientist and archaeology. N.Y., 1964.
Arc 400.27 Pallottino, Massimo. Che cos'è l'archeologia. Firenze, 1963.
Arc 400.28.2 La préhistoire par André Leroi-Gourhan. 2. éd. Paris, 1968.
Arc 400.30 Philip Phillips: lower Mississippi survey, 1940-1970. Cambridge, Mass., 1970.
Arc 401.1 Quicherat, Jules. Mélanges d'archéologie et d'histoire. Paris, 1885.
Arc 401.1.2 Quicherat, Jules. Mélanges d'archéologie du Moyen Age. Paris, 1886.
Arc 401.1.8 Quicherat, Jules. Jules Quicherat, 1814-1882. Paris, 1882.

Arc 385 - 410 Archaeology - General works - Individual authors (A-Z) - cont.

Arc 401.2.5 Quennell, Marjorie (Courtney). Everyday life in the new stone, bronze, and early iron ages. 2. ed. London, 1931.
Arc 401.2.10 Quennell, Marjorie (Courtney). Everyday life in prehistoric times. 4. ed. London, 1952.
Arc 402.1 Rayet, O. Études d'archéologie et d'art. Paris, 1888.
Arc 402.2 Reinach, S. Chroniques d'Orient. Paris, 1891. 2v.
Arc 402.2.2 Reinach, S. Esquisses archéologiques. Paris, 1888.
Arc 402.2.9 Reinach, S. Le mirage oriental. Paris, 1893.
Arc 402.2.25 Reinach, S. Bibliographie de S. Reinach. Paris, 1936.
Arc 402.3 Robiou, F. Chefs-d'oeuvre de l'art antique. 1st ser., 1-3; 2d ser., 1-4. Paris, 1867. 7v.
Arc 402.4 Ross, L. Archaeologische Aufsaetze. Leipzig, 1855. 2v.
Arc 402.5 Rossignol, J.P. Services de l'archéologie aux études classiques. Paris, 1878.
Arc 402.6 Ruins of sacred and historic lands. London, 1853.
Arc 402.7 Robert, Charles. Mélanges d'archéologie. Paris, 1875.
Arc 402.8 Roger-Milès, L. Vingt siècles de travail. Paris, 1902.
Arc 402.9.25 Maspero, G. Notice biographique du vicomte Emmanuel de Rouge. Paris, 1908.
Arc 402.10 Pamphlet vol. Reinach, Theodore. Pamphlets on art, archaeology and ancient history. 25 pam.
Arc 402.10.25 Jamot, Paul. Theodore Reinach, (1860-1928). Paris, 1928.
Arc 402.11 Dalton, O.M. Sir Hercules Read. London, 1936.
Arc 402.12 Vernadskii, G.V. M.I. Rostovtsev. Praga, 1951.
Htn Arc 402.13* Vasconcellos, Joaquim de. Conde de Raczynski (Athanasius). Porto, 1875.
Arc 402.14 Sammarco, Angelo. Alessandro Ricci e il suo giornale dei viaggi. v.2. Cairo, 1930.
Arc 402.15 Pamphlet vol. Reisner, G.A. Miscellaneous papers. 14 pam.
Arc 402.16 Pamphlet vol. Reisner, G.A. Miscellaneous papers. 10 pam.
Arc 402.18 Rumpf, A. Archäologie. Berlin, 1953-56. 2v.
Arc 402.19 Romaios, K.A. Mikra meletēmata. Thessalonikē, 1955.
Arc 402.20 Rapport, S.B. Archaeology. N.Y., 1963.
Arc 402.22 Rehork, Joachim. Faszinierende Funde; Archäologie heute. Bergisch Gladbach, 1971.
Arc 403.1 Seabird, H. Element of archaeology. n.p., 1878.
Arc 403.2 Smith, C.R. Collectanea antiqua. London, 1848-80. 7v.
Arc 403.3 Stark, K.B. Handbuch der Archäologie der Kunst. Leipzig, 1880.
Arc 403.4 Spon, J. Recherche curieuse d'antiquité. Lyon, 1683.
Arc 403.5 Stevens, E.T. Flint chips. A guide to pre-historical archaeology. London, 1870.
Arc 403.6 Salinas, A. Miscellanea di archaeologia, storia, e filologia. Palermo, 1907.
Arc 403.7.3 Strzygowski, J. Die Baukunst der Armenier und Europa. Wien, 1918. 2v.
Arc 403.8 Simpson, J.Y. Archaeological essays. Edinburgh, 1872. 2v.
Arc 403.9 Smolin, V.F. Opyt instruktsii po sostaleniiu arkheologicheskikh kart. Kazan', 1921.
Arc 403.10 Silva, J.P.N. da. Noções elementares de archeologia. Lisboa, 1878.
Arc 403.12.2 Société Préhistorique de France. Manuel de recherches préhistoriques. 2. éd. Paris, 1929.
Arc 403.13F Schumacher-Festschrift. Mainz, 1930.
Arc 403.14 Oudheidkundig Genootschap, Amsterdam. Bibliographie der geschriften van Jhr. Dr. Jan Six. Amsterdam, 1933.
Arc 403.16.5 Schliemann, Heinrich. Selbstbiographie bis zu seinem Tod vervollständigt. 2. Aufl. Leipzig, 1936.
Arc 403.16.10 Schliemann, Heinrich. Heinrich Schliemann. 3. Aufl. Leipzig, 1939.
Arc 403.16.15 Schliemann, Heinrich. Heinrich Schliemann. Selbstbiographie. 7. Aufl. Leipzig, 1949.
Arc 403.16.17 Schliemann, Heinrich. Heinrich Schliemann. 8. Aufl. Wiesbaden, 1955.
Arc 403.16.20 Schliemann, Heinrich. Briefwechsel. Berlin, 1953. 2v.
Arc 403.16.25 Stoll, Heinrich A. Die Traum von Troja. Berlin, 1957.
Arc 403.16.30 Payne, R. The gold of Troy. N.Y., 1959.
Arc 403.16.35 Schliemann, Heinrich. Kein Troja ohne Homer. Nürnberg, 1960.
Arc 403.16.36 Lavater-Sloman, Mary. Das Gold von Troja. Zürich, 1969.
Arc 403.16.40 Poole, Lynn. One passion, two loves; the story of Heinrich and Sophia Schliemann. N.Y., 1966.
Arc 403.17 Sukhov, P.A. Arkheologicheskie pamiatniki. Moskva, 1941.
Arc 403.18 Schuckhartt, C. Aus Leben und Arbeit. Berlin, 1944.
Arc 403.19 Piggott, Stuart. William Stukely. Oxford, 1950.
Arc 403.20 Schweitzer, B. Zur Kunst der Antike. Tübingen, 1963. 2v.
Arc 403.21 Silverberg, R. Great adventures in archaeology. N.Y., 1964.
Arc 403.22 Statistiko-kombinatornye metody v arkheologii. Moskva, 1970.
Arc 403.23 Santos Rocha, Antonio dos. Memórias e exploraçoes arquelógicas. Coimbra, 1971-
Arc 403.24 Scientific methods in medieval archaeology. Berkeley, 1970.
Arc 403.25 Zenner, Klaus. Gang durch versunkene Städte; ein Ausflug ins Reich der Archäologie. Leipzig, 1974.
Arc 404.1.5A Tyskiewicz, M. Memories of an old collector. London, 1898.
Arc 404.1.5B Tyskiewicz, M. Memories of an old collector. London, 1898.
Arc 404.1.30 Thompson, Alexander Hamilton. A bibliography of the published writings of Sir William St. John Hope. Leeds, 1929.
Arc 404.2 Driver, Godfrey Rolles. Reginald Cambell Thompson. London, 1944.
Arc 404.3 Trapsh, M.M. Trudy. v.2. Sukhumi, 1969.
Arc 404.4 Touchard, Michel C. L'archéologie mystérieuse. Paris, 1972.
Arc 405.1.25 Pamiati grafa Alekseia Sergeevicha Uvarova. Kazan, 1885.
Arc 405.1.30 Uvarov, Aleksei S. Katalog sobraniia drevnostei. v.1,3-11. Moskva, 1887- 10v.
Arc 405.1.35 Nezabvennoi pamiati grafa Alekseia Sergeevicha Uvarova. Moskva, 1885.
Arc 405.1.40F Ardashev, Nikolai N. Grat A.S. Uvarov, kak teoretik arkheologii. Moskva, 1911.
Arc 405.2F UNESCO. Monuments et sites d'art. Paris, 1950.
Arc 405.3 Usov, S.A. Sochineniia. Moskva, 1892. 2v.
Arc 406.1 Vecchi, M.M. Il Mediterraneo illustrato. Firenze, 1841.
Arc 406.2 Sforza, G. Ennio Quirion Visconti Giacobino. n.p., n.d. 2 pam.

Arc 385 - 410 Archaeology - General works - Individual authors (A-Z) - cont.

Arc 406.3F Conestabile, G. Della vita degli studî, e delle opere di Giambattista Vermiglioli discorso. Perugia, 1855.
Arc 406.4 Vayson de Pradenne, A. La préhistoire. Paris, 1938.
Arc 406.4.5 Vayson de Pradenne, A. Prehistory. London, 1940.
Arc 406.5 Métral, D. Blaise de Vigenère, archéologue et critique d'art, 1523-1596. Thèse. Paris, 1839.
Arc 406.6 Viana, Abel. Algumas noções elementares do arqueologia pratica. Beja, 1962.
Arc 407.1 Walpole, R. Memoirs relating to European and Asiatic Turkey. London, 1817-20. 2v.
Htn Arc 407.2* Wise, F. Letter to Dr. Mead. Oxford, 1738-64. 4 pam.
Arc 407.3 Wright, G.F. Early man. Cleveland, 1883.
Arc 407.4A Wright, T. Essays on archaeological subjects. v.1-2. London, 1861.
Arc 407.4B Wright, T. Essays on archaeological subjects. London, 1861. 2v.
Arc 407.5 Wussow, A. von. Der Erhaltung der Denkmäler. Berlin, 1885.
Arc 407.5.2 Wussow, A. von. Die Erhaltung der Denkmäler. Berlin, 1885.
Arc 407.6 Wilson, John Albert. Prehistoric art. Washington, 1898.
Arc 407.6.5 Wilson, John Albert. Study of prehistoric anthropology. Washington, 1890.
Arc 407.6.10 Wilson, John Albert. Thousands of years. N.Y., 1972.
Arc 407.7 Werveke, N. van. Mélanges archéologiques. Luxembourg, 1882.
Arc 407.9.2 Westropp, Hodder Michael. Handbook of archaeology. 2. ed. London, 1878.
Arc 407.10 Woolley, Charles L. Dead towns and living men. London, 1920.
Arc 407.10.5 Woolley, Charles L. Digging up the past. Harmondsworth, 1937.
Arc 407.10.7 Woolley, Charles L. Digging up the past. Harmondsworth, 1956.
Arc 407.10.10 Woolley, Charles L. Spadework in archaeology. N.Y., 1953.
Arc 407.10.11 Woolley, Charles L. Spadework. London, 1953.
Arc 407.10.15 Woolley, Charles L. History unearthed. London, 1958.
Arc 407.10.18 Woolley, Charles L. History unearthed. N.Y., 1962.
Arc 407.10.20 Woolley, Charles L. As I seem to remember. London, 1962.
Arc 407.11 Wirth, Herman. Der Aufgang der Menschheit. Jena, 1928.
Arc 407.12 Wieringen, J.H. van. De voor historische mens. Zutphen, 1938.
Arc 407.14 Watzinger, C. Theodor Wiegand. München, 1944.
Arc 407.15 Wegner, Max. Altertumskunde. Freiburg, 1951.
Arc 407.16 Wheeler, Robert Eric Mortimer. Archaeology from the earth. Oxford, 1954.
Arc 407.17 Wheeler, Robert Eric Mortimer. Still digging. London, 1955.
Arc 407.18 Wheeler, Robert Eric Mortimer. Rome beyond the imperial frontiers. London, 1954.
Arc 407.19 White, Anne Terry. Lost worlds; the romance of archaeology. N.Y., 1941.
Arc 407.20 Wheeler, Robert Eric Mortimer. Alms for oblivion: an antiquary's scrapbook. London, 1966.
Arc 407.25 Westropp, Hodder Michael. Pre-historic phases. London, 1872.
Arc 407.30 Leppmann, Wolfgang. Winckelmann. 1. ed. N.Y., 1970.
Arc 407.30.5 Schadewaldt, Wolfgang. Winckelmann und Rilke: zwei Beschreibungen des Apollon. Pfullingen, 1968.
Arc 407.30.10 Johann Joachim Winckelmann, 1768-1968. Bad Godesberg, 1968.
Arc 407.30.15 Rein, Ulrike G.M. Winckelmanns Begriff der Schönheit. Bonn, 1972.
Arc 407.31 Wilkinson, Edward M. Technische und naturwissenschaftliche Beiträge zur Feldarchäologie. Köln, 1974.
Arc 410.1.18 Welcker, F.G. Zoega's Leben. Stuttgart, 1819. 2v.

Arc 412 Archaeology - General special

Arc 412.1 Bass, George Fletcher. Archaeology under water. London, 1966.
Arc 412.1.5 Bass, George Fletcher. A history of seafaring based on underwater archaeology. London, 1972.
Arc 412.1.10 Flemming, Nicholas C. Cities in the sea. 1. ed. Garden City, N.Y., 1971.
Arc 412.1.15 Bass, George Fletcher. Archaeology beneath the sea. N.Y., 1975.
Arc 412.2 Taylor, Joan du Plat. Marine archaeology. London, 1965.
Arc 412.3 Dzhus, Vsevolod E. My-gedronavty. Leningrad, 1974.
Arc 412.5 Pannell, John Percival Masterman. The technology of industrial archaeology. Newton Abbot, 1966.
Arc 412.5.5 Brolin, Per Erik. Gamla fynd och glömda folk. Göteborg, 1969.
Arc 412.7 Symposium on Archaeological Chemistry. Science and archaeology. Cambridge, Mass., 1971.
Arc 412.8 García y Bellido, Antonio. Urbanistica de las grandes ciudades del mundo antiguo. Madrid, 1966.
Arc 412.9 Clarke, David L. Models in archaeology. London, 1972.
VArc 412.11 Jażdżewski, Konrad. Ochrona zabytków archeologicznych. Warszawa, 1966.
Arc 412.12 Rieth, Adolf. Vorzeit gefälscht. Tübingen, 1967.
Arc 412.14 Goguey, René. De l'aviation à l'archéologie. Paris, 1968.
Arc 412.16 Throckmorton, Peter. Shipwrecks and archaeology: the unharvested sea. 1. ed. Boston, 1970.
Arc 412.18 Devel, Leo. Flights into yesterday. N.Y., 1969.
Arc 412.20 Dating techniques for the archaeologist. Cambridge, 1971.
Arc 412.22 Kondratov, Aleksandr M. Tainy tsekh okeanov. Leningrad, 1971.
Arc 412.22.1 Kondratov, Aleksandr M. The riddles of three oceans. Moscow, 1974.
Arc 412.24 Animals in archaeology. N.Y., 1972.
Arc 412.25 Problemy absoliutnogo datirovaniia v arkheologii. Moskva, 1972.
Arc 412.26 Cleator, Philip. Underwater archaeology. London, 1973.
Arc 412.27 Selhus, Wilhelm. Und sie waren doch da: wissenschaftliche Beweise für den Besuch aus dem All. München, 1975.
Arc 412.28 Alpözen, Oğuz. Türkuiye'de sualt, arkeolojisi. İstanbul, 1975.

Arc 415 Archaeology - Local - Asia in general - Folios [Discontinued]

Arc 415.1 Heger, Franz. Alte Metalltrommeln aus Südost-Asien. Leipzig, 1902. 2v.

Classified Listing

Arc 416 Archaeology - Local - Asia in general - General works, Special topics

Arc 416.1 Babelon, E. Manuel d'archéologie orientale. Paris, 1888.
Arc 416.1.2 Babelon, E. Manual of Oriental antiquities. N.Y., 1889.
Arc 416.1.3A Babelon, E. Manual of Oriental antiquities. N.Y., 1906.
Arc 416.1.3B Babelon, E. Manual of Oriental antiquities. N.Y., 1906.
VArc 416.2 Clermont-Ganneau, Charles. Recueil d'archéologie orientale. Paris, 1888-1924, 8v.
Arc 416.2.2 Clermont-Ganneau, Charles. Études d'archéologie orientale. Paris, 1880. 2v.
Arc 416.3 Fischer, H. Stone implements in Asia. Worcester, 1884.
Arc 416.4 Lunet de Lajonquière, E.E. Rapport...mission archéologique (Cambodge, Siam, presqu'île Malaise, Inde). Paris, 1907-08.
Arc 416.5 Asie centrale et Tibet. Missions Pelliot et Bacot, documens exposés au Musée Guimet. Paris, 1921.
Arc 416.6 Contenau, Georges. Manuel d'archéologie orientale depuis les origines jusqu'a l'époque d'Alexandre. Paris, 1927-47. 4v.
Arc 416.7F Moskovskoe Arkheologicheskoe Obshchestvo. Drevnosti vostoch'iia trudi vostochnoi kommissii. Moskva, 1889-1915. 5v.
Arc 416.8 Hackin, J. Recherches archéologiques en Asie centrale (1931). Paris, 1936.
Arc 416.9 Carleton, P. Buried empires; the earliest civilizations of the Middle East. London, 1939.
Arc 416.10 Beylié, Léon de. Prome et Samara; voyage archéologique en Birmanie et en Mesopotamie. Paris, 1907.
Arc 416.11 Nag, K. India and the Pacific world. Calcutta, 1941.
Arc 416.13 Pamphlet vol. Stein, Mark. Reprints. 13 pam.
Arc 416.15 Pamphlet box. Stein, Mark. Reprints.
Arc 416.17F Rozanthal, A. Arts antiques de l'Asie occidentale. Nice, 1948.
Arc 416.19 Schaeffer, C.F. Stratigraphie comparée. London, 1848-
Arc 416.20 Mellaart, James. The Neolithic of the Near East. London, 1975.
Arc 416.21 Miles, G.C. Archaeologica orientalia in memoriam Ernst Herzfeld. Locust Valles, N.Y., 1952.
Arc 416.23 Parrot, A. Découverte des mondes ensevelés. Neuchâtel, 1952.
Arc 416.23.5 Parrot, A. Discovering buried worlds. 1. ed. N.Y., 1955.
Arc 416.24 Deuel, Leo. The treasures of time. 1. ed. Cleveland, 1961.
Arc 416.25 Burton-Brown, Theodore. Early Mediterranean migration; an essay in archaeological interpretation. Manchester, 1959.
Arc 416.26 Akishev, K.A. Drevniaia kul'tura sakov i usunei doliny reki Ili. Alma Ata, 1963.
Arc 416.27 Andrae, Walter. Alte Feststrassen im Nahen Orient. Stuttgart, 1964.
Arc 416.28 Masson, V.M. Sredniaia Aziia i drevnii Vostok. Leningrad, 1964.
Arc 416.30 Kantor, H.J. The Aegean and the Orient in the second millennium B.C. Bloomington, 1947.
Arc 416.32 Hierche, Henri. Manuel d'archéologie d'Extrême-Orient. Paris, 1966- 2v.
Arc 416.33 Akademiia nauk SSSR. Institut narodov Azii. Deshifrovka i interpretatsiia pis'mennostei drevnego Vostoka. Moskva, 1966.
Arc 416.35 Loofs, Helmut Hermann Ernst. Elements of the megalithic complex in Southeast Asia. Canberra, 1967.
Arc 416.36 Mellaart, James. Earliest civilizations of the Near East. N.Y., 1965.
Arc 416.38 Brentjes, Burchard. Von Schanidar bis Akkad. 1. Aufl. Leipzig, 1968.
Arc 416.40 Studia z archeologii Azji Przedniej i Starożytnego Wschodu. Wyd. 1. Kraków, 1970.
Arc 416.42 Laricheo, Vitalii E. Paleolit Severnoi, Tsentral'noi i Vostochnoi Azii. Novosibirsk, 1969- 2v.
Arc 416.44 Lloyd, Seton Howard Frederick. Mounds of the Near East. Edinburgh, 1963.
Arc 416.46 Borisovskii, Pavel I. Drevnii kamennyi vek Iuzhnoi i Iuga-Vostochnoi Azii. Leningrad, 1971.
Arc 416.47 South Asian archaeology; papers. 1. U.S. ed. Park Ridge, N.Y., 1973.
Arc 416.48 Drevnii Vostok. Erevan, 1973.
Arc 416.49 Korfmann, Manfred. Schleuder und Bogen in Südwestasien; von der frühesten Belagen bis zum Beginn der historischen Stadtstaaten. Bonn, 1972.

Arc 419 Archaeology - Local - China - Pamphlet volumes

Arc 419.1 Pamphlet box. China. Miscellaneous pamphlets.

Arc 420 Archaeology - Local - China - Folios [Discontinued]

Arc 420.5F Chavannes, E. Mission archéologique dans la Chine septentrionale. v.1-2; planches, pt.3. Paris, 1909-15. 4v.
Arc 420.7 Radloff, W. Tpya...Atraer. St. Petersburg, 1892.
Arc 420.8F Segalen, V. Mission archéologique en Chine (1914 et 1917). Atlas. Paris, 1923-24. 2v.

Arc 421 Archaeology - Local - China - General works; Local; Special topics

Arc 421.1 Dumontier, G. Le grand-Bouddha de Hanoi. Hanoi, 1888.
Arc 421.4 Ferguson, J.C. A bronze table with accompanying vessels. Peking, 1924.
Arc 421.4.5 Ferguson, J.C. The four bronze vessels of the Marquis. Peking, 1928.
Arc 421.4.10 Ferguson, J.C. Two bronze drums. Peking, 1932.
Arc 421.5 Godfrey, E.F. Die Kaiserspräher der Tsing Dynastie in China. Berlin, 1930.
Arc 421.6 Stockholm. Astasiatiska bulletin. v.1-30,35-42. Stockholm, 1929-58.
Arc 421.8 Ségalen, V. Mission archéologique en Chine (1914). Paris, 1935.
Arc 421.9F Houo-Ming-Tse, P. Preuves des antiquités. Pekin, 1930.
Arc 421.10 Andersson, J. Preliminary report on archaeological research in Kansu. Pekin, 1925.
Arc 421.10.15 Andersson, J. Children of the yellow earth. London, 1934.
Arc 421.11 White, W.C. Tombs of old Lo-yang. Shanghai, 1934.
Arc 421.12 Creel, H.G. Studies in early Chinese culture. London, 1938.
Arc 421.14 Reischauer, E.O. Japanese archaeological work on the Asiatic continent. Baltimore, 1940.
Arc 421.16 Bunakov, I.V. Tadatel'nie kosti iz Khznani. Moskva, 1935.
Arc 421.18 Torü, P. Sculptured stone tombs of the Lion dynasty. Peking, 1942.
Arc 421.20 Yale University. Gallery of Fine Arts. An exhibition of Chinese antiquities from Ch'ang Sha. New Haven, 1939.
Arc 421.22 Chêng, Tê-k'un. Archaeology in China. v.1-3. Cambridge, Eng., 1959-

Arc 421 Archaeology - Local - China - General works; Local; Special topics - cont.

Arc 421.23 Watson, William. China before the Han dynasty. London, 1961.
Arc 421.24 Watson, William. Archaeology in China. London, 1960.
Arc 421.25 Yu. Inschrift des Yu. Halle, 1811.
Arc 421.26 Crump, J. Dragon bones in the yellow earth. N.Y., 1963.
Arc 421.27 Tung, Tso-pin. Fifty years of studies in oracle inscriptions. Tokyo, 1964.
Arc 421.28 Chaung, K. The archaeology of ancient China. New Haven, 1963.
Arc 421.30 Hentze, Carl. Funde in Alt-China. Göttingen, 1967.
Arc 421.31.2 Li, Chi. The beginnings of Chinese civilization. Seatle, 1968.
Arc 421.32 Watson, William. Cultural frontiers in ancient east Asia. Edinburgh, 1971.
Arc 421.33 Hay, John. Ancient China. London, 1973.

Arc 424 Archaeology - Local - Japan - Pamphlet volumes

Arc 424.01 Pamphlet box. Japan. Miscellaneous pamphlets.

Arc 426 Archaeology - Local - Japan - General works; Local; Special topics

Arc 426.1 Morse, E.S. Traces of an early race in Japan. N.Y., 1879.
Arc 426.2A Kanda, T. Notes on ancient stone implements...of Japan. Tokio, 1884.
Arc 426.2B Kanda, T. Notes on ancient stone implements...of Japan. Tokio, 1884.
Arc 426.3 Munro, N.G. Prehistoric Japan. Yokohama, 1908.
Arc 426.3.5 Munro, N.G. Prehistoric Japan. Yokohama, 1911.
Arc 426.4 Arai, Hakuseki. The sword book, in Honiko Gunkiko. Reading, 1913. 2 pam.
Arc 426.5 Kyoto. University. Archaeological Institute. Report upon archaeological research. Tokyo. 3-10,1919-1927 4v.
Arc 426.7F Gowland, William. The dolmens and burial mounds in Japan. London, 1897.
Arc 426.8 Hitchcoke, R. The ancient burial mounds of Japan. Washington, 1893.
Arc 426.9 Reischauer, E.O. The thunder-weapon in ancient Japan. Baltimore, 1940.
Arc 426.10 Groot, G.J. The prehistory of Japan. N.Y., 1951.
Arc 426.12 Kidder, J.E. Japan before Buddhism. London, 1959.
Arc 426.15 Vorob'ev, M.V. Drevniaia Iaponiia. Moskva, 1958.

Arc 428 Archaeology - Local - Korea

Arc 428.5PF Archaeology of Korea. Plates and maps. Tokyo, 1913. 7v.
Arc 428.10 Vorob'ev, M.V. Drevniaia Korea. Moskva, 1961.

Arc 430 Archaeology - Local - India - Folios [Discontinued]

Arc 430.2F Rájendralála Mitra. Antiquities of Orissa. Calcutta, 1875-80. 2v.
Arc 430.3 Griffin, L. Famous monuments of central India. London, 1886.
Arc 430.5 Gruenwedel, A. Buddhistische Studien. Berlin, 1897.
Arc 430.10F Stein, Mark A. Archaeological reconnaissances in north-western India and south-eastern Iran. London, 1937.
Arc 430.201 Lebon, G. Les monuments de l'Inde. Paris, 1893.
Arc 430.202 Bird, James. Historical researches...caves of western India. Bombay, 1847.

Arc 432 Archaeology - Local - India - General works

Arc 432.01 Pamphlet box. India. Miscellaneous pamphlets.
Arc 432.07F Annual bibliography of Indian archaeology. Leyden. 1-17 17v.
Arc 432.1 Fergusson, J. Cave temples of India. London, 1880.
Arc 432.1.2 Fergusson, F. Rock-cut temples of India. London, 1864.
Arc 432.1.3 Fergusson, J. Rock-cut temples of India. London, 1864.
Arc 432.1.5 Fergusson, J. Archaeology in India. London, 1884.
Arc 432.2A Maurice, G. Indian antiquities. London, 1800. 7v.
Arc 432.2B Maurice, G. Indian antiquities. v.7. London, 1800.
Arc 432.3 Cloquet, L. L'art munumental des Indous et des Perses. Bruxelles, 1896.
Arc 432.4 Pinto, Christoram. India prehistorica. Lisboa, 1909.
Arc 432.5.2 Mitra, Panchanan. Prehistoric India. 2. ed. Calcutta, 1927.
Arc 432.6 Crinwasa Aiyangar, P.T. The stone age in India. Madras, 1926.
Arc 432.7 Jouveau-Dubreuil, D. Vedic antiquities. London, 1922.
Arc 432.8 Cumming, John. Revealing India's past. London, 1939.
Arc 432.9 Bruhl, O. Indian temples. Calcutta, 1937.
Arc 432.10 Dikshit, K.N. Prehistoric civilization of the Indus Valley. Madras, 1939.
Arc 432.11 Burgess, J. Indian architecture. Oxford, 1907.
Arc 432.12 Mode, Heinz. Indische Frühkulturen und ihre Beziehungen zum Westen. Basel, 1944.
Arc 432.12.5 Mode, Heinz. Das frühe Indien. Stuttgart, 1959.
Arc 432.13 Piggott, Stuart. Some ancient cities of India. London, 1945.
Arc 432.14 Punja, P.R.R. India's legacy. Mangalore, 1948.
Arc 432.15 Sivaramamurto, C. Indian epigraphy and south Indian scripts. Madra, 1952.
Arc 432.16 Shakur, M.A. A handbook to the Inscription Gallery in the Peshhawar Museum. Peshawar, 1946.
Arc 432.17 India. Department of Archaeology. Ancient monuments. Delhi, 1957. 6 pam.
Arc 432.18 Combaz, Gisbert. L'Inde et l'Orient classique. Paris, 1937. 2v.
Arc 432.19 Gupta, Swarajya Prakash. Disposal of the dead and physical types in ancient India. 1. ed. Delhi, 1972.
Arc 432.20 Gordon, Douglas Hamilton. The pre-historic background of Indian culture. Bombay, 1958.
Arc 432.20.2 Gordon, Douglas Hamilton. The pre-historic background of Indian culture. 2. ed. Bombay, 1960.
Arc 432.22 Dani, A.H. Prehistory and protohistory of east India. Calcutta, 1960.
Arc 432.23 Akademiia Nauk SSSR. Institut Narodov Azii. Indiia v drevnosti; sbornik statei. Moskva, 1964.
Arc 432.24 Sankalis, Hasmukh Dhirajlal. Prehistory and protohistory in India and Pakistan. Bombay, 1962.
Arc 432.25 Chhabra, Bahadur Chand. Expansion of Indo-Aryan culture during Pallava rule as evidenced by inscriptions. Delhi, 1965.
Arc 432.26 Wheeler, Robert Eric Mortimer. Civilizations of the Indus Valley and beyond. London, 1966.
Arc 432.27 Lal, Braj Basi. Indian archaeology since independence. 1. ed. Delhi, 1964.
Arc 432.28 Banerjee, N.R. The iron age in India. Delhi, 1965.
Arc 432.29 Roy, Sourindranath. The story of Indian archaeology, 1784-1947. New Delhi, 1961.

Classified Listing

Arc 432 Archaeology - Local - India - General works - cont.

Arc 432.30 Chattopadhyay, Kshitis Prasad. Ancient Indian culture contacts and migration. Calcutta, 1965.
Arc 432.31 Agrawal, Dharma Pal. Prehistoric chronology and radiocarbon dating in India. New Delhi, 1974.
Arc 432.32 Seminar on Indian Prehistory and Protohistory, Deccan College Post Graduate and Research Institute, 1964. Indian prehistory. 1. ed. Poona, 1965.
Arc 432.34 Abu, Imam. Sir Alexander Cunningham and...Indian archaeology. Dacca, 1966.
Arc 432.35 Indologische Arbeitstagung, Museum für Indische Kunst, Berlin, 1971. Indologen-Tagung 1971. Weisbaden, 1973.

Arc 435 Archaeology - Local - India - Archaeological Survey reports

Arc 435.1.1 India. Archaeological Survey. Reports. Varanasi, 1966-72. 24v.
Arc 435.1.5 Pamphlet box. Indian inscriptions.
Arc 435.1.10 Indian Museum, Calcutta. Catalogue raisonné of the prehistoric antiquities. Simla, 1917.
Arc 435.1.15F India. Archaeological Survey. Memoirs. Calcutta. 1-73,1919-1955 14v.
Arc 435.1.18 India. Archaeological Survey. Library. Classified catalogue of the library of the director general of archaeology. Calcutta, 1908.
Arc 435.1.20 India. Archaeological Survey. Library. Consolidated catalogue. New Delhi, 1940.
Arc 435.2 India. Archaeological Survey. Report. London. 1-5,1874-1883// 4v.
X Cg Arc 435.2 India. Archaeological Survey. Report. London. 3
Arc 435.2.6F Burgess, James. The Buddhist stupas of Amarayati and Jaggayyapeta. London, 1887.
Arc 435.2.7F Sewell, Robert. Lists of the antiquarian remains in the presidency of Madras. Madras, 1882.
Arc 435.2.8F Sewell, Robert. Lists of inscriptions and sketch...dynasties of southern India. Madras, 1884.
Arc 435.2.9F India. Department of Archaeology. South-Indian inscriptions. Madras. 1890-1949 16v.
Arc 435.2.11F Führer, A.A. The Sharqi architecture of Jaunpur. Calcutta, 1889.
Arc 435.2.12F Führer, A.A. Monumental antiquities and inscriptions. Allahabad, 1891.
Arc 435.2.15F Rea, Alexander. South Indian Buddhist antiquities. Madras, 1894.
Arc 435.2.16F Burgess, James. Revised lists of antiquarian remains in the Bombay presidency. Bombay, 1897.
Arc 435.2.17F Rea, Alexander. List of architectural and archaeological remains in Coorg. Madras, 1894.
Arc 435.2.19F Cousens, Henry. Lists of antiquarian remains in the central provinces and Berâr. Calcutta, 1897.
X Cg Arc 435.2.20F Smith, V.A. The Jain stûpa and other antiquities of Mathûra. Allahabad, 1901.
Arc 435.2.21F Rea, Alexander. Châlukyan architecture. Madras, 1898.
Arc 435.2.22F Hoernle, A.F.R. The Bower manuscript. Calcutta, 1893-1912.
Arc 435.2.23F Burgess, James. On the Muhammadan architecture of Bharoch, Cambay. London, 1896.
Arc 435.2.24F Burgess, James. The Muhammadan architecture of Ahmadabad. London, 1900.
Arc 435.2.25F Rea, Alexander. Monumental remains of the Dutch East India Company in the presidency of Madras. Madras, 1897.
Arc 435.2.26F Purna Chandra, Mukhopâdhyâya. Report of a tour of exploration of the antiquities in the Tarai, Nepal. Calcutta, 1901.
Arc 435.2.30F Smith, E.W. Moghul colour decoration of Agra. Allahabad, 1901.
X Cg Arc 435.2.32F Burgess, James. The architectural antiquities of northern Gujarat. London, 1903.
Arc 435.2.32.1 Burgess, James. The architectural antiquities of northern Gujarat. 1. Indian ed. Varanasi, 1975.
Arc 435.2.33F Burgess, James. The Muhammadan architecture. pt.2. London, 1905.
Arc 435.2.34F Rea, Alexander. Pallava architecture. Madras, 1909.
Arc 435.2.35F Smith, E.W. Akbar's tomb, Sikandarah, near Agra. Allahabad, 1909.
Arc 435.2.36F Vogel, J.P. Antiquities of Chamba state. Calcutta, 1911.
Arc 435.2.38F Francke, A.H. Antiquities of Indian Tibet. Calcutta, 1914-26. 2v.
Arc 435.2.39F Rice, B.S. Epigraphia caratica. Madras, 1914.
Arc 435.2.40F Kaye, G.R. The astronomical observatories of Jai Singh. Calcutta, 1918.
Arc 435.2.41F Vogel, J.P. Tile-mosaics of the Lahore fort. Calcutta, 1920.
Arc 435.2.42F Cousens, Henry. Chalukyan architecture. Calcutta, 1926.
Arc 435.2.43F Kaye, G.R. Bakhshali manuscript. pt.1-3. Calcutta, 1927-33. 2v.
Arc 435.2.51F Ķuraishi, M.M.Ḥ. List of ancient monuments protected in Bihar and Orissa. Calcutta, 1931.
Arc 435.2.53 Sen, B. Some historical aspects of the inscriptions of Bengal. Calcutta, 1942.
Arc 435.3F India. Archaeological Survey. Annual report. Calcutta. 1902-1916// 14v.
Arc 435.3.5F India. Archaeological Survey. Annual report. Index, 1902-1916. Calcutta, 1924.
Arc 435.4F India. Archaeological Survey. Annual report of the director-general of archaeology. pt.1. Calcutta. 1902-1921// 11v.
Arc 435.4.25F India. Archaeological Survey. Annual report of the Archaeological Survey of India. Calcutta. 1916-1936 18v.
Htn Arc 435.8.6* Führer, A.A. Monograph on Buddha Sâkyamuni's birth-place in the Nepalese Tarâi. Allahabad, 1897.
Arc 435.9.3 Burgess, James. Notes on the Amarâvati stûpa. Madras, 1882.
Arc 435.9.5 Burgess, James. Notes on the Amarâvati stûpa. Madras, 1882. 2 pam.
Arc 435.11.10 Burgess, James. Inscriptions from cave-temples of western India. Bombay, 1881.
Arc 435.11.11 Burgess, James. Lists of antiquarian remains in the Bombay presidency. Bombay, 1885.
Arc 435.11.12 Cousens, Henry. An account of the caves at Nadsur and Karsambla. Bombay, 1891.
Arc 435.12F Fleet, J.F. Pâli, Sanskrit and old Canarese inscriptions. London, 1878.
Arc 435.12.4F Burgess, James. Memorandum on the survey of architecture and other archaeological remians...Sindh, Berar. Bombay, 1870. 2 pam.
Arc 435.13 Hirâlâl, Rai Bahâdur. Descriptive lists of inscriptions in the central provinces and Berar. Nagpur, 1916.

Arc 435 Archaeology - Local - India - Archaeological Survey reports - cont.

NEDL Arc 435.16 India. Curator of Ancient Monuments. Preservation of national monuments. v.1-3. Simla, 1882-84.
Arc 435.16.2F India. Curator of Ancient Monuments. Plan of Delhi. v.1-15. n.p., 1881.
Arc 435.20 India. Archaeological Survey. Epigraphia Indica. 1,1888+ 35v.
Arc 435.20.1F Corpus inscriptionum Indicarum. Calcutta, 1877.
Arc 435.20.2F Corpus inscriptionum Indicarum. v.1-4. Calcutta, 1879-1929. 5v.
Arc 435.20.3 India. Archaeological Survey. Epigraphia Indo-Moslemica. Arabic and Persian supplement. 1927+ 7v.
Arc 435.20.5 Corpus inscriptionum Indicarum. Oxford, 1925.
Arc 435.20.45 Rangâchârya, V. A topographical list of the inscirptions of the Madras presidency (collected till 1915) with notes. Madras, 1919. 3v.
Arc 435.21 Rice, B.L. Epigraphia carnatica. v.1-2. Bangalore, 1889- 15v.
Arc 435.21.5F Rice, B.L. Epigraphia carnatica. Bangalore, 1923.
Arc 435.22 Narasimhachar, R. Architecture and sculpture in Mysore. v.2. Bangalore, 1919.
Arc 435.25 Cole, H.H. Mixed Hindu-Mahamedan style. London, 1873.
Arc 435.25.3F Indian Museum, Calcutta. A list of the photographic negatives of Indian antiquities. Calcutta, 1900.
Arc 435.25.4F Conference of Orientalists, Simla. The conference...including museums and archaeological conference...Simla, 1911. Simla, 1911.
Arc 435.25.5F India. Archaeological Survey. Illustrations of ancient buildings of Kashmir. London, 1869.
Arc 435.25.6 Burgess, James. Descriptive account of the rock temples of western India. Bombay, 187-?
Arc 435.25.7F India. Archaeological Survey. Loan exhibition of antiquities, Coronation Durbar, 1911. Calcutta, 1912.
Arc 435.25.8F Sanchi, Bhopal State. Museum of Archaeology. Catalogue of the Museum of Archaeology at Sanchi, Bhopal State. Calcutta, 1922.
Arc 435.26 India. Archaeological Survey. Archaeological remains. v.1-2. New Delhi, 1964.
Arc 435.51F Burma. Archaeological Survey. Report of the superintendent. Rangoon. 1901-1939 5v.
Arc 435.52 India. Archaeological Survey. Eastern Circle, Bengal. Annual report. Calcutta. 1888-1921 2v.
Arc 435.53F India. Archaeological Survey. Northern Circle, Punjab. Annual progress report of the superintendent. 1906-1916
Arc 435.53.2F India. Archaeological Survey. Northern Circle, Punjab. Annual progress report of the superintendent, Hindu and Buddhist monuments. 1911-1921
Arc 435.53.3F India. Archaeological Survey. Northern Circle, Punjab. Annual progress report of the superintendent, Muhammadan and British monuments. Allahabad. 1910-1921// 5v.
Arc 435.54F India. Archaeological Survey. Southern Circle, Madras. Annual report. Madras. 1858-1921 7v.
Arc 435.54.3F India. Archaeological Survey. Southern Circle, Madras. Annual report of the assistant superintendent for epigraphy. Madras. 1881-1945 9v.
Arc 435.54.10F India. Department of Archaeology. Annual report on Indian epigraphy. Delhi. 1945-1964 2v.
Arc 435.55F Mysore. Archaeological Survey. Annual report. Bangalore. 1909-1946 22v.
Arc 435.55.2F Mysore. Archaeological Survey. Index to the annual reports of the Mysore Archaeological Department for the years 1906-1922. Bangalore, 1929.
Arc 435.56F India. Archaeological Survey. Uttar Pradesh. Progress reports of the epigraphical and architectural branches. Allahabad. 1887-1905 2v.
Arc 435.57 India. Archaeological Survey. Punjab Circle. Report. Calcutta. 1888-1889
Arc 435.58F India. Archaeological Survey. Western Circle, Bombay. Progress report. 1889-1921 3v.
Arc 435.59F India. Archaeological Survey. Frontier Circle, Peshawar. Annual report. Peshawar. 1904-1921 3v.
Arc 435.60F India. Archaeological Survey. Central Circle. Annual progress report. Patna. 1920-1921
Arc 435.70F Ceylon. Archaeological Survey. Annual report. Colombo. 1904-1947 6v.
Arc 435.70.2F Ceylon. Archaeological Survey. Annual report, 1903. Preliminary proof. n.p., 1903.
Arc 435.70.3F Ceylon. Archaeological Survey. Annual report. Colombo. 1892-1912 3v.
Arc 435.70.5F Ceylon. Archaeological Survey. Memoirs. Colombo. 1-6,1924-1953 7v.
Arc 435.70.9F Pamphlet box. Ceylon. Archaeological Survey.
Arc 435.71F Ceylon. Archaeological Survey. Progress report. Colombo. 1-7
Arc 435.72F Epigraphia zeylanica. London. 1-4,1904-1941 5v.
Arc 435.85 Kashmir. Archaeological Survey. Memoirs. Mysore City. 1-2 2v.
Arc 435.86 Sircar, Dineschandra. Indian epigraphy. 1. ed. Delhi, 1965.

Arc 440 - 465 Archaeology - Local - India - Local; Special topics (A-Z by place or topic)

Arc 440.1 Sewell, R. Report on the Amarâvati Tope. London, 1880.
Arc 440.2F Crawley-Boevey, A.W. A scheme for the protection and conservation of antient buildings...city of Ahmedabad. Bombay, 1886.
Arc 440.3 Subramanian, K. Buddhist remains in Andhra. Madras, 1932.
Arc 440.4 Ancient monuments of India. Bombay. 1-4,1957-1958
Arc 440.7 Centro scavi e ricerche archeologiche in Asia. Altinità archeologica italiana in Asia. Roma, 1960.
Arc 440.8 Casal, Jean Marie. Fouilles d'Amri. Paris, 1964. 2v.
Arc 440.10 Das Gupta, Kalyan Kumar. The Audumbaras. Calcutta, 1965.
Arc 440.11 Sankalia, Hasmukh Dhirajlal. Excavations at Ahar (Tambavati) [1961-62]. 1. ed. Poona, 1969.
Arc 441.1F Rájendralála Mitra. Buddha Gayá. Calcutta, 1878.
Arc 441.1.3 Indraje, B. Antiquarian remains at Sopârâ and Padana, being an account of the Buddhist Stûpa and Asoka edict. Bombay, 1882.
Arc 441.1.7 Barua, B.M. Gaya and Buddha-Gaya. Calcutta, 1931-34. 2v.
Arc 441.2.3 Epigraphia Birmanica. Rangoon. 2-4,1921-1936 3v.
Arc 441.2.9 Kathiawar. Department for an Archaeological and Antiquarian Survey. Bhavanagar pracina sodh a samgraha. Bhavanagar, 1885.
Arc 441.3F Bengal. Public Works Department. Revised list of ancient monuments in Bengal, 1886. Calcutta, 1887.

Arc 440 - 465 Archaeology - Local - India - Local; Special topics (A-Z by place or topic) - cont.

Arc 441.3.2F Bengal. Public Works Department. List of ancient monuments in Bengal. Calcutta, 1896.
Arc 441.3.10 Maitra, Akshay Kumar. The ancient monuments of Varendra (North Bengal). Rajshahi, 1949?
Arc 441.4 Vakil, K.H. Rock-cut temples around Bombay. Bombay, 1932.
Arc 441.5 Stein, Mark A. Detailed report of an archaeological tour with the Buner Field Force. Lahore, 1898.
Arc 441.6F Cunningham, Alexander. The stûpa of Bharhut. London, 1879.
Arc 441.7 Doreau, Jean Louis. Les bains dans l'Inde antique; monuments et textes médicaux. Paris, 1936.
Arc 441.9 Gadre, A.S. Important inscriptions from the Baroda state. Baroda, 1943.
Arc 441.9.5 Gadre, A.S. Archaeology in Baroda, 1934-1947. Baroda, 1947.
Arc 441.9.10F Baroda (State). Archaeological Department. Annual report. Baroda. 1935-1939 4v.
Arc 441.10 Subbarao, B. Stone age cultures of Bellary. 1. ed. Poona, 1948.
Arc 441.15 Subbarao, B. Baroda through the ages. Baroda, 1953.
Arc 441.22 Patil, Devendrakumar Rajaram. The antiquarian remains in Bihar. Patna, 1963.
Arc 441.23 Misra, Virendra Nath. Pre- and proto-history of the Berach Basin, South Rajasthan. 1. ed. Poona, 1967.
Arc 442.2 Wheeler, Robert. Chārsada. London, 1962.
Arc 442.5 Deo, Shantavam Bhalchandra. Chalcolithic Chandoli. Poona, 1965.
Arc 442.10 Wauchope, Robert S. Buddhist cave temples of India. Calcutta, 1933.
Arc 442.15 Mackay, Ernest J.H. Excavations at Chanhu-Daro...1935-36. Washington, 1938.
Arc 443.2 Ansari, Zainuddin. Excavations at Dwarka. 1. ed. Poona, 1966.
Arc 443.3 Sarkar, Sasanka Sekhar. Ancient races of the Deccan. New Delhi, 1972.
Arc 443.4 Joseph, P. The Dravidian problem in the south Indian culture complex. Bombay, 1972.
Arc 443.5 Allchin, F.R. Neolithic cattle-keepers of south India; a study of the Deccan ashmounds. Cambridge, Eng., 1963.
Arc 443.6 Shchetenko, Anatolii I. Drevneishie zemledel'cheskie kul'tury Dekana. Leningrad, 1968.
Arc 444.1 Burgess, James. Rock-temples of Elephanta. Bombay, 1871.
Arc 444.1.10 Pearse and Company, ltd. Pearse guide to Elephanta, or Gharapuri. Devonport, 1884.
Arc 444.1.15 Hirananda, Sastri. A guide to Elephanta. Delhi, 1934.
Arc 444.2 Burgess, James. Rock temples of Elurâ or Verul. Bombay, 1877.
Arc 444.2.5 Burgess, James. Rock temples of Elurâ or Verul. Bombay, 1877.
Arc 444.2.10 Balasaheb, Pant Pratinidhi. Ellora; a handbook of Verul (Ellora caves). Bombay, 1929.
Arc 446.5 Garde, M.B. Archaeology in Gwalior. 2. ed. Gwalior, 1934.
Arc 446.10 Zluner, F.E. Stone age and Pleistocene chronology in Gujarat. 1. ed. Poona, 1950.
Arc 446.12 Abid Ali Khan, M. Memoirs of Gaur and Pandua. Calcutta, 1931.
Arc 447.1F Hyderabad, India (State). Archaeological Department. Annual report. Calcutta. 1323-1349,1914-1940 11v.
Arc 447.1.5 Hyderabad, India (State). Archaeological Department. Antiquarian remains in Hyderabad State. Hyderabad, 1953.
Arc 447.2 Bilgrami, S.A.A. Landmarks of the Deccan; a comprehensive guide to the archaeological remains of the city and suburbs of Hyderabad. Hyderabad, 1927.
Arc 447.5 Chand, Amar. Hastināpura. Banoras, 1952.
Arc 447.6 Mode, Heinz Adolph. The Harappa culture and the West. Calcutta, 1961.
Arc 447.6.5F Vats, Madho Sarup. Excavations at Harappa. Delhi, 1940. 2v.
Arc 448.1 Mackay, Ernest. The Indus civilization. London, 1935.
Arc 448.1.2 Mackay, Ernest. Early Indus civilization. 2. ed. London, 1948.
Arc 448.1.10 Indian Museum, Calcutta. Catalogue and hand-book of the archaeological collections in the Indian Museum. Calcutta, 1883. 2v.
Arc 448.1.15 Heros, Henry. Studies in proto-Indo-Mediterranean culture. Bombay, 1933.
Arc 448.1.20 Deshmukh, P.R. The Indus civilization in the Rgveda. Yeotmal, 1954.
Arc 448.1.25 Khan, F.A. The Indus Valley and early Iran. Karachi, 1964.
Arc 448.1.30 Sastri, K.N. New light on the Indus civilization. Delhi, 1957-65. 2v.
Arc 448.1.35 Casal, Jean Marie. La civilisation de l'Indus et ses énigmes. Paris, 1969.
Arc 448.1.40 Mughal, M. Rafique. Present state of research on the Indus Valley civilization. Karachi, 1973.
Arc 450.1 Swarup, B. Konarka. Bengal, 1910.
Arc 450.2A Kak, Ram C. Ancient monuments of Kashmir. London, 1933.
Arc 450.2B Kak, Ram C. Ancient monuments of Kashmir. London, 1933.
Arc 450.5 Sankalia, Hasmukh Dhirajlal. Excavations at Brahmapuri, 1945-46. Poona, 1952.
Arc 450.10 Dhama, B.L. Khajuraho. Delhi, 1953.
Arc 450.30 Altekar, Anant L. Report on Humrahar excavations. Patna, 1959.
Arc 450.32 Sharma, G.R. The excavations at Kauśāmbī (1957-59). Allahabad, 1960.
Arc 450.34 Mujumdar, Ganesh. Ashmound excavations at Kupgal. 1. ed. Poona, 1966.
Arc 450.38 Roy, Sita Ram. Karian excavations, 1955. Patna, 1965.
Arc 451.1F Lucknow Exhibit. A memorandum of suggestions for use of contributors to the Loan Collection Department of the Exhibit. Lucknow, 1885.
Arc 451.3 Sankalia, Hasmukh Dhirajlal. Excavations at Langhnaj, 1944-63. 1. ed. v.1-2. Poona, 1965.
Arc 451.5 Rao, Shikaripur R. Lothal and the Indus civilization. N.Y., 1973.
Arc 452.1F Marshall, John. Mohenjo-daro and the Indus civilization. London, 1931. 3v.
Arc 452.1.15 Puri, K.N. La civilisation de Mohen-Jo-Daro. Thèse. Paris? 1938.
Arc 452.1.25F Mackay, Ernest. Further excavations at Mohenjo-daro. Delhi, 1938. 2v.
Arc 452.3 Brown, William N. A pillared hall from a temple at Madura, India. Philadelphia, 1940.
Arc 452.10 Sankalia, Hasmukh Dhirajlal. The excavations at Maheshwar and Navdatoli. Baroda, 1958.

Arc 440 - 465 Archaeology - Local - India - Local; Special topics (A-Z by place or topic) - cont.

Arc 453.1 Bendall, C. Journey in Nepal and northern India. Cambridge, 1886.
Arc 453.5 Fleet, J.F. Indian epigraphy. Oxford, 1907.
Arc 453.10 Bendrey, F. A study of Muslim inscriptions. Bombay, 1944?
Arc 453.15 Sankalia, Hasmukh Dhirajlal. Report on the excavations at Nasik and Jorve. 1. ed. Poona, 1955.
Arc 453.16 Sankalia, Hasmukh Dhirajlal. From history to pre-history at Nevasa. Poona, 1960.
Arc 453.18 Sankalia, Hasmukh Dhirajlal. Chalcolithic Navdatoli; the excavations at Navdatoli, 1957-59. 1. ed. Poona, 1971.
Arc 454.1 Ganguly, M.M. Orissa and her remains. Calcutta, 1912.
Arc 454.1.5 Mohapatra, Gopal Chandra. The stone age cultures of Orissa. 1. ed. Poona, 1962.
Arc 455.1 Waddell, L.A. Discovery of Pātaliputra. Calcutta, 1892.
Arc 455.1.5 Waddell, L.A. Report on the excavations at Pātaliputra. Calcutta, 1903.
Arc 455.2 Jouveau-Dubreuil, G. Pallava antiquites. v.1-2. Pondicherry, 1916-18.
Arc 455.3 Wheeler, R.E. Five thousand years of Pakistan. London, 1950.
Arc 455.5 Casal, Jean Marie. Site urbain et sites funéraires des environs de Pondichéry. Paris, 1956.
Arc 455.10 Istituto Italiano per il Medio ed Estremo Oriente, Rome. Italian archaeological researches in Asia...Pakistan and Afghanistan, 1956-1959.. Turin, 1960.
Arc 457.5 Banerji, R.D. The age of the imperial Guptas. Banares, 1933.
Arc 457.10 Ḳuraishi, M.M.H. Rājgir. 4. ed. Delhi, 1956.
Arc 457.15 Ṛydh, Hanna. Ṛang Mahal. Lund, 1959.
Arc 457.20 Temple, Richard C. Notes on antiquities in Ramannadesa. Bombay, 1894.
Arc 458.1 Maisey, F.C. Sanchi and its remains. London, 1892.
Arc 458.1.5 Foucher, A. La porte orientale du stûpa de Sânchi. Paris, 1910.
Arc 458.1.9 Marshall, John. A guide to Sanchi. Calcutta, 1918.
Arc 458.1.10 Marshall, John. A guide to Sanchi. 2. ed. Delhi, 1936.
Arc 458.1.12 Marshall, John. A guide to Sanchi. 3. ed. Delhi, 1955.
Arc 458.2 Ritter, C. Die Stupa's (Topes). Berlin, 1838.
Arc 458.2.2 Ritter, C. Die Stupa's (Topes). Berlin, 1838.
Arc 458.2.10 Combaz, Gisbert. L'évolution du Stūpa en Asie. Bruxelles, 1933. 3 pam.
Arc 458.3 Gough, Richard. Comparative view of antient monuments of India...island of Salset. London, 1785.
Arc 458.4 Carr, Mark William. Descriptive and historical papers...the seven pagodas on the Coromandel coast. Madras, 1869.
Arc 458.4.5 Temple, Richard C. Notes on the seven pagodas. London, 1928-29.
Arc 458.5 Wilson, Thomas. Minute stone implements from India. n.p., 1892.
Arc 458.7 Vogel, J.P. Indian serpent-lore. London, 1926.
Arc 458.8A Stein, Mark A. On Alexander's track to the Indus. London, 1929.
Arc 458.8B Stein, Mark A. On Alexander's track to the Indus. London, 1929.
Arc 458.8C Stein, Mark A. On Alexander's track to the Indus. London, 1929.
Arc 458.8D Stein, Mark A. On Alexander's track to the Indus. London, 1929.
Arc 458.9 Sahni, Daya Ram. Guide to the Buddhist ruins of Sarnath. 5. ed. Delhi, 1933.
Arc 458.12 Sircar, Dineschandra. Indian epigraphical glossary. 1. ed. Delhi, 1966.
Arc 458.14 Ansari, Z.D. Excavations at Sanganakallu and Songaon. Poona, 1969. 3 pam.
Arc 459.2F Travancore. Archaeological Survey. Annual report for M.E. 1085 (1909-1910). n.p., 191-?
Arc 459.3 Marshall, John. A guide to Taxila. Calcutta, 1918.
Arc 459.3.15 Marshall, John. A guide to Taxila. 3. ed. Delhi, 1936.
Arc 459.3.19 Marshall, John. A guide to Taxila. 4. ed. Cambridge, 1960.
Arc 459.3.20 Marshall, John. Taxila. Cambridge, 1951. 3v.
Arc 459.3.30 Il'in, G.F. Drevnii indiiskii gorod Taksila. Moskva, 1918.
Arc 459.5 Nagaraja Rao, M.S. The stone age hill dwellers of Tekkalakota. Poona, 1965.
Arc 459.20 Tirumalai-Tirupati Devasthanem epigraphical series. Madras. 1-6,1930-1938 8v.
Arc 461.2 Mathur, J.C. Homage to Vaisali. Vaisali, 1948.
Arc 461.4 Casal, Jean Marie. Fouilles de Virampatnam Arikamedu. Paris, 1949.
Arc 462.5 Das Gupta, Paresh Chandra. Archaeological discovery in West Bengal. Alipore, 1963.

Arc 482 Archaeology - Local - Mesopotamia, Iraq - Since 650 A.D., Islamic period - General works

Arc 482.201F-482.206 Forschungen zur Islamische Kunst

Arc 482.201F Sarre, Friedrich. Archäologische Reise im Euphrat. Berlin, 1911-20. 4v.
Arc 482.202F Herzfeld, Ernst E. Der Wandschmuck der Bauten. Berlin, 1923.
Arc 482.202.2F Sarre, Friedrich. Die Keramik von Samarra. Berlin, 1925.
Arc 482.202.3F Herzfeld, Ernst E. Die Malereien von Samarra. Berlin, 1927.
Arc 482.202.4F Lamm, C.J. Das Glas von Samarra. Berlin, 1928.
Arc 482.202.5F Herzfeld, Ernst E. Die vorgeschichtlichen Töpfereien von Samarra. Berlin, 1930.
Arc 482.202.6F Herzfeld, Ernst E. Geschichte der Stadt Samarra. Hamburg, 1948.
Arc 482.203PF Herzfled, Ernst E. Paikuli. Berlin, 1924. 2v.
Arc 482.204F Spanner, H. Rusafa. Berlin, 1926.
Arc 482.205F Lamm, C.J. Mittelalterliche Gläser und Steinschnittarbeiten aus dem Nahen Osten. Berlin, 1930. 2v.
Arc 482.206 Schmidt, J.H. Friedrich Sarre Schriften. Berlin, 1935.

Arc 483 Archaeology - Local - Mesopotamia, Iraq - Since 650 A.D., Islamic period - Local; Special topics

Arc 483.5 Iraq. Department of Antiquities. Harba bridge. Baghdad, 1935.
Arc 483.7.2 Iraq. Department of Antiquities. Some works on the antiquities in the Abbasid Palace. 2. ed. Baghdad, 1956.
Arc 483.10 Iraq. Department of Antiquities. Excavations at Samarra, 1936-1939. Baghdad, 1940.

Arc 483 Archaeology - Local - Mesopotamia, Iraq - Since 650 A.D., Islamic period - Local; Special topics - cont.

Arc 483.11 al-'Amid, Tahir Mudhaffar. The 'Abbasid architecture of Samarra in the reign of both al-Mu'tasim and al-Mutawakkil. Baghdad, 1973.

Arc 485 Archaeology - Local - Persia, Iran - Folios [Discontinued]

Arc 485.4F Diez, Ernst. Churasaniche Baudenkmäler. Berlin, 1918.
Arc 485.200 Dieulafoy, M. L'art antique de la Perse. Paris, 1884-89. 5v.
Arc 485.201 Dieulafoy, M. L'acropole de Suse. Paris, 1890-92. 4v.
Arc 485.202 Persepolis illustrata. London, 1739.
Arc 485.202.5 Godard, André. Persepolis. Teheran, 1950.

Arc 487 Archaeology - Local - Persia, Iran - Pamphlet volumes

Arc 487.1 Pamphlet box. Archaeology. Persia. Tracts.

Arc 488 Archaeology - Local - Persia, Iran - General works

Arc 488.1 Price, W. Journal of the British embassy to Persia. v.1-2. London, 1832.
Arc 488.1.5 Price, W. Journal of the British embassy to Persia. London, 1832.
Arc 488.5F Herzfeld, Ernst E. Am Tor von Asien. Berlin, 1920.
Arc 488.9F France. Délégation Archéologique en Iran. Mémoires. Paris. 1,1900+ 35v.
Arc 488.10F Herzfeld, Ernst E. Iran in the ancient East. London, 1941.
Arc 488.13 Stein, Mark A. Archaeological reconnaissances in southern Persia. London, 1934.
Arc 488.14A Stein, Mark A. Old routes of western Iran. London, 1940.
Arc 488.14B Stein, Mark A. Old routes of western Iran. London, 1940.
Arc 488.14.10 Karimi, B.M. Rapport résumé de quinze mai de voyage. Teheran, 1950?
Arc 488.15 Herzfeld, Ernst E. Archaeological history of Iran. London, 1935.
Arc 488.16 Sanadi, H.A. Les découvertes fortuites. n.p., 1960.
Arc 488.17F Schmidt, E.F. Flights over ancient cities of Iran. Chicago, 1940.
Arc 488.18 Coon, Carleton Stevens. Cave explorations in Iran, 1949. Philadelphia, 1951.
Arc 488.19F McCown, D.E. The comparative stratigraphy of early Iran. Chicago, 1942.
Arc 488.20 Mellink, M.J. Dark ages and nomads c.1000 B.C. Istanbul, 1964.
Arc 488.21F Herzfeld, Ernst E. Iranische Denkmäler. v.1-4. Berlin, 1932-
Arc 488.23 Porada, Edith. Alt-Iran. Baden-Baden, 1962.
Arc 488.24 Culican, William. The Medes and Persians. London, 1965.
Arc 488.25 Bittal, Kurt. Vorderasiatische Archäologie. Berlin, 1964.
Arc 488.28 Hinz, Walther. Altiranische Funde und Forschungen. Berlin, 1969.
Arc 488.30 Matheson, Sylvia A. Persia; an archaeological guide. London, 1972.
Arc 488.31 Schippmann, Klaus. Die iranischen Feuerheiligtümer. Habilitationsschrift. Berlin, 1971.
Arc 488.32 Excavations in Iran: the British contribution. Oxford, 1972.

Arc 493 Archaeology - Local - Persia, Iran - Local; Special topics

Arc 493.1 Easton, M.W. Observations on the platform at Persepolis. Philadelphia, 1892.
Arc 493.2 Adler, C. Two Persepolitan casts in the U.S. National Museum. Washington, 1893.
Arc 493.2.5 Sami, A. Persepolis. 2. ed. Shiraz, 1955.
Arc 493.2.10F Schmidt, E.F. Persepolis. Chicago, 1953-70. 3v.
Arc 493.2.15 Herzfeld, Ernst E. Rapport sur l'état actuel des ruines de Persépole. Berlin, 1928.
Arc 493.2.20 Sami, A. Persepolis. Shiraz, 1954.
Arc 493.2.25 Wheeler, Robert E. Flames over Persepolis: turning point in history. London, 1962.
Arc 493.2.30 Wilber, Donald Newton. Persepolis, the archaelogy of Parsa. N.Y., 1969.
Arc 493.3 Morgan, J. de. Le délégation en Perse. Paris, 1902.
Arc 493.4 Pillet, M.L. Le palais de Darius. Paris, 1914.
Arc 493.5 Minorekii, V. Kelianshchin, stela u Topuzava. Petrograd, 1917.
Arc 493.6 Burton Brown, T. Excavations in Azerbaijan. 1. ed. London, 1951.
Arc 493.6.10 Baku. Muzei Istorii Azerbaidzhana. Material'naia kultura Azerbaidzhana. v.2. Baku, 1949-
Arc 493.6.15 Akademiia Nauk Azerbaidzhanskoi SSR, Baku. Ockerki po drevnei istorii Azerbaidzhana SSR. Baku, 1956.
Arc 493.6.20 Trever, K.V. Ocherki po istorii i kul'ture Kavkozskoi Albanii. Moskva, 1959.
Arc 493.6.22 Akademiia Nauk Azerbaidzhanskoi SSR, Baku. Institut Istorii. Voprosy istorii Kavkazskoi Albanii; sbornik statei. Baku, 1962.
Arc 493.6.25 Ismizade, O.S. Ialoilutepinskaia kul'tura. Baku, 1950.
Arc 493.6.30 Selimkhanov, I.S. Istoriko-khimicheskie i analiticheskie issledovaniia drevnikh predmetov iz mednykh splavov. Baku, 1960.
Arc 493.6.35F Aslanov, G.M. Drevnii Mingechaur. Baku, 1959.
Arc 493.6.40 Akademiia Nauk Azerbaidzhanskoi SSR, Baku. Institut Istorii. Arkheologicheskie issledoveniia v Azerbaidzhane. Baku, 1965.
Arc 493.6.45 Sadykhzade, S.G. Drevnie ukrashcheniia Azerbaidzhana. Baku, 1971.
Arc 493.6.50 Dzhafarzade, Iskhak M. Gobustan. Baku, 1973.
Arc 493.9 Ivanov, V.A. Alamut and Lamasar. Teheran, 1960.
Arc 493.15F Langsdorff, A. Tall-i-Bakun A, season of 1932. Chicago, 1942.
Arc 493.20 Stein, Mark A. An archaeological tour in the ancient Persis. Oxford, 1936.
Arc 493.25 Godard, André. Le trésor de Ziwiyè. Haarlem, 1950.
Arc 493.25.5 Godard, André. Le trésor de Ziwiyè. Teheran, 1949.
Arc 493.26 Laessøe, Jørgen. The Shemshāra tablets. København, 1959.
Arc 493.30 Sami, A. Pasargadae. Shiraz, 1956.
Arc 493.35 Jaenichen, H. Bildzeichen der königlichen Hoheit bei den iranischen Völkern. Bonn, 1956.
Arc 493.40F Paris. Musée National du Louvre. Fouilles de Chapour. v.2. Paris, 1956.
Arc 493.45F Conténau, G. Fouilles du Tépé-Giyan. Paris, 1935.
Arc 493.50 Sauvaget, J. Quatre décrets seldjoukides. Beyrouth, 1947.
Arc 493.55 Baghdaden Mitteilungen. Berlin. 1,1960+ 4v.
Arc 493.60.5 Ellis, Richard Stephens. A bibliography of Mesopotamian archaeological sites. Wiesbaden, 1972.

Arc 493 Archaeology - Local - Persia, Iran - Local; Special topics - cont.

Arc 493.62 Minasian, Caro Owen. Shah Diz of Isma'ili fame. London, 1971.

Arc 495 Archaeology - Local - Palestine and Syria - Folios [Discontinued]

Arc 495.3.5F Croly, George. The Holy Land, Syria, Idumea, Arabia, Egypt and Nubia. London, 1855-56. 3v.
Arc 495.5.5F Wiegand, Theodor. Baalbek. v.1-3; atlas. Berlin, 1921-25. 4v.
NEDL Arc 495.6PF Vogue, M. de. Le temple de Jérusalem. Paris, 1864.
Arc 495.7 Renan, E. Mission de Phénicie. Paris, 1864. 2v.
Arc 495.13FA Reisner, George A. Harvard excavations at Samaria 1908-1910. Cambridge, 1924. 2v.
Arc 495.13FB Reisner, George A. Harvard excavations at Samaria 1908-1910. Cambridge, 1924. 2v.
Arc 495.200 Luynes, H.T.P.J. d'Albert de. Voyage d'exploration à la Mer Morte. Paris, 1874. 3v.
Arc 495.201 Pierotti, E. Jerusalem explored. London, 1864. 2v.
Arc 495.203 Paine, T.O. Solomon's Temple. Boston, 1886.
Arc 495.204 Garrett, Robert. Topography and itinerary (American archaeological exedition to Syria). N.Y., 1914.
Arc 495.204.2 Butler, H.C. Architecture and other arts. N.Y., 1903.
Arc 495.204.3 Prentice, William K. Greek and Latin inscriptions. N.Y., 1908.
Arc 495.204.4 Littman, Enno. Semitic inscriptions. N.Y., 1904.
Arc 495.205 Brünnow, R.E. Die Provincia Arabia. Strassburg, 1904. 3v.
Arc 495.206F Kondakov, N.P. Arkheologicheskoe puteshestvie in Sirii. Sankt Peterburg, 1904.
Arc 495.207F Vincent L.H. Hebron le haram el-Khalîl, sépulture des patriachs. Paris, 1923. 2v.
Arc 495.208F Breasted, J.H. Oriental forerunners of Byzantine painting...wall-paintings from the fortress of Dura. Chicago, 1924.
Arc 495.210F Ghirshman, Roman. Fouilles de Sialk près de Kashan. Paris, 1938-39. 2v.

Arc 496 Archaeology - Local - Palestine and Syria - Pamphlet volumes

Arc 496 Pamphlet box. Archaeology. Syria and Palestine.
Arc 496.1 Pamphlet box. Archaeology. Syria and Palestine.

Arc 497 Archaeology - Local - Palestine and Syria - General works

Arc 497.1 American Palestine Exploration Society. Catalogue of photographs. N.Y., 1876.
Arc 497.2 Clermont-Ganneau, Charles. Premiers rapports sur une mission en Palestine et en Phénicie. Paris, 1882.
Arc 497.3 Reeland, Adriaan. Palaestina. Utrecht, 1714. 2v.
Arc 497.4 Rey, E.G. Rapport sur une mission scientifique. Paris, 1867.
Arc 497.5 Conder, C.R. Palestine. London, 1889.
Arc 497.5.3 Conder, C.R. Palestine. N.Y., 1889.
Arc 497.6 Tristram, H.B. The land of Moab. London, 1873.
Arc 497.7 Vogüé, M. de. Fragments d'un journal de voyage en Orient. Paris, 1855.
Arc 497.8 Sachau, E. Reise in Syrien und Mesopotamien. Leipzig, 1883.
Arc 497.9 Guérin, V. Description de la Palestine. pt.1-3. Paris, 1868-80. 7v.
Arc 497.11 Bliss, F.J. The development of Palestine exploration. N.Y., 1906.
Arc 497.12 Musil, A. Arabia Petraca. v.1-3. Wien, 1907. 4v.
Arc 497.13A Driver, S.R. Modern research as illustrating the Bible. London, 1909.
Arc 497.13B Driver, S.R. Modern research as illustrating the Bible. London, 1909.
Arc 497.14 St. Aignan, L. de. Découvertes récentes en Terre-Sainte. n.p., 1874.
Arc 497.15 Héron de Villefosse, A. Notice des monuments de la Palestine conservés au Musée du Louvre. 2. éd. Paris, 1879.
Arc 497.16 Sepp, J.N. Neue architektonische Studien...Forschungen in Palästina. Würzburg, 1867.
Arc 497.17 Dawson, J.W. Modern science in Bible lands. N.Y., 1889.
Arc 497.18 Handcock, P.S.P. Archaeology of the Holy Land. London, 1916.
Arc 497.19 Redding, M.W. Antiquities of the Orient unveiled. N.Y., 1872.
Arc 497.20.5 Harper, H.A. The Bible and modern discoveries. 4. ed. London, 1891.
Arc 497.21 Jaussen, Antonin J. Mission archéologique en Arabie. v.1-3 et Atlas. Paris, 1909-22. 4v.
Arc 497.23 Peters, John B. Bible and spade. N.Y., 1922.
Arc 497.24 Cumont, Franz. Études syriennes. Paris, 1917.
Arc 497.25 Macalister, R.A.S. A century of excavation in Palestine. London, 1925.
Arc 497.26F Kennedy, A.B. William. Petra; its history and monuments. London, 1925.
Arc 497.27F Nielsen, D. Handbuch der altarabischen Altertumskunde. Kopenhagen, 1927.
Arc 497.28A Robinson, George L. The sarcophagus of an ancient civilization. N.Y., 1930.
Arc 497.28B Robinson, George L. The sarcophagus of an ancient civilization. N.Y., 1930.
Arc 497.29 Kyle, M.G. Moses and the monuments. London, 1920.
Arc 497.30 Albright, William Foxwell. The archaeology of Palestine and the Bible. N.Y., 1932.
Arc 497.30.3 Albright, William Foxwell. The archaeology of Palestine. London, 1954.
Arc 497.30.5 Du Buit, Michel. Archéologie du peuple d'Israël. Paris, 1960.
Arc 497.31 Duncan, J.G. Digging up Biblical history. N.Y., 1931- 2v.
Arc 497.31.5 Wright, G.E. Biblical archaeology. Philadelphia, 1962.
Arc 497.31.10 Albright, William Foxwell. New horizons in Biblical research. London, 1966.
Arc 497.34 Köppel, Robert. Untersuchungen über die Steinzeit Palästina-Syriens. Inaug. Diss. Rom, 1933.
Arc 497.35 Courtin, Louis. Collection de Louis Courtin. Paris, 189-.
Arc 497.36 Watzinger, Carl. Denkmäler Palästinas. v.1-2. Leipzig, 1933-35.
Arc 497.37 Woolley, C.L. The wilderness of Zin. London, 1936.
Arc 497.38 Simons, J.J. Opgravingen in Palestina. Roermond-Maaseik, 1935.
Arc 497.39 Stekelis, M. Les monuments megalithiques de Palestine. Thèse. Paris, 1935.
Arc 497.40A Caiger, S.L. Bible and spade. London, 1938.
Arc 497.40B Caiger, S.L. Bible and spade. London, 1938.

Classified Listing

Arc 497 Archaeology - Local - Palestine and Syria - General works - cont.

Arc 497.41 Richardson, George H. Biblical archaeology, its use and abuse. London, 1938.
Arc 497.43 Thomsen, P. Palästina und seine Kultur in fünf Jahrtausenden. 2. Aufl. Leipzig, 1917.
Arc 497.44 Kenyon, F.G. The Bible and archaeology. London, 1940.
Arc 497.45 Gordon, Cyrus H. The living past. N.Y., 1941.
Arc 497.46 McGown, J.C. The ladder of progress in Palestine. N.Y., 1943.
Arc 497.47 Burrows, M. What mean these stones? New Haven, 1941.
Arc 497.48 Needler, W. Palestine, ancient and modern...guide to the Palestinian collection...Royal Ontario Museum. Toronto, 1949.
Arc 497.49 Reifenberg, A. Ancient Hebrew arts. N.Y., 1950.
Arc 497.50 Corswant, Willy. Dictionnaire d'archéologie biblique. Neuchâtel, 1956.
Arc 497.50.5 Corswant, Willy. A dictionary of life in Bible times. N.Y., 1960.
Arc 497.51 Jirku, Anton. Der Ausgrabungen in Palästina und Syrien. Halle, 1956.
Arc 497.51.5 Jirku, Anton. Von Jerusalem nach Ugarit. Graz, 1966.
Arc 497.52 Yeivin, Samuel. Archaeological activities in Israel. Jerusalem, 1955.
Arc 497.53 Ilton, Paul. Digging in the Holy Land. London, 1959.
Arc 497.55 Bentwich, Norman de Mattos. The new-old land of Israel. London, 1960.
Arc 497.60 Kenyon, Kathleen Mary. Archaeology in the Holy Land. N.Y., 1960.
Arc 497.60.3 Kenyon, Kathleen Mary. Archaeology in the Holy Land. 3. ed. N.Y., 1970.
Arc 497.65 Yeivin, Samuel. A decade of archaeology in Israel, 1948-1958. Istanbul, 1960.
Arc 497.67 Franken, Hedricus J. Van aartsvaders tot prafeten. Amsterdam, 1967.
Arc 497.71 Anati, E. Palestine before the Hebrews. 1. ed. N.Y., 1962.
Arc 497.72 Biblical Archaeologist. The Biblical archaeologist reader. Chicago, 1961.
Arc 497.72.1 Biblical Archaeologist. The Biblical archaeologist reader. Garden City, 1961-70. 3v.
Arc 497.73 Gryglewicz, F. Archeologiczne odkrycia w egzegezie Nowego Testamentu. Lublin, 1962.
Arc 497.74 Williams, Walter George. Archaeology in Biblical research. N.Y., 1965.
Arc 497.75 Kryvelev, Iosif A. Raskopki v bibleiskikh stranakh. Moskva, 1965.
Arc 497.76.2 Markovski, Ivan S. Bibleiska arkheologiia. 2. izd. Sofiia, 1948.
Arc 497.77 Views of the Biblical world. Jerusalem, 1958- 4v.
Arc 497.78 Cohen, Lenore. Biblical treasure in Bible lands. Los Angeles, 1965.
Arc 497.79 Palestine Exploration Fund. World of the Bible. South Kensington, 1965?
Arc 497.80 Archaeological discoveries in the Holy Land. N.Y., 1967.
Arc 497.81F Hennessy, John Basil. The foreign relations of Palestine during the early bronze age. London, 1967.
Arc 497.85 Applebaum, Shimon. Israel and her vicinity in the Roman and Byzantine periods. Tel-Aviv, 1967.
Arc 497.86 Thomas, David Winton. Archaeology and Old Testament study. Oxford, 1967.
Arc 497.88 New direction in Biblical archaeology. 1. ed. Garden City, N.Y., 1969.
VArc 497.90 Ackermann, Peter Fourier. Bibliai régiségtan. Eger, 1889.
Arc 497.92 Szekrényi, Lajos. A bibliai régiségtudomány kézikönyve. Szeged, 1894.
Arc 497.94 Near Eastern archaeology in the twentieth century. 1. ed. Garden City, N.Y., 1970.
Arc 497.96 Kenyon, Kathleen Mary. Royal cities of the Old Testament. N.Y., 1971.
Arc 497.98 Archaeologie und Altes Testament. Festschrift für Kurt Galling 28. Jan. 1970. Tübingen, 1970.
Arc 497.99 Encyclopedia of archaeological excavations in the Holy Land. Englewood Cliffs, N.J., 1975- 2v.
Arc 497.100 Landay, Jerry M. Silent cities, sacred stones: archaeological discovery in the land of the Bible. London, 1971.
Arc 497.101 Rehork, Joachim. Archäologie und biblisches Leben. Bergish Gladbach, 1972.
Arc 497.102 Negev, Avraham. Archaeological encyclopedia of the Holy Land. N.Y., 1972.
Arc 497.103 Harker, Ronald. Digging up the Bible lands. London, 1972.
Arc 497.104 Paul, Sholom. Biblical archaeology. Jerusalem, 1973.

Arc 500 Archaeology - Local - Palestine and Syria - Palestine Exploration Fund publications - Folios [Discontinued]

Arc 500.1 Warren, C. Jerusalem. London, 1884.
X Cg Arc 500.2 Wilson, C. Special papers. London, 1881.
Arc 500.3 Conder, C.R. Arabic and English name lists. London, 1881.
Arc 500.4 Conder, C.R. Memoirs of the topography. London, 1881-83. 3v.
Arc 500.5 Conder, C.R. Memoirs of the topography. London, 1889.
Arc 500.5.5 Hull, E. The survey of Western Palestine. Adelphi, 1886.
Arc 500.6 Clermont-Ganneau, C. Archaeological researches in Palestine. London, 1896. 2v.
X Cg Arc 500.7 Bliss, F.J. Excavations in Palestine, 1895-1900. London, 1902.
Arc 500.8 Peters, John P. Painted tombs in the necropolis of Marissa. London, 1905.

Arc 501 Archaeology - Local - Palestine and Syria - Palestine Exploration Fund publications - General publications of the Fund

Arc 501.1 Palestine exploration quarterly. London. 1,1869+ 67v.
Arc 501.1.2 Palestine exploration quarterly. Index, 1869-1881. London, 1882.
Arc 501.1.3 Palestine exploration quarterly. Index, 1869-1892. London, n.d.
Arc 501.1.4 Palestine exploration quarterly. Index, 1911-1963. London, n.d.
Arc 501.1.5 Pamphlet box. Palestine Exploration Fund.
Arc 501.1.7 Palestine Exploration Fund. Annual report and accounts with list of subscriptions. 1910-1923
Arc 501.1.12 Palestine Exploration Fund. Annual. London. 1-6,1911-1953 6v.
Arc 501.2 Saunders, T. Brief geographical account of the survey of Western Palestine. London, 1882.
Arc 501.3 Saunders, T. Introduction to the survey of Western Palestine. London, 1881.

Arc 501 Archaeology - Local - Palestine and Syria - Palestine Exploration Fund publications - General publications of the Fund - cont.

Arc 501.4 Committee of the Fund. Our work in Palestine. London, 1873.
Arc 501.5A Besant, W. Twenty-one years' work in the Holy Land. London, 1886.
Arc 501.5.2 Besant, W. Palestine Exploration Fund. Thirty years' work in the Holy Land, 1865-1895. London, 1895.
Arc 501.6.3 The city and the land. Seven lectures. London, 1894.
Arc 501.7 Watson, C.M. Fifty years' work in the Holy Land, 1924-1948. London, 1915. 2v.
Arc 501.15 Schumacher, G. Across the Jordan. London, 1886.
Arc 501.15.2 Schumacher, G. Across the Jordan. London, 1889.
Arc 501.15.4 Schumacher, G. Abila of the Decapolis. London, 1889. 3 pam.
Arc 501.15.5 Schumacher, G. Northern Ajlûn. London, 1890.
Arc 501.15.8 Schumacher, G. The Jaulân. London, 1888.
Arc 501.16 Conder, C.R. Heth and Moab. London, 1885.
Arc 501.16.2 Conder, C.R. Heth and Moab. London, 1892.
Arc 501.16.5 Conder, C.R. Tent work in Palestine. London, 1878. 2v.
Arc 501.16.7 Conder, C.R. Tent work in Palestine. London, 1887.
Arc 501.16.8 Conder, C.R. Syrian stone-lore. N.Y., 1887.
Arc 501.16.11 Conder, C.R. The Tell Amarna tablets. London, 1893.
Arc 501.16.12 Conder, C.R. The Tell Amarna tablets. London, 1893.
Arc 501.16.13A Conder, C.R. The Tell Amarna tablets. 2. ed. London, 1894.
Arc 501.16.13B Conder, C.R. The Tell Amarna tablets. 2. ed. London, 1894.
Arc 501.17 Bliss, F.J. A mound of many cities. London, 1894.
X Cg Arc 501.17.5A Bliss, F.J. Excavations at Jerusalem 1894-1897. London, 1898.
Arc 501.17.5B Bliss, F.J. Excavations at Jerusalem 1894-1897. London, 1898.
Arc 501.18 Hull, E. Mount Seir. London, 1885.
Arc 501.19 Morrison, W. The recovery of Jerusalem. London, 1871.

Arc 502 Archaeology - Local - Palestine and Syria - Palestine Exploration Fund publications - Publications of local Fund societies

Arc 502.1 Palestine Exploration Society, New York. Statements. N.Y. 1-4,1871-1877 4v.
Arc 502.1.5 Pamphlet box. Palestine Exploration Society, New York.

Arc 503 Archaeology - Local - Palestine and Syria - Publications of other exploration societies

Arc 503.1 Tell El Mutesellim. Leipzig, 1908-1929. 3v.
Arc 503.2.2F Princeton University Archaeological Expeditions to Syria in 1904-1905 and 1909. Publications. Leyden, 1907-1934. 18v.
Arc 503.3F Deutsch-Turkischer Denkmalschutz-Kommando. Wissenschaftliche Veröffentlichungen. v.1-6. Berlin, 1920-
Arc 503.4 Gesellschaft für Palästina. Forschung. Veröffentlichung. Wien. 1,1910
Arc 503.5 Grant, Elihu. Beth Shemesh (Palestine). Haverford, Pa., 1929.
Arc 503.5.10F Grant, Elihu. Ain Shems excavations (Palestine), 1933. Pt.3. Haverford, 1934.
Arc 503.6 Palestine. Department of Antiquities. Quarterly. 1-14,1931-1950 10v.
Arc 503.6.5 Palestine. Department of Antiquities. Quarterly. Index, v.1-14 (1931-1950). Jerusalem, 1964.
Arc 503.7F Colt Archaeological Institute. Excavations at Nessana. Princeton, 1950. 3v.
Arc 503.8F Svenske Syrien expeditionem, 1952-1953. Lund, 1956.

Arc 505 Archaeology - Local - Palestine and Syria - Local; Special topics

Arc 505.1 Mueller, K.O. Antiquitates Antiochenae. Goettingen, 1839.
Arc 505.1.9F Antioch-on-the-Orontes. v.1-4. Princeton, 1934-48. 5v.
Arc 505.2 Simonsen, D. Sculptures et inscriptions de Palmyre. Copenhagen, 1889.
Arc 505.2.5F Wiegand, T. Palmyra; Ergebnisse der Expeditionen von 1902 und 1917. Text and plates. Berlin, 1932. 2v.
Arc 505.2.10 Schlumberger, D. La Palmyrène du Nord-Ouest. Thèse. Paris, 1951.
Arc 505.2.15F Bibliothèque Nationale. Département des Médailles et Antiques. Les tessères et les monnaies de Palmyre, 1944. Paris, 1962. 2v.
Arc 505.2.20 Mission Archeologique Suisse en Syrie. Le sanctuaire de Baalshamin à Palmyre. Rome, 1969- 4v.
Arc 505.3 Fergusson, J. Notes on the site of the Holy Sepulchre. London, 1861.
Arc 505.3.5 Fergusson, J. The Holy Sepulchre and Temple at Jerusalem. London, 1865.
Arc 505.3.9 Cyprien. Le vraie forme primitive...du Saint Sépulcre. Paris, 1879.
Arc 505.3.12 Clermont-Ganneau, Charles. L'authenticité du Saint-Sépulcre. Paris, 1877.
Arc 505.4 Berton, J. de. La topographie de Tyr. Paris, 1881.
Arc 505.4.2 Berton, J. de. Essai sur la topographie de Tyr. Paris, 1843.
Arc 505.4.8 Sepp, J.N. Meerfahrt nach Tyrus zur Ausgrabung der Kathedrale mit Barbarossa's Grab. Leipzig, 1879.
Arc 505.5 Fergusson, J. The temples of the Jews. London, 1878.
Arc 505.5.3 Prestel, J. Baugeschichte des Jüdischen Heiligthums...Tempel Salomons. Strassburg, 1902.
Htn Arc 505.5.5* Lightfoot, J. The temple. London, 1650.
Arc 505.5.6 Paine, T.O. Solomon's temple. Boston, 1861.
Arc 505.5.7 Wolff, P.O. Der Tempel von Jerusalem. Graz, 1887.
Arc 505.5.8 Reeland, Adriaan. De spoliis templi Hierosolymitani. Utrecht, 1716.
Arc 505.5.9 Rossi, J.B. de. Verre colorie representant le temple de Jerusalem. Paris, 1882.
Arc 505.5.10 Rossi, J.B. de. Verre representant le temple de Jerusalem. Genes, 1883.
Arc 505.5.15 Osgood, P.E. The Temple of Solomon. Chicago, 1910.
Arc 505.5.19 Rosen, G. Das Harom von Jerusalem und Tempelplatz des Maria. Gotha, 1866.
Arc 505.5.23 Vogüé. Note sur le Temple de Jerusalem. n.p., n.d.
Arc 505.5.25 Bartolini, D. Sull'antico Tempio Salomone. Roma, 1868.
Arc 505.5.30 Lindberg, N. Templet i Jerusalem. Kolding, 1880.
Arc 505.5.32 Lindberg, N. Templet i Jerusalem. Stockholm, 1881.
Arc 505.5.35 Parrat, André. Le Temple de Jérusalem. Neuchâtel, 1954.
Arc 505.5.37 Jehuda Leon, J. De templo Hierosolymitano. Helmaestadi, 1665.
Arc 505.5.40 Estevan, M. Compendio del Rico Aparato, y Hermosa del templo de Salomon. Alcala, 1615.

Classified Listing

Arc 505 Archaeology - Local - Palestine and Syria - Local; Special topics - cont.

Arc 505.5.42 Holtzfuss, V.S. Dissertatio historico-theologica de templi Hierosolymitani Iuliani. Halae Magdeburgicae, 1751. 2 pam.

Arc 505.5.44 Münter, F. Om den Davidische families begravelse under Zions bierg. Kjobenhavn, 1804.

Arc 505.5.48 Sturm, L.C. Sciagraphia templi Hierosolymitano. Lipsiae, 1694.

Arc 505.5.50 Herrmann, J. Temple de Jérusalem. Valenciennes, 1882.

Arc 505.5.52 Saint-Aignan. Temple de Salomon; sa description d'après découvertes récentes. Paris, 1875.

Arc 505.5.54 Isambert, E. Visite au temple de Jerusalem et à la Mosquée d'Omar. Paris, 1860.

Arc 505.5.60 Paton, Lewis B. Jerusalem in Bible times. Chicago, 1913.

Arc 505.5.65F Vincent, Louis H. Jérusalem sous terre. Londres, 1911.

Arc 505.5.66 Vincent, Louis H. Jérusalem de l'Ancien Testament. Pt.1-3. Paris, 1954. 3v.

Arc 505.5.67 Le Lithostrotos d'après des fouilles récentes. Paris, 1933.

Arc 505.5.70 Lanvy, B. De tabernaculo foederis...Jerusalem. Paris, 1720.

Arc 505.5.75 Möblenbrinck, K. Studien zum Salomonischen Tempel. Inaug. Diss. Stuttgart, 1931.

Arc 505.5.81 King, J. Recent discoveries on the Temple Hill at Jerusalem. 2. ed. London, 1885.

Arc 505.5.85 Macalister, R.A.S. Excavations...Ophel, Jerusalem, 1923-1925. London, 1926.

Arc 505.5.90 Crowfoot, J.W. Excavations...Tyropoeon Valley, Jerusalem, 1927. London, 1929.

Arc 505.5.95 Creswell, K.A. La mosquée Al Aqsa et la Néa de Justinien. Liege, 1929.

Arc 505.5.100F Adler, Cyrus. Memorandum on the Western Wall. Jerusalem, 1930.

Arc 505.5.105 Kenyon, Kathleen M. Jerusalem: excavating 3000 years of history. London, 1967.

Arc 505.5.110 Busink, T.A. Der Tempel von Jerusalem von Salomo bis Herodes. Leiden, 1970.

Arc 505.5.115 Cornfeld, Gaalyahu. The mystery of the Temple Mount. Tel Aviv, 1972.

Arc 505.5.120 Simons, Jan Jozef. Jerusalem in the Old Testament; researches and theories. Leiden, 1952.

Arc 505.6 Clermont-Ganneau, Charles. Fraudes archeologiques en Palestine. (Bibliothéque Orientale Elzevirienne). Paris, 1885.

Arc 505.7 Clermont-Ganneau, Charles. La présentation du Christ au Temple. Paris, 1877.

Arc 505.7.5 Clermont-Ganneau, Charles. Resultats...archéologies des fouilles entreprises à Jérusalem. n.p., 1872.

Arc 505.8 Clermont-Ganneau, Charles. La pierre de Bethphagé. Paris, 1877.

Arc 505.9 Dussaud, René. Voyage archéologique au Safâ. Paris, 1901.

Arc 505.10 Raint. Lettre sur un plan du Haram El-Khalil. Paris, 1886.

Arc 505.11 Bechstein, O. 30 Ansichten der deutschen Ausgraben Baalbek. Berlin, 1905.

Arc 505.11.5 Puchstein, O. Führer durch die Ruinen von Baalbek. Berlin, 1905.

Arc 505.11.10 Harding, G.L. Baalbek. Khayats, 1963.

Arc 505.12 Petrie, W.M.F. Researches in Sinai. London, 1906.

Arc 505.12.5 Petrie, W.M.F. Till el Hesy (Lachish). London, 1891.

Arc 505.12.10F Torczyner, H. Lachish I (Tell Ed Durveir). v.1-4. London, 1938-1940. 6v.

Arc 505.12.10.5 Balazs, György. Egy feltárt bibliai város. Budapest, 1940.

Arc 505.12.15F Momumenta Sinaitica. pt.1- Leningrad, 1912-1925. 2v.

Arc 505.13 Kittel, D.R. Schlaugenstein im Kidrontal bei Jerusalem. Leipzig, 1907.

X Cg Arc 505.14 Macalister, R.A.S. Excavation of Gezer, 1902-1905, 1907-1909. London, 1912. 3v.

Arc 505.15 Groot, J. de. Palestijnsche masseben (Opgerichte Steenen). Groningen, 1913.

Arc 505.16 Bourquenond, A. Mémoire sur les ruines de Séleucie de Piérie. Paris, 1860.

Arc 505.17 Guérin, V. Tombeau de Josué. Note sur le Khirbet-Tibneh. Paris, 1865.

Arc 505.18 Saulcy. Memoire sur...maçonneril...du Haram-Ech-Cherif de Jerusalem. Paris, 1866.

Arc 505.18.7 Saulcy. Recherches sur l'emplacement...du tombeau d'Hélène. Paris, 1869.

Arc 505.19 Notice historique sur...sanctuaire d'Emmans. Paris, 1862.

Arc 505.19.5 Barnabas. Deux questions d'archéologie palestinienne. Jérusalem, 1902. 2v.

Arc 505.20 Pierotti, E. Macpela, ou Tombeau des patriarches à Hebron. Lausanne, 1869.

Arc 505.21 Cramer, F. Scythische Denkmahlen in Palästina. Kiel, 1777.

Arc 505.22.2 Petrie, W.M.F. Eastern exploration past and future. London, 1918.

Arc 505.25 Weill, Raymond. La cité de David. Plans and atlas. Paris, 1920. 2v.

Arc 505.25.5 Meistermann, B. La ville de David. Paris, 1905.

Arc 505.27F Turville-Petre, F. Researches in prehistoric Galilee, 1925-1926. London, 1927.

Arc 505.29 Wiener, H.M. The altars of the Old Testament. Leipzig, 1927.

Arc 505.31 Meistermann, Barnabé. Questions de topographie palestinienne. Jerusalem, 1903.

Arc 505.35 Meistermann, Barnabé. Capharnaüm et Bethsaïde, suivi d'une étude sur l'âge de la synagogue de Tell Houm. Paris, 1921.

Arc 505.35.5 Loffreda, Stanislao. A visit to Capharnaum. Jerusalem, 1972.

Arc 505.35.7 Loffreda, Stanislao. A visit to Capharnaum. 2d ed. Jerusalem, 1973.

Arc 505.35.10 Sapir, Baruch. Capernaum (Kfar-Nochum). Tel Aviv, 1967.

Arc 505.39A Jack, J.M. Samaria in Ahab's time. Edinburgh, 1929.

Htn Arc 505.39*B Jack, J.M. Samaria in Ahab's time. Edinburgh, 1929.

Arc 505.39.5 Samaria-Sebaste; reports of the work of the joint expedition in 1931-1933. London, 1938-42. 3v.

Arc 505.39.10 Parrot, André. Samarie. Neuchatel, 1955.

Arc 505.39.12 Parrot, André. Samaria. N.Y., 1958.

Arc 505.42 Montet, Pierre. Les reliques de l'art syrien dans l'Égypte du nouvel empire. Paris, 1937.

Arc 505.45A Baur, P.V.C. The excavations at Dura-Europas. pt.1-9. New Haven, 1929-1946. 9v.

Arc 505.45B Baur, P.V.C. The excavations at Dura-Europas. pt.1. New Haven, 1929.

Arc 505.45.5 Johnson, J. Dura studies. Philadelphia, 1932.

Arc 505 Archaeology - Local - Palestine and Syria - Local; Special topics - cont.

Arc 505.45.10 Ehrenstein, Theodor. Über die Fresken der Synagoge von Dura Europas. Wien, 1937.

Arc 505.45.15 Rostovtsen, M.I. Dura-Europas and its art. Oxford, 1938.

Arc 505.45.20 Yale University. The excavations at Dura-Europas. New Haven, 1943-1949. 13v.

Arc 505.45.25 Christian church at Dura-Europas. New Haven, 1934.

Arc 505.49F Iukenik, Eleazar L. The ancient synagogue of Beth Alpha. Jeruselem, 1932.

Arc 505.51 Mesnil du Buisson, R. du. Le site archéologique de Mishrifé-Qatna. Thèse. Paris, 1935.

Arc 505.53 Waterman, Leroy. Preliminary report of the University of Michigan excavations at Sepphoris, Palestine, in 1931. Ann Arbor, 1937.

Arc 505.55 New York. Metropolitan Museum of Art. A crusaders' fortress in Palestine. N.Y., 1927.

Arc 505.57 Joint Expedition of the British School of Archaeology in Jerusalem. The stone age of Mount Carmel. Oxford, 1937-1939. 2v.

Arc 505.58 Vaux, R. de. Fouilles à Qaryet el-'Enab Abu-Gôch. Paris, 1950.

Arc 505.59 Parrot, André. Mari, une ville perdue...et retrouvée par l'archéologie française. Paris, 1936.

Arc 505.61F Lamon, R.S. Megiddo I. Chicago, 1939.

Arc 505.61.5 Guy, P.L.O. Megiddo tombs. Chicago, 1938.

Arc 505.61.10F Chicago. Oriental Institute. Megiddo Expedition. Megiddo II. Chicago, 1948. 2v.

Arc 505.63F Rome. Pontifico Istituto Biblico. Teleilát Ghassúl. Roma, 1934.

Arc 505.65F Fitzgerald, G.M. A sixth century monastery at Beth-Shan (Scythopolis). Philadelphia, 1939.

Arc 505.66 Garstang, John. The story of Jericho. London, 1940.

Arc 505.66.5 Kenyon, K.M. Digging up Jericho. N.Y., 1957.

Arc 505.66.10 Joint Expedition of the British School of Archaeology. Excavations at Jerico. London, 1960. 2v.

Arc 505.67 Glueck, N. The other side of the Jordan. New Haven, Conn., 1940.

Arc 505.68 Kraeling, C.H. Gerasa, city of the Decapolis. New Haven, Conn., 1938.

Arc 505.68.5 Harding, Gerald. The antiquities of Jordan. London, 1959.

Arc 505.68.6 Harding, Gerald. The antiquities of Jordan. London, 1967.

Arc 505.68.10 Jordan. Department of Antiquities. Official guide to Jerash. Jerusalem, 194-?

Arc 505.68.15 Abalmelck-Lazarev, Semen S. Dzherash (Gerasa). Sankt Peterburg, 1897.

Arc 505.69 Broome, E.C. The dolmens of Palestine and Transjordania. Philadelphia, 1940.

Arc 505.70 Solomiac, Michel. Les tours royales de Josèphe Flavius. Jérusalem, 1936.

Arc 505.71 Dussaud, René. L'art phénicien du IIe millenaire. Paris, 1949.

Arc 505.72 Carlsbergfondet, Copenhagen. Hama. v.2,4. København, 1948. 2v.

Arc 505.72.5F Lassus, Jean. Inventoire archéologique de la région au nord-est de Hama. v.1-2. Damas, 1935-1936.

Arc 505.73.5 Mouterde, René. Beyrouth, ville romaine. Beyrouth, 1952.

Arc 505.74 Jordan. Department of Antiquities. Annual. 1-9 2v.

Arc 505.75 Altheim, F. Das erste Auftreten der Hunnen das Alter der Jesaja-Rolle. Baden-Baden, 1953.

Arc 505.77F Dunand, Maurice. Fouilles de Byblos. Paris, 1937- 3v.

Arc 505.77.5 Jidejian, Nina. Byblos through the ages. Beirut, 1968.

Arc 505.80 Saadé, Gabriel. Ras-Shamra. Beyrouth, 1954.

Arc 505.82 Mader, Andreas E. Mambre. v.1, text; v.2, plates. Freiburg im Breisgau, 1957. 2v.

Arc 505.84F Jerusalem. Hebrew Community. Hazor. v.1-4. Jerusalem, 1958. 3v.

Arc 505.84.5 Yadin, Yigael. Hazor; the head of all those kingdoms. London, 1972.

Arc 505.86 Kleemann, Ilse. Der Satrapen-Sarkophag aus Sidon. Berlin, 1958.

Arc 505.88 Pritchard, James B. Hebrew inscriptions and stamps from Gibeon. Philadelphia, 1959.

Arc 505.90F Hamilton, R.W. Khirbat al Mafjar. Oxford, 1959.

Arc 505.92 Murray, Margaret A. Petra, the rock city of Edom. London, 1939.

Arc 505.92.5 Hammond, Philip C. The excavation of the main theater at Petra, 1961-1962, final report. London, 1965.

Arc 505.95PF Musil, Alois. Kusejr 'Amra. Wien, 1907.

Arc 505.97 Bagatti, Bellarmino. L'archeologia cristiana in Palestina. Firenze, 1962.

Arc 505.100 Damascus. Musée National Syrien. Etat de Syree. Damas, 1931.

Arc 505.100.2 Damascus. Musée National Syrien. Catalogue illustré du Departement des antiquités gréco-romaines. Damas, 1951.

Arc 505.102F Excavations in the Plain of Antioch. Chicago, 1960- 2v.

Arc 505.105F Delougaz, Pinhas. A Byzantine church at Khirbat al-Karak. Chicago, 1960.

Arc 505.107 Mayerson, Philip. The ancient agricultural regime of Nessana and the Central Negeb. London, 1961.

Arc 505.110 Michalowski, Kazimierz. Palmyre. Warszawa, 1960. 6v.

Arc 505.115 Moortgat, Anton. Tell Chuēra in Nordost-Syrien. Köln, 1960.

Arc 505.115.2 Moortgat, Anton. Tell Chuēra in Nordost-Syrien. Köln, 1962.

Arc 505.115.3 Moortgat, Anton. Tell Chuēra in Nordost-Syrien. Köln, 1965.

Arc 505.116 Mécérian, Jean. Expedition archéologique dans l'Antiochène occidentale. Beyrouth, 1965.

Arc 505.120 Presbyterian Theological Seminary, Chicago, Illinois. The citadel of Beth-Zur. Philadelphia, 1933.

Arc 505.121 Pritchard, James. Gibeon, where the sun stood still. Princeton, 1962.

Arc 505.121.10 Pritchard, James. The Bronze Age Cemetery at Gibeon. Philadelphia, 1963.

Arc 505.123F Missione Archeologica. Caesarea Maritima (Israele). Milano, 1959.

Arc 505.124F Joint Expedition of the University of Rome and the Hebrew University. Excavations at Ramat Rahel, seasons 1959 and 1960. Rome, 1962.

Arc 505.124.2F Joint Expedition of the University of Rome and the Hebrew University. Excavations at Ramat Rahel, seasons 1961 and 1962. Rome, 1964.

Arc 505.124.5F Rome (City). Università. Missione Archeologica. Il colle de Rachele. Roma, 1960.

Arc 505.125 Israel Exploration. The expedition to the Judean desert, 1960-1961. Jerusalem, 1963.

Classified Listing

Arc 505 Archaeology - Local - Palestine and Syria - Local; Special topics - cont.

Arc 505.126F Missione archeologica italiana in Siria. Roma, 1964- 3v.
Arc 505.127 Wilson, Charles. The recovery of Jerusalem. London, 1871.
Arc 505.128 Yadin, Yigael. Masada; Herod's fortress and the Zealot's last stand. N.Y., 1966.
Arc 505.128.1 Yadin, Yigael. Masada: Herod's fortress and the Zealot's last stand. London, 1966.
Arc 505.129 Negev, Avraham. Cities of the desert. Tel-Aviv, 1966.
Arc 505.130 Lafontaine-Dosogne, Jacqueline. Itinéraires archéologiques dans la région d'Antioche. Bruxelles, 1967.
Arc 505.131 Buhl, Marie Louise. Shiloh; the Danish excavations at Tall Sailūn, Palestine, in 1926, 1929, 1932, and 1963. Copenhagen, 1969.
Arc 505.132 Dunand, Maurice. Oumm el-'Amed. Text and atlas. Paris, 1962. 2v.
Arc 505.133 Stékélis, Moshé. Archaeological excavations at Ubeidiya, 1964-1966. Jerusalem, 1969.
Arc 505.134 Ehrich, Ann M. Early pottery of the Jebeleh region. Philadelphia, 1939.
Arc 505.136 Hachmann, Rolf. Vademecum der Grabung Kamid-el-Loz. Bonn, 1969.
Arc 505.136.5 Kamid el-Loz-Kumidi. Bonn, 1970.
Arc 505.138 Mittmann, Siegfried. Beiträge zur Siedlungs- und Territorialgeschichte des nördlichen Ostjordanlandes. Wiesbaden, 1970.
Arc 505.140 Hachmann, Rolf. Bericht über die Ergebnisse der Ausgrabungen in Kamid el-Loz (Libanon) in den Jahren 1963 und 1964. Bonn, 1966.
Arc 505.140.5 Hachmann, Rolf. Bericht über die Ergebnisse der Ausgrabungen in Kamid el-Loz (Libanon) in den Jahren 1966 und 1967. Bonn, 1970.
Arc 505.144 Miroschedji, Pierre R. de. L'époque que pré-urbaine en Palestine. Paris, 1971.
Arc 505.146 Queen Elizabeth of Belgium Institute of Archaeology, Hebrew University, Jerusalem. Livre d'or de l'Institute d'archéologie. Bruxelles, 1965.
Arc 505.147.1 Mazar, Benjamin. The excavations in the old city of Jerusalem near the Temple Mount. Jerusalem, 1971.
Arc 505.148 Prausnitz, Moshe W. Studies in the lithic industries of Israel and adjacent countries. Jerusalem, 1970.
Arc 505.149 Meyers, Eric Mark. Jewish ossuaries: reburial and rebirth. Rome, 1971.
Arc 505.150 Beth She'arim; report on the excavations during 1936-1940. New Brunswick, 1973-76. 3v.
Arc 505.150.1 Beth She'arim; report on the excavations during 1936-1940. Jerusalem, 1973.
Arc 505.151 Stékélis, Moshé. The Yarmukian culture of the Neolithic period. Jerusalem, 1972.
Arc 505.152 Boraas, Roger S. Heshbon 1971: the second campaign at Tell Hesbân. Berrien Spring, Mich., 1973.
Arc 505.153 College of Wooster Expedition to Pella. Pella of the Decapolis. Wooster, 1973-
Arc 505.154 Kenyon, Kathleen Mary. Digging up Jerusalem. London, 1974.
Arc 505.155F Callaway, Joseph A. The early bronze age sanctuary at Ai (et-Tell). London, 1972.

Arc 510 Archaeology - Local - Asia Minor - Folios [Discontinued]

Arc 510.1 Salzmann, A. Nécropole de Camiros. Paris, 1875.
Arc 510.2 Deutsches Archäologisches Institut. Altertümer von Pergamon. Berlin. 1,1912+ 18v.
Arc 510.2PF Deutches Archäologisches Institut. Altertümer von Pergamon. Atlases. 9v.
Arc 510.2.9F Boehringer, C. Das Temenos für den Herrscher Kult. Berlin, 1937.
Arc 510.2.10F Szalay, Akos. Die hellenistischen Arsenale. Berlin, 1937.
Arc 510.3 Laborde, L. de. Voyate de l'Asie Mineure. Paris, 1838.
Arc 510.4 Texier, Charles. Description de l'Asie Mineure. Paris, 1839-1849. 3v.
Arc 510.5 Newton, C.T. Halicarnassus, Cnidas and Branchidae. v.1; v.2, pt.1-2. London, 1862-1863. 3v.
Arc 510.6 Benndorf, O. Das Heroon von Gjoelbaschi-Trysa. Vienna, 1889. 2v.
Arc 510.7 Rayet, O. Milet et le golfe latmique. Paris, 1877-85.
X Cg Arc 510.8 American Archaeological Institute. Investigations at Assos. v.1-2. Cambridge, 1902-21.
Arc 510.9 Texier, Charles. Principal ruins of Asia Minor. London, 1865.
X Cg Arc 510.10 Schliemann, H. Altas des antiquités troyennes. Leipzig, 1874.
Arc 510.201 Benndorf, O. Reisen in Lykien und Karien. Vienna, 1884.
Arc 510.201.2 Petersen, E. Reiden in Lykien, Milyas und Kibyratis. Vienna, 1889.
X Cg Arc 510.202 Humann, K. Reisen in Kleinasien und Nordsyrien. Text and atlas. Berlin, 1890. (Changed to XP 9867) 2v.
Arc 510.203 Gell, W. The topography of Troy. London, 1804.
Arc 510.204 Thiersch, F. Die Koenigsburg von Pergamon. Stuttgart, 1883.
X Cg Arc 510.206 Niemann, S. Les villes de la Pamphylie et de la Pisidie. Paris, 1890-1893. 2v.
Arc 510.207 Pottier, E. La Nécropole de Myrina. Paris, 1888. 2v.
Arc 510.208 Conze, A. Die Ergebnisse der Ausgrabungen zu Pergamon. Berlin, 1880.
Arc 510.208.2 Conze, A. Die Ergebnisse der Ausgrabungen zu Pergamon, 1880-1881. Berlin, 1882.
Arc 510.209 Normand, Charles. La Troie d'Homère. Paris, 1892.
Arc 510.210 Forchhammer, P.W. Das homerische Troja. n.p., 1874.
Arc 510.211 Hamdy Bey, O. Le Tumulus de Nemroud-Dagh. Constantinople, 1883.
Arc 510.212 Sabatier, J. Chronologie du Royaume de Bosphore. St. Petersbourg, 1849.
Arc 510.213 Ussing, J.L. Pergamos seine Geschichte und Monumente. Berlin, 1899
Arc 510.214 Collignon, M. Pergame restauration des monuments de l'Aropole. Paris, 1900.
Arc 510.215 Brosset. Les ruines d'Ani, capitale de l'Arménie. Text and atlas. St. Petersbourg, 1860. 2v.
Arc 510.215.5 Marr, N. Raskopki...1904 godu. Sankt Peterburg, 1906.
X Cg Arc 510.216 Wiegand, Theodor. Prierre. Berlin, 1904.
X Cg Arc 510.217 Humann, Carl. Magnesia am Maeander. Berlin, 1904.
Arc 510.218F Wiegand, Theodor. Milet-Ergebnisse der Ausgrabungen. Berlin, 1906- 18v.
Arc 510.218PF Milet. Bd.1, Heft 5 (Tafeln); Bd.4, Atlas. Berlin, n.d. 3v.
Arc 510.219F Österreichisches Archäologisches Institut. Forschungen in Ephesop. v.1-4, pt.1-3; v.5. Wien, 1906-51. 8v.

Arc 510 Archaeology - Local - Asia Minor - Folios [Discontinued] - cont.

Arc 510.220F Kinch, K.F. Vroulia [Rhodes]. Berlin, 1914.

Arc 513 Archaeology - Local - Asia Minor - General works

Arc 513.01 Pamphlet box. Archaeology. Asia Minor. General works.
Arc 513.02 Pamphlet vol. Archaeology. Asia Minor. General works. 10 pam.
Arc 513.1 Sterrett, J.R.S. Leaflets from the notebook of an archaeological traveller in Asia Minor. Austin, 1889.
Arc 513.1.5 Sterrett, J.R.S. A plea for research in Asia Minor. Ithaca, 1911.
Arc 513.1.10 Ugarit-Bibliographie/Manfried Dietrich. Neukirchen, 1973. 4v.
Htn Arc 513.2* Beaufort, F. Karamania. London, 1817.
Arc 513.4 Fellows, C. Asia Minor. London, 1839.
Arc 513.4.2 Fellows, C. Discoveries in Lycia. London, 1841.
Arc 513.4.5 Fellows, C. Travels and researches in Asia Minor. London, 1852.
Arc 513.4.6 Fellows, C. Travels and researches in Asia Minor. Hildesheim, 1975.
Arc 513.5 Hamilton, W.J. Researches in Asia Minor, Pontus and Armenia. London, 1842. 2v.
Arc 513.6 Haynes, J.H. Descriptive catalogue to accompany a series of photographs of Asia Minor. N.Y., 1892.
Arc 513.7 Newton, C.T. Travels and discoveries in the Levant. London, 1865. 2v.
Arc 513.8 Franz, J. Fuenf Inschriften und fuenf Staedte in Kleinasien. Berlin, 1840.
Arc 513.9 Ross, L. Reisen nach Kos, Halikarnassos, Rhodos. Halle, 1852.
NEDL Arc 513.10 Spratt, T.A.B. Travels in Lycia, Milyas, and the Cibyratis. London, 1847. 2v.
Arc 513.11 Arundell, F.V.J. Discoveries in Asia Minor. v.2, photoreproduction. London, 1834. 2v.
Arc 513.11.1 Arundell, F.V.J. Discoveries in Asia Minor. v.1-2. Hildesheim, 1975.
Arc 513.12 Leake, William M. Journal of a tour in Asia Minor. London, 1824.
Arc 513.13 Ramsay, W.M. The historical geography of Asia Minor. v.1-2. Photoreproduction. London, 1890.
X Cg Arc 513.13 Ramsay, W.M. The historical geography of Asia Minor. v.1-2. London, 1890.
Arc 513.13.5 Ramsay, W.M. Studies in history and art...Eastern Provinces, Roman Empire. Aberdeen, 1906.
Arc 513.14 Maps. Asia Minor (1899). Archäologische Karte von Kleinasien. Halle, 1899.
Arc 513.15 Jüthner, J. Vorläufiger Bericht...Expeditionen Kleinasien. Prag, 1903.
Arc 513.16 Gallois, E. Asie-Mineure et Syrie. Paris, n.d.
Arc 513.17 Dussaud, René. Les civilisations prehelléniques. Paris, 1910.
Arc 513.17.2 Dussaud, René. Les civilisations prehelléniques. 2. éd. Paris, 1914.
Arc 513.17.15 Dussaud, René. La Lydie et ses voisins aus hautes époques. Paris, 1930.
Arc 513.17.20 Dussaud, René. Prélydiens Hittites et Achéens. Paris, 1953.
Arc 513.18 Sartiaux, Félix. Villes mortes d'Asie Mineure. Paris, 1911.
Arc 513.18.5 Sartiaux, Félix. L'archéologie française en Asie Mineure et l'expansion allemande. Paris, 1918.
Arc 513.19.5 Ximinez, S. Asia Minor in ruins. N.Y., 1925.
Arc 513.20 Calder, W.M. Monumenta Asiae Minoris antiqua. London, 1928-39. 8v.
Arc 513.20.5 Ülgen, Ali Saim. Anitlaria koranmasi ve onarilmasi. Ankara, 1943.
Arc 513.21 Bittel, Kurt. Prähistorische Forschung in Kleinasien. Istanbul, 1934.
Arc 513.21.10 Bittel, Kurt. Kleinasiatische Studien. Istanbul, 1942.
Arc 513.22 Robert, L. Villes d'Asie Mineure. Paris, 1935.
Arc 513.22.2 Robert, L. Villes d'Asie Mineure. 2. éd. Paris, 1962.
Arc 513.24F Gabriel, Albert. Voyages archeologiques dans la Turquie orientale. Paris, 1940. 2v.
Arc 513.25 Deutsches Archäologisches Institut. Neue deutsche Ausgrabungen im Mittelmeergebiet. Berlin, 1959.
Arc 513.26 Akurgal, E. Arkeoloji arastirmalari. Ankara, 1945.
Arc 513.28 Duyuran, Rüstem. The ancient cities of Western Anatolia. n.p., 195-?
Arc 513.28.5 Duyuran, Rüstem. Carte archeologique de l'Anatolie occidentale. Izmir, 1952.
Arc 513.30 Diez, E. Die Sprache der Ruinen. Wien, 1962.
Arc 513.32A Mellaart, James. The Chaleolithic and early Bronze Ages in the Near East and Anatolia. Beirut, 1966.
Arc 513.32B Mellaart, James. The Chaleolithic and early Bronze Ages in the Near East and Anatolia. Beirut, 1966.
Arc 513.34 Duyuran, Rüstem. Bati Anoidolu'da eski şehirler. İstanbul, 1948.
Arc 513.38 Erder, Cevat. Hellenistik devir Anadolu nimorisinde kyma. Ankara, 1967.
Arc 513.40 Kink, Khilida A. Vostochnoe sredizemnamor'e v drevneishuiu epokhu. Moskva, 1970.
Arc 513.41 Orient and Occident. Kevelaer, 1973.
Arc 513.42 Pfannenstiel, Max. Die altsteinzeitlichen Kulturen Anatoliens. Berlin, 1941.

Arc 518 Archaeology - Local - Asia Minor - Ephesus

Arc 518.1 Wood, J.T. Discoveries at Ephesus. London, 1877.
Arc 518.1.3 Wood, J.T. Discoveries at Ephesus. Boston, 1877.
Arc 518.1.5 Wood, J.T. Modern discoveries on the site of ancient Ephesus. London, 1890.
Arc 518.2 Curtius, E. Ephesos. Berlin, 1874.
Arc 518.3 Falkener, E. Ephesus and the Temple of Diana. London, 1862.
Arc 518.4 Fergusson, J. The Temple of Diana at Ephesus. London, 1883.
Arc 518.5 Clarke, Hyde. Ephesus. Smyrna, 1863.
Arc 518.6 Murray, A.S. Sculptured columns...Temple of Diana at Ephesus. London, 1895-96.
Arc 518.7 Vienna. Kaiserhaus. Ausstellung von Fundstücken aus Ephesos im unteren Belvedere. Wien, 1905.
Arc 518.8 Keil, Josef. Ephesos. Wien, 1915.
Arc 518.8.5 Keil, Josef. Ephesos. Wien, 1955.
Arc 518.8.7 Keil, Josef. Ephesos. 4. Aufl. Wien, 1957.
Arc 518.9 Lauria, G.A. Efeso; studj. Napoli, 1874.
Arc 518.10 Duyuran, Rüstem. Ephèse. Ankara, 1951.
Arc 518.11 Miltner, Franz. Ephesos, Stadt der Artemis. Wien, 1958.
Arc 518.12 Alzinger, Wilhelm. Die Stadt des siebenten Weltwunders. Wien, 1962.

Classified Listing

Arc 518 Archaeology - Local - Asia Minor - Ephesus - cont.

Arc 518.12.5F Alzinger, Wilhelm. Augusteische Architektur in Ephesos. v.1-2. Wien, 1974.

Arc 518.13 Menestrier, C.F. Symbolica Dianae Ephesiae statua a Claudio Menetreio exposita. Romae, 1657. 3 pam.

Arc 520 Archaeology - Local - Asia Minor - Pergamon

Arc 520.1 Bohn, R. Tempel des Athena Polias zu Pergamon. Berlin, 1881.

Arc 520.2 Graeber, F. Die Wasserleitungen von Pergamon. Berlin, 1888.

Arc 520.3 Conze, A. Pergamon. Berlin, 1880.

Arc 520.4 Mitchell, L.M. (Mrs.). Sculptures of the Great Pergamon Altar. N.Y., 1882.

Arc 520.5 Urlichs, L. Pergamon - Geschichte und Kunst. Leipzig, 1883.

Arc 520.6 Berlin. Königliches Museum. Führer durch die Ruinen von Pergamon. Berlin, 1887.

Arc 520.6.5 Berlin. Königliches Museum. Führer durch die Ruinen von Pergamon. 5. Aufl. Berlin, 1911.

Arc 520.7 Habich, G. Die Amazonengruppe die attalischen Weihgeschenks. Berlin, 1896.

Arc 520.8 Hachtmann, K. Pergamon. Pflanzstätte Hellenisches Kunst. Gütersloh, 1900.

Arc 520.9 Schmidt. Pergamon. Lübeck, 1899.

Arc 520.10 Berlin. Königliches Museum. Beschreibung der Skulpturen aus Pergamon. Berlin, 1904.

Arc 520.10.5 Berlin. Königliches Museum. Beschreibung der Skulpturen aus Pergamon. Berlin, 1895.

Arc 520.11 Berlin. Königliches Museum. Guide to the Pergamon Museum. Berlin, 1904. 2v.

Arc 520.11.5 Berlin. Königliches Museum. Führer durch das Pergamon Museum. Berlin, 1904.

Arc 520.11.6 Berlin. Königliches Museum. Führer durch die Ruinen von Pergamon. 6. Aufl. Berlin, 1922.

Arc 520.12 Salis, A. von. Der Altar von Pergamon. Berlin, 1912.

Arc 520.13 Schwabe, L. von. Pergamon und seine Kunst. Tubingen, 1882.

Arc 520.14F Schuchhardt, W.H. Die Meister des grossen Frieses von Pergamon. Berlin, 1925.

Arc 520.15A Stier, Hans Erich. Aus der Welt des Pergamonaltars. Berlin, 1932.

Arc 520.15B Stier, Hans Erich. Aus der Welt des Pergamonaltars. Berlin, 1932.

Arc 520.16 Dopp, W. Eine Altisdarstellung am grossen Fries von Pergamon. Inaug. Diss. Rostock, 1934.

Arc 520.17 Napp, A.E. Das Altar von Pergamon. München, 1936.

Arc 520.18 Humann, K. Der Entdecker von Pergamon. Berlin, 1930.

Arc 520.18.10 Schulte, Eduard. Carl Humann. Dortmund, 1971.

Arc 520.19 Kähler, Heinz. Der grosse Fries von Pergamon. Berlin, 1948.

Arc 520.19.5 Kähler, Heinz. Pergamon. Berlin, 1949.

Arc 520.20 Schober, A. Die Kunst von Pergamon. Wien, 1951.

Arc 520.25 Belov, G.D. Altar' Zevsa v Pergame. Leningrad, 1958.

Arc 520.25.2 Belov, G.D. Altar' Zevsa v Pergame. Leningrad, 1959.

Arc 520.30 Humann, Karl. Der Pergamon Altar. Dortmund, 1959.

Arc 520.35 Rohde, Elisabeth. Pergamon: Burgberg und Altar. 2. Aufl. Berlin, 1961.

Arc 520.36 Schulte, Eduard. Chronik der Ausgrabung von Pergamon. Dortmund, 1963.

Arc 520.37 Szczepański, Jan A. Ołtarz i miasto. Wyd. 1. Kraków, 1974.

Arc 522 Archaeology - Local - Asia Minor - Troy

Arc 522.1 Lechevalier, Jean Baptiste. Description of the plain of Troy. Edinburgh, 1791.

Arc 522.1.2 Lechevalier, Jean Baptiste. Voyage de la Troade. Paris, 1802. 3v.

Arc 522.1.2.3 Lechevalier, Jean Baptiste. Voyage dans la Troade. 2. éd. Paris, 1799.

Arc 522.2 Bryant, Jacob. Observations upon a treatise entitled A description of the plain of Troy. Eton, 1795.

Htn Arc 522.2.3* Bryant, Jacob. Observations upon a treatise: Description of plain of Troy. Eton, 1795.

Arc 522.3 Lenormant, F. Les antiquités de la Troade. Paris, 1876.

Arc 522.4 Schliemann, H. Troia und seine Ruinen. Rostock, 1875?

Arc 522.4.2 Schliemann, H. Trojanische Alterthuemer. Leipzig, 1874.

Arc 522.4.3A Schliemann, H. Troy and its remains. London, 1875.

Arc 522.4.3B Schliemann, H. Troy and its remains. London, 1875.

Arc 522.4.3C Schliemann, H. Troy and its remains. London, 1875.

Arc 522.4.4A Schliemann, H. Troja. London, 1884.

Arc 522.4.4B Schliemann, H. Troja. London, 1884.

Arc 522.4.4.2 Schliemann, H. Troja. London, 1884.

Arc 522.4.5 Schliemann, H. Ilios. Leipzig, 1881.

Arc 522.4.5.3 Schliemann, H. Ilios. London, 1880.

Arc 522.4.6 Schliemann, H. Ilios. N.Y., 1881.

Arc 522.4.7 Schliemann, H. Bericht ueber der Ausgrabungen in Troja im Jahre 1890. Leipzig, 1891.

Arc 522.4.9 Berlin. Königliches Museum. Heinrich Schliemanns Sammlung Trojanischer Altertümer. Berlin, 1902.

Arc 522.4.15 Boetticher, E. Hissarlik wie es ist. Berlin, 1890.

Arc 522.4.18 Boetticher, E. Der Trojanische Humbug. Berlin, 1911.

Arc 522.5 Salisbury, S. Troy and Homer. Worcester, 1875.

Arc 522.6 Virchow, R. Beitraege zur Landeskunde der Troas. Berlin, 1879.

Arc 522.7 Rennell, J. Observations on the topography of the plain of Troy. London, 1814.

Htn Arc 522.8* Barker-Webb, P. Topographie de la Troade. Paris, 1844.

Arc 522.9 Keller, O. Die Entdeckung Ilions zu Hissarlik. Freiburg in Baden, 1875.

Arc 522.10 Brentano, E. Zur Loesung der Troianischen Frage. Heilbronn, 1881.

Arc 522.10.2 Brentano, E. Alt-Ilion im Dumbrekthal. Heilbronn, 1877?

Arc 522.10.3 Brentano, E. Troia und Neu-Ilion. Heilbronn, 1882.

Arc 522.11 Lenz, C.G. Die Ebene von Troja. Neu-Strelitz, 1798.

Arc 522.12 Dörpfeld, W. Troja 1893. Leipzig, 1894.

Arc 522.13 Hildebrand, H.H. Fynden i Troas och Homeroe' Troja. Stockholm, 1878.

Arc 522.15 Dörpfeld, W. Troja und Ilion. Athen, 1902. 2v.

Arc 522.16A Tolman, H.C. Mycenaean Troy. N.Y., 1903.

Arc 522.16B Tolman, H.C. Mycenaean Troy. N.Y., 1903.

Arc 522.17 Sartiaux, Felix. Troie, la guerre de Troie. Paris, 1915.

Arc 522.18 Seyk, V. Das Wahre und richtige Troja-Illion. Prag, 1926.

Arc 522.19 Vellay, Charles. Les nouveaux aspects de la question de Troie. Paris, 1930.

Arc 522.19.2 Vellay, Charles. Les nouveaux aspects de la question de Troie. Paris, 1930.

Arc 522 Archaeology - Local - Asia Minor - Troy - cont.

Arc 522.19.5 Vellay, Charles. La question de Troie. Chartres, 1931. 4 pam.

Arc 522.19.10 Vellay, Charles. Controverses autour de Troie. Paris, 1936.

Arc 522.20 Kosay, Hamit. "Troad" da dört yerleş me yeri. Istanbul, 1936.

Arc 522.25 Mey, Oscar. Das Schlachtfeld vor Troja, eine Untersuchung. Berlin, 1926.

Arc 522.30 Perret, J. Les origines de la legende troyenne de Rome. Thèse. Paris, 1942.

Arc 522.35F Blegen, Carl William. Troy. v.1-4, pt.1-2. Princeton, N.J., 1950-51. 8v.

Arc 522.35.5F Troy. Supplementary monographs. Princeton, N.J. 1-3,1951-1963 3v.

Arc 522.36 Blegen, Carl William. Troy and the Trojans. London, 1963.

Arc 522.37 Holden, B.M. The metopes of the Temple of Athena at Ilion. Northampton, 1964.

Arc 522.40 Kandemir, Selâhattin. Tarova harabesi. 2. basi. Istanbul, 1938.

Arc 522.40.5 Kandemir, Selâhattin. Turova harabeleri ve skalor. Izmir, 1933.

Arc 522.41 Cook, John Manuel. The Troad; an archaeological and topographical study. Oxford, 1973.

Arc 530 Archaeology - Local - Asia Minor - Other Local; Special topics

Arc 530.1 Hirschfeld, G. Paphlagonische Felsengraeber. Berlin, 1885.

Arc 530.1.5 Hirschfeld, G. Felsenreliefs in Kleinasien und die Volk der Hitteter. Berlin, 1887.

Arc 530.2 Olfers, J.F.M. Lydische Koenigsgraeber bei Sardes. Berlin, 1859.

Arc 530.2.4F Morey, Charles B. Roman and Christian sculpture. Princeton, 1924.

Arc 530.2.6 Archaeological Exploration of Sardis. Monograph. Cambridge. 1,1971+ 4v.

Arc 530.2.8 Sardis newsletter. Cambridge, Mass. 1958+

Arc 530.2.10 Hanfmann, George M.A. Letters from Sardis. Cambridge, 1972.

Arc 530.3 Fellows, C. The Xanthian marbles. London, 1843.

Arc 530.3.5 Lloyd, W.W. The Xanthian marbles. Londdon, 1845.

Arc 530.4 Preger, T. Anonymi Byzantini. München, 1898.

Arc 530.5 Papodopoulos, A. Phōkaika. Smyrnē, 1899.

Arc 530.6 Langlois, Victor. Rapport...de la Cilicie et de la Petite-Arménie. Paris, 1854.

Arc 530.6.5F Alfoldi-Rosenbaum, Elizabeth. A survey of coastal cities in Western Cilicia. Ankara, 1967.

Arc 530.6.10F Alfoldi-Rosenbaum, Elizabeth. Anamur nekropolu. The necropolis Anemurium. Ankara, 1971.

Arc 530.8 Dickson, W.K. The life of Major General Sir R.M. Smith. Edinburgh, 1901.

Arc 530.9 Anderson, J.G.C. Journey of exploration in Pontus. v.1. Bruxelles, 1903.

Arc 530.9.2 Anderson, J.G.C. Journey of exploration in Pontus. v.2. Bruxelles, 1903.

Arc 530.9.3 Anderson, J.G.C. Journey of exploration in Pontus. v.3. Bruxelles, 1903.

Arc 530.10 Herkenrath, E. Der Fries des Artemisions von Magnesia. Berlin, 1902.

Arc 530.10.15 Gerkan, Armin von. Der Altar des Artemis-Tempels in Magnesia am Mäander. Berlin, 1929.

Arc 530.11 Joubin, André. De sarcophagis Clazomeniis. Paris, 1901.

Arc 530.12 Garstang, John. The land of the Hittites. London, 1910.

Arc 530.12.5 Osten, H.H. von der. Explorations in Hittite Asia Minor. Chicago, 1927.

Arc 530.12.10 Osten, H.H. von der. Explorations in Hittite Asia Minor, 1927-28. Chicago, 1929.

Arc 530.12.25 Bittel, Kurt. Die Felsbilder von Yazilikaya. Bamberg, 1934.

Arc 530.12.28F Boğazköy. v.3-5. Berlin, 1935- 3v.

Arc 530.12.30 Bittel, Kurt. Die Ruinen von Boğazköy, der Hauptstadt des Hethiterreiches. Berlin, 1937.

Arc 530.12.32 Krause, K. Boğazköy. Berlin, 1940.

Arc 530.12.35 Marek, Kurt W. The secret of the Hittites. N.Y., 1956.

Arc 530.12.40 Marek, Kurt W. Enge Schlucht und Schwarzer Berg. Hamburg, 1955.

Arc 530.12.42 Marek, Kurt W. Enge Schlucht und Schwarzer Berg. Reinbek, 1966.

Arc 530.13 Radet, G. Cybébé. Paris, 1909.

Arc 530.14 Wiegand, Theodor. Priene. Leipzig, 1910.

Arc 530.14.5F Wiegand, Theodor. Priene: Ergebnisse der Ausgrabungen. Berlin, 1904.

Arc 530.14.15F Gerkan, Armin von. Das Theater von Priene. München, 1921.

Arc 530.14.25 Schede, Martin. Die Ruinen von Priene. Berlin, 1934.

Arc 530.14.26 Schede, Martin. Die Ruinen von Priene. 2. Aufl. Berlin, 1964.

Arc 530.15 Wedel, F. Skizzierte Gedanken eines Kunst freundes. Neustadt, 1905.

Arc 530.16F Chantre, E. Mission en Cappadoce. Paris, 1898.

Arc 530.17 Sartiaux, Felix. Les sculptures et la restauration du temple d'Assos. Paris, 1915.

Arc 530.18 Viollet, H. Description du palais de al-Montasim. Paris, 1909.

Arc 530.19F Pontrenioli, E. Didymes fouilles de 1895 et 1896. Paris, 1904.

Arc 530.22F Marr, H. Arkheologicheskiia ekspeditsiia 1916 g. Sankt Peterburg, 1922.

Arc 530.22.10 Piotrovskii, Boris Borisovich. Vanskoe tsarstvo (Urartu). 2. Izd. Moskva, 1959.

Arc 530.22.11 Piotrovskii, Boris Borisovich. Urartu. London, 1969.

Arc 530.22.15 Arutiunian, Nikolai V. Zemledelic i skotovodstvo Urartu. Erevan, 1964.

Arc 530.25 Bezobrazov, P.V. Trapezunt', ego sviatyni i drevnosti. Petrograd, 1916.

Arc 530.29 Shober, Arnold. Der Fries des Hekateions von Lagina. Baden, 1933.

Arc 530.35F Osten, H.H. von der. The Alishar Hüyük, seasons of 1930-32. Chicago, 1937.

Arc 530.37 Schede, Martin. Ankara und Augustus. Berlin, 1937.

Arc 530.39F Swoboda, H. Denkmäler aus Lykaonien, Pamphylien und Isaurien. Brunn, 1935.

Arc 530.45 Berlin. Tell Halaf Museum. Führer durch das Tell Halaf Maueum. Berlin, 1934.

Arc 530.47 Berlin. Staatliche Museen. Die Ausgrabungen der zweiten Ktesiphon-Expedition. Berlin, 1933.

Arc 530.49 Schneider, A.M. Die Stadtmauer von Iznik. Berlin, 1938.

Arc 530.51F Mansel, A.M. Pergede kazilar ne arastumalar. Ankara, 1949.

Classified Listing

Arc 530 Archaeology - Local - Asia Minor - Other Local; Special topics - cont.

Arc 530.52 Özgüc, T. Ön tarih'te Qnadolu'da dü Gomme Adetleri. Basimevi, 1948.
Arc 530.53 Akurgal, E. Remarques stylistiques sur les reliefs de Malatya. Istanbul, 1946.
Arc 530.54 Landsberger, Benno. Samial. Ankara, 1948.
Arc 530.54.5 Landsberger, Benno. Samial. Photoreproduction. Ankara, 1948.
Arc 530.55F Özgüc, T. Türk Tarih kurumu tarafindan yapelan karakoyuk hafreyate raporu. Ankara, 1947.
Arc 530.60 Garstang, John. Prehistoric Mersin. Oxford, 1953.
Arc 530.65 Akademiia nauk Armianskoi SSR, Erevan. Institut Istorii. Garni. Erevan, 1951- 4v.
Arc 530.65.5 Akademiia nauk Armianskoi SSR, Erevan. Institut Istorii. Karmir-blur. Erevan, 1955- 4v.
Arc 530.65.10 Martirosian, A. Gorod Teishenbaini po raskopkam 1947-1958 gg. Erevan, 1961.
Arc 530.65.15 Martirosian, A. Armeniia v epokhu bronzy i rannego zheleza. Erevan, 1964.
Arc 530.65.20 Arin-berd. Erevan, 1961.
Arc 530.70 Woolley, C.L. A forgotten kingdom. Baltimore, 1953.
Arc 530.75 Özgüc, T. Türk Tarih kurumu tarafindan yapelan Kültepe kazisi raporu, 1948. Ankara, 1950.
Arc 530.76F Özgüc, T. Türk Tarih kurumu tarafindan yapelan Kültepe kazisi raporu, 1949. Ankara, 1953.
Arc 530.80A Trever, K.V. Ocherki po istorii kultur' Erevnei Armenii. Moskva, 1953.
Arc 530.80B Trever, K.V. Ocherki po istorii kultur' Erevnei Armenii. Moskva, 1953.
Arc 530.80.5 Khachatrian, T.S. Materialnaia Kul'tura drevnego Artika. Erevan, 1963.
Arc 530.81 Akademiia nauk Armianskoi SSR, Erevan. Institut Istorii. Dzhrvezh. Erevan, 1959. 2v.
Arc 530.82 Martirosian, A. Raskopki v golovino. Erevan, 1954.
Arc 530.85 Doerner, F.K. Inschriften und Denkmäler aus Bithynien. Berlin, 1941.
Arc 530.90 Jacopi, G. Esplorazioni e studi in Paflagonia e Cappadocia. Roma, 1937.
Arc 530.90.5 Jacopi, G. Dalla Paflagonia alla Commagene. Roma, 1936.
Arc 530.95F Akademiia nauk Gruz SSR, Tiflis. Institut Istorii. Mtskheta; itogi arkheologicheskikh issledovanii. Tbilisi, 1955.
Arc 530.95.2F Akademiia nauk Gruz SSR, Tiflis. Institut Istorii. Mtskheta; itogi arkheologicheskikh issledovanii. Tbilisi, 1958.
Arc 530.95.5 Tkeshelashvili, G. Mtskheta; putevaditel'. Tbilisi, 1958.
Arc 530.95.10 Apakidze, A.M. Mtskheta. Tbilisi, 1959.
Arc 530.96 Lomatidze, C.A. Arkheologicheskie raskopki v srevnegruziiskoi storitse Mtskheta. Tbilisi, 1955.
Arc 530.97 Chubinishvili, T.N. Drevneiskie arkheologicheskie...Mtskheta. Tbilisi, 1957.
Arc 530.100 Otto-Dorn, K. Das Islamische Iznik. Berlin, 1941.
Arc 530.105 Lloyd, Seton. Early Anatolia. Harmondsworth, 1956.
Arc 530.110 Schneider, A.M. Die römischen und byzantinischen Denkmäler von Iznik-Nicaea. Berlin, 1943.
Arc 530.115 Irag. Department of Antiquities. Ctesiphon and Hatra. Baghdad, 1943.
Arc 530.120 Egiazarian, O. Pamiatniki kul'tury...raiona. Erevan, 1955.
Arc 530.125 Le sanctuaire de Sinuri prés de Mylasa. Paris, 1945.
Arc 530.130 Moraux, Paul. Une imprécation funéraire a néocésarée. Paris, 1959.
Arc 530.135F Arik, Remri Ogur. Ankara-Konya. Ankara, 1956.
Arc 530.135.5 Arik, Remri Ogur. Turkiye de 1936 yelendaki arkeoloji isleri. Istanbul, 1938.
Arc 530.135.10 Arik, Remri Ogur. Turk muzeciliéine bir bakis. Istanbul, 1953.
Arc 530.140F Kosay, H.Z. Büyük Güllücek karisi. Ankara, 1957.
Arc 530.141F Kosay, H.Z. Guzelova karisi. Ankara, 1967.
Arc 530.145F Mansel, A.M. Side agorasi ve civarindaki binalar. Ankara, 1956.
Arc 530.150 Institut Français d'Archéologie, Istanbul. Phrygie, exploration archéologique. v.1-3. Paris, 1941- 2v.
Arc 530.151 Haspels, Caroline H.E. The highlands of Phrygia: sites and monuments. Princeton, 1971. 2v.
Arc 530.155 Ülgen, Ali Saim. Collection of cuttings from Turkish archeological periodicals. n.p., n.d.
Arc 530.160 Tuchelt, Klaus Franz. Tiergefässe in Kopf- und Protomengestalt. Berlin, 1962.
Arc 530.162 Robert, Louis. Nouvelles inscriptions de Sardes. Paris, 1964.
Arc 530.163 Dupont-Sommer, André. La déesse de Hiérapolis Castabala (Cilicie). Paris, 1964.
Arc 530.164 Labraunda; Swedish excavations and researches. v.1, pt.1-2; v.2, pt.1; v.3, pt.1. Lund, 1955- 4v.
Arc 530.165 Matthiae, Paolo. Studi sui rilie vi di Karatepe. Roma, 1963.
Arc 530.166 Przeworski, Stefan. Opera selecta. Wrocław, 1967.
Arc 530.167 Yesaian, Stepan. Oruzhie i voennoe delo drevnei Armenii. Greoan, 1966.
Arc 530.168 Ankara. Universite Enstitusu. Arkeoloji arasturmalari. Istanbul, 1941.
Arc 530.169 Orthmann, Winfried. Das Gräberfeld bei Ilica. Wiesbaden, 1967.
Arc 530.171 Pekmon, A. Son kari ve arasturmalann i syei altinda Penge tanhi. Ankara, 1973.
Arc 530.172 Contributions to the archaeology of Armenia. Cambridge, 1968.
Arc 530.173 Person, Kenneth. The Dorak affair. N.Y., 1968.
Arc 530.174 Yesaian, Stepan. Erevan. Erevan, 1969.
Arc 530.176 Bean, George Ewart. Turkey beyond the Maeander, an archaeological guide. London, 1971.
Arc 530.178F Arik, Remri Ogur. Türk Tarih kurumu tarafindan yapilan Alaca noyük nafriyoti. Ankara, 1937.
Arc 530.180 Laodicée du Lycos; le nymphée; campagnes 1961-1963. Québec, 1969.
Arc 530.181 Mollaart, James. Çatal Hüyük. N.Y., 1967.
Arc 530.182 Khach'atryan, Telemak S. Drevnaia kul'tura Shiraka. Erevan, 1975.
Arc 530.183 Korucutepe; final report on the excavations of the Universities of Chicago, California (Los Angeles). Amsterdam, 1975.

Arc 535 Archaeology - Local - Cyprus - Folios [Discontinued]

Arc 535.3 Cyprus. Department of Antiquities. Report. Nicosia. 1936+ 6v.
Arc 535.4 Cyprus. Department of Antiquities. Annual report of the director. Nicosia. 1949+
Arc 535.200 Ohnefalsch-Richter, M. Kypros, the Bible and Homer. London, 1893. 2v.
Arc 535.201 Doell, J. Die Sammlung Cesnola. St. Petersburg, 1873.

Arc 537 Archaeology - Local - Cyprus - General works

Arc 537.1 Hogarth, D.G. Devia Cypria. London, 1889.
Arc 537.2 Cesnola, L.P. Cyprus. London, 1877.
Arc 537.2.3A Cesnola, L.P. Cyprus. N.Y., 1878.
Arc 537.2.3B Cesnola, L.P. Cyprus. N.Y., 1878.
Arc 537.2.7 New York (City). Metropolitan Museum of Art. Cesnola Collection. Guide to the Cesnola collection...Island of Cyprus. N.Y., 1876.
Arc 537.2.12 Metropolitan Museum of Art. Handbook of th Cesnola collection of antiquities from Cyprus. N.Y., 1914.
Arc 537.3 Regaldi, G. Le antichita di Cipro. Roma, 1879.
Arc 537.3.2 Feuardent, G.L. Answer to L.P. di Cesnola. N.Y., 1881.
Arc 537.3.3 Cook, C. Transformations and migrations of certain statues in the Cesnola collection. N.Y., 1882.
Arc 537.4 Holwerda, A.E.J. Die alten Kyprier in Kunst und Cultur. Leiden, 1885.
Arc 537.6 Gjerstad, Einar. Studies on prehistoric Cyprus. Inaug. Diss. Uppsala, 1926.
Arc 537.7F Gjerstad, Einar. The Swedish Cyprus expedition...1927-1931. v.1-4. Stockholm, 1934-48. 8v.
Arc 537.8A Casson, S. Ancient Cyprus; its art and archaeology. London, 1937.
Arc 537.8B Casson, S. Ancient Cyprus; its art and archaeology. London, 1937.
Arc 537.9 Schaeffer, C.F.A. Missions en Chypre, 1932-1935. Paris, 1936.
Arc 537.10 Sjoeqvist, Erik. Reports on excavations in Cyprus. Stockholm, 1947. 2v.
Arc 537.11 Melbourne. University. Cyprus Expedition. Publication. 1-2,1957-1964// 2v.
Arc 537.12 Karageorghis, Basos. Cyprus. London, 1949.
Arc 537.13.1PF British Museum. Department of Greek and Roman Antiquities. Excavations in Cyprus. 1. ed. London, 1970.
Arc 537.14 Mission Archéologique d'Alasia. Mission archéologique d'Alasia. Paris, 19- .

Arc 540 Archaeology - Local - Cyprus - Local; Special topics

Arc 540.1 Cesnola, L.P. Scoperta del tempio di Venere a Golgos. Turin, 1871.
Arc 540.1.5 Cesnola, L.P. Gaston L. Feuardent vs. L.P. Cesnola - testimony of the defendant. N.Y., 1884.
Arc 540.1.12 Cesnola, L.P. Extraits de l'histoire générale des hommes vivants. Genève, 1869.
Arc 540.2 Cesnola, L.P. Salaminia. London, 1882.
Arc 540.4 Marti, I.I. Raskopki goradishcha kiteia v 1928 g. Simferopol, 1929.
Arc 540.5F Westholm, A. The temples of Soli. Stockholm, 1936.
Arc 540.6 Dikaios, P. The excavations at Vounous-Bellapais in Cyprus. London, 1940.
Arc 540.6.5 Dikaios, P. Khirakitia. London, 1953.
Arc 540.7 Schaeffer, C.F.A. Enkomè-Alasia. Paris, 1952.
Arc 540.8F Stewart, E.M. Vounous 1937-38. Lund, 1950.
Arc 540.9F Aastroem, Paul. The Middle Cypriote Bronze Age. Lund, 1957.
Arc 540.10F Taylor, Joan. Myrton-Pigadhes. Oxford, 1957.
Arc 540.11F Hennessy, J.B. Stephania; a middle and late bronze-age cemetery in Cyprus. London, 1964.
Arc 540.12 Catling, H.W. Cypriot bronzework in the Mycenaean world. Oxford, 1964.
Arc 540.14 Karageōrgēs, Basos. Salamis; recent discoveries in Cyprus. N.Y., 1969.
Arc 540.14.5F Salamine de Chypre. Paris. 1,1969+ 6v.
Arc 540.15 Masson, Oliviér. Recherches sur les pheniciens a Chypre. Genève, 1972.
Arc 540.16F Benson, Jack L. Bamboula at Kourion. Philadelphia, 1972.

Arc 542 Archaeology - Local - Other Asia - Folios [Discontinued]

Arc 542.2 Leemans, C. Boro-Boudour dans l'Isle de Jara. Leyden, 1874. 5v.
Arc 542.200 Pleyte, C.M. Die Buddha-Legende. Amsterdam, 1901.
Arc 542.200.5 Mus, Paul. Barabudur. v.1, pt.1-2; v.2. Hanoi, 1935. 3v.
Arc 542.205 Mission Henri Dufour. Bayon d'Angkor Thom. Paris, 1910.
Arc 542.207F Stein, Mark Aurel. Serindia. Oxford, 1921.

Arc 543 Archaeology - Local - Other Asia - General works; Local; Special topics

Arc 543.01 Pamphlet box. Archaeology. Other Asiatic. General and special.
Arc 543.1 Cave, H.W. The ruined cities of Ceylon. London, 1897.
Arc 543.1.4 Cave, H.W. The ruined cities of Ceylon. 4th ed. London, 1907.
Arc 543.2 Lunet de Lagonquiere, E. Inventaire descriptif des monuments du Cambodge. v.1-3 and map. Paris, 1902. 4v.
Arc 543.2.5 Groslier, Bernard P. The arts and civilization of Angkor. N.Y., 1957.
Arc 543.2.6 Groslier, Bernard P. Angkor: art and civilization. N.Y., 1966.
Arc 543.2.10 Boisselier, Jean. La statuaire khmère son évolution. Saigon, 1955. 2v.
Arc 543.3A Stein, Mark Aurel. Sand-buried ruins of Khotan. London, 1903.
Arc 543.3B Stein, Mark Aurel. Sand-buried ruins of Khotan. London, 1903.
Arc 543.3C Stein, Mark Aurel. Sand-buried ruins of Khotan. London, 1903.
Arc 543.3.1 International Conference on the History, Archaeology and Culture of Central Asia in the Kushan Period, Dushanbe, 1968. Sovetskaiia arkheologiia frednei Azii i Kushanskaia problema. v.1-2. Moskva, 1968.
Arc 543.3.1.5 International Conference on the History, Archeology and Culture of Central Asia in the Kushan Period, Dushanbe, 1968. Tsentral'naia Aziia v kushanskuiu spokhu. Moskva, 1974- 2v.
Arc 543.3.2 Stein, Mark Aurel. Sand-buried ruins of Khotan. London, 1904.
Arc 543.3.3 Stein, Mark Aurel. Preliminary report on a journey of archaeological exploration...Turkestan. London, 1901.
Arc 543.3.5A Stein, Mark Aurel. Ancient Khotan. Oxford, 1907. 2v.

Arc 543 Archaeology - Local - Other Asia - General works; Local; Special topics - cont.

Arc 543.3.5B Stein, Mark Aurel. Ancient Khotan. Oxford, 1907. 2v.

Arc 543.3.8A Stein, Mark Aurel. Ruins of desert Cathay. London, 1912. 2v.

Arc 543.3.8B Stein, Mark Aurel. Ruins of desert Cathay. London, 1912. 2v.

Arc 543.3.10 Stein, Mark Aurel. A third journey of exploration in Central Asia, 1913-16. London, 1916.

Htn Arc 543.3.15F* Stein, Mark Aurel. Innermost Asia. Oxford, 1928. 4v.

Arc 543.3.17F Stein, Mark Aurel. Innermost Asia. Oxford, 1928. 4v.

Arc 543.3.19A Stein, Mark Aurel. On Central-Asian tracks. London, 1933.

Arc 543.3.19B Stein, Mark Aurel. On Central-Asian tracks. London, 1933.

Arc 543.3.20 Stein, Mark Aurel. On ancient Central-Asian tracks. N.Y., 1964.

Arc 543.3.50F Field, Henry. Archaeological investigations in Central Asia, 1917-37. n.p., 1938.

Arc 543.3.55F Field, Henry. Recent excavations at Khawazm. Ann Arbor, 1948.

Arc 543.3.57 Nerazik, Elena E. Sel'skie poseleniia afriyid skogo Khorezma. Moskva, 1966.

Arc 543.3.60 Staviskii, Boris Ia. Mezhdu Pamirom i Kaspiem. Moskva, 1966.

Arc 543.3.65 Akademiia nauk SSSR. Institut Arkheologod. Sredniaia Aziia v epokhu Kamnia i bronzy. Leningrad, 1966.

Arc 543.3.70 Akademiia nauk SSSR. Institut Etnografii. Material'naia Kul'tura narodov Srednei Azii i Kazakustana. Moskva, 1966.

Arc 543.3.75 Litvinskii, Boris A. Kangiuisko-sarmatskii farn. Dushanbe, 1968.

Arc 543.3.80 Staviskii, Boris Ia. Arkheologicheskie raboty muzeia v Srednei Azii. Moskva, 1969.

Arc 543.3.85 Novgorodova, Eleonora A. Tsentral'naia Aziia i karasukskaia problema. Moskva, 1970.

Arc 543.3.90 Masson, Vadim Mikhailovich. Central Asia. London, 1972.

Arc 543.3.95 Litvinskii, Boris A. Drevnie kochevniki "Kryshi mira". Moskva, 1972.

Arc 543.3.100 Bulatova, Vera A. Drevnaia kuva. Tashkent, 1972.

Arc 543.3.105 Ginzburg, Vul'f V. Paleoantropologiia Srednei Azii. Moskva, 1972.

Arc 543.3.110 Kasymov, M.R. Kremneobrabatyvaiushchie masterskie i shakhty Kamennogo veka Srednii Azii. Tashkent, 1972.

Arc 543.3.115 Babaev, Aktam D. Kreposti drevnego Vakhana. Dushanbe, 1973.

Arc 543.4FA Pumpelly, R. Exploration in Turkestan. Expedition of 1904. Washington, 1908. 2v.

Arc 543.4FB Pumpelly, R. Exploration in Turkestan. Expedition of 1904. Washington, 1908.

Arc 543.4.13 LeCoq, Albert. Auf Hellas spuren in Ostturkistan. Leipzig, 1926.

Arc 543.4.14 LeCoq, Albert. Buried treasures of Chinese Turkestan. London, 1928.

Arc 543.4.15 Tai, Tse tsan. The cradle of humanity. n.p., 1926.

Arc 543.4.17 Herrmann, A. Lou-lan. Leipzig, 1931.

Arc 543.4.20F Conrady, A. Die chinesischen Handschriften..Sven Hedins in Lou-lan. Stockholm, 1920.

Arc 543.4.25F Pelliot, Paul. Toumchoug. v.2. Paris, 1961-1964.

Arc 543.4.50 Castagné, J. Les monuments funeraires de la steppe des Kirghizes. Orenburg, 1911.

Arc 543.5 Parmentier, H. Inventaires des monuments Čams de l'Annam. Paris, 1909. 2v.

Arc 543.5.15 École Française d'Extrême-Orient, Hanoi, Indo-China. L'École française d'Extrême Orient. Hanoi, 1930.

Arc 543.5.16 Malleret, L. Le cinquantenaire de l'École française d'Extrême-Orient. Paris, 1953.

Arc 543.5.25 Colani, M. Mégalithes du Haut-Laos. Paris, 1935. 2v.

Arc 543.6 Hough, W. The Bernadou collection in the United States National Museum. n.p., n.d.

Arc 543.7 Carpeaux, C. Les ruines d'Angkor. Paris, 1908.

Arc 543.7.5 Beerski, A. (Mrs.). Angkor; ruins in Cambodia. London, 1923.

Arc 543.7.7A Candee, H.C. Angkor the magnificent. N.Y., 1924.

Arc 543.7.7B Candee, H.C. Angkor the magnificent. N.Y., 1924.

Arc 543.7.9 Groslier, G. Angkor. Paris, 1924.

Arc 543.7.13 Marchal, H. Guide archéologique aux temples d'Angkor. Paris, 1928.

Arc 543.7.15 Naudin, G. Le groupe d'Angkor vu par les ecrivains et les étrangers. Saigon, 1928.

Arc 543.7.17A Casey, R.J. Four faces of Siva. Indianapolis, 1929.

Arc 543.7.17B Casey, R.J. Four faces of Siva. Indianapolis, 1929.

Arc 543.7.19F École Française d'Extrême-Orient, Hanoi, Indo-China. Le temple d'Angkor Vat. pt.2. Paris, 1930. 2v.

Arc 543.7.21F Angkor. Paris, 1931.

Arc 543.7.23 Coedès, George. Les bas-reliefs d'Angkor-Vat. Paris, 1911.

Arc 543.7.25F Cohen, Joan Lebold. Angkor monuments of the god-kings. London, 1975.

Arc 543.7.30 Delvert, Jean. Recherches sur l'érosin des gres des monuments d'Angkor. Paris, 1963.

Arc 543.7.50 Parmentier, H. L'art khmèr primitif. Paris, 1927. 2v.

Arc 543.8 Daubrée, Auguste. Rapport sur une collection d'instrument en pierre. Paris, 1868.

Arc 543.9 Kondakov, N.P. Puteshestvie na Cinai. Odessa, 1882.

Arc 543.10 Tobler, T. Golgatha, seine Kirchen und Kloster. St. Gallen, 1851.

Arc 543.11F Kondakov, N.P. Opic' pamiatnikov' drevnosti. Sankt Peterburg, 1890.

Arc 543.12F France. Délégation Archéologique Française en Afghanistan. Mémoires. Paris. 1-19 14v.

Arc 543.12.5 Hackin, Joseph. L'oeuvre de la délégation archéologique française en Afghanistan, 1922-1932. Tokyo, 1933.

Arc 543.25 Groneman, I. The Tyandi-Barabudur in Central Java. Samarang, 1901.

Arc 543.25.5 Groneman, I. The Tyandi-Barabudur in Central Java. 2. ed. Samarang, 1906.

Arc 543.25.10 Bernet Kempers, A. Borobudur, mysteriegebeuren in steen. Den Haag, 1960.

Arc 543.25.15 Sivaramamenti, C. Le stupa du Barabudur. Paris? 1961.

Arc 543.27A Nelsen, F.C. Die Buddha-Legende auf den Flachreliefs der ersten Galerie des Stupa von Boro-Budur, Java. Leipzig, 1923.

Arc 543.27B Nelsen, F.C. Die Buddha-Legende auf den Flachreliefs der ersten Galerie des Stupa von Boro-Budur, Java. Leipzig, 1923.

Arc 543.27.5 Krom, N.J. Barabudur. The Hague, 1927. 2v.

Arc 543 Archaeology - Local - Other Asia - General works; Local; Special topics - cont.

Arc 543.27.15 Krom, N.J. De levensgeschiedenis van den Buddha op Barabudur. 's Gravenhage, 1926.

Arc 543.29 Evans, Ivor H.N. Papers on the ethnology and archaeology of the Malay Peninsula. Cambridge, Eng., 1927.

Arc 543.32 Perry, William J. The megalithic culture of Indonesia. Manchester, 1918.

Arc 543.35 Stutterheim, W.F. Oudheden van Bali I. Singaradja, 1930.

Arc 543.35.15 Stutterheim, W.F. Indian influences in old Balinese art. London, 1935.

Arc 543.40F Thomassen à Thuessink van der Hoop, A.N.J. Megalithische oudheden in Zuid-Sumatra. Proefschrift. Zutphen, 1932.

Arc 543.40.15 Schnitger, F.M. Forgotten kingdoms in Sumatra. Leiden, 1939.

Arc 543.45A Shakur, M.A. A dash through the heart of Afghanistan. Peshawar, 1947.

Arc 543.45B Shakur, M.A. A dash through the heart of Afghanistan. Peshawar, 1947.

Arc 543.50 Rudenko, Sergei I. Der zweite Kurgen von Pasyryk. Berlin, 1951.

Arc 543.52 Rudenko, Sergei I. Kul'tura khunnov i Noinulinskie kurzany. Moskva, 1962.

Arc 543.52.1 Rudenko, Sergei I. Die Kultur der Hsiung-nu und die Hügelgräber von Noin Ula. Bonn, 1969.

Arc 543.55A Akademiia nauk SSSR. Institut Istorii Materialii Kul'tura. Zhivopis drevnogo Piandzhikenta. Moskva, 1954. 2v.

Arc 543.55B Akademiia nauk SSSR. Institut Istorii Materialii Kul'tura. Zhivopis drevnogo Piandzhikenta. Moskva, 1954.

Arc 543.60F Iakhry, A. Anarchaeological journey to Yemen. v.1-3. Cairo, 1951-52. 2v.

Arc 543.65 Akademiia nauk Tadzhikskoi SSSR, Stalinabad. Institut Istorii, Arkheologii i Etnografii. Arkheologicheskie i numzmaticheskie kollektsii. Stalinabad, 1956.

Arc 543.65.5 Ranov, V.A. Kamennye rek Tadzhikistana. Dushambe, 1965.

Arc 543.65.10 Material'naia kul'tura Tadzhikistana. Dushambe. 1,1968+

Arc 543.65.15 Mandel'shtam, Anatolii M. Pamiatniki epokhi bronzy v Iuzhnom Tadzhikistane. Leningrad, 1968.

Arc 543.65.20 Akademiia nauk Tadzhikskoi SSSR, Dushambe. Institut Istorii, Arkheologii i Etnografii. Arkheologicheskie raboty v Tadzhikistane. Stalinabad. 10,1970+

Arc 543.66 Abademiia nauk Uzbek SSSR, Tashkend. Institut Istorii i Arkheologii. Istoriia material'noi kul'tury uzbekistana. Taskhend, 1953- 12v.

Arc 543.66.5 Al'baum, L.I. Balalyk-tepe. Tashkend, 1960.

Arc 543.66.10 Masson, M.E. Akhangeran. Tashkend, 1953.

Arc 543.66.13 Ovezov, D.M. Akadenik Akademii nauk Turkmenskoi SSR Mikhail Evgen'evich Masson. Ashkhabad, 1970.

Arc 543.66.15 Gudkova, A.V. Tok-kala. Tashkend, 1964.

Arc 543.66.20 Termezskaia Arkheologicheskaia Kompleksnaia Ekspeditsiia, 1937, 1961-1962. Kara-tepe. Moskva, 1964.

Arc 543.66.23 Termezskaia Arkheologicheskaia Kompleksnaia Ekspeditsiia, 1937, 1961-1962. Buddiiskie peshchery Kara-tepe v starom Termeze. Moskva, 1969.

Arc 543.66.24 Termezskaia Arkheologicheskaia Kompleksnaia Ekspeditsiia, 1937, 1961-1962. Buddiiskii kul'tovyi tsentr Kara-tepe v starom Termeze. Moskva, 1972.

Arc 543.66.25 Puga-Chenkova, Galina A. Khalchaian. Tashkent, 1966.

Arc 543.66.30 Guliamov, Iukliia G. Pervobytnaia kul'tura i vorniknovenie oroshaemogo zemledeliia v mizov'iakh Zara Fsbana. Tashkend, 1966.

Arc 543.66.35 Afrasiabskaia Kompleksnaia Arkheologicheskaia Ekspeditsiia. Afrasiab. Tashkent, 1969- 3v.

Arc 543.66.40 Iagadin, V.N. Nekropol' drevnego Mizdakhana. Tashkent, 1970.

Arc 543.66.45 Suleimanov, R.K. Statisticheskoe izuchenie kul'tury grota Obi-Rakhmat. Tashkent, 1972.

Arc 543.66.50 Iuzhno-Turkmenistanskaia Arkheologicheskaia Ekspeditsiia, 1946-. Perechen' opublikovannykh rabot i materialov po tematike Iuzhno-Turkmenistanskoi Arkheologicheskoi Kompleksnoi Ekspeditsii. Ashkhabad, 1970.

Arc 543.66.55 Iz istorii antichnoi kul'tury Uzbekistana. Tashkent, 1973.

Arc 543.66.60 Askarov, A.A. Sapallitepa. Tashkent, 1973.

Arc 543.66.65 Mirsaatov, T. Drevnie shakhty Uchtuta. Tashkent, 1973.

Arc 543.70 Lysjsms, Philippe. Expédition en Arabie centrale. Paris, 1956. 3v.

Arc 543.70.5F Rathjens, Carl. Sabaeica. Hamburg, 1953.

Arc 543.70.10 Expédition Philhy-Ryckmans-Lippens en Arabie. Expédition Philhy-Ryskmane-Lippens en Arabie. v.3. Louvain, 1962- 3v.

Arc 543.75 Stutterheim, W.F. Studies in Indonesian archaeology. The Hague, 1956.

Arc 543.75.5 Bosch, Frederick D.K. Selected studies in Indonesian archaeology. The Hague, 1961.

Arc 543.78F Janse, Olov R.T. Archaeological research in Indo-China. Cambridge, 1947- 2v.

Arc 543.79 Rathjens, Carl. Vorislamische Altertümer. Hamburg, 1932.

Arc 543.80 Bowen, R. Archaeological discoveries in South Arabia. Baltimore, 1958.

Arc 543.81 Harding, Gerald Lankester. Archaeology in the Aden Protectorates. London, 1964.

Arc 543.82 Cleveland, Ray L. An ancient South Arabian necropolis. Baltimore, 1965.

Arc 543.83 Gerlach, Eva. Sand über den Tempeln Arabiens. 2. Aufl. Leipzig, 1967.

Arc 543.83.5 Wissmann, Hermann. Zur Archäologie und antiken Geographie von Südarabien. Istanbul, 1968.

Arc 543.83.10 Doe, Brian. Southern Arabia. London, 1971.

Arc 543.85 Zuniatov, T.A. Zemledelie i skotovodstvo u Azerbaidzhane v epokhu bronzy. Baku, 1957.

Arc 543.88 Bibby, Geoffrey. Looking for Dilmun. 1st ed. N.Y., 1969.

Arc 543.95 Akademiia nauk Tazhikskoi SSSR, Stalinabad. Institut Istorii, Arkheologii i Etnografii. Sektor Arkheologi i Numizmatiki. Arkheologi rasskazy-vaiut. Stalinabad, 1959.

Arc 543.96 Knobloch, Edgar. Beyond the Oxus; archaeology, art and architecture of Central Asia. London, 1972.

Arc 543.100 École Française d'Extrême-Orient, Hanoi. Indochina Musée. Louis Premier. Paris, 1960.

Arc 543.105 Ziablin, L.L. Vtoroi buddiiskii khram Ak-Beshimskogo gorodishcha. Frunze, 1961.

Arc 543.110 Solá Solé, J.M. Las dos grandes inscripciones sudarabigas del dique de Marib. Barcelona, 1960.

Arc 543.115F Braidwood, Robert John. Prehistoric investigations in Iraqi Kurdistan. Chicago, 1960.

Arc 543.116 Zehren, Erich. The cresent and the bull; a survey. N.Y., 1962.

Arc 543.116.1 Zehren, Erich. Die biblischen Hügel. Berlin, 1961.

Arc 543.120 Akademiia nauk SSSR. Mongol'skii arkheologicheskii sbornik. Moskva, 1962.

Classified Listing

Arc 543 Archaeology - Local - Other Asia - General works; Local; Special topics - cont.

Arc 543.120.5 Kiselev, Sergei. Drevnemongol'skie goroda. Moskva, 1965.
Arc 543.120.10 Lubo-Lesnichenko, Evgenii. Mertvyi gorod Khara-Khoto. Moskva, 1968.
Arc 543.125 Klements, D.A. Arkheologicheskii dnevnik poezdki v Sredniuiu Mongoliiu v 1891 godu. Sankt Peterburg, 1895.
Arc 543.130 Schlumberger, D. The excavations at Surkh Kotal and the problem of Hellenism in Bactria and India. London, 1961.
Arc 543.131 Malleret, Louis. L'archéologie du Delta du Nékoug. v.1-4. Paris, 1959- 7v.
Arc 543.131.5 Wales, Horace Geoffrey Q. Towards Angkor in the footsteps of the Indian invaders. London, 1937.
Arc 543.132 Boriskovskii, Pavel Io. Pervobytnoe proshloe B'etnama. Leningrad, 1966.
Arc 543.135 Dupont, P. L'archéologie moue de Dváravati. Paris, 1959. 2v.
Arc 543.136 Dupree, Louis Benjamin. Deh Morasi Ghunelai: a cholcolithic site in south-central Afghanistan. N.Y., 1963.
Arc 543.138 Belenitskii, Aleksandr Markovich. Central Asia. London, 1969.
Arc 543.138.5 Belenitskii, Aleksandr Markovich. Srednevekovyi gorod Srednei Azii. Leningrad, 1973.
Arc 543.142 Matheson, S. Time off to dig. London, 1961.
Arc 543.145 Negmatov, Numan. Srednevekovyi Shakhristan. Dushambe, 1966.
Arc 543.146 Sarianidi, Viktor I. Za barkhanami, proshloe. Moskva, 1966.
Arc 543.146.5 Sarianidi, Viktor I. Tainy ischeznuvshego iskusstva Karakumov. Moskva, 1967.
Arc 543.146.10 Karakumskie drevnosti. Photoreproduction. Ashkhabad, 1968- 4v.
Arc 543.146.15 Khlopin, Igor N. Geoksiurskaia gruppa poselenii epokhi eneolita. Leningrad, 1964.
Arc 543.146.20 Neoliticheskie poseleniia i srednevekovye goroda. Ashkhabad, 1971.
Arc 543.146.25 Berdyev, Ovliabuli. Drevneishie zemledel'tsy Iuzhnogo Turkmenistana. Ashkhabad, 1969.
Arc 543.146.30 Masson, Vadim M. Karakumyi zavia tsivilizatsii. Moskva, 1972.
Arc 543.146.35 Poliakov, Sergei P. Etnicheskaia istoriia Severo-Zapadnoi Turkmenii v srednie veka. Moskva, 1973.
Arc 543.146.40 Arazov, O. Arkheologicheskie i arkhitekturnye pamiatniki Serakhskogo oazisa. Ashkhabad, 1973.
Arc 543.146.45 Atagarryev, Egen. Material'naia kul'tura Shekhr-Islama. Ashkhabad, 1973.
Arc 543.147 Larichev, Vitalii E. Aziia dalekaia i tainstvennaia. Novosibirsk, 1968.
Arc 543.148 Istoriia, arkheologiia i etnografiia srednei Azii. Moskva, 1968.
Arc 543.150 Van Beek, Gus Willard. Hajar Cin Humeid. Baltimore, 1969.
VArc 543.152 Bendefy, Lásylo. Syallam tolmács kůldetése Naagy Sändor folokog. Budapest, 1941.
Arc 543.153 Sarianidi, Viktor I. Raskopki Tillia-tepe v Severnom Afganistane. Moskva, 1972.
Arc 543.154 Brykina, Galina A. Karabulak. Moskva, 1974.
Arc 543.155 Pulatov, Uktam P. Chil'khudzhra. Dushanbe, 1975.
Arc 543.156 Buriakov, Iurii F. Gornoe delo i metallurgia srednevekovogo Ilaka, V-nachalo XIII v. Moskva, 1974.
Arc 543.157 Iz istorii iskusstva velikogo goroda. Tashkent, 1972.

Arc 545 Archaeology - Local - Egypt - Folios [Discontinued]

Arc 545.2 Champollion, J.F. Monuments de l'Égypte et de la Nubie. Paris, 1835-45.
Arc 545.8.3 London. Institution Library. Bibliographical account...of La description de l'Egypt. London, 1838.
Arc 545.14 Belzoni, G.B. Narrative of the operations...in Egypt and Nubia. 3. ed. London, 1822. 2v.
Arc 545.14PF Belzoni, G.B. Narrative of the operations...in Egypt and Nubia. 3. ed. Atlas. London, 1822.
Arc 545.15F Denon, V. Voyages dans la Basse et la Haute Égypte. London, 1807.
Arc 545.15PF Denon, V. Voyages dans la Basse et la Haute Égypte. Atlas. London, 1807.
Arc 545.15.2PF Planches du Voyage dans la Basse et la Haute Égypte. Atlas. London, 18- ?
Arc 545.16 Cailliand, F. Voyage à l'Oasis de Thèbes. pt.1-2. Paris, 1821.
Arc 545.17 Jomard, E.F. Description générale de Memphis et des Pyramides. Paris, 1829.
Arc 545.20 Zoega, G. De origine et usu obeliscorum. Rome, 1797.
Arc 545.28.3 Mariette, A. Monuments divers..en Égypte et en Nubie. Paris, 1872-1889. 2v.
Htn Arc 545.200* Kircher, A. Oedipus Aegyptiacus. v.1-3. Romae, 1652-54. 4v.
Arc 545.201 Das Pyramidenfeld von Abusir. n.p., n.d.
Arc 545.202FA Gorringe, H.H. Egyptian obelisks. N.Y., 1882.
Arc 545.202FB Gorringe, H.H. Egyptian obelisks. N.Y., 1882.
Arc 545.203 Morgan, J. Fouilles à Dahchour. Vienna, 1895.
Arc 545.204 Pickering, C. The Gliddon mummy-case. Washington, 1869.
Arc 545.205 Duemichen, J. Bangeschichte des Denderatempels. Strassburg, 1877.
Arc 545.205.2 Duemichen, J. Bauurkunde der Tempelanlagen von Dendera. Leipzig, 1865.
Htn Arc 545.206* Le Musée Egyptien. v.1-4. Cairo, 1890-1924.
Arc 545.207F Berlin Museum. Mitteilungen aus der Aegyptischen Sammlung. Berlin, 1910- 6v.
Arc 545.208FA Petrie, William M.F. Hawara, Biahmu and Arsinoe. London, 1889.
Arc 545.208FB Petrie, William M.F. Hawara, Biahmu and Arsinoe. London, 1889.
Arc 545.210 Lyons, H.G. Report on the island and temples of Philae. Cairo, 1896.
Arc 545.210.5 Lyons, H.G. Report on the temples of Philae. Cairo, 1908.
Arc 545.215 Forrer, R. Die Graeber- und Textilfunde von Achmim-Panopolis. Strassburg, 1891.
X Cg Arc 545.216 Forrer, R. Roemische und Byzantinische Seiden-Textilien aus.....Achmim-Panopolis. Strassburg, 1891.
Arc 545.217 Forrer, R. Die fruehchristliche Alterthuemer aus....Achmim Panopolis. Strassburg, 1893.
Arc 545.222 Brugsch, E. La trouvaille de Deir-el-Bahari. Cairo, 1881.
Arc 545.223 Abney, W. de W. Thebes and its five greater temples. London, 1876.
Arc 545.224 Mook, F. Aegyptens vormetallische Zeit. Wuerzburg, 1880.
Arc 545.225 Haynes, H.W. Egyptian Palaeolithic implements. Cambridge, 1882.
Arc 545.226 Mariette, A. Catalogue général des monuments d'Abydos. Paris, 1880.

Arc 545 Archaeology - Local - Egypt - Folios [Discontinued] - cont.

Arc 545.226.5F Mariette, A. Les mastabas de l'ancien empire. Paris, 1884.
Arc 545.227F Cairo. Musée des Antiquités Égyptiennes. Catalogue général des antiquités égyptiennes Ostraca. Le Caire. 1-100,1901-1937 77v.
X Cg Arc 545.227F Cairo. Musée des Antiquités Égyptiennes. Catalogue général des antiquités égyptiennes Ostraca. Le Caire. 10
Arc 545.227.5 Weigal, A.E.P. Report on antiquities of Lower Nubia. Oxford, 1907.
Arc 545.227.10F Firth, C.M. The step pyramid. Le Caire, 1935-36. 2v.
Arc 545.227.11A Lauer, J.P. Fouilles à Saqqarah, la pyramide à degrés. v.1-2, 4-5. La Caire, 1936. 4v.
Arc 545.227.11B Lauer, J.P. Fouilles à Saqqarah, la pyramide à degrés. La Caire, 1936. 2v.
Arc 545.227.13 Lefebvre, G. Recueil des inscriptions grecques. Le Caire, 1907.
Arc 545.227.15 Kamal, A.B. Livre des perles enfoneio. Leipzig, 1907. 2v.
Arc 545.227.19 Legrain, G. Repertoire genealogique et onomastique. Genève, 1908.
Arc 545.227.21F Lefebvre, G. Le tombeau de Petosiris. v.1-3. Le Caire, 1923-1924.
Arc 545.227.25 Maspero, Gaston. Rapports. Le Caire, 1909. 2v.
Arc 545.227.29 Gauthier, M.H. Le temple de Kalabach. Le Caire, 1911. 2v.
Arc 545.227.31 Roeder, G. Debod bis Bal Kalabach. Le Caire, 1911. 3v.
Arc 545.227.33 Blackman, A.M. Temple of Dendûr. Le Caire, 1911.
Arc 545.227.35 Maspero, Gaston. Documents. Le Caire, 1912.
Arc 545.227.36 Gauthier, H. Temple de Ouadi Es-Seboua. Le Caire, 1912.
Arc 545.227.38 Gauthier, H. Le temple d'Amada. Le Caire, 1913.
Arc 545.227.40 Blackman, A.M. The temple of Derr. Le Caire, 1913.
Arc 545.227.42F Zippert, Erwin. Der Gedächtnistempel Sethos' Izu Abydos. Berlin, 1931.
Arc 545.227.44F Griffith, F.L. Catalogue of demotic graffiti of the Dodecaschoenus. Oxford, 1935.
Arc 545.227.44PF Griffith, F.L. Catalogue of demotic graffiti of the Dodecaschoenus. v.2. Oxford, 1937.
Arc 545.228 Egypt. Antiquities Department. Catalogue des monuments et inscriptions de l'Egypte antique. Vienne, 1894-1909. 3v.
Arc 545.229 University of California. Hearst Egyptian Expedition. Egyptian archaeology. Leipzig. 1-7 6v.
Arc 545.230 Müller, W.M. Egyptological researches. Results, 1904. Washington, 1906. 3v.
Arc 545.231 Burlington Five Arts Club, London. The art of ancient Egypt. London, 1895.
Arc 545.231.7F Burlington Five Arts Club, London. Catalogue of an exhibition of ancient Egyptian art. London, 1922.
Arc 545.232 Naville, E. Tomb of Hâtshopsitu. Life and monuments of queen. London, 1906.
Arc 545.232.5 Davis, T.M. The tomb of Iouiya and Touiyou. London, 1907.
Arc 545.232.9 Davis, T.M. The tomb of Queen Tiyi. London, 1910.
Arc 545.232.13 Davis, T.M. The tomb of Siptah. London, 1908.
Arc 545.233 Capart, J. Recueil de monuments egyptiens. Bruxelles, 1902-05. 2v.
Arc 545.233.5FA Capart, J. Une rue de tombeaux a Saqqarah. Bruxelles, 1907. 2v.
Arc 545.233.5FB Capart, J. Une rue de tombeaux a Saqqarah. Bruxelles, 1907. 2v.
Arc 545.234 Marius of Northampton. Report on some excavations...Theban necropolis. London, 1908.
X Cg Arc 545.235F Petrie, W.M.F. Scarabs and cylinders with names. London, 1917. (Changed to XP 9838 F)
Arc 545.236 Bissing, F.W. Die Mastaba des Gem-Ni-Kai. Berlin, 1905- 2v.
Arc 545.236.5F Bissing, F.W. Das Re-Heiligtum des Ne-Woser-Re. Berlin, 1905-23. 2v.
Arc 545.237 Pörtner, B. Aegyptische Grabsteine und Denksteine aus Athen und Konstantinople. Strassburg, 1908.
Arc 545.238 Carter, H. Five years' explorations at Thebes. London, 1912.
Arc 545.240F Wreszinski, Walter. Atlas zur altaegyptischen Kulturgeschichte. Leipzig, 1914. 4v.
Arc 545.240PF Wreszinski, Walter. Atlas zur altaegyptischen Kulturgeschichte. v.2. Leipzig, 1939.
Arc 545.241F Budge, Ernest A. The Rosetta stone. London, 1913.
Arc 545.242F Junker, Hermann. Bericht über die Grabungen der Akademie des Wissenschaften in Wien. Wien, 1919.
Arc 545.243F Pagenstrecher, R. Nekropolis. Leipzig, 1919.
Arc 545.244F Lugn, Pehr. Ausgewählte Denkmäler aus ägyptischen Sammlungen in Schweden. Leipzig, 1922.

Arc 547 Archaeology - Local - Egypt - Archaeological museums and collections [Discontinued]

Arc 547.1 Abbott, H. Catalogue of a collection of Egyptian antiquities. N.Y., 1853.
Arc 547.2 Brugsch, H. Uebersichtliche Erklaerung Aegyptischer Denkmaeler des Koenigliche Neuen Museum zu Berlin. Berlin, 1850.
Arc 547.2.2 Berlin. Staatliche Museen. Ausführliches Verzeichniss der Aegyptischen Altertuemer, Gipsabguesse und Papyrus. Berlin, 1894.
Arc 547.2.15 Berlin. Staatliche Museen. Abtheilung der Aegyptischen Alterthümer - Die Wandgemaelde. Berlin, 1855.
Arc 547.2.16 Berlin. Staatliche Museen. Abtheilung der Aegyptischen Alterthümer - Die Wandgemaelde. Berlin, 1870.
Arc 547.3 Prisse d'Avennes. Notice sur les antiquités égyptiennes du Musée Britannique. Paris, 1847.
Arc 547.4 Rougé, E. de. Notice sommaire des monuments égyptiens du Musée du Louvre. Paris, 1855.
Arc 547.4.10 Paris. Musée Nationale du Louvre. Département des Antiquités Égyptiennes. Notice sommaire des monuments égyptiens. Paris, 1873.
Arc 547.5 Passalacqua, J. Catalogue des antiquités découvertes en Egypte. Paris, 1826.
Arc 547.5.25 Geoffroy Saint Hillaire, E. Rapport fait à l'Académie royale des sciences. Paris, 1826.
Arc 547.6 Boolak Museum. Guide du visiteur au Musée de Boulaq. Boolak, 1883.
Arc 547.6.5 Cairo. Musée des Antiquités Égyptiennes. Notice des principaux monuments...à Boulaq. Alexandrie, 1864.
Arc 547.6.7 Cairo. Musée des Antiquités Égyptiennes. Notice des principaux monuments...du Musée d'Antiquités Égyptiennes à Boulaq. 3. éd. Paris, 1869.

Classified Listing

Arc 547 Archaeology - Local - Egypt - Archaeological museums and collections [Discontinued] - cont.

Arc 547.6.9 A short description of the objects from the tomb of Tutankhamun now exhibited in the Cairo Museum. Cairo, 1926.
Arc 547.6.10 Cairo. Musée des Antiquités Égyptiennes. A brief description of the principal monuments. Cairo, 1927.
Arc 547.6.12 Cairo. Musée des Antiquités Égyptiennes. Guide du visiteur au Musée du Caire. Caire, 1902.
Arc 547.6.13 Cairo. Musée des Antiquités Égyptiennes. Guide du visiteur au Musée du Caire. 2. éd. Caire, 1912.
Arc 547.6.15 Cairo. Musée des Antiquités Égyptiennes. A brief description of the principal monuments. Cairo, 1961.
Arc 547.6.20F Hickmann, Hans. Instruments de musique. Le Caire, 1949.
Arc 547.6.25 Cairo. Musée des Antiquités Égyptiennes. Guide to the Cairo Museum. 4. ed. Cairo, 1908.
Arc 547.6.27 Egypt. State Tourists. Egyptian museum. Cairo, 1962.
Arc 547.6.35F Borchardt, Ludwig. Denkmäler des alten Reiches. Berlin, 1937-1964. 2v.
Arc 547.7 Jones, O. Description of the Egyptian court erected in the Crystal Palace. London, 1854.
Arc 547.8 Hay, J. Catalogue of the collection of Egyptian antiquities belonging to the late Robert Hay, Esq. London, 1869.
Arc 547.9 Champollion, J.F. Notice descriptive des monumens égyptiens du Musée Charles X. Paris, 1827.
Arc 547.10 Florence, Italy. Guida del Museo Archeologico I. Antichita Egiziane. Florence, 1880.
Arc 547.11 Bergmann, E. Uebersichtung der Sammlung Aegyptischen Alterthuemer des Allerhöchsten Kaiserhauses. Vienna, 1880.
Arc 547.12 British Museum. A guide to the 1st and 2nd Egyptian rooms. London, n.d.
Arc 547.12.2 British Museum. A guide to the 3rd and 4th Egyptian rooms. London, 1904.
Arc 547.13 British Museum. A guide to the Egyptian collections. London, 1909.
Arc 547.14 Schreiber, T. Der Gallier. Leipzig, 1896.
Arc 547.15 Aegyptische Gräber. v.2. Strassburg, 1904.
Arc 547.16 Schmidt, V. Den aegyptiske samlung. Copenhagen, 1899.
Arc 547.17 British Museum. Hieroglyphic Texts from Egyptian Stelae. Pt.1-7, 9. London, 1911-25. 8v.
Arc 547.18 Musée de Gizeh. Notice des principaux monuments. Le Caire, 1897.
Arc 547.19 Turin. R. Museo di Antichità. Catalogo illustrato dei monumenti egizii. pt. 2. Torino, 1855.
Arc 547.19.5 Farina, G. Il R. Museo di Antichità di Torino. 2. ed. Roma, 1938.
Arc 547.20 New York (City). Metropolitan Museum of Art. A handbook of Egyptian rooms. N.Y., 1920.
Arc 547.21 Pamphlet box. New York (City). Metropolitan Museum of Art. Egyptian antiquities.
Arc 547.22F New York (City). Metropolitan Museum of Art. Egyptian Expedition. Publications. N.Y. 1-18,1916-1955 14v.
Arc 547.22.10F New York (City). Metropolitan Museum of Art. Department of Egyptian Art. Publication. N.Y. 1-5,1921-1936 3v.
Arc 547.23 Marucchi, O. Gli antichi oggetti egiziani. Roma, 1901.
Arc 547.24F Alexandria. Musée Gréco-Romain. Le Musée Gréco-Romain du cours de l'année 1922-23. Alexandrie, 1924.
Arc 547.24.10F Alexandria. Musée Gréco-Romain. Le Musée Gréco-Romain, 1925-1931. Bergamo, 1932.
Arc 547.24.12F Alexandria. Musée Gréco-Romain. Annuaire. 1932-1950 3v.
Arc 547.24.15 Breccia, E. Sculture inedite del Museo Greco-Romano. Alexandrie, 1931.
Arc 547.25F British Museum. Department of Egyptian and Assyrian Antiquities. Egyptian sculptures in the British Museum. London, 1914.
Arc 547.25.5 British Museum. Department of Egyptian and Assyrian Antiquities. Gallery of antiquities. London, 1842.
Arc 547.26 British Museum. Department of Egyptian and Assyrian Antiquities. A general introductory guide to the Egyptian collections in the British Museum. London, 1964.
Arc 547.27 Mogensen, M. Inscriptions hiéroglyphiques du Musée national de Copenhague. Copenhague, 1918.
Arc 547.28 Smith, W.S. Ancient Egypt as represented in the Museum of Fine Arts. Boston, 1942.
Arc 547.29 Botti, Giuseppe. Le casse di mummie e i sarcofagi da el Hibeh. Fienze, 1958.
Arc 547.30 Cambridge. University. Fitzwilliam Museum. A catalogue of the Egyptian collection. Cambridge, Eng., 1893.
Arc 547.35F Brunner-Traut, Emma. Die altägyptischen Scherbenbilder. Wiesbaden, 1956.
Arc 547.40 Bankes, Ralph. Egyptian Stelae in the Bankes collection. Oxford, 1958.
Arc 547.41F Goedicke, Hans. Ostraka Michaeliders. Wiesbaden, 1962.
Arc 547.42 Brussels. Musées Coyaux d'Art et d'Histoire. Fondation Égyptologique Reine Elisabeth. Département égyptien; album. Bruxelles, 1934.
Arc 547.43 Cairo, Egypt. Coptic Museum. The Coptic Museum and the fortress of Babylon at old Cairo. Cairo, 1962.
Arc 547.44 Botti, Giuseppe. I cimeli egizi del Museo. Firenze, 1964.
Arc 547.45 Zayid, Abd al-Hamid. Egyptian antiquities. Cairo, 1962.
Arc 547.46 Leyden. Rijksmuseum van Oudheden. Inleiding lot de oud-Egyptische beschaving. 's-Gravenhage, 1959.
Arc 547.50F British Museum. Department of Egyptian Antiquities. Catalogue of Egyptian antiquities in the British Museum. London, 1968- 2v.

Arc 548 Archaeology - Local - Egypt - Bibliographies [Discontinued]

Arc 548.5 Porter, Bertha. Topographical bibliography of ancient Egyptian hieroglyphic texts, reliefs. Oxford, 1927-39. 7v.
Arc 548.5.10A Porter, Bertha. Topographical bibliography of ancient Egyptian hieroglyphic texts. v.1, pt.1-2; v.2; v.3, pt.1. 2. ed. Oxford, 1960- 4v.
Arc 548.5.10B Porter, Bertha. Topographical bibliography of ancient Egyptian hieroglyphic texts. v.1, pt.2. 2. ed. Oxford, 1960-

Arc 549 Archaeology - Local - Egypt - Pamphlet volumes

Arc 549 Pamphlet box. Archaeology. Egypt.
Arc 549.1 Pamphlet box. Archaeology. Egypt.
Arc 549.5 Fuscaldo, Perla. Egyptian archaeology. n.p., n.d. 3 pam.

Arc 550 - 575 Archaeology - Local - Egypt - General works (A-Z)

Arc 550.5 Aboudi, M. Guide book to the antiquities of upper Egypt and Nubia. 4. ed. Cairo, 1946.
Arc 550.10F Angioletti, Giovanni B. Testimane in Egittto. Firenze, 1958.
Arc 551.1 Belzoni, G.B. Narrative of the operations in Egypt and Nubia. Brussels, 1835.
Arc 551.1.5 Belzoni, G.B. G.B. Belzoni. Padova, 1960.
Arc 551.2 Blanc, C. Voyage de la Haute Egypte. Paris, 1876.
Arc 551.3 Brodrick, M. A concise dictionary of Egyptian archaeology. London, 1902.
Arc 551.4 Bissing, F.W. Die Kunst der alten Ägypter. Leipzig, 1911.
Arc 551.5 Budge, Ernest A. By Nile and Tigris. London, 1920. 2v.
Arc 551.6 Baikie, James. Egyptian antiquities in the Nile Valley. London, 1932.
Arc 551.6.5 Baikie, James. A century of excavation in the land of the Pharaohs. London, 1924.
Arc 551.9F Baumgartel, Elise J. The cultures of prehistoric Egypt. London, 1947.
Arc 551.10 Borchardt, L. Allerhand Kleinigkeiten. Leipzig, 1933?
Arc 551.20 Bratton, Fred Gladstone. A history of Egyptian archaeology. London, 1967.
Arc 552.1 Champollion, J.F. Lettres écrites d'Egypte et de Nubie. Paris, 1833.
Arc 552.1.2 Champollion, J.F. Lettres à M. le Duc de Blacas d'Aulps. Paris, 1824.
Arc 552.1.4 Champollion, J.F. Lettres écrites d'Égypte et de Nubie en 1828 et 1829. Paris, 1868.
Arc 552.1.6 Champollion-Figeac, J.J. Les deux Champollion, leur vie. Grenoble, 1887.
Arc 552.2 Cloquet, L. L'art monumental des Égyptiens et des Assyriens. n.p., n.d.
Arc 552.3 Clark, Edward L. Daleth; or The homestead of the nations. Boston, 1864.
Arc 552.4 Cottrell, L. The lost Pharaohs. N.Y., 1951.
Arc 552.5 Combined Pre-Historic Expedition to Egyptian and Sudanese Nubia. The prehistory of Nubia. Taos, N.M., 1968. 2v.
Arc 553.1 Dawson, W.R. Who was who in Egyptology. London, 1951.
Arc 553.5 Dawson, John W. Notes on prehistoric man in Egypt and Lebanon. London, 1884.
Arc 554.1 Edwards, A.B. Pharaohs, fellahs and explorers. N.Y., 1891.
Arc 554.1.3 Edwards, A.B. Pharaohs, fellahs and explorers. N.Y., 1891.
Arc 554.1.5 Edwards, A.B. Pharaohs, fellahs and explorers. N.Y., 1892.
Arc 554.1.15 Winslow, William C. The queen of Egyptology. n.p., 1892.
Arc 554.5 Erdöse, K. Mumiäk es minarétek. Budapest, 1937.
Arc 554.6 Emery, Walter. Archaic Egypt. Baltimore, 1963.
Arc 554.7.2 Engelbach, Reginald. Introduation to Egyptian archaeology. 2. ed. Cairo, 1961.
Arc 555.1 Forrer, R. Besuch in El-Achmem. Reisebriefe aus Aegypten. Strassburg, 1895.
Arc 555.2 Fagan, Brian M. The rape of the Nile. N.Y., 1975.
Arc 556.1 Griffith, Francis L. The study of Egyptology. Oxford, 1901.
Arc 556.2 Glanville, Stephen A.K. The growth and nature of Egyptology. Cambridge, 1947.
Arc 556.3 Galassi, G. Tehena. Roma, 1942.
Arc 556.4 Grapow, Hermann. Meine Begegnung mit einigen Agyptologen. Berlin, 1973.
Arc 556.5 Greener, Leslie. The discovery of Egypt. London, 1966.
Arc 557.1 Hawks, F.L. The monuments of Egypt. N.Y., 1850.
Arc 557.2 Hamilton, W. Aegyptiaca. London, 1809.
Arc 557.3 Hichens, Robert. Egypt and its monuments. London, 1908.
Arc 557.3.2A Hichens, Robert. Egypt and its monuments. N.Y., 1908.
Arc 557.3.2B Hichens, Robert. Egypt and its monuments. N.Y., 1908.
Arc 557.3.2.5 Hichens, Robert. Egypt and its monuments. N.Y., 1909.
Arc 557.3.3 Hichens, Robert. The spell of Egypt. London, 1910.
Arc 557.3.5 Hichens, Robert. The spell of Egypt. Leipzig, 1910.
Arc 557.4 Hayes, William Christopher. The scepter of Egypt. N.Y., 1953. 2v.
Arc 557.4.5 Hayes, William Christopher. The scepter of Egypt. Cambridge, 1960.
Arc 557.5 Hayes, William Christopher. Most ancient Egypt. Chicago, 1965.
Arc 557.8 Hornung, Erik. Einführung in die Ägyptologie. Darmstadt, 1967.
Arc 557.10 Helck, Hans Wolfgang. Ägyptologie an deutschen Universitäten. Wiesbaden, 1969.
Arc 559.1 Jéquier, G. Manuele d'archéologie egyptienne. Paris, 1924.
Arc 559.4 James, Thomas Garnet Henry. The archaeology of ancient Egypt. London, 1972.
Arc 560.1 King, L.W. Egypt and Western Asia. London, 1907.
Arc 560.2 Kink, Khil'da A. Egipet do faraonov. Moskva, 1964.
Arc 560.4 Kayser, Hans. Ägyptisches Kunstlandwerk. Braunschweig, 1969.
Arc 561.1 Lepsius, R. Discoveries in Egypt, Ethiopia and the Peninsula of Sinai. London, 1853.
Arc 561.1.2 Lepsius, R. Briefe aus Aegypten. Berlin, 1852.
Arc 561.1.5 Pierret, Paul. Explication des monuments de l'Égypte et de l'Ethiopie. Paris, 1885.
Arc 561.1.10 Ebers, George. Richard Lepsius. N.Y., 1887.
Arc 561.2 Letronne, J.A. Recherches pour servir à l'histoire de l'Égypte. Paris, 1823.
Arc 561.3 Long, G. British Museum. Egyptian antiquities. London, 1832. 2v.
Arc 561.3.3 Long, G. Egyptian antiquities in British Museum. London, 1846. 2v.
Arc 561.4 Lieblein, J. Die aegyptischen Denkmäler. Christiania, 1873.
Arc 561.4.5 Lieblein, J. Egypten i dess minnesmärken o chi dess fărhållande till Palestine och Grekland. Stockholm, 1877.
Arc 561.5 Lagier, Camille. A travers la Haute Égypte. Bruxelles, 1921.
Arc 561.5.5 Lagier, Camille. L'Égypte monumentale et pittoresque. 2. éd. Paris, 1922.
Arc 561.6 Leemans, Conrad. L'égyptologue Conrad Leemans et sa correspondance. Leiden, 1973.
Arc 562.1 Mariette, A. Itinéraire de la Haute-Égypte. Paris, 1880.
Arc 562.1.3 Chèlu, Alfred Jacques. Mariette Pacha. Le Caire, 1911.
Arc 562.1.5 Mariette, A. The monuments of upper Egypt. Boston, 1890.
Arc 562.1.6 Mariette, A. The monuments of upper Egypt. Alexandria, 1877.

Arc 550 - 575 Archaeology - Local - Egypt - General works (A-Z) - cont.

Arc 562.1.20 Maspero, Gaston. Notice biographique sur Auguste Mariette. Paris, 1904.
Arc 562.2 Maspero, Gaston. L'archéologie égyptienne (in Bibliothèque de l'Enseignement des Beaux-Arts). Paris, 1887.
Arc 562.2.5 Maspero, Gaston. Egyptian archaeology. N.Y., 1887.
Arc 562.2.6 Maspero, Gaston. Egyptian archaeology. 2. ed. N.Y., 1892.
Arc 562.2.7 Maspero, Gaston. Egyptian archaeology. London, 1893.
Arc 562.2.8 Maspero, Gaston. Manual of Egyptian archaeology. N.Y., 1895.
Arc 562.2.9 Maspero, Gaston. Manual of Egyptian archaeology. London, 1895.
Arc 562.2.10 Cordier, Henri. Bibliographie des oeuvres de Gaston Maspero. Paris, 1922.
Arc 562.2.13 Maspero, Gaston. Manual of Egyptian archaeology. London, 1902.
Arc 562.2.14 Maspero, Gaston. Manual of Egyptian archaeology. London, 1902.
Arc 562.2.16A Maspero, Gaston. Manual of Egyptian archaeology. 6. ed. N.Y., 1914.
Arc 562.2.16B Maspero, Gaston. Manual of Egyptian archaeology. 6. ed. N.Y., 1914.
Arc 562.2.16C Maspero, Gaston. Manual of Egyptian archaeology. 6. ed. N.Y., 1914.
Arc 562.2.20A Maspero, Gaston. Manual of Egyptian archaeology. 6th English ed. N.Y., 1926.
Arc 562.2.20B Maspero, Gaston. Manual of Egyptian archaeology. 6th English ed. N.Y., 1926.
Arc 562.2.20C Maspero, Gaston. Manual of Egyptian archaeology. 6th English ed. N.Y., 1926.
Arc 562.2.26 Maspero, Gaston. New light on ancient Egypt. London, 1908.
Arc 562.2.27 Maspero, Gaston. New light on ancient Egypt. N.Y., 1909.
Arc 562.2.35 Maspero, Gaston. Causeries d'Égypte. 2. éd. Paris, 1907.
Arc 562.2.40 Maspero, Gaston. Egypt: ancient sites and modern scenes. N.Y., 1911.
Arc 562.2.45F Miscellanea gregoriana. Roma, 1941.
Arc 562.3 Morgan, J. Recherches sur les origines de l'Égypte. Paris, 1896-97.
Arc 562.4 Mélanges d'archéologie égyptienne et assyrienne. v.1-3. Paris, 1873-78.
Arc 562.5 Meyer, Eduard. Bericht über eine Expedition nach Ägypten zur Erforschung der Darstellungen der Fremdvolker. Berlin, 1913. 9v.
Arc 562.6 Masters, D. The romance of excavation. N.Y., 1923.
Arc 562.7 Montet, Pierre. Isis; ou, A la recherche de l'Egypte ensevelie. Paris, 1956.
Arc 565.1 Petrie, W.M.F. Ten years' digging in Egypt. N.Y., 1892.
Arc 565.1.2 Petrie, W.M.F. Ten years' digging in Egypt. 2. ed. London, 1893.
Arc 565.1.5 Petrie, W.M.F. Seventy years in archaeology. London, 1931.
Arc 565.1.6A Petrie, W.M.F. Seventy years in archaeology. N.Y., 1932.
Arc 565.1.6B Petrie, W.M.F. Seventy years in archaeology. N.Y., 1932.
Arc 565.2 Pierret, Paul. Dictionnaire d'archéologie égyptienne. Paris, 1875.
Arc 565.3 Pendlebury, J.D.S. Aegyptiaca. Cambridge, Eng., 1930.
Arc 565.5 Put, Thomas C. Egypt and the Old Testament. Liverpool, 1924.
Arc 567.1.5 Rosellini, Ippolito. Ippolito Rosellini e il suo giornale della spedizione letteraria toscana in Egitto. Roma, 1925.
Arc 567.1.10 Pisa. Università. Studi in memoria di Ippolito Rosellini nel primo centerario della morte. Pisa, 1949. 2v.
Arc 567.1.15F Florence. Università. Scritti dedicati alla memoria di Ippolito Rosellini. Firenze, 1945.
Arc 567.3 Pamphlet vol. Reisner, George Andrew. 13 pam.
Arc 567.3.5 Pamphlet vol. Reisner, George Andrew. 9 pam.
Arc 568.1 Stuart, V. Nile gleanings. London, 1879.
X Cg Arc 568.1.2 Stuart, V. The funeral tent of an Egyptian queen. London, 1882.
Arc 568.2 Schenkel, W. Frühmittelägyptische Studien. Bonn, 1962.
Arc 570.1A Uhlemann, M. Handbuch der gesammten aegyptischen Alterthumskunde. v.1-4. Leipzig, 1857. 2v.
Arc 570.1B Uhlemann, M. Handbuch der gesammten aegyptischen Alterthumskunde. v.1-2. Leipzig, 1857.
Arc 571.5 Vandier, Jacques. Manuel d'archéologie égyptienne. v.1-5; atlases. Paris, 1952. 10v.
Arc 572.1 Weigall, Arthur Edward Pearse Brome. Guide to the antiquities of upper Egypt. London, 1910.
Arc 572.1.2 Weigall, Arthur Edward Pearse Brome. A guide to the antiquities of upper Egypt from Abydos to the Sudan frontier. N.Y., 1910.
Arc 572.1.5A Weigall, Arthur Edward Pearse Brome. The glory of the Pharaohs. N.Y., 1923.
Arc 572.1.5B Weigall, Arthur Edward Pearse Brome. The glory of the Pharaohs. N.Y., 1923.
Arc 572.1.10 Weigall, Arthur Edward Pearse Brome. Tutankhamen, and other essays. London, 1923.
Arc 572.1.15 Weigall, Arthur Edward Pearse Brome. The treasury of ancient Egypt. Chicago, 1912.
Arc 572.1.20 Weigall, Arthur Edward Pearse Brome. Ancient Egyptian works of art. London, 1924.
Arc 572.2 Wilson, John Albert. Signs and wonders upon Pharaoh. Chicago, 1964.
Arc 572.5 Wilbour, Charles E. Travels in Egypt. December 1880-May 1891. Brooklyn, 1936.
Arc 572.10 Wortham, John David. The genesis of British Egyptology, 1549-1906. 1st ed. Norman, 1971.
Arc 572.10.5 Wortham, John David. British Egyptology, 1549-1906. Newton Abbot, 1971.
Arc 572.11 Wolf, Walther. Funde in Ägypten. Göttingen, 1966.

Arc 580 Archaeology - Local - Egypt - Institut Français d'Archéologie Orientale du Caire - General reports

Arc 580.1 France. Mission Archéologique Française au Caire. Mémoires. Paris. 1-31,1889-1934 25v.
Arc 580.1.2 Institut Français d'Archéologie Orientale du Caire. Mémoires. Le Caire. 1,1902+ 92v.

Arc 582 Archaeology - Local - Egypt - Institut Français d'Archéologie Orientale du Caire - Special reports

Arc 582.1 Institut Français d'Archéologie Orientale du Caire. Bulletin. Le Caire. 1,1901+ 48v.
Arc 582.2 Institut Français d'Archéologie Orientale du Caire. Bibliothèque d'étude. Le Caire. 1+ 53v.
Arc 582.4F Institut Français d'Archéologie Orientale du Caire. Rapport sur les fouilles d'Abou-Roarch. Le Caire. 1922-1924

Arc 582 Archaeology - Local - Egypt - Institut Français d'Archéologie Orientale du Caire - Special reports - cont.

Arc 582.5F Institut Français d'Archéologie Orientale du Caire. Rapport sur les fouilles de Dair el Médineh. Le Caire. 1922-1951 10v.
Arc 582.6F Institut Français d'Archéologie Orientale du Caire. Rapport sur les fouilles de Médamoud. Le Caire. 1925-1932 7v.
Arc 582.7F Institut Français d'Archéologie Orientale du Caire. Rapport sur les fouilles de Tell Edfou. La Caire. 1921-1933 2v.
Arc 582.9 Institut Français d'Archéologie Orientale du Caire. Fouilles franco-suisses. Rapports. 1-2 2v.

Arc 583 Archaeology - Local - Egypt - Bibliothèque de l'École des Hautes Études reports

Arc 583.1 Berend, W.B. Principaux monuments du Musée Égyptienne de Florence. no.51. Paris, 1882.
Arc 583.2F Gayet, E. Musée du Louvre - Stèles de la XIIe Dynastie. pt.1-2. no.68. Paris, 1886.
Arc 583.3 Leedrain, E. Monumens égyptiens de la Bibliothèque Nationale. pt.1-3. no.38. Paris, 1879-81.

Arc 584.1 - .90 Archaeology - Local - Egypt - Egypt. Service des Antiquités reports

Arc 584.1 Egypt. Antiquities Department. Rapports sur la Marche, 1899-1910. Le Caire, 1912.
Arc 584.1.5 Egypt. Antiquities Department. Catalogue des publications du Service des Antiquités, mars 1961. Le Caire, 1961.
Arc 584.2 Société d'Archéologie Copte, Cairo. Bulletin. 4,1938+ 10v.
Arc 584.2.2 Société d'Archéologie Copte, Cairo. Bulletin. Index, 1-10, 1935-44. Le Caire, n.d.
Arc 584.3F Emery, W.B. Great tombs of the First Dynasty. Cairo, 1949. 3v.
Arc 584.3.5F Emery, W.B. Excavations at Saqqara. Cairo, 1938.
Arc 584.3.10 Emery, W.B. Excavations at Saqqara, 1937-1938. Cairo, 1939.
Arc 584.4F Dunbar, J.H. The rock-picutres of Lower Nubia. Cairo, 1941.
Arc 584.5F Egypt. Antiquities Department. The cheops boats. Cairo, 1960-
Arc 584.6F Pennsylvania-Yale Expedition to Egypt. Publications. New Haven. 1,1963+ 4v.

Arc 584.100 Archaeology - Local - Egypt - Société Archéologique d'Alexandrie reports

Arc 584.100 Société Royale d'Archéologie d'Alexandrie. Bulletin. Alexandrie. 1-41,1898-1956 11v.
Arc 584.100.3 Société Royale d'Archéologie d'Alexandrie. Bulletin. Index analytique, 1-41 (1898-1956). Alexandrie, 1937-63. 2v.
Arc 584.100.5 Société Royale d'Archéologie d'Alexandrie. Conférence. Alexandrie. 1,1964+
Arc 584.100.10 Société Royale d'Archéologie d'Alexandrie. Mémoires. Le Caire. 1-8,1922-1936 4v.
Arc 584.100.15 Lackany, Rudames Sany. La Société archéologique d'Alexandrie à 80 ans. Alexandrie, 1973.
Arc 584.100.20F Société Royale d'Archéologie d'Alexandrie. Monuments de l'Egypte gréco-romaine. Bergamo. 1-2,1926-1934 3v.

Arc 585 Archaeology - Local - Egypt - Egypt Exploration Society or Fund - Memoirs

Arc 585.1 Naville, E.H. The store-city of Pithom. 3. ed. London, 1888.
Arc 585.2A Petrie, W.M.F. Tannis. Pt.1-2. London, 1885-88. 2v.
Arc 585.2B Petrie, W.M.F. Tannis. Pt.1-2. London, 1885-88. 2v.
Arc 585.2.2F Petrie, W.M.F. Tanis. Pt.1. 2. ed. London, 1889.
Arc 585.3 Petrie, W.M.F. Naukratis. Pt.1-2. London, 1886-88. 2v.
Arc 585.5F Naville, E.H. The shrine of Saft el Henneh. Malagny, 1887.
NEDL Arc 585.7 Naville, E.H. Mound of the Jew and City of Onias. London, 1890.
Arc 585.8 Naville, E.H. Bubastis. London, 1891.
Arc 585.9 Griffith, F.L. Two hieroglyphic papyri from Tanis. London, 1889.
Arc 585.10A Naville, E.H. Festival-Hall of Osorkon II in the Great Temple of Bubastis. London, 1892.
Arc 585.10B Naville, E.H. Festival-Hall of Osorkon II in the Great Temple of Bubastis. London, 1892.
Arc 585.11A Naville, E.H. Ahnas el Medinek. London, 1894.
Arc 585.11B Naville, E.H. Ahnas el Medinek. London, 1894.
Arc 585.12.2 Naville, E.H. The temple of Deir el Bahari. London, 1894.
Htn Arc 585.14F* Naville, E.H. The temple of Deir el Bahari. London, 1895-1908. 7v.
Arc 585.15A Petrie, W.M.F. Deshashek. 1897. London, 1898.
Arc 585.15B Petrie, W.M.F. Deshashek. 1897. London, 1898.
Arc 585.15C Petrie, W.M.F. Deshashek. 1897. London, 1898.
Arc 585.17A Petrie, W.M.F. Dendereh. 1898. London, 1900.
Arc 585.17B Petrie, W.M.F. Dendereh. 1898. London, 1900.
Arc 585.18A Petrie, W.M.F. The royal tombs of the First Dynasty. v.1; v.2, pt.1-2. London, 1900. 3v.
Arc 585.18B Petrie, W.M.F. The royal tombs of the First Dynasty. v.1; v.2, pt.1. London, 1900. 2v.
Arc 585.18C Petrie, W.M.F. The royal tombs of the First Dynasty. v.1; v.2, pt.1. London, 1900. 2v.
Arc 585.19 Petrie, W.M.F. Diospolis Parva...1898-99. London, 1901.
Arc 585.20A Petrie, W.M.F. Abydos. Pt.1-3. London, 1902-04. 3v.
Arc 585.20B Petrie, W.M.F. Abydos. Pt.1-2. London, 1902-03. 2v.
Arc 585.21 Randall-MacIver, D. Amrah and Abydos. 1899-1901. London, 1902.
Arc 585.22 Crum, W.E. Coptic Ostraca. London, 1902.
Arc 585.23A Petrie, W.M.F. Ehnasya. 1904. London, 1905.
Arc 585.23B Petrie, W.M.F. Ehnasya. 1904. London, 1905.
Arc 585.23.2 Petrie, W.M.F. Roman Ehnasya. 1904. Supplement. London, 1905.
Arc 585.25 Naville, E.H. XI Dynasty temple at Deir El-Bahari. London, 1907-13. 3v.
Arc 585.26F Ayrton, Edward R. Pre-dynastic cemetery at El Mahasna. London, 1911.
Arc 585.27 Peet, T.E. The cemeteries of Abydos. London, 1913-14. 3v.
Arc 585.28F Caminos, Ricardo A. The New Kingdom temples of Buhen. London, 1974. 2v.

Arc 585 Archaeology - Local - Egypt - Egypt Exploration Society or Fund - Memoirs - cont.

Arc 585.29F Wainwright, G.A. Balabish. London, 1920.
Arc 585.30F The city of Akhenaten. v.1-3. London, 1923-33. 4v.
Arc 585.31F Frankfort, H. The cenotaph of Seti I at Abydos. London, 1933. 2v.
Arc 585.32F Mond, Robert. The Bucheum. London, 1934. 3v.
Arc 585.34F Mond, Robert. Cemeteries of Armant. London, 1937. 2v.
Arc 585.37F Gardiner, Alan H. Egyptian letters to the dead. London, 1928.
Htn Arc 585.38F* Frankfort, H. The mural painting of El-Amarneh. London, 1929.
Arc 585.40F Egypt Exploration Society. Studies presented to F.L. Griffith. London, 1932.
Arc 585.47 Mond, Robert. Temples of Armant. London, 1940. 2v.

Arc 586 Archaeology - Local - Egypt - Egypt Exploration Society or Fund - Miscellaneous publications

Arc 586.1 Egypt Exploration Society. Reports of annual meetings. London. 1884-1937 6v.
Arc 586.2 Egypt Exploration Society. Archaeological reports. London. 1890-1912 5v.
Arc 586.5 Egypt Exploration Society. The proposed excavations at Tell-el-Amarna. n.p., n.d.
Arc 586.7 Egypt Exploration Society. Guide to the temple of Deir el Bahari. London? 1895?
Arc 586.15F The Theban tombs series. London. 1-5,1915-1933 5v.
Arc 586.40 Pamphlet box. Egypt Exploration Society.
Arc 586.60 Winslow, W.C. The truth about the Egypt Exploration Society. Boston, 1903.

Arc 587 Archaeology - Local - Egypt - Egypt Exploration Society or Fund - Archaeological Survey reports

Arc 587.1A Newberry, P.E. Beni Hasan. London, 1893. 4v.
Arc 587.1B Newberry, P.E. Beni Hasan. London, 1893. 3v.
Arc 587.3 Newberry, P.E. El Bersheh. Pt.1-2. London, 1894-95. 2v.
Arc 587.4 Griffith, F.L. Hieroglyphs. London, 1898.
Arc 587.5 Griffith, F.L. The Mastabo of Ptalshetep and Alsbrethetep. London, 1900. 2v.
Arc 587.6 Davies, N. de Garis. The rock tombs of Sheikh Said. London, 1901.
Arc 587.7 Davies, N. de Garis. The rock tombs of Deir el Gebrâevi. London, 1902. 2v.
Arc 587.8 Davies, N. de Garis. The rock tombs of El Amarna. London, 1903. 6v.
Arc 587.8.5F Martin, Geoffrey Torndike. The royal tomb at El-Amana. London, 1974.
Arc 587.9 Griffith, F.L. Meroitic inscriptions. London, 1911. 2 pam.
Arc 587.9.15 Davies, N. de Garis. Five Theban tombs. London, 1913.
Arc 587.10F Blackman, A.M. The rock tombs of Meir. London, 1914-24. 6v.
Arc 587.10.15 Winkler, Hans A. Rock drawings of southern upper Egypt. London, 1938-39. 2v.
Arc 587.11 James, Thomas Garnet H. The mastaba of Khentika called Ikhekhi. London, 1953.
Arc 587.12F Caminos, Ricardo A. Gebel es-Silsilah. London, 1963.
Arc 587.13 Caminos, Ricardo A. The shrines and rock-inscriptions of Ibrim. London, 1968.
Arc 587.50 Newberry, P.E. The life of Rekhmara. Westminster, 1900.
Arc 587.85 Egypt. Ministry of Finance. Archaeological survey of Nubia. v.1-7. Cairo, 1908.
Arc 587.87F Egypt. Ministry of Finance. Archaeological survey of Nubia; report. Cairo. 1907-1911 8v.
Arc 587.89 Egypt Exploration Society. Preliminary reports of the Egypt Exploration Society's Nubian Survey. Cairo, 1962.

Arc 588 Archaeology - Local - Egypt - British School of Archaeology in Egypt - Research accounts

Arc 588.1 Petrie, W.M.F. Ollahum, Kahun, and Gurob. 1889-90. London, 1891.
Arc 588.2 Petrie, W.M.F. Kahum, Gurob, and Hawara. London, 1890.
Arc 588.3 Petrie, W.M.F. Medum. London, 1892.
Arc 588.4 Petrie, W.M.F. Nagada and Ballas. London, 1895.
Arc 588.5 Petrie, W.M.F. Koptos. London, 1896.
Arc 588.6 Petrie, W.M.F. Six temples at Thebes. 1896. London, 1897.
Arc 588.7 Quibell, J.E. Teh Rainesseum. 1896. London, 1898.
Arc 588.8 Quibell, J.E. El Kab. 1897. London, 1898.
Arc 588.10 Quibell, J.E. Hierakonpolis. Pt.1-2. London, 1900-1902.
NEDL Arc 588.10 Quibell, J.E. Hierakonpolis. Pt.1-2. London, 1900-1902.
Arc 588.11 Garstang, John. El Arâbah. London, 1901.
Arc 588.12 Garstang, John. Mahâsna and Bêt Khalfâf. London, 1902.
Arc 588.13 Caulfield, A.S.G. Temple of the Kings at Abydos. London, 1902.
Arc 588.14 Murray, M. The Osireron at Abydos. London, 1904.
Arc 588.15 Murray, M. Saqqara Mastabas. London, 1905-37. 2v.
Arc 588.17 Petrie, W.M.F. Hyksos and Graelite cities. London, 1906.
Arc 588.18 Petrie, W.M.F. Gizeh and Rifeh. London, 1907.
Arc 588.19 Petrie, W.M.F. Athribis. London, 1908.
Arc 588.20 Petrie, W.M.F. Memphis. London, 1909-1915. 7 pam.
Arc 588.21 Petrie, W.M.F. Qurneh. London, 1909.
Arc 588.23 Petrie, W.M.F. Historical studies. London, 1911.
Arc 588.24 Petrie, W.M.F. Labyrinth Gerzeh and Mazghumeh. London, 1912.
Arc 588.25A Petrie, W.M.F. Hawara portfolio; paintings. London, 1913.
Arc 588.25B Petrie, W.M.F. Hawara portfolio; paintings. London, 1913.
Arc 588.26 Petrie, W.M.F. Heliopolis. London, 1915.
Arc 588.27 Petrie, W.M.F. Heliopolis. London, 1915.
Arc 588.28 Brunton, Guy. Lahun I, II; the treasure. London, 1920. 2v.
Arc 588.29F Engelbach, R. Harageh. London, 1923.
Arc 588.30A Petrie, W.M.F. Tools and weapons. London, 1917.
Arc 588.30B Petrie, W.M.F. Tools and weapons. London, 1917.
Arc 588.31 Petrie, W.M.F. Prehistoric Egypt. London, 1920.
Arc 588.34 Petrie, W.M.F. Sedment I, II. London, 1924. 2v.
Arc 588.36 Thompson, H. The gospel of St. John. London, 1924.
Arc 588.37 Petrie, W.M.F. Tombs of the courtiers and oxyrhynkhos. London, 1925.
Arc 588.38F Petrie, W.M.F. Buttons and design scarabs. London, 1925.
Arc 588.39F Petrie, W.M.F. Ancient weights and measures. London, 1926.
Arc 588.40F Petrie, W.M.F. Glass stamps and weights. London, 1926.
Arc 588.41F Brunton, Guy. Gurob. London, 1927.
Arc 588.42F Petrie, W.M.F. Objects of daily use. London, 1927.
Arc 588.43F Petrie, W.M.F. Gerar. London, 1928.
Arc 588.44F Brunton, Guy. Qau and Badari. London, 1927-30. 3v.

Arc 588 Archaeology - Local - Egypt - British School of Archaeology in Egypt - Research accounts - cont.

Arc 588.46F Brunton, Guy. The Badarian civilization. London, 1928.
Arc 588.47F MacKay, Ernest. Bahrein and Hemamieh. London, 1929.
Arc 588.48F Petrie, W.M.F. Beth-Pelet. London, 1930-32. 2v.
Arc 588.49F Duncan, J.G. Corpus of dated Palestinian pottery. London, 1930.
Arc 588.51F Petrie, W.M.F. Antaeopolis. London, 1930.
Arc 588.53F Petrie, W.M.F. Ancient Gaza. London, 1931-34. 4v.
Arc 588.57F Petrie, W.M.F. Shabtis. London, 1935.
Arc 588.58F Petrie, W.M.F. Anthedon. London, 1937.
Arc 588.59F Petrie, W.M.F. The funeral furniture of Egypt. London, 1937.
Arc 588.60 Petrie, W.M.F. Egyptian architecture. London, 1938.
Arc 588.62F Murray, M.A. A street in Petra. London, 1940.
Arc 588.63 Petrie, W.M.F. Wisdom of the Egyptians. London, 1940.
Arc 588.64F Petrie, W.M.F. City of shepherd kings. London, 1952.
Arc 588.65F Petrie, W.M.F. Seven Memphite tomb chapels. London, 1952.
Arc 588.66F Petrie, W.M.F. Flinders Petrie centenary...ceremonial slate palettes. London, 1953.

Arc 589 Archaeology - Local - Egypt - British School of Archaeology in Egypt - Other series

Arc 589.1 Murray, M.A. Index of names and titles of the old kingdoms. London, 1908.
Arc 589.1.3 Petrie, W.M.F. The formation of the alphabet. London, 1912.
Arc 589.5 British School of Archaeology in Egypt. Report. London. 13-20,1907-1914
Arc 589.7 Garstang, J. The third Egyptian dynasty. Westminster, 1904.
Arc 589.75F Ernst von Sieglin Expedition in Ägypten. Veröffentlichungen. Leipzig. 1-6,1912-1936 6v.

Arc 590 Archaeology - Local - Egypt - Special topics - Mummies and sarcophagi

Arc 590.01 Pamphlet box. Egyptian mummies and sarcophagi.
Arc 590.1A Budge, E.A.W. The mummy. Chapters on Egyptian funereal archaeology. Cambridge, 1893.
Arc 590.1B Budge, E.A.W. The mummy. Chapters on Egyptian funereal archaeology. Cambridge, 1893.
Arc 590.1.4 Budge, E.A.W. The mummy. 2. ed. N.Y., 1974.
Arc 590.1.5 Budge, E.A.W. The mummy. 2. ed. Cambridge, 1925.
Arc 590.2 Warren, J.C. Description of an Egyptian mummy. Boston, n.d.
Arc 590.3 Perrot, J.F.A. Essai sur les momies. Nimes, 1844.
Arc 590.4 Sharpe, S. Triple mummy case of Aroeri-Ao. London, 1858.
Arc 590.4.2 Sharpe, S. Alabaster sarcophagus of Oimenepthah. London, 1864.
Arc 590.5 Szedlo, G. Le grand sarcophage du Musée civique de Bologne. Bologne, 1876.
Arc 590.6 Champollion, J.F. Notice sur le papyrus hiératique et les peintures du cercueil de Pétaménoph. Paris, 1827.
Arc 590.7 Kettner, F.G. Moymia tōn Aigyptian. 2. ed. Lipsiae, 1703. 3 pam.
Arc 590.8F Smith, G. Elliot. Mémoires présentés à l'Institut Égyptien. Le Caire, 1906.
Arc 590.9F Schmidt, Valdemar. Sarkofager, muniekister og muniehylstre i det gamle a Egypten. København, 1919.
Arc 590.10 Clark, Edward. The tomb of Alexander. Cambridge, 1805.
Arc 590.10.5 Breccia, E. La tomba di Alessandro Magno. Alexandria, 1930.
Arc 590.11 Birch, Samuel. Remarks upon the cover of the granite sarcophagus of Rameses III in the Fitzwilliam Museum. Cambridge, Eng., 1876.
Arc 590.12 Buberl, Paul. Die griechisch-ägyptischen Mumienbildnisse der Sammlung T. Graf. Wien, 1922.
Arc 590.13.1 Drerup, Heinrich. Die Datierung der Mumienporträts. Paderborn, 1968.
Arc 590.14 Hayes, William C. Royal sarcophagi of the XVIII Dynasty. Princeton, 1935.
Arc 590.15 Wilson, E. The recent discovery of ancient Egyptian mummies at Thebes. London, 1883.
Arc 590.16F Buhl, Marie Louise. The late Egyptian anthropoid stone sarcophagi. København, 1959.
Arc 590.18 Muhammad, Ahmad Rajab. Lights on the royal mummies in the Egyptian Museum. Cairo, 1964.
Arc 590.20 Donadoni Roveri, Anna Maria. I sarcofagi egizi dalle origini alla fine dell'antico regno. Roma, 1969.
Arc 590.22 Harris, James E. X-raying the pharaohs. N.Y., 1973.

Arc 593 Archaeology - Local - Egypt - Special topics - Obelisks

Arc 593.1 Moldenke, C.E. The New York obelisk. N.Y., 1891.
Arc 593.1.2 Moldenke, C.E. The New York obelisk. N.Y., 1891.
Arc 593.2 Julien, A.A. Notes of research on the New York obelisk. N.Y., 1893.
Arc 593.3 Engelbach, R. The problem of the obelisks. London, 1923.
Arc 593.4 Budge, E.A.W. Cleopatra's needles and other Egyptian obelisks. London, 1926.
Arc 593.5 Wilson, E. Cleopatra's needle. London, 1878.
Arc 593.6 Noakes, Aubrey. Cleopatra's needles. London, 1962.

Arc 595 Archaeology - Local - Egypt - Special topics - Pyramids

Arc 595.01F Pyramids. Haverhill, 1943.
Arc 595.1 Ballard, R. The solution of the Pyramid problem. N.Y., 1882.
Arc 595.2 Grobert, J. Description des pyramides de Ghizé. Paris, 1801.
Arc 595.3 Dissertation of the antiquity...of the principal pyramids of Egypt. London, 1833.
Arc 595.4 James, H. Notes on the Great Pyramid of Egypt. Southampton, 1869. 2 pam.
X Cg Arc 595.5 Petrie, W.M.F. Pyramids and temples of Gizeh. London, 1883.
Arc 595.6 Proctor, R.A. The Great Pyramid. London, 1883.
Arc 595.6.2 Proctor, R.A. The Great Pyramid. N.Y., 1883.
Arc 595.6.5 Mencken, A. Designing and building the Great Pyramid. Baltimore, 1963.
Arc 595.7 Seiss, J.A. A miracle in stone, or The Great Pyramid of Egypt. Philadelphia, 1877?
Arc 595.7.4 Seiss, J.A. A miracle in stone, or The Great Pyramid of Egypt. 4th ed. Philadelphia, 1877.
Arc 595.8 Skinner, J.R. The Great Pyramid of Jizeh. Cincinnati, 1871. 2 pam.
Arc 595.9 Smyth, C.P. Our inheritance in the Great Pyramid. London, 1877.
Arc 595.9.2 Smyth, C.P. Our inheritance in the Great Pyramid. London, 1864.

Classified Listing

Arc 595 Archaeology - Local - Egypt - Special topics - Pyramids - cont.

Arc 595.9.3 Smyth, C.P. Our inheritance in the Great Pyramid. 4. ed. London, 1880.
Arc 595.9.5 Smyth, C.P. Life and work at the Great Pyramid. Edinburgh, 1867. 3v.
Arc 595.10 Totten, C.A.L. The metrology of the Great Pyramid. N.Y., 1884.
Arc 595.11 Vyse, H. Operations carried on at the pyramids of Gizeh in 1837. London, 1840. 2v.
Arc 595.12 Grossi, V. Le leggende delle piramidi. Genova, 1890.
Arc 595.13 Greaves, John. Pyramidographia. London, 1646.
Arc 595.16 Borchardt, Ludwig. Gegen die Zahlenmystik an der grossen Pyramide bei Gise. Berlin, 1922.
Arc 595.16.10 Borchardt, Ludwig. Längen und Richtungen der vier Grandkanten der grossen Pyramide bei Gise. Berlin, 1926.
Arc 595.17 Denslow, Van Buren. The pyramid of Gizeh. N.Y., 18- .
Arc 595.18 Bart, J.Y.S. On some points in certain theories...of the great Pyramid of Jeeseh. Glasgow, 1868.
Arc 595.19 MacDari, C. Irish wisdom preserved in bibles and pyramids. Boston, 1923.
Arc 595.20 MacHuisdean, Hamish. The great law, told simply in seven visits. v.2. Glasgow, 1928.
Arc 595.23FA Reisner, G.A. Mycerinus; the temples of the third pyramid at Giza. Cambridge, 1931.
Arc 595.23FB Reisner, G.A. Mycerinus; the temples of the third pyramid at Giza. Cambridge, 1931.
Arc 595.23.5F Reisner, G.A. A history of the Giza mecropolis. Cambridge, Mass., 1942- 2v.
Arc 595.26 Meier-Graefe, J. Pyramid and temple. London, 1931.
Arc 595.27 Kingsland, William. The Great Pyramid in fact and in theory. London, 1932-35. 2v.
Arc 595.28 Davie, John G. Phythagoras takes the second step, and other works on the pyramids. Griffin, 1935.
Arc 595.29 Fish, E.W. The Egyptian pyramids. Chicago, 1880.
Arc 595.30F Schiaparelli, E. Il significato simbolico delle piramidi egiziane. Roma, 1884.
Arc 595.31 Bache, R.M. The latest phase of the Great Pyramid discussion. Philadelphia, 1885.
Arc 595.32.15 Davidson, D. The Great Pyramid; its divine message. 8th ed. London, 1940.
Arc 595.33.5 Haberman, F. Armageddon has come; the climax of the ages is near. 2. ed. St. Petersburg, 1940.
Arc 595.34.5 Marks, T.S. The Great Pyramid. 2. ed. London, 1879?
Arc 595.35 Grinsell, Leslie V. Egyptian pyramids. Gloucester, 1947.
Arc 595.40 Lauer, J.P. Le problème des pyramides d'Égypte. Paris, 1948.
Arc 595.41 Lauer, J.P. Le mystère des pyramides. Paris, 1974.
Arc 595.45 Goneim, M. The buried pyramid. London, 1956.
Arc 595.50 Borchardt, Ludwig. Die Entstehung der Pyramide an der Baugeschichte. Berlin, 1928.
Arc 595.51 Borchardt, Ludwig. Einiges zur dritten Bauperiode der grossen Pyramide bei Gise. Berlin, 1932.
Arc 595.55 Cottrell, Leonard. The mountains of Pharaoh. N.Y., 1956.
Arc 595.59 Edwards, L.E.S. The pyramids of Egypt. London, 1954.
Arc 595.60 Edwards, L.E.S. The pyramids of Egypt. London, 1961.
Arc 595.62 Fakhry, A. The pyramids. Chicago, 1961.
Arc 595.63 Tompkins, Peter. Secrets of the great pyramid. London, 1973.
Arc 595.64 United Arab Republic. Ministry of Culture and National Guidance. Nocturnal magic of the pyramids. Paris, 1961.
Arc 595.65 Cormack, Maribelle. Imhotep, builder in stone. N.Y., 1965.
Arc 595.66 Lauer, Jean Philippe. Les pyramides de Sakkarah. Le Caire, 1961.
Arc 595.66.4 Lauer, Jean Philippe. Les pyramides de Sakkarah. 4. éd. Le Caire, 1972.
Arc 595.67F Maragioglio, Vito. L'archittura delle piramidi menfite. v.2-7; plates. Torino, 1963- 9v.
Arc 595.68 Kink, Khil'da A. Kak stroilis' egipetskte piramidy. Moskva, 1967.
Arc 595.69 Mendelssohn, Kurt. The riddle of the pyramids. London, 1974.
Arc 595.70.1 Wake, Charles Staniland. The origin and significance of the great pyramid. Minneapolis, 1975.

Arc 600 Archaeology - Local - Egypt - Local; Other Special topics

Arc 600.1 Kiepert, H. Zur Topographie des alten Alexandria. Berlin, n.d.
Arc 600.1.2 Néroutsos-Bey, T.D. L'ancienne Alexandrie. Paris, 1888.
Arc 600.1.3 Hogarth, D.G. Report on prospects of research in Alexandria. London, 1895.
Arc 600.1.5 Botti, G. Plan du Quartier "Rhacotis" dans l'Alexandrie. Alexandrie, 1897.
Arc 600.1.9 Strzygowski, J. Hellenistische und koptische Kunst in Alexandria. Wien, 1902.
Arc 600.1.13 Togheb, A.M. de. Études sur l'ancienne Alexandrie. Paris, 1909.
Arc 600.1.15 Breccia, E. Alexandrea ad Aegyptum. Bergamo, 1914.
Arc 600.1.17 Breccia, E. Una statuetta del Buon Pastore da Marsa Matruh. Alexandria, 1931.
Arc 600.2 Brugsch-Bey, H. Reise nach der grossen Oase El-Khargeh. Leipzig, 1878.
Arc 600.3 Mariette, A. Choix de monuments et de dessins...Sérapéum de Memphis. Paris, 1856.
Arc 600.3.5 Heuser, G. Die Katochëim Sarapieion bei Memphis. Inaug. Diss. Marburg, 1935.
Arc 600.3.10 Hermann, A. Führer durch die Altertümer von Memphis und Sakkara. Berlin, 1938.
Arc 600.3.15 Vercoutter, J. Textes biographiques du Sérapéum de Memphis. Paris, 1962.
Arc 600.4 Winslow, W.C. Naukratis - a Greek city in Egypt. Boston, 1887.
Arc 600.4.5 Prinz, H. Funde aus Naukratis. Leipzig, 1906.
Arc 600.4.9 Jong, E.F.P. Scherben aus Naukratis. Proefschrift. n.p., 1925.
Arc 600.4.13 Smith, E.M. Naukratis. Diss. Vienna, 1926.
Arc 600.5 Brown, R.H. The Fayûm and Lake Moeris. London, 1892.
Arc 600.5.2 Bellefonds, L. de. Mémoire sur le Lac Moeris. Alexandrie, 1843.
Arc 600.5.3 Whitehouse, F.C. Lake Moeris and the pyramids. n.p., 1884?
Arc 600.5.15F Caton-Thompson, G. The desert Fayum. London, 1934. 2v.
Arc 600.5.20 Missione di Scavo a Medinet Madi. Rapporto preliminare delle campagine di Scavo 1966-1967. Milano, 1968.
Arc 600.6A Rhind, A.H. Thebes. London, 1862.
Arc 600.6B Rhind, A.H. Thebes. London, 1862.
Arc 600.6.5 Campbell, C. Two Theben queens. London, 1909.

Arc 600 Archaeology - Local - Egypt - Local; Other Special topics - cont.

Arc 600.6.9 Chenillon, A. Terres mortes. Paris, 1897.
Arc 600.6.15F Capart, Jean. Thèbes. Bruxelles, 1925.
Arc 600.6.20F Carlier, A. Thèbes. Paris, 1948.
Arc 600.6.25F Carter, H. The tomb of Thoutmôsis. Westminster, 1904.
Arc 600.6.30 Leclant, Jean. Recherches sur les monuments thébains de la XXVe dynastie dite éthiopienne. Le Caire, 1965. 2v.
Arc 600.7 Karabaček. Die Theodor Graf'schen Funde in Aegypten. Wien, 1883.
Arc 600.8 Wendel, F.C.H. Über die in altägyptischen Texten erwähnten Bau- und Edelsteine. Leipzig, 1888.
Arc 600.9 Foucart, G. Histoire de l'Ordre Lotiforme. Paris, 1897.
Arc 600.10 Winslow, W.C. Egyptian antiquities for our museums. n.p., 1900.
Arc 600.11 Amélineau, E. Les nouvelles fouilles d'Abydos, seconde campagne 1896-1897. Paris, 1902.
Arc 600.11.2 Amélineau, E. Les nouvelles fouilles d'Abydos 1897-1898. Paris, 1904-05. 2v.
Arc 600.12.5A Newberry, P.E. Scarabs. London, 1906.
Arc 600.12.5B Newberry, P.E. Scarabs. London, 1906.
Arc 600.12.10F Palestine. Archaeological Museum. A catalogue of Egyptian scarabs by Alan Rowe. La Caire, 1936.
Arc 600.13 Köster, A. Die ägyptische Pflanzensäule der Spätzeit. Paris, 1903.
Arc 600.14 Kaufmann, C.M. Die Ausgrabung des Menas-Heiligtümes. v.1-3. Cairo, 1906.
Arc 600.14.5 Kaufmann, C.M. La découverte des sanctuaires. Alexandrie, 1908.
Arc 600.15 Garstang, J. The burial customs of ancient Egypt. London, 1907.
Arc 600.15.5 Daninos, A. Les monuments funéraires de l'Egypte ancienne. Paris, 1899.
Arc 600.15.15 Speleers, L. Les figurines funéraires égyptiennes. Bruxelles, 1923.
Arc 600.15.20 Hooper, Finley A. Funerary stelae from Kom Abour Billow. Ann Arbor, 1961.
Arc 600.15.25 Emery, Walter Bryan. A funerary repast in an Egyptian tomb of the archaic period. Leiden, 1962.
Htn Arc 600.16*A Nichols, C.L. The library of Rameses the Great. Boston, 1909.
Htn Arc 600.16*B Nichols, C.L. The library of Rameses the Great. Boston, 1909.
Arc 600.17 Naville, E. Les têtes de pierre...tombeaux égyptiens. Genève, 1909.
Arc 600.18A Mogensen, Maria. Le mastaba égyptien de la glyphtothèque de Carlsberg. Copenhagen, 1921.
Arc 600.18B Mogensen, Maria. Le mastaba égyptien de la glyphtothèque de Carlsberg. Copenhagen, 1921.
Arc 600.18.15F Junker, H. Gîza. Leipzig, 1929-38. 3v.
Arc 600.20 Theban ostraca. Toronto, 1913.
Arc 600.21 Lucas, Alfred. Ancient Egyptian materials. N.Y., 1926.
Arc 600.21.5 Lucas, Alfred. Ancient Egyptian materials and industries. 3. ed. London, 1948.
Arc 600.21.6 Lucas, Alfred. Ancient Egyptian materials. London, 1962.
Arc 600.26 Elkab. Bruxelles. 1,1971+
Arc 600.30 Benson, Margaret. The temple of Mut in Asher. London, 1899.
Arc 600.35 Suys, Émile. Vie de Petasiris, grand prêtre di That à Hermopolis-la-Grande. Bruxelles, 1927.
Arc 600.35.5 Roeder, Günther. Vorläufiger Bericht über die Ausgrabungen in Hermopolis 1929-30. Augsburg, 1931 .
Arc 600.35.10 Roeder, Günther. Vorläufiger Bericht über die detsche Hermopolis-Expedition, 1931-32. Augsburg, 1932.
Arc 600.35.15 Roeder, Günther. Ein Jahrzehnt deutscher Ausgrabungen in einer ägyptischen Stadtruine. Hildesheim, 1951.
Arc 600.35.20F Wace, Alan John. Hermopolis Magna. Alexandria, 1959.
Arc 600.36 Boak, A.E.R. Karanis. Ann Arbor, 1931.
Arc 600.36.5 Boak, A.E.R. Karanis. Ann Arbor, 1933.
Arc 600.37A Murray, M.A. Egyptian temples. London, 1931.
Arc 600.37B Murray, M.A. Egyptian temples. London, 1931.
Arc 600.38 New York (City). Metropolitan Museum of Art. The tomb of Perneb. N.Y., 1916.
Arc 600.39 Montet, Pierre. Les nouvelles fouilles de Tanis (1929-32). Paris, 1933.
Arc 600.40 Boak, A.E.R. Soknopaiou Nesos. Ann Arbor, 1935.
Arc 600.41FA Reisner, George A. The development of the Egyptian tomb down to the accession of Cheops. Cambridge, 1936.
Arc 600.41FB Reisner, George A. The development of the Egyptian tomb down to the accession of Cheops. Cambridge, 1936.
Arc 600.43 Vogliano, A. Primo rapporto degli scavi condotti dalla Missione archeologica d'Egitto della R. Università di Milano. Milano, 1936-37. 2v.
Arc 600.44 Winkler, H.A. Völker und Völkerbewegungen im vorgeschichtlichen Oberägypten im Lichte neuer Felshilderfunde. Stuttgart, 1937.
Arc 600.45F Borchardt, Ludwig. Ägyptische Tempel mit Umgang. Kairo, 1938.
Arc 600.46F Hassan, S. Excavations at Giza, 1929-1930. v.1-10. Oxford, 1932. 13v.
Arc 600.46.5F Abd el Monem, Joussef Abubakr. Excavations at Giza, 1945-50. Cairo, 1953.
Arc 600.46.10F Giza mastabas. Boston, 1974- 2v.
Arc 600.47F Edgar, C.A. Der Isistempel von Behbet. pt.2. Rom, 1913.
Arc 600.48 Johnson, J. de M. Antinoë and its papyri; excavations by the Graeco-Roman branch, 1913-14. London, 1914.
Arc 600.49 Menghin, O. The excavations of the Egyptian university in the neolithic site at Maadi. Cairo, 1932.
Arc 600.51F Hayes, William C. The burial chamber of the treasurer Sobk-Mosĕ from Er Rizeikât. N.Y., 1939.
Arc 600.52 Posener, G. Princes et pays d'Asie et de Nubie. Bruxelles, 1940.
Arc 600.53F MacAdam, M.F.L. The temples of Kawa. v.1-2; plates. London, 1949- 4v.
Arc 600.54 Winlock, H.E. Excavations at Deir el Bahri, 1911-1931. N.Y., 1942.
Arc 600.54.5 Deir el-Bahari. Varsovic, 1974-
Arc 600.55F Varille, Alexandre. Karnak. v.1,3-4. Le Caire, 1943-51. 4v.
Arc 600.55.5 Barguet, Paul. Le temple d'Amon-Rê à Karnak. Le Caire, 1962.
Arc 600.60F Mewberry, P.E. El Bersheh. London, 1894-95. 2v.
Arc 600.65F Winlock, H.E. The slain soldiers of Neb-hebek-Re' Mentu-hotpe. N.Y., 1945.
Arc 600.70 Jéquier, Gustave. Douze ans de fouilles dans la nécropole memphite, 1924-1936. Neuchâtel, 1940.
Arc 600.71F Jéquier, Gustave. Fouilles à Saqqarah. Le Caire, 1928.
Arc 600.72F Jéquier, Gustave. Fouilles à Saqqarah. La Caire, 1928.

Classified Listing

Arc 600 Archaeology - Local - Egypt - Local; Other Special topics - cont.

Arc 600.75 Montet, Pierre. Tanis, douze années de fouilles. Paris, 1942.
Arc 600.75.5F Montet, Pierre. La nécropole royale de Tanis. Paris, 1947. 3v.
Arc 600.80F Brunton, Guy. Matmar. London, 1948.
Arc 600.85F Schweitzer, U. Löwe und Sphinx im alten Ägypten. Glückstadt, 1948.
Arc 600.90F Paujade, J. Trois flottilles de la VIIème dynastie des pharaons. Djibouti, 1948.
Arc 600.95 Breccia, E. Nuovi scari nelle necropoli di Hadra. Alexandria, 1930.
Arc 600.100 Ward, J. The sacred beetle. London, 1902.
Arc 600.105F Stefanski, E. Coptic ostraca from Medinet Habu. Chicago, 1952.
Arc 600.105.5F Lichtheim, M. Demotic ostraca from Medinet Habu. Chicago, 1957.
Arc 600.110F Černý, Jaroslav. Répertoire onomastique de Deir et Médineh. Le Caire, 1949.
Arc 600.112 Hoelsche, Uvo. Die Wiedergewinnung von Medinet Habu im westlichen Theben. Tübingen, 1958.
Arc 600.115 Drioton, E. Sakkarah. Le Caire, 1939.
Arc 600.120 Pesce, Gennaro. Il Palazzo delle calonne in Talemaide di Cirenaria. Roma, 1950.
Arc 600.130 Reuterswaerd, Patrick. Studien zur Polychromie der Plaskik. Stockholm, 1958- 2v.
Arc 600.135 Schwaller de Lubicz, R.A. Le Temple de l'homme. Paris, 1957. 3v.
Arc 600.140 Goyon, Georges. Nouvelles inscriptions rupestres du Wadi Hammamat. Paris, 1957.
Arc 600.145F Junker, Hermann. Der Grosse Pylon des Tempels der Isis in Philä. Wien, 1958.
Arc 600.155F Vaudier, Jacques. Catalogue des ostraca figurés de Deir el Médineh. Pt. 4. Le Caire, 1959.
Arc 600.156F Sauneron, Serge. Catalogue des ostraca hiératiques littéraires de Deir el Médineh. Le Caire, 1959- 2v.
Arc 600.156.5F Posener, Georges. Catalogue des ostraca hiératiques littéraires de Deir el Médineh. Le Caire, 1972-
Arc 600.156.10F Valbelle, Dominique. Ouchebtis de Deir el-Médineh. Le Caire, 1972.
Arc 600.160F Ranke, Hermann. Koptische Friedhöfe bei Karâra und der Amontempel Schesehonks I bei El Hibe. Berlin, 1926.
Arc 600.165 Chubb, Mary. Nefertiti lived here. N.Y., 1954.
Arc 600.170 Maczamallah, R. Fouilles à Saqqarah. Le Caire, 1935.
Arc 600.172 Bisson de la Roque, Fernand. Tôd, 1934 à 1936. Le Caire, 1937.
Arc 600.175 Firth, Cecil M. Excavations at Saqqara. Le Caire, 1926. 2v.
Arc 600.180F Morzan, J. de. Carte de la nécropole memphite. n.p., 1897.
Arc 600.184 Schott, Siegfried. Wall scenes from the mortuary chapel of the Mayor Poser at Medinet Habu. Chicago, 1957.
Arc 600.185F Daumot, F. Les mammisis de Dendara, le mammisi de Nectanébo. Le Caire, 1955.
Arc 600.188 Sauneron, Serge. Esna. Le Caire, 1959- 5v.
Arc 600.188.5 Sauneron, Serge. Les ermitages chrétiens du désert d'Esna. Le Caire, 1972.
Arc 600.190 Bachatly, C. Le monastère de Phoebammon. Le Caire, 1964- 2v.
Arc 600.191 Petrie, W.M.F. The arts of ancient Egypt. London, 1884.
Arc 600.193 Haykal, Fa'iza. Tombeau de Pannout à Aniba. Le Caire, 196-.
Arc 600.194F Bahgat, Aly. Fouilles d'al Foustât. Paris, 1921.
Arc 600.195 United Arab Republic. Ministry of Culture and National Guidance. The salvation of the Nubian monuments. Cairo, 196-
Arc 600.200F Farid, Shafik. Exavations at Ballana, 1958-1959. Cairo, 1963.
Arc 600.205 Edel, Elmar. Die Felsengräber der Qubbet el Hawa bei Assuan. Wiesbaden, 1970- 2v.
Arc 600.210F Bruyère, Bernard. Fouilles de Clysma-Qolzoum (Suez) 1930-1932. Le Caire, 1966.
Arc 600.215 United Arab Republic. Centre of Documentation and Studies on Ancient Egypt. Kalabsha. Cairo, n.d.
Arc 600.215.5 Daumas, François. La ouabet de Kalabcha. Le Caire, 1970.
Arc 600.220F Missione Archeologica in Egitto. Tamit, 1964. Roma, 1967.
Arc 600.222 Gamer-Wallert, Ingrid. Der verziete Löffel; seine Formgeschichte und Verwendung im alten Ägypten. Wiesbaden, 1967.
Arc 600.225 Saad, Zaki Yusef. The excavations at Helwan. 1st ed. Norman, 1969.
Arc 600.230F Daumas, François. Kellia I. Le Caire, 1969- 2v.
Arc 600.235 Virey, Philippe. Quelques observations sur l'épisode d'Aristée; à propos d'un monument égyptien. Paris, 1889. Paris, 1889.
Arc 600.236 Michelucci, Maurizio. La collezione di lucerne del Museo egizio di Firenze. Firenze, 1975.
Arc 600.240F Baumgaertel, Elise J. Petrie's Nagada excavation; a supplement. London, 1970.
Arc 600.241 Abitz, Friedrich. Die religiöse Bedeutung der sogenannten Grabräuberschächte in den ägyptischen Königsgräbern der 18. bis 20. Dynastie. Wiesbaden, 1974.
Arc 600.242 Kaplony, Peter. Beschriftete Kleinfunde in der Sammlung Georges Michailidis. Istanbul, 1973.
Arc 600.243 Cabra, Sami. Chez les derniers adorateurs du Trismegiste. Cairo, 1971.
Arc 600.244F Adams, Barbara. Ancient Hierakonpolis. Warminster, 1974.
Arc 600.244.1F Adams, Barbara. Ancien Hierakonpolis. Supplement. Warminster, 1974.

Arc 603 Archaeology - Local - Africa in general

Arc 603.5 Vaufrey, Raymond. Prehistoire de l'Afrigue. Paris, 1955.
Arc 603.6.5 Alimen, Henriette. The prehistory of Africa. London, 1957.
Arc 603.7A Background to evolution in Africa. Chicago, 1968.
Arc 603.7B Background to evolution in Africa. Chicago, 1968.

Arc 605 Archaeology - Local - North Africa except Egypt - Folios [Discontinued]

Arc 605.1 Pacho, J.R. Relation d'un voyage dans la Marmarique. Text, plates. Paris, 1827. 2v.
Arc 605.201 Smith, R.M. History of the recent discovery at Cyrene. London, 1864.
Arc 605.202 France. Ministère de l'Instruction Publique. Musées de l'Algérie. Paris. 1-21,1890-1928 24v.
Arc 605.203 Playfair, R.L. Travels in the footsteps of Bruce in Algeria and Tunis. London, 1877.

Arc 605 Archaeology - Local - North Africa except Egypt - Folios [Discontinued] - cont.

Arc 605.204 Cagnet, R. Les monuments historiques de la Tunise. Paris, 1898-99. 2v.
Arc 605.204.5F Renault, Jules. Cahiers d'archéologie tunisienne. v.1-4. Tunis, 1908-11.
Arc 605.205 Boeswillwald, E. Timgad, une cité africaine. Londres, 1892-
Arc 605.205.5 Holtzinger, H. Timgad und die römische Provinzial-Architektur. Berlin, 1906.

Arc 606 Archaeology - Local - North Africa except Egypt - Coxe Expedition to Nubia reports

Arc 606.1 Randall-MacIver, David. Areika. Oxford, 1909.
Arc 606.2 Mileham, G.S. Churches in lower Nubia. Philadelphia, 1910.
Arc 606.3 Woolley, C.L. Karanòg, the Romano-Nubian cemetery. Philadelphia, 1910. 2v.
Arc 606.5 Woolley, C.L. Karanòg, the town. Philadelphia, 1911.
Arc 606.6 Griffith, F.L. Karanòg, the Meroitic inscriptions. Philadelphia, 1911.
Arc 606.7 Randall-MacIver, David. Buhen. Philadelphia, 1911. 2v.

Arc 608 Archaeology - Local - North Africa except Egypt - General works; Local; Special topics

Arc 608.1 Carton, Louis B.C. Découvertes épigraphiques et archéologiques faites en Tunisie. Paris, 1895.
Arc 608.1.3 Gauckler, Paul. L'archéologie de la Tunisie. Paris, 1896.
Arc 608.1.5 Cagnat, R. Explorations épigraphiques et archéologiques en Tunise. v.1-3. Paris, 1883-6.
Arc 608.1.15 Tunis. Compte rendu de la marche du service. Tunis, 1898.
Arc 608.1.25 Gauckler, Paul. Enquête sur les installations hydrologiques romaines en Tunisie. Tunis, 1897-
Arc 608.1.27 Perrot, G. La musée du Bardo à Tunis et les fouilles de M. Gauckler. Paris, 1899.
Arc 608.1.28 Carton, Louis B.C. Le sanctuaire de Base-Saturne à Dougga. Paris, 1896.
Arc 608.1.29 Carton, Louis B.C. Le théâtre de Dougga. Paris, 1902.
Arc 608.1.30 Carton, Louis B.C. La colonisation romaine dans le pays de Dougga. Tunis, 1904.
Arc 608.1.31 Tunis. Direction des Antiquités et Arts. Notes et documents. Paris. 1,1908+ 9v.
Arc 608.1.35 Balut, Georges. Tunisie. Tunis, 1903.
Arc 608.1.37F Massigli, T. Musée de Sfax. Paris, 1912.
Arc 608.1.37.5 Fandri, Muhammed. Découverte archéologigue dans la région de Sfax: mosaique des océans. Tunis, 1963.
Arc 608.1.39 Hérisson, M. d'. Relation d'une mission archéologique en Tunisie. Paris, 1881.
Arc 608.1.41F Berger, P. Stèles trouvées à Hadrumète. Paris, 1884.
Arc 608.1.43 Foucher, Louis. La maison de la procession dionysiaque à el Jem. Paris, 1963.
Arc 608.1.50 Cintas, Pierre. Éléments d'étude pour une protohistoire de la Tunisie. Paris, 1961.
Arc 608.1.55 Baratte, François. Recherches archéologiques à Haïdra. Paris, 1974.
Arc 608.2 Sainte-Marie, E. de. Mission à Carthage. Paris, 1884.
Arc 608.2.2 Davis, N. Carthage and her remains. London, 1861.
Arc 608.2.3 Delattre, A.L. Souvenir de la Croisade de Saint-Louis trouvé à Carthage. Lyon, 1888.
Arc 608.2.5 Delattre, R.P. Notice sur les plombs chrétiens trouvés à Carthage. Lyon, 1887.
Arc 608.2.8 Moore, M. Carthage of the Phoenicians. London, 1905.
Arc 608.2.9 Gauckler, Paul. Nécropoles puniques de Carthage. pt.1-2. Paris, 1915. 2v.
Arc 608.2.10 Delattre, R.P. Un pélerinage aux ruines de Carthage. Lyon, 1906.
Arc 608.2.12 Dureau de la Malle, Adolphe. Recherches sur la topographie de Carthage. Paris, 1835.
Arc 608.2.15 Babelon, E. Carthage. Paris, 1896.
Arc 608.2.17 Lavigerie, C.M.A. De l'utilité d'une mission archéologique permanente à Carthage. Alger, 1881.
Arc 608.2.19 Vives y Escudero, Antonio. Estudio de arqueología cartaginesa. Madrid, 1917.
Arc 608.2.23 Kelsey, Francis W. Excavations at Carthage 1925. N.Y., 1926.
Arc 608.2.25 Gielly, Paul. Quelques lueurs nouvelles sur l'emplacement de la Carthage punique et de ses ports. Casablanca, 1927.
X Cg Arc 608.2.27 Carthage. Carthage, 19- .
Arc 608.2.37 Lapeyre, Gabriel G. Carthage punique. Paris, 1942.
Arc 608.2.38 Lapeyre, Gabriel G. Carthage latine et chrétienne. Paris, 1950.
Arc 608.2.39 Khun de Prorot, Byron. Fouilles à Carthage. Paris, 1923.
Arc 608.2.41 Cahiérs de Byrsa. Paris. 1-10,1951-1965// 6v.
Arc 608.2.45 Meunié, Jacques. Recherches archéologiques à Marrakech. Paris, 1952.
Arc 608.2.45.5 Meunié, Jacques. Nouvelles recherches archéologiques à Marrakech. Paris, 1957.
Arc 608.2.50 Marec, Erwan. Hippone la Royale. Alger, 1954.
Arc 608.2.52 Marec, Erwan. Monuments chrétiens d'Hippone. Paris, 1958.
Arc 608.2.55 Cintas, Pierre. Amulettes puniques. Tunis, 1946.
Arc 608.2.60 Acquaro, Enrico. I rasoi punici. Roma, 1971.
Arc 608.2.65 Lézine, Alexandre. Les thermes d'Antonin à Carthage. Tunis, 1969.
Arc 608.2.70 Carton, Louis B.C. Carthage. Strasbourg, 1926.
Arc 608.2.75 Carthage: Cirque, Colline dite de Junon, Douar Chott. Wrocław, 1974.
Arc 608.2.80F Collection cahiers de Byrsa. Série monographies. Paris. 1,1974+ 2v.
Arc 608.5 Barth, H. Wanderungen...Kuestenlaender...Mittelmeeres. Berlin, 1849.
Arc 608.6 Cagnat, R. Guides en Algérie...Lambèse. Paris, 1893.
Arc 608.6.3 Renier, Léon. Rapports adressés à M. le ministre de l'instruction publique et des cultes. Paris, 1852.
Arc 608.6.4 Courtois, C. Timgad. Alger, 1951.
Arc 608.6.5 Ballu, Albert. Les ruines de Timgad. Paris, 1897.
Arc 608.6.6 Ballu, Albert. Guide illustré de Timgad (antique Thamrigadi). 2. éd. Paris, 1910.
Arc 608.6.7 Ballu, Albert. Les ruines de Timgad. Paris, 1911.
Arc 608.6.9 Ruines romaines au nord de l'Aurès. Rome, 1894. 2 pam.
Arc 608.6.13 Gsell, Stéphane. Fouilles de Gouraya. Paris, 1903.
Arc 608.6.18 Algeria. Directoire de l'Intérieur et de Beaux-Arts. Villes d'or. Alger, 1951.
Arc 608.6.21F Gsell, Stéphane. Khamissa, Mdaourouch, Announa. Alger, 1914-22.
Arc 608.6.22 Exploration scientifique de l'Algérie. Paris, 1912. 2v.

Arc 608 Archaeology - Local - North Africa except Egypt - General works; Local; Special topics - cont.

Arc 608.6.23	Gsell, Stéphane. Promenades archéologiques aux environs d'Alger. Paris, 1926.
Arc 608.6.24	Gsell, Stéphane. Cherchel. Alger, 1952.
Arc 608.6.25	Blanchet, P. La porte de Sidi Oqba. Paris, 1900.
Arc 608.6.27	Note sur quelques villes romaines de l'Algérie. Paris, 1849?
Arc 608.6.29	Leschi, Louis. Djemila Cuicul de Numidie. Alger, 1938.
Arc 608.6.30	Leschi, Louis. Djemila. Alger, 1953.
Arc 608.6.31	Gsell, Stéphane. Guide archéologique des environs d'Alger. Alger, 1896.
Arc 608.6.35	Gsell, Stéphane. Recherches archéologiques en Algérie. Paris, 1893.
Arc 608.6.40	Picard, G.C. Castellum Dimmidi. Paris, 1947.
Arc 608.6.45	Leschi, Louis. Algérie antique. Paris, 1952.
Arc 608.6.46	Leschi, Louis. Études d'épigraphie. Paris, 1957.
Arc 608.6.50	Berthier, A. Tiddis. Alger, 1951.
Arc 608.6.55	Christople, M. Le tombeau de la Chrétienne. Paris, 1951.
Arc 608.6.60	Luiks, A.G. Cathedra en mensa. Franeker, 1955.
Arc 608.6.65	Mercier, Maurice. Prière sur le Tombeau de la Chrétienne. Paris, 1954.
Arc 608.6.70	Brahime, Claude. Initiation à la préhistoire de l'Algérie. Alger, 1972.
Arc 608.6.75	Monceaux, Paul. Tingad chrétien. Paris, 1911.
Arc 608.7	Schulten, A. Das römische Afrika. Leipzig, 1899.
Arc 608.7.5	Université de l'Instruction Publique. Recherches des antiquités dans le nord de l'Afrique. Paris, 1890.
Arc 608.7.9	Pallary, P. Instituts pour les recherches préhistoriques. Alger, 1909.
Arc 608.7.15	Tissot. Recherches sur la géographie comparée de la Maurétanie Tingitane. Paris, 1877.
Arc 608.7.25	Ruhlmann, A. Les grottes préhistoriques d'"El Khenzira" (région de Mazagan). Thèse. Nogent-le-Rotrou, 1936.
Arc 608.10	Bibliothèque d'archéologie africaine. Paris, 1897-1906. 7v.
Arc 608.11	Cagnot, R. Carthage, Timgad Febessa. Paris, 1909.
Arc 608.12	Cowper, H.S. The hill of the Graces...Tripoli. London, 1897.
Arc 608.12.15	Bartoccini, R. Guida di Sabratha. Roma, 1927.
Arc 608.13	Mesnege, P.J. L'Afrique chrétienne...ruines antiques. Paris, 1912.
Arc 608.15	Béylié, Leon. La Kaloa des Beni-Hammad. Paris, 1909.
Arc 608.16	Gsell, Stéphane. De Tipasa, Mauretaniae Caesariensis urbe. Diss. Algerii, 1894.
Arc 608.16.7	Waille, Victor. De Caesareae monumentis quae supersunt. Alger, 1891.
Arc 608.16.10	Douël, M. L'Algérie romaine; forums et basiliques. Paris, 1930.
Arc 608.16.15	Baradez, J.L. Tipasa. Alger, 1952.
Arc 608.17	Norton, Richard. The excavations at Cyrene. N.Y., 1911.
Arc 608.17.3	Norton, Richard. From Bengazi to Cyrene. n.p., 1911.
Arc 608.17.5	Ferri, Silvio. Contributi di Cirene alla storia della religione greca. Roma, 1923.
Arc 608.17.9F	Ferri, Silvio. Divinità ignate. Firenze, 1929.
Arc 608.17.11	Caputo, Giacomo. Lo scultore del grande bassorilievo. Roma, 1948.
Arc 608.17.13	Wilamowitz-Moellendorff, U. Cirene. Bergamo, 1930.
Arc 608.17.15	Vitali, L. Fonti per la storia della religione cyrenaica. Padova, 1932.
Arc 608.17.19F	Pernier, Luigi. Il tempio e l'altare di Apollo a Cirene. Bergamo, 1935.
Arc 608.17.21	Rowe, Alan. Cyrenaican expedition of the University of Manchester. Manchester, Eng., 1956.
Arc 608.17.25F	Kraeling, C.H. Ptolemais, city of the Libyan Pentapolis. Chicago, 1962.
Arc 608.17.30F	Arkell, A.J. Wanyanga. London, 1964.
Arc 608.17.35	Stucchi, Sandro. L'Agorà di Cirene. Roma, 1965.
Arc 608.18F	Romanelli, P. Leptis Magna. Roma, 1925.
Arc 608.18.5F	Bartoccini, R. Le terme di Lepcis (Leptis Magna). Bergamo, 1929.
Arc 608.19	Khun de Prorok, Byron. Digging for lost African gods. N.Y., 1926.
Arc 608.20	Corò, Francesco. Vestigia di colonie agricole romane Gebel Nefusa. Roma, 1928.
Arc 608.21	La Blanchère, R. du C. Voyage d'étude dans une partie de la Maurétanie césarienne. Paris, 1883.
Arc 608.22	Perret, Robert. Recherches archéologiques et ethnographiques au Tassili des Ajjers (Sahara Central). Paris, 1936.
Arc 608.23	Emery, Walter B. Nubian treasure. London, 1948.
Arc 608.23.5	Akademiia Nauk SSSR. Institut Arkheologii. Drevniaia Nubiia. Leningrad, 1964.
Arc 608.23.10	Vantini, Giovanni. The exavations at Faras. Thesis. Bologna, 1970.
Arc 608.24F	Dunham, D. The Royal cemeteries of Kush. Hambridge, 1950-63. 5v.
Arc 608.24.5F	Dunham, D. Second cataract forts. Boston, 1960-67. 2v.
Arc 608.25F	Addison, F. Jebel Moya. London, 1949. 2v.
Arc 608.26F	Crawfard, O.G.S. Abu Geili. London, 1951.
Arc 608.28	Thouvenat, R. Volubilis. Paris, 1949.
Arc 608.30F	Pesce, G. Il tempio d'Iside in Sabratha. Roma, 1953.
Arc 608.30.5	Caputa, Giacomo. Il teatro di Sabatha e l'architettura teatrale africana. Roma, 1959.
Arc 608.31	Tarradell, M. Guia arqueológica del Marruecos Español. Tetuán, 1953.
Arc 608.32	Reyniers, F.L.M. Port à Utique. Alger, 1952.
Arc 608.32.5	Lézine, Alexandre. Utique. Tunis, 1970.
Arc 608.33	Neukom, Tolantha T. Pitture rupestri del Tasili degli Azger. Firenze, 1955.
Arc 608.33.5	Neukom, Tolantha T. Les peintures rupestres du Tassili-n-Ajjer. Neuchâtel, 1956.
Arc 608.33.10	Lajoux, Jean D. Merveilles du Tassili n'Ajjer. Paris, 1962.
Arc 608.33.15	Savary, Jean Pierre. Monuments en pierres sèches du Fadnoun, Tassili n'Ajjer. Paris, 1966.
Arc 608.35	Golvin, Lucien. Le Magrib central à l'époque des Zerides. Paris, 1957.
Arc 608.35.5	Golvin, Lucien. Recherches archéologiques à la Qal'a des Banû Hammâd. Paris, 1965.
Arc 608.36	Poinssot, Claude. Les ruines de Dougga. Tunis, 1958.
Arc 608.37	Haynes, D.E.L. An archaeological and historical guide to the pre-Islamic antiquities of Tripolitania. Tripoli, 1956.
Arc 608.38	Sérée de Roch. Tebessa. Alger, 1952.
Arc 608.39	Lhote, Henri. The search for the Tassili frescoes. London, 1959.

Arc 608 Archaeology - Local - North Africa except Egypt - General works; Local; Special topics - cont.

Arc 608.40	Forde-Johnston. Neolithic culture of North Africa. Liverpool, 1959.
Arc 608.42	McBurney, Charles. The stone age of Northern Africa. Harmondsworth, 1960.
Arc 608.42.5	McBurney, Charles. The Hana Fteah (Cyrenaica) and the Stone Age of the South-East Mediterranean. London, 1967.
Arc 608.45F	Paribeni, Enrico. Catalogo delle sculture di Cirene. Roma, 1959.
Arc 608.48	Goodchild, Richard G. Cyrene and Apollonia. Tripoli? 1959.
Arc 608.50	Etienne, Robert. Le guarbier nord-est de Volubilis. Paris, 1960. 2v.
Arc 608.52F	Traversari, Gustavo. L'altorilievo di Afrodite a Cirene. Roma, 1959.
Arc 608.54	Fernandez de Castro y Pedrera, R. Historia y exploración de las ruinas de Cazaza. Larache, 1943.
Arc 608.64	Meanié, Djinn. Cités anciennes de Mauritanie. Paris, 1961.
Arc 608.65	Foncher, L. Hodrumetum. Paris, 1964.
Arc 608.66	Hugot, Henri J. Recherches préhistoriques dans l'Ahazzar nord-occidental. Paris, 1963.
Arc 608.67	Tixier, Jacques. Typologie de l'épipaléolithique du Maghreb. Paris, 1963.
Arc 608.68	Birebent, Jean. Aquae Romanae. Alger, 1962.
Arc 608.69	Precleur-Canonge, Thérèse. La vie rurale en Afrique romaine d'après les mosaiques. Paris, 1962.
Arc 608.70	Leglay, Marcel. Saturne africain; monuments. Paris, 1961. 2v.
Arc 608.72	Camps, Gabriel. La nécropole mégalithique du Djebel Mazela à Bou Nouara. Paris, 1964.
Arc 608.73	Thamurida, fouilles du Service des antiquités du Maroc. v.1-2. Paris, 1965. 3v.
Arc 608.75	Aksha. Paris, 1966- 3v.
Arc 608.76	Camps-Fabrer, Henriette. Matière et art mobilier dans la préhistoire nord-africaine. Thèse. Paris, 1966.
Arc 608.78	Lefebvre, Gillette. Corpus des gravures et des peintures rupestres de la région de Constantine. Paris, 1967.
Arc 608.82	Katsnel'son, Isidor S. Napata i meroe-drevnie tsarstva sudzna. Moskva, 1970.
Arc 608.84	Ziegert, Helmut. Gebel Ben Ghnema und Nord-Tibesti; Habilitationsschrift. Wiesbaden, 1969.
Arc 608.86	Pamphlet vol. Carthage. 3 pam.
Arc 608.88.5	Ponsich, Michel. Recherches archéologiques à Tanger et dans sa région. Paris, 1970.
Arc 608.90	Mission Michela Schiff Giorgini. Soleb. Firenze, 1965- 2v.
Arc 608.92	Moscati, Sabatino. Tra Cartagine e Roma. Milano, 1971.
Arc 608.93	Lézine, Alexandre. Deux villes d'Ifriqiya: Sousse, Tunis. Paris, 1971.
Arc 608.94F	Solignac, Marcel. Les pierres écrites de la Berbérie orientale. Tunis, 1928.

Arc 609 Archaeology - Local - Subsaharan Africa

Arc 609.1	Bent, J.T. The ruined cities of Mashonaland. London, 1892.
Arc 609.1.4	Dillmann, A. Über die geschichtlichen Ergebnisse der Th. Bent'schen Reisen in Ostafrica. Berlin, 1894.
Arc 609.1.5	Willoughby, J.C. A narrative of further excavations at Zimbabye (Mashonaland). London, 1893.
Arc 609.1.7	Lenz, Oskar. Ophir und die Ruinen von Zimbabye. Prag, 1896.
Arc 609.1.9	Hall, R.N. The ancient ruins of Rhodesia. London, 1902.
Arc 609.1.10	Hall, R.N. The ancient ruins of Rhodesia. London, 1904.
Arc 609.1.13	Hall, R.N. Great Zimbabwe. London, 1905.
Arc 609.1.15	Hall, R.N. Pre-historic Rhodesia. Philadelphia, 1910.
Arc 609.1.17F	Maciver, D.R. Mediaeval Rhodesia. London, 1906.
Arc 609.1.20	Johnson, J.P. The pre-historic period in South Africa. London, 1912.
Arc 609.1.25	Rhodesia (Southern). Bureau of Publicity. The great Zimbabwe ruins. Bulawayo, 1930.
Arc 609.1.27	Jones, Neville. The prehistory of southern Rhodesia. Cambridge, Eng., 1949.
Arc 609.1.29	Fort Victoria, Southern Rhodesia. Town Management. Fort Victoria and the great Zimbabwe ruins. Bulawayo, 1929.
Arc 609.1.35	O'Brien, T.P. The prehistory of Uganda Protectorate. Cambridge, Eng., 1939.
Arc 609.1.40	Bruwer, Andries Johannes. Zimbabwe; Rhodesia's ancient greatness. Johannesburg, 1965.
Arc 609.1.45	Summers, Roger. Zimbabwe. Johannesburg, 1963.
Arc 609.1.50	Fletcher, Harold Clarkson. Psychic episodes of Great Zimbabwe. Johannesburg, 1941.
Arc 609.1.57	Caton-Thompson, Gertrude. The Zimbabwe culture: ruins and reactions. 2. ed. London, 1971.
Arc 609.2F	Littmann, Enno. Deutsche Aksum-Expedition. v.1-4. Berlin, 1913.
Arc 609.2.7F	Azaïs, R.P. Cinq années de recherches archéologiques en Ethiopie. Paris, 1931. 2v.
Arc 609.2.15	Garstang, John. Meroë, the city of the Ethiopians. Oxford, 1911.
Arc 609.2.20	Leroy, Jules. L'Éthiopie. Paris, 1973.
Arc 609.3F	Lebzelter, Viktor. Die Vorgeschichte von Süd- und Südwestafrica. Leipzig, 1930-34. 2v.
Arc 609.5	Seekirchner, A. Die geographischen und geopolitischen Grundlagen der sudafrikanischen Ruinenkultur. Memmingen, 1933.
Arc 609.6F	Fouché, Leo. Mapungubwe, ancient Bantu civilization on the Limpopo. Cambridge, Eng., 1937. 2v.
Arc 609.7	Davies, Oliver. Natal archaeological studies. Pietermaritzburg, 1952.
Arc 609.8	Kirkman, James Spedding. The Arab city of Gedi. London, 1954.
Arc 609.8.5	Kirkman, James Spedding. The tomb of the dated inscription at Gedi. London, 1960.
Arc 609.9	Clark, John Desmond. The prehistory of southern Africa. Harmondsworth, Middlesex, Eng., 1959.
Arc 609.9.6	Clark, John Desmond. The prehistoric cultures of the Horn of Africa. N.Y., 1972.
Arc 609.10	Davidson, Basil. Old Africa rediscovered. London, 1959.
Arc 609.12F	Rosenkranz, Ingrid. Rock paintings and petroglyphs of south and central Africa. Capetown, 1958.
Arc 609.13	Cole, Sonia Mary. The prehistory of east Africa. Harmondsworth, 1954.
Arc 609.13.2	Cole, Sonia Mary. The prehistory of east Africa. N.Y., 1963.
Arc 609.13.5	Cole, Sonia Mary. Early man in east Africa. London, 1958.

Classified Listing

Arc 609 Archaeology - Local - Subsaharan Africa - cont.

Arc 609.13.10 East African Vocation School in Pre-European African History and Archaeology. Prelude to East African history: a collection of papers given at the first East African Vocation School in Pre-European History and Archaeology, in December, 1962. London, 1966.

Arc 609.15 Johnson, Townley. Rock painting of the southwest Cape. Capetown, 1959.

Arc 609.16F Clark, John Desmond. Further paleo-anthropological studies in northern Lunda. Lisboa, 1968.

Arc 609.17F Shaw, Thurstan. Excavation at Dawu. Edinburgh, 1961.

Arc 609.17.10 Shaw, Thurstan. A bibliography of Nigerian archaeology. Ibadan, 1969.

Arc 609.17.15 Allison, Philip. Cross River monoliths. Laejos, 1968.

Arc 609.17.20 Lectures on Nigerian prehistory and archaeology. Ibadan, 1969.

Arc 609.18 Green, L.G. Something rich and strange. Capetown, 1962.

Arc 609.19 Gabd, Creighton. Stone age hunters of the Kafue. Boston, 1965.

Arc 609.20 Jaeger, Otto. Antiquities of north Ethiopia. Brockhaus, 1965.

Arc 609.20.5 Wendorf, Fred. A Middle Stone Age sequence from the Central Riff Valley, Ethiopia. Wrocław, 1974.

Arc 609.21 Brokensha, David W. Applied anthropology in English speaking Africa. Lexington, Ky., 1966.

Arc 609.22.5 Woodhouse, Herbert Charles. Archaelogy in southern Africa. Capetown, 1971.

Arc 609.23 Galloway, Alexander. The skeletal remains of Bambandyanalo. Johannesburg, 1959.

Arc 609.24 Fagan, Brian. Iron Age cultures in Zambia. London, 1967- 2v.

Arc 609.24.5 Vogel, Joseph O. Kamanejoza: an introduction to the Iron Age cultures of the Victoria Falls region. London, 1971.

Arc 609.28 Willett, Frank. Ife in the history of west African sculpture. N.Y., 1967.

Arc 609.30 Guide to the rock paintings of Tanzania. Dar es Salaam, 1965.

Arc 609.32 Shinnie, Peter L. The African Iron Age. Oxford, 1971.

Arc 609.34 Summers, Roger. Ancient ruins and vanished civilizations of southern Africa. Capetown, 1971.

Arc 609.35 Robinson, Keith Radcliffe. The Iron Age of the southern lake area of Malawi. Zomba, 1970.

Arc 609.36 Cole-King, P.A. Mwalawolemba on Mikolongwe Hill. Zomba, 1968.

Arc 609.37 Robinson, Keith Radcliffe. The early Iron Age in Malawi: an appraisal. Zomba, 1969.

Arc 609.38 Sandelowsky, B.H. Fingira; preliminary report. Zomba, 1968.

Arc 609.39 Inskeep, R.R. Preliminary investigation of a proto-historic cemetery at Nkudzi Bay, Malawi. Livingstone, 1965.

Arc 609.40 Davies, Oliver. Archaeology in Ghana. Edinburgh, 1961.

Arc 609.41 Davies, Oliver. The quarternary in the coastlands of Guinea. Glasgow, 1964.

Arc 610 Archaeology - Local - Europe in general - Folios [Discontinued]

Arc 610.5F Kemble, John M. Horae ferales. London, 1863.

Arc 612 Archaeology - Local - Europe in general - General works; Special topics

Arc 612.1 Undset, F. Jernalderens Begyndelse i nord Europa. Kristiania, 1881.

Arc 612.2 Hoernes, M. Urgeschichte der bildenden Kunst in Europa. Wien, 1898.

Arc 612.2.2 Hoernes, M. Urgeschichte der bildenden Kunst in Europa. 2. Aufl. Wien, 1915.

Arc 612.3 Munro, Robert. The lake-dwellings of Europe. London, 1890.

Arc 612.4 Müller, S. Urgeschichte Europas. Strassburg, 1905.

Arc 612.5 Müller, S. L'Europe préhistorique. Paris, 1907.

Arc 612.6 Hahne, Hans. Das vorgeschichtliche Europa. Bielefeld, 1910.

Arc 612.6.5 Hahne, Hans. 25 Jahre Siedlungsarchäologie. Leipzig, 1922.

Arc 612.7 Baring-Gould, S. Cliff castles and cave dwellings of Europe. London, 1911.

Arc 612.8 Cotteau, G.H. Le préhistorique en Europe. Paris, 1889.

Arc 612.9 Sacken, Eduard. Leitfaden zur Kunde des heidnischen Alterthümes. Wien, 1865.

Arc 612.10 Kimakowicz-Winnicki, M. Spinn und Webewerkzeuge. Würzburg, 1910.

Arc 612.11 Schuchhardt, Carl. Alteuropa. Strassburg, 1919.

Arc 612.11.2 Schuchhardt, Carl. Alteruopa; eine Vorgeschichte unseres Erdteils. 2. Aufl. Leipzig, 1926.

Arc 612.11.4 Schuchhardt, Carl. Alteuropa. Berlin, 1941.

Arc 612.12A Tyler, John Mason. The new stone age in northern Europe. N.Y., 1921.

Arc 612.12B Tyler, John Mason. The new stone age in northern Europe. N.Y., 1921.

Arc 612.13 Dottin, Georges. Les anciens peuples de l'Europe. Paris, 1916. 2v.

Arc 612.14 Neubert, Max. Die dorische Wanderung in ihren europaischen Zusammenhängen. Stuttgart, 1920.

Arc 612.15 Macalister, R.A.S. A text-book of European archaeology. Cambridge, Eng., 1921.

Arc 612.16 Åberg, Nils. Die Franken und Westgoten in der Volkewanderungszeit. Uppsala, 1922.

Arc 612.17 Johansen, K. Friis. De forhistoriske tider i Europa. København, 1927. 2v.

Arc 612.18 Gotbe, I.V. Ocherki po istorii...Evropy. Leningrad, 1925.

Arc 612.19 Childe, Vere G. The Danube in prehistory. Oxford, 1929.

Arc 612.19.5 Childe, Vere G. The prehistory of European society. Harmondsworth, 1958.

Arc 612.20 Much, M. Die Trugspiegelung orientalischer Kultur in den vorgeschichtlichen Zeitaltern Nord- und Mitteleuropas. Jena, 1907.

Arc 612.21 Åberg, Nils. Studier öfver den yngre stenildern i Norden och Vosteuropa. Norrköping, 1912.

Arc 612.21.7F Åberg, Nils. Bronzezeitliche und früheisenzeitliche Chronologie. v.4-5. Stockholm, 1933-35. 2v.

Arc 612.22F Baye, Joseph. De l'influence de l'art des Goths en Occident. Paris, 1891.

Arc 612.23 Clark, John Desmond. The mesolithic settlement of northern Europe. Cambridge, Eng., 1936.

Arc 612.24 Dellenbach, M.E. La conquête du massif alpin et de ses abords. Thèse. Grenoble, 1935.

Arc 612.25 Hahne, Hans. Totenehre im alten Norden. Jena, 1929.

Arc 612.26 Fock, G. Die steinzeitlichen Keulen Mitteleuropas. Inaug. Diss. Düsseldorf, 1937.

Arc 612 Archaeology - Local - Europe in general - General works; Special topics - cont.

Arc 612.27 Rydh, H. Grott-människornas årtusenden. Stockholm, 1926.

Arc 612.28 Hawkes, C.F.C. The prehistoric foundations of Europe to the Mycenean age. London, 1940.

Arc 612.29 Philipp, H. Vor- und Frühgeschichte des Nordens und des Mittelmeerraumes. Berlin, 1937.

Arc 612.30 Bumüller, J. Leitfaden der Vorgeschichte Europas. Augsburg, 1925. 2v.

Arc 612.31 Pittioni, Richard. Die urgeschichtlichen Grundlagen der europäischen Kultur. Wien, 1949.

Arc 612.32 Zatz, L.F. Altsteinzeitkunde Mitteleuropas. Stuttgart, 1951.

Arc 612.33 Clark, John Desmond. Prehistoric Europe. London, 1952.

Arc 612.34 Laming, A. L'art préhistorique. Paris, 1951.

Arc 612.34.5 Laming, A. La signification de l'art rupestre paléolithique. Paris, 1962.

Arc 612.36 Kühn, Herbert. Die Felsbilder Europas. Zürich, 1952.

Arc 612.36.5 Kühn, Herbert. Die Kunst Alteuropas. Stuttgart, 1958.

Arc 612.37 Rust, Alfred. Werkzeuge des Frühmenschen in Europa. Neumünster, 1971.

Arc 612.38 Behn, Friedrich. Aus europäischer Vorzeit. Stuttgart, 1957.

Arc 612.40 Laviosa, Zambotti. Il mediterraneo. Torino, 1954.

Arc 612.42 Briard, Jacques. L'Age du Bronze. Paris, 1959.

Arc 612.44 Koztowski, J.K. Próba klasyfikacji górnopaleolitycznych przemysłów z płoszczami lesciowatymi w Europie. Krakow, 1961.

Arc 612.45 Holmqvist, Wilhelm. Germanic art during the first millenium. Stockholm, 1955.

Arc 612.46 Symposium Consacre aux Problèmes du Neolithique Européen. L'Europe à la fin de l'âge de la pierre. Praha, 1961.

Arc 612.47 Frost, H. Under the Mediterranean. London, 1963.

Arc 612.48 Akademiia Nauk SSSR. Institut Arkheologii. Pamiatniki kamennogo i bronz. vekov Evrazii. Moskva, 1964.

Arc 612.49 Stacul, Giorgio. La grande madre. Roma, 1963.

Arc 612.50 Piggott, Stuart. Ancient Europe from the beginings of agriculture to classical antiquity. Edinburgh, 1965.

Arc 612.51 Lukan, Karl. Alpenwanderungen in die Vorzeit zu Drachenhöhlen und Druidensteinen. Wien, 1965.

Arc 612.52F Dieck, Alfred. Die europäischen Moorleichenfunde. Neumünster, 1965.

Arc 612.53 Filip, Jan. Evropský pravěk. Praha, 1962.

Arc 612.53.5 Filip, Jan. Enzyklopädisches Handbuch zur Ur- und Frühgeschichte Europas. Stuttgart, 1966. 2v.

Arc 612.55F Gimbutas, Marija Alseikaites. Bronze age kultures in central and eastern Europe. The Hague, 1965.

Arc 612.55.5 Gimbutas, Marija Alseikaites. The gods and goddesses of old Europe, 7000 to 3500 B.C. London, 1974.

Arc 612.56 Abramova, Zoia. Izobrasheniia cheloveka v paleoliticheskom iskusstve Evrazii. Leningrad, 1966.

Arc 612.57 Chernych, Evgenii N. Istoriia drevneishei metallurgii Vostochnoi Evropy. Moskva, 1966.

Arc 612.57.5 Ryndina, Nataliia Vadimovna. Drevneishee metalloobrabatyvainshchee proiznodstno Vostochnoi Evropy. Moskva, 1971.

Arc 612.60 Laplace, Georges. Recherches sur l'origine et l'évolution des complexes leptolithiques. Paris, 1966.

Arc 612.65 Behn, Friedrich. Die Bronzezeit in Nordeuropa. Bildnis einer prähistorischen Hochkultur. Stuttgart, 1967.

Arc 612.66 Congrès International d'Archéologie Slave, 1st, Warsaw, 1965. I międzynarodoury kongres Archeologii Słowianskiej. Wrocław, 1968. 7v.

Arc 612.66.5 Congrès International d'Archéologie Slave, 2d. Berichte. Berlin, 1970. 3v.

Arc 612.67 Grigor'ev, Gennadii P. Machalo verkhnego paleolita i proiskhozhdenie Homo Sapiens. Leningrad, 1968.

Arc 612.68 Studies in ancient Europe. Leicester, 1968.

Arc 612.69 Sympozjum Paleolityczne, 3d, Kraków, 1967. III. sympozjum paleolityczne, Kraków 30 XI-2 XII, 1967. v.1-2. Kraków, 1967.

Arc 612.70 Archaeologia urbiom. Warszawa, 1966. 2v.

Arc 612.71 Bachelot de la Pylaie, Auguste Jean Marie. Études archéologiques et géographiques. Quimper, 1970.

Arc 612.72 L'archéologie du village médiéval. Louvain, 1967.

Arc 612.73 Tabaczyński, Stanisław. Neolit środkowaeuropejski. Wrocław, 1970.

Arc 612.74 Studien zur europäischen Vor- und Frühgeschichte. Neumünster, 1968.

Arc 612.76 Krueger, Karl Heinrich. Königsgrabkirchen der Franken. München, 1971.

Arc 612.77 Medieval pottery from excavations. London, 1974.

Arc 612.78 Kowalczyk, Jan. Zmierzch epoki kamicnia. Wrocław, 1971.

Arc 612.79 Recent archaeological excavations in Europe. London, 1975.

Arc 612.80 Murray, Jacqueline. The first European agriculture. Edinburgh, 1970.

Arc 612.82 Kozłowski, Janusz. Munj cyklopów. Wrocław, 1971.

Arc 612.83 Background to archaeology; Britain in its European setting. Cambridge, 1973.

Arc 612.86 Albrecht, Gerd. Merkmalanalyse von Geschossspitzen des mittleren Jungpleistozäns im Mittel- und Osteuropa. Stuttgart, 1972.

Arc 612.87 Lange, Elsbeth. Botanisch Beiträge zur mitteleuropäischen Siedlungsgeschichte. Berlin, 1971.

Arc 612.88 International Archaeological Symposium on the Mesolithic in Europe. The mesolithic in Europe. Wyd. 1. Warsaw, 1973.

Arc 612.89 Renfrew, Colin. Before civilization; the radiocarbon revolution and prehistoric Europe. London, 1973.

Arc 612.90 Mongait, Aleksandr L. Arkheologiia Zapadnoi Evropy. Moskva, 1973- 2v.

Arc 612.91 Woźniak, Zenon. Wschodnie pogranicze kultury lateńskiej. Wrocław, 1974.

Arc 612.92 Symposium über die Entstehung und Chronologie der Badener Kultur, Archäologisches Institut der Slowakischen Akademie der Wissenschaften, 1969. Symposium über die Entstehung und Chronologie der Badener Kultur. Bratislava, 1973.

Arc 612.93 Schneider, Renate-Ursula. Zur Südabgrenzung des Bereichs der nordischen jüngeren Bronzezeit in Periode IV nach Montelius. Hamburg, 1971.

Arc 615 Archaeology - Local - Celtic in general - Folios [Discontinued]

Arc 615.5 Waring, J.B. Stone monuments...of remote ages. London, 1870.

Arc 618 Archaeology - Local - Celtic in general - General works; Special topics

Arc 618.1 Reinach, S. Les celtes dans les vallées du Po et du Danube. Paris, 1894.
Arc 618.2 Roger, J.C. Celticism a myth. 2. ed. London, 1889.
Arc 618.3 Mallet, J.W. Account of a chemical examination of the Celtic antiquities. Dublin, 1852.
Htn Arc 618.4* Keysler, J.G. Antiquitas...septentrionales et celticae. Hannover, 1720.
Arc 618.5 Martin, Henri. Études d'archéologie celtique. Paris, 1872.
Arc 618.6A Allen, J. Romilly. Celtic art in pagan and Christian times. London, 1904.
Arc 618.6B Allen, J. Romilly. Celtic art in pagan and Christian times. London, 1904.
Arc 618.7 Higgins, G. The Celtic druids. London, 1827.
Arc 618.7.3 Higgins, G. The Celtic druids. London, 1829.
Arc 618.8 Jacobsthal, P. Imagery in early Celtic art. London, 1941.
Arc 618.9 Verworm, M. Keltische Kunst. Berlin, 1919.
Arc 618.10 Fox, Cyril. Pattern and purpose. Cardiff, 1958.
Arc 618.11 Todorovic, Jovan. Kelti u jugoistočnoj Evropi. Beograd, 1968.

Arc 625 Archaeology - Local - Greek and Roman together - Folios [Discontinued]

Arc 625.2 Ivanoff, S.A. Architektonische Studien. Berlin, 1892-95. 3v.
Arc 625.2PF Ivanoff, S.A. Architektonische Studien. Berlin, 1892-95. 4v.
Arc 625.4 Gerhard, E. Antike Bildwerke. Text. München, 1828.
Arc 625.5.2 Erklaren der Text. v.1-2. 2. Aufl. Leipzig, 1901.
Arc 625.7 Fongères, G. La vie...des Grecs et des Romains. Paris, 1894.
Arc 625.8 Festschrift für Johannes Overbeck. Leipzig, 1893.
Arc 625.9 Sturgis, R. Classical archaeology on the shores of the Mediterranean. Rochester, n.d.
Arc 625.10 Festschrift für Otto Benndorf. Wien, 1898.
Arc 625.11 Antiquités grecques et romaines. Paris, 1904.
Arc 625.12 Delestre, M. Collection d'antiquités, grecques et romaines. Paris, 1901.
Arc 625.13 Schneider, R. von. Album...Antike-Sammlung. Wien, 1895.

Arc 628 Archaeology - Local - Greek and Roman together - General works

Arc 628.1 Nissen, H. Pompeji. 2. Aufl. Berlin, 1827. 22 pam.
Arc 628.2 Jahn, O. Socrate et Diotime. Greifswald, 1846. 9 pam.
Arc 628.3 Oehler, R. Klassisches Bilderbuch. n.p., 1892?
Arc 628.4 Müller, K.O. Denkmäler der alten Kunst. Göttingen, 1854-81. 2v.
Arc 628.4.2 Müller, K.O. Denkmäler der alten Kunst. v.1-2. Göttingen, 1832.
Arc 628.5 Schreiber, T. Atlas of classical antiquities. London, 1895.
Arc 628.6 Rheinhard, H. Album des klassischen Alterthums. Stuttgart, 1882.
Arc 628.7 Biagi, C. Monumenta Graeca ex Museo Jacobi Nanni. Monumenta Graeca et Latina Jacobi Nanni. Roma, 1785-87. 2v.
Arc 628.8 Welcker, F.G. Alte Denkmäler. v.1-5. Göttingen, 1849-64. 4v.
Arc 628.9 Lovatelli-Caetani, E. Antichi monumenti illustrati. Roma, 1889.
Arc 628.10 Spon, J. Voyage d'Italie, de Dalmatie, de Grèce. La Haye, 1724. 2v.
Arc 628.11 Urlichs, L. von. Beiträge zur Kunstgeschichte. Leipzig, n.d.
Arc 628.12 Brunn, H. Kleine Schriften. Leipzig, 1898. 3v.
Arc 628.13 Luckenbach, H. Abbildungen zur Alten Geschichte der Oberen Klassen. München, 1898.
Arc 628.13.5 Luckenbach, H. Kunst und Geschichte. München, 1902-03. 3v.
Arc 628.13.7 Luckenbach, H. Kunst und Geschichte. München, 1904.
Arc 628.13.8 Luckenbach, H. Kunst und Geschichte. 6. Aufl. München, 1906.
Arc 628.14 Strema Helbigiana. Leipzig, 1900.
Arc 628.16 Lang, G. Von Rom nach Sardes. Stuttgart, 1900.
Arc 628.17 Luckenbach, H. Antike Kunstwerke im klassischen Unterricht. München, 1901.
Arc 628.18 Melanges Perrot; recueil de memoires. Paris, 1903.
Arc 628.19 Olenin', A.N. Arkheologicheskie trudy. v.1-3. Sankt Peterburg, 1877-82.
Arc 628.20 Couch, Herbert N. The treasuries of the Greeks and Romans. Menasha, 1929.
Arc 628.20.5 Couch, Herbert N. Treasure of the Greeks and Romans. Thesis. Menasha, 1929.
Arc 628.21 Visconti, Pietro E. La stazione della coorte VII dei vigili e i ricordi istorici. 2. ed. Roma, 1867. 19 pam.
Arc 628.22 Pamphlet vol. Hübner, E. Opuscules. 16 pam.
Arc 628.23 Elderkin, G.W. Archeological papers. v.1-5, 6-10. Springfield, Mass., 1941- 2v.
Arc 628.24 Knell, Heiner. Archäologie. Darmstadt, 1972.
Arc 628.25F Corolla archaeologica principi hereditario regni sueciae Gustavo Adolpho dedicata. Lund, 1932.
Arc 628.27 Paribeni, R. Filologia classica. Milano, 1945.
Arc 628.28 Onofrio, Cesare d'. Quando il cielo stava quaggiù. Roma, 1960.
Arc 628.30 Calderini, A. Dizionario di antichità greche e romane. Milano, 1960.
Arc 628.32 Nemirovskii, Aleksandr I. Nit' Ariadny. Voronesh, 1972.

Arc 630 Archaeology - Local - Greek and Roman together - Special topics

Arc 630.1 Fink, J. Der Verschluss bei den Griechen und Römern. Regensburg, 1890.
Arc 630.2 Castan, Auguste. Les capitoles provinciaux du monde romain. Besançon, 1886.
Arc 630.3 Jordt, H. Untersuch über Silikat und Carbenatbiblung in antiken Morteln. Leipzig, 1906.
Arc 630.4 Sybel, L. von. Die klassische Archäologie und die altchristliche Kunst. Marburg, 1906.
Arc 630.5 Sumbolae Leitt. im Honorem Julii de Petra. Neapoli, 1911.
Arc 630.6 British Museum. Catalogue of Greek and Roman lamps in the British Museum. London, 1914.
Arc 630.7 Spoor, Henricus. Favissae utriusque antiqtam Romanae quam Graecae. Ultrajecti, 1707.
Arc 630.8 Woelcke, Karl. Beiträge zur Geschichte des Tropaions. Bonn, 1911.
Arc 630.9 Cook, Arthur B. Rise and progress of classical archaeology. Cambridge, Eng., 1931.
Arc 630.10 Martini, G.H. Antiquorum monimentorum, sylloge altera. Lipsiae, 1787.

Arc 630 Archaeology - Local - Greek and Roman together - Special topics - cont.

Arc 630.11F Herbig, R. Ganymed; Heidelberger Beiträge zur antiken Kunstgeschichte. Heidelberg, 1949.
Arc 630.11.5 Herbig, R. Vermächtnis der antiken Kunst. Heidelberg, 1950.
Arc 630.12 Schefold, Karl. Orient, Hellas und Rom in der archäologischen Forschungszeit 1939. Bern, 1949.
Arc 630.13 Stevens, G.P. Restorations of classical buildings. Princeton, N.J., 1955.
Arc 630.15 Schefold, Karl. Basler Antiken im Bild. Basel, 1958.
Arc 630.17 Oikonomes, Georgios P. De profusionum receptaeulis sepulchalilus. Athenis, 1921.
Arc 630.20 Thieman, Eugen. Hellenistische Vatergottheiten. Münster, 1959.
Arc 630.22 Simon, Erika. Die Geburt der Aphrodite. Berlin, 1959.

Arc 632 Archaeology - Local - Greek and Roman together - Miscellany [Discontinued]

Arc 632 Pamphlet box. Archaeology. Greece and Rome. 39 pam.
Arc 632.4 Pamphlet box. Archaeology. Greece and Rome. 7 pam.

Arc 635 Archaeology - Local - Greece - Folios [Discontinued]

Arc 635.4 Curtius, E. Die Funde von Olympia. Berlin, 1882.
Arc 635.10 Strack, J.H. Das Altgriechisches Theatergebäude. Potsdam, 1843.
Arc 635.13 Cavvadias, P. Fouilles d'Épidaure. Athène, 1893.
Arc 635.17 Lebas, P. Voyage archéologique en Grèce et en Asie Mineure. Paris, 1847-77. 5v.
Arc 635.20F Hiller von Gärtringen. Thera 1895-. Berlin, 1899- 4v.
Arc 635.24 Maraghiannio, G. Antiquités crétoises. Vienne, n.d.
Arc 635.24.5 Maraghiannio, G. Antiquités crétoises. 2. série. Athène, 1911.
Arc 635.200 Conze, A. Archäologische Untersuchungen auf Samothrake. Wien, 1875-80. 2v.
Arc 635.201 Normand, C. Corpus des monuments grecs. Livre II: Lycosoura. Paris, n.d.
Arc 635.203 Bröndsted, P.O. Voyages dans la Gréce. Paris, 1826.
Arc 635.204 Heuzey, L. Mission archéologique de Macédoine. Paris, 1876.
Arc 635.205 Benndorf, O. Die Metopen von Selinunt. Berlin, 1873.
Arc 635.206 Dumon, K. Le théâtre de Polyclète. Paris, 1889.
Arc 635.207 Furtwängler, A. Archäologische Studien...Heinrich Brunn...dargebracht. Berlin, 1893.
Arc 635.207.5 Furtwängler, A. Ägena, das Heiligtum der Aphaia. Text and atlas. München, 1906. 2v.
Arc 635.207.9 Fiechter, E.R. Der Tempel der Aphaia auf Aegena. München, 1906.
Arc 635.208 Association pour l'Encouragement des Études Grècques en France, Paris. Monuments grècs. Paris, 1882-97. 2v.
Arc 635.209 Kabbadias, P. Fouilles de Lycosoura. Série 1. Athène, 1893.
Arc 635.210 Kinch, K.F. L'Arc de Triomphe de Salonique. Paris, 1890.
Arc 635.211 Cabrol, E. Voyage en Grèce. Paris, 1890.
Arc 635.212 Carapanos, C. Dodone et ses ruines. Paris, 1878. 2v.
Arc 635.213 Sittl, C. Parerga zur alten Kunstgeschichte. Würzburg, 1893.
Arc 635.214 Stillman, W.J. On the track of Ulysses. Boston, 1888.
Htn Arc 635.215* Wheler, G. A journey into Greece. London, 1682.
Arc 635.216 Curtius, E. Zur Geschichte des Wegebaus bei den Griechen. Berlin, 1855.
Arc 635.217 Homolle, T. Fouilles de Delphes. 1902+ 19v.
Arc 635.217.5F Homolle, T. Exploratoire archéologique de Délos. Paris. 1-30 7v.
Arc 635.217.10 Deonna, W. La vie privée des Déliens. Paris, 1948.
Arc 635.218 Skovgaard, N.K. Apollon - Gavlgruppen fra Zeustemp. Olympia. København, 1905.
Arc 635.219 Mnémeia. Tēs Ellados. Athēnai, 1906.
Arc 635.220 Tsoynta, C. Ai Proistorikai...diménioy kaiseskloy. Athēnai, 1900.
Arc 635.221 Seta, A.D. La genesi dello Scorcio nell'arte greca. Roma, 1907.
Arc 635.222 Wace, A.J.B. Prehistoric Thessaly. Cambridge, 1912.
Arc 635.223F Frickenhaus, A. Tiryns. v.1-8. Athēnai, 1912- 9v.
Arc 635.224F Schwab, G.H. An archaeological cruise in the Levant. N.Y.? 1904.
Arc 635.225F Vogell, A. Griechische Alterthümer südrussischen Fundorts. Cassel, 1908.
Arc 635.226F Blegen, Carl W. Korakou, a prehistoric settlement near Corinth. Boston, 1921.

Arc 638 Archaeology - Local - Greece - Pamphlet volumes

Arc 638.1 Hesselmeyer, E. Die Ursprunge der Stadt Pergamos in Kleinasien. Tübingen, 1884-85. 7 pam.
Arc 638.3 Michaelis, A.T.F. Il Leone Nemeo. Roma, 1859. 7 pam.
Arc 638.4 Kirckhoff, C. Der Rhombus in der Orchestra des Dionysustheaters zu Athen. Altona, 1885. 3 pam.
Arc 638.5 Pamphlet vol. Greek Archaeology. 36 pam.
Arc 638.5.2 Pamphlet vol. Greek archaeology. 7 pam.
Arc 638.6 Pamphlet vol. Mykenische Archäologie 1875-1903. 2 pam.
Arc 638.7 Pamphlet vol. Greek archaeology. Furtwängler pamphlets. 8 pam.
Arc 638.7.2 Pamphlet vol. Greek archaeology. Furtwängler pamphlets. 20 pam.
Arc 638.7.3 Pamphlet vol. Greek archaeology. Furtwängler pamphlets. 11 pam.
Arc 638.8 Pamphlet box. Greek archaeology. Miscellaneous pamphlets.

Arc 640 - 665 Archaeology - Local - Greece - General works (A-Z)

Arc 641.1 Blenkenberg, C. Archäologische Studien. Leipzig, 1904.
Arc 641.2 Börger, Hans. Griechische Reisetage. Hamburg, 1925.
Arc 641.4A Bouzek, Jan. Homerisches Griechenland im Lichte der archäologischen Quellen. Praha, 1969.
Arc 641.4B Bouzek, Jan. Homerisches Griechenland im Lichte der archäologischen Quellen. Praha, 1969.
Arc 641.5 Buchholz, Hans-Günter. Prehistoric Greece and Cyprus: an archaeological handbook. London, 1973.
Arc 642.1 Chase, T. Hellas. Cambridge, 1863.
Arc 642.2A Collignon, Maxime. Manuel d'archéologie grecque. Paris, 1881.
Arc 642.2B Collignon, Maxime. Manuel d'archéologie grecque. Paris, 1881.
Arc 642.2.3 Collignon, Maxime. Manuel d'archéologie grecque. Paris, 188-.
Arc 642.2.5A Collignon, Maxime. A manual of Greek archaeology. London, 1886.

Classified Listing

Arc 640 - 665 Archaeology - Local - Greece - General works (A-Z) - cont.

Arc 642.2.5B Collignon, Maxime. A manual of Greek archaeology. London, 1886.
Arc 642.2.6 Collignon, Maxime. A manual of Greek archaeology. N.Y., 1886.
Arc 642.2.15 Collignon, Maxime. L'archéologie grecque. Paris, n.d.
Arc 642.3 Conze, A. Rapporto d'un viaggio fatto nella Grecia nel 1860. Roma, 1861.
Arc 642.3.2 Conze, A. Reise auf Inseln des Thrak. Meeres. Hannover, 1860.
Arc 642.4 Cousinéry, E.M. Voyage dans la Macédoine. Paris, 1831. 2v.
Arc 642.5 Ciriacus, Pizzicolli. Itinerarium. Florentiae, 1742.
Arc 642.6 Casson, S. Essays in Aegean archaeology. Oxford, 1927.
Arc 642.7F Chisholm, H.J. Hellas. N.Y., 1943.
Arc 642.8 Cottrell, Leonard. The bull of Minos. London, 1953.
Arc 642.8.1 Cottrell, Leonard. The bull of Minos. London, 1971.
Arc 642.8.5 Cottrell, Leonard. The bull of Minos. London, 1962.
Arc 642.9 Carpenter, Rhys. The humanistic value of archaeology. Cambridge, Mass., 1933.
Arc 642.10 Cook, R.M. The Greeks till Alexander. London, 1961.
Arc 642.11 Colloquium on Bronze Age Migrations in the Aegean Region, Sheffield, Eng., 1970. Bronze Age migrations in the Aegean. London, 1973.
Arc 643.1 Diehl, C. Excursions archéologiques en Grèce. Paris, 1890.
Arc 643.1.4 Diehl, C. Excursions archéologiques en Grèce. 5. éd. Paris, 1903.
Arc 643.1.5A Diehl, C. Excursions in Greece. London, 1893.
Arc 643.1.5B Diehl, C. Excursions in Greece. London, 1893.
Arc 643.2 Dodwell, E. A classical and topographical tour through Greece. London, 1819. 2v.
Arc 645.1 Forchhammer, P.W. Hellenika. Berlin, 1837.
Arc 645.2.2A Fowler, H.N. Handbook of Greek archaeology. N.Y., 1909.
Arc 645.2.2B Fowler, H.N. Handbook of Greek archaeology. N.Y., 1909.
Arc 645.3 Fuchs, Siegfried. Die griechischen Fundgruppen der frühen Bronzezeit und ihre auswärtigen Beziehungen. Berlin, 1937.
Arc 646.1 Gell, W. The itinerary of Greece: the geography of Ithaca. v.1-2. London, 1810.
Arc 646.2 Gerhard, E. Archäologischer Nachlass aus Rom. Berlin, 1952.
Arc 646.3 Guillet de St.-George, George. Lettres écrites sur une dissertation d'un voyage de Grèce. Paris, 1679.
Arc 646.4 Gennadios, I. O Lordoz Elgin. Athēnai, 1930.
Arc 647.1 Heuzey, L. Le Mont Olympe et l'Acarnanie. Paris, 1860.
Arc 647.2 Herzog, A. Studien zur Geschichte der griechischen Kunst. Leipzig, 1888.
Arc 647.3A Hall, H.R. Aegean archaeology. London, 1915.
Arc 647.3B Hall, H.R. Aegean archaeology. London, 1915.
Arc 647.3.2A Hall, H.R. Aegean archaeology. London, 1915.
Arc 647.3.2B Hall, H.R. Aegean archaeology. London, 1915.
Arc 647.3.5 Hall, H.R. The civilization of Greece in the bronze age. London, 1928.
Arc 650.1 Klenze, L. von. Aphoristische Bemerkungen gesammelt...Reise nach Griechenland. Berlin, 1838.
Arc 650.10 Kirsten, Ernst. Griechenlandkunde. Heidelberg, 1955.
Arc 650.10.5 Kirsten, Ernst. Griechenlandkunde; ein Führer zu klassischen Stätten. Heidelberg, 1956.
Arc 650.10.7 Kirsten, Ernst. Griechenlandkunde. 3. Aufl. Heidelberg, 1957.
Arc 650.11 Kultura materialna starożytnej Grecji. Wrocław, 1975.
X Cg Arc 651.1 Le Bas, P. Voyage archéologique en Grèce et en Asie Mineure. Paris, 1888.
Arc 651.2 Lethaby, W.R. Greek buildings. London, 1908.
Arc 651.3 Lichtenberg, R.F. Die ägäische Kultur. Leipzig, 1911.
Arc 651.3.2 Lichtenberg, R.F. Die ägäische Kultur. 2. Aufl. Leipzig, 1918.
Arc 652.1 Mure, W. Journal of a tour in Greece. Edinburgh, 1842. 2v.
Arc 652.2 Mahaffy, J.P. Rambles and studies in Greece. London, 1876.
Arc 652.3 Mélanges Holleaux - recueil de memoires concernant l'antiquité grecque offert à Maurice Holleaux. Paris, 1913.
Arc 652.4 Marshall, Fred H. Discovery in Greek lands. Cambridge, 1920.
Arc 652.5F Montelius, Oscar. La Grèce préclassique. Stockholm, 1924-28. 2v.
Arc 652.6 Mylonas, G.E. Hē neolithike epoche en Helladi. Athēnai, 1928.
Arc 652.7F Majewski, K. Kultura materialna starozytnej Grecji. Warszawa, 1956.
Arc 652.8 MacKendrick, P.L. The Greek stories speak. N.Y., 1962.
Arc 653.1 Nebraska. University. Catalogue of Greece and Sicily. Lincoln, Neb., 1905.
Arc 653.2 Neue Ausgrabungen in Griechenland. Olten, 1963.
Arc 654.1 Kunze, Emil. Olympische Forschungen. Berlin, 1944-8v.
Arc 654.1PF Olympische Forschungen. Plates. Berlin, 1944-50.
Arc 655.1 Philios, Demetrios. Peri tou pōs graphontai ta tōn araskaphōn. Athēnai, 1890.
Arc 655.5 Pannati, Ulrico. L'archeologia in Grecia. Napoli, 1965.
Arc 655.6 Perowne, Stewart. The archaeology of Greece and the Aegean. London, 1974.
Arc 657.1 Reinach, S. Conseils aux voyageurs archéologues en Grèce. Paris, 1886.
Arc 657.2 Pasch van Krienen. Abdruck seiner italienischer Beschreibung des griechisches Archipelagus. Halle, 1860.
Arc 657.2.2 Ross, L. Reisen und Reiseronten durch Griechenland. Berlin, 1841.
Arc 657.2.3 Ross, L. Reisen und der griechischen Inseln. v.1-3. Stuttgart, 1840-45.
Arc 658.3 Schliemann, H. Ithaka, der Peleponnes und Troja. Leipzig, 1869.
Arc 658.3.1 Schliemann, H. Briefe von Heinrich Schliemann. Berlin, 1936.
Arc 658.3.2 Chase, T. Dr. Schliemann and the archaeological value of his discoveries. Worcester, 1891.
Arc 658.3.3A Schuchhardt, K. Schliemann's excavations. London, 1891.
Arc 658.3.3B Schuchhardt, K. Schliemann's excavations. London, 1891.
Arc 658.3.3C Schuchhardt, K. Schliemann's excavations. London, 1891.
NEDL Arc 658.3.4 Schuchhardt, K. Schliemanns Ausgrabungen. Leipzig, 1890.
Arc 658.3.5A Schuchhardt, K. Schliemanns Ausgrabungen. Leipzig, 1891.
Arc 658.3.5B Schuchhardt, K. Schliemanns Ausgrabungen. Leipzig, 1891.
Arc 658.3.7 Schliemann, Heinrich. Abenteuer meines Lebens. Leipzig, 1960.
Arc 658.3.8 Schliemann, Heinrich. Schliemann in Indianapolis. Indianapolis, 1961.

Arc 640 - 665 Archaeology - Local - Greece - General works (A-Z) - cont.

Arc 658.3.9 Nelson, J. Heinrich Schliemann und die Homersche Welt. Leipzig, 1900.
Arc 658.3.11 Brinckmeier. Heinrich Schliemann und die Ausgrabungen auf Hissarlik. Burg, 1901.
Arc 658.3.14 Ludwig, Emil. Schliemann. Berlin, 1932.
Arc 658.3.15A Ludwig, Emil. Schliemann. Boston, 1932.
Arc 658.3.15B Ludwig, Emil. Schliemann. Boston, 1932.
Arc 658.3.16 Ludwig, Emil. Schliemann. Boston, 1931.
Arc 658.3.17 Ludwig, Emil. Schliemann of Troy. London, 1931.
Arc 658.3.20 Weber, Shirley H. Schliemann's first visit to America, 1850-1851. Cambridge, 1942.
Arc 658.3.22 Meyer, Ernst. Heinrich Schliemann: Kaufmann und Forscher. Göttingen, 1969.
Arc 658.3.25 Brusti, Franz Georg. Heinrich Schliemann. München, 1971.
Arc 658.10 Styrenius, Carl Gustaf. Submycenaean studies. Lund, 1967.
Arc 658.15 Stubbings, Frank Henry. Prehistoric Greece. London, 1972.
Arc 659.3 Tsountas, Chrēstos. The Mycenaean age. London, 1897.
Arc 659.5 Tsountas, Chrēstos. Istoria tēs archaias Hellēnikēs technēs. Athēnai, 1928.
Arc 659.10 Terzaghi, Nicola. Prometeo; scritti di archeologia e filologia. Torino, 1966.
Arc 659.12 Titov, Valerii S. Neolit Gretsii. Moskva, 1969.
Arc 659.15 Tagung das Problem der Klassik im Alten Orient und in der Antike, Halle, 1966. Das Problem der klassik im Alten Orient und in der Antike. Berlin, 1967.
Arc 659.20F Theocharēs, Dēmētrios R. Neolithikē Hellas. Athēnai, 1973.
Arc 660.1 Ulrichs, H.N. Reisen und Forschungen in Griechenland. pt.1-2. Bremen, 1840.
Arc 662.1 Wyse, T. An excursion in the Peloponnesus. London, 1865-2v.
Arc 662.2 Wordsworth, C. Athens and Attica. Journal of a residence there. London, 1837.
Arc 662.3 Woodhouse, W.J. Aetolia, its geography and antiquities. Oxford, 1897.
Arc 662.4 Weissmann, K. Beiträge zur Erklärung...griechische Kunstwerke. Schweinfurt, 1903.
Arc 662.5 Wheeler, J.R. Archaeology. N.Y., 1908.
Arc 662.6 Warner, R. Eternal Greece. N.Y., 1962.
Arc 665.1 Ziebarth, E. Kulturbilder aus griechischen Städten. Leipzig, 1907.

Arc 670 - 695 Archaeology - Local - Greece - Local except Athens (A-Z by place)

Arc 670.1 Rangabé, A.R. Souvenirs d'une excursion d'Athènes en Arcadie. Paris, 1857.
Arc 670.2 Schildt, A. Die Giebelgruppen von Aegina. Leipzig, 1895.
Arc 670.2.3 Furtwängler, A. Die Ägineten der Glypotothek König Ludwigs I. München, 1906.
Arc 670.2.5 Groote, M. von. Ägineten und Archäologen. Strassburg, 1912.
Arc 670.2.7 Harland, J.P. Prehistoric Aigina. Diss. Paris, 1925.
Arc 670.2.9 Weeter, G. Aigina. Berlin, 1938.
Arc 670.3 Hastings, H.R. Relations between inscriptions and sculptured representations on Attica tombstones. Madison, 1912.
Arc 670.3.5 Gerando, A. de. Gróf teleki Emma Görögorszagi a Rége Attikanak. Pest, 1873.
Arc 670.3.10 Wrede, W. Attika. Athens, 1934.
Arc 670.4F Walston, Charles. Excavations at the Heraion of Argos. 1892. Boston, 1892.
Arc 670.4.5F Walston, Charles. The Argive Heraeum. Boston, 1902-05. 2v.
Arc 670.5F Frödin, Otto. Asine; results of the Swedish excavations 1922-1930. Stockholm, 1938.
Arc 670.6 Broneer, O. The lion monument at Amphipolis. Cambridge, Mass., 1941.
Arc 670.7F Holmberg, E.J. The Swedish excavations at sea in Arcadia. Lund, 1944.
Arc 670.8 Rutkowski, Bogdan. Cult places in the Aegean world. Wrocław, 1972.
Arc 670.9 Branigan, Keith. Aegean metalwork of the early and middle Bronze Age. Oxford, 1974.
Arc 671.10 Rōmaios, K.A. Ho Makedonikoi taros tēs Berginas. Athēnai, 1951.
Arc 671.15 Fraser, F.M. Boeotian and west Greek tombstones. Lund, 1954.
Arc 672.1 Pashley, R. Travels in Crete. Cambridge, 1837. 2v.
Arc 672.1.4 Mosso, Angelo. The palaces of Crete and their builders. N.Y., 1907.
Arc 672.1.5 Mosso, Angelo. Palaces of Crete and their builders. London, 1907.
Arc 672.1.6 Mosso, Angelo. Le origini della civilta Mediterranea. Milano, 1910.
Arc 672.1.7 Mosso, Angelo. Dawn of Mediterranean civilization. London, 1910.
Arc 672.1.7.5 Mosso, Angelo. Dawn of Mediterranean civilization. N.Y., 1911.
Arc 672.1.8 Lagrange, M.J. La Crete ancienne. Paris, 1908.
Arc 672.1.9.5 Hawes, C.H. Crete, the forerunner of Greece. London, 1922.
X Cg Arc 672.1.11 Belli, Onorio. A description of some theatres in Crete. London, 1854.
Arc 672.1.13 Burrows, R.M. The discoveries in Crete. London, 1907.
Arc 672.1.15 Burrows, R.M. The discoveries in Crete; with addenda. London, 1908.
Arc 672.1.16A Burrows, R.M. The discoveries in Crete and their bearing. N.Y., 1907.
Arc 672.1.16B Burrows, R.M. The discoveries in Crete and their bearing. N.Y., 1907.
Arc 672.1.19A Baikie, James. The sea-kings of Crete. London, 1910.
Arc 672.1.19B Baikie, James. The sea-kings of Crete. London, 1910.
Arc 672.1.21 Baikie, James. The sea-kings of Crete. 3. ed. London, 1920.
Arc 672.1.22 Baikie, James. The sea-kings of Crete. 4. ed. London, 1926.
Arc 672.1.25 Noack, F. Ovalhaus und Palást in Kreta. Leipzig, 1908.
Arc 672.1.26 Evans, Arthur John. Early Nilotic, Libyan, and Egyptian relations with Minoan Crete. London, 1925.
Arc 672.1.27 Evans, Arthur John. The palace of Minos. v.1; v.2, pt.1-2; v.3; v.4, pt.1-2. London, 1921-35. 6v.
Arc 672.1.27.5 Evans, Arthur John. Index to the palace of Minos. London, 1936.
Arc 672.1.28 Pendlebury, J.D.S. Handbook to the palace of Minos at Knossos. London, 1933.
Arc 672.1.28.5 Pendlebury, J.D.S. The archaeology of Crete. London, 1939.

Classified Listing

Arc 670 - 695 Archaeology - Local - Greece - Local except Athens (A-Z by place) - cont.

Arc 672.1.28.6 Pendlebury, J.D.S. The archaeology of Crete. N.Y., 1963.
NEDL Arc 672.1.28.10 Pendlebury, J.D.S. Hodēgos tōn minoikou anaktoro tēs knōsa. Hērakleì, 1950.
Arc 672.1.29 Hazzidakis, J. Étude de préhistorie crétoise. Paris, 1921.
Arc 672.1.29.5 Chatzidakēs, I. Istoria tou Krētikou Monseiou kai tōn archaiologikōn ereynōn en Krēte. Athēnai, 1931.
Arc 672.1.31F Halbherr, F. Relazione sugli scavi...in Gortyna. Roma, 1889.
X Cg Arc 672.1.33 Bossert, H.T. Alt Kreta. Berlin, 1921.
Arc 672.1.34 Bossert, H.T. Alt Kreta. 3. Aufl. Berlin, 1937.
Arc 672.1.35 Xanthoudídes, S. The vaulted tombs of Mesará. London, 1924.
Arc 672.1.37 Bell, Edward. Prehellenic architecture in the Aegean. London, 1926.
Arc 672.1.45 Oulié, Marthe. Les animaux dans la peinture de la Crete préhellénique. Thèse. Paris, 1926.
Htn Arc 672.1.47F* Oulié, Marthe. Decoration égéenne. Paris, 1927.
Arc 672.1.49F Gerola, G. Monumenti veneti nell'isola di Creta. v.1, pt.1-2, v.2-4. Venezia, 1905-32. 5v.
Arc 672.1.51F Wace, A.J.B. A Cretan statuette in the Fitzwilliam Museum. Cambridge, Eng., 1927.
Arc 672.1.52F Kunze, Emil. Kretische Bonzereliefs. Text and plates. Stuttgart, 1931. 2v.
Arc 672.1.53 Glasgow, George. The Minoans. London, 1923.
Arc 672.1.55 Athens. École Française. Études crétoises. Paris. 1-19 16v.
Arc 672.1.57A Burn, A.R. Minoans, Philistines, and Greeks, B.C. 1400-900. N.Y., 1930.
Arc 672.1.57B Burn, A.R. Minoans, Philistines, and Greeks, B.C. 1400-900. N.Y., 1930.
Arc 672.1.59 Forsdyke, E.J. Minoan art. London, 1931.
Arc 672.1.61 Snijder, G.A.S. Kretische Kunst. Berlin, 1936.
Arc 672.1.63 Charbonneaux, J. L'art égéen. Paris, 1929.
Arc 672.1.65F Pernier, Luigi. Il palazzo minoico di Festos. Roma, 1935-51. 3v.
Arc 672.1.67 Matz, F. Forschungen auf Kreta 1942. Berlin, 1951.
Arc 672.1.70 Pernier, Luigi. Guida degli scavi italiani in Creta. Roma, 1947.
Arc 672.1.72F Karo, G.H. Greifen am Thron. Baden-Baden, 1959.
Arc 672.1.73 Matton, Raymond. La Crète antique. Athènes, 1955.
Arc 672.1.75F Marinatos, Spyridon. Kreta und das mykenische Hellas. München, 1959.
Arc 672.1.80F Marinatos, Spyridon. Crete and Mycenae. N.Y., 1960.
Arc 672.1.85 Maltezos, G.P. Das alte Kreta. Kaiserslautern, 1957.
Arc 672.1.90 Honour, Alan. Secrets of Minos. 1. ed. N.Y., 1961.
Arc 672.1.92 Deshayes, J. Les quatier Z à Mallia. Paris, 1959.
Arc 672.1.94 Graham, J.W. The palace of Crete. Princeton, N.J., 1962.
Arc 672.1.96 Demargne, P. La Crète dédalique. Paris, 1947.
Arc 672.1.105 Faure, Paul. Fonctions des cavernes crétoises. Paris, 1964.
Arc 672.1.110 Palmer, Leonard R. On the Knossos tablets. Oxford, 1963.
Arc 672.1.112 Stibbe, C.M. Kreta en Mykene. Zeist, 1964.
Arc 672.1.114 Tiré, Claire. Guide des fouilles francaises en Crète. Athènes, 1966.
Arc 672.1.116 Pini, Ingo. Beiträge zur minoischen Gräberkunde. Wiesbaden, 1968.
Arc 672.1.118 Warren, Peter. Minoan stone vases. Cambridge, Eng., 1969.
Arc 672.1.120 Branigan, Keith. The tombs of Mesara; a study of funerary architecture and ritual in southern Crete, 2800-1700 B.C. London, 1970.
Arc 672.1.122 Platon, Nikolaos Eleutheriou. Zakros: the discovery of a lost places of ancient Crete. N.Y., 1971.
Arc 672.1.125 Coldstream, John Nicolas. Knossos. London, 1973.
Arc 672.1.130 Evans, Arthur John. The palace of Minos. N.Y., 1964. 6v.
Arc 672.1.131 Evans, Arthur John. The palace of Minos. Index. N.Y., 1964.
Arc 672.1.135 Palmer, Leonard R. A new guide to the palace of Knossos. London, 1969.
Arc 672.1.140 Vaughan, Agnes C. The house of the Double Axe; the palace at Knossos. Garden City, 1959.
Arc 672.1.146 Wunderlich, Hans-Georg. The secret of Crete. N.Y., 1974.
Arc 672.1.150 Wunderlich, Hans-Georg. Wohin der Stier Europa trug. Reinbek bei Hamburg, 1972.
Arc 672.2 Schmidt, B. Korkyraeische Studien. Leipzig, 1890. 2v.
Arc 672.2.5F Korkya. Berlin. 1-2,1939-1940
Arc 672.2.10 Sordinas, Augustus John. Stone implements from northwestern Corfu, Greece. Memphis, 1970.
Arc 672.4 Staïs,V. Ta ez antikythēren eyrēmata. Athēnai, 1905.
Arc 672.5 Wilisch, E. Beiträge zur Geschichte des alten Korinth. Zittau, 1901.
Arc 672.5.5 American School of Classical Studies at Athens. Ancient Corinth. Macon, 1928.
Arc 672.5.7F American School of Classical Studies at Athens. Corinth. 2-16,1932-1957 26v.
Arc 672.5.7PF American School of Classical Studies at Athens. Corinth. 1-6,1952-1964 4v.
Arc 672.5.10 O'Neill, J.G. Ancient Corinth. Photoreproduction. Baltimore, 1930.
Arc 672.5.15F Payne, H. Perachora, the sanctuaries of Hera Akraia and Lemenia. Oxford, 1940. 2v.
Arc 672.5.20F Kosmopoulos, L.W. The prehistoric inhabitation of Corinth. Munich, 1948.
Arc 672.5.25 American School of Classical Studies at Athens. Ancient Corinth. 4. ed. Athens, 1947.
Arc 672.6F Kos. Berlin. 1,1932
Arc 672.7 Dyggve, E. Das heroon von Kalydon. København, 1934.
Arc 672.10 Rutkowski, Bogdan. Larnaksy egejskie. Wrocław, 1966.
Arc 672.11 Boardman, John. Excavations in Chios, 1952-1955. London, 1967.
Arc 673:1 Pomtow, H. Beiträge zur Topographie von Delphi. Berlin, 1889.
Arc 673.1.2 Witte, J. de Baron. Monumens de Delphes. Roma, 1842.
Arc 673.1.3 Bourguet, E. Les ruines de Delphes. Paris, 1914.
Arc 673.1.4 Bourguet, E. L'aurige de Delphes. Paris, 1912.
Arc 673.1.6 Malteros, G.T. Delphi. Kaiserslautern, 1958.
Arc 673.1.7 Preuner, E. Ein Delphische Weihgeschenk. Bonn, 1899.
Arc 673.1.8 Preuner, E. Ein Delphische Weihgeschenk. Leipzig, 1900.
Arc 673.1.9 Trendelenburg, A. Die Anfangsstreke der heiligen Strasse in Delphi. Berlin, 1908.
Arc 673.1.12 Michałowski, K. Delfy. Warszawa, 1959.
X Cg Arc 673.1.13 Poulson, F. Delphi. London, 1920.
Arc 673.1.15 Frotier de la Coste Messelière, P. Au musée de Delphes. Thèse. Paris, 1936.

Arc 670 - 695 Archaeology - Local - Greece - Local except Athens (A-Z by place) - cont.

Arc 673.1.17 Graindor, P. Delphes et son oracle. Le Caire, 1930.
Arc 673.1.20F Bousquet, Jean. Le trésor de Cyrène à Delphes. Thèse. Paris, 1952.
Arc 673.1.22F Amandry, P. La colonne des Naxiens et le partique des Athéneéns. Thèse. Paris, 1953.
Arc 673.1.25F Jannosay, J. Le gymnase de Delphes. Thèse. Paris, 1953.
Arc 673.1.29 Mylonas, George Emmanuel. Eleusis and the Eleusinian mysteries. Princeton, 1972.
Arc 673.1.30 Keramopoullos, A.D. Topographia tōn Delphōn. Athēnai, 1917.
Arc 673.1.35 Poulsen, Frederik. Delphi. Washington, 1973.
Arc 673.1.35F Pouilloux, Jean. Énigmes à Delphes. Paris, 1963.
Arc 673.1.40F Pouilloux, Jean. La région nord du sanctuaire de l'épogue archaïque à la fin du sanctuaire. Paris, 1960. 2v.
Arc 673.1.50 Karouzos, Chrēstos Iōannou. Delphoi. Athēnai, 1974.
Arc 673.2 Gerlach, F.D. Dodona. Basel, 1859.
Arc 673.3 Lebègue, J.A. Recherches sur Délos. Paris, 1876.
Arc 673.5 Bulletin de Correspondance Hellénique. Fouilles de Délos exécutées de M. de Loubat 1904-1907. Paris, n.d.
Arc 673.7 Fritsch, O. Delos, die Insel des Apolon. Gütersloh, 1908.
Arc 673.10 Pamphlet box. Delos.
Arc 673.11F Plassart, A. Les sanctuaires et les cultes du Mont Cynthe a Délos. Thèse. Paris, 1928.
Arc 673.12F Chapouthier, F. Exploration archéologique de Délos. Paris, 1935.
Arc 674.1 Rubensohn, O. Die Mysterienheiligtuemer in Eleusis und Samothrake. Berlin, 1892.
Arc 674.1.5F Noack, F. Eleusis. Text and plates. Berlin, 1927. 2v.
Arc 674.1.6 Strube, Carl. Studien über den Bilderkreis von Eleusis. Leipzig, 1870.
Arc 674.1.9F Kourouniotos, K. Eleusiniaka. Athēnai, 1932.
Arc 674.1.10 Kourouniotos, K. Eleusis. Athēnai, 1934.
Arc 674.1.12 Kourouniotos, K. Eleusis. Athens, 1936.
Arc 674.1.13F Mylonas, George E. Ho prōtoattikos amphoreni tēs Eleusinos. Athēnai, 1957.
Arc 674.1.25 Pamphlet box. Eleusis.
Arc 674.2.5 Falcon-Barker, T. 1600 years under the sea. London, 1960.
Arc 674.3 Herrlich, S. Epidaurus, eine antike Heilstätte. Berlin, 1898.
Arc 674.3.3 Crome, J.F. Die Skulpturen des Asklepiostempels von Epidauros. Berlin, 1951.
Arc 674.3.5 Kabbaria. Toieron toy asklēpioy. Athēnai, 1900.
Arc 674.3.8F Gerhan, Armen. Das Theater von Epidauros. Stuttgart, 1961.
Arc 674.3.15 Burford, Alison. The Greek temple builders at Epidauros. Liverpool, 1969.
Arc 674.10F Papabasileios, G.A. Peri tōn en Euboia archaiōn taphōn. Athēnai, 1910.
Arc 674.15F Goldman, Hetty. Excavations at Eutresis in Boeotia. Cambridge, Mass., 1931.
Arc 674.20 Schroeder, Johan. Epidauros en Kreta. Amsterdam, 1960.
Arc 676.5F Die deutschen Ausgrabungen auf der Argissa-Magula in Thessalien. Bonn, 1962.
Arc 677.1 Forchhammer, P.W. Halkyoma. Berlin, 1857.
Arc 677.5F Mylonas, George E. Aghios Kosmas. Princeton, 1959.
Arc 678.5 Isthmia; excavations by the University of Chicago. Princeton, N.J., 1971. 2v.
Arc 680.1 Kythera - excavations and studies. London, 1972.
Arc 681.1 Conze, A. Reise auf der Insel Lesbos. Hannover, 1865.
Arc 681.1.5 Lamb, Winifred. Excavations at Thermi in Lesbos. Cambridge, Eng., 1936.
Arc 681.1.10 Weickert, Carl. Das lesbische Kymation. Leipzig, 1913.
Arc 681.5 Benson, Jack L. Ancient Leros. Durham, 1963.
Arc 681.7F Brae, Luigi Bernabo. Poliochni. v.1-2. Roma, 1964.
Arc 681.10 Milojčić, Vladmir. Paläolithikum um Larissa in Thessalien. Bonn, 1965.
Arc 681.10.5 Die deutschen Ausgrabungen auf der Otzaki-Magula in Thessalien. Bonn, 1971- 2v.
Arc 681.15 American School of Classical Studies at Athens. Lerna, a preclassical site in the Argolid. Princeton, N.J., 1969. 2v.
Arc 681.15.5 Angel, John Lawrence. The people of Lerna. Princeton, N.J., 1971.
Arc 681.20 Popham, Mervyn R. Excavations at Lefkandi, Euboea, 1964-66. London, 1968.
Arc 682.1 Schliemann, Heinrich. Mycenae; a narrative of researches and discoveries at Mycenae and Tiryns. London, 1878.
Arc 682.1.2 Schliemann, Heinrich. Mycenae; a narrative. N.Y., 1880.
Arc 682.1.3A Schliemann, Heinrich. Mycenae; a narrative. N.Y., 1878.
Arc 682.1.3B Schliemann, Heinrich. Mycenae; a narrative. N.Y., 1878.
Arc 682.1.5 Schliemann, Heinrich. Mykenae; Bericht über meine Forschungen und Entdeckungen in Mykenae und Tiryns. Faksimile. Darmstadt, 1964.
Arc 682.1.8 Schliemann, Heinrich. Tiryns; the prehistoric palace of the kings of Tiryns. N.Y., 1885.
Arc 682.1.9 Schliemann, Heinrich. Tiryns; the prehistoric palace of the kings of Tiryns. London, 1886.
Arc 682.1.15 Schulze, E. Mykenai - eine kritische Untersuchung der Schliemannschen Alterthümer. St. Petersburg, 1880.
Arc 682.1.16 Schliemann, Heinrich. Catalogue des trésors de Mycènes au Musée d'Athènes. Leipzig, 1882.
Arc 682.1.17 Schliemann, Heinrich. Catalogue des trésors de Mycènes au Musée d'Athènes. Leipzig, 1882.
Arc 682.2 Tsountas, C. Mukyrai. Athēnai, 1893.
Arc 682.3 Reber, F. von. Und die Verhältniss der mykenischen zur dorischen Baustiel. München, 1896.
Arc 682.4 Hall, H.R. The oldest civilization of Greece. London, 1901. 2v.
Arc 682.5 Marcks, F. Die mykenische Zeit. Cöln, 1902.
Arc 682.6 The Mycenae tablets. v.4. Phildelphia, 1953.
Arc 682.7 Seunig, Vingenz. Die kritisch-mykenische Kultur. Graz, 1921.
Arc 682.8 Papachatzēs, N. Mykēnes kai Tirynthа. Athēnai, 1951.
Arc 682.9 Fimmen, Diedrich. Die kritisch-mykenische Kultur. Leipzig, 1921.
Arc 682.10F Rodenwaldt, G. Der Fries des Megarons von Mykenai. Halle an der Saale, 1921.
Arc 682.11 Evans, Arthur. The shaft graves and bee-hive tombs of Mycenae and their interrelation. London, 1929.
Arc 682.12F Karo, Georg. Die Schachtgräber von Mykenai. Text and plates. München, 1930-33. 2v.
Arc 682.13F Persson, A.W. The royal tombs at Dendra near Midea. Lund, 1931.
Arc 682.14F Archäologisches Institut des Deutschen Reichs-Athenische Zweigeanstalt. Das Kuppelgrab bei Menidi. Athen, 1880.

Classified Listing

Arc 670 - 695 Archaeology - Local - Greece - Local except Athens (A-Z by place) - cont.

Arc 682.15A Seager, R.B. Explorations in the island of Mochlos. Boston, 1912.
Arc 682.15B Seager, R.B. Explorations in the island of Mochlos. Boston, 1912.
Arc 682.20 Olkonomlkes, S. Ta sōzomena Ithōmēs Messenes kai tōn Perix. Athēnai, 1879.
Arc 682.20.5F Valmin, M.N. The Swedish Messenia expedition. Lund, 1938.
Arc 682.25 Kondakov, N.P. Makedoniia arkheologiia putesh. Sankt Peterburg, 1909.
Arc 682.25.15 Ivanov, Iordan. Bulgarski starini iz Makedoniia. Sofiia, 1908.
VArc 682.25.17 Ivanov, Iordan. Bulgarski starini iz Makedoniia. 2. izd. Sofiia, 1931.
VArc 682.25.19 Ivanov, Iordan. Bulgarski starini iz Makedoniia. 2. izd. Sofiia, 1970.
Arc 682.25.25 Rey, Léon. Observations sur les premiers habitats de la Macédoine. Paris, 1921-22. 2v.
Arc 682.25.35F Heurtley, W.A. Prehistoric Macedonia. Cambridge, Eng., 1939.
Arc 682.25.40 Skeat, T.C. The Dorians in archaeology. London, 1932?
Arc 682.30 Mylonas, George E. Ancient Mycenae. Princeton, 1957.
Arc 682.30.5 Mylonas, George E. Mycenae's last century of greatness. Sydney, 1968.
Arc 682.31F Desborough, V.R. d'. The last Mycenaeans and their successors. Oxford, 1964.
Arc 682.32 Hope Simpson, Richard. A gazetteer and atlas of Mycenaean sites. London, 1965.
Arc 682.35 Evans, John Davies. Excavations at Saliagos near Antiparos. London, 1968.
Arc 682.40 Papastamos, Dēmētrios. Melische amphoren. Münster, 1970.
Arc 682.42 Warren, Peter. Myrtos: an early Bronze Age settlement in Crete. London, 1972.
X Cg Arc 684.1 Boetticher, A. Olympia - das Fest und seine Stätte. Berlin, 1883. (Changed to XP 9960)
Arc 684.1.2 Curtius, E. Die Altere von Olympia. Berlin, 1882.
Arc 684.1.3 Curtius, E. Olympia und Umgegend. Berlin, 1882.
Arc 684.1.4 Urlichs, K.L. Bemerkungen über den olympischen Tempel und seine Bildwerke. Würzburg, 1877.
Arc 684.1.5 Boetticher, A. Olympia. Berlin, 1886.
Arc 684.1.7 Leonardos, B. Hē Olympia. Athēnai, 1901.
Arc 684.1.11 Luckerrbach, H. Olympia und Delphi. München, 1904.
Arc 684.1.12 Wernick, F. Olympia. Leipzig, 1877.
Arc 684.1.15 Die Ernst Curtius-Büste. Berlin, 1895.
Arc 684.1.19 Gardiner, E.N. Olympia; its history and remains. Oxford, 1925.
Arc 684.1.25 Buschor, E. Die Skulpturen des Zeustempels zu Olympia. Giessen, 1924. 2v.
Arc 684.1.29 Wolters, Paul. Der Westgiebel des olympischen Zeustempels. München, 1908.
Arc 684.1.33 Schlief, Hans. Der Zeus-Altar in Olympia. Diss. Berlin, 1935.
Arc 684.1.37 Dörpfeld, Wilhelm. Alt-Olympia. Berlin, 1935. 2v.
Arc 684.1.38 Dörpfeld, Wilhelm. Alt-Olympia. Beiheft. Berlin, 1935.
Arc 684.1.45F Rodenwaldt, G. Olympia. Berlin, 1926.
Arc 684.1.48 Kunze, Emil. Neue Meisterwerke griechischer Kunst aus Olympia. München, 1948.
Arc 684.1.50 Kontes, I.D. To Hieron tēs Olympias. Athēnai, 1958.
Arc 684.1.55 100 Jahre deutsche Ausgrabung in Olympia. München, 1972.
Htn Arc 684.2* Schliemann, Heinrich. Orchomenos. Athēnai, 1883.
Arc 684.3 Schliemann, Heinrich. Orchomenos. Leipzig, 1881.
Arc 684.4 Finlay, G. Remarks on the topography of Oropia and Diacria. Athens, 1838. 2 pam.
Arc 684.5 Schwarzstein, A. Eine Gebäudegruppe in Olympia. Strassburg, 1909.
Arc 684.5.10F Curtius, Ernst. Olympia: die Ergebnisse. v.5. Berlin, 1896.
Arc 684.6 Quaatz, H. Wie sind die Figuren im Ostgiebel des Zeustempels zu Olympia anzuordnen. Berlin, 1908.
Arc 684.7 Kourouniotos, K. Hodēgos tēs Olympias. Athēnai, 1904.
Arc 684.7.5 Kourouniotos, K. Katalogos tōn mouseiou Lukosouras. Athēnai, 1911.
Arc 684.9 John Hopkins University. Excavations at Olynthus. Baltimore, 1929-52. 14v.
Arc 684.9.5 Mylonas, George E. The neolithic settlement at Olynthus. Baltimore, 1929.
Arc 684.9.10 Gude, Mabel. A history of Olynthus. Baltimore, 1933.
Arc 685.1 Wide, S. Ausgrabungen auf Kalaureia. n.p., n.d.
Arc 685.1.5 Welter, Gabriel. Troizen und Kalaureia. Berlin, 1941.
Arc 685.2FA Blegen, C.W. Prosymna; the Helladic settlement preceding the Argive Heraeum. Cambridge, Eng., 1937. 2v.
Arc 685.2FB Blegen, C.W. Prosymna; the Helladic settlement preceding the Argive Heraeum. Cambridge, Eng., 1937. 2v.
Arc 685.4 Bosanquet, Robert. The unpublished objects from the Palaikastro excavations, 1902-06. London, 1923.
Arc 685.5 Syriopoulos, K. Hē proistoria...Peloponnēsou. Athēnai, 1964.
Arc 687.1F Blinkenberg, C. Lindos; fouilles et recherches, 1902-1914. Berlin, 1931. 4v.
Arc 687.1.5 Blinkenberg, C. Exploration archéologique de Rhodes. v.1-6. København, 1903-12.
Arc 687.1.10 Dietz, Søren. Arkaelogens Rhodos. København, 1974.
Arc 687.2 Montesanto, M. La città sacra (Lindo). Roma, 1930.
Arc 688.1 Schinas, D. Archaiologia tēs Nesou Sikinou. Athēnai, 1837.
Arc 688.2 Dressel, H. Die antiken Kunstwerke aus Sparta und Umgebung. Athen, 1878.
Arc 688.3F Courby, F. Recherches archéologiques à Stratos d'Acarnanie. Paris, 1924.
Arc 688.4 Fouqué, F. Premier rapport sur une mission scientifique à l'Ile Santorin. Paris, 1867.
Arc 688.5 Béquignon, Y. La vallée du Spercheios des origines au IVe siècle. Thèse. Paris, 1937.
Arc 688.6 Lehmann, Karl. Samothrace. N.Y., 1955.
Arc 688.6.5F Lehmann, Karl. Samothrace. v.1-4,6. N.Y., 1959-64. 5v.
Arc 688.6.7 Lehmann, Phyllis. The pedimental sculpture of the Hieron. N.Y., 1962.
Arc 688.7F Reuther, Oskar. Der Heratempel von Samos. Berlin, 1957.
Arc 688.7.5F Deutsches Archäologisches Institut. Samos. v.1,5-8,12,14. Bonn, 1961- 7v.
Arc 688.7.10 Tölle-Kastenbein, Renate. Die antike Stadt Samos. Mainz am Rhein, 1969.
Arc 688.8 Staés, B. To Eounion. Athēnai, 1920.
Arc 688.8.5 Oikonomides, A.N. Eounion. Athēnai, 1957.
Arc 689.2 Granidor, P. Les fouilles de Tēnos. Louvain, 1906.
Arc 689.3 Arvanitopoulas, A.S. Thessalika Mnēmeia. Athēnai, 1909.

Arc 670 - 695 Archaeology - Local - Greece - Local except Athens (A-Z by place) - cont.

Arc 689.3.10 Hansen, H.D. Early civilization in Thessaly. Baltimore, 1933.
Arc 689.3.15 Béquignon, Y. Recherches archéologiques à Phères de Thessalie. Paris, 1937.
Arc 689.3.17 Bequignon, Y. Recherches archéologiques à Phères de Thessalie. Thèse. Strasbourg, 1937.
Arc 689.3.20F Soteriou, G.A. Ai Christianikai Thebai tēs Thessalias kai at palaiochristianikai basilikai tēs Ellados. Athēnai, 1931.
Arc 689.5F Dugas, C. Le sanctuaire d'Aléa Athéna à Tégée au IVe siècle. Text and atlas. Paris, 1924. 2v.
Arc 689.6 Braun, I. De theraeorum rebus sacris. Inaug. Diss. Halis Saxonum, 1932.
Arc 689.7.5 Karo, G. Fürhrer durch Tiryns. 2. Aufl. Athen, 1934.
Arc 689.8 Nolters, P. Das Kabirenheiligtum bei Theben. Berlin, 1940.
Arc 689.9 Lazarides, D.I. Hē Thasos. Thessalonikē, 1958.
Arc 689.10 Thorikos. Bruxelles. 1,1963+ 3v.
Arc 689.12 Hauptmann, Harald. Die Funde der früher Dimini-Zeit aus der Arapi-Magula. Diss. Bonn, 1969.
Arc 691.2 Weller. The cave at Vari. n.p., n.d.
Arc 691.5F Arbanitopoulos, A.S. Graptai stēlai Dēmetriidos-Palasōn. Athēnai, 1928.
Arc 695.1F Blegen, Carl W. Zygouries. Cambridge, 1928.
Arc 695.2 Zagora I; excavation season 1967. Sydney, 1971.

Arc 700 Archaeology - Local - Greece - Special topics

Arc 700.1 Gell, W. Probestuecke von Städtemanern des Alten Griechenlands. München, 1831.
Arc 700.2 Rangabé, A.R. Ausgrabung beim Tempel der Hera Unweit Argos. Halle, 1855.
Arc 700.3 Belger, C. Beiträge zur Kenntnis der Griechischen Kuppelgraeber. Berlin, 1887.
Htn Arc 700.4* Belger, C. Die Mykenische Lokalsage von den Gräbern Agamemnons und der Seinen. Berlin, 1893.
Arc 700.5 Haussoullier, B. Quomodo sepulera Tanagraei decoravirent. Paris, 1884.
Arc 700.6 Dörpfeld, W. Das Griechische Theater. Athen, 1896.
Arc 700.7 Gardner, P. Sculptured tombs of Hellas. London, 1896.
Arc 700.8 Lenormant, F. Monographie de la voie sacrée éleusinienne. Paris, 1884.
Arc 700.9 Kietz, G. Agonistische Studien I, Der Diskoswurf bei der Grechen. München, 1892.
Arc 700.10 Brueckner, A. Ornament und Form der altischen Grabstelen. Weimar, 1886.
Arc 700.10.15F Moebius, Hans. Die Ornamente der griechischen Grabstelen. Berlin, 1929.
Arc 700.11 Gropengiesser, H. Die Gräber von Attika. Athen, 1907.
Arc 700.12 Holwerda, J.H. Die altischen Gräber der Bluethezeit. Leiden, 1899.
Arc 700.12.15 Wiesner, J. Grab und Jenseits. Berlin, 1938.
Arc 700.13 Dumont, Albert. De plumbeis apud graecos tesseris. Paris, 1870.
Arc 700.14 Calderini, A. Di un'ara greca. Milano, 1907.
Arc 700.15 Pottier, Edmond. Quam ab causam Graeci in sepulcris figlina na sigilla deposuerint. Parisiis, 1883.
Arc 700.16 Kairo. Ägyptischen Museums. Griechische Urkunden. Strassburg, 1911.
Arc 700.17 Foerster, R. Die Hochzeit des Zeus und der Hera; Relief der Schaubert'schen Sammlung. Breslau, 1867.
Arc 700.18 Overbeck, J. Über die Lade des Kypselos. Leipzig, 1865.
Arc 700.19 Scranton, R.L. Greek walls. Cambridge, 1941.
Arc 700.19.5 Scranton, R.L. The chronology of Greek walls. Thesis. Chicago, 1941.
Arc 700.19.10 Winter, F.E. Greek fortifications. London, 1971.
Arc 700.19.11 Winter, F.E. Greek fortifications. Toronto, 1971.
Arc 700.20 McDonald, W.A. The political meeting places of the Greeks. Baltimore, 1943.
Arc 700.21 Hall, Elise von. Over den oorsprong van de griekse grafstele. Proefschrift. Amsterdam, 1941.
Arc 700.25F Adriani, A. Le gobelet en argent des amours vendangeurs du musée d'Alexandrie. n.p., 1939.
Arc 700.30 Burton-Brown, T. The coming of iron to Greece. Wincle, 1954.
Arc 700.33 Jantzen, Ulf. Griechische Greifenkessel. Berlin, 1955.
Arc 700.35 Richter, G.M.A. Archaic attic gravestones. Cambridge, 1944.
Arc 700.40A Brock, James K. Fortetsa. Cambridge, Eng., 1957.
Arc 700.40B Brock, James K. Fortetsa. Cambridge, Eng., 1957.
Arc 700.50 Niemeyer, Hans G. Promachos. Waldsassen, 1960.
Arc 700.52 Kallipolites, B.G. Chronologikē katataxis. Athēnai, 1958.
Arc 700.55 Delorme, Jean. Gymnasion. Paris, 1960.
Arc 700.56 Alsop, J. From the silent earth. N.Y., 1964.
Arc 700.57 Cook, R.M. Niobe and her children. Cambridge, 1964.
Arc 700.58 Boardman, J. The Greeks overseas. Harmondsworth, 1964.
Arc 700.58.2 Boardman, J. The Greeks overseas. 2. ed. Harmondsworth, 1973.
Arc 700.59 Wąsowicz, Aleksandra. Obróbka drewna w Starożytnej Grecji. Wrocław, 1966.
Arc 700.60 Zlatkovskaia, Tat'iana D. U istokov evropeiskoi kul'tury. Moskva, 1961.
Arc 700.62 Heres, Gerald. Die punischen und griechischen Tonlampen der Staatlichen Museen zu Berlin. Amsterdam, 1969.
Arc 700.64 Sinos, Stefan. Die vorklassischen Hausformen in der Ägäis. Mainz, 1971.
Arc 700.68A Snodgrass, Anthony M. The dark age of Greece: an archaeological survey of the eleventh to the eighth centuries B.C. Edinburgh, 1971.
Arc 700.68B Snodgrass, Anthony M. The dark age of Greece: an archaeological survey of the eleventh to the eighth centuries B.C. Edinburgh, 1971.
Arc 700.69 Bouzek, Jan. Graeco-Macedonian bronzes. Praha, 1974.
Arc 700.70 Schoder, Raymond Victor. Ancient Greece from the air. London, 1974.

Arc 705 Archaeology - Local - Greece - Athens - Folios [Discontinued]

Htn Arc 705.5* Stuart, J. Antiquities of Athens. London, 1762-1816. 4v.
Htn Arc 705.6* Cockerell, C.R. Antiquities of Athens and other places in Greece and Sicily. London, 1830.
Arc 705.7 Stillman, W.J. The acropolis of Athens. London, 1870.
Arc 705.11 Curtius, E. Sieben Karten zur Topographie von Athen. Gotha, 1868.
Arc 705.11PF Curtius, E. Sieben Karten zur Topographie von Athen. Atlas. Gotha, 1868.

Arc 705 Archaeology - Local - Greece - Athens - Folios [Discontinued] - cont.

Arc 705.14 Heller, B.R. Archäologisch-artische Mittheilungen...über die Ausgrabungen auf der Akropolis zu Athen. Nuremberg, 1852.
Arc 705.15A Michaelis, A. Der Parthenon. Text and atlas. Leipzig, 1871. 2v.
Arc 705.15B Michaelis, A. Der Parthenon. Text and atlas. Leipzig, 1871. 2v.
Arc 705.200 Kekulé, R. Die Reliefs an der Balustrade der Athena Nike. Stuttgart, 1881.
Arc 705.200.5F Blümel, Carl. Der Fries des Tempels der Athena Nike. Berlin, 1923.
Arc 705.201A Maps, Athens. Atlas von Athen. Berlin, 1878.
Arc 705.201B Maps, Athens. Atlas von Athen. Berlin, 1878.
Arc 705.202 Durm, J. Der Zustand der Antiken Athenischen Bauwerke. Berlin, 1895.
Arc 705.203 Sayer, R. Ruinen und Überbleibsel von Athen. Augsburg, 1764.
Arc 705.204 Sauer, B. Das Sergenannte Theseion. Berlin, 1899.
Arc 705.205 Polites, N.G. To ranathēnaikon stadion. Athēnai, 1896.
Arc 705.207 Schwerzek, Karl. Erläuterungen...Rekonstruktion des östlichen Parthenongiebels. Wien, 1904.
Arc 705.208 Schwerzek, Karl. Erläuterungen...Rekonstruktion Westgiebels des Parthenongiebels. Wien, 1896.
Arc 705.209 Bienkowski, P. von. Die Darstellungen der Gallier in der Hellenistischen Kunst. Wien, 1908.
Arc 705.210 Brueckner, A. Der Friedhof am Eridanos...zu Athen. Berlin, 1909.
Arc 705.211F Maurras, Charles. Athènes antique. Paris, 1918.

Arc 708 Archaeology - Local - Greece - Athens - General works

Arc 708.1 Barker, H.A. Description of the view of Athens. n.p., n.d.
Arc 708.2 Baumgarten, Fritz. Ein Rundgang durch die Ruinen Athens. Wertheim, 1887.
Arc 708.2.3 Baumgarten, Fritz. Ein Rundgang durch die Ruinen Athens. Leipzig, 1888.
Arc 708.3 Burnouf, E. La ville et l'acropole d'Athènes. Paris, 1877.
Arc 708.5 Dyer, T.H. Ancient Athens. London, 1873.
Arc 708.6 Forchhammer, P. Zur Topographie von Athen. Göttingen, 1873.
Arc 708.6.2 Forchhammer, P. Zur Topographie Athens. Göttingen, 1833. 2 pam.
Arc 708.8 Laborde, L.E.S.J. Athènes aux XVe, XVIe et XVIIe siècles. Paris, 1854. 2v.
Arc 708.9 Leake, W.M. Topographie von Athen. Halle, 1829.
Arc 708.9.2 Leake, W.M. The topography of Athens. London, 1821.
Arc 708.9.3 Leake, W.M. The topography of Athens. London, 1841. 2v.
Arc 708.9.9 Leake, W.M. Athènes d'après le colonel Leake. Paris, 1876.
Arc 708.11 Mommsen, A. Athenae Christianae. Leipzig, 1868.
Arc 708.12 Moüy, Charles. Lettres athéniennes. Paris, 1887.
Arc 708.13 Notes descriptive of panoramic sketch of Athens. Coventry, 1836? 3 pam.
Arc 708.14 Pittakys, K.S. L'ancienne Athènes. Athens, 1835.
Arc 708.15 Stuart, J. Die Alterthuemer von Athen. Darmstadt, 1829-31. 2v.
Arc 708.15.5 Souvenirs d'Athènes. Trieste, 186-?
Arc 708.16 Wachsmuth, C. Die Stadt Athen im Alterthum. Leipzig, 1874- 2v.
Arc 708.17 Warsberg, A. von. Die Kunstwerke Athens. Wien, 1892.
Arc 708.18 Wilkins, W. Atheniensia, or Remarks on the topography and buildings of Athens. London, 1816.
Arc 708.19 Broughton, V. Delves (Mrs.). Handbook to antiquities of Athens. Athens, 1896.
Arc 708.20 Maps, Athens. Athen mit Umgebung (1877). Berlin, 1881.
Arc 708.21 Ambrosoli, G. Atene. Brevi cenni sulla città antica e moderna. Milano, 1901.
Arc 708.22A Gardner, E.A. Ancient Athens. N.Y., 1902.
Arc 708.22B Gardner, E.A. Ancient Athens. N.Y., 1902.
Arc 708.22.3 Gardner, E.A. Ancient Athens. London, 1902.
Arc 708.22.5 Gardner, E.A. Ancient Athens. London, 1907.
Arc 708.23 Fougères, G. Athènes et ses environs. Paris, 1906.
Arc 708.23.7 Fougères, G. Athènes. Paris, 1914.
Arc 708.23.9 Gougères, G. Athènes. 4e éd. Paris, 1923.
Arc 708.24 Sybel, L. von. Katalog der Sculpturen zu Athen. Marburg, 1881.
Arc 708.25 Petersen, E. Athen. Leipzig, 1908.
Arc 708.26 Sophoules, T. Peritou Archaioterou Attikou Ergastēriou. Athēnai, 1887.
Arc 708.27 Weller, C.H. Athens and its monuments. N.Y., 1913.
Arc 708.27.5 Weller, C.H. Athens and its monuments. N.Y., 1924.
Arc 708.30 Hill, I.C.T. The ancient city of Athens. London, 1953.
Arc 708.30.2A Hill, I.C.T. The ancient city of Athens. Cambridge, 1953.
Arc 708.30.2B Hill, I.C.T. The ancient city of Athens. Cambridge, 1953.
Arc 708.35 Kolobova, K.M. Drevnii gorod Afiny i ego pamiatniki. Leningrad, 1961.
Arc 708.36 Prokopiou, Angelos G. Athens, city of the Gods. N.Y., 1964.
Arc 708.38 Pantazēs, Dēmētrios. Periēgētēs Athēnōn. Athēnai, 1868.

Arc 710 Archaeology - Local - Greece - Athens - Acropolis

Arc 710.01 Pamphlet box. Athens. Acropolis.
Arc 710.1 Beulé, E. L'acropole d'Athènes. Paris, 1853-54. 2v.
Arc 710.2 Boetticher, C. Bericht über die Untersuchungen auf der Akropolis von Athen. n.p., n.d.
Arc 710.2.2 Boetticher, C. Die Akropolis von Athen. Berlin, 1888.
Arc 710.2.4 Buschor, Ernst. Winke für Akropolis-Pilger. München, 1960.
Arc 710.3 Curtius, E. Die Akropolis von Athen. Berlin, 1844.
Arc 710.4 Michaelis, A. Über den jetzigen Zustand der Akropolis von Athen. Frankfurt, 1861.
Arc 710.4.2 Michaelis, A. A brief explanation of the ground plan of the akropolis of Athens. Cambridge, 1882.
Arc 710.5 Luckenbach, H. Die Akropolis von Athen. München, 1896.
Arc 710.5.2 Luckenbach, H. Die Akropolis von Athen. München, 1905.
Arc 710.7 Milchhoefer, A. Rede zum Winckelmann-Zage. Kiel, 1898.
Arc 710.7.5 Milchhoefer, A. Über die alten Burgheiligthümer in Athen. Kiliae, 1899.
Arc 710.8 Hachtmann, K. Akropolis von Athen im Zeitalter des Perikles. Gütersloh, 1903.
Arc 710.9 Freericks, H. Die drei Athenetempel der Akropolis. Münster, 1905.
Arc 710.9.5 Petersen, E. Die Burgtempel der Athenaia. Berlin, 1907.
X Cg Arc 710.10 D'Ooge, M.L. The acropolis of Athens. N.Y., 1908.

Arc 710 Archaeology - Local - Greece - Athens - Acropolis - cont.

Arc 710.11 Köster, A. Das Pelargikon. Strasburg, 1909.
Arc 710.12 Schede, Martin. Die Burg von Athen. Berlin, 1922.
Arc 710.12.5 Schede, Martin. The acropolis of Athens. Berlin, 1924.
Arc 710.13 Merezhkovskii, D.S. The acropolis, from the Russian of Merejkowski. London, 1909.
Arc 710.14F Rodenwaldt, Gerhart. Die Akropolis. Berlin, 1930.
Arc 710.14.2 Rodenwaldt, Gerhart. The acropolis. 2. ed. Oxford, 1957.
Arc 710.15A Walter, Otto. Athen, Akropolis. Wien, 1929.
Arc 710.15B Walter, Otto. Athen, Akropolis. Wien, 1929.
Arc 710.16 Thibaudet, A. L'acropole. Paris, 1929.
Arc 710.17 White, John W. The apisthodomus on the acropolis at Athens. Boston, 1895.
Arc 710.18F Balanos, N. Les monuments de l'acropole. Paris, 1936.
Arc 710.19FA Stevens, G.P. The Periclean entrance court of the acropolis of Athens. Cambridge, 1936.
Arc 710.19FB Stevens, G.P. The Periclean entrance court of the acropolis of Athens. Cambridge, 1936.
Arc 710.20F Kakkadin, P. He anaskaphē tēs Akropoleōs apo tou 1885 mechri tou 1890. Athēnai, 1906.
Arc 710.22 Rubió y Lluch, Antonio. La acrópolis de Atenas en la época catalana. Barcelona, 1908.
Arc 710.24 Iakōbidēs, S.E. E Mykēnaikē Akropolis tōn Athēnōn. Athēnai, 1962.
Arc 710.26 Hopper, Robert John. The acropolis. London, 1971.
Arc 710.27F Kawerau, Georg. The excavation of the Athenian Acropolis 1882-1890. v.1-2. Copenhagen, 1974.
Arc 710.28 Des Gagniers, Jean. L'acropole d'Athènes. Québec, 1971.

Arc 712 Archaeology - Local - Greece - Athens - Parthenon

Arc 712.1 Boetticher, K. Der Zophorus am Parthenon. Berlin, 1875.
Arc 712.2 Petersen, C. Die Feste der Pallas Athene in Athen. Hamburg, 1855.
Arc 712.3 Ronchaud, L. de. Au Parthénon. Paris, 1886.
Arc 712.4 Choisy, A. Note sur la courbure dissymétrique des degrés qui limitent au couchant la plate-forme du Parthénon. Paris, 1865.
Arc 712.5 Visconti, E.Q. Mémoires sur des ouvrages de sculpture du Parthénon. Paris, 1818.
Arc 712.6 Flasch, A. Zum Parthenonfries. Wuerzburg, 1877.
Arc 712.7 Marchal. Le Parthénon. Paris, 1864.
Arc 712.8 Davidson, T. The Parthenon frieze and other essays. London, 1882.
Arc 712.9 Fielitz, W. Der Parthenon. Ein Vortag. Stralsund, 1871.
Arc 712.10 Michaelis, A. Über die Composition der Giebelgruppen am Parthenon. Tübingen, 1870.
Arc 712.11 Magne, L. Le Parthénon. Paris, 1895.
Arc 712.12 British Museum. Sculpures...Parthenon. London, 1900.
Arc 712.14 Sauer, B. Der...Kopf und die Giebelgruppen der Parthenon. Berlin, 1903.
Arc 712.15 Mot, J. de. Le frontal orientale du Parthenon. Bruxelles, 1906.
Arc 712.16 Hertz, A.P. Parthenons Kvindefigurer. n.p., 1905.
Arc 712.17 Pousopoulos, A. O Parthenōn. Athēnai, 1895.
Arc 712.18 Michaelis, A. Dei due figure alate sul fregio del Partenone. Lipsia, 1865.
Arc 712.19 Fergusson, J. The Parthenon. London, 1883.
Arc 712.21A Hambidge, Jay. The Parthenon and other Greek temples. New Haven, 1924.
Arc 712.21B Hambidge, Jay. The Parthenon and other Greek temples. New Haven, 1924.
Arc 712.22 Lloyd, W.W. On the general theory of proportion in archaeological design and its exemplification in detail in the Parthenon. London, 1863.
Arc 712.23 Praschniker, C. Parthenonstudien. Augsburg, 1928.
Arc 712.25 Stevens, G.P. The setting of the Periclean Parthenon. Baltimore, 1940.
Arc 712.28 Syriopoulos, K.T. Ho stereobatēs toy Parthenonos. Athēnai, 1951.
Arc 712.30 Berger, Ernst. Parthenon-Ostgiebel. Bonn, 1959.
Arc 712.32 Corbett, Peter Edgar. The sculpture of the Parthenon. Harmondsworth, 1959.
Arc 712.34 Buschor, E. Der Parthenonfries. München, 1961.
Arc 712.36 Brommer, F. Die Giebel des Parthenon. Mainz, 1959.
Arc 712.37 Orlandos, Anastasios K. Ta charagmata tou Parthenōuos. Athēnai, 1973.

Arc 716 Archaeology - Local - Greece - Athens - Other special topics

Arc 716.1 Welcker, F.G. Der Felsaltar des Höchsten Zens oder das Pelasgikon zu Athen. Berlin, 1852.
Arc 716.2 Kirchhoff, F.C. Vergleichung der Überreste vom Theater des Dionysuszu Athen. Altona, 1882.
Arc 716.2.2 Kirchhoff, F.C. Neue Messungen der Überreste vom Theater des Dionysus zu Athen. Altona, 1883.
Arc 716.2.5 Wheeler, James R. The theatre of Dionysus. n.p., n.d.
Arc 716.2.10F Das Dionysos Theater in Athen. v.1-3,4. Stuttgart, 1935-50. 2v.
Arc 716.2.15 Pickard-Cambridge, Arthur Wallace. The theater of Dionysus in Athens. Oxford, 1946.
Arc 716.2.20 Maass, Michael. Die Prohedrie des Dionysostheaters in Athen. München, 1952.
Arc 716.3 Bötticher, Karl. Die Thymele der Athena Nike. Berlin, 1880.
Arc 716.3.2 Kekulé, R. Die Balustrade des Templs der Athena-Nike. Leipzig, 1869.
Arc 716.3.5 Carpenter, Rhys. The sculpture of the Nike temple parapet. Cambridge, 1929.
Arc 716.4 Bursian, C. De Foro Atheniensium Disputatio. Zürich, 1865.
Arc 716.4.5 Dörpfeld, W. Alt-Athen und seine Agora. Berlin, 1937-39. 2v.
Arc 716.4.10 American School of Classical Studies at Athens. The Athenian Agora. Princeton, n.d. 18v.
Arc 716.4.12 American School of Classical Studies at Athens. Excavations of the Athenian Agora. Princeton. 1-9
Arc 716.4.20 American School of Classical Studies at Athens. The Athenian Agora. 2. ed. Athens, 1962.
Arc 716.5 White, J.W. The Opisthodomus on the Acropolis at Athens. n.p., 1894?
Arc 716.6 Mueller, R.O. Minervae Poliadis Sacra et Aedem in Arce Athenarum. Göttingen, 1820.
Arc 716.7 Forchhammer, P.W. Das Erechtheion. Kiel, 1879.
Arc 716.7.5A Bötticher, Karl. Das Poliastempel als Wohnhaus des Königs Erechtheus. Berlin, 1851.
Arc 716.7.5B Bötticher, Karl. Das Poliastempel als Wohnhaus des Königs Erechtheus. Berlin, 1851.
Arc 716.7.10F Paton, James M. The Erechtheum. Cambridge, 1927.
Arc 716.7.10PF Paton, James M. The Erechtheum. Atlas. Cambridge, 1927.

Arc 716 Archaeology - Local - Greece - Athens - Other special topics - cont.

Arc 716.7.15F Dörpfeld, W. Erechtheion. Berlin, 1942.
Arc 716.7.20 Kontoleon, N.M. To Erehtheion ôs iokodomema chthonias latreias. Athênai, 1949.
Arc 716.8 Pervanoglu, P. Die Grabsteine der alten Griechen. Leipzig, 1863.
Arc 716.9 Köster, A. Das Stadion von Athen. Berlin, n.d.
Arc 716.10 Ross, Ludwig. Das Theseion und der Tempel des Ares in Athen. Halle, 1852.
Arc 716.12A Karo, G.H. An Attic cemetery. Philadelphia, 1943.
Arc 716.12B Karo, G.H. An Attic cemetery. Philadelphia, 1943.
Arc 716.14.2 Brunnsaaker, Sture. The tyrant slayers of Kritios and Nesiotes: a critical study of the sources and restorations. 2. ed. Stockholm, 1971.

Arc 720 Archaeology - Local - Italy - Folios [Discontinued]

Htn Arc 720.7.5* Major, T. Les ruines de Paestum. Londres, 1769.
Arc 720.9 Micali, G. Storia degli antichi popoli italiani. v.1-3; atlas. Firenze, 1832. 4v.
Arc 720.9.2 Micali, G. Storia degli antichi popoli italiani. 2. ed. Firenze, 1833.
Arc 720.9.2.5F Micali, G. Antichi monumenti per servire all'opera...l'Italia. Firenze, 1810.
Arc 720.9.7 Micali, G. Storia degli antichi popoli italiani. 3. ed. v.1-4. Firenze, 1849. 2v.
Arc 720.11 Vermiglioli, G.B. Dei monumenti di Perugia etrusca e romana. pts.1-4. Perugia, 1855-70. 2v.
Arc 720.11PF Vermiglioli, G.B. Dei monumenti di Perugia etrusca e romana. Table. Perugia, 1870.
Arc 720.11.5 Vermiglioli, G.B. Dei monumenti di Perugia etrusca e romana. Pt.1. Perugia, 1855.
Htn Arc 720.12* Middleton, J. Grecian remains in Italy. London, 1812.
Htn Arc 720.14* Fontana, D. Del modo tenuto...liobelisco vaticano. Roma, 1590.
Arc 720.16PF Alvino, Francesco. Amfiteatro campano illustrato. Napoli, 1842. 2v.
Arc 720.18PF Promis, Carlo. Le antichità di Aosta. Torino, 1862. 2v.
NEDL Arc 720.200 Graevuis, J.G. Thesaurus antiquitatum et historiarum Italiae. Lugdunum Batavorum, 1704-23. 16v.
NEDL Arc 720.200.2 Graevius, J.G. Thesaurus antiquitatum et historiarum Siciliae. v.1-15. Lugdunum Batavorum, 1723-25. 8v.
Arc 720.200.5 Poleni, G. Catalogi...ad thesauros antiquitatum. Bononiae, 1853.
Arc 720.201 Montfaucon, B. de. The antiquities of Italy. 2. ed. London, 1725.
Arc 720.202 Bartolini, D. L'antico cassino e il primitivo monasterio. Montecassino, 1880.
Htn Arc 720.203* Sallengre, A. de. Novus thesaurus antiquitatum romanorum. The Hague, 1716. 3v.
Htn Arc 720.204* Panvini, O. Antiquitatum veronensium libri VIII. Padua, 1648.
Arc 720.205 Vila, G. de. Thesaurus antiquitatum beneventanarum. Romae, 1754.
Arc 720.206 Maps. Pozzuoli. Pozzuoli e contorni. Napoli, 1810.
Arc 720.207 Massazza, P.A. L'arco antico di Susa. Torino, 1750.
NEDL Arc 720.208 Ferrero, E. L'arc d'Auguste à Suse. Turin, 1901.
Arc 720.209 Livy, P. Le abitazioni Lacustri di Fimon. Venezia, 1876.
Arc 720.210 Nottingham. Museum. Illustrated catalogue of classical antiquities. Nottingham, n.d.
Arc 720.211 Rome. Istituto di Archeologia. Instituto archeologica centrum semertria. Roma, 1879.
Arc 720.212 Monteluis, O. La civilization primitive en Italie. pt.1-2; plates. Stockholm, 1895. 5v.
Arc 720.212.5 Monteluis, O. Die vorklassiche Chronologie Italiens. Stockholm, 1912. 2v.
Arc 720.213 Gusmann, P. La villa imperiale de Tibur. Paris, 1904.
Arc 720.214F Grassi. Rappresentazione...edifizi...di Piza. Piza, 1839.
Arc 720.215 Mayer, M. La coppa tarantina di argento dorato. Bari, 1910.
Arc 720.216 Fiorelli, G. Monumenti cumani. Napoli, 1853.
Arc 720.217 Pallastrelli, B. La città d'Umbria. Piacenza, 1864.
Arc 720.218F Minto, Antonio. Marsiliana d'Albegna. Firenze, 1921.
Arc 720.219F Nibby, Antonio. Viaggio antiquario ad Ostia. Roma, 1829.
Arc 720.220F Gastaldi, B. Nuovi cenni sugli oggetti di alta antichità. Torino, 1862.

Arc 722 Archaeology - Local - Italy - Pamphlet volumes

Arc 722.1 Pamphlet box. Italy. Archeology.
Arc 722.5 Pamphlet box. Archeology. Italy.

Arc 723 Archaeology - Local - Italy - General works

Arc 723.1 Abeken, W. Mittelitalien. Stuttgart, 1843.
Arc 723.2 Eustace, J.C. A classical tour through Italy. London, 1841. 3v.
Arc 723.3 Hoare, R.C. A classical tour through Italy and Sicily. London, 1819. 2v.
Arc 723.4 Forsyth, J. Remarks on antiquities, arts and letters. Boston, 1818.
Arc 723.4.2 Forsyth, J. Remarks on antiquities, arts and letters. 3. ed. London, 1824. 2v.
Arc 723.4.4 Forsyth, J. Remarks on antiquities, arts and letters. 4. ed. London, 1835.
Arc 723.5A Helbig, W. Beiträge zur altitalischen Kultur und Kunstgeschichte. Leipzig, 1879.
Arc 723.5B Helbig, W. Beiträge zur altitalischen Kultur und Kunstgeschichte. Leipzig, 1879.
Arc 723.6 Martha, Jules. Manuel d'archéologie étrusque et romaine. Paris, 1884.
Arc 723.8 Gentile, I. Trattato di archeologia e storia dell'arte italiano. Milano, 1901. 2v.
Arc 723.9 Antiquités romaines...mémoires de comte de B. La Haye, 1750.
Arc 723.10A Peet, T.E. Stone and bronze ages in Italy and Sicily. Oxford, 1909.
Arc 723.10B Peet, T.E. Stone and bronze ages in Italy and Sicily. Oxford, 1909.
Arc 723.11 Frothingham, Arthur L. Roman cities in Italy and Dalmatia. N.Y., 1910.
Arc 723.11.5 Frothingham, Arthur L. Roman cities in Northern Italy and Dalmatia. London, 1910.
Arc 723.12 Kelsall, Charles. Classical excursion from Rome to Arpino. Geneva, 1820.
Arc 723.14 Barthélemy, J.J. Voyage en Italie. Paris, 1801.
Arc 723.15F Randall-McIver, David. Villanovans and early Etruscans. Oxford, 1924.
Arc 723.15.7 Randall-McIver, David. The iron age in Italy. Oxford, 1927.

Arc 723 Archaeology - Local - Italy - General works - cont.

Arc 723.15.15 Randall-McIver, David. Italy before the Romans. Oxford, 1928.
Arc 723.16PF Pinza, Giovanni. Storia della civitá latina dalle origini al secolo V avante Christo. Roma, 1924.
Arc 723.17 Sergi, Giuseppi. Italia, le origini. Torino, 1919.
Arc 723.18 Toscanelli, Nello. Le origini italiche. Milano, 1914.
Arc 723.19.2 Seta, Alessandro. Italia antica. 2a ed. Bergamo, 1928.
Arc 723.20.10F Forma Italiae. Roma, 1926- 17v.
Arc 723.20.12F Forma Italiae. Sardinia. v.1-2. Roma, 1952-54.
Arc 723.20.14F Forma Italiae. Serie II documenti. Firenze, 1972-
Arc 723.22 Messerschmidt, Franz. Bronzezeit und frühe Eisenzeit in Italien. Berlin, 1935.
Arc 723.23A Whatmough, J. The foundations of Roman Italy. London, 1937.
Arc 723.23B Whatmough, J. The foundations of Roman Italy. London, 1937.
Arc 723.23C Whatmough, J. The foundations of Roman Italy. London, 1937.
Arc 723.24 Haftmann, W. Das italienische Säulenmonument. Leipzig, 1939.
Arc 723.25 Patroni, G. Storia politica d'Italia. Milano, 1937. 2v.
Arc 723.25.5 Patroni, G. La preistoria. Milano, 1951. 2v.
Arc 723.26 Comitato esecutivo per le fete del 1911, Rome. Per una esposizione di etnografia italiana in Roma nel 1911. 2a ed. Firenze, 1909.
Arc 723.28F Blake, Marion E. Ancient Roman construction in Italy from the pre-historica period to Augustus. Washington, 1947.
Arc 723.30 Blake, Marion E. Roman construction in Italy from Tiberius through the Flavians. Washington, 1959.
Arc 723.30.5 Blake, Marion E. Roman construction in Italy from Nerva through the Antonines. Philadelphia, 1973.
Arc 723.33 Grimal, Pierre. In search of Ancient Italy. 1st American ed. N.Y., 1964.
Arc 723.34 Istituto Italiano di Preistoria e Protostoria. Atti della VII riunione scientifica. Firenze, 1963.
Arc 723.34.5 Istituto Italiano di Preistoria e Protostoria. Atti della XI e XII riunione scientifica. Firenze, 1968.
Arc 723.36 Centro Studi Ciociaria. Gli archeologi italiani in onore di Amedeo Maiuri. Cava dei Tirreni, 1965.
Arc 723.38 Simposia Internazionale di Protostoria Italiana. Atti. Roma, 1969.
Arc 723.40 Rodmilli, Antonio M. La preistoria d'Italia alla luce delle ultime scoperte. Firenze, 1963.
Arc 723.42 Weiss, Robert. The Renaissance discovery of classical antiquity. Oxford, 1969.
Arc 723.44 Peroni, Renato. L'età del bronzo nella penisola italiana. Firenze, 1971-
Arc 723.46 Barfield, Lawrence. Northern Italy before Rome. London, 1971.

Arc 726 Archaeology - Local - Italy - Local; Special topics

Arc 726.1 Chienci, G. Antichi monumenti della Pianosa. Reggio, 1875.
Arc 726.2 Lasena, P. Dell'antico ginnasio napoletano. n.p., n.d.
Arc 726.2.2 Lasena, P. Dell'antico ginnasio napoletano. n.p., n.d.
Arc 726.2.4 Capasso, B. Sull'antico sito di Napoli e Palepoli dubbie e conghietture. Napoli, 1855.
Arc 726.2.5 Capasso, B. Napoli greca-romana. Topografia. Napoli, 1905.
Arc 726.2.9 Günther, R.T. Contributions to a study of earth movements in the Bay of Naples. Oxford, 1903.
Arc 726.2.15 Günther, R.T. Pausilypon...imperial villa near Naples. Oxford, 1913.
Arc 726.2.19 Antiquités des environs de Naples. Naples, 1913.
Arc 726.2.25 Panvini, P. Il forestiere alle antichità e curiosità nationali Pozzuoli. Napoli, 1818.
Arc 726.2.30 Caterino, Antonio. Bibliografia sulle catacombe napoletane. Firenze, 1957.
Arc 726.3 Persichetti, N. Viaggio archeologico sulla Via Salaria. Roma, 1893.
Arc 726.4 Jorio, A. de. Scheletri cumani. Napoli, 1810.
Arc 726.4.5 Minieri Riccio, C. Cenni storici sulla distrutta città di Cuma. Napoli, 1846.
Arc 726.4.10 Guidobaldi, D. de. Intorno ad una imagine cerea. Napoli, 1853.
Arc 726.4.15A Consoli Fiego, G. Cumae and the Phlegraean fields. Naples, 1927.
Arc 726.4.15B Consoli Fiego, G. Cumae and the Phlegraean fields. Naples, 1927.
Arc 726.4.20 Maiuri, Amedeo. The Phlegraean fields, from Virgil's tomb to the grotto of the Cumaean Sibyl. Rome, 1937.
Arc 726.5 Cabral, S. Delle ville e de' più notabili monumenti. Roma, 1779.
Htn Arc 726.6* Orsati, S. Monumenta patavina. Padova, 1652.
Arc 726.7 Visconti, E.A. Monumenti gabini della Villa Pinciana. Milano, 1835.
Arc 726.7.5 Visconti, E.A. Monumenti gabini della Villa Pinciana. Roma, 1797.
Arc 726.8 Pigorini, L. Le abitazioni Palustri di Fontanellato. Parma, 1865.
Arc 726.9 Montfaucon, B. de. Diarium italicum. Paris, 1702.
Htn Arc 726.9.15* Montjaucon, B. de. Diarium italicum. London, 1711.
Arc 726.10 Schumacher, K. Eine Praenestinische Ciste. Heidelberg, 1891.
Arc 726.10.2 Brunn, H. Cista prenestina. Roma, 1864.
Arc 726.10.4 Barthélemy, J.J. Explication de la mosaique de Palestrine. Paris, 1760.
Arc 726.10.5 Marucchi, Orazio. Guida archeologica dell'antica Preneste. Roma, 1885.
Arc 726.10.9 Behn, F. Die ficoronische Cista. Diss. Rostock, 1907.
Arc 726.10.10 Behn, F. Die ficoronische Cista. Leipzig, 1907.
Arc 726.10.11 Dernan Mugoffin, R. Study of the topography of Preneste. Baltimore, 1908.
Arc 726.10.14 Marucchi, Orazio. Guida archeologica della città di Palestrina. Roma, 1912.
Arc 726.10.17 Marucchi, Orazio. Il tempio della fortuna prenestina. Roma, 1908.
Arc 726.11 Michaelis, A. Der Silberschatz von Boscoreale. Berlin, 1896.
Arc 726.11.5 Héron de Villefosse, Antoine. L'argenterie et les bijoux d'or du trésor de Boscoreale. Paris, 1903.
Arc 726.11.7 Héron de Villefosse, Antoine. Le trésor d'argenterie de Boscoreale. Paris, 189-.
Arc 726.11.9 Corte, M. della. Cleopatra, M. Antonio e Ottaviano nelle allegorie storico-umoristiche delle argenterie del tesoro di Boscoreale. Pompei, 1951.

Classified Listing

Arc 726 **Archaeology - Local - Italy - Local; Special topics - cont.**

Arc 726.12.5 Mayer, M. Molfetta und Matera. Leipzig, 1924.
Arc 726.13 Voigt, M. Über das römische System der Wege in alten Italien. n.p., 1872.
Arc 726.14 Remedi, A.A. Relazione delli scari fatti in Luni. Sarzana, 1860.
Arc 726.16 Monteluis, O. Tombe ed antichità galliche in Italia. Roma, 1877.
Arc 726.17 Johanneau, E. Lettre...sur l'inscription...du Lion de Venise. n.p., 1808.
Arc 726.18 Saccardo, G. I pilastri acritani. Venezia, 1887.
Arc 726.19 Angelucci, A. I cannoni veneti di Famagosta. Venezia, n.d.
Arc 726.20 Tononi, A.G. Documenti inediti...scoperta di Velleia. Modena, 1881.
Arc 726.20.3 Tononi, A.G. Velleia studiata da un erudita francese. n.p., 1887.
Arc 726.20.7PF Antolini, G. Le rovine di Veleia misurate e disegnate. Pt.1-2. Milano, 1819-22.
Arc 726.21 Bertrand, A. Sepultures à l'incinération de Poggio Renzo. n.p., 1874.
Arc 726.22 Visconti, A. Lettera al signor Giuseppe Carnevali di Albano. Roma, 1817.
Arc 726.22.5A Bryan, W.R. Italic hut urns and hut urn cemeteries. Rome, 1925.
Arc 726.22.5B Bryan, W.R. Italic hut urns and hut urn cemeteries. Rome, 1925.
Arc 726.22.9 Duhn, F. von. Italische Gräberkunde. Heidelberg, 1924-39. 2v.
Arc 726.23 Vercelli, C. di. Per un ricordo al padre L. Bruzza. Vercelli, 1884.
Arc 726.24 Müller, G.A. Tempel zu Tivoli bei Rom. Leipzig, 1899.
Arc 726.24.7 Sanctis, D. de. Dissertazioni...la villa d'Orazio, il mausoleo di Plauzj in Tivoli. Ravenna, 1784.
Arc 726.24.8 Bardi, Giovanni de'. Della imp. villa Adriana. Firenze, 1825.
Arc 726.24.9 Nibby, Antonio. Descrizione della villa Adriana. Roma, 1827.
Arc 726.24.11 Lanciani, R. La villa Adriana; guida e descrizione. Roma, 1906.
Arc 726.24.13FA Kähler, H. Hadrian und seine Villa bei Tivoli. Berlin, 1950.
Arc 726.24.13FB Kähler, H. Hadrian und seine Villa bei Tivoli. Berlin, 1950.
Arc 726.24.15 Paribeni, R. The villa of the emperor Hadrian at Tivoli. Milan, 1930?
Arc 726.24.17 Aurigemma, S. La villa Adriana presso Tivoli. Tivoli, 1948.
Arc 726.24.20 Aurigemma, S. La villa Adriana. 2a ed. Tivoli, 1953.
Arc 726.24.22 Aurigemma, S. Die Hadriansvilla bei Tivoli. Tivoli, 1955.
Arc 726.24.24F Aurigemma, S. Villa Adriana. Roma, 1961.
Arc 726.25 Fea, Carlo. Relazione di un viaggio ad Ostia. Roma, 1802.
Arc 726.25.5 Vagliere, Dante. Piccola giuda di Ostia. Roma, 1914.
Arc 726.25.7 Vagliere, Dante. Ostia; cenni storici e guida. Roma, 1914.
Arc 726.25.13 Calza, Guido. Il teatro romano di Ostia. Roma, 1927.
Arc 726.25.15F Calza, Guido. La necropoli del porto di Roma nell'isola sacra. Roma, 1940.
Arc 726.25.16F Lugli, G. Il porto di Roma imperiale e l'agro portuense. Roma, 1935.
Arc 726.25.17 Calza, Guido. Ostia, guida storico monumentale. Milano, 1925?
Arc 726.25.18 Calza, Guido. Ostia; historical guide to the monuments. Milano, 1926.
Arc 726.25.25A Carcopino, J. Ostie. Paris, 1929.
Arc 726.25.25B Carcopino, J. Ostie. Paris, 1929.
Arc 726.25.30 Schaal, Hans. Ostia, der Welthafen Roms. Bremen, 1957.
Arc 726.25.35 Calza, Raissa. Ostia. Firenze, 1959.
Arc 726.26 Borgia, S. Breve i storia dell'antica città di Tadino. Roma, 1751.
Arc 726.27 Rossi, G.B. de. Porticus triumphi. Roma, 1889.
Arc 726.27.3 Schmatz, Joseph. Baiae, das erste luxusbad der Römer. Regensburg, 1905-06.
Arc 726.27.10 Paget, Robert F. In the footsteps of Orpheus. N.Y., 1968.
Arc 726.28 Altmann, W. Die italischen Rundbauten. Berlin, 1906.
Arc 726.29 Willers, H. Römische Bronzeindustrie von Capua und von Niedergermanien. Hannover, 1907.
Htn Arc 726.30* Zuzzeri, G.L. D'una antica villa. Venezia, 1746.
Arc 726.31 Ghirardini, G. Il museo nazionale atestino. Padova, 1903.
Arc 726.32 Pagenstecher, R. Unteritalische Grabdenkmäler. Strassburg, 1912.
Arc 726.33 Milani, L.A. Le recenti scoperte di antichita in Verona. Verona, 1891.
Arc 726.34 Centurione, P.A.M. Studie recenti sopra i Nuraghi. Prato, 1886.
Arc 726.34.5 Waltzan, H. Reise auf der Insel Sardinien. Leipzig, 1869.
Arc 726.35 Giorgi, Antonio. Dissertazione...monumento etrusco...di Volterra. Firenze, 1752.
Arc 726.36 Rosso, G. del. Saggio...sui monumenti della antica città di Fiesole. Firenze, 1814.
Arc 726.36.5 Galli, Edoardo. Fiesole. Gli scair, il museo civico. Milano, 1914.
Arc 726.36.10 Otto, prince of Hesse. Die langobardenzeitlichen Grabfunde aus Fiesole bei Florenz. München, 1966.
Arc 726.37F Maye, M. Apulien vor und während der Hellenisirung. Leipzig, 1914.
Arc 726.38 Marchisio, A.F. Per l'archeologia del territorio albese. Alba, 1913.
Arc 726.39 Venuti, R. Osservazioni sopra il fiume Clitunno. Roma, 1753.
NEDL Arc 726.40 Meomartini, A. I monumenti e le opere d'arte. Benevento, 1889.
Arc 726.41 Bourguet, Louis. Spiegazione di alcuni monumenti degli antichi Palasgi. Pesaro, 1735.
Arc 726.42 Schulz, Bruno. Das Grabmal des Theoderich zu Ravenna. Würzburg, 1911.
Arc 726.42.5 Savini, Gaetano. Per i monumenti e per la storia di Ravenna. Ravenna, 1914.
Arc 726.44 Colini, Giuseppe A. Il sepolcreto de Remedello-Sotto. Parma, 1899-1902.
Arc 726.45 Lupi, Clemente. Nuovi studi sulle antiche terme pisane. Pisa, 1885.
Arc 726.45.15 Toscanelli, N. Pisa nell'antichità dalle età preistoriche alla caduta dell'impero romano. Pisa, 1933. 2v.
Htn Arc 726.46* Ficorini, Francesco de. Le memorie ritrovate...de Labrico. Roma, 1745.
Arc 726.47 Åberg, Nils. Die Gothen und Langobarden in Italien. Uppsala, 1923.

Arc 726 **Archaeology - Local - Italy - Local; Special topics - cont.**

Arc 726.48 Colucci, G. Sulle antiche città picene Falera e Tignio. Fermo, 1777.
Arc 726.48.2 Colucci, G. Alla dissertazione epistolare sulle antiche città picene Falera e Tignio. Appendice. Macerata, 1778.
Arc 726.49 Guarini, R. Ricerche sull'antica città di Eclano. 2a ed. Appendice. Napoli, 1814-15.
Arc 726.50 Tonini, Luigi. Rimini avanti il principio. v.1-2. Rimini, 1848.
Arc 726.51F Caruana, A.A. Report on the Phoenician and Roman antiquities in the group of the islands of Malta. Malta, 1882.
Arc 726.52 Holland, Louise. The Faliscans in prehistoric times. Rome, 1925.
Arc 726.53 Neppi Modona, A. Cortona etrusca e romana. Firenze, 1925.
Arc 726.54 Iozzi, Oliviero. Cenno storico della antica Libarna. Pisa, 1890.
Htn Arc 726.55* Mazzella, S. Sito, et antichita della città di Pozzuolo e del sus amenissimo distretto. Napoli, 1606.
Arc 726.56 Albert, Maurice. De villis Tiburtinis, principe Augusto Thesim proponebat. Parisios, 1883.
Arc 726.58 Colini, Giuseppe A. Necropoli de Pianello presso Genza (Ancona). Parma, 1913.
Arc 726.59 Zammit, Themistocles. Prehistoric Malta; the Tarxien temples. London, 1930.
Arc 726.59.5 Ceschi, Carlo. Architettura dei templi magalitici di Malta. Roma, 1939.
Arc 726.59.15 Ugolini, L.M. Malta; origini della civiltà mediterranea. Roma, 1934.
Arc 726.59.25 Barbaro, C.A. Degli avanzi d'alcuni antichissimi edifizi, scoperti in Malta l'anno 1768. Malta, 1794.
Arc 726.59.30 Evans, John D. Malta. London, 1959.
Arc 726.59.35 Missione archeologica italiana a Malta. Rapporto preliminare della campagna. Roma. 1963+ 6v.
Arc 726.59.40 Frost, Honor. The mortar wreck in Mellieha Bay. London, 1969.
Arc 726.59.45 Trump, David H. Malta: an archaeological guide. London, 1972.
Arc 726.60 Dumitrescu, V. L'età del ferro nel Piceno. Tesi. Bucarest, 1929.
Arc 726.60.5 Speranza, G. Il Piceno dalle origini alla fine d'ogni sua autonomia sotto Augusto. v.1-2. Ancona, 1934.
Arc 726.61 Michaelis, Adolf. Das corsinische Silbergefäss. Leipzig, 1859.
Arc 726.62 Terra d'Otranto. Commissione Conservatrice dei Monumenti Storici e di Belle Arti. Relazione. Lecci.
Arc 726.63 Miceli, Salvatore. Vicovaro e la villa di Q. Orazio Flacco. Roma, 1929.
Arc 726.64 Nibby, Antonio. Della via portuense. Roma, 1827.
Arc 726.65F Nibby, Antonio. Del monumento sepolcrale detto volgarmente degli Orazii e Curiazii; discurso. Roma, 1834.
Arc 726.66 Passeri, G.B. De marmoreo sepulcrali cinerario. Romae, 1773.
Arc 726.67F Marchi, G. La stipe tributata alle divinità delle acque Apollinari. Roma, 1852.
Htn Arc 726.68* Nazari, G.B. Bressa anticha. Bressa, 1562.
Arc 726.68.5 Nazari, G.B. Brescia antica. Brescia, 1658.
Arc 726.69F Pennsylvania. University. University Museum. Excavations at Minturnae. Rome, 1933-35. 2v.
Arc 726.70F American School of Classical Studies in Rome. The triumphal arch of Trajan at Beneventum. Rome, 1896.
Arc 726.70.5 American School of Classical Studies in Rome. The triumphal arch of Trajan at Beneventum. Rome, 19- ?
Arc 726.70.10F Garger, E. Der Trajansbogen in Benevent. Berlin, 1943.
Arc 726.71 Bucciolotti, A. Della origine e delle antiche città de' Sabini. Roma, 1825.
Arc 726.71.10 Guattani, G.A. Monumenti Sabini. Roma, 1827-28. 3v.
Arc 726.72 Tolomei, Antonio. La cappella degli Scrovigni e l'arena di Padova. Padova, 1881.
Arc 726.73 Hadrawa, N. Ragguagli di varii scavi. Napoli, 1793.
Arc 726.73.5 Hadrawa, N. Ragguagli di varii scavi. Dresda, 1794.
Htn Arc 726.73.15* Douglas, N. Some antiquarian notes. Napoli, 1907.
Arc 726.74F Crespellani, A. Del sepolcreto e degli altri monumenti antichi scoperti presso Bazzano. Modena, 1875.
Arc 726.75F Lanci, Fortunato. Intorno un antico specchio metallico epistola...Cavaaliere Odoardo Gerhard in occasion di sue nozze...Emilia de Riess. Roma, 1842.
Arc 726.76F Klumbach, H. Tarentiner Grabkunst. Reuttingen, 1937.
Arc 726.77F Marescalchi, A. Storia della vite e del vino in Italia. Milano, 1931-37. 3v.
Arc 726.78F Savignoni, L. Relazione sopra gli scavi eseguiti a Norba nell'estate dell'anno 1901. Roma, 1902.
Arc 726.79 Marzulla, A. Tombe dipinte scoperte nel territorio Pestano. Salerno, 1935.
Arc 726.81F Dohan, Edith H. Italic tomb-groups in the University Museum. Philadelphia, 1942.
Arc 726.83 Conestabile, Giancarlo. Sopra un cista in bronzo con rapparesentanze a graffito. Firenze, 1866.
Arc 726.85 Lamb, Carl. Die Tempel von Paestum. Leipzig, 1944.
Arc 726.87 Antonielli, U. La prima nave imperiale del lago di Nemi. Roma, 1930.
Arc 726.89 Ferrare, F. Relazione sulle antichita prehistoriche rinvenute nella contrado comino presso Guardeagrele. Guardeagrele, 1913.
Arc 726.91 Bertoni, G. La cattedrale modenese. Modena, 1914.
Arc 726.93F Price, F. A restoration of "Horace's Sabine Villa". n.p., 1932.
Arc 726.95F Brusin, G. Aquileia. n.p., n.d.
Arc 726.97F Zancani Montuoro, P. Heraion. v.1-2, atlases. Roma, 1951. 4v.
Arc 726.99 Consortini, L. Volterra nell'antichità. Volterra, 1940.
Arc 726.101 Calderini, A. L'anfiteatro romano. Milano, 1940.
Arc 726.103 Maetzke, G. Florentia (Firenze). Rome, 1941.
Arc 726.105 Cressedi, G. Velitrae. Roma, 1953.
Arc 726.107 Pietrangeli, Carlo. Mevania. Roma, 1953.
Arc 726.108 Pietrangeli, Carlo. Scavi e scoperte di antichità il pontificato di Pio VI. 2. ed. Roma, 1958.
Arc 726.110 Lenotti, T. L'arena di Verona. Verona, 1954.
Arc 726.112 Levi, Doro. L'ipogeo di San Salvatore di Cabras in Sardegna. Roma, 1949.
Arc 726.115 Orsi, Libero d'. Gli scavi di Stabia a cura del Comitato per gli scavi di Stabia. Napoli, 1954.
Arc 726.120 Maiuri, Amedeo. Saggi di varia antichità. Venezia, 1954.
Arc 726.122 Maiuri, Amedeo. Vita d'archeologo. Napoli, 1959.
Arc 726.125F Säflund, G. Le terremare delle provincie di Modena. Lund, 1939.
Arc 726.130 Akerstrom, A. Der geometrische Stil in Italien. Lund, 1943.

Classified Listing

Arc 726 Archaeology - Local - Italy - Local; Special topics - cont.

Arc 726.135 Battisti, C. La Venezia Tridentina nella preistoria. Firenze, 1954.
Arc 726.135.5 Lunz, Reimo. Ur- und Frühgeschichte Südtirols. Bozen, 1973.
Arc 726.140 Marconi, Pirro. Verona romana. Bergamo, 1937.
Arc 726.140.10 Grancelli, Umberto. Il piano di fondazione di Verona romana. Verona, 1964.
Arc 726.145 Convegno di Studi Plorici e Archeologici Veleiati, 1st, Piacenza. Studi veleiati. Piacenza, 1955.
Arc 726.150 Gentili, Gino Vinicio. Auximum (Osimo) regio V. Picenum. Roma, 1955.
Arc 726.155 Giorgi, Gello. Suasa senonum. Parma, 1953.
Arc 726.160 Buccolini, Geralberto. Il problema archeologico di Orvieto antica. Orvieto, 1935.
Arc 726.165 Berti, Leo. Scoperte paletnologiche e archeologiche nella provincia di Treviso. 1. ed. Firenze, 1956.
Arc 726.170 Schiavo, Armando. Acquedotti romani e medioevali. Napoli, 1935.
Arc 726.175 Toti, Odoardo. La città medioevale di Centocelle. Allumicre, 1958.
Arc 726.180 Forno, Federico dal. Il teatro romano di Verona. Verona, 1954.
Arc 726.185 Franciscis, Alfonso de. Mausolei romani di Campania. Napoli, 1957.
Arc 726.195 Pesce, Gennaro. Sarcafagi romani di Sardegna. Roma, 1957.
Arc 726.200 Willemsen, C.A. Apulia, imperial splendor in southern Italy. N.Y., 1959.
Arc 726.202 Oliver, Andrew. The reconstruction of two Apulian tomb groups. Bern, 1968.
Arc 726.205F Pesce, Gennaro. I rilievi dell'anfiteatro Campano. Roma, 1941.
Arc 726.206F Capua preromana; le antichita etrusche di Santa Maria Capua Vetere. v.1, pt.7. v.2, pt.1,2. Firenze, 1965- 3v.
Arc 726.210 Jacopi, Giulio. I ritrovamenti dell'antro cosiddetto "di Tiberio" a Sperlongo. Roma, 1958.
Arc 726.215 Pallottino, Massimo. Turquinia. Milano, 1959.
Arc 726.215.5 Hencken, Hugh O'Neill. Tarquinia and Etruscan origins. London, 1968.
Arc 726.216 Zecchini, Michelangelo. L'archeologia nell'Arcipelago toscano. Pisa, 1971.
Arc 726.220 Jacopi, Giulio. L. Munazio Planco e il suo mausoleo a Gaeta. Milano, 1960.
Arc 726.225F Degani, Mario. Il tesoro romano barbarico di Reggio Emilia. Firenze, 1959.
Arc 726.235F Studi storici; topografici ed archeologici sul Portus Augusti di Ravenna e sul territorio classicano. Firenze, 1961.
Arc 726.235.5 Convegno internazionale di studi sulle antichità di classe. Atti del Convegno internazionale di studi sulle antichità di classe. Ravenna, 1968.
Arc 726.235.10 Cortesi, Giuseppe. Il porto e la città di classe. Alfonsine, 1967.
Arc 726.237 Visscher, Fernand de. Héraclès Epitrapezios. Paris, 1962.
Arc 726.237.5 Alba fucens. Rapports et études présentes par J. Mercens. Bruxelles, 1969. 2v.
Arc 726.240 Paroscandola, A. I fenomeni fra disisneici del Serapeo di pozzuoli. Napoli, 1947.
Arc 726.241 Huelsen, Hans von. Funde in der Magna Graecia. Gottingen, 1962.
Arc 726.242 Cassani, Lino. Repertorio di antichità. Novara, 1962.
Arc 726.245 Guido, M. Sardinia. London, 1963.
Arc 726.246 Pesce, Gennaro. Sardegna punica. Cagliari, 1961.
Arc 726.246.5 Moscati, Sabatino. Le stele puniche di Nora nel museo nazionale di Cagliari. Roma, 1970.
Arc 726.247 Rome. Università. Monte Sirai. Roma, 1964. 4v.
Arc 726.248 Pesce, Gennaro. Le statuette puniche di Bithia. Roma, 1965.
Arc 726.249 Aurigemma, Salvatore. I monumenti della necropoli romana di Sarsina. Roma, 1963.
Arc 726.250 Gierow, Pär Göran. The iron age culture of Latium. v.2, pt.1. Lund, 1964.
Arc 726.251 Susini, Giancarlo. Fonti per la storia greca e romana del Salento. Bologna, 1962.
Arc 726.252 Bindi, Vincenzo. Castel S. Flaviano. Napoli, 1879-82. 4v.
Arc 726.253 Mertens, Jozef. Ordona. Bruxelles, 1965. 4v.
Arc 726.254 Trump, David H. Central and suthern Italy before Rome. London, 1966.
Arc 726.255 Radmilli, Antonio Mario. Abruzzo preistorico. Firenze, 1965.
Arc 726.258 Östenberg, Carl Eric. Luni sul Mignone e problemi della preistoria d'Italia. Lund, 1967.
Arc 726.258.5 Luni sul Mignone. Lund, 1969.
Arc 726.260 Rome (City). Università. Istituto di Topografia Antica. Saggio di fotointerpretazione archeologica. Roma, 1964.
Arc 726.261 Stoop, Maria W. Floral figurines from south Italy. Assen, 1960.
Arc 726.262 Gasperini, Lidio. Aletrium. Roma, 1964.
Arc 726.263 Les églises piévanes de Corse, de l'époque romaine au Moyen Age. Bastia, 1972-
Arc 726.263.5 Découvertes archéologiques fortuites en Corse. v.1-2. Bastia, 1971-
Arc 726.264 Fois, Foiso. I ponti romani in Sardegna. Sassari, 1964.
Arc 726.265 Pennucci, Umberto. Bisenzo e le antiche civiltà intorno al lago di Bolsena. Grotte di Castro, 1964.
Arc 726.270 Giordano, Nicola. Civiltà millenarie in terra di Bari. Bari, 1963.
Arc 726.275 Usai, Angelino. Il villaggio nuragico di Seleni, Lanusei. Cagliari, 1966.
Arc 726.280 Sarsina: la cita romana, il museo archeologico. Faenza, 1967.
Arc 726.285 Grillo, Francesco. Antichità storiche e monumentali di Corigliano Calabro. Cosenza, 1965.
Arc 726.290 Pesce, Gennaro. Tharros. Cagliari, 1966.
Arc 726.295 Rittatore Vonwiller, Ferrante. La necropoli preromana della Ca'Morta, Scavi 1955-1965. Como, 1966.
Arc 726.296 Bondi, Sandro Filippo. Le stele di Monte Sirai. Roma, 1972.
Arc 726.300 Sommella, Paolo. Antichi campi di battaglia in Italia. Roma, 1967.
Arc 726.305 Venetia. Padova, 1967- 2v.
Arc 726.310 Fellmann, Rudolf. Das Grab des Lucius Munatius Plancus bei Gaeta. Basel, 1957.
Arc 726.315 Cecchini, Serena Maria. I ritrovamenti fenici e punici in Sardegna. Roma, 1969.
Arc 726.318 Schumacher, Erich. Die Protovillanova-Fundgruppe. Bonn, 1967.

Arc 726 Archaeology - Local - Italy - Local; Special topics - cont.

Arc 726.319 Coradazzi, Giovanni. Le rete stradale romana fra Brescia, Bergamo e Milano. Brescia, 1974.
Arc 726.320 Ricerche puniche nel Mediterraneo centrale. Roma, 1970.
Arc 726.322 Otto, prince of Hesse. Primo contributo alla archeologia longobarda in Toscana: Le necropoli. Firenze, 1971.
Arc 726.323 Davison, Jean M. Seven Italic tomb-groups from Narce. Firenze, 1972.
Arc 726.324 Garoffolo, Francesco. Ipponion; saggio storico-archeologico e nuove osservazioni. Reggio Calabria, 1969.
Arc 726.325 Archeologia e storia nella Lombardia padana. Bedriacum nel XIX centenario delle Battaglie. Como, 1972.
Arc 726.326 Franciosa, Nicola. La villa romana di Minori. Minori, 1968.
Arc 726.327 Bovini, Giuseppe. Antichità cristiane di San Canzian d'Isonzo. Bologna, 1973.
Arc 726.328 Convegno su Archeologia e Storia nella Lombardia Pedemontana Occidentale. Archeologia e storia nella Lombardia pedemontana occidentale. Como, 1969.
Arc 726.329 Cannas, Vincenzo Mario. I nuraghi Aleri e Nastasi e le nuove scoperte archeologiche nel territorio di Tertenia. Cagliari, 1972.
Arc 726.330 Scarani, Renato. Civiltà preromane del territorio parmense. Parma, 1971.
Arc 726.331 Galliazzo, Vittorio. I ponti di Padova romana. Padova, 1971.
Arc 726.332 Pohl, Ingrid. The iron age necropolis of Sorbo at Cerveteri. Lund, 1972.
Arc 726.333 Italy. Soprintendenza alle Antichità della Basilicata. Popoli anellenici in Basilicata. Napoli, 1971.
Arc 726.334 Angrisani, Mario. La Villa Augustea in Somma Vesuviana. Aversa, 1936.
Arc 726.335 Bonghi Jovino, Maria. La necropoli di Nola preromana. Napoli, 1969.
Arc 726.336 Chiostri, Frido. Le tombe a Tholos di Quinto nel comune di Sesto Fiorentino. n.p., 1969.
Arc 726.337 Holloway, Robert Ross. Satrianum. Providence, 1970.
Arc 726.338 Colonna di Paolo, Elena. Castel d'Asso. Roma, 1970. 2v.
Arc 726.339 Rome, Italy. Università. Istituto di Topografia Antica. Lavinium. Roma, 1972- 2v.
Arc 726.340 San Giovenale. Results of excavations conducted by the Swedish Institute of Classical Studies. Stockholm, 1972-
Arc 726.341 Arrigo, Agatino d'. Premessa geofisica alla ricerca di Sibari. Napoli, 1959.
Arc 726.341.5 Rainey, Froelich G. The search for Sybaris, 1960-1965. Roma, 1967.
Arc 726.342 Franciscis, Alfonso. Ricerche sulla topografia e i monumenti di Locri. Napoli, 1971-
Arc 726.342.5 Franciscis, Alfonso. Stato e società in Loori. Napoli, 1972.
Arc 726.343 Roth, Helmut. Die Ornamentik der Langobarden in Italien. Bonn, 1973.

Arc 730 Archaeology - Local - Sicily - Folios [Discontinued]

Arc 730.2 Cavallari, F.S. Atlante. Topografia archaeologica. Siracusa. Palermo, 1883. 2v.
Arc 730.2.2 Cavallari, F.S. Appendice. Topografia archaeologica. Siracusa. Torino, 1891.
Arc 730.2.3 Cavallari, F.S. Euryalos e le opere di difesa di Siracusa. Palermo, 1893.
Arc 730.5.3 Politi, R. Lettera di...Grove-Olympico in Agrigento. Palermo, 1819.
Arc 730.6 Hulot, J. Sélimonte. Paris, 1910.
Arc 730.6.5 Santangelo, M. Selinunte. Roma, 1953.
Arc 730.200 Pancrazi, G.M. Antichita siciliane spiegate. Naples, 1751. 2v.
Arc 730.201 Serradifalco. Le antichita della Sicilia. Palermo, 1834. 5v.
Arc 730.202 Orville, J.P. d'. Sicula, guibus Sicilae veritis ruderd. Amsterdam, 1764.
Arc 730.203 Scarabelli, Gommi. Stazione prehistorica sul monte del Castel. Imola, 1887.
Arc 730.204 Riolo, G. La porta arabo-normanna. Palermo, 1871.
Arc 730.205 Orsi, P. L'olympieion di Siracusa. Roma, 1903.
Arc 730.206 Salinas, A. Relazione sommaria intorno agli. Roma, 1894.
Arc 730.207 Salinas, A. Nuove metope arcaiche selinantine. Roma, 1892.
Arc 730.208 White, J.W. Oeri tou pelaryikon epiperikleous. Athēnai, 1894.
Arc 730.209F Rizzo, G.E. Il teatro greco di Siracusa. Milano, 1923.

Arc 733 Archaeology - Local - Sicily - General works

Arc 733.1 Cavallari, F.S. Sulla topografia di Talune città greche. Palermo, 1879.
Arc 733.2 Rivela, A. The dead cities of Sicily. Palermo, 1905.
Arc 733.3 Sicilia antiqua. Catania. 1-2,1925-1927 2v.
Arc 733.4.5 Paterno, I.V. Viaggio per tutte le antichita della Sicilia. 3a ed. Palermo, 1817.
Arc 733.6 Belgiorno, Franco Libero. I Siciliani di 15 mila anni fa. Catania, 1965.

Arc 736 Archaeology - Local - Sicily - Local; Special topics

Arc 736.1 Sehnbring, J. Historische Topographie von Akragas in Sicilien. Leipzig, 1870.
Arc 736.1.5 Bonfiglio, S. Su l'akropoli Akragantina. Girgenti, 1897.
Arc 736.1.9F Marconi, Pirro. Agrigento. Firenze, 1929.
Arc 736.1.10 Dara, G. Sulla topografia d'Agrigento del F.S. Cavallari. Girgenti, 1883.
Arc 736.1.12 Marconi, Pirro. Agrigento. Roma, 1933.
Arc 736.1.15 Griffo, Pietro. Sulla collocazione dei Telamoni nel Tempio. Agrigento, 1952.
Arc 736.2 Beulé, C.E. Les temples de Syracuse. n.p., n.d.
Arc 736.2.2 Politi, G. Siracusa pei Viaggiatori. Siracusa, 1835.
Arc 736.2.3 Letronne, A. Essai critique sur la topographie de Syracuse. Paris, 1812.
Arc 736.2.4 Lupus, B. Die Stadt Skyrakus im Alterthum. Strassburg, 1887.
Arc 736.2.9 Mirabella a Alagona, V. Dichiarazioni della pianta dell'antiche Siracuse. Napoli, 1625.
Arc 736.2.10F Mauceri, L. Il castello Eurialo. Syracuse. Roma, 1912.
Arc 736.3 Fraccia, G. Ricerche ed osservazioni. Fatte in Segesta. Palermo, 1855.
Arc 736.4 Tummarello, F. Su le origini di Erice. Trapini, 1898.
Arc 736.5 Garafalo, F.B. Le vie romane in Sicilia. Napoli, 1901.
Arc 736.6 Coglitore, I. Mozia, studi storico-archeologico. Catania, 1894.

Classified Listing

Arc 736 Archaeology - Local - Sicily - Local; Special topics - cont.
Arc 736.6.5 Whitaker, J.I.S. Motya. London, 1921.
Arc 736.6.10 Isserlin, B.S.J. Motya, a Phoenician and Carthaginian city in Sicily. Leiden, 1974.
Arc 736.7 Rossbach, Otto. Castrogiovanni...nebst einer Untersuchung. Leipzig, 1912.
Arc 736.8F Libertini, Guido. Centuripe. Catania, 1926.
Arc 736.9F Strazzeri, Niccolo. Teatro di Taormina. n.p., n.d.
Arc 736.11 Marconi, P. Himera; lo scavo del Tempio della Vittoria e del temenos. Roma, 1931.
Arc 736.11.5 Himera I. Campagne di scavo 1963-1965. Roma, 1970.
Arc 736.12 Naselli, S. L'inesplorato Monte Albura o Albuchia. Castelbuono, 1952.
Arc 736.15 Canale, C.G. Engyon. Catania, 1955.
Arc 736.17 Margani, M.N. Casmene ritrovata? Comiso, 1955.
Arc 736.19 Kayser, Hans. Paestum. Heidelburg, 1958.
Arc 736.20 Missione Archeologica della Soprintendenza alle Antichità della Sicilia Occidentale e dell'Università di Roma. Mozia. Roma, 1964- 8v.
Arc 736.22 Vallet, Georges. Megara Hyblaca. v.2,4. Text and atlas. Paris, 1964- 4v.
Arc 736.24 Ciancio, Salvatore. Leontinoi: anni di ricerche archeologiche. Lentini, 1965.
Arc 736.26 Grotta Regina. Roma, 1969.

Arc 740 Archaeology - Local - Etruria - Folios [Discontinued]
Arc 740.6 Zannoni, A. Gli scavi della Certosa in Bologna. Bologna, 1876-84. 2v.
Arc 740.6.5 Zannoni, A. Sugli scavi della Certosa. Bologna, 1871.
Arc 740.8 Visconti, C.P.E. Antichi monumenti sepolcrali nel ducato di Ceri. Roma, 1836.
Arc 740.10PF Pinza, G. Materiali per la etnologia antica toscana laziale. Milano, 1915.
Htn Arc 740.200* Gorio, A.F. Museum Etruscum. Florence, 1737. 3v.
Arc 740.201 Gerhard, E. Etruskische Spiegel. v.1-2,3,4,5. Berlin, 1843- 4v.
Arc 740.202 Brunn, H. I relievi delle urne etrusche. Rome, 1870-1916. 3v.
Htn Arc 740.203* Dempster, T. De Etruria regali libri VII. Florence, 1723-24. 2v.
Arc 740.204 Inghirami, F. Monumenti etruschi. Badia, 1821-25. 9v.
Arc 740.204.2 Inghirami, F. Indici dei monumenti etruschi. Badia, 1826.
Arc 740.205 Gsell, S. Fouilles...nécropole de Vulci. Paris, 1891.

Arc 742 Archaeology - Local - Etruria - Pamphlet volumes
Arc 742.01 Pamphlet box. Etruscan antiquities.

Arc 743 Archaeology - Local - Etruria - General works
Arc 743.1 Dennis, G. The cities and cemeteries of Etruria. London, 1848. 2v.
Arc 743.1.2 Dennis, G. The cities and cemeteries of Etruria. London, 1878. 2v.
Arc 743.1.3 Dennis, G. The cities and cemeteries of Etruria. 3. ed. London, 1883. 2v.
Arc 743.1.5 Dennis, G. The cities and cemeteries of Etruria. London, 1906. 2v.
Arc 743.1.9 Dennis, G. The cities and cemeteries of Etruria. London, 19- . 2v.
Arc 743.2 Gray, H. (Mrs.). Tour to the sepulchres of Etruria. London, 1840.
Arc 743.3 Koch, M. Die Alpen-Etrusker. Leipzig, 1853.
Arc 743.4 Taylor, G.L. The stones of Etruria and marbles of ancient Rome. London, 1859.
Arc 743.5 Gori, A.F. Risposta. Firenze, 1739.
Arc 743.6 Solari, A. Topografia storica dell'Etruria. Pisa, 1914-18. 3v.
Arc 743.6.2 Solari, A. Topografia storica dell'Etruria. Appendix. Pisa, 1915.
Arc 743.7 Inghirami, F. Lettere di Etrusca erudizione. Poligrafia, 1828.
Arc 743.9 Seymour, F. Up hill and down dale in ancient Etruria. London, 1910.
Arc 743.10 Cameron, M.L. Old Etruria and modern Tuscany. London, 1909.
Arc 743.11 Randall-MacIver, D. The Etruscans. Oxford, 1927.
Arc 743.13 Comitato Permanente per l'Etruria. Studi etruschi. Firenze. 1,1927+ 41v.
Arc 743.13.5 Comitato Permanente per l'Etruria. Studi etruschi. Indici, v.1-40, 1927-1972. Firenze, 1968- 2v.
Arc 743.14 Covegno Nazionale Etrusco. Atti. Firenze. 1-2
Arc 743.15 Congresso Internazionale Etrusco. Miscellaneous pamphlets. 1,1928+ 2v.
Arc 743.16 Congresso Internazionale Etrusco. Atti. Firenze. 1,1928
X Cg Arc 743.17 Lawrence, D.H. Etruscan places. London, 1932.
Arc 743.17.10 Lawrence, D.H. Etruscan places. Middlesex, 1950.
Arc 743.18 Hanfmann, G.M.A. The Etruscans and their art. n.p., 1940.
Arc 743.19 Nogara, B. Les Etrusques et leur civilisation. Paris, 1936.
Arc 743.20 Cles-Reden, S. Das versunkene Volk. Innsbruck, 1948.
Arc 743.21 Neppi Modona, Aldo. Guide des antiquités éstrusques. Florence, 1958.
Arc 743.23 Lerici, C.M. Nuove testimonianze dell'arte e della civiltà etrusca. Milano, 1960.
Arc 743.26 Guzzo, Piero G. Le fibule in Etruria dal VI al I secolo. Firenze, 1973.
Arc 743.27 Mostra del restauro archeologico. Grosseto, 1970.

Arc 746 Archaeology - Local - Etruria - Local; Special topics
Arc 746.1 Brunn, H. Über die Ausgrabungen der Certosa von Bologna. München, 1887.
Arc 746.1.2 Burton, R.F. Etruscan Bologna. London, 1876.
Arc 746.2 Gerhard, E. Über die Metallspriegel der Etrusker. Berlin, 1838.
Arc 746.2.9 Matthies, S. Die Praenestinischen Spiegel. Strassburg, 1912.
Arc 746.3 Osservazioni sopra un'Etrusco Lampadario. Montepulciano, 1844.
Arc 746.4 Gerhard, E. Dionysos und Semele. v.1. Berlin, 1833. 2 pam.
Arc 746.5 Forchhammer, P.W. Apollon's Ankunft in Delphi. Kiel, 1840.
Arc 746.6 Dasti, L. Notizie storiche archeologiche di Tarquinia e Corneto. Roma, 1878.
Arc 746.7 Stryk, F. von. Studien über etruskischen Kammagräber. Dorpat, 1910.
Arc 746.7.9F Åkerström, Åke. Studien über die etruskischen Gräber. Uppsala, 1934.

Arc 746 Archaeology - Local - Etruria - Local; Special topics - cont.
Arc 746.8 Bellucci, G. L'ipoge della famiglia etrusca "Rufia". Perugia, 1911.
Arc 746.9 Bienkowski, P. De speculis Etruscis et cista in museo. . Cracoviae, 1912.
Arc 746.9.15 Ulisse (pseud.). Figure mitologiche degli specchi "Etruschi". pt.1-7. Roma, 1929-37.
Arc 746.9.20F Olfieri, Nereo. Spina. München, 1958.
Arc 746.9.25F Scavi di Spina. v.1, pt.1-2. Roma, 1960- 2v.
Arc 746.10 Minto, Antonio. Populonia; la necropoli arcaica. Firenze, 1922.
Arc 746.11F Jacobsthal, Paul. Die Bronzeschnabelkannen. Berlin, 1929.
Arc 746.11.10F Langsdorff, A. Die Grabfunde mit Bronzeschnabelkannen. Inaug. Diss. Berlin, 1929.
Arc 746.12 Sauer, Hertha. Die archaischen etruskischen Terracottasarkophage aus Caere. Diss. Rendsburg, 1930.
Arc 746.12.10F Grifi, L. Monumenti di cere antica. Roma, 1841.
Arc 746.13 Bianchi-Bandinelli, R. Sovana, topografia ed arte. Firenze, 1929.
Arc 746.14 Brizio, E. Una Pompei etrusca a Marzabotto nel Bolognese. Bologna, 1928.
Arc 746.15 DeWitte, J. Description d'une collection de vases peints et bronzes. Paris, 1837.
Arc 746.16 Fontani, Giusto. De antiquitatibus Hortae coloniae etruscorum. 3a ed. Roma, 1723.
Arc 746.17 Tononi, A.G. Scoperta di un bronzo etrusco. Milano, 1879.
Arc 746.18F Orvieto, Italy. Orvieto etrusca. Roma, 1928.
Arc 746.18.5 Puglisi, S. Studi e ricerche su Orvieto etrusca. Catania, 1934.
Arc 746.19 Consortini, P.L. Le necropoli etrusche di Volterra. Lucca, 1933.
Arc 746.20 Shaw, C. Etruscan Perugia. Baltimore, 1939.
Arc 746.22 Bastianelli, S. Centumcellae (Civitavecchia). Roma, 1954.
Arc 746.24 Lombardi, M. Faesulae (Fiesole) Regio VII Etruria. Roma, 1941.
Arc 746.25F Andrèn, A.Architectural terracottas from Etrusco-Italic temples. Leipzig, 1939-40. 2v.
Arc 746.27 Riis, Poul J. Tyrrhenika, an archaeological study of the Etruscan sculpture in the archaic and classical periods. Copenhagen, 1941.
Arc 746.30F Banti, Luisa. Luni. Firenze, 1937.
Arc 746.40F Canina, Luigi. L'antica città di Veil. Roma, 1847.
Arc 746.40.5F Vagnetti, Lucia. Il deposito votivo di Competti a Veio. Firenze, 1971.
Arc 746.45 Decouflé, Pierre. La notion d'ex-voto anatomique chez les Etrusco Romains. Bruxelles, 1964.
Arc 746.46 Hanfmann, George Maxim Anossov. Altetruskische Plastik. Würzburg, 1936.
Arc 746.47 Cristofani, Mauro. La tomba delle iscrizioni a Cerveteri. Firenze, 1965.
Arc 746.47.5 Roncalli, Francesco. Le lastre dipinte da Cerveteri. Firenze, 1965.
Arc 746.48F Falchi, Isidoro. Vetulonia e la sua necropoli antichissima ed anastatica. Roma, 1965.
Arc 746.50 Rilli, Nicola. Gli estruschi a Sesto Fiorentino. Firenze, 1964.
Arc 746.52 Poggio civitate (Murlo, Siena), il santuario arcaico. Firenze, 1970.
Arc 746.54 Camporeale, Giovannangelo. I commerci di Vetulonia in età orientalizzante. Firenze, 1969.
Arc 746.56 Staccioli, Romolo Augusto. Modelli di edifici etrusco-italici. Firenze, 1968.
Arc 746.58 Neppi Modona, Aldo. I: Gli alfabeti etruschi; II: La scultura etrusca. Genova, 1970.
Arc 746.60 Hus, Alain. Vulci étrusque et étrusco-romaine. Paris, 1971.
Arc 746.61 Wetter, Erik. Med kungen på Acquarossa. Malmö, 1972.

Arc 750 Archaeology - Local - Rome (City) - Folios [Discontinued]
Arc 750.1.5 Cichorius, C. Die Reliefs der Trajanssäule. v.1,2, plates. v.2,3, text. Berlin, 1896-1900. 4v.
Htn Arc 750.5* Pianesi, G.B. Campus Martius. Roma, 1762.
Htn Arc 750.25* Bellori, G.A. Veteres Arcus Augustorum. Roma, 1690.
Arc 750.29 Jordan, Henri. Forma urbis Romae. Berolino, 1874.
Arc 750.30 Cassini, G.M. Pitture antiche. Roma, 1783.
Arc 750.30.5 Collection de peintures antiques...Rome. Rome, 1781.
Htn Arc 750.31* DuPerac, E. I vestigi dell'antichità di Roma. Roma, 1575.
Arc 750.37.1 Rostovtsev, Mikhail Ivanovich. Tesserarum urbis Romae et suburbi plumbearum sylloge. Supplement. St. Petersbourgh, 1905.
Arc 750.38 Narducci, P. Sulla fognatura della città di Roma. Roma, 1889. 2v.
Arc 750.39F Canina, Luigi. Esposizione storica e topografica del foro romano. 2a ed. Roma, 1845.
Arc 750.39PF Canina, Luigi. Tavole...foro romano. Atlas. Roma, 1845.
Arc 750.200 Magnan, D. La città di Roma. Roma, 1779. 2v.
Arc 750.201 Dionisi, F.L. Sacr. Vat. Basilicae. Roma, 1773.
Arc 750.202 Canina, Luigi. La prima parte della Via Appia. Roma, 1853. 2v.
Arc 750.203 Suardi, B. Le rovine di Roma. Milano, 1875.
Arc 750.204 Lanciani, R. L'itinerario di Einsiedeln. Roma, 1891.
Arc 750.205 Beltzami, L. Il pantheon. Milano, 1898.
Arc 750.206 Petersen, E. Ara Pacis Augustae. Wien, 1902. 2v.
Arc 750.206.10 Kraus, Theodor. Die Ranken der Ara Pacis. Berlin, 1953.
Arc 750.207 Rodocanachi, E. Le capitole romain. Paris, 1904.
Arc 750.208 Sambon, Arthur. Les fresques de Boscoreale. Paris, 1903.
Arc 750.208.5F Sambon, Arthur. Catalogue des fresques de Boscoreale. Macon, 1903.
Arc 750.209 Thédenat, H. Le forum romain et la voie sacrée. Paris, 1905.
Arc 750.211 Delbrück, R. Hellenistische Bauten in Latium. Strassburg, 1907.
Htn Arc 750.212* Fabretti, R. De columna traiani syntaqua. Roma, 1683.
Arc 750.213 Delbrück, R. Das Capitolium von Signia. Rom, 1903.
Arc 750.217F Rodacanchi, E. Les monuments de Rome après la chute de l'empire. Paris, 1914.
Arc 750.218F Pamphlet box. Bellissima, G.B.
Htn Arc 750.219* Venuti, Ridolfino. Veteris Latii antiqua vestigia urbis moenia. Romae, 1751.
Htn Arc 750.220F* Bellori, G.P. Fragmenta vestigii veteris Romae. Colophon, 1673.
Htn Arc 750.221F* Chausse, M.A. de la. Le grand cabinet romain. Amsterdam, 1706.
Arc 750.222F Canina, Luigi. Sugli antichi edifizj. Roma, 1840.
Arc 750.223F Riccy, G.A. Dell'antico pago Lemonio in oggi Roma Vecchia. Roma, 1802.

Classified Listing

Arc 750 Archaeology - Local - Rome (City) - Folios [Discontinued] - cont.
Arc 750.224F Italy. Commissione reale per la zona monumentale di Roma. La zona monumentale di Roma e l'opera della Commissione reale. Roma, 1914.

Arc 754 Archaeology - Local - Rome (City) - Pamphlet volumes
Arc 754 Pamphlet box. Archaeology. Rome.
Arc 754.1 Pamphlet vol. Rom, 1880-1901. 14 pam.
Arc 754.2 Pamphlet vol. Rom. Provincial Kunst, 1890-1903. 22 pam.
Arc 754.3 Pamphlet vol. Provincial Römisches, 1847-1899. 6 pam.
Arc 754.4 Pamphlet vol. Roman Archaeology. 16 pam.
Arc 754.5 Pamphlet box. Archaeology. Rome.
Arc 754.6 Piale, S. Roman archaeology in the city of Rome. Diss. Rome, 1832-33. 12 pam.

Arc 755 - 780 Archaeology - Local - Rome (City) - General works (A-Z)
Arc 755.1 Cumelung, W. Museums and ruins of Rome. London, 1906. 2v.
Arc 755.3.2 Ashby, Thomas. The Roman campagna in classical times. London, 1970.
Arc 755.4 Associazione artistica fra i cultori di architecttura. La zona monumentale di Roma. Roma, 1910.
Arc 755.6 Aucler, Paul. Rome; restauration archéologique. Paris, 1899.
Arc 756.1 Becker, W.A. Die römische Topographie in Rom. Leipzig, 1844.
Arc 756.1.2 Becker, W.A. Zur römischen Topographie. Leipzig, 1845.
Htn Arc 756.2* Boissard, J.J. Topographia Romae. pt.1-6. Frankfort, 1627. 2v.
Arc 756.3 Braun, Emil. Die Ruinen und Museen Roms. Braunschweig, 1854.
Arc 756.3.4 Braun, Emil. The ruins and museums of Rome. Brunswick, 1854.
Arc 756.3.5 Braun, Emil. Handbook...ruins and museums of Rome. London, 1855.
Arc 756.4 Burgess, R. The topography and antiquities of Rome. London, 1831. 2v.
Arc 756.5 Burn, R. Rome and the campagna. Cambridge, 1871.
Arc 756.5.2 Burn, R. Old Rome. London, 1880.
Arc 756.5.3 Burn, R. Ancient Rome and its neighborhood. London, 1895.
Arc 756.6 Burton, Edward. A description of the antiquities and other curiosities of Rome. 2. ed. London, 1828. 2v.
Arc 756.6.3 Burton, Edward. A description of the antiquities and other curiosities of Rome. v.1-2. Florence, 1830.
Arc 756.7 Boissier, Gaston. Promenades archéologiques, Rome et Pompéi. Paris, 1880.
Arc 756.7.1 Boissier, Gaston. Promenades archéologiques, Rome et Pompéi. 2. éd. Paris, 1881.
Arc 756.7.2A Boissier, Gaston. Rome and Pompeii. N.Y., 1896.
Arc 756.7.2B Boissier, Gaston. Rome and Pompeii. N.Y., 1896.
Arc 756.7.3 Boissier, Gaston. Promenades archéologiques, Rome et Pompéi. 3. éd. Paris, 1887.
Arc 756.7.8 Boissier, Gaston. Promenades archéologiques, Rome et Pompéi. 8. éd. Paris, 1904.
Arc 756.8 Borsari, L. Topografia di Roma antica. Milano, 1897.
Arc 756.10 Bigot, P. Rome imperiale. Rome, 1911.
Arc 756.11 Bertaux, Émile. Rome; l'antiquité. 2. éd. Paris, 1907.
Arc 756.11.2 Bertaux, Émile. Rome, l'antiquité. Paris, 1904.
Arc 756.11.3 Bertaux, Émile. Rome, l'antiquité. 3. éd. Paris, 1913.
Arc 756.11.4 Bertaux, Émile. Rome, l'antiquité. 4. éd. Paris, 1924.
Arc 756.12 Brtnický, L. Topografie starověkého Říma. Praha, 1925.
Arc 756.13 Bühlmann, J. Das alte Rom mit dem Triumphzuge Kaiser Constantins im Jahre 312 n. Chr. München, 1892.
Arc 756.13.5 Bühlmann, J. Rom mit dem Triumphzuge Constantins im Jahre 312. 4. Aufl. München, 1894.
Arc 757.1 Canina, Luigi. Indicazione topografica di Roma antica. 3. ed. Roma, 1841.
Arc 757.2 Canina, Luigi. Pianta topografica di Roma antica. Roma? 1844?
Arc 757.2.2 Canina, Luigi. Pianta topografica di Roma antica. Roma? 1851?
Arc 757.3 Cookesley, W.G. Explanatory index to the map of ancient Rome. Eton, 1851.
Arc 757.4 Cyriacus. Anconitanus. La Roma antica...desegnii inedite. Roma, 1907.
Arc 757.5 Carnevale, C.G. Roma nel III secolo - era volgare. Roma, 1896.
Arc 757.6 Caetani Lovatelli, E. Passeggiate nella Roma antica. Roma, 1909.
Arc 757.6.5 Caetani Lovatelli, E. Aurea Roma. Roma, 1915.
Arc 757.7 Clementi, F. Roma imperiale nelle XIV regioni Agustee secondo. Roma, 1935. 2v.
Arc 757.8 Cozzo, G. Il luogo primitivo di Roma. Roma, 1935.
Arc 757.9F Curtius, Ludwig. Das antike Rom. 3. Aufl. Wien, 1957.
Arc 757.10 Chester, England. Museum. An account of the Roman antiquities. 2. ed. London, 1907.
Arc 758.1 Dyer, T.H. Ancient Rome. London, 1864.
Htn Arc 758.2* Dosio, G.A. Urbis Romae aedificae illustrae quae supersunt reliquiae. n.p., n.d.
Arc 758.2.5F Dosio, G.A. Das Skizzenbuch des G. Dosio im staatlichen Kupferstichkabinett zu Berlin. Berlin, 1933.
Arc 758.3 Descrittione di Roma antica e moderna. Roma, 1650.
Arc 758.4 Diehl, Ernst. Das alte Rom sein Werden. Leipzig, 1909.
Arc 758.5 Dennie, John. Rome of to-day and yesterday. Boston, 1894.
Arc 758.5.5 Dennie, John. Rome of to-day and yesterday. 5. ed. N.Y., 1910.
Arc 758.6 Deseine, F. L'ancienne Rome. v.1-4. Leide, 1713. 2v.
Arc 759.1 Elter, A. Das alte Rom im Mittelalter. Bonn, 1904.
Arc 759.2 Egger, Rudolf. Römische Antike und frühes Christentum. Klagenfurt, 1962-63. 2v.
Htn Arc 760.1* Faunus, L. Delle antichità della città di Roma. Venice? 1548.
Htn Arc 760.1.5* Faunus, L. De antiquitiae Romae. Venetiis, 1549.
Htn Arc 760.2* Ficoroni, F. de. Le vestigia e rarità di Roma antica. Rome, 1744.
Htn Arc 760.4* Fulvio, A. Antiquitates urbis. Roma, 1527.
Htn Arc 760.4.5* Fulvio, A. De urbis antiquitatibus. Roma, 1545.
Htn Arc 760.4.8* Fulvio, A. L'antichita di Roma. Venetia, 1588.
Arc 760.6 Fea, Carlo. Varieta di notizie economiche fisiche antiquarie. Rome, 1820.
Arc 760.6.2 Pamphlet vol. Fea, Carlo. Opuscoli. 10 pam.
Arc 760.6.5 Fea, Carlo. Miscellanea filologica critica e antiquaria. Roma, 1790-1836. 2v.
Arc 760.6.7 Fea, Carlo. Nuova descrizione de' monumenti antichi. Roma, 1819.
Arc 760.6.11 Fea, Carlo. Annotazioni alla memoria sui diritti del principato. Roma, 1806.

Arc 755 - 780 Archaeology - Local - Rome (City) - General works (A-Z) - cont.
Arc 760.6.15 Fea, Carlo. Ossequiosissimo rapporto alla Santità. Roma, 1826. 2 pam.
Arc 760.6.17 Fea, Carlo. Eccellentissima congregazione diputata da sua Santità Papa Leone XII. Roma, 1827.
Arc 760.7 Forbes, S. Russell. Rambles in Rome. London, 1882.
Arc 761.1 Gell, W. The topography of RomeAnd its vicinity. London, 1846. 2v.
Arc 761.1.2 Gell, W. The topography of Rome and its vicinity. London, 1834. 3v.
Arc 761.2 Gsell-Fels, T. Roemische Ausgrabungen. Hildburghausen, 1870.
Arc 761.3PF Restauro grafico del Monte Capitalino. Maps and text. Roma, 1897.
Htn Arc 761.4* Gamucci, B. Le antichita della città di Roma. Venetia, 1565.
Htn Arc 761.4.3* Gamucci, B. Le antichita della città di Roma. 2. ed. Vinegia, 1569.
Htn Arc 761.4.5* Gamucci, B. Le antichita della città di Roma. Vinegia, 1580.
Htn Arc 761.4.9* Gamucci, B. Le antichita della città di Roma. Vinegia, 1588. 2 pam.
Htn Arc 761.5.2* Guattani, G.A. Roma descritta ed illustrata. 2. ed. v.1-2. Roma, 1805.
Arc 761.6F Gatteschi, Giuseppe. Restauri della Roma imperiale. Roma, 1924.
Arc 761.7 Gabrici, Ettore. Il problema delle origini di Roma secondo le recenti scoperti archeologiche. Padova, 1906.
Arc 761.8F Gjerstadt, E. Early Rome. v.1-6. Lund, 1953. 5v.
Arc 762.1 Hare, A.J.C. Walks in Rome. London, 1871. 2v.
Arc 762.1.2 Hare, A.J.C. Walks in Rome. 4. ed. London, 1874. 2v.
Arc 762.1.2.5 Hare, A.J.C. Walks in Rome. 4. American ed. N.Y., 1874.
Arc 762.1.3 Hare, A.J.C. Walks in Rome. N.Y., 1875.
Arc 762.1.3.5 Hare, A.J.C. Walks in Rome. 6. American ed. N.Y., 1877.
Arc 762.1.3.7 Hare, A.J.C. Walks in Rome. 7. American ed. N.Y., 187-.
Arc 762.1.3.9 Hare, A.J.C. Walks in Rome. 8. American ed. N.Y., 1882.
Arc 762.1.4 Hare, A.J.C. Walks in Rome. London, 1878. 2v.
Arc 762.1.4.5 Hare, A.J.C. Walks in Rome. 13th ed. London, 1893. 2v.
Arc 762.1.5 Hare, A.J.C. Walks in Rome. 14th ed. N.Y., 1899. 2v.
Arc 762.1.5.5 Hare, A.J.C. Walks in Rome. 15th ed. N.Y., 190-?
Arc 762.1.6 Hare, A.J.C. Walks in Rome. 16th ed. London, 1903. 2v.
Arc 762.1.9 Hare, A.J.C. Walks in Rome. 20th ed. London, 1913.
Arc 762.1.10 Hare, A.J.C. Walks in Rome. 21st ed. London, 1923.
Arc 762.1.20 Hare, A.J.C. Days near Rome. v.1-2. Philadelphia, 1875.
Arc 762.1.25 Hare, A.J.C. Days near Rome. 3. ed. N.Y., 1902.
Arc 762.1.30 Hare, A.J.C. Days near Rome. 4. ed. London, 1906.
Arc 762.1.35 Hare, A.J.C. Days near Rome. 5. ed. London, 1907.
Arc 762.2 Homo, L. Lexique de topographie romaine. Paris, 1900.
Arc 762.3 Hula, E. Römische Altertümer. Leipzig, 1901.
Htn Arc 762.4* Hobhouse, J. Historical illustrations of 4th canto of Childe Harold. London, 1818.
Arc 762.4.2 Broughton, J.C.H. Historical illustrations of 4th canto of Childe Harold. 2. ed. London, 1818.
Arc 762.5 Huelsen, C. La pianta di Roma dell'anonimo einsidlense. Roma, 1907.
Arc 762.6 Hill, Ida T. Rome of the kings. N.Y., 1925.
Arc 762.7 Huelsen, Hans von. Römische Funde. Göttingen, 1960.
Arc 764.1 Jordan, Henri. Topographie der Stadt Rom in Alterthum. v.1-2. Berlin, 1878. 4v.
Arc 764.1.2 Jordan, Henri. De formae urbis Romae...novo disputatio. Roma, 1883.
Arc 765.5 Kaehler, Heinz. Rom und seine Welt. München, 1958.
Arc 766.1 Lanciani, R. Topografia di Roma antica. Roma, 1880.
Arc 766.1.2A Lanciani, R. Ancient Rome in the light of recent excavations. Boston, 1888.
Arc 766.1.2B Lanciani, R. Ancient Rome in the light of recent excavations. Boston, 1888.
Arc 766.1.2C Lanciani, R. Ancient Rome in the light of recent excavations. Boston, 1888.
Arc 766.1.2D Lanciani, R. Ancient Rome in the light of recent excavations. Boston, 1888.
Htn Arc 766.1.2.7* Lanciani, R. Ancient Rome in the light of recent discoveries. 7. ed. Boston, 1888.
Arc 766.1.2.8 Lanciani, R. Ancient Rome in the light of recent discoveries. Boston, 1888.
Arc 766.1.2.10 Lanciani, R. Ancient Rome in the light of recent discoveries. London, 1888.
Arc 766.1.2.11 Lanciani, R. Ancient Rome in the light of recent discoveries. London, 1888.
Arc 766.1.2.12 Lanciani, R. Ancient Rome in the light of recent discoveries. 5. ed. Boston, 1889.
Arc 766.1.2.15 Lanciani, R. Ancient Rome in the light of recent discoveries. 10. ed. Boston, 1894.
Arc 766.1.2.30 Lanciani, R. Pagan and Christian Rome. Boston, 1892.
Arc 766.1.3 Lanciani, R. Pagan and Christian Rome. Boston, 1893.
Arc 766.1.3.5 Lanciani, R. Pagan and Christian Rome. London, 1893.
Htn Arc 766.1.4* Lanciani, R. Pagan and Christian Rome. Boston, 1893.
Arc 766.1.5A Lanciani, R. Ruins and excavations of ancient Rome. Boston, 1897.
Arc 766.1.5B Lanciani, R. Ruins and excavations of ancient Rome. Boston, 1897.
Arc 766.1.6 Lanciani, R. The ruins and excavations of ancient Rome. London, 1897.
Arc 766.1.9 Lanciani, R. The destruction of ancient Rome. N.Y., 1899.
Arc 766.1.9.1 Lanciani, R. The destruction of ancient Rome. N.Y., 1967.
Arc 766.1.9.5 Lanciani, R. La distruzione di Roma antica. Milano, 1971.
Arc 766.1.10 Lanciani, R. The ruins and excavations of ancient Rome. Boston, 1900.
Arc 766.1.13A Lanciani, R. New tales of old Rome. Boston, 1901.
Arc 766.1.13B Lanciani, R. New tales of old Rome. Boston, 1901.
Arc 766.1.14 Lanciani, R. New tales of old Rome. Boston, 1902.
Arc 766.1.15 Lanciani, R. New tales of old Rome. London, 1901.
Arc 766.1.17A Lanciani, R. Storia degli scavi di Roma. v.1-4. Roma, 1902. 5v.
Arc 766.1.17B Lanciani, R. Storia degli scavi di Roma. Roma, 1902. 2v.
Arc 766.1.19 Lanciani, R. Wanderings in the Roman campagns. Boston, 1909.
Arc 766.2 Lumisden, A. Remarks on the antiquities of Rome and its environs. London, 1797.
Arc 766.3 Le Blant, Edmond. Les ateliers de sculpture chez les premiers chrétiens. Rome, 1884.
Arc 766.4 Lugli, Giuseppe. La zona archeologica di Roma. Roma, 1924.

Classified Listing

Arc 755 - 780 Archaeology - Local - Rome (City) - General works (A-Z) - cont.

Arc 766.4.5 Lugli, Giuseppe. I monumenti antichi di Roma e suburbio. Roma, 1930-40. 4v.
Arc 766.4.10 Lugli, Giuseppe. Roma antica. Roma, 1946.
Arc 766.4.15 Lugli, Giuseppe. Fontes ad topographism veteris urbis Romae pertinentes. v.1-4; v.6, pt.1-2; v.8, pt.1. Roma, 1953. 7v.
Arc 766.4.20 Lugli, Giuseppe. Studi minori di topografia antica. Roma, 1965.
Arc 766.4.25 Lugli, Giuseppe. Itinerario di Roma antica. Milano, 1970.
Arc 767.1.5 Maps, Rome. Ancient (1896). Formae urbis Romae antiquae. Berolino, 1896.
Arc 767.1.7A Maps, Rome. Ancient (1912). Formae urbis Romae antiquae. Berolino, 1912.
Arc 767.1.7B Maps, Rome. Ancient (1912). Formae urbis Romae antiquae. Berolino, 1912.
Htn Arc 767.2* Marliani, B. L'antichità di Roma. Roma, 1622.
Htn Arc 767.2.2* Marliani, B. Urbis Romae topographia. Colophon, 1544.
Arc 767.2.5 Marliani, B. Descrizione di Roma antica. Roma, 1697.
Arc 767.2.7 Marliani, B. Descrizione di Roma antica. Roma, 1708. 2v.
Arc 767.2.10 Marliani, B. Descrizione di Roma antica. Roma, 1739.
Arc 767.3 Mayerhoefer, A. Studien über das alte Rom. München, 1887.
Arc 767.4 Middleton, J.H. Ancient Rome in 1885. Edinburgh, 1885.
Arc 767.4.2 Middleton, J.H. The remains of ancient Rome. London, 1892. 2v.
Arc 767.5 Muentz, E. Les antiquités de la ville de Rome. Paris, 1886.
Htn Arc 767.6* Liber de vilitate coditionis humane Mirabilia Romae. Paris, 1509.
Htn Arc 767.6.2* Mirabilia urbis Romae nova. Roma, 1550.
Arc 767.6.3 Mirabilia Romae. Berlin, 1869.
Arc 767.6.5 Mirabilia urbis Romae. London, 1889.
Arc 767.10 Mauro, L. Le antichità della città di Roma. Venetia, 1562.
Arc 768.1 Nardini, F. Roma antica. Roma, 1666.
Arc 768.1.25 Nardini, F. Roma antica. 4. ed. Roma, 1818-20. 4v.
Arc 768.2 Nispi-Landi, Ciro. Roma monumentale dinanzi all'umanita. Roma, 1892.
Arc 768.2.15 Nibby, Antonio. Analisi storico...dentorni di Roma. Roam, 1837. 3v.
Arc 768.2.16 Nibby, Antonio. Analisi storico...dentorni di Roma. Roma, 1837. 4v.
Arc 768.3 Nibby, Antonio. Analisi della carta de' dentorni di Roma. Roma, 1848. 3v.
Arc 768.3.5 Nibby, Antonio. Roma nell'anno 1838. Roma, 1838-41. 4v.
Arc 768.5 Nuova raccolta...antiche e moderne...Roma. Roma, 18- .
Arc 768.6F Nash, Ernest. Pictorial dictionary of ancient Rome. London, 1961-62. 2v.
Arc 769.1 Rolli, P. Degli avanzi dell'antica Roma. Londra, 1739.
Arc 770.1 Parker, J.H. The archaeology of Rome. v.1-2, 4-11. Oxford, 1874. 12v.
Arc 770.1.5 Parker, J.H. Description of the plan of Rome. Oxford, 1878.
Arc 770.2 Parker, J.H. Catalogue of a series of photographs illustrative of the archaeology of Rome. n.p., 1867.
Arc 770.2.2 Pamphlet vol. Parker, J.H. Antiquities of Rome in danger. 6 pam.
Arc 770.2.5 Parker, J.H. De variis structurarum generibus penes romanos veteres. Romae, 1868.
Arc 770.3A Preller, L. Die Regionen der Stadt Rom. Jena, 1846.
Arc 770.3B Preller, L. Die Regionen der Stadt Rom. Jena, 1846.
Arc 770.4A Platner, S.B. Topography and monuments of ancient Rome. Boston, 1904.
Arc 770.4B Platner, S.B. Topography and monuments of ancient Rome. Boston, 1904.
Arc 770.4.2 Platner, S.B. Topography and monuments of ancient Rome. 2. ed. Boston, 1911.
Arc 770.4.10 Platner, S.B. A topographical dictionary of ancient Rome. London, 1929.
Arc 770.5 Pinarolo, G. L'antichita di Roma. Roma, 1703. 2v.
Arc 770.6.2 Petersen, Eugen. Vom alten Rom. 2. Aufl. Leipzig, 1900.
Arc 770.6.5 Petersen, Eugen. Vom alten Rom. 3. Aufl. Leipzig, 1904.
Arc 770.7 Paléologue, M. Rome, notes d'histoire et d'art. 11. éd. Paris, 1921.
Arc 770.7.5 Paléologue, M. Rome, notes d'histoire et d'art. 22. éd. Paris, 1935.
Arc 770.8 Piroli, T. Gli edifici antichi di Roma. Roma, 1800?
Arc 770.9 Piale, Stefano. Delle porte del recinto di servio Tullio nella parte orientale di Roma. Roma, 1833. 13 pam.
Arc 772.1 Reber, F. von. Die Ruinen Roms. Leipzig, 1879.
Arc 772.1.2 Reber, F. von. Die Ruinen Roms. Leipzig, 1863.
Htn Arc 772.2* Roma antica e moderna. Roma, 1750. 3v.
Htn Arc 772.2.5* Roma antica e moderna. Roma, 1765. 3v.
Htn Arc 772.3* Albertini, F. De Roma prisca et nova varii auctores. Romae, 1523?
Arc 772.4 Rossi, G.B. de. Note di topographia romana. Roma, 1882.
Arc 772.4.5 Rossi, G.B. de. Note di Ruderi e monumenti antico di Roma. Roma, 1883.
Arc 772.5 Richter, O. Geographie und Geschichte des Römischen Altertums. Nordlingen, 1889.
Arc 772.5.5 Richter, O. Topographie der Stadt Rom. Nordlingen, 1889.
Arc 772.6 Holtzinger, H. Die Ruinen Roms. 2. Aufl. Stuttgart, 1912.
Arc 772.6.2 Amelung, W. Die antiken Sammlungen. 2. Aufl. Stuttgart, 1913.
Arc 772.7 Riva, Giuseppe. Sito di Roma e la carta. 2. ed. Vicenza, 1846.
Arc 772.8 Ruggiero, E. de. Lo stato e le opere pubbliche in Roma antica. Torino, 1925.
Arc 772.9F Italy. Commissione reale per la zona monumentale di Roma. La zona monumentale di Roma e l'opera commissione reale. Roma, 1910.
Arc 772.10 Rome (City). Istituto di studi romani. Campania romana. Napoli, 1938.
Arc 772.11 Roma medio republicana. Aspetti culturali di Roma e del Lazio. Roma, 1973.
Arc 772.12 Ryberg, Inez. An archaeological record of Rome from the seventh to the second century B.C. v.1-2. Philadelphia, 1940.
Arc 772.14 Robathan, D. The monuments of ancient Rome. Rome, 1950.
Arc 772.16 Richmond, Ian A. The archaeology of the Roman empire. Oxford, 1957.
Arc 773.1 Sachse, K. Geschichte und Beschreibung der alten Stadt Rom. Hannover, 1824.
Arc 773.3 Scaglia, S. La promenade archéologique. Rome, 1911.
Htn Arc 773.5F* Sadeler, Marco. Nestigi della antichita di Roma. Roma, 1660.
Arc 773.6F Shipley, F.W. Chronology of the building operations in Rome from the death of Caesar. n.p., 1931.
Arc 773.7 Scherer, M.R. Marvels of ancient Rome. N.Y., 1955.
Arc 774.1 Tomassetti, G. La campagna romana. Roma, 1910. 4v.
Arc 774.3 Tomassetti, G. Della campagna romana. Roma, 1885.
Arc 774.3.5 Tomassetti, G. Della campagna romana. Roma, 1907.
NEDL Arc 775.1 Urlichs, K.L. Roemische Topographie in Leipzig. Stuttgart, 1845.
Arc 775.1.2 Urlichs, K.L. Codex urbis Romae topographicus. Wirceburg, 1871.
Htn Arc 776.1.2* Venuti, R. Accurata e succinta descrizione topografica delle antichità di Roma. 2. ed. Roma, 1803. 2v.
Arc 776.1.3 Venuti, R. Accurata e succinta descrizione topografica delle antichità di Roma. Roma, 1824. 2v.
Arc 776.1.7 Venuti, R. Accurata e succinta descrizione topografica delle antichità di Roma moderna. Roma, 1767. 4v.
Arc 776.2A Van Buren, A.W. Ancient Rome as revealed by recent discoveries. London, 1936.
Arc 776.2B Van Buren, A.W. Ancient Rome as revealed by recent discoveries. London, 1936.
Arc 776.2C Van Buren, A.W. Ancient Rome as revealed by recent discoveries. London, 1936.
Arc 777.1 Westphal, J.H. Die Roemische Kampagne. Berlin, 1829.
Arc 777.1.5 Westphal, Enrico. Guida per la campagna di Roma. Roma, 1854.
Arc 777.2 Westropp, H.M. Early and imperial Rome. London, 1884.
Arc 777.3 Wissowa, G. Analecta Romana topographica. Halis, 1897.
Arc 777.4 Wiesel, Julius Maxim. Das alte Rom zur konstantinischen Zeit undHeute. Mainz, 1964.
Arc 780.1 Ziegler, C. Das alte Rom. Stuttgart, 1882.

Arc 785 Archaeology - Local - Rome (City) - Special topics

Arc 785.1 Jordan, Henri. Tempel der Vesta und das Haus der Vestalinnen. Berlin, 1886.
Arc 785.1.3 Meschler, M. Der Vestatempel und der Vestalenhof am römische Forum. Freiburg, 1898.
Arc 785.1.5 Piale, Stefano. Del tempio volgarmente detto di Vesta. Roma, 1817.
Arc 785.1.8 Maes, C. Vesta e vestali. 2. ed. Roma, 1884.
Htn Arc 785.2* Fontana, C. Discorsa sopra l'antico Monte Citabrio. Roma, 1708.
Arc 785.3 Brizio, E. Pitture e sipolcri scoperti sull'Esquilino. Roma, 1876.
Arc 785.4 Mullooly, J. Breve notizie delle antiche pitture. Roma, 1866.
Arc 785.5 Sturm, J. Das kaiserliches Stadium auf dem Palatin. Würzburg, 1888.
Arc 785.6 Fabretti, R. De aquis et aquaeductis veteris Romae. Romae, 1680.
Arc 785.6.5 Blumenstihl, B. Brevi notizie sull'acqua pia (antica Marcia). Roma, 1872.
Arc 785.6.10 Forbes, S.R. Aqueducts fountains of ancient Rome. Rome, 1899.
Arc 785.6.13 Borgnana, C. Dell'acqua di Q. Marcio Ré e del suo acquedotto. Roma, 1861.
Arc 785.6.17F Van Deman, E.B. The building of the Roman aqueducts. Washington, 1934.
Arc 785.6.19 Ashby, T. The aqueducts of ancient Rome. Oxford, 1935.
Arc 785.7 Wells, C.L. The amphitheatres of ancient Rome. Boston, 1884.
Arc 785.8 Parker, J.H. The Colosseum at Rome. London, 1882.
Arc 785.8.5 Viola, Joseph. Das Kolosseum. Rom, 1913.
Arc 785.8.7F Colgrossi, P. L'anfiteatro Flavio nei suoi venti secoli di storia. Firenze, 1913.
Arc 785.9 Lanciani, R. Ricerche sulle XIV regioni urbane. Roma, 1890.
Htn Arc 785.10* Oliva, G. In Marmor Isiacum...exercitationes. Rome, 1719.
Arc 785.11 Mazois, F. Le palais de Scaurus. Paris, 1822.
Arc 785.11.4 Mazois, F. Le palais de Scaurus. 4. éd. Paris, 1869.
Arc 785.11.5 Mazois, F. Il palazzo di Scauro. 2. ed. Milano, 1825.
Arc 785.12 Jordan, Henri. Der capitolinische Plan der Stadt Rom. Berlin, 1867.
Arc 785.13 Michelet, C.L. Das Forum Romanum, oder Die...Region des alten Rom. Berlin, 1877.
Arc 785.13.3 Levy, L. Das Forum Romanum der Kaiser Zeit. München, 1895.
Arc 785.13.5 Thédenat, Henry. Le Forum Romain et les Forum impériaux. Paris, 1900.
Arc 785.13.7 Vaglieri, Dante. Gli scavi recenti nel Foro Romano. Roma, 1903.
Arc 785.13.8 Vaglieri, Dante. Gli scavi recenti nel Foro Romano. Supplemento. Roma, 1903.
Arc 785.13.9 Burton Brown, E. Recent excavations in the Roman Forum. 1898-1904. N.Y., 1904.
Arc 785.13.11 Burton Brown, E. Recent excavations in the Roman Forum. N.Y., 1905.
Arc 785.13.13 Maes, C. Primo trofeo della croce nel Foro Romano. Roma, 1901.
Arc 785.13.15 Borsari, Luigi. Le Forum Romain selon les dernières fouilles. Rome, 1900.
Arc 785.13.17 Braddeley, S.C. Recent discoveries in the Forum. N.Y., 1904.
Arc 785.13.17.5 Braddeley, S.C. Recent discoveries in the Forum, 1898-1904. London, 1904.
Arc 785.13.20 Huelsen, Christian. Die Ausgrabungen auf dem Forum Romanum. v.1-2. Roma, 1902-05.
Arc 785.13.21 Huelsen, Christian. Das Forum Romanum. Rom, 1904.
Arc 785.13.22 Huelsen, Christian. Das Forum Romanum. Rom, 1905.
Arc 785.13.22.5 Huelsen, Christian. Die neuesten Ausgrabungen...Nachtrag. Rom, 1910.
Arc 785.13.22.15 Huelsen, Christian. Le Forum Romain, son histoire et ses monuments. Rome, 1906.
Arc 785.13.23 Huelsen, Christian. The Roman Forum. Rome, 1906.
Arc 785.13.24 Huelsen, Christian. The Roman Forum. Rome, 1906.
Arc 785.13.24.5 Huelsen, Christian. The Roman Forum. Rome, 1909.
Arc 785.13.24.7 Huelsen, Christian. Il Foro Romano; storia e monumenti. Roma, 1905.
Arc 785.13.24.9 Huelsen, Christian. Forum und Palatin. München, 1926.
Arc 785.13.24.13 Huelsen, Christian. The Forum and the Palatine. N.Y., 1928.
Arc 785.13.25 Visconti, C.L. Deux actes de Domitien. Rome, 1873.
Arc 785.13.27 Ravioli, Camillo. Regionamento del Foro Romano. Roma, 1859.
Arc 785.13.28 Marucchi, O. Description du Forum Romain et guide pour le visiteur. Rome, 1885.
Arc 785.13.29 Marucchi, O. Nova descrizione della casa dell Vestali. Roma, 1887.

Arc 785 Archaeology - Local - Rome (City) - Special topics - cont.

Arc 785.13.31 Marucchi, O. Nova scoperte nella casa dell Vestali. Roma, 1884.
Arc 785.13.35 Marucchi, O. Le Forum Romain et le Palatin. Paris, 1902.
Arc 785.13.35.5 Marucchi, O. The Roman Forum and the Palatine. Rome, 1906.
Arc 785.13.39 Van Deman, E.B. The Atrium Vestae. Washington, 1909.
Arc 785.13.40 Canina, Luigi. Descrizione storica del Foro Romano. Roma, 1834.
Arc 785.13.42 A Christian corner in the Roman Forum. Rome, 1901.
Arc 785.13.45 Thiele, Richard. Das Forum Romanum. 2. Aufl. Erfurt, 1906.
Arc 785.13.48 Ruggiero, E. de. Il Foro Romano. Roma, 1913.
Arc 785.13.50 Augé de Lassus, L. Le Forum. Paris, 1892.
Arc 785.13.51 Artioli, Romolo. The Roman Forum. Rome, 19- .
Arc 785.13.53A Lansiani, Rodolfo. The Roman forum. Rome, 1910.
Arc 785.13.53B Lansiani, Rodolfo. The Roman Forum. Rome, 1910.
Arc 785.13.55 Bartoli, Alfonso. Il Foro Romano, il Palatino. Milano, 1924.
Arc 785.13.57 Bartoli, Alfonso. The Roman Forum; the Palatine. Milan, 1924.
Htn Arc 785.13.60* Palletus, F. Historia Fori Romani restituto et aucta per Philippum Broidaeum Ariensem. Buaci, 1576.
Arc 785.13.63 Nichols, Francis M. A revised history of the column of Phocas in the Roman Forum. Westminster, 1890.
Arc 785.13.65 Owen, A.S. Excerpta ex antiquis scriptoribus quae ad Forum Romanum spectant. Oxonii, 1930.
Arc 785.13.70 Carettoni, G. A short guide to the Roman Forum. Bologna, 1948.
Arc 785.13.75 Welin, Erik. Studien zur Topographie des Forum Romanum. Lund, 1953.
Arc 785.13.80F Castagnoli, F. Foro romano. Milano, 1957.
Arc 785.13.85 Stucchi, S. I monumenti della parte meridionale del Foro Romano. Roma, 1958.
Arc 785.13.90 Staderini, G. The Roman Forum. Rome, 19- .
Arc 785.13.95 Grant, Michael. The Roman Forum. London, 1970.
Arc 785.13.200F Tolonei, Arnaldo. La via Cavour e i fori imperiali. Roma, 1903.
Arc 785.13.205 Paribeni, R. I fori imperiali. Roma, 1930.
Arc 785.14 Jordan, Henri. Capitol, Forum und Sacra Via in Rom. Berlin, 1881.
Arc 785.14.5 Rodocanachi, E. The Roman capitol in ancient and modern times. N.Y., 1906.
Arc 785.14.9 Maes, Costantino. Tutte le rovine, le memorie storiche. Roma, 1900.
Arc 785.15 Froehner, W. La colonne trajane. Paris, 1865.
Arc 785.15.5 Petersen, E. Trajans Dakische Kriege. Leipzig, 1899.
Arc 785.15.9 Boni, G. Trajan's column. (The British Academy). London, n.d.
Arc 785.15.11FA Lehmann-Hartleben, Karl. Die Trajanssaule. Text and Atlas. Berlin, 1926. 2v.
Arc 785.15.11FB Lehmann-Hartleben, Karl. Die Trajanssaule. v.1-2. Berlin, 1926.
Arc 785.15.13 Reinach, S. La colonne trajane au Musee de Saint-Germain. Paris, 1886.
Arc 785.15.15 Bartoli, P.S. Die Traianssäule. Voorburg, 1941.
Arc 785.15.20 Stucchi, S. Contributo alla conoscenza della topografia dell'arte e della storia nella Colonna Traiana. Udine, 1960.
Arc 785.15.50 Calcografia di Roma. v.6-7. Roma, 1779.
Arc 785.16 Bayer, J. Stuck-Reliefs...Casa Farnesina in Rom. Wien, 1897.
Arc 785.17 Steinmetz, G. Die römischen Glasspiegel. n.p., 1897.
Arc 785.18 Delbrück, R. Die drei Tempel am Forum Holitorium in Rom. Rom, 1903.
Arc 785.19 Richter, O. Beiträge zur römischen Topographie. v.1-2,3. Berlin, 1903. 2v.
Arc 785.20 Itinerario. Descrizione dei monumenti...Via Appia. Roma, 1854.
Arc 785.20.5 Ripostelli, Giuseppe. La Via Appia en ruine et en reconstruction. Rome, 1904.
Arc 785.20.7 Ripostelli, Giuseppe. La Via Appia, à l'époque romaine et de nos jours. Rome, 1908.
Arc 785.20.9A Leoni, N. On the Appian Way. Florence, 1907.
Arc 785.20.9B Leoni, N. On the Appian Way. Florence, 1907.
Arc 785.20.13 Fea, Carlo. Osservazioni suo ristabilimento della Via Appia da Roma a Brindisi. Roma, 1833.
Arc 785.20.15F Castagnoli, F. Appia antica. Milano, 1957.
Arc 785.21 Oberlin, J.J. Exposé Diene découverte...le Chévalier de Freden. Strasbourg, 1796.
Arc 785.22 Haugwitz, E. Der Palatin seine Geschichte und seine Ruinen. Rom, 1901.
Arc 785.22.2 Haugwitz, E. Der Palatin. Rom, 1901.
Arc 785.22.5 Lanciani, Visconti de. Guida del Palatino. Roma, 1873.
Arc 785.22.8 Gori, Fabio. Sugli edifizi palatini. Roma, 1867.
Arc 785.22.10F Thon, C. Il palazzo de' Cesari sul monte Palatino. Roma, 1828.
Arc 785.22.15 Carettoni, G. A short guide to the Palatine. Bologna, 1948.
Arc 785.22.20 Lugli, G. Regio urbis decima. Roma, 1960.
Arc 785.23 Rossi, G.B. de. Ricerche archeologico e topografico nel monto Albano. Roma, 1874.
Arc 785.23.3 Rossi, M.S. de. Scavi e studi nel tempio di Giove Laziale. Roma, 1876.
Arc 785.23.5 Rossi, M.S. de. Collare di servo fuggitivo novo Scoperto. Roma, 1892.
Arc 785.24 Pullen, H.W. Handbooks of ancient Rome. London, 1894.
Arc 785.25 Mémoire sur les fouilles exécutées à Santa Sabina. 1855-1857
Arc 785.26 Prestel, J. Des Marcus Vitruvius Pollio Basilika zu Fanum Fortunae. Strassburg, 1900.
Arc 785.27 Dressel, H. Untersuchungen über Ziegelstempel des Geno Domitia. Berlin, 1886.
Arc 785.28 Corsi, F. Delle pietre antiche. Roma, 1845.
Arc 785.28.5 Corsi, F. Delle pietre antiche. 2. ed. Roma, 1833.
Arc 785.29 Nibby, A. Le mura di Roma. Roma, 1820.
Arc 785.29.5 Quarenghi, G. Le mura di Roma. Roma, 1880.
Arc 785.29.10 Richmond, Ian A. The city wall of imperial Rome. Oxford, 1930.
Arc 785.29.15F Säflund, G. Le mura di Roma republicana. Uppsala, 1932.
Arc 785.29.20 Quaderni dellimpero. Al linies romano. Romano. 1-10
Arc 785.30 Petersen, Eugen. Comitium, rostra, Grab des Romulus. Rom, 1904.
Arc 785.30.5 Pinza, G. Il comizio romano...ed i suoi monumenti. Roma, 1905.
Arc 785.31 Marucchi, O. Recenti scoperte dell'Iseo Compense. Roma, 1883.

Arc 785 Archaeology - Local - Rome (City) - Special topics - cont.

Arc 785.32 Rossi, G.B. de. L'ara massima ed il tempio d'Ercole. Roma, 1854.
Arc 785.33 Altmann, W. Die römischen Grabaltäre der Kaiserzeit. Berlin, 1905.
Arc 785.33.1 Altmann, W. Die römischen Grabaltäre der Kaiserzeit. N.Y., 1975.
Arc 785.34 Cannizzaro, M.E. Ara Pacis Augustae. Roma, 1907.
Arc 785.34.5 Dissel, Karl. Der Opferzug der Ara Pacis Augustae. Hamburg, 1907.
Arc 785.34.9 Gardthausen, V. Der Altar des Kaiserfriedens Ara Pacis Augustae. Leipzig, 1908.
Arc 785.34.13 Paribeni, R. Ara Pacis Augustae. Roma, 1932.
Arc 785.34.14 Bowerman, H.C. Roman sacrificial altars. Lancaster, Pa., 1913.
Arc 785.34.20 Herman, Werner. Römische Götteraltaere. Kallmuerz, 1961.
Arc 785.34.25 Toynbee, Jocelyn M.C. The Ara Pacia reconsidered and historical art in Roman Italy. London, 1954.
Arc 785.35 Porter, M.W. What Rome was built with. London, 1907.
Arc 785.36 Pfretzschner, E. Die Grundrissentwicklung der römischen Thermen. Strassburg, 1909.
Arc 785.37 Fonteanive, R. Sui munimenti ed altre costruzione poligonie...provincia romana. Roma, 1887.
Arc 785.38 Huelsen, C. Die Thermen des Agrippa. Rom, 1910.
Arc 785.38.7 Maes, Constantino. Le terme di Agrippa. Roma, 1882.
Arc 785.39.10 Ripostelli, Giuseppe. Les Thermes de Caracalla. 4. éd. Rome, 191- .
Arc 785.39.45 Pellegrini, A. Scavi nelle terme di Novato ed in altri luoghi di Roma. Roma, 1870.
Arc 785.39.50 Broedner, Erika. Untersuchungen an der Caracallathermen. Berlin, 1951.
Arc 785.40 Cancellieri, F. Notizie del carcere Tulliano. Roma, 1855.
Arc 785.40.5 Cancellieri, F. Notizie del carcere Tulliano. Roma, 1788.
Htn Arc 785.40.10* Palladio, A. Le terme dei Romani disegnate. Vicenza, 1797.
Arc 785.40.15 Bertotti Scamozzi, Ottavio. Les thermes des Romains. v.5. Vicenza, 1797.
Arc 785.41 Piale, Stefano. Degli antichi templi di Vespasiano e della concordia. Roma, 1821. 2 pam.
Arc 785.42 Valadier, G. Narrazione artistica dell'operato finora nel ristauro dell'arco di Tito. Roma, 1822.
Arc 785.42.5 Knight, William. The arch of Titus. London, 1896.
Arc 785.43 Préchac, F. Le colosse de Néron. Paris, 1920.
Arc 785.44 Crellius, C. Priteal libonis ex antquus erutis. Wittenberg, 1729.
Arc 785.45 Munoz, A. Il restauro del tiempo della Fortuna Virile. Roma, 1925.
Arc 785.45.5 Lafontaine, Jacqueline. Peintures médiévales dans le temple de la Fortune Virile à Rome. Bruxelles, 1959.
Arc 785.46 Gauckler, P. Le sanctuaire syrien du Janicule. Paris, 1912.
Arc 785.46.5 Nicole, Georges. Le sanctuaire des dieux orientaux au Janicule. Rome, 1909.
Arc 785.47 Carcopino, J. La basilique pythagoricienne de la Porte Majeure. Paris, 1927.
Arc 785.48 Fea, Carlo. La Fossa Trajana confermata al Ludovico Linotte. Roma, 1824.
Arc 785.49 Fea, Carlo. I reclami del Foro Trajano esposti al pubblico e giustificati. Roma, 1832.
Arc 785.50 Bigot, Paul. Recherche des limites du Grand Arque. Rome, 1909.
Arc 785.51 Sabatini, F. La torre delle milizie, erroneamente denominala torre di Nerone. Roma, 1914.
Arc 785.52F Monaci, Alfredo. Nuovi studi sull'arco di Constantino. Roma, 1904.
Arc 785.52.5 L'Orange, N.P. Der spätantike Bildschmuch. Berlin, 1939.
Arc 785.52.5PF L'Orange, N.P. Der spätantike Bildschmuch. Tafeln. Berlin. 10,1939
Arc 785.53 Gori, Fabio. La torre del Monzone presso il Ponte Ratto. Roma, 1872.
Arc 785.54 Barsari, Luigi. Del Pons Agruppae sul Tevere tra le regioni IX e XIII. Roma, 1888.
Arc 785.55 Martinori, E. Via Cassia. Roma, 1930.
Arc 785.56 Pickett, Cora Aileen. Temple of Quirinus. Thesis. Philadelphia, 1930.
Arc 785.57 Bologna. Università. Per un centro di studi di archeologia dell'Impero Romano. Bologna, 1932.
Arc 785.58F Vaudoyer. Description du théâtre de Marcellus à Rome. Paris, 1812.
Arc 785.59F Munoz, A. Via dei trionfi isolamento del Campidoglio. 2a ed. Roma, 1933.
Arc 785.60 Ricci, Corrado. Via dell'impero. Roma, 1933.
Arc 785.61 Chevalier, N. Remarques sur la pièce antique de bronze. Amsterdam, 1694.
Arc 785.62F Van Buren, A.W. The Aqua Traiana and the mills on the Janiculum. Bergamo, 1917.
Arc 785.63 Broderick, B.F. The so-called Altar of Calvinus on the Palatine hill, in Rome. N.Y., 1930. 3 pam.
Arc 785.64 Peebles, Bernard M. La "Meta Romuli" e una lettera di Michele Ferno. Roma, 1936.
Arc 785.67F Munoz, A. I templi della Zona Argentina. Roma, 1929.
Arc 785.68 Marchetti-Longhi, G. L'"area sacra" ed i templi repubblicani del Largo Argentina. Roma, 1930.
Arc 785.69.5F Munoz, A. La via del Circo Massimo. 2. ed. Roma, 1934.
Arc 785.69.10F Munoz, A. Il Parco di Traiano. Roma, 1936.
Arc 785.70F Haynes, D.E.L. Porta Argentoriorum. London, 1939.
Arc 785.71 Lyngby, H. Die Tempel der Fortuna und der Mater Matuta am Forum Boarium in Rom. Berlin, 1939.
Arc 785.72A Lehmann-Hartleben, K. Dionysiac sarcophagi in Baltimore. Baltimore, 1942.
Arc 785.72B Lehmann-Hartleben, K. Dionysiac sarcophagi in Baltimore. Baltimore, 1942.
Arc 785.73 Munoz, A. L'isolamento del Colle Capitolino. Roma, 1943.
Arc 785.74F Esplorazioni sotto la confessione di San Pietro in Vaticano. Città del Vaticano, 1951. 2v.
Arc 785.75 Calderini, A. La zona di piazza S. Sepolcro. Milano, 1940.
Arc 785.76 Recherches sur les amphores romains. Rome, 1972.
Arc 785.77 Toynbee, J.M. The shrine of St. Peter. London, 1956.
Arc 785.80 Salomonson, Jan Willem. Chair, sceptre and wreath. Amsterdam, 1956.
Arc 785.82 Quaderni dell'impero. Le grandi strade del mondo romano. Roma. 1-15
Arc 785.83 Hagen, Victor Wolfgang von. The roads that led to Rome. London, 1967.
Arc 785.83.5 Pekáry, Thomas. Untersuchungen zu den römischer Reichsstrassen. Bonn, 1968.

Classified Listing

Arc 785 Archaeology - Local - Rome (City) - Special topics - cont.

Arc 785.83.10 Hyde, Walter Woodburn. Roman Alpine routes (with map showing chief Roman passes). Philadelphia, 1935.
Arc 785.83.15 Bosio, Luciano. Itinerari e strade della Venetia Romana. Padova, 1970.
Arc 785.92 Hanson, John A. Roman theater-temples. Princeton, 1959.
Arc 785.102 Kristensen, W.B. De Romeinsche fascas. Amsterdam, 1932.
Arc 785.103 Winslow, E.M. A libation to the gods. London, 1963.
Arc 785.104 Nogara, Bartolomeo. Monumenti romani scoperti negli anni 1938-XVI-1939-XVII nell'area del Palazzo della Cancelleria. Roma, 1942.
Arc 785.107 Itinera Romana; Beitrage zur Strassengeschichte des römischen Reiches. Bern. 1-3,1967-1970// 2v.
Arc 785.110 Wielowiejski, Jerzy. Kontakty Noricum i Pannonii z ludami połnochymi. Wrocław, 1970.
Arc 785.115 Testaguzza, Otello. Portus. Roma, 1970.
Arc 785.118 Biernacka-Lukańska, Małgorzata. Wodociągi rzymskie i wczesnobizantyjskie z obszaru Mezji Dolnej i Północnej Tracji. Wrocław, 1973.
Arc 785.119.1F Rostovtsev, Milchail Ivanovich. Tesserarum urbis Romae et suburbi plumbearum sylloge. Text and atlas. Leipzig, 1975. 2v.

Arc 790 Archaeology - Local - Herculaneum and Pompeii together - Folios [Discontinued]

Arc 790.6 Zahn, W. New Entdeckte Wandgemälde in Pompeji. München, 1828.
Htn Arc 790.9* Ternite, W. Wandgemälde aus Pompeii und Herculanum. Berlin, 1858?
Arc 790.35 Comparette, D. Villa ercolanese dei Pisoni i suoi monumenti. Torino, 1888.
Arc 790.200 Avellino, F.M. Descrizione di una lasa disotterrata in Pompeii. Naples, 1837. 2 pam.
Arc 790.201 Fiorelli, G. Gli scavi di Pompei dal 1861 al 1872. Napoli, 1873.
Arc 790.203 Helbig, W. Wandgemaelde der...Staedte Campaniens. Leipzig, 1868. 2v.
Arc 790.204 Persuhn, E. Pompeji. Leipzig, 1878-82. 2v.
Arc 790.205 Presuhn, E. Die Wanddekoration in Pompeji. Leipzig, 1877.
Arc 790.206 Gusman, P. Pompei. Paris, n.d.
Arc 790.206.3 Gusman, P. Pompei; la ville, les moeurs, les arts. Paris, 1906.
Arc 790.206.5 Gusman, P. Pompei; the city, its life and art. London, 1900.
Arc 790.207 Cocchia, E. La forma del Vesuvio nelle pitture...antiche. n.p., n.d.
Arc 790.208 Barnabei, F. La villa pompeiana. Roma, 1901.
Arc 790.210 Ruggiero, Michele. Storia degli scavi di Ercolano. Napoli, 1885.
Arc 790.210.5F Ruggiero, Michele. Discorso pronunziato in Pompei. Napoli, 1879.
Arc 790.211F Fischetti, Luigi. Pompei com'era e com'è. Milano, 19- ? 2v.
Arc 790.212F Carini, P.B. Pompei principali monumenti e nuovissimi scavi. Milano, 1921.
Arc 790.213F Italy. Ufficio Tecnico degli Scavi delle Province Meridionale. Pompei e la regione sotterrata dal Vesuvio nell'anno LXXXIX. Napoli, 1879.
Arc 790.214F Sogliano, A. Le pitture murali campane. Napoli, 1880.

Arc 793 Archaeology - Local - Herculaneum and Pompeii together - General works

Arc 793.1 Hoepli, U. Bibliography of Vesuvius, Pompeii, Herculaneum. Milan, 1883.
Arc 793.1.2 Furchheim, F. Bibliografia di Pompei, Ercolano e Stabia. Napoli, 1891.
Arc 793.2 Adams, W.H.D. Pompeii and Herculaneum. London, n.d.
Arc 793.2.5 Adams, W.H.D. The buried cities of Campania. London, 1870.
Arc 793.3 Beulé, C.E. Le drame du Vésuve. Paris, 1872.
Arc 793.3.8 Miola, Alfonso. Ricordi Vesuviani. n.p., 1879.
Arc 793.4 Romanelli, D. Viaggio a Pompei a Pesto e di ritorno ad Ercolano ed a Pozzuoli. Napoli, 1817.
Arc 793.4.5 Romanelli, D. Voyage à Pompéi. Paris, 1829.
Arc 793.5 Barré, L. Herculanum et Pompéi. Paris, 1840. 7v.
Htn Arc 793.5* Barré, L. Herculanum et Pompéi. v.8. Paris, 1840.
Arc 793.5.5 Barré, L. Herculanum et Pompéi. Paris, 1863-72. 7v.
Htn Arc 793.5.5* Barré, L. Herculanum et Pompéi. v.8. Paris, 1872.
Arc 793.6 Naples. Museo Nazionale. Raccolta...pinture e di...musaici...di Ercolano, di Pompei, e di Stabia. Napoli, 183-.
Arc 793.6.5 Naples. Museo Nazionale. Raccolta...pinture e di...musaici...di Ercolano, di Pompei, e di Stabia. Napoli, 1843.
Arc 793.6.9F Naples. Museo Nazionale. Raccolta...pinture...musaici...Ercolano, di Pompei, e di Stabia. Napoli, 1854.
Arc 793.7 Horne, J.F. The mirage of two buried cities. London, 1900.
Arc 793.9 Breton, Ernest. Pompeia. 3. éd. Paris, 1870.
Arc 793.9.2 Breton, Ernest. Pompeia. 3. éd. Paris, 1869.
Arc 793.10F Kraus, Theodor. Pompeii and Herculaneum: the living cities of the dead. N.Y., 1975.
Arc 793.11 Reale Accademia Ercolanese di Archeologia, Naples. Memorie. v.1-9. Napoli, 1822-62. 10v.
Arc 793.12 Ellaby, Christopher G. Pompeii and Herculaneum. London, 1930.
Arc 793.13 Van Buren, Albert W. A companion to the study of Pompeii and Herculaneum. Rome, 1933.
Arc 793.14.5A Corti, Egon C. Untergang und Auferstehung von Pompeji und Herculaneum. 3. Aufl. München, 1941.
Arc 793.14.5B Corti, Egon C. Untergang und Auferstehung von Pompeji und Herculaneum. 3. Aufl. München, 1941.
Arc 793.15 Corti, E.C. The destruction and resurection of Pompeii and Herculaneum. London, 1951.
Arc 793.17 Brion, Marcel. Pompeii and Herculaneum. N.Y., 1961.
Arc 793.19 Maiuri, Amedeo. Pompei, Ercolano e Stabia. Novara, 1961.
Arc 793.22 Grant, Michael. Cities of Vesuvius: Pompeii and Herculaneum. London, 1971.

Arc 796 Archaeology - Local - Herculaneum and Pompeii together - Special topics

Arc 796.1 Helbig, W. Untersuchungen über die campanische Wandmalerei. Leipzig, 1873.
Arc 796.2F Beyen, Hendrik G. Über Stilleben aus Pompeji und Herculaneum. 's-Gravenhage, 1928.
Arc 796.2.10F Beyen, Hendrik G. Die pompejanischen Wanddekoration. v.1-2. Haag, 1938. 4v.

Arc 796 Archaeology - Local - Herculaneum and Pompeii together - Special topics - cont.

Arc 796.5 Bogaerts, T. Kunst der illusie; antieke wandschilderungen uit Campanie. Den Haag, 1958.

Arc 800 Archaeology - Local - Herculaneum - General works

Arc 800.1 Bellicard, J.C. Observations on the antiques of the town of Herculaneum. London, 1753.
Arc 800.2 Maréchal, P.S. Antiquités d'Herculanum. Paris, 1780-1803. 12v.
Arc 800.2.5 Maréchal, P.S. Antiquités d'Herculanum. Paris, 1871. 8v.
Htn Arc 800.3* Winckelmann, J. Sendschreiben von den Herculanischen Entdeckungen. Dresden, 1762. 4 pam.
Arc 800.3.5 Winckelmann, J. Recueil de lettres de M. Winckelmann. Paris, 1784.
Arc 800.3.7 Winckelmann, J. Lettre à Monsieur le Comte de Brühl. Dresde, 1764.
Arc 800.3.13 Winckelmann, J. Critical account of the situation and destruction by the first eruptions of Mount Vesuvius. London, 1771.
Arc 800.4 Pagano, N. Description des fouilles d'Herculanum. Naples, 1871.
Htn Arc 800.5* Venuti, N.M. de. Descrizione delle prime scoperte dell'antica città d'Ercolano. Venezia, 1749.
Arc 800.5.2 Venuti, N.M. de. Descrizione delle prime scoperte dell'antica città d'Ercolano. Roma, 1748.
Arc 800.5.10 Venuti, N.M. de. A description of the first discoveries of...ancient city of Heraclea. London, 1750.
Arc 800.6A Waldstein, C. Herculaneum, past, present and future. London, 1908.
Arc 800.6B Waldstein, C. Herculaneum, past, present and future. London, 1908.
Arc 800.7 Barker, E.R. Buried Herculaneum. London, 1908.
Arc 800.8.2 Cochin, Charles N. Observations sur les antiquités d'Herculanum. 2e éd. Paris, 1755.
Arc 800.8.3 Cochin, Charles N. Observations sur les antiquités d'Herculanum. 2e éd. Paris, 1757.
Arc 800.9F Maiuri, Amedeo. Ercolano. Roma, 1932.
Arc 800.9.5 Maiuri, Amedeo. Ercolano. 2. ed. Roma, 1937.
Arc 800.9.8F Maiuri, Amedeo. Ercolano. Roma, 1958.
Arc 800.10 Bondaroy, F. de. Recherches sur les ruines d'Herculanum. Paris, 1770.
Arc 800.11 Brosses, Charles de. Lettres sur l'état actuel de la ville souterraine d'Herculée. Dijon, 1750.
Arc 800.12 Lettre sur les peintures d'Herculanum. Bruxelles, 1751.
Arc 800.13 Mémoire sur la ville. Paris, 1748. 3 pam.
Arc 800.14 Fordyce, W. Memoirs concerning Herculaneum. London, 1750.
Arc 800.15 Catalano, V. Storia di Ercolano. Napoli, 1953.
Arc 800.16 Kusch, Eugen. Herculaneum. Nürnberg, 1960.

Arc 805 Archaeology - Local - Herculaneum - Special topics

Arc 805.2 Forti, Lidia. Le danzatrici di Ercolano. Napoli, 1959.
Arc 805.3 Koehler, H.K.E. von. Description de deux monumens antiques. St. Petersbourg, 1810.

Arc 810 Archaeology - Local - Pompeii - General works

Arc 810.1 Aloe, Stanislas d'. Les ruines de Poméi. Naples, 1852.
Arc 810.1.2 Aloe, Stanislas d'. Les ruines de Pompéi. Naples, 1851.
Arc 810.1.3 Aloe, Stanislas d'. Les ruines de Pompéi. Naples, 1850-51. 3 pam.
Arc 810.2 Bonucci, Carlo. Pompéi. Naples, 1828.
Arc 810.2.5 Bonucci, Carlo. Pompéi. 2. éd. Naples, 1830.
Arc 810.3 Clarke, W. Pompeii (in library of entertaining knowledge). London, 1831-32. 2v.
Arc 810.4 Dyer, T.H. Pompeii: its history, buildings and antiquities. London, 1867.
Arc 810.5 Fiorelli, G. Pompeianarum antiquitatum historia. Naples, 1860-62. 3v.
Arc 810.5.2A Fiorelli, G. Descrizione di Pompei. Naples, 1875.
Arc 810.5.2B Fiorelli, G. Descrizione di Pompei. Naples, 1875.
Arc 810.6 Gell, William. Pompeiana. London, 1817-19.
Arc 810.6.2 Gell, William. Pompeiana. London, 1837. 2v.
Arc 810.6.3A Gell, William. Pompeiana. London, 1852.
Arc 810.6.3B Gell, William. Pompeiana. London, 1852.
Arc 810.6.5 Gell, William. Pompeiana. London, 1832. 2v.
Arc 810.6.7 Gell, William. Pompeiana; the topography, edifices, and ornaments of Pompeii. London, 1835. 2v.
Arc 810.7 Guide de Pompéi. Naples, 1866.
Arc 810.8 Lagrèze, G.B. de. Pompéi, les catacombes, l'Alhambra. Paris, 1889.
Arc 810.10 Monnier, Marc. Pompéi et les Pompéiens. 3. éd. Paris, 1873.
Arc 810.10.5 Monnier, Marc. The wonders of Pompeii. N.Y., 1870.
Arc 810.11 Mau, August. Pompejanische Beitraege. Berlin, 1879.
Arc 810.11.2 Mau, August. Fuehrer durch Pompeji. Naples, 1893.
Arc 810.11.3 Mau, August. Fuehrer durch Pompeji. 2. Aufl. Leipzig, 1896.
Arc 810.11.4 Mau, August. Fuehrer durch Pompeji. 3. Aufl. Leipzig, 1898.
Arc 810.11.4.5 Mau, August. Fuehrer durch Pompeji. 4e Aufl. Leipzig, 1903.
Arc 810.11.5 Mau, August. Fuehrer durch Pompeji. 6. Aufl. Leipzig, 1928.
Arc 810.11.6 Mau, August. Pompeji in Leben und Kunst. Leipzig, 1900.
Arc 810.11.7 Mau, August. Pompeji in Leben und Kunst. 2. Aufl. Leipzig, 1908.
Arc 810.11.7.2 Mau, August. Pompeji in Leben und Kunst. 2. Aufl. Leipzig, 1913.
Arc 810.11.8 Mau, August. Pompeii, its life and art. N.Y., 1899.
Arc 810.11.9 Mau, August. Pompeii, its life and art. N.Y., 1902.
Arc 810.11.10 Mau, August. Pompeii, its life and art. N.Y., 1907.
Arc 810.11.11 Mau, August. Pompeii, its life and art. Washington, D.C., 1973.
Arc 810.12 Nissen, H. Pompeianische Studien zur Staedtekunde des Altertums. Leipzig, 1877.
Arc 810.13 Overbeck, J. Pompeji. Leipzig, 1856.
Arc 810.13.2A Overbeck, J. Pompeji. Leipzig, 1884.
Arc 810.13.2B Overbeck, J. Pompeji. Leipzig, 1884.
Arc 810.13.5 Overbeck, J. Pompeji in seinen Gebäuden. 3. Aufl. Leipzig, 1875.
Arc 810.14 Wall, J.W. Naples and Pompeii. Burlington, 1856.
Arc 810.15 Ziegeler, E. Aus Pompeji. Guetersloh, 1895.
Arc 810.16 Marriott, H.P.F. Facts about Pompeii. London, 1895.
Arc 810.17 Weichardt, C. Pompeii before its destruction. Leipzig, n.d.
Arc 810.17.13 Weichardt, C. Pompei vor der Zerstoerung. 3. Aufl. München, 1909.
Arc 810.18 Hubik, J. Pompeji im Gymnasialunterricht. Wien, 1900.

Arc 810 Archaeology - Local - Pompeii - General works - cont.

Arc 810.19 Guillaume, Paul. Une excursion à Pompéi. Paris, 1880.
Arc 810.20 Mayer, E. von. Pompeji in seiner Kunst. Berlin, n.d.
Arc 810.21 Engelmann, R. Pompeii. London, 1904.
Arc 810.22 Thédenat, H. Pompéi. Vie privée. Histoire. Paris, 1906.
Arc 810.22.2 Thédenat, H. Pompéi. Vie publique. Paris, 1906.
Arc 810.22.5 Thédenat, H. Pompéi. Vie publique. Paris, 1910.
Arc 810.23 Duhn, F. von. Pompeii, eine hellenistische Stadt in Italien. Leipzig, 1906.
Arc 810.24 Schoener, R. Pompeii. Beschreibung der Stadt. Stuttgart, n.d.
Arc 810.25 Fiorelli, G. Guida di Pompei. Roma, 1877.
Arc 810.26 Mackenzie, W.M. Pompeii. London, 1910.
Arc 810.27 Nuova pianta degli scavi di Pompei. n.p., n.d.
Arc 810.28 Monod, Jules. La cité antique de Pompéi. Paris, 1911.
Arc 810.29 Pompeii: its destruction and re-discovery. London, 1853.
Arc 810.30 Pompeii. N.Y., n.d.
Arc 810.31 Garrucci, Räffaele. Questioni Pompeiane. Napoli, 1853.
Arc 810.32 Pernice, Erich. Pompejiforschung und Archäologie nach dem Kriege. Griefswald, 1920.
Arc 810.32.5 Pernice, Erich. Pompeji. Leipzig, 1926.
Arc 810.33 Beccarini, Paolo. Un decennio di nuovi scavi in Pompei. Milano, 1922.
Arc 810.34 Curti, Pier A. Pompei e le sue rovine. Milano, 1872-74. 3v.
Arc 810.35 Twelve photographs of Pompeii. n.p., n.d.
Arc 810.36F Die hellenistische Kunst in Pompeji. Berlin. 4-6,1925-1938 3v.
Arc 810.37 Ippel, Albert. Pompeji. Leipzig, 1925.
Arc 810.38 Engelmann, W. Neuer Führer durch Pompeji. Leipzig, 1925.
Arc 810.38.5 Engelmann, W. New guide to Pompeii. Leipzig, 1925.
Arc 810.39 Warscher, Tatiana. Pompeji; ein Führer durch die Ruinen. Berlin, 1925.
Arc 810.40 Corte, Matteo della. Pompéi; les nouvelles fouilles. Pompéi, 1926.
Arc 810.40.3 Corte, Matteo della. Pompéi. Pompéi, 1935.
Arc 810.40.5 Corte, Matteo della. Pompeji. Pompeji, 1926.
Arc 810.40.10 Corte, Matteo della. Pompei; i nuovi scavi e l'anfiteatro. Pompei, 1930.
Arc 810.41 Van Buren, A.W. A companion to Pompeian studies. Rome, 1927.
Arc 810.42F Maiuri, Amedeo. Pompeii. Roma, 1929.
Arc 810.42.5 Maiuri, Amedeo. Introduzione alla studio di Pompei. Napoli, 1949.
Arc 810.42.10 Maiuri, Amedeo. L'ultima fase edilizia di Pompei. Roma, 1942.
Arc 810.44 Neville-Rolfe, Eustace. Pompeii, popular and practical. Naples, 1888.
Arc 810.45 Warsher, Tatiana. Pompeii in three hours. Rome, 1930.
Arc 810.46 Bruun, Carl. Pompeji, dets historie og mindesmärker. Kjøbenhavn, 1881.
Arc 810.47 Pagano, N. Guide de Pompéi tirée de toutes les ouvrages les plus intéressantes. 4. éd. Naples, 1874.
Arc 810.47.5 Pagano, N. Guide de Pompéi. 5. éd. Naples, 1875.
Arc 810.47.7 Pagano, N. Guide de Pompéi. 17. éd. Scafati, 1886.
Arc 810.48 Jorio, Andrea. Plan de Pompéi. Naples, 1828.
Arc 810.48.10 Jorio, Andrea. Guida di Pompei. Napoli, 1836.
Arc 810.49 Clarac, Frédéric. Fouille faite a Pompéi en présence de S.M. la reine des deux Siciles. n.p., 1813.
Arc 810.50A Carrington, R.C. Pompeii. Oxford, 1936.
Arc 810.50B Carrington, R.C. Pompeii. Oxford, 1936.
Arc 810.51 Sogliano, A. Pompei nel suo sviluppo storico. Roma, 1937.
Arc 810.52 Seymour-Browne, C. Notes on Pompei. Naples, 1913.
Arc 810.53 Morlicchio, F. Guide to Pompei illustrated. Pompei, 1901.
Arc 810.54 Corte, Matteo della. Piccola guida di Pompei. Pompei, 1939.
Arc 810.54.5 Corte, Matteo della. Case ed abitanti di Pompei. 2. ed. Pompei, 1954.
Arc 810.54.7 Corte, Matteo della. Case ed abitanti di Pompei. 3. ed. Napoli, 1965.
Arc 810.56 Pompeiana. Napoli, 1950.
Arc 810.57F Spinazzola, Vittorio. Pompei alla luce degli scavi novi di Via dell'Abondanza (anni 1910-1923). Roma, 1953. 2v.
Arc 810.58 Man, Ivonne de. Dag faun. Amsterdam, 1960.
Arc 810.60 Lindsay, J. The writing on the wall. London, 1960.
Arc 810.62 Ciprotti, Pio. Conoscere Pompei. Roma, 1959.
Arc 810.63.2 Aafjes, B. Dag van gramschap in Pompeji. 2. druk. Amsterdam, 1961.
Arc 810.64 Jashemski, Stanley A. Pompeii and the region destroyed by Vesuvius in A.D. 79. Garden City, 1965.
Arc 810.65 Etienne, Robert. La vie quotidienne à Pompéi. Paris, 1966.
Arc 810.66 Guerdan, René. Pompei. Paris, 1973.
Arc 810.68 Seedorff Pedersen, Hans H.O. Pompeji. København, 1966.

Arc 815 Archaeology - Local - Pompeii - Special topics

Arc 815.1 Ruggiero, Michele. Studi sopra gli edifizi e le arti meccaniche dei Pompeiani. Napoli, 1872.
Arc 815.2 Smith, F.W. The Pompeia. Saratoga, 1890.
Arc 815.3 Scharf, G.J. The Pompeian court in the Crystal Palace. London, 1854.
Htn Arc 815.4* Gautier, T. Le palais pompéien. Paris, 1866.
Arc 815.5 Comes, O. Illustrazione delle piante rappresentativa nei diputi Pompeiani. Napoli, 1879.
Arc 815.5.5 Cube, G. von. Die römische "Scenae Frons". Berlin, 1906.
Arc 815.6 Czechowski, D. Die Hausgötter in Pompeji. Peremyal, 1900.
Arc 815.7 Rodenwaldt, G. Komposition der Pompejanischen Wandgewälde. Berlin, 1909.
Arc 815.8 Ippel, Albert. Der dritte pompejanische Stil. Berlin, 1910.
Arc 815.9F Comparetti, D. Le nozze di Bacco et Arianna. Firenze, 1921.
Arc 815.10 Corte, Matteo della. Inventus. Arpino, 1924.
Arc 815.12 Rostovtsev, M.I. Mifologicheskii peizazh 3-go pompeiaiskago stilia. n.p., n.d.
NEDL Arc 815.13 Macchiaro, V. Die Villa des Mysterien in Pompei. Neapel, 1926?
Htn Arc 815.13.15F* Maiuri, Amedeo. La villa dei misteri. Roma, 1931.
Htn Arc 815.13.15PF* Maiuri, Amedeo. La villa dei misteri. Plates. Roma, 1931.
Arc 815.13.20 Feiler, Leopold. Mysterion Gedanken vor den dionysischen Fresken der Mysterienvilla in Pompeji. Wien, 1946.
Arc 815.14 Feis, Leopoldo. Di alcune memorie bibliche scaperte a Pompei. Firenze, 1906.
Arc 815.15 Curtius, Ludwig. Die Wandmalerei Pompejis. Leipzig, 1929.
Arc 815.15.2 Curtius, Ludwig. Die Wandmalerei Pompejis. Darmstadt, 1960.
Arc 815.16F Sogliano, A. La Basilica di Pompei. Napoli, 1911. 6 pam.

Arc 815 Archaeology - Local - Pompeii - Special topics - cont.

Arc 815.18F Paribeni, R. Pompei. n.p., 1902.
Arc 815.19 Millin, A.L. Description des tombeaux qui ont été découverts à Pompéi dans l'année 1812. Naples, 1813.
Arc 815.19.5 Borrelli, L. Le tombe di Pompei a schola semicircolare. Napoli, 1937.
Arc 815.20 Burrascano, N. I misteri orfici nell'antica Pompei. Roma, 1928.
Arc 815.21 Baizini, G.B. Due lettere sopra il musaico di Pompei. Bergamo, 1836.
Arc 815.22F Van Buren, A.W. Studies in the archaeology of the forum at Pompeii. Bergamo, 1918.
Arc 815.23F Petra, Giulio de. Le tavolette cerate di Pompei. Roma, 1876.
Arc 815.24F Maiuri, Amedeo. La casa del Menandro e il suo tesoro di Argenteria. Roma, 1933. 2v.
Arc 815.25 Bicentenario degli scavi di Pompei. Napoli, 1948.
Arc 815.26 Schefold, Karl. Pompejanische Malerei. Basel, 1952.
Arc 815.26.2 Schefold, Karl. La peinture pompéienne; essai sur l'évolution de sa signification. Bruxelles, 1972.
Arc 815.26.5 Schefold, Karl. Die Wände Pompejis. Berlin, 1957.
Arc 815.26.10 Schefold, Karl. Vergessene Pompeji. Bern, 1962.
Arc 815.27 Ragghianti, C.L. Pittori di Pompei. Milano, 1963.
Arc 815.28 Maiuri, Amedeo. Pompejanische Wandgemälde. Bern, 1959.
Arc 815.30 Leppmann, Wolfgang. Pompeji. Eine Stadt in Literatur und Leben. München, 1966.
Arc 815.35 Leppmann, Wolfgang. Pompeii in fact and fiction. London, 1968.
Arc 815.36 Little, Alan. A Roman bridal drama at the Villa of the Mysteries. Wheaton, Md., 1972.

Arc 820 Archaeology - Local - France - Folios [Discontinued]

Arc 820.2 Chantre, Ernest. Études paléoethnologiques dans le bassin du Rhône. Âge du bronze. Paris, 1875-76. 4v.
Arc 820.5 Borrel, E.L. Les monuments anciens de la Tarentaise (Savoie). Paris, 1884. 2v.
Arc 820.6PF Bibliotheque Nationale, Paris. Département des Médailles et Antiques. Le trésor d'argenterie de Berthouville, près Bernay. Paris, 1916.
Arc 820.8F Société Nationale des Antiquaires de France. Rapport de la commission...sur les antiquaires gallo-romaines. Paris, 1830.
Arc 820.11PF Huber, Émile. La ville de Rouhling. Texte et atlas. Metz, 1905.
Arc 820.200 Perrin, A. Etude préhistorique sur la Savoie. Paris, 1870.
Arc 820.201 Bernard, A. Le temple d'Auguste et la nationalité. Lyon, 1863.
Arc 820.202 Moreau, F. Collection Caranda. St. Quentin, 1877. 4v.
Arc 820.202.2 Pilloy, J. Table générale de la Collection Caranda. Paris, 1908.
Arc 820.203 France. Ministère de l'Instruction. Dictionnaire archéologique de la Gaule. Paris, 1875-1923. 2v.
Arc 820.204 Barrière-Flavy, Casimir. Les arts industriels. Paris, 1901. 3v.
Arc 820.205 Mantellier, P. Mémoire sur les bronzes antiques. Paris, 1865.
Arc 820.206F Deane, John Bathurst. Dracontia. London, 1834.
Arc 820.207F Barrière-Flavy, Casimir. Étude sur les sépultures barbares du midi et de l'ouest de la France. Toulouse, 1892.
Arc 820.208F Delort, J.B. Dix années de fouilles en Auvergne. Lyon, 1901.
Arc 820.210F Champollion-Figeac, Jacques J. Antiquités de Grenoble. Grenoble, 1807.
Arc 820.211F Lacour, Pierre. Tombeaux antiques. Bordeaux, 1806.
Arc 820.212F Jollois, J.B.P. Mémoire sur les antiquités du départment du Loiret. Paris, 1836.
Arc 820.212.5F Jollois, J.B.P. Mémoire sur guelques antiquités...des Vosges. Paris, 1843.
Arc 820.213F Tudot, Edmond. Carte des voies romaines du départment de l'Allier. Paris, 1859.
Arc 820.214F Côte-d'Or. Commission des Antiquités. Voies romaines...de la Côte-d'Or. Dijon, 1872.
Arc 820.215F Maupercher. Paris ancien, Paris moderne. Paris, 1814.
Arc 820.216F Flouest, E. Notice archéologique sur le camp de Chassey. Chalon-sur-Saône, 1869.
Arc 820.217F Morel-Macler, F. Antiquités Mandeure. Montbéliard, 1847.
Arc 820.218F Tardieu, A. La ville gallo-romaine de Beauclair. Clermont-Ferrand, 1882.
Arc 820.219F Vasseur, G. L'origine de Marseille. Marseille, 1914.
Arc 820.220F Leclere, J.B. Archéologie celto-romaine de l'arrondissement de Chatillon-sur-Seine. pt.1-2. Paris, 1840-1843.
Arc 820.221F Bonstetten, W. Carte archéologique du départment du Var. Toulon, 1873. 2 pam.
Arc 820.222F Roussel, Jules. Atlas monumental de la France. Paris, 1922.

Arc 822 Archaeology - Local - France - Pamphlet volumes

Arc 822 Pamphlet box. Archeology. France.
Arc 822.01 Pamphlet box. Archeology. France.
Arc 822.1 Baudry, F. Recherches archéologiques à Pareds. La-Roche-sur-Yon, 1874. 21 pam.
Arc 822.2 Cellerier. Notice relative à la découverte d'un tombeau. Paris, 1818. 25 pam.
Arc 822.3 Pamphlet vol. Archéologie Gauloise. 17 pam.
Arc 822.4 Pamphlet vol. Archéologie Gauloise. 21 pam.
Arc 822.5 Pamphlet vol. Antiquités de la Gaule. v.1. 6 pam.
Arc 822.6 Pamphlet vol. Antiquités de la Gaule. v.2. 12 pam.
Arc 822.7 Pamphlet vol. Inscriptions antiques. 15 pam.
Arc 822.8 Pamphlet vol. Mémoires archéologiques. 13 pam.
Arc 822.9 Pamphlet vol. Mélanges d'archéologie nationale. 9 pam.

Arc 823 Archaeology - Local - France - General works

Arc 823.1 Bertrand, A. Nos origines - La Gaule avant les Gaulois. Paris, 1891.
Arc 823.1.3 Bertrand, A. Nos origines - La religion des Gaulois. Paris, 1897.
Arc 823.1.5 Bertrand, A. Archéologie celtique et gaulois. Paris, 1889.
Arc 823.2 Blanchet, J.A. Mélanges d'archéologie gallo-romaine. fasc.1-2. Paris, 1893. 2v.
Arc 823.2.7 Pamphlet box. Blanchet, A. Miscellaneous pamphlets.
Arc 823.3 Fleury, E. Civilisation et art des Romains...Gaule-Belgique. Paris, 1860-1861.

Arc 823 Archaeology - Local - France - General works - cont.

Arc 823.4 D'Arbois de Jubainville. Répertoire archéologique du département de l'Aube. Paris, 1861.
Arc 823.4.2 Woillez, E. Répertoire archéologique du département de l'Oise. Paris, 1862.
Arc 823.4.3 Rosenzweig, L. Répertoire archéologique du département du Morbihan. Paris, 1863.
Arc 823.4.4 Croyes, H. Répertoire archéologique du département du Tarn. Paris, 1865.
Arc 823.4.5 Quantin, M. Répertoire archéologique du département de l'Yonne. Paris, 1868.
Arc 823.4.6 Cochet, J.B.D. Répertoire archéologique du département de la Seine-Inférieure. Paris, 1871.
Arc 823.4.7 Souttrait, J.H. Répertoire archéologique du département de la Niène. Paris, 1875.
Arc 823.4.8 Roman, M.J. Répertoire archéologique du département du Hautes-Alpes. Paris, 1887.
Arc 823.6 L'Empereur, J. Dissertations historiques sur divers sujets. Paris, 1706.
Arc 823.7 Pasumot, Francois. Dissertations et mémoires sur differens sujets d'antiquité et d'histoire. Paris, 1810-1813.
Arc 823.7.5 Pasumot, Francois. Mémoires géographiques sur quelques antiquités de la Gaule. Paris, 1765. 2 pam.
Arc 823.8 Hirshfeld, O. Gallische Studien. Wien, 1883-1884.
Arc 823.9A Enlart, C. Manuel d'archéologie française. Paris, 1902-1904. 3v.
Arc 823.9B Enlart, C. Manuel d'archéologie française. Paris, 1902-1904. 2v.
Arc 823.9.2 Enlart, C. Manuel d'archéologie française. v.1, pts.1-3. Paris, 1919-1920. 3v.
Arc 823.9.3 Enlart, C. Manuel d'archéologie française. 3e éd. pt.2. Paris, 1929.
Arc 823.10 Blanchet, A. Cronique archéologique de la France. Paris, 1902.
Arc 823.10.2 Blanchet, A. Cronique archéologique de la France. Paris, 1903.
Arc 823.10.5 Blanchet, A. Les enceintes Romaines de la Gaule. Paris, 1907.
Arc 823.10.15 Blanchet, A. Carte archéologique de la Gaule romaine. pts.1-3,5-8,10-11,14. Paris, 1931- 10v.
Arc 823.10.15PF Blanchet, A. Carte archéologique de la Gaule romaine. pts.8-9. Paris, n.d.
Arc 823.11 Déchelette, Joseph. Manuel d'archéologie. v.1-2. Paris, 1908-14. 5v.
Arc 823.11.3F Blăzej, Benadík. Keltské pohrebiská na juhozápadnom Slovensku. Bratislava, 1957.
Arc 823.11.5 Déchelette, Joseph. Manuel d'archéologie préhistorique, celtique et gallo-romaine. v.1-2. Paris, 1913-1924. 4v.
Arc 823.11.9 Grenier, Albert. Manuel d'archéologie gallo-romaine. v.1-4. Paris, 1931-1934. 6v.
NEDL Arc 823.12 Molin, Jean. Archéologie de la Gaule. Paris, 1908.
Htn Arc 823.13* Ledain, A. Lettres et notices d'archéologie. Metz, 1869.
Arc 823.14 Courcelle-Seneuil, Jean L. Les dieux gaulois d'après les monuments figurés. Paris, 1910.
Arc 823.15 Millon, Henry E. La collection Millon. Paris, 1913.
Arc 823.16 Grivaud de la Vincelle, C.M. Recueil de monumens antiques. v.1-2. Paris, 1817.
Arc 823.17 Maffei, Scipione. Galliae antiguitates quaedam selectae atque in plures epistolas distributaes. Parisiis, 1733.
Arc 823.18 La Sauvagère, F. Recueil d'antiquités dans les Gaules. Paris, 1770.
Arc 823.19.4F Thédenat, H. Cognitio cognitionibus. Parisiis, 1873.
Arc 823.19.5F Thédenat, H. Commentariensis a commentarus commentarius. Parisiis, 1873.
Arc 823.19.10 Thédenat, H. Cachet d'oculiste. Paris, 1879.
Arc 823.19.15 Thédenat, H. L'epigraphie romaine en France. Paris, 1879.
Arc 823.19.20 Thédenat, H. Les noms des deux premiers Gordiens par Sallet. Paris, 1883.
Arc 823.19.25 Thédenat, H. Critique 1880. Paris, 1880.
Arc 823.19.30 Thédenat, H. Droit latin de O. Hirschfeld. Paris, 1880.
Arc 823.19.35 Thédenat, H. Notes sur deux inscriptions fausses. Paris, 1880.
Arc 823.19.40 Thédenat, H. Cachet du médecin Feror. Paris, 1880.
Arc 823.19.45 Thédenat, H. Antiquaires 1880. Paris, 1880.
Arc 823.19.50 Thédenat, H. Les médecins Magillius et D. Gallius Sextus. Paris, 1880.
Arc 823.19.55 Thédenat, H. Observations sur l'èpigraphie des Alpes maritimes de M.E. Blanc. Paris, 1881.
Arc 823.19.60 Thédenat, H. Antiquaires 1881. Paris, 1881.
Arc 823.19.65 Thédenat, H. 14 juillet, 1881. Paris, 1881.
Arc 823.19.70 Thédenat, H. Etvi à collyre égyptien. Paris, 1881.
Arc 823.19.75 Thédenat, H. Exposition d'Utique. Paris, 1881.
Arc 823.19.80 Thédenat, H. Lettre a M. Ernest Desjardins. Paris, 1881.
Arc 823.19.85 Thédenat, H. De Villefosse. Inscription de Gordien. Vienne, 1881.
Arc 823.19.90 Thédenat, H. Antiquités romaines trouvées aux Lilas-Romainville. Paris, 1881.
Arc 823.19.95 Thédenat, H. Critique, 1881. Paris, 1881.
Arc 823.19.100 Thédenat, H. Extrait des procès-verbaux. Nogent-le-Rotrou, 1881.
Arc 823.19.105 Thédenat, H. Zénobie vaballathus...Philippe le Jeune par Mommsen. Paris, 1882.
Arc 823.19.110 Thédenat, H. Critique, 1882. Paris, 1882.
Arc 823.19.115 Thédenat, H. Inscriptions latines des fouilles d'Utique. Vienne, 1882.
Arc 823.19.120 Thédenat, H. Şur une inscription inédite. Paris, 1884.
Arc 823.19.125 Thédenat, H. Etude sur Lambèse par Wilmanns. Paris, 1884.
Arc 823.19.130 Thédenat, H. Diffusion du droit latin. Paris, 1885.
Arc 823.19.145F Thédenat, H. Les trésors d'argenteuie trouvés en Gaule. Paris, 1885. 3v.
Arc 823.19.150 Thédenat, H. Milliaires du Var. Paris, 1886.
Arc 823.19.155 Thédenat, H. Deux masques d'enfants. Paris, 1886.
Arc 823.19.165 Pamphlet vol. Thédenat, H. 1888-1902. 9 pam.
Arc 823.19.168 Thédenat, H. M. Henri Thélier et Mlle Henriette Filhos. Paris, 1903.
Arc 823.19.170 Thédenat, H. Inscription de la caserne des Vigiles à Ostie. Paris, 1904.
Arc 823.20 Sketla segobrani. v.1-3. Sant-Brieg, 1923-25.
Arc 823.21.5F Goury, Georges. L'enceinte d'Haulzy et sa nécropole. Nancy, 1911.
Arc 823.21.10F Goury, Georges. Essai sur l'époque barbare dans la Marne. Nancy, 1908.
Arc 823.22 Bleicher, G. Guide pour les recherches archéologiques. Nancy, 1896.
Arc 823.25 Jullian, C. Au seuil de notre histoire. Paris, 1930-1931. 3v.
X Cg Arc 823.30 Hubert, J. L'art pré-roman. Paris, 1938.

Arc 823 Archaeology - Local - France - General works - cont.

Arc 823.35 Durand-Lefebvre, M. Art gallo-romain et sculpture romane. Paris, 1937.
Arc 823.35.5 Durand-Lefebvre, M. Art gallo-romain et sculpture romane. Thèse. Paris, 1937.
Arc 823.40 France. Centre National de la Recherche Scientifique. Gallia. Paris. 1,1943+ 28v.
Arc 823.41 Gallia. Supplément. Paris. 1+ 18v.
Arc 823.42 Gallia préhistoire. Paris. 1,1958+ 22v.
Arc 823.42.5 Gallia préhistoire. Supplément. Paris. 1,1963+ 8v.
Arc 823.45 Déchelette, Joseph. Manuel d'archéologie prêhistorique, celtique et gallo-romaine. v.1-6; v.1-4, 2. éd. Paris, 1924-34. 7v.
Arc 823.45.5 Déchelette, Joseph. Manuel d'archéologie préhistorique, celtique et gallo-romaine. v.1-2, pt.1-3. Westmead, Eng., 1971. 5v.
Arc 823.50 Sandars, Nancy K. Bronze Age cultures in France. Cambridge, Eng., 1957.
Arc 823.55 Laubenheimer-Leenhardt, F. Recherches sur les lingots de cuivre et de plomb d'époque romaine dans les régions de Languedoc-Roussillon et de Provence-Corse. Paris, 1973.
Arc 823.60F Pobé, Marcel. Kelten-Römer. Olten, 1958. 2v.
Arc 823.65 Eydoux, Henri Paul. Lumières sur la Gaule. Paris, 1960.
Arc 823.70 Eydoux, Henri Paul. Hommes et dieux de la Gaule. Paris, 1961.
Arc 823.75 Eydoux, Henri Paul. Rescurrection de la Gaule. Paris, 1961.
Arc 823.80 Eydoux, Henri Paul. Monuments et trésors de la Gaule. Paris, 1962.
Arc 823.81 Laming, Annette. Origines de l'archéologie préhistorique en France. Paris, 1964.

Arc 825 Archaeology - Local - France - Nîmes

Arc 825.1 Deyron, J. Des antiquités de la ville de Nismes. Nîmes, 1663.
Arc 825.2 Ménard, L. Histoire des antiquités de la ville de Nismes. Nîmes, 1803.
Arc 825.2.2 Ménard, L. Histoire des antiquités de la ville de Nismes. Nîmes, 1814.
Arc 825.2.4 Ménard, L. Supplément à l'édition de 1829 de l'Histoire des antiquités de la ville de Nismes. Nîmes, 1830.
Arc 825.2.5 Ménard, L. Histoire des antiquités de la ville de Nismes. Nîmes, 1832.
Arc 825.2.9 Ménard, L. Histoire des antiquités de la ville de Nismes. 7e éd. Nismes, 1838.
Arc 825.2.10 Ménard, L. Histoire des antiquités de la ville de Nismes. 9e éd. Nismes, 1842. 3 pam.
Arc 825.2.11 Ménard, L. Histoire des antiquités de la ville de Nîmes. 11e éd. Nîmes, 1856.
Arc 825.3 Pelet, Auguste. Description de l'amphithéâtre de Nîmes. Nîmes, 1853.
Arc 825.3.1 Pelet, Auguste. Description de l'amphithéâtre de Nîmes. 2e éd. Nîmes, 1859. 9 pam.
Arc 825.3.2 Pelet, Auguste. Description de l'amphithéâtre de Nîmes. 3e éd. Nîmes, 1866.
Arc 825.3.5 Nîmes. Musée des Antiques et Cabinet des Médailles. Catalogue de Musée de Nîmes. 6e éd. Nîmes, 1863.
Arc 825.3.8 Nîmes. Musée des Antiques et Cabinet des Médailles. Catalogue de Musée de Nîmes. 6e éd. Nîmes, 1863-75.
Arc 825.3.15 Espéraudieu, E. La maison carrée a Nîmes. Paris, 1929.
Arc 825.3.20 Segni, Emile, Le trésor de la Maison Carrée. Nîmes, 1937?
Arc 825.3.25 Balty, J.C. Etudes sur la Maison Carrée de Nîmes. Bruxelles, 1960.
Arc 825.4 Boucoiran, L. Guide...dans Nîmes et les environs. Nîmes, 1863.
Arc 825.4.4 Boucoiran, L. Guide aux monuments de Nîmes et au Pont du Gard. Nîmes, 1863.
Arc 825.6 Bazin, H. Nîmes gallo-romain. Paris, 1892.
Arc 825.7.2 Description...des antiquités. 2. éd. Nismes, 1786.
Arc 825.8 Germer-Durand, E. Découvertes archéologiques faites à Nîmes, 1870-72. Nîmes, 1871-73.
Arc 825.8.3 Germer-Durand, E. Notes épigraphiques. Nîmes, 1869. 6 pam.
Arc 825.8.5 Germer-Durand, E. Découvertes archéologiques faites a Nîmes. 1873. Nîmes, 1876.
Arc 825.8.6 Germer-Durand, E. Enceintes successives de Nîmes depuis les Romains. 2e éd. Nîmes, 1877.
Arc 825.9 Perrot, J.F.A. Lettres sur Nismes et le Midi. Nismes, 1840. 2v.
Htn Arc 825.10F* Poldo d'Albenas, J. Discours historial de l'antique et illustrie cité de Nismes. Lyon, 1560.
Arc 825.11 Seguin, J.F. L'ancienne inscription de la Maison Carrée. Paris, 1759. 4 pam.
Arc 825.12 Maucomble, Jean François Dieudonné. Description historique et abrégée des antiquités de Nismes. Nismes, 1789.

Arc 830 Archaeology - Local - France - Other Local; Special topics

Arc 830.1 Freminville. Antiquités de la Bretagne. Brest, 1834.
Arc 830.1.4 Pamphlet vol. Bizeul, de Blain. Géographie ancienne de la Bretagne. 7 pam.
Arc 830.1.5 Jéhan, L.F. La Bretagne. Tours, 1863.
Arc 830.1.7 Grand, Roger. Mélanges d'archéologie bretonne. Série I. Nantes, 1921.
Arc 830.1.9 Waquet, H. Vieilles pierres bretonnes. Quimper, 1920.
Arc 830.2 Delandre, M.C. Le Morbihan son histoire et ses monuments. Paris, 1847. 2v.
Arc 830.2.5 Hirmenech, H.P. Morbihan antiquités. Paris, n.d. 5 pam.
Arc 830.2.6 Hirmenech, H.P. Le dolmen royal de Gavrénis près d'Auray. Le Mans, 1908.
Arc 830.2.7 Hirmenech, H.P. Le Men-letonniec de Locmariaquer, Morbihan. Paris? 1911.
Arc 830.2.13 Marsille, Louis. Le déput de l'age du bronze dans le Morbihan. Vannes, 1913.
Arc 830.2.15 Marsille, Louis. Le tumulus de cote-er-garf, en elven et les sépulture de l'age du bronze dans le Morbihan. Vannes, 1913.
Arc 830.2.19 Le Rouzic, Z. Locmariaquer. La table des marchands. 2e ed. Vannes, 1923.
Arc 830.3 Cenac-Moncaut, J.E.M. Voyage archéologique et historique dans l'ancien Comté de Comminges. Tarbes, 1856.
Arc 830.3.15 Lizop, Raymond. Les convenae et les consoranni. Thèse. Toulouse, 1931.
Arc 830.3.20 Lizop, Raymond. Le Comminges et le Censeraus avant la domination romaine. Thèse. Toulouse, 1931.
Arc 830.4 Compiègne, France. Société Historique. Excursions archéologiques dans les environs de Compiègne. 1869-74, 1875-1900. Compiègne, 1875. 2v.

Arc 830 Archaeology - Local - France - Other Local; Special topics - cont.

Arc 830.5 Revon, L. La Haute-Savoie avant les Romains. Paris, 1878.
Arc 830.5.3 Ducis, Claude A. Mémoire sur les voies romaines de la Savoie. Annecy, 1863.
Arc 830.5.15 Gras-Bourguet. Antiquités de l'arrondissement de Castellanne. 2e éd. Digne, 1842.
Arc 830.6 Bazin, H. Villes antiques - Vienne et Lyon gallo-romain. Paris, 1891.
Arc 830.6.8 Niepce, L. Archéologie lyonnaise. Lyon, n.d.
Arc 830.6.13 Martin-Daussigny, E.C. Description d'une voie romaine. Lyon, 1855. 12 pam.
Arc 830.6.17 Germain de Montauzen, C. Les aqueducs antiques de Lyon. Paris, 1908.
Arc 830.6.19 Colonia, Dominique de. Dissertation sur un monument antique decouvert a Lyon. Lyon, 1705.
Htn Arc 830.7* Mérimée, Prosper. Notes d'un voyage dans le midi de la France. Paris, 1835.
Arc 830.8 Mérimée, Prosper. Notes d'un voyage dans l'ouest de la France. Paris, 1836.
Arc 830.8.3A Mérimée, Prosper. Notes d'un voyage dans l'ouest de la France. Bruxelles, 1837.
Arc 830.8.3B Mérimée, Prosper. Notes d'un voyage dans l'ouest de la France. Bruxelles, 1837.
Arc 830.9 Mérimée, Prosper. Notes d'un voyage en Auvergne. Paris, 1838.
Arc 830.10 Mérimée, Prosper. Notes d'un voyage en Corse. Paris, 1840.
Arc 830.11 Le Rouzic, Z. Carnac et ses monuments. Morlaix, 1897.
Arc 830.11.5 Le Rouzic, Z. Les monuments mégalithiques de Carnac et de Locmariaquer. n.p., 1901?
Arc 830.11.7 Le Rouzic, Z. Carnac; restaurations faites dans la région. Vannes, 1930.
Arc 830.11.8 Le Rouzic, Z. Carnac; menhirs, statues. Nantes, 1931.
Arc 830.11.9 Le Rouzic, Z. Carnac; fouilles faites dans la région. Vannes. 1897-1902
Arc 830.11.9.5 Le Rouzic, Z. Carnac. Vannes, 1932.
Arc 830.11.9.9 Le Rouzic, Z. Carnac. Nancy, 1922.
Arc 830.11.9.10 Le Rouzic, Z. Carnac; fouilles faites dans la région. Campagne 1922. Paris, 1931.
Arc 830.11.10 Miln, James. Fouilles faites a Carnac. Paris, 1877.
Arc 830.11.15 Miln, James. Excavations at Carnac. Edinburgh, 1877.
Arc 830.11.19 Miln, James. Excavations at Carnac. Edinburgh, 1881.
Arc 830.11.25 Daniel, G.E. Lascaux and Carnac. London, 1955.
Arc 830.12 Sauvage, H.E. Notes d'archéologie gallo-romaine. Boulogne, n.d.
Arc 830.13 Hermann, M.J. Le Théâtre d'Orange. Paris, 1897.
Arc 830.13.5 Chatelain, L. Bibliothéque d'école des hautes études. Monuments romains d'Orange. Paris, 1908.
Arc 830.13.10 Grube, G. Die Attika an römischen Triumphbogen...Bogens von Orange. Karlsruhe-Baden, 1931.
Arc 830.14 Fillion, B. Lettre à M.J. Quicherat...sur une decouverte...dans l'etang de Nesmy. La Roche-sur-Yon, 1879.
Arc 830.15 Estrangin, J.J. Études archéologiques, histoire et statistique sur Arles. Zix, 1838.
Arc 830.15.5 Bazin, H. Arles gallo-romain. Guide du touriste archéologue. Paris, 1896.
Arc 830.15.7 Seguin, J. Les antiquités d'Arles. Avignon, 1877.
Arc 830.15.9 Constans, L.A. Arles antique. Thèse. Paris, 1921.
Arc 830.15.13 Constans, L.A. Arles. Paris, 1928.
Arc 830.15.15 Véran, Auguste. Arles antique. Tours, 1876.
Arc 830.16 Hamerton, P.G. The mount. Boston, 1897.
Arc 830.16.5 Société Eduenne. Autun archéologique. Autun, 1848.
Arc 830.16.7 Thomas, Edme. Histoire de l'antique cité d'Autun. Autun, 1846.
Arc 830.16.9 De Fontenay, H. Notice des tableaux, Dessins. Autun, n.d.
Arc 830.16.11 Ladonne, E. Augustoduni amplissimae civitatis. Augustoduni, 1640.
Arc 830.17 Bulliot, J.G. Fouilles du Mont Beuvray. Autun, 1899. 3v.
Arc 830.17.3 Déchelette, J. Fouilles du Mont Beuvray 1897-1901. Paris, 1904.
Arc 830.17.5 Bircher, H. Bibracte. Aarau, 1904.
Arc 830.18 Bertrand, Alexandre. Les voies romaines en Gaule. Paris, 1864.
Arc 830.18.3 Arbaud, Damase. Alaunium Catuiaca. n.p., 1868.
Arc 830.18.5 Lievre, A.F. Les chemins gaulois et romains. 2e éd. Niort, 1893.
Arc 830.18.7 Peigné-Delacourt, A. Recherche sur divers lieux du pays des Silvanectes. Amiens, 1864.
Arc 830.18.9 Lion, J. Les voies romaines après la table Théodosienne. Amiens, 1907.
Arc 830.18.10 Gilles, Isidore. Les voies romaines et massiliennes. Avignon, 1884.
Arc 830.18.11 Gilles, Isidore. Saint Gens, ermite et Boèce. Supplément. v.1-2. Avignon, 1885.
Arc 830.18.15 Rochetin, L. Étude sur la viabilité romaine dans le département de Vauclus. Avignon, 1883.
Arc 830.18.19 Gobin, Léon. Viae, apud arvenos Romanae. Thesis. Augustonemeti, 1896.
Arc 830.18.23 Müller, Reiner. Die Angaben der römischen Itinerare über die Heerstrasse Köln-Eifel-Reims. Münstereifel, 1933.
Arc 830.18.27 Charvet, G. Les voies romaines chez les Volkes-Arécomiques. Alais, 1874.
Arc 830.19 Rochebrune, R. de. Sépulture d'un légionnaire romain. Niort, 1878.
Arc 830.20 Boucher de Molandon. Le tumulus de Reuilly. Orléans, 1887.
Arc 830.21 Castan, Auguste. Les arènes de Vesontio. Besançon, 1886.
Arc 830.21.3 Castan, Auguste. Le capitole de Vesontio et les capitoles provinciaux du monde romain. Paris, 1869.
Arc 830.21.5 Castan, Auguste. Le théâtre de Vesontio. Besançon, 1873.
Arc 830.22 Du Seigneur, M. Les arènes de Lutèce. Paris, 1886.
Arc 830.22.3 Normand, Charles. Nouvelles antiquités gallo-romaines de Paris. Paris, 1894. 2v.
Arc 830.22.5 Bournon, Fernand. Les arènes de Lutèce. Paris, 1908.
Arc 830.22.9 Moreau de Mantour, Philibert B. Observations sur des monuments d'antiquité trouvez dans l'eglise cathedrale de Paris. Paris, 1711.
Arc 830.22.11 Toulouze, Eugène. Mes fouilles dans le sol du vieux Paris. Dunkerque, 1888.
Arc 830.22.13 Nagne, Charles. Les voies romaines de l'antique Lutèce. Paris, 189-?
Arc 830.22.14 Grivaud de la Vincelle, C.M. Antiquités gauloises et romaines. Texte. Paris, 1807.
Arc 830.22.14F Grivaud de la Vincelle, C.M. Antiquités gauloises et romaines. Atlas. Paris, 1807.

Arc 830 Archaeology - Local - France - Other Local; Special topics - cont.

Arc 830.22.16 Bernard, Eugene. Découverte d'une statue de Bacchus dans la rue de Fossés Saint Jacques. Paris, 1883.
Arc 830.23 Piette, Edouard. Note sur les tumulus de Bartrès et d'Ossun. Toulouse, 1881. 2 pam.
Arc 830.25 Hahn, Alexandre. Monuments celtiques des environs de Luzarches. Paris, 1867.
Arc 830.26 Barranger, A. Étude d'archéologie celtique...Seine-et-Oise. Paris, 1864.
Arc 830.26.15 Notice archéologique sur le département de l'Oise. Beauvais, 1839.
Arc 830.26.20 Toussaint, M. Répertoire archéologique du département de Seine-et-Oise. Paris, 1951.
Arc 830.27 Bertrand, Alexandre. L'autel de saintes et les triades gauloises. Paris, 1880.
Arc 830.28 Travers, Emile. Une voie Saxonne à Caen. Caen, 1875.
Arc 830.29 Spencer-Smith, I. Précis...monument arabe du moyen âge en Normandie. Caen, n.d.
Arc 830.29.4 Cochet, J.B.D. La Normandie souterraine. Rouen, 1854.
Arc 830.29.5 Cochet, J.B.D. Sépultures gauloises, romaines. Paris, 1857.
Arc 830.29.10 Pamphlet vol. Rever, F. Mémoires sur diverses antiquités de la Normandie. 6 pam.
Arc 830.30 Bertrand, Alexandre. Les bijoux de Jouy-le-Comte. Paris, 1879.
Arc 830.31 Chabouillet, A. Notice sur dea inscriptions...Bourbonne-les-Bains. Paris, 1881.
Arc 830.31.5 Berger de Xivrey, Jules. Lettre à Monsieur Hase sur une inscription latine du second siècle. Paris, 1833.
Arc 830.32 Cochet, J.B.D. Notice sur une sépulture gauloise. Rouen, 1866.
Arc 830.32.5 Cochet, J.B.D. Le tombeau de Childéric. Paris, 1859.
Arc 830.32.8 Cochet, J.B.D. La Seine-Inférieure historique et archéologique. 2e éd. Paris, 1866.
Arc 830.33 Galles, René. Manné-er-H'roëk; dolmen découvert. Vannes, 1863.
Arc 830.34 Nicaise, Auguste. L'époque gauloise dans...la Marne. Paris, 1884.
Arc 830.35 Piette, Edouard. La montagne d'Espiaup. Paris, 1877.
Arc 830.36 Ollier de Marichard, J. Les Carthaginois en France. Montpellier, 1870.
Arc 830.37 Peigné-Delacourt, A. Recherches sur le lieu...bataille d'Attila en 451. Paris, 1860. 2v.
Arc 830.38 Moreau, Frédéric. Catalogue de la collection Caranda. v.1-2. Supplément. St. Quentin, 1895-96.
Arc 830.38.2 Moreau, Frédéric. Petit album suite au Caranda. St. Quentin, 1896.
Arc 830.39 Coutil, Léon. Inventaire des monuments megalithiques du Calvados. Caen, 1902.
Arc 830.40 Coutil, Léon. Inventaire des menhirs et dolmens de France. Eure. Louviers, 1897.
Arc 830.40.5 Coutil, Léon. Archéologie gauloise, gallo-romaine, franque et carolingienne. v.1-2, 3-5. Paris, 1895-1925. 2v.
Arc 830.40.9 Coutil, Léon. Les ruines romaines de Noyers-sur-Andelys (Eure); villa rustica et théatre. Évreux, 1928. 2 pam.
Arc 830.40.15 Lenormant, François. De la découverte d'un prétendu cimitière mérovingien a la Chapelle-Saint-Eloi (Eure). Evreux, 1855. 2 pam.
Arc 830.40.17 Lenormant, François. De l'authenticité des monuments découverts a la Chapelle-Saint-Eloi. Paris, 1855.
Arc 830.41 Manteyer, G. de. Le nom et les 2 premières encientes de Gap. Gap, 1905.
Arc 830.42 Grenier, A. Habitations gauloises et villas latines. Paris, 1906.
Arc 830.43 Verneau, R. L'homme de la Barma-Grande. 2e éd. Baoussé-Roussé, 1908.
Arc 830.44 Blanchet, A. Recherches sur les aqueducs et cloaques de la Gaule. Paris, 1908.
Arc 830.44.5 Julliot, Gustave. Notice sur l'aqueduc romain de Sens. Paris, 1875.
Arc 830.45 Thiellen, A. Hommage à Boucher de Perthes. Paris, 1904.
Arc 830.46 Gilles, Isidore. Précis historique et chronique des monuments triomphaux. Paris, 1873.
Arc 830.47 Fabre, Gabrielle. Les civilisations protohistoriques de l'Aquitaine. Paris, 1952.
Arc 830.47.10 Fabre, Gabrielle. Inventaire des découvertes prohistoriques. Thèse. Paris, 1951.
Arc 830.48 Fraysse, Jean. Les troglodytes en Anjou à travers les âges. Cholet, 1963.
Arc 830.49 Société Historique et Archéologique du Périgord. Questionnaire. Périgueux, 1874.
Arc 830.49.15F Taillefer, W. Antiquités de Vésone. Périgneux, 1826. 2v.
Arc 830.49.25 Barrière, P. Vesunna Petrucoriorum. Périgueux, 1930.
Arc 830.50 Société Historique et Archéologique de Langres. Catalogue du Musée. Langres, 1902.
Arc 830.51 La Scava...excavation of a Roman town on the hill of Chatelet. London, 1818.
Arc 830.51.5 Phulpin, A. Notes archéologiques sur les fouilles et les monuments découverts sur la montagne du Chatêlet. Neufchateau, 1840.
Arc 830.52 Du Chatellier, Paul. Le bronze dans le Finistère. Quimper, 1899.
Arc 830.53 Du Chatellier, Paul. Époques préhistoriques...dans le Finistère. 2e éd. Rennes, 1907.
Arc 830.53.25 Le Pontois, B. Le Finistère préhistorique. Paris, 1929.
Arc 830.54 Montauzan, C. Germain de. Les fouilles de fourvière en 1911. Lyon, 1912.
Arc 830.55 Zocco-Rosa, A. La Tavola Bronzea di Narbona. Catania, 1912.
Arc 830.56 Barbey, A. Les grottes préhistoriques du village de Jouaignes. v.1-3. Chateau-Thierry, 1870-75.
Arc 830.57 Cauchemè, V. Description des fouilles archéologiques...Compiègne. pt.1-4. Compiègne, 1900-12.
Arc 830.58 Gerin-Ricard, H. de. Antiquités de la vallée de l'Arc en Provence. Aix, 1907.
Arc 830.59 Morin-Jean. La verrerie en Gaule à l'époque romaine. Le Mans, 1913.
Arc 830.59.2 Morin-Jean. La verrerie en Gaule sous l'empire romain. Paris, 1913.
Arc 830.59.5 Morin-Jean. La verrerie en Gaule sous l'empire romain. Paris, 1923.
Arc 830.60 Allmer, Auguste. Trion. Lyon, 1888.
Arc 830.61 Toulmoudre, Adolphe. Histoire archéologique de l'époque gallo-romaine de la ville de Rennes. Rennes, 1847.
Arc 830.62 Musset, Georges. La Charente-Inferieure avant l'histoire. La Rochelle, 1885.

Classified Listing

Arc 830 **Archaeology - Local - France - Other Local; Special topics - cont.**

Arc 830.63 Bousrez, Louis. Les monuments mégalithiques. Tours, 1894.
Arc 830.63.5 Contades, G. Les monuments mégalithiques. Paris, 1886.
Arc 830.63.9 Léon des Ormeaux, A. La Roche aux Feés. Laval, 188-?
Arc 830.64 Barbe, Henri. Jublains, Mayenne. Mayenne, 1865.
Arc 830.65 Baudry, Ferdinand. Puits funéraires gallo-romains. La Roche-sur-Yon, 1873.
Arc 830.66 Greppo, J.G.H. Études archéologiques sur les Eaux Thermalès. Paris, 1846.
Arc 830.66.9 Bonnard, Louis. La Gaule thermale. Paris, 1908.
Arc 830.67 La Croix, Camille. Les origines des anciens monuments...de Poitiers. Poitiers, 1906.
Arc 830.67.5 Brouillet, A. Époques antédiluvienne et celtique du Poitu. pt.1-2. Poitiers, 1865.
Arc 830.67.10 Brouillet, A. Mémoire sur l'enceinte gallo-romaine de Poitiers. Poitiers, 1872.
Arc 830.68 Bousrez, Louis. L'Anjou aux âges de la pierre...bronze. Paris, 1897.
Arc 830.69 Hauser, Otto. La Micoque; die Kultur einer neuen Diluvialrasse. Leipzig, 1916.
Arc 830.70 Hutinel, F. La préhistoire dans la région lyonnaise. Lyon, 1913.
Arc 830.70.5 Bernard, Auguste. Description du pays des Ségusiaves. Paris, 1858. 11 pam.
Arc 830.70.7 Lafon, M.A. Amphithéatre de Fourvière. Lyon, 1896.
Arc 830.70.10 Wuilleumier, P. L'eglise et la nécropole Saint-Laurent dans le quartier lyonnais de Chaueand. Lyon, 1949.
Arc 830.71 Allou, Charles N. Descriptions des monumens des differeus âges observés dans le département de la Haute-Vienne. Paris, 1821.
Arc 830.72 Reser, François. Mémoires sur les ruines de Lillebonne. Evreux, 1821.
Arc 830.73 Guillaume, Paul. La station préhistorique de Panacelle. Gap, 1878.
Arc 830.74 Sirand, Alexandre. Antiquités générales de l'Ain. Bourg-en-Bresse, 1855.
Arc 830.75 Duvernoy, Clement. Notice sur le pays de Montbéliard. Montbéliard, 1869.
Arc 830.76 Saint-Amans, J.F.B. Essai sur les antiquités du département de Lot-et-Garonne. Agen, 1859.
Arc 830.77 Lacoste, Pierre F. Observations sur les travaux qui doivent être faits pour la recherche des objets d'antiquité. Clermont, 1824.
Arc 830.78 Lisle, Pitre de. Dictionnaire archéologique de la Loire-Inférieure. Nantes, 1882.
Arc 830.78.5 Maitre, Léon. Geographie historique et descriptive de la Loire-Inférieure. Nantes, 1893.
Arc 830.78.15A Mangou de la Lande, C.F.J. Essais historiques sur les antiquités du département de la Haute-Loire. Saint-Quentin, 1826.
Arc 830.78.15B Mangou de la Lande, C.F.J. Essais historiques sur les antiquités du département de la Haute-Loire. Saint-Quentin, 1826.
Arc 830.78.20PF Chevalier, Pierre. Nantes et la Loire-Inférieure. Nantes, 1850.
Arc 830.78.100F Société Archéologique d'Eure-et-Loire. Dallas tumulaires et pierres tombales du département d'Eure-et-Loire. Chartres, 1895-1930. 2v.
Arc 830.79 Roget de Belloguet, Dominique F.L. Origines dijonnaises. Dijon, 1851.
Arc 830.79.5 Le Goux de Gerland. Dissertations sur l'origine de la ville de Dijon. Dijon, 1771.
Arc 830.80 Gregoire d'Essigny, L.A.J. Mémoire sur la question des voies romaines. Paris, 1811. 2 pam.
Arc 830.81 Venuti, Niccolo M. Dissertations sur les anciens monumens de la ville de Bordeaux. Bordeaux, 1754.
Arc 830.82 Vachon, Marius. Les ruines de Sanxay découvertes en 1882. Paris, 1883.
Arc 830.82.5 La Croix, C. de. Mémoire archéologique sur les découvertes d'Herbord dites de Sanxay. Niort, 1883.
Arc 830.83 Grossen, J.B.B. Recueil des antiquités et monumens marseillos. Marseille, 1773.
Arc 830.83.5 Mery, Louis. De vetere Massilia disquisitiones. Massillae, 1849.
Arc 830.84 Moreau de Néris, E. Néris, capitale des Gaules. Paris, 1902.
Arc 830.84.5 Esmonnot, L. Néris. Vicus Neriomagus. Recherches sur ses monuments. Moulins, 1885.
Arc 830.85 Rever, Marie F. Mémoire sur les ruines du Vieil-Évreux. Évreux, 1827.
Arc 830.86 Loriquet, Charles. Reims pendant la domination romaine. Reims, 1860.
Arc 830.86.5 Brunette, N. Notice sur les antiquités de Reims. Reims, 1861.
Arc 830.87 Mathieu, P.P. Le Puy deDome. Clermont-Ferrand, 1876.
Arc 830.88 Audollent, A. Clermont gallo-romain. Clermont-Ferrand, 19- .
Arc 830.88.5 Audollent, A. Les tombes à l'incinération du Musée de Clermont-Ferrand. Paris, 1911. 3 pam.
Arc 830.89 Villeneuve-Bargemon, Christophe. Fragment d'un voyage dans les Basses-Alpes. Agen, 1811. 3 pam.
Arc 830.89.7 Henry, Dominique M.J. Recherches sur la géographie ancienne et les antiquités du département des Basses-Alpes. 2e éd. Digne, 1842.
Arc 830.90 Martin, Jean C. Antiquités et inscriptions des villes de Die, d'Orange. Orange, 1818.
Arc 830.91 Piette, Amédée. Itinéraires gallo-romains dans le département de l'Aisne. Léon, 1856-62.
Arc 830.91.10 Pilloy, Jules. Études sur d'anciens lieux de sépultre dans l'Aisne. Saint-Quentin, 1880-99. 3v.
Arc 830.92 Hure, Auguste. Le sénonais préhistorique. Sens, 1921.
Arc 830.93 Boissieu, A. de. Ainay; son autel, son amphithéatre, ses martyrs. Lyon, 1864.
Arc 830.94 Danicourt, A. Étude sur quelques antiquités trouvées en Picardie. Paris, 1886.
Arc 830.95 Fiancette d'Agos, L. de. Étude sur la basilique de Saint-Just. Saint-Gaudens, 1856.
Arc 830.96 Joulin, Léon. Les établissements gallo-romaines de la plaine de Martres-Tolosanes. Paris, 1901.
Arc 830.97 Porte, J.F. Aix ancien et moderne. 2e éd. Aix, 1833.
Arc 830.97.5 Gibelin, Antoine. Lettre sur les tours antiques qu'on a démoliés à Aix en Provence et sur les antiquités qu'elles renfermoient. Aix, 1787.
Arc 830.98 Voisin, F. Monuments gallo-romains du département de l'Jndre. Chateauroux, 1877.
Arc 830.99 Cassan, A. Antiquités gauloises et gallo-romaines de l'arrondissement de Mantes. Mantes, 1835.

Arc 830 **Archaeology - Local - France - Other Local; Special topics - cont.**

Arc 830.100 Gasser, A. Recherches archéologiques sur le térritoire de Mantoche. Gray, 1901.
Arc 830.101 Aurès, Auguste. Monographie des bornes milliaires du département du Gard. Nîmes, 1877.
Arc 830.101.7 Louis, Maurice. Le néolithique dans le Gard. Thèse. Nîmes, 1932.
Arc 830.103 Beaulieu, J.L.D. Antiquités des eaux minérales de Vichy. Paris, 1851.
Arc 830.103.5 Chauvet, J.M. Notice...des antiquités de Vichy-les-Bains. Cusset, 1851.
Arc 830.104 Lalande P. Ruines romaines de Tintignac (Corrèze). Brive, 1885.
Arc 830.105 La Sauvagère, F. Recherches sur la nature et l'etendue d'un ancien ouvrage des Romains. Paris, 1740.
Arc 830.106 Scheurer, F. Fouilles du cimetière barbare de Bourgogne. Paris, 1914.
Arc 830.107 Salin, Édouard. Le cimetière barbare de Lezéville. Nancy, 1922.
Arc 830.107.5 Salin, Édouard. Manuel des fouilles archéologiques. 1e éd. Paris, 1946.
Arc 830.108 Augey, Edmond. Suite de recherches archéologiques relatives à la préhistoire du département de la Gironde. 7e série. Bordeaux, 1910.
Arc 830.109 Dubreuil-Chambardel, Louis. La Touraine préhistorique. Paris, 1923.
Arc 830.110 George, J. Cachette d'objets en bronze découverte à Vénat. Angoulême, 1895.
Arc 830.111 Clerc, E. La Franche-Comté à l'époque romaine. Besançon, 1847.
Arc 830.112 Roche, J.J. Notices historiques sur les anciens cintrons. Moutiers, 1819.
Arc 830.113F Ferry, H. de. Le Maconnais préhistorique. Macon, 1870.
Arc 830.114 Raymond, Paul. L'arrondissement d'Uzès avant l'histoire. Paris, 1900.
Arc 830.115 Lunet, B. La ville de Rodez à l'époque romaine. Rodez, 1888.
Arc 830.116 Thomas, Henri. Une nouvelle page ajoutèe à l'histoire de Rosny-sur-Seine. Paris, 1893.
Arc 830.117 Lévesque, L. Inscriptions da la ville de Saint-Maixent du Xe au XIXe siècle. n.p., n.d.
Arc 830.118 La Croix, C. de. Notes archéologiques sur Nouaillé. Poitiers, 1910.
Arc 830.119 Sautel, Joseph. Vaison dans l'antiquité. Avignon, 1926-27. 2v.
Arc 830.119.5 Sautel, Joseph. Vaison dans l'antiquité. v.1-2. Avignon, 1926.
Arc 830.119.7 Sautel, Joseph. Vaison dans l'antiquité. pts.1-3. Lyon, 1926.
Arc 830.119.10 Pellerin, Pierre. En ressuscitant Vaison-la-Romaine. Paris, 1962.
Arc 830.120 Sawtell, R.O. Primitive hearths in the Pyrenees. N.Y., 1927.
Arc 830.121 Linckenheld, E. Les stèles funéraires enforme de maison chez les médiomatriques et en Gaule. Paris, 1927.
Arc 830.122F Piette, Édouard. L'art pendant l'âge du Renne. Paris, 1907.
Arc 830.123 Straub, A. Le cimetière gallo-romain de Strasbourg. Strasbourg, 1881.
Arc 830.124 Wolff, F. Handbuch der staatlichen Denkmalpflege in Elsass-Lothringen. Strassburg, 1903.
Arc 830.124.5 Forrer, Robert. Bauernfarmen der Steinzeit. Strassburg, 1903.
Arc 830.124.15 Schaeffer, F.A. Un dépôt d'outils et un trésor de bronzes...à Seltz. Haguenau, 1927.
Arc 830.125 Weise, Georg. Zwei fränkische Königspfalzen. Tübingen, 1923.
Arc 830.126 Donnadieu, A. La Pompéi de la Provence, Fréjus. Paris, 1927.
Arc 830.126.3 Donnadieu, A. Fréjus le port militaire du Forum Julii. Paris, 1935.
Arc 830.126.5 Pottier, Raimond. Fréjus et les carrières...de l'Esterel. Draguignan, 1885.
Arc 830.127 D'Ardé, J. Musée lapidaire, l'histoire de Béziers. Béziers, 1912.
Arc 830.128 Borel, Pierre. Les antiquités de Castres. Paris, 1868.
Arc 830.129 Chalieu, Alexis. Mémoires sur diverses antiquités du département de la Drôme. Valence, 1811.
Arc 830.130 Dussaud, René. Autour des inscriptions de Glozel. Paris, 1927.
Arc 830.130.10 Cartereau, E. La mise au point de Glozel. Paris, 1928.
Arc 830.130.15 Cartereau, E. Glozel et sa signification. Paris, 1928.
Arc 830.130.20 Côle, Léon. Glozel, trente ans après. St.-Etienne, 1959.
Arc 830.130.23 Morlet, Antonin. Glozel. v.2. Macon, 1962.
Arc 830.130.25 Morlet, Antonin. Petit historique de l'affaire de Glozel. Marsat, 1970.
Arc 830.130.30 Veelter, Daniel. Glozel, und die Einwanderung von Semiten im heutigen französischen Departement. Strassburg, 1929.
Arc 830.137 Pathier, Edgard L.F. Les tumulus du plateau de Ger. Paris, 1900.
Arc 830.138 Henry, Françoise. Les tumulus du département de la Côte-d'Or. Thèse. Paris, 1932.
Arc 830.139 Sacaze, Julien. Histoire ancienne de Luchon. Saint-Gaudens, 1887.
Arc 830.140 Petit, Ange. Dissertation sur Genabum-Gien. Orléans, 1863.
Arc 830.141F Aix. Commission d'Archéologie. Rapport sur les fouilles d'antiquités. pts.1-3. Aix, 1841-44.
Arc 830.142 Lebreton, J. Archéologie de Mons Seleucus. Gap, 1806.
Arc 830.143 Cougny, G. de. Chinon et ses monuments. 3. éd. Chinon, 1889.
Arc 830.144F Comarmond, A. Description de l'écrin d'une dame romaine. Paris, 1844.
Arc 830.145 Lebeuf, Jean. Mémoire sur quelques antiquités du diocese de Bayeux. n.p., 1747.
Arc 830.146 Bottin, S. Mélangés d'archéologie. Paris, 1831.
Arc 830.147F Catalogue du trésor de Chaource. Paris, 1888.
Arc 830.148 Dujardin, A. Estampes mythologiques des Celtes. Étampes, 1904.
Arc 830.149 Plat, Ernest. L'abbaye royale du Lieu-Notre-Dame-les-Romorantin. Romorantin, 1886.
Arc 830.150 Boyer, H. Noviodunum Biturigum et ses graffiti. Bourges, 1861.
Arc 830.151 Gazan, A. Notice sur une pierre tumulaire découverte aux environs de Solliès-Pont. Antibes, 1873.
Arc 830.152 Macon, Gustave. Une fondation du connétable Henri de Montmorency. Senlis, 1908.
Arc 830.153 Pamphlet vol. Sarmarobriva. 4 pam.

Arc 830 Archaeology - Local - France - Other Local; Special topics - cont.

Arc 830.155 Société des Antiquaires du Centre, Bourges. Catalogue du Musée lapidaire de Bourges. Bourges, 1873.
Arc 830.156 Pamphlet vol. Inscription d'Auch. 4 pam.
Arc 830.157 Pamphlet vol. Histoire et inscriptions de Vence. 2 pam.
Arc 830.158 Fallue, Léon. Sur les mouvements stratégiques de César...avant le siége d'Alise. n.p., 1856. 12 pam.
Arc 830.158.5 Toutain, Jules. Les fouilles d'Alésia de 1909-10. Semur-en-Auxois, 1912.
Arc 830.158.10 Le Gall, J. Alésia. Paris, 1963.
Arc 830.158.15F Sénéchal, Robert. Contribution à l'étude de la céramique à reflects métalliques recueillie à Alésia. Dijon, 1972.
Arc 830.159 Mignard, T.J.A.P. Histoire de différents cultes. Dijon, 1851.
Arc 830.160 Saurel, Ferdinand. Aeria. Recherches sur son emplacement. Paris, 1885.
Arc 830.160.5 Chevalier, Alexandre. Altonum, fille d'Aeria, origines gallo-romaines de Montbrison. Valence, 1968.
Arc 830.160.10 Chevalier, Alexandre. Le site d'Aeria. Valence, 1968.
Arc 830.161 Casimir, Philippe. Le trophée d'Auguste a la Turbie. Marseille, 1932.
Arc 830.162 Forrer, Robert. L'Alsace romaine. Paris, 1935.
Arc 830.163 Busset, Maurice. Gergovia, capitale des Gaules. Paris, 1933.
Arc 830.164 Temple, P. La préhistoire du département de l'Avignon. Thèse. Nîmes, 1935.
Arc 830.165 La Grange, E. de. Notice sur des antiquités romaines découvertes en 1834 à Chandai (Orne). Caen, 1835.
Arc 830.165.5 Caumont, Arcisse de. Les monuments historiques de l'Orne. Caen, 187-. 2v.
Arc 830.166 Forrer, Robert. Strasbourg-Argentorate. Strasbourg, 1927. 2v.
Arc 830.167 Société d'Histoire et d'Archéologie de Châlon-sur-Saône. Musée Denon. Catalogue des collections lapidaires. Châlon-sur-Saône, 1936.
Arc 830.168 Bonnet, E. Périodes wisigothique, carolingienne et romane. Montpellier, 1938.
Arc 830.169 Quelques notes sur Noviodurum Biturigum. Bourges, n.d.
Arc 830.170 Taffanel, O. Le cayla de Mailhac, Aube. Carcassonne, 1938.
Arc 830.171 Gruyer, Paul. Les calvaires bretons. Paris, 1920.
Arc 830.172 Cumont, Franz. La stèle du danseur d'Antibes et son decor végétal. Paris, 1942.
Arc 830.173 Ydier, F. Découverte de trois sarcophages merovingiens du VIIe siècle aux Sables-d'Olonne. La Roche-sur-Yon, 1925.
Arc 830.174 Bonsor, G. Les colonies agricoles pré-romaines de la vallée du betes. Paris, 1899.
Arc 830.175.10 Rolland, Henri. Glanum. Paris, 1949.
Arc 830.175.11 Rolland, Henri. Glanum. Saint-Remy-de-Provence, 1974.
Arc 830.176 Cousset, A. Découverte de gravures de sabots d'équides sur Rocher. Paris, 1911.
Arc 830.177 Cousset, A. Communications. Le Mans, 1913.
Arc 830.178 Baudouin, M. Le Rocher aux pieds du mas d'île à Lessac. Paris, 1915.
Arc 830.179 Segret, Gabriel. Une maison d'époque romaine à Blesle. Clermont-Ferrand, 1925.
Arc 830.180 Letelié, J.A. Les Arenes de Saints en 1882. Pons, 1883.
Arc 830.181 Huguenotte, A. Les mosaïques de Clervae. Besançon, 1925.
Arc 830.181.2 Audiat, L. Le capitole de Saintes. Paris, 1881.
Arc 830.182 Peyrony, D. Le périgord préhistorique. Perigneux, 1949.
Arc 830.183 Clerc, Michele. Découvertes archéologiques à Marseille. Marseille, 1904.
Arc 830.184 Hatt, Jean J. La tombe gallo-romaine. Thèse. Paris, 1951.
Arc 830.185 Toussaint, M. Répertoire archéologique du département de la Seine. Paris, 1953.
Arc 830.186 Wuilleumier, P. Les médaillons d'applique gallo-romain. Paris, 1952.
Arc 830.190 Toussaint, M. Répertoire archéologique du département de la Seine-et-Marne. Paris, 1953.
Arc 830.192 Werner, J. Der Fund von Ittenheim. Strassburg, 1943.
Arc 830.194 Toussaint, M. Répertoire archéologique du département de Meurthe-et-Moselle. Nancy, 1947.
Arc 830.196 Toussaint, M. Répertoire archéologique du département de la Moselle. Nancy, 1950.
Arc 830.198 Toussaint, M. Répertoire archéologique du département de la Meuse. Bar-le-Duc, 1946.
Arc 830.199 Toussaint, M. Répertoire archéologique du département des Ardennes. Paris, 1955.
Arc 830.200 Société Nationale des Antiquaires de France. Mémorial d'un voyage d'études. Paris, 1953.
Arc 830.201 Thévenot, Emile. Le Beaunois gallo-romain; ouvrage présenté et complété. Bruxelles, 1971.
Arc 830.205 Hatt, Jean J. Strasbourg au temps des Romaims. Strasbourg, 1953.
Arc 830.210 Forrer, Robert. Das römische Zabern. Strassburg, 1918.
Arc 830.215 Toussaint, M. Répertoire archéologique du département de l'Aube. Paris, 1954.
Arc 830.220 Guérin, Gérard. Découverte du Baptistère de Sanctus Martinus de Joulle. Fontenay-le-Comte, 1954.
Arc 830.225 Baurés, Jacques. L'aventure souterraine. Paris, 1958.
Arc 830.230 Morlet, Antonin. Vichy gallo-romain. Macon, 1957.
Arc 830.235 Lestocquoy, Jean. Nécropoles et civilisation en Artois et Boulounais. Arras, 1957.
Arc 830.240 Besançon, France. Musée des Beaux-Arts. Exposition. Besançon, 1958.
Arc 830.245 Lille. Palais des Beaux-Arts. Baoai, cité gallo-romaine. Lille, 1957.
Arc 830.250 Meroc, L. Cougnac, grotte peinte. Stuttgart, 1956.
Arc 830.260 Couture, Claude Paul. A l'assaut de la carrière du Puits. Le Havre, 1957.
Arc 830.265 Boudon-Fashermes, Albert. Le Velay gallo-grec. Rodez, 1958.
Arc 830.270 Lelièvre, Léon. Menhirs et marches sacrées. Caen, 195-.
Arc 830.275 Benoît, Fernand. Entremont, capitale celto-ligure des Salyens de Provence. Aix-en-Provence, 1957.
Arc 830.275.10 Benoît, Fernand. Entremont, capitale celto-ligure des Salyens de Provence. Gap, 1969.
Arc 830.275.15 Cornet, Jean M. Entremont et l'impérium arverne. Romans, 1972- 2v.
Arc 830.280 Giot, Pierre Roland. Brittany. London, 1960.
Arc 830.285F Zervos, Christian. L'art de l'époque du Renne en France. Paris, 1959.
Arc 830.290 Croix, Charles. Les anciennes fortifications d'Avesnes. Cholet, 1957.
Arc 830.300 Bolnat, Georges. La nécropole protohistorique de La Colombine à Champlay-Yonne. Paris, 1957.
Arc 830.305 Harmand, Jacques. Les origines des recherches francaises sur l'habitat rural gallo-romain. Bruxelles, 1961.

Arc 830 Archaeology - Local - France - Other Local; Special topics - cont.

Arc 830.310 Blouet, L. Le chrismale de Mortain. Coutances, 1955.
Arc 830.315 Rolland, Henri. Glanum. Paris, 1960.
Arc 830.320 Niort, France. Bibliothèque Municipale. Répertoire des dessins archéologiques. Niort, 1915.
Arc 830.325 Duval, Paul M. Paris antique des origines au troisième siécle. Paris, 1961.
Arc 830.330F Bégouën, Henri. Les cavernes du Volp. Paris, 1958.
Arc 830.331 Baudot, L.B. Observations sur la passage de M. Millin à Dijon. Dijon, 1808.
Arc 830.332 Nouel, André. La civilisation néolithique. Orléans, 1961.
Arc 830.333 Helena, T. Les origines de Narbonne. Toulouse, 1937.
Arc 830.334F Liénard, F. Archéologie de la Meuse. v.1-3, texte. v.4-6, carte. Verdun, 1881-85. 6v.
Arc 830.335 Daniel, G.E. The hungry archaeologist in France. London, 1963.
Arc 830.336 Prévost, R. Répertoire bibliographique. Arras, 1958.
Arc 830.337 Dupont, J. Le site et les lampes votives du Chasterland de Lardiers. Cavaillon, 1962?
Arc 830.338 Commission Historique du Département du Nord. Statistique archéologique du département du Nord. Lille, 1867. 2v.
Arc 830.339 Gilbert, Max. Menhirs et dolmens dans le nord-est de la Bretagne. Guernsey, 1964.
Arc 830.340F Guimet, Emile. Les isiaques de la Gaule. Paris, 1900.
Arc 830.341 Clébert, Jean Paul. Provence antique. Paris, 1966. 2v.
Arc 830.342 Nouel, André. Manuel de préhistoire par le sud du Bassin parisien. Orléans, 1966.
Arc 830.343 Bourdier, Franck. Préhistoire de France. Paris, 1967.
Arc 830.344F Perrault, Ernest. Note sur un foyer de l'âge de la Pierre Polie découvert an camp de Chassey en septembre 1869. Chalons-sur-Saône, 1870.
Arc 830.345 Richard, Jean-Claude M. La région montpelliévaine à l'époque préromaine (750-121 avant J.-C.). Bruxelles, 1973.
Arc 830.346 Joffroy, René. Le trésor de Vix; histoire et portée d'une grande découverte. Paris, 1962.
Arc 830.348 Haensch, Wolf. Die paläolithischen Menschendarstellungen. Bonn, 1968.
Arc 830.350 Frantin, Jean Marie. Notice sur les origines de Dijon et sur les fragments romains découverts dans les substructions de l'ancien palais ducal de Dijon. Dijon, 1854?
Arc 830.352 Maury, Jean. Les étapes du peuplement sur les grands causses des origines à l'époque gallo-romaine. Millau, 1967.
Arc 830.354 Thevenon, Urbain. La nécropole du monastier à Vagnas. Saint-Etienne, 1961.
Arc 830.356 Fixot, Michel. Les fortifications de terre et les origines féodales dans le Cinglais. Caen, 1968.
Arc 830.357 Ballet, Pierre. Le Haute-Marne antique. Chaumont, 1971.
Arc 830.358 Nouvelles recherches sur les origines de Clermont-Ferrand. Clermont-Ferrand, 1970.
Arc 830.360 Foramitti, Hans. Wiederbelebung historischer Stadtviertel; die Lösing in Frankreich als mögliches Vorbild. Graz, 1965.
Arc 830.362 MacKendrick, Paul Lachlan. Roman France. N.Y., 1972.
Arc 830.364 Audiat, Louis. Fouilles dans les remparts gallo-romains de saintes. Paris, 1887.
Arc 830.366 Truc, J.B. Osmin. Forum Voconii aux Arc sur Argens. Paris, 1864.
Arc 830.367 Stahl-Weber, Martine. Dix ans de recherches archéologiques région de Mulhouse. Mulhouse, 1972.
Arc 830.368 Bordes, François. A tale of two caves. N.Y., 1972.
Arc 830.369 Veillard, Jean Yves. Celtes et Armorique. Rennes, 1971.
Arc 830.370 Archéologie du village déserté. Paris, 1970.
Arc 830.371 Pruvot, Georges. Epave antique étrusco-punique? Antibes, 1971.

Arc 835 Archaeology - Local - Spain and Portugal - Folios [Discontinued]

Arc 835.5 Siret, H. Les premiers ages du métal dans le sud-est de l'Espagne. Antwerp, 1887. 2v.
Arc 835.200 Cean-Bermudez, J.A. Sumario de las antiqüedades Romanas que hay en España. Madrid, 1832.
Arc 835.201F Mastorelly Peña, F. Apuntes arqueologicos. Barcelona, 1879.
Arc 835.202F Santos Rocha, A. dos. Antiquidades prehistoricas do conselho da Figueira. v.1-4. Coimbra, 1888-1900. 2v.
Arc 835.203FA Veiga, Estacio da. Antiquidades de Mafra. Lisboa, 1879.
Arc 835.203FB Veiga, Estacio da. Antiquidades de Mafra. Lisboa, 1879.
Arc 835.205F Pereira da Costa, Francisco. Noções sobre o estado prehistorico de terra e do homein. Lisboa, 1868. 2v.

Arc 837 Archaeology - Local - Spain and Portugal - Pamphlet volumes

Arc 837 Pamphlet box. Archaeology. Spain and Portugal.
Arc 837.1 Pamphlet box. Archaeology. Spain and Portugal.
Arc 837.2 Pamphlet vol. Hübner, E. Géographie et archéologie anciennes de l'Espagne. 5 pam.

Arc 838 Archaeology - Local - Spain and Portugal - General works

Arc 838.1 Cartailhac, E. Les âges préhistoriques de l'Espagne et du Portugal. Paris, 1886.
Arc 838.2 Hübner, E. La arqueologia de España. Barcelona, 1888.
Arc 838.3 Leite de Vasconcellos, J. Portugal pre-historico. Lisboa, 1885.
Arc 838.3.5 Leite de Vasconcellos, J. Religiões da Lusitania. Lisboa, 1897. 3v.
Arc 838.3.7 Leite de Vasconcellos, J. Historia do museu etnologico português (1893-1914). Lisboa, 1915.
Arc 838.3.13 Leite de Vasconcellos, J. De terra em terra. v.1-2. Lisboa, 1927.
Arc 838.4 Paris, Pierre. Essai sur l'art et l'industrie de l'Espagne primitive. Paris, 1903. 2v.
Arc 838.5 Paris, Pierre. Promenades archéologiques en Espagne. Paris, 1910-1921. 2v.
Arc 838.6 Gomes-Moreno, M. Materiales de arqueologia española. Madrid, 1912.
Arc 838.9 Mélida, José R. Iberia arqueológica ante-romana, discursos. Madrid, 1906.
Arc 838.9.10 Mélida, José R. Arqueológica española. 2. ed. Barcelona, 1942.
Arc 838.11 Åberg, Nils. La civilisation énéolithique dans la péninsule ibérique. Uppsala, 1921.
Arc 838.12 Simões, A.F. Escriptos diversos. Coimbra, 1888.
Arc 838.13 Simões, A.F. Introducção à archeologia da Peninsula Iberica. pt.1. Lisboa, 1878.
Arc 838.15 Obermaier, H. Fossil man in Spain. New Haven, 1924.

Classified Listing

Arc 838 Archaeology - Local - Spain and Portugal - General works - cont.

Arc 838.16F Sociedad Española de Amigos del Arte. Exposición de arte prehistórico español. Madrid, 1921.

Arc 838.17 Mendes Corrêa, A.A. Os povos primitivos da Lusitânia. Porto, 1924.

Arc 838.18 Carpenter, Rhys. The Greeks in Spain. Bryn Mawr, 1925.

Arc 838.19.2 Manjarrés, J. de. Nociones de arqueologia españolas. 2. ed. Barcelona, 1874.

Arc 838.20 Fortes, José. Lagar de Mouros. Porto, 1901-08. 6 pam.

Arc 838.22F Madrid. Museo Arqueológico Nacional. Falcata iberica. N.Y., 1916.

Arc 838.23 Boutroue, A. Rapport...sur une mission archéologique en Portugal et dans le sud de l'Espagne. Paris, 1893.

Arc 838.24F Zeiss, Hans. Die Grabfunde aus dem spanischen Westgotenreich. Berlin, 1934.

Arc 838.25 Dixon, P. The Iberians of Spain. London, 1940.

Arc 838.26 Montey, P. Historia da arquitectura primitiva em Portugal. Lisboa, 1943.

Arc 838.27 Sociedad Española de Antropología, Etnografía y Prehistoria. Corona de estudios. Madrid, 1941.

Arc 838.28 Garcia y Bellido, A. La dama de Elche. Madrid, 1943.

Arc 838.30 Camon Aznar, J. Los artes y los pueblos de la España primitiva. Madrid, 1954.

Arc 838.32 Pericat y Garcia, Luis. La España primiva. Barcelona, 1950.

Arc 838.35 Wiseman, F.J. Roman Spain. London, 1956.

Arc 838.36 Gómez Tabanera, José Manuel. Las raices de España. Madrid, 1967.

Arc 838.38F Raddatz, Klaus. Die Schaftzfunde der Iberischen Halbinsel. Berlin, 1969. 2v.

Arc 838.39 Llobregat Conesa, Enrique. Contestanía Ibérica. Alicante, 1972.

Arc 838.40 Jornadas Arqueológicas. Actas. Lisboa, 1970. 2v.

Arc 838.40.2 Jornadas Arqueológicas, 2nd, Lisbon, 1972. Actas. Lisboa, 1973.

Arc 838.41 Mendes, Maria Teresa Pinto. Bibliografia arqueológica portuguesa 1960-1969. Coimbra, 1970.

Arc 843 Archaeology - Local - Spain and Portugal - Local; Special topics

Arc 843.2 Ramis y Ramis, J. Inscripciones romanas que existen en Menorca. Mahon, 1817.

Arc 843.2.5 Murray, M.A. Cambridge evcavations in Minorca. London, 1932- 2v.

Arc 843.3 Henao, G. de. Averignaciones de las antiguedades de Cantabria. Salamanca, 1689-91. 2v.

Arc 843.3.5 Hernandez Morales, Angel. Juliobriga, ciudad romana en Cantabria. Santander, 1946.

Arc 843.4 Engel, A. Une forteresse ibérique...de 1903. Paris, 1906.

Arc 843.5 Teixidor, J. Antiquedades de Valencia. Valencia, 1895. 2v.

Arc 843.5.15 Valcarcel, A. Lucentum, oy La ciudad de Alicante. Valencia, 1780.

Arc 843.5.25 Almarche, V.F. La antigua civilización ibérica en el reino de Valencia. Valencia, 1918.

Arc 843.5.30 Fletcher y Valls, D. Repertorio de bibliografía arqueológica. v.1-2, 4-6. Valencia, 1951. 4v.

Arc 843.7 Giraud, C. Les bronzes d'Osuna. Paris, 1874.

Arc 843.7.5 Rodriquez de Berlanga, M. Los bronces de Osuna. Malaga, 1873.

Arc 843.7.7 Rodriquez de Berlanga, M. Los nuevos bronces de Osuna. Malaga, 1876.

Arc 843.8 Whishaw, B. Illustrated descriptive account of the museum of Andalucian pottery and lace. Seville, 1912.

Arc 843.8.5F Bonson, J.E. The archaeological expedition along the Guadalquivir, 1889-1901. N.Y., 1931. 2v.

Arc 843.9 Aguilera y Gamboa, E. El alto Jalón. Madrid, 1909.

Arc 843.9.5 Aguilera y Gamboa, E. Las necropolis ibéricas. Madrid, 1916.

Arc 843.11 Bardavíu Ponz, V. Estaciones prehistoricas...desiertos. Zaragoza, 1918.

Arc 843.12 Morán Bardon, C. Investigaciones acerca de arqueologia y prehistoria de la region salamantina. Salamanca, 1919.

Arc 843.13F Gomez de Somorrostro y Martin, A. El acueducto y otras antigüedades de Segovia. Madrid, 1820.

Arc 843.13.2 Gomez de Somorrostro y Martin, A. El acueducto y otras antigüedades de Segovia. 2. ed. Segovia, 1861.

Arc 843.14 Botet y Sisó, J. Monumento sepulcral romano de Lloret de Mar. Gerona, 1892.

Arc 843.15 Gibert y Olivé, A.M. Excursions arqueológicas. Ciutats focenses del litoral coseta. Barcelona, 1900.

Arc 843.15.9 Bosch Gimpera, P. Prehistoria catalana. Barcelona, 1919.

Arc 843.15.12 Serra-Vilars, J. El vas companiforme a Catalunya i las caves sepulcrals eneolitequeis. Solsona, 1923.

Arc 843.15.14 Serra-Vilars, J. De mental-lurgia prehistorica a Catalunya. Solsona, 1924.

Arc 843.16 Memoria sobre las notables escavaciones hechas en el Cerrode los Santos. Madrid, 1871.

Arc 843.17 Estacio da Veiga, S.P.M. Memoria da antiquidades de Mertola. Lisboa, 1880.

Arc 843.18 Pereira, Gabriel. Notas d'archeologia. Erora, 1879.

Arc 843.19 Rada y Delgado, Juan de Dios de la. Necropolis de Carmona; memoria. Madrid, 1885.

Arc 843.19.15FA Bonson, J.E. An archaeological sketch-book of the Roman necropolis at Carmona. N.Y., 1931.

Arc 843.19.15FB Bonson, J.E. An archaeological sketch-book of the Roman necropolis at Carmona. N.Y., 1931.

Arc 843.20 Rocha Peixoto, A.A. da. A pedra dos namorados. Porto, 1903. 4 pam.

Arc 843.21F Rada y Delgado, Juan de Dios de la. Discursos leidos ante la Academia de la Historia. Madrid, 1875.

Arc 843.22 Hübner, E. Citania. Porto, 1879.

Arc 843.23 Ferraz de Macedo, F. Luzitanos e romanos en Villa Franca de Xira. Lisboa, 1893.

Arc 843.24 Carvalho, M. O dolmen da Barroza. Porto, 1898.

Arc 843.25 Brenha, José. Dolmens ou antas de ville ponco d'Aguir. (Traz-os-montes). Porto, 1903.

Arc 843.26 Sousa Maia. A necropole de condidello (Terrada-Maia). Porto, 1908.

Arc 843.27 Santos Rocha, A. dos. Estações pre-romanas da idade do ferre nas visinhanças da figueira. Porto, 1908.

Arc 843.28 Severo, Ricardo. Os braceletes d'ouro de arnozella. Porto, 1905. 2 pam.

Arc 843.29 Fouilles de Belo Bolonia, Province de Cadix (1917-1921). Bordeaux, 1923-26. 2v.

Arc 843.30 Mancheño y Olivares, Miguel. Antigüedades del partido oficial de Arcos de la Frontera. Arcos de la Frontera, 1901.

Arc 843 Archaeology - Local - Spain and Portugal - Local; Special topics - cont.

Arc 843.32F Spain. Comisión ejecutiva de las excavaciones de Numancia. Excavaciones de Numancia. Madrid, 1912.

Arc 843.35 Serra-Vilaró, J. Escornalbou prehistòrich. Castell de Sant Miquel d'Escornalbou, 1925.

Arc 843.40 Ansoleaga, F. de. El cementerio franco de Pamplona (Navarra). Pamplona, 1914.

Arc 843.45 Teixeira de Aragão, A.C. Relatorio sobre o comiterio romano. Lisboa, 1868.

Arc 843.50 Gibert, Augusté M. Tarragona prehistòrica i protohistòrica. Barcelona, 1909.

Arc 843.50.5 Martorell, Jeroni. Tarragona i els seus antics monuments. Barcelona, 1920.

Arc 843.50.10 Schulter, Adolf. Tarraco. Barcelona, 1948.

Arc 843.55 Suarez de Salazar, Juan B. Grandezas y antiguedades de la isla y ciudad de Cadiz. Cadiz, 1610.

Arc 843.55.10 Quintero, P. Necropolis ante-romana de Cadiz. Madrid, 1915.

Arc 843.56 Boix, Vicente. Memorias de Sagunto. Valencia, 1865.

Arc 843.56.5 Gomzalez Simancos, M. Sagunto. 1. ed. Sagunto? n.d.

Arc 843.57 Aranzadi, T. de. Exploraciones prehistóricas en Guepiezcoa los años 1924-1927. San Sebastian, 1928.

Arc 843.58 Paris, Pierre. Fouilles dans la région d'Alcañis, province de Teruel. Bordeaux, 1926.

Arc 843.59 Aranzadi, T. Exploración de calorce dolmenes del Aralar. Pamplona, 1918.

Arc 843.60 Monsalad, M.C.S.G. Arqueología romana y visigotica de extremadura. Madrid, 1900.

Arc 843.61 Zuazo y Palacios, J. Meca. Madrid, 1916.

Arc 843.62 Bosch-Gimpera, P. La prehistoria de las Iberas y la etnologia vasca. San Sebastian, 1926.

Arc 843.62.10 Bosch-Gimpera, P. Two Celtic waves in Spain. London, 1939.

Arc 843.63F Cartailhac, Émile. La caverne d'Altamira à Santillane près Santander (Espagne). Monaco, 1906.

Arc 843.64 Biscay, Sain. Disputación Provincial. Junta de Cultura. Exploraciones de la caverna de Santimamiñe. Basondo: Cortezubi. Memoria 2-3. Bilbao, 1931-35. 2v.

Arc 843.65.2 Pla y Cargol, J. Empúries i roses. 2. ed. Girona, 1934.

Arc 843.65.4 Pla y Cargol, J. Ampurios y rosas. 4. ed. Gerona, 1953.

Arc 843.66 Lopez Martí, L. Santa Eulalia de Bóveda. Lugo, 1934.

Arc 843.67 Hernández-Pecheco, E. La caverna de la Peña de Candamo (Asturias). Madrid, 1919.

Arc 843.68 Obermaier, H. Las pinturas rupestres del Barranco de Valltorta (Castellón). Madrid, 1919.

Arc 843.69 Oliveira, M. De Talabriga a Lancobriga pela via militar romano. Coimbra, 1943.

Arc 843.70 Mattos, A. de. Dois estudos: "Manis Pallas"; "Giral Cabrom". Porto, 1943.

Arc 843.71 Vives, José. Inscripciones cristianas de la España romana y visigoda. Barcelona, 1942.

Arc 843.71.2 Vives, José. Inscripciones cristianas de la España romana y visigoda. 2. ed. Barcelona, 1969.

Arc 843.72 Carro, Jesús. Otesouro de Toxados. Santiago, 1933.

Arc 843.73 Mélida, José R. Les fouilles de Merida. n.p., 19- ?

Arc 843.73.5F Mélida, José R. El disco de Teodosio. Madrid, 1930.

Arc 843.74 Mélida, José R. El teatro de Mérida. Madrid, 1915.

Arc 843.75 Bonser, J.E. El coto de Doña Ana. Madrid, 1922.

Arc 843.77 Fernandez, L.M. Excavaciones en Italica. Sevilla, 1904.

Arc 843.77.5 García y Bellido, Antonio. Colonia Aelia Augusta Halica. Madrid, 1960.

Arc 843.77.10 Yali Lassaletta, Aurelio. Historia de Italica. Sevilla, 1892.

Arc 843.77.15 Amador de los Ríos, Rodrigo. El anfiteatro de Italica. Madrid, 1916.

Arc 843.79 Vielva, M. De re arqueologica. Valencia, 1924.

Arc 843.81F Masriera y Manovens, J. Apuntes sobre la villa de Tossa de Mar. Barcelona, 1923.

Arc 843.82 Galia y Sarañana, José. Prehistoria de Aragón. Zaragoza, 1945.

Arc 843.83 Madrid. Museo Arqueologico Nacional. Catalogo de las exvatos de bronce. Madrid, 1941. 2v.

Arc 843.85 Institución Principe de Viana Pamplona. Excavaciones en Navarra. Pamplona, 1947. 7v.

Arc 843.90 García y Bellido, Antonio. Hispania graeca. v.1-2, atlas. Barcelona, 1948. 3v.

Arc 843.95 Karst, Josef. Essai sur l'origine des Basques Ibères et peuples apparentés. Strasbourg, 1954.

Arc 843.100 Leisner, G.K. Antas nas herdades da Casa de Braganca no concelho de Estremoz. Lisboa, 1955.

Arc 843.100.5F Leisner, G.K. Die Negalithgräber der Iberischen Halbinsel. v.1-3; atlas. Berlin, 1956. 4v.

Arc 843.105 Almeida, Fernando de. Egitânia. Lisboa, 1956.

Arc 843.105.5 Almeida, Fernando de. Ruinas de Mirobriga dos Célticos. Lisboa, 1964.

Arc 843.110 Rileas i Bertran, Marià. El poblament d'Ilduro. Barcelona, 1952.

Arc 843.115 Ruig y Cadafalch, José. Noves des cobertes a la catedral d'Égara. Barcelona, 1948.

Arc 843.120 López Cuevillas, Florentino. La civilización céltica en Galicia. Santiago, 1953.

Arc 843.125 Nieto Gallo, Gratiniano. El oppedum de Iruña. Victória, 1958.

Arc 843.130 Monteagudo, Luis. Galicia legendaria y arqueologica. Madrid, 1957.

Arc 843.135 Rico García, Manuel. Memoria relativa a los nuevos descubrimientos de la antigua Lucantum, 1892. Aicante, 1958.

Arc 843.140 Hernandez-Pacheco, Eduardo. Las pinturas prehistoricas de las cuevas de la Araña (Valencia). Madrid, 1924.

Arc 843.145 Hernandez-Pacheco, Eduardo. Las pinturas prehistoricas de Peña Tú. Madrid, 1914.

Arc 843.147 Cabre-Aguilo, Juan. El arte rupestre en España. Madrid, 1915.

Arc 843.149 Cabre-Aguilo, Juan. Avance al estudio de las pinturas. Madrid, 1915.

Arc 843.150 Quintero y de Atuuci, Pelayo. Cadiz; primeros pobladores. Cadiz, 1917.

Arc 843.151 Gimenez, Reyna. La Cueva de la Pileta. Málaga, 1958.

Arc 843.153 Museo, Canario. El Museo Canario. Las Palmas de Gran Canaria, 1957.

Arc 843.155 Madrid. Museo Archeologica. Catáloga de las antigüedades que se conservan en el Patio Arabe. Madrid, 1932.

Arc 843.160 Carballo, Jesús. El descubrimiento de la cueva y pinturas de altamira por Marcelino S. de Sauteola. Santander, 1950.

Arc 843.165 Frankowski, Eugeniusz. Estelas discoideas de la Peninsula Iberica. Madrid, 1920.

Arc 843 Archaeology - Local - Spain and Portugal - Local; Special topics - cont.

Arc 843.170 Mascaró i Pasarius, J. Els monuments megalitics a l'illa de Menorca. Barcelona, 1958.
Arc 843.175 Costa, J.M. da. Novos elementos para a lócalização de Cetóbriga.Setúbal, 1960.
Arc 843.180 Vega de la Sella, Ricardo. El dolmen de la capilla de Santa Cruz. Madrid, 1919.
Arc 843.181 Vega de la Sella, Ricardo. Astucias. v.1-4. Madrid, 1916.
Arc 843.182 Obermaier, Hugo. La cueva del Buar. Madrid, 1918.
Arc 843.185 Hernández-Pacheco, E. La vida de nuestros antecesores paleolíticos. Madrid, 1923.
Arc 843.186 Cabré-Aguiló, Juan. El paleolítico inferior de Puento Mochs. Madrid, 1916.
Arc 843.190 Alvarez-Ossori, F. Bronces ibericas o hispancion del Mueso Arquelogico Nacional. Madrid, 1935.
Arc 843.192 Ewert, Christian. Islamische Funde in Balaguer und die Aljaferia in Zaragoza. Berlin, 1971.
Arc 843.195 Román, Carlos. Antigüedades ebusitanas. Barcelona, 1913.
Arc 843.197 Barandiaran, J.M. Excavaciones en Atxeta. Bilbao, 1961.
Arc 843.198 Tarradell, M. Les arrels de Catalunya. Barcelona, 1962.
Arc 843.199F Jordá Cerdá, F. Las murias de Beloño. Oviedo, 1957.
Arc 843.205 Balil, Alberto. Colonia Iblia Augusta Paterna Farentia Barcino. Madrid, 1964.
Arc 843.208 Pavón Maldonado, Basilio. Memoria de la excavación de la Mezquita de Medinat al-Zahra. Madrid, 1966.
Arc 843.210 Almagro Basch, Martin. El ajuar del 'Dolmen de la pastora' de Valentina del Alcor (Sevilla). Madrid, 1962.
Arc 843.212 Sousa Gomes, A. A citânia de briteiros através dos séculos. Lisboa, 1967.
Arc 843.214 Niemeyer, Hans G. Toscanos, die altpunische Faktorei an der Mündung des Rio de Vélez. Berlin, 1969.
Arc 843.215 Pamphlet vol. Málaga. Antigüedad. 4 pam.
Arc 843.218 Martinez Hombre, Eduardo. Vindius; el lado septentrional clasico de Hispania. Madrid, 1964.
Arc 843.220 Ribeiro, Fernando Nunes. O bronze meridional português. Beja, 1965.
Arc 843.222 Schuele, Wilhelm. Die Meseta-Kulturen der iberischen Halbinsel. Berlin, 1969. 2v.
Arc 843.223F Fouilles de Conimbriga. Paris, 1974- 3v.
Arc 843.224 Prat Puig, Francisco. L'aqueducte Romà de Pineda. Barcelona, 1936.
Arc 843.225 Martín Aguado, Máximo. El yacimiento prehistórico de Pinedo, Toledo, y su industria triedrica. Toledo, 1963.
Arc 843.226 Martínez Fernandez, Jesus. Ensayo biologico sobre los hombres y los pueblos de la Asturias primativa. Oviedo, 1969.
Arc 843.227 Jimenez Cisneros, Maria Josefa. Historia de Cadiz en la antigüedad. Cadiz, 1973.
Arc 843.228 Blanco, A. Excavaciones arqueológicas en el cerro Salomón. Madrid, 1970.
Arc 843.229 Guerra y Gómez, Manuel. Constantes religiosas europeas y sotocuevenses (Ojo Guareña, cuna de Castilla). Burgos, 1973.
Arc 843.230 Nicolini, Gerard. Les bronzes figurés des sanctuaires ibériques. 1. éd. Paris, 1969.
Arc 843.231 Correia, Vergilio. Estudos arqueologicos. Coimbra, 1972.
Arc 843.232 Julia, Dolorès. Étude épigraphique et iconographique des stèles funéraires de Vigo. Heidelberg, 1971.
Arc 843.233 García Guinea, Miguel Angel. El asentamiento cántabra de Celada Marlantes. Santander, 1970.
Arc 843.234.4 Pericot Garcia, Luis. The Balearic Islands. London, 1972.
Arc 843.235 Martinez i Hualde, Angel. El poblat ibèric de Puig Castellar. Barcelona, 1966.

Arc 845 Archaeology - Local - Germany - Folios [Discontinued]

Arc 845.1 Chlingensnsperg-Berg, M. von. Das Graeberfeld von Reichenhall. Reichenhall, 1890.
Arc 845.1.5 Chlingensnsperg-Berg, M. von. Die Römischen Brandgräber. Braunsch, 1896.
Arc 845.2 Frankfurt am Main. Verein für Geschichte und Alterthumskunde. Mittheilungen über Römische Funde in Heddernheim. Frankfurt, 1894. 6v.
Arc 845.3 Kempten. Allgaüer Alterthumsverein. Bericht ueber die...Ausgrabungen. v.1-4. Kempten, 1888. 2v.
Arc 845.4 Mainz, Germany. Römisch-Germanische Centralmuseum. Das Römisch-Germanische Centralmuseum. Mainz, 1889.
Arc 845.5 Germany. Reichskommission. Limes. Der obergermanisch-raetische Limes. Abteilung A und B. Heidelberg. 1894-1910 14v.
Arc 845.200 Quilling, F. Die Nauheimer Funde. Frankfurt am Main, 1903.
Arc 845.201 Nürnberg. Deutschen Anthropologischen Gesellschaft. Festschrift zur Begrüssung des XVIII. Kongresses der Gesellschaft. Nürnberg, 1887.
Arc 845.202 Grempler, Wilhelm. Der Fund von Sackrau. pts.1-3. Berlin, 1887-88.
Arc 845.203 Frankfurt am Main. Historisches Museum. Einzelforschungen über Kunst- undAltertumsgegenstände zu Frankfurt am Main. Frankfurt, 1908.
Arc 845.204 Saalburg Museum. Saalburg Jahrbuch 1910-1913. Frankfurt am Main. 1,1910+ 25v.
Arc 845.205F Henkel, F. Die Römischen Fingerringe der Rheinlande. Berlin, 1913. 2v.
Arc 845.206F Jacob, Karl H. Zur Prähistorie Nordwest-Sachsens. Halle an der Saale, 1911.
Arc 845.207F Hahne, Hans. Vorzeitfunde aus Niedersachsen. Hannover, 1915-25.
Arc 845.208F Wurttembergisches Landesamt für Denkmalpflege. Cannstatt zur Römerzeit. Stuttgart, 1921.
Arc 845.209F Houben, P. Denkmaeler von Castra Vetera. Xanten, 1839.
Htn Arc 845.210F* Velser, Marcus. Rerum Augustanar. Vindelicar. Libri octo. Venetiis, 1594.
Arc 845.211F Architekten und Ingenieur-Verein für Niederrhein und Westfalen, Cologne. Cölner Thorburgen und Befestigungen, 1180-1882. Cöln, 1883.

Arc 847 Archaeology - Local - Germany - Pamphlet volumes

Arc 847 Pamphlet box. Archaeology. Germany. Miscellaneous pamphlets.
Arc 847.1 Pamphlet box. Archaeology. Germany. Miscellaneous pamphlets.
Arc 847.2 Pamphlet box. Archaeology. German dissertations.
Arc 847.10 Pamphlet vol. Die jungsteinzeitlichen Felsgeräte des Landes Braun und der Nachbargebiete. 7 pam.

Arc 848 Archaeology - Local - Germany - General works

Arc 848.1 Lindenschmit, L. Handbuch der Deutsche Alterthumskunde. Braunschweig, 1880.
Arc 848.2 Hettner, Felix. Die römischen Steindenkmäler der Provinzialmuseum zu Trier. Trier, 1893.
Arc 848.4 Hoops, J. Reallexikon der germanischen Altertumskunde. Strassburg, 1911. 4v.
Arc 848.4.2 Reallexikon der germanischen Altertumskunde. v.1-2, pt.1-5. 2. Aufl. Berlin, 1968-
Arc 848.5 Koepp, F. Die Römer in Deutschland. Bielefeld, 1912.
Arc 848.6 Kauffmann, F. Deutsche Altertumskunde. München, 1913-23. 2v.
Arc 848.8.2 Kossinna, Gustaf. Die deutsche Vorgeschichte. 2. Aufl. Würzburg, 1914.
Arc 848.8.4 Kossinna, Gustaf. Die deutsche Vorgeschichte. 7. Aufl. Leipzig, 1936.
Arc 848.8.5 Kossinna, Gustaf. Die Herkunft der Germanen. Würzburg, 1911.
Arc 848.8.9 Kossinna, Gustaf. Altgermanische Kulturhöhe. München, 1927.
Arc 848.8.10 Kossinna, Gustaf. Altgermanische Kulturhöhe. 8. Aufl. Leipzig, 1942.
Arc 848.8.11 Kossinna, Gustaf. Germanische Kultur im letzten Jahrtausend nach Christus. Leipzig, 1932.
Arc 848.8.13 Kossinna, Gustaf. Ursprung und Verbreitung der Germanen in vor-und frühgeschichtlicher Zeit. Leipzig, 1928.
Arc 848.9.3 Schwantes, G. Aus Deutschlands Urgeschichts. 3. Aufl. Leipzig, 1921.
Arc 848.10 Kataloge west- und süddeutscher Altertumssamlungen. Frankfurt am Main. 1-6,1911-1926 5v.
Arc 848.11 Erbt, Wilhelm. Germanische Kultur im Bronzezeitalter (2200-800 v. Chr.) Leipzig, 1926.
Arc 848.12 Blümlein, Carl. Bilder aus dem römisch-germanischen Kulturleben. 2. Aufl. München, 1926.
Arc 848.13 Wels, K.H. Die germanische Vorzeit. Leipzig, 1923.
Arc 848.14F Deutsches Archäologisches Institut. Germania romana. Bamberg, 1922.
Arc 848.14.35 Espérandieu, Émile. Recueil général des bas-reliefs. Paris, 1931.
Arc 848.15 Schuchhardt, C. Vorgeschichte von Deutschland. München, 1928.
Arc 848.15.5 Schuchhardt, C. Vorgeschichte von Deutschland. 3. Aufl. München, 1935.
Arc 848.15.7 Schuchhardt, C. Vorgeschichte von Deutschland. 5. Aufl. München, 1943.
Arc 848.15.10 Schuchhardt, C. Deutsche Vor- und Frühgeschichte in Bildern. München, 1936.
Arc 848.16.2 Wilser, Ludwig. Deutsche Vorzeit. 2. Aufl. Steglitz, 1918.
Arc 848.17 Teudt, Wilhelm. Germanische Heiligtümer. Jena, 1929.
Arc 848.17.5 Teudt, Wilhelm. Germanische Heiligtümer. 4. Aufl. Jena, 1936.
Arc 848.18 Führer zur Urgeschichte. Augsburg. 1,1928
Arc 848.19 Brown, Gerard Baldwin. The arts and crafts of our Teutonic forefathers. London, 1910.
Arc 848.20 Schulz, Walther. Die germanische Familie in der Vorzeit. Leipzig, 1925.
Arc 848.20.5 Schulz, Walther. Staat und Gesellschaft in germanischer Vorzeit. Leipzig, 1926.
Arc 848.21 Kadig, Werner. Der Wohnbau im jungsteinzeitlichen Deutschland. pt.1-2. Inaug. Diss. Leipzig, 1930.
Arc 848.22 Schuchhardt, C. Nordwestdeutschland und die Frage des Germanenursprungs. n.p., 1928.
Arc 848.23 Wahle, Ernst. Deutsche Vorzeit. Leipzig, 1932.
Arc 848.23.3 Wahle, Ernst. Deutsche Vorzeit. 3. Aufl. Bad Homburg, 1962.
Arc 848.24F Mainz. Römisch-germanische Zentralmuseum. Die Altertümer unserer heidnischen Vorzeit. v.5. Mainz, 1911.
Arc 848.25 Neckel, Gustav. Deutsche Ur- und Vorgeschichtswissenschaft der Gegenwart. Berlin, 1934.
Arc 848.26 Stemmermann, P.H. Die Anfänge der deutschen Vorgeschichtsforschung. Inaug. Diss. Quakenbrück, 1934
Arc 848.27 Balch, E.S. Roman and pre-historic remains in central Germany. Philadelphia, 1903.
Arc 848.28.5 Hohne, Hans. Deutsche Vorzeit. 6. Aufl. Bielefeld, 1937.
Arc 848.29.5 Radig, Werner. Germanischer Lebensraum. 4. Aufl. Stuttgart, 1934.
Arc 848.30.4 Schultz, W. Altgermanische Kultur in Wort und Bild. 3. Aufl. München, 1935.
Arc 848.30.5 Schultz, W. Altgermanische Kultur in Wort und Bild. 4. Aufl. München, 1937.
Arc 848.31 Behn, Friedrich. Altgermanische Kultur. Leipzig, 1935.
Arc 848.31.5 Behn, Friedrich. Altmordisches Leben vor 3000 Jahren. München, 1935.
Arc 848.32 Frenzel, W. Grundzüge der Vorgeschichte Deutschlands. Stuttgart, 1935.
Arc 848.33 Dittmann, K.H. Untersuchungen zur Geschichte der ältern Bronzezeit im Nordwestdeutschland. Inaug. Diss. Hamburg, 1938.
Arc 848.34 Gummel, H. Forschungsgeschichte in Deutschland. Berlin, 1938.
Arc 848.35 Uslar, R. von. Westgermanische Bodenfunde. Berlin, 1938.
Arc 848.36 Hofmeister, H. Germanenkunde. Frankfurt am Main, 1936.
Arc 848.37 Diekmann, H. Steinzeitseidlungen im Teutoburger Walde. Bielefeld, 1931.
Arc 848.38 Reinerth, Hans. Vorgeschichte der deutschen Stämme. Leipzig, 1940. 3v.
Arc 848.40 Behn, Friedrich. Altgermanische Kunst. 2. Aufl. München, 1930.
Arc 848.46 Mähling, W. Die frühgermanische Landnahme im mitteldeutsch-sächsisch-nordböhmischen Gebiet. Prag, 1944.
Arc 848.48 Adama van Scheltema, Z. Die Kunst der Vorzeit. Stuttgart, 1950.
Arc 848.50 Akademie der Wissenschaften, Berlin. Frühe Burger und Städte. Berlin, 1954.
Arc 848.52 Mueller, Adriaan von. Formenkreise der älteren römischen Kaiserzeit im Raum zwischen Havelseinplatte und Ostsee. Berlin, 1957.
Arc 848.54 Deutsches Archäologisches Institut. Neue Ausgrabungen im Deutschland. Berlin, 1958.
Arc 848.55 Paertner, Rudolf. Mit dem Fahrstuhl in die Römerzeit. Düsseldorf, 1963.
Arc 848.56 Schrickel, Waldtraut. Westeuropäische Elemente im neolithischen Grabbau Mitteldeutschlands und die Galeriegräber Westdeutschlands und ihre Inventare. Bonn, 1966. 2v.
Arc 848.57 Kellermann, Volkmar. Germanische Altertumskunde. Berlin, 1966.

Arc 848 Archaeology - Local - Germany - General works - cont.

Arc 848.58 Corpus archäologischer Quellen zur Frühgeschichte auf dem Gebiet der Deutschen Demokratischen Republik (7. bis 12. Jahrhundert). Berlin, 1973- 2v.
Arc 848.61 Hachmann, Rolf. The Germanic peoples. London, 1971.
Arc 848.61.5 Hachmann, Rolf. Die Germanen. München, 1971.

Arc 853 Archaeology - Local - Germany - Local; Special topics

Arc 853.1 Mestorf, J. Vorgeschichtliche Alterthuemer. Hamburg, 1885.
Arc 853.2 Jaumann, V. Colonia Sumlocenne-Rottenburg am Neckar unter die Roemern. Stuttgart, 1840.
Arc 853.3 Klein, C. Die römischen Denkmäler in und bei Mainz. Mainz, 1861.
Arc 853.3.15 Grenier, Albert. Etudes d'archéologie rhénane. Paris, 1925.
Arc 853.4 Becker, J. Drei römische Votivhaende aus den Rheinlanden. Frankfurt am Main, 1862.
Arc 853.4.2 Becker, J. Die Heddernheimer Votivhand. Frankfurt am Main, 1861.
Arc 853.4.13 Becker, J. Castellum Mattiacorum. Wiesbaden, 1863. 6 pam.
Arc 853.4.15 Hofmann, H. Römische Militärgrabsteine der Donauländer. Wien, 1905.
Arc 853.4.20 Fischer, Ulrich. Grabungen im romischen Steinkastell von Heddernheim 1957-1959. Frankfurt am Main, 1973.
Arc 853.5 Rupp, T. Aus der Verzeit Reuthingens. 2. Aufl. Stuttgart, 1869.
Arc 853.6 Suettich, S. Der 'Puestrich' zu Sondershausen. Naumburg an der Saale, 1894.
Arc 853.7.1 Cohausen, August. Der römische Grenzwall in Deutschland. Text, atlas. Faksimile. Walluf bei Weisbaden, 1973 2v.
Arc 853.8 Kröhnke, O. Chemische Untersuchung an Vorgeschichts Bronzen Schleswig-Holsteins. Kiel, 1897.
Arc 853.8.5F Hellmich, Max. Die Besiedlungschlesiens in vor- und frühgeschichtlicher Zeit. 2. Aufl. Breslau, 1923.
Arc 853.8.10 Hofmeister, H. Urholstein. Glückstadt, 1932.
Arc 853.9 Krause E. Die megalithischen Gräber...Deutschlands. Berlin, 1893.
Arc 853.10 Simony, F. Die Alterthümer vovon Hallstätter Salzberg. Wien, 1851.
Arc 853.10.5 Jacobi, H. Führer durch das Römerkastell Saalburg. 4. Aufl. Homburg, 1908.
Arc 853.10.15 Cohausen, August. Das Römerkastell Saalburg. 4. Aufl. Homburg vor der Höhe, 1893.
Arc 853.10.20 Schoeberger, H. Führer durch das Römerkastell Saalburg. Bad Homburg, 1957.
Arc 853.11 Jacobi, L. Das Römerkastell Saalburg. Text und plates. Homburg vor der Höhe, 1897 2v.
Arc 853.11.15 Steger, Adrian. De vis militaribus romanorum in vetiri Germania. Lipsiae, 1738.
Arc 853.12 Naelier, J. Die römischen Militarstrassen. Strassburg, 1887.
Arc 853.13 Hang, F. Die römischen Inschriften und Bildwerke Württembergs. v.1-2. Stuttgart, 1898-1900.
Arc 853.13.2 Hang, F. Die römischen Inschriften und Bildwerke Württembergs. v.1-3. Stuttgart, 1913.
Arc 853.13.3 Hang, F. Die römischen Inschriften und Bildwerke Württembergs. 2. Aufl. Stuttgart, 1914-15.
Arc 853.13.25 Hertlein, F. Die Römer in Württemberg. pt.1-3. Stuttgart, 1928-32. 3v.
Arc 853.13.30F Veeck, Walther. Die Alamannen in Württemberg. Berlin, 1931. 2v.
Arc 853.13.35 Zuern, Hartwig. Hallstattforschungen in Nordwürttemberg. Stuttgart, 1970.
Arc 853.13.40 Field guide to prehistoric sites in Württemberg and Bavaria. Wiesbaden, 1969.
Arc 853.14 Seyler, E. Die Drusenverschanzungen bei Deisenhofen. München, 1900.
Arc 853.15 Lische, G. Pfahlbauten in Mechlenberg. Schwerin, 1865.
Arc 853.15.5 Lütjen-Janssen, Hans. Die Germanen in Mecklenburg im 2. Jahrtausend vor Christus. Leipzig, 1935.
Arc 853.16 Mayer, Anton. Ein paar Worte über ein paar Drudenbäume. Eichstatt, 1826.
Arc 853.17 Der Externstein aus Zeit des Heithenthums in Westfalen. Detmold, 1879.
Arc 853.17.15F Albrecht, C. Frühgeschichtliche Funde aus Westfalen im städtischen Kunst- und Gewerbemuseum Dortmund. Dortmund, 1936.
Arc 853.18 Ranke, Johannes. Die akademische Kommission. München, 1900.
Arc 853.19 Weynand, R. De cipporum germaniae romanorum ornamentis. Bonnae, 1902.
Arc 853.20 Wyttenback, J.H. Neue Forschungen über Römischen architektonisch Alterhümer. Trier, 1835.
Arc 853.20.2 Wyttenback, J.H. Forschungen über die römischen Alterthümer. 2. Aufl. Trier, 1844.
Arc 853.20.5 Hettner, F. Illustrierter Führer...Provinzialmuseum in Trier. Trier, 1903.
Arc 853.20.7 Krencher, D. Das römische Trier. Berlin, 1923.
Arc 853.20.8 Wyttenback, J.H. Stranger's guide to Roman antiquities of the city of Treves. London, 1839.
Arc 853.20.9 Wyttenback, J.H. Recherches sur les antiquités romaines dans la vallée de la Moselle de Trèves. Trèves, 1840.
Arc 853.20.10 Hetzrodt, J.B.M. Notices sur les anciens Trévirois. Trèves, 1809.
Arc 853.20.12 Treves. Rheinisches Landesmuseum. Aus der Schatzkammer des antiken Trier. Trier, 1951.
Arc 853.20.12.5 Treves. Rheinisches Landesmuseum. Aus der Schatzkammer des antiken Trier. 2. Aufl. Trier, 1959.
Arc 853.20.15 Trierer Grabungen und Forschungen. Augsburg. 2,1955+ 12v.
Arc 853.20.19 Steinhausen, J. Archäologische Siedlungskunde des trierer Landes. Trier, 1936.
Arc 853.20.25F Loeschcke, S. Der Tempelbezirk im Altbachtale zu Trier. Berlin, 1938-42.
Arc 853.20.27 Loeschcke, S. Bedeutung und Gefährdung der grossen Tempelgrabung in Trier. Trier, 1930.
Arc 853.20.29 Loeschcke, S. Die Erforschung des Tempelbezirkes im Altbachtale zu Trier. Berlin, 1928.
Arc 853.20.32 Böhner, Kurt. Die fränkischen Altertümer des trierer Landes. v.1-2. Berlin, 1958.
Arc 853.20.35F Mahr, Gustav. Die jüngere Latènekultur des trierer Landes. Berlin, 1967.
Arc 853.21 Hartmann, A. Becherstatuen in Ostpreussen. Braunschweig, 1892.
Arc 853.21.5 Lissauer, A. Alterthümer der Bronzezeit in Westpreussen. Danzig, 1891.

Arc 853 Archaeology - Local - Germany - Local; Special topics - cont.

Arc 853.21.15 LaBaume, W. Vorgeschichte von Westpreussen in ihren Grundzügen allgemeinverstandlich dargestellt. Danzig, 1920.
Arc 853.21.20 Kiekebusch, A. Die Ausgrabung des bronzezeitlichen Dorfes Buch bei Berlin. Berlin, 1923.
Arc 853.21.25 Kraft, Georg. Die Kultur der Bronzezeit in Süddeutschland auf Grund der Funde in Württemberg. Augsburg, 1926.
Arc 853.22 Schreiner, P.W. Eining die Dortigen Römerausgrabungen. Landsbut, 1882. 2v.
Arc 853.23 Wilhelmi, K. Beschreibung der 14alten deutschen Todtenhügel. Heidelberg, 1830.
Arc 853.23.5 Wilhelmi, K. Les anciens tombeaux germaniques. Heidelberg, 1831.
Arc 853.24 Hefner, J. von. Das römische Bayern, in antiquarischer Hinsicht. München, 1842.
Arc 853.24.5 Wagner, F. Die Römer in Bayern. München, 1928.
Arc 853.24.7 Torbruegge, Walter. Bilder zur Vorgeschichte Bayerns. Konstanz, 1968.
Arc 853.24.9 Hülle, Werner. Grundzüge der vorrömischen Besiedelung Bayerns. Inaug. Diss. Augsburg, 1932.
Arc 853.24.12F Abbildungen zu dem I. u II. Heft der Römischen Alterthümer in Baiern. n.p., n.d.
Arc 853.24.15F Schweighauser, J.G. Antiquités de Rheinzabern. Strasbourg, 181-.
Arc 853.24.22 Kellner, Hans-Jörg. Die Römer in Bayern. 2. Aufl. München, 1972.
Arc 853.24.25 Vor- und frühgeschichtliche Archäologie in Bayern: Beiträge. München, 1972.
Arc 853.25 Mehlis, C. Studien zur ältesten Geschichte der Rheinlands. v.1-9. Leipzig, 1875-1886. 2v.
Arc 853.26 Blume, T. The treasure-trove of Hildesheim. Hildesheim, n.d.
Arc 853.26.5 Lindemann, Kurt. Der Hildesheimer Silberfund. Hildesheim, 1967.
Arc 853.27 Schuchhardt, C. Aliso...Ausgrabungen bei Haltern. Haltern, 1906.
Arc 853.27.5 Prein, Otto. Aliso bei Oberaden und Vernusschlacht. Münster, 1930.
Arc 853.27.10F Albrecht, C. Das Römerlager in Oberaden. Dortmund, 1938. 2v.
Arc 853.28 Kickebunde, A. Einfluss der Römischen Kultur. Berlin, 1908.
Arc 853.29 Wolff, G. Die Römerstadt Nida bei Heddernheim. Frankfurt, 1908.
Arc 853.30 Loeschcke, S. Heraniesche Funde in Haltern. Münster, 1909.
Arc 853.30.5 Dragendorff, Hans. II. Ausgrabungen bei Haltern. n.p., 1902.
Arc 853.31 Götze. Die vor- und frühgeschichtlichen altertümer Thüringens. Würzburg, 1902.
Arc 853.31.5 Cämmerer, E. Die Alteburg bei Armstadt. Leipzig, 1924.
Arc 853.31.10 Knack, H. Die Latènekulter in Thüringen. Inaug. Diss. Stettin, 1929?
Arc 853.31.15 Timpel, Wolfgang. Burgen, Gräber, alte Kreuze. Weimar, 1970.
Arc 853.33 Luschan, F. von. Die Karl Knorrsche Sammlung von Benin-Altertümern. Stuttgart, 1901.
Arc 853.35 Korhl, C. Neue prähistorische Funde aus Worms und Augsburg. n.p., n.d.
Arc 853.36 Fredrich. Die in Ostdeutschland gefundenen römischen Bronzestatuellen. Cüstrin, 1912. 3 pam.
Arc 853.37 Hertlein, F. Die Juppitergigantensäulen. Stuttgart, 1910.
Arc 853.38 Hauptmann, Carl. Die strategischen Rheinübergange der Römer bei Bonn. Bonn, 1912.
Arc 853.38.5 Sadie, Emil. Das römische Bonn. Bonn, 1925.
Arc 853.40 Hauptmann, Carl. Die Erhaltung der Römerstrassen. Bonn, 1912.
Arc 853.40.5 Maassen, F. Die römische Staatsstrasse. Bonn, 1881.
Arc 853.41 Baden-Baden. Städtischen historischen Sammlungen. Baden-Baden. 1908-1910
Arc 853.41.5F Wagner, E. Hügelgräber und Urnen-Friedhöfe. Karlsruhe, 1885.
Arc 853.41.9 Calliano, G. Prähistorische Funde in der Umgebung von Baden. Wein, 1894.
Arc 853.41.15 Garscha, Friedrich. Die Alamannen in Sudbaden. Berlin, 1970. 2v.
Arc 853.43 Kasiski, F.W. Beschreibung der vaterländischen Alterthümer. Danzig, 1881.
Arc 853.44 Blume, Erich. Die germanischen Stämme und die Kulturen. Würzburg, 1912-15. 2v.
Arc 853.45 Lienau, M.M. Über Megalithgräber und sonstige Grabformen der Lüneburger Gegend. Würzburg, 1914.
Arc 853.46 Åberg, Nils. Ostpreussen in der Völkerwanderungszeit. Uppsala, 1919.
Arc 853.47 Bartelt, Wilhelm. Die Burgwälle des Ruppiner Kreises. Würzburg, 1910.
Arc 853.48 Kropp, Philipp. Latenezeitliche Funde an der keltischgermanischen Völkergrenze. Würzburg, 1911.
Arc 853.50 Kostrzewski, J. Die ostgermanische Kultur. Leipzig, 1919. 2v.
Arc 853.51 Rademacher, C. Die vorgeschichtliche Besiedelung. Leipzig, 1920.
Arc 853.52 Dutschmann, G. Literatur zur Vor- und Frühgeschichte Sachsens. Leipzig, 1921.
Arc 853.53.3 Kiekebusch, A. Bilder aus der märkischen Vorzeit. 3. Aufl. Berlin, 1921.
Arc 853.54 Schumacher, P. Der Ringwälle in der früheren preusischen Provinz Posen. Leipzig, 1924.
Arc 853.55F Deutsches Archaeologisches Institut. Römisch-Germanische Kommission. Römische Grabmäler des Mosellandes. Trier. 1-2,1924-1932 3v.
Arc 853.56 Krebs, Albert. Die vorrömische Metallzeit im östlichen Westfalen. Leipzig, 1925.
Arc 853.56.7 Andree, Julius. Das Paläolithikum der Höhlen des Hönnetales in Westfalen. Leipzig, 1928.
Arc 853.57 Behn, Friedrich. Führer durch die römische Granitindustrie auf dem Felsberg im Odenwald. Mainz, 1925.
Arc 853.58 Kunkel, Otto. Oberhessens vorgeschichtliche Altertümer. Marburg, 1926.
Arc 853.58.5 Helmke, Paul. Hügelgräber im Vorderwald von Muschenheim. Giessen, 1919. 2v.
Arc 853.58.10 Kunkel, Otto. Vorgeschichtliches aus dem Lumdstale. Giessen, 1919.
Arc 853.59 Gumpert, Carl. Fränkisches Mesolithikum. Leipzig, 1927.
Arc 853.60 Eichhorn, G. Der Urnenfriedhof auf der Schanze bei Grossromstedt. Leipzig, 1927.

Arc 853 **Archaeology - Local - Germany - Local; Special topics - cont.**

Arc 853.61F Schliz, A. Das steinzeitliche Dorf Grossgartach. Stuttgart, 1901.
Arc 853.62 Jungklaus, Ernst. Römische Funde in Pommein. Greifswald, 1924.
Arc 853.62.7 Kunkel, Otto. Pommersche Urgeschichte in Bildern. Stettin, 1931. 2v.
Arc 853.63 Matthes, W. Die nördlichen Elbgermanen in spätrömischer Zeit. Leipzig, 1931.
Arc 853.63.7 Matthes, W. Die Germanen in der Prignitz zur Zeit der Völkerwanderung. Leipzig, 1931.
Arc 853.64 Andree, Julius. Beiträge zur Kenntnis des norddeutschen Paläolithikums und Mesolithikums. Leipzig, 1932.
Arc 853.65 Geschwendt, F. Die steinurnen Streitäxte und Keulen Schlesiens. Inaug. Diss. Breslau, 1931.
Arc 853.65.5 Rothert. Die mittlere Steinzeit in Schlesien. Leipzig, 1936.
Arc 853.65.10 Seger, Hans. Schlesiens Urgeschichte. Leipzig, 1913.
Arc 853.65.15 Zatz, Lothar. Die Altsteinzeit in Niederschlesien. Leipzig, 1939.
Arc 853.65.20 Polskie Towarzystwo Archeologiczne. Z przesztośći Sląska. Wrocław, 1960.
Arc 853.65.25 Heckowa, K.W. Pod znakiem świętego słońca. Wrocław, 1961.
Arc 853.65.30 Badura-Simonides, D. Baśń i podanie górno-sląskie. Katowice, 1961. 4 pam.
Arc 853.65.35 Kaletyn, Marta. Grodziska wczesnośredniowieczne województwa wrocławskiego. Wrocław, 1968.
Arc 853.65.40 Godłowski, Kazimierz. Kultura przeworska na Górnym Sląsku. Wyd. 1. Katowice, 1969.
Arc 853.65.45 Kostrzewski, Józef. Pradzieje Śląska. Wrocław, 1970.
Arc 853.65.50 Kramarek, Janusz. Wczesnośredniowieczne grodziska nyczyńskie na Śląsku. Wrocław, 1969.
Arc 853.65.55 Śląsk w pradziejach Polski. Wrocław, 1970.
Arc 853.65.60 Bagniewski, Zbigniew. Dzieje zierni wydarte. Wrocław, 1970.
Arc 853.65.65 Gardawski, Aleksander. Z pradzisjćw zieme dolnosląskiej lod około. Wrocław, 1973.
Arc 853.66 Grimm, Paul. Die vor- und frühgeschichtliche Besiedlung des Unterharzes und seines Vorlandes auf Grund der Bodenfunde. Inaug. Diss. Halle an der Saale, 1931.
Arc 853.67 Raiser, J.N. von. Die römischen Alterthümer zu Augsburg. Augsburg, 1820.
Arc 853.68F Gätze, A. Die altthüringischen Funde von Weimar (5.-7. Jahrhundert nach Christus.) Berlin, 1912.
Arc 853.69.15 Reith, A. Vorgeschichte der Schwäbischen Alb. Leipzig, 1938.
Arc 853.70 Piesker, Hans. Vorneolithische Kulturen der südlichen Lüneburger Heide. Inaug. Diss. Hildesheim, 1932.
Arc 853.71 Holter, F. Die Hallesche Kultur der frühen Eisenzeit. Inaug. Diss. Halle, 1934.
Arc 853.71.5F Grimm, Paul. Die vor- und frühgeschichtlichen Burgwälle der Bezirke Halle und Magdeburg. Berlin, 1958. 2v.
Arc 853.72 Bicker, F.K. Dünenmesolithikum aus dem Fiener Bruch. Inaug. Diss. Halle an der Saale, 1934.
Arc 853.73 Hofmeister, Hans. Die Chalten. Frankfurt am Main, 1930.
Arc 853.74 Lehner, Hans. Das Römerlager Vetera bei Hauten. Bonn, 1926.
Arc 853.75F Schmidt, R.R. Jungsteinzeit-Siedlungen im Federseemoor. Augsburg, 1930-37.
Arc 853.76 Umbreit, Carl. Neue Forschungen zur ostdeutschen Steinzeit und frühen Bronzezeit. Leipzig, 1937.
Arc 853.76.5 Umbreit, Carl. Die Ausgrabung des steinzeitlichen Dorfes von Berlin-Britz. Inaug. Diss. Leipzig, 1936.
Arc 853.77 Scheuermayer. Auffindung eines römischen Bades in Augsburg. n.p., 1867?
Arc 853.78 Guthjahr, R. Die Semnonen im Havelland zur frühen Kaiserzeit. Diss. Greifswald, 1934.
Arc 853.79 Witter, W. Die älteste Erzgewinnung im nordischgermanischen Lehenskreis. Leipzig, 1938. 2v.
Arc 853.80 Kropf, W. Die Billendorfer Kultur auf Grund der Grabfunde. Leipzig, 1938.
Arc 853.81 Stofar, Walter. Spinnen und Weben. Leipzig, 1938.
Arc 853.82 Kuchenbuch, F. Die altmärkisch-osthannöverschen Schalenurnenfelder der spätrömischen Zeit. Inaug. Diss. Halle an der Saale, 1938.
Arc 853.83 Fuchs, Alois. Im Streit um die Externsteine. Paderborn, 1934.
Arc 853.83.5 Gsaenger, Hans. Die Externsteine. Freiburg, 1964.
Arc 853.83.10 Giefers, Wilhelm. Die Externsteine im Fürstenthum Lippe-Detmold. Paderborn, 1851.
Arc 853.83.15 Hamkens, F.H. Der Externstein. Tübingen, 1971.
Arc 853.84 Weiershausen, P. Vorgeschichtliche Eisenbütten Deutschlands. Leipzig, 1939.
Arc 853.85 Meier-Böke, A. Die frühe Altsteinzeit am der Weser. Leipzig, 1940.
Arc 853.90 Crefeld, Germany. Städtischen Kulturamt Schriftenreihe. Krefeld. 1-2,1937-1938 2v.
Arc 853.91 Ströbel, R. Die Feuersteingeröte der Pfahlbaukultur. Leipzig, 1939.
Arc 853.92 Nickel, E. Die Steinwerkzeuge der jüngeren Steinzeit. Inaug. Diss. Würzburg, 1938.
Arc 853.93F Behmer, E. Das zweischneidige Schwert der germanischen völkerwanderungszeit. Stockholm, 1939.
Arc 853.94 Tergast. Die beidniscken Alterthümer Ostfrieslands. Emden, 1879.
Arc 853.95 Beck, F. Der Karlsgraben. Nürnberg, 1911.
Arc 853.96 Thärigen, Günter. Die Nordharzgruppe der Elbgermanen bis zur sächsischen Überlagerung. Berlin, 1939.
Arc 853.96.10 Capelle, Torsten. Studien über elbgermanische Gräber felder im der ausgehenden Latènezeit und der alteren Kaiserzeit. Habilitationsschrift. Hildesheim, 1971.
Arc 853.97 Colin, Jean. Les antiquités romaines de la Rhenanie. Paris, 1927.
Arc 853.98 Hertlein, F. Die Alterthümer des Oberamts Heidenheims. Eszlingen, 1912.
Arc 853.99F Franken, M. Die Alamannen zwischen iller und lech. Berlin, 1944.
Arc 853.101F Fremersdorf, F. Die Denkmäler des römischen Köln. v.1-8,22. Köln, 1950- 9v.
Arc 853.101.2F Fremersdorf, F. Die Denkmäler des römischen Köln. 2. Aufl. Köln, 1958-63. 2v.
Arc 853.101.5 Fremersdorf, F. Das römische Hans mit dem Dionysos-Mosaik vor dem Sudportal des Kölner Domes. Berlin, 1956.
Arc 853.101.10F Fremersdorf, F. Das fränkische Reichengräberfeld Köln-Mungersdorf. Text and plates. Berlin, 1955. 2v.
Arc 853.103F Grohne, E. Mohndorf. Bremen, 1953.
Arc 853.105 Wolff, G. Der römische Grenzwald bei Hanau mit dem Kastellen zu Rückingen und Markäbel. Hanau, 1885.

Arc 853 **Archaeology - Local - Germany - Local; Special topics - cont.**

Arc 853.108 Geidel, H. Münchens Vorzeit. München, 1930.
Arc 853.110 Brunn, W.A. von. Steinpockungsgräber von Köthen. Berlin, 1954.
Arc 853.112 Kramert, K. Ausgrabungen unter der St. Jakobskirche Dokumertieren. n.p., 1954.
Arc 853.115 Schuldt, E. Pritzier. Berlin, 1955.
Arc 853.117 Arbeits- und Forschungsberichte zur sächsischen Bodendenkmalspflege. Dresden. 2,1950+ 11v.
Arc 853.117.5 Arbeits- und Forschungsberichte zur sächsischen Bodendenkmalspflege. Beiheft, 1-9, 1956-1971. n.p., n.d.
Arc 853.120 Hachmann, Rolf. Studien zur Geschichte Mitteldeutschlands während der älteren Latènezeit. Hamburg, 1950.
Arc 853.125 Reusch, Wilhelm. Augusta Treverorum. Trier, 1958.
Arc 853.130F Stroh, Armin. Katalog Günzburg. Kallmünz, 1952.
Arc 853.135F Stroh, Armin. Die Reihengräber der karolingisch-ottonischen Zeit. Kallmünz, 1954. 2 pam.
Arc 853.136 Torbruegge, Walter. Die Hallstattzeit in der Oberpfalz. v.2. Kallmünz, 1965.
Arc 853.140F Müller-Karpe, H. Das Arnenfeld von Kelheim. Kallmünz, 1954.
Arc 853.145F Cambodunumforschungen, 1953- Kallmünz, 1957- 2v.
Arc 853.150F Schwarz, Klaus. Die vor- und frühgeschichtlichen Gebäudedenkmäler Oberfrankens. Kallmünz, 1955. 2v.
Arc 853.155F Dohn, Wolfgang. Die Steinzeit im kieslische Katalog der steinzeitlichen Altertümer. Kallmünz, 1954.
Arc 853.160F Werner, Joachim. Das alamannische Gräberfeld von Mindelheim. Kallmünz, 1955.
Arc 853.165 Schindler, Reinhard. Ausgrabungen in alt Hamburg. Hamburg, 1958.
Arc 853.165.5 Schindler, Reinhard. Studien zum vorgeschichtlichen Siedlungs- und Befestigungswesen des Saarlandes. Trier, 1968.
Arc 853.165.10 Maisant, Hermann. Der Kreis Saarlouis in vor- und frühgeschichtlichen Zeit. Bonn, 1971. 2v.
Arc 853.170 Schleiermacher, Wilhelm. Der römische Limes in Deutschland. Berlin, 1959.
Arc 853.175 Endrich, Peter. Vor- und Frühgeschichts des bayerischen Untermaingebietes. Aschaffenburg, 1961.
Arc 853.180F Billig, Gerhard. Die Aunjebitzer Kultur in Sachsen. Leipzig, 1958.
Arc 853.185 Hahn, Heinrich. Die Ausgrabungen am Fuldaer Donaplatz. Fulda, 1956.
Arc 853.190 Mildenberger, Gerhard. Mitteldentschlands Ur- und Frühgeschichte. Leipzig, 1959.
Arc 853.195 Lehmann, F. Aus der Frühgeschichte der Oberlausitz. Berlin, 1958.
Arc 853.200 Konik, E. Ślask starożytny a Imperium Rzymskie. Warszawa, 1959.
Arc 853.205 Łosiński, Władysław. Z badań nad rzemiostem we wczesnośredniowiecznym Kotobrzegu. Poznań, 1959.
Arc 853.205.5 Leciyewicz, Leah. Kołobrzeg we wczesnymsredniowieczu. Wrocław, 1961.
Arc 853.205.10 Łosinski, Władysław. Pouzątki wczesnośredniowiecznego. Wrocław, 1972.
Arc 853.210F Brunn, Wilhelm Albert von. Bronzezeitliche Hortfunde. Berlin, 1959.
Arc 853.215 Schoppa, Helmut. Die fränkischen Friedhöfe von Weilbach Maintaunuskreis. Weisbaden, 1959.
Arc 853.220 Cämmerer, Erich. Vor- und Frühgeschichte Arnstadts und seiner weiteren Umgebung. Jena, 1956.
Arc 853.225F Torbruegge, Walter. Die Bronzezeit in der Oberpfalz. Kallmünz, 1959.
Arc 853.230F Hundt, Hans Jürgen. Katalog Stromling. Kallmünz, 1958. 2v.
Arc 853.232 Archaeologische Funde und Denkmäler des Rheinlandes. Köln. 1,1960+ 3v.
Arc 853.234F Nierhaus, Rolf. Das römische Brand- und Körpergräberfeld. Stuttgart, 1959.
Arc 853.236 Bogen, Alfred. Die Vorgeschichte des magdeburger Landes. Magdeburg, 1937.
Arc 853.236.5F Nickel, Ernest. Der alte Markt in Magdeburg. Berlin, 1964.
Arc 853.238 Saarland. Staatliches Konservatoramt. Bericht der Staatlichen Denkmalpflege im Saarland. Saarbrücken. 6,1953+ 5v.
Arc 853.240 Röder, J. Toutonenstein und Heinesäulen bei Mildenburg. Kallmünz, 1960.
Arc 853.242F Funk, A. Bilder aus der Vor- und Frühgeschichte des Hegaus. Singen, 1960.
Arc 853.244F Linder, H. Die altsteinzeitlichen Kulturen der Räuberhöhle am Schelmeengraben bei Sinzing. Kallmünz, 1961.
Arc 853.246F Schuldt, Ewald. Hohen Viecheln. Berlin, 1961.
Arc 853.248 Haermann, S. Die dritte Hallstattstufe im Gebeit. Nürnberg, 1925.
Arc 853.250 Vollrath, Friedrich. Die Hunbirg. Nürnberg, 1961.
Arc 853.252F Die Ausgrabungen in Haithabu. Neumünster. 2,1959+ 4v.
Arc 853.254F Grenz, Rudolf. Die slawischen Funde aus dem hanoverschen Wendland. Neumünster, 1961.
Arc 853.256F Krueger, Heinrich. Die Jastorf Kultur in der Kreisen. Neumünster, 1961.
Arc 853.258 Sprater, Friedrich. Die Urgeschichte der Pfalz. Speier, 1928.
Arc 853.259 Spindler, Konrad. Magdalenenberg. Villingen, 1971. 3v.
Arc 853.260 Sprater, Friedrich. Die Pfalz unter den Römern. Speier, 1929-30. 2v.
Arc 853.262F Dannheimer, H. Die germanischen Funde der späten Kaiserzeit und des frühen Mittelalters in Mittelfranken. Text and atlas. Berlin, 1962. 2v.
Arc 853.264F Reinbacker, E. Börnicke. Berlin, 1963.
Arc 853.265F Fiedler, R. Katalog Kirchheim unter Teck. Stuttgart, 1962.
Arc 853.266 Engel, Carl. Typen ostpreussischer Hügelgräber. Neumünster, 1962.
Arc 853.267 Roth, H. Wetterauer Fundberichte, 1941-49. Friedberg, 1951
Arc 853.268F Müller, A. von. Fohrde und Hohenferchesar; zwei germanische Gräberfelder der frühen römischen Kaiserzeit aus der Mark Brandenburg. Berlin, 1962.
Arc 853.269F Müller-Karpe, H. Die spätneolithische Siedlung. Kallmünz, 1961.
Arc 853.270F Nowothnig, Walter. Brandgräber des Völkeswandernugszeit im siedlichen Niedersachsen. Neumünster, 1964.
Arc 853.270.10 Sudholz, Gisela. Die ältere Bronzezeit zwischen Niederrhein und Mittelwesen. Hildesheim, 1964.

Classified Listing

Arc 853 Archaeology - Local - Germany - Local; Special topics - cont.

Arc 853.271F Ziegart, Helmut. Zur Chronologie und Gruppengliederung des westlichen Hügelgräberkultur. Berlin, 1963.
Arc 853.272F Müller, Hanns H. Die Haustiere der mitteldeutschen Bandkiramiker. Berlin, 1964.
Arc 853.273F Müller, Adriaan. Die jungbronzezeitliche Siedlung von Berlin-Lichterfelde. Berlin, 1964.
Arc 853.273.5 Müller, Adriaan. Berlins Urgeschichte. Berlin, 1964.
Arc 853.274 Schuldt, Ewald. Behren-Lübchin. Berlin, 1965.
Arc 853.275F Rempel, Heinrich. Reihengräberfriedhofe des 8. bis 11. Jahrhunderts. Berlin, 1966.
Arc 853.276F Sprockhoff, Ernst. Atlas der Megalithgräber Deutschlands. Text and atlas. Bonn, 1965-75. 4v.
Arc 853.277 Cologne. Römisch-Germanisches Museum. Frühchristliches Köln. Köln, 1965.
Arc 853.278 Kühn, Herbert. Die germanischen Bügelfibeln der Völkerwanderungszeit. v.1-2. Graz, 1965- 3v.
Arc 853.280F Koerber-Grohne, Udelgard. Geobotanische Untersuchungen auf der Feddersen Wierde. Wiesbaden, 1967. 2v.
Arc 853.282 Christlein, Rainer. Das alamannische Reihengräberfeld von Marktoberdorf im Allgäu. Kallmünz, 1966.
Arc 853.283 Schmid, Armin. Die Römer am Rein und Main. Frankfurt, 1972.
Arc 853.284F Koch, Robert. Bodenfunde der Völkerwanderungszeit aus dem Main-Tauber-Gebiet. Diss. Berlin, 1967. 2v.
Arc 853.286 Pirling, Renate. Das römisch-fränkische Gräberfeld vor Krefeld-Gellep. Berlin, 1966. 2v.
Arc 853.287 La Baume, Peter. Das fränkische Gräberfeld von Junkersdorf bei Köln. Berlin, 1967.
Arc 853.290 Zuern, Hartwig. Das jungsteinzeitliche Dorf Ehrenstein. Stuttgart, 1965. 3v.
Arc 853.292 Wegewitz, Willi. Reihengräberfriedhöfe. Neumünster, 1968.
Arc 853.294 Neuffer-Müller, Christiane. Ein Reihengräberfriedhof in Sontheim an der Brenz. Stuttgart, 1966.
Arc 853.294.5 Neuffer-Müller, Christiane. Das fränkische Gräberfeld von Iversheim, Kreis Euskirchen. Berlin, 1972.
Arc 853.296 Hinz, Hermann. Das fränkische Gräberfeld von Eick. Berlin, 1969.
Arc 853.298 Krämer, Wolfgang. Neue Beiträge zur Vor- und Frühgeschichte von Gauting. München, 1967.
Arc 853.300 Koester, Hans. Die mittlere Bronzezeit im nördlichen Rheingraben. Bonn, 1968.
Arc 853.302F Heiligendorff, Wolfgang. Das latènezeitliche Gräberfeld von Berlin-Blankenfelde. Berlin, 1965.
Arc 853.304 Wightman, Edith Mary. Roman Trier and the Treveri. London, 1970.
Arc 853.306 Bohnsack, Dietrich. Die Burgunden in Ostdeutschland und Palen während des letzten Jahrhunderts vor Christus. Inaug. Diss. Leipzig, 1938.
Arc 853.308 Hoof, Dieter. Die Steinbeile und Steinarte im Gebiet der Niederrheins und der Maas. Bonn, 1970.
Arc 853.309 Herrmann, Joachim. Der germanischen und slawischen Siedlungen und das mittelalterliche Dorf von Tornow. Berlin, 1973.
Arc 853.315 Engels, Heinz-Josef. Die Hallstatt und Latènekultur in der Pfalz. Diss. n.p., 1967.
Arc 853.316 Materialhefte zur Vor- und Frühgeschichte der Pfalz. Speyer, 1974.
Arc 853.317 Kossack, Georg. Gräberfelder dur Hallstattzeit an Main und Fränkischer Saale. Kallmünz, 1970.
Arc 853.320 Mildenberger, Gerhard. Die thuringischen Brandgräber der spätrömischen Zeit. Köln, 1970.
Arc 853.325 Krueger, Bruno. Dessau-Mosigkau. Berlin, 1967.
Arc 853.330 Mauser-Goller, Katharina. Die relative Chronologie des Neolithikums in Südwestdeutschland und der Schweiz. Diss. Basel, 1969.
Arc 853.335 Die Bremer Hanse-Kogge. Bremen, 1969.
Arc 853.338 Lindenschmit, Wilhelm. Das germanische Todtenlager bei Selzen. Faksimile. Mainz an Rhein, 1969.
Arc 853.340 Schach-Dörges, Helga. Das jungkaiserzeitliche Gräberfeld von Wilhelmsaue in Brandenburg. Berlin, 1969.
Arc 853.341 Rau, Hermann Gunther. Das urnenfelderzeitliche Gräberfeld von Aschaffenburg-Streitwald. Kallmünz, 1972.
Arc 853.342 Bergmann, Joseph. Die altere Bronzezeit Nordwestdeutschlands. Marburg, 1970. 2v.
Arc 853.343F Behm-Blancke, Günter. Gesellschaft und Kunst der Germanen. Dresden, 1973.
Arc 853.344 Schrickel, Waldtraut. Die Funde vom Wartberg in Hessen. Marburg, 1969.
Arc 853.345.1 Stoll, Hermann. Die Alamannengräber von Hailfingen. Photoreproduction. Berlin, 1939.
Arc 853.346 Seitz, Hermann Josf. Die Steinzeit im Donaumoos. Augsburg, 1965.
Arc 853.347 Grenz, Rudolf. Die Anfänge der Stadt Münden nach den Ausgrabungen in der St. Blasius-Kirche. Hannoversch Münden, 1973.
Arc 853.348 Hennig, Hilke. Die Grab- und Hortfunde der Urnenfelderkultur aus Ober- und Mittelfranken. Kallmünz, 1970.
Arc 853.349 Kolling, Alfons. Funde aus der Römerstadt Schwarzenacke und ihrer nahen Ungebung. Homburg-Saar, 1971.
Arc 853.350 Christlein, Rainer. Das alamannische Gräberfeld von Dirlewang bei Minchelheim. Kallmünz, 1971.
Arc 853.351F Elisenhof: die Ergebnisse der Ausgrabung der frühgeschichtlichen Marschersiedlung beim Elisenhof in Eiderstedt 1957/58 und 1961/64. Bern, 1975-
Arc 853.353 Schleier, Wilhelm. Cambodunum-Kempten. Bonn, 1972.
Arc 853.354 Wetzel, Robert. Die Bocksteinschmiede im Lonetal (Markung Ramminger, Kreis Ulm). Stuttgart, 1969. 2v.
Arc 853.355 Müller, Adriaan von. Gesicherte Spuren. 1. Aufl. Berlin, 1972.
Arc 853.356 Brandt, Karl Heinz. Studien über steinerne Äxte und Beile der jüngeren Steinzeit und der Stein-Kupferzeit Nordwestdeutschlands. Hildesheim, 1967.
Arc 853.357 Findeisen, Jürgen. Spuren römerzeitlicher Siedlungsvorgänger im Dorfund Stadtbild Südeutschlands und seiner Nachbargebiete. Bonn, 1970.
Arc 853.358 Spätkaiserzeitliche Funde in Westfalen. Münster, 1970.
Arc 853.359 Stein, Frauke. Adelsgräber des achten Jahrhunderts in Deutschland. Berlin, 1967. 2v.
Arc 853.360 Koch, Ursula. Die Grabfunde der Merowingerzeit aus dem Donautal um Regensberg. Berlin, 1968. 2v.
Arc 853.361 Fingerlin, Gerhard. Die alamannischen Gräberfelder von Guttingen und Merdingen in Südbaden. Berlin, 1971. 2v.
Arc 853.362 Krämer, Werner. Die Ausgrabungen in Manching 1955-1961. Wiesbaden, 1970.
Arc 853.363 Fehr, Horst. Die vor- und frühgeschichtliche Besiedlung der Kreise. Speyer, 1972.
Arc 853.364 Kleemann, Otto. Vor- und Frühgeschichte des Kreises Ahrweiler. Bonn, 1971.
Arc 853.365 Bantelmann, Niels. Die Urgeschichte des Kreises Kusel. Speyer, 1972.
Arc 853.366 Mildenberger, Berhard. Römerzeitliche Siedlungen in Nordhessen. Marburg, 1972.
Arc 853.367 Seidel, Martin Fredrich. Thesaurus Orcivus Marchicus. Faksimile. Berlin, 1972.
Arc 853.368 Körner, Gerhard. Vorgeschichte im Landkreis Lüneburg. Lüneburg, 1971.
Arc 853.369 La Baume, Peter. Die Römer am Rhein. Bonn, 1973.
Arc 853.370 Bayer, Heinrich. Die ländliche Besiedlung Rheinhessens. Inaug. Diss. Mainz, 1967?
Arc 853.371 Neuffer-Müller, Christiane. Das fränkische Gräberfeld von Rübenach. Berlin, 1973.
Arc 853.372 Fischer, Ulrich. Aus Frankfurts Vorgeschichte. Frankfurt am Main, 1971.
Arc 853.373 Stolberg, Friedrich. Befastigungsanlagen im und am Harz von der Frühgeschichte bis zur Neuzeit. Ein Handbuch. Hildesheim, 1968.
Arc 853.374 Neuhof, Elias. Nachricht von den Alterthümern in der Gegend und auf dem Gebürge bey Homburg vor der Höhe. Homburg, 1780.
Arc 853.375 Zotz, Lothar F. Die mittelpaläolithische Geröllgeräteindustrie aus der Umgebung von Kronach in Oberfranken. Kallmünz, 1973.
Arc 853.376F Huebener, Wolfgang. Die römischen Metallfunde von Augsburg-Oberhausen. Kallmünz, 1973.
Arc 853.377 Vorgeschichte und römische Zeit zwischen Main und Lahn. Beiträge. Bonn, 1972.

Arc 855 Archaeology - Local - Great Britain - Folios [Discontinued]

Arc 855.01F Pamphlet box. English antiquities.
Arc 855.2 Skelton, J. The Royal House of Stuart. London, 1890.
Arc 855.3 Artis, E.T. The Durobrivae of Antoninus. London, 1828.
Arc 855.4 Stuart, J. Sculptured stones of Scotland. Aberdeen, 1856. 2v.
Arc 855.5 Small, J.W. Scottish market crosses. Stirling, 1900.
Arc 855.6 White, T.P. Architectural sketches in Scotland - Kintyre. Edinburgh, 1873.
Arc 855.6.2 White, T.P. Architectural sketches in Scotland - Knapdale. Edinburgh, 1875.
Arc 855.7 Lapidarium Septentrionale, or A description of the monument of Roman rule. London, 1875.
X Cg Arc 855.8 Smith, A.C. Guide to British and Roman antiquities in north Wiltshire. n.p., 1884. 2v.
Arc 855.9 Curle, James. A Roman frontier post and its people. Glasgow, 1911.
Arc 855.11 MacLauchlan, H. Memoir...survey of eastern branch of Watling Street. London, 1864. 2v.
Htn Arc 855.14F* Douglas, J. Nenia Britannica, or Sepulchral history of Great Britain. London, 1793.
Arc 855.200 Horsley, J. Britannia Romana, or The Roman antiquities of Britain. London, 1732.
Arc 855.201 Lukis, W.C. The prehistoric stone monuments of the British Isles - Cornwall. London, 1885.
Arc 855.202 Baye, J. de. The industrial arts of the Anglo-Saxons. London, 1893.
Arc 855.203 Bevan, J.O. Architectural survey of Herefordshire. Westminster, 1896. 2 pam.
Arc 855.204 MacLagan, C. Hill forts, stone circles...Scotland. Edinbrugh, 1875.
Arc 855.205 Tite, Will. Notes on Roman architectural remains. London, 1867. 2 pam.
NEDL Arc 855.206 Allen, J.R. The early Christian monuments of Scotland. Edinburgh, 1903.
Arc 855.207 Robertson, D.H. The sculptured stones of Leith. Leith, 1851.
Arc 855.208 Westwood, J.O. Lapidarium Walliae. Oxford, 1876-79.
Arc 855.209F Dymond, C.W. Worlebury - an ancient stronghold. Bristol, 1902.
Arc 855.209.2F Dymond, C.W. Worlebury - an ancient stronghold. Bristol, 1886.
Arc 855.210 Whichcord, J. Roman antiquities recently discovered. London, 1873.
Arc 855.211 Faussett, B. Inventorium sepulchrale. London, 1856.
Arc 855.212 James, H. Plans and photographs of Stonehenge. n.p., 1867.
Arc 855.214 Stukeley, William. Albury. Temple of the British Druids. London, 1743.
Arc 855.215 Jones, I. Most notable antiquity of Great Britain called Stone-Heng. London, 1725.
Arc 855.216 Warne, C. The Celtic Tumuli of Dorset. London, 1866.
Arc 855.217F Bulleid, A. The Glastonbury Lake village. n.p., 1911. 2v.
Arc 855.218 Warne, Charles. Ancient Dorset. Bournemouth, 1872.
Arc 855.219 Fox-Pitt-Rivers. King John's house, Tollard Royal, Wilts. n.p., 1890.
Arc 855.219.5F Fox-Pitt-Rivers. Excavations in Cranbone Chase. London, 1887-1905. 5v.
Arc 855.220 Griffith, J.E. Portfolio of photographs of Cromlechs of Anglesey and Carnarvonshire. Derby, 1900.
Arc 855.221 Stokes, Margaret. Notes on the Cross of Cong. Dublin, 1895.
Arc 855.222F Drummond, James. Archaeologia scotica; sculptured monuments in Iona. Edinbrugh, 1881.
Arc 855.223F Malcolm, J.P. Lives of topographers and antiquaries. London, 1815.
Arc 855.224F Ashby, Thomas. Excavations at Caerwent, Monmouthshire 1901-1903. London, 1902-1904.
Arc 855.225F Great Britain. Commissions. Ancient and Historical Monuments and Constructions in Wales and Monmouthshire. A inventory of the ancient monuments in Wales and Monmouthshire. v.1-5,7-8. London, 1911-37. 4v.
Arc 855.226F Dymond, Charles W. The ancient remains at Stanton Drew. Bristol, 1896.
Arc 855.227F Cunnington, M.E. (Mrs.) The early iron age inhabited site at All Cannings Cross farm, Wiltshire. Devizes, 1923.
Arc 855.228F Moir, J. Reid. The great flint implements of Cromer, Norfolk. Ipswich, 1923?

Arc 857 Archaeology - Local - Great Britain - Pamphlet volumes

Arc 857 Pamphlet box. Archaeology. Great Britain.
Arc 857.1 Pamphlet box. Archaeology. Great Britain.
Arc 857.5 Windle, Bertram. A collection of archaeological pamphlets on Roman remains...Great Britain. n.p., n.d. 12v.
Arc 857.15 Pamphlet box. Archaeology. Great Britain. Miscellaneous pamphlets by T. McKenny Hughes.

Arc 858 Archaeology - Local - Great Britain - General works

Arc 858.1 Akerman, J.Y. Remains of Pagan Saxondom. London, 1855.
Arc 858.1.5 Akerman, J.Y. An archaeological index. London, 1847.
Arc 858.2 Dawkins, W.B. Early man in Britain. London, 1880.
Arc 858.3 Godwin, H. The English archaeologist's hand-book. Oxford, 1867.
Arc 858.4 Hodgetts, J.F. Older England. London, 1884.
Arc 858.4.2 Hodgetts, J.F. Older England. 2. series. London, 1884.
Arc 858.5 Kains-Jackson, C.P. Our ancient monuments and the land around them. London, 1880.
Arc 858.6 Murray, D. An archaeological survey of the United Kingdom. Glasgow, 1896.
Arc 858.7 Smith, C.R. Etchings of ancient remains. London, 1852.
Arc 858.8 Armitage, E.S. Key to English antiquities. Sheffield, 1897.
Arc 858.9 Windle, B.C.A. Life in early Britain. London, 1897.
Arc 858.9.3 Windle, B.C.A. Life in early Britain. N.Y., 1897.
Arc 858.9.5 Windle, B.C.A. Remains of the Prehistoric Age in England. London, 1904.
Arc 858.9.6 Windle, B.C.A. Remains of the Prehistoric Age in England. London, 1909.
Arc 858.10 Greenwell, G. British barrows. Oxford, 1877.
Arc 858.11 Bateman, T. Ten years' diggings in Celtic and Saxon grave hills. London, 1861.
Arc 858.12 Wright, T. The archaeological album; or Museum of National Antiquities. London, 1845.
Htn Arc 858.13* Stackhouse, T. Two lectures on the remains of ancient pagan Britain. London, 1833.
Arc 858.14 Johnson, W. Folk-memory. Oxford, 1908.
Arc 858.15 Relics of antiquity in Great Britain. London, 1811.
Arc 858.16 The gentleman's magazine library - Romano-British remains. London, 1887. 2v.
Arc 858.17 Clinch, George. Handbook of English antiquities. London, 1905.
Arc 858.20 Bloxam, M.H. Fragmenta sepulchralia. Sepulchral and early monumental remains of Great Britain. n.p., n.d.
Arc 858.21 Munro, Robert. Prehistoric Britain. London, n.d.
Arc 858.22 Rimmer, Alfred. Ancient stone crosses of England. London, 1875.
Arc 858.22.5 Vallance, A. Old crosses and lychgates. London, 1920.
Arc 858.23 Cox, R.H. The green roads of England. London, 1914.
Arc 858.24F Great Britain. Royal Commission on Ancient and Historical Monuments. Interim report. London. 1-22 2v.
Arc 858.24.5F Great Britain. Ancient Monuments Advisory Committee. Report of the committee. London, n.d.
Arc 858.24.9 Great Britain. Commissions. Ancient and Historical Monuments and Constructions of England. An inventory of the historical monuments in Hertfordshire. London, 1911.
Arc 858.24.10 Great Britain. Commissions. Ancient and Historical Monuments and Constructions of England. An inventory of the historical monuments in Hertfordshire. London, 1910.
Arc 858.24.11 Great Britain. Commissions. Ancient and Historical Monuments and Constructions of England. An inventory of the historical monuments in Buckinghamshire. London, 1912-13. 2v.
Arc 858.24.13 Great Britain. Commissions. Ancient and Historical Monuments and Constructions of England. An inventory of the historical monuments in Essex. London, 1916-23. 4v.
Arc 858.24.15 Great Britain. Commissions. Ancient and Historical Monuments and Constructions of England. An inventory of the historical monuments in Huntingdonshire. London, 1926.
Arc 858.24.17 Great Britain. Commissions. Ancient and Historical Monuments and Constructions of England. An inventory of the historical monuments in Herefordshire. London, 1931-34. 3v.
Arc 858.24.19 Great Britain. Commissions. Ancient and Historical Monuments and Constructions of England. An inventory of the historical monuments in Westmorland. London, 1936.
Arc 858.24.21 Great Britain. Commissions. Ancient and Historical Monuments and Constructions of England. An inventory of the historical monuments in Middlesex. London, 1937.
Arc 858.24.23 Great Britain. Commissions. Ancient and Historical Monuments and Constructions of England. An inventory of the historical monuments in the city of Oxford. London, 1939.
Arc 858.24.25 Great Britain. Commissions. Ancient and Historical Monuments and Constructions of England. An inventory of the historical monuments in Dorset. v.1,3. London, 1952- 3v.
Arc 858.24.30F Royal Institute of British Architects, London. Library. Royal Commission on Historical Monuments. London, 1958.
Arc 858.25 Haverfield, F. Roman Britain in 1913- v.1-2. Oxford, 1914- 5v.
Arc 858.26 Rust, J. Druidism exhumed. Edinburgh, 1871.
Arc 858.27 Norman, A. Glossary of archaeology. London, 1915. 2v.
Arc 858.28 Smith, Charles R. Retrospections, social and archaeological. London, 1883-91. 3v.
Arc 858.29 Wright, Thomas. Wa5derings of an antiquary. London, 1854.
Arc 858.30 Stukely, William. Palaeographia brittanica. London, 1743. 2 pam.
Arc 858.31 Bigsley, R. Old places revisited. London, 1851. 3v.
Arc 858.31.5 Bigsley, R. Visions of the times of old. London, 1848. 3v.
Arc 858.32 Bayley, Harold. Archaic England. London, 1919.
Arc 858.33 Ault, Norman. Life in ancient Britain. London, 1920.
Arc 858.34 Bevan, J.O. The towns of Roman Britain. London, 1917.
Arc 858.35 Mackenzie, D.A. Ancient man in Britain. London, 1922.
Arc 858.36 Quennell, M. (Mrs.) Everyday life in Roman Britain. London, 1924.
Arc 858.37.2 Massingham, H.J. Downland man. London, 1927.
Arc 858.37.5 Massingham, H.J. Fee, fi, fo, fum, or, The giants in England. London, 1926.
Arc 858.38 Garrod, D.A.E. The upper palaeolithic age in Britain. Oxford, 1926.
Arc 858.39 Weigall, A.E.P.B. Wanderings in Roman Britain. London, 1926.
Arc 858.40 Watkins, A. The old straight track. London, 1925.
Arc 858.41 Clarke, W.G. Our homeland prehistoric antiquities and how to study them. London, 1924.

Arc 858 Archaeology - Local - Great Britain - General works - cont.

Arc 858.42 Collingwood, Robin George. The archaeology of Roman Britain. N.Y., 1930.
Arc 858.42.1 Collingwood, Robin George. The archaeology of Roman Britain. London, 1969.
Arc 858.43 Jewitt, L. Half-hours among some English antiquities. London, 1877.
Arc 858.44 Sumner, H. Local papers. London, 1931.
Arc 858.45 Macdonald, George. Roman Britain, 1914-1928. London, 1931.
Arc 858.46 Kendrick, T.D. Archaeology in England and Wales, 1914-1931. London, 1932.
Arc 858.47 Great Britain. Office of Works. Ancient monuments. London. 1932-1958 7v.
Arc 858.47.5A Great Britain. Ministry of Works. Illustrated regional guides to ancient monuments. London, 1936-48. 5v.
Arc 858.47.5B Great Britain. Ministry of Works. Illustrated regional guides to ancient monuments. London, 1936-48. 5v.
Arc 858.47.10 Great Britain. Ministry of Works. Illustrated regional guides to ancient monuments. v.2-6. 2. ed. London, 1949- 5v.
Arc 858.47.12 Great Britain. Ministry of Works. Illustrated regional guides to ancient monuments. v.1-2,4,6. London, 1954. 4v.
Arc 858.47.14 Great Britain. Ministry of Works. Illustrated guide to ancient monuments. Edinburgh, 1961.
Arc 858.47.16.5 Great Britain. Ministry of Works. Illustrated guide to ancient monuments. Edinburgh, 1967.
Arc 858.48 London Museum. Catalogue of an exhibition of recent archaeological discoveries in Great Britain. London, 1932.
Arc 858.49 Macdonald, George. Agricola in Britain. London, 1932.
Arc 858.50A Childe, V.G. Prehistoric communities of the British Isles. London, 1940.
Arc 858.50B Childe, V.G. Prehistoric communities of the British Isles. London, 1940.
Arc 858.50.5 Childe, V.G. Prehistoric communities of the British Isles. 2. ed. London, 1947.
Arc 858.51 Clark, John Grahame Douglas. Prehistoric England. London, 1940.
Arc 858.51.2 Clark, John Grahame Douglas. Prehistoric England. 2. ed. London, 1941.
Arc 858.52 Wright, G.R. Archaeologic and historic fragments. London, 1887.
Arc 858.53 Harris, James R. Caravan essays. no.1-12. Cambridge, 1929.
Arc 858.54 Beaumont, Comyns. The riddle of prehistoric Britain. London, 1946.
Arc 858.54.5 Beaumont, Comyns. Britain, the key to world history. London, 1949.
Arc 858.55.3 Hawkes, Jacquette. Early Britain. London, 1946.
Arc 858.56 Shètelig, H. Viking antiquities in Great Britain and Ireland. pts.1-3, 4-6. Oslo, 1940. 2v.
Arc 858.57 Lethbridge, Thomas C. Merlin's Island. London, 1948.
Arc 858.58 Piggott, Stuart. British prehistory. London, 1949.
Arc 858.58.5 Piggott, Stuart. The neolithic cultures of the British Isles. Cambridge, Eng., 1954.
Arc 858.59 Daniel, G. The prehistoric chamber tombs. Cambridge, Eng., 1950.
Arc 858.59.50 Meaney, A. A gazetteer of early Anglo-Saxon burial sites. London, 1964.
Arc 858.60 Hawkes, Jacquette. A guide to the prehistoric and Roman monuments in England and Wales. London, 1951.
Arc 858.60.5 Hawkes, Jacquette. History in earth and stone. Cambridge, Mass., 1952.
Arc 858.62 Winbolt, S.E. Britain B.C. Harmondsworth, Eng., 1945.
Arc 858.63 Bruce-Mitford, R.L.S. Recent archaeological excavations in Britain. London, 1956.
Arc 858.66 Fox, Cyril. Life and death in the bronze age. London, 1959.
Arc 858.70A Wilson, David McKenzie. The Anglo-Saxons. London, 1960.
Arc 858.70B Wilson, David McKenzie. The Anglo-Saxons. London, 1960.
Arc 858.72 Grimes, W.F. Excavations on defence sites. London, 1960.
Arc 858.73 Wood, E.S. Collins field guide to archaeology. London, 1964.
Arc 858.74 Fox, Aileen H. South west England. London, 1964.
Arc 858.77 Conference on Romano-British Cantonal Capitals, University of Leicester, 1963. The civitas capitals of Roman Britain. Leicester, 1966.
Arc 858.78 British Museum. Guide to the antiquities of Roman Britain. 3. ed. London, 1964.
Arc 858.80 Thomas, Nicholas. A guide to prehistoric England. London, 1960.
Arc 858.82 Council for British Archaeology, London. Iron Age and Roman Research Committees. The Iron Age in Northern Britain. Edinbrugh, 1967.
Arc 858.83 The Iron Age and its hill-forts. Southampton, 1971.
Arc 858.84 Thom, Alexander. Megalithic sites in Britain. Oxford, 1967.
Arc 858.86 Jessup, Ronald Frederick. Age by age. London, 1967.
Arc 858.88 Jessup, Ronald Frederick. The story of archaeology in Britain. London, 1964.
Arc 858.91 The small towns of Roman Britain. Oxford, 1975.
Arc 858.92 Great Britain. Commissions. Ancient and Historical Monuments and Constructions of England. A matter of time; an archaeological survey of the river gravels of England. London, 1960-61.
Arc 858.93F Sedgley, Jeffrey. The Roman milestones of Britain. Oxford, 1975.
Arc 858.94 Megalithic enquiries in the West of Britain: a Liverpool symposium. Liverpool, 1969.
Arc 858.95 Swanton, M.J. A corpus of pagan Anglo-Saxon spear-types. Oxford, 1974.
Arc 858.96 Thomas, Stanley E. Pre-Roman Britain. London, 1965.
Arc 858.97 Harbison, Peter. Some Iron Age Mediterranean imports in England. Oxford, 1974.
Arc 858.98 Cambrian Archaeological Association, London. The Irish Sea province in archaeology and history. Cardiff, 1970.
Arc 858.99 Laing, Lloyd Robert. The archaeology of late Celtic Britain and Ireland, c. 400-1200. London, 1975.
Arc 858.100 Bowen, Emrys George. Britain and the western seaways. London, 1972.
Arc 858.101 Cunliffe, Barry W. Cradle of England: an introduction through archaeology to the early history of England and a brief guide to selected sites in the South. London, 1972.
Arc 858.102 Gąssowski, Jerzy. Irlandia i Brytania w początkach średniowiecza w świetle badań archeologicznyćh. Warszawa, 1973.
Arc 858.103 Cunliffe, Barry W. Iron Age communities in Britain. London, 1974.

Classified Listing

Arc 858 Archaeology - Local - Great Britain - General works - cont.

Arc 858.104 Coles, John M. Field archaeology in Britain. London, 1972.
Arc 858.105 Thomas, Charles. The early Christian archaeology of Northern Britain. London, 1971.

Arc 861 Archaeology - Local - Great Britain - England and neighboring islands - Local

Arc 861.1.3 Rowlands, Henry. Mona antiqua restaurata. Dublin, 1723.
Arc 861.1.6 Rowlands, Henry. Mona antiqua restaurata. 2. ed. London, 1766.
Htn Arc 861.2* Somner, W. The antiquities of Canterbury. London, 1640.
Arc 861.2.5 Roman Canterbury. London. 1-7
Arc 861.3 Hume, A. Ancient meols, or Some account of the antiquities found near Dove Point. London, 1863.
Arc 861.3.9 Watkin, W.T. Roman Cheshire. Liverpool, 1886.
Arc 861.3.10 Watkin, W.T. Roman Cheshire. Wakefield, Eng., 1974.
Arc 861.4 Earwaker, J.P. The recent discoveries of Roman remains found in the...City of Chester. Manchester, 1888.
Arc 861.4.3 Lawson, P.H. Schedule of the Roman remains of Chester. Chester, 1928.
Arc 861.4.5 Classical Association. Melandra Castle. Manchester, 1906.
Arc 861.4.9 Brutton, F.A. Classical Association...Roman fort at Manchester. Manchester, 1909.
Arc 861.5 Borlase, W.C. Naema Cornubiae. London, 1872.
Arc 861.5.5 Blight, J.T. Ancient crosses and antiquities east of Cornwall. London, 1858.
Arc 861.5.9 Hingston, F.C. Specimens of ancient Cornish crosses, fonts. London, 1850.
Arc 861.5.15 Hencken, H.O. The archaeology of Cornwall and Scilly. London, 1932.
X Cg Arc 861.6 Smith, C.R. Report on excavations made on the site of the Roman Castrum at Lymne. London, 1852.
Htn Arc 861.6.5* Marriott, William. The antiquities of Lyme. Stockport, 1810.
Arc 861.7 Brown, J.A. Paleolithic man in northwest Middlesex. London, 1887.
Arc 861.7.5 Vulliamy, Colwyn E. The archaeology of Middlesex and London. London, 1930.
Arc 861.8 Smith, C.R. The antiquities of Richborough, Reculver, and Lyme. London, 1850.
Arc 861.8.5 Battely, J. Antiquitates rutupinae. Oxoniae, 1811.
Arc 861.8.6 Battely, J. Antiquitates rutupinae. 2. ed. Oxoniae, 1745. 2 pam.
Arc 861.8.9 Battely, J. The antiquities of Richborough and Reculver. London, 1774.
Arc 861.9 Allies, J. The British, Roman, and Saxon antiquities and folklore of Worcestershire. London, 1856.
Arc 861.10 Halliwell, J.O. Round about notes...Isle of Man. London, 1863.
Arc 861.10.5 Cumming, J.G. Runic and other monumental remains...Isle of Man. London, 1857.
Arc 861.10.7 Kinnebrook, William. Etchings of the Runic monuments in Isle of Man. London, 1841.
Arc 861.10.9 Kermode, P.M. Catalogue of the Manks crosses. London, 1892.
Arc 861.10.11 Kinnebrook, William. Manx crosses...monuments...Isle of Man. London, 1907.
Arc 861.10.13 Kinnebrook, William. Traces of the Norse mythology. London, 1904.
Arc 861.10.15 Kinnebrook, William. List of Manx antiquities. Douglas, 1930.
Arc 861.10.17 Kinnebrook, William. Manks antiquities. 2. ed. Liverpool, 1914.
Arc 861.10.20F Isle of Man. Natural History and Antiquarian Society. The Manx archaeological survey; reports. pt.1-6. Douglas, 1909-35.
Arc 861.10.22 Bersu, Gerhard. Three Viking graves in the Isle of Man. London, 1966.
Arc 861.10.24 Liverpool. Public Libraries, Museum and Art Gallery. Handbook and guide to the replicas and casts of Manx crosses on exhibition in the Free Public Museums. 2. ed. Liverpool, 1920.
Arc 861.11 Hope, W.H. St. J. Excavations...Roman city at Silchester, Hants in 1895. Westminster, 1896.
Arc 861.11.3 Fox, G.E. Excavations...Roman city at Silchester, Hants in 1890. Westminster, 1891.
Arc 861.11.5 Davis, F. The Romano-British city of Silchester. London, 1898.
Arc 861.11.7F Thomson, James. A great free city; the book of Silchester. London, 1924. 2v.
Arc 861.11.10 Boon, George Counsell. Roman Silchester. London, 1957.
Arc 861.11.11 Boon, George Counsell. Silchester, the Roman town of Calleva. Newton Abbot, 1974.
Arc 861.12 Bruce, J.C. The handbook to the Roman wall. 4. ed. London, 1895.
Arc 861.12.2 Bruce, J.C. The handbook to the Roman wall. 9. ed. Newcastle-upon-Tyne, 1933.
Arc 861.12.2.5 Bruce, J.C. Handbook to the Roman wall. 10. ed. Newcastle-upon-Tyne, 1947.
Arc 861.12.3 Abbatt, Richard. History of the Picts or Roman British wall. London, 1849.
Arc 861.12.9 Warburton, J. Vallum Romanum...Cumberland and Northumberland. London, 1753.
Arc 861.12.12 Hutton, W. History of the Roman wall. London, 1802.
Arc 861.12.15 Clayton, J. Observations on centurial stones found on the Roman wall in Northumberland and Cumberland. Newcastle-on-Tyne, 1880.
Arc 861.12.18 Hardy, James. On urns and other antiquities found round the southern skirts of the Cheviot Hills. n.p., 1886.
Arc 861.13 Calverley, W.S. Notes on the early sculptured crosses...present diocese of Carlisle. Kendal, 1899.
Arc 861.13.5 Parker, C.A. The ancient crosses at Gosforth, Cumberland. London, 1896.
Arc 861.13.9 Collingwood, W.G. On some ancient sculptures of the devil bound. Kendal, 1903.
Arc 861.13.15 Cook, A.S. Some accounts of the Bewcastle Cross. N.Y., 1914.
Arc 861.14 Glastonbury, England. Antiquarian Society. British lake-village near Glastonbury. Taunton, 1899.
Arc 861.15 Ives, J. Remarks on the Garianorum...Romans. 2. ed. Yarmouth, 1803.
Arc 861.15.5 Ives, J. Remarks on the Garianorum...Romans. 2. ed. London, 1774.
Arc 861.16 Miller, S.H. Illustrations of the traces...Romans and Saxons. n.p., 1871.
Arc 861.16.2 Little, W.C. Roman fen road in Cambridgeshire. n.p., n.d.

Arc 861 Archaeology - Local - Great Britain - England and neighboring islands - Local - cont.

Arc 861.16.5 Fox, Cyril. The archaeology of the Cambridge region. Cambridge, Eng., 1923.
Arc 861.16.7 Smith, F. Prehistoric man and the Cambridge gravels. Cambridge, Eng., 1926.
Arc 861.16.10 Watkins, A. Archaic tracks round Cambridge. London, 1932.
Arc 861.17 Haverfield, F. Catalogue of the Roman inscribed and sculptured stones...ms. of Tullie House. Kendal, 1899.
Arc 861.17.9 Tite, William. Descriptive catalogue of antiquities...Roman London. London, 1848.
Arc 861.18 Smith, C.R. Illustrations of Roman London. London, 1858.
Arc 861.18.3 Tylor, Alfred. New points in the history of Roman Britain, as illustrated by discoveries at Warwick Square. Westminster, 1884.
Arc 861.18.5 Price, J.E. On a bastion of London Wall. Westminster, 1880.
Arc 861.18.9 Bruce, J.C. The wall of Hadrian. Newcastle-upon-Tyne, 1874.
Arc 861.18.13 Smith, Washington G. On a palaeolithic floor at north east London. London, 1884.
Arc 861.18.15 Gordon, E.O. Prehistoric London; its mounds. London, 1914.
Arc 861.18.16 Home, Gordon. Roman London. London, 1926.
Arc 861.18.16.5 Home, Gordon. Roman London. N.Y., 1926.
Arc 861.18.16.10 Home, Gordon. Roman London. London, 1948.
Arc 861.18.16.15 Merrifield, Ralph. The Roman city of London. London, 1965.
Arc 861.18.16.20 Merrifield, Ralph. The archaeology of London. Park Ridge, 1975.
Htn Arc 861.18.17* Woodward, J. Account of some urns. London, 1713. 2 pam.
Arc 861.18.19 Bayley, Harold. The lost language of London. London, 1935.
Arc 861.19 Crossing, W. The ancient stone crosses of Dartmoor. Exeter, 1902.
Arc 861.19.5 Shortt, W.T.P. Collectanea curiosa antiqua Dunmonia. Londinium, n.d.
Arc 861.20 Kerslake, T. Caer Pensauelcoit. London, 1882.
Arc 861.21 Wellbeloved, C. Eburacum, or York under the Romans. York, 1842.
Arc 861.21.5 Colls, J.M.N. Letters upon some early remains discovered in Yorkshire. v.1-2. n.p., n.d.
Arc 861.21.9 Mortimer, J.P. Forty years' research in British and Saxon burial grounds of East Yorkshire. London, 1879.
Arc 861.21.12 Simpson, H.T. Archaeologia Adelensis...West Riding of Yorkshire. London, 1879.
Arc 861.21.15 Home, Gordon. Roman York. London, 1924.
Arc 861.21.17 Andrew, S. Excavation of the Roman forts at Castleshaw. Manchester, 1911.
Arc 861.21.19 Elgee, Frank. Early man in north east Yorkshire. Gloucester, 1930.
Arc 861.21.21 Elgee, Frank. The archaeology of Yorkshire. London, 1933.
Arc 861.21.25F Smith, Henry E. Reliquae isurianae; remains of Roman Isurium. London, 1852.
Arc 861.21.30 Butler, Ronald Morley. Soldier and civilian in Roman Yorkshire; essay to commemorate the nineteenth century of the foundation of York. Leicester, 1971.
Arc 861.21.35 Garlick, Tom. Roman sites in Yorkshire. Lancaster, 1971.
Arc 861.21.40 Le Patourel, John Herbert. The moated sites of Yorkshire. London, 1973.
Arc 861.21.45 Manby, Terence George. Grooved ware sites in Yorkshire and the north of England. Oxford, 1974.
Arc 861.22 Lyttelton. Description of an ancient font in Bridekirk. n.p., 1767.
Arc 861.23 Flower, J.W. Notices of an Anglo-Saxon cemetery...Surrey. London, 1872.
Arc 861.23.5 Johnston, P.M. Schedule of antiquities in the county of Surrey. London, 1913.
Arc 861.23.7 Johnson, Walter. Neolithic man in northeast Surrey. London, 1903.
Arc 861.23.9 Whimster, D.C. The archaeology of Surrey. London, 1931.
Arc 861.23.15 Oakley, K.P. A survey of the prehistory of the Farnham district, Surrey. Guildford, 1939.
Arc 861.24 Somner, W. Treatise of Roman ports and forts. Oxford, 1693.
Arc 861.25 Pope, Alfred. The old stone crosses of Dorset. London, 1906.
Arc 861.25.5 Hill-Forts Study Group. Hill-forts in Dorset. Bristol, 1966.
Arc 861.26 Newmarch, C.H. Remains of Roman art Corinum. London, n.d.
Arc 861.27 Bateman, T. Vestiges of the antiquities of Derbyshire. London, 1848.
Arc 861.28 Bathurst, W.H. Roman antiquities at Lyndney Park. London, 1879.
Arc 861.29.5 Wright, Thomas. Unriconium. London, 1872.
Arc 861.29.15 Kenyon, K.M. Excavations at Wroxeter, 1936. Shrewsbury, 1936.
Arc 861.29.20 Kenyon, K.M. Excavations at Virsconium (Wroxeter), 1937. Shrewsbury, 1937.
Arc 861.30 Pooley, C. Notes on the old crosses of Gloucester. London, 1868.
Htn Arc 861.30.5* Burrow, E.J. The ancient entrenchments and camps of Gloucester. Cheltenham, 1919.
Arc 861.31 Twining, T. Avebury in Wiltshire. London, 1723.
Arc 861.31.5 Merewether, J. Diary of a dean. London, 1851.
Arc 861.31.10 Cunnington, M.E. (Mrs.) Avebury; a guide. Devizes, 19- .
Arc 861.31.15F Smith, Alfred Charles. Guide to the British and Roman antiquities of the North Wiltshire downs. 2. ed. Devizes, 1885.
Arc 861.31.20 Cunnington, M.E. (Mrs.). Introduction to the archaeology of Wiltshire. Devizes, 1933.
Arc 861.31.25 Smith, Isobel F. Windmill Hill and Avebury. Oxford, 1965.
Arc 861.31.30 Atkinson, Richard J.C. Silbury Hill: background information on the Silbury dig. London, 1968.
Arc 861.32 Davidson, J. British and Roman remains in Axminster. London, 1833.
Arc 861.33 Rauthmell, R. Antiquitates Bremetonacenses. London, 1746.
Arc 861.33.3 Rauthmell, R. Antiquitates Bremetonacenses, or Roman antiquitites of Overborough. Kirkby Lonsdale, 1824.
Arc 861.34 Wylie, W.M. Fairford graves. Oxford, 1852.
Arc 861.35 Ely, Talfourd. Roman Hayling. London, 1914.
Arc 861.35.5 Ely, Talfourd. Roman Hayling. 2. ed. London, 1908.
Arc 861.36 Michell-Whitley, H. Discovery of Roman-British remains. n.p., 1890.
Arc 861.37.3 Williamson, W.C. Description of the Tumulus. 3. ed. Scarborough, 1872.

Classified Listing

Arc 861 Archaeology - Local - Great Britain - England and neighboring islands - Local - cont.

Arc 861.38 Pooley, C. An historical and descriptive account of the old stone crosses of Somerset. London, 1877.
Arc 861.38.5 Rutter, John. Delineations of the northwest division of the county of Somerset. London, 1829.
Arc 861.38.6 Rutter, John. Delineations of the northwest division of the county of Somerset. London, 1829.
Arc 861.38.7 Burrow, E.J. Ancient earthworks and camps of Somerset. Cheltenham, 1924.
Arc 861.38.8 Bath and Camerton Archaeological Society. A north Somerset miscellany. Bath, 1966.
Arc 861.38.9 Dobson, Dina P. The archaeology of Somerset. London, 1931.
Arc 861.38.10 Wedlake, William. Excavations at Camerton, Somerset. Camerton, 1958.
Arc 861.39 Ward, John. Romano-British buildings and earthworks. London, 1911.
Arc 861.39.5 Ward, John. The Roman era in Britain. London, 1911.
Arc 861.40 Scarth, H.M. Aquae solis...Roman Bath. London, 1864.
Arc 861.40.5 Warner, Richard. An illustration of the Roman antiquities discovered at Bath. Bath, 1797.
Arc 861.40.10 Taylor, A.J. The Roman baths of Bath. Bath, 1923.
Arc 861.40.15 Gilyard-Beer, R. The Romano-British baths at Well. Leeds, 1951.
Arc 861.40.20 Cunliffe, Barry W. Roman Bath discovered. London, 1971.
Arc 861.41 Smith, H. Notes on prehistoric burial in Sussex. n.p., n.d.
Arc 861.41.9 Winbolt, S.E. The Roman villa at Bignor, Sussex. Oxford, 1925.
Arc 861.41.10 Winbolt, S.E. The Roman villa at Bignor, Sussex. Oxford, 1930.
Arc 861.41.20 Curwen, E. Cecil. Prehistoric Sussex. London, 1929.
Arc 861.41.25 Curwen, E. Cecil. The archaeology of Sussex. London, 1937.
Arc 861.42 Neville, R.C. Antiqua explorata. Chesterford. Walden Saffron, 1847.
Arc 861.43 George, W. On an inscribed stone at Orchard Wyndham, Somerset. Bristol, 1879.
Arc 861.44 Stevens, J. On newly discovered Roman remains at Finkley near Andover. London, n.d.
Arc 861.45 Hooppell, R.E. On the discovery...of Roman remains at South Shields. London, 1878.
Arc 861.47 Nixon, J. Marmor Estonianum...in agro Northamptoniensi. Londinium, 1744.
Arc 861.47.5 Markham, C.A. Stone crosses of county of Northampton. London, 1901.
Arc 861.48 Ormerod, George. Archaeological memoirs...district of the Severn and the Wye. London, 1861.
Arc 861.49 Watkin, W.J. Roman Lancashire. Liverpool, 1883.
Arc 861.49.5 Taylor, H. Ancient crosses and holy wells of Lancashire. Manchester, 1906.
Arc 861.50 Brighton and Hove Archaeological Club. Brighton and Hove archaeologist, 1914. Hove, 1914.
Arc 861.51 Williams-Freeman, J.P. Introduction to field archaeology...Hampshire. London, 1915.
Arc 861.52 Glasscock, J.L. The ancient crosses of Stortford. Bishops, 1905.
Arc 861.53 Richardson, G.B. Pons Aelii; the site of the Roman station. Newcastle-upon-Tyne, 1852.
Arc 861.54 Miles, William A. A description of the deverel barrow. London, 1826.
Arc 861.55 Summer, H. Excavations on Rockbourne Downs, Hampshire. London, 1914.
Arc 861.56 Parkin, Charles. An answer to...Dr. Stukeley's Origines Roystonianae. London, 1744. 2 pam.
Arc 861.57F Balch, H.E. Wookey Hole; its caves and cave dwellers. London, 1914.
Arc 861.58 Addy, S.O. The hall of Waltheof...Hallamshire. London, 1893.
Arc 861.59 Turner, William. Ancient remains near Buxton. Buxton, 1899.
Arc 861.60 Atkinson, Donald. The Romano-British site on Lowbury Hill in Berkshire. Reading, 1916.
Arc 861.61 Jack, G.H. Excavations on the site of the Romano-British town of Magna, Kenchester. Hereford, 1916.
Arc 861.62 Wardell, James. Antiquities of the borough of Leeds. London, 1853.
Htn Arc 861.62.10* Wardell, James. Historical notices of Ilkley, Rombald's Moor, Baildon Common. 2. ed. Leeds, 1881.
Arc 861.63 Chambers, J. The stone age and Lake Lothing. Norwich, 1911.
Arc 861.65 Payne, George. Collectanea cantiana. London, 1893.
Arc 861.65.15 Winbolt, S.E. Roman Folkestone. London, 1925.
Arc 861.66 Sumner, H. The ancient earthworks of New Forest. London, 1917.
Arc 861.67F Lee, John Edward. Delineations of Roman antiquities...at Caerleon. London, 1845.
Arc 861.68 Gray, Harold St. George. Maumbury Rings excavations. Interim report. Dorchester, 1913.
Htn Arc 861.69* Stapleton, A. A history of the public crosses of old Nottingham. Nottingham, 1893.
Arc 861.70 May, Thomas. The Roman forts of Templeborough near Rotherham. Rotherham, 1922.
Arc 861.71 Tate, George. The ancient British sculptured rocks of Northumberland. Alnwick, 1865.
Arc 861.71.5F Collingwood, W.G. Northumbrian crosses of the pre-Norman age. London, 1927.
Arc 861.72 Elgee, Frank. The Romans in Cleveland. Middlesbrough, 1923.
Arc 861.73 Chudleigh, J. Devonshire antiquities. 2. ed. Exeter, 1893.
Arc 861.74 Ravenhill, T.H. The Rollright stones and the men who erected them. Birmingham, 1926.
Arc 861.75 Prehistoric Society of East Anglia. Report on excavations at Grime's Graves, Weeting, Norfolk, March-May, 1914. London, 1915.
Arc 861.76 Dutt, W.A. The ancient mark-stones of East Anglia. Lowestoft, 1926.
Arc 861.77.5 Parker, C.A. The Gosforth district. Kendal, 1926.
Arc 861.78 Davies, J.A. Early life in the West. Clifton, 1927.
Arc 861.80 Bullen, R.A. Harlyn Bay and the discoveries of its prehistoric remains. 3. ed. Harlyn Padstow, 1912.
Arc 861.81 Buckler, Geroge. Colchester castle, a Roman building. Colchester, 1876.
Arc 861.82F Crawford, O.G.S. Wessex from the air. Oxford, 1928.
Arc 861.83 Kendrick, T.D. The archaeology of the Channel Islands. London, 1928.

Arc 861 Archaeology - Local - Great Britain - England and neighboring islands - Local - cont.

Arc 861.84 Hopkinson, J.H. The Roman fort at Ribchester. 3. ed. Manchester, 1928.
Arc 861.86F Cunnington, M.E. (Mrs.) Woodhenge. Devizes, 1929.
Arc 861.87F Neville, R.C. Saxon obsequies illustrated by ornaments and weapons. London, 1851.
Arc 861.88 Watkins, Alfred. The old standing crosses of Herefordshire. London, 1930.
Arc 861.89 Jessup, Ronald F. Archaeology of Kent. London, 1930.
Arc 861.89.5 Wright, Thomas. A lecture on the antiquities of the Anglo-Saxon cemeteries of the ages of paganism. Liverpool, 1854.
Arc 861.90 Yorkshire Archaeolgical Society. Roman Malton and district. Report. York. 2-7 6v.
Arc 861.91 Peake, Harold. The archaeology of Berkshire. London, 1931.
Arc 861.92 Mitchell, E.H. The crosses of Monmouthshire. Newport, 1893.
Arc 861.93 Corder, Philip. Excavations at the Roman fort at Brough-on-Humber. Hull, 1934.
Arc 861.93.5 Corder, Philip. Excavations at the Roman town at Brough-Petuaria, 1937. Hull, 1938.
Arc 861.95 Moule, H.J. Dorchester antiquities. Dorchester, 1906.
Arc 861.96 Hurd, Howard. Some notes on recent archaeological discoveries at Broadstairs. Broadstairs, 1913.
Arc 861.97 Fieldhouse, William J. A Romano-British industrial settlement near Tiddington, Stratford-upon-Avon. Birmingham, 1931.
Arc 861.100 British Museum. Department of British and Mediaeval Antiquities. The Sutton-Hoo ship burial. 1. ed. London, 1947.
Arc 861.100.2 Bruce-Mitford, Rupert Leo. The Sutton-Hoo ship burial. London, 1951.
Arc 861.100.5 Magoren, F.P. The Sutton-Hoo ship burial. Cambridge, Mass., 1952.
Arc 861.100.10 Green, C. Sutton-Hoo. London, 1963.
Arc 861.100.15 Bruce-Mitford, Rupert Leo. The Sutton-Hoo ship burial. London, 1968.
Arc 861.100.20 Grohskoph, Bernice. The treasure of Sutton-Hoo. 1. ed. N.Y., 1970.
Arc 861.100.25 Bruce-Mitford, Rupert Leo. Aspects of Anglo-Saxon archaeology. London, 1974.
Arc 861.101 Pettit, Paul. Prehistoric Dartmoor. Newton Abbot, 1974.
Arc 861.102F Longhurst, M.H. The Easby cross. Oxford, 1931.
Arc 861.104 Clapham, A.W. St. John of Jerusalem, Clerkenwell. London, 1912.
Arc 861.106F Clapham, A.W. On the topography of the Dominican Priory of London. Oxford, 1912.
Arc 861.108F Clapham, A.W. On the topography of the Cistercian Abbey of Tower Hill. Oxford, 1915.
Arc 861.109 Grimes, William F. The excavation of Roman and mediaeval London. London, 1968.
Arc 861.110 Corder, Philip. The Roman town and villa at Great Casterton. Nottingham, 1951.
Arc 861.118 Atkinson, Donald. Report on excavations at Wroxeter...1923-1927. Oxford, 1942.
Arc 861.120 Clark, J.G.D. Excavations at Star Caer. Cambridge, Eng., 1954.
Arc 861.125 Fullbrook-Leggatt, Lawrence Edward Wells Outen. Roman Gloucester. Gloucester, 1950.
Arc 861.126 Fullbrook-Leggatt, Lawrence Edward Wells Outen. Roman Gloucester. Lansdown, 1968.
Arc 861.130 Lincoln Archaeological Research Committee. Ten seasons digging, 1945-1954. Lincoln, 1955.
Arc 861.135 Cotton, M. Aylwin. Excavations at Clausentum (Southampton). London, 1958.
Arc 861.135.5 Excavations in medieval Southampton 1953-1969. Leicester, Eng., 1975. 2v.
Arc 861.140 Grinsell, L.V. The archaeology of Wessex. London, 1958.
Arc 861.141 Stone, J.F.S. Wessex before the Celts. London, 1958.
Arc 861.145 Anthony, I.E. The Iron Age camp at Poston. Hereford, 1958.
Arc 861.147 Meates, Geoffrey W. Lullingstone Roman villa. London, 1955.
Arc 861.150 Frere, Sheppard. The city of Durovernum. Canterbury, 1957.
Arc 861.153 Frere, Sheppard. The city of Durovernum. Canterbury, 1962.
Arc 861.155 Thompson, F.D. Deva: Roman Chester. Chester, Eng., 1959.
Arc 861.160 Great Britain. Commissions. Ancient and Historical Monuments and Constructions of England. An inventory of the historical monuments in the city of York. London, 1962. 3v.
Arc 861.160.10 Yorkshire Architectural and Archaeological Society. A short guide to Roman York. York, 1962.
Arc 861.160.20 Wenham, Leslie. The Romano-British cemetery at Trentholm Drive. London, 1968.
Arc 861.165 Piggot, Stuart. The west Kennet long barrow. London, 1962.
Arc 861.166 British Museum. Department of British and Mediaeval Antiquities. Hox Hill. London, 1962.
Arc 861.167 Clarke, R. East Anglia. London, 1960.
Arc 861.168 Brewster, Thomas. Excavation of Staple Howe. Wentringham, 1963.
Arc 861.169F Bulleid, Arthur. The Meare Lake village. v.1,3. Taunton, 1948- 2v.
Arc 861.170 Feachem, Richard. The North Britons. London, 1965.
Arc 861.171 Winchester, England. Winchester excavations, 1949-1960. Winchester, Hants, 1964.
Arc 861.172 Workers' Educational Association. Slough and Eton Branch. The Middle Thames in antiquity. Slough, Bucks, 1966.
Arc 861.172.5 Harding, Derek William. The Iron Age in the Upper Thames basin. Oxford, 1972.
Arc 861.174 Thomas, Charles. Christian antiquities of Camborne. St. Austell, Cornwall, 1967.
Arc 861.175 Colchester, England. Museum and Muniment Committee. Colonia-Claudia Victricensis: the story of Roman Colchester. Colchester, 1967.
Arc 861.178 Hencken, Thalassa Cruso. The excavation of the Iron Age camp on Bredon Hill. London, 1939.
Arc 861.180 Brodribb, Arthur Charles Conant. Excavations at Shakenoak Farm. v.1-4. Oxford, Eng., 1968- 3v.
Arc 861.188 Calkin, John Bernard. Discovering prehistoric Bournemouth and Christchurch: a record of local finds in the twentieth century. Christchurch, Hants, 1966.
Arc 861.189F Matthews, C.L. Occupation sites on a Chiltern ridge. Oxford, 1976.

Classified Listing

Arc 861 Archaeology - Local - Great Britain - England and neighboring islands - Local - cont.

Arc 861.190 Great Britain. Commissions. Ancient and Historical Monuments and Constructions of England. Peterborough New town. London, 1969.
Arc 861.191F Woodhouse, Jayne. Barrow Mead, Bath, 1964: excavation of a medieval peasant house. Oxford, 1976.
Arc 861.192 Joint Excavation Committee of the Wakefield Corporation and the Wakefield Historical Society. Sandal Castle; a short account of the history of the site and the 1964 excavations. Wakefield, Eng., 1965.
Arc 861.192.5 Joint Excavation Committee of the Wakefield Corporation and the Wakefield Historical Society. Sandal Castle excavations, 1967. Wakefield, Eng., 1967?.
Arc 861.193F Froom, F.R. Wawcott II, a stratified Mesolithic succession. Oxford, 1976.
Arc 861.194 Rahtz, Philip. Excavations at King John's hunting lodge, Writtle, Essex, 1955-57. London, 1969.
Arc 861.195 Branigan, Keith. Town and country. Bourne End, 1973.
Arc 861.196 Meany, Audrey. Two Anglo-Saxon cemeteries at Winnall, Winchester, Hampshire. London, 1970.
Arc 861.197 Dickinson, Tania M. Cuddesdon and Dorcester-on-Thames, Oxfordshire. Oxford, 1974.
Arc 861.198 Jessup, Ronald-Ferederick. South east England. London, 1970.
Arc 861.199.1 Pearson, Frederick Richard. Roman Yorkshire. 1. ed. Wakefield, 1973.
Arc 861.200 Garlick, Tom. Romans in the Lake counties. Clapham, 1970.
Arc 861.200.5 Fell, Clare. Early settlement in the Lake counties. Clapham, 1972.
Arc 861.201 Rahtz, Philip. Beckery Chapel, Glastonbury, 1967-68. Glastonbury, 1974.
Arc 861.202 Barker, P.A. The mediaeval pottery of Shropshire from the conquest to 1400. Shropshire, 1970.
Arc 861.203 Ashbee, Paul. Ancient Scilly from the first farmers to the early Christians. Newton Abbot, 1974.
Arc 861.204 Blank, Elizabeth. A guide to Leicestershire archaeology. Leicester, 1970.
Arc 861.205 Woolf, Charles William. An introduction to the archaeology of Cornwall. Truro, 1970.
Arc 861.206 Fox, Aileen Mary Henderson. Exeter in Roman times. Exeter, 1973.
Arc 861.207 Alcock, Leslie. By South Cadbury is that Camelot. London, 1970.
Arc 861.208 Uhthoff-Kaufmann, Raymond R. The archaeology of Jodrell Hall (Terra Nova), Cheshire. Wilmslow, 1971.
Arc 861.209 Brixworth excavations. Northampton, Eng., 1972?
Arc 861.210 Down, Alec. Chichester excavations. Chichester, 1971- 2v.
Arc 861.211 Hassall, Tom Grafton. Oxford, the city beneath your feet. Oxford, 1972.
Arc 861.212 Shotter, David Colin Arthur. Romans in Lancashire. Yorkshire, 1973.

Arc 865 Archaeology - Local - Great Britain - England and neighboring islands - Stonehenge

X Cg Arc 865.1 Barclay, E. Stonehenge and its earth works. London, 1895.
Arc 865.1.10 Barclay, E. The ruined temple Stonehenge. London, 1911.
Arc 865.2 Petrie, W.M.F. Stonehenge; plans, descriptions and theories. London, 1880.
Arc 865.3 Browne, H. An illustration of Stonehenge and Abury. 4. ed. Salisbury, 1854.
Arc 865.4 Clapperton, W. Stonehenge handbook. Salisbury, n.d.
Arc 865.5 Herbert, A. Cyclops Christianus; disprove...Stonehenge. London, 1849.
Htn Arc 865.6* Charleton, W. Chorea gigantum, or...Stone-Heng restored to the Danes. London, 1663.
Arc 865.7 Ireland, A.J. Stonehenge: story of its building and its legends. London, 1903.
Arc 865.8 Lockyer, N. Stonehenge and other British stone monuments. London, 1906.
Htn Arc 865.9* Jones, Inigo. The most notable antiquity of Great Britain. London, 1655. 2 pam.
Htn Arc 865.9.5* Jones, Inigo. The most notable antiquity of Great Britain. London, 1655.
Htn Arc 865.9.10F* Jones, Inigo. The most notable antiquity of Great Britain called Stone-Heng. London, 1725.
Arc 865.9.11 Jones, Inigo. The most notable antiquity of Great Britain called Stone-Heng. Farnborough, 1971.
Arc 865.10 Long, william. Stonehenge and its barrows. Devizes, 1876.
Arc 865.11 Gidley, L. Stonehenge...by the light of ancient history. London, 1873.
Arc 865.13 Smith, John. Choir Gaur...Orrery of Druids...Stonehenge. 2. ed. Salisbury, 1771. 2 pam.
Arc 865.13.2 Smith, John. Choir Gaur...Orrery of Druids...Stonehenge. 2. ed. Salisbury, 1771.
Arc 865.14 Brown and Company, Salisbury, publishers. Illustrated guide to Old Sarum and Stonehenge. London, 1888.
Arc 865.14.5 Brown and Company, Salisbury, publishers. The illustrated guide to Old Sarum and Stonehenge. Salisbury, 1877.
Arc 865.15 Stevens, Frank. Stonehenge today and yesterday. London, 1916.
Arc 865.15.5 Stevens, Frank. Stonehenge today and yesterday. London, 1924.
Arc 865.16 Stevens, E.T. Jottings on some of the objects of interest in the Stonehenge excursion. Salisbury, 1882.
Arc 865.17 Stone, E.H. The stones of Stonehenge. London, 1924.
Arc 865.18 Wood, John. Choir Gaure, vulgarly called Stonehenge. Oxford, 1747.
Arc 865.19 Grover, Henry M. A voice from Stonehenge. pt.1. London, 1847.
Arc 865.21 Cunnington, R.H. Stonehenge and its date. London, 1935.
Arc 865.22 Atkinson, R.J.C. Stonehenge. London, 1956.
Arc 865.23 Twist, Richard Marsden. Stonehenge. Truro, 1964.
Arc 865.24 Hawkins, Gerald Stanley. Stonehenge decoded. 1. ed. Garden City, N.Y., 1965.
Arc 865.26 Crampton, Patrick. Stonehenge of the kings: a people appear. London, 1967.
Arc 865.27 Peach, Wystan A. Stonehenge; a new theory. Cardiff, 1961.
Arc 865.28 Twist, Richard Marsden. Stonehenge: a classical interpretation. St. Anthony, 1971.
Arc 865.29 Bergström, Theo. Stonehenge. London, 1974.

Arc 870 Archaeology - Local - Great Britain - England and neighboring islands - Special topics

Arc 870.1 Evans, J. The ancient stone implements, weapons and ornaments of Great Britain. N.Y., 1872.
Arc 870.1.1 Evans, J. The ancient stone implements, weapons and ornaments of Great Britain. London, 1897.
Arc 870.1.2 Evans, J. The ancient bronze implements, weapons and ornaments of Great Britain. London, 1881.
Arc 870.1.3 Evans, J. The ancient bronze implements, weapons and ornaments of Great Britain. N.Y., 1881.
Arc 870.1.9 Stevens, J. Descriptive lists of flint implements. St. Mary Bourne. London, 1867.
Arc 870.2 Plenderleath, W.C. The white horses of the west of England. London, 1886.
Arc 870.3 Hamper, William. Observations on certain ancient pillars of memoir called Hoar-Stones. Birmingham, 1820.
Arc 870.4 Codrington, Thomas. Roman roads in Britain. London, 1903.
Arc 870.4.2 Codrington, Thomas. Roman roads in Britain. 2. ed. London, 1905.
Arc 870.4.3 Codrington, Thomas. Roman roads in Britain. 3. ed. London, 1918.
Arc 870.4.4 Codrington, Thomas. Roman roads in Britain. 3. ed. N.Y., 1919.
Arc 870.4.15 Hughes, G.M. Roman roads in south-east Britain. London, 1936.
Arc 870.4.20 Margary, Ivan D. Roman ways in the Weald. London, 1948.
Arc 870.4.21 Margary, Ivan D. Roman roads in Britain. London, 1955. 2v.
Arc 870.4.21.2 Margary, Ivan D. Roman roads in Britain. London, 1967.
Arc 870.4.21.3 Margary, Ivan D. Roman roads in Britain. 3. ed. London, 1973.
Arc 870.4.22 Margary, Ivan D. Roman ways in the Weald. London, 1965.
Arc 870.5 Hubbard, A.J. Neolithic dew-ponds and cattle ways. London, 1905.
Arc 870.5.3 Hubbard, A.J. Neolithic dew-ponds and cattle ways. 3. ed. London, 1916.
Arc 870.5.5 Martin, E. A. Dew-ponds; history, observation and experiment. London, 1915.
Arc 870.5.7 Pugsley, A.J. Dew-ponds in fable and fact. London, 1939.
Htn Arc 870.6* Pointer, J. Britannia Romana, or Romans in Britain. Oxford, 1724. 4 pam.
Arc 870.7 Simpson, J.Y. Archaic sculpturings of cups, circles. Edinbrugh, 1867.
Arc 870.8 Duke, E. The druidical temples of the county of Wilts. London, 1846.
Arc 870.9 Allcroft, A.H. Earthwork of England. London, 1908.
Arc 870.9.10 Allcroft, A.H. The circle and the cross. London, 1927-30. 2v.
Arc 870.10 Woolls, C. Barrow diggers. London, 1839.
Arc 870.10.5 Crawford, O.G.S. The long barrows of Cotswolds. Gloucester, Eng., 1925.
Arc 870.10.9 Grinsell, L.V. The ancient burial-mounds of England. London, 1936.
Arc 870.10.9.5 Grinsell, L.V. The ancient burial-mounds of England. 2. ed. London, 1955.
Arc 870.10.15 Ashbee, Paul. The bronze age round barrow in Britain. London, 1960.
Arc 870.10.20 Ashbee, Paul. The earthen long barrow in Britain. Toronto, 1970.
Arc 870.11 Smith, Frederick. The stone ages in northern Britain and Ireland. London, 1909.
Arc 870.12 Leeds, E.T. The archaeology of the Anglo-Saxon settlements. Oxford, 1913.
Arc 870.12.10 Leeds, E.T. The corpus of early Anglo-Saxon great square-headed broaches. Oxford, 1949.
Arc 870.12.15A Leeds, E.T. Early Anglo-Saxon art and archaeology. Oxford, 1936.
Arc 870.12.15B Leeds, E.T. Early Anglo-Saxon art and archaeology. Oxford, 1936.
Arc 870.12.19 Leeds, E.T. The Anglo-Saxon cemetery at Abingdon, Berkshire. Oxford, 1936. 2v.
Arc 870.13 Styan, K.E. Short history of sepulchral cross-slabs. London, 1902.
Arc 870.14F Bruce, John C. The Roman wall. 3. ed. London, 1867.
Arc 870.14.3 Bruce, John C. Hadrian, the builder of the Roman wall. London, 1853.
Arc 870.14.5 Hoyer, M.A. By the Roman wall. London, 1908.
Arc 870.14.9 Mothersole, Jessie. Hadrian's wall. London, 1922.
Arc 870.14.12 Mariette, E. The Roman walls. 2. ed. Paris, 1906.
Arc 870.14.15 Brown, Paul. The great wall of Hadrian in Roman times. London, 1932.
Arc 870.15 Ross, Percival. Roman road from Rochester to low barrow bridge. Bradford, 1916.
Arc 870.15.5 MacLauchlan, H. Memoir written during a survey of the Watling Street. London, 1852.
Arc 870.15.7 Mothersole, Jessie. Agricola's road into Scotland. London, 1927.
Arc 870.15.11 Dunning, J.E. The Roman road to Portslade. London, 1925.
Arc 870.15.15 Winholt, S.E. With a spade on Stane Street. London, 1936.
Arc 870.16 Haslam, William. Perran-zabuloe. London, 1844.
Arc 870.17F Major, Albany F. The mystery of Wansdyke. Cheltenham, 1926.
Arc 870.18F Crawford, O.G.S. Air survey and archaeology. Southampton, 1924.
Arc 870.19 Bristol. University. Spelaeological Society. Proceedings. Bristol, Eng. 1,1919+ 6v.
Arc 870.20 Marples, M. White horses. London, 1949.
Arc 870.22F Lilienthal-Gesellschaft für Luft. Lufthild und Vorgeschichte. Berlin, 1938.
Arc 870.23 O'Dwyer, Stanhope. The Roman roads of Cheshire. Newtown, 1935.
Arc 870.24 Berry, B. A lost Roman road. London, 1963.
Arc 870.25 Bowen, H.C. Ancient fields. London, 1963.
Arc 870.26 Rural settlement in Roman Britain. London, 1966.
Arc 870.27 Henig, Martin. A corpus of Roman engraved gemstones from British sites. v.1-2. Oxford, 1974.
Arc 870.28 King, Alan. Early Pennine settlement: a field study. Lancaster, 1970.
Arc 870.29 Evison, Vera I. The fifth-century invasions south of the Thames. London, 1965.
Arc 870.30 Wildman, Samuel Gerald. The black horsemen: English inns and King Arthur. London, 1971.
Arc 870.31F Elsdon, Sheila M. Stamp and roulette decorated pottery of the La Tème period in Eastern England. Oxford, 1975.
Arc 870.33 Harding, Derek William. The Iron Age in lowland Britain. London, 1974.
Arc 870.34 Rivet, Albert L.F. The Roman villa in Britain. London, 1969.

Classified Listing

Arc 870 Archaeology - Local - Great Britain - England and neighboring islands - Special topics - cont.

Arc 870.35 — Marsden, Barry M. The early barrow-diggers. Park Ridge, N.J., 1974.

Arc 875 Archaeology - Local - Great Britain - Scotland

Arc 875.2 — Small, A. Interesting Roman antiquities recently discovered in Fife. Edinbrugh, 1823.
Arc 875.3 — Anderson, Joseph. Scotland in early Christian times. Edinburgh, 1881.
Arc 875.3.2 — Anderson, Joseph. Scotland in early Christian times. 2. series. Edinburgh, 1881.
Arc 875.4 — Anderson, Joseph. Scotland in Pagan times. The Iron Age. Edinburgh, 1883.
Arc 875.4.2 — Anderson, Joseph. Scotland in Pagan times. The Bronze and Stone Ages. Edinburgh, 1886.
X Cg Arc 875.5 — Munro, R. Ancient Scottish lake-dwellings. Edinburgh, 1882.
Arc 875.5.5 — Munro, R. Prehistoric Scotland. Edinburgh, 1899.
Arc 875.6 — Wilson, D. The archaeology and prehistoric annals of Scotland. Edinburgh, 1851.
Arc 875.7 — Maclagan, C. Catalogue...British Museum...sculptured stones...Scotland. Edinburgh, 1898.
Arc 875.8 — Annandale, C. A history of the Scottish people from the earliest times. London, 1892.
Arc 875.9 — Macdonald, J. Tituli Hunteriani, an account of the Roman stones in the Hunterian Museum. Glasgow, 1897.
Arc 875.10 — Glasgow, Scotland. Archaeological Society. The Antonine wall report. Glasgow, 1899.
Arc 875.10.7 — Miller, S.N. The Roman fort at Balmuildy. Glasgow, 1922.
Arc 875.10.13 — Clarke, John. The Roman fort at Cadder near Glasgow. Glasgow, 1933.
Arc 875.11 — Christison, D. Early fortifications in Scotland. London, 1898.
Arc 875.11.7 — Christison, D. Account of the excavation of the Roman station at Ardoch. Edinburgh, 1898.
Arc 875.12 — Munro, Robert. Archaeology and false antiquities. London, 1905.
Arc 875.12.2 — Munro, Robert. Archaeology and false antiquities. Philadelphia, 1906.
Arc 875.13 — Macdonald, G. The Roman forts on the Bar Hill, Dumbartonshire. Glasgow, 1906.
Arc 875.13.5 — Macdonald, G. The Roman wall in Scotland. Glasgow, 1911.
Arc 875.13.7 — Macdonald, G. The Roman wall in Scotland. 2. ed. Oxford, 1934.
Arc 875.13.10 — Robertson, Anne S. Bar Will. Oxford, 1975.
Arc 875.14 — Dietrichson, L. Monumenta orcadica. Kristiania, 1906.
Arc 875.14.7 — Childe, V.G. Ancient dwellings at Skara Brae. Edinburgh, 1933.
Arc 875.14.10 — Childe, V.G. Skara Brae. London, 1931.
Arc 875.14.15 — Childe, V.G. The prehistory of Scotland. London, 1935.
Arc 875.14.20 — Childe, V.G. Scotland before the Scots. London, 1946.
Arc 875.14.25 — Roussell, Aage. Norse building customs in the Scottish isles. Copenhagen, 1934.
Arc 875.15 — Leslie, Forbes. The early races of Scotland and their monuments. Edinburgh, 1866. 2v.
Arc 875.16 — Thomas, F.L.W. Primitive dwellings and hypogea of the Outer Hebrides. Edinburgh, 1869.
Arc 875.17 — Mann, L.M. Prehistoric pile-structures in pits. Edinburgh, 1904.
Arc 875.18 — Mackenzie, G.S. A letter to Sir Walter Scott, Baronet. Edinburgh, 1824.
Arc 875.19 — Barclay, A. Perthia Romana: line or chain of forts erected by Agricola. Perth, 1883.
Arc 875.20 — Sutherland, G. Outlines of Scottish archaeology. Edinburgh, 1870.
Arc 875.21 — Brydall, R. The monumental effigies of Scotland. Glasgow, 1895.
Arc 875.22 — Balfour, J.A. Book of Arran - archaeology. Glasgow, 1910. 2v.
Arc 875.23 — Laing, S. Prehistoric remains of Caithness. Edinburgh, 1866.
Arc 875.24 — Beveridge, E. Coll and Tiree - their prehistoric forts. Edinburgh, 1903.
Arc 875.25 — Williams, J. An account of some remarkable ancient ruins. Edinburgh, 1777.
Arc 875.26 — Stuart, Robert. Caledonia romana. Edinburgh, 1845.
Arc 875.26.2 — Stuart, Robert. Caledonia Romana...Roman antiquities of Scotland. Edinburgh, 1852.
Arc 875.28 — Graham, R.C. The carved stones of Islay. Glasgow, 1895.
Arc 875.29 — Black, William G. Glasgow cross. Glasgow, 1913.
Arc 875.29.7 — Black, William G. The Scots mercat "cross"; an inquiry as to its history and meaning. Glasgow, 1928.
Arc 875.30 — McFarlan, J. The Ruthwell cross. Dumfries, 1896.
Arc 875.31 — Hewison, J.K. Runic roods of Ruthwell and Bewcastle. Glasgow, 1914.
Arc 875.31.5F — Brown, G.F. Ancient cross shafts at Bewcastle and Ruthwell. Cambridge, 1916.
Arc 875.31.7 — Hewison, J.K. The romance of Bewcastle cross. Glasgow, 1923.
Arc 875.31.10 — Dinwiddie, J. The Ruthwell cross and its story. Dumfries, 1927.
Arc 875.32 — Carnegie, J. Origins of Pictish symbolism. Edinburgh, 1893.
Arc 875.32.5 — Diack, F.C. The Newton stone and other Pictish inscriptions. Paisley, 1922.
Arc 875.32.10 — Diack, F.C. The inscription of Pictland. Aberdeen, 1944.
Arc 875.33 — Lang, Andrew. The Clyde mystery. Glasgow, 1905.
Arc 875.34 — Smith, Frederick. Some investigations into palaeolithic remains in Scotland. Glasgow, 1898-99.
Arc 875.35 — Fergusson, James. Short essay on age and uses of brochs...Orkeney Islands. London, 1877.
Htn Arc 875.36* — Wilson, Wilson D. Description of an ancient cross at Kilmory. Edinburgh, 1839.
Arc 875.37 — Maclagan, Christian. What means these stones? Edinburgh, 1894.
Arc 875.37.5 — Maclagan, Christian. Chips from old stones. Edinburgh, 1881.
Arc 875.38 — Black, George F. Descriptive catalogue of antiquities in Ayrshire. n.p., n.d.
Arc 875.39 — Graham, H.D. Antiquities of Iona. London, 1850.
Arc 875.40 — Cordiner, Charles. Remarkable ruins and romantic prospects of North Britain. London, 1788-95.
Arc 875.41 — Mothersole, Jessie. In Roman Scotland. London, 1927.
Arc 875.42.5 — Waldie, G. Walks along the northern Roman wall. Linlithgow, 1913.
Arc 875.43 — Hutcheson, Alexander. Old stories in stones and other papers. Dundee, 1927.

Arc 875 Archaeology - Local - Great Britain - Scotland - cont.

Arc 875.44 — Simpson, William D. The province of Mar. Aberdeen, 1943.
Arc 875.45 — Small, Alan. Craig Phadrig; interim report on 1971 excavation. Dundee, 1972.
Arc 875.50 — Great Britain. Commissions. Ancient and Historical Monuments of Scotland. Report and inventory of monuments and constructions. Edinburgh. 1-13,1909-1957 11v.
Arc 875.52 — Great Britain. Commissions. Ancient and Historical Monuments of Scotland. An inventory of the ancient and historical monuments of Roxburghshire. Edinburgh, 1956. 2v.
Arc 875.53 — Great Britain. Commissions. Ancient and Historical Monuments of Scotland. An inventory of the ancient and historical monuments of Selkirkshire. Edinburgh, 1956.
Arc 875.54 — Great Britain. Commissions. Ancient and Historical Monuments of Scotland. Ancient and historical monuments of Stirlingshire. Edinburgh, 1963. 2v.
Arc 875.55 — Spence, James. Ruined castles. Edinburgh, 1873.
Arc 875.56 — Great Britain. Commissions. Ancient and Historical Monuments of Scotland. Peeblesshire: an inventory of the ancient monuments. Edinburgh, 1967. 2v.
Arc 875.60 — The Drostin stone at St. Vigeans and its inscription. Aberdeen, 1928.
Arc 875.65 — Ogston, Alexander. The prehistoric antiquities of the Howe of Cromar. Aberdeen, 1931.
Arc 875.75 — Lethbridge, T. Herdsmen and hermits. Cambridge, Eng., 1950.
Arc 875.80 — Miller, S.N. The Roman occupation of southwestern Scotland. Glasgow, 1952.
Arc 875.85 — Lacaille, A.D. The Stone Age in Scotland. London, 1954.
Arc 875.90 — Simpson, William D. Dundarg Castle. Edinburgh, 1954.
Arc 875.95 — Simpson, William D. The Viking congress. Edinburgh, 1954.
Arc 875.100 — Robertson, Anne. An Antonine fort. Edinburgh, 1957.
Arc 875.100.5 — Robertson, Anne. The Roman fort at Castledykes. Edinburgh, 1964.
Arc 875.105 — Hamilton, J.R.C. Excavations at Jarlshof. Edinburgh, 1956.
Arc 875.110 — Cruden, Stewart. The early Christian and Pictish monuments of Scotland. Edinburgh, 1957.
Arc 875.115F — O'Dell, Andrew. St. Ninian's isle treasure. Edinburgh, 1960.
Arc 875.120 — Taylor, B. Archaeology of Tayside. Dundee, 196-?
Arc 875.122 — Wainwright, Frederick Threlfall. The northern isles. Edinburgh, 1962.
Arc 875.124 — Wainwright, Fredrick Threlfall. The souterrains of southern Pictland. London, 1963.
Arc 875.126 — Feachem, R. A guide to prehistoric Scotland. London, 1963.
Arc 875.127 — Piggott, Stuart. The prehistoric peoples of Scotland. London, 1962.
Arc 875.128 — Newall, Frank. Excavation of prehistoric and mediaeval homesteads at Knapps, Renfrewshire. Paisley, 1965.
Arc 875.129 — Laing, Lloyd Robert. Settlement types in post-Roman Scotland. Oxford, 1975.
Arc 875.130 — Hamilton, John. Excavations at Clicknimin, Shetland. Edinburgh, 1968.
Arc 875.131 — Henshall, Audrey Shore. The chambered tombs of Scotland. Edinburgh, 1963-72. 2v.
Arc 875.132 — Ritchie, James Neil Graham. Edinburgh and southeast Scotland. London, 1972.
Arc 875.133 — Small, Alan. St. Ninian's Isle and its treasure. London, 1973. 2v.
Arc 875.134 — Dundee, Scotland. Museum and Art Gallery. Tayside before history. Dundee, 1971.

Arc 880 Archaeology - Local - Great Britain - Ireland

Arc 880.1 — O'Brien, H. The round towers of Ireland. London, 1834.
Arc 880.2 — Borlase, W.C. The dolmens of Ireland. London, 1897. 3v.
Arc 880.3 — Wood-Martin, W.G. Pagan Ireland. An archaeological sketch. London, 1895.
Arc 880.4 — Wakeman, W.F. Wakeman's handbook of Irish antiquities. Dublin, 1903.
Arc 880.4.8 — Wakeman, W.F. Archaeologia Hibernica. Dublin, 1848.
Arc 880.5 — O'Neill, Henry. Fine arts and civilization of ancient Ireland. London, 1863.
Arc 880.7 — Keane, Marcus. Towers and temples of ancient Ireland. Dublin, 1867.
X Cg Arc 880.8 — Coffey, George. New Grange and other incised tumuli. Dublin, 1912.
Arc 880.9 — Ffrench, J.F.M. Prehistoric faith and worship. London, 1912.
Arc 880.10 — Coffey, George. The bronze age in Ireland. Dublin, 1913.
Arc 880.11 — Doherty, W.J. Round towers of Ireland. Dublin, 1881.
Arc 880.12.2 — Wright, Thomas. Louthiana, or Introduction to antiquities of Ireland. London, 1758.
Arc 880.13 — Conwell, E.A. Discovery of tomb of Ollamh Fodhla. Dublin, 1873.
Htn Arc 880.14* — Graves, James. Church and shrine of St. Manchan. Dublin, 1875.
Arc 880.15 — Wakeman, W.F. A survey of antiquarian periods on...Inismurray. London, 1893.
Arc 880.16 — Notices of the round tower of Ulster. Belfast, 1854.
Arc 880.17 — Morres, Hervey Montmorency. A historical and critical inquiry into the origin and primitive use of the Irish pillar-tower. London, 1821.
NEDL Arc 880.19 — Stokes, William. The life and labors in art and archaeology of George Petrie. London, 1868.
Arc 880.20A — Wood-Martin, W.G. The lake-dwellings of Ireland. Dublin, 1886.
Arc 880.20B — Wood-Martin, W.G. The lake-dwellings of Ireland. Dublin, 1886.
Arc 880.21 — Poe, J.W. The cromlechs of county Dublin. Dublin, 1918?
Arc 880.22 — Cochrane, Robert. List of ancient and national monuments in county of Cork. Cork, 1913.
Arc 880.23 — Macalister, R.A.S. The memorial slabs of Clonmacnois, King's County. Dublin, 1909.
Arc 880.24 — Macalister, R.A.S. Ireland in pre-Celtic times. Dublin, 1921.
Arc 880.25 — Macalister, R.A.S. The present and future of archaeology in Ireland. Dublin, 1925.
Arc 880.25.7 — Macalister, R.A.S. The archaeology of Ireland. London, 1928.
Arc 880.25.8A — Macalister, R.A.S. The archaeology of Ireland. 2. ed. London, 1949.
Arc 880.25.8B — Macalister, R.A.S. The archaeology of Ireland. 2. ed. London, 1949.
Arc 880.25.9A — Macalister, R.A.S. Ancient Ireland. London, 1935.

Classified Listing

Arc 880 Archaeology - Local - Great Britain - Ireland - cont.

Arc 880.25.9B Macalister, R.A.S. Ancient Ireland. London, 1935.
Arc 880.25.10 Macalister, R.A.S. Cluain Maccu Nois [Clonmacmois]. Dublin, 1911.
Arc 880.29 Lawlor, H.C. The monastery of St. Mochaoi of Nendrum. Belfast, 1925.
Arc 880.31 Power, P. Early Christian Ireland. Dublin, 1925.
Arc 880.32 Evans, Emyr Estyn. Prehistoric and early Christian Ireland. London, 1966.
Arc 880.33F Burchell, J.P.T. The early Mousterian implements of Sligo, Ireland. Ipswich, 1928.
Arc 880.35 Lawlor, H.C. Ulster. Belfast, 1928.
Arc 880.36 Bremer, Walther. Ireland's place in prehistoric and early historic Europe. Dublin, 1928.
Arc 880.37A Porter, Arthur Kingsley. The crosses and culture of Ireland. New Haven, 1931.
Arc 880.37B Porter, Arthur Kingsley. The crosses and culture of Ireland. New Haven, 1931.
Arc 880.38A Hencken, H.O. Cahercomnaun, a stone fort in county Clare. Dublin, 1938.
Arc 880.38B Hencken, H.O. Cahercomnaun, a stone fort in county Clare. Dublin, 1938.
Arc 880.38.15 Hencken, H.O. A tumulus at Carrowlesdooaun, County Mayo. n.p., 1935. 2 pam.
Arc 880.39 Movius, H.L. Kilgreany cove, county Waterford. Dublin? 1935.
Arc 880.39.5A Movius, H.L. The Irish Stone Age. Cambridge, Eng., 1942.
Arc 880.39.5B Movius, H.L. The Irish Stone Age. Cambridge, Eng., 1942.
Arc 880.40 Ancient Monuments Advisory Council for Northern Ireland. A preliminary survey of the ancient monuments of Northern Ireland. Belfast, 1940.
Arc 880.42 Northern Ireland. Ministry of Finance. An account of the ancient monuments in state charge. Belfast, 1947.
Arc 880.43 Northern Ireland. Ministry of Finance. Ancient monuments of Northern Ireland. v.1-2. Belfast, 1966-69.
Arc 880.44 Raftery, J. Prehistoric Ireland. London, 1951.
Arc 880.46 O'Riordain, Sean P. Antiquities of the Irish countryside. 3. ed. London, 1953.
Arc 880.46.5 O'Riordain, Sean P. New Grange and the bend of the Boyne. London, 1964.
Arc 880.47F Herity, Michael. Irish passage graves. Dublin, 1974.
Arc 880.48 Dublin. National Museum of Ireland. A brief guide to the collection of Irish antiquities. Dublin, 1960.
Arc 880.49 Royal Irish Academy, Dublin. Museum. A descriptive catalogue of the antiquities. Dublin, 1857.
Arc 880.50 Norman, Edward R. The early development of Irish society: the evidence of aerial photography. Cambridge, Eng., 1969.

Arc 885 Archaeology - Local - Great Britain - Wales

Arc 885.1 Langdon, A.G. Old Cornish crosses. Truro, 1896.
Htn Arc 885.2* Halliwell, J.O. An ancient survey of Pen Maen Maur. London, 1859.
Arc 885.3 Blight, J.C. Antiquities...Kirrier and Penwith, West Cornwall. Truro, 1862.
Arc 885.4 Owen, E. Old stone crosses...ancient manners. London, 1886.
Arc 885.5 James, C.H. Excavations at Gelli Gaer camp. Cardiff, 1899?
Arc 885.6 Ward, John. Roman fort of Gelly Gaer in...Glamorgan. London, 1903.
Arc 885.7 Morgan, W.D. An antiquarian survey of East Gower, Glamorganshire. London, 1899.
Arc 885.7.5 Rutter, Joseph G. Prehistoric Gower; early archaeology of West Glamorgan. Swansea, 1948.
Arc 885.8 Wheeler, R.E.M. Prehistoric and Roman Wales. Oxford, 1925.
Arc 885.8.5 Wheeler, R.E.M. Wales and archaeology. London, 1929.
Arc 885.9 Wheeler, R.E.M. The Roman fort near Brecon. London, 1926.
Arc 885.10 Evans, William. The Meini Hirion and Sarns of Anglesey. Llangefni, 1927.
Arc 885.11 Hughes, I.T. Out of the dark. Wrexham, 1930.
Arc 885.12 Paget, Clara. Some ancient stone forts in Carnarvonshire. Cambridge, 1896.
Arc 885.12.5 Wheeler, R.E.M. Segontium and the Roman occupation of Wales. London, 1923.
Arc 885.13 Stanley, W.O. Memoirs on remains of ancient dwellings in Holyhead Island. London, 1871.
Arc 885.14 Lee, J.E. Description of a Roman building and other remains...at Caerleon. London, 1850. 5 pam.
Arc 885.15 Morgan, O. Notice of a tessellated pavement. Newport, 1866.
Arc 885.15.8 Boon, George C. Isca, the Roman legionaryfortress at Caerleon. 3. ed. Cardiff, 1972.
Arc 885.16 O'Dwyer, S. The Roman roads of Wales. Newtown, 1936.
Arc 885.17 Great Britain. Commissions. Ancient and Historical Monuments and Constructions of Wales and Monmouthshire. Interim report. London. 9-11,1920-1956
Arc 885.18 Cambrian Archaeological Association. A hundred years of Welsh archaeology. Gloucester, 1949.
Arc 885.19.5 Nash-Williams, Victor Erle. The Roman frontier in Wales. Cardiff, 1954.
Arc 885.19.7 Nash-Williams, Victor Erle. The Roman frontier in Wales. Cardiff, 1969.
Arc 885.20 Grimes, W.F. The prehistory of Wales. 2. ed. Cardiff, 1951.
Arc 885.22 Reynolds, P.K.B. Excavations on the site of the Roman fort of Kanovium at Caerhun. Cardiff, 1938.
Arc 885.23 North, F.J. Sunken cities. Cardiff, 1957.
Arc 885.24 Alcock, L. Dinas Powys. Cardiff, 1963.
Arc 885.25 Gardner, Willoughby. Dinorben. Cardiff, 1964.
Arc 885.25.5 Savory, Hubert Newman. Excavations at Dinorben, 1965-69. Cardiff, 1971.
Arc 885.26 Foster, Idris L. Prehistoric and early Wales. London, 1965.
Arc 885.28 Wainwright, G. Coygan Camp; a prehistoric Romano-British and Dark Age settlemant in Carmarthenshire. Cwmgwyn, 1967.
Arc 885.30 Lewis, Ewart Thomas. Mynachlogddu: a guide to its antiquities. Clunderwen, 1967.
Arc 885.32 Prehistoric man in Wales and the west. Bath, 1972.

Arc 887 Archaeology - Local - Low Countries - Folios [Discontinued]

Arc 887.1F Bast, M.J. de. Receueil d'antiquités romaines et gauloises trouvées dans la Flandre. Gand, 1808.

Arc 888 Archaeology - Local - Low Countries - General works

Arc 888.1 Åberg, Nils. Die Steinzeit in der Niederlanden. Uppsala, 1916.
Arc 888.5F Bursch, F.C. Die Becherkultur in den Niederlanden. Inaug. Diss. Leiden, 1933.
Arc 888.6 Willems, W.J.A. Een bijdrage tot de kennis der vóór-Romeinsche urnenvelden in Nederland. Proefschrift. Maastricht, 1935.
Arc 888.10 Byvonck, A.W. De voorgeschiedenis nou Nederland. Leiden, 1944.
Arc 888.15 Giffen, Albert Egges van. Oudheidkundige perspectieven in het bijzonder ten aanzien van de vaderlandsche Prae en protohistorie. Groningen, 1947.
X Cg Arc 888.17 Giffen, Albert Egges van. Inheemse en Romeinse terpen. Atlas and plates. Groningen, 1950. 2v.
Arc 888.20 Heemskerck Düker, W.F. van. Wat aarde bewaarde. Den Haag, 1942?
Arc 888.25 Popping, H.J. Onze voorhistorie. Zutphen, 1952.
Arc 888.30 Een kwart eeun. Meppal, 1947.
Arc 888.35 Boeles, P.C.J.A. De aldste kultuer yn de sânen feankriten fen Fryspân. Boalsert, 1930.
Arc 888.40F Pleyte, Willem. Nederlandsche oudheden van de vroegste tijden tot op Karel dan Groote. Leiden, 1902. 2v.
Arc 888.45 Laet, Siegfried J. de. The Low Countries. London, 1958.
Arc 888.45.5 Laet, Siegfried J. de. De voorgeschiedenis der Lage Landen. Groningen, 1959.
Arc 888.50 Klok, R.H.J. Archeologie en monument. Bussum, 1969.
Arc 888.55 Narr, Karl J. Studien zur älteren und mittleren Steinzeit der Niederen Lande. Habilitationsschrift. Bonn, 1968.

Arc 889 Archaeology - Local - Low Countries - Local; Special topics

Arc 889.1 Schuermans, H. Objets étrusques découvertes en Belgique. pt.1-5. Bruxelles, 1872.
Arc 889.2 Delvaux, Emile. Les alhuions de l'escault et les tourbières...d'Audenarde. Liége, 1885.
Arc 889.3 Dessel, Camille. Topographie des voies romaines de la Belgiqye. Bruxelles, 1877.
Arc 889.4.2 Dupont, Édouard. Les temps préhistoriques en Belgique. 2. éd. Bruxelles, 1872.
Arc 889.4.10 Maeyer, R. de. De Romeinsche villa's in België. Antwerpen, 1937.
Arc 889.4.15 Maeyer, R. de. De overblijfselev der Romainsche villa's in België. Antwerpen, 1940.
Arc 889.5 Giffen, Albert Egges van. Die Bauart der Einzelgräber. Text and atlas. Leipzig, 1930. 2v.
Arc 889.6 Loë, Alfred de. Le dolmen de Solwaster. Bruxelles, 1889.
Arc 889.7 Loë, Alfred de. Les roches-polissoirs du "Bruzel" à Saint-Mard, province de Luxembourg. Bruxelles, 1896.
Arc 889.8 Brunsting, H. Het grafveld onder hees bij Nijmegen. Amsterdam, 1937.
Arc 889.8.5 Daniels, M.P.M. Noviomagus. Nijmegen, 195-.
Arc 889.9 Weerd, H. van de. Inleiding tot de Gallo-Romeinsche archeologie der Nederlanden. Antwerpen, 1944.
Arc 889.10 Brom, Leo H.M. The Stevensweert Kantharos. The Hague, 1952.
Arc 889.12 Tourneur, V. Les Belges avant César. Bruxelles, 1944.
Arc 889.15 Hondius-Crone, Ada. The temple of Nehalennia at Domburg. Amsterdam, 1955.
Arc 889.17 Bogaers, J.E.A.T. De Gallo-Romeinse tempels te Elst in de Over Betuive. 's-Gravenhage, 1955.
Arc 889.20F Friesch Genootschap van Geschied-Oudheid en Taalkunde te Leeuwarden. Friesche oudheden. Leeuwarden, 1875.
Arc 889.22 Mariën, M.E. Oud-België. Antwerpen, 1952.
Arc 889.24 Damme, Daniel van. Promenades archéologiques à Anderlecht. Bruxelles, 1958.
Arc 889.26 Beckers, H.J. Voorgeschiedenis van Zuid Limburg. Maastricht, 1940.
Arc 889.28 Leblois, C. Le cimetière merovingien de Cuesmes. Cuesmes, 1960.
Arc 889.30 Faider-Feytmans, Germaine. La nécropole gallo-romaine de Thuin. Morlanwelz, 1965.
Arc 889.30.5 Faider-Feytmans, Germaine. Le site sacré de Fontaine-Valmont. Morlanwelz? 196-.
Arc 889.32 Es, William Albertus van. Wijster; a native village beyond the imperial frontier, 150-425 A.D. Text and atlas. Groningen, 1967. 2v.
Arc 889.33 Raepsuet, Georges. La céramique en terre sigillée de la ville belgo-romaine de Robelmont, campagnes 1968-1971. Bruxelles, 1974.
Arc 889.34 Madderman, Pieter Jan Remees. Linearbandkeramik aus Elsloo und Stein. v.1-2. 's-Gravenhage, 1970.
Arc 889.35 Stadskernonderzoek in Amsterdam (1954-1962). Groningen, 1966.
Arc 889.36 Clason, Antje Trientje. Animal and man in Holland's past. v.1-2. Groningen, 1967.
Arc 889.37 Laurent, René. L'habitat rural à l'époque romaine. Bruxelles, 1972.

Arc 890 Archaeology - Local - Scandinavia - Folios [Discontinued]

Arc 890.203 Copenhagen. Kongeligi Nordiske Oldskrift-Selskab. Altas de l'archéologie du nord. Copenhagen, 1857.
Arc 890.206 Mueller, S. Ordnung af Danmark's oldsager stenalderen. Paris, 1888. 2v.
Arc 890.207 Rygh, O. Norske oldsager. Christiania, 1885.
Arc 890.208 Vedel, E. Bornholms oldtidsminder og oldsager. Kjøbenhavn, 1886.
Arc 890.208.2 Vedel, E. Efterskrift oldtidsminder og oldsager. Kjøbenhavn, 1897.
Arc 890.209 Holmberg, A.E. Skandinairens hällristningar. Stockholm, 1848.
Arc 890.210F Stockholm. Svenska Statens Historiska Museum. Techningar. v.1-3. Stockholm, 1873-83.
Arc 890.214 Gustafson, G. Norges oldtid. Mindesmärker og oldsager. Kristiania, 1906.

Arc 891 Archaeology - Local - Scandinavia - Pamphlet volumes

Arc 891 Pamphlet box. Archaeology. Scandinavia.

Arc 893 Archaeology - Local - Scandinavia - General works

Arc 893.1A Mueller, S. Nordische Altertumskunde. Strassburg, 1896. 2v.
Arc 893.1B Mueller, S. Nordische Altertumskunde. Strassburg, 1896. 2v.
X Cg Arc 893.1.5 Mueller, S. Vor oldtisminder Danmarks. Kjøbenhavn, 1897.
Arc 893.2 Copenhagen. Kongelige Nordiske Oldskrift-Selskab. Report addressed by the Royal Society of Northern Antiquaries ot its British and American members. Copenhagen, 1836.

Arc 893 Archaeology - Local - Scandinavia - General works - cont.

Arc 893.3 Copenhagen. Kongelige Nordiske Oldskrift-Selskab. Guide to northern archaeology. v.1-10. London, 1848.
Arc 893.3.2 Copenhagen. Kongelige Nordiske Oldskrift-Selskab. Guide to northern archaeology. London, 1848.
Arc 893.3.3 Copenhagen. Kongelige Nordiske Oldskrift-Selskab. Ledetraad til nordisk oldkyndighed. Kjøbenhavn, 1836.
Arc 893.3.5 Nordiske Oldskrift-Selskab. Leitfaden zur Nordischen Alterthumskunde. Copenhagen, 1837.
Arc 893.4 Undset, I.M. Norske oldsager i fremmede museer. Christiania, 1878.
Arc 893.5.2A Worsaae, J.J.A. The primeval antiquities of Denmark. London, 1849.
Arc 893.5.2B Worsaae, J.J.A. The primeval antiquities of Denmark. London, 1849.
NEDL Arc 893.5.3 Worsaae, J.J.A. The pre-history of the North. London, 1886.
Arc 893.5.4 Worsaae, J.J.A. Nordene forhistorie. Kjøbenhavn, 1881.
Arc 893.8 Nilsson, S. Skandinaviska nordens ur-invånare. Stockholm, 1862-66. 2v.
Arc 893.8.5 Nilsson, S. Die Ureinwohner des Scandinavischen Nordens. Hamburg, 1863-68. 2v.
Arc 893.8.6 Nilsson, S. Die Ureinwohner des Scandinavischen Nordens. pt.1-2. Hamburg, 1865-66.
Arc 893.12 Montelius, Oscar. Kulturgeschichte Schwedens von den ältesten Zeiten bis zum elften Jahrhundert nach Christus. Leipzig, 1906.
Arc 893.13 Adama van Scheltema, F. Die altnordische Kunst. Berlin, 1923.
Arc 893.13.5 Adama van Scheltema, F. Die altnordische Kunst. 2. Aufl. Leipzig, 1923.
Arc 893.13.15 Adama van Scheltema, F. Die Kunst unserer Vorzeit. Leipzig, 1936.
Arc 893.14 Brøgger, A.W. Universitetets oldsakamlings skrifter. Oslo, 1929.
Arc 893.15F Åberg, Nils. Den nordiska folkvandringstidens kronologi. Stockholm, 1924.
Arc 893.16F Copenhagen. Nationalmuseet. Affaldsdynger faa stenalderen i Denmark undersögte for Nationalmuseet. Paris, 1900.
Arc 893.17 Engelhardt, C. Influence classique sur le nord pendant l'antiquité. Copenhagen, 1876.
Arc 893.18 Hildebrand, H. Den äldre jernåldern i Norrland. Stockholm, 1869.
Arc 893.19 Winkel Horn, F. Kort udsigt over Nordens oldtidsminder. Kjøbenhavn, 1883.
Arc 893.20 Forssander, J.E. Der Ostskandinavische Norden während der ältesten Metallzeit Europas. Lund, 1936.
Arc 893.21 Shetelig, H. Scandinavian archaeology. Oxford, 1937.
Arc 893.23F Montelius, Oscar. Från jernåldern. Stockholm, 1869.
Arc 893.24 Fra Danmarksungtid. København, 1940.
Arc 893.25 Sprockhoff, E. Und zeugen von einem stolzen Geschlecht. Oslo, 1945.
Arc 893.26 Oxenstierna, E.C.G. Die Nordgermanen. Stuttgart, 1957.
Arc 893.27F Jankuhn, H. Denkmaler der Vorzeit zwischen Nord- und Ostsee. Schleswig, 1957.
Arc 893.28 Aeve, Astrid. I stider och märmiskor i Norden. Uppsala, 1960.
Arc 893.29 Malmer, Mats P. Jungneolithische Studien. Habelt, 1968.
Arc 893.30F Randsborg, Klavs. From period III to period IV. Copenhagen, 1972.
Arc 893.31 Klindt-Jensen, Ole. A history of Scandinavian archaeology. London, 1975.

Arc 895 Archaeology - Local - Scandinavia - Local; Special topics

Arc 895.5 Montelius, Oscar. La Suède préhistorique. Stockholm, n.d.
Arc 895.5.3 Montelius, Oscar. Les temps préhistoriques en Suède. Paris, 1895.
Arc 895.5.4F Montelius, Oscar. Minnen från vår forntide. Stockholm, 1917.
Arc 895.5.5 Montelius, Oscar. Bibliographie de l'archéologie préhistorique de la Suède. Stockholm, 1875.
Arc 895.5.25 Montelius, Oscar. Studier tillägnade Oscar Montelius. Stockholm, 1903.
Arc 895.5.27F Montelius, Oscar. Swedish antiquities. Stockholm, 1922.
Arc 895.7 Worsaae, J.J.A. The industrial arts of Denmark. London, 1882.
Arc 895.7.5 Worsaae, J.J.A. Danmarks oldtid oplyst ved oldsager og gravhøie. Kjøbenhavn, 1843.
Arc 895.7.9 Worsaae, J.J.A. Om jernålderen i Denmark. Kjøbenhavn, 1858.
Arc 895.7.25F Brøndsted, J. Danmarks oldtid. Kjøbenhavn, 1938-40. 3v.
Arc 895.7.25.2F Brøndsted, J. Danmarks oldtid. Kjøbenhavn, 1957- 3v.
Arc 895.7.26 Brøndsted, J. Danmarks stengrave og gravhøge i forhold til landets jordbund. Kjøbenhavn, 1939.
Arc 895.7.30 Gabrielsen, S.V. De forhistoriske tider i Danmark. København, 1948.
Arc 895.7.35 Klindt-Jensen, Ole. Denmark before the Vikings. London, 1957.
Arc 895.7.35.2 Klindt-Jensen, Ole. Le Danemark avant les Vikings. Grenoble, 1960.
Arc 895.11 Undset, F. Fra Norges aeldre jernalder. Kjøbenhavn, 1880.
Arc 895.12 Nicolaysen, N. Norske fornlevninger. Hefte 1-5. Kristiania, 1862-65.
Arc 895.14 Zinck, L. Nordisk archaelogi. Kjøbenhavn, 1890.
Arc 895.15 Worsaae, J.J.A. Blekingske mindemaerker fra hedenold. Kjøbenhavn, 1846.
Arc 895.15.25 Bagge, A. Stenåldersboplatserna vid Siretorp i Blekinge. Stockholm, 1939.
Arc 895.17 Brøgger, A.W. Studier over Norges stenalder. Christiania, 1906.
Arc 895.17.9 Shetelig, Haakon. Primitive tider i Norge. Bergen, 1922.
Arc 895.17.12 Shetelig, Haakon. Préhistoire de la Norvège. Oslo, 1926.
Arc 895.17.15F Engelstad, E.S. Ostnorske ristninger og malinger av den arktiske gruppe. Oslo, 1934.
Arc 895.17.20 Hallström, Gustaf. Monumental art of Northern Europe from the Stone Age. Stockholm, 1938. 2v.
Arc 895.19 Schnittger, Bror. Förhistoriska flintgrufvor och kulturlager vid kvarn. Stockholm, 1910.
Arc 895.20 Stolpe, H. Naturhistoriska och arkaeologiska undersökninger pa Björkö i Mälaren. Stockholm, 1872.
Arc 895.20.10F Birka. Stockholm. 1,1913 2v.
Arc 895.20.15F Birka. Stockholm.
Arc 895.21.15 Hallenberg, J. Quatuor monumenta aenea e terra i Suecia eruta. Stockholm, 1802.
Arc 895.21.25 Montelius, Oscar. Minnen från lapparnes stenålder i Sverige. Stockholm, 1875-76.

Arc 895 Archaeology - Local - Scandinavia - Local; Special topics - cont.

Arc 895.21.30 Rydh, Hanna. Hos stenåldersfolket. Stockholm, 1933.
Arc 895.22 Lithberg, Nils. Gotlands stenalder. Stockholm, 1914.
Arc 895.22.3 Stenberger, M. Das Grabfeld von Västerbjers auf Gotland. Stockholm, 1943.
Arc 895.22.5F Nordén, Arthur. Östergötlands bronsälder. Linköping, 1925.
Arc 895.22.10F Almgren, Oscar. Die ältere Eisenzeit Gotlands. pt.1-2. Stockholm, 1914-23.
Arc 895.22.17F Newman, B. Die Volkerwanderungszeit Gotlands. Stockholm, 1935.
Arc 895.22.20F Post, Linnart. Bronsaldersmanteln fran Gerumsberget i Vastergötland. Stockholm, 1924-25.
Arc 895.22.25 Sahlström, K.E. Om Våstergötlands stenålders bebyggelse. Stockholm, 1915.
Arc 895.22.27F Nylén, Erik. Die jungere vorrömische Eisenzeit Gotlands. Stockholm, 1956.
Arc 895.23 Ekholm, Gunnar. Studier i Upplands bebyggelse-historia. Uppsala, 1915.
Arc 895.23.10F Arne, T.J. Das Bootgräberfeld von Tuna in Alsike, Uppland. Stockholm, 1934.
Arc 895.25 Enquist, Arvid. Stenaldersbebyggeken på Arnst och Tjöm. Uppsala, 1922.
Arc 895.26 Janse, Olov Robert. Le travail de l'or en Suède à l'époque mérovingienne. Orléans, 1922.
Arc 895.28 Gihl, Gunnar. Sigtunna och Norrsunda. Uppsala, 1925.
Arc 895.29 Steenstrup, Japetus. Det store sølofund ved Gundestrup i Jylland 1891. Kjøbenhavn, 1895.
Arc 895.29.15 Worsaae, J.J.A. Om Sleswigs eller Sønderjyllands oldtidsminder. Kjøbenhavn, 1865.
Arc 895.30F Stolpe, Hjalmar. Graffältet oid Vendel. Stockholm, 1912.
Arc 895.32 Åberg, Nils. Nordische Ornamentik in vorgeschichtlicher Zeit. Leipzig, 1931.
Arc 895.34F Stenberger, Mårten. Öland under äldre järnaldern. Stockholm, 1933.
Arc 895.34.5F Stenberger, Mårten. Öland under äldre järnaldern. Stockholm, 1933.
Arc 895.35 Gjessing, H.J. Rogalands stenalder. Stavanger, 1920.
Arc 895.36 Forssenius, A.C. Specimen historicum de monumento Kiwikensi. Londini Gothorum, 1780.
Arc 895.36.5 Montelius, Oscar. Bohulänska hällristningar. Stockholm, 1876.
Arc 895.36.7F Lohse, E. Versuch einer Typologie der Felszeichnungen von Bohuslän. Inaug. Diss. Dresden, 1934.
Arc 895.36.9 Bruzelius, N.G. Sur des rochers sculptés decouverts en Scanie. Stockholm, 1875.
Arc 895.36.15F Schwedische Felsbilder von Göteborg zu Strömstad. Hagen, 1919.
Arc 895.36.20 Rydh, Hanna. En ristning på lös skifferplatta. n.p., 1921. 2 pam.
Arc 895.37 Montelius, Oscar. Sur les différents types des haches en Silex suédoise. Stockholm, 1875. 5 pam.
Arc 895.37.5 Åberg, Nils. Die Typologie der nordischen Streitäxte. Würzburg, 1918.
Arc 895.38F Rydbeck, Otto. Den medeltida borgen i Skanör. Lund, 1935.
Arc 895.39F Rydh, Hanna. Förhistoriska undersökningar på Adelso. Stockholm, 1936.
Arc 895.39.5 Rydh, Hanna. Ett bidrag till frågan om suöroornamentiken på stenålders boplatsernas lerkärl. Lund, 1937.
Arc 895.40 Swenska Farnminnesföreningen. Arkeologiska studier tillägnade H.K.H. kronprins Gustaf Adrolf. Stockholm, 1932.
Arc 895.41 Mathiassen, T. Studier over Vestjyllands oldtidsbebyggelse. København, 1948.
Arc 895.42 Becker, C. Mosefund lerkar fra yngre stenalder. København, 1948.
Arc 895.43 Lindqvist, Sune. Den helige Eskils buskopsdöme. Stockholm, 1924.
Arc 895.44F Bagge, A. Die Funde aus Dolman. v.1-2. Stockholm, 1950-52.
Arc 895.45F Oldeberg, A. Studien über die schwedische Bootaxtkultur. Stockholm, 1952.
Arc 895.46 Paulsen, P. Schwertartbänder der Wikingerzeit. Stuttgart, 1953.
Arc 895.47 Broholm, Hans Christian. Studier over den yngre Bronzealder Danmark. København, 1933.
Arc 895.47.5F Broholm, Hans Christian. Kulturforbindelser mellem Danmark og syden i aeldre. København, 1960.
Arc 895.50F Flarin, Sten. Vråkulturen. Stockholm, 1958.
Arc 895.52 Oxenstierna, E.C.G. Die altere Eisenzeit im Ostergötland. Lidingö, 1958.
Arc 895.54 Hallström, Gustaf. Monumental art of Northern Sweden from the Stone Age. Stockholm, 1960.
Arc 895.56 Strömberg, Märta. Untersuchungen zur jüngeren Eisenzeit in Schonen. Bonn, 1961.
Arc 895.56.6 Strömberg, Märta. Die Megalithgräber von Hagestad. Lund, 1971.
Arc 895.58 Gudnitz, F. Broncealderens monumentalkunst. København, 1962.
Arc 895.60 Lidén, Oskar L. Hällgröpningstudier i arsbetring till nya sydsverska fynd. Lund, 1938.
Arc 895.61 Stenberger, Marten. Sweden. London, 1942?
Arc 895.62 Sjoevold, T. The iron age settlement of Arctic Norway. v.1-2. Tromsö, 1962-74.
Arc 895.63 Malmer, M.P. Metodproblem inom järnålderns konsthistoria. Bonn, 1963.
Arc 895.64 Moberg, Carl Axel. Innan Sverige blev Sverige. Stockholm, 1964.
Arc 895.65 Brunius, Carl Georg. Försök till förklaringar öfver hällristningar. Lund, 1968.
Arc 895.66 Oldeberg, Andreas. Die ältere Metallzeit in Schweden. Stockholm, 1974.
Arc 895.67 Moberg, Carl Axel. Spår från tusentals år. Stockholm, 1966.
Arc 895.70 Hagberg, Ulf Eric. The archaeology of Skedemosse. Stockholm, 1967. 3v.
Arc 895.72 Cullberg, Carl. On artifact analysis. Bonn, 1968.
Arc 895.74 Strömberg, Märta. Der Dolmen Trollasten in St. Köpinge, Schonen. Bonn, 1968.
Arc 895.76 Knuth, Eigil. Archaeology of the musk-ox way. Paris, 1967.
Arc 895.78 Stjernquist, Berta. Beiträge zum Studium von bronzeitlichen Siedlungen. Bonn, 1969.
Arc 895.79 Arkaeologisk ABC. Handbog i dansk forhistorie. København, 1972.
Arc 895.80 Munksgaard, Elisabeth. Oldtidsdragter. København, 1974.

Classified Listing

Arc 900 Archaeology - Local - Austria and Hungary - Folios [Discontinued]

Arc 900.2.5F Austria. Zentral Kommission für Enforschung und Erhaltung der Kunst- und Historischen Denkmäle in Wien. Articles on the palace of Diocletian in Spalato. Wien? 1903.
Arc 900.200 Magyar, Yudo. Monumenta Hungariae archaeologica. Pesth, 1869-79. 4v.
Arc 900.201 Nyáry, Jenö. Az aggteleki Barlang mint orkori temetö. Budapest, 1881.
Arc 900.202 Lanza, F. Dell'antico Palazzo di Dioclez in Spalato. Trieste, 1855.
Htn Arc 900.203* Bertoli, G. Le antichità d'Aquileja. Venice, 1739.
Arc 900.204 Jabornegg-Altenfels. Kärnten's römischen Alterthümer. Klagenfurt, 1870.
Arc 900.205 Austria. K.K. Central Commission. Kunst historischer Atlas. Wien. 1-10,1889-1894 2v.
Arc 900.206 Ballif, P. Römische Strasen in Bosnien. Wien, 1893.
Arc 900.207 Lepkowski, J. Monumenta epigraphica Cracoviensia. Krakow, 1883.
Arc 900.208 Jenny, S. Die römische Begräbnisstätte von Bugant. Wien, 1898.
Arc 900.209 Vienna. Akademie. Der römische Limes in Österreich. Wien, 1900- 20v.
Arc 900.210 Bericht des Vereins Carnuntum. Wien. 1887-1911 11v.
Arc 900.211F Hueber, P. Austria exarchivis mellicensilus. Lipsiae, 1722.
Arc 900.212 Premerstein, A. Römischen Strassen und Befestigungen in Krain. Wien, 1899.
Arc 900.213 Klose, O. Die römischen Meilensteine in Salzberg. Wien, 1902.
Arc 900.214 Sacken, E. von. Das Grabfeld von Hallstatt. Wien, 1868.
Arc 900.215F Pič, Josef L. Archaeologický víyzhum. pt.1-3. Praha, 1893-97.
Arc 900.215.5 Pič, Josef L. Le Hradischt de Stradonitz en Bohême. Leipzig, 1906.

Arc 902 Archaeology - Local - Austria and Hungary - Pamphlet volumes

Arc 902.01 Pamphlet box. Archaeology. Austrian Empire.
Arc 902.05F Pamphlet box. Archaeology. Austrian Empire.

Arc 903 Archaeology - Local - Austria and Hungary - General works

Arc 903.1 Undset, F. Etudes sur l'age de bronze...Hongrie. Christiana, 1880.
Arc 903.4 Franz, Leonhard. Lexikon ur- und frühgeschichtlicher Fundstätten Österreichs. Wien, 1965.
Arc 903.5 Schreiber, Georg. Den Funden nach zu Schliessen. Wien, 1960.
Arc 903.5.1 Schreiber, Georg. Den Funden nach zu schliessen. 2. Aufl. Wien, 1965.

Arc 905 Archaeology - Local - Austria and Hungary - Local; Special topics

Arc 905.1 Munro, Robert. Rambles and studies in Bosnia. Edinburgh, 1895.
Arc 905.1.5 Munro, Robert. Rambles and studies in Bosnia-Herzegovina and Dalmatia, with an account of the proceedings of the congress of archaeologists and anthropologists. 2. ed. Edinburgh, 1900.
Arc 905.2 Knabl, R. Wo stand das "Flavium Solvense?" n.p., n.d.
Arc 905.3 Stancovick, P. Dello anfiteatro di Pola. Venice, 1822.
Arc 905.4 Carrara, F. Topografia e scavi di Salona. Trieste, 1850.
Arc 905.4.5 Carrara, F. Di scavi di Salona nel 1850. Memoria. Praga, 1852.
Arc 905.4.10 Bulić, Frane. Po ruševinama staroga Salina. Zagreb, 1900.
Arc 905.4.15 Jelić, Luka. Raccolta di documenti relativi ai monumenti artistici di Spalato e Salona. Spalato, 1894.
Arc 905.5 Burton, R.F. Notes on the castellieri or prehistoric ruins of the Istrian Peninsula. Trieste, n.d.
Arc 905.5.5 Trieste. Il museo civico di antichita. Trieste, 1879.
Arc 905.5.7 Gnirs, Anton. Istria praeromana. Karlsbad, 1925.
Arc 905.5.9 Degrassi, A. Abitati preistorici e romani nell'agro di Capodistria. Parenzo, 1933.
Arc 905.6 Hauser, A. Spalato und die römischen Monumente Dalmatiens. Wien, 1883.
Arc 905.7 Wosinsky, M. Das prähistorische Schanzwerk von Lengyel. Budapest, 1888.
Arc 905.8 Przyborowski, J. Wycieczki archeologizne po...Wisly. Warszawa, 1874.
Arc 905.9 Fischbach, O. Römische Lampen aus Poetovio. Graz, 1896.
Arc 905.10 Rodlow, O.W. von. Die Brennerstrasse im Alterthum und Mittelalter. Prag, 1900.
Arc 905.11 Rodlow, O.W. von. Der Verkehr...Pass von Pontelba-Pontafel...Predil. Prag, 1898.
Arc 905.12 List, G. Der Wiederauflau von Carnuntum. Wien, 1900.
Arc 905.12.5 Kubitschek, W. Führer durch Carnuntum. Wien, 1904.
Arc 905.12.9 Verein Carnuntum, Wien. Carnuntum 1885-1910. Wien, 1911.
Arc 905.12.9.5 Verein Carnuntum, Wien. Carnuntum 1885-1910. Wien, 1935.
Arc 905.12.12 Swoboda, Erich. Carnuntum. Wien, 1949.
Arc 905.12.15 Miltner, F. Das zweite Amphitheater von Carnuntum. Wien, 1939.
Arc 905.12.20 Swoboda, Erich. Carnuntum. Wien, 1953.
Arc 905.12.23 Swoboda, Erich. Carnuntum. 3. Aufl. Graz, 1958.
Arc 905.12.25 Gollob, Hedwig. Karnuntums Wiederaufbau. Wien, 1956.
Arc 905.12.26 Gollob, Helwig. Gäbber in Karnuntum. Wien, 1957.
Arc 905.12.35 Obermayr, August. Römerstadt Carnuntum. Wien, 1967.
Arc 905.13 Rosenegger, J. Tabellarisische Ubersicht der Alterthumer in Roseneggers Garten. Salzburg, 1824.
Arc 905.14 Historischer Verein für Innerösterreich. Schriften. Graz, 1848.
Arc 905.15 Wocel, J.E. Grundzüge der böhmischen Alterthumskunde. Prag, 1845.
Arc 905.15.5 Menghin, Oswald. Einführung in der Urgeschichte Böhmens und Mährens. Reichenberg, 1926.
Arc 905.15.9 Gnirs, Anton. Die römischen Schutzbezirke an der Oberen Donau. Augsburg, 1929.
Arc 905.17 Meyer. Die Römerstadt Agunt. Berlin, 1908.
Arc 905.17.5 Swoboda, Erich. Führer durch Aguntum. Baden, 1935.
Arc 905.17.10F Alzinger, Wilhelm. Kleinfunde von Aguntum aus den Jahren 1850 bis 1952. Wien, 1955.
Arc 905.17.12 Alzinger, Wilhelm. Aguntum. Wien, 1958.
Arc 905.18 Aigner, A. Hallstatt. München, n.d.
Arc 905.18.5 Mahr, Adolf. Das vorgeschichtliche Hallstatt. Wien, 1925.
Arc 905.18.10 Morton, F. Hallstatt. Hallstatt, 1953. 2v.
Arc 905.19 Patsch, Carl. Bosnien und Herzegowina in Römischer Zeit. Sarajevo, 1911.
Arc 905.20 Österreichisches Archäologisches Institut. Führer durch das K.K. Staatsmuseum in S. Donato in Zara. Wien, 1912.
Arc 905.21 Kalina, M. Böhmens...Opferplätz, Gräber und Alterthümer. Prag, 1836.

Arc 905 Archaeology - Local - Austria and Hungary - Local; Special topics - cont.

Arc 905.22 Müllner, Alfons. Emona; archaeologischen Studien aus Krain. Laibach, 1879.
Arc 905.23F Tappeiner, Franz. Zum Schluss der Majafrage. Muan, 1897.
Arc 905.24 Schlechter, Max. Beiträge zur alten Geschichte des Obergailthales in Kärnten. Wien, 1885.
Arc 905.24.5 Egger, Rudolf. Teurnia; die römischen und frühchristlichen Altertümer Oberkärntens. Wien, 1924.
Arc 905.24.6 Egger, Rudolf. Teurnia. 2. Aufl. Wien, 1926.
Arc 905.24.13 Egger, Rudolf. Führer druch die Ausgrabungen und das Museum auf dem Magdalensberg. 3. Aufl. Klagenfurt, 1956.
Arc 905.24.14 Egger, Rudolf. Teurnia. 4. Aufl. Klagenfurt, 1955.
Arc 905.24.15 Egger, Rudolf. Führer durch die Ausgrabungen und das Museum auf dem Magdalensberg. 5. Aufl. Klagenfurt, 1958.
Arc 905.24.20 Obermayr, August. Kelten und Römer am Magdalensberg. Wien, 1971.
Arc 905.24.25 Leber, Paul Siegfried. Aus Kärntens römischer Vergangenheit. v.1-5. Wolfsberg, 1971-
Arc 905.25 Schmid, Walter. Flavia Solva. 2. Aufl. Graz, 1917.
Arc 905.26 Hampel, J. Der Goldfund von Nagy-Szent-Miklos. Budapest, 1885.
Arc 905.27F Kubinyi, August von. Szekszár der Alterthümer. Pest, 1857.
Arc 905.29F Archaeologia Hungarica. Budapest. 1,1926+ 25v.
Arc 905.29.5 Fitz, Jeno. Les Syriens à Intercisa. Bruxelles, 1972.
Arc 905.30 Dissertationes Pannonicae. Ser. 1. Budapest. 1-14,1932-1944 12v.
Arc 905.30F Dissertationes Pannonicae. Ser. 2. Budapest. 1-23
Arc 905.31 Hampel, J. Alterthümer des frühen Mittelalters in Ungarn. Braunschweig, 1905. 3v.
Arc 905.35 Brusin, G. Gli scavi di Aquileia. Udine, 1934.
Arc 905.37 Wankel, Jindřich. Die prähistorische Jagd in Mähren. Olmütz, 1892.
Arc 905.40 Kuzsinszky, V. Aquincum; Ausgrabungen und Funde. Budapest, 1934.
Arc 905.41 Hampel, J. A Bronzkor emlékei magyarhonban. Budapest, 1886. 3v.
Arc 905.42 Hampel, J. Ujabb tanulmányok a honfoglalasi kor emlékeiral. Budapest, 1907.
Arc 905.50 Gaheis, Alexander. Lauriacum; Führer durch die Altertümer von Enns. Linz, 1937.
Arc 905.55 Forschungen in Lauriacum. Linz. 1,1953+ 7v.
Arc 905.60 Banner, János. Népvándorlás koté sérok Nagykamaráson. Szeged, 1927.
Arc 905.65 Beninger, E. Die Wasserburg Neydharting. Linz, 1959.
Arc 905.70 Mozsolics, Anália. Der Goldfund von Velem-Szentvid. Basel, 1950.
Arc 905.75 Jandaurek, H. Die Strassen der Römer. Wels, 1951.
Arc 905.76 Neumann, Alfred. Vindobona. Die römische Vergangenheit Wiens. Wien, 1972.
Arc 905.78 Kreuz, Trans. Rätsel um Carnuntum. Wien, 1939.
Arc 905.80 Neumann, Alfred. Die römischen Ruinen unter dem Hohen Markt. Wien, 1950.
Arc 905.80.3 Neumann, Alfred. Die römischen Ruinen unter dem Hohen Markt. 2. Aufl. Wien, 1957.
Arc 905.80.5 Neumann, Alfred. Ausgrabungen und Funde. v.1-3. Wien, 1951.
Arc 905.85 Csallány, Dezsö. Archäologische Denkmäler der Awarenzeit in Mitteleuropa. Budapest, 1956.
Arc 905.86 Tot, Tibor A. Antropologicheskie dannye k voprosu o velikom peseselenii narodov. Leningrad, 1970.
Arc 905.90 Folteny, Stephan. Zur Cronologie der Bronzezeit des Karpatenbeckens. Bonn, 1955.
Arc 905.90.5 Haensel, Bernhard. Beiträge zur Chronologie der Mittleren Bronzezeit im Karpatenbecken. Bonn, 1968. 2v.
Arc 905.95F Szilágyi, János. Aquencum. Budapest, 1956.
Arc 905.98 Sausgruber, L. Sammlung der bisher erschienenen Aufsätze. Feldhirch, 1918.
Arc 905.100F Thomas, Baja. Archäologische Funde in Ungarn. Budapest, 1956.
Arc 905.105 Pittioni, Richard. Der frühmittelalterliche Gräberfund von Köttloch. Brun, 1943.
Arc 905.110 László, Gyula. A honfoglaló magyar nép élete. 2. biadás. Budapest, 1944.
Arc 905.115F Töräh, Gyula. Die Bewohner vor Halimbacseres noch. Leipzig, 1959.
Arc 905.120 Meysels, T.F. Auf Römerstrassen durch Osterreich von Aguntum nach Carnuntum. Wien, 1960.
Arc 905.120.5 Miltner, Franz. Lavant und Aguntum. Lienz, 1951.
Arc 905.125 Kratzschmer, F. Die Entwicklungsgeschichte des antiken Bades und das Bad auf dem Maydalensberg. Düsseldorf, 1961.
Arc 905.126 Kromer, Karl. Von frühen Eisen und reichen Salzherren die Hallstattkultur in Osterreich. Wien, 1964.
Arc 905.126.1 Rieth, Adolf. Die Eisentechnik der Hallstattzeit. Photoreproduction. Leipzig, 1942.
Arc 905.128 Mozsolics, Anália. Bronzefunde des Karpatenbeckens. Budapest, 1967.
Arc 905.130 Gábori-Csánk, V. La station du paléolithique moyen d'Erd-Hongrie. Budapest, 1968.
Arc 905.132 Denk, Stefan. Das Erlaufgebiet im ur- und frühgeschichtlicher Zeit. Wien, 1962.
Arc 905.134 Bamberger, Anton. Tergolape. Linz, 1966.
Arc 905.136 Menghin, Osmund. Beiträge zur Urgeschichte Tirols. Innsbruck, 1969.
Arc 905.138 Merhart, Gero von. Hallstatt und Italien. Bonn, 1969.
Arc 905.140 Fehér, Géza. A Közép-Duna-medence magyar honfoglalás. Budapest, 1962.
Arc 905.142 Gabori, Miklos. Akésöi paleolitikum Magyarországon. Budapest, 1964.
Arc 905.144 Gyor története a tizenharmadik század közepéig. Györ, 1942.
Arc 905.145 Lippert, Andreas. Das Gräberfeld von Welzelach. Bonn, 1972.
Arc 905.146 Burgstaller, Ernst. Felsbilder in Österreich. Linz, 1972.
Arc 905.147 Lichardus, Ján. Studien zur Bükker Kultur. Bonn, 1974.
Arc 905.148 Die Römer an der Donau. Wien, 1973.

Arc 910 Archaeology - Local - Switzerland - Folios [Discontinued]

Arc 910.1 Zeller-Werdmüller, H. Denkmäler aus der Feudalzeit im Lande Uri. Zürich, 1884.
Arc 910.4 Gross, V. Les protohelvètes. Paris, 1883.
Arc 910.8F Loeschcke, Siegfried. Lampen aus Vindonissa. Zürich, 1919.
Arc 910.9F Bonstetten, W. Carte archeologique du canton de Fribourg. Genève, 1878.
Arc 910.10F Messikommer, H. Die Pfahlbauten von Robenhausen. Zürich, 1913.

Arc 913 Archaeology - Local - Switzerland - General works

Arc 913.5 Keller, F. Lake dwellings of Switzerland and other parts of Europe. London, 1878. 2v.
Arc 913.5.5 Keller, F. Beilage zur archäologischen Karte den Ostschweiz. 2. Aufl. Frauenfeld, 1873.
Arc 913.7 Staub, Johannes. Die Pfahlbauten in den Schweizerseen bei Fluntern. Zürich, 1864.
Arc 913.8 Bandi, Hans. Die Schweiz zur Rentierzeit. Frauenfeld, 1947.
Arc 913.15 Viollier, David. Les sépultures du second âge. Thèse. Genève, 1916.
Arc 913.16 Viollier, David. Essai sur les rites funéraires en Suisse des origines à la conquête romaine. Paris, 1911.
Arc 913.17 Tschumi, O. Urgeschichte der Schweiz. Frauenfeld, 1926.
Arc 913.17.10 Tschumi, O. Urgeschichte der Schweiz. Frauenfeld, 1949-
Arc 913.18 Degen, Rudolf. Helvetia antiqua. Uitikon, 1966.
Arc 913.19 Heierli, J. Urgeschichte der Schweiz. Zürich, 1901.
Arc 913.21 Franz, L. Vorgeschichtliches Leben in den Alpen. Wien, 1929.
Arc 913.23 Tschumi, O. Einführung in die Vorgeschichte der Schweiz. 2. Aufl. Bern, 1918.
Arc 913.25 Moosbrugger, Leu Rudolf. Die Schweiz zur Merowingerzeit. Bern, 1971. 2v.

Arc 915 Archaeology - Local - Switzerland - Local; Special topics

Arc 915.1 Thioly, F. Epoques antéhistoriques an Mont Salève. Genève, 1867.
Arc 915.2 Schnarrenberger. Die Pfahlbauten des Bodensees. Konstanz, 1891.
Arc 915.3 Naef, A. Le cimetiere Gallo-Helvète de Vevey. n.p., 1903.
Arc 915.4 Frey, F. Führer durch die Ruinen vor Augusta Raurica. Liestal, 1907.
Arc 915.4.5 Jacob-Kolb, G. Recherches historiques sur les antiquités d'Augst. Rheims, 1823.
Arc 915.4.10 Laur-Belart, Rudolf. Führer durch Augusta Raurica. Basel, 1937.
Arc 915.4.11 Laur-Belart, Rudolf. Führer durch Augusta Raurica. 2. Aufl. Basel, 1948.
Arc 915.4.14 Laur-Belart, Rudolf. Führer durch Augusta Raurica. 4. Aufl. Basel, 1966.
Arc 915.4.20 Provincialia; Festschrift für Rudolf Laur-Belart. Basel, 1968.
Arc 915.5 Mayor, J. Fragments d'archeologie genevoise. Genève, 1892.
Htn Arc 915.6* Schmidt, F.S. Recueil d'antiquités trouvées à Avenches...de la Suisse. Berne, 1760.
Arc 915.6.2 Schmidt, F.S. Recueil d'antiquités de la Suisse. Francfort sur le Meyn, 1771.
Arc 915.7 Dunant, Émile. Guide illustrative du Musée d'Avenches. Genève, 1900.
Arc 915.8 Secretan, Eugène. Aventicum. Lausanne, 1905.
Arc 915.8.5 Secretan, Eugène. Aventicum. Lausanne, 1896.
Arc 915.9 Viollier, David. Carte archéologique du Canton de Vaud des origines à l'époque de Charlemagne. Lausanne, 1927.
Arc 915.10 Morel, C. Genève et la colonie de Vienne sous les Romains. pt.1. Genève, 1879? 2 pam.
Arc 915.11F Vogt, Emil. Der Lindenhof in Zürich. Zürich, 1948.
Arc 915.15 Guyan, Walter Ulrich. Das Grabhügelfeld im Sankert bei Hemishofen. Basel, 1951.
Arc 915.20 Forrer, Robert. Die helvetishen und helvetarömischen Votivbeilchen der Schweiz. Basel, 1948.
Arc 915.25 Stehlin, Karl. Die spätrömischen Wachthürme am Rhein von Basel bis zum Bodensee. Basel, 1957.
Arc 915.30 Spahni, Jean Christian. Les megálithes de la Suisse. Basel, 1950.
Arc 915.32 Laur-Belart, Rudolf. Uber die Colonia Raurica und den Ursprung von Basel. 2. Aufl. Basel, 1959.
Arc 915.34 Fellmann, Rudolf. Die Principia des Legionslageos Vindonissa und das Zentralgeläude der römischen Lager und Kastelle. Brugg, 1958.
Arc 915.35 Berger, L. Die Ausgrabungen am Petersberg in Basel. Basel, 1963.
Arc 915.36 Bocksberger, Olivier Jean. Age du Bronze en Valais et dans le chablais vaudois. Lausanne, 1964.
Arc 915.37 Traininas, Davidas. Beiträge zur Kenntnis der Haustiere der romischkeltischen Ansiedlung auf der Engehalbinsel bei Bern. Bern, 1933.
Arc 915.40.3 International Congress of Roman Frontier Studies, 3d, Rheinfelden, Switzerland. Limes-Studien; Vorträge des 3. Internationalen Limes-Kongresses in Rheinfelden. Basel, 1957.
Arc 915.42 Wandeler, Max. LuzernStadt und Land in römischer Zeit. Luzern, 1968.
Arc 915.44 Guyan, Walter Ulrich. Das alamannische Gräberfeld von Beggingen-Löbern. Basel, 1958.
Arc 915.46 Keller-Tarnuzzer, Karl. Urgeschichte des Thurgaus. Frauenfeld, 1925.
Arc 915.48.2 Wyss, René. Die Egolzwiler Kultur. 2. Aufl. Bern, 1971.
Arc 915.48.5 Wyss, René. Wirtschaft und Gesellschaft in der Jungsteinzeit. Bern, 1973.
Arc 915.50 Lambert, André. Führer durch die römische Schweiz. Zürich, 1973.
Arc 915.51 Colloque International sur les Cols des Alpes (Antiquité et Moyen-Age), Bourg-en-Bresse, France, 1969. Actes du Colloque International sur les Cols des Alpes, Antiquité et Moyen-Age, Bourg-en-Bresse, 1969. Orléans, 1971.
Arc 915.52 Schwab, Hanni. Jungsteinzeitliche Fundstellen im Kanton Freiburg. Basel, 1971.
Arc 915.53 Fischer, Franz. Die fruhbronzezeitliche Ansiedlung in der Bleiche bei Arbon T.G. Basel, 1971.
Arc 915.54F Ettlinger, Elisabeth. Die römischen Fibeln in der Schweiz. Bern, 1973.

Arc 920 Archaeology - Local - Russia - Folios [Discontinued]

Arc 920.2 Russia. Commission Impériale Archéologique. Recueil d'antiquités de la Scythie. St. Petersbourg, 1866. 2v.
Arc 920.4 Armtiunov, Sergei A. Drevnie kul'tury aziatskikh eskimosov. Moskva, 1969.
Arc 920.7 Virchow, R. Das Gräberfeld von Koban. Text und Atlas. Berlin, 1883. 2v.
Arc 920.8 Berzhe, A. Zapiski...knigai. Tiflis, 1875.
Arc 920.9 Kieseritzky, G. von. Griechische Grabreliefs aus Südrussland. Berlin, 1909.
Arc 920.203F Kondakov, N. Antiquités de la Russie méridionale. Paris, 1891.
Arc 920.204F Pósta, Béla. Régészeti tanulmányok az Oroszföldon. v.3-4. Leipzig, 1905. 2v.

Arc 920 Archaeology - Local - Russia - Folios [Discontinued] - cont.

Arc 920.206F Bobrinskii, A. Kurgany i sluchainyia arkheologicheskiia nakhodki. Sankt Petersburg, 1887.
Arc 920.207F Tolstoi, I. Russkiia drebnosti b' pamiatnikakh iskusstva. v.1-3, 4-6. Sankt Petersburg, 1889-99. 2v.
Arc 920.208F Samokbasov, D.Ia. Opisanie arkheologicheskich raskopok. Moskva, 1908.

Arc 922 Archaeology - Local - Russia - Pamphlet volumes

Arc 922.1 Pamphlet vol. Russia - Antiquities. 6 pam.

Arc 923 Archaeology - Local - Russia - General works

Arc 923 Pamphlet box. Archaeology. Russia.
Arc 923.1 Pamphlet box. Archaeology. Russia and Slavic.
Arc 923.4 Tishchenko, Andrei V. A.V. Tishchenko. Petrograd, 1916.
Arc 923.5 Turaeb, B.A. Drevnii mir' na Iug' Rossii. Moskva, 1918.
Arc 923.7 Arkhivnye kursy. pt.1-3. Sankt Petersburg, 1920.
Arc 923.11 Tolstoi, I. Rossiiskii istoricheskii muzei. Moskva, 1893.
Arc 923.11.5F Shchukinym, P.I. Kratkoe opisanie novago vladaniia imperatopskago rossiiskago istoricheskago muzeia. Moskva, 1906.
Arc 923.13 Sbornik' arkheologicheskikh statei. Sankt Petersburg, 1911.
Arc 923.15.2 Ebert, Max. Südrussland im Altertum. Aalen, 1973.
Arc 923.20F Kondakov, N. Russkie klady. Sankt Petersburg, 1896.
Arc 923.25F Uvarob, A.S. Arkheologiia Rossii. Moskva, 1881. 2v.
Arc 923.30 Shliapkin, I.A. Russkaia paleograiuiia. Sankt Petersburg, 1913.
Arc 923.35F Golomshtok, E.A. The old stone age in European Russia. Diss. Philadelphia, 1938.
Arc 923.37 Artsikhovskii, A.V. Osnovy arkheologii. Moskva, 1954.
Arc 923.37.5 Artsikhovskii, A.V. Osnovy arkheologii. Izd. 2. Moskva, 1955.
Arc 923.40 Sbornik statei po arkheologii SSSR. Moskva, 1938. 2v.
Arc 923.45F Anuchin, D.N. K' voprosu o sostavlenii legendy dlia arkheologicheskoi karty Rossii. Moskva, 1885.
Arc 923.50 Preidel, Helmut. Slawische Altertumskunde das östlichen Mitteleuropa im 9. und 10. Jahrhundert. v.1-3. Grafeling bei München, 1961-
Arc 923.55 Miller, M.A. Arkheologiia v SSSR. Miunchen, 1954.
Arc 923.60 Miller, M.A. Archaeology in the U.S.S.R. N.Y., 1956.
Arc 923.65 Obladnikov, A.P. Uspekhi sovetskoi arkheologii. Leningrad, 1950.
Arc 923.70 Arkheologicheskii sbornik. Moskva, 1960.
Arc 923.75 Formozov, A.A. Ocherki po istorii russkoi arkheologii. Moskva, 1961.
Arc 923.75.5 Formazov, Aleksandr A. Arkheologicheskie puteshestviia. Moskva, 1974.
Arc 923.80 Akademiia Nauk SSSR. Institut Arkheologii. Arkheologicheskie ekspechtsii gosudarstvennoi akademii istorii material'noi kul'tury instituta arkheologii Akademii nauk SSSR. Moskva, 1962.
Arc 923.85 Rabinovich, M.G. Arkheologicheskie materialy v ekspozitsii kraevedcheskikh muzeev. v.2. Moskva, 1961.
Arc 923.90 Gorodtsov, V.A. Bytovaia arkheologiia. Moskva, 1910.
Arc 923.95 Russkoe arkheologicheskoe obshchestvo, Leningrad. Zapiska dlia obozreniia russkikh drevnostei. Sankt Petersburg, 1851.
Arc 923.100 Uspenskii, L.V.P. Za sem'iu pechatiami. Izd. 2. Moskva, 1962.
Arc 923.105 Ilarionov, V.T. Opyt istoriografii paleolita SSSR. Gor'kei, 1947.
Arc 923.106 Les rapports et les informations des archéologues de l'URSS. Moscou, 1962.
Arc 923.107 Vsesoiuznaia Arkheologicheskaia Studencheskaia Konferentsiia, 6th, Moscw, 1960. Sbornik dokladov na VI i VII vsesoiuznykh arkheologicheskikh studencheskikh konferentsiiakh. Moskva, 1963.
Arc 923.108 Vsesoiuznaia Arkheologicheskaia Studencheskaia Konferentsiia, 8th, Leningrad, 1962. Arkheologicheskii sbornik trudy. Leningrad, 1964.
Arc 923.109 Vsesoiuznaia Arkheologicheskaia Studencheskaia Konferentsiia, 11th, Erevan, 1965. Doklady, prochitannye na XI Vsesoiuznoi studencheskoi arkheologicheskoi konferentsii 1965 g. v Erevane. Erevan, 1968.
Arc 923.110 Iskhizov, M.D. Zagadki drevnikh Kurganov. Saratov, 1961.
Arc 923.111F Korzukhina, G.F. Russkie klady IX-XIII vv. Moskva, 1954.
Arc 923.112 International Congress of Prehistoric and Protohistoric Sciences. 7th, Moscow, 1966. Doklady i soobshchenia arkheologov SSSR. Moskva, 1966.
Arc 923.113 Beregovaia, Nina Aleksandrovna. Contributions to the archaeology of the Soviet Union. Cambridge, 1966.
Arc 923.114 Vsesoiuznaia Sessiia, Posviashchennaia Itogam Arkheologicheskikh i Etnograficheskikh Issledovanii 1966 goda. Tezisy dokladov. Kishinev, 1967.
Arc 923.115 Arkheologicheskii sbornik. Moskva, 1966.
Arc 923.116 Avdusin, Daniil A. Arkheologiia SSSR. Moskva, 1967.
Arc 923.117 Fedorov-Davydov, German A. Kurgany, idoly, monety. Moskva, 1968.
Arc 923.118 Slaviane i Rus'. Moskva, 1968.
Arc 923.120 Sulimirski, Tadeusz. Prehistoric Russia; an outline. N.Y., 1970.
Arc 923.122 Leninskie idei v izuchenii istorii pervobytnogo obshchestva, rabovladeniia i feodalizma. Moskva, 1970.
Arc 923.123.1 Arkheologicheskie issledovaniia na iuge Vostochnoi Evropy. Photoreproduction. Moskva, 1974.
Arc 923.124 Vsesoiuznaia Arkheologicheskaia Studencheskaia Konferentsiia, 9th, Moscow, 1963. Sbornik dokladov na IX i X vsesoiuznykh arkheologicheskikh studencheskikh konferentsiiakh. Moskva, 1968.
Arc 923.125 Arkheologicheskii sbornik. Photoreproduction. Moskva, 1953.
Arc 923.126 Moscow. Gosudarstvennyi Istoricheskii Muzei. Raboty arhheologicheskikh ekspeditsii. Moskva, 1941. 2v.
Arc 923.127 Avdusin, Daniil A. Polevaia arkheologiia SSSR. Moskva, 1972.
Arc 923.128 Novoe v arkheologii. Moskva, 1972.
Arc 923.129 Problemy arkheologii i drevnei istorii ugrov. Moskva, 1972.
Arc 923.130 Kirpicknikov, Anatolii N. Snariazhenie vsadnika i verkhovogo konia na Rusi IX-XIII vv. Leningrad, 1973.
Arc 923.131 Martynov, Anatolii I. Arkheologiia SSSR. Moskva, 1973.
Arc 923.132 Akademiia nauk SSSR. Institut Arkheologii. Stogi i perspektivy razvitiia sovetskoi arkheologii. Moskva, 1945.
Arc 923.133 Istoriko-arkheologicheskii sbornik. Moskva, 1962.
Arc 923.134 Leningrad. Universitet. Issledovaniia po arkheologii SSSR. Leningrad, 1961.

Classified Listing

Arc 923 Archaeology - Local - Russia - General works - cont.

Arc 923.135 Voprosy okhrany, klassifikatsii i ispol'zovaniia arkheologicheskikh pamiatnikov. Moskva, 1974.

Arc 925 Archaeology - Local - Russia - Local; Special topics

Arc 925.1 Bibliotheque des Monuments Figurés. Antiquités du Bosphore Cimmérien. Paris, 1892.
Arc 925.2 Spasskii, Grigorii I. Bostor Kimmeriiskii sego drevnostiami i dostopamiasnostiami. Moskva, 1846.
Arc 925.3 Maury, A. Des monuments de la Russie connus sous le nom de Tumulus Tchoudes. Paris, n.d.
Arc 925.4 Heikel, A. Antiquités de la Sibérie Occidentale. Helsingfors, 1894.
Arc 925.4.3F Savenkov, I.T. O drevnikh pamiatnikakh na Enisev. Moskva, 1910.
Arc 925.4.5 Merhart, Gero von. The palaeolithic period in Siberia contributions to the prehistory of the Yenisei region. n.p., 1923.
Arc 925.4.7 Khlobystina, M.D. Bronzovye nozhi minusinskogo kraia i nekotorye voprosy razvitiia karasukskoi kul'tury. Leningrad, 1962.
Arc 925.4.9 Merhard, Gero von. Bronzezeit am Janissei. Wien, 1926.
Arc 925.4.13F Jochelsen, W. Archaeological investigations in Kamchatka. Washington, 1928.
Arc 925.4.18 Tomsk, Siberia. Oblastnoi Kraevedcheskii Muzei. Nekotorye voprosy drevnei istorii Zapadnoi Sibiri. Tomsk, 1959.
Arc 925.4.20 Okladnikov, A.P. Olen' zolotye goda. Leningrad, 1964.
Arc 925.4.25 Martynov, Anatolii O. Lodki, v strany predkov. Kemerovo, 1966.
Arc 925.4.29 Martynov, Anatolii I. Shestakovskie kurgany. Kemerovo, 1971.
Arc 925.4.30 Larichev, Vitalii E. Okhotniki za mamontanii. Novosibirsk, 1968.
Arc 925.4.35 Drevnie pis'mena khakarii. Abakan, 1970.
Arc 925.4.40 Soveshchanie po Problemam Khronologii i Kul'turnoi Prinadlezhnosti Arkheologicheskikh Pamiatnikov Zapadnoi Sibiri. Tomsk, 1970. Problemy khronologii i kul'turnoi prinadlezhnosti arkheologicheskikh pamiatnikov Zapadnoi Sibiri. Tomsk, 1970.
Arc 925.4.45 Problemy arkheologii Urala i Sibiri. Moskva, 1973.
Arc 925.4.50 Rizhskii, Mikhail I. Iz glubiny vekov. Irkutsk, 1965.
Arc 925.4.55 Khamzina, Evgeniia A. Arkheologicheskie pamiatniki zapadnogo zabaikal'ia. Ulan-Ude, 1970.
Arc 925.4.60 Kosarev, Mikhail F. Drevnie kul'tury Tomsko-Narymskogo Priob'ia. Moskva, 1974.
Arc 925.5 Spasskii, Grigorii I. De antiquis quibusdam sculptures. Petropoli, 1822.
Arc 925.5.5 Spasskii, Grigorii I. Odastoporimiechatel'ineishikh pamatnikakh sibirskikh drevnatei. Sankt Petersburg, 1857.
Arc 925.5.10 Zuikov, B.B. Pod volnami Issyk-Kuha. Moskva, 1962.
Arc 925.6 Frähn, C.M.J. Über alte süd-sibirische Gräberfunde. St. Petersburg, 1837.
Arc 925.6.10 Talko-Hryncewicz, J. Suzhdenskoe doietoricheskoe kladbishche. Moskva, 1899.
Arc 925.7 Wapel, Leon de. Recueil de quelques antiquités. Berlin, 1803.
Arc 925.8 Brun. Chernomorek. Gotyieledy dolgago ikh prebyv. Sankt Petersburg, 1874. 2 pam.
Arc 925.8.15F Khersonesskii sbornik. Sevastopol. 1,1926+ 4v.
Arc 925.8.20 Knipovick, T.N. Tamaie. Moskva, 1949.
Arc 925.8.25 Marti, Iu.Iu. Problema raskopok drevnego pantikapeia. n.p., 1928?
Arc 925.8.30 Koehne, B. Beiträge zur Geschichte und Archäologie von Cherronesos in Taurien. St. Petersburg, 1850.
Arc 925.8.35 Belov, G.D. Muzei i raskopki khersonesa. Simferopol, 1936.
Arc 925.8.37 Belov, G.D. Khersones tavricheskii. Leningrad, 1948.
Arc 925.8.40 Blavatskii, Vladimir D. Iskusstvo severnoi prichernomoriia. Moskva, 1946.
Arc 925.8.45 Zhebelev, S.A. Severnoe prichernomor. Moskva, 1953.
Arc 925.8.50 Blavatskii, Vladimir D. Pantikapei; Ocherki istorii stolitsy Bospora. Moskva, 1964.
Arc 925.9 Mourier, J. L'archéologie au Caucase. Paris, 1887.
Arc 925.9.5 Vyrubov, V. Predmety drevnosti. Tiflis, 1877.
Arc 925.9.7 Vladimirova, N. Drevnosti chernomorskia poberezh'ia kavkaza. Sankt Petersburg, 1900.
Arc 925.9.9 Viviendekt-Martin, Louis. Recherches sur les populations primitives. Paris, 1847.
Arc 925.9.10 Bapst, Y. Souvenirs de deux missions an Caucase. Paris, 1886.
Arc 925.9.12 Hančar, Franz. Urgeschichte Kaukasuns. Wien, 1937.
Arc 925.9.15 Krupnov, E.T. Drevniaia istoriia Severnogo Kavkaza. Moskva, 1960.
Arc 925.9.25 Akademiia nauk SSSR. Institut Arkheologii. Drevnosti checheno-ingushetii. Moskva, 1963.
Arc 925.9.30 Semenov, L.P. Arkheologicheskie i etnograficheskie razyskaniia v Ingushetii v 1925-32 gg. Groznyi, 1963.
Arc 925.9.35 Tekhov, Bagrat V. K istorii izucheniia pamiatnikov epokhi eneolita i bronzy v nizhnem. Tbilisi, 1963.
Arc 925.9.40 Pachulia, Vianor P. V kraiu zolotogo runa. Moskva, 1964.
Arc 925.9.41 Pachulia, Vianor P. V kraiu zolotogo runa. Izd. 2. Moskva, 1968.
Arc 925.9.45 Karakashly, K.T. Material'naia kul'tura azerbaidzhantsev severo-vostochnoi i Tsentral'noi zon Malogo Kavkaza. Balzu, 1964.
Arc 925.9.50 Markovin, Vladimir I. V ushchel'iakh Arguna i Fortangi. Moskva, 1965.
Arc 925.9.52 Markovin, Vladimir I. V strane vainakhor. Moskva, 1969.
Arc 925.9.55 Lavrov, L.I. Epigraficheskie pamiatniki severnogo Kavkaza. Moskva, 1966- 2v.
Arc 925.9.60 Iessen, Aleksandr A. Mozdokskii mogil'nik. Leningrad, 1940.
Arc 925.9.65 Materia'ly no arkheologii abkhazii. Tbilisi, 1970.
Arc 925.9.70 Kushmareva, Karinek. Drevnie kultury Izhnogo Kavkaza. Leningrad, 1970.
Arc 925.9.75 Kakhetskaia arkheologicheskaia ekspeditniia, 1965. Trudy. Tbilisi, 1969.
Arc 925.9.80 Shamba, G.K. Akhachcharkhu-drevnii mogil'nik nagornoi Abkhazii. Sukhumi, 1970.
Arc 925.9.90 Virchow, Rudolf. Über die culturgeschtliche Stellung des Kaukasus. Berlin, 1895.
Arc 925.9.95PF Dorn, Boris A. Atlas k puteshestviiu po Kavkazu i iuzknomu poberezh'iu kaspiskago moria. Sankt Petersburg, 1895. 2v.
Arc 925.9.100 Vinogradov, Vitalii B. Cherez khrebty vekov. Grozny, 1970.
Arc 925.9.105 Chubinishvili, Taniel. K drevnei istorii Iuzhnogo Kavkaza. Tbilisi, 1971.

Arc 925 Archaeology - Local - Russia - Local; Special topics - cont.

Arc 925.9.110 Turchaninov, Georgii F. Pamiatniki pis'nu i iazyka narodov Kavkaza i vostochnoi Evropy. Leningrad, 1971.
Arc 925.9.115 Lordkipanidze, Guram A. K istorii drevnei Kolkhidy. Tbilisi, 1970.
Arc 925.9.120 Krupnov, Evgenii I. Srednovekoraia Ingushetiia. Moskva, 1971.
Arc 925.9.125 Tekhov, Bagrat V. Ocherki drevnei istorii i arkheologii Iugo-Osetri. Tbilisi, 1971.
Arc 925.9.130 Vinogradov, Vitalii B. Tsentral'nyi i severo-vostochnyi Kavkaz v skitskoe vremia. Groznyi, 1972.
Arc 925.9.135 Kuznetsov, Vladimir A. Alaniia v X-XIII vv. Ordzhonikidze, 1971.
Arc 925.9.140 Kashkai, Mir-Ali. Iz istorii drevnei metallurgii Kavkaza. Baku, 1973.
Arc 925.9.145 Dzhavakhishvili, Aleksandr I. Stroitel'noe delo i arkhitektura poselenii Iuzhnogo Kavkaza. Tbilisi, 1973.
Arc 925.9.151 Solov'ev, L.N. Pervobytnoe obshchestvo na territorii Abkhazii. Photoreproduction. Sukhumi, 1971.
Arc 925.10 Krupnov, Evgenii I. Kratkii ocherk arkheologii kabardinskoi ASSR. Nal'chik, 1946.
Arc 925.10.5 Miziev, Ismail M. Srednevekovye bashni i sklepy Balkarii i Karachaia (XIII-XVIII vv). Nal'chik, 1970.
Arc 925.11 Shchtern, E. von. K voproscho proiskhozhdenii gotskago stilia. Odessa, 1897.
Arc 925.12 Minns, E.H. Scythians and Greeks...ancient history and archaeology. Cambridge, 1913.
Arc 925.12.3 Minns, E.H. The art of the northern nomads. London, 1942.
Arc 925.12.5 Ashik, Anton. Vosporskoe tsarstvo. Odessa, 1848.
Arc 925.12.6 Shevchenko, V. Sokrovishcha ischeznuvshikh gorodov. Moskva, 1948.
Arc 925.12.7 Gaidukevich, V.F. Bosporskoe tsarstvo. Moskva, 1949.
Arc 925.12.7.2 Gaidukevich, V.F. Das bosporanische Reich. 2. Aufl. Berlin, 1971.
Arc 925.12.10 Gerts, K.K. Arkheologicheskaia tipografiia tapanskago poluostrova. pts. 1-9. Sankt Peterburg, 1898-1901. 8v.
Arc 925.12.15 Ivanova, A.P. Skul'ptura i zhivopis' Bospora. Kiev, 1961.
Arc 925.12.20F Minns, Ellis Hovell. Scythians and Greeks. N.Y., 1971.
Arc 925.13 Rostovtsev, M.I. Ellinstvo i iranstvo na iuge Rossii. Petrograd, 1918.
Arc 925.13.5 Rostovtsev, M.I. Iranians and Greeks in south Russia. Oxford, 1922.
Arc 925.13.6 Blavatskii, V.D. Iskusstvo severnogo Prichernomor'ia. Moskva, 1947.
Arc 925.13.7 Vaksel, H.C.L. Izobrazheniia raznykh' pamiashchnikov drevnosti. Sankt Petersburg, 1801.
Arc 925.13.8 Rudenko, S.I. Iskusstvo. Moskva, 1949.
Arc 925.13.8.10 Rudenko, S.I. Gornoaltaiskie nachadki iskify. Moskva, 1952.
Arc 925.13.10 Rostovtsev, M.I. Skifiia i Bospor". Leningrad, 1925.
Arc 925.13.12 Rostovtsev, M.I. Skythien und der Bosporus. Berlin, 1931.
Arc 925.13.15 Latyshev, V.V. Pontika...skifiia, Kavkaz. Sankt Petersburg, 1909.
Arc 925.13.25 Toll', N.R. Skify i gunny. Praga, 1928.
Arc 925.13.50 Borovka, Grigorii I. Scythian art. London, 1927.
Arc 925.13.52 Borovka, Grigorii I. Scythian art. London, 1928.
Arc 925.13.55 Rostovtsev, M.I. The animal style in south Russia and China. Princeton, 1929.
Arc 925.13.60 Seminar Kondakovianum, Prague. Ekufika. Praha. 1-4,1929-1931 2v.
Arc 925.13.65 Domanovszky, G. Steppenvölker und Germanen. Budapest, 1939.
Arc 925.13.70 Blavatskaia, T.V. Zapadnopontiiskie gopoda. Moskva, 1952.
Arc 925.13.75 Iatsenko, I.V. Skifiia VII-V vekov do nashei ery. Moskva, 1959.
Arc 925.13.80 Blavatskii, V.D. Antichnaia arkheologiia Severnogo Prichernomor'ia. Moskva, 1961.
Arc 925.13.85 Viaz'mitina, M.I. Zalsta balka. Kyiv, 1962.
Arc 925.13.90 Materialy po arkheologii Severnago Prichernomor'ia. Odessa. 2,1959
Arc 925.13.95 Trapsh, M.M. Pamiatniki kolkhidskoi i skifskoi kul'tur v sele kulanurkhva abkhazskoi ASSR. Sukhumi, 1962.
Arc 925.13.100F Ozols, Jekabs. Ursprung und Herkunft der zentralrussischen Fatjanowo Kultur. Berlin, 1962.
Arc 925.13.105 Boriskovskii, P.I. Pamiatniki drevneishei chelovesheskoi kul'tury Severo-Zapadnogo Prichernomor'ia. Odessa, 1961.
Arc 925.13.110 Smirnov, K.F. Savromaty. Moskva, 1964.
Arc 925.13.115 Semenov-Zuser, Semen A. Opyt istoriografii skifov. Khar'kov, 1947.
Arc 925.13.120 Smirnov, Aleksei P. Skify. Moskva, 1966.
Arc 925.13.125 Lapin, Vladimir V. Grecheskaia kolonizatsiia Severnogo Prichernomor'ia. Kiev, 1966.
Arc 925.13.130 Brashinskii, I. Sokrovishcha skifskikh tsarei. Moskva, 1967.
Arc 925.13.140 Il'inskaia, Vervara A. Skify dneprovskogo lesostepnogo Levoberezh'ia. Kiev, 1968.
Arc 925.13.145 Shtambok, Anatoii A. Iz tsarstva Ateia v Neapol' Skifskii. Moskva, 1968.
Arc 925.13.150 Antichnaia istoriia i kul'tura Sredizemnomor'ia i Prichernomor'ia. Leningrad, 1968.
Arc 925.13.155 Chernenko, Evgenii V. Skifskii dospekh. Kiev, 1968.
Arc 925.13.160 Petrov, Viktor P. Skifi. Kyiv, 1968.
Arc 925.13.165 Tsvetaeva, Galina A. Sokrovishcha prichernomorskikh kurganov. Moskva, 1968.
Arc 925.13.170 Sulimirski, Tadeusz. The Sarmatians. London, 1970.
Arc 925.13.175 Grakov, Boris N. Skify. Moskva, 1971.
Arc 925.13.180 Khazanov, Anatolii M. Ocherki noennogo dela sarmatov. Moskva, 1971.
Arc 925.13.186 Bakay, Kornél. Scythian rattles in the Carpathian Basin and their eastern connections. Amsterdam, 1971.
Arc 925.13.190 Terrakotovye statuetki. v.3- Moskva, 1974- 2v.
Arc 925.13.195 Skifskie drevnosti. Kiev, 1973.
Arc 925.13.200 Moshkova, Marina G. Proiskhazhdenie rannesarmatskoi (prokhorovskoi) kul'tury. Moskva, 1974.
Arc 925.13.205 Drachuk, Viktor S. Sistemy znakov Severnogo Prichernomoria. Kiev, 1975.
Arc 925.14F Materialy po arkheologii Kavkaza. Moskva. 1-13,1888-1916 5v.
Arc 925.15F Moskovskoe Arkheologicheskoe Obshchestvo. Materialy po...Rossii. Moskva, 1893- 2v.
Arc 925.16 Moskovskoe Arkheologicheskoe Obshchestvo. Izviestiia Kavkazskago otdieleniia. Vyp. 6 (1921). Tifilis, n.d.
Arc 925.16.5 Tavadze, F. Bronzy drevnei Gruzii. Tbilisi, 1959.
Arc 925.16.10 Rubinshtein, N.L. Arkheologicheskii sbornik. Moskva, 1947.
Arc 925.16.15 Margulan, A.K. Iz istorii gorodov i stroitel'nogo isskustva drevnego Kazakhstana. Alma-Ata, 1950.

Arc 925 Archaeology - Local - Russia - Local; Special topics - cont.

Arc 925.16.17	Margulan, A.K. Drevniaia kul'tura Tsentral'nogo Kazakhstana. Alma-Ata, 1966.
Arc 925.16.20	Chernikov, Sergei. Zagadka zolotogo kurgana. Moskva, 1965.
Arc 925.16.25	Sher, Iakov A. Kamennye iz vaianiia Semirech'ia. Leningrad, 1966.
Arc 925.16.30	Novoe v arkheologii Kazakhstana. Alma-Ata, 1968.
Arc 925.16.35	Drevnosti chandary. Alma-Ata, 1968.
Arc 925.16.40	Kul'tura drevnikh skotovodov i zemledel'tsev Kazakhstana. Alma-Ata, 1969.
Arc 925.16.45	Po sledam drevnikh kul'tur Kazakhstana. Alma-Ata, 1970.
Arc 925.16.50	Musabaev, Gainetdin G. Epigrafika Kazakhstana. Alma-Ata, 1971.
Arc 925.16.55	Poiski i raskopki v Kazakhstane. Alma-Ata, 1972.
Arc 925.16.60	Akishev, Kemal' A. Drevnii Otrar. Alma-Ata, 1972.
Arc 925.16.65	Senigova, Taisiia N. Srednevekovyi taraz. Alma-Ata, 1972.
Arc 925.16.70	V glub' vekov. Alma-Ata, 1974.
Arc 925.17	Veselovskii, N.I. Pervobytnyia drevnosti. Tuapse, 1904.
Arc 925.18F	Prokhorov, V. Materialy po istorii russkikh odezhd. Sankt Petersburg, 1881-85. 3v.
Arc 925.19F	Bulychov, N. Kourgans et Gorodietz. Moskva, 1900. 3 pam.
Arc 925.20	Knipovich, Tatiana N. Tanais. Moskva, 1949.
Arc 925.20.5	Shelov, Dmitrii B. Tanais, poteriannyi i naidennyi gorod. Moskva, 1967.
Arc 925.20.10	Shelov, Dmitrii B. Tanais i Nizhnii Don v III-I vv. do n.e. Moskva, 1970.
Arc 925.20.15	Shelov, Dmitrii B. Tanais i Nizhnyi Don v peroye veka nashei erg. Moskva, 1972.
Arc 925.21	Ballod, F.V. Privolzhskie Pompei. Moskva, 1923.
Arc 925.23	Kallistov, D.P. Sev. Prichernomor'e v antich. epolu. Moskva, 1952.
Arc 925.25	Spitsyn, A. Arkheologicheskii razvedki. St. Peterburg, 1908.
Arc 925.27F	Samokvasov, D. Sbornik topograffiia sved. o kurgana. St. Peterburg, 1888.
Arc 925.30	Prozorovskii, D.I. Opisanie smolenskago klada. St. Peterburg, 1870.
Arc 925.35	Matsulevich, L.A. Pogrebenie varvarskogo kniazia v vostochnoi Evrope. Moskva, 1934.
Arc 925.35.5F	Samoksavov, D.I. Atlas gochevskikh drevnostei. Moskva, 1915.
Arc 925.37	Blavatskaia, T.V. Ocherki politicheskii istorii Vospora v V-IV vv. do n.e. Moskva, 1959.
Arc 925.38	Griaznov, M.P. Pazyrykskii kurgan. Moskva, 1937.
Arc 925.38.5	Griaznov, M.P. Pervyi pazyrykskii kurgan. Leningrad, 1950.
Arc 925.38.10	Leningrad. Ermitazh. Drevnee iskusstov Altaia. Leningrad, 1958.
Arc 925.38.15	Rudenko, Sergei Ivanovich. Kul'tura naseleniia Gornogo Altaia v skifskoe vremiia. Moskva, 1953.
Arc 925.38.16	Rudenko, Sergei Ivanovich. Frozen tombs of Siberia. 1. English ed. Berkeley, 1970.
Arc 925.38.20	Gavrilova, Antonina. Mogil'nik kudyrge kak istochnik po istorii altaiskikh plemen. Leningrad, 1965.
Arc 925.39	Savvateev, Iurii A. Risunki na skalakh. Petrozavodsk, 1967.
Arc 925.40	Linevskii, A.M. Petroglify Karelii. Petrozavodsk, 1939.
Arc 925.41	Pomiatniki epokhi bronzy inga Evropeiskoi chasti SSSR. Kiev, 1967.
Arc 925.45F	McPherson, Duncan. Antiquities of Kertch. London, 1857.
Arc 925.50	Rudins'kyi, M. Materialy...stantsiia. Bila Hira pid Poltavoiu. Kyïv, 1926.
Arc 925.50.01	Pamphlet vol. Archaeology. Russia. Ukraine. 4 pam.
Arc 925.50.1	Shovkoplias, Ivan H. Rozvitok radians'koi arkheolohii na Ukraini. Kyiv, 1969.
Arc 925.50.3	Arkheolochichni pam"iatky Ukrains'koi RSR. Kyïv, 1966.
Arc 925.50.5	Ratych, O.O. Drevnorus'ki arkheologii pam'iatky na teryt. Kyïv, 1957.
Arc 925.50.10	Sorokina, N.P. Tuzlinskii nekropol'. Moskva, 1957.
Arc 925.50.15	Piatysheva, Natalia V. Iuvelirnye izdeliia Khersonesa. Moskva, 1956.
Arc 925.50.18	Piatysheva, Natalia V. Zheleznaia maska iz Khersonesa. Moskva, 1964.
Arc 925.50.20	Sebastopol'. Khersoneskii Gosudarstvennyi Istoriko-Arkheologicheskii Muzei. Soobshcheniia. v.1-3. Simferopol', n.d. 2v.
Arc 925.50.25	Shovkoplias, Ivan H. Arkheolohichni doslidzheniia na Ukraini 1917-1957. Kyïv, 1957.
Arc 925.50.27	Shovkoplias, Ivan H. Mezinskaia stoianka. Kiev, 1965.
Arc 925.50.30	Akademiia Nauk URSR, Kiev. Kryms'kyi Filologicheskii. Istoriia i arkheologiia drev. Kryma. Kiev, 1957.
Arc 925.50.33	Shchepinskii, Askold A. Severnoe prisivash'e v V-I tysiacheleliiakh do nashei ery. Simferopol', 1969.
Arc 925.50.35	Smirnov, A.P. Istoriia ii arkheologiia srednevek. Kryma. Moskva, 1958.
Arc 925.50.40	Belov, G.D. Khersones Tavricheskii. Simferopol', 1958.
Arc 925.50.42	Sebastopol. Khersoneskii Gosudarstvennyi Istoriko-Arkheologicheskii Muzei. Khersones Tavricheskii. Simferopol', 1962.
Arc 925.50.45	Miller, Mykhailo O. Don i Priazov'e u drevnosti. v.1,3. Moskva, 1958- 2v.
Arc 925.50.47	Rostov on the Don (Province). Muzei Kraevedeniia. Arkheologicheskie raskopki na Donu. v.2, photoreproduction. Rostov na Donu, 1962- 2v.
Arc 925.50.48	Liberov, Petr D. Plemena srednego Dona v epokhu bronzy. Moskva, 1964.
Arc 925.50.50	Smirniv, A.P. Problemy istorii Sever. Prichernomor'ia. Moskva, 1959.
Arc 925.50.55	Smishko, M.I. Karpats'ki kurhany pershoi polov. I tysiacholettia nash. ery. Kyïv, 1960.
Arc 925.50.60	Chernysh, K.K. Rannotrypil's'ke poselennia lenkivtsi seredn'omu Dnistri. Kyïv, 1959.
Arc 925.50.65	Bondar, M.M. Pam'iatky starodavnoho Prydniprov'ia. Kyïv, 1959.
Arc 925.50.70	Grabowski, M. Ukraina davna i terazniejsza. Kijów, 1850.
Arc 925.50.75	Rudyns'kyi, M.I. Kam'iana Mohyla. Kyïv, 1961.
Arc 925.50.80	Pasternak, I. Arkheolohiia Ukraïny. Toronto, 1961.
Arc 925.50.85	Materialy z antropolohii Ukraïny. Kyïv. 1960-1964 5v.
Arc 925.50.90	Terenozhkin, A.I. Predskifskii period na Dneprovskom Pravoberezh'e. Kiev, 1961.
Arc 925.50.93	Miller, Mykhailo O. Pervobytnyi period v istorii Nizhego Dnepra. Miunkhen, 1965.
Arc 925.50.95	Nabodovs'ka, O.F. Mykhailivs'ke poselennia. Kyïv, 1962.
Arc 925.50.100	Chachkovs'kyi, L. Kniazhii galich. 2. vyd. Chikago, 1959.
Arc 925.50.105	Iakobson, A.L. Srednevekovyi Krym. Leningrad, 1964.

Arc 925 Archaeology - Local - Russia - Local; Special topics - cont.

Arc 925.50.110	Braichevs'kyi, Mykhailo I. Bilia dzherel plov'ians'koi derzhevnosti. Kyïv, 1964.
Arc 925.50.115F	Smilenko, Alla T. Hlodos'ki skarby. Kyïv, 1965.
Arc 925.50.120	Leskov, Aleksandr M. Gornyi Krym v I tysicacheletii do nashei coy. Kiev, 1965.
Arc 925.50.125	Khvoika, V.V. Drevnie obitateli Sredniago Pridneprov'ia. Kiev, 1913.
Arc 925.50.130	Surov, E.G. Khersones Tavricheskii. Sverdlovsk, 1961.
VArc 925.50.135	Shovkoplias, Ivan H. Osnovy arkheolohii. Kyïv, 1964.
Arc 925.50.137	Shovkoplias, Ivan H. Osnovy arkheolohii. 2. vyd. Kyïv, 1972.
Arc 925.50.140	Kovpanenko, Halyna T. Plemena skifs'koho chasu na Vorskli. Kyïv, 1967.
Arc 925.50.145	Dovzhenok, Vasyl' I. Drevn'orus'ke misto Voin. Kyïv, 1966.
Arc 925.50.155	Arkheologicheskie issledovaniia srednevekovogo Kryma. Kiev, 1968.
Arc 925.50.160	Kam'iana Mohyla. Kyïv, 1967. 2 pam.
Arc 925.50.165	Mezentseva, Galina G. Drevn'orus'ke misto Roden', Kniazha hora. Kyïv, 1968.
Arc 925.50.170	Telehin, Dmytro I. Dnipro-donets'ka kul'tura. Kyïv, 1968.
Arc 925.50.175	Pidoplichko, Ivan G. Pozdnepaleoliticheskie zhilizhcha iz kostei mamontz na Ukraine. Kiev, 1969.
Arc 925.50.180	Slov'iano-rus'ki starozhytnosti. Kyïv, 1969.
Arc 925.50.185	Danilenko, Valentin N. Eneolit Ukrainy. Kiev, 1969.
Arc 925.50.185.5	Danilenko, Valentin N. Eneolit Ukrainy. Kiev, 1974.
Arc 925.50.190F	Samokvasev, Dmitrii I. Raskopki severianskikh kurganov v Chernigove vo vremiia XIV arkheologicheskago s"ezda. Moskva, 1916.
Arc 925.50.195	Drevnosti vostochnogo kryma. Kiev, 1970.
Arc 925.50.200	Humenna, Dokiia. Rodynnyi al'bom. Niu-Iork, 1971.
Arc 925.50.205	Bidzilia, Vasyl' I. Istoriia kul'tury Zakarpattia na rubezhi nashoi ery. Kyïv, 1971.
Arc 925.50.210	Seredni viky na Ukraini. Kyïv, 1971.
Arc 925.50.215	Onaiko, Nadezhda A. Antichnyi import v Pridneprov'e i pobuzh'e v IV-II vv. do n.e. Moskva, 1970.
Arc 925.50.220	Pasternak, Iaroslav. Staryi Halych. Krakiv, 1944.
Arc 925.50.225	Knyzhitskii, Sergei D. Zhilye ansambli drevnei Ol'vii IV-II vv. do n.e. Kiev, 1971.
Arc 925.50.230	Arkheolohiia Ukrains'koi RSR. Kyïv, 1971. 2v.
Arc 925.50.235	Lisin, V. Kratkii putevoditel' po antichnomu otdelu i vaskopkam khersonesa. Sevastopol', 1939.
Arc 925.50.240	Kolosov, Iurii H. Shaitan-Koba - mustievs'ka stoianka Knymii. Kyïv, 1972.
Arc 925.50.245	Bevezans'ka, Sofiia S. Srednii period bronzovogo veka v Severnoi Ukraine. Kiev, 1972.
Arc 925.50.250	Vynokur, Ion S. Istoriia da kul'tura cherniakhivs'kykh veemen dnistro-din'provs'koho mezhyrichchia. Kyïv, 1972.
Arc 925.50.255	Aulikh, Vitold V. Zymnivs'ke horodyshche-slov'ians'ka pam'iatka. Kyïv, 1972.
Arc 925.50.260	Kurinnyi, Petro. Istoriia arkheolohichnoho znannia pro Ukrainu. Miunkhen, 1970.
Arc 925.50.265	Baran, Volodymyr D. Ranni slov'iany mizh Dnistrom i pnypiatkii. Kyïv, 1972.
Arc 925.50.270	Pol', Aleksandr N. Katalog kolleztni drevnostei A.N. Pol', v Ekaterinoslave. Kiev, 1893.
Arc 925.50.275	Vysotskaia, Tat'iana N. Pozdnie skify viugo-zapadnom Kryma. Kiev, 1972.
Arc 925.50.280	Viaz'mitina, Mariia I. Zolotobalkovskii mogil'nik. Kiev, 1972.
Arc 925.50.285F	Antonovich, V.B. Arkheologicheskaia karta Kievskoi gubernii. Moskva, 1895.
Arc 925.50.290	Telehin, Dnytro I. Seredn'ostohivs'ka kul'tura epokhy midi. Kyïv, 1973.
Arc 925.50.295	Cynkałowski, Aleksandr. Materiały do pradziejów Wołynia i Polesia Wołyńskiego. Warszawa, 1961.
Arc 925.50.300	Pletneva, Svetlana A. Drevnosh Chernykh Klobukov. Moskva, 1973.
Arc 925.50.305	Doslidzhennia starodavn'oï istoriï Zakarpattia. Uzhhorod, 1972.
Arc 925.50.310	Rusanova, Irina P. Slavianskie drevnosti VI-IX vv. mezhdu Dneprom i Zapadnym Bugom. Moskva, 1973.
Arc 925.50.315	Iakavenko, Ieleonora V. Skify skhidnego Krymu v V-III st. do n.e. Kyïv, 1974.
Arc 925.50.320	Smyrnov, Stanislav V. Paleolit Dniprovs'koho Nadporizhzhia. Kyïv, 1973.
Arc 925.50.325	Pislarii, Ivan A. Tainy stepnykh kurganov. Donetsk, 1972.
Arc 925.50.330	Kezub, Iuliia I. Nekropol' Ol'viï V-VI st. do n.e. Kyïv, 1974.
Arc 925.50.335	Dombrovskii, Oleg I. Stolitsa feodoritov. Simferopol', 1973.
Arc 925.50.340	Belov, Grigorii D. Otchet o raskopkakh v Khersonese za 1935-36 gg. Sevastopol', 1938.
Arc 925.50.345	Svieshnikov, Ihor K. Istoriia naselennia Peredkarpattia, Podillia i Volyni v kintsi III-na pochatku II tysiacholittia do nashoï ery. Kyïv, 1974.
Arc 925.50.350	Maksimov, Evgenii V. Srednes Podneprov's na rubezhe nashei ery. Kiev, 1972.
Arc 925.50.355	Parovich-Peshikan, Maia. Nekropol' Ol'vii ellinisticheskogo vremeni. Kiev, 1974.
Arc 925.50.360	Feodal'naia Tavrika. Kiev, 1974.
Arc 925.50.365	Ol'viia. Kiev, 1975.
Arc 925.50.370	Savych, Volodymyr P. Pizn'opaleolitychne naselennia pivdenno-zakhidnoï Volyni. Kyïv, 1975.
Arc 925.50.375	Pletneva, Svetlana A. Polovetskie kamennye izvaianiia. Moskva, 1974.
Arc 925.50.380	Bondar', Mykola M. Poseleniia srednego podneprov'ia epokhi rannei bronzy. Kiev, 1974.
Arc 925.50.385	Smilenko, Alla T. Slov'iany ta ïkh susidy v stepovomu Podniprov'ï II-XIII st. Kyïv, 1975.
Arc 925.50.390	Sukhobokov, Oleg V. Slaviane Dneprovskogo Levoberezh'ia. Kiev, 1975.
Arc 925.55	Akademiia Nauk URSR, Kyïv. Khronyka arkheolohyi ta mystetstva. Kyïv, 1930.
Arc 925.60	Khakovskii, V.F. Pamiatniki material'noi kul'tury Chuvashskoi ASSR. Cheboksary, 1957.
Arc 925.60.5	Gorodishche Khulash i pamiatniki srednevekov'ia chuvashskogo Povolzh'ia. Cheboksary, 1972.
Arc 925.65	Akademii Nauk URSR, Kyïv. Vseukrains'kii arkheologichnii komitet Tripil'ska kul'tura na Ukraini. Kyïv, n.d.
Arc 925.68	Bogaevskii, B.L. Druzhiia proiz. i dom. zhivotn. tripol'ia. Leningrad, 1937.
Arc 925.70	Akademii Nauk URSR, Kyïv. Vseukrains'kii arkheologichnii komitet. Zapiski. Kyïv, n.d.
Arc 925.75	Ziebell, W. Olbia. Hamburg, 1937.
Arc 925.75.3FA	Akademiia Nauk URSR, Kiev. Institut Arkheologicheskaia. Ol'viia. Kiev, 1940.

Classified Listing

Arc 925 Archaeology - Local - Russia - Local; Special topics - cont.

Arc 925.75.3B Akademiia Nauk URSR, Kiev. Institut Arkheologicheskaia. Ol'viia. Kiev, 1940.
Arc 925.75.4 Ol'viiskaia Ekspeditsiia, 1946. Ol'viia; temenos i agora. Leningrad, 1964.
Arc 925.75.5 Lapin, V.V. Ol'viia. Kiev, 1959.
Arc 925.75.10 Gansiniec, Z. Olbia. Kraków, 1962.
Arc 925.75.20 Belinde Ballu, Eugéne. Olbia. Leiden, 1972.
Arc 925.80 Przeworski, S. Zagadnienie wpływów Bl. wschodnie. Warszawa, 1933.
Arc 925.85 Shul'ts, P. Maveolei neapole skifskogo. Moskva, 1953.
Arc 925.90A Blavatskii, V.D. Ocherki voen. dela. v antich. gosud. seleriogo Prichernomord. Moskva, 1954.
Arc 925.90B Blavatskii, V.D. Ocherki voen. dela. v antich. gosud. seleriogo Prichernomord. Moskva, 1954.
Arc 925.90.5 Blavatskii, V.D. Zemdsd v antichnikh gorodov severnogo Prichernomor'ia. Moskva, 1953.
Arc 925.92 Iranova, A.P. Iskusstvo antichnikh gorodov severnogo Prichernomoria. Petrograd, 1953.
Arc 925.93 Popova, Tat'iana B. Plemena katakombnoi kul'tury. Photoreproduction. Moskva, 1955.
Arc 925.95 Kolchin, B.A. Tekhnika obra botki metala v drev. ruhssi. Moskva, 1953.
Arc 925.95.5 Nikitin, Arkadii. Russkoe kwznechmoe remeslo XVI-XVII vv. Moskva, 1971.
Arc 925.97 Smirnov, K.F. Severskii kurgan. Moskva, 1953.
Arc 925.100 Akademiia Nauk SSSR. Institut Istorii Materialy Kul'tury. Voprosy skifo-sarmatskoi arkheologicheskoi. Moskva, 1954.
Arc 925.105 Kotsevalov, A.S. Antichnikh istoria i kul'tura severi Prichernomor'ia. Miunkhon, 1955.
Arc 925.107 Fedorov, G.B. Po sledam drevnik kul'tur. Moskva, 1954.
Arc 925.107.5 Lebende Vergangenheit; deutsche Übertragen von Alexander Becker und Ruth Kalinowski. 1. Aufl. Berlin, 1954.
Arc 925.110 Mongait, A.L. Arkheologiia v SSSR. Moskva, 1955.
Arc 925.110.5 Mongait, A.L. Archaeology in USSR. Moscow, 1959.
Arc 925.113 Akademiia Nauk SSSR. Institut Istorii Materialy Kul'tury. Antichnye goroda severnogo Prichernomoria. Moskva, 1955.
Arc 925.115 Golubtsova, E.S. Severnoe Prichernomor'e i Rim. Moskva, 1951.
Arc 925.120 Shelov, D.B. Monetnoe delo Bospora. Moskva, 1956.
Arc 925.121 Haavio Martti, Henrikki. Bjarmien vallan kukoistur ja tuho. Porvoo, 1965.
Arc 925.125 Shelov, D.B. Antichnyi mir v severnom Prichernomor'e. Moskva, 1956.
Arc 925.126 Solomonik, E.I. Sarmatskie znaki severnogo Prichernomor'ia. Kiev, 1959.
Arc 925.130 Tsvetkova, I.K. Volosovskii klad. Moskva, 1957.
Arc 925.134.5 Kanivets, Viacheslav I. Kaninskaia peshchera. Moskva, 1964.
Arc 925.134.10 Lashuk, L. P. Ocherk etnicheskoi istorii Pechorskogo kraia. Syktyvkar, 1958.
Arc 925.135 Smirnov, A.P. Novaia nakhodka vostochnogo serebra v Priural'e. Moskva, 1957.
Arc 925.136 Bader, Otto N. Drevneishie metallurgi Priural'ia. Moskva, 1964.
Arc 925.136.5 Sal'nikov, Konstantin V. Ocherki drevnei istorii Iuzhnogo Urala. Moskva, 1967.
Arc 925.136.10 Sal'nikov, Konstantin V. Drevnieshie pamiatniki istorii Urala. Sverdlovsk, 1952.
Arc 925.136.15 Stokolos, Vladimir S. Kul'tura naseleniia bronzovogo veka Iuzhnogo Zaural'ia. Moskva, 1972.
Arc 925.140 Bers, E.M. Arkheologicheskie pamiatniki Sverdlovska i ego obrestnostei. Sverdlovsk, 1954.
Arc 925.140.2 Bers, E.M. Arkheologicheskie pamiatniki Sverdlovska i ego obrestnostei. 2. izd. Sverdlovsk, 1963.
Arc 925.150 Akademiia Nauk BSSR, Minsk. Institut Historyi. Materialy po arkheologii BSSR. Minsk, 1957.
Arc 925.150.5 Gurevich, F.D. Drevnosti Belorusskogo ponemania. Leningrad, 1962.
Arc 925.150.10 Zagorul'ski, Edward M. Arkheologiia Belorussii. Minsk, 1965.
Arc 925.150.15 Mel'nikovskaia, Ol'ga N. Plemena Iuzhnoi Belorussii v rannem zheleznom veke. Moskva, 1967.
Arc 925.150.20 Polikarpovich, Konstantin M. Paleolit verkhego podneptovia. Minsk, 1968.
Arc 925.150.23 Konferentsiia no Arkheologii Belorussii i Smezhnykh Territorii, Minsk, 1966. Drevnosti Belorussii. Minsk, 1966.
Arc 925.150.25 Konferentsiia po Arkheologii Belorussii, Minsk, 1968. Belorusskie drevnosti. Minsk, 1967.
Arc 925.150.30 Konferentsiia po Arkheologii Belorussii, Minsk, 1969. Drevnosti Belorussii. Minsk, 1969.
Arc 925.150.35 Arkheologicheskaia karta Belorussii. Minsk, 1968- 2v.
Arc 925.150.40 Ocherki po arkheologii Belorussii. Minsk, 1970- 2v.
Arc 925.150.45 Pobol', Leonid D. Slavianskie drevnosti Belorussii. Minsk, 1971.
Arc 925.150.46 Pobol', Leonid D. Slavianskie drevnosti Belorussii. Minsk, 1973.
Arc 925.150.47 Pobol', Leonid D. Slavianskie drevnosti Belorussii. Minsk, 1974.
Arc 925.150.50 Konferentsiia po Arkheologii Belorussii i Smezhnykh Territorii, Minsk, 1972. Belorusskiia starazhytnastsi. Minsk, 1972.
Arc 925.151 Dal'nevostochnaia Arkheologicheskaia Ekspeditsiia. Materialy polevykh izsledovanii Dal'nevostochnoi arkheologicheskoi ekspeditsii. Novosibirsk, 1970- 2v.
Arc 925.151.5 Derevianko, Anatolii P. Pannii zheleznyi vek Dal'nego Vostoka. v.2- Novosibirsk, 1972-
Arc 925.152 Pobol', Leonid D. Drevnosti Turovshching. Minsk, 1969.
Arc 925.155F Mykopalicka polsko-radzi eckie w Mirmeki. Warszawa, n.d. 2v.
Arc 925.155.5 Sztetyllo, Zofia. Rola Mirmekionu w zyciu gospoelarczym państwa bosforskiego. 1. wyd. Warszawa, 1972.
Arc 925.160 Chilashvili, L.A. Gorod Rustavi. Tbilisi, 1958.
Arc 925.165 Datsiak, B.D. Pervobytnoe obshchestvo na territorii nashei strang. Moskva, 1954.
Arc 925.170 Bader, Otto N. Nazare istorii Piskam'ia. Perm', 1958.
Arc 925.170.5 Charnoluskii, Vladimir V. Legenda ob olene-chelovcke. Moskva, 1965.
Arc 925.170.11 Nizhnekamskaia Arkheologicheskaia Ekspeditsiia, 1968-1969? Otchety Nizhnekamskoi arkheologicheskoi ekspeditsii. Photoreproduction. Moskva, 1972.
Arc 925.172 Bader, Otto N. Baranovskii nogil'nik. Moskva, 1963.
Arc 925.173F Bulychov, Nikolai I. Raskopki po chasti vodorazdela verkhnikh pritokov Dnepra i Volgi, 1903 g. Moskva, 1903.
Arc 925.173.5F Bulychov, Nikolai I. Zhurnal raskopok po chasti vodorazdela verkhnikh pritokov Volgi i Dnepra. Moskva, 1899.

Arc 925 Archaeology - Local - Russia - Local; Special topics - cont.

Arc 925.175 Smipnov, A.P. Arkheologicheskie pamiatniki na territorii Mariiskoi ASSR. Kozmodem'iansk, 1949-
Arc 925.175.5 Mariiskaia Arkheologicheskaia Ekspeditsiia, 1956-59. Materialy k arkheologicheskoi karte Mariiskoi ASSR. Ioshkar-Ola, 1960.
Arc 925.175.10 Arkhipov, Gennadii A. Mariitsy IX-XI vv. Ioshkar-Ola, 1973.
Arc 925.180 Okladnikov, Aleksei Pavlovich. Dalekoe proshloe Primor'ia. Vladivostok, 1959-
Arc 925.180.5F Okladnikov, Aleksei Pavlovich. Petroglify Angary. Leningrad, 1966.
Arc 925.180.10 Okladnikov, Aleksei Pavlovich. The Soviet Far East in antiquity. Toronto, 1965.
Arc 925.180.15 Shavkunov, Ernst V. Gosudarstvo bokhai i pamiatniki ego kul'tury v Primor'e. Leningrad, 1968.
Arc 925.180.20 Okladnikov, Aleksei Pavlovich. Liki drevnego Amura. Novosibirsk, 1968.
Arc 925.180.25 Larichev, Vitalii E. Taina kamennoi cherepakhi. Novosibirsk, 1966.
Arc 925.180.30 Okladnikov, Aleksei Pavlovich. Dalekoe proshloe Primor'ia i Priamur'ia. Vladivostok, 1973.
Arc 925.185 Gaprindashvili, Givi M. Kldis sakhli skal'nye doma selishcha Pia. Tbilisi, 1959.
Arc 925.187 Gaprindashvili, Givi M. Peshchernyi ansambl' Vardzia, 1156-1213 gg. Tbilisi, 1960.
Arc 925.190 Leningrad. Ermitazh. New archaeological material relating to the history of the Soviet East. Leningrad, 1960.
Arc 925.195 Piatysheva, N.V. Tamanskii sarkofag. Moskva, 1949.
Arc 925.200 Maksimenkov, G.A. Verkhne-metliaevskii klad. Irkutsk, 1960.
Arc 925.205 Mongait, A.L. Riazanskaia zemlia. Moskva, 1961.
Arc 925.210 Polesskikh, M.R. Pamiatniki material'noi kul'tury Penzenskoi oblasti. Penza, 1960.
Arc 925.215 Khalikov, A.K. Materialy k drevnei istorii Povetluzh'ia. Gor'kii, 1960.
Arc 925.220 Erdniev, U.E. Gorodishche maiak. Kemerovo, 1960.
Arc 925.225 Grach, A.D. Drevnetiurkskie izvaianiia Tuvy. Moskva, 1961.
Arc 925.225.5 Mannai-ool, Mongush. Tuva v skifskoe vremia. Moskva, 1970.
Arc 925.230 Vologda, Russia (City). Ablastnoi Kraevedcheskii Muzei. Sbornik po arkheologii Vologdskoi oblasti. Vologda, 1961.
Arc 925.230.5 Golubeva, Leonilla A. Ves' i Slaviane na Belom ozere X-XIII vv. Moskva, 1973.
Arc 925.235F Urusov, V.P. Raskopki kurganov Eniseiskoi gubernii. Moskva, 1902.
Arc 925.237 Vadetskaia, El'ga B. Drevnie idoly Eniseia. Leningrad, 1967.
Arc 925.240 Divov, N.N. Bronzovyi vek Zabaikal'ia. Ulan-Ude, 1958.
Arc 925.245 Khudiak, M.M. Iz istorii Nimfeia VI-III vekov. Leningrad, 1962.
Arc 925.250 Nowicka, M. Ad Fanagorii do Apollonii. Warszawa, 1962.
Arc 925.255 Kartsov, V.G. O chem govoriat kurgany Eniseia. Abakhan, 1961.
Arc 925.255.5F Krasnoiarsk, Siberia (City). Kraevoi Kraevedcheskii Muzei. Materialy i issledovaniia po arkheologii etnografii i istorii Krasnoiarskogo kraia. Krasnoiarsk, 1963.
Arc 925.255.10 Toettermann, A. Fünf Sulfekinschriften. Helsingfors, 1891.
Arc 925.260 Kazan, Russia (City). Universitet. Arkheologicheskie pamiatniki u sela Rozhdestveno. Kazan, 1962.
Arc 925.265 Ural'skoe Arkheologicheskogo Soveshchanie. 2d, Sverdlovsk, 1961. Materialy. Sverdlovsk, 1961.
Arc 925.267 Raushenbakh, V.M. Srednee Zaural'e v epokhu neolita i bronzy. Moskva, 1956.
Arc 925.268 Konstantinov, Ivan V. Material'naia kul'tura iakutov XVIII veka. Iakutsk, 1971.
Arc 925.269 Konstantinov, Ivan V. Material'naia kul'tura Iakutov XVIII veka. Photoreproduction. Novosibirsk, 1967.
Arc 925.280 Shramko, B.A. Drevnosti Severskogo Dontsa. Khar'kov, 1962.
Arc 925.285 Kozyreva, Rimma V. Drevneishee proshloe Sakhalina. Iuzhno, 1960.
Arc 925.285.5 Kozyreva, Rimma V. Drevnii Sakhalin. Leningrad, 1967.
Arc 925.290 Gening, V.F. Arkheologicheskie pamiatniki Udmurtii. Izhevsk, 1958.
Arc 925.295 Kafoev, A.Z. Adygskie pamiatniki. Nal'chik, 1963.
Arc 925.295.5 Maikop. Adygeiskogo Nauchno-Issledovatel'skogo Instituta Iazyka, Literatury, Istorii i Ekonomiki. Sbornik materialov po arkheologii adygei. Maikop, 1961.
Arc 925.296F Nat, Daniel. Éléments de préhistoire et d'archéologie nord-sibériennes. Paris, 1971-
Arc 925.300 Autlev, P.U. Abadzekhskaia nizhnepaleoliticheskaia stoianka. Maikop, 1963.
Arc 925.300.5 Popova, T.B. Dol'meny stanitsy Novosvobodnoi. Moskva, 1963.
Arc 925.300.10 Formozov, Aleksandr A. Kamennyi vek i eneolit Prikubania. Moskva, 1965.
Arc 925.301 Tret'iakov, P.N. Drevnii gorodishcha Smolenshchiny. Leningrad, 1963.
Arc 925.305 Andreev, N.V. O chëm rasskazyvaiut kurgany. Smolensk, 1951.
Arc 925.310 Alekseeva, Evgeniia P. O chem rasskazyvaiut arkheologicheskie pamiatniki Karachaevo-Cherkesii. Cherkessk, 1960.
Arc 925.310.5 Alekseeva, Evgeniia P. Karachaevtsy i balkartsy, drevnii narod Kavkaza. Cherkessk, 1963.
Arc 925.310.10 Alekseeva, Evgeniia P. Drevniaia i srednevekovaia istoriia Karachaevo-Cherkesii. Moskva, 1971.
Arc 925.320 Moscow. Gosudarstvennyi Istoricheskii Muzei. Iaroslavskoe Povolzh'e X-XI vv. po materialam Timerevskogo Mikhailovskogo i Petrovskogo mogil'nikov. Moskva, 1963.
Arc 925.321 Akademiia Nauk SSSR. Karel'skii Filial, Petrozavedsk. Instituta Iazyka, Literatury i Istorii. Novye pamiatniki istorii drevnei Karelii. Leningrad, 1966.
Arc 925.321.5 Pankrushev, Grigorii A. Plemena Karelii v epokhu neolita i rannego metalla. Leningrad, 1964.
Arc 925.321.10 Briusov, Aleksandr I. Istoriia drevnei Karelii. Moskva, 1940.
Arc 925.321.15 Arkheologicheskie issledovaniia v Karelii. Leningrad, 1972.
Arc 925.321.20 Kochkurkina, Svetlana I. Iugo-Vostochnoe Priladozh'e v desiatomtrinadtsatom vekakh. Leningrad, 1973.
Arc 925.322 Ataev, Dibir M. Nagornyi Dagestan v rannem srednevekove. Makhachkala, 1963.

Classified Listing

Arc 925 Archaeology - Local - Russia - Local; Special topics - cont.

Arc 925.322.5 Isakov, Magomed I. Arkheologicheskie pamiatniki Dagestana. Makhachkala, 1966.
Arc 925.322.10 Kotovich, Vladimir G. Kamennyi vek Dagestana. Makhachkala, 1964.
Arc 925.322.15 Pikul', Milifsa I. Epokha rannego zheleza v Dagestane. Makhachkala, 1967.
Arc 925.322.20 Kotovich, Valentina M. Verkhnegunibskoe poselenie-pamiatnik epokhi bronzy gornogo Dagestana. Makhachkala, 1965.
Arc 925.322.25 Gadzhiev, Magomed G. Iz istorii kul'tury Dagestana v epokhu bronzy. Makhachkala, 1969.
Arc 925.322.30 Shikhsaidov, Amri Rzaevich. Nadpisi rasskazyvaiut. Dagknigoizdat, 1969.
Arc 925.323.5 Gening, Vladimir F. Rannie bolgary na Volge. Moskva, 1964.
Arc 925.324 Mezentseva, Galina G. Kanivs'ke poselennia polian. Kyïv, 1965.
Arc 925.325 Bader, Otto N. Kapovaia peshchera. Moskva, 1965.
Arc 925.325.5 Mazhitov, Niiaz A. Bakhmutinskaia kul'tura. Moskva, 1968.
Arc 925.325.10 Drevnosti Bashkirii. Moskva, 1970.
Arc 925.326 Samokrasov, Dmitrii I. Severianskaia zumlia i severiane po gorodishcham i mogilam. Moskva, 1908.
Arc 925.327 Minaeva, Tat'iana M. Ocherki po arkheologii Stavropol'ia. Stavropol', 1965.
Arc 925.328 Vitkov, Z.A. Pervobytnye liudi na Kol'skom poluostrove. Murmansk, 1960.
Arc 925.329 Thompson, Michael W. Novgorod the Great. London, 1967.
Arc 925.330 Chlenova, Natalia L. Proiskhozhdenie i ranniaia istoriia plemen Tagarskoi kul'tury. Moskva, 1967.
Arc 925.331 Burov, Grigorii M. Vychegodskii krai. Moskva, 1965.
Arc 925.331.5 Burov, Grigorii M. Arkheologicheskie pamiatniki Vychegodskoi doliny. Syktyvkar, 1967.
Arc 925.331.10 Burov, Grigorii M. Drevnii Sindar. Moskva, 1967.
Arc 925.332F Ivanov, Petr P. Materialy po istorii Mordvy VIII-IX vv. Moskva, 1952.
Arc 925.332.5 Stepanov, Pavel D. Osh Paudo. Saransk, 1967.
Arc 925.332.10 Material'naia kul'tura sredne-tsninskoi Mordvy VIII-XIVV. Saransk, 1969.
Arc 925.332.15 Materialy po arkheologii i etnografii Mordevii. Saransk, 1974.
Arc 925.333 Fedoseeva, Svetlana A. Drevnie kul'tury verkhnego Viliuia. Moskva, 1968.
Arc 925.334 Nikitin, Andrei L. Golubye doragi vekov. Moskva, 1968.
Arc 925.335 Mezolit Verkhnego Priangar'ia. Irkutsk, 1971-
Arc 925.336 Mochanov, I.A. Mnogosloinaia stoianka Bel'kachi I. i periodizatsiia kamennogo veka Iakutii. Moskva, 1969.
Arc 925.337 Priakhin, Anatolii D. Abashevskaia kul'tura v Podon'e. Voronezh, 1971.
Arc 925.337.5 Artamonov, Mikhail I. Srednevekovye poseleniia na Nizhnem Donu. Leningrad, 1935.
Arc 925.337.10 Kiiashko, Vladimir I. Legenda i byl' donskikh kurganov. Rostov-na-Donu, 1972.
Arc 925.337.15 Arkheologicheskie pamiatniki Nizhnego Podon'ia. Moskva. 1,1974+
Arc 925.338 Khalikov, Al'fred K. Drevniaia istoriia Srednego Povolzhia. Moskva, 1969.
Arc 925.338.5 Krainov, Dmitrii A. Drevneishaia istoriia Volgo-Okskogo mezhdurech'ia. Moskva, 1972.
Arc 925.338.10 Merpert, Nikolai I. Drevneishie skotovody Volzhsko-Uraliskogo mezhdurech'ia. Moskva, 1974.
Arc 925.339 Inadze, Meri P. Prichernomorskie goroda drevnei Kolkhidy. Tbilisi, 1968.
Arc 925.340 Ranshenbakh, Vera M. Novye nakhodki na chetyrekhstolbovom ostrove. Moskva, 1969.
Arc 925.341 Okladnikov, Aleksei P. Petroglify zabaikal'ia. Leningrad, 1969- 2v.
Arc 925.341.5 Okladnikov, Aleksei P. Petroglify srednei Leny. Leningrad, 1972.
Arc 925.341.10 Okladnikov, Aleksei P. Petroglify Baikala - pamiatniki drevnei kul'tury narodov Sibiri. Novosibirsk, 1974.
Arc 925.342 Bader, Otto N. Bassein Oki v epokhu bronzy. Moskva, 1970.
Arc 925.342.5 Okskii bassein v epokhu kamnia i bronzy. Moskva, 1970.
Arc 925.343F Spitsyn, Aleksandr A. Gdovskie kurgany v raskopkakh U.N. Glazova. Sankt Petersburg, 1903.
Arc 925.344 Kropotkin, Vladislav V. Rinskie importnye izdeliia v Vostochnoi Evrope. Moskva, 1970.
Arc 925.345 Andrianov, Boris V. Drevnie orositel'nye sistemy Priaral'ia. Moskva, 1969.
Arc 925.346 Dikov, Nikolai N. Drevnie kostry Kamchatki i Chukotki. Magadan, 1969.
Arc 925.347 Derevianko, Anatolii P. V strane srekh solnts. Khabarovsk, 1970.
Arc 925.347.5 Derevianko, Anatolii P. Novopetrovskaia kul'tura Srednego Amura. Novosibirsk, 1970.
Arc 925.347.10 Okladnikov, Aleksei P. Petroglify Nizhnego Amura. Leningrad, 1971.
Arc 925.348 Sedov, Valentin V. Novgorodskie sopki. Moskva, 1970.
Arc 925.349 Chernetsov, Valerii Nikolaevich. Prehistory of western Siberia. Montreal, 1974.
Arc 925.350 Luzgin, Valerii E. Drevnie kul'tury Izhmy. Moskva, 1972.
Arc 925.351 Tret'iakov, Viktor P. Kul'tura iamochno-grebenchatoi keramiki v lesnoi polose evropeiskoi chasti SSSR. Leningrad, 1972.
Arc 925.352 Pletnev, V.A. Ob ostatkakh drevnosti i stariny v Tserskoi Gubernii. Tver', 1903.
Arc 925.353 Minaeva, Tat'iana M. K istorii alan Verkhnego Prikuban'ia po arkheologicheskim dannym. Staviopol', 1971.
Arc 925.354 Priakhin, Anatolii D. Drevnes naselenie Peschanki. Voronezh, 1973.
Arc 925.355 Sedov, Valentin V. Dlinnye kurgany krivichei. Moskva, 1974.
Arc 925.356.1 Fisenko, Vladimir A. Plemena iamnoi kul'tury Iugo-Vostoka. Photoreproduction. Saratov, 1970.
Arc 925.357 Pitskhelauri, Konstantin. Osnovnye problemy istorii plemen Vostochnoi Gruzii v XV-VII vv. do n.e. Tbilisi, 1973.

Arc 930 Archaeology - Local - Other Europe - Folios [Discontinued]

Arc 930.200 Tocilescou, G.G. Das Monument von Adamklissi. Wien, 1895.
Arc 930.200.5F Tocilescou, G.G. Fouilles et recherches archéologiques en Roumanie. Bucarest, 1900.
Arc 930.201 Ossowski, G. Zabytki przedhistoryczne Ziem Polskich. Krakow, 1879-88.
Arc 930.202 Ciampinus, Joan. De sacris aêdificiis a Constantino Magno constr. Romae, 1693.
Arc 930.203 Dethier. Nouvelles découvertes archéologiques à Constantinople. Constantinople, 1867.

Arc 930 Archaeology - Local - Other Europe - Folios [Discontinued] - cont.

Arc 930.204 Schlumberger, G. Monuments byzantins inédits. Macon, 1884.
Arc 930.205F Akademie der Wissenschaften in Wien. Schriften der Balkancommission. Antiquarische Abtheilung. v.1-7,9-10,13. Wien, 1900-39. 10v.
Arc 930.206F Praschniker, C. Archäologische Forschungen in Albanien und Montenegro. Wien, 1919.

Arc 933 Archaeology - Local - Other Europe - General works

Arc 933.2F Kruegar, Bruno. Die Kietzsiedlungen im nordlichen Mitteleuropa. Berlin, 1962.
Arc 933.5 Kropotkin, Vladislav V. Ekonomicheskie sviazi Vostochnoi Evropy v I tysiacheletii neshei ery. Moskva, 1967.
Arc 933.7 Istoriia i kul'tura Vostochnoi Evropy po arkheologicheskim dannym. Moskva, 1971.
Arc 933.10 Deutsche Historiker Gesellschaft. Fachgruppe Ur- und Frühgeschichte. Problem des frühen Mittelalters in archäologischer und historischer Sicht. Berlin, 1966.

Arc 935 Archaeology - Local - Other Europe - Turkey

Arc 935.01 Pamphlet box. Archaeology. Constantinople.
Arc 935.1 Tafel, G.L. Via militaris Romanorum Egnatia. Tubingae, 1841.
Arc 935.2.5 Constantiniade, ou Description de Constantinople. Constantinople, 1861.
Arc 935.3 Brunet de Presle. Extrait d'un notice sur les tombeaux des empereurs de Constantinople. Paris, 1856.
Arc 935.4 Montucci, Henry. Les coupes du palais des empereurs byzantins. Paris, 1877.
Arc 935.5 Paspati, A.G. Byzantinai meletai topographikai kai istorikai. Konstantinople, 1877.
Arc 935.6 Mordtmann, J. Das Denkmal des Porphyrius. Athen, 1880.
Arc 935.7 Bourquelot, Félix. La colonne serpentine à Constantinople. Paris, n.d.
Arc 935.8 Constantinople, Turkey. Hellēnikos Philologikos Syllogos. Archaiologikē Epitropē. Archaiologikos chartēs. Konstantinople, 1884.
Arc 935.9 Grosvenor, E.A. The hippodrome of Constantinople. London, 1889.
Arc 935.9.25 British Academy. Report upon the excavations carried out in and near the hippodrome of Constantinople. London. 1-2,1927-1928
Arc 935.9.30 Bruns, G. Der Obelisk und seine Basis auf dem Hippodrom zu Konstantinopel. Istanbul, 1935.
Arc 935.9.40F Demangel, Robert. Le quartier des Manganes et la première région de Constantinople. Paris, 1939.
Arc 935.10 Mordtmann, J. Esquisse topographique de Constantinople. Lille, 1892.
Arc 935.10.3 Ebersolt, Jean. Mission archéologique de Constantinople. Paris, 1921.
Arc 935.10.5 Pamphlet box. Musée Imperial Ottoman.
Arc 935.11 Mas Latrie. Rapport. Paris, 1846.
Arc 935.12 Heuzy, Leon. Reconnaissance archéologique...cours de l'Erigon et des ruines de Stobi. Paris, 1873.
Arc 935.15 Heuzy, Leon. Panthéon des rochers de Philippes. Paris, n.d.
Arc 935.16 Gedeon, M.J. Eggraphoi liphoi kai keramia. Konstantinople, 1892.
Arc 935.18 Pamphlet vol. Troesmis, 1864-1868. 8 pam.
Arc 935.19F Mamboury, Ernest. Die Kaiserpaläste von Konstantinopel zwischen Hippodrom und Marmara-Meer. Berlin, 1934.
Arc 935.20 Schneider, A.M. Byzanz; Vorarbeiten zur Topographie und Archäologie der Stadt. Berlin, 1936.
Arc 935.23F St. Andrews. University. The great palace of the Byzantine emperors. London, 1947-58. 2v.
Arc 935.23.5F Miranda, S. El Gran Palacio Sagrado de Bizancio. Mexico, 1955.
Arc 935.24F Kosay, Hâmit Z. Türk Tarih Kurumu tarafindan yapilan Alaca Höyük kafriyati. Ankara, 1938.
Arc 935.24.5 Kosay, Hâmit Z. Alacahöyük. n.p., 195-?
Arc 935.24.10 Kosay, Hâmit Z. Türk Tarih Kurumu tarafindan yapilan Alaca Höyük karisi. Ankara, 1973.
Arc 935.26F Kosay, Hâmit Z. Türk Tarih Kurumu tarafindan apilan Pazarli kafreyati raporu. Ankara, 1941.
Arc 935.28F Kansu, S. Türk Tarih Kurumu tarafindan yapilan Etiyrkusu kafiryati raporu. Ankara, 1940.
Arc 935.29 Dörner, Friedrich K. Arsameia am Nymphaios. Berlin, 1963.
Arc 935.30 Firatli, Nezih. Les stiles funéraires de Byzance gréco-romaine. Paris, 1964.
Arc 935.31 Arutiunian, Varazdat. Gorod Ani. Erevan, 1964.
Arc 935.31.5 Kipshidze, David A. Peshckery Ani. Erevan, 1972.
Arc 935.32 Tezcan, Burhan. 1962 iki 1963. Ankara, 1904.
Arc 935.32.5 Tezcan, Burhan. 1964 yalencak köyü çaleşmalare. Ankara, 1966.
Arc 935.32.10 Tezcan, Burhan. 1964 kaçumbeli kazese. Ankara, 1966.
Arc 935.32.15 Turkey. Maarif Vekaleli Antikiteler ve Muzeler Direktorlügü. Aniflari Koruma Kurulu. Kilavuzlar. v.1,4,6. Ankara, 1935- 7v.
Arc 935.33 Sartiaux, Felix. Eski foca, foca taukin koker. Izmir, 1952.
Arc 935.33.5 Resit Mazhar Ertüzün. Kapidagi Yariniadasi ve Cevresindeki Adalar. Ankara, 1964.
Arc 935.34 Boysal, Yusuf. Uzuncaburç ve Ura kilavuzu. Istanbul, 1962.
Arc 935.40 Sakir, M. Sinop ta candar ogullarizamanina. Istanbul, 1934.
Arc 935.45 Duyaran, Rüstem. 1952 yilinda arkeolojik. Istanbul, 1953.
Arc 935.50 Taslikliogiu, Zafer. Trokya'da epigrafya arastirmalari. Istanbul, 1961-71. 2v.
Arc 935.60 Taslikliogiu, Zafer. Anadolu'da Apollon kültu ile ilgili kaynaklar. Istanbul, 1963.
Arc 935.70 Kosay, Hâmit Zübeyr. Pulur kazisi; 1960 mersimi çalişmalari raporu. Ankara, 1964.
Arc 935.75 Başar, Zeki. Evrurumda eski merorliklarve resimli mezar taşlari. Ankara, 1973.
Arc 935.80 Türk Tarih Kurumu. Mansel'e armagan. Melanges mansel. Ankara, 1974. 3v.

Arc 936 Archaeology - Local - Other Europe - Other Local; Special topics

Arc 936.01 Pamphlet box. Balkan states. Archaeology.
Arc 936.02 Pamphlet vol. Balkan states. Archaeology.
Arc 936.1 Tafrali, O. Mélanges d'archéologie et d'epigraphie byzantines. Paris, 1913.
Arc 936.1.5 Tafrali, O. Topographie de Thessalonique. Paris, 1912.
Arc 936.1.6 Tafrali, O. Topographie de Thessalonique. Paris, 1913.
Arc 936.1.7 Tafrali, O. La cité pontique de Dionysopolis. Paris, 1927.

Classified Listing

Arc 936 Archaeology - Local - Other Europe - Other Local; Special topics - cont.

Arc 936.1.8 Stählin, F. Pharsalos. Nürnberg, 1914.
Arc 936.1.15 Kalliga, M. Die Hagia Sophia von Thessalonike. Inaug. Diss. Würzburg, 1935.
Arc 936.3F Ugalini, L.U. Albania antica. Roma, 1927-42. 3v.
Arc 936.3.5 Jubani, Bep. Bibliographi arkeologjisë dhe historisë së lashtë të Shqipërisë, 1945-71. Tiranë, 1972.
Arc 936.3.10F Shqiperia arkeologjike - Archaeological Albania. Tiranë, 1971.
Arc 936.4 Szafrański, W. Skarby brązowe z epoki wspólnoty. Warszawa, 1955.
Arc 936.5 Tanusz, Bohdan. Kultura przedhistoryczne podola. Lwów, 1919.
Arc 936.6 Kostrzewski, Józef. Wielkopolska w czasach. Poznań, 1914.
Arc 936.6.3 Kostrzewski, Józef. Z dziejów badań archeologja w Wielkopolsce. Wrocław, 1958.
Arc 936.6.5 Kostrzewski, Józef. Wielkopolska w czasach. Poznań, 1923.
Arc 936.6.10 Kostrzewski, Józef. Wielkopolska w pradziejach. 3. wyd. Warszawa, 1955.
Arc 936.6.15 Kostrzewski, Józef. Kultura łużycka na Pomorzu. Poznań, 1958.
Arc 936.6.20 Gedl, Marek. Uwagi v gospodarce i strukturze społecznej ludności kultury łuzyckiej. Kraków, 1961.
Arc 936.6.25 Filip, Jan. Pocatkij slovanskeho osidlene. Praha, 1946.
Arc 936.6.30 Wiklak, Henryk. Początki kultury łuzyckiej w Polsce Środkowej. Łodź, 1963.
Arc 936.6.35 Gediga, Bogusław. Plemiona kultury łuzyckiej w epoce brazu na ślasku środkowym. Text and atlas. Wrocław, 1967.
Arc 936.6.36 Gediza, Bogusław. Motyiwj tiguralne w sztuce ludnosci kultury luzyckiej. Wrocław, 1970.
Arc 936.6.40 Bukowski, Zbigniew. Studia nad południowym i południowowschodnim pograniczem kultury łuzyckiej. Wrocław, 1969.
Arc 936.6.45 Dąbrowski, Jan. Zabytki metalowe epoki brązu między dolną wisłą a Niemnem. Wrocław, 1968.
Arc 936.7 Zawisza, Jan. Recherches archéologiques en Pologne? Warszawa, 1874.
Arc 936.7.10 Szymański, W. Kontakty handlowe Wielkopolski w IX-XI wieku. Poznań, 1958.
Arc 936.8 Czarnowski, S.J. Siedziba paleolityczna. Warszawa, 1910-14. 4 pam.
Arc 936.9 Spostrzeżenia lat ostatnich w dziedzinie starozytnoşci krajowych. v.1-2. Warszawa, 1875-76.
Arc 936.10 Studia wczesnośredniowieczne. Warszawa. 1-5,1952-1962 5v.
Arc 936.11F Materiały wczesnośredniowieczne (1949). Warszawa. 1,1951+ 4v.
Arc 936.12 Hołowińska, Z. Wczesnośredniowieczne grodziska w Bonikowie. Poznań, 1956.
Arc 936.12.5 Sobociński, M. Materiał kostny zwierzecy z wykopalisk wczesnośredniowiecznego grodziska w Bonikowie. Poznań, 1963.
Arc 936.13 Gardanski, A. Archeologia i pradzieje Polski. Warszawa, 1957.
Arc 936.14 Hensel, Witold. Archäologische Forschungen in Polen. Warschau, 1958.
Arc 936.14.01 Pamphlet vol. Z badań nad przeszłością Ziemi Lubuskiej. 5 pam.
Arc 936.14.02 Pamphlet vol. Z badań nad przeszłością Ziemi Lubuskiej. 6 pam.
Arc 936.14.03 Pamphlet vol. Volumes on archaeology and numismatics in Poland. 6 pam.
Arc 936.14.04 Pamphlet vol. Poland - Antiquities. 4 pam.
Arc 936.14.5 Kostrzewski, Józef. Zagadnienie ciągłosci zaludnienia ziem polskich co pradziejach. Poznań, 1961.
Arc 936.14.8 Kostrzewski, Józef. Zur Frage der Siedlungsstetigkeit in der Geschichte Polens. Wrocław, 1965.
Arc 936.14.9 Polish archaeological abstracts. Wroclaw. 1,1972+
Arc 936.14.10 Rajewski, Z. Biskupin. Varsovie, 1959.
Arc 936.14.15F Majewski, K. Importy rzymskie w Polsce. Warszawa, 1960.
Arc 936.14.20 Hensel, Witold. Najdawniejsje stolice Polski. Warszawa, 1960.
Arc 936.14.25 Woźnicka, Z. Wyroby bednarskie i tokarskie średniowiécznego Medzurzecza. Poznań, 1961.
Arc 936.14.30 Tasienica, P. Sławianski rodowod. Warszawa, 1961.
Arc 936.14.35 Burzyński, R. Polska na więcej niz 1000 lat. Wrocław, 1961.
Arc 936.14.35.5 Blaszczyk, Włodzimierz. Die Anfänge der polnischen Städt im Lichte der Bodenforschung. Poznań, 1974.
Arc 936.14.40 Hensel, Witold. Starodawna kruszwica. Wrocław, 1961.
Arc 936.14.45 Paris. Université. Les origines de l'etat polonais. Paris, 1961.
Arc 936.14.50 Chmielewski, W. Civilisation de Jerzmanowice. Wrocław, 1961.
Arc 936.14.55 Polska Akademia Nauk. Oddział w Krakowie. Prace Komisji Archeologicznej. Igołomia. Wrocław, 1961.
Arc 936.14.60 Krzak, Zygmunt. Materiały doznajomości kyltury złockiej. Wrocław, 1961.
Arc 936.14.61 Krzak, Zygmunt. Cmentarzysko kultury słockiej "nad Wawrem" w Złotej. Wrocław, 1970.
Arc 936.14.65 Kurnatowski, S. Z przeszłości międzyrzecza. Poznań, 1961.
Arc 936.14.70 Zak, Jan. Importy skandynawskie na ziemiach zachodnioslowianskich. Poznań, 1963. 3v.
Arc 936.14.75 Kostrzewski, B. Z najdawniejszych dziejow Giecza. Wrocław, 1962.
Arc 936.14.80 Jamka, Rudolf. Kraków w pradziejach. Wrocław, 1963.
Arc 936.14.85 Wystawa Objazdowa Kielecczyzna w Swietle Wykopolisk. Przewodnik. Kielce, 1962.
Arc 936.14.90F Kostrzewski, Józef. Odkrycia archeologja na ziemaich zachodnich i północnych Polski. Warszawa, 1962.
Arc 936.14.92 Kostrzewski, Józef. Pradzieje Pomorza. Wrocław, 1966.
Arc 936.14.95 Posen (City). Museum Archeologicznej Oddział w Gnieznie. Ziemia gnieźnieńska w okresie powstawania państwa polskiego. Poznań, 1961.
Arc 936.14.100 Polska Akademia Nauk. Oddział w Krakowie. Prace Komisja Archeologicznej. Studia i materiały do badań nad Neolitem Małopolski. Wrocław, 1964.
Arc 936.14.103 Z badnań nad neolotem i wczesną epoką bręcu w Małopolsce. Wrocław, 1973.
Arc 936.14.105 Nosek, Stefan. Zarys historii badań archeologicznych w Małopolsce. Wrocław, 1967.
Arc 936.14.110 Urbańska, A. Wytwórczość włokiennicza predniowiecznego międzyrzeeza. Poznań, 1964.
Arc 936.14.115 Rzeszow, Poland. Muzeum. Rzeszowskie w zaraniu dziejów. Rzeszów, 1961.
Arc 936.14.120 Warsaw. Uniwersytet. Zespoł Badan nad Polskim Sredniowieczem. Odrycia w wiślecy. Warszawa, 1963-64.
Arc 936.14.125 Warsaw. Uniwersytet. Zespoł Badan nad Polskim Sredniowieczem. Badania archeologiczne w okolicy wislicy. Warszawa, 1963-64.
Arc 936.14.130 Polskie Towarzystwo Archeologiczne. Z przeszłósci Pomorza Wschodniego. Wrocław, 1962.
Arc 936.14.134 Warsaw. Uniwersytet. Zespoł Badan nad Polskim Srezniowieczem. I konferencja naukowa w Warszawie...1968. Warszawa, 1962.
Arc 936.14.135 Warsaw. Uniwersytet. Zespoł Badan nad Polskim Sredniowieczem. II konferencja naukowa w Warszawie...1961. Warszawa, 1963.
Arc 936.14.136 Warsaw. Uniwersytet. Zespoł Badan nad Polskim Sredniowieczem. III konferencja naukowa w Warszawie. Warszawa, 1964.
Arc 936.14.137 Warsaw. Uniwersytet. Zespoł Badan nad Polskim Sredniowieczem. IV konferencja w kielcach, 5 kwietnia 1963. Warszawa, 1965.
Arc 936.14.138 Warsaw. Uniwersytet. Zespoł Badan nad Polskim Sredniowieczem. V konferencja naukowa w Busknzdroju i w Wislicy, 19-20 maja, 1966. Vyd. 1. Warszawa, 1968.
Arc 936.14.139 Warsaw. Uniwersytet. Zespoł Badan nad Polskim Sredniowieczem. VI konferencja naukowa w Warszawie 10-11 stycznia 1969. Warszawa, 1970.
Arc 936.14.140 Polskie Towarzystwo Archeologiczne. Pradzieje Rzeszowszczyzny. Rzeszów, 1963.
Arc 936.14.142 Moskwa, Kazimierz. Pradzieje powiatu rzeszowskiego. Lublin, 1964.
Arc 936.14.145 Kaminska, Janina. Z dziejów prednowiecz sieradza. Wrocław, 1964.
Arc 936.14.149 Kostrzewski, Józef. Pradzieje Polski. Poznań, 1949.
Arc 936.14.150 Kostrzewski, Józef. Pradzieje Polski. wyd. 2. Wrocław, 1965.
Arc 936.14.155 Dabrowski, Krzysztof. Przymierze z archeologią. Warszawa, 1964.
Arc 936.14.160 Koszalin, Poland (City). Muzeum. Pradzieje pomorza srodkowego. Koszalin, 1964.
Arc 936.14.165A Jazdzewski, Konrad. Poland. London, 1965.
Arc 936.14.165B Jazdzewski, Konrad. Poland. London, 1965.
Arc 936.14.170 Przeworska, Janina. Tradycje celtyckie w obrzędowości Protosłowian. Wrocław, 1964.
Arc 936.14.175 Potemski, Gzesław. Pradzieje Bydgoszczy i powiatu bydgoskiego. Bydgoszcz, 1963.
Arc 936.14.180 Olczak, Jerzy. Zrodła archeologiczne do studiow nad wczesnosredniowiecznym osadnictwem grodowym na terenie wojewodztwa. Poznań, 1966- 4v.
Arc 936.14.185 Jamka, Rudolf. Pierwsi mieszkancy Gornego Slaska w swietle badan archeologicznych. Katowice, 1965.
Arc 936.14.190 Cnotliwy, Eugeniusz. Powiat kamicński w starozytności. Szczecin, 1966.
Arc 936.14.195 Łuka, Leon J. Kultura wschodniopomorska na Pomorzu Odańskim. Wrocław, 1966.
Arc 936.14.200 Danzig (City). Muzeum Archeologiczne. Pomerania antiqua. Gdynia, 1965- 6v.
Arc 936.14.203 Malinowski, Tadewsz. Obrzadek pogrzebowy ludności kultury pomorskiej. Wrocław, 1969.
Arc 936.14.205 Zoll-Adamikowa, Helena. Wczesnośredniowieczne cmentarzyska szkieltowe Małopolski. Wrocław, 1966-71. 2v.
Arc 936.14.210 Kozłowski, Janusz K. Paleolit na Gónnym Śląsku. Wrocław, 1964.
Arc 936.14.215 Warsaw. Uniwersytet. Zespól Badań nad Polskim Średniowieczem. Kolegiata wislicka. Kielce, 1965.
Arc 936.14.220 Gabałówna, Lidia. Zé studiów nad grupą brzesko-kujawską kultury lendzielskiej. Łódź, 1966.
Arc 936.14.225 Machnik, Jan. Studia nad kulturą ceramiki sznurowej w Małopolsce. Wrocław, 1966.
Arc 936.14.230 Kołodziejski, Adam. Rozwój archeologii województwa zielonogórskiego w dwudziestoleciu Polski Ludowej. Zielona Góra, 1965.
Arc 936.14.235 Nadolski, Andrzej. Sciezki archeologów. Łódź, 1967.
Arc 936.14.240 Nosek, Stefan. Kultura amfor kulistych. Wrocław, 1967.
Arc 936.14.243 Nosek, Stefan. Słowianie w pradziejach siem polskich. Kraków, 1946.
Arc 936.14.245 Chmtelewski, Waldemar. Materiały do prahistorii plejstocenu i wczesnego holocenu Polski. Wrocław, 1967.
Arc 936.14.250 Szymański, Wojciech. Szeligi pod Płockiem na początku wczesnego średniowiecza. Wrocław, 1967.
Arc 936.14.255 Metodyka naukowo-techniczna badań archeologicznych i antropologicznych. Warszawa, 1967.
Arc 936.14.260 Hilczerówna, Zofia. Dorzecze górnej i środkowej Obry od VI do początków XI wieku. Wrocław, 1967.
Arc 936.14.265 Polska Akademia Nauk. Oddział w Krakowie. Prace Komisja Archeologicznej. Zagadnienia okresu lateńskiego w Polsce. Wrocław, 1968.
Arc 936.14.270 Łomnicki, Jerzy. Ostrów Lednicki. Wyd 1. Poznań, 1968.
Arc 936.14.275 Kmieciński, Jerzy. Odry. Wrocław, 1968.
Arc 936.14.280 Karpińska, Aleksandra. Kurhany, zokresu rzymskiego w Polsce ze szczegolnem uwzględnieniem typu siedlemińskiego. Poznań, 1926.
Arc 936.14.285 Z badań nad kulturą ceramiki promienistej. Kraków, 1968.
Arc 936.14.286 Z badań nad kulturą ceramiki nytej. Wyd. 1. Kraków, 1970.
Arc 936.14.290 Wojtasik, Jerzy. Cmentarzysko wczesnośredniowieczne na wzgárzu "Młynówka" w Wolinie. Szczecin, 1968.
Arc 936.14.295 Siuchniński, Kazimierz. Klasyfikacja czasowo-przestrzenna kultur neolitycznych na Pomorzu zachodnim. wyd. 1. Szczecin, 1969.
Arc 936.14.296 Kiersnowska, Teresa. Zycie codzienne na Pomorzu wczesnośredniowiecznym, wiek X-XII. Warszawa, 1970.
Arc 936.14.297 Cnotliwy, Eugeniusz. Rzemiosło rogounicze na Pomorzu wczesnośredniowiecznym. Wrocław, 1973.
Arc 936.14.300 Wiślański, Tadeusz. Podstawy gospodarcze plemion neolitycznych w Polsce połnocno-zachodniej. Wrocław, 1969.
Arc 936.14.305 Kukharenko, I.V. Arkheologiia Pol'ski. Moskva, 1969.
Arc 936.14.310 Jaskanis, Danuta. Pradzieje Białostocczyzny. wyd. 1. Warszawa, 1969.
Arc 936.14.315 The neolithic in Poland. Ossolinskich, 1970.
Arc 936.14.320 Szkice z najdawniejszej przesstosci Mazausza. Wrocław, 1968.
Arc 936.14.325 Woyda, Stefan. Bibliografia archeologiczna Mazowsza. wyd. 1. Warszawa, 1970.
Arc 936.14.330 Hensel, Witold. Ziemie polskie w pradziejach. wyd. 1. Warszawa, 1969.
Arc 936.14.332 Hensel, Witold. Ur- und Frühgeschichte Polens. Berlin, 1974.
Arc 936.14.333 Hensel, Witold. Archeologia i prahistoria. Wrocław, 1971.
Arc 936.14.334 Hensel, Witold. Polska starozytna. Wrocław, 1973.
Arc 936.14.335 Sarnowska, Wanda. Kultura unietycka w Polsce. Wrocław, 1969-1975. 2v.

Classified Listing

Arc 936 Archaeology - Local - Other Europe - Other Local; Special topics - cont.

Arc 936.14.340 Kramarkowa, Irena. Stosunki społeczno-gospodarcze i polityczne. Opole, 1969.

Arc 936.14.345 Rajewski, Zolzisław. Biskupin. wyd. 1. Warszawa, 1970.

Arc 936.14.350 Z dziejsw regionu koninskiego. Wrocław, 1970.

Arc 936.14.355 Polskie Towarzystwo Archeologiczne. Polskie towarzystwo archeologiczne społeczeństwu. Wrocław, 1970.

Arc 936.14.360 Polska Akademia Nauk. Instytut Historii Kultury Materialnej. Badania archeologiczne w Polsce w latach 1944-64. Wrocław, 1965.

Arc 936.14.365 Woźniak, Zenon. Osadnictwo celtyckie w Pobie. Wrocław, 1970.

Arc 936.14.370 Okulicz, Łucja. Kultura kushanów zachodniobałtyjskich we wezesnej epoce zelasa. Wrocław, 1970.

Arc 936.14.375 Gąsgowski, Jerzy. Z dziejów polskiej archeologii. wyd. 1. Warszawa, 1970.

Arc 936.14.380 Głosek, Marian. Miecze średniowieczne z ziem polskich. Łódź, 1970.

Arc 936.14.380.5 Głosek, Marian. Znaki i napisy na mieczach średniowiecznych w Polsce. Wrocław, 1973.

Arc 936.14.385 25 lat archeologii na Dolnym Śląsku, 1945-70. Wrocław, 1971.

Arc 936.14.390 Malinowska, Marie. Wczesnósredniowieczne skarby srebrne z Wielkopolski. Poznań, 1970.

Arc 936.14.395 Malinowski, Tadeusz. Prasłowiańskie osadnictur w słupcy. Poznań, 1969.

Arc 936.14.400 Chmielowska, Aldona. Grebienie starozytne i sredniowieczne z ziem polskich. Łódź, 1971.

Arc 936.14.405 Kozłowski, Stefan. Pradzieje ziem polskich od IX do V tysiąclecia. wyd. 1. Warszawa, 1972.

Arc 936.14.410 Sesja naukowa Zorzanizowana Zokazji 50- Lecia Katedry Archeologii Pradziejavej i Wczesnoś Redniowiecznej UAM, Poznań, 1969. Problemy badań archeologicznych Polski połnocnozachodniej. 1. wyd. Poznań, 1972.

Arc 936.14.415 Pyrgała, Jerzy. Mikroregion osadniczy między wisłą a Dolną Wkrą w obresie rzymskini. Wrocław, 1972.

Arc 936.14.420 Dąbrowski, Jan. Powiązanie ziem polskich z terenami uschodnimi w epoce brązu. Wrocław, 1972.

Arc 936.14.425 Sprawozdania z badań archeologicznych prowadzonych na terenie województwa koszolińskiego w Labach 1967-1968. Koszolin, 1969.

Arc 936.14.430 Nowakowski, Andrej. Gorne Pobuze w wiskach VIII-XI. Łódź, 1972.

Arc 936.14.435 Niewęgłowski, Andrej. Mazowsze na przełomie er. Wrocław, 1972.

Arc 936.14.440 Ogólnopolska Konferencja Konserwatorów Zabytkow Archeologicznych. Wspolpraca z Przemyslem w Dziedzinie Ochrony Zabytkow Archeologicznych, Poznań, 1969. Przemysł a archeologia. Poznań, 1971.

Arc 936.14.445 Węgzynowicz, Teresa. Wędrowki po wjkopaliskach. wyd. 1. Warszawa, 1972.

Arc 936.14.450 Kaletyn, Marta. Pierwsze lokacje miast w dorzeczu orli w XIII wieku. Wrocław, 1973.

Arc 936.14.455 Lodowski, Jerzy. Sądowel we wczesnym średniowieczu. Wrocław, 1972.

Arc 936.14.460 Gedl, Marek. Cmentarzysko halsztackie w kietrzue. Wrocław, 1973.

Arc 936.14.460.5 Gedl, Marek. Kultura przedłużycka. Wrocław, 1975.

Arc 936.14.465 Kruk, Janusz. Studia osadnicze nad neolitem wyżym lessowych. Wrocław, 1973.

Arc 936.14.470 Malinowski, Tadeusz. Wielkopolska wdobie Prasłowian. wyd. 1. Poznań, 1973.

Arc 936.14.475 Romanow, Jerzy. Tomice, pow. Wrocław, 1973.

Arc 936.14.480 Okulicz, Jerzy. Pradzieje ziem pruskich od późnego paleolitu do VII w.n.e. Wrocław, 1973.

Arc 936.14.485 Gąssowski, Jerzy. Przewodnik archeologiczny po Polsce. Wrocław, 1973.

Arc 936.14.490 Chudziakowa, Jadwiga. Kultura lużycka na terenie nięzdyrzecza Wisły, Drwęcy i Osy. wyd. 1. Warszawa, 1974.

Arc 936.14.495 Abramowicz, Andrzej. Dalecy i bliscy. Łódź, 1974.

Arc 936.14.500 Dąbrowska, Elżbieta. Wielkie grody dorzecza góinej Wisły. Wrocław, 1973.

Arc 936.14.505 Lachowicz, Franciszek J. Dorobek archeologii koszalińskiej w latach 1945-70. Koszalin, 1973.

Arc 936.14.510 Żaki, Andrzej. Wędrówki Sącza. Kraków, 1974.

Arc 936.14.515 Żaki, Andrzej. Archeologia Małopolski wczesnośredniowiecznej. Wrocław, 1947.

Arc 936.14.522 Godłowski, Kazimierz. Historia starożytna ziem polskich. 2. wyd. Kraków, 1973.

Arc 936.14.525 Chudziakowa, Jadwiga. Źródła archeologiczne zterenu zamku krzyżackiego w Towniu. 1. wyd. Warszawa, 1974.

Arc 936.14.530 Tyszkiewicz, Jan. Mozowsze północno-wschodnie we wczesnym średniowieczu. 1. wyd. Warszawa, 1974.

Arc 936.14.535 Przewoźna, Krystyna. Struktura i rozwój zasiedlenia południowowschedniej strefy nadbałtyckiej u sckyłku starożytności. 1. wyd. Warszawa, 1974.

Arc 936.14.540 Materiały do studiów nad osadnictwem bnińskim. Poznań, 1975.

Arc 936.14.545 Muzeum Ziemi Przemyskiej w Przemyślu. Historia badań archeologicznych i zbiorów Muzeum Ziemi Przemyskiej. Przemyśl, 1973.

Arc 936.14.550 Gierlach, Bogusław. Studia nad archeologią średniewiecznego Mazowsza. Wyd. 1. Warszawa, 1975.

Arc 936.14.555 Wachowski, Krzysztof. Cmentarzyska doby wczesnopiastowskiej na Śląsku. Wrocław, 1975.

Arc 936.15 Pamphlet vol. Fewkes, V.J. Archaeology. 6 pam.

Arc 936.15.5 Fewkes, V.J. Neolithic sites in the Mozavo-Danubian area. n.p., 1936.

Arc 936.15.10 Fewkes, V.J. Neolithic sites in the Yugoslavian portion of the lower Danube valley. Lancaster, 1937?

Arc 936.15.20 Pelikan, 'Old. Slovensko a rémske impérium. Bratislava, 1960.

Arc 936.15.25 Kongres archeologa Jugoslavije, 6th, Ljubljana, 1963. Kongrresni materijali VI Kongresa Jugoslovinskih arheoloya. Beograd, 1964. 2v.

Arc 936.20 Pârvan, Vasile. Dacia. Cambridge, 1928.

Arc 936.20.5 Ionitâ, Ian. Das Gräberfeld von Independenta. Bonn, 1971.

Arc 936.20.10 Tonescu, G.M. Etiopienii in Dacia preistorica. Bucureşti, 1926.

Arc 936.20.30 Pârvan, Vasile. Inseputurite vietii romane. Bucureşti, 1923.

Arc 936.20.40 Tudor, D. Sucidara; une cité daco-romaine en Dacie. Bruxelles, 1965.

Arc 936.20.50 Berciu, Dumitru. Neue Forschungsergebnisse zur Vorgeschichte Rumäniens. Bonn, 1966.

Arc 936.20.60 Fedorov, Georgii B. Arkheologiia Rumynii. Moskva, 1973.

Arc 936.20.65 Pârvan, Vasile. Dacia. Bucureşti, 1972.

Arc 936 Archaeology - Local - Other Europe - Other Local; Special topics - cont.

Arc 936.20.71 Gajewska, Halina. Topographie des fortifications romaines en Dobroudja. Wrocław, 1974.

Arc 936.20.75 Barbu, V. Adamclisi. Bucuresti, 1965.

Arc 936.24 Berciu, Dumitru. Romania. N.Y., 1967.

Arc 936.24.5 Condurachi, Emil. Romania. London, 1971.

Arc 936.24.10 Horedt, Kurt. Die prähistorische Ansiedlung auf dem Wietenberg bei Sighisoara-Schässburg. Bonn, 1971.

Arc 936.25 Gooss, Carl. Chronik der Archäologischenfund Siebenbürgens. Hermanstadt, 1876.

Arc 936.26 Notice sur les antiquités de la Roumanie. Paris, 1868.

Arc 936.26.10 György, L. Az Erdelyi Múzeum-Egyesület. Kolozsvár, 1937.

Arc 936.27 Hachhausen und Hachlaus, S.J. Die Alterthümer Daciens in dem heutigen Siebenbürgen. Wien, 1775.

Arc 936.28F Romstorfer, K.A. Cetalea Sucerii. Bucureşti, 1913.

Arc 936.29 Popov, R. Peshterata Temnata dupka. Sofiia, 1936.

Arc 936.29.5F Popov, R. Peshterata Mirezlivka. Sofiia, 1933.

Arc 936.30 Stanchev, S. Neuropolüt do novi pazar. Sofiia, 1958.

Arc 936.35F Filov, B. Die archäische Nekropole von Trebenischte am Ochrida-See. Leipzig, 1927.

Arc 936.35.5 Lahtov, Vasil. Problem trebeniške kulture. Ohrid, 1965.

Arc 936.38 Dimitrov, D. Bulgaria. Sofiia, 1961.

Arc 936.38.5 Böttger, Burkhard. Bulgarien; eine Reise zu antiken Kulturstätten. 1. Aufl. Berlin, 1971.

Arc 936.39F Filov, Bogdan. Die Grabhügelnekropole bei Duvanlij in Südbulgarien. Sofiia, 1934.

Arc 936.39.5 Filov, Bogdan. Nadgrobnité mogili pri Duvanlii v Plovdivsko. Sofiia, 1934.

Arc 936.40 Mikov, Vasil. Devetashkata peshtera. Sofiia, 1960.

Arc 936.40.5 Vuzharova, Z. Slaviano-bulgarskato selishte brai selo Popina. Sofiia, 1956.

Arc 936.40.10 Bulgarska Akademiia na Naukite, Sofia. Arkheologicheskikh Institut. Apoloniía. Sofiia, 1963.

Arc 936.40.15F Tsonchev, D. Prinosi kum "starata ist. na Ploadir". Sofiia, 1938.

Arc 936.40.16 Tsonchev, D. Contributions a l'histoire du stade antique de Philippopolis. Sofia, 1947.

Arc 936.40.20 Ivanova-Mavrodinova, Vera. Preslav. Sofiia, 1963.

Arc 936.40.25F Tsonchev, D. Le sanctuaire thrace prés du village de Batkoun. Sofia, 1941.

Arc 936.40.30F Sofia. Naroden Arkheologicheski Muzei. Madara. Sofiia, 1934.

Arc 936.40.35 Vüzharova, Zhivka N. Slavianski i slavianobulgarski selishta v bulgarskite semi. Sofiia, 1965.

Arc 936.40.41 Venedikov, Ivan. Nessebre. Sofia, 1971.

Arc 936.40.45 Tsarevgrad Turnov. Dvoretsutna bulgarskite tsare prez Utorata bulgarska durzhava. Sofiia, 1973-74. 2v.

Arc 936.40.50 Féher, Géza. Roliata i kulturata na prabulgarite. Sofiia, 1940.

Arc 936.42F Ivanov, T. Rimska mozaika ot Ulpiia Eskus. Sofiia, 1954.

Arc 936.43 Litsov, Khristo. Rimskiiat grad Abritus pri Razgrad. Razgrad, 1959.

Arc 936.50 Bulić, France. L'archéologie en Dalmatie du Xe siècle. n.p., 1924-25.

Arc 936.50.5 Bulić, France. Povodom pedestgod jubileja "Vjesnika za arh. hist. Dalmatinsku". Split, 1931.

Arc 936.50.10 Nin. Zadar, 1968.

Arc 936.55 Rostovtsev, M. Une tablette votive thraco-mithriaque du Louvre. Paris, 1923.

Arc 936.65F Mansel, A.M. Trakya-Kirklareli. Ankara, 1943.

Arc 936.65.5 Velkov, V.I. Gradût v Trakiia i Dakiia prez küsnata antichnost. Sofiia, 1959.

Arc 936.65.10 Tudor, D. Oltenia romănă. Bucureşti, 1968.

Arc 936.70 Spomenitse kulture. Beograd, 1951.

Arc 936.75 Kostrzewski, J. Les origines de la civilisation polonaise. Paris, 1949.

Arc 936.80F Mikov, Vasil. Le tombeau antique près de Kazanlak. Sofia, 1954.

Arc 936.80.5F Mikov, Vasil. Antichnata grobnitsa pri Kazanlak. Sofiia, 1954.

Arc 936.85 Schneider, A.M. Die Grabung in Westhofler Sophienkirche zu Istanbul. Berlin, 1941.

Arc 936.100 Karaman, L. Živa stariua. Zagreb, 1943.

Arc 936.100.10 Karaman, L. Baštiva djedova. Zagreb, 1944.

Arc 936.100.15 Karaman, L. Iz kdijerke hrvatsbe prostosti. Zagreb, 1930.

Arc 936.100.20 Gunjaca, S. Novi naucni rezultati u hrvatskoj arheologiji. Zagreb, 1958.

Arc 936.100.25 Horvat, L.A. Konzervatorski rad kod Hrvata. Zagreb, 1944.

Arc 936.100.30 Kukuljevic-Sakcinski, I. Nadpisi sredovječni i novovjeki na crkvah. Zagreb, 1891.

Arc 936.100.35 Vinkovci. Gradski Muzej. 20 godina Muzeja Vinkovci 1946-66. Vinkovci, 1966.

Arc 936.100.40 Valentic, Mirko. Kameni spomenici hrvatsko XIII-XIX stoljeća. Zagreb, 1969.

Arc 936.100.45 Škobalj, Ante. Obredne gomile. Sveti Križ na Čiovu, 1970.

Arc 936.100.50 Dimitrijevic, Stojan. Sopotsko-lendjelska kultura. Zagreb, 1968.

Arc 936.105 Srpska Akademia Nauka Belgrade. Arkheol. Institut. Arkheologika slomenichi i malazishta u Srbiji. v.1-2. Beograd, 1953.

Arc 936.110F Poulék, J. Pravěké umení. Praha, 1956.

Arc 936.115 Histria monografie archeologică. Bucureşti, 1954. 3v.

Arc 936.115.5 Cercetari privind istoria veche ARPR. Bucureşti, 1954.

Arc 936.115.10 Stoian, Iorgu. Etudes histriennes. Bruxelles, 1972.

Arc 936.120 Antonescu, Teohari. Le trophée d'Adamclissi. Jarsy, 1905.

Arc 936.120.5 Studniozka, Franz. Tropaeum Traiani. Leipzig, 1904.

Arc 936.120.10 Florescu, Florea B. Monumentul de la Adamklissi Tropaeum Traiani. Bucureşti, 1959.

Arc 936.140 Todorov, Ianko. Antichna kultura v Bulgariia. Sofiia, 1942?

Arc 936.140.01 Pamphlet vol. Bulgaria. Antiquities. 4 pam.

Arc 936.140.5 Velkov, Ivan. Murtvi gradove. Sofiia, 1933.

Arc 936.140.10 Škorpil, Hermeneyild. Mogili Ot. Kh. i K. Shkorpil. Plovdiv, 1898.

Arc 936.140.15 Dimitrov, Dimitur P. Nadgrobnite plochi ot rimsko vreme. Sofiia, 1942.

Arc 936.140.20 Majewski, Kazimierz. Kultura rzymska w Bułgarii. Wrocław, 1969.

Arc 936.140.25 Chichikova, Mariia. Sevtopolis. Sofiia, 1970.

Arc 936.140.30 Changova, Iordanka. Srednovekovnoto selishte nad trakiiskiia grad Sevtopolis. Sofiia, 1972.

Arc 936.140.35 Novae-sektor zachodni 1970. Poznań, 1973.

Arc 936.140.35.5 Novae-sektor zachodni 1972. Wyd. 1. Poznań, 1975.

Arc 936.140.40 Vuzharova, Zhivka N. O proiskhczhdenii bolgarskikh pakhotnykh orudii. Moskva, 1956.

Arc 936.140.45 Arkheologicheski otkritiia v Bulgariia. Sofiia, 1957.

Classified Listing

Arc 936 Archaeology - Local - Other Europe - Other Local; Special topics - cont.

Arc 936.140.50 Krusteva-Nozharova, Gina. Ukazatel na predmeti izobrazeni vurkhu antichni pametnitsi ot Bulgariia. Sofiia, 1958.
Arc 936.140.55 Vasiliev, Asen. Ivanovskite stenopisi. Sofiia, 1953.
Arc 936.140.60 Vuzharova, Zhivka N. Ruskite ucheni i bulgarskite starini. Sofiia, 1960.
Arc 936.150 Ondrouch, Vojtech. Bohaté hroby z doby rímskej na Slovensku. Bratislava, 1957.
Arc 936.150.5 Limes Romanus Konferenz, Nitra, Slovakia, 1957. Limes Romanus Konferenz. Bratislava, 1959.
Arc 936.150.10 Novotný, B. Počiatky výtvarnéreo prejavu na Slovensku. Bratislava, 1958.
Arc 936.155 Bernshtam, A.N. Istoriko-kul'turnoe proshloe severnoi Kirgizii. Frunze, 1943.
Arc 936.155.5 Kozhemiako, P.N. Radnesrednevekovye goroda i pos. Chuiskoi doliny. Frunze, 1959.
Arc 936.155.10 Baruzdin, J.D. Arkheologicheskie pamiatniki Batkena i Liailiaka, Jugo-Zapadnaia Kirgiziia. Frunze, 1962.
Arc 936.155.15 Akademiia Nauk Kirgizskoi SSR, Frunze. Institut Istorii. Arkheologicheskie pamiatniki Talasskoi dolny. Frunze, 1963.
Arc 936.155.20 Akademiia Nauk Kirgizskoi SSR, Frunze. Institut Istorii. Drevniaia i rannesrednevekovaia kul'tura Kirgizstana. Frunze, 1967.
Arc 936.165 Vulpe, Radu. Le vallum de la Moldavie inférieure et le mur d'Athanaric. 's-Gravenhage, 1957.
Arc 936.165.5 Materialy i issledovaniia po arkheologii Jugo-Zapada SSSR i Rumynskoi narodniki Respubliki. Kishinev, 1960.
Arc 936.165.10 Rikman, Emmanuil A. Pamiatniki drevnego iskusstva Moldavii. Kishinev, 1961.
Arc 936.165.12 Rikman, Emmanuil A. Khudozhestvennye sokrovishcha drevnei Moldavii. Kishinev, 1969.
Arc 936.165.15 Akademiia Nauk Moldavskoi SSSR, Kishinev. Institut Istorii. Materialy i issledovanii po arkheologii i ethnografii Moldavskoi SSR. Kishinev, 1964.
Arc 936.165.20 Arkheologiia, etnografiia i iskusstvovedenie Moldavii. Kishinev, 1968.
Arc 936.165.25 Dalekoe proshloe Moldavii. Kishinev, 1969.
Arc 936.165.30 Polevoi, Lazar' L'. Gorodskoe goncharstvo Pruto-Dnestrov'ia v XIV v. Kishinev, 1969.
Arc 936.165.35 Antropogen Moldavii. Kishinev, 1969.
Arc 936.165.40 Rikman, Emmanuil A. Ocherki istorii kul'tury Moldavii (II-XIV vv). Kishinev, 1971.
Arc 936.165.45 Ratalovich, Isak A. Slaviane VI-IX wkov v Moldavii. Kishinev, 1972.
Arc 936.165.50 Arkheologicheskaia karta Moldavskoi SSR. Kishinev, 1973- 5v.
Arc 936.165.55 Chebotarenko, Georgii T. Kal'fa-gorodishche vos'mogo-desiatego v.v. na Dnestre. Kishinev, 1973.
Arc 936.165.60 Khynku, Ivan G. Kepreriia-pamiatnik kul'tury X-XII vv. Kishinev, 1973.
Arc 936.165.65 Ketraru, Nikolai A. Sokrovishcha pyrkolaba Gangura. Kishinev, 1973.
Arc 936.170 Zontschew, Dimiter. Der Goldschatz von Panagjurischte. Berlin, 1959.
Arc 936.172F Venechikov, Ivan. The Panagynoishte gold treasure. Sofia, 1961.
Arc 936.175 Bešlagić, Š. Stećci na Blidinju. Zagreb, 1959.
Arc 936.180 Klemenc, J. Archäologische Karte von Jugoslavien. Beograd, 1938.
Arc 936.180.5 Mikulčić, Ivan. Pelagonija u svetlosti arheoloških nalaza. Beograd, 1966.
Arc 936.180.10 Aleksova, Blaga. Prosek-Demir Kapija. Skopje, 1966.
Arc 936.180.15 Batović, Šime. Stariji neolit u Dalmaciji. Zadar, 1966.
Arc 936.180.20 Tasić, Nikola. Badenski i vučedolski kulturni kompleks u Jugoslaviji. Beograd, 1967.
Arc 936.180.25 Tasić, Nikola. Crnokalačka bara. Kruševac, 1969.
Arc 936.180.30 Letića, Zagorka. Antropomorfne figurine bronzanog doba u Jugoslaviji. Beograd, 1973.
Arc 936.180.35 Wisaman, James. Stobi; a guide to the excavations. Beograd, 1973.
Arc 936.180.36 Studies in the antiquities of Stobi. Beograd. 1,1973+
Arc 936.185 Daicoviciu, C. Sarmizegetusa. București, 1960.
Arc 936.185.5 Antonescu, T. Cetatea Sarmizegetusa reconstitutiă. Iasi, 1966.
Arc 936.190 Beshevliev, V. Antike und Mittelalter in Bulgarien. Berlin, 1960.
Arc 936.195 Neustupny, E. Czechoslovakia before the Slavs. London, 1961.
Arc 936.195.5 Ceskoslovenska Academie Ved. Archeologichy Ustav. Nouvelles fouilles archéologiques en Tchécoslovaque. Prague, 1960.
Arc 936.195.10F Adámek, F. Pravěké Hradisko u Obřan. Brno, 1961.
Arc 936.195.15 Poulík, Josef. Zivot a umenie doby železnej na Slovensku. Bratislava, 1962.
Arc 936.195.20 Filip, Jan. Uměleckí řemeslo v pravěku. Praha, 1941.
Arc 936.195.25 Novotný, B. Luzianska skukina a pociatky malovanej keramiky na Slovensku. Bratislava, 1962.
Arc 936.195.30F Polla, B. Stredoveká zaniknuta osada na Spiši. Bratislava, 1962.
Arc 936.195.35 Poulík, Josef. Staří Moravané budiyí svůj stát. Gottwaldov, 1960.
Arc 936.195.37F Chropovský, Bohuslav. Pohrebiská zo staršej doby bronzovej na Slovensku. Bratislava, 1960.
Arc 936.195.37.5 Chropovský, Bohuslav. Slovensko na úsvite dejím. 1. vyd. Bratislava, 1970.
Arc 936.195.40F Budinsky-Krička, V. Slovanské mohyly v Skalici. Bratislava, 1959.
Arc 936.195.45 Turek, R. Čechy na úsvitě dějin. Praha, 1963.
Arc 936.195.50F Tučik, Aňton. Opevnina osada z doby bronzovej vo Veselom. Bratislava, 1964.
Arc 936.195.55 Tinelka, Karel. Cezavy u Bluciny ve svetle archeologickych vyskumů a nalezů. Brno, 1957.
Arc 936.195.60 Janšak, Stefan. Základy archeolog. vyskumu v teréne. Bratislava, 1955.
Arc 936.195.65 Novotný, B. Slovensko v mladšij dobe kaminej. Bratislava, 1958.
Arc 936.195.70 Boehn, Jároslav. Kronika objeveného véku. Praha, 1941.
Arc 936.195.75 Ondrouch, Vojtěch. Limes Romanus na Slovensku. Bratislava, 1938.
Arc 936.195.80 Poulík, Josef. Průvodce po výzkumech na staroslovanskim hradisku staré zámky u Lišně. Praha, 1949.
Arc 936.195.85 Borkovský, Ivan. Levý Hradec. Praha, 1965.
Arc 936.195.90 Volovek, V. Pravek vychodnich a severovychodnich Cech. Hradec Králové, 1962.
Arc 936.195.93 Volovek, V. Pohřebiště a súdliště lidu popelnicóvych poh v Třebešově. Hradec Králové, 1966.

Arc 936 Archaeology - Local - Other Europe - Other Local; Special topics - cont.

Arc 936.195.95 Balaša, Gejza. Praveké osídlenie stredného Slovenska. Bratislava, 1960.
Arc 936.195.96 Balaša, Gejza. Zvolen v období lužickej kultúry. Banská Bystrica, 1964.
Arc 936.195.100F Dostál, Bořivoj. Slovanská pohřebiště za střední doby hradištní na Moravě. Praha, 1966.
Arc 936.195.105 Slovenská Akademia Vied. Archeologický Ústav, Nitra. Pravek Slovenska. Bratislava, 1965- 2v.
Arc 936.195.110 Štěpánek, Miroslav. Opevněná sídliště 8.-12. století ve střední Ezvropě. Praha, 1965.
Arc 936.195.115F Dušek, Mikuláš. Thrakisches Gräberfeld der Hallstattzeit in Chotín. Bratislava, 1966.
Arc 936.195.120 Soudský, Bohumil. Bylany. Praha, 1966.
Arc 936.195.125 Hrubý, Vilém. Velkomoravské hradisko sv. Klimenta u Osvětiman. Brno, 1961.
Arc 936.195.130 Jansová, Libuše. Hrazany, Keltské oppidum na Sedlčansku. Praha, 1965.
Arc 936.195.135 Pravek východného Slovenska. Košice, 1966.
Arc 936.195.140 Filip, Jan. Recent archaeological finds in Czechoslavakia. Prague, 1966.
Arc 936.195.145 Pamphlet vol. Pamphlets on antiquities of Slovakia. 10 pam.
Arc 936.195.150 International Congress of Prehistoric and Protohistoric Sciences, 7th, Prague. Investigations archéologiques en Tchécoslovaquie. Prague, 1966.
Arc 936.195.155 Točík, Anton. Altmagyarische Gräberfelder in der Südwestslowakei. Bratislava, 1968.
Arc 936.195.160 Točík, Anton. Slawisch-awarisches Gräberfeld in Šturovo. 1. Aufl. Bratislava, 1968.
Arc 936.195.165 Poulík, Josef. Pevnost v lužním lese. 1. vyd. Praha, 1967.
Arc 936.195.165.5 Poulík, Josef. Velkomoravské hradiště Mikulčice. 1. vyd. Gottwaldov, 1959.
Arc 936.195.170 Preidel, Helmut. Das grossmährische Reich im Spiegel der Bodenfunde. Gräfelfing, 1968.
Arc 936.195.175 Skutil, Josef. Pravěké nálezy na Kloboucku. Klobuka, 1939.
Arc 936.195.180 Pichlerová, Magda. Nové košariská. 1. vyd. Bratislava, 1969.
Arc 936.195.185 Lichardus, Jan. Taskjňa Domica, najuznačnejšie sidlisko i udu bukovohorskej kultúry. 1. vyd. Bratislava, 1968.
Arc 936.195.190 Huml, Václav. Zaniklá turz Semonice. Hradec Králové, 1967.
Arc 936.195.195 Bánesz, Ladislav. Barca bei Košice - paläolithische Fundstelle. Bratislava, 1968.
Arc 936.195.200 Poláček, Josef. Divčě kámen. České Budějovice, 1960.
Arc 936.195.205 Barth, Fritz Eckart. Die hallstattzeitlichen Grabhügel im Bereiche der Kutscher bei Podsemel (Slowenien). Bonn, 1969.
Arc 936.195.210 Castelin, Karel O. Die Goldprägung der Kelten in den böhmischen Ländern. Graz, 1965.
Arc 936.195.215 Čilinská, Zlata. Slawisch-awarisches Gräberfeld in Nové Zámky. Bratislava, 1966.
Arc 936.195.220 Polla, Belo. Kežmarok. 1. vyd. Bratislava, 1971.
Arc 936.195.225 Novotná, Mária. Die Bronzehortfunde in der Slowakei. 1. vyd. Bratislava, 1970.
Arc 936.195.230 Davidek, Vácalv. Co bylo préd Prahon. 1. vyd. Praha, 1971.
Arc 936.195.235 Peškař, Ivan. Fibeln aus der römischen Kaiserzeit in Mähren. Prag, 1972.
Arc 936.195.240 Bolecek, B.V. Ancient Slovakia. n.p., 1973.
Arc 936.195.245 Čilinská, Zlata. Frühmittelalterliches Gräberfeld in Želovce. Bratislava, 1973.
Arc 936.195.250 Budinsky-Kricka, Vojtech. Das altungarische Fürstengral von Zemplén. Bratislava, 1973.
Arc 936.195.255 Dušek, Mikuláš. Bronzezeitliche Gräberfelder in der Südwestslowakei. Bratislava, 1969.
Arc 936.195.260 Vladár, Josef. Pohrebiská zo staršej doby bronzovej v Branči. 1. vyd. Bratislava, 1973.
Arc 936.195.265 Celostátní Seminář o Problematice Zaniklých Středověkých Vesnic, 3rd, Uherské Hradiště, Czechoslovak Republic, 1971. Zaniklé středověké vesnice v ČSSR ve svetle archeologických výzkumů. Uherské Hradiště, 1972.
Arc 936.195.270 Stocký, Albin. La Bohême préhistorique. Prague, 1929.
Arc 936.195.275 Prague. Národní Muzeum. Prehistorické Oddeleni. The prehistory of Czechoslovakia; exhibition, 1958. Prague, 1958.
Arc 936.195.280 Kraskovská, L'udmila. Slovansko-avarské pohrebisko pri Z'ahoiskej Bystrici. 1. vyd. Bratislava, 1972.
Arc 936.195.285 Hrubý, Vilém. Staré Město-Velehrad. 1. vyd. Praha, 1964.
Arc 936.195.285.5 Hrubý, Vilém. Staré Město-Veligrad. Gottwaldov, 1955.
Arc 936.195.290 Turek, Rudolf. Slavníkova Libice. Praha, 1946.
Arc 936.195.295 Vocel, Jan E. Pravěk země české. Praha, 1866-68.
Arc 936.195.300 Neustupný, Jiří. Pravěk Ceskoslovenska. 1. vyd. Praha, 1960.
Arc 936.195.305 Svoboda, Bedřich. Neuerworbene römische Metallgefässe aus Stáže bei Piešťany. 1. Aufl. Bratislava, 1972.
Arc 936.195.310 Adámsk, František. Důkaz pravosti metodějských nálezů z "Hrobů" u Osvětiman. Brno, 1934.
Arc 936.195.315 Krolmus, Wácslaw. Poslední bčžiště Černoboha s runami na Skalsku, v kraji Boleslavském, v Čechach, na své archaeologické cestě vypátral Václeslav Krolmus. Praha, 1857.
Arc 936.200 Hilczerowna, Z. Wczesnosredniowieczne grodzisko w Daleszynie (st. 2) w pow. gostynskim. Poznań, 1960.
Arc 936.205F Pašalić, E. Antička naselja i komunikacije u Bosni i Hercegovini. Sarajevo, 1960.
Arc 936.205.5 Čremošnik, Gregor. Nalazi iz rimskog doba na stupu kod. Sarajeva. Sarajevo, 1930.
Arc 936.205.10 Bešlagić, Šefik. Grborezi srednjovjckovna nekropola. Sarajevo, 1964.
Arc 936.205.15 Andjelić, Pavao. Bobovac i Kraljeva Sutjeska. Sarajevo, 1973.
Arc 936.215 Kovačević, J. Arheologija i istorija varvarske kolonizacije juzroslov. oblasti. Novi Sad, 1960.
Arc 936.215.5 Hoeckmann, Olaf. Die menschengestaltige Figuralplastik der südosteuropäischen Jungsteinzeit und Steinkupferzeit. v.1-2. Hildesheim, 1968.
Arc 936.215.10 Les Illyriens et la genèse des Albanais; travaux de la session du 3-4 mars, 1969. Tirana, 1971.
Arc 936.220F Garašanin, Milutin V. Arheološka nalazišta u Srbiji. Beograd, 1951.
Arc 936.220.01 Pamphlet vol. Serbia. Antiquities. 5 pam.
Arc 936.220.3 Garašanin, Milutin V. Arheološki nalazi u Jugoslaviji. Beograd, 1966.
Arc 936.220.5 Bajalović-Biztašević, Marya. Srednjevekovna nekropola w Mirijevu. Beograd, 1960.

Arc 936 Archaeology - Local - Other Europe - Other Local; Special topics - cont.

Arc 936.220.10 Todorović, Jovan. Banjica, naselje vinčanske kulture. Beograd, 1961.
Arc 936.220.15 Garašanin, Milutin V. Pregled materijame kulture juznih slovena u ranom s rednem veku. Beograd, 1950.
Arc 936.220.20 Todorović, Jovan. Stare kulture i narodi na tlu Beograd. Beograd, 1963.
Arc 936.220.22 Todorović, Jovan. Katalog praistorijskih metalmih predmeta. Beograd, 1971.
Arc 936.220.25 Pamphlet vol. Yugoslavia. Antiquities. 6 pam.
Arc 936.220.30 Belgrade. Narodni Muzej. Lepenski vir. Beograd, 1967.
Arc 936.220.32 Srejović, Dragoslav. Lepenski vir. Beograd, 1969.
Arc 936.220.35 Mijović, Pavle. Monodija o kamenu. Kruševac, 1967.
Arc 936.220.38 Mijović, Pavle. Tragam drevnih kultura Crme Gore. Titograd, 1970.
Arc 936.220.40 Djuhnić, Milena. Ilirska kneževsha nekropola u atenici. Čačak, 1966.
Arc 936.220.45 Todorović, Jovan. Kelti na tlu Beograda. Beograd, 1968.
Arc 936.220.50 Brukner, Bogdan. Neolit n Vojvodini. Beograd, 1968.
Arc 936.220.55 Srpska Akademija Nauka i Umetnosti, Belgrade, Galerije. Stare kul'ture u Djerdapu. Beograd, 1969.
Arc 936.220.60 Mano-Zisi, Djordje. Novi Pazar. Beograd, 1969.
Arc 936.220.65 Trbuhović, Vojislav B. Problemi porekla i datovanja bronzanog doba u Srbiji. Beograd, 1968.
Arc 936.220.70 Trbuhović, Vojislav B. Donja toponica. Prokuplje, 1970.
Arc 936.220.75 McPherron, Alan. Early farming cultures in Central Serbia (Eastern Yugoslavia). Krazujevać, 1971.
Arc 936.220.80 Girić, Milorad. Mokim. Washington, 1971-72. 2v.
Arc 936.220.85 Todorović, Jovan. Praistorijska Karaburma. Beograd, 1972.
Arc 936.220.90 Alexander, John. Jugoslavia before the Roman conquest. London, 1972.
Arc 936.220.91 Alexander, John. Yugoslavia before the Roman conquest. N.Y., 1972.
Arc 936.220.95 Srpska Akademija Nauka i Umetnosti, Belgrade. Arheološki Institut. Caričin Grad, 1912-62. Beograd, 1962.
Arc 936.220.100 Stalio, Blaženka. Gradac. Beograd, 1972.
Arc 936.220.105 Garašanin, Milutin V. Praistorija na thu SR Srbije. Beograd, 1973. 2v.
Arc 936.220.110 Vasić, Rastko. Kulturne grupe starijeg grozdenog doba u Jugoslaviji. Beograd, 1973.
Arc 936.220.115 Mano-Zisi, Djordje. Sliri i Grci, njihcvi kulturni odnosi u prošlosti naše zemlje na osnovu arheološkog materijala. Beograd, 1959.
Arc 936.220.120 Sirmium. Beograd, 1971- 3v.
Arc 936.220.125 Zotovič, Ljubica. Mitraizam na thu Jugoslavije. Beograd, 1973.
Arc 936.221 Čerškov, Emil. Rimljani na kosovu i Metohiji. Beograd, 1969.
Arc 936.221.5 Čerškov, Emil. Municipium DD kod Sočanice. Priština, 1970.
Arc 936.222 Adriatica praehistorica et antigua. Zagreb, 1970.
Arc 936.223 Pavlovič, L. Neki spomenici kulture; osvrti i Zapožanja. v.1-2. Smedrevo, 1962- 3v.
Arc 936.225 Šašel, Jaro. Vodnik po Emoni. Ljubljana, 1955.
Arc 936.225.5 Pirković, Ivo. Crucium. Ljubljana, 1968.
Arc 936.225.10 Petru, Peter. Hišaste žare Latobikov. Ljubljana, 1971.
Arc 936.225.15F Petru, Sonja. Emonske nekropole. Ljubljana, 1972.
Arc 936.225.20F Pahić, Stanka. Pobrežje. Lujbljana, 1972.
Arc 936.225.25F Plesničar-Gec, Ljudmila. Severno emonsko grobišče. Ljubljana, 1972.
Arc 936.225.30 Arheološka najdišča Slovenije. Ljubljana, 1975.
Arc 936.230 Klemenc, J. Rimske izkopanine v Šempetru. Ljubljana, 1961.
Arc 936.235 Gabrovec, S. Najstarejša zgodovina Dolenjske. Novo Mesto, 1956.
Arc 936.238 Knez, Tone. Novo Mesto v davnini. Maribar, 1972.
Arc 936.238.5 Novo Mesto, Yugoslavia. Dolenjski Muzej. Prazgodovina Novego Mesta. Novo Mesto, 1971.
Arc 936.240 Abramič, M. Poetovio. Ptuj, 1925.
Arc 936.241 Zemun. Narodni Muzej. Seoba naroda. Zemun, 1962.
Arc 936.242F Köhler, Ralf. Untersuchungen zu Grabkomplexam der älteren römischen Kaiserzeit in Böhmen unter Aspekten der religiösen und sozialen Gliederung. Neumünster, 1975.
Arc 936.250 Gzelishvili, Iosif. Zhelezoplavil'noe proizvodstvo v drevnei Gruzii. Tbilisi, 1964.
Arc 936.250.5 Kuftin, Boris A. Materialy k arkheologii kolkhidy. v.2. Tbilisi, 1950.
Arc 936.251 Benae, Alojz. Studije o kamenom i bakarnom dobu u sjeverozapadnom Balkanu. Sarajevo, 1964.
Arc 936.251.5 Belgrade. Narodni Muzej. Neolit centralnog Balkana. Beograd, 1968.
Arc 936.251.10 Jovanović, Borislav. Metalurgija eneolitskog perioda Yugoslavije. Beograd, 1971.
Arc 936.252 Melitauri, Konstantin N. Kreposti dofeodal'noi i rannefeodal'noi Gruzii. Tbilisi, 1969- 2v.
Arc 936.253 Symposium zu Problemen der Jüngeren Hallstattzeit in Mitteleuropa, Smolenice, 1970. Symposium zu Problemen der jüngeren Hallstattzeit. Bratislava, 1974.
Arc 936.260 Bŭlgarska Akademiia na Naukite, Sofia. Arkheologicheski Institut. Nessébre. Sofia, 1969.
Arc 936.261 Korošec, Paola. Predistariska naselba Barutnica kaj anzibegovo vo Makedonija. Prilep, 1973.
Arc 936.262 Pachkova, Svitlana P. Hospodarstvo skhidnoslov'ians'kykh plemen na rubezhi nashoï ery. Kyïv, 1974.

Arc 938 Archaeology - Local - Other Europe - Finland and Baltic States

Arc 938.5 Archäologischer Kongress, 10th, Riga, 1896. Katalog der Ausstellung. Riga, 1896.
Arc 938.5.5 Archäologischer Kongress, 10th, Riga, 1896. Klusie liecinieki; senlietu albums. Lincoln, Nebraska, 1964.
Arc 938.9 Archäologischer Kongress. Baltischen...Komitee. Baltische Studien zur Archäologie und Geschichte. Berlin, 1914.
Arc 938.11 Litzka, J. Verzeichnis archäologischer Fundorte in Liv-, Est- und Kurland. Jurjew, 1896.
Arc 938.13 Lincke, B. Eine baltische Halsringform der Volkerwanderungszeit. Inaug. Diss. Berlin, 1937.
Arc 938.15F Aspelin, J.R. Antiquités du Nord-Finno-Ougrien. v.1-5. St. Pétersbourg, 1877.
Arc 938.17 Balodis, F. L'ancienne frontiére slavo-latvienne. n.p., 192-.
Arc 938.17.5 Graudonis, J. Senatnes pédás. Riga, 1961.
Arc 938.17.10 Graudonis, Jánis. Latviia v epokhu pozdnei bronzy i rannego sheleza. Riga, 1967.
Arc 938.17.15 Vankina, Lutsiia V. Tortianikovaia stoiankor Sarnate. Riga, 1970.
Arc 938.19F Kruse, F.K.H. Necrolivonica. Dorpat, 1842.
Arc 938.25F Bahr, Johann K. Die Gräber der Liven. Dresden, 1850.

Arc 938 Archaeology - Local - Other Europe - Finland and Baltic States - cont.

Arc 938.27 Aspelin, Johan R. Suomalais-Ugrilaisen muinaistutkinnon alkeita. Helsingissä, 1875.
Arc 938.27.5 Aspelin, Johan R. Suomen asukkaat pakanuuden aikana. Helsingissä, 1885.
Arc 938.30 Hackman, A. Die ältere Eisenzeit in Finnland. Helsingfors, 1905.
Arc 938.50 Puzinas, Jonas. Vorgeschichtsforschung und Nationalbewusstsein in Litauen. Inaug. Diss. Kaunas, 1935.
Arc 938.50.5 Tarasenka, P. Priešistorine lieluwa. Kaunas, 1927.
Arc 938.55 Bielenstein, A. Die Holzbauten und Holzgeräte der Litten. pt.1-2. n.p., 1907-18.
Arc 938.60F Nerman, Burger. Grobin-Seeburg. Stockholm, 1958.
Arc 938.65 Volkerite-Kulikauskiené, R. Lietuvos archeologiniai pominklai ir jų tyrinejimai. Vil'nius, 1958.
Arc 938.65.5 Volkaitė-Kulikauskienė, Regina. Punios piliakalnis. Vilnius, 1974.
Arc 938.68 Daugudis, V. Stakliškių lobis. Vil'nius, 1968.
Arc 938.70 Kulikauskar, P. Lietuvos archeologijos bruočai. Vil'nius, 1961.
Arc 938.75F Kivikoski, Ella. Suomen rantakauden kuoasto. Helsinki, 1947-51. 2v.
Arc 938.80F Racz, István. Kivikirves ja hapearisti. Helsingissä, 1961.
Arc 938.85 Kivikoski, Ella. Suomen esihistoria. Helsinki, 1961.
Arc 938.85.5 Kivikoski, Ella. Finland. London, 1967.
Arc 938.85.10 Kivikoski, Ella. Suomen kiinteät muinaisjäännökset. Helsinki, 1966.
Arc 938.95 Selirand, J. Läbi aastatuhandete. Tallinn, 1963.
Arc 938.95.5 Selirand, Jüri. Estlaste matmiskombed varafeodaalsete suhete tärkamise perioodil (11.-13. sajand). Tallinn, 1974.
Arc 938.96F Kivikoski, Ella. Kvaonbacken. Helsinki, 1963.
Arc 938.97 Eesti NSV Teaduste Akadeemia. Ajaloo Institut. Pronksiajast varase feodalisimini. Tallinn, 1966.
Arc 938.98 Lietuvos BR Mokslų Akademije, Vilna. Istorijas Institutas. Zo let. Vil'nius, 1968.
Arc 938.99 Lietuvos archeologikiai paminklai. Vil'nius, 1968.
Arc 938.100 Dolukhanov, Pavel M. Istoriia Baltiki. Moskva, 1969.
Arc 938.101 Sauvateev, Iurii A. Zalavruga. Leningrad, 1970.
Arc 938.102 Studia archaelogica in memoriam Harri Moora. Tallinn, 1970.
Arc 938.104 Indreko, Richard. Mesolithische und frühneolithische Kulturen in Osteuropa und Westsebirien. Stockholm, 1964.
Arc 938.106 Šturms, Edward. Die steinzeitlichen Kulturen des Baltikums. Bonn, 1970.
Arc 938.107 Tönisson, Evald. Die Gauja-Liven und ihre materielle Kultur. Tallinn, 1974.
Arc 938.108 Pagirienė, L. Lietuvos TSR archeologija 1940-1967. Vil'nius, 1970.
Arc 938.109 Rimantienė, Rimutė Jablonskytė. Pirmieji Lietuvos gyventojai. Vil'ius, 1972.
Arc 938.110 Volkaitė-Kulikauskienė, Regina. Lietuvio kario žirgas. Vil'nius, 1971.
Arc 938.111 Lietuvos TSR archeologijos atlasas. Vil'nius, 1974- 3v.
Arc 938.112 Latvijas PSR arheologija. Riga, 1974.

Arc 942 Archaeology - Local - Americas in general - Pamphlet volumes

Arc 942.1 Pamphlet vol. Archaeology. American. 1880- 32 pam.
Arc 942.2 Pamphlet vol. Archaeology. American. 5 pam.
Arc 942.3 Pamphlet vol. Archaeology. American. 7 pam.
Arc 942.4 Pamphlet vol. Topics in American archaeology. 9 pam.
Arc 942.5 Pamphlet vol. Archaeology. American. 17 pam.
Arc 942.6 Pamphlet vol. American antiquities and archaeology. 26 pam.
Arc 942.7 Pamphlet vol. Archaeology. Aboriginal America. 31 pam.
Arc 942.8 Pamphlet box. Archaeology. American. Miscellaneous pamphlets.
Arc 942.9 Pamphlet vol. Willoughby, C. Archaeological and ethnological papers. 22 pam.

Arc 943 Archaeology - Local - Americas in general - General works

Arc 943.2 Phillips, H. A brief account of the more important public collections of American archaeology in the United States. n.p., n.d.
Arc 943.3 Baldwin, J.D. Ancient America. N.Y., 1878.
Arc 943.3.5 Baldwin, J.D. Ancient America. N.Y., 1872.
Arc 943.4 Kabell, S.K. America for Columbus. Roenne, 1892.
Arc 943.5 Larkin, F. Ancient man in America. n.p., 1880.
Arc 943.6 Larrainzar, M. Estudios sobre la historia de America. Mexico, 1875-78. 5v.
Arc 943.7 Pouget, J.F.A. du Nadaillac. L'Amérique préhistorique. Paris, 1883.
Arc 943.7.5A Pouget, J.F.A. du Nadaillac. Prehistoric America. N.Y., 1884.
Arc 943.7.5B Pouget, J.F.A. du Nadaillac. Prehistoric America. N.Y., 1884.
Arc 943.8 Rafn, K.C. Cabinet d'antiquités americaines. Copenhagen, 1858.
Arc 943.9.5 Thomas, C. Introduction...study North American archaeology. Cincinnati, 1903.
Arc 943.10.1 Hamy, Jules. Mémoires d'archéologie et d'ethnographié americaines. Graz, 1971.
Arc 943.11 Pamphlet box. MacCurdy, G.G. American archaeology pamphlets.
Arc 943.12 Beuchat, H. Manuel d'archéologie americaine. Paris, 1912.
Arc 943.13 Shipp, B. The Indian and antiquities of America. Philadelphia, 1897.
Arc 943.14 N.Y. Museum of the American Indian. Heye Foundation. Contributions. N.Y. 1-18 13v.
Arc 943.14.3 N.Y. Museum of the American Indian. Heye Foundation. Indian notes and monographs. N.Y. 1-10,1919-1928 9v.
Arc 943.14.4 N.Y. Museum of the American Indian. Heye Foundation. Indian notes and monographs. N.Y. 1-53,1920-1943 20v.
Arc 943.14.5F N.Y. Museum of the American Indian. Heye Foundation. Leaflets. N.Y. 1-5,1919-1926
Arc 943.14.8 N.Y. Museum of the American Indian. Heye Foundation. Indian notes. N.Y. 1-7,1924-1930 6v.
Arc 943.14.9 N.Y. Museum of the American Indian. Heye Foundation. Indian notes. Index, v.1-7. N.Y., 1949.
Arc 943.15 Pamphlet box. Putnam, F.W. American archaeology.
Arc 943.17 Pamphlet box. Holmes, W.H. American archaeology.
Arc 943.18 Pamphlet box. Fewkes, J.W. American archaeology.
Arc 943.25 Utzinger, Rudolf. Indianer-Kunst. München, 1921.
Arc 943.26 Hill, Ira. Antiquities of America explained. Hagerstown, 1831.

Classified Listing

Arc 943 Archaeology - Local - Americas in general - General works - cont.

Arc 943.27 Hudlicka, A. Recent discoveries attributed to early man in America. Washington, 1918.
Arc 943.28 Brown, F.M. America's yesterday. Philadelphia, 1937.
Arc 943.29 Brown, A. Indian relics and their values. Chicago, 1942.
Arc 943.31 Panneton, P. Un monde était leur empire. Montréal, 1943.
Arc 943.32 Hibben, F.C. Treasure in the dust. 1. ed. Philadelphia, 1951.
Arc 943.34 Verrill, A.H. America's ancient civilizations. N.Y., 1953.
Arc 943.36F Appleton, LeRoy H. Indian art of the Americas. N.Y., 1950.
Arc 943.38 Covarrubias, M. The eagle. 1. ed. N.Y., 1954.
Arc 943.40 Kinzhalov, R.V. Pamiatniki kul'tury i iskusstva drevnei Ameriki. Leningrad, 1958.
Arc 943.42 Trimborn, Hermann. Das alte Amerika. Stuttgart, 1959.
Arc 943.44 Lothrop, S.K. Essays in pre-Columbian art and archaeology. Cambridge, Mass., 1961.
Arc 943.45 Rice University. Prehistoric man in the new world. Chicago, 1964.
Arc 943.46 Alcina Franch, José. Manual de arqueologia americana. Madrid, 1965.
Arc 943.50 Cusack, Betty Bugbee. Collector's luck: giant steps into prehistory. 1. ed. Stoneham, Mass., 1968.
Arc 943.51 Guliaev, Valerii I. Amerika i Staryi svet v dokolumbovu epokhu. Moskva, 1968.
Arc 943.53 Comas, Juan. Origen de las culturas precolombinas. 1. ed. México, 1975.
Arc 943.54 Judd, Neil Morton. Men met along the trail. 1. ed. Norman, 1968.

Arc 945 Archaeology - Local - Americas in general - Special topics

Arc 945.1 Hough, W. The lamp of the Eskimo. Washington, 1898.
Arc 945.2 Grossi, V. Teocalli e piramidi. Torino, 1888.
Arc 945.3 Squier, E.G. Serpent symbol and worship of nature in America. N.Y., 1851.
Arc 945.4 Mason, Otis J. Aboriginal American harpoons. Washington, 1900.
Arc 945.5F Capitan, Louis. Décades américaines. Levallois-Perret, 1907.
Arc 945.6 Posnansky, Arthur. Las Americas son un nuevo mundo. La Paz, Bolivia, 1943.
Arc 945.7 Peterson, Clarence S. America's rune stone of A.D. 1362 gains favor. N.Y., 1946.
Arc 945.8 Nantes. Trésors d'archéologie américaine et océanienne. Nantes, 1958?

Arc 950 Archaeology - Local - United States and Canada - Folios [Discontinued]

Htn Arc 950.5* Harris, W.P. Brief account of the discovery of the brass plates...Kinderbrook, Illinois. Nauvoo, Illinois, 1843.
Arc 950.10F Hewett, E.L. Les communautés anciennes dans le désert américain. Genève, 1908.
Arc 950.200 Nordenskiold, G. The cliff dwellers of the Mesa Verde. Stockholm, 1893.
Arc 950.200.9 Moore, C.B. Certain aboriginal mounds. Philadelphia, 1898.
Arc 950.201A Moore, C.B. Certain sand mounds of the St. John's River. pt.1-2. Philadelphia, 1894.
Arc 950.201B Moore, C.B. Certain sand mounds of the St. John's River. pt.1-2. Philadelphia, 1894.
Arc 950.202 Moore, C.B. Certain river mounds of Duval County, Florida. Philadelphia, 1895.
Arc 950.202.2 Moore, C.B. Additional mounds of Duval and of Clay Counties, Florida. n.p., 1896.
Arc 950.202.5 Moore, C.B. Certain aboriginal mounds of the Georgia coast. Philadelphia, 1897.
Arc 950.202.9 Moore, C.B. Certain aboriginal remains...Alabama River. Philadelphia, 1899.
Arc 950.202.11 Moore, C.B. Certain aborginal remains of the northwestern Florida coast. pt.1-2. Philadelphia, 1901. 2v.
Arc 950.202.12F Moore, C.B. The northwestern Florida coast revisited. Philadelphia, 1918.
Arc 950.202.13 Moore, C.B. Certain antiquities of the Florida west coast. Philadelphia, 1900.
Arc 950.202.15 Moore, C.B. Certain aboriginal remains...Florida coast. Philadelphia, 1903.
Arc 950.202.17 Moore, C.B. Certain aboriginal remains of the Black Warrior River. Philadelphia, 1905.
Arc 950.202.21 Moore, C.B. Moundville revisited. Philadelphia, 1907.
Arc 950.202.23 Moore, C.B. Certain mounds of Arkansas and Mississippi. Philadelphia, 1908.
Arc 950.202.25 Moore, C.B. Antiquities of the Onachita Valley. Philadelphia, 1909.
Arc 950.202.29 Moore, C.B. Antiquities of the St. Francis, White and Black rivers, Arkansas. Philadelphia, 1910.
Arc 950.202.32 Moore, C.B. Some aboriginal sites on the Red River. Philadelphia, 1912.
Arc 950.202.33 Moore, C.B. Some aboriginal sites on Mississippi River. Philadelphia, 1911.
Arc 950.202.35 Moore, C.B. Some aboriginal sites in Louisiana and Arkansas. Philadelphia, 1913.
Arc 950.202.38F Moore, C.B. Aboriginal sites on Tennessee River. Philadelphia, 1915.
Arc 950.203 Lapham, I.A. The antiquities of Wisconsin. Washington, 1855?
Arc 950.204 Terry, J. Sculptured anthropoid ape heads. N.Y., 1891.
Arc 950.205 Haldeman, S.S. On the contents of a rock retreat in Southeast Pennsylvania. n.p., n.d.
Arc 950.206 United States. Report upon geographical surveys west of the one hundredth meridian. v.7. Archaeology. Washington, 1879.
Arc 950.207 Brower, J.V. Memoirs of explorations...basin...Mississippi. v.1-3,4-5,6-7,8. St. Paul, Minn., 1898. 7v.
Arc 950.208 Thomas, C. Report of mound explorations of Bureau of Ethnology. Washington, 1894.
Arc 950.209 Pinart, A.L. La caverne d'Aknanh, ile d'Ounga. Paris, 1875.
Arc 950.210 Mackenzie, A. Descriptive notes on certain implements...Graham Island. n.p., 1891.
Arc 950.211 Putnam anniversary volume. N.Y., 1909. 2v.
Arc 950.212F Ancient monuments of...Mississippi Valley. Prospectus. N.Y., 1848.

Arc 953 Archaeology - Local - United States and Canada - General works

Arc 953.01 Pamphlet box. Archaeology. United States and Canada.
Arc 953.1 Abbott, C.C. Primitive industry. Salem, 1881.
Arc 953.1.50 Foster, J.W. Prehistoric races of U.S.A. Chicago, 1873.
Arc 953.2 Foster, J.W. Prehistoric races of the United States of America. 4. ed. Chicago, 1878.
Arc 953.2.3 Foster, J.W. Prehistoric races of the United States of America. 5. ed. Chicago, 1881.
Arc 953.3 Haynes, H.W. The prehistoric archaeology of North America. Boston, 1889.
NEDL Arc 953.4 Lewis, T.H. Tracts for archaeologists. First series, 1880-91. St. Paul, 1892.
Arc 953.5 MacLean, J.P. The mound builders. Cincinnati, 1879.
Arc 953.6 Mason, O.T. Miscellaneous papers relating to anthropology. Washington, 1883.
Arc 953.7 Morris, C. Extinct races of America - the mound builders. Review. n.p., n.d.
Arc 953.8 Peet, S.D. Prehistoric America. v.1, The mound builders. v.3, Cliff dwellers. v.4, Ancient monuments. v.5, Myths and symbols. Chicago, 1890-1905. 4v.
Arc 953.9 Pidgeon, W. Traditions of De-coo-dah and antiquarian researches. N.Y., 1858.
Arc 953.10 Schmidt, E. Vorgeschichte Nordamerikas im Gebiet der Vereinigten Staaten. Braunschweig, 1894.
Arc 953.11 Short, J.F. The North Americans of antiquity. N.Y., 1879-80.
Arc 953.13 Warden, D.B. Recherches sur les antiquités de l'Amérique. Paris, 1827.
Arc 953.14 Holmes, William H. Art in shell of ancient Americans. Washington, 1880-81.
Arc 953.15 Boston Society of Natural History. Palaeolithic implements of...Delaware. v.1-3. Cambridge, 1881.
Arc 953.17 Pamphlet vol. Archaeology. United States. 15 pam.
Arc 953.18 Moorehead, W.K. The stone age in North America. Boston, 1910. 2v.
Arc 953.18.5 Moorehead, W.K. A narrative of explorations of New Mexico, Arizona, Indiana. Andover, 1906.
Arc 953.19 Pamphlet box. Smith, Harlan I. Archaeology. United States and Canada.
Arc 953.19.5 Smith, Harlan I. An album of prehistoric Canadian art. Ottawa, 1923.
Arc 953.20F Haven, S.F. Archaeology of the United States. Washington, 1856.
Arc 953.21 Fowke, G. Archaeological investigations. Washington, 1922.
Arc 953.22 United States. Department of the Interior. Annual report of department archaeologist. Washington. 1928-1931
Arc 953.23A Ewers, J.C. Plains Indian painting. Stanford, 1939.
Arc 953.23B Ewers, J.C. Plains Indian painting. Stanford, 1939.
Arc 953.24A Douglas, F.H. Indian art of the United States. N.Y., 1941.
Arc 953.24B Douglas, F.H. Indian art of the United States. N.Y., 1941.
Arc 953.25 Renaud, E.B. Classification and description of Indian stone artifacts. Gunnison, 1941.
Arc 953.26 Speck, F.G. Eastern Algonkian block stamp decoration. Trenton, New Jersey, 1947.
Arc 953.28F Griffin, James. Archaeology of eastern United States. Chicago, 1952.
Arc 953.29 McGregor, John Charles. Southwestern archaeology. 2. ed. Urbana, 1965.
Arc 953.30 Baldwin, Gordon Cortis. Race against time. N.Y., 1966.
Arc 953.32 Nöel Hume, Ivor. A guide to artifacts of colonial America. 1. ed. N.Y., 1970.
Arc 953.34 Marek, Kurt W. The first American. 1. ed. N.Y., 1971.
Arc 953.34.1 Marek, Kurt W. Der erste Amerikaner. Reinbek bei Hamburg, 1972.

Arc 955 - 980 Archaeology - Local - United States and Canada - Local (A-Z by state of the U.S. or province of Canada]

Arc 955.01 Pamphlet box. Archaeology. United States and Canada. Miscellaneous pamphlets.
Arc 955.1 Burns, Frank. The Crump burial cave (Blount County, Alabama). n.p., 1892.
Arc 955.2 Hough, W. Antiquities of the Upper Gila...(Arizona). Washington, 1907.
Arc 955.2.4 Fewkes, J.W. Excavations at Casa Grande, Arizona in 1906-07. v.1-2. Washington, 1907.
Arc 955.2.5 Fewkes, J.W. Preliminary report on a visit to Navaha national monument Arizona. Washington, 1911.
Arc 955.2.7 Fewkes, J.W. A preliminary account of archaeological field work in Arizona in 1897. Washington, 1898.
Arc 955.2.9 Fewkes, J.W. Casa Grande, Arizona (28th report of the Bureau of American Ethnology). Washington, 1913.
Arc 955.2.11 Fewkes, J.W. Basket-maker, caves of northeastern Arizona. Cambridge, 1921.
Arc 955.2.12 Guernsey, S.J. Explorations in northeastern Arizona. Cambridge, Mass., 1931.
Arc 955.2.13 Mindeleff, C. The repair of Casa Grande ruin, Arizona, in 1891. Washington, n.d. 2 pam.
Arc 955.2.20 Oakland, California. Museum. The Doheny scientific expedition to the Hava Supai Canyon, northern Arizona...1924. San Francisco, 1925.
Arc 955.5 Cummings, B. Kinishba. Phoenix, Arizona, 1940.
Arc 956.1 Smith, Harlan I. Archaeological collection from the southern interior of British Columbia. Museum of Geological Survey, Canada. Ottawa, 1913.
Arc 956.2 Okladnikov, Aleksei P. Drevnie poseleniia Baranova mysa. Novosibirsk, 1971.
Arc 957.1 Fewkes, J.W. Antiquities of the Mesa Verde National Park Cliff Palace (Colorado). Washington, 1911.
Arc 957.1.5 Fewkes, J.W. Antiquities of the Mesa Verde National Park Spruce Tree House. Washington, 1909.
Arc 957.1.8A Fewkes, J.W. Prehistoric villages, castles, and towers of southwestern Colorado. Washington, 1919.
Arc 957.1.8B Fewkes, J.W. Prehistoric villages, castles, and towers of southwestern Colorado. Washington, 1919.
Arc 957.1.15 Jeancon, J.A. Archaeological research in the northeast San Juan basin of Colorado. Denver, 1922.
Arc 957.1.25 Roberts, Frank H.H. Early pueblo in the Piedra district. Washington, 1930.
Arc 957.2 Holmes, William H. Anthropological studies in California. n.p., n.d.
Arc 958.1 Abbott, Charles C. Recent archaeological explorations in the Valley of the Delaware. Boston, 1892.
Arc 958.1.3 Abbott, Charles C. Researches upon antiquities of man, Delaware Valley. Boston, 1897.

Classified Listing

Arc 955 - 980 Archaeology - Local - United States and Canada - Local (A-Z by state of the U.S. or province of Canada] - cont.

	Arc 958.1.5	Volk, E. The archaeology of the Delaware Valley. Cambridge, 1911.
	Arc 958.1.8	Abbott, C.C. Ten years' diggings in Lenâpè Sand, Delaware. Trenton, New Jersey, 1912.
	Arc 958.1.15	Weslager, Clinton Alfred. Delaware's buried past. Philadelphia, 1944.
	Arc 958.2	Kengla, L.A. Contributions to the archaeology of the District of Columbia. Washington, 1883.
	Arc 960.1	Kunz, G.F. Gold and silver ornaments from mounds of Florida. Chicago, 1887.
	Arc 960.2	Wyman, J. Fresh-water shell mounds...St. John's River, Florida. Salem, 1875.
	Arc 960.2.5	Fewkes, J.W. Preliminary archaeological explorations at Weeden Island, Florida. Washington, 1924.
	Arc 960.2.15F	Moore, C.B. As to Cooper from the mounds of the St. John's River, Florida. Philadelphia, 1894.
	Arc 961.1	Jones, C.C. Aboriginal structures in Georgia. Washington, 1878. 2 pam.
	Arc 961.1.3	Jones, C.C. Indian remains in southern Georgia. Savannah, 1859.
	Arc 961.1.4	Jones, C.C. Monumental remains of Georgia. Savannah, 1861.
	Arc 961.1.5	Jones, C.C. Antiquities of the southern Indians. N.Y., 1873.
	Arc 961.1.15	Fewkes, J.W. W.P.A. excavations at Irene Mound, Savannah, Georgia, May 4, 1938. Savannah, 1938.
	Arc 961.1.20	Caldwell, Joseph. Irene Mound site, Chatham County, Georgia. Athens, 1941.
	Arc 961.1.25	Sears, William H. Excavations at Kolomoki. v.1-2. Athens, 1950?
	Arc 963.1	Lewis, T.H. Stone monuments in northwestern Iowa and southwestern Minnesota. n.p., 1890?
	Arc 963.2	Baker, Frank C. The Cahokia mounds. [Illinois]. Urbana, 1923.
	Arc 963.2.15	Crook, A.R. The origin of the Cahokia mounds. Springfield, 1922.
	Arc 963.2.20	Cole, Fay C. Rediscovering Illinois. Chicago, 1937.
	Arc 963.3	McAllister, J.G. The archaeology of Porter County, Indiana. Indianapolis, 1932.
	Arc 963.3.5	Lilly, Eli. Prehistoric antiquities of Indiana. Indianapolis, 1937.
	Arc 965.1	Whiteford, Guy L. Indian archaeology in Saline County, Kansas. Salina, 1941.
	Arc 967.1	Squier, E.G. Observations on the aboriginal monuments of the Mississippi Valley. N.Y., 1847.
	Arc 967.1.2	McAdams, William. Records of ancient races. St. Louis, 1887.
	Arc 967.1.3	Carr, L. The mounds of the Mississippi Valley. Cambridge, 188-?
	Arc 967.1.4	Carr, L. The mounds of the Mississippi Valley. Washington, 1893.
	Arc 967.1.5	Carr, L. The mounds of the Mississippi Valley. Frankfort, 1883.
	Arc 967.1.9	Conant, Alban J. Foot-prints of vanished races in the Mississippi Valley. St. Louis, 1879.
	Arc 967.1.11	Conference on Midwestern Archaeology, St. Louis. Report. Washington, 1929.
	Arc 967.1.13	Brown, C.S. Archaeology of Mississippi. University, 1926.
	Arc 967.2	Folvke, G. Antiquities of central and southeastern Missouri. Washington, 1910.
	Arc 967.2.5	Peabody, Charles. The exploration of Jacobs Cavern, McDonald County, Missouri. Norwood, 1904.
	Arc 967.2.10	Graves, H.B. The pre-Cambrian structure of Missouri. Diss. St. Louis, 1938.
	Arc 967.3	Moorehead, W.K. Certain peculiar earthworks near Andover, Massachusetts. Andover, 1912.
	Arc 967.3.5	Sheldon, J.M.A. (Mrs.). Pitted stones. Deerfield, 1925.
	Arc 967.4	Peabody, Charles. The exploration of Bushey Cavern near Cavetown, Maryland. Andover, 1908.
	Arc 967.5	Moorehead, W.K. The Merrimack archaeological survey. Salem, Mass., 1931.
	Arc 967.6	Miller, J. Jefferson. Eighteenth-century ceramics from Fort Michilimackinac, Michigan. Washington, 1970.
	Arc 967.7	Voices from the rapids: an underwater search for fur trade artifacts, 1960-73 (Minnesota). St. Paul, 1975.
	Arc 968.1	Squier, E.G. Antiquities of the state of New York. Buffalo, 1851.
	Arc 968.1.2	Conover, G.S. Reasons why the state should acquire the famous burial mound of the Seneca Indians. n.p., n.d.
	Arc 968.1.5	Beauchamp, W.M. Metallic ornaments of the New York Indians. n.p., n.d.
	Arc 968.1.5.5	Beauchamp, W.M. Wampum and shell articles used by the New York Indians. Albany, 1901. 2 pam.
	Arc 968.1.9	Parker, A.C. Excavations in an Erie Indian village. n.p., 1907.
	Arc 968.1.15	Ferguson, Henry L. Archaeological exploration of Fishers Island, New York. N.Y., 1935.
	Arc 968.2	Morgan, L.H. On the ruins of a stone pueblo on the Animas River in New Mexico. Salem, 1879.
	Arc 968.2.5	Hodge, F.W. The enchanted Mesa. v.1-2. Washington, 1897.
	Arc 968.2.10	Hewett, E.L. Antiquities of the Jemez Plateau, New Mexico. Washington, 1906.
	Arc 968.2.12	Hewett, E.L. Pajarito Plateau and its ancient people. Albuquerque, 1938.
	Arc 968.2.15	Fewkes, J.W. Archaeological investigations in New Mexico, Colorado, and Utah. Washington, 1917.
	Arc 968.2.20	Fewkes, J.W. Archaeology of the lower Mimbres Valley, New Mexico. Washington, 1914.
	Arc 968.2.23	Bradfield, W. Cameron Creek village...New Mexico. Santa Fé, 1931.
	Arc 968.2.25	Cosgrove, H.S. The Swarts ruin...New Mexico. Cambridge, 1932.
	Arc 968.2.30	Roberts, Frank H.H. Shabik'eschee village. Washington, 1929.
	Arc 968.2.32	Roberts, Frank H.H. The village of the great Kivas on the Zuñi reservation, New Mexico. Washington, 1932.
	Arc 968.2.35	Roberts, Frank H.H. A survey of southwestern archaeology. Washington, 1936.
	Arc 968.2.40F	New Mexico. University. Bulletin survey series. Albuquerque. 1,1931
	Arc 968.2.45	Kidder, Alfred V. An introduction to the study of southwestern archaeology. New Haven, 1924.
	Arc 968.2.50	Kidder, Alfred V. The artifacts of Pecas. New Haven, 1932.
	Arc 968.2.55	Howard, E.B. Evidence of early man in North America...archaeological work in New Mexico. Philadelphia, 1935.
	Arc 968.2.60	Prince, Le B.B. The stone lions of Cochite. Santa Fe, 1903.
	Arc 968.2.65	Nesbitt, Paul H. Starkweather ruin: a Mogollon-Pueblo site in the Upper Gila area of New Mexico. Diss. Chicago, 1938.
	Arc 968.2.70	Morris, E.H. Archaeological studies in the La Plata district, southwestern Colorado and northwestern New Mexico. Washington, 1939.
Htn	Arc 968.2.75*	Baumann, G. Frijoles Canyon pictographs. Santa Fe, 1939.
	Arc 968.2.80	Hendron, J.W. Prehistory of El Rito de los Frijoles, Bandelier national monument. Phoenix, 1940.
	Arc 968.2.85	Vivian, G. Gran Quivira. Washington, 1964.
	Arc 968.4	Abbott, Charles C. Archaeologia nova caesarea, 1907-09. Trenton, New Jersey, 1907-08.
	Arc 968.4.5	Abbott, Charles C. Stone age in New Jersey. Washington, 1877.
	Arc 968.10	Will, G.F. The Mandans. [North Dakota]. Cambridge, 1906.
	Arc 968.11	Bell, Earl Hoyt. Chapters in Nebraska archaeology. Lincoln, Nebraska, 1936.
	Arc 968.12A	Goodwin, William B. The ruins of Great Ireland in New England. Boston, 1946.
	Arc 968.12B	Goodwin, William B. The ruins of Great Ireland in New England. Boston, 1946.
	Arc 969.1	Read, M.C. Archaeology of Ohio. Cleveland, 1888.
	Arc 969.1.05	Morgan, Richard G. Bibliography of Ohio archaeology. Columbus, 1947.
	Arc 969.1.2	Moorehead, W.K. Primitive man in Ohio. N.Y., 1892.
	Arc 969.1.3	Moorehead, W.K. Fort Ancient. Cincinnati, 1890.
	Arc 969.1.3.7	Griffin, James B. The Fort Ancient aspect. Ann Arbor, 1943.
	Arc 969.1.6	Clarke, R. The pre-historic remains...of the city of Cincinnati, Ohio. Cincinnati, 1876.
	Arc 969.1.7	Putnam, F.W. Iron from the Ohio mounds. v.2. n.p., n.d.
Htn	Arc 969.1.8*	Manuscripts. English. Effigy, or Symbolic mound in Licking County, Ohio. n.p., n.d.
Htn	Arc 969.1.9*	Sargent, W. Papers relative to certain American antiquities. Philadelphia, 1796.
	Arc 969.1.10	Force, M.F. Indians of Ohio. Cincinnati, 1879.
	Arc 969.1.12	Willoughby, C.C. The Turner group of earthworks, Hamilton County, Ohio. Cambridge, 1922.
	Arc 969.1.15	Thomas, Cyrus. The problem of the Ohio mounds. Washington, 1889.
	Arc 969.1.17	Vietzen, R.C. Ancient man in northern Ohio. Lorain, Ohio, 1941.
	Arc 969.9	Cressman, L.S. Archaeological researches in the northern great basin. Washington, 1942.
	Arc 969.15	Wright, James V. The laurel tradition and the middle woodland period. Ottawa, 1967.
	Arc 969.15.5	Kidd, Kenneth E. The excavations of Sainte-Marie I. Toronto, 1949.
	Arc 969.15.10	Jury, Wilfrid. Sainte-Marie among the Hurons. Toronto, 1954.
	Arc 970.1	Holmes, W.H. Stone implements; Potomac-Chesapeake Province. Washington, 1893-94.
	Arc 970.2	Society for Pennsylvania Archaeology. Publications. Athens. 1,1931
	Arc 970.2.5	Cadzow, D.A. Petroglyphs (rock carvings) in the Susquehanna River near Safe Harbor, Pennsylvania. Harrisburg, 1934.
	Arc 971.1	Wallbridge, T.C. On some ancient mounds upon the shores of the Bay of Quinte. Toronto, 1860.
	Arc 971.5	Pendergast, James F. Cartier's Hochelaga and the Dawson site. Montreal, 1972.
	Arc 973.10	Smith, Carl S. The two Teeth site [South Dakota]. Lincoln, 1968.
	Arc 974.1	Thruston, G.P. The antiquities of Tennessee. Cincinnati, 1890.
	Arc 974.1.5	Webb, William S. An archaeological survey of the Norris Basen in eastern Tennessee. Washington, 1938.
	Arc 974.2	Pearce, J.E. A prehistoric rock shelter in Val Verde County, Tennessee. Austin, Texas, 1933.
	Arc 974.3	Lewis, Thomas M. Hiwassee Island: an archaeological account of 4 Tennessee Indian peoples. Knoxville, 1946.
	Arc 975.1	Morss, Noel. The ancient culture of the Fremont River in Utah. Cambridge, Mass., 1931.
	Arc 975.2	Gillin, John. Archaeological investigations in Nine Mile Canyon, Utah, during the year 1936. Salt Lake City, 1938?
	Arc 975.5	Gillin, John. Archaeological investigations in central Utah. Cambridge, 1941.
	Arc 975.10	Smith, E.R. The archaeology of Deadman Cave, Utah. Salt Lake City, 1941.
	Arc 975.12	Judd, Neil M. Archaeological observations north of the Rio Colorado, Utah. Washington, 1926.
	Arc 976.5	Cotter, J.L. Archaeological excavations at Jamestown. Washington, 1958.
	Arc 976.7	Noël Hume, Ivor. Here lies Virginia. N.Y., 1963.
	Arc 976.8	United States. National Park Service. Excavations at Green Spring Plantation. Yorktown, 1955.
	Arc 976.9	Benthall, Joseph L. Archaeological investigation of the Shannon site, Montgomery County, Virginia. Richmond, 1969.
	Arc 977.1	Peet, S.D. The emblematic mounds of Wisconsin. n.p., n.d.
	Arc 977.2	Renaud, E.B. Archaeological survey of eastern Wyoming, summer 1931. Denver, 1932.

Arc 983 Archaeology - Local - United States and Canada - Special topics

	Arc 983.1	Green, C.H. Catalogue of a unique collection of cliff dweller relics. Chicago? n.d.
	Arc 983.1.2	Henderson, P. The cliff dwellers. St. Paul, 1893.
	Arc 983.2	Hemenway, S.W. Catalogo de los objetos etnológicos y arqueológicos. Madrid, 1892.
	Arc 983.2.5	Catálogo...objetos...Estados Unidos de América. Madrid, 1892.
	Arc 983.2.7	United States. Commission. Report to the Columbian historical exposition at Madrid. Washington, 1895.
	Arc 983.3	Putnam, C.E. Elephant pipes and inscribed tablets in the Museum of the Academy of Natural Sciences. Davenport, 1886.
	Arc 983.3.2	Putnam, C.E. Elephant pipes and inscribed tablets. Davenport, 1885.
	Arc 983.3.5	Henshaw, H.W. Animal carvings from mounds of the Mississippi Valley. Washington, 1881?
	Arc 983.4	Peet, S.D. Ancient village architecture in America. n.p., n.d.

Classified Listing

Arc 983 Archaeology - Local - United States and Canada - Special topics - cont.

Arc 983.5 Putnam, F.W. Remarks upon chipped stone implements. Salem, 1885.
Arc 983.6 Slafter, E.F. Prehistoric copper implements. Boston, 1879.
Arc 983.7 Dall, William H. On masks, labrets and certain aboriginal customs. Washington, 1881-82.
Arc 983.8 Peabody, Charles. The so called "gorgets". Andover, 1906.
Arc 983.9 Moore, C.B. Aboriginal urn-burial in the United States. Lancaster, 1904.
Arc 983.9.9 Snyder, J.F. A primitive urn-burial. Washington, 1891.
Arc 983.10 Brinton, D.G. The Taki, the Swastika, and the Cross in America. Philadelphia, 1889.
Arc 983.11 Mercer, H.C. The Lenape stone. N.Y., 1885.
Arc 983.12 Thomas, C. Burial mounds of the northern sections of the United States. Washington? 1884?
Arc 983.12.5 Thomas, C. Work in mound exploration of the Bureau of Ethnology. Washington, 1887.
Arc 983.13 Steward, J.H. Petroglyphs of the United States. Washington, 1937.
Arc 983.14 American Society of Naturalists. Early man in America with particular reference to the southwestern United States. n.p., 1936.
Arc 983.15 United States. Inter-Agency Archaeological Salvage Program. River basin surveys papers. Washington, 1958.
Arc 983.17 Dewdney, Selwya. Indian rock paintings of the Great Lakes. Toronto, 1962.
Htn Arc 985.01PF* Pamphlet box. Archaeology. Mexico and Central America.
Arc 985.210F Hamy, M.E.T. Recherches historiques et archéologiques. Paris, 1885.

Arc 1010 Archaeology - Local - Pacific Islands - Local; Special topics

Arc 1010.5 Hirmenech, H.P. Une tablette de l'ile de Pâques. Paris, 1912.
Arc 1010.10 Peabody Museum of Salem, Salem, Massachusetts. The Hervey Islands adzes in the Peabody Museum of Salem. Salem, 1937.
Arc 1010.15 Ponosov, V.V. Results of an archaeological survey of the southern region of Moreten Bay and of Moreten Island, 1963-64. St. Lucian, Brisbane, 1967.
Arc 1010.17 Jacob, Teuku. Some problems pertaining to the racial history of the Indonesian region. Utrecht, 1967.
Arc 1010.20 Chêng, Tê-k'un. Archaeology in Sarawak. Cambridge, 1969.
Arc 1010.25 Fox, Robert B. The Calatagan excavations. Manila, 1965.
Arc 1010.26 Garanger, José. Archéologie des Nouvelles Hébrides. Paris, 1972.
Arc 1010.27 Vasil'evskii, Ruslan S. Drevnie kul'tury Tikhookeanskogo Severa. Novosibirsk, 1973.
Arc 1010.28 Hutterer, Karl. An archaeological picture of a pre-Spanish Cebuano community. Cebu City, 1973.
Arc 1010.29F The recent archaeology of the Sydney district: excavations, 1964-1967. Canberra, 1974.

Arc 1015 Archaeology - Christian antiquities - Folios - Catacombs [Discontinued]

Arc 1015F Pamphlet box. Christian. Folios. Catacombs.
Arc 1015.5 Moretto, P. De S'Callisto pp. etm ejusque Basilica. Romae, 1767.
Arc 1015.5.5 Wilpert, J. Die Papstgräber und di Cäciliengruf. Freiburg, 1909.
Arc 1015.202 Bosio, A. Roma scotterranea. Roma, 1651. 2v.
Arc 1015.202.5 Bosio, A. Roma scotterranea. Paris, 1658.
Arc 1015.203 Bottari, G.G. Sculture e pitture sagre estratte dai cimitery de Roma. Roma, 1737-54. 3v.
Arc 1015.204 Roller, T. Les catacombes di Rome. Paris, 1881. 2v.
Arc 1015.205 Rossi, G.B. de. La Roma scotterranea christiana. Roma, 1864-77. 4v.
Arc 1015.205.2 Rossi, M.S. de. Appendice...al tomo terzo della Roma sotterranea. Roma, 1877.
Arc 1015.205.5 Roma sotterranea cristiana. pt.1-2. Roma, 1909-14.
Arc 1015.205.9 Rossi, G.B. de. Verre representant le temple de Jerusalem. Genes, 1883.
Arc 1015.205.13 Rossi, G.B. de. Il museo epigrafico cristiano pio-sateranense. Roma, 1877.
Arc 1015.205.15 Rossi, M.S. de. Analsi geologica ed archilettonica de Cemet de Callisto. Roma, 1867.
Arc 1015.206 Iozzi, Oliviero. Supplementa alla Roma sotterranea cristiana. Roma, 1898.
Arc 1015.206.5 Iozzi, Oliviero. Roma sotterranea; il cimitero di S. Castolo M. Roma, 1904.
Arc 1015.206.9 Iozzi, Oliviero. Cryptae Carciliae trans Tiberim descriptio. 2. ed. Romae, 1902.
Arc 1015.207 Boldetti, M.A. Osservazioni sopra i cimitery. Roma, 1720.
Arc 1015.208 Garrucci, R. Vetri ornati di figura in oro. Roma, 1858.
Arc 1015.208.2 Garrucci, R. Vetri ornati di figure in oro. Roma, 1864.
Arc 1015.208.5 Garrucci, R. Dissertazioni archaeologiche di vario argomento. v.1-2. Roma, 1864.
Arc 1015.208.8 Garrucci, R. Tre sepolcri con pitture ed iscrizione. Napoli, 1852.
Arc 1015.208.13 Garrucci, R. Relazione generale degli scavi e scoperte...via Satina. Roma, 1859.
Arc 1015.209 Lugari, G.B. Le catacombe ossia il sepolcro. Roma, 1888.
Arc 1015.210 Marchi, Giuseppe. Monumenti delle arti cristiane primitive nella metropoli del cristianismo. Roma, 1844.
Arc 1015.210.5 Marchi, Giuseppe. Il sepolcro dei ss martiri Proto e Giacinta. Roma, 1845.
Arc 1015.211 Settele, G. Illustrazione di un antico monumento cristiano. Roma, 1829.
Arc 1015.212 Scognamiglio, A. Notice sur deux catacombs. Paris, 1863.
Arc 1015.213 Wilpert, J. Die Katakombengemalde. Ihre alten Copiers. Freiburg, 1891.
Arc 1015.213.9 Wilpert, J. Fractio Panis. Freiburg, 1895.
Arc 1015.213.12 Wilpert, J. La cripta dei Papi et la capella di Santa Cecilia. Roma, 1910.
Arc 1015.215 Giovanni, V. di. Palermo sotterranea. Palermo, n.d.
Arc 1015.216 Armellini, M.J. Vetri cristiani della collezione di Campo-Santo. n.p., n.d.
Arc 1015.217 Waal, A. de. La platonia ossia il sepolcro apostolico della via Appia. Roma, 1892.
Arc 1015.217.5 Waal, A. de. Valeria; historische Erzahlung. Regensburg, 1884.
Arc 1015.221 Caruana, A.A. Ancient pagan tombs and Christian cemeteries in Malta. Malta, 1898.
Arc 1015.222 Franconi, F. La catacomba e la basilica costantiniana. Roma, 1877.
Arc 1015.223 Orsi, P. Esplorazioni nelle catacombe. Siracusa. Roma, 1893.
Arc 1015.224 Grisar, H. Tombe apostoliche di Roma. Roma, 1892.
Arc 1015.225 Marucchi, O. Il sepolcro gentilizio di Sant'Ambrogio. Milano, 1897.

Arc 1015 Archaeology - Christian antiquities - Folios - Catacombs [Discontinued] - cont.

Arc 1015.225.5 Marucchi, O. Di un nuovo cimitero giudaico. Roma, 1884.
Arc 1015.225.9 Marucchi, O. Scavi nella Platonia. Roma, 1892.
Arc 1015.226 Carini, I. Catacombe di S. Giovanni in Siracusa. Roma, 1890.
Arc 1015.227 Rossi, M.S. de. Duale metodo tecnico per dirigere l'escavazione. Roma, 1880.
Arc 1015.228 Galante, G.A. Cemetero di S. Ipolisto in Atripalda. Napoli, 1893.
Arc 1015.229 Stevenson, H. Escavazioni in un ipogeo cristiano de Bolsena. Roma, 1881.
Arc 1015.230 Dionysius, P.L. Sacrarum vaticanae...cryptarum. Romae, 1773.
Arc 1015.231 Obermann, H.T. De oud-christelijke sarkophagen. 's-Gravenhage, 1911.
Arc 1015.232F Wilpert, J. Ein Cyclus christologischer Gemälde. Freiburg, 1891.

Arc 1016 Archaeology - Christian antiquities - Folios - Others [Discontinued]

Arc 1016.1 Molinier, E. Le trésor de la cathédrale de Coire. Paris, 1895.
Arc 1016.3 Barbier de Montault, X. Étude archéologique sur le reliquaire du chef de S. Laurent. Rome, 1864.
Arc 1016.4 Busiri Vici, A. La colonna santa. Tempio de Gerusalemme. Roma, 1888.
Arc 1016.6F Rossi, J. de. Inscriptionae christianae urbis Romae. Romae. 1-3 7v.
Arc 1016.6.3F Rossi, J. de. Inscriptionae christianae urbis Romae. Supplement. Romae. 1,1925
Arc 1016.8 Hager, Joseph. Monument de Yu, ou La plus ancienne inscription de la Chine. Paris, 1802.
Arc 1016.9 Lugari, G.B. Intorno ad alcuni monumenti antichi. Roma, 1882.
Arc 1016.9.5 Lugari, G.B. L'aventino e le origine pagane e Christian di Roma. Roma, 1886.
Arc 1016.9.9 Lugari, G.B. S. Bonifazio e S. Alessio sull'aventino. Roma, 1894.
Arc 1016.9.15 Lugari, G.B. L'anfiteatro Flavio rivendicato ai martiri. Roma, 1899.
Arc 1016.10 Odorici, F. Antichita cristiane di Brescia. Brescia, 1845.
Arc 1016.12 Wittig, Joseph. Die altchristlichen Skulpturen...deutschen Nationalstiftung am Campo Santo. Rom, 1906.
Arc 1016.13.5 David, J. Sainte Marie antigue. Roma, 1911.
Arc 1016.200 Kaufmann, C.I. Die sepulcralen Jenseits Denkmäler. Mainz, 1900.
Arc 1016.201 Palustre, L. Le trésor de Trèves. Paris, 1886.
Arc 1016.202 Casano, A. Del sotterraneo della chiesa cattedrale di Palermo. Palermo, 1849.
Arc 1016.204 Kraus, F.X. Die altchristlichen Inschriften der Rheinlande. Freiburg, 1890.
Arc 1016.205 Hübner, A. Inscritione hispaniae christianae. Berlolini, 1871.
Arc 1016.205.5 Hübner, A. Inscritione hispaniae christianarum. Supplement. Berolini, 1900.
Arc 1016.206 Iozzi, Oliviero. Vetri cimiteriali con figure in oro conservati nell Museo Britannico. Roma, 1900.
Arc 1016.206.3 Iozzi, Oliviero. Vetri cimiteriali con figure in oro conservati nell Museo Sacro Vaticano. Roma, 1900.
Arc 1016.206.9 Iozzi, Oliviero. Basilica di S. Maria Maggiore. Roma, 1903.
Arc 1016.207 Rohault de Fleury, C. La messe études archéologiques sur ses monuments. v.3-7. Paris, 1883- 5v.
X Cg Arc 1016.207 Rohault de Fleury, C. La messe études archéologiques sur ses monuments. v.1-2,8. Paris, 1883- 3v.
X Cg Arc 1016.207.5 Rohault de Fleury, C. La Sainte Vierge. Paris, 1878. 2v.
Arc 1016.208 Roulin, E. L'ancien trésor de l'Abbaye de Silos. Paris, 1901.
Arc 1016.209 Wilpert, J. Die Gottgeweihten Jungfrauen. Freiburg, 1892.
Arc 1016.210 Richter, J.P. The golden age of classic Christian art. London, 1904.
Arc 1016.211 Waal, A. de. Sarkophag des Junius Bassus. Rom, 1900.
Arc 1016.211.5F Gerke, F. Der Sarkophag des Iunius Bassus. Berlin, 1936.
Arc 1016.212 Gazzera, C. Delle iscrizioni cristiani del Piemonte. Torino, 1847.
Arc 1016.212.3 Gazzera, C. Delle iscrizioni cristiani del Piemonte. Torino, 1849.
Arc 1016.213 Nibby, A. Della forma degli antichi templi cristiani. Roma, 1825.
Arc 1016.215 Rossi, G.B. de. Dell'antichissimo codice della Bibbia Graeca. Roma, 1860.
Arc 1016.215.5 Rossi, G.B. de. Iscrizione in scritta e lingua Nabatea...Madaba. Roma, 1893.
Arc 1016.216 Moreschi, L. Sulla sedia pontificale della basilica di S. Paolo. Roma, 1838.
Arc 1016.216.3 Moreschi, L. Sulla sedia pontificale della basilica di S. Paolo. n.p., n.d.
Arc 1016.217 Cancellieri, F. Memorie storiche delle sacre teste. 2. ed. Roma, 1852.
Arc 1016.218 Belloni, P. Sulla grandezza della primitiva basilica ostiense. Roma, 1853.
Arc 1016.219 Rampolla, M. De cathedra romana B. Petri. Roma, 1868.
Arc 1016.220A Galante, G.A. Memorie dell'antico cenobio di S. Severino. Napoli, 1869.
Arc 1016.220B Galante, G.A. Memorie dell'antico cenobio di S. Severino. Napoli, 1869.
Arc 1016.221 Lugari, G.B. La pontificia accademia romana di archeologia. Roma, 1900.
Arc 1016.222 Rasponi, C. De basilica et patriarchio Lateranensi. Roma, 1656.
Arc 1016.223 Bartolini, D. Atti del martiro della S. Agnese. Roma, 1858.
Arc 1016.224 Garrucci, R. Esame della numismatica costantiniana. Roma, 1858.
Arc 1016.225 Odorici, F. Di un antico sarcofago cristiano...Mantova. Brescia, 1855.
Arc 1016.226 Visconti, A. Dissertazione...cristianita di Costantino Magno. Roma, 1835.
Arc 1016.227 Visconti, P.E. Dissertazione...iscrizione cristiana. Roma, 1833.
Arc 1016.228 Laderchi, J. Acta passionis SS. Crescii et S. Martyrum. Florentiae, 1707.
Arc 1016.229 Legati, L. Museo Cospiano. Bologna, 1677.
Arc 1016.230 Catholic Church. Congregatio Indulgentiarum et Sacrarum Reliquiarum. Acta congregationis praeparatoriae habitae die 4 iulii 1901. De authenticitate S. Sindonis Taurinensis. Roma, 1901.

Classified Listing

Arc 1016 Archaeology - Christian antiquities - Folios - Others [Discontinued] - cont.

Arc 1016.230.2 Catholic Church. Congregatio Indulgentiarum et Sacrarum Reliquiarum. Excellentissimo ac revmo dño Aloisio Tripepi. De authenticitate S. Sindonis Taurinensis. Roma, 1901.
Arc 1016.231 Adriano I. Lettera...sul culto delle sacre immagini. Roma, 1885.
Arc 1016.232 Lupi, A.M. Dissertatio...severae martyris epitaphium. Panormi, 1734.
Arc 1016.232.2 Lupi, A.M. Dissertatio...severae martyris epitaphium. Panormi, 1734.
Arc 1016.233 Visconti, P.E. Sposizione di alcune antiche iscrizione cristiane. Roma, 1824.
Arc 1016.233.5 Visconti, F.A. Sopra una iscrizione cimiteriale. Roma, 1831.
Arc 1016.235 Marini, G. Iscrizioni antiche doliari. Roma, 1884.
Arc 1016.236 Kaufmann, K.W. Die Menasstadt. Leipzig, 1910.
Arc 1016.237 Secchi, P.G. La cattedra Alessandrina di San Marco Evangelista e Martire. Venezia, 1853.
Arc 1016.238 Bellomo, G. La pala d'oro dell...basilica di San Marco. Venezia, 1847.
Arc 1016.239 Dragoni, A. Sul dittico eburneo de santi martiri Teodoro ed Acacio. Parma, 1810.
Htn Arc 1016.240* Apianus, P. Inscriptiones sacrosanctae vetustatis...Romanae. Ingolstadii, 1534.
Arc 1016.241 Peyrat, G. du. L'histoire ecclesiastico...les antiquitez...de la chapelle et oratoire du Roy de France. Paris, 1645.
Arc 1016.242 Heideloff, C. Der Christliche Altar. Nürnberg, 1838.
Arc 1016.243 Balasko, F. Majesticus...Delatio...S. Stephani Manus Dexterae. Budae, n.d.
Htn Arc 1016.244* Crux triumphans et gloriosa. Antwerp, 1617.
Arc 1016.245F Weiss, Karl. Der romanische Speisekelch. Wien, 1860.
Arc 1016.246F Barbier de Montault, X. La trésor liturgique de Cherves en Angoumois. Angoulême, 1897.

Arc 1018 Archaeology - Christian antiquities - General works

Arc 1018.01 Dictionnaire d'archéologie chrétienne et littérature. v.1-15. Paris, 1903-52. 28v.
Arc 1018.02 Martigny, J.A. Dictionnaire des antiquités chrétiennes. Paris, 1877.
Arc 1018.05 Kraus, Franz X. Real-Encyclopädie der Christlichen Alterthümer. Freiburg, 1882-86. 2v.
Arc 1018.1 Bourassé, J.J. Archéologie chrétienne. Tours, 1878.
Arc 1018.2 Lefort, L. Études sur les monuments primitifs. Paris, 1885.
Arc 1018.3 Pératé, A. L'archéologie chrétienne. Paris, 1892.
Arc 1018.4 Reusens, E. Eléments d'archéologie chrétienne. Louvain, 1871-75. 2v.
Arc 1018.5 Schultze, Victor. Archäologie der altchristlichen Kunst. München, 1895.
Arc 1018.5.5 Schultze, Victor. Archäologische Studien über altchristliche Monumente. Wien, 1880.
Arc 1018.5.9 Schultze, Victor. Grundriss der christlichen Archäologie. München, 1919.
Arc 1018.6 Armellini, M. Lezioni di archaeologici cristiana. Roma, 1898.
Arc 1018.6.3 Armellini, M. Lezioni popolari di archaeologici cristiana. Roma, 1903.
Arc 1018.6.18 Stevenson, E. Lettera intorno...premessa all...Armellini. Roma, 1898.
Arc 1018.6.21 Bartolini, A. Elogio del cavalier professore Mariano Armellini. Roma, 1896.
Arc 1018.7.2 Lourie, W. Monuments of the early church. N.Y., 1901.
Arc 1018.7.5 Lourie, W. Monuments of the early church. N.Y., 1906.
Arc 1018.9 Ficker, J. Studien über christliche Denkmäler. Leipzig. 1-24,1902-1937 19v.
Arc 1018.10 Rome, Italy. Collections. Stromation archaiologikon. Rome, 1900.
Arc 1018.11 Mazochuis, A.S. Mélanges de litterature et d'histoire religieuses. Paris, 1899. 3v.
Arc 1018.12 Wilpert, J. Principienfragen der christliche Archäologie. Freiburg, 1889.
Arc 1018.12.8 Wilpert, J. Nochmals Principienfragen. Rom, 1890.
Arc 1018.14 Belloc, J.T. de. Ste. Agnès et son siècle. Lille, 1893.
Arc 1018.15 Mamachi, T.M. De' costumi de' primitivi cristiani. Venezia, 1757. 3v.
Arc 1018.15.3 Mamachi, T.M. De' costumi de' primitivi cristiani. v.1-2. Firenze, 1853.
Arc 1018.16 Rinaldi, P. De falea veterum christianorum rituum. Romae, 1777.
Arc 1018.17 Selvaggio, J.L. Antiquitatum christianarum institutiones. Vercellis, 1778. 3v.
Arc 1018.18 Garrucci, R. Opuscoli archeologici profana e cristiana. Roma, 1860-77.
Arc 1018.18.2 Garrucci, R. Opuscoli di archeologia christiana e profana. Roma, n.d.
Arc 1018.18.18 Montescaglioro, F. Commemorazione di P. Raffaele Garucci. Napoli, 1885.
Arc 1018.19 Haufmann, C.M. Handbuch der christlichen Archäologie. Paderborn, 1905.
Arc 1018.19.2 Haufmann, C.M. Handbuch der christlichen Archäologie. 2. Aufl. Paderborn, 1913.
Arc 1018.19.3 Kaufmann, C.M. Handbuch der christlichen Archäologie. 3. Aufl. Paderborn, 1922.
Arc 1018.19.10 Haufmann, C.M. Amerika und Urchristentum. München, 1924.
Arc 1018.20 Bonavenia. Una pittura di basilica di Antiochia. Roma, 1888.
Arc 1018.22 Tacchi-Venturi, P. Correspondenza di L.A. Muratori. Roma, 1901.
Arc 1018.23 Sybel, L. von. Christliche Antike. Marburg, 1906. 2v.
Arc 1018.24 LeClercq, H. Manuel d'archéologie chrétienne. Paris, 1907. 2v.
Arc 1018.25 Augusti, J.C.W. Denkwürdigkeiten und der christlichen Archäologie. Leipzig, 1817-26. 12v.
Arc 1018.25.5 Augusti, J.C.W. Handbuch der christlichen Archäologie. Leipzig, 1838. 3v.
Arc 1018.25.25 Coleman, Lyman. Antiquities of the Christian church. Andover, 1841.
Arc 1018.26 Siegel, C.C.F. Handbuch der christlich-kirchlichen Alterthümer. Leipzig, 1836-38. 4v.
Arc 1018.27 Piper, F. Einleitung in die Monumentale Theologie. Gotha, 1867.
Arc 1018.28 Wolcott, M.E.C. Sacred archaeology...dictionary. London, 1868.
Arc 1018.29 Guericke, H. Lehrbuch der christlich kirchlichen Archäologie. Berlin, 1859.

Arc 1018 Archaeology - Christian antiquities - General works - cont.

Arc 1018.29.7 Guericke, H. Manual of the antiquities of the church. London, 1851.
Arc 1018.30 Böhmer, W. Die socialen Verhältnisse. Breslau, 1836.
Arc 1018.31 Scaglia, P.S. Manuale di archeologia cristiana. Roma, 1911.
Arc 1018.31.3 Scaglia, P.S. Manuel d'archéologie chrétienne. Turin, 1916.
Arc 1018.32 Kraus, F.X. Über Begriff...christlichen Archäologie. Freiburg, 1879.
Arc 1018.32.7 Kraus, F.X. Die christliche Kunst in ihren frühesten Anfängen. Leipzig, 1872.
Arc 1018.33 Reichensperger. Bermischte Schriften über christliche Kunst. Leipzig, 1856.
Arc 1018.35 Kraus, F.X. Archäologie...Christliche Archäologie, 1880-86. Stuttgart, 1882. 2v.
Arc 1018.36 Syxtus, P. Notiones archaeologiae christianae. v.1-2. Romae, 1909-10. 4v.
Arc 1018.37 Barnes, A.S. The early church in the light of monuments. London, 1913.
Arc 1018.38 Bruyn, H. de. Archéologie religieuse. v.1-2. Bruxelles, 1869.
Arc 1018.39 Chiefletius, J.J. De linteis sepulchralibus. Antverpiae, 1688. 4 pam.
Arc 1018.40 Volbeding, J.E. Thesaurus commentationum...antiquiorum...illustrandis antiquitatibus christianis. Lipsiae, 1847. 2v.
Arc 1018.41 Heales, Alfred. The archaeology...Christian altar...western Europe. London, 1881.
Arc 1018.42 Pamphlet vol. Carini, Isidoro. Writings. 23 pam.
Arc 1018.43 Pamphlet vol. Carini, Isidoro. Writings. 6 pam.
Arc 1018.44 Marucchi, O. Manuale di archeologia cristiana. 3. ed. Roma, 1923.
Arc 1018.44.15 Marucchi, O. Manuel of Christian archaeology. 4. Italian ed. Paterson, N.J., 1935.
Arc 1018.44.17 Marucchi, O. Manuel of Christian archaeology. 4. Italian ed. Paterson, N.J., 1949.
Arc 1018.45 Villa Amil y Castro, J. Rudimentos de arqueología sagrada. Lugo, 1867.
Arc 1018.46 Jerphanion, G. de. La voix des monuments. Paris, 1930.
Arc 1018.46.5 Jerphanion, G. de. La voix des monuments. Rome, 1938.
Arc 1018.47 Von der Antike zum Christentum. Stettin, 1931.
Arc 1018.49 Cobern, C.M. The new archaeological discoveries and their bearing upon the New Testament. N.Y., 1917.
Arc 1018.49.5 Cobern, C.M. The new archaeological discoveries and their bearing upon the New Testament. 3. ed. N.Y., 1918.
Arc 1018.50 Ferretto, Giuseppe. Note storico-bibliografiche di archeologia cristiana. Città del Vaticano, 1942.
Arc 1018.52 Grossi-Gondi, F. I monumenti cristiani. Roma, 1920-23. 2v.
Arc 1018.53 Aragón Fernández, A. Tratado de arqueología eclesiástica. Barcelona, 1935.
Arc 1018.55 Testini, P. Archeologia cristiana. Roma, 1958.
Arc 1018.58 Cecchelli, Carlo. Il cenacolo filippino e l'archeologia cristiana. Roma, 1938.
Arc 1018.60 Aebischer, Paul. Linguistique romane et histoire religieuse. Abadía de San Cugat del Valles, 1968.
Arc 1018.62 Mancini, Ignazio. Le scoperte archeologiche sui giudeo-cristiani. Assisi, 1968.
Arc 1018.64 Die Attribute der Heiligen, alphabetisch Geordnet. Hannover, 1843.

Arc 1020 Archaeology - Christian antiquities - Local

Arc 1020.1 Bock, F. Das Heiligthum zu Aachen. Köln, 1867.
Arc 1020.1.3 Bock, F. Der Reliquienschatz des Leibfrauen-Münsters zu Aachen in seinen Kunstreichen Behältern. Aachen, 1860.
Arc 1020.1.5 Vienna. St. Stephansdom. Das Wiener Heiligthumbuch. Wien, 1882.
Htn Arc 1020.2* Prost, B. Le trésor de l'Abbaye St. Bénique de Dijon. Dijon, 1894.
Arc 1020.3 Bruges, Belgium. Commission Provinciale. Inventaire des objets d'art et d'antique...Bruges. Bruges, 1848.
Arc 1020.4 Girardot. Histoire et inventaire du trésor Bourges. Paris, 1859.
Arc 1020.4.5 Boissoudy, A. de. La sainte-chapelle de Bourges. n.p., 1884.
Arc 1020.5 Van Drival, E. Le trésor sacré de la cathédrale d'Arras. Arras, 1860.
Arc 1020.6 Durand, J. Trésor de l'église Saint-Marc à Venise. Paris, 1862.
Arc 1020.6.3 Passini, A. Sul frontale dell'altar maggiore in San Marco. Venezia, 1881.
Arc 1020.6.5 Breve descrittione del sacro thesoro...San Marco. Milano, 1617.
Arc 1020.6.7 Passini, A. Il tesoro di San Marco in Venezia. Venezia, 1878.
Arc 1020.6.9 Veludo, G. Dichiarazione di un monumento sepolcrale cristiano. Venezia, 1877.
Arc 1020.6.12 Cappelletti, G. La chiesa di S. Simone profeta. Venezia, 1860.
Htn Arc 1020.6.15* Schioppalalba, I.B. In perantiquam sacram tabulam...S. Mariae Caritatis. Venetiis, 1767.
Arc 1020.7 Lebarte, J. L'église cathedrale de Sienne...trésor. Paris, 1868.
Arc 1020.8 Legrand, E. Description...de l'église des Saints Apotres de Constantinople. Paris, 1896.
Arc 1020.9 Mazzolari, G.M. Diario sacro le sacre vie, le sacre basilicho. Roma, 1779-81. 5v.
Arc 1020.9.01 Pamphlet vol. Christian archaeology of Rome.
Arc 1020.9.5 Mazzolari, G.M. Diario sacro. 2. ed. Roma, 1805-06. 4v.
Arc 1020.9.5.25 Fea, Carlo. Dei diritti del principato. Roma, 1806.
Arc 1020.9.6 Fea, Carlo. L'integrita del panteon di M. Agrippa. Roma, 1807.
Arc 1020.9.6.2 Fea, Carlo. L'integrita del panteon rivendicata a Marco Agrippo. 2a ed. Roma, 1820.
Arc 1020.9.7 Fea, Carlo. Conclusione per l'integrita del panteon. Roma, 1807.
Arc 1020.9.8 Eroli, Giovanni. Raccolta generale delle iscrizioni pagne e cristiane...nel panteon di Roma. Narni, 1895.
Arc 1020.9.9 Nibby, A. Del tempio della pace e della basilica di Costantino. Roma, 1819.
Arc 1020.9.11 Bonties, G.B. Brevi notitie archeologici sull'origine delle chiese di Roma. Roma, 1825.
Arc 1020.9.12 Torres, C.A. Cenni sulla forma primitiva del panteon di Roma. Roma, 1838.
Arc 1020.9.13 Baracconi, G. Il panteon e la tomba reale monografia. Roma, 1878. 3 pam.

Arc 1020 Archaeology - Christian antiquities - Local - cont.

Arc 1020.9.15 Bartolomei, L. Memorie autentiche sulla chiesa di S. Paolo alla Regola. Roma, 1858.
Arc 1020.9.20 Caterbi, G. La chiesa di S. Onofrio. Roma, 1858.
Arc 1020.9.25 Cancellieri, F. Sagrestica vaticana eretta...Pio Sesto. Roma, 1784.
Arc 1020.9.28 Sindone, R. Altarium et reliquarum...basilicae vaticanae. Romae, 1744.
Arc 1020.9.30 Bossi, G. La chiesa di Santa Marta al Vaticano. Roma, 1883.
Arc 1020.9.32 Barbier de Montault, X. La bibliothèque vaticane et ses annexes. Rome, 1867.
Arc 1020.9.33 Barbier de Montault, X. Inventaire de la chapelle papale sous Paul III en 1547. Tours, 1878.
Arc 1020.9.35 Armellini, M. Notizie istoriche...Domine Quo Vadis. Roma, 1874.
Arc 1020.9.40 Gianuizzi, P. La chiesa di Santa Maria di Loreto IV. Sacre notizio V. Roma, 1884.
Arc 1020.9.43 Biasiotti, G. La basilica esquilina di Santa Maria ed il palazzo apostolico. Roma, 1911.
Arc 1020.9.45 Rossi, G.B. di. Miscellania...la topografia...dei monumenti de Roma. Roma, 1889.
Arc 1020.9.47 Rossi, G.B. di. Panorama circolari di Roma, deliniato nu 1534. Roma, 1892.
Arc 1020.9.50 Severano, G. Memorie sacre delle sette chiese di Roma. Roma, 1630.
Arc 1020.9.51 Fioravanti, G.A. Visita...delle sette chiese. Fermo, 1763.
Arc 1020.9.55 Contarino, F.L. Dell antiquita sito, chiese...di Roma. Napoli, 1678.
Arc 1020.9.60 Iozzi, Oliviero. Le chiese di Roma...nel secolo XIX. Roma, 1900. 4 pam.
Arc 1020.9.63 Iozzi, Oliviero. La veneranda antica chiesa di S. Andrea e Gregoria. Roma, 1902.
Arc 1020.9.64 Iozzi, Oliviero. La reale chiesa del SS. Sudario in Roma. Roma, 1910.
Arc 1020.9.65 Marucchi, O. Conferenze della società di cultura della cristianità archeologia. Roma, 1877.
Arc 1020.9.70 Marucchi, O. Di un nuovo cippo del pomerio urbano. Roma, 1900.
Htn Arc 1020.9.75* Gesualdo, E. Osservazione...storia via Appia di Pratelle. Napoli, 1754.
Arc 1020.9.80 Rossi, G.B. di. Incrementi del museo sacro della Biblioteca Vaticana di Leone XIII. Roma, n.d.
Arc 1020.9.85 Vannitelli, V. Memorie sacre Lateranensi. Roma, 1900.
Arc 1020.9.90 Pellegrini, A. Anni storici intorno ad una basilica di S. Pietro in Campo di Mirlo. Roma, 1860.
Arc 1020.9.95 Wolff. Geschichtsbilder aus alt christlicher Zeit. Roms. Berlin, 1907.
Arc 1020.9.97 Kirsch, Johann P. Die römischen Titelkirchen im Altertum. Paderborn, 1918.
Arc 1020.9.99 Landucci, A. Origine del tempio. Roma, 1646.
Arc 1020.9.102 Phoebeus, F. De indentitate cathedral...Sanct. Petrus Romae. Romae, 1666.
Arc 1020.9.103 Barbier de Montault, X. Les souterrains et le tresor...St. Pierre à Rome. Rome, 1866.
Htn Arc 1020.9.106* Panvinus, Onuphrus. Veronesia fatris...de praecipius urbis. Romae, 1570.
Arc 1020.9.110 Costanzi, G. Le instituzioni di Pieta...in Roma. v.1-2. Roma, 1825.
Htn Arc 1020.9.114* Albertini, F. Mirabilia Roma. Firenze, 1520.
Htn Arc 1020.9.115* Les merveilles de la ville de Rome. Rome, 1690.
Htn Arc 1020.9.116* Léon, François. Les merveilles de la ville de Rome. Rome, 1646.
Arc 1020.9.117 Albertini, F. Mirabilibus...Romae. Heilbron, 1886.
Arc 1020.9.118 Léon, François. Les merveilles de la ville de Rome. Rome, 1750.
Arc 1020.9.120 Barbier de Montault, X. Observations archéologique...les églises de Rome. Arras, 1878.
Arc 1020.9.125 Scognamiglio, A. Cripta di S. Gennaro nel cimeterio. Roma, 1863.
Arc 1020.9.127 Barbier de Montault, X. L'année liturgique à Rome. Paris, 1857.
Arc 1020.9.128 Barbier de Montault, X. L'année liturgique à Rome. 2. éd. Rome, 1862.
Arc 1020.9.130 Barbier de Montault, X. L'année liturgique à Rome. Rome, 1870.
Arc 1020.9.131 Barbier de Montault, X. L'année liturgique à Rome. Rome, 1902.
Arc 1020.9.135 Barbier de Montault, X. Exposition religieuse de Rome 1870. Antiquités chrétiennes. Rome, 1870.
Arc 1020.9.137 Barbier de Montault, X. Exposition religieuse de Rome 1870. L'archéologie et l'art chrétien. Arras, 1877.
Arc 1020.9.142 Bartolini, D. Sopra l'antichissimo altare di legno...Lateranense. Roma, 1852.
Arc 1020.9.145 Leitzmann, Hans. Petrus und Paulus in Rom. Bonn, 1915.
Arc 1020.9.146 Leitzmann, Hans. Petrus und Paulus in Rom. 2. Aufl. Berlin, 1927.
Arc 1020.9.147 Lanciani, R. Wanderings through ancient Roman churches. Boston, 1924.
Arc 1020.9.153 Armailhacq. L'eglise nationale de Saint Louis des Français à Rome. Rome, 1894.
Arc 1020.9.163 Tani, A.D. Le chiese di Roma. Torino, 1922.
Arc 1020.9.164F Hendrichs, F. La voce delle chiese antichissime di Roma. Roma, 1933.
Arc 1020.9.169 Dattoli, M. L'aula del senato romano e la chiesa di S. Adriano. Roma, 1921.
Arc 1020.9.175 Bevan, Gladys M. Early Christians of Rome. London, 1927.
Arc 1020.9.179 Gerardi, F.M. Bella congregazione illirica e de' nuovi affreschi. Roma, 1853.
Arc 1020.9.183 Masetti, Pio. Memorie istoriche della chiesa di S. Maria. Roma, 1855.
Arc 1020.9.187 Biasiotti, G. Le diaconie cardinatizie e la diaconia "S. Vite in Macello". Roma, 1911.
Arc 1020.10 Valeri, A. Monumenti cristiani del Foro Romano. Roma, 1900.
Arc 1020.10.5 La Gournerie, E. de. Rome chrétienne. Paris, 1843. 2v.
Arc 1020.10.9 La Gournerie, E. de. Christian Rome. London, 1898. 2v.
Arc 1020.10.15 Dandolo, C.J. Roma christiana nei primi secoli. Asisi, 1865-67. 3v.
Arc 1020.10.19 A Christian corner in Roman Forum. Rome, 1901.
Arc 1020.10.23 Duchesne, L. Le forum chrétien. Rome, 1899.
Arc 1020.10.29 Bertaux, E. Rome. Paris, 1905.
Arc 1020.10.33 Nibby, A. Del Foro Romano e de' luoghi adjacenti. Roma, 1819.
Arc 1020.10.37 Cruickshank, J.W. Christian Rome. London, 1906.

Arc 1020 Archaeology - Christian antiquities - Local - cont.

Arc 1020.10.38 Cruickshank, J.W. Christian Rome. 2. ed. London, 1911.
Arc 1020.10.39 Favshingham, A.L. The monuments of Christian Rome. N.Y., 1908.
Arc 1020.10.43 Notizie compendiose delle sagre stazioni e chiese stazionali di Roma. Roma, 1833.
Arc 1020.10.46 Gerbet, O.P. Esquisse de Rome chrétienne. Paris, 1889. 3v.
Arc 1020.10.50F Goyau, Georges. Le visage de Rome chrétienne. Genève, 1926.
Htn Arc 1020.11* Relazione dello scuoprimento...in Ancona. Roma, 1756.
Arc 1020.12 Lorenzo, Giuseppe di. Antichi monumenti di religioni cristiani in Toscanella. Rocca, 1883.
Arc 1020.13 Molinier, E. Inventaire du trésor du Saint Siège. Paris, 1888.
Arc 1020.14 Kaufmann, C.M. Ein altchristliches Pompeji. Mainz, 1902.
Arc 1020.15 Wall, J.C. Shrines of British saints. London, 1905.
Arc 1020.16 Orsi, P. Monumenti cristiani del Trentino. Roma, 1883.
Arc 1020.17 Pannelli, D. Ragguaglio della univerzione...dei S.S. Martue. Pesaro, 1751.
Arc 1020.18 Bendixen, B.E. Aus der mittelalterlichen Sammlung des Museums in Bergen. Bergen, 1889-
Arc 1020.19 Biragus, A. Datiana historica ecclesiastica Mediolanensis. Mediolani, 1848.
Arc 1020.19.5 Gratiolio, P. De praeclaris Mediolani aedificiciis. Mediolani, 1735.
Arc 1020.20 Bonelli, G.A. Memorie storiche della Basilica Costantiniana. Roma, 1879.
Arc 1020.20.5 Fea, C. La Basilica di Costantino. Roma, 1819.
Arc 1020.21 Ruggieri, C. De portuensi S. Hippolyti. Romae, 1771.
Arc 1020.22 Lampake, G. Christianichē archaiologia. Athēnai, 1889.
X Cg Arc 1020.22.5 Lampake, G. Hē monē daphnioy. Athēnai, 1889.
Arc 1020.23 Martinelli, F. Diaconia S. Agathae in subura. Roma, 1638.
Arc 1020.24 Pulignani, M.F. Chiesa...Pietro e Paolo...Cancelli. Foligno, 1882.
Arc 1020.25 Olivieri, Abati. Munorie della Chiesa S. Maria di Monte Granaro. Pesaro, 1777.
Arc 1020.26 Bartolini, D. Su l'antica basilica di S. Nicola in Bari. Roma, 1882.
Arc 1020.26.5 Barbier de Montault, X. Les manuscrits du trésor de Bari. Toulouse, 1876.
Arc 1020.27 Rossi, G.B. de. Spiciligio d'archeologia cristiana nell'Umbria. Roma, 1871.
Arc 1020.28 Rossi, G.B. de. Découvertes de divers monuments chrétiens en Sardaigne. Rome, 1873.
Arc 1020.29 Marucchi, O. Le recenti scoperte nel Duomo di Parinzo. Roma, 1896.
Arc 1020.30 Dütschke, H. Ravennatische Studien. Leipzig, 1909.
Arc 1020.30.5 Diehl, Charles. Ravenne. Paris, 1907.
Arc 1020.31 Alger, C. L'antica chiesa S. Anna...Gerusalemma. Gerusalemma, 1863.
Arc 1020.31.9 Mariti, Giovanni. Istoria del tempio della resurrezione. Livorno, 1784.
Arc 1020.31.15 Besozzi, R. La storia della Basilica di Santa Croce in Gerusalemma. Roma, 1750.
Arc 1020.31.17 Baumstark, Anton. Die Modestianischen...zu Jerusalem. Paderborn, 1915.
Arc 1020.31.19 Schmaltz, Karl. Mater ecclesiarum. Strassburg, 1918.
Arc 1020.31.23 Lagrange, Marie. Saint Étienne et son sanctuaire à Jérusalem. Paris, 1894.
Arc 1020.31.25 Mommert, Carl. Saint Étienne et ses sanctuaires à Jérusalem. Jérusalem, 1912.
Htn Arc 1020.32* Allegranza, G. Spiegazione...sacri monumenti antichi di Milano. Milano, 1757.
Htn Arc 1020.32.5* Morigi, P. Santuario della città e diocesi di Milano. Milano, 1603.
Arc 1020.32.8 Caffi, M. Della chiesa di Sant'Eustorgio in Milano. Milano, 1841.
Arc 1020.32.12 Biraghi, L. I tre sepolcri santambrisiani scoperti...1864. Milano, 1864.
Arc 1020.34 Mader, Andreas E. Altchristliche Basiliken und Lokaltraditionen in Südjudäa. Paderborn, 1918.
Arc 1020.35 Delattre, R.P. Archéologie chrétienne de Carthage. Lyon, 1886.
Arc 1020.45 Deirnel, T. Christliche Römerfunde in Carnuntum. Wien, 1911.
Arc 1020.47 Franciotti, C. Historia delle Miracolose Imagni...città di Lucca. Lucca, 1613.
Arc 1020.48 Nitzhammer, R. Die christlichen Altertümer der Dobrogia. Bukarest, 1906.
Arc 1020.49 Barbier de Montault, X. Le trésor du dame d'Aix-La-Chapelle. Tours, 1877.
Arc 1020.49.1 Recueil...reliques...Nôtre Dame d'Aix la Chapelle. Aix, 1776?
Arc 1020.49.3 Trésor d'Aix-la-Chapelle. 1.-3. éd. Aix, 1818-20? 3 pam.
Arc 1020.50 Barbier de Montault, X. Le trésor de la cathédrale de Bénévent. Arras, 1879.
Arc 1020.51 Bock, Franz. Les trésors sacrés de Cologne. Paris, 1862.
Arc 1020.51.5 Winkeim, Erharde. Sacrarium Agrippinae...praecipuarum reliquarum. Coloniae, 1607. 2 pam.
Arc 1020.51.10 Winheim, Erharde. Sacrarium Agrippinae...praecipuarum reliquarum. Coloniae Agrippinae, 1736. 2 pam.
Arc 1020.52 Mély, F. de. Le trésor de Chartres. Paris, 1886.
Arc 1020.52.5 Merlet, L. Catalogue des reliques...Notre Dame de Chartres. Chartres, 1885.
Arc 1020.52.9 Mély, F. de. Les inventaires de l'Abbaye Saint Pére en Vallés de Chartres. Paris, 1887.
Arc 1020.53 Dusevel, M.H. Histoire...du trésor...de Saint Pierre de Corbie. Amiens, 1861.
Arc 1020.54 Van de Putte, F. La Chapelle des Comtes de Flandre à Courtrai. Bruges, 1875.
Arc 1020.55 Barbier de Montault, X. La visite de la Cathédrale St. Bertrand de Comminges. Montpélier, 1877.
Arc 1020.56 Salore, Charles. Le trésor de Clairvaux. Paris, 1875.
Arc 1020.57 Dechristé, Louis. Les tableaux...appartenant aux églises...de Douai. Douai, 1877.
Arc 1020.58 Cionacci, T. Relazione delle Sante Relique...della città di Firenze. Bologna, 1685.
Arc 1020.59 Martinov, J. Le trésor de la cathédrale de Gran. Arras, 1881.
Arc 1020.60 Besançon, B. Description des monuments de l'Abbaye de Rosières. n.p., 1714.
Arc 1020.61 Chavannes, E. Le trésor de l'église cathédrale de Lausanne. Lausanne, 1873.
Arc 1020.62 Richard, J.M. Le trésor...de Notre Dame de Lens au XVe siècle. Arras, 1876.

Arc 1020 Archaeology - Christian antiquities - Local - cont.

Arc 1020.63 Van Drival. Catalogue de l'exposition d'objets d'art...à Lille en 1874. 2. éd. Lille, 1874.
Arc 1020.64 Notice sur les reliques...l'église de lYon. Lyon, 1865.
Arc 1020.64.5 Valouse, V. de. Inventaires du trésor de l'église de Lyon. Lyon, 1877.
Arc 1020.65 Weale, W.H.J. Catalogue des objets d'art religieux...à l'Hotel Liederkerke à Malines. 2. éd. Bruxelles, 1864.
Arc 1020.66 Falk, V.A.F. Heiliges Mainz...Heiligenthümer. Mainz, 1877.
Arc 1020.67 Feraud, J.J.M. Les saintes reliques...chateau de Manosque. Digne, 1885.
Arc 1020.68 Barbier de Montault, X. Le trésor de la cathédrale de Moutiers. Tours, n.d.
Arc 1020.68.9 Barbier de Montault, X. Notes archéologiques sur Moutiers et la Tarentaise. Montiers, 1877.
Arc 1020.69 Deblaye, L.F. Reliques de l'église de Moyenmoutier. Nancy, 1856.
Arc 1020.70 Notre Dame de Myans. Chambéry, 1856.
Arc 1020.71 Gonzati, B. Il santuario delle relique...di Padova. Padova, 1851.
Arc 1020.72 Barbier de Montault, X. Le martyrium de Poitiers. Poitiers, 1885.
Arc 1020.72.5 Barbier de Montault, X. Le trésor de l'abbaye de Ste. Croix de Poitiers. Poitiers, 1883.
Arc 1020.72.9 Chamard, F. L'hypogée des dunes à Poitiers. Paris, 1884.
Arc 1020.72.15 La Croix, C. de. L'autel de Sainte-Sixte et ses reliques. Poitiers, 1907.
Arc 1020.73 Notice historique sur les saintes reliques...de S. Jacques-des-Hauts-Pas à Paris. Paris, 1835.
Arc 1020.73.5 Fagniez, G. Inventaires du trésor de Notre Dame de Paris. Paris, 1874.
Arc 1020.73.6 Gosselin, J.E.A. Notice historique et critique sur le sainte couronne d'épines...l'église metropolitaine de Paris. Paris, 1828.
Arc 1020.73.9 Molinier, E. Fragments d'un inventaire du trésor de l'abbaye de Saint Victor de Paris. Paris, 1882.
Arc 1020.73.12 Molinier, E. Inventaire du trésor...de Saint-Sépulchre de Paris. Paris, 1883.
Arc 1020.73.14 Troche, N.M. Sainte-Chapelle de Paris. Notice historique, archéologique et descriptive. Paris, 1853.
Arc 1020.73.15 Douet d'Arco, L.C. Inventaire des reliques de la Sainte-Chapelle. Paris, 1848.
Arc 1020.73.17 Wailly, J.N. de. Récit...sur les translations...1239 et 1241...reliques de la Passion. Nogent-le-Rotrou, n.d.
Arc 1020.74 Nampoon, P. Histoire de Notre Dame de France. Puy, 1868.
Arc 1020.75 Le Puy et Rome. Souvenirs et monuments. Paris, 1877.
Arc 1020.76 Le tresor, les corps saints...dans l'eglise royale de S. Denys. Paris, 1715.
Arc 1020.77 Delisle, Léopold. Authentiques de reliques...decouvertes à Vergy. Rome, 1884.
Arc 1020.78 Petracchi, C. Della insigne di S. Stefano di Bologna. Bologna, 1747.
Arc 1020.79 Promis, V. Reliquiario armeno...convento...Alessandria in Piemonte. Torino, 1883.
Arc 1020.80 Julliot, M.G. Inventaire des reliques...l'église metropolitaine de Sens. Sens, 1877.
Arc 1020.80.5 Julliot, M.G. Inventaire des sainctes reliques...de St. Pierre-le-Vif de Sens. Sens, 1877.
Arc 1020.80.7 Geoffroy de Couleron. Livre des reliques de l'abbaye de St. Pierre-le-Vif de Sens. Sens, 1887.
Arc 1020.81 Galeron, F. Sur un reliquare...monastère de St. Évroult. n.p., n.d.
Arc 1020.82 Lecocq, G. Notice sur un reliquare de St. Quentin. St. Quentin, 1875.
Arc 1020.83 Jadart, H. Les anciens pupitres de Rheims. n.p., n.d.
Arc 1020.83.5 Notice sur le mobilier de l'église cathedrale de Reims. Reims, 1856.
Arc 1020.84 Le Brun Dalbaune. Les aumonières du trésor...cathedrale de Troyes. Troyes, 1864.
Arc 1020.84.5 Le Brun Dalbaune. Recherches...emaux du trésor de la Cathedrale de Troyes. Troyes, 1862.
Arc 1020.84.9 Coffinet, L'Abbé. Trésor de St. Etienne...collegiale de Troyes. Paris, 1860.
Arc 1020.84.13 Salore, Charles. Probationes cultus sanctorum Diocesis Trecensis. Troyes, 1869.
Arc 1020.85 Guélou, P.F. Un reliquare romano Byzantin (Auveregne). Clermont-Ferrand, 1883.
Arc 1020.86 Monographie de l'insigne Basilique de St. Saturnin. Paris, 1854.
Arc 1020.87 Brocchi, G.M. Descrizione delle reliquare di Santi...Rocca di Lutiano. Firenze, 1744.
Arc 1020.88 Barbier de Montault, X. Inventaires de la Basilique Royale de Monza. Paris, 1886. 3 pam.
Arc 1020.89 Bock. Antiquités sacrées...S. Servais et de Notre Dame à Maestricht. Maestricht, 1873.
Htn Arc 1020.90* Farnese. Il santoario di Parma. Parma, 1593.
Arc 1020.91 Diehl, P. Die St. Matthias-Kirche bei Trier. Trier, 1881.
Arc 1020.92 Recherches sur precieuses reliques...dans la Sainte Eglise de Vienne. Vienne, 1876.
Arc 1020.92.3 Caccia, Franciscus. Mater dolorosa et gratiosa. Wienn, 1703.
Arc 1020.93 Salore, Charles. Reliques de trois tombeaux saints de Clairvoux...a Ville-sous-la-Ferté (Aubé). Troyes, 1877.
Arc 1020.94 Helbig, Jules. Reliques...données par St. Louis, roi de France, au couvent des Dominicains de Liége. Bruxelles, 1881.
Arc 1020.95 Fabiani, G. Sulla Cattedra Alessandria di S. Marco. Modena, 1869.
Arc 1020.95.11 Tiepolo, G. Trattato delle sanctissime reliquie...San Marco. Venet, 1617.
Htn Arc 1020.96* Bagatas, R. SS. episcoparum...antiqua monumenta. Venetiis, 1576.
Arc 1020.97 Morales, Ambrosio de. Viage...para reconocer las reliquias de santos, sepulcros reales. Madrid, 1765.
Arc 1020.99 Kaufmann, C.M. Der Menastempel und die Heiligtümer von Karm Abu Mina. Frankfurt, 1909.
Arc 1020.99.9 Kaufmann, C.M. Die heilige Stadt der Wüste. 2.-3. Aufl. Kempten, 1921.
Arc 1020.99.10 Kaufmann, C.M. Die heilige Stadt der Wüste. 4e Aufl. Kempten, 1921.
Arc 1020.99.15 Kaufmann, C.M. Zur Ikonographie des Menas-Ampullen. Cairo, 1910.
Arc 1020.100 Mutio, Mario. Delle reliquie insigni...chiesa de Bergamo. Bergamo, 1616.
Arc 1020.101 Récit de la fondation de l'Eglise de Notre Dame de Long-Pré. Abbéville, 1818.

Arc 1020 Archaeology - Christian antiquities - Local - cont.

Arc 1020.102 Breve distinta relazione...sacre relique... S. Maria...città di Siena. Siena, 1750.
Arc 1020.102.3 Angelis, L. de. Osservazioni critici...Siena...sopra croce di rame intagliata...1129. Siena, 1814.
Arc 1020.103 Bartoletti, T. Privato santuario atessano...de'santi, beati. Napoli, 1835.
Arc 1020.104 Rohault de Fleury, G. Un tabernacle chrétien du Ve siècle. Arras, 1880.
Arc 1020.105 Capece, G. Dissertazione...intorno alle due campane della chiesa parochiale di S. Giovanni. Napoli, 1750.
Arc 1020.106 Bled, O. Livre d'or de Notre Dame des miracles à Saint Omer. St. Omer, 1913.
Arc 1020.107 Payne, J.O. St. Paul's Cathedral...account of the treasures. London, 1893.
Arc 1020.108 Fabre, A. Trésor de la ste. chapelle des ducs de Savoie. Lyon, 1875.
Arc 1020.110 Brouillet, A. Description des reliquaires...abboye de Charroux. Poitiers, 1856.
Htn Arc 1020.111* Croques reliques. Poéme burlesque. Paris, 1876.
Arc 1020.112 Fleury, E. Trésor de Notre-Dame-de-Liesse...de 1655 à 1790. Paris, 1854.
Arc 1020.113 Furno, A. Breve istoria del santuario di Belmonte presso Valperga. Torino, 1788.
Arc 1020.114 Schenkel, I.I. Die Reliquien des Klosters Allerheiligen. Schaffhausen, 1866.
Arc 1020.115 Poquet, A.E. De terra iheroslimitana...allate sunt relique. n.p., n.d.
Arc 1020.116 Les corps saints de l'insigne Basilique Saint Saturnin de Toulouse. Toulouse, n.d.
Arc 1020.117 Stokes, Margaret. Six months in the Apennines. London, 1892.
Arc 1020.118 Holahan, J. Notes on the antiquities of united parishes of Ballycollan, Kilmaugh and Killaloe, Kilkenny, 1875.
Arc 1020.119 Gudiol y Cunill, J. Nocions d'arqueologia sagrada catalana. Vich, 1911.
Arc 1020.119.5 Gudiol y Cunill, J. Nocions d'arqueologia sagrada catalana. 2a ed. Vich, 1931-33. 2v.
Htn Arc 1020.120* Campos, Manoel de. Relaçam do solenne recebimento que se fez em Lisboa. Lisboa, 1588.
Arc 1020.120.15 Telfer, William. The treasure of São Roque. London, 1932.
Arc 1020.122 La Croix, C. de. Une dalle mérovingienne trouvée à Challans (Vendée). Poitiers, 1909.
Arc 1020.123 Swoboda, H. Neue Funde aus dem altchristlichen Österreich. Wien, 1909.
Arc 1020.124 Huidobro Serna, Luciano. Nuestra Señora del Espino en Santa Gadea del Cid Burgos. Lérida, 1922. 3 pam.
Arc 1020.124.5 Hergueta y Martin, Domingo. Santa María la mayor de la catedral de Burgos y su culto. Lérida, 1922.
Arc 1020.125 Darcel, Alfred. Trésor de l'église de conques. Paris, 1861.
Htn Arc 1020.126* López Madera, G. Discursos de la certidumbre de las reliquias descubiertas en Granada. Madrid, 1601.
Arc 1020.126.5 López Madera, G. Historia y discursos de la certidumbre de las reliquias, láminas. Granada, 1602.
Arc 1020.127 Más, Joseph. Les reliquies del Monastir de Sant Cugat del Vallès. Barcelona, 1908.
Arc 1020.128F Pappageorgios, P. Un édit de l'empereur Justinien II. Leipzig, 1900.
Arc 1020.129F Falke, Otto von. Der Welfenschatz. Frankfurt, 1930.
Arc 1020.130 Neuss, Wilhelm. Die Anfänge des Christentums im Rheinlande. 2. Aufl. Bonn, 1933.
Arc 1020.131 Kollwitz, J. Die Lipsanothek von Brescia. Berlin, 1933.
Arc 1020.131PF Kollwitz, J. Die Lipsanothek von Brescia. Atlas. Berlin, 1933.
Arc 1020.132 Le Prevost, A. Notice sur la châsse de Saint Taurin d'Évreux. Évreux, 1838.
Arc 1020.133 Schnyder, William. Acht Studien zur christlichen Altertumswissenschaft und zur Kirchengeschichte. Luzern, 1937.
Arc 1020.134F Das hallesche Heiltum. Berlin, 1931.
Arc 1020.135 Camprubi Alemany, Francisco. El monumento paleocristiano de Centcelles. Barcelona, 1952.
Arc 1020.136 Agnello, G. Gli studi di archeologia cristiana in Sicilia. Catania, 1950.
Arc 1020.137 Bovini, G. Sarcofagi paleocristiani della Spagna. Roma, 1954.
Arc 1020.138 Gavrilova, A. Sviatyni Egipta; zemlia egipet kak sad gospoden. Buenos Aires, 1960.
Arc 1020.140 Friken, A. Rimskaia katakomby i pamiatniki pervonachal'nago Khristianskago iskusstva. Moskva, 1872-
Arc 1020.142 Cagiano de Azevedo, Michelangelo. Testimonianze archaeologiche della tradizione paolina a Malta. Roma, 1966.
Arc 1020.144 Czober, Béla. Egyházi emlékek a törtenelmi kiállitison. Budapest, 1898.
Arc 1020.146 Kollautz, Arnulf. Denkmäler byzantinischen Christentums aus der Awarenzeit der Donauländer. Amsterdam, 1970.
Arc 1020.150 Fink, Josef. Der Mars Camulus-Stein in der Pfarrkirche zu Rindern. Kevelaer, 1970.

Arc 1025 Archaeology - Christian antiquities - Catacombs - General works

Arc 1025.01 Pamphlet box. Christian catacombs.
Arc 1025.1 Rip, W.I. The catacombs of Rome. N.Y., 1854.
Arc 1025.2 Kraus, F.K. Roma Sotterranea, die römischen Katakomben. Freiburg, 1879.
Arc 1025.3 Ludwig, C. Ein Blick in die römischen Katakomben. Bern, 1876.
Arc 1025.4 Northcote, J.S. The Roman catacombs. London, 1857.
Arc 1025.4.2 Northcote, J.S. The Roman catacombs. Philadelphia, 1857.
Arc 1025.4.5 Northcote, J.S. A visit to the Roman catacombs. London, 1877.
Arc 1025.4.7 Northcote, J.S. Visite aux catacombes de Rome. Paris, 1878.
Arc 1025.4.9 Northcote, J.S. Les catacombes romaines. Rome, 1859.
Arc 1025.5 Northcote, J.S. Roma sotterranea. pts.1-3. London, 1879. 2v.
Arc 1025.6 Northcote, J.S. Rome souterraine. 2. éd. Paris, 1874.
Arc 1025.7 Raoul-Rochette, D. Troisième mémoire sur les antiquités chrétiennes des catacombes. Paris, 1838.
Arc 1025.7.5 Raoul-Rochette, D. Tabelau des catacombes de Rome. Paris, n.d.
Arc 1025.7.7 Raoul-Rochette, D. Tableau des catacombes de Rome. Paris, 1853.
Arc 1025.7.11 Raoul-Rochette, D. Le catacombe di Roma. Milano, 1841.
Arc 1025.8 Schultze, V. Die Katakomben. Photoreproduction. Leipzig, 1882.

Arc 1025 Archaeology - Christian antiquities - Catacombs - General works - cont.

Arc 1025.9 Smyth, E. Recent excavations in American Christian cemeteries. Worcester, 1882.
Arc 1025.10 Maitland, C. Church in the catacombs. London, 1847.
Arc 1025.11 Withrow, W.H. Catacombs of Rome. London, 1877.
Arc 1025.12 Marriott, W.B. Testimony of the catacombs. London, 1870.
Arc 1025.13 Liell, H.F.J. Die Darstellungen...Maria...Katakomben. Freiburg, 1887.
Arc 1025.14 Housse, L. Die Katakomben über das Unterirdische. Lurenburg, 1867.
Arc 1025.15 Romeke, K. Rom's christliche Katakomben. Leipzig, 1886.
Arc 1025.16 Wolter, M. Die römischen Katakomben. Frankfurt, 1866.
Arc 1025.17 Scott, B. Contents...catacombs of Rome. London, 1873.
Arc 1025.18 Wiegand, F. Eine Wanderung...römischen Katakomben. Erlangen, 1893.
Arc 1025.20 L'Epinovis, H. de. Les catacombes de Rome. Paris, 1875.
Arc 1025.21 Scherillo, G. Archeologia sacra. v.1-2. Napoli, 1875.
Arc 1025.22 Janssen, L.J.F. Over de catacomben van Rome. Utrecht, 1854.
Arc 1025.23 Angelini, A. Genni sopra i primi cimiteri...Roma christiana. Roma, 1840.
Arc 1025.24 Martorelli, I. Le catacombe di Roma. Vercelli, 1881.
Arc 1025.25 Desbassayns de Richemont, M.C. Les nouvelles études...catacombes romaines. Paris, 1870.
Arc 1025.26 Strazzula, V. Museum epigraphicum. Panormi, 1897.
Arc 1025.27 Cavedoni, Celestino. Ragguaglio critico dei monumenti delle arti cristiane. Modena, 1849.
Arc 1025.28.3 Marucchi, O. Eléments d'archélogie chrétienne. v.1-2. Paris, 1899. 3v.
Arc 1025.28.4 Marucchi, O. Eléments d'archéologie chrétienne. Paris, 1903. 2v.
Arc 1025.28.6 Marucchi, O. Handbuch der christlichen Archäologie. N.Y., 1912.
Arc 1025.28.8 Marucchi, O. Come lo studio dell'archeologia cristiana giovi grandemente. Roma, 1903.
Arc 1025.28.15 Le tombe dei martiri nelle catacombe romane. Roma, 1896.
Arc 1025.28.19 Marucchi, O. Come lo studio dell'archeologia cristiana. Roma, 1900.
Arc 1025.28.25 Marucchi, O. La catacombe romane a proposito della recente opera del Roller. Roma, 1883.
Arc 1025.28.27 Marucchi, O. Guide des catacombes romaines. 2. éd. Paris, 1903.
Arc 1025.28.30 Marucchi, O. Scavi nelle catacombe romane. Roma, 1899.
Arc 1025.28.35 Marucchi, O. Esame di un opuscolo di Mons. G. Wilpert. Roma, 1909.
Arc 1025.28.40 Marucchi, O. Compendio storico e topografico delle catacombe romane. Albano Laziale, 1928.
Arc 1025.28.45 Marucchi, O. The evidencce of the catacombs for the doctrines and organization of the primitive church. London, 1929.
Arc 1025.28.50F Marucchi, O. Le catacombe romane. Roma, 1933.
Arc 1025.29 Rossi, G.B. de. Del luogo appellato ad Caprean. Roma, 1888.
Arc 1025.29.5 Rossi, G.B. de. Aperçu général sur les catacombes de Rome. Paris, 1867.
Arc 1025.29.18 Odorici, F. Sulla Roma sotterranea dal G.B. de Rossi. Milano, 1866.
Arc 1025.29.21 Tonini, P. La Roma sotterranea cristiana...dal G.B. de Rossi. Firenze, 1879.
Arc 1025.30 Armellini, M. Gli antichi cimiteri cristiani di Roma e d'Italia. Roma, 1893.
Arc 1025.30.5 Armellini, M. Le catacombe romane. Roma, 1880.
Arc 1025.31 Gaume, J. Histoire des catacombes. Paris, 1848.
Arc 1025.31.3 Gaume, J. Histoire des catacombes de Rome. Paris, n.d.
Arc 1025.32 Lefort, Louis. Chronologie des peintures des catacombes romaines. Paris, 1881.
Arc 1025.33 Treat, J.H. The catacombs of Rome. n.p., n.d.
Arc 1025.34 Cyprian, E.S. De ecclesia subterranea liber. Helmstedt, 1699. 8 pam.
Arc 1025.35 Bosio, A. Roma subterranea novissima. Arnhemi, 1671.
Arc 1025.35.20 Valeri, A. Cenni biografici di Antonio Bosio. Roma, 1900.
Arc 1025.36 Agincourt, G.B.L.G. d'. Viaggio nelle catacombe di Roma. Milano, 1835.
Arc 1025.37 Lampake, G. Christianikē gechnē...katakombai. Athēnai, 1900.
Arc 1025.38 Partenio, G.M. Vie sacre. 2a ed. Roma, 1806-07. 2v.
Arc 1025.39 Cancellieri, F. Dissertazione epistolare. Roma, 1819.
Arc 1025.40 Fontana, G. Le notti cristiane. Colle, 1829.
Arc 1025.41 Scognamiglio, A. In Roma i cristianai...soterranei cimiteri. Roma, 1863.
Arc 1025.42 Emiliani, A. Ricordi di viaggio ad catacumbas. Livorno, 1883.
Arc 1025.43 Crostarosa, P. Notizie sullo stato delle catacombe romane. Roma, 1901.
Arc 1025.44 Prina, B. Le catacombe. Firenze, 1894.
Arc 1025.45 Mommesen, T. The Roman catacombs. Londin, 1871.
Arc 1025.46 Minoccheri, L. Le catacombe. Roma, 1897.
Arc 1025.47 Les catacombes de Rome. Conférence. Paris, n.d.
Arc 1025.48 Besnier, M. Les catacombes de Rome. Paris, 1904.
Arc 1025.48.3 Besnier, M. Les catacombes de Rome. Paris, 1909.
Arc 1025.50 Treat, J.H. The catacombs of Rome. Boston, 1907.
Arc 1025.51 Schmid, G. Das unterirdische Rom. Brixen, 1908.
Arc 1025.52 Grillwitzer, A. Die bildischen Darstellungen in die römischen Katakomben. Graz, 1876.
Arc 1025.53 Becker, T. Rom's altchristliche Coemeterien. Düsseldorf, 1874.
Arc 1025.54 Desimoni, C. Le catacombe romane. Firenze, 1870.
Arc 1025.55 Hasenclever, A. Der altchristliche Gräberschmuck. Braunschweig, 1886.
Arc 1025.56 Schultze, M.V. De christianorum viterum rebus sepulchralibus. Gothae, 1879.
Arc 1025.57 Nicolai, Joannis. De luctie christianorum. Lugdnum Batavorum, 1739.
Arc 1025.58 MacFarlane, Charles. The catacombs of Rome. London, 1852.
Arc 1025.59 Artaud de Montor, A.F. Voyages dans les catacombes de Rome. Paris, 1810.
Arc 1025.60 Davin, V. Les sanctuaires primitifs de Rome et des Gaules. Paris, 1873?
Arc 1025.61 Henderson, Alexander. The lesson of the catacombs. London, 1920.
Arc 1025.62 Styger, Paul. Die altchristliche Grabeskunst. München, 1927.
Arc 1025.62.10F Styger, Paul. Die römischen Katakomben. Berlin, 1933.
Arc 1025.62.15F Styger, Paul. Römische Märtyrergrüfte. Berlin, 1935. 2v.
Arc 1025.63 Beyer, Oskar. Die Katakombenwelt. Tübingen, 1927.
Arc 1025.65 Wilpert, Josef. Erlebnisse und Ergebnisse im Dienste der christlichen Archäologie. Freiburg, 1930.

Arc 1025 Archaeology - Christian antiquities - Catacombs - General works - cont.

Htn Arc 1025.66* Englefield, T.B. Some of the notes...on various subjects, especially the catacombs. n.p., n.d.
Arc 1025.67 Collezione "Amici della catacombe". Roma. 1-25,1933-1956 13v.
Arc 1025.68 Bosio, Antonio. Abgebildetes unterirdisches Rom. Arnheim, 1668.
Arc 1025.69 Bakhuitzen van den Brink, J.N. De romeinsche catacomben en haar frescos. 's-Gravenhage, 1933.
Arc 1025.70 Cecchelli, C. La chiesa delle catacombe. Roma, 1943.
Arc 1025.71.2 Bock, Emil. Die Katakomben. 2. Aufl. Stuttgart, 1961.
Arc 1025.72 Hertling, Ludwig. Die römischen Katakomben und ihre Martyrer. Wien, 1950.
Arc 1025.72.5 Hertling, Ludwig. Die römischen Katakomben und ihre Martyrer. 2. Aufl. Wien, 1950.
Arc 1025.73 Kirsch, G.P. The catacombs of Rome. Rome, 1946.
Arc 1025.74 Carcopino, J. De Pythagore aux apôtres. Paris, 1956.
Arc 1025.75 Denis-Boulet, Noële M. Rome souterraine. Paris, 1965.

Arc 1027 Archaeology - Christian antiquities - Catacombs - Special topics

Arc 1027 Pamphlet box. Christian catacombs.
Arc 1027.01 Pamphlet box. Christian catacombs.
Arc 1027.1 Kaus, F.X. Die Blutampullen der römischen Katakomben. Frankfurt, 1868.
Arc 1027.1.5 Kraus, F.X. Über den gegenwärtigenStand der Frage. Freiburg, 1872.
Arc 1027.1.13 Gaetani, V. Trina comunicazione...vasello col sangui. Palermo, 1895.
Arc 1027.1.17 Bartolini, D. Relazione severamente i vasi...sangue dei martiri. Roma, 1863.
Arc 1027.2 Morcelli, S.A. Agapea Michaëleia. Bononiae, 1822.
Arc 1027.2.5 Morcelli, S.A. Comento sull'iscrizione sepolcrale. Modena, 1824.
Arc 1027.2.15 Polidori, L. Dei conviti effigiati a simbolo ne' monumenti cristiani. Milano, 1844.
Arc 1027.2.19 Lefort, L. Les scènes de banquets. Paris, 1883.
Arc 1027.3 Wilpert, G. La croce sui monumenti delle catacombe. Roma, 1902.
Arc 1027.3.5 Carini, I. Il crocifesso negli antichi monumenti. Roma, 1889.
Arc 1027.4 De Rossi, G.B. Fouilles et découverts...cimetière de Priscille. Rome, 1880.
Arc 1027.4.5 Davin, V. Les antiquités chrétiennes...Cappella greca. Paris, 1892.
Arc 1027.4.9 Paoli. Notizie...S. Feliciano...cimitero di Priscilla. Roma, 1796.
Arc 1027.4.11 Marucchi, O. Le nuove scoperte nelle catacombe di Priscilla. v.1-2. Roma, 1888.
Arc 1027.4.13 Marucchi, O. Di un battistero scoperto nel cimitero di Priscilla. Roma, 1901.
Arc 1027.4.15 Marucchi, O. Guida del cimitero di Priscilla. Paris, 1903.
Arc 1027.4.17 Bonavenia, G. L'antichissima imagine della B. Vergine nel cimitero di Priscilla. Siena, 1897.
Arc 1027.4.19 Bonavenia, G. Soluzione di un problema...cimitero di Priscilla. Roma, 1903.
Arc 1027.4.21 Bonavenia, G. La cuestione...controversia filumeniana. Roma, 1907.
Arc 1027.4.25 Santucci, S. Sulla lapide sepolcrale di S. Filomena. Roma, 1837.
Arc 1027.4.27 Povèda, G. de. Memorie...S. Filomena e l'invenzione del suo corpo. Foligno, 1834.
Arc 1027.4.29 Marucchi, O. Studio archaeologico...iscrizione di Filomena. Roma, 1907.
Arc 1027.4.35 Rossi, G.B. de. La basilica di S. Silvestro nel cimitero di Priscilla. Roma, 1890.
Arc 1027.4.40 Marucchi, O. La basilica papale del cimitero di Priscilla. Roma, 1908.
Arc 1027.5 Rossi, G.B. de. Importantes decouvertes...cimetiere de Domitille. Paris, 1875.
Arc 1027.5.2 Rossi, G.B. de. Isigni scoperte nel cimitero di Domitilla. Roma, n.d.
Arc 1027.5.3 Rossi, G.B. de. Roma; scavi nel cimitero de Domitilla. Roma, 1877.
Arc 1027.5.4 Rossi, G.B. de. Il cubicolo di Ampliato nel cimitero di Domitilla. Roma, 1900.
Arc 1027.5.13 Marucchi, O. Guida del cimitero di Domitilla. Paris, 1902.
Arc 1027.5.15 Marucchi, O. Di un gruppo di antiche iscrizioni...Domitilla. Roma, 1902.
Arc 1027.5.18 Marucchi, O. La memoria dei santi...cimitero di Domitilla. n.p., n.d.
Arc 1027.5.25 Stevenson, H. Scavi nel cimitero di Domitilla. Roma, 1898.
Arc 1027.5.55 Petit guide du cimetière de Domitille. Rome, 1900.
Arc 1027.5.59 Monumenta subterranea selecta urbis Romae praesertim ex coemeterio Domitillae. Roma, n.d.
Arc 1027.6 Marucchi, O. Sepolcro apostolico delle catacombe. Roma, 1892.
Arc 1027.7.5 Visconti, P.E. Di un nuovo tratto catacombe San Marcellino Pietro. Roma, 1839.
Arc 1027.7.9 Wilpert, J. Di un cielo di rappresent cristianità...SS. Pietro ed Marcelino. Roma, 1892.
Arc 1027.7.13 Laderchu, J. De sacris Basilicis S. Martyrum. Roma, 1705.
Arc 1027.7.17 Rossi, G.B. de. Escavazioni nel cimitero dei SS. Pietro e Marcellino. Roma, 1882.
Arc 1027.8 Grisar, H. Die römische Sebastianuskirche. Rom, 1895.
Arc 1027.8.9 Marucchi, O. Di un ipogeo scoperto nel cimitero di S. Sebastian. Roma, 1879.
Arc 1027.8.13 Chéramy, H. Saint-Sébastien hors les murs. Paris, 1925.
Arc 1027.9 Armellini, M. Le catacombe e il protestantesimo. Roma, 1875.
Arc 1027.9.5 Marucchi, O. Gli errori della scuola protestante. n.p., 1884.
Arc 1027.9.9 Marucchi, O. Le catacombe ed il protestantesimo. Roma, 1911.
Arc 1027.10 Tizzani, V. Commissione de archeologia sagrada...Basilica di San Clemente. Roma, 1886.
Arc 1027.11 Michettoni, V. Memorie archeologica su di S. Aurelia Procope vergine e martire. Ripatransone, 1845.
Arc 1027.12 DeWaal, A. Die Apostelgruft ad Catacumbas S. Peter und S. Paul. Rom, 1894.
Arc 1027.12.5 Battandier, A. La Platonia...sepulcre des Sts. Pierre et Paul. Paris, 1896.
Arc 1027.12.9 Bufalieré, P. La basilica apostolorum e la critta apostolica. Roma, 1891.
Arc 1027.12.11 Sindone. Della sacrosanta basilica di S. Pietro. Roma, 1750.

Arc 1027 Archaeology - Christian antiquities - Catacombs - Special topics - cont.

Arc 1027.12.13 Mecchi, F.E. La tomba di San Pietro. Roma, 1893.
Arc 1027.12.15 Lugari, G.B. I varii seppellimenti...Pietro e Paolo. Roma, 1898.
Arc 1027.12.17 Armellini, M. D'una transl...SS. Pietro e Paolo in...le catacombe. Roma, 1874.
Arc 1027.12.19 La Piana, George. The tombs of Peter and Paul ad catacumbas. Cambridge, 1920.
Arc 1027.12.20 Guarducci, Margherita. The tomb of Saint Peter. N.Y., 1960.
Arc 1027.12.26 Carsopino, Jérôme. Les fouilles de Saint Pierre et la tradition. Paris, 1963.
Arc 1027.13 Tarantini, G. Di alcunce cripte nell'agro di Brindisi. Napoli, 1878.
Arc 1027.14 Billaud, Pelissier B. Pelerinage au cauc du Pape S. Alexandre I. Rome, 1856.
Arc 1027.14.5 Atti...S. Alessandro I...memorie del suo sepolcro. Roma, 1858.
X Cg Arc 1027.15 Marucchi, O. Il cimitero e la Basilica di San Valentino. Roma, 1890.
Arc 1027.15.5 Marucchi, O. La cripta sepolceale di San Valentio sulla Flaminia. Roma, 1878.
Arc 1027.15.9 Marucchi, O. Le recenti scoperte presso il cimitero di San Valentino. Roma, 1888.
Arc 1027.15.19 Rossi, G.B. de. Fibula d'oro aquiliforme. Roma, 1894.
Arc 1027.16 Strazzulla, V. Nouvi studi su alcuni elemente Pagani. Messina, 1900.
Arc 1027.17 Stevenson, H. Das Coerneterium de H. Christina zu Bolsena. n.p., n.d.
Arc 1027.18 Garruci, R. Cimitero degli antichi ebrei. Roma, 1862.
Arc 1027.18.5 Müller, Nikolaus. Le catacombe degli ebrei...via Appia. Roma, 1885?
Arc 1027.18.6 Müller, Nikolaus. Die Inschriften der jüdischen Katakombe. Leipzig, 1919.
Arc 1027.18.7 Müller, Nikolaus. Die jüdische Katakombe am Monteverde zu Rom. Leipzig, 1912.
Arc 1027.18.9 Marucchi, O. Di un nuovo cimitero giudaico. Roma, 1884.
Arc 1027.18.12 Engeström, Adolf von. Om Judarne i Rom...och deras...katakomber. Upsala, 1876.
Arc 1027.18.15 Beyer, Hermann W. Die jüdische Katakombe der Villa Torlonia in Rom. Berlin, 1930.
Arc 1027.18.20 Frey, J.B. Nouvelles inscriptions inedites de la cata-combe juive de la via Appia. n.p., 193-.
Arc 1027.19 Nortet. Les catacombes de Saint Calixte. Rome, 1887.
Arc 1027.19.2 Nortet. Cimetière de Saint Calixte. 3e éd. Rome, 1888.
Arc 1027.19.3 Nortet. Cimetière de Saint Calixte. 3e éd. Rome, 1899.
Arc 1027.19.5 Nortet. Cimetière de Saint Calixte. 3e éd. Rome, 1900.
Arc 1027.19.13 Pillet, A. Souvenirs du cimetière de Saint Calliste. Arras, 1881.
Arc 1027.19.17 Marucchi, O. Guida del cimitero di Callisto. Paris, 1902.
Arc 1027.19.21 Marucchi, O. Osservazioni sulla iscrizione della madre del papa Damaso. Roma, 1903.
Arc 1027.19.29 Wilpert, J. Die Malerein der Sacramentskapellen in der Katakombe des honorable Callistus. Freiburg, 1897.
Arc 1027.19.33 Huthmacher, L. Ein Besuch in der römischen Katakomben...S. Kallisto. Mainz, 1861.
Arc 1027.19.35 Trappists. Selecta ex coemeterio Si Callisti. Roma, 189-?
Arc 1027.19.40F Reekmans, Louis. La tombe du Pape Corneille et su région cimetriale. Città del Vaticano, 1964.
Arc 1027.20 Stevenson, E. Il cimitero di Zotico. Dec miglio...Labicana. Modena, 1876.
Arc 1027.21 Schultze, V. Die Katakomben von San Gennaro die Poveri. Jena, 1877.
Arc 1027.21.5 Jorio, A. de. Notzie sulle crepte...San Gennaro di Poveri. v.1-2. Napoli, 1833-39.
Arc 1027.21.9 Stornaiolo, C. Alcuni recenti scavi nelle catacombe di San Gennaro. Roma, 1879.
Arc 1027.22 Achelis, H. Das Symbol des Fisches...Fischi der Römische Katakombe. Marburg, 1888.
Arc 1027.22.5 Rossi, J.B. de. De christianis monumentes Ichthys. Paris, 1855.
Arc 1027.22.9 Majocchi, R. L'Ichthys eucaristico nei monumenti. Milano, 1895.
Arc 1027.22.13 Calori Cesis, F. Un insigne monumento cristiano del secolo III. Bologna, 1873.
Arc 1027.22.17 Das Christliche Fischsymbol. Freiburg, 1905.
Arc 1027.23 Becker, F. Die Darstellung Jesu Christi...Bilde des Fisches. Gero, 1876.
Arc 1027.23.5 Becker, F. Die Waud- und Decken-Gernälde Römischen Katakomben. Düsseldorf, 1874.
Arc 1027.23.9 Hennecke, E. Altchristliche Malerei...römischen Katacomben. Leipzig, 1896.
Arc 1027.23.13 Ghignoni, A. Le pitture della catacombe romane. Firenze, 1905.
Arc 1027.23.17 Schulke, V. Die altchristlichen Bildwerke. Erlangen, 1889.
Arc 1027.23.20 Lamberton, C.D. Themes from St. John's gospel in early Roman catacomb painting. Princeton, 1905.
Arc 1027.23.23 Kampffmeyer, K. Die Landschaft in der altchristlichen Katakombenmalerei. Greifswald, 1933.
Arc 1027.24 Bellermann, C.F. Über die ältesten christlichen Begrabnifsstätten. Hamburg, 1839.
Arc 1027.24.5 Taglialatela, G. Di una imagine de S. Protasio, nella catacombe severiana. Napoli, 1874.
Arc 1027.24.9 Lefort, L. Chronologie des peintures des catacombes de Naples. Rome, 1883.
Arc 1027.24.13 Scherillo, G. Archeologia sacra: Catacombe napolitane. Napoli, 1875.
Htn Arc 1027.24.25F* Achelis, Hans. Die Katakomben von Neapel. Leipzig, 1935-36.
Arc 1027.25 Scognamiglio, A. De phiala cruenta...Christo martyrii. Paris, 1867.
Arc 1027.25.5 Pitra, J.B. Inscriptions des...Rome chretienne. Paris, 1862-92. 3 pam.
Arc 1027.25.9 Rossi, J.B. de. Albo dei sottoscrittori...medaglio d'oro. Roma, 1882.
Arc 1027.25.11 Geffroy, A. Une fête archéologique à Rome. Paris, 1883.
Arc 1027.25.13 Cozza, Luzi G. Per un busto...G.B. de Rossi. Roma, 1883-3 pam.
Arc 1027.25.15 Rossi, G.B. de. Albo dei sottoscrittori pel busto marmoreo. Roma, 1892.
Arc 1027.25.17 Adunanza della Pontificia accademia romana d'archeologia dedicata alla memoria di G.B. de Rossi. Roma, 1894.
Arc 1027.25.19 Baumgarten, P.M. Giovanni Battista de Rossi. Köln, 1892.
Arc 1027.25.20 Baumgarten, P.M. Giovanni Battista de Rossi. Roma, 1892.
Arc 1027.25.24 Rossi, G.B. de. Melanges G.B. Rossi. Paris, 1892.
Arc 1027.25.27 Marucchi, O. Solenne festa in onore del Comm. G.B. de Rossi. Roma, 1883.

Arc 1027 Archaeology - Christian antiquities - Catacombs - Special topics - cont.

Arc 1027.25.29 Marucchi, O. Giovanni Battista de Rossi. Roma, 1895.
Arc 1027.25.31 Marucchi, O. Giovanni Battista de Rossi. Roma, 1901.
Arc 1027.25.33 Stevensen, H. Giovanni Battista de Rossi. Roma, 1895.
Arc 1027.25.37 Grossi-Gondi, A. Giovanni Battista de Rossi, archeologo romano. Roma, 1894.
Arc 1027.25.41 Archäologische Ehren-Gabe zur 70. Geburtstage De Rossi. Rom, 1892.
Arc 1027.25.45 Galante, G.A. Giovanni Battista de Rossi e l'archeologia cristiana. Napoli, 1900.
Arc 1027.25.51 Des travaux de M. de Rossi. Arras, n.d.
Arc 1027.25.55 Buck, V. de. M. de Rossi ets ses récents travaux...catacombes. v.1-2. Paris, 1865.
Arc 1027.25.61 LeBlant, E. Jean-Baptiste de Rossi. Paris, 1894.
Arc 1027.25.65 Bellesheim, A. Der heilige Johannes Baptista de Rossi. Mainz, 1882.
Arc 1027.26 Bartolini, D. Le catacombe di Siracusa. Roma, 1847.
Arc 1027.26.5 Orsi, Paolo. Nuove esplorazioni nelle catacombe di S. Giovanni Battista de Rossi nell 1894 in Siracusa. Roma, 1896.
Arc 1027.26.9 Cavallari, S. Osservazioni sulle basiliche e le catacombe...Siracusa. Palermo, 1874.
Arc 1027.26.15 Carini, I. Rassegna archeologica. Iscrizioni cristiana dei catacombe di Siracusa. Palermo, 1876.
Arc 1027.26.25 Führer, J. Forschungen zur Sicilia sotterranea. München, 1897.
Arc 1027.27 Bartolini, D. Le nuove catacombe di Chiusi. Roma, 1852.
Arc 1027.27.2 Bartolini, D. Le nuove catacombe di Chiusi. Roma, 1853.
Arc 1027.27.5 Pasquini, G. Relazione...cimitero di cristiani. Montepulciano, 1833.
Arc 1027.27.9 Liverani, F. Catacombe e antichità cristiana di Chiusi. Siena, 1872.
Arc 1027.27.13 Cavedoni, C. Ragguaglio di due antichi cimiteri. Modena, 1853.
Arc 1027.28 Rampolla, M. Catalogo cimiteriale romano. Roma, 1900.
Arc 1027.28.5 Stevenson, Enrico. Di un nuovo insigne esemplare...indice dei cimiteri cristiani di Roma. Roma, 1897.
Arc 1027.29 Rossi, M.S. Dell'ampiezza. Romane catacombe macchina. Roma, 1860.
Arc 1027.30.5 Gori, F. Della porta e basilica di S. Lorenzo dell catacombe. Roma, 1862.
Arc 1027.30.9 Salvatore da Morrovalle, P. La basilica di S. Lorenzo fuor delle mura. Bologna, 1861.
Arc 1027.30.15 Bartolini, D. Inscrizione S. Martire Fortissima nel cimitero...Ciriaca. Roma, 1842.
Arc 1027.30.19 Rossi, G.B. de. Arcosolio dipinto del cimitero di Ciriaca. Roma, 1876.
Arc 1027.31 Santoni, M. La cripta di S. Angelo de Profoglio...Camerino. Camerino, 1892.
Arc 1027.32 Dufresne, D. Les cryptes vaticanes. Paris, 1902.
Arc 1027.32.10 Kirschbaum, E. Die Graeber der Apostelfürsten. Frankfurt, 1957.
Arc 1027.32.12 Kirschbaum, E. Die Graeber der Apostelfürsten. 2. Aufl. Frankfurt, 1959.
Arc 1027.33 Appell, J.W. Monuments of early Christian art. London, 1872.
Htn Arc 1027.34* Marangoni, J. Acta S. Victorini episcopi amiterni et martyres. Rome, 1740.
Arc 1027.35 Armellini, M. Il cimiterio di S. Agnese sulla via nomentana. Roma, 1880.
Arc 1027.36 Volpi, A.T. Dell'indentila dei S. Corpi dei S. Fermo Rustico, e Procolo. Milano, 1761.
Arc 1027.36.5 Dionisi, G.J. Della città di Preconi nominata negli atti di SS. MM. fermo e rustico. Vinegia, 1782.
Arc 1027.37 Armellini, M. I cemeteri cristiano della via latina. Roma, 1874.
Arc 1027.38 Cassini da Perinaldo, F. Le veglie notturne al cimitero di Cimella. Genova, 1858.
Arc 1027.39 Armellini, M. Scoperta d'un graffito storico...cimiteri di Pretestato. Roma, 1874.
Arc 1027.39.5 Baruffaldi, G. Dissertazione intorno...sepolcro...cimitero di Prestato. Venezia? 1747?
Arc 1027.39.9 Marucchi, O. Scavi eseguiti nell'antica Basilica di S. Agapito. Roma, 1899.
Arc 1027.40 Armellini, M. Scoperta...cripta S. Emerenziana...cimiteri Ostriano. Roma, 1877.
Arc 1027.40.5 Marucchi, O. La recente condroversia sul cimitero Ostriano. Roma, 1903.
Arc 1027.41 Marucchi, O. Il cimitero di Commodilla. Roma, 1904.
Arc 1027.41.3F Bagatti, B. Il cimitero di Commodilla. Città del Vaticano, 1936.
Arc 1027.41.9 Stevenson, H. Osservazione sulla topografia della via Ostiense. Roma, 1897.
Arc 1027.41.15 Stevenson, H. L'area di Lucina sulla via Ostiense. Roma, 1898.
Arc 1027.41.25 Moreschi, L. Indicazione dei dipinti a buon presco dell'Apostolo S. Paolo. Roma, 1867.
Arc 1027.41.35 Grisar, H. Die Grabplatte des H. Paulus. Rom, 1892.
Arc 1027.41.39 Lugari, G.B. Il "Dolocenum" della XIII regione. Roma, 1893.
Arc 1027.42 Atti del collegium cultorum martyrum. Romae, 1888.
Arc 1027.43 Bulic, F. Necropoli antica cristiana a Slanɔ di Ragusa. Roma, 1901.
Arc 1027.44 Marucchi, O. Di alcune iscrizioni...Basilia de S. Petronella. Roma, n.d.
Arc 1027.45 Galt Said, G. Grotta di San Paolo a Malta. Malta, 1863.
Arc 1027.45.5 Becker, Erich. Malta Sotterranea...Sepulkralkunst. Strassburg, 1913.
Arc 1027.46 Fortunati, L. Brevi cenni...scoprimento...martire...S. Stefano. Roma, 1858.
Arc 1027.46.5 Nardoni, L. Dell'antica chiesa di S. Stefano sulla via Cassia. Roma, 1859.
Arc 1027.47 Bufalieri da Montécelio, P. Ricersa...tomba S. Cecilia. Roma, 1891.
Arc 1027.48 Germano di S. Stanislalo, P. Memorie archeologico...il cimitero S. Eutizio di Ferento. Roma, 1886.
Arc 1027.49 Marucchi, O. Osservazioni intorno al cimitero delle catacombe. n.p., n.d.
Arc 1027.50 Pellegrini, C. Il pensiero e il dogma cristiano. n.p., n.d.
Arc 1027.50.5 Schulke, V. Theologische Etrag...Katakombenforschung. Leipzig, 1882.
Arc 1027.51 Cascioli, C.G. S. Damaso poeta insigne di martiri. Roma, 1898.
Arc 1027.52 Carmelo, D. Guida delle catacombe e dei monumenti. Roma, 1900.
Arc 1027.52.5 Spadoni, O.L. Tombs and catacombs of the Appian Way. Rome, 1892.

Arc 1027 Archaeology - Christian antiquities - Catacombs - Special topics - cont.

Arc 1027.53	Taglialatela, G. Dell'antica basilica e della catacomba di Prata. n.p., n.d.
Arc 1027.54	Benigni, U. Le madonne delle catacombe. Roma, 1904.
Arc 1027.54.5	Cavedoni, C. Sacra imagine della beata Virgine Maria. Modena, 1855.
Arc 1027.54.9	Montenovesi, O. Le madonne antiche delle catacombe. Roma, 1904.
Arc 1027.55	Pinza, G. Notizie sul cimitero cristiano di Bonaria [Sardini]. Roma, 1902.
Arc 1027.56	Marucchi, O. Guida delle catacombe di Albano. Roma, 1903.
Arc 1027.57	Colasanti, A. Le stagione nell'antichità...arte christiano. Roma, 1901.
Arc 1027.58	De Feis, L. La bocca della verita. Roma, 1885.
Arc 1027.59	Labanca, B. Gesù Cristo nelle catacombe di Roma. Roma, 1902.
Arc 1027.60	Bartolini, D. Sopra l'antico oratorio...regione de Marsi. Roma, 1855.
Arc 1027.61	Precis recitandae in recognitione, et extractione Corporum S. Martyrum. Romae, 1774.
Arc 1027.61.5	Ansaldi, P.C. De caussis inopiae veterum monument. pro copia Martyrum. Medina, 1740.
Arc 1027.62	Diamilla. I monumenti degli antichi cristiani in relazione col progresso. Roma, 1850.
Arc 1027.63	Rossi, G.B. de. Decouvertes dans l'arenaire situé...sur la voie Salaria. Rome, 1873.
Arc 1027.64	Bruzza, L. Oggetti ritrovati in un sepolcro della via Prinistina. Roma, 1882.
Arc 1027.65	Rossi, G.B. de. Le horrea sotto l'aventino. Roma, 1885.
Arc 1027.66	Huelsen, C. Di una iscrizione monumentale al cimitero di Generosa. Roma, 1900.
Arc 1027.68	Servanzi-Collis, S. Relazione della chiesa sotterranea di S. Lorenzo in Sanseverino. Macerata, 1838.
Arc 1027.69	Rossi, G.B. de. Scoperte nell'arenaria tra i cimiteri di Trasone e dei Giordani sulla via Salaria. Roma, 1872.
Arc 1027.69.5	Rossi, G.B. de. Epigrafi rinvenute nell'arenaria tra i cimiteri di Trasone e dei Giordani sulla via Salaria. Roma, 1873.
Arc 1027.70	Stevenson, H. Escavazione di un antico diverticolo della via Tiburtina. Roma, 1878.
Arc 1027.71	Rossi, G.B. de. Il cimitero di S. Ippolito presso la via Tiburtina. Roma, 1882.
Arc 1027.72	Leynaud, A.F. Rapports sur les fouilles des catacombes d'Hadrumète. Paris, 1905.
Arc 1027.72.3	Carton, Louis B.C. Les catacombes d'Hadrumète. Sousse, 1905.
Arc 1027.73	Hoferdt, E. Ursprung und Entwickelung der Chorkrypta. Breslau, 1905.
Arc 1027.74	Bartolini, D. Il cimitero d'Aproniano di anche della S. Eugenia. Roma, 1840.
Arc 1027.75	Pietro, A.C. Ancora del sepolero originario di San Domnio. Zara, 1906.
Arc 1027.76	Berbrugger, M. Le tombeau de la chrétienne. Alger, 1867.
Arc 1027.78	Leynaud, A.F. Les catacombes africaines. Sousse, 1910.
Arc 1027.78.2	Leynaud, A.F. Les catacombes africaines. 2e éd. Alger, 1922.
Arc 1027.79	Bassi, A. Della torre Antonia d'una stupenda galleria...in Gerusalemme. Gerusalemme, 1860.
Arc 1027.80	Stückelberg, E.A. Die Katakombenheiligen der Schweiz. Kempten, 1907.
Arc 1027.85F	LaCroix, Camille. Monographie de l'hypogée-martyrium. Paris, 1883. 2v.
Arc 1027.87	Scaglia, Sisto. Osservazioni sopra i recenti studi intorne ai cimiteri di Marco e Marcelliano. Saronno, 1909. 3 pam.
Arc 1027.88F	Prandi, A. La memoria apostolorum in catacombas. Città del Vaticano, 1936.
Arc 1027.89	Gabrieli, Giuseppe. Inventario topografico e bibliografico delle cripte eremitiche basiliane di Puglia. Roma, 1936.
Arc 1027.90	Achelis, H. Römische Katakombenbilder in Catania. Berlin, 1932.

Arc 1030 Archaeology - Christian antiquities - Christian inscriptions

Arc 1030.1	Galante, G.A. Lapida sepolcrale di Teofilatto. Napoli, 1867.
Arc 1030.2	Brunatius, J. Musei kircheriani inscript. ethnicae et christianae. Mediolani, 1837.
Arc 1030.3	Cavedoni, C. Cenni sopra alcume antiche iscrizioni cristiane. Modena, 1839.
Arc 1030.3.5	Cavedoni, C. Dichiarazione dell'iscrizione sepolcrale di San Decenzio Martire. Modena, 1839.
Arc 1030.3.9	Cavedoni, C. Sopra l'iscrizione sepolcrale di S. Gemello. Modena, 1839.
Arc 1030.3.11	Cavedoni, C. Dichiarazione di due antiche gemme incise. Modena, n.d.
Arc 1030.3.13	Cavedoni, C. Dichiarazione dell'epetaffo di S. Georgio Martire. Modena, 1843.
Arc 1030.4	Marucchi, O. Di una...iscrizione cristiana. Roma, 1883.
Arc 1030.4.5	Marucchi, O. Di una rarissima epigrafe cristiana. Roma, 1878.
Arc 1030.4.9	Marucchi, O. Silloge di alcune iscrizioni. Roma, 1881.
Arc 1030.4.15	Marucchi, O. Dell'importanza dell'epigrafia romana. Roma, 1898.
Arc 1030.4.19	Marucchi, O. L'iscrizione di Quirinio. Siena, 1897.
Arc 1030.4.25	Marucchi, O. Di alcuni antiche monumenti. Roma, 1899-1900.
Arc 1030.4.29	Marucchi, O. Epigrafia christiana. Milano, 1910.
Arc 1030.4.30	Marucchi, O. Christian epigraphy. Cambridge, 1912.
Arc 1030.4.32	Marucchi, O. Il pontificato del papa Damaso. Roma, 1905.
Arc 1030.5.3	Rossi, G.B. de. Il tomo secondo delle conferenze di Chiusura. Roma, 1888.
Arc 1030.5.5	Rossi, G.B. de. Sepolcri del secolo ottavo...di S. Lorenzo in Lucina. Roma, 1872.
Arc 1030.5.9	Rossi, G.B. de. Frammenti di fasti di Ludi Capenati. Roma, 1884.
Arc 1030.5.13	Rossi, G.B. de. D'una mutila epigrafe...nel torrione della porta flaminia. Roma, 1877.
Arc 1030.5.15	Rossi, G.B. de. Memorie degli apostoli Pietro e Paolo. Roma, 1877.
Arc 1030.5.17	Rossi, G.B. de. Della praepositus della via flaminia. n.p., 1888.
Arc 1030.5.21	Rossi, G.B. de. L'elogio funebre di Turia...Q. Lucrezio Vespillone. Roma, 1880.
Arc 1030.5.25	Rossi, G.B. de. Delle sillogi epigrafiche di Smezio e di Panvinio. Roma, 1862.
Arc 1030.5.29	Rossi, G.B. de. Il sarcofago di S. Siro. Roma, 1876.
Arc 1030.5.31	Rossi, G.B. de. L'inscription du tombeau d'Hadrien I. Rome, 1888.

Arc 1030 Archaeology - Christian antiquities - Christian inscriptions - cont.

Arc 1030.5.35	Rossi, G.B. de. Iscrizione in un spillo d'oso, trovato a Bolsena. Roma, 1890.
Arc 1030.5.40	Rossi, G.B. de. Iscrizione della statua...di Nicomaco Flaviano Seniore. Roma, 1849.
Arc 1030.5.43	Rossi, G.B. de. Del arco fabiano nel foro. Roma, 1859.
Arc 1030.5.50	Rossi, G.B. de. Adunanze solenne in commemorazione di Guglielmo Henzen. Roma, 1887.
Arc 1030.5.55	Rossi, G.B. de. Scavi nell'orto di S. Sabina sull'Aventino. Roma, 1856.
Arc 1030.5.59	Rossi, G.B. de. Iscrizione cristiana di Tropea in Calabria. Roma, 1857. 2v.
Arc 1030.5.62	Garruci, P.R. Il crocifisso graffito. Roma, 1857.
Arc 1030.6	Bayet, C. De titulis atticae christianis. Paris, 1878.
Arc 1030.7	Millet, G. Inscriptions byzantines de Mistra. Athènes, 1899.
Arc 1030.8.12	Saeki, P.Y. The Nestorian monument in China. London, 1916.
Arc 1030.8.13	Nestorian Tablet of Sian-fu. The Nestorian monument of Hsian Fu in Shen-hsi, China, 7th and 8th centuries. London, 1888.
Arc 1030.8.14	Carus, P. The Nestorian monument; an ancient record of Christianity in China. Chicago, 1909.
Arc 1030.8.15	Holm, F.W. My Nestorian adventure in China. N.Y., 1923.
Arc 1030.8.17	Pauthier, G. L'inscription syro-chinois de Si-Ngan-Fou. Paris, 1858. 2 pam.
Arc 1030.8.21	Dabry de Thiessaut. La catholicisme en Chine au VIIIe siècle de notre ère. Paris, 1877.
Arc 1030.9	Le Blant, E. L'épigraphie chrétienne en Gaule. n.p., 1890.
Arc 1030.9.5	Le Blant, E. Sur une pierre tumulaire. Arras, 1877.
Arc 1030.11	Bourquelot, M.F. Inscriptions chrétiennes trouvées en Italie. n.p., n.d.
Arc 1030.12	Delattre, R.P. Inscriptions chrétiennes. Constantine, 1887.
Arc 1030.13	Adami, L. Dell culto, A.S.S.M.M., cemeteriali e dell'antichita. Roma, 1815.
Arc 1030.14	Bruzza, L. Iscrizione in onore di Iallia Bassia. Roma, 1883.
Arc 1030.14.5	Bruzza, L. Fistula plumbea acquaria di Porto. Roma, 1878.
Arc 1030.15	Bruzza, L. Iscrizione antiche vercellesi. Roma, 1874.
Arc 1030.16	Allegrantia, J. De sepulcris christianis. Mediolani, 1773.
Arc 1030.17	McCaul, J. Christian epitaphs. Toronto, 1869.
Arc 1030.18	Riant, Paul de. Trois inscriptions...rapportées de Constantinople. Paris, 1880.
Arc 1030.19	Zaccheri, G. L'iscrizione di Abercio. Roma, 1898.
Arc 1030.20	Strazzulla, V. Studio critico sulle iscrizioni cristiane di Siracusa. Siracusa, 1895.
Arc 1030.21	Manni, D.M. Antichissima lapida cristiana. Firenze, 1763.
Arc 1030.22	Secchi, G. Epigramma greco christiano...Autun. Roma, 1840.
Arc 1030.23	Amati, G. Monumenti gentileschi e cristiani...Lorio nell'Aurelia. Roma, 1824.
Arc 1030.24	Carini, I. Dell'utilità che la teologia può trarre dall'epigrafia. Roma, 1891.
Arc 1030.25	Pasini, P. Sovra un'antica lapida cristiana. n.p., 1843.
Arc 1030.26	Rome. Italy. Santa Maria in Via Lata. Tabularium. pt.1-3; plates. Vienna, 1895. 4v.
Arc 1030.27	Ciofi, A. Lectio inscriptionum...sulpicii maximi. Roma, 1872.
Arc 1030.29	Gazzera, C. Ragguaglio critico del discorso sopra le iscrizioni cristiane. Modena, 1851.
Arc 1030.30	Vettori, P. Dissertatio philologica qua nonnulla monimenta sacrae vetera ex museo Vict. Roma, 1751.
Arc 1030.31	Cantarelli, L. Un frammento epigrafico cristiano dell'isola Portuense. Roma, 1896.
Arc 1030.32	Reumont, A. Inscriptiones christianae urbis Romae. n.p., 1862.
Arc 1030.33	Becker, F. Inschriften der römischen Coemeterien. Gera, 1878.
Arc 1030.34	Le Blant, E. Manuel d'épigraphie chrétienne. Paris, 1869.
Arc 1030.36	Carrière, A. Inscriptions d'un reliquare arménien. Paris, 1883.
Arc 1030.37	Romano, C.C. Dell'arte...le iscrizione lapidarie. Roma, 1846.
Arc 1030.38	Aigrain, R. Manuel d'épigraphie chrétienne. Paris, 1912.
Arc 1030.39	Kaufmann, Carl M. Handbuch der altchristlichen Epigraphik im Breisgau. Freiburg, 1917.
Arc 1030.40	Cavedoni, C. Ragguaglio critico delle iscrizioni cristiane. Modena, 185-?
Arc 1030.41	Galletthio, P.A. Inscriptiones Bononienses. Roma, 1759.
Arc 1030.42	Smit, E.L. De oud christelijke monumenten van Spanje. 's-Gravenhage, 1916.
Arc 1030.44	Cunha de Almeida, Jeronymo. Quizo historico sobre o letreiro que se achon em hua pedra que estaua no celeiro do Monst. de Vayrão. Pôrto, 1918.
Arc 1030.46	Bakhuizen van den Brink, J.N. De aid-christelijke monumenten van Ephesus. Haag, 1923.
Arc 1030.47	Diehl, Ernst. Inscriptiones latinae christianae veteres. Berolini, 1924-31. 3v.
Arc 1030.47.5	Diehl, Ernst. Inscriptiones latinae christianae veteres. Berolini, 1961- 4v.
Arc 1030.48	Le Blant, E. Inscriptions chrétiennes de la Gaule antérieure au VIIIe siècle. Paris, 1856-65. 2v.
Arc 1030.48.5	Recueil des inscriptions de la Gaule antérieures à la Renaissance carolingienne. Paris, 1975-
Arc 1030.49	Cordeiro de Sousa, J.M. Inscrições sepulcrais da sé de Lisboa. Lisboa, 1927.
Arc 1030.49.5	Cordeiro de Sousa, J.M. Apontamentos de epigrafia portuguesa. 2a ed. Lisboa, 1937.
Arc 1030.50	Latyshchev', B.B. Sbornik' grech. nadlisei Chrisi bre.-men'. Sankt Peterburg, 1896.
Arc 1030.51	Wessel, C. Inscriptiones graecae christianae veteres occidentes. Diss. inaug. Halae Saxonum, 1936.
Arc 1030.52	Cantini, Giuseppe. Inscriptiones. Colle, 1844.
Arc 1030.53	Patten, A.W. Early Christian inscriptions in the Bennett Museum of Christian archaeology. Evanston, 1915.
Arc 1030.54F	Lietzmann, Hans. Corpus der griechisch-christlichen Inschriften von Hellas. Athen, 1941.
Arc 1030.55PF	Silvagni, Angelo. Monumenta epigraphica christiana saeculo XIII. v.1-2. Civitate Vaticana, 1943-
Arc 1030.56	Milan. Castillo Sforzesco. Il castillo sforzesco in Milano. Milano, 1915.
Arc 1030.57	Deschamps, P. Étude sur la paléographie des inscriptions lapidaires de la fin de l'époque mérovingienne aux dernières années du XIIe siècle. Paris, 1929.

Classified Listing

Arc 1030 Archaeology - Christian antiquities - Christian inscriptions - cont.
Arc 1030.58F Hubner, E. Inscriptiones Britanniae christianae. Berolini, 1876.
Arc 1030.59 Nunn, H.P.V. Christian inscriptions. N.Y., 1952.
Arc 1030.60 Beyer, Oskar. Fruhchristliche Sinnbilder und Inschriften. Kassel, 1954.
Arc 1030.61 Schneider, Fedor. Die Epitaphien der Päpste und andere stadtrömische Inschriften des Mittelalters. Rom, 1933.

Arc 1033 Archaeology - Christian antiquities - Other Special topics
Arc 1033.01 Pamphlet box. Archaeology. Christian.
Arc 1033.02 Pamphlet box. Archaeology. Christian.
Htn Arc 1033.1* Buonarroti, F. Osservazioni sopra alcune frammenti di vasi antichi. Firenze, 1716.
Arc 1033.1.4 Rossi, G.B. de. Insigne...Battesimo d'una fanciulla. Roma, 1872.
Arc 1033.1.5 Rossi, G.B. de. Frammento di Becchiere Vitreo. Roma, 1885.
Arc 1033.1.7 Rossi, G.B. de. Vetro graffito con immagini di santi. Roma, 1878.
Arc 1033.1.9 Cavedoni, C. Osservazioni sopra alcuni frammenti di vasi. Modena, 1859.
Arc 1033.2 Crostarosa, P. Osservazioni sul musaico di S. Pudenziana. Roma, 1895.
Arc 1033.3 Bottazzi, G.A. Emblemi...del...sarcofago...di Tortona. Tortona, 1824.
Arc 1033.3.3 Amati, G. Emblemi sepolcrali degli antichi cristiani. Roma, 1825.
Arc 1033.3.5 Ratti, N. Sopra un sarcofago cristiano con travole. Roma, 1828.
Arc 1033.3.9 Marucchi, O. Un frammento di sarcofago cristiano del Museo Laterano. Roma, 1896.
Arc 1033.3.13 Marucchi, O. Un frammento di sarcofago cristiano. Roma, 1897.
Arc 1033.3.17 Torlonia, L. Di un sarcofago cristiano del palazzo torlonia. Roma, 1897.
Arc 1033.3.21 Minicis, G. de. Sarcofago cristiano nel templo di Fermo. Roma, 1848.
Arc 1033.3.23 Cavedoni, C. Sarcofago cristiano nel templo di Fermo. Roma, 1843.
Arc 1033.3.27 Visconti, C.L. Dichiarazione di un sarcofago cristiano ostiense. Roma, 1859.
Arc 1033.3.33 Le sarcophage chrétien de Luc de Biarn. Paris, 1880.
Arc 1033.3.37 Stuhlfauth, G. Un frammento di sarcofago cristiano. Roma, 1897.
Arc 1033.3.41 Goldmann, K. Die ravennatischen Sarkophage. Strassburg, 1906.
Arc 1033.3.42A Hanfmann, G.M. The season sarcophagus in Dumbarton Oakes. Cambridge, 1951. 2v.
Arc 1033.3.42B Hanfmann, G.M. The season sarcophagus in Dumbarton Oakes. Cambridge, 1951. 2v.
Arc 1033.3.45 Campenhausen, Hans von. Die Passionssarkophage. Marburg, 1929.
Arc 1033.3.46 Roosval, J. Petrus- och Moses-gruppen bland Roms sarkofagy. Stockholm, 1932.
Arc 1033.3.47 Roosval, J. Junius Bassus sarkofag och dess datering. Stockholm, 1932.
Arc 1033.4 Bucci, P. Sulla comunione christiana nei primi secoli. Roma, 1862.
Arc 1033.4.5 Cavedoni, C. La credenza della primitiva chiesa del Sacramento dell'Eucaristia. Modena, 1869.
Arc 1033.5 Marucchi, O. La supremazia della sede romana considerata nei monumenti dei primi secoli. Roma, 1897.
Arc 1033.5.5 Luzi, G.C. Le chiavi di S. Pietro. Roma, 1884.
Arc 1033.5.9 Rich, Anthony. The legend of Saint Peter's chair. London, 1851.
Arc 1033.6 Germano, Stanislao P. La casa celimontana...Giovanni e Paolo. Roma, 1894.
Arc 1033.6.10 Gasdia, U.E. La casa pagano cristiana del Celio (Titulus Byzantis sive Pammachii). Roma, 1937.
Arc 1033.6.25 Gatti, Giuseppe. La casa celimontana dei Valerii e il Monastero di S. Erasmo. Roma, 1902.
Arc 1033.7 Fita y Colomé, Fidel. Recuerdos de un viaje a Santiago de Galicia. Madrid, 1880.
Arc 1033.8 Manni, D.M. Dell'errore che persiste...al Santo Evangelista. Firenze, 1766.
Arc 1033.9 Garrucci, R. Nuova interpretazione di un vetro cimiteriale. n.p., n.d.
Arc 1033.9.5 Garrucci, R. Descrizioni dei vetri ornati di figure in oro. n.p., n.d.
Arc 1033.10 Ebers, G. Sinnbildliches die koptische Kunst. Leipzig, 1892.
Arc 1033.10.10 Carcopino, Jérome. Le mystère d'un symbole chrétien. Paris, 1955.
Arc 1033.11 Gaborel de Rossillon, J. Alma Mater. Paris, 1877.
Arc 1033.12 Cozza-Luzi. Le memorie...dell'infanzia di Gesù Cristo. Roma, 1894.
Arc 1033.12.1 Liverani, F. Del nome di S. Maria ad Praesepe. Roma, 1854.
Arc 1033.12.2 Notizie intorno alla novena...di natale. Roma, 1788.
Arc 1033.12.4 Breve racconta del SS. Prepuzio di Gesu Christi. Roma, 1728.
Arc 1033.12.5 Narrazione critico storica...Prepuzio de Gesu. Roma, 1802.
Arc 1033.12.6 Jesus Christ. Narrazione critico storica della reliquia...Santissimo Prepuzio. Roma, 1802.
Arc 1033.12.8 Gourgues, A. de. Le Saint Suaire. Perigueux, 1868.
Arc 1033.12.9 Vignon, P. The shroud of Christ. Westminster, 1902.
Arc 1033.12.9.5F Vignon, P. Le Saint Suaire de Turin devant la science. 2. éd. Paris, 1939.
Arc 1033.12.9.10 Walsh, J.E. The shroud. N.Y., 1963.
Arc 1033.12.9.15 Bachinger, Rudolf. Das Leichentuch von Turin. Stein am Rhein, 1967.
Arc 1033.12.10 Carles, A. Histoire du Saint Suaire de Cadouin. Perigueux, 1868.
Arc 1033.12.11 Carles, A. Histoire du Saint Suaire de Notre Seigneur. Paris, 1875. 2 pam.
Arc 1033.12.16 Gauthier, J. Notes iconographique sur le Saint Suaire de Besançon. Besançon, 1884.
Arc 1033.12.17 Eberlé, L. Confrérie du Saint Suaire. Besançon, 1886.
Arc 1033.12.21 Notice historique et critique de Saint Suaire. Poitiers, 1882.
Arc 1033.12.22 Baffico, G.F. Istoria del Santo Sudario. Genova, n.d.
Arc 1033.12.23 Calcagnino, A. Dell'imagine Edessena. Genova, 1639.
Arc 1033.12.24 Chubinashvili, G.N. Siriiskaia chasha v Ushgule. n.p., 1941.
Arc 1033.12.25 Cyprian, E.S. Facias Christi. Helmestad, n.d.
Arc 1033.12.27 Barnate, C. Il furto del "Santo Sudario" nel 1507. Genova, 1915.

Arc 1033 Archaeology - Christian antiquities - Other Special topics - cont.
Arc 1033.12.30 Chifflet, J.J. De linteis sepulchralibus Cristi servatoris crisis historica. Antverpiae, 1624.
Arc 1033.12.31 Buonafede, G. Panegirici sacri a i misterii della S. Sindone. Asti, 1654.
Htn Arc 1033.12.32* Pingone, E.F. Sindon evangelica. Augustae Taurinorum, 1581.
Arc 1033.12.32.2 Pingone, E.F. Sindon evangelica. Augustae Taurinorum, 1777.
Arc 1033.12.33 Berta, G. Della sacra sindone di Nostro Signor. Torino, 1826?
Arc 1033.12.34F Piano, L.G. Commentarii critico archeologici sopra la SS. Sindone. Torino, 1833. 2v.
Arc 1033.12.35 Vigo, G.B. Ad carolum...de Sindone Taurinensi. Augustae Taurinorum, 1768.
Arc 1033.12.36 Pellegrini, C. Sermone sulla SS. Sindone di Torino. Torino, 1844.
Arc 1033.12.37 Pietro, S. di. Santa sindone. Sermone. Torino, 1884.
Arc 1033.12.38 Balliani, C. Ragionamenti della sacra sindone. Torino, 1610.
Arc 1033.12.39 Narrazione della solennita...Torino...SS. Sindone. Torino, n.d.
Arc 1033.12.40F Vassalli, M. Discorso sopra la sacra sindone...Torino. Parma, n.d.
Arc 1033.12.41 Solaro, A. Sindone evangelica, historica e theologica. Torino, 1627.
Arc 1033.12.42 Talamini, G. Della Santissima Sindone e la vanda dei piedi. Torino, n.d.
Arc 1033.12.43 Cenni sulla Santissima Sindone. Torino, 1842?
Arc 1033.12.44 Lombardo, V.G. Panegirico della Sacra Sindone. Torino, 1884.
Htn Arc 1033.12.48* Pratique pour honorer le St. Suaire de...Jésus Crist. Cain, 1881.
Htn Arc 1033.12.49*A Paleotti, A. Esplicatione del sacro lenzvolo ove fu involto il Signore. Bologna, 1599.
Htn Arc 1033.12.49*B Paleotti, A. Esplicatione del sacro lenzvolo ove fu involto il Signore. Bologna, 1599.
Arc 1033.12.50 Paleotti, A. Tableau de mortification...stigmates...Christ...S. Suaire. Paris, 1609.
Arc 1033.12.51 Curtius, C. De clavis Dominicis liber. Antverpiae, 1670.
Arc 1033.12.51.3 Curtius, C. De clavis Dominicis liber. Antverpiae, 1634.
Arc 1033.12.52 Fontanini, J. Dissertatio de corona ferrea Langobardoum. Romae, 1717.
Arc 1033.12.53F Rohault de Fleury, C. Memoire sur les instruments de la Passion. Paris, 1870.
Htn Arc 1033.12.54* Ista sunt queda notabilia de passione Christi...de biblia hebreorum. Venetiis, 1506.
Arc 1033.12.55 Anguissola, G.B. Stromenti che servirono alla Passione...nostro signori. Piacenza, 1812.
Arc 1033.12.56 Corrieris, L. de. De sessorianis praecepuis passionis...reliquiis commentariis. Romae, 1830.
Arc 1033.12.57 Paleotti, A. Historia de Jesu Christi stigmatibus. Antverpiae, 1616.
Htn Arc 1033.12.58* Vigerius, M. Controversia de excellentia instrumentorum passionis. Roma, 1512.
Arc 1033.12.59 Ciprian, E.S. Diss. eccl. pentas. De sudore Christi. Jenae, n.d.
Htn Arc 1033.12.64* Ludecus, M. Historia von der Erfindung, Wunderwerken und Zerstörung der vermeinten Heiligenbluts zur Wilssnagk. Wittenberg, 1586.
Htn Arc 1033.12.65* Domenechi, D. De sanguine Christi tractatus. Venetiis, 1557.
Arc 1033.12.66 Quiroga, M.P. de. Bellum de sanguine Christi. Valladolid, 1721.
Arc 1033.12.67 Rossi, B. de. Teatro dell'umana rendenzione...relazione istorica del...sangue...Sarzana. Massa, 1708.
Arc 1033.12.68 Rota, S.A. Verita trionfante...della fede in...narrazione delle reliquie del Sangue...Venezia. Venezia, 1763.
Arc 1033.12.69 Vergaro, G.C. Racconto dell'apparato...espositione del Sangue Venetia...1617. Venezia, 1617.
Arc 1033.12.70 Cimatti, E. Cenni storici intorno al Sangue Mirae...Ferrara. Ferrara, 1857.
Arc 1033.12.71 Aquilini, H. De pretiosissimo Jesu Christi Sanguine Mantuae asservato. Venezia, 1782.
Arc 1033.12.72 Histoire du précieux sang de Jésus-Christ...à Fécamp. Fécamp, 1874.
Arc 1033.12.73 Haignere, D. Notre-Dame de Saint-Sang. 2e éd. Paris, 1884.
Arc 1033.12.74 Messe du précieux Sang...Fécamp. Fécamp, 1874.
Arc 1033.12.75 Recueil historique...du...sang...Bruges. Bruges, 1761.
Arc 1033.12.76 Déscription de la relique...du...sang...Bruges. Bruges, 1782.
Arc 1033.12.77 The miraculous host tortured by the Jew. 3. ed. London, 1822.
Arc 1033.12.80 Erfreulicher Ursprung...am Semmering. Neustadt, 1738.
Arc 1033.12.83 Diehl, C. Un nouveau trésor d'argenterie syrienne. Paris, 1926.
Arc 1033.12.85 Filson, F.V. Who are the figures on the chalice of Antioch? n.p., 1942.
Arc 1033.12.87 Arnason, H. The history of the chalice of Antioch. n.p., 1941.
Arc 1033.12.89 Bréhier, L. The treasures of Syrian silverwar. Paris, 1921.
Arc 1033.12.100 Lindovius, J. Rubram Jesu Christi chlamydem...exponent...respondens. Jenae, 1772?
Htn Arc 1033.12.101* Anno domini 1512. Reliquie plurimorū. n.p., n.d.
Arc 1033.12.102 Hommer, J. von. Geschichte des heiligen Rockes...Trier. v.1-2. Bonn, 1844.
Arc 1033.12.103 Marx, J. Ausstellung des heiligen Roches in die Domkirche zur Trier. Trier, 1845.
Arc 1033.12.104 Gildemeister, J. Heilige Rock zu Trier. Düsseldorf, 1845.
Arc 1033.12.105 Wilmowsky, J.N. von. Heilige Rock; eine archäologische Prüfung...Trier. Trier, 1876.
Arc 1033.12.106 Clarke, R.F. A pilgrimage to the Holy Coat of Treves. London, 1892.
Arc 1033.12.107 Sauren, J. Pilgerbuchlein zum heiligen Rock in Trier. Köln, 1891. 2 pam.
Arc 1033.12.111 Gerberon, G. Histoire de la robe sans couture de...J.-C....Argenteuil. Paris, 1677.
Arc 1033.12.112 Histoire de la robe sans couture de...Jésus Christ. 4e éd. Paris, 1838.
Arc 1033.12.113 Davin, V. Sainte tunique. Discours...Argeteuil...1865. Paris, n.d.
Arc 1033.12.114 Guérin, L.F. Notice abrégée sur la sainte tunique de...Christ. Paris, 1864.
Arc 1033.12.121 Seelen, I.H. Memorabilium...specimen sive de festo lanceae et clavorum. Flensburgi, 1715.

Classified Listing

Arc 1033 Archaeology - Christian antiquities - Other Special topics - cont.

Arc 1033.12.122 Lange, P. De lancea qua perfossum latus...Christi. Jena, 1673.

Arc 1033.12.126 Schreck, J.A. Jesu...coronam spineam. Lipsiae, n.d.

Arc 1033.12.127 Bortolan, D. S. spina di Vicenza. Vicenza, 1887.

Arc 1033.12.128 Gonzati, L. Sopra un patrio monumento di antica oreficeria. Vicenza, 1871.

Arc 1033.12.132 Lecomte, A. Sainte-face de la cathédrale de Laon. Laon, 1885.

Arc 1033.12.133 Janvier. Culte de la sainte-face à S. Pierre du Vatican. Tours, 1883.

Arc 1033.12.134 Sacro pellegrinaggio al Monte Sano per adorar il volto...del Salutor. Genova, 1660.

Arc 1033.12.135 Apparizione del santo volto. Napoli, 1849.

Arc 1033.12.136 Soresinus, J.M. De imagine SS. Salvatoris...ad Sancta Sanctorum. Roma, 1675.

Arc 1033.12.137 Mencacci, P. Alcune memorie sull'imagine acheropita del SS. Salvatore di Sancta Santorum. Roma, 1863.

Arc 1033.12.138 Memorie istoriche...miracolosa crocifisso...Chiavari. Chiavari, 1856.

Arc 1033.12.139 Mese di luglio ovvero esercizii divoti...giorni...miracolosa immagine di Gesu. Venezia, 1867.

Arc 1033.12.140 Notizie storiche intorno al SS. Crocifisso...in Trastevere. Roma, 1801.

Arc 1033.12.141 Notizie istoriche...della immagine del...Salvatore. Roma, 1798.

Arc 1033.12.142 Histoire de la sainte-face de...Christ. Laon, 1884.

Htn Arc 1033.12.143* Historia de como fue hallada la ymage del Sancto Crucifixo. Burgos? 1554?

Arc 1033.12.144 Cerqueira Pinto, Antonio. Historia da prodigiosa imagem de Christo crucificado. Lisboa, 1737.

Htn Arc 1033.12.156* Historia del santissimo Volto di S. Croce di Lucca. Lucca, 1582.

Arc 1033.12.157 Tofanelli, S. Primo ritratto del crofifisso...historia della miracolosa scultura. Napoli, 1644.

Arc 1033.12.158 Serantoni, G.M. Apologia del Volto santo di Lucca. Lucca, 1765.

Arc 1033.12.159 Conti, G.B. Dell'origine invenzione...simulacro di Gesu Crocifisso...Volto santo. Lucca, n.d.

Arc 1033.12.160 Conti, G.B. Dell'origine invenzione...del...simulacro di...Gesu Crocifisso...volto santo. Lucca, 1834.

Arc 1033.12.161 Pera, P. Della lampada d'oro offerta dai Lucchssi al volto santo. Lucca, 1836. 2 pam.

Arc 1033.12.163 Serantoni, G.M. Risposta...alla seconda replica del celebre autore delle letterarie di Firenze. Lucca, 1767.

Arc 1033.12.166 Barbier de Montault, X. Saint Clou à la cathédrale de Toul. Nancy, 1885.

Arc 1033.12.166.15 Le Saint Clou de Toul. Nancy, 1888. 3 pam.

Arc 1033.12.167 Buonafede, G. Sacro chiodo del redentore. Siena, 1653.

Arc 1033.12.168 Cateni, P.F. Notizie della reliquia...del sacro chiodo. Colle, 1821.

Arc 1033.12.169 Kraus, F.X. Heilige Nagel...zu Trier. Trier, 1868.

Arc 1033.12.170 Terris, F. Saint mors de Carpentras et son reliquaire. Carpentras, 1874.

Arc 1033.12.171 Terris, F. Saint mors de Carpentras et son reliquaire. n.p., n.d.

Arc 1033.12.172 Collection de pièces sur le saint clou veneri à Tours. n.p., n.d.

Arc 1033.12.175 Eufrasio. Memorie storico-critiche...lagrime di...Dongo. Lugano, 1808.

Arc 1033.12.181 Muratori, L.A. De corona ferrea...commentarius. Mediolani, 1719.

Arc 1033.12.182 Zucchi, B. Historia della corona ferrea...Monza descritta. Milano, 1707.

Arc 1033.12.183 Bacci, G. Corona di ferro. Ferrara, 1884.

Arc 1033.12.184 Bianconi, A. Memoria intorno la corona di ferro longobardo. Milano, 1860.

Arc 1033.12.185 Articolo sulla corona ferrea...dal Geornale. Venezia, 1821.

Arc 1033.12.186 Bombelli, R. Storia della corona ferrea dei re d'Italia. Firenze, 1870.

Arc 1033.12.187 Zerbi, L. Corona ferrea al funebri nazionali di Vittorio Emanuele. Monza, 1878.

Arc 1033.12.188 Cathalogus authorum, qui de corona. Roma, 1715.

Arc 1033.12.191 Thiers, J.B. Dissertation sur la sainte larme de Vendome. Amsterdam, 1751.

Arc 1033.12.192 Thiers, J.B. Réponse à la lettre du père Mabillon...prétendue sur larme. Cologne, 1700.

Arc 1033.12.193 Lettre d'un Benedictin...touchant le discernement. Diss. Paris, 1700.

Arc 1033.12.194 Rochambeau, E.A. de. Voyage à la sainte-larme de Vendome. Vendome, 1874.

Arc 1033.12.195 Métais, C. Processions de la sainte-larme à Vendome. Orléans, 1886.

Arc 1033.12.196 Sainte-larme de Selincourt. Notice historique et bibliographique. Amiens, 1876.

Arc 1033.12.197 Le Mercier, J. Histoire de la larme sainte...Selincourt. Amiens, 1707.

Arc 1033.12.210 Jacob, J.N. Disputatio theologica de Vulneribus Christi. Wittenbergae, 1663.

Htn Arc 1033.12.211* Bartholini, T. De latere Christi aperto. Lugdunum Batavorum, 1646.

Arc 1033.12.234 Murray, D. A small brass cup...Rodil, Harris. Glasgow, 1898.

Arc 1033.12.235 Sanchis y Sivera, José. El santo cáliz de la cena (santo grial) venerado en Valencia. Valencia, 1914.

Arc 1033.12.239 Jerphanion, G. de. Le calice d'Antioche. Rome, 1926.

Arc 1033.12.243 Gogan, L.S. The Ardagh chalice. Dublin, 1932.

Arc 1033.13.5 Marucchi, O. Le memorie dei SS. apostoli Pietro e Paolo nella città di Roma. Roma, 1894.

Arc 1033.13.13 Bartolini, D. Sopra l'anno LXII dell'era...Pietro e Paolo. 2. ed. Roma, 1867.

Arc 1033.14 Una controversia famosa di archeologia cristiana. n.p., 1872.

Arc 1033.15 De Lucca, A.A. Annali delli scienze religiose. Roma, 1841.

Arc 1033.16 Cavedoni, C. Atti dei tre santi martiri Sarace, Probo e Andronico. Modena, 1839.

NEDL Arc 1033.17.3 Strumz, Franz. Unsere liebe Frau in Österreich. Zürich, 1921.

Arc 1033.17.5 Griscembeni, G.M. Memorie istoriche della miracolosa immagine di S. Maria in Portico. Roma, 1716.

Arc 1033.17.10 Marracci, L. Memorie di Santa Maria in Portico di Roma. Roma, 1675.

Arc 1033.17.12 Notizie dell'origine e dell'antichità del Monastero di S. Ambrozio. Roma, 1755.

Arc 1033 Archaeology - Christian antiquities - Other Special topics - cont.

Arc 1033.17.14 Notizie...miracolosa immagine Bma Vergine...di S. Maria in Cosmedin. Roma, 1835.

Arc 1033.17.18 Teodoro di Santa Maria. Memorie...miracolosa immagine della Madonna Ssma detta della Vittoria. Roma, 1796.

Arc 1033.17.20 Historia breve della miracolosa imagine della Madre di Dio. Napoli, 1638.

Arc 1033.17.22 Erra, C.A. Storia dell'imagine...Santa Maria in portico di Campitelli. Roma, 1750.

Arc 1033.17.25 Zocca, I.M. Apparitione della Madonna Santissima di Misericordia di Savona. Modena, 1632.

Arc 1033.17.26 Storia dell'apparizione...di Nostra Signora di Misericordia di Savona. Genova, 1760.

Arc 1033.17.27 Storia dell'apparizione di Nostra Signora di Misericordia in Savona. Napoli, 1838.

Arc 1033.17.29 Relazione del prodigioso...aprimento di Occhi di una immagine di Maria...Ancona. Venezia, 1796.

Arc 1033.17.30 Raccolta di varie lettere...relique ed immagine...Santissima Vergine Maria Cattedrale...Ancona. Roma, 1796.

Arc 1033.17.31 Miracolo...Maria...Ancona. n.p., n.d. 2 pam.

Arc 1033.17.33 Garruba, M. Eoniade della translazione...miracolosa immagine di Santa Maria...Constantinopoli. Napoli, 1834.

Arc 1033.17.34 Gregorio. Storia della translazione...immagine di Santa Maria di Constantinopoli. 2a ed. Napoli, 1813.

Arc 1033.17.35 Gregorio. Storia della translazione...immagine di Santa Maria di Constantinopoli. 2a ed. Napoli, 1824.

Arc 1033.17.36 Bambacari, C. La città di refugio panegirico...greca imagine di Maria da Constantinopoli. Forli, 1678.

Arc 1033.17.45 Orsini, Mathieu. La Virgen. 4. ed. Barcelona, 1867. 2v.

Arc 1033.17.49 Vandel, R.P. Les impressions d'un pelerinou l'ecole de Marie à Pontmain. Issoudun, 1872.

Arc 1033.17.50 Kiedrzynski, A. Mensa nazaraea...seu historia imagine divae Claromontanae. Claromontanae, 1763.

Arc 1033.17.51 Kiedrzynski, A. Mensa nazaraea...seu historia imagine divae Claromontanae. Cracoviae, 1760.

Htn Arc 1033.17.52* Kordecki, A. Nova gigantomachia contra...imagine...virgine...Lucea depictam. Czestochovia, n.d.

Arc 1033.17.53 Nieszporkowicz, A. Analecta mensae reginalis seu historia imaginis...virginis...Claromontanae. Cracoviae, 1681.

Arc 1033.17.54 Goldonowski, A. Historia...B.V. Maria Claromontanae s. imaginis origine Jerosolymis Constantinopolim. n.p., n.d.

Arc 1033.17.55 Schlichter, C.L. Ecloga historia qua fabula pontificia de Luca Pictore exploditur. Halae, 1734.

Arc 1033.17.56 Milochau, A. Vierge de Saint Luc à S.-Marie Majeure. Paris, 1862.

Arc 1033.17.57 Hilaire. Madone de Saint Luc. Paris, 1886.

Arc 1033.17.58 Crispi, L. Dissertazione anti-critica...S. Luca evangelista fosse pittore. Faenza, 1776.

Arc 1033.17.59 Bocchi, M.F. Opera sopra l'imagine. Fiorenza, 1592.

Arc 1033.17.60 Klein, Dorothee. St. Lukas als Maler der Maria. Berlin, 1933.

Arc 1033.17.70 Malvasia, D. Venuta, et i progressi miracolosi della S. Madonna...S. Luca...1160-1617. Bononia, 1617.

Arc 1033.17.71 Istoria della miraclosa immagine...della...vergine di S. Luca. Bologna, 1783.

Arc 1033.17.72 Prospetto storico dell'imagine di Maria vergine...S.Luca. Bologna, 1812.

Arc 1033.17.73 Prospetto storico dell'immagine di Maria vergine dipinta dall'evangelista S. Luca. Bologna, 1826.

Arc 1033.17.85 Cornaro, F. Notizie...delle apparizioni e delle immagini di Maria...di Bergamo. Bergamo, 1868.

Arc 1033.17.88 Chigi, A. La città diletta di Maria...miracolosa immagine di Nostra Donna. Roma, 1716.

Arc 1033.17.90 Ranaldi, Giuseppe. Memorie storiche di S. Maria del Glorioso. Macerata, 1837.

Arc 1033.17.92 Marracci, Lodovico. Memorie di Santa Maria in Portico. Roma, 1871.

Arc 1033.17.95 Francisco de San Joseph. Historia universal...Nuestra Señora de Guadalupe. Madrid, 1743.

Arc 1033.17.95.2F Francisco de San Joseph. Historia universal...Nuestra Señora de Guadalupe. Madrid, 1743.

Arc 1033.17.95.5 Triduo in ossequio di Maria santissima di Guadalupe. Roma, 1792.

Htn Arc 1033.17.96.3* Becerra Tanco, Luis. Felicidad de México...Nuestra Señora de Guadalupe. México, 1780.

Arc 1033.17.96.6 Becerra Tanco, Luis. Nuestra Señora de Guadalupe y origen. 6. ed. México, 1883.

Htn Arc 1033.17.97* Sánchez, Miguel. Imagen de la virgen Maria...de Guadalupe. México, 1648.

Arc 1033.17.97.5 Guridi, José M. Apología de la aparición de Nuestra Señora de Guadalupe de Méjico. Méjico, 1820.

Arc 1033.17.97.8 Sotomayor, José F. Reflecciones sobre la aparición de la santísima virgen de Guadalupe. México, 1870.

Arc 1033.17.98 Rosa, Agustin de. Dissertatio historico-theologica de apparitione B.M.V. de Guadalupe. Guadalaxarae, 1887.

Arc 1033.17.98.3 Rosa, Agustin de. Defensa de la aparición de Nuestra Señora de Guadalupe. Guadalajara, 1896.

Arc 1033.17.98.5 Conde y Oquendo, F. Dissertación histórica sobre la aparición de Nuestra Señora de Guadalupe. México, 1852. 2v.

Arc 1033.17.98.7 García, Juan C. Rasgo histórico acerca de nuestra Señora de la antigua de Guadalajara. Guadalajara, 1884.

Arc 1033.17.99 Vera, Fortino Hipólito. Informaciones sobre la milagrosa aparición de la virgen de Guadalupe. Amecameca, 1889.

Arc 1033.17.99.5 Vera, Fortino Hipólito. Tesoro guadalupano. Amecameca, 1887.

Arc 1033.17.100 Cuevas, J. de J. La santissima virgen de Guadalupe. México, 1887.

Arc 1033.17.100.5 Keyer, F.P.W. (Mrs.). The grace of Guadalupe. N.Y., 1941.

Arc 1033.17.101 Astolfi, G.F. Historia universale delle imagini miracolose...Madre di Dio...tutte le parti del Mondo. Venezia, 1623.

Arc 1033.17.102 Gumppenberg, G. Atlas Marianus sive de imaginibus deiparae per orbem. Monachii, 1657. 2v.

Arc 1033.17.102.2 Gumppenberg, G. Atlas Marianus sive de imaginibus deiparae. v.1-2. Ingaldeladii, 1657.

Arc 1033.17.104 Stengel, K. Hoedoporicum Mariana Benedictinum seu historia de imaginibus. Augsbourg, 1659.

Arc 1033.17.105 Delattre, A.L. Le culte de la Sainte Vierge en Afrique. Paris, 1907.

Arc 1033.17.106 Historia de Nuestra Señora de Lujan. Buenos Aires, 1885. 2v.

Arc 1033.17.107 Agostinho de Santa Maria. Santuario Mariano e historia das imagẽs milagrosas de Nossa Senhora. Lisboa, 1707-23. 10v.

Arc 1033 Archaeology - Christian antiquities - Other Special topics - cont.

Arc 1033.17.109 Soveral, Roque do. Historia do insigne aparecimento de N. Senhora da Luz. Lisboa, 1610.
Arc 1033.17.131 Compendio dell'origine...della sacra cintura. Verona, 1642.
Arc 1033.17.132 Cerbelli, D. Opuscoletti varii ovvero monografia di Mottafollone storia della sacra cinta. Napoli, 1857.
Arc 1033.17.133 Buenchini, G.M. Notizie istoriche intorno alla sma. Cintola. Prato, 1795.
Arc 1033.17.134 Gervasi, F.A. Sorte invidiabile di Prato...della sagra Cintola. Firenze, 1742.
Arc 1033.17.135 Russo, M. dello. Storia della sma. Cintola de Prato. Napoli, 1858.
Arc 1033.17.136 Bédouet, Z. Pélérinage de la sainte ceinture au Puy-Notre Dame. Paris, n.d.
Arc 1033.17.137 Notre-Dame de Déliverance et la ceinture de la S. Vierge. Quintin, 1872.
Arc 1033.17.138 Cavedoni, C. Cenni storici e critici intorno alla S. Zona della...Vergine. Modena, 1842.
Arc 1033.17.151 Cerf. Notice sur la relique...Cathédrale de Reims. n.p., n.d.
Arc 1033.17.152 Paris, L. Chapelle dans la Cathédrale de Reims. Epernay, 1885.
Arc 1033.17.153 Sigoni, I. Relazione della venta a Montevarchi del socrosanto latte. Firenze, 1653.
Arc 1033.17.161 Lauro, G.B. De annulo pronubo...virginis...Perusiae. Roma, 1622.
Arc 1033.17.162 Lauro, G.B. De annulo proniebo...virginis...Perusiae. Colonia Agrippina, 1626.
Arc 1033.17.163 Cavallucci, V. Istoria critica del sagro anello...Perugia. Perugia, 1783.
Arc 1033.17.181 Mély, F. de. Chemises de la Vierge. Chartres, n.d.
Arc 1033.17.201 Mouls, X. Pélérinage de Notre-Dame d'Arcachon. Bordeaux, 1857.
Arc 1033.17.202 Relación verdadera de la imagen...Alcay. Valencia, 1665.
Arc 1033.17.203 Terninck, A. Notre-Dame du Joyel, ou Histoire légendaire et numismatique de la chandelle d'Arras. Arras, 1853.
Arc 1033.17.221 Le Roy, A. Histoire de Notre-Dame de Boulogne. Boulogne, 1704.
Arc 1033.17.222 Haigneré, D. Couronnement de Notre-Dame de Boulogne. Boulogne, 1885.
Arc 1033.17.223 Gazulla, F.D. La patrona de Barcelona y su santuario. Barcelona, 1918.
Arc 1033.17.241 Calvi, D. Delle grandezze della Madonna di Carvaggio. v.3. Napoli, 1749.
Arc 1033.17.242 Ronzini, D. Brevi notizie sul celebre santuario di Maria sma. nel Sacro Monte di Novi. Napoli, 1853.
Arc 1033.17.243 Lomonaco, V. Monografia sul santuario di Nostra Donna della Grotta nella Praja della Schiavi. 3a ed. Napoli, 1858.
Arc 1033.17.244 Saggio storico della portentosa immagine di S. Maria di Campiglione. Napoli, 1848.
Arc 1033.17.245 Ruggieri, S. Istoria dell'immagine di S. Maria di Pozzano. Napoli, 1743.
Htn Arc 1033.17.247* Chifflet, J.J. De sacris inscriptionibus, quibus tabella D. Viginis Cameracensis. Antverp, 1749.
Arc 1033.17.248 Lambert, R. Diva Virgo de Cortenbosch, eius miracula. Leodii, 1656.
Arc 1033.17.249 Bronte, G. da. Santuario di Maria Sma. di Gibilmanna. Catania, 1856.
Arc 1033.17.250 Castellano, U. Ave Maria. La milagrosa imagen de Nuestra Señora del Rosario. Córdoba, 1891.
Arc 1033.17.253 Estratto di una lettera di Ancona di 27 giugno 1796. n.p., 1796.
Arc 1033.17.255 Histoire des images miraculeuses. Paris, 1850.
Arc 1033.17.301 Memorie del ritrovamento della santissima immagine della...annunziata. Firenze, 1733.
Arc 1033.17.302 Ciabilli, G. Notizie risguardanti lo stato antico e moderno del sacro eratorio....miracolosa immagine di Maria. Firenze, 1802.
Arc 1033.17.303 Per la icona vetere di Maria sma. Venerata in Foggia. Napoli, 1850.
Arc 1033.17.304 Spada, G.N. Saggio istorico e coroncina della taumalurga immagine di Maria Sma. Napoli, 1839.
Arc 1033.17.304.5 Spada, G.N. Saggio storico con coroncina di Maria Sma. l'aconavetere. Foggia, 1917.
Arc 1033.17.305 Guelfone. Orazione...Foggia...dell'icona...Santa Maria. Foggia, 1669.
Arc 1033.17.321 Ciappolini, D. Divoto compendio della storia...s. immagine di Maria...Scutari. Napoli, 1810.
Arc 1033.17.322 Orgio. Istoriche notizie...dell'immagine di Maria...di Genazzano. 3. ed. Roma, 1790.
Arc 1033.17.323 Fera di Plati, D. Sul santuario di Polsi sito...Gerace memorie. Napoli, 1851.
Arc 1033.17.325 Cavalieri, M. Il Pellegrino al Gargano...di San Michele. Napoli, 1690.
Arc 1033.17.326 Ragguaglio...della arcangelo San Michele. Napoli, 1846.
Arc 1033.17.330 Fries, Felix. Histoire de Notre Dame de Foy. Namur, 1909.
Htn Arc 1033.17.361* Lipsius, I. Diva virgo hallensis. Antverp, 1604.
Htn Arc 1033.17.362* Denaise, Pierre. Dissertatio deidolo hallensi. n.p., 1605.
Arc 1033.17.421 Cenno storico dell'insigne di Santa Maria a Pareta. Napoli, 1857.
Arc 1033.17.422 Relazione della...coronazione della miracolosa imagine dell Sma. Vergine di Monte Nero. Pistoia, 1694.
Arc 1033.17.423 Nocelli. Cenno istorico sul duomo e sagra immagine di Santa Maria...in Lucera. Napoli, 1843.
Arc 1033.17.424 Charpentier, L.F. Nouveau histoire de l'image miraculeux de Notre-Dame-de-Liesse. Soissons, 1888.
Arc 1033.17.425 Villette, E.N. Histoire de Notre-Dame de Liesse. Laon, 1708?
Arc 1033.17.441 Portenico, E. Cenno storico della Taumaturga efficie di Santa Maria dell'Arco...Miano. Napoli, 1851.
Arc 1033.17.442 Oberhausen, G. Istoria della miracolosa immagine di Nostra Signora di Montenero. Lucca, 1745.
Arc 1033.17.443 Andrea, G.A. Breve istoria della miracolosa immagine di Maria Sma...di Montenero. Livorno, 1774.
Arc 1033.17.444 Cenno storico del culto di Santa Maria dell'abbondanza...Marzano. Napoli, 1855.
Arc 1033.17.445 Cenni storici della taumaturga effigie di Santa Maria di Monserrato. Napoli, 1848.
Arc 1033.17.446 Mastelloni, A. Memorie istoriche della Madonna de' bagno di Magliano. Napoli, 1711.
Arc 1033.17.447 Notice sur le temple et l'hospice du Mont Carmel dédiés à la Vierge. Paris, 1843.
Arc 1033.17.448 Blot, F. Notre Dame du Mont Carmel. Paris, 1878.
Arc 1033.17.449 Ricci, A.M. Septenaire ou sept allégresses de Notre Dame de Mont Carmel. Paris, 1839.

Arc 1033 Archaeology - Christian antiquities - Other Special topics - cont.

Arc 1033.17.450 Officium commemorationis solemnis beatae virginis Maria de Monte Carmelo. Ulysarpone, 1679.
Arc 1033.17.455 Patiño, P.P. Disertación critico-theo-filosófica sobre la conservación de la santa imagen de Nuestra Señora de los Angeles. México, 1801.
Arc 1033.17.461 Coronella in onore della G. Madre di Dio....Santa Maria di Caravaggio...Porta Reale. Napoli, 1748.
Arc 1033.17.462 Montorio, S. Zodiaco di Maria...Napoli. Napoli, 1715.
Arc 1033.17.463 Corvino, R. Tesoro nascosto minifestato per la miracolosa invenzione di Santa Maria...Napoli. Napoli, 1831.
Arc 1033.17.464 Istoria della miracolosa immagine della...Maria del Carmine...Napoli. Napoli, 1788.
Arc 1033.17.465 Ossequi e preghiere onde meritarsi...di Maria...Napoli. Napoli, 1839.
Arc 1033.17.466 Libretto che contiene l'istoria...di Santa Maria...Nocera-Pagani. Napoli, 1834.
Arc 1033.17.481 Eroli, G. Narrazione storica sopra il santuario della madonna del Ponte. Roma, 1856.
Arc 1033.17.501 Rienzo, G. de. Notizie storiche sulla...effigie di Maria...Paterno. Napoli, 1829.
Arc 1033.17.502 Notizie istoriche...alla transformazione di una immagine della B.V...Palazzolo. Brescia, 1805.
Arc 1033.17.503 Oliveira Lemos, F.J. de. Livro do romeiro ao sumptuoso sanctuario da Senhora do Porto Ava. n.p., 1875.
Arc 1033.17.504 Brito Alão, M. de. Antiguidade da sagrada imagem de Nossa S. de Nazareth...Pederneira. Lisboa, 1628.
Arc 1033.17.531 Pla, José. Historia de Queralt. Barcelona, 1893.
Arc 1033.17.541 Mary mother of Christ. Facsimile. London, 1878.
Arc 1033.17.542 Novena in preparazione alla...festa...in Rapallo Nostra Signora sue Montallegro. Rapallo, 1878.
Arc 1033.17.542.5 Mariano, Filoteo. La miracolosa imagine della B.V. Maria del Mont'Allegro in Rapello. Venezia, 1688.
Arc 1033.17.543 Bagnari, P. Divozioni..in onore di Nostra Signora del Carmine. Roma, 1728.
Arc 1033.17.544 Diotallevi, D. Notizie della prodigiosa immagine di Maria Sma. della Grazie a Pta Angelica in Roma. Roma, 1887.
Arc 1033.17.545 Santelamazza, M. Cenni intorno la chiesa di S. Salvatore alle Coppelle. Roma, 1863.
Arc 1033.17.547 Grossi-Gondi, F. La dormitio B. Mariae. Roma, 1910.
Arc 1033.17.548 Saggio di notizie istoriche relative ai tre sagri monumenti, che si portano in processione la Mallina del di 17. gennajo 1798. n.p., 1798? 2 pam.
Arc 1033.17.549F Lauer, Philippe. Le trésor du Sancta Sanctorum. Paris, 1906.
Arc 1033.17.560 Más, Joseph. Nota historica de la Mare de Deu de la Cisa. Barcelona, 1908.
Arc 1033.17.581 Relazione del principio, e cause della venerazione dell'immagine..vergine. Firenze, 1704.
Arc 1033.17.582 Sassi, G.A. Notizie istoriche intorno alla miracolosa immagine...Maria. Milano, 1765.
Htn Arc 1033.17.583* Gonzalez de Mendoza, P. Historia del Monte Celia de Nuestra Señora de la Salceda. Granada, 1616.
Arc 1033.17.601 Galizia, C.M. Rapporto cronistorico della formazione...del simolacro...Vergine Maria di Trapani. Palermo, 1733.
Arc 1033.17.621 Venezia favorita da Maria. Relazione delle imagine...di Maria...in Venezia. Venezia, 1758.
Arc 1033.17.622 Apparitionum et celebriorum imaginum...Mariae...Venetiis. Venetia, 1760.
Arc 1033.17.623 Molin, A. Dell'antica immagine di Maria...S. Marco in Venezia. Venezia, 1821.
Arc 1033.17.624 Nelli, A. Origine della Madonna della Quercia di Viterbo. n.p., n.d.
Arc 1033.17.625 Notizie storiche intorno al santuario...Madonna della croce de Varazze. Varazze, 1875.
Arc 1033.17.626 Sangiovanni, V. Storia della Madre di Dio...del Monte Berico. Vicenza, 1776.
Arc 1033.17.650 Dörffel, F. St. Maria Culm das ist Bremdliche Historia. n.p., 1721.
Arc 1033.18.5 Bartolini, A. Gli atti della Passione degli ss. Abdon e Sennen. Roma, 1859.
Arc 1033.19 Du Camp, M. Iconographie chrétienne. n.p., n.d.
Arc 1033.19.9 Durand, Paul. Étude sur l'étimacia symbole du jugement dernier dans l'iconographie grecque chrétienne. Chartres, 1867.
Htn Arc 1033.20* Analdi, E. Delle basiliche antiche. Vincenza, 1767.
Arc 1033.20.5 Carini, I. Le basiliche cristiane. Roma, 1893.
Arc 1033.20.9 Sarnelli, Pompeo. Antica basilicografia. Napoli, 1686.
Arc 1033.20.13 Hessel, C. Die altchristlichen Basiliken Roms. Weslau, 1873.
Arc 1033.20.17 Globočnik, G.N. Le sette basiliche di Roma. Venesia, 1877.
Arc 1033.20.19 Paulinus a S. Barthol. De Basilica S. Paneratii M. Christi. Roma, 1703.
Arc 1033.20.25 Mullooly, Joseph. Saint Clement, pope and martyr and his Basilica in Rome. Rome, 1869.
Arc 1033.20.25.2 Mullooly, Joseph. Saint Clement, pope and martyr. 2. ed. Rome, 1873.
Arc 1033.20.26 Brownlow. Basilica of St. Clement in Rome. London, 1900.
Arc 1033.20.28 Nolan, Louis. The Basilica of Saint Clemente in Rome. Rome, 1910.
Arc 1033.20.29 Nolan, Louis. The Basilica of Saint Clemente in Rome. 2. ed. Rome, 1914.
Arc 1033.21 Arnellini, M. Scoperta oratorio presso Via Appia. Roma, 1875.
Arc 1033.21.5 Victorius Franciscus. Sanctorum septem dormientium...Musei Victorii. Roma, 1741.
Arc 1033.22 Gori, F. Sul tesoro di antiche suppellettili sacre. Spoleto, 1891.
Arc 1033.23 Grisar, H. Il sancta sanctorum...tesoro sacro. Roma, 1907.
Arc 1033.23.5 Scaglia, Sisto. Nova circa thesaurum sacelli Palalini "sancta sanctorum". Roma, 1909
Arc 1033.24 Di Carlo. Risposta al P. Grisar...contre il sacro tesoro. Tivoli, 1896. 3 pam.
Arc 1033.24.5 Vecchi, G. de. Una rarita del secolo XIX...sacro tesoro del G.C. Rossi. Roma, 1896.
Arc 1033.25 Taglialatela, G. L'arte cristiana nello studio della storia della chiesa. Napoli, 1901.
Arc 1033.25.5 Héron de Villefosse. Lampes chrétiennes inédites. Paris, 1875.
Arc 1033.25.7 Troppanneger, C. De lucernis veterum christianorum sepulcralibus. Vitembergae, 1710?
Arc 1033.25.8 Delattré, Alfred Louis. Lampes chrétiennes de Carthage. Lyon, 1880.
Arc 1033.26 Rossi, G.B. de. Dissertazione postume del P. Luigi Bruzza. Roma, 1889.
Arc 1033.26.5 Pamphlet box. P.L. Bruzza.

Classified Listing

Arc 1033 Archaeology - Christian antiquities - Other Special topics - cont.

Arc 1033.27 Nardoni. Di alcune sotterrance confessoni...Basiliche di Roma. Roma, 1881.
Arc 1033.27.5 Bartolini, D. La sotterranea confessoni...di San Marco. Roma, 1844.
Arc 1033.28 Pelka, O. Altchristliche Ehredenkmäler. Strassburg, 1901.
Arc 1033.28.5 Marucchi, O. Il matrimonio cristiano sopra antico monumento. Roma, 1882.
Arc 1033.28.8 Marucchi, O. La santità del matrimonio. Roma, 1902.
Arc 1033.28.15 Tori, G. Dei riti nuziali degli antichi cristiani. Perugia, 1793.
Arc 1033.29 Miracles et bien-faits obtenus...invocation du...T. Xavier en ses reliques. Malines, 1661.
Arc 1033.30 Armellini, Mariano. Scoperta della cripta di Santa Emerenziana e di una memoria relativa alla cattedra di San Pietro. Roma, 1877.
Arc 1033.31 Mély, F. de. Le Saint Suaire de Turin. Paris, 1902?
Arc 1033.32 Polidori, L. Illustrazione di due monumenti cristiani. Verona, 1843.
Arc 1033.33 Müller, N. Koimeterien die altchristlichen Begrabnis. Leipzig, 1901.
Arc 1033.34 Merracci P. Les chaines de Saint Pierre. Rome, 1877.
Arc 1033.34.1 Palmieri, N. Notizie istoriche delle sacre catene del principe degli apostoli. Orvieto, 1846.
Arc 1033.34.2 Palmieri, N. Notizie istoriche delle sacre catene del principe degli apostoli. n.p., n.d.
Arc 1033.34.3 Monsacrati, M.A. De catenis San Petri dissertatio. Roma, 1828.
Arc 1033.34.5 Caprara, C. Venuta di San Pietro in Roma. Roma, 1872.
Arc 1033.34.7 Resoconto...della disputa...fra sacerdoti e ministri...venuta di San Pietro. Roma, 1872.
Arc 1033.34.8 Resoconto...della disputa...fra sacerdoti e ministri...venuta di San Pietro. Roma, 1872.
Arc 1033.34.9 Lugari, J.B. Lieu du crucifiement de Saint Pierre. Tours, 1898.
Arc 1033.34.11F Lugari, J.B. Il culto di San Pietro sul Gianicolo. Roma, 1907.
Arc 1033.34.13 Cornoldi, G.M. San Pietro a Roma. Roma, 1872.
Arc 1033.34.17 Wiseman, N. Remarks on...Saint Peter's chair. Rome, 1833. 2v.
Arc 1033.34.19 Wiseman, N. Sul ragguaglio...cattedra di San Pietro. Roma, 1832.
Arc 1033.34.21 Cascioli, J. De aeneo simulacro divi Petri apostoli. Roma, 1895.
Arc 1033.34.25 Giovanni, V. di. San Pietro in Roma. Monumenti e testimoni. Palermo, 1895.
Arc 1033.34.29 Stocchi, P. Viaggio ed episopato romano di San Pietro. Roma, 1867. 2 pam.
Arc 1033.34.35 Grissar, H. Della statua di bronzo di San Pietro. Roma, 1898.
Arc 1033.34.39 Mauro di Polvica, Francesco di. Storia di San Pietro apostolo. Bologna, 1872.
Arc 1033.34.41 Marucchi, O. La crocifisione di San Pietro nel Vaticano. Roma, 1905.
Arc 1033.34.43 Zwölger, Theodor. Die Verehrung des Heiligen Petrus bei den Franken und Angelsachsen. Inaug. Diss. Stuttgart, 1929.
Arc 1033.34.45 Mancini, Pietro. Del primato e della residenza in Roma dell'apostolo Pietro. Roma, 1898.
Arc 1033.34.50 Wenzel, P. Die Ausgrabbungen unter der Peterskirche in Rom. Leipzig, 1953.
Arc 1033.34.55 Kioschbaum, Engelbert. La tumba de San Pedro y las catacumbas romanas. Madrid, 1954.
Arc 1033.34.60 Corte, Nicola. San Pietro e sepolto in Vaticano? Roma, 1957.
Arc 1033.34.65 Bagatti, Bellarmino. San Pietro nei monumenti di Palestina. Cairo, 1960.
Arc 1033.34.70 Corbo, Virgilio. Ricordi di San Pietro sul lago di Tiberiade. Jerusalem, 1969.
Arc 1033.35 Regazzi, A. De sacrosancta...cruce...quae in S. Crucis osservantur. Roma, 1777.
Arc 1033.35.3 Barrau, J.B. Notice historique sur la vraie croix de Baugé. Angers, 1874.
Arc 1033.35.5 Combes, L. de. Finding of the Cross. London, 1907.
Arc 1033.35.7F Van de Putte, F. Collégiale de S. Walburge à Furnes. Relique de la croix. Bruges, 1864. 3 pam.
Arc 1033.35.9 Brunati. Di un antica stauroteca istoriata...Brescia. Roma, 1839.
Arc 1033.35.11 Fulda, H. Freuz und die Kreuzigung. Breslau, 1878.
Htn Arc 1033.35.13F* Borgia, S. De cruce vaticana...commentarius. Roma, 1779.
Htn Arc 1033.35.15F* Borgia, S. De cruce veliterna. Roma, 1780.
Arc 1033.35.17 Colá, C. Memorie historiche dell'apparitione delle croci. Napoli, 1661.
Arc 1033.35.19 Michele, I. de. Sopra un'antica croce nel duomo di Termini-Imerese. Palermo, 1859.
Htn Arc 1033.35.21F* Bosio, I. Trionfante e gloriosa croce trattato. Roma, 1610.
Arc 1033.35.23 Velentini, A. Santissime croci di Brescia. Brescia, 1882.
Arc 1033.35.25 Camers, A.R. De particula ex pretioso...crucis...commentarius. Roma, 1609.
Arc 1033.35.27 Venuti, F. De cruce cortonensi dissertatio. Florenzia, 1781.
Arc 1033.35.29 Triumphe van het heilig kruise Christi. Brugge, 1871.
Arc 1033.35.31 Magrini, A. Sopra la insigne reliquia della S. Croce. Thiene, 1860.
Arc 1033.35.33 Taglialatela, G. Stauroteca di San Leonzio...Napoli. Napoli, 1877.
Arc 1033.35.35 Notizia storica sulla croce del Carroccio. Milano, 1870.
Arc 1033.35.37 Kohler, C. Réfugié à Jérusalem au VIe siècle. Nogent-le-Rotrou, n.d.
Arc 1033.35.39 Reinartz, J.L. Notice sur le reliquaire de la sainte croix...à Tongres. n.p., n.d.
Arc 1033.35.41 Bastelaer, D.A. Étude sur les précieux reliquaire phylactère du XIIe siècle. Anvers, 1880.
Arc 1033.35.43 Sévérac, G. Notice sur la vraie croix de St. Guilhelm-du-Désert. Lodève, 1861.
Arc 1033.35.45 Barbier de Montault, X. Lettres testimoniales...portant donation d'un morceau de la vrai croix...Angers. Tours, n.d.
Arc 1033.35.47 Barbier de Montault, X. Croix-reliquiare de l'eglise de S. Florent-les-Saumur. Angers, n.d.
Arc 1033.35.49 Drach, P.L.B. Inscription hébräique du titre de S. Croix. 2e éd. Rome, 1831.
Arc 1033.35.51 Cellier. La sainte vraie croix de Douchy. Valenciennes, 1863.
Arc 1033.35.53 Velasco, Alfonso A. Historia de la milagrosa renovación. México, 1845.

Arc 1033 Archaeology - Christian antiquities - Other Special topics - cont.

Arc 1033.35.55 Cavedoni, C. Dichiarazione de' tre antiche Stauroteche. Modena, 1847.
Arc 1033.35.61 Ceva Grimaldi, F. Su la vera forma delle croce di N. Signore. Medina, n.d.
Arc 1033.35.66 Exposé historique de l'honneur...du culte...au bois de la vraie croix. Bruxelles, 1790. 2 pam.
Arc 1033.35.71 Sionnet, A. Lettre à...Piolin sur la legende hébraïque du titre de la viaie croix. n.p., n.d.
Arc 1033.35.81 Rioja, F. de. Titulo de la cruz de Christi. n.p., n.d.
Arc 1033.35.85 Gretser, J. Hortus S. Crucis. Ingolstadii, 1610.
Arc 1033.35.101 Ciampini, G.G. De cruce stationale investigatio historica. Roma, 1737.
Arc 1033.35.121 Sorio, B. Sunto storica della croce e del crocefisso nel suo svolgimento. n.p., n.d.
Htn Arc 1033.35.141* Gretser, J. De cruce Christi. Inglodstadii, 1600. 3v.
Arc 1033.35.145 Zöckler, Otto. Das Kreuz Christi. Gütersloh, 1875.
Arc 1033.35.146 Zöckler, Otto. The cross of Christ. London, 1877.
Arc 1033.35.147 Almeida, R.V. d'. A cruz de vila Viçosa. Lisboa, 1908.
Arc 1033.35.147.2 Almeida, R.V. d'. A cruz de vila Viçosa. 2. ed. Lisboa, 1957.
Arc 1033.35.149 Garces Teixeira, F.A. Acruz Manoelina do covento de Cristo. Lisboa, 1922.
Arc 1033.35.151 Prime, W.C. Holy Cross. London, 1877.
Arc 1033.35.153 Gualzetti, G.B. Pel giorno dell'invenzione di S. Croce, 1848. Milano, 1848.
Arc 1033.35.155 Braun, J. Die Reliquiare des christlichen Kultes und ihre Entwicklung. Freiburg, 1940.
Arc 1033.35.160 Frolow, Anatole. La relique de la Vraie Croix. Paris, 1961.
Arc 1033.35.161 Frolow, Anatole. Les reliquaires de la Vraie Croix. Paris, 1965.
Arc 1033.36 Zardetti, C. Monumenti cristiani. Milano, 1843.
Arc 1033.37 Abbati Olivieri Giordani, Annibale degli. Di alcune antichità cristiane...in Pesaro nel Museo Olivieri. Pesaro, 1781.
Arc 1033.37.3 Abbati Olivieri Giordani, Annibale degli. Di alcune altre antichità cristiane. Pesaro, 1784.
Arc 1033.38 Giorgi, Calisto. Sull'autenticità del capo di S. Lorenzo. Roma, 1864.
Arc 1033.38.5 Memorie della Vita del Martirio...S. Lorenzo. Roma, 1756.
Arc 1033.38.9 Bresnicio, C.B. Historia de Insigni Martyrio...Laurentii. Leipzig, 1572.
Arc 1033.38.15 Pérez Báyes, F. Damascus et Laurentius. Rome, 1756.
Arc 1033.39 Bulic, F. Frammento di pettine son reppresentanze cristiane. Roma, 1902.
Arc 1033.40 Bartolini, D. Gli atti del martirio...S. Cecilia. Roma, 1867.
Arc 1033.40.5 Bartolini, D. Istoria del Martirio di S. Cecilia. Roma, 1759.
Arc 1033.40.9 Bianchi-Cagliesi. Santa Cecilia et La Sua Basilica nel Trastevere. Roma, 1902. 2 pam.
Arc 1033.40.15 Picarelli, T. Basilica e Casa Romana di S. Cecilia in Trastevere. Roma, 1904.
Arc 1033.41 Bobone, G. Apologia di protomartiri...Tolomeo e Romano. Roma, 1865.
Arc 1033.42 Brunatio, J. De Christianorum veterum monumentorum im rem biblicam utilitate. Diss. Mediolani, 1838.
Arc 1033.43 Annali...degli Apostoli Pietro e Paolo. v.1-3. Torino, 1883. 2v.
Arc 1033.43.5 Ruggieri, E. Dell'antico Pellegrinaggio XVIII centenario Martirio Pietro e Paolo. Roma, 1867.
Arc 1033.43.9 Breve Notizia dell'Orato in Memoria Abitazione. Roma, 1770.
Arc 1033.43.11 Sybel, L. von. Der Herr der Seligkeit. Archäologische Studie. Marburg, 1913.
Arc 1033.43.13 Soresinas, I.M. De capitibus S. apostolorum Petri et Pauli in Lateran. Roma, 1673.
Arc 1033.44 Georgius, D. De monogrammate Christi Domini. Diss. Roma, 1738.
Arc 1033.44.5 De monogrammate sanetissimi nominis Jesu. Roma, 1747.
Arc 1033.44.9 Cavedoni, C. Dell'origine...IHS del SS. Nome de Gesú. Modena, n.d.
Arc 1033.44.13 Cavedoni, C. Ricerche critiche...medaglie di Constantino. Modena, 1858.
Arc 1033.44.15 Sodo, G. Il monogramma del nome ss. di Gesú. Napoli, 1885.
Arc 1033.44.19 De monogrammate D.N. Jesu Christe. n.p., n.d.
Arc 1033.44.27 Garrucci, R. Deux monuments des premiers siècles. Rome, 1862.
Arc 1033.44.33 Allegranza, J. De monogrammate D.N. Jesu Christe. Milano, 1773.
Arc 1033.45 Persus, L. de. Del pontificato di S. Sisto I. Alatri, 1884.
Arc 1033.46 Bartolini, D. Cenni biografici di S. Giacomo apostolo il maggiore. Roma, 1885.
Arc 1033.46.8 Os miragres de Santiago. Valladolid, 1918.
Arc 1033.47 Profumo, A. L'incendio neroniano ed i Cristiani. Roma, 1903.
Arc 1033.47.8 Abbatescianni, G. Primi Christiani e Nerone aproposito dell'opuscolo di Carlo Pascal. Bari, 1901.
Arc 1033.47.12 Negri, G. Nerone e il cristianesimo. Roma, 1899.
Arc 1033.47.17 Mapelli, L. L'incendio di Roma e i primi Cristiani. Milano, 1900.
Arc 1033.47.21 Coen, J.A. La persecuzione neroniana dei Cristiani. Firenze, 1900.
Arc 1033.47.25 Fea, C. Della Casa Aurea di Nerone. Roma, 1832.
Htn Arc 1033.47.28* Cardani, H. Neronis encomium. Amstelodami, 1640.
Arc 1033.48 Sandellius, D. De Priscorum Christianorum Synaxibus. Venetiis, 1770.
Arc 1033.49 Canallotti, G.B. Vita di S. Severino e di S. Vittorio. Pariso, 1643.
Arc 1033.50 Tizzani, V. La celebre contesa fra S. Stefano e S. Cipriano. Roma, 1862.
Arc 1033.51 Angelini, N. Brevi notizie intorno San Rufino. Frascati, 1885.
Arc 1033.51.3 Angelini, N. Brevi notizie intorno San Rufino ves e Martire. Roma, 1862.
Arc 1033.51.5 Vincenti, D. de. Nitizie dei Sante Rufino e Cesidio Martire. Avezzano, 1885.
Arc 1033.52 Angelini, N. Vita, martiro e culto di S. Ambrogio. Frascati, 1884.
Arc 1033.53 Marucchi, O. Un nuovo monumento della persecuzione diocleziana. Roma, 1893.
Arc 1033.53.5 Scognamiglio, A. Ne' primi tre secoli di persecuzione cristiane. Napoli, 1869.

Classified Listing

Arc 1033 Archaeology - Christian antiquities - Other Special topics - cont.

Arc 1033.53.9 Cavedoni, C. Cenni cronologica...rescritti di Traiano e di Adriano. Modena, 1855.

Arc 1033.53.15 Cavedoni, C. L'era de' martiri osia di Diocleziano. Modena, 1848.

Arc 1033.53.19 Miscellanea in onore di S. Maurizio. Roma, 1847.

Arc 1033.53.20 Ducis, C.A. Saint Maurice et le Légion Thébéenne. Annecy, 1882.

Arc 1033.53.22 Peissard, N. La découverte du tombeau du tombeau de St. Maurice. St. Maurice, 1922.

Arc 1033.53.23 Dupraz, Louis. Les passions de S. Maurice d'Agaune. Fribourg, 1961.

Arc 1033.53.24 Berchem, D. van. Le martyre de la Légion Thébaine. Basel, 1956.

Arc 1033.54 Gori, A.F. Dissertazioni...di S. Giuseppe. Modena, 1865.

Arc 1033.55 Romano, G.B. Memorie sacre della cappella...e di...la Scola Santa. Roma, 1798.

Arc 1033.55.3 Marangoni, G. Istoria dell'...oratorio...Lateran...Sancta Sanctorum. Roma, 1798.

Arc 1033.55.5 Soresini, I.M. De scala sancta ante S. Sanctorum in Lateran. Roma, 1672.

Arc 1033.55.6 Soresini, G.M. Compendio istorico cronologico delle cose più cospicul concernenti la Scala Santa. Roma, 1674.

Arc 1033.55.7 Mazzucconi, L. Memorie storiche della scala santa...di Sancto Sanctorum. Roma, 1840.

Arc 1033.56 Marucchi, O. Guida del Museo Christiano Christiano Lateranense. Roma, 1898.

Arc 1033.57 Cozza-Luzi, G. Di un antico filiatterio christiano. Napoli, 1887.

Arc 1033.58 Lugari, G.B. S. Sebastiano; memorie. Roma, 1889.

Arc 1033.58.5 Lucatelli, G. Notizie istoriche...la testa di S. Sebastiano. Roma, 1757.

Arc 1033.58.9 Brevi racconto sopra immagini S. Sebastiano. Roma, 1830.

Arc 1033.58.15 Styger, Paolo. Il monumento apostolico a San Sebastiano sulla Via Appia. Roma, 1925.

Arc 1033.59 Ferrari, G. de. Panegirico di S. Vittoria. Roma, 1850.

Arc 1033.59.5 Pennesi, A. Cenni storici sul culto di S. Vittoria. S. Vittoria, 1893.

Arc 1033.60 Calo, Luigi. S. Beatrice vergine e martire. Napoli, 1894.

Arc 1033.61 Franchi de Cavalieri, P. S. Agnese nella tradizione e nella leggenda. Roma, 1899.

Arc 1033.62 Franchi de' Cavalieri, P. La Passio SS. Perpetuae et Felicitatis. Roma, 1896.

Arc 1033.62.2 Fanchi de' Cavalieri, P. La Passio SS. Perpetuae et Felicitatis. Roma, 1896.

Arc 1033.62.7 Perpetua, Saint Legend. Passio Sanctarum Perpetuae et Felicitatis. Noviomagi, 1936.

Arc 1033.62.9 Führer, Joseph. Ein Beitrag zur Lösung zer Felicitas-Frage. Leipzig, 1890.

Arc 1033.62.40 Wetzel, A. Die Translatie S. Alexandri. Kiel, 1881.

Htn Arc 1033.63* Magi, H. De Tintinnabulis. Amstelodami, 1664. 2 pam.

Arc 1033.63.5 Visconti, C.L. Dell'uso...dei monumenti cristiani cronologici. Roma, 1856.

Arc 1033.63.9 Gallonio, A. Traité des instruments de martyre. Paris, 1904.

Arc 1033.64 Levera, F. De invicta veritate anni, mensis, et diei. Roma, 1668.

Arc 1033.65 Ferrari, L.F. dei. Sul valore storico del'atti S.S. Flavia Domitilla, Nereo, Achilleo. Roma, 1880.

Arc 1033.65.5 Lais, G. Memoire del titolo di Fasciola. Roma, 1880.

Arc 1033.66 Bonet, F.R. Breve notizia...d'alcuni Santi del Colosseo. Roma, 1796.

Arc 1033.66.5 Bonet, F.R. Breve notizia...di alcuni Santi del Colosseo. Roma, 1759.

Arc 1033.67 Rossi, G.B. de. Antichi Mulini in Roma e nel Lazio. Roma, 1857.

Arc 1033.68 Rossi, G.B. de. Esame...dell'Immagine di Urbano II. Roma, 1881.

Arc 1033.69 Arcangeli, P. Della interpretazione del Monogramma. Roma, 1879.

Arc 1033.69.5 Bruzza, L. Della interpretazione del Monogramma. Roma, 1877.

Arc 1033.69.20 Becker, F. Die Heidnische Weiheformel Diis Manibus. Gera, 1881.

Arc 1033.70 Armellini, M. Scoperta d'una pittura nel Laterno. Roma, 1880.

Arc 1033.70.5 Taeggi, O.P. Avanzi di pitture del secolo IX in una cripta. n.p., 1885.

Arc 1033.70.9 Mullooly, J. Brief notice of the ancient paintings...Rome. Rome, 1866.

Arc 1033.70.13 Lefort, L. Peintures inédites de L'Église St. Nicolas. Paris, 1879.

Arc 1033.70.19 Nardoni, L. L'antico oratorio di S. Agnese. Roma, 1870.

Arc 1033.70.23 Wilpert, G. Le pitture della Basilica primitiva di S. Clemente. Roma, 1906.

Arc 1033.71 Rossi, J.B. de. La capsella d'argent africaine. Caen, 1890.

Arc 1033.72 Ciampini, J. Explicatio 2 sarcophagorum...baptismatis. Roma, 1597.

Arc 1033.72.5 Mundt, A. Die Erztaufen Norddeutschlands. Leipzig, 1908.

Arc 1033.73 Cavedoni, C. Ricerche...del sacro pallio ecclesiastico. Modena, 1856.

Arc 1033.74 Fortini, E. Solenne Ricevimento della testa di S. Andrea Apostolo. Roma, 1848.

Arc 1033.75 Andreucci, A.G. Notizie...SS. Valentino Prete ed Flario Diacono. Roma, 1740.

Arc 1033.76 Notizie, regole...ss. Martire della ss. Basilica Vaticana. Roma, 1756.

Arc 1033.77 Navarro, G. Il corpo di S. Leonzio Martire. Napoli, 1846.

Arc 1033.78 Taglialatela, G. Le solenni feste della traslazione dei martiri di Atripalda. Pompei, 1888.

Arc 1033.79 Taglialatela, G. Del primo vescovo di Napoli Sant'Aspreno. Napoli, 1879.

Arc 1033.80 Castro, V. de. Difesa della causa di S. Marcellino. Roma, 1819.

Arc 1033.81 Stornaiuolo, C. Ricerche...SS. Eutichete ed Acuzio. Napoli, 1874.

Arc 1033.82 Pollidoro, J.B. Vita...S. Pardi...de SS. Primiano, Firmiano et Casto. Roma, 1741.

Arc 1033.83 Mannerini, L. Memorie del Martiro, S. Vitale e Valeria. Roma, 1848.

Arc 1033.84 Pellino, G. Trattenimento...S. Igino Papa e Martire. Napoli, 1831.

Arc 1033.85 Cavedoni, C. Osservazioni...sepolcro di Maria. Modena, 1865.

Arc 1033.86 Rossi, G.B. de. Oratorio privato del secolo IV...nel Monte della Giustizia. Roma, 1876.

Arc 1033 Archaeology - Christian antiquities - Other Special topics - cont.

Arc 1033.87 Marucchi, O. Brevi compendio di memorie...martire S. Agapito. Roma, 1898.

Arc 1033.88 Baruffaldi, G. Del Colpo di Spada...la morte a i Martiri. Venezia, 1759.

Arc 1033.89 Bassich, A. Della vita e del martirio di San Trifone. Vienna, 1845.

Arc 1033.90 Heredia del Rio, P.M. Historia Sanctorum Martyrum...Ruderici, et Salomonis. Romae, 1838.

Arc 1033.91 Florentinio, M. Hetruscae...Pietates...de Prima Thusciae Christianae. Lucae, 1701.

Arc 1033.92 Rossi, G.B. de. Commemorazione del P. Luigi Bruzza. Roma, 1883.

Arc 1033.93 Cavedoni, C. Dichiarazione di 5 bassirilievi biblici...Modena. Modena, 1855.

Arc 1033.94 Laurenti, V. Vita SS. Apostoli Filippo et Giacono Minore. Roma, 1873.

Arc 1033.95 Le Blant, E. D'un nouveau monument...Sainte Félicité. Rome, 1888.

Arc 1033.96 Salomoni, P. De Liminibus Apostolorum. Romae, 1775.

Arc 1033.97 Le Blant, E. Des voies d'exception...contre les martyrs. Rome, 1884.

Arc 1033.98 Mauro, G.D. Historia sacra. Roma, 1682.

Arc 1033.99 Carini, Isidoro. La passione di Cristo. Milano, 1894.

Arc 1033.100 Carini, Isidoro. Simbolismo dei primi secoli. Romae, 1890.

Arc 1033.101 Barreca, C. Santa Lucia di Siracusa. Roma, 1902.

Arc 1033.102 Carpini, J. Sacro-historica disquisitio emblematibus in Cimelio. Roma, 1691.

Arc 1033.103 Liberati, D.P. Processo belle reliquie false. Roma, 1871.

Arc 1033.104 Acta...de identitate SS. Corporum Ambrosii Episcopatum...et...Cristi martyrum Gervasii et Protasii. Romae, 1873.

Arc 1033.104.5 Cenni storici sulla sepoltura...Gervasi e Protasi. Milano, 1873.

Arc 1033.105 Coppola, G. Relazione dello scoprimento del corpo del...martire S. Eusanio. Roma, 1749.

Arc 1033.106 Bartolomei. Della scuola di S. Paolo. Roma, 1850.

Arc 1033.107 Fratini, G. Gli atti più antichi del martirio di S. Felice. Foligno, 1881.

Arc 1033.108 Guazzugli, M. Notizie riguardanti il culto di S. Irene. Osimo, 1783.

Arc 1033.109 Uccelli, P.A. Dei santi martiri Domno, Domnione ed Eusebia. Bergamo, 1874.

Arc 1033.110 Le Blant, E. Les premiers Chrétiens et le Démon. Rome, 1888.

Arc 1033.111 Le Blant, E. Les songes et les visions des martyrs. Rome, 1892.

Arc 1033.112 Wilpert, J. Die Gewandung der Christen in den ersten Jahrhunderten. Köln, 1898.

Arc 1033.112.5 Swoboda, Franz. Die liturgischen Kämme. Thesis. n.p., 1963?

Arc 1033.113 Leport, L. Deux mosaiques chrétiennes du IVe siècle. Paris, 1894.

Arc 1033.113.3 Leport, L. Nouvelles observations sur la Mosaique de S. Pudentienne. Rome, 1896.

Arc 1033.114 Lugari, G.B. Sopra l'età di alcuni Bolli di figuline. Roma, 1895.

Arc 1033.115 Emerton, E. The religious environment of early Christianity. Cambridge, 1910.

Arc 1033.116 Collin de Plancy, J.A.S. Dictionnaire des reliques. Paris, 1821-1822. 3v.

Arc 1033.118 Ancessi, V. Atlas géographique et archéologique...Testament. Paris, 1876.

Arc 1033.119 Charles, archbishop of Alger. Sainte Anne de Jérusalem et Sainte Anne d'Auray. Alger, 1879.

Arc 1033.120 Beheim, J.C. Dissertatio...de archeiois sive tabulariis sacris. Norimburgi, n.d.

Arc 1033.121 Guillaume, P. Le navi cavensi nel Mediterraneo...vita di S. Costabile de Lucania. Napoli, 1876.

Arc 1033.122 Sanna Solaro, G. Acquisito conservazione, ristaurato degli arredi sacri. Torino, 1886.

Arc 1033.123 Wieland, F. Altar und Altargrab der christlichen Kirchen...Mensa und Confessio. v.1-2. München, 1906-12.

Arc 1033.123.5 Wieland, F. Schrift Mensa und Confessio und P. Emil Dorsch. München, 1909.

Arc 1033.123.9 Wieland, F. Der vorirenäische Obferbegriff. München, 1909.

Arc 1033.124 Bargès, Jean. Notice sur quelques antels chrétiens. Paris, 1890.

Arc 1033.130 Calcagnino, A. Historia del glorioso precursore di N.S.S. G. Battista. Genova, 1648.

Htn Arc 1033.131* Du Cange, C. du F. Traite historique du chef de S. Jean Baptiste. Paris, 1665.

Htn Arc 1033.133* Viseur, R. Recueil de la vie, mort, invention et miracles de S. Jean Baptiste. Amyens, 1618.

Arc 1033.135 Lettre circulaire de M....d'Amiens...de la reception de la face de S. Jean Baptiste. Amiens, 1879.

Htn Arc 1033.137* Paciandi, P. De cultu S. J. Baptistae...commentarius. Roma, 1755.

Arc 1033.141 Razy, E. Saint Jean-Baptiste, sa vie, son culte. Paris, 1880.

Arc 1033.143 Salmon, C. Histoire du chef de S. J.-Baptiste...Amiens. Amiens, 1876.

Arc 1033.145 Odvardo a S. Francisco Xaverio. Dissertatio storico-critico-dogmatico...mano destra di S. Giovanni Battista...Repagnano. Roma, 1738.

Arc 1033.147 San Giovanni Battista e i Genovesi. Genova, 1879.

Arc 1033.150 Favilli, A. Relazione dell'origine...Firenze...Bastone del S.P. Giuseppe. Lucca, 1721.

Arc 1033.160 Boulgaris, N.T. Alēthēs ekthesis...thaymatourchou...touachiouspyridōnos. Benetia, 1880.

Arc 1033.161 Liquefaction of the blood of St. Januarius. N.Y., 1872.

Arc 1033.162 Molini, A.M. De vita et Lipsanis S. Marci Evangelistae. Romae, 1864.

Arc 1033.162.5F Manin, Leonardo. Memorie storico-critiche...di S. Marco. Venezia, 1835.

Arc 1033.163 Kardag. Die Geschichte des Mâr Abhdiso und seines Jüngers Mâr Quardagh. Kiel, 1889.

Arc 1033.164 Usener, H.K. Acta martyris Anastasii Persae. Bonnae, 1894.

Arc 1033.165 Aubé, Benjamin. Polyeucte dans l'histoire. Paris, 1882.

Arc 1033.166 La passio Ss. Mariani et Iacobi. Roma, 1900.

Arc 1033.167 Eleuterio. I martirii di S. Teodoto e di S. Ariadne. Roma, 1901.

Arc 1033.168 Stentrup, F. Die Translatio sancti viti. Münster, 1906.

Arc 1033 Archaeology - Christian antiquities - Other Special topics - cont.

Arc 1033.169 Dini, F. Dissertatio...de translatio...S. Bartholomaei. Venetiis, 1700.
Arc 1033.169.5 Benedictus XIII. Discorso nel quale si prova...S. Bartholomeo. Benevento, 1695.
Arc 1033.170 Der heilige Märtyrer - Apollonius von Rom. Mainz, 1903.
Arc 1033.171 Usener, H.K. Acta S. Timothei. Bonn, 1877.
Arc 1033.172 Acta iberica...Speusippi, Eleusippi. Sankt Peterburg, 1906.
Arc 1033.173 Albarellio, G. Il cimitero "In clivum cucumeris". Aquila, 1909.
Arc 1033.175 Stuiber, Alfred. Refrigerium interim. Bonn, 1957.
Arc 1033.177 Cecchelli, Carlo. Lezioni di archeologia cristiana; liturgia ed archeologia. Roma, 1958.
Arc 1033.178 Gotsmick, A. Proserpina - virgo sacrata Dei; ein fruhchristlichen Antithese. München, 1962.
Arc 1033.180 Doelger, Franz J. Ichthys. v.2-5. Münster, 1910-43. 4v.
Arc 1033.181 Kriss-Rettenbeck, Lenz. Ex voto. Zürich, 1972.
Arc 1033.182 Nussbaum, Otto. Der Standort des Liturgen am christlichen Altar vor dem Jahre 1000. Diss. Bonn, 1965.

Arc 1045 Archaeology - Islamic antiquities - Local

X Cg Arc 1045.5 Marçais, W. Les monumens arabes. Paris, 1903.

Arc 1048 Archaeology - Islamic antiquities - Special topics

Arc 1048.1 Fraehn, C.M. Antiquitatis Muhammedanae monumenta varia. pt.1-2. Petropoli, 1820-22.

Arc 1050 Archaeology - Iconography - Folios [Discontinued]

Htn Arc 1050.201* Canini, G.A. Iconografia. Romae, 1669.
Arc 1050.202 Portraits I. Roman emperors. n.p., n.d.
Arc 1050.203 Virchow, R. Porträt-Munzen und Grafs...Porträt Gallerie. Berlin, 1903.
Htn Arc 1050.204* Icones, vitae et elogia...Romanorum. Antwerp, 1645.

Arc 1053 Archaeology - Iconography - General works

Arc 1053 Pamphlet box. Archaeology. Iconography.
Arc 1053.1 Canini, G.A. Images des héros et des grandes hommes de l'antiquité. Amsterdam, 1731.
Arc 1053.2 Winter, F. Über die griechische Porträtkunst. Berlin, 1894.
Arc 1053.2.2 Bernoulli, J.J. Die erhaltenen Bildnisse berühmter Griechen. Basel, 1877.
Arc 1053.2.5 Bernoulli, J.J. Griechische Ikonographie. München, 1901. 2v.
X Cg Arc 1053.3 Bernoulli, J.J. Römische Ikonographie. v.2, pt.1. Stuttgart, 1882-94.
Arc 1053.3.1 Bernoulli, J.J. Römische Ikonographie. v.1-2. Hildesheim, 1969. 4v.
Htn Arc 1053.4* Faber, Johannes. Illustrium imagines ex...Fuliri Ursini. Antwerpiae, 1606.
Arc 1053.5 Dietrichson, L. Antinoos. Christiania, 1884.
Arc 1053.5.2 Laban, F. Der Gemüthsansdruck des Antinous. Berlin, 1891.
Arc 1053.5.3 Levezow, R. Ueber den Antinous. Berlin, 1808.
Arc 1053.5.7 Holm, Erich. Das Bildnis des Antinous. Inaug. Diss. Würzburg, 1933.
Arc 1053.6 Ebers, G. Antike. Portraits. Leipzig, 1893.
Arc 1053.6.2 Ebers, G. The Hellenic portraits from the Fayum. N.Y., 1893.
Arc 1053.6.4 Catalogue of...Theodor Graf collection. n.p., n.d.
Arc 1053.6.6F Graul, Richard. Die antiken Porträtgemälde aus den Grabstätten des Fayum. Leipzig, 1888.
Arc 1053.6.7F Strelkov, A. Faymskii portret. Moskva, 1936.
Htn Arc 1053.6.9* Patarolo, Lorenzo. Series Augustorum, Augustarum, Caesarum. Venetiis, 1702.
Arc 1053.6.12 Patarolo, Lorenzo. Series Augustorum, Augustarum, Caesarum. 3. ed. Venetiis, 1740.
Arc 1053.6.25 Delbrück, R. Spätantike Kaiserporträts. Berlin, 1933.
Arc 1053.7 Patarolo, Lorenzo. Series Augustorum, Augustarum, Caesarum. 4. ed. Venetiis, 1743.
Arc 1053.7.5 Patarolo, Lorenzo. Opera omnia. Venetiis, 1743. 2v.
Arc 1053.8 Schuster, P. Über die erhaltenen Porträts der griechischen Philosophen. Leipzig, 1876.
Arc 1053.10 Lichteuber, G.R. von. Das Porträt an Grabdenkmalen. Strassburg, 1902.
Arc 1053.11 Stenersen, L.B. De historia variisque generibus statuarum iconicarum. Christianiae, 1877.
Arc 1053.13 Longpérier, A. de. Mémoires sur la chronologie et l'iconographie des rois parthes arsacides. Paris, 1853-82.
Arc 1053.15 Martinov, Jean. Un tétraptique russe. Arras, 1877.
Arc 1053.16 Barbier de Montault, X. Solution d'un problème iconographique. Poitiers, 1877.
Htn Arc 1053.18* Boehringer, E. Der Caesar von Acireale. Stuttgart, 1933.
Arc 1053.19F Paribeni, R. Il ritratto nell'arte antica. Milano, 1934.
Arc 1053.20 Visconti, E.Q. Iconografia greca. Milano, 1923-25. 3v.
Arc 1053.21F Bréhier, L. Les visions apocalyptiques dans l'art byzantin. Bucarest, 1930?
Arc 1053.22 Bianchi Bandinelli, Ranuccio. Il problema del ritratto greco. Firenze, 1952.
Arc 1053.23 Budde, Ludwig. Der Ertstehung des antiken Reprasentationsbildes. Berlin, 1957.
Arc 1053.25 Stommel, Edward. Beiträge zur Ikonographie der konstantinischen Sarkophagplastik. Bonn, 1954.

Arc 1070 Archaeology - Other special topics - Folios [Discontinued]

Arc 1070.200 Graser, B. Das Model eines athenischen Fuenfreihenschiffs Pentere. Berlin, 1866.
Htn Arc 1070.201* Liceti, F. De lucernis antiquorum reconditis libb. sex. Utini, 1653.
Arc 1070.201.9F Bartoli, P.S. Gli antichi sepolcri. Roma, 1697.
Arc 1070.202 Bartoli, P.S. Gli antichi sepolcri. Roma, 1727.
Arc 1070.202.3 Bartoli, P.S. Le antiche lucerne. Roma, 1691.
Arc 1070.203 Bartoli, P.S. Le antiche lucerne. Roma, 1729.
Arc 1070.204 Gozzadini, G. De quelques mors de cheval italiques et de l'épée de Ronzano en bronze. Bologne, 1875.
Arc 1070.205 Passeri, J.B. Lucernae futiles Musei Passerii. Pisauri, 1739-51. 3v.
Arc 1070.206 Thiele, G. Antike Himmelsbilder. Berlin, 1898.
Arc 1070.207 Furtwängler, A. Neuere Faelschungen von Antiken. Berlin, 1899.
Arc 1070.208 Marchant, Louis. Ampoules de pèlerinages en plomb...Bourgogne. Dijon, 1873.

Arc 1075 - 1099 Archaeology - Other special topics - Monographs (A-Z by topic)

Arc 1075.2 Grabar, André. Ampoules de Terre Sainte. Paris, 1958.
Arc 1075.5F Tyler, Alan. Neolithic flint axes from the Cotswold Hills. Oxford, 1976.
Arc 1076.1 Heuzey, Léon. Recherches sur les lits antiques. Paris, 1873.
Arc 1076.2 Foster, J.R. Liber singularis de Bysso antiquorum. Londini, 1776.
Arc 1076.3 Bergner, H.H. Zur Glockenkunde Thürigens. Jena, 1896.
Htn Arc 1076.3.5* Downman, E.A. Ancient church bells in England. London, 1899.
Arc 1076.3.9 Otte, H. Glockenkunde. Leipzig, 1884.
Arc 1076.3.13 Stahlschmidt, J.C.L. Surrey bells and London bell-founders. London, 1884.
Arc 1076.3.13.5 Stahlschmidt, J.C.L. The church bells of Kent. London, 1887.
Arc 1076.3.14 Tyack, G.S. A book about bells. London, 1898.
Arc 1076.3.17 Walters, Henry Beauchamp. Church bells. London, 1908.
Arc 1076.3.18 Walters, Henry Beauchamp. Church bells of England. London, 1912.
Arc 1076.3.18.10 Walters, Henry Beauchamp. Church bells of Wiltshire. Devizes, 1927-29.
Arc 1076.3.18.15 Walter, Henry Beauchamp. The church bells of Shropshire. Oswestry, 1915.
Arc 1076.3.19 Maggi, G. De tintinnalbulis. Hanoviae, 1608.
Arc 1076.3.23 Morillot, L. Étude sur l'emploi de clochettes. Dijon, 1888.
Arc 1076.3.27 Blavignac, J.D. La cloche, études. Genève, 1877.
Arc 1076.3.31 Raven, J.J. The bells of England. London, 1906.
Arc 1076.3.35 Thiers, J.B. Traitez des cloches. Paris, 1721.
Arc 1076.3.37 Caminada, Christian. Die bündner Glocken. Zürich, 1915.
Arc 1076.3.38 Berthele, J. Mélanges. Montpellier, 1906.
Arc 1076.3.39 Berthele, J. La famille Cavillier et les fonderies de cloches de Carrepuits. Caen, 1901. 2 pam.
Arc 1076.3.41 Schubart, F.W. Die Glocken in herzogtum Anhalt. Dessau, 1896.
Arc 1076.3.43 Olovianishnikov, N. Istoriia kolokolov i kolokitenoe iskusstvo. Moskva, 1912.
Arc 1076.3.47 Verband Deutscher Vereine für Volkskunde. Bericht über die Sammlung der Glockensprüche, Glockensagen und Glockenbräuche. Freiburg, 1918.
Arc 1076.3.48 Metzger, O.H. Die Glocken im Friedländischen. Friedland, 1912.
Arc 1076.3.49 Haas, A. Glockensagen im pommerschen Volksmunde. Stettin, 1919.
Arc 1076.3.50 Pamphlet box. Bells. Miscellaneous pamphlets.
Arc 1076.3.52 Ephemeris campanographica. Montpellier.
Arc 1076.3.53 L'Estrange, John. The church bells of Norfolk. Norwich, 1874.
Arc 1076.3.55 Raven, John J. The church bells of Suffolk. London, 1890.
Arc 1076.3.60 Tyssen, A.D. The church bells of Sussex. Lewes, 1915.
Arc 1076.3.65 North, Thomas. The church bells of Rutland. Leicester, 1880.
Arc 1076.3.67F Lyman, Charles. The church bells of the county of Stafford. London, 1889.
Arc 1076.3.70 Cocks, A.H. The church bells of Buckinghamshire. London, 1897.
Arc 1076.3.75 Tilley, H.T. The church bells of Warwickshire. Birmingham, 1910.
Arc 1076.3.77F Ellacombe, H.T. Bells of the church. Exeter, 1872.
Arc 1076.3.78 Ellacombe, H.T. The church bells of Somerset. Exeter, 1875.
Arc 1076.3.79F Ellacombe, H.T. The church bells of Gloucestershire. Exeter, 1881.
Arc 1076.3.85 Jadart, Henri. Le Bourdon de Notre-Dame de Reims. Reims, 1884.
Arc 1076.3.89 Edel, Friederich W. Von den Glocken. pt.1-2. Strassburg, 1862-63.
Arc 1076.3.90 Fehrmann, Christiaan Nathanaël. De Kamper klokgieters. Kampen, 1967.
Arc 1076.3.93 Nichols, J.R. Bells thro' the ages. London, 1928.
Arc 1076.3.95 Coleman, Satis N. (Barton). Bells; their history, legends, making, and uses. Chicago, 1928.
Arc 1076.3.97 Briscoe, J.P. Curiosities of the belfry. London, 1883.
Arc 1076.3.99 Andrews, H.C. A Hertfordshire worthy, John Briant. St. Albans, 1930.
Arc 1076.3.103 Staercke, Alphonse E. de. Cloches et carillons. Bruxelles, 1947.
Arc 1076.3.105 Morris, E. Legends o' the bells. London, 1935.
Htn Arc 1076.3.110* Rocca, Angelo. De campanis commentarius. Romae, 1612.
Arc 1076.3.115 Walter, Karl. Glockenkunde. Regensburg, 1913.
Arc 1076.3.120 Glade, Heinz. Erdentiefe-Turmeshöhe; von Glocken und Glockengiessern. Berlin, 1965.
Arc 1076.4 Morse, E.S. On the so-called bow puller of antiquity. Salem, 1894.
Arc 1076.4.5 Kuuliala, Vilji K. Kellot temppelin. Sortavala, 1943.
Arc 1076.4.10 Rausing, Gad. The bow; some notes on its origin and development. Bonn, 1967.
Arc 1076.8 Kybalová, L. Pražské zvony. Praha, 1958.
Arc 1076.10 Grundmann, Günther. Deutschen Glockenatlas. München, 1959- 3v.
Arc 1076.12 Gribsoe, Erland. Frederiksborg amts kirkekloffer. Hillerød, 1934.
Arc 1076.14 Weidenbaeck, A. Tönendes Erz. Graz, 1961.
Arc 1076.16 Heuven, Englebert W. van. Accoustical measurements on church-bells and carillons. 's-Gravenhage, 1949.
Arc 1076.20 Potratz, Johannes Albert Heinrich. Die Pferdetrensen des alten Orient. Roma, 1966.
Arc 1076.21 Avent, Richard. Anglo-Saxon garnet inlaid and composite brooches. v.1-2. Oxford, 1975.
Arc 1076.22 Brensztejn, Michał E. Zarys dziejów lvdwisarstwa na ziemiach b. Wielkiego Księstwa Litewskiego. Wilno, 1924.
Arc 1076.23 Spiritza, Juraj. Spišské zvony. Vyd. 1. Bratislava, 1972.
Arc 1076.24 Pukhnachev, Iurii V. Zagadki zvuchashchego metalla. Moskva, 1974.
Arc 1077.1 Much, M. Die Kupferzeit in Europa. Jena, 1893.
Arc 1077.1.9 Moore, C.B. Sheet-copper from the mounds. Washington, 1903.
Htn Arc 1077.2* Lipsius, J. De cruce libri tres. Antverpiae, 1594.
Htn Arc 1077.2.1* Lipsius, J. De cruce libri tres...cum notis. 3. ed. Antverpiae, 1597.
Htn Arc 1077.2.2* Lipsius, J. De cruce libri tres. Parisiis, 1598.
Arc 1077.2.3 Mortillet, G. de. Le signe de la croix avant de Christianité. Paris, 1866.
Arc 1077.2.5 Seymour, W.W. The cross. N.Y., 1898.
Arc 1077.2.9 Brunet y Bellet, J. La creu els monuments megalitics. Barcelona, 1892.

Classified Listing

Arc 1075 - 1099 Archaeology - Other special topics - Monographs (A-Z by topic) - cont.

Arc 1077.2.13 Cavedoni, C. Di tre antiche stauroteche...cattedrale di Modena. Modena, 1847.
Arc 1077.2.21 Strazzulla, V. Indagini archeologiche del "Signum Christi". Palermo, 1899.
Arc 1077.2.23 Calfhill, J. An answer to John Martiall's Treatise of the cross. Cambridge, Eng., 1846.
Htn Arc 1077.2.25* Gori, A.F. Crux dominica adorabile christianae religionis vexillum observationibus. Florentiae, 1749.
Arc 1077.2.28 Cutts, E.L. Manuel...sepulchral slabs and crosses of the Middle Ages. London, 1849.
Arc 1077.2.30 Stockbauer, J. Kunstgeschichte des Kreuzes. Schaffhausen, 1870.
Arc 1077.2.33 Tyack, G.S. The cross in ritual architecture and art. 2. ed. London, 1900.
Arc 1077.2.35 Bunsen, E. von. Das Symbol des Kreuzes. Berlin, 1876.
Arc 1077.2.39F Gudiol y Cunill, José. Les creus d'Argenteria a Catalunya. Barcelona, 1920.
Arc 1077.2.41 Rapp, Edward. Das Labarum und der Sonnen-Cultus. Bonn, 1865.
Arc 1077.2.42 Bergmann, Alois. Die Schmiedkreuze Westböhmens. Elbogen, 1926.
Arc 1077.2.43 Benson, G.W. The cross, its history and symbolism. Buffalo, 1934.
Arc 1077.2.44 Cecchelli, Carlo. Il trionfo della croce. Roma, 1954.
Arc 1077.2.45 Chauncey Ross, M. La croix Gaillard de la Dionnerie au Musée metropolitan. Poitiers, 1934.
Arc 1077.2.46F King, E.S. The date and provenance of a bronze reliquary cross in the Museo Cristiano. Rome, 1928.
Arc 1077.2.47 Guénon, René. Le symbolisme de la croix. Paris, 1931.
Arc 1077.2.47.2 Guénon, René. Le symbolisme de la croix. Paris, 1970.
Arc 1077.2.49 Müller, Ludvig. Det saakaldte Hagekors's Anvendelse og Betydning i Aldtiden. København, 1877.
Arc 1077.2.51 Miller, M. (Sweeney). My hobby of the cross. N.Y., 1939.
Arc 1077.2.53.2 Baus, Karl. Der Kranz in Antike und Christentum. Bonn, 1965.
Arc 1077.2.60 Foerster, Else. Das irische Hochkreuz. Inaug. Diss. München, 1965.
Arc 1077.2.65 Füglister, Robert L. Das Lebende Kreuz. Einsiedeln, 1964.
Arc 1077.3 Reinaud, J. Rapport sur la chape arabe de Chinon. Paris, 1856.
Arc 1077.3.2 Cavallari, S. Lettre sur la chape arabe de Chinon. Paris, 1857.
Arc 1077.4 Archaic rock inscriptions...cup and ring markings. London, 1891.
Arc 1077.5 Johns, C.H.W. Ur-Engur. Treatise on canephorous statues. N.Y., 1908.
Arc 1077.6 Nelson, E.M. The cult of the circle-builders. London, 1909.
Arc 1077.7 Mercklin, E. von. Der Rennwagen in Griechenland. Leipzig, 1909.
Arc 1077.7.5 Nachod, H. Der Rennwagen bei ben Italikern. Leipzig, 1909.
Arc 1077.10 Thoby, Paul. Le crucifix. Nantes, 1959.
Arc 1077.10.2 Thoby, Paul. Le crucifix. Supplément. Nantes, 1963.
Arc 1077.12 Brockpaehler,W. Steinkreuze in Westfalen. Münster, 1963.
Arc 1077.13 Stjernqvist, Berta. Cesta a cordoni (Rippenzisten); Produktion-Funktion-Diffusion. v.1-2. Bonn, 1967.
Arc 1078.1 Wieseler, F. Das Diptychon Quirinianum zu Brescia. Göttingen, 1868.
Arc 1078.3 Niel, Fernand. Dolmens et menhirs. 3. éd. Paris, 1966.
Arc 1079.2 Hardaker, Ron. A corpus of early Bronze Age dagger pommels from Great Britain and Ireland. Oxford, 1974.
Arc 1080.5 Sundwall, J. Die älteren italischen Fibeln. Berlin, 1943.
Arc 1080.10F Deutsches Archäologisches Institut. Die langobardischen Fibeln aus Italien. Berlin, 1950.
Arc 1081.1 Jewett, L. Grave mounds and their contents. London, 1870.
Arc 1081.1.5 Duhn, F. von. Ein Rückblick auf die Gräberforschung. Heidelberg, 1911.
Arc 1082.5F Steensberg, Axel. Ancient harvesting implements. København, 1943.
Arc 1082.10 Lethbridge, T.C. Gogmagog. London, 1957.
Arc 1082.15 Verbrugge, A.R. Le symbole de la main. Courauces, 1958.
Arc 1083.1 Undset, I. Das erste Auftreten des Eisens in Nord-Europa. Hamburg, 1882.
Arc 1083.2 Wigand, Karl. Thymiateria. Inaug. Diss. Bonn, 1912.
Arc 1084.1 Kunz, G.F. H.R. Bishop and his jade collection. Lancaster, 1903.
Htn Arc 1084.3PF* New York (City). Metropolitan Museum of Art. The Bishop collections. N.Y., 1906. 2v.
Arc 1084.5 Getz, John. The Woodward collection of jades and other hard stones. n.p., 1913.
Arc 1084.7 Alexander, R. Jade; its philosophy. N.Y., 1928.
Arc 1084.10 Pope-Hennessy, U. (Mrs.). Early Chinese jades. London, 1923.
Arc 1084.12 Field Museum of Natural History, Chicago. Archaic Chinese jades collections in China. N.Y., 1927.
Arc 1084.15F Wu, Henry H. Ancient Chinese jade. n.p., 1933.
Arc 1084.17F Nott, S.C. Chinese jades in the S.C. Nott collection. St. Augustine, 1942.
Arc 1084.19 Goette, J.A. Jade lore. N.Y., 1937.
Arc 1086.1 Hartmann, A. Zur Hochächerfrage. München, 1876.
Arc 1086.2 Bachofen, J.J. Römische Grablampen. Basel, 1890.
Arc 1086.2.9F Bartoli, Pietro. Veterum lucernae sepulcrales. Lugduni Batavorum, 1723. 2 pam.
Arc 1086.5 Coimbra. Museu Machado de Castro. Catálogo de lucernas romanas. Coimbra, 1952.
Arc 1086.10 Hula, Franz. Mittelalterliche Kultmale. Wien, 1970.
Arc 1087.1 Garofalo, Biagio. De antiquis marmoribus opusculum. Ad Rhenum, 1743.
Arc 1087.1.2 Garofalo, Biagio. De antiquis marmoribus. 2. ed. Oxonii, 1828.
Arc 1087.2 Engelmann, R. Die antiken Mühlen. Berlin, 1904.
Arc 1087.3 Kugnezow, S. Die Sepulkralmasken, ihre Gebrauch und Bedeutung. Kasan, 1906.
Arc 1087.4F Benndorf, Otto. Antike Gesichtshelme und Sepulcralmasken. Wien, 1878.
Arc 1087.5 Chernykh, Evgenii N. Metall-chelovsk-vremia. Moskva, 1972.
Arc 1088.1 Breusing, A. Die Nautik der Alten. Bremen, 1886.
Arc 1088.1.2 Graser, B. Untersuchungen und das Seewesen des Alterthums. Göttingen, 1867.
Arc 1088.1.3 Graser, B. De veterum re navali. Berolini, 1864.
Arc 1088.1.4 Graser, B. De veterum trirenium fabrica. Berolini, 1864.
Arc 1088.1.5 Weber, L. Die Lösung der Frierenrätsels. Danzig, 1896.
Arc 1088.1.6 Jal, A. Archéologie navale. Paris, 1840. 2v.
Arc 1088.1.7 Torr, Cecil. Ancient ships. Chicago, 1964.

Arc 1075 - 1099 Archaeology - Other special topics - Monographs (A-Z by topic) - cont.

Arc 1088.1.8 Torr, Cecil. Ancient ships. Cambridge, 1894.
Arc 1088.1.9A Torr, Cecil. Ancient ships. Cambridge, 1895.
Arc 1088.1.9B Torr, Cecil. Ancient ships. Cambridge, 1895.
NEDL Arc 1088.1.10 Vars, J. L'art nautique dans l'antiquité. Paris, 1887.
Arc 1088.1.11 Casson, Lionel. Ships and seamanship in the ancient world. Princeton, N.J., 1971.
Arc 1088.1.15 Stahlecker, R. Über die verrchiedenen Versuche der Rekonstruktion. Ravensburg, 1897.
Arc 1088.1.17 Serre, Paul. Les marines de guerre. Paris, 1885.
Arc 1088.1.19 Malfatti, V. Le navi romane del lago di Nemi. Roma, 1896.
Arc 1088.1.20F Maes, Constantino. La nave di Tiberio sommersa nel lago di Nemi. Roma, 1895. 2 pam.
Arc 1088.1.20.5 Maes, Constantino. Trionfo navale ovvero prassima estrazione. Roma, 1899.
Arc 1088.1.21 Levi, C.A. Navi venete. Venezia, 1892.
Arc 1088.1.23 Boisacq, E. La trière antique et la guerre navale. Bruxelles, 1905.
Arc 1088.1.25 Köster, August. Das antike Seewesen. 1. Aufl. Berlin, 1923.
Arc 1088.4 Mariani, Lucilla. Le nave di Nemi nella bibliografia. Roma, 1942.
Arc 1088.5 Dionisi, Francesco. Le navi sacre di Claudio nel lago di Nemi. Roma, 1956.
Arc 1088.7F Ucelli, Guido. Le navi di Nemi. 2. ed. Roma, 1950.
Arc 1090.1 Behlen, H. Der Pflug und der Pflügen. Dillenburg, 1904.
Arc 1090.5A New York (City). Museum of Modern Art. Prehistoric rock pictures in Europe and Africa. N.Y., 1937.
Arc 1090.5B New York (City). Museum of Modern Art. Prehistoric rock pictures in Europe and Africa. N.Y., 1937.
Arc 1090.6F Oswald, Adrian. Clay pipes for the archaeologists. Oxford, 1975.
Arc 1092.1 Longpérier, H. Note sur les rouelles antiques de bronze. Paris, 1867.
Arc 1092.1.2 Longpérier, H. Des rouelles et des anneaux antiques. Paris, 1867.
Htn Arc 1093.1* Chimentelli, V. Marmor pisanum. Bononiae, 1666.
Arc 1093.2 Fergusson, J. Rude stone monuments. London, 1872.
Arc 1093.2.2 Petit-Radel, L.C.F. Recherches sur les monuments cyclopéens. Paris, 1841.
Arc 1093.2.3 Frederik VII, king of Denmark. Sur la construction des ralles dites des géants. Copenhague, 1857.
Arc 1093.2.3.5 Frederik VII, king of Denmark. Om bygningsmaaden af oldtidens jaettestuer. 2. udg. København, 1862.
Arc 1093.2.3.7 Frederik VII, king of Denmark. Über den Bau des Riesenbetten der Vorzeit. Kopenhagen, 1863.
Arc 1093.2.4 McGuire, J.D. The stone hammer and its various uses. Washington, 1891.
Arc 1093.2.5 Clodd, E. The later stone age in Europe. London, 1880.
Arc 1093.2.6 Baye, J. de. Les instruments en pierre à l'epoque de métaux. Paris, 1881.
Arc 1093.2.8 Wilke, Georg. Südwesteuropäische Megalithkultur. Würzburg, 1912.
Arc 1093.2.9F Peigne-Delacourt, M. Un tranche-tête. Paris, 1866.
Arc 1093.2.11 Baudon, T. Des silex perforés naturellement. Paris, 1909.
Arc 1093.2.13 Paniagua, A. Les monuments mégalithiques. Paris, 1912.
Arc 1093.2.15 Menghin, O. Weltgeschichte der Steinzeit. Wien, 1931.
Arc 1093.2.17 Pei Wen Chung. Le rôle des phénomènes naturels dans l'éclatement. Thèse. Paris, 1936.
Arc 1093.2.19 Brjussow, A. Geschichte der neolithischen Stämme im europäischen Teil der Ud SSR. Berlin, 1957.
Arc 1093.2.30 Cles-Reden, Sibylle. The realm of the great goddess; the story of the megalith builders. London, 1961.
Arc 1093.2.35 Hirsch, Friedrich. Der Sonnwendbogen. Lahr, 1965.
Arc 1093.2.40 Bar, Henry. Les pierres levées. Paris, 1973.
Htn Arc 1093.3* Martini, G.H. Abhandlung von den Sonnenuhren der Alten. Leipzig, 1877.
Arc 1093.4 Altmann, W. Architectur und Ornamentik der antiken Sarkophage. Berlin, 1902.
Arc 1093.5 Redslob, E. Die fränkischen Epitaphen im 4. und 5. Jahrhundert. Inaug. Diss. Nürnberg, 1907.
Arc 1093.6 Wilson, Thomas. The swastika, the earliest known symbol. Washington, 1896.
Arc 1093.6.5 Murray-Aynsley, L.H.G.M. The swastika. Margate, 1891.
Arc 1093.6.9 Doering, J.F. The swastika. Kitchner, Ontario, 1936.
Arc 1093.6.12 Paegle, Eduard. Salktis, Progenitor der Svastika. Würzburg, 1957.
Arc 1093.6.15 Wilser, L. Das Hakenkreuz nach Ursprung, Vorkommen und Bedeutung. 5. Aufl. Leipzig, 1922.
Arc 1093.6.18 Scheuermann, W. Woher kommt das Hakenkreuz? Berlin, 1933.
Arc 1093.6.20 Lecher, Jörg. Vom Hakenkreuz. Leipzig, 1921.
Arc 1093.6.22 Lecher, Jörg. Vom Hakenkreuz. 2. Aufl. Leipzig, 1934.
Arc 1093.7.2 Koch, Rudolf. Das Zeichenbuch. 2. Aufl. Offenbach am Main, 1926.
Arc 1093.8 Müfid, Arif. Katalog der Bleisarkophage. Istanbul, 1932.
Arc 1093.9 Sankalia, Hasmukh Dhirajlal. Stone age tools. 1. ed. Poona, 1964.
Arc 1093.11 Hald, Margrethe. Primitive shoes. København, 1972.
Arc 1096.1 Scheffer, J. De re vehiculari veterum libri duo. Francofurti, 1671.
Arc 1096.2 Krause, J.H. Angeiologie. Halle, 1854.
Arc 1097.5 Waals, Johannes D. van der. Prehistoric disc wheels in the Netherlands. Proefschrift. Groningen, 1964.

Arc 1125 Palaeography - Periodicals and Society publications

Arc 1125.3 Archivalische Zeitschrift. Stuttgart. 1876+ 47v.
Arc 1125.3.10 Archivalische Zeitschrift. Beiheft. Stuttgart. 1-4,1925-1932 4v.
Arc 1125.5 Archiv für Urkundenforschung. Leipzig. 1-18,1907-1944 14v.
Arc 1125.10 Scriptorium; international review of manuscript studies. Bruxelles. 1,1946+ 35v.
Arc 1125.11 Bulletin codiocologique; bibliographie courante des études relatives aux manuscrits. Bruxelles. 1959-1960
Arc 1125.28PF Ireland. Manuscripts Commission. Facsimiles in collotype of Irish manuscripts. Dublin. 1-6,1931-1954 6v.
Arc 1125.30 Cairo, Egypt. Ayn Shams University. Ibrahim University studies in papyrology.
Arc 1125.35 The Edwards lectures. Glasgow. 2,1966+
Arc 1125.40 Zeitschrift für Papyrologie und Epigraphik. Bonn. 1,1967+ 7v.
Arc 1125.42 Tabulae palaeographicae. Amsterdam. 1,1968+

Classified Listing

Arc 1130 Palaeography - Bibliographies

Arc 1130.5 Moore, Margaret F. Two select bibliographies mediaeval historical study. London, 1912.
Arc 1130.10 Cairo, Egypt. National Library. A bibliography of works about papyrology. Cairo, 1960.
Arc 1130.15F London. University. Library. The palaeography collection. Boston, 1968. 2v.

Arc 1135 Palaeography - Folios [Discontinued]

Arc 1135.200.5 Papyrus Erzherzog Rainer; Führer...Ausstellung. Wien, 1894.
Arc 1135.201.2 Berlin. Staatliche Museum. Aegyptische Urkunden. Koptische Urkunden. Berlin. 1,1904+ 3v.
Arc 1135.201.3 Berlin. Staatliche Museum. Aegyptische Urkunden. Arabische Urkunden. Berlin. 1896-1900//
Arc 1135.202 Prou, Maurice. Recueil de facsimiles d'écritures du XIIe au XVIIe siècle. Paris, 1892.
Arc 1135.202.5 Prou, Maurice. Recueil de facsimiles d'écritures du XIIe au XVIIe siècle. Paris, 1896.
Arc 1135.206FA Prou, Maurice. Manuel de paléographie. Paris, 1904.
Arc 1135.206FB Prou, Maurice. Manuel de paléographie. Paris, 1904.
Arc 1135.206FC Prou, Maurice. Manuel de paléographie. Paris, 1904.
Htn Arc 1135.209* Spicilegium palimpsestorum. Bevronae, 1913.

Arc 1138 Palaeography - General works

Arc 1138.1 Thoyts, E.E. How to decipher and study old documents. London, 1893.
Arc 1138.3 Grand, E. Daniel. Leçon d'ouverture du cours de paléographie. Montpellier, 1890.
Arc 1138.4.4A Prou, Maurice. Manuel de paléographie latine et française. 3. éd. Paris, 1910.
Arc 1138.4.4B Prou, Maurice. Manuel de paléographie latine et française. 3. éd. Paris, 1910.
Arc 1138.4.5 Prou, Maurice. Manuel de paléographie latine et française avec atlas. 4. éd. Paris, 1924. 2v.
Arc 1138.5 Chassant, Alphonse. Paléographie des chartes. 7. éd. Paris, 1876.
Arc 1138.5.2 Chassant, Alphonse. Paléographie des chartes. 8. éd. Paris, 1885.
Arc 1138.5.3 Chassant, Alphonse. Paléographie des chartes. 5. éd. Paris, 1862.
Arc 1138.5.4 Chassant, Alphonse. Paléographie des chartes. 4. éd. Paris, 1854.
Arc 1138.6 Gloria, A. Compendio delle lezioni teorico-pratiche di paleografia e diplomatica. Padova, 1870.
Arc 1138.6F Gloria, A. Compendio delle lezioni teorico-pratiche di paleografia e diplomatica. Atlas. Padova, 1870.
Arc 1138.7 Silvestre, J.B. Universal palaeography. London, 1850. 2v.
Arc 1138.8 Pfeiffer, A.F. Ueber Buecher-Handschriften. Erlangen, 1810.
Arc 1138.9 Kopp, U.F. Palaeographia critica. Mannheim, 1817-29. 4v.
Arc 1138.13 Gautier, Léon. Quelques mots sur l'étude de la paléographie. Paris, 1864.
Arc 1138.15 Madan, F. Books in manuscript. London, 1893.
Arc 1138.17 Ebert, F.A. Zur Handschriftenkunde. v.1-2. Leipzig, 1825.
Arc 1138.18 Astle, Thomas. Origin and progress of writing. London, 1803.
Arc 1138.19 Sinks, Perry W. The reign of the manuscript. Boston, 1917.
Arc 1138.23 Kantorowicz, Hermann. Einführung in die Textkritik. Leipzig, 1921.
Arc 1138.25 Bauckner, A. Einführung in das mittelalterliche Schriftum. München, 1923.
Arc 1138.27.5 Natale, Alfio Rosario. Ludwig Traube e la nuova metodologia paleografica. Milano, 1957.
Arc 1138.28 Greg, Walter W. The calculus of variants, an essay on textual criticism. Oxford, 1927.
Arc 1138.29 Quentin, Henri. Essais de critique textuelle. Paris, 1926.
Arc 1138.30 Coellen, Ludwig. Die Stilentwicklung der Schrift im christlichen Abendlande. Darmstadt, 1922.
Arc 1138.32 Löffler, Karl. Einführung in die Handschriftenkunde. Leipzig, 1929.
Arc 1138.33 Collomp, Paul. La critique des textes. Paris, 1931.
Arc 1138.36 Stieg, Lewis. An introduction to palaeography for librarians. Chicago, 1938.
Arc 1138.37 Dobiaš-Rozhdestvenskaia, O.A. Istoriia pis'ma v srednie veka. Moskva, 1936.
Arc 1138.40 Scritti di paleografia e diplomatica in onore de Vincenzo Federici. Firenze, 1944.
Arc 1138.50 Berlin. Staatliche Museen. Zur Einführung in die Papyrusausstellung. Berlin, 1908.
Arc 1138.55 Dain, A. Les manuscrits. Paris, 1949.
Arc 1138.55.2 Dain, A. Les manuscrits. Paris, 1964.
Arc 1138.60 Floriano, A.C. Curso general de paleografia y diplomatica españolas. v.1-2. Oviedo, 1946.
Arc 1138.65 Friedrich, Johannes. Entzifferung verschollener Schriften und Sprachen. Berlin, 1954.
Arc 1138.65.2 Friedrich, Johannes. Entzifferung verschollener Schriften und Sprachen. 2. Aufl. Berlin, 1966.
Arc 1138.65.5 Friedrich, Johannes. Extinct languages. N.Y., 1957.
Arc 1138.70 Raalte, James van. De schrijfkunst in de Bijbellanden. Baarn, 1955.
Arc 1138.75 Doblhofer, Ernst. Zeichen und Wunder. Wien, 1957.
Arc 1138.75.5 Doblhofer, Ernst. Voices in stone. N.Y., 1961.
Arc 1138.80.6 Hector, Leonard Charles. The handwriting of English documents. 2. ed. London, 1966.
Arc 1138.85 Navascués y de Juan, Joaquin Maria de. El concepto de la epigrafia consideraciones sobre la necesidad de su ampliación. Madrid, 1953.
Arc 1138.90 Velazquez de Velasco, L.J. Ensayo sobre los alphabetos de las letras des conocidas. Madrid, 1952.
Arc 1138.100 Cleator, Philip. Lost languages. London, 1959.
Arc 1138.105F Strubbe, Egied I. Groudbegrippen van de paleografie. 3. druk. Gent, 1961. 2v.
Arc 1138.108F Awad, G. Report in search of the condition of manuscripts in Egypt. n.p., 1957?
Arc 1138.110 Ekschmitt, Werner. Das Gedächtnis der Völker. Berlin, 1964.
Arc 1138.112.2 Brouwer, Hans. Geschreven verleden. 2. druk. 's-Gravenhage, 1963.
Arc 1138.115 Gordon, Cyrus Herzl. Forgotten scripts. N.Y., 1968.
Arc 1138.115.2 Gordon, Cyrus Herzl. Forgotten scripts. Harmondsworth, 1971.
Arc 1138.120 Kondratov, Aleksandr Mikhailovich. Kogda molchat pis'mena. Moskva, 1970.

Arc 1138 Palaeography - General works - cont.

Arc 1138.121 König, Marie E.P. Am Anfang der Kultur. Berlin, 1973.
Arc 1138.122 Lowe, Elias Avery. Handwriting. Our medieval legacy. Rome, 1969.
Arc 1138.122.5 Lowe, Elias Avery. Palaeographical papers, 1907-1965. Oxford, 1972. 2v.
Arc 1138.123 Cope, Emma Elizabeth T. How to decipher and study old documents. Chicago, 1974.
Arc 1138.124 Stipišić, Jakov. Pomoćne povijesne znanosti u teoriji i praksi. Zagreb, 1972.
Arc 1138.125 Millares Carlo, Agustín. Consideraciones sobre la escritura visigótica cursiva. León, 1973.
Arc 1138.126 Epigrafika Vostochnoi i Iuzhnoi Azii. Moskva, 1972.
Arc 1138.127 Sparrow, John. Visible words. London, 1969.
Arc 1138.128 Problemy paleografii i kodikologii v SSSR. Moskva, 1974.
Arc 1138.129 Polák, Stanislav. Studium novověkého písma. Příbram, 1973.
Arc 1138.130 Norman, James. Ancestral voices. N.Y., 1975.

Arc 1143 Palaeography - Greek and Latin together - General works

Arc 1143.1 Mone, F. De libris palimpsestis. Carlsruhae, 1855.
Arc 1143.2 Thompson, Edward Maunde. Handbook of Greek and Latin palaeography. N.Y., 1893.
Arc 1143.2.3 Thompson, Edward Maunde. Handbook of Greek and Latin palaeography. Ann Arbor, 1973.
Arc 1143.2.5A Thompson, Edward Maunde. Introduction to Greek and Latin palaeography. Oxford, 1912.
Arc 1143.2.5B Thompson, Edward Maunde. Introduction to Greek and Latin palaeography. Oxford, 1912.
Arc 1143.2.5C Thompson, Edward Maunde. Introduction to Greek and Latin palaeography. Oxford, 1912.
Arc 1143.2.7 Thompson, Edward Maunde. Paleografia greca e latina. Milano, 1899.
Arc 1143.2.11 Thompson, Edward Maunde. Hencheiridion Hellēnikēs. Athēnai, 1903.
Arc 1143.3.2 Wattenbach, W. Schriftwesen im Mittelalter. 2. Aufl. Leipzig, 1875.
Arc 1143.3.4 Wattenbach, W. Das Schriftwesen in Mittelalter. 4. Aufl. Graz, 1958.
Arc 1143.4.1 Birt, Theodor. Das antike Buchwesen in seinem Verhältnis zur Literatur. Aalen, 1974.
Arc 1143.4.5 Birt, Theodor. Die Buchrolle in der Kunst. Leipzig, 1907.
Arc 1143.9 Schwarz, M.C.G. Ornamentis librorum apud veteres usitatis. v.1-3. Lipsiae, 1705-
Htn Arc 1143.9.5* Schwarz, M.C.G. Ornamentis librorum. Lipsiae, 1756.
Arc 1143.10 Dziatzko, K. Untersuchungen...antiken Buchwesens. Leipzig, 1900.
Arc 1143.12 Hanger, H. Studien zur griechischen Paläographie. Wien, 1954.
Arc 1143.14F Bassi, Stelio. Monumenta Italiae graphica. Cremona, 1956-57.

Arc 1145 Palaeography - Greek - Folios [Discontinued]

Arc 1145.1 Graux, C. Facsimiles de manuscrits grecs d'Espagne. Paris, 1897. 2v.
Arc 1145.3 Omont, H. Facsimiles des manuscrits grecs datés de la Bibliothèque Nationale. Paris, 1891.
Arc 1145.206 Hodgkin, J. Calligraphia Graeca et poecilographia Graeca. Londini, 1794.
Arc 1145.207 Steffens, Franz. Proben aus griechischen Handscriften und Urkunden. Trier, 1912.

Arc 1148 Palaeography - Greek - General works

Arc 1148.1.5 Allen, T.W. Greek abbreviation in the 15th century. London, n.d.
Arc 1148.2 Lehmann, O. Die Tachygraphischen Abkürzungen der griechischen Handschriften. Leipzig, 1880.
Arc 1148.4 Gomperz, T. Ueber eine bisher Unbekanntes griechisches Schriftsystem. Wien, 1884.
NEDL Arc 1148.5 Gardthausen, V. Griechische Palaeographie. v.1-2. Leipzig, 1879.
Arc 1148.5.2 Gardthausen, V. Griechische Palaeographie. 2. Aufl. Leipzig, 1911. 2v.
Arc 1148.5.5 Gardthausen, V. Geschichte der griechischen Tachygraphie. Berlin, 1906.
Arc 1148.12 Gitlbauer, M. Studien zur griechischen Tachygraphie. Berlin, 1903.
Arc 1148.13 Mentz, A. Geschichte...der griechischen Tachygraphie. Berlin, 1907.
Arc 1148.14 Franchi de' Cavalieri, P. Specimina codicum graecorum vaticanorum. Bonniae, 1910.
Arc 1148.14.5 Franchi de' Cavalieri, P. Specimina codicum graecorum vaticanorum. Berolini, 1929.
Arc 1148.16 Amphilochii, A. Snimki ne" Kondakaria XII-XIII. Moskva, 1869.
Arc 1148.17 Sreznevskii, I.I. Paleograficheskiia navliudeniia. v.1-2. Sankt Peterburg, 1876.
Arc 1148.19 Engelhes, W. Het Griehsche boek in voor. Amsterdam, 1926.
Arc 1148.20 Groningen, B.A. Short manual of Greek palaeography. Leiden, 1940.
Arc 1148.20.2 Groningen, B.A. Short manual of Greek palaeography. 2. ed. Leiden, 1955.
Arc 1148.20.3 Groningen, B.A. Short manual of Greek palaeography. 3. ed. Leyden, 1963.
Arc 1148.22 Breccia, E. Note epigrafiche. Alexandria, 1931.
Arc 1148.25 Bataille, A. Pour une terminologie in paléographie grecque. Paris, 1954.
Arc 1148.25.5 Bataille, A. Les papyrus. 1. éd. Paris, 1955.
Arc 1148.27 Rémondon, R. Papyrus grecs d'Apollônos anô. Le Caire, 1953.
Arc 1148.28F Wittek, Martin. Album de paléographie grecque. Gand, 1967.
Arc 1148.30 Roberts, C.H. Greek literary hands. Oxford, 1955.
Arc 1148.32 Plagiannēs, D.I. Byzantinoi sēmeiographoi. Athēnia, 1940.
Arc 1148.33 Sarros, D.M. Palaiographikos eranos. Konstantinoypolei, 1914.
Arc 1148.34 Polites, L.N. Ōdēgos katalogoy cheirographōn. Athēnia, 1961.
Arc 1148.35 Boge, Herbert. Griechische Tachygraphie und tironische Noten. Hildesheim, 1974.
Arc 1148.36 Turner, Eric Gardiner. Greek manuscripts of the ancient world. Oxford, 1971.
Arc 1148.37 Rainò, Beniamino. Giovanni Onorio da Maglie, trascrittore di codici greci. Bari, 1972.
Arc 1148.38 Mioni, Elpidio. Introduzione alla paleografia greca. Padova, 1973.

Arc 1150 Palaeography - Latin - Folios [Discontinued]

Arc 1150.1.9 Mélanges offert à M. Émile Chatelain. Paris, 1910.
Arc 1150.14 Staerk, Antonio. Monuments de l'abbaye celtique. Tournai, 1914.
Arc 1150.202 Schmitz, W. Commentarii notarum tironianarum. Lipsiae, 1893. 2v.
Arc 1150.203 Schmitz, W. Monumenta tachygraphica codicus parisienis Latini. Hannoverae, 1882.
Arc 1150.208 Delisle, L. Notice sur un manuscript Mérovingun. Paris, 1875.
Arc 1150.208.5 Delisle, L. Notice sur un manuscript Mérovingun. Paris, 1878.
Arc 1150.208.9F Delisle, L. L'evangeliaire de Saint-Vaast d'Arras. Paris, 1888.

Arc 1153 Palaeography - Latin - General works

Arc 1153.1 Delisle, L. Forme des abréviations et des liaisons dans les lettres des papes. Paris, 1887.
Arc 1153.1.5 Delisle, L. Mémoire sur l'école calligraphique de Tours au IXe siècle. Paris, 1885.
Arc 1153.2 Paoli, Cesare. Programma scolastico di paleografia latina. Firenze, 1888.
Arc 1153.2.2 Paoli, Cesare. Programma scolastico di paleografia latina. 3. ed. Firenze, 1901.
Arc 1153.2.3 Paoli, Cesare. Grundriss der lateinischen Palaeographie und der Urkundenlehre. Innsbruck, 1885.
Arc 1153.2.5 Paoli, Cesare. Le abbreviatore nella paleografia latina del Medio Evo. Firenze, 1891.
Arc 1153.2.9 Paoli, Cesare. Grundriss - lateinische Palaeographie. Innsbruck, 1889-95.
Arc 1153.2.15 Paoli, Cesare. Grundriss - lateinische Palaeographie. Innsbruck, 1902.
Arc 1153.4.5 Breidenbach, H. Zwei Abhandlungen...tironischen Noten. Darmstadt, 1900.
Arc 1153.4.7 Traube, L. Die Geschichte der tironischen Noten. Berlin, 1901.
Arc 1153.4.23 Wikenhauser, A. Der heilige Cassian. Berlin, 1906.
Arc 1153.4.25 Molina, E. Grammatica tironiana. Padova, 1933.
Arc 1153.5 Massmann, H.P. Libellus aurarius sivi tabulae ceratae. Lipsaie, 1840.
Arc 1153.6 Muñoz y Rivero, J. Paleografía visigoda. Madrid, 1881.
Arc 1153.6.5 Muñoz y Rivero, J. Paleografía visigoda. Madrid, 1919.
Arc 1153.7 Wattenbach, W. Anleitung zur lateinischen Palaeographie. Leipzig, 1869.
Arc 1153.7.4 Wattenbach, W. Anleitung zur lateinischen Palaeographie. 4. Aufl. Leipzig, 1886.
Arc 1153.8.5 Lindsay, W.M. Contractions in early Latin miniscule MSS. Oxford, 1908.
Arc 1153.8.7A Lindsay, W.M. Notae Latinae...abbreviation in Latin MSS...miniscule period. Cambridge, 1915.
Arc 1153.8.7B Lindsay, W.M. Notae Latinae...abbreviation in Latin MSS...miniscule period. Cambridge, 1915.
Arc 1153.9 Vries, S.G. de. Boethii fragmentum notis Tironianis descript. Lugduni Batavorum, 1893.
Arc 1153.11 Lupi, C. Manuale di paleografia delle carte. Firenze, 1875.
Arc 1153.12 Cappelli, A. Dizionario di abbreviature latine ed italiane. Milano, 1899.
Arc 1153.12.3 Cappelli, A. Lexicon abbreviaturarum. Leipzig, 1901.
Arc 1153.12.10A Cappelli, A. Lexicon abbreviaturarum. 2. Aufl. Leipzig, 1928.
Arc 1153.12.10B Cappelli, A. Lexicon abbreviaturarum. 2. Aufl. Leipzig, 1928.
Arc 1153.12.15 Cappelli, A. Lexicon abbreviaturarum. 3. ed. Milano, 1929.
Arc 1153.12.20 Cappelli, A. Lexicon abbreviaturarum. 4. ed. Milano, 1949.
Arc 1153.13 Monaci, E. Esempj di scrittura latina. Roma, 1898.
Arc 1153.14 Vianini, G. Raccolta...abbreviazioni e frasi abbreviate. Roma, 1898.
Arc 1153.18 Friedrich, G. Učebna kniha palaeografie latinskě. Praha, 1898.
Arc 1153.19 Federici, V. Esempi di corsiva antico del secolo I...al IV. Roma, 1908.
Arc 1153.21 Guénin, L.P. Histoire de la sténographie...notes tironiennes. Paris, 1908.
Arc 1153.23 Bretholtz, B. Lateinische Paläographie. 2. Aufl. Leipzig, 1912.
Arc 1153.24.2F Ehrle, Franz. Specimina codicum latinorum Vaticanorum. Berolini, 1932.
Arc 1153.25 Voss, Ulrich. Lateinische Stenographie...Wilhelm Stolze. Berlin, 1907.
Arc 1153.27 Lowe, E.A. The Benevetan script. Oxford, 1914.
Arc 1153.29.2 Chassant, A. Dictionnaire des abréviations latines et françaises. 2. éd. Paris, 1862.
Arc 1153.29.3 Chassant, A. Dictionnaire des abréviations latines et françaises. 3. éd. Paris, 1866.
Arc 1153.29.4 Chassant, A. Dictionnaire des abréviations latines et françaises. 4. éd. Paris, 1876.
Arc 1153.29.5 Chassant, A. Dictionnaire des abréviations latines et françaises. 5. éd. Paris, 1884.
Arc 1153.31 Hulákovsky, J.M. Abbreviaturae vocabulorum. Pragae, 1913.
Arc 1153.32 Söldner, Georg. Die abgeleiteten Verba in den tironischen Noten. Inaug. Ddiss. Borna, 1916.
Arc 1153.33 Millares Carlo, A. Estudios paleográficos. Madrid, 1918.
Arc 1153.34 Mentz, Arthur. Geschichte der griechisch-römischen Schrift. Leipzig, 1920.
Arc 1153.35 Bosseboeuf, L.A. École de calligraphie et de miniature de Tours. Tours, 1891.
Arc 1153.41 Ruess, F. Ueber die Tachygraphie der Römer. Inaug. Diss. München, 1879.
Arc 1153.43.7 Schiaparelli, L. Avviamento allo studio delle abbreviature latine nel medievo. Firenze, 1926.
Arc 1153.44.5F Rand, Edward K. The earliest book of Tours. Cambridge, Mass., 1934.
Arc 1153.44.25 Rand, Edward K. A preliminary study of Alcuin's Bible. Cambridge, 1931.
Arc 1153.45 Gerrard, John. Siglarium romanum. Londini, 1792.
Arc 1153.46 Sarpe, Gustav. Prolegomena ad tachygraphiam Romanam. Rostochii, 1829.
Arc 1153.47PF Catholic Church. Pope. Pontificum Romanorum diplomata. Romae, 1928.
Arc 1153.53 Ullmann, B.L. Ancient writing and its influence. N.Y., 1932.
Arc 1153.53.5 Ullmann, B.L. The origin and development of humanistic script. Rome, 1960.
Arc 1153.58 Rauh, Rudolf. Paläographie des mainfränkischen Monumentalinscriften. Inaug. Diss. München, 1935.

Arc 1153 Palaeography - Latin - General works - cont.

Arc 1153.59 Allamoda, H. Beiträge zur Geschichte der äusseren Merkmale des ältesten Breslauer Bischofsurkunden bis zum Jahre 1319. Inaug. Diss. Oblau, 1924.
Htn Arc 1153.60* Peignot, G. Lettres à M.C.N. Amanton sur deux manuscrits précieux des temps de Charlemagne. Dijon, 1829.
Arc 1153.61 Venturini, T. Ricerche paleografiche intorno all'arcidiacono pacifico di Verona. Verona, 1929.
Arc 1153.61.5 Venturini, M. Vita ed attività dello "Scriptorium" veronese nel secolo XI. Verona, 1930.
Arc 1153.62 Giuliano, M.L. Coltura e attività calligrafica nel secolo XII a Verona. Padova, 1933.
Arc 1153.65 Fichtenau, Heinrich. Mensch und Schrift im Mittelalter. Wien, 1946.
Arc 1153.69 Zazo, Alfredo. Paleografia latina e diplomatica. 6. ed. Napoli, 1946.
Arc 1153.72 Boson, G.G. Paléographie valdôtaine. v.1-3. Aoste, 1950-52.
Arc 1153.73 Kirchner, J. Scriptura latina libraria. Monachii, 1955.
Arc 1153.81 Moschetti, G. Primordi esegetici sulla legislazione longobardo. Spoleto, 1954.
Arc 1153.82 Colloque International de Paléographie Latine, 1st, Paris, 1953. Nomenclature des écritures livresques du IXe au XVIe siècle. Photoreproduction. Paris, 1954.
Arc 1153.84 Guarducci, M. I graffiti sotto la confessione di San Petro in Vaticano. Città del Vaticano, 1958. 3v.
Arc 1153.85 Politzer, R.L. A study of the language of eighth century Lombardic documents. N.Y., 1949.
Arc 1153.87F Gordon, Arthur Ernest. Album of dated Latin inscriptions. v.1-4. Berkeley, 1958- 6v.
Arc 1153.90F Umbrae codicum acidentalium. Amsterdam. 1,1961+ 10v.
Arc 1153.92 Foerster, H. Abriss der lateinische Paläographie. 2. Aufl. Stuttgart, 1963.
Arc 1153.93 Wagner, L. Proba centum scripturarum. Leipzig, 1963. 2v.
Arc 1153.94 Pelzer, Auguste. Abréviations latines médiévales. Louvain, 1964.
Arc 1153.95 Mazzoleni, Jole. Lezioni di paleografia latina e diplomatica. Napoli, 1964?
Arc 1153.95.1 Mazzoleni, Jole. Paleografia e diplomatica e scienze ausiliarie. Napoli, 1970.
Arc 1153.96 Merkelbach, Reinhold. Lateinisches Leseheft zur Einführung in Paläographie und Textkritik. Göttingen, 1969.
Arc 1153.98F Thomson, Samuel Harrison. Latin bookhands of the later Middle Ages, 1110-1500. Cambridge, Eng., 1969.
Arc 1153.100 Apianus, Petrus. Abbrevationes vetustorum monumentorum, in ordinem alphabeticum digestae. München, 1968.
Arc 1153.102 Orlandelli, Gainfranco. Rinascimento giuridico e scrittura carolina a Bologna nel secolo XII. Bologna, 1965.
Arc 1153.104.2 Lazzarini, Vittorio. Scritti di paleografia e diplomatica. 2. ed. Padova, 1969.
Arc 1153.106 Scriptorum opus: Schreiber-Mönche am Werk. Wiesbaden, 1971.
Arc 1153.108F Mazzoleni, Jole. Esempi di scritture cancelleresche. Napoli, 1972.
Arc 1153.109F Gilissen, Léon. L'expertise des éscritures médiévales. Gand, 1973.
Arc 1153.110 Costamagna, Giorgio. Tachigrafia notarile e scritture segrete medioevali in Italia. Roma, 1968.
Arc 1153.111 Thiel, Helmut van. Mittellateinische Texte: ein Handschriften-Lesebuch. Göttingen, 1972.
Arc 1153.112PF Codices latini antiquiores. pt.2. 2. ed. Oxford, 1972.
Arc 1153.113 Gasparri, Françoise. L'écriture des actes de Louis VI, Louis VII et Philippe Auguste. Genève, 1973.
Arc 1153.114 Costamagna, Giorgio. Studi di paleografia e diplomatica. Roma, 1972.
Arc 1153.115 Stiennon, Jacques. Paléographie du Moyen Age. Paris, 1973.

Arc 1160 Palaeography - Other individual languages - Folios [Discontinued]

Arc 1160.11 Kaulek, J. Recueil de fac-simile...paléographie moderne. Paris, 1889.
Arc 1160.12 Brugmans, H. Atlas der Nederlandsche palaeographie. 's Gravenhage, 1910.
Arc 1160.13F Ojha, Gaurishankar. The palaeography of India. 2. ed. Ajmer, 1918.
Arc 1160.201 Peper, P. Otfrid...Weissenburg. Schreiber XIX Jahrhundert. Frankfurt, 1899.
Arc 1160.202 Alvera Delgras, A. Compendio de paleografia española. Madrid, 1857.
Htn Arc 1160.202.5* Merino, Andres. Escuela paleographica...letras antiguas. Madrid, 1780.
Arc 1160.202.9F Colomera y Rodriguez, V. Paleografía castellana. Valladolid, 1862.
Arc 1160.204 Foerster, W. Sulla questione...codice di Arborea. Torino, 1905.
Htn Arc 1160.206* Clemen, O. Handschriftenproben aus der Reformationzeit. Zwickau, 1911.
Arc 1160.209F Lavrov, P.A. Paleograficheskie snimki. Sankt Peterburg, n.d.
Arc 1160.210F Moskovskii Arkheologicheskii Institut. Sbornik snimkov s russkago pis'ma. Moskva, 1913. 2v.
Arc 1160.210.5F Moskovskii Arkheologicheskii Institut. Sbornik snimkov s russkago pis'ma XIII-XVIII vv. Moskva, 1908.

Arc 1163 Palaeography - Other individual languages - General works

Arc 1163.1 Muñoz y Rivero, J. Idioma y escritura de España. Madrid, 1888.
Arc 1163.2 Muñoz y Rivero, J. Scripturae hispanae veteris. Matriti, 1890.
Htn Arc 1163.2.3* Terreros y Pando, E. Paleografía española. Madrid, 1758.
Arc 1163.2.9 Tos, Joaquin. Paleografía que para inteligencia de les manuscrites. Barcelona, 1820.
Arc 1163.2.14 Muñoz y Rivero, J. Manual de paleografía diplomática española. Madrid, 1880.
Arc 1163.2.15 Muñoz y Rivero, J. Manual de paleografía diplomática española. Madrid, 1889.
Arc 1163.2.17 Muñoz y Rivero, J. Manual de paleografía diplomática española. 2. ed. Madrid, 1917.
Arc 1163.2.17.1 Muñoz y Rivero, J. Manual de paleografía diplomática española. 2. ed. Madrid, 1917.
Arc 1163.2.21F Paluzie y Cantalozella, Esteban. Paleografía española. Barcelona, 1846.
Arc 1163.2.22 Paluzie y Cantelozella, Esteban. Escritura y lenguaje de España. Barcelona, 1935.
Arc 1163.2.23 Moriano, F. Ortografía general paleográfica-bibliográfica de la lengua castellana. Sevilla, 1866.

Arc 1163 Palaeography - Other individual languages - General works - cont.

Arc 1163.2.25 Millares Carlo, A. Paleografía española. Barcelona, 1929. 2v.
Arc 1163.2.29 Millares Carlo, A. Nuevos estudios de paleografía española. Mexico, 1941.
Arc 1163.2.32 Millares Carlo, A. Contribución al "corpus" de códices visigoticos. Madrid, 1931.
Arc 1163.3 Sreznevski, T.T. Slavjano-russkaja paleografija. Sankt Peterburg, 1885.
Arc 1163.3.3 Beliaev, Ivan S. Prakticheskii kurs izucheniia drevnei russkoi skoropisi dlia chteniia rukopisei XV-XVIII stoletii. 2. izd. Reproduction. Mqskva, 1911.
Arc 1163.3.4 Shchepkin, Viacheslav N. Russkaia paleografiia. Moskva, 1967.
Arc 1163.3.5 Shchepkin, Viacheslav N. Uchebnik russkoi paleografii. Moskva, 1918.
Arc 1163.3.6 Savva, archbishop of Tver. Paleograficheskie snimki. Moskva, 1863.
Arc 1163.3.7 Druzhinin, V.G. Pomorskie paleografy 18 stol. Petrograd, 1921.
Arc 1163.3.10 Karskii, E.F. Obraztsy slavianskago kirillovskago pis'ma. Varshava, 1902.
Arc 1163.3.15 Karskii, E.F. Slavianskaia kirillovskaia paleografiia. Leningrad, 1928.
Arc 1163.3.17 Vajs, Josef. Rukovět hlaholské paleografie. Praha, 1932.
Htn Arc 1163.3.20PF* Karinskii, N.M. Obraztsy pis'ma brevneishego perioda istorii russkoi knigi. Leningrad, 1925.
Arc 1163.3.25 Azbuka i skoropis' XVII. Moskva, 1875.
Arc 1163.3.30 Moskovskii Arkheologicheskii Institut. Bukvitsa na 77 listakh. Moskva, 1909.
Arc 1163.3.35 Ivanov, P.I. Sbornik paleograficheskikh snimkov. Moskva, 1844.
Arc 1163.3.38 Orlov, A.S. Bibliografiia russkikh nadpisei XI-XV vv. Moskva, 1936.
Arc 1163.3.40 Orlov, A.S. Bibliografiia russkikh nadpisei XI-XV vv. Moskva, 1952.
Arc 1163.3.45 Chaev, N.S. Russkaia paleografiia. Moskva, 1946.
Arc 1163.3.50 Horodyski, Bogden. Podrecznik paleografii ruskiej. Kraków, 1951.
Arc 1163.3.55 Cherepnin, L.V. Russkaia paleografiia. Moskva, 1956.
Arc 1163.3.60 Sololevskii, A.I. Slaviano-russkaia paleografiia. Sankt Peterburg, 1908.
Arc 1163.3.65F Goskev, Ivan. Starobulgarski glayolicheski i kirilski nadpisi ot IX i X v. Sofiia, 1961.
Arc 1163.3.70 Zhukovskaia, L.P. Razvitie slaviano-russkoi paleografii v dosrevoluitsionnoi Rossii. Moskva, 1963.
Arc 1163.3.75 Koppen, P.I. Spisok. russkim pamiatnikam, sluzhashchim k postavleniiu istorii khudozhestv i otechestvennoi paleografii. Moskva, 1822.
Arc 1163.3.80 Mortero y Simón, C. Apuntes de iniciacion a la paleografia española de los siglos XII a XVII. Madrid, 1963.
Arc 1163.3.85 Tikhomlrov, Mikhail N. Russkaia paleografiia. Moskva, 1966.
Arc 1163.3.90 Paleografiia. Moskva, 1967.
Arc 1163.3.95 Paleograficheskii al'bom. Leningrad, 1968.
Arc 1163.3.100 Mongait, Aleksandr L. Nadpis'na kamne. Moskva, 1969.
Arc 1163.3.105 Nikolaeva, Tat'iana V. Proizvedeniia russkogo prikladnogo iskusstvo s nadpisiami XV- pervoi chetverti XVI v. Mosvka, 1971.
Arc 1163.3.110 Panaskenko, Vira V. Paleohrafiia ukraïns'koho skoiopysii durkoï polovyny XVII st. Kyïv, 1974.
Arc 1163.3.115F Tomović, Gordana. Morfologija ćiriličkih natpisa na Balkanu. Beograd, 1974.
Arc 1163.3.120 Zapisi i letopisi. Skopje, 1975.
Arc 1163.4 Cherbonneau, A. Exercises pour la lecture des manuscrits arabes. Paris, 1853.
Arc 1163.4.5 Combarel, E. Cahier d'écritures arabes. Paris, 1848.
Arc 1163.4.10 India Office Library. Specimens of Arabic and Persian palaeography. London, 1939.
Arc 1163.4.13F Delhi. Museum of Archaeology. Specimens of calligraphy in the Delhi Museum of Archaeology. Calcutta, 1926.
Arc 1163.4.20F Vajda, Georges. Album de paléographie arabe. Paris, 1958.
Arc 1163.4.25F Abbott, N. The rise of the north Arabic script and its Kur'ānic development. Chicago, 1939.
Arc 1163.4.32 Kühnel, Ernst. Islamische Schriftkunst. 2. Aufl. Graz, 1972.
Arc 1163.5 Ojha, G.H. The palaeography of India (in Sansk). Oodeypore, 1894.
Arc 1163.5.5 Burnell, A.C. Elements of south-Indian palaeography. 2. ed. London, 1878.
Arc 1163.5.6 Burnell, A.C. Elements of south-Indian palaeography. 2. ed. London, 1878.
Arc 1163.5.10 Bühler, G. Indische Palaeographie von Arca. Strassburg, 1896.
NEDL Arc 1163.5.15 Bühler, G. Indian paleography. Bombay, 1904.
Arc 1163.5.20 Pandey, R.B. Indian palaeography. Banaras, 1952.
Arc 1163.5.25 Dani, A.H. Indian palaeography. Oxford, 1963.
Arc 1163.5.30 Arif, Aida S. Arabic lapidary Kūfic in Africa. London, 1967.
Arc 1163.6 Lindsay, W.M. Early Irish minuscule script. Oxford, 1910.
Arc 1163.7 Vries, S.G. de. Middeleeuwsche handschriften kunde. Leiden, 1909.
Arc 1163.8 Mentz, G. Handschriften der Reformationszeit. Bonn, 1912.
Arc 1163.8.10 Ziemer, Meline. Datierung und Lokalisierung nach den Schreibformen von K und Z im Althochdeutschen. Inaug. Diss. Breslau, 1933.
Arc 1163.9 Lindsay, W.M. Early Welsh script. Oxford, 1912.
Arc 1163.10A Tisserant, E. Specimena codicum orientalium. Bonnae, 1914.
Arc 1163.10B Tisserant, E. Specimena codicum orientalium. Bonnae, 1914.
Arc 1163.11 Franke, O. Epigraphische Denkmäler aus China. Berlin, 1914. 2v.
Arc 1163.12 Pillito, I. Analisi paleografia di...codici...secoli XIV e XV...in Cagliari. Cagliari, 1879.
Arc 1163.13 Cordeiro de Sausa, J.M. Algunas siglas e abreviaturas usadas. Lisboa, 1926.
Arc 1163.14 Rademacher, M. Die Worttrennung in angelsächsischen Handschriften. Inaug. Diss. Münster, 1921.
Arc 1163.14.6 Keller, Wolfgang. Angelsächsiche Palaeographie. N.Y., 1970-71. 2v.
Arc 1163.15 Spehr, Harald. Der Ursprung der isländischen Schrift und ihre Weiterbildung bis zur Mitte des 13. Jahrhunderts. Inaug. Diss. Halle, 1929.
Arc 1163.16F Bianu, I. Album de paleografie românească. București, 1929.
Arc 1163.17 Skeat, W.W. Twelve facsimiles of old English manuscripts. Oxford, 1892.

Arc 1163 Palaeography - Other individual languages - General works - cont.

Arc 1163.17.5 Essex, England. Record Office. Some examples of English handwriting. Chelmsford, 1949.
Arc 1163.17.7 Essex, England. Record Office. Examples of English handwriting. Essex? 1954.
Htn Arc 1163.17.10* Sisson, C.J. Photographic slides of English manuscripts. n.p., n.d.
Arc 1163.17.15A Tannenbaum, S.A. The handwriting of the Renaissance. N.Y., 1930.
Arc 1163.17.15B Tannenbaum, S.A. The handwriting of the Renaissance. N.Y., 1930.
Arc 1163.17.20FA Judge, C.B. Specimens of sixteenth-century English handwriting. Cambridge, 1925.
Arc 1163.17.20FB Judge, C.B. Specimens of sixteenth-century English handwriting. Cambridge, 1925.
Arc 1163.17.25 Wright, Cyril Ernest. English vernacular hands from the twelfth to the fifteenth centuries. Oxford, 1960.
Arc 1163.17.30 Parkes, Malcolm Beckwith. English cursive book hands, 1250-1500. Oxford, 1969.
Arc 1163.17.35 Hector, Leonard C. The handwriting of English documents. London, 1958.
Arc 1163.18 Arens, Fritz V. Mainzer Inschriften. Stuttgart, 1945.
Arc 1163.19 Eis, Gerhard. Altdeutsche Handschriften. München, 1949.
Arc 1163.20 Laurent, M. De abbreviationibus et signis scripturae gothicae. Romae, 1939.
Arc 1163.21 Pagnin, B. Le origini della scriturra gotica padovana. Padova, 1933.
Arc 1163.21.5F De la Mare, Albinia Cathérine. The handwriting of Italian humanists. Oxford, 1973-
Arc 1163.22 Kirchner, J. Germanistische Handschriftenpraxis. München, 1950.
Arc 1163.23 Grun, Paul A. Leseschlüssel zu unserer alten Schrift. Görlitz, 1935.
Arc 1163.25F Deimel, Anton. Keilschrift-Palaeographie. Roma, 1929.
Arc 1163.30PF Guboglu, Mihail. Paleografia si diplomatica Turco-Osmană. București, 1958.
Arc 1163.32 Kirkham, E. Kay. How to read the handwriting and records of early America. Salt Lake City, 1961.
Arc 1163.34F Garcia Villada, Zacarias. Paleografia española. Album. Barcelona, 1974. 2v.
Arc 1163.35 Codices Hungarici. Budapest. 4-7 4v.
Arc 1163.36 Bernheimer, K. Paleografia ebraica. Firenze, 1924.
Arc 1163.37 Colloque International sur la Paléographie Hébraïque Médiévale, Paris, 1972. La paléographie hébraïque médiévale, Paris, 11-13 septembre 1972. Paris, 1974.
Arc 1163.38F Poulle, Emmanuel. Paléographie des écritures cursives en France du 15e au 17e siècle. Genève, 1966.
Arc 1163.39 Garcés G, Jorge A. Cómo han de traducirse los documentos paleográficos de Hispanoámerica. Quinto, 1961.
Arc 1163.40.2 Duelfer, Kurt. Schrifttafeln zur deutschen Paläographie. v.1-2. 2. Aufl. Marburg, 1967.
Arc 1163.41.5 Aaberg, Alf. Läsning av gamla handstilar. 5. uppl. Stockholm, 1971.

Arc 1166 Palaeography - Special topics - Monographs

Arc 1166.1 Harris, J.R. Stichometry. Baltimore, 1883.
Arc 1166.1.5 Ohly, Kurt. Stichometrische Untersuchungen. Leipzig, 1928.
Arc 1166.2 Paoli, Cesare. Carta di cotone e carta di lino. Firenze, 1885.
Arc 1166.3 Brigiuti, R. La paleografia ed i Raggi di Röntgen. Roma, 1899.
Arc 1166.4 Peignot, G. Essai sur l'histoire du parchemin. Paris, 1812.
Arc 1166.5 Finzi, A.M. La fotografia quale mezzo di scoperta della falsità in documenti. Firenze, 1911.
Arc 1166.6 Thompson, D.V. Medieval parchment-making. London, 1935.
Arc 1166.7 Cramer, Maria. Koptische Inschriften im Kaiser-Friedrich Museum zu Berlin. Le Caire, 1949.
Arc 1166.7.10 Cramer, Maria. Archäologische und epigraphische Klassifikation koptischer Denkmäler des Metropolitan Museum of Art, N.Y. und des Museum of Fine Arts, Boston, Mass. Wiesbaden, 1957.
Arc 1166.7.15F Cramer, Maria. Koptische Paläographie. Wiesbaden, 1964.
Arc 1166.8 Norlén, Saga-Marianne. Alt datera manuskript. Stockholm, 1973.

Arc 1175 Diplomatics - Folios [Discontinued]

Arc 1175.1 Sybel, H. von. Kaiserurkunden in Abbildungen. v.1-11 and atlas. Berlin, 1880-91. 12v.
Arc 1175.3 Pertz, G.H. Schrifttafeln zum Gebrauch bei diplomatischen Vorlesungen. Hannover, 1844.
Arc 1175.5F Mabillon, J. De re diplomatica libri VI. Luteciae Parisiorum, 1681.
Arc 1175.7 Voigt, Karl. Beiträge zur Diplomatik der langodardischen Fürsten. Göttingen, 1902.
Arc 1175.10 Marini, G.L. I papiri diplomatici. Roma, 1805.
Arc 1175.11 Anderson, J. Selectus diplomatum et numismatum Scotiae Thesaurus. Edinburgi, 1739.
Arc 1175.12FA Jenkinson, H. Palaeography and...study of court hand. Cambridge, 1915.
Arc 1175.12FB Jenkinson, H. Palaeography and...study of court hand. Cambridge, 1915.

Arc 1178 Diplomatics - Pamphlet volumes

Arc 1178 Pamphlet box. Diplomatics. Miscellaneous pamphlets.
Arc 1178.2 Pamphlet box. Diplomatics. Miscellaneous pamphlets.

Arc 1180 Diplomatics - Dictionaries

Arc 1180.1 Brinckmeier, E. Glossarium diplomaticum. Gotha, 1856-63. 2v.
Arc 1180.2 Vaines, J. de. Dictionnaire raisonnè de diploéatique. Paris, 1774. 2v.
Arc 1180.5 Demundt, Karl Ernst. Lateinisch-deutsche Interpretationshilfen für spätmittelalterliche und frühneuzeitliche Archivalien. Marburg, 1970.

Arc 1185 Diplomatics - General works

Arc 1185.1 Tassin, R.P. Nouveau traité de diplomatique. Paris, 1750-65. 6v.
Arc 1185.1.5 Archiv für Diplomatik, Schriftgeschichte, Siegel- und Wappenkunde. Münster. 1,1955+ 14v.
Arc 1185.3 Leist, F. Urkundenlehre. Leipzig, 1882.
Arc 1185.3.2 Leist, F. Urkundenlehre. 2. Aufl. Leipzig, 1893.
Arc 1185.4A Giry, Arthur. Manuel de diplomatique. Paris, 1894.
Arc 1185.4B Giry, Arthur. Manuel de diplomatique. Paris, 1894.
Arc 1185.4C Giry, Arthur. Manuel de diplomatique. Paris, 1894.

Arc 1185 Diplomatics - General works - cont.

Arc 1185.4.5 Giry, Arthur. Manuel de diplomatique. Paris, 1925. 2v.

Arc 1185.5.1 Posse, Otto. Die Lehre von der Privaturkunden. Berlin, 1974.

Arc 1185.6 Ficker, J. Beitraege zur Urkundenlehre. Innsbruck, 1877-78. 2v.

Arc 1185.7 Spangenberg, E. Lehre von dem Urkundenbeweise. Heidelberg, 1827. 2v.

Arc 1185.8 Gatterer, J.C. Abriss der Diplomatik. Göttingen, 1798.

Arc 1185.8.2 Gatterer, J.C. Praktische Diplomatik. Göttingen, 1799.

Arc 1185.9 Erben, Wilhelm. Urkundenlehre. v.1,3. München, 1907. 2v.

Arc 1185.9.5 Erben, Wilhelm. Die Kaiser- und Königsurkunden des Mittelalters in Deutschland, Frankreich und Italien. München, 1967.

Arc 1185.10 Baring, D.E. Clavis diplomatica. Hanoverae, 1737.

Arc 1185.10.5 Baring, D.E. Clavis diplomatica. Hanoverae, 1754.

Arc 1185.10.15 Redlich, Oswald. Der Privaturkunden des Mittelalters. München, 1967.

Arc 1185.11 Rietsch, K.F. Handbuch der Urkundwissen. Berlin, 1904.

Arc 1185.13 Lustro, G.N. di. Degli archivii, ricerche archaeologiche, storiche , critiche, diplomatiche. Napoli, 1880.

Arc 1185.14 Frazer, P. Manual of the study of documents. Philadelphia, 1894.

Arc 1185.15 Zinkernagel, K.F.B. Handbuch für angehende Archivare und Registratoren. Nördlingen, 1800.

Arc 1185.16 Brandi, Karl. Urkunden und Akten. Leipzig, 1913.

Arc 1185.18 Rosenmund, R. Die Fortschritte der Diplomatik seit Mabillon. München, 1897.

Arc 1185.19.3 Barone, N. Paleografia latina diplomatica. 3. ed. Napoli, 1923.

Arc 1185.19.3F Barone, N. Paleografia latina diplomatica. Atlas. 3. ed. Napoli, 1923.

Arc 1185.20 Likhachev, N.P. Diplomatika. Sankt Peterburg, 1901.

Arc 1185.21 Lodolini, A. Elementi di diplomatica. Milano, 1926.

Arc 1185.22 Zatschek, Heinz. Studien zur mittelterlicher Urkundenlehre. Brünn, 1929.

Arc 1185.23 Lemoine, P.C. Diplomatique-pratique. Metz, 1765.

Arc 1185.26 Valenti, Filippo. Il documento medioevale. Modena, 1961.

Arc 1185.28 Mabillon, Jean. Histoire des contestations sur la diplomatique. Naples, 1767.

Arc 1185.29 Pratesi, A. Elementi di diplomatica generale. Bari, 1963?

Arc 1185.30 Battheney. L'archiviste françois. 2. éd. Paris, 1775.

Arc 1185.30.2 Tessier, Georges. La diplomatique. 2. éd. Paris, 1962.

Arc 1185.32.2 Paoli, Cesare. Diplomatica. Firenze, 1969.

Arc 1185.33.3 Santifaller, Leo. Urkundenforschung. 3. Aufl. Darmstadt, 1968.

Arc 1185.34 Vittani, Giovanni. Scritti di diplomatica e archivistica. Milano, 1974-

Arc 1190 Diplomatics - Local

Arc 1190.1 Bresslau, H. Handbuch der Urkundenlehre fuer Deutschland und Italien. Leipzig, 1889.

Arc 1190.1.2 Bresslau, H. Diplomata centum. Berlin, 1872.

Arc 1190.1.3 Bresslau, H. Handbuch der Urkundenlehre. 3. Aufl. Berlin, 1958. 2v.

Arc 1190.1.9 Jaffé, P. Diplomata quadraginta. Berlin, 1863.

Arc 1190.1.12 Schulze, H. Handbuch der Urkundenlehre für Deutschland und Italien. 2. und 3. Aufl. Berlin, 1960.

Arc 1190.2 Aronius, J. Diplomatische Studien über die älteren angelsächischen Urkunden. Inaug. Diss. Königsberg, 1883.

Arc 1190.3 Wright, Andrew. Court hand restored. 2. ed. London, 1778.

Arc 1190.3.2 Wright, Andrew. Court hand restored. 8. ed. London, 1867.

Arc 1190.3.3 Wright, Andrew. Court hand restored. 9. ed. London, 1879.

NEDL Arc 1190.3.5 Wright, Andrew. Court hand restored. 10. ed. London, 1912.

Arc 1190.3.6 Wright, Andrew. Court-hand restored, or The student's assistant in reading old deeds. London, 1974.

Arc 1190.4 Müller, Karl. Unsere Kanzleisprache. Dresden, 1926.

Arc 1190.4.15 Sprenger, G. Diplomatische und rechtsgeschichtliche Untersuchungen über Immunität und Königsschutz in Deutschland seit dem 12. Jahrhundert. Inaug. Diss. Breslau, 1936.

Arc 1190.5 Hall, Hubert. A formula book of English historical documents. Cambridge, 1908. 2v.

Arc 1190.7 Russi, M. Paleografia e diplomatica...province napolitane. Napoli, 1883.

Arc 1190.9 Hajnal, Istvan. Írástörténet az írásbeliség felujulása korából. Budapest, 1921.

Arc 1190.10F Jenkinson, H. The later court hands in England. Test and atlas. Cambridge, 1927. 2v.

Arc 1190.25 Kern, Fritz. Dorsualkonzept und Imbreviatur in Italien. Stuttgart, 1906.

Arc 1190.25.10 Maffei, Scipione. Istoria diplomatica che serve d'introduzione all'arte critica in tal materia. Mantova, 1727.

Arc 1190.25.12 Maffei, Scipione. Istoria diplomatica che serve d'introduzione all'arte critica in tal materia. Roma, 1964.

Arc 1190.30 Boüard, Alain de. Manuel de diplomatique française et pontificale. Paris, 1929-52. 2v.

Arc 1190.30F Boüard, Alain de. Manuel de diplomatique française et pontificale. Atlas. Paris, 1929-52. 2v.

Arc 1190.35 Meisner, H.O. Aktenkunde. Berlin, 1935.

Arc 1190.35.5 Meisner, H.O. Urkunden- und Aktenlehre der Neuzeit. Leipzig, 1950.

Arc 1190.35.7 Meisner, H.O. Urkunden- und Aktenlehre der Neuzeit. 2. Aufl. Leipzig, 1952.

Arc 1190.40 Ruddiman, T. A introduction to James Anderson's Diplomata Scotiae. Edinburgh, 1773.

Arc 1190.45 Luzzatto, G.I. Epigrafia giuridica greca e romana. Milano, 1942.

Arc 1190.50 Cheney, C. English bishops' chanceries. Manchester, 1950.

Arc 1190.55 Santifaller, Leo. Bozner Schreibschriften der Neuzeit. Jena, 1930.

Arc 1190.60 Zajączkowski, Anan. Zarys dyplomatyki osmánsko-tureckiej. Warszawa, 1955.

Arc 1190.65 Doelger, Franz. Byzantinische Diplomatik. Ettal, 1956.

Arc 1190.65.5 Karagiannopoulos, Iōannēs E. Byzantinē diplomatikē. Thessalonikē, 1969.

Arc 1190.65.10 Mazal, Otto. Die Prooimien der byzantinischen Patriarchenurkunden. Wien, 1974.

Arc 1190.70 Szentpetery, Imre. Magyar oklevéltan. Budapest, 1930.

Arc 1190.75 Purvis, John Stanley. Notarial signs from the York archiepescopal records. London, 1957.

Arc 1190.77 Chhabra, Bahadur C. Diplomatic of Sanskrit copper-plate grants. Delhi? 1961?

Arc 1190 Diplomatics - Local - cont.

Arc 1190.80 Fekete, Lajos. Die Siyâquat-Schrift in der türkischen Finanzverwaltung. Budapest, 1955.

Arc 1190.80.5 Irānshahr Husayn, Kazimz ādah. Les chiffres siyâk et la comptabilitié persane. Paris, 1915.

Arc 1190.82 Yazir, Mahmud. Siyakat yazisi. Istanbul, 1941.

Arc 1190.82.5 Yazir, Mahmud. Eski yazilari okuma anahtari. Istanbul, 1942.

Arc 1190.84 Strennon, Jacques. L'écriture diplomatique dans le diocèse de Liège. Paris, 1960.

Arc 1190.85 Schwarz, Klaus. Osmanische Sultansurkunden des Sinai-Klosters in türkischer Sprache. Freiburg, 1970.

Arc 1190.86 Elker, Salâhaddin. Divan rakamlari. Ankara, 1953.

Arc 1190.86.5 Nedkov, Boris K. Osmanotwiska diplomatika: paleografiia. Sofiia, 1966-72. 2v.

Arc 1190.86.10 Reychman, Jan. Handbook of Ottoman-Turkish diplomatics. The Hague, 1968.

Arc 1190.87 Tessier, Georges. Diplomatique royale française. Paris, 1962.

Arc 1190.88F Fekete, Lajos. Beveztés a hodoltśag török diplomatikájála. Budapest, 1926.

Arc 1190.90 Dyplomatyka wieków średnich. Wyd. 1. Warszawa, 1971.

Arc 1190.90.5 Maleczyński, Karol. Studia nad dokumentem polskim. Wrocław, 1971.

Arc 1200 Diplomatics - Special topics

Arc 1200.3 Heinemann, O. Beiträge zur Diplomatik der ältern Bischoefe von Hildesheim. Inaug. Diss. Marburg, 1895.

Arc 1200.4 Lewinski, L. Die Brandenburgische Kanzlei und die Urkundenwesen. Inaug. Diss. Strassburg, 1893.

Arc 1200.5 Kaiser, H. Der collectarus perpeturom formorum des Johann von Gelnhausen. Strassburg, 1898.

Arc 1200.5.5 Kaiser, H. Collection perpetuorum formorum. Innsbruck, 1900.

Arc 1200.6 Pflugh-Harttung, J. Bullen der Päpste. Gotha, 1901.

Arc 1200.8 Schillmann, F. Beiträge zum Urkundenwesen der ältern Bischöfe. Leipzig, 1908.

Arc 1200.9 Boüard, A. de. Études de diplomatique sur les actes, des iquenotaires de Paris. Paris, 1910.

Htn Arc 1200.10* Guigue, M.C. De l'origine de la signature...au Moyen Âge. Paris, 1863.

Arc 1200.12 Krüger, P. Bedeutung der Salutatio...14. Jahrhundert. Greifswald, 1912.

Arc 1200.13 Schmitz, Karl. Ursprung und Geschichte der Devotionsformeln. Stuttgart, 1913.

Arc 1200.14 Huillard-Bréholles. Examen des chartes de l'eglise romaine. Paris, 1865.

Arc 1200.15 MasLatrie, L. Les éléments de la diplomatique pontificale. Paris, 1886.

Arc 1200.16 Madras. Government Museum. Catalogue of copper-plate grants. Madras, 1918.

Arc 1200.17 Millares Carlo, A. Documentos pontificios en papiro de archivos. pt.1. Madrid, 1918.

Arc 1200.17.5 Millares Carlo, A. Documentos pontificios en papiro de archivos. Madrid, 1918.

Arc 1200.18 Alter, Franz K. Beitrag zur praktischen Diplomatik für Slaven. Wien, 1801.

Arc 1200.19 Schütt, Otto. Heusburgen Akten- und Urkundensprache im 14., 15., und 16. Jahrhundert. Heusburg, 1919.

Arc 1200.20 Schütt, Otto. Die Geschichte der Schriftsprache im ehemaligen Amt und in der Stadt Heusburg bis 1650. Heusburg, 1919.

Arc 1200.21 Björkman, Walther. Beiträge zur Geschichte der Staatskanzlei im islamischen Ägypten. Hamburg, 1928.

Arc 1200.22 Curschmann, Fritz. Die älteren Papsturkunden des Erzbistums Hamburg. Hamburg, 1909.

Arc 1200.23 Menzer, Anne. Die Jahresmerkmale in den Datierungen der Papsturkunden bis zum Ausgang des 11. Jahrhundert. Inaug. Diss. Berlin, 1932.

Arc 1200.24 Kopczynski, M. Die Arengen der Papsturkunden nach ihrer Bedeutung und Verwendung bis zu Gregor VII. Inaug. Diss. Bottrop, 1936.

Arc 1200.25 Purvis, J.S. An introduction to ecclesiastical records. London, 1953.

Arc 1200.26 William of Hoo, S. The letter-book of William of Hoo. Ipswich, 1963.

Arc 1200.28 Schiaparelli, Luigi. Raccolta di documenti latini. Torino, 1969.

Arc 1205 Sigillography - Bibliographies

Arc 1205.5 Tourneur-Nicodème, Mariette. Bibliographie générale de la sigillographie. Besançon, 1933.

Arc 1207 Sigillography - Folios [Discontinued]

Arc 1207.1PF Hare, Thomas. Engravings from ancient seals attached to deeds. Stowe-Bardolph, 1847.

Arc 1207.200F Garrucci, R. I piombi antichi. Roma, 1847.

Arc 1208 Sigillography - Museums and Private collections

Arc 1208.1 British Museum. Catalogue of seals in the department of manuscripts. London, 1887-1900. 6v.

Arc 1208.2 Le Clert, Louis. Catalogue de sigillographie du Musée de Troyes. Troyes, 1887.

Arc 1208.4 Dissard, Paul. Catalogues des plombs antiques. Paris, 1905.

Htn Arc 1208.5.15* Seals of Gianfrancesco Pico della Mirandola. n.p., n.d.

Arc 1208.6 Schlumberger, G. Collections sigillographiques de G. Schlumberger. Paris, 1914.

Arc 1208.7 France. Archives Nationales. Le service sigillographique et les collections d'empreintes de sceaux des archives. Paris, 1916.

Arc 1208.8 Vatican. Biblioteca Vaticana. Le bolle d'oro dell'archivio vaticano. Città del Vaticano, 1934.

Htn Arc 1208.9PF* Pamphlet box. Collection of the seals of various individuals, cities and institutions mounted on sheets.

Arc 1208.10 Dongé, E. Description des collections de sceaux matrices. Paris, 1872.

Arc 1208.11F Committee of Ancient Near Eastern Seals. Corpus of ancient Near Eastern seals in North American collections. pt.1-2. N.Y., 1948-

Arc 1208.12 Academia...Bucharest. Documents de sigillographie byzantine. Paris, 1952.

Arc 1208.13F Aulock, Hans von. Altorientalische Siegelsteine der Sammlung Hans Silvius von Aulock. Uppsala, 1957.

Arc 1208.14F British Museum. Department of Western Asiatic Antiquities. Catalogue of the Western Asiatic seals in the British Museum. London, 1962.

Classified Listing

Arc 1208 Sigillography - Museums and Private collections - cont.
Arc 1208.15 Borisov, Andrei Ivan Iakovlevich. Sasanidskie gemmy. Leningrad, 1963.

Arc 1209 Sigillography - Dictionaries
Arc 1209.1 Chassant, A.A.L. Dictionnaire de sigillographie pratique. Paris, 1860.

Arc 1210 Sigillography - Pamphlet volumes
Arc 1210.01 Pamphlet box. Archaeology. Sigillography.

Arc 1212 Sigillography - General works
Arc 1212.1 Lecoy de la Marche, A. Les sceaux. Paris, 1889.
Arc 1212.2 Seyler, Gustav A. Geschichte der Siegel. Leipzig, 1894.
X Cg Arc 1212.3 Birch, William de Gray. Seals. London, 1907?
Arc 1212.4 Ewald, W. Siegelkunde. München, 1914.
Arc 1212.5 Poole, Reginald Lane. Seals and documents. London, 1919?
Arc 1212.6 Rittel, Erich. Siegel. Braunschweig, 1970.

Arc 1213 Sigillography - Special periods - Ancient
Arc 1213.1 Winnefeld, H. Hellenistische Silberreliefs. Berlin, 1908.

Arc 1215 Sigillography - Special periods - Medieval
Arc 1215.1 Migieu. Recueil des sceaux du Moyen Âge dits sceaux gothiques. Paris, 1779.
Arc 1215.2 Eitel, Anton. Ueber Blei- und Goldbullen im Mittelalter. Freiburg, 1912.

Arc 1220 Sigillography - Local - Asia in general - Folios [Discontinued]
Arc 1220.5F Hogarth, D.G. Hittite seals. Oxford, 1920.

Arc 1221 Sigillography - Local - Asia in general - General works
Arc 1221.1 Hammer-Purgstall. Abhandlung über die Siegel der Araber, Perser. n.p., n.d.
Arc 1221.4F Brett, Agnes B. Ancient oriental seals in the collection of Mrs. Agnes Baldwin Brett. Chicago, 1936.
Arc 1221.5F Newell, E.T. Ancient oriental seals in the collection of Mr. E.T. Newell. Chicago, 1934.
Arc 1221.6 Moore, Ada S. Ancient oriental cylinder and other seals with a description of the collection of Mrs. William H. Moore. Chicago, 1940.
Arc 1221.7 Ward, William Hayes. The seal cylinders of western Asia. Washington, 1910.

Arc 1223 Sigillography - Local - China
Arc 1223.2 Ledderhose, Lothar. Die Siegelschrift (Chuan-shu) in der Ch'ing-Zeit. Wiesbaden, 1970.
Arc 1223.3 Hsiang, Huai-shu. Recueil de cachets sur la Montagne jeune. Saigon, 1932?

Arc 1227 Sigillography - Local - India
Arc 1227.5 India. National Archives. Indian seals; problems and prospects. New Delhi? 1960.

Arc 1229 Sigillography - Local - Palestine and Syria
Arc 1229.1 Conteneau, G. La glyptique syro-hittite. Thèse. Paris, 1922.
Arc 1229.5 Bossert, H.T. Die hethitisches Königssiegel. Berlin, 1944.
Arc 1229.10 Welfen, Peter. Die Königs-Stempel. Wiesbaden, 1969.

Arc 1232 Sigillography - Local - Asia Minor
Arc 1232.1 Schlumberger, G. Sceaux et bulles de l'Orient Latin au Moyen Age. Paris, 1879.
Arc 1232.5 Wisemar, D.J. Gotter und Menschen im Rollsiegel. Prague, 1958.
Arc 1232.10 Alp, Sedat. Zylinder- und Stempelsiegel aus Karahöyük bei Konya. Ankara, 1968.

Arc 1237 Sigillography - Local - Other Asia
Arc 1237.1 Seals of Siam. n.p., n.d.
Arc 1237.5.2 Frankfort, Henri. Stratified cylinder seals from the Diyala region. Chicago, 1964.
Arc 1237.10 Thailand. Ministry of Interior. Changwat seals. Bangkok, 1968.

Arc 1247 Sigillography - Local - Europe in general - Folios [Discontinued]
Arc 1247.1 Heffner, Carl. Die deutschen Kaiser- und Königs-Siegel. Würzburg, 1875.
Arc 1247.2 Demay, G. Inventaire des sceaux de la Flandre. v.1-2. Paris, 1873.

Arc 1248 Sigillography - Local - Europe in general - General works
Arc 1248.2 Ewe, Herbert. Schiffe auf Siegeln. 1. Aufl. Rostock, 1972.

Arc 1251 Sigillography - Local - Greek - Ancient
Arc 1251.1 Pappadopoulos, G.G. Perigraphē ektypōmatōn archaiōn sphragidolithōn. Athēnai, 1855.
Arc 1251.2 Xenakē-Sakellariou, Agnē. Mykēnaike Zphragidoglyphia. Athēnai, 1966.
Arc 1251.3 Cardoni, B. De siglis veterum graecorum. v.1-3. Romae, 1757.
Arc 1251.10F Kenna, V.E.G. Cretan seals. Oxford, 1960.
Arc 1251.12 Corpus der minoischen und mykenischen Siegel. Berlin. 1,1964+ 10v.
Arc 1251.25 Matz, F. Die frühkretischen Siegel. Berlin, 1928.
Arc 1251.26 Biesantz, Hagen. Kretisch-mykenische Siegelbilder. Marburg, 1954.
Arc 1251.27 Kroll, John Hennig. Athenian bronze allotment plates. Thesis. Cambridge, 1972.

Arc 1254 Sigillography - Local - Greek - Byzantine and Modern Greece
Arc 1254.1 Carrara, F. Teodora Ducaina Paleologhina. Vienna, 1840.
Arc 1254.2 Sabatier, J. Plombs, bulles et sceaux byzantins. Paris, 1858.
Arc 1254.3 Miller, E. Bulles byzantines de la collection de M...de Köhne. Paris, 1867.
Arc 1254.4 Mordtmann, A.D. Sur les sceaux et plombs byzantins. Constantinople, 1873.
Arc 1254.5 Mordtmann, A.D. Peri byzantinōn molybdoboyllōn. n.p., n.d.
Arc 1254.6 Schlumberger, G. Sceaux byzantins; les églises, les couvents, les palais. n.p., n.d.
Arc 1254.7 Schlumberger, G. Deux chefs normands des armées byzantines. Paris, 1881.
Arc 1254.8 Schlumberger, G. Sceaux en plomb de chefs des Manglavites impériaux. Paris, 1882.

Arc 1254 Sigillography - Local - Greek - Byzantine and Modern Greece - cont.
Arc 1254.9 Schlumberger, G. Cinq sceaux de l'époque byzantine. Paris, 1883.
Arc 1254.10 Schlumberger, G. Documents pour servir à l'histoire des thémes byzantines. Paris, 1883.
Arc 1254.11 Schlumberger, G. La vierge, le Christ, les saints sur les sceaux byzantins. Paris, 1883.
Arc 1254.12 Schlumberger, G. Deux epagia...sceau d'un capitaine arménien. Paris, 1884.
Arc 1254.13 Sorlin-Dorigny, A. Sceaux et bulles des comnènes. Paris, 1876.
Arc 1254.14 Ebersolt, Jean. Catalogue des sceaux byzantins. Paris, 1922.
Arc 1254.15 Taurent, Vitalieu. Les bulles métriques dans la sigillographie byzantine. Eetjia, 1932.
Arc 1254.16F Schlumberger, G. Sigillographie de l'empire byzantin. Paris, 1884.

Arc 1255 Sigillography - Local - Roman
Arc 1255.1F Poggi, Vittorio. Sigilli antichi romani raccolti e publicati da Vittorio Poggi. Torino, 1876.

Arc 1259 Sigillography - Local - Italy - Papal States
Arc 1259.1 Rossi, G.B. de. Di una bolla plumbea papale. Roma, 1882.
Arc 1259.2 Chamard, François. Les bulles de plomb des lettres pontificales. Paris, 1883.
Arc 1259.3F Vatican. Archivio Vaticano. I sigilli dell'archivio vaticano. v.1-3. Città del Vaticano, 1937- 5v.

Arc 1260 Sigillography - Local - Italy - Other
Arc 1260.1 Daugnon, F.F. La vera arma della città di Crema. v.1-2. Fermo, 1874.
Arc 1260.2 Schlumberger. G. Sceau inédit de Boniface de Montferrat. Paris, 1886.
Arc 1260.3 Manno, Antonio. Sopra alcuni piombi sardi. Torino, 1878.
Arc 1260.4 Cecchetti, B. Bolle dei dogi di Venezia. Venezia, 1888.
Arc 1260.4.5 Cecchetti, B. Bolle dei dogi di Venezia. Venezia, 1865.

Arc 1261 Sigillography - Local - Spain and Portugal
Arc 1261.1 Travers, Émile. Le sceau de Loja et la sigillographie pittoresque. Paris, 1885.
Arc 1261.2F Sagarra, Ferran de. Sigillografía catalana. v.1-3. Barcelona, 1916-32. 5v.
Arc 1261.3 Spain. Archivo Historico Nacional, Madrid. Sección de Sigilografía. Catálogo i sellos españoles de la edad media por Juan Menéndez Pidal. Madrid, 1907.
Arc 1261.3.5 Spain. Archivo Historico Nacional, Madrid. Sección de Sigilografía. Catálogo. Madrid, 1918.
Arc 1261.3.10 Spain. Archivo General de Simancas. Registro general del sello. Valladolid. 1,1950+ 12v.
Arc 1261.3.15 Spain. Archivo Histórico Nacional, Madrid. Sección de Sigilografía. Catálogo de sellos de la Sección de Sigilografía del Archivo Histórico Nacional. Madrid, 1974- 3v.
Arc 1261.4 Escudero de la Penna, José Marie. Sigilografía española. Madrid, 1875.
Arc 1261.50 Tovar. Esfragistica medieval portuguesa. Lisboa, 1937.

Arc 1263 Sigillography - Local - France - Folios
Arc 1263.1 Douët d'Arcq, L.C. Collection de sceaux. Paris, 1863-67. 2v.
Arc 1263.2 Demay, G. Inventaire des sceaux de l'Artois et de la Picardie. v.1-2. Paris, 1877-81.
Arc 1263.3 Bosredon, P. de. Sigillographie du Périgord. Perigneux, 1880.
Arc 1263.4 France. Direction des Archives. Inventaire des sceaux de la Bourgogné. Paris, 1912.

Arc 1264 Sigillography - Local - France - General works
Arc 1264.1 Forgeais, Arthur. Collection de plombs historiés trouvés dans la Seine. v.1-3. Paris, 1858-66. 2v.
Arc 1264.1.3 Forgeais, Arthur. Blasons et chevaliers du Moyen Âge. Paris, 1877.
Arc 1264.2 Lalore, C. Le sceau et les armoiries...Saint Pierre de Troyes. Troyes, 1887.
Arc 1264.3 Prost, A. Notice sur un sceau de Landfriede du XIVe siècle. Paris, 1879.
Arc 1264.4 Barbier de Montault, X. Le grand sceau de Raoul du Fou. Reims, n.d.
Arc 1264.5 Hucher, Eugène. Catalogue de la collection de sceaux matrices. Paris, 1863.
Arc 1264.6 Gauthier, Jules. L'origine des armoiries de l'église de Besançon. n.p., 1880.
Arc 1264.7 Blanchet, A. Sigillographie française. Paris, 1902.
Arc 1264.7.5 Blanchet, A. Les drapiers de Beauvais et leurs plombs de contrôle. Beauvais, 1927.
Arc 1264.8A Roman, J. Manuel de sigillographie française. Paris, 1912.
Arc 1264.8B Roman, J. Manuel de sigillographie française. Paris, 1912.
Arc 1264.9 Barabé, A. Recherches historiques sur le tabellionage royal. Rouen, 1863.
Arc 1264.10 Hermand, A. Histoire sigillaire de la ville de Saint-Omer. Paris, 1860.
Arc 1264.11 Farcy, Paul de. Sigillographie de la Normandie. Caen, 1875.
Arc 1264.11.5F Mancel, G. Les anciennes abbayes de Normandie. Caen, 1834.
Arc 1264.12 Eygun, F. Sigillographie du Poitou jusqu'en 1515. Poitiers, 1938.
Arc 1264.12.5 Eygun, F. Sigillographie du Poitou jusqu'en 1515. Thèse. Macon, 1938.
Arc 1264.13 Guesnon, A. Sigillographie de la ville d'Arras. Arras, 1865.
Arc 1264.15 Gardilhon, R. Sigillographie des universités de France. Paris, 1952.
Arc 1264.22F Bouches-du-Rhone. Archives. Iconographie des sceaux et bulles conservés dans la partie antérieure à 1790 des archives départementales des Bouches-du-Rhone. Marseille, 1860.

Arc 1268 Sigillography - Local - Germany - Folios [Discontinued]

Htn Arc 1268.5* A collection of seals - mostly German. n.p., n.d.

Arc 1269 Sigillography - Local - Germany - General works

Arc 1269.5 Siferlinger, C. Die Siegel der Beschöfe von Freising. Inaug. Diss. München, 1925.

Arc 1269.10F Posse, Otto. Die Siegel der deutschen Kaiser und Könige von 751 bis 1913. Dresden, 1909-13. 5v.

Arc 1269.15F Albrecht, J. Die hohenlohischen Siegel des Mittelalters. Oehringen, 1859.

Arc 1269.20 Kiefhaber, J.K.S. Historisch-diplomatische Beschreibung der Nürnbergischen Kloster-Siegel. Nürnberg, 1797.

Arc 1269.22.3 Berchem, E.F. von. Siegel. 2. Aufl. Berlin, 1923.

Arc 1269.27 Kaufmann, E. Studien über Amtssiegel des 13. und 14. Jahrhunderts vornehmlich in Hessen. Inaug. Diss. Marburg, 1937.

Arc 1269.30 Engel, W. Würzburger Zunftsiegel aus fünf Jahrhunderten. Würzburg, 1950.

Arc 1269.35 Korn, Otto. Rheinisches Siegel- und Urkundenbuch. Brühl, 1952.

Arc 1269.40 Wittmer, C. Inventaire des sceaux des archives de la ville de Strasbourg de 1050 à 1300. Strasbourg, 1946.

Arc 1269.45 Vossberg, F.A. Siegel des Mittelalters von Polen, Lithauen, Schiesien, Pommern und Preussen. Berlin, 1854.

Arc 1271 Sigillography - Local - Low Countries

Htn Arc 1271.1.5* Wree, Olivier de. Les sceaux des comtes de Flandre. Bruge, 1641.

Arc 1271.2 Nederlandsche kloosterzegels voor 1600. v.1-23. 's Gravenhage, 1935-52. 4v.

Arc 1273 Sigillography - Local - Great Britain - Folios [Discontinued]

Arc 1273.1 Wyon, A. The great seals of England. London, 1887.

Htn Arc 1273.2F* Vertue, G. Medals, coins, great seals, impressions from the elaborate works of Thomas Simon. London, 1753.

Arc 1274 Sigillography - Local - Great Britain - General works

Arc 1274.1 Deville, J. Achille. Dissertation sur les sceaux de Richard-Coeur-de-Lion. Rouen, 1828.

Arc 1274.2.3 Laing, Henry. Supplemental descriptive catalogue of ancient Scottish seals. Edinburgh, 1866.

Arc 1274.3 Pedrick, G. Monastic seals of the XIIIth century. London, 1902.

Arc 1274.3.5 Pedrick, G. Borough seals of the Gothic period. London, 1904.

Arc 1274.4 Birch de Gray, W. History of Scottish seals. London, 1905. 2v.

Arc 1274.5 Blood, J.H. English seals. London, n.d.

Arc 1274.6 Porteous, A. The town council seals. Edinburgh, 1906.

Arc 1274.7 Caulfield, R. Sigilla ecclesiae Hibernicae illustrata. pt.1-4. Dublin, 1853.

Arc 1274.9 Morgan, Frederick Charles. A concise list of seals belonging to the Dean and Chapter of Hereford Cathedral. Hereford, 1966.

Arc 1276 Sigillography - Local - Scandinavian Countries

Arc 1276.5 Grandjean, P.B. Danske haandvaerkerlavs segl. København, 1950.

Arc 1276.10F Grandjean, P.B. Danske konggelige segl fra Frederik ILS. København, 1951.

Arc 1276.15F Grandjean, P.B. Slesvigske kobstaeders og herreders segl indtil 1660. København, 1953.

Arc 1276.20F Grandjean. P.B. Danske gilders segl fra middelaldesen. København, 1948.

Arc 1276.25F Grandjean, P.B. Danske herreders segl indtil 1660. København, 1946.

Arc 1276.30F Grandjean, P.B. Danske kobstaeders segl indtil 1660. København, 1937.

Arc 1276.31F Petersen, H. Danske adelige sigiller. København, 1897.

Arc 1279 Sigillography - Local - Austria and Hungary

Arc 1279.2 Hungary. K. Orszagos Leveltar. A Magy. Kiral. Orszagos Leveltar diplom. osztalyaban orzalt. Budapest, 1909.

Arc 1279.5 Melly, Edward. Beiträge zur Siegelkunde des Mittelalters. Wien, 1850. 2v.

Arc 1279.5F Melly, Edward. Beiträge zur Siegelkunde des Mittelalters. Supplement. Wien, 1850.

Arc 1279.6 Lind, Karl. Blaetter für altere Sphragiotik. Wien, 1878.

Arc 1279.10 Czobor, Béla. Magyarország világi és egyházi hatóságai kiadott pecseteinek jegyzeke. Pest, 1872.

Arc 1281 Sigillography - Local - Russia - Folios [Discontinued]

Arc 1281.1F Russia. Commission d'Impression des Lettres Patentes et Traités. Reproduction d'anciens cachets russes. Moscou, 1880.

Arc 1282 Sigillography - Local - Russia - General works

Arc 1282.5 Likhachen, N.I. Drenieishiia bully i nechati shiriully. Sankt Peterburg, 1907.

Arc 1282.7 Likhachen, N.I. Zemskaia nechat' Moskovskago gosudarstva. Moskva, 1914.

Arc 1282.9F Ivanov, I. Sbornik' snimkov's' drevnikh' pechatei. Moskva, 1858.

Arc 1282.10 Kamentseva, Elena I. Russkaia spagistika i geral'dika. Moskva, 1963.

Arc 1282.12 Ianin, Valentin L. Aktovye pechati drevnei Rusi X-XV vv. Moskva, 1970. 2v.

Arc 1285 Sigillography - Local - Other Europe

Arc 1285.1 Delaville Le Roulx, J. Note sur les sceaux de l'ordre de Saint Jean de Jérusalem. Paris, 1881.

Arc 1285.2 Delaville Le Roulx, J. Des sceaux des prieurs anglais de l'ordre de l'hôpital. Rome, 1881.

Arc 1285.2.3 Delaville Le Roulx, J. Des sceaux des prieurs anglais de l'ordre de l'hôpital. Rome, 1881. 2 pam.

Arc 1285.10 Haisig, Marian. Studia nad legendą pieczęci miejskiej. Wrocław, 1953.

Arc 1285.10.5 Gumowski, M. Pieczęcie i herby miejscowosci wojew lubelskiego. Lublin, 1959.

Arc 1285.10.6 Gumowski, M. Herby miast polskich. Warszawa, 1960.

Arc 1285.10.7 Gumowski, M. Sfragistyka. Warszawa, 1960.

Arc 1285.10.8 Gumowski, M. Handbuch der polnischen Siegelkunde. Graz, 1966.

Arc 1285.10.10 Fudalej, Aleksander. Pieczęcie kręstw głogowskigeo [sic] i Żagańskiego. Nova Sól, 1973.

Arc 1285.25 Nehmiz, H. Untersuchungen über die Besiegelung der schlesichen Herzogsurkunden im 13. Jahrhundert. Inaug. Diss. Breslau, 1938.

Arc 1285 Sigillography - Local - Other Europe - cont.

Arc 1285.25.5 Tomczyk, Damian. Pieczęcie górnośląskich cechów rzemieslniczych z XV-XVIII wisku i ich znaczenie historyczne. Wyd. 1. Opolu, 1975.

Arc 1285.27F Pfotenhauer, P. Die schlesischen Siegel von 1250 bis 1300 beziehentlich 1324. Breslau, 1849.

Arc 1285.30 Vojtišek, V. O pečetech a erbech měst pražskych a jinych českych. Praha, 1928.

Arc 1285.30.5 Beneš, František. Pečeti v českých zemích a jejich cena jako dějepisného pramene. Praha, 1949.

Arc 1285.30.10 Pamphlet vol. "Pečete". 2 pam.

Arc 1285.35 Solovjev, A.V. Istorija srpskog grba. Melburn, 1958.

Arc 1285.35.5 Ivić, Aleksa. Stari srpski pečati i grbovi. Novi Sad, 1910.

Arc 1297 Sigillography - Special topics - Folios [Discontinued]

Arc 1297.5 Leist, F. Die Notariats-Signete. Leipzig, n.d.

Arc 1298 Sigillography - Special topics - Monographs

Arc 1298.1 Guenther, M. Ins sigillorum mediiaevi. Lipsiae, 1813.

Arc 1298.1.5 Guenther, M. Das Siegelrecht des Mittelalters. Stuttgart, 1870.

Arc 1298.2 Eitel, Anton. Über Blei- und Goldbullen. Freiburg, 1912.

Arc 1300 - 1325 Numismatics - Periodicals and Societies (A-Z)

Arc 1300.01 Pamphlet box. American Numismatic and Archaeological Society. Miscellaneous pamphlets.

Arc 1300.1 American Numismatic Society. American journal of numismatics. N.Y. 1-53,1866-1919 28v.

Arc 1300.1.5 American Numismatic Society. The American Numismatic Society. N.Y., 195-

Arc 1300.1.7 American Numismatic Society. Centennial publication. N.Y., 1958.

Arc 1300.1.8 American Numismatic Society. Centennial celebration. N.Y., 1958.

Arc 1300.1.9 American Numismatic Society. Proceedings of annual meetings. 20-104,1878-1962 11v.

NEDL Arc 1300.1.10 American Numismatic Society. Proceedings.

Arc 1300.1.11 American Numismatic Society. Annual report. N.Y. 1962+ 2v.

Arc 1300.1.12 American Numismatic Society. Numismatic notes and monographs. N.Y. 1-157 40v.

Arc 1300.1.15 American Numismatic Society. Numismatic studies. N.Y. 1-12 5v.

Arc 1300.1.17 American Numismatic Society. Museum notes. N.Y. 1-15 8v.

Arc 1300.2 American Numismatic Society. Membership list. N.Y. 1930

Arc 1300.3 Numismatic literature. N.Y. 1,1947+ 13v.

Arc 1300.4 Archiv für Medaillen- und Plaketten-Kunde. Halle an der Saale. 1-5,1913-1926 3v.

Arc 1300.5 Academia...Bucharest. Academia Republicii Populare Romêne, Bucharest. Studii si certcetari de numismatica. 1-5 5v.

Arc 1300.6 Aureus; Zeitschrift für Numismatik und Geldwesen. München. 3-16,1960-1971//

Arc 1300.8 Arte e moneta. Roma. 3

Arc 1300.9 Antike Münzen und Geschnittere Steine. Berlin. 1,1969+ 9v.

Arc 1300.30 Adelson, Howard L. The American Numismatic Society. N.Y., 1958.

Arc 1300.32 Az érem. Budapest. 1922+

Arc 1300.34 Acta numismática. Barcelona. 1,1971+ 5v.

Arc 1301.1 British Numismatic Society. British numismatic journal. London. 1,1905+ 39v.

Arc 1301.1.9 Rules of the British Numismatic Society. London, 1908.

Arc 1301.1.15 Pamphlet box. The British Numismatic Society. Miscellaneous pamphlets.

Arc 1301.2 Pamphlet box. The Boston Numismatic Society. Miscellaneous pamphlets.

Arc 1301.2.5 Lewis, Winslow. Address...on resigning the presidency of the Boston Numismatic Society, January 5, 1865. N.Y., 1866.

Arc 1301.3 Bulletin de numisnatique. v.1-3,4-7,8-13. Paris, 1891-1906. 3v.

Arc 1301.4 Bullettino di numismatica e sfragistica per la storia d'Italia. Camerino. 1-3,1882-1887 5v.

Arc 1301.6 Bayerische Numismatische Gesellschaft. Mitteilungen. München. 1-52,1882-1934

Arc 1301.6.2 Bayerische Numismatische Gesellschaft. Mitteilungen. Register. München. 1-48,1882-1930

Arc 1301.8 Blätter für Münzfreunde und Münzforschung. Lübeck. 1,1865+ 19v.

Arc 1301.10 Biuletyn numizmatyczny. Warszawa. 2,1965+ 2v.

Arc 1302.1 The coin collector's journal 1876-1882. N.Y. 1876-1888 10v.

Arc 1302.4 Numismatický časopis československý. Praha. 1-21 9v.

Arc 1302.5 Österreich Gesellschaft für Münz und Medaillenkunde. Mitteilungen. Wien. 1890-1905 3v.

Arc 1302.6 Cercle d'Études Numismatiques. Travaux. Bruxelles. 1,1964+

Arc 1302.7 Cercle d'Études Numismatiques. Bulletin. Bruxelles. 1,1964+

Arc 1302.8 Cahiers numismatiques. Paris. 1,1964+

Arc 1302.9 Cunobelin; the yearbook of the British Association of Numismatic Societies. Leeds. 3-14,1956-1968//

Arc 1302.10 Coin hoards. London. 1,1975+

Arc 1303.2 Deutsches Jahrbuch für Numismatik. München. 1-4,1938-1941 3v.

Arc 1303.3 Deutsche Münzblätter. Berlin. 26-62,1905-1943 14v.

Arc 1304.5 Exposición Iberoamericana de Numismatica y Medallistica. Boletin. Barcelona. 1,1958

Arc 1304.10 Études numismatiques. Bruxelles. 1-4,1960-1967//

Arc 1305.2 Frank Caucey Wilson's monthly rare coin bulletin. Chicago. 63,1943

Arc 1305.3 Die Fundmünzen der römischen Zeit in Österreich. Burgenland. Eisenstadt. 1,1970+

Arc 1306.3 La gazette numismatique. Bruxelles.

Arc 1306.4 Gazette numismatique française. Paris. 1897

Arc 1306.6 Geldgeschichtliche Nachrichten. Frankfurt am Main. 1,1966+

Arc 1307.5 Handbook of United States coins. Racine, Wis. 2,1943

Arc 1307.7 Hamburger Beiträge zur Numismatik. Hamburg. 6,1947+ 9v.

Arc 1307.9 Hispanic numismatic series. N.Y. 3v.

Arc 1307.11 Hautes études numismatiques. Paris. 1,1966+ 4v.

Arc 1307.13 Historia; the journal of the Historical Medal Society of Australia and New Zealand. Sydney. 1,1968+

Classified Listing

Arc 1300 - 1325 Numismatics - Periodicals and Societies (A-Z) - cont.

Arc 1307.15 Handbuecker der mittelasiatischen Numismatik. Braunschweig. 1-4,1968-1973// 5v.
Arc 1308.2 Istituto Italiano di Numismatica, Rome. Atti e memorie. Roma. 1-4,1913-1921 2v.
Arc 1308.3 Istituto Italiano di Numismatica, Rome. Annali. 1-24 10v.
Arc 1308.5 Numismatic Society of India. Journal. Calcutta. 1,1939+ 12v.
Arc 1308.7 International Numismatic Congress. Congrès international de numismatique. Paris, 1953-57. 2v.
Arc 1308.7.6 International Numismatic Congress, 6th, Rome, 1961. Congresso internazionale di numismatica, Roma, 11-16 sett., 1961. Roma, 1961-65. 2v.
Arc 1308.10 Israel numismatic journal. Tel-Aviv. 1,1963
Arc 1309.1 Journal international d'archéologie numismatique. Athenes. 1-21,1898-1927// 12v.
Arc 1309.1.5 Journal international d'archéologie numismatique. Analytical index. 1898-1927. N.Y., 1967.
Arc 1309.5 Jahrbuch für Numismatik und Geldgeschichte. München. 1,1949+ 8v.
Arc 1311.1 Liverpool Numismatic Society. Journal. Liverpool. 1-2,1873-1877
Arc 1311.1.3 Liverpool Numismatic Society. Report, proceedings. Liverpool. 1,1871
Arc 1311.2 Leningrad. Ermitazh. Trutsy otts. numizmatiki. Leningrad. 1,1945 4v.
Arc 1312.1 Liverpool Numismatic Society. Melanges numismatique. Le Mens. 1-3,1874-1882 3v.
Arc 1312.2 Manchester Numismatic Society. Proceedings. Manchester.
Arc 1312.3 Mason's monthly illustrated coin collectors' magazine. Boston.
Arc 1312.4 Mehl's numismatic monthly. Fort Worth, Texas.
Arc 1312.5 Muenzstudien. Halle an der Saale. 1-7,1923-1929 4v.
Arc 1312.6 Moskovskoe Numizmaticheskoe Obshchestvo. Numizmaticheskii sbornik. Moskva. 3,1915
Arc 1312.7 Münzstudien. Leipzig. 1-9,1857-1877 7v.
Arc 1312.8 Der Münzen- und Medaillensammler. Freiburg im Breisgau. 1,1961+ 3v.
Arc 1312.9 Minerva numismatic handbooks. Newcastle-upon-Tyne. 1,1967+
Arc 1312.10 Memorial numismático español. Barcelona. 1-2,1866-1868
Arc 1312.12 Moravské numismatické zprávy. Brno. 1,1956+
Arc 1313.1 Royal Numismatic Society. Numismatic chronicle. London. 1,1894+ 105v.
Arc 1313.1.9 Pamphlet box. Royal Numismatic Society. Miscellaneous pamphlets.
Arc 1313.1.10 Royal Numismatic Society. Special publications. 1-8 8v.
Arc 1313.2 Royal Numismatic Society. Proceedings. London. 1836-1837
Arc 1313.2.25 Royal Numismatic Society. Transactions of the International Numismatic Congress. London, 1938.
Arc 1313.3 Numismatic journal. London. 1887
Arc 1313.3.5 Nummus; numismática - medalhística - arqueologia. Porto. 1,1952+ 7v.
Arc 1313.4 The numismatist. Federalsburg. 1,1894+ 99v.
Arc 1313.5 Blätter für Münzkunde. Leipzig. 1-4,1834-1844 2v.
Arc 1313.5.3 Numismatischer Anzeiger. Hannover. 1-2,1868-1869
Arc 1313.5.6 Numismatisch-sphragistischer Anzeiger. Hannover. 1-29,1870-1898 5v.
Arc 1313.7 Numismatische Gesellschaft in Wien. Monatsblatt. Wien. 69,1956
Arc 1313.8 Numismatische Zeitschrift. Wien. 1-88 41v.
Arc 1313.9 Numisma. Irvington, N.Y.
Arc 1313.10 Numismatic review. N.Y. 2-4,1944-1947 2v.
Arc 1313.11 Numismatic and philatelic journal of Japan. Yokohama. 1-4,1913-1914 4v.
Arc 1313.12 Numismatic gallery monthly. California? 1-6,1948-1953
Arc 1313.14 Numismatische Studien. Hamburg. 1-7 3v.
Arc 1313.15 Numisma. Madrid. 1,1951+ 9v.
Arc 1313.15.5 Periodico di numismatica e sfragistica per la storia d'Italia. Firenze. 1-6,1868-1874 3v.
Arc 1313.18 Nordisk numismatisk årsskrift. Stockholm. 1936+ 14v.
Arc 1313.19 Numismatisches Nachrichtenblatt; Organ des Verbandes der westdeutschen Münzvereine und der numismatischen Kommissio der Länder in der Bundesrepublik Deutschland. Hamburg. 6,1957+ 9v.
Arc 1313.20 Numismatický sborník. Praha. 1-8,1953-1964 10v.
Arc 1313.21 Numismatické listý. Praha. 1+ 8v.
Arc 1313.22 Numismática. Madrid. 2-3
Arc 1313.25 Numizmaticheskii sbornik. Moskva. 1-2,1955-1957 2v.
Arc 1313.30 Numizmatika i epigrafika. Moskva. 1-4,1960-1963 11v.
Arc 1313.32 Numizmatika i sfragistika. Kiev. 1,1963 4v.
Arc 1313.35 Numizmatičke vijesti. Zagreb. 15+ 2v.
Arc 1313.36 Nálezy mincé na Slovensku. Bratislava. 2,1968+
Arc 1313.40 Österreichische Numismatische Gesellschaft. Mitteilungen. Wien. 1,1937+ 6v.
Arc 1313.44 Numismatique romaine. Wetteren. 1,1965+ 3v.
Arc 1313.46 Nomismatika chronika. Athēnai. 1,1972+
Arc 1315.1 Société Francaise de Numismatique. Annuaire. Paris. 1-20,1866-1896 20v.
Arc 1315.1.5 Société Francaise de Numismatique. Comptes rendu. Paris, 1869-75. 7v.
Arc 1315.5 Strozzi, Carlo. Periodico di numismatica e sfragistica per la storia d'Italia. Firenze, 1868-74. 6v.
Arc 1317.1 Revue de la numismatique françoise. Blois. 1,1836+ 94v.
Arc 1317.1.5 Dieudonné, A. Table de la revue numismatique. Paris. 1836-1915 2v.
Arc 1317.2 Revue Charlemagne. Paris. 1911 2v.
Arc 1317.3 Revue belge de numismatique. Bruxelles. 1842+ 91v.
Arc 1317.3.2 Revue belge de numismatique. Table alphabetique. 1842-1880 3v.
Arc 1317.4 Ambrosoli, S. Revista italiana di numismatica. Milano. 1,1888+ 43v.
Arc 1317.4F Ambrosoli, S. Revista italiana di numismatica. Milano. 37,1924
Arc 1317.4.12 Rassegna numismatica. Orbetello. 1-38,1904-1941 12v.
Arc 1317.5 Rossiiskaia Akademiia Istorii Material'noi Kul'tury. Trudy Numizmaticheskoi Kommissii. Sankt Peterburg. 1-6,1921-1927
Arc 1318.2 Svenska Numismatika Föreningen. Numismatiska meddelanden. Stockholm. 1-29,1874-1943 7v.
Arc 1318.3 Société Suisse de Numismatique. Bulletin. Fribourg. 1-11,1882-1892 4v.
Arc 1318.3.5 Société Suisse de Numismatique. Revue suisse de numismatique. Genève. 1,1891+ 19v.

Arc 1300 - 1325 Numismatics - Periodicals and Societies (A-Z) - cont.

Arc 1318.3.6 Société Suisse de Numismatique. Regiser zu Bulletin, v.1-11; Revue suisse de numismatique, v.1-24. Bern, 1929.
Arc 1318.3.7 Société Suisse de Numismatique. La Société Suisse...de 1879 à 1896, notices divers. Genève, 1896.
Arc 1318.4 The shekel. N.Y. 1,1968+ 3v.
Arc 1318.5 Steigerwalt's coin journal. Lancaster, Pa. 1-2,1883-1884
Arc 1318.6 Schweizer Münzblätter. Basel. 1-14,1950-1964 7v.
Arc 1318.7 Spain. Consejo Superior de Investigaciones Cientificas. Instituto Antonio Agustin de Numismatica. Numario hispánico. 1-10,1952-1961 5v.
Arc 1318.8 Seaby's coin and medal bulletin. London. 1958+ 16v.
Arc 1318.9 Slovenská numizmatika. Bratislava. 1,1970+ 2v.
Arc 1319.1 K. Nederlandsch Genootschap voor Munt en Penningkunde. Tijdschrift van het (Koninklyk) genootschap. Amsterdam. 1-21,1893-1913 14v.
Arc 1319.1.5 K. Nederlandsch Genootschap voor Munt en Penningknude. Tijdschrift van het (Koninklyk) genootschap. Index, 1-20, 1893-1912. Amsterdam, 1903.
Arc 1319.2 K. Nederlandsch Genootschap voor Munt en Penningkunde. Jaarboek. Amsterdam. 1-26,1914-1939 9v.
Arc 1322.5 Wiadomości numizmatyczne. Warszawa. 1+ 6v.
Arc 1322.10F Wiadomości numizmatyczno-archeologiczne. Krakowie. 1-21,1889-1948 8v.
Arc 1322.15 Whitman numismatic journal. Racine, Wis. 1,1964+ 2v.
Arc 1324.1 Yorkshire Numismatic Society. Transactions. Hull. 1,1913
Arc 1324.2 Yorkshire Numismatic Fellowship. Annual report. Hull. 1,1909
Arc 1324.3 Pamphlet box. Yorkshire Numismatic Society.
Arc 1325.1 Sallet, A. von. Zeitschrift für Numismatik. Berlin. 1-42,1894-1935 37v.
Arc 1325.1.5 Sallet, A. von. Register. Berlin. 1-20,1884-1898
Arc 1325.2 Kölme, B. Zeitschrift für Münz, Siegel und Wappenkunde. Berlin. 1-6 3v.

Arc 1329 Numismatics - Bibliographies - Folios [Discontinued]

Arc 1329.1 Hirsch, J.C. Bibliotheca numismatica. Nuremberg, 1760.
Arc 1329.2 AmericanNumismatic Society. Catalogue of numismatic books in the library. N.Y., 1883.
Arc 1329.3 Riechmann, A. and Co. Numismatische Literatur. Halle am der Saale, 1926.

Arc 1330 Numismatics - Bibliographies - General works

Arc 1330.1 Banduri, A. Bibliotheca nummaria. Hamburg, 1719.
Arc 1330.2 Lipsius, J.G. Bibliotheca numaria. Leipzig, 1801. 2v.
Arc 1330.3 Leitzmann, J. Bibliotheca numaria. Weissensee, 1867.
Arc 1330.4 New York Public Library. List of works relating to numismatics. N.Y., 1914.
Arc 1330.5F American Numismatic Society. Auction catalogue. Boston, 1962.
Arc 1330.6F American Numismatic Society. Dictionary catalogue. Boston, 1962. 6v.
Arc 1330.6.2F American Numismatic Society. Library. Dictionary and auction catalogues of the Library of the American Numismatic Society. First and second supplement. Boston, 1967. 2v.
Arc 1330.7 Clain-Stepanelli, Elvira Eliza. Select numismatic bibliography. N.Y., 1965.
Arc 1330.8 Numismatische Literatur Osteuropas und des Balkans. Graz. 1,1960+
Arc 1330.9 Janovský, Hubert. Katalog knihovny. Numismatické společnosti československé v Praze. vyd. 1. Praha, 1967.
Arc 1330.10 A survey of numismatic research 1960-1965. v.1-3. Copenhagen, 1967.
Arc 1330.11 Sigler, Phares O. Numismatic bibliography. Dearborn, Mich., 1951.
Arc 1330.15 Singhal, C.R. Bibliography of Indian coins. v.1-2. Bombay, 1950-52.
Arc 1330.18 Mayer, Leo Ary. A bibliography of Jewish numismatics. Jerusalem, 1966.
Arc 1330.20 Mayer, Leo Ary. Bibliography of Moslem numismatics, India excepted. London, 1939.
Arc 1330.20.2 Mayer, Leo Ary. Bibliography of Moslem numismatics, India excepted. 2. ed. London, 1954.
Arc 1330.25 Noble, Fiona Virginia. South African numismatics, 1652-1965; a bibliography. Capetown, 1967.
Arc 1330.30 Malter, Joel L. Byzantine numismatic bibliography, 1950-1965. Chicago, 1968.
Arc 1330.35 Ciferri, Raffaello. Saggio di bibliografia numismata medioevale italiana. Pavia, 1961.
Arc 1330.40 Roda y Delgada, Juan de Dios de la. Bibliografia numismatica española. Madrid, 1886.
Arc 1330.45 Camont, Georges. Bibliographie générale et raisonnée de la numismatique belge. Bruxelles, 1883.
Arc 1330.55 Canadian numismatic bibliography. A review of R.W. McLachlan's Canadian numismatics and other books and pamphlets describing Canadian coins and medals. Montreal, 1866.
Arc 1330.56.1 Gromachevskii, Semen G. Bibliografìcheskii ukajatel' literatury po russkoi numizmatike. Ann Arbor, Mich., 1965.

Arc 1333 Numismatics - Museums and Private collections - Folios [Discontinued]

Arc 1333.01F Pamphlet box. Numismatic collections.
Arc 1333.1 Venuti, R. Antiqua numismata. v.1-2. Rome, 1739-44.
Arc 1333.2 Wise, F. Numismata antiqua. Scriniis bodleianis rec. catalogus. Oxford, 1750.
Arc 1333.3 British Museum. Nummi veteres - in Museo R.P. Knight asservati. London, 1830.
Arc 1333.4 British Museum. Veteres pop. et reg. numi. London, 1814.
Htn Arc 1333.5* Herbert, T. Numismata antiqua. n.p., 1746.
Arc 1333.6 Koehne. Description. Musée...Prince Basile Kotschoubey. St. Petersbourg, 1857. 2v.
Arc 1333.7 Erdmann, F. Numi asiatici musei univ. caes. liter. Casanensis. Casani, 1834.
Arc 1333.8 Dudik, Beda. Des hohen deutschen Ritter-Ordens Münz-Sammlung in Wien. Wien, 1858.
Arc 1333.9 Smith, Harlan P. Catalogue...coins of the U.S. Philadelphia, 1906.
Arc 1333.10 Chapman, H. Catalogue of collections of coins of M.A. Trickney. Philadelphia, 1907.
Arc 1333.11 Serafini, C. Monete e bolle plumbee...del Medaghere Vaticano. Milano, 1910. 4v.
Arc 1333.13F Lockhart, J.H.S. The S. Lockhart collection of Chinese copper coins. Shanghai, 1915.
Arc 1333.14F Spink and Son, Ltd. Numismatic circular. London. 1-72,1893-1964 36v.

Arc 1333 Numismatics - Museums and Private collections - Folios [Discontinued] - cont.

Arc 1333.14.7 Spink and Son, Ltd. Numismatic circular of coins, medals, war medals, books, offered for sale. London. 1,1940+ 19v.
Arc 1333.15F St. Florian, Austria. Die Münzsammlung. Wien, 1871.
Arc 1333.16F Bahrfeldt, Emil. Die Münzen- und Medaillen-Sammlung. Danzig, 1901-10. 6v.
Arc 1333.17F Vienna. U.L.F. zu den Schotten. Benedictine Monastery. Die Münzensammlung des Stiftes Schotten in Wien. Wien, 1910-20. 2v.

Arc 1334 Numismatics - Museums and Private collections - Pamphlet volumes

Arc 1334.02 Pamphlet vol. Coin catalogue. A-Z, by collector.
Arc 1334.04 Pamphlet vol. Coin catalogue. A-Z, by dealer.
Arc 1334.06 Pamphlet vol. Coin catalogue of miscellaneous dealers and special collectors, A-Z. 12 pam.
Htn Arc 1334.5* Pamphlet vol. Coins and medals, 1749-1756.
Htn Arc 1334.6* Pamphlet vol. Coins and medals, 1860-1865. 4 pam.
Arc 1334.6.10 Catalogue de monnaies royales francaise en or. Paris, 1864. 9 pam.
Arc 1334.8 Phillips, H. Numismatics. Philadelphia, 1863-80. 12 pam.

Arc 1335 Numismatics - Museums and Private collections - General works

Arc 1335.1 Catalogue raisonné d'une collection de médailles. Leipzig, 1774.
Arc 1335.2 Chadbourne, S.H. Catalogue of a collection of coins and medals. Boston, 1867.
Arc 1335.3 Curtis, J.K. Priced catalogue of coins, medals and numismatic works. v.1-2. N.Y., 1858-59.
Arc 1335.4 Harzfeld, S.K. Catalogue of choice English, French, and American coins and medals. Boston, 1878.
Arc 1335.5 Hodges, D.M. Gold and silver coin chart manual. N.Y., n.d.
Arc 1335.6 Woodward, W.E. Catalogue of the numismatic collection of F.S. Hoffman. N.Y., 1866.
Arc 1335.7 Leavitt, Strebeigh and Company. Catalogue of an excellent choice and select collection of coins, medals, and autographs. n.p., 1870.
Arc 1335.8 Groux, D.E. Descriptive catalogue of coins belonging to the Historical Society of Maryland. n.p., n.d.
Arc 1335.9 Hansen von Ehrencron, F.A. Numophylacium Ehrencronianum. n.p., 1730.
Htn Arc 1335.10* Lefroy, A. Catalogus numism. mus. Lefroyani. Livorno, 1763.
Arc 1335.11 Leipzig. Stadtbibliothek. Katalog des Münzkabinets. Leipzig, 1853.
Arc 1335.11.5 Friedlander. Das königliche Münzkabinet. 2. Aufl. Berlin, 1877.
Htn Arc 1335.12* Mead, R. Museum Meadianum. London, n.d.
Htn Arc 1335.12.2* Mead, R. Museum Meadianum. London, n.d.
Arc 1335.13 Wesener, F.J. Die Gotthard mimus'sche Thaler und Medaillensammlung. Wien, 1874.
Arc 1335.14 Du Mersan, T.M. Notice sur la bibliothèque royale...sur le cabinet des médailles. Paris, 1836.
Arc 1335.14.2 Du Mersan, T.M. Histoire du cabinet des médailles. Paris, 1838.
Arc 1335.14.3 Du Mersan, T.M. Notice des monuments exposés dans le cabinet des médailles. Paris, 1840.
Arc 1335.14.4 Babelon, E. Guide illustré au cabinet des médailles. Paris, 1900.
Arc 1335.15 Thott, O. Thesaurus numismatum. Copenhagen, 1789.
Arc 1335.16 United States Mint, Philadelphia. A description of ancient and modern coins. Philadelphia, 1860.
Arc 1335.16.5 United States Mint, Philadelphia. Guide. Washington, 1913.
Arc 1335.17 Yates, J. Descriptive catalogue of a collection of current coins of all countries. London, 1862.
Arc 1335.18 Leonard and Company. Catalogue of American coins. Boston, 1860-70. 4 pam.
Arc 1335.19 Charvet, Jules. Collection Charvet. Paris, 1883.
Arc 1335.20 Werveke, N. van. Catalogue descriptive des monnaies luxembourgeoises. Luxembourg, 1880.
Arc 1335.21 Morbio, Carlo. VI catalogo dei duplicati delle raccolte. Milano, 1876.
Arc 1335.22 Stickel, J.G. Die grossherzogliche morgenländische Münzsammlung in Jena. Jena, 1846.
Arc 1335.23 Nesselmann, G.H.F. Die orientalischen Münzen...in Königsberg. Leipzig, 1858.
Arc 1335.24 Museum Munterianum. v.1-3. Hauniae, n.d.
Arc 1335.25 Tychsen, T.C. De numis cuficis in biblio. regia Gottingense. n.p., n.d.
Arc 1335.26 Wilmersdörffer, M. von. Max Ritter von Wilmersdörfferische Münzen-Sammlung. Frankfurt am Main, 1905-07. 2v.
Arc 1335.27.25 Bibliothèque Nationale, Paris. Département des Médailles et Antiques. Les monnaies. Paris, 1929.
Arc 1335.28 Judice dos Santos, J.J. Collection. pt.1,3. Amsterdam, 1906. 2v.
Arc 1335.29 Ulex, G.F. Sammlung des G.F. Ulex; Münzen und Medaillen von Nord-, Central-, und Süd-Amerika. Frankfurt, 1908.
Arc 1335.30 Antoine-Feill. Münzen- und Medaillen-Sammlung. Frankfurt, 1908.
Arc 1335.31 Boudeau, E. Catalogue général illustré de monnaies antiques. 2. ed. Paris, n.d.
Arc 1335.31.3 Boudeau, E. Catalogue général illustré de monnaies françaises. Paris, n.d.
Arc 1335.32 Zabriskie, A.C. Catalogue of the collection of American coins and medals. N.Y., 1909.
Arc 1335.33 D'Angers, D. Catalogue général de monnaies, médailles et jetons. Paris, n.d.
Arc 1335.34 Neumann, J. Beschreibung der Bekanntesten. v.1,2,3-4,5,6. Prag, 1858-72. 5v.
Arc 1335.36 Montélhet, A. Musée crozatier - catalogue du médaillier. v.1-2. Paris, 1912.
Arc 1335.37 Sambon, G. Catalogo delle monete italiane...collezione A. Cantoni di Milano. Milano, 1887.
Arc 1335.38 Young, Matthew. Catalogue of...coins and medals in gold, silver, and copper. pt.1. London, 1839.
Arc 1335.39 Elder, Thomas L. Rare coins and medals of William S. Appleton. N.Y., 1913.
Arc 1335.40 Erbstein, J. Die Schellhass'sche Münzsammlung. Dresden, 1870.
Arc 1335.41.5 Robinson, John. Oriental numismatics - catalogue of collections of books related to coinage of the east presented to Essex Institute, Salem. Salem, 1913.
Arc 1335.42 Quelen, E. de. Collection de M. le Vicomte de...monnaies. Paris, 1883.

Arc 1335 Numismatics - Museums and Private collections - General works - cont.

Arc 1335.43 Borrell, H.P. Catalogue of...Greek, Roman, Byzantine and Mediterranean coins. v.1-2. London? 1852?
Arc 1335.44 Borioni, T. Collana di medaglie antiche e moderne. Loreto, 1835.
Arc 1335.45.9 Alexander and Company, Boston. Alexander and Company's Hub coin book. Boston, 1910.
Arc 1335.46 Bonnet, Emile. Médaillier de la Société archéologique de Montpellier. Montpellier, 1896.
Arc 1335.47 Coins and their values. London, 1917.
Arc 1335.48 Helbing, Otto. Auktions-Katalog. München, 1910.
Arc 1335.49 Hirsch, J. Sammlung Gustav Philipsen. München, 1909.
Arc 1335.50 Thomsen, C.J. Catalogue de la collection de monnaies. v.1, pt.1-2; v.2, pt.1-3; v.3, pt.1-2. Copenhague, 1869-76. 7v.
Arc 1335.51 Bellissima, G.B. Riordinamento del museo numismatico. v.1-2. Siena, 1914.
Arc 1335.52 Stephanik, J.W. Cabinet de monnaies. Amsterdam, 1904.
Arc 1335.53 Stroehlin, P.C. Collections numismatiques. Genève, 1909.
Arc 1335.54 Fiala, Eduard. Collection Ernest Prinz zu Windisch Gratz. Prag, 1895-99. 7v.
Arc 1335.55 Murray, David. The Hunterian Museum in the old college of Glasgow. Glasgow, 1925.
Arc 1335.56.2 Bataviaasch Genootschap van Kunsten en Wetenschappen. Museum. Catalogus der numismatische afdeeling. 2. druk. Batavia, 1877.
Arc 1335.56.3 Bataviaasch Genootschap van Kunsten en Wetenschappen. Museum. Catalogus der numismatische versameling. 3. druk. Batavia, 1886.
Arc 1335.57F Gohl, Ödön. Gróf Dessewffy Miklos barbár pénzei. pt.1-2. Budapest, 1910-11.
Arc 1335.58 Yale College. Catalogue of the cabinet of coins belonging to Yale College. New Haven, 1863.
Arc 1335.59 Cahn, A.E. Versteigerungskatalog nr. 57. Frankfurt, 1926.
Arc 1335.59.5 Cahn, A.E. Versteigerungskatalog nr. 63. v.2. Frankfurt am Main, 1929.
Arc 1335.59.10 Cahn, A.E. Versteigerungskatalog nr. 71. v.2. Frankfurt am Main, 1931.
Arc 1335.60 Hutchins. A catalogue of the collection of curious...coins. London, 1790.
Arc 1335.61 Dupriez, C. La grande guerre. Bruxelles, 19- ?
Arc 1335.62 André, Leon. Importante collection de monnaies et médailles. Paris, 1926.
Arc 1335.63.3 British Museum. Department of Coins and Medals. A guide to the department of coins and medals. London, 1922.
Arc 1335.64 Jandolo et Lavazzi, Rome, auctioneers. Vente aux enchères publiques de la collection de médailles grecques. Roma, 1908.
Arc 1335.65 Berlin. Staatliche Museum. Kaiser Friedrich Museum. Die Schausammlung des Münzkabinetts im Kaiser Friedrich Museum Berlin, 1919.
Arc 1335.70 Mikocki, Leon. Verzeichniss einer grossen und sehr gewählten polnischen Münz- und Medaillen-Sammlung. Wien, 1850.
Arc 1335.75 Wallraf, F.F. Beschreibung der köllnischen Munzsammlung des domherrn und kurfürstlich-weltlichen Hofgerichts Präsidenten von Merle. Kölln am Rhein, 1792.
Arc 1335.76.3 Athens. Ethnikon Nomismatikon Mouseion. Katalogos. Athēnai, 1910.
Arc 1335.76.5 Athens. Ethnikon Nomismatikon Mouseion. Ekthesis ōerilēotikē. Athēnai, 1857.
Arc 1335.76.10F Athens. Ethnikon Nomismatikon Mouseion. Katalogos. Athēnai, 1868.
Arc 1335.76.11F Athens. Ethnikon Nomismatikon Mouseion. Katalogos. Athēnai, 1872.
Arc 1335.76.13F Athens. Ethnikon Nomismatikon Mouseion. Synopsis numorum veterum. Athenes, 1878.
Arc 1335.76.14 Athens. Ethnikon Nomismatikon Mouseion. Karmatia symbolika. Athēnai, 1880.
Arc 1335.76.16 Athens. Ethnikon Nomismatikon Mouseion. Nomismata. Athēnai, 1885.
Arc 1335.77 Colombo Museum. Colombo, Ceylon. Catalogue of coins in the Colombo Museum. Hertford, 1914.
Arc 1335.80 Tizengauzen', V. Novyia numizmaticheskiia priobreteniia N.P. Linevicha. Sankt Peterburg, 1896.
Arc 1335.81 MacDonald, G. The Hunterian coin cabinet. Glasgow, 1933.
Arc 1335.82F Chapman, H. Catalogue of J.S. Jenks collection of coins. Philadelphia, 1921.
Arc 1335.83 Pertusi, G., firm, auctioneer, Milan. Catalogo della collezione A. Ancona di Milano. Milano, 1892.
Arc 1335.84.5 Gnecchi, F. Guida numismatica universale. 4. ed. Milano, 1903.
Arc 1335.85F Haverkamp, S. Nummophylacium reginae Christinae. Comitum Hagae, 1742.
Arc 1335.86.5 Stockvis, Albert. Standard coin and medal catalogue of the world. Cleveland. 1940-1945 3v.
Arc 1335.87 Helbing, Otto. Auktions-Katalog enthaltend die Münzen- und Medaillen-Bestände der aufgelösten Firma zschiesche und Köder. München, 1913.
Arc 1335.88F Rollin et Teuardent, firm, Paris. Monnaies d'or romaines et byzantines. Paris, 1887.
Arc 1335.88.25F Rollin et Teuardent, firm, Paris. Monnaies d'or romaines et byzantines vente aux enchères publiques 20-28 avril, 1896. Paris, 1896.
Arc 1335.89 Sotheby, W. Catalogue of the collection of Greek coins in gold. London, 1894.
Arc 1335.90 Kündig, W. Monnaies romaines impériales provenant des collections de Paul Vautier. Genève, 1922.
Arc 1335.91 Kündig, W. Monnaies grecques antiques provenant des collection de S.A.I. le grand-duc Alexandra Michäilouit. Genève, 1922.
Arc 1335.91.25 Kündig, W. Monnaies grecques antiques provenant des doubles du British Museum des collections de feu le Gen. A.L. Bertier. Genève, 1923.
Arc 1335.101 Hirsch, Jacob. Auctions-Catalog der bedeutenden Sammlung römischer und byzantinischer Münzen. München, 1907.
Arc 1335.101.25 Hirsch, Jacob. Griechische, römische und byzantinische Münzen aus dem Besitze von Friedrich von Schennis. München, 1913.
Arc 1335.101.51 Hirsch, Jacob. Griechische, römische, byzantinische Münzen. München, 1914.
Arc 1335.101.71 Hirsch, Jacob. Sammlung Consul Eduard Friedrich Weber, Hamburg. München, 1908-09. 2v.
Arc 1335.103 Poulhariez, P.N. Histoire métallique de l'Europe, ou Catalogue des médailles modernes. Lyon, 1767.
Arc 1335.105 Devegge, Ole. Ole Devegge's mynt-og medaille-samling. Kjøbenhavn, 1851.

Arc 1335 Numismatics - Museums and Private collections - General works - cont.

Arc 1335.107 Moscow. Gosudarstvennyi Rumiantsovskii Muzei. Numizmaticheskii kabinet. Moskva, 1884.
Arc 1335.110 American Numismatic Society. International medallic exhibition. N.Y., 1910.
Arc 1335.112PF American Numismatic Society. Sylloge nummoium Graecorum. v.1, pt.2. N.Y., 1961.
Arc 1335.115 Signorelli, A. Collezione del Prof. Angelo Signorelli. pt.1-2. Roma, 1951-52.
Arc 1335.120 Hollschek, Karl. Sammlung Hollschek. v.4-20. Wien, 1956? 4v.
Arc 1335.120F Hollschek, Karl. Sammlung Hollschek. v.1-3. Wien, 1956? 2v.
Arc 1335.125 Enzenberg, Arthur. Katalog der Münzensammlung Arthur Graf Enzenberg. Luzern, 1935.
Arc 1335.130 Landowne, William P. A catalogue of a valuable collection. London, 18- ?
Arc 1335.135 Madrid. Museo Argueológico Nacional. Catalago. Madrid, 1925.
Arc 1335.140 Escorial. Biblioteca. Catalago de las monedas y medallas de la biblioteca de San Lorenzo de el Escorial. Madrid, 1935.
Arc 1335.145 Götz, Christian. Beyträge zum Groschen-Cabinet. Dresden, 1810. 3v.
Arc 1335.150F Gesellschaft der Freunde. Die Siegelsammlung des Mannheimer. Manheim, 1897.
Arc 1335.151 Jewish Theological Seminary. Great Jewish portraits in metal. N.Y., 1963.
Arc 1335.153 Erlangen. Universität. Bibliothek. Die Voit von Salzburg'sche Münz. München, 1933.
Arc 1335.154 Wambolt, F. von. Katalog des grossen Freiherrlich von Wambolt'schen Münzkabinets in Heidelberg. v.1-2. Heidelberg, 1833.
Arc 1335.155 Chalon, Renier. Collection de feu M. Renier Chalon. v.2. Bruxelles, 1889.
Arc 1335.156 Reinfeld, Fred. Catalogue of the world's most popular coins. Garden City, 1965.
Arc 1335.157.2 Friedberg, Robert. Gold coins of the world, complete from 600 A.D. to the present. N.Y., 1965.
Arc 1335.158 Kiel. Universität. Museum für Vor- und Frühgeschichte. Kieler Münzkatalog. Verzeichniss der Münzsammlung des Schleswig-Holsteinischen Museum Vaterländischer Alterthümer. 1863-1887//
Arc 1335.159 American University of Beirut. Archaeological Museum. The coins exhibited in the Archaeological Museum of the American University of Beirut. Beirut, 1968.
Arc 1335.161 Dickmann-Secherau, Johanna N. Dickmann's Münzsammlung in Wien. Wien, 1836.
Arc 1335.164F American University of Beirut. Museum of Archaeology. The coin collection. Beirut, 1974.
Arc 1335.165 Kapossy, Balázs. Münzen und Medaillen aus dem Bernischen Historischen Museum. Bern, 1969.

Arc 1340 Numismatics - Dictionaries

Arc 1340.1 Rasche, J.C. Lex. univ. rei nummariae. v.1-5, pt.1-2; v.6, pt.1. Leipzig, 1785-95. 11v.
Arc 1340.1.2 Rasche, J.C. Lex. univ. rei numariae veterum. Supplement. Leipzig, 1802-05. 3v.
Arc 1340.2 Stevenson, Seth William. A dictionary of Roman coins. London, 1889.
Arc 1340.2.2 Stevenson, Seth William. A dictionary of Roman coins, republican and imperial. London, 1964.
Arc 1340.3F Martinori, E. Moneta; vocabolario. Roma, 1915.
Arc 1340.4 Boutkowski, Alex. Dictionnaire numismatique. Leipzig, 1877.
Arc 1340.5 Pamphlet box. First part of a German numismatic dictionary.
Arc 1340.6 Girod, Joseph. Dictionnaire spécial et classique des monnaies. Paris, 1827.
Arc 1340.7 Smith, Alfred M. Illustrated encyclopedia of gold and silver coins of the world. Philadelphia, 1886.
Arc 1340.8 Schrotter, F. Wörterbuch der Münzkunde. Berlin, 1930.
Arc 1340.9 Holtz, Walter. Abkürzungen auf Münzen. Braunschweig, 1972.
Arc 1340.10 Zvarych, Volodymyr V. Numizmatychnyi slovnyk. L'viv, 1972.

Arc 1345 Numismatics - General works - Folios [Discontinued]

Arc 1345.1 Trésor de numismatique et glyptique, numismatique des rois grecs. Paris, 1858.
Arc 1345.1.2 Nouvelle galerie mythologique. Paris, 1858.
Arc 1345.1.3 Bas-reliefs du Parthénon. Paris, 1858.
Arc 1345.1.4 Iconographie des empereurs romains. Paris, 1858.
Arc 1345.1.5 Histoire de l'art monétaires...modernes. Paris, 1858.
Arc 1345.1.6 Choix histoires des médailles des papes. Paris, 1858.
Arc 1345.1.7 Recueil de médailles italiennes, XVe et XVIe siècles. Paris, 1858. 2v.
Arc 1345.1.8 Recueil de médailles allemandes, XVIe et XVIIe siècles. Paris, 1858.
Arc 1345.1.9 Sceaux des rois et reines d'Angleterre. Paris, 1858.
Arc 1345.1.10 Sceaux des rois et des reines de France. Paris, 1858.
Arc 1345.1.11 Sceaux des grands feudataires de la couronne. Paris, 1858.
Arc 1345.1.12 Sceaux des communes, communautés, évêques. Paris, 1858.
Arc 1345.1.13 Histoire de France par médailles: Charles VII-Louis XVI. Paris, 1858. 3v.
Arc 1345.1.14 Histoire de France par médailles: Révolution française. Paris, 1858.
Arc 1345.1.15 Histoire de France par médailles: Empire français. Paris, 1858.
Arc 1345.1.16 Recueil général de bas-reliefs et d'ornements. Paris, 1858. 2v.
Arc 1345.5F Mangeart, Thomas. Introduction a la science des médailles. Paris, 1763.

Arc 1347 Numismatics - General works - Pamphlet volumes

Arc 1347 Pamphlet box. Numismatics.
Arc 1347.1 Ruhe, C.F. Specimen philolgiae numismatico-latinae primum. Frankfort, 1708-29. 3 pam.
Arc 1347.2 Bytemeister, H.J. Delineatio rei numismaticae. Helmstadt, 1738? 3 pam.
Arc 1347.3 Scott, W.H. On the Parthian coins. London, 1836-54. 28 pam.
Arc 1347.4 Pamphlet vol. Numismatik. 27 pam.

Arc 1348 Numismatics - General works - Monographs

Arc 1348.1 Akerman, J.Y. Numismatic manual. London, 1840.
Arc 1348.1.5 Akerman, J.Y. Introductory study of ancient and modern coins. London, 1848.
Arc 1348.2 Dubois, P. Moneta: a study. n.p., 1884.

Arc 1348 Numismatics - General works - Monographs - cont.

Arc 1348.4A Hazlitt, W.C. The coin collector. N.Y., 1896.
Arc 1348.4B Hazlitt, W.C. The coin collector. N.Y., 1896.
Arc 1348.5 Hoffmann, L.W. Alter und neuer Münz-Schlüssel. Nuremberg, 1692.
NEDL Arc 1348.6 Humphreys, H.N. The coin collector's manual. London, 1875. 2v.
Arc 1348.7 Jobert, L. La science des médailles. Paris, 1715.
Arc 1348.7.1 Jobert, L. La scienza delle medaglie. Venezia, 1756. 2v.
Arc 1348.7.2 Jobert, L. The knowledge of medals. London, 1697.
Arc 1348.7.3 Jobert, L. Notitia rei nummariae. Leipzig, 1695.
Arc 1348.8 Poole, S. Lane. Coins and medals. London, 1885.
Arc 1348.9 Lenormant, F. Monnaies et médailles. Paris, 1883.
Arc 1348.10 Pinkerton, John. An essay on medals. London, 1784.
Arc 1348.10.3 Pinkerton, John. An essay on medals. London, 1808. 2v.
Arc 1348.11 Phillips, H. Pamphlets on numismatics. Philadelphia, 1867-83. 4 pam.
Arc 1348.12 Prime, W.C. Coins, medals and seals. N.Y., 1861. 4 pam.
Arc 1348.13 Gleichius, J. Historia numismatum succincta. Lipsiae, 1698.
Arc 1348.14 Marsy, Arthur. Cueilloir numismatique. n.p., 1887.
Arc 1348.15 Stuckelburg, E.A. Der Münzsammler. Zürich, 1899.
Arc 1348.16 Halke, H. Einleitung in das Studium des Numismatik. Berlin, 1889.
Arc 1348.16.2 Halke, H. Einleitung in das Studium des Numismatik. 3. Aufl. Berlin, 1905.
Arc 1348.17 Luschin von Elengreuth, A. Allgemeine Münzkunde. München, 1904.
Arc 1348.17.2 Luschin von Elengreuth, A. Allgemeine Münzkunde und Geldgeschichte. 2. Aufl. München, 1926.
Arc 1348.18 Joachim, J.F. Unterricht von dem Münzwesen. Halle, 1754.
Arc 1348.19 Babelon, E. Mélanges numismatiques. Paris, 1892-1912. 5v.
Arc 1348.20 McDonald, George. Coin types, their origin and development. Glasgow, 1905.
Arc 1348.21 Rawlings, G.B. Coins and how to know them. N.Y., n.d.
Arc 1348.22 Friedensburg, F. Die Münze in der Kulturgeschichte. Berlin, 1909.
Arc 1348.23 Blanchet, A. Mémoires et notes de numismatique. Paris, 1909.
Arc 1348.23.5 Pamphlet box. Blanchet, A. Numismatics.
Arc 1348.24 Escher, A. Schweizerische Münz- und Geldgeschichte. Bern, 1881.
Arc 1348.25 McDonald, George. Evolution of coinage. Cambridge, 1916.
Arc 1348.26 Pamphlet box. Abbott, G.H. Numismatics.
Arc 1348.27 Burgess, F.W. Chats on old coins. London, 1913.
Htn Arc 1348.28* Agustin, Antonius. Dialogos de medallas, inscriciones y otras antiquedades. Madrid, 1744.
Arc 1348.29.3 Ambrosoli, S. Manuale di numismatica. 3. ed. Milano, 1904.
Arc 1348.30 Sbōronos, I.N. Articles on numismatics. Athenes, 1898-1903. 16 pam.
Arc 1348.31 Butkovskii. Numismatika ili istoriia monet'. Moskva, 1861.
Arc 1348.32 Icard, Séverin. Identification des monnaies. Paris, 1927.
Arc 1348.33F Bonneville, P.F. Traité des monnaies d'or et d'argent qui circulent chez les différens peuples. Paris, 1806.
Arc 1348.34 Pfister, J.G. Stray leaves from the journal of a traveler. London, 1857.
Arc 1348.36 The coin chart manual. St. Louis, 1848?
Arc 1348.37 Markov', A.K. O chistk' drevnikh' monet'. Sankt Peterburg, 1908.
Htn Arc 1348.38* Het thres oor aft schat van alle de specien. Gheprint Tautluerpen, 1580.
Arc 1348.39 Mathews, George D. The coinages of the world. N.Y., 1876.
Arc 1348.40 Magnan, D. Miscellanea numismatica. Romae, 1772-74. 3v.
Arc 1348.41 Strozzi, Carlo. Quadro di geografia numismatica da servire. Firenze, 1836.
Arc 1348.42PF Collezione di tavole monetarie. Venezia, 1796.
Arc 1348.43 Darier, Hugues. Tableau du titre. Geneve, 1807.
Arc 1348.44 Chase National Bank, N.Y. The Chase architrave. N.Y., 19-
Arc 1348.46 Dye, John S. Dye's coin encyclopaedia. Philadelphia, 1883.
Arc 1348.48 Grote, Hermann. Münzstudien. v.1-2. Leipzig, 1857-62.
Arc 1348.50 Gardner, Percy. Macedonian and Greek coins of the Seleucidae. London, 1878.
Arc 1348.51 Milne, J.G. Coin collecting. London, 1951.
Arc 1348.52 Gebhart, H. Numismatik und Geldgeschichte. Heidelberg, 1949.
Arc 1348.53F Babelon, Jean. Portraits en médaille. Paris, 1946.
Arc 1348.55 Sutherland, C.H.V. Art in coinage. London, 1955.
Arc 1348.55.2 Sutherland, C.H.V. Art in coinage. N.Y., 1956.
Arc 1348.60 Roubier, Jean. Dauernder als Erz. Wien, 1958.
Arc 1348.65 Deutscher Numismatikertag, Göttingen. Wissenschaftliche Abhandlunger des deutschen Numismatikertages. Göttingen, 1959.
Arc 1348.70 Fliessbach, Ferdinand. Münzsammlung, Enthaltend. Leipzig, 1853. 2v.
Arc 1348.74 Ferreira Barros, A. Numismática. Porto, 1961.
Arc 1348.76 Lagerqvist, Lars. Myntoch medaljer. Stockholm, 1960.
Arc 1348.77 Grierson, Philip. Numismatics. London, 1975.
Arc 1348.78 Carson, Robert. Coins of the world. N.Y., 1962.
Arc 1348.79 Tourneur, Victor. Initiation à la numismatique. Bruxelles, 1945.
Arc 1348.80 Del Monte, Jacques. Fell's international coin book. N.Y., 1953.
Arc 1348.81 Bosch, Enin. Eski sikkeler rehberi. Istanbul, 1951.
Arc 1348.82.5 Kroha, Tyll. Münzen sammeln. 5. Aufl. Braunschweig, 1968.
Arc 1348.83F Coins and the archaeologist. Oxford, 1974.
Arc 1348.84.2 Suhle, Arthur. Die Münze von der Anfängen bis zur europäischen Neuzeit. 2. Aufl. Leipzig, 1970.
Arc 1348.85 Nau, Elisabeth. Epochen der Geldgeschichte. Stuttgart, 1972.

Arc 1349.01 - .099 Numismatics - Biographies of numismatists - Pamphlet volumes

Arc 1349.01 Pamphlet box. Numismatics. Biography.

Arc 1349.1 - .19 Numismatics - Biographies of numismatists - Collected

Arc 1349.5 Forrer, L. Biographical dictionary of medallists. London, 1904-30. 8v.

Classified Listing

Arc 1349.20 - .299 Numismatics - Biographies of numismatists - Individual

Arc 1349.25 Pinder, Moritz. Numismatique beckerienne. Paris, 1853.
Arc 1349.30 Ricci, Serafino. L'opera numismatica di Solone Ambrosoli. Milano, 1908.
Arc 1349.35F Calabi, A. Matteo dei Pasti. Milano, 1926.
Arc 1349.45 Fayolle, A. Evrard. Recherches sur Bertrand Andrieu de Bordeau. Chalon-sur-Saone, 1902.
Arc 1349.55 Ciampi, Ignazio. Benedetto Pistrucci. n.p., n.d.
Arc 1349.55.5 Azzurri, Francesco. Cenni biografici di Bennedetto Pistrucci. Roma, 1887.
Arc 1349.60F Hujer, L. Mein Leben und Streben. Wien, 1954.
Arc 1349.65 Więcek, A. Sebastian Dadler. Gdańsk, 1962.
Arc 1349.70 Grigor'ev, V.V. Zhizn' i trudy P.S. Savel'eva. Sankt Peterburg, 1861.
Arc 1349.72 Domanig, K. Anton Scharff, K. und K. Kammer-Medaillen. Wien, 1895.
Arc 1349.73 Gumowski, Marian. Wspomnienia numizmatyka. Kraków, 1966.
Arc 1349.75 Brunetti, Lodovico. Opus monetale cigoi. Bologna, 1966.
Arc 1349.80 Quesada, Ernesto. Enrique Peña. Buenos Aires, 1924.

Arc 1350 Numismatics - Special periods - Ancient in general - Folios [Discontinued]

Htn Arc 1350.1* Spanheim, E. Dissertation de praestantia et usu numismatum. Londoni, 1706-17. 2v.
Htn Arc 1350.2* Agostini, A. Dialoghi - intorno alle medaglie...altre antichità. Rome, 1592.
Htn Arc 1350.4* Arbuthnot, J. Tables of ancient coins, weights and measures. London, 1727.
Arc 1350.4.2 Langwith, B. Observations on Doctor Arbuthnot's dissertation. London, 1754.
Htn Arc 1350.5F* Pembroke, T.H. Numismata antiqua. London, 1746.

Arc 1353 Numismatics - Special periods - Ancient in general - Catalogues of collections

Arc 1353.1X Berlin. Königliche Museen. Beschreibung der antiken Münzen. Berlin, 1888- 3v.
Arc 1353.1.5 Berlin. Staatliche Museen. Die antiken Münzen. Berlin, 1851.
Arc 1353.2.2 British Museum. Department of Coins and Medals. A guide to the principal gold and silver coins of the ancients. London, 1886.
Arc 1353.2.3 British Museum. Department of Coins and Medals. A guide to the principal gold and silver coins of the ancients. London, 1881.
Arc 1353.2.5 British Museum. Department of Coins and Medals. A guide to the gold and silver coins of the ancients. 4. ed. London, 1895.
Arc 1353.2.10 British Museum. Department of Coins and Medals. A guide to the gold and silver coins of the ancients. 5. ed. London, 1909.
Arc 1353.2.15 British Museum. Department of Coins and Medals. Greek coins acquired by the British Museum. London. 1887-1896
Arc 1353.3 DuBois, W.E. A brief account of the collection of coins belonging to the mint of the United States. Philadelphia, 1846.
NEDL Arc 1353.4 Ramus, Christian. Catalogus numorum veterum graecorum et latinorum. pt. 1-2. Hafniae, 1816.
Arc 1353.5 Eckhel, J. Thesauro Caesarum...Numorun Gemmarumque. Budae, 1799.
Arc 1353.6 Jonge, J.C. de. Notice sur le cabinet des médailles et des pierres gravées de...roi des Pays-Bas. La Haye, 1824.
Arc 1353.7F Copenhagen. National Museet. Sylloge nummorum Graecorum. v.1-30,41-42. Copenhagen, 1942- 20v.
Arc 1353.7.5 Copenhagen. National Museet. Catalogus numorum veterum graecorum et Latinorum musei. Hafniae, 1816. 3v.
Arc 1353.12 Copenhagen. National Museet. Orientalske, graeske og romerske. Kjøbenhavn, 1952.
Arc 1353.15 Zeno, Apostalo. Sonder Münzenouktion. v.1-2,3. Wien, 1955. 2v.
Arc 1354 Pamphlet box. Numismatics. Ancient.

Arc 1355 - 1380 Numismatics - Special periods - Ancient in general - Monographs (A-Z)

Htn Arc 1355.1* Addison, J. Dialogue upon the usefulness of ancient medals. Glasgow, 1751.
Arc 1355.1.5 Addison, J. Dialogue upon the usefulness of ancient medals. Glasgow, 1769.
Arc 1355.2 Ackerman, J.Y. Ancient coins of cities and princes. London, 1846.
Arc 1356.1 Barthélemy, A.J.B.A. Nouveau manuel complete de numismatique ancienne. Text and atlas. Paris, 1866. 2v.
Arc 1356.1.3 Barthélemy, A.J.B.A. Nouveau manuel complete de numismatique ancienne. Paris, 1866.
Arc 1356.2 Babelon, E. Les collections de monnaies anciennes. Paris, 1897.
Arc 1356.3 Blancard, Louis. Le trésor d'Auriol et les dieux nègres de la Grèce. Marseille, n.d.
Arc 1356.4 Bible coins...facsimile of coins in...scripture. London, n.d.
Arc 1356.5 Babelon, Jean. Le portrait dans l'antiquité d'apres les monnaies. Paris, 1942.
Arc 1356.6 Beltrán Martinez, A. Curso de numismatica. 2. ed. Cartagena, 1950.
Arc 1356.7 Brabich, Vladimir M. Puteshestire s drevnei monetoi. Leningrad, 1970.
Arc 1356.8.3 Bernareggi, Ernesto. Istituzioni di numismatica antica. 3. ed. Milano, 1973.
Arc 1357.5 Christ, Karl. Antike Numismatik. Darmstadt, 1967.
Arc 1359.1 Eckhel, J.H. Doctrina numorum veterum. Viennae, 1792-98. 8v.
Htn Arc 1359.2* Erizzo, S. Discorso sopra le medaglie de gli antichi. Venice, 1568.
Arc 1360.1 Friedlaender, J. Repertorium zur antiken Numismatik. Berlin, 1885.
Arc 1360.2 Froelich, E. Utilitas rei numariae veteris. Viennae, 1733.
Arc 1360.2.5 Froelich, E. Quatuor tentamina in re. numaria vetere. Viennae, 1737.
Arc 1360.2.7 Froelich, E. Ad numismata regum veterum anecdota. Viennae, 1756. 2 pam.
Htn Arc 1360.3* Ficoroni, F. de. I piombi antichi. Roma, 1740.
Arc 1360.4 Farkas, Sandor. Antik érmészet. Aiud, 1932.
Arc 1361.1 Grässe, J.G.T. Handbuch der alten Numismatik. Leipzig, 1854.
Arc 1361.2 Green, B.R. A lecture on the study of ancient coins. London, 1829.

Arc 1355 - 1380 Numismatics - Special periods - Ancient in general - Monographs (A-Z) - cont.

Arc 1361.3 Gardner, Percy. A history of ancient coinage. 700-300 B.C. Oxford, 1918.
Arc 1361.4 Giesecke, W. Antikes Geldwesen. Leipzig, 1938.
Arc 1362.1 Harduin, J. Nummi antiqui pop. et urb. illustrati. Parisii, 1684.
Arc 1362.2 Hennin, M. Manuel de numismatique ancienne. Paris, 1830-69. 3v.
Htn Arc 1364.1* Jennings, D. An introduction to the knowledge of medals. London, 1764.
Htn Arc 1364.1.2* Jennings, D. An introduction to the knowledge of medals. 2. ed. Birmingham, 1775.
Arc 1364.2 Janssen, A.J. Het antieke tropaion. Ledeberg, 1957.
Arc 1364.3 Jeločnik, Aleksander. Čenturska zakladna najdba folisov maksencija in tetrarhije. Ljubljana, 1973.
Arc 1365.1 Khevenhueller, F.A. Regum veterum numismata. v.1-2. Vienna, 17- .
Arc 1365.2 King, Charles W. Early Christian numismatics. London, 1873.
Arc 1365.4 Kraft, Konrad. Der goldene Kranz Caesars und der Kampf um die Entlassung des "Tyrannen". 2. Aufl. Darmstadt, 1969.
Arc 1365.5 Kazamanova, Liudmila N. Vvedenie v antichnaia numizmatiku. Moskva, 1969.
Arc 1366.1A Lenormant, F. La monnaie dans l'antiquité. Paris, 1878-79. 3v.
Arc 1366.1B Lenormant, F. La monnaie dans l'antiquité. Paris, 1878-79. 3v.
Arc 1366.2 Lederer, Philipp. Neue Beiträge zur antike Münzkunde. Bern, 1943.
Arc 1367.1 Morel, Andre. Specimen universae rei nummariae antiquae. Paris, 1683.
Arc 1367.2 Miller, Max. Die Münzen des Altertums. Berlin, 1933.
Arc 1367.2.2 Miller, Max. Die Münzen des Altertums. 2. Aufl. Braunschweig, 1963.
Arc 1367.3 Magnaguti, A.G. Ex nummis historia. Roma, 1949-53. 12v.
Arc 1368.1 Nestle, W. Funde antiker Münzen im königrieche Württemberg. Stuttgart, 1893.
Arc 1369.1 Oesel, J. Thesaurus sel. numismata antiqua. Amsterdam, 1677.
Arc 1370.1 Patin, C. Thesaurus numismatum. Amsterdam? 1672.
Htn Arc 1370.2* Patin, C. Thesaurus numismatum. v.1-2. Amsterdam? 1672.
Arc 1370.3 Pinder, M. Beiträge zur älteren Münzkunde. Berlin, 1851.
Arc 1370.4 Pellerin, J. Recueil de médailles de rois. Paris, 1762.
Arc 1370.4.2 Pellerin, J. Recueil de médailles de peuples. Paris, 1763. 3v.
Arc 1370.4.3 Pellerin, J. Mélange de diverses médailles. Paris, 1765. 2v.
Arc 1370.4.4 Pellerin, J. Suppléments aux six volumes. Paris, 1767.
Arc 1371.1 Queipo, V.V. Essai sur les systèmes métriques et monétaires. v.1-2, tables. Paris, 1859. 3v.
NEDL Arc 1372.1 Reinach, T. L'histoire par les monnaies. Paris, 1902.
Arc 1372.1.5 Pamphlet vol. Reinach, T. Numismatics. 7 pam.
Arc 1372.2 Ridgeway, W. The origin of metallic currency and weight standards. Cambridge, 1892.
Arc 1372.3 Regling, Kurt. Die antike Münze als Kunstwerk. 1. Aufl. Berlin, 1924.
Arc 1373.01 Pamphlet box. Seltman, E.J.
Arc 1373.1 Sabatier, P.J. Production de l'or, de l'argent et du cuivre. St. Petersbourg, 1850.
Htn Arc 1373.2* Savot, L. Discours sur les médailles antiques. Paris, 1627.
Arc 1373.3 Scotti, V.N. Della rarità delle medaglie antiche. Florence, 1809.
Arc 1373.3.3 Scotti, V.N. Della rarità delle medaglie antiche. Roma, 1838.
Htn Arc 1373.4* Seguin, P. Sel. numismata antiqua. Paris, 1684.
Arc 1373.4.2 Seguin, P. Sel. numismata antiqua. Paris, 1684.
Htn Arc 1373.5* Spanheim, E. Diss. de praestantia et usu numismata antiqua. Rome, 1664.
Htn Arc 1373.6* Swinton, J. Metilia: sive de quinario gentis metiliae. Oxford, 1750.
Htn Arc 1373.7* Strada, J. de. Epitome du thresor des antiquitez. Lyon, 1553.
Arc 1373.8 Steuer. Die Geschichte im Lichte der Münzen. Luckenwalde, 1911.
Arc 1373.9 Smith, W. Literae de re nummaria. Newcastle-upon-Tyne, 1729.
Arc 1373.10 Sestini, Domenico. Classes generales seu moneta vetus urbium populorum et regum ordine. Florentiae, 1821.
Arc 1373.11 Sutherland, Carol H.V. Ancient numismatics. N.Y., 1958.
Arc 1377.1 Walsh, R. An essay on ancient coins, medals, and gems. 2. ed. London, 1828.

Arc 1388 Numismatics - Special periods - Medieval in general - Catalogues of collections

Arc 1388.1 Tornberg, C.J. Fölhagen-fyndet. Stockholm, 1870.

Arc 1390 Numismatics - Special periods - Medieval in general - Monographs

Arc 1390.1 Barthélemy, A.J.B.A. Nouveau manuel complet de numismatique du moyen age et moderne. Text et atlas. Paris, n.d. 2v.
Arc 1390.1.3 Barthélemy, A.J.B.A. Nouveau manuel complet de numismatique du moyen age et moderne. Text et atlas. Paris, 1874. 2v.
Arc 1390.1.5 Blanchet, J.A. Nouveau manuel de numismatique du moyen age et moderne. Text et atlas. Paris, 1890. 3v.
Arc 1390.3 Blancard, Louis. Le saiga mérovingien dérive de la silique byzantine. v.1-2. Marseille, 1883.
Arc 1390.4 Blancard, Louis. L'origine du marc. Macon, 1888.
Arc 1390.5 Blancard, Louis. Rapport...concernant le trésor de Vallon. Marseille, n.d.
Arc 1390.6 Morbio, Carlo. Delle monete battute da Carlo Magno in Italia. Milano, 1866.
Arc 1390.7 Marchant, N.D. Mélanges de numismatique et d'histoire. Paris, 1818.
Arc 1390.8 Engel, A. Traite de numismatique en moyen age. Paris, 1891. 3v.
X Cg Arc 1390.9 Keary, C.F. Coinage of western Europe. London, 1879.
Arc 1390.10 Friedensburg, F. Münzkunde und Geldgeschichte der Einzelstaaten des Mittelalters und der neuer Zeit. München, 1926.
Arc 1390.11 Lange, Kurt. Münzkunst des Mittelalters. Leipzig, 1942.
Arc 1390.12 Rasmusson, Nils L. Commentationes de nummis saeculorum IX-XI in suecia repertis. Stockholm, 1961- 2v.
Arc 1390.15 Stockvis, Albert. Effective research on unknown mediaeval coinage. 1. ed. Cleveland, 1955.

Classified Listing

Arc 1390 Numismatics - Special periods - Medieval in general - Monographs - cont.

Arc 1390.15.5 Stockvis, Albert. Critical survey of mediaeval Teutonic and Spanish coinage. Cleveland, 1960.
Arc 1390.17 Berghaus, Peter. Dona numismatica. Hamburg, 1965.
Arc 1390.18 Seifedolini, M.A. Monety il'khakov XIV veka. Baku, 1968.
Arc 1390.19 Kmietowicz, Anna. Wczesnośredniowieczny skarb srebrny z zalesia powiat słupca. Wrocław, 1969-74. 2v.
Arc 1390.20 Kotliar, Mykola F. Hroskovyi sbih na terytorii Ukrainy doby teodalizma. Kyïv, 1971.

Arc 1400 Numismatics - Special periods - Modern in general - Monographs

Arc 1400.1 Eckfeldt, J.R. New varieties of gold and silver coins. N.Y., 1851.
Arc 1400.1.2 Eckfeldt, J.R. A manual of gold and silver coins. Philadelphia, 1851.
Arc 1400.2 Taylor, S. Gold and silver coin examiner. N.Y., 1846-57. 3 pam.
Arc 1400.3 Morbio, Carlo. Monete franco-italiche ossidionali. Asti, 1865.
Arc 1400.4 Neueste Münzkunde. Leipzig, 1853. 2v.
Arc 1400.5 Martin, Leopold Charles. The current gold and silver coins of all countries. London, 1863?
Arc 1400.6 Comencini, M. Coins of the modern world, 1870-1936. London, 1937.
Arc 1400.7 Coins of the world; the standard catalogue of twentieth century issues. 1. ed. N.Y., 1938.
Arc 1400.7.2 Raymond, Wayte. Coins of the world, twentieth century issues. 2. ed. N.Y., 1945.
Arc 1400.8 Altz, Charles G. Foreign coins struck at United States mints. Racine, Wis., 1965.

Arc 1405 Numismatics - Local - Asia in general - Folios [Discontinued]

Arc 1405.1 Thomas, E. Marsden's Numismata orientalia. v.1. London, 1874.
Arc 1405.1.2 Madden, F.W. Coins of the Jews. v.2. London, 1881.
Arc 1405.1.3 Phayre, A.P. Numismata orientalia. v.3. pt.1-3. n.p., n.d.

Arc 1406 Numismatics - Local - Asia in general - Pamphlet volumes

Arc 1406 Pamphlet box. Numismatics. Asia. 4 pam.

Arc 1408 Numismatics - Local - Asia in general - General works

Arc 1408.1 Brandis, J. Das Münz-, Mass- und Gewichtswesen in Vorderasien. Berlin, 1866.
Arc 1408.2 Tornberg, E.J. Sur un Dirhem Kakweïhide inédit. Bruxelles, 1858.
X Cg Arc 1408.3 Lockhart, James H.S. Currency of the Farther East from earliest times up to 1895. Hong Kong, 1895-1907. 3v.
Arc 1408.4 Morgan, J. de. Manuel de numismatique orientale de l'antiquité et du moyen-age. Paris, 1923-36.
X Cg Arc 1408.5 British Museum. Department of Coins and Medals. Catalogue of Oriental coins. London, 1875-90. 10v.
Arc 1408.6 Thomas, E. On the coins of the kings of Ghazni. London, 1848.
Arc 1408.7 Moshniagin, D.I. Monety stran zarubezhnoi Azii i Afriki XIX-XX veka. Moskva, 1967.
Arc 1408.10 L'Ecluse, Charles de. Monnaies orientales. Paris, 1888.

Arc 1411 Numismatics - Local - China - General works

Arc 1411.1 Bushell, S.W. Coins of the present dynesty in China. n.p., 1880.
Arc 1411.2 Kainz, C. Die ältesten chinesischen Staatsmünzen. Berlin, 1894.
Arc 1411.3 Wylie, A. Coins of the Ta-ts'ing dynasty. Shanghai, 1858.
Arc 1411.4 Hopkins, L.C. Origin and earlier history of Chinese coinage. n.p., n.d.
Arc 1411.5 Manuals of Far Eastern numismatics. Yokohama, 1911.
Arc 1411.6 Davis, Andrew. Ancient Chinese paper money. Boston, 1918.
Arc 1411.7 Batairaasch Genootschap van Kunsten in Wetenschappen. Catalogus der munten en amuletten van China. Batavia, 1904.
Arc 1411.8 Terrien de Lacouperie, A.E.J.B. Catalogue of Chinese coins from the 7th century B.C. to A.D. 621. London, 1892.
Arc 1411.9F Hager, Joseph. Description des médailles chinoises du cabinet imperial de France. Paris, 1805.
Arc 1411.10F Schjöth, F. The currency of the Far East. London, 1929.
Arc 1411.11 Higgins, F.C. The Chinese numismatic riddle. N.Y., 1910.
Arc 1411.12 Jorgensen, Holgar. Old coins of China. n.p., 19- .
Arc 1411.13 Kann, Eduard. Illustrated catalog of Chinese coins, gold, silver, nickel and aluminum. Los Angeles, 1954.
Arc 1411.14 Coole, Arthur Braddan. An encyclopedia of Chinese coins. 1. ed. Denver, 1967.
Arc 1411.15 Bykov, Aleksei A. Monety Kitaia. Leningrad, 1969.

Arc 1412 Numismatics - Local - Japan - Folios [Discontinued]

Arc 1412.1 Bramsen, W. The coins of Japan. pt.1. Yokohama, 1880.
Arc 1412.5 Fonahn, Adolf. Japanische Bildermünze. Leipzig, 1934.

Arc 1413 Numismatics - Local - Japan - General works

Arc 1413.01 Pamphlet box. Numismatics. Japan.
X Cg Arc 1413.09 Munro, N.G. Coins of Japan. 1. ed. Yokohama, 1904.
Arc 1413.1 Munro, N.G. Coins of Japan. London, 1905.
Arc 1413.2 Polder, L. Abridged history of copper coins in Japan. n.p., 1891.
Arc 1413.3 Tsukamoto, Toyojino. The old and new coins of Japan. Tokyo, 1930.
Arc 1413.5 Jacobs, N.G. Japanese coinage. N.Y., 1953.
Arc 1413.25 Ramsden, H.A. Corean coin charms and amulets. Yokohama, 1910.

Arc 1418 Numismatics - Local - India - General works

Arc 1418.01 Pamphlet box. Numismatics. India.
Arc 1418.1 British Museum. Department of Coins and Medals. Catalogue of Indian coins. v.1-5,7. London, 1884-1936. 6v.
Arc 1418.2 Cunningham, A. Coins of ancient India. London, 1891.
Arc 1418.2.2 Cunningham, A. Coins of mediaeval India. London, 1894.
Htn Arc 1418.2.4* Cunningham, A. Coins of Alexander's succesors in the East. London, 1884?
Arc 1418.2.7 British Museum. Department of Coins and Medals. Catalogue of the coins of the Gupta dynasties and of Sásānka. London, 1914.
Arc 1418.3 Prinsep, J. Essays on Indian antiquities. London, 1858. 2v.
Arc 1418.4 Reinaud, J.T. Explication de cinq médailles...du Bengale. Paris, 1823.
Arc 1418.5A Indian Museum. Catalogue of coins in the Indian Museum, Calcutta. Oxford, 1906-08. 3v.

Arc 1418 Numismatics - Local - India - General works - cont.

Arc 1418.5B Indian Museum. Catalogue of coins in the Indian Museum, Calcutta. Oxford, 1906.
Arc 1418.6 Lucknow, India. Provincial Museum. Catalogue of coins in the Provincial Museum. Oxford, 1920. 2v.
Arc 1418.6.5 Brown, C.J. The coins of India. Calcutta, 1922.
Arc 1418.7 Campos, M.J. da C. Numismatica indo-portuguesa. Lisboa, 1901.
Arc 1418.8F Phayre Provincial Museum, Rangoon. Catalogue of coins in the museum. Rangoon, 1924.
Arc 1418.9 Webb, W.W. The currencies of Hindu states of Réjputána. Westminster, 1893.
Arc 1418.10 Bhandarkar, D.R. Lectures on ancient Indian numismatics. Calcutta, 1921.
Arc 1418.11 Chakrabortty, S.K. A study of ancient Indian numismatics. Calcutta, 1931.
Arc 1418.12 Rapson, E.J. Indian coins. Strassburg, 1897.
Arc 1418.13 Sivaramamurti, C. Numismatic parallels of Kālidāsa. Madras, 1945.
Arc 1418.15 Altekar, A.S. Catalogue of the Gupta gold coins in the Bayana Hoard. Bombay, 1954.
Arc 1418.15.5 Numismatic Society of India. Corpus of Indian coins. Banaras, 1957.
Arc 1418.20 Lahore Museum. Catalogue of coins in the Punjab Museum. Oxford, 1914-34. 3v.
Arc 1418.22 Karim, A. Corpus of the Muslim coins of Bengal. Decca, 1960.
Arc 1418.24 Chattopadhyay, Bhaskar. The age of the Kushānas; a numismatic study. 1. ed. Calcutta, 1967.
Arc 1418.26 Hussain, M.K. Catalogue of coins of the Mughal emperors. Bombay, 1968.

Arc 1420 Numismatics - Local - Palestine and Syria - Folios [Discontinued]

Htn Arc 1420.1* Froelich, E. Annales compendiarii regum et rerum Syriae. 2. ed. Vienna, 1754.
Arc 1420.1.5F Froelich, E. Annales compendiarii regum et rerum Syriae. Vienna, 1744.
Htn Arc 1420.2F* Pérez Báyer, F. F. Perezii Bayerii. De numis hebraeo-samaritanis. Valentia, 1781.

Arc 1423 Numismatics - Local - Palestine and Syria - General works

Arc 1423.1 Waserus, C. De antiquis numis. Zürich, 1605.
Arc 1423.2 Révillout, Eugène. Note sur les plus anciennes monnaies hébraiques. Macon, 1884.
Arc 1423.3 Lindberg, J.C. Commentatio de numis punicis sextorum. Havniae, 1824.
Arc 1423.4 Tychsen, T.C. De numis Hasmonaeorum paralipomena. n.p., 1792.
Arc 1423.5 Saulcy, L.F.J.C. de. Numismatique de la Terre-Sainte. Paris, 1877.
Arc 1423.6 Schlumberger, G. Monnaie inédite des seigneurs du Toron, en Syrie. Paris, 1875.
Arc 1423.7 Lavoix, Henri. Monnaies à légendes arabes frappées en Syrie. Paris, 1877.
Arc 1423.8 Pfaffenhoffen, F. von. Le prince croisé Baudouin. Paris, 1863.
Arc 1423.9 Madden, Frederic W. History of Jewish coinage. London, 1864.
Arc 1423.9.5F Madden, Frederic W. Coins of the Jews. Boston, 1881.
Arc 1423.9.6 Madden, Frederic W. History of Jewish coinage, and of money. San Diego, 1967.
Arc 1423.9.7 Madden, Frederic W. History of Jewish coinage. N.Y., 1967.
Arc 1423.10 Reinach, Théodore. Les monnaies juives. Paris, 1887.
Arc 1423.10.5 Reinach, Théodore. Jewish coins. London, 1903.
Arc 1423.11 Newell, E.T. The Seleucid mint of Antioch. N.Y., 1918.
Arc 1423.11.5F Foy-Vaillant, J. Seleucidarum imperium. Hagae-Comitum, 1732.
Arc 1423.12.5 Cavedoni, C. Biblische Numismatik. Hannover, 1855-56. 2v.
Arc 1423.13 Wruck, W. Die Syrische Provinzialprägung von Augustus bis Klaudius. Inaug. Diss. Stuttgart, 1931.
Arc 1423.13.5 Wruck, W. Die Syrische Provinzialprägung von Augustus. Stuttgart, 1931.
Arc 1423.14 Williamson, G.C. The money of the Bible illustrated by numerous woodcuts. London, 1894.
Arc 1423.14.5 Williamson, G.C. The money of the Bible. N.Y., 18- ?
Arc 1423.15 Levy, Moritz Abraham. Geschichte der jüdischen Münzen. Breslau, 1862.
Arc 1423.15.1 Levy, Moritz Abraham. Geschichte der jüdischen Münzen. Leipzig, 1862.
Arc 1423.16 Rogers, Edgar. A handy guide to Jewish coins. London, 1914.
Arc 1423.17 Romanoff, P. Jewish symbols on ancient Jewish coins. Philadelphia, 1944.
Arc 1423.18 Reifenberg, A. Ancient Jewish coins. 2. ed. Jerusalem, 1947.
Arc 1423.18.4 Reifenberg, A. Ancient Jewish coins. Jerusalem, 1965.
Arc 1423.18.5 Reifenberg, A. Ancient Hebrew seals. London, 1950.
Arc 1423.18.10 Reifenberg, A. Israel's history in coins from the Maccabees to the Roman conquest. London, 1953.
Arc 1423.19 Corpus nummorum Palaestinensium; publications of the Israel Numismatic Society. Jerusalem. 1-4,1956-1961 4v.
Arc 1423.20 Kindler, A. The coins of Tiberias. Tiberias, 1961.
Arc 1423.21 Israel Numismatic Society. The dating and meaning of ancient Jewish coins and symbols. Tel-Aviv, 1958.
Arc 1423.22 Muehsam, Alice. Coin and temple; a study of the architectural representation on ancient Jewish coins. Leeds, 1966.
Arc 1423.23 Meshorer, Va'akov. Jewish coins of the second temple period. Tel-Aviv, 1967.
Arc 1423.25 Haffner, Sylvia. The history of modern Israel's money, 1917 to 1967, including state medals and Palestine mandate. 1st ed. La Mesa? 1967.
Arc 1423.26 International Numismatic Convention, Jerusalem, 1963. The patterns of monetary development in Phoenicia and Palestine in antiquity. Tel-Aviv, 1967.
Arc 1423.27 Baldus, Hans Roland. Uranius Antoninius. Bonn, 1971.
Arc 1423.28 Meyshan, Josef. Essays in Jewish numismatics. Jerusalem, 1968.
Arc 1423.30 Bertram, Fred. Israel's 20-year catalog of coins and currency. N.Y., 1968.
Arc 1423.32 Rosen, Josef. Münzen aus biblischer Zeit. Basel, 1968.
Arc 1423.32.1 Rosen, Josef. Münzen aus biblischer Zeit. n.p., 1969.

Arc 1425 Numismatics - Local - Asia Minor - Folios [Discontinued]

Arc 1425.1 Luynes, H.T.P.J. Numismatique et inscription Cypriotes. Paris, 1852.
Arc 1425.2 Schlumberger, G. Numismatique de l'Orient Latin. Paris, 1878.
Arc 1425.2.2 Schlumberger, G. Numismatique de l'Orient Latin. Paris, 1882.
Arc 1425.3 Saulcy, L.F.J.C. de. Numismatique de Croisades. Paris, 1847.
Arc 1425.4F Bell, H.W. Sardis, coins. v.11. Leiden, 1916.

Arc 1428 Numismatics - Local - Asia Minor - General works

Arc 1428.1 Langlois, Victor. Monnaies inédites, ou Peu connues de la Cilicie. Paris, 1854.
Arc 1428.2 Schlumberger, G. Les monnaies à légendes grecques. Paris, 1880.
Arc 1428.3 Dechant, Norbert. Kreuzfahrer-Münzen. Wien, 1868.
Arc 1428.4 Friedländer, J. Frankische im Orient geprägte Münzen. n.p., n.d.
Arc 1428.5 Münter, F.C.K.H. Om Frankernes mynter i Orienten. v.1-2. n.p., n.d.
Arc 1428.6 Schlumberger, G. Les principautés Franques du Levant. Paris, 1877.
Arc 1428.7 Vogué, C.J. Monnaies inédites des Croisades. Paris, 1864.
Arc 1428.8 Furse, E.H. Mémories numismatiques de l'ordre...St. Jean de Jerusalem. Rome, 1889.
Htn Arc 1428.9* Mead, Richard. Oratio dissertio de nummis...a Symrnaeis. Londoni, 1724.
Htn Arc 1428.9.2* Mead, Richard. Oratio dissertio de nummis...a Symrnaeis. Londoni, 1724.
Arc 1428.10 Waddington, W.H. Voyage en Asie-Mineure au point du vie numismatique. Paris, 1853.
Arc 1428.11F Berlin. Staatliche Museen. Die Münzen von Priene. Berlin, 1927.
Arc 1428.13F Bosch, C. Die kleinasiatischen Münzen der römischen Kaiserzeit. Stuttgart, 1935.
Arc 1428.14 Imhoof-Blumer, Friedrich. Lydische Stadtmünzen. Genf, 1897.
Arc 1428.15 Akademie der Wissenschaften, Berlin. Die antiken Münzen Mysiens. Berlin, 1913.
Arc 1428.21 Fellows, Charles. Coins of ancient Lycia before the reign of Alexander. London, 1855.
Arc 1428.23 Sydenham, E.A. The coinage of Caesarea in Cappadocia. London, 1933.
Arc 1428.25 Cairo. Egyptian Library. Catalogue of the collection of Arabic coins...in the Khedivial Library at Cairo. London, 1897.
Arc 1428.27 Brett, A. The electrum coinage of Lampakos. N.Y., 1914.
Arc 1428.29 Vacquier, Polydore. Numismatique des Scythes et des Sarmates. Paris, 1881.
Arc 1428.30 Petrowicz, A. von. Arsaciden-Münzen. Wien, 1904.
Arc 1428.32 Akarca, A. Les monnaies grecques de Mylasa. Paris, 1959.
Arc 1428.33 Franke, Peter R. Kleinasien zur Römerzeit; griechisches Leben im Spiegel der Münzen. München, 1968.

Arc 1430 Numismatics - Local - Other Asia - Folios [Discontinued]

Arc 1430.1 Schlumberger, G. Le trésor de San'a. Paris, 1880.
Arc 1430.2 Mainoni, S. de. Descrizione di alcune monete cufiche del Museo. Milano, 1820.
Arc 1430.10 Ghiron, I. Monete arabiche del gabinetto numismatico di Milano. Milano, 1878.
Arc 1430.200 Imhoof-Blumer, Friedrich. Kleinasiatische Münzen. Wien, 1901-02. 2v.

Arc 1433 Numismatics - Local - Other Asia - General works; Local

Arc 1433.1 Bibliothèque Nationale, Paris. Catalogue des monnaies musulmanes. Paris, 1887-96. 3v.
Arc 1433.2 Palermo. Biblioteca Comunale. Catalogo delle monete arabe. Palermo, 1892.
Arc 1433.2.2 Murr, C.G. von. Drei Abhandlungen von der Geschichte der Araber. Nüremberg, 1770.
Arc 1433.2.5 Nützel, Heinrich. Münzen der Rasuliden. Berlin, 1891.
Arc 1433.3 Tychsen, O.G. Introductio in rem numariam Muhammedanorum. Rostock, 1794. 2 pam.
Arc 1433.4 Cunningham, A. Coins of the Indo-Scythians. pt.1-2. London, 1888.
Arc 1433.5 Wilson, H. A descriptive account of antiquity and coins of Afghanistan. London, 1841.
Arc 1433.5.10 Prinsep, H.T. Note on the historical results deducible from recent discoveries in Afghanistan. London, 1844.
Arc 1433.5.15 Hamidi, Hakim. A catalog of modern coins of Afghanistan. 1. English ed. Kabal, 1967.
Htn Arc 1433.6* Adler, I.G.C. Collectio nova numorum cuficum. Hafniae, 1782-92. 2v.
Arc 1433.7 Fraehn, C.M.J. Numophylacium orientale Pototianum. Casani, 1813.
Arc 1433.8 Fraehn, C.M.J. Numi Muhammedani...Museo Asiatico. Petropoli, 1826.
Arc 1433.8.3 Fraehn, C.M.J. Nova supplementa ad recesionem numorum Muhammedanum. Petropoli, 1855.
Arc 1433.8.5 Fraehn, C.M.J. Das Muhammedanische Münzkabinet. St. Petersburg, 1821.
Arc 1433.9 Fraehn, C.M.J. Novae symbolae ad rem numariam Muhammedanorum. Petropoli, 1819.
Arc 1433.9.3 Fraehn, C.M.J. De aliquot numis Kuficis. n.p., 1824.
Arc 1433.9.4 Fraehn, C.M.J. De Musei Sprewitziani Mosquae numis Kuficis. Petropoli, 1825.
Arc 1433.10 Fraehn, C.M.J. Beiträge zur Muhammedanischen Münzkunde. Berlin, n.d.
Arc 1433.11 Hallenberg, Jonas. Collectio nummorum cuficorum. Stockholm, 1800.
Arc 1433.11.3 Hallenberg, Jonas. Numismata orientalia aere expressa. pt. 1-2. Upsaliae, 1822.
Arc 1433.12 Tornberg, Carl Johan. Numi cufici regii numophylacii Holmiensis. Upsaliae, 1848.
Arc 1433.12.3 Tornberg, Carl Johan. Découvertes récentes de monnaies koufiques. Bruxelles, n.d.
Arc 1433.12.5 Tornberg, Carl Johan. Om de i Svensk jord funna Österländska mynt. Stockholm, 1857.
Arc 1433.13 Tornberg, Carl Johan. Symbolae ad rem numariam Muhammedan. Upsaliae, 1846-62.
Arc 1433.14 Winbom, Jonas A. Dissertatio de recentioribus numis Arabicis. Upsaliae, 1815.
Arc 1433.15 Cipelli, Luigi. Di una moneta Turca coniata nella zecca di Parma. Parma, 1868.
Arc 1433.16 Blancard, Louis. Sur l'origine du monnayage musulman. Paris, n.d.

Arc 1433 Numismatics - Local - Other Asia - General works; Local - cont.

Arc 1433.17 Blancard, Louis. Le besant d'or sarrazinas pendant les croisades. Marseille, 1880.
Arc 1433.18 Dirks, J. Souveniers numismatiques des croisades. Photoreproduction. Bruxelles, 1861.
Arc 1433.19 Saulcy, L.F.J.C. de. Lettres sur quelques points de la numismatique arabe. Lettres 4,5, et 6. Paris, 1841.
Arc 1433.20 Moeller, J.H. De numis Orientalibus in numophylacio Gothano. Erford, 1826-31. 2v.
Arc 1433.21 Kehr, G. Jacob. Monarchiae Asiatico-Saracenicae status. Lipsiae, 1724.
Arc 1433.22 Pietraszewski, Ignatius. Numi Mohammedani. Berolini, 1843.
Arc 1433.23 Erdmann, F. von. Zur Muhammedanischen Münzkunde. St. Petersburg, 1856.
Arc 1433.24 Grigorbev, V.V. Opisanie kuficheskikh monet' X veka. Sankt Peterburg, 1841.
Arc 1433.24.5 Schott, W. W. Grigorjew's Beschreibung kufischer Münzen. n.p., n.d.
Arc 1433.25 Dresden. K. Münzkabinett. De numis Muhammadanis in Numophylacio regio Dresdensi. Lipsiae, 1856.
Arc 1433.26 Loerve, L. Observations on a unique Cufic gold coin. London, 1849.
Arc 1433.27 Bohlen, P. von. Über die wissenschaftlichen Werth...Arabischen Münzen. n.p., 1835.
Arc 1433.28 Langlois, Victor. Numismatique général de l'Armenie. v.1-2. Paris, 1855-59.
Arc 1433.28.2 Langlois, Victor. Numismatique général. v.2. Paris, 1855.
Arc 1433.28.5 Mushegian, K. Denezhnoe obrashchenie Dvina po numizmaticheskim dannym. Erevan, 1962.
Arc 1433.29 Mubarek, Ghalib Bey. Notices sur les monnaies turques. Bruxelles, 1899.
Arc 1433.30 Lacroix, D. Numismatique annamite. Text and atlas. Saigon, 1900. 2v.
Arc 1433.31 Codrington, O. Manuel of Musalman numismatics. London, 1904.
Arc 1433.32 Ghiron, I. Di alcuni conii osmani della museo di Modena. Firenze, 1870.
X Cg Arc 1433.33 Babelon, E. Perses achemenides les satrapes. Paris, 1893.
Arc 1433.34 Casanova, Paul. Inventaire sommaire des monnaies musulmanes. Paris, 1896.
Arc 1433.35 Gardner, Percy. Gold coinage of Asia before Alexander the Great. London, 1908.
Arc 1433.36 Valentine, W.H. Modern copper coins of the Muhammadan states. London, 1911.
Arc 1433.37 Codera y Zaidin, F. Titulos y nombres propios monedas arábigo-españolas. Madrid, 1878.
Arc 1433.37.10 Vives y Escudero, A. Monedas de las dinastiás arábigo-españolas. Madrid, 1893.
Arc 1433.38 Morgan, J. de. Contribution à l'étude des ateliers monétaires...rois Sassanides. Paris, 1913.
Arc 1433.38.10F Paruck, F.D.J. Sassanian coins. Bombay, 1924.
Arc 1433.39 Krotkov', A.A. Klad' serebianykh' monet' s" vodianskago gorodishcha. Saragov', 1913.
Arc 1433.40 Savelbev', P. Monety dzhuchidov' dzhagataidov", I.D.R. Sankt Peterburg, 1858.
Arc 1433.40.5 Savelbev', P. Topogafiia kladov' s' vosiochnymi monetami. Sankt Peterburg, 1846.
Arc 1433.41 Fraehn, C.M.J. Monety khanov' uluea dzhuchieva. Sankt Peterburg, 1832.
Arc 1433.41.5 Fraehn, C.M.J. Die Münzen des Chane vom Ulus. St. Petersburg, 1832.
Arc 1433.42F Tizengauzen', V. Monety bostochnago khalifata. Sankt Peterburg, 1873.
Arc 1433.43 British Museum. Department of Coins and Medals. A catalogue of the Muhammadan coins in the British Museum. London, 1941. 2v.
Arc 1433.44 Leningrad. Ermitazh. Katakog' dzhelairidskiu' monety Sost. A. Markov'. Sankt Peterburg, 1897.
Arc 1433.45F Leningrad. Ermitazh. Inventarnyi katalog musulbmanskikh monet. Sankt Peterburg, 1896.
Arc 1433.46F Near Eastern numismatics, iconography, epigraphy and history. Beirut, 1974.
Arc 1433.50 Le May, R.S. The coinage of Siam. Bangkok, 1932.
Arc 1433.52 Schroeder, Albert. Annam; études numismatiques. Text et atlas. Paris, 1905. 2v.
Arc 1433.55 Guthrie, C.S. Catalogue of the collection of oriental coins belonging to C. Sefan Guthrie. Hertford, 1874.
Arc 1433.60 Rabino, Hyacinth L. Coins, medals, and seals of the shâhs of Irân. Hertford, 1945.
Arc 1433.60.5 Frye, Richard N. Sasanian remains from Qasr-i Abu Nasr; seals, sealings, and coins. Cambridge, 1973.
Arc 1433.62F Unvala, Jamshedji M. Coins of Tabaristän and some Sassenian coins from Susa. Paris, 1938.
Arc 1433.64 Farkas, Sándor. Die Ikonographie der Partherkönige. Aiud, 1933.
Arc 1433.65 Prokesch-Osten, A. Les monnaies des rois Parthes. Paris, 1874-75.
Arc 1433.65.5 McDowell, Robert H. Coins from Seleucia on the Tigris. Ann Arbor, 1935.
Arc 1433.67 Istanbul. Asari Atika Müzeleri. Catalcgue dis monnaies turcomanes. Constantinople, 1894.
Arc 1433.67.2 Istanbul. Asari Atika Müzeleri. Catalogue des monnaies turcomanes. Bologne, 1965.
Arc 1433.70 Sourdel, D. Inventaire des monnaies musulmanes anciennes du musée de Caboul. Damas, 1953.
Arc 1433.71F Zambaur, Edward K.M. von. Die Münzprägungen des Islams. Wiesbaden, 1968.
Arc 1433.73 Artuk, S. Demýhoci definesi. Ankara, 1966.
Arc 1433.73.5 Artuk, S. Istanbul arkeoloji murelen teşhirdeki islami sikkeler kotalogu. Istanbul, 1970. 2v.
Arc 1433.75 Czapkicwicz, A. Skarb dirhemov arabskich z Czechowa. Warszawa, 1957.
Arc 1433.80 Allouche-Le Page, M.T. L'art monétaire des royaumes bactriens. Paris, 1956.
Arc 1433.85 Bibliothèque Nationale, Paris. Département des Médailles et Antiques. Catalogue des étalons monétaires. Paris, 1960.
Arc 1433.90 Davidovich, Elena A. Istoriia monetnogo dela Srednei Azii XVII-XVIII vv. Dushanbe, 1964.
Arc 1433.91 Smirnova, O.I. Katalog monet s gorodischa Pendzhikent...1949-1956 gg. Moskva, 1963.
Arc 1433.92F Miles, George Carpenter. Trésor de dirhems du IXe siècle. Paris, 1960.
Arc 1433.96 Goebl, Robert. Dokumente zur Geschichte der iranischen Hunnen in Baktrien und Indien. v.1,2,3-4. Wiesbaden, 1967. 3v.
Arc 1433.99 Tosun, Mebrure. Mejopotamya silindir muhurlerinder hurri mitanni usulü. Ankara, 1956.

Classified Listing

Arc 1433 Numismatics - Local - Other Asia - General works; Local - cont.

Arc 1433.100 Selcuklulonn nadir paralarendon borilom. Istanbul, 1972.
Arc 1433.101 Davidovich, Elena A. Denezhnoe khoziaistvo Srednei Azii posle mongol'skaia zavoevaniia i reforma Mas'ud-beka. Moskva, 1972.
Arc 1433.102 Tolunogullan ve povalan. Istanbul, 1972.

Arc 1435 Numismatics - Local - Africa in general - Folios [Discontinued]

Arc 1435.1 Mueller, L. Numismatique de l'ancienne Afrique. v.1 and supplement. Copenhague, 1860-94. 2v.
Arc 1435.1.5 Mueller, L. Numismatique de l'ancienne Afrique. v.1-3. Copenhague, 1860-62.

Arc 1438 Numismatics - Local - Africa in general - General works

Arc 1438.2 Mueller, L. Numismatique de l'ancienne Afrique. v.1-3. Bologne, 1964. 2v.

Arc 1440 Numismatics - Local - Egypt - Folios [Discontinued]

Arc 1440.200 Sborōnos, I.N. Ta nomiomata toy kratoys tōn ptolemaiōn. Athēnai, 1904. 2v.

Arc 1443 Numismatics - Local - Egypt - General works

Arc 1443.1 Rougé, Jacques de. Description de quelques monnaies nouveaux des nomes d'Égypte. Paris, 1882.
Arc 1443.2 Revillout, Eugène. Lettre à M.P. Charles Robert sur les monnaies égyptiennes. Macon, 1884.
Arc 1443.3 Langlois, V. Numismatique des nomes d'Égypte. Paris, 1852.
Arc 1443.4 Giesecke, Walther. Das Ptalemäergeld. Leipzig, 1930.
Arc 1443.5F Oxford. University. Ashmolean Museum. Catalogue of Alexandrian coins. Oxford, 1933.
Arc 1443.6 Launois, Aimée. Estampilles et poids musulmans en verre du cabinet des médailles. Caire, 1959.

Arc 1445 Numismatics - Local - Other Africa - Folios [Discontinued]

Arc 1445.5 Milan. I.R. Museo. Monete cufiche dell'I.R. Museo di Milano. Milano, 1819.

Arc 1448 Numismatics - Local - Other Africa - General works; Local

Arc 1448.1 Charrier, Louis. Description des monnaies de la Numidie et de la Maurétanie. Macon, 1912.
Arc 1448.5 Mazard, Jean. Corpus nummorum Nunudiae nauretaniaeque. Paris, 1955.
Arc 1448.6 Becklake, J.T. From real to rand. South Africa, 1963?
Arc 1448.8 Vaccaro, Francesco. Le monete di Aksum. Casteldario, 1967.
Arc 1448.10 Naville, Lucien. Les monnaies d'or de la Cyrenaïque de 450 à 250 avant J.C. Genève, 1951.

Arc 1453 Numismatics - Local - Europe in general - General works

Arc 1453.1 Hazlitt, William Carew. The coinage of the European continent. London, 1893.
Arc 1453.1.1 Hazlitt, William Carew. The coinage of the European continent. Chicago, 1974.
Arc 1453.2F Bellinger, A.R. Catalogue of the coins found at Corinth, 1925. New Haven, 1930.
Arc 1453.3 Morgenroth, Sigmund. Medals and plaquettes from the S. Morgenroth collection. Chicago, 1944.
Arc 1453.5 Soothe, J.C. von. Auserlesenes und hochstansehnliches Ducatenkabinett. Hamburg, 1784.
Arc 1453.7 Wilcke, Julius. Daler. Kjøbenhavn, 1931.
Arc 1453.8 Davenport, J.S. European crowns, 1700-1800. Galenburg, Ill., 1961.
Arc 1453.9 Russkoe Arkheologischeskoe Obshchestvo, Leningrad. Muzei. Katalog evropeiskikh medalei i monet. Sankt Peterburg, 1864.
Arc 1453.10 Suchodolski, Stanisław. Początki mennictwa w Europie Środkowej, Wschodniej i Połnocnej. Wrocław, 1971.
Arc 1453.11 Kargel, Adolf. Münzen erzählen. Bielefeld, 1971.
Arc 1453.13 Schlumberger, Hans. Goldmünzen Europas seit 1800. 3. Aufl. München, 1973.

Arc 1454 Numismatics - Local - Celtic

Arc 1454.200 Forrer, Robert. Keltische Numismatik der Rhein. Strassburg, 1908.
Arc 1454.205 Ondrouch, V. Keltské mince typu Biatec z Bratislavy. Bratislava, 1958.
Arc 1454.210F Göbl, Robert. Ostkeltischer Typenatlas. Braunschweig, 1973.

Arc 1455 Numismatics - Local - Greek and Roman together - Folios [Discontinued]

Htn Arc 1455.1* Beger, L. Thesaurus Brandenburgicus. Colonia Marchica, 1696. 3v.
Htn Arc 1455.2* Havercamp, S. Nummophylacium Reginae Christinae. The Hague, 1742.
Htn Arc 1455.3F* Goltzius, H. De re nummaria antiqua opera. Antwerp, 1708. 5v.
Htn Arc 1455.4* Vaillant, J. Numismata imperatorum. Amsterdam, 1700.
Arc 1455.5 Rizzo, G.E. Vasi greci della Sicilia. Roma, 1904.
Arc 1455.6F Sartiges. Collection du vicomte de Sartiges. Paris, 19- ?

Arc 1456 Numismatics - Local - Greek and Roman together - Pamphlet volumes

Arc 1456 Pamphlet box. Numismatics. Greek and Roman.
Arc 1456.1 Pamphlet box. Numismatics. Greek and Roman.

Arc 1458 Numismatics - Local - Greek and Roman together - General works

Arc 1458.1 Mionnet, T.E. Description de médailles antiques. Paris, 1806-08. 7v.
Arc 1458.1.2 Mionnet, T.E. Description de médailles antiques. Supplément. Paris, 1819-37. 10v.
Arc 1458.2 Yale College. Catalogue of the Greek and Roman coins in the numismatic collection. New Haven, 1880.
Arc 1458.3 Hartmann, H.L. Tabellarische Übersicht der gewoehnlichsten Altrömische Münzen. Leipzig, 1828.
Arc 1458.4 Letronne, J.A. Considerations générales sur l'évaluation des monnaies grecques et romaines. Paris, 1817.
Arc 1458.5 Haym, N.F. Del tesoro britannico. London, 1719-20. 2v.
Arc 1458.6 Raper, M. An inquiry into the value of the ancient Greek and Roman money. London, 1772.
Arc 1458.7 Cardwell, E. Lectures on the coinage of the Greeks and Romans. Oxford, 1832.
Htn Arc 1458.8* Woltereck, C. Electa rei numariae. Hamburgi, 1709.
Arc 1458.8.5 Woltereck, C. Electa rei numariae. Hamburgi, 1709.
Arc 1458.9 Hill, G.F. A handbook of Greek and Roman coins. London, 1899.
Arc 1458.10 Boston. Museum of Fine Arts. Guide to the C.P. Perkins collection of Greek and Roman coins. Boston, 1902.

Arc 1458 Numismatics - Local - Greek and Roman together - General works - cont.

Arc 1458.11 Corolla numismatica...in honour of B.V. Head. London, 1906.
Arc 1458.12 Hammer, J. Der Feingehalt die griechischen und römischen Münzen. Berlin, 1906.
Arc 1458.13 Babelon, E. Traite des monnaies grecques et romaines. Paris, 1901-33. 8v.
Arc 1458.14 Imhoof-Blumer, Friedrich. Zur griechischen und römischen Münzkunde. Genf, 1908.
Arc 1458.15 Jameson, R. Collection of monnaies grecques et romaines. v.1-2. Paris, 1913. 3v.
Arc 1458.16 Strozzi. Collection Strozzi. Médailles grecques et romaines aes grave. Paris, 1907.
Arc 1458.17 Wren, C. Numismatum antiquorum sylloge populis Graecis. Londini, 1708.
Arc 1458.18 Bibliothèque Nationale, Paris. Département des Médailles et Antiques. Collections Armand-Valton. Paris, 1912.
Arc 1458.19 Badeigts de Laborde. Description des médailles grecques. Paris, 1869.
Arc 1458.20 Naville et Cie, Geneva. Monnaies grecques et romaines. Genève, 1925.
Arc 1458.21 Ars Classica, Geneva. Monnaies antiques grecques et romaines. Genève, 1933.
Arc 1458.21.5 Ars Classica, Geneva. Monnaies antiques grecques, romaines, byzantines. Genève, 1930.
Arc 1458.22 Milne, Joseph G. Greek and Roman coins and the study of history. London, 1939.
Arc 1458.23 McGill University, Montreal. The McGill University collection of Greek and Roman coins. v.1-2. Amsterdam, 1975-

Arc 1460 Numismatics - Local - Greek and Roman together - Special topics

Arc 1460.1 Gronovius, J.F. De sestertiis. Leyden, 1691.
Htn Arc 1460.2* Walker, O. The Greek and Roman history illustrated by coins and medals. London, 1692.
Arc 1460.3 Bernhard, O. Griechische und römische Münzbilder. Zürich, 1926.
Arc 1460.4 Lacroix, L. Les reproductions des statues. Liège, 1949.
Arc 1460.5 Haak, A.C. Gold coins of the Royal Netherlands Academy. Amsterdam, 1964.
Arc 1460.6 Orlov, Georgije. Vimi nacijum. Beograd, 1970.
Arc 1460.7.1 Imhoof-Blumer, Friedrich. Tier- und Pflanzenbilder auf Münzen und Gemmen des klassischen Altertums. Hildesheim, 1972.
Arc 1460.8 Baldus, Hans Roland. Mor(eta) urb(is)-Antiona. Frankfurt am Main, 1969.

Arc 1465 Numismatics - Local - Greek - Ancient - Folios [Discontinued]

Arc 1465.1 Imhoof-Blumer, Friedrich. Choix de monnaies grecques. 2. ed. Paris, 1883.
Arc 1465.2 Gardner, P. The types of Greek coins. Cambridge, Eng., 1883.
Arc 1465.3 Imhoof-Blumer, Friedrich. Porträtköpfe auf antiken Münzen. Leipzig, 1885.
Arc 1465.4 Beulé, E. Les monnaies d'Athènes. Paris, 1858.
Arc 1465.5 Leake, W.M. Numismata Hellenica. London, 1854.
Arc 1465.6 MacDonald, G. Catalogue of Greek coins in the Hunterian collection. Glasgow, 1899. 3v.
Arc 1465.76 Gabrici, E. Topografia e numismatica dell'antica Imera, Sicily. Napoli, 1893.
Arc 1465.77 Fritze. Nomisma, Untersuchungen auf dem gebiete. Berlin, 1907-12. 12v.
Arc 1465.78 Anson, L. Numismata Graeca. pt.1-6. Londoni, 1910-16. 2v.
Arc 1465.79 Imhoof-Blumer, Friedrich. Griechische Münzen. München, 1890.
Arc 1465.80F Seltman, Charles Theodore. Athens, its history and coinage before the Persian invasion. Cambridge, 1924.
Arc 1465.80.1 Seltman, Charles Theodore. Athens; its history and coinage before the Persian invasion. Chicago, 1974.

Arc 1468 Numismatics - Local - Greek - Ancient - General works

Arc 1468.1 British Museum. Department of Coins and Medals. A catalogue of the Greek coins. London, 1873-94. 29v.
Arc 1468.2 British Museum. Department of Coins and Medals. A guide to the select Greek coins. London, 1872.
Arc 1468.2.10 British Museum. Department of Coins and Medals. A guide to the principal coins of Greeks from circa 700 B.C. to A.D. 270. London, 1932.
Arc 1468.3 Arneth, J. Synopsis numorum Graecorum. Vienna, 1837.
Arc 1468.4 Frochner, W. Monnaies grecques de la collection Photiadès Pacha. Paris, 1890.
Arc 1468.5 Bibliothèque Nationale, Paris. Département des Médailles et Antiques. Catalogue des monnaies grecques. Les rois de Syrie, d'Arménie et de Commagène. Paris, 1890.
X Cg Arc 1468.5.5 Bibliothèque Nationale, Paris. Département des Médailles et Antiques. Catalogue de la collection de Luynes. v.1-3 and plates. Paris, 1924. 6v.
Arc 1468.5.6 Bibliothèque Nationale, Paris. Département des Médailles et Antiques. Catalogue de la collection de Luynes. pt.2-3 and plates. Paris, 1925-30. 2v.
Arc 1468.6 Head, B.V. Historia numorum. Oxford, 1887.
Arc 1468.6.5A Head, B.V. Historia numorum. Oxford, 1911.
Arc 1468.6.5B Head, B.V. Historia numorum. Oxford, 1911.
Arc 1468.7 Imhoof-Blumer, Friedrich. Monnaies grecques. Amsterdam, 1883.
Arc 1468.7.5 Imhoof-Blumer, Friedrich. Monnaies grecques. Paris, 1883.
Arc 1468.8 Grunauer, E. Altgriechischen Münzorten. Basel, 1877.
Arc 1468.9 Dominicis, F. de. Repertorio numismatico. v.1-2. Naples, 1826.
Arc 1468.10 Raoul-Rachette. Mémories de numismatique et d'antiquité. Paris, 1840.
Arc 1468.11 Ward, J. Greek coins and their parent cities. London, 1902.
Arc 1468.12 Pick, Bekrendt. Die antiken Münzen von Dacien. Berlin, 1898-1910. 2v.
Arc 1468.12.2 Münzer, Friedrich. Die antiken Münzen von Thrakien. Berlin, 1912.
Arc 1468.12.3 Gaebler, Hugo. Die antiken Münzen von Makedonia. Berlin, 1906-35. 2v.
Arc 1468.13A Hill, G.F. Historical Greek coins. London, 1906.
Arc 1468.13B Hill, G.F. Historical Greek coins. London, 1906.
Arc 1468.13.2 Hill, G.F. Historical Greek coins. N.Y., 1906.
Arc 1468.13.5F Hill, G.F. Select Greek coins. Paris, 1927.
Arc 1468.14 Regling, H. Griechischen Münzen der Sammlung Warren. Text and plates. Berlin, 1906. 2v.
Arc 1468.15 Hands, A.W. Common Greek coins. London, 1907.
Arc 1468.16 Hirsch, F. Auctions-Katalog XIII. München, 1905.

Arc 1468 Numismatics - Local - Greek - Ancient - General works - cont.

Arc 1468.16.2 Hirsch, F. Auctions-Catalog XIV, XV. Greek and Roman coins. München, 1905-06.
Arc 1468.17 Weston, S. Historic notices of coins in Greece. London, 1826.
Arc 1468.18 Sundwall, J. Attischen Münzen des neueren Stiles. Helsingfors, 1907.
Arc 1468.19 Sestini, D. Descrizione d'alcune medaglie greche. Firenze, 1821.
Arc 1468.20 Lambros, J.P. Griechische Münzen. München, 1910.
Arc 1468.21 Sborōnos, Ioannēs N. Synopsis de mille coins faux du faussaire C. Christopoulos. Athènes, 1922.
Arc 1468.21.6 Sborōnos, Ioannēs N. Numismatique de la Crète ancienne. Bonn, 1972.
Arc 1468.22 Babelon, E. Les monnaies grecques. Paris, 1921.
Arc 1468.23 Weber, Hermann. The Weber collection...Greek coins. v.1-3. London, 1922-29. 6v.
Arc 1468.24 Cambridge, Eng. University. Fitzwilliam Museum. Catalogue of the McClean collection of Greek coins. Cambridge, 1923-29. 3v.
Arc 1468.25 Greenwell, W. Rare Greek coins. London, 1893.
Arc 1468.26 Börger, Hans. Griechische Münzen. Leipzig, 1922.
Arc 1468.27 Milne, Joseph G. Greek coinage. Oxford, 1931.
Arc 1468.27.5 Milne, Joseph G. The first stages in the development of Greek coinage. Oxford, 1934.
Arc 1468.28F British Academy. Sylloge nummorum Graecorum. London, 1931-51. 4v.
Arc 1468.28.5F Sylloge nummorum Graecorum. pt.1-18. Berlin, 1957- 13v.
Arc 1468.29.10 Seltman, C.T. A book of Greek coins. London, 1952.
Arc 1468.30 Dumersan, T.M. Description des médailles antiques du cabinet de feu M. Allier de Hauteroche. Paris, 1829.
Arc 1468.32 Newell, E.T. Alexander Loards. v.3. N.Y., 1921-23.
Arc 1468.34 Robert, Louis. Études de numismatique grecque. Paris, 1951.
Arc 1468.36 Pierfitte, G. Les monnaies grecques du musée Saint Raymond de Toulouse. Toulouse, 1939.
Arc 1468.38 Schlumberger, P. L'argent grec l'empire achémenide. Thèse. Paris, 1953.
Arc 1468.40 Gabrici, E. Tecnica e cronologia delle monete greche. Roma, 1951.
Arc 1468.42 Klawans, Zander H. An outline of ancient Greek coins. Racine, Wis. , 1959.
Arc 1468.45 Allotte de la Fuÿe, F.M. Monnaies grecques. Paris, 1925.
Arc 1468.48 Nanteuil, H. de. Collection de monnaies grecques. Paris, 1925. 2v.
Arc 1468.50 Boston. Museum of Fine Arts. Greek coins, 1950-1963. Boston, 1964.
Arc 1468.52 Gardner, Percy. Archaeology and the types of Greek coins. Chicago, 1965.
Arc 1468.53 Ars Classica, Geneva. Monnaies grecques. Genève, 1929.
Arc 1468.54 Naville et Cie, Geneva. Monnaies grecques antiques en or en argent. pt. 2. Genève, 1924.
Arc 1468.55 Schwarz, Dietrich Wallo Horman. Aus einer Sammlung griechischer Münzen. Zürich, 1961.
Arc 1468.58 Essays in Greek coinage. Oxford, 1968.
Arc 1468.59 Weidauer, Liselotte. Probleme der frühen Elektronprägung. n.p., n.d.
Arc 1468.60F Sylloge numorum Graecorum. v.1-3. Berlin, 1968.
Arc 1468.61 Lacroix, Léon. Études d'archéologie numismatique. Paris, 1974.
Arc 1468.62 Greek coins in North American collections. N.Y. 1,1969+
Arc 1468.63 Jenkins, G. Kenneth. Ancient Greek coins. London, 1972.
Arc 1468.64 Thompson, Margaret. An inventory of Greek coin hoards. N.Y., 1973.
Arc 1468.65.1 Münsterberg, Rudolf. Die Beamtennamen auf den griechischen Münzen. Hildesheim, 1973.
Arc 1468.66F Sylloge nummorum Graecorum Gréce. Athènes, 1970- 2v.
Arc 1468.67F Sylloge nummorum Graecorum, Sweden. Stockholm, 1974-

Arc 1470 Numismatics - Local - Greek - Ancient - Local; Special topics

Arc 1470.1 Mueller, L. Numismatique d'Alexander le Grand. Text and atlas. Copenhagen, 1855. 2v.
Arc 1470.2 Sallet, A. von. Die Nachfolger Alexanders des Grossen. Berlin, 1879.
Arc 1470.3 Imhoof-Blumer, Friedrich. Zur Münzkunde Grossgriechenlands. Wien, 1887.
Arc 1470.3.5 Hands, A.W. Coins of Magna Graecia. London, 1909.
Arc 1470.4 Head, B.V. On the chronological sequence of the coins of Syracuse. London, 1874.
Arc 1470.4.5F Gallatin, A.E. Syracusan dekadrachmas. Cambridge, 1930.
Arc 1470.4.15 Evans, A.J. Syracusan "medallions" and their engravers in the light of recent finds. London, 1892.
Arc 1470.5 Sallet, A. von. Die Künstlerinschriften auf Griechischen Münzen. Berlin, 1871.
Arc 1470.6 Warren, J.L. An essay on Greek federal coinage. London, 1863.
Arc 1470.7 Phillips, H. Remarks upon a coin of Sicyon. Philadelphia, 1882.
Arc 1470.8 Rathgeber, G. Neumundneunzig Silberne Münzen der Athenaier. Weissensee, 1858.
Arc 1470.8.5 Starr, Chester. Athenian coinage, 480-449 B.C. Oxford, 1970.
Arc 1470.9 Sestini, D. Descrizione degli stateri antichi. Florence, 1817.
Arc 1470.10 Clerk, M.G. Catalogue of coins of the Achaean League. London, 1895.
Arc 1470.11 Sallet, A. von. Beiträge zur Geschichte und Numismatik...des Pontus. Berlin, 1866.
Arc 1470.12 Levezow, J.A.K. Über mehrere im...Posen...griechische Münzen. n.p., 1833.
Arc 1470.13 Lampros, Paulos. Nomismata tēs nēsoy Amorgy. Athēnai, 1870.
Arc 1470.14 Waddington, W.H. Recueil général des monnaies grecques d'Asie Mineure. Paris, 1904. 4v.
Arc 1470.14.13 Bibliothèque Nationale, Paris. Département des Médailles et Antiques. Inventaire sommaire de la collection Waddington...1897. Paris, 1897.
Arc 1470.14.15 Bibliothèque Nationale, Paris. Département des Médailles et Antiques. Inventaire sommaire de la collection Waddington...1897. Paris, 1898.
Arc 1470.15 Regling, K. Terina. Berlin, 1906.
Arc 1470.20 Königliche Academie der Wissenschaft zu Amsterdam. Beschreibung der Griechischen Autonomen Münzen. Amsterdam, 1912.
Arc 1470.21 Müller, L. Den thraciske konge Lysimachus's mynter. Kjøbenhavn, 1857.

Arc 1470 Numismatics - Local - Greek - Ancient - Local; Special topics - cont.

Arc 1470.21.5 Müller, L. Die Münzen des thracischen Königs Lysimachus. Kopenhagen, 1858.
Htn Arc 1470.21.6* Müller, L. Die Münzen des thracischen Königs Lysimachus. Kopenhagen, 1858.
Arc 1470.22 Pansa, G. La moneta di P. Ovidio Nasone. Milano, 1912.
Arc 1470.24 Baldwin, Agnes. Symbolism on Greek coins. N.Y., 1916.
Arc 1470.25 Landon, Charles P. Numismatique du voyage du jeune Anacharsis. Paris, 1846. 2v.
Arc 1470.26 MacDonald, George. The silver coinage of Crete. London, 1919?
Arc 1470.26.5 Le Rider, Georges. Monnaies crétoises du Ve au Ier siècle avant J.C. Thèse. Paris, 1966.
Arc 1470.27 Seltman, C.J. The temple coins of Olympia. Cambridge, Eng., 1921. 2v.
Arc 1470.28 Bompois, H.F. Les médailles restitutées par M.F. Lenormant à Lyncus ou Héraclée de Lyncestide. Paris, 1867-76. 3 pam.
Arc 1470.28.5 Bompois, H.F. Médailles grecques autonomes. Paris, 1869.
X Cg Arc 1470.29 Vogt, Joseph. Die alexandrinischen Münzen. v.1-2. Stuttgart, 1924. (Changed to XP 9970)
Arc 1470.30 Mavrogordato, J. A chronological arrangement of the coins of Chios. pt.1-5. London, 1915-18.
Arc 1470.31 Newell, E.T. The coinage of Demetrius Poliorcetes. London, 1927.
Arc 1470.31.5 Newell, E.T. Tyrus rediviva. N.Y., 1923.
Arc 1470.31.10 Newell, E.T. Royal Greek portrait coins. N.Y., 1937.
Arc 1470.32F Burachkov', P. Obshchagi katalog' monety. Odessa, 1884.
Arc 1470.32.7 Beribe-Delagart, A.L. Popravki obshchagi kataloga monet. P.O. Burachkov'. Moskva, 1907.
Arc 1470.34 Schmitz, Hermann. Ein Gesetz der Stadt Olbia zum Schulze ihres Silbergeldes. Freiburg, 1925.
Arc 1470.35 Koch, Cornelius D. De Aristotle in nummo aureo. Helmestadi, 1703.
Arc 1470.37 Lampros, Paulos. Anagraphē tōn nomismatōn tēs kypies Hellados. Athēnai, 1891.
Arc 1470.38 Head, B.V. On the chronological sequence of the coins of Ephesus. London, 1880.
Arc 1470.39 Head, B.V. On the chronological sequence of the coins of Boeotia. London, 1881.
Arc 1470.40 Evans, A.J. The "Horsemen" of Tarentum. London, 1889.
Arc 1470.41 Ravel, O.E. Les "Poulains" de Corinthe; monographie des statères corinthiens. Bâle, 1936-48. 2v.
Arc 1470.42 Gardner, Percy. Samos and Samian coins. London, 1882.
Arc 1470.43 May, J.M.F. The coinage of Damastion and the lesser coinages of the Illyra-Paeonian region. London, 1939.
Arc 1470.43.5 Ceka, Hasan. Questions de numismatique illyrie. Tirana, 1972.
Arc 1470.44 Lange, Kurt. Götter Griechenlands. Berlin, 1941.
Arc 1470.45 Milne, J.G. Finds of Greek coins in the British Isles. London, 1948.
Arc 1470.47 Caley, Earle R. The composition of ancient Greek bronze coins. Philadelphia, 1939.
Arc 1470.50 May, J.M.F. Ainos. London, 1950.
Arc 1470.55 Kerényi, K. Der Mythos der Hellenen. Amsterdam, 1941.
Arc 1470.60 Oreshnikov, A. Zkskursy v oblast' drevnsi numizmatiki cherno morskago pobereniia. Moskva, 1914.
Arc 1470.70 Lauckoranski, Leo Maria. Mythen und Münzen. 1. Aufl. München, 1958.
Arc 1470.80 Brussels. Bibliothèque Royale. La collection Lucien de Hirsch. v.1-2. Bruxelles, 1959.
Arc 1470.82 Franke, P.R. Die antiken Münzen von Epirus. v.1-2. Wiesbaden, 1961.
Arc 1470.83 Le Rider, Georges. Deux trésors de monnaies. Paris, 1963.
Arc 1470.84 Schoenert-Geiss, E. Griechisches Münzwerk. Berlin, 1965. 2v.
Arc 1470.86 Kraay, Colin M. The composition of Greek silver coins. Oxford, 1962.
Arc 1470.87 Centro Internazionale di Studi Numismatici. Atti del IIo Convegno del Centro internazionale di studi numismatici. Roma, 1971.
Arc 1470.88 Centro Internazionale di Studi Numismatici. La circolazione della moneta ateniese in Sicilia e in Magna Grecia. Roma, 1969.
Arc 1470.89 Davis, Norman. The Hellenistic kingdoms. London, 1973.

Arc 1473 Numismatics - Local - Greek - Byzantine and Modern Greece

Arc 1473.1 Lampros, Paulos. Anekdota nomismata tēs kuprhoy. Athēnai, 1876.
Arc 1473.1.3 Lampros, Paulos. Anekdota nomismata en Glarentsa. Athēnai, 1876.
Arc 1473.1.3.5 Lampros, Paulos. Anekdota nomismata kopenta en Glarentsa kata mimēsin tōn Henetikōn. Oak Park, 1969.
Arc 1473.1.5 Lampros, Paulos. Anekdota nomismata tēs Hellados. Athēnai, 1880.
Arc 1473.1.8 Lampros, Paulos. Nomismata tōn ademiōn Zachariōn. Athēnai, 1884.
Arc 1473.1.9 Lampros, Paulos. Mesaiōnika nomismara tēs Chiny. Athēnai, 1886.
Arc 1473.1.10 Lampros, Paulos. Anekdoton nomisma Saroykchan Emiry tēs Iōnias. n.p., n.d.
Arc 1473.2 Pfaffenhoffen, F. Essai sur les arpres comnénats...de Trébisonde. Paris, 1847.
Arc 1473.3 Schlumberger, G. Monuments numismatiques et sphragistiques...byzantin. Paris, 1880.
Arc 1473.4 Pfaffenhoffen, F. Lettre...sur quelques monnaies byzantines. Paris, 1865.
Arc 1473.5 Soret, Frédéric. Trois lettres sur des monnaies byzantines. Genève, 1837.
Arc 1473.6A Wroth, W. Catalogue of imperial Byzantine coins in the British Museum. London, 1908. 2v.
Arc 1473.6B Wroth, W. Catalogue of imperial Byzantine coins in the British Museum. London, 1908. 2v.
Arc 1473.6.5 British Museum. Department of Coins and Medals. Catalogue of coins of vandals, ostrogoths. London, 1911.
Arc 1473.7 Tolstoi, Jean. Monnaies byzantines. v.1-4,8-9. St. Petersbourg, 1912-14. 4v.
Arc 1473.8 Goodacre, H.G. A handbook of the coinage of the Byzantine empire. pt.1-3. London, 1928-33.
Arc 1473.8.2 Goodacre, H.G. A handbook of the coinage of the Byzantine empire. London, 1957.
Arc 1473.9 Du Cange, C. du F. De imperatorum constantinopalitanorum. Romae, 1755.
Arc 1473.12 Metcalf, David Michael. The origins of the Anastasian currency reforms. Amsterdam, 1969.
Arc 1473.14 Hendy, Michael. Coinage and money in the Byzantine empire, 1081-1261. Washington, 1969.

Classified Listing

Arc 1473 Numismatics - Local - Greek - Byzantine and Modern Greece - cont.

Arc 1473.16 Bibliothèque Nationale, Paris. Département des Médailles et Antiques. Catalogue des monnaies byzantines de la Bibliothèque Nationale. Paris, 1970. 2v.
Arc 1473.18 Whitting, Philip David. Byzantine coins. London, 1973.
Arc 1473.19 Dumbarton Oaks. Catalogue of the Byzantine coins in the Dumbarton Oaks collection and in the Whittemore collection. v. 1-3. Washington, 1966- 5v.
Arc 1473.50 Lampros, Paulos. Nomismata tēs Hepianēdon politeias. Athēnai, 1884.
Arc 1473.50.5 Lampros, Paulos. Coins and medals of the Ionian Islands. Amsterdam, 1968.

Arc 1474 Numismatics - Local - Etruscan

Arc 1474.5 Cesano, Secondina L. Tipi monetali etruschi. Roma, 1926.

Arc 1475 Numismatics - Local - Roman - Folios [Discontinued]

Htn Arc 1475.1F* Occo, A. Imperatorum romanorum numismata. Milan, 1730.
Htn Arc 1475.1.2F* Occo, A. Imperatorum romanorum numismata. Milan, n.d.
Htn Arc 1475.2* Banduri, A. Numismata imperatorum romanorum. Paris, 1718. 2v.
Htn Arc 1475.3* Morelli, A. Thesaurus Morellianus. Amsterdam, 1734. 2v.
Htn Arc 1475.4* Patin, C. Familiae Romanae. Paris, 1663.
Arc 1475.4.5 Patin, C. Imperatorum romanorum numismata. Paris, 1697.
Htn Arc 1475.5* Orsini, F. Familiae Romanae. Rome, 1577.
Htn Arc 1475.6* Vaillant, J. Numi antiqui familiae romanarum. Amsterdam, 1703. 2v.
Arc 1475.7 Hobler, F. Records of Roman history. Westminster, 1860. 2v.
Arc 1475.7.2 Hobler, F. Records of Roman history. n.p., n.d. 2v.
Arc 1475.8 Morris, R. The twelve Caesars. La Grange, Ky., 1877.
Arc 1475.9 Imhoof-Blumer, Friedrich. Porträtköpfe auf Römischen Münzen. Leipzig, 1892.
Arc 1475.10 Naples. Museo Nazionale. Medagliere II. Monete Romane. pt.1-2. Naples, 1870-71. 3v.
Arc 1475.11 Häberlin, J.E.J. Aes grove das Schwergeld Roms und Mittelitaliens. v. 1, Text; v. 2, Plates. Frankfurt, 1910. 2v.
Htn Arc 1475.12F* Pedrusi, Paolo. I Cesari in oro. Parma, 1694-1727. 10v.
Arc 1475.201 Vernazza de Freney, J. Recensio nummorum qui secusii. Augustae Taurinorum, 1812.

Arc 1476 Numismatics - Local - Roman - Pamphlet volumes

Arc 1476.5 Pamphlet vol. Tractatus tres de nummis antiquorum. 3 pam.

Arc 1478 Numismatics - Local - Roman - General works

Arc 1478.1 Ackerman, J.Y. A descriptive catalogue of rare Roman coins. London, 1834. 2v.
Arc 1478.2 A catalogue of medals from Julius Caesar to Heraclius. London, 1716.
Arc 1478.3 Cohen, H. Description générale des monnaies de la Republique Romaine. Paris, 1857.
Arc 1478.3.2 Cohen, H. Description historique des monnaies frappées sons l'Empire Romain. Paris, 1859. 7v.
Arc 1478.3.3 Cohen, H. Description historique des monnaies frappées sons l'Empire Romain. Paris, 1880-92. 8v.
Arc 1478.3.10 Crawford, Michael H. Roman Republican coinage. N.Y., 1974. 2v.
Arc 1478.4 Sabatier, J. Description générale des monnaies byzantines. Text and plates. Paris, 1862. 2v.
Htn Arc 1478.5* Hulsius, L. Impp. Romanorum numismatum series. Frankfort, 1603.
Arc 1478.6 Landi, C. Selectiorum numismatum, praecipue Romanorum expositiones. Leyden, 1695.
Arc 1478.7 Madden, F.W. The handbook of Roman numismatics. London, 1861.
Arc 1478.8 Mionnet, T.E. De la rareté et du prix des médailles romaines. Paris, 1858. 2v.
Arc 1478.9 Mommsen, T. Über das römische Münzwesen. Leipzig, 1850.
Arc 1478.10 Mommsen, T. Geschichte des römisches Münzwesens. Berlin, 1860.
Arc 1478.10.5 Mommsen, T. Histoire de la monnaie romaine. Paris, 1865. 4v.
Arc 1478.11 Pfeiffer, A. Antike Münzbilder. Winterthur, 1895.
Arc 1478.12 Blanchet, A. Les monnaies romaines. Paris, 1896.
Arc 1478.13 Bahrfeldt, M. Nachträge und Bericht zur Münzkunde. Wien, 1897.
Arc 1478.14 Gruman, G. Inschriften und Darstellungen Römus. Biel, 1899.
Arc 1478.15 Gnecchi, F. Monete romane. Milano, 1900.
Arc 1478.15.2 Gnecchi, F. Monete romane. Milano, 1896.
Arc 1478.15.4 Gnecchi, F. Monetazione romana. Genève, 1897.
Arc 1478.15.5 Gnecchi, F. Roman coins. London, 1903.
Arc 1478.15.10 Gnecchi, F. I medaglioni romani. Bologna, 1968. 3v.
Arc 1478.16 Samer, K. Geschichte älteren römischen Münzwesens...200 B.C. Wien, 1883.
Arc 1478.17 Babelon, Ernest. Description historique et chronologique des monnaies de la République romaine vulgairement appelées monnaies consulaires. Paris, 1885-86. 2v.
Arc 1478.17.5 Babelon, Ernest. Description historique et chronologique des monnaies de la République romaine vulgairement appelées monnaies consulaires. Bologna, 1963. 2v.
Arc 1478.18 Hill, G.F. Historical Roman coins. London, 1909.
Arc 1478.19 Foy-Vaillant, J. Numismata imperatorum romanorum. Romae, 1743. 3v.
Arc 1478.19.2 Susomni, J.B. Numismata imperatorum romanorum. Supplementum. Vindobonae, 1767.
Arc 1478.19.5 Foy-Vaillant, J. Numismata imperatorum Augustarum et Caesarum. Amsterdami, 1700.
Arc 1478.20 Grueber, H.A. Coins of the Roman Republic in the British Museum. v.1-3,5; pt.1-2. London, 1910. 5v.
Arc 1478.21 British Museum. Department of Coins and Medals. Coins of the Roman Empire in the British Museum. v.1-4,6. London, 1923-40. 5v.
Arc 1478.21.2 British Museum. Department of Coins and Medals. Coins of the Roman Empire. v.1-3; v.4, pt.1-2; v.6. London, 1966. 6v.
Arc 1478.21.5 British Museum. Department of Coins and Medals. A guide to the exhibition of Roman coins in the British Museum. London, 1927.
Arc 1478.23 Bernhart, Max. Münzkunde der römischen Kaiserzeit. Genève, 1922.
Arc 1478.23.5 Bernhart, Max. Handbuch zur Münzkunde der römischen Kaiserzeit. Halle an der Saale, 1926. 2v.
Arc 1478.24 Mattingly, Harold. The Roman imperial coinage. v.1-9. London, 1923-38. 10v.

Arc 1478 Numismatics - Local - Roman - General works - cont.

Arc 1478.24.7 Mattingly, Harold. Roman coins from the earliest times to the fall of the Western Empire. London, 1928.
Arc 1478.24.7.2 Mattingly, Harold. Roman coins from the earliest times to the fall of the Western Empire. 2. ed. London, 1960.
Arc 1478.24.13 Mattingly, Harold. The date of the Roman denarius. London, 1933.
Arc 1478.24.15 Mattingly, Harold. Roman numismatics. London, 195-?
Arc 1478.25 Coimbra. Universidade. Biblioteca. Moedas romanas da Biblioteca da Universidade de Coimbra. Coimbra, 1905.
Arc 1478.26F Augustin, A. Antiquitatum romanorum Hispanarumque in nummis veterum dialogi XI. Antverpiae, 1617.
Arc 1478.27 Teixeira de Aragão, Augusto. Descripção historica das moedas romanas existentes no gabinete numismatico de S.M. el Rei o Senhor Dom Luiz I. Lisboa, 1870.
Arc 1478.28F Strack, Paul L. Untersuchungen zur römischen Reichsprägung des zweiten Jahrhunderts. Stuttgart, 1931-37. 3v.
Arc 1478.29 Robinson, A.E. False and imitation Roman coins. n.p., 1932.
Arc 1478.30 Catalogue d'une collection de médailles romaines. pt.1-2,3. Paris, 18- . 2v.
Arc 1478.32F Pizzamiglio, Luigi. Saggio cronologico, ossia storia della moneta romana. Roma, 1867.
Arc 1478.33A Milne, J.G. The development of Roman coinage. Oxford, 1937.
Arc 1478.33B Milne, J.G. The development of Roman coinage. Oxford, 1937.
Arc 1478.34 Mickwitz, G. Die Systeme des römischen Silbergeldes. Helsingfors, 1933.
Htn Arc 1478.35F* Phillipps, Thomas. Numismata vetera et inscriptiones ex voto. Medio-Montana, 1855.
Arc 1478.36 Belfort, A. Recherches des monnaies impériales romaines non décrites dans l'ouvrage de H. Cohen. Macon, 1884.
Arc 1478.38 Brown, D.F. Temples of Rome as coin types. N.Y., 1940.
Arc 1478.39 Hirmer, Max. Römische Kaisermünzen. Leipzig, 1941.
Arc 1478.40 Grant, Michael. Roman anniversary issues. Cambridge, Eng., 1950.
Arc 1478.40.2 Grant, Michael. Roman imperial money. London, 1954.
Arc 1478.40.5 Grant, Michael. Roman history from coins. Cambridge, Eng., 1958.
Arc 1478.42 Sutherland, C.H.V. Coinage in Roman imperial policy. London, 1951.
Arc 1478.45 Breglia, L. La prima fase della coniozione romana dell'argento. Roma, 1952.
Arc 1478.50 West, Louis. Gold and silver coin standards in the Roman empire. N.Y., 1941.
Arc 1478.55 Carson, R.A.G. Essays in Roman coinage. Oxford, 1956.
Arc 1478.60 Elmer, Georg. Verzeichnis der römischen Reichsprägungen von Augustus bis Anastasius. 2. Aufl. Graz, 1956.
Arc 1478.65F Thomsen, Rudi. Early Roman coinage. København, 1957. 3v.
Arc 1478.70 Quaderni dell'impero. L'impero di Roma nella sua moneta. Roma. 1,1939.
Arc 1478.75 Goebl, Robert. Einführung in die Münzprägung der römischen Kaiserzeit. Wien, 1957.
Arc 1478.80 Bruck, Guide. Die spatrömische Kupferprägung. Graz, 1961.
Arc 1478.81F Oxford. University. Ashmolean Museum. Catalogue of coins of the Roman Empire in the Ashmolean Museum. Oxford, 1975
Arc 1478.82F Milano. Gabinetto Numismatico. Le monete romane dell'età republicana. Milano, 1960.
Arc 1478.83 Naville et Cie, Geneva. Monnaies romaines antiques. Genève, 1924.
Arc 1478.83.5 Naville et Cie, Geneva. Monnaies romaines antiques. Genève, 1925.
Arc 1478.84 Uhlich, Gottfried. Versuch einer Numismatik für Künstler. Lemberg, 1792.
Arc 1478.85 Klawans, Zander H. Reading and dating Roman imperial coins. 3. ed. Racine, Wis., 1963.
Arc 1478.86 Carney, Thomas Francis. A catalogue of the Roman and related foreign coins in the collections of Sir Stephen Courtland at the University College of Rhodesia and Nyasaland. Salisbury, 1963.
Arc 1478.87 Sutherland, Carol H.V. Roman coins. London, 1974.
Arc 1478.88.1F Bahrfeldt, Max von. Sammlung römischer Münzen der Republik und des West-Kaiserreichs. Aalen, 1972.
Arc 1478.89 Banti, Alberto. Corpus nummorum romanorum. Firenze, 1972- 8v.

Arc 1480 Numismatics - Local - Roman - Special topics

Arc 1480.1 Venutis, P. de. Duodenorum nomismatum antehac ineditorum brevis expositio. Leghorn, 1760.
Arc 1480.2 Riccio, G.G. Le monete delle antiche famiglie di Roma. 2. ed. Naples, 1843.
Arc 1480.3 Riccio, G.G. Catalogo di antiche medaglie consolari e di famiglie romane. Naples, 1855.
Arc 1480.4 Rome. Museo Kircheriano. L'aes grave del Museo Kircheriano. Text and atlas. Roma, 1839. 2v.
Arc 1480.5 Paciandi, P.M. Ad nummos consulares III viri M. Antonii. Rome, 1757.
Arc 1480.6 Medals of the Caesars. n.p., n.d.
Arc 1480.7 London, England. Society of Antiquaries. Catalogue of Roman coins. London? 1852.
Arc 1480.8 Blancard, Louis. L'aureus romain se divisait en six-millièmes. v.1-2. Marseille, n.d.
Arc 1480.10 Blancard, Louis. Sur les chiffres romaines ou grecs...des monnaies impériales. Marseille, n.d.
Arc 1480.11 Mowat, Robert. Explication d'une marque monétaire du tempe de Constantin. Paris, 1886.
Arc 1480.12 Haeberlin, E.J. Zum corpus numorum aeris gravis. Berlin, 1905.
Arc 1480.13 Akerman, J.Y. Coins of the Romans relative to Britain. London, 1844.
Arc 1480.14 Willers, H. Geschichte der römischen Kupferprägung. Leipzig, 1909.
Arc 1480.15.1 Maurice, Jules. Numismatique constantinienne. Bruxelles, 1965. 3v.
Htn Arc 1480.16* Bruce, J.C. The story...of the Thorngrafton "Find". n.p., 1871.
Arc 1480.17 Shortt, W.T.P. Sylva antiqua iscana. Londini, n.d.
Htn Arc 1480.18* Zelada, F.X. de. De nummis aliquot...epistola. Romae, 1778.
Arc 1480.19 Sydenham, E.A. Historical references on coins of the Roman empire. London, 1917.
Arc 1480.19.10 Sydenham, E.A. The coinage of the Roman republic. London, 1952.
NEDL Arc 1480.20 Gnecchi, Francesco. The fauna and flora on the coin-types of...Rome. London, 1919.
Arc 1480.21 Pinder, Moritz. Die Münzen Justinians. Berlin, 1843.

Classified Listing

Arc 1480 Numismatics - Local - Roman - Special topics - cont.

Arc 1480.22 Kubitschek, Wilhelm. Zur Geschichte von Städten des römischen Kaiserreiches. Wien, 1916.
Arc 1480.23 Tochon D'Annecy, J.F. Mémoire sur les médailles de Marinus. Paris, 1817.
Arc 1480.24 Babelon, E. L'iconographie monetaire de Julien l'Apostat. Paris, 1903.
Arc 1480.25.1 Schulz, Otto Theodor. Die Rechtstitel und Regierungsprogramme auf römischen Kaisermünzen. N.Y., 1968.
Arc 1480.26 Sydenham, E.A. Aes grave; a study of the cast coinage of Rome and Central Italy. London, 1926.
Arc 1480.27 Pansa, Giovanni. Il tipo.di Roma dei denari consolari. Milano, 1911.
Arc 1480.28F Strack, Paul L. Untersuchungen zur Geschichte der Kaiser Nerva, Traian und Hadrian. Inaug. Diss. Stuttgart, 1930.
Arc 1480.29 Longpérier, Adrien. Recherches sur les insignes de la questure et sur les récipients monétaires. Paris, 1868.
Arc 1480.30F Caylus, A.C.P. Numismata aurea imperatorum Romanorum. n.p., n.d.
Arc 1480.31F Artaud, F. Discours sur les médailles d'Auguste et de Tibère. Lyon, 1818.
Arc 1480.32 Mabbott, T.O. A small bronze of Nero. Rome, 1936.
Arc 1480.33 Rohde, T. Die Münzen des Kaisers Aurelianus. v.1-2. Miskoloz, 1881-82.
Arc 1480.34 Manns, F. Münzkundliche und historische Unterschungen über die Zeit der Illyrerkaiser. Inaug. Diss. Würzburg, 1939.
Htn Arc 1480.35F* Croy, Charles. Regum et imperatorum Romanorum numismata. Antverpiae, 1654.
Arc 1480.36F Northumberland, A.P. Descriptive catalogue of a cabinet of Roman family coins belonging to...the Duke of Northumberland. London, 1856.
Arc 1480.38 Vallemont, P. Nouvelle explication d'une médaille d'or du cabinet du roy. Paris, 1699.
Arc 1480.40 Grant, Michael. From imperium to auctoritas. Cambridge, 1946.
Arc 1480.40.1 Grant, Michael. From imperium to auctoritas. 1. ed. London, 1969.
Arc 1480.42F Grunwald, Michael. Die römischen Bronze- und Kupfermünzen mit schlagmarken um legionslager Vindonissa. Basel, 1946.
Arc 1480.42.10F Kraay, C.W. Die Münzfunde von Vindonissa bis Trafar. Basel, 1962.
Arc 1480.42.15 Pekary, Thomas. Die Fundmünzen von Vindonissa von Hadrian bis zum Ausgang der Römerherrschaft. Brugg, 1971.
Arc 1480.44 Lanckorónski, L.M. Das römische Bildnis in Meisterwerken der Münzkunst. Amsterdam, 1944.
Arc 1480.46 Leeds, Edward T. A hoard of Roman folles from Diocletian's reform. Oxford, 1946.
Arc 1480.48 Grant, Michael. Aspects of the principate of Tiberius. N.Y., 1950.
Arc 1480.50 Rajic, H.P. Ilustrovani katalog novaca rimskih i vizantiskih vladaoca. Beograd, 1939?
Arc 1480.54 Grant, Michael. The six main AES coinages of Augustus. Edinburgh, 1953.
Arc 1480.54.5 Mattingly, Harold. Some new studies of the Roman republican coinage. London, 195-.
Arc 1480.56 Deutsches Archäologisches Institut. Die Fundmünzen der römischen Zeit in Deutschland. Berlin, 1960- 17v.
Arc 1480.58 Callu, Jean Pierre. Genio populi romani, 295-316. Paris, 1960.
Arc 1480.60 Ondrouch, V. Der römische Denarfund von Vyşkovce aus der Frühkaiserzeit. Bratislava, 1934.
Arc 1480.62 Es, W.A. van. De romeinse muntvondsten uit de drie noordelijke provincies. Groningen, 1960.
Arc 1480.63 Late Roman bronze coinage, A.D. 324-498. London, 1960.
Arc 1480.64F Kropotkin, V.V. Klady rimskikh monet na teriitorii SSSR. Moskva, 1961.
Arc 1480.65 Wosnik, Bernhard. Untersuchungen zur Geschichte Sullas. Inaug. Diss. Würzburg, 1963.
Arc 1480.66 Franke, Peter. Römische Kaiserporträts im Münzbild. München, 1961.
Arc 1480.67 Cappelli, R. Profili imperiali romani. Milano, 1963.
Arc 1480.68 Konik, Eugeniusz. Znaleziska monet rzymskich na Śląsku. Wrocław, 1965.
Arc 1480.71 Hill, Philip V. The coinage of Septimius Severus and his family of the mint of Rome, A.D. 193-217. London, 1964.
Arc 1480.72 Hill, Philip V. The dating and arrangement of the undated coins of Rome, A.D. 98-148. London, 1970.
Arc 1480.75 Turcan, Robert. Le trésor de Guelma. Thèse. Paris, 1963.
Arc 1480.80 Kellner, Wendelin. Libertas und Christogramm. Thesis. Karlsruhe, 1968.
Arc 1480.84 Alföldi, András. Caesar in 44 v. Chr. Bonn, 1974.
Arc 1480.85 Burzio, Humberto F. La marina en la moneda romana. Buenos Aires, 1961.
Arc 1480.86 Weissgerber, Clemens. Der Fröndenberger Münzschatzfund römischer Denare. Dortmund, 1969?

Arc 1485 Numismatics - Local - Italy - Folios [Discontinued]

Arc 1485.1 Buonanni, P. Numismata pontificum romanorum. Rome, 1699. 2v.
Arc 1485.1.2 Buonanni, P. Numismata summorum pontificum. Rome, 1715.
Arc 1485.2 Beger, L. Numismata...Brandenburgici sectio prima. Brandenburgi, 1704.
Arc 1485.3 Schweitzer, F. Serie delle monete e medaglie d'Aquilya e di Venezia. v.1-2. Trieste, 1848-52.
Arc 1485.4 Cinagli, Angelo. Le monete de' papi. Fermo, 1848.
Arc 1485.4.5F Vitalini, O. Supplemento alle monete dei papi. Camerino, 1892.
Arc 1485.5 Friedländer, Julius. Die italienischen Schaumünzen der fünfzehnten Jahrhundert. Berlin, 1882.
Arc 1485.6 Paruta, F. Sicilia numismatica. v.1-3. Lugdunum Batavorum, 1723. 2v.
Arc 1485.7F Corpus nummorum italicorum. Roma, 1910-29. 15v.
Arc 1485.7.5 Dotti, E. Tariffa di monete medioevale e moderne italiane. Milano, 1913.
Arc 1485.8 Argelati, P. De monetis italiae variorum illustrium virorum. Mediolani, 1750. 6v.
Arc 1485.9F Zanetti, G.A. Nuova raccolta delle monete e zecche d'Italia. Bologna, 1775-89. 5v.

Arc 1486 Numismatics - Local - Italy - Pamphlet volumes

Arc 1486.1 Pamphlet box. Numismatics. Italy.
Arc 1486.2 Pamphlet vol. Italian medals. 16 pam.

Arc 1488 Numismatics - Local - Italy - General works

Arc 1488.3 Società Numismatica Italiana. Bibliografia numismatica. Milano, 1918-20.
Arc 1488.5 Sambon, Arthur. Les monnaies antiques. Paris, 1903.
Htn Arc 1488.6* Bellini, V. De monetis Italiae medii aeirhactenus. Ferrariae, 1755.
Arc 1488.7 Ambrosoli, Solone. Atlante numismatico italiano. Milano, 1906.
Arc 1488.8F Giesecke, Walther. Italia numismatica. Leipzig, 1928.
Arc 1488.9 Cagiati, Memmo. Manuale per il raccoglitore di monete del regno d'Italia. Napoli, 1918.
Arc 1488.10 Ricci, S. Storia della moneta in Italia. Padova, 1937.
Arc 1488.11F Sambon, Giulio. Repertoiro generale delle monete coniate in Italia. Parigi, 1912.
Arc 1488.15F Gennarelli, Achille. La moneta primitiva e i monumenti dell'Italia antica. Diss. Roma, 1843.
Arc 1488.18 Simonetti, Luigi. Manuale di numismatica ialiana medioevale e moderna dalla caduta dell'impero romano alla rivoluzione francese. v.1, pt. 1. Firenze, 1965.
Arc 1488.20 Secchi, Alberto. Le monete decimali sabaude. Milano, 1955.
Arc 1488.25 Pagani, Antonio. Monete italiane moderne a sistema decimale da Napoleone console alla Repubblica Italiana. 2. ed. Milano, 1953.
Arc 1488.26F Venice. Museo. Catalogo della raccolta numismatica Papadopoli-Aldobandino. Venezia, 1925. 2v.
Arc 1488.27 Ciferra, Raffaello. Repertorio alfabetico di numismatica medioevale e moderna. Pavia, 1963. 2v.
Arc 1488.32 Pagani, Antonio. Monete italiane dall'invasione napoleonica ai giorni nostri, 1796-1963. 2. ed. Milano, 1965.
Arc 1488.34 Cainola, Aldo. Le antiche zecche d'Italia. Roma, 1971.

Arc 1490 Numismatics - Local - Italy - Local; Special topics

Arc 1490.2 Gandolfi, G.C. Della moneta antica di Genova. v.1-2. Genova, 1841-42.
Arc 1490.3 Friedländer, Julius. Die Oskischen Münzen. Leipzig, 1850.
Arc 1490.4 Schweitzer, F. Indice delle Zecche d'Italia. Trieste, 1857.
Arc 1490.4.5 Carli, G.R. Delle monete e dell'istituzione delle Zecche d'Italia. Mantova, 1754. 3v.
Arc 1490.4.7 Carli, G.R. Delle monete e dell'istituzione delle Zecche d'Italia. L'Aja, 1754-57. 2v.
Arc 1490.5 Lazari, V. Le monete dei possedimenti veneziani. Venezia, 1851.
Htn Arc 1490.5.5* Palati, J. Fasti ducales ab Anafesto I. Venetiis, 1696.
Arc 1490.5.7 Papadopoli, Nicolo. Le monete di Venezia. pt.1-3. Venezia, 1893-1919. 4v.
Arc 1490.5.10 Gian, M.L. dal. Il Leone di S. Marco. Venezia, 1958.
Arc 1490.6 Morbio, C. Opere storico-numismatiche. Bologna, 1870.
Arc 1490.7 Mayr, A. Die antiken Münzen...Malta. München, 1895.
Arc 1490.8 Garufi, C.A. Monete econii nella storia del diritto siculo. Palermo, 1898.
Arc 1490.8.5 Hill, G.F. Coins of ancient Sicily. Westminster, 1903.
Arc 1490.8.9 Lederer, Philipp. Die Tetrodrachmenprägung von Segesta. München, 1910.
Arc 1490.8.10 Pennisi, Agostino. Siciliae veteres nummi. Acireale, 1940.
Arc 1490.8.15 Consolo Langher, S. Contributo alla storia della...moneta. Milano, 1964.
Arc 1490.8.20 Holm, Adolf. Storia della moneta siciliana. Bologna, 1965.
Arc 1490.9 Vignoli, Giovanni. Antiquiores pontificum romanorum denarii. Romae, 1709.
Arc 1490.10 Vettori, Francesco. Il fiorino d'oro antico illustrato. Firenze, 1738.
Arc 1490.11 Marks von Marksfeld, J. Vierzig Münzen der Normannen Hohenstaufen. Mailand, 1858.
Arc 1490.12 Camera, Matteo. Importante scoperta del famoso Tarèno di Amalfi. Napoli, 1872.
Arc 1490.13 Promis, Domenico. Monete dei romani pontefici avanti il mille. Torino, 1858.
Arc 1490.13.10 Hamburger, L. Katalog alte Sammlung päpstlicher Münzen. Frankfurt, 1921.
Arc 1490.14 Maguan, A.P.D. Lucania numismatica. Roma, 1775.
Arc 1490.15 Engel, A. Recherches sur la numismatique...des nomands de Sicile. Paris, 1882.
Arc 1490.16 Schembri, H.C. Coins and medals of knights of Malta. London, 1908.
Htn Arc 1490.17* Bellini, Y. Delle monete di Ferrara. Ferrara, 1761.
Arc 1490.18 Diodati, D. Illustrazione delle monete. 2. ed. Napoli, 1849.
Arc 1490.19 Perini, L. La repubblica di San Marino sue monete medaglie decorazioni. Roverto, 1900.
Arc 1490.20 Vermiglioli, G.B. Di un quadrante unico ed inedito. Perugia, 1825.
Arc 1490.21 Martinori, Edoardo. Annali della zecca di Roma. v.1-11,12-16,17-24. Roma, 1917-20. 3v.
Arc 1490.22 Minicis, Gaetano de. Numismatica ascolana...ascoli nel piceno. Fermo, 1853.
Arc 1490.23 Bompois, H.F. Les types monétaires de la guerre sociale. Paris, 1873.
Arc 1490.24 Cagiati, Memmo. Le monete del reame delle Due Sicilie da Carlo I d'Angio a Vittorio Emanuele II. Napoli, 1911-16.
Arc 1490.24.2 Supplemento all'opera Le monete del reame de Due Sicilie. Napoli. 2-3,1912-1913
Arc 1490.25 Benedictus Floravantensis. Antiqui romanorum pontificum denarii a Benedicto XI ad Paulum III. Romae, 1738.
Arc 1490.27 Perini, Quintilio. La repubblica romana del 1849 e le sue monete. Rovereto, 1903.
Arc 1490.27.5 Perini, Quintilio. Le monete di Verona. Rovereto, 1902.
Arc 1490.28F Promis, D. Monete dei reali di Savoia. Torino, 1841. 2v.
Arc 1490.30 Parisio, Prospero. Rariora magnae Graeciae numismata...1592. n.p., 1683.
Arc 1490.31 Strada, M. La zecca di Milano e le sue monete. Milano, 1930.
Arc 1490.32 Ulrich-Bansa, O. Monete mediolanensis. Venezia, 1949.
Arc 1490.35 Brambilla, C. Monete di Pavia. Pavia, 1883.
Arc 1490.37 Friedländer, Julius. Die Münzen der Ostgothen. Berlin, 1844.
Arc 1490.40F Vermiglioli, G.B. Della zecca e delle monete perugine. Perugia, 1816.
Arc 1490.45 Vergare, Cesare A. Monete del regno di Napoli da Roggiero. Roma, 1715.
Arc 1490.50F Fusco, G.V. Intorno alle zecche ed alle monete battute nel reame di Napoli da Re Carlo VIII di Francia. Napoli, 1846.
Arc 1490.55F Schweitzer, F. Serie dei nummi aquilejesi. Trieste, 1848.

Classified Listing

Arc 1490 Numismatics - Local - Italy - Local; Special topics - cont.

Arc 1490.60 Särström, M. A study in the coinage of the Mamertines. Lund, 1940.
Arc 1490.65F Bernareggi, E. Monete d'oro con ritratto del rinascimento italiano. Milano, 1954.
Arc 1490.68 Horzfelder, Hubert. Les monnaies d'argent de Rhegion frappées entre 461 et le milieu du IVe siècle avant J.-C. Paris, 1957.
Arc 1490.75 Gamberini, Cesare. Prontuario pezzario delle monete. Bologna, 1960.
Arc 1490.80 Spahr, Rodolfo. Le monete siciliane dagli Aragonisi ai Borboni. Palermo, 1959.
Arc 1490.82 Pagani, Antonio. I bersaglieri nelle medaglie 1836-1936. Milano, 1937.
Arc 1490.85 Weiss, Roberto. The medals of Pope Sixtus IV, 1471-1484. Rome, 1961.
Arc 1490.90 Patrignani, Antonio. Le medaglie di Pio VII, 1829-1830. Catania, 1933.
Arc 1490.92 Shuhaievs'kyi, Valentyn. Funde venezianischer Münzen des 13. Jahrhundert in der Ostukraine als geschichtliche Quelle. Berlin, 1944.
Arc 1490.94.1 Gnecchi, Francesco. Monete di Milano; inedite supplemento all'opera: Le monete di Milano da Carlo Magno a Vittorio Emanuele II. Milano, 1894.
Arc 1490.96 Rinaldi, Alfio. Catalogo delle medaglie papali annuali da Pio VII a Paolo VI. Verona, 1967.
Arc 1490.98 Salinas Gargotta, Antonino. Su di alcune monete puniche di Mozia. Palermo, 1858.
Arc 1490.98.5F Salinas Gargotta, Antonino. Le monete dell'antiche città di Sicilia. Palermo, 1867-72.
Arc 1490.98.10F Giesecke, Walther. Sicilia numismata. Leipzig, 1923.
Arc 1490.98.15 Cirami, Giacomo. La monetazione greca della Sicilia antica. Bologna, 1959. 2v.

Arc 1492 Numismatics - Local - Spain and Portugal - Folios [Discontinued]

Arc 1492.200 Heiss, Aloiss. Descripcion generale de las monedas hispanicas cristianas. Madrid, 1865. 3v.
Arc 1492.201 Heiss, Aloiss. Description générale des monnaies antiques de l'Espagne. Paris, 1870.
Arc 1492.202 Heiss, Aloiss. Description générale des monnaies des rois wisigoths. Paris, 1872.
Arc 1492.203F Saez, Liciniano. Demonstración histórica del verdadero valor detodas las monedas que corrian en Castilla. Madrid, 1796.

Arc 1493 Numismatics - Local - Spain and Portugal - General works

Arc 1493 Pamphlet box. Numismatics. Spain and Portugal. 2 pam.
Arc 1493.2 Aragão, A.C. de. Descripção...das moedas cunhadas en home dos reis. Lisboa, 1874-80. 3v.
Arc 1493.3 Allen, E.A. Monnaies d'or suévo-lusitaniennes. Paris, 1865.
Arc 1493.4 Zobel de Zangroniz, J. Estudio de la moneda antigua española. Madrid, 1878. 2v.
Arc 1493.5 Lopes Fernandes, M.B. Memoria das moedas correntes em Portugal. Lisboa, 1856.
Arc 1493.6 Delgado, Antonio. Nuevo método de clasificacion de las medallas autonomas de España. Sevilla, 1871-76. 3v.
Arc 1493.7F Saez, Liciniano. Apendice á la crónica nuevamente impressa del señor rey don Juan el II. Madrid, 1786.
Arc 1493.8 Saez, Liciniano. Demostración histórica del verdadero valor de todas las monedas que corrián en Castilla. Madrid, 1805.
Arc 1493.9 Leite de Vasconcellos, J. Da numismatica em Portugal. Lisboa, 1923.
Arc 1493.10 Catalogo descriptivo das moedas portuguesas. Lisboa, 1903.
Arc 1493.11 Lamas, Arthur. Medalhas portuguesas e estrangeiras referentes a Portugal. Lisboa, 1916.
Arc 1493.12 Martin Minquez, Bernardino. Datos epigráficos y numismáticos de España. Valladolid, 1883.
Arc 1493.13 Vives y Escudero, Antonio. La moneda hispánica. Madrid, 1926. 2v.
Arc 1493.14 Ferrandis Torres, J. Les monnaies hispaniques. Barcelona, 1929.
Arc 1493.15 Yriarte, José de. Catalogo de los reales de a ocho espanoles. Madrid, 1955.
Arc 1493.17 Gracia de la Fuente, Arturo. Resumen historico. Madrid, 1934.
Arc 1493.20 Perelada, Spain. Castillo de los Condes de Perelada. Museo. Monetario. Perelada, 1957.
Arc 1493.22 Ortega Galindo, Julio. La España firmitiva a través de las monedas ibéricas. Bilbao, 1963.
Arc 1493.23 Brazão, Arnaldo. Numismatalogos contemporaneas. Lisboa, 1963.
Arc 1493.24 Guadan, Antonio M. de. Numismatica iberica e iberoromana. Madrid, 1969.
Arc 1493.25 Vicenti, Jose A. España, 1869-1973: la peseta. 8. ed. Madrid, 1973.
Arc 1493.26 Navascués y de Juan, Joaquin Maria de. Las monedas hispanicas del Museo arqueologico nacional de Madrid. Barcelona, 1969. 2v.
Arc 1493.27 Coelho, Antonio D.S. Numária da Lusitânia. Lisboa, 1972.

Arc 1494 Numismatics - Local - Spain and Portugal - Local; Special topics

Arc 1494.1 Velazquez, L.J. Congeturae sobre las medallos. Malaga, 1759.
Arc 1494.2 Blancard, Louis. Essai d'interpretation des lettres B.N.M...dinars. Marseille, n.d.
Arc 1494.3 Markl, M. Die Münzen, Medaillen, und Prägungen. Prag, 1896. 2v.
Arc 1494.4 Salat, Josef. Tratado de las monedas labradas...de Cataluña. v.1-2. Barcelona, 1818.
Arc 1494.4.9 Botet y Sisó, Joaquim. Les monedes Catalanes. Barcelona, 1908-11. 3v.
Arc 1494.5 Reis de Sanches Ferreira, M. Opataco apontamentos para a sua historia. Coimbra, 1911.
Arc 1494.6 Batalha Reis, Pedro. Moedas de Toro. Lisboa, 1933.
Arc 1494.7 Ferreira Barros, A. Moedas portuguesas dos reinados de D. Carlos I. e de D. Manuel II. Pôrto, 1943.
Arc 1494.8 Codera y Zaiden, F. Tratado de numismática. Madrid, 1879.
Arc 1494.9 Mateu y Llopis, Felipe. Glosario hispanico de numismatica. Barcelona, 1946.
Arc 1494.10 Fernandez Lopez, M. El tesoro visigotico de la Capilla. Sevilla, 1895.
Arc 1494.15 Castejan, R. Medina Zahira. Cordoba, 1924.
Arc 1494.20F Herrera y Chiesanova, A. El duro. Madrid, 1914. 2v.
Arc 1494.25 Costa Couvreur, Raul de. Uma reproducão em cabre de moeda de retrato datado de 1630. Lisboa, 1956.

Arc 1494 Numismatics - Local - Spain and Portugal - Local; Special topics - cont.

Arc 1494.30 Prieto y Vives, Antonio. Los reyes de Taijas. Madrid, 1926.
Arc 1494.35 Madrid. Museo Arqueologico Nacional. Catalogo de las monedas previsigadas. Madrid, 1936.
Arc 1494.40 Mateu y Llopis, Felipe. El ius monetae en el condado de Ampurias. Perelada, 1957.
Arc 1494.45 Lastanosa, V.J. de. Tratado de la moneda jaquesa y otras de oro. Zaragozana, 1681.
Arc 1494.50 Fontecha y Sanchez, Ramon de. La reforma monetaria de 1868; catalogo de monedas. Madrid, 1965.
Arc 1494.55 Garcia de la Fuente, Arturo. La numismática española en el reinado de Felipe II. Escorial, 1927.
Arc 1494.57 Gil Farres, Octavia. La moneda hispanica en la edad antigua. Madrid, 1966.
Arc 1494.59 Campaner y Fuertes, Alvaro. Numismática balear. Palma de Mallorca, 1879.
Arc 1494.60 Vaz, Joaquin Ferraro. Livro das moedas de Portugal. Book of the coins of Portugal. Braga, 1969-70. 2v.
Arc 1494.62 Calbató de Grau, Gabriel. Compendio de las piezas de ocho reales. San Juan, 1970. 2v.

Arc 1495 Numismatics - Local - France - Folios [Discontinued]

Arc 1495.1 Marx, R. Les médailleurs français contemporains. Paris, 1898.
Arc 1495.2 De Sauley, F. Recherches sur les monnaies. Paris, 1843.
Arc 1495.4F Plantet, L. Essai sur les monnaies du Comte de Bourgogne. Paris, 1865.

Arc 1496 Numismatics - Local - France - Pamphlet volumes

Arc 1496.01 Pamphlet box. Numismatics. France.

Arc 1498 Numismatics - Local - France - General works

Arc 1498.1 Engel, A. Répertoire...de la numismatique française. Paris, 1887-89. 2v.
Arc 1498.1.2 Engel, A. Répertoire...de la numismatique française. Supplément et table. Paris, 1889.
Arc 1498.2 Leblanc, F. Traité historique des monnayes de France. Amsterdam, 1692.
Arc 1498.2.5 Leblanc, F. Traité historique des monnayes de France. Paris, 1690.
Arc 1498.3 Saulcy, L.F.J.C. de. Recueil de documents...monnaies frappées par les rois de France depuis Philippe II jusqu'à François I. Paris, 1879-92. 4v.
Arc 1498.4 Barthélemy, A. de. Numatisque de la France. Paris, 1891.
Arc 1498.6 Caron, E. Monnaies féodales françaises. fasc. 1-3. Paris, 1882.
Arc 1498.7 Blanchet, A. Manuel de numismatique francaise. Paris, 1912-36. 4v.
Arc 1498.8 Poey d'Avant, F. Monnaies féodales de France. Paris, 1858. 4v.
Arc 1498.9 Dieudonné, A. Les monnaies françaises. Paris, 1923.
Arc 1498.10 Ciani, Louis. Catalogue de monnaies françaises. pt.1-3. Paris, 1927-29.
Arc 1498.11 Fillon, B. Considérations historiques et artistiques sur les monnaies de France. Fontenay, 1850.
Arc 1498.15 Lafaurie, Jean. Les monnaies des rois de France. Paris, 1951. 2v.
Arc 1498.20 Ernst, Barbara. Les monnaies françaises depuis 1848. Braunschweig, 1968.

Arc 1500 Numismatics - Local - France - Local; Special topics

Arc 1500.1 Jeuffrain, A. Essai d'interpretation...médailles...celtes-gaulois. Tours, 1846.
Arc 1500.2 Duchalais, A. Description des médailles gauloises...de la Bibliothèque Royale. Paris, 1846.
Arc 1500.3 Morel-Fatio, A. Catalogue raisonné de la collection de deniers merovingiens. Paris, 1890.
Arc 1500.4 Blancard, Louis. Essai sur les monnaies de Charles Ier, comté de Provence. Paris, 1868.
Arc 1500.5 Ponton d'Amécourt, G. de. Monnaies mérovingiennes du palais et de l'ecole. Paris, 1862.
Arc 1500.5.3 Ponton d'Amécourt, G. de. Description raisonnée des monnaies mérovingiennes de Châlon-sur-Saône. Paris, 1874-83. 3 pam.
Arc 1500.5.5 Ponton d'Amécourt, G. de. Monnaies mérovingiennes de Saint-Denis. Macon, 1884.
Arc 1500.5.25 Prou, Maurice. Catalogue des deniers mérovingiens de la trouvaille de Bais (Ille et Vilaine). Paris, 1908.
Arc 1500.5.35 Bibliothèque Nationale, Paris. Département des Médailles et Antiques. Inventaire sommaire des monnaies mérovingiennes de la collection d'Amécourt. Paris, 1890.
Arc 1500.6 Germain, A. Mémoire sur les anciennes monnaies seigneuriales. Montpellier, 1852.
Arc 1500.6.3 Germain, A. De la monnaie Mahométane atribuée à um évêque. Montpellier, 1854.
Arc 1500.7 Blancard, Louis. Les marcs de la ville et de la cour romaine d'Avignon. Tours, n.d. 2 pam.
Arc 1500.8.5 Blancard, Louis. Monnaies féodales françaises par M.E. Caron. Résumé. Draguignan, 1885.
Arc 1500.10 Blancard, Louis. Nouveau classement des monnaies bretonnes. Marseille, 1888-89.
Arc 1500.11 Blancard, Louis. Des monogrammes...deniers capétiens. Marseille, n.d.
Arc 1500.12 Blancard, Louis. Sur quelques points obscurs de la numismatique de Charles VIII. Paris, n.d.
Arc 1500.13 Blancard, Louis. La médaille d'argent de Fauquembergue...dame au faucon. Marseille, 1883.
Arc 1500.14 Barthélemy, Anatole de. Note sur les monnaies trouvées au Mont César. Paris, 1881.
Arc 1500.15 Barthélemy, Anatole de. Monnaie gauloise inédite de Luctérius, chef Cadurque. n.p., 1880.
Arc 1500.16 Barthélemy, Anatole de. Liste des noms d'hommes gravés sur les monnaies. Paris, 1881.
Arc 1500.17 Robert, Charles. Monnaies gauloises. Paris, 1880.
Arc 1500.18 Maxe-Werly, L. Note sur l'origine du gros tournois. Paris, 1880.
Arc 1500.19 Blancard, Louis. Le gros tournois est imite du sarrazinas Chrétien d'Acre. n.p., n.d.
Arc 1500.20 Holmboe, C.A. Im vildsvintypen fraa galliske mynter. Kjøbenhavn, 1868.
Arc 1500.21 Blanchet, A. Traité des monnaies gauloises. v.1-2. Paris, 1905.
Arc 1500.22 Rigollot, M.J. Monnaies inconnues des évêques des innocens. Paris, 1857.
Arc 1500.23 Florange, J. Armorial du jetonophile. Paris, 1907. 2v.

Classified Listing

Arc 1500 Numismatics - Local - France - Local; Special topics - cont.

Arc 1500.24 Leblond, V. Le pays des Bellovaques. Essai...numismatique. Caen, 1906.
Arc 1500.25 Rossignol. Jetons des états de Bourgogne. Autun, 1851.
Arc 1500.26 Fontenay, J. de. Nouvelle étude de jetons. Autun, 1850.
Arc 1500.27 Roman, J. Classement des monnaies épiscopales. Paris, 1886.
Arc 1500.28 Bascle de Lagrèze, G. Essai sur l'histoire monetaire...de Béarn. Toulouse, 1855.
Arc 1500.28.5 Blanchet, J.A. Histoire monetaire du Béarn et description des monnaies...Béarn. v.1-2. Paris, 1893.
X Cg Arc 1500.29F Witte, Jean. Recherches sur les empereurs qui ont régné dans les Gaules. n.p., 1920.
Arc 1500.30 Grappin, Pierre-Philippe. Recherches sur les anciennes monnaies du comté de Bourgogne. Paris, 1782.
Arc 1500.31 Ducrocq, T. Les nouveaux types monétaires de la France. Poitiers, 1900.
Arc 1500.34 Robert, M.P.C. Sur la prétendue restauration du pouvoir de Maurice Tibère. Paris, 1883.
Arc 1500.35 Colson, Achille. Recherches sur les monnaiss qui ont en cours en Roussillon. Perpignan, 1853.
Arc 1500.36 Florange, C. Étude sur les messageries et les postes. Paris, 1925.
Arc 1500.37 Bompois, H.F. Notice sur un dèpot de monnaies carlovingiennes. Paris, 1871.
Arc 1500.39 Changarnier, A. Monnaies des Boïens de la Germanie. Dijon, 1914.
Arc 1500.40 Lecoq-Kerneven, J. Monnaies du moyen-age (Gaule). Rennes, 1870.
Arc 1500.40.5 Lecoq-Kerneven, J. Étude historique sur la numismatique bretonne. Rennes, 1868.
Arc 1500.40.10 Buisson, Honoré. Monnaies féodales bretonnes de Charles le Chauve a Anne de Bretagne. Perigueux, 1961.
Arc 1500.41 Lelewel, Joachim. Réapparitions du type gaulois dans le coin du moyen age. Bruxelles, 1841.
Arc 1500.43 Bigot, A. Essai sur les monnaies du royaume. Paris, 1857.
Arc 1500.45 Bibliothèque Nationale, Paris. Département des Médailles et Antiques. Catalogue des jetons. Paris, 1897.
Arc 1500.46 Recamier, E. Monnaies romaines. Paris, 1925.
Arc 1500.47.5 Fillioux, A. Nouvel essai d'interprétation et de classification des monnaies de la Gaule. 2. éd. Paris, 1867.
Arc 1500.48 Garnier, Alphonse. La monnaie de Troyes de 1422 à 1434. n.p., n.d.
Arc 1500.49 Joubert, André. Les monnaies anglo-françaises. Mamers, 1886.
Arc 1500.50 Saunier, Charles. Augustin Dupré: ofèvre, médailleur et graveur général des monnaies. Paris, 1894.
Arc 1500.51 Chalon, Rénier. Recherches sur les monnaies de Wallincourt en Cambrésis. Bruxelles, 1847.
Arc 1500.52 Rybat, N.V.L. Armorican art. Jersey, 1952.
Arc 1500.53F Lengyel, L. L'art gaulais dans les médailles. Montrange-Seine, 1954.
Arc 1500.54 Chevallier, Guy. Les trésors de monnaies romaines découverts dans le départément du Loiret. Gien, 1958.
Arc 1500.55 Babelon, Jean. Histoire de Paris d'après les médailles de la Renaissance au XX. siècle. Paris, 1951.
Arc 1500.56 Richebé, C. Les monnaies féodales d'artois. Paris, 1963.
Arc 1500.57 Rolland, Henri. Monnaies des comtés de Provence, XII-XV siècles. Paris, 1956.
Arc 1500.59 Paris. Musée Monétaire et des Médailles. Entente cordiale. v.1-2. Paris, 1957.
Arc 1500.60F Tricou, Jean. Médailles lyonnaises du XVe au XVIIIe siècle. Paris, 1958.
Arc 1500.61 Tricou, Jean. Numismatique des corporations. Paris, 1957.
Arc 1500.62 Gamberini, Cesare. Prontuario. Bologna, 1952.
Arc 1500.63 Dancoisne, Louis. Recueil de monnaies...de Douai. Douai, 1836.
Arc 1500.64 Le Gentilhomme, P. Melanges de numismatique merovingienne. Paris, 1940.
Arc 1500.66 Scheers, Simone. Les monnaies de la Gaule inspirées de celles de la republique romaine. Leuven, 1969.
Arc 1500.68 Saulcy, Felicien de. Recherches sur les monnaies des ducs hereditaires de Lorraine. Metz, 1841.
Arc 1500.69 Dumas-Dubourg, Françoise. Le trésor de Fécamp et la monnayage en Francie occidentale pendant la seconde moitié du Xe siècle. Paris, 1971.

Arc 1503 Numismatics - Local - Switzerland - General works

Arc 1503.1 Haller, G.E. von. Schweizerisches Münz- und Medaillenkabinet. v.1-2. Bern, 1780-81.
Arc 1503.2F Caraggioni, L. Münzgeschichte der Schweiz. Geneve, 1896.
Arc 1503.5 Schweizerische Münzkataloge. Bern. 1-3
Arc 1503.7 Divo, Jean-Paul. Die Münzen der Schweiz im 19. und 20. Jahrhundert. Zürich, 1967.
Arc 1503.8 Divo, Jean-Paul. Die neueren Münzen der Schweiz und des Fürstentums Leichtenstein. 1850-1970. 4. Aufl. Freiburg, 1971.
Arc 1503.9 Grossmann, Theodor. Sammlung Schweizer Münzen und Medaillen des Herrn Theodor Grossmann. Frankfurt, 1926?

Arc 1504 Numismatics - Local - Switzerland - Local; Special topics

Arc 1504.5 Fluri, Adolf. Die Berner Schulpfennige und die Tischlivierer. Bern, 1910.
Arc 1504.10 Girtamner-Solchli, H. Das Münzwesen im Kanton St. Gallen. Genf, 1923.
Arc 1504.15 Wielandt, Friedrich. Schaffhausen Münz- und Geldgeschichte. Schaffhausen, 1959?
Arc 1504.20 Divo, Jean-Paul. Die neueren Münzen der Schweiz und des Fürstentums Liechtenstein, 1850-1963. Freiburg, 1965.
Arc 1504.20.5 Jaeger, Kurt. Die Münzprägungen der letzten Monarchien des teutschen Bundes von 1815. Fürstentum Liechtenstein. Basel, 1963.
Arc 1504.25 Wielandt, Friedrich. Münz- und Geldgeschichte des Standes Schuyz. Schuyz, 1964.
Arc 1504.30 Wielandt, Friedrich. Münz- und Geldgeschichte des Standes Luzern. Luzern, 1969.

Arc 1505 Numismatics - Local - Germany - Folios [Discontinued]

Arc 1505.1 Dannenberg, H. Die deutschen Münzender Saeschischen und Frankischen Kaiserzeit. Text und Plates. Berlin, 1876. 2v.
Arc 1505.2 Dannenberg, H. Pommerns Münzen im Mittelalter. Berlin, 1864.
Arc 1505.3 Dollinger, F. Furstenbergischen Münzen und Medaillen. Donaueschingen, 1903.
Arc 1505.6 Engel, Arthur. Numismatique de l'Alsace. Paris, 1887.

Arc 1505 Numismatics - Local - Germany - Folios [Discontinued] - cont.

Arc 1505.201 Domanig, K. Die deutsche Medaille in Kunst oc Hinsicht. Wien, 1907.
Arc 1505.203 Buchenau, H. Der Bracteatenfund von Seega. Marburg, 1905.
Arc 1505.205 Fiola, Eduard. Münzen und Medaillen der Wellischenlande. v.1-8. Prag, 1916. 6v.

Arc 1506 Numismatics - Local - Germany - Pamphlet volumes

Arc 1506 Pamphlet box. Numismatics. Germany.
Arc 1506.01 Pamphlet box. Numismatics. Germany.

Arc 1508 Numismatics - Local - Germany - General works

Arc 1508.5 Schönemann, C.P.C. Zur vaterländischen Münzkunde. Walfenbüttel, 1852.
Arc 1508.7 Gebhart, H. Die deutschen Münzen des Mittelalters. 4. Aufl. Berlin, 1929.
Arc 1508.8 Habich, Georg. Die deutschen Medailleure des XVI. Jahrhunderts. Halle an der Saale, 1916.
Arc 1508.10 Suhle, Arthur. Die deutschen Renaissance-Medaille. Leipzig, 1950.
Arc 1508.11 Suhle, Arthur. Deutsche Münz- und Geldgeschichte von den Anfanger bis zum 15. Jahrhundert. Berlin, 1955.
Arc 1508.15 Jaeger, Kurt. Die neuren Münzprägungen der deutschen Staaten. pt.1-2,3-4,8,9,10,11,12. Stuttgart, 1951-72. 12v.
Arc 1508.15.5 Jaeger, Kurt. Die deutschen Reichsmünzen seit 1871. Basel, 1956.
Arc 1508.15.10 Jaeger, Kurt. Berwertungstablellen der deutschen Reichsmünzen seit 1871. Basel, 1957.
Arc 1508.15.15 Jaeger, Kurt. Die Münzprägungen der deutschen Staaten von Einführung des Reichswährung. v.3. Basel, 1967.
Arc 1508.15.20 Jaeger, Kurt. Die deutschen Münzen seit 1871. 6. Aufl. Basel, 1967.
Arc 1508.20 Fiorino, Alexander. Sammlung des Herrn Alexander Fiorino in Cassel. Frankfurt am Main, 1917.
Arc 1508.25 Deutsche Bundesbank. Deutsche Taler von den Anfängen der Talerprägung bis zum Dreissigjährigen Krieg aus der Münzensammlung der Deutschen Bundesbank. Frankfurt, 1966?-67? 2v.
Arc 1508.29 Knigge, Wilhelm. Münz- und Medaillen-Kabinet des Freiherrn Wilhelm Knigge. Bielefeld, 1972.
Arc 1508.30 Göetz, Christian Jacob. Deutschlands Kayser-Münzen des Mittel-Alters. Leipzig, 1968.
Arc 1508.31 Kahl, Hans Dietrich. Hauptlinien der deutschen Münzgeschichte vom Ende des 18. Jahrhunderts bis 1878. Frankfurt, 1972.

Arc 1510 Numismatics - Local - Germany - Local; Special topics

Arc 1510.1 Widmer, M.J. von. Domus Wittelbachensis numismatica. Munich, 1784-85.
Arc 1510.1.2 Widmer, M.J. von. Dormus Wittelbachensis numismatica. Munich, 1784.
Arc 1510.1.5 Munich. Medaillen und Münzen des Gesammthauses Wittelsbach. v.1, pt.1-2. München, 1897. 2v.
Arc 1510.2 Tentzel, W.E. Saxonia Numismatica, oder Medaillen-Cabinet von Bedächtnissmünzen. Dresden, 1705. 2v.
Arc 1510.3 Tentzel, W.E. Saxonia Numismatica, oder Medaillen-Cabinet von Münzen. Dresden, 1705. 2v.
Htn Arc 1510.3.7* Stürmer, Wolff. Vortzeichnus und Gedräge der groben und kleinen Müntzsorten. Leipzig, 1572.
Arc 1510.3.10 Posern-Klett, Karl Friedrich von. Sachens Münzen im Mittelalter. Leipzig, 1970.
Arc 1510.4 Langermann, J.P. Die neuren Hamburgischen Münzen und Medaillen. Hamburg, 1843.
Arc 1510.5 Bürkel, L. von. Die Bilder der Süddeutschen. München, 1903.
Arc 1510.5.5 Goessler, Peter. Beiträge zur süddeutschen Münzgeschichte. Stuttgart, 1927.
Arc 1510.6 Müller, J.H. Deutsche Münzgeschichte biz zu der Ottonenzeit. Leipzig, 1860.
Arc 1510.7 Cerexhe, M. Les monnaies de Charlemagne. Gand, 1887.
Arc 1510.8 Cappe, H.P. Münzen der deutschen Kaiser des Mittelalters. v.1,3. Dresden, 1848-57.
Arc 1510.8.5 Cappe, H.P. Münzen der Herzöge von Baiern. Dresden, 1850.
Arc 1510.8.10 Cappe, H.P. Die Mittelalter-Münzen von Münster. Dresden, n.d.
Arc 1510.9 Jungk, H. Die bremischen Münzen. Bremen, 1875.
Arc 1510.10 Bahrfeldt, Max von. Die Münzen der Stadt Stade. Wien, 1879.
Arc 1510.10.5F Bahrfeldt, Max von. Niedersachsisches Münzarchiv. Halle, 1927. 4v.
Arc 1510.11 Finauer, P.P. Münzreihe der Herzoge in Baiern. München, 1777.
Arc 1510.11.5 Kull, J.V. Repertorium zur Münzkunde Bayerns und Forzetz. v.1-3. München, 1894. 2v.
Arc 1510.11.10 Bayerische Münzkataloge. Günwald. 1,1957 4v.
Arc 1510.11.15 Och, Friedrich. Münzen bayerischer Klöster, Kirchen. München, 1897.
Arc 1510.11.20 Hahn, Wolfgang Reinhard Otto. Typenkatalog der Münzer der bayerischen Herzöge und Kurfürsten, 1506-1805. Braunschweig, 1971.
Arc 1510.12 Heusinger, F. Versuch einer Abhandlung von den Nutzen der teutschen Münzwissenschaft. Nürnberg, 1750.
Arc 1510.13 Schlegel, C. Schediasma de nummis antiquis. Dresdae, 1518.
Arc 1510.14.3 Rudolph, E. Ergänzungen und Berichtigungen. Dresden, 1908.
Arc 1510.14.5 Rudolph, E. Zusammenstellung der Taler. Dresden, 1904.
Arc 1510.15 Grimm, E. Münzen und Medaillen der Stadt Wismar. Berlin, 1897.
Arc 1510.16 Schrötter, F.F. von. Die Münzen F. Wilhelms des Grossen Kurfürst und Friedrichs III von Brandenberg. Berlin, 1913.
Arc 1510.16.2 Berlin. Staatliche Museen. Die Münzen Friedrich Wilhelms des Grossen Kurfürsten und Friedrichs III. Berlin, 1922.
Arc 1510.17 Rhon, G. Exercitatio historica de Joh. Uratislaviensibus. Uratslaviae, 1693.
Arc 1510.18 Wibel, Ferdinand. Zur Münzgeschichte der Grafen von Wertheim. Hamburg, 1880.
Arc 1510.19F Suchier, Reinhard. Die Münzen der Grafen von Hanau. Hanau, 1897.
Arc 1510.20 Scholler, Ernst. Der Reichsstadt Nürnberg. Nürnberg, 1916.
Arc 1510.20.5 Verzaichnus der Bösessmüntzsortens. n.p., 1571.
Arc 1510.21 Scholtz, Henrico. Sancta colonia numis antiquissimis illustrata et monumentis historicis explicata. Ploenae, 1738.
Arc 1510.22 Berstett, A. Versuch einer Münzgeschichte des Elsasses. Freiburg, 1840. 2 pam.

Arc 1510 Numismatics - Local - Germany - Local; Special topics - cont.

Arc 1510.22.5 Lehr, Ernest. Les monnaies des landgraves autrichiens de la Haute Alsace. Supplement. Mulhouse, 1896. 2 pam.
Arc 1510.22.10 Bibliothèque Nationale, Paris. Département des Médailles et Antiques. Collection de monnaies et médailles d'Alsace. Paris, 1902.
Arc 1510.23 Joseph, Paul. Die Münzen von Worms. Darmstadt, 1906.
Arc 1510.23.5 Joseph, Paul. Die Medaillen und Münzen der Wild- und Rheingrafen Fürsten zu Salm. Frankfurt am Main, 1914.
Arc 1510.24 Sperl, Karl. Die Münzgeschichte Regensburgs. Inaug. Diss. Kallmünz, 1928.
Arc 1510.25 Mertens, E. Münz- und Geldgeschichte der Stadt Northeim. Diss. Halle an der Saale, 1928.
Arc 1510.26 Schwinkowski, Walter. Münz- und Geldgeschichte der Mark Meissen und Münzen. Frankfurt am Main, 1931.
Arc 1510.28 Hauser, Josef. Die Münzen und Medaillen der im Jahre 1156 gegründeten (seit 1255). München, 1905.
Arc 1510.29 Bahrfeldt, Max von. Das Gepräge amtliche Notgeld der Provinz Schlesien, 1917-1921. Breslau, 1935.
Arc 1510.30F Buck, H. Die Münzen der Stadt Hannover. Hannover, 1935.
Arc 1510.31F Cologne. Die Münzen und Medaillen von Köln. Köln, 1913-35. 4v.
Arc 1510.32F Lange, C.C.A. Sammlung schleswig-holsteinischer Münzen und Medaillen. Berlin, 1908-12. 2v.
Arc 1510.33 Cappe, H.P. Beschreibung des Mainzer Münzen des Mittelalters. Dresden, 1856.
Arc 1510.34 Pfeiffer, L. Pestilantia in nummis. Tübingen, 1882.
Arc 1510.35 Hamburger, L. Sammlung Pfalzischer. Frankfurt am Main, 1929.
Arc 1510.36 Cahn, Julius. Der Rappenmünzbund. Heidelberg, 1901.
Arc 1510.37 Mader, Joseph. Versuch über die Brakteaten. v.2. Prag, 1808.
Arc 1510.38 Kennepohl, K. Die Münzen von Osnabrück. München, 1938.
Arc 1510.39 Jesse, Wilhelm. Der zweite Brakteatenfund von Mödesse und die Kunst der Brakteaten zur Zeit Heinrichs des Löwen. Braunschweig, 1957.
Arc 1510.40 Haeberle, Adolf. Ulmer Münz- und Geldgeschichte des Mittelalters. n.p., 1935.
Arc 1510.41 Erman, Adolf. Deutsche Medailleure des sechzehnten und siebzehnten Jahrhunderts. Berlin, 1884.
Arc 1510.45 Badische Gesellschaft für Münzkunde. Münzkunde und Münzkabinette am Oberrheim. Karlsruhe am Rhein, 1951.
Arc 1510.50 Jesse, Wilhelm. Münz- und Geldgeschichte Niedersachsens. Braunschweig, 1952.
Arc 1510.55 Binder, C. Württembergische Münz- und Medaillen-Kunde. Stuttgart, 1846.
Arc 1510.60F Tornau, Otto. Münzwesen und Münzen der Grafschaft Mansfeld von der Mitte. Prag, 1937.
Arc 1510.65F Gaettens, R. Das Geld- und Münzwesen der Abtei Fulda im Hoch. Fulda, 1957.
Arc 1510.65.5 Gaettens, R. Münzporträts im 11. Jahrhundert? Heidelberg, 1956.
Arc 1510.70 Wintz, Hermann. Erlangen in Spiegel der Münze. Erlangen, 1936.
Arc 1510.75 Hohenlohe Waldenburg, Friedrich. Sphragistische Aphorismen. Heilbronn, 1882.
Arc 1510.80 Behrens, Heinrich. Münzen und Medaillen der Stadt und des Bisthums Siebeck. Berlin, 1905.
Arc 1510.85 Blaschke, Karlheinz. Siegel und Wappen in Sachsen. Leipzig, 1960.
Arc 1510.90 Christ, Karl. Antike Münzfunde Südwestdeutschlands. pt.1-5. Heidelberg, 1960.
Arc 1510.95 Erbstein, H.A. Der Münzfund von Trebitz bei Wittenberg. Halle an der Saale, 1924.
Arc 1510.100 Neu, Heinrich. Die Münzen und Medaillen des Herrogstums und des herroglichen Hauses Arenberg. Bonn, 1959.
Arc 1510.105F Friedensburg, F. Die schlesischen Münzen des Mittelalters. Breslau, 1931.
Arc 1510.107 Dewerdeck, G. Silesia numismatica. Jauer, 1711.
Arc 1510.110 Gumowski, M. Pieniądz gdański. Gdańsk, 1960.
Arc 1510.115F Horn, Otto. Die Münzen und Medaillen. Leipzig, 1923.
Arc 1510.120F Die Münzen des Bistums und der Stadt Hildesheim. Hildesheim, 1937.
Arc 1510.122 Schwarzenau, J.L. Ansehnlichen Vorrath von Thalern und Schaustücken des langraflich-hessischen Gesamthauses. n.p., 1776.
Arc 1510.125 Bernhart, Max. Die Münzen und Medaillen der Stadt Kaufbeureh nebst einer münzgeschichtlichen Einleitung. n.p., 1923.
Arc 1510.126 Kraemer, Georg. Bayerns Ehrenbuch. Nürnberg, 1834.
Arc 1510.127 Obermayr, J. Historische Nachricht von bayerischen Münzen. Frankfurt, 1763.
Arc 1510.128F Hess, Adolph. Münzen der Hohenstauffenzeit. Zürich, 1959?
Arc 1510.130 Kundmann, J.C. Numuni jubilaei, oder Jubel Schau-Stücke. Bresslau, 1735.
Arc 1510.131 Gaettens, R. Die Münzen der Grafschaft Lüchow. Halle, 1937.
Arc 1510.132 Rehle, Q. Die Münzen der Stadt Kaufbeuren. Kaufbeuren, 1880.
Arc 1510.133 Jesse, W. Die Münzen der Stadt Braunschweig von 1499 bis 1680. Braunschweig, 1962.
Arc 1510.134F Buck, H. Die Münzen der Stadt Einbeck. Hildesheim, 1939.
Arc 1510.135 Kundmann, J.C. Silesii in nummis, oder Berühmte Schlesier in Müntzen. Bresslau, 1738.
Arc 1510.136 Metcalf, D. The coinage of South Germany in the thirteenth century. London, 1961.
Arc 1510.137 Leuckfeld, J.G. Antiquitates nummariae, oder Historische Beschreibung vieleralten. Leipzig, 1721.
Arc 1510.138 Rueppell, E. Beschreibung der Münzen und Medaillen. Frankfurt am Main, 1857.
Arc 1510.139 Albrecht, J. Mittheilungen zur Geschichte der Reichs-Münzstaetten. Heilbronn, 1835.
Arc 1510.140 Gebert, Carl Friedrich. Die Brandenburg Frankischen Kippermünzstätten, 1620-1622. München, 1901.
Arc 1510.141 Schurnkowski, Walter. Zur Münzgeschichte der chemaligen Wettinischen Lande um 1180-1230. Halle, 1936.
Arc 1510.142 Hagen, Johann Georg Friedrich von. Münzbeschreibung des gräflich und fürstlichen Hauses Mansfeld. Nürnberg, 1778.
Arc 1510.143 Buchenau, H. Beiträge zur schwäbisch-fränkischen Münzkunde des späteren Mittelalters. n.p., 19- .
Arc 1510.144F Bally, Otto. Beschreibung von Münzen und Medaillen des Fürsten-Hauses und Landes Baden in chronologischer Folge. Aarau, 1896- 2v.
Arc 1510.145 Erbstein, Karl Friedrich Wilhelm. Numismatische Bruchstücke in Bezug auf sächsische Geschichte. v.1-3. Dresden, 1816.
Arc 1510.146 Beyschlag, Daniel Eberhardt. Versuch einer Münzgeschichte Augsburgs in dem Mittelalter. Stuttgart, 1835.

Arc 1510 Numismatics - Local - Germany - Local; Special topics - cont.

Arc 1510.147 Klotzsch, Johann Friedrich. Versuch einer chur-sächsischen Münzgeschichte von den Altesten, bis auf jetzige Zeiten. v.1-2. Chemnitz, 1779-80.
Arc 1510.148 Weidhas, J.F. Die Brandenburger Denare von Heinrich König der Wenden bis auf Friedrich I. Kurfürst aus dem Hause Hohenzollern. Berlin, 1855.
Arc 1510.150 Dudik, Beda. Des hahen deutschen Ritterordens Münz-Sammlung in Wien. Bonn, 1966.
Arc 1510.152.5 Funck, Walter. Die Notmünzen der deutschen Städt, Gemeinden, Kreise, Länder. 5. Aufl. Münster, 1966.
Arc 1510.152.7 Funck, Walter. Die Notmünzen der deutschen Städt, Gemeinden, Kreise, Länder. 2. Aufl. Münster, 1973.
Arc 1510.154 Duve, Gebhard. History of the redeemable, multiple and mining talers of Brunswick-Luneburg. 1. ed. Johannesburg, 1966.
Arc 1510.154.5 Duve, Gebhard. Dicktaler-Prägungen, 1544-1679. v.2. Frankfurt am Main, 1974-
Arc 1510.156 Wielandt, Friedrich. Münze und Geld in Pforzheim. Pforzheim, 1968.
Arc 1510.158 Erbstein, Julius. Zur mittelalterlichen Münzgeschichte der Grafen von Mansfeld und der Edlen Hessen von Querfurt. Dresden, 1876.
Arc 1510.160 Alexander, Prince of Messe and of the Rhine, 1823-1888. Mainzisches Münzcabinet des Prinzen Alexander von Hessen. Faksimile. Münster, 1968.
Arc 1510.162 Braun von Stumm, Gustaf. Die Münzen der Abtei Hornbach nebst Beiträgen zur Münzkunde von Speyergau und Elsass im 12-14. Halle an der Saale, 1926.
Arc 1510.164 Welter, Gerhard. Die Münzen der Welfen seit Heinrich dem Löwen. Braunschweig, 1971-73. 2v.
Arc 1510.166 Schwalbach, Carl. Die neueren deutschen Taler. Lübeck, 1962.
Arc 1510.167 Meyer, Adolf. Prägungen Brandenburg-Preussens. Berlin, 1885.
Arc 1510.168 Isenbeck, Julius. Das nassauische Münzwesen. Münster, 1970.
Arc 1510.169 Friedrich, Karl. Ein Beitrag zur Geschichte des Kontermarkenwesens. Münster, 1970.
Arc 1510.170 Hoffmeister, Jacob Christoph Carl. Historisch-kritische Beschreibung aller bis jetzt bekannt gewordenen nessischen Münzen. v.1-4. Leipzig, 1974. 3v.
Arc 1510.171.1 Tergast, Pefrus. Die Münzen Ostfrieslands. Leer, 1974.
Arc 1510.172 Haas, Rudolf. Die Prägungen der Mannheimer Münzstätten. Mannheim, 1974.
Arc 1510.173F Vossberg, Friedrich August. Münzgeschichte der Stadt Berlin. Berlin, 1869.
Arc 1510.174F Bahrfeldt, Emil. Das Münzwesen der Mark Brandenburg. Berlin, 1889- 2v.

Arc 1512 Numismatics - Local - Low Countries in general

Arc 1512.2F Rathgeber, Georg. Aufbau der niederländischen Kunstgeschichte und Museologie...Niederländische Münzen und Medaillen dis Herzoglichen Museums zu Gotha. Weissensee, 1839.

Arc 1518 Numismatics - Local - Belgium - General works

Arc 1518.2 Piot, C. Catalogue des coins, poincons et matrices. 2. ed. Bruxelles, 1880.
Arc 1518.3 Tourneur, Victor. Catalogue des medailles du Royaume de Belgique. Bruxelles, 1911.
Arc 1518.4 Serrure, Raymond. Dictionaire géographique de l'histoire monétaire belge. Bruxelles, 1880.
Arc 1518.5 Serrure, Raymond. Elements de l'histoire monétaire de Flandre. Gand, 1879.
Arc 1518.6 Morin, Francois. Monnaies de Belgique de 1832 à 1963. Boom, 1964.
Arc 1518.6.5 Morin, Francois. Monnaies de Belgique de 1832 à 1967. Anvers, 1968.
Arc 1518.10 Société Royale de Numismatique de Belgique. Exposition numismatique, Bruxelles, Bibliothèque Albert I., 30 avril-24 mai, 1966. Bruxelles, 1966.

Arc 1520 Numismatics - Local - Belgium - Local; Special topics

Htn Arc 1520.1* Carte ou liste contenant le pris de chascun marcq. Anvers, 1621. 5 pam.
Arc 1520.3 Carte ou liste contenant le pris de chascun marcq. Anvers, 1627.
Arc 1520.5 Vandenpeereboom, A. Essai de numismatique yproise. Bruxelles, 1877.
Arc 1520.12 Chalon, Renier. Recherches sur les monnaies des Comtes de Hainout. Supplement. Bruxelles, 1848-54. 2v.
Arc 1520.15 Brussels. Bibliothèque Royale. Mille ans de monnayage Bruxellois, 1965. Bruxelles, 1965.
Arc 1520.20 Crab, Jan. De munt to Leuven tot het einde der XVe eeuw. Leuven, 1967.
Arc 1520.25 Hoc, Marcel. Histoire monétaire de Tournai. Bruxelles, 1970.

Arc 1522 Numismatics - Local - Luxemburg

Arc 1522.3 Harpes, Jean. Médailles et jetons du pays de Luxembourg. Luxembourg, 1955.
Arc 1522.5 Weiller, Raymond. Monnaies antiques découvertes au Grand-Duché de Luxembourg. Berlin, 1972.
Arc 1522.6 Reding, Lucien. Les monnaies gauloises du Tetelbierg. Luxembourg, 1972.

Arc 1525 Numismatics - Local - Netherlands, Holland - Folios [Discontinued]

Arc 1525.1 Loon, Gerard van. Histoire metallique des XVII provinces des Pays-Bas. La Haye, 1732-37. 5v.

Arc 1528 Numismatics - Local - Netherlands, Holland - General works

Arc 1528.1 Bizot, P. Histoire metallique de la Republique de Hollande. Amsterdam, 1688. 2v.
Arc 1528.1.5 Bizot, P. Histoire metallique de la Republique de Hollande. Amsterdam, 1688. 2v.
Arc 1528.1.7 Bizot, P. Histoire metallique de la Republique de Hollande. Supplément. Amsterdam, 1690.
Arc 1528.2 Muller, F. Cabinet de monnaies, J.W. Stephanik. Amsterdam, 1904.
Arc 1528.3 Dingniolle, J.F. Le jeton historique des dix-sept provinces des Pays-Bas. Bruxelles, 1876-77. 2v.
Arc 1528.5PF Akademie...Amsterdam. Akademie von Wetenschappen, Amsterdam. Beschrijving van Nederlandsche historie-penningen. v.1-4,6-10. Amsterdam, 1821-69. 6v.
Arc 1528.5.5PF Loon, Gerard van. Beschrijving der Nederlandsche historie-penningen. 's-Gravenhage, 1723-31. 4v.

Arc 1528 Numismatics - Local - Netherlands, Holland - General works - cont.

Arc 1528.7 Chijs, P.O. van der. De munten. Haarlem, 1851-66. 9v.
Arc 1528.8.5 Gelder, Hendrik Enno van. De Nederlandse munten. 5. druk. Utrecht, 1972.
Arc 1528.9 Loehr, August. Die niederlandische Medaille des 17. Wien, 1921.
Arc 1528.10.5 Voogt, W.J. de. Bijdragen tot de numismatiek van Gelderland. Arnhem, 1869.
Arc 1528.11 Handleiding tot de kennis der Nederlandsche munten. Amsterdam, 1850.
Arc 1528.12 Schulman, Jacques. Handboek van de Nederlandsche munten van 1795-1945. Amsterdam, 1946.
Arc 1528.12.1 Schulman, Jacques. Handboek van de Nederlandsche munten van 1795 tot 1969. 4. druk. Amsterdam, 1969.
Arc 1528.14 Frederiks, J.W. Penningen. Amsterdam, 1947.

Arc 1530 Numismatics - Local - Netherlands, Holland - Local; Special topics

Arc 1530.5 Gelder, Hendrik Enno van. De Nederlandse noodmunten van de tachtigjarige vorlog. 's-Gravenhage, 1955.
Arc 1530.5.5 Gelder, Hendrik Enno van. Les monnaies des Pays-Bas bourguigons et espagnols. Amsterdam, 1960.
Arc 1530.10 Scholten, C. The coins of the Dutch overseas territories, 1601-1948. Amsterdam, 1953.
Arc 1530.15 Polak, Arthur. Joodse penningen in de Nederlanden. Amsterdam, 1958.
Arc 1530.20 Dirks, Jacob. De noord-Nederlandsche gildepenningen. Haarlem, 1878. 2v.

Arc 1535 Numismatics - Local - Great Britain - Folios [Discontinued]

Htn Arc 1535.1* Snelling, T. A view of the silver coin and coinage of England. London, 1762.
Arc 1535.2 British Museum. Department of Coins and Medals. Description of the Anglo-Gallic coins. London, 1826.
Htn Arc 1535.3* Folkes, M. Tables of English silver and gold coins. London, 1763. 2v.
Arc 1535.4 Ruding, R. Annals of the coinage of Great Britain. London, 1817. 4v.
Arc 1535.4.2 Ruding, R. Annals of the coinage of Great Britain. 3. ed. London, 1840. 3v.
Arc 1535.5 Illustrations of the Anglo French coinage. London, 1830.
Htn Arc 1535.6* Twelve plates of English silver coins. London, 1756.
Arc 1535.7 Pye, Charles. Provincial copper coins or tokens, 1787-1796. London, 1795.
Arc 1535.7.2 Pye, Charles. Provincial copper coins, tokens of trade...1787-1801. 2. ed. London, 1801.
Arc 1535.8 Cochran-Patrick, R.W. Records of the coinage of Scotland. Edinburgh, 1876. 2v.
Arc 1535.9 Davis, W.J. Old Warwickshire coins, tokens and medals. n.p., 1896.
Arc 1535.10F Burns, Edward. The coinage of Scotland. Edinburgh, 1837. 3v.
Arc 1535.200F Milford Haven, L. British naval medals. London, 1919.
Arc 1535.205F Mudie, James. An historical and critical account...medals. London, 1820.
Arc 1535.207F Chetwynd, George. A catalogue of provincial copper coins, tokens, tickets, medals issued in Great Britain, Ireland and the colonies...18th century. London, 1834.

Arc 1536 Numismatics - Local - Great Britain - Pamphlet volumes

Arc 1536 Pamphlet box. Numismatics. Great Britain.
Arc 1536.01 Pamphlet box. Numismatics. Great Britain.

Arc 1538 Numismatics - Local - Great Britain - General works

Htn Arc 1538.1* Clarke, W. The connexion of the Roman, Saxon, and English coins. London, 1767.
Arc 1538.2 British Museum. Department of Coins and Medals. Catalogue of English coins in the British Museum. London, 1916. 2v.
Arc 1538.2.15 British Museum. Department of Coins and Medals. A catalogue of English coins in the British Museum. Anglo-Saxon series. London, 1887-93. 2v.
Arc 1538.2.20 British Museum. Department of Coins and Medals. English copper, tin, and bronze coins in the British Museum. London, 1960.
Arc 1538.2.22 British Museum. Department of Coins and Medals. English copper, tin and bronze coins in the British Museum. 2. ed. London, 1964.
Arc 1538.3 Humphreys, H.N. The coinage of the British empire. London, 1854.
Htn Arc 1538.3.2* Humphreys, H.N. The coinage of the British empire. London, 1855.
Arc 1538.3.5 Humphreys, H.N. The gold, silver, and copper coins of England. 6. ed. London, 1849.
Arc 1538.4 Batty, D.T. Catalogue of the copper coinage of Great Britain. Manchester, 1868-98. 4v.
Htn Arc 1538.5* Leake, S.M. Historical account of English money from the conquest. London, 1745.
Arc 1538.6 Lindsay, J. View of the coinage of Ireland. Cork, 1839.
Arc 1538.7.2 British Museum. Department of Coins and Medals. Handbook of the coins of Great Britain and Ireland in the British Museum. 2. ed. London, 1970.
Arc 1538.8 Hawkins, E. The silver coins of England. London, 1887.
X Cg Arc 1538.9 Kenyon, R.L. Gold coins of England, sequel to the silver coins of England. London, 1884.
Arc 1538.10 Nummi Britannici historia. London, 1626.
Arc 1538.11 Evans, J. Coins of the ancient Britons. v.1 and supplement. London, 1864-90. 2v.
Arc 1538.12 Montagu, H. Copper coins of England. London, 1893.
Arc 1538.13 Conder, James. An arrangement of provincial coins...Great Britain, Ireland. Ipswich, 1799.
Arc 1538.14 Leigh, Sotheby, and Son. Collection of 28 plates illustrating ancient coins of Great Britain. London, 1803.
Arc 1538.15 Stukeley, W.M. Twenty-three plates of the coins of the ancient British kings. London, 17- .
Arc 1538.17 Oman, C.W.C. The coinage of England. Oxford, 1931.
Arc 1538.18 Brooke, George C. English coins from the seventh century to the present day. London, 1932.
Arc 1538.18.10 Brooke, George C. English coins. 3. ed. London, 1950.
Arc 1538.19 Jewitt, L. Handbook of English coins. London, 1879.
Arc 1538.20 Mack, R.P. The coinage of ancient Britain. London, 1953.
Arc 1538.21 Sutherland, Carol Humphrey Vivian. Anglo-Saxon gold coinage in the light of the Crondall hoard. London, 1948.
Arc 1538.21.5 Sutherland, Carol Humphrey Vivian. English coinage, 600-1900. London, 1973.
Arc 1538.23 Sylloge of coins of the British Isles. Series A. London, 1958- 23v.

Arc 1538 Numismatics - Local - Great Britain - General works - cont.

Arc 1538.23.2 Sylloge of coins of the British Isles. Series B. London, 1966.
Arc 1538.23.6 Sylloge of coins of the British Isles. London, 1968.
Arc 1538.25 North, J.J. English hammered coinage. London, 1960-63. 2v.
Arc 1538.27.3 Seaby, Herbert Allen. The English silver coinage from 1649. 3. ed. London, 1968.
Arc 1538.28 Seaby's standard catalogue of British coins. pt.1-2. London. 14,1975+

Arc 1540 Numismatics - Local - Great Britain - Local; Special topics

Arc 1540.1 Stukeley, W. The medallic history of M.A.V. Carausins. London, 1757-89.
Arc 1540.2 Shafter, E.F. The copper coinage of the Earl of Stirling. Boston, 1874.
Arc 1540.3 Holmboe, C.A. De numis MD medii aevi in Norvegia nuper repertis. Christiania, 1837.
Arc 1540.4 Keder, N. De argento runis siu lit. Lipsiae, 1703-08. 4 pam.
Arc 1540.5 Mayo, J. Medals and decorations of the army and navy. Westminster, 1897. 2v.
Arc 1540.6A Chalmers, R. History of currency in the British colonies. London, n.d.
Arc 1540.6B Chalmers, R. History of currency in the British colonies. London, n.d.
Arc 1540.7 Head, B.V. An account of the hoard of Anglo-Saxon coins found at Chancton farm, Sussex. n.p., n.d.
Arc 1540.9 Schröder, J.H. De moneta Anglo-Saxonica. Upsaliae, 1849.
Arc 1540.9.5 Schröder, J.H. Numismata Angliae vetusta. pt.1. Upsaliae, 1833.
Arc 1540.10 Stainer, C.L. Oxford silver pennies, 925-1272. Oxford, 1904.
Arc 1540.11 Haigh, D.H. Essay on the numismatic history of the East Angles. Leeds, 1845.
Arc 1540.12 Andrew, W.J. A numismatic history of the reign of Henry I. v.1-2. London, 1901.
Arc 1540.12.5 Andrew, W.J. Notes on numismatic history of the reign of Henry I. v.1-2. London, 1903.
Htn Arc 1540.13* Perry, Francis. Series of English medals. London, 1762.
Arc 1540.14 Henfrey, H.W. Numismata Cromwelliana. Londini, 1877.
Arc 1540.15 Wingate, James. Illustrations of coinage of Scotland. Glasgow, 1868.
Arc 1540.16 Lindsay, John. View of coinage of Scotland, tables. Cork, 1845.
Arc 1540.17 Robertson, John D. Handbook to coinage of Scotland. London, 1878.
Arc 1540.17.10 Cochran-Patrick, R.W. Catalogue of the medals of Scotland. Edinburgh, 1884.
Arc 1540.17.15 Stewart, Ian Halley. The Scottish coinage. London, 1955.
Arc 1540.18 Atkins, James. The coins and tokens of the possessions and colonies of the British empire. London, 1889.
Arc 1540.19 Cardonnel-Lawson, Adam. Numismata Scotiae. Edinburgi, 1786.
Arc 1540.20 Davis, William John. Tickets and passes of Great Britain and Ireland struck or engraved on metal, ivory. Leamington Spa, 1922.
Arc 1540.20.1 Davis, William John. Tickets and passes of Great Britain and Ireland. N.Y., 1973.
Arc 1540.21 Poste, Beale. Celtic inscriptions on Gaulish and British coins. London, 1861.
Arc 1540.21.5 Poste, Beale. A vindication of the Celtic inscription on Gaulish and British coins. London, 1862.
Arc 1540.22 Noble, Mark. Two dissertations upon the mint and coins of Durham. Birmingham, 1780.
Arc 1540.22.7 Bartlet, B. The episcopal coins of Durham. Newcastle, 1817.
Arc 1540.23 Sutherland, Carol Humphrey Vivian. Coinage and currency in Roman Britain. London, 1937.
Arc 1540.24F Medina, J.T. Las medallas del almirante Vernon. Santiago, 1919.
Arc 1540.25 Golding, Charles. The coinage of Suffolk. London, 1868.
Arc 1540.26 Wright, L.V.W. Colonial and commonwealth coins. London, 1959.
Arc 1540.27 Dolley, Reginald Hugh Michael. Anglo-Saxon coins. London, 1961.
Arc 1540.27.5 Dolley, Reginald Hugh Michael. The Norman conquest and the English coinage. London, 1966.
Arc 1540.28 Boundy, W.S. Bushell and Harman of Lundy. Bideford, 1961.
Arc 1540.29 Duveen, G.E. The history of the gold sovereign. London, 1962.
Arc 1540.30 O'Sullivan, W. The earliest Irish coinage. Dublin, 1961.
Arc 1540.31 Mathias, Peter. The English trade tokens. London, 1962.
Arc 1540.32 Watson, J.H. Ancient trial plates, a description of the ancient gold and silver. London, 1962.
Arc 1540.33 Petersson, H. Bertil A. Anglo-Saxon currency: King Edgar's reform to the Norman conquest. Lund, 1969.
Arc 1540.35 Schreier, Ulrich. Die Münzen der Kanal-Inseln. Dortmund, 1965?
Arc 1540.36 Cleveland. Museum of Art. English gold coins. Cleveland, 1968.
Arc 1540.37 Askew, Gilbert. The coinage of Roman Britain. London, 1951.
Arc 1540.38 Cardiff, Wales. National Museum of Wales. Welsh tokens of the seventeenth century. Cardiff, 1973.

Arc 1542 Numismatics - Local - Scandinavia in general

Arc 1542.2 Malmer, Brita. Nordiska mynt före år 1000. Bonn, 1966.
Arc 1542.2.5 Malmer, Brita. Mynt och människor. Stockholm, 1968.
Arc 1542.3F Galster, Georg. Unionstidens udmøntninger. København, 1972.

Arc 1548 Numismatics - Local - Denmark - General works

Arc 1548.2F Hede, Holger. Danmarks og Norges mønter, 1541-1814-1963. Udgivet of Dansk numisatisk forening. Kjøbenhavn, 1964.
Arc 1548.5 Soemod, Jørgen. Danmarks og Norges mønter, 1448-1540. Kjøbenhavn, 1967.

Arc 1550 Numismatics - Local - Denmark - Local; Special topics

Arc 1550.1 Holmboe, C.A. Et guldbracteat-praeg som ofte forekommer. Kjøbenhavn, 1869.
Arc 1550.2 Holmboe, C.A. Et lidet fund af mynter fra 11. aaehundrede. Kjøbenhavn, 1871.
Arc 1550.3 Mansfeld-Bûllner, H.V. Afbildninger af danske mønter, 1241-1377. Kjøbenhavn, 1887.
Arc 1550.4 Hauberg, Peter C. Myntforhold og utmyntninger i Danmark indtil 1146. Kjøbenhavn, 1900.
Arc 1550.5 Wilcke, Julius. Sølo-og guldmøntfod. Kjøbenhavn, 1930.

Classified Listing

Arc 1550 Numismatics - Local - Denmark - Local; Special topics - cont.

Arc 1550.6 Wilcke, Julius. Kurantmønten. Kjøbenhavn, 1927.
Arc 1550.7 Wilcke, Julius. Montvaesenet under Christian IV og Frederik III i tidsrummet, 1625-70. Kjøbenhavn, 1924.
Arc 1550.8 Galster, Georg. Danske og norske medailler og jetons. Kjøbenhavn, 1936.
Arc 1550.8.5 Galster, Georg. Coins and history. Kopenhagen, 1959.
Arc 1550.8.10 Lauring, P. Regis Daniae. København, 1961.
Arc 1550.8.15 Golster, Georg. Flensborg mønt, 14. og 16. århundrede. Udg. af numismatisk forening for nord-og sydslesvig. Sønderborg, 1967.
Arc 1550.9 Wilcke, Julius. Specie. Kjøbenhavn, 1929.
Arc 1550.10 Mansfeld-Bûllner, H.V. Afbildninger af panstlege indtil kjendte danske mønter. 2. Opl. Kjøbenhavn, 1964.
Arc 1550.11F Schou, Hans Henrich. Beskrivelse of danske og norske mønter. Kjøbenhavn, 1926.

Arc 1552 Numismatics - Local - Iceland

Arc 1552.1 Bjoerkman, S. Myntic Islands, 1836-1922-1963. Stockholm, 1965.

Arc 1558 Numismatics - Local - Sweden - General works

Arc 1558.1 Stiernstedt, A.V. Description des monnaies de Cuivre...Suedois. Stockholm, 1871-72.
Arc 1558.2 Stockholm. Statens Historiske Museum och Myntkabinett. Anglosachsiska mynt i svenska kongliga myntkabinette funna i sveriges jord. Stockholm, 1881.
Arc 1558.5 Nathorst-Böös, E. Atto samla numismatica. Stockholm, 1958.
Arc 1558.6.14 Glück, Harry. Artalsförtecknia over soenskamynt med varderingspriser. Stockholm, 1968.
Arc 1558.6.15 Glück, Harry. Årtalsförteckning över svenska mynt. Stockholm, 1974.
Arc 1558.8.2 Tingström, Bertel. Svensk numismatisk uppslagsbok. 2. upp. Stockholm, 1968.

Arc 1560 Numismatics - Local - Sweden - Local; Special topics

Arc 1560.1 Hildebrand, H. Sveriges mynt under medeltiden. Stockholm, 1887.
Arc 1560.2 Humbles, C.P. Förteckning öfver C.P. Humbles. Stockholm, 1852.
Arc 1560.3.1 Cavalli, Gustaf. Gustaf Cavallis samlung av svenska kopparmynt. Facsimile. Stockholm, 1971.
Arc 1560.4 Platbarzdis, Aleksander. Die königlich schwedische Münze in Livland. Stockholm, 1968.

Arc 1565 Numismatics - Local - Norway - Folios [Discontinued]

Arc 1565.1 Stenersen, L.B. Myntfundet fra Graeslid i Thydalen. Christiania, 1881.
Arc 1565.2 Schive, C.I. Norges mynter i middetalderen. pt.1-6. Christiania, 1858-65.

Arc 1568 Numismatics - Local - Norway - General works

Arc 1568.1 Holmboe, C.A. De prisca re monetaria Norvegiae. 2. ed. Christiania, 1854.
Arc 1568.1.3 Holmboe, C.A. De prisca re monetaria Norvegiae. Christiania, 1841.
Arc 1568.5 Skaare, Kolbjørn. Moneta Norwei. Oslo, 1966.
Arc 1568.6 Rønning, Bjørn R. Norges mynter. Oslo, 1971.
Arc 1568.7 Rønning, Bjørn R. Norges mynter og pengesedler etter 1874. Oslo, 1972.

Arc 1570 Numismatics - Local - Norway - Local; Special topics

Arc 1570.1 Holmboe, C.A. Et frar fund af norske mynter. Kjøbenhavn, 1866.
Arc 1570.1.5 Holmboe, C.A. Om nogle norske pengeten. Kjøbenhavn, 1868.
Arc 1570.1.9 Holmboe, C.A. Das älteste Münzwesen Norwegens. Berlin, 1846.
Arc 1570.2 Schive, C. Im et fund af norske mynter fraa Sando. Kjøbenhavn, 1866.
Arc 1570.5 Rønning, Bjørn R. Norges mynter i 150 år, 1816-1966. Oslo, 1967.
Arc 1570.8 Hansen, Per. Norsk numismatisk forenings historie: 1927-1967. Oslo, 1967.

Arc 1576 Numismatics - Local - Austria - Pamphlet volumes

Arc 1576.01 Pamphlet box. Numismatics. Austria.

Arc 1578 Numismatics - Local - Austria - General works

Arc 1578.1 Melle, Jakob von. Sylloge nummorum ex arg. uncialium. v.1-3. Lubeck, 1697-98.
Arc 1578.2 Melle, Jakob von. Sylloge nummorum ex arg. uncialium. v.1-3. Lubeck, 1698-99.
Arc 1578.3 Kolb, J. von. Die Münzen, Medaillen und Jetone. Linz, 1882.
Arc 1578.4F Miller zu Aicholz, V. von. Österreichische Münzprägungen, 1519-1918. Wien, 1920.
Arc 1578.5F Miller zu Aichholz, V. von. Österreichische Münzprägungen. 2. Aufl. Wien, 1948. 2v.
Arc 1578.6 Probszt, Günther. Quellenkunde der Münz- und Geldgeschichte. Graz, 1954.
Arc 1578.6.5 Probszt, Günther. Quellenkunde der Münz- und Geldgeschichte. Nachtrag. Graz. 1,1960+
Arc 1578.6.10 Probszt, Günther. Österreichische Münz- und Geldgeschichte. Wien, 1973.
Arc 1578.10 Austria. Haupt Münzamt in Wien. Katalog der Münzen- und Medaillen-Stampel. Wien, 1901-06. 4v.
Arc 1578.15 Mort, Selwyn R. Coins of the Hapsburg emperors and related issues. Melbourne, 1959.
Arc 1578.20 Herinek, Ludwig. Österreichische Münzprägungen von Ergänzungen, 1740-1969. Wien, 1970.
Arc 1578.20.1 Herinek, Ludwig. Österreichische Münzprägungen von Ergänzungen, 1740-1969. Wien, 1972.
Arc 1578.20.5 Herinek, Ludwig. Österreichische Münzprägungen von 1657-1740. Wien, 1972.

Arc 1580 Numismatics - Local - Austria - Local; Special topics

Arc 1580.5 Donebauer, Max. Beschreibung der Sammlung böhmischer Münzen. pt.1-2. Prag, 1889-90.
Arc 1580.7 Voigt, A. Beschreibung der bisher bekaunten böhmischen Münzen. v.1-2,3-4. Prag, 1771-87. 2v.
Arc 1580.8 Fiala, E. České denáry. Praha, 1895-
Arc 1580.10 Hanthaler, C. Verzeichnung...wiennerischer...Müntzen. Lintz, 1745.
Arc 1580.15 Höfken, Rudolf von. Numismatische Denkmale...in Österreich. Wien, 1904.
Arc 1580.20 Hess, A. Die Siebenbürgischen Münzen des furstlich Montenuoro'schen Münzcabinets. Frankfurt, 1880.

Arc 1580 Numismatics - Local - Austria - Local; Special topics - cont.

Arc 1580.30 Probszt, Günther. Die Münzen Salzburgs. Bâle, 1959.
Arc 1580.35 Cejnek, Josef. Österreichische, ungarische, böhmische, und schlesische Münzen. v.2. Wien, 1936.
Arc 1580.40 Roll, Karl. Die Schaumünzen auf die Salzburger Emigration. Halle, 1925.
Arc 1580.45 Hans, Josef. Maria-Theresien-Taler. 2. Aufl. Leiden, 1961.
Arc 1580.46 Innsbruck, F. Der Tiroler Taler. Innsbruck, 1963.
Arc 1580.48 Bernhart, Max. Die Münzen und Medaillen des Erzstiftes Salzburg. München, 1929-30.
Arc 1580.50 Luschin von Ebengreath, Arnold. Steirische Münzfunde. Graz, 1971.
Arc 1580.51.2 Polívka, Eduard. Mince Františka Josefa I., 1848-1916. 2. vyd. Praha, 1968.

Arc 1582 Numismatics - Local - Russia - Folios [Discontinued]

Arc 1582.1 Tilesius von Tilenau, Adolf. Explication de la figure problématique. St. Petersbourg, 1864.
Arc 1582.5F Tolstoi, I.I. Russkaia dopetrovenaia numismatika. Sankt Peterburg, 1884-86. 2v.
Arc 1582.7 Shubert, Fedor F. Monnayes russes, 1547-1855. Leipsic, 1857.
Arc 1582.7.2PF Shubert, Fedor F. Monnayes russes, 1547-1855. Atlas. Leipsic, 1857.
Arc 1582.9PF Tolstoi, I.I. Monety vel. kniazhestva Kievskago. Sankt Peterburg, 1882.

Arc 1583 Numismatics - Local - Russia - General works

Arc 1583.01 Pamphlet box. Numismatics. Russia.
Arc 1583.1 Shubert, Fedor F. Opisanie Russkikh monet. Sankt Peterburg, 1843.
Arc 1583.2 Fraehn, C.M.J. Aperçu sur les monnaies russes. n.p., n.d. 2 pam.
Arc 1583.5 Chertkov, A. Opisanie drevnikh Russkik' monet'. Moskva, 1834.
Arc 1583.5.2 Chertkov, A. Pribavlenie. Moskva, 1837-42. 3v.
Arc 1583.6 Demmeni, M. Sbornik' ukazov' po monetnomu delu. Sankt Peterburg, 1887. 3v.
Arc 1583.7 Shrapeznikov', A.N. Katalog' monet' chekannyk' v' Rossii. Sankt Peterburg, 1909.
Arc 1583.8 Gutten'-Chalskii, F.K. Chdel'n. velikokn. idsarsk. den'gi drevn. Rusi. Sankt Peterburg, 1875.
Arc 1583.9 Krug, A.L. Zur Münzkunde Russlands. St. Petersburg, 1805.
Arc 1583.10 Prozarovskii, D.I. Moneta i vec' v' Rossii do kontsa XVIII stoletiia. Sankt Peterburg, 1865.
Arc 1583.14 Oreshnikov, A.V. Denezhnye znaki domongol'. Rusi. Moskva, 1936.
Arc 1583.19.1 Georgii Mikhailovich, Grand Duke of Russia. Monnaies de l'empire de Russie, 1725-1894. Boston, 1973.
Arc 1583.22 Chaudoir, S. Aperçu sur les monnaies russes et sur les monnaies étrangères. v.1-3. St. Petersbourg, 1836. 2v.
Arc 1583.24 Fedorov-Davydov, German A. Monety rasskazy-vaiut. Moskva, 1963.
VArc 1583.24.5 Fedorov-Davydov, German A. Monety opowiadają o historii. Warszawa, 1966.
Arc 1583.26 Potin, Vsevolod M. Drevniaia Rus' i evropeiskie gosudarstva. Leningrad, 1968.
Arc 1583.28 Kaim, Reinhold. Russische Numismatik. Braunschweig, 1968.
RRC Arc 1583.30 Harris, Robert P. A guidebook of Russian coins, 1725 to 1970. 1. ed. Santa Cruz, California, 1971.
Arc 1583.32 Moscow. Gosudarstvennyi Istoricheskii Muzei. Monety SSSR. Moskva, 1971.

Arc 1584 Numismatics - Local - Russia - Local; Special topics

Arc 1584.1.3 Langlois, Victor. Numismatique de la Géorgie au moyen âge. Paris, 1852.
Arc 1584.1.4 Kapanadze, D.G. Gruzinskia numizmatika. Moskva, 1955.
Arc 1584.1.5 Dzhalaganiia, I.L. Iz istorii monetnogo dela v gruzii XIII veha. Tbilisi, 1958.
Arc 1584.1.6 Brosset, M.F. Rapport sur l'ouvrage intitulé. St. Petersbourg, 1847.
Arc 1584.1.9 Karst, J. Précis de numismatique géorgienne. Paris, 1938.
Arc 1584.1.10 Abramishvili, T.I. Zapadno-gruzinskie monety XIII-XIV vv. Tbilisi, 1959.
Arc 1584.1.15 Golenko, Konstantin V. Denizhnoe obrashchenie kolkhidy v rimskoe vremia. Leningrad, 1964.
Arc 1584.1.20 Pakhomov, Evgenii A. Monety Gruzii. Tbilisi, 1970.
Arc 1584.3 Gille, F. Lettre...sur une monnaie attribuée à Oleg. Paris, 1861.
Arc 1584.4 Pakhomov, Evgenii A. Monetnye klady Azerbaidzhana. pt.6,8. Baku, 1954.
Arc 1584.4.5 Pakhomov, Evgenii A. Monety Azerbaidzhana. Baku, 1959- 2v.
Arc 1584.5F Bulychev, N.I. Imennye serebrian. kop. i denezhki Ivana IV. Sankt Peterburg, 1906.
Arc 1584.10 Hrbas, M. Antike Münzen aus Olbia und Pantikapaum. Prag, 1959.
Arc 1584.12 Opeshnikov, A.V. Russkiia monety do 1547 g. Moskva, 1896.
Arc 1584.15 Braichevs'kyi, M.I. Ryms'ka moneta naterytorii Ukraïny. Kyïv, 1959.
Arc 1584.20 Spasskii, Ivan G. Talery v russkom denezhnom obrashchenii 1654-59 godov. Leningrad, 1960.
Arc 1584.25 Iaroslavskaia Uchenaia Arkhivnaia Kommissii. Opisanie russikh monet muzeia Iaroslavskoi uchenoi arkkivnoi kommissii. Iaroslav, 1898.
Arc 1584.26 Spasskii, Ivan G. Po sledam odnoi redkoi monety. Leningrad, 1964.
Arc 1584.27 Spasskii, Ivan G. Denezhnoe khoziaistvo Russkogo gosudarstva. Leningrad, 1961.
Arc 1584.28 Chizhov, Sergei I. Azbabskii klad'. Moskva, 1911. 2 pam.
Arc 1584.29 Kunik, Anst A. O russko-vizantiiskikh monetakh Iaroslava I Vladiminovicha. Sankt Peterburg, 1860.
Arc 1584.30 Kairn, Reinhold. Russische Münzstätten, Münzzeichen, Münzmeisterzeichen. Braunschweig, 1971.
Arc 1584.31 Veksler, Aleksandr G. Moskovskie klady. Moskva, 1973.
Arc 1584.32.1 Kotliar, Mykola F. Kladoiskatel'stvo i numizmatika. Kiev, 1974.

Arc 1588 Numismatics - Local - Other Europe - General works

Arc 1588.1 Lelewel, J. Notice sur la monnaie de Pologne. Bruxelles, 1842.
Arc 1588.1.9 Polkowski, J. Decouverte à Gtebokie de monnaies polonaises. Gnesen, 1876.
Arc 1588.1.11 Kirmis, M. Handbuch der polnischen Münzkunde. Posen, 1892.

Classified Listing

Arc 1588 Numismatics - Local - Other Europe - General works - cont.

Arc 1588.1.13 Tyszkiewicz, J. Guide de l'amateur de monnaies polonaises. Posen, 1890.
Arc 1588.1.14 Bandtki, K.W.S. Numismatyka Krajowa. Warszawa, 1839. 2v.
Arc 1588.1.15 Zagorski, I. Monety fawney Polski jakotez prowincyj i nuast. Warszawa, 1845.
Arc 1588.1.16 Zagorski, I. Tablice do dziela o monetach dawnej Polski. Warszawa, 1845.
Arc 1588.1.18 Dawne monety Polskie dynastyi Piasłow Jagiełłonow. Piotrkow, 1883-85. 3v.
Arc 1588.1.19 Gumowski, Marian. Podrecznik numiznatyki Polskiej. Kraków, 1914.
Arc 1588.1.20 Gumowski, Marian. Zarys numizmatyki Polskiej. Łódź, 1952.
Arc 1588.1.21 Gumowski, Marian. Numizmatyczno-historyczne z wieku. Poznań, 1924.
Arc 1588.1.22 Gumowski, Marian. Corpus numniorum Poloniae. Kraków, 1939.
Arc 1588.1.23 Gumowski, Marian. Monety polskie. Warszawa, 1924.
Arc 1588.1.24 Gumowski, Marian. Handbuch der polnischen Numismatik. Graz, 1960.
Arc 1588.1.25F Wittyg, W. Pieczecie miast dawnej Polski. Kraków, 1905.
Arc 1588.1.27 Gartman, V.G. Pol'skiia i litobskiia star. monety. Syzran, 1901.
Arc 1588.1.30 Gutten Czapskii, E.K. Catalogue de la collection des medailles et monnaies polonaises. Graz, 1957. 5v.
Arc 1588.1.31 Jabłoński, Tadeusz. Katalog monet polskich, 1765-1864. Warszawa, 1965.
Arc 1588.1.32 Terlecki, W. The catalogue of Polish coins. Warsaw, 1960.
Arc 1588.1.33 Terlecki, W. Ilustrowany katalog monet polskich bitych w okresie 1916-1965. 2. wyd. Warszawa, 1965.
Arc 1588.1.34 Terlecki, W. Katalog monet polskich. Warszawa, 1960.
Arc 1588.1.36 Wojtulewicz, H. Moneta polska od X-XX wieku. Lublin, 1960.
Arc 1588.1.37 Lublin (City). Museum Lubelskie. Tysiąc lat monety polskiej. Lublin, 1966.
Arc 1588.1.38 Czapkiewicz, Maria. Skarb monet arabskich z okolic Drohiczyna nad Bugiem. Kraków, 1960.
Arc 1588.1.40 Kmietowicz, A. Skarb srebrny z miejscowosci Ochle. Wrocław, 1962.
Arc 1588.1.42 Kiersnowski, R. Początki pieniadza polskiego. Warszawa, 1962.
Arc 1588.1.44F Kałkowski, Tadeusz. Tysiac lat monety polskiej. Kraków, 1963.
Arc 1588.1.44.2 Kałkowski, Tadeusz. Tysiac lat monety polskiej. Wyd. 2. Kraków, 1974.
Arc 1588.1.50 Polskiej Akademja Nauk. Instytut Historyjka Kultury Materialnej. Skarb monet arabskich z klukowicz powiat siemiatycze. Wrocław, 1964.
Arc 1588.1.55 Kiersnowski, Ryszard. Wstęp do numizmatyki polskiej wieków średnich. Warszawa, 1964.
Arc 1588.1.60 Breslau. Zakład Narodowy im Ossalińskikh. Biblioteka. Tysiąc lat monety na ziemiach poliskich. Wrocław, 1966.
Arc 1588.1.65 Kamiński, Czesław. Katalog banknotów i monet Polskiej Rzeczy pospolitej Ludowej. pt.1-2. Warszawa, 1966-68.
Arc 1588.1.65.7 Kamiński, Czesław. Ilustrowany katakog monet polskich, 1916-1972. wyd. 2. Warszawa, 1973.
Arc 1588.1.65.8 Kamiński, Czesław. Ilustrowany katalog monet polskich, 1916-1974. Wyd. 3. Warszawa, 1974.
Arc 1588.1.66 Kunisz, A. Chronologia naptywu pieniądza vzymskiegs na ziemie Matspoblei. Wyd. 1. Wrocław, 1969.
Arc 1588.1.70 Terlecki, W. Mennica warszawska 1765-1965. Wrocław, 1970.
Arc 1588.1.75 Kubiak, Stanisława. Monety pierwszych Jagiellonów 1386-1444. Wyd. 1. Wrocław, 1970.
Arc 1588.1.80 Gumowski, Marian. Biskupstwo kniszwickie w XI wieku. Poznań, 1921.
Arc 1588.1.85 Suchodolski, Stanisław. Mennictwo polskie w XI-XII wieku. Wrocław, 1973.
Arc 1588.1.91 Zagórski, Ignacy. Monety dawnej Polski. Warszawa, 1969.
Arc 1588.1.96 Beyer, Karol. Skorowidz monet polskich od 1506 do 1825. Warszawa, 1973.
Arc 1588.1.101 Plage, Karol. Monety bite dla Królestwa Polskiego w latach 1815-1864 i monety bite dla miasta Krakowa w roku 1835. Warszawa, 1972.
Arc 1588.1.105 Sesja Numizmatyczna, 3rd, Nowa Sól, 1970. III Sesja Numizmatyczna w Nowej Soli poświęcona monecie i mennicom Wielkopolski, 10-11 listopada 1970 r. Nowa Sól, 1972.
Arc 1588.1.110 Kopicki, Edmund. Katalog podstawowych typów monet i banknotów Polski oraz ziem historycznie z Polską związanych. v.1, pt.1-2. Warszawa, 1974- 2v.
Arc 1588.2 Fraehn, C.M.J. De numorum Bulgharicorum forte antiguissimo. Casani, 1816.
Arc 1588.2.5 Pamphlet vol. Numismatics. Bulgaria.
Arc 1588.2.10 Mushmov, N.A. Monety i pechatite na bolg. Acare. Sofiia, 1924.
Arc 1588.2.11 Mushmov, N.A. Antichnite moneti na Balkanskiia polustrov i monetite. Sofiia, 1912.
Arc 1588.3 Luczenbacher, J. A' szerb zsupánok királyok es ezárok. Budán, 1843.
Arc 1588.3.5 Dimitrijević, Sergije. Novac kneza Lasara. Kruševac, 1971.
Arc 1588.4 Skalsky, G. Denár knizete Vacłava Svatého a. Praha, 1929.
Arc 1588.4.10 Cermák, K. Mince kralowstvi Českéko za panováné rodu Habsburskeho od voku 1526. n.p., 1891-1913. 3v.
Arc 1588.4.15 Chaura, K. Die Wahrheit übes den St. Wenzel-Denar. Praha, 1929.
Arc 1588.4.17 Nohejlova, Eman. Nálezi minci v Cechacle na Morave a ve slezsku. Praha, 1955. 4v.
Arc 1588.4.20F Turnwald, K. Česki a Moravské denary a brakteaty. Praha, 1949.
Arc 1588.4.25 Castelin, K.O. Česka drobna mince v doly predhus, a husitske, 1300-1471. Praha, 1953.
Arc 1588.4.30 Nohejlová, Emanuela. Krasa česke mince. Praha, 1955.
Arc 1588.4.35 Nohejlová, Emanuela. Kratký přehled českého mincovnictví a tabulky cen a mezd. Praha, 1964.
Arc 1588.4.38 Nohejlová, Emanuela. Dvě stoleti vědecké numismatiky v českých Zemich. 1771-1971. Praha, 1971.
Arc 1588.4.40 Gumowski, Marian. Bolesław Chrobry v Czechach. Poznań, 1934.
Arc 1588.4.45 Katz, Viktor. Ocuronolozu denaru Boleslava I a II. Praha, 1935.
Arc 1588.4.45.5 Katz, Viktor. Tisíc let české vládní mince (929-1929). Praha, 1929.
Arc 1588.4.50 Vereine für Numismatik. Beschreibung. Prag, 1852-70.
Arc 1588.4.55 Ondrouch, Vojtech. Nálezy keltských, antických a byzantských mincí na Slovensku. Bratislava, 1964.
Arc 1588.4.60 Nemeškal, Lubomir. Jáchymovská mincovna v první polovině 16. století, 1519/20-1561. Praha, 1964.

Arc 1588 Numismatics - Local - Other Europe - General works - cont.

Arc 1588.4.62 Nemeškal, Lubomir. Českobudějovická mincovina v letech 1569-1611. Vyd. 1. Česke Budějovice, 1969.
Arc 1588.4.65F Horák, Jan. Kremnická mincovňa. Banska Bystrica, 1965.
Arc 1588.4.70 Sejbal, Jiří. Moravská mince doby husitské. Brno, 1965.
Arc 1588.4.73 Pŏsvář, Jaroslav. Moravské mincovny. Vyd. 1. Brno, 1970.
Arc 1588.4.75 Pŏsvář, Jaroslav. Měna v českých zemích od 10. do poč 20. století. Opava, 1962.
Arc 1588.4.80 Radoměřský, Pavel. Nález přemyslovských denárů iz století v Hodkově u Kutné Hory. Kutná Hora, 1964.
Arc 1588.4.85 Horák, Ján. Kremnické dukáty. Vyd. 1. Bratislava, 1968.
Arc 1588.4.90 Hlinka, Jozef. Vývgpeňazi a medailí na Slovensku. Bratislava, 1970.
Arc 1588.4.95 Polivka, Eduard. Československé mince 1918-1968. Vyd. 1. Hradec Králové, 1969.
Arc 1588.4.100 Hásková, Jarmila. Chebské mince z 12. a 13. století. Cheb, 1972.
Arc 1588.5.5 Metcalf, David Michael. Coinage in the Balkans. Thessaloniki, 1965.
Arc 1588.5.6 Metcalf, David Michael. Coinage in the Balkans, 820-1355. Chicago, 1966.
Arc 1588.5.8 Metcalf, David Michael. Classification of Byzantine stamena in the light of a hoard found in southern Serbia. Ljubljana, 1967.
Arc 1588.5.10 Fedorov, Dimitrii I. Monety pribaltiki XIII-XVIII stoletii. Tallin, 1966.
Arc 1588.6 Artuk, Ibrah. Fatik sikke re madalyalari. Istanbul, 1946.
Arc 1588.6.1 Artuk, Ibrah. Konuni Sultan Suleymon adena basilon sikkeler. Ankara, 1972.
Arc 1588.6.2 Ölçer, Cüneyt. Sovyet Rusya Müzelerindeki, Moskova ve Leningrad, Nardir Osmanli raralon. Istanbul, 1972.
Arc 1588.6.2.5 Ölçer, Cüneyt. Sultan Mohmut II zamomuda darpedilen osmanli madeni porolori. Istanbul, 1970.
Arc 1588.6.2.10 Ölçer, Cüneyt. San alti osmanli padişahi zamaninda Istanbulda basilan gümuç paralor. Istanbul, 1966.
Arc 1588.6.2.15 Ölçer, Cüneyt. Yildivim Bayezid'in agullanu ait akçe ve mangirlav. Istanbul, n.d.
Arc 1588.6.2.20 Olçer, Cüneyt. Nakışlį Osmanlį mangirlarį. Istanbul, 1975.
Arc 1588.6.5 Kolerkilic, Eksen. Osmarli inpatatorlugurda pava. Ankara, 1958.
Arc 1588.6.15 Butak, Bekzad. Resimli Turk paralari. Istanbul, 1947.
Arc 1588.6.20 Saglani, O.F. Simdiye kadar görülmiyen Cimri Sikkesi. n.p., 1949.
Arc 1588.6.25 Kocaer, Remje. Osmanli altinlari. Istanbul, 1967.
Arc 1588.6.30 Butak, Bekzad. Cumhuriyet devrinde madeni para bois. Istanbul, 1955.
Arc 1588.6.35 Tesla-Zarić, Dobrila. Katalog novca Osmanske imperije sakupljenog- na području SFR Jugoslavije. Beograd, 1974.
Arc 1588.7.5F Floca, Ochaviau. Coutributic la cunoasterea Syauselar de arguil doeice. Bucureşti, 1956.
Arc 1588.8 Bosch, E. Turkizenin ankils deviedeke meskukatina. Ankara, 1949.
Arc 1588.9 Sengbusch, R. von. Heinrich Jochumsen. Verzeichnis aller bisher nachweisbaren boltischen Münzen und der Desiderata der Sammlung Anton Buchholtz. Riga, 1928.
Arc 1588.10 Budapest. Magyar Eremmuveszet Nemzeti Galeria. Medailles hongroises aux XIXe et XXe siècles. Budapest, 1959.
Arc 1588.10.5 Rethy, Landislaus. Corpus nummorum Hungariae. Graz, 1958.
Arc 1588.10.10 Huszár, Lajos. Munzkunst in Ungarn. Budapest, 1963.
Arc 1588.10.12 Huszár, Lajos. A budai pénzverés története a középkorban. Budapest, 1958.
Arc 1588.10.15 Budapest. Orszagos Széchenyi-Könyvtár. Catalogus numorum Hungariae ac Transiwaniae Instituti Nationalis Széchényrani. Pestini, 1807. 2v.
Arc 1588.10.20 Hlinka, Jozef. Bratislavské korunovačné medaily a žetóny. Vyd. 1. Bratislava, 1966.
Arc 1588.10.25 Tözen, Ibrahim. Türkiye cumhuriyeti madeni ponohr. Istanbul, 1973.
Arc 1588.10.30 Hóman, Bálint. Magyar pénztörténet, 1000-1325. Budapest, 1916.
Arc 1588.10.35 Rupp, Jakab. Magyarorszag ekkorig ismeretes pénzei. Budan, 1841.
Arc 1588.11 Karys, Jonas K. Senoues lietuviu pinigai. Bridgeport, Conn., 1959.
Arc 1588.11.5 Gumowski, Marian. Mennica wileńska w XVI i XVII wieku. Warszawa, 1921.
Arc 1588.12 Horvath, Henrik. A Budai penzverde muveszett orterenete a kesoi kozepkorban. Budapest, 1932.
Arc 1588.13 Ered, Serafeddin. Nadir hirkaç sikke. Ankara? 1967.
Arc 1588.13.5 Erel, Serafeddin. Nadir hirkaç sikke. Istanbul, 1963.
Arc 1588.14 Pere, Nuri. Osmanhlarda madeni paralar. Istanbul, 1968.
Arc 1588.15 Numismatika. Rigā, 1968.

Arc 1590 Numismatics - Local - Other Europe - Local; Special topics

Arc 1590.1 Schlumberger, G. Une nouvelle monnaie a legende grecque...de Cappadoce. Paris, 1887.
Arc 1590.2 Lambros, P. Monete inedite dei gran maestri...in Rodi. Venezia, 1865.
Arc 1590.2.3 Lambros, P. Monete inedite dei gran maestri. Primo supplemento. Venezia, 1866.
Arc 1590.2.5 Lambros, P. Monnaies inédites de Raimond Zacosta. Athènes, 1877.
Arc 1590.3 Friedlaender, J. Recherches sur les monnaies frappées dans l'île de Rhodes. Paris, 1855.
Arc 1590.4 Schlumberger, G. Deux plombs satiriques. Paris, 1878. 3 pam.
Arc 1590.5 Laugier. Étude historique sur les monnaies...de l'ordre de Saint Jean de Jérusalem. Marseille, 1868.
Arc 1590.6 Lambros, Paulos. Monnaies de Chypre et de Salona. n.p., 1866.
Arc 1590.7 Schweitzer, F. Brevi cenni storici...una medagliā di Ugone III. Trieste, 1846.
Arc 1590.8 Farkas, Sandor. Az erdélyi érmek müvészete. Aiud, 1936.
Htn Arc 1590.8.5* Farkas, Sandor. Die Kunst und der Wert...Münzen. Aiud, 1938.
Arc 1590.9 Rajić, N.P. Illustr. katal. nov. srpekhikh tsareva, 700-1710 g. Beograd, 1940.
Arc 1590.9.5 Rengjeo, Ivan. Corpus der mittelalterlichen Münzen von Kroatien, Slavozien, Dalmatien und Bosnien. Graz, 1959.
Arc 1590.10 Mihailović, Vojislav. Katalog novca Srbije i Crne Gore 1868-1918. Beograd, 1973.
Arc 1590.20 Mirchev, M. Amfornite pechati ot Muzeia vuv Varna. Sofiia, 1958.
Arc 1590.25 Resch, Adolf. Siebenbürgishe Münzen und Medaillen von 1538 bis zur Gegenwart. Montreal, 1965.
Arc 1590.30 Pošvář, Jaroslav. Die Währung in der Ländern der böhmischen Krone. Graz, 1970.

Classified Listing

Arc 1590 Numismatics - Local - Other Europe - Local; Special topics - cont.
Arc 1590.31 Katz, Viktor. Kontramarky na pražských groších. Praha, 1927.

Arc 1598 Numismatics - Local - Americas in general - General works
Arc 1598.15 Riddell, J.L. A monograph of the silver dollar, good and bad. New Orleans, 1845.

Arc 1601 Numismatics - Local - Canada - Pamphlet volumes
Arc 1601 Pamphlet box. Numismatics. Canada. 3 pam.

Arc 1603 Numismatics - Local - Canada - General works
Arc 1603.1 Breton, P.N. Le collectionneur...des mqnnaies canadiennes. Montreal, 1890.
Arc 1603.1.5 Breton, P.N. Popular illustrated guide to Canadian coins. Montreal, 1912.
Arc 1603.3.5 Sandham, Alfred. Coins, tokens and medals of the Dominion of Canada. Montreal, 1869.
Arc 1603.3.6 Sandham, Alfred. Coins, tokens and medals of the Dominion of Canada. Montreal, 1962.
Arc 1603.3.7 Sandham, Alfred. Supplement to coins, tokens and medals. Montreal, 1872.
X Cg Arc 1603.4 Lerouv, J. Le médaillier du Canada. Montreal, 1888.
Arc 1603.5 Standard catalogue of Canadian coins, tokens, and paper money. Racine, Wis. 15,1967

Arc 1605 Numismatics - Local - Canada - Local; Special topics
Htn Arc 1605.1* Wood, H. Canadian blacksmith coppers. Philadelphia, 1910.

Arc 1610 Numismatics - Local - United States - Folios [Discontinued]
Arc 1610.1 Dickeson, M.W. The American numismatic manual. 2. ed. Philadelphia, 1860.
Arc 1610.2 Crosby, S.S. The early coins of America. Boston, 1875.
Arc 1610.2.1 Crosby, S.S. The early coins of America. Lawrence, 1974.
Arc 1610.3 Bangs, Merwin C. Catalogue of coins and medals. Roxbury, 1863.

Arc 1611 Numismatics - Local - United States - Pamphlet volumes
Arc 1611.1 Pamphlet box. Numismatics. United States. 5 pam.

Arc 1613 Numismatics - Local - United States - General works
Arc 1613.1 Hickcox, J.H. An historical account of American coinage. Albany, 1858.
Arc 1613.2 Evans, G.G. Illustrated history of the United States mint. Philadelphia, 1890.
Arc 1613.2.2 Evans, G.G. Illustrated history of the United States mint. Philadelphia, 1892.
Arc 1613.2.3 Evans, G.G. Illustrated history of the United States mint. Philadelphia, 1889.
Arc 1613.2.4 Evans, G.G. Illustrated history of the United States mint. Philadelphia, 1891.
Arc 1613.2.5 Evans, G.G. Illustrated history of the United States mint. Philadelphia, 1893.
Arc 1613.3 Appleton, W.S. Description of a selection of coins and medals relating to America. Cambridge, 1870-76. 2 pam.
Arc 1613.4 Phillips, H. The coinage of the United States of America. Philadelphia, 1883.
Arc 1613.5 Vattemare, A. Collection de monnaies et médailles de l'Amérique. Paris, 1861.
Arc 1613.6 Woodward, W.E. Catalogue of American and foreign coins, medals, tokens. Providence, 1866.
Arc 1613.6.2 Woodward, W.E. Catalogue of American and foreign coins, medals, tokens. Roxbury, 1867.
Arc 1613.7 Adams, E.H. Adams' official premium list. United States gold coins. N.Y., 1909.
Arc 1613.7.5 Adams, E.H. United States pattern, trial, and experimental pieces. N.Y., 1913.
Arc 1613.8 Hart, C.H. A historical sketch of the national medals. Philadelphia, 1867.
Arc 1613.9 United States Mint. Catalogue of coins of the United States. Washington, 1928.
Arc 1613.10F Dickeson, M.W. The American numismatical manual of the currency or money of the aborigines. Philadelphia, 1859.
Arc 1613.11F Bushnell, C.I. Catalogue of...American coins and medals of C.I. Bushnell. Philadelphia, 1882.
Arc 1613.12 Smith, A.M. Coins and coinage. The United States Mint, Philadelphia. Philadelphia, 1884.
Arc 1613.13 American Numismatic Society, N.Y. Exhibition of United States and colonial coins, Jan. 17 to Feb. 18, 1914. Catalogue. N.Y., 1914.
Arc 1613.14 Lewis, E.A. Laws authorizing issuance of medals. Washington, 1936.
Arc 1613.14.5 Lewis, E.A. Laws authorizing issuance of medals and commerative coins. Washington, 1936.
Arc 1613.17 Coffin, J. Our American money. N.Y., 1940.
Arc 1613.18 The standard catalogue of United States coins and tokens from 1652 to present day. N.Y. 1941
Arc 1613.19 Von Bergen, W. The rare coins of America, England, Ireland, Scotland, France, Germany, and Spain. Cambridge, Mass., 1899.
Arc 1613.20 Johnson, J.B. Auction prices: "United States coins." 3. ed. Cincinnati, 1944.
Arc 1613.21 Venn, T.J. Large United States cents. Chicago, 1915.
Arc 1613.22 Mumey, N. Clark, Gruber and Co. Denver, 1950.
Arc 1613.23 Del Monte, J. Fell's United States coin books. N.Y., 1952.
Arc 1613.24 Judd, T. Hewitt. United States pattern. Racine, 1959.
Arc 1613.25 Belden, Bauman. United States war medals. N.Y., 1916.
Arc 1613.28 Massey, Joseph Earl. America's money. N.Y., 1968.
Arc 1613.29 United States. Domestic and foreign coins manufactured by mints of the United States, 1793-1973. Washington, 1974.
Arc 1613.30 Vermeule, Cornelius Clarkson. Numismatic art in America. Cambridge, 1971.

Arc 1615 Numismatics - Local - United States - Local; Special topics
Arc 1615.1 Slafter, E.F. The Vermont coinage. Montpelier, 1870.
Arc 1615.2 Crosby, S.S. United States coinage of 1793, cents and half cents. Boston, 1897.
Arc 1615.3 Newlin, H.P. A classification of early half-dimes in the United States. Philadelphia, 1883.
Arc 1615.4 United States Mint. Catalogue of coins, tokens, and medals. Washington, 1912.
Arc 1615.4.2 United States Mint. Catalogue of coins, tokens, and medals. 2. ed. Washington, 1913.
Arc 1615.4.3 United States Mint. Catalogue of coins, tokens, and medals. 3. ed. Washington, 1914.
Arc 1615.4.10 United States Mint. Medals of the United States Mint. Washington, 1969.

Arc 1615 Numismatics - Local - United States - Local; Special topics - cont.
Arc 1615.4.11 United States Mint. Medals of the United States Mint. Washington, 1972.
Arc 1615.5 Adams, E.H. Private gold coinage of California, 1849-55, its history and issues. Brooklyn, 1913.
Arc 1615.6 Gilbert, Ebenezer. The United States half cents. N.Y., 1916.
Arc 1615.7 Frossard, E. Monograph of United States cents and half cents issued between the years 1793 and 1857. Irvington, 1879.
Arc 1615.8 Foster, Charles W. Historical arrangement of United States commemorative coins. Rochester, 1936.
Arc 1615.9 Mosher, S. United States commemorative coins, 1892-1939. N.Y., 1940.
Arc 1615.10 Sheldon, W.H. Early American cents, 1793-1814. 1. ed. N.Y., 1949.
Arc 1615.14 Newman, Eric. The fantastic 1804 dollar. Racine, 1962.
Arc 1615.16 Gould, Maurice M. Alaska's coinage through the years. 2. ed. Racine, 1965.

Arc 1623 Numismatics - Local - Mexico - General works
Arc 1623.1 Fisher, A. Catalogue of coins, medals, and tokens of Mexico. N.Y., 1891.
Arc 1623.5 Prudeau, A.F. Historia numismatica de Mexico desde la epoca precortesiana hasta 1823. Mexico, 1950.
Arc 1623.6 Sobrino, Jose Manuel. La moneda mexicana. Mexico, 1972.

Arc 1625 Numismatics - Local - Mexico - Local; Special topics
Arc 1625.1 Low, Lyman H. Sketch of coinage of Mexican revolutionary General Morelos. N.Y., 1886.
Arc 1625.2 Romero de Terreros y Vinent, Manuel. Los tlacos coloniales. México, 1935.
Arc 1625.3 Raymond, W. The coins of Mexico in silver and copper, 1536-1939. N.Y., 1940.
Arc 1625.5 Moreno, Alvaro. El signo de pesos. México, 1965.

Arc 1631 Numismatics - Local - Central America - Pamphlet volumes
Arc 1631.01 Pamphlet box. Numismatics. South America.

Arc 1635 Numismatics - Local - Central America - Local; Special topics
Arc 1635.5 Prober, Kurt. Historia numismática de Guatemala. Guatemala, 1957.

Arc 1640 Numismatics - Local - South America - Folios [Discontinued]
Arc 1640.5 Medina, J.T. Las monedas chilenas. Santiago, 1902.
Arc 1640.7F Meili, Julius. Die auf das Kaiserreich Brasilien...1822 bis 1889. Zürich, 1890.

Arc 1643 Numismatics - Local - South America - General works
Arc 1643.1 Medina, J.T. Monedas y medallas hispano-americanas. Santiago, 1891.
Arc 1643.1.5 Medina, J.T. Medallas coloniales hispano-americanas. Santiago, 1900.
Arc 1643.1.10F Medina, J.T. Las monedas coloniales hispano-americanas. Santiago, 1919.
Arc 1643.1.15F Medina, J.T. Las monedas obsidionales hispano-americanas. Santiago, 1919.
Arc 1643.2 Rosa, A. Monetario americano. Buenos Aires, 1892.
Arc 1643.4F Burzio, Humberto F. Diccionario de la moneda hispano-americana. Santiago, 1956-58. 2v.
Arc 1643.5 Posada, Eduardo. Numismatica colombiana. Bogotá, 1937.

Arc 1645 Numismatics - Local - South America - Local; Special topics
Arc 1645.1 Azeredo, C. de. Apreciação do medalheiro da casa da Moeda. Rio de Janeiro, 1862.
Arc 1645.1.5 Meili, Julius. Die Münzen der Colonie Brasilien, 1645-1822. Zürich, 1895.
Arc 1645.1.7 Meili, Julius. Die Münzen des Kaiserreichs Brasilien, 1822-1889. Leipzig, 1890.
Arc 1645.1.10 Prober, Kurt. Catalogo das moedas brasileiras. Rio de Janeiro, 1960.
Arc 1645.1.15 Meili, Julius. Das brasilianische Geldwesen. Zürich, 1897-1905. 2v.
Arc 1645.2 Raymond, Wayte. The coins of South America; silver and copper. British Guiana, Dutch Guiana, French Guiana. N.Y., 1942.
Arc 1645.3 Medina, J.T. Manual ilustrado de numismatica chilena. Santiago, 1919.
Arc 1645.3.5F Medina, J.T. Las monedas coloniales de Chile. Santiago, 1919. 2 pam.
Arc 1645.5 Ferrari, Jorge N. La revolución de Mayo en la medalla. Buenos Aires, 1960.
Arc 1645.6F Salazar Bondy, Sebastian. Lima, su moneda y su ceca. v.1-2. Lima, 1964.

Arc 1655 Numismatics - Local - Pacific Islands - Local; Special topics
Arc 1655.5 Dutton, M.K. The case of the elusive hubs and dies. Honolulu, 1959.

Arc 1660 Numismatics - Special topics - Historical coins and medals - Folios [Discontinued]
Arc 1660.1 Loubat, J.F. The medallic history of the United States of America, 1776-1876. Text and plates. N.Y., 1878. 2v.
Arc 1660.2 Pinkerton, J. The medallic history of England. London, 1790.
Arc 1660.3 Liesville, A.R. de. Histoire numismatique de la révolution de 1848. Paris, 1877-83.
Htn Arc 1660.4F* Loehr, August. Wiener Medailleure, 1899. Wien, 1899.
Arc 1660.4.2F Loehr, August. Wiener Medailleure. Nachtrag, 1901. Wien, 1902.
Htn Arc 1660.5* Menestrier, C.F. Histoire du Roy Louis le Grand. Paris, 1691.
Htn Arc 1660.5.2* France. Institut. Médailles sur les principaux evenements du règne de Louis le Grand. Baden, 1705.
Htn Arc 1660.6* Fleurimont, G.R. Médailles du règne de Louis XV. n.p., n.d.
Arc 1660.7 Myer, I. The Waterloo medal. Philadelphia, 1885.
Arc 1660.8 Snowden, J.R. A description of the medals of Washington. Philadelphia, 1861.
Arc 1660.9 Medallic illustrations. History of Great Britain and Ireland. v.1-50,101-120. London, 1904. 7v.
Arc 1660.11 Luckius, J.J. Sylloge numismatum elegantiorum. Argentina, 1620.
Arc 1660.12 Rosa, A. Estudios numismaticos. Buenos Aires, n.d.
Arc 1660.13 Medina, J.T. Las medallas chilenas. Santiago, 1601.
Arc 1660.14F Welch, Charles. Medals struck by the corporation of London. London, 1894.

Arc 1660 Numismatics - Special topics - Historical coins and medals - Folios [Discontinued] - cont.

Arc 1660.15F Duby, P.A.T. Recueil général des pieces obsidionales. Paris, 1786.
Arc 1660.15.5F Duby, P.A.T. Trauté des monnaies des barons. Paris, 1790. 2v.
Arc 1660.16F Hill, George F. Medals of the renaissance. Oxford, 1920.
Arc 1660.17F Gnechi, Francesco. Le monete dei Trivulzio. Milano, 1887.
Arc 1660.18F Edwards, Edward. The Napoleon medals. London, 1837.
Arc 1660.19F Lefebure, Charles. Contribution à la documentation du temps de guerre. Bruxelles, 1923.

Arc 1661 Numismatics - Special topics - Historical coins and medals - Pamphlet volumes

Arc 1661 Pamphlet box. Numismatics. Special.

Arc 1663 Numismatics - Special topics - Historical coins and medals - Monographs

Arc 1663.1 Wyatt, T. A description of the national medals of America. N.Y., 1854. 2 pam.
Arc 1663.2 Betts, C.W. - American colonial history illustrated by contemporary medals. N.Y., 1894.
Arc 1663.3 Hawkins, E. Medallic illustrations of the history of Great Britain and Ireland. London, 1885. 2v.
Arc 1663.4 Henfrey, H.W. Numismata Cromwelliana. London, 1873.
Arc 1663.5 Sandham, Alfred. Medals commemorative of the visit of H.R.H. the Prince of Wales to Montreal. Montreal, 1871.
Arc 1663.5.5 Sandham, Alfred. Historic medals of Canada. Quebec, 1873.
Arc 1663.6 Storer, H.R. Les médailles de la Princesse Charlotte d'Angleterre. Bruxelles, 1888-91. 2 pam.
Arc 1663.6.15 Widdington, M. Catalogue of Jacobite medals and touch pieces. Leeds, 1938.
Arc 1663.6.20 Whiting, John Roger Scott. Commemorative medals. Newton Abbot, 1972.
Arc 1663.7 Grande museo rivoluzionario. Roma, 1850.
Arc 1663.7.5F Camozzi Vertova, G. Dissertazione sul medagliere relativo alla storia mederna d'Italia. Bergamo, 1879.
Arc 1663.7.7F Camozzi Vertova, G. Dissertazione sul medagliere relativo alla storia moderna d'Italia. Bergamo, 1880.
Arc 1663.8 Clarke, H. The early history of the Mediterranean populations. London, 1882.
Arc 1663.9 Cessac. Un trésor de monnaies des comtes de la Marche. v.1-2. Paris, 1882.
Arc 1663.10 Perreau, A. Recherches sur les comtes de Looz et sur leurs monnaies. Bruxelles, 1845.
Arc 1663.11 Arnold, H.P. The evolution of the Boston medal. Boston, 1901.
Arc 1663.12 Hildebrand, B.E. Sveriges konungahusets minnespenningar. Stockholm, 1874. 2v.
Arc 1663.13 Ludwig I. von Bayern und sein Wirken. Leipzig, 1853.
Arc 1663.14 Belts, Benjamin. Descriptive list of medals relating to John Law. n.p., 1907.
Arc 1663.15 Laverrenz, C. Die Medaillen und Gedachtniszeichen der deutschen Hochschulen. Berlin, 1887. 2v.
Arc 1663.15.5 Hesse, Waldemar E. Die tragbaren Ehrenzeichen des Deutschen Reiches. Berlin, 1940.
Arc 1663.15.10 Więcek, Adam. Medale Piastów Śląskich. Wyd. 1. Warszawa, 1958.
Arc 1663.16 Ricciardi, E. Medaglie del Regno delle due Sicilie 1735-1861. Napoli, 1900.
Arc 1663.16.5F Ricciardi, E. Medaglie del Regno delle due Sicilie 1735-1861. 2. ed. Napoli, 1930.
Arc 1663.16.10 Majorca Mortillaro, L.M. Ventitre medaglie borboniche napoletane. Pitigliano, 1889.
Arc 1663.17 Saulcy, Félecien. Souvenirs numismatiques de la révolution de 1848. Paris, 1850.
Arc 1663.18 Madrid. Real Biblioteca. Medallas de la casa de Borbón. Madrid, 1916.
Arc 1663.19 Herrera y Chiesanova, A. Medallos de los gobernadores. Madrid, 1901.
Arc 1663.20 Greppo, J.G.H. Mémoire sur les voyages de...Hadrien et sur les médailles. Paris, 1842.
Arc 1663.21 Müller, Bernhard. Medaillen und Münzen im Dienste der Religion. Berlin, 1915.
Arc 1663.22 Satterlee, Alfred H. An arrangement of medals and tokens struck in honor of the presidents of the United States. N.Y., 1862.
Arc 1663.23 Cunha, Xavier. A medalha de Casimiro José de Lima em homenagem a Sousa Martins. Coimbra, 1903.
Arc 1663.24 Cunha, Xavier. A medalha escolar do coll. do Corpo-Santo noticia numismatic. Coimbra, 1907.
Arc 1663.25 Florange, Charles. Les assemblées du clergé de France avant 1789. Paris, 1927.
Arc 1663.26 Barnard, F.P. Saterical and controversial medals of the reformation. Oxford, 1927.
Arc 1663.27 Laskey, John C. A description of the series of medals struck at the national medal mint by...Napoleon Bonaparte. London, 1818.
Arc 1663.28 Camozzi Vertova, G. Medaglie coniate in onore del generale Giuseppe Garibaldi. Bergamo, 1885.
Arc 1663.28.2 Camozzi Vertova, G. Medaglie coniate in onore del generale Giuseppe Garibaldi. Bergamo, 1885.
Arc 1663.28.10 Romussi, Carlo. Garibaldi nelle medaglie del Museo del Risorgimento in Milano. Milano, 1905.
Arc 1663.30 Delbrueck, Richard. Die Münzbildnisse von Maximinus bis Carenus. Berlin, 1940.
Arc 1663.31 Lange, Kurt. Charakterkopfe der Weltgeschichte. München, 1949.
Arc 1663.33 Quinot, Henri. Recueil illustré des ordres de chevalerie et decorations belges de 1830 à 1963. 5. éd. Bruxelles, 1963.
Arc 1663.34 African Museum. Commemorative medals of the Z.A.R. Johannesburg, 1958.
Arc 1663.45 Fuld, George. Patriotic Civil War tokens. Racine, 1960.
Arc 1663.52F Frede, Lothar. Das klassische Weimar in Medaillen. Leipzig, 1959.
Arc 1663.55 Bauquier, Henri. Histoire numismatique du comte de Chanbord. Paris, 1911-40.
Arc 1663.56 Lesser, Friedrich Christian. Besondere Münzen. Frankfurt, 1739.
Arc 1663.57 Koernlein, Melchior. Thesaurus numismatum modernorum huius seculi, sive numismata mnemonica et iconica qui bus praecipui eventus et res gestae ab anno MDCC illustrantur. Norimbergae, 1711-17?
Arc 1663.58 Belden, Bauman Lowe. Indian peace medals issued in the United States. New Milford, Conn., 1966.
Arc 1663.60 Gumowski, Marian. Medale polskie. Warszawa, 1925.
Arc 1663.61 Gumowski, Marian. Medale Tagiellonów. Kraków, 1906.

Arc 1663 Numismatics - Special topics - Historical coins and medals - Monographs - cont.

Arc 1663.62 Wojtulewicz, Henryk. Medale polskie XVI-XX w. Lublin, 1968.
Arc 1663.63 Gumowski, Marian. Medale Zygmunta III. Kraków, 1924.
Arc 1663.64 Jaworski, Franciszek. Medalionej polskie. Lwow, 1911.

Arc 1665 Numismatics - Special topics - Special aspects - Folios [Discontinued]

X Cg Arc 1665.1 Imhoof-Blumer, F. Tier- und Pflanzenbilder auf Münzen und Gemmen. Leipzig, 1889.
Arc 1665.2 Knifer, Gijsbert. De elephantis in numis obviis exercitationes duae. Hagae, 1719. 2 pam.
Arc 1665.3 Rentzmann, W. Numismatisches Wappen-Lexicon. Berlin, 1876.
Arc 1665.3.5 Rentzmann, W. Numismatisches Wappen-Lexicon. Index. Berlin, 1876.
Arc 1665.4F Babelon, Ernest. Les medailles historique...Napoléon le Grand. Paris, 1912.

Arc 1666 Numismatics - Special topics - Special aspects - Pamphlet volumes

Arc 1666 Pamphlet box. Numismatics. Special.

Arc 1668 Numismatics - Special topics - Special aspects - Monographs

NEDL Arc 1668.1 Donaldson, T.L. Architectura numismatica. London, 1859.
Arc 1668.2 Bolton, H.C. Contribution of alchemy to numismatics. N.Y., 1890.
Arc 1668.3 Schlickeysen, F.W.A. Erklärung der Abkürzungen auf Münzen der neueren Zeit. Berlin, 1882.
Arc 1668.3.2 Schlickeysen, F.W.A. Erklärung der Abkürzungen auf Münzen der neueren Zeit. Graz, 1961.
Arc 1668.4 Keller, D. Biltnusse der Rhömischen Keyseren. Zürich, 1558.
Arc 1668.5 Rentzmann, W. Numismatisches Legenden-Lexicon. v.1-2. Berlin, 1865-66.
Arc 1668.5.3 Rentzmann, W. Numismatisches Legenden-Lexicon. Berlin, 1881.
Arc 1668.6 Sperling, Otto. De nummorum bracteatorum et cavorum. Lubecae, 1700.
Arc 1668.7 Casali, J. De nummulis Peioesa inscriptis. Romae, 1796.
Arc 1668.8 Perez Varela, H. Ensayo de un catalogo...de las medallas. Habana, 1863.
Arc 1668.10 Friedensburg, F. Die Symbolik der Mittlaltermünzen. v.1,2-3. Berlin, 1913-22. 2v.
Arc 1668.12 Klotz, C.A. Historia numorum contumeliosorum. Altenburgi, 1765. 2 pam.

Arc 1670 Numismatics - Special topics - Medals, Tokens, and Jetons - Folios [Discontinued]

Arc 1670.1 Heiss, A. Les médailleurs de la Renaissance. v.3,8. Paris, 1883. 2v.
Htn Arc 1670.2* Evelyn, J. Numismata. A discourse of medals. London, 1697.
Arc 1670.3 Iversen, J. Unedited and rare Russian medals. St. Petersburg, 1874.
Arc 1670.4 Durand, Anthony. Médailles et jetons des numismates. Genève, 1865.
Arc 1670.5 Fournie, H. Les jetons des Doyens...de Paris. Chalon-sur-Saone, 1907.
Arc 1670.6F Hague. Koninklijk Kabinet van Munten. Les médailles et plaquettes modernes. v.1-6. Haarlem, 1899-1900.
Arc 1670.7F Milford Haven, L.A.M. Naval medals. London, 1921-28. 2v.
Arc 1670.50F Mazerolle, Fernand. Claude de Héry, médailleur du roi Henri III. Paris, 18- ?
Arc 1670.51 Feuardent, F. Jetons et méreaux depuis Louis IX...consulat. Paris, 1904. 2v.
Arc 1670.51.2 Feuardent, F. Jetons et méreaux depuis Louis IX...plandres. London, 1907.
Arc 1670.52 Hirsch, Jacob. Kunstmedaillen und Plaketten des XV. bis XVII. Jahrhunderts. München, 1908.
Arc 1670.53 Lorichs, G.D. de. Recherches numismatiques...les médailles celtiberiennes. Paris, 1852.
Arc 1670.54F Barnard, F.P. The casting-counter and the counting board...numismatics. Oxford, 1916.
Htn Arc 1670.56F* Hedlinger, J.K. Oeuvre du chevalier Hedlinger. Basle, 1776.
Htn Arc 1670.56.5F* Hedlinger, J.K. Explication historique et critique des médailles de l'oeuvre du Chevalier Hedlinger. Basle, 1778.
Arc 1670.57F Habich, Georg. De Medaillon der italienischen Renaissance. Stuttgart, 1924.

Arc 1671 Numismatics - Special topics - Medals, Tokens, and Jetons - Pamphlet volumes

Arc 1671 Pamphlet box. Numismatics. Medals.
Arc 1671.01 Pamphlet box. Numismatics. Medals.

Arc 1675 Numismatics - Special topics - Medals, Tokens, and Jetons - General works

Arc 1675.1 Lawrence, R.H. Medals by Giovanni Carino. N.Y., 1883.
Arc 1675.2 Armand, A. Les médailleurs italiens. Paris, 1879.
Arc 1675.3 Armand, A. Les médailleurs italiens. v.1-2. 2. éd. Paris, 1883.
Arc 1675.3.7 Fabriczy, C. von. Italian medal. London, 1904.
Arc 1675.3.9 Johnson, Stephen C. Le rivendicazioni italiane del Trentino...nelle medaglie. Milano, 1919-20.
Arc 1675.4 Robert, Charles. Les médailleurs de la Renaissance. Paris, 1882.
Arc 1675.5 Vallet de Viriville, A. Notice historique sur la médaille...en souvenir de l'expulsion. Paris, n.d.
Htn Arc 1675.6* Roville, G. Prima-seconda parte del prontuario de le medaglie de piu illustri et fulgenti huomini et donne. Lione, 1553.
Htn Arc 1675.6.5* Roville, G. Promtuarii iconum insigniorum a secule homenum. pt.1-2. 2. ed. Lugduni, 1581.
Arc 1675.7 Serie dei conj di medaglie pontificie da Martino V. Roma, 1824.
Arc 1675.7.5 Lincoln, W.S. and Son, firm, auctioneers, London. A descriptive catalogue of papal medals. London, 1898.
Arc 1675.8 Hildebrand, B.E. Minnespenningar öfver svenska män och qvinnor. Stockholm, 1860.
Arc 1675.9 Bildt. Les médailles romaines de Christine de Suède. Rome, 1908.
Arc 1675.10 Foville, J. de. Pisanello et les médailleurs italiens. Paris, 1908.
Arc 1675.10.5 Hill, G.F. Pisanello. London, 1905.
Arc 1675.10.7 Calabi, A. Pisanello. Milano, 1928.
Arc 1675.10.9 Olivieri, A. Monete e medaglie degli Spinola di Tassarolo. Genova, 1860.

Arc 1675 Numismatics - Special topics - Medals, Tokens, and Jetons - General works - cont.

Arc 1675.11 Rosenberg, S. Medaillen auf Privat-Personen. Frankfurt, n.d.
Arc 1675.12 Rondot, N. Les médailleurs et l. graveurs de monnaies. Paris, 1904.
Arc 1675.13 Bernhart, M. Medaillen und Plaketten. Berlin, 1911.
Arc 1675.14 Rosa, A. Coleccion de leyes, decretos. Buenos Aires, 1891.
Arc 1675.15 Longpérier, A. de. Médailles de rois Perses de la Dynastie Sassanide. Paris, 1840.
Arc 1675.16 De La Tour, H. Jean de Candida. Paris, 1895.
Arc 1675.17 Storer, H.R. Medals and tokens of Rhode Island. Boston, 1895.
Arc 1675.17.5 Storer, H.R. Medals, jetons and tokens illustrative of obstetrics and gynaecology. Bridgeport, Conn., 1887.
Arc 1675.17.10 Storer, H.R. Medicina in nummis. Boston, 1931.
Arc 1675.19 Russia. Monetnyi. Opisanie russkikh medalei. Sankt Peterburg, 1908.
Arc 1675.19.5 Iversen, I. Beitrag zur russischen Medaillenkunde. St. Petersburg, 1870.
Arc 1675.19.10F Iversen, I. Medaillen auf die Thaten Peter des Grossen. St. Petersburg, 1872.
Arc 1675.19.15 Shaten, Anatolii V. Sovetskaia memorial'naia medal', 1917-1967. Moskva, 1970.
Arc 1675.19.20 Rikhter, Vladimir G. Sobranie trudov po russkoi voennoi medalistike i istorii. v.1-2. Parizh, 1972.
Arc 1675.20F British Museum. Department of Coins and Medals. Select Italian medals of the Renaissance. London, 1915.
Arc 1675.20.10 Hill, George F. Portrait medals of Italian artists of the Renaissance. London, 1912.
Arc 1675.20.25F Italy. Esercito Corpo di Stato Maggiore. Ufficio Storico. Nel I. centenario della istituzione delle medaglie al valore. Roma, 1933.
Arc 1675.21 Velazquez, L.J. Congeturas sobre las medallas de los reyes godos y suevos de España. Malaga, 1759. 2 pam.
Arc 1675.22F American Numismatic Society. Catalogue of international exhibition of contemporary medals. N.Y., 1911.
Arc 1675.22.5 American Numismatic Society. International medallic exhibition of the American Numismatic Society. N.Y., 1910.
Arc 1675.22.10 American Numismatic Society. International medallic exhibition of the American Numismatic Society. Catalogue. N.Y., 1910.
Arc 1675.23 Froehner, Vilhelm. Les medaillons de l'Empire romain depuis le règne d'Auguste jusqu'à Priscus Attale. Paris, 1878.
Htn Arc 1675.23.5* Morganti, Bento. Nummismalogia, ou Breve recopilação de algunas medalhas dos emperadores romanos de ouro. Lisboa, 1737.
Arc 1675.24 Fleming, J.W. Medals, clasps, and crosses, military and naval in the collection of J.W. Fleming. Brighton, 1871.
Arc 1675.25 Nocz, Henry. Les Duvivier. Paris, 1911.
Htn Arc 1675.26* Florez, Enrique. Medallas de la colonias, municipios y pueblos antiguos de España. Madrid, 1757-73. 3v.
Arc 1675.27 Andorfer, Karl. Musica in nummis. Wien, 1907.
Arc 1675.27.5F Andorfer, Karl. Musica in nummis. Wien, 1901.
X Cg Arc 1675.29 Marx, Roger. Les medailleurs modernes, 1789-1900. Paris, 190-.
Arc 1675.30 Salgado, Vicente. Conjecturas sobre huma medallia de bronze. Lisboa, 1784.
Arc 1675.31 Lopes Fernandes, Manuel Bernardo. Memoria das medallias e condecorações port. Lisboa, 1861.
Arc 1675.35 Meili, Julius. Die Werke des Medailleur's Hans Frei in Basel, 1894-1906. Zürich, 1906.
Arc 1675.36 Lamas, A. Portuguese medals. Lisbon, 1905-10. 12 pam.
Arc 1675.37 Costa, Luiz X. da. Domingos Antonio de Sequeira e Francesco Vieira Lusitano. Lisboa, 1923. 2 pam.
Arc 1675.37.15 Oporto, Portugal. Museu Municipal. Catalogo das moedas portuguesas. Porto. 1-2,1929-1934
Arc 1675.38 Victoria and Albert Museum. Catalogue of Italian placquettes. London, 1924.
Arc 1675.45 Patin, Charles. Introduction à l'histoire par la connoissance des medailles. Paris, 1665.
Arc 1675.47 Ribagarza, Martin de Gurrea y Aragon. Discursos de medallas y antiguedades. Madrid, 1903.
Arc 1675.49F Mazzuchelli, G.M. Museum Mazzuchellianum. Venetiis, 1761-63. 2v.
Arc 1675.49.5F Mazzuchelli, G.M. Museum Mazzuchellianum. Venetiis, 1761-63. 2v.
Arc 1675.50 Mondini, R. Spigolando tra medaglie e date, 1848-71. Livorno, 1913.
Arc 1675.51 Poland. Mennica Panstwowa. Katalog wejborów. Warszawa, 19- ?
Arc 1675.51.5 Bentkowski, F. Spis medalów poliskich lub z dziejami krainy polskiej stycznych. Warszawa, 1830.
Arc 1675.51.10 Raczynski, E. Le médailleur de Pologne. Berlin, 1845. 4v.
Arc 1675.51.15F Tyszkiewicz, E. Sammlung von Medaillen. Riga, 1871.
Arc 1675.51.25 Wichura-Zajdel, E. Sląski medalier Jan Wysocki. Katowia, 1961.
Arc 1675.52 Sambon, Giulio. Catalogo delle medaglie del rinascimento e moderne di uomini illustri. Roma, 1883.
Arc 1675.53F Jocelyn, Arthur. The orders, decorations and medals of the world. London, 1934.
Arc 1675.54 Samlung merkwürdiger Medaillen. Nürnbueg. 1-8,1737-1744 8v.
Arc 1675.55 British Museum. Department of Coins and Medals. Synopsis of the contents of the British Museum. London, 1881.
Arc 1675.56 Gray, J.M. James and William Tassie. Edinburgh, 1894.
Arc 1675.57 Storelli, A. Jean-Baptiste Nini. Tours, 1896.
Arc 1675.58 Brenner, V.D. The art of the medal. N.Y., 1910.
Arc 1675.59 De Kay, Charles. A brief word on medals. N.Y., 1910.
Arc 1675.63 Morin, Victor. Les médailles décerniés aux Indien. Ottawa, 1916.
Arc 1675.65 Grotemeyer, Paul. Da ich het die gestalt. München, 1957.
Arc 1675.70 Günzburger, Julius. Medaillen badischer Klöster. Nürnberg, 1930.
Arc 1675.75 Bibliothèque Nationale, Paris. Exposition: Effigies et portraits. Paris? 1957.
Arc 1675.80 Bahrfeldt, Max. Die Schaumünzen der Universität Halle-Wittenberg. Halle, 1926.
Arc 1675.85 Katz, Viktor. Die erzgebirgische Prägmedaille des XVI. Jahrhundert. Praha, 1932.
Arc 1675.86 Katz, Viktor. Medaile na přátelstir a při buzné památky. Praha, 1938.
Arc 1675.90 Probszt, Günther. Ludwig Neufahrer. Wien, 1960.
Arc 1675.91 Pachinger, A.M. Wallfahrts-, Bruderschafts- und Weihe. Wien, 1908.

Arc 1675 Numismatics - Special topics - Medals, Tokens, and Jetons - General works - cont.

Arc 1675.92 Probszt, Günther. Die Kärntner Medaillen. Klagenfurt, 1964.
Arc 1675.93 Chamberlain, G.S. American medals and medalists. Annandale, Va., 1963.
Arc 1675.94 Respublička Izložba Hrvatskih Medalja i Plaketa. 1st, Zagreb, 1964-65. Medalja u hrvatskoj. Zagreb, 1964?
Arc 1675.95 Todorović, Nada. Jugoslovenske i inostrane medalje. Beograd, 1964.
Arc 1675.96F Johns Hopkins University. Medals relating to medicine and allied sciences in the numismatic collection. Baltimore, 1964.
Arc 1675.97 Dresden. Historisches Museum. Order und Ehrenzeichen der Deutschen Demokratischen Republik. Dresden, 1964.
Arc 1675.98 Zaretti, Vincenzo. Della medaglie di Murano. Bologna, 1965.
Arc 1675.99 Patrignani, Antonio. Le medaglie di Leone XII, 1823-1829. Catania, 1938.
Arc 1675.100 Marvin, William Theophilus Rogers. Materials for a catalogue of masonic medals. Boston, 1877.
Arc 1675.102 Hauek, Karl. Goldbrakteaten aus Sievern. München, 1970.
Arc 1675.104 Probszt, Günther. Die geprägten Schaumünzen Innerösterreichs; Steinmark, Kärnten, Krain. Zürich, 1928.
Arc 1675.106 Nikolić, Desanka. Naša odlikovanja do 1941. Beograd, 1971.

Arc 1680 Numismatics - Special topics - Medals, Tokens, and Jetons - Tokens

Arc 1680.1 Burn, J.H. A descriptive catalogue of the London traders, tavern and coffee-house tokens. London, 1855.
Arc 1680.2 Bushnell, C.I. An arrangement of tradesmen's cards, political tokens; also election medals. N.Y., 1858.
Arc 1680.3 Bushnell, C.I. An historical account of the first three business tokens issued in N.Y. N.Y., 1859.
Arc 1680.4 Waters, A.W. Notes...eighteenth century tokens. Leamington, 1906.
Htn Arc 1680.4.5* Waters, A.W. Token coinage of South London...eighteenth and nineteenth centuries. Leamington, 1904.
Arc 1680.5 Stainsfield, C.W. Descriptive catalogue of Australian tradesmen's tokens. London, 1883.
Arc 1680.6 Davis, William John. The nineteenth century token coinage. London, 1904.
Arc 1680.6.1 Davis, William John. The nineteenth century token coinage of Great Britain. London, 1969.
NEDL Arc 1680.6.5 Davis, William John. The token coinage of Warwickshire. Birmingham, 1895.
X Cg Arc 1680.7 Dalton, R. The provincial token - coinage of the eighteenth century. 1-9 2v.
Arc 1680.8 Brief particulars...eighteenth century tokens...county of Middlesex. n.p., 1914?
Arc 1680.9 Boyne, William. Tokens issued in seventeenth century England...by corporations. London, 1858.
Arc 1680.9.3 Boyne, William. Trade tokens...seventeenth century...England, Wales and Ireland. London, 1889. 2v.
Arc 1680.10 Shiells, Robert. Story of the token. N.Y., 1891.
Arc 1680.10.5 Brook, A.J.S. Communion tokens of the established Church of Scotland. Edinburgh, 1907.
Arc 1680.10.9 Tenney, M.M. Communion tokens. Grand Rapids, 1936.
Arc 1680.11 Photographs of merchant and political medals...of the United States...1825-1845. n.p., n.d.
Arc 1680.12 Longman, W. Tokens of the eighteenth century connected with booksellers. London, 1916.
Arc 1680.13 Simpson, Justin. List of the Lincolnshire series of tradesmen's tokens. London, 1880.
Arc 1680.14 Atkins, James. The tradesmen's tokens of the eighteenth century. London, 1892.
Arc 1680.15 Ramsden, H.A. Siamese porcelain and other tokens. Yokohama, 1911.
Arc 1680.16 Wiltshire Archaeological and Natural History Society, Devizes. Museum. Catalogue of the collection of Wiltshire trade tokens. Devizes, 1893.
Arc 1680.16.5 Whiting, John Roger Scott. Trade tokens; a social and economic history. Newton Abbot, 1971.
Arc 1680.17 Bibliothèque Nationale, Paris. Département des Médailles et Antiques. Collection Rouyer. Catalogue de la collection Rouyer. Paris, 1899-1910. 2v.
Arc 1680.18 Bell, Robert Charles. Tradesmen's tickets and private tokens: 1785-1819. Newcastle-upon-Tyne, 1966.
Arc 1680.20 Africana Museum, Johannesburg. Tokens of South Africa. Johannesburg, 1966.

WIDENER LIBRARY SHELFLIST, 56

ARCHAEOLOGY

CHRONOLOGICAL LISTING

Chronological Listing

No date

	Call number	Entry
	Arc 853.24.12F	Abbildungen zu dem I. u II. Heft der Römischen Alterthümer in Baiern. n.p., n.d.
	Arc 273.2.5	Académie Royale d'Archéologie de Belgique. Table des publications de l'Académie Royale d'Archéologie de Belgique, 1843 à 1900. Anvers? n.d.
	Arc 793.2	Adams, W.H.D. Pompeii and Herculaneum. London, n.d.
	Arc 905.18	Aigner, A. Hallstatt. München, n.d.
	Arc 925.70	Akademii Nauk URSR, Kyïv. Vseukrains'kii arkheologichnii komitet. Zapiski. Kyïv, n.d.
	Arc 925.65	Akademii Nauk URSR, Kyïv. Vseukrains'kii arkheologichnii komitet Tripil'ska kul'tura na Ukraini. Kyïv, n.d.
	Arc 66.1.127	Albertini, E. La composition dans les ouvrages philosophiques de Sévèque. n.p., n.d.
	Arc 1148.1.5	Allen, T.W. Greek abbreviation in the 15th century. London, n.d.
	Arc 30.1.2	Der alte Orient. Ergänzungsband. Leipzig, n.d. 2v.
	Arc 1.6.15	American journal of archaeology. Index to I-X and appendix to XI. Princeton, n.d.
	Arc 1.6.16	American journal of archaeology. Index to 2nd series. v.1-10, (1897-1906); v.11-70 (1907-66). N.Y., n.d. 2v.
	Arc 716.4.10	American School of Classical Studies at Athens. The Athenian Agora. Princeton, n.d. 18v.
	Arc 726.19	Angelucci, A. I cannoni veneti di Famagosta. Venezia, n.d.
	Arc 30.3.2	Annales du service des antiquités de l'Égypte. Index, 1-30. Le Caire, n.d. 3v.
Htn	Arc 1033.12.101*	Anno domini 1512. Reliquie plurimorū. n.p., n.d.
	Arc 1.16.5	Antiquity. General index, v.1-25, 1927-1951. Gloucester, Eng., n.d.
	Arc 853.117.5	Arbeits- und Forschungsberichte zur sächsischen Bodendenkmalspflege. Beiheft, 1-9, 1956-1971. n.p., n.d.
	Arc 1015.216	Armellini, M.J. Vetri cristiani della collezione di Campo-Santo. n.p., n.d.
	Arc 1033.12.22	Baffico, G.F. Istoria del Santo Sudario. Genova, n.d.
	Arc 1016.243	Balasko, F. Majesticus...Delatio...S. Stephani Manus Dexterae. Budae, n.d.
	Arc 1033.35.47	Barbier de Montault, X. Croix-reliquiare de l'eglise de S. Florent-les-Saumur. Angers, n.d.
	Arc 1264.4	Barbier de Montault, X. Le grand sceau de Raoul du Fou. Reims, n.d.
	Arc 1033.35.45	Barbier de Montault, X. Lettres testimoniales...portant donation d'un morceau de la vrai croix...Angers. Tours, n.d.
	Arc 1020.68	Barbier de Montault, X. Le trésor de la cathédrale de Moutiers. Tours, n.d.
	Arc 708.1	Barker, H.A. Description of the view of Athens. n.p., n.d.
	Arc 1390.1	Barthélemy, A.J.B.A. Nouveau manuel complet de numismatique du moyen age et moderne. Text et atlas. Paris, n.d. 2v.
	Arc 968.1.5	Beauchamp, W.M. Metallic ornaments of the New York Indians. n.p., n.d.
	Arc 1033.17.136	Bédouet, Z. Pélérinage de la sainte ceinture au Puy-Notre Dame. Paris, n.d.
	Arc 1033.120	Beheim, J.C. Dissertatio...de archeiois sive tabulariis sacris. Norimburgi, n.d.
	Arc 736.2	Beulé, C.E. Les temples de Syracuse. n.p., n.d.
	Arc 1356.4	Bible coins...facsimile of coins in...scripture. London, n.d.
	Arc 875.38	Black, George F. Descriptive catalogue of antiquities in Ayrshire. n.p., n.d.
	Arc 1480.8	Blancard, Louis. L'aureus romain se divisait en six-millièmes. v.1-2. Marseille, n.d.
	Arc 1500.11	Blancard, Louis. Des monogrammes...deniers capétiens. Marseille, n.d.
	Arc 1494.2	Blancard, Louis. Essai d'interpretation des lettres B.N.M...dinars. Marseille, n.d.
	Arc 1500.19	Blancard, Louis. Le gros tournois est imite du sarrazinas Chrétien d'Acre. n.p., n.d.
	Arc 1500.7	Blancard, Louis. Les marcs de la ville et de la cour romaine d'Avignon. Tours, n.d. 2 pam.
	Arc 1390.5	Blancard, Louis. Rapport...concernant le trésor de Vallon. Marseille, n.d.
	Arc 1480.10	Blancard, Louis. Sur les chiffres romaines ou grecs...des monnaies impériales. Marseille, n.d.
	Arc 1433.16	Blancard, Louis. Sur l'origine du monnayage musulman. Paris, n.d.
	Arc 1500.12	Blancard, Louis. Sur quelques points obscurs de la numismatique de Charles VIII. Paris, n.d.
	Arc 1356.3	Blancard, Louis. Le trésor d'Auriol et les dieux nègres de la Grèce. Marseille, n.d.
	Arc 823.10.15PF	Blanchet, A. Carte archéologique de la Gaule romaine. pts.8-9. Paris, n.d.
	Arc 1274.5	Blood, J.H. English seals. London, n.d.
	Arc 858.20	Bloxam, M.H. Fragmenta sepulchralia. Sepulchral and early monumental remains of Great Britain. n.p., n.d.
	Arc 853.26	Blume, T. The treasure-trove of Hildesheim. Hildesheim, n.d.
	Arc 710.2	Boetticher, C. Bericht über die Untersuchungen auf der Akropolis von Athen. n.p., n.d.
	Arc 785.15.9	Boni, G. Trajan's column. (The British Academy). London, n.d.
	Arc 1335.31	Boudeau, E. Catalogue général illustré de monnaies antiques. 2. ed. Paris, n.d.
	Arc 1335.31.3	Boudeau, E. Catalogue général illustré de monnaies françaises. Paris, n.d.
	Arc 66.1.126	Boulanger, André. Relius Aristide. n.p., n.d.
	Arc 935.7	Bourquelot, Félix. La colonne serpentine à Constantinople. Paris, n.d.
	Arc 1030.11	Bourquelot, M.F. Inscriptions chrétiennes trouvées en Italie. n.p., n.d.
	Arc 547.12	British Museum. A guide to the 1st and 2nd Egyptian rooms. London, n.d.
	Arc 66.8.2	British School at Athens. British School at Athens...index, 1-32. London, n.d. 2v.
	Arc 726.95F	Brusin, G. Aquileia. n.p., n.d.
	Arc 673.5	Bulletin de Correspondance Hellénique. Fouilles de Délos exécutées de M. de Loubat 1904-1907. Paris, n.d.
	Arc 66.4.1	Bulletino di archeologia cristiana. Indici generali, 1882-1889. 4. serie. Roma, n.d.
	Arc 66.7.2	Bulletino di commissione archeologico municipale. Indici, 1872-1885. Roma, n.d. 3v.
	Arc 905.5	Burton, R.F. Notes on the castellieri or prehistoric ruins of the Istrian Peninsula. Trieste, n.d.
	Arc 1510.8.10	Cappe, H.P. Die Mittelalter-Münzen von Münster. Dresden, n.d.

No date - cont.

	Call number	Entry
	Arc 1025.47	Les catacombes de Rome. Conférence. Paris, n.d.
	Arc 1053.6.4	Catalogue of...Theodor Graf collection. n.p., n.d.
	Arc 1033.44.9	Cavedoni, C. Dell'origine...IHS del SS. Nome de Gesú. Modena, n.d.
	Arc 1030.3.11	Cavedoni, C. Dichiarazione di due antiche gemme incise. Modena, n.d.
	Arc 1480.30F	Caylus, A.C.P. Numismata aurea imperatorum Romanorum. n.p., n.d.
	Arc 390.3.25	Cenni biografici di Carlo Fea. Roma, n.d.
	Arc 1033.17.151	Cerf. Notice sur la relique...Cathédrale de Reims. n.p., n.d.
	Arc 1033.35.61	Ceva Grimaldi, F. Su la vera forma delle croce di N. Signore. Medina, n.d.
	Arc 1540.6A	Chalmers, R. History of currency in the British colonies. London, n.d.
	Arc 380.207	Chevalier, N. Recherche curieuse d'antiquité. Utrecht, n.d.
	Arc 1349.55	Ciampi, Ignazio. Benedetto Pistrucci. n.p., n.d.
	Arc 1033.12.59	Ciprian, E.S. Diss. eccl. pentas. De sudore Christi. Jenae, n.d.
	Arc 865.4	Clapperton, W. Stonehenge handbook. Salisbury, n.d.
	Arc 552.2	Cloquet, L. L'art monumental des Égyptiens et des Assyriens. n.p., n.d.
	Arc 790.207	Cocchia, E. La forma del Vesuvio nelle pitture...antiche. n.p., n.d.
	Arc 1033.12.172	Collection de pièces sur le saint clou veneri à Tours. n.p., n.d.
Htn	Arc 1268.5*	A collection of seals - mostly German. n.p., n.d.
	Arc 642.2.15	Collignon, Maxime. L'archéologie grecque. Paris, n.d.
	Arc 861.21.5	Colls, J.M.N. Letters upon some early remains discovered in Yorkshire. v.1-2. n.p., n.d.
	Arc 968.1.2	Conover, G.S. Reasons why the state should acquire the famous burial mound of the Seneca Indians. n.p., n.d.
	Arc 66.1.128	Constant, G. Confession a l'Allemagne. n.p., n.d. 2v.
	Arc 1033.12.159	Conti, G.B. Dell'origine invenzione...simulacro di Gesu Crocifisso...Volto santo. Lucca, n.d.
	Arc 247.4.2	Copenhagen. Mémoires de la Société Royale des Antiquaires du Nord (1840-44). Copenhagen, n.d.
	Arc 1020.116	Les corps saints de l'insigne Basilique Saint Saturnin de Toulouse. Toulouse, n.d.
	Arc 66.1.125	Courby, Fernand. Les vases grecs à reliefs. n.p., n.d.
	Arc 1033.12.25	Cyprian, E.S. Facias Christi. Helmestad, n.d.
	Arc 1335.33	D'Angers, D. Catalogue général de monnaies, médailles et jetons. Paris, n.d.
	Arc 1033.12.113	Davin, V. Sainte tunique. Discours...Argeteuil...1865. Paris, n.d.
	Arc 1033.44.19	De monogrammate D.N. Jesu Christe. n.p., n.d.
	Arc 830.16.9	De Fontenay, H. Notice des tableaux, Dessins. Autun, n.d.
	Arc 1027.25.51	Des travaux de M. de Rossi. Arras, n.d.
Htn	Arc 758.2*	Dosio, G.A. Urbis Romae aedificae illustrae quae supersunt reliquiae. n.p., n.d.
	Arc 1033.19	Du Camp, M. Iconographie chrétienne. n.p., n.d.
	Arc 586.5	Egypt Exploration Society. The proposed excavations at Tell-el-Amarna. n.p., n.d.
Htn	Arc 1025.66*	Englefield, T.B. Some of the notes...on various subjects, especially the catacombs. n.p., n.d.
Htn	Arc 1660.6*	Fleurimont, G.R. Médailles du règne de Louis XV. n.p., n.d.
	Arc 1583.2	Fraehn, C.M.J. Aperçu sur les monnaies russes. n.p., n.d. 2 pam.
	Arc 1433.10	Fraehn, C.M.J. Beiträge zur Muhammedanischen Münzkunde. Berlin, n.d.
	Arc 1428.4	Friedländer, J. Frankische im Orient geprägte Münzen. n.p., n.d.
	Arc 549.5	Fuscaldo, Perla. Egyptian archaeology. n.p., n.d. 3 pam.
	Arc 1020.81	Galeron, F. Sur un reliquare...monastère de St. Évroult. n.p., n.d.
	Arc 513.16	Gallois, E. Asie-Mineure et Syrie. Paris, n.d.
	Arc 1500.48	Garnier, Alphonse. La monnaie de Troyes de 1422 à 1434. n.p., n.d.
	Arc 1033.9.5	Garrucci, R. Descrizioni dei vetri ornati di figure in oro. n.p., n.d.
	Arc 1033.9	Garrucci, R. Nuova interpretazione di un vetro cimiteriale. n.p., n.d.
	Arc 1018.18.2	Garrucci, R. Opuscoli di archeologia christiana e profana. Roma, n.d.
	Arc 1025.31.3	Gaume, J. Histoire des catacombes de Rome. Paris, n.d.
	Arc 7.1	Gazette archéologique. Paris, n.d. 14v.
	Arc 7.1.2	Gazette archéologique. v.7. Paris, n.d.
	Arc 1015.215	Giovanni, V. di. Palermo sotterranea. Palermo, n.d.
	Arc 1033.17.54	Goldonowski, A. Historia...B.V. Maria Claromontanae s. imaginis origine Jerosolymis Constantinopolim. n.p., n.d.
	Arc 843.56.5	Gomzalez Simancos, M. Sagunto. 1. ed. Sagunto? n.d.
	Arc 858.24.5F	Great Britain. Ancient Monuments Advisory Committee. Report of the committee. London, n.d.
	Arc 983.1	Green, C.H. Catalogue of a unique collection of cliff dweller relics. Chicago? n.d.
	Arc 1335.8	Groux, D.E. Descriptive catalogue of coins belonging to the Historical Society of Maryland. n.p., n.d.
	Arc 790.206	Gusman, P. Pompei. Paris, n.d.
	Arc 950.205	Haldeman, S.S. On the contents of a rock retreat in Southeast Pennsylvania. n.p., n.d.
	Arc 1221.1	Hammer-Purgstall. Abhandlung über die Siegel der Araber, Perser. n.p., n.d.
	Arc 1540.7	Head, B.V. An account of the hoard of Anglo-Saxon coins found at Chancton farm, Sussex. n.p., n.d.
	Arc 935.15	Heuzy, Leon. Panthéon des rochers de Philippes. Paris, n.d.
	Arc 830.2.5	Hirmenech, H.P. Morbihan antiquités. Paris, n.d. 5 pam.
	Arc 66.1.120	Hirschauer, C. La politique de St. Pie V en France. Paris, n.d.
	Arc 1475.7.2	Hobler, F. Records of Roman history. n.p., n.d. 2v.
	Arc 1335.5	Hodges, D.M. Gold and silver coin chart manual. N.Y., n.d.
	Arc 957.2	Holmes, William H. Anthropological studies in California. n.p., n.d.
	Arc 1411.4	Hopkins, L.C. Origin and earlier history of Chinese coinage. n.p., n.d.
	Arc 543.6	Hough, W. The Bernadou collection in the United States National Museum. n.p., n.d.
	Arc 293.3PF	Istanbul. Russkii Arkheologicheskii Institut. Izvestiia. Atlas. Sofiia, n.d.
	Arc 1020.83	Jadart, H. Les anciens pupitres de Rheims. n.p., n.d.

No date - cont.

	Arc 194.1.2	Jahresschrift für die Vorgeschichte der sächsisch-thüringischen Länder. Register. v.1-32, 1954. Halle, n.d.
	Arc 600.1	Kiepert, H. Zur Topographie des alten Alexandria. Berlin, n.d.
	Arc 905.2	Knabl, R. Wo stand das "Flavium Solvense?" n.p., n.d.
	Arc 716.9	Köster, A. Das Stadion von Athen. Berlin, n.d.
	Arc 1033.35.37	Kohler, C. Réfugié à Jérusalem au VIe siècle. Nogent-le-Rotrou, n.d.
Htn	Arc 1033.17.52*	Kordecki, A. Nova gigantomachia contra...imagine...virgine...Lucea depictam. Czestochovia, n.d.
	Arc 853.35	Korhl, C. Neue prähistorische Funde aus Worms und Augsburg. n.p., n.d.
	Arc 1473.1.10	Lampros, Paulos. Anekdoton nomisma Saroykchan Emiry tēs Iōnias. n.p., n.d.
	Arc 726.2.2	Lasena, P. Dell'antico ginnasio napoletano. n.p., n.d.
	Arc 726.2	Lasena, P. Dell'antico ginnasio napoletano. n.p., n.d.
	Arc 1160.209F	Lavrov, P.A. Paleograficheskie snimki. Sankt Peterburg, n.d.
	Arc 1297.5	Leist, F. Die Notariats-Signete. Leipzig, n.d.
	Arc 830.117	Lévesque, L. Inscriptions da la ville de Saint-Maixent du Xe au XIXe siècle. n.p., n.d.
	Arc 861.16.2	Little, W.C. Roman fen road in Cambridgeshire. n.p., n.d.
	Arc 74.4.25	MacMillan, G.A. History of the Society for the promotion of Hellenic studies. n.p., n.d.
Htn	Arc 969.1.8*	Manuscripts. English. Effigy, or Symbolic mound in Licking County, Ohio. n.p., n.d.
	Arc 635.24	Maraghiannio, G. Antiquités crétoises. Vienne, n.d.
	Arc 1027.44	Marucchi, O. Di alcune iscrizioni...Basilia de S. Petronella. Roma, n.d.
	Arc 1027.5.18	Marucchi, O. La memoria dei santi...cimitero di Domitilla. n.p., n.d.
	Arc 1027.49	Marucchi, O. Osservazioni intorno al cimitero delle catacombe. n.p., n.d.
	Arc 925.3	Maury, A. Des monuments de la Russie connus sous le nom de Tumulus Tchoudes. Paris, n.d.
	Arc 810.20	Mayer, E. von. Pompeji in seiner Kunst. Berlin, n.d.
Htn	Arc 1335.12*	Mead, R. Museum Meadianum. London, n.d.
Htn	Arc 1335.12.2*	Mead, R. Museum Meadianum. London, n.d.
	Arc 1480.6	Medals of the Caesars. n.p., n.d.
	Arc 137.6	Mediaeval archaeology. Index. v.1-5, (1957-61). London, n.d.
	Arc 1033.17.181	Mély, F. de. Chemises de la Vierge. Chartres, n.d.
	Arc 510.218PF	Milet. Bd.1, Heft 5 (Tafeln); Bd.4, Atlas. Berlin, n.d. 3v.
	Arc 386.24.5	Millin, A.L. Notice sur la vie du Cardinal Borgia. n.p., n.d.
	Arc 955.2.13	Mindeleff, C. The repair of Casa Grande ruin, Arizona, in 1891. Washington, n.d. 2 pam.
	Arc 1033.17.31	Miracolo...Maria...Ancona. n.p., n.d. 2 pam.
	Arc 895.5	Montelius, Oscar. La Suède préhistorique. Stockholm, n.d.
	Arc 1027.5.59	Monumenta subterranea selecta urbis Romae praesertim ex coemeterio Domitillae. Roma, n.d.
	Arc 1254.5	Mordtmann, A.D. Peri byzantinōn molybdoboyllōn. n.p., n.d.
	Arc 1016.216.3	Moreschi, L. Sulla sedia pontificale della basilica di S. Paolo. n.p., n.d.
	Arc 953.7	Morris, C. Extinct races of America - the mound builders. Review. n.p., n.d.
	Arc 925.16	Moskovskoe Arkheologicheskoe Obshchestvo. Izviestiia Kavkazskago otdieleniia. Vyp. 6 (1921). Tiflis, n.d.
	Arc 1428.5	Münter, F.C.K.H. Om Frankernes mynter i Orienten. v.1-2. n.p., n.d.
	Arc 858.21	Munro, Robert. Prehistoric Britain. London, n.d.
	Arc 1335.24	Museum Munterianum. v.1-3. Hauniae, n.d.
	Arc 925.155F	Mykopalicka polsko-radzi eckie w Mirmeki. Warszawa, n.d. 2v.
	Arc 1033.12.39	Narrazione della solennita...Torino...SS. Sindone. Torino, n.d.
	Arc 1033.17.624	Nelli, A. Origine della Madonna della Quercia di Viterbo. n.p., n.d.
	Arc 861.26	Newmarch, C.H. Remains of Roman art Corinum. London, n.d.
	Arc 830.6.8	Niepce, L. Archéologie lyonnaise. Lyon, n.d.
	Arc 635.201	Normand, C. Corpus des monuments grecs. Livre II: Lycosoura. Paris, n.d.
	Arc 720.210	Nottingham. Museum. Illustrated catalogue of classical antiquities. Nottingham, n.d.
	Arc 810.27	Nuova pianta degli scavi di Pompei. n.p., n.d.
Htn	Arc 1475.1.2F*	Occo, A. Imperatorum romanorum numismata. Milan, n.d.
	Arc 1588.6.2.15	Ölçer, Cüneyt. Yildivim Bayezid'in agullanu ait akçe ve mangirlav. Istanbul, n.d.
	Arc 501.1.3	Palestine exploration quarterly. Index, 1869-1892. London, n.d.
	Arc 501.1.4	Palestine exploration quarterly. Index, 1911-1963. London, n.d.
	Arc 1033.34.2	Palmieri, N. Notizie istoriche delle sacre catene del principe degli apostoli. n.p., n.d.
	Arc 983.4	Peet, S.D. Ancient village architecture in America. n.p., n.d.
	Arc 977.1	Peet, S.D. The emblematic mounds of Wisconsin. n.p., n.d.
	Arc 1027.50	Pellegrini, C. Il pensiero e il dogma cristiano. n.p., n.d.
	Arc 1405.1.3	Phayre, A.P. Numismata orientalia. v.3. pt.1-3. n.p., n.d.
	Arc 943.2	Phillips, H. A brief account of the more important public collections of American archaeology in the United States. n.p., n.d.
	Arc 1680.11	Photographs of merchant and political medals...of the United States...1825-1845. n.p., n.d.
	Arc 810.30	Pompeii. N.Y., n.d.
	Arc 1020.115	Poquet, A.E. De terra iheroslimitana...allate sunt relique. n.p., n.d.
	Arc 1050.202	Portraits I. Roman emperors. n.p., n.d.
	Arc 140.1.10	Prehistoric Society of East Anglia. Minor publications. n.p., n.d.
	Arc 969.1.7	Putnam, F.W. Iron from the Ohio mounds. v.2. n.p., n.d.
	Arc 545.201	Das Pyramidenfeld von Abusir. n.p., n.d.
	Arc 830.169	Quelques notes sur Noviodurum Biturigum. Bourges, n.d.
	Arc 1025.7.5	Raoul-Rochette, D. Tabelau des catacombes de Rome. Paris, n.d.
	Arc 1348.21	Rawlings, G.B. Coins and how to know them. N.Y., n.d.
	Arc 1033.35.39	Reinartz, J.L. Notice sur le reliquaire de la sainte croix...à Tongres. n.p., n.d.
	Arc 18.1.2	Revue archéologique. Index, 1860-1869. Paris, n.d.
	Arc 1033.35.81	Rioja, F. de. Titulo de la cruz de Christi. n.p., n.d.

No date - cont.

	Arc 82.1.2	Rome, Italy. École Française. Mélanges d'archéologie et d'histoire. Tables des tomes 58-72, 1941-60. Paris, n.d.
	Arc 1660.12	Rosa, A. Estudios numismaticos. Buenos Aires, n.d.
	Arc 1675.11	Rosenberg, S. Medaillen auf Privat-Personen. Frankfurt, n.d.
	Arc 1027.5.2	Rossi, G.B. de. Isigni scoperte nel cimitero di Domitilla. Roma, n.d.
	Arc 1020.9.80	Rossi, G.B. di. Incrementi del museo sacro della Biblioteca Vaticana di Leone XIII. Roma, n.d.
	Arc 815.12	Rostovtsev, M.I. Mifologicheskii peizazh 3-go pompeiaiskago stilia. n.p., n.d.
	Arc 66.1.122	Roussel, Louis. Grammaire descriptive du Roméique littéraire. Paris, n.d.
	Arc 292.40PF	Russia. Arkheologicheskaia Kommissiia. Compte rendu. St. Petersbourg, n.d.
	Arc 830.12	Sauvage, H.E. Notes d'archéologie gallo-romaine. Boulogne, n.d.
	Arc 1254.6	Schlumberger, G. Sceaux byzantins; les églises, les couvents, les palais. n.p., n.d.
	Arc 810.24	Schoener, R. Pompeii. Beschreibung der Stadt. Stuttgart, n.d.
	Arc 1433.24.5	Schott, W. W. Grigorjew's Beschreibung kufischer Münzen. n.p., n.d.
	Arc 1033.12.126	Schreck, J.A. Jesu...coronam spineam. Lipsiae, n.d.
Htn	Arc 1208.5.15*	Seals of Gianfrancesco Pico della Mirandola. n.p., n.d.
	Arc 1237.1	Seals of Siam. n.p., n.d.
	Arc 925.50.20	Sebastopol'. Khersoneskii Gosudarstvennyi Istoriko-Arkheologicheskii Muzei. Soobshcheniia. v.1-3. Simferopol', n.d. 2v.
	Arc 406.2	Sforza, G. Ennio Quirion Visconti Giacobino. n.p., n.d. 2 pam.
	Arc 861.19.5	Shortt, W.T.P. Collectanea curiosa antiqua Dunmonia. Londinium, n.d.
	Arc 1480.17	Shortt, W.T.P. Sylva antiqua iscana. Londini, n.d.
	Arc 1033.35.71	Sionnet, A. Lettre à...Piolin sur la legende hébraïque du titre de la viaie croix. n.p., n.d.
Htn	Arc 1163.17.10*	Sisson, C.J. Photographic slides of English manuscripts. n.p., n.d.
	Arc 861.41	Smith, H. Notes on prehistoric burial in Sussex. n.p., n.d.
	Arc 584.2.2	Société d'Archéologie Copte, Cairo. Bulletin. Index, 1-10, 1935-44. Le Caire, n.d.
	Arc 41.1.5	Society of Biblical Archaeology. Proceedings. Index, v.11-30. London, n.d. 2v.
	Arc 41.2.2	Society of Biblical Archaeology. Transactions. Index, v.1-9. London, n.d.
	Arc 1033.35.121	Sorio, B. Sunto storica della croce e del crocefisso nel suo svolgimento. n.p., n.d.
	Arc 830.29	Spencer-Smith, I. Précis...monument arabe du moyen âge en Normandie. Caen, n.d.
	Arc 861.44	Stevens, J. On newly discovered Roman remains at Finkley near Andover. London, n.d.
	Arc 1027.17	Stevenson, H. Das Coerneterium de H. Christina zu Bolsena. n.p., n.d.
	Arc 736.9F	Strazzeri, Niccolo. Teatro di Taormina. n.p., n.d.
	Arc 625.9	Sturgis, R. Classical archaeology on the shores of the Mediterranean. Rochester, n.d.
	Arc 1027.53	Taglialatela, G. Dell'antica basilica e della catacomba di Prata. n.p., n.d.
	Arc 1033.12.42	Talamini, G. Della Santissima Sindone e la vanda dei piedi. Torino, n.d.
	Arc 1033.12.171	Terris, F. Saint mors de Carpentras et son reliquaire. n.p., n.d.
	Arc 1433.12.3	Tornberg, Carl Johan. Découvertes récentes de monnaies koufiques. Bruxelles, n.d.
	Arc 1025.33	Treat, J.H. The catacombs of Rome. n.p., n.d.
	Arc 810.35	Twelve photographs of Pompeii. n.p., n.d.
	Arc 1335.25	Tychsen, T.C. De numis cuficis in biblio. regia Gottingense. n.p., n.d.
	Arc 530.155	Ülgen, Ali Saim. Collection of cuttings from Turkish archeological periodicals. n.p., n.d.
	Arc 600.215	United Arab Republic. Centre of Documentation and Studies on Ancient Egypt. Kalabsha. Cairo, n.d.
	Arc 628.11	Urlichs, L. von. Beiträge zur Kunstgeschichte. Leipzig, n.d.
	Arc 1675.5	Vallet de Viriville, A. Notice historique sur la médaille...en souvenir de l'expulsion. Paris, n.d.
	Arc 1033.12.40F	Vassalli, M. Discorso sopra la sacra sindone...Torino. Parma, n.d.
	Arc 273.9	Vereeniging tot Bevordering der Kennis van de Antieke Beschaving. Bulletin. Index, v.1-40, 1926-1965. Leiden, n.d.
	Arc 505.5.23	Vogüé. Note sur le Temple de Jerusalem. n.p., n.d.
	Arc 1020.73.17	Wailly, J.N. de. Récit...sur les translations...1239 et 1241...reliques de la Passion. Nogent-le-Rotrou, n.d.
	Arc 590.2	Warren, J.C. Description of an Egyptian mummy. Boston, n.d.
	Arc 810.17	Weichardt, C. Pompeii before its destruction. Leipzig, n.d.
	Arc 1468.59	Weidauer, Liselotte. Probleme der frühen Elektronprägung. n.p., n.d.
	Arc 691.2	Weller. The cave at Vari. n.p., n.d.
	Arc 716.2.5	Wheeler, James R. The theatre of Dionysus. n.p., n.d.
	Arc 685.1	Wide, S. Ausgrabungen auf Kalaureia. n.p., n.d.
	Arc 857.5	Windle, Bertram. A collection of archaeological pamphlets on Roman remains...Great Britain. n.p., n.d. 12v.
	Arc 399.2	Zaratti-Bianco, Umberto. Paolo Orsi. n.p., n.d.
	Arc 55.1.3	Zeitschrift der Deutschen Palaestina-Vereins. Index, v.6-25. Leipzig, n.d. 2v.

1500-1509

Htn	Arc 1033.12.54*	Ista sunt queda notabilia de passione Christi...de biblia hebreorum. Venetiis, 1506.
Htn	Arc 767.6*	Liber de vilitate coditionis humane Mirabilia Romae. Paris, 1509.

1510-1519

Htn	Arc 1033.12.58*	Vigerius, M. Controversia de excellentia instrumentorum passionis. Roma, 1512.
	Arc 1510.13	Schlegel, C. Schediasma de nummis antiquis. Dresdae, 1518.

Chronological Listing

1520-1529

Htn	Arc 1020.9.114*	Albertini, F. Mirabilia Roma. Firenze, 1520.
Htn	Arc 772.3*	Albertini, F. De Roma prisca et nova varii auctores. Romae, 1523?
Htn	Arc 760.4*	Fulvio, A. Antiquitates urbis. Roma, 1527.

1530-1539

Htn	Arc 1016.240*	Apianus, P. Inscriptiones sacrosanctae vetustatis...Romanae. Ingolstadii, 1534.

1540-1549

Htn	Arc 767.2.2*	Marliani, B. Urbis Romae topographia. Colophon, 1544.
Htn	Arc 760.4.5*	Fulvio, A. De urbis antiquitatibus. Roma, 1545.
Htn	Arc 760.1*	Faunus, L. Delle antichità della città di Roma. Venice? 1548.
Htn	Arc 760.1.5*	Faunus, L. De antiquitiae Romae. Venetiis, 1549.

1550-1559

Htn	Arc 767.6.2*	Mirabilia urbis Romae nova. Roma, 1550.
Htn	Arc 1675.6*	Roville, G. Prima-seconda parte del prontuario de le medaglie de piu illustri et fulgenti huomini et donne. Lione, 1553.
Htn	Arc 1373.7*	Strada, J. de. Epitome du thresor des antiquitez. Lyon, 1553.
Htn	Arc 1033.12.143*	Historia de como fue hallada la ymage del Sancto Crucifixo. Burgos? 1554?
Htn	Arc 1033.12.65*	Domenechi, D. De sanguine Christi tractatus. Venetiis, 1557.
	Arc 1668.4	Keller, D. Biltnusse der Rhömischen Keyseren. Zürich, 1558.

1560-1569

Htn	Arc 825.10F*	Poldo d'Albenas, J. Discours historial de l'antique et illustrie cité de Nismes. Lyon, 1560.
	Arc 767.10	Mauro, L. Le antichità della città di Roma. Venetia, 1562.
Htn	Arc 726.68*	Nazari, G.B. Bressa anticha. Bressa, 1562.
Htn	Arc 761.4*	Gamucci, B. Le antichita della città di Roma. Venetia, 1565.
Htn	Arc 1359.2*	Erizzo, S. Discorso sopra le medaglie de gli antichi. Venice, 1568.
Htn	Arc 761.4.3*	Gamucci, B. Le antichita della città di Roma. 2. ed. Vinegia, 1569.

1570-1579

Htn	Arc 1020.9.106*	Panvinus, Onuphrus. Veronesia fatris...de praecipius urbis. Romae, 1570.
	Arc 1510.20.5	Verzaichnus der Bösessmüntzsortens. n.p., 1571.
	Arc 1033.38.9	Bresnicio, C.B. Historia de Insigni Martyrio...Laurentii. Leipzig, 1572.
Htn	Arc 1510.3.7*	Stürmer, Wolff. Vortzeichnus und Gedräge der groben und kleinen Müntzsorten. Leipzig, 1572.
Htn	Arc 750.31*	DuPerac, E. I vestigi dell'antichità di Roma. Roma, 1575.
Htn	Arc 1020.96*	Bagatas, R. SS. episcoparum...antiqua monumenta. Venetiis, 1576.
Htn	Arc 785.13.60*	Palletus, F. Historia Fori Romani restituto et aucta per Philippum Broidaeum Ariensem. Buaci, 1576.
Htn	Arc 1475.5*	Orsini, F. Familiae Romanae. Rome, 1577.

1580-1589

Htn	Arc 761.4.5*	Gamucci, B. Le antichita della città di Roma. Vinegia, 1580.
Htn	Arc 1348.38*	Het thres oor aft schat van alle de specien. Gheprint Tautluerpen, 1580.
Htn	Arc 1033.12.32*	Pingone, E.F. Sindon evangelica. Augustae Taurinorum, 1581.
Htn	Arc 1675.6.5*	Roville, G. Promtuarii iconum insigniorum a secule homenum. pt.1-2. 2. ed. Lugduni, 1581.
Htn	Arc 1033.12.156*	Historia del santissimo Volto di S. Croce di Lucca. Lucca, 1582.
Htn	Arc 1033.12.64*	Ludecus, M. Historia von der Erfindung, Wunderwerken und Zerstörung der vermeinten Heiligenbluts zur Wilssnagk. Wittenberg, 1586.
Htn	Arc 1020.120*	Campos, Manoel de. Relaçam do solenne recebimento que se fez em Lisboa. Lisboa, 1588.
Htn	Arc 760.4.8*	Fulvio, A. L'antichita di Roma. Venetia, 1588.
Htn	Arc 761.4.9*	Gamucci, B. Le antichita della città di Roma. Vinegia, 1588. 2 pam.

1590-1599

Htn	Arc 720.14*	Fontana, D. Del modo tenuto...liobelisco vaticano. Roma, 1590.
Htn	Arc 1350.2*	Agostini, A. Dialoghi - intorno alle medaglie...altre antichità. Rome, 1592.
	Arc 1033.17.59	Bocchi, M.F. Opera sopra l'imagine. Fiorenza, 1592.
Htn	Arc 1020.90*	Farnese. Il santoario di Parma. Parma, 1593.
Htn	Arc 1077.2*	Lipsius, J. De cruce libri tres. Antverpiae, 1594.
Htn	Arc 845.210F*	Velser, Marcus. Rerum Augustanar. Vindelicar. Libri octo. Venetiis, 1594.
	Arc 1033.72	Ciampini, J. Explicatio 2 sarcophagorum...baptismatis. Roma, 1597.
Htn	Arc 1077.2.1*	Lipsius, J. De cruce libri tres...cum notis. 3. ed. Antverpiae, 1597.
Htn	Arc 1077.2.2*	Lipsius, J. De cruce libri tres. Parisiis, 1598.
Htn	Arc 1033.12.49*A	Paleotti, A. Esplicatione del sacro lenzvolo ove fu involto il Signore. Bologna, 1599.

1600-1609

Htn	Arc 1033.35.141*	Gretser, J. De cruce Christi. Inglodstadii, 1600. 3v.
Htn	Arc 1020.126*	López Madera, G. Discursos de la certidumbre de las reliquias descubiertas en Granada. Madrid, 1601.
	Arc 1660.13	Medina, J.T. Las medallas chilenas. Santiago, 1601.
	Arc 1020.126.5	López Madera, G. Historia y discursos de la certidumbre de las reliquias, láminas. Granada, 1602.
Htn	Arc 1478.5*	Hulsius, L. Impp. Romanorum numismatum series. Frankfort, 1603.
Htn	Arc 1020.32.5*	Morigi, P. Santuario della città e diocesi di Milano. Milano, 1603.

1600-1609 - cont.

Htn	Arc 1033.17.361*	Lipsius, I. Diva virgo hallensis. Antverp, 1604.
Htn	Arc 1033.17.362*	Denaise, Pierre. Dissertatio deidolo hallensi. n.p., 1605.
Htn	Arc 382.1*	Pignoria, L. Vetustissimae tabulae aeneae. Venetiis, 1605.
	Arc 1423.1	Waserus, C. De antiquis numis. Zürich, 1605.
Htn	Arc 1053.4*	Faber, Johannes. Illustrium imagines ex...Fuliri Ursini. Antwerpiae, 1606.
Htn	Arc 726.55*	Mazzella, S. Sito, et antichita della città di Pozzuolo e del sus amenissimo distretto. Napoli, 1606.
	Arc 1020.51.5	Winkeim, Erharde. Sacrarium Agrippinae...praecipuarum reliquarum. Coloniae, 1607. 2 pam.
	Arc 1076.3.19	Maggi, G. De tintinnalbulis. Hanoviae, 1608.
	Arc 1033.35.25	Camers, A.R. De particula ex pretioso...crucis...commentarius. Roma, 1609.
	Arc 1033.12.50	Paleotti, A. Tableau de mortification...stigmates...Christ...S. Suaire. Paris, 1609.

1610-1619

	Arc 1033.12.38	Balliani, C. Ragionamenti della sacra sindone. Torino, 1610.
Htn	Arc 1033.35.21F*	Bosio, I. Trionfante e gloriosa croce trattato. Roma, 1610.
	Arc 1033.35.85	Gretser, J. Hortus S. Crucis. Ingolstadii, 1610.
	Arc 1033.17.109	Soveral, Roque do. Historia do insigne aparecimento de N. Senhora da Luz. Lisboa, 1610.
	Arc 843.55	Suarez de Salazar, Juan B. Grandezas y antiguedades de la isla y ciudad de Cadiz. Cadiz, 1610.
Htn	Arc 1076.3.110*	Rocca, Angelo. De campanis commentarius. Romae, 1612.
	Arc 1020.47	Franciotti, C. Historia delle Miracolose Imagni...città di Lucca. Lucca, 1613.
	Arc 505.5.40	Estevan, M. Compendio del Rico Aparato, y Hermosa del templo de Salomon. Alcala, 1615.
Htn	Arc 1033.17.583*	Gonzalez de Mendoza, P. Historia del Monte Celia de Nuestra Señora de la Salceda. Granada, 1616.
	Arc 1020.100	Mutio, Mario. Delle reliquie insigni...chiesa de Bergamo. Bergamo, 1616.
	Arc 1033.12.57	Paleotti, A. Historia de Jesu Christi stigmatibus. Antverpiae, 1616.
	Arc 1478.26F	Augustin, A. Antiquitatum romanorum Hispanarumque in nummis veterum dialogi XI. Antverpiae, 1617.
	Arc 1020.6.5	Breve descrittione del sacro thesoro...San Marco. Milano, 1617.
Htn	Arc 1016.244*	Crux triumphans et gloriosa. Antwerp, 1617.
	Arc 1033.17.70	Malvasia, D. Venuta, et i progressi miracolosi della S. Madonna...S. Luca...1160-1617. Bononia, 1617.
	Arc 1020.95.11	Tiepolo, G. Trattato delle sanctissime reliquie...San Marco. Venet, 1617.
	Arc 1033.12.69	Vergaro, G.C. Racconto dell'apparato...espositione del Sangue Venetia...1617. Venezia, 1617.
Htn	Arc 1033.133*	Viseur, R. Recueil de la vie, mort, invention et miracles de S. Jean Baptiste. Amyens, 1618.

1620-1629

	Arc 1660.11	Luckius, J.J. Sylloge numismatum elegantiorum. Argentina, 1620.
Htn	Arc 1520.1*	Carte ou liste contenant le pris de chascun marcq. Anvers, 1621. 5 pam.
	Arc 1033.17.161	Lauro, G.B. De annulo pronubo...virginis...Perusiae. Roma, 1622.
Htn	Arc 767.2*	Marliani, B. L'antichità di Roma. Roma, 1622.
	Arc 1033.17.101	Astolfi, G.F. Historia universale delle imagini miracolose...Madre di Dio...tutte le parti del Mondo. Venezia, 1623.
	Arc 1033.12.30	Chifflet, J.J. De linteis sepulchralibus Cristi servatoris crisis historica. Antverpiae, 1624.
	Arc 736.2.9	Mirabella a Alagona, V. Dichiarazioni della pianta dell'antiche Siracuse. Napoli, 1625.
	Arc 1033.17.162	Lauro, G.B. De annulo proniebo...virginis...Perusiae. Colonia Agrippina, 1626.
	Arc 1538.10	Nummi Britannici historia. London, 1626.
Htn	Arc 756.2*	Boissard, J.J. Topographia Romae. pt.1-6. Frankfort, 1627. 2v.
	Arc 1520.3	Carte ou liste contenant le pris de chascun marcq. Anvers, 1627.
Htn	Arc 1373.2*	Savot, L. Discours sur les médailles antiques. Paris, 1627.
	Arc 1033.12.41	Solaro, A. Sindone evangelica, historica e theologica. Torino, 1627.
	Arc 1033.17.504	Brito Alão, M. de. Antiguidade da sagrada imagem de Nossa S. de Nazareth...Pederneira. Lisboa, 1628.

1630-1639

	Arc 1020.9.50	Severano, G. Memorie sacre delle sette chiese di Roma. Roma, 1630.
	Arc 1033.17.25	Zocca, I.M. Apparitione della Madonna Santissima di Misericordia di Savona. Modena, 1632.
	Arc 1033.12.51.3	Curtius, C. De clavis Dominicis liber. Antverpiae, 1634.
	Arc 1033.17.20	Historia breve della miracolosa imagine della Madre di Dio. Napoli, 1638.
	Arc 1020.23	Martinelli, F. Diaconia S. Agathae in subura. Roma, 1638.
	Arc 1033.12.23	Calcagnino, A. Dell'imagine Edessena. Genova, 1639.

1640-1649

Htn	Arc 1033.47.28*	Cardani, H. Neronis encomium. Amstelodami, 1640.
	Arc 830.16.11	Ladonne, E. Augustoduni amplissimae civitatis. Augustoduni, 1640.
Htn	Arc 861.2*	Somner, W. The antiquities of Canterbury. London, 1640.
Htn	Arc 1271.1.5*	Wree, Olivier de. Les sceaux des comtes de Flandre. Bruge, 1641.
	Arc 1033.17.131	Compendio dell'origine...della sacra cintura. Verona, 1642.
	Arc 1033.49	Canallotti, G.B. Vita di S. Severino e di S. Vittorio. Pariso, 1643.
	Arc 1033.12.157	Tofanelli, S. Primo ritratto del crofifisso...historia della miracolosa scultura. Napoli, 1644.
Htn	Arc 1050.204*	Icones, vitae et elogia...Romanorum. Antwerp, 1645.
	Arc 1016.241	Peyrat, G. du. L'histoire ecclesiastico...les antiquitez...de la chapelle et oratoire du Roy de France. Paris, 1645.

1640-1649 - cont.

Htn	Arc 1033.12.211*	Bartholini, T. De latere Christi aperto. Lugdunum Batavorum, 1646.
	Arc 595.13	Greaves, John. Pyramidographia. London, 1646.
	Arc 1020.9.99	Landucci, A. Origine del tempio. Roma, 1646.
Htn	Arc 1020.9.116*	Léon, François. Les merveilles de la ville de Rome. Rome, 1646.
	Arc 1033.130	Calcagnino, A. Historia del glorioso precursore di N.S.S. G. Battista. Genova, 1648.
Htn	Arc 720.204*	Panvini, O. Antiquitatum veronensium libri VIII. Padua, 1648.
Htn	Arc 1033.17.97*	Sánchez, Miguel. Imagen de la virgen Maria...de Guadalupe. México, 1648.

1650-1659

	Arc 758.3	Descrittione di Roma antica e moderna. Roma, 1650.
Htn	Arc 505.5.5*	Lightfoot, J. The temple. London, 1650.
Htn	Arc 362.1.20*	Manilli, Jacomo. Villa Borghese. Roma, 1650.
	Arc 1015.202	Bosio, A. Roma scotterranea. Roma, 1651. 2v.
Htn	Arc 545.200*	Kircher, A. Oedipus Aegyptiacus. v.1-3. Romae, 1652-54. 4v.
Htn	Arc 726.6*	Orsati, S. Monumenta patavina. Padova, 1652.
	Arc 1033.12.167	Buonafede, G. Sacro chiodo del redentore. Siena, 1653.
Htn	Arc 1070.201*	Liceti, F. De lucernis antiquorum reconditis libb. sex. Utini, 1653.
	Arc 1033.17.153	Sigoni, I. Relazione della venta a Montevarchi del socrosanto latte. Firenze, 1653.
	Arc 1033.12.31	Buonafede, G. Panegirici sacri a i misterii della S. Sindone. Asti, 1654.
Htn	Arc 1480.35F*	Croy, Charles. Regum et imperatorum Romanorum numismata. Antverpiae, 1654.
Htn	Arc 865.9.5*	Jones, Inigo. The most notable antiquity of Great Britain. London, 1655.
Htn	Arc 865.9*	Jones, Inigo. The most notable antiquity of Great Britain. London, 1655. 2 pam.
	Arc 1033.17.248	Lambert, R. Diva Virgo de Cortenbosch, eius miracula. Leodii, 1656.
	Arc 1016.222	Rasponi, C. De basilica et patriarchio Lateranensi. Roma, 1656.
	Arc 1033.17.102.2	Gumppenberg, G. Atlas Marianus sive de imaginibus deiparae. v.1-2. Ingaldeladii, 1657.
	Arc 1033.17.102	Gumppenberg, G. Atlas Marianus sive de imaginibus deiparae per orbem. Monachii, 1657. 2v.
	Arc 518.13	Menestrier, C.F. Symbolica Dianae Ephesiae statua a Claudio Menetreio exposita. Romae, 1657. 3 pam.
	Arc 1015.202.5	Bosio, A. Roma scotterranea. Paris, 1658.
	Arc 726.68.5	Nazari, G.B. Brescia antica. Brescia, 1658.
	Arc 1033.17.104	Stengel, K. Hoedoporicum Mariana Benedictinum seu historia de imaginibus. Augsbourg, 1659.

1660-1669

	Arc 1033.12.134	Sacro pellegrinaggio al Monte Sano per adorar il volto...del Salutor. Genova, 1660.
Htn	Arc 773.5F*	Sadeler, Marco. Nestigi della antichita di Roma. Roma, 1660.
	Arc 1033.35.17	Colá, C. Memorie historiche dell'apparitione delle croci. Napoli, 1661.
	Arc 1033.29	Miracles et bien-faits obtenus...invocation du...T. Xavier en ses reliques. Malines, 1661.
Htn	Arc 865.6*	Charleton, W. Chorea gigantum, or...Stone-Heng restored to the Danes. London, 1663.
	Arc 825.1	Deyron, J. Des antiquités de la ville de Nismes. Nîmes, 1663.
	Arc 1033.12.210	Jacob, J.N. Disputatio theologica de Vulneribus Christi. Wittenbergae, 1663.
Htn	Arc 1475.4*	Patin, C. Familiae Romanae. Paris, 1663.
Htn	Arc 1033.63*	Magi, H. De Tintinnabulis. Amstelodami, 1664. 2 pam.
Htn	Arc 1373.5*	Spanheim, E. Diss. de praestantia et usu numismata antiqua. Rome, 1664.
Htn	Arc 1033.131*	Du Cange, C. du F. Traite historique du chef de S. Jean Baptiste. Paris, 1665.
	Arc 505.5.37	Jehuda Leon, J. De templo Hierosolymitano. Helmaestadi, 1665.
	Arc 1675.45	Patin, Charles. Introduction à l'histoire par la connoissance des medailles. Paris, 1665.
	Arc 1033.17.202	Relación verdadera de la imagen...Alcay. Valencia, 1665.
Htn	Arc 1093.1*	Chimentelli, V. Marmor pisanum. Bononiae, 1666.
	Arc 768.1	Nardini, F. Roma antica. Roma, 1666.
	Arc 1020.9.102	Phoebeus, F. De indentitate cathedral...Sanct. Petrus Romae. Romae, 1666.
	Arc 1025.68	Bosio, Antonio. Abgebildetes unterirdisches Rom. Arnheim, 1668.
	Arc 1033.64	Levera, F. De invicta veritate anni, mensis, et diei. Roma, 1668.
Htn	Arc 1050.201*	Canini, G.A. Iconografia. Romae, 1669.
	Arc 1033.17.305	Guelfone. Orazione...Foggia...dell'icona...Santa Maria. Foggia, 1669.

1670-1679

	Arc 1033.12.51	Curtius, C. De clavis Dominicis liber. Antverpiae, 1670.
	Arc 1025.35	Bosio, A. Roma subterranea novissima. Arnhemi, 1671.
	Arc 1096.1	Scheffer, J. De re vehiculari veterum libri duo. Francofurti, 1671.
	Arc 1370.1	Patin, C. Thesaurus numismatum. Amsterdam? 1672.
Htn	Arc 1370.2*	Patin, C. Thesaurus numismatum. v.1-2. Amsterdam? 1672.
	Arc 1033.55.5	Soresini, I.M. De scala sancta ante S. Sanctorum in Lateran. Roma, 1672.
Htn	Arc 750.220F*	Bellori, G.P. Fragmenta vestigii veteris Romae. Colophon, 1673.
	Arc 1033.12.122	Lange, P. De lancea qua perfossum latus...Christi. Jena, 1673.
	Arc 1033.43.13	Soresinas, I.M. De capitibus S. apostolorum Petri et Pauli in Lateran. Roma, 1673.
	Arc 1033.55.6	Soresini, G.M. Compendio istorico cronologico delle cose più cospicul concernenti la Scala Santa. Roma, 1674.
	Arc 1033.17.10	Marracci, L. Memorie di Santa Maria in Portico di Roma. Roma, 1675.
	Arc 1033.12.136	Soresinus, J.M. De imagine SS. Salvatoris...ad Sancta Sanctorum. Roma, 1675.
	Arc 1033.12.111	Gerberon, G. Histoire de la robe sans couture de...J.-C....Argenteuil. Paris, 1677.
	Arc 1016.229	Legati, L. Museo Cospiano. Bologna, 1677.
	Arc 1369.1	Oesel, J. Thesaurus sel. numismata antiqua. Amsterdam, 1677.

1670-1679 - cont.

	Arc 1033.17.36	Bambacari, C. La città di refugio panegirico...greca imagine di Maria da Constantinopoli. Forli, 1678.
	Arc 1020.9.55	Contarino, F.L. Dell antiquita sito, chiese...di Roma. Napoli, 1678.
	Arc 646.3	Guillet de St.-George, George. Lettres écrites sur une dissertation d'un voyage de Grèce. Paris, 1679.
	Arc 1033.17.450	Officium commemorationis solemnis beatae virginis Maria de Monte Carmelo. Ulysarpone, 1679.

1680-1689

	Arc 785.6	Fabretti, R. De aquis et aquaeductis veteris Romae. Romae, 1680.
	Arc 1494.45	Lastanosa, V.J. de. Tratado de la moneda jaquesa y otras de oro. Zaragozana, 1681.
	Arc 1175.5F	Mabillon, J. De re diplomatica libri VI. Luteciae Parisiorum, 1681.
	Arc 1033.17.53	Nieszporkowicz, A. Analecta mensae reginalis seu historia imaginis...virginis...Claromontanae. Cracoviae, 1681.
	Arc 1033.98	Mauro, G.D. Historia sacra. Roma, 1682.
Htn	Arc 635.215*	Wheler, G. A journey into Greece. London, 1682.
Htn	Arc 750.212*	Fabretti, R. De columna traiani syntaqua. Roma, 1683.
	Arc 1367.1	Morel, Andre. Specimen universae rei nummariae antiquae. Paris, 1683.
	Arc 1490.30	Parisio, Prospero. Rariora magnae Graeciae numismata...1592. n.p., 1683.
	Arc 403.4	Spon, J. Recherche curieuse d'antiquité. Lyon, 1683.
	Arc 1362.1	Harduin, J. Nummi antiqui pop. et urb. illustrati. Parisii, 1684.
	Arc 1373.4.2	Seguin, P. Sel. numismata antiqua. Paris, 1684.
Htn	Arc 1373.4*	Seguin, P. Sel. numismata antiqua. Paris, 1684.
	Arc 1020.58	Cionacci, T. Relazione delle Sante Relique...della città di Firenze. Bologna, 1685.
	Arc 386.14	Baudelot de Dairval, C.C. De l'utilité des voyages...la recherche des antiquitéz. Paris, 1686. 2v.
	Arc 1033.20.9	Sarnelli, Pompeo. Antica basilicografia. Napoli, 1686.
	Arc 1528.1.5	Bizot, P. Histoire metallique de la Republique de Hollande. Amsterdam, 1688. 2v.
	Arc 1528.1	Bizot, P. Histoire metallique de la Republique de Hollande. Amsterdam, 1688. 2v.
	Arc 1018.39	Chiefletius, J.J. De linteis sepulchralibus. Antverpiae, 1688. 4 pam.
	Arc 1033.17.542.5	Mariano, Filoteo. La miracolosa imagine della B.V. Maria del Mont'Allegro in Rapello. Venezia, 1688.
	Arc 843.3	Henao, G. de. Averignaciones de las antiguedades de Cantabria. Salamanca, 1689-91. 2v.

1690-1699

Htn	Arc 750.25*	Bellori, G.A. Veteres Arcus Augustorum. Roma, 1690.
	Arc 1528.1.7	Bizot, P. Histoire metallique de la Republique de Hollande. Supplément. Amsterdam, 1690.
	Arc 1033.17.325	Cavalieri, M. Il Pellegrino al Gargano...di San Michele. Napoli, 1690.
	Arc 1498.2.5	Leblanc, F. Traité historique des monnayes de France. Paris, 1690.
Htn	Arc 1020.9.115*	Les merveilles de la ville de Rome. Rome, 1690.
	Arc 1070.202.3	Bartoli, P.S. Le antiche lucerne. Roma, 1691.
	Arc 1033.102	Carpini, J. Sacro-historica disquisitio emblematibus in Cimelio. Roma, 1691.
	Arc 1460.1	Gronovius, J.F. De sestertüs. Leyden, 1691.
Htn	Arc 1660.5*	Menestrier, C.F. Histoire du Roy Louis le Grand. Paris, 1691.
Htn	Arc 380.208*	Beger, L. Spiciligium antiquitates. Coloniae Brandenburgicae, 1692.
Htn	Arc 343.225F*	Du Molinet, Claude. Le cabinet de la bibliothèque de Sainte Geneviève. Paris, 1692.
	Arc 1348.5	Hoffmann, L.W. Alter und neuer Münz-Schlüssel. Nuremberg, 1692.
	Arc 1498.2	Leblanc, F. Traité historique des monnayes de France. Amsterdam, 1692.
Htn	Arc 1460.2*	Walker, O. The Greek and Roman history illustrated by coins and medals. London, 1692.
	Arc 930.202	Ciampinus, Joan. De sacris aêdificiis a Constantino Magno constr. Romae, 1693.
	Arc 1510.17	Rhon, G. Exercitatio historica de Joh. Uratislaviensibus. Uratslaviae, 1693.
	Arc 861.24	Somner, W. Treatise of Roman ports and forts. Oxford, 1693.
	Arc 785.61	Chevalier, N. Remarques sur la pièce antique de bronze. Amsterdam, 1694.
Htn	Arc 1475.12F*	Pedrusi, Paolo. I Cesari in oro. Parma, 1694-1727. 10v.
	Arc 1033.17.422	Relazione della...coronazione della miracolosa imagine dell Sma. Vergine di Monte Nero. Pistoia, 1694.
	Arc 505.5.48	Sturm, L.C. Sciagraphia templi Hierosolymitano. Lipsiae, 1694.
	Arc 1033.169.5	Benedictus XIII. Discorso nel quale si prova...S. Bartholomeo. Benevento, 1695.
	Arc 1348.7.3	Jobert, L. Notitia rei nummariae. Leipzig, 1695.
	Arc 1478.6	Landi, C. Selectiorum numismatum, praecipue Romanorum expositiones. Leyden, 1695.
Htn	Arc 1455.1*	Beger, L. Thesaurus Brandenburgicus. Colonia Marchica, 1696. 3v.
Htn	Arc 1490.5.5*	Palati, J. Fasti ducales ab Anafesto I. Venetiis, 1696.
	Arc 1070.201.9F	Bartoli, P.S. Gli antichi sepolcri. Roma, 1697.
Htn	Arc 1670.2*	Evelyn, J. Numismata. A discourse of medals. London, 1697.
	Arc 1348.7.2	Jobert, L. The knowledge of medals. London, 1697.
	Arc 767.2.5	Marliani, B. Descrizione di Roma antica. Roma, 1697.
	Arc 1578.1	Melle, Jakob von. Sylloge nummorum ex arg. uncialium. v.1-3. Lubeck, 1697-98.
	Arc 1475.4.5	Patin, C. Imperatorum romanorum numismata. Paris, 1697.
	Arc 1348.13	Gleichius, J. Historia numismatum succincta. Lipsiae, 1698.
	Arc 1578.2	Melle, Jakob von. Sylloge nummorum ex arg. uncialium. v.1-3. Lubeck, 1698-99.
	Arc 1485.1	Buonanni, P. Numismata pontificum romanorum. Rome, 1699. 2v.
	Arc 1025.34	Cyprian, E.S. De ecclesia subterranea liber. Helmstedt, 1699. 8 pam.
	Arc 1480.38	Vallemont, P. Nouvelle explication d'une médaille d'or du cabinet du roy. Paris, 1699.

Chronological Listing

17-

	Arc 1365.1	Khevenhueller, F.A. Regum veterum numismata. v.1-2. Vienna, 17- .
	Arc 1538.15	Stukeley, W.M. Twenty-three plates of the coins of the ancient British kings. London, 17- .

1700-1709

	Arc 1033.169	Dini, F. Dissertatio...de translatio...S. Bartholomaei. Venetiis, 1700.
	Arc 1478.19.5	Foy-Vaillant, J. Numismata imperatorum Augustarum et Caesarum. Amsterdami, 1700.
	Arc 1033.12.193	Lettre d'un Benedictin...touchant le discernement. Diss. Paris, 1700.
	Arc 1668.6	Sperling, Otto. De nummorum bracteatorum et cavorum. Lubecae, 1700.
	Arc 1033.12.192	Thiers, J.B. Réponse à la lettre du père Mabillon...prétendue sur larme. Cologne, 1700.
Htn	Arc 1455.4*	Vaillant, J. Numismata imperatorum. Amsterdam, 1700.
	Arc 1033.91	Florentinio, M. Hetruscae...Pietates...de Prima Thusciae Christianae. Lucae, 1701.
	Arc 726.9	Montfaucon, B. de. Diarium italicum. Paris, 1702.
Htn	Arc 1053.6.9*	Patarolo, Lorenzo. Series Augustorum, Augustarum, Caesarum. Venetiis, 1702.
	Arc 1020.92.3	Caccia, Franciscus. Mater dolorosa et gratiosa. Wienn, 1703.
	Arc 1540.4	Keder, N. De argento runis siu lit. Lipsiae, 1703-08. 4 pam.
	Arc 590.7	Kettner, F.G. Moymia tōn Aigyptian. 2. ed. Lipsiae, 1703. 3 pam.
	Arc 1470.35	Koch, Cornelius D. De Aristotle in nummo aureo. Helmestadi, 1703.
	Arc 1033.20.19	Paulinus a S. Barthol. De Basilica S. Paneratii M. Christi. Roma, 1703.
	Arc 770.5	Pinarolo, G. L'antichita di Roma. Roma, 1703. 2v.
Htn	Arc 1475.6*	Vaillant, J. Numi antiqui familiae romanarum. Amsterdam, 1703. 2v.
	Arc 1485.2	Beger, L. Numismata...Brandenburgici sectio prima. Brandenburgi, 1704.
NEDL	Arc 720.200	Graevuis, J.G. Thesaurus antiquitatum et historiarum Italiae. Lugdunum Batavorum, 1704-23. 16v.
	Arc 1033.17.221	Le Roy, A. Histoire de Notre-Dame de Boulogne. Boulogne, 1704.
	Arc 1033.17.581	Relazione del principio, e cause della venerazione dell'immagine..vergine. Firenze, 1704.
	Arc 830.6.19	Colonia, Dominique de. Dissertation sur un monument antique decouvert a Lyon. Lyon, 1705.
Htn	Arc 1660.5.2*	France. Institut. Médailles sur les principaux evenements du règne de Louis le Grand. Baden, 1705.
	Arc 1027.7.13	Laderchu, J. De sacris Basilicis S. Martyrum. Roma, 1705.
	Arc 1143.9	Schwarz, M.C.G. Ornamentis librorum apud veteres usitatis. v.1-3. Lipsiae, 1705-
	Arc 1510.2	Tentzel, W.E. Saxonia Numismatica, oder Medaillen-Cabinet von Bedächtnissmünzen. Dresden, 1705. 2v.
	Arc 1510.3	Tentzel, W.E. Saxonia Numismatica, oder Medaillen-Cabinet von Münzen. Dresden, 1705. 2v.
Htn	Arc 750.221F*	Chausse, M.A. de la. Le grand cabinet romain. Amsterdam, 1706.
	Arc 823.6	L'Empereur, J. Dissertations historiques sur divers sujets. Paris, 1706.
Htn	Arc 1350.1*	Spanheim, E. Dissertation de praestantia et usu numismatum. Londoni, 1706-17. 2v.
	Arc 1033.17.107	Agostinho de Santa Maria. Santuario Mariano e historia das imagẽs milagrosas de Nossa Senhora. Lisboa, 1707-23. 10v.
	Arc 1016.228	Laderchi, J. Acta passionis SS. Crescii et S. Martyrum. Florentiae, 1707.
	Arc 1033.12.197	Le Mercier, J. Histoire de la larme sainte...Selincourt. Amiens, 1707.
	Arc 630.7	Spoor, Henricus. Favissae utriusque antiqtam Romanae quam Graecae. Ultrajecti, 1707.
	Arc 1033.12.182	Zucchi, B. Historia della corona ferrea...Monza descritta. Milano, 1707.
Htn	Arc 785.2*	Fontana, C. Discorsa sopra l'antico Monte Citabrio. Roma, 1708.
Htn	Arc 1455.3F*	Goltzius, H. De re nummaria antiqua opera. Antwerp, 1708. 5v.
	Arc 767.2.7	Marliani, B. Descrizione di Roma antica. Roma, 1708. 2v.
	Arc 1033.12.67	Rossi, B. de. Teatro dell'umana rendenzione...relazione istorica del...sangue...Sarzana. Massa, 1708.
	Arc 1347.1	Ruhe, C.F. Specimen philolgiae numismatico-latinae primum. Frankfort, 1708-29. 3 pam.
	Arc 1033.17.425	Villette, E.N. Histoire de Notre-Dame de Liesse. Laon, 1708?
	Arc 1458.17	Wren, C. Numismatum antiquorum sylloge populis Graecis. Londini, 1708.
	Arc 1490.9	Vignoli, Giovanni. Antiquiores pontificum romanorum denarii. Romae, 1709.
	Arc 1458.8.5	Woltereck, C. Electa rei numariae. Hamburgi, 1709.
Htn	Arc 1458.8*	Woltereck, C. Electa rei numariae. Hamburgi, 1709.

1710-1719

	Arc 1033.25.7	Troppanneger, C. De lucernis veterum christianorum sepulcralibus. Vitembergae, 1710?
	Arc 1510.107	Dewerdeck, G. Silesia numismatica. Jauer, 1711.
	Arc 1663.57	Koernlein, Melchior. Thesaurus numismatum modernorum huius seculi, sive numismata mnemonica et iconica qui bus praecipui eventus et res gestae ab anno MDCC illustrantur. Norimbergae, 1711-17?
	Arc 1033.17.446	Mastelloni, A. Memorie istoriche della Madonna de' bagno di Magliano. Napoli, 1711.
Htn	Arc 726.9.15*	Montjaucon, B. de. Diarium italicum. London, 1711.
	Arc 830.22.9	Moreau de Mantour, Philibert B. Observations sur des monuments d'antiquité trouvez dans l'eglise cathedrale de Paris. Paris, 1711.
	Arc 758.6	Deseine, F. L'ancienne Rome. v.1-4. Leide, 1713. 2v.
Htn	Arc 861.18.17*	Woodward, J. Account of some urns. London, 1713. 2 pam.
	Arc 1020.60	Besançon, B. Description des monuments de l'Abbaye de Rosières. n.p., 1714.
	Arc 497.3	Reeland, Adriaan. Palaestina. Utrecht, 1714. 2v.
	Arc 1485.1.2	Buonanni, P. Numismata summorum pontificum. Rome, 1715.
	Arc 1033.12.188	Cathalogus authorum, qui de corona. Roma, 1715.
	Arc 1348.7	Jobert, L. La science des médailles. Paris, 1715.
	Arc 1033.17.462	Montorio, S. Zodiaco di Maria...Napoli. Napoli, 1715.

1710-1719 - cont.

	Arc 1033.12.121	Seelen, I.H. Memorabilium...specimen sive de festo lanceae et clavorum. Flensburgi, 1715.
	Arc 1020.76	Le tresor, les corps saints...dans l'eglise royale de S. Denys. Paris, 1715.
	Arc 1490.45	Vergare, Cesare A. Monete del regno di Napoli da Roggiero. Roma, 1715.
Htn	Arc 1033.1*	Buonarroti, F. Osservazioni sopra alcune frammenti di vasi antichi. Firenze, 1716.
	Arc 1478.2	A catalogue of medals from Julius Caesar to Heraclius. London, 1716.
	Arc 1033.17.88	Chigi, A. La città diletta di Maria...miracolosa immagine di Nostra Donna. Roma, 1716.
	Arc 1033.17.5	Griscembeni, G.M. Memorie istoriche della miracolosa immagine di S. Maria in Portico. Roma, 1716.
	Arc 505.5.8	Reeland, Adriaan. De spoliis templi Hierosolymitani. Utrecht, 1716.
Htn	Arc 720.203*	Sallengre, A. de. Novus thesaurus antiquitatum romanorum. The Hague, 1716. 3v.
	Arc 1033.12.52	Fontanini, J. Dissertatio de corona ferrea Langobardoum. Romae, 1717.
Htn	Arc 1475.2*	Banduri, A. Numismata imperatorum romanorum. Paris, 1718. 2v.
	Arc 1330.1	Banduri, A. Bibliotheca nummaria. Hamburg, 1719.
	Arc 1458.5	Haym, N.F. Del tesoro britannico. London, 1719-20. 2v.
	Arc 1665.2	Knifer, Gijsbert. De elephantis in numis obviis exercitationes duae. Hagae, 1719. 2 pam.
	Arc 1033.12.181	Muratori, L.A. De corona ferrea...commentarius. Mediolani, 1719.
Htn	Arc 785.10*	Oliva, G. In Marmor Isiacum...exercitationes. Rome, 1719.

1720-1729

	Arc 1015.207	Boldetti, M.A. Osservazioni sopra i cimitery. Roma, 1720.
Htn	Arc 618.4*	Keysler, J.G. Antiquitas...septentrionales et celticae. Hannover, 1720.
	Arc 505.5.70	Lanvy, B. De tabernaculo foederis...Jerusalem. Paris, 1720.
	Arc 380.199	Noris, Enrico. Lettere sopra vari punti di erudizione. n.p., 1720.
	Arc 1033.17.650	Dörffel, F. St. Maria Culm das ist Bremdliche Historia. n.p., 1721.
	Arc 1033.150	Favilli, A. Relazione dell'origine...Firenze...Bastone del S.P. Giuseppe. Lucca, 1721.
	Arc 1510.137	Leuckfeld, J.G. Antiquitates nummariae, oder Historische Beschreibung vieleralten. Leipzig, 1721.
	Arc 380.201	Montfaucon, B. de. Antiquity explained. London, 1721. 7v.
	Arc 1033.12.66	Quiroga, M.P. de. Bellum de sanguine Christi. Valladolid, 1721.
	Arc 1076.3.35	Thiers, J.B. Traitez des cloches. Paris, 1721.
	Arc 900.211F	Hueber, P. Austria exarchivis mellicensilus. Lipsiae, 1722.
	Arc 380.200	Montfaucon, B. de. L'antiquité expliquée. 2. éd. v.1-5. Paris, 1722. 10v.
	Arc 1086.2.9F	Bartoli, Pietro. Veterum lucernae sepulcrales. Lugduni Batavorum, 1723. 2 pam.
Htn	Arc 740.203*	Dempster, T. De Etruria regali libri VII. Florence, 1723-24. 2v.
	Arc 746.16	Fontani, Giusto. De antiquitatibus Hortae coloniae etruscorum. 3a ed. Roma, 1723.
NEDL	Arc 720.200.2	Graevius, J.G. Thesaurus antiquitatum et historiarum Siciliae. v.1-15. Lugdunum Batavorum, 1723-25. 8v.
	Arc 1528.5.5PF	Loon, Gerard van. Beschrijving der Nederlandsche historie-penningen. 's-Gravenhage, 1723-31. 4v.
	Arc 1485.6	Paruta, F. Sicilia numismatica. v.1-3. Lugdunum Batavorum, 1723. 2v.
	Arc 861.1.3	Rowlands, Henry. Mona antiqua restaurata. Dublin, 1723.
	Arc 861.31	Twining, T. Avebury in Wiltshire. London, 1723.
	Arc 1433.21	Kehr, G. Jacob. Monarchiae Asiatico-Saracenicae status. Lipsiae, 1724.
Htn	Arc 1428.9*	Mead, Richard. Oratio dissertio de nummis...a Symrnaeis. Londoni, 1724.
Htn	Arc 1428.9.2*	Mead, Richard. Oratio dissertio de nummis...a Symrnaeis. Londoni, 1724.
	Arc 380.200.2	Montfaucon, B. de. L'antiquité expliquée. Supplément. Paris, 1724. 5v.
Htn	Arc 870.6*	Pointer, J. Britannia Romana, or Romans in Britain. Oxford, 1724. 4 pam.
	Arc 628.10	Spon, J. Voyage d'Italie, de Dalmatie, de Grèce. La Haye, 1724. 2v.
	Arc 855.215	Jones, I. Most notable antiquity of Great Britain called Stone-Heng. London, 1725.
Htn	Arc 865.9.10F*	Jones, Inigo. The most notable antiquity of Great Britain called Stone-Heng. London, 1725.
	Arc 720.201	Montfaucon, B. de. The antiquities of Italy. 2. ed. London, 1725.
Htn	Arc 1350.4*	Arbuthnot, J. Tables of ancient coins, weights and measures. London, 1727.
	Arc 1070.202	Bartoli, P.S. Gli antichi sepolcri. Roma, 1727.
	Arc 386.14.5	Baudelot de Dairval, C.C. De l'utilité des voyages...la recherche des antiquitéz. Rouen, 1727. 2v.
	Arc 1190.25.10	Maffei, Scipione. Istoria diplomatica che serve d'introduzione all'arte critica in tal materia. Mantova, 1727.
	Arc 1033.17.543	Bagnari, P. Divozioni..in onore di Nostra Signora del Carmine. Roma, 1728.
	Arc 1033.12.4	Breve racconta del SS. Prepuzio di Gesu Christi. Roma, 1728.
	Arc 1070.203	Bartoli, P.S. Le antiche lucerne. Roma, 1729.
	Arc 785.44	Crellius, C. Priteal libonis ex antquus erutis. Wittenberg, 1729.
	Arc 1373.9	Smith, W. Literae de re nummaria. Newcastle-upon-Tyne, 1729.

1730-1739

	Arc 1335.9	Hansen von Ehrencron, F.A. Numophylacium Ehrencronianum. n.p., 1730.
Htn	Arc 1475.1F*	Occo, A. Imperatorum romanorum numismata. Milan, 1730.
	Arc 1053.1	Canini, G.A. Images des héros et des grandes hommes de l'antiquité. Amsterdam, 1731.
	Arc 1423.11.5F	Foy-Vaillant, J. Seleucidarum imperium. Hagae-Comitum, 1732.
	Arc 855.200	Horsley, J. Britannia Romana, or The Roman antiquities of Britain. London, 1732.

Chronological Listing

1730-1739 - cont.

Arc 1525.1 — Loon, Gerard van. Histoire metallique des XVII provinces des Pays-Bas. La Haye, 1732-37. 5v.

Arc 1360.2 — Froelich, E. Utilitas rei numariae veteris. Viennae, 1733.

Arc 1033.17.601 — Galizia, C.M. Rapporto cronistorico della formazione...del simolacro...Vergine Maria di Trapani. Palermo, 1733.

Arc 823.17 — Maffei, Scipione. Galliae antiguitates quaedam selectae atque in plures epistolas distributaes. Parisiis, 1733.

Arc 1033.17.301 — Memorie del ritrovamento della santissima immagine della...annunziata. Firenze, 1733.

Arc 1016.232.2 — Lupi, A.M. Dissertatio...severae martyris epitaphium. Panormi, 1734.

Arc 1016.232 — Lupi, A.M. Dissertatio...severae martyris epitaphium. Panormi, 1734.

Htn Arc 1475.3* — Morelli, A. Thesaurus Morellianus. Amsterdam, 1734. 2v.

Arc 1033.17.55 — Schlichter, C.L. Ecloga historia qua fabula pontificia de Luca Pictore exploditur. Halae, 1734.

Arc 726.41 — Bourguet, Louis. Spiegazione di alcuni monumenti degli antichi Palasgi. Pesaro, 1735.

Arc 1020.19.5 — Gratiolio, P. De praeclaris Mediolani aedificiciis. Mediolani, 1735.

Arc 1510.130 — Kundmann, J.C. Numuni jubilaei, oder Jubel Schau-Stücke. Bresslau, 1735.

Arc 1020.51.10 — Winheim, Erharde. Sacrarium Agrippinae...praecipuarum reliquarum. Coloniae Agrippinae, 1736. 2 pam.

Arc 1185.10 — Baring, D.E. Clavis diplomatica. Hanoverae, 1737.

Arc 1015.203 — Bottari, G.G. Sculture e pitture sagre estratte dai cimitery de Roma. Roma, 1737-54. 3v.

Arc 1033.12.144 — Cerqueira Pinto, Antonio. Historia da prodigiosa imagem de Christo crucificado. Lisboa, 1737.

Arc 1033.35.101 — Ciampini, G.G. De cruce stationale investigatio historica. Roma, 1737.

Arc 1360.2.5 — Froelich, E. Quatuor tentamina in re. numaria vetere. Viennae, 1737.

Htn Arc 740.200* — Gorio, A.F. Museum Etruscum. Florence, 1737. 3v.

Htn Arc 1675.23.5* — Morganti, Bento. Nummismalogia, ou Breve recopilação de algunas medalhas dos emperadores romanos de ouro. Lisboa, 1737.

Arc 1490.25 — Benedictus Floravantensis. Antiqui romanorum pontificum denarii a Benedicto XI ad Paulum III. Romae, 1738.

Arc 1347.2 — Bytemeister, H.J. Delineatio rei numismaticae. Helmstadt, 1738? 3 pam.

Arc 1033.12.80 — Erfreulicher Ursprung...am Semmering. Neustadt, 1738.

Arc 1033.44 — Georgius, D. De monogrammate Christi Domini. Diss. Roma, 1738.

Arc 1510.135 — Kundmann, J.C. Silesii in nummis, oder Berühmte Schlesier in Müntzen. Bresslau, 1738.

Arc 1033.145 — Odvardo a S. Francisco Xaverio. Dissertatio storico-critico-dogmatico...mano destra di S. Giovanni Battista...Repagnano. Roma, 1738.

Arc 1510.21 — Scholtz, Henrico. Sancta colonia numis antiquissimis illustrata et monumentis historicis explicata. Ploenae, 1738.

Arc 853.11.15 — Steger, Adrian. De vis militaribus romanorum in vetiri Germania. Lipsiae, 1738.

Arc 1490.10 — Vettori, Francesco. Il fiorino d'oro antico illustrato. Firenze, 1738.

Htn Arc 407.2* — Wise, F. Letter to Dr. Mead. Oxford, 1738-64. 4 pam.

Arc 1175.11 — Anderson, J. Selectus diplomatum et numismatum Scotiae Thesaurus. Edinburgi, 1739.

Htn Arc 900.203* — Bertoli, G. Le antichità d'Aquileja. Venice, 1739.

Arc 743.5 — Gori, A.F. Risposta. Firenze, 1739.

Arc 1663.56 — Lesser, Friedrich Christian. Besondere Münzen. Frankfurt, 1739.

Arc 767.2.10 — Marliani, B. Descrizione di Roma antica. Roma, 1739.

Arc 1025.57 — Nicolai, Joannis. De luctie christianorum. Lugdnum Batavorum, 1739.

Arc 1070.205 — Passeri, J.B. Lucernae futiles Musei Passerii. Pisauri, 1739-51. 3v.

Arc 485.202 — Persepolis illustrata. London, 1739.

Arc 769.1 — Rolli, P. Degli avanzi dell'antica Roma. Londra, 1739.

Arc 1333.1 — Venuti, R. Antiqua numismata. v.1-2. Rome, 1739-44.

1740-1749

Arc 1033.75 — Andreucci, A.G. Notizie...SS. Valentino Prete ed Flario Diacono. Roma, 1740.

Arc 1027.61.5 — Ansaldi, P.C. De caussis inopiae veterum monument. pro copia Martyrum. Medina, 1740.

Htn Arc 1360.3* — Ficoroni, F. de. I piombi antichi. Roma, 1740.

Arc 830.105 — La Sauvagère, F. Recherches sur la nature et l'etendue d'un ancien ouvrage des Romains. Paris, 1740.

Htn Arc 1027.34* — Marangoni, J. Acta S. Victorini episcopi amiterni et martyres. Rome, 1740.

Arc 1053.6.12 — Patarolo, Lorenzo. Series Augustorum, Augustarum, Caesarum. 3. ed. Venetiis, 1740.

Arc 1033.82 — Pollidoro, J.B. Vita...S. Pardi...de SS. Primiano, Firmiano et Casto. Roma, 1741.

Arc 1033.21.5 — Victorius Franciscus. Sanctorum septem dormientium...Musei Victorii. Roma, 1741.

Arc 642.5 — Ciriacus, Pizzicolli. Itinerarium. Florentiae, 1742.

Arc 1033.17.134 — Gervasi, F.A. Sorte invidiabile di Prato...della sagra Cintola. Firenze, 1742.

Htn Arc 1455.2* — Havercamp, S. Nummophylacium Reginae Christinae. The Hague, 1742.

Arc 1335.85F — Haverkamp, S. Nummophylacium reginae Christinae. Comitum Hagae, 1742.

Arc 1478.19 — Foy-Vaillant, J. Numismata imperatorum romanorum. Romae, 1743. 3v.

Arc 1033.17.95.2F — Francisco de San Joseph. Historia universal...Nuestra Señora de Guadalupe. Madrid, 1743.

Arc 1033.17.95 — Francisco de San Joseph. Historia universal...Nuestra Señora de Guadalupe. Madrid, 1743.

Arc 1087.1 — Garofalo, Biagio. De antiquis marmoribus opuculum. Ad Rhenum, 1743.

Arc 1053.7.5 — Patarolo, Lorenzo. Opera omnia. Venetiis, 1743. 2v.

Arc 1053.7 — Patarolo, Lorenzo. Series Augustorum, Augustarum, Caesarum. 4. ed. Venetiis, 1743.

Arc 1033.17.245 — Ruggieri, S. Istoria dell'immagine di S. Maria di Pozzano. Napoli, 1743.

Arc 855.214 — Stukeley, William. Albury. Temple of the British Druids. London, 1743.

Arc 858.30 — Stukely, William. Palaeographia brittanica. London, 1743. 2 pam.

1740-1749 - cont.

Htn Arc 1348.28* — Agustin, Antonius. Dialogos de medallas, inscriciones y otras antiquedades. Madrid, 1744.

Arc 1020.87 — Brocchi, G.M. Descrizione delle reliquare di Santi...Rocca di Lutiano. Firenze, 1744.

Htn Arc 760.2* — Ficoroni, F. de. Le vestigia e rarità di Roma antica. Rome, 1744.

Arc 1420.1.5F — Froelich, E. Annales compendiarii regum et rerum Syriae. Vienna, 1744.

Arc 861.47 — Nixon, J. Marmor Estonianum...in agro Northamptoniensi. Londinium, 1744.

Arc 861.56 — Parkin, Charles. An answer to...Dr. Stukeley's Origines Roystonianae. London, 1744. 2 pam.

Arc 1020.9.28 — Sindone, R. Altarium et reliquarum...basilicae vaticanae. Romae, 1744.

Arc 861.8.6 — Battely, J. Antiquitates rutupinae. 2. ed. Oxoniae, 1745. 2 pam.

Htn Arc 726.46* — Ficorini, Francesco de. Le memorie ritrovate...de Labrico. Roma, 1745.

Arc 1580.10 — Hanthaler, C. Verzeichnung...wiennerischer...Müntzen. Lintz, 1745.

Htn Arc 1538.5* — Leake, S.M. Historical account of English money from the conquest. London, 1745.

Arc 1033.17.442 — Oberhausen, G. Istoria della miracolosa immagine di Nostra Signora di Montenero. Lucca, 1745.

Htn Arc 1333.5* — Herbert, T. Numismata antiqua. n.p., 1746.

Htn Arc 1350.5F* — Pembroke, T.H. Numismata antiqua. London, 1746.

Arc 861.33 — Rauthmell, R. Antiquitates Bremetonacenses. London, 1746.

Htn Arc 726.30* — Zuzzeri, G.L. D'una antica villa. Venezia, 1746.

Arc 1027.39.5 — Baruffaldi, G. Dissertazione intorno...sepolcro...cimitero di Prestato. Venezia? 1747?

Arc 1033.44.5 — De monogrammate sanetissimi nominis Jesu. Roma, 1747.

Arc 830.145 — Lebeuf, Jean. Mémoire sur quelques antiquités du diocese de Bayeux. n.p., 1747.

Arc 1020.78 — Petracchi, C. Della insigne di S. Stefano di Bologna. Bologna, 1747.

Arc 865.18 — Wood, John. Choir Gaure, vulgarly called Stonehenge. Oxford, 1747.

Arc 1033.17.461 — Coronella in onore della G. Madre di Dio....Santa Maria di Caravaggio...Porta Reale. Napoli, 1748.

Arc 391.3 — Gori, A.F. Symbolia litterariae. Decas I. Florentiae, 1748-53. 10v.

Arc 800.13 — Mémoire sur la ville. Paris, 1748. 3 pam.

Arc 800.5.2 — Venuti, N.M. de. Descrizione delle prime scoperte dell'antica città d'Ercolano. Roma, 1748.

Arc 1033.17.241 — Calvi, D. Delle grandezze della Madonna di Carvaggio. v.3. Napoli, 1749.

Htn Arc 1033.17.247* — Chifflet, J.J. De sacris inscriptionibus, quibus tabella D. Viginis Cameracensis. Antverp, 1749.

Arc 1033.105 — Coppola, G. Relazione dello scoprimento del corpo del...martire S. Eusanio. Roma, 1749.

Htn Arc 1077.2.25* — Gori, A.F. Crux dominica adorabile christianae religionis vexillum observationibus. Florentiae, 1749.

Htn Arc 800.5* — Venuti, N.M. de. Descrizione delle prime scoperte dell'antica città d'Ercolano. Venezia, 1749.

1750

Arc 723.9 — Antiquités romaines...mémoires de comte de B. La Haye, 1750.

Arc 1485.8 — Argelati, P. De monetis italiae variorum illustrium virorum. Mediolani, 1750. 6v.

Arc 1020.31.15 — Besozzi, R. La storia della Basilica di Santa Croce in Gerusalemma. Roma, 1750.

Arc 1020.102 — Breve distinta relazione...sacre relique... S. Maria...città di Siena. Siena, 1750.

Arc 800.11 — Brosses, Charles de. Lettres sur l'état actuel de la ville souterraine d'Herculée. Dijon, 1750.

Arc 1020.105 — Capece, G. Dissertazione...intorno alle due campane della chiesa parochiale di S. Giovanni. Napoli, 1750.

Arc 1033.17.22 — Erra, C.A. Storia dell'imagine...Santa Maria in portico di Campitelli. Roma, 1750.

Arc 800.14 — Fordyce, W. Memoirs concerning Herculaneum. London, 1750.

Arc 1510.12 — Heusinger, F. Versuch einer Abhandlung von den Nutzen der teutschen Münzwissenschaft. Nürnberg, 1750.

Arc 1020.9.118 — Léon, François. Les merveilles de la ville de Rome. Rome, 1750.

Arc 720.207 — Massazza, P.A. L'arco antico di Susa. Torino, 1750.

Htn Arc 772.2* — Roma antica e moderna. Roma, 1750. 3v.

Arc 1027.12.11 — Sindone. Della sacrosanta basilica di S. Pietro. Roma, 1750.

Htn Arc 1373.6* — Swinton, J. Metilia: sive de quinario gentis metiliae. Oxford, 1750.

Arc 1185.1 — Tassin, R.P. Nouveau traité de diplomatique. Paris, 1750-65. 6v.

Arc 800.5.10 — Venuti, N.M. de. A description of the first discoveries of...ancient city of Heraclea. London, 1750.

Arc 1333.2 — Wise, F. Numismata antiqua. Scriniis bodleianis rec. catalogus. Oxford, 1750.

1751

Htn Arc 1355.1* — Addison, J. Dialogue upon the usefulness of ancient medals. Glasgow, 1751.

Arc 726.26 — Borgia, S. Breve i storia dell'antica città di Tadino. Roma, 1751.

Arc 391.3.5 — Gori, A.F. Symbolia litterariae. Decas II. v.1-10. Romae, 1751-54. 5v.

Arc 505.5.42 — Holtzfuss, V.S. Dissertatio historico-theologica de templi Hierosolymitani Iuliani. Halae Magdeburgicae, 1751. 2 pam.

Arc 800.12 — Lettre sur les peintures d'Herculanum. Bruxelles, 1751.

Arc 730.200 — Pancrazi, G.M. Antichita siciliane spiegate. Naples, 1751. 2v.

Arc 1020.17 — Pannelli, D. Ragguaglio della univerzione...dei S.S. Martue. Pesaro, 1751.

Arc 1033.12.191 — Thiers, J.B. Dissertation sur la sainte larme de Vendome. Amsterdam, 1751.

Htn Arc 750.219* — Venuti, Ridolfino. Veteris Latii antiqua vestigia urbis moenia. Romae, 1751.

Arc 1030.30 — Vettori, P. Dissertatio philologica qua nonnulla monimenta sacrae vetera ex museo Vict. Roma, 1751.

Chronological Listing

1752

Arc 387.1 Caylus, A.C.P. Recueil d'antiquités égyptiennes. Paris, 1752. 7v.

Arc 726.35 Giorgi, Antonio. Dissertazione...monumento etrusco...di Volterra. Firenze, 1752.

1753

Arc 800.1 Bellicard, J.C. Observations on the antiques of the town of Herculaneum. London, 1753.

Arc 726.39 Venuti, R. Osservazioni sopra il fiume Clitunno. Roma, 1753.

Htn Arc 1273.2F* Vertue, G. Medals, coins, great seals, impressions from the elaborate works of Thomas Simon. London, 1753.

Arc 861.12.9 Warburton, J. Vallum Romanum...Cumberland and Northumberland. London, 1753.

1754

Arc 1185.10.5 Baring, D.E. Clavis diplomatica. Hanoverae, 1754.

Arc 1490.4.7 Carli, G.R. Delle monete e dell'istituzione delle Zecche d'Italia. L'Aja, 1754-57. 2v.

Arc 1490.4.5 Carli, G.R. Delle monete e dell'istituzione delle Zecche d'Italia. Mantova, 1754. 3v.

Htn Arc 1420.1* Froelich, E. Annales compendiarii regum et rerum Syriae. 2. ed. Vienna, 1754.

Htn Arc 1020.9.75* Gesualdo, E. Osservazione...storia via Appia di Pratelle. Napoli, 1754.

Arc 1348.18 Joachim, J.F. Unterricht von dem Münzwesen. Halle, 1754.

Arc 1350.4.2 Langwith, B. Observations on Doctor Arbuthnot's dissertation. London, 1754.

Arc 830.81 Venuti, Niccolo M. Dissertations sur les anciens monumens de la ville de Bordeaux. Bordeaux, 1754.

Arc 720.205 Vila, G. de. Thesaurus antiquitatum beneventanarum. Romae, 1754.

1755

Htn Arc 1488.6* Bellini, V. De monetis Italiae medii aeirhactenus. Ferrariae, 1755.

Arc 800.8.2 Cochin, Charles N. Observations sur les antiquités d'Herculanum. 2e éd. Paris, 1755.

Arc 1473.9 Du Cange, C. du F. De imperatorum constantinopalitanorum. Romae, 1755.

Arc 1033.17.12 Notizie dell'origine e dell'antichità del Monastero di S. Ambrozio. Roma, 1755.

Htn Arc 1033.137* Paciandi, P. De cultu S. J. Baptistae...commentarius. Roma, 1755.

1756

Arc 1360.2.7 Froelich, E. Ad numismata regum veterum anecdota. Viennae, 1756. 2 pam.

Arc 1348.7.1 Jobert, L. La scienza delle medaglie. Venezia, 1756. 2v.

Arc 1033.38.5 Memorie della Vita del Martirio...S. Lorenzo. Roma, 1756.

Arc 1033.76 Notizie, regole...ss. Martire della ss. Basilica Vaticana. Roma, 1756.

Arc 1033.38.15 Pérez Báyes, F. Damascus et Laurentius. Rome, 1756.

Htn Arc 1020.11* Relazione dello scuoprimento...in Ancona. Roma, 1756.

Htn Arc 1143.9.5* Schwarz, M.C.G. Ornamentis librorum. Lipsiae, 1756.

Htn Arc 1535.6* Twelve plates of English silver coins. London, 1756.

1757

Htn Arc 1020.32* Allegranza, G. Spiegazione...sacri monumenti antichi di Milano. Milano, 1757.

Arc 1251.3 Cardoni, B. De siglis veterum graecorum. v.1-3. Romae, 1757.

Arc 800.8.3 Cochin, Charles N. Observations sur les antiquités d'Herculanum. 2e éd. Paris, 1757.

Htn Arc 1675.26* Florez, Enrique. Medallas de la colonias, municipios y pueblos antiguos de España. Madrid, 1757-73. 3v.

Arc 1033.58.5 Lucatelli, G. Notizie istoriche...la testa di S. Sebastiano. Roma, 1757.

Arc 1018.15 Mamachi, T.M. De' costumi de' primitivi cristiani. Venezia, 1757. 3v.

Arc 1480.5 Paciandi, P.M. Ad nummos consulares III viri M. Antonii. Rome, 1757.

Arc 1540.1 Stukeley, W. The medallic history of M.A.V. Carausins. London, 1757-89.

1758

Htn Arc 1163.2.3* Terreros y Pando, E. Paleografía española. Madrid, 1758.

Arc 1033.17.621 Venezia favorita da Maria. Relazione delle imagine...di Maria...in Venezia. Venezia, 1758.

Arc 880.12.2 Wright, Thomas. Louthiana, or Introduction to antiquities of Ireland. London, 1758.

1759

Arc 1033.40.5 Bartolini, D. Istoria del Martirio di S. Cecilia. Roma, 1759.

Arc 1033.88 Baruffaldi, G. Del Colpo di Spada...la morte a i Martiri. Venezia, 1759.

Arc 1033.66.5 Bonet, F.R. Breve notizia...di alcuni Santi del Colosseo. Roma, 1759.

Arc 1030.41 Gallethio, P.A. Inscriptiones Bononienses. Roma, 1759.

Arc 825.11 Seguin, J.F. L'ancienne inscription de la Maison Carrée. Paris, 1759. 4 pam.

Arc 1494.1 Velazquez, L.J. Congeturae sobre las medallos. Malaga, 1759.

Arc 1675.21 Velazquez, L.J. Congeturas sobre las medallas de los reyes godos y suevos de España. Malaga, 1759. 2 pam.

1760

Arc 1033.17.622 Apparitionum et celebriorum imaginum...Mariae...Venetiis. Venetia, 1760.

Arc 726.10.4 Barthélemy, J.J. Explication de la mosaique de Palestrine. Paris, 1760.

Arc 1329.1 Hirsch, J.C. Bibliotheca numismatica. Nuremberg, 1760.

Arc 1033.17.51 Kiedrzynski, A. Mensa nazaraea...seu historia imagine divae Claromontanae. Cracoviae, 1760.

Htn Arc 915.6* Schmidt, F.S. Recueil d'antiquités trouvées à Avenches...de la Suisse. Berne, 1760.

1760 - cont.

Arc 1033.17.26 Storia dell'apparizione...di Nostra Signora di Misericordia di Savona. Genova, 1760.

Arc 1480.1 Venutis, P. de. Duodenorum nomismatum antehac ineditorum brevis expositio. Leghorn, 1760.

1761

Htn Arc 1490.17* Bellini, Y. Delle monete di Ferrara. Ferrara, 1761.

Arc 387.1.2 Caylus, A.C.P. Recueil d'antiquités. Paris, 1761.

Arc 1675.49F Mazzuchelli, G.M. Museum Mazzuchellianum. Venetiis, 1761-63. 2v.

Arc 1675.49.5F Mazzuchelli, G.M. Museum Mazzuchellianum. Venetiis, 1761-63. 2v.

Arc 1033.12.75 Recueil historique...du...sang...Bruges. Bruges, 1761.

Arc 1027.36 Volpi, A.T. Dell'indentila dei S. Corpi dei S. Fermo Rustico, e Procolo. Milano, 1761.

1762

Arc 1370.4 Pellerin, J. Recueil de médailles de rois. Paris, 1762.

Htn Arc 1540.13* Perry, Francis. Series of English medals. London, 1762.

Htn Arc 750.5* Pianesi, G.B. Campus Martius. Roma, 1762.

Htn Arc 1535.1* Snelling, T. A view of the silver coin and coinage of England. London, 1762.

Htn Arc 705.5* Stuart, J. Antiquities of Athens. London, 1762-1816. 4v.

Htn Arc 800.3* Winckelmann, J. Sendschreiben von den Herculanischen Entdeckungen. Dresden, 1762. 4 pam.

1763

Arc 1020.9.51 Fioravanti, G.A. Visita...delle sette chiese. Fermo, 1763.

Htn Arc 1535.3* Folkes, M. Tables of English silver and gold coins. London, 1763. 2v.

Arc 1033.17.50 Kiedrzynski, A. Mensa nazaraea...seu historia imagine divae Claromontanae. Claromontanae, 1763.

Htn Arc 1335.10* Lefroy, A. Catalogus numism. mus. Lefroyani. Livorno, 1763.

Arc 1345.5F Mangeart, Thomas. Introduction a la science des médailles. Paris, 1763.

Arc 1030.21 Manni, D.M. Antichissima lapida cristiana. Firenze, 1763.

Arc 1510.127 Obermayr, J. Historische Nachricht von bayerischen Münzen. Frankfurt, 1763.

Arc 1370.4.2 Pellerin, J. Recueil de médailles de peuples. Paris, 1763. 3v.

Arc 1033.12.68 Rota, S.A. Verita trionfante...della fede in...narrazione delle reliquie del Sangue...Venezia. Venezia, 1763.

1764

Htn Arc 1364.1* Jennings, D. An introduction to the knowledge of medals. London, 1764.

Arc 730.202 Orville, J.P. d'. Sicula, guibus Sicilae veritis ruderd. Amsterdam, 1764.

Arc 705.203 Sayer, R. Ruinen und Überbleibsel von Athen. Augsburg, 1764.

Arc 800.3.7 Winckelmann, J. Lettre à Monsieur le Comte de Brühl. Dresde, 1764.

1765

Arc 1668.12 Klotz, C.A. Historia numorum contumeliosorum. Altenburgi, 1765. 2 pam.

Arc 1185.23 Lemoine, P.C. Diplomatique-pratique. Metz, 1765.

Arc 1020.97 Morales, Ambrosio de. Viage...para reconocer las reliquias de santos, sepulcros reales. Madrid, 1765.

Arc 823.7.5 Pasumot, Francois. Mémoires géographiques sur quelques antiquités de la Gaule. Paris, 1765. 2 pam.

Arc 1370.4.3 Pellerin, J. Mélange de diverses médailles. Paris, 1765. 2v.

Htn Arc 772.2.5* Roma antica e moderna. Roma, 1765. 3v.

Arc 1033.17.582 Sassi, G.A. Notizie istoriche intorno alla miracolosa immagine...Maria. Milano, 1765.

Arc 1033.12.158 Serantoni, G.M. Apologia del Volto santo di Lucca. Lucca, 1765.

1766

Arc 395.10 Klotz, C.A. Ueber das Studium des Alterthums. Halle, 1766.

Arc 1033.8 Manni, D.M. Dell'errore che persiste...al Santo Evangelista. Firenze, 1766.

Arc 861.1.6 Rowlands, Henry. Mona antiqua restaurata. 2. ed. London, 1766.

1767

Htn Arc 1033.20* Analdi, E. Delle basiliche antiche. Vincenza, 1767.

Htn Arc 1538.1* Clarke, W. The connexion of the Roman, Saxon, and English coins. London, 1767.

Arc 861.22 Lyttelton. Description of an ancient font in Bridekirk. n.p., 1767.

Arc 1185.28 Mabillon, Jean. Histoire des contestations sur la diplomatique. Naples, 1767.

Arc 1015.5 Moretto, P. De S'Callisto pp. etm ejusque Basilica. Romae, 1767.

Arc 1370.4.4 Pellerin, J. Suppléments aux six volumes. Paris, 1767.

Arc 1335.103 Poulhariez, P.N. Histoire métallique de l'Europe, ou Catalogue des médailles modernes. Lyon, 1767.

Htn Arc 1020.6.15* Schioppalalba, I.B. In perantiquam sacram tabulam...S. Mariae Caritatis. Venetiis, 1767.

Arc 1033.12.163 Serantoni, G.M. Risposta...alla seconda replica del celebre autore delle letterarie di Firenze. Lucca, 1767.

Arc 1478.19.2 Susomni, J.B. Numismata imperatorum romanorum. Supplementum. Vindobonae, 1767.

Arc 776.1.7 Venuti, R. Accurata e succinta descrizione topografica delle antichità di Roma moderna. Roma, 1767. 4v.

Htn Arc 380.209* Winckelmann, J. Monumenti antichi inedite. v.1-2. Roma, 1767.

Chronological Listing

1768

Arc 1033.12.35 Vigo, G.B. Ad carolum...de Sindone Taurinensi. Augustae Taurinorum, 1768.

1769

Arc 1355.1.5 Addison, J. Dialogue upon the usefulness of ancient medals. Glasgow, 1769.

Htn Arc 720.7.5* Major, T. Les ruines de Paestum. Londres, 1769.

1770

Arc 800.10 Bondaroy, F. de. Recherches sur les ruines d'Herculanum. Paris, 1770.

Arc 1033.43.9 Breve Notizia dell'Orato in Memoria Abitazione. Roma, 1770.

Arc 823.18 La Sauvagère, F. Recueil d'antiquités dans les Gaules. Paris, 1770.

Arc 1433.2.2 Murr, C.G. von. Drei Abhandlungen von der Geschichte der Araber. Nüremberg, 1770.

Arc 1033.48 Sandellius, D. De Priscorum Christianorum Synaxibus. Venetiis, 1770.

1771

Arc 830.79.5 Le Goux de Gerland. Dissertations sur l'origine de la ville de Dijon. Dijon, 1771.

Arc 1020.21 Ruggieri, C. De portuensi S. Hippolyti. Romae, 1771.

Arc 915.6.2 Schmidt, F.S. Recueil d'antiquités de la Suisse. Francfort sur le Meyn, 1771.

Arc 865.13 Smith, John. Choir Gaur...Orrery of Druids...Stonehenge. 2. ed. Salisbury, 1771. 2 pam.

Arc 865.13.2 Smith, John. Choir Gaur...Orrery of Druids...Stonehenge. 2. ed. Salisbury, 1771.

Arc 1580.7 Voigt, A. Beschreibung der bisher bekaunten böhmischen Münzen. v.1-2,3-4. Prag, 1771-87. 2v.

Arc 800.3.13 Winckelmann, J. Critical account of the situation and destruction by the first eruptions of Mount Vesuvius. London, 1771.

1772

Arc 1033.12.100 Lindovius, J. Rubram Jesu Christi chlamydem...exponent...respondens. Jenae, 1772?

Arc 1348.40 Magnan, D. Miscellanea numismatica. Romae, 1772-74. 3v.

Arc 1458.6 Raper, M. An inquiry into the value of the ancient Greek and Roman money. London, 1772.

1773

Arc 1030.16 Allegrantia, J. De sepulcris christianis. Mediolani, 1773.

Arc 1033.44.33 Allegranza, J. De monogrammate D.N. Jesu Christe. Milano, 1773.

Arc 750.201 Dionisi, F.L. Sacr. Vat. Basilicae. Roma, 1773.

Arc 1015.230 Dionysius, P.L. Sacrarum vaticanae...cryptarum. Romae, 1773.

Arc 830.83 Grossen, J.B.B. Recueil des antiquités et monumens marseillos. Marseille, 1773.

Arc 726.66 Passeri, G.B. De marmoreo sepulcrali cinerario. Romae, 1773.

Arc 1190.40 Ruddiman, T. A introduction to James Anderson's Diplomata Scotiae. Edinburgh, 1773.

1774

Arc 1033.17.443 Andrea, G.A. Breve istoria della miracolosa immagine di Maria Sma...di Montenero. Livorno, 1774.

Arc 861.8.9 Battely, J. The antiquities of Richborough and Reculver. London, 1774.

Arc 1335.1 Catalogue raisonné d'une collection de médailles. Leipzig, 1774.

Arc 861.15.5 Ives, J. Remarks on the Garianorum...Romans. 2. ed. London, 1774.

Arc 1027.61 Precis recitandae in recognitione, et extractione Corporum S. Martyrum. Romae, 1774.

Arc 1180.2 Vaines, J. de. Dictionnaire raisonnè de diploéatique. Paris, 1774. 2v.

1775

Arc 1185.30 Battheney. L'archiviste françois. 2. éd. Paris, 1775.

Arc 936.27 Hachhausen und Hachlaus, S.J. Die Alterthümer Daciens in dem heutigen Siebenbürgen. Wien, 1775.

Htn Arc 1364.1.2* Jennings, D. An introduction to the knowledge of medals. 2. ed. Birmingham, 1775.

Arc 380.212 Lubersac, M. Discours sur les monumens publics. Paris, 1775.

Arc 1490.14 Maguan, A.P.D. Lucania numismatica. Roma, 1775.

Arc 1033.96 Salomoni, P. De Liminibus Apostolorum. Romae, 1775.

Arc 1485.9F Zanetti, G.A. Nuova raccolta delle monete e zecche d'Italia. Bologna, 1775-89. 5v.

1776

Arc 1033.17.58 Crispi, L. Dissertazione anti-critica...S. Luca evangelista fosse pittore. Faenza, 1776.

Arc 1076.2 Foster, J.R. Liber singularis de Bysso antiquorum. Londini, 1776.

Htn Arc 1670.56F* Hedlinger, J.K. Oeuvre du chevalier Hedlinger. Basle, 1776.

Arc 1020.49.1 Recueil...reliques...Nôtre Dame d'Aix la Chapelle. Aix, 1776?

Arc 1033.17.626 Sangiovanni, V. Storia della Madre di Dio...del Monte Berico. Vicenza, 1776.

Arc 1510.122 Schwarzenau, J.L. Ansehnlichen Vorrath von Thalern und Schaustücken des langraflich-hessischen Gesamthauses. n.p., 1776.

1777

Arc 726.48 Colucci, G. Sulle antiche città picene Falera e Tignio. Fermo, 1777.

Arc 505.21 Cramer, F. Scythische Denkmahlen in Palästina. Kiel, 1777.

1777 - cont.

Arc 1510.11 Finauer, P.P. Münzreihe der Herzoge in Baiern. München, 1777.

Arc 1020.25 Olivieri, Abati. Munorie della Chiesa S. Maria di Monte Granaro. Pesaro, 1777.

Arc 1033.12.32.2 Pingone, E.F. Sindon evangelica. Augustae Taurinorum, 1777.

Arc 1033.35 Regazzi, A. De sacrosancta...cruce...quae in S. Crucis osservantur. Roma, 1777.

Arc 1018.16 Rinaldi, P. De falea veterum christianorum rituum. Romae, 1777.

Arc 875.25 Williams, J. An account of some remarkable ancient ruins. Edinburgh, 1777.

1778

Arc 726.48.2 Colucci, G. Alla dissertazione epistolare sulle antiche città picene Falera e Tignio. Appendice. Macerata, 1778.

Arc 1510.142 Hagen, Johann Georg Friedrich von. Münzbeschreibung des gräflich und fürstlichen Hauses Mansfeld. Nürnberg, 1778.

Htn Arc 1670.56.5F* Hedlinger, J.K. Explication historique et critique des médailles de l'oeuvre du Chevalier Hedlinger. Basle, 1778.

Arc 1018.17 Selvaggio, J.L. Antiquitatum christianarum institutiones. Vercellis, 1778. 3v.

Arc 1190.3 Wright, Andrew. Court hand restored. 2. ed. London, 1778.

Htn Arc 1480.18* Zelada, F.X. de. De nummis aliquot...epistola. Romae, 1778.

1779

Htn Arc 1033.35.13F* Borgia, S. De cruce vaticana...commentarius. Roma, 1779.

Arc 726.5 Cabral, S. Delle ville e de' più notabili monumenti. Roma, 1779.

Arc 785.15.50 Calcografia di Roma. v.6-7. Roma, 1779.

Arc 1510.147 Klotzsch, Johann Friedrich. Versuch einer chur-sächsischen Münzgeschichte von den Ältesten, bis auf jetzige Zeiten. v.1-2. Chemnitz, 1779-80.

Arc 750.200 Magnan, D. La città di Roma. Roma, 1779. 2v.

Arc 1020.9 Mazzolari, G.M. Diario sacro le sacre vie, le sacre basilicho. Roma, 1779-81. 5v.

Arc 1215.1 Migieu. Recueil des sceaux du Moyen Âge dits sceaux gothiques. Paris, 1779.

1780

Htn Arc 1033.17.96.3* Becerra Tanco, Luis. Felicidad de México...Nuestra Señora de Guadalupe. México, 1780.

Htn Arc 1033.35.15F* Borgia, S. De cruce veliterna. Roma, 1780.

Arc 895.36 Forssenius, A.C. Specimen historicum de monumento Kiwikensi. Londini Gothorum, 1780.

Arc 1503.1 Haller, G.E. von. Schweizerisches Münz- und Medaillenkabinet. v.1-2. Bern, 1780-81.

Arc 800.2 Maréchal, P.S. Antiquités d'Herculanum. Paris, 1780-1803. 12v.

Htn Arc 1160.202.5* Merino, Andres. Escuela paleographica...letras antiguas. Madrid, 1780.

Arc 853.374 Neuhof, Elias. Nachricht von den Alterthümern in der Gegend und auf dem Gebürge bey Homburg vor der Höhe. Homburg, 1780.

Arc 1540.22 Noble, Mark. Two dissertations upon the mint and coins of Durham. Birmingham, 1780.

Arc 843.5.15 Valcarcel, A. Lucentum, oy La ciudad de Alicante. Valencia, 1780.

1781

Arc 1033.37 Abbati Olivieri Giordani, Annibale degli. Di alcune antichità cristiane...in Pesaro nel Museo Olivieri. Pesaro, 1781.

Arc 386.25 Burgess, Thomas. An essay on the study of antiquities. Oxford, 1781.

Arc 750.30.5 Collection de peintures antiques...Rome. Rome, 1781.

Htn Arc 1420.2F* Pérez Báyer, F. F. Perezii Bayerii. De numis hebraeo-samaritanis. Valentia, 1781.

Arc 1033.35.27 Venuti, F. De cruce cortonensi dissertatio. Florenzia, 1781.

1782

Htn Arc 1433.6* Adler, I.G.C. Collectio nova numorum cuficum. Hafniae, 1782-92. 2v.

Arc 1033.12.71 Aquilini, H. De pretiosissimo Jesu Christi Sanguine Mantuae asservato. Venezia, 1782.

Arc 1033.12.76 Déscription de la relique...du...sang...Bruges. Bruges, 1782.

Arc 1027.36.5 Dionisi, G.J. Della città di Preconi nominata negli atti di SS. MM. fermo e rustico. Vinegia, 1782.

Arc 1500.30 Grappin, Pierre-Philippe. Recherches sur les anciennes monnaies du comté de Bourgogne. Paris, 1782.

Arc 400.8 Pownall, T. Treatise on the study of antiquities. London, 1782.

1783

Arc 750.30 Cassini, G.M. Pitture antiche. Roma, 1783.

Arc 1033.17.163 Cavallucci, V. Istoria critica del sagro anello...Perugia. Perugia, 1783.

Arc 1033.108 Guazzugli, M. Notizie riguardanti il culto di S. Irene. Osimo, 1783.

Arc 1033.17.71 Istoria della miraclosa immagine...della...vergine di S. Luca. Bologna, 1783.

1784

Arc 1033.37.3 Abbati Olivieri Giordani, Annibale degli. Di alcune altre antichità cristiane. Pesaro, 1784.

Arc 1020.9.25 Cancellieri, F. Sagrestica vaticana eretta...Pio Sesto. Roma, 1784.

Arc 136.1.60 Fenn, John. Three...tables...exhibiting a state of...Society of Antiquaries. London, 1784. 2 pam.

Arc 136.1.63 King, Edward. A speech...23rd April 1784. London, 1784.

Arc 1020.31.9 Mariti, Giovanni. Istoria del tempio della resurrezione. Livorno, 1784.

Arc 1348.10 Pinkerton, John. An essay on medals. London, 1784.

Arc 1675.30 Salgado, Vicente. Conjecturas sobre huma medallia de bronze. Lisboa, 1784.

Chronological Listing

1784 - cont.

Arc 726.24.7 — Sanctis, D. de. Dissertazioni...la villa d'Orazio, il mausoleo di Plauzj in Tivoli. Ravenna, 1784.

Arc 1453.5 — Soothe, J.C. von. Auserlesenes und hochstansehnliches Ducatenkabinett. Hamburg, 1784.

Arc 1510.1 — Widmer, M.J. von. Domus Wittelbachensis numismatica. Munich, 1784-85.

Arc 1510.1.2 — Widmer, M.J. von. Dormus Wittelbachensis numismatica. Munich, 1784.

Arc 800.3.5 — Winckelmann, J. Recueil de lettres de M. Winckelmann. Paris, 1784.

1785

Arc 628.7 — Biagi, C. Monumenta Graeca ex Museo Jacobi Nanni. Monumenta Graeca et Latina Jacobi Nanni. Roma, 1785-87. 2v.

Arc 458.3 — Gough, Richard. Comparative view of antient monuments of India...island of Salset. London, 1785.

Arc 1340.1 — Rasche, J.C. Lex. univ. rei nummariae. v.1-5, pt.1-2; v.6, pt.1. Leipzig, 1785-95. 11v.

1786

Arc 1540.19 — Cardonnel-Lawson, Adam. Numismata Scotiae. Edinburgi, 1786.

Arc 825.7.2 — Description...des antiquités. 2. éd. Nismes, 1786.

Arc 1660.15F — Duby, P.A.T. Recueil général des pieces obsidionales. Paris, 1786.

Arc 1493.7F — Saez, Liciniano. Apendice á la crónica nuevamente impressa del señor rey don Juan el II. Madrid, 1786.

1787

Arc 830.97.5 — Gibelin, Antoine. Lettre sur les tours antiques qu'on a démoliés à Aix en Provence et sur les antiquités qu'elles renfermoient. Aix, 1787.

Arc 630.10 — Martini, G.H. Antiquorum monimentorum, sylloge altera. Lipsiae, 1787.

1788

Arc 785.40.5 — Cancellieri, F. Notizie del carcere Tulliano. Roma, 1788.

Arc 875.40 — Cordiner, Charles. Remarkable ruins and romantic prospects of North Britain. London, 1788-95.

Arc 1020.113 — Furno, A. Breve istoria del santuario di Belmonte presso Valperga. Torino, 1788.

Arc 1033.17.464 — Istoria della miracolosa immagine della...Maria del Carmine...Napoli. Napoli, 1788.

Arc 1033.12.2 — Notizie intorno alla novena...di natale. Roma, 1788.

1789

Arc 825.12 — Maucomble, Jean François Dieudonné. Description historique et abrégée des antiquités de Nismes. Nismes, 1789.

Arc 1335.15 — Thott, O. Thesaurus numismatum. Copenhagen, 1789.

1790

Arc 1660.15.5F — Duby, P.A.T. Trauté des monnaies des barons. Paris, 1790. 2v.

Arc 1033.35.66 — Exposé historique de l'honneur...du culte...au bois de la vraie croix. Bruxelles, 1790. 2 pam.

Arc 760.6.5 — Fea, Carlo. Miscellanea filologica critica e antiquaria. Roma, 1790-1836. 2v.

Arc 1335.60 — Hutchins. A catalogue of the collection of curious...coins. London, 1790.

Arc 1033.17.322 — Orgio. Istoriche notizie...dell'immagine di Maria...di Genazzano. 3. ed. Roma, 1790.

Arc 1660.2 — Pinkerton, J. The medallic history of England. London, 1790.

1791

Arc 522.1 — Lechevalier, Jean Baptiste. Description of the plain of Troy. Edinburgh, 1791.

1792

Arc 1359.1 — Eckhel, J.H. Doctrina numorum veterum. Viennae, 1792-98. 8v.

Arc 1153.45 — Gerrard, John. Siglarium romanum. Londini, 1792.

Arc 143.2 — Society of Antiquaries of Scotland. Archaeologia Scotica. Edinburgh, 1792- 5v.

Arc 1033.17.95.5 — Triduo in ossequio di Maria santissima di Guadalupe. Roma, 1792.

Arc 1423.4 — Tychsen, T.C. De numis Hasmonaeorum paralipomena. n.p., 1792.

Arc 1478.84 — Uhlich, Gottfried. Versuch einer Numismatik für Künstler. Lemberg, 1792.

Arc 1335.75 — Wallraf, F.F. Beschreibung der köllnischen Munzsammlung des domherrn und kurfürstlich-weltlichen Hofgerichts Präsidenten von Merle. Kölln am Rhein, 1792.

1793

Htn Arc 855.14F* — Douglas, J. Nenia Britannica, or Sepulchral history of Great Britain. London, 1793.

Arc 726.73 — Hadrawa, N. Ragguagli di varii scavi. Napoli, 1793.

Arc 1033.28.15 — Tori, G. Dei riti nuziali degli antichi cristiani. Perugia, 1793.

1794

Arc 726.59.25 — Barbaro, C.A. Degli avanzi d'alcuni antichissimi edifizi, scoperti in Malta l'anno 1768. Malta, 1794.

Arc 726.73.5 — Hadrawa, N. Ragguagli di varii scavi. Dresda, 1794.

Arc 1145.206 — Hodgkin, J. Calligraphia Graeca et poecilographia Graeca. Londini, 1794.

Arc 1433.3 — Tychsen, O.G. Introductio in rem numariam Muhammedanorum. Rostock, 1794. 2 pam.

1795

Htn Arc 522.2.3* — Bryant, Jacob. Observations upon a treatise: Description of plain of Troy. Eton, 1795.

Arc 522.2 — Bryant, Jacob. Observations upon a treatise entitled A description of the plain of Troy. Eton, 1795.

Arc 1033.17.133 — Buenchini, G.M. Notizie istoriche intorno alla sma. Cintola. Prato, 1795.

Arc 1535.7 — Pye, Charles. Provincial copper coins or tokens, 1787-1796. London, 1795.

1796

Arc 1033.66 — Bonet, F.R. Breve notizia...d'alcuni Santi del Colosseo. Roma, 1796.

Arc 1668.7 — Casali, J. De nummulis Peioesa inscriptis. Romae, 1796.

Arc 1348.42PF — Collezione di tavole monetarie. Venezia, 1796.

Arc 1033.17.253 — Estratto di una lettera di Ancona di 27 giugno 1796. n.p., 1796.

Arc 785.21 — Oberlin, J.J. Exposé Diene découverte...le Chévalier de Freden. Strasbourg, 1796.

Arc 1027.4.9 — Paoli. Notizie...S. Feliciano...cimitero di Priscilla. Roma, 1796.

Arc 1033.17.30 — Raccolta di varie lettere...relique ed immagine...Santissima Vergine Maria Cattedrale...Ancona. Roma, 1796.

Arc 1033.17.29 — Relazione del prodigioso...aprimento di Occhi di una immagine di Maria...Ancona. Venezia, 1796.

Arc 1492.203F — Saez, Liciniano. Demonstración histórica del verdadero valor detodas las monedas que corrian en Castilla. Madrid, 1796.

Htn Arc 969.1.9* — Sargent, W. Papers relative to certain American antiquities. Philadelphia, 1796.

Arc 1033.17.18 — Teodoro di Santa Maria. Memorie...miracolosa immagine della Madonna Ssma detta della Vittoria. Roma, 1796.

1797

Arc 785.40.15 — Bertotti Scamozzi, Ottavio. Les thermes des Romains. v.5. Vicenza, 1797.

Arc 1269.20 — Kiefhaber, J.K.S. Historisch-diplomatische Beschreibung der Nürnbergischen Kloster-Siegel. Nürnberg, 1797.

Arc 766.2 — Lumisden, A. Remarks on the antiquities of Rome and its environs. London, 1797.

Htn Arc 785.40.10* — Palladio, A. Le terme dei Romani disegnate. Vicenza, 1797.

Arc 726.7.5 — Visconti, E.A. Monumenti gabini della Villa Pinciana. Roma, 1797.

Arc 861.40.5 — Warner, Richard. An illustration of the Roman antiquities discovered at Bath. Bath, 1797.

Arc 545.20 — Zoega, G. De origine et usu obeliscorum. Rome, 1797.

1798

Arc 1185.8 — Gatterer, J.C. Abriss der Diplomatik. Göttingen, 1798.

Arc 522.11 — Lenz, C.G. Die Ebene von Troja. Neu-Strelitz, 1798.

Arc 1033.55.3 — Marangoni, G. Istoria dell'...oratorio...Lateran...Sancta Sanctorum. Roma, 1798.

Arc 1033.12.141 — Notizie istoriche...della immagine del...Salvatore. Roma, 1798.

Arc 1033.55 — Romano, G.B. Memorie sacre della cappella...e di...la Scola Santa. Roma, 1798.

Arc 1033.17.548 — Saggio di notizie istoriche relative ai tre sagri monumenti, che si portano in processione la Mallina del di 17. gennajo 1798. n.p., 1798? 2 pam.

1799

Arc 1538.13 — Conder, James. An arrangement of provincial coins...Great Britain, Ireland. Ipswich, 1799.

Arc 1353.5 — Eckhel, J. Thesauro Caesarum...Numorun Gemmarumque. Budae, 1799.

Arc 1185.8.2 — Gatterer, J.C. Praktische Diplomatik. Göttingen, 1799.

Arc 522.1.2.3 — Lechevalier, Jean Baptiste. Voyage dans la Troade. 2. éd. Paris, 1799.

18-

Arc 1478.30 — Catalogue d'une collection de médailles romaines. pt.1-2,3. Paris, 18- . 2v.

Arc 595.17 — Denslow, Van Buren. The pyramid of Gizeh. N.Y., 18- .

Arc 1335.130 — Landowne, William P. A catalogue of a valuable collection. London, 18- ?

Arc 1670.50F — Mazerolle, Fernand. Claude de Héry, médailleur du roi Henri III. Paris, 18- ?

Arc 768.5 — Nuova raccolta...antiche e moderne...Roma. Roma, 18- .

Arc 545.15.2PF — Planches du Voyage dans la Basse et la Haute Egypte. Atlas. London, 18- ?

Arc 1423.14.5 — Williamson, G.C. The money of the Bible. N.Y., 18- ?

1800

Arc 385.2 — Astle, Thomas. Observations on stone pillars. London, 1800.

Arc 1433.11 — Hallenberg, Jonas. Collectio nummorum cuficorum. Stockholm, 1800.

Arc 136.1.50 — London Society of Antiquaries. A copy of the royal charter and statutes. London, 1800.

Arc 432.2A — Maurice, G. Indian antiquities. London, 1800. 7v.

Arc 770.8 — Piroli, T. Gli edifici antichi di Roma. Roma, 1800?

Arc 1185.15 — Zinkernagel, K.F.B. Handbuch für angehende Archivare und Registratoren. Nördlingen, 1800.

1801

Arc 1200.18 — Alter, Franz K. Beitrag zur praktischen Diplomatik für Slaven. Wien, 1801.

Arc 723.14 — Barthélemy, J.J. Voyage en Italie. Paris, 1801.

Arc 595.2 — Grobert, J. Description des pyramides de Ghizé. Paris, 1801.

Arc 1330.2 — Lipsius, J.G. Bibliotheca numaria. Leipzig, 1801. 2v.

Arc 1033.12.140 — Notizie storiche intorno al SS. Crocifisso...in Trastevere. Roma, 1801.

Arc 1033.17.455 — Patiño, P.P. Disertación crítico-theo-filosófica sobre la conservación de la santa imagen de Nuestra Señora de los Angeles. México, 1801.

Chronological Listing

1801 - cont.

Arc 1535.7.2 — Pye, Charles. Provincial copper coins, tokens of trade...1787-1801. 2. ed. London, 1801.

Arc 925.13.7 — Vaksel, H.C.L. Izobrazheniia raznykh' pamiashchnikov drevnosti. Sankt Petersburg, 1801.

1802

Arc 1033.17.302 — Ciabilli, G. Notizie risguardanti lo stato antico e moderno del sacro eratorio....miracolosa immagine di Maria. Firenze, 1802.

Arc 726.25 — Fea, Carlo. Relazione di un viaggio ad Ostia. Roma, 1802.

Arc 1016.8 — Hager, Joseph. Monument de Yu, ou La plus ancienne inscription de la Chine. Paris, 1802.

Arc 895.21.15 — Hallenberg, J. Quatuor monumenta aenea e terra i Suecia eruta. Stockholm, 1802.

Arc 861.12.12 — Hutton, W. History of the Roman wall. London, 1802.

Arc 1033.12.6 — Jesus Christ. Narrazione critico storica della reliquia...Santissimo Prepuzio. Roma, 1802.

Arc 522.1.2 — Lechevalier, Jean Baptiste. Voyage de la Troade. Paris, 1802. 3v.

Arc 397.1 — Millin, A.L. Monumens antiques. Paris, 1802-06. 2v.

Arc 1033.12.5 — Narrazione critico storica...Prepuzio de Gesu. Roma, 1802.

Arc 400.23 — Paciaudi, Paolo M. Lettres au comte de Caylus. Paris, 1802.

Arc 1340.1.2 — Rasche, J.C. Lex. univ. rei numariae veterum. Supplement. Leipzig, 1802-05. 3v.

Arc 750.223F — Riccy, G.A. Dell'antico pago Lemonio in oggi Roma Vecchia. Roma, 1802.

1803

Arc 1138.18 — Astle, Thomas. Origin and progress of writing. London, 1803.

Arc 861.15 — Ives, J. Remarks on the Garianorum...Romans. 2. ed. Yarmouth, 1803.

Arc 1538.14 — Leigh, Sotheby, and Son. Collection of 28 plates illustrating ancient coins of Great Britain. London, 1803.

Arc 825.2 — Ménard, L. Histoire des antiquités de la ville de Nismes. Nîmes, 1803.

Htn Arc 776.1.2* — Venuti, R. Accurata e succinta descrizione topografica delle antichità di Roma. 2. ed. Roma, 1803. 2v.

Arc 925.7 — Wapel, Leon de. Recueil de quelques antiquités. Berlin, 1803.

1804

Arc 510.203 — Gell, W. The topography of Troy. London, 1804.

Arc 505.5.44 — Münter, F. Om den Davidische families begravelse under Zions bierg. Kjobenhavn, 1804.

1805

Arc 590.10 — Clark, Edward. The tomb of Alexander. Cambridge, 1805.

Htn Arc 761.5.2* — Guattani, G.A. Roma descritta ed illustrata. 2. ed. v.1-2. Roma, 1805.

Arc 1411.9F — Hager, Joseph. Description des médailles chinoises du cabinet imperial de France. Paris, 1805.

Arc 1583.9 — Krug, A.L. Zur Münzkunde Russlands. St. Petersburg, 1805.

Arc 1175.10 — Marini, G.L. I papiri diplomatici. Roma, 1805.

Arc 1020.9.5 — Mazzolari, G.M. Diario sacro. 2. ed. Roma, 1805-06. 4v.

Arc 1033.17.502 — Notizie istoriche...alla transformazione di una immagine della B.V...Palazzolo. Brescia, 1805.

Arc 1493.8 — Saez, Liciniano. Demostración histórica del verdadero valor de todas las monedas que corrián en Castilla. Madrid, 1805.

1806

Arc 386.5 — Böttiger, Carl August. Archäologie. Dresden, 1806.

Arc 1348.33F — Bonneville, P.F. Traité des monnaies d'or et d'argent qui circulent chez les différens peuples. Paris, 1806.

Arc 760.6.11 — Fea, Carlo. Annotazioni alla memoria sui diritti del principato. Roma, 1806.

Arc 1020.9.5.25 — Fea, Carlo. Dei diritti del principato. Roma, 1806.

Arc 820.211F — Lacour, Pierre. Tombeaux antiques. Bordeaux, 1806.

Arc 830.142 — Lebreton, J. Archéologie de Mons Seleucus. Gap, 1806.

Arc 1458.1 — Mionnet, T.E. Description de médailles antiques. Paris, 1806-08. 7v.

Arc 1025.38 — Partenio, G.M. Vie sacre. 2a ed. Roma, 1806-07. 2v.

1807

Arc 1588.10.15 — Budapest. Orszagos Széchenyi-Könyvtár. Catalogus numorum Hungariae ac Transiwaniae Instituti Nationalis Szechényrani. Pestini, 1807. 2v.

Arc 820.210F — Champollion-Figeac, Jacques J. Antiquités de Grenoble. Grenoble, 1807.

Arc 1348.43 — Darier, Hugues. Tableau du titre. Geneve, 1807.

Arc 545.15F — Denon, V. Voyages dans la Basse et la Haute Égypte. London, 1807.

Arc 545.15PF — Denon, V. Voyages dans la Basse et la Haute Égypte. Atlas. London, 1807.

Arc 1020.9.7 — Fea, Carlo. Conclusione per l'integrita del panteon. Roma, 1807.

Arc 1020.9.6 — Fea, Carlo. L'integrita del panteon di M. Agrippa. Roma, 1807.

Arc 830.22.14F — Grivaud de la Vincelle, C.M. Antiquités gauloises et romaines. Atlas. Paris, 1807.

Arc 830.22.14 — Grivaud de la Vincelle, C.M. Antiquités gauloises et romaines. Texte. Paris, 1807.

Arc 390.7F — Notice sur Jules-Francois-Paul Fauris Saint-Vincens. Aix, 1807.

1808

Arc 887.1F — Bast, M.J. de. Receueil d'antiquités romaines et gauloises trouvées dans la Flandre. Gand, 1808.

Arc 830.331 — Baudot, L.B. Observations sur la passage de M. Millin à Dijon. Dijon, 1808.

Arc 1033.12.175 — Eufrasio. Memorie storico-critiche...lagrime di...Dongo. Lugano, 1808.

Arc 726.17 — Johanneau, E. Lettre...sur l'inscription...du Lion de Venise. n.p., 1808.

Arc 1053.5.3 — Levezow, R. Ueber den Antinous. Berlin, 1808.

1808 - cont.

Arc 1510.37 — Mader, Joseph. Versuch über die Brakteaten. v.2. Prag, 1808.

Arc 1348.10.3 — Pinkerton, John. An essay on medals. London, 1808. 2v.

Arc 400.4 — Pronti, D. Nuova raccolta representante i costumi. Roma, 1808.

1809

Arc 557.2 — Hamilton, W. Aegyptiaca. London, 1809.

Arc 853.20.10 — Hetzrodt, J.B.M. Notices sur les anciens Trévirois. Trèves, 1809.

Arc 136.1.2 — London Society of Antiquaries. Index to Archaeologia. v.1-30. London, 1809-44. 2v.

Arc 1373.3 — Scotti, V.N. Della rarità delle medaglie antiche. Florence, 1809.

181-

Arc 853.24.15F — Schweighauser, J.G. Antiquités de Rheinzabern. Strasbourg, 181-.

1810

Arc 1025.59 — Artaud de Montor, A.F. Voyages dans les catacombes de Rome. Paris, 1810.

Arc 1033.17.321 — Ciappolini, D. Divoto compendio della storia...s. immagine di Maria...Scutari. Napoli, 1810.

Arc 1016.239 — Dragoni, A. Sul dittico eburneo de santi martiri Teodoro ed Acacio. Parma, 1810.

Arc 646.1 — Gell, W. The itinerary of Greece: the geography of Ithaca. v.1-2. London, 1810.

Arc 1335.145 — Götz, Christian. Beyträge zum Groschen-Cabinet. Dresden, 1810. 3v.

Arc 726.4 — Jorio, A. de. Scheletri cumani. Napoli, 1810.

Arc 805.3 — Koehler, H.K.E. von. Description de deux monumens antiques. St. Petersbourg, 1810.

Arc 720.206 — Maps. Pozzuoli. Pozzuoli e contorni. Napoli, 1810.

Htn Arc 861.6.5* — Marriott, William. The antiquities of Lyme. Stockport, 1810.

Arc 720.9.2.5F — Micali, G. Antichi monumenti per servire all'opera...l'Italia. Firenze, 1810.

Arc 823.7 — Pasumot, Francois. Dissertations et mémoires sur differens sujets d'antiquité et d'histoire. Paris, 1810-1813.

Arc 1138.8 — Pfeiffer, A.F. Ueber Buecher-Handschriften. Erlangen, 1810.

1811

Arc 861.8.5 — Battely, J. Antiquitates rutupinae. Oxoniae, 1811.

Arc 830.129 — Chalieu, Alexis. Mémoires sur diverses antiquités du département de la Drôme. Valence, 1811.

Arc 830.80 — Gregoire d'Essigny, L.A.J. Mémoire sur la question des voies romaines. Paris, 1811. 2 pam.

Arc 858.15 — Relics of antiquity in Great Britain. London, 1811.

Arc 830.89 — Villeneuve-Bargemon, Christophe. Fragment d'un voyage dans les Basses-Alpes. Agen, 1811. 3 pam.

Arc 421.25 — Yu. Inschrift des Yu. Halle, 1811.

1812

Arc 1033.12.55 — Anguissola, G.B. Stromenti che servirono alla Passione...nostro signori. Piacenza, 1812.

Arc 736.2.3 — Letronne, A. Essai critique sur la topographie de Syracuse. Paris, 1812.

Htn Arc 720.12* — Middleton, J. Grecian remains in Italy. London, 1812.

Arc 1166.4 — Peignot, G. Essai sur l'histoire du parchemin. Paris, 1812.

Arc 1033.17.72 — Prospetto storico dell'imagine di Maria vergine...S.Luca. Bologna, 1812.

Arc 785.58F — Vaudoyer. Description du théâtre de Marcellus à Rome. Paris, 1812.

Arc 1475.201 — Vernazza de Freney, J. Recensio nummorum qui secusii. Augustae Taurinorum, 1812.

1813

Arc 810.49 — Clarac, Frédéric. Fouille faite a Pompéi en présence de S.M. la reine des deux Siciles. n.p., 1813.

Arc 1433.7 — Fraehn, C.M.J. Numophylacium orientale Pototianum. Casani, 1813.

Arc 1033.17.34 — Gregorio. Storia della translazione...immagine di Santa Maria di Constantinopoli. 2a ed. Napoli, 1813.

Arc 1298.1 — Guenther, M. Ins sigillorum mediiaevi. Lipsiae, 1813.

Arc 815.19 — Millin, A.L. Description des tombeaux qui ont été découverts à Pompéi dans l'année 1812. Naples, 1813.

1814

Arc 1020.102.3 — Angelis, L. de. Osservazioni critici...Siena...sopra croce di rame intagliata...1129. Siena, 1814.

Arc 1333.4 — British Museum. Veteres pop. et reg. numi. London, 1814.

Arc 726.49 — Guarini, R. Ricerche sull'antica città di Eclano. 2a ed. Appendice. Napoli, 1814-15.

Arc 820.215F — Maupercher. Paris ancien, Paris moderne. Paris, 1814.

Arc 825.2.2 — Ménard, L. Histoire des antiquités de la ville de Nismes. Nîmes, 1814.

Arc 522.7 — Rennell, J. Observations on the topography of the plain of Troy. London, 1814.

Arc 726.36 — Rosso, G. del. Saggio...sui monumenti della antica città di Fiesole. Firenze, 1814.

1815

Arc 1030.13 — Adami, L. Dell culto, A.S.S.M.M., cemeteriali e dell'antichita. Roma, 1815.

Arc 855.223F — Malcolm, J.P. Lives of topographers and antiquaries. London, 1815.

Arc 1433.14 — Winbom, Jonas A. Dissertatio de recentioribus numis Arabicis. Upsaliae, 1815.

Chronological Listing

1816

Arc 1353.7.5 — Copenhagen. National Museet. Catalogus numorum veterum graecorum et Latinorum musei. Hafniae, 1816. 3v.

Arc 1510.145 — Erbstein, Karl Friedrich Wilhelm. Numismatische Bruchstücke in Bezug auf sächsische Geschichte. v.1-3. Dresden, 1816.

Arc 1588.2 — Fraehn, C.M.J. De numorum Bulgharicorum forte antiguissimo. Casani, 1816.

NEDL Arc 1353.4 — Ramus, Christian. Catalogus numorum veterum graecorum et latinorum. pt. 1-2. Hafniae, 1816.

Arc 1490.40F — Vermiglioli, G.B. Della zecca e delle monete perugine. Perugia, 1816.

Arc 708.18 — Wilkins, W. Atheniensia, or Remarks on the topography and buildings of Athens. London, 1816.

1817

Arc 1018.25 — Augusti, J.C.W. Denkwürdigkeiten und der christlichen Archäologie. Leipzig, 1817-26. 12v.

Arc 1540.22.7 — Bartlet, B. The episcopal coins of Durham. Newcastle, 1817.

Htn Arc 513.2* — Beaufort, F. Karamania. London, 1817.

Arc 810.6 — Gell, William. Pompeiana. London, 1817-19.

Arc 823.16 — Grivaud de la Vincelle, C.M. Recueil de monumens antiques. v.1-2. Paris, 1817.

Arc 1138.9 — Kopp, U.F. Palaeographia critica. Mannheim, 1817-29. 4v.

Arc 1458.4 — Letronne, J.A. Considerations générales sur l'évaluation des monnaies grecques et romaines. Paris, 1817.

Arc 733.4.5 — Paterno, I.V. Viaggio per tutte le antichita della Sicilia. 3a ed. Palermo, 1817.

Arc 785.1.5 — Piale, Stefano. Del tempio volgarmente detto di Vesta. Roma, 1817.

Arc 843.2 — Ramis y Ramis, J. Inscripciones romanas que existen en Menorca. Mahon, 1817.

Arc 793.4 — Romanelli, D. Viaggio a Pompei a Pesto e di ritorno ad Ercolano ed a Pozzuoli. Napoli, 1817.

Arc 1535.4 — Ruding, R. Annals of the coinage of Great Britain. London, 1817. 4v.

Arc 1470.9 — Sestini, D. Descrizione degli stateri antichi. Florence, 1817.

Arc 1480.23 — Tochon D'Annecy, J.F. Mémoire sur les médailles de Marinus. Paris, 1817.

Arc 726.22 — Visconti, A. Lettera al signor Giuseppe Carnevali di Albano. Roma, 1817.

Arc 407.1 — Walpole, R. Memoirs relating to European and Asiatic Turkey. London, 1817-20. 2v.

1818

Arc 1480.31F — Artaud, F. Discours sur les médailles d'Auguste et de Tibère. Lyon, 1818.

Arc 762.4.2 — Broughton, J.C.H. Historical illustrations of 4th canto of Childe Harold. 2. ed. London, 1818.

Arc 822.2 — Cellerier. Notice relative à la découverte d'un tombeau. Paris, 1818. 25 pam.

Arc 723.4 — Forsyth, J. Remarks on antiquities, arts and letters. Boston, 1818.

Htn Arc 762.4* — Hobhouse, J. Historical illustrations of 4th canto of Childe Harold. London, 1818.

Arc 830.51 — La Scava...excavation of a Roman town on the hill of Chatelet. London, 1818.

Arc 1663.27 — Laskey, John C. A description of the series of medals struck at the national medal mint by...Napoleon Bonaparte. London, 1818.

Arc 1390.7 — Marchant, N.D. Mélanges de numismatique et d'histoire. Paris, 1818.

Arc 830.90 — Martin, Jean C. Antiquités et inscriptions des villes de Die, d'Orange. Orange, 1818.

Arc 768.1.25 — Nardini, F. Roma antica. 4. ed. Roma, 1818-20. 4v.

Arc 726.2.25 — Panvini, P. Il forestiere alle antichità e curiosità nationali Pozzuoli. Napoli, 1818.

Arc 1020.101 — Récit de la fondation de l'Eglise de Notre Dame de Long-Pré. Abbéville, 1818.

Arc 1494.4 — Salat, Josef. Tratado de las monedas labradas...de Cataluña. v.1-2. Barcelona, 1818.

Arc 1020.49.3 — Trésor d'Aix-la-Chapelle. 1.-3. éd. Aix, 1818-20? 3 pam.

Arc 712.5 — Visconti, E.Q. Mémoires sur des ouvrages de sculpture du Parthénon. Paris, 1818.

1819

Arc 726.20.7PF — Antolini, G. Le rovine di Veleia misurate e disegnate. Pt.1-2. Milano, 1819-22.

Arc 1025.39 — Cancellieri, F. Dissertazione epistolare. Roma, 1819.

Arc 1033.80 — Castro, V. de. Difesa della causa di S. Marcellino. Roma, 1819.

Arc 643.2 — Dodwell, E. A classical and topographical tour through Greece. London, 1819. 2v.

Arc 1020.20.5 — Fea, C. La Basilica di Costantino. Roma, 1819.

Arc 760.6.7 — Fea, Carlo. Nuova descrizione de' monumenti antichi. Roma, 1819.

Arc 1433.9 — Fraehn, C.M.J. Novae symbolae ad rem numariam Muhammedanorum. Petropoli, 1819.

Arc 723.3 — Hoare, R.C. A classical tour through Italy and Sicily. London, 1819. 2v.

Arc 1445.5 — Milan. I.R. Museo. Monete cufiche dell'I.R. Museo di Milano. Milano, 1819.

Arc 1458.1.2 — Mionnet, T.E. Description de médailles antiques. Supplément. Paris, 1819-37. 10v.

Arc 1020.10.33 — Nibby, A. Del Foro Romano e de' luoghi adjacenti. Roma, 1819.

Arc 1020.9.9 — Nibby, A. Del tempio della pace e della basiilica di Costantino. Roma, 1819.

Arc 730.5.3 — Politi, R. Lettera di...Grove-Olympico in Agrigento. Palermo, 1819.

Arc 830.112 — Roche, J.J. Notices historiques sur les anciens cintrons. Moutiers, 1819.

Arc 410.1.18 — Welcker, F.G. Zoega's Leben. Stuttgart, 1819. 2v.

1820

Arc 386.5.6 — Böttiger, Carl August. Amalthea. v.1-3. Leipzig, 1820-25. 2v.

Arc 1020.9.6.2 — Fea, Carlo. L'integrita del panteon rivendicata a Marco Agrippo. 2a ed. Roma, 1820.

1820 - cont.

Arc 760.6 — Fea, Carlo. Varieta di notizie economiche fisiche antiquarie. Rome, 1820.

Arc 1048.1 — Fraehn, C.M. Antiquitatis Muhammedanae monumenta varia. pt.1-2. Petropoli, 1820-22.

Arc 843.13F — Gomez de Somorrostro y Martin, A. El acueducto y otras antiqüedades de Segovia. Madrid, 1820.

Arc 1033.17.97.5 — Guridi, José M. Apología de la aparición de Nuestra Señora de Guadalupe de Méjico. Méjico, 1820.

Arc 870.3 — Hamper, William. Observations on certain ancient pillars of memoir called Hoar-Stones. Birmingham, 1820.

Arc 723.12 — Kelsall, Charles. Classical excursion from Rome to Arpino. Geneva, 1820.

Arc 1430.2 — Mainoni, S. de. Descrizione di alcune monete cufiche del Museo. Milano, 1820.

Arc 1535.205F — Mudie, James. An historical and critical account...medals. London, 1820.

Arc 716.6 — Mueller, R.O. Minervae Poliadis Sacra et Aedem in Arce Athenarum. Göttingen, 1820.

Arc 785.29 — Nibby, A. Le mura di Roma. Roma, 1820.

Arc 853.67 — Raiser, J.N. von. Die römischen Alterthümer zu Augsburg. Augsburg, 1820.

Arc 1163.2.9 — Tos, Joaquin. Paleografía que para inteligencia de les manuscrites. Barcelona, 1820.

1821

Arc 1528.5PF — Akademie...Amsterdam. Akademie von Wetenschappen, Amsterdam. Beschrijving van Nederlandsche historie-penningen. v.1-4,6-10. Amsterdam, 1821-69. 6v.

Arc 830.71 — Allou, Charles N. Descriptions des monumens des differeus âges observés dans le département de la Haute-Vienne. Paris, 1821.

Arc 1033.12.185 — Articolo sulla corona ferrea...dal Geornale. Venezia, 1821.

Arc 545.16 — Cailliand, F. Voyage à l'Oasis de Thèbes. pt.1-2. Paris, 1821.

Arc 1033.12.168 — Cateni, P.F. Notizie della reliquia...del sacro chiodo. Colle, 1821.

Arc 1033.116 — Collin de Plancy, J.A.S. Dictionnaire des reliques. Paris, 1821-1822. 3v.

Arc 1433.8.5 — Fraehn, C.M.J. Das Muhammedanische Münzkabinet. St. Petersburg, 1821.

Arc 740.204 — Inghirami, F. Monumenti etruschi. Badia, 1821-25. 9v.

Arc 708.9.2 — Leake, W.M. The topography of Athens. London, 1821.

Arc 1033.17.623 — Molin, A. Dell'antica immagine di Maria...S. Marco in Venezia. Venezia, 1821.

Arc 880.17 — Morres, Hervey Montmorency. A historical and critical inquiry into the origin and primitive use of the Irish pillar-tower. London, 1821.

Arc 785.41 — Piale, Stefano. Degli antichi templi di Vespasiano e della concordia. Roma, 1821. 2 pam.

Arc 400.3 — Porter, R.K. Travels in Georgia, Persia. London, 1821-22. 2v.

Arc 830.72 — Reser, François. Mémoires sur les ruines de Lillebonne. Evreux, 1821.

Arc 1468.19 — Sestini, D. Descrizione d'alcune medaglie greche. Firenze, 1821.

Arc 1373.10 — Sestini, Domenico. Classes generales seu moneta vetus urbium populorum et regum ordine. Florentiae, 1821.

1822

Arc 545.14 — Belzoni, G.B. Narrative of the operations...in Egypt and Nubia. 3. ed. London, 1822. 2v.

Arc 545.14PF — Belzoni, G.B. Narrative of the operations...in Egypt and Nubia. 3. ed. Atlas. London, 1822.

Arc 1433.11.3 — Hallenberg, Jonas. Numismata orientalia aere expressa. pt. 1-2. Upsaliae, 1822.

Arc 1163.3.75 — Koppen, P.I. Spisok. russkim pamiatnikam, sluzhashchim k postavleniiu istorii khudozhestv i otechestvennoi paleografii. Moskva, 1822.

Arc 785.11 — Mazois, F. Le palais de Scaurus. Paris, 1822.

Arc 380.205 — Millingen, J. Ancient unedited monuments. London, 1822.

Arc 1033.12.77 — The miraculous host tortured by the Jew. 3. ed. London, 1822.

Arc 1027.2 — Morcelli, S.A. Agapea Michaëleia. Bononiae, 1822.

Arc 793.11 — Reale Accademia Ercolanese di Archeologia, Naples. Memorie. v.1-9. Napoli, 1822-62. 10v.

Arc 925.5 — Spasskii, Grigorii I. De antiquis quibusdam sculptures. Petropoli, 1822.

Arc 905.3 — Stancovick, P. Dello anfiteatro di Pola. Venice, 1822.

Arc 785.42 — Valadier, G. Narrazione artistica dell'operato finora nel ristauro dell'arco di Tito. Roma, 1822.

1823

Arc 915.4.5 — Jacob-Kolb, G. Recherches historiques sur les antiquités d'Augst. Rheims, 1823.

Arc 561.2 — Letronne, J.A. Recherches pour servir à l'histoire de l'Égypte. Paris, 1823.

Arc 1418.4 — Reinaud, J.T. Explication de cinq médailles...du Bengale. Paris, 1823.

Arc 875.2 — Small, A. Interesting Roman antiquities recently discovered in Fife. Edinbrugh, 1823.

1824

Arc 1030.23 — Amati, G. Monumenti gentileschi e cristiani...Lorio nell'Aurelia. Roma, 1824.

Arc 1033.3 — Bottazzi, G.A. Emblemi...del...sarcofago...di Tortona. Tortona, 1824.

Arc 552.1.2 — Champollion, J.F. Lettres à M. le Duc de Blacas d'Aulps. Paris, 1824.

Arc 785.48 — Fea, Carlo. La Fossa Trajana confermata al Ludovico Linotte. Roma, 1824.

Arc 723.4.2 — Forsyth, J. Remarks on antiquities, arts and letters. 3. ed. London, 1824. 2v.

Arc 1433.9.3 — Fraehn, C.M.J. De aliquot numis Kuficis. n.p., 1824.

Arc 1033.17.35 — Gregorio. Storia della translazione...immagine di Santa Maria di Constantinopoli. 2a ed. Napoli, 1824.

Arc 1353.6 — Jonge, J.C. de. Notice sur le cabinet des médailles et des pierres gravées de...roi des Pays-Bas. La Haye, 1824.

Arc 830.77 — Lacoste, Pierre F. Observations sur les travaux qui doivent être faits pour la recherche des objets d'antiquité. Clermont, 1824.

1824 - cont.

Arc 513.12 Leake, William M. Journal of a tour in Asia Minor. London, 1824.
Arc 1423.3 Lindberg, J.C. Commentatio de numis punicis sextorum. Havniae, 1824.
Arc 875.18 Mackenzie, G.S. A letter to Sir Walter Scott, Baronet. Edinburgh, 1824.
Arc 1027.2.5 Morcelli, S.A. Comento sull'iscrizione sepolcrale. Modena, 1824.
Arc 861.33.3 Rauthmell, R. Antiquitates Bremetonacenses, or Roman antiquitites of Overborough. Kirkby Lonsdale, 1824.
Arc 905.13 Rosenegger, J. Tabellarisische Ubersicht der Alterthumer in Roseneggers Garten. Salzburg, 1824.
Arc 773.1 Sachse, K. Geschichte und Beschreibung der alten Stadt Rom. Hannover, 1824.
Arc 1675.7 Serie dei conj di medaglie pontificie da Martino V. Roma, 1824.
Arc 776.1.3 Venuti, R. Accurata e succinta descrizione topografica delle antichità di Roma. Roma, 1824. 2v.
Arc 1016.233 Visconti, P.E. Sposizione di alcune antiche iscrizione cristiane. Roma, 1824.

1825

Arc 1033.3.3 Amati, G. Emblemi sepolcrali degli antichi cristiani. Roma, 1825.
Arc 726.24.8 Bardi, Giovanni de'. Della imp. villa Adriana. Firenze, 1825.
Arc 1020.9.11 Bonties, G.B. Brevi notitie archeologici sull'origine delle chiese di Roma. Roma, 1825.
Arc 726.71 Bucciolotti, A. Della origine e delle antiche città de' Sabini. Roma, 1825.
Arc 1020.9.110 Costanzi, G. Le instituzioni di Pieta...in Roma. v.1-2. Roma, 1825.
Arc 1138.17 Ebert, F.A. Zur Handschriftenkunde. v.1-2. Leipzig, 1825.
Arc 375.2 Fosbroke, T.D. Encyclopaedia of Antiquities. London, 1825. 2v.
Arc 1433.9.4 Fraehn, C.M.J. De Musei Sprewitziani Mosquae numis Kuficis. Petropoli, 1825.
Arc 785.11.5 Mazois, F. Il palazzo di Scauro. 2. ed. Milano, 1825.
Arc 1016.213 Nibby, A. Della forma degli antichi templi cristiani. Roma, 1825.
Arc 1490.20 Vermiglioli, G.B. Di un quadrante unico ed inedito. Perugia, 1825.

1826

Arc 1033.12.33 Berta, G. Della sacra sindone di Nostro Signor. Torino, 1826?
Arc 1535.2 British Museum. Department of Coins and Medals. Description of the Anglo-Gallic coins. London, 1826.
Arc 635.203 Bröndsted, P.O. Voyages dans la Gréce. Paris, 1826.
Arc 1468.9 Dominicis, F. de. Repertorio numismatico. v.1-2. Naples, 1826.
Arc 760.6.15 Fea, Carlo. Ossequiosissimo rapporto alla Santità. Roma, 1826. 2 pam.
Arc 1433.8 Fraehn, C.M.J. Numi Muhammedani...Museo Asiatico. Petropoli, 1826.
Arc 547.5.25 Geoffroy Saint Hillaire, E. Rapport fait à l'Académie royale des sciences. Paris, 1826.
Arc 740.204.2 Inghirami, F. Indici dei monumenti etruschi. Badia, 1826.
Arc 830.78.15A Mangou de la Lande, C.F.J. Essais historiques sur les antiquités du département de la Haute-Loire. Saint-Quentin, 1826.
Arc 853.16 Mayer, Anton. Ein paar Worte über ein paar Drudenbäume. Eichstatt, 1826.
Arc 861.54 Miles, William A. A description of the deverel barrow. London, 1826.
Arc 1433.20 Moeller, J.H. De numis Orientalibus in numophylacio Gothano. Erford, 1826-31. 2v.
Arc 547.5 Passalacqua, J. Catalogue des antiquités découvertes en Egypte. Paris, 1826.
Arc 1033.17.73 Prospetto storico dell'immagine di Maria vergine dipinta dall'evangelista S. Luca. Bologna, 1826.
Arc 830.49.15F Taillefer, W. Antiquités de Vésone. Périgneux, 1826. 2v.
Arc 1468.17 Weston, S. Historic notices of coins in Greece. London, 1826.

1827

Arc 547.9 Champollion, J.F. Notice descriptive des monumens égyptiens du Musée Charles X. Paris, 1827.
Arc 590.6 Champollion, J.F. Notice sur le papyrus hiératique et les peintures du cercueil de Pétaménoph. Paris, 1827.
Arc 760.6.17 Fea, Carlo. Eccellentissima congregazione diputata da sua Santità Papa Leone XII. Roma, 1827.
Arc 1340.6 Girod, Joseph. Dictionnaire spécial et classique des monnaies. Paris, 1827.
Arc 726.71.10 Guattani, G.A. Monumenti Sabini. Roma, 1827-28. 3v.
Arc 618.7 Higgins, G. The Celtic druids. London, 1827.
Arc 726.64 Nibby, Antonio. Della via portuense. Roma, 1827.
Arc 726.24.9 Nibby, Antonio. Descrizione della villa Adriana. Roma, 1827.
Arc 628.1 Nissen, H. Pompeji. 2. Aufl. Berlin, 1827. 22 pam.
Arc 605.1 Pacho, J.R. Relation d'un voyage dans la Marmarique. Text, plates. Paris, 1827. 2v.
Arc 830.85 Rever, Marie F. Mémoire sur les ruines du Vieil-Évreux. Évreux, 1827.
Arc 1185.7 Spangenberg, E. Lehre von dem Urkundenbeweise. Heidelberg, 1827. 2v.
Arc 953.13 Warden, D.B. Recherches sur les antiquités de l'Amérique. Paris, 1827.

1828

Arc 855.3 Artis, E.T. The Durobrivae of Antoninus. London, 1828.
Arc 386.5.2 Böttiger, Carl August. Archäologie und Kunst. Breslau, 1828.
Arc 810.2 Bonucci, Carlo. Pompéi. Naples, 1828.
Arc 756.6 Burton, Edward. A description of the antiquities and other curiosities of Rome. 2. ed. London, 1828. 2v.
Arc 1274.1 Deville, J. Achille. Dissertation sur les sceaux de Richard-Coeur-de-Lion. Rouen, 1828.
Arc 375.2.2 Fosbroke, T.D. Foreign topography. Encyclopaedia of antiquites. v.3. London, 1828.

1828 - cont.

Arc 1087.1.2 Garofalo, Biagio. De antiquis marmoribus. 2. ed. Oxonii, 1828.
Arc 625.4 Gerhard, E. Antike Bildwerke. Text. München, 1828.
Arc 1020.73.6 Gosselin, J.E.A. Notice historique et critique sur le sainte couronne d'épines...l'église metropolitaine de Paris. Paris, 1828.
Arc 1458.3 Hartmann, H.L. Tabellarische Übersicht der gewoehnlichsten Altrömische Münzen. Leipzig, 1828.
Arc 743.7 Inghirami, F. Lettere di Etrusca erudizione. Poligrafia, 1828.
Arc 810.48 Jorio, Andrea. Plan de Pompéi. Naples, 1828.
Arc 1033.34.3 Monsacrati, M.A. De catenis San Petri dissertatio. Roma, 1828.
Arc 1033.3.5 Ratti, N. Sopra un sarcofago cristiano con travole. Roma, 1828.
Arc 785.22.10F Thon, C. Il palazzo de' Cesari sul monte Palatino. Roma, 1828.
Arc 1377.1 Walsh, R. An essay on ancient coins, medals, and gems. 2. ed. London, 1828.
Arc 790.6 Zahn, W. New Entdeckte Wandgemälde in Pompeji. München, 1828.

1829

Arc 1468.30 Dumersan, T.M. Description des médailles antiques du cabinet de feu M. Allier de Hauteroche. Paris, 1829.
Arc 1025.40 Fontana, G. Le notti cristiane. Colle, 1829.
Arc 1361.2 Green, B.R. A lecture on the study of ancient coins. London, 1829.
Arc 618.7.3 Higgins, G. The Celtic druids. London, 1829.
Arc 545.17 Jomard, E.F. Description générale de Memphis et des Pyramides. Paris, 1829.
Arc 708.9 Leake, W.M. Topographie von Athen. Halle, 1829.
Arc 720.219F Nibby, Antonio. Viaggio antiquario ad Ostia. Roma, 1829.
Htn Arc 1153.60* Peignot, G. Lettres à M.C.N. Amanton sur deux manuscrits précieux des temps de Charlemagne. Dijon, 1829.
Arc 380.210 Quatremère de Quincy, A.C. Monuments et ouvrages d'art antiques. Paris, 1829.
Arc 1033.17.501 Rienzo, G. de. Notizie storiche sulla...effigie di Maria...Paterno. Napoli, 1829.
Arc 793.4.5 Romanelli, D. Voyage à Pompéi. Paris, 1829.
Arc 861.38.5 Rutter, John. Delineations of the northwest division of the county of Somerset. London, 1829.
Arc 861.38.6 Rutter, John. Delineations of the northwest division of the county of Somerset. London, 1829.
Arc 1153.46 Sarpe, Gustav. Prolegomena ad tachygraphiam Romanam. Rostochii, 1829.
Arc 1015.211 Settele, G. Illustrazione di un antico monumento cristiano. Roma, 1829.
Arc 708.15 Stuart, J. Die Alterthuemer von Athen. Darmstadt, 1829-31. 2v.
Arc 777.1 Westphal, J.H. Die Roemische Kampagne. Berlin, 1829.

183-

Arc 793.6 Naples. Museo Nazionale. Raccolta...pinture e di...musaici...di Ercolano, di Pompei, e di Stabia. Napoli, 183-.

1830

Arc 386.24 Baraldi, Giuseppe. Notizia biografica sul cardinale S. Borgia. Modena, 1830.
Arc 1675.51.5 Bentkowski, F. Spis medalów poliskich lub z dziejami krainy polskiej stycznych. Warszawa, 1830.
Arc 810.2.5 Bonucci, Carlo. Pompéi. 2. éd. Naples, 1830.
Arc 1033.58.9 Brevi racconto sopra immagini S. Sebastiano. Roma, 1830.
Arc 1333.3 British Museum. Nummi veteres - in Museo R.P. Knight asservati. London, 1830.
Arc 756.6.3 Burton, Edward. A description of the antiquities and other curiosities of Rome. v.1-2. Florence, 1830.
Htn Arc 705.6* Cockerell, C.R. Antiquities of Athens and other places in Greece and Sicily. London, 1830.
Arc 1033.12.56 Corrieris, L. de. De sessorianis praecepuis passionis...reliquiis commentariis. Romae, 1830.
Arc 1362.2 Hennin, M. Manuel de numismatique ancienne. Paris, 1830-69. 3v.
Arc 1535.5 Illustrations of the Anglo French coinage. London, 1830.
Arc 825.2.4 Ménard, L. Supplément à l'édition de 1829 de l'Histoire des antiquités de la ville de Nismes. Nîmes, 1830.
Arc 820.8F Société Nationale des Antiquaires de France. Rapport de la commission...sur les antiquaires gallo-romaines. Paris, 1830.
Arc 853.23 Wilhelmi, K. Beschreibung der 14alten deutschen Todtenhügel. Heidelberg, 1830.

1831

Arc 830.146 Bottin, S. Mélangés d'archéologie. Paris, 1831.
Arc 756.4 Burgess, R. The topography and antiquities of Rome. London, 1831. 2v.
Arc 810.3 Clarke, W. Pompeii (in library of entertaining knowledge). London, 1831-32. 2v.
Arc 1033.17.463 Corvino, R. Tesoro nascosto minifestato per la miracolosa invenzione di Santa Maria...Napoli. Napoli, 1831.
Arc 642.4 Cousinéry, E.M. Voyage dans la Macédoine. Paris, 1831. 2v.
Arc 1033.35.49 Drach, P.L.B. Inscription hébräique du titre de S. Croix. 2e éd. Rome, 1831.
Arc 700.1 Gell, W. Probestuecke von Städtemanern des Alten Griechenlands. München, 1831.
Arc 391.1 Gurlitt, J. Archäologische Schriften. Altona, 1831.
Arc 943.26 Hill, Ira. Antiquities of America explained. Hagerstown, 1831.
Arc 1033.84 Pellino, G. Trattenimento...S. Igino Papa e Martire. Napoli, 1831.
Arc 1016.233.5 Visconti, F.A. Sopra una iscrizione cimiteriale. Roma, 1831.
Arc 853.23.5 Wilhelmi, K. Les anciens tombeaux germaniques. Heidelberg, 1831.

Chronological Listing

1832

Arc 1458.7 Cardwell, E. Lectures on the coinage of the Greeks and Romans. Oxford, 1832.

Arc 835.200 Cean-Bermudez, J.A. Sumario de las antiqüedades Romanas que hay en España. Madrid, 1832.

Arc 1033.47.25 Fea, C. Della Casa Aurea di Nerone. Roma, 1832.

Arc 785.49 Fea, Carlo. I reclami del Foro Trajano esposti al pubblico e giustificati. Roma, 1832.

Arc 1433.41 Fraehn, C.M.J. Monety khanov' uluea dzhuchieva. Sankt Peterburg, 1832.

Arc 1433.41.5 Fraehn, C.M.J. Die Münzen des Chane vom Ulus. St. Petersburg, 1832.

Arc 810.6.5 Gell, William. Pompeiana. London, 1832. 2v.

Arc 561.3 Long, G. British Museum. Egyptian antiquities. London, 1832. 2v.

Arc 825.2.5 Ménard, L. Histoire des antiquités de la ville de Nismes. Nîmes, 1832.

Arc 720.9 Micali, G. Storia degli antichi popoli italiani. v.1-3; atlas. Firenze, 1832. 4v.

Arc 628.4.2 Müller, K.O. Denkmäler der alten Kunst. v.1-2. Göttingen, 1832.

Arc 754.6 Piale, S. Roman archaeology in the city of Rome. Diss. Rome, 1832-33. 12 pam.

Arc 488.1.5 Price, W. Journal of the British embassy to Persia. London, 1832.

Arc 488.1 Price, W. Journal of the British embassy to Persia. v.1-2. London, 1832.

Arc 1033.34.19 Wiseman, N. Sul ragguaglio...cattedra di San Pietro. Roma, 1832.

1833

Arc 830.31.5 Berger de Xivrey, Jules. Lettre à Monsieur Hase sur une inscription latine du second siècle. Paris, 1833.

Arc 552.1 Champollion, J.F. Lettres écrites d'Egypte et de Nubie. Paris, 1833.

Arc 785.28.5 Corsi, F. Delle pietre antiche. 2. ed. Roma, 1833.

Arc 861.32 Davidson, J. British and Roman remains in Axminster. London, 1833.

Arc 595.3 Dissertation of the antiquity...of the principal pyramids of Egypt. London, 1833.

Arc 785.20.13 Fea, Carlo. Osservazioni suo ristabilimento della Via Appia da Roma a Brindisi. Roma, 1833.

Arc 708.6.2 Forchhammer, P. Zur Topographie Athens. Göttingen, 1833. 2 pam.

Arc 746.4 Gerhard, E. Dionysos und Semele. v.1. Berlin, 1833. 2 pam.

Arc 1027.21.5 Jorio, A. de. Notzie sulle crepte...San Gennaro di Poveri. v.1-2. Napoli, 1833-39.

Arc 1470.12 Levezow, J.A.K. Über mehrere im...Posen...griechische Münzen. n.p., 1833.

Arc 720.9.2 Micali, G. Storia degli antichi popoli italiani. 2. ed. Firenze, 1833.

Arc 1020.10.43 Notizie compendiose delle sagre stazioni e chiese stazionali di Roma. Roma, 1833.

Arc 1027.27.5 Pasquini, G. Relazione...cimitero di cristiani. Montepulciano, 1833.

Arc 770.9 Piale, Stefano. Delle porte del recinto di servio Tullio nella parte orientale di Roma. Roma, 1833. 13 pam.

Arc 1033.12.34F Piano, L.G. Commentarii critico archeologici sopra la SS. Sindone. Torino, 1833. 2v.

Arc 830.97 Porte, J.F. Aix ancien et moderne. 2e éd. Aix, 1833.

Arc 1540.9.5 Schröder, J.H. Numismata Angliae vetusta. pt.1. Upsaliae, 1833.

Htn Arc 858.13* Stackhouse, T. Two lectures on the remains of ancient pagan Britain. London, 1833.

Arc 380.202 Steinbüchel, A. von. Antiquarischer Atlas. Wien, 1833.

Arc 1016.227 Visconti, P.E. Dissertazione...iscrizione cristiana. Roma, 1833.

Arc 1335.154 Wambolt, F. von. Katalog des grossen Freiherrlich von Wambolt'schen Münzkabinets in Heidelberg. v.1-2. Heidelberg, 1833.

Arc 1033.34.17 Wiseman, N. Remarks on...Saint Peter's chair. Rome, 1833. 2v.

1834

Arc 1478.1 Ackerman, J.Y. A descriptive catalogue of rare Roman coins. London, 1834. 2v.

Arc 513.11 Arundell, F.V.J. Discoveries in Asia Minor. v.2, photoreproduction. London, 1834. 2v.

Arc 785.13.40 Canina, Luigi. Descrizione storica del Foro Romano. Roma, 1834.

Arc 1583.5 Chertkov, A. Opisanie drevnikh Russkik' monet'. Moskva, 1834.

Arc 1535.207F Chetwynd, George. A catalogue of provincial copper coins, tokens, tickets, medals issued in Great Britain, Ireland and the colonies...18th century. London, 1834.

Arc 387.4 Compendio completo di archeologia. Milano, 1834. 2v.

Arc 1033.12.160 Conti, G.B. Dell'origine invenzione...del...simulacro di...Gesu Crocifisso...volto santo. Lucca, 1834.

Arc 820.206F Deane, John Bathurst. Dracontia. London, 1834.

Arc 1333.7 Erdmann, F. Numi asiatici musei univ. caes. liter. Casanensis. Casani, 1834.

Arc 830.1 Freminville. Antiquités de la Bretagne. Brest, 1834.

Arc 1033.17.33 Garruba, M. Eoniade della translazione...miracolosa immagine di Santa Maria...Constantinopoli. Napoli, 1834.

Arc 761.1.2 Gell, W. The topography of Rome and its vicinity. London, 1834. 3v.

Arc 1510.126 Kraemer, Georg. Bayerns Ehrenbuch. Nürnberg, 1834.

Arc 1033.17.466 Libretto che contiene l'istoria...di Santa Maria...Nocera-Pagani. Napoli, 1834.

Arc 1264.11.5F Mancel, G. Les anciennes abbayes de Normandie. Caen, 1834.

Arc 726.65F Nibby, Antonio. Del monumento sepolcrale detto volgarmente degli Orazii e Curiazii; discurso. Roma, 1834.

Arc 880.1 O'Brien, H. The round towers of Ireland. London, 1834.

Arc 1027.4.27 Povèda, G. de. Memorie...S. Filomena e l'invenzione del suo corpo. Foligno, 1834.

Arc 730.201 Serradifalco. Le antichita della Sicilia. Palermo, 1834. 5v.

1835

Arc 1025.36 Agincourt, G.B.L.G. d'. Viaggio nelle catacombe di Roma. Milano, 1835.

1835 - cont.

Arc 1510.139 Albrecht, J. Mittheilungen zur Geschichte der Reichs-Münzstaetten. Heilbronn, 1835.

Arc 1020.103 Bartoletti, T. Privato santuario atessano...de'santi, beati. Napoli, 1835.

Arc 551.1 Belzoni, G.B. Narrative of the operations in Egypt and Nubia. Brussels, 1835.

Arc 1510.146 Beyschlag, Daniel Eberhardt. Versuch einer Münzgeschichte Augsburgs in dem Mittelalter. Stuttgart, 1835.

Arc 1433.27 Bohlen, P. von. Über die wissenschaftlichen Werth...Arabischen Münzen. n.p., 1835.

Arc 1335.44 Borioni, T. Collana di medaglie antiche e moderne. Loreto, 1835.

Arc 830.99 Cassan, A. Antiquités gauloises et gallo-romaines de l'arrondissement de Mantes. Mantes, 1835.

Arc 545.2 Champollion, J.F. Monuments de l'Égypte et de la Nubie. Paris, 1835-45.

Arc 608.2.12 Dureau de la Malle, Adolphe. Recherches sur la topographie de Carthage. Paris, 1835.

Arc 723.4.4 Forsyth, J. Remarks on antiquities, arts and letters. 4. ed. London, 1835.

Arc 810.6.7 Gell, William. Pompeiana; the topography, edifices, and ornaments of Pompeii. London, 1835. 2v.

Arc 830.165 La Grange, E. de. Notice sur des antiquités romaines découvertes en 1834 à Chandai (Orne). Caen, 1835.

Arc 1033.162.5F Manin, Leonardo. Memorie storico-critiche...di S. Marco. Venezia, 1835.

Htn Arc 830.7* Mérimée, Prosper. Notes d'un voyage dans le midi de la France. Paris, 1835.

Arc 1020.73 Notice historique sur les saintes reliques...de S. Jacques-des-Hauts-Pas à Paris. Paris, 1835.

Arc 1033.17.14 Notizie...miracolosa immagine Bma Vergine...di S. Maria in Cosmedin. Roma, 1835.

Arc 708.14 Pittakys, K.S. L'ancienne Athènes. Athens, 1835.

Arc 736.2.2 Politi, G. Siracusa pei Viaggiatori. Siracusa, 1835.

Arc 1016.226 Visconti, A. Dissertazione...cristianita di Costantino Magno. Roma, 1835.

Arc 726.7 Visconti, E.A. Monumenti gabini della Villa Pinciana. Milano, 1835.

Arc 853.20 Wyttenback, J.H. Neue Forschungen über Römischen architektonisch Alterhümer. Trier, 1835.

1836

Arc 815.21 Baizini, G.B. Due lettere sopra il musaico di Pompei. Bergamo, 1836.

Arc 1018.30 Böhmer, W. Die socialen Verhältnisse. Breslau, 1836.

Arc 1583.22 Chaudoir, S. Aperçu sur les monnaies russes et sur les monnaies étrangères. v.1-3. St. Petersbourg, 1836. 2v.

Arc 893.3.3 Copenhagen. Kongelige Nordiske Oldskrift-Selskab. Ledetraad til nordisk oldkyndighed. Kjøbenhavn, 1836.

Arc 893.2 Copenhagen. Kongelige Nordiske Oldskrift-Selskab. Report addressed by the Royal Society of Northern Antiquaries ot its British and American members. Copenhagen, 1836.

Arc 1500.63 Dancoisne, Louis. Recueil de monnaies...de Douai. Douai, 1836.

Arc 1335.161 Dickmann-Secherau, Johanna N. Dickmann's Münzsammlung in Wien. Wien, 1836.

Arc 1335.14 Du Mersan, T.M. Notice sur la bibliothèque royale...sur le cabinet des médailles. Paris, 1836.

Arc 391.2 Gerhard, Eduard. Über die Metallspiegel der Etrusker. Berlin, 1836. 11 pam.

Arc 820.212F Jollois, J.B.P. Mémoire sur les antiquités du départment du Loiret. Paris, 1836.

Arc 810.48.10 Jorio, Andrea. Guida di Pompei. Napoli, 1836.

Arc 905.21 Kalina, M. Böhmens...Opferplätz, Gräber und Alterthümer. Prag, 1836.

Arc 830.8 Mérimée, Prosper. Notes d'un voyage dans l'ouest de la France. Paris, 1836.

Arc 708.13 Notes descriptive of panoramic sketch of Athens. Coventry, 1836? 3 pam.

Arc 1033.12.161 Pera, P. Della lampada d'oro offerta dai Lucchssi al volto santo. Lucca, 1836. 2 pam.

Arc 1347.3 Scott, W.H. On the Parthian coins. London, 1836-54. 28 pam.

Arc 1018.26 Siegel, C.C.F. Handbuch der christlich-kirchlichen Alterthümer. Leipzig, 1836-38. 4v.

Arc 1348.41 Strozzi, Carlo. Quadro di geografia numismatica da servire. Firenze, 1836.

Arc 740.8 Visconti, C.P.E. Antichi monumenti sepolcrali nel ducato di Ceri. Roma, 1836.

1837

Arc 1468.3 Arneth, J. Synopsis numorum Graecorum. Vienna, 1837.

Arc 790.200 Avellino, F.M. Descrizione di una lasa disotterrata in Pompeii. Naples, 1837. 2 pam.

Arc 386.5.4A Böttiger, Carl August. Kleine Schriften. Dresden, 1837-38. 3v.

Arc 386.5.18 Böttiger, Carl Wilhelm. Karl August Böttiger. Leipzig, 1837.

Arc 1030.2 Brunatius, J. Musei kircheriani inscript. ethnicae et christianae. Mediolani, 1837.

Arc 1535.10F Burns, Edward. The coinage of Scotland. Edinburgh, 1837. 3v.

Arc 1583.5.2 Chertkov, A. Pribavlenie. Moskva, 1837-42. 3v.

Arc 746.15 DeWitte, J. Description d'une collection de vases peints et bronzes. Paris, 1837.

Arc 1660.18F Edwards, Edward. The Napoleon medals. London, 1837.

Arc 645.1 Forchhammer, P.W. Hellenika. Berlin, 1837.

Arc 925.6 Frähn, C.M.J. Über alte süd-sibirische Gräberfunde. St. Petersburg, 1837.

Arc 810.6.2 Gell, William. Pompeiana. London, 1837. 2v.

Arc 1540.3 Holmboe, C.A. De numis MD medii aevi in Norvegia nuper repertis. Christiania, 1837.

Arc 830.8.3A Mérimée, Prosper. Notes d'un voyage dans l'ouest de la France. Bruxelles, 1837.

Arc 768.2.15 Nibby, Antonio. Analisi storico...dentorni di Roma. Roam, 1837. 3v.

Arc 768.2.16 Nibby, Antonio. Analisi storico...dentorni di Roma. Roma, 1837. 4v.

Arc 893.3.5 Nordiske Oldskrift-Selskab. Leitfaden zur Nordischen Alterthumskunde. Copenhagen, 1837.

Arc 672.1 Pashley, R. Travels in Crete. Cambridge, 1837. 2v.

Arc 1033.17.90 Ranaldi, Giuseppe. Memorie storiche di S. Maria del Glorioso. Macerata, 1837.

Chronological Listing

1837 - cont.

Arc 1027.4.25 — Santucci, S. Sulla lapide sepolcrale di S. Filomena. Roma, 1837.
Arc 688.1 — Schinas, D. Archaiologia tês Nesou Sikinou. Athênai, 1837.
Arc 1473.5 — Soret, Frédéric. Trois lettres sur des monnaies byzantines. Genève, 1837.
Arc 662.2 — Wordsworth, C. Athens and Attica. Journal of a residence there. London, 1837.

1838

Arc 1018.25.5 — Augusti, J.C.W. Handbuch der christlichen Archäologie. Leipzig, 1838. 3v.
Arc 1033.42 — Brunatio, J. De Christianorum veterum monumentorum im rem biblicam utilitate. Diss. Mediolani, 1838.
Arc 1335.14.2 — Du Mersan, T.M. Histoire du cabinet des médailles. Paris, 1838.
Arc 830.15 — Estrangin, J.J. Études archéologiques, histoire et statistique sur Arles. Zix, 1838.
Arc 684.4 — Finlay, G. Remarks on the topography of Oropia and Diacria. Athens, 1838. 2 pam.
Arc 746.2 — Gerhard, E. Über die Metallspriegel der Etrusker. Berlin, 1838.
Arc 1016.242 — Heideloff, C. Der Christliche Altar. Nürnberg, 1838.
Arc 1033.90 — Heredia del Rio, P.M. Historia Sanctorum Martyrum...Ruderici, et Salomonis. Romae, 1838.
Arc 1033.12.112 — Histoire de la robe sans couture de...Jésus Christ. 4e éd. Paris, 1838.
Arc 650.1 — Klenze, L. von. Aphoristische Bemerkungen gesammelt...Reise nach Griechenland. Berlin, 1838.
Arc 510.3 — Laborde, L. de. Voyate de l'Asie Mineure. Paris, 1838.
Arc 1020.132 — Le Prevost, A. Notice sur la châsse de Saint Taurin d'Évreux. Évreux, 1838.
Arc 545.8.3 — London. Institution Library. Bibliographical account...of La description de l'Egypt. London, 1838.
Arc 825.2.9 — Ménard, L. Histoire des antiquités de la ville de Nismes. 7e éd. Nismes, 1838.
Arc 830.9 — Mérimée, Prosper. Notes d'un voyage en Auvergne. Paris, 1838.
Arc 1016.216 — Moreschi, L. Sulla sedia pontificale della basilica di S. Paolo. Roma, 1838.
Arc 768.3.5 — Nibby, Antonio. Roma nell'anno 1838. Roma, 1838-41. 4v.
Arc 1025.7 — Raoul-Rochette, D. Troisième mémoire sur les antiquités chrétiennes des catacombes. Paris, 1838.
Arc 458.2 — Ritter, C. Die Stupa's (Topes). Berlin, 1838.
Arc 458.2.2 — Ritter, C. Die Stupa's (Topes). Berlin, 1838.
Arc 1373.3.3 — Scotti, V.N. Della rarità delle medaglie antiche. Roma, 1838.
Arc 1027.68 — Servanzi-Collis, S. Relazione della chiesa sotterranea di S. Lorenzo in Sanseverino. Macerata, 1838.
Arc 1033.17.27 — Storia dell'apparizione di Nostra Signora di Misericordia in Savona. Napoli, 1838.
Arc 1020.9.12 — Torres, C.A. Cenni sulla forma primitiva del panteon di Roma. Roma, 1838.

1839

Arc 1588.1.14 — Bandtki, K.W.S. Numismatyka Krajowa. Warszawa, 1839. 2v.
Arc 1027.24 — Bellermann, C.F. Über die ältesten christlichen Begrabnifsstätten. Hamburg, 1839.
Arc 1033.35.9 — Brunati. Di un antica stauroteca istoriata...Brescia. Roma, 1839.
Arc 1033.16 — Cavedoni, C. Atti dei tre santi martiri Sarace, Probo e Andronico. Modena, 1839.
Arc 1030.3 — Cavedoni, C. Cenni sopra alcume antiche iscrizioni cristiane. Modena, 1839.
Arc 1030.3.5 — Cavedoni, C. Dichiarazione dell'iscrizione sepolcrale di San Decenzio Martire. Modena, 1839.
Arc 1030.3.9 — Cavedoni, C. Sopra l'iscrizione sepolcrale di S. Gemello. Modena, 1839.
Arc 513.4 — Fellows, C. Asia Minor. London, 1839.
Arc 720.214F — Grassi. Rappresentazione...edifizi...di Piza. Piza, 1839.
Arc 845.209F — Houben, P. Denkmaeler von Castra Vetera. Xanten, 1839.
Arc 1538.6 — Lindsay, J. View of the coinage of Ireland. Cork, 1839.
Arc 406.5 — Métral, D. Blaise de Vigenère, archéologue et critique d'art, 1523-1596. Thèse. Paris, 1839.
Arc 505.1 — Mueller, K.O. Antiquitates Antiochenae. Goettingen, 1839.
Arc 830.26.15 — Notice archéologique sur le département de l'Oise. Beauvais, 1839.
Arc 1033.17.465 — Ossequi e preghiere onde meritarsi...di Maria...Napoli. Napoli, 1839.
Arc 1512.2F — Rathgeber, Georg. Aufbau der niederländischen Kunstgeschichte und Museologie...Niederländische Münzen und Medaillen dis Herzoglichen Museums zu Gotha. Weissensee, 1839.
Arc 1033.17.449 — Ricci, A.M. Septenaire ou sept allégresses de Notre Dame de Mont Carmel. Paris, 1839.
Arc 1480.4 — Rome. Museo Kircheriano. L'aes grave del Museo Kircheriano. Text and atlas. Roma, 1839. 2v.
Arc 113.1 — Société Française pour la Conservation des Monuments Historiques, Séances tennes en 1839. Caen, 1839.
Arc 1033.17.304 — Spada, G.N. Saggio istorico e coroncina della taumalurga immagine di Maria Sma. Napoli, 1839.
Arc 510.4 — Texier, Charles. Description de l'Asie Mineure. Paris, 1839-1849. 3v.
Arc 1027.7.5 — Visconti, P.E. Di un nuovo tratto catacombe San Marcellino Pietro. Roma, 1839.
Htn Arc 875.36* — Wilson, Wilson D. Description of an ancient cross at Kilmory. Edinburgh, 1839.
Arc 870.10 — Woolls, C. Barrow diggers. London, 1839.
Arc 853.20.8 — Wyttenback, J.H. Stranger's guide to Roman antiquities of the city of Treves. London, 1839.
Arc 1335.38 — Young, Matthew. Catalogue of...coins and medals in gold, silver, and copper. pt.1. London, 1839.

1840

Arc 1348.1 — Akerman, J.Y. Numismatic manual. London, 1840.
Arc 1025.23 — Angelini, A. Genni sopra i primi cimiteri...Roma christiana. Roma, 1840.
Arc 793.5 — Barré, L. Herculanum et Pompéi. Paris, 1840. 7v.
Htn Arc 793.5* — Barré, L. Herculanum et Pompéi. v.8. Paris, 1840.
Arc 1027.74 — Bartolini, D. Il cimitero d'Aproniano di anche della S. Eugenia. Roma, 1840.

1840 - cont.

Arc 1510.22 — Berstett, A. Versuch einer Münzgeschichte des Elsasses. Freiburg, 1840. 2 pam.
Arc 386.7 — Bucke, C. Ruins of ancient cities. London, 1840. 2v.
Arc 750.222F — Canina, Luigi. Sugli antichi edifizj. Roma, 1840.
Arc 1254.1 — Carrara, F. Teodora Ducaina Paleologhina. Vienna, 1840.
Arc 1335.14.3 — Du Mersan, T.M. Notice des monuments exposés dans le cabinet des médailles. Paris, 1840.
Arc 746.5 — Forchhammer, P.W. Apollon's Ankunft in Delphi. Kiel, 1840.
Arc 513.8 — Franz, J. Fuenf Inschriften und fuenf Staedte in Kleinasien. Berlin, 1840.
Arc 743.2 — Gray, H. (Mrs.). Tour to the sepulchres of Etruria. London, 1840.
Arc 1088.1.6 — Jal, A. Archéologie navale. Paris, 1840. 2v.
Arc 853.2 — Jaumann, V. Colonia Sumlocenne-Rottenburg am Neckar unter die Roemern. Stuttgart, 1840.
Arc 820.220F — Leclere, J.B. Archéologie celto-romaine de l'arrondissement de Chatillon-sur-Seine. pt.1-2. Paris, 1840-1843.
Arc 1675.15 — Longpérier, A. de. Médailles de rois Perses de la Dynastie Sassanide. Paris, 1840.
Arc 1153.5 — Massmann, H.P. Libellus aurarius sivi tabulae ceratae. Lipsaie, 1840.
Arc 1033.55.7 — Mazzucconi, L. Memorie storiche della scala santa...di Sancto Sanctorum. Roma, 1840.
Arc 830.10 — Mérimée, Prosper. Notes d'un voyage en Corse. Paris, 1840.
Arc 825.9 — Perrot, J.F.A. Lettres sur Nismes et le Midi. Nismes, 1840. 2v.
Arc 830.51.5 — Phulpin, A. Notes archéologiques sur les fouilles et les monuments découverts sur la montagne du Chatêlet. Neufchateau, 1840.
Arc 1468.10 — Raoul-Rachette. Mémories de numismatique et d'antiquité. Paris, 1840.
Arc 657.2.3 — Ross, L. Reisen und der griechischen Inseln. v.1-3. Stuttgart, 1840-45.
Arc 1535.4.2 — Ruding, R. Annals of the coinage of Great Britain. 3. ed. London, 1840. 3v.
Arc 1030.22 — Secchi, G. Epigramma greco christiano...Autun. Roma, 1840.
Arc 660.1 — Ulrichs, H.N. Reisen und Forschungen in Griechenland. pt.1-2. Bremen, 1840.
Arc 595.11 — Vyse, H. Operations carried on at the pyramids of Gizeh in 1837. London, 1840. 2v.
Arc 853.20.9 — Wyttenback, J.H. Recherches sur les antiquités romaines dans la vallée de la Moselle de Trèves. Trèves, 1840.

1841

Arc 830.141F — Aix. Commission d'Archéologie. Rapport sur les fouilles d'antiquités. pts.1-3. Aix, 1841-44.
Arc 1020.32.8 — Caffi, M. Della chiesa di Sant'Eustorgio in Milano. Milano, 1841.
Arc 757.1 — Canina, Luigi. Indicazione topografica di Roma antica. 3. ed. Roma, 1841.
Arc 1018.25.25 — Coleman, Lyman. Antiquities of the Christian church. Andover, 1841.
Arc 1033.15 — De Lucca, A.A. Annali delli scienze religiose. Roma, 1841.
Arc 723.2 — Eustace, J.C. A classical tour through Italy. London, 1841. 3v.
Arc 513.4.2 — Fellows, C. Discoveries in Lycia. London, 1841.
Arc 1490.2 — Gandolfi, G.C. Della moneta antica di Genova. v.1-2. Genova, 1841-42.
Arc 87.1 — Gerhard, E. Kunstgeschichtliche Vasenbilder. Berlin, 1841.
Arc 746.12.10F — Grifi, L. Monumenti di cere antica. Roma, 1841.
Arc 1433.24 — Grigorbev, V.V. Opisanie kuficheskikh monet' X veka. Sankt Peterburg, 1841.
Arc 1568.1.3 — Holmboe, C.A. De prisca re monetaria Norvegiae. Christiania, 1841.
Arc 861.10.7 — Kinnebrook, William. Etchings of the Runic monuments in Isle of Man. London, 1841.
Arc 708.9.3 — Leake, W.M. The topography of Athens. London, 1841. 2v.
Arc 1500.41 — Lelewel, Joachim. Réapparitions du type gaulois dans le coin du moyen age. Bruxelles, 1841.
Arc 397.3.2 — Müller, K.O. Nouveau manuel d'archéologie. v.1-2 and atlas. Paris, 1841. 3v.
Arc 1093.2.2 — Petit-Radel, L.C.F. Recherches sur les monuments cyclopéens. Paris, 1841.
Arc 1490.28F — Promis, D. Monete dei reali di Savoia. Torino, 1841. 2v.
Arc 1025.7.11 — Raoul-Rochette, D. Le catacombe di Roma. Milano, 1841.
Arc 657.2.2 — Ross, L. Reisen und Reiseronten durch Griechenland. Berlin, 1841.
Arc 1588.10.35 — Rupp, Jakab. Magyarorszag ekkorig ismeretes pénzei. Budan, 1841.
Arc 1500.68 — Saulcy, Felicien de. Recherches sur les monnaies des ducs hereditaires de Lorraine. Metz, 1841.
Arc 1433.19 — Saulcy, L.F.J.C. de. Lettres sur quelques points de la numismatique arabe. Lettres 4,5, et 6. Paris, 1841.
Arc 935.1 — Tafel, G.L. Via militaris Romanorum Egnatia. Tubingae, 1841.
Arc 406.1 — Vecchi, M.M. Il Mediterraneo illustrato. Firenze, 1841.
Arc 1433.5 — Wilson, H. A descriptive account of antiquity and coins of Afghanistan. London, 1841.

1842

Arc 720.16PF — Alvino, Francesco. Amfiteatro campano illustrato. Napoli, 1842. 2v.
Arc 1027.30.15 — Bartolini, D. Inscrizione S. Martire Fortissima nel cimitero...Ciriaca. Roma, 1842.
Arc 547.25.5 — British Museum. Department of Egyptian and Assyrian Antiquities. Gallery of antiquities. London, 1842.
Arc 1033.17.138 — Cavedoni, C. Cenni storici e critici intorno alla S. Zona della...Vergine. Modena, 1842.
Arc 1033.12.43 — Cenni sulla Santissima Sindone. Torino, 1842?
Arc 87.1.2 — Gerhard, E. Phrixos der Herold. Berlin, 1842.
Arc 830.5.15 — Gras-Bourguet. Antiquités de l'arrondissement de Castellanne. 2e éd. Digne, 1842.
Arc 1663.20 — Greppo, J.G.H. Mémoire sur les voyages de...Hadrien et sur les médailles. Paris, 1842.
Arc 513.5 — Hamilton, W.J. Researches in Asia Minor, Pontus and Armenia. London, 1842. 2v.

Chronological Listing

1842 - cont.

Arc 853.24 Hefner, J. von. Das römische Bayern, in antiquarischer Hinsicht. München, 1842.

Arc 830.89.7 Henry, Dominique M.J. Recherches sur la géographie ancienne et les antiquités du département des Basses-Alpes. 2e éd. Digne, 1842.

Arc 938.19F Kruse, F.K.H. Necrolivonica. Dorpat, 1842.

Arc 726.75F Lanci, Fortunato. Intorno un antico specchio metallico epistola...Cavaaliere Odoardo Gerhard in occasion di sue nozze...Emilia de Riess. Roma, 1842.

Arc 1588.1 Lelewel, J. Notice sur la monnaie de Pologne. Bruxelles, 1842.

Arc 825.2.10 Ménard, L. Histoire des antiquités de la ville de Nismes. 9e éd. Nismes, 1842. 3 pam.

Arc 652.1 Mure, W. Journal of a tour in Greece. Edinburgh, 1842. 2v.

Arc 861.21 Wellbeloved, C. Eburacum, or York under the Romans. York, 1842.

Arc 673.1.2 Witte, J. de Baron. Monumens de Delphes. Roma, 1842.

1843

Arc 723.1 Abeken, W. Mittelitalien. Stuttgart, 1843.

Arc 380.206 Allan, J.H. Pictorial tour in the Mediterranean. London, 1843.

Arc 1018.64 Die Attribute der Heiligen, alphabetisch Geordnet. Hannover, 1843.

Arc 600.5.2 Bellefonds, L. de. Mémoire sur le Lac Moeris. Alexandrie, 1843.

Arc 505.4.2 Berton, J. de. Essai sur la topographie de Tyr. Paris, 1843.

Arc 1030.3.13 Cavedoni, C. Dichiarazione dell'epetaffo di S. Georgio Martire. Modena, 1843.

Arc 1033.3.23 Cavedoni, C. Sarcofago cristiano nel templo di Fermo. Roma, 1843.

Arc 1495.2 De Sauley, F. Recherches sur les monnaies. Paris, 1843.

Arc 530.3 Fellows, C. The Xanthian marbles. London, 1843.

Arc 1488.15F Gennarelli, Achille. La moneta primitiva e i monumenti dell'Italia antica. Diss. Roma, 1843.

Arc 740.201 Gerhard, E. Etruskische Spiegel. v.1-2,3,4,5. Berlin, 1843- 4v.

Arc 87.1.3 Gerhard, E. Die Heilung des Telephos. Berlin, 1843-

Htn Arc 950.5* Harris, W.P. Brief account of the discovery of the brass plates...Kinderbrook, Illinois. Nauvoo, Illinois, 1843.

Arc 820.212.5F Jollois, J.B.P. Mémoire sur guelques antiquités...des Vosges. Paris, 1843.

Arc 1020.10.5 La Gournerie, E. de. Rome chrétienne. Paris, 1843. 2v.

Arc 1510.4 Langermann, J.P. Die neuren Hamburgischen Münzen und Medaillen. Hamburg, 1843.

Arc 1588.3 Luczenbacher, J. A' szerb zsupánok királyok es ezárok. Budán, 1843.

Arc 793.6.5 Naples. Museo Nazionale. Raccolta...pinture e di...musaici...di Ercolano, di Pompei, e di Stabia. Napoli, 1843.

Arc 1033.17.423 Nocelli. Cenno istorico sul duomo e sagra immagine di Santa Maria...in Lucera. Napoli, 1843.

Arc 1033.17.447 Notice sur le temple et l'hospice du Mont Carmel dédiés à la Vierge. Paris, 1843.

Arc 1030.25 Pasini, P. Sovra un'antica lapida cristiana. n.p., 1843.

Arc 1433.22 Pietraszewski, Ignatius. Numi Mohammedani. Berolini, 1843.

Arc 1480.21 Pinder, Moritz. Die Münzen Justinians. Berlin, 1843.

Arc 1033.32 Polidori, L. Illustrazione di due monumenti cristiani. Verona, 1843.

Arc 1480.2 Riccio, G.G. Le monete delle antiche famiglie di Roma. 2. ed. Naples, 1843.

Arc 1583.1 Shubert, Fedor F. Opisanie Russkikh monet. Sankt Peterburg, 1843.

Arc 635.10 Strack, J.H. Das Altgriechisches Theatergebäude. Potsdam, 1843.

Arc 895.7.5 Worsaae, J.J.A. Danmarks oldtid oplyst ved oldsager og gravhøie. Kjøbenhavn, 1843.

Arc 1033.36 Zardetti, C. Monumenti cristiani. Milano, 1843.

1844

Arc 1480.13 Akerman, J.Y. Coins of the Romans relative to Britain. London, 1844.

Htn Arc 522.8* Barker-Webb, P. Topographie de la Troade. Paris, 1844.

Arc 1033.27.5 Bartolini, D. La sotterranea confessoni...di San Marco. Roma, 1844.

Arc 756.1 Becker, W.A. Die römische Topographie in Rom. Leipzig, 1844.

Arc 757.2 Canina, Luigi. Pianta topografica di Roma antica. Roma? 1844?

Arc 1030.52 Cantini, Giuseppe. Inscriptiones. Colle, 1844.

Arc 830.144F Comarmond, A. Description de l'écrin d'une dame romaine. Paris, 1844.

Arc 710.3 Curtius, E. Die Akropolis von Athen. Berlin, 1844.

Arc 1.7 Didron, A.N. Annales archéologiques. Paris, 1844-1870. 27v.

Arc 1490.37 Friedländer, Julius. Die Münzen der Ostgothen. Berlin, 1844.

Arc 870.16 Haslam, William. Perran-zabuloe. London, 1844.

Arc 1033.12.102 Hommer, J. von. Geschichte des heiligen Rockes...Trier. v.1-2. Bonn, 1844.

Arc 1163.3.35 Ivanov, P.I. Sbornik paleograficheskikh snimkov. Moskva, 1844.

Arc 290.1 Kruse, F. Russische Alterthümer 1844. Dorpat, 1844.

Arc 1015.210 Marchi, Giuseppe. Monumenti delle arti cristiane primitive nella metropoli del cristianismo. Roma, 1844.

Arc 746.3 Osservazioni sopra un'Etrusco Lampadario. Montepulciano, 1844.

Arc 1033.12.36 Pellegrini, C. Sermone sulla SS. Sindone di Torino. Torino, 1844.

Arc 590.3 Perrot, J.F.A. Essai sur les momies. Nimes, 1844.

Arc 1175.3 Pertz, G.H. Schrifttafeln zum Gebrauch bei diplomatischen Vorlesungen. Hannover, 1844.

Arc 1027.2.15 Polidori, L. Dei conviti effigiati a simbolo ne' monumenti cristiani. Milano, 1844.

Arc 1433.5.10 Prinsep, H.T. Note on the historical results deducible from recent discoveries in Afghanistan. London, 1844.

Arc 853.20.2 Wyttenback, J.H. Forschungen über die römischen Alterthümer. 2. Aufl. Trier, 1844.

1845

Arc 1033.89 Bassich, A. Della vita e del martirio di San Trifone. Vienna, 1845.

Arc 756.1.2 Becker, W.A. Zur römischen Topographie. Leipzig, 1845.

Arc 750.39F Canina, Luigi. Esposizione storica e topografica del foro romano. 2a ed. Roma, 1845.

Arc 750.39PF Canina, Luigi. Tavole...foro romano. Atlas. Roma, 1845.

Arc 785.28 Corsi, F. Delle pietre antiche. Roma, 1845.

Arc 1033.12.104 Gildemeister, J. Heilige Rock zu Trier. Düsseldorf, 1845.

Arc 1540.11 Haigh, D.H. Essay on the numismatic history of the East Angles. Leeds, 1845.

Arc 861.67F Lee, John Edward. Delineations of Roman antiquities...at Caerleon. London, 1845.

Arc 1540.16 Lindsay, John. View of coinage of Scotland, tables. Cork, 1845.

Arc 530.3.5 Lloyd, W.W. The Xanthian marbles. Londdon, 1845.

Arc 1015.210.5 Marchi, Giuseppe. Il sepolcro dei ss martiri Proto e Giacinta. Roma, 1845.

Arc 1033.12.103 Marx, J. Ausstellung des heiligen Roches in die Domkirche zur Trier. Trier, 1845.

Arc 1027.11 Michettoni, V. Memorie archeologica su di S. Aurelia Procope vergine e martire. Ripatransone, 1845.

Arc 1016.10 Odorici, F. Antichita cristiane di Brescia. Brescia, 1845.

Arc 87.1.5 Panofka, T.S. Antikenkranz. Berlin, 1845-

Arc 1663.10 Perreau, A. Recherches sur les comtes de Looz et sur leurs monnaies. Bruxelles, 1845.

Arc 1675.51.10 Raczynski, E. Le médailleur de Pologne. Berlin, 1845. 4v.

Arc 1598.15 Riddell, J.L. A monograph of the silver dollar, good and bad. New Orleans, 1845.

Arc 136.1.6 Society of Noviomagus. Momentores minutes of the meeting. London, 1845.

Arc 875.26 Stuart, Robert. Caledonia romana. Edinburgh, 1845.

NEDL Arc 775.1 Urlichs, K.L. Roemische Topographie in Leipzig. Stuttgart, 1845.

Arc 1033.35.53 Velasco, Alfonso A. Historia de la milagrosa renovación. México, 1845.

Arc 905.15 Wocel, J.E. Grundzüge der böhmischen Alterthumskunde. Prag, 1845.

Arc 858.12 Wright, T. The archaeological album; or Museum of National Antiquities. London, 1845.

Arc 1588.1.15 Zagorski, I. Monety fawney Polski jakotez prowincyj i nuast. Warszawa, 1845.

Arc 1588.1.16 Zagorski, I. Tablice do dziela o monetach dawnej Polski. Warszawa, 1845.

1846

Arc 1355.2 Ackerman, J.Y. Ancient coins of cities and princes. London, 1846.

Arc 1510.55 Binder, C. Württembergische Münz- und Medaillen-Kunde. Stuttgart, 1846.

Arc 125.4.5 British Archaeological Association. Transactions at its 2nd Congress, 1845. London, 1846.

Arc 1077.2.23 Calfhill, J. An answer to John Martiall's Treatise of the cross. Cambridge, Eng., 1846.

Arc 387.4.7 Catalogo di tutte le produzioni letterarie...dell'abate Francesco Girolamo Cancellieri. Roma, 1846. 2 pam.

Arc 1353.3 DuBois, W.E. A brief account of the collection of coins belonging to the mint of the United States. Philadelphia, 1846.

Arc 1500.2 Duchalais, A. Description des médailles gauloises...de la Bibliothèque Royale. Paris, 1846.

Arc 870.8 Duke, E. The druidical temples of the county of Wilts. London, 1846.

Arc 1490.50F Fusco, G.V. Intorno alle zecche ed alle monete battute nel reame di Napoli da Re Carlo VIII di Francia. Napoli, 1846.

Arc 761.1 Gell, W. The topography of RomeAnd its vicinity. London, 1846. 2v.

Arc 87.1.6 Gerhard, E. Das Orakel der Themis. Berlin, 1846.

Arc 830.66 Greppo, J.G.H. Études archéologiques sur les Eaux Thermalès. Paris, 1846.

Arc 1570.1.9 Holmboe, C.A. Das älteste Münzwesen Norwegens. Berlin, 1846.

Arc 628.2 Jahn, O. Socrate et Diotime. Greifswald, 1846. 9 pam.

Arc 1500.1 Jeuffrain, A. Essai d'interpretation...médailles...celtes-gaulois. Tours, 1846.

Arc 1470.25 Landon, Charles P. Numismatique du voyage du jeune Anacharsis. Paris, 1846. 2v.

Arc 87.2.45 Lersch, J.H.L. Das coelner Mosaik. Bonn, 1846.

Arc 561.3.3 Long, G. Egyptian antiquities in British Museum. London, 1846. 2v.

Arc 935.11 Mas Latrie. Rapport. Paris, 1846.

Arc 726.4.5 Minieri Riccio, C. Cenni storici sulla distrutta città di Cuma. Napoli, 1846.

Arc 1033.77 Navarro, G. Il corpo di S. Leonzio Martire. Napoli, 1846.

Arc 1033.34.1 Palmieri, N. Notizie istoriche delle sacre catene del principe degli apostoli. Orvieto, 1846.

Arc 1163.2.21F Paluzie y Cantalozella, Esteban. Paleografía española. Barcelona, 1846.

Arc 770.3A Preller, L. Die Regionen der Stadt Rom. Jena, 1846.

Arc 1033.17.326 Ragguaglio...della arcangelo San Michele. Napoli, 1846.

Arc 772.7 Riva, Giuseppe. Sito di Roma e la carta. 2. ed. Vicenza, 1846.

Arc 1030.37 Romano, C.C. Dell'arte...le iscrizione lapidarie. Roma, 1846.

Arc 1433.40.5 Savelbev', P. Topogafiia kladov' s' vosiochnymi monetami. Sankt Peterburg, 1846.

Arc 1590.7 Schweitzer, F. Brevi cenni storici...una medaglià di Ugone III. Trieste, 1846.

Arc 925.2 Spasskii, Grigorii I. Bostor Kimmeriiskii sego drevnostiami i dostopamiasnostiami. Moskva, 1846.

Arc 1335.22 Stickel, J.G. Die grossherzogliche morgenländische Münzsammlung in Jena. Jena, 1846.

Arc 1400.2 Taylor, S. Gold and silver coin examiner. N.Y., 1846-57. 3 pam.

Arc 830.16.7 Thomas, Edme. Histoire de l'antique cité d'Autun. Autun, 1846.

Arc 1433.13 Tornberg, Carl Johan. Symbolae ad rem numariam Muhammedan. Upsaliae, 1846-62.

Arc 87.2.46 Urlichs, K.L. Dreizehn Gemmen. Bonn, 1846.

Arc 895.15 Worsaae, J.J.A. Blekingske mindemaerker fra hedenold. Kjøbenhavn, 1846.

Chronological Listing

1847

Arc 858.1.5 Akerman, J.Y. An archaeological index. London, 1847.

Arc 1027.26 Bartolini, D. Le catacombe di Siracusa. Roma, 1847.

Arc 1016.238 Bellomo, G. La pala d'oro dell...basilica di San Marco. Venezia, 1847.

Arc 430.202 Bird, James. Historical researches...caves of western India. Bombay, 1847.

Arc 1584.1.6 Brosset, M.F. Rapport sur l'ouvrage intitulé. St. Petersbourg, 1847.

Arc 746.40F Canina, Luigi. L'antica città di Veil. Roma, 1847.

Arc 1077.2.13 Cavedoni, C. Di tre antiche stauroteche...cattedrale di Modena. Modena, 1847.

Arc 1033.35.55 Cavedoni, C. Dichiarazione de' tre antiche Stauroteche. Modena, 1847.

Arc 1500.51 Chalon, Rénier. Recherches sur les monnaies de Wallincourt en Cambrésis. Bruxelles, 1847.

Arc 830.111 Clerc, E. La Franche-Comté à l'époque romaine. Besançon, 1847.

Arc 830.2 Delandre, M.C. Le Morbihan son histoire et ses monuments. Paris, 1847. 2v.

Arc 1207.200F Garrucci, R. I piombi antichi. Roma, 1847.

Arc 1016.212 Gazzera, C. Delle iscrizioni cristiani del Piemonte. Torino, 1847.

Arc 865.19 Grover, Henry M. A voice from Stonehenge. pt.1. London, 1847.

Arc 1207.1PF Hare, Thomas. Engravings from ancient seals attached to deeds. Stowe-Bardolph, 1847.

Arc 635.17 Lebas, P. Voyage archéologique en Grèce et en Asie Mineure. Paris, 1847-77. 5v.

Arc 1025.10 Maitland, C. Church in the catacombs. London, 1847.

Arc 1033.53.19 Miscellanea in onore di S. Maurizio. Roma, 1847.

Arc 820.217F Morel-Macler, F. Antiquités Mandeure. Montbéliard, 1847.

Arc 861.42 Neville, R.C. Antiqua explorata. Chesterford. Walden Saffron, 1847.

Arc 1473.2 Pfaffenhoffen, F. Essai sur les arpres comnénats...de Trébisonde. Paris, 1847.

Arc 547.3 Prisse d'Avennes. Notice sur les antiquités égyptiennes du Musée Britannique. Paris, 1847.

Arc 1425.3 Saulcy, L.F.J.C. de. Numismatique de Croisades. Paris, 1847.

NEDL Arc 513.10 Spratt, T.A.B. Travels in Lycia, Milyas, and the Cibyratis. London, 1847. 2v.

Arc 967.1 Squier, E.G. Observations on the aboriginal monuments of the Mississippi Valley. N.Y., 1847.

Arc 830.61 Toulmoudre, Adolphe. Histoire archéologique de l'époque gallo-romaine de la ville de Rennes. Rennes, 1847.

Arc 925.9.9 Viviendekt-Martin, Louis. Recherches sur les populations primitives. Paris, 1847.

Arc 1018.40 Volbeding, J.E. Thesaurus commentationum...antiquiorum...illustrandis antiquitatibus christianis. Lipsiae, 1847. 2v.

1848

Arc 1348.1.5 Akerman, J.Y. Introductory study of ancient and modern coins. London, 1848.

Arc 950.212F Ancient monuments of...Mississippi Valley. Prospectus. N.Y., 1848.

Arc 925.12.5 Ashik, Anton. Vosporskoe tsarstvo. Odessa, 1848.

Arc 861.27 Bateman, T. Vestiges of the antiquities of Derbyshire. London, 1848.

Arc 858.31.5 Bigsley, R. Visions of the times of old. London, 1848. 3v.

Arc 1020.19 Biragus, A. Datiana historica ecclesiastica Mediolanensis. Mediolani, 1848.

Arc 1020.3 Bruges, Belgium. Commission Provinciale. Inventaire des objets d'art et d'antique...Bruges. Bruges, 1848.

Arc 1510.8 Cappe, H.P. Münzen der deutschen Kaiser des Mittelalters. v.1,3. Dresden, 1848-57.

Arc 1033.53.15 Cavedoni, C. L'era de' martiri osia di Diocleziano. Modena, 1848.

Arc 1033.17.445 Cenni storici della taumaturga effigie di Santa Maria di Monserrato. Napoli, 1848.

Arc 1520.12 Chalon, Renier. Recherches sur les monnaies des Comtes de Hainout. Supplement. Bruxelles, 1848-54. 2v.

Arc 1485.4 Cinagli, Angelo. Le monete de' papi. Fermo, 1848.

Arc 1348.36 The coin chart manual. St. Louis, 1848?

Arc 1163.4.5 Combarel, E. Cahier d'écritures arabes. Paris, 1848.

Arc 893.3.2 Copenhagen. Kongelige Nordiske Oldskrift-Selskab. Guide to northern archaeology. London, 1848.

Arc 893.3 Copenhagen. Kongelige Nordiske Oldskrift-Selskab. Guide to northern archaeology. v.1-10. London, 1848.

Arc 743.1 Dennis, G. The cities and cemeteries of Etruria. London, 1848. 2v.

Arc 1020.73.15 Douet d'Arco, L.C. Inventaire des reliques de la Sainte-Chapelle. Paris, 1848.

Arc 1033.74 Fortini, E. Solenne Ricevimento della testa di S. Andrea Apostolo. Roma, 1848.

Arc 1025.31 Gaume, J. Histoire des catacombes. Paris, 1848.

Arc 1033.35.153 Gualzetti, G.B. Pel giorno dell'invenzione di S. Croce, 1848. Milano, 1848.

Arc 905.14 Historischer Verein für Innerösterreich. Schriften. Graz, 1848.

Arc 890.209 Holmberg, A.E. Skandinairens hällristningar. Stockholm, 1848.

Arc 1033.83 Mannerini, L. Memorie del Martiro, S. Vitale e Valeria. Roma, 1848.

Arc 1033.3.21 Minicis, G. de. Sarcofago cristiano nel templo di Fermo. Roma, 1848.

Arc 768.3 Nibby, Antonio. Analisi della carta de' dentorni di Roma. Roma, 1848. 3v.

Arc 1033.17.244 Saggio storico della portentosa immagine di S. Maria di Campiglione. Napoli, 1848.

Arc 416.19 Schaeffer, C.F. Stratigraphie comparée. London, 1848-

Arc 1490.55F Schweitzer, F. Serie dei nummi aquilejesi. Trieste, 1848.

Arc 1485.3 Schweitzer, F. Serie delle monete e medaglie d'Aquilya e di Venezia. v.1-2. Trieste, 1848-52.

Arc 403.2 Smith, C.R. Collectanea antiqua. London, 1848-80. 7v.

Arc 830.16.5 Société Eduenne. Autun archéologique. Autun, 1848.

Arc 1408.6 Thomas, E. On the coins of the kings of Ghazni. London, 1848.

Arc 861.17.9 Tite, William. Descriptive catalogue of antiquities...Roman London. London, 1848.

Arc 726.50 Tonini, Luigi. Rimini avanti il principio. v.1-2. Rimini, 1848.

1848 - cont.

Arc 1433.12 Tornberg, Carl Johan. Numi cufici regii numophylacii Holmiensis. Upsaliae, 1848.

Arc 880.4.8 Wakeman, W.F. Archaeologia Hibernica. Dublin, 1848.

1849

Arc 861.12.3 Abbatt, Richard. History of the Picts or Roman British wall. London, 1849.

Arc 1033.12.135 Apparizione del santo volto. Napoli, 1849.

Arc 608.5 Barth, H. Wanderungen...Kuestenlaender...Mittelmeeres. Berlin, 1849.

Arc 87.2.49 Braun, J.W.J. Die Kapitole. Bonn, 1849-

Arc 1016.202 Casano, A. Del sotterraneo della chiesa cattedrale di Palermo. Palermo, 1849.

Arc 1025.27 Cavedoni, Celestino. Ragguaglio critico dei monumenti delle arti cristiane. Modena, 1849.

Arc 1077.2.28 Cutts, E.L. Manuel...sepulchral slabs and crosses of the Middle Ages. London, 1849.

Arc 1490.18 Diodati, D. Illustrazione delle monete. 2. ed. Napoli, 1849.

Arc 1016.212.3 Gazzera, C. Delle iscrizioni cristiani del Piemonte. Torino, 1849.

Arc 865.5 Herbert, A. Cyclops Christianus; disprove...Stonehenge. London, 1849.

Arc 1538.3.5 Humphreys, H.N. The gold, silver, and copper coins of England. 6. ed. London, 1849.

Arc 87.2.48 Lersch, J.H.L. Schwert des Giberins. Bonn, 1849.

Arc 1433.26 Loerve, L. Observations on a unique Cufic gold coin. London, 1849.

Arc 830.83.5 Mery, Louis. De vetere Massilia disquisitiones. Massillae, 1849.

Arc 720.9.7 Micali, G. Storia degli antichi popoli italiani. 3. ed. v.1-4. Firenze, 1849. 2v.

Arc 608.6.27 Note sur quelques villes romaines de l'Algérie. Paris, 1849?

Arc 1285.27F Pfotenhauer, P. Die schlesischen Siegel von 1250 bis 1300 beziehentlich 1324. Breslau, 1849.

Arc 1030.5.40 Rossi, G.B. de. Iscrizione della statua...di Nicomaco Flaviano Seniore. Roma, 1849.

Arc 510.212 Sabatier, J. Chronologie du Royaume de Bosphore. St. Petersbourg, 1849.

Arc 1540.9 Schröder, J.H. De moneta Anglo-Saxonica. Upsaliae, 1849.

Arc 393.1 Vegni, V. de. Notizie biografiche del cavaliere Francesco Inghirami. Volterra, 1849.

Arc 628.8 Welcker, F.G. Alte Denkmäler. v.1-5. Göttingen, 1849-64. 4v.

Arc 893.5.2A Worsaae, J.J.A. The primeval antiquities of Denmark. London, 1849.

185-

Arc 1030.40 Cavedoni, C. Ragguaglio critico delle iscrizioni cristiane. Modena, 185-?

1850

Arc 810.1.3 Aloe, Stanislas d'. Les ruines de Pompéi. Naples, 1850-51. 3 pam.

Arc 938.25F Bahr, Johann K. Die Gräber der Liven. Dresden, 1850.

Arc 1033.106 Bartolomei. Della scuola di S. Paolo. Roma, 1850.

Arc 386.5.3 Böttiger, Carl August. Kleine Schriften. 2. Aufl. Leipzig, 1850. 3v.

Arc 547.2 Brugsch, H. Uebersichtliche Erklaerung Aegyptischer Denkmaeler des Koenigliche Neuen Museum zu Berlin. Berlin, 1850.

Arc 1510.8.5 Cappe, H.P. Münzen der Herzöge von Baiern. Dresden, 1850.

Arc 905.4 Carrara, F. Topografia e scavi di Salona. Trieste, 1850.

Arc 830.78.20PF Chevalier, Pierre. Nantes et la Loire-Inférieure. Nantes, 1850.

Arc 1027.62 Diamilla. I monumenti degli antichi cristiani in relazione col progresso. Roma, 1850.

Arc 1033.59 Ferrari, G. de. Panegirico di S. Vittoria. Roma, 1850.

Arc 1498.11 Fillon, B. Considérations historiques et artistiques sur les monnaies de France. Fontenay, 1850.

Arc 1500.26 Fontenay, J. de. Nouvelle étude de jetons. Autun, 1850.

Arc 1490.3 Friedländer, Julius. Die Oskischen Münzen. Leipzig, 1850.

Arc 925.50.70 Grabowski, M. Ukraina davna i terazniejsza. Kijów, 1850.

Arc 875.39 Graham, H.D. Antiquities of Iona. London, 1850.

Arc 1663.7 Grande museo rivoluzionario. Roma, 1850.

Arc 1528.11 Handleiding tot de kennis der Nederlandsche munten. Amsterdam, 1850.

Arc 557.1 Hawks, F.L. The monuments of Egypt. N.Y., 1850.

Arc 861.5.9 Hingston, F.C. Specimens of ancient Cornish crosses, fonts. London, 1850.

Arc 1033.17.255 Histoire des images miraculeuses. Paris, 1850.

Arc 925.8.30 Koehne, B. Beiträge zur Geschichte und Archäologie von Cherronesos in Taurien. St. Petersburg, 1850.

Arc 885.14 Lee, J.E. Description of a Roman building and other remains...at Caerleon. London, 1850. 5 pam.

Arc 1279.5 Melly, Edward. Beiträge zur Siegelkunde des Mittelalters. Wien, 1850. 2v.

Arc 1279.5F Melly, Edward. Beiträge zur Siegelkunde des Mittelalters. Supplement. Wien, 1850.

Arc 1335.70 Mikocki, Leon. Verzeichniss einer grossen und sehr gewählten polnischen Münz- und Medaillen-Sammlung. Wien, 1850.

Arc 1478.9 Mommsen, T. Über das römische Münzwesen. Leipzig, 1850.

Arc 1033.17.303 Per la icona vetere di Maria sma. Venerata in Foggia. Napoli, 1850.

Arc 1373.1 Sabatier, P.J. Production de l'or, de l'argent et du cuivre. St. Petersbourg, 1850.

Arc 1663.17 Saulcy, Félecien. Souvenirs numismatiques de la révolution de 1848. Paris, 1850.

Arc 1138.7 Silvestre, J.B. Universal palaeography. London, 1850. 2v.

Arc 861.8 Smith, C.R. The antiquities of Richborough, Reculver, and Lyme. London, 1850.

1851

Arc 810.1.2 Aloe, Stanislas d'. Les ruines de Pompéi. Naples, 1851.

Arc 830.103 Beaulieu, J.L.D. Antiquités des eaux minérales de Vichy. Paris, 1851.

Arc 1353.1.5 Berlin. Staatliche Museen. Die antiken Münzen. Berlin, 1851.

Arc 858.31 Bigsley, R. Old places revisited. London, 1851. 3v.

Chronological Listing

1851 - cont.

Arc 716.7.5A Bötticher, Karl. Das Poliastempel als Wohnhaus des Königs Erechtheus. Berlin, 1851.
Arc 757.2.2 Canina, Luigi. Pianta topografica di Roma antica. Roma? 1851?
Arc 830.103.5 Chauvet, J.M. Notice...des antiquités de Vichy-les-Bains. Cusset, 1851.
Arc 1528.7 Chijs, P.O. van der. De munten. Haarlem, 1851-66. 9v.
Arc 757.3 Cookesley, W.G. Explanatory index to the map of ancient Rome. Eton, 1851.
Arc 1335.105 Devegge, Ole. Ole Devegge's mynt-og medaille-samling. Kjøbenhavn, 1851.
Arc 1400.1.2 Eckfeldt, J.R. A manual of gold and silver coins. Philadelphia, 1851.
Arc 1400.1 Eckfeldt, J.R. New varieties of gold and silver coins. N.Y., 1851.
Arc 1033.17.323 Fera di Plati, D. Sul santuario di Polsi sito...Gerace memorie. Napoli, 1851.
Arc 1030.29 Gazzera, C. Ragguaglio critico del discorso sopra le iscrizioni cristiane. Modena, 1851.
Arc 853.83.10 Giefers, Wilhelm. Die Externsteine im Fürstenthum Lippe-Detmold. Paderborn, 1851.
Arc 1020.71 Gonzati, B. Il santuario delle relique...di Padova. Padova, 1851.
Arc 1018.29.7 Guericke, H. Manual of the antiquities of the church. London, 1851.
Arc 400.12.25 Herberger, T. Conrad Peutinger in seinem Verhältnisse zum Kaiser Maximilian I. Augsburg, 1851.
Arc 1490.5 Lazari, V. Le monete dei possedimenti veneziani. Venezia, 1851.
Arc 861.31.5 Merewether, J. Diary of a dean. London, 1851.
Arc 830.159 Mignard, T.J.A.P. Histoire de différents cultes. Dijon, 1851.
Arc 861.87F Neville, R.C. Saxon obsequies illustrated by ornaments and weapons. London, 1851.
Arc 87.2.51 Overbeck, J.A. Roemische Villa bei Weingarten. Bonn, 1851.
Arc 1370.3 Pinder, M. Beiträge zur älteren Münzkunde. Berlin, 1851.
Arc 1033.17.441 Portenico, E. Cenno storico della Taumaturga efficie di Santa Maria dell'Arco...Miano. Napoli, 1851.
Arc 380.203 Rathgeber, D.G. Archäologische Schriften. Gotha, 1851-57.
Arc 1033.5.9 Rich, Anthony. The legend of Saint Peter's chair. London, 1851.
Arc 855.207 Robertson, D.H. The sculptured stones of Leith. Leith, 1851.
Arc 830.79 Roget de Belloguet, Dominique F.L. Origines dijonnaises. Dijon, 1851.
Arc 1500.25 Rossignol. Jetons des états de Bourgogne. Autun, 1851.
Arc 923.95 Russkoe arkheologicheskoe obshchestvo, Leningrad. Zapiska dlia obozreniia russkikh drevnostei. Sankt Petersburg, 1851.
Arc 853.10 Simony, F. Die Alterthümer vovon Hallstätter Salzberg. Wien, 1851.
Arc 968.1 Squier, E.G. Antiquities of the state of New York. Buffalo, 1851.
Arc 945.3 Squier, E.G. Serpent symbol and worship of nature in America. N.Y., 1851.
Arc 543.10 Tobler, T. Golgatha, seine Kirchen und Kloster. St. Gallen, 1851.
Arc 875.6 Wilson, D. The archaeology and prehistoric annals of Scotland. Edinburgh, 1851.

1852

Arc 810.1 Aloe, Stanislas d'. Les ruines de Poméi. Naples, 1852.
Arc 1027.27 Bartolini, D. Le nuove catacombe di Chiusi. Roma, 1852.
Arc 1020.9.142 Bartolini, D. Sopra l'antichissimo altare di legno...Lateranense. Roma, 1852.
Arc 1335.43 Borrell, H.P. Catalogue of...Greek, Roman, Byzantine and Mediterranean coins. v.1-2. London? 1852?
Arc 386.8 Buckley, T.A. Great cities of the ancient world. London, 1852.
Arc 1016.217 Cancellieri, F. Memorie storiche delle sacre teste. 2. ed. Roma, 1852.
Arc 905.4.5 Carrara, F. Di scavi di Salona nel 1850. Memoria. Praga, 1852.
Arc 1033.17.98.5 Conde y Oquendo, F. Dissertación histórica sobre la aparición de Nuestra Señora de Guadalupe. México, 1852. 2v.
Arc 87.1.12 Curtius, E. Herakles der Satyr und Dreifussränber. Berlin, 1852.
Arc 513.4.5 Fellows, C. Travels and researches in Asia Minor. London, 1852.
Arc 1015.208.8 Garrucci, R. Tre sepolcri con pitture ed iscrizione. Napoli, 1852.
Arc 810.6.3A Gell, William. Pompeiana. London, 1852.
Arc 1500.6 Germain, A. Mémoire sur les anciennes monnaies seigneuriales. Montpellier, 1852.
Arc 705.14 Heller, B.R. Archäologisch-artische Mittheilungen...über die Ausgrabungen auf der Akropolis zu Athen. Nuremberg, 1852.
Arc 1560.2 Humbles, C.P. Förteckning öfver C.P. Humbles. Stockholm, 1852.
Arc 1443.3 Langlois, V. Numismatique des nomes d'Égypte. Paris, 1852.
Arc 1584.1.3 Langlois, Victor. Numismatique de la Géorgie au moyen âge. Paris, 1852.
Arc 561.1.2 Lepsius, R. Briefe aus Aegypten. Berlin, 1852.
Arc 1480.7 London, England. Society of Antiquaries. Catalogue of Roman coins. London? 1852.
Arc 1670.53 Lorichs, G.D. de. Recherches numismatiques...les médailles celtiberiennes. Paris, 1852.
Arc 1425.1 Luynes, H.T.P.J. Numismatique et inscription Cypriotes. Paris, 1852.
Arc 1025.58 MacFarlane, Charles. The catacombs of Rome. London, 1852.
Arc 870.15.5 MacLauchlan, H. Memoir written during a survey of the Watling Street. London, 1852.
Arc 618.3 Mallet, J.W. Account of a chemical examination of the Celtic antiquities. Dublin, 1852.
Arc 726.67F Marchi, G. La stipe tributata alle divinità delle acque Apollinari. Roma, 1852.
Arc 608.6.3 Renier, Léon. Rapports adressés à M. le ministre de l'instruction publique et des cultes. Paris, 1852.
Arc 861.53 Richardson, G.B. Pons Aelii; the site of the Roman station. Newcastle-upon-Tyne, 1852.

1852 - cont.

Arc 513.9 Ross, L. Reisen nach Kos, Halikarnassos, Rhodos. Halle, 1852.
Arc 716.10 Ross, Ludwig. Das Theseion und der Tempel des Ares in Athen. Halle, 1852.
Arc 1508.5 Schönemann, C.P.C. Zur vaterländischen Münzkunde. Walfenbüttel, 1852.
Arc 858.7 Smith, C.R. Etchings of ancient remains. London, 1852.
X Cg Arc 861.6 Smith, C.R. Report on excavations made on the site of the Roman Castrum at Lymne. London, 1852.
Arc 861.21.25F Smith, Henry E. Reliquae isurianae; remains of Roman Isurium. London, 1852.
Arc 875.26.2 Stuart, Robert. Caledonia Romana...Roman antiquities of Scotland. Edinburgh, 1852.
Arc 1588.4.50 Vereine für Numismatik. Beschreibung. Prag, 1852-70.
Arc 716.1 Welcker, F.G. Der Felsaltar des Höchsten Zens oder das Pelasgikon zu Athen. Berlin, 1852.
Arc 861.34 Wylie, W.M. Fairford graves. Oxford, 1852.

1853

Arc 547.1 Abbott, H. Catalogue of a collection of Egyptian antiquities. N.Y., 1853.
Arc 1027.27.2 Bartolini, D. Le nuove catacombe di Chiusi. Roma, 1853.
Arc 1016.218 Belloni, P. Sulla grandezza della primitiva basilica ostiense. Roma, 1853.
Arc 710.1 Beulé, E. L'acropole d'Athènes. Paris, 1853-54. 2v.
Arc 870.14.3 Bruce, John C. Hadrian, the builder of the Roman wall. London, 1853.
Arc 750.202 Canina, Luigi. La prima parte della Via Appia. Roma, 1853. 2v.
Arc 1274.7 Caulfield, R. Sigilla ecclesiae Hibernicae illustrata. pt.1-4. Dublin, 1853.
Arc 1027.27.13 Cavedoni, C. Ragguaglio di due antichi cimiteri. Modena, 1853.
Arc 1163.4 Cherbonneau, A. Exercises pour la lecture des manuscrits arabes. Paris, 1853.
Arc 1500.35 Colson, Achille. Recherches sur les monnaiss qui ont en cours en Roussillon. Perpignan, 1853.
Arc 720.216 Fiorelli, G. Monumenti cumani. Napoli, 1853.
Arc 1348.70 Fliessbach, Ferdinand. Münzsammlung, Enthaltend. Leipzig, 1853. 2v.
Arc 810.31 Garrucci, Räffaele. Questioni Pompeiane. Napoli, 1853.
Arc 1020.9.179 Gerardi, F.M. Bella congregazione illirica e de' nuovi affreschi. Roma, 1853.
Arc 726.4.10 Guidobaldi, D. de. Intorno ad una imagine cerea. Napoli, 1853.
Arc 743.3 Koch, M. Die Alpen-Etrusker. Leipzig, 1853.
Arc 1335.11 Leipzig. Stadtbibliothek. Katalog des Münzkabinets. Leipzig, 1853.
Arc 561.1 Lepsius, R. Discoveries in Egypt, Ethiopia and the Peninsula of Sinai. London, 1853.
Arc 1053.13 Longpérier, A. de. Mémoires sur la chronologie et l'iconographie des rois parthes arsacides. Paris, 1853-82.
Arc 1663.13 Ludwig I. von Bayern und sein Wirken. Leipzig, 1853.
Arc 1018.15.3 Mamachi, T.M. De' costumi de' primitivi cristiani. v.1-2. Firenze, 1853.
Arc 1490.22 Minicis, Gaetano de. Numismatica ascolana...ascoli nel piceno. Fermo, 1853.
Arc 1400.4 Neueste Münzkunde. Leipzig, 1853. 2v.
Arc 87.1.13 Panofka, T.S. Zur Erklärung der Plinius. Berlin, 1853.
Arc 825.3 Pelet, Auguste. Description de l'amphithéâtre de Nîmes. Nîmes, 1853.
Arc 1349.25 Pinder, Moritz. Numismatique beckerienne. Paris, 1853.
Arc 720.200.5 Poleni, G. Catalogi...ad thesauros antiquitatum. Bononiae, 1853.
Arc 810.29 Pompeii: its destruction and re-discovery. London, 1853.
Arc 1025.7.7 Raoul-Rochette, D. Tableau des catacombes de Rome. Paris, 1853.
Arc 1033.17.242 Ronzini, D. Brevi notizie sul celebre santuario di Maria sma. nel Sacro Monte di Novi. Napoli, 1853.
Arc 402.6 Ruins of sacred and historic lands. London, 1853.
Arc 1016.237 Secchi, P.G. La cattedra Alessandrina di San Marco Evangelista e Martire. Venezia, 1853.
Arc 1033.17.203 Terninck, A. Notre-Dame du Joyel, ou Histoire légendaire et numismatique de la chandelle d'Arras. Arras, 1853.
Arc 1020.73.14 Troche, N.M. Sainte-Chapelle de Paris. Notice historique, archéologique et descriptive. Paris, 1853.
Arc 1428.10 Waddington, W.H. Voyage en Asie-Mineure au point du vie numismatique. Paris, 1853.
Arc 861.62 Wardell, James. Antiquities of the borough of Leeds. London, 1853.
Arc 382.2 Williams, John. On Carn Goch in Caermarthenshire. London, 1853. 17 pam.

1854

X Cg Arc 672.1.11 Belli, Onorio. A description of some theatres in Crete. London, 1854.
Arc 756.3 Braun, Emil. Die Ruinen und Museen Roms. Braunschweig, 1854.
Arc 756.3.4 Braun, Emil. The ruins and museums of Rome. Brunswick, 1854.
Arc 386.6 Braun, J. Studien und Skizzen. Mannheim, 1854.
Arc 865.3 Browne, H. An illustration of Stonehenge and Abury. 4. ed. Salisbury, 1854.
Arc 1138.5.4 Chassant, Alphonse. Paléographie des chartes. 4. éd. Paris, 1854.
Arc 830.29.4 Cochet, J.B.D. La Normandie souterraine. Rouen, 1854.
Arc 1020.112 Fleury, E. Trésor de Notre-Dame-de-Liesse...de 1655 à 1790. Paris, 1854.
Arc 830.350 Frantin, Jean Marie. Notice sur les origines de Dijon et sur les fragments romains découverts dans les substructions de l'ancien palais ducal de Dijon. Dijon, 1854?
Arc 87.1.14 Gerhard, E. Danae. Berlin, 1854.
Arc 1500.6.3 Germain, A. De la monnaie Mahométane atribuée à um évêque. Montpellier, 1854.
Arc 1361.1 Grässe, J.G.T. Handbuch der alten Numismatik. Leipzig, 1854.
Arc 1568.1 Holmboe, C.A. De prisca re monetaria Norvegiae. 2. ed. Christiania, 1854.
Arc 1538.3 Humphreys, H.N. The coinage of the British empire. London, 1854.
Arc 785.20 Itinerario. Descrizione dei monumenti...Via Appia. Roma, 1854.

Chronological Listing

1854 - cont.

Arc 1025.22 Janssen, L.J.F. Over de catacomben van Rome. Utrecht, 1854.
Arc 547.7 Jones, O. Description of the Egyptian court erected in the Crystal Palace. London, 1854.
Arc 1096.2 Krause, J.H. Angeiologie. Halle, 1854.
Arc 708.8 Laborde, L.E.S.J. Athènes aux XVe, XVIe et XVIIe siècles. Paris, 1854. 2v.
Arc 1428.1 Langlois, Victor. Monnaies inédites, ou Peu connues de la Cilicie. Paris, 1854.
Arc 530.6 Langlois, Victor. Rapport...de la Cilicie et de la Petite-Arménie. Paris, 1854.
Arc 1465.5 Leake, W.M. Numismata Hellenica. London, 1854.
Arc 1033.12.1 Liverani, F. Del nome di S. Maria ad Praesepe. Roma, 1854.
Arc 1020.86 Monographie de l'insigne Basilique de St. Saturnin. Paris, 1854.
Arc 628.4 Müller, K.O. Denkmäler der alten Kunst. Göttingen, 1854-81. 2v.
Arc 793.6.9F Naples. Museo Nazionale. Raccolta...pinture...musaici...Ercolano, di Pompei, e di Stabia. Napoli, 1854.
Arc 880.16 Notices of the round tower of Ulster. Belfast, 1854.
Arc 1025.1 Rip, W.I. The catacombs of Rome. N.Y., 1854.
Arc 785.32 Rossi, G.B. de. L'ara massima ed il tempio d'Ercole. Roma, 1854.
Arc 815.3 Scharf, G.J. The Pompeian court in the Crystal Palace. London, 1854.
Arc 1269.45 Vossberg, F.A. Siegel des Mittelalters von Polen, Lithauen, Schiesien, Pommern und Preussen. Berlin, 1854.
Arc 777.1.5 Westphal, Enrico. Guida per la campagna di Roma. Roma, 1854.
Arc 861.89.5 Wright, Thomas. A lecture on the antiquities of the Anglo-Saxon cemeteries of the ages of paganism. Liverpool, 1854.
Arc 858.29 Wright, Thomas. Wa5derings of an antiquary. London, 1854.
Arc 1663.1 Wyatt, T. A description of the national medals of America. N.Y., 1854. 2 pam.

1855

Arc 858.1 Akerman, J.Y. Remains of Pagan Saxondom. London, 1855.
Arc 1027.60 Bartolini, D. Sopra l'antico oratorio...regione de Marsi. Roma, 1855.
Arc 1500.28 Bascle de Lagrèze, G. Essai sur l'histoire monetaire...de Béarn. Toulouse, 1855.
Arc 547.2.15 Berlin. Staatliche Museen. Abtheilung der Aegyptischen Alterthümer - Die Wandgemaelde. Berlin, 1855.
Arc 756.3.5 Braun, Emil. Handbook...ruins and museums of Rome. London, 1855.
Arc 1680.1 Burn, J.H. A descriptive catalogue of the London traders, tavern and coffee-house tokens. London, 1855.
Arc 785.40 Cancellieri, F. Notizie del carcere Tulliano. Roma, 1855.
Arc 726.2.4 Capasso, B. Sull'antico sito di Napoli e Palepoli dubbie e conghietture. Napoli, 1855.
Arc 1423.12.5 Cavedoni, C. Biblische Numismatik. Hannover, 1855-56. 2v.
Arc 1033.53.9 Cavedoni, C. Cenni cronologica...rescritti di Traiano e di Adriano. Modena, 1855.
Arc 1033.93 Cavedoni, C. Dichiarazione di 5 bassirilievi biblici...Modena. Modena, 1855.
Arc 1027.54.5 Cavedoni, C. Sacra imagine della beata Virgine Maria. Modena, 1855.
Arc 1033.17.444 Cenno storico del culto di Santa Maria dell'abbondanza...Marzano. Napoli, 1855.
Arc 406.3F Conestabile, G. Della vita degli studî, e delle opere di Giambattista Vermiglioli discorso. Perugia, 1855.
Arc 495.3.5F Croly, George. The Holy Land, Syria, Idumea, Arabia, Egypt and Nubia. London, 1855-56. 3v.
Arc 635.216 Curtius, E. Zur Geschichte des Wegebaus bei den Griechen. Berlin, 1855.
Arc 1428.21 Fellows, Charles. Coins of ancient Lycia before the reign of Alexander. London, 1855.
Arc 736.3 Fraccia, G. Ricerche ed osservazioni. Fatte in Segesta. Palermo, 1855.
Arc 1433.8.3 Fraehn, C.M.J. Nova supplementa ad recesionem numorum Muhammedanum. Petropoli, 1855.
Arc 1590.3 Friedlaender, J. Recherches sur les monnaies frappées dans l'île de Rhodes. Paris, 1855.
Htn Arc 1538.3.2* Humphreys, H.N. The coinage of the British empire. London, 1855.
Arc 1433.28.2 Langlois, Victor. Numismatique général. v.2. Paris, 1855.
Arc 1433.28 Langlois, Victor. Numismatique général de l'Armenie. v.1-2. Paris, 1855-59.
Arc 900.202 Lanza, F. Dell'antico Palazzo di Dioclez in Spalato. Trieste, 1855.
Arc 950.203 Lapham, I.A. The antiquities of Wisconsin. Washington, 1855?
Arc 830.40.15 Lenormant, François. De la découverte d'un prétendu cimitière mérovingien a la Chapelle-Saint-Eloi (Eure). Evreux, 1855. 2 pam.
Arc 830.40.17 Lenormant, François. De l'authenticité des monuments découverts a la Chapelle-Saint-Eloi. Paris, 1855.
Arc 830.6.13 Martin-Daussigny, E.C. Description d'une voie romaine. Lyon, 1855. 12 pam.
Arc 1020.9.183 Masetti, Pio. Memorie istoriche della chiesa di S. Maria. Roma, 1855.
Arc 1143.1 Mone, F. De libris palimpsestis. Carlsruhae, 1855.
Arc 1470.1 Mueller, L. Numismatique d'Alexander le Grand. Text and atlas. Copenhagen, 1855. 2v.
Arc 1016.225 Odorici, F. Di un antico sarcofago cristiano...Mantova. Brescia, 1855.
Arc 1251.1 Pappadopoulos, G.G. Perigraphē ektypōmatōn archaiōn sphragidolithōn. Athēnai, 1855.
Arc 712.2 Petersen, C. Die Feste der Pallas Athene in Athen. Hamburg, 1855.
Htn Arc 1478.35F* Phillipps, Thomas. Numismata vetera et inscriptiones ex voto. Medio-Montana, 1855.
Arc 700.2 Rangabé, A.R. Ausgrabung beim Tempel der Hera Unweit Argos. Halle, 1855.
Arc 1480.3 Riccio, G.G. Catalogo di antiche medaglie consolari e di famiglie romane. Naples, 1855.
Arc 402.4 Ross, L. Archaeologische Aufsaetze. Leipzig, 1855. 2v.
Arc 1027.22.5 Rossi, J.B. de. De christianis monumentes Ichthys. Paris, 1855.

1855 - cont.

Arc 547.4 Rougé, E. de. Notice sommaire des monuments égyptiens du Musée du Louvre. Paris, 1855.
Arc 830.74 Sirand, Alexandre. Antiquités générales de l'Ain. Bourg-en-Bresse, 1855.
Arc 547.19 Turin. R. Museo di Antichità. Catalogo illustrato dei monumenti egizii. pt. 2. Torino, 1855.
Arc 720.11.5 Vermiglioli, G.B. Dei monumenti di Perugia etrusca e romana. Pt.1. Perugia, 1855.
Arc 720.11 Vermiglioli, G.B. Dei monumenti di Perugia etrusca e romana. pts.1-4. Perugia, 1855-70. 2v.
Arc 497.7 Vogüé, M. de. Fragments d'un journal de voyage en Orient. Paris, 1855.
Arc 1510.148 Weidhas, J.F. Die Brandenburger Denare von Heinrich König der Wenden bis auf Friedrich I. Kurfürst aus dem Hause Hohenzollern. Berlin, 1855.

1856

Arc 861.9 Allies, J. The British, Roman, and Saxon antiquities and folklore of Worcestershire. London, 1856.
Arc 1027.14 Billaud, Pelissier B. Pelerinage au cauc du Pape S. Alexandre I. Rome, 1856.
Arc 1180.1 Brinckmeier, E. Glossarium diplomaticum. Gotha, 1856-63. 2v.
Arc 1033.17.249 Bronte, G. da. Santuario di Maria Sma. di Gibilmanna. Catania, 1856.
Arc 1020.110 Brouillet, A. Description des reliquaires...abboye de Charroux. Poitiers, 1856.
Arc 935.3 Brunet de Presle. Extrait d'un notice sur les tombeaux des empereurs de Constantinople. Paris, 1856.
Arc 1510.33 Cappe, H.P. Beschreibung des Mainzer Münzen des Mittelalters. Dresden, 1856.
Arc 1033.73 Cavedoni, C. Ricerche...del sacro pallio ecclesiastico. Modena, 1856.
Arc 830.3 Cenac-Moncaut, J.E.M. Voyage archéologique et historique dans l'ancien Comté de Comminges. Tarbes, 1856.
Arc 1020.69 Deblaye, L.F. Reliques de l'église de Moyenmoutier. Nancy, 1856.
Arc 1433.25 Dresden. K. Münzkabinett. De numis Muhammadanis in Numophylacio regio Dresdensi. Lipsiae, 1856.
Arc 1433.23 Erdmann, F. von. Zur Muhammedanischen Münzkunde. St. Petersburg, 1856.
Arc 1033.17.481 Eroli, G. Narrazione storica sopra il santuario della madonna del Ponte. Roma, 1856.
Arc 830.158 Fallue, Léon. Sur les mouvements stratégiques de César...avant le siége d'Alise. n.p., 1856. 12 pam.
Arc 855.211 Faussett, B. Inventorium sepulchrale. London, 1856.
Arc 830.95 Fiancette d'Agos, L. de. Étude sur la basilique de Saint-Just. Saint-Gaudens, 1856.
Arc 953.20F Haven, S.F. Archaeology of the United States. Washington, 1856.
Arc 1030.48 Le Blant, E. Inscriptions chrétiennes de la Gaule antérieure au VIIIe siècle. Paris, 1856-65. 2v.
Arc 1493.5 Lopes Fernandes, M.B. Memoria das moedas correntes em Portugal. Lisboa, 1856.
Arc 600.3 Mariette, A. Choix de monuments et de dessins...Sérapéum de Memphis. Paris, 1856.
Arc 1033.12.138 Memorie istoriche...miracolosa crocifisso...Chiavari. Chiavari, 1856.
Arc 825.2.11 Ménard, L. Histoire des antiquités de la ville de Nîmes. 11e éd. Nîmes, 1856.
Arc 1480.36F Northumberland, A.P. Descriptive catalogue of a cabinet of Roman family coins belonging to...the Duke of Northumberland. London, 1856.
Arc 1020.83.5 Notice sur le mobilier de l'église cathedrale de Reims. Reims, 1856.
Arc 1020.70 Notre Dame de Myans. Chambéry, 1856.
Arc 810.13 Overbeck, J. Pompeji. Leipzig, 1856.
Arc 830.91 Piette, Amédée. Itinéraires gallo-romains dans le département de l'Aisne. Léon, 1856-62.
Arc 1018.33 Reichensperger. Bermischte Schriften über christliche Kunst. Leipzig, 1856.
Arc 1077.3 Reinaud, J. Rapport sur la chape arabe de Chinon. Paris, 1856.
Arc 1030.5.55 Rossi, G.B. de. Scavi nell'orto di S. Sabina sull'Aventino. Roma, 1856.
Arc 855.4 Stuart, J. Sculptured stones of Scotland. Aberdeen, 1856. 2v.
Arc 1033.63.5 Visconti, C.L. Dell'uso...dei monumenti cristiani cronologici. Roma, 1856.
Arc 810.14 Wall, J.W. Naples and Pompeii. Burlington, 1856.

1857

Arc 1160.202 Alvera Delgras, A. Compendio de paleografia española. Madrid, 1857.
Arc 1335.76.5 Athens. Ethnikon Nomismatikon Mouseion. Ekthesis ōerilēotikē. Athēnai, 1857.
Arc 1020.9.127 Barbier de Montault, X. L'année liturgique à Rome. Paris, 1857.
Arc 1500.43 Bigot, A. Essai sur les monnaies du royaume. Paris, 1857.
Arc 1077.3.2 Cavallari, S. Lettre sur la chape arabe de Chinon. Paris, 1857.
Arc 1033.17.421 Cenno storico dell'insigne di Santa Maria a Pareta. Napoli, 1857.
Arc 1033.17.132 Cerbelli, D. Opuscoletti varii ovvero monografia di Mottafollone storia della sacra cinta. Napoli, 1857.
Arc 1033.12.70 Cimatti, E. Cenni storici intorno al Sangue Mirae...Ferrara. Ferrara, 1857.
Arc 830.29.5 Cochet, J.B.D. Sépultures gauloises, romaines. Paris, 1857.
Arc 1478.3 Cohen, H. Description générale des monnaies de la Republique Romaine. Paris, 1857.
Arc 890.203 Copenhagen. Kongeligi Nordiske Oldskrift-Selskab. Altas de l'archéologie du nord. Copenhagen, 1857.
Arc 861.10.5 Cumming, J.G. Runic and other monumental remains...Isle of Man. London, 1857.
Arc 677.1 Forchhammer, P.W. Halkyoma. Berlin, 1857.
Arc 1093.2.3 Frederik VII, king of Denmark. Sur la construction des ralles dites des géants. Copenhague, 1857.
Arc 1030.5.62 Garruci, P.R. Il crocifisso graffito. Roma, 1857.
Arc 1348.48 Grote, Hermann. Münzstudien. v.1-2. Leipzig, 1857-62.
Arc 1333.6 Koehne. Description. Musée...Prince Basile Kotschoubey. St. Petersbourg, 1857. 2v.

Chronological Listing

1857 - cont.

Arc 936.195.315 Krolmus, Wácslaw. Poslední bcžiště Černoboha s runami na Skalsku, v kraji Boleslavském, v Čechach, na své archaeologické cestě vypátral Václeslav Krolmus. Praha, 1857.

Arc 905.27F Kubinyi, August von. Szekszár der Alterthümer. Pest, 1857.

Arc 925.45F McPherson, Duncan. Antiquities of Kertch. London, 1857.

Arc 1033.17.201 Mouls, X. Pélérinage de Notre-Dame d'Arcachon. Bordeaux, 1857.

Arc 1470.21 Müller, L. Den thraciske konge Lysimachus's mynter. Kjøbenhavn, 1857.

Arc 1025.4 Northcote, J.S. The Roman catacombs. London, 1857.

Arc 1025.4.2 Northcote, J.S. The Roman catacombs. Philadelphia, 1857.

Arc 375.4 Otte, H. Archäologisches Wörterbuch. Leipzig, 1857.

Arc 87.1.17 Panofka, T.S. Poseidon Basileus und Athene Sthenias. Berlin, 1857.

Arc 1348.34 Pfister, J.G. Stray leaves from the journal of a traveler. London, 1857.

Arc 670.1 Rangabé, A.R. Souvenirs d'une excursion d'Athènes en Arcadie. Paris, 1857.

Arc 1500.22 Rigollot, M.J. Monnaies inconnues des évêques des innocens. Paris, 1857.

Arc 1033.67 Rossi, G.B. de. Antichi Mulini in Roma e nel Lazio. Roma, 1857.

Arc 1030.5.59 Rossi, G.B. de. Iscrizione cristiana di Tropea in Calabria. Roma, 1857. 2v.

Arc 880.49 Royal Irish Academy, Dublin. Museum. A descriptive catalogue of the antiquities. Dublin, 1857.

Arc 1510.138 Rueppell, E. Beschreibung der Münzen und Medaillen. Frankfurt am Main, 1857.

Arc 1490.4 Schweitzer, F. Indice delle Zecche d'Italia. Trieste, 1857.

Arc 1582.7 Shubert, Fedor F. Monnayes russes, 1547-1855. Leipsic, 1857.

Arc 1582.7.2PF Shubert, Fedor F. Monnayes russes, 1547-1855. Atlas. Leipsic, 1857.

Arc 925.5.5 Spasskii, Grigorii I. Odastoporimiechatel'ineishikh pamatnikakh sibirskikh drevnatei. Sankt Petersburg, 1857.

Arc 1433.12.5 Tornberg, Carl Johan. Om de i Svensk jord funna Österländska mynt. Stockholm, 1857.

Arc 570.1A Uhlemann, M. Handbuch der gesammten aegyptischen Alterthumskunde. v.1-4. Leipzig, 1857. 2v.

1858

Arc 1027.14.5 Atti...S. Alessandro I...memorie del suo sepolcro. Roma, 1858.

Arc 1016.223 Bartolini, D. Atti del martiro della S. Agnese. Roma, 1858.

Arc 1020.9.15 Bartolomei, L. Memorie autentiche sulla chiesa di S. Paolo alla Regola. Roma, 1858.

Arc 1345.1.3 Bas-reliefs du Parthénon. Paris, 1858.

Arc 830.70.5 Bernard, Auguste. Description du pays des Ségusiaves. Paris, 1858. 11 pam.

Arc 1465.4 Beulé, E. Les monnaies d'Athènes. Paris, 1858.

Arc 861.5.5 Blight, J.T. Ancient crosses and antiquities east of Cornwall. London, 1858.

Arc 87.1.18 Boetticher, C. Grab des Dionysos. Berlin, 1858.

Arc 1680.9 Boyne, William. Tokens issued in seventeenth century England...by corporations. London, 1858.

Arc 1680.2 Bushnell, C.I. An arrangement of tradesmen's cards, political tokens; also election medals. N.Y., 1858.

Arc 1027.38 Cassini da Perinaldo, F. Le veglie notturne al cimitero di Cimella. Genova, 1858.

Arc 1020.9.20 Caterbi, G. La chiesa di S. Onofrio. Roma, 1858.

Arc 1033.44.13 Cavedoni, C. Ricerche critiche...medaglie di Constantino. Modena, 1858.

Arc 1345.1.6 Choix histoires des médailles des papes. Paris, 1858.

Arc 1335.3 Curtis, J.K. Priced catalogue of coins, medals and numismatic works. v.1-2. N.Y., 1858-59.

Arc 1333.8 Dudik, Beda. Des hohen deutschen Ritter-Ordens Münz-Sammlung in Wien. Wien, 1858.

Arc 1264.1 Forgeais, Arthur. Collection de plombs historiés trouvés dans la Seine. v.1-3. Paris, 1858-66. 2v.

Arc 1027.46 Fortunati, L. Brevi cenni...scoprimento...martire...S. Stefano. Roma, 1858.

Arc 1016.224 Garrucci, R. Esame della numismatica costantiniana. Roma, 1858.

Arc 1015.208 Garrucci, R. Vetri ornati di figura in oro. Roma, 1858.

Arc 1613.1 Hickcox, J.H. An historical account of American coinage. Albany, 1858.

Arc 1345.1.13 Histoire de France par médailles: Charles VII-Louis XVI. Paris, 1858. 3v.

Arc 1345.1.15 Histoire de France par médailles: Empire français. Paris, 1858.

Arc 1345.1.14 Histoire de France par médailles: Révolution française. Paris, 1858.

Arc 1345.1.5 Histoire de l'art monétaires...modernes. Paris, 1858.

Arc 1345.1.4 Iconographie des empereurs romains. Paris, 1858.

Arc 1282.9F Ivanov, I. Sbornik' snimkov's' drevnikh' pechatei. Moskva, 1858.

Arc 1033.17.243 Lomonaco, V. Monografia sul santuario di Nostra Donna della Grotta nella Praja della Schiavi. 3a ed. Napoli, 1858.

Arc 1490.11 Marks von Marksfeld, J. Vierzig Münzen der Normannen Hohenstaufen. Mailand, 1858.

Arc 1478.8 Mionnet, T.E. De la rareté et du prix des médailles romaines. Paris, 1858. 2v.

Htn Arc 1470.21.6* Müller, L. Die Münzen des thracischen Königs Lysimachus. Kopenhagen, 1858.

Arc 1470.21.5 Müller, L. Die Münzen des thracischen Königs Lysimachus. Kopenhagen, 1858.

Arc 1335.23 Nesselmann, G.H.F. Die orientalischen Münzen...in Königsberg. Leipzig, 1858.

Arc 1335.34 Neumann, J. Beschreibung der Bekanntesten. v.1,2,3-4,5,6. Prag, 1858-72. 5v.

Arc 1345.1.2 Nouvelle galerie mythologique. Paris, 1858.

Arc 1030.8.17 Pauthier, G. L'inscription syro-chinois de Si-Ngan-Fou. Paris, 1858. 2 pam.

Arc 953.9 Pidgeon, W. Traditions of De-coo-dah and antiquarian researches. N.Y., 1858.

Arc 1498.8 Poey d'Avant, F. Monnaies féodales de France. Paris, 1858. 4v.

Arc 1418.3 Prinsep, J. Essays on Indian antiquities. London, 1858. 2v.

1858 - cont.

Arc 1490.13 Promis, Domenico. Monete dei romani pontefici avanti il mille. Torino, 1858.

Arc 943.8 Rafn, K.C. Cabinet d'antiquités americaines. Copenhagen, 1858.

Arc 1470.8 Rathgeber, G. Neumundneunzig Silberne Münzen der Athenaier. Weissensee, 1858.

Arc 1345.1.8 Recueil de médailles allemandes, XVIe et XVIIe siècles. Paris, 1858.

Arc 1345.1.7 Recueil de médailles italiennes, XVe et XVIe siècles. Paris, 1858. 2v.

Arc 1345.1.16 Recueil général de bas-reliefs et d'ornements. Paris, 1858. 2v.

Arc 1033.17.135 Russo, M. dello. Storia della sma. Cintola de Prato. Napoli, 1858.

Arc 1254.2 Sabatier, J. Plombs, bulles et sceaux byzantins. Paris, 1858.

Arc 1490.98 Salinas Gargotta, Antonino. Su di alcune monete puniche di Mozia. Palermo, 1858.

Arc 1433.40 Savelbev', P. Monety dzhuchidov' dzhagataidov", I.D.R. Sankt Peterburg, 1858.

Arc 1345.1.12 Sceaux des communes, communautés, évêques. Paris, 1858.

Arc 1345.1.11 Sceaux des grands feudataires de la couronne. Paris, 1858.

Arc 1345.1.10 Sceaux des rois et des reines de France. Paris, 1858.

Arc 1345.1.9 Sceaux des rois et reines d'Angleterre. Paris, 1858.

Arc 1565.2 Schive, C.I. Norges mynter i middetalderen. pt.1-6. Christiania, 1858-65.

Arc 590.4 Sharpe, S. Triple mummy case of Aroeri-Ao. London, 1858.

Arc 861.18 Smith, C.R. Illustrations of Roman London. London, 1858.

Htn Arc 790.9* Ternite, W. Wandgemälde aus Pompeii und Herculanum. Berlin, 1858?

Arc 1408.2 Tornberg, E.J. Sur un Dirhem Kakweïhide inédit. Bruxelles, 1858.

Arc 1345.1 Trésor de numismatique et glyptique, numismatique des rois grecs. Paris, 1858.

Arc 895.7.9 Worsaae, J.J.A. Om jernålderen i Denmark. Kjøbenhavn, 1858.

Arc 1411.3 Wylie, A. Coins of the Ta-ts'ing dynasty. Shanghai, 1858.

1859

Arc 1269.15F Albrecht, J. Die hohenlohischen Siegel des Mittelalters. Oehringen, 1859.

Arc 1033.18.5 Bartolini, A. Gli atti della Passione degli ss. Abdon e Sennen. Roma, 1859.

Arc 87.1.19 Boetticher, C. Omphalos der Zeus zu Delphi. Berlin, 1859.

Arc 1680.3 Bushnell, C.I. An historical account of the first three business tokens issued in N.Y. N.Y., 1859.

Arc 1033.1.9 Cavedoni, C. Osservazioni sopra alcuni frammenti di vasi. Modena, 1859.

Arc 830.32.5 Cochet, J.B.D. Le tombeau de Childéric. Paris, 1859.

Arc 1478.3.2 Cohen, H. Description historique des monnaies frappées sons l'Empire Romain. Paris, 1859. 7v.

Arc 1613.10F Dickeson, M.W. The American numismatical manual of the currency or money of the aborigines. Philadelphia, 1859.

NEDL Arc 1668.1 Donaldson, T.L. Architectura numismatica. London, 1859.

Arc 1015.208.13 Garrucci, R. Relazione generale degli scavi e scoperte...via Satina. Roma, 1859.

Arc 673.2 Gerlach, F.D. Dodona. Basel, 1859.

Arc 1020.4 Girardot. Histoire et inventaire du trésor Bourges. Paris, 1859.

Arc 1018.29 Guericke, H. Lehrbuch der christlich kirchlichen Archäologie. Berlin, 1859.

Htn Arc 885.2* Halliwell, J.O. An ancient survey of Pen Maen Maur. London, 1859.

Arc 961.1.3 Jones, C.C. Indian remains in southern Georgia. Savannah, 1859.

Arc 638.3 Michaelis, A.T.F. Il Leone Nemeo. Roma, 1859. 7 pam.

Arc 726.61 Michaelis, Adolf. Das corsinische Silbergefäss. Leipzig, 1859.

Arc 1033.35.19 Michele, I. de. Sopra un'antica croce nel duomo di Termini-Imerese. Palermo, 1859.

Arc 1027.46.5 Nardoni, L. Dell'antica chiesa di S. Stefano sulla via Cassia. Roma, 1859.

Arc 1025.4.9 Northcote, J.S. Les catacombes romaines. Rome, 1859.

Arc 530.2 Olfers, J.F.M. Lydische Koenigsgraeber bei Sardes. Berlin, 1859.

Arc 825.3.1 Pelet, Auguste. Description de l'amphithéâtre de Nîmes. 2e éd. Nîmes, 1859. 9 pam.

Arc 1371.1 Queipo, V.V. Essai sur les systèmes métriques et monétaires. v.1-2, tables. Paris, 1859. 3v.

Arc 785.13.27 Ravioli, Camillo. Regionamento del Foro Romano. Roma, 1859.

Arc 1030.5.43 Rossi, G.B. de. Del arco fabiano nel foro. Roma, 1859.

Arc 830.76 Saint-Amans, J.F.B. Essai sur les antiquités du département de Lot-et-Garonne. Agen, 1859.

Arc 743.4 Taylor, G.L. The stones of Etruria and marbles of ancient Rome. London, 1859.

Arc 820.213F Tudot, Edmond. Carte des voies romaines du départment de l'Allier. Paris, 1859.

Arc 1033.3.27 Visconti, C.L. Dichiarazione di un sarcofago cristiano ostiense. Roma, 1859.

186-

Arc 708.15.5 Souvenirs d'Athènes. Trieste, 186-?

1860

Arc 1027.79 Bassi, A. Della torre Antonia d'una stupenda galleria...in Gerusalemme. Gerusalemme, 1860.

Arc 1033.12.184 Bianconi, A. Memoria intorno la corona di ferro longobardo. Milano, 1860.

Arc 1020.1.3 Bock, F. Der Reliquienschatz des Leibfrauen-Münsters zu Aachen in seinen Kunstreichen Behältern. Aachen, 1860.

Arc 1264.22F Bouches-du-Rhone. Archives. Iconographie des sceaux et bulles conservés dans la partie antérieure à 1790 des archives départementales des Bouches-du-Rhone. Marseille, 1860.

Arc 505.16 Bourquenond, A. Mémoire sur les ruines de Séleucie de Piérie. Paris, 1860.

Arc 510.215 Brosset. Les ruines d'Ani, capitale de l'Arménie. Text and atlas. St. Petersbourg, 1860. 2v.

Arc 1020.6.12 Cappelletti, G. La chiesa di S. Simone profeta. Venezia, 1860.

Chronological Listing

1860 - cont.

Arc 1209.1 Chassant, A.A.L. Dictionnaire de sigillographie pratique. Paris, 1860.

Arc 1020.84.9 Coffinet, L'Abbé. Trésor de St. Etienne...collegiale de Troyes. Paris, 1860.

Arc 642.3.2 Conze, A. Reise auf Inseln des Thrak. Meeres. Hannover, 1860.

Arc 1610.1 Dickeson, M.W. The American numismatic manual. 2. ed. Philadelphia, 1860.

Arc 390.1 Falkener, E. Museum of classical antiquities. London, 1860.

Arc 810.5 Fiorelli, G. Pompeianarum antiquitatum historia. Naples, 1860-62. 3v.

Arc 823.3 Fleury, E. Civilisation et art des Romains...Gaule-Belgique. Paris, 1860-1861.

Arc 1018.18 Garrucci, R. Opuscoli archeologici profana e cristiana. Roma, 1860-77.

Arc 391.2.5 Gerhard, Eduard. Über archäologische Sammlungen und Studien. Berlin, 1860.

Arc 1264.10 Hermand, A. Histoire sigillaire de la ville de Saint-Omer. Paris, 1860.

Arc 647.1 Heuzey, L. Le Mont Olympe et l'Acarnanie. Paris, 1860.

Arc 1675.8 Hildebrand, B.E. Minnespenningar öfver svenska män och qvinnor. Stockholm, 1860.

Arc 1475.7 Hobler, F. Records of Roman history. Westminster, 1860. 2v.

Arc 505.5.54 Isambert, E. Visite au temple de Jerusalem et à la Mosquée d'Omar. Paris, 1860.

Arc 1584.29 Kunik, Anst A. O russko-vizantiiskikh monetakh Iaroslava I Vladiminovicha. Sankt Peterburg, 1860.

Arc 1335.18 Leonard and Company. Catalogue of American coins. Boston, 1860-70. 4 pam.

Arc 87.1.20 Lohde, L. Die Skene der Alten. Berlin, 1860.

Arc 830.86 Loriquet, Charles. Reims pendant la domination romaine. Reims, 1860.

Arc 1033.35.31 Magrini, A. Sopra la insigne reliquia della S. Croce. Thiene, 1860.

Arc 1478.10 Mommsen, T. Geschichte des römisches Münzwesens. Berlin, 1860.

Arc 1510.6 Müller, J.H. Deutsche Münzgeschichte biz zu der Ottonenzeit. Leipzig, 1860.

Arc 1435.1 Mueller, L. Numismatique de l'ancienne Afrique. v.1 and supplement. Copenhague, 1860-94. 2v.

Arc 1435.1.5 Mueller, L. Numismatique de l'ancienne Afrique. v.1-3. Copenhague, 1860-62.

Arc 1675.10.9 Olivieri, A. Monete e medaglie degli Spinola di Tassarolo. Genova, 1860.

Arc 657.2 Pasch van Krienen. Abdruck seiner italienischer Beschreibung des griechisches Archipelagus. Halle, 1860.

Arc 830.37 Peigné-Delacourt, A. Recherches sur le lieu...bataille d'Attila en 451. Paris, 1860. 2v.

Arc 1020.9.90 Pellegrini, A. Anni storici intorno ad una basilica di S. Pietro in Campo di Mirlo. Roma, 1860.

Arc 726.14 Remedi, A.A. Relazione delli scari fatti in Luni. Sarzana, 1860.

Arc 1016.215 Rossi, G.B. de. Dell'antichissimo codice della Bibbia Graeca. Roma, 1860.

Arc 1027.29 Rossi, M.S. Dell'ampiezza. Romane catacombe macchina. Roma, 1860.

Arc 1335.16 United States Mint, Philadelphia. A description of ancient and modern coins. Philadelphia, 1860.

Arc 1020.5 Van Drival, E. Le trésor sacré de la cathédrale d'Arras. Arras, 1860.

Arc 971.1 Wallbridge, T.C. On some ancient mounds upon the shores of the Bay of Quinte. Toronto, 1860.

Arc 1016.245F Weiss, Karl. Der romanische Speisekelch. Wien, 1860.

1861

Arc 858.11 Bateman, T. Ten years' diggings in Celtic and Saxon grave hills. London, 1861.

Arc 853.4.2 Becker, J. Die Heddernheimer Votivhand. Frankfurt am Main, 1861.

Arc 785.6.13 Borgnana, C. Dell'acqua di Q. Marcio Ré e del suo acquedotto. Roma, 1861.

Arc 830.150 Boyer, H. Noviodunum Biturigum et ses graffiti. Bourges, 1861.

Arc 830.86.5 Brunette, N. Notice sur les antiquités de Reims. Reims, 1861.

Arc 1348.31 Butkovskii. Numismatika ili istoriia monet'. Moskva, 1861.

Arc 935.2.5 Constantiniade, ou Description de Constantinople. Constantinople, 1861.

Arc 642.3 Conze, A. Rapporto d'un viaggio fatto nella Grecia nel 1860. Roma, 1861.

Arc 823.4 D'Arbois de Jubainville. Répertoire archéologique du département de l'Aube. Paris, 1861.

Arc 1020.125 Darcel, Alfred. Trésor de l'église de conques. Paris, 1861.

Arc 608.2.2 Davis, N. Carthage and her remains. London, 1861.

Arc 1433.18 Dirks, J. Souveniers numismatiques des croisades. Photoreproduction. Bruxelles, 1861.

Arc 1020.53 Dusevel, M.H. Histoire...du trésor...de Saint Pierre de Corbie. Amiens, 1861.

Arc 505.3 Fergusson, J. Notes on the site of the Holy Sepulchre. London, 1861.

Arc 87.1.21 Friederichs, K. Apollon mit den Lamm. Berlin, 1861.

Arc 1584.3 Gille, F. Lettre...sur une monnaie attribuée à Oleg. Paris, 1861.

Arc 843.13.2 Gomez de Somorrostro y Martin, A. El acueducto y otras antigüedades de Segovia. 2. ed. Segovia, 1861.

Arc 1349.70 Grigor'ev, V.V. Zhizn' i trudy P.S. Savel'eva. Sankt Peterburg, 1861.

Arc 1027.19.33 Huthmacher, L. Ein Besuch in der römischen Katakomben...S. Kallisto. Mainz, 1861.

Arc 961.1.4 Jones, C.C. Monumental remains of Georgia. Savannah, 1861.

Arc 853.3 Klein, C. Die römischen Denkmäler in und bei Mainz. Mainz, 1861.

Arc 1675.31 Lopes Fernandes, Manuel Bernardo. Memoria das medallias e condecorações port. Lisboa, 1861.

Arc 1478.7 Madden, F.W. The handbook of Roman numismatics. London, 1861.

Arc 710.4 Michaelis, A. Über den jetzigen Zustand der Akropolis von Athen. Frankfurt, 1861.

Arc 861.48 Ormerod, George. Archaeological memoirs...district of the Severn and the Wye. London, 1861.

1861 - cont.

Arc 505.5.6 Paine, T.O. Solomon's temple. Boston, 1861.

Arc 1540.21 Poste, Beale. Celtic inscriptions on Gaulish and British coins. London, 1861.

Arc 1348.12 Prime, W.C. Coins, medals and seals. N.Y., 1861. 4 pam.

Arc 1027.30.9 Salvatore da Morrovalle, P. La basilica di S. Lorenzo fuor delle mura. Bologna, 1861.

Arc 1033.35.43 Sévérac, G. Notice sur la vraie croix de St. Guilhelm-du-Désert. Lodève, 1861.

Arc 1660.8 Snowden, J.R. A description of the medals of Washington. Philadelphia, 1861.

Arc 1613.5 Vattemare, A. Collection de monnaies et médailles de l'Amérique. Paris, 1861.

Arc 87.2.61 Weerth, E. Bad der roemische Villa bei Allenz. Bonn, 1861-1870.

Arc 407.4A Wright, T. Essays on archaeological subjects. v.1-2. London, 1861.

1862

Arc 1033.51.3 Angelini, N. Brevi notizie intorno San Rufino ves e Martire. Roma, 1862.

Arc 1645.1 Azeredo, C. de. Apreciação do medalheiro da casa da Moeda. Rio de Janeiro, 1862.

Arc 1020.9.128 Barbier de Montault, X. L'année liturgique à Rome. 2. éd. Rome, 1862.

Arc 853.4 Becker, J. Drei römische Votivhaende aus den Rheinlanden. Frankfurt am Main, 1862.

Arc 382.4 Benndorf, O. De anthologiae Graecae epigrammatis. Bonn, 1862. 20 pam.

Arc 885.3 Blight, J.C. Antiquities...Kirrier and Penwith, West Cornwall. Truro, 1862.

Arc 1020.51 Bock, Franz. Les trésors sacrés de Cologne. Paris, 1862.

Arc 386.4 Borghesi, Bartolomeo. Oeuvres complètes. Paris, 1862-72. 10v.

Arc 125.4.8 British Archaeological Association. Communications made to the association. London, 1862. 2v.

Arc 1033.4 Bucci, P. Sulla comunione christiana nei primi secoli. Roma, 1862.

Arc 1153.29.2 Chassant, A. Dictionnaire des abréviations latines et françaises. 2. éd. Paris, 1862.

Arc 1138.5.3 Chassant, Alphonse. Paléographie des chartes. 5. éd. Paris, 1862.

Arc 1160.202.9F Colomera y Rodriguez, V. Paleografía castellana. Valladolid, 1862.

Arc 387.3 Curtius, E. Festrede. Göttingen, 1862.

Arc 1020.6 Durand, J. Trésor de l'église Saint-Marc à Venise. Paris, 1862.

Arc 1076.3.89 Edel, Friederich W. Von den Glocken. pt.1-2. Strassburg, 1862-63.

Arc 518.3 Falkener, E. Ephesus and the Temple of Diana. London, 1862.

Arc 1093.2.3.5 Frederik VII, king of Denmark. Om bygningsmaaden af oldtidens jaettestuer. 2. udg. København, 1862.

Arc 87.2.62 Frendenberg, J. Denkmal der Hercules Saxanus. Bonn, 1862.

Arc 1033.44.27 Garrucci, R. Deux monuments des premiers siècles. Rome, 1862.

Arc 1027.18 Garruci, R. Cimitero degli antichi ebrei. Roma, 1862.

Arc 720.220F Gastaldi, B. Nuovi cenni sugli oggetti di alta antichità. Torino, 1862.

Arc 1027.30.5 Gori, F. Della porta e basilica di S. Lorenzo dell catacombe. Roma, 1862.

Arc 1020.84.5 Le Brun Dalbaune. Recherches...emaux du trésor de la Cathedrale de Troyes. Troyes, 1862.

Arc 1423.15 Levy, Moritz Abraham. Geschichte der jüdischen Münzen. Breslau, 1862.

Arc 1423.15.1 Levy, Moritz Abraham. Geschichte der jüdischen Münzen. Leipzig, 1862.

Arc 1033.17.56 Milochau, A. Vierge de Saint Luc à S.-Marie Majeure. Paris, 1862.

Arc 510.5 Newton, C.T. Halicarnassus, Cnidas and Branchidae. v.1; v.2, pt.1-2. London, 1862-1863. 3v.

Arc 895.12 Nicolaysen, N. Norske fornlevninger. Hefte 1-5. Kristiania, 1862-65.

Arc 893.8 Nilsson, S. Skandinaviska nordens ur-invånare. Stockholm, 1862-66. 2v.

Arc 505.19 Notice historique sur...sanctuaire d'Emmans. Paris, 1862.

Arc 1027.25.5 Pitra, J.B. Inscriptions des...Rome chretienne. Paris, 1862-92. 3 pam.

Arc 1500.5 Ponton d'Amécourt, G. de. Monnaies mérovingiennes du palais et de l'ecole. Paris, 1862.

Arc 1540.21.5 Poste, Beale. A vindication of the Celtic inscription on Gaulish and British coins. London, 1862.

Arc 720.18PF Promis, Carlo. Le antichità di Aosta. Torino, 1862. 2v.

Arc 1030.32 Reumont, A. Inscriptiones christianae urbis Romae. n.p., 1862.

Arc 600.6A Rhind, A.H. Thebes. London, 1862.

Arc 1030.5.25 Rossi, G.B. de. Delle sillogi epigrafiche di Smezio e di Panvinio. Roma, 1862.

Arc 1478.4 Sabatier, J. Description générale des monnaies byzantines. Text and plates. Paris, 1862. 2v.

Arc 1663.22 Satterlee, Alfred H. An arrangement of medals and tokens struck in honor of the presidents of the United States. N.Y., 1862.

Arc 1033.50 Tizzani, V. La celebre contesa fra S. Stefano e S. Cipriano. Roma, 1862.

Arc 823.4.2 Woillez, E. Répertoire archéologique du département de l'Oise. Paris, 1862.

Arc 1335.17 Yates, J. Descriptive catalogue of a collection of current coins of all countries. London, 1862.

1863

Arc 1020.31 Alger, C. L'antica chiesa S. Anna...Gerusalemma. Gerusalemma, 1863.

Arc 1610.3 Bangs, Merwin C. Catalogue of coins and medals. Roxbury, 1863.

Arc 1264.9 Barabé, A. Recherches historiques sur le tabellionage royal. Rouen, 1863.

Arc 793.5.5 Barré, L. Herculanum et Pompéi. Paris, 1863-72. 7v.

Arc 1027.1.17 Bartolini, D. Relazione severamente i vasi...sangue dei martiri. Roma, 1863.

Arc 853.4.13 Becker, J. Castellum Mattiacorum. Wiesbaden, 1863. 6 pam.

Chronological Listing

1863 - cont.

Arc 820.201 Bernard, A. Le temple d'Auguste et la nationalité. Lyon, 1863.
Arc 825.4 Boucoiran, L. Guide...dans Nîmes et les environs. Nîmes, 1863.
Arc 825.4.4 Boucoiran, L. Guide aux monuments de Nîmes et au Pont du Gard. Nîmes, 1863.
Arc 382.6 Carus, K.G. Ueber die typisch gewordenen Abbildungen menschlichen Kopfformen. Jena, 1863. 15 pam.
Arc 1033.35.51 Cellier. La sainte vraie croix de Douchy. Valenciennes, 1863.
Arc 642.1 Chase, T. Hellas. Cambridge, 1863.
Arc 518.5 Clarke, Hyde. Ephesus. Smyrna, 1863.
Arc 1263.1 Douët d'Arcq, L.C. Collection de sceaux. Paris, 1863-67. 2v.
Arc 830.5.3 Ducis, Claude A. Mémoire sur les voies romaines de la Savoie. Annecy, 1863.
Arc 87.2.63 Fiedler, F. Gripswalder Matronen- und Mereurius-Statuen. Bonn, 1863.
Arc 113.2 France. Mémoires lus à la Sorbonne. Archéologie, 1861, 63-68. Paris, 1863-69. 7v.
Arc 1093.2.3.7 Frederik VII, king of Denmark. Über den Bau des Riesenbetten der Vorzeit. Kopenhagen, 1863.
Arc 830.33 Galles, René. Manné-er-H'roëk; dolmen découvert. Vannes, 1863.
Arc 1027.45 Galt Said, G. Grotta di San Paolo a Malta. Malta, 1863.
Itn Arc 1200.10* Guigue, M.C. De l'origine de la signature...au Moyen Âge. Paris, 1863.
Arc 861.10 Halliwell, J.O. Round about notes...Isle of Man. London, 1863.
Arc 1264.5 Hucher, Eugène. Catalogue de la collection de sceaux matrices. Paris, 1863.
Arc 861.3 Hume, A. Ancient meols, or Some account of the antiquities found near Dove Point. London, 1863.
Arc 1190.1.9 Jaffé, P. Diplomata quadraginta. Berlin, 1863.
Arc 830.1.5 Jéhan, L.F. La Bretagne. Tours, 1863.
Arc 610.5F Kemble, John M. Horae ferales. London, 1863.
Arc 712.22 Lloyd, W.W. On the general theory of proportion in archaeological design and its exemplification in detail in the Parthenon. London, 1863.
Arc 1400.5 Martin, Leopold Charles. The current gold and silver coins of all countries. London, 1863?
Arc 1033.12.137 Mencacci, P. Alcune memorie sull'imagine acheropita del SS. Salvatore di Sancta Santorum. Roma, 1863.
Arc 893.8.5 Nilsson, S. Die Ureinwohner des Scandinavischen Nordens. Hamburg, 1863-68. 2v.
Arc 825.3.5 Nîmes. Musée des Antiques et Cabinet des Médailles. Catalogue de Musée de Nîmes. 6e éd. Nîmes, 1863.
Arc 825.3.8 Nîmes. Musée des Antiques et Cabinet des Médailles. Catalogue de Musée de Nîmes. 6e éd. Nîmes, 1863-75.
Arc 880.5 O'Neill, Henry. Fine arts and civilization of ancient Ireland. London, 1863.
Arc 1668.8 Perez Varela, H. Ensayo de un catalogo...de las medallas. Habana, 1863.
Arc 716.8 Pervanoglu, P. Die Grabsteine der alten Griechen. Leipzig, 1863.
Arc 830.140 Petit, Ange. Dissertation sur Genabum-Gien. Orléans, 1863.
Arc 1423.8 Pfaffenhoffen, F. von. Le prince croisé Baudouin. Paris, 1863.
Arc 1334.8 Phillips, H. Numismatics. Philadelphia, 1863-80. 12 pam.
Arc 772.1.2 Reber, F. von. Die Ruinen Roms. Leipzig, 1863.
Arc 823.4.3 Rosenzweig, L. Répertoire archéologique du département du Morbihan. Paris, 1863.
Arc 1033.17.545 Santelamazza, M. Cenni intorno la chiesa di S. Salvatore alle Coppelle. Roma, 1863.
Arc 1163.3.6 Savva, archbishop of Tver. Paleograficheskie snimki. Moskva, 1863.
Arc 1020.9.125 Scognamiglio, A. Cripta di S. Gennaro nel cimeterio. Roma, 1863.
Arc 1025.41 Scognamiglio, A. In Roma i cristianai...soterranei cimiteri. Roma, 1863.
Arc 1015.212 Scognamiglio, A. Notice sur deux catacombs. Paris, 1863.
Arc 1470.6 Warren, J.L. An essay on Greek federal coinage. London, 1863.
Arc 1335.58 Yale College. Catalogue of the cabinet of coins belonging to Yale College. New Haven, 1863.

1864

Arc 1016.3 Barbier de Montault, X. Étude archéologique sur le reliquaire du chef de S. Laurent. Rome, 1864.
Arc 830.26 Barranger, A. Étude d'archéologie celtique...Seine-et-Oise. Paris, 1864.
Arc 830.18 Bertrand, Alexandre. Les voies romaines en Gaule. Paris, 1864.
Arc 1020.32.12 Biraghi, L. I tre sepolcri santambrisiani scoperti...1864. Milano, 1864.
Arc 87.1.24 Boetticher, C. Dirke. Berlin, 1864.
Arc 830.93 Boissieu, A. de. Ainay; son autel, son amphithéatre, ses martyrs. Lyon, 1864.
Arc 726.10.2 Brunn, H. Cista prenestina. Roma, 1864.
Arc 83.1 Bulletino di commissione di antichita in Sicilia. Palermo, 1864.
Arc 547.6.5 Cairo. Musée des Antiquités Égyptiennes. Notice des principaux monuments...à Boulaq. Alexandrie, 1864.
Arc 1334.6.10 Catalogue de monnaies royales francaise en or. Paris, 1864. 9 pam.
Arc 552.3 Clark, Edward L. Daleth; or The homestead of the nations. Boston, 1864.
Arc 1505.2 Dannenberg, H. Pommerns Münzen im Mittelalter. Berlin, 1864.
Arc 758.1 Dyer, T.H. Ancient Rome. London, 1864.
Arc 1538.11 Evans, J. Coins of the ancient Britons. v.1 and supplement. London, 1864-90. 2v.
Arc 432.1.2 Fergusson, F. Rock-cut temples of India. London, 1864.
Arc 432.1.3 Fergusson, J. Rock-cut temples of India. London, 1864.
Arc 1015.208.5 Garrucci, R. Dissertazioni archaeologiche di vario argomento. v.1-2. Roma, 1864.
Arc 1015.208.2 Garrucci, R. Vetri ornati di figure in oro. Roma, 1864.
Arc 1138.13 Gautier, Léon. Quelques mots sur l'étude de la paléographie. Paris, 1864.
Arc 1033.38 Giorgi, Calisto. Sull'autenticità del capo di S. Lorenzo. Roma, 1864.
Arc 1088.1.3 Graser, B. De veterum re navali. Berolini, 1864.
Arc 1088.1.4 Graser, B. De veterum trirenium fabrica. Berolini, 1864.

1864 - cont.

Arc 1033.12.114 Guérin, L.F. Notice abrégée sur la sainte tunique de...Christ. Paris, 1864.
Arc 1020.84 Le Brun Dalbaune. Les aumonières du trésor...cathedrale de Troyes. Troyes, 1864.
Arc 855.11 MacLauchlan, H. Memoir...survey of eastern branch of Watling Street. London, 1864. 2v.
Arc 1423.9 Madden, Frederic W. History of Jewish coinage. London, 1864.
Arc 712.7 Marchal. Le Parthénon. Paris, 1864.
Arc 1033.162 Molini, A.M. De vita et Lipsanis S. Marci Evangelistae. Romae, 1864.
Arc 720.217 Pallastrelli, B. La città d'Umbria. Piacenza, 1864.
Arc 830.18.7 Peigné-Delacourt, A. Recherche sur divers lieux du pays des Silvanectes. Amiens, 1864.
Arc 495.201 Pierotti, E. Jerusalem explored. London, 1864. 2v.
Arc 495.7 Renan, E. Mission de Phénicie. Paris, 1864. 2v.
Arc 1015.205 Rossi, G.B. de. La Roma scotterranea christiana. Roma, 1864-77. 4v.
Arc 1453.9 Russkoe Arkheologischeskoe Obshchestvo, Leningrad. Muzei. Katalog evropeiskikh medalei i monet. Sankt Peterburg, 1864.
Arc 861.40 Scarth, H.M. Aquae solis...Roman Bath. London, 1864.
Arc 590.4.2 Sharpe, S. Alabaster sarcophagus of Oimenepthah. London, 1864.
Arc 605.201 Smith, R.M. History of the recent discovery at Cyrene. London, 1864.
Arc 595.9.2 Smyth, C.P. Our inheritance in the Great Pyramid. London, 1864.
Arc 913.7 Staub, Johannes. Die Pfahlbauten in den Schweizerseen bei Fluntern. Zürich, 1864.
Arc 1582.1 Tilesius von Tilenau, Adolf. Explication de la figure problématique. St. Petersbourg, 1864.
Arc 830.366 Truc, J.B. Osmin. Forum Voconii aux Arc sur Argens. Paris, 1864.
Arc 1033.35.7F Van de Putte, F. Collégiale de S. Walburge à Furnes. Relique de la croix. Bruges, 1864. 3 pam.
Arc 1428.7 Vogué, C.J. Monnaies inédites des Croisades. Paris, 1864.
NEDL Arc 495.6PF Vogue, M. de. Le temple de Jérusalem. Paris, 1864.
Arc 1020.65 Weale, W.H.J. Catalogue des objets d'art religieux...à l'Hotel Liederkerke à Malines. 2. éd. Bruxelles, 1864.

1865

Arc 1493.3 Allen, E.A. Monnaies d'or suévo-lusitaniennes. Paris, 1865.
Arc 830.64 Barbe, Henri. Jublains, Mayenne. Mayenne, 1865.
Arc 1033.41 Bobone, G. Apologia di protomartiri...Tolomeo e Romano. Roma, 1865.
Arc 843.56 Boix, Vicente. Memorias de Sagunto. Valencia, 1865.
Arc 830.67.5 Brouillet, A. Époques antédiluvienne et celtique du Poitu. pt.1-2. Poitiers, 1865.
Arc 1027.25.55 Buck, V. de. M. de Rossi ets ses récents travaux...catacombes. v.1-2. Paris, 1865.
Arc 716.4 Bursian, C. De Foro Atheniensium Disputatio. Zürich, 1865.
Arc 1033.85 Cavedoni, C. Osservazioni...sepolcro di Maria. Modena, 1865.
Arc 1260.4.5 Cecchetti, B. Bolle dei dogi di Venezia. Venezia, 1865.
Arc 712.4 Choisy, A. Note sur la courbure dissymétrique des degrés qui limitent au couchant la plate-forme du Parthénon. Paris, 1865.
Arc 681.1 Conze, A. Reise auf der Insel Lesbos. Hannover, 1865.
Arc 823.4.4 Croyes, H. Répertoire archéologique du département du Tarn. Paris, 1865.
Arc 1020.10.15 Dandolo, C.J. Roma christiana nei primi secoli. Asisi, 1865-67. 3v.
Arc 545.205.2 Duemichen, J. Bauurkunde der Tempelanlagen von Dendera. Leipzig, 1865.
Arc 1670.4 Durand, Anthony. Médailles et jetons des numismates. Genève, 1865.
Arc 505.3.5 Fergusson, J. The Holy Sepulchre and Temple at Jerusalem. London, 1865.
Arc 785.15 Froehner, W. La colonne trajane. Paris, 1865.
Arc 1033.54 Gori, A.F. Dissertazioni...di S. Giuseppe. Modena, 1865.
Arc 505.17 Guérin, V. Tombeau de Josué. Note sur le Khirbet-Tibneh. Paris, 1865.
Arc 1264.13 Guesnon, A. Sigillographie de la ville d'Arras. Arras, 1865.
Arc 1492.200 Heiss, Aloiss. Descripcion generale de las monedas hispanicas cristianas. Madrid, 1865. 3v.
Arc 1200.14 Huillard-Bréholles. Examen des chartes de l'eglise romaine. Paris, 1865.
Arc 87.1.25 Jordan, Henri. Vesta und die Laren auf einem pompischen Wandgemälde. Berlin, 1865.
Arc 1590.2 Lambros, P. Monete inedite dei gran maestri...in Rodi. Venezia, 1865.
Arc 853.15 Lische, G. Pfahlbauten in Mechlenberg. Schwerin, 1865.
Arc 820.205 Mantellier, P. Mémoire sur les bronzes antiques. Paris, 1865.
Arc 382.5 Michaelis, A. Anaglyphi vaticani explicatio. Tubingae, 1865. 15 pam.
Arc 712.18 Michaelis, A. Dei due figure alate sul fregio del Partenone. Lipsia, 1865.
Arc 1478.10.5 Mommsen, T. Histoire de la monnaie romaine. Paris, 1865. 4v.
Arc 1400.3 Morbio, Carlo. Monete franco-italiche ossidionali. Asti, 1865.
Arc 513.7 Newton, C.T. Travels and discoveries in the Levant. London, 1865. 2v.
Arc 893.8.6 Nilsson, S. Die Ureinwohner des Scandinavischen Nordens. pt.1-2. Hamburg, 1865-66.
Arc 1020.64 Notice sur les reliques...l'église de lYon. Lyon, 1865.
Arc 700.18 Overbeck, J. Über die Lade des Kypselos. Leipzig, 1865.
Arc 1473.4 Pfaffenhoffen, F. Lettre...sur quelques monnaies byzantines. Paris, 1865.
Arc 726.8 Pigorini, L. Le abitazioni Palustri di Fontanellato. Parma, 1865.
Arc 1495.4F Plantet, L. Essai sur les monnaies du Comte de Bourgogne. Paris, 1865.
Arc 1583.10 Prozarovskii, D.I. Moneta i vec' v' Rossii do kontsa XVIII stoletiia. Sankt Peterburg, 1865.
Arc 1077.2.41 Rapp, Edward. Das Labarum und der Sonnen-Cultus. Bonn, 1865.
Arc 1668.5 Rentzmann, W. Numismatisches Legenden-Lexicon. v.1-2. Berlin, 1865-66.

Chronological Listing

1865 - cont.

Arc 73.4 Rome. Istituto. Nuove memorie dell'instituto. Leipzig, 1865. 2v.

Arc 612.9 Sacken, Eduard. Leitfaden zur Kunde des heidnischen Alterthümes. Wien, 1865.

Arc 861.71 Tate, George. The ancient British sculptured rocks of Northumberland. Alnwick, 1865.

Arc 510.9 Texier, Charles. Principal ruins of Asia Minor. London, 1865.

Arc 895.29.15 Worsaae, J.J.A. Om Sleswigs eller Sønderjyllands oldtidsminder. Kjøbenhavn, 1865.

Arc 662.1 Wyse, T. An excursion in the Peloponnesus. London, 1865- 2v.

1866

Arc 1020.9.103 Barbier de Montault, X. Les souterrains et le tresor...St. Pierre à Rome. Rome, 1866.

Arc 1356.1.3 Barthélemy, A.J.B.A. Nouveau manuel complete de numismatique ancienne. Paris, 1866.

Arc 1356.1 Barthélemy, A.J.B.A. Nouveau manuel complete de numismatique ancienne. Text and atlas. Paris, 1866. 2v.

Arc 1408.1 Brandis, J. Das Münz-, Mass- und Gewichtswesen in Vorderasien. Berlin, 1866.

Arc 1330.55 Canadian numismatic bibliography. A review of R.W. McLachlan's Canadian numismatics and other books and pamphlets describing Canadian coins and medals. Montreal, 1866.

Arc 387.12.30 Cappeli, A. Monsignor Celestino Cavedoni. Firenze, 1866.

Arc 387.12.31 Cappeli, A. Necrologia di Mons. Celestino Cavedoni. 2. ed. Modena, 1866.

Arc 1153.29.3 Chassant, A. Dictionnaire des abréviations latines et françaises. 3. éd. Paris, 1866.

Arc 830.32 Cochet, J.B.D. Notice sur une sépulture gauloise. Rouen, 1866.

Arc 830.32.8 Cochet, J.B.D. La Seine-Inférieure historique et archéologique. 2e éd. Paris, 1866.

Arc 726.83 Conestabile, Giancarlo. Sopra un cista in bronzo con rapparesentanze a graffito. Firenze, 1866.

Htn Arc 815.4* Gautier, T. Le palais pompéien. Paris, 1866.

Arc 1070.200 Graser, B. Das Model eines athenischen Fuenfreihenschiffs Pentere. Berlin, 1866.

Arc 810.7 Guide de Pompéi. Naples, 1866.

Arc 1570.1 Holmboe, C.A. Et frar fund af norske mynter. Kjøbenhavn, 1866.

Arc 87.1.26 Huebner, E. Relief eines roemischen Kriegers. Berlin, 1866.

Arc 1274.2.3 Laing, Henry. Supplemental descriptive catalogue of ancient Scottish seals. Edinburgh, 1866.

Arc 875.23 Laing, S. Prehistoric remains of Caithness. Edinburgh, 1866.

Arc 1590.2.3 Lambros, P. Monete inedite dei gran maestri. Primo supplemento. Venezia, 1866.

Arc 1590.6 Lambros, Paulos. Monnaies de Chypre et de Salona. n.p., 1866.

Arc 875.15 Leslie, Forbes. The early races of Scotland and their monuments. Edinburgh, 1866. 2v.

Arc 1301.2.5 Lewis, Winslow. Address...on resigning the presidency of the Boston Numismatic Society, January 5, 1865. N.Y., 1866.

Arc 1390.6 Morbio, Carlo. Delle monete battute da Carlo Magno in Italia. Milano, 1866.

Arc 885.15 Morgan, O. Notice of a tessellated pavement. Newport, 1866.

Arc 1163.2.23 Moriano, F. Ortografia general paleográfica-bibliográfica de la lengua castellana. Sevilla, 1866.

Arc 1077.2.3 Mortillet, G. de. Le signe de la croix avant de Christianité. Paris, 1866.

Arc 785.4 Mullooly, J. Breve notizie delle antiche pitture. Roma, 1866.

Arc 1033.70.9 Mullooly, J. Brief notice of the ancient paintings...Rome. Rome, 1866.

Arc 1025.29.18 Odorici, F. Sulla Roma sotterranea dal G.B. de Rossi. Milano, 1866.

Arc 1093.2.9F Peigne-Delacourt, M. Un tranche-tête. Paris, 1866.

Arc 825.3.2 Pelet, Auguste. Description de l'amphithéâtre de Nîmes. 3e éd. Nîmes, 1866.

Arc 505.5.19 Rosen, G. Das Harom von Jerusalem und Tempelplatz des Maria. Gotha, 1866.

Arc 920.2 Russia. Commission Impériale Archéologique. Recueil d'antiquités de la Scythie. St. Petersbourg, 1866. 2v.

Arc 1470.11 Sallet, A. von. Beiträge zur Geschichte und Numismatik...des Pontus. Berlin, 1866.

Arc 505.18 Saulcy. Memoire sur...maçonneril...du Haram-Ech-Cherif de Jerusalem. Paris, 1866.

Arc 1020.114 Schenkel, I.I. Die Reliquien des Klosters Allerheiligen. Schaffhausen, 1866.

Arc 1570.2 Schive, C. Im et fund af norske mynter fraa Sando. Kjøbenhavn, 1866.

Arc 936.195.295 Vocel, Jan E. Pravěk země české. Praha, 1866-68.

Arc 855.216 Warne, C. The Celtic Tumuli of Dorset. London, 1866.

Arc 1025.16 Wolter, M. Die römischen Katakomben. Frankfurt, 1866.

Arc 1613.6 Woodward, W.E. Catalogue of American and foreign coins, medals, tokens. Providence, 1866.

Arc 1335.6 Woodward, W.E. Catalogue of the numismatic collection of F.S. Hoffman. N.Y., 1866.

1867

Arc 1020.9.32 Barbier de Montault, X. La bibliothèque vaticane et ses annexes. Rome, 1867.

Arc 1033.40 Bartolini, D. Gli atti del martirio...S. Cecilia. Roma, 1867.

Arc 1033.13.13 Bartolini, D. Sopra l'anno LXII dell'era...Pietro e Paolo. 2. ed. Roma, 1867.

Arc 1027.76 Berbrugger, M. Le tombeau de la chrétienne. Alger, 1867.

Arc 1020.1 Bock, F. Das Heiligthum zu Aachen. Köln, 1867.

Arc 1470.28 Bompois, H.F. Les médailles restitutées par M.F. Lenormant à Lyncus ou Héraclée de Lyncestide. Paris, 1867-76. 3 pam.

Arc 870.14F Bruce, John C. The Roman wall. 3. ed. London, 1867.

Arc 1335.2 Chadbourne, S.H. Catalogue of a collection of coins and medals. Boston, 1867.

Arc 830.338 Commission Historique du Département du Nord. Statistique archéologique du département du Nord. Lille, 1867. 2v.

1867 - cont.

Arc 930.203 Dethier. Nouvelles découvertes archéologiques à Constantinople. Constantinople, 1867.

Arc 1033.19.9 Durand, Paul. Étude sur l'étimacia symbole du jugement dernier dans l'iconographie grecque chrétienne. Chartres, 1867.

Arc 810.4 Dyer, T.H. Pompeii: its history, buildings and antiquities. London, 1867.

Arc 1500.47.5 Fillioux, A. Nouvel essai d'interprétation et de classification des monnaies de la Gaule. 2. éd. Paris, 1867.

Arc 700.17 Foerster, R. Die Hochzeit des Zeus und der Hera; Relief der Schaubert'schen Sammlung. Breslau, 1867.

Arc 688.4 Fouqué, F. Premier rapport sur une mission scientifique à l'Ile Santorin. Paris, 1867.

Arc 1030.1 Galante, G.A. Lapida sepolcrale di Teofilatto. Napoli, 1867.

Arc 858.3 Godwin, H. The English archaeologist's hand-book. Oxford, 1867.

Arc 785.22.8 Gori, Fabio. Sugli edifizi palatini. Roma, 1867.

Arc 1088.1.2 Graser, B. Untersuchungen und das Seewesen des Alterthums. Göttingen, 1867.

Arc 830.25 Hahn, Alexandre. Monuments celtiques des environs de Luzarches. Paris, 1867.

Arc 1613.8 Hart, C.H. A historical sketch of the national medals. Philadelphia, 1867.

Arc 1025.14 Housse, L. Die Katakomben über das Unterirdische. Lurenburg, 1867.

Arc 855.212 James, H. Plans and photographs of Stonehenge. n.p., 1867.

Arc 785.12 Jordan, Henri. Der capitolinische Plan der Stadt Rom. Berlin, 1867.

Arc 880.7 Keane, Marcus. Towers and temples of ancient Ireland. Dublin, 1867.

Arc 1330.3 Leitzmann, J. Bibliotheca numaria. Weissensee, 1867.

Arc 1092.1.2 Longpérier, H. Des rouelles et des anneaux antiques. Paris, 1867.

Arc 1092.1 Longpérier, H. Note sur les rouelles antiques de bronze. Paris, 1867.

Arc 1033.12.139 Mese di luglio ovvero esercizii divoti...giorni...miracolosa immagine di Gesu. Venezia, 1867.

Arc 1254.3 Miller, E. Bulles byzantines de la collection de M...de Köhne. Paris, 1867.

Arc 1027.41.25 Moreschi, L. Indicazione dei dipinti a buon presco dell'Apostolo S. Paolo. Roma, 1867.

Arc 1033.17.45 Orsini, Mathieu. La Virgen. 4. ed. Barcelona, 1867. 2v.

Arc 770.2 Parker, J.H. Catalogue of a series of photographs illustrative of the archaeology of Rome. n.p., 1867.

Arc 1348.11 Phillips, H. Pamphlets on numismatics. Philadelphia, 1867-83. 4 pam.

Arc 1018.27 Piper, F. Einleitung in die Monumentale Theologie. Gotha, 1867.

Arc 1478.32F Pizzamiglio, Luigi. Saggio cronologico, ossia storia della moneta romana. Roma, 1867.

Arc 497.4 Rey, E.G. Rapport sur une mission scientifique. Paris, 1867.

Arc 402.3 Robiou, F. Chefs-d'oeuvre de l'art antique. 1st ser., 1-3; 2d ser., 1-4. Paris, 1867. 7v.

Arc 1025.29.5 Rossi, G.B. de. Aperçu général sur les catacombes de Rome. Paris, 1867.

Arc 1015.205.15 Rossi, M.S. de. Analsi geologica ed archilettonica de Cemet de Callisto. Roma, 1867.

Arc 1033.43.5 Ruggieri, E. Dell'antico Pellegrinaggio XVIII centenario Martirio Pietro e Paolo. Roma, 1867.

Arc 1490.98.5F Salinas Gargotta, Antonino. Le monete dell'antiche città di Sicilia. Palermo, 1867-72.

Arc 853.77 Scheuermayer. Auffindung eines römischen Bades in Augsburg. n.p., 1867?

Arc 1027.25 Scognamiglio, A. De phiala cruenta...Christo martyrii. Paris, 1867.

Arc 497.16 Sepp, J.N. Neue architektonische Studien...Forschungen in Palästina. Würzburg, 1867.

Arc 870.7 Simpson, J.Y. Archaic sculpturings of cups, circles. Edinbrugh, 1867.

Arc 595.9.5 Smyth, C.P. Life and work at the Great Pyramid. Edinburgh, 1867. 3v.

Arc 870.1.9 Stevens, J. Descriptive lists of flint implements. St. Mary Bourne. London, 1867.

Arc 1033.34.29 Stocchi, P. Viaggio ed episopato romano di San Pietro. Roma, 1867. 2 pam.

Arc 915.1 Thioly, F. Epoques antéhistoriques an Mont Salève. Genève, 1867.

Arc 855.205 Tite, Will. Notes on Roman architectural remains. London, 1867. 2 pam.

Arc 87.2.67 Urlichs, L. Die Gruppe des Pasquino. Bonn, 1867.

Arc 1018.45 Villa Amil y Castro, J. Rudimentos de arqueología sagrada. Lugo, 1867.

Arc 628.21 Visconti, Pietro E. La stazione della coorte VII dei vigili e i ricordi istorici. 2. ed. Roma, 1867. 19 pam.

Arc 1613.6.2 Woodward, W.E. Catalogue of American and foreign coins, medals, tokens. Roxbury, 1867.

Arc 1190.3.2 Wright, Andrew. Court hand restored. 8. ed. London, 1867.

1868

Arc 830.18.3 Arbaud, Damase. Alaunium Catuiaca. n.p., 1868.

Arc 1335.76.10F Athens. Ethnikon Nomismatikon Mouseion. Katalogos. Athēnai, 1868.

Arc 595.18 Bart, J.Y.S. On some points in certain theories...of the great Pyramid of Jeeseh. Glasgow, 1868.

Arc 505.5.25 Bartolini, D. Sull'antico Tempio Salomone. Roma, 1868.

Arc 1538.4 Batty, D.T. Catalogue of the copper coinage of Great Britain. Manchester, 1868-98. 4v.

Arc 1500.4 Blancard, Louis. Essai sur les monnaies de Charles Ier, comté de Provence. Paris, 1868.

Arc 830.128 Borel, Pierre. Les antiquités de Castres. Paris, 1868.

Arc 1033.12.10 Carles, A. Histoire du Saint Suaire de Cadouin. Perigueux, 1868.

Arc 552.1.4 Champollion, J.F. Lettres écrites d'Égypte et de Nubie en 1828 et 1829. Paris, 1868.

Arc 1433.15 Cipelli, Luigi. Di una moneta Turca coniata nella zecca di Parma. Parma, 1868.

Arc 1033.17.85 Cornaro, F. Notizie...delle apparizioni e delle immagini di Maria...di Bergamo. Bergamo, 1868.

Chronological Listing

1868 - cont.

Arc 705.11 Curtius, E. Sieben Karten zur Topographie von Athen. Gotha, 1868.
Arc 705.11PF Curtius, E. Sieben Karten zur Topographie von Athen. Atlas. Gotha, 1868.
Arc 543.8 Daubrée, Auguste. Rapport sur une collection d'instrument en pierre. Paris, 1868.
Arc 1428.3 Dechant, Norbert. Kreuzfahrer-Münzen. Wien, 1868.
Arc 1540.25 Golding, Charles. The coinage of Suffolk. London, 1868.
Arc 1033.12.8 Gourgues, A. de. Le Saint Suaire. Perigueux, 1868.
Arc 497.9 Guérin, V. Description de la Palestine. pt.1-3. Paris, 1868-80. 7v.
Arc 790.203 Helbig, W. Wandgemaelde der...Staedte Campaniens. Leipzig, 1868. 2v.
Arc 1500.20 Holmboe, C.A. Im vildsvintypen fraa galliske mynter. Kjøbenhavn, 1868.
Arc 1570.1.5 Holmboe, C.A. Om nogle norske pengeten. Kjøbenhavn, 1868.
Arc 87.1.28 Huebner, E. Augustus. Berlin, 1868.
Arc 394.1 Jahn, Otto. Aus der Alterthumswissenschaft. Bonn, 1868.
Arc 391.2.17 Jahn, Otto. Eduard Gerhard. Berlin, 1868.
Arc 1027.1 Kaus, F.X. Die Blutampullen der römischen Katakomben. Frankfurt, 1868.
Arc 1033.12.169 Kraus, F.X. Heilige Nagel...zu Trier. Trier, 1868.
Arc 1590.5 Laugier. Étude historique sur les monnaies...de l'ordre de Saint Jean de Jérusalem. Marseille, 1868.
Arc 1020.7 Lebarte, J. L'église cathedrale de Sienne...trésor. Paris, 1868.
Arc 1500.40.5 Lecoq-Kerneven, J. Étude historique sur la numismatique bretonne. Rennes, 1868.
Arc 1480.29 Longpérier, Adrien. Recherches sur les insignes de la questure et sur les récipients monétaires. Paris, 1868.
Arc 708.11 Mommsen, A. Athenae Christianae. Leipzig, 1868.
Arc 1020.74 Nampoon, P. Histoire de Notre Dame de France. Puy, 1868.
Arc 936.26 Notice sur les antiquités de la Roumanie. Paris, 1868.
Arc 708.38 Pantazēs, Dēmētrios. Periēgētēs Athēnōn. Athēnai, 1868.
Arc 770.2.5 Parker, J.H. De variis structurarum generibus penes romanos veteres. Romae, 1868.
Arc 835.205F Pereira da Costa, Francisco. Noções sobre o estado prehistorico de terra e do homein. Lisboa, 1868. 2v.
Arc 400.5 Petersen, C. Ueber dea Verhaltniss des Broncealters. Hamburg, 1868.
Arc 861.30 Pooley, C. Notes on the old crosses of Gloucester. London, 1868.
Arc 823.4.5 Quantin, M. Répertoire archéologique du département de l'Yonne. Paris, 1868.
Arc 1016.219 Rampolla, M. De cathedra romana B. Petri. Roma, 1868.
Arc 900.214 Sacken, E. von. Das Grabfeld von Hallstatt. Wien, 1868.
NEDL Arc 880.19 Stokes, William. The life and labors in art and archaeology of George Petrie. London, 1868.
Arc 1315.5 Strozzi, Carlo. Periodico di numismatica e sfragistica per la storia d'Italia. Firenze, 1868-74. 6v.
Arc 843.45 Teixeira de Aragão, A.C. Relatorio sobre o comiterio romano. Lisboa, 1868.
Arc 1078.1 Wieseler, F. Das Diptychon Quirinianum zu Brescia. Göttingen, 1868.
Arc 87.2.68 Wieseler, F. Hildesheimer Silberfund. Bonn, 1868.
Arc 1540.15 Wingate, James. Illustrations of coinage of Scotland. Glasgow, 1868.
Arc 1018.28 Wolcott, M.E.C. Sacred archaeology...dictionary. London, 1868.

1869

Arc 1148.16 Amphilochii, A. Snimki ne" Kondakaria XII-XIII. Moskva, 1869.
Arc 1458.19 Badeigts de Laborde. Description des médailles grecques. Paris, 1869.
Arc 1470.28.5 Bompois, H.F. Médailles grecques autonomes. Paris, 1869.
Arc 793.9.2 Breton, Ernest. Pompeia. 3. éd. Paris, 1869.
Arc 1018.38 Bruyn, H. de. Archéologie religieuse. v.1-2. Bruxelles, 1869.
Arc 547.6.7 Cairo. Musée des Antiquités Égyptiennes. Notice des principaux monuments...du Musée d'Antiquités Égyptiennes à Boulaq. 3. éd. Paris, 1869.
Arc 458.4 Carr, Mark William. Descriptive and historical papers...the seven pagodas on the Coromandel coast. Madras, 1869.
Arc 830.21.3 Castan, Auguste. Le capitole de Vesontio et les capitoles provinciaux du monde romain. Paris, 1869.
Arc 1033.4.5 Cavedoni, C. La credenza della primitiva chiesa del Sacramento dell'Eucaristia. Modena, 1869.
Arc 540.1.12 Cesnola, L.P. Extraits de l'histoire générale des hommes vivants. Genève, 1869.
Arc 830.75 Duvernoy, Clement. Notice sur le pays de Montbéliard. Montbéliard, 1869.
Arc 1020.95 Fabiani, G. Sulla Cattedra Alessandria di S. Marco. Modena, 1869.
Arc 820.216F Flouest, E. Notice archéologique sur le camp de Chassey. Chalon-sur-Saône, 1869.
Arc 1016.220A Galante, G.A. Memorie dell'antico cenobio di S. Severino. Napoli, 1869.
Arc 387.10 Gallo, Francesco. Biografia del generale americano e console in Cipro, Luigi Palma di Cesnola. Vercelli, 1869.
Arc 825.8.3 Germer-Durand, E. Notes épigraphiques. Nîmes, 1869. 6 pam.
Arc 547.8 Hay, J. Catalogue of the collection of Egyptian antiquities belonging to the late Robert Hay, Esq. London, 1869.
Arc 893.18 Hildebrand, H. Den äldre jernåldern i Norrland. Stockholm, 1869.
Arc 1550.1 Holmboe, C.A. Et guldbracteat-praeg som ofte forekommer. Kjøbenhavn, 1869.
Arc 435.25.5F India. Archaeological Survey. Illustrations of ancient buildings of Kashmir. London, 1869.
Arc 595.4 James, H. Notes on the Great Pyramid of Egypt. Southampton, 1869. 2 pam.
Arc 716.3.2 Kekulé, R. Die Balustrade des Templs der Athena-Nike. Leipzig, 1869.
Arc 1030.34 Le Blant, E. Manuel d'épigraphie chrétienne. Paris, 1869.
Htn Arc 823.13* Ledain, A. Lettres et notices d'archéologie. Metz, 1869.
Arc 1030.17 McCaul, J. Christian epitaphs. Toronto, 1869.
Arc 900.200 Magyar, Yudo. Monumenta Hungariae archaeologica. Pesth, 1869-79. 4v.
Arc 785.11.4 Mazois, F. Le palais de Scaurus. 4. éd. Paris, 1869.
Arc 767.6.3 Mirabilia Romae. Berlin, 1869.
Arc 893.23F Montelius, Oscar. Från jernåldern. Stockholm, 1869.

1869 - cont.

Arc 1033.20.25 Mullooly, Joseph. Saint Clement, pope and martyr and his Basilica in Rome. Rome, 1869.
Arc 87.2.69 Peters, F. Burg-Kapelle zu Iben. Bonn, 1869.
Arc 545.204 Pickering, C. The Gliddon mummy-case. Washington, 1869.
Arc 505.20 Pierotti, E. Macpela, ou Tombeau des patriarches à Hebron. Lausanne, 1869.
Arc 853.5 Rupp, T. Aus der Verzeit Reuthingens. 2. Aufl. Stuttgart, 1869.
Arc 1020.84.13 Salore, Charles. Probationes cultus sanctorum Diocesis Trecensis. Troyes, 1869.
Arc 1603.3.5 Sandham, Alfred. Coins, tokens and medals of the Dominion of Canada. Montreal, 1869.
Arc 505.18.7 Saulcy. Recherches sur l'emplacement...du tombeau d'Hélène. Paris, 1869.
Arc 658.3 Schliemann, H. Ithaka, der Peleponnes und Troja. Leipzig, 1869.
Arc 1033.53.5 Scognamiglio, A. Ne' primi tre secoli di persecuzione cristiane. Napoli, 1869.
Arc 1315.1.5 Société Francaise de Numismatique. Comptes rendu. Paris, 1869-75. 7v.
Arc 875.16 Thomas, F.L.W. Primitive dwellings and hypogea of the Outer Hebrides. Edinburgh, 1869.
Arc 1335.50 Thomsen, C.J. Catalogue de la collection de monnaies. v.1, pt.1-2; v.2, pt.1-3; v.3, pt.1-2. Copenhague, 1869-76. 7v.
Arc 1528.10.5 Voogt, W.J. de. Bijdragen tot de numismatiek van Gelderland. Arnhem, 1869.
Arc 1510.173F Vossberg, Friedrich August. Münzgeschichte der Stadt Berlin. Berlin, 1869.
Arc 726.34.5 Waltzan, H. Reise auf der Insel Sardinien. Leipzig, 1869.
Arc 1153.7 Wattenbach, W. Anleitung zur lateinischen Palaeographie. Leipzig, 1869.

187-

Arc 435.25.6 Burgess, James. Descriptive account of the rock temples of western India. Bombay, 187-?
Arc 830.165.5 Caumont, Arcisse de. Les monuments historiques de l'Orne. Caen, 187-. *2v.
Arc 762.1.3.7 Hare, A.J.C. Walks in Rome. 7. American ed. N.Y., 187-.

1870

Arc 793.2.5 Adams, W.H.D. The buried cities of Campania. London, 1870.
Arc 1613.3 Appleton, W.S. Description of a selection of coins and medals relating to America. Cambridge, 1870-76. 2 pam.
Arc 830.56 Barbey, A. Les grottes préhistoriques du village de Jouaignes. v.1-3. Chateau-Thierry, 1870-75.
Arc 1020.9.130 Barbier de Montault, X. L'année liturgique à Rome. Rome, 1870.
Arc 1020.9.135 Barbier de Montault, X. Exposition religieuse de Rome 1870. Antiquités chrétiennes. Rome, 1870.
Arc 547.2.16 Berlin. Staatliche Museen. Abtheilung der Aegyptischen Alterthümer - Die Wandgemaelde. Berlin, 1870.
Arc 1033.12.186 Bombelli, R. Storia della corona ferrea dei re d'Italia. Firenze, 1870.
Arc 387.12.25 Brandoli, Placido. Monsignor Celestino Cavedoni. Modena, 1870.
Arc 793.9 Breton, Ernest. Pompeia. 3. éd. Paris, 1870.
Arc 740.202 Brunn, H. I relievi delle urne etrusche. Rome, 1870-1916. 3v.
Arc 435.12.4F Burgess, James. Memorandum on the survey of architecture and other archaeological remians...Sindh, Berar. Bombay, 1870. 2 pam.
Arc 87.1.29 Curtius, E. Die knieenden Figuren der altgriechische Kunst. Berlin, 1870.
Arc 388.1 Demarsy, A. Le congrès international d'archéologie préhistorique de Copenhague en 1869. Arras, 1870.
Arc 1025.25 Desbassayns de Richemont, M.C. Les nouvelles études...catacombes romaines. Paris, 1870.
Arc 1025.54 Desimoni, C. Le catacombe romane. Firenze, 1870.
Arc 700.13 Dumont, Albert. De plumbeis apud graecos tesseris. Paris, 1870.
Arc 1335.40 Erbstein, J. Die Schellhass'sche Münzsammlung. Dresden, 1870.
Arc 830.113F Ferry, H. de. Le Maconnais préhistorique. Macon, 1870.
Arc 1433.32 Ghiron, I. Di alcuni conii osmani della museo di Modena. Firenze, 1870.
Arc 1138.6 Gloria, A. Compendio delle lezioni teorico-pratiche di paleografia e diplomatica. Padova, 1870.
Arc 1138.6F Gloria, A. Compendio delle lezioni teorico-pratiche di paleografia e diplomatica. Atlas. Padova, 1870.
Arc 761.2 Gsell-Fels, T. Roemische Ausgrabungen. Hildburghausen, 1870.
Arc 1298.1.5 Guenther, M. Das Siegelrecht des Mittelalters. Stuttgart, 1870.
Arc 1492.201 Heiss, Aloiss. Description générale des monnaies antiques de l'Espagne. Paris, 1870.
Arc 87.1.30 Heydemann, H. Humoristische Vasenbilder. Berlin, 1870.
Arc 1675.19.5 Iversen, I. Beitrag zur russischen Medaillenkunde. St. Petersburg, 1870.
Arc 900.204 Jabornegg-Altenfels. Kärnten's römischen Alterthümer. Klagenfurt, 1870.
Arc 1081.1 Jewett, L. Grave mounds and their contents. London, 1870.
Arc 1470.13 Lampros, Paulos. Nomismata tēs nēsoy Amorgy. Athēnai, 1870.
Arc 1335.7 Leavitt, Strebeigh and Company. Catalogue of an excellent choice and select collection of coins, medals, and autographs. n.p., 1870.
Arc 1500.40 Lecoq-Kerneven, J. Monnaies du moyen-age (Gaule). Rennes, 1870.
Arc 1025.12 Marriott, W.B. Testimony of the catacombs. London, 1870.
Arc 712.10 Michaelis, A. Über die Composition der Giebelgruppen am Parthenon. Tübingen, 1870.
Arc 810.10.5 Monnier, Marc. The wonders of Pompeii. N.Y., 1870.
Arc 1490.6 Morbio, C. Opere storico-numismatiche. Bologna, 1870.
Arc 1475.10 Naples. Museo Nazionale. Medagliere II. Monete Romane. pt.1-2. Naples, 1870-71. 3v.
Arc 1033.70.19 Nardoni, L. L'antico oratorio di S. Agnese. Roma, 1870.
Arc 1033.35.35 Notizia storica sulla croce del Carroccio. Milano, 1870.
Arc 830.36 Ollier de Marichard, J. Les Carthaginois en France. Montpellier, 1870.
Arc 785.39.45 Pellegrini, A. Scavi nelle terme di Novato ed in altri luoghi di Roma. Roma, 1870.

Chronological Listing

1870 - cont.

Arc 830.344F Perrault, Ernest. Note sur un foyer de l'âge de la Pierre Polie découvert an camp de Chassey en septembre 1869. Chalons-sur-Saône, 1870.
Arc 820.200 Perrin, A. Etude préhistorique sur la Savoie. Paris, 1870.
Arc 925.30 Prozorovskii, D.I. Opisanie smolenskago klada. St. Peterburg, 1870.
Arc 1033.12.53F Rohault de Fleury, C. Memoire sur les instruments de la Passion. Paris, 1870.
Arc 736.1 Sehnbring, J. Historische Topographie von Akragas in Sicilien. Leipzig, 1870.
Arc 1615.1 Slafter, E.F. The Vermont coinage. Montpelier, 1870.
Arc 1033.17.97.8 Sotomayor, José F. Reflecciones sobre la aparición de la santísima virgen de Guadalupe. México, 1870.
Arc 403.5 Stevens, E.T. Flint chips. A guide to pre-historical archaeology. London, 1870.
Arc 705.7 Stillman, W.J. The acropolis of Athens. London, 1870.
Arc 1077.2.30 Stockbauer, J. Kunstgeschichte des Kreuzes. Schaffhausen, 1870.
Arc 674.1.6 Strube, Carl. Studien über den Bilderkreis von Eleusis. Leipzig, 1870.
Arc 875.20 Sutherland, G. Outlines of Scottish archaeology. Edinburgh, 1870.
Arc 1478.27 Teixeira de Aragão, Augusto. Descripção historica das moedas romanas existentes no gabinete numismatico de S.M. el Rei o Senhor Dom Luiz I. Lisboa, 1870.
Arc 1388.1 Tornberg, C.J. Fölhagen-fyndet. Stockholm, 1870.
Arc 720.11PF Vermiglioli, G.B. Dei monumenti di Perugia etrusca e romana. Table. Perugia, 1870.
Arc 615.5 Waring, J.B. Stone monuments...of remote ages. London, 1870.

1871

Arc 87.1.31 Adler, F. Das Pantheon zu Rom. Berlin, 1871.
Arc 1500.37 Bompois, H.F. Notice sur un dèpot de monnaies carlovingiennes. Paris, 1871.
Htn Arc 1480.16* Bruce, J.C. The story...of the Thorngrafton "Find". n.p., 1871.
Arc 444.1 Burgess, James. Rock-temples of Elephanta. Bombay, 1871.
Arc 756.5 Burn, R. Rome and the campagna. Cambridge, 1871.
Arc 540.1 Cesnola, L.P. Scoperta del tempio di Venere a Golgos. Turin, 1871.
Arc 823.4.6 Cochet, J.B.D. Répertoire archéologique du département de la Seine-Inférieure. Paris, 1871.
Arc 1493.6 Delgado, Antonio. Nuevo método de clasificacion de las medallas autonomas de España. Sevilla, 1871-76. 3v.
Arc 712.9 Fielitz, W. Der Parthenon. Ein Vortag. Stralsund, 1871.
Arc 1675.24 Fleming, J.W. Medals, clasps, and crosses, military and naval in the collection of J.W. Fleming. Brighton, 1871.
Arc 825.8 Germer-Durand, E. Découvertes archéologiques faites à Nîmes, 1870-72. Nîmes, 1871-73.
Arc 1033.12.128 Gonzati, L. Sopra un patrio monumento di antica oreficeria. Vicenza, 1871.
Arc 762.1 Hare, A.J.C. Walks in Rome. London, 1871. 2v.
Arc 1550.2 Holmboe, C.A. Et lidet fund af mynter fra 11. aaehundrede. Kjøbenhavn, 1871.
Arc 1016.205 Hübner, A. Inscritione hispaniae christianae. Berlolini, 1871.
Arc 87.2.71 Keller, O. Vicus Aurelii. Bonn, 1871.
Arc 1033.103 Liberati, D.P. Processo belle reliquie false. Roma, 1871.
Arc 800.2.5 Maréchal, P.S. Antiquités d'Herculanum. Paris, 1871. 8v.
Arc 1033.17.92 Marracci, Lodovico. Memorie di Santa Maria in Portico. Roma, 1871.
Arc 843.16 Memoria sobre las notables escavaciones hechas en el Cerrode los Santos. Madrid, 1871.
Arc 705.15A Michaelis, A. Der Parthenon. Text and atlas. Leipzig, 1871. 2v.
Arc 861.16 Miller, S.H. Illustrations of the traces...Romans and Saxons. n.p., 1871.
Arc 1025.45 Mommesen, T. The Roman catacombs. Londin, 1871.
Arc 501.19 Morrison, W. The recovery of Jerusalem. London, 1871.
Arc 800.4 Pagano, N. Description des fouilles d'Herculanum. Naples, 1871.
Arc 292.155 Polenov, D. Bibliografiia obozrenie trydov. Sankt Peterburg, 1871.
Arc 1018.4 Reusens, E. Eléments d'archéologie chrétienne. Louvain, 1871-75. 2v.
Arc 730.204 Riolo, G. La porta arabo-normanna. Palermo, 1871.
Arc 1020.27 Rossi, G.B. de. Spiciligio d'archeologia cristiana nell'Umbria. Roma, 1871.
Arc 858.26 Rust, J. Druidism exhumed. Edinburgh, 1871.
Arc 1333.15F St. Florian, Austria. Die Münzsammlung. Wien, 1871.
Arc 1470.5 Sallet, A. von. Die Künstlerinschriften auf Griechischen Münzen. Berlin, 1871.
Arc 1663.5 Sandham, Alfred. Medals commemorative of the visit of H.R.H. the Prince of Wales to Montreal. Montreal, 1871.
Arc 595.8 Skinner, J.R. The Great Pyramid of Jizeh. Cincinnati, 1871. 2 pam.
Arc 885.13 Stanley, W.O. Memoirs on remains of ancient dwellings in Holyhead Island. London, 1871.
Arc 1558.1 Stiernstedt, A.V. Description des monnaies de Cuivre...Suedois. Stockholm, 1871-72.
Arc 1033.35.29 Triumphe van het heilig kruise Christi. Brugge, 1871.
Arc 1675.51.15F Tyszkiewicz, E. Sammlung von Medaillen. Riga, 1871.
Arc 775.1.2 Urlichs, K.L. Codex urbis Romae topographicus. Wirceburg, 1871.
Arc 505.127 Wilson, Charles. The recovery of Jerusalem. London, 1871.
Arc 391.2.15 Witte, J. Notice sur Edouard Gerhard. Bruxelles, 1871.
Arc 740.6.5 Zannoni, A. Sugli scavi della Certosa. Bologna, 1871.

1872

Arc 1027.33 Appell, J.W. Monuments of early Christian art. London, 1872.
Arc 1335.76.11F Athens. Ethnikon Nomismatikon Mouseion. Katalogos. Athênai, 1872.
Arc 943.3.5 Baldwin, J.D. Ancient America. N.Y., 1872.
Htn Arc 793.5.5* Barré, L. Herculanum et Pompéi. v.8. Paris, 1872.
Arc 793.3 Beulé, C.E. Le drame du Vésuve. Paris, 1872.
Arc 785.6.5 Blumenstihl, B. Brevi notizie sull'acqua pia (antica Marcia). Roma, 1872.
Arc 861.5 Borlase, W.C. Naema Cornubiae. London, 1872.
Arc 1190.1.2 Bresslau, H. Diplomata centum. Berlin, 1872.

1872 - cont.

Arc 1468.2 British Museum. Department of Coins and Medals. A guide to the select Greek coins. London, 1872.
Arc 830.67.10 Brouillet, A. Mémoire sur l'enceinte gallo-romaine de Poitiers. Poitiers, 1872.
Arc 1490.12 Camera, Matteo. Importante scoperta del famoso Tarèno di Amalfi. Napoli, 1872.
Arc 1033.34.5 Caprara, C. Venuta di San Pietro in Roma. Roma, 1872.
Arc 1030.27 Ciofi, A. Lectio inscriptionum...sulpicii maximi. Roma, 1872.
Arc 505.7.5 Clermont-Ganneau, Charles. Resultats...archéologies des fouilles entreprises à Jérusalem. n.p., 1872.
Arc 1033.14 Una controversia famosa di archeologia cristiana. n.p., 1872.
Arc 1033.34.13 Cornoldi, G.M. San Pietro a Roma. Roma, 1872.
Arc 820.214F Côte-d'Or. Commission des Antiquités. Voies romaines...de la Côte-d'Or. Dijon, 1872.
Arc 810.34 Curti, Pier A. Pompei e le sue rovine. Milano, 1872-74. 3v.
Arc 1279.10 Czobor, Béla. Magyarország világi és egyházi hatóságai kiadott pecseteinek jegyzeke. Pest, 1872.
Arc 1208.10 Dongé, E. Description des collections de sceaux matrices. Paris, 1872.
Arc 382.3 Dümichen, J. Über die Tempel und Gräber im alten Ägypten. Strassburg, 1872. 7 pam.
Arc 889.4.2 Dupont, Édouard. Les temps préhistoriques en Belgique. 2. éd. Bruxelles, 1872.
Arc 1076.3.77F Ellacombe, H.T. Bells of the church. Exeter, 1872.
Arc 870.1 Evans, J. The ancient stone implements, weapons and ornaments of Great Britain. N.Y., 1872.
Arc 1093.2 Fergusson, J. Rude stone monuments. London, 1872.
Arc 861.23 Flower, J.W. Notices of an Anglo-Saxon cemetery...Surrey. London, 1872.
Arc 1020.140 Friken, A. Rimskaia katakomby i pamiatniki pervonachal'nago Khristianskago iskusstva. Moskva, 1872-
Arc 785.53 Gori, Fabio. La torre del Monzone presso il Ponte Ratto. Roma, 1872.
Arc 1492.202 Heiss, Aloiss. Description générale des monnaies des rois wisigoths. Paris, 1872.
Arc 87.1.32 Hirschfeld, G. Athena und Marsyas. Berlin, 1872.
Arc 1675.19.10F Iversen, I. Medaillen auf die Thaten Peter des Grossen. St. Petersburg, 1872.
Arc 1018.32.7 Kraus, F.X. Die christliche Kunst in ihren frühesten Anfängen. Leipzig, 1872.
Arc 1027.1.5 Kraus, F.X. Über den gegenwärtigenStand der Frage. Freiburg, 1872.
Arc 1033.161 Liquefaction of the blood of St. Januarius. N.Y., 1872.
Arc 1027.27.9 Liverani, F. Catacombe e antichità cristiana di Chiusi. Siena, 1872.
Arc 545.28.3 Mariette, A. Monuments divers..en Égypte et en Nubie. Paris, 1872-1889. 2v.
Arc 618.5 Martin, Henri. Études d'archéologie celtique. Paris, 1872.
Arc 1033.34.39 Mauro di Polvica, Francesco di. Storia di San Pietro apostolo. Bologna, 1872.
Arc 1033.17.137 Notre-Dame de Déliverance et la ceinture de la S. Vierge. Quintin, 1872.
Arc 497.19 Redding, M.W. Antiquities of the Orient unveiled. N.Y., 1872.
Arc 1033.34.7 Resoconto...della disputa...fra sacerdoti e ministri...venuta di San Pietro. Roma, 1872.
Arc 1033.34.8 Resoconto...della disputa...fra sacerdoti e ministri...venuta di San Pietro. Roma, 1872.
Arc 1033.1.4 Rossi, G.B. de. Insigne...Battesimo d'una fanciulla. Roma, 1872.
Arc 1027.69 Rossi, G.B. de. Scoperte nell'arenaria tra i cimiteri di Trasone e dei Giordani sulla via Salaria. Roma, 1872.
Arc 1030.5.5 Rossi, G.B. de. Sepolcri del secolo ottavo...di S. Lorenzo in Lucina. Roma, 1872.
Arc 815.1 Ruggiero, Michele. Studi sopra gli edifizi e le arti meccaniche dei Pompeiani. Napoli, 1872.
Arc 1603.3.7 Sandham, Alfred. Supplement to coins, tokens and medals. Montreal, 1872.
Arc 889.1 Schuermans, H. Objets étrusques découvertes en Belgique. pt.1-5. Bruxelles, 1872.
Arc 403.8 Simpson, J.Y. Archaeological essays. Edinburgh, 1872. 2v.
Arc 895.20 Stolpe, H. Naturhistoriska och arkaeologiska undersökninger pa Björkö i Mälaren. Stockholm, 1872.
Arc 1033.17.49 Vandel, R.P. Les impressions d'un pelerinou l'ecole de Marie à Pontmain. Issoudun, 1872.
Arc 726.13 Voigt, M. Über das römische System der Wege in alten Italien. n.p., 1872.
Arc 855.218 Warne, Charles. Ancient Dorset. Bournemouth, 1872.
Arc 407.25 Westropp, Hodder Michael. Pre-historic phases. London, 1872.
Arc 861.37.3 Williamson, W.C. Description of the Tumulus. 3. ed. Scarborough, 1872.
Arc 861.29.5 Wright, Thomas. Unriconium. London, 1872.

1873

Arc 1033.104 Acta...de identitate SS. Corporum Ambrosii Episcopatum...et...Cristi martyrum Gervasii et Protasii. Romae, 1873.
Arc 830.65 Baudry, Ferdinand. Puits funéraires gallo-romains. La Roche-sur-Yon, 1873.
Arc 635.205 Benndorf, O. Die Metopen von Selinunt. Berlin, 1873.
Arc 386.3 Beulé, C.E. Fouilles et découvertes. Paris, 1873. 2v.
Arc 1020.89 Bock. Antiquités sacrées...S. Servais et de Notre Dame à Maestricht. Maestricht, 1873.
Arc 1490.23 Bompois, H.F. Les types monétaires de la guerre sociale. Paris, 1873.
Arc 820.221F Bonstetten, W. Carte archéologique du départment du Var. Toulon, 1873. 2 pam.
Arc 1468.1 British Museum. Department of Coins and Medals. A catalogue of the Greek coins. London, 1873-94. 29v.
Arc 1027.22.13 Calori Cesis, F. Un insigne monumento cristiano del secolo III. Bologna, 1873.
Arc 830.21.5 Castan, Auguste. Le théâtre de Vesontio. Besançon, 1873.
Arc 1033.104.5 Cenni storici sulla sepoltura...Gervasi e Protasi. Milano, 1873.
Arc 387.2 Chabas, F. Études sur l'antiquité historique. Paris, 1873.
Arc 1020.61 Chavannes, E. Le trésor de l'église cathédrale de Lausanne. Lausanne, 1873.

Chronological Listing

1873 - cont.

Arc 435.25 Cole, H.H. Mixed Hindu-Mahamedan style. London, 1873.
Arc 501.4 Committee of the Fund. Our work in Palestine. London, 1873.
Arc 880.13 Conwell, E.A. Discovery of tomb of Ollamh Fodhla. Dublin, 1873.
Arc 1025.60 Davin, V. Les sanctuaires primitifs de Rome et des Gaules. Paris, 1873?
Arc 1247.2 Demay, G. Inventaire des sceaux de la Flandre. v.1-2. Paris, 1873.
Arc 535.201 Doell, J. Die Sammlung Cesnola. St. Petersburg, 1873.
Arc 708.5 Dyer, T.H. Ancient Athens. London, 1873.
Arc 790.201 Fiorelli, G. Gli scavi di Pompei dal 1861 al 1872. Napoli, 1873.
Arc 708.6 Forchhammer, P. Zur Topographie von Athen. Göttingen, 1873.
Arc 953.1.50 Foster, J.W. Prehistoric races of U.S.A. Chicago, 1873.
Arc 380.204 Gaedechens, R. Unedirte antike Bildwerke. Jena, 1873.
Arc 830.151 Gazan, A. Notice sur une pierre tumulaire découverte aux environs de Solliès-Pont. Antibes, 1873.
Arc 670.3.5 Gerando, A. de. Gróf teleki Emma Görögorszagi a Rége Attikanak. Pest, 1873.
Arc 865.11 Gidley, L. Stonehenge...by the light of ancient history. London, 1873.
Arc 830.46 Gilles, Isidore. Précis historique et chronique des monuments triomphaux. Paris, 1873.
Arc 796.1 Helbig, W. Untersuchungen über die campanische Wandmalerei. Leipzig, 1873.
Arc 1663.4 Henfrey, H.W. Numismata Cromwelliana. London, 1873.
Arc 1033.20.13 Hessel, C. Die altchristlichen Basiliken Roms. Weslau, 1873.
Arc 1076.1 Heuzey, Léon. Recherches sur les lits antiques. Paris, 1873.
Arc 935.12 Heuzy, Leon. Reconnaissance archéologique...cours de l'Érigon et des ruines de Stobi. Paris, 1873.
Arc 87.1.33 Huebner, E. Bildniss einer Roemerin. Berlin, 1873.
Arc 961.1.5 Jones, C.C. Antiquities of the southern Indians. N.Y., 1873.
Arc 913.5.5 Keller, F. Beilage zur archäologischen Karte den Ostschweiz. 2. Aufl. Frauenfeld, 1873.
Arc 1365.2 King, Charles W. Early Christian numismatics. London, 1873.
Arc 785.22.5 Lanciani, Visconti de. Guida del Palatino. Roma, 1873.
Arc 1033.94 Laurenti, V. Vita SS. Apostoli Filippo et Giacono Minore. Roma, 1873.
Arc 561.4 Lieblein, J. Die aegyptischen Denkmäler. Christiania, 1873.
Arc 1070.208 Marchant, Louis. Ampoules de pèlerinages en plomb...Bourgogne. Dijon, 1873.
Arc 562.4 Mélanges d'archéologie égyptienne et assyrienne. v.1-3. Paris, 1873-78.
Arc 810.10 Monnier, Marc. Pompéi et les Pompéiens. 3. éd. Paris, 1873.
Arc 1254.4 Mordtmann, A.D. Sur les sceaux et plombs byzantins. Constantinople, 1873.
Arc 397.3 Müller, K.O. Kunstarchaeologische Werke. v.1-5. Berlin, 1873. 2v.
Arc 1033.20.25.2 Mullooly, Joseph. Saint Clement, pope and martyr. 2. ed. Rome, 1873.
Arc 547.4.10 Paris. Musée Nationale du Louvre. Départément des Antiquités Égyptiennes. Notice sommaire des monuments égyptiens. Paris, 1873.
Arc 843.7.5 Rodriquez de Berlanga, M. Los bronces de Osuna. Malaga, 1873.
Arc 1027.63 Rossi, G.B. de. Decouvertes dans l'arenaire situé...sur la voie Salaria. Rome, 1873.
Arc 1020.28 Rossi, G.B. de. Découvertes de divers monuments chrétiens en Sardaigne. Rome, 1873.
Arc 1027.69.5 Rossi, G.B. de. Epigrafi rinvenute nell'arenaria tra i cimiteri di Trasone e dei Giordani sulla via Salaria. Roma, 1873.
Arc 1663.5.5 Sandham, Alfred. Historic medals of Canada. Quebec, 1873.
Arc 1025.17 Scott, B. Contents...catacombs of Rome. London, 1873.
Arc 830.155 Société des Antiquaires du Centre, Bourges. Catalogue du Musée lapidaire de Bourges. Bourges, 1873.
Arc 875.55 Spence, James. Ruined castles. Edinburgh, 1873.
Arc 890.210F Stockholm. Svenska Statens Historiska Museum. Techningar. v.1-3. Stockholm, 1873-83.
Arc 823.19.4F Thédenat, H. Cognitio cognitionibus. Parisiis, 1873.
Arc 823.19.5F Thédenat, H. Commentariensis a commentarus commentarius. Parisiis, 1873.
Arc 1433.42F Tizengauzen', V. Monety bostochnago khalifata. Sankt Peterburg, 1873.
Arc 497.6 Tristram, H.B. The land of Moab. London, 1873.
Arc 785.13.25 Visconti, C.L. Deux actes de Domitien. Rome, 1873.
Arc 855.210 Whichcord, J. Roman antiquities recently discovered. London, 1873.
Arc 855.6 White, T.P. Architectural sketches in Scotland - Kintyre. Edinburgh, 1873.

1874

NEDL Arc 87.1.34 Adler, F. Stoa der Koenigs Attalos. Berlin, 1874.
Arc 1493.2 Aragão, A.C. de. Descripção...das moedas cunhadas en home dos reis. Lisboa, 1874-80. 3v.
Arc 1027.37 Armellini, M. I cemeteri cristiano della via latina. Roma, 1874.
Arc 1027.12.17 Armellini, M. D'una transl...SS. Pietro e Paolo in...le catacombe. Roma, 1874.
Arc 1020.9.35 Armellini, M. Notizie istoriche...Domine Quo Vadis. Roma, 1874.
Arc 1027.39 Armellini, M. Scoperta d'un graffito storico...cimiteri di Pretestato. Roma, 1874.
Arc 1033.35.3 Barrau, J.B. Notice historique sur la vraie croix de Baugé. Angers, 1874.
Arc 1390.1.3 Barthélemy, A.J.B.A. Nouveau manuel complet de numismatique du moyen age et moderne. Text et atlas. Paris, 1874. 2v.
Arc 822.1 Baudry, F. Recherches archéologiques à Pareds. La-Roche-sur-Yon, 1874. 21 pam.
Arc 1027.23.5 Becker, F. Die Waud- und Decken-Gernälde Römischen Katakomben. Düsseldorf, 1874.
Arc 1025.53 Becker, T. Rom's altchristliche Coemeterien. Düsseldorf, 1874.
Arc 726.21 Bertrand, A. Sepultures à l'incinération de Poggio Renzo. n.p., 1874.

1874 - cont.

Arc 861.18.9 Bruce, J.C. The wall of Hadrian. Newcastle-upon-Tyne, 1874.
Arc 925.8 Brun. Chernomorek. Gotyieledy dolgago ikh prebyv. Sankt Petersburg, 1874. 2 pam.
Arc 1030.15 Bruzza, L. Iscrizione antiche vercellesi. Roma, 1874.
Arc 1027.26.9 Cavallari, S. Osservazioni sulle basiliche e le catacombe...Siracusa. Palermo, 1874.
Arc 830.18.27 Charvet, G. Les voies romaines chez les Volkes-Arécomiques. Alais, 1874.
Arc 518.2 Curtius, E. Ephesos. Berlin, 1874.
Arc 1260.1 Daugnon, F.F. La vera arma della città di Crema. v.1-2. Fermo, 1874.
Arc 1020.73.5 Fagniez, G. Inventaires du trésor de Notre Dame de Paris. Paris, 1874.
Arc 510.210 Forchhammer, P.W. Das homerische Troja. n.p., 1874.
Arc 87.2.74 Gaedechens, R. Medusenhaupt von Blariacum. Bonn, 1874.
Arc 843.7 Giraud, C. Les bronzes d'Osuna. Paris, 1874.
Arc 1433.55 Guthrie, C.S. Catalogue of the collection of oriental coins belonging to C. Sefan Guthrie. Hertford, 1874.
Arc 762.1.2.5 Hare, A.J.C. Walks in Rome. 4. American ed. N.Y., 1874.
Arc 762.1.2 Hare, A.J.C. Walks in Rome. 4. ed. London, 1874. 2v.
Arc 1470.4 Head, B.V. On the chronological sequence of the coins of Syracuse. London, 1874.
Arc 1663.12 Hildebrand, B.E. Sveriges konungahusets minnespenningar. Stockholm, 1874. 2v.
Arc 1033.12.72 Histoire du précieux sang de Jésus-Christ...à Fécamp. Fécamp, 1874.
Arc 1670.3 Iversen, J. Unedited and rare Russian medals. St. Petersburg, 1874.
Arc 750.29 Jordan, Henri. Forma urbis Romae. Berolino, 1874.
Arc 518.9 Lauria, G.A. Efeso; studj. Napoli, 1874.
Arc 542.2 Leemans, C. Boro-Boudour dans l'Isle de Jara. Leyden, 1874. 5v.
Arc 1076.3.53 L'Estrange, John. The church bells of Norfolk. Norwich, 1874.
Arc 495.200 Luynes, H.T.P.J. d'Albert de. Voyage d'exploration à la Mer Morte. Paris, 1874. 3v.
Arc 838.19.2 Manjarrés, J. de. Nociones de arqueologia españolas. 2. ed. Barcelona, 1874.
Arc 1033.12.74 Messe du précieux Sang...Fécamp. Fécamp, 1874.
Arc 1025.6 Northcote, J.S. Rome souterraine. 2. éd. Paris, 1874.
Arc 810.47 Pagano, N. Guide de Pompéi tirée de toutes les ouvrages les plus intéressantes. 4. éd. Naples, 1874.
Arc 770.1 Parker, J.H. The archaeology of Rome. v.1-2, 4-11. Oxford, 1874. 12v.
Arc 1500.5.3 Ponton d'Amécourt, G. de. Description raisonnée des monnaies mérovingiennes de Châlon-sur-Saône. Paris, 1874-83. 3 pam.
Arc 1433.65 Prokesch-Osten, A. Les monnaies des rois Parthes. Paris, 1874-75.
Arc 905.8 Przyborowski, J. Wycieczki archeologizne po...Wisly. Warszawa, 1874.
Arc 1033.12.194 Rochambeau, E.A. de. Voyage à la sainte-larme de Vendome. Vendome, 1874.
Arc 785.23 Rossi, G.B. de. Ricerche archeologico e topografico nel monto Albano. Roma, 1874.
Arc 497.14 St. Aignan, L. de. Découvertes récentes en Terre-Sainte. n.p., 1874.
X Cg Arc 510.10 Schliemann, H. Altas des antiquités troyennes. Leipzig, 1874.
Arc 522.4.2 Schliemann, H. Trojanische Alterthuemer. Leipzig, 1874.
Arc 1540.2 Shafter, E.F. The copper coinage of the Earl of Stirling. Boston, 1874.
Arc 830.49 Société Historique et Archéologique du Périgord. Questionnaire. Périgueux, 1874.
Arc 1033.81 Stornaiuolo, C. Ricerche...SS. Eutichete ed Acuzio. Napoli, 1874.
Arc 1027.24.5 Taglialatela, G. Di una imagine de S. Protasio, nella catacombe severiana. Napoli, 1874.
Arc 1033.12.170 Terris, F. Saint mors de Carpentras et son reliquaire. Carpentras, 1874.
Arc 1405.1 Thomas, E. Marsden's Numismata orientalia. v.1. London, 1874.
Arc 1033.109 Uccelli, P.A. Dei santi martiri Domno, Domnione ed Eusebia. Bergamo, 1874.
Arc 1020.63 Van Drival. Catalogue de l'exposition d'objets d'art...à Lille en 1874. 2. éd. Lille, 1874.
Arc 708.16 Wachsmuth, C. Die Stadt Athen im Alterthum. Leipzig, 1874- 2v.
Arc 1335.13 Wesener, F.J. Die Gotthard mimus'sche Thaler und Medaillensammlung. Wien, 1874.
Arc 936.7 Zawisza, Jan. Recherches archéologiques en Pologne? Warszawa, 1874.

1875

Arc 87.2.75 Aldenkirchen, J. Mittelalterliche Kunst in Soest. Bonn, 1875.
Arc 1027.9 Armellini, M. Le catacombe e il protestantesimo. Roma, 1875.
Arc 1033.21 Arnellini, M. Scoperta oratorio presso Via Appia. Roma, 1875.
Arc 938.27 Aspelin, Johan R. Suomalais-Ugrilaisen muinaistutkinnon alkeita. Helsingissä, 1875.
Arc 1163.3.25 Azbuka i skoropis' XVII. Moskva, 1875.
Arc 386.10 Bertrand, A. Rapport sur les questions archéologiques...Congrès de Stockholm. Paris, 1875.
Arc 920.8 Berzhe, A. Zapiski...knigai. Tiflis, 1875.
Arc 712.1 Boetticher, K. Der Zophorus am Parthenon. Berlin, 1875.
X Cg Arc 1408.5 British Museum. Department of Coins and Medals. Catalogue of Oriental coins. London, 1875-90. 10v.
Arc 895.36.9 Bruzelius, N.G. Sur des rochers sculptés decouverts en Scanie. Stockholm, 1875.
Arc 1033.12.11 Carles, A. Histoire du Saint Suaire de Notre Seigneur. Paris, 1875. 2 pam.
Arc 820.2 Chantre, Ernest. Études paléoethnologiques dans le bassin du Rhône. Âge du bronze. Paris, 1875-76. 4v.
Arc 726.1 Chienci, G. Antichi monumenti della Pianosa. Reggio, 1875.
Arc 830.4 Compiègne, France. Société Historique. Excursions archéologiques dans les environs de Compiègne. 1869-74, 1875-1900. Compiègne, 1875. 2v.
Arc 635.200 Conze, A. Archäologische Untersuchungen auf Samothrake. Wien, 1875-80. 2v.

Chronological Listing

1875 - cont.

Arc 726.74F Crespellani, A. Del sepolcreto e degli altri monumenti antichi scoperti presso Bazzano. Modena, 1875.

Arc 1610.2 Crosby, S.S. The early coins of America. Boston, 1875.

Arc 1150.208 Delisle, L. Notice sur un manuscript Mérovingun. Paris, 1875.

Arc 1076.3.78 Ellacombe, H.T. The church bells of Somerset. Exeter, 1875.

Arc 1261.4 Escudero de la Penna, José Marie. Sigilografía española. Madrid, 1875.

Arc 1020.108 Fabre, A. Trésor de la ste. chapelle des ducs de Savoie. Lyon, 1875.

Arc 1264.11 Farcy, Paul de. Sigillographie de la Normandie. Caen, 1875.

Arc 810.5.2A Fiorelli, G. Descrizione di Pompei. Naples, 1875.

Arc 820.203 France. Ministère de l'Instruction. Dictionnaire archéologique de la Gaule. Paris, 1875-1923. 2v.

Arc 889.20F Friesch Genootschap van Geschied-Oudheid en Taalkunde te Leeuwarden. Friesche oudheden. Leeuwarden, 1875.

Arc 1070.204 Gozzadini, G. De quelques mors de cheval italiques et de l'épée de Ronzano en bronze. Bologne, 1875.

Htn Arc 880.14* Graves, James. Church and shrine of St. Manchan. Dublin, 1875.

Arc 1583.8 Gutten'-Chalskii, F.K. Chdel'n. velikokn. idsarsk. den'gi drevn. Rusi. Sankt Peterburg, 1875.

Arc 762.1.20 Hare, A.J.C. Days near Rome. v.1-2. Philadelphia, 1875.

Arc 762.1.3 Hare, A.J.C. Walks in Rome. N.Y., 1875.

Arc 1247.1 Heffner, Carl. Die deutschen Kaiser- und Königs-Siegel. Würzburg, 1875.

Arc 1033.25.5 Héron de Villefosse. Lampes chrétiennes inédites. Paris, 1875.

Arc 1020.118 Holahan, J. Notes on the antiquities of united parishes of Ballycollan, Kilmaugh and Killaloe. Kilkenny, 1875.

NEDL Arc 1348.6 Humphreys, H.N. The coin collector's manual. London, 1875. 2v.

Arc 830.44.5 Julliot, Gustave. Notice sur l'aqueduc romain de Sens. Paris, 1875.

Arc 1510.9 Jungk, H. Die bremischen Münzen. Bremen, 1875.

Arc 522.9 Keller, O. Die Entdeckung Ilions zu Hissarlik. Freiburg in Baden, 1875.

Arc 855.7 Lapidarium Septentrionale, or A description of the monument of Roman rule. London, 1875.

Arc 943.6 Larrainzar, M. Estudios sobre la historia de America. Mexico, 1875-78. 5v.

Arc 1020.82 Lecocq, G. Notice sur un reliquare de St. Quentin. St. Quentin, 1875.

Arc 1025.20 L'Epinovis, H. de. Les catacombes de Rome. Paris, 1875.

Arc 1153.11 Lupi, C. Manuale di paleografia delle carte. Firenze, 1875.

Arc 855.204 MacLagan, C. Hill forts, stone circles...Scotland. Edinbrugh, 1875.

Arc 853.25 Mehlis, C. Studien zur ältesten Geschichte der Rheinlands. v.1-9. Leipzig, 1875-1886. 2v.

Arc 895.5.5 Montelius, Oscar. Bibliographie de l'archéologie préhistorique de la Suède. Stockholm, 1875.

Arc 895.21.25 Montelius, Oscar. Minnen från lapparnes stenålder i Sverige. Stockholm, 1875-76.

Arc 895.37 Montelius, Oscar. Sur les différents types des haches en Silex suédoise. Stockholm, 1875. 5 pam.

Arc 1033.17.625 Notizie storiche intorno al santuario...Madonna della croce de Varazze. Varazze, 1875.

Arc 1033.17.503 Oliveira Lemos, F.J. de. Livro do romeiro ao sumptuoso sanctuario da Senhora do Porto Ava. n.p., 1875.

Arc 810.13.5 Overbeck, J. Pompeji in seinen Gebäuden. 3. Aufl. Leipzig, 1875.

Arc 810.47.5 Pagano, N. Guide de Pompéi. 5. éd. Naples, 1875.

Arc 400.2 Perrot, G. Mémoires d'archéologie. Paris, 1875.

Arc 565.2 Pierret, Paul. Dictionnaire d'archéologie égyptienne. Paris, 1875.

Arc 950.209 Pinart, A.L. La caverne d'Aknanh, ile d'Ounga. Paris, 1875.

Arc 843.21F Rada y Delgado, Juan de Dios de la. Discursos leidos ante la Academia de la Historia. Madrid, 1875.

Arc 430.2F Rájendralála Mitra. Antiquities of Orissa. Calcutta, 1875-80. 2v.

Arc 858.22 Rimmer, Alfred. Ancient stone crosses of England. London, 1875.

Arc 402.7 Robert, Charles. Mélanges d'archéologie. Paris, 1875.

Arc 1027.5 Rossi, G.B. de. Importantes decouvertes...cimetiere de Domitille. Paris, 1875.

Arc 505.5.52 Saint-Aignan. Temple de Salomon; sa description d'après découvertes récentes. Paris, 1875.

Arc 522.5 Salisbury, S. Troy and Homer. Worcester, 1875.

Arc 1020.56 Salore, Charles. Le trésor de Clairvaux. Paris, 1875.

Arc 510.1 Salzmann, A. Nécropole de Camiros. Paris, 1875.

Arc 1027.24.13 Scherillo, G. Archeologia sacra: Catacombe napolitane. Napoli, 1875.

Arc 1025.21 Scherillo, G. Archeologia sacra. v.1-2. Napoli, 1875.

Arc 522.4 Schliemann, H. Troia und seine Ruinen. Rostock, 1875?

Arc 522.4.3A Schliemann, H. Troy and its remains. London, 1875.

Arc 1423.6 Schlumberger, G. Monnaie inédite des seigneurs du Toron, en Syrie. Paris, 1875.

Arc 823.4.7 Souttrait, J.H. Répertoire archéologique du département de la Niène. Paris, 1875.

Arc 936.9 Spostrzeżenia lat ostatnich w dziedzinie starozytnoşci krajowych. v.1-2. Warszawa, 1875-76.

Arc 750.203 Suardi, B. Le rovine di Roma. Milano, 1875.

Arc 830.28 Travers, Emile. Une voie Saxonne à Caen. Caen, 1875.

Arc 87.1.35 Tren, G. Grosse Thongefaesse in Statuetten- und Buestenform. Berlin, 1875.

Arc 1020.54 Van de Putte, F. La Chapelle des Comtes de Flandre à Courtrai. Bruges, 1875.

Htn Arc 402.13* Vasconcellos, Joaquim de. Conde de Raczynski (Athanasius). Porto, 1875.

Arc 1143.3.2 Wattenbach, W. Schriftwesen im Mittelalter. 2. Aufl. Leipzig, 1875.

Arc 855.6.2 White, T.P. Architectural sketches in Scotland - Knapdale. Edinburgh, 1875.

Arc 960.2 Wyman, J. Fresh-water shell mounds...St. John's River, Florida. Salem, 1875.

Arc 1033.35.145 Zöckler, Otto. Das Kreuz Christi. Gütersloh, 1875.

1876

Arc 545.223 Abney, W. de W. Thebes and its five greater temples. London, 1876.

1876 - cont.

Arc 497.1 American Palestine Exploration Society. Catalogue of photographs. N.Y., 1876.

Arc 1033.118 Ancessi, V. Atlas géographique et archéologique...Testament. Paris, 1876.

Arc 80.8 Archaiologikē Hetairia, Athens. Organismos. Athēnai, 1876.

Arc 1020.26.5 Barbier de Montault, X. Les manuscrits du trésor de Bari. Toulouse, 1876.

Arc 1027.23 Becker, F. Die Darstellung Jesu Christi...Bilde des Fisches. Gero, 1876.

Arc 590.11 Birch, Samuel. Remarks upon the cover of the granite sarcophagus of Rameses III in the Fitzwilliam Museum. Cambridge, Eng., 1876.

Arc 551.2 Blanc, C. Voyage de la Haute Egypte. Paris, 1876.

Arc 785.3 Brizio, E. Pitture e sipolcri scoperti sull'Esquilino. Roma, 1876.

Arc 861.81 Buckler, Geroge. Colchester castle, a Roman building. Colchester, 1876.

Arc 1077.2.35 Bunsen, E. von. Das Symbol des Kreuzes. Berlin, 1876.

Arc 746.1.2 Burton, R.F. Etruscan Bologna. London, 1876.

Arc 1027.26.15 Carini, I. Rassegna archeologica. Iscrizioni cristiana dei catacombe di Siracusa. Palermo, 1876.

Arc 1153.29.4 Chassant, A. Dictionnaire des abréviations latines et françaises. 4. éd. Paris, 1876.

Arc 1138.5 Chassant, Alphonse. Paléographie des chartes. 7. éd. Paris, 1876.

Arc 969.1.6 Clarke, R. The pre-historic remains...of the city of Cincinnati, Ohio. Cincinnati, 1876.

Arc 1535.8 Cochran-Patrick, R.W. Records of the coinage of Scotland. Edinburgh, 1876. 2v.

Htn Arc 1020.111* Croques reliques. Poéme burlesque. Paris, 1876.

Arc 1505.1 Dannenberg, H. Die deutschen Münzender Saeschischen und Frankischen Kaiserzeit. Text und Plates. Berlin, 1876. 2v.

Arc 1528.3 Dingniolle, J.F. Le jeton historique des dix-sept provinces des Pays-Bas. Bruxelles, 1876-77. 2v.

Arc 893.17 Engelhardt, C. Influence classique sur le nord pendant l'antiquité. Copenhagen, 1876.

Arc 1027.18.12 Engeström, Adolf von. Om Judarne i Rom...och deras...katakomber. Upsala, 1876.

Arc 1510.158 Erbstein, Julius. Zur mittelalterlichen Münzgeschichte der Grafen von Mansfeld und der Edlen Hessen von Querfurt. Dresden, 1876.

Arc 825.8.5 Germer-Durand, E. Découvertes archéologiques faites a Nîmes. 1873. Nîmes, 1876.

Arc 936.25 Gooss, Carl. Chronik der Archäologischenfund Siebenbürgens. Hermanstadt, 1876.

Arc 1025.52 Grillwitzer, A. Die bildischen Darstellungen in die römischen Katakomben. Graz, 1876.

Arc 1033.121 Guillaume, P. Le navi cavensi nel Mediterraneo...vita di S. Costabile de Lucania. Napoli, 1876.

Arc 1086.1 Hartmann, A. Zur Hochächerfrage. München, 1876.

Arc 635.204 Heuzey, L. Mission archéologique de Macédoine. Paris, 1876.

Arc 1030.58F Hubner, E. Inscriptiones Britanniae christianae. Berolini, 1876.

Arc 1473.1.3 Lampros, Paulos. Anekdota nomismata en Glarentsa. Athēnai, 1876.

Arc 1473.1 Lampros, Paulos. Anekdota nomismata tēs kuprhoy. Athēnai, 1876.

Arc 708.9.9 Leake, W.M. Athènes d'après le colonel Leake. Paris, 1876.

Arc 673.3 Lebègue, J.A. Recherches sur Délos. Paris, 1876.

Arc 522.3 Lenormant, F. Les antiquités de la Troade. Paris, 1876.

Arc 720.209 Livy, P. Le abitazioni Lacustri di Fimon. Venezia, 1876.

Arc 865.10 Long, william. Stonehenge and its barrows. Devizes, 1876.

Arc 1025.3 Ludwig, C. Ein Blick in die römischen Katakomben. Bern, 1876.

Arc 652.2 Mahaffy, J.P. Rambles and studies in Greece. London, 1876.

Arc 1348.39 Mathews, George D. The coinages of the world. N.Y., 1876.

Arc 830.87 Mathieu, P.P. Le Puy deDome. Clermont-Ferrand, 1876.

Arc 895.36.5 Montelius, Oscar. Bohulänska hällristningar. Stockholm, 1876.

Arc 1335.21 Morbio, Carlo. VI catalogo dei duplicati delle raccolte. Milano, 1876.

Arc 537.2.7 New York (City). Metropolitan Museum of Art. Cesnola Collection. Guide to the Cesnola collection...Island of Cyprus. N.Y., 1876.

Arc 815.23F Petra, Giulio de. Le tavolette cerate di Pompei. Roma, 1876.

Arc 1255.1F Poggi, Vittorio. Sigilli antichi romani raccolti e publicati da Vittorio Poggi. Torino, 1876.

Arc 1588.1.9 Polkowski, J. Decouverte à Gtebokie de monnaies polonaises. Gnesen, 1876.

Arc 82.1.10 Ravaisson-Mollien, F. Lettre à Mollien le directeur de la Revue archéologique. Paris, 1876.

Arc 1020.92 Recherches sur precieuses reliques...dans la Sainte Eglise de Vienne. Vienne, 1876.

Arc 1665.3 Rentzmann, W. Numismatisches Wappen-Lexicon. Berlin, 1876.

Arc 1665.3.5 Rentzmann, W. Numismatisches Wappen-Lexicon. Index. Berlin, 1876.

Arc 1020.62 Richard, J.M. Le trésor...de Notre Dame de Lens au XVe siècle. Arras, 1876.

Arc 843.7.7 Rodriquez de Berlanga, M. Los nuevos bronces de Osuna. Malaga, 1876.

Arc 1027.30.19 Rossi, G.B. de. Arcosolio dipinto del cimitero di Ciriaca. Roma, 1876.

Arc 1033.86 Rossi, G.B. de. Oratorio privato del secolo IV...nel Monte della Giustizia. Roma, 1876.

Arc 1030.5.29 Rossi, G.B. de. Il sarcofago di S. Siro. Roma, 1876.

Arc 785.23.3 Rossi, M.S. de. Scavi e studi nel tempio di Giove Laziale. Roma, 1876.

Arc 1033.12.196 Sainte-larme de Selincourt. Notice historique et bibliographique. Amiens, 1876.

Arc 1033.143 Salmon, C. Histoire du chef de S. J.-Baptiste...Amiens. Amiens, 1876.

Arc 1053.8 Schuster, P. Über die erhaltenen Porträts der griechischen Philosophen. Leipzig, 1876.

Arc 1254.13 Sorlin-Dorigny, A. Sceaux et bulles des comnènes. Paris, 1876.

Arc 1148.17 Sreznevski, I.I. Paleograficheskiia navliudeniia. v.1-2. Sankt Peterburg, 1876.

Arc 1027.20 Stevenson, E. Il cimitero di Zotico. Dec miglio...Labicana. Modena, 1876.

Chronological Listing

1876 - cont.

Arc 590.5 Szedlo, G. Le grand sarcophage du Musée civique de Bologne. Bologne, 1876.
Arc 87.1.36 Trendelenburg, A. Der Musenchor. Berlin, 1876.
Arc 830.15.15 Véran, Auguste. Arles antique. Tours, 1876.
Arc 855.208 Westwood, J.O. Lapidarium Walliae. Oxford, 1876-79.
Arc 1033.12.105 Wilmowsky, J.N. von. Heilige Rock; eine archäologische Prüfung...Trier. Trier, 1876.
Arc 740.6 Zannoni, A. Gli scavi della Certosa in Bologna. Bologna, 1876-84. 2v.

1877

Arc 968.4.5 Abbott, Charles C. Stone age in New Jersey. Washington, 1877.
Arc 1027.40 Armellini, M. Scoperta...cripta S. Emerenziana...cimiteri Ostriano. Roma, 1877.
Arc 1033.30 Armellini, Mariano. Scoperta della cripta di Santa Emerenziana e di una memoria relativa alla cattedra di San Pietro. Roma, 1877.
Arc 938.15F Aspelin, J.R. Antiquités du Nord-Finno-Ougrien. v.1-5. St. Pétersbourg, 1877.
Arc 830.101 Aurès, Auguste. Monographie des bornes milliaires du département du Gard. Nîmes, 1877.
Arc 1020.9.137 Barbier de Montault, X. Exposition religieuse de Rome 1870. L'archéologie et l'art chrétien. Arras, 1877.
Arc 1020.68.9 Barbier de Montault, X. Notes archéologiques sur Moutiers et la Tarentaise. Montiers, 1877.
Arc 1053.16 Barbier de Montault, X. Solution d'un problème iconographique. Poitiers, 1877.
Arc 1020.49 Barbier de Montault, X. Le trésor du dame d'Aix-La-Chapelle. Tours, 1877.
Arc 1020.55 Barbier de Montault, X. La visite de la Cathédrale St. Bertrand de Comminges. Montpélier, 1877.
Arc 1335.56.2 Bataviaasch Genootschap van Kunsten en Wetenschappen. Museum. Catalogus der numismatische afdeeling. 2. druk. Batavia, 1877.
Arc 1053.2.2 Bernoulli, J.J. Die erhaltenen Bildnisse berühmter Griechen. Basel, 1877.
Arc 1076.3.27 Blavignac, J.D. La cloche, études. Genève, 1877.
Arc 1340.4 Boutkowski, Alex. Dictionnaire numismatique. Leipzig, 1877.
Arc 522.10.2 Brentano, E. Alt-Ilion im Dumbrekthal. Heilbronn, 1877?
Arc 865.14.5 Brown and Company, Salisbury, publishers. The illustrated guide to Old Sarum and Stonehenge. Salisbury, 1877.
Arc 1033.69.5 Bruzza, L. Della interpretazione del Monogramma. Roma, 1877.
Arc 444.2 Burgess, James. Rock temples of Elurâ or Verul. Bombay, 1877.
Arc 444.2.5 Burgess, James. Rock temples of Elurâ or Verul. Bombay, 1877.
Arc 708.3 Burnouf, E. La ville et l'acropole d'Athènes. Paris, 1877.
Arc 537.2 Cesnola, L.P. Cyprus. London, 1877.
Arc 505.3.12 Clermont-Ganneau, Charles. L'authenticité du Saint-Sépulcre. Paris, 1877.
Arc 505.8 Clermont-Ganneau, Charles. La pierre de Bethphagé. Paris, 1877.
Arc 505.7 Clermont-Ganneau, Charles. La présentation du Christ au Temple. Paris, 1877.
Arc 66.1.2 Collignon, M. Essai sur les monuments grecs et romains relatifs au mythe de psyché. Paris, 1877.
Arc 435.20.1F Corpus inscriptionum Indicarum. Calcutta, 1877.
Arc 1030.8.21 Dabry de Thiessaut. La catholicisme en Chine au VIIIe siècle de notre ère. Paris, 1877.
Arc 1020.57 Dechristé, Louis. Les tableaux...appartenant aux églises...de Douai. Douai, 1877.
Arc 1263.2 Demay, G. Inventaire des sceaux de l'Artois et de la Picardie. v.1-2. Paris, 1877-81.
Arc 889.3 Dessel, Camille. Topographie des voies romaines de la Belgique. Bruxelles, 1877.
Arc 66.1 Duchesne, L. Étude sur le liber pontificalis. Paris, 1877.
Arc 545.205 Duemichen, J. Bangeschichte des Denderatempels. Strassburg, 1877.
Arc 1020.66 Falk, V.A.F. Heiliges Mainz...Heiligenthümer. Mainz, 1877.
Arc 875.35 Fergusson, James. Short essay on age and uses of brochs...Orkeney Islands. London, 1877.
Arc 1185.6 Ficker, J. Beitraege zur Urkundenlehre. Innsbruck, 1877-78. 2v.
Arc 810.25 Fiorelli, G. Guida di Pompei. Roma, 1877.
Arc 712.6 Flasch, A. Zum Parthenonfries. Wuerzburg, 1877.
Arc 1264.1.3 Forgeais, Arthur. Blasons et chevaliers du Moyen Âge. Paris, 1877.
Arc 1015.222 Franconi, F. La catacomba e la basilica costantiniana. Roma, 1877.
Arc 1335.11.5 Friedlander. Das königliche Münzkabinet. 2. Aufl. Berlin, 1877.
Arc 1033.11 Gaborel de Rossillon, J. Alma Mater. Paris, 1877.
Arc 825.8.6 Germer-Durand, E. Enceintes successives de Nîmes depuis les Romains. 2e éd. Nîmes, 1877.
Arc 1033.20.17 Globočnik, G.N. Le sette basiliche di Roma. Venesia, 1877.
Arc 307.3.12 Grairer, Gabriel. Allocution fait à la Société de Géographie...sur la 2e session des Congrés international de Americanistes. Rouen, 1877.
Arc 858.10 Greenwell, G. British barrows. Oxford, 1877.
Arc 1468.8 Grunauer, E. Altgriechischen Münzorten. Basel, 1877.
Arc 762.1.3.5 Hare, A.J.C. Walks in Rome. 6. American ed. N.Y., 1877.
Arc 1540.14 Henfrey, H.W. Numismata Cromwelliana. Londini, 1877.
Arc 858.43 Jewitt, L. Half-hours among some English antiquities. London, 1877.
Arc 1020.80 Julliot, M.G. Inventaire des reliques...l'église metropolitaine de Sens. Sens, 1877.
Arc 1020.80.5 Julliot, M.G. Inventaire des sainctes reliques...de St. Pierre-le-Vif de Sens. Sens, 1877.
Arc 395.1 Kenward, J. Place of archaeology in science. Birmingham, 1877.
Arc 1590.2.5 Lambros, P. Monnaies inédites de Raimond Zacosta. Athènes, 1877.
Arc 1423.7 Lavoix, Henri. Monnaies à légendes arabes frappées en Syrie. Paris, 1877.
Arc 1030.9.5 Le Blant, E. Sur une pierre tumulaire. Arras, 1877.
Arc 561.4.5 Lieblein, J. Egypten i dess minnesmärken o chi dess färhållande till Palestine och Grekland. Stockholm, 1877.

1877 - cont.

Arc 1660.3 Liesville, A.R. de. Histoire numismatique de la révolution de 1848. Paris, 1877-83.
Arc 562.1.6 Mariette, A. The monuments of upper Egypt. Alexandria, 1877.
Arc 1018.02 Martigny, J.A. Dictionnaire des antiquités chrétiennes. Paris, 1877.
Htn Arc 1093.3* Martini, G.H. Abhandlung von den Sonnenuhren der Alten. Leipzig, 1877.
Arc 1053.15 Martinov, Jean. Un tétraptique russe. Arras, 1877.
Arc 1020.9.65 Marucchi, O. Conferenze della società di cultura della cristianità archeologia. Roma, 1877.
Arc 1675.100 Marvin, William Theophilus Rogers. Materials for a catalogue of masonic medals. Boston, 1877.
Arc 1033.34 Merracci P. Les chaines de Saint Pierre. Rome, 1877.
Arc 785.13 Michelet, C.L. Das Forum Romanum, oder Die...Region des alten Rom. Berlin, 1877.
Arc 830.11.15 Miln, James. Excavations at Carnac. Edinburgh, 1877.
Arc 830.11.10 Miln, James. Fouilles faites a Carnac. Paris, 1877.
Arc 726.16 Monteluis, O. Tombe ed antichità galliche in Italia. Roma, 1877.
Arc 935.4 Montucci, Henry. Les coupes du palais des empereurs byzantins. Paris, 1877.
Arc 820.202 Moreau, F. Collection Caranda. St. Quentin, 1877. 4v.
Arc 1475.8 Morris, R. The twelve Caesars. La Grange, Ky., 1877.
Arc 375.1 Müller, H.A. Archäologisches Wörterbuch. Leipzig, 1877-78. 2v.
Arc 1077.2.49 Müller, Ludvig. Det saakaldte Hagekors's Anvendelse og Betydning i Aldtiden. København, 1877.
Arc 810.12 Nissen, H. Pompeianische Studien zur Staedtekunde des Altertums. Leipzig, 1877.
Arc 1025.4.5 Northcote, J.S. A visit to the Roman catacombs. London, 1877.
Arc 628.19 Olenin', A.N. Arkheologicheskie trudy. v.1-3. Sankt Peterburg, 1877-82.
Arc 935.5 Paspati, A.G. Byzantinai meletai topographikai kai istorikai. Konstantinople, 1877.
Arc 830.35 Piette, Edouard. La montagne d'Espiaup. Paris, 1877.
Arc 605.203 Playfair, R.L. Travels in the footsteps of Bruce in Algeria and Tunis. London, 1877.
Arc 861.38 Pooley, C. An historical and descriptive account of the old stone crosses of Somerset. London, 1877.
Arc 790.205 Presuhn, E. Die Wanddekoration in Pompeji. Leipzig, 1877.
Arc 1033.35.151 Prime, W.C. Holy Cross. London, 1877.
Arc 1020.75 Le Puy et Rome. Souvenirs et monuments. Paris, 1877.
Arc 510.7 Rayet, O. Milet et le golfe latmique. Paris, 1877-85.
Arc 1030.5.13 Rossi, G.B. de. D'una mutila epigrafe...nel torrione della porta flaminia. Roma, 1877.
Arc 1030.5.15 Rossi, G.B. de. Memorie degli apostoli Pietro e Paolo. Roma, 1877.
Arc 1015.205.13 Rossi, G.B. de. Il museo epigrafico cristiano pio-sateranense. Roma, 1877.
Arc 1027.5.3 Rossi, G.B. de. Roma; scavi nel cimitero de Domitilla. Roma, 1877.
Arc 1015.205.2 Rossi, M.S. de. Appendice...al tomo terzo della Roma sotterranea. Roma, 1877.
Arc 1020.93 Salore, Charles. Reliques de trois tombeaux saints de Clairvoux...a Ville-sous-la-Ferté (Aubé). Troyes, 1877.
Arc 1423.5 Saulcy, L.F.J.C. de. Numismatique de la Terre-Sainte. Paris, 1877.
Arc 87.1.37 Schillbach, D. Beitrag zur griechischen Gewichtskunde. Berlin, 1877.
Arc 1428.6 Schlumberger, G. Les principautés Franques du Levant. Paris, 1877.
Arc 1027.21 Schultze, V. Die Katakomben von San Gennaro die Poveri. Jena, 1877.
Arc 387.15 Sclopis de Salerano, F. Notizie degli studi conte Giancarlo Conestabile della Staffa. Torino, 1877.
Arc 830.15.7 Seguin, J. Les antiquités d'Arles. Avignon, 1877.
Arc 595.7 Seiss, J.A. A miracle in stone, or The Great Pyramid of Egypt. Philadelphia, 1877?
Arc 595.7.4 Seiss, J.A. A miracle in stone, or The Great Pyramid of Egypt. 4th ed. Philadelphia, 1877.
Arc 595.9 Smyth, C.P. Our inheritance in the Great Pyramid. London, 1877.
Arc 1053.11 Stenersen, L.B. De historia variisque generibus statuarum iconicarum. Christianiae, 1877.
Arc 1033.35.33 Taglialatela, G. Stauroteca di San Leonzio...Napoli. Napoli, 1877.
Arc 608.7.15 Tissot. Recherches sur la géographie comparée de la Maurétanie Tingitane. Paris, 1877.
Arc 684.1.4 Urlichs, K.L. Bemerkungen über den olympischen Tempel und seine Bildwerke. Würzburg, 1877.
Arc 1033.171 Usener, H.K. Acta S. Timothei. Bonn, 1877.
Arc 1020.64.5 Valouse, V. de. Inventaires du trésor de l'église de Lyon. Lyon, 1877.
Arc 1520.5 Vandenpeereboom, A. Essai de numismatique yproise. Bruxelles, 1877.
Arc 1020.6.9 Veludo, G. Dichiarazione di un monumento sepolcrale cristiano. Venezia, 1877.
Arc 830.98 Voisin, F. Monuments gallo-romains du département de l'Jndre. Chateauroux, 1877.
Arc 925.9.5 Vyrubov, V. Predmety drevnosti. Tiflis, 1877.
Arc 684.1.12 Wernick, F. Olympia. Leipzig, 1877.
Arc 1025.11 Withrow, W.H. Catacombs of Rome. London, 1877.
Arc 518.1.3 Wood, J.T. Discoveries at Ephesus. Boston, 1877.
Arc 518.1 Wood, J.T. Discoveries at Ephesus. London, 1877.
Arc 1033.35.146 Zöckler, Otto. The cross of Christ. London, 1877.

1878

Arc 1335.76.13F Athens. Ethnikon Nomismatikon Mouseion. Synopsis numorum veterum. Athenes, 1878.
Arc 943.3 Baldwin, J.D. Ancient America. N.Y., 1878.
Arc 1020.9.13 Baracconi, G. Il panteon e la tomba reale monografia. Roma, 1878. 3 pam.
Arc 1020.9.33 Barbier de Montault, X. Inventaire de la chapelle papale sous Paul III en 1547. Tours, 1878.
Arc 1020.9.120 Barbier de Montault, X. Observations archéologique...les églises de Rome. Arras, 1878.
Arc 386.1 Bartlett, T.H. About monuments. Boston, 1878?
Arc 1030.6 Bayet, C. De titulis atticae christianis. Paris, 1878.
Arc 1030.33 Becker, F. Inschriften der römischen Coemeterien. Gera, 1878.
Arc 1087.4F Benndorf, Otto. Antike Gesichtshelme und Sepulcralmasken. Wien, 1878.

Chronological Listing

1878 - cont.

Arc 1033.17.448 Blot, F. Notre Dame du Mont Carmel. Paris, 1878.
Arc 910.9F Bonstetten, W. Carte archeologique du canton de Fribourg. Genève, 1878.
Arc 1018.1 Bourassé, J.J. Archéologie chrétienne. Tours, 1878.
Arc 600.2 Brugsch-Bey, H. Reise nach der grossen Oase El-Khargeh. Leipzig, 1878.
Arc 1030.14.5 Bruzza, L. Fistula plumbea acquaria di Porto. Roma, 1878.
Arc 1163.5.6 Burnell, A.C. Elements of south-Indian palaeography. 2. ed. London, 1878.
Arc 1163.5.5 Burnell, A.C. Elements of south-Indian palaeography. 2. ed. London, 1878.
Arc 635.212 Carapanos, C. Dodone et ses ruines. Paris, 1878. 2v.
Arc 537.2.3A Cesnola, L.P. Cyprus. N.Y., 1878.
Arc 113.2.5 Chabouillet. Discours et compte rendu des lectures...section d'archéologie. Réunion annuelle des délégués de société savantes à la Sorbonne. Paris, 1878-81. 3v.
Arc 1433.37 Codera y Zaidin, F. Titulos y nombres propios monedas arábigo-españolas. Madrid, 1878.
Arc 66.1.3 Collignon, M. Catalogue des vases peints du musée. Paris, 1878.
Arc 501.16.5 Conder, C.R. Tent work in Palestine. London, 1878. 2v.
Arc 87.1.38 Conze, Alexander. Thesens und Minotauros. Berlin, 1878.
Arc 746.6 Dasti, L. Notizie storiche archeologiche di Tarquinia e Corneto. Roma, 1878.
Arc 1150.208.5 Delisle, L. Notice sur un manuscript Mérovingun. Paris, 1878.
Arc 743.1.2 Dennis, G. The cities and cemeteries of Etruria. London, 1878. 2v.
Arc 1530.20 Dirks, Jacob. De noord-Nederlandsche gildepenningen. Haarlem, 1878. 2v.
Arc 688.2 Dressel, H. Die antiken Kunstwerke aus Sparta und Umgebung. Athen, 1878.
Arc 505.5 Fergusson, J. The temples of the Jews. London, 1878.
Arc 435.12F Fleet, J.F. Pâli, Sanskrit and old Canarese inscriptions. London, 1878.
Arc 953.2 Foster, J.W. Prehistoric races of the United States of America. 4. ed. Chicago, 1878.
Arc 1675.23 Froehner, Vilhelm. Les medaillons de l'Empire romain depuis le règne d'Auguste jusqu'à Priscus Attale. Paris, 1878.
Arc 1033.35.11 Fulda, H. Freuz und die Kreuzigung. Breslau, 1878.
Arc 1348.50 Gardner, Percy. Macedonian and Greek coins of the Seleucidae. London, 1878.
Arc 1430.10 Ghiron, I. Monete arabiche del gabinetto numismatico di Milano. Milano, 1878.
Arc 830.73 Guillaume, Paul. La station préhistorique de Panacelle. Gap, 1878.
Arc 762.1.4 Hare, A.J.C. Walks in Rome. London, 1878. 2v.
Arc 1335.4 Harzfeld, S.K. Catalogue of choice English, French, and American coins and medals. Boston, 1878.
Arc 522.13 Hildebrand, H.H. Fynden i Troas och Homeroe' Troja. Stockholm, 1878.
Arc 861.45 Hooppell, R.E. On the discovery...of Roman remains at South Shields. London, 1878.
Arc 961.1 Jones, C.C. Aboriginal structures in Georgia. Washington, 1878. 2 pam.
Arc 764.1 Jordan, Henri. Topographie der Stadt Rom in Alterthum. v.1-2. Berlin, 1878. 4v.
Arc 913.5 Keller, F. Lake dwellings of Switzerland and other parts of Europe. London, 1878. 2v.
Arc 1366.1A Lenormant, F. La monnaie dans l'antiquité. Paris, 1878-79. 3v.
Arc 1279.6 Lind, Karl. Blaetter für altere Sphragiotik. Wien, 1878.
Arc 1660.1 Loubat, J.F. The medallic history of the United States of America, 1776-1876. Text and plates. N.Y., 1878. 2v.
Arc 1260.3 Manno, Antonio. Sopra alcuni piombi sardi. Torino, 1878.
Arc 705.201A Maps, Athens. Atlas von Athen. Berlin, 1878.
Arc 1027.15.5 Marucchi, O. La cripta sepolceale di San Valentio sulla Flaminia. Roma, 1878.
Arc 1030.4.5 Marucchi, O. Di una rarissima epigrafe cristiana. Roma, 1878.
Arc 1033.17.541 Mary mother of Christ. Facsimile. London, 1878.
Arc 66.1.4 Muentz, E. Arts à la cour des papes. Paris, 1878-82. 3v.
Arc 1025.4.7 Northcote, J.S. Visite aux catacombes de Rome. Paris, 1878.
Arc 1033.17.542 Novena in preparazione alla...festa...in Rapallo Nostra Signora sue Montallegro. Rapallo, 1878.
Arc 770.1.5 Parker, J.H. Description of the plan of Rome. Oxford, 1878.
Arc 1020.6.7 Passini, A. Il tesoro di San Marco in Venezia. Venezia, 1878.
Arc 790.204 Persuhn, E. Pompeji. Leipzig, 1878-82. 2v.
Arc 441.1F Rájendralála Mitra. Buddha Gayá. Calcutta, 1878.
Arc 830.5 Revon, L. La Haute-Savoie avant les Romains. Paris, 1878.
Arc 1540.17 Robertson, John D. Handbook to coinage of Scotland. London, 1878.
Arc 830.19 Rochebrune, R. de. Sépulture d'un légionnaire romain. Niort, 1878.
X Cg Arc 1016.207.5 Rohault de Fleury, C. La Sainte Vierge. Paris, 1878. 2v.
Arc 1033.1.7 Rossi, G.B. de. Vetro graffito con immagini di santi. Roma, 1878.
Arc 402.5 Rossignol, J.P. Services de l'archéologie aux études classiques. Paris, 1878.
Arc 682.1.3A Schliemann, Heinrich. Mycenae; a narrative. N.Y., 1878.
Arc 682.1 Schliemann, Heinrich. Mycenae; a narrative of researches and discoveries at Mycenae and Tiryns. London, 1878.
Arc 1590.4 Schlumberger, G. Deux plombs satiriques. Paris, 1878. 3 pam.
Arc 1425.2 Schlumberger, G. Numismatique de l'Orient Latin. Paris, 1878.
Arc 403.1 Seabird, H. Element of archaeology. n.p., 1878.
Arc 403.10 Silva, J.P.N. da. Noções elementares de archeologia. Lisboa, 1878.
Arc 838.13 Simões, A.F. Introducção à archeologia da Peninsula Iberica. pt.1. Lisboa, 1878.
Arc 1027.70 Stevenson, H. Escavazione di un antico diverticolo della via Tiburtina. Roma, 1878.
Arc 1027.13 Tarantini, G. Di alcunce cripte nell'agro di Brindisi. Napoli, 1878.
Arc 893.4 Undset, I.M. Norske oldsager i fremmede museer. Christiania, 1878.

1878 - cont.

Arc 407.9.2 Westropp, Hodder Michael. Handbook of archaeology. 2. ed. London, 1878.
Arc 593.5 Wilson, E. Cleopatra's needle. London, 1878.
Arc 1033.12.187 Zerbi, L. Corona ferrea al funebri nazionali di Vittorio Emanuele. Monza, 1878.
Arc 1493.4 Zobel de Zangroniz, J. Estudio de la moneda antigua española. Madrid, 1878. 2v.

1879

Arc 1033.69 Arcangeli, P. Della interpretazione del Monogramma. Roma, 1879.
Arc 1675.2 Armand, A. Les médailleurs italiens. Paris, 1879.
Arc 1510.10 Bahrfeldt, Max von. Die Münzen der Stadt Stade. Wien, 1879.
Arc 1020.50 Barbier de Montault, X. Le trésor de la cathédrale de Bénévent. Arras, 1879.
Arc 861.28 Bathurst, W.H. Roman antiquities at Lyndney Park. London, 1879.
Arc 66.1.10 Bayet, C. Peinture et sculpture chrétiennes en Orient. Paris, 1879.
Arc 66.1.6 Berger, E. Notice sur des manuscrits de la Bibliothèque Vaticane. Paris, 1879.
Arc 386.11 Bertrand, A. De la valeur historique des documents archéologiques. Chartres, 1879.
Arc 830.30 Bertrand, Alexandre. Les bijoux de Jouy-le-Comte. Paris, 1879.
Arc 726.252 Bindi, Vincenzo. Castel S. Flaviano. Napoli, 1879-82. 4v.
Arc 1020.20 Bonelli, G.A. Memorie storiche della Basilica Costantiniana. Roma, 1879.
Arc 386.9 Burnouf, E. Mémoires sur l'antiquité. Paris, 1879.
Arc 1663.7.5F Camozzi Vertova, G. Dissertazione sul medagliere relativo alla storia mederna d'Italia. Bergamo, 1879.
Arc 1494.59 Campaner y Fuertes, Álvaro. Numismática balear. Palma de Mallorca, 1879.
Arc 733.1 Cavallari, F.S. Sulla topografia di Talune città greche. Palermo, 1879.
Arc 1033.119 Charles, archbishop of Alger. Sainte Anne de Jérusalem et Sainte Anne d'Auray. Alger, 1879.
Arc 66.1.7 Clédat, L. Role historique de Bertrand de Born. Paris, 1879.
Arc 1494.8 Codera y Zaiden, F. Tratado de numismática. Madrid, 1879.
Arc 815.5 Comes, O. Illustrazione delle piante rappresentativa nei diputi Pompeiani. Napoli, 1879.
Arc 967.1.9 Conant, Alban J. Foot-prints of vanished races in the Mississippi Valley. St. Louis, 1879.
Arc 435.20.2F Corpus inscriptionum Indicarum. v.1-4. Calcutta, 1879-1929. 5v.
Arc 441.6F Cunningham, Alexander. The stûpa of Bharhut. London, 1879.
Arc 505.3.9 Cyprien. Le vraie forme primitive...du Saint Sépulcre. Paris, 1879.
Arc 853.17 Der Externstein aus Zeit des Heithenthums in Westfalen. Detmold, 1879.
Arc 66.1.5 Fernique, E. Inscriptions du pays des marses. Paris, 1879.
Arc 830.14 Fillion, B. Lettre à M.J. Quicherat...sur une decouverte...dans l'etang de Nesmy. La Roche-sur-Yon, 1879.
Arc 969.1.10 Force, M.F. Indians of Ohio. Cincinnati, 1879.
Arc 716.7 Forchhammer, P.W. Das Erechtheion. Kiel, 1879.
Arc 1615.7 Frossard, E. Monograph of United States cents and half cents issued between the years 1793 and 1857. Irvington, 1879.
NEDL Arc 1148.5 Gardthausen, V. Griechische Palaeographie. v.1-2. Leipzig, 1879.
Arc 861.43 George, W. On an inscribed stone at Orchard Wyndham, Somerset. Bristol, 1879.
Arc 723.5A Helbig, W. Beiträge zur altitalischen Kultur und Kunstgeschichte. Leipzig, 1879.
Arc 497.15 Héron de Villefosse, A. Notice des monuments de la Palestine conservés au Musée du Louvre. 2. éd. Paris, 1879.
Arc 843.22 Hübner, E. Citania. Porto, 1879.
Arc 790.213F Italy. Ufficio Tecnico degli Scavi delle Province Meridionale. Pompei e la regione sotterrata dal Vesuvio nell'anno LXXXIX. Napoli, 1879.
Arc 1538.19 Jewitt, L. Handbook of English coins. London, 1879.
Arc 80.1 Kastorkes, E. Historikē ekthesis tōn praxeon tēs Archaiologikēs Hetairias. Athēnai, 1879.
X Cg Arc 1390.9 Keary, C.F. Coinage of western Europe. London, 1879.
Arc 1025.2 Kraus, F.K. Roma Sotterranea, die römischen Katakomben. Freiburg, 1879.
Arc 1018.32 Kraus, F.X. Über Begriff...christlichen Archäologie. Freiburg, 1879.
Arc 583.3 Leedrain, E. Monumens égyptiens de la Bibliothèque Nationale. pt.1-3. no.38. Paris, 1879-81.
Arc 1033.70.13 Lefort, L. Peintures inédites de L'Eglise St. Nicolas. Paris, 1879.
Arc 1033.135 Lettre circulaire de M....d'Amiens...de la reception de la face de S. Jean Baptiste. Amiens, 1879.
Arc 953.5 MacLean, J.P. The mound builders. Cincinnati, 1879.
Arc 595.34.5 Marks, T.S. The Great Pyramid. 2. ed. London, 1879?
Arc 1027.8.9 Marucchi, O. Di un ipogeo scoperto nel cimitero di S. Sebastian. Roma, 1879.
Arc 835.201F Mastorelly Peña, F. Apuntes arqueologicos. Barcelona, 1879.
Arc 810.11 Mau, August. Pompejanische Beitraege. Berlin, 1879.
Arc 73.15 Michaelis, A. Geschichte des deutschen archäologisches Institut. Berlin, 1879.
Arc 73.15.5 Michaelis, A. Storia dell'Instituto archeologico germanico, 1829-1879. Roma, 1879.
Arc 793.3.8 Miola, Alfonso. Ricordi Vesuviani. n.p., 1879.
Arc 915.10 Morel, C. Genève et la colonie de Vienne sous les Romains. pt.1. Genève, 1879? 2 pam.
Arc 968.2 Morgan, L.H. On the ruins of a stone pueblo on the Animas River in New Mexico. Salem, 1879.
Arc 426.1 Morse, E.S. Traces of an early race in Japan. N.Y., 1879.
Arc 861.21.9 Mortimer, J.P. Forty years' research in British and Saxon burial grounds of East Yorkshire. London, 1879.
Arc 905.22 Müllner, Alfons. Emona; archaeologischen Studien aus Krain. Laibach, 1879.
Arc 1025.5 Northcote, J.S. Roma sotterranea. pts.1-3. London, 1879. 2v.

Chronological Listing

1879 - cont.

Arc 682.20 Olkonomlkes, S. Ta sōzomena Ithōmēs Messenes kai tōn Perix. Athēnai, 1879.
Arc 930.201 Ossowski, G. Zabytki przedhistoryczne Ziem Polskich. Krakow, 1879-88.
Arc 843.18 Pereira, Gabriel. Notas d'archeologia. Erora, 1879.
Arc 1163.12 Pillito, I. Analisi paleografia di...codici...secoli XIV e XV...in Cagliari. Cagliari, 1879.
Arc 1264.3 Prost, A. Notice sur un sceau de Landfriede du XIVe siècle. Paris, 1879.
Arc 772.1 Reber, F. von. Die Ruinen Roms. Leipzig, 1879.
Arc 537.3 Regaldi, G. Lę antichita di Cipro. Roma, 1879.
Arc 66.1.11 Riemann, O. Études sur la langue de Yite-Live. Paris, 1879.
Arc 66.1.8 Riemann, O. Les îles ioniennes. Paris, 1879-80. 3v.
Arc 87.1.39 Robert, C. Thanatos. Berlin, 1879.
Arc 720.211 Rome. Istituto di Archeologia. Instituto archeologica centrum semertria. Roma, 1879.
Arc 1153.41 Ruess, F. Ueber die Tachygraphie der Römer. Inaug. Diss. München, 1879.
Arc 790.210.5F Ruggiero, Michele. Discorso pronunziato in Pompei. Napoli, 1879.
Arc 1470.2 Sallet, A. von. Die Nachfolger Alexanders des Grossen. Berlin, 1879.
Arc 1033.147 San Giovanni Battista e i Genovesi. Genova, 1879.
Arc 1498.3 Saulcy, L.F.J.C. de. Recueil de documents...monnaies frappées par les rois de France depuis Philippe II jusqu'à François I. Paris, 1879-92. 4v.
Arc 1232.1 Schlumberger, G. Sceaux et bulles de l'Orient Latin au Moyen Age. Paris, 1879.
Arc 1025.56 Schultze, M.V. De christianorum viterum rebus sepulchralibus. Gothae, 1879.
Arc 505.4.8 Sepp, J.N. Meerfahrt nach Tyrus zur Ausgrabung der Kathedrale mit Barbarossa's Grab. Leipzig, 1879.
Arc 1518.5 Serrure, Raymond. Elements de l'histoire monétaire de Flandre. Gand, 1879.
Arc 953.11 Short, J.F. The North Americans of antiquity. N.Y., 1879-80.
Arc 861.21.12 Simpson, H.T. Archaeologia Adelensis...West Riding of Yorkshire. London, 1879.
Arc 983.6 Slafter, E.F. Prehistoric copper implements. Boston, 1879.
Arc 1027.21.9 Stornaiolo, C. Alcuni recenti scavi nelle catacombe di San Gennaro. Roma, 1879.
Arc 568.1 Stuart, V. Nile gleanings. London, 1879.
Arc 1033.79 Taglialatela, G. Del primo vescovo di Napoli Sant'Aspreno. Napoli, 1879.
Arc 853.94 Tergast. Die beidnischen Alterthümer Ostfrieslands. Emden, 1879.
Arc 823.19.10 Thédenat, H. Cachet d'oculiste. Paris, 1879.
Arc 823.19.15 Thédenat, H. L'epigraphie romaine en France. Paris, 1879.
Arc 1025.29.21 Tonini, P. La Roma sotterranea cristiana...dal G.B. de Rossi. Firenze, 1879.
Arc 746.17 Tononi, A.G. Scoperta di un bronzo etrusco. Milano, 1879.
Arc 905.5.5 Trieste. Il museo civico di antichita. Trieste, 1879.
Arc 950.206 United States. Report upon geographical surveys west of the one hundredth meridian. v.7. Archaeology. Washington, 1879.
Arc 835.203FA Veiga, Estacio da. Antiquidades de Mafra. Lisboa, 1879.
Arc 522.6 Virchow, R. Beitraege zur Landeskunde der Troas. Berlin, 1879.
Arc 1190.3.3 Wright, Andrew. Court hand restored. 9. ed. London, 1879.

188-

Arc 967.1.3 Carr, L. The mounds of the Mississippi Valley. Cambridge, 188-?
Arc 642.2.3 Collignon, Maxime. Manuel d'archéologie grecque. Paris, 188-.
Arc 830.63.9 Léon des Ormeaux, A. La Roche aux Feés. Laval, 188-?

1880

Arc 180.1.501 Antiquarische Gesellschaft in Zürich-Bibliothek. Liederchronik der Antiquarischen Gesellschaft in Zürich. Frauenfeld, 1880.
Arc 682.14F Archäologisches Institut des Deutschen Reichs-Athenische Zweigeanstalt. Das Kuppelgrab bei Menidi. Athen, 1880.
Arc 1025.30.5 Armellini, M. Le catacombe romane. Roma, 1880.
Arc 1027.35 Armellini, M. Il cimiterio di S. Agnese sulla via nomentana. Roma, 1880.
Arc 1033.70 Armellini, M. Scoperta d'una pittura nel Laterno. Roma, 1880.
Arc 1335.76.14 Athens. Ethnikon Nomismatikon Mouseion. Karmatia symbolika. Athēnai, 1880.
Arc 1500.15 Barthélemy, Anatole de. Monnaie gauloise inédite de Luctérius, chef Cadurque. n.p., 1880.
Arc 720.202 Bartolini, D. L'antico cassino e il primitivo monasterio. Montecassino, 1880.
Arc 1033.35.41 Bastelaer, D.A. Étude sur les précieux reliquaire phylactère du XIIe siècle. Anvers, 1880.
Arc 547.11 Bergmann, E. Uebersichtung der Sammlung Aegyptischen Alterthuemer des Allerhöchsten Kaiserhauses. Vienna, 1880.
Arc 830.27 Bertrand, Alexandre. L'autel de saintes et les triades gauloises. Paris, 1880.
Arc 1433.17 Blancard, Louis. Le besant d'or sarrazinas pendant les croisades. Marseille, 1880.
Arc 716.3 Bötticher, Karl. Die Thymele der Athena Nike. Berlin, 1880.
Arc 756.7 Boissier, Gaston. Promenades archéologiques, Rome et Pompéi. Paris, 1880.
Arc 1263.3 Bosredon, P. de. Sigillographie du Périgord. Perigneux, 1880.
Arc 1033.160 Boulgaris, N.T. Alēthēs ekthesis...thaymatourchou...touachiouspyridōnos. Benetia, 1880.
Arc 1412.1 Bramsen, W. The coins of Japan. pt.1. Yokohama, 1880.
Arc 756.5.2 Burn, R. Old Rome. London, 1880.
Arc 1411.1 Bushell, S.W. Coins of the present dynesty in China. n.p., 1880.
Arc 1663.7.7F Camozzi Vertova, G. Dissertazione sul medagliere relativo alla storia moderna d'Italia. Bergamo, 1880.
Arc 66.1.14 Chatelain, E. Manuscrits des poesies de S. Paulin de Nole. Paris, 1880.
Arc 861.12.15 Clayton, J. Observations on centurial stones found on the Roman wall in Northumberland and Cumberland. Newcastle-on-Tyne, 1880.

1880 - cont.

Arc 416.2.2 Clermont-Ganneau, Charles. Études d'archéologie orientale. Paris, 1880. 2v.
Arc 1093.2.5 Clodd, E. The later stone age in Europe. London, 1880.
Arc 1478.3.3 Cohen, H. Description historique des monnaies frappées sons l'Empire Romain. Paris, 1880-92. 8v.
Arc 510.208 Conze, A. Die Ergebnisse der Ausgrabungen zu Pergamon. Berlin, 1880.
Arc 520.3 Conze, A. Pergamon. Berlin, 1880.
Arc 858.2 Dawkins, W.B. Early man in Britain. London, 1880.
Arc 66.1.19 Delaborde, H.F. Chartes de terre sainte. Paris, 1880.
Arc 1033.25.8 Delattré, Alfred Louis. Lampes chrétiennes de Carthage. Lyon, 1880.
Arc 1027.4 De Rossi, G.B. Fouilles et découverts...cimetière de Priscille. Rome, 1880.
Arc 66.1.15 Descemet, C. Inscriptions doliaires latines. Paris, 1880.
Arc 66.1.13 Duchesne, L. De codd. mss. graecis Pü II in Biblioteca Vaticana. Paris, 1880.
Arc 843.17 Estacio da Veiga, S.P.M. Memoria da antiquidades de Mertola. Lisboa, 1880.
Arc 432.1 Fergusson, J. Cave temples of India. London, 1880.
Arc 66.1.17 Fernique, E. Étude sur prénestė. Paris, 1880.
Arc 1033.65 Ferrari, L.F. dei. Sul valore storico del'atti S.S. Flavia Domitilla, Nereo, Achilleo. Roma, 1880.
Arc 595.29 Fish, E.W. The Egyptian pyramids. Chicago, 1880.
Arc 1033.7 Fita y Colomé, Fidel. Recuerdos de un viaje a Santiago de Galicia. Madrid, 1880.
Arc 547.10 Florence, Italy. Guida del Museo Archeologico I. Antichita Egiziane. Florence, 1880.
Arc 87.1.40 Furtwaengler, A. Der Satyr aus Pergamon. Berlin, 1880.
Arc 1264.6 Gauthier, Jules. L'origine des armoiries de l'église de Besançon. n.p., 1880.
Arc 810.19 Guillaume, Paul. Une excursion à Pompéi. Paris, 1880.
Arc 1470.38 Head, B.V. On the chronological sequence of the coins of Ephesus. London, 1880.
Arc 1580.20 Hess, A. Die Siebenbürgischen Münzen des furstlich Montenuoro'schen Münzcabinets. Frankfurt, 1880.
Arc 953.14 Holmes, William H. Art in shell of ancient Americans. Washington, 1880-81.
Arc 858.5 Kains-Jackson, C.P. Our ancient monuments and the land around them. London, 1880.
Arc 1033.65.5 Lais, G. Memoire del titolo di Fasciola. Roma, 1880.
Arc 1473.1.5 Lampros, Paulos. Anekdota nomismata tēs Hellados. Athēnai, 1880.
Arc 766.1 Lanciani, R. Topografia di Roma antica. Roma, 1880.
Arc 943.5 Larkin, F. Ancient man in America. n.p., 1880.
Arc 1148.2 Lehmann, O. Die Tachygraphischen Abkürzungen der griechischen Handschriften. Leipzig, 1880.
Arc 505.5.30 Lindberg, N. Templet i Jerusalem. Kolding, 1880.
Arc 848.1 Lindenschmit, L. Handbuch der Deutsche Alterthumskunde. Braunschweig, 1880.
Arc 1185.13 Lustro, G.N. di. Degli archivii, ricerche archaeologiche, storiche , critiche, diplomatiche. Napoli, 1880.
Arc 545.226 Mariette, A. Catalogue général des monuments d'Abydos. Paris, 1880.
Arc 562.1 Mariette, A. Itinéraire de la Haute-Égypte. Paris, 1880.
Arc 66.1.16 Martha, J. Catalogue des figurines en terre cuite. Paris, 1880.
Arc 1500.18 Maxe-Werly, L. Note sur l'origine du gros tournois. Paris, 1880.
Arc 397.2 Mitchell, A. The past in the present. Edinburgh, 1880.
Arc 545.224 Mook, F. Aegyptens vormetallische Zeit. Wuerzburg, 1880.
Arc 935.6 Mordtmann, J. Das Denkmal des Porphyrius. Athen, 1880.
Arc 1163.2.14 Muñoz y Rivero, J. Manual de paleografía diplomática española. Madrid, 1880.
Arc 398.2 Newton C.T. Essays on art and archaeology. London, 1880.
Arc 1076.3.65 North, Thomas. The church bells of Rutland. Leicester, 1880.
Arc 865.2 Petrie, W.M.F. Stonehenge; plans, descriptions and theories. London, 1880.
Arc 830.91.10 Pilloy, Jules. Études sur d'anciens lieux de sépultre dans l'Aisne. Saint-Quentin, 1880-99. 3v.
Arc 1518.2 Piot, C. Catalogue des coins, poincons et matrices. 2. ed. Bruxelles, 1880.
Arc 861.18.5 Price, J.E. On a bastion of London Wall. Westminster, 1880.
Arc 785.29.5 Quarenghi, G. Le mura di Roma. Roma, 1880.
Arc 1033.141 Razy, E. Saint Jean-Baptiste, sa vie, son culte. Paris, 1880.
Arc 1510.132 Rehle, Q. Die Münzen der Stadt Kaufbeuren. Kaufbeuren, 1880.
Arc 1030.18 Riant, Paul de. Trois inscriptions...rapportées de Constantinople. Paris, 1880.
Arc 1500.17 Robert, Charles. Monnaies gauloises. Paris, 1880.
Arc 1020.104 Rohault de Fleury, G. Un tabernacle chrétien du Ve siècle. Arras, 1880.
Arc 1030.5.21 Rossi, G.B. de. L'elogio funebre di Turia...Q. Lucrezio Vespillone. Roma, 1880.
Arc 1015.227 Rossi, M.S. de. Duale metodo tecnico per dirigere l'escavazione. Roma, 1880.
Arc 1281.1F Russia. Commission d'Impression des Lettres Patentes et Traités. Reproduction d'anciens cachets russes. Moscou, 1880.
Arc 1033.3.33 Le sarcophage chrétien de Luc de Biarn. Paris, 1880.
Arc 522.4.5.3 Schliemann, H. Ilios. London, 1880.
Arc 682.1.2 Schliemann, Heinrich. Mycenae; a narrative. N.Y., 1880.
Arc 1428.2 Schlumberger, G. Les monnaies à légendes grecques. Paris, 1880.
Arc 1473.3 Schlumberger, G. Monuments numismatiques et sphragistiques...byzantin. Paris, 1880.
Arc 1430.1 Schlumberger, G. Le trésor de San'a. Paris, 1880.
Arc 1018.5.5 Schultze, Victor. Archäologische Studien über altchristliche Monumente. Wien, 1880.
Arc 682.1.15 Schulze, E. Mykenai - eine kritische Untersuchung der Schliemannschen Alterthümer. St. Petersburg, 1880.
Arc 1518.4 Serrure, Raymond. Dictionaire géographique de l'histoire monétaire belge. Bruxelles, 1880.
Arc 440.1 Sewell, R. Report on the Amarävati Tope. London, 1880.
Arc 1680.13 Simpson, Justin. List of the Lincolnshire series of tradesmen's tokens. London, 1880.
Arc 595.9.3 Smyth, C.P. Our inheritance in the Great Pyramid. 4. ed. London, 1880.
Arc 790.214F Sogliano, A. Le pitture murali campane. Napoli, 1880.
Arc 403.3 Stark, K.B. Handbuch der Archäologie der Kunst. Leipzig, 1880.
Arc 1175.1 Sybel, H. von. Kaiserurkunden in Abbildungen. v.1-11 and atlas. Berlin, 1880-91. 12v.

Chronological Listing

1880 - cont.

Arc 823.19.45 Thédenat, H. Antiquaires 1880. Paris, 1880.
Arc 823.19.40 Thédenat, H. Cachet du médecin Feror. Paris, 1880.
Arc 823.19.25 Thédenat, H. Critique 1880. Paris, 1880.
Arc 823.19.30 Thédenat, H. Droit latin de O. Hirschfeld. Paris, 1880.
Arc 823.19.50 Thédenat, H. Les médecins Magillius et D. Gallius Sextus. Paris, 1880.
Arc 823.19.35 Thédenat, H. Notes sur deux inscriptions fausses. Paris, 1880.
Arc 903.1 Undset, F. Etudes sur l'age de bronze...Hongrie. Christiana, 1880.
Arc 895.11 Undset, F. Fra Norges aeldre jernalder. Kjøbenhavn, 1880.
Arc 1335.20 Werveke, N. van. Catalogue descriptive des monnaies luxembourgeoises. Luxembourg, 1880.
Arc 1510.18 Wibel, Ferdinand. Zur Münzgeschichte der Grafen von Wertheim. Hamburg, 1880.
Arc 1458.2 Yale College. Catalogue of the Greek and Roman coins in the numismatic collection. New Haven, 1880.

1881

Arc 953.1 Abbott, C.C. Primitive industry. Salem, 1881.
Arc 875.3 Anderson, Joseph. Scotland in early Christian times. Edinburgh, 1881.
Arc 875.3.2 Anderson, Joseph. Scotland in early Christian times. 2. series. Edinburgh, 1881.
Arc 830.181.2 Audiat, L. Le capitole de Saintes. Paris, 1881.
Arc 1.7.2 Barbier de Montault. Annales archéologiques. Index, v.28. Paris, 1881.
Arc 1500.16 Barthélemy, Anatole de. Liste des noms d'hommes gravés sur les monnaies. Paris, 1881.
Arc 1500.14 Barthélemy, Anatole de. Note sur les monnaies trouvées au Mont César. Paris, 1881.
Arc 1093.2.6 Baye, J. de. Les instruments en pierre à l'epoque de métaux. Paris, 1881.
Arc 1033.69.20 Becker, F. Die Heidnische Weiheformel Diis Manibus. Gera, 1881.
Arc 505.4 Berton, J. de. La topographie de Tyr. Paris, 1881.
Arc 520.1 Bohn, R. Tempel des Athena Polias zu Pergamon. Berlin, 1881.
Arc 756.7.1 Boissier, Gaston. Promenades archéologiques, Rome et Pompéi. 2. éd. Paris, 1881.
Arc 375.10 Bosc, E. Dictionnaire général de l'archéologie. Paris, 1881.
Arc 953.15 Boston Society of Natural History. Palaeolithic implements of...Delaware. v.1-3. Cambridge, 1881.
Arc 522.10 Brentano, E. Zur Loesung der Troianischen Frage. Heilbronn, 1881.
Arc 1353.2.3 British Museum. Department of Coins and Medals. A guide to the principal gold and silver coins of the ancients. London, 1881.
Arc 1675.55 British Museum. Department of Coins and Medals. Synopsis of the contents of the British Museum. London, 1881.
Arc 545.222 Brugsch, E. La trouvaille de Deir-el-Bahari. Cairo, 1881.
Arc 810.46 Bruun, Carl. Pompeji, dets historie og mindesmärker. Kjøbenhavn, 1881.
Arc 435.11.10 Burgess, James. Inscriptions from cave-temples of western India. Bombay, 1881.
Arc 66.1.20 Cartault, A. La trière athénienne. Paris, 1881.
Arc 830.31 Chabouillet, A. Notice sur dea inscriptions...Bourbonne-les-Bains. Paris, 1881.
Arc 642.2A Collignon, Maxime. Manuel d'archéologie grecque. Paris, 1881.
Arc 500.3 Conder, C.R. Arabic and English name lists. London, 1881.
Arc 500.4 Conder, C.R. Memoirs of the topography. London, 1881-83. 3v.
Arc 66.1.21 Cuq, E. Études d'epigraphie juridique. Paris, 1881.
Arc 983.7 Dall, William H. On masks, labrets and certain aboriginal customs. Washington, 1881-82.
Arc 66.1.22 Delaborde, H.F. Étude sur la chronique de Guillaume le Breton. Paris, 1881.
Arc 1285.2.3 Delaville Le Roulx, J. Des sceaux des prieurs anglais de l'ordre de l'hôpital. Rome, 1881. 2 pam.
Arc 1285.2 Delaville Le Roulx, J. Des sceaux des prieurs anglais de l'ordre de l'hôpital. Rome, 1881.
Arc 1285.1 Delaville Le Roulx, J. Note sur les sceaux de l'ordre de Saint Jean de Jérusalem. Paris, 1881.
Arc 1020.91 Diehl, P. Die St. Matthias-Kirche bei Trier. Trier, 1881.
Arc 87.1.41 Doerpfeld, W. Die Verwendung von Terrakotten. Berlin, 1881.
Arc 880.11 Doherty, W.J. Round towers of Ireland. Dublin, 1881.
Arc 855.222F Drummond, James. Archaeologia scotica; sculptured monuments in Iona. Edinbrugh, 1881.
Arc 1076.3.79F Ellacombe, H.T. The church bells of Gloucestershire. Exeter, 1881.
Arc 1348.24 Escher, A. Schweizerische Münz- und Geldgeschichte. Bern, 1881.
Arc 870.1.2 Evans, J. The ancient bronze implements, weapons and ornaments of Great Britain. London, 1881.
Arc 870.1.3 Evans, J. The ancient bronze implements, weapons and ornaments of Great Britain. N.Y., 1881.
Arc 537.3.2 Feuardent, G.L. Answer to L.P. di Cesnola. N.Y., 1881.
Arc 953.2.3 Foster, J.W. Prehistoric races of the United States of America. 5. ed. Chicago, 1881.
Arc 1033.107 Fratini, G. Gli atti più antichi del martirio di S. Felice. Foligno, 1881.
Arc 66.1.23 Girard, P. L'asclépicion d'Athènes. Paris, 1881.
Arc 392.6 Hanno, Georges. Les villes retrouvées. Paris, 1881.
Arc 1470.39 Head, B.V. On the chronological sequence of the coins of Boeotia. London, 1881.
Arc 1018.41 Heales, Alfred. The archaeology...Christian altar...western Europe. London, 1881.
Arc 1020.94 Helbig, Jules. Reliques...données par St. Louis, roi de France, au couvent des Dominicains de Liége. Bruxelles, 1881.
Arc 983.3.5 Henshaw, H.W. Animal carvings from mounds of the Mississippi Valley. Washington, 1881?
Arc 608.1.39 Hérisson, M. d'. Relation d'une mission archéologique en Tunisie. Paris, 1881.
Arc 435.16.2F India. Curator of Ancient Monuments. Plan of Delhi. v.1-15. n.p., 1881.
Arc 307.3.2 International Congress of Americanists, 4th, Madrid, 1881. Congreso international de Americanistas. Madrid, 1881.
Arc 785.14 Jordan, Henri. Capitol, Forum und Sacra Via in Rom. Berlin, 1881.
Arc 853.43 Kasiski, F.W. Beschreibung der vaterländischen Alterthümer. Danzig, 1881.

1881 - cont.

Arc 705.200 Kekulé, R. Die Reliefs an der Balustrade der Athena Nike. Stuttgart, 1881.
Arc 608.2.17 Lavigerie, C.M.A. De l'utilité d'une mission archéologique permanente à Carthage. Alger, 1881.
Arc 1025.32 Lefort, Louis. Chronologie des peintures des catacombes romaines. Paris, 1881.
Arc 830.334F Liénard, F. Archéologie de la Meuse. v.1-3, texte. v.4-6, carte. Verdun, 1881-85. 6v.
Arc 505.5.32 Lindberg, N. Templet i Jerusalem. Stockholm, 1881.
Arc 136.1.11 London Society of Antiquaries. Review of Archaeologia. London, 1881.
Arc 853.40.5 Maassen, F. Die römische Staatsstrasse. Bonn, 1881.
Arc 875.37.5 Maclagan, Christian. Chips from old stones. Edinburgh, 1881.
Arc 1405.1.2 Madden, F.W. Coins of the Jews. v.2. London, 1881.
Arc 1423.9.5F Madden, Frederic W. Coins of the Jews. Boston, 1881.
Arc 708.20 Maps, Athens. Athen mit Umgebung (1877). Berlin, 1881.
Arc 66.1.24 Martin, A. Manuscrit d'Isocrate, Urbinas CXI. Paris, 1881.
Arc 1020.59 Martinov, J. Le trésor de la cathédrale de Gran. Arras, 1881.
Arc 1025.24 Martorelli, I. Le catacombe di Roma. Vercelli, 1881.
Arc 1030.4.9 Marucchi, O. Silloge di alcune iscrizioni. Roma, 1881.
Arc 830.11.19 Miln, James. Excavations at Carnac. Edinburgh, 1881.
Arc 387.4.8 Moroni, A. Nuovo catalogo delle opere...dell'abate Francesco Cancellieri. Roma, 1881.
Arc 397.5 Müntz, Eugène. Richerche intorno...Grimaldi. Firenze, 1881. 8 pam.
Arc 1153.6 Muñoz y Rivero, J. Paleografía visigoda. Madrid, 1881.
Arc 398.1 Nadaillac, J.F.A. du Pouget de. Les premiers hommes. Paris, 1881. 2v.
Arc 1033.27 Nardoni. Di alcune sotterrance confessoni...Basiliche di Roma. Roma, 1881.
Arc 900.201 Nyáry, Jenö. Az aggteleki Barlang mint orkori temetö. Budapest, 1881.
Arc 1020.6.3 Passini, A. Sul frontale dell'altar maggiore in San Marco. Venezia, 1881.
Arc 830.23 Piette, Edouard. Note sur les tumulus de Bartrès et d'Ossun. Toulouse, 1881. 2 pam.
Arc 1027.19.13 Pillet, A. Souvenirs du cimetière de Saint Calliste. Arras, 1881.
Htn Arc 1033.12.48* Pratique pour honorer le St. Suaire de...Jésus Crist. Cain, 1881.
Arc 925.18F Prokhorov, V. Materialy po istorii russkikh odezhd. Sankt Petersburg, 1881-85. 3v.
Arc 1668.5.3 Rentzmann, W. Numismatisches Legenden-Lexicon. Berlin, 1881.
Arc 1480.33 Rohde, T. Die Münzen des Kaisers Aurelianus. v.1-2. Miskoloz, 1881-82.
Arc 1015.204 Roller, T. Les catacombes di Rome. Paris, 1881. 2v.
Arc 1033.68 Rossi, G.B. de. Esame...dell'Immagine di Urbano II. Roma, 1881.
Arc 501.3 Saunders, T. Introduction to the survey of Western Palestine. London, 1881.
Arc 522.4.5 Schliemann, H. Ilios. Leipzig, 1881.
Arc 522.4.6 Schliemann, H. Ilios. N.Y., 1881.
Arc 684.3 Schliemann, Heinrich. Orchomenos. Leipzig, 1881.
Arc 1254.7 Schlumberger, G. Deux chefs normands des armées byzantines. Paris, 1881.
Arc 1565.1 Stenersen, L.B. Myntfundet fra Graeslid i Thydalen. Christiania, 1881.
Arc 1015.229 Stevenson, H. Escavazioni in un ipogeo cristiano de Bolsena. Roma, 1881.
Arc 1558.2 Stockholm. Statens Historiske Museum och Myntkabinett. Anglosachisiska mynt i svenska kongliga myntkabinette funna i sveriges jord. Stockholm, 1881.
Arc 830.123 Straub, A. Le cimetière gallo-romain de Strasbourg. Strasbourg, 1881.
Arc 708.24 Sybel, L. von. Katalog der Sculpturen zu Athen. Marburg, 1881.
Arc 823.19.60 Thédenat, H. Antiquaires 1881. Paris, 1881.
Arc 823.19.90 Thédenat, H. Antiquités romaines trouvées aux Lilas-Romainville. Paris, 1881.
Arc 823.19.95 Thédenat, H. Critique, 1881. Paris, 1881.
Arc 823.19.85 Thédenat, H. De Villefosse. Inscription de Gordien. Vienne, 1881.
Arc 823.19.70 Thédenat, H. Etvi à collyre égyptien. Paris, 1881.
Arc 823.19.75 Thédenat, H. Exposition d'Utique. Paris, 1881.
Arc 823.19.100 Thédenat, H. Extrait des procès-verbaux. Nogent-le-Rotrou, 1881.
Arc 823.19.80 Thédenat, H. Lettre a M. Ernest Desjardins. Paris, 1881.
Arc 823.19.55 Thédenat, H. Observations sur l'èpigraphie des Alpes maritimes de M.E. Blanc. Paris, 1881.
Arc 823.19.65 Thédenat, H. 14 juillet, 1881. Paris, 1881.
Arc 726.72 Tolomei, Antonio. La cappella degli Scrovigni e l'arena di Padova. Padova, 1881.
Arc 726.20 Tononi, A.G. Documenti inediti...scoperta di Velleia. Modena, 1881.
Arc 612.1 Undset, F. Jernalderens Begyndelse i nord Europa. Kristiania, 1881.
Arc 923.25F Uvarob, A.S. Arkheologiia Rossii. Moskva, 1881. 2v.
Arc 1428.29 Vacquier, Polydore. Numismatique des Scythes et des Sarmates. Paris, 1881.
Htn Arc 861.62.10* Wardell, James. Historical notices of Ilkley, Rombald's Moor, Baildon Common. 2. ed. Leeds, 1881.
Arc 1033.62.40 Wetzel, A. Die Translatie S. Alexandri. Kiel, 1881.
X Cg Arc 500.2 Wilson, C. Special papers. London, 1881.
Arc 893.5.4 Worsaae, J.J.A. Nordene forhistorie. Kjøbenhavn, 1881.

1882

Arc 635.208 Association pour l'Encouragement des Études Grècques en France, Paris. Monuments grècs. Paris, 1882-97. 2v.
Arc 1033.165 Aubé, Benjamin. Polyeucte dans l'histoire. Paris, 1882.
Arc 595.1 Ballard, R. The solution of the Pyramid problem. N.Y., 1882.
Arc 1020.26 Bartolini, D. Su l'antica basilica di S. Nicola in Bari. Roma, 1882.
Arc 1027.25.65 Bellesheim, A. Der heilige Johannes Baptista de Rossi. Mainz, 1882.
Arc 583.1 Berend, W.B. Principaux monuments du Musée Égyptienne de Florence. no.51. Paris, 1882.
X Cg Arc 1053.3 Bernoulli, J.J. Römische Ikonographie. v.2, pt.1. Stuttgart, 1882-94.
Arc 522.10.3 Brentano, E. Troia und Neu-Ilion. Heilbronn, 1882.

Chronological Listing

1882 - cont.

Arc 1027.64 Bruzza, L. Oggetti ritrovati in un sepolcro della via Prinistina. Roma, 1882.

Arc 435.9.3 Burgess, James. Notes on the Amarâvati stûpa. Madras, 1882.

Arc 435.9.5 Burgess, James. Notes on the Amarâvati stûpa. Madras, 1882. 2 pam.

Arc 1613.11F Bushnell, C.I. Catalogue of...American coins and medals of C.I. Bushnell. Philadelphia, 1882.

Arc 1498.6 Caron, E. Monnaies féodales françaises. fasc. 1-3. Paris, 1882.

Arc 726.51F Caruana, A.A. Report on the Phoenician and Roman antiquities in the group of the islands of Malta. Malta, 1882.

Arc 540.2 Cesnola, L.P. Salaminia. London, 1882.

Arc 1663.9 Cessac. Un trésor de monnaies des comtês de la Marche. v.1-2. Paris, 1882.

Arc 1663.8 Clarke, H. The early history of the Mediterranean populations. London, 1882.

Arc 497.2 Clermont-Ganneau, Charles. Premiers rapports sur une mission en Palestine et en Phénicie. Paris, 1882.

Arc 510.208.2 Conze, A. Die Ergebnisse der Ausgrabungen zu Pergamon, 1880-1881. Berlin, 1882.

Arc 537.3.3 Cook, C. Transformations and migrations of certain statues in the Cesnola collection. N.Y., 1882.

Arc 684.1.2 Curtius, E. Die Altere von Olympia. Berlin, 1882.

Arc 635.4 Curtius, E. Die Funde von Olympia. Berlin, 1882.

Arc 684.1.3 Curtius, E. Olympia und Umgegend. Berlin, 1882.

Arc 712.8 Davidson, T. The Parthenon frieze and other essays. London, 1882.

Arc 1033.53.20 Ducis, C.A. Saint Maurice et le Légion Thébéenne. Annecy, 1882.

Arc 1490.15 Engel, A. Recherches sur la numismatique...des nomands de Sicile. Paris, 1882.

Arc 760.7 Forbes, S. Russell. Rambles in Rome. London, 1882.

Arc 1485.5 Friedländer, Julius. Die italienischen Schaumünzen der fünfzehnten Jahrhundert. Berlin, 1882.

Arc 1470.42 Gardner, Percy. Samos and Samian coins. London, 1882.

Arc 545.202FA Gorringe, H.H. Egyptian obelisks. N.Y., 1882.

Arc 762.1.3.9 Hare, A.J.C. Walks in Rome. 8. American ed. N.Y., 1882.

Arc 545.225 Haynes, H.W. Egyptian Palaeolithic implements. Cambridge, 1882.

Arc 505.5.50 Herrmann, J. Temple de Jérusalem. Valenciennes, 1882.

Arc 1510.75 Hohenlohe Waldenburg, Friedrich. Sphragistische Aphorismen. Heilbronn, 1882.

NEDL Arc 435.16 India. Curator of Ancient Monuments. Preservation of national monuments. v.1-3. Simla, 1882-84.

Arc 441.1.3 Indraje, B. Antiquarian remains at Sopârâ and Padana, being an account of the Buddhist Stûpa and Asoka edict. Bombay, 1882.

Arc 861.20 Kerslake, T. Caer Pensauelcoit. London, 1882.

Arc 716.2 Kirchhoff, F.C. Vergleichung der Überreste vom Theater des Dionysuszu Athen. Altona, 1882.

Arc 1578.3 Kolb, J. von. Die Münzen, Medaillen und Jetone. Linz, 1882.

Arc 543.9 Kondakov, N.P. Puteshestvie na Cinai. Odessa, 1882.

Arc 1018.35 Kraus, F.X. Archäologie...Christliche Archäologie, 1880-86. Stuttgart, 1882. 2v.

Arc 1018.05 Kraus, Franz X. Real-Encyclopädie der Christlichen Alterthümer. Freiburg, 1882-86. 2v.

Arc 1185.3 Leist, F. Urkundenlehre. Leipzig, 1882.

Arc 830.78 Lisle, Pitre de. Dictionnaire archéologique de la Loire-Inférieure. Nantes, 1882.

Arc 1016.9 Lugari, G.B. Intorno ad alcuni monumenti antichi. Roma, 1882.

Arc 785.38.7 Maes, Constantino. Le terme di Agrippa. Roma, 1882.

Arc 66.1.26 Martha, J. Sacerdoces anthéniens. Paris, 1882.

Arc 66.1.27 Martin, A. Scolies du ms. d'Aristophane à Ravenne. Paris, 1882.

Arc 1033.28.5 Marucchi, O. Il matrimonio cristiano sopra antico monumento. Roma, 1882.

Arc 710.4.2 Michaelis, A. A brief explanation of the ground plan of the akropolis of Athens. Cambridge, 1882.

Arc 87.1.42 Milchhoefer, A. Befreining des Prometheus. Berlin, 1882.

Arc 520.4 Mitchell, L.M. (Mrs.). Sculptures of the Great Pergamon Altar. N.Y., 1882.

Arc 1020.73.9 Molinier, E. Fragments d'un inventaire du trésor de l'abbaye de Saint Victor de Paris. Paris, 1882.

X Cg Arc 875.5 Munro, R. Ancient Scottish lake-dwellings. Edinburgh, 1882.

Arc 1033.12.21 Notice historique et critique de Saint Suaire. Poitiers, 1882.

Arc 501.1.2 Palestine exploration quarterly. Index, 1869-1881. London, 1882.

Arc 785.8 Parker, J.H. The Colosseum at Rome. London, 1882.

Arc 1510.34 Pfeiffer, L. Pestilantia in nummis. Tübingen, 1882.

Arc 1470.7 Phillips, H. Remarks upon a coin of Sicyon. Philadelphia, 1882.

Arc 1020.24 Pulignani, M.F. Chiesa...Pietro e Paolo...Cancelli. Foligno, 1882.

Arc 401.1.8 Quicherat, Jules. Jules Quicherat, 1814-1882. Paris, 1882.

Arc 628.6 Rheinhard, H. Album des klassischen Alterthums. Stuttgart, 1882.

Arc 1675.4 Robert, Charles. Les médailleurs de la Renaissance. Paris, 1882.

Arc 1027.71 Rossi, G.B. de. Il cimitero di S. Ippolito presso la via Tiburtina. Roma, 1882.

Arc 1259.1 Rossi, G.B. de. Di una bolla plumbea papale. Roma, 1882.

Arc 1027.7.17 Rossi, G.B. de. Escavazioni nel cimitero dei SS. Pietro e Marcellino. Roma, 1882.

Arc 772.4 Rossi, G.B. de. Note di topographia romana. Roma, 1882.

Arc 1027.25.9 Rossi, J.B. de. Albo dei sottoscrittori...medaglio d'oro. Roma, 1882.

Arc 505.5.9 Rossi, J.B. de. Verre colorie representant le temple de Jerusalem. Paris, 1882.

Arc 1443.1 Rougé, Jacques de. Description de quelques monnaies nouveaux des nomes d'Égypte. Paris, 1882.

Arc 501.2 Saunders, T. Brief geographical account of the survey of Western Palestine. London, 1882.

Arc 1668.3 Schlickeysen, F.W.A. Erklärung der Abkürzungen auf Münzen der neueren Zeit. Berlin, 1882.

Arc 682.1.16 Schliemann, Heinrich. Catalogue des trésors de Mycènes au Musée d'Athènes. Leipzig, 1882.

Arc 682.1.17 Schliemann, Heinrich. Catalogue des trésors de Mycènes au Musée d'Athènes. Leipzig, 1882.

1882 - cont.

Arc 1425.2.2 Schlumberger, G. Numismatique de l'Orient Latin. Paris, 1882.

Arc 1254.8 Schlumberger, G. Sceaux en plomb de chefs des Manglavites impériaux. Paris, 1882.

Arc 1150.203 Schmitz, W. Monumenta tachygraphica codicus parisienis Latini. Hannoverae, 1882.

Arc 853.22 Schreiner, P.W. Eining die Dortigen Römerausgrabungen. Landsbut, 1882. 2v.

Arc 1027.50.5 Schulke, V. Theologische Etrag...Katakombenforschung. Leipzig, 1882.

Arc 1025.8 Schultze, V. Die Katakomben. Photoreproduction. Leipzig, 1882.

Arc 520.13 Schwabe, L. von. Pergamon und seine Kunst. Tubingen, 1882.

Arc 435.2.7F Sewell, Robert. Lists of the antiquarian remains in the presidency of Madras. Madras, 1882.

Arc 1025.9 Smyth, E. Recent excavations in American Christian cemeteries. Worcester, 1882.

Arc 865.16 Stevens, E.T. Jottings on some of the objects of interest in the Stonehenge excursion. Salisbury, 1882.

X Cg Arc 568.1.2 Stuart, V. The funeral tent of an Egyptian queen. London, 1882.

Arc 820.218F Tardieu, A. La ville gallo-romaine de Beauclair. Clermont-Ferrand, 1882.

Arc 823.19.110 Thédenat, H. Critique, 1882. Paris, 1882.

Arc 823.19.115 Thédenat, H. Inscriptions latines des fouilles d'Utique. Vienne, 1882.

Arc 823.19.105 Thédenat, H. Zénobie vaballathus...Philippe le Jeune par Mommsen. Paris, 1882.

Arc 66.1.25 Thomas, A. Recherches sur l'entrée de Spagne. Paris, 1882.

Arc 1582.9PF Tolstoi, I.I. Monety vel. kniazhestva Kievskago. Sankt Peterburg, 1882.

Arc 1083.1 Undset, I. Das erste Auftreten des Eisens in Nord-Europa. Hamburg, 1882.

Arc 1033.35.23 Velentini, A. Santissime croci di Brescia. Brescia, 1882.

Arc 1020.1.5 Vienna. St. Stephansdom. Das Wiener Heiligthumbuch. Wien, 1882.

Arc 407.7 Werveke, N. van. Mélanges archéologiques. Luxembourg, 1882.

Arc 895.7 Worsaae, J.J.A. The industrial arts of Denmark. London, 1882.

Arc 780.1 Ziegler, C. Das alte Rom. Stuttgart, 1882.

NEDL Arc 180.1.2 Zürich. Antiquarische Gesellschaft. Denkschrift zu fuenfzigjaehrigen Stiftungsfeier. Zürich, 1882?

1883

Arc 66.1.31 Albert, M. Culte de castor et pollux en Italie. Paris, 1883.

Arc 726.56 Albert, Maurice. De villis Tiburtinis, principe Augusto Thesim proponebat. Parisios, 1883.

Arc 1329.2 AmericanNumismatic Society. Catalogue of numismatic books in the library. N.Y., 1883.

Arc 875.4 Anderson, Joseph. Scotland in Pagan times. The Iron Age. Edinburgh, 1883.

Arc 1033.43 Annali...degli Apostoli Pietro e Paolo. v.1-3. Torino, 1883. 2v.

Arc 845.211F Architekten und Ingenieur-Verein für Niederrhein und Westfalen, Cologne. Cölner Thorburgen und Befestigungen, 1180-1882. Cöln, 1883.

Arc 1675.3 Armand, A. Les médailleurs italiens. v.1-2. 2. éd. Paris, 1883.

Arc 1190.2 Aronius, J. Diplomatische Studien über die älteren angelsächischen Urkunden. Inaug. Diss. Königsberg, 1883.

Arc 1020.72.5 Barbier de Montault, X. Le trésor de l'abbaye de Ste. Croix de Poitiers. Poitiers, 1883.

Arc 875.19 Barclay, A. Perthia Romana: line or chain of forts erected by Agricola. Perth, 1883.

Arc 1033.17.96.6 Becerra Tanco, Luis. Nuestra Señora de Guadalupe y origen. 6. ed. México, 1883.

Arc 830.22.16 Bernard, Eugene. Découverte d'une statue de Bacchus dans la rue de Fossés Saint Jacques. Paris, 1883.

Arc 1500.13 Blancard, Louis. La médaille d'argent de Fauquembergue...dame au faucon. Marseille, 1883.

Arc 1390.3 Blancard, Louis. Le saiga mérovingien dérive de la silique byzantine. v.1-2. Marseille, 1883.

Arc 66.1.29 Bloch, G. Origines du sénat romain. Paris, 1883.

X Cg Arc 684.1 Boetticher, A. Olympia - das Fest und seine Stätte. Berlin, 1883. (Changed to XP 9960)

Arc 547.6 Boolak Museum. Guide du visiteur au Musée de Boulaq. Boolak, 1883.

Arc 1020.9.30 Bossi, G. La chiesa di Santa Marta al Vaticano. Roma, 1883.

Arc 1490.35 Brambilla, C. Monete di Pavia. Pavia, 1883.

Arc 1076.3.97 Briscoe, J.P. Curiosities of the belfry. London, 1883.

Arc 1030.14 Bruzza, L. Iscrizione in onore di Iallia Bassia. Roma, 1883.

Arc 608.1.5 Cagnat, R. Explorations épigraphiques et archéologiques en Tunise. v.1-3. Paris, 1883-6.

Arc 1330.45 Camont, Georges. Bibliographie générale et raisonnée de la numismatique belge. Bruxelles, 1883.

Arc 967.1.5 Carr, L. The mounds of the Mississippi Valley. Frankfort, 1883.

Arc 1030.36 Carrière, A. Inscriptions d'un reliquare arménien. Paris, 1883.

Arc 730.2 Cavallari, F.S. Atlante. Topografia archaeologica. Siracusa. Palermo, 1883. 2v.

Arc 1259.2 Chamard, François. Les bulles de plomb des lettres pontificales. Paris, 1883.

Arc 1335.19 Charvet, Jules. Collection Charvet. Paris, 1883.

Arc 1027.25.13 Cozza, Luzi G. Per un busto...G.B. de Rossi. Roma, 1883- 3 pam.

Arc 736.1.10 Dara, G. Sulla topografia d'Agrigento del F.S. Cavallari. Girgenti, 1883.

Arc 1588.1.18 Dawne monety Polskie dynastyi Piasłow Jagiełłonow. Piotrkow, 1883-85. 3v.

Arc 66.1.32 Delaville Le Roulx, J. Les archives...à Malte. Paris, 1883.

Arc 743.1.3 Dennis, G. The cities and cemeteries of Etruria. 3. ed. London, 1883. 2v.

Arc 1348.46 Dye, John S. Dye's coin encyclopaedia. Philadelphia, 1883.

Arc 1025.42 Emiliani, A. Ricordi di viaggio ad catacumbas. Livorno, 1883.

Arc 712.19 Fergusson, J. The Parthenon. London, 1883.

Chronological Listing

1883 - cont.

Arc 518.4 Fergusson, J. The Temple of Diana at Ephesus. London, 1883.

Arc 87.1.43 Furtwaengler, A. Goldfund von Vettersfelde. Berlin, 1883.

Arc 1465.2 Gardner, P. The types of Greek coins. Cambridge, Eng., 1883.

Arc 1027.25.11 Geffroy, A. Une fête archéologique à Rome. Paris, 1883.

Arc 910.4 Gross, V. Les protohelvètes. Paris, 1883.

Arc 1020.85 Guélou, P.F. Un reliquare romano Byzantin (Auverogne). Clermont-Ferrand, 1883.

Arc 510.211 Hamdy Bey, O. Le Tumulus de Nemroud-Dagh. Constantinople, 1883.

Arc 1166.1 Harris, J.R. Stichometry. Baltimore, 1883.

Arc 905.6 Hauser, A. Spalato und die römischen Monumente Dalmatiens. Wien, 1883.

Arc 1670.1 Heiss, A. Les médailleurs de la Renaissance. v.3,8. Paris, 1883. 2v.

Arc 823.8 Hirshfeld, O. Gallische Studien. Wien, 1883-1884.

Arc 793.1 Hoepli, U. Bibliography of Vesuvius, Pompeii, Herculaneum. Milan, 1883.

Arc 1465.1 Imhoof-Blumer, Friedrich. Choix de monnaies grecques. 2. ed. Paris, 1883.

Arc 1468.7 Imhoof-Blumer, Friedrich. Monnaies grecques. Amsterdam, 1883.

Arc 1468.7.5 Imhoof-Blumer, Friedrich. Monnaies grecques. Paris, 1883.

Arc 448.1.10 Indian Museum, Calcutta. Catalogue and hand-book of the archaeological collections in the Indian Museum. Calcutta, 1883. 2v.

Arc 1033.12.133 Janvier. Culte de la sainte-face à S. Pierre du Vatican. Tours, 1883.

Arc 764.1.2 Jordan, Henri. De formae urbis Romae...novo disputatio. Roma, 1883.

Arc 600.7 Karabaček. Die Theodor Graf'schen Funde in Aegypten. Wien, 1883.

Arc 958.2 Kengla, L.A. Contributions to the archaeology of the District of Columbia. Washington, 1883.

Arc 716.2.2 Kirchhoff, F.C. Neue Messungen der Überreste vom Theater des Dionysus zu Athen. Altona, 1883.

Arc 395.1.2 Kulturhistorischer Bilder-Atlas. Leipzig, 1883-85. 2v.

Arc 608.21 La Blanchère, R. du C. Voyage d'étude dans une partie de la Maurétanie césarienne. Paris, 1883.

Arc 830.82.5 La Croix, C. de. Mémoire archéologique sur les découvertes d'Herbord dites de Sanxay. Niort, 1883.

Arc 1027.85F LaCroix, Camille. Monographie de l'hypogée-martyrium. Paris, 1883. 2v.

Arc 1675.1 Lawrence, R.H. Medals by Giovanni Carino. N.Y., 1883.

Arc 1027.24.9 Lefort, L. Chronologie des peintures des catacombes de Naples. Rome, 1883.

Arc 1027.2.19 Lefort, L. Les scènes de banquets. Paris, 1883.

Arc 1348.9 Lenormant, F. Monnaies et médailles. Paris, 1883.

Arc 900.207 Lepkowski, J. Monumenta epigraphica Cracoviensia. Krakow, 1883.

Arc 830.180 Letelié, J.A. Les Arenes de Saints en 1882. Pons, 1883.

Arc 396.1 Longpérier, A. de. Oeuvres. Paris, 1883-87. 7v.

Arc 1020.12 Lorenzo, Giuseppe di. Antichi monumenti di religioni cristiani in Toscanella. Rocca, 1883.

Arc 1493.12 Martin Minquez, Bernardino. Datos epigráficos y numismáticos de España. Valladolid, 1883.

Arc 1025.28.25 Marucchi, O. La catacombe romane a proposito della recente opera del Roller. Roma, 1883.

Arc 1030.4 Marucchi, O. Di una...iscrizione cristiana. Roma, 1883.

Arc 785.31 Marucchi, O. Recenti scoperte dell'Iseo Compense. Roma, 1883.

Arc 1027.25.27 Marucchi, O. Solenne festa in onore del Comm. G.B. de Rossi. Roma, 1883.

Arc 953.6 Mason, O.T. Miscellaneous papers relating to anthropology. Washington, 1883.

Arc 1020.73.12 Molinier, E. Inventaire du trésor...de Saint-Sépulchre de Paris. Paris, 1883.

Arc 1615.3 Newlin, H.P. A classification of early half-dimes in the United States. Philadelphia, 1883.

Arc 1020.16 Orsi, P. Monumenti cristiani del Trentino. Roma, 1883.

Arc 375.4.2 Otte, H. Archäologisches Wörterbuch. Leipzig, 1883.

Arc 400.1 Perkins, F.B. Prehistoric man. San Francisco, 1883.

X Cg Arc 595.5 Petrie, W.M.F. Pyramids and temples of Gizeh. London, 1883.

Arc 1613.4 Phillips, H. The coinage of the United States of America. Philadelphia, 1883.

Arc 66.1.30 Pottier, E. Étude sur les lécythes blancs attiques. Paris, 1883.

Arc 700.15 Pottier, Edmond. Quam ab causam Graeci in sepulcris figlina na sigilla deposuerint. Parisiis, 1883.

Arc 943.7 Pouget, J.F.A. du Nadaillac. L'Amérique préhistorique. Paris, 1883.

Arc 595.6 Proctor, R.A. The Great Pyramid. London, 1883.

Arc 595.6.2 Proctor, R.A. The Great Pyramid. N.Y., 1883.

Arc 1020.79 Promis, V. Reliquiario armeno...convento...Alessandria in Piemonte. Torino, 1883.

Arc 1335.42 Quelen, E. de. Collection de M. le Vicomte de...monnaies. Paris, 1883.

Arc 1500.34 Robert, M.P.C. Sur la prétendue restauration du pouvoir de Maurice Tibère. Paris, 1883.

Arc 830.18.15 Rochetin, L. Étude sur la viabilité romaine dans le département de Vauclus. Avignon, 1883.

X Cg Arc 1016.207 Rohault de Fleury, C. La messe études archéologiques sur ses monuments. v.1-2,8. Paris, 1883- 3v.

Arc 1016.207 Rohault de Fleury, C. La messe études archéologiques sur ses monuments. v.3-7. Paris, 1883- 5v.

Arc 1033.92 Rossi, G.B. de. Commemorazione del P. Luigi Bruzza. Roma, 1883.

Arc 772.4.5 Rossi, G.B. de. Note di Ruderi e monumenti antico di Roma. Roma, 1883.

Arc 1015.205.9 Rossi, G.B. de. Verre representant le temple de Jerusalem. Genes, 1883.

Arc 505.5.10 Rossi, J.B. de. Verre representant le temple de Jerusalem. Genes, 1883.

Arc 1190.7 Russi, M. Paleografia e diplomatica...province napolitane. Napoli, 1883.

Arc 497.8 Sachau, E. Reise in Syrien und Mesopotamien. Leipzig, 1883.

Arc 1675.52 Sambon, Giulio. Catalogo delle medaglie del rinascimento e moderne di uomini illustri. Roma, 1883.

Arc 1478.16 Samer, K. Geschichte älteren römischen Münzwesens...200 B.C. Wien, 1883.

Htn Arc 684.2* Schliemann, Heinrich. Orchomenos. Athēnai, 1883.

Arc 1254.9 Schlumberger, G. Cinq sceaux de l'époque byzantine. Paris, 1883.

Arc 1254.10 Schlumberger, G. Documents pour servir à l'histoire des thémes byzantines. Paris, 1883.

Arc 1254.11 Schlumberger, G. La vierge, le Christ, les saints sur les sceaux byzantins. Paris, 1883.

Arc 858.28 Smith, Charles R. Retrospections, social and archaeological. London, 1883-91. 3v.

Arc 1680.5 Stainsfield, C.W. Descriptive catalogue of Australian tradesmen's tokens. London, 1883.

Arc 823.19.20 Thédenat, H. Les noms des deux premiers Gordiens par Sallet. Paris, 1883.

Arc 510.204 Thiersch, F. Die Koenigsburg von Pergamon. Stuttgart, 1883.

Arc 66.1.35 Thomas, A. Francesco da Barberino. Paris, 1883.

Arc 520.5 Urlichs, L. Pergamon - Geschichte und Kunst. Leipzig, 1883.

Arc 830.82 Vachon, Marius. Les ruines de Sanxay découvertes en 1882. Paris, 1883.

Arc 920.7 Virchow, R. Das Gräberfeld von Koban. Text und Atlas. Berlin, 1883. 2v.

Arc 861.49 Watkin, W.J. Roman Lancashire. Liverpool, 1883.

Arc 590.15 Wilson, E. The recent discovery of ancient Egyptian mummies at Thebes. London, 1883.

Arc 893.19 Winkel Horn, F. Kort udsigt over Nordens oldtidsminder. Kjøbenhavn, 1883.

Arc 407.3 Wright, G.F. Early man. Cleveland, 1883.

1884

Arc 1033.52 Angelini, N. Vita, martiro e culto di S. Ambrogio. Frascati, 1884.

Arc 340.1 Archaeological book lists. n.p., 1884-1891.

Arc 1033.12.183 Bacci, G. Corona di ferro. Ferrara, 1884.

Arc 66.1.36 Beaudoin, M. Étude du dialecte chypriote. Paris, 1884.

Arc 1478.36 Belfort, A. Recherches des monnaies impériales romaines non décrites dans l'ouvrage de H. Cohen. Macon, 1884.

Arc 510.201 Benndorf, O. Reisen in Lykien und Karien. Vienna, 1884.

Arc 608.1.41F Berger, P. Stèles trouvées à Hadrumète. Paris, 1884.

Arc 1020.4.5 Boissoudy, A. de. La sainte-chapelle de Bourges. n.p., 1884.

Arc 820.5 Borrel, E.L. Les monuments anciens de la Tarentaise (Savoie). Paris, 1884. 2v.

Arc 1418.1 British Museum. Department of Coins and Medals. Catalogue of Indian coins. v.1-5,7. London, 1884-1936. 6v.

Arc 1470.32F Burachkov', P. Obshchagi katalog' monety. Odessa, 1884.

Arc 540.1.5 Cesnola, L.P. Gaston L. Feuardent vs. L.P. Cesnola - testimony of the defendant. N.Y., 1884.

Arc 1020.72.9 Chamard, F. L'hypogée des dunes à Poitiers. Paris, 1884.

Arc 1153.29.5 Chassant, A. Dictionnaire des abréviations latines et françaises. 5. éd. Paris, 1884.

Arc 1540.17.10 Cochran-Patrick, R.W. Catalogue of the medals of Scotland. Edinburgh, 1884.

Arc 935.8 Constantinople, Turkey. Hellēnikos Philologikos Syllogos. Archaiologikē Epitropē. Archaiologikos chartēs. Konstantinople, 1884.

Htn Arc 1418.2.4* Cunningham, A. Coins of Alexander's succesors in the East. London, 1884?

Arc 553.5 Dawson, John W. Notes on prehistoric man in Egypt and Lebanon. London, 1884.

Arc 1020.77 Delisle, Léopold. Authentiques de reliques...decouvertes à Vergy. Rome, 1884.

Arc 1053.5 Dietrichson, L. Antinoos. Christiania, 1884.

Arc 485.200 Dieulafoy, M. L'art antique de la Perse. Paris, 1884-89. 5v.

Arc 1348.2 Dubois, P. Moneta: a study. n.p., 1884.

Arc 1510.41 Erman, Adolf. Deutsche Medailleure des sechzehnten und siebzehnten Jahrhunderts. Berlin, 1884.

Arc 432.1.5 Fergusson, J. Archaeology in India. London, 1884.

Arc 416.3 Fischer, H. Stone implements in Asia. Worcester, 1884.

Arc 1033.17.98.7 García, Juan C. Rasgo histórico acerca de nuestra Señora de la antigua de Guadalajara. Guadalajara, 1884.

Arc 1033.12.16 Gauthier, J. Notes iconographique sur le Saint Suaire de Besançon. Besançon, 1884.

Arc 82.1.5 Geffroy, M.A. L'école française de Rome. Paris, 1884.

Arc 1020.9.40 Gianuizzi, P. La chiesa di Santa Maria di Loreto IV. Sacre notizio V. Roma, 1884.

Arc 830.18.10 Gilles, Isidore. Les voies romaines et massiliennes. Avignon, 1884.

Arc 1148.4 Gomperz, T. Ueber ein bisher Unbekanntes griechisches Schriftsystem. Wien, 1884.

Arc 1033.12.73 Haignere, D. Notre-Dame de Saint-Sang. 2e éd. Paris, 1884.

Arc 700.5 Haussoullier, B. Quomodo sepulera Tanagraei decoravirent. Paris, 1884.

Arc 66.1.38 Haussoullier, B. La vie municipale en Attique. Paris, 1884.

Arc 638.1 Hesselmeyer, E. Die Urspruenge der Stadt Pergamos in Kleinasien. Tübingen, 1884-85. 7 pam.

Arc 1033.12.142 Histoire de la sainte-face de...Christ. Laon, 1884.

Arc 858.4 Hodgetts, J.F. Older England. London, 1884.

Arc 858.4.2 Hodgetts, J.F. Older England. 2. series. London, 1884.

Arc 1076.3.85 Jadart, Henri. Le Bourdon de Notre-Dame de Reims. Reims, 1884.

Arc 66.1.37 Jullian, C. Transformations politiques de l'Italie. Paris, 1884.

Arc 426.2A Kanda, T. Notes on ancient stone implements...of Japan. Tokio, 1884.

X Cg Arc 1538.9 Kenyon, R.L. Gold coins of England, sequel to the silver coins of England. London, 1884.

Arc 66.1.34 La Blanchere, M.R. de. Terracine. Paris, 1884.

X Cg Arc 66.1.33 Lafaye, G. Histoire du culte des divinités d'Alexandre. Paris, 1884. (Changed to XP 9785)

Arc 66.1.33 Lafaye, G. Histoire du culte des divinités d'Alexandre. Photoreproduction. Paris, 1884.

Arc 1473.50 Lampros, Paulos. Nomismata tēs Hepianēdon politeias. Athēnai, 1884.

Arc 1473.1.8 Lampros, Paulos. Nomismata tōn ademiōn Zachariōn. Athēnai, 1884.

Arc 1033.97 Le Blant, E. Des voies d'exception...contre les martyrs. Rome, 1884.

Arc 766.3 Le Blant, Edmond. Les ateliers de sculpture chez les premiers chrétiens. Rome, 1884.

Arc 700.8 Lenormant, F. Monographie de la voie sacrée éleusinienne. Paris, 1884.

Arc 1033.12.44 Lombardo, V.G. Panegirico della Sacra Sindone. Torino, 1884.

Arc 1033.5.5 Luzi, G.C. Le chiavi di S. Pietro. Roma, 1884.

Chronological Listing

1884 - cont.

Arc 785.1.8 Maes, C. Vesta e vestali. 2. ed. Roma, 1884.
Arc 545.226.5F Mariette, A. Les mastabas de l'ancien empire. Paris, 1884.
Arc 1016.235 Marini, G. Iscrizioni antiche doliari. Roma, 1884.
Arc 723.6 Martha, Jules. Manuel d'archéologie étrusque et romaine. Paris, 1884.
Arc 1015.225.5 Marucchi, O. Di un nuovo cimitero giudaico. Roma, 1884.
Arc 1027.18.9 Marucchi, O. Di un nuovo cimitero giudaico. Roma, 1884.
Arc 1027.9.5 Marucchi, O. Gli errori della scuola protestante. n.p., 1884.
Arc 785.13.31 Marucchi, O. Nova scoperte nella casa dell Vestali. Roma, 1884.
Arc 1335.107 Moscow. Gosudarstvennyi Rumiantsovskii,Muzei. Numizmaticheskii kabinet. Moskva, 1884.
Arc 77.1 Museo Italiano di antichita classica. v.1-3 and atlas. Florence, 1884-90. 4v.
Arc 830.34 Nicaise, Auguste. L'époque gauloise dans...la Marne. Paris, 1884.
Arc 1076.3.9 Otte, H. Glockenkunde. Leipzig, 1884.
Arc 810.13.2A Overbeck, J. Pompeji. Leipzig, 1884.
Arc 444.1.10 Pearse and Company, ltd. Pearse guide to Elephanta, or Gharapuri. Devonport, 1884.
Arc 1033.45 Persus, L. de. Del pontificato di S. Sisto I. Alatri, 1884.
Arc 600.191 Petrie, W.M.F. The arts of ancient Egypt. London, 1884.
Arc 1033.12.37 Pietro, S. di. Santa sindone. Sermone. Torino, 1884.
Arc 1500.5.5 Ponton d'Amécourt, G. de. Monnaies mérovingiennes de Saint-Denis. Macon, 1884.
Arc 943.7.5A Pouget, J.F.A. du Nadaillac. Prehistoric America. N.Y., 1884.
Arc 1443.2 Revillout, Eugène. Lettre à M.P. Charles Robert sur les monnaies égyptiennes. Macon, 1884.
Arc 1423.2 Révillout, Eugène. Note sur les plus anciennes monnaies hébraiques. Macon, 1884.
Arc 1030.5.9 Rossi, G.B. de. Frammenti di fasti di Ludi Capenati. Roma, 1884.
Arc 608.2 Sainte-Marie, E. de. Mission à Carthage. Paris, 1884.
Arc 595.30F Schiaparelli, E. Il significato simbolico delle piramidi egiziane. Roma, 1884.
Arc 522.4.4A Schliemann, H. Troja. London, 1884.
Arc 522.4.4.2 Schliemann, H. Troja. London, 1884.
Arc 1254.12 Schlumberger, G. Deux epagia...sceau d'un capitaine arménien. Paris, 1884.
Arc 930.204 Schlumberger, G. Monuments byzantins inédits. Macon, 1884.
Arc 1254.16F Schlumberger, G. Sigillographie de l'empire byzantin. Paris, 1884.
Arc 435.2.8F Sewell, Robert. Lists of inscriptions and sketch...dynasties of southern India. Madras, 1884.
X Cg Arc 855.8 Smith, A.C. Guide to British and Roman antiquities in north Wiltshire. n.p., 1884. 2v.
Arc 1613.12 Smith, A.M. Coins and coinage. The United States Mint, Philadelphia. Philadelphia, 1884.
Arc 861.18.13 Smith, Washington G. On a palaeolithic floor at north east London. London, 1884.
Arc 1076.3.13 Stahlschmidt, J.C.L. Surrey bells and London bell-founders. London, 1884.
Arc 823.19.125 Thédenat, H. Étude sur Lambèse par Wilmanns. Paris, 1884.
Arc 823.19.120 Thédenat, H. Sur une inscription inédite. Paris, 1884.
Arc 983.12 Thomas, C. Burial mounds of the northern sections of the United States. Washington? 1884?
Arc 1582.5F Tolstoi, I.I. Russkaia dopetrovenaia numismatika. Sankt Peterburg, 1884-86. 2v.
Arc 595.10 Totten, C.A.L. The metrology of the Great Pyramid. N.Y., 1884.
Arc 861.18.3 Tylor, Alfred. New points in the history of Roman Britain, as illustrated by discoveries at Warwick Square. Westminster, 1884.
Arc 726.23 Vercelli, C. di. Per un ricordo al padre L. Bruzza. Vercelli, 1884.
Arc 1015.217.5 Waal, A. de. Valeria; historische Erzahlung. Regensburg, 1884.
Arc 500.1 Warren, C. Jerusalem. London, 1884.
Arc 87.1.44 Weil, R. Kuenstlerinschriften der sicilienischen Muenzen. Berlin, 1884.
Arc 785.7 Wells, C.L. The amphitheatres of ancient Rome. Boston, 1884.
Arc 777.2 Westropp, H.M. Early and imperial Rome. London, 1884.
Arc 600.5.3 Whitehouse, F.C. Lake Moeris and the pyramids. n.p., 1884?
Arc 910.1 Zeller-Werdmüller, H. Denkmäler aus der Feudalzeit im Lande Uri. Zürich, 1884.

1885

Arc 1016.231 Adriano I. Lettera...sul culto delle sacre immagini. Roma, 1885.
Arc 1033.51 Angelini, N. Brevi notizie intorno San Rufino. Frascati, 1885.
Arc 923.45F Anuchin, D.N. K' voprosu o sostavlenii legendy dlia arkheologicheskoi karty Rossii. Moskva, 1885.
Arc 938.27.5 Aspelin, Johan R. Suomen asukkaat pakanuuden aikana. Helsingissä, 1885.
Arc 1335.76.16 Athens. Ethnikon Nomismatikon Mouseion. Nomismata. Athênai, 1885.
Arc 1478.17 Babelon, Ernest. Description historique et chronologique des monnaies de la République romaine vulgairement appelées monnaies consulaires. Paris, 1885-86. 2v.
Arc 595.31 Bache, R.M. The latest phase of the Great Pyramid discussion. Philadelphia, 1885.
Arc 1020.72 Barbier de Montault, X. Le martyrium de Poitiers. Poitiers, 1885.
Arc 1033.12.166 Barbier de Montault, X. Saint Clou à la cathédrale de Toul. Nancy, 1885.
Arc 1033.46 Bartolini, D. Cenni biografici di S. Giacomo apostolo il maggiore. Roma, 1885.
Arc 1500.8.5 Blancard, Louis. Monnaies féodales françaises par M.E. Caron. Résumé. Draguignan, 1885.
Arc 386.23 Brunn, H. von. Archäologie und Anschauung. München, 1885.
Arc 435.11.11 Burgess, James. Lists of antiquarian remains in the Bombay presidency. Bombay, 1885.
Arc 1663.28 Camozzi Vertova, G. Medaglie coniate in onore del generale Giuseppe Garibaldi. Bergamo, 1885.
Arc 1663.28.2 Camozzi Vertova, G. Medaglie coniate in onore del generale Giuseppe Garibaldi. Bergamo, 1885.

1885 - cont.

Arc 1138.5.2 Chassant, Alphonse. Paléographie des chartes. 8. éd. Paris, 1885.
Arc 505.6 Clermont-Ganneau, Charles. Fraudes archeologiques en Palestine. (Bibliothéque Orientale Elzevirienne). Paris, 1885.
Arc 501.16 Conder, C.R. Heth and Moab. London, 1885.
Arc 1027.58 De Feis, L. La bocca della verita. Roma, 1885.
Arc 1153.1.5 Delisle, L. Mémoire sur l'école calligraphique de Tours au IXe siècle. Paris, 1885.
Arc 889.2 Delvaux, Emile. Les alhuions de l'escault et les tourbières...d'Audenarde. Liége, 1885.
Arc 66.1.40 Dubois, M. Les ligues étolienne et achéenne. Paris, 1885.
Arc 830.84.5 Esmonnot, L. Néris. Vicus Neriomagus. Recherches sur ses monuments. Moulins, 1885.
Arc 1020.67 Feraud, J.J.M. Les saintes reliques...chateau de Manosque. Digne, 1885.
Arc 1360.1 Friedlaender, J. Repertorium zur antiken Numismatik. Berlin, 1885.
Arc 830.18.11 Gilles, Isidore. Saint Gens, ermite et Boèce. Supplément. v.1-2. Avignon, 1885.
Arc 66.1.42 Grousset, R. Étude sur l'histoire des sarcophages chrétiens. Paris, 1885.
Arc 1033.17.222 Haigneré, D. Couronnement de Notre-Dame de Boulogne. Boulogne, 1885.
Arc 905.26 Hampel, J. Der Goldfund von Nagy-Szent-Miklos. Budapest, 1885.
Arc 985.210F Hamy, M.E.T. Recherches historiques et archéologiques. Paris, 1885.
Arc 66.1.41 Hauvette-Besnault, A. Les stratèges athéniens. Paris, 1885.
Arc 1663.3 Hawkins, E. Medallic illustrations of the history of Great Britain and Ireland. London, 1885. 2v.
Arc 530.1 Hirschfeld, G. Paphlagonische Felsengraeber. Berlin, 1885.
Arc 1033.17.106 Historia de Nuestra Señora de Lujan. Buenos Aires, 1885. 2v.
Arc 537.4 Holwerda, A.E.J. Die alten Kyprier in Kunst und Cultur. Leiden, 1885.
Arc 501.18 Hull, E. Mount Seir. London, 1885.
Arc 1465.3 Imhoof-Blumer, Friedrich. Porträtköpfe auf antiken Münzen. Leipzig, 1885.
NEDL Arc 136.2.3 Index Society. Index to engravings in proceedings of Society of Antiquaries. London, 1885.
Arc 93.25F Italy. Direzione generale della antichità e belle arti. Sull'ordinamento del servizio archeologico. Roma, 1885.
Arc 441.2.9 Kathiawar. Department for an Archaeological and Antiquarian Survey. Bhavanagar pracina sodh a samgraha. Bhavanagar, 1885.
Arc 505.5.81 King, J. Recent discoveries on the Temple Hill at Jerusalem. 2. ed. London, 1885.
Arc 638.4 Kirckhoff, C. Der Rhombus in der Orchestra des Dionysustheaters zu Athen. Altona, 1885. 3 pam.
Arc 830.104 Lalande P. Ruines romaines de Tintignac (Corrèze). Brive, 1885.
Arc 1033.12.132 Lecomte, A. Sainte-face de la cathédrale de Laon. Laon, 1885.
Arc 380.213 Leemans, C. Études archéologiques, linguistiques. Leide, 1885.
Arc 1018.2 Lefort, L. Études sur les monuments primitifs. Paris, 1885.
Arc 838.3 Leite de Vasconcellos, J. Portugal pre-historico. Lisboa, 1885.
Arc 451.1F Lucknow Exhibit. A memorandum of suggestions for use of contributors to the Loan Collection Department of the Exhibit. Lucknow, 1885.
Arc 855.201 Lukis, W.C. The prehistoric stone monuments of the British Isles - Cornwall. London, 1885.
Arc 726.45 Lupi, Clemente. Nuovi studi sulle antiche terme pisane. Pisa, 1885.
Arc 785.13.28 Marucchi, O. Description du Forum Romain et guide pour le visiteur. Rome, 1885.
Arc 726.10.5 Marucchi, Orazio. Guida archeologica dell'antica Preneste. Roma, 1885.
Arc 983.11 Mercer, H.C. The Lenape stone. N.Y., 1885.
Arc 1020.52.5 Merlet, L. Catalogue des reliques...Notre Dame de Chartres. Chartres, 1885.
Arc 853.1 Mestorf, J. Vorgeschichtliche Alterthuemer. Hamburg, 1885.
Arc 1510.167 Meyer, Adolf. Prägungen Brandenburg-Preussens. Berlin, 1885.
Arc 767.4 Middleton, J.H. Ancient Rome in 1885. Edinburgh, 1885.
Arc 1018.18.18 Montescaglioro, F. Commemorazione di P. Raffaele Garucci. Napoli, 1885.
Arc 1027.18.5 Müller, Nikolaus. Le catacombe degli ebrei...via Appia. Roma, 1885?
Arc 830.62 Musset, Georges. La Charente-Inferieure avant l'histoire. La Rochelle, 1885.
Arc 1660.7 Myer, I. The Waterloo medal. Philadelphia, 1885.
Arc 405.1.35 Nezabvennoi pamiati grafa Alekseia Sergeevicha Uvarova. Moskva, 1885.
Arc 405.1.25 Pamiati grafa Alekseia Sergeevicha Uvarova. Kazan, 1885.
Arc 1166.2 Paoli, Cesare. Carta di cotone e carta di lino. Firenze, 1885.
Arc 1153.2.3 Paoli, Cesare. Grundriss der lateinischen Palaeographie und der Urkundenlehre. Innsbruck, 1885.
Arc 1033.17.152 Paris, L. Chapelle dans la Cathédrale de Reims. Epernay, 1885.
Arc 585.2A Petrie, W.M.F. Tannis. Pt.1-2. London, 1885-88. 2v.
Arc 561.1.5 Pierret, Paul. Explication des monuments de l'Égypte et de l'Ethiopie. Paris, 1885.
Arc 1348.8 Poole, S. Lane. Coins and medals. London, 1885.
Arc 830.126.5 Pottier, Raimond. Fréjus et les carrières...de l'Esterel. Draguignan, 1885.
Arc 983.3.2 Putnam, C.E. Elephant pipes and inscribed tablets. Davenport, 1885.
Arc 983.5 Putnam, F.W. Remarks upon chipped stone implements. Salem, 1885.
Arc 401.1 Quicherat, Jules. Mélanges d'archéologie et d'histoire. Paris, 1885.
Arc 843.19 Rada y Delgado, Juan de Dios de la. Necropolis de Carmona; memoria. Madrid, 1885.
Arc 87.1.45 Richter, O. Antike Steinmetzzeichen. Berlin, 1885.
Arc 1033.1.5 Rossi, G.B. de. Frammento di Becchiere Vitreo. Roma, 1885.
Arc 1027.65 Rossi, G.B. de. Le horrea sotto l'aventino. Roma, 1885.

Chronological Listing

1885 - cont.

Arc 790.210 Ruggiero, Michele. Storia degli scavi di Ercolano. Napoli, 1885.

Arc 890.207 Rygh, O. Norske oldsager. Christiania, 1885.

Arc 830.160 Saurel, Ferdinand. Aeria. Recherches sur son emplacement. Paris, 1885.

Arc 905.24 Schlechter, Max. Beiträge zur alten Geschichte des Obergailthales in Kärnten. Wien, 1885.

Arc 682.1.8 Schliemann, Heinrich. Tiryns; the prehistoric palace of the kings of Tiryns. N.Y., 1885.

Arc 1088.1.17 Serre, Paul. Les marines de guerre. Paris, 1885.

Arc 861.31.15F Smith, Alfred Charles. Guide to the British and Roman antiquities of the North Wiltshire downs. 2. ed. Devizes, 1885.

Arc 1033.44.15 Sodo, G. Il monogramma del nome ss. di Gesú. Napoli, 1885.

Arc 1163.3 Sreznevski, T.T. Slavjano-russkaja paleografija. Sankt Peterburg, 1885.

Arc 1033.70.5 Taeggi, O.P. Avanzi di pitture del secolo IX in una cripta. n.p., 1885.

Arc 823.19.130 Thédenat, H. Diffusion du droit latin. Paris, 1885.

Arc 823.19.145F Thédenat, H. Les trésors d'argenteuie trouvés en Gaule. Paris, 1885. 3v.

Arc 774.3 Tomassetti, G. Della campagna romana. Roma, 1885.

Arc 1261.1 Travers, Émile. Le sceau de Loja et la sigillographie pittoresque. Paris, 1885.

Arc 87.2.85 Veith, C. Das roemische Koeln. Bonn, 1885.

Arc 1033.51.5 Vincenti, D. de. Nitizie dei Sante Rufino e Cesidio Martire. Avezzano, 1885.

Arc 853.41.5F Wagner, E. Hügelgräber und Urnen-Friedhöfe. Karlsruhe, 1885.

Arc 853.105 Wolff, G. Der römische Grenzwald bei Hanau mit dem Kastellen zu Rückingen und Markäbel. Hanau, 1885.

Arc 407.5 Wussow, A. von. Der Erhaltung der Denkmäler. Berlin, 1885.

Arc 407.5.2 Wussow, A. von. Die Erhaltung der Denkmäler. Berlin, 1885.

1886

Arc 1020.9.117 Albertini, F. Mirabilibus...Romae. Heilbron, 1886.

Arc 1.5.6 American School of Classical Studies at Athens. Annual report, 1-3. Reprint ed. Cambridge, 1886.

Arc 875.4.2 Anderson, Joseph. Scotland in Pagan times. The Bronze and Stone Ages. Edinburgh, 1886.

Arc 925.9.10 Bapst, Y. Souvenirs de deux missions an Caucase. Paris, 1886.

Arc 1020.88 Barbier de Montault, X. Inventaires de la Basilique Royale de Monza. Paris, 1886. 3 pam.

Arc 1335.56.3 Bataviaasch Genootschap van Kunsten en Wetenschappen. Museum. Catalogus der numismatische versameling. 3. druk. Batavia, 1886.

Arc 453.1 Bendall, C. Journey in Nepal and northern India. Cambridge, 1886.

Arc 501.5A Besant, W. Twenty-one years' work in the Holy Land. London, 1886.

Arc 684.1.5 Boetticher, A. Olympia. Berlin, 1886.

Arc 1088.1 Breusing, A. Die Nautik der Alten. Bremen, 1886.

Arc 1353.2.2 British Museum. Department of Coins and Medals. A guide to the principal gold and silver coins of the ancients. London, 1886.

Arc 700.10 Brueckner, A. Ornament und Form der altischen Grabstelen. Weimar, 1886.

Arc 838.1 Cartailhac, É. Les âges préhistoriques de l'Espagne et du Portugal. Paris, 1886.

Arc 830.21 Castan, Auguste. Les arènes de Vesontio. Besançon, 1886.

Arc 630.2 Castan, Auguste. Les capitoles provinciaux du monde romain. Besançon, 1886.

Arc 726.34 Centurione, P.A.M. Studie recenti sopra i Nuraghi. Prato, 1886.

Arc 642.2.5A Collignon, Maxime. A manual of Greek archaeology. London, 1886.

Arc 642.2.6 Collignon, Maxime. A manual of Greek archaeology. N.Y., 1886.

Arc 830.63.5 Contades, G. Les monuments mégalithiques. Paris, 1886.

Arc 440.2F Crawley-Boevey, A.W. A scheme for the protection and conservation of antient buildings...city of Ahmedabad. Bombay, 1886.

Arc 830.94 Danicourt, A. Étude sur quelques antiquités trouvées en Picardie. Paris, 1886.

Arc 1020.35 Delattre, R.P. Archéologie chrétienne de Carthage. Lyon, 1886.

Arc 66.1.44 Delaville Le Roulx, J. La France en Orient au XIVe siècle. Paris, 1886. 2v.

Arc 785.27 Dressel, H. Untersuchungen über Ziegelstempel des Geno Domitia. Berlin, 1886.

Arc 66.1.46 Durrieu, P. Archives angevines de Naples. Paris, 1886-1887. 2v.

Arc 830.22 Du Seigneur, M. Les arènes de Lutèce. Paris, 1886.

Arc 855.209.2F Dymond, C.W. Worlebury - an ancient stronghold. Bristol, 1886.

Arc 1033.12.17 Eberlé, L. Confrérie du Saint Suaire. Besançon, 1886.

Arc 66.1.43 Faucon, M. Libraire des papes d'Avignon. Paris, 1886. 2v.

Arc 583.2F Gayet, E. Musée du Louvre - Stèles de la XIIe Dynastie. pt.1-2. no.68. Paris, 1886.

Arc 1027.48 Germano di S. Stanislalo, P. Memorie archeologico...il cimitero S. Eutizio di Ferento. Roma, 1886.

Arc 430.3 Griffin, L. Famous monuments of central India. London, 1886.

Arc 905.41 Hampel, J. A Bronzkor emlékei magyarhonban. Budapest, 1886. 3v.

Arc 861.12.18 Hardy, James. On urns and other antiquities found round the southern skirts of the Cheviot Hills. n.p., 1886.

Arc 1025.55 Hasenclever, A. Der altchristliche Gräberschmuck. Braunschweig, 1886.

Arc 1033.17.57 Hilaire. Madone de Saint Luc. Paris, 1886.

Arc 87.1.46 Huelsen, C. Septizonim des Septimius Severus. Berlin, 1886.

Arc 500.5.5 Hull, E. The survey of Western Palestine. Adelphi, 1886.

Arc 785.1 Jordan, Henri. Tempel der Vesta und das Haus der Vestalinnen. Berlin, 1886.

Arc 1500.49 Joubert, André. Les monnaies anglo-françaises. Mamers, 1886.

Arc 1473.1.9 Lampros, Paulos. Mesaiōnika nomismara tēs Chiny. Athēnai, 1886.

1886 - cont.

Arc 1625.1 Low, Lyman H. Sketch of coinage of Mexican revolutionary General Morelos. N.Y., 1886.

Arc 1016.9.5 Lugari, G.B. L'aventino e le origine pagane e Christian di Roma. Roma, 1886.

Arc 66.1.47 Martin, A. Les cavaliers athéniens. Paris, 1886.

Arc 1200.15 MasLatrie, L. Les éléments de la diplomatique pontificale. Paris, 1886.

Arc 1020.52 Mély, F. de. Le trésor de Chartres. Paris, 1886.

Arc 1033.12.195 Métais, C. Processions de la sainte-larme à Vendome. Orléans, 1886.

Arc 1480.11 Mowat, Robert. Explication d'une marque monétaire du tempe de Constantin. Paris, 1886.

Arc 767.5 Muentz, E. Les antiquités de la ville de Rome. Paris, 1886.

Arc 885.4 Owen, E. Old stone crosses...ancient manners. London, 1886.

Arc 810.47.7 Pagano, N. Guide de Pompéi. 17. éd. Scafati, 1886.

Arc 495.203 Paine, T.O. Solomon's Temple. Boston, 1886.

Arc 1016.201 Palustre, L. Le trésor de Trèves. Paris, 1886.

Arc 585.3 Petrie, W.M.F. Naukratis. Pt.1-2. London, 1886-88. 2v.

Arc 830.149 Plat, Ernest. L'abbaye royale du Lieu-Notre-Dame-les-Romorantin. Romorantin, 1886.

Arc 870.2 Plenderleath, W.C. The white horses of the west of England. London, 1886.

Arc 983.3 Putnam, C.E. Elephant pipes and inscribed tablets in the Museum of the Academy of Natural Sciences. Davenport, 1886.

Arc 401.1.2 Quicherat, Jules. Mélanges d'archéologie du Moyen Age. Paris, 1886.

Arc 505.10 Raint. Lettre sur un plan du Haram El-Khalil. Paris, 1886.

Arc 785.15.13 Reinach, S. La colonne trajane au Musee de Saint-Germain. Paris, 1886.

Arc 657.1 Reinach, S. Conseils aux voyageurs archéologues en Grèce. Paris, 1886.

Arc 1330.40 Roda y Delgada, Juan de Dios de la. Bibliografia numismatica española. Madrid, 1886.

Arc 1500.27 Roman, J. Classement des monnaies épiscopales. Paris, 1886.

Arc 78.3.2 Rome. Accademia dei Lincei. Notizie degli Scavi. Indici epigrafici. 1876-85. Rome, 1886.

Arc 1025.15 Romeke, K. Rom's christliche Katakomben. Leipzig, 1886.

Arc 712.3 Ronchaud, L. de. Au Parthénon. Paris, 1886.

Arc 1033.122 Sanna Solaro, G. Acquisito conservazione, ristaurato degli arredi sacri. Torino, 1886.

Arc 682.1.9 Schliemann, Heinrich. Tiryns; the prehistoric palace of the kings of Tiryns. London, 1886.

Arc 1260.2 Schlumberger. G. Sceau inédit de Boniface de Montferrat. Paris, 1886.

Arc 501.15 Schumacher, G. Across the Jordan. London, 1886.

Arc 1340.7 Smith, Alfred M. Illustrated encyclopedia of gold and silver coins of the world. Philadelphia, 1886.

Arc 823.19.155 Thédenat, H. Deux masques d'enfants. Paris, 1886.

Arc 823.19.150 Thédenat, H. Milliaires du Var. Paris, 1886.

Arc 1027.10 Tizzani, V. Commissione de archeologia sagrada...Basilica di San Clemente. Roma, 1886.

Arc 890.208 Vedel, E. Bornholms oldtidsminder og oldsager. Kjøbenhavn, 1886.

Arc 1.1.3 Ward, W.H. Report on the Wolfe Expedition to Babylonia, 1884-85. Boston, 1886.

Arc 861.3.9 Watkin, W.T. Roman Cheshire. Liverpool, 1886.

Arc 1153.7.4 Wattenbach, W. Anleitung zur lateinischen Palaeographie. 4. Aufl. Leipzig, 1886.

Arc 880.20A Wood-Martin, W.G. The lake-dwellings of Ireland. Dublin, 1886.

NEDL Arc 893.5.3 Worsaae, J.J.A. The pre-history of the North. London, 1886.

1887

Arc 830.364 Audiat, Louis. Fouilles dans les remparts gallo-romains de saintes. Paris, 1887.

Arc 1349.55.5 Azzurri, Francesco. Cenni biografici di Bennedetto Pistrucci. Roma, 1887.

Arc 708.2 Baumgarten, Fritz. Ein Rundgang durch die Ruinen Athens. Wertheim, 1887.

Arc 700.3 Belger, C. Beiträge zur Kenntnis der Griechischen Kuppelgraeber. Berlin, 1887.

Arc 441.3F Bengal. Public Works Department. Revised list of ancient monuments in Bengal, 1886. Calcutta, 1887.

Arc 520.6 Berlin. Königliches Museum. Führer durch die Ruinen von Pergamon. Berlin, 1887.

Arc 1433.1 Bibliothèque Nationale, Paris. Catalogue des monnaies musulmanes. Paris, 1887-96. 3v.

Arc 920.206F Bobrinskii, A. Kurgany i sluchainyia arkheologicheskiia nakhodki. Sankt Petersburg, 1887.

Arc 756.7.3 Boissier, Gaston. Promenades archéologiques, Rome et Pompéi. 3. éd. Paris, 1887.

Arc 1033.12.127 Bortolan, D. S. spina di Vicenza. Vicenza, 1887.

Arc 830.20 Boucher de Molandon. Le tumulus de Reuilly. Orléans, 1887.

Arc 1208.1 British Museum. Catalogue of seals in the department of manuscripts. London, 1887-1900. 6v.

Arc 1538.2.15 British Museum. Department of Coins and Medals. A catalogue of English coins in the British Museum. Anglo-Saxon series. London, 1887-93. 2v.

Arc 861.7 Brown, J.A. Paleolithic man in northwest Middlesex. London, 1887.

Arc 746.1 Brunn, H. Über die Ausgrabungen der Certosa von Bologna. München, 1887.

Arc 435.2.6F Burgess, James. The Buddhist stupas of Amarayati and Jaggayyapeta. London, 1887.

Arc 1510.7 Cerexhe, M. Les monnaies de Charlemagne. Gand, 1887.

Arc 552.1.6 Champollion-Figeac, J.J. Les deux Champollion, leur vie. Grenoble, 1887.

Arc 501.16.8 Conder, C.R. Syrian stone-lore. N.Y., 1887.

Arc 501.16.7 Conder, C.R. Tent work in Palestine. London, 1887.

Arc 1033.57 Cozza-Luzi, G. Di un antico filiatterio christiano. Napoli, 1887.

Arc 1033.17.100 Cuevas, J. de J. La santissima virgen de Guadalupe. México, 1887.

Arc 1030.12 Delattre, R.P. Inscriptions chrétiennes. Constantine, 1887.

Arc 608.2.5 Delattre, R.P. Notice sur les plombs chrétiens trouvés à Carthage. Lyon, 1887.

Chronological Listing

1887 - cont.

Arc 1153.1 Delisle, L. Forme des abréviations et des liaisons dans les lettres des papes. Paris, 1887.
Arc 1583.6 Demmeni, M. Sbornik' ukazov' po monetnomu delu. Sankt Peterburg, 1887. 3v.
Arc 1033.17.544 Diotallevi, D. Notizie della prodigiosa immagine di Maria Sma. della Grazie a Pta Angelica in Roma. Roma, 1887.
Arc 561.1.10 Ebers, George. Richard Lepsius. N.Y., 1887.
Arc 1498.1 Engel, A. Répertoire...de la numismatique française. Paris, 1887-89. 2v.
Arc 1505.6 Engel, Arthur. Numismatique de l'Alsace. Paris, 1887.
Arc 785.37 Fonteanive, R. Sui munimenti ed altre costruzione poligonie...provincia romana. Roma, 1887.
Arc 855.219.5F Fox-Pitt-Rivers. Excavations in Cranbone Chase. London, 1887-1905. 5v.
Arc 375.3F Gay, V. Glossaire archéologique. Paris, 1887-1928. 2v.
Arc 858.16 The gentleman's magazine library - Romano-British remains. London, 1887. 2v.
Arc 1020.80.7 Geoffroy de Couleron. Livre des reliques de l'abbaye de St. Pierre-le-Vif de Sens. Sens, 1887.
Arc 1660.17F Gnechi, Francesco. Le monete dei Trivulzio. Milano, 1887.
Arc 845.202 Grempler, Wilhelm. Der Fund von Sackrau. pts.1-3. Berlin, 1887-88.
Arc 1538.8 Hawkins, E. The silver coins of England. London, 1887.
Arc 1468.6 Head, B.V. Historia numorum. Oxford, 1887.
Arc 1560.1 Hildebrand, H. Sveriges mynt under medeltiden. Stockholm, 1887.
Arc 530.1.5 Hirschfeld, G. Felsenreliefs in Kleinasien und die Volk der Hitteter. Berlin, 1887.
Arc 66.1.49 Homolle, T. Archives de l'intendance sacrée à Délos. Paris, 1887.
Arc 1470.3 Imhoof-Blumer, Friedrich. Zur Münzkunde Grossgriechenlands. Wien, 1887.
Arc 960.1 Kunz, G.F. Gold and silver ornaments from mounds of Florida. Chicago, 1887.
Arc 1264.2 Lalore, C. Le sceau et les armoiries...Saint Pierre de Troyes. Troyes, 1887.
Arc 1663.15 Laverrenz, C. Die Medaillen und Gedachtniszeichen der deutschen Hochschulen. Berlin, 1887. 2v.
Arc 1208.2 Le Clert, Louis. Catalogue de sigillographie du Musée de Troyes. Troyes, 1887.
Arc 1025.13 Liell, H.F.J. Die Darstellungen...Maria...Katakomben. Freiburg, 1887.
Arc 736.2.4 Lupus, B. Die Stadt Skyrakus im Alterthum. Strassburg, 1887.
Arc 967.1.2 McAdams, William. Records of ancient races. St. Louis, 1887.
Arc 1550.3 Mansfeld-Bûllner, H.V. Afbildninger af danske mønter, 1241-1377. Kjøbenhavn, 1887.
Arc 397.6 March, H.C. An examination of the tithe. Rochdale, 1887. 5 pam.
Arc 1348.14 Marsy, Arthur. Cueilloir numismatique. n.p., 1887.
Arc 785.13.29 Marucchi, O. Nova descrizione della casa dell Vestali. Roma, 1887.
Arc 562.2 Maspero, Gaston. L'archéologie égyptienne (in Bibliothèque de l'Enseignement des Beaux-Arts). Paris, 1887.
Arc 562.2.5 Maspero, Gaston. Egyptian archaeology. N.Y., 1887.
Arc 767.3 Mayerhoefer, A. Studien über das alte Rom. München, 1887.
Arc 1020.52.9 Mély, F. de. Les inventaires de l'Abbaye Saint Pére en Vallés de Chartres. Paris, 1887.
Arc 925.9 Mourier, J. L'archéologie au Caucase. Paris, 1887.
Arc 708.12 Moüy, Charles. Lettres athéniennes. Paris, 1887.
Arc 66.1.48 Muentz, E. Bibliothèque du Vatican au XVe siècle. Paris, 1887.
Arc 397.4 Müntz, Eugène. Études iconographiques et archéologiques. Paris, 1887.
Arc 853.12 Naelier, J. Die römischen Militarstrassen. Strassburg, 1887.
Arc 585.5F Naville, E.H. The shrine of Saft el Henneh. Malagny, 1887.
Arc 1027.19 Nortet. Les catacombes de Saint Calixte. Rome, 1887.
Arc 845.201 Nürnberg. Deutschen Anthropologischen Gesellschaft. Festschrift zur Begrüssung des XVIII. Kongresses der Gesellschaft. Nürnberg, 1887.
Arc 87.1.47 Puchstein, O. Das ionische Capitell. Berlin, 1887.
Arc 1423.10 Reinach, Théodore. Les monnaies juives. Paris, 1887.
Arc 1335.88F Rollin et Teuardent, firm, Paris. Monnaies d'or romaines et byzantines. Paris, 1887.
Arc 823.4.8 Roman, M.J. Répertoire archéologique du département du Hautes-Alpes. Paris, 1887.
Arc 1033.17.98 Rosa, Agustin de. Dissertatio historico-theologica de apparitione B.M.V. de Guadalupe. Guadalaxarae, 1887.
Arc 1030.5.50 Rossi, G.B. de. Adunanze solenne in commemorazione di Guglielmo Henzen. Roma, 1887.
Arc 830.139 Sacaze, Julien. Histoire ancienne de Luchon. Saint-Gaudens, 1887.
Arc 726.18 Saccardo, G. I pilastri acritani. Venezia, 1887.
Arc 1335.37 Sambon, G. Catalogo delle monete italiane...collezione A. Cantoni di Milano. Milano, 1887.
Arc 730.203 Scarabelli, Gommi. Stazione prehistorica sul monte del Castel. Imola, 1887.
Arc 1590.1 Schlumberger, G. Une nouvelle monnaie a legende grecque...de Cappadoce. Paris, 1887.
Arc 835.5 Siret, H. Les premiers ages du métal dans le sud-est de l'Espagne. Antwerp, 1887. 2v.
Arc 94.7 Sociedad Arqueologica de Carmona. Memorias de la sociedad arqueologica de Carmona. Carmona, 1887. 9v.
Arc 708.26 Sophoules, T. Peritou Archaioterou Attikou Ergastēriou. Athēnai, 1887.
Arc 1076.3.13.5 Stahlschmidt, J.C.L. The church bells of Kent. London, 1887.
Arc 1675.17.5 Storer, H.R. Medals, jetons and tokens illustrative of obstetrics and gynaecology. Bridgeport, Conn., 1887.
Arc 983.12.5 Thomas, C. Work in mound exploration of the Bureau of Ethnology. Washington, 1887.
Arc 726.20.3 Tononi, A.G. Velleia studiata da un erudita francese. n.p., 1887.
Arc 405.1.30 Uvarov, Aleksei S. Katalog sobraniia drevnostei. v.1,3-11. Moskva, 1887- 10v.
NEDL Arc 1088.1.10 Vars, J. L'art nautique dans l'antiquité. Paris, 1887.
Arc 1033.17.99.5 Vera, Fortino Hipólito. Tesoro guadalupano. Amecameca, 1887.
Arc 600.4 Winslow, W.C. Naukratis - a Greek city in Egypt. Boston, 1887.
Arc 505.5.7 Wolff, P.O. Der Tempel von Jerusalem. Graz, 1887.

1887 - cont.

Arc 858.52 Wright, G.R. Archaeologic and historic fragments. London, 1887.
Arc 1273.1 Wyon, A. The great seals of England. London, 1887.

1888

Arc 1027.22 Achelis, H. Das Symbol des Fisches...Fischi der Römische Katakombe. Marburg, 1888.
Arc 830.60 Allmer, Auguste. Trion. Lyon, 1888.
Arc 1.8 Archeological review. London, 1888-90. 4v.
Arc 1027.42 Atti del collegium cultorum martyrum. Romae, 1888.
Arc 416.1 Babelon, E. Manuel d'archéologie orientale. Paris, 1888.
Arc 785.54 Barsari, Luigi. Del Pons Agruppae sul Tevere tra le regioni IX e XIII. Roma, 1888.
Arc 708.2.3 Baumgarten, Fritz. Ein Rundgang durch die Ruinen Athens. Leipzig, 1888.
Arc 386.2 Baye, J. de. L'archéologie préhistorique. Paris, 1888.
Arc 395.1.5 Bernhardi, K. Textbuch zu Th. Sc[illegible]eibers Kulturhistorischem Bilderatlas des klassischen Altertums. Leipzig, 1888.
Arc 1500.10 Blancard, Louis. Nouveau classement des monnaies bretonnes. Marseille, 1888-89.
Arc 1390.4 Blancard, Louis. L'origine du marc. Macon, 1888.
Arc 710.2.2 Boetticher, C. Die Akropolis von Athen. Berlin, 1888.
Arc 1018.20 Bonavenia. Una pittura di basilica di Antiochia. Roma, 1888.
Arc 865.14 Brown and Company, Salisbury, publishers. Illustrated guide to Old Sarum and Stonehenge. London, 1888.
Arc 1016.4 Busiri Vici, A. La colonna santa. Tempio de Gerusalemme. Roma, 1888.
Arc 830.147F Catalogue du trésor de Chaource. Paris, 1888.
Arc 1260.4 Cecchetti, B. Bolle dei dogi di Venezia. Venezia, 1888.
Arc 1033.17.424 Charpentier, L.F. Nouveau histoire de l'image miraculeux de Notre-Dame-de-Liesse. Soissons, 1888.
VArc 416.2 Clermont-Ganneau, Charles. Recueil d'archéologie orientale. Paris, 1888-1924. 8v.
Arc 790.35 Comparette, D. Villa ercolanese dei Pisoni i suoi monumenti. Torino, 1888.
Arc 1433.4 Cunningham, A. Coins of the Indo-Scythians. pt.1-2. London, 1888.
Arc 608.2.3 Delattre, A.L. Souvenir de la Croisade de Saint-Louis trouvé à Carthage. Lyon, 1888.
Arc 1150.208.9F Delisle, L. L'evangeliaire de Saint-Vaast d'Arras. Paris, 1888.
X Cg Arc 66.1.53 Diehl, C. Études sur l'administration Byzantine. Paris, 1888.
Arc 421.1 Dumontier, G. Le grand-Bouddha de Hanoi. Hanoi, 1888.
Arc 861.4 Earwaker, J.P. The recent discoveries of Roman remains found in the...City of Chester. Manchester, 1888.
Arc 520.2 Graeber, F. Die Wasserleitungen von Pergamon. Berlin, 1888.
Arc 1053.6.6F Graul, Richard. Die antiken Porträtgemälde aus den Grabstätten des Fayum. Leipzig, 1888.
Arc 945.2 Grossi, V. Teocalli e piramidi. Torino, 1888.
Arc 87.1.48 Herrmann, P. Graeberfeld von Marion. Berlin, 1888.
Arc 647.2 Herzog, A. Studien zur Geschichte der griechischen Kunst. Leipzig, 1888.
Arc 838.2 Hübner, E. La arqueologia de España. Barcelona, 1888.
Arc 845.3 Kempten. Allgaüer Alterthumsverein. Bericht ueber die...Ausgrabungen. v.1-4. Kempten, 1888. 2v.
Arc 766.1.2.8 Lanciani, R. Ancient Rome in the light of recent discoveries. Boston, 1888.
Arc 766.1.2.10 Lanciani, R. Ancient Rome in the light of recent discoveries. London, 1888.
Arc 766.1.2.11 Lanciani, R. Ancient Rome in the light of recent discoveries. London, 1888.
Htn Arc 766.1.2.7* Lanciani, R. Ancient Rome in the light of recent discoveries. 7. ed. Boston, 1888.
Arc 766.1.2A Lanciani, R. Ancient Rome in the light of recent excavations. Boston, 1888.
X Cg Arc 651.1 Le Bas, P. Voyage archéologique en Grèce et en Asie Mineure. Paris, 1888.
Arc 1033.95 Le Blant, E. D'un nouveau monument...Sainte Félicité. Rome, 1888.
Arc 1033.110 Le Blant, E. Les premiers Chrétiens et le Démon. Rome, 1888.
Arc 1408.10 L'Ecluse, Charles de. Monnaies orientales. Paris, 1888.
Arc 66.1.52 Lécrivain, C. Le Sénat Romain depuis Dioclétien. Paris, 1888.
X Cg Arc 1603.4 Lerouv, J. Le médaillier du Canada. Montreal, 1888.
Arc 1015.209 Lugari, G.B. Le catacombe ossia il sepolcro. Roma, 1888.
Arc 830.115 Lunet, B. La ville de Rodez à l'époque romaine. Rodez, 1888.
Arc 1027.4.11 Marucchi, O. Le nuove scoperte nelle catacombe di Priscilla. v.1-2. Roma, 1888.
Arc 1027.15.9 Marucchi, O. Le recenti scoperte presso il cimitero di San Valentino. Roma, 1888.
Arc 1020.13 Molinier, E. Inventaire du trésor du Saint Siège. Paris, 1888.
Arc 1076.3.23 Morillot, L. Étude sur l'emploi de clochettes. Dijon, 1888.
Arc 890.206 Mueller, S. Ordnung af Danmark's oldsager stenalderen. Paris, 1888. 2v.
Arc 1163.1 Muñoz y Rivero, J. Idioma y escritura de España. Madrid, 1888.
Arc 585.1 Naville, E.H. The store-city of Pithom. 3. ed. London, 1888.
Arc 600.1.2 Néroutsos-Bey, T.D. L'ancienne Alexandrie. Paris, 1888.
Arc 1030.8.13 Nestorian Tablet of Sian-fu. The Nestorian monument of Hsian Fu in Shen-hsi, China, 7th and 8th centuries. London, 1888.
Arc 810.44 Neville-Rolfe, Eustace. Pompeii, popular and practical. Naples, 1888.
Arc 1027.19.2 Nortet. Cimetière de Saint Calixte. 3e éd. Rome, 1888.
Arc 1153.2 Paoli, Cesare. Programma scolastico di paleografia latina. Firenze, 1888.
Arc 510.207 Pottier, E. La Nécropole de Myrina. Paris, 1888. 2v.
Arc 402.1 Rayet, O. Études d'archéologie et d'art. Paris, 1888.
Arc 969.1 Read, M.C. Archaeology of Ohio. Cleveland, 1888.
Arc 402.2.2 Reinach, S. Esquisses archéologiques. Paris, 1888.
Arc 87.2.88 Roemische Lager in Bonn. Bonn, 1888.
Arc 1025.29 Rossi, G.B. de. Del luogo appellato ad Caprean. Roma, 1888.
Arc 1030.5.17 Rossi, G.B. de. Della praepositus della via flaminia. n.p., 1888.

1888 - cont.

Arc 1030.5.31 Rossi, G.B. de. L'inscription du tombeau d'Hadrien I. Rome, 1888.
Arc 1030.5.3 Rossi, G.B. de. Il tomo secondo delle conferenze di Chiusura. Roma, 1888.
Arc 1033.12.166.15 Le Saint Clou de Toul. Nancy, 1888. 3 pam.
Arc 925.27F Samokvasov, D. Sbornik topograffiia sved. o kurgana. St. Peterburg, 1888.
Arc 835.202F Santos Rocha, A. dos. Antiquidades prehistoricas do conselho da Figueira. v.1-4. Coimbra, 1888-1900. 2v.
Arc 501.15.8 Schumacher, G. The Jaulân. London, 1888.
Arc 838.12 Simões, A.F. Escriptos diversos. Coimbra, 1888.
Arc 74.4.2F Society for the Promotion of Hellenic Studies. Journal. Plates 1-83. v.1-8. London, 1888?
Arc 635.214 Stillman, W.J. On the track of Ulysses. Boston, 1888.
Arc 1663.6 Storer, H.R. Les médailles de la Princesse Charlotte d'Angleterre. Bruxelles, 1888-91. 2 pam.
Arc 785.5 Sturm, J. Das kaiserliches Stadium auf dem Palatin. Würzburg, 1888.
Arc 1033.78 Taglialatela, G. Le solenni feste della traslazione dei martiri di Atripalda. Pompei, 1888.
Arc 830.22.11 Toulouze, Eugène. Mes fouilles dans le sol du vieux Paris. Dunkerque, 1888.
Arc 600.8 Wendel, F.C.H. Über die in altägyptischen Texten erwähnten Bau- und Edelsteine. Leipzig, 1888.
Arc 905.7 Wosinsky, M. Das prähistorische Schanzwerk von Lengyel. Budapest, 1888.

1889

VArc 497.90 Ackermann, Peter Fourier. Bibliai régiségtan. Eger, 1889.
Arc 1540.18 Atkins, James. The coins and tokens of the possessions and colonies of the British empire. London, 1889.
Arc 416.1.2 Babelon, E. Manual of Oriental antiquities. N.Y., 1889.
Arc 1510.174F Bahrfeldt, Emil. Das Münzwesen der Mark Brandenburg. Berlin, 1889- 2v.
Arc 1020.18 Bendixen, B.E. Aus der mittelalterlichen Sammlung des Museums in Bergen. Bergen, 1889-
Arc 510.6 Benndorf, O. Das Heroon von Gjoelbaschi-Trysa. Vienna, 1889. 2v.
Arc 823.1.5 Bertrand, A. Archéologie celtique et gaulois. Paris, 1889.
Arc 1680.9.3 Boyne, William. Trade tokens...seventeenth century...England, Wales and Ireland. London, 1889. 2v.
Arc 1190.1 Bresslau, H. Handbuch der Urkundenlehre fuer Deutschland und Italien. Leipzig, 1889.
Arc 983.10 Brinton, D.G. The Taki, the Swastika, and the Cross in America. Philadelphia, 1889.
Arc 1027.3.5 Carini, I. Il crocifesso negli antichi monumenti. Roma, 1889.
Arc 1335.155 Chalon, Renier. Collection de feu M. Renier Chalon. v.2. Bruxelles, 1889.
Arc 500.5 Conder, C.R. Memoirs of the topography. London, 1889.
Arc 497.5 Conder, C.R. Palestine. London, 1889.
Arc 497.5.3 Conder, C.R. Palestine. N.Y., 1889.
Arc 612.8 Cotteau, G.H. Le préhistorique en Europe. Paris, 1889.
Arc 830.143 Cougny, G. de. Chinon et ses monuments. 3. éd. Chinon, 1889.
Arc 497.17 Dawson, J.W. Modern science in Bible lands. N.Y., 1889.
Arc 66.1.55 Diehl, C. L'église...du Couvent de Saint-Luc en Procide. Paris, 1889.
Arc 1580.5 Donebauer, Max. Beschreibung der Sammlung böhmischer Münzen. pt.1-2. Prag, 1889-90.
Arc 635.206 Dumon, K. Le théâtre de Polyclète. Paris, 1889.
Arc 1498.1.2 Engel, A. Répertoire...de la numismatique française. Supplément et table. Paris, 1889.
Arc 1470.40 Evans, A.J. The "Horsemen" of Tarentum. London, 1889.
Arc 1613.2.3 Evans, G.G. Illustrated history of the United States mint. Philadelphia, 1889.
Arc 435.2.11F Führer, A.A. The Sharqi architecture of Jaunpur. Calcutta, 1889.
Arc 1428.8 Furse, E.H. Mémories numismatiques de l'ordre...St. Jean de Jerusalem. Rome, 1889.
Arc 1020.10.46 Gerbet, O.P. Esquisse de Rome chrétienne. Paris, 1889. 3v.
Arc 585.9 Griffith, F.L. Two hieroglyphic papyri from Tanis. London, 1889.
Arc 935.9 Grosvenor, E.A. The hippodrome of Constantinople. London, 1889.
Arc 672.1.31F Halbherr, F. Relazione sugli scavi...in Gortyna. Roma, 1889.
Arc 1348.16 Halke, H. Einleitung in das Studium des Numismatik. Berlin, 1889.
Arc 953.3 Haynes, H.W. The prehistoric archaeology of North America. Boston, 1889.
Arc 537.1 Hogarth, D.G. Devia Cypria. London, 1889.
X Cg Arc 1665.1 Imhoof-Blumer, F. Tier- und Pflanzenbilder auf Münzen und Gemmen. Leipzig, 1889.
Arc 1033.163 Kardag. Die Geschichte des Mâr Abhdiso und seines Jüngers Mâr Quardagh. Kiel, 1889.
Arc 1160.11 Kaulek, J. Recueil de fac-simile...paléographie moderne. Paris, 1889.
Arc 87.1.49 Kekule, R. Bronzestatue des sogenannten Idolino. Berlin, 1889.
Arc 810.8 Lagrèze, G.B. de. Pompéi, les catacombes, l'Alhambra. Paris, 1889.
Arc 1020.22 Lampake, G. Christianichē archaiologia. Athēnai, 1889.
X Cg Arc 1020.22.5 Lampake, G. Hē monē daphnioy. Athēnai, 1889.
Arc 766.1.2.12 Lanciani, R. Ancient Rome in the light of recent discoveries. 5. ed. Boston, 1889.
Arc 1212.1 Lecoy de la Marche, A. Les sceaux. Paris, 1889.
Arc 889.6 Loë, Alfred de. Le dolmen de Solwaster. Bruxelles, 1889.
Arc 136.1.3 London Society of Antiquaries. Index to Archaeologia. v.1-50. London, 1889.
Arc 628.9 Lovatelli-Caetani, E. Antichi monumenti illustrati. Roma, 1889.
Arc 1033.58 Lugari, G.B. S. Sebastiano; memorie. Roma, 1889.
Arc 1076.3.67F Lyman, Charles. The church bells of the county of Stafford. London, 1889.
Arc 845.4 Mainz, Germany. Römisch-Germanische Centralmuseum. Das Römisch-Germanische Centralmuseum. Mainz, 1889.
Arc 1663.16.10 Majorca Mortillaro, L.M. Ventitre medaglie borboniche napoletane. Pitigliano, 1889.
NEDL Arc 726.40 Meomartini, A. I monumenti e le opere d'arte. Benevento, 1889.

1889 - cont.

Arc 767.6.5 Mirabilia urbis Romae. London, 1889.
Arc 416.7F Moskovskoe Arkheologicheskoe Obshchestvo. Drevnosti vostoch'iia trudi vostochnoi kommissii. Moskva, 1889-1915. 5v.
Arc 1163.2.15 Muñoz y Rivero, J. Manual de paleografía diplomática española. Madrid, 1889.
Arc 750.38 Narducci, P. Sulla fognatura della città di Roma. Roma, 1889. 2v.
Arc 66.1.54 Noiret, H. Lettres inedites de Michel Apostolis. Paris, 1889.
Arc 1153.2.9 Paoli, Cesare. Grundriss - lateinische Palaeographie. Innsbruck, 1889-95.
Arc 510.201.2 Petersen, E. Reiden in Lykien, Milyas und Kibyratis. Vienna, 1889.
Arc 585.2.2F Petrie, W.M.F. Tanis. Pt.1. 2. ed. London, 1889.
Arc 545.208FA Petrie, William M.F. Hawara, Biahmu and Arsinoe. London, 1889.
Arc 673.1 Pomtow, H. Beiträge zur Topographie von Delphi. Berlin, 1889.
Arc 435.21 Rice, B.L. Epigraphia carnatica. v.1-2. Bangalore, 1889- 15v.
Arc 772.5 Richter, O. Geographie und Geschichte des Römischen Altertums. Nordlingen, 1889.
Arc 772.5.5 Richter, O. Topographie der Stadt Rom. Nordlingen, 1889.
Arc 387.1.25 Rocheblave, S. Essai sur le comte de Caylus. Paris, 1889.
Arc 618.2 Roger, J.C. Celticism a myth. 2. ed. London, 1889.
Arc 1033.26 Rossi, G.B. de. Dissertazione postume del P. Luigi Bruzza. Roma, 1889.
Arc 726.27 Rossi, G.B. de. Porticus triumphi. Roma, 1889.
Arc 1020.9.45 Rossi, G.B. di. Miscellania...la topografia...dei monumenti de Roma. Roma, 1889.
Arc 1027.23.17 Schulke, V. Die altchristlichen Bildwerke. Erlangen, 1889.
Arc 501.15.4 Schumacher, G. Abila of the Decapolis. London, 1889. 3 pam.
Arc 501.15.2 Schumacher, G. Across the Jordan. London, 1889.
Arc 505.2 Simonsen, D. Sculptures et inscriptions de Palmyre. Copenhagen, 1889.
Arc 513.1 Sterrett, J.R.S. Leaflets from the notebook of an archaeological traveller in Asia Minor. Austin, 1889.
Arc 1340.2 Stevenson, Seth William. A dictionary of Roman coins. London, 1889.
Arc 969.1.15 Thomas, Cyrus. The problem of the Ohio mounds. Washington, 1889.
Arc 920.207F Tolstoi, I. Russkiia drebnosti b' pamiatnikakh iskusstva. v.1-3, 4-6. Sankt Petersburg, 1889-99. 2v.
Arc 1033.17.99 Vera, Fortino Hipólito. Informaciones sobre la milagrosa aparición de la virgen de Guadalupe. Amecameca, 1889.
Arc 600.235 Virey, Philippe. Quelques observations sur l'épisode d'Aristée; à propos d'un monument égyptien. Paris, 1889. Paris, 1889.
Arc 1018.12 Wilpert, J. Principienfragen der christliche Archäologie. Freiburg, 1889.

189-

Arc 497.35 Courtin, Louis. Collection de Louis Courtin. Paris, 189-.
Arc 726.11.7 Héron de Villefosse, Antoine. Le trésor d'argenterie de Boscoreale. Paris, 189-.
Arc 830.22.13 Nagne, Charles. Les voies romaines de l'antique Lutèce. Paris, 189-?
Arc 400.16 Pietto, E. Études d'ethnographie préhistorique. Paris, 189-. 9 pam.
Arc 1027.19.35 Trappists. Selecta ex coemeterio Si Callisti. Roma, 189-?

1890

Arc 275.16 Arkheologicheskii s"ezd, 8th, Moscow, 1890. Katalog vystavki VIII Arkheologicheskago s"ezda v Moskve, 1890 g. Pt.1-10. Moskva, 1890.
Arc 385.1 Aus der Anomia; archaeologische Beitraege. Berlin, 1890.
Arc 1086.2 Bachofen, J.J. Römische Grablampen. Basel, 1890.
Arc 1033.124 Bargès, Jean. Notice sur quelques antels chrétiens. Paris, 1890.
Arc 1468.5 Bibliothèque Nationale, Paris. Département des Médailles et Antiques. Catalogue des monnaies grecques. Les rois de Syrie, d'Arménie et de Commagène. Paris, 1890.
Arc 1500.5.35 Bibliothèque Nationale, Paris. Département des Médailles et Antiques. Inventaire sommaire des monnaies mérovingiennes de la collection d'Amécourt. Paris, 1890.
Arc 1390.1.5 Blanchet, J.A. Nouveau manuel de numismatique du moyen age et moderne. Text et atlas. Paris, 1890. 3v.
Arc 522.4.15 Boetticher, E. Hissarlik wie es ist. Berlin, 1890.
Arc 1668.2 Bolton, H.C. Contribution of alchemy to numismatics. N.Y., 1890.
Arc 1603.1 Breton, P.N. Le collectionneur...des monnaies canadiennes. Montreal, 1890.
Arc 635.211 Cabrol, E. Voyage en Grèce. Paris, 1890.
Arc 1015.226 Carini, I. Catacombe di S. Giovanni in Siracusa. Roma, 1890.
Arc 1033.100 Carini, Isidoro. Simbolismo dei primi secoli. Romae, 1890.
Arc 845.1 Chlingensperg-Berg, M. von. Das Graeberfeld von Reichenhall. Reichenhall, 1890.
Arc 643.1 Diehl, C. Excursions archéologiques en Grèce. Paris, 1890.
Arc 485.201 Dieulafoy, M. L'acropole de Suse. Paris, 1890-92. 4v.
Arc 66.1.57 Duerrbach, F. L'orateur Lycurgue. Paris, 1890.
Arc 389.2 Ely, Talfourd. Manual of archaeology. N.Y., 1890.
Arc 1613.2 Evans, G.G. Illustrated history of the United States mint. Philadelphia, 1890.
Arc 630.1 Fink, J. Der Verschluss bei den Griechen und Römern. Regensburg, 1890.
Arc 855.219 Fox-Pitt-Rivers. King John's house, Tollard Royal, Wilts. n.p., 1890.
Arc 1468.4 Frochner, W. Monnaies grecques de la collection Photiadès Pacha. Paris, 1890.
Arc 1033.62.9 Führer, Joseph. Ein Beitrag zur Lösung zer Felicitas-Frage. Leipzig, 1890.
Arc 1138.3 Grand, E. Daniel. Leçon d'ouverture du cours de paléographie. Montpellier, 1890.
Arc 595.12 Grossi, V. Le leggende delle piramidi. Genova, 1890.
X Cg Arc 510.202 Humann, K. Reisen in Kleinasien und Nordsyrien. Text and atlas. Berlin, 1890. (Changed to XP 9867) 2v.

Chronological Listing

1890 - cont.

Arc 1465.79 Imhoof-Blumer, Friedrich. Griechische Münzen. München, 1890.

Arc 726.54 Iozzi, Oliviero. Cenno storico della antica Libarna. Pisa, 1890.

Arc 635.210 Kinch, K.F. L'Arc de Triomphe de Salonique. Paris, 1890.

Arc 543.11F Kondakov, N.P. Opic' pamiatnikov' drevnosti. Sankt Peterburg, 1890.

Arc 1016.204 Kraus, F.X. Die altchristlichen Inschriften der Rheinlande. Freiburg, 1890.

Arc 785.9 Lanciani, R. Ricerche sulle XIV regioni urbane. Roma, 1890.

Arc 1030.9 Le Blant, E. L'épigraphie chrétienne en Gaule. n.p., 1890.

Arc 963.1 Lewis, T.H. Stone monuments in northwestern Iowa and southwestern Minnesota. n.p., 1890?

Arc 562.1.5 Mariette, A. The monuments of upper Egypt. Boston, 1890.

X Cg Arc 1027.15 Marucchi, O. Il cimitero e la Basilica di San Valentino. Roma, 1890.

Arc 1640.7F Meili, Julius. Die auf das Kaiserreich Brasilien...1822 bis 1889. Zürich, 1890.

Arc 1645.1.7 Meili, Julius. Die Münzen des Kaiserreichs Brasilien, 1822-1889. Leipzig, 1890.

Arc 861.36 Michell-Whitley, H. Discovery of Roman-British remains. n.p., 1890.

Arc 275.101 Miliukov, P.N. VIII Arkheologicheskii s"ezd v Moskve. Moskva, 1890.

Arc 969.1.3 Moorehead, W.K. Fort Ancient. Cincinnati, 1890.

Arc 1500.3 Morel-Fatio, A. Catalogue raisonné de la collection de deniers merovingiens. Paris, 1890.

Arc 1163.2 Muñoz y Rivero, J. Scripturae hispanae veteris. Matriti, 1890.

Arc 612.3 Munro, Robert. The lake-dwellings of Europe. London, 1890.

Htn Arc 545.206* Le Musée Egyptien. v.1-4. Cairo, 1890-1924.

NEDL Arc 585.7 Naville, E.H. Mound of the Jew and City of Onias. London, 1890.

Arc 785.13.63 Nichols, Francis M. A revised history of the column of Phocas in the Roman Forum. Westminster, 1890.

X Cg Arc 510.206 Niemann, S. Les villes de la Pamphylie et de la Pisidie. Paris, 1890-1893. 2v.

Arc 953.8 Peet, S.D. Prehistoric America. v.1, The mound builders. v.3, Cliff dwellers. v.4, Ancient monuments. v.5, Myths and symbols. Chicago, 1890-1905. 4v.

Arc 588.2 Petrie, W.M.F. Kahum, Gurob, and Hawara. London, 1890.

Arc 655.1 Philios, Demetrios. Peri tou pōs graphontai ta tōn araskaphōn. Athēnai, 1890.

X Cg Arc 513.13 Ramsay, W.M. The historical geography of Asia Minor. v.1-2. London, 1890.

Arc 513.13 Ramsay, W.M. The historical geography of Asia Minor. v.1-2. Photoreproduction. London, 1890.

Arc 1076.3.55 Raven, John J. The church bells of Suffolk. London, 1890.

Arc 87.1.50 Robert, C. Homerische Becher. Berlin, 1890.

Arc 1027.4.35 Rossi, G.B. de. La basilica di S. Silvestro nel cimitero di Priscilla. Roma, 1890.

Arc 1030.5.35 Rossi, G.B. de. Iscrizione in un spillo d'oso, trovato a Bolsena. Roma, 1890.

Arc 1033.71 Rossi, J.B. de. La capsella d'argent africaine. Caen, 1890.

Arc 672.2 Schmidt, B. Korkyraeische Studien. Leipzig, 1890. 2v.

NEDL Arc 658.3.4 Schuchhardt, K. Schliemanns Ausgrabungen. Leipzig, 1890.

Arc 501.15.5 Schumacher, G. Northern Ajlûn. London, 1890.

Arc 855.2 Skelton, J. The Royal House of Stuart. London, 1890.

Arc 815.2 Smith, F.W. The Pompeia. Saratoga, 1890.

Arc 974.1 Thruston, G.P. The antiquities of Tennessee. Cincinnati, 1890.

Arc 1588.1.13 Tyszkiewicz, J. Guide de l'amateur de monnaies polonaises. Posen, 1890.

Arc 608.7.5 Université de l'Instruction Publique. Recherches des antiquités dans le nord de l'Afrique. Paris, 1890.

Arc 1018.12.8 Wilpert, J. Nochmals Principienfragen. Rom, 1890.

Arc 407.6.5 Wilson, John Albert. Study of prehistoric anthropology. Washington, 1890.

Arc 518.1.5 Wood, J.T. Modern discoveries on the site of ancient Ephesus. London, 1890.

Arc 895.14 Zinck, L. Nordisk archaelogi. Kjøbenhavn, 1890.

1891

Arc 1.1.5 Archaeological Institute of America. Index to publications, 1879-89. Cambridge, 1891.

Arc 1077.4 Archaic rock inscriptions...cup and ring markings. London, 1891.

Arc 1498.4 Barthélemy, A. de. Numatisque de la France. Paris, 1891.

Arc 612.22F Baye, Joseph. De l'influence de l'art des Goths en Occident. Paris, 1891.

Arc 830.6 Bazin, H. Villes antiques - Vienne et Lyon gallo-romain. Paris, 1891.

Arc 823.1 Bertrand, A. Nos origines - La Gaule avant les Gaulois. Paris, 1891.

Arc 1153.35 Bosseboeuf, L.A. École de calligraphie et de miniature de Tours. Tours, 1891.

Arc 1027.12.9 Bufalieré, P. La basilica apostolorum e la critta apostolica. Roma, 1891.

Arc 1027.47 Bufalieri da Montécelio, P. Ricersa...tomba S. Cecilia. Roma, 1891.

Arc 1301.3 Bulletin de numisnatique. v.1-3,4-7,8-13. Paris, 1891-1906. 3v.

Arc 66.1.59 Cadier, L. Essai sur l'administration du Royaume de Sicile. Paris, 1891.

Arc 1030.24 Carini, I. Dell'utilità che la teologia può trarre dall'epigrafia. Roma, 1891.

Arc 1033.17.250 Castellano, U. Ave Maria. La milagrosa imagen de Nuestra Señora del Rosario. Córdoba, 1891.

Arc 730.2.2 Cavallari, F.S. Appendice. Topografia archaeologica. Siracusa. Torino, 1891.

Arc 1588.4.10 Cermák, K. Mince kralowstvi Českéko za panováné rodu Habsburskeho od voku 1526. n.p., 1891-1913. 3v.

Arc 658.3.2 Chase, T. Dr. Schliemann and the archaeological value of his discoveries. Worcester, 1891.

Arc 435.11.12 Cousens, Henry. An account of the caves at Nadsur and Karsambla. Bombay, 1891.

Arc 1418.2 Cunningham, A. Coins of ancient India. London, 1891.

Arc 554.1.3 Edwards, A.B. Pharaohs, fellahs and explorers. N.Y., 1891.

1891 - cont.

Arc 554.1 Edwards, A.B. Pharaohs, fellahs and explorers. N.Y., 1891.

Arc 1390.8 Engel, A. Traite de numismatique en moyen age. Paris, 1891. 3v.

Arc 1613.2.4 Evans, G.G. Illustrated history of the United States mint. Philadelphia, 1891.

Arc 1623.1 Fisher, A. Catalogue of coins, medals, and tokens of Mexico. N.Y., 1891.

Arc 545.215 Forrer, R. Die Graeber- und Textilfunde von Achmim-Panopolis. Strassburg, 1891.

X Cg Arc 545.216 Forrer, R. Roemische und Byzantinische Seiden-Textilien aus.....Achmim-Panopolis. Strassburg, 1891.

Arc 861.11.3 Fox, G.E. Excavations...Roman city at Silchester, Hants in 1890. Westminster, 1891.

Arc 435.2.12F Führer, A.A. Monumental antiquities and inscriptions. Allahabad, 1891.

Arc 793.1.2 Furchheim, F. Bibliografia di Pompei, Ercolano e Stabia. Napoli, 1891.

Arc 1033.22 Gori, F. Sul tesoro di antiche suppellettili sacre. Spoleto, 1891.

Arc 740.205 Gsell, S. Fouilles...nécropole de Vulci. Paris, 1891.

Arc 497.20.5 Harper, H.A. The Bible and modern discoveries. 4. ed. London, 1891.

Arc 307.3.6 International Congress of Americanists, 9th, Madrid, 1892. Congreso internacional de Americanistas. Madrid, 1891.

Arc 87.1.51 Koldewery, R. Neandrid. Berlin, 1891.

Arc 920.203F Kondakov, N. Antiquités de la Russie méridionale. Paris, 1891.

Arc 936.100.30 Kukuljevic-Sakcinski, I. Nadpisi sredovječni i novovjeki na crkvah. Zagreb, 1891.

Arc 1053.5.2 Laban, F. Der Gemüthsansdruck des Antinous. Berlin, 1891.

Arc 1470.37 Lampros, Paulos. Anagraphē tōn nomismatōn tēs kypies Hellados. Athēnai, 1891.

Arc 750.204 Lanciani, R. L'itinerario di Einsiedeln. Roma, 1891.

Arc 66.1.58 Langlois, E. Origines et sources du Roman de la Rose. Paris, 1891.

Arc 853.21.5 Lissauer, A. Alterthümer der Bronzezeit in Westpreussen. Danzig, 1891.

Arc 1093.2.4 McGuire, J.D. The stone hammer and its various uses. Washington, 1891.

Arc 950.210 Mackenzie, A. Descriptive notes on certain implements...Graham Island. n.p., 1891.

Arc 1643.1 Medina, J.T. Monedas y medallas hispano-americanas. Santiago, 1891.

Arc 726.33 Milani, L.A. Le recenti scoperte di antichita in Verona. Verona, 1891.

Arc 593.1 Moldenke, C.E. The New York obelisk. N.Y., 1891.

Arc 593.1.2 Moldenke, C.E. The New York obelisk. N.Y., 1891.

Arc 1093.6.5 Murray-Aynsley, L.H.G.M. The swastika. Margate, 1891.

Arc 585.8 Naville, E.H. Bubastis. London, 1891.

Arc 1433.2.5 Nützel, Heinrich. Münzen der Rasuliden. Berlin, 1891.

Arc 1145.3 Omont, H. Facsimiles des manuscrits grecs datés de la Bibliothèque Nationale. Paris, 1891.

Arc 1153.2.5 Paoli, Cesare. Le abbreviatore nella paleografia latina del Medio Evo. Firenze, 1891.

Arc 588.1 Petrie, W.M.F. Ollahum, Kahun, and Gurob. 1889-90. London, 1891.

Arc 505.12.5 Petrie, W.M.F. Till el Hesy (Lachish). London, 1891.

Arc 1413.2 Polder, L. Abridged history of copper coins in Japan. n.p., 1891.

Arc 402.2 Reinach, S. Chroniques d'Orient. Paris, 1891. 2v.

Arc 1675.14 Rosa, A. Coleccion de leyes, decretos. Buenos Aires, 1891.

Arc 1033.12.107 Sauren, J. Pilgerbuchlein zum heiligen Rock in Trier. Köln, 1891. 2 pam.

Arc 522.4.7 Schliemann, H. Bericht ueber der Ausgrabungen in Troja im Jahre 1890. Leipzig, 1891.

Arc 915.2 Schnarrenberger. Die Pfahlbauten des Bodensees. Konstanz, 1891.

Arc 658.3.5A Schuchhardt, K. Schliemanns Ausgrabungen. Leipzig, 1891.

Arc 658.3.3A Schuchhardt, K. Schliemann's excavations. London, 1891.

Arc 726.10 Schumacher, K. Eine Praenestinische Ciste. Heidelberg, 1891.

Arc 1680.10 Shiells, Robert. Story of the token. N.Y., 1891.

Arc 983.9.9 Snyder, J.F. A primitive urn-burial. Washington, 1891.

Arc 74.4.14 Society for the Promotion of Hellenic Studies. Rules and list of members. London, 1891. 2 pam.

Arc 950.204 Terry, J. Sculptured anthropoid ape heads. N.Y., 1891.

Arc 925.255.10 Toettermann, A. Fünf Sulfekinschriften. Helsingfors, 1891.

Arc 608.16.7 Waille, Victor. De Caesareae monumentis quae supersunt. Alger, 1891.

Arc 1015.232F Wilpert, J. Ein Cyclus christologischer Gemälde. Freiburg, 1891.

Arc 1015.213 Wilpert, J. Die Katakombengemalde. Ihre alten Copiers. Freiburg, 1891.

1892

Arc 958.1 Abbott, Charles C. Recent archaeological explorations in the Valley of the Delaware. Boston, 1892.

Arc 875.8 Annandale, C. A history of the Scottish people from the earliest times. London, 1892.

Arc 1027.25.41 Archäologische Ehren-Gabe zur 70. Geburtstage De Rossi. Rom, 1892.

Arc 1680.14 Atkins, James. The tradesmen's tokens of the eighteenth century. London, 1892.

Arc 785.13.50 Augé de Lassus, L. Le Forum. Paris, 1892.

Arc 66.1.56 Auvray, L. Manuscrits de Dante des Bibliothèques de France. Paris, 1892.

Arc 1348.19 Babelon, E. Mélanges numismatiques. Paris, 1892-1912. 5v.

Arc 820.207F Barrière-Flavy, Casimir. Étude sur les sépultures barbares du midi et de l'ouest de la France. Toulouse, 1892.

Arc 1027.25.19 Baumgarten, P.M. Giovanni Battista de Rossi. Köln, 1892.

Arc 1027.25.20 Baumgarten, P.M. Giovanni Battista de Rossi. Roma, 1892.

Arc 825.6 Bazin, H. Nîmes gallo-romain. Paris, 1892.

Arc 609.1 Bent, J.T. The ruined cities of Mashonaland. London, 1892.

Arc 925.1 Bibliotheque des Monuments Figurés. Antiquités du Bosphore Cimmérien. Paris, 1892.

Arc 605.205 Boeswillwald, E. Timgad, une cité africaine. Londres, 1892-

Arc 843.14 Botet y Sisó, J. Monumento sepulcral romano de Lloret de Mar. Gerona, 1892.

Arc 600.5 Brown, R.H. The Fayûm and Lake Moeris. London, 1892.

1892 - cont.

Arc 1077.2.9 Brunet y Bellet, J. La creu els monuments megalitics. Barcelona, 1892.

Arc 756.13 Bühlmann, J. Das alte Rom mit dem Triumphzuge Kaiser Constantins im Jahre 312 n. Chr. München, 1892.

Arc 955.1 Burns, Frank. The Crump burial cave (Blount Courty, Alabama). n.p., 1892.

Arc 983.2.5 Catálogo...objetos...Estados Unidos de América. Madrid, 1892.

Arc 1033.12.106 Clarke, R.F. A pilgrimage to the Holy Coat of Treves. London, 1892.

Arc 501.16.2 Conder, C.R. Heth and Moab. London, 1892.

Arc 3.2 Congrès International d'Archéologie Prehistorique et d'Anthropologie, 11th, Moscow, 1892. Congrès internationatonal d'archéologie préhistorique et d'anthropologie. v.1-2. Moscou, 1892-93.

Arc 1027.4.5 Davin, V. Les antiquités chrétiennes...Cappella greca. Paris, 1892.

Arc 388.4 Dumont, A. Mélanges d'archéologie et d'épigraphie. Paris, 1892.

Arc 493.1 Easton, M.W. Observations on the platform at Persepolis. Philadelphia, 1892.

Arc 1033.10 Ebers, G. Sinnbildliches die koptische Kunst. Leipzig, 1892.

Arc 554.1.5 Edwards, A.B. Pharaohs, fellahs and explorers. N.Y., 1892.

Arc 1470.4.15 Evans, A.J. Syracusan "medallions" and their engravers in the light of recent finds. London, 1892.

Arc 1613.2.2 Evans, G.G. Illustrated history of the United States mint. Philadelphia, 1892.

Arc 66.1.62 Fabre, P. Étude sur le liber censuum. Paris, 1892.

Arc 935.16 Gedeon, M.J. Eggraphoi liphoi kai keramia. Konstantinople, 1892.

Arc 1027.41.35 Grisar, H. Die Grabplatte des H. Paulus. Rom, 1892.

Arc 1015.224 Grisar, H. Tombe apostoliche di Roma. Roma, 1892.

Arc 853.21 Hartmann, A. Becherstatuen in Ostpreussen. Braunschweig, 1892.

Arc 513.6 Haynes, J.H. Descripitive catalogue to accompany a series of photographs of Asia Minor. N.Y., 1892.

Arc 983.2 Hemenway, S.W. Catalogo de los objetos etnológicos y arqueológicos. Madrid, 1892.

Arc 392.1 Hunter-Duvar, J. Stone, bronze and iron ages. London, 1892.

Arc 1475.9 Imhoof-Blumer, Friedrich. Porträtköpfe auf Römischen Münzen. Leipzig, 1892.

Arc 335.3 Index of archaeological papers, 1891-1908. London, 1892- 2v.

Arc 625.2 Ivanoff, S.A. Architektonische Studien. Berlin, 1892-95. 3v.

Arc 625.2PF Ivanoff, S.A. Architektonische Studien. Berlin, 1892-95. 4v.

Arc 943.4 Kabell, S.K. America for Columbus. Roenne, 1892.

Arc 861.10.9 Kermode, P.M. Catalogue of the Manks crosses. London, 1892.

Arc 700.9 Kietz, G. Agonistische Studien I, Der Diskoswurf bei der Grechen. München, 1892.

Arc 1588.1.11 Kirmis, M. Handbuch der polnischen Münzkunde. Posen, 1892.

Arc 87.1.52 Koepp, F. Das Bildnis Alexanders des Grossen. Berlin, 1892.

Arc 766.1.2.30 Lanciani, R. Pagan and Christian Rome. Boston, 1892.

Arc 1033.111 Le Blant, E. Les songes et les visions des martyrs. Rome, 1892.

Arc 1088.1.21 Levi, C.A. Navi venete. Venezia, 1892.

NEDL Arc 953.4 Lewis, T.H. Tracts for archaeologists. First series, 1880-91. St. Paul, 1892.

Arc 196.1 Limesblatt, 1892-1903. Trien, 1892.

Arc 458.1 Maisey, F.C. Sanchi and its remains. London, 1892.

Arc 1015.225.9 Marucchi, O. Scavi nella Platonia. Roma, 1892.

Arc 1027.6 Marucchi, O. Sepolcro apostolico delle catacombe. Roma, 1892.

Arc 562.2.6 Maspero, Gaston. Egyptian archaeology. 2. ed. N.Y., 1892.

Arc 915.5 Mayor, J. Fragments d'archeologie genevoise. Genève, 1892.

Arc 767.4.2 Middleton, J.H. The remains of ancient Rome. London, 1892. 2v.

Arc 969.1.2 Moorehead, W.K. Primitive man in Ohio. N.Y., 1892.

Arc 935.10 Mordtmann, J. Esquisse topographique de Constantinople. Lille, 1892.

Arc 398.1.2 Nadaillac, J.F.A. du Pouget de. Prehistoric peoples. N.Y., 1892.

Arc 585.10A Naville, E.H. Festival-Hall of Osorkon II in the Great Temple of Bubastis. London, 1892.

Arc 768.2 Nispi-Landi, Ciro. Roma monumentale dinanzi all'umanita. Roma, 1892.

Arc 510.209 Normand, Charles. La Troie d'Homère. Paris, 1892.

Arc 628.3 Oehler, R. Klassisches Bilderbuch. n.p., 1892?

Arc 1433.2 Palermo. Biblioteca Comunale. Catalogo delle monete arabe. Palermo, 1892.

Arc 66.1.60 Paris, P. Élatée. Paris, 1892.

Arc 1018.3 Pératé, A. L'archéologie chrétienne. Paris, 1892.

Arc 1335.83 Pertusi, G., firm, auctioneer, Milan. Catalogo della collezione A. Ancona di Milano. Milano, 1892.

Arc 588.3 Petrie, W.M.F. Medum. London, 1892.

Arc 565.1 Petrie, W.M.F. Ten years' digging in Egypt. N.Y., 1892.

Arc 1135.202 Prou, Maurice. Recueil de facsimiles d'écritures du XIIe au XVIIe siècle. Paris, 1892.

Arc 420.7 Radloff, W. Tpya...Atraer. St. Petersburg, 1892.

Arc 1372.2 Ridgeway, W. The origin of metallic currency and weight standards. Cambridge, 1892.

Arc 1643.2 Rosa, A. Monetario americano. Buenos Aires, 1892.

Arc 1027.25.15 Rossi, G.B. de. Albo dei sottoscrittori pel busto marmoreo. Roma, 1892.

Arc 1027.25.24 Rossi, G.B. de. Melanges G.B. Rossi. Paris, 1892.

Arc 1020.9.47 Rossi, G.B. di. Panorama circolari di Roma, deliniato nu 1534. Roma, 1892.

Arc 785.23.5 Rossi, M.S. de. Collare di servo fuggitivo novo Scoperto. Roma, 1892.

Arc 674.1 Rubensohn, O. Die Mysterienheiligtuemer in Eleusis und Samothrake. Berlin, 1892.

Arc 730.207 Salinas, A. Nuove metope arcaiche selinantine. Roma, 1892.

Arc 1027.31 Santoni, M. La cripta di S. Angelo de Profoglio...Camerino. Camerino, 1892.

Arc 1163.17 Skeat, W.W. Twelve facsimiles of old English manuscripts. Oxford, 1892.

1892 - cont.

Arc 1027.52.5 Spadoni, O.L. Tombs and catacombs of the Appian Way. Rome, 1892.

Arc 1020.117 Stokes, Margaret. Six months in the Apennines. London, 1892.

Arc 1411.8 Terrien de Lacouperie, A.E.J.B. Catalogue of Chinese coins from the 7th century B.C. to A.D. 621. London, 1892.

Arc 405.3 Usov, S.A. Sochineniia. Moskva, 1892. 2v.

Arc 1485.4.5F Vitalini, O. Supplemento alle monete dei papi. Camerino, 1892.

Arc 1015.217 Waal, A. de. La platonia ossia il sepolcro apostolico della via Appia. Roma, 1892.

Arc 455.1 Waddell, L.A. Discovery of Pātaliputra. Calcutta, 1892.

Arc 670.4F Walston, Charles. Excavations at the Heraion of Argos. 1892. Boston, 1892.

Arc 905.37 Wankel, Jindřich. Die prähistorische Jagd in Mähren. Olmütz, 1892.

Arc 708.17 Warsberg, A. von. Die Kunstwerke Athens. Wien, 1892.

Arc 1027.7.9 Wilpert, J. Di un cielo di rappresent cristianità...SS. Pietro ed Marcelino. Roma, 1892.

Arc 1016.209 Wilpert, J. Die Gottgeweihten Jungfrauen. Freiburg, 1892.

Arc 458.5 Wilson, Thomas. Minute stone implements from India. n.p., 1892.

Arc 554.1.15 Winslow, William C. The queen of Egyptology. n.p., 1892.

Arc 843.77.10 Yali Lassaletta, Aurelio. Historia de Italica. Sevilla, 1892.

1893

Arc 861.58 Addy, S.O. The hall of Waltheof...Hallamshire. London, 1893.

Arc 493.2 Adler, C. Two Persepolitan casts in the U.S. National Museum. Washington, 1893.

Arc 1025.30 Armellini, M. Gli antichi cimiteri cristiani di Roma e d'Italia. Roma, 1893.

X Cg Arc 1433.33 Babelon, E. Perses achemenides les satrapes. Paris, 1893.

Arc 900.206 Ballif, P. Römische Strasen in Bosnien. Wien, 1893.

Arc 855.202 Baye, J. de. The industrial arts of the Anglo-Saxons. London, 1893.

Htn Arc 700.4* Belger, C. Die Mykenische Lokalsage von den Gräbern Agamemnons und der Seinen. Berlin, 1893.

Arc 1018.14 Belloc, J.T. de. Ste. Agnès et son siècle. Lille, 1893.

Arc 1500.28.5 Blanchet, J.A. Histoire monetaire du Béarn et description des monnaies...Béarn. v.1-2. Paris, 1893.

Arc 823.2 Blanchet, J.A. Mélanges d'archéologie gallo-romaine. fasc.1-2. Paris, 1893. 2v.

Arc 838.23 Boutroue, A. Rapport...sur une mission archéologique en Portugal et dans le sud de l'Espagne. Paris, 1893.

Arc 590.1A Budge, E.A.W. The mummy. Chapters on Egyptian funereal archaeology. Cambridge, 1893.

Arc 608.6 Cagnat, R. Guides en Algérie...Lambèse. Paris, 1893.

Arc 547.30 Cambridge. University. Fitzwilliam Museum. A catalogue of the Egyptian collection. Cambridge, Eng., 1893.

Arc 1033.20.5 Carini, I. Le basiliche cristiane. Roma, 1893.

Arc 875.32 Carnegie, J. Origins of Pictish symbolism. Edinburgh, 1893.

Arc 967.1.4 Carr, L. The mounds of the Mississippi Valley. Washington, 1893.

Arc 730.2.3 Cavallari, F.S. Euryalos e le opere di difesa di Siracusa. Palermo, 1893.

Arc 635.13 Cavvadias, P. Fouilles d'Épidaure. Athène, 1893.

Arc 861.73 Chudleigh, J. Devonshire antiquities. 2. ed. Exeter, 1893.

Arc 66.1.64 Clerc, M. Les meteques atheniens. Paris, 1893.

Arc 853.10.15 Cohausen, August. Das Römerkastell Saalburg. 4. Aufl. Homburg vor der Höhe, 1893.

Arc 501.16.11 Conder, C.R. The Tell Amarna tablets. London, 1893.

Arc 501.16.12 Conder, C.R. The Tell Amarna tablets. London, 1893.

Arc 643.1.5A Diehl, C. Excursions in Greece. London, 1893.

Arc 1053.6 Ebers, G. Antike. Portraits. Leipzig, 1893.

Arc 1053.6.2 Ebers, G. The Hellenic portraits from the Fayum. N.Y., 1893.

Arc 1613.2.5 Evans, G.G. Illustrated history of the United States mint. Philadelphia, 1893.

Arc 843.23 Ferraz de Macedo, F. Luzitanos e romanos en Villa Franca de Xira. Lisboa, 1893.

Arc 625.8 Festschrift für Johannes Overbeck. Leipzig, 1893.

Arc 545.217 Forrer, R. Die fruehchristliche Alterthuemer aus....Achmim Panopolis. Strassburg, 1893.

Arc 635.207 Furtwängler, A. Archäologische Studien...Heinrich Brunn...dargebracht. Berlin, 1893.

Arc 1465.76 Gabrici, E. Topografia e numismatica dell'antica Imera, Sicily. Napoli, 1893.

Arc 1015.228 Galante, G.A. Cemetero di S. Ipolisto in Atripalda. Napoli, 1893.

Arc 1468.25 Greenwell, W. Rare Greek coins. London, 1893.

Arc 608.6.35 Gsell, Stéphane. Recherches archéologiques en Algérie. Paris, 1893.

Arc 762.1.4.5 Hare, A.J.C. Walks in Rome. 13th ed. London, 1893. 2v.

Arc 1453.1 Hazlitt, William Carew. The coinage of the European continent. London, 1893.

Arc 983.1.2 Henderson, P. The cliff dwellers. St. Paul, 1893.

Arc 848.2 Hettner, Felix. Die römischen Steindenkmäler der Provinzialmuseum zu Trier. Trier, 1893.

Arc 426.8 Hitchcoke, R. The ancient burial mounds of Japan. Washington, 1893.

Arc 435.2.22F Hoernle, A.F.R. The Bower manuscript. Calcutta, 1893-1912.

Arc 970.1 Holmes, W.H. Stone implements; Potomac-Chesapeake Province. Washington, 1893-94.

Arc 593.2 Julien, A.A. Notes of research on the New York obelisk. N.Y., 1893.

Arc 635.209 Kabbadias, P. Fouilles de Lycosoura. Série 1. Athène, 1893.

Arc 87.1.53 Kalkmann, A. Proportionen des Gesichts in der Grosse Kunst. Berlin, 1893.

Arc 853.9 Krause E. Die megalithischen Gräber...Deutschlands. Berlin, 1893.

Htn Arc 766.1.4* Lanciani, R. Pagan and Christian Rome. Boston, 1893.

Arc 766.1.3 Lanciani, R. Pagan and Christian Rome. Boston, 1893.

Arc 766.1.3.5 Lanciani, R. Pagan and Christian Rome. London, 1893.

Arc 430.201 Lebon, G. Les monuments de l'Inde. Paris, 1893.

Arc 1185.3.2 Leist, F. Urkundenlehre. 2. Aufl. Leipzig, 1893.

Arc 1200.4 Lewinski, L. Die Brandenburgische Kanzlei und die Urkundenwesen. Inaug. Diss. Strassburg, 1893.

Chronological Listing

1893 - cont.

Arc 830.18.5 Lievre, A.F. Les chemins gaulois et romains. 2e éd. Niort, 1893.
Arc 1027.41.39 Lugari, G.B. Il "Dolocenum" della XIII regione. Roma, 1893.
Arc 1138.15 Madan, F. Books in manuscript. London, 1893.
Arc 830.78.5 Maitre, Léon. Geographie historique et descriptive de la Loire-Inférieure. Nantes, 1893.
Arc 1033.53 Marucchi, O. Un nuovo monumento della persecuzione diocleziana. Roma, 1893.
Arc 562.2.7 Maspero, Gaston. Egyptian archaeology. London, 1893.
Arc 810.11.2 Mau, August. Fuehrer durch Pompeji. Naples, 1893.
Arc 1027.12.13 Mecchi, F.E. La tomba di San Pietro. Roma, 1893.
Arc 861.92 Mitchell, E.H. The crosses of Monmouthshire. Newport, 1893.
Arc 1538.12 Montagu, H. Copper coins of England. London, 1893.
Arc 925.15F Moskovskoe Arkheologicheskoe Obshchestvo. Materialy po...Rossii. Moskva, 1893- 2v.
Arc 1077.1 Much, M. Die Kupferzeit in Europa. Jena, 1893.
Arc 1368.1 Nestle, W. Funde antiker Münzen im königrieche Württemberg. Stuttgart, 1893.
Arc 587.1A Newberry, P.E. Beni Hasan. London, 1893. 4v.
Arc 950.200 Nordenskiold, G. The cliff dwellers of the Mesa Verde. Stockholm, 1893.
Arc 535.200 Ohnefalsch-Richter, M. Kypros, the Bible and Homer. London, 1893. 2v.
Arc 1015.223 Orsi, P. Esplorazioni nelle catacombe. Siracusa. Roma, 1893.
Arc 1490.5.7 Papadopoli, Nicolo. Le monete di Venezia. pt.1-3. Venezia, 1893-1919. 4v.
Arc 861.65 Payne, George. Collectanea cantiana. London, 1893.
Arc 1020.107 Payne, J.O. St. Paul's Cathedral...account of the treasures. London, 1893.
Arc 1033.59.5 Pennesi, A. Cenni storici sul culto di S. Vittoria. S. Vittoria, 1893.
Arc 726.3 Persichetti, N. Viaggio archeologico sulla Via Salaria. Roma, 1893.
Arc 565.1.2 Petrie, W.M.F. Ten years' digging in Egypt. 2. ed. London, 1893.
Arc 900.215F Pič, Josef L. Archaeologický výzhum. pt.1-3. Praha, 1893-97.
Arc 1033.17.531 Pla, José. Historia de Queralt. Barcelona, 1893.
Arc 925.50.270 Pol', Aleksandr N. Katalog kolleztni drevnostei A.N. Pol', v Ekaterinoslave. Kiev, 1893.
Arc 66.1.63 Radet, Georges. La Lydie et le monde grec. Paris, 1893.
Arc 402.2.9 Reinach, S. Le mirage oriental. Paris, 1893.
Arc 18.1.3 Revue archéologique. Index, v.23, 1870-1890. 3d series. Paris, 1893.
Arc 82.2.2 Römische Quartalschrift für...Kirch. Supplementheft. v.1-31. Rom, 1893. 14v.
Arc 1016.215.5 Rossi, G.B. de. Iscrizione in scritta e lingua Nabatea...Madaba. Roma, 1893.
Arc 1150.202 Schmitz, W. Commentarii notarum tironianarum. Lipsiae, 1893. 2v.
Arc 635.213 Sittl, C. Parerga zur alten Kunstgeschichte. Würzburg, 1893.
Htn Arc 861.69* Stapleton, A. A history of the public crosses of old Nottingham. Nottingham, 1893.
Arc 830.116 Thomas, Henri. Une nouvelle page ajoutèe à l'histoire de Rosny-sur-Seine. Paris, 1893.
Arc 1143.2 Thompson, Edward Maunde. Handbook of Greek and Latin palaeography. N.Y., 1893.
Arc 1138.1 Thoyts, E.E. How to decipher and study old documents. London, 1893.
Arc 923.11 Tolstoi, I. Rossiiskii istoricheskii muzei. Moskva, 1893.
Arc 682.2 Tsountas, C. Mukyrai. Athēnai, 1893.
Arc 1433.37.10 Vives y Escudero, A. Monedas de las dinastiás arábigo-españolas. Madrid, 1893.
Arc 1153.9 Vries, S.G. de. Boethii fragmentum notis Tironianis descript. Lugduni Batavorum, 1893.
Arc 880.15 Wakeman, W.F. A survey of antiquarian periods on...Inismurray. London, 1893.
Arc 1418.9 Webb, W.W. The currencies of Hindu states of Réjputána. Westminster, 1893.
Arc 1025.18 Wiegand, F. Eine Wanderung...römischen Katakomben. Erlangen, 1893.
Arc 609.1.5 Willoughby, J.C. A narrative of further excavations at Zimbabye (Mashonaland). London, 1893.
Arc 1680.16 Wiltshire Archaeological and Natural History Society, Devizes. Museum. Catalogue of the collection of Wiltshire trade tokens. Devizes, 1893.

1894

Arc 1027.25.17 Adunanza della Pontificia accademia romana d'archeologia dedicata alla memoria di G.B. de Rossi. Roma, 1894.
Arc 1020.9.153 Armailhacq. L'eglise nationale de Saint Louis des Français à Rome. Rome, 1894.
Arc 66.1.68 Baudrillart, A. Divinités de la victoire en Grèce et en Italie. Paris, 1894.
Arc 66.1.67 Bérard, V. Origine des cultes arcadiens. Paris, 1894.
Arc 547.2.2 Berlin. Staatliche Museen. Ausführliches Verzeichniss der Aegyptischen Altertuemer, Gipsabguesse und Papyrus. Berlin, 1894.
Arc 1663.2 Betts, C.W. American colonial history illustrated by contemporary medals. N.Y., 1894.
Arc 501.17 Bliss, F.J. A mound of many cities. London, 1894.
Arc 830.63 Bousrez, Louis. Les monuments mégalithiques. Tours, 1894.
Arc 756.13.5 Bühlmann, J. Rom mit dem Triumphzuge Constantins im Jahre 312. 4. Aufl. München, 1894.
Arc 853.41.9 Calliano, G. Prähistorische Funde in der Umgebung von Baden. Wein, 1894.
Arc 1033.60 Calo, Luigi. S. Beatrice vergine e martire. Napoli, 1894.
Arc 1033.99 Carini, Isidoro. La passione di Cristo. Milano, 1894.
Arc 501.6.3 The city and the land. Seven lectures. London, 1894.
Arc 736.6 Coglitore, I. Mozia, studi storico-archeologico. Catania, 1894.
Arc 501.16.13A Conder, C.R. The Tell Amarna tablets. 2. ed. London, 1894.
Arc 1033.12 Cozza-Luzi. Le memorie...dell'infanzia di Gesù Cristo. Roma, 1894.
Arc 1418.2.2 Cunningham, A. Coins of mediaeval India. London, 1894.
Arc 758.5 Dennie, John. Rome of to-day and yesterday. Boston, 1894.
Arc 1027.12 DeWaal, A. Die Apostelgruft ad Catacumbas S. Peter und S. Paul. Rom, 1894.
Arc 609.1.4 Dillmann, A. Über die geschichtlichen Ergebnisse der Th. Bent'schen Reisen in Ostafrica. Berlin, 1894.

1894 - cont.

Arc 522.12 Dörpfeld, W. Troja 1893. Leipzig, 1894.
Arc 396.3.18 Le duc de Loubat, 1831-1894. Paris, 1894.
Arc 545.228 Egypt. Antiquities Department. Catalogue des monuments et inscriptions de l'Egypte antique. Vienne, 1894-1909. 3v.
Arc 66.1.66 Enlart, C. Origines françaises de l'architecture gothique en Italie. Paris, 1894.
Arc 625.7 Fongères, G. La vie...des Grecs et des Romains. Paris, 1894.
Arc 845.2 Frankfurt am Main. Verein für Geschichte und Alterthumskunde. Mittheilungen über Römische Funde in Heddernheim. Frankfurt, 1894. 6v.
Arc 1185.14 Frazer, P. Manual of the study of documents. Philadelphia, 1894.
Arc 1033.6 Germano, Stanislao P. La casa celimontana...Giovanni e Paolo. Roma, 1894.
Arc 1185.4A Giry, Arthur. Manuel de diplomatique. Paris, 1894.
Arc 1490.94.1 Gnecchi, Francesco. Monete di Milano; inedite supplemento all'opera: Le monete di Milano da Carlo Magno a Vittorio Emanuele II. Milano, 1894.
Arc 1675.56 Gray, J.M. James and William Tassie. Edinburgh, 1894.
Arc 1027.25.37 Grossi-Gondi, A. Giovanni Battista de Rossi, archeologo romano. Roma, 1894.
Arc 66.1.65 Gsell, S. Essai sur Domitien. Paris, 1894.
Arc 608.16 Gsell, Stéphane. De Tipasa, Mauretaniae Caesariensis urbe. Diss. Algerii, 1894.
Arc 925.4 Heikel, A. Antiquités de la Sibérie Occidentale. Helsingfors, 1894.
Arc 1433.67 Istanbul. Asari Atika Müzeleri. Catalogue dis monnaies turcomanes. Constantinople, 1894.
Arc 905.4.15 Jelić, Luka. Raccolta di documenti relativi ai monumenti artistici di Spalato e Salona. Spalato, 1894.
Arc 1411.2 Kainz, C. Die ältesten chinesischen Staatsmünzen. Berlin, 1894.
Arc 87.1.54 Kekule, R. Ueber einen bisher Marcellus genannten Kopf. Berlin, 1894.
Arc 1510.11.5 Kull, J.V. Repertorium zur Münzkunde Bayerns und Forzetz. v.1-3. München, 1894. 2v.
Arc 1020.31.23 Lagrange, Marie. Saint Étienne et son sanctuaire à Jérusalem. Paris, 1894.
Arc 766.1.2.15 Lanciani, R. Ancient Rome in the light of recent discoveries. 10. ed. Boston, 1894.
Arc 1027.25.61 LeBlant, E. Jean-Baptiste de Rossi. Paris, 1894.
Arc 1033.113 Leport, L. Deux mosaiques chrétiennes du IVe siècle. Paris, 1894.
Arc 1016.9.9 Lugari, G.B. S. Bonifazio e S. Alessio sull'aventino. Roma, 1894.
Arc 875.37 Maclagan, Christian. What means these stones? Edinburgh, 1894.
Arc 1033.13.5 Marucchi, O. Le memorie dei SS. apostoli Pietro e Paolo nella città di Roma. Roma, 1894.
Arc 600.60F Mewberry, P.E. El Bersheh. London, 1894-95. 2v.
Arc 960.2.15F Moore, C.B. As to Cooper from the mounds of the St. John's River, Florida. Philadelphia, 1894.
Arc 950.201A Moore, C.B. Certain sand mounds of the St. John's River. pt.1-2. Philadelphia, 1894.
Arc 1076.4 Morse, E.S. On the so-called bow puller of antiquity. Salem, 1894.
Arc 585.11A Naville, E.H. Ahnas el Medinek. London, 1894.
Arc 585.12.2 Naville, E.H. The temple of Deir el Bahari. London, 1894.
Arc 587.3 Newberry, P.E. El Bersheh. Pt.1-2. London, 1894-95. 2v.
Arc 830.22.3 Normand, Charles. Nouvelles antiquités gallo-romaines de Paris. Paris, 1894. 2v.
Arc 1163.5 Ojha, G.H. The palaeography of India (in Sansk). Oodeypore, 1894.
Arc 1135.200.5 Papyrus Erzherzog Rainer; Führer...Ausstellung. Wien, 1894.
Arc 1025.44 Prina, B. Le catacombe. Firenze, 1894.
Htn Arc 1020.2* Prost, B. Le trésor de l'Abbaye St. Bénique de Dijon. Dijon, 1894.
Arc 100.1.25 Prow, M. Table alphabétique...l'Académie Celtique...Antiquaires de France. Paris, 1894. 2v.
Arc 785.24 Pullen, H.W. Handbooks of ancient Rome. London, 1894.
Arc 435.2.17F Rea, Alexander. List of architectural and archaeological remains in Coorg. Madras, 1894.
Arc 435.2.15F Rea, Alexander. South Indian Buddhist antiquities. Madras, 1894.
Arc 618.1 Reinach, S. Les celtes dans les vallées du Po et du Danube. Paris, 1894.
Arc 66.1.69 Ridder, A. de. Catalogue des bronzes de la société archeologique d'Athènes. Paris, 1894.
Arc 1027.15.19 Rossi, G.B. de. Fibula d'oro aquiliforme. Roma, 1894.
Arc 608.6.9 Ruines romaines au nord de l'Aurès. Rome, 1894. 2 pam.
Arc 730.206 Salinas, A. Relazione sommaria intorno agli. Roma, 1894.
Arc 1500.50 Saunier, Charles. Augustin Dupré: ofèvre, médailleur et graveur général des monnaies. Paris, 1894.
Arc 953.10 Schmidt, E. Vorgeschichte Nordamerikas im Gebiet der Vereinigten Staaten. Braunschweig, 1894.
Arc 1212.2 Seyler, Gustav A. Geschichte der Siegel. Leipzig, 1894.
Arc 1335.89 Sotheby, W. Catalogue of the collection of Greek coins in gold. London, 1894.
Arc 853.6 Suettich, S. Der 'Puestrich' zu Sondershausen. Naumburg an der Saale, 1894.
Arc 497.92 Szekrényi, Lajos. A bibliai régiségtudomány kézikönyve. Szeged, 1894.
Arc 457.20 Temple, Richard C. Notes on antiquities in Ramannadesa. Bombay, 1894.
Arc 950.208 Thomas, C. Report of mound explorations of Bureau of Ethnology. Washington, 1894.
Arc 1088.1.8 Torr, Cecil. Ancient ships. Cambridge, 1894.
Arc 1033.164 Usener, H.K. Acta martyris Anastasii Persae. Bonnae, 1894.
Arc 400.6 Voss, Albert. Merkbuch. 2. Aufl. Berlin, 1894.
Arc 1660.14F Welch, Charles. Medals struck by the corporation of London. London, 1894.
Arc 730.208 White, J.W. Oeri tou pelaryikon epiperikleous. Athēnai, 1894.
Arc 716.5 White, J.W. The Opisthodomus on the Acropolis at Athens. n.p., 1894?
Arc 1423.14 Williamson, G.C. The money of the Bible illustrated by numerous woodcuts. London, 1894.
Arc 1053.2 Winter, F. Über die griechische Porträtkunst. Berlin, 1894.

Chronological Listing

1895

Arc 925.50.285F Antonovich, V.B. Arkheologicheskaia karta Kievskoi gubernii. Moskva, 1895.

Arc 1.15 Archaeologische Studien zum Christlichen Altertum. Freiburg, 1895.

X Cg Arc 865.1 Barclay, E. Stonehenge and its earth works. London, 1895.

Arc 66.1.70 Berger, E. Histoire de Blanche de Castile. Paris, 1895.

Arc 520.10.5 Berlin. Königliches Museum. Beschreibung der Skulpturen aus Pergamon. Berlin, 1895.

Arc 501.5.2 Besant, W. Palestine Exploration Fund. Thirty years' work in the Holy Land, 1865-1895. London, 1895.

Arc 1353.2.5 British Museum. Department of Coins and Medals. A guide to the gold and silver coins of the ancients. 4. ed. London, 1895.

Arc 861.12 Bruce, J.C. The handbook to the Roman wall. 4. ed. London, 1895.

Arc 875.21 Brydall, R. The monumental effigies of Scotland. Glasgow, 1895.

Arc 545.231 Burlington Five Arts Club, London. The art of ancient Egypt. London, 1895.

Arc 756.5.3 Burn, R. Ancient Rome and its neighborhood. London, 1895.

Arc 608.1 Carton, Louis B.C. Découvertes épigraphiques et archéologiques faites en Tunisie. Paris, 1895.

Arc 1033.34.21 Cascioli, J. De aeneo simulacro divi Petri apostoli. Roma, 1895.

Arc 1470.10 Clerk, M.G. Catalogue of coins of the Achaean League. London, 1895.

Arc 830.40.5 Coutil, Léon. Archéologie gauloise, gallo-romaine, franque et carolingienne. v.1-2, 3-5. Paris, 1895-1925. 2v.

Arc 1033.2 Crostarosa, P. Osservazioni sul musaico di S. Pudenziana. Roma, 1895.

NEDL Arc 1680.6.5 Davis, William John. The token coinage of Warwickshire. Birmingham, 1895.

Arc 1675.16 De La Tour, H. Jean de Candida. Paris, 1895.

Arc 1349.72 Domanig, K. Anton Scharff, K. und K. Kammer-Medaillen. Wien, 1895.

Arc 925.9.95PF Dorn, Boris A. Atlas k puteshestviiu po Kavkazu i iuzknomu poberezh'iu kaspiskago moria. Sankt Petersburg, 1895. 2v.

Arc 705.202 Durm, J. Der Zustand der Antiken Athenischen Bauwerke. Berlin, 1895.

Arc 586.7 Egypt Exploration Society. Guide to the temple of Deir el Bahari. London? 1895?

Arc 684.1.15 Die Ernst Curtius-Büste. Berlin, 1895.

Arc 1020.9.8 Eroli, Giovanni. Raccolta generale delle iscrizioni pagne e cristiane...nel panteon di Roma. Narni, 1895.

Arc 1494.10 Fernandez Lopez, M. El tesoro visigotico de la Capilla. Sevilla, 1895.

Arc 1580.8 Fiala, E. České denáry. Praha, 1895-

Arc 1335.54 Fiala, Eduard. Collection Ernest Prinz zu Windisch Gratz. Prag, 1895-99. 7v.

Arc 555.1 Forrer, R. Besuch in El-Achmem. Reisebriefe aus Aegypten. Strassburg, 1895.

Arc 1027.1.13 Gaetani, V. Trina comunicazione...vasello col sangui. Palermo, 1895.

Arc 830.110 George, J. Cachette d'objets en bronze découverte à Vénat. Angoulême, 1895.

Arc 1033.34.25 Giovanni, V. di. San Pietro in Roma. Monumenti e testimoni. Palermo, 1895.

Arc 875.28 Graham, R.C. The carved stones of Islay. Glasgow, 1895.

Arc 1027.8 Grisar, H. Die römische Sebastianuskirche. Rom, 1895.

Arc 1200.3 Heinemann, O. Beiträge zur Diplomatik der ältern Bischoefe von Hildesheim. Inaug. Diss. Marburg, 1895.

Arc 600.1.3 Hogarth, D.G. Report on prospects of research in Alexandria. London, 1895.

Arc 307.3.7 International Congress of Americanists, 11th, Mexico, 1895. Congreso de Americanistas. Reunion en Mexico. México, 1895.

Arc 543.125 Klements, D.A. Arkheologicheskii dnevnik poezdki v Sredniuiu Mongoliiu v 1891 godu. Sankt Peterburg, 1895.

Arc 785.13.3 Levy, L. Das Forum Romanum der Kaiser Zeit. München, 1895.

X Cg Arc 1408.3 Lockhart, James H.S. Currency of the Farther East from earliest times up to 1895. Hong Kong, 1895-1907. 3v.

Arc 1033.114 Lugari, G.B. Sopra l'età di alcuni Bolli di figuline. Roma, 1895.

Arc 1088.1.20F Maes, Constantino. La nave di Tiberio sommersa nel lago di Nemi. Roma, 1895. 2 pam.

Arc 712.11 Magne, L. Le Parthénon. Paris, 1895.

Arc 1027.22.9 Majocchi, R. L'Ichthys eucaristico nei monumenti. Milano, 1895.

Arc 810.16 Marriott, H.P.F. Facts about Pompeii. London, 1895.

Arc 1027.25.29 Marucchi, O. Giovanni Battista de Rossi. Roma, 1895.

Arc 562.2.9 Maspero, Gaston. Manual of Egyptian archaeology. London, 1895.

Arc 562.2.8 Maspero, Gaston. Manual of Egyptian archaeology. N.Y., 1895.

Arc 1490.7 Mayr, A. Die antiken Münzen...Malta. München, 1895.

Arc 1645.1.5 Meili, Julius. Die Münzen der Colonie Brasilien, 1645-1822. Zürich, 1895.

Arc 1016.1 Molinier, E. Le trésor de la cathédrale de Coire. Paris, 1895.

Arc 895.5.3 Montelius, Oscar. Les temps préhistoriques en Suède. Paris, 1895.

Arc 720.212 Monteluis, O. La civilization primitive en Italie. pt.1-2; plates. Stockholm, 1895. 5v.

Arc 950.202 Moore, C.B. Certain river mounds of Duval County, Florida. Philadelphia, 1895.

Arc 830.38 Moreau, Frédéric. Catalogue de la collection Caranda. v.1-2. Supplément. St. Quentin, 1895-96.

Arc 545.203 Morgan, J. Fouilles à Dahchour. Vienna, 1895.

Arc 905.1 Munro, Robert. Rambles and studies in Bosnia. Edinburgh, 1895.

Arc 518.6 Murray, A.S. Sculptured columns...Temple of Diana at Ephesus. London, 1895-96.

Htn Arc 585.14F* Naville, E.H. The temple of Deir el Bahari. London, 1895-1908. 7v.

Arc 588.4 Petrie, W.M.F. Nagada and Ballas. London, 1895.

Arc 1478.11 Pfeiffer, A. Antike Münzbilder. Winterthur, 1895.

Arc 712.17 Pousopoulos, A. O Parthenōn. Athēnai, 1895.

Arc 66.1.71 Rolland, R. Histoire de l'Opera en Europe. Paris, 1895.

Arc 1030.26 Rome. Italy. Santa Maria in Via Lata. Tabularium. pt.1-3; plates. Vienna, 1895. 4v.

Arc 670.2 Schildt, A. Die Giebelgruppen von Aegina. Leipzig, 1895.

Arc 625.13 Schneider, R. von. Album...Antike-Sammlung. Wien, 1895.

Arc 628.5 Schreiber, T. Atlas of classical antiquities. London, 1895.

1895 - cont.

Arc 1018.5 Schultze, Victor. Archäologie der altchristlichen Kunst. München, 1895.

Arc 830.78.100F Société Archéologique d'Eure-et-Loire. Dallas tumulaires et pierres tombales du département d'Eure-et-Loire. Chartres, 1895-1930. 2v.

Arc 895.29 Steenstrup, Japetus. Det store sølofund ved Gundestrup i Jylland 1891. Kjøbenhavn, 1895.

Arc 1027.25.33 Stevensen, H. Giovanni Battista de Rossi. Roma, 1895.

Arc 855.221 Stokes, Margaret. Notes on the Cross of Cong. Dublin, 1895.

Arc 1675.17 Storer, H.R. Medals and tokens of Rhode Island. Boston, 1895.

Arc 1030.20 Strazzulla, V. Studio critico sulle iscrizioni cristiane di Siracusa. Siracusa, 1895.

Arc 843.5 Teixidor, J. Antiquedades de Valencia. Valencia, 1895. 2v.

Arc 930.200 Tocilescou, G.G. Das Monument von Adamklissi. Wien, 1895.

Arc 1088.1.9A Torr, Cecil. Ancient ships. Cambridge, 1895.

Arc 983.2.7 United States. Commission. Report to the Columbian historical exposition at Madrid. Washington, 1895.

Arc 925.9.90 Virchow, Rudolf. Über die culturgeschtliche Stellung des Kaukasus. Berlin, 1895.

Arc 710.17 White, John W. The apisthodomus on the acropolis at Athens. Boston, 1895.

Arc 1015.213.9 Wilpert, J. Fractio Panis. Freiburg, 1895.

Arc 87.1.55 Winter, F. Eine attische Lekythos. Berlin, 1895.

Arc 880.3 Wood-Martin, W.G. Pagan Ireland. An archaeological sketch. London, 1895.

Arc 810.15 Ziegeler, E. Aus Pompeji. Guetersloh, 1895.

1896

Arc 726.70F American School of Classical Studies in Rome. The triumphal arch of Trajan at Beneventum. Rome, 1896.

Arc 938.5 Archäologischer Kongress, 10th, Riga, 1896. Katalog der Ausstellung. Riga, 1896.

Arc 608.2.15 Babelon, E. Carthage. Paris, 1896.

Arc 1510.144F Bally, Otto. Beschreibung von Münzen und Medaillen des Fürsten-Hauses und Landes Baden in chronologischer Folge. Aarau, 1896- 2v.

Arc 1018.6.21 Bartolini, A. Elogio del cavalier professore Mariano Armellini. Roma, 1896.

Arc 1027.12.5 Battandier, A. La Platonia...sepulcre des Sts. Pierre et Paul. Paris, 1896.

Arc 830.15.5 Bazin, H. Arles gallo-romain. Guide du touriste archéologue. Paris, 1896.

Arc 441.3.2F Bengal. Public Works Department. List of ancient monuments in Bengal. Calcutta, 1896.

Arc 1076.3 Bergner, H.H. Zur Glockenkunde Thürigens. Jena, 1896.

Arc 855.203 Bevan, J.O. Architectural survey of Herefordshire. Westminster, 1896. 2 pam.

Arc 1478.12 Blanchet, A. Les monnaies romaines. Paris, 1896.

Arc 823.22 Bleicher, G. Guide pour les recherches archéologiques. Nancy, 1896.

Arc 756.7.2A Boissier, Gaston. Rome and Pompeii. N.Y., 1896.

Arc 1335.46 Bonnet, Emile. Médaillier de la Société archéologique de Montpellier. Montpellier, 1896.

Arc 708.19 Broughton, V. Delves (Mrs.). Handbook to antiquities of Athens. Athens, 1896.

Arc 1163.5.10 Bühler, G. Indische Palaeographie von Arca. Strassburg, 1896.

Arc 435.2.23F Burgess, James. On the Muhammadan architecture of Bharoch, Cambay. London, 1896.

Arc 1030.31 Cantarelli, L. Un frammento epigrafico cristiano dell'isola Portuense. Roma, 1896.

Arc 1503.2F Caraggioni, L. Münzgeschichte der Schweiz. Geneve, 1896.

Arc 757.5 Carnevale, C.G. Roma nel III secolo - era volgare. Roma, 1896.

Arc 608.1.28 Carton, Louis B.C. Le sanctuaire de Base-Saturne à Dougga. Paris, 1896.

Arc 1433.34 Casanova, Paul. Inventaire sommaire des monnaies musulmanes. Paris, 1896.

Arc 845.1.5 Chlingesnsperg-Berg, M. von. Die Römischen Brandgräber. Braunsch, 1896.

Arc 750.1.5 Cichorius, C. Die Reliefs der Trajanssäule. v.1,2, plates. v.2,3, text. Berlin, 1896-1900. 4v.

Arc 500.6 Clermont-Ganneau, C. Archaeological researches in Palestine. London, 1896. 2v.

Arc 432.3 Cloquet, L. L'art munumental des Indous et des Perses. Bruxelles, 1896.

Arc 684.5.10F Curtius, Ernst. Olympia: die Ergebnisse. v.5. Berlin, 1896.

Arc 1535.9 Davis, W.J. Old Warwickshire coins, tokens and medals. n.p., 1896.

Arc 1033.24 Di Carlo. Risposta al P. Grisar...contre il sacro tesoro. Tivoli, 1896. 3 pam.

Arc 700.6 Dörpfeld, W. Das Griechische Theater. Athen, 1896.

Arc 855.226F Dymond, Charles W. The ancient remains at Stanton Drew. Bristol, 1896.

Arc 1033.62.2 Fanchi de' Cavalieri, P. La Passio SS. Perpetuae et Felicitatis. Roma, 1896.

Arc 905.9 Fischbach, O. Römische Lampen aus Poetovio. Graz, 1896.

Arc 1033.62 Franchi de' Cavalieri, P. La Passio SS. Perpetuae et Felicitatis. Roma, 1896.

Arc 700.7 Gardner, P. Sculptured tombs of Hellas. London, 1896.

Arc 608.1.3 Gauckler, Paul. L'archéologie de la Tunisie. Paris, 1896.

Arc 1478.15.2 Gnecchi, F. Monete romane. Milano, 1896.

Arc 830.18.19 Gobin, Léon. Viae, apud arvenos Romanae. Thesis. Augustonemeti, 1896.

Arc 608.6.31 Gsell, Stéphane. Guide archéologique des environs d'Alger. Alger, 1896.

Arc 66.1.73 Guiraud, J. L'état pontificale après le grand schisme. Paris, 1896.

Arc 520.7 Habich, G. Die Amazonengruppe die attalischen Weihgeschenks. Berlin, 1896.

Arc 1348.4A Hazlitt, W.C. The coin collector. N.Y., 1896.

Arc 1027.23.9 Hennecke, E. Altchristliche Malerei...römischen Katacomben. Leipzig, 1896.

Arc 861.11 Hope, W.H. St. J. Excavations...Roman city at Silchester, Hants in 1895. Westminster, 1896.

Arc 785.42.5 Knight, William. The arch of Titus. London, 1896.

Arc 923.20F Kondakov, N. Russkie klady. Sankt Petersburg, 1896.

Arc 830.70.7 Lafon, M.A. Amphithéatre de Fourvière. Lyon, 1896.

Arc 885.1 Langdon, A.G. Old Cornish crosses. Truro, 1896.

Arc 1030.50 Latyshchev', B.B. Sbornik' grech. nadlisei Chrisi bre.-men'. Sankt Peterburg, 1896.

Chronological Listing

1896 - cont.

Arc 1020.8 Legrand, E. Description...de l'église des Saints Apotres de Constantinople. Paris, 1896.

Arc 1510.22.5 Lehr, Ernest. Les monnaies des landgraves autrichiens de la Haute Alsace. Supplement. Mulhouse, 1896. 2 pam.

Arc 1433.45F Leningrad. Ermitazh. Inventarnyi katalog musulbmanskikh monet. Sankt Peterburg, 1896.

Arc 609.1.7 Lenz, Oskar. Ophir und die Ruinen von Zimbabye. Prag, 1896.

Arc 1033.113.3 Leport, L. Nouvelles observations sur la Mosaique de S. Pudentienne. Rome, 1896.

Arc 938.11 Litzka, J. Verzeichnis archäologischer Fundorte in Liv-, Est- und Kurland. Jurjew, 1896.

Arc 889.7 Loë, Alfred de. Les roches-polissoirs du "Bruzel" à Saint-Mard, province de Luxembourg. Bruxelles, 1896.

Arc 710.5 Luckenbach, H. Die Akropolis von Athen. München, 1896.

Arc 545.210 Lyons, H.G. Report on the island and temples of Philae. Cairo, 1896.

Arc 875.30 McFarlan, J. The Ruthwell cross. Dumfries, 1896.

Arc 1088.1.19 Malfatti, V. Le navi romane del lago di Nemi. Roma, 1896.

Arc 767.1.5 Maps, Rome. Ancient (1896). Formae urbis Romae antiquae. Berolino, 1896.

Arc 1494.3 Markl, M. Die Münzen, Medaillen, und Prägungen. Prag, 1896. 2v.

Arc 1033.3.9 Marucchi, O. Un frammento di sarcofago cristiano del Museo Laterano. Roma, 1896.

Arc 1020.29 Marucchi, O. Le recenti scoperte nel Duomo di Parinzo. Roma, 1896.

Arc 810.11.3 Mau, August. Fuehrer durch Pompeji. 2. Aufl. Leipzig, 1896.

Arc 726.11 Michaelis, A. Der Silberschatz von Boscoreale. Berlin, 1896.

Arc 950.202.2 Moore, C.B. Additional mounds of Duval and of Clay Counties, Florida. n.p., 1896.

Arc 830.38.2 Moreau, Frédéric. Petit album suite au Caranda. St. Quentin, 1896.

Arc 562.3 Morgan, J. Recherches sur les origines de l'Égypte. Paris, 1896-97.

Arc 893.1A Mueller, S. Nordische Altertumskunde. Strassburg, 1896. 2v.

Arc 858.6 Murray, D. An archaeological survey of the United Kingdom. Glasgow, 1896.

Arc 1584.12 Opeshnikov, A.V. Russkiia monety do 1547 g. Moskva, 1896.

Arc 1027.26.5 Orsi, Paolo. Nuove esplorazioni nelle catacombe di S. Giovanni Battista de Rossi nell 1894 in Siracusa. Roma, 1896.

Arc 885.12 Paget, Clara. Some ancient stone forts in Carnarvonshire. Cambridge, 1896.

Arc 861.13.5 Parker, C.A. The ancient crosses at Gosforth, Cumberland. London, 1896.

Arc 66.1.75 Pélissier, L.G. Louis XII et Ludovic Sforza. Paris, 1896. 3v.

Arc 87.1.56 Pernice, E. Griechisches Pferdegeschirr...Königlichen Museum. Berlin, 1896.

Arc 588.5 Petrie, W.M.F. Koptos. London, 1896.

Arc 705.205 Polites, N.G. To ranathēnaikon stadion. Athēnai, 1896.

Arc 1135.202.5 Prou, Maurice. Recueil de facsimiles d'écritures du XIIe au XVIIe siècle. Paris, 1896.

Arc 682.3 Reber, F. von. Und die Verhältniss der mykenischen zur dorischen Baustiel. München, 1896.

Arc 66.1.74 Ridder, A. de. Catalogue des bronzes trouvés sur l'Acropole. Paris, 1896. 2v.

Arc 1335.88.25F Rollin et Teuardent, firm, Paris. Monnaies d'or romaines et byzantines vente aux enchères publiques 20-28 avril, 1896. Paris, 1896.

Arc 1033.17.98.3 Rosa, Agustin de. Defensa de la aparición de Nuestra Señora de Guadalupe. Guadalajara, 1896.

Arc 547.14 Schreiber, T. Der Gallier. Leipzig, 1896.

Arc 1076.3.41 Schubart, F.W. Die Glocken in herzogtum Anhalt. Dessau, 1896.

Arc 705.208 Schwerzek, Karl. Erläuterungen...Rekonstruktion Westgiebels des Parthenongiebels. Wien, 1896.

Arc 915.8.5 Secretan, Eugène. Aventicum. Lausanne, 1896.

Arc 1318.3.7 Société Suisse de Numismatique. La Société Suisse...de 1879 à 1896, notices divers. Genève, 1896.

Arc 1675.57 Storelli, A. Jean-Baptiste Nini. Tours, 1896.

Arc 1335.80 Tizengauzen', V. Novyia numizmaticheskiia priobreteniia N.P. Linevicha. Sankt Peterburg, 1896.

Arc 1025.28.15 Le tombe dei martiri nelle catacombe romane. Roma, 1896.

Arc 1033.24.5 Vecchi, G. de. Una rarita del secolo XIX...sacro tesoro del G.C. Rossi. Roma, 1896.

Arc 1088.1.5 Weber, L. Die Lösung der Frierenrätsels. Danzig, 1896.

Arc 1093.6 Wilson, Thomas. The swastika, the earliest known symbol. Washington, 1896.

1897

Arc 505.68.15 Abalmelck-Lazarev, Semen S. Dzherash (Gerasa). Sankt Peterburg, 1897.

Arc 958.1.3 Abbott, Charles C. Researches upon antiquities of man, Delaware Valley. Boston, 1897.

Arc 858.8 Armitage, E.S. Key to English antiquities. Sheffield, 1897.

Arc 1356.2 Babelon, E. Les collections de monnaies anciennes. Paris, 1897.

Arc 1478.13 Bahrfeldt, M. Nachträge und Bericht zur Münzkunde. Wien, 1897.

Arc 608.6.5 Ballu, Albert. Les ruines de Timgad. Paris, 1897.

Arc 1016.246F Barbier de Montault, X. La trésor liturgique de Cherves en Angoumois. Angoulême, 1897.

Arc 785.16 Bayer, J. Stuck-Reliefs...Casa Farnesina in Rom. Wien, 1897.

Arc 823.1.3 Bertrand, A. Nos origines - La religion des Gaulois. Paris, 1897.

Arc 608.10 Bibliothèque d'archéologie africaine. Paris, 1897-1906. 7v.

Arc 1500.45 Bibliothèque Nationale, Paris. Département des Médailles et Antiques. Catalogue des jetons. Paris, 1897.

Arc 1470.14.13 Bibliothèque Nationale, Paris. Département des Médailles et Antiques. Inventaire sommaire de la collection Waddington...1897. Paris, 1897.

Arc 1027.4.17 Bonavenia, G. L'antichissima imagine della B. Vergine nel cimitero di Priscilla. Siena, 1897.

Arc 736.1.5 Bonfiglio, S. Su l'akropoli Akragantina. Girgenti, 1897.

Arc 880.2 Borlase, W.C. The dolmens of Ireland. London, 1897. 3v.

Arc 756.8 Borsari, L. Topografia di Roma antica. Milano, 1897.

1897 - cont.

Arc 600.1.5 Botti, G. Plan du Quartier "Rhacotis" dans l'Alexandrie. Alexandrie, 1897.

Arc 830.68 Bousrez, Louis. L'Anjou aux âges de la pierre...bronze. Paris, 1897.

Arc 435.2.16F Burgess, James. Revised lists of antiquarian remains in the Bombay presidency. Bombay, 1897.

Arc 1428.25 Cairo. Egyptian Library. Catalogue of the collection of Arabic coins...in the Khedivial Library at Cairo. London, 1897.

Arc 543.1 Cave, H.W. The ruined cities of Ceylon. London, 1897.

Arc 387.7 Champollion, J.F. Champollion inconnu. Paris, 1897.

Arc 600.6.9 Chenillon, A. Terres mortes. Paris, 1897.

Arc 1076.3.70 Cocks, A.H. The church bells of Buckinghamshire. London, 1897.

Arc 435.2.19F Cousens, Henry. Lists of antiquarian remains in the central provinces and Berâr. Calcutta, 1897.

Arc 830.40 Coutil, Léon. Inventaire des menhirs et dolmens de France. Eure. Louviers, 1897.

Arc 608.12 Cowper, H.S. The hill of the Graces...Tripoli. London, 1897.

Arc 1615.2 Crosby, S.S. United States coinage of 1793, cents and half cents. Boston, 1897.

Arc 870.1.1 Evans, J. The ancient stone implements, weapons and ornaments of Great Britain. London, 1897.

Arc 600.9 Foucart, G. Histoire de l'Ordre Lotiforme. Paris, 1897.

Htn Arc 435.8.6* Führer, A.A. Monograph on Buddha Sâkyamuni's birth-place in the Nepalese Tarâi. Allahabad, 1897.

Arc 1027.26.25 Führer, J. Forschungen zur Sicilia sotterranea. München, 1897.

Arc 608.1.25 Gauckler, Paul. Enquête sur les installations hydrologiques romaines en Tunisie. Tunis, 1897-

Arc 1335.150F Gesellschaft der Freunde. Die Siegelsammlung des Mannheimer. Manheim, 1897.

Arc 1478.15.4 Gnecchi, F. Monetazione romana. Genève, 1897.

Arc 426.7F Gowland, William. The dolmens and burial mounds in Japan. London, 1897.

Arc 1145.1 Graux, C. Facsimiles de manuscrits grecs d'Espagne. Paris, 1897. 2v.

Arc 1510.15 Grimm, E. Münzen und Medaillen der Stadt Wismar. Berlin, 1897.

Arc 430.5 Gruenwedel, A. Buddhistische Studien. Berlin, 1897.

Arc 830.16 Hamerton, P.G. The mount. Boston, 1897.

Arc 830.13 Hermann, M.J. Le Théâtre d'Orange. Paris, 1897.

Arc 968.2.5 Hodge, F.W. The enchanted Mesa. v.1-2. Washington, 1897.

Arc 392.2 Hutchinson, H.N. Prehistoric man and beast. N.Y., 1897.

Arc 1428.14 Imhoof-Blumer, Friedrich. Lydische Stadtmünzen. Genf, 1897.

Arc 853.11 Jacobi, L. Das Römerkastell Saalburg. Text und plates. Homburg vor der Höhe, 1897 2v.

Arc 87.1.57 Kekule, R. Ueber Copien einer Frauenstatue. Berlin, 1897.

Arc 853.8 Kröhnke, O. Chemische Untersuchung an Vorgeschichts Bronzen Schleswig-Holsteins. Kiel, 1897.

Arc 766.1.5A Lanciani, R. Ruins and excavations of ancient Rome. Boston, 1897.

Arc 766.1.6 Lanciani, R. The ruins and excavations of ancient Rome. London, 1897.

Arc 838.3.5 Leite de Vasconcellos, J. Religiões da Lusitania. Lisboa, 1897. 3v.

Arc 1433.44 Leningrad. Ermitazh. Katakog' dzhelairidskiu' monety Sost. A. Markov'. Sankt Peterburg, 1897.

Arc 830.11 Le Rouzic, Z. Carnac et ses monuments. Morlaix, 1897.

Arc 875.9 Macdonald, J. Tituli Hunteriani, an account of the Roman stones in the Hunterian Museum. Glasgow, 1897.

Arc 1033.3.13 Marucchi, O. Un frammento di sarcofago cristiano. Roma, 1897.

Arc 1030.4.19 Marucchi, O. L'iscrizione di Quirinio. Siena, 1897.

Arc 1015.225 Marucchi, O. Il sepolcro gentilizio di Sant'Ambrogio. Milano, 1897.

Arc 1033.5 Marucchi, O. La supremazia della sede romana considerata nei monumenti dei primi secoli. Roma, 1897.

Arc 1540.5 Mayo, J. Medals and decorations of the army and navy. Westminster, 1897. 2v.

Arc 1645.1.15 Meili, Julius. Das brasilianische Geldwesen. Zürich, 1897-1905. 2v.

Arc 1025.46 Minoccheri, L. Le catacombe. Roma, 1897.

Arc 950.202.5 Moore, C.B. Certain aboriginal mounds of the Georgia coast. Philadelphia, 1897.

Arc 600.180F Morzan, J. de. Carte de la nécropole memphite. n.p., 1897.

X Cg Arc 893.1.5 Mueller, S. Vor oldtisminder Danmarks. Kjøbenhavn, 1897.

Arc 1510.1.5 Munich. Medaillen und Münzen des Gesammthauses Wittelsbach. v.1, pt.1-2. München, 1897. 2v.

Arc 547.18 Musée de Gizeh. Notice des principaux monuments. Le Caire, 1897.

Arc 1510.11.15 Och, Friedrich. Münzen bayerischer Klöster, Kirchen. München, 1897.

Arc 1276.31F Petersen, H. Danske adelige sigiller. København, 1897.

Arc 588.6 Petrie, W.M.F. Six temples at Thebes. 1896. London, 1897.

Arc 1418.12 Rapson, E.J. Indian coins. Strassburg, 1897.

Arc 435.2.25F Rea, Alexander. Monumental remains of the Dutch East India Company in the presidency of Madras. Madras, 1897.

Arc 761.3PF Restauro grafico del Monte Capitalino. Maps and text. Roma, 1897.

Arc 1185.18 Rosenmund, R. Die Fortschritte der Diplomatik seit Mabillon. München, 1897.

Arc 925.11 Shchtern, E. von. K voproscho proiskhozhdenii gotskago stilia. Odessa, 1897.

Arc 943.13 Shipp, B. The Indian and antiquities of America. Philadelphia, 1897.

Arc 143.1.5 Society of Antiquaries of Scotland. Proceedings. Index. v.25-81. Edinburgh, 1897-1968. 2v.

Arc 1088.1.15 Stahlecker, R. Über die verrchiedenen Versuche der Rekonstruktion. Ravensburg, 1897.

Arc 785.17 Steinmetz, G. Die römischen Glasspiegel. n.p., 1897.

Arc 1027.28.5 Stevenson, Enrico. Di un nuovo insigne esemplare...indice dei cimiteri cristiani di Roma. Roma, 1897.

Arc 1027.41.9 Stevenson, H. Osservazione sulla topografia della via Ostiense. Roma, 1897.

Arc 1025.26 Strazzula, V. Museum epigraphicum. Panormi, 1897.

Arc 1033.3.37 Stuhlfauth, G. Un frammento di sarcofago cristiano. Roma, 1897.

Arc 1510.19F Suchier, Reinhard. Die Münzen der Grafen von Hanau. Hanau, 1897.

Arc 905.23F Tappeiner, Franz. Zum Schluss der Majafrage. Muan, 1897.

Arc 1033.3.17 Torlonia, L. Di un sarcofago cristiano del palazzo torlonia. Roma, 1897.

Chronological Listing

1897 - cont.

Arc 659.3 Tsountas, Chrēstos. The Mycenaean age. London, 1897.
Arc 890.208.2 Vedel, E. Efterskrift oldtidsminder og oldsager. Kjøbenhavn, 1897.
Arc 1027.19.29 Wilpert, J. Die Malerein der Sacramentskapellen in der Katakombe des honorable Callistus. Freiburg, 1897.
Arc 858.9 Windle, B.C.A. Life in early Britain. London, 1897.
Arc 858.9.3 Windle, B.C.A. Life in early Britain. N.Y., 1897.
Arc 777.3 Wissowa, G. Analecta Romana topographica. Halis, 1897.
Arc 662.3 Woodhouse, W.J. Aetolia, its geography and antiquities. Oxford, 1897.

1898

Arc 1018.6 Armellini, M. Lezioni di archaeologici cristiana. Roma, 1898.
Arc 750.205 Beltzami, L. Il pantheon. Milano, 1898.
Arc 1470.14.15 Bibliothèque Nationale, Paris. Département des Médailles et Antiques. Inventaire sommaire de la collection Waddington...1897. Paris, 1898.
X Cg Arc 501.17.5A Bliss, F.J. Excavations at Jerusalem 1894-1897. London, 1898.
Arc 950.207 Brower, J.V. Memoirs of explorations...basin...Mississippi. v.1-3,4-5,6-7,8. St. Paul, Minn., 1898. 7v.
Arc 628.12 Brunn, H. Kleine Schriften. Leipzig, 1898. 3v.
Arc 605.204 Cagnet, R. Les monuments historiques de la Tunise. Paris, 1898-99. 2v.
Arc 1015.221 Caruana, A.A. Ancient pagan tombs and Christian cemeteries in Malta. Malta, 1898.
Arc 843.24 Carvalho, M. O dolmen da Barroza. Porto, 1898.
Arc 1027.51 Cascioli, C.G. S. Damaso poeta insigne di martiri. Roma, 1898.
Arc 530.16F Chantre, E. Mission en Cappadoce. Paris, 1898.
Arc 875.11.7 Christison, D. Account of the excavation of the Roman station at Ardoch. Edinburgh, 1898.
Arc 875.11 Christison, D. Early fortifications in Scotland. London, 1898.
Arc 1020.144 Czober, Béla. Egyházi emlékek a törtenelmi kiállitison. Budapest, 1898.
Arc 861.11.5 Davis, F. The Romano-British city of Silchester. London, 1898.
Arc 625.10 Festschrift für Otto Benndorf. Wien, 1898.
Arc 955.2.7 Fewkes, J.W. A preliminary account of archaeological field work in Arizona in 1897. Washington, 1898.
Arc 66.1.78 Fougères, G. Mantinée et l'arcadie orientale. Paris, 1898.
Arc 1153.18 Friedrich, G. Učebna kniha palaeografie latinskě. Praha, 1898.
Arc 1490.8 Garufi, C.A. Monete econii nella storia del diritto siculo. Palermo, 1898.
Arc 925.12.10 Gerts, K.K. Arkheologicheskaia tipografiia tapanskago poluostrova. pts. 1-9. Sankt Peterburg, 1898-1901. 8v.
Arc 587.4 Griffith, F.L. Hieroglyphs. London, 1898.
Arc 1033.34.35 Grissar, H. Della statua di bronzo di San Pietro. Roma, 1898.
Arc 853.13 Hang, F. Die römischen Inschriften und Bildwerke Württembergs. v.1-2. Stuttgart, 1898-1900.
Arc 674.3 Herrlich, S. Epidaurus, eine antike Heilstätte. Berlin, 1898.
Arc 612.2 Hoernes, M. Urgeschichte der bildenden Kunst in Europa. Wien, 1898.
Arc 945.1 Hough, W. The lamp of the Eskimo. Washington, 1898.
Arc 1584.25 Iaroslavskaia Uchenaia Arkhivnaia Kommissii. Opisanie russikh monet muzeia Iaroslavskoi uchenoi arkkivnoi kommissii. Iaroslav, 1898.
Arc 1015.206 Iozzi, Oliviero. Supplementa alla Roma sotterranea cristiana. Roma, 1898.
Arc 900.208 Jenny, S. Die römische Begräbnisstätte von Bugant. Wien, 1898.
Arc 1200.5 Kaiser, H. Der collectarus perpeturom formorum des Johann von Gelnhausen. Strassburg, 1898.
Arc 1020.10.9 La Gournerie, E. de. Christian Rome. London, 1898. 2v.
Arc 66.1.79 Legrand, P.E. Étude sur Théocrite. Paris, 1898.
Arc 1675.7.5 Lincoln, W.S. and Son, firm, auctioneers, London. A descriptive catalogue of papal medals. London, 1898.
Arc 628.13 Luckenbach, H. Abbildungen zur Alten Geschichte der Oberen Klassen. München, 1898.
Arc 1027.12.15 Lugari, G.B. I varii seppellimenti...Pietro e Paolo. Roma, 1898.
Arc 1033.34.9 Lugari, J.B. Lieu du crucifiement de Saint Pierre. Tours, 1898.
Arc 875.7 Maclagan, C. Catalogue...British Museum...sculptured stones...Scotland. Edinburgh, 1898.
Arc 1033.34.45 Mancini, Pietro. Del primato e della residenza in Roma dell'apostolo Pietro. Roma, 1898.
Arc 1033.87 Marucchi, O. Brevi compendio di memorie...martire S. Agapito. Roma, 1898.
Arc 1030.4.15 Marucchi, O. Dell'importanza dell'epigrafia romana. Roma, 1898.
Arc 1033.56 Marucchi, O. Guida del Museo Christiano Christiano Lateranense. Roma, 1898.
Arc 1495.1 Marx, R. Les médailleurs français contemporains. Paris, 1898.
Arc 810.11.4 Mau, August. Fuehrer durch Pompeji. 3. Aufl. Leipzig, 1898.
Arc 785.1.3 Meschler, M. Der Vestatempel und der Vestalenhof am römische Forum. Freiburg, 1898.
Arc 710.7 Milchhoefer, A. Rede zum Winckelmann-Zage. Kiel, 1898.
Arc 1153.13 Monaci, E. Esempj di scrittura latina. Roma, 1898.
Arc 950.200.9 Moore, C.B. Certain aboriginal mounds. Philadelphia, 1898.
Arc 1033.12.234 Murray, D. A small brass cup...Rodil, Harris. Glasgow, 1898.
Arc 87.1.58 Pernice, E. Hellenistische Silbergefässe...Königlichen Museum. Berlin, 1898.
Arc 585.15A Petrie, W.M.F. Deshashek. 1897. London, 1898.
Arc 1468.12 Pick, Bekrendt. Die antiken Münzen von Dacien. Berlin, 1898-1910. 2v.
Arc 530.4 Preger, T. Anonymi Byzantini. München, 1898.
Arc 588.8 Quibell, J.E. El Kab. 1897. London, 1898.
Arc 588.7 Quibell, J.E. Teh Rainesseum. 1896. London, 1898.
Arc 66.2.85 Radet, G. Correspondance d'Emmanuel Roux. Bordeaux, 1898.
Arc 435.2.21F Rea, Alexander. Châlukyan architecture. Madras, 1898.
Arc 905.11 Rodlow, O.W. von. Der Verkehr...Pass von Pontelba-Pontafel...Predil. Prag, 1898.

1898 - cont.

Arc 1348.30 Sbōronos, I.N. Articles on numismatics. Athenes, 1898-1903. 16 pam.
Arc 1077.2.5 Şeymour, W.W. The cross. N.Y., 1898.
Arc 936.140.10 Škorpil, Hermeneyild. Mogili Ot. Kh. i K. Shkorpil. Plovdiv, 1898.
Arc 875.34 Smith, Frederick. Some investigations into palaeolithic remains in Scotland. Glasgow, 1898-99.
Arc 74.4.1 Society for the Promotion of Hellenic Studies. Journal. Index. v.9-42. London, 1898-1923. 3v.
Arc 441.5 Stein, Mark A. Detailed report of an archaeological tour with the Buner Field Force. Lahore, 1898.
Arc 1018.6.18 Stevenson, E. Lettera intorno...premessa all...Armellini. Roma, 1898.
Arc 1027.41.15 Stevenson, H. L'area di Lucina sulla via Ostiense. Roma, 1898.
Arc 1027.5.25 Stevenson, H. Scavi nel cimitero di Domitilla. Roma, 1898.
Arc 1070.206 Thiele, G. Antike Himmelsbilder. Berlin, 1898.
Arc 736.4 Tummarello, F. Su le origini di Erice. Trapini, 1898.
Arc 608.1.15 Tunis. Compte rendu de la marche du service. Tunis, 1898.
Arc 1076.3.14 Tyack, G.S. A book about bells. London, 1898.
Arc 404.1.5A Tyskiewicz, M. Memories of an old collector. London, 1898.
Arc 1153.14 Vianini, G. Raccolta...abbreviazioni e frasi abbreviate. Roma, 1898.
Arc 1033.112 Wilpert, J. Die Gewandung der Christen in den ersten Jahrhunderten. Köln, 1898.
Arc 407.6 Wilson, John Albert. Prehistoric art. Washington, 1898.
Arc 1030.19 Zaccheri, G. L'iscrizione di Abercio. Roma, 1898.

1899

Arc 755.6 Aucler, Paul. Rome; restauration archéologique. Paris, 1899.
Arc 600.30 Benson, Margaret. The temple of Mut in Asher. London, 1899.
Arc 1680.17 Bibliothèque Nationale, Paris. Département des Médailles et Antiques. Collection Rouyer. Catalogue de la collection Rouyer. Paris, 1899-1910. 2v.
Arc 386.12 Blanchet, A. Guide pratique de l'antiquaire. Paris, 1899.
Arc 830.174 Bonsor, G. Les colonies agricoles pré-romaines de la vallée du betes. Paris, 1899.
Arc 1166.3 Brigiuti, R. La paleografia ed i Raggi di Röntgen. Roma, 1899.
Arc 830.17 Bulliot, J.G. Fouilles du Mont Beuvray. Autun, 1899. 3v.
Arc 925.173.5F Bulychov, Nikolai I. Zhurnal raskopok po chasti vodorazdela verkhnikh pritokov Volgi i Dnepra. Moskva, 1899.
Arc 861.13 Calverley, W.S. Notes on the early sculptured crosses...present diocese of Carlisle. Kendal, 1899.
Arc 1153.12 Cappelli, A. Dizionario di abbreviature latine ed italiane. Milano, 1899.
Arc 726.44 Colini, Giuseppe A. Il sepolcreto de Remedello-Sotto. Parma, 1899-1902.
Arc 66.1.81 Courbaud, E. Le Bas-Relief Romain a représentations historiques. Paris, 1899.
Arc 600.15.5 Daninos, A. Les monuments funéraires de l'Egypte ancienne. Paris, 1899.
Htn Arc 1076.3.5* Downman, E.A. Ancient church bells in England. London, 1899.
Arc 830.52 Du Chatellier, Paul. Le bronze dans le Finistère. Quimper, 1899.
Arc 1020.10.23 Duchesne, L. Le forum chrétien. Rome, 1899.
Arc 785.6.10 Forbes, S.R. Aqueducts fountains of ancient Rome. Rome, 1899.
Arc 1033.61 Franchi de Cavalieri, P. S. Agnese nella tradizione e nella leggenda. Roma, 1899.
Arc 1070.207 Furtwängler, A. Neuere Faelschungen von Antiken. Berlin, 1899.
Arc 875.10 Glasgow, Scotland. Archaeological Society. The Antonine wall report. Glasgow, 1899.
Arc 861.14 Glastonbury, England. Antiquarian Society. British lake-village near Glastonbury. Taunton, 1899.
Arc 1478.14 Gruman, G. Inschriften und Darstellungen Römus. Biel, 1899.
Arc 1670.6F Hague. Koninklijk Kabinet van Munten. Les médailles et plaquettes modernes. v.1-6. Haarlem, 1899-1900.
Arc 762.1.5 Hare, A.J.C. Walks in Rome. 14th ed. N.Y., 1899. 2v.
Arc 861.17 Haverfield, F. Catalogue of the Roman inscribed and sculptured stones...ms. of Tullie House. Kendal, 1899.
Arc 1458.9 Hill, G.F. A handbook of Greek and Roman coins. London, 1899.
Arc 635.20F Hiller von Gärtringen. Thera 1895-. Berlin, 1899- 4v.
Arc 392.3 Hogarth, David George. Authority and archaeology. N.Y., 1899.
Arc 700.12 Holwerda, J.H. Die altischen Gräber der Bluethezeit. Leiden, 1899.
Arc 885.5 James, C.H. Excavations at Gelli Gaer camp. Cardiff, 1899?
Arc 766.1.9 Lanciani, R. The destruction of ancient Rome. N.Y., 1899.
Htn Arc 1660.4F* Loehr, August. Wiener Medailleure, 1899. Wien, 1899.
Arc 66.1.80 Loye, J. de. Les archives de la chambre apostolique XIVe siècle. Paris, 1899.
Arc 1016.9.15 Lugari, G.B. L'anfiteatro Flavio rivendicato ai martiri. Roma, 1899.
Arc 1465.6 MacDonald, G. Catalogue of Greek coins in the Hunterian collection. Glasgow, 1899. 3v.
Arc 1088.1.20.5 Maes, Constantino. Trionfo navale ovvero prassima estrazione. Roma, 1899.
Arc 513.14 Maps. Asia Minor (1899). Archäologische Karte von Kleinasien. Halle, 1899.
Arc 1030.4.25 Marucchi, O. Di alcuni antiche monumenti. Roma, 1899-1900.
Arc 1025.28.3 Marucchi, O. Eléments d'archélogie chrétienne. v.1-2. Paris, 1899. 3v.
Arc 1027.39.9 Marucchi, O. Scavi eseguiti nell'antica Basilica di S. Agapito. Roma, 1899.
Arc 1025.28.30 Marucchi, O. Scavi nelle catacombe romane. Roma, 1899.
Arc 810.11.8 Mau, August. Pompeii, its life and art. N.Y., 1899.
Arc 1018.11 Mazochuis, A.S. Mélanges de litterature et d'histoire religieuses. Paris, 1899. 3v.
Arc 19.1 Milani, L.A. Studi e materiali di archeologia e numismatica. v.1-3. Firenze, 1899. 4v.

Chronological Listing

1899 - cont.

Arc 710.7.5 Milchhoefer, A. Über die alten Burgheiligthümer in Athen. Kiliae, 1899.
Arc 1030.7 Millet, G. Inscriptions byzantines de Mistra. Athènes, 1899.
Arc 950.202.9 Moore, C.B. Certain aboriginal remains...Alabama River. Philadelphia, 1899.
Arc 885.7 Morgan, W.D. An antiquarian survey of East Gower, Glamorganshire. London, 1899.
Arc 1433.29 Mubarek, Ghalib Bey. Notices sur les monnaies turques. Bruxelles, 1899.
Arc 726.24 Müller, G.A. Tempel zu Tivoli bei Rom. Leipzig, 1899.
Arc 875.5.5 Munro, R. Prehistoric Scotland. Edinburgh, 1899.
Arc 1033.47.12 Negri, G. Nerone e il cristianesimo. Roma, 1899.
Arc 1027.19.3 Nortet. Cimetière de Saint Calixte. 3e éd. Rome, 1899.
Arc 530.5 Papodopoulos, A. Phōkaika. Smyrnē, 1899.
Arc 1160.201 Peper, P. Otfrid...Weissenburg. Schreiber XIX Jahrhundert. Frankfurt, 1899.
Arc 608.1.27 Perrot, G. La musée du Bardo à Tunis et les fouilles de M. Gauckler. Paris, 1899.
Arc 785.15.5 Petersen, E. Trajans Dakische Kriege. Leipzig, 1899.
Arc 900.212 Premerstein, A. Römischen Strassen und Befestigungen in Krain. Wien, 1899.
Arc 673.1.7 Preuner, E. Ein Delphische Weihgeschenk. Bonn, 1899.
Arc 705.204 Sauer, B. Das Sergenannte Theseion. Berlin, 1899.
Arc 547.16 Schmidt, V. Den aegyptiske samlung. Copenhagen, 1899.
Arc 520.9 Schmidt. Pergamon. Lübeck, 1899.
Arc 608.7 Schulten, A. Das römische Afrika. Leipzig, 1899.
Arc 1077.2.21 Strazzulla, V. Indagini archeologiche del "Signum Christi". Palermo, 1899.
Arc 1348.15 Stuckelburg, E.A. Der Münzsammler. Zürich, 1899.
Arc 925.6.10 Talko-Hryncewicz, J. Suzhdenskoe doietoricheskoe kladbishche. Moskva, 1899.
Arc 1143.2.7 Thompson, Edward Maunde. Paleografia greca e latina. Milano, 1899.
Arc 861.59 Turner, William. Ancient remains near Buxton. Buxton, 1899.
Arc 510.213 Ussing, J.L. Pergamos seine Geschichte und Monumente. Berlin, 1899
Arc 387.10.5 Vedova, Giuseppe. Il conte L. Palma di Cesnola e il Museo metropolitano di Nuova York. Roma, 1899.
Arc 1613.19 Von Bergen, W. The rare coins of America, England, Ireland, Scotland, France, Germany, and Spain. Cambridge, Mass., 1899.
Arc 87.1.59 Winnefeld, H. Altgriechisches Bronzebecken aus Leontini. Berlin, 1899.

19-

Arc 726.70.5 American School of Classical Studies in Rome. The triumphal arch of Trajan at Beneventum. Rome, 19- ?
Arc 785.13.51 Artioli, Romolo. The Roman Forum. Rome, 19- .
Arc 830.88 Audollent, A. Clermont gallo-romain. Clermont-Ferrand, 19- .
Arc 1510.143 Buchenau, H. Beiträge zur schwäbisch-fränkischen Münzkunde des späteren Mittelalters. n.p., 19- .
X Cg Arc 608.2.27 Carthage. Carthage, 19- .
Arc 1348.44 Chase National Bank, N.Y. The Chase architrave. N.Y., 19-
Arc 861.31.10 Cunnington, M.E. (Mrs.) Avebury; a guide. Devizes, 19- .
Arc 743.1.9 Dennis, G. The cities and cemeteries of Etruria. London, 19- . 2v.
Arc 1335.61 Dupriez, C. La grande guerre. Bruxelles, 19- ?
Arc 790.211F Fischetti, Luigi. Pompei com'era e com'è. Milano, 19- ? 2v.
Arc 1411.12 Jorgensen, Holgar. Old coins of China. n.p., 19- .
Arc 843.73 Mélida, José R. Les fouilles de Merida. n.p., 19- ?
Arc 537.14 Mission Archéologique d'Alasia. Mission archéologique d'Alasia. Paris, 19- .
Arc 1675.51 Poland. Mennica Panstwowa. Katalog wejborów. Warszawa, 19- ?
Arc 1455.6F Sartiges. Collection du vicomte de Sartiges. Paris, 19- ?
Arc 785.13.90 Staderini, G. The Roman Forum. Rome, 19- .

190-

Arc 762.1.5.5 Hare, A.J.C. Walks in Rome. 15th ed. N.Y., 190-?
X Cg Arc 1675.29 Marx, Roger. Les medailleurs modernes, 1789-1900. Paris, 190-.

1900

Arc 1.14.2 Accademia...Rome. Accademia Romana di Archeologia. Indice delle dissertazioni e communicazioni. Roma, 1900.
Arc 930.205F Akademie der Wissenschaften in Wien. Schriften der Balkancommission. Antiquarische Abtheilung. v.1-7,9-10,13. Wien, 1900-39. 10v.
Arc 1335.14.4 Babelon, E. Guide illustré au cabinet des médailles. Paris, 1900.
Arc 608.6.25 Blanchet, P. La porte de Sidi Oqba. Paris, 1900.
Arc 785.13.15 Borsari, Luigi. Le Forum Romain selon les dernières fouilles. Rome, 1900.
Arc 1153.4.5 Breidenbach, H. Zwei Abhandlungen...tironischen Noten. Darmstadt, 1900.
Arc 712.12 British Museum. Sculpures...Parthenon. London, 1900.
Arc 1033.20.26 Brownlow. Basilica of St. Clement in Rome. London, 1900.
Arc 905.4.10 Bulić, Frane. Po ruševinama staroga Salina. Zagreb, 1900.
Arc 925.19F Bulychov, N. Kourgans et Gorodietz. Moskva, 1900. 3 pam.
Arc 435.2.24F Burgess, James. The Muhammadan architecture of Ahmadabad. London, 1900.
Arc 1027.52 Carmelo, D. Guida delle catacombe e dei monumenti. Roma, 1900.
Arc 830.57 Cauchemè, V. Description des fouilles archéologiques...Compiègne. pt.1-4. Compiègne, 1900-12.
Arc 1033.47.21 Coen, J.A. La persecuzione neroniana dei Cristiani. Firenze, 1900.
Arc 510.214 Collignon, M. Pergame restauration des monuments de l'Aropole. Paris, 1900.
Arc 893.16F Copenhagen. Nationalmuseet. Affaldsdynger faa stenalderen i Denmark undersögte for Nationalmuseet. Paris, 1900.
Arc 815.6 Czechowski, D. Die Hausgötter in Pompeji. Peremyal, 1900.
Arc 340.2 Deutsches Archäologisches Institut. Römische Abteilung. Bibliothek. Katalog der Bibliothek. Rom, 1900-02. 2v.
Arc 66.1.83 Dofourco, A. Etudes sur les gesta martyrum. Paris, 1900.
Arc 1500.31 Ducrocq, T. Les nouveaux types monétaires de la France. Poitiers, 1900.

1900 - cont.

Arc 915.7 Dunant, Émile. Guide illustrative du Musée d'Avenches. Genève, 1900.
Arc 1143.10 Dziatzko, K. Untersuchungen...antiken Buchwesens. Leipzig, 1900.
Arc 1027.25.45 Galante, G.A. Giovanni Battista de Rossi e l'archeologia cristiana. Napoli, 1900.
Arc 843.15 Gibert y Olivé, A.M. Excursions arqueológicas. Ciutats focenses del litoral coseta. Barcelona, 1900.
Arc 1478.15 Gnecchi, F. Monete romane. Milano, 1900.
Arc 587.5 Griffith, F.L. The Mastabo of Ptalshetep and Alsbrethetep. London, 1900. 2v.
Arc 855.220 Griffith, J.E. Portfolio of photographs of Cromlechs of Anglesey and Carnarvonshire. Derby, 1900.
Arc 830.340F Guimet, Émile. Les isiaques de la Gaule. Paris, 1900.
Arc 790.206.5 Gusman, P. Pompei; the city, its life and art. London, 1900.
Arc 520.8 Hachtmann, K. Pergamon. Pflanzstätte Hellenisches Kunst. Gütersloh, 1900.
Arc 1550.4 Hauberg, Peter C. Myntforhold og utmyntninger i Danmark indtil 1146. Kjøbenhavn, 1900.
Arc 762.2 Homo, L. Lexique de topographie romaine. Paris, 1900.
Arc 793.7 Horne, J.F. The mirage of two buried cities. London, 1900.
Arc 810.18 Hubik, J. Pompeji im Gymnasialunterricht. Wien, 1900.
Arc 1016.205.5 Hübner, A. Inscritione hispaniae christianarum. Supplement. Berolini, 1900.
Arc 1027.66 Huelsen, C. Di una iscrizione monumentale al cimitero di Generosa. Roma, 1900.
Arc 435.25.3F Indian Museum, Calcutta. A list of the photographic negatives of Indian antiquities. Calcutta, 1900.
Arc 73.100 International Congress of Christian Archaeology, 2nd, Rome, 1900. Commentarius authenticus. v.1-6. Rome, 1900.
Arc 1020.9.60 Iozzi, Oliviero. Le chiese di Roma...nel secolo XIX. Roma, 1900. 4 pam.
Arc 1016.206 Iozzi, Oliviero. Vetri cimiteriali con figure in oro conservati nell Museo Britannico. Roma, 1900.
Arc 1016.206.3 Iozzi, Oliviero. Vetri cimiteriali con figure in oro conservati nell Museo Sacro Vaticano. Roma, 1900.
Arc 80.1.5 Kabbadias, P. Historia tēs Archaiologikēs Hetairias. Athēnai, 1900.
Arc 674.3.5 Kabbaria. Toieron toy asklēpioy. Athēnai, 1900.
Arc 1200.5.5 Kaiser, H. Collection perpetuorum formorum. Innsbruck, 1900.
Arc 1016.200 Kaufmann, C.I. Die sepulcralen Jenseits Denkmäler. Mainz, 1900.
Arc 1433.30 Lacroix, D. Numismatique annamite. Text and atlas. Saigon, 1900. 2v.
Arc 1025.37 Lampake, G. Christianikē gechnē...katakombai. Athēnai, 1900.
Arc 766.1.10 Lanciani, R. The ruins and excavations of ancient Rome. Boston, 1900.
Arc 628.16 Lang, G. Von Rom nach Sardes. Stuttgart, 1900.
Arc 905.12 List, G. Der Wiederauflau von Carnuntum. Wien, 1900.
Arc 1016.221 Lugari, G.B. La pontificia accademia romana di archeologia. Roma, 1900.
Arc 66.1.82 Macé, A. Essai sur Suétone. Paris, 1900.
Arc 785.14.9 Maes, Costantino. Tutte le rovine, le memorie storiche. Roma, 1900.
Arc 1033.47.17 Mapelli, L. L'incendio di Roma e i primi Cristiani. Milano, 1900.
Arc 1025.28.19 Marucchi, O. Come lo studio dell'archeologia cristiana. Roma, 1900.
Arc 1020.9.70 Marucchi, O. Di un nuovo cippo del pomerio urbano. Roma, 1900.
Arc 945.4 Mason, Otis J. Aboriginal American harpoons. Washington, 1900.
Arc 810.11.6 Mau, August. Pompeji in Leben und Kunst. Leipzig, 1900.
Arc 1643.1.5 Medina, J.T. Medallas coloniales hispano-americanas. Santiago, 1900.
Arc 843.60 Monsalad, M.C.S.G. Arqueología romana y visigotica de extremadura. Madrid, 1900.
Arc 950.202.13 Moore, C.B. Certain antiquities of the Florida west coast. Philadelphia, 1900.
Arc 905.1.5 Munro, Robert. Rambles and studies in Bosnia-Herzegovina and Dalmatia, with an account of the proceedings of the congress of archaeologists and anthropologists. 2. ed. Edinburgh, 1900.
Arc 658.3.9 Nelson, J. Heinrich Schliemann und die Homersche Welt. Leipzig, 1900.
Arc 587.50 Newberry, P.E. The life of Rekhmara. Westminster, 1900.
Arc 1027.19.5 Nortet. Cimetière de Saint Calixte. 3e éd. Rome, 1900.
Arc 1020.128F Pappageorgios, P. Un édit de l'empereur Justinien II. Leipzig, 1900.
Arc 1033.166 La passio Ss. Mariani et Iacobi. Roma, 1900.
Arc 830.137 Pathier, Edgard L.F. Les tumulus du plateau de Ger. Paris, 1900.
Arc 1490.19 Perini, L. La repubblica di San Marino sue monete medaglie decorazioni. Roverto, 1900.
Arc 770.6.2 Petersen, Eugen. Vom alten Rom. 2. Aufl. Leipzig, 1900.
Arc 1027.5.55 Petit guide du cimetière de Domitille. Rome, 1900.
Arc 585.17A Petrie, W.M.F. Dendereh. 1898. London, 1900.
Arc 585.18A Petrie, W.M.F. The royal tombs of the First Dynasty. v.1; v.2, pt.1-2. London, 1900. 3v.
Arc 785.26 Prestel, J. Des Marcus Vitruvius Pollio Basilika zu Fanum Fortunae. Strassburg, 1900.
Arc 673.1.8 Preuner, E. Ein Delphische Weihgeschenk. Leipzig, 1900.
Arc 588.10 Quibell, J.E. Hierakonpolis. Pt.1-2. London, 1900-1902.
NEDL Arc 588.10 Quibell, J.E. Hierakonpolis. Pt.1-2. London, 1900-1902.
Arc 1027.28 Rampolla, M. Catalogo cimiteriale romano. Roma, 1900.
Arc 853.18 Ranke, Johannes. Die akademische Kommission. München, 1900.
Arc 830.114 Raymond, Paul. L'arrondissement d'Uzès avant l'histoire. Paris, 1900.
Arc 1663.16 Ricciardi, E. Medaglie del Regno delle due Sicilie 1735-1861. Napoli, 1900.
Arc 905.10 Rodlow, O.W. von. Die Brennerstrasse im Alterthum und Mittelalter. Prag, 1900.
Arc 1018.10 Rome, Italy. Collections. Stromation archaiologikon. Rome, 1900.
Arc 1027.5.4 Rossi, G.B. de. Il cubicolo di Ampliato nel cimitero di Domitilla. Roma, 1900.
Arc 87.1.60 Schrader, H. Sechziges Program zum Winckelmannsfeste. Berlin, 1900.
Arc 853.14 Seyler, E. Die Drusenverschanzungen bei Deisenhofen. München, 1900.
Arc 855.5 Small, J.W. Scottish market crosses. Stirling, 1900.

Chronological Listing

1900 - cont.

Arc 1027.16 Strazzulla, V. Nouvi studi su alcuni elemente Pagani. Messina, 1900.
Arc 628.14 Strema Helbigiana. Leipzig, 1900.
Arc 785.13.5 Thédenat, Henry. Le Forum Romain et les Forum impériaux. Paris, 1900.
Arc 930.200.5F Tocilescou, G.G. Fouilles et recherches archéologiques en Roumanie. Bucarest, 1900.
Arc 635.220 Tsoynta, C. Ai Proistorikai...diménioy kaisesklоy. Athēnai, 1900.
Arc 1077.2.33 Tyack, G.S. The cross in ritual architecture and art. 2. ed. London, 1900.
Arc 1025.35.20 Valeri, A. Cenni biografici di Antonio Bosio. Roma, 1900.
Arc 1020.10 Valeri, A. Monumenti cristiani del Foro Romano. Roma, 1900.
Arc 1020.9.85 Vannitelli, V. Memorie sacre Lateranensi. Roma, 1900.
Arc 292.150 Veselovskii, H.I. Istorii. Sankt Peterburg, 1900.
Arc 900.209 Vienna. Akademie. Der römische Limes in Österreich. Wien, 1900- 20v.
Arc 925.9.7 Vladimirova, N. Drevnosti chernomorskia poberezh'ia kavkaza. Sankt Petersburg, 1900.
Arc 1016.211 Waal, A. de. Sarkophag des Junius Bassus. Rom, 1900.
Arc 600.10 Winslow, W.C. Egyptian antiquities for our museums. n.p., 1900.

1901

Arc 1033.47.8 Abbatescianni, G. Primi Christiani e Nerone apropositо dell'opuscolo di Carlo Pascal. Bari, 1901.
Arc 708.21 Ambrosoli, G. Atene. Brevi cenni sulla città antica e moderna. Milano, 1901.
Arc 1675.27.5F Andorfer, Karl. Musica in nummis. Wien, 1901.
Arc 1540.12 Andrew, W.J. A numismatic history of the reign of Henry I. v.1-2. London, 1901.
Arc 1663.11 Arnold, H.P. The evolution of the Boston medal. Boston, 1901.
Arc 1578.10 Austria. Haupt Münzamt in Wien. Katalog der Münzen- und Medaillen-Stampel. Wien, 1901-06. 4v.
Arc 1458.13 Babelon, E. Traite des monnaies grecques et romaines. Paris, 1901-33. 8v.
Arc 1333.16F Bahrfeldt, Emil. Die Münzen- und Medaillen-Sammlung. Danzig, 1901-10. 6v.
Arc 790.208 Barnabei, F. La villa pompeiana. Roma, 1901.
Arc 820.204 Barrière-Flavy, Casimir. Les arts industriels. Paris, 1901. 3v.
Arc 968.1.5.5 Beauchamp, W.M. Wampum and shell articles used by the New York Indians. Albany, 1901. 2 pam.
Arc 1053.2.5 Bernoulli, J.J. Griechische Ikonographie. München, 1901. 2v.
Arc 1076.3.39 Berthele, J. La famille Cavillier et les fonderies de cloches de Carrepuits. Caen, 1901. 2 pam.
Arc 658.3.11 Brinckmeier. Heinrich Schliemann und die Ausgrabungen auf Hissarlik. Burg, 1901.
Arc 1027.43 Bulic, F. Necropoli antica cristiana a Slano di Ragusa. Roma, 1901.
Arc 1510.36 Cahn, Julius. Der Rappenmünzbund. Heidelberg, 1901.
Arc 1418.7 Campos, M.J. da C. Numismatica indo-portuguesa. Lisboa, 1901.
Arc 1153.12.3 Cappelli, A. Lexicon abbreviaturarum. Leipzig, 1901.
Arc 1016.230 Catholic Church. Congregatio Indulgentiarum et Sacrarum Reliquiarum. Acta congregationis praeparatoriae habitae die 4 iulii 1901. De authenticitate S. Sindonis Taurinensis. Roma, 1901.
Arc 1016.230.2 Catholic Church. Congregatio Indulgentiarum et Sacrarum Reliquiarum. Excellentissimo ac revmo dño Aloisio Tripepi. De authenticitate S. Sindonis Taurinensis. Roma, 1901.
Arc 1020.10.19 A Christian corner in Roman Forum. Rome, 1901.
Arc 785.13.42 A Christian corner in the Roman Forum. Rome, 1901.
Arc 1027.57 Colasanti, A. Le stagione nell'antichità...arte christiano. Roma, 1901.
Arc 1025.43 Crostarosa, P. Notizie sullo stato delle catacombe romane. Roma, 1901.
Arc 587.6 Davies, N. de Garis. The rock tombs of Sheikh Said. London, 1901.
Arc 625.12 Delestre, M. Collection d'antiquités, grecques et romaines. Paris, 1901.
Arc 820.208F Delort, J.B. Dix années de fouilles en Auvergne. Lyon, 1901.
Arc 530.8 Dickson, W.K. The life of Major General Sir R.M. Smith. Edinburgh, 1901.
Arc 505.9 Dussaud, René. Voyage archéologique au Safâ. Paris, 1901.
Arc 1033.167 Eleuterio. I martirii di S. Teodoto e di S. Ariadne. Roma, 1901.
Arc 625.5.2 Erklaren der Text. v.1-2. 2. Aufl. Leipzig, 1901.
NEDL Arc 720.208 Ferrero, E. L'arc d'Auguste à Suse. Turin, 1901.
Arc 838.20 Fortes, José. Lagar de Mouros. Porto, 1901-08. 6 pam.
Arc 736.5 Garafalo, F.B. Le vie romane in Sicilia. Napoli, 1901.
Arc 588.11 Garstang, John. El Arábah. London, 1901.
Arc 1588.1.27 Gartman, V.G. Pol'skiia i litobskiia star. monety. Syzran, 1901.
Arc 830.100 Gasser, A. Recherches archéologiques sur le térritoire de Mantoche. Gray, 1901.
Arc 1510.140 Gebert, Carl Friedrich. Die Brandenburg Frankischen Kippermünzstätten, 1620-1622. München, 1901.
Arc 723.8 Gentile, I. Trattato di archeologia e storia dell'arte italiano. Milano, 1901. 2v.
Arc 556.1 Griffith, Francis L. The study of Egyptology. Oxford, 1901.
Arc 543.25 Groneman, I. The Tyandi-Barabudur in Central Java. Samarang, 1901.
Arc 682.4 Hall, H.R. The oldest civilization of Greece. London, 1901. 2v.
Arc 785.22.2 Haugwitz, E. Der Palatin. Rom, 1901.
Arc 785.22 Haugwitz, E. Der Palatin seine Geschichte und seine Ruinen. Rom, 1901.
Arc 913.19 Heierli, J. Urgeschichte der Schweiz. Zürich, 1901.
Arc 1663.19 Herrera y Chiesanova, A. Medallos de los gobernadores. Madrid, 1901.
Arc 762.3 Hula, E. Römische Altertümer. Leipzig, 1901.
Arc 1430.200 Imhoof-Blumer, Friedrich. Kleinasiatische Münzen. Wien, 1901-02. 2v.
Arc 530.11 Joubin, André. De sarcophagis Clazomeniis. Paris, 1901.
Arc 830.96 Joulin, Léon. Les établissements gallo-romaines de la plaine de Martres-Tolosanes. Paris, 1901.
Arc 87.1.61 Kekule, R. Über ein Bildnis des Perikles in den Königlichen Museum. Berlin, 1901.

1901 - cont.

Arc 766.1.13A Lanciani, R. New tales of old Rome. Boston, 1901.
Arc 766.1.15 Lanciani, R. New tales of old Rome. London, 1901.
Arc 684.1.7 Leonardos, B. Hē Olympia. Athēnai, 1901.
Arc 830.11.5 Le Rouzic, Z. Les monuments mégalithiques de Carnac et de Locmariaquer. n.p., 1901?
Arc 1185.20 Likhachev, N.P. Diplomatika. Sankt Peterburg, 1901.
Arc 1018.7.2 Lourie, W. Monuments of the early church. N.Y., 1901.
Arc 628.17 Luckenbach, H. Antike Kunstwerke im klassischen Unterricht. München, 1901.
Arc 853.33 Luschan, F. von. Die Karl Knorrsche Sammlung von Benin-Altertümern. Stuttgart, 1901.
Arc 785.13.13 Maes, C. Primo trofeo della croce nel Foro Romano. Roma, 1901.
Arc 843.30 Mancheño y Olivares, Miguel. Antigüedades del partido oficial de Arcos de la Frontera. Arcos de la Frontera, 1901.
Arc 861.47.5 Markham, C.A. Stone crosses of county of Northampton. London, 1901.
Arc 547.23 Marucchi, O. Gli antichi oggetti egiziani. Roma, 1901.
Arc 1027.4.13 Marucchi, O. Di un battistero scoperto nel cimitero di Priscilla. Roma, 1901.
Arc 1027.25.31 Marucchi, O. Giovanni Battista de Rossi. Roma, 1901.
Arc 950.202.11 Moore, C.B. Certain aborginal remains of the northwestern Florida coast. pt.1-2. Philadelphia, 1901. 2v.
Arc 810.53 Morlicchio, F. Guide to Pompei illustrated. Pompei, 1901.
Arc 1033.33 Müller, N. Koimeterien die altchristlichen Begrabnis. Leipzig, 1901.
Arc 1153.2.2 Paoli, Cesare. Programma scolastico di paleografia latina. 3. ed. Firenze, 1901.
Arc 1033.28 Pelka, O. Altchristliche Ehredenkmäler. Strassburg, 1901.
Arc 585.19 Petrie, W.M.F. Diospolis Parva...1898-99. London, 1901.
Arc 1200.6 Pflugh-Harttung, J. Bullen der Päpste. Gotha, 1901.
Arc 542.200 Pleyte, C.M. Die Buddha-Legende. Amsterdam, 1901.
Arc 435.2.26F Purna Chandra, Mukhopâdhyâya. Report of a tour of exploration of the antiquities in the Tarai, Nepal. Calcutta, 1901.
Arc 66.2.80 Radet, G. L'histoire et l'oeuvre de l'école française d'Athènes. Paris, 1901.
Arc 1016.208 Roulin, E. L'ancien trésor de l'Abbaye de Silos. Paris, 1901.
Arc 387.10.10 Roversi, Luigi. Ricordi Canavesani. Luigi Palma di Cesnola. N.Y., 1901.
Arc 853.61F Schliz, A. Das steinzeitliche Dorf Grossgartach. Stuttgart, 1901.
Arc 435.2.30F Smith, E.W. Moghul colour decoration of Agra. Allahabad, 1901.
X Cg Arc 435.2.20F Smith, V.A. The Jain stûpa and other antiquities of Mathûra. Allahabad, 1901.
Arc 543.3.3 Stein, Mark Aurel. Preliminary report on a journey of archaeological exploration...Turkestan. London, 1901.
Arc 1018.22 Tacchi-Venturi, P. Correspondenza di L.A. Muratori. Roma, 1901.
Arc 1033.25 Taglialatela, G. L'arte cristiana nello studio della storia della chiesa. Napoli, 1901.
Arc 1153.4.7 Traube, L. Die Geschichte der tironischen Noten. Berlin, 1901.
Arc 672.5 Wilisch, E. Beiträge zur Geschichte des alten Korinth. Zittau, 1901.

1902

Arc 1093.4 Altmann, W. Architectur und Ornamentik der antiken Sarkophage. Berlin, 1902.
Arc 600.11 Amélineau, E. Les nouvelles fouilles d'Abydos, seconde campagne 1896-1897. Paris, 1902.
X Cg Arc 510.8 American Archaeological Institute. Investigations at Assos. v.1-2. Cambridge, 1902-21.
Arc 855.224F Ashby, Thomas. Excavations at Caerwent, Monmouthshire 1901-1903. London, 1902-1904.
Arc 1020.9.131 Barbier de Montault, X. L'année liturgique à Rome. Rome, 1902.
Arc 505.19.5 Barnabas. Deux questions d'archéologie palestinienne. Jérusalem, 1902. 2v.
Arc 1033.101 Barreca, C. Santa Lucia di Siracusa. Roma, 1902.
Arc 522.4.9 Berlin. Königliches Museum. Heinrich Schliemanns Sammlung Trojanischer Altertümer. Berlin, 1902.
X Cg Arc 66.1.87 Besiner, M. L'ile tiberine dans l'antiquité. Paris, 1902.
Arc 1033.40.9 Bianchi-Cagliesi. Santa Cecilia et La Sua Basilica nel Trastevere. Roma, 1902. 2 pam.
Arc 1510.22.10 Bibliothèque Nationale, Paris. Département des Médailles et Antiques. Collection de monnaies et médailles d'Alsace. Paris, 1902.
Arc 823.10 Blanchet, A. Cronique archéologique de la France. Paris, 1902.
Arc 1264.7 Blanchet, A. Sigillographie française. Paris, 1902.
X Cg Arc 500.7 Bliss, F.J. Excavations in Palestine, 1895-1900. London, 1902.
Arc 1458.10 Boston. Museum of Fine Arts. Guide to the C.P. Perkins collection of Greek and Roman coins. Boston, 1902.
Arc 551.3 Brodrick, M. A concise dictionary of Egyptian archaeology. London, 1902.
Arc 1033.39 Bulic, F. Frammento di pettine son reppresentanze cristiane. Roma, 1902.
Arc 547.6.12 Cairo. Musée des Antiquités Égyptiennes. Guide du visiteur au Musée du Caire. Caire, 1902.
Arc 545.233 Capart, J. Recueil de monuments egyptiens. Bruxelles, 1902-05. 2v.
Arc 608.1.29 Carton, Louis B.C. Le théâtre de Dougga. Paris, 1902.
Arc 588.13 Caulfield, A.S.G. Temple of the Kings at Abydos. London, 1902.
Arc 66.1.85 Collignon, M. Catalogue des vases peints. Paris, 1902. 4v.
Arc 830.39 Coutil, Léon. Inventaire des monuments megalithiques du Calvados. Caen, 1902.
Arc 861.19 Crossing, W. The ancient stone crosses of Dartmoor. Exeter, 1902.
Arc 585.22 Crum, W.E. Coptic Ostraca. London, 1902.
Arc 587.7 Davies, N. de Garis. The rock tombs of Deir el Gebrâevi. London, 1902. 2v.
Arc 66.1.86 Déprez, E. Les préliminaires de la guerre de cents ans. Paris, 1902.
Arc 73.6.2 Deutsches Archäologisches Institut. Römische Abteilung. Mittheilungen. Register, Bd. I-X. Rom, 1902.
Arc 522.15 Dörpfeld, W. Troja und Ilion. Athen, 1902. 2v.
Arc 853.30.5 Dragendorff, Hans. II. Ausgrabungen bei Haltern. n.p., 1902.

Chronological Listing

1902 - cont.

Arc 1027.32 Dufresne, D. Les cryptes vaticanes. Paris, 1902.
Arc 855.209F Dymond, C.W. Worlebury - an ancient stronghold. Bristol, 1902.
Arc 823.9A Enlart, C. Manuel d'archéologie française. Paris, 1902-1904. 3v.
Arc 1349.45 Fayolle, A. Evrard. Recherches sur Bertrand Andrieu de Bordeau. Chalon-sur-Saone, 1902.
Arc 708.22.3 Gardner, E.A. Ancient Athens. London, 1902.
Arc 708.22A Gardner, E.A. Ancient Athens. N.Y., 1902.
Arc 588.12 Garstang, John. Mahâsna and Bêt Khalfâf. London, 1902.
Arc 1033.6.25 Gatti, Giuseppe. La casa celimontana dei Valerii e il Monastero di S. Erasmo. Roma, 1902.
Arc 853.31 Götze. Die vor- und frühgeschichtlichen altertümer Thüringens. Würzburg, 1902.
Arc 609.1.9 Hall, R.N. The ancient ruins of Rhodesia. London, 1902.
Arc 762.1.25 Hare, A.J.C. Days near Rome. 3. ed. N.Y., 1902.
Arc 415.1 Heger, Franz. Alte Metalltrommeln aus Südost-Asien. Leipzig, 1902. 2v.
Arc 530.10 Herkenrath, E. Der Fries des Artemisions von Magnesia. Berlin, 1902.
Arc 785.13.20 Huelsen, Christian. Die Ausgrabungen auf dem Forum Romanum. v.1-2. Roma, 1902-05.
Arc 73.100.5 International Congress of Christian Archaeology, 2nd, Rome, 1900. Atti del II Congresso internazionale...tenuto in Roma nell'aprile 1900. Roma, 1902.
Arc 1015.206.9 Iozzi, Oliviero. Cryptae Carciliae trans Tiberim descriptio. 2. ed. Romae, 1902.
Arc 1020.9.63 Iozzi, Oliviero. La veneranda antica chiesa di S. Andrea e Gregoria. Roma, 1902.
Arc 93.25 Italy. Ministero dell'Istruzione Pubblica. L'amministrazione delle antichità e belle arti in Italia. Roma, 1902.
Arc 1163.3.10 Karskii, E.F. Obraztsy slavianskago kirillovskago pis'ma. Varshava, 1902.
Arc 1020.14 Kaufmann, C.M. Ein altchristliches Pompeji. Mainz, 1902.
Arc 900.213 Klose, O. Die römischen Meilensteine in Salzberg. Wien, 1902.
Arc 1027.59 Labanca, B. Gesù Cristo nelle catacombe di Roma. Roma, 1902.
Arc 766.1.14 Lanciani, R. New tales of old Rome. Boston, 1902.
Arc 766.1.17A Lanciani, R. Storia degli scavi di Roma. v.1-4. Roma, 1902. 5v.
Arc 1053.10 Lichteuber, G.R. von. Das Porträt an Grabdenkmalen. Strassburg, 1902.
Arc 1660.4.2F Loehr, August. Wiener Medailleure. Nachtrag, 1901. Wien, 1902.
Arc 628.13.5 Luckenbach, H. Kunst und Geschichte. München, 1902-03. 3v.
Arc 543.2 Lunet de Lagonquiere, E. Inventaire descriptif des monuments du Cambodge. v.1-3 and map. Paris, 1902. 4v.
Arc 682.5 Marcks, F. Die mykenische Zeit. Cöln, 1902.
Arc 1027.5.15 Marucchi, O. Di un gruppo di antiche iscrizioni...Domitilla. Roma, 1902.
Arc 785.13.35 Marucchi, O. Le Forum Romain et le Palatin. Paris, 1902.
Arc 1027.19.17 Marucchi, O. Guida del cimitero di Callisto. Paris, 1902.
Arc 1027.5.13 Marucchi, O. Guida del cimitero di Domitilla. Paris, 1902.
Arc 1033.28.8 Marucchi, O. La santità del matrimonio. Roma, 1902.
Arc 562.2.13 Maspero, Gaston. Manual of Egyptian archaeology. London, 1902.
Arc 562.2.14 Maspero, Gaston. Manual of Egyptian archaeology. London, 1902.
Arc 810.11.9 Mau, August. Pompeii, its life and art. N.Y., 1902.
Arc 1640.5 Medina, J.T. Las monedas chilenas. Santiago, 1902.
Arc 1033.31 Mély, F. de. Le Saint Suaire de Turin. Paris, 1902?
Arc 830.84 Moreau de Néris, E. Néris, capitale des Gaules. Paris, 1902.
Arc 493.3 Morgan, J. de. Le délégation en Perse. Paris, 1902.
Arc 1153.2.15 Paoli, Cesare. Grundriss - lateinische Palaeographie. Innsbruck, 1902.
Arc 815.18F Paribeni, R. Pompei. n.p., 1902.
Arc 1274.3 Pedrick, G. Monastic seals of the XIIIth century. London, 1902.
Arc 1490.27.5 Perini, Quintilio. Le monete di Verona. Rovereto, 1902.
Arc 750.206 Petersen, E. Ara Pacis Augustae. Wien, 1902. 2v.
Arc 585.20A Petrie, W.M.F. Abydos. Pt.1-3. London, 1902-04. 3v.
Arc 1027.55 Pinza, G. Notizie sul cimitero cristiano di Bonaria [Sardini]. Roma, 1902.
Arc 888.40F Pleyte, Willem. Nederlandsche oudheden van de vroegste tijden tot op Karel dan Groote. Leiden, 1902. 2v.
Arc 505.5.3 Prestel, J. Baugeschichte des Jüdischen Heiligthums...Tempel Salomons. Strassburg, 1902.
Arc 585.21 Randall-MacIver, D. Amrah and Abydos. 1899-1901. London, 1902.
NEDL Arc 1372.1 Reinach, T. L'histoire par les monnaies. Paris, 1902.
Arc 402.8 Roger-Milès, L. Vingt siècles de travail. Paris, 1902.
Arc 726.78F Savignoni, L. Relazione sopra gli scavi eseguiti a Norba nell'estate dell'anno 1901. Roma, 1902.
Arc 830.50 Société Historique et Archéologique de Langres. Catalogue du Musée. Langres, 1902.
Arc 600.1.9 Strzygowski, J. Hellenistische und koptische Kunst in Alexandria. Wien, 1902.
Arc 870.13 Styan, K.E. Short history of sepulchral cross-slabs. London, 1902.
Arc 925.235F Urusov, V.P. Raskopki kurganov Eniseiskoi gubernii. Moskva, 1902.
Arc 1033.12.9 Vignon, P. The shroud of Christ. Westminster, 1902.
Arc 1175.7 Voigt, Karl. Beiträge zur Diplomatik der langodardischen Fürsten. Göttingen, 1902.
Arc 670.4.5F Walston, Charles. The Argive Heraeum. Boston, 1902-05. 2v.
Arc 1468.11 Ward, J. Greek coins and their parent cities. London, 1902.
Arc 600.100 Ward, J. The sacred beetle. London, 1902.
Arc 853.19 Weynand, R. De cipporum germaniae romanorum ornamentis. Bonnae, 1902.
Arc 1027.3 Wilpert, G. La croce sui monumenti delle catacombe. Roma, 1902.

1903

NEDL Arc 855.206 Allen, J.R. The early Christian monuments of Scotland. Edinburgh, 1903.
Arc 530.9 Anderson, J.G.C. Journey of exploration in Pontus. v.1. Bruxelles, 1903.

1903 - cont.

Arc 530.9.2 Anderson, J.G.C. Journey of exploration in Pontus. v.2. Bruxelles, 1903.
Arc 530.9.3 Anderson, J.G.C. Journey of exploration in Pontus. v.3. Bruxelles, 1903.
Arc 1540.12.5 Andrew, W.J. Notes on numismatic history of the reign of Henry I. v.1-2. London, 1903.
Arc 1018.6.3 Armellini, M. Lezioni popolari di archaeologici cristiana. Roma, 1903.
Arc 900.2.5F Austria. Zentral Kommission für Enforschung und Erhaltung der Kunst- und Historischen Denkmäle in Wien. Articles on the palace of Diocletian in Spalato. Wien? 1903.
Arc 1480.24 Babelon, E. L'iconographie monetaire de Julien l'Apostat. Paris, 1903.
Arc 848.27 Balch, E.S. Roman and pre-historic remains in central Germany. Philadelphia, 1903.
Arc 608.1.35 Balut, Georges. Tunisie. Tunis, 1903.
Arc 875.24 Beveridge, E. Coll and Tiree - their prehistoric forts. Edinburgh, 1903.
Arc 823.10.2 Blanchet, A. Cronique archéologique de la France. Paris, 1903.
Arc 687.1.5 Blinkenberg, C. Exploration archéologique de Rhodes. v.1-6. København, 1903-12.
Arc 1027.4.19 Bonavenia, G. Soluzione di un problema...cimitero di Priscilla. Roma, 1903.
Arc 843.25 Brenha, José. Dolmens ou antas de ville ponco d'Aguir. (Traz-os-montes). Porto, 1903.
Arc 1510.5 Bürkel, L. von. Die Bilder der Süddeutschen. München, 1903.
Arc 925.173F Bulychov, Nikolai I. Raskopki po chasti vodorazdela verkhnikh pritokov Dnepra i Volgi, 1903 g. Moskva, 1903.
X Cg Arc 435.2.32F Burgess, James. The architectural antiquities of northern Gujarat. London, 1903.
Arc 495.204.2 Butler, H.C. Architecture and other arts. N.Y., 1903.
Arc 1493.10 Catalogo descriptivo das moedas portuguesas. Lisboa, 1903.
Arc 435.70.2F Ceylon. Archaeological Survey. Annual report, 1903. Preliminary proof. n.p., 1903.
Arc 870.4 Codrington, Thomas. Roman roads in Britain. London, 1903.
Arc 861.13.9 Collingwood, W.G. On some ancient sculptures of the devil bound. Kendal, 1903.
Arc 1663.23 Cunha, Xavier. A medalha de Casimiro José de Lima em homenagem a Sousa Martins. Coimbra, 1903.
Arc 587.8 Davies, N. de Garis. The rock tombs of El Amarna. London, 1903. 6v.
Arc 750.213 Delbrück, R. Das Capitolium von Signia. Rom, 1903.
Arc 785.18 Delbrück, R. Die drei Tempel am Forum Holitorium in Rom. Rom, 1903.
Arc 1018.01 Dictionnaire d'archéologie chrétienne et littérature. v.1-15. Paris, 1903-52. 28v.
Arc 643.1.4 Diehl, C. Excursions archéologiques en Grèce. 5. éd. Paris, 1903.
Arc 1505.3 Dollinger, F. Furstenbergischen Münzen und Medaillen. Donaueschingen, 1903.
Arc 830.124.5 Forrer, Robert. Bauernfarmen der Steinzeit. Strassburg, 1903.
Arc 726.31 Ghirardini, G. Il museo nazionale atestino. Padova, 1903.
Arc 1148.12 Gitlbauer, M. Studien zur griechischen Tachygraphie. Berlin, 1903.
Arc 1335.84.5 Gnecchi, F. Guida numismatica universale. 4. ed. Milano, 1903.
Arc 1478.15.5 Gnecchi, F. Roman coins. London, 1903.
Arc 608.6.13 Gsell, Stéphane. Fouilles de Gouraya. Paris, 1903.
Arc 726.2.9 Günther, R.T. Contributions to a study of earth movements in the Bay of Naples. Oxford, 1903.
Arc 710.8 Hachtmann, K. Akropolis von Athen im Zeitalter des Perikles. Gütersloh, 1903.
Arc 762.1.6 Hare, A.J.C. Walks in Rome. 16th ed. London, 1903. 2v.
Arc 1033.170 Der heilige Märtyrer - Apollonius von Rom. Mainz, 1903.
Arc 726.11.5 Héron de Villefosse, Antoine. L'argenterie et les bijoux d'or du trésor de Boscoreale. Paris, 1903.
Arc 853.20.5 Hettner, F. Illustrierter Führer...Provinzialmuseum in Trier. Trier, 1903.
Arc 1490.8.5 Hill, G.F. Coins of ancient Sicily. Westminster, 1903.
Arc 1016.206.9 Iozzi, Oliviero. Basilica di S. Maria Maggiore. Roma, 1903.
Arc 865.7 Ireland, A.J. Stonehenge: story of its building and its legends. London, 1903.
Arc 861.23.7 Johnson, Walter. Neolithic man in northeast Surrey. London, 1903.
Arc 513.15 Jüthner, J. Vorläufiger Bericht...Expeditionen Kleinasien. Prag, 1903.
Arc 1319.1.5 K. Nederlandsch Genootschap voor Munt en Penningknude. Tijdschrift van het (Koninklyk) genootschap. Index, 1-20, 1893-1912. Amsterdam, 1903.
Arc 600.13 Köster, A. Die ägyptische Pflanzensäule der Spätzeit. Paris, 1903.
Arc 1084.1 Kunz, G.F. H.R. Bishop and his jade collection. Lancaster, 1903.
X Cg Arc 1045.5 Marçais, W. Les monumens arabes. Paris, 1903.
Arc 1025.28.8 Marucchi, O. Come lo studio dell'archeologia cristiana giovi grandemente. Roma, 1903.
Arc 1025.28.4 Marucchi, O. Eléments d'archéologie chrétienne. Paris, 1903. 2v.
Arc 1027.4.15 Marucchi, O. Guida del cimitero di Priscilla. Paris, 1903.
Arc 1027.56 Marucchi, O. Guida delle catacombe di Albano. Roma, 1903.
Arc 1025.28.27 Marucchi, O. Guide des catacombes romaines. 2. éd. Paris, 1903.
Arc 1027.19.21 Marucchi, O. Osservazioni sulla iscrizione della madre del papa Damaso. Roma, 1903.
Arc 1027.40.5 Marucchi, O. La recente condroversia sul cimitero Ostriano. Roma, 1903.
Arc 810.11.4.5 Mau, August. Fuehrer durch Pompeji. 4e Aufl. Leipzig, 1903.
Arc 505.31 Meistermann, Barnabé. Questions de topographie palestinienne. Jerusalem, 1903.
Arc 628.18 Melanges Perrot; recueil de memoires. Paris, 1903.
Arc 895.5.25 Montelius, Oscar. Studier tillägnade Oscar Montelius. Stockholm, 1903.
Arc 950.202.15 Moore, C.B. Certain aboriginal remains...Florida coast. Philadelphia, 1903.
Arc 1077.1.9 Moore, C.B. Sheet-copper from the mounds. Washington, 1903.
Arc 915.3 Naef, A. Le cimetiere Gallo-Helvète de Vevey. n.p., 1903.
Arc 730.205 Orsi, P. L'olympieion di Siracusa. Roma, 1903.

Chronological Listing

1903 - cont.

Arc 838.4 Paris, Pierre. Essai sur l'art et l'industrie de l'Espagne primitive. Paris, 1903. 2v.
Arc 1490.27 Perini, Quintilio. La repubblica romana del 1849 e le sue monete. Rovereto, 1903.
Arc 925.352 Pletnev, V.A. Ob ostatkakh drevnosti i stariny v Tserskoi Gubernii. Tver', 1903.
Arc 968.2.60 Prince, Le B.B. The stone lions of Cochite. Santa Fe, 1903.
Arc 1033.47 Profumo, A. L'incendio neroniano ed i Cristiani. Roma, 1903.
Arc 845.200 Quilling, F. Die Nauheimer Funde. Frankfurt am Main, 1903.
Arc 1423.10.5 Reinach, Théodore. Jewish coins. London, 1903.
Arc 1675.47 Ribagarza, Martin de Gurrea y Aragon. Discursos de medallas y antiguedades. Madrid, 1903.
Arc 785.19 Richter, O. Beiträge zur römischen Topographie. v.1-2,3. Berlin, 1903. 2v.
Arc 843.20 Rocha Peixoto, A.A. da. A pedra dos namorados. Porto, 1903. 4 pam.
Arc 292.30.5 Russia. Arkheologicheskaia Kommissiia. Ukazateli k otchetame za 1882-98. Sankt Peterburg, 1903.
Arc 750.208.5F Sambon, Arthur. Catalogue des fresques de Boscoreale. Macon, 1903.
Arc 750.208 Sambon, Arthur. Les fresques de Boscoreale. Paris, 1903.
Arc 1488.5 Sambon, Arthur. Les monnaies antiques. Paris, 1903.
Arc 712.14 Sauer, B. Der...Kopf und die Giebelgruppen der Parthenon. Berlin, 1903.
Arc 925.343F Spitsyn, Aleksandr A. Gdovskie kurgany v raskopkakh U.N. Glazova. Sankt Petersburg, 1903.
Arc 543.3A Stein, Mark Aurel. Sand-buried ruins of Khotan. London, 1903.
Arc 823.19.168 Thédenat, H. M. Henri Thélier et Mlle Henriette Filhos. Paris, 1903.
Arc 943.9.5 Thomas, C. Introduction...study North American archaeology. Cincinnati, 1903.
Arc 1143.2.11 Thompson, Edward Maunde. Hencheiridion Hellēnikēs. Athēnai, 1903.
Arc 522.16A Tolman, H.C. Mycenaean Troy. N.Y., 1903.
Arc 785.13.200F Tolonei, Arnaldo. La via Cavour e i fori imperiali. Roma, 1903.
Arc 785.13.7 Vaglieri, Dante. Gli scavi recenti nel Foro Romano. Roma, 1903.
Arc 785.13.8 Vaglieri, Dante. Gli scavi recenti nel Foro Romano. Supplemento. Roma, 1903.
Arc 1050.203 Virchow, R. Porträt-Munzen und Grafs...Porträt Gallerie. Berlin, 1903.
Arc 455.1.5 Waddell, L.A. Report on the excavations at Pātaliputra. Calcutta, 1903.
Arc 880.4 Wakeman, W.F. Wakeman's handbook of Irish antiquities. Dublin, 1903.
Arc 885.6 Ward, John. Roman fort of Gelly Gaer in...Glamorgan. London, 1903.
Arc 87.1.63 Watzinger, C. Das Relief des Archelaos von Priene. Berlin, 1903.
Arc 662.4 Weissmann, K. Beiträge zur Erklärung...griechische Kunstwerke. Schweinfurt, 1903.
Arc 586.60 Winslow, W.C. The truth about the Egypt Exploration Society. Boston, 1903.
Arc 830.124 Wolff, F. Handbuch der staatlichen Denkmalpflege in Elsass-Lothringen. Strassburg, 1903.
X Cg Arc 66.1.88 Yver, G. Le commerce et les marchands. Paris, 1903.

1904

Arc 547.15 Aegyptische Gräber. v.2. Strassburg, 1904.
Arc 618.6A Allen, J. Romilly. Celtic art in pagan and Christian times. London, 1904.
Arc 1348.29.3 Ambrosoli, S. Manuale di numismatica. 3. ed. Milano, 1904.
Arc 600.11.2 Amélineau, E. Les nouvelles fouilles d'Abydos 1897-1898. Paris, 1904-05. 2v.
Arc 625.11 Antiquités grecques et romaines. Paris, 1904.
Arc 73.11.10 Archäologisches Institut des Deutschen Reichs. Jahrbuch. Bibliographie, Register, 1-50. Berlin, 1904-21. 4v.
Arc 1411.7 Batairaasch Genootschap van Kunsten in Wetenschappen. Catalogus der munten en amuletten van China. Batavia, 1904.
Arc 1090.1 Behlen, H. Der Pflug und der Pflügen. Dillenburg, 1904.
Arc 1027.54 Benigni, U. Le madonne delle catacombe. Roma, 1904.
Arc 520.10 Berlin. Königliches Museum. Beschreibung der Skulpturen aus Pergamon. Berlin, 1904.
Arc 520.11.5 Berlin. Königliches Museum. Führer durch das Pergamon Museum. Berlin, 1904.
Arc 520.11 Berlin. Königliches Museum. Guide to the Pergamon Museum. Berlin, 1904. 2v.
Arc 756.11.2 Bertaux, Émile. Rome, l'antiquité. Paris, 1904.
Arc 1025.48 Besnier, M. Les catacombes de Rome. Paris, 1904.
Arc 830.17.5 Bircher, H. Bibracte. Aarau, 1904.
Arc 641.1 Blenkenberg, C. Archäologische Studien. Leipzig, 1904.
Arc 756.7.8 Boissier, Gaston. Promenades archéologiques, Rome et Pompéi. 8. éd. Paris, 1904.
Arc 785.13.17.5 Braddeley, S.C. Recent discoveries in the Forum, 1898-1904. London, 1904.
Arc 785.13.17 Braddeley, S.C. Recent discoveries in the Forum. N.Y., 1904.
Arc 547.12.2 British Museum. A guide to the 3rd and 4th Egyptian rooms. London, 1904.
Arc 87.1.64 Brueckner, A. Anakabypteria. Berlin, 1904.
Arc 495.205 Brünnow, R.E. Die Provincia Arabia. Strassburg, 1904. 3v.
NEDL Arc 1163.5.15 Bühler, G. Indian paleography. Bombay, 1904.
Arc 785.13.9 Burton Brown, E. Recent excavations in the Roman Forum. 1898-1904. N.Y., 1904.
Arc 600.6.25F Carter, H. The tomb of Thoutmôsis. Westminster, 1904.
Arc 608.1.30 Carton, Louis B.C. La colonisation romaine dans le pays de Dougga. Tunis, 1904.
Arc 830.183 Clerc, Michele. Découvertes archéologiques à Marseille. Marseille, 1904.
Arc 1433.31 Codrington, O. Manuel of Musalman numismatics. London, 1904.
Arc 1680.6 Davis, William John. The nineteenth century token coinage. London, 1904.
Arc 830.17.3 Déchelette, J. Fouilles du Mont Beuvray 1897-1901. Paris, 1904.
Arc 830.148 Dujardin, A. Estampes mythologiques des Celtes. Étampes, 1904.

1904 - cont.

Arc 759.1 Elter, A. Das alte Rom im Mittelalter. Bonn, 1904.
Arc 1087.2 Engelmann, R. Die antiken Mühlen. Berlin, 1904.
Arc 810.21 Engelmann, R. Pompeii. London, 1904.
Arc 1675.3.7 Fabriczy, C. von. Italian medal. London, 1904.
Arc 843.77 Fernandez, L.M. Excavaciones en Italica. Sevilla, 1904.
Arc 1670.51 Feuardent, F. Jetons et méreaux depuis Louis IX...consulat. Paris, 1904. 2v.
Arc 1349.5 Forrer, L. Biographical dictionary of medallists. London, 1904-30. 8v.
Arc 1033.63.9 Gallonio, A. Traité des instruments de martyre. Paris, 1904.
Arc 589.7 Garstang, J. The third Egyptian dynasty. Westminster, 1904.
Arc 720.213 Gusmann, P. La villa imperiale de Tibur. Paris, 1904.
Arc 609.1.10 Hall, R.N. The ancient ruins of Rhodesia. London, 1904.
Arc 1580.15 Höfken, Rudolf von. Numismatische Denkmale...in Österreich. Wien, 1904.
Arc 66.1.89 Homo, Leon. Essai sur le regne de l'empereur Aurélien. Paris, 1904.
Arc 785.13.21 Huelsen, Christian. Das Forum Romanum. Rom, 1904.
X Cg Arc 510.217 Humann, Carl. Magnesia am Maeander. Berlin, 1904.
Arc 1015.206.5 Iozzi, Oliviero. Roma sotterranea; il cimitero di S. Castolo M. Roma, 1904.
Arc 861.10.13 Kinnebrook, William. Traces of the Norse mythology. London, 1904.
Arc 495.206F Kondakov, N.P. Arkheologicheskoe puteshestvie in Sirii. Sankt Peterburg, 1904.
Arc 684.7 Kourouniotos, K. Hodēgos tēs Olympias. Athēnai, 1904.
Arc 905.12.5 Kubitschek, W. Führer durch Carnuntum. Wien, 1904.
Arc 66.1.92 Lechat, Henri. La sculpture attique avant Phidias. Paris, 1904.
Arc 495.204.4 Littman, Enno. Semitic inscriptions. N.Y., 1904.
Arc 628.13.7 Luckenbach, H. Kunst und Geschichte. München, 1904.
Arc 684.1.11 Luckerrbach, H. Olympia und Delphi. München, 1904.
Arc 1348.17 Luschin von Elengreuth, A. Allgemeine Münzkunde. München, 1904.
Arc 875.17 Mann, L.M. Prehistoric pile-structures in pits. Edinburgh, 1904.
Arc 1027.41 Marucchi, O. Il cimitero di Commodilla. Roma, 1904.
Arc 562.1.20 Maspero, Gaston. Notice biographique sur Auguste Mariette. Paris, 1904.
Arc 1660.9 Medallic illustrations. History of Great Britain and Ireland. v.1-50,101-120. London, 1904. 7v.
Arc 66.1.91 Millet, J. Recueil des inscriptiosn chrétiennes du Mont Athos. Paris, 1904.
Arc 785.52F Monaci, Alfredo. Nuovi studi sull'arco di Constantino. Roma, 1904.
Arc 1027.54.9 Montenovesi, O. Le madonne antiche delle catacombe. Roma, 1904.
Arc 983.9 Moore, C.B. Aboriginal urn-burial in the United States. Lancaster, 1904.
Arc 1528.2 Muller, F. Cabinet de monnaies, J.W. Stephanik. Amsterdam, 1904.
X Cg Arc 1413.09 Munro, N.G. Coins of Japan. 1. ed. Yokohama, 1904.
Arc 588.14 Murray, M. The Osireron at Abydos. London, 1904.
Arc 967.2.5 Peabody, Charles. The exploration of Jacobs Cavern, McDonald County, Missouri. Norwood, 1904.
Arc 1274.3.5 Pedrick, G. Borough seals of the Gothic period. London, 1904.
Arc 785.30 Petersen, Eugen. Comitium, rostra, Grab des Romulus. Rom, 1904.
Arc 770.6.5 Petersen, Eugen. Vom alten Rom. 3. Aufl. Leipzig, 1904.
Arc 400.24 Petrie, William M. Flinders. Methods and aims in archaeology. London, 1904.
Arc 1428.30 Petrowicz, A. von. Arsaciden-Münzen. Wien, 1904.
Arc 1033.40.15 Picarelli, T. Basilica e Casa Romana di S. Cecilia in Trastevere. Roma, 1904.
Arc 770.4A Platner, S.B. Topography and monuments of ancient Rome. Boston, 1904.
Arc 530.19F Pontrenioli, E. Didymes fouilles de 1895 et 1896. Paris, 1904.
Arc 1135.206FA Prou, Maurice. Manuel de paléographie. Paris, 1904.
Arc 1016.210 Richter, J.P. The golden age of classic Christian art. London, 1904.
Arc 1185.11 Rietsch, K.F. Handbuch der Urkundwissen. Berlin, 1904.
Arc 785.20.5 Ripostelli, Giuseppe. La Via Appia en ruine et en reconstruction. Rome, 1904.
Arc 1455.5 Rizzo, G.E. Vasi greci della Sicilia. Roma, 1904.
Arc 750.207 Rodocanachi, E. Le capitole romain. Paris, 1904.
Arc 78.3.3 Rome. Accademia dei Lincei. Notizie degli Scavi. Indici generali, 1876-1955. Milano, 1904-1961. 3v.
Arc 1675.12 Rondot, N. Les médailleurs et 1. graveurs de monnaies. Paris, 1904.
Arc 1510.14.5 Rudolph, E. Zusammenstellung der Taler. Dresden, 1904.
Arc 1440.200 Sborōnos, I.N. Ta nomiomata toy kratoys tōn ptolemaiōn. Athēnai, 1904. 2v.
Arc 635.224F Schwab, G.H. An archaeological cruise in the Levant. N.Y.? 1904.
Arc 705.207 Schwerzek, Karl. Erläuterungen...Rekonstruktion des östlichen Parthenongiebels. Wien, 1904.
Arc 100.1.7 Société Nationale des Antiquaires de France. Centenaire (1804-1904). Compte-rendu de la journée du 11 avril 1904. Paris, 1904.
Arc 100.1.6 Société Nationale des Antiquaires de France. Centenaire 1804-1904. Recueil de mémoires. Paris, 1904.
Arc 1540.10 Stainer, C.L. Oxford silver pennies, 925-1272. Oxford, 1904.
Arc 543.3.2 Stein, Mark Aurel. Sand-buried ruins of Khotan. London, 1904.
Arc 1335.52 Stephanik, J.W. Cabinet de monnaies. Amsterdam, 1904.
Arc 936.120.5 Studniozka, Franz. Tropaeum Traiani. Leipzig, 1904.
Arc 935.32 Tezcan, Burhan. 1962 iki 1963. Ankara, 1904.
Arc 823.19.170 Thédenat, H. Inscription de la caserne des Vigiles à Ostie. Paris, 1904.
Arc 830.45 Thiellen, A. Hommage à Boucher de Perthes. Paris, 1904.
Arc 925.17 Veselovskii, N.I. Pervobytnyia drevnosti. Tuapse, 1904.
Arc 1470.14 Waddington, W.H. Recueil général des monnaies grecques d'Asie Mineure. Paris, 1904. 4v.
Htn Arc 1680.4.5* Waters, A.W. Token coinage of South London...eighteenth and nineteenth centuries. Leamington, 1904.
Arc 530.14.5F Wiegand, Theodor. Priene: Ergebnisse der Ausgrabungen. Berlin, 1904.
X Cg Arc 510.216 Wiegand, Theodor. Prierre. Berlin, 1904.
Arc 858.9.5 Windle, B.C.A. Remains of the Prehistoric Age in England. London, 1904.

Chronological Listing

1905

Arc 785.33 Altmann, W. Die römischen Grabaltäre der Kaiserzeit. Berlin, 1905.
Arc 936.120 Antonescu, Teohari. Le trophée d'Adamclissi. Jarsy, 1905.
Arc 505.11 Bechstein, O. 30 Ansichten der deutschen Ausgraben Baalbek. Berlin, 1905.
Arc 1510.80 Behrens, Heinrich. Münzen und Medaillen der Stadt und des Bisthums Siebeck. Berlin, 1905.
Arc 1020.10.29 Bertaux, E. Rome. Paris, 1905.
Arc 1274.4 Birch de Gray, W. History of Scottish seals. London, 1905. 2v.
Arc 545.236 Bissing, F.W. Die Mastaba des Gem-Ni-Kai. Berlin, 1905- 2v.
Arc 545.236.5F Bissing, F.W. Das Re-Heiligtum des Ne-Woser-Re. Berlin, 1905-23. 2v.
Arc 1500.21 Blanchet, A. Traité des monnaies gauloises. v.1-2. Paris, 1905.
Arc 1088.1.23 Boisacq, E. La trière antique et la guerre navale. Bruxelles, 1905.
Arc 386.4.25 Borghesi, Bartolomeo. Bartolomeo Borghesi. Firenze, 1905.
Arc 66.1.95 Bourquet, E. L'administration financiere du sanctuaire pythique. Paris, 1905.
Arc 386.13 Brown, G.B. The care of ancient monuments. Cambridge, 1905.
Arc 1505.203 Buchenau, H. Der Bracteatenfund von Seega. Marburg, 1905.
Arc 435.2.33F Burgess, James. The Muhammadan architecture. pt.2. London, 1905.
Arc 785.13.11 Burton Brown, E. Recent excavations in the Roman Forum. N.Y., 1905.
Arc 726.2.5 Capasso, B. Napoli greca-romana. Topografia. Napoli, 1905.
Arc 1027.72.3 Carton, Louis B.C. Les catacombes d'Hadrumète. Sousse, 1905.
Arc 1027.22.17 Das Christliche Fischsymbol. Freiburg, 1905.
Arc 858.17 Clinch, George. Handbook of English antiquities. London, 1905.
Arc 870.4.2 Codrington, Thomas. Roman roads in Britain. 2. ed. London, 1905.
Arc 1478.25 Coimbra. Universidade. Biblioteca. Moedas romanas da Biblioteca da Universidade de Coimbra. Coimbra, 1905.
Arc 66.1.93 Colin, G. Le culte d'Apollon Pythien à Athènes. Paris, 1905.
Arc 66.1.94 Colin, G. Rome et la Grèce de 200 a 146 avant Jésus-Christ. Paris, 1905.
Arc 3.1.21 Congrès International d'Archéologie Classique, 1st, Athens, 1905. Comptes rendus du Congrès International d'Archéologie Ire Session, Athènes, 1905. Athènes, 1905.
Arc 1208.4 Dissard, Paul. Catalogues des plombs antiques. Paris, 1905.
Arc 1160.204 Foerster, W. Sulla questione...codice di Arborea. Torino, 1905.
Arc 710.9 Freericks, H. Die drei Athenetempel der Akropolis. Münster, 1905.
Arc 672.1.49F Gerola, G. Monumenti veneti nell'isola di Creta. v.1, pt.1-2, v.2-4. Venezia, 1905-32. 5v.
Arc 1027.23.13 Ghignoni, A. Le pitture della catacombe romane. Firenze, 1905.
Arc 861.52 Glasscock, J.L. The ancient crosses of Stortford. Bishops, 1905.
Arc 938.30 Hackman, A. Die ältere Eisenzeit in Finnland. Helsingfors, 1905.
Arc 1480.12 Haeberlin, E.J. Zum corpus numorum aeris gravis. Berlin, 1905.
Arc 1348.16.2 Halke, H. Einleitung in das Studium des Numismatik. 3. Aufl. Berlin, 1905.
Arc 609.1.13 Hall, R.N. Great Zimbabwe. London, 1905.
Arc 905.31 Hampel, J. Alterthümer des frühen Mittelalters in Ungarn. Braunschweig, 1905. 3v.
Arc 1018.19 Haufmann, C.M. Handbuch der christlichen Archäologie. Paderborn, 1905.
Arc 1510.28 Hauser, Josef. Die Münzen und Medaillen der im Jahre 1156 gegründeten (seit 1255). München, 1905.
Arc 395.7.2 Hauviller, E. Franz Xaver Kraus. München, 1905.
Arc 712.16 Hertz, A.P. Parthenons Kvindefigurer. n.p., 1905.
Arc 1675.10.5 Hill, G.F. Pisanello. London, 1905.
Arc 1468.16.2 Hirsch, F. Auctions-Catalog XIV, XV. Greek and Roman coins. München, 1905-06.
Arc 1468.16 Hirsch, F. Auctions-Katalog XIII. München, 1905.
Arc 1027.73 Hoferdt, E. Ursprung und Entwickelung der Chorkrypta. Breslau, 1905.
Arc 853.4.15 Hofmann, H. Römische Militärgrabsteine der Donauländer. Wien, 1905.
Arc 870.5 Hubbard, A.J. Neolithic dew-ponds and cattle ways. London, 1905.
Arc 820.11PF Huber, Émile. La ville de Rouhling. Texte et atlas. Metz, 1905.
Arc 785.13.24.7 Huelsen, Christian. Il Foro Romano; storia e monumenti. Roma, 1905.
Arc 785.13.22 Huelsen, Christian. Das Forum Romanum. Rom, 1905.
Arc 87.1.65 Kekule, R. Echelos und Basile. Berlin, 1905.
Arc 1675.36 Lamas, A. Portuguese medals. Lisbon, 1905-10. 12 pam.
Arc 1027.23.20 Lamberton, C.D. Themes from St. John's gospel in early Roman catacomb painting. Princeton, 1905.
Arc 875.33 Lang, Andrew. The Clyde mystery. Glasgow, 1905.
Arc 1027.72 Leynaud, A.F. Rapports sur les fouilles des catacombes d'Hadrumète. Paris, 1905.
Arc 710.5.2 Luckenbach, H. Die Akropolis von Athen. München, 1905.
Arc 1348.20 McDonald, George. Coin types, their origin and development. Glasgow, 1905.
Arc 830.41 Manteyer, G. de. Le nom et les 2 premières encientes de Gap. Gap, 1905.
Arc 1033.34.41 Marucchi, O. La crocifisione di San Pietro nel Vaticano. Roma, 1905.
Arc 1030.4.32 Marucchi, O. Il pontificato del papa Damaso. Roma, 1905.
Arc 505.25.5 Meistermann, B. La ville de David. Paris, 1905.
Arc 950.202.17 Moore, C.B. Certain aboriginal remains of the Black Warrior River. Philadelphia, 1905.
Arc 608.2.8 Moore, M. Carthage of the Phoenicians. London, 1905.
Arc 612.4 Müller, S. Urgeschichte Europas. Strassburg, 1905.
Arc 1413.1 Munro, N.G. Coins of Japan. London, 1905.
Arc 875.12 Munro, Robert. Archaeology and false antiquities. London, 1905.
Arc 588.15 Murray, M. Saqqara Mastabas. London, 1905-37. 2v.
Arc 653.1 Nebraska. University. Catalogue of Greece and Sicily. Lincoln, Neb., 1905.
Arc 398.3 Nicole, J. Mélanges Nicole...recueil de mémoires. Genève, 1905.

1905 - cont.

Arc 400.13 Pallu de Lessert, A.C. Julien Poinssot; souvenirs 1844-1900. Paris, 1905.
Arc 500.8 Peters, John P. Painted tombs in the necropolis of Marissa. London, 1905.
Arc 585.23A Petrie, W.M.F. Ehnasya. 1904. London, 1905.
Arc 585.23.2 Petrie, W.M.F. Roman Ehnasya. 1904. Supplement. London, 1905.
Arc 785.30.5 Pinza, G. Il comizio romano...ed i suoi monumenti. Roma, 1905.
Arc 920.204F Pósta, Béla. Régészeti tanulmányok az Oroszföldon. v.3-4. Leipzig, 1905. 2v.
Arc 505.11.5 Puchstein, O. Führer durch die Ruinen von Baalbek. Berlin, 1905.
Arc 733.2 Rivela, A. The dead cities of Sicily. Palermo, 1905.
Arc 1663.28.10 Romussi, Carlo. Garibaldi nelle medaglie del Museo del Risorgimento in Milano. Milano, 1905.
Arc 750.37.1 Rostovtsev, Mikhail Ivanovich. Tesserarum urbis Romae et suburbi plumbearum sylloge. Supplement. St. Petersbourgh, 1905.
Arc 66.1.96 Samarin, C.M.D. La fiscalité pontificale en France XIVe siècle. Paris, 1905.
Arc 726.27.3 Schmatz, Joseph. Baiae, das erste luxusbad der Römer. Regensburg, 1905-06.
Arc 1433.52 Schroeder, Albert. Annam; études numismatiques. Text et atlas. Paris, 1905. 2v.
Arc 915.8 Secretan, Eugène. Aventicum. Lausanne, 1905.
Arc 843.28 Severo, Ricardo. Os braceletes d'ouro de arnozella. Porto, 1905. 2 pam.
Arc 635.218 Skovgaard, N.K. Apollon - Gavlgruppen fra Zeustemp. Olympia. København, 1905.
Arc 672.4 Staïs,V. Ta ez antikythēren eyrēmata. Athēnai, 1905.
Arc 750.209 Thédenat, H. Le forum romain et la voie sacrée. Paris, 1905.
Arc 387.10.15 Toesca di Castellazzo, G. Commemoriazione del generale Luigi Palma di Cesnola. Torino, 1905.
Arc 518.7 Vienna. Kaiserhaus. Ausstellung von Fundstücken aus Ephesos im unteren Belvedere. Wien, 1905.
Arc 1020.15 Wall, J.C. Shrines of British saints. London, 1905.
Arc 530.15 Wedel, F. Skizzierte Gedanken eines Kunst freundes. Neustadt, 1905.
Arc 380.214 Wieland, C.A. Der Denkmal und Heimatschutz...der Gegenwart. Basel, 1905.
Arc 1335.26 Wilmersdörffer, M. von. Max Ritter von Wilmersdörfferische Münzen-Sammlung. Frankfurt am Main, 1905-07. 2v.
Arc 1588.1.25F Wittyg, W. Pieczecie miast dawnej Polski. Kraków, 1905.

1906

Arc 1033.172 Acta iberica...Speusippi, Eleusippi. Sankt Peterburg, 1906.
Arc 726.28 Altmann, W. Die italischen Rundbauten. Berlin, 1906.
Arc 1488.7 Ambrosoli, Solone. Atlante numismatico italiano. Milano, 1906.
Arc 416.1.3A Babelon, E. Manual of Oriental antiquities. N.Y., 1906.
Arc 1076.3.38 Berthele, J. Mélanges. Montpellier, 1906.
Arc 497.11 Bliss, F.J. The development of Palestine exploration. N.Y., 1906.
Arc 895.17 Brøgger, A.W. Studier over Norges stenalder. Christiania, 1906.
Arc 1584.5F Bulychev, N.I. Imennye serebrian. kop. i denezhki Ivana IV. Sankt Peterburg, 1906.
Arc 843.63F Cartailhac, Émile. La caverne d'Altamira à Santillane près Santander (Espagne). Monaco, 1906.
Arc 861.4.5 Classical Association. Melandra Castle. Manchester, 1906.
Arc 1458.11 Corolla numismatica...in honour of B.V. Head. London, 1906.
Arc 1020.10.37 Cruickshank, J.W. Christian Rome. London, 1906.
Arc 815.5.5 Cube, G. von. Die römische "Scenae Frons". Berlin, 1906.
Arc 755.1 Cumelung, W. Museums and ruins of Rome. London, 1906. 2v.
Arc 608.2.10 Delattre, R.P. Un pélerinage aux ruines de Carthage. Lyon, 1906.
Arc 743.1.5 Dennis, G. The cities and cemeteries of Etruria. London, 1906. 2v.
Arc 875.14 Dietrichson, L. Monumenta orcadica. Kristiania, 1906.
Arc 810.23 Duhn, F. von. Pompeii, eine hellenistische Stadt in Italien. Leipzig, 1906.
Arc 843.4 Engel, A. Une forteresse ibérique...de 1903. Paris, 1906.
Arc 815.14 Feis, Leopoldo. Di alcune memorie bibliche scaperte a Pompei. Firenze, 1906.
Arc 635.207.9 Fiechter, E.R. Der Tempel der Aphaia auf Aegena. München, 1906.
Arc 708.23 Fougères, G. Athènes et ses environs. Paris, 1906.
Arc 635.207.5 Furtwängler, A. Ägena, das Heiligtum der Aphaia. Text and atlas. München, 1906. 2v.
Arc 670.2.3 Furtwängler, A. Die Ägineten der Glypotothek König Ludwigs I. München, 1906.
Arc 761.7 Gabrici, Ettore. Il problema delle origini di Roma secondo le recenti scoperti archeologiche. Padova, 1906.
Arc 1468.12.3 Gaebler, Hugo. Die antiken Münzen von Makedonia. Berlin, 1906-35. 2v.
Arc 1148.5.5 Gardthausen, V. Geschichte der griechischen Tachygraphie. Berlin, 1906.
Arc 1033.3.41 Goldmann, K. Die ravennatischen Sarkophage. Strassburg, 1906.
Arc 689.2 Granidor, P. Les fouilles de Tēnos. Louvain, 1906.
Arc 830.42 Grenier, A. Habitations gauloises et villas latines. Paris, 1906.
Arc 543.25.5 Groneman, I. The Tyandi-Barabudur in Central Java. 2. ed. Samarang, 1906.
Arc 1663.61 Gumowski, Marian. Medale Tagiellonów. Kraków, 1906.
Arc 790.206.3 Gusman, P. Pompei; la ville, les moeurs, les arts. Paris, 1906.
Arc 890.214 Gustafson, G. Norges oldtid. Mindesmärker og oldsager. Kristiania, 1906.
Arc 1458.12 Hammer, J. Der Feingehalt die griechischen und römischen Münzen. Berlin, 1906.
Arc 762.1.30 Hare, A.J.C. Days near Rome. 4. ed. London, 1906.
Arc 968.2.10 Hewett, E.L. Antiquities of the Jemez Plateau, New Mexico. Washington, 1906.
Arc 1468.13A Hill, G.F. Historical Greek coins. London, 1906.
Arc 1468.13.2 Hill, G.F. Historical Greek coins. N.Y., 1906.
Arc 605.205.5 Holtzinger, H. Timgad und die römische Provinzial-Architektur. Berlin, 1906.
Arc 785.13.22.15 Huelsen, Christian. Le Forum Romain, son histoire et ses monuments. Rome, 1906.

Chronological Listing

1906 - cont.

Arc 785.13.24 Huelsen, Christian. The Roman Forum. Rome, 1906.
Arc 785.13.23 Huelsen, Christian. The Roman Forum. Rome, 1906.
Arc 1418.5A Indian Museum. Catalogue of coins in the Indian Museum, Calcutta. Oxford, 1906-08. 3v.
Arc 630.3 Jordt, H. Untersuch über Silikat und Carbenatbiblung in antiken Morteln. Leipzig, 1906.
Arc 1510.23 Joseph, Paul. Die Münzen von Worms. Darmstadt, 1906.
Arc 1335.28 Judice dos Santos, J.J. Collection. pt.1,3. Amsterdam, 1906. 2v.
Arc 710.20F Kakkadin, P. He anaskaphē tēs Akropoleōs apo tou 1885 mechri tou 1890. Athēnai, 1906.
Arc 600.14 Kaufmann, C.M. Die Ausgrabung des Menas-Heiligtümes. v.1-3. Cairo, 1906.
Arc 1190.25 Kern, Fritz. Dorsualkonzept und Imbreviatur in Italien. Stuttgart, 1906.
Arc 1087.3 Kugnezow, S. Die Sepulkralmasken, ihre Gebrauch und Bedeutung. Kasan, 1906.
Arc 830.67 La Croix, Camille. Les origines des anciens monuments...de Poitiers. Poitiers, 1906.
Arc 726.24.11 Lanciani, R. La villa Adriana; guida e descrizione. Roma, 1906.
Arc 396.2 Lange, Konrad. Grundsätze der modernen Denkmalpflege. Tübingen, 1906.
Arc 1033.17.549F Lauer, Philippe. Le trésor du Sancta Sanctorum. Paris, 1906.
Arc 1500.24 Leblond, V. Le pays des Bellovaques. Essai...numismatique. Caen, 1906.
Arc 865.8 Lockyer, N. Stonehenge and other British stone monuments. London, 1906.
Arc 1018.7.5 Lourie, W. Monuments of the early church. N.Y., 1906.
Arc 628.13.8 Luckenbach, H. Kunst und Geschichte. 6. Aufl. München, 1906.
Arc 875.13 Macdonald, G. The Roman forts on the Bar Hill, Dumbartonshire. Glasgow, 1906.
Arc 609.1.17F Maciver, D.R. Mediaeval Rhodesia. London, 1906.
Arc 870.14.12 Mariette, E. The Roman walls. 2. ed. Paris, 1906.
Arc 510.215.5 Marr, N. Raskopki...1904 godu. Sankt Peterburg, 1906.
Arc 785.13.35.5 Marucchi, O. The Roman Forum and the Palatine. Rome, 1906.
Arc 1675.35 Meili, Julius. Die Werke des Medailleur's Hans Frei in Basel, 1894-1906. Zürich, 1906.
Arc 838.9 Mélida, José R. Iberia arqueológica ante-romana, discursos. Madrid, 1906.
Arc 66.1.97 Merlin, A. L'aventin dans l'antiquité. Paris, 1906.
Arc 397.7 Michaelis, A. Die archäologischen Entdeckungen des 19. Jahrhunderts. Leipzig, 1906.
Arc 635.219 Mnémeia. Tés Ellados. Athēnai, 1906.
Arc 893.12 Montelius, Oscar. Kulturgeschichte Schwedens von den ältesten Zeiten bis zum elften Jahrhundert nach Christus. Leipzig, 1906.
Arc 953.18.5 Moorehead, W.K. A narrative of explorations of New Mexico, Arizona, Indiana. Andover, 1906.
Arc 712.15 Mot, J. de. Le frontal orientale du Parthenon. Bruxelles, 1906.
Arc 861.95 Moule, H.J. Dorchester antiquities. Dorchester, 1906.
Arc 545.230 Müller, W.M. Egyptological researches. Results, 1904. Washington, 1906. 3v.
Arc 875.12.2 Munro, Robert. Archaeology and false antiquities. Philadelphia, 1906.
Arc 545.232 Naville, E. Tomb of Hâtshopsitu. Life and monuments of queen. London, 1906.
Htn Arc 1084.3PF* New York (City). Metropolitan Museum of Art. The Bishop collections. N.Y., 1906. 2v.
Arc 600.12.5A Newberry, P.E. Scarabs. London, 1906.
Arc 1020.48 Nitzhammer, R. Die christlichen Altertümer der Dobrogia. Bukarest, 1906.
Arc 510.219F Österreichisches Archäologisches Institut. Forschungen in Ephesop. v.1-4, pt.1-3; v.5. Wien, 1906-51. 8v.
Arc 983.8 Peabody, Charles. The so called "gorgets". Andover, 1906.
Arc 588.17 Petrie, W.M.F. Hyksos and Graelite cities. London, 1906.
Arc 505.12 Petrie, W.M.F. Researches in Sinai. London, 1906.
Arc 900.215.5 Pič, Josef L. Le Hradischt de Stradonitz en Bohême. Leipzig, 1906.
Arc 1027.75 Pietro, A.C. Ancora del sepolero originario di San Domnio. Zara, 1906.
Arc 861.25 Pope, Alfred. The old stone crosses of Dorset. London, 1906.
Arc 1274.6 Porteous, A. The town council seals. Edinburgh, 1906.
Arc 600.4.5 Prinz, H. Funde aus Naukratis. Leipzig, 1906.
Arc 513.13.5 Ramsay, W.M. Studies in history and art...Eastern Provinces, Roman Empire. Aberdeen, 1906.
Arc 1076.3.31 Raven, J.J. The bells of England. London, 1906.
Arc 1468.14 Regling, H. Griechischen Münzen der Sammlung Warren. Text and plates. Berlin, 1906. 2v.
Arc 1470.15 Regling, K. Terina. Berlin, 1906.
Arc 785.14.5 Rodocanachi, E. The Roman capitol in ancient and modern times. N.Y., 1906.
Arc 853.27 Schuchhardt, C. Aliso...Ausgrabungen bei Haltern. Haltern, 1906.
Arc 923.11.5F Shchukinym, P.I. Kratkoe opisanie novago vladaniia imperatopskago rossiiskago istoricheskago muzeia. Moskva, 1906.
Arc 590.8F Smith, G. Elliot. Mémoires présentés à l'Institut Égyptien. Le Caire, 1906.
Arc 1333.9 Smith, Harlan P. Catalogue...coins of the U.S. Philadelphia, 1906.
Arc 1033.168 Stentrup, F. Die Translatio sancti viti. Münster, 1906.
Arc 1018.23 Sybel, L. von. Christliche Antike. Marburg, 1906. 2v.
Arc 630.4 Sybel, L. von. Die klassische Archäologie und die altchristliche Kunst. Marburg, 1906.
Arc 861.49.5 Taylor, H. Ancient crosses and holy wells of Lancashire. Manchester, 1906.
Arc 810.22 Thédenat, H. Pompéi. Vie privée. Histoire. Paris, 1906.
Arc 810.22.2 Thédenat, H. Pompéi. Vie publique. Paris, 1906.
Arc 785.13.45 Thiele, Richard. Das Forum Romanum. 2. Aufl. Erfurt, 1906.
Arc 1680.4 Waters, A.W. Notes...eighteenth century tokens. Leamington, 1906.
Arc 510.218F Wiegand, Theodor. Milet-Ergebnisse der Ausgrabungen. Berlin, 1906- 18v.
Arc 1033.123 Wieland, F. Altar und Altargrab der christlichen Kirchen...Mensa und Confessio. v.1-2. München, 1906-12.
Arc 1153.4.23 Wikenhauser, A. Der heilige Cassian. Berlin, 1906.
Arc 968.10 Will, G.F. The Mandans. [North Dakota]. Cambridge, 1906.

1906 - cont.

Arc 1033.70.23 Wilpert, G. Le pitture della Basilica primitiva di S. Clemente. Roma, 1906.
Arc 1016.12 Wittig, Joseph. Die altchristlichen Skulpturen...deutschen Nationalstiftung am Campo Santo. Rom, 1906.

1907

Arc 968.4 Abbott, Charles C. Archaeologia nova caesarea, 1907-09. Trenton, New Jersey, 1907-08.
Arc 1675.27 Andorfer, Karl. Musica in nummis. Wien, 1907.
Arc 1.1.6 Archaeological Institute of America. Report of the fellow in American archaeology. N.Y., 1907.
Arc 726.10.10 Behn, F. Die ficoronische Cista. Leipzig, 1907.
Arc 726.10.9 Behn, F. Die ficoronische Cista. Diss. Rostock, 1907.
Arc 1663.14 Belts, Benjamin. Descriptive list of medals relating to John Law. n.p., 1907.
Arc 1470.32.7 Beribe-Delagart, A.L. Popravki obshchagi kataloga monet. P.O. Burachkov'. Moskva, 1907.
Arc 756.11 Bertaux, Émile. Rome; l'antiquité. 2. éd. Paris, 1907.
Arc 416.10 Beylié, Léon de. Prome et Samara; voyage archéologique en Birmanie et en Mesopotamie. Paris, 1907.
Arc 938.55 Bielenstein, A. Die Holzbauten und Holzgeräte der Litten. pt.1-2. n.p., 1907-18.
X Cg Arc 1212.3 Birch, William de Gray. Seals. London, 1907?
Arc 1143.4.5 Birt, Theodor. Die Buchrolle in der Kunst. Leipzig, 1907.
Arc 823.10.5 Blanchet, A. Les enceintes Romaines de la Gaule. Paris, 1907.
Arc 1027.4.21 Bonavenia, G. La cuestione...controversia filumeniana. Roma, 1907.
Arc 1680.10.5 Brook, A.J.S. Communion tokens of the established Church of Scotland. Edinburgh, 1907.
Arc 87.1.62 Brueckner, A. Lebensregeln auf Athens. Hochzeitsgeschenken. Berlin, 1907.
Arc 432.11 Burgess, J. Indian architecture. Oxford, 1907.
Arc 672.1.13 Burrows, R.M. The discoveries in Crete. London, 1907.
Arc 672.1.16A Burrows, R.M. The discoveries in Crete and their bearing. N.Y., 1907.
Arc 700.14 Calderini, A. Di un'ara greca. Milano, 1907.
Arc 785.34 Cannizzaro, M.E. Ara Pacis Augustae. Roma, 1907.
Arc 545.233.5FA Capart, J. Une rue de tombeaux a Saqqarah. Bruxelles, 1907. 2v.
Arc 945.5F Capitan, Louis. Décades américaines. Levallois-Perret, 1907.
Arc 543.1.4 Cave, H.W. The ruined cities of Ceylon. 4th ed. London, 1907.
Arc 1333.10 Chapman, H. Catalogue of collections of coins of M.A. Trickney. Philadelphia, 1907.
Arc 66.1.99 Chapot, V. La frontière de l'Euphrate de Pompée à la Conquête Arabe. Paris, 1907.
Arc 757.10 Chester, England. Museum. An account of the Roman antiquities. 2. ed. London, 1907.
Arc 1033.35.5 Combes, L. de. Finding of the Cross. London, 1907.
Arc 1663.24 Cunha, Xavier. A medalha escolar do coll. do Corpo-Santo noticia numismatic. Coimbra, 1907.
Arc 757.4 Cyriacus. Anconitanus. La Roma antica...desegnii inedite. Roma, 1907.
Arc 545.232.5 Davis, T.M. The tomb of Iouiya and Touiyou. London, 1907.
Arc 1033.17.105 Delattre, A.L. Le culte de la Sainte Vierge en Afrique. Paris, 1907.
Arc 750.211 Delbrück, R. Hellenistische Bauten in Latium. Strassburg, 1907.
Arc 1020.30.5 Diehl, Charles. Ravenne. Paris, 1907.
Arc 785.34.5 Dissel, Karl. Der Opferzug der Ara Pacis Augustae. Hamburg, 1907.
Arc 1505.201 Domanig, K. Die deutsche Medaille in Kunst oc Hinsicht. Wien, 1907.
Htn Arc 726.73.15* Douglas, N. Some antiquarian notes. Napoli, 1907.
Arc 66.1.98 Dubois, C. Pouzzoles antique. Paris, 1907.
Arc 830.53 Du Chatellier, Paul. Époques préhistoriques...dans le Finistère. 2e éd. Rennes, 1907.
Arc 1185.9 Erben, Wilhelm. Urkundenlehre. v.1,3. München, 1907. 2v.
Arc 1670.51.2 Feuardent, F. Jetons et méreaux depuis Louis IX...plandres. London, 1907.
Arc 955.2.4 Fewkes, J.W. Excavations at Casa Grande, Arizona in 1906-07. v.1-2. Washington, 1907.
Arc 453.5 Fleet, J.F. Indian epigraphy. Oxford, 1907.
Arc 1500.23 Florange, J. Armorial du jetonophile. Paris, 1907. 2v.
Arc 375.6 Forrer, R. Reallexikon der prähistorischen, klassischen...Altertümer. Berlin, 1907.
Arc 1670.5 Fournie, H. Les jetons des Doyens...de Paris. Chalon-sur-Saone, 1907.
Arc 915.4 Frey, F. Führer durch die Ruinen vor Augusta Raurica. Liestal, 1907.
Arc 1465.77 Fritze. Nomisma, Untersuchungen auf dem gebiete. Berlin, 1907-12. 12v.
Arc 708.22.5 Gardner, E.A. Ancient Athens. London, 1907.
Arc 600.15 Garstang, J. The burial customs of ancient Egypt. London, 1907.
Arc 830.58 Gerin-Ricard, H. de. Antiquités de la vallée de l'Arc en Provence. Aix, 1907.
Arc 335.2 Gomme, G.L. Index of archaeological papers, 1665-1890. London, 1907.
Arc 1033.23 Grisar, H. Il sancta sanctorum...tesoro sacro. Roma, 1907.
Arc 700.11 Gropengiesser, H. Die Gräber von Attika. Athen, 1907.
Arc 905.42 Hampel, J. Ujabb tanulmányok a honfoglalasi kor emlékeiral. Budapest, 1907.
Arc 1468.15 Hands, A.W. Common Greek coins. London, 1907.
Arc 762.1.35 Hare, A.J.C. Days near Rome. 5. ed. London, 1907.
Arc 1335.101 Hirsch, Jacob. Auctions-Catalog der bedeutenden Sammlung römischer und byzantinischer Münzen. München, 1907.
Arc 955.2 Hough, W. Antiquities of the Upper Gila...(Arizona). Washington, 1907.
Arc 762.5 Huelsen, C. La pianta di Roma dell'anonimo einsidlense. Roma, 1907.
Arc 392.4 Hunter, R. Preservation of places of interest or beauty. Manchester, 1907.
Arc 545.227.15 Kamal, A.B. Livre des perles enfoneio. Leipzig, 1907. 2v.
Arc 560.1 King, L.W. Egypt and Western Asia. London, 1907.
Arc 861.10.11 Kinnebrook, William. Manx crosses...monuments...Isle of Man. London, 1907.
Arc 505.13 Kittel, D.R. Schlaugenstein im Kidrontal bei Jerusalem. Leipzig, 1907.

Chronological Listing

1907 - cont.

Arc 1020.72.15 La Croix, C. de. L'autel de Sainte-Sixte et ses reliques. Poitiers, 1907.
Arc 1018.24 LeClercq, H. Manuel d'archéologie chrétienne. Paris, 1907. 2v.
Arc 545.227.13 Lefebvre, G. Recueil des inscriptions grecques. Le Caire, 1907.
Arc 785.20.9A Leoni, N. On the Appian Way. Florence, 1907.
Arc 1282.5 Likhachen, N.I. Drenieishiia bully i nechati shiriully. Sankt Peterburg, 1907.
Arc 830.18.9 Lion, J. Les voies romaines après la table Théodosienne. Amiens, 1907.
Arc 1033.34.11F Lugari, J.B. Il culto di San Pietro sul Gianicolo. Roma, 1907.
Arc 416.4 Lunet de Lajonquière, É.E. Rapport...mission archéologique (Cambodge, Siam, presqu'île Malaise, Indo). Paris, 1907-08.
Arc 1027.4.29 Marucchi, O. Studio archaeologico...iscrizione di Filomena. Roma, 1907.
Arc 562.2.35 Maspero, Gaston. Causeries d'Égypte. 2. éd. Paris, 1907.
Arc 810.11.10 Mau, August. Pompeii, its life and art. N.Y., 1907.
Arc 1148.13 Mentz, A. Geschichte...der griechischen Tachygraphie. Berlin, 1907.
Arc 950.202.21 Moore, C.B. Moundville revisited. Philadelphia, 1907.
Arc 672.1.5 Mosso, Angelo. Palaces of Crete and their builders. London, 1907.
Arc 672.1.4 Mosso, Angelo. The palaces of Crete and their builders. N.Y., 1907.
Arc 612.20 Much, M. Die Trugspiegelung orientalischer Kultur in den vorgeschichtlichen Zeitaltern Nord- und Mitteleuropas. Jena, 1907.
Arc 612.5 Müller, S. L'Europe préhistorique. Paris, 1907.
Arc 497.12 Musil, A. Arabia Petraca. v.1-3. Wien, 1907. 4v.
Arc 505.95PF Musil, Alois. Kusejr 'Amra. Wien, 1907.
Arc 585.25 Naville, E.H. XI Dynasty temple at Deir El-Bahari. London, 1907-13. 3v.
Arc 968.1.9 Parker, A.C. Excavations in an Erie Indian village. n.p., 1907.
Arc 710.9.5 Petersen, E. Die Burgtempel der Athenaia. Berlin, 1907.
Arc 588.18 Petrie, W.M.F. Gizeh and Rifeh. London, 1907.
Arc 830.122F Piette, Édouard. L'art pendant l'âge du Renne. Paris, 1907.
Arc 785.35 Porter, M.W. What Rome was built with. London, 1907.
Arc 503.2.2F Princeton University Archaeological Expeditions to Syria in 1904-1905 and 1909. Publications. Leyden, 1907-1934. 18v.
Arc 1093.5 Redslob, E. Die fränkischen Epitaphen im 4. und 5. Jahrhundert. Inaug. Diss. Nürnberg, 1907.
Arc 403.6 Salinas, A. Miscellanea di archaeologia, storia, e filologia. Palermo, 1907.
Arc 87.1.67 Schröder, Bruno. Die Victoria von Calvatone. Berlin, 1907.
Arc 635.221 Seta, A.D. La genesi dello Scorcio nell'arte greca. Roma, 1907.
Arc 1261.3 Spain. Archivo Historico Nacional, Madrid. Sección de Sigilografía. Catálogo i sellos españoles de la edad media por Juan Menéndez Pidal. Madrid, 1907.
Arc 543.3.5A Stein, Mark Aurel. Ancient Khotan. Oxford, 1907. 2v.
Arc 1458.16 Strozzi. Collection Strozzi. Médailles grecques et romaines aes grave. Paris, 1907.
Arc 1027.80 Stückelberg, E.A. Die Katakombenheiligen der Schweiz. Kempten, 1907.
Arc 1468.18 Sundwall, J. Attischen Münzen des neueren Stiles. Helsingfors, 1907.
Arc 774.3.5 Tomassetti, G. Della campagna romana. Roma, 1907.
Arc 1025.50 Treat, J.H. The catacombs of Rome. Boston, 1907.
Arc 1153.25 Voss, Ulrich. Lateinische Stenographie...Wilhelm Stolze. Berlin, 1907.
Arc 545.227.5 Weigal, A.E.P. Report on antiquities of Lower Nubia. Oxford, 1907.
Arc 726.29 Willers, H. Römische Bronzeindustrie von Capua und von Niedergermanien. Hannover, 1907.
Arc 1020.9.95 Wolff. Geschichtsbilder aus alt christlicher Zeit. Roms. Berlin, 1907.
Arc 665.1 Ziebarth, E. Kulturbilder aus griechischen Städten. Leipzig, 1907.

1908

Arc 870.9 Allcroft, A.H. Earthwork of England. London, 1908.
Arc 1033.35.147 Almeida, R.V. d'. A cruz de vila Viçosa. Lisboa, 1908.
Arc 1335.30 Antoine-Feill. Münzen- und Medaillen-Sammlung. Frankfurt, 1908.
Arc 800.7 Barker, E.R. Buried Herculaneum. London, 1908.
Arc 1138.50 Berlin. Staatliche Museen. Zur Einführung in die Papyrusausstellung. Berlin, 1908.
Arc 705.209 Bienkowski, P. von. Die Darstellungen der Gallier in der Hellenistischen Kunst. Wien, 1908.
Arc 1675.9 Bildt. Les médailles romaines de Christine de Suède. Rome, 1908.
Arc 830.44 Blanchet, A. Recherches sur les aqueducs et cloaques de la Gaule. Paris, 1908.
Arc 830.66.9 Bonnard, Louis. La Gaule thermale. Paris, 1908.
Arc 1494.4.9 Botet y Sisó, Joaquim. Les monedes Catalanes. Barcelona, 1908-11. 3v.
Arc 830.22.5 Bournon, Fernand. Les arènes de Lutèce. Paris, 1908.
Arc 672.1.15 Burrows, R.M. The discoveries in Crete; with addenda. London, 1908.
Arc 547.6.25 Cairo. Musée des Antiquités Égyptiennes. Guide to the Cairo Museum. 4. ed. Cairo, 1908.
Arc 543.7 Carpeaux, C. Les ruines d'Angkor. Paris, 1908.
Arc 66.1.100 Cavaignac, E. Études sur l'histoire financière d'Athènes au Ve siècle. Paris, 1908.
Arc 830.13.5 Chatelain, L. Bibliothèque d'école des hautes études. Monuments romains d'Orange. Paris, 1908.
Arc 545.232.13 Davis, T.M. The tomb of Siptah. London, 1908.
Arc 823.11 Déchelette, Joseph. Manuel d'archéologie. v.1-2. Paris, 1908-14. 5v.
Arc 726.10.11 Dernan Mugoffin, R. Study of the topography of Preneste. Baltimore, 1908.
X Cg Arc 710.10 D'Ooge, M.L. The acropolis of Athens. N.Y., 1908.
Arc 587.85 Egypt. Ministry of Finance. Archaeological survey of Nubia. v.1-7. Cairo, 1908.
Arc 861.35.5 Ely, Talfourd. Roman Hayling. 2. ed. London, 1908.
Arc 1020.10.39 Favshingham, A.L. The monuments of Christian Rome. N.Y., 1908.

1908 - cont.

Arc 1153.19 Federici, V. Esempi di corsiva antico del secolo I...al IV. Roma, 1908.
Arc 1454.200 Forrer, Robert. Keltische Numismatik der Rhein. Strassburg, 1908.
Arc 1675.10 Foville, J. de. Pisanello et les médailleurs italiens. Paris, 1908.
Arc 845.203 Frankfurt am Main. Historisches Museum. Einzelforschungen über Kunst- undAltertumsgegenstände zu Frankfurt am Main. Frankfurt, 1908.
Arc 673.7 Fritsch, O. Delos, die Insel des Apolon. Gütersloh, 1908.
Arc 1433.35 Gardner, Percy. Gold coinage of Asia before Alexander the Great. London, 1908.
Arc 785.34.9 Gardthausen, V. Der Altar des Kaiserfriedens Ara Pacis Augustae. Leipzig, 1908.
Arc 830.6.17 Germain de Montauzen, C. Les aqueducs antiques de Lyon. Paris, 1908.
Arc 823.21.10F Goury, Georges. Essai sur l'époque barbare dans la Marne. Nancy, 1908.
Arc 1153.21 Guénin, L.P. Histoire de la sténographie...notes tironiennes. Paris, 1908.
Arc 1190.5 Hall, Hubert. A formula book of English historical documents. Cambridge, 1908. 2v.
Arc 950.10F Hewett, E.L. Les communautés anciennes dans le désert américain. Genève, 1908.
Arc 557.3 Hichens, Robert. Egypt and its monuments. London, 1908.
Arc 557.3.2A Hichens, Robert. Egypt and its monuments. N.Y., 1908.
Arc 830.2.6 Hirmenech, H.P. Le dolmen royal de Gavrénis près d'Auray. Le Mans, 1908.
Arc 1670.52 Hirsch, Jacob. Kunstmedaillen und Plaketten des XV. bis XVII. Jahrhunderts. München, 1908.
Arc 1335.101.71 Hirsch, Jacob. Sammlung Consul Eduard Friedrich Weber, Hamburg. München, 1908-09. 2v.
Arc 870.14.5 Hoyer, M.A. By the Roman wall. London, 1908.
Arc 1458.14 Imhoof-Blumer, Friedrich. Zur griechischen und römischen Münzkunde. Genf, 1908.
Arc 435.1.18 India. Archaeological Survey. Library. Classified catalogue of the library of the director general of archaeology. Calcutta, 1908.
Arc 682.25.15 Ivanov, Iordan. Bulgarski starini iz Makedoniia. Sofiia, 1908.
Arc 853.10.5 Jacobi, H. Führer durch das Römerkastell Saalburg. 4. Aufl. Homburg, 1908.
Arc 1335.64 Jandolo et Lavazzi, Rome, auctioneers. Vente aux enchères publiques de la collection de médailles grecques. Roma, 1908.
Arc 1077.5 Johns, C.H.W. Ur-Engur. Treatise on canephorous statues. N.Y., 1908.
Arc 858.14 Johnson, W. Folk-memory. Oxford, 1908.
Arc 600.14.5 Kaufmann, C.M. La découverte des sanctuaires. Alexandrie, 1908.
Arc 853.28 Kickebunde, A. Einfluss der Römischen Kultur. Berlin, 1908.
Arc 672.1.8 Lagrange, M.J. La Crete ancienne. Paris, 1908.
Arc 1510.32F Lange, C.C.A. Sammlung schleswig-holsteinischer Münzen und Medaillen. Berlin, 1908-12. 2v.
Arc 545.227.19 Legrain, G. Repertoire genealogique et onomastique. Genève, 1908.
Arc 651.2 Lethaby, W.R. Greek buildings. London, 1908.
Arc 1153.8.5 Lindsay, W.M. Contractions in early Latin miniscule MSS. Oxford, 1908.
NEDL Arc 136.2.15 London Society of Antiquaries. Index. v.1-20. 2d series. London, 1908.
Arc 545.210.5 Lyons, H.G. Report on the temples of Philae. Cairo, 1908.
Arc 830.152 Macon, Gustave. Une fondation du connétable Henri de Montmorency. Senlis, 1908.
Arc 545.234 Marius of Northampton. Report on some excavations...Theban necropolis. London, 1908.
Arc 1348.37 Markov', A.K. O chistk' drevnikh' monet'. Sankt Peterburg, 1908.
Arc 1027.4.40 Marucchi, O. La basilica papale del cimitero di Priscilla. Roma, 1908.
Arc 726.10.17 Marucchi, Orazio. Il tempio della fortuna prenestina. Roma, 1908.
Arc 1033.17.560 Más, Joseph. Nota historica de la Mare de Deu de la Cisa. Barcelona, 1908.
Arc 1020.127 Más, Joseph. Les reliquies del Monastir de Sant Cugat del Vallès. Barcelona, 1908.
Arc 402.9.25 Maspero, G. Notice biographique du vicomte Emmanuel de Rouge. Paris, 1908.
Arc 562.2.26 Maspero, Gaston. New light on ancient Egypt. London, 1908.
Arc 810.11.7 Mau, August. Pompeji in Leben und Kunst. 2. Aufl. Leipzig, 1908.
Arc 905.17 Meyer. Die Römerstadt Agunt. Berlin, 1908.
Arc 397.8 Michaelis, A. A century of archaeological discoveries. London, 1908.
NEDL Arc 823.12 Molin, Jean. Archéologie de la Gaule. Paris, 1908.
Arc 950.202.23 Moore, C.B. Certain mounds of Arkansas and Mississippi. Philadelphia, 1908.
Arc 1160.210.5F Moskovskii Arkheologicheskii Institut. Sbornik snimkov s russkago pis'ma XIII-XVIII vv. Moskva, 1908.
Arc 1033.72.5 Mundt, A. Die Erztaufen Norddeutschlands. Leipzig, 1908.
Arc 426.3 Munro, N.G. Prehistoric Japan. Yokohama, 1908.
Arc 589.1 Murray, M.A. Index of names and titles of the old kingdoms. London, 1908.
Arc 672.1.25 Noack, F. Ovalhaus und Paläst in Kreta. Leipzig, 1908.
Arc 1675.91 Pachinger, A.M. Wallfahrts-, Bruderschafts- und Weihe. Wien, 1908.
Arc 967.4 Peabody, Charles. The exploration of Bushey Cavern near Cavetown, Maryland. Andover, 1908.
Arc 66.1.101 Perdrizet, P. La vierge de miséricorde. Paris, 1908.
Arc 708.25 Petersen, E. Athen. Leipzig, 1908.
Arc 588.19 Petrie, W.M.F. Athribis. London, 1908.
Arc 820.202.2 Pilloy, J. Table générale de la Collection Caranda. Paris, 1908.
Arc 545.237 Pörtner, B. Aegyptische Grabsteine und Denksteine aus Athen und Konstantinople. Strassburg, 1908.
Arc 495.204.3 Prentice, William K. Greek and Latin inscriptions. N.Y., 1908.
Arc 1500.5.25 Prou, Maurice. Catalogue des deniers mérovingiens de la trouvaille de Bais (Ille et Vilaine). Paris, 1908.
Arc 543.4FA Pumpelly, R. Exploration in Turkestan. Expedition of 1904. Washington, 1908. 2v.
Arc 684.6 Quaatz, H. Wie sind die Figuren im Ostgiebel des Zeustempels zu Olympia anzuordnen. Berlin, 1908.

Chronological Listing

1908 - cont.

Arc 605.204.5F Renault, Jules. Cahiers d'archéologie tunisienne. v.1-4. Tunis, 1908-11.

Arc 1349.30 Ricci, Serafino. L'opera numismatica di Solone Ambrosoli. Milano, 1908.

Arc 785.20.7 Ripostelli, Giuseppe. La Via Appia, à l'époque romaine et de nos jours. Rome, 1908.

Arc 710.22 Rubió y Lluch, Antonio. La acrópolis de Atenas en la época catalana. Barcelona, 1908.

Arc 1510.14.3 Rudolph, E. Ergänzungen und Berichtigungen. Dresden, 1908.

Arc 1301.1.9 Rules of the British Numismatic Society. London, 1908.

Arc 1675.19 Russia. Monetnyi. Opisanie russkikh medalei. Sankt Peterburg, 1908.

Arc 920.208F Samokbasov, D.Ia. Opisanie arkheologicheskich raskopok. Moskva, 1908.

Arc 925.326 Samokrasov, Dmitrii I. Severianskaia zumlia i severiane po gorodishcham i mogilam. Moskva, 1908.

Arc 843.27 Santos Rocha, A. dos. Estações pre-romanas da idade do ferre nas visinhanças da figueira. Porto, 1908.

Arc 1490.16 Schembri, H.C. Coins and medals of knights of Malta. London, 1908.

Arc 1200.8 Schillmann, F. Beiträge zum Urkundenwesen der ältern Bischöfe. Leipzig, 1908.

Arc 375.5 Schlemm, J. Wörterbuch zur Vorgeschichte. Berlin, 1908.

Arc 1025.51 Schmid, G. Das unterirdische Rom. Brixen, 1908.

Arc 1163.3.60 Sololevskii, A.I. Slaviano-russkaia paleografiia. Sankt Peterburg, 1908.

Arc 843.26 Sousa Maia. A necropole de condidello (Terrada-Maia). Porto, 1908.

Arc 925.25 Spitsyn, A. Arkheologicheskii razvedki. St. Peterburg, 1908.

Arc 503.1 Tell El Mutesellim. Leipzig, 1908-1929. 3v.

Arc 673.1.9 Trendelenburg, A. Die Anfangsstreke der heiligen Strasse in Delphi. Berlin, 1908.

Arc 1335.29 Ulex, G.F. Sammlung des G.F. Ulex; Münzen und Medaillen von Nord-, Central-, und Süd-Amerika. Frankfurt, 1908.

Arc 830.43 Verneau, R. L'homme de la Barma-Grande. 2e éd. Baoussé-Roussé, 1908.

Arc 635.225F Vogell, A. Griechische Alterthümer südrussischen Fundorts. Cassel, 1908.

Arc 800.6A Waldstein, C. Herculaneum, past, present and future. London, 1908.

Arc 1076.3.17 Walters, Henry Beauchamp. Church bells. London, 1908.

Arc 662.5 Wheeler, J.R. Archaeology. N.Y., 1908.

Arc 1213.1 Winnefeld, H. Hellenistische Silberreliefs. Berlin, 1908.

Arc 853.29 Wolff, G. Die Römerstadt Nida bei Heddernheim. Frankfurt, 1908.

Arc 684.1.29 Wolters, Paul. Der Westgiebel des olympischen Zeustempels. München, 1908.

Arc 1473.6A Wroth, W. Catalogue of imperial Byzantine coins in the British Museum. London, 1908. 2v.

1909

Arc 1613.7 Adams, E.H. Adams' official premium list. United States gold coins. N.Y., 1909.

Arc 843.9 Aguilera y Gamboa, E. El alto Jalón. Madrid, 1909.

Arc 1033.173 Albarellio, G. Il cimitero "In clivum cucumeris". Aquila, 1909.

Arc 689.3 Arvanitopoulas, A.S. Thessalika Mnēmeia. Athēnai, 1909.

Arc 1093.2.11 Baudon, T. Des silex perforés naturellement. Paris, 1909.

Arc 1025.48.3 Besnier, M. Les catacombes de Rome. Paris, 1909.

Arc 608.15 Béylié, Leon. La Kaloa des Beni-Hammad. Paris, 1909.

Arc 785.50 Bigot, Paul. Recherche des limites du Grand Arque. Rome, 1909.

Arc 1348.23 Blanchet, A. Mémoires et notes de numismatique. Paris, 1909.

Arc 66.1.102 Bourgin, G. La France et Rome de 1788 à 1797. Paris, 1909.

Arc 547.13 British Museum. A guide to the Egyptian collections. London, 1909.

Arc 1353.2.10 British Museum. Department of Coins and Medals. A guide to the gold and silver coins of the ancients. 5. ed. London, 1909.

Arc 705.210 Brueckner, A. Der Friedhof am Eridanos...zu Athen. Berlin, 1909.

Arc 861.4.9 Brutton, F.A. Classical Association...Roman fort at Manchester. Manchester, 1909.

Arc 757.6 Caetani Lovatelli, E. Passeggiate nella Roma antica. Roma, 1909.

Arc 608.11 Cagnot, R. Carthage, Timgad Febessa. Paris, 1909.

Arc 743.10 Cameron, M.L. Old Etruria and modern Tuscany. London, 1909.

Arc 600.6.5 Campbell, C. Two Theben queens. London, 1909.

Arc 1030.8.14 Carus, P. The Nestorian monument; an ancient record of Christianity in China. Chicago, 1909.

Arc 420.5F Chavannes, E. Mission archéologique dans la Chine septentrionale. v.1-2; planches, pt.3. Paris, 1909-15. 4v.

Arc 723.26 Comitato esecutivo per le fete del 1911, Rome. Per una esposizione di etnografia italiana in Roma nel 1911. 2a ed. Firenze, 1909.

Arc 3.1.22 Congrès International d'Archéologie Classique, 2d, Cairo, 1909. Comptes rendus. Le Caire, 1909.

Arc 1200.22 Curschmann, Fritz. Die älteren Papsturkunden des Erzbistums Hamburg. Hamburg, 1909.

Arc 758.4 Diehl, Ernst. Das alte Rom sein Werden. Leipzig, 1909.

Arc 497.13A Driver, S.R. Modern research as illustrating the Bible. London, 1909.

Arc 1020.30 Dütschke, H. Ravennatische Studien. Leipzig, 1909.

Arc 957.1.5 Fewkes, J.W. Antiquities of the Mesa Verde National Park Spruce Tree House. Washington, 1909.

Arc 645.2.2A Fowler, H.N. Handbook of Greek archaeology. N.Y., 1909.

Arc 1348.22 Friedensburg, F. Die Münze in der Kulturgeschichte. Berlin, 1909.

Arc 1033.17.330 Fries, Felix. Histoire de Notre Dame de Foy. Namur, 1909.

Arc 843.50 Gibert, Augusté M. Tarragona prehistòrica i protohistòrica. Barcelona, 1909.

Arc 1470.3.5 Hands, A.W. Coins of Magna Graecia. London, 1909.

Arc 557.3.2.5 Hichens, Robert. Egypt and its monuments. N.Y., 1909.

Arc 1478.18 Hill, G.F. Historical Roman coins. London, 1909.

Arc 1335.49 Hirsch, J. Sammlung Gustav Philipsen. München, 1909.

Arc 785.13.24.5 Huelsen, Christian. The Roman Forum. Rome, 1909.

Arc 1279.2 Hungary. K. Orszagos Leveltar. A Magy. Kiral. Orszagos Leveltar diplom. osztalyaban orzalt. Budapest, 1909.

1909 - cont.

Arc 861.10.20F Isle of Man. Natural History and Antiquarian Society. The Manx archaeological survey; reports. pt.1-6. Douglas, 1909-35.

Arc 497.21 Jaussen, Antonin J. Mission archéologique en Arabie. v.1-3 et Atlas. Paris, 1909-22. 4v.

Arc 1020.99 Kaufmann, C.M. Der Menastempel und die Heiligtümer von Karm Abu Mina. Frankfurt, 1909.

Arc 87.1.69 Kekule, R. Bronzes. Berlin, 1909.

Arc 920.9 Kieseritzky, G. von. Griechische Grabreliefs aus Südrussland. Berlin, 1909.

Arc 710.11 Köster, A. Das Pelargikon. Strasburg, 1909.

Arc 682.25 Kondakov, N.P. Makedoniia arkheologiia putesh. Sankt Peterburg, 1909.

Arc 1020.122 La Croix, C. de. Une dalle mérovingienne trouvée à Challans (Vendée). Poitiers, 1909.

Arc 766.1.19 Lanciani, R. Wanderings in the Roman campagns. Boston, 1909.

Arc 925.13.15 Latyshev, V.V. Pontika...skifiia, Kavkaz. Sankt Petersburg, 1909.

Arc 853.30 Loeschcke, S. Heraniesche Funde in Haltern. Münster, 1909.

Arc 880.23 Macalister, R.A.S. The memorial slabs of Clonmacnois, King's County. Dublin, 1909.

Arc 1025.28.35 Marucchi, O. Esame di un opuscolo di Mons. G. Wilpert. Roma, 1909.

Arc 562.2.27 Maspero, Gaston. New light on ancient Egypt. N.Y., 1909.

Arc 545.227.25 Maspero, Gaston. Rapports. Le Caire, 1909. 2v.

Arc 1077.7 Mercklin, E. von. Der Rennwagen in Griechenland. Leipzig, 1909.

Arc 710.13 Merezhkovskii, D.S. The acropolis, from the Russian of Merejkowski. London, 1909.

Arc 950.202.25 Moore, C.B. Antiquities of the Onachita Valley. Philadelphia, 1909.

Arc 131.1 Moore, William. The Gentlemen's Society at Spalding. Cambridge, 1909. 2 pam.

Arc 1163.3.30 Moskovskii Arkheologicheskii Institut. Bukvitsa na 77 listakh. Moskva, 1909.

Arc 390.2.8 Münchener archäologische Studien...A. Furtwängler. München, 1909.

Arc 1077.7.5 Nachod, H. Der Rennwagen bei ben Italikern. Leipzig, 1909.

Arc 600.17 Naville, E. Les têtes de pierre...tombeaux égyptiens. Genève, 1909.

Arc 1077.6 Nelson, E.M. The cult of the circle-builders. London, 1909.

Htn Arc 600.16*A Nichols, C.L. The library of Rameses the Great. Boston, 1909.

Arc 785.46.5 Nicole, Georges. Le sanctuaire des dieux orientaux au Janicule. Rome, 1909.

Arc 608.7.9 Pallary, P. Instituts pour les recherches préhistoriques. Alger, 1909.

Arc 543.5 Parmentier, H. Inventaires des monuments Čams de l'Annam. Paris, 1909. 2v.

Arc 723.10A Peet, T.E. Stone and bronze ages in Italy and Sicily. Oxford, 1909.

Arc 588.20 Petrie, W.M.F. Memphis. London, 1909-1915. 7 pam.

Arc 588.21 Petrie, W.M.F. Qurneh. London, 1909.

Arc 785.36 Pfretzschner, E. Die Grundrissentwicklung der römischen Thermen. Strassburg, 1909.

Arc 432.4 Pinto, Christoram. India prehistorica. Lisboa, 1909.

Arc 1269.10F Posse, Otto. Die Siegel der deutschen Kaiser und Könige von 751 bis 1913. Dresden, 1909-13. 5v.

Arc 950.211 Putnam anniversary volume. N.Y., 1909. 2v.

Arc 530.13 Radet, G. Cybébé. Paris, 1909.

Arc 606.1 Randall-MacIver, David. Areika. Oxford, 1909.

Arc 435.2.34F Rea, Alexander. Pallava architecture. Madras, 1909.

Arc 815.7 Rodenwaldt, G. Komposition der Pompejanischen Wandgewälde. Berlin, 1909.

Arc 1015.205.5 Roma sotterranea cristiana. pt.1-2. Roma, 1909-14.

Arc 1033.23.5 Scaglia, Sisto. Nova circa thesaurum sacelli Palalini "sancta sanctorum". Roma, 1909

Arc 1027.87 Scaglia, Sisto. Osservazioni sopra i recenti studi intorne ai cimiteri di Marco e Marcelliano. Saronno, 1909. 3 pam.

Arc 684.5 Schwarzstein, A. Eine Gebäudegruppe in Olympia. Strassburg, 1909.

Arc 1583.7 Shrapeznikov', A.N. Katalog' monet' chekannyk' v' Rossii. Sankt Peterburg, 1909.

Arc 435.2.35F Smith, E.W. Akbar's tomb, Sikandarah, near Agra. Allahabad, 1909.

Arc 870.11 Smith, Frederick. The stone ages in northern Britain and Ireland. London, 1909.

Arc 1335.53 Stroehlin, P.C. Collections numismatiques. Genève, 1909.

Arc 1020.123 Swoboda, H. Neue Funde aus dem altchristlichen Österreich. Wien, 1909.

Arc 1018.36 Syxtus, P. Notiones archaeologiae christianae. v.1-2. Romae, 1909-10. 4v.

Arc 600.1.13 Togheb, A.M. de. Études sur l'ancienne Alexandrie. Paris, 1909.

Arc 785.13.39 Van Deman, E.B. The Atrium Vestae. Washington, 1909.

Arc 530.18 Viollet, H. Description du palais de al-Montasim. Paris, 1909.

Arc 1163.7 Vries, S.G. de. Middeleeuwsche handschriften kunde. Leiden, 1909.

Arc 810.17.13 Weichardt, C. Pompei vor der Zerstoerung. 3. Aufl. München, 1909.

Arc 1033.123.5 Wieland, F. Schrift Mensa und Confessio und P. Emil Dorsch. München, 1909.

Arc 1033.123.9 Wieland, F. Der vorirenäische Obferbegriff. München, 1909.

Arc 1480.14 Willers, H. Geschichte der römischen Kupferprägung. Leipzig, 1909.

Arc 1015.5.5 Wilpert, J. Die Papstgräber und di Cäciliengruf. Freiburg, 1909.

Arc 858.9.6 Windle, B.C.A. Remains of the Prehistoric Age in England. London, 1909.

Arc 1335.32 Zabriskie, A.C. Catalogue of the collection of American coins and medals. N.Y., 1909.

191-

Arc 785.39.10 Ripostelli, Giuseppe. Les Thermes de Caracalla. 4. éd. Rome, 191- .

Arc 459.2F Travancore. Archaeological Survey. Annual report for M.E. 1085 (1909-1910). n.p., 191-?

Chronological Listing

1910

Arc 1335.45.9 Alexander and Company, Boston. Alexander and Company's Hub coin book. Boston, 1910.

Arc 1335.110 American Numismatic Society. International medallic exhibition. N.Y., 1910.

Arc 1675.22.5 American Numismatic Society. International medallic exhibition of the American Numismatic Society. N.Y., 1910.

Arc 1675.22.10 American Numismatic Society. International medallic exhibition of the American Numismatic Society. Catalogue. N.Y., 1910.

Arc 1465.78 Anson, L. Numismata Graeca. pt.1-6. Londoni, 1910-16. 2v.

Arc 305.3.5 Archaeological Institute of America. Southwest Society, Los Angeles. Two great gifts. The Lummies Library and collections; the Munk Library. Los Angeles, 1910.

Arc 755.4 Associazione artistica fra i cultori di architecttura. La zona monumentale di Roma. Roma, 1910.

Arc 1335.76.3 Athens. Ethnikon Nomismatikon Mouseion. Katalogos. Athēnai, 1910.

Arc 830.108 Augey, Edmond. Suite de recherches archéologiques relatives à la préhistoire du département de la Gironde. 7e série. Bordeaux, 1910.

Arc 672.1.19A Baikie, James. The sea-kings of Crete. London, 1910.

Arc 875.22 Balfour, J.A. Book of Arran - archaeology. Glasgow, 1910. 2v.

Arc 608.6.6 Ballu, Albert. Guide illustré de Timgad (antique Thamrigadi). 2. éd. Paris, 1910.

Arc 853.47 Bartelt, Wilhelm. Die Burgwälle des Ruppiner Kreises. Würzburg, 1910.

Arc 545.207F Berlin Museum. Mitteilungen aus der Aegyptischen Sammlung. Berlin, 1910- 6v.

Arc 1200.9 Boüard, A. de. Etudes de diplomatique sur les actes, des iquenotaires de Paris. Paris, 1910.

Arc 1675.58 Brenner, V.D. The art of the medal. N.Y., 1910.

Arc 848.19 Brown, Gerard Baldwin. The arts and crafts of our Teutonic forefathers. London, 1910.

Arc 1160.12 Brugmans, H. Atlas der Nederlandsche palaeographie. 's Gravenhage, 1910.

Arc 66.1.103 Celier, Léonce. Les dataires du XVe siècle et les origines de la daterie apostolique. Paris, 1910.

Arc 1485.7F Corpus nummorum italicorum. Roma, 1910-29. 15v.

Arc 823.14 Courcelle-Seneuil, Jean L. Les dieux gaulois d'après les monuments figurés. Paris, 1910.

Arc 307.3.8 Currier, C.W. Seventeenth international congress of Americanists. Washington, 1910?

Arc 936.8 Czarnowski, S.J. Siedziba paleolityczna. Warszawa, 1910-14. 4 pam.

Arc 545.232.9 Davis, T.M. The tomb of Queen Tiyi. London, 1910.

Arc 1675.59 De Kay, Charles. A brief word on medals. N.Y., 1910.

Arc 758.5.5 Dennie, John. Rome of to-day and yesterday. 5. ed. N.Y., 1910.

Arc 1033.180 Doelger, Franz J. Ichthys. v.2-5. Münster, 1910-43. 4v.

Arc 513.17 Dussaud, René. Les civilisations prehelléniques. Paris, 1910.

Arc 1033.115 Emerton, E. The religious environment of early Christianity. Cambridge, 1910.

Arc 136.4.5 Excavation Committee. Report for 1909. Oxford, 1910.

Arc 1504.5 Fluri, Adolf. Die Berner Schulpfennige und die Tischlivierer. Bern, 1910.

Arc 967.2 Folvke, G. Antiquities of central and southeastern Missouri. Washington, 1910.

Arc 458.1.5 Foucher, A. La porte orientale du stûpa de Sânchi. Paris, 1910.

Arc 1148.14 Franchi de' Cavalieri, P. Specimina codicum graecorum vaticanorum. Bonniae, 1910.

Arc 723.11 Frothingham, Arthur L. Roman cities in Italy and Dalmatia. N.Y., 1910.

Arc 723.11.5 Frothingham, Arthur L. Roman cities in Northern Italy and Dalmatia. London, 1910.

Arc 530.12 Garstang, John. The land of the Hittites. London, 1910.

Arc 1335.57F Gohl, Ödön. Gróf Dessewffy Miklos barbár pénzei. pt.1-2. Budapest, 1910-11.

Arc 923.90 Gorodtsov, V.A. Bytovaia arkheologiia. Moskva, 1910.

Arc 858.24.10 Great Britain. Commissions. Ancient and Historical Monuments and Constructions of England. An inventory of the historical monuments in Hertfordshire. London, 1910.

Arc 1033.17.547 Grossi-Gondi, F. La dormitio B. Mariae. Roma, 1910.

Arc 1478.20 Grueber, H.A. Coins of the Roman Republic in the British Museum. v.1-3,5; pt.1-2. London, 1910. 5v.

Arc 1475.11 Häberlin, J.E.J. Aes grove das Schwergeld Roms und Mittelitaliens. v. 1, Text; v. 2, Plates. Frankfurt, 1910. 2v.

Arc 612.6 Hahne, Hans. Das vorgeschichtliche Europa. Bielefeld, 1910.

Arc 609.1.15 Hall, R.N. Pre-historic Rhodesia. Philadelphia, 1910.

Arc 1335.48 Helbing, Otto. Auktions-Katalog. München, 1910.

Arc 853.37 Hertlein, F. Die Juppitergigantensäulen. Stuttgart, 1910.

Arc 557.3.5 Hichens, Robert. The spell of Egypt. Leipzig, 1910.

Arc 557.3.3 Hichens, Robert. The spell of Egypt. London, 1910.

Arc 1411.11 Higgins, F.C. The Chinese numismatic riddle. N.Y., 1910.

Arc 785.38 Huelsen, C. Die Thermen des Agrippa. Rom, 1910.

Arc 785.13.22.5 Huelsen, Christian. Die neuesten Ausgrabungen...Nachtrag. Rom, 1910.

Arc 730.6 Hulot, J. Sélimonte. Paris, 1910.

Arc 307.3.4 International Congress of Americanists, 17th, Buenos Aires, 1910. Sumarios de la conferencias y memorias presentadas al congreso. Buenos Aires, 1910.

Arc 1020.9.64 Iozzi, Oliviero. La reale chiesa del SS. Sudario in Roma. Roma, 1910.

Arc 815.8 Ippel, Albert. Der dritte pompejanische Stil. Berlin, 1910.

Arc 772.9F Italy. Commissione reale per la zona monumentale di Roma. La zona monumentale di Roma e l'opera commissione reale. Roma, 1910.

Arc 1285.35.5 Ivić, Aleksa. Stari srpski pečati i grbovi. Novi Sad, 1910.

Arc 1020.99.15 Kaufmann, C.M. Zur Ikonographie des Menas-Ampullen. Cairo, 1910.

Arc 1016.236 Kaufmann, K.W. Die Menasstadt. Leipzig, 1910.

Arc 612.10 Kimakowicz-Winnicki, M. Spinn und Webewerkzeuge. Würzburg, 1910.

Arc 830.118 La Croix, C. de. Notes archéologiques sur Nouaillé. Poitiers, 1910.

Arc 1468.20 Lambros, J.P. Griechische Münzen. München, 1910.

Arc 785.13.53A Lansiani, Rodolfo. The Roman forum. Rome, 1910.

1910 - cont.

Arc 1490.8.9 Lederer, Philipp. Die Tetrodrachmenprägung von Segesta. München, 1910.

Arc 1027.78 Leynaud, A.F. Les catacombes africaines. Sousse, 1910.

Arc 1163.6 Lindsay, W.M. Early Irish minuscule script. Oxford, 1910.

Arc 810.26 Mackenzie, W.M. Pompeii. London, 1910.

Arc 1030.4.29 Marucchi, O. Epigrafia christiana. Milano, 1910.

Arc 720.215 Mayer, M. La coppa tarantina di argento dorato. Bari, 1910.

Arc 1150.1.9 Mélanges offert à M. Émile Chatelain. Paris, 1910.

Arc 606.2 Mileham, G.S. Churches in lower Nubia. Philadelphia, 1910.

Arc 542.205 Mission Henri Dufour. Bayon d'Angkor Thom. Paris, 1910.

Arc 950.202.29 Moore, C.B. Antiquities of the St. Francis, White and Black rivers, Arkansas. Philadelphia, 1910.

Arc 953.18 Moorehead, W.K. The stone age in North America. Boston, 1910. 2v.

Arc 672.1.7 Mosso, Angelo. Dawn of Mediterranean civilization. London, 1910.

Arc 672.1.6 Mosso, Angelo. Le origini della civilta Mediterranea. Milano, 1910.

Arc 1033.20.28 Nolan, Louis. The Basilica of Saint Clemente in Rome. Rome, 1910.

Arc 505.5.15 Osgood, P.E. The Temple of Solomon. Chicago, 1910.

Arc 674.10F Papabasileios, G.A. Peri tōn en Euboia archaiōn taphōn. Athēnai, 1910.

Arc 838.5 Paris, Pierre. Promenades archéologiques en Espagne. Paris, 1910-1921. 2v.

Arc 1138.4.4A Prou, Maurice. Manuel de paléographie latine et française. 3. éd. Paris, 1910.

Arc 1413.25 Ramsden, H.A. Corean coin charms and amulets. Yokohama, 1910.

Arc 925.4.3F Savenkov, I.T. O drevnikh pamiatnikakh na Enisev. Moskva, 1910.

Arc 895.19 Schnittger, Bror. Förhistoriska flintgrufvor och kulturlager vid kvarn. Stockholm, 1910.

Arc 1333.11 Serafini, C. Monete e bolle plumbee...del Medaghere Vaticano. Milano, 1910. 4v.

Arc 743.9 Seymour, F. Up hill and down dale in ancient Etruria. London, 1910.

Arc 746.7 Stryk, F. von. Studien über etruskischen Kammagräber. Dorpat, 1910.

Arc 450.1 Swarup, B. Konarka. Bengal, 1910.

Arc 810.22.5 Thédenat, H. Pompéi. Vie publique. Paris, 1910.

Arc 1076.3.75 Tilley, H.T. The church bells of Warwickshire. Birmingham, 1910.

Arc 774.1 Tomassetti, G. La campagna romana. Roma, 1910. 4v.

Arc 87.1.70 Trendelenburg, A. Phantasiai. Berlin, 1910.

Arc 1333.17F Vienna. U.L.F. zu den Schotten. Benedictine Monastery. Die Münzensammlung des Stiftes Schotten in Wien. Wien, 1910-20. 2v.

Arc 1221.7 Ward, William Hayes. The seal cylinders of western Asia. Washington, 1910.

Arc 572.1 Weigall, Arthur Edward Pearse Brome. Guide to the antiquities of upper Egypt. London, 1910.

Arc 572.1.2 Weigall, Arthur Edward Pearse Brome. A guide to the antiquities of upper Egypt from Abydos to the Sudan frontier. N.Y., 1910.

Arc 530.14 Wiegand, Theodor. Priene. Leipzig, 1910.

Arc 1015.213.12 Wilpert, J. La cripta dei Papi et la capella di Santa Cecilia. Roma, 1910.

Htn Arc 1605.1* Wood, H. Canadian blacksmith coppers. Philadelphia, 1910.

Arc 606.3 Woolley, C.L. Karanòg, the Romano-Nubian cemetery. Philadelphia, 1910. 2v.

1911

Arc 32.2F Almstead, A.T. Travels and studies in...nearer East. Ithaca, N.Y., 1911.

Arc 1675.22F American Numismatic Society. Catalogue of international exhibition of contemporary medals. N.Y., 1911.

Arc 861.21.17 Andrew, S. Excavation of the Roman forts at Castleshaw. Manchester, 1911.

Arc 405.1.40F Ardashev, Nikolai N. Grat A.S. Uvarov, kak teoretik arkheologii. Moskva, 1911.

Arc 830.88.5 Audollent, A. Les tombes à l'incinération du Musée de Clermont-Ferrand. Paris, 1911. 3 pam.

Arc 585.26F Ayrton, Edward R. Pre-dynastic cemetery at El Mahasna. London, 1911.

Arc 608.6.7 Ballu, Albert. Les ruines de Timgad. Paris, 1911.

Arc 865.1.10 Barclay, E. The ruined temple Stonehenge. London, 1911.

Arc 612.7 Baring-Gould, S. Cliff castles and cave dwellings of Europe. London, 1911.

Arc 1663.55 Bauquier, Henri. Histoire numismatique du comte de Chanbord. Paris, 1911-40.

Arc 853.95 Beck, F. Der Karlsgraben. Nürnberg, 1911.

Arc 1163.3.3 Beliaev, Ivan S. Prakticheskii kurs izucheniia drevnei russkoi skoropisi dlia chteniia rukopisei XV-XVIII stoletii. 2. izd. Reproduction. Moskva, 1911.

Arc 746.8 Bellucci, G. L'ipoge della famiglia etrusca "Rufia". Perugia, 1911.

Arc 520.6.5 Berlin. Königliches Museum. Führer durch die Ruinen von Pergamon. 5. Aufl. Berlin, 1911.

Arc 1675.13 Bernhart, M. Medaillen und Plaketten. Berlin, 1911.

Arc 1020.9.43 Biasiotti, G. La basilica esquilina di Santa Maria ed il palazzo apostolico. Roma, 1911.

Arc 1020.9.187 Biasiotti, G. Le diaconie cardinalizie e la diaconia "S. Vite in Macello". Roma, 1911.

Arc 756.10 Bigot, P. Rome imperiale. Rome, 1911.

Arc 551.4 Bissing, F.W. Die Kunst der alten Ägypter. Leipzig, 1911.

Arc 545.227.33 Blackman, A.M. Temple of Dendûr. Le Caire, 1911.

Arc 522.4.18 Boetticher, E. Der Trojanische Humbug. Berlin, 1911.

Arc 547.17 British Museum. Hieroglyphic Texts from Egyptian Stelae. Pt.1-7, 9. London, 1911-25. 8v.

Arc 1473.6.5 British Museum. Department of Coins and Medals. Catalogue of coins of vandals, ostrogoths. London, 1911.

Arc 855.217F Bulleid, A. The Glastonbury Lake village. n.p., 1911. 2v.

Arc 1490.24 Cagiati, Memmo. Le monete del reame delle Due Sicilie da Carlo I d'Angio a Vittorio Emanuele II. Napoli, 1911-16.

Arc 543.4.50 Castagné, J. Les monuments funeraires de la steppe des Kirghizes. Orenburg, 1911.

Arc 861.63 Chambers, J. The stone age and Lake Lothing. Norwich, 1911.

Arc 562.1.3 Chèlu, Alfred Jacques. Mariette Pacha. Le Caire, 1911.

Arc 1584.28 Chizhov, Sergei I. Azbabskii klad'. Moskva, 1911. 2 pam.

Chronological Listing

1911 - cont.

	Call number	Entry
Htn	Arc 1160.206*	Clemen, O. Handschriftenproben aus der Reformationzeit. Zwickau, 1911.
	Arc 543.7.23	Coedès, George. Les bas-reliefs d'Angkor-Vat. Paris, 1911.
	Arc 435.25.4F	Conference of Orientalists, Simla. The conference...including museums and archaeological conference...Simla, 1911. Simla, 1911.
	Arc 830.176	Cousset, A. Découverte de gravures de sabots d'équides sur Rocher. Paris, 1911.
	Arc 1020.10.38	Cruickshank, J.W. Christian Rome. 2. ed. London, 1911.
	Arc 855.9	Curle, James. A Roman frontier post and its people. Glasgow, 1911.
	Arc 1016.13.5	David, J. Sainte Marie antigue. Roma, 1911.
	Arc 1020.45	Deirnel, T. Christliche Römerfunde in Carnuntum. Wien, 1911.
	Arc 1081.1.5	Duhn, F. von. Ein Rückblick auf die Gräberforschung. Heidelberg, 1911.
	Arc 957.1	Fewkes, J.W. Antiquities of the Mesa Verde National Park Cliff Palace (Colorado). Washington, 1911.
	Arc 955.2.5	Fewkes, J.W. Preliminary report on a visit to Navaha national monument Arizona. Washington, 1911.
	Arc 1166.5	Finzi, A.M. La fotografia quale mezzo di scoperta della falsità in documenti. Firenze, 1911.
	Arc 87.1.71	Gaertringen, F.H. Hira und Andania...zum Winckelmannsfeste. Berlin, 1911.
	Arc 1148.5.2	Gardthausen, V. Griechische Palaeographie. 2. Aufl. Leipzig, 1911. 2v.
	Arc 609.2.15	Garstang, John. Meroë, the city of the Ethiopians. Oxford, 1911.
	Arc 545.227.29	Gauthier, M.H. Le temple de Kalabach. Le Caire, 1911. 2v.
	Arc 823.21.5F	Goury, Georges. L'enceinte d'Haulzy et sa nécropole. Nancy, 1911.
	Arc 858.24.9	Great Britain. Commissions. Ancient and Historical Monuments and Constructions of England. An inventory of the historical monuments in Hertfordshire. London, 1911.
	Arc 855.225F	Great Britain. Commissions. Ancient and Historical Monuments and Constructions in Wales and Monmouthshire. A inventory of the ancient monuments in Wales and Monmouthshire. v.1-5,7-8. London, 1911-37. 4v.
	Arc 606.6	Griffith, F.L. Karanòg, the Meroitic inscriptions. Philadelphia, 1911.
	Arc 587.9	Griffith, F.L. Meroitic inscriptions. London, 1911. 2 pam.
	Arc 1020.119	Gudiol y Cunill, J. Nocions d'arqueologia sagrada catalana. Vich, 1911.
	Arc 1468.6.5A	Head, B.V. Historia numorum. Oxford, 1911.
	Arc 830.2.7	Hirmenech, H.P. Le Men-letonniec de Locmariaquer, Morbihan. Paris? 1911.
	Arc 848.4	Hoops, J. Reallexikon der germanischen Altertumskunde. Strassburg, 1911. 4v.
	Arc 845.206F	Jacob, Karl H. Zur Prähistorie Nordwest-Sachsens. Halle an der Saale, 1911.
	Arc 1663.64	Jaworski, Franciszek. Medalionej polskie. Lwow, 1911.
	Arc 66.1.104	Jouguet, P. La vie municipale dans l'Égypte Romaine. Paris, 1911.
	Arc 700.16	Kairo. Ägyptischen Museums. Griechische Urkunden. Strassburg, 1911.
	Arc 395.3	Körte, G. Archäologie und Geschichts Wissenschaft. Göttingen, 1911.
	Arc 848.8.5	Kossinna, Gustaf. Die Herkunft der Germanen. Würzburg, 1911.
	Arc 684.7.5	Kourouniotos, K. Katalogos tōn mouseiou Lukosouras. Athēnai, 1911.
	Arc 853.48	Kropp, Philipp. Latenezeitliche Funde an der keltischgermanischen Völkergrenze. Würzburg, 1911.
	Arc 651.3	Lichtenberg, R.F. Die ägäische Kultur. Leipzig, 1911.
	Arc 880.25.10	Macalister, R.A.S. Cluain Maccu Nois [Clonmacmois]. Dublin, 1911.
	Arc 875.13.5	Macdonald, G. The Roman wall in Scotland. Glasgow, 1911.
	Arc 848.24F	Mainz. Römisch-germanische Zentralmuseum. Die Altertümer unserer heidnischen Vorzeit. v.5. Mainz, 1911.
	Arc 1411.5	Manuals of Far Eastern numismatics. Yokohama, 1911.
	Arc 635.24.5	Maraghiannio, G. Antiquités crétoises. 2. série. Athène, 1911.
	Arc 1027.9.9	Marucchi, O. Le catacombe ed il protestantesimo. Roma, 1911.
	Arc 562.2.40	Maspero, Gaston. Egypt: ancient sites and modern scenes. N.Y., 1911.
	Arc 608.6.75	Monceaux, Paul. Tingad chrétien. Paris, 1911.
	Arc 810.28	Monod, Jules. La cité antique de Pompéi. Paris, 1911.
	Arc 950.202.33	Moore, C.B. Some aboriginal sites on Mississippi River. Philadelphia, 1911.
	Arc 672.1.7.5	Mosso, Angelo. Dawn of Mediterranean civilization. N.Y., 1911.
	Arc 426.3.5	Munro, N.G. Prehistoric Japan. Yokohama, 1911.
	Arc 1675.25	Nocz, Henry. Les Duvivier. Paris, 1911.
	Arc 608.17	Norton, Richard. The excavations at Cyrene. N.Y., 1911.
	Arc 608.17.3	Norton, Richard. From Bengazi to Cyrene. n.p., 1911.
	Arc 1015.231	Obermann, H.T. De oud-christelijke sarkophagen. 's-Gravenhage, 1911.
	Arc 1480.27	Pansa, Giovanni. Il tipo.di Roma dei denari consolari. Milano, 1911.
	Arc 905.19	Patsch, Carl. Bosnien und Herzegowina in Römischer Zeit. Sarajevo, 1911.
	Arc 588.23	Petrie, W.M.F. Historical studies. London, 1911.
	Arc 770.4.2	Platner, S.B. Topography and monuments of ancient Rome. 2. ed. Boston, 1911.
	Arc 1680.15	Ramsden, H.A. Siamese porcelain and other tokens. Yokohama, 1911.
	Arc 606.7	Randall-MacIver, David. Buhen. Philadelphia, 1911. 2v.
	Arc 1494.5	Reis de Sanches Ferreira, M. Opataco apontamentos para a sua historia. Coimbra, 1911.
	Arc 545.227.31	Roeder, G. Debod bis Bal Kalabach. Le Caire, 1911. 3v.
	Arc 482.201F	Sarre, Friedrich. Archäologische Reise im Euphrat. Berlin, 1911-20. 4v.
	Arc 513.18	Sartiaux, Félix. Villes mortes d'Asie Mineure. Paris, 1911.
	Arc 923.13	Sbornik' arkheologicheskikh statei. Sankt Petersburg, 1911.
	Arc 1018.31	Scaglia, P.S. Manuale di archeologia cristiana. Roma, 1911.
	Arc 773.3	Scaglia, S. La promenade archéologique. Rome, 1911.
	Arc 726.42	Schulz, Bruno. Das Grabmal des Theoderich zu Ravenna. Würzburg, 1911.
	Arc 815.16F	Sogliano, A. La Basilica di Pompei. Napoli, 1911. 6 pam.
	Arc 513.1.5	Sterrett, J.R.S. A plea for research in Asia Minor. Ithaca, 1911.
	Arc 1373.8	Steuer. Die Geschichte im Lichte der Münzen. Luckenwalde, 1911.
	Arc 630.5	Sumbolae Leitt. im Honorem Julii de Petra. Neapoli, 1911.
	Arc 1518.3	Tourneur, Victor. Catalogue des medailles du Royaume de Belgique. Bruxelles, 1911.
	Arc 1433.36	Valentine, W.H. Modern copper coins of the Muhammadan states. London, 1911.
	Arc 905.12.9	Verein Carnuntum, Wien. Carnuntum 1885-1910. Wien, 1911.
	Arc 505.5.65F	Vincent, Louis H. Jérusalem sous terre. Londres, 1911.
	Arc 913.16	Viollier, David. Essai sur les rites funéraires en Suisse des origines à la conquête romaine. Paris, 1911.
	Arc 435.2.36F	Vogel, J.P. Antiquities of Chamba state. Calcutta, 1911.
	Arc 958.1.5	Volk, E. The archaeology of the Delaware Valley. Cambridge, 1911.
	Arc 861.39.5	Ward, John. The Roman era in Britain. London, 1911.
	Arc 861.39	Ward, John. Romano-British buildings and earthworks. London, 1911.
	Arc 630.8	Woelcke, Karl. Beiträge zur Geschichte des Tropaions. Bonn, 1911.
	Arc 606.5	Woolley, C.L. Karanòg, the town. Philadelphia, 1911.

1912

	Call number	Entry
	Arc 612.21	Åberg, Nils. Studier öfver den yngre stenildern i Norden och Vosteuropa. Norrköping, 1912.
	Arc 958.1.8	Abbott, C.C. Ten years' diggings in Lenâpè Sand, Delaware. Trenton, New Jersey, 1912.
	Arc 1030.38	Aigrain, R. Manuel d'épigraphie chrétienne. Paris, 1912.
	Arc 1665.4F	Babelon, Ernest. Les medailles historique...Napoléon le Grand. Paris, 1912.
	Arc 943.12	Beuchat, H. Manuel d'archéologie americaine. Paris, 1912.
	Arc 1458.18	Bibliothèque Nationale, Paris. Département des Médailles et Antiques. Collections Armand-Valton. Paris, 1912.
	Arc 746.9	Bienkowski, P. De speculis Etruscis et cista in museo. Cracoviae, 1912.
	Arc 1498.7	Blanchet, A. Manuel de numismatique francaise. Paris, 1912-36. 4v.
	Arc 853.44	Blume, Erich. Die germanischen Stämme und die Kulturen. Würzburg, 1912-15. 2v.
	Arc 673.1.4	Bourguet, E. L'aurige de Delphes. Paris, 1912.
	Arc 1153.23	Bretholtz, B. Lateinische Paläographie. 2. Aufl. Leipzig, 1912.
	Arc 1603.1.5	Breton, P.N. Popular illustrated guide to Canadian coins. Montreal, 1912.
	Arc 861.80	Bullen, R.A. Harlyn Bay and the discoveries of its prehistoric remains. 3. ed. Harlyn Padstow, 1912.
	Arc 547.6.13	Cairo. Musée des Antiquités Égyptiennes. Guide du visiteur au Musée du Caire. 2. éd. Caire, 1912.
	Arc 545.238	Carter, H. Five years' explorations at Thebes. London, 1912.
	Arc 1448.1	Charrier, Louis. Description des monnaies de la Numidie et de la Maurétanie. Macon, 1912.
	Arc 861.106F	Clapham, A.W. On the topography of the Dominican Priory of London. Oxford, 1912.
	Arc 861.104	Clapham, A.W. St. John of Jerusalem, Clerkenwell. London, 1912.
X Cg	Arc 880.8	Coffey, George. New Grange and other incised tumuli. Dublin, 1912.
	Arc 3.1.23	Congrès International d'Archéologie Classique, 3d, Rome, 1912. Bolletino riassuntivo. Roma, 1912.
	Arc 830.127	D'Ardé, J. Musée lapidaire, l'histoire de Béziers. Béziers, 1912.
	Arc 375.7	Deinard, S.N. Descriptive charts of ancient monuments. no.1-5. Minneapolis, 1912.
	Arc 396.3.20	Le duc de Loubat, 1894-1912. Paris, 1912.
	Arc 584.1	Egypt. Antiquities Department. Rapports sur la Marche, 1899-1910. Le Caire, 1912.
	Arc 1298.2	Eitel, Anton. Über Blei- und Goldbullen. Freiburg, 1912.
	Arc 1215.2	Eitel, Anton. Ueber Blei- und Goldbullen im Mittelalter. Freiburg, 1912.
	Arc 608.6.22	Exploration scientifique de l'Algérie. Paris, 1912. 2v.
	Arc 880.9	Ffrench, J.F.M. Prehistoric faith and worship. London, 1912.
	Arc 1263.4	France. Direction des Archives. Inventaire des sceaux de la Bourgogné. Paris, 1912.
	Arc 853.36	Fredrich. Die in Ostdeutschland gefundenen römischen Bronzestatuellen. Cüstrin, 1912. 3 pam.
	Arc 87.1.72	Frickenhaus, A. Lenäenvasen. Berlin, 1912.
	Arc 635.223F	Frickenhaus, A. Tiryns. v.1-8. Athēnai, 1912- 9v.
	Arc 390.2.12	Furtwängler, Adolf. Kleine Schriften. München, 1912. 2v.
	Arc 853.68F	Gätze, A. Die altthüringischen Funde von Weimar (5.-7. Jahrhundert nach Christus.) Berlin, 1912.
	Arc 454.1	Ganguly, M.M. Orissa and her remains. Calcutta, 1912.
	Arc 785.46	Gauckler, P. Le sanctuaire syrien du Janicule. Paris, 1912.
	Arc 545.227.36	Gauthier, H. Temple de Ouadi Es-Seboua. Le Caire, 1912.
	Arc 838.6	Gomes-Moreno, M. Materiales de arqueologia española. Madrid, 1912.
	Arc 858.24.11	Great Britain. Commissions. Ancient and Historical Monuments and Constructions of England. An inventory of the historical monuments in Buckinghamshire. London, 1912-13. 2v.
	Arc 66.1.106	Grenier, A. Bologne villanovienne et etrusque. Paris, 1912.
	Arc 670.2.5	Groote, M. von. Ägineten und Archäologen. Strassburg, 1912.
	Arc 670.3	Hastings, H.R. Relations between inscriptions and sculptured representations on Attica tombstones. Madison, 1912.
	Arc 853.40	Hauptmann, Carl. Die Erhaltung der Römerstrassen. Bonn, 1912.
	Arc 853.38	Hauptmann, Carl. Die strategischen Rheinübergange der Römer bei Bonn. Bonn, 1912.
	Arc 66.1.105	Hautecoeur, L. Rome et la Renaissance de l'antiquite. Photoreproduction. Paris, 1912.
	Arc 853.98	Hertlein, F. Die Alterthümer des Oberamts Heidenheims. Eszlingen, 1912.

Chronological Listing

1912 - cont.

Arc 1675.20.10 Hill, George F. Portrait medals of Italian artists of the Renaissance. London, 1912.
Arc 1010.5 Hirmenech, H.P. Une tablette de l'île de Pâques. Paris, 1912.
Arc 772.6 Holtzinger, H. Die Ruinen Roms. 2. Aufl. Stuttgart, 1912.
Arc 435.25.7F India. Archaeological Survey. Loan exhibition of antiquities, Coronation Durbar, 1911. Calcutta, 1912.
Arc 307.3.9 International Congress of Americanists, 17th, May 1910 (2d meeting, Mexico, Sept. 1910). Reseña de la segunda sesion del XVII Congresso...de Americanistes. México, 1912.
Arc 609.1.20 Johnson, J.P. The pre-historic period in South Africa. London, 1912.
Arc 1470.20 Königliche Academie der Wissenschaft zu Amsterdam. Beschreibung der Griechischen Autonomen Münzen. Amsterdam, 1912.
Arc 848.5 Koepp, F. Die Römer in Deutschland. Bielefeld, 1912.
Arc 1200.12 Krüger, P. Bedeutung der Salutatio...14. Jahrhundert. Greifswald, 1912.
Arc 1163.9 Lindsay, W.M. Early Welsh script. Oxford, 1912.
Arc 136.4 London Society of Antiquaries. Report for 1909-1911. Old Sarum Excavation fund. Oxford, 1912.
Arc 340.17 Lyell, Arthur H. A bibliographical list descriptive of Romano-British architectural remains in Great Britain. Cambridge, 1912.
Cg Arc 505.14 Macalister, R.A.S. Excavation of Gezer, 1902-1905, 1907-1909. London, 1912. 3v.
Arc 767.1.7A Maps, Rome. Ancient (1912). Formae urbis Romae antiquae. Berolino, 1912.
Arc 1030.4.30 Marucchi, O. Christian epigraphy. Cambridge, 1912.
Arc 1025.28.6 Marucchi, O. Handbuch der christlichen Archäologie. N.Y., 1912.
Arc 726.10.14 Marucchi, Orazio. Guida archeologica della città di Palestrina. Roma, 1912.
Arc 545.227.35 Maspero, Gaston. Documents. Le Caire, 1912.
Arc 608.1.37F Massigli, T. Musée de Sfax. Paris, 1912.
Arc 746.2.9 Matthies, S. Die Praenestinischen Spiegel. Strassburg, 1912.
Arc 736.2.10F Mauceri, L. Il castello Eurialo. Syracuse. Roma, 1912.
Arc 1163.8 Mentz, G. Handschriften der Reformationszeit. Bonn, 1912.
Arc 608.13 Mesnege, P.J. L'Afrique chrétienne...ruines antiques. Paris, 1912.
Arc 1076.3.48 Metzger, O.H. Die Glocken im Friedländischen. Friedland, 1912.
Arc 1020.31.25 Mommert, Carl. Saint Étienne et ses sanctuaires à Jérusalem. Jérusalem, 1912.
Arc 505.12.15F Momumenta Sinaitica. pt.1- Leningrad, 1912-1925. 2v.
Arc 830.54 Montauzan, C. Germain de. Les fouilles de fourvière en 1911. Lyon, 1912.
Arc 1335.36 Montélhet, A. Musée crozatier - catalogue du médaillier. v.1-2. Paris, 1912.
Arc 720.212.5 Monteluis, O. Die vorklassiche Chronologie Italiens. Stockholm, 1912. 2v.
Arc 950.202.32 Moore, C.B. Some aboriginal sites on the Red River. Philadelphia, 1912.
Arc 1130.5 Moore, Margaret F. Two select bibliographies mediaeval historical study. London, 1912.
Arc 967.3 Moorehead, W.K. Certain peculiar earthworks near Andover, Massachusetts. Andover, 1912.
Arc 1027.18.7 Müller, Nikolaus. Die jüdische Katakombe am Monteverde zu Rom. Leipzig, 1912.
Arc 1468.12.2 Münzer, Friedrich. Die antiken Münzen von Thrakien. Berlin, 1912.
Arc 1588.2.11 Mushmov, N.A. Antichnite moneti na Balkanskiia polustrov i monetite. Sofiia, 1912.
Arc 905.20 Österreichisches Archäologisches Institut. Führer durch das K.K. Staatsmuseum in S. Donato in Zara. Wien, 1912.
Arc 1076.3.43 Olovianishnikov, N. Istoriia kolokolov i kolokitenoe iskusstvo. Moskva, 1912.
Arc 726.32 Pagenstecher, R. Unteritalische Grabdenkmäler. Strassburg, 1912.
Arc 1093.2.13 Paniagua, A. Les monuments mégalithiques. Paris, 1912.
Arc 1470.22 Pansa, G. La moneta di P. Ovidio Nasone. Milano, 1912.
Arc 589.1.3 Petrie, W.M.F. The formation of the alphabet. London, 1912.
Arc 588.24 Petrie, W.M.F. Labyrinth Gerzeh and Mazghumeh. London, 1912.
Arc 1264.8A Roman, J. Manuel de sigillographie française. Paris, 1912.
Arc 736.7 Rossbach, Otto. Castrogiovanni...nebst einer Untersuchung. Leipzig, 1912.
Arc 520.12 Salis, A. von. Der Altar von Pergamon. Berlin, 1912.
Arc 1488.11F Sambon, Giulio. Repertoiro generale delle monete coniate in Italia. Parigi, 1912.
Arc 682.15A Seager, R.B. Explorations in the island of Mochlos. Boston, 1912.
Arc 396.4.20 Société des Antiquaires de l'Ouest, Poitiers. Monument érigé à la mémoire de R.P. de la Croix. Poitiers, 1912.
Arc 843.32F Spain. Comisión ejecutiva de las excavaciones de Numancia. Excavaciones de Numancia. Madrid, 1912.
Arc 1145.207 Steffens, Franz. Proben aus griechischen Handscriften und Urkunden. Trier, 1912.
Arc 543.3.8A Stein, Mark Aurel. Ruins of desert Cathay. London, 1912. 2v.
Arc 895.30F Stolpe, Hjalmar. Graffältet oid Vendel. Stockholm, 1912.
Arc 18.1.10 Tables générales de l'année épigraphique. 1901-1950. Paris, 1912-1932.
Arc 936.1.5 Tafrali, O. Topographie de Thessalonique. Paris, 1912.
Arc 1143.2.5A Thompson, Edward Maunde. Introduction to Greek and Latin palaeography. Oxford, 1912.
Arc 1473.7 Tolstoi, Jean. Monnaies byzantines. v.1-4,8-9. St. Petersbourg, 1912-14. 4v.
Arc 830.158.5 Toutain, Jules. Les fouilles d'Alésia de 1909-10. Semur-en-Auxois, 1912.
Arc 1615.4 United States Mint. Catalogue of coins, tokens, and medals. Washington, 1912.
Arc 635.222 Wace, A.J.B. Prehistoric Thessaly. Cambridge, 1912.
Arc 1076.3.18 Walters, Henry Beauchamp. Church bells of England. London, 1912.
Arc 572.1.15 Weigall, Arthur Edward Pearse Brome. The treasury of ancient Egypt. Chicago, 1912.
Arc 843.8 Whishaw, B. Illustrated descriptive account of the museum of Andalucian pottery and lace. Seville, 1912.
Arc 1083.2 Wigand, Karl. Thymiateria. Inaug. Diss. Bonn, 1912.
Arc 1093.2.8 Wilke, Georg. Südwesteuropäische Megalithkultur. Würzburg, 1912.

1912 - cont.

NEDL Arc 1190.3.5 Wright, Andrew. Court hand restored. 10. ed. London, 1912.
Arc 830.55 Zocco-Rosa, A. La Tavola Bronzea di Narbona. Catania, 1912.

1913

Arc 1615.5 Adams, E.H. Private gold coinage of California, 1849-55, its history and issues. Brooklyn, 1913.
Arc 1613.7.5 Adams, E.H. United States pattern, trial, and experimental pieces. N.Y., 1913.
Arc 1428.15 Akademie der Wissenschaften, Berlin. Die antiken Münzen Mysiens. Berlin, 1913.
Arc 772.6.2 Amelung, W. Die antiken Sammlungen. 2. Aufl. Stuttgart, 1913.
Arc 726.2.19 Antiquités des environs de Naples. Naples, 1913.
Arc 426.4 Arai, Hakuseki. The sword book, in Honiko Gunkiko. Reading, 1913. 2 pam.
Arc 428.5PF Archaeology of Korea. Plates and maps. Tokyo, 1913. 7v.
Arc 1018.37 Barnes, A.S. The early church in the light of monuments. London, 1913.
Arc 1027.45.5 Becker, Erich. Malta Sotterranea...Sepulkralkunst. Strassburg, 1913.
Arc 756.11.3 Bertaux, Émile. Rome, l'antiquité. 3. éd. Paris, 1913.
Arc 875.29 Black, William G. Glasgow cross. Glasgow, 1913.
Arc 545.227.40 Blackman, A.M. The temple of Derr. Le Caire, 1913.
Arc 1020.106 Bled, O. Livre d'or de Notre Dame des miracles à Saint Omer. St. Omer, 1913.
Arc 785.34.14 Bowerman, H.C. Roman sacrificial altars. Lancaster, Pa., 1913.
Arc 1185.16 Brandi, Karl. Urkunden und Akten. Leipzig, 1913.
Arc 545.241F Budge, Ernest A. The Rosetta stone. London, 1913.
Arc 1348.27 Burgess, F.W. Chats on old coins. London, 1913.
Arc 880.22 Cochrane, Robert. List of ancient and national monuments in county of Cork. Cork, 1913.
Arc 880.10 Coffey, George. The bronze age in Ireland. Dublin, 1913.
Arc 785.8.7F Colgrossi, P. L'anfiteatro Flavio nei suoi venti secoli di storia. Firenze, 1913.
Arc 726.58 Colini, Giuseppe A. Necropoli de Pianello presso Genza (Ancona). Parma, 1913.
Arc 1510.31F Cologne. Die Münzen und Medaillen von Köln. Köln, 1913-35. 4v.
Arc 830.177 Cousset, A. Communications. Le Mans, 1913.
Arc 587.9.15 Davies, N. de Garis. Five Theban tombs. London, 1913.
Arc 823.11.5 Déchelette, Joseph. Manuel d'archéologie préhistorique, celtique et gallo-romaine. v.1-2. Paris, 1913-1924. 4v.
Arc 340.2.5 Deutsches Archäologisches Institut. Römische Abteilung. Bibliothek. Katalog der Bibliothek. v.1-2. Rom, 1913-32. 4v.
Arc 1485.7.5 Dotti, E. Tariffa di monete medioevale e moderne italiane. Milano, 1913.
Arc 600.47F Edgar, C.A. Der Isistempel von Behbet. pt.2. Rom, 1913.
Arc 1335.39 Elder, Thomas L. Rare coins and medals of William S. Appleton. N.Y., 1913.
Arc 726.89 Ferrare, F. Relazione sulle antichita prehistoriche rinvenute nella contrado comino presso Guardeagrele. Guardeagrele, 1913.
Arc 955.2.9 Fewkes, J.W. Casa Grande, Arizona (28th report of the Bureau of American Ethnology). Washington, 1913.
Arc 1668.10 Friedensburg, F. Die Symbolik der Mittlaltermünzen. v.1,2-3. Berlin, 1913-22. 2v.
Arc 545.227.38 Gauthier, H. Le temple d'Amada. Le Caire, 1913.
Arc 1084.5 Getz, John. The Woodward collection of jades and other hard stones. n.p., 1913.
Arc 861.68 Gray, Harold St. George. Maumbury Rings excavations. Interim report. Dorchester, 1913.
Arc 505.15 Groot, J. de. Palestijnsche masseben (Opgerichte Steenen). Groningen, 1913.
Arc 726.2.15 Günther, R.T. Pausilypon...imperial villa near Naples. Oxford, 1913.
Arc 853.13.2 Hang, F. Die römischen Inschriften und Bildwerke Württembergs. v.1-3. Stuttgart, 1913.
Arc 762.1.9 Hare, A.J.C. Walks in Rome. 20th ed. London, 1913.
Arc 1018.19.2 Haufmann, C.M. Handbuch der christlichen Archäologie. 2. Aufl. Paderborn, 1913.
Arc 1335.87 Helbing, Otto. Auktions-Katalog enthaltend die Münzen- und Medaillen-Bestände der aufgelösten Firma zschiesche und Köder. München, 1913.
Arc 845.205F Henkel, F. Die Römischen Fingerringe der Rheinlande. Berlin, 1913. 2v.
Arc 1335.101.25 Hirsch, Jacob. Griechische, römische und byzantinische Münzen aus dem Besitze von Friedrich von Schennis. München, 1913.
Arc 1153.31 Hulákovsky, J.M. Abbreviaturae vocabulorum. Pragae, 1913.
Arc 861.96 Hurd, Howard. Some notes on recent archaeological discoveries at Broadstairs. Broadstairs, 1913.
Arc 830.70 Hutinel, F. La préhistoire dans la région lyonnaise. Lyon, 1913.
Arc 1458.15 Jameson, R. Collection of monnaies grecques et romaines. v.1-2. Paris, 1913. 3v.
Arc 861.23.5 Johnston, P.M. Schedule of antiquities in the county of Surrey. London, 1913.
Arc 848.6 Kauffmann, F. Deutsche Altertumskunde. München, 1913-23. 2v.
Arc 925.50.125 Khvoika, V.V. Drevnie obitateli Sredniago Pridneprov'ia. Kiev, 1913.
Arc 1433.39 Krotkov', A.A. Klad' serebianykh' monet' s" vodianskago gorodishcha. Saragov', 1913.
Arc 870.12 Leeds, E.T. The archaeology of the Anglo-Saxon settlements. Oxford, 1913.
Arc 66.1.108 Leroux, Gabriel. Les origines de l'édifice hypostyle. Paris, 1913.
Arc 609.2F Littmann, Enno. Deutsche Aksum-Expedition. v.1-4. Berlin, 1913.
Arc 726.38 Marchisio, A.F. Per l'archeologia del territorio albese. Alba, 1913.
Arc 830.2.13 Marsille, Louis. Le déput de l'age du bronze dans le Morbihan. Vannes, 1913.
Arc 830.2.15 Marsille, Louis. Le tumulus de cote-er-garf, en elven et les sépulture de l'age du bronze dans le Morbihan. Vannes, 1913.
Arc 810.11.7.2 Mau, August. Pompeji in Leben und Kunst. 2. Aufl. Leipzig, 1913.

Chronological Listing

1913 - cont.

	Arc 652.3	Mélanges Holleaux - recueil de memoires concernant l'antiquité grecque offert à Maurice Holleaux. Paris, 1913.
	Arc 910.10F	Messikommer, H. Die Pfahlbauten von Robenhausen. Zürich, 1913.
	Arc 562.5	Meyer, Eduard. Bericht über eine Expedition nach Ägypten zur Erforschung der Darstellungen der Fremdvolker. Berlin, 1913. 9v.
	Arc 394.1.20	Michaelis, A. Otto Jahn in seinen Briefen. Leipzig, 1913.
	Arc 823.15	Millon, Henry E. La collection Millon. Paris, 1913.
	Arc 925.12	Minns, E.H. Scythians and Greeks...ancient history and archaeology. Cambridge, 1913.
	Arc 1675.50	Mondini, R. Spigolando tra medaglie e date, 1848-71. Livorno, 1913.
	Arc 950.202.35	Moore, C.B. Some aboriginal sites in Louisiana and Arkansas. Philadelphia, 1913.
	Arc 1433.38	Morgan, J. de. Contribution à l'étude des ateliers monétaires...rois Sassanides. Paris, 1913.
	Arc 830.59	Morin-Jean. La verrerie en Gaule à l'époque romaine. Le Mans, 1913.
	Arc 830.59.2	Morin-Jean. La verrerie en Gaule sous l'empire romain. Paris, 1913.
	Arc 1160.210F	Moskovskii Arkheologicheskii Institut. Sbornik snimkov s russkago pis'ma. Moskva, 1913. 2v.
	Arc 287.2F	Moskovskoe Arkheologicheskoe Obshchestvo. Slisok izdanii. Moskva, 1913.
	Arc 505.5.60	Paton, Lewis B. Jerusalem in Bible times. Chicago, 1913.
	Arc 585.27	Peet, T.E. The cemeteries of Abydos. London, 1913-14. 3v.
	Arc 588.25A	Petrie, W.M.F. Hawara portfolio; paintings. London, 1913.
	Arc 400.9	Piper, Otto. Bedenken zur Vorgeschichts-Forschung. München, 1913.
	Arc 1335.41.5	Robinson, John. Oriental numismatics - catalogue of collections of books related to coinage of the east presented to Essex Institute, Salem. Salem, 1913.
	Arc 843.195	Román, Carlos. Antigüedades ebusitanas. Barcelona, 1913.
	Arc 936.28F	Romstorfer, K.A. Cetalea Sucerii. București, 1913.
	Arc 785.13.48	Ruggiero, E. de. Il Foro Romano. Roma, 1913.
	Arc 1200.13	Schmitz, Karl. Ursprung und Geschichte der Devotionsformeln. Stuttgart, 1913.
	Arc 1510.16	Schrötter, F.F. von. Die Münzen F. Wilhelms des Grossen Kurfürst und Friedrichs III von Brandenberg. Berlin, 1913.
	Arc 853.65.10	Seger, Hans. Schlesiens Urgeschichte. Leipzig, 1913.
	Arc 810.52	Seymour-Browne, C. Notes on Pompei. Naples, 1913.
	Arc 923.30	Shliapkin, I.A. Russkaia paleograiuiia. Sankt Petersburg, 1913.
	Arc 956.1	Smith, Harlan I. Archaeological collection from the southern interior of British Columbia. Museum of Geological Survey, Canada. Ottawa, 1913.
Htn	Arc 1135.209*	Spicilegium palimpsestorum. Bevronae, 1913.
	Arc 1033.43.11	Sybel, L. von. Der Herr der Seligkeit. Archäologische Studie. Marburg, 1913.
	Arc 936.1	Tafrali, O. Mélanges d'archéologie et d'epigraphie byzantines. Paris, 1913.
	Arc 936.1.6	Tafrali, O. Topographie de Thessalonique. Paris, 1913.
	Arc 600.20	Theban ostraca. Toronto, 1913.
	Arc 1335.16.5	United States Mint, Philadelphia. Guide. Washington, 1913.
	Arc 1615.4.2	United States Mint. Catalogue of coins, tokens, and medals. 2. ed. Washington, 1913.
	Arc 785.8.5	Viola, Joseph. Das Kolosseum. Rom, 1913.
	Arc 875.42.5	Waldie, G. Walks along the northern Roman wall. Linlithgow, 1913.
	Arc 1076.3.115	Walter, Karl. Glockenkunde. Regensburg, 1913.
	Arc 681.1.10	Weickert, Carl. Das lesbische Kymation. Leipzig, 1913.
	Arc 708.27	Weller, C.H. Athens and its monuments. N.Y., 1913.
	Arc 87.1.73	Wiegand, Theodore. Bronzefigur einer Spinnerin. Berlin, 1913.

1914

Arc 895.22.10F	Almgren, Oscar. Die ältere Eisenzeit Gotlands. pt.1-2. Stockholm, 1914-23.
Arc 1.13.6F	American Academy, Rome. The American Academy in Rome, 1894-1914. N.Y., 1914.
Arc 1613.13	American Numismatic Society, N.Y. Exhibition of United States and colonial coins, Jan. 17 to Feb. 18, 1914. Catalogue. N.Y., 1914.
Arc 843.40	Ansoleaga, F. de. El cementerio franco de Pamplona (Navarra). Pamplona, 1914.
Arc 938.9	Archäologischer Kongress. Baltischen...Komitee. Baltische Studien zur Archäologie und Geschichte. Berlin, 1914.
Arc 861.57F	Balch, H.E. Wookey Hole; its caves and cave dwellers. London, 1914.
Arc 1335.51	Bellissima, G.B. Riordinamento del museo numismatico. v.1-2. Siena, 1914.
Arc 726.91	Bertoni, G. La cattedrale modenese. Modena, 1914.
Arc 587.10F	Blackman, A.M. The rock tombs of Meir. London, 1914-24. 6v.
Arc 673.1.3	Bourguet, E. Les ruines de Delphes. Paris, 1914.
Arc 600.1.15	Breccia, E. Alexandrea ad Aegyptum. Bergamo, 1914.
Arc 1428.27	Brett, A. The electrum coinage of Lampakos. N.Y., 1914.
Arc 1680.8	Brief particulars...eighteenth century tokens...county of Middlesex. n.p., 1914?
Arc 861.50	Brighton and Hove Archaeological Club. Brighton and Hove archaeologist, 1914. Hove, 1914.
Arc 630.6	British Museum. Catalogue of Greek and Roman lamps in the British Museum. London, 1914.
Arc 1418.2.7	British Museum. Department of Coins and Medals. Catalogue of the coins of the Gupta dynasties and of Sásānka. London, 1914.
Arc 547.25F	British Museum. Department of Egyptian and Assyrian Antiquities. Egyptian sculptures in the British Museum. London, 1914.
Arc 1500.39	Changarnier, A. Monnaies des Boïens de la Germanie. Dijon, 1914.
Arc 1335.77	Colombo Museum. Colombo, Ceylon. Catalogue of coins in the Colombo Museum. Hertford, 1914.
Arc 861.13.15	Cook, A.S. Some accounts of the Bewcastle Cross. N.Y., 1914.
Arc 858.23	Cox, R.H. The green roads of England. London, 1914.
Arc 188.1.5F	Die Denkmalpflege. Inhattsverzeichnis der Jahrg, 1899-1913. Berlin, 1914.
Arc 513.17.2	Dussaud, René. Les civilisations prehelléniques. 2. éd. Paris, 1914.
Arc 861.35	Ely, Talfourd. Roman Hayling. London, 1914.

1914 - cont.

Arc 1212.4	Ewald, W. Siegelkunde. München, 1914.
Arc 968.2.20	Fewkes, J.W. Archaeology of the lower Mimbres Valley, New Mexico. Washington, 1914.
Arc 708.23.7	Fougères, G. Athènes. Paris, 1914.
Arc 435.2.38F	Francke, A.H. Antiquities of Indian Tibet. Calcutta, 1914-26. 2v.
Arc 1163.11	Franke, O. Epigraphische Denkmäler aus China. Berlin, 1914. 2v.
Arc 726.36.5	Galli, Edoardo. Fiesole. Gli scair, il museo civico. Milano, 1914.
Arc 495.204	Garrett, Robert. Topography and itinerary (American archaeological exedition to Syria). N.Y., 1914.
Arc 861.18.15	Gordon, E.O. Prehistoric London; its mounds. London, 1914.
Arc 608.6.21F	Gsell, Stéphane. Khamissa, Mdaourouch, Announa. Alger, 1914-22.
Arc 1588.1.19	Gumowski, Marian. Podrecznik numiznatyki Polskiej. Kraków, 1914.
Arc 853.13.3	Hang, F. Die römischen Inschriften und Bildwerke Württembergs. 2. Aufl. Stuttgart, 1914-15.
Arc 858.25	Haverfield, F. Roman Britain in 1913- v.1-2. Oxford, 1914- 5v.
Arc 843.145	Hernandez-Pacheco, Eduardo. Las pinturas prehistoricas de Peña Tú. Madrid, 1914.
Arc 1494.20F	Herrera y Chiesanova, A. El duro. Madrid, 1914. 2v.
Arc 875.31	Hewison, J.K. Runic roods of Ruthwell and Bewcastle. Glasgow, 1914.
Arc 1335.101.51	Hirsch, Jacob. Griechische, römische, byzantinische Münzen. München, 1914.
Arc 400.17	In onore di Luigi Pigorini, Roma, 11 gennaio 1914. Roma, 1914.
Arc 750.224F	Italy. Commissione reale per la zona monumentale di Roma. La zona monumentale di Roma e l'opera della Commissione reale. Roma, 1914.
Arc 600.48	Johnson, J. de M. Antinoë and its papyri; excavations by the Graeco-Roman branch, 1913-14. London, 1914.
Arc 1510.23.5	Joseph, Paul. Die Medaillen und Münzen der Wild- und Rheingrafen Fürsten zu Salm. Frankfurt am Main, 1914.
Arc 395.5	Kabbadias, P. Proistorikē archaiologia. Athēnai, 1914.
Arc 510.220F	Kinch, K.F. Vroulia [Rhodes]. Berlin, 1914.
Arc 861.10.17	Kinnebrook, William. Manks antiquities. 2. ed. Liverpool, 1914.
Arc 848.8.2	Kossinna, Gustaf. Die deutsche Vorgeschichte. 2. Aufl. Würzburg, 1914.
Arc 936.6	Kostrzewski, Józef. Wielkopolska w czasach. Poznań, 1914.
Arc 1418.20	Lahore Museum. Catalogue of coins in the Punjab Museum. Oxford, 1914-34. 3v.
Arc 853.45	Lienau, M.M. Über Megalithgräber und sonstige Grabformen der Lüneburger Gegend. Würzburg, 1914.
Arc 1282.7	Likhachen, N.I. Zemskaia nechat' Moskovskago gosudarstva. Moskva, 1914.
Arc 895.22	Lithberg, Nils. Gotlands stenalder. Stockholm, 1914.
Arc 1153.27	Lowe, E.A. The Benevetan script. Oxford, 1914.
Arc 562.2.16A	Maspero, Gaston. Manual of Egyptian archaeology. 6. ed. N.Y., 1914.
Arc 726.37F	Maye, M. Apulien vor und während der Hellenisirung. Leipzig, 1914.
Arc 537.2.12	Metropolitan Museum of Art. Handbook of th Cesnola collection of antiquities from Cyprus. N.Y., 1914.
Arc 397.10	Mortel, Victor. Mélanges d'archéologie; antiquité romaine et moyen âge. Paris, 1914-15. 2v.
Arc 1330.4	New York Public Library. List of works relating to numismatics. N.Y., 1914.
Arc 1033.20.29	Nolan, Louis. The Basilica of Saint Clemente in Rome. 2. ed. Rome, 1914.
Arc 1470.60	Oreshnikov, A. Zkskursy v oblast' drevnsi numizmatiki cherno morskago pobereniia. Moskva, 1914.
Arc 493.4	Pillet, M.L. Le palais de Darius. Paris, 1914.
Arc 435.2.39F	Rice, B.S. Epigraphia caratica. Madras, 1914.
Arc 750.217F	Rodacanchi, E. Les monuments de Rome après la chute de l'empire. Paris, 1914.
Arc 1423.16	Rogers, Edgar. A handy guide to Jewish coins. London, 1914.
Arc 785.51	Sabatini, F. La torre delle milizie, erroneamente denominala torre di Nerone. Roma, 1914.
Arc 1033.12.235	Sanchis y Sivera, José. El santo cáliz de la cena (santo grial) venerado en Valencia. Valencia, 1914.
Arc 1148.33	Sarros, D.M. Palaiographikos eranos. Konstantinoypolei, 1914.
Arc 726.42.5	Savini, Gaetano. Per i monumenti e per la storia di Ravenna. Ravenna, 1914.
Arc 830.106	Scheurer, F. Fouilles du cimetière barbare de Bourgogne. Paris, 1914.
Arc 1208.6	Schlumberger, G. Collections sigillographiques de G. Schlumberger. Paris, 1914.
Arc 87.1.74	Schröder, Bruno. Griechische Bronzeeimer im berlinen Antiquarium. Berlin, 1914.
Arc 74.4.17	Society for the Promotion of Hellenic Studies. First supplementary catalogue of lantern slides. London, 1914.
Arc 743.6	Solari, A. Topografia storica dell'Etruria. Pisa, 1914-18. 3v.
Arc 936.1.8	Stählin, F. Pharsalos. Nürnberg, 1914.
Arc 1150.14	Staerk, Antonio. Monuments de l'abbaye celtique. Tournai, 1914.
Arc 861.55	Summer, H. Excavations on Rockbourne Downs, Hampshire. London, 1914.
Arc 1163.10A	Tisserant, E. Specimena codicum orientalium. Bonnae, 1914.
Arc 723.18	Toscanelli, Nello. Le origini italiche. Milano, 1914.
Arc 1615.4.3	United States Mint. Catalogue of coins, tokens, and medals. 3. ed. Washington, 1914.
Arc 726.25.7	Vagliere, Dante. Ostia; cenni storici e guida. Roma, 1914.
Arc 726.25.5	Vagliere, Dante. Piccola giuda di Ostia. Roma, 1914.
Arc 820.219F	Vasseur, G. L'origine de Marseille. Marseille, 1914.
Arc 545.240F	Wreszinski, Walter. Atlas zur altaegyptischen Kulturgeschichte. Leipzig, 1914. 4v.

1915

Arc 275.17	Arkheologicheskii s"ezd, 16th, Pskov, 1915. Katalog vystaki. Pskov, 1915.
Arc 1033.12.27	Barnate, C. Il furto del "Santo Sudario" nel 1507. Genova, 1915.
Arc 830.178	Baudouin, M. Le Rocher aux pieds du mas d'île à Lessac. Paris, 1915.

1915 - cont.

Arc 1020.31.17 Baumstark, Anton. Die Modestianischen...zu Jerusalem. Paderborn, 1915.

Arc 1675.20F British Museum. Department of Coins and Medals. Select Italian medals of the Renaissance. London, 1915.

Arc 843.147 Cabre-Aguilo, Juan. El arte rupestre en España. Madrid, 1915.

Arc 843.149 Cabre-Aguilo, Juan. Avance al estudio de las pinturas. Madrid, 1915.

Arc 757.6.5 Caetani Lovatelli, E. Aurea Roma. Roma, 1915.

Arc 1076.3.37 Caminada, Christian. Die bündner Glocken. Zürich, 1915.

Arc 861.108F Clapham, A.W. On the topography of the Cistercian Abbey of Tower Hill. Oxford, 1915.

Arc 388.2 Droop, J.P. Archaeological excavation. Cambridge, Eng., 1915.

Arc 895.23 Ekholm, Gunnar. Studier i Upplands bebyggelse-historia. Uppsala, 1915.

Arc 608.2.9 Gauckler, Paul. Nécropoles puniques de Carthage. pt.1-2. Paris, 1915. 2v.

Arc 845.207F Hahne, Hans. Vorzeitfunde aus Niedersachsen. Hannover, 1915-25.

Arc 647.3A Hall, H.R. Aegean archaeology. London, 1915.

Arc 647.3.2A Hall, H.R. Aegean archaeology. London, 1915.

Arc 612.2.2 Hoernes, M. Urgeschichte der bildenden Kunst in Europa. 2. Aufl. Wien, 1915.

Arc 1190.80.5 Irānshahr Husayn, Kazimz ādah. Les chiffres siyâk et la comptabilitié persane. Paris, 1915.

Arc 1175.12FA Jenkinson, H. Palaeography and...study of court hand. Cambridge, 1915.

Arc 518.8 Keil, Josef. Ephesos. Wien, 1915.

Arc 1.13.15 La Farge, C.G. History of the American Academy in Rome. N.Y., 1915.

Arc 396.5 Leite de Vasconcellos, J. De Campolide a Melrose. Lisboa, 1915.

Arc 838.3.7 Leite de Vasconcellos, J. Historia do museu etnologico português (1893-1914). Lisboa, 1915.

Arc 1020.9.145 Leitzmann, Hans. Petrus und Paulus in Rom. Bonn, 1915.

Arc 1153.8.7A Lindsay, W.M. Notae Latinae...abbreviation in Latin MSS...miniscule period. Cambridge, 1915.

Arc 1333.13F Lockhart, J.H.S. The S. Lockhart collection of Chinese copper coins. Shanghai, 1915.

Arc 870.5.5 Martin, E. A. Dew-ponds; history, observation and experiment. London, 1915.

Arc 1340.3F Martinori, E. Moneta; vocabolario. Roma, 1915.

Arc 1470.30 Mavrogordato, J. A chronological arrangement of the coins of Chios. pt.1-5. London, 1915-18.

Arc 843.74 Mélida, José R. El teatro de Mérida. Madrid, 1915.

Arc 1030.56 Milan. Castillo Sforzesco. Il castillo sforzesco in Milano. Milano, 1915.

Arc 950.202.38F Moore, C.B. Aboriginal sites on Tennessee River. Philadelphia, 1915.

Arc 1663.21 Müller, Bernhard. Medaillen und Münzen im Dienste der Religion. Berlin, 1915.

Arc 830.320 Niort, France. Bibliothèque Municipale. Répertoire des dessins archéologiques. Niort, 1915.

Arc 858.27 Norman, A. Glossary of archaeology. London, 1915. 2v.

Arc 400.7 Parkyn, E.A. An introduction to the study of prehistoric art. London, 1915.

Arc 1030.53 Patten, A.W. Early Christian inscriptions in the Bennett Museum of Christian archaeology. Evanston, 1915.

Arc 588.26 Petrie, W.M.F. Heliopolis. London, 1915.

Arc 588.27 Petrie, W.M.F. Heliopolis. London, 1915.

Arc 740.10PF Pinza, G. Materiali per la etnologia antica toscana laziale. Milano, 1915.

Arc 861.75 Prehistoric Society of East Anglia. Report on excavations at Grime's Graves, Weeting, Norfolk, March-May, 1914. London, 1915.

Arc 843.55.10 Quintero, P. Necropolis ante-romana de Cadiz. Madrid, 1915.

Arc 895.22.25 Sahlström, K.E. Om Våstergötlands stenålders bebyggelse. Stockholm, 1915.

Arc 925.35.5F Samoksavov, D.I. Atlas gochevskikh drevnostei. Moskva, 1915.

Arc 530.17 Sartiaux, Felix. Les sculptures et la restauration du temple d'Assos. Paris, 1915.

Arc 522.17 Sartiaux, Felix. Troie, la guerre de Troie. Paris, 1915.

Arc 87.1.75 Scenika 75. Programm zum Winckelmannsfeste der Achäologischen Gesellschaft zu Berlin. Berlin, 1915.

Arc 743.6.2 Solari, A. Topografia storica dell'Etruria. Appendix. Pisa, 1915.

Arc 94.5 Spain. Junta Superior de Excavaciones y Antiguedades. Memoria. Madrid, 1915-1926. 7v.

Arc 1076.3.60 Tyssen, A.D. The church bells of Sussex. Lewes, 1915.

Arc 1613.21 Venn, T.J. Large United States cents. Chicago, 1915.

Arc 1076.3.18.15 Walter, Henry Beauchamp. The church bells of Shropshire. Oswestry, 1915.

Arc 501.7 Watson, C.M. Fifty years' work in the Holy Land, 1924-1948. London, 1915. 2v.

Arc 861.51 Williams-Freeman, J.P. Introduction to field archaeology...Hampshire. London, 1915.

1916

Arc 888.1 Åberg, Nils. Die Steinzeit in der Niederlanden. Uppsala, 1916.

Arc 843.9.5 Aguilera y Gamboa, E. Las necropolis ibéricas. Madrid, 1916.

Arc 843.77.15 Amador de los Ríos, Rodrigo. El anfiteatro de Italica. Madrid, 1916.

Arc 340.5 American Academy in Rome. Library. A bibliographical guide to Latium and southern Eturia. Rome, 1916.

Arc 861.60 Atkinson, Donald. The Romano-British site on Lowbury Hill in Berkshire. Reading, 1916.

Arc 1470.24 Baldwin, Agnes. Symbolism on Greek coins. N.Y., 1916.

Arc 1670.54F Barnard, F.P. The casting-counter and the counting board...numismatics. Oxford, 1916.

Arc 1613.25 Belden, Bauman. United States war medals. N.Y., 1916.

Arc 1425.4F Bell, H.W. Sardis, coins. v.11. Leiden, 1916.

Arc 530.25 Bezobrazov, P.V. Trapezunt', ego sviatyni i drevnosti. Petrograd, 1916.

Arc 820.6PF Bibliotheque Nationale, Paris. Département des Médailles et Antiques. Le trésor d'argenterie de Berthouville, près Bernay. Paris, 1916.

Arc 1538.2 British Museum. Department of Coins and Medals. Catalogue of English coins in the British Museum. London, 1916. 2v.

1916 - cont.

Arc 875.31.5F Brown, G.F. Ancient cross shafts at Bewcastle and Ruthwell. Cambridge, 1916.

Arc 843.186 Cabré-Aguiló, Juan. El paleolítico inferior de Puento Mochs. Madrid, 1916.

Arc 612.13 Dottin, Georges. Les anciens peuples de l'Europe. Paris, 1916. 2v.

Arc 1505.205 Fiola, Eduard. Münzen und Medaillen der Wellischenlande. v.1-8. Prag, 1916. 6v.

Arc 1208.7 France. Archives Nationales. Le service sigillographique et les collections d'empreintes de sceaux des archives. Paris, 1916.

Arc 1615.6 Gilbert, Ebenezer. The United States half cents. N.Y., 1916.

Arc 858.24.13 Great Britain. Commissions. Ancient and Historical Monuments and Constructions of England. An inventory of the historical monuments in Essex. London, 1916-23. 4v.

Arc 1508.8 Habich, Georg. Die deutschen Medailleure des XVI. Jahrhunderts. Halle an der Saale, 1916.

Arc 497.18 Handcock, P.S.P. Archaeology of the Holy Land. London, 1916.

Arc 830.69 Hauser, Otto. La Micoque; die Kultur einer neuen Diluvialrasse. Leipzig, 1916.

Arc 435.13 Hirālāl, Rai Bahādur. Descriptive lists of inscriptions in the central provinces and Berar. Nagpur, 1916.

Arc 1588.10.30 Hóman, Bálint. Magyar pénztörténet, 1000-1325. Budapest, 1916.

Arc 870.5.3 Hubbard, A.J. Neolithic dew-ponds and cattle ways. 3. ed. London, 1916.

Arc 861.61 Jack, G.H. Excavations on the site of the Romano-British town of Magna, Kenchester. Hereford, 1916.

Arc 455.2 Jouveau-Dubreuil, G. Pallava antiquites. v.1-2. Pondicherry, 1916-18.

Arc 1480.22 Kubitschek, Wilhelm. Zur Geschichte von Städten des römischen Kaiserreiches. Wien, 1916.

Arc 1493.11 Lamas, Arthur. Medalhas portuguesas e estrangeiras referentes a Portugal. Lisboa, 1916.

Arc 1680.12 Longman, W. Tokens of the eighteenth century connected with booksellers. London, 1916.

Arc 1348.25 McDonald, George. Evolution of coinage. Cambridge, 1916.

Arc 838.22F Madrid. Museo Arqueológico Nacional. Falcata iberica. N.Y., 1916.

Arc 1663.18 Madrid. Real Biblioteca. Medallas de la casa de Borbón. Madrid, 1916.

Arc 397.14 Marini, G. Lettere inedite. v.1-3. Roma, 1916-40. 2v.

Arc 66.1.109 Millet, G. Recherches sur l'conographie de l'évangile aux XIV, XV et XVI siècles. Paris, 1916.

Arc 1675.63 Morin, Victor. Les médailles décerniés aux Indien. Ottawa, 1916.

Arc 600.38 New York (City). Metropolitan Museum of Art. The tomb of Perneb. N.Y., 1916.

Arc 870.15 Ross, Percival. Roman road from Rochester to low barrow bridge. Bradford, 1916.

Arc 66.1.111 Roussel, Pierre. Délos; colonie athénienne. Paris, 1916.

Arc 1030.8.12 Saeki, P.Y. The Nestorian monument in China. London, 1916.

Arc 1261.2F Sagarra, Ferran de. Sigillografía catalana. v.1-3. Barcelona, 1916-32. 5v.

Arc 925.50.190F Samokvasev, Dmitrii I. Raskopki severianskikh kurganov v Chernigove vo vremia XIV arkheologicheskago s"ezda. Moskva, 1916.

Arc 1018.31.3 Scaglia, P.S. Manuel d'archéologie chrétienne. Turin, 1916.

Arc 1510.20 Scholler, Ernst. Der Reichsstadt Nürnberg. Nürnberg, 1916.

Arc 1030.42 Smit, E.L. De oud christelijke monumenten van Spanje. 's-Gravenhage, 1916.

Arc 1153.32 Söldner, Georg. Die abgeleiteten Verba in den tironischen Noten. Inaug. Ddiss. Borna, 1916.

Arc 543.3.10 Stein, Mark Aurel. A third journey of exploration in Central Asia, 1913-16. London, 1916.

Arc 865.15 Stevens, Frank. Stonehenge today and yesterday. London, 1916.

Arc 923.4 Tishchenko, Andrei V. A.V. Tishchenko. Petrograd, 1916.

Arc 843.181 Vega de la Sella, Ricardo. Astucias. v.1-4. Madrid, 1916.

Arc 913.15 Viollier, David. Les sépultures du second âge. Thèse. Genève, 1916.

Arc 843.61 Zuazo y Palacios, J. Meca. Madrid, 1916.

1917

Arc 858.34 Bevan, J.O. The towns of Roman Britain. London, 1917.

Arc 386.16 Beyermann, Erich. Das Recht an Denkmälern. Inaug. Diss. Halle, 1917.

Arc 1018.49 Cobern, C.M. The new archaeological discoveries and their bearing upon the New Testament. N.Y., 1917.

Arc 1335.47 Coins and their values. London, 1917.

Arc 497.24 Cumont, Franz. Études syriennes. Paris, 1917.

Arc 968.2.15 Fewkes, J.W. Archaeological investigations in New Mexico, Colorado, and Utah. Washington, 1917.

Arc 1508.20 Fiorino, Alexander. Sammlung des Herrn Alexander Fiorino in Cassel. Frankfurt am Main, 1917.

Arc 435.1.10 Indian Museum, Calcutta. Catalogue raisonné of the prehistoric antiquities. Simla, 1917.

Arc 1030.39 Kaufmann, Carl M. Handbuch der altchristlichen Epigraphik im Breisgau. Freiburg, 1917.

Arc 673.1.30 Keramopoullos, A.D. Topographia tōn Delphōn. Athēnai, 1917.

Arc 1490.21 Martinori, Edoardo. Annali della zecca di Roma. v.1-11,12-16,17-24. Roma, 1917-20. 3v.

Arc 493.5 Minorekii, V. Kelianshchin, stela u Topuzava. Petrograd, 1917.

Arc 895.5.4F Montelius, Oscar. Minnen från vår forntide. Stockholm, 1917.

Arc 1163.2.17 Muñoz y Rivero, J. Manual de paleografía diplomática española. 2. ed. Madrid, 1917.

Arc 1163.2.17.1 Muñoz y Rivero, J. Manual de paleografía diplomática española. 2. ed. Madrid, 1917.

X Cg Arc 545.235F Petrie, W.M.F. Scarabs and cylinders with names. London, 1917. (Changed to XP 9838 F)

Arc 588.30A Petrie, W.M.F. Tools and weapons. London, 1917.

Arc 843.150 Quintero y de Atuuci, Pelayo. Cadiz; primeros pobladores. Cadiz, 1917.

Arc 905.25 Schmid, Walter. Flavia Solva. 2. Aufl. Graz, 1917.

Arc 1138.19 Sinks, Perry W. The reign of the manuscript. Boston, 1917.

Chronological Listing

1917 - cont.

Arc 1033.17.304.5 Spada, G.N. Saggio storico con coroncina di Maria Sma. l'aconavetere. Foggia, 1917.

Arc 861.66 Sumner, H. The ancient earthworks of New Forest. London, 1917.

Arc 1480.19 Sydenham, E.A. Historical references on coins of the Roman empire. London, 1917.

Arc 497.43 Thomsen, P. Palästina und seine Kultur in fünf Jahrtausenden. 2. Aufl. Leipzig, 1917.

Arc 785.62F Van Buren, A.W. The Aqua Traiana and the mills on the Janiculum. Bergamo, 1917.

Arc 608.2.19 Vives y Escudero, Antonio. Estudio de arqueología cartaginesa. Madrid, 1917.

1918

Arc 895.37.5 Åberg, Nils. Die Typologie der nordischen Streitäxte. Würzburg, 1918.

Arc 843.5.25 Almarche, V.F. La antigua civilización ibérica en el reino de Valencia. Valencia, 1918.

Arc 843.59 Aranzadi, T. Exploración de calorce dolmenes del Aralar. Pamplona, 1918.

Arc 843.11 Bardavíu Ponz, V. Estaciones prehistoricas...desiertos. Zaragoza, 1918.

Arc 1488.9 Cagiati, Memmo. Manuale per il raccoglitore di monete del regno d'Italia. Napoli, 1918.

Arc 1018.49.5 Cobern, C.M. The new archaeological discoveries and their bearing upon the New Testament. 3. ed. N.Y., 1918.

Arc 870.4.3 Codrington, Thomas. Roman roads in Britain. 3. ed. London, 1918.

Arc 1030.44 Cunha de Almeida, Jeronymo. Quizo historico sobre o letreiro que se achon em hua pedra que estaua no celeiro do Monst. de Vayrão. Pôrto, 1918.

Arc 1411.6 Davis, Andrew. Ancient Chinese paper money. Boston, 1918.

Arc 485.4F Diez, Ernst. Churasaniche Baudenkmäler. Berlin, 1918.

Arc 830.210 Forrer, Robert. Das römische Zabern. Strassburg, 1918.

Arc 1361.3 Gardner, Percy. A history of ancient coinage. 700-300 B.C. Oxford, 1918.

Arc 1033.17.223 Gazulla, F.D. La patrona de Barcelona y su santuario. Barcelona, 1918.

Arc 66.1.113 Holleaux, Maurice. Stratēgos Ypatos. Paris, 1918.

Arc 943.27 Hudlicka, A. Recent discoveries attributed to early man in America. Washington, 1918.

Arc 459.3.30 Il'in, G.F. Drevnii indiiskii gorod Taksila. Moskva, 1918.

Arc 435.2.40F Kaye, G.R. The astronomical observatories of Jai Singh. Calcutta, 1918.

Arc 1020.9.97 Kirsch, Johann P. Die römischen Titelkirchen im Altertum. Paderborn, 1918.

Arc 651.3.2 Lichtenberg, R.F. Die ägäische Kultur. 2. Aufl. Leipzig, 1918.

Arc 1020.34 Mader, Andreas E. Altchristliche Basiliken und Lokaltraditionen in Südjudäa. Paderborn, 1918.

Arc 1200.16 Madras. Government Museum. Catalogue of copper-plate grants. Madras, 1918.

Arc 458.1.9 Marshall, John. A guide to Sanchi. Calcutta, 1918.

Arc 459.3 Marshall, John. A guide to Taxila. Calcutta, 1918.

Arc 705.211F Maurras, Charles. Athènes antique. Paris, 1918.

Arc 1200.17.5 Millares Carlo, A. Documentos pontificios en papiro de archivos. Madrid, 1918.

Arc 1200.17 Millares Carlo, A. Documentos pontificios en papiro de archivos. pt.1. Madrid, 1918.

Arc 1153.33 Millares Carlo, A. Estudios paleográficos. Madrid, 1918.

Arc 547.27 Mogensen, M. Inscriptions hiéroglyphiques du Musée national de Copenhague. Copenhague, 1918.

Arc 950.202.12F Moore, C.B. The northwestern Florida coast revisited. Philadelphia, 1918.

Arc 1423.11 Newell, E.T. The Seleucid mint of Antioch. N.Y., 1918.

Arc 843.182 Obermaier, Hugo. La cueva del Buar. Madrid, 1918.

Arc 1160.13F Ojha, Gaurishankar. The palaeography of India. 2. ed. Ajmer, 1918.

Arc 1033.46.8 Os miragres de Santiago. Valladolid, 1918.

Arc 543.32 Perry, William J. The megalithic culture of Indonesia. Manchester, 1918.

Arc 505.22.2 Petrie, W.M.F. Eastern exploration past and future. London, 1918.

Arc 880.21 Poe, J.W. The cromlechs of county Dublin. Dublin, 1918?

Arc 925.13 Rostovtsev, M.I. Ellinstvo i iranstvo na iuge Rossii. Petrograd, 1918.

Arc 513.18.5 Sartiaux, Félix. L'archéologie française en Asie Mineure et l'expansion allemande. Paris, 1918.

Arc 905.98 Sausgruber, L. Sammlung der bisher erschienenen Aufsätze. Feldhirch, 1918.

Arc 1020.31.19 Schmaltz, Karl. Mater ecclesiarum. Strassburg, 1918.

Arc 1163.3.5 Shchepkin, Viacheslav N. Uchebnik russkoi paleografii. Moskva, 1918.

Arc 1488.3 Società Numismatica Italiana. Bibliografia numismatica. Milano, 1918-20.

Arc 1261.3.5 Spain. Archivo Historico Nacional, Madrid. Sección de Sigilografía. Catálogo. Madrid, 1918.

Arc 403.7.3 Strzygowski, J. Die Baukunst der Armenier und Europa. Wien, 1918. 2v.

Arc 913.23 Tschumi, O. Einführung in die Vorgeschichte der Schweiz. 2. Aufl. Bern, 1918.

Arc 923.5 Turaeb, B.A. Drevnii mir' na Iug' Rossii. Moskva, 1918.

Arc 815.22F Van Buren, A.W. Studies in the archaeology of the forum at Pompeii. Bergamo, 1918.

Arc 1076.3.47 Verband Deutscher Vereine für Volkskunde. Bericht über die Sammlung der Glockensprüche, Glockensagen und Glockenbräuche. Freiburg, 1918.

Arc 848.16.2 Wilser, Ludwig. Deutsche Vorzeit. 2. Aufl. Steglitz, 1918.

Arc 66.1.112 Zeiller, Jacques. Les origines chrétiennes...provinces danubiennes. Paris, 1918.

1919

Arc 853.46 Åberg, Nils. Ostpreussen in der Völkerwanderungszeit. Uppsala, 1919.

Arc 858.32 Bayley, Harold. Archaic England. London, 1919.

Arc 1335.65 Berlin. Staatliche Museum. Kaiser Friedrich Museum. Die Schausammlung des Münzkabinetts im Kaiser Friedrich Museum Berlin, 1919.

Arc 843.15.9 Bosch Gimpera, P. Prehistoria catalana. Barcelona, 1919.

Htn Arc 861.30.5* Burrow, E.J. The ancient entrenchments and camps of Gloucester. Cheltenham, 1919.

1919 - cont.

Arc 870.4.4 Codrington, Thomas. Roman roads in Britain. 3. ed. N.Y., 1919.

Arc 823.9.2 Enlart, C. Manuel d'archéologie française. v.1, pts.1-3. Paris, 1919-1920. 3v.

Arc 957.1.8A Fewkes, J.W. Prehistoric villages, castles, and towers of southwestern Colorado. Washington, 1919.

NEDL Arc 1480.20 Gnecchi, Francesco. The fauna and flora on the coin-types of...Rome. London, 1919.

Arc 1076.3.49 Haas, A. Glockensagen im pommerschen Volksmunde. Stettin, 1919.

Arc 853.58.5 Helmke, Paul. Hügelgräber im Vorderwald von Muschenheim. Giessen, 1919. 2v.

Arc 843.67 Hernández-Pecheco, E. La caverna de la Peña de Candamo (Asturias). Madrid, 1919.

Arc 1675.3.9 Johnson, Stephen C. Le rivendicazioni italiane del Trentino...nelle medaglie. Milano, 1919-20.

Arc 545.242F Junker, Hermann. Bericht über die Grabungen der Akademie des Wissenschaften in Wien. Wien, 1919.

Arc 853.50 Kostrzewski, J. Die ostgermanische Kultur. Leipzig, 1919. 2v.

Arc 853.58.10 Kunkel, Otto. Vorgeschichtliches aus dem Lumdstale. Giessen, 1919.

Arc 66.1.117 Laurent, J. L'arménie entre Byzance et l'Islam. Paris, 1919.

Arc 910.8F Loeschcke, Siegfried. Lampen aus Vindonissa. Zürich, 1919.

Arc 1470.26 MacDonald, George. The silver coinage of Crete. London, 1919?

Arc 1645.3 Medina, J.T. Manual ilustrado de numismatica chilena. Santiago, 1919.

Arc 1540.24F Medina, J.T. Las medallas del almirante Vernon. Santiago, 1919.

Arc 1645.3.5F Medina, J.T. Las monedas coloniales de Chile. Santiago, 1919. 2 pam.

Arc 1643.1.10F Medina, J.T. Las monedas coloniales hispano-americanas. Santiago, 1919.

Arc 1643.1.15F Medina, J.T. Las monedas obsidionales hispano-americanas. Santiago, 1919.

Arc 1535.200F Milford Haven, L. British naval medals. London, 1919.

Arc 843.12 Morán Bardon, C. Investigaciones acerca de arqueologia y prehistoria de la region salamantina. Salamanca, 1919.

Arc 1027.18.6 Müller, Nikolaus. Die Inschriften der jüdischen Katakombe. Leipzig, 1919.

Arc 1153.6.5 Muñoz y Rivero, J. Paleografía visigoda. Madrid, 1919.

Arc 435.22 Narasimhachar, R. Architecture and sculpture in Mysore. v.2. Bangalore, 1919.

Arc 843.68 Obermaier, H. Las pinturas rupestres del Barranco de Valltorta (Castellón). Madrid, 1919.

Arc 545.243F Pagenstrecher, R. Nekropolis. Leipzig, 1919.

Arc 1212.5 Poole, Reginald Lane. Seals and documents. London, 1919?

Arc 930.206F Praschniker, C. Archäologische Forschungen in Albanien und Montenegro. Wien, 1919.

Arc 435.20.45 Rangāchārya, V. A topographical list of the inscirptions of the Madras presidency (collected till 1915) with notes. Madras, 1919. 3v.

Arc 87.1.76 Rodenwaldt, Gerhart. Griechische Porträts aus dem Ausgang der Antike. Berlin, 1919.

Arc 590.9F Schmidt, Valdemar. Sarkofager, muniekister og muniehylstre i det gamle a Egypten. København, 1919.

Arc 612.11 Schuchhardt, Carl. Alteuropa. Strassburg, 1919.

Arc 1200.20 Schütt, Otto. Die Geschichte der Schriftsprache im ehemaligen Amt und in der Stadt Heusburg bis 1650. Heusburg, 1919.

Arc 1200.19 Schütt, Otto. Heusburgen Akten- und Urkundensprache im 14., 15., und 16. Jahrhundert. Heusburg, 1919.

Arc 1018.5.9 Schultze, Victor. Grundriss der christlichen Archäologie. München, 1919.

Arc 895.36.15F Schwedische Felsbilder von Göteborg zu Strömstad. Hagen, 1919.

Arc 723.17 Sergi, Giuseppi. Italia, le origini. Torino, 1919.

Arc 936.5 Tanusz, Bohdan. Kultura przedhistoryczne podola. Lwów, 1919.

Arc 843.180 Vega de la Sella, Ricardo. El dolmen de la capilla de Santa Cruz. Madrid, 1919.

Arc 618.9 Verworm, M. Keltische Kunst. Berlin, 1919.

192-

Arc 938.17 Balodis, F. L'ancienne frontiére slavo-latvienne. n.p., 192-.

1920

Arc 1.13.7F American Academy, Rome. Twenty fifth anniversary. N.Y.? 1920?

Arc 923.7 Arkhivnye kursy. pt.1-3. Sankt Petersburg, 1920.

Arc 858.33 Ault, Norman. Life in ancient Britain. London, 1920.

Arc 672.1.21 Baikie, James. The sea-kings of Crete. 3. ed. London, 1920.

Arc 588.28 Brunton, Guy. Lahun I, II; the treasure. London, 1920. 2v.

Arc 551.5 Budge, Ernest A. By Nile and Tigris. London, 1920. 2v.

Arc 543.4.20F Conrady, A. Die chinesischen Handschriften..Sven Hedins in Lou-lan. Stockholm, 1920.

Arc 66.1.118 De Boüard, A. Le régime politique et les institutions de Rome au Moyen-Age, 1252-1347. Paris, 1920.

Arc 503.3F Deutsch-Turkischer Denkmalschutz-Kommando. Wissenschaftliche Veröffentlichungen. v.1-6. Berlin, 1920-

Arc 843.165 Frankowski, Eugeniusz. Estelas discoideas de la Peninsula Iberica. Madrid, 1920.

Arc 895.35 Gjessing, H.J. Rogalands stenalder. Stavanger, 1920.

Arc 1018.52 Grossi-Gondi, F. I monumenti cristiani. Roma, 1920-23. 2v.

Arc 830.171 Gruyer, Paul. Les calvaires bretons. Paris, 1920.

Arc 1077.2.39F Gudiol y Cunill, José. Les creus d'Argenteria a Catalunya. Barcelona, 1920.

Arc 1025.61 Henderson, Alexander. The lesson of the catacombs. London, 1920.

Arc 488.5F Herzfeld, Ernst E. Am Tor von Asien. Berlin, 1920.

Arc 1660.16F Hill, George F. Medals of the renaissance. Oxford, 1920.

Arc 1220.5F Hogarth, D.G. Hittite seals. Oxford, 1920.

Arc 395.4 Koepp, Friedrich. Archäologie. 2. Aufl. v.2,4. Berlin, 1920. 2v.

Chronological Listing

1920 - cont.

Arc 395.6 Koldewey, Robert. Heitere und ernst Briefe aus einem deutschen Archäologenleben. Berlin, 1920.

Arc 497.29 Kyle, M.G. Moses and the monuments. London, 1920.

Arc 853.21.15 LaBaume, W. Vorgeschichte von Westpreussen in ihren Grundzügen allgemeinverstandlich dargestellt. Danzig, 1920.

Arc 1027.12.19 La Piana, George. The tombs of Peter and Paul ad catacumbas. Cambridge, 1920.

Arc 861.10.24 Liverpool. Public Libraries, Museum and Art Gallery. Handbook and guide to the replicas and casts of Manx crosses on exhibition in the Free Public Museums. 2. ed. Liverpool, 1920.

Arc 1418.6 Lucknow, India. Provincial Museum. Catalogue of coins in the Provincial Museum. Oxford, 1920. 2v.

Arc 652.4 Marshall, Fred H. Discovery in Greek lands. Cambridge, 1920.

Arc 843.50.5 Martorell, Jeroni. Tarragona i els seus antics monuments. Barcelona, 1920.

Arc 1153.34 Mentz, Arthur. Geschichte der griechisch-römischen Schrift. Leipzig, 1920.

Arc 1578.4F Miller zu Aicholz, V. von. Österreichische Münzprägungen, 1519-1918. Wien, 1920.

Arc 612.14 Neubert, Max. Die dorische Wanderung in ihren europaischen Zusammenhängen. Stuttgart, 1920.

Arc 547.20 New York (City). Metropolitan Museum of Art. A handbook of Egyptian rooms. N.Y., 1920.

Arc 810.32 Pernice, Erich. Pompejiforschung und Archäologie nach dem Kriege. Griefswald, 1920.

Arc 588.31 Petrie, W.M.F. Prehistoric Egypt. London, 1920.

X Cg Arc 673.1.13 Poulson, F. Delphi. London, 1920.

Arc 785.43 Préchac, F. Le colosse de Néron. Paris, 1920.

Arc 853.51 Rademacher, C. Die vorgeschichtliche Besiedelung. Leipzig, 1920.

Arc 688.8 Staés, B. To Eounion. Athēnai, 1920.

Arc 858.22.5 Vallance, A. Old crosses and lychgates. London, 1920.

Arc 435.2.41F Vogel, J.P. Tile-mosaics of the Lahore fort. Calcutta, 1920.

Arc 585.29F Wainwright, G.A. Balabish. London, 1920.

Arc 830.1.9 Waquet, H. Vieilles pierres bretonnes. Quimper, 1920.

Arc 505.25 Weill, Raymond. La cité de David. Plans and atlas. Paris, 1920. 2v.

X Cg Arc 1500.29F Witte, Jean. Recherches sur les empereurs qui ont régné dans les Gaules. n.p., 1920.

Arc 407.10 Woolley, Charles L. Dead towns and living men. London, 1920.

1921

Arc 838.11 Åberg, Nils. La civilisation énéolithique dans la péninsule ibérique. Uppsala, 1921.

Arc 416.5 Asie centrale et Tibet. Missions Pelliot et Bacot, documens exposés au Musée Guimet. Paris, 1921.

Arc 1468.22 Babelon, E. Les monnaies grecques. Paris, 1921.

Arc 600.194F Bahgat, Aly. Fouilles d'al Foustât. Paris, 1921.

Arc 1418.10 Bhandarkar, D.R. Lectures on ancient Indian numismatics. Calcutta, 1921.

Arc 635.226F Blegen, Carl W. Korakou, a prehistoric settlement near Corinth. Boston, 1921.

X Cg Arc 672.1.33 Bossert, H.T. Alt Kreta. Berlin, 1921.

Arc 1033.12.89 Bréhier, L. The treasures of Syrian silverwar. Paris, 1921.

Arc 790.212F Carini, P.B. Pompei principali monumenti e nuovissimi scavi. Milano, 1921.

Arc 1335.82F Chapman, H. Catalogue of J.S. Jenks collection of coins. Philadelphia, 1921.

Arc 815.9F Comparetti, D. Le nozze di Bacco et Arianna. Firenze, 1921.

Arc 66.1.119 Constans, L.A. Arles antique. Paris, 1921.

Arc 830.15.9 Constans, L.A. Arles antique. Thèse. Paris, 1921.

Arc 387.5 Crawford, Osbert Guy S. Man and his past. London, 1921.

Arc 1020.9.169 Dattoli, M. L'aula del senato romano e la chiesa di S. Adriano. Roma, 1921.

Arc 1163.3.7 Druzhinin, V.G. Pomorskie paleografy 18 stol. Petrograd, 1921.

Arc 853.52 Dutschmann, G. Literatur zur Vor- und Frühgeschichte Sachsens. Leipzig, 1921.

Arc 935.10.3 Ebersolt, Jean. Mission archéologique de Constantinople. Paris, 1921.

Arc 672.1.27 Evans, Arthur John. The palace of Minos. v.1; v.2, pt.1-2; v.3; v.4, pt.1-2. London, 1921-35. 6v.

Arc 66.1.121 Fawtier, Robert. Sainte Catherine de Sienne. Paris, 1921.

Arc 955.2.11 Fewkes, J.W. Basket-maker, caves of northeastern Arizona. Cambridge, 1921.

Arc 682.9 Fimmen, Diedrich. Die kritisch-mykenische Kultur. Leipzig, 1921.

Arc 530.14.15F Gerkan, Armin von. Das Theater von Priene. München, 1921.

Arc 830.1.7 Grand, Roger. Mélanges d'archéologie bretonne. Série I. Nantes, 1921.

Arc 1588.1.80 Gumowski, Marian. Biskupstwo kniszwickie w XI wieku. Poznań, 1921.

Arc 1588.11.5 Gumowski, Marian. Mennica wileńska w XVI i XVII wieku. Warszawa, 1921.

Arc 1190.9 Hajnal, Istvan. Írástörténet az írásbeliség felujulása korából. Budapest, 1921.

Arc 1490.13.10 Hamburger, L. Katalog alte Sammlung päpstlicher Münzen. Frankfurt, 1921.

Arc 672.1.29 Hazzidakis, J. Étude de préhistorie crétoise. Paris, 1921.

Arc 66.1.124 Holleaux, Maurice. Rome, la Grèce, et les monarchies hellénistiques. Paris, 1921.

Arc 830.92 Hure, Auguste. Le sénonais préhistorique. Sens, 1921.

Arc 1138.23 Kantorowicz, Hermann. Einführung in die Textkritik. Leipzig, 1921.

Arc 1020.99.9 Kaufmann, C.M. Die heilige Stadt der Wüste. 2.-3. Aufl. Kempten, 1921.

Arc 1020.99.10 Kaufmann, C.M. Die heilige Stadt der Wüste. 4e Aufl. Kempten, 1921.

Arc 853.53.3 Kiekebusch, A. Bilder aus der märkischen Vorzeit. 3. Aufl. Berlin, 1921.

Arc 561.5 Lagier, Camille. A travers la Haute Égypte. Bruxelles, 1921.

Arc 1093.6.20 Lecher, Jörg. Vom Hakenkreuz. Leipzig, 1921.

Arc 1528.9 Loehr, August. Die niederlandische Medaille des 17. Wien, 1921.

Arc 880.24 Macalister, R.A.S. Ireland in pre-Celtic times. Dublin, 1921.

1921 - cont.

Arc 612.15 Macalister, R.A.S. A text-book of European archaeology. Cambridge, Eng., 1921.

Arc 392.7.80 MacDonald, G. F. Haverfield, 1860-1919. London, 1921.

Arc 505.35 Meistermann, Barnabé. Capharnaüm et Bethsaïde, suivi d'une étude sur l'âge de la synagogue de Tell Houm. Paris, 1921.

Arc 1670.7F Milford Haven, L.A.M. Naval medals. London, 1921-28. 2v.

Arc 720.218F Minto, Antonio. Marsiliana d'Albegna. Firenze, 1921.

Arc 383.66 Miscellanea di studi sicelioti ed italioti in onore di Paolo Orsi. Catania, 1921.

Arc 600.18A Mogensen, Maria. Le mastaba égyptien de la glyphtothèque de Carlsberg. Copenhagen, 1921.

Arc 1468.32 Newell, E.T. Alexander Loards. v.3. N.Y., 1921-23.

Arc 630.17 Oikonomes, Georgios P. De profusionum receptaeulis sepulchalilus. Athenis, 1921.

Arc 770.7 Paléologue, M. Rome, notes d'histoire et d'art. 11. éd. Paris, 1921.

Arc 1163.14 Rademacher, M. Die Worttrennung in angelsächsischen Handschriften. Inaug. Diss. Münster, 1921.

Arc 682.25.25 Rey, Léon. Observations sur les premiers habitats de la Macédoine. Paris, 1921-22. 2v.

Arc 682.10F Rodenwaldt, G. Der Fries des Megarons von Mykenai. Halle an der Saale, 1921.

Arc 895.36.20 Rydh, Hanna. En ristning på lös skifferplatta. n.p., 1921. 2 pam.

Arc 848.9.3 Schwantes, G. Aus Deutschlands Urgeschichts. 3. Aufl. Leipzig, 1921.

Arc 1470.27 Seltman, C.J. The temple coins of Olympia. Cambridge, Eng., 1921. 2v.

Arc 682.7 Seunig, Vingenz. Die kritisch-mykenische Kultur. Graz, 1921.

Arc 403.9 Smolin, V.F. Opyt instruktsii po sostaleniiu arkheologicheskikh kart. Kazan', 1921.

Arc 838.16F Sociedad Española de Amigos del Arte. Exposición de arte prehistórico español. Madrid, 1921.

Arc 542.207F Stein, Mark Aurel. Serindia. Oxford, 1921.

NEDL Arc 1033.17.3 Strumz, Franz. Unsere liebe Frau in Österreich. Zürich, 1921.

Arc 612.12A Tyler, John Mason. The new stone age in northern Europe. N.Y., 1921.

Arc 943.25 Utzinger, Rudolf. Indianer-Kunst. München, 1921.

Arc 736.6.5 Whitaker, J.I.S. Motya. London, 1921.

Arc 495.5.5F Wiegand, Theodor. Baalbek. v.1-3; atlas. Berlin, 1921-25. 4v.

Arc 845.208F Wurttembergisches Landesamt für Denkmalpflege. Cannstatt zur Römerzeit. Stuttgart, 1921.

1922

Arc 612.16 Åberg, Nils. Die Franken und Westgoten in der Volkewanderungszeit. Uppsala, 1922.

Arc 810.33 Beccarini, Paolo. Un decennio di nuovi scavi in Pompei. Milano, 1922.

Arc 520.11.6 Berlin. Königliches Museum. Führer durch die Ruinen von Pergamon. 6. Aufl. Berlin, 1922.

Arc 1510.16.2 Berlin. Staatliche Museen. Die Münzen Friedrich Wilhelms des Grossen Kurfürsten und Friedrichs III. Berlin, 1922.

Arc 1478.23 Bernhart, Max. Münzkunde der römischen Kaiserzeit. Genève, 1922.

Arc 1468.26 Börger, Hans. Griechische Münzen. Leipzig, 1922.

Arc 843.75 Bonser, J.E. El coto de Doña Ana. Madrid, 1922.

Arc 595.16 Borchardt, Ludwig. Gegen die Zahlenmystik an der grossen Pyramide bei Gise. Berlin, 1922.

Arc 1335.63.3 British Museum. Department of Coins and Medals. A guide to the department of coins and medals. London, 1922.

Arc 1418.6.5 Brown, C.J. The coins of India. Calcutta, 1922.

Arc 590.12 Buberl, Paul. Die griechisch-ägyptischen Mumienbildnisse der Sammlung T. Graf. Wien, 1922.

Arc 545.231.7F Burlington Five Arts Club, London. Catalogue of an exhibition of ancient Egyptian art. London, 1922.

Arc 387.6 Capitan, Louis. La préhistoire. Paris, 1922.

Arc 1138.30 Coellen, Ludwig. Die Stilentwicklung der Schrift im christlichen Abendlande. Darmstadt, 1922.

Arc 1229.1 Conteneau, G. La glyptique syro-hittite. Thèse. Paris, 1922.

Arc 562.2.10 Cordier, Henri. Bibliographie des oeuvres de Gaston Maspero. Paris, 1922.

Arc 963.2.15 Crook, A.R. The origin of the Cahokia mounds. Springfield, 1922.

Arc 1540.20 Davis, William John. Tickets and passes of Great Britain and Ireland struck or engraved on metal, ivory. Leamington Spa, 1922.

Arc 388.3 Deonna, Waldemar. L'archéologie, son domaine, son but. Paris, 1922.

Arc 848.14F Deutsches Archäologisches Institut. Germania romana. Bamberg, 1922.

Arc 875.32.5 Diack, F.C. The Newton stone and other Pictish inscriptions. Paisley, 1922.

Arc 1254.14 Ebersolt, Jean. Catalogue des sceaux byzantins. Paris, 1922.

Arc 895.25 Enquist, Arvid. Stenaldersbebyggeken på Arnst och Tjöm. Uppsala, 1922.

Arc 953.21 Fowke, G. Archaeological investigations. Washington, 1922.

Arc 1033.35.149 Garces Teixeira, F.A. Acruz Manoelina do convento de Cristo. Lisboa, 1922.

Arc 612.6.5 Hahne, Hans. 25 Jahre Siedlungsarchäologie. Leipzig, 1922.

Arc 672.1.9.5 Hawes, C.H. Crete, the forerunner of Greece. London, 1922.

Arc 1020.124.5 Hergueta y Martin, Domingo. Santa María la mayor de la catedral de Burgos y su culto. Lérida, 1922.

Arc 1020.124 Huidobro Serna, Luciano. Nuestra Señora del Espino en Santa Gadea del Cid Burgos. Lérida, 1922. 3 pam.

Arc 895.26 Janse, Olov Robert. Le travail de l'or en Suède à l'époque mérovingienne. Orléans, 1922.

Arc 957.1.15 Jeancon, J.A. Archaeological research in the northeast San Juan basin of Colorado. Denver, 1922.

Arc 432.7 Jouveau-Dubreuil, D. Vedic antiquities. London, 1922.

Arc 1018.19.3 Kaufmann, C.M. Handbuch der christlichen Archäologie. 3. Aufl. Paderborn, 1922.

Arc 1335.91 Kündig, W. Monnaies grecques antiques provenant des collection de S.A.I. le grand-duc Alexandra Michäilouit. Genève, 1922.

Arc 1335.90 Kündig, W. Monnaies romaines impériales provenant des collections de Paul Vautier. Genève, 1922.

Chronological Listing

1922 - cont.

Arc 561.5.5 Lagier, Camille. L'Égypte monumentale et pittoresque. 2. éd. Paris, 1922.
Arc 830.11.9.9 Le Rouzic, Z. Carnac. Nancy, 1922.
Arc 1027.78.2 Leynaud, A.F. Les catacombes africaines. 2e éd. Alger, 1922.
Arc 545.244F Lugn, Pehr. Ausgewählte Denkmäler aus ägyptischen Sammlungen in Schweden. Leipzig, 1922.
Arc 858.35 Mackenzie, D.A. Ancient man in Britain. London, 1922.
Arc 530.22F Marr, H. Arkheologicheskiia ekspeditsiia 1916 g. Sankt Peterburg, 1922.
Arc 861.70 May, Thomas. The Roman forts of Templeborough near Rotherham. Rotherham, 1922.
Arc 875.10.7 Miller, S.N. The Roman fort at Balmuildy. Glasgow, 1922.
Arc 746.10 Minto, Antonio. Populonia; la necropoli arcaica. Firenze, 1922.
Arc 895.5.27F Montelius, Oscar. Swedish antiquities. Stockholm, 1922.
Arc 870.14.9 Mothersole, Jessie. Hadrian's wall. London, 1922.
Arc 1033.53.22 Peissard, N. La découverte du tombeau du tombeau de St. Maurice. St. Maurice, 1922.
Arc 497.23 Peters, John B. Bible and spade. N.Y., 1922.
Arc 66.1.123 Picard, Charles. Éphèse et Claros. Paris, 1922.
Arc 925.13.5 Rostovtsev, M.I. Iranians and Greeks in south Russia. Oxford, 1922.
Arc 820.222F Roussel, Jules. Atlas monumental de la France. Paris, 1922.
Arc 830.107 Salin, Edouard. Le cimetière barbare de Lezéville. Nancy, 1922.
Arc 435.25.8F Sanchi, Bhopal State. Museum of Archaeology. Catalogue of the Museum of Archaeology at Sanchi, Bhopal State. Calcutta, 1922.
Arc 1468.21 Sborōnos, Ioannēs N. Synopsis de mille coins faux du faussaire C. Christopoulos. Athènes, 1922.
Arc 710.12 Schede, Martin. Die Burg von Athen. Berlin, 1922.
Arc 895.17.9 Shetelig, Haakon. Primitive tider i Norge. Bergen, 1922.
Arc 1020.9.163 Tani, A.D. Le chiese di Roma. Torino, 1922.
Arc 1468.23 Weber, Hermann. The Weber collection...Greek coins. v.1-3. London, 1922-29. 6v.
Arc 969.1.12 Willoughby, C.C. The Turner group of earthworks, Hamilton County, Ohio. Cambridge, 1922.
Arc 1093.6.15 Wilser, L. Das Hakenkreuz nach Ursprung, Vorkommen und Bedeutung. 5. Aufl. Leipzig, 1922.

1923

Arc 726.47 Åberg, Nils. Die Gothen und Langobarden in Italien. Uppsala, 1923.
Arc 893.13 Adama van Scheltema, F. Die altnordische Kunst. Berlin, 1923.
Arc 893.13.5 Adama van Scheltema, F. Die altnordische Kunst. 2. Aufl. Leipzig, 1923.
Arc 963.2 Baker, Frank C. The Cahokia mounds. [Illinois]. Urbana, 1923.
Arc 1030.46 Bakhuizen van den Brink, J.N. De aid-christelijke monumenten van Ephesus. Haag, 1923.
Arc 925.21 Ballod, F.V. Privolzhskie Pompei. Moskva, 1923.
Arc 1185.19.3F Barone, N. Paleografia latina diplomatica. Atlas. 3. ed. Napoli, 1923.
Arc 1185.19.3 Barone, N. Paleografia latina diplomatica. 3. ed. Napoli, 1923.
Arc 1138.25 Bauckner, A. Einführung in das mittelalterliche Schriftum. München, 1923.
Arc 543.7.5 Beerski, A. (Mrs.). Angkor; ruins in Cambodia. London, 1923.
Arc 1269.22.3 Berchem, E.F. von. Siegel. 2. Aufl. Berlin, 1923.
Arc 1510.125 Bernhart, Max. Die Münzen und Medaillen der Stadt Kaufbeureh nebst einer münzgeschichtlichen Einleitung. n.p., 1923.
Arc 705.200.5F Blümel, Carl. Der Fries des Tempels der Athena Nike. Berlin, 1923.
Arc 685.4 Bosanquet, Robert. The unpublished objects from the Palaikastro excavations, 1902-06. London, 1923.
Arc 1478.21 British Museum. Department of Coins and Medals. Coins of the Roman Empire in the British Museum. v.1-4,6. London, 1923-40. 5v.
Arc 1468.24 Cambridge, Eng. University. Fitzwilliam Museum. Catalogue of the McClean collection of Greek coins. Cambridge, 1923-29. 3v.
Arc 585.30F The city of Akhenaten. v.1-3. London, 1923-33. 4v.
Arc 1675.37 Costa, Luiz X. da. Domingos Antonio de Sequeira e Francesco Vieira Lusitano. Lisboa, 1923. 2 pam.
Arc 855.227F Cunnington, M.E. (Mrs.) The early iron age inhabited site at All Cannings Cross farm, Wiltshire. Devizes, 1923.
Arc 1498.9 Dieudonné, A. Les monnaies françaises. Paris, 1923.
Arc 830.109 Dubreuil-Chambardel, Louis. La Touraine préhistorique. Paris, 1923.
Arc 861.72 Elgee, Frank. The Romans in Cleveland. Middlesbrough, 1923.
Arc 588.29F Engelbach, R. Harageh. London, 1923.
Arc 593.3 Engelbach, R. The problem of the obelisks. London, 1923.
Arc 608.17.5 Ferri, Silvio. Contributi di Cirene alla storia della religione greca. Roma, 1923.
Arc 843.29 Fouilles de Belo Bolonia, Province de Cadix (1917-1921). Bordeaux, 1923-26. 2v.
Arc 861.16.5 Fox, Cyril. The archaeology of the Cambridge region. Cambridge, Eng., 1923.
Arc 1490.98.10F Giesecke, Walther. Sicilia numismata. Leipzig, 1923.
Arc 1504.10 Girtamner-Solchli, H. Das Münzwesen im Kanton St. Gallen. Genf, 1923.
Arc 672.1.53 Glasgow, George. The Minoans. London, 1923.
Arc 708.23.9 Gougères, G. Athènes. 4e éd. Paris, 1923.
Arc 762.1.10 Hare, A.J.C. Walks in Rome. 21st ed. London, 1923.
Arc 853.8.5F Hellmich, Max. Die Besiedlungschlesiens in vor- und frühgeschichtlicher Zeit. 2. Aufl. Breslau, 1923.
Arc 843.185 Hernández-Pacheco, E. La vida de nuestros antecesores paleolíticos. Madrid, 1923.
Arc 482.202F Herzfeld, Ernst E. Der Wandschmuck der Bauten. Berlin, 1923.
Arc 875.31.7 Hewison, J.K. The romance of Bewcastle cross. Glasgow, 1923.
Arc 1030.8.15 Holm, F.W. My Nestorian adventure in China. N.Y., 1923.
Arc 1510.115F Horn, Otto. Die Münzen und Medaillen. Leipzig, 1923.
Arc 386.17 Howard Crosby Butler, 1872-1922. Princeton, 1923.
Arc 608.2.39 Khun de Prorot, Byron. Fouilles à Carthage. Paris, 1923.
Arc 853.21.20 Kiekebusch, A. Die Ausgrabung des bronzezeitlichen Dorfes Buch bei Berlin. Berlin, 1923.

1923 - cont.

Arc 1088.1.25 Köster, August. Das antike Seewesen. 1. Aufl. Berlin, 1923.
Arc 936.6.5 Kostrzewski, Józef. Wielkopolska w czasach. Poznań, 1923.
Arc 853.20.7 Krencher, D. Das römische Trier. Berlin, 1923.
Arc 1335.91.25 Kündig, W. Monnaies grecques antiques provenant des doubles du British Museum des collections de feu le Gen. A.L. Bertier. Genève, 1923.
Arc 1660.19F Lefebure, Charles. Contribution à la documentation du temps de guerre. Bruxelles, 1923.
Arc 545.227.21F Lefebvre, G. Le tombeau de Petosiris. v.1-3. Le Caire, 1923-1924.
Arc 1493.9 Leite de Vasconcellos, J. Da numismatica em Portugal. Lisboa, 1923.
Arc 830.2.19 Le Rouzic, Z. Locmariaquer. La table des marchands. 2e ed. Vannes, 1923.
Arc 595.19 MacDari, C. Irish wisdom preserved in bibles and pyramids. Boston, 1923.
Arc 397.11 Marshall, John. Conservation manual. Calcutta, 1923.
Arc 1018.44 Marucchi, O. Manuale di archeologia cristiana. 3. ed. Roma, 1923.
Arc 843.81F Masriera y Manovens, J. Apuntes sobre la villa de Tossa de Mar. Barcelona, 1923.
Arc 562.6 Masters, D. The romance of excavation. N.Y., 1923.
Arc 1478.24 Mattingly, Harold. The Roman imperial coinage. v.1-9. London, 1923-38. 10v.
Arc 925.4.5 Merhart, Gero von. The palaeolithic period in Siberia contributions to the prehistory of the Yenisei region. n.p., 1923.
Arc 855.228F Moir, J. Reid. The great flint implements of Cromer, Norfolk. Ipswich, 1923?
Arc 1408.4 Morgan, J. de. Manuel de numismatique orientale de l'antiquité et du moyen-age. Paris, 1923-36.
Arc 830.59.5 Morin-Jean. La verrerie en Gaule sous l'empire romain. Paris, 1923.
Arc 543.27A Nelsen, F.C. Die Buddha-Legende auf den Flachreliefs der ersten Galerie des Stupa von Boro-Budur, Java. Leipzig, 1923.
Arc 1470.31.5 Newell, E.T. Tyrus rediviva. N.Y., 1923.
Arc 936.20.30 Pârvan, Vasile. Inseputurite vietii romane. București, 1923.
Arc 400.19 Peyrony, D. Éléments de préhistoire. Ussel, 1923.
Arc 1084.10 Pope-Hennessy, U. (Mrs.). Early Chinese jades. London, 1923.
Arc 435.21.5F Rice, B.L. Epigraphia carnatica. Bangalore, 1923.
Arc 730.209F Rizzo, G.E. Il teatro greco di Siracusa. Milano, 1923.
Arc 936.55 Rostovtsev, M. Une tablette votive thraco-mithriaque du Louvre. Paris, 1923.
Arc 420.8F Segalen, V. Mission archéologique en Chine (1914 et 1917). Atlas. Paris, 1923-24. 2v.
Arc 843.15.12 Serra-Vilars, J. El vas companiforme a Catalunya i las caves sepulcrals eneolitequeis. Solsona, 1923.
Arc 823.20 Sketla segobrani. v.1-3. Sant-Brieg, 1923-25.
Arc 953.19.5 Smith, Harlan I. An album of prehistoric Canadian art. Ottawa, 1923.
Arc 600.15.15 Speleers, L. Les figurines funéraires égyptiennes. Bruxelles, 1923.
Arc 861.40.10 Taylor, A.J. The Roman baths of Bath. Bath, 1923.
Arc 386.18 Touzeskul, V. Otkrytyia XIX i nachala XX v. Sankt Peterburg, 1923.
Arc 495.207F Vincent L.H. Hebron le haram el-Khalîl, sépulture des patriachs. Paris, 1923. 2v.
Arc 1053.20 Visconti, E.Q. Iconografia greca. Milano, 1923-25. 3v.
Arc 572.1.5A Weigall, Arthur Edward Pearse Brome. The glory of the Pharaohs. N.Y., 1923.
Arc 572.1.10 Weigall, Arthur Edward Pearse Brome. Tutankhamen, and other essays. London, 1923.
Arc 830.125 Weise, Georg. Zwei fränkische Königspfalzen. Tübingen, 1923.
Arc 848.13 Wels, K.H. Die germanische Vorzeit. Leipzig, 1923.
Arc 885.12.5 Wheeler, R.E.M. Segontium and the Roman occupation of Wales. London, 1923.

1924

Arc 893.15F Åberg, Nils. Den nordiska folkvandringstidens kronologi. Stockholm, 1924.
Arc 547.24F Alexandria. Musée Gréco-Romain. Le Musée Gréco-Romain du cours de l'année 1922-23. Alexandrie, 1924.
Arc 1153.59 Allamoda, H. Beiträge zur Geschichte der äusseren Merkmale des ältesten Breslauer Bischofsurkunden bis zum Jahre 1319. Inaug. Diss. Oblau, 1924.
Arc 551.6.5 Baikie, James. A century of excavation in the land of the Pharaohs. London, 1924.
Arc 785.13.55 Bartoli, Alfonso. Il Foro Romano, il Palatino. Milano, 1924.
Arc 785.13.57 Bartoli, Alfonso. The Roman Forum; the Palatine. Milan, 1924.
Arc 1163.36 Bernheimer, K. Paleografia ebraica. Firenze, 1924.
Arc 756.11.4 Bertaux, Émile. Rome, l'antiquité. 4. éd. Paris, 1924.
X Cg Arc 1468.5.5 Bibliothèque Nationale, Paris. Département des Médailles et Antiques. Catalogue de la collection de Luynes. v.1-3 and plates. Paris, 1924. 6v.
Arc 495.208F Breasted, J.H. Oriental forerunners of Byzantine painting...wall-paintings from the fortress of Dura. Chicago, 1924.
Arc 1076.22 Brensztejn, Michał E. Zarys dziejów lvdwisarstwa na ziemiach b. Wielkiego Księstwa Litewskiego. Wilno, 1924.
Arc 936.50 Bulić, France. L'archéologie en Dalmatie du Xe siècle. n.p., 1924-25.
Arc 861.38.7 Burrow, E.J. Ancient earthworks and camps of Somerset. Cheltenham, 1924.
Arc 684.1.25 Buschor, E. Die Skulpturen des Zeustempels zu Olympia. Giessen, 1924. 2v.
Arc 853.31.5 Cämmerer, E. Die Alteburg bei Armstadt. Leipzig, 1924.
Arc 543.7.7A Candee, H.C. Angkor the magnificent. N.Y., 1924.
Arc 1494.15 Castejan, R. Medina Zahira. Cordoba, 1924.
Arc 858.41 Clarke, W.G. Our homeland prehistoric antiquities and how to study them. London, 1924.
Arc 815.10 Corte, Matteo della. Inventus. Arpino, 1924.
Arc 688.3F Courby, F. Recherches archéologiques à Stratos d'Acarnanie. Paris, 1924.
Arc 870.18F Crawford, O.G.S. Air survey and archaeology. Southampton, 1924.

Chronological Listing

1924 - cont.

Arc 823.45 Déchelette, Joseph. Manuel d'archéologie prêhistorique, celtique et gallo-romaine. v.1-6; v.1-4, 2. éd. Paris, 1924-34. 7v.

Arc 1030.47 Diehl, Ernst. Inscriptiones latinae christianae veteres. Berolini, 1924-31. 3v.

Arc 689.5F Dugas, C. Le sanctuaire d'Aléa Athéna à Tégée au IVe siècle. Text and atlas. Paris, 1924. 2v.

Arc 726.22.9 Duhn, F. von. Italische Gräberkunde. Heidelberg, 1924-39. 2v.

Arc 375.8 Ebert, Max. Reallexikon der Vorgeschichte. v.1-15. Berlin, 1924-32. 16v.

Arc 905.24.5 Egger, Rudolf. Teurnia; die römischen und frühchristlichen Altertümer Oberkärntens. Wien, 1924.

Arc 1510.95 Erbstein, H.A. Der Münzfund von Trebita bei Wittenberg. Halle an der Saale, 1924.

Arc 421.4 Ferguson, J.C. A bronze table with accompanying vessels. Peking, 1924.

Arc 960.2.5 Fewkes, J.W. Preliminary archaeological explorations at Weeden Island, Florida. Washington, 1924.

Arc 761.6F Gatteschi, Giuseppe. Restauri della Roma imperiale. Roma, 1924.

Arc 543.7.9 Groslier, G. Angkor. Paris, 1924.

Arc 1663.63 Gumowski, Marian. Medale Zygmunta III. Kraków, 1924.

Arc 1588.1.23 Gumowski, Marian. Monety polskie. Warszawa, 1924.

Arc 1588.1.21 Gumowski, Marian. Numizmatyczno-historyczne z wieku. Poznań, 1924.

Arc 1670.57F Habich, Georg. De Medaillon der italienischen Renaissance. Stuttgart, 1924.

Arc 712.21A Hambidge, Jay. The Parthenon and other Greek temples. New Haven, 1924.

Arc 1018.19.10 Haufmann, C.M. Amerika und Urchristentum. München, 1924.

Arc 843.140 Hernandez-Pacheco, Eduardo. Las pinturas prehistoricas de las cuevas de la Araña (Valencia). Madrid, 1924.

Arc 482.203PF Herzfled, Ernst E. Paikuli. Berlin, 1924. 2v.

Arc 861.21.15 Home, Gordon. Roman York. London, 1924.

Arc 435.3.5F India. Archaeological Survey. Annual report. Index, 1902-1916. Calcutta, 1924.

Arc 559.1 Jéquier, G. Manuele d'archéologie egyptienne. Paris, 1924.

Arc 853.62 Jungklaus, Ernst. Römische Funde in Pommein. Greifswald, 1924.

Arc 968.2.45 Kidder, Alfred V. An introduction to the study of southwestern archaeology. New Haven, 1924.

Arc 1020.9.147 Lanciani, R. Wanderings through ancient Roman churches. Boston, 1924.

Arc 386.17.5 Leach, H.S. A bibliography of Howard Crosby Butler, 1872-1922. Princeton, 1924.

Arc 396.6 Linde, Richard. Alte Kulturstätten. 2. Aufl. Bielefeld, 1924.

Arc 895.43 Lindqvist, Sune. Den helige Eskils buskopsdöme. Stockholm, 1924.

Arc 396.9 Lucas, A. Antiques, their restoration and preservation. London, 1924.

Arc 766.4 Lugli, Giuseppe. La zona archeologica di Roma. Roma, 1924.

Arc 726.12.5 Mayer, M. Molfetta und Matera. Leipzig, 1924.

Arc 838.17 Mendes Corrêa, A.A. Os povos primitivos da Lusitânia. Porto, 1924.

Arc 652.5F Montelius, Oscar. La Grèce préclassique. Stockholm, 1924-28. 2v.

Arc 530.2.4F Morey, Charles B. Roman and Christian sculpture. Princeton, 1924.

Arc 1588.2.10 Mushmov, N.A. Monety i pechatite na bolg. Acare. Sofiia, 1924.

Arc 1468.54 Naville et Cie, Geneva. Monnaies grecques antiques en or en argent. pt. 2. Genève, 1924.

Arc 1478.83 Naville et Cie, Geneva. Monnaies romaines antiques. Genève, 1924.

Arc 395.9 Nikodim Pavlovich Kondakov, 1844-1924. Praga, 1924.

Arc 838.15 Obermaier, H. Fossil man in Spain. New Haven, 1924.

Arc 1433.38.10F Paruck, F.D.J. Sassanian coins. Bombay, 1924.

Arc 588.34 Petrie, W.M.F. Sedment I, II. London, 1924. 2v.

Arc 1418.8F Phayre Provincial Museum, Rangoon. Catalogue of coins in the museum. Rangoon, 1924.

Arc 723.16PF Pinza, Giovanni. Storia della civitá latina dalle origini al secolo V avante Christo. Roma, 1924.

Arc 895.22.20F Post, Linnart. Bronsaldersmanteln fran Gerumsberget i Vastergötland. Stockholm, 1924-25.

Arc 1138.4.5 Prou, Maurice. Manuel de paléographie latine et française avec atlas. 4. éd. Paris, 1924. 2v.

Arc 565.5 Put, Thomas C. Egypt and the Old Testament. Liverpool, 1924.

Arc 858.36 Quennell, M. (Mrs.) Everyday life in Roman Britain. London, 1924.

Arc 1349.80 Quesada, Ernesto. Enrique Peña. Buenos Aires, 1924.

Arc 723.15F Randall-McIver, David. Villanovans and early Etruscans. Oxford, 1924.

Arc 1372.3 Regling, Kurt. Die antike Münze als Kunstwerk. 1. Aufl. Berlin, 1924.

Arc 495.13FA Reisner, George A. Harvard excavations at Samaria 1908-1910. Cambridge, 1924. 2v.

Arc 710.12.5 Schede, Martin. The acropolis of Athens. Berlin, 1924.

Arc 853.54 Schumacher, P. Der Ringwälle in der früheren preusischen Provinz Posen. Leipzig, 1924.

Arc 1465.80F Seltman, Charles Theodore. Athens, its history and coinage before the Persian invasion. Cambridge, 1924.

Arc 843.15.14 Serra-Vilars, J. De mental-lurgia prehistorica a Catalunya. Solsona, 1924.

Arc 74.4.15 Society for the Promotion of Hellenic Studies. A classified catalogue of the books, pamphlets and maps in the library. London, 1924.

Arc 865.15.5 Stevens, Frank. Stonehenge today and yesterday. London, 1924.

Arc 865.17 Stone, E.H. The stones of Stonehenge. London, 1924.

Arc 386.19F Strena Buliciana; commentationes gratulatoriae F. Bulić. Zagrebiae, 1924.

Arc 588.36 Thompson, H. The gospel of St. John. London, 1924.

Arc 861.11.7F Thomson, James. A great free city; the book of Silchester. London, 1924. 2v.

Arc 1675.38 Victoria and Albert Museum. Catalogue of Italian placquettes. London, 1924.

Arc 843.79 Vielva, M. De re arqueologica. Valencia, 1924.

X Cg Arc 1470.29 Vogt, Joseph. Die alexandrinischen Münzen. v.1-2. Stuttgart, 1924. (Changed to XP 9970)

Arc 572.1.20 Weigall, Arthur Edward Pearse Brome. Ancient Egyptian works of art. London, 1924.

Arc 708.27.5 Weller, C.H. Athens and its monuments. N.Y., 1924.

Arc 1550.7 Wilcke, Julius. Montvaesenet under Christian IV og Frederik III i tidsrummet, 1625-70. Kjøbenhavn, 1924.

Arc 672.1.35 Xanthoudídes, S. The vaulted tombs of Mesará. London, 1924.

1925

Arc 936.240 Abramič, M. Poetovio. Ptuj, 1925.

Arc 1468.45 Allotte de la Fuÿe, F.M. Monnaies grecques. Paris, 1925.

Arc 340.5.2 American Academy in Rome. Library. A bibliographical guide to Latium and southern Eturia. 2. ed. Rome, 1925.

Arc 421.10 Andersson, J. Preliminary report on archaeological research in Kansu. Pekin, 1925.

Arc 853.57 Behn, Friedrich. Führer durch die römische Granitindustrie auf dem Felsberg im Odenwald. Mainz, 1925.

Arc 1468.5.6 Bibliothèque Nationale, Paris. Département des Médailles et Antiques. Catalogue de la collection de Luynes. pt.2-3 and plates. Paris, 1925-30. 2v.

Arc 641.2 Börger, Hans. Griechische Reisetage. Hamburg, 1925.

Arc 756.12 Brtnický, L. Topografie starověkého Říma. Praha, 1925.

Arc 726.22.5A Bryan, W.R. Italic hut urns and hut urn cemeteries. Rome, 1925.

Arc 590.1.5 Budge, E.A.W. The mummy. 2. ed. Cambridge, 1925.

Arc 612.30 Bumüller, J. Leitfaden der Vorgeschichte Europas. Augsburg, 1925. 2v.

Arc 726.25.17 Calza, Guido. Ostia, guida storico monumentale. Milano, 1925?

Arc 600.6.15F Capart, Jean. Thèbes. Bruxelles, 1925.

Arc 838.18 Carpenter, Rhys. The Greeks in Spain. Bryn Mawr, 1925.

Arc 1027.8.13 Chéramy, H. Saint-Sébastien hors les murs. Paris, 1925.

Arc 435.20.5 Corpus inscriptionum Indicarum. Oxford, 1925.

Arc 870.10.5 Crawford, O.G.S. The long barrows of Cotswolds. Gloucester, Eng., 1925.

Arc 66.1.129 Dugas, Charles. La céramique des cyclades. Paris, 1925.

Arc 870.15.11 Dunning, J.E. The Roman road to Portslade. London, 1925.

Arc 810.38 Engelmann, W. Neuer Führer durch Pompeji. Leipzig, 1925.

Arc 810.38.5 Engelmann, W. New guide to Pompeii. Leipzig, 1925.

Arc 672.1.26 Evans, Arthur John. Early Nilotic, Libyan, and Egyptian relations with Minoan Crete. London, 1925.

Arc 1500.36 Florange, C. Étude sur les messageries et les postes. Paris, 1925.

Arc 684.1.19 Gardiner, E.N. Olympia; its history and remains. Oxford, 1925.

Arc 895.28 Gihl, Gunnar. Sigtunna och Norrsunda. Uppsala, 1925.

Arc 1185.4.5 Giry, Arthur. Manuel de diplomatique. Paris, 1925. 2v.

Arc 905.5.7 Gnirs, Anton. Istria praeromana. Karlsbad, 1925.

Arc 612.18 Gotbe, I.V. Ocherki po istorii...Evropy. Leningrad, 1925.

Arc 853.3.15 Grenier, Albert. Etudes d'archéologie rhénane. Paris, 1925.

Arc 1663.60 Gumowski, Marian. Medale polskie. Warszawa, 1925.

Arc 853.248 Haermann, S. Die dritte Hallstattstufe im Gebeit. Nürnberg, 1925.

Arc 392.5 Hammerton, J.A. Wonders of the past; the romance of antiquity and its splendours. N.Y., 1925-26. 4v.

Arc 670.2.7 Harland, J.P. Prehistoric Aigina. Diss. Paris, 1925.

Arc 762.6 Hill, Ida T. Rome of the kings. N.Y., 1925.

Arc 726.52 Holland, Louise. The Faliscans in prehistoric times. Rome, 1925.

Arc 830.181 Huguenotte, A. Les mosaïques de Clervae. Besançon, 1925.

Arc 810.37 Ippel, Albert. Pompeji. Leipzig, 1925.

Arc 66.1.130 Jardé, A. Les céréales dans l'antiquité grecque. Paris, 1925.

Arc 600.4.9 Jong, E.F.P. Scherben aus Naukratis. Proefschrift. n.p., 1925.

Arc 1163.17.20FA Judge, C.B. Specimens of sixteenth-century English handwriting. Cambridge, 1925.

Htn Arc 1163.3.20PF* Karinskii, N.M. Obraztsy pis'ma brevneishego perioda istorii russkoi knigi. Leningrad, 1925.

Arc 915.46 Keller-Tarnuzzer, Karl. Urgeschichte des Thurgaus. Frauenfeld, 1925.

Arc 497.26F Kennedy, A.B. William. Petra; its history and monuments. London, 1925.

Arc 853.56 Krebs, Albert. Die vorrömische Metallzeit im östlichen Westfalen. Leipzig, 1925.

Arc 880.29 Lawlor, H.C. The monastery of St. Mochaoi of Nendrum. Belfast, 1925.

Arc 497.25 Macalister, R.A.S. A century of excavation in Palestine. London, 1925.

Arc 880.25 Macalister, R.A.S. The present and future of archaeology in Ireland. Dublin, 1925.

Arc 1335.135 Madrid. Museo Argueológico Nacional. Catalago. Madrid, 1925.

Arc 905.18.5 Mahr, Adolf. Das vorgeschichtliche Hallstatt. Wien, 1925.

Arc 785.45 Munoz, A. Il restauro del tiempo della Fortuna Virile. Roma, 1925.

Arc 1335.55 Murray, David. The Hunterian Museum in the old college of Glasgow. Glasgow, 1925.

Arc 1468.48 Nanteuil, H. de. Collection de monnaies grecques. Paris, 1925. 2v.

Arc 1458.20 Naville et Cie, Geneva. Monnaies grecques et romaines. Genève, 1925.

Arc 1478.83.5 Naville et Cie, Geneva. Monnaies romaines antiques. Genève, 1925.

Arc 726.53 Neppi Modona, A. Cortona etrusca e romana. Firenze, 1925.

Arc 895.22.5F Nordén, Arthur. Östergötlands bronsälder. Linköping, 1925.

Arc 955.2.20 Oakland, California. Museum. The Doheny scientific expedition to the Hava Supai Canyon, northern Arizona...1924. San Francisco, 1925.

Arc 588.38F Petrie, W.M.F. Buttons and design scarabs. London, 1925.

Arc 588.37 Petrie, W.M.F. Tombs of the courtiers and oxyrhynkhos. London, 1925.

Arc 880.31 Power, P. Early Christian Ireland. Dublin, 1925.

Arc 1500.46 Recamier, E. Monnaies romaines. Paris, 1925.

Arc 1580.40 Roll, Karl. Die Schaumünzen auf die Salzburger Emigration. Halle, 1925.

Arc 608.18F Romanelli, P. Leptis Magna. Roma, 1925.

Arc 567.1.5 Rosellini, Ippolito. Ippolito Rosellini e il suo giornale della spedizione letteraria toscana in Egitto. Roma, 1925.

Arc 925.13.10 Rostovtsev, M.I. Skifiia i Bospor". Leningrad, 1925.

Arc 772.8 Ruggiero, E. de. Lo stato e le opere pubbliche in Roma antica. Torino, 1925.

Arc 853.38.5 Sadie, Emil. Das römische Bonn. Bonn, 1925.

Arc 482.202.2F Sarre, Friedrich. Die Keramik von Samarra. Berlin, 1925.

Chronological Listing

1925 - cont.

Arc 1470.34 Schmitz, Hermann. Ein Gesetz der Stadt Olbia zum Schulze ihres Silbergeldes. Freiburg, 1925.
Arc 520.14F Schuchhardt, W.H. Die Meister des grossen Frieses von Pergamon. Berlin, 1925.
Arc 848.20 Schulz, Walther. Die germanische Familie in der Vorzeit. Leipzig, 1925.
Arc 830.179 Segret, Gabriel. Une maison d'époque romaine à Blesle. Clermont-Ferrand, 1925.
Arc 843.35 Serra-Vilaró, J. Escornalbou prehistòrich. Castell de Sant Miquel d'Escornalbou, 1925.
Arc 967.3.5 Sheldon, J.M.A. (Mrs.). Pitted stones. Deerfield, 1925.
Arc 1269.5 Siferlinger, C. Die Siegel der Beschöfe von Freising. Inaug. Diss. München, 1925.
Arc 391.4 Studien zur vorgeschichtlichen Archäologie Alfred Götze. Leipzig, 1925.
Arc 1033.58.15 Styger, Paolo. Il monumento apostolico a San Sebastiano sulla Via Appia. Roma, 1925.
Arc 1488.26F Venice. Museo. Catalogo della raccolta numismatica Papadopoli-Aldobandino. Venezia, 1925. 2v.
Arc 810.39 Warscher, Tatiana. Pompeji; ein Führer durch die Ruinen. Berlin, 1925.
Arc 858.40 Watkins, A. The old straight track. London, 1925.
Arc 885.8 Wheeler, R.E.M. Prehistoric and Roman Wales. Oxford, 1925.
Arc 861.65.15 Winbolt, S.E. Roman Folkestone. London, 1925.
Arc 861.41.9 Winbolt, S.E. The Roman villa at Bignor, Sussex. Oxford, 1925.
Arc 513.19.5 Ximinez, S. Asia Minor in ruins. N.Y., 1925.
Arc 830.173 Ydier, F. Découverte de trois sarcophages merovingiens du VIIe siècle aux Sables-d'Olonne. La Roche-sur-Yon, 1925.

1926

Arc 1335.62 André, Leon. Importante collection de monnaies et médailles. Paris, 1926.
Arc 396.8 Aubert, M. Notice nécrologique sur le comte Robert de Lesteyrie du Saillant, 1849-1919. Paris, 1926.
Arc 1675.80 Bahrfeldt, Max. Die Schaumünzen der Universität Halle-Wittenberg. Halle, 1926.
Arc 672.1.22 Baikie, James. The sea-kings of Crete. 4. ed. London, 1926.
Arc 66.1.132.5 Bayet, J. Herclé, étude critique. Paris, 1926.
Arc 66.1.132 Bayet, J. Les origines de l'Hercule Romain. Paris, 1926.
Arc 672.1.37 Bell, Edward. Prehellenic architecture in the Aegean. London, 1926.
Arc 1077.2.42 Bergmann, Alois. Die Schmiedkreuze Westböhmens. Elbogen, 1926.
Arc 1460.3 Bernhard, O. Griechische und römische Münzbilder. Zürich, 1926.
Arc 1478.23.5 Bernhart, Max. Handbuch zur Münzkunde der römischen Kaiserzeit. Halle an der Saale, 1926. 2v.
Arc 848.12 Blümlein, Carl. Bilder aus dem römisch-germanischen Kulturleben. 2. Aufl. München, 1926.
Arc 595.16.10 Borchardt, Ludwig. Längen und Richtungen der vier Grandkanten der grossen Pyramide bei Gise. Berlin, 1926.
Arc 843.62 Bosch-Gimpera, P. La prehistoria de las Iberas y la etnologia vasca. San Sebastian, 1926.
Arc 1510.162 Braun von Stumm, Gustaf. Die Münzen der Abtei Hornbach nebst Beiträgen zur Münzkunde von Speyergau und Elsass im 12-14. Halle an der Saale, 1926.
Arc 967.1.13 Brown, C.S. Archaeology of Mississippi. University, 1926.
Arc 593.4 Budge, E.A.W. Cleopatra's needles and other Egyptian obelisks. London, 1926.
Arc 66.1.131 Bulard, M. La religion domestique. Paris, 1926.
Arc 386.20A Burkitt, M.C. Our early ancestors. Cambridge, 1926.
Arc 1335.59 Cahn, A.E. Versteigerungskatalog nr. 57. Frankfurt, 1926.
Arc 1349.35F Calabi, A. Matteo dei Pasti. Milano, 1926.
Arc 726.25.18 Calza, Guido. Ostia; historical guide to the monuments. Milano, 1926.
Arc 608.2.70 Carton, Louis B.C. Carthage. Strasbourg, 1926.
Arc 1474.5 Cesano, Secondina L. Tipi monetali etruschi. Roma, 1926.
Arc 1163.13 Cordeiro de Sausa, J.M. Algunas siglas e abreviaturas usadas. Lisboa, 1926.
Arc 810.40 Corte, Matteo della. Pompéi; les nouvelles fouilles. Pompéi, 1926.
Arc 810.40.5 Corte, Matteo della. Pompeji. Pompeji, 1926.
Arc 435.2.42F Cousens, Henry. Chalukyan architecture. Calcutta, 1926.
Arc 432.6 Crinwasa Aiyangar, P.T. The stone age in India. Madras, 1926.
Arc 1163.4.13F Delhi. Museum of Archaeology. Specimens of calligraphy in the Delhi Museum of Archaeology. Calcutta, 1926.
Arc 1033.12.83 Diehl, C. Un nouveau trésor d'argenterie syrienne. Paris, 1926.
Arc 861.76 Dutt, W.A. The ancient mark-stones of East Anglia. Lowestoft, 1926.
Arc 905.24.6 Egger, Rudolf. Teurnia. 2. Aufl. Wien, 1926.
Arc 1148.19 Engelhes, W. Het Griehsche boek in voor. Amsterdam, 1926.
Arc 848.11 Erbt, Wilhelm. Germanische Kultur im Bronzezeitalter (2200-800 v. Chr.) Leipzig, 1926.
Arc 1190.88F Fekete, Lajos. Beveztés a hodoltśag török diplomatikájála. Budapest, 1926.
Arc 600.175 Firth, Cecil M. Excavations at Saqqara. Le Caire, 1926. 2v.
Arc 723.20.10F Forma Italiae. Roma, 1926- 17v.
Arc 1390.10 Friedensburg, F. Münzkunde und Geldgeschichte der Einzelstaaten des Mittelalters und der neuer Zeit. München, 1926.
Arc 858.38 Garrod, D.A.E. The upper palaeolithic age in Britain. Oxford, 1926.
Arc 537.6 Gjerstad, Einar. Studies on prehistoric Cyprus. Inaug. Diss. Uppsala, 1926.
Arc 1020.10.50F Goyau, Georges. Le visage de Rome chrétienne. Genève, 1926.
Arc 858.24.15 Great Britain. Commissions. Ancient and Historical Monuments and Constructions of England. An inventory of the historical monuments in Huntingdonshire. London, 1926.
Arc 1503.9 Grossmann, Theodor. Sammlung Schweizer Münzen und Medaillen des Herrn Theodor Grossmann. Frankfurt, 1926?
Arc 608.6.23 Gsell, Stéphane. Promenades archéologiques aux environs d'Alger. Paris, 1926.
Arc 861.18.16 Home, Gordon. Roman London. London, 1926.
Arc 861.18.16.5 Home, Gordon. Roman London. N.Y., 1926.
Arc 785.13.24.9 Huelsen, Christian. Forum und Palatin. München, 1926.
Arc 1033.12.239 Jerphanion, G. de. Le calice d'Antioche. Rome, 1926.
Arc 975.12 Judd, Neil M. Archaeological observations north of the Rio Colorado, Utah. Washington, 1926.

1926 - cont.

Arc 936.14.280 Karpińska, Aleksandra. Kurhany, zokresw rzymskiego w Polsce ze szczegolnem uwzględnieniem typu siedlemińskiego. Poznań, 1926.
Arc 608.2.23 Kelsey, Francis W. Excavations at Carthage 1925. N.Y., 1926.
Arc 608.19 Khun de Prorok, Byron. Digging for lost African gods. N.Y., 1926.
Arc 1093.7.2 Koch, Rudolf. Das Zeichenbuch. 2. Aufl. Offenbach am Main, 1926.
Arc 853.21.25 Kraft, Georg. Die Kultur der Bronzezeit in Süddeutschland auf Grund der Funde in Württemberg. Augsburg, 1926.
Arc 543.27.15 Krom, N.J. De levensgeschiedenis van den Buddha op Barabudur. 's Gravenhage, 1926.
Arc 853.58 Kunkel, Otto. Oberhessens vorgeschichtliche Altertümer. Marburg, 1926.
Arc 543.4.13 LeCoq, Albert. Auf Hellas spuren in Ostturkistan. Leipzig, 1926.
Arc 785.15.11FA Lehmann-Hartleben, Karl. Die Trajanssaule. Text and Atlas. Berlin, 1926. 2v.
Arc 853.74 Lehner, Hans. Das Römerlager Vetera bei Hauten. Bonn, 1926.
Arc 736.8F Libertini, Guido. Centuripe. Catania, 1926.
Arc 1185.21 Lodolini, A. Elementi di diplomatica. Milano, 1926.
Arc 600.21 Lucas, Alfred. Ancient Egyptian materials. N.Y., 1926.
Arc 1348.17.2 Luschin von Elengreuth, A. Allgemeine Münzkunde und Geldgeschichte. 2. Aufl. München, 1926.
Arc 505.5.85 Macalister, R.A.S. Excavations...Ophel, Jerusalem, 1923-1925. London, 1926.
NEDL Arc 815.13 Macchiaro, V. Die Villa des Mysterien in Pompei. Neapel, 1926?
Arc 870.17F Major, Albany F. The mystery of Wansdyke. Cheltenham, 1926.
Arc 562.2.20A Maspero, Gaston. Manual of Egyptian archaeology. 6th English ed. N.Y., 1926.
Arc 858.37.5 Massingham, H.J. Fee, fi, fo, fum, or, The giants in England. London, 1926.
Arc 905.15.5 Menghin, Oswald. Einführung in der Urgeschichte Böhmens und Mährens. Reichenberg, 1926.
Arc 925.4.9 Merhard, Gero von. Bronzezeit am Janissei. Wien, 1926.
Arc 522.25 Mey, Oscar. Das Schlachtfeld vor Troja, eine Untersuchung. Berlin, 1926.
Arc 1190.4 Müller, Karl. Unsere Kanzleisprache. Dresden, 1926.
Arc 672.1.45 Oulié, Marthe. Les animaux dans la peinture de la Crete préhellénique. Thèse. Paris, 1926.
Arc 400.15 Paniagua, A. de. L'âge du renne. Paris, 1926.
Arc 843.58 Paris, Pierre. Fouilles dans la région d'Alcañis, province de Teruel. Bordeaux, 1926.
Arc 861.77.5 Parker, C.A. The Gosforth district. Kendal, 1926.
Arc 810.32.5 Pernice, Erich. Pompeji. Leipzig, 1926.
Arc 588.39F Petrie, W.M.F. Ancient weights and measures. London, 1926.
Arc 588.40F Petrie, W.M.F. Glass stamps and weights. London, 1926.
Arc 1494.30 Prieto y Vives, Antonio. Los reyes de Taijas. Madrid, 1926.
Arc 1138.29 Quentin, Henri. Essais de critique textuelle. Paris, 1926.
Arc 600.160F Ranke, Hermann. Koptische Friedhöfe bei Karâra und der Amontempel Schesehonks I bei El Hibe. Berlin, 1926.
Arc 861.74 Ravenhill, T.H. The Rollright stones and the men who erected them. Birmingham, 1926.
Arc 1329.3 Riechmann, A. and Co. Numismatische Literatur. Halle am der Saale, 1926.
Arc 684.1.45F Rodenwaldt, G. Olympia. Berlin, 1926.
Arc 925.50 Rudins'kyi, M. Materialy...stantsiia. Bila Hira pid Poltavoiu. Kyïv, 1926.
Arc 612.27 Rydh, H. Grott-människornas årtusenden. Stockholm, 1926.
Arc 830.119 Sautel, Joseph. Vaison dans l'antiquité. Avignon, 1926-27. 2v.
Arc 830.119.7 Sautel, Joseph. Vaison dans l'antiquité. pts.1-3. Lyon, 1926.
Arc 830.119.5 Sautel, Joseph. Vaison dans l'antiquité. v.1-2. Avignon, 1926.
Arc 1153.43.7 Schiaparelli, L. Avviamento allo studio delle abbreviature latine nel medievo. Firenze, 1926.
Arc 1550.11F Schou, Hans Henrich. Beskrivelse of danske og norske mønter. Kjøbenhavn, 1926.
Arc 612.11.2 Schuchhardt, Carl. Alteruopa; eine Vorgeschichte unseres Erdteils. 2. Aufl. Leipzig, 1926.
Arc 848.20.5 Schulz, Walther. Staat und Gesellschaft in germanischer Vorzeit. Leipzig, 1926.
Arc 522.18 Seyk, V. Das Wahre und richtige Troja-Illion. Prag, 1926.
Arc 895.17.12 Shetelig, Haakon. Préhistoire de la Norvège. Oslo, 1926.
Arc 547.6.9 A short description of the objects from the tomb of Tutankhamun now exhibited in the Cairo Museum. Cairo, 1926.
Arc 600.4.13 Smith, E.M. Naukratis. Diss. Vienna, 1926.
Arc 861.16.7 Smith, F. Prehistoric man and the Cambridge gravels. Cambridge, Eng., 1926.
Arc 482.204F Spanner, H. Rusafa. Berlin, 1926.
Arc 1480.26 Sydenham, E.A. Aes grave; a study of the cast coinage of Rome and Central Italy. London, 1926.
Arc 543.4.15 Tai, Tse tsan. The cradle of humanity. n.p., 1926.
Arc 936.20.10 Tonescu, G.M. Etiopienii in Dacia preistorica. Bucureşti, 1926.
Arc 913.17 Tschumi, O. Urgeschichte der Schweiz. Frauenfeld, 1926.
Arc 1493.13 Vives y Escudero, Antonio. La moneda hispánica. Madrid, 1926. 2v.
Arc 458.7 Vogel, J.P. Indian serpent-lore. London, 1926.
Arc 858.39 Weigall, A.E.P.B. Wanderings in Roman Britain. London, 1926.
Arc 885.9 Wheeler, R.E.M. The Roman fort near Brecon. London, 1926.

1927

Arc 870.9.10 Allcroft, A.H. The circle and the cross. London, 1927-30. 2v.
Arc 1510.10.5F Bahrfeldt, Max von. Niedersachsisches Münzarchiv. Halle, 1927. 4v.
Arc 905.60 Banner, János. Népvándorlás koté sérok Nagykamaráson. Szeged, 1927.
Arc 1663.26 Barnard, F.P. Saterical and controversial medals of the reformation. Oxford, 1927.
Arc 608.12.15 Bartoccini, R. Guida di Sabratha. Roma, 1927.
Arc 1428.11F Berlin. Staatliche Museen. Die Münzen von Priene. Berlin, 1927.
Arc 1020.9.175 Bevan, Gladys M. Early Christians of Rome. London, 1927.

Chronological Listing

1927 - cont.

Arc 1025.63 Beyer, Oskar. Die Katakombenwelt. Tübingen, 1927.
Arc 447.2 Bilgrami, S.A.A. Landmarks of the Deccan; a comprehensive guide to the archaeological remains of the city and suburbs of Hyderabad. Hyderabad, 1927.
Arc 1264.7.5 Blanchet, A. Les drapiers de Beauvais et leurs plombs de contrôle. Beauvais, 1927.
Arc 925.13.50 Borovka, Grigorii I. Scythian art. London, 1927.
Arc 1478.21.5 British Museum. Department of Coins and Medals. A guide to the exhibition of Roman coins in the British Museum. London, 1927.
Arc 588.41F Brunton, Guy. Gurob. London, 1927.
Arc 588.44F Brunton, Guy. Qau and Badari. London, 1927-30. 3v.
Arc 547.6.10 Cairo. Musée des Antiquités Égyptiennes. A brief description of the principal monuments. Cairo, 1927.
Arc 726.25.13 Calza, Guido. Il teatro romano di Ostia. Roma, 1927.
Arc 785.47 Carcopino, J. La basilique pythagoricienne de la Porte Majeure. Paris, 1927.
Arc 642.6 Casson, S. Essays in Aegean archaeology. Oxford, 1927.
Arc 1498.10 Ciani, Louis. Catalogue de monnaies françaises. pt.1-3. Paris, 1927-29.
Arc 853.97 Colin, Jean. Les antiquités romaines de la Rhenanie. Paris, 1927.
Arc 861.71.5F Collingwood, W.G. Northumbrian crosses of the pre-Norman age. London, 1927.
Arc 726.4.15A Consoli Fiego, G. Cumae and the Phlegraean fields. Naples, 1927.
Arc 416.6 Contenau, Georges. Manuel d'archéologie orientale depuis les origines jusqu'a l'époque d'Alexandre. Paris, 1927-47. 4v.
Arc 1030.49 Cordeiro de Sousa, J.M. Inscrições sepulcrais da sé de Lisboa. Lisboa, 1927.
Arc 861.78 Davies, J.A. Early life in the West. Clifton, 1927.
Arc 875.31.10 Dinwiddie, J. The Ruthwell cross and its story. Dumfries, 1927.
Arc 830.126 Donnadieu, A. La Pompéi de la Provence, Fréjus. Paris, 1927.
Arc 830.130 Dussaud, René. Autour des inscriptions de Glozel. Paris, 1927.
Arc 853.60 Eichhorn, G. Der Urnenfriedhof auf der Schanze bei Grossromstedt. Leipzig, 1927.
Arc 543.29 Evans, Ivor H.N. Papers on the ethnology and archaeology of the Malay Peninsula. Cambridge, Eng., 1927.
Arc 885.10 Evans, William. The Meini Hirion and Sarns of Anglesey. Llangefni, 1927.
Arc 1084.12 Field Museum of Natural History, Chicago. Archaic Chinese jades collections in China. N.Y., 1927.
Arc 936.35F Filov, B. Die archäische Nekropole von Trebenischte am Ochrida-See. Leipzig, 1927.
Arc 1663.25 Florange, Charles. Les assemblées du clergé de France avant 1789. Paris, 1927.
Arc 830.166 Forrer, Robert. Strasbourg-Argentorate. Strausbourg, 1927. 2v.
Arc 1494.55 Garcia de la Fuente, Arturo. La numismática española en el reinado de Felipe II. Escorial, 1927.
Arc 608.2.25 Gielly, Paul. Quelques lueurs nouvelles sur l'emplacement de la Carthage punique et de ses ports. Casablanca, 1927.
Arc 1510.5.5 Goessler, Peter. Beiträge zur süddeutschen Münzgeschichte. Stuttgart, 1927.
Arc 1138.28 Greg, Walter W. The calculus of variants, an essay on textual criticism. Oxford, 1927.
Arc 853.59 Gumpert, Carl. Fränkisches Mesolithikum. Leipzig, 1927.
Arc 482.202.3F Herzfeld, Ernst E. Die Malereien von Samarra. Berlin, 1927.
Arc 1468.13.5F Hill, G.F. Select Greek coins. Paris, 1927.
Arc 875.43 Hutcheson, Alexander. Old stories in stones and other papers. Dundee, 1927.
Arc 1348.32 Icard, Séverin. Identification des monnaies. Paris, 1927.
Arc 1190.10F Jenkinson, H. The later court hands in England. Test and atlas. Cambridge, 1927. 2v.
Arc 612.17 Johansen, K. Friis. De forhistoriske tider i Europa. København, 1927. 2v.
Arc 1590.31 Katz, Viktor. Kontramarky na pražských groších. Praha, 1927.
Arc 435.2.43F Kaye, G.R. Bakhshali manuscript. pt.1-3. Calcutta, 1927-33. 2v.
Arc 395.8 Kondakov, N.P. Vospominaniia i dumy. Praga, 1927.
Arc 848.8.9 Kossinna, Gustaf. Altgermanische Kulturhöhe. München, 1927.
Arc 543.27.5 Krom, N.J. Barabudur. The Hague, 1927. 2v.
Arc 838.3.13 Leite de Vasconcellos, J. De terra em terra. v.1-2. Lisboa, 1927.
Arc 1020.9.146 Leitzmann, Hans. Petrus und Paulus in Rom. 2. Aufl. Berlin, 1927.
Arc 830.121 Linckenheld, E. Les stèles funéraires enforme de maison chez les médiomatriques et en Gaule. Paris, 1927.
Arc 383.53.10F Mainz. Römisch Germanisches Zentralmuseum. Festschrift zur Feier des fünfundsiebzigjährigen Bestehens. Mainz, 1927.
Arc 858.37.2 Massingham, H.J. Downland man. London, 1927.
Arc 432.5.2 Mitra, Panchanan. Prehistoric India. 2. ed. Calcutta, 1927.
Arc 870.15.7 Mothersole, Jessie. Agricola's road into Scotland. London, 1927.
Arc 875.41 Mothersole, Jessie. In Roman Scotland. London, 1927.
Arc 505.55 New York. Metropolitan Museum of Art. A crusaders' fortress in Palestine. N.Y., 1927.
Arc 1470.31 Newell, E.T. The coinage of Demetrius Poliorcetes. London, 1927.
Arc 497.27F Nielsen, D. Handbuch der altarabischen Altertumskunde. Kopenhagen, 1927.
Arc 674.1.5F Noack, F. Eleusis. Text and plates. Berlin, 1927. 2v.
Arc 530.12.5 Osten, H.H. von der. Explorations in Hittite Asia Minor. Chicago, 1927.
Htn Arc 672.1.47F* Oulié, Marthe. Decoration égéenne. Paris, 1927.
Arc 543.7.50 Parmentier, H. L'art khmèr primitif. Paris, 1927. 2v.
Arc 716.7.10F Paton, James M. The Erechtheum. Cambridge, 1927.
Arc 716.7.10PF Paton, James M. The Erechtheum. Atlas. Cambridge, 1927.
Arc 400.11 Peake, Harold J.E. Hunters and artists. New Haven, 1927.
Arc 588.42F Petrie, W.M.F. Objects of daily use. London, 1927.
Arc 383.18 Plovdiv, Bulgaria. Durzhavna biblioteka "Ivan Vazov". Sbornik Boris Liabovich. Plovdiv, 1927.
Arc 548.5 Porter, Bertha. Topographical bibliography of ancient Egyptian hieroglyphic texts, reliefs. Oxford, 1927-39. 7v.
Arc 743.11 Randall-MacIver, D. The Etruscans. Oxford, 1927.

1927 - cont.

Arc 723.15.7 Randall-McIver, David. The iron age in Italy. Oxford, 1927.
Arc 830.120 Sawtell, R.O. Primitive hearths in the Pyrenees. N.Y., 1927.
Arc 830.124.15 Schaeffer, F.A. Un dépôt d'outils et un trésor de bronzes...à Seltz. Haguenau, 1927.
Arc 390.6 Stephaniskos. Ernst Fabricius. Freiburg, 1927.
Arc 1025.62 Styger, Paul. Die altchristliche Grabeskunst. München, 1927.
Arc 600.35 Suys, Émile. Vie de Petasiris, grand prêtre di That à Hermopolis-la-Grande. Bruxelles, 1927.
Arc 936.1.7 Tafrali, O. La cité pontique de Dionysopolis. Paris, 1927.
Arc 938.50.5 Tarasenka, P. Priešistorine lieſuwa. Kaunas, 1927.
Arc 505.27F Turville-Petre, F. Researches in prehistoric Galilee, 1925-1926. London, 1927.
Arc 936.3F Ugalini, L.U. Albania antica. Roma, 1927-42. 3v.
Arc 810.41 Van Buren, A.W. A companion to Pompeian studies. Rome, 1927.
Arc 915.9 Viollier, David. Carte archéologique du Canton de Vaud des origines à l'époque de Charlemagne. Lausanne, 1927.
Arc 672.1.51F Wace, A.J.B. A Cretan statuette in the Fitzwilliam Museum. Cambridge, Eng., 1927.
Arc 1076.3.18.10 Walters, Henry Beauchamp. Church bells of Wiltshire. Devizes, 1927-29.
Arc 505.29 Wiener, H.M. The altars of the Old Testament. Leipzig, 1927.
Arc 1550.6 Wilcke, Julius. Kurantmønten. Kjøbenhavn, 1927.

1928

Arc 1084.7 Alexander, R. Jade; its philosophy. N.Y., 1928.
Arc 672.5.5 American School of Classical Studies at Athens. Ancient Corinth. Macon, 1928.
Arc 853.56.7 Andree, Julius. Das Paläolithikum der Höhlen des Hönnetales in Westfalen. Leipzig, 1928.
Arc 843.57 Aranzadi, T. de. Exploraciones prehistóricas en Guepiezcoa los años 1924-1927. San Sebastian, 1928.
Arc 691.5F Arbanitopoulos, A.S. Graptai stēlai Dēmetriidos-Palasōn. Athēnai, 1928.
Arc 796.2F Beyen, Hendrik G. Über Stilleben aus Pompeji und Herculaneum. 's-Gravenhage, 1928.
Arc 1200.21 Björkman, Walther. Beiträge zur Geschichte der Staatskanzlei im islamischen Ägypten. Hamburg, 1928.
Arc 875.29.7 Black, William G. The Scots mercat "cross"; an inquiry as to its history and meaning. Glasgow, 1928.
Arc 695.1F Blegen, Carl W. Zygouries. Cambridge, 1928.
Arc 595.50 Borchardt, Ludwig. Die Entstehung der Pyramide an der Baugeschichte. Berlin, 1928.
Arc 925.13.52 Borovka, Grigorii I. Scythian art. London, 1928.
Arc 880.36 Bremer, Walther. Ireland's place in prehistoric and early historic Europe. Dublin, 1928.
Arc 746.14 Brizio, E. Una Pompei etrusca a Marzabotto nel Bolognese. Bologna, 1928.
Arc 588.46F Brunton, Guy. The Badarian civilization. London, 1928.
Arc 880.33F Burchell, J.P.T. The early Mousterian implements of Sligo, Ireland. Ipswich, 1928.
Arc 815.20 Burrascano, N. I misteri orfici nell'antica Pompei. Roma, 1928.
Arc 1675.10.7 Calabi, A. Pisanello. Milano, 1928.
Arc 513.20 Calder, W.M. Monumenta Asiae Minoris antiqua. London, 1928-39. 8v.
Arc 1153.12.10A Cappelli, A. Lexicon abbreviaturarum. 2. Aufl. Leipzig, 1928.
Arc 830.130.15 Cartereau, E. Glozel et sa signification. Paris, 1928.
Arc 830.130.10 Cartereau, E. La mise au point de Glozel. Paris, 1928.
Arc 1153.47PF Catholic Church. Pope. Pontificum Romanorum diplomata. Romae, 1928.
Arc 387.8A Cleland, H.F. Our prehistoric ancestors. N.Y., 1928.
Arc 1076.3.95 Coleman, Satis N. (Barton). Bells; their history, legends, making, and uses. Chicago, 1928.
Arc 830.15.13 Constans, L.A. Arles. Paris, 1928.
Arc 608.20 Corò, Francesco. Vestigia di colonie agricole romane Gebel Nefusa. Roma, 1928.
Arc 830.40.9 Coutil, Léon. Les ruines romaines de Noyers-sur-Andelys (Eure); villa rustica et théatre. Évreux, 1928. 2 pam.
Arc 861.82F Crawford, O.G.S. Wessex from the air. Oxford, 1928.
Arc 875.60 The Drostin stone at St. Vigeans and its inscription. Aberdeen, 1928.
Arc 421.4.5 Ferguson, J.C. The four bronze vessels of the Marquis. Peking, 1928.
Arc 390.8 Feron, R. La préhistoire. Paris, 1928.
Arc 585.37F Gardiner, Alan H. Egyptian letters to the dead. London, 1928.
Arc 392.12.80 Georg Habich zum 60. Geburtstag. München, 1928.
Arc 1488.8F Giesecke, Walther. Italia numismatica. Leipzig, 1928.
Arc 1473.8 Goodacre, H.G. A handbook of the coinage of the Byzantine empire. pt.1-3. London, 1928-33.
Arc 647.3.5 Hall, H.R. The civilization of Greece in the bronze age. London, 1928.
Arc 392.8.80 Harrison, E.R. Harrison of Ightham. London, 1928.
Arc 853.13.25 Hertlein, F. Die Römer in Württemberg. pt.1-3. Stuttgart, 1928-32. 3v.
Arc 493.2.15 Herzfeld, Ernst E. Rapport sur l'état actuel des ruines de Persépole. Berlin, 1928.
Arc 861.84 Hopkinson, J.H. The Roman fort at Ribchester. 3. ed. Manchester, 1928.
Arc 785.13.24.13 Huelsen, Christian. The Forum and the Palatine. N.Y., 1928.
Arc 402.10.25 Jamot, Paul. Theodore Reinach, (1860-1928). Paris, 1928.
Arc 600.72F Jéquier, Gustave. Fouilles à Saqqarah. La Caire, 1928.
Arc 600.71F Jéquier, Gustave. Fouilles à Saqqarah. Le Caire, 1928.
Arc 925.4.13F Jochelsen, W. Archaeological investigations in Kamchatka. Washington, 1928.
Arc 1163.3.15 Karskii, E.F. Slavianskaia kirillovskaia paleografiia. Leningrad, 1928.
Arc 861.83 Kendrick, T.D. The archaeology of the Channel Islands. London, 1928.
Arc 1077.2.46F King, E.S. The date and provenance of a bronze reliquary cross in the Museo Cristiano. Rome, 1928.
Arc 848.8.13 Kossinna, Gustaf. Ursprung und Verbreitung der Germanen in vor-und frühgeschichtlicher Zeit. Leipzig, 1928.
Arc 482.202.4F Lamm, C.J. Das Glas von Samarra. Berlin, 1928.
Arc 880.35 Lawlor, H.C. Ulster. Belfast, 1928.

Chronological Listing

1928 - cont.

Arc 861.4.3 Lawson, P.H. Schedule of the Roman remains of Chester. Chester, 1928.
Arc 543.4.14 LeCoq, Albert. Buried treasures of Chinese Turkestan. London, 1928.
Arc 396.20 Leopold, Hendrik M.R. Uit de school van de spade. Zutphen, 1928-34. 6v.
Arc 853.20.29 Loeschcke, S. Die Erforschung des Tempelbezirkes im Altbachtale zu Trier. Berlin, 1928.
Arc 880.25.7 Macalister, R.A.S. The archaeology of Ireland. London, 1928.
Arc 595.20 MacHuisdean, Hamish. The great law, told simply in seven visits. v.2. Glasgow, 1928.
Arc 543.7.13 Marchal, H. Guide archéologique aux temples d'Angkor. Paris, 1928.
Arc 925.8.25 Marti, Iu.Iu. Problema raskopok drevnego pantikapeia. n.p., 1928?
Arc 1025.28.40 Marucchi, O. Compendio storico e topografico delle catacombe romane. Albano Laziale, 1928.
Arc 1478.24.7 Mattingly, Harold. Roman coins from the earliest times to the fall of the Western Empire. London, 1928.
Arc 1251.25 Matz, F. Die frühkretischen Siegel. Berlin, 1928.
Arc 810.11.5 Mau, August. Fuehrer durch Pompeji. 6. Aufl. Leipzig, 1928.
Arc 1510.25 Mertens, E. Münz- und Geldgeschichte der Stadt Northeim. Diss. Halle an der Saale, 1928.
Arc 652.6 Mylonas, G.E. Hē neolithike epoche en Helladi. Athēnai, 1928.
Arc 543.7.15 Naudin, G. Le groupe d'Angkor vu par les ecrivains et les étrangers. Saigon, 1928.
Arc 93.16 Neppi Modona, Aldo. I fasti dell'Accademia Etrusca di Cortona. Cortona, 1928.
Arc 1076.3.93 Nichols, J.R. Bells thro' the ages. London, 1928.
Arc 1166.1.5 Ohly, Kurt. Stichometrische Untersuchungen. Leipzig, 1928.
Arc 746.18F Orvieto, Italy. Orvieto etrusca. Roma, 1928.
Arc 936.20 Pârvan, Vasile. Dacia. Cambridge, 1928.
Arc 588.43F Petrie, W.M.F. Gerar. London, 1928.
Arc 673.11F Plassart, A. Les sanctuaires et les cultes du Mont Cynthe a Délos. Thèse. Paris, 1928.
Arc 66.1.133 Pocquet, J. du Haut-Jusse. Les papes et les ducs de Bretagne. Paris, 1928. 2v.
Arc 712.23 Praschniker, C. Parthenonstudien. Augsburg, 1928.
Arc 1675.104 Probszt, Günther. Die geprägten Schaumünzen Innerösterreichs; Steinmark, Kärnten, Krain. Zürich, 1928.
Arc 723.15.15 Randall-McIver, David. Italy before the Romans. Oxford, 1928.
Arc 392.3.25 Sayce, A.H. David George Hogarth, 1862-1927. London, 1928.
Arc 848.22 Schuchhardt, C. Nordwestdeutschland und die Frage des Germanenursprungs. n.p., 1928.
Arc 848.15 Schuchhardt, C. Vorgeschichte von Deutschland. München, 1928.
Arc 1588.9 Sengbusch, R. von. Heinrich Jochumsen. Verzeichnis aller bisher nachweisbaren boltischen Münzen und der Desiderata der Sammlung Anton Buchholtz. Riga, 1928.
Arc 723.19.2 Seta, Alessandro. Italia antica. 2a ed. Bergamo, 1928.
Arc 608.94F Solignac, Marcel. Les pierres écrites de la Berbérie orientale. Tunis, 1928.
Arc 1510.24 Sperl, Karl. Die Münzgeschichte Regensburgs. Inaug. Diss. Kallmünz, 1928.
Arc 853.258 Sprater, Friedrich. Die Urgeschichte der Pfalz. Speier, 1928.
Arc 543.3.17F Stein, Mark Aurel. Innermost Asia. Oxford, 1928. 4v.
Htn Arc 543.3.15F* Stein, Mark Aurel. Innermost Asia. Oxford, 1928. 4v.
Arc 458.4.5 Temple, Richard C. Notes on the seven pagodas. London, 1928-29.
Arc 925.13.25 Toll', N.R. Skify i gunny. Praga, 1928.
Arc 659.5 Tsountas, Chrēstos. Istoria tēs archaias Hellēnikēs technēs. Athēnai, 1928.
Arc 1613.9 United States Mint. Catalogue of coins of the United States. Washington, 1928.
Arc 1285.30 Vojtišek, V. O pečetech a erbech měst pražskych a jinych českych. Praha, 1928.
Arc 853.24.5 Wagner, F. Die Römer in Bayern. München, 1928.
Arc 407.11 Wirth, Herman. Der Aufgang der Menschheit. Jena, 1928.

1929

Arc 1468.53 Ars Classica, Geneva. Monnaies grecques. Genève, 1929.
Arc 444.2.10 Balasaheb, Pant Pratinidhi. Ellora; a handbook of Verul (Ellora caves). Bombay, 1929.
Arc 608.18.5F Bartoccini, R. Le terme di Lepcis (Leptis Magna). Bergamo, 1929.
Arc 505.45A Baur, P.V.C. The excavations at Dura-Europas. pt.1-9. New Haven, 1929-1946. 9v.
Arc 1580.48 Bernhart, Max. Die Münzen und Medaillen des Erzstiftes Salzburg. München, 1929-30.
Arc 746.13 Bianchi-Bandinelli, R. Sovana, topografia ed arte. Firenze, 1929.
Arc 1163.16F Bianu, I. Album de paleografie românească. București, 1929.
Arc 1335.27.25 Bibliothèque Nationale, Paris. Département des Médailles et Antiques. Les monnaies. Paris, 1929.
Arc 1190.30 Boüard, Alain de. Manuel de diplomatique française et pontificale. Paris, 1929-52. 2v.
Arc 1190.30F Boüard, Alain de. Manuel de diplomatique française et pontificale. Atlas. Paris, 1929-52. 2v.
Arc 386.15.5 British Museum. How to observe in archaeology. 2. ed. London, 1929.
Arc 893.14 Brøgger, A.W. Universitetets oldsakamlings skrifter. Oslo, 1929.
Arc 66.1.134 Cahen, Emile. Callimaque. Paris, 1929.
Arc 1335.59.5 Cahn, A.E. Versteigerungskatalog nr. 63. v.2. Frankfurt am Main, 1929.
Arc 389.1 Camille, Enlart, 1862-1927. Paris, 1929.
Arc 1033.3.45 Campenhausen, Hans von. Die Passionssarkophage. Marburg, 1929.
Arc 1153.12.15 Cappelli, A. Lexicon abbreviaturarum. 3. ed. Milano, 1929.
Arc 726.25.25A Carcopino, J. Ostie. Paris, 1929.
Arc 716.3.5 Carpenter, Rhys. The sculpture of the Nike temple parapet. Cambridge, 1929.
Arc 543.7.17A Casey, R.J. Four faces of Siva. Indianapolis, 1929.
Arc 672.1.63 Charbonneaux, J. L'art égéen. Paris, 1929.

1929 - cont.

Arc 1588.4.15 Chaura, K. Die Wahrheit übes den St. Wenzel-Denar. Praha, 1929.
Arc 612.19 Childe, Vere G. The Danube in prehistory. Oxford, 1929.
Arc 967.1.11 Conference on Midwestern Archaeology, St. Louis. Report. Washington, 1929.
Arc 3.1.24 Congrès International d'Archéologie Classique, 4th, Barcelona, 1929. IV Congresso internazionale d'archéologia; 23-29 settembre 1929. Barcelona? 1929.
Arc 93.38F Convegno Archeologico in Sardegna. Il Convegno archeologico en Sardegna. 2. ed. Reggio nell'Emilia, 1929.
Arc 628.20.5 Couch, Herbert N. Treasure of the Greeks and Romans. Thesis. Menasha, 1929.
Arc 628.20 Couch, Herbert N. The treasuries of the Greeks and Romans. Menasha, 1929.
Arc 505.5.95 Creswell, K.A. La mosquée Al Aqsa et la Néa de Justinien. Liege, 1929.
Arc 505.5.90 Crowfoot, J.W. Excavations...Tyropoeon Valley, Jerusalem, 1927. London, 1929.
Arc 861.86F Cunnington, M.E. (Mrs.) Woodhenge. Devizes, 1929.
Arc 815.15 Curtius, Ludwig. Die Wandmalerei Pompejis. Leipzig, 1929.
Arc 861.41.20 Curwen, E. Cecil. Prehistoric Sussex. London, 1929.
Arc 1163.25F Deimel, Anton. Keilschrift-Palaeographie. Roma, 1929.
Arc 1030.57 Deschamps, P. Étude sur la paléographie des inscriptions lapidaires de la fin de l'époque mérovingienne aux dernières années du XIIe siècle. Paris, 1929.
Arc 726.60 Dumitrescu, V. L'età del ferro nel Piceno. Tesi. Bucarest, 1929.
Arc 823.9.3 Enlart, C. Manuel d'archéologie française. 3e éd. pt.2. Paris, 1929.
Arc 825.3.15 Espéraudieu, E. La maison carrée a Nîmes. Paris, 1929.
Arc 682.11 Evans, Arthur. The shaft graves and bee-hive tombs of Mycenae and their interrelation. London, 1929.
Arc 1493.14 Ferrandis Torres, J. Les monnaies hispaniques. Barcelona, 1929.
Arc 608.17.9F Ferri, Silvio. Divinità ignate. Firenze, 1929.
Arc 609.1.29 Fort Victoria, Southern Rhodesia. Town Management. Fort Victoria and the great Zimbabwe ruins. Bulawayo, 1929.
Arc 1148.14.5 Franchi de' Cavalieri, P. Specimina codicum graecorum vaticanorum. Berolini, 1929.
Htn Arc 585.38F* Frankfort, H. The mural painting of El-Amarneh. London, 1929.
Arc 913.21 Franz, L. Vorgeschichtliches Leben in den Alpen. Wien, 1929.
Arc 1508.7 Gebhart, H. Die deutschen Münzen des Mittelalters. 4. Aufl. Berlin, 1929.
Arc 530.10.15 Gerkan, Armin von. Der Altar des Artemis-Tempels in Magnesia am Mäander. Berlin, 1929.
Arc 905.15.9 Gnirs, Anton. Die römischen Schutzbezirke an der Oberen Donau. Augsburg, 1929.
Arc 503.5 Grant, Elihu. Beth Shemesh (Palestine). Haverford, Pa., 1929.
Arc 392.15F Haeberlin, Ernst Justus. Ernst Justus Haeberlin, sein Wirken. München, 1929. 2v.
Arc 612.25 Hahne, Hans. Totenehre im alten Norden. Jena, 1929.
Arc 1510.35 Hamburger, L. Sammlung Pfalzischer. Frankfurt am Main, 1929.
Arc 858.53 Harris, James R. Caravan essays. no.1-12. Cambridge, 1929.
Arc 505.39A Jack, J.M. Samaria in Ahab's time. Edinburgh, 1929.
Arc 746.11F Jacobsthal, Paul. Die Bronzeschnabelkannen. Berlin, 1929.
Arc 684.9 John Hopkins University. Excavations at Olynthus. Baltimore, 1929-52. 14v.
Arc 600.18.15F Junker, H. Gîza. Leipzig, 1929-38. 3v.
Arc 1588.4.45.5 Katz, Viktor. Tisíc let české vládní mince (929-1929). Praha, 1929.
Arc 853.31.10 Knack, H. Die Latènekulter in Thüringen. Inaug. Diss. Stettin, 1929?
Arc 746.11.10F Langsdorff, A. Die Grabfunde mit Bronzeschnabelkannen. Inaug. Diss. Berlin, 1929.
Arc 830.53.25 Le Pontois, B. Le Finistère préhistorique. Paris, 1929.
Arc 1138.32 Löffler, Karl. Einführung in die Handschriftenkunde. Leipzig, 1929.
Arc 588.47F MacKay, Ernest. Bahrein and Hemamieh. London, 1929.
Arc 397.16 Magoffin, Rolf V.D. Magic spades. N.Y., 1929.
Arc 810.42F Maiuri, Amedeo. Pompeii. Roma, 1929.
Arc 736.1.9F Marconi, Pirro. Agrigento. Firenze, 1929.
Arc 540.4 Marti, I.I. Raskopki goradishcha kiteia v 1928 g. Simferopol, 1929.
Arc 1025.28.45 Marucchi, O. The evidencce of the catacombs for the doctrines and organization of the primitive church. London, 1929.
Arc 726.63 Miceli, Salvatore. Vicovaro e la villa di Q. Orazio Flacco. Roma, 1929.
Arc 1163.2.25 Millares Carlo, A. Paleografía española. Barcelona, 1929. 2v.
Arc 700.10.15F Moebius, Hans. Die Ornamente der griechischen Grabstelen. Berlin, 1929.
Arc 785.67F Munoz, A. I templi della Zona Argentina. Roma, 1929.
Arc 684.9.5 Mylonas, George E. The neolithic settlement at Olynthus. Baltimore, 1929.
Arc 435.55.2F Mysore. Archaeological Survey. Index to the annual reports of the Mysore Archaeological Department for the years 1906-1922. Bangalore, 1929.
Arc 530.12.10 Osten, H.H. von der. Explorations in Hittite Asia Minor, 1927-28. Chicago, 1929.
Arc 770.4.10 Platner, S.B. A topographical dictionary of ancient Rome. London, 1929.
Arc 968.2.30 Roberts, Frank H.H. Shabik'eschee village. Washington, 1929.
Arc 925.13.55 Rostovtsev, M.I. The animal style in south Russia and China. Princeton, 1929.
Arc 1411.10F Schjöth, F. The currency of the Far East. London, 1929.
Arc 1588.4 Skalsky, G. Denár knizete Vaclava Svatého a. Praha, 1929.
Arc 403.12.2 Société Préhistorique de France. Manuel de recherches préhistoriques. 2. éd. Paris, 1929.
Arc 1318.3.6 Société Suisse de Numismatique. Regiser zu Bulletin, v.1-11; Revue suisse de numismatique, v.1-24. Bern, 1929.
Arc 1163.15 Spehr, Harald. Der Ursprung der isländischen Schrift und ihre Weiterbildung bis zur Mitte des 13. Jahrhunderts. Inaug. Diss. Halle, 1929.
Arc 853.260 Sprater, Friedrich. Die Pfalz unter den Römern. Speier, 1929-30. 2v.
Arc 458.8A Stein, Mark A. On Alexander's track to the Indus. London, 1929.
Arc 421.6 Stockholm. Astasiatiska bulletin. v.1-30,35-42. Stockholm, 1929-58.

1929 - cont.

Arc 936.195.270 Stocký, Albin. La Bohême préhistorique. Prague, 1929.
Arc 848.17 Teudt, Wilhelm. Germanische Heiligtümer. Jena, 1929.
Arc 710.16 Thibaudet, A. L'acropole. Paris, 1929.
Arc 404.1.30 Thompson, Alexander Hamilton. A bibliography of the published writings of Sir William St. John Hope. Leeds, 1929.
Arc 746.9.15 Ulisse (pseud.). Figure mitologiche degli specchi "Etruschi". pt.1-7. Roma, 1929-37.
Arc 830.130.30 Veelter, Daniel. Glozel, und die Einwanderung von Semiten im heutigen französischen Departement. Strassburg, 1929.
Arc 1153.61 Venturini, T. Ricerche paleografiche intorno all'arcidiacono pacifico di Verona. Verona, 1929.
Arc 710.15A Walter, Otto. Athen, Akropolis. Wien, 1929.
Arc 885.8.5 Wheeler, R.E.M. Wales and archaeology. London, 1929.
Arc 1550.9 Wilcke, Julius. Specie. Kjøbenhavn, 1929.
Arc 1185.22 Zatschek, Heinz. Studien zur mittelterlicher Urkundenlehre. Brünn, 1929.
Arc 1033.34.43 Zwölger, Theodor. Die Verehrung des Heiligen Petrus bei den Franken und Angelsachsen. Inaug. Diss. Stuttgart, 1929.

193-

Arc 1027.18.20 Frey, J.B. Nouvelles inscriptions inedites de la cata-combe juive de la via Appia. n.p., 193-.

1930

Arc 505.5.100F Adler, Cyrus. Memorandum on the Western Wall. Jerusalem, 1930.
Arc 925.55 Akademiia Nauk URSR, Kyïv. Khronyka arkheolohyi ta mystetstva. Kyïv, 1930.
Arc 1076.3.99 Andrews, H.C. A Hertfordshire worthy, John Briant. St. Albans, 1930.
Arc 726.87 Antonielli, U. La prima nave imperiale del lago di Nemi. Roma, 1930.
Arc 73.20.15F Archäologisches Institut des Deutschen Reichs. Funfundzwanzig Jahre Römisch-Germanische Kommission. Römische-germanische Kommission. Berlin, 1930.
Arc 1458.21.5 Ars Classica, Geneva. Monnaies antiques grecques, romaines, byzantines. Genève, 1930.
Arc 830.49.25 Barrière, P. Vesunna Petrucoriorum. Périgueux, 1930.
Arc 848.40 Behn, Friedrich. Altgermanische Kunst. 2. Aufl. München, 1930.
Arc 1453.2F Bellinger, A.R. Catalogue of the coins found at Corinth, 1925. New Haven, 1930.
Arc 1027.18.15 Beyer, Hermann W. Die jüdische Katakombe der Villa Torlonia in Rom. Berlin, 1930.
Arc 888.35 Boeles, P.C.J.A. De aldste kultuer yn de sânen feankriten fen Fryslân. Boalsert, 1930.
Arc 600.95 Breccia, E. Nuovi scari nelle necropoli di Hadra. Alexandria, 1930.
Arc 590.10.5 Breccia, E. La tomba di Alessandro Magno. Alexandria, 1930.
Arc 1053.21F Bréhier, L. Les visions apocalyptiques dans l'art byzantin. Bucarest, 1930?
Arc 785.63 Broderick, B.F. The so-called Altar of Calvinus on the Palatine hill, in Rome. N.Y., 1930. 3 pam.
Arc 672.1.57A Burn, A.R. Minoans, Philistines, and Greeks, B.C. 1400-900. N.Y., 1930.
Arc 66.1.134.5 Cahen, Emile. Les hymes de Callimaque. Paris, 1930.
Arc 387.9 Childe, Vere Gordon. Bronze age. Cambridge, Eng., 1930.
Arc 858.42 Collingwood, Robin George. The archaeology of Roman Britain. N.Y., 1930.
Arc 810.40.10 Corte, Matteo della. Pompei; i nuovi scavi e l'anfiteatro. Pompei, 1930.
Arc 936.205.5 Čremošnik, Gregor. Nalazi iz rimskog doba na stupu kod. Sarajeva. Sarajevo, 1930.
Arc 340.2.7 Deutsches Archäologisches Institut. Römische Abteilung. Bibliothek. Katalog der Bibliothek. Supplement. Berlin, 1930.
Arc 608.16.10 Douël, M. L'Algérie romaine; forums et basiliques. Paris, 1930.
Arc 588.49F Duncan, J.G. Corpus of dated Palestinian pottery. London, 1930.
Arc 513.17.15 Dussaud, René. La Lydie et ses voisins aus hautes époques. Paris, 1930.
Arc 543.5.15 École Française d'Extrême-Orient, Hanoi, Indo-China. L'École française d'Extrême Orient. Hanoi, 1930.
Arc 543.7.19F École Française d'Extrême-Orient, Hanoi, Indo-China. Le temple d'Angkor Vat. pt.2. Paris, 1930. 2v.
Arc 861.21.19 Elgee, Frank. Early man in north east Yorkshire. Gloucester, 1930.
Arc 793.12 Ellaby, Christopher G. Pompeii and Herculaneum. London, 1930.
Arc 1020.129F Falke, Otto von. Der Welfenschatz. Frankfurt, 1930.
Arc 66.1.135 Fawtier, Robert. Sainte Catherine de Sienne. Paris, 1930.
Arc 1470.4.5F Gallatin, A.E. Syracusan dekadrachmas. Cambridge, 1930.
Arc 853.108 Geidel, H. Münchens Vorzeit. München, 1930.
Arc 646.4 Gennadios, I. O Lordoz Elgin. Athēnai, 1930.
Arc 1443.4 Giesecke, Walther. Das Ptalemäergeld. Leipzig, 1930.
Arc 889.5 Giffen, Albert Egges van. Die Bauart der Einzelgräber. Text and atlas. Leipzig, 1930. 2v.
Arc 421.5 Godfrey, E.F. Die Kaiserspräher der Tsing Dynastie in China. Berlin, 1930.
Arc 673.1.17 Graindor, P. Delphes et son oracle. Le Caire, 1930.
Arc 1675.70 Günzburger, Julius. Medaillen badischer Klöster. Nürnberg, 1930.
Arc 482.202.5F Herzfeld, Ernst E. Die vorgeschichtlichen Töpfereien von Samarra. Berlin, 1930.
Arc 853.73 Hofmeister, Hans. Die Chalten. Frankfurt am Main, 1930.
Arc 421.9F Houo-Ming-Tse, P. Preuves des antiquités. Pekin, 1930.
Arc 885.11 Hughes, I.T. Out of the dark. Wrexham, 1930.
Arc 520.18 Humann, K. Der Entdecker von Pergamon. Berlin, 1930.
Arc 307.3.10 International Congress of Americanists, 24th, Hamburg, 1930. Internationale Amerikanisten Kongress. Vorläufiges Program. n.p., 1930.
Arc 93.27 International Mediterranean Research Association. The International Mediterranean Research Association of Rome, Villa Celeniontana. Roma, 1930.
Arc 30.12.10 Iranian Institute of America. Announcement and outline of program. N.Y., 1930.
Arc 1018.46 Jerphanion, G. de. La voix des monuments. Paris, 1930.
Arc 861.89 Jessup, Ronald F. Archaeology of Kent. London, 1930.
Arc 823.25 Jullian, C. Au seuil de notre histoire. Paris, 1930-1931. 3v.

1930 - cont.

Arc 848.21 Kadig, Werner. Der Wohnbau im jungsteinzeitlichen Deutschland. pt.1-2. Inaug. Diss. Leipzig, 1930.
Arc 936.100.15 Karaman, L. Iz kdijerke hrvatsbe prostosti. Zagreb, 1930.
Arc 682.12F Karo, Georg. Die Schachtgräber von Mykenai. Text and plates. München, 1930-33. 2v.
Arc 861.10.15 Kinnebrook, William. List of Manx antiquities. Douglas, 1930.
Arc 482.205F Lamm, C.J. Mittelalterliche Gläser und Steinschnittarbeiten aus dem Nahen Osten. Berlin, 1930. 2v.
Arc 609.3F Lebzelter, Viktor. Die Vorgeschichte von Süd- und Südwestafrica. Leipzig, 1930-34. 2v.
Arc 830.11.7 Le Rouzic, Z. Carnac; restaurations faites dans la région. Vannes, 1930.
Arc 853.20.27 Loeschcke, S. Bedeutung und Gefährdung der grossen Tempelgrabung in Trier. Trier, 1930.
Arc 766.4.5 Lugli, Giuseppe. I monumenti antichi di Roma e suburbio. Roma, 1930-40. 4v.
Arc 397.12 Magoffin, Rolf V.D. Romance of archaeology. London, 1930.
Arc 785.68 Marchetti-Longhi, G. L'"area sacra" ed i templi repubblicani del Largo Argentina. Roma, 1930.
Arc 785.55 Martinori, E. Via Cassia. Roma, 1930.
Arc 843.73.5F Mélida, José R. El disco de Teodosio. Madrid, 1930.
Arc 687.2 Montesanto, M. La città sacra (Lindo). Roma, 1930.
Arc 672.5.10 O'Neill, J.G. Ancient Corinth. Photoreproduction. Baltimore, 1930.
Arc 785.13.65 Owen, A.S. Excerpta ex antiquis scriptoribus quae ad Forum Romanum spectant. Oxonii, 1930.
Arc 785.13.205 Paribeni, R. I fori imperiali. Roma, 1930.
Arc 726.24.15 Paribeni, R. The villa of the emperor Hadrian at Tivoli. Milan, 1930?
Arc 565.3 Pendlebury, J.D.S. Aegyptiaca. Cambridge, Eng., 1930.
Arc 588.51F Petrie, W.M.F. Antaeopolis. London, 1930.
Arc 588.48F Petrie, W.M.F. Beth-Pelet. London, 1930-32. 2v.
Arc 785.56 Pickett, Cora Aileen. Temple of Quirinus. Thesis. Philadelphia, 1930.
Arc 853.27.5 Prein, Otto. Aliso bei Oberaden und Vernusschlacht. Münster, 1930.
Arc 609.1.25 Rhodesia (Southern). Bureau of Publicity. The great Zimbabwe ruins. Bulawayo, 1930.
Arc 1663.16.5F Ricciardi, E. Medaglie del Regno delle due Sicilie 1735-1861. 2. ed. Napoli, 1930.
Arc 785.29.10 Richmond, Ian A. The city wall of imperial Rome. Oxford, 1930.
Arc 957.1.25 Roberts, Frank H.H. Early pueblo in the Piedra district. Washington, 1930.
Arc 497.28A Robinson, George L. The sarcophagus of an ancient civilization. N.Y., 1930.
Arc 710.14F Rodenwaldt, Gerhart. Die Akropolis. Berlin, 1930.
Arc 402.14 Sammarco, Angelo. Alessandro Ricci e il suo giornale dei viaggi. v.2. Cairo, 1930.
Arc 1190.55 Santifaller, Leo. Bozner Schreibschriften der Neuzeit. Jena, 1930.
Arc 746.12 Sauer, Hertha. Die archaischen etruskischen Terracottasarkophage aus Caere. Diss. Rendsburg, 1930.
Arc 853.75F Schmidt, R.R. Jungsteinzeit-Siedlungen im Federseemoor. Augsburg, 1930-37.
Arc 196.2 Schoenenberg, J. Festschrift zum 50 Jährigen Jubiläum des Lahnsteiner Altertumsvereins. Oberlahnstein, 1930.
Arc 1340.8 Schrotter, F. Wörterbuch der Münzkunde. Berlin, 1930.
Arc 403.13F Schumacher-Festschrift. Mainz, 1930.
Arc 1480.28F Strack, Paul L. Untersuchungen zur Geschichte der Kaiser Nerva, Traian und Hadrian. Inaug. Diss. Stuttgart, 1930.
Arc 1490.31 Strada, M. La zecca di Milano e le sue monete. Milano, 1930.
Arc 543.35 Stutterheim, W.F. Oudheden van Bali I. Singaradja, 1930.
Arc 1190.70 Szentpetery, Imre. Magyar oklevéltan. Budapest, 1930.
Arc 1163.17.15A Tannenbaum, S.A. The handwriting of the Renaissance. N.Y., 1930.
Arc 392.9.80 Thompson, R.C. Harry R.H. Hall, 1873-1930. London, 1930.
Arc 1413.3 Tsukamoto, Toyojino. The old and new coins of Japan. Tokyo, 1930.
Arc 522.19 Vellay, Charles. Les nouveaux aspects de la question de Troie. Paris, 1930.
Arc 522.19.2 Vellay, Charles. Les nouveaux aspects de la question de Troie. Paris, 1930.
Arc 1153.61.5 Venturini, M. Vita ed attività dello "Scriptorium" veronese nel secolo XI. Verona, 1930.
Arc 861.7.5 Vulliamy, Colwyn E. The archaeology of Middlesex and London. London, 1930.
Arc 810.45 Warsher, Tatiana. Pompeii in three hours. Rome, 1930.
Arc 861.88 Watkins, Alfred. The old standing crosses of Herefordshire. London, 1930.
Arc 608.17.13 Wilamowitz-Moellendorff, U. Cirene. Bergamo, 1930.
Arc 1550.5 Wilcke, Julius. Sølo-og guldmøntfod. Kjøbenhavn, 1930.
Arc 1025.65 Wilpert, Josef. Erlebnisse und Ergebnisse im Dienste der christlichen Archäologie. Freiburg, 1930.
Arc 861.41.10 Winbolt, S.E. The Roman villa at Bignor, Sussex. Oxford, 1930.
Arc 726.59 Zammit, Themistocles. Prehistoric Malta; the Tarxien temples. London, 1930.

1931

Arc 895.32 Åberg, Nils. Nordische Ornamentik in vorgeschichtlicher Zeit. Leipzig, 1931.
Arc 446.12 Abid Ali Khan, M. Memoirs of Gaur and Pandua. Calcutta, 1931.
Arc 543.7.21F Angkor. Paris, 1931.
Arc 609.2.7F Azaïs, R.P. Cinq années de recherches archéologiques en Ethiopie. Paris, 1931. 2v.
Arc 441.1.7 Barua, B.M. Gaya and Buddha-Gaya. Calcutta, 1931-34. 2v.
Arc 843.64 Biscay, Sain. Disputación Provincial. Junta de Cultura. Exploraciones de la caverna de Santimamiñe. Basondo: Cortezubi. Memoria 2-3. Bilbao, 1931-35. 2v.
Arc 823.10.15 Blanchet, A. Carte archéologique de la Gaule romaine. pts.1-3,5-8,10-11,14. Paris, 1931- 10v.
Arc 687.1F Blinkenberg, C. Lindos; fouilles et recherches, 1902-1914. Berlin, 1931. 4v.
Arc 600.36 Boak, A.E.R. Karanis. Ann Arbor, 1931.
Arc 843.8.5F Bonson, J.E. The archaeological expedition along the Guadalquivir, 1889-1901. N.Y., 1931. 2v.
Arc 843.19.15FA Bonson, J.E. An archaeological sketch-book of the Roman necropolis at Carmona. N.Y., 1931.

Chronological Listing

1931 - cont.

Arc 968.2.23 Bradfield, W. Cameron Creek village...New Mexico. Santa Fé, 1931.
Arc 1148.22 Breccia, E. Note epigrafiche. Alexandria, 1931.
Arc 547.24.15 Breccia, E. Sculture inedite del Museo Greco-Romano. Alexandrie, 1931.
Arc 600.1.17 Breccia, E. Una statuetta del Buon Pastore da Marsa Matruh. Alexandria, 1931.
Arc 1468.28F British Academy. Sylloge nummorum Graecorum. London, 1931-51. 4v.
Arc 936.50.5 Bulić, France. Povodom pedestgod jubileja "Vjesnika za arh. hist. Dalmatinsku". Split, 1931.
Arc 1335.59.10 Cahn, A.E. Versteigerungskatalog nr. 71. v.2. Frankfurt am Main, 1931.
Arc 1418.11 Chakrabortty, S.K. A study of ancient Indian numismatics. Calcutta, 1931.
Arc 672.1.29.5 Chatzidakēs, I. Istoria tou Krētikou Monseiou kai tōn archaiologikōn ereynōn en Krēte. Athēnai, 1931.
Arc 875.14.10 Childe, V.G. Skara Brae. London, 1931.
Arc 1138.33 Collomp, Paul. La critique des textes. Paris, 1931.
Arc 630.9 Cook, Arthur B. Rise and progress of classical archaeology. Cambridge, Eng., 1931.
Arc 505.100 Damascus. Musée National Syrien. Etat de Syree. Damas, 1931.
Arc 848.37 Diekmann, H. Steinzeitseidlungen im Teutoburger Walde. Bielefeld, 1931.
Arc 861.38.9 Dobson, Dina P. The archaeology of Somerset. London, 1931.
Arc 497.31 Duncan, J.G. Digging up Biblical history. N.Y., 1931- 2v.
Arc 390.5 Elliger, W. Forschungen zur Kirchengeschichte...Johannes Ficker als Festgabe. Leipzig, 1931.
Arc 848.14.35 Espérandieu, Émile. Recueil général des bas-reliefs. Paris, 1931.
Arc 861.97 Fieldhouse, William J. A Romano-British industrial settlement near Tiddington, Stratford-upon-Avon. Birmingham, 1931.
Arc 672.1.59 Forsdyke, E.J. Minoan art. London, 1931.
Arc 1510.105F Friedensburg, F. Die schlesischen Münzen des Mittelalters. Breslau, 1931.
Arc 853.65 Geschwendt, F. Die steinurnen Streitäxte und Keulen Schlesiens. Inaug. Diss. Breslau, 1931.
Arc 674.15F Goldman, Hetty. Excavations at Eutresis in Boeotia. Cambridge, Mass., 1931.
Arc 858.24.17 Great Britain. Commissions. Ancient and Historical Monuments and Constructions of England. An inventory of the historical monuments in Herefordshire. London, 1931-34. 3v.
Arc 823.11.9 Grenier, Albert. Manuel d'archéologie gallo-romaine. v.1-4. Paris, 1931-1934. 6v.
Arc 853.66 Grimm, Paul. Die vor- und frühgeschichtliche Besiedlung des Unterharzes und seines Vorlandes auf Grund der Bodenfunde. Inaug. Diss. Halle an der Saale, 1931.
Arc 830.13.10 Grube, G. Die Attika an römischen Triumphbogen...Bogens von Orange. Karlsruhe-Baden, 1931.
Arc 1020.119.5 Gudiol y Cunill, J. Nocions d'arqueologia sagrada catalana. 2a ed. Vich, 1931-33. 2v.
Arc 1077.2.47 Guénon, René. Le symbolisme de la croix. Paris, 1931.
Arc 955.2.12 Guernsey, S.J. Explorations in northeastern Arizona. Cambridge, Mass., 1931.
Arc 1020.134F Das hallesche Heiltum. Berlin, 1931.
Arc 543.4.17 Herrmann, A. Lou-lan. Leipzig, 1931.
VArc 682.25.17 Ivanov, Iordan. Bulgarski starini iz Makedoniia. 2. izd. Sofiia, 1931.
Arc 303.25 Kongress Baltischer Archäologen, 2d, Riga, 1930. Congressus secundus archaeologorum balticorum. Riga, 1931.
Arc 853.62.7 Kunkel, Otto. Pommersche Urgeschichte in Bildern. Stettin, 1931. 2v.
Arc 672.1.52F Kunze, Emil. Kretische Bonzereliefs. Text and plates. Stuttgart, 1931. 2v.
Arc 435.2.51F Ḳuraishi, M.M.Ḥ. List of ancient monuments protected in Bihar and Orissa. Calcutta, 1931.
Arc 830.11.9.10 Le Rouzic, Z. Carnac; fouilles faites dans la région. Campagne 1922. Paris, 1931.
Arc 830.11.8 Le Rouzic, Z. Carnac; menhirs, statues. Nantes, 1931.
Arc 830.3.20 Lizop, Raymond. Le Comminges et le Censeraus avant la domination romaine. Thèse. Toulouse, 1931.
Arc 830.3.15 Lizop, Raymond. Les convenae et les consoranni. Thèse. Toulouse, 1931.
Arc 861.102F Longhurst, M.H. The Easby cross. Oxford, 1931.
Arc 658.3.16 Ludwig, Emil. Schliemann. Boston, 1931.
Arc 658.3.17 Ludwig, Emil. Schliemann of Troy. London, 1931.
Arc 858.45 Macdonald, George. Roman Britain, 1914-1928. London, 1931.
Htn Arc 815.13.15F* Maiuri, Amedeo. La villa dei misteri. Roma, 1931.
Htn Arc 815.13.15PF* Maiuri, Amedeo. La villa dei misteri. Plates. Roma, 1931.
Arc 736.11 Marconi, P. Himera; lo scavo del Tempio della Vittoria e del temenos. Roma, 1931.
Arc 726.77F Marescalchi, A. Storia della vite e del vino in Italia. Milano, 1931-37. 3v.
Arc 452.1F Marshall, John. Mohenjo-daro and the Indus civilization. London, 1931. 3v.
Arc 853.63.7 Matthes, W. Die Germanen in der Prignitz zur Zeit der Völkerwanderung. Leipzig, 1931.
Arc 853.63 Matthes, W. Die nördlichen Elbgermanen in spätrömischer Zeit. Leipzig, 1931.
Arc 595.26 Meier-Graefe, J. Pyramid and temple. London, 1931.
Arc 1093.2.15 Menghin, O. Weltgeschichte der Steinzeit. Wien, 1931.
Arc 1163.2.32 Millares Carlo, A. Contribución al "corpus" de códices visigoticos. Madrid, 1931.
Arc 1468.27 Milne, Joseph G. Greek coinage. Oxford, 1931.
Arc 505.5.75 Möblenbrinck, K. Studien zum Salomonischen Tempel. Inaug. Diss. Stuttgart, 1931.
Arc 967.5 Moorehead, W.K. The Merrimack archaeological survey. Salem, Mass., 1931.
Arc 975.1 Morss, Noel. The ancient culture of the Fremont River in Utah. Cambridge, Mass., 1931.
Arc 600.37A Murray, M.A. Egyptian temples. London, 1931.
Arc 875.65 Ogston, Alexander. The prehistoric antiquities of the Howe of Cromar. Aberdeen, 1931.
Arc 1538.17 Oman, C.W.C. The coinage of England. Oxford, 1931.
Arc 861.91 Peake, Harold. The archaeology of Berkshire. London, 1931.
Arc 400.11.10 Peake, Harold J.E. Merchant venturers in bronze. New Haven, 1931.
Arc 682.13F Persson, A.W. The royal tombs at Dendra near Midea. Lund, 1931.
Arc 588.53F Petrie, W.M.F. Ancient Gaza. London, 1931-34. 4v.
Arc 565.1.5 Petrie, W.M.F. Seventy years in archaeology. London, 1931.
Arc 400.21 Pick, Behrendt. Aufsätze zur Numismatik und Archäologie. Jena, 1931.
Arc 880.37A Porter, Arthur Kingsley. The crosses and culture of Ireland. New Haven, 1931.
Arc 401.2.5 Quennell, Marjorie (Courtney). Everyday life in the new stone, bronze, and early iron ages. 2. ed. London, 1931.
Arc 1153.44.25 Rand, Edward K. A preliminary study of Alcuin's Bible. Cambridge, 1931.
Arc 595.23FA Reisner, G.A. Mycerinus; the temples of the third pyramid at Giza. Cambridge, 1931.
Arc 600.35.5 Roeder, Günther. Vorläufiger Bericht über die Ausgrabungen in Hermopolis 1929-30. Augsburg, 1931.
Arc 925.13.12 Rostovtsev, M.I. Skythien und der Bosporus. Berlin, 1931.
Arc 1510.26 Schwinkowski, Walter. Münz- und Geldgeschichte der Mark Meissen und Münzen. Frankfurt am Main, 1931.
Arc 773.6F Shipley, F.W. Chronology of the building operations in Rome from the death of Caesar. n.p., 1931.
Arc 689.3.20F Soteriou, G.A. Ai Christianikai Thebai tēs Thessalias kai at palaiochristianikai basilikai tēs Ellados. Athēnai, 1931.
Arc 1675.17.10 Storer, H.R. Medicina in nummis. Boston, 1931.
Arc 1478.28F Strack, Paul L. Untersuchungen zur römischen Reichsprägung des zweiten Jahrhunderts. Stuttgart, 1931-37. 3v.
Arc 858.44 Sumner, H. Local papers. London, 1931.
Arc 390.4 Swanton, J.R. Jesse Walter Fewkes. Washington, 1931.
Arc 853.13.30F Veeck, Walther. Die Alamannen in Württemberg. Berlin, 1931. 2v.
Arc 522.19.5 Vellay, Charles. La question de Troie. Chartres, 1931. 4 pam.
Arc 1018.47 Von der Antike zum Christentum. Stettin, 1931.
Arc 861.23.9 Whimster, D.C. The archaeology of Surrey. London, 1931.
Arc 1453.7 Wilcke, Julius. Daler. Kjøbenhavn, 1931.
Arc 1423.13.5 Wruck, W. Die Syrische Provinzialprägung von Augustus. Stuttgart, 1931.
Arc 1423.13 Wruck, W. Die Syrische Provinzialprägung von Augustus bis Klaudius. Inaug. Diss. Stuttgart, 1931.
Arc 545.227.42F Zippert, Erwin. Der Gedächtnistempel Sethos' Izu Abydos. Berlin, 1931.

1932

Arc 1027.90 Achelis, H. Römische Katakombenbilder in Catania. Berlin, 1932.
Arc 497.30 Albright, William Foxwell. The archaeology of Palestine and the Bible. N.Y., 1932.
Arc 547.24.10F Alexandria. Musée Gréco-Romain. Le Musée Gréco-Romain, 1925-1931. Bergamo, 1932.
Arc 30.12.5 American Institute of Persian Art and Archaeology. What it is, etc. N.Y., 1932.
Arc 853.64 Andree, Julius. Beiträge zur Kenntnis des norddeutschen Paläolithikums und Mesolithikums. Leipzig, 1932.
Arc 551.6 Baikie, James. Egyptian antiquities in the Nile Valley. London, 1932.
Arc 785.57 Bologna. Università. Per un centro di studi di archeologia dell'Impero Romano. Bologna, 1932.
Arc 595.51 Borchardt, Ludwig. Einiges zur dritten Bauperiode der grossen Pyramide bei Gise. Berlin, 1932.
Arc 689.6 Braun, I. De theraeorum rebus sacris. Inaug. Diss. Halis Saxonum, 1932.
Arc 1468.2.10 British Museum. Department of Coins and Medals. A guide to the principal coins of Greeks from circa 700 B.C. to A.D. 270. London, 1932.
Arc 1538.18 Brooke, George C. English coins from the seventh century to the present day. London, 1932.
Arc 870.14.15 Brown, Paul. The great wall of Hadrian in Roman times. London, 1932.
Arc 830.161 Casimir, Philippe. Le trophée d'Auguste a la Turbie. Marseille, 1932.
Arc 628.25F Corolla archaeologica principi hereditario regni sueciae Gustavo Adolpho dedicata. Lund, 1932.
Arc 968.2.25 Cosgrove, H.S. The Swarts ruin...New Mexico. Cambridge, 1932.
Arc 66.1.136 Demangel, R. La frise ionique. Paris, 1932.
Arc 585.40F Egypt Exploration Society. Studies presented to F.L. Griffith. London, 1932.
Arc 1153.24.2F Ehrle, Franz. Specimina codicum latinorum Vaticanorum. Berolini, 1932.
Arc 1360.4 Farkas, Sandor. Antik érmészet. Aiud, 1932.
Arc 421.4.10 Ferguson, J.C. Two bronze drums. Peking, 1932.
Arc 1033.12.243 Gogan, L.S. The Ardagh chalice. Dublin, 1932.
Arc 600.46F Hassan, S. Excavations at Giza, 1929-1930. v.1-10. Oxford, 1932. 13v.
Arc 861.5.15 Hencken, H.O. The archaeology of Cornwall and Scilly. London, 1932.
Arc 830.138 Henry, Françoise. Les tumulus du département de la Côte-d'Or. Thèse. Paris, 1932.
Arc 488.21F Herzfeld, Ernst E. Iranische Denkmäler. v.1-4. Berlin, 1932-
Arc 853.8.10 Hofmeister, H. Urholstein. Glückstadt, 1932.
Arc 1588.12 Horvath, Henrik. A Budai penzverde muveszett orterenete a kesoi kozepkorban. Budapest, 1932.
Arc 1223.3 Hsiang, Huai-shu. Recueil de cachets sur la Montagne jeune. Saigon, 1932?
Arc 853.24.9 Hülle, Werner. Grundzüge der vorrömischen Besiedelung Bayerns. Inaug. Diss. Augsburg, 1932.
Arc 505.49F Iukenik, Eleazar L. The ancient synagogue of Beth Alpha. Jeruselem, 1932.
Arc 505.45.5 Johnson, J. Dura studies. Philadelphia, 1932.
Arc 1675.85 Katz, Viktor. Die erzgebirgische Prägmedaille des XVI. Jahrhundert. Praha, 1932.
Arc 858.46 Kendrick, T.D. Archaeology in England and Wales, 1914-1931. London, 1932.
Arc 968.2.50 Kidder, Alfred V. The artifacts of Pecas. New Haven, 1932.
Arc 595.27 Kingsland, William. The Great Pyramid in fact and in theory. London, 1932-35. 2v.
Arc 848.8.11 Kossinna, Gustaf. Germanische Kultur im letzten Jahrtausend nach Christus. Leipzig, 1932.
Arc 674.1.9F Kourouniotos, K. Eleusiniaka. Athēnai, 1932.
Arc 785.102 Kristensen, W.B. De Romeinsche fascas. Amsterdam, 1932.

1932 - cont.

Arc 180.1.25 Largiader, Anton. Hundert Jahre Antiquarische Gesellschaft in Zürich, 1832-1932. Zürich, 1932.
X Cg Arc 743.17 Lawrence, D.H. Etruscan places. London, 1932.
Arc 1433.50 Le May, R.S. The coinage of Siam. Bangkok, 1932.
Arc 830.11.9.5 Le Rouzic, Z. Carnac. Vannes, 1932.
Arc 858.48 London Museum. Catalogue of an exhibition of recent archaeological discoveries in Great Britain. London, 1932.
Arc 830.101.7 Louis, Maurice. Le néolithique dans le Gard. Thèse. Nîmes, 1932.
Arc 396.9.5 Lucas, A. Antiques, their restoration and preservation. 2. ed. London, 1932.
Arc 658.3.14 Ludwig, Emil. Schliemann. Berlin, 1932.
Arc 658.3.15A Ludwig, Emil. Schliemann. Boston, 1932.
Arc 963.3 McAllister, J.G. The archaeology of Porter County, Indiana. Indianapolis, 1932.
Arc 858.49 Macdonald, George. Agricola in Britain. London, 1932.
Arc 843.155 Madrid. Museo Archeologica. Catáloga de las antigüedades que se conservan en el Patio Arabe. Madrid, 1932.
Arc 800.9F Maiuri, Amedeo. Ercolano. Roma, 1932.
Arc 600.49 Menghin, O. The excavations of the Egyptian university in the neolithic site at Maadi. Cairo, 1932.
Arc 1200.23 Menzer, Anne. Die Jahresmerkmale in den Datierungen der Papsturkunden bis zum Ausgang des 11. Jahrhundert. Inaug. Diss. Berlin, 1932.
Arc 1093.8 Müfid, Arif. Katalog der Bleisarkophage. Istanbul, 1932.
Arc 843.2.5 Murray, M.A. Cambridge evcavations in Minorca. London, 1932- 2v.
Arc 785.34.13 Paribeni, R. Ara Pacis Augustae. Roma, 1932.
Arc 565.1.6A Petrie, W.M.F. Seventy years in archaeology. N.Y., 1932.
Arc 853.70 Piesker, Hans. Vorneolithische Kulturen der südlichen Lüneburger Heide. Inaug. Diss. Hildesheim, 1932.
Arc 726.93F Price, F. A restoration of "Horace's Sabine Villa". n.p., 1932.
Arc 543.79 Rathjens, Carl. Vorislamische Altertümer. Hamburg, 1932.
Arc 977.2 Renaud, E.B. Archaeological survey of eastern Wyoming, summer 1931. Denver, 1932.
Arc 968.2.32 Roberts, Frank H.H. The village of the great Kivas on the Zuñi reservation, New Mexico. Washington, 1932.
Arc 1478.29 Robinson, A.E. False and imitation Roman coins. n.p., 1932.
Arc 600.35.10 Roeder, Günther. Vorläufiger Bericht über die detsche Hermopolis-Expedition, 1931-32. Augsburg, 1932.
Arc 1033.3.47 Roosval, J. Junius Bassus sarkofag och dess datering. Stockholm, 1932.
Arc 1033.3.46 Roosval, J. Petrus- och Moses-gruppen bland Roms sarkofagy. Stockholm, 1932.
Arc 785.29.15F Säflund, G. Le mura di Roma republicana. Uppsala, 1932.
Arc 682.25.40 Skeat, T.C. The Dorians in archaeology. London, 1932?
Arc 520.15A Stier, Hans Erich. Aus der Welt des Pergamonaltars. Berlin, 1932.
Arc 440.3 Subramanian, K. Buddhist remains in Andhra. Madras, 1932.
Arc 895.40 Swenska Farnminnesföreningen. Arkeologiska studier tillägnade H.K.H. kronprins Gustaf Adrolf. Stockholm, 1932.
Arc 1254.15 Taurent, Vitalieu. Les bulles métriques dans la sigillographie byzantine. Eetjia, 1932.
Arc 386.22 Tea, Eva. Giacomo Boni nella vita del suo tempo. Milano, 1932. 2v.
Arc 1020.120.15 Telfer, William. The treasure of São Roque. London, 1932.
Arc 543.40F Thomassen à Thuessink van der Hoop, A.N.J. Megalithische oudheden in Zuid-Sumatra. Proefschrift. Zutphen, 1932.
Arc 1153.53 Ullmann, B.L. Ancient writing and its influence. N.Y., 1932.
Arc 1163.3.17 Vajs, Josef. Rukovět hlaholské paleografie. Praha, 1932.
Arc 441.4 Vakil, K.H. Rock-cut temples around Bombay. Bombay, 1932.
Arc 608.17.15 Vitali, L. Fonti per la storia della religione cyrenaica. Padova, 1932.
Arc 848.23 Wahle, Ernst. Deutsche Vorzeit. Leipzig, 1932.
Arc 861.16.10 Watkins, A. Archaic tracks round Cambridge. London, 1932.
Arc 505.2.5F Wiegand, T. Palmyra; Ergebnisse der Expeditionen von 1902 und 1917. Text and plates. Berlin, 1932. 2v.

1933

Arc 612.21.7F Åberg, Nils. Bronzezeitliche und früheisenzeitliche Chronologie. v.4-5. Stockholm, 1933-35. 2v.
Arc 340.5.3 American Academy in Rome. Library. A bibliographical guide to Latium and southern Eturia. 3. ed. Rome, 1933.
Arc 1458.21 Ars Classica, Geneva. Monnaies antiques grecques et romaines. Genève, 1933.
Arc 1025.69 Bakhuizen van den Brink, J.N. De romeinsche catacomben en haar frescos. 's-Gravenhage, 1933.
Arc 457.5 Banerji, R.D. The age of the imperial Guptas. Banares, 1933.
Arc 1494.6 Batalha Reis, Pedro. Moedas de Toro. Lisboa, 1933.
Arc 530.47 Berlin. Staatliche Museen. Die Ausgrabungen der zweiten Ktesiphon-Expedition. Berlin, 1933.
Arc 600.36.5 Boak, A.E.R. Karanis. Ann Arbor, 1933.
Htn Arc 1053.18* Boehringer, E. Der Caesar von Acireale. Stuttgart, 1933.
Arc 551.10 Borchardt, L. Allerhand Kleinigkeiten. Leipzig, 1933?
Arc 895.47 Broholm, Hans Christian. Studier over den yngre Bronzealder Danmark. København, 1933.
Arc 861.12.2 Bruce, J.C. The handbook to the Roman wall. 9. ed. Newcastle-upon-Tyne, 1933.
Arc 386.20.10 Burkitt, M.C. The old stone age. Cambrige, 1933.
Arc 888.5F Bursch, F.C. Die Becherkultur in den Niederlanden. Inaug. Diss. Leiden, 1933.
Arc 830.163 Busset, Maurice. Gergovia, capitale des Gaules. Paris, 1933.
Arc 642.9 Carpenter, Rhys. The humanistic value of archaeology. Cambridge, Mass., 1933.
Arc 843.72 Carro, Jesús. Otesouro de Toxados. Santiago, 1933.
Arc 875.14.7 Childe, V.G. Ancient dwellings at Skara Brae. Edinburgh, 1933.
Arc 875.10.13 Clarke, John. The Roman fort at Cadder near Glasgow. Glasgow, 1933.
Arc 458.2.10 Combaz, Gisbert. L'évolution du Stūpa en Asie. Bruxelles, 1933. 3 pam.
Arc 3.1.25 Congrès International d'Archéologie Classique, 5th, Algiers, 1930. Cinquième Congrès international d'archéologie, Alger, 14-16 avril 1930. Alger, 1933.
Arc 746.19 Consortini, P.L. Le necropoli etrusche di Volterra. Lucca, 1933.
Arc 861.31.20 Cunnington, M.E. (Mrs.). Introduction to the archaeology of Wiltshire. Devizes, 1933.

1933 - cont.

Arc 905.5.9 Degrassi, A. Abitati preistorici e romani nell'agro di Capodistria. Parenzo, 1933.
Arc 1053.6.25 Delbrück, R. Spätantike Kaiserporträts. Berlin, 1933.
Arc 758.2.5F Dosio, G.A. Das Skizzenbuch des G. Dosio im staatlichen Kupferstichkabinett zu Berlin. Berlin, 1933.
Arc 861.21.21 Elgee, Frank. The archaeology of Yorkshire. London, 1933.
Arc 1335.153 Erlangen. Universität. Bibliothek. Die Voit von Salzburg'sche Münz. München, 1933.
Arc 1433.64 Farkas, Sándor. Die Ikonographie der Partherkönige. Aiud, 1933.
Arc 585.31F Frankfort, H. The cenotaph of Seti I at Abydos. London, 1933. 2v.
Arc 1153.62 Giuliano, M.L. Coltura e attività calligrafica nel secolo XII a Verona. Padova, 1933.
Arc 684.9.10 Gude, Mabel. A history of Olynthus. Baltimore, 1933.
Arc 543.12.5 Hackin, Joseph. L'oeuvre de la délégation archéologique française en Afghanistan, 1922-1932. Tokyo, 1933.
Arc 689.3.10 Hansen, H.D. Early civilization in Thessaly. Baltimore, 1933.
Arc 1020.9.164F Hendrichs, F. La voce delle chiese antichissime di Roma. Roma, 1933.
Arc 448.1.15 Heros, Henry. Studies in proto-Indo-Mediterranean culture. Bombay, 1933.
Arc 1053.5.7 Holm, Erich. Das Bildnis des Antinous. Inaug. Diss. Würzburg, 1933.
Arc 1675.20.25F Italy. Esercito Corpo di Stato Maggiore. Ufficio Storico. Nel I. centenario della istituzione delle medaglie al valore. Roma, 1933.
Arc 450.2A Kak, Ram C. Ancient monuments of Kashmir. London, 1933.
Arc 1027.23.23 Kampffmeyer, K. Die Landschaft in der altchristlichen Katakombenmalerei. Greifswald, 1933.
Arc 522.40.5 Kandemir, Selâhattin. Turova harabeleri ve skalor. Izmir, 1933.
Arc 1033.17.60 Klein, Dorothee. St. Lukas als Maler der Maria. Berlin, 1933.
Arc 497.34 Köppel, Robert. Untersuchungen über die Steinzeit Palästina-Syriens. Inaug. Diss. Rom, 1933.
Arc 1020.131 Kollwitz, J. Die Lipsanothek von Brescia. Berlin, 1933.
Arc 1020.131PF Kollwitz, J. Die Lipsanothek von Brescia. Atlas. Berlin, 1933.
Arc 505.5.67 Le Lithostrotos d'après des fouilles récentes. Paris, 1933.
Arc 1335.81 MacDonald, G. The Hunterian coin cabinet. Glasgow, 1933.
Arc 815.24F Maiuri, Amedeo. La casa del Menandro e il suo tesoro di Argenteria. Roma, 1933. 2v.
Arc 736.1.12 Marconi, Pirro. Agrigento. Roma, 1933.
Arc 1025.28.50F Marucchi, O. Le catacombe romane. Roma, 1933.
Arc 1478.24.13 Mattingly, Harold. The date of the Roman denarius. London, 1933.
Arc 1478.34 Mickwitz, G. Die Systeme des römischen Silbergeldes. Helsingfors, 1933.
Arc 1367.2 Miller, Max. Die Münzen des Altertums. Berlin, 1933.
Arc 1153.4.25 Molina, E. Grammatica tironiana. Padova, 1933.
Arc 600.39 Montet, Pierre. Les nouvelles fouilles de Tanis (1929-32). Paris, 1933.
Arc 397.13 Morin, Jean. Les artistes préhistoriques. Paris, 1933.
Arc 830.18.23 Müller, Reiner. Die Angaben der römischen Itinerare über die Heerstrasse Köln-Eifel-Reims. Münstereifel, 1933.
Arc 785.59F Munoz, A. Via dei trionfi isolamento del Campidoglio. 2a ed. Roma, 1933.
Arc 1020.130 Neuss, Wilhelm. Die Anfänge des Christentums im Rheinlande. 2. Aufl. Bonn, 1933.
Arc 403.14 Oudheidkundig Genootschap, Amsterdam. Bibliographie der geschriften van Jhr. Dr. Jan Six. Amsterdam, 1933.
Arc 1443.5F Oxford. University. Ashmolean Museum. Catalogue of Alexandrian coins. Oxford, 1933.
Arc 1163.21 Pagnin, B. Le origini della scriturra gotica padovana. Padova, 1933.
Arc 1490.90 Patrignani, Antonio. Le medaglie di Pio VII, 1829-1830. Catania, 1933.
Arc 400.11.20 Peake, Harold J.E. The horse and the sword. New Haven, 1933.
Arc 974.2 Pearce, J.E. A prehistoric rock shelter in Val Verde County, Tennessee. Austin, Texas, 1933.
Arc 672.1.28 Pendlebury, J.D.S. Handbook to the palace of Minos at Knossos. London, 1933.
Arc 726.69F Pennsylvania. University. University Museum. Excavations at Minturnae. Rome, 1933-35. 2v.
Arc 936.29.5F Popov, R. Peshterata Mirezlivka. Sofiia, 1933.
Arc 505.120 Presbyterian Theological Seminary, Chicago, Illinois. The citadel of Beth-Zur. Philadelphia, 1933.
Arc 925.80 Przeworski, S. Zagadnienie wpływów Bl. wschodnie. Warszawa, 1933.
Arc 785.60 Ricci, Corrado. Via dell'impero. Roma, 1933.
Arc 895.21.30 Rydh, Hanna. Hos stenåldersfolket. Stockholm, 1933.
Arc 458.9 Sahni, Daya Ram. Guide to the Buddhist ruins of Sarnath. 5. ed. Delhi, 1933.
Arc 1093.6.18 Scheuermann, W. Woher kommt das Hakenkreuz? Berlin, 1933.
Arc 1030.61 Schneider, Fedor. Die Epitaphien der Päpste und andere stadtrömische Inschriften des Mittelalters. Rom, 1933.
Arc 609.5 Seekirchner, A. Die geographischen und geopolitischen Grundlagen der sudafrikanischen Ruinenkultur. Memmingen, 1933.
Arc 530.29 Shober, Arnold. Der Fries des Hekateions von Lagina. Baden, 1933.
Arc 543.3.19A Stein, Mark Aurel. On Central-Asian tracks. London, 1933.
Arc 895.34F Stenberger, Mårten. Öland under äldre järnaldern. Stockholm, 1933.
Arc 895.34.5F Stenberger, Mårten. Öland under äldre järnaldern. Stockholm, 1933.
Arc 1025.62.10F Styger, Paul. Die römischen Katakomben. Berlin, 1933.
Arc 1428.23 Sydenham, E.A. The coinage of Caesarea in Cappadocia. London, 1933.
Arc 726.45.15 Toscanelli, N. Pisa nell'antichità dalle età preistoriche alla caduta dell'impero romano. Pisa, 1933. 2v.
Arc 1205.5 Tourneur-Nicodème, Mariette. Bibliographie générale de la sigillographie. Besançon, 1933.
Arc 915.37 Traininas, Davidas. Beiträge zur Kenntnis der Haustiere der romischkeltischen Ansiedlung auf der Engehalbinsel bei Bern. Bern, 1933.
Arc 793.13 Van Buren, Albert W. A companion to the study of Pompeii and Herculaneum. Rome, 1933.
Arc 936.140.5 Velkov, Ivan. Murtvi gradove. Sofiia, 1933.
Arc 497.36 Watzinger, Carl. Denkmäler Palästinas. v.1-2. Leipzig, 1933-35.

Chronological Listing

1933 - cont.

Arc 442.10 Wauchope, Robert S. Buddhist cave temples of India. Calcutta, 1933.

Arc 1084.15F Wu, Henry H. Ancient Chinese jade. n.p., 1933.

Arc 1163.8.10 Ziemer, Meline. Datierung und Lokalisierung nach den Schreibformen von K und Z im Althochdeutschen. Inaug. Diss. Breslau, 1933.

1934

Arc 746.7.9F Åkerström, Åke. Studien über die etruskischen Gräber. Uppsala, 1934.

Arc 936.195.310 Adámsk, František. Důkaz pravosti metodějských nálezů z "Hrobů" u Osvětiman. Brno, 1934.

Arc 421.10.15 Andersson, J. Children of the yellow earth. London, 1934.

Arc 505.1.9F Antioch-on-the-Orontes. v.1-4. Princeton, 1934-48. 5v.

Arc 136.2.5.3 Antiquaries journal. General index. v.1-10. London, 1934.

Arc 895.23.10F Arne, T.J. Das Bootgräberfeld von Tuna in Alsike, Uppland. Stockholm, 1934.

Arc 1077.2.43 Benson, G.W. The cross, its history and symbolism. Buffalo, 1934.

Arc 530.45 Berlin. Tell Halaf Museum. Führer durch das Tell Halaf Maueum. Berlin, 1934.

Arc 853.72 Bicker, F.K. Dünenmesolithikum aus dem Fiener Bruch. Inaug. Diss. Halle an der Saale, 1934.

Arc 530.12.25 Bittel, Kurt. Die Felsbilder von Yazilikaya. Bamberg, 1934.

Arc 513.21 Bittel, Kurt. Prähistorische Forschung in Kleinasien. Istanbul, 1934.

Arc 905.35 Brusin, G. Gli scavi di Aquileia. Udine, 1934.

Arc 547.42 Brussels. Musées Coyaux d'Art et d'Histoire. Fondation Égyptologique Reine Elisabeth. Département égyptien; album. Bruxelles, 1934.

Arc 970.2.5 Cadzow, D.A. Petroglyphs (rock carvings) in the Susquehanna River near Safe Harbor, Pennsylvania. Harrisburg, 1934.

Arc 387.11 Casson, Stanley. Progress of archaeology. London, 1934.

Arc 600.5.15F Caton-Thompson, G. The desert Fayum. London, 1934. 2v.

Arc 1077.2.45 Chauncey Ross, M. La croix Gaillard de la Dionnerie au Musée metropolitan. Poitiers, 1934.

Arc 505.45.25 Christian church at Dura-Europas. New Haven, 1934.

Arc 861.93 Corder, Philip. Excavations at the Roman fort at Brough-on-Humber. Hull, 1934.

Arc 520.16 Dopp, W. Eine Altisdarstellung am grossen Fries von Pergamon. Inaug. Diss. Rostock, 1934.

Arc 672.7 Dyggve, E. Das heroon von Kalydon. København, 1934.

Arc 895.17.15F Engelstad, E.S. Ostnorske ristninger og malinger av den arktiske gruppe. Oslo, 1934.

Arc 936.39F Filov, Bogdan. Die Grabhügelnekropole bei Duvanlij in Südbulgarien. Sofiia, 1934.

Arc 936.39.5 Filov, Bogdan. Nadgrobnité mogili pri Duvanlii v Plovdivsko. Sofiia, 1934.

Arc 1412.5 Fonahn, Adolf. Japanische Bildermünze. Leipzig, 1934.

Arc 853.83 Fuchs, Alois. Im Streit um die Externsteine. Paderborn, 1934.

Arc 446.5 Garde, M.B. Archaeology in Gwalior. 2. ed. Gwalior, 1934.

Arc 302.2.7 Gerasimov, T. Ukaz, kumuizv na bulgarekoto archeologichesko. Sofiia, 1934.

Arc 537.7F Gjerstad, Einar. The Swedish Cyprus expedition...1927-1931. v.1-4. Stockholm, 1934-48. 8v.

Arc 1493.17 Gracia de la Fuente, Arturo. Resumen historico. Madrid, 1934.

Arc 503.5.10F Grant, Elihu. Ain Shems excavations (Palestine), 1933. Pt.3. Haverford, 1934.

Arc 1076.12 Gribsoe, Erland. Frederiksborg amts kirkekloffer. Hillerød, 1934.

Arc 1588.4.40 Gumowski, Marian. Bolesław Chrobry v Czechach. Poznań, 1934.

Arc 853.78 Guthjahr, R. Die Semnonen im Havelland zur frühen Kaiserzeit. Diss. Greifswald, 1934.

Arc 444.1.15 Hirananda, Sastri. A guide to Elephanta. Delhi, 1934.

Arc 853.71 Holter, F. Die Hallesche Kultur der frühen Eisenzeit. Inaug. Diss. Halle, 1934.

Arc 9.2.1 International Congress of Prehistoric and Protohistoric Sciences, 1st, London, 1932. Proceedings. London, 1934.

Arc 1675.53F Jocelyn, Arthur. The orders, decorations and medals of the world. London, 1934.

Arc 689.7.5 Karo, G. Fürhrer durch Tiryns. 2. Aufl. Athen, 1934.

Arc 674.1.10 Kourouniotos, K. Eleusis. Athēnai, 1934.

Arc 905.40 Kuzsinszky, V. Aquincum; Ausgrabungen und Funde. Budapest, 1934.

Arc 1093.6.22 Lecher, Jörg. Vom Hakenkreuz. 2. Aufl. Leipzig, 1934.

Arc 895.36.7F Lohse, E. Versuch einer Typologie der Felszeichnungen von Bohuslän. Inaug. Diss. Dresden, 1934.

Arc 843.66 Lopez Martí, L. Santa Eulalia de Bóveda. Lugo, 1934.

Arc 875.13.7 Macdonald, G. The Roman wall in Scotland. 2. ed. Oxford, 1934.

Arc 935.19F Mamboury, Ernest. Die Kaiserpaläste von Konstantinopel zwischen Hippodrom und Marmara-Meer. Berlin, 1934.

Arc 925.35 Matsulevich, L.A. Pogrebenie varvarskogo kniazia v vostochnoi Evrope. Moskva, 1934.

Arc 1468.27.5 Milne, Joseph G. The first stages in the development of Greek coinage. Oxford, 1934.

Arc 585.32F Mond, Robert. The Bucheum. London, 1934. 3v.

Arc 785.69.5F Munoz, A. La via del Circo Massimo. 2. ed. Roma, 1934.

Arc 848.25 Neckel, Gustav. Deutsche Ur- und Vorgeschichtswissenschaft der Gegenwart. Berlin, 1934.

Arc 1221.5F Newell, E.T. Ancient oriental seals in the collection of Mr. E.T. Newell. Chicago, 1934.

Arc 1480.60 Ondrouch, V. Der römische Denarfund von Vyşkovce aus der Frühkaiserzeit. Bratislava, 1934.

Arc 1053.19F Paribeni, R. Il ritratto nell'arte antica. Milano, 1934.

Arc 843.65.2 Pla y Cargol, J. Empúries i roses. 2. ed. Girona, 1934.

Arc 400.14.25 Porter, Lucy W. Kingsley. Writings of A. Kingsley Porter. Cambridge, 1934.

Arc 746.18.5 Puglisi, S. Studi e ricerche su Orvieto etrusca. Catania, 1934.

Arc 848.29.5 Radig, Werner. Germanischer Lebensraum. 4. Aufl. Stuttgart, 1934.

Arc 1153.44.5F Rand, Edward K. The earliest book of Tours. Cambridge, Mass., 1934.

Arc 93.24.3 Rivista archeologica della provincia e antica diocesi di Como. Indice generale, 85-139, 1923-1957. Como, 1934-1958. 2v.

Arc 505.63F Rome. Pontifico Istituto Biblico. Teleilát Ghassúl. Roma, 1934.

1934 - cont.

Arc 875.14.25 Roussell, Aage. Norse building customs in the Scottish isles. Copenhagen, 1934.

Arc 935.40 Sakir, M. Sinop ta candar ogullarizamanina. Istanbul, 1934.

Arc 530.14.25 Schede, Martin. Die Ruinen von Priene. Berlin, 1934.

Arc 936.40.30F Sofia. Naroden Arkheologicheski Muzei. Madara. Sofiia, 1934.

Arc 726.60.5 Speranza, G. Il Piceno dalle origini alla fine d'ogni sua autonomia sotto Augusto. v.1-2. Ancona, 1934.

Arc 488.13 Stein, Mark A. Archaeological reconnaissances in southern Persia. London, 1934.

Arc 848.26 Stemmermann, P.H. Die Anfänge der deutschen Vorgeschichtsforschung. Inaug. Diss. Quakenbrück, 1934

Arc 726.59.15 Ugolini, L.M. Malta; origini della civiltà mediterranea. Roma, 1934.

Arc 785.6.17F Van Deman, E.B. The building of the Roman aqueducts. Washington, 1934.

Arc 1208.8 Vatican. Biblioteca Vaticana. Le bolle d'oro dell'archivio vaticano. Città del Vaticano, 1934.

Arc 421.11 White, W.C. Tombs of old Lo-yang. Shanghai, 1934.

Arc 670.3.10 Wrede, W. Attika. Athens, 1934.

Arc 838.24F Zeiss, Hans. Die Grabfunde aus dem spanischen Westgotenreich. Berlin, 1934.

1935

Htn Arc 1027.24.25F* Achelis, Hans. Die Katakomben von Neapel. Leipzig, 1935-36.

Arc 843.190 Alvarez-Ossori, F. Bronces ibericas o hispancion del Mueso Arquelogico Nacional. Madrid, 1935.

Arc 1018.53 Aragón Fernández, A. Tratado de arqueología eclesiástica. Barcelona, 1935.

Arc 925.337.5 Artamonov, Mikhail I. Srednevekovye poseleniia na Nizhnem Donu. Leningrad, 1935.

Arc 785.6.19 Ashby, T. The aqueducts of ancient Rome. Oxford, 1935.

Arc 1510.29 Bahrfeldt, Max von. Das Geprägte amtliche Notgeld der Provinz Schlesien, 1917-1921. Breslau, 1935.

Arc 861.18.19 Bayley, Harold. The lost language of London. London, 1935.

Arc 848.31 Behn, Friedrich. Altgermanische Kultur. Leipzig, 1935.

Arc 848.31.5 Behn, Friedrich. Altmordisches Leben vor 3000 Jahren. München, 1935.

Arc 600.40 Boak, A.E.R. Soknopaiou Nesos. Ann Arbor, 1935.

Arc 530.12.28F Boğazköy. v.3-5. Berlin, 1935- 3v.

Arc 1428.13F Bosch, C. Die kleinasiatischen Münzen der römischen Kaiserzeit. Stuttgart, 1935.

Arc 935.9.30 Bruns, G. Der Obelisk und seine Basis auf dem Hippodrom zu Konstantinopel. Istanbul, 1935.

Arc 726.160 Buccolini, Geralberto. Il problema archeologico di Orvieto antica. Orvieto, 1935.

Arc 1510.30F Buck, H. Die Münzen der Stadt Hannover. Hannover, 1935.

Arc 421.16 Bunakov, I.V. Tadatel'nie kosti iz Khznani. Moskva, 1935.

Arc 66.1.137 Chapouthier, F. Les dioscures au service d'une déesse. Paris, 1935.

Arc 673.12F Chapouthier, F. Exploration archéologique de Délos. Paris, 1935.

Arc 875.14.15 Childe, V.G. The prehistory of Scotland. London, 1935.

Arc 757.7 Clementi, F. Roma imperiale nelle XIV regioni Agustee secondo. Roma, 1935. 2v.

Arc 543.5.25 Colani, M. Mégalithes du Haut-Laos. Paris, 1935. 2v.

Arc 493.45F Conténau, G. Fouilles du Tépé-Giyan. Paris, 1935.

Arc 810.40.3 Corte, Matteo della. Pompéi. Pompéi, 1935.

Arc 757.8 Cozzo, G. Il luogo primitivo di Roma. Roma, 1935.

Arc 865.21 Cunnington, R.H. Stonehenge and its date. London, 1935.

Arc 595.28 Davie, John G. Phythagoras takes the second step, and other works on the pyramids. Griffin, 1935.

Arc 612.24 Dellenbach, M.E. La conquête du massif alpin et de ses abords. Thèse. Grenoble, 1935.

Arc 716.2.10F Das Dionysos Theater in Athen. v.1-3,4. Stuttgart, 1935-50. 2v.

Arc 684.1.37 Dörpfeld, Wilhelm. Alt-Olympia. Berlin, 1935. 2v.

Arc 684.1.38 Dörpfeld, Wilhelm. Alt-Olympia. Beiheft. Berlin, 1935.

Arc 830.126.3 Donnadieu, A. Fréjus le port militaire du Forum Julii. Paris, 1935.

Arc 1335.125 Enzenberg, Arthur. Katalog der Münzensammlung Arthur Graf Enzenberg. Luzern, 1935.

Arc 1335.140 Escorial. Biblioteca. Catalago de las monedas y medallas de la biblioteca de San Lorenzo de el Escorial. Madrid, 1935.

Arc 968.1.15 Ferguson, Henry L. Archaeological exploration of Fishers Island, New York. N.Y., 1935.

Arc 545.227.10F Firth, C.M. The step pyramid. Le Caire, 1935-36. 2v.

Arc 830.162 Forrer, Robert. L'Alsace romaine. Paris, 1935.

Arc 848.32 Frenzel, W. Grundzüge der Vorgeschichte Deutschlands. Stuttgart, 1935.

Arc 545.227.44F Griffith, F.L. Catalogue of demotic graffiti of the Dodecaschoenus. Oxford, 1935.

Arc 1163.23 Grun, Paul A. Leseschlüssel zu unserer alten Schrift. Görlitz, 1935.

Arc 1510.40 Haeberle, Adolf. Ulmer Münz- und Geldgeschichte des Mittelalters. n.p., 1935.

Arc 590.14 Hayes, William C. Royal sarcophagi of the XVIII Dynasty. Princeton, 1935.

Arc 880.38.15 Hencken, H.O. A tumulus at Carrowlesdooaun, County Mayo. n.p., 1935. 2 pam.

Arc 488.15 Herzfeld, Ernst E. Archaeological history of Iran. London, 1935.

Arc 600.3.5 Heuser, G. Die Katochëim Sarapieion bei Memphis. Inaug. Diss. Marburg, 1935.

Arc 968.2.55 Howard, E.B. Evidence of early man in North America...archaeological work in New Mexico. Philadelphia, 1935.

Arc 785.83.10 Hyde, Walter Woodburn. Roman Alpine routes (with map showing chief Roman passes). Philadelphia, 1935.

Arc 307.3.15 International Congress of Americanists, 26th, Seville, 1935. Programa. Madrid, 1935.

Arc 483.5 Iraq. Department of Antiquities. Harba bridge. Baghdad, 1935.

Arc 936.1.15 Kalliga, M. Die Hagia Sophia von Thessalonike. Inaug. Diss. Würzburg, 1935.

Arc 1588.4.45 Katz, Viktor. Ocuronolozu denaru Boleslava I a II. Praha, 1935.

Arc 505.72.5F Lassus, Jean. Inventoire archéologique de la région au nord-est de Hama. v.1-2. Damas, 1935-1936.

Chronological Listing

1935 - cont.

Arc 396.12 Lemaire, Raymond. La restauration des monuments anciens. Anvers, 1935.
Arc 340.3F London. University. Library. Catalogue of books on archaeology and art. London, 1935-37. 2v.
Arc 853.15.5 Lütjen-Janssen, Hans. Die Germanen in Mecklenburg im 2. Jahrtausend vor Christus. Leipzig, 1935.
Arc 726.25.16F Lugli, G. Il porto di Roma imperiale e l'agro portuense. Roma, 1935.
Arc 880.25.9A Macalister, R.A.S. Ancient Ireland. London, 1935.
Arc 1433.65.5 McDowell, Robert H. Coins from Seleucia on the Tigris. Ann Arbor, 1935.
Arc 448.1 Mackay, Ernest. The Indus civilization. London, 1935.
Arc 600.170 Maczamallah, R. Fouilles à Saqqarah. Le Caire, 1935.
Arc 1018.44.15 Marucchi, O. Manuel of Christian archaeology. 4. Italian ed. Paterson, N.J., 1935.
Arc 726.79 Marzulla, A. Tombe dipinte scoperte nel territorio Pestano. Salerno, 1935.
Arc 1190.35 Meisner, H.O. Aktenkunde. Berlin, 1935.
Arc 505.51 Mesnil du Buisson, R. du. Le site archéologique de Mishrifé-Qatna. Thèse. Paris, 1935.
Arc 723.22 Messerschmidt, Franz. Bronzezeit und frühe Eisenzeit in Italien. Berlin, 1935.
Arc 1076.3.105 Morris, E. Legends o' the bells. London, 1935.
Arc 880.39 Movius, H.L. Kilgreany cove, county Waterford. Dublin? 1935.
Arc 542.200.5 Mus, Paul. Barabudur. v.1, pt.1-2; v.2. Hanoi, 1935. 3v.
Arc 1271.2 Nederlandsche kloosterzegels voor 1600. v.1-23. 's Gravenhage, 1935-52. 4v.
Arc 895.22.17F Newman, B. Die Volkerwanderungszeit Gotlands. Stockholm, 1935.
Arc 870.23 O'Dwyer, Stanhope. The Roman roads of Cheshire. Newtown, 1935.
Arc 770.7.5 Paléologue, M. Rome, notes d'histoire et d'art. 22. éd. Paris, 1935.
Arc 1163.2.22 Paluzie y Cantelozella, Esteban. Escritura y lenguaje de España. Barcelona, 1935.
Arc 672.1.65F Pernier, Luigi. Il palazzo minoico di Festos. Roma, 1935-51. 3v.
Arc 608.17.19F Pernier, Luigi. Il tempio e l'altare di Apollo a Cirene. Bergamo, 1935.
Arc 588.57F Petrie, W.M.F. Shabtis. London, 1935.
Arc 938.50 Puzinas, Jonas. Vorgeschichtsforschung und Nationalbewusstsein in Litauen. Inaug. Diss. Kaunas, 1935.
Arc 1153.58 Rauh, Rudolf. Paläographie des mainfränkischen Monumentalinscriften. Inaug. Diss. München, 1935.
Arc 513.22 Robert, L. Villes d'Asie Mineure. Paris, 1935.
Arc 1625.2 Romero de Terreros y Vinent, Manuel. Los tlacos coloniales. México, 1935.
Arc 895.38F Rydbeck, Otto. Den medeltida borgen i Skanör. Lund, 1935.
Arc 726.170 Schiavo, Armando. Acquedotti romani e medioevali. Napoli, 1935.
Arc 684.1.33 Schlief, Hans. Der Zeus-Altar in Olympia. Diss. Berlin, 1935.
Arc 482.206 Schmidt, J.H. Friedrich Sarre Schriften. Berlin, 1935.
Arc 848.15.5 Schuchhardt, C. Vorgeschichte von Deutschland. 3. Aufl. München, 1935.
Arc 848.30.4 Schultz, W. Altgermanische Kultur in Wort und Bild. 3. Aufl. München, 1935.
Arc 421.8 Ségalen, V. Mission archéologique en Chine (1914). Paris, 1935.
Arc 497.38 Simons, J.J. Opgravingen in Palestina. Roermond-Maaseik, 1935.
Arc 395.11.5 Stampfuss, Rudolf. Gustav Kossinna. Leipzig, 1935.
Arc 497.39 Stekelis, M. Les monuments megalithiques de Palestine. Thèse. Paris, 1935.
Arc 543.35.15 Stutterheim, W.F. Indian influences in old Balinese art. London, 1935.
Arc 1025.62.15F Styger, Paul. Römische Märtyrergrüfte. Berlin, 1935. 2v.
Arc 905.17.5 Swoboda, Erich. Führer durch Aguntum. Baden, 1935.
Arc 530.39F Swoboda, H. Denkmäler aus Lykaonien, Pamphylien und Isaurien. Brunn, 1935.
Arc 830.164 Temple, P. La préhistoire du département de l'Avignon. Thèse. Nîmes, 1935.
Arc 1166.6 Thompson, D.V. Medieval parchment-making. London, 1935.
Arc 935.32.15 Turkey. Maarif Vekaleli Antikiteler ve Muzeler Direktorlügü. Aniflari Koruma Kurulu. Kilavuzlar. v.1,4,6. Ankara, 1935- 7v.
Arc 905.12.9.5 Verein Carnuntum, Wien. Carnuntum 1885-1910. Wien, 1935.
Arc 888.6 Willems, W.J.A. Een bijdrage tot de kennis der vóór-Romeinsche urnenvelden in Nederland. Proefschrift. Maastricht, 1935.

1936

Arc 893.13.15 Adama van Scheltema, F. Die Kunst unserer Vorzeit. Leipzig, 1936.
Arc 853.17.15F Albrecht, C. Frühgeschichtliche Funde aus Westfalen im städtischen Kunst- und Gewerbemuseum Dortmund. Dortmund, 1936.
Arc 983.14 American Society of Naturalists. Early man in America with particular reference to the southwestern United States. n.p., 1936.
Arc 726.334 Angrisani, Mario. La Villa Augustea in Somma Vesuviana. Aversa, 1936.
Arc 1027.41.3F Bagatti, B. Il cimitero di Commodilla. Città del Vaticano, 1936.
Arc 710.18F Balanos, N. Les monuments de l'acropole. Paris, 1936.
Arc 968.11 Bell, Earl Hoyt. Chapters in Nebraska archaeology. Lincoln, Nebraska, 1936.
Arc 925.8.35 Belov, G.D. Muzei i raskopki khersonesa. Simferopol, 1936.
Arc 66.1.139 Boüard, Michel de. La France et l'Italie au temps du Grand Schisme d'Occident. Paris, 1936.
Arc 1221.4F Brett, Agnes B. Ancient oriental seals in the collection of Mrs. Agnes Baldwin Brett. Chicago, 1936.
Arc 810.50A Carrington, R.C. Pompeii. Oxford, 1936.
Arc 1580.35 Cejnek, Josef. Österreichische, ungarische, böhmische, und schlesische Münzen. v.2. Wien, 1936.
Arc 394.2 Cheynier, A. Jovannet, grand-père de la préhistoire. Brive, 1936.
Arc 612.23 Clark, John Desmond. The mesolithic settlement of northern Europe. Cambridge, Eng., 1936.
Arc 402.11 Dalton, O.M. Sir Hercules Read. London, 1936.

1936 - cont.

Arc 66.1.140 Daux, Georges. Delphes au IIe et au Ier siècle. Paris, 1936.
Arc 1138.37 Dobiaš-Rozhdestvenskaia, O.A. Istoriia pis'ma v srednie veka. Moskva, 1936.
Arc 1093.6.9 Doering, J.F. The swastika. Kitchner, Ontario, 1936.
Arc 441.7 Doreau, Jean Louis. Les bains dans l'Inde antique; monuments et textes médicaux. Paris, 1936.
Arc 672.1.27.5 Evans, Arthur John. Index to the palace of Minos. London, 1936.
Arc 1590.8 Farkas, Sandor. Az erdélyi érmek müvészete. Aiud, 1936.
Arc 936.15.5 Fewkes, V.J. Neolithic sites in the Mozavo-Danubian area. n.p., 1936.
Arc 893.20 Forssander, J.E. Der Ostskandinavische Norden während der ältesten Metallzeit Europas. Lund, 1936.
Arc 1615.8 Foster, Charles W. Historical arrangement of United States commemorative coins. Rochester, 1936.
Arc 673.1.15 Frotier de la Coste Messelière, P. Au musée de Delphes. Thèse. Paris, 1936.
Arc 1027.89 Gabrieli, Giuseppe. Inventario topografico e bibliografico delle cripte eremitiche basiliane di Puglia. Roma, 1936.
Arc 1550.8 Galster, Georg. Danske og norske medailler og jetons. Kjøbenhavn, 1936.
Arc 1016.211.5F Gerke, F. Der Sarkophag des Iunius Bassus. Berlin, 1936.
Arc 858.24.19 Great Britain. Commissions. Ancient and Historical Monuments and Constructions of England. An inventory of the historical monuments in Westmorland. London, 1936.
Arc 858.47.5A Great Britain. Ministry of Works. Illustrated regional guides to ancient monuments. London, 1936-48. 5v.
Arc 870.10.9 Grinsell, L.V. The ancient burial-mounds of England. London, 1936.
Arc 416.8 Hackin, J. Recherches archéologiques en Asie centrale (1931). Paris, 1936.
Arc 746.46 Hanfmann, George Maxim Anossov. Altetruskische Plastik. Würzburg, 1936.
Arc 848.36 Hofmeister, H. Germanenkunde. Frankfurt am Main, 1936.
Arc 870.4.15 Hughes, G.M. Roman roads in south-east Britain. London, 1936.
Arc 530.90.5 Jacopi, G. Dalla Paflagonia alla Commagene. Roma, 1936.
Arc 861.29.15 Kenyon, K.M. Excavations at Wroxeter, 1936. Shrewsbury, 1936.
Arc 1200.24 Kopczynski, M. Die Arengen der Papsturkunden nach ihrer Bedeutung und Verwendung bis zu Gregor VII. Inaug. Diss. Bottrop, 1936.
Arc 522.20 Kosay, Hamit. "Troad" da dört yerleş me yeri. Istanbul, 1936.
Arc 848.8.4 Kossinna, Gustaf. Die deutsche Vorgeschichte. 7. Aufl. Leipzig, 1936.
Arc 674.1.12 Kourouniotos, K. Eleusis. Athens, 1936.
Arc 66.1.138 La Coste-Messelière, P. de. Au musée de Delphes. Paris, 1936.
Arc 681.1.5 Lamb, Winifred. Excavations at Thermi in Lesbos. Cambridge, Eng., 1936.
Arc 545.227.11A Lauer, J.P. Fouilles à Saqqarah, la pyramide à degrés. v.1-2, 4-5. La Caire, 1936. 4v.
Arc 870.12.19 Leeds, E.T. The Anglo-Saxon cemetery at Abingdon, Berkshire. Oxford, 1936. 2v.
Arc 870.12.15A Leeds, E.T. Early Anglo-Saxon art and archaeology. Oxford, 1936.
Arc 1613.14 Lewis, E.A. Laws authorizing issuance of medals. Washington, 1936.
Arc 1613.14.5 Lewis, E.A. Laws authorizing issuance of medals and commerative coins. Washington, 1936.
Arc 1480.32 Mabbott, T.O. A small bronze of Nero. Rome, 1936.
Arc 1494.35 Madrid. Museo Arqueologico Nacional. Catalogo de las monedas previsigadas. Madrid, 1936.
Arc 458.1.10 Marshall, John. A guide to Sanchi. 2. ed. Delhi, 1936.
Arc 459.3.15 Marshall, John. A guide to Taxila. 3. ed. Delhi, 1936.
Arc 785.69.10F Munoz, A. Il Parco di Traiano. Roma, 1936.
Arc 520.17 Napp, A.E. Das Altar von Pergamon. München, 1936.
Arc 743.19 Nogara, B. Les Etrusques et leur civilisation. Paris, 1936.
Arc 885.16 O'Dwyer, S. The Roman roads of Wales. Newtown, 1936.
Arc 1583.14 Oreshnikov, A.V. Denezhnye znaki domongol'. Rusi. Moskva, 1936.
Arc 1163.3.38 Orlov, A.S. Bibliografiia russkikh nadpisei XI-XV vv. Moskva, 1936.
Arc 600.12.10F Palestine. Archaeological Museum. A catalogue of Egyptian scarabs by Alan Rowe. La Caire, 1936.
Arc 505.59 Parrot, André. Mari, une ville perdue...et retrouvée par l'archéologie française. Paris, 1936.
Arc 785.64 Peebles, Bernard M. La "Meta Romuli" e una lettera di Michele Ferno. Roma, 1936.
Arc 1093.2.17 Pei Wen Chung. Le rôle des phénomènes naturels dans l'éclatement. Thèse. Paris, 1936.
Arc 1033.62.7 Perpetua, Saint Legend. Passio Sanctarum Perpetuae et Felicitatis. Noviomagi, 1936.
Arc 608.22 Perret, Robert. Recherches archéologiques et ethnographiques au Tassili des Ajjers (Sahara Central). Paris, 1936.
Arc 936.29 Popov, R. Peshterata Temnata dupka. Sofiia, 1936.
Arc 1027.88F Prandi, A. La memoria apostolorum in catacombas. Città del Vaticano, 1936.
Arc 843.224 Prat Puig, Francisco. L'aqueducte Romà de Pineda. Barcelona, 1936.
Arc 1470.41 Ravel, O.E. Les "Poulains" de Corinthe; monographie des statères corinthiens. Bâle, 1936-48. 2v.
Arc 402.2.25 Reinach, S. Bibliographie de S. Reinach. Paris, 1936.
Arc 600.41FA Reisner, George A. The development of the Egyptian tomb down to the accession of Cheops. Cambridge, 1936.
Arc 968.2.35 Roberts, Frank H.H. A survey of southwestern archaeology. Washington, 1936.
Arc 853.65.5 Rothert. Die mittlere Steinzeit in Schlesien. Leipzig, 1936.
Arc 608.7.25 Ruhlmann, A. Les grottes préhistoriques d'"El Khenzira" (région de Mazagan). Thèse. Nogent-le-Rotrou, 1936.
Arc 895.39F Rydh, Hanna. Förhistoriska undersökningar på Adelso. Stockholm, 1936.
Arc 537.9 Schaeffer, C.F.A. Missions en Chypre, 1932-1935. Paris, 1936.
Arc 658.3.1 Schliemann, H. Briefe von Heinrich Schliemann. Berlin, 1936.
Arc 403.16.5 Schliemann, Heinrich. Selbstbiographie bis zu seinem Tod vervollständigt. 2. Aufl. Leipzig, 1936.
Arc 935.20 Schneider, A.M. Byzanz; Vorarbeiten zur Topographie und Archäologie der Stadt. Berlin, 1936.

1936 - cont.

Arc 848.15.10 Schuchhardt, C. Deutsche Vor- und Frühgeschichte in Bildern. München, 1936.
Arc 1510.141 Schurnkowski, Walter. Zur Münzgeschichte der chemaligen Wettinischen Lande um 1180-1230. Halle, 1936.
Arc 672.1.61 Snijder, G.A.S. Kretische Kunst. Berlin, 1936.
Arc 830.167 Société d'Histoire et d'Archéologie de Châlon-sur-Saône. Musée Denon. Catalogue des collections lapidaires. Châlon-sur-Saône, 1936.
Arc 505.70 Solomiac, Michel. Les tours royales de Josèphe Flavius. Jérusalem, 1936.
Arc 1190.4.15 Sprenger, G. Diplomatische und rechtsgeschichtliche Untersuchungen über Immunität und Königsschutz in Deutschland seit dem 12. Jahrhundert. Inaug. Diss. Breslau, 1936.
Arc 493.20 Stein, Mark A. An archaeological tour in the ancient Persis. Oxford, 1936.
Arc 853.20.19 Steinhausen, J. Archäologische Siedlungskunde des trierer Landes. Trier, 1936.
Arc 710.19FA Stevens, G.P. The Periclean entrance court of the acropolis of Athens. Cambridge, 1936.
Arc 1053.6.7F Strelkov, A. Faymskii portret. Moskva, 1936.
Arc 1680.10.9 Tenney, M.M. Communion tokens. Grand Rapids, 1936.
Arc 848.17.5 Teudt, Wilhelm. Germanische Heiligtümer. 4. Aufl. Jena, 1936.
Arc 390.5.5 Thulin, Oskar. Johannes Ficker. Halle, 1936.
Arc 853.76.5 Umbreit, Carl. Die Ausgrabung des steinzeitlichen Dorfes von Berlin-Britz. Inaug. Diss. Leipzig, 1936.
Arc 776.2A Van Buren, A.W. Ancient Rome as revealed by recent discoveries. London, 1936.
Arc 522.19.10 Vellay, Charles. Controverses autour de Troie. Paris, 1936.
Arc 600.43 Vogliano, A. Primo rapporto degli scavi condotti dalla Missione archeologica d'Egitto della R. Università di Milano. Milano, 1936-37. 2v.
Arc 1030.51 Wessel, C. Inscriptiones graecae christianae veteres occidentes. Diss. inaug. Halae Saxonum, 1936.
Arc 540.5F Westholm, A. The temples of Soli. Stockholm, 1936.
Arc 572.5 Wilbour, Charles E. Travels in Egypt. December 1880-May 1891. Brooklyn, 1936.
Arc 870.15.15 Winholt, S.E. With a spade on Stane Street. London, 1936.
Arc 1510.70 Wintz, Hermann. Erlangen in Spiegel der Münze. Erlangen, 1936.
Arc 497.37 Woolley, C.L. The wilderness of Zin. London, 1936.

1937

Arc 530.178F Arik, Remri Ogur. Türk Tarih kurumu tarafindan yapilan Alaca noyük nafriyoti. Ankara, 1937.
Arc 746.30F Banti, Luisa. Luni. Firenze, 1937.
Arc 689.3.15 Béquignon, Y. Recherches archéologiques à Phères de Thessalie. Paris, 1937.
Arc 689.3.17 Bequignon, Y. Recherches archéologiques à Phères de Thessalie. Thèse. Strasbourg, 1937.
Arc 688.5 Béquignon, Y. La vallée du Spercheios des origines au IVe siècle. Thèse. Paris, 1937.
Arc 66.1.144 Béquignon, Yves. La Vallée du spercheios. Paris, 1937.
Arc 600.172 Bisson de la Roque, Fernand. Tôd, 1934 à 1936. Le Caire, 1937.
Arc 530.12.30 Bittel, Kurt. Die Ruinen von Boğazköy, der Hauptstadt des Hethiterreiches. Berlin, 1937.
Arc 685.2FA Blegen, C.W. Prosymna; the Helladic settlement preceding the Argive Heraeum. Cambridge, Eng., 1937. 2v.
Arc 510.2.9F Boehringer, C. Das Temenos für den Herrscher Kult. Berlin, 1937.
Arc 925.68 Bogaevskii, B.L. Druzhiia proiz. i dom. zhivotn. tripol'ia. Leningrad, 1937.
Arc 853.236 Bogen, Alfred. Die Vorgeschichte des magdeburger Landes. Magdeburg, 1937.
Arc 547.6.35F Borchardt, Ludwig. Denkmäler des alten Reiches. Berlin, 1937-1964. 2v.
Arc 815.19.5 Borrelli, L. Le tombe di Pompei a schola semicircolare. Napoli, 1937.
Arc 672.1.34 Bossert, H.T. Alt Kreta. 3. Aufl. Berlin, 1937.
Arc 66.1.141 Boyancé, Pierre. Le culte des muses. Paris, 1937.
Arc 943.28 Brown, F.M. America's yesterday. Philadelphia, 1937.
Arc 432.9 Bruhl, O. Indian temples. Calcutta, 1937.
Arc 889.8 Brunsting, H. Het grafveld onder hees bij Nijmegen. Amsterdam, 1937.
Arc 537.8A Casson, S. Ancient Cyprus; its art and archaeology. London, 1937.
Arc 963.2.20 Cole, Fay C. Rediscovering Illinois. Chicago, 1937.
Arc 432.18 Combaz, Gisbert. L'Inde et l'Orient classique. Paris, 1937. 2v.
Arc 1400.6 Comencini, M. Coins of the modern world, 1870-1936. London, 1937.
Arc 1030.49.5 Cordeiro de Sousa, J.M. Apontamentos de epigrafia portuguesa. 2a ed. Lisboa, 1937.
Arc 387.13F Corolia Ludwig Curtius zum sechzigsten Geburtstag dargebracht. Stuttgart, 1937. 2v.
Arc 861.41.25 Curwen, E. Cecil. The archaeology of Sussex. London, 1937.
Arc 716.4.5 Dörpfeld, W. Alt-Athen und seine Agora. Berlin, 1937-39. 2v.
Arc 505.77F Dunand, Maurice. Fouilles de Byblos. Paris, 1937- 3v.
Arc 823.35 Durand-Lefebvre, M. Art gallo-romain et sculpture romane. Paris, 1937.
Arc 823.35.5 Durand-Lefebvre, M. Art gallo-romain et sculpture romane. Thèse. Paris, 1937.
Arc 505.45.10 Ehrenstein, Theodor. Über die Fresken der Synagoge von Dura Europas. Wien, 1937.
Arc 554.5 Erdöse, K. Mumiäk es minarétek. Budapest, 1937.
Arc 936.15.10 Fewkes, V.J. Neolithic sites in the Yugoslavian portion of the lower Danube valley. Lancaster, 1937?
Arc 66.1.143 Flacelière, Robert. Les Aitoliens a Dalphes. Paris, 1937.
Arc 612.26 Fock, G. Die steinzeitlichen Keulen Mitteleuropas. Inaug. Diss. Düsseldorf, 1937.
Arc 609.6F Fouché, Leo. Mapungubwe, ancient Bantu civilization on the Limpopo. Cambridge, Eng., 1937. 2v.
Arc 645.3 Fuchs, Siegfried. Die griechischen Fundgruppen der frühen Bronzezeit und ihre auswärtigen Beziehungen. Berlin, 1937.
Arc 1510.131 Gaettens, R. Die Münzen der Grafschaft Lüchow. Halle, 1937.
Arc 905.50 Gaheis, Alexander. Lauriacum; Führer durch die Altertümer von Enns. Linz, 1937.

1937 - cont.

Arc 1033.6.10 Gasdia, U.E. La casa pagano cristiana del Celio (Titulus Byzantis sive Pammachii). Roma, 1937.
Arc 1084.19 Goette, J.A. Jade lore. N.Y., 1937.
Arc 1276.30F Grandjean, P.B. Danske kobstaeders segl indtil 1660. København, 1937.
Arc 858.24.21 Great Britain. Commissions. Ancient and Historical Monuments and Constructions of England. An inventory of the historical monuments in Middlesex. London, 1937.
Arc 925.38 Griaznov, M.P. Pazyrykskii kurgan. Moskva, 1937.
Arc 545.227.44PF Griffith, F.L. Catalogue of demotic graffiti of the Dodecaschoenus. v.2. Oxford, 1937.
Arc 936.26.10 György, L. Az Erdelyi Múzeum-Egyesület. Kolozsvár, 1937.
Arc 392.5.7 Hammerton, J.A. Wonders of the past. N.Y., 1937. 2v.
Arc 925.9.12 Hancăr, Franz. Urgeschichte Kaukasuns. Wien, 1937.
Arc 830.333 Helena, T. Les origines de Narbonne. Toulouse, 1937.
Arc 391.6 Hill, George. Percy Gardner, 1846-1937. London, 1937.
Arc 848.28.5 Hohne, Hans. Deutsche Vorzeit. 6. Aufl. Bielefeld, 1937.
Arc 530.90 Jacopi, G. Esplorazioni e studi in Paflagonia e Cappadocia. Roma, 1937.
Arc 505.57 Joint Expedition of the British School of Archaeology in Jerusalem. The stone age of Mount Carmel. Oxford, 1937-1939. 2v.
Arc 1269.27 Kaufmann, E. Studien über Amtssiegel des 13. und 14. Jahrhunderts vornehmlich in Hessen. Inaug. Diss. Marburg, 1937.
Arc 861.29.20 Kenyon, K.M. Excavations at Virsconium (Wroxeter), 1937. Shrewsbury, 1937.
Arc 726.76F Klumbach, H. Tarentiner Grabkunst. Reuttingen, 1937.
Arc 915.4.10 Laur-Belart, Rudolf. Führer durch Augusta Raurica. Basel, 1937.
Arc 963.3.5 Lilly, Eli. Prehistoric antiquities of Indiana. Indianapolis, 1937.
Arc 938.13 Lincke, B. Eine baltische Halsringform der Volkerwanderungszeit. Inaug. Diss. Berlin, 1937.
Arc 340.3.5F London. University. Library. Catalogue of books on archaeology and art. Index. London, 1937.
Arc 340.3.2F London. University. Library. Catalogue of books on archaeology and art. Supplement. London, 1937.
Arc 889.4.10 Maeyer, R. de. De Romeinsche villa's in België. Antwerpen, 1937.
Arc 800.9.5 Maiuri, Amedeo. Ercolano. 2. ed. Roma, 1937.
Arc 726.4.20 Maiuri, Amedeo. The Phlegraean fields, from Virgil's tomb to the grotto of the Cumaean Sibyl. Rome, 1937.
Arc 726.140 Marconi, Pirro. Verona romana. Bergamo, 1937.
Arc 1478.33A Milne, J.G. The development of Roman coinage. Oxford, 1937.
Arc 585.34F Mond, Robert. Cemeteries of Armant. London, 1937. 2v.
Arc 505.42 Montet, Pierre. Les reliques de l'art syrien dans l'Égypte du nouvel empire. Paris, 1937.
Arc 1510.120F Die Münzen des Bistums und der Stadt Hildesheim. Hildesheim, 1937.
Arc 1090.5A New York (City). Museum of Modern Art. Prehistoric rock pictures in Europe and Africa. N.Y., 1937.
Arc 1470.31.10 Newell, E.T. Royal Greek portrait coins. N.Y., 1937.
Arc 530.35F Osten, H.H. von der. The Alishar Hüyük, seasons of 1930-32. Chicago, 1937.
Arc 1490.82 Pagani, Antonio. I bersaglieri nelle medaglie 1836-1936. Milano, 1937.
Arc 723.25 Patroni, G. Storia politica d'Italia. Milano, 1937. 2v.
Arc 1010.10 Peabody Museum of Salem, Salem, Massachusetts. The Hervey Islands adzes in the Peabody Museum of Salem. Salem, 1937.
Arc 588.58F Petrie, W.M.F. Anthedon. London, 1937.
Arc 588.59F Petrie, W.M.F. The funeral furniture of Egypt. London, 1937.
Arc 612.29 Philipp, H. Vor- und Frühgeschichte des Nordens und des Mittelmeerraumes. Berlin, 1937.
Arc 1643.5 Posada, Eduardo. Numismatica colombiana. Bogotá, 1937.
Arc 66.1.142 Recueil Edmond Pottier. Paris, 1937.
Arc 1488.10 Ricci, S. Storia della moneta in Italia. Padova, 1937.
Arc 895.39.5 Rydh, Hanna. Ett bidrag till frågan om suöroornamentiken på stenålders boplatsernas lerkärl. Lund, 1937.
Arc 530.37 Schede, Martin. Ankara und Augustus. Berlin, 1937.
Arc 1020.133 Schnyder, William. Acht Studien zur christlichen Altertumswissenschaft und zur Kirchengeschichte. Luzern, 1937.
Arc 848.30.5 Schultz, W. Altgermanische Kultur in Wort und Bild. 4. Aufl. München, 1937.
Arc 398.4 Scritti in onore di Bartolomeo Nogara. Città del Vaticano, 1937.
Arc 825.3.20 Segni, Emile. Le trésor de la Maison Carrée. Nîmes, 1937?
Arc 893.21 Shetelig, H. Scandinavian archaeology. Oxford, 1937.
Arc 391.5 Simony, C. de. Un curieuse figure d'artiste, Girault de Prangey, 1802-1892. Dijon, 1937.
Arc 584.100.3 Société Royale d'Archéologie d'Alexandrie. Bulletin. Index analytique, 1-41 (1898-1956). Alexandrie, 1937-63. 2v.
Arc 810.51 Sogliano, A. Pompei nel suo sviluppo storico. Roma, 1937.
Arc 430.10F Stein, Mark A. Archaeological reconnaissances in north-western India and south-eastern Iran. London, 1937.
Arc 983.13 Steward, J.H. Petroglyphs of the United States. Washington, 1937.
Arc 1540.23 Sutherland, Carol Humphrey Vivian. Coinage and currency in Roman Britain. London, 1937.
Arc 510.2.10F Szalay, Akos. Die hellenistischen Arsenale. Berlin, 1937.
Arc 1510.60F Tornau, Otto. Münzwesen und Münzen der Grafschaft Mansfeld von der Mitte. Prag, 1937.
Arc 1261.50 Tovar. Esfragistica medieval portuguesa. Lisboa, 1937.
Arc 853.76 Umbreit, Carl. Neue Forschungen zur ostdeutschen Steinzeit und frühen Bronzezeit. Leipzig, 1937.
Arc 1259.3F Vatican. Archivio Vaticano. I sigilli dell'archivio vaticano. v.1-3. Città del Vaticano, 1937- 5v.
Arc 543.131.5 Wales, Horace Geoffrey Q. Towards Angkor in the footsteps of the Indian invaders. London, 1937.
Arc 505.53 Waterman, Leroy. Preliminary report of the University of Michigan excavations at Sepphoris, Palestine, in 1931. Ann Arbor, 1937.
Arc 723.23A Whatmough, J. The foundations of Roman Italy. London, 1937.
Arc 600.44 Winkler, H.A. Völker und Völkerbewegungen im vorgeschichtlichen Oberägypten im Lichte neuer Felshilderfunde. Stuttgart, 1937.
Arc 407.10.5 Woolley, Charles L. Digging up the past. Harmondsworth, 1937.
Arc 925.75 Ziebell, W. Olbia. Hamburg, 1937.

Chronological Listing

1938

Arc 853.27.10F — Albrecht, C. Das Römerlager in Oberaden. Dortmund, 1938. 2v.

Arc 80.1.6 — Archaiologikē Hetairia, Athens. To ergon tēs en Athēnais, Archaiologikēs Hetairias kata ten prōten autēs hekatontaetias. Athēnai, 1938.

Arc 530.135.5 — Arik, Remri Ogur. Turkiye de 1936 yelendaki arkeoloji isleri. Istanbul, 1938.

Arc 925.50.340 — Belov, Grigorii D. Otchet o raskopkakh v Khersonese za 1935-36 gg. Sevastopol', 1938.

Arc 796.2.10F — Beyen, Hendrik G. Die pompejanischen Wanddekoration. v.1-2. Haag, 1938. 4v.

Arc 853.306 — Bohnsack, Dietrich. Die Burgunden in Ostdeutschland und Palen während des letzten Jahrhunderts vor Christus. Inaug. Diss. Leipzig, 1938.

Arc 830.168 — Bonnet, E. Périodes wisigothique, carolingienne et romane. Montpellier, 1938.

Arc 600.45F — Borchardt, Ludwig. Ägyptische Tempel mit Umgang. Kairo, 1938.

Arc 895.7.25F — Brøndsted, J. Danmarks oldtid. Kjøbenhavn, 1938-40. 3v.

Arc 497.40A — Caiger, S.L. Bible and spade. London, 1938.

Arc 1018.58 — Cecchelli, Carlo. Il cenacolo filippino e l'archeologia cristiana. Roma, 1938.

Arc 1400.7 — Coins of the world; the standard catalogue of twentieth century issues. 1. ed. N.Y., 1938.

Arc 861.93.5 — Corder, Philip. Excavations at the Roman town at Brough-Petuaria, 1937. Hull, 1938.

Arc 421.12 — Creel, H.G. Studies in early Chinese culture. London, 1938.

Arc 848.33 — Dittmann, K.H. Untersuchungen zur Geschichte der ältern Bronzezeit im Nordwestdeutschland. Inaug. Diss. Hamburg, 1938.

Arc 66.1.146 — Durry, Marcel. Les cohortes prétoriennes. Paris, 1938.

Arc 584.3.5F — Emery, W.B. Excavations at Saqqara. Cairo, 1938.

Arc 1264.12 — Eygun, F. Sigillographie du Poitou jusqu'en 1515. Poitiers, 1938.

Arc 1264.12.5 — Eygun, F. Sigillographie du Poitou jusqu'en 1515. Thèse. Macon, 1938.

Arc 547.19.5 — Farina, G. Il R. Museo di Antichità di Torino. 2. ed. Roma, 1938.

Htn Arc 1590.8.5* — Farkas, Sandor. Die Kunst und der Wert...Münzen. Aiud, 1938.

Arc 383.67 — Festschrift für August Oxé. Darmstadt, 1938.

Arc 961.1.15 — Fewkes, J.W. W.P.A. excavations at Irene Mound, Savannah, Georgia, May 4, 1938. Savannah, 1938.

Arc 543.3.50F — Field, Henry. Archaeological investigations in Central Asia, 1917-37. n.p., 1938.

Arc 387.14.5 — Folkers, T. Liste des publications de Jean Capart. Leiden, 1938.

Arc 670.5F — Frödin, Otto. Asine; results of the Swedish excavations 1922-1930. Stockholm, 1938.

Arc 495.210F — Ghirshman, Roman. Fouilles de Sialk près de Kashan. Paris, 1938-39. 2v.

Arc 1361.4 — Giesecke, W. Antikes Geldwesen. Leipzig, 1938.

Arc 975.2 — Gillin, John. Archaeological investigations in Nine Mile Canyon, Utah, during the year 1936. Salt Lake City, 1938?

Arc 923.35F — Golomshtok, E.A. The old stone age in European Russia. Diss. Philadelphia, 1938.

Arc 967.2.10 — Graves, H.B. The pre-Cambrian structure of Missouri. Diss. St. Louis, 1938.

Arc 848.34 — Gummel, H. Forschungsgeschichte in Deutschland. Berlin, 1938.

Arc 505.61.5 — Guy, P.L.O. Megiddo tombs. Chicago, 1938.

Arc 895.17.20 — Hallström, Gustaf. Monumental art of Northern Europe from the Stone Age. Stockholm, 1938. 2v.

Arc 880.38A — Hencken, H.O. Cahercomnaun, a stone fort in county Clare. Dublin, 1938.

Arc 600.3.10 — Hermann, A. Führer durch die Altertümer von Memphis und Sakkara. Berlin, 1938.

Arc 968.2.12 — Hewett, E.L. Pajarito Plateau and its ancient people. Albuquerque, 1938.

X Cg Arc 823.30 — Hubert, J. L'art pré-roman. Paris, 1938.

Arc 1018.46.5 — Jerphanion, G. de. La voix des monuments. Rome, 1938.

Arc 522.40 — Kandemir, Selâhattin. Tarova harabesi. 2. basi. Istanbul, 1938.

Arc 1584.1.9 — Karst, J. Précis de numismatique géorgienne. Paris, 1938.

Arc 1675.86 — Katz, Viktor. Medaile na přátelstir a při buzné památky. Praha, 1938.

Arc 1510.38 — Kennepohl, K. Die Münzen von Osnabrück. München, 1938.

Arc 936.180 — Klemenc, J. Archäologische Karte von Jugoslavien. Beograd, 1938.

Arc 935.24F — Kosay, Hâmit Z. Türk Tarih Kurumu tarafindan yapilan Alaca Höyük kafriyati. Ankara, 1938.

Arc 505.68 — Kraeling, C.H. Gerasa, city of the Decapolis. New Haven, Conn., 1938.

Arc 853.80 — Kropf, W. Die Billendorfer Kultur auf Grund der Grabfunde. Leipzig, 1938.

Arc 853.82 — Kuchenbuch, F. Die altmärkisch-osthannöverschen Schalenurnenfelder der spätrömischen Zeit. Inaug. Diss. Halle an der Saale, 1938.

Arc 608.6.29 — Leschi, Louis. Djemila Cuicul de Numidie. Alger, 1938.

Arc 895.60 — Lidén, Oskar L. Hällgröpningstudier i arsbetring till nya sydsverska fynd. Lund, 1938.

Arc 870.22F — Lilienthal-Gesellschaft für Luft. Lufthild und Vorgeschichte. Berlin, 1938.

Arc 853.20.25F — Loeschcke, S. Der Tempelbezirk im Altbachtale zu Trier. Berlin, 1938-42.

Arc 452.1.25F — Mackay, Ernest. Further excavations at Mohenjo-daro. Delhi, 1938. 2v.

Arc 442.15 — Mackay, Ernest J.H. Excavations at Chanhu-Daro...1935-36. Washington, 1938.

Arc 383.94F — Mnemosynon Theodor Wiegand. München, 1938.

Arc 1285.25 — Nehmiz, H. Untersuchungen über die Besiegelung der schlesichen Herzogsurkunden im 13. Jahrhundert. Inaug. Diss. Breslau, 1938.

Arc 968.2.65 — Nesbitt, Paul H. Starkweather ruin: a Mogollon-Pueblo site in the Upper Gila area of New Mexico. Diss. Chicago, 1938.

Arc 853.92 — Nickel, E. Die Steinwerkzeuge der jüngeren Steinzeit. Inaug. Diss. Würzburg, 1938.

Arc 80.1.7F — Oikonomos, G.P. Ta hekaton etē tēs en Athēnais Archaiologikēs Hetaireias. Athēnai, 1938.

Arc 936.195.75 — Ondrouch, Vojtěch. Limes Romanus na Slovensku. Bratislava, 1938.

Arc 400.18 — Passemard, L. (Mme). Les statuettes feminines paléolithiques dites venus stéatophyges. Thèse. Nimes, 1938.

1938 - cont.

Arc 1675.99 — Patrignani, Antonio. Le medaglie di Leone XII, 1823-1829. Catania, 1938.

Arc 588.60 — Petrie, W.M.F. Egyptian architecture. London, 1938.

Arc 452.1.15 — Puri, K.N. La civilisation de Mohen-Jo-Daro. Thèse. Paris? 1938.

Arc 853.69.15 — Reith, A. Vorgeschichte der Schwäbischen Alb. Leipzig, 1938.

Arc 885.22 — Reynolds, P.K.B. Excavations on the site of the Roman fort of Kanovium at Caerhun. Cardiff, 1938.

Arc 497.41 — Richardson, George H. Biblical archaeology, its use and abuse. London, 1938.

Arc 772.10 — Rome (City). Istituto di studi romani. Campania romana. Napoli, 1938.

Arc 505.45.15 — Rostovtsen, M.I. Dura-Europas and its art. Oxford, 1938.

Arc 1313.2.25 — Royal Numismatic Society. Transactions of the International Numismatic Congress. London, 1938.

Arc 505.39.5 — Samaria-Sebaste; reports of the work of the joint expedition in 1931-1933. London, 1938-42. 3v.

Arc 923.40 — Sbornik statei po arkheologii SSSR. Moskva, 1938. 2v.

Arc 530.49 — Schneider, A.M. Die Stadtmauer von Iznik. Berlin, 1938.

Arc 1138.36 — Stieg, Lewis. An introduction to palaeography for librarians. Chicago, 1938.

Arc 853.81 — Stofar, Walter. Spinnen und Weben. Leipzig, 1938.

Arc 830.170 — Taffanel, O. Le cayla de Mailhac, Aube. Carcassonne, 1938.

Arc 505.12.10F — Torczyner, H. Lachish I (Tell Ed Durveir). v.1-4. London, 1938-1940. 6v.

Arc 936.40.15F — Tsonchev, D. Prinosi kum "starata ist. na Ploadir". Sofiia, 1938.

Arc 1433.62F — Unvala, Jamshedji M. Coins of Tabaristān and some Sassenian coins from Susa. Paris, 1938.

Arc 848.35 — Uslar, R. von. Westgermanische Bodenfunde. Berlin, 1938.

Arc 682.20.5F — Valmin, M.N. The Swedish Messenia expedition. Lund, 1938.

Arc 406.4 — Vayson de Pradenne, A. La préhistoire. Paris, 1938.

Arc 974.1.5 — Webb, William S. An archaeological survey of the Norris Basen in eastern Tennessee. Washington, 1938.

Arc 670.2.9 — Weeter, G. Aigina. Berlin, 1938.

Arc 1663.6.15 — Widdington, M. Catalogue of Jacobite medals and touch pieces. Leeds, 1938.

Arc 407.12 — Wieringen, J.H. van. De voor historische mens. Zutphen, 1938.

Arc 700.12.15 — Wiesner, J. Grab und Jenseits. Berlin, 1938.

Arc 587.10.15 — Winkler, Hans A. Rock drawings of southern upper Egypt. London, 1938-39. 2v.

Arc 853.79 — Witter, W. Die älteste Erzgewinnung im nordischgermanischen Lehenskreis. Leipzig, 1938. 2v.

1939

Arc 1163.4.25F — Abbott, N. The rise of the north Arabic script and its Kur'ānic development. Chicago, 1939.

Arc 700.25F — Adriani, A. Le gobelet en argent des amours vendangeurs du musée d'Alexandrie. n.p., 1939.

Arc 746.25F — Andrèn, A.Architectural terracottas from Etrusco-Italic temples. Leipzig, 1939-40. 2v.

Arc 895.15.25 — Bagge, A. Stenåldersboplatserna vid Siretorp i Blekinge. Stockholm, 1939.

Htn Arc 968.2.75* — Baumann, G. Frijoles Canyon pictographs. Santa Fe, 1939.

Arc 853.93F — Behmer, E. Das zweischneidige Schwert der germanischen völkerwanderungszeit. Stockholm, 1939.

Arc 843.62.10 — Bosch-Gimpera, P. Two Celtic waves in Spain. London, 1939.

Arc 895.7.26 — Brøndsted, J. Danmarks stengrave og gravhøge i forhold til landets jordbund. Kjøbenhavn, 1939.

Arc 1510.134F — Buck, H. Die Münzen der Stadt Einbeck. Hildesheim, 1939.

Arc 1470.47 — Caley, Earle R. The composition of ancient Greek bronze coins. Philadelphia, 1939.

Arc 416.9 — Carleton, P. Buried empires; the earliest civilizations of the Middle East. London, 1939.

Arc 726.59.5 — Ceschi, Carlo. Architettura dei templi magalitici di Malta. Roma, 1939.

Arc 3.1.26 — Congrès International d'Archéologie Classique, 6th, Berlin, 1939. Vorläufiges Programm. Berlin? 1939?

Arc 810.54 — Corte, Matteo della. Piccola guida di Pompei. Pompei, 1939.

Arc 432.8 — Cumming, John. Revealing India's past. London, 1939.

Arc 935.9.40F — Demangel, Robert. Le quartier des Manganes et la première région de Constantinople. Paris, 1939.

Arc 432.10 — Dikshit, K.N. Prehistoric civilization of the Indus Valley. Madras, 1939.

Arc 925.13.65 — Domanovszky, G. Steppenvölker und Germanen. Budapest, 1939.

Arc 600.115 — Drioton, E. Sakkarah. Le Caire, 1939.

Arc 505.134 — Ehrich, Ann M. Early pottery of the Jebeleh region. Philadelphia, 1939.

Arc 584.3.10 — Emery, W.B. Excavations at Saqqara, 1937-1938. Cairo, 1939.

Arc 953.23A — Ewers, J.C. Plains Indian painting. Stanford, 1939.

Arc 505.65F — Fitzgerald, G.M. A sixth century monastery at Beth-Shan (Scythopolis). Philadelphia, 1939.

Arc 858.24.23 — Great Britain. Commissions. Ancient and Historical Monuments and Constructions of England. An inventory of the historical monuments in the city of Oxford. London, 1939.

Arc 1588.1.22 — Gumowski, Marian. Corpus numniorum Poloniae. Kraków, 1939.

Arc 723.24 — Haftmann, W. Das italienische Säulenmonument. Leipzig, 1939.

Arc 600.51F — Hayes, William C. The burial chamber of the treasurer Sobk-Mosē from Er Rizeikāt. N.Y., 1939.

Arc 785.70F — Haynes, D.E.L. Porta Argentoriorum. London, 1939.

Arc 861.178 — Hencken, Thalassa Cruso. The excavation of the Iron Age camp on Bredon Hill. London, 1939.

Arc 682.25.35F — Heurtley, W.A. Prehistoric Macedonia. Cambridge, Eng., 1939.

Arc 1163.4.10 — India Office Library. Specimens of Arabic and Persian palaeography. London, 1939.

Arc 905.78 — Kreuz, Trans. Rätsel um Carnuntum. Wien, 1939.

Arc 505.61F — Lamon, R.S. Megiddo I. Chicago, 1939.

Arc 1163.20 — Laurent, M. De abbreviationibus et signis scripturae gothicae. Romae, 1939.

Arc 925.40 — Linevskii, A.M. Petroglify Karelii. Petrozavodsk, 1939.

Arc 925.50.235 — Lisin, V. Kratkii putevoditel' po antichnomu otdelu i vaskopkam khersonesa. Sevastopol', 1939.

Arc 785.52.5 — L'Orange, N.P. Der spätantike Bildschmuch. Berlin, 1939.

Chronological Listing

1939 - cont.

Arc 396.15F Lugli, Giuseppe. Saggi di explorazione archeologica. Roma, 1939.

Arc 785.71 Lyngby, H. Die Tempel der Fortuna und der Mater Matuta am Forum Boarium in Rom. Berlin, 1939.

Arc 1480.34 Manns, F. Münzkundliche und historische Unterschungen über die Zeit der Illyrerkaiser. Inaug. Diss. Würzburg, 1939.

Arc 1470.43 May, J.M.F. The coinage of Damastion and the lesser coinages of the Illyra-Paeonian region. London, 1939.

Arc 1330.20 Mayer, Leo Ary. Bibliography of Moslem numismatics, India excepted. London, 1939.

Arc 1077.2.51 Miller, M. (Sweeney). My hobby of the cross. N.Y., 1939.

Arc 1458.22 Milne, Joseph G. Greek and Roman coins and the study of history. London, 1939.

Arc 905.12.15 Miltner, F. Das zweite Amphitheater von Carnuntum. Wien, 1939.

Arc 968.2.70 Morris, E.H. Archaeological studies in the La Plata district, southwestern Colorado and northwestern New Mexico. Washington, 1939.

Arc 505.92 Murray, Margaret A. Petra, the rock city of Edom. London, 1939.

Arc 861.23.15 Oakley, K.P. A survey of the prehistory of the Farnham district, Surrey. Guildford, 1939.

Arc 609.1.35 O'Brien, T.P. The prehistory of Uganda Protectorate. Cambridge, Eng., 1939.

Arc 672.1.28.5 Pendlebury, J.D.S. The archaeology of Crete. London, 1939.

Arc 1468.36 Pierfitte, G. Les monnaies grecques du musée Saint Raymond de Toulouse. Toulouse, 1939.

Arc 870.5.7 Pugsley, A.J. Dew-ponds in fable and fact. London, 1939.

Arc 1480.50 Rajic, H.P. Ilustrovani katalog novaca rimskih i vizantiskih vladaoca. Beograd, 1939?

Arc 66.1.147 Robert, Fernand. Thymélè. Paris, 1939.

Arc 726.125F Säflund, G. Le terremare delle provincie di Modena. Lund, 1939.

Arc 403.16.10 Schliemann, Heinrich. Heinrich Schliemann. 3. Aufl. Leipzig, 1939.

Arc 543.40.15 Schnitger, F.M. Forgotten kingdoms in Sumatra. Leiden, 1939.

Arc 746.20 Shaw, C. Etruscan Perugia. Baltimore, 1939.

Arc 936.195.175 Skutil, Josef. Pravěké nálezy na Kloboucku. Klobuka, 1939.

Arc 853.345.1 Stoll, Hermann. Die Alamannengräber von Hailfingen. Photoreproduction. Berlin, 1939.

Arc 853.91 Ströbel, R. Die Feuersteingeröte der Pfahlbaukultur. Leipzig, 1939.

Arc 853.96 Thärigen, Günter. Die Nordharzgruppe der Elbgermanen bis zur sächsischen Überlagerung. Berlin, 1939.

Arc 1033.12.9.5F Vignon, P. Le Saint Suaire de Turin devant la science. 2. éd. Paris, 1939.

Arc 853.84 Weiershausen, P. Vorgeschichtliche Eisenbütten Deutschlands. Leipzig, 1939.

Arc 66.1.148 Wirilleumier, Pierre. Tarente; des origines a la conquête romaine. Paris, 1939. 2v.

Arc 545.240PF Wreszinski, Walter. Atlas zur altaegyptischen Kulturgeschichte. v.2. Leipzig, 1939.

Arc 421.20 Yale University. Gallery of Fine Arts. An exhibition of Chinese antiquities from Ch'ang Sha. New Haven, 1939.

Arc 853.65.15 Zatz, Lothar. Die Altsteinzeit in Niederschlesien. Leipzig, 1939.

194-

Arc 505.68.10 Jordan. Department of Antiquities. Official guide to Jerash. Jerusalem, 194-?

1940

Arc 925.75.3FA Akademiia Nauk URSR, Kiev. Institut Arkheologicheskaia. Ol'viia. Kiev, 1940.

Arc 880.40 Ancient Monuments Advisory Council for Northern Ireland. A preliminary survey of the ancient monuments of Northern Ireland. Belfast, 1940.

Arc 505.12.10.5 Balazs, György. Egy feltárt bibliai város. Budapest, 1940.

Arc 889.26 Beckers, H.J. Voorgeschiedenis van Zuid Limburg. Maastricht, 1940.

Arc 1033.35.155 Braun, J. Die Reliquiare des christlichen Kultes und ihre Entwicklung. Freiburg, 1940.

Arc 925.321.10 Briusov, Aleksandr I. Istoriia drevnei Karelii. Moskva, 1940.

Arc 505.69 Broome, E.C. The dolmens of Palestine and Transjordania. Philadelphia, 1940.

Arc 1478.38 Brown, D.F. Temples of Rome as coin types. N.Y., 1940.

Arc 452.3 Brown, William N. A pillared hall from a temple at Madura, India. Philadelphia, 1940.

Arc 726.101 Calderini, A. L'anfiteatro romano. Milano, 1940.

Arc 785.75 Calderini, A. La zona di piazza S. Sepolcro. Milano, 1940.

Arc 726.25.15F Calza, Guido. La necropoli del porto di Roma nell'isola sacra. Roma, 1940.

Arc 858.50A Childe, V.G. Prehistoric communities of the British Isles. London, 1940.

Arc 858.51 Clark, John Grahame Douglas. Prehistoric England. London, 1940.

Arc 1613.17 Coffin, J. Our American money. N.Y., 1940.

Arc 3.1.26.5 Congrès International d'Archéologie Classique, 6th, Berlin, 1939. Bericht über den VI. Internationalen Kongress für Archäologie, Berlin, 21.-26. August, 1939. Berlin, 1940.

Arc 726.99 Consortini, L. Volterra nell'antichità. Volterra, 1940.

Arc 955.5 Cummings, B. Kinishba. Phoenix, Arizona, 1940.

Arc 595.32.15 Davidson, D. The Great Pyramid; its divine message. 8th ed. London, 1940.

Arc 1663.30 Delbrueck, Richard. Die Münzbildnisse von Maximinus bis Carenus. Berlin, 1940.

Arc 540.6 Dikaios, P. The excavations at Vounous-Bellapais in Cyprus. London, 1940.

Arc 838.25 Dixon, P. The Iberians of Spain. London, 1940.

Arc 936.40.50 Féher, Géza. Roliata i kulturata na prabulgarite. Sofiia, 1940.

Arc 893.24 Fra Danmarksungtid. København, 1940.

Arc 513.24F Gabriel, Albert. Voyages archeologiques dans la Turquie orientale. Paris, 1940. 2v.

Arc 505.66 Garstang, John. The story of Jericho. London, 1940.

Arc 505.67 Glueck, N. The other side of the Jordan. New Haven, Conn., 1940.

1940 - cont.

Arc 1148.20 Groningen, B.A. Short manual of Greek palaeography. Leiden, 1940.

Arc 595.33.5 Haberman, F. Armageddon has come; the climax of the ages is near. 2. ed. St. Petersburg, 1940.

Arc 743.18 Hanfmann, G.M.A. The Etruscans and their art. n.p., 1940.

Arc 612.28 Hawkes, C.F.C. The prehistoric foundations of Europe to the Mycenean age. London, 1940.

Arc 968.2.80 Hendron, J.W. Prehistory of El Rito de los Frijoles, Bandelier national monument. Phoenix, 1940.

Arc 1663.15.5 Hesse, Waldemar E. Die tragbaren Ehrenzeichen des Deutschen Reiches. Berlin, 1940.

Arc 925.9.60 Iessen, Aleksandr A. Mozdokskii mogil'nik. Leningrad, 1940.

Arc 435.1.20 India. Archaeological Survey. Library. Consolidated catalogue. New Delhi, 1940.

Arc 483.10 Iraq. Department of Antiquities. Excavations at Samarra, 1936-1939. Baghdad, 1940.

Arc 600.70 Jéquier, Gustave. Douze ans de fouilles dans la nécropole memphite, 1924-1936. Neuchâtel, 1940.

Arc 935.28F Kansu, Ş. Türk Tarih Kurumu tarafindan yapilan Etiyrkusu kafiryati raporu. Ankara, 1940.

Arc 497.44 Kenyon, F.G. The Bible and archaeology. London, 1940.

Arc 530.12.32 Krause, K. Boğazköy. Berlin, 1940.

Arc 1500.64 Le Gentilhomme, P. Melanges de numismatique merovingienne. Paris, 1940.

Arc 889.4.15 Maeyer, R. de. De overblijfselev der Romainsche villa's in België. Antwerpen, 1940.

Arc 853.85 Meier-Böke, A. Die frühe Altsteinzeit am der Weser. Leipzig, 1940.

Arc 585.47 Mond, Robert. Temples of Armant. London, 1940. 2v.

Arc 1221.6 Moore, Ada S. Ancient oriental cylinder and other seals with a description of the collection of Mrs. William H. Moore. Chicago, 1940.

Arc 1615.9 Mosher, S. United States commemorative coins, 1892-1939. N.Y., 1940.

Arc 588.62F Murray, M.A. A street in Petra. London, 1940.

Arc 689.8 Nolters, P. Das Kabirenheiligtum bei Theben. Berlin, 1940.

Arc 672.5.15F Payne, H. Perachora, the sanctuaries of Hera Akraia and Lemenia. Oxford, 1940. 2v.

Arc 1490.8.10 Pennisi, Agostino. Siciliae veteres nummi. Acireale, 1940.

Arc 588.63 Petrie, W.M.F. Wisdom of the Egyptians. London, 1940.

Arc 1148.32 Plagiannēs, D.I. Byzantinoi sēmeiographoi. Athēnia, 1940.

Arc 600.52 Posener, G. Princes et pays d'Asie et de Nubie. Bruxelles, 1940.

Arc 1590.9 Rajić, N.P. Illustr. katal. nov. srpekhikh tsareva, 700-1710 g. Beograd, 1940.

Arc 1625.3 Raymond, W. The coins of Mexico in silver and copper, 1536-1939. N.Y., 1940.

Arc 848.38 Reinerth, Hans. Vorgeschichte der deutschen Stämme. Leipzig, 1940. 3v.

Arc 421.14 Reischauer, E.O. Japanese archaeological work on the Asiatic continent. Baltimore, 1940.

Arc 426.9 Reischauer, E.O. The thunder-weapon in ancient Japan. Baltimore, 1940.

Arc 772.12 Ryberg, Inez. An archaeological record of Rome from the seventh to the second century B.C. v.1-2. Philadelphia, 1940.

Arc 1490.60 Särström, M. A study in the coinage of the Mamertines. Lund, 1940.

Arc 488.17F Schmidt, E.F. Flights over ancient cities of Iran. Chicago, 1940.

Arc 858.56 Shètelig, H. Viking antiquities in Great Britain and Ireland. pts.1-3, 4-6. Oslo, 1940. 2v.

Arc 383.53 Société Nationale des Antiquaires de France. Mélanges en hommage à la mémoire de Fr. Martroye. Paris, 1940.

Arc 488.14A Stein, Mark A. Old routes of western Iran. London, 1940.

Arc 712.25 Stevens, G.P. The setting of the Periclean Parthenon. Baltimore, 1940.

Arc 66.1.149 Thouvenot, R. Essai sur le province romaine de Béteque. Paris, 1940.

Arc 447.6.5F Vats, Madho Sarup. Excavations at Harappa. Delhi, 1940. 2v.

Arc 406.4.5 Vayson de Pradenne, A. Prehistory. London, 1940.

1941

Arc 530.168 Ankara. Universite Enstitusu. Arkeoloji arasturmalari. Istanbul, 1941.

Arc 1033.12.87 Arnason, H. The history of the chalice of Antioch. n.p., 1941.

Arc 785.15.15 Bartoli, P.S. Die Traianssäule. Voorburg, 1941.

VArc 543.152 Bendefy, Lásylo. Syallam tolmács kůldetése Naagy Sändor folokog. Budapest, 1941.

Arc 66.1.150 Bérard, Jean. La colonisation grecque de l'Italie meridionale et de la Sicilie. Paris, 1941.

Arc 936.195.70 Boehn, Jároslav. Kronika objeveného věku. Praha, 1941.

Arc 1433.43 British Museum. Department of Coins and Medals. A catalogue of the Muhammadan coins in the British Museum. London, 1941. 2v.

Arc 670.6 Broneer, O. The lion monument at Amphipolis. Cambridge, Mass., 1941.

Arc 497.47 Burrows, M. What mean these stones? New Haven, 1941.

Arc 961.1.20 Caldwell, Joseph. Irene Mound site, Chatham County, Georgia. Athens, 1941.

Arc 1033.12.24 Chubinashvili, G.N. Siriiskaia chasha v Ushgule. n.p., 1941.

Arc 858.51.2 Clark, John Grahame Douglas. Prehistoric England. 2. ed. London, 1941.

Arc 793.14.5A Corti, Egon C. Untergang und Auferstehung von Pompeji und Herculaneum. 3. Aufl. München, 1941.

Arc 397.15 Curle, Alexander O. Sir George Macdonald, 1862-1940. London, 1941?

Arc 530.85 Doerner, F.K. Inschriften und Denkmäler aus Bithynien. Berlin, 1941.

Arc 953.24A Douglas, F.H. Indian art of the United States. N.Y., 1941.

Arc 584.4F Dunbar, J.H. The rock-picutres of Lower Nubia. Cairo, 1941.

Arc 628.23 Elderkin, G.W. Archeological papers. v.1-5, 6-10. Springfield, Mass., 1941- 2v.

Arc 936.195.20 Filip, Jan. Umělecký řemeslo v pravěku. Praha, 1941.

Arc 609.1.50 Fletcher, Harold Clarkson. Psychic episodes of Great Zimbabwe. Johannesburg, 1941.

Chronological Listing

1941 - cont.

Arc 340.37 — Frontier Forts and Trails Survey. A partial bibliography of the archaeology of Pennsylvania and adjacent states. Harrisburg, 1941.
Arc 975.5 — Gillin, John. Archaeological investigations in central Utah. Cambridge, 1941.
Arc 391.8 — Giovannoni, G. Il restauro dei monumenti. Roma, 1941?
Arc 497.45 — Gordon, Cyrus H. The living past. N.Y., 1941.
Arc 700.21 — Hall, Elise von. Over den oorsprong van de grieksche grafstele. Proefschrift. Amsterdam, 1941.
Arc 488.10F — Herzfeld, Ernst E. Iran in the ancient East. London, 1941.
Arc 1478.39 — Hirmer, Max. Römische Kaisermünzen. Leipzig, 1941.
Arc 530.150 — Institut Français d'Archéologie, Istanbul. Phrygie, exploration archéologique. v.1-3. Paris, 1941- 2v.
Arc 618.8 — Jacobsthal, P. Imagery in early Celtic art. London, 1941.
Arc 1470.55 — Kerényi, K. Der Mythos der Hellenen. Amsterdam, 1941.
Arc 1033.17.100.5 — Keyer, F.P.W. (Mrs.). The grace of Guadalupe. N.Y., 1941.
Arc 935.26F — Kosay, Hâmit Z. Türk Tarih Kurumu tarafindan apilan Pazarli kafreyati raporu. Ankara, 1941.
Arc 1470.44 — Lange, Kurt. Götter Griechenlands. Berlin, 1941.
Arc 1030.54F — Lietzmann, Hans. Corpus der griechisch-christlichen Inschriften von Hellas. Athen, 1941.
Arc 746.24 — Lombardi, M. Faesulae (Fiesole) Regio VII Etruria. Roma, 1941.
Arc 843.83 — Madrid. Museo Arqueologico Nacional. Catalogo de las exvatos de bronce. Madrid, 1941. 2v.
Arc 726.103 — Maetzke, G. Florentia (Firenze). Rome, 1941.
Arc 1163.2.29 — Millares Carlo, A. Nuevos estudios de paleografía española. Mexico, 1941.
Arc 562.2.45F — Miscellanea gregoriana. Roma, 1941.
Arc 923.126 — Moscow. Gosudarstvennyi Istoricheskii Muzei. Raboty arhheologicheskikh ekspeditsii. Moskva, 1941. 2v.
Arc 416.11 — Nag, K. India and the Pacific world. Calcutta, 1941.
Arc 340.4 — Orlinsky, H.M. An indexed bibliography of the writings of W.F. Albright. New Haven, 1941.
Arc 530.100 — Otto-Dorn, K. Das Islamische Iznik. Berlin, 1941.
Arc 726.205F — Pesce, Gennaro. I rilievi dell'anfiteatro Campano. Roma, 1941.
Arc 513.42 — Pfannenstiel, Max. Die altsteinzeitlichen Kulturen Anatoliens. Berlin, 1941.
Arc 953.25 — Renaud, E.B. Classification and description of Indian stone artifacts. Gunnison, 1941.
Arc 66.1.151 — Renouard, Yves. Les relations des papes d'Avignon. Paris, 1941.
Arc 746.27 — Riis, Poul J. Tyrrhenika, an archaeological study of the Etruscan sculpture in the archaic and classical periods. Copenhagen, 1941.
Arc 936.85 — Schneider, A.M. Die Grabung in Westhofler Sophienkirche zu Istanbul. Berlin, 1941.
Arc 612.M.4 — Schuchhardt, Carl. Alteuropa. Berlin, 1941.
Arc 700.19.5 — Scranton, R.L. The chronology of Greek walls. Thesis. Chicago, 1941.
Arc 700.19 — Scranton, R.L. Greek walls. Cambridge, 1941.
Arc 975.10 — Smith, E.R. The archaeology of Deadman Cave, Utah. Salt Lake City, 1941.
Arc 838.27 — Sociedad Española de Antropología, Etnografía y Prehistoria. Corona de estudios. Madrid, 1941.
Arc 403.17 — Sukhov, P.A. Arkheologicheskie pamiatniki. Moskva, 1941.
Arc 936.40.25F — Tsonchev, D. Le sanctuaire thrace prés du village de Batkoun. Sofia, 1941.
Arc 969.1.17 — Vietzen, R.C. Ancient man in northern Ohio. Lorain, Ohio, 1941.
Arc 685.1.5 — Welter, Gabriel. Troizen und Kalaureia. Berlin, 1941.
Arc 1478.50 — West, Louis. Gold and silver coin standards in the Roman empire. N.Y., 1941.
Arc 407.19 — White, Anne Terry. Lost worlds; the romance of archaeology. N.Y., 1941.
Arc 965.1 — Whiteford, Guy L. Indian archaeology in Saline County, Kansas. Salina, 1941.
Arc 1190.82 — Yazir, Mahmud. Siyakat yazisi. Istanbul, 1941.

1942

Arc 861.118 — Atkinson, Donald. Report on excavations at Wroxeter...1923-1927. Oxford, 1942.
Arc 1356.5 — Babelon, Jean. Le portrait dans l'antiquité d'apres les monnaies. Paris, 1942.
Arc 513.21.10 — Bittel, Kurt. Kleinasiatische Studien. Istanbul, 1942.
Arc 943.29 — Brown, A. Indian relics and their values. Chicago, 1942.
Arc 66.7.3 — Bulletino di commissione archeologico municipale. Indici generali dal 1922-1938. Roma, 1942.
Arc 1353.7F — Copenhagen. National Museet. Sylloge nummorum Graecorum. v.1-30,41-42. Copenhagen, 1942- 20v.
Arc 969.9 — Cressman, L.S. Archaeological researches in the northern great basin. Washington, 1942.
Arc 830.172 — Cumont, Franz. La stèle du danseur d'Antibes et son decor végétal. Paris, 1942.
Arc 936.140.15 — Dimitrov, Dimitur P. Nadgrobnite plochi ot rimsko vreme. Sofiia, 1942.
Arc 716.7.15F — Dörpfeld, W. Erechtheion. Berlin, 1942.
Arc 726.81F — Dohan, Edith H. Italic tomb-groups in the University Museum. Philadelphia, 1942.
Arc 225.1.5 — Erdélyi Muzéum-Egyesület, Cluj. Emlékkünyv az Erdélyi Muzeum-Egyesületjélszázados ünnepére, 1859-1909. Kolozsvár, 1942.
Arc 1018.50 — Ferretto, Giuseppe. Note storico-bibliografiche di archeologia cristiana. Città del Vaticano, 1942.
Arc 66.1.152 — Feyel, Michel. Palybe et l'histoire de Biotre. Paris, 1942.
Arc 1033.12.85 — Filson, F.V. Who are the figures on the chalice of Antioch? n.p., 1942.
Arc 556.3 — Galassi, G. Tehena. Roma, 1942.
Arc 905.144 — Gyor története a tizenharmadik század közepéig. Györ, 1942.
Arc 888.20 — Heemskerck Düker, W.F. van. Wat aarde bewaarde. Den Haag, 1942?
Arc 66.1.154 — Heurgon, J. Recherches sur l'histoire, la religion et la civilisation. Paris, 1942.
NEDL Arc 307.3.25F — International Congress of Americanists, 27th, Mexico and Lima, 1939. Actas. México, 1942-47.
Arc 848.8.10 — Kossinna, Gustaf. Altgermanische Kulturhöhe. 8. Aufl. Leipzig, 1942.
Arc 1390.11 — Lange, Kurt. Münzkunst des Mittelalters. Leipzig, 1942.
Arc 493.15F — Langsdorff, A. Tall-i-Bakun A, season of 1932. Chicago, 1942.
Arc 608.2.37 — Lapeyre, Gabriel G. Carthage punique. Paris, 1942.

1942 - cont.

Arc 785.72A — Lehmann-Hartleben, K. Dionysiac sarcophagi in Baltimore. Baltimore, 1942.
Arc 1190.45 — Luzzatto, G.I. Epigrafia giuridica greca e romana. Milano, 1942.
Arc 488.19F — McCown, D.E. The comparative stratigraphy of early Iran. Chicago, 1942.
Arc 810.42.10 — Maiuri, Amedeo. L'ultima fase edilizia di Pompei. Roma, 1942.
Arc 1088.4 — Mariani, Lucilla. Le nave di Nemi nella bibliografia. Roma, 1942.
Arc 838.9.10 — Mélida, José R. Arqueológica española. 2. ed. Barcelona, 1942.
Arc 925.12.3 — Minns, E.H. The art of the northern nomads. London, 1942.
Arc 600.75 — Montet, Pierre. Tanis, douze années de fouilles. Paris, 1942.
Arc 880.39.5A — Movius, H.L. The Irish Stone Age. Cambridge, Eng., 1942.
Arc 785.104 — Nogara, Bartolomeo. Monumenti romani scoperti negli anni 1938-XVI-1939-XVII nell'area del Palazzo della Cancelleria. Roma, 1942.
Arc 1084.17F — Nott, S.C. Chinese jades in the S.C. Nott collection. St. Augustine, 1942.
Arc 522.30 — Perret, J. Les origines de la legende troyenne de Rome. Thèse. Paris, 1942.
Arc 1645.2 — Raymond, Wayte. The coins of South America; silver and copper. British Guiana, Dutch Guiana, French Guiana. N.Y., 1942.
Arc 595.23.5F — Reisner, G.A. A history of the Giza mecropolis. Cambridge, Mass., 1942- 2v.
Arc 905.126.1 — Rieth, Adolf. Die Eisentechnik der Hallstattzeit. Photoreproduction. Leipzig, 1942.
Arc 435.2.53 — Sen, B. Some historical aspects of the inscriptions of Bengal. Calcutta, 1942.
Arc 547.28 — Smith, W.S. Ancient Egypt as represented in the Museum of Fine Arts. Boston, 1942.
Arc 895.61 — Stenberger, Marten. Sweden. London, 1942?
Arc 936.140 — Todorov, Ianko. Antichna kultura v Bulgariia. Sofiia, 1942?
Arc 421.18 — Torü, P. Sculptured stone tombs of the Lion dynasty. Peking, 1942.
Arc 843.71 — Vives, José. Inscripciones cristianas de la España romana y visigoda. Barcelona, 1942.
Arc 658.3.20 — Weber, Shirley H. Schliemann's first visit to America, 1850-1851. Cambridge, 1942.
Arc 600.54 — Winlock, H.E. Excavations at Deir el Bahri, 1911-1931. N.Y., 1942.
Arc 1190.82.5 — Yazir, Mahmud. Eski yazilari okuma anahtari. Istanbul, 1942.

1943

Arc 726.130 — Akerstrom, A. Der geometrische Stil in Italien. Lund, 1943.
Arc 936.155 — Bernshtam, A.N. Istoriko-kul'turnoe proshloe severnoi Kirgizii. Frunze, 1943.
Arc 386.26 — Breasted, C. Pioneer to the past. N.Y., 1943.
Arc 1025.70 — Cecchelli, C. La chiesa delle catacombe. Roma, 1943.
Arc 642.7F — Chisholm, H.J. Hellas. N.Y., 1943.
Arc 396.16 — Conference on the Future of Archaeology, University of London, 1943. Conference on the future of archaeology held at the University of London. London, 1943?
Arc 389.3 — Evans, Joan. Time and chance; story of Arthur Evans and his forebears. London, 1943.
Arc 608.54 — Fernandez de Castro y Pedrera, R. Historia y exploración de las ruinas de Cazaza. Larache, 1943.
Arc 1494.7 — Ferreira Barros, A. Moedas portuguesas dos reinados de D. Carlos I. e de D. Manuel II. Pôrto, 1943.
Arc 441.9 — Gadre, A.S. Important inscriptions from the Baroda state. Baroda, 1943.
Arc 838.28 — Garcia y Bellido, A. La dama de Elche. Madrid, 1943.
Arc 726.70.10F — Garger, E. Der Trajansbogen in Benevent. Berlin, 1943.
Arc 969.1.3.7 — Griffin, James B. The Fort Ancient aspect. Ann Arbor, 1943.
Arc 66.1.155 — Grimal, Pierre. Las jardins romains. Paris, 1943.
Arc 66.1.153 — Guillon, P. Les trépieds du Ptoion. Paris, 1943.
Arc 392.10.5 — Hewett, Edgar Lee. Campfire and trail. Albuquerque, 1943.
Arc 530.115 — Irag. Department of Antiquities. Ctesiphon and Hatra. Baghdad, 1943.
Arc 936.100 — Karaman, L. Živa stariua. Zagreb, 1943.
Arc 716.12A — Karo, G.H. An Attic cemetery. Philadelphia, 1943.
Arc 1076.4.5 — Kuuliala, Vilji K. Kellot temppelin. Sortavala, 1943.
Arc 1366.2 — Lederer, Philipp. Neue Beiträge zur antike Münzkunde. Bern, 1943.
Arc 700.20 — McDonald, W.A. The political meeting places of the Greeks. Baltimore, 1943.
Arc 497.46 — McGown, J.C. The ladder of progress in Palestine. N.Y., 1943.
Arc 936.65F — Mansel, A.M. Trakya-Kirklareli. Ankara, 1943.
Arc 843.70 — Mattos, A. de. Dois estudos: "Manis Pallas"; "Giral Cabrom". Porto, 1943.
Arc 838.26 — Montey, P. Historia da arquitectura primitiva em Portugal. Lisboa, 1943.
Arc 785.73 — Munoz, A. L'isolamento del Colle Capitolino. Roma, 1943.
Arc 843.69 — Oliveira, M. De Talabriga a Lancobriga pela via militar romano. Coimbra, 1943.
Arc 943.31 — Panneton, P. Un monde était leur empire. Montréal, 1943.
Arc 905.105 — Pittioni, Richard. Der frühmittelalterliche Gräberfund von Köttloch. Brun, 1943.
Arc 945.6 — Posnansky, Arthur. Las Americas son un nuevo mundo. La Paz, Bolivia, 1943.
Arc 400.20 — Powell, D. The traveller's journey is done. London, 1943.
Arc 595.01F — Pyramids. Haverhill, 1943.
Arc 530.110 — Schneider, A.M. Die römischen und byzantinischen Denkmäler von Iznik-Nicaea. Berlin, 1943.
Arc 848.15.7 — Schuchhardt, C. Vorgeschichte von Deutschland. 5. Aufl. München, 1943.
Arc 1030.55PF — Silvagni, Angelo. Monumenta epigraphica christiana saeculo XIII. v.1-2. Civitate Vaticana, 1943-
Arc 875.44 — Simpson, William D. The province of Mar. Aberdeen, 1943.
Arc 1082.5F — Steensberg, Axel. Ancient harvesting implements. København, 1943.
Arc 895.22.3 — Stenberger, M. Das Grabfeld von Västerbjers auf Gotland. Stockholm, 1943.
Arc 1080.5 — Sundwall, J. Die älteren italischen Fibeln. Berlin, 1943.
Arc 513.20.5 — Ülgen, Ali Saim. Anitlaria koranmasi ve onarilmasi. Ankara, 1943.

1943 - cont.

Arc 600.55F Varille, Alexandre. Karnak. v.1,3-4. Le Caire, 1943-51. 4v.

Arc 830.192 Werner, J. Der Fund von Ittenheim. Strassburg, 1943.

Arc 505.45.20 Yale University. The excavations at Dura-Europas. New Haven, 1943-1949. 13v.

1944

Arc 453.10 Bendrey, F. A study of Muslim inscriptions. Bombay, 1944?

Arc 1229.5 Bossert, H.T. Die hethitisches Königssiegel. Berlin, 1944.

Arc 66.1.156 Boulet, Marquerite. Questiones Johannes Galli. Paris, 1944.

Arc 888.10 Byvonck, A.W. De voorgeschiedenis nou Nederland. Leiden, 1944.

Arc 66.1.160 Chatelain, Louis. Le Maroc des romains. Paris, 1944. 2v.

Arc 387.9.5A Childe, Vere Gordon. Progress and archaeology. London, 1944.

Arc 875.32.10 Diack, F.C. The inscription of Pictland. Aberdeen, 1944.

Arc 404.2 Driver, Godfrey Rolles. Reginald Cambell Thompson. London, 1944.

Arc 853.99F Franken, M. Die Alamannen zwischen iller und lech. Berlin, 1944.

Arc 670.7F Holmberg, E.J. The Swedish excavations at sea in Arcadia. Lund, 1944.

Arc 936.100.25 Horvat, L.A. Konzervatorski rad kod Hrvata. Zagreb, 1944.

Arc 1613.20 Johnson, J.B. Auction prices: "United States coins." 3. ed. Cincinnati, 1944.

Arc 936.100.10 Karaman, L. Baštiva djedova. Zagreb, 1944.

Arc 654.1 Kunze, Emil. Olympische Forschungen. Berlin, 1944- 8v.

Arc 726.85 Lamb, Carl. Die Tempel von Paestum. Leipzig, 1944.

Arc 1480.44 Lanckorónski, L.M. Das römische Bildnis in Meisterwerken der Münzkunst. Amsterdam, 1944.

Arc 905.110 László, Gyula. A honfoglaló magyar nép élete. 2. biadás. Budapest, 1944.

Arc 848.46 Mähling, W. Die frühgermanische Landnahme im mitteldeutsch-sächsisch-nordböhmischen Gebiet. Prag, 1944.

Arc 432.12 Mode, Heinz. Indische Frühkulturen und ihre Beziehungen zum Westen. Basel, 1944.

Arc 1453.3 Morgenroth, Sigmund. Medals and plaquettes from the S. Morgenroth collection. Chicago, 1944.

Arc 654.1PF Olympische Forschungen. Plates. Berlin, 1944-50.

Arc 925.50.220 Pasternak, Iaroslav. Staryi Halych. Krakiv, 1944.

Arc 700.35 Richter, G.M.A. Archaic attic gravestones. Cambridge, 1944.

Arc 1423.17 Romanoff, P. Jewish symbols on ancient Jewish coins. Philadelphia, 1944.

Arc 403.18 Schuckhartt, C. Aus Leben und Arbeit. Berlin, 1944.

Arc 1138.40 Scritti di paleografia e diplomatica in onore de Vincenzo Federici. Firenze, 1944.

Arc 1490.92 Shuhaievs'kyi, Valentyn. Funde venezianischer Münzen des 13. Jahrhundert in der Ostukraine als geschichtliche Quelle. Berlin, 1944.

Arc 889.12 Tourneur, V. Les Belges avant César. Bruxelles, 1944.

Arc 66.1.157 Vallois, René. L'architecture hellénique et hellenistique a Délos. Paris, 1944-53. 2v.

Arc 407.14 Watzinger, C. Theodor Wiegand. München, 1944.

Arc 889.9 Weerd, H. van de. Inleiding tot de Gallo-Romeinsche archeologie der Nederlanden. Antwerpen, 1944.

Arc 958.1.15 Weslager, Clinton Alfred. Delaware's buried past. Philadelphia, 1944.

1945

Arc 923.132 Akademiia nauk SSSR. Institut Arkheologii. Stogi i perspektivy razvitiia sovetskoi arkheologii. Moskva, 1945.

Arc 513.26 Akurgal, E. Arkeoloji arastirmalari. Ankara, 1945.

Arc 1163.18 Arens, Fritz V. Mainzer Inschriften. Stuttgart, 1945.

Arc 567.1.15F Florence. Università. Scritti dedicati alla memoria di Ippolito Rosellini. Firenze, 1945.

Arc 843.82 Galia y Sarañana, José. Prehistoria de Aragón. Zaragoza, 1945.

Arc 66.1.161 Mahor, J.B. L'ordre cistercien et son gouvernement. Paris, 1945.

Arc 628.27 Paribeni, R. Filologia classica. Milano, 1945.

Arc 432.13 Piggott, Stuart. Some ancient cities of India. London, 1945.

Arc 1433.60 Rabino, Hyacinth L. Coins, medals, and seals of the shâhs of Irân. Hertford, 1945.

Arc 1400.7.2 Raymond, Wayte. Coins of the world, twentieth century issues. 2. ed. N.Y., 1945.

Arc 530.125 Le sanctuaire de Sinuri prés de Mylasa. Paris, 1945.

Arc 1418.13 Sivaramamurti, C. Numismatic parallels of Kālidāsa. Madras, 1945.

Arc 893.25 Sprockhoff, E. Und zeugen von einem stolzen Geschlecht. Oslo, 1945.

Arc 1348.79 Tourneur, Victor. Initiation à la numismatique. Bruxelles, 1945.

Arc 858.62 Winbolt, S.E. Britain B.C. Harmondsworth, Eng., 1945.

Arc 600.65F Winlock, H.E. The slain soldiers of Neb-hebek-Re' Mentu-hotpe. N.Y., 1945.

1946

Arc 550.5 Aboudi, M. Guide book to the antiquities of upper Egypt and Nubia. 4. ed. Cairo, 1946.

Arc 530.53 Akurgal, E. Remarques stylistiques sur les reliefs de Malatya. Istanbul, 1946.

Arc 1588.6 Artuk, Ibrah. Fatik sikke re madalyalari. Istanbul, 1946.

Arc 1348.53F Babelon, Jean. Portraits en médaille. Paris, 1946.

Arc 858.54 Beaumont, Comyns. The riddle of prehistoric Britain. London, 1946.

Arc 925.8.40 Blavatskii, Vladimir D. Iskusstvo severnoi prichernomoriia. Moskva, 1946.

Arc 1163.3.45 Chaev, N.S. Russkaia paleografiia. Moskva, 1946.

Arc 875.14.20 Childe, V.G. Scotland before the Scots. London, 1946.

Arc 608.2.55 Cintas, Pierre. Amulettes puniques. Tunis, 1946.

Arc 815.13.20 Feiler, Leopold. Mysterion Gedanken vor den dionysischen Fresken der Mysterienvilla in Pompeji. Wien, 1946.

Arc 1153.65 Fichtenau, Heinrich. Mensch und Schrift im Mittelalter. Wien, 1946.

Arc 936.6.25 Filip, Jan. Pocatkij slovanskeho osidlene. Praha, 1946.

Arc 1138.60 Floriano, A.C. Curso general de paleografia y diplomatica españolas. v.1-2. Oviedo, 1946.

1946 - cont.

Arc 391.7 Garrod, Dorothy A.E. Environment, tools and man. Cambridge, 1946.

Arc 968.12A Goodwin, William B. The ruins of Great Ireland in New England. Boston, 1946.

Arc 1276.25F Grandjean, P.B. Danske herreders segl indtil 1660. København, 1946.

Arc 1480.40 Grant, Michael. From imperium to auctoritas. Cambridge, 1946.

Arc 1480.42F Grunwald, Michael. Die römischen Bronze- und Kupfermünzen mit schlagmarken um legionslager Vindonissa. Basel, 1946.

Arc 858.55.3 Hawkes, Jacquette. Early Britain. London, 1946.

Arc 843.3.5 Hernandez Morales, Angel. Juliobriga, ciudad romana en Cantabria. Santander, 1946.

Arc 1.5.10 Hesperia. Index 1-10, supplements 1-6. Baltimore, Md., 1946.

Arc 1025.73 Kirsch, G.P. The catacombs of Rome. Rome, 1946.

Arc 925.10 Krupnov, Evgenii I. Kratkii ocherk arkheologii kabardinskoi ASSR. Nal'chik, 1946.

Arc 1480.46 Leeds, Edward T. A hoard of Roman folles from Diocletian's reform. Oxford, 1946.

Arc 974.3 Lewis, Thomas M. Hiwassee Island: an archaeological account of 4 Tennessee Indian peoples. Knoxville, 1946.

Arc 766.4.10 Lugli, Giuseppe. Roma antica. Roma, 1946.

Arc 1494.9 Mateu y Llopis, Felipe. Glosario hispanico de numismatica. Barcelona, 1946.

Arc 936.14.243 Nosek, Stefan. Słowianie w pradziejach siem polskich. Kraków, 1946.

Arc 945.7 Peterson, Clarence S. America's rune stone of A.D. 1362 gains favor. N.Y., 1946.

Arc 716.2.15 Pickard-Cambridge, Arthur Wallace. The theater of Dionysus in Athens. Oxford, 1946.

Arc 830.107.5 Salin, Édouard. Manuel des fouilles archéologiques. 1e éd. Paris, 1946.

Arc 1528.12 Schulman, Jacques. Handboek van de Nederlandsche munten van 1795-1945. Amsterdam, 1946.

Arc 66.1.162 Seston, William. Dioclétien et la tétrarchie. Paris, 1946. 2v.

Arc 432.16 Shakur, M.A. A handbook to the Inscription Gallery in the Peshhawar Museum. Peshawar, 1946.

Arc 830.198 Toussaint, M. Répertoire archéologique du département de la Meuse. Bar-le-Duc, 1946.

Arc 936.195.290 Turek, Rudolf. Slavníkova Libice. Praha, 1946.

Arc 386.27 Vale, Giuseppe. Gian Domenico Bertoli. Aquileia, 1946.

Arc 1269.40 Wittmer, C. Inventaire des sceaux des archives de la ville de Strasbourg de 1050 à 1300. Strasbourg, 1946.

Arc 1153.69 Zazo, Alfredo. Paleografia latina e diplomatica. 6. ed. Napoli, 1946.

1947

Arc 672.5.25 American School of Classical Studies at Athens. Ancient Corinth. 4. ed. Athens, 1947.

Arc 340.36 An anthropological bibliography of the eastern seaboard. New Haven, 1947-63. 2v.

Arc 385.3.5 Artsikhovshii, A.V. Vvedenie v arkheologiiu. 3. izd. Moskva, 1947.

Arc 913.8 Bandi, Hans. Die Schweiz zur Rentierzeit. Frauenfeld, 1947.

Arc 551.9F Baumgartel, Elise J. The cultures of prehistoric Egypt. London, 1947.

Arc 723.28F Blake, Marion E. Ancient Roman construction in Italy from the pre-historica period to Augustus. Washington, 1947.

Arc 925.13.6 Blavatskii, V.D. Iskusstvo severnogo Prichernomor'ia. Moskva, 1947.

Arc 861.100 British Museum. Department of British and Mediaeval Antiquities. The Sutton-Hoo ship burial. 1. ed. London, 1947.

Arc 861.12.2.5 Bruce, J.C. Handbook to the Roman wall. 10. ed. Newcastle-upon-Tyne, 1947.

Arc 1588.6.15 Butak, Bekzad. Resimli Turk paralari. Istanbul, 1947.

Arc 858.50.5 Childe, V.G. Prehistoric communities of the British Isles. 2. ed. London, 1947.

Arc 387.21A Clark, John Grahame Douglas. Archaeology and society. 2. ed. London, 1947.

Arc 672.1.96 Demargne, P. La Crète dédalique. Paris, 1947.

Arc 66.1.164 Demargne, Pierre. La Crète dédalique. Paris, 1947. 2v.

Arc 383.9.5 Drack, Walter. Beiträge zur Kulturgeschichte; Festschrfit Reinhold Bosch. Aarau, 1947.

Arc 1528.14 Frederiks, J.W. Penningen. Amsterdam, 1947.

Arc 441.9.5 Gadre, A.S. Archaeology in Baroda, 1934-1947. Baroda, 1947.

Arc 888.15 Giffen, Albert Egges van. Oudheidkundige perspectieven in het bijzonder ten aanzien van de vaderlandsche Prae en protohistorie. Groningen, 1947.

Arc 556.2 Glanville, Stephen A.K. The growth and nature of Egyptology. Cambridge, 1947.

Arc 595.35 Grinsell, Leslie V. Egyptian pyramids. Gloucester, 1947.

Arc 923.105 Ilarionov, V.T. Opyt istoriografii paleolita SSSR. Gor'kei, 1947.

Arc 843.85 Institución Principe de Viana Pamplona. Excavaciones en Navarra. Pamplona, 1947. 7v.

Arc 543.78F Janse, Olov R.T. Archaeological research in Indo-China. Cambridge, 1947- 2v.

Arc 416.30 Kantor, H.J. The Aegean and the Orient in the second millennium B.C. Bloomington, 1947.

Arc 938.75F Kivikoski, Ella. Suomen rantakauden kuoasto. Helsinki, 1947-51. 2v.

Arc 888.30 Een kwart eeun. Meppal, 1947.

Arc 66.1.165 Lapalus, Etienne. Le fronton sculpté en Grèce. Paris, 1947. 2v.

Arc 600.75.5F Montet, Pierre. La nécropole royale de Tanis. Paris, 1947. 3v.

Arc 969.1.05 Morgan, Richard G. Bibliography of Ohio archaeology. Columbus, 1947.

Arc 880.42 Northern Ireland. Ministry of Finance. An account of the ancient monuments in state charge. Belfast, 1947.

Arc 530.55F Özgüc, T. Türk Tarih kurumu tarafindan yapelan karakoyuk hafreyate raporu. Ankara, 1947.

Arc 726.240 Paroscandola, A. I fenomeni fra disisneici del Serapeo di pozzuoli. Napoli, 1947.

Arc 672.1.70 Pernier, Luigi. Guida degli scavi italiani in Creta. Roma, 1947.

Arc 608.6.40 Picard, G.C. Castellum Dimmidi. Paris, 1947.

Arc 1423.18 Reifenberg, A. Ancient Jewish coins. 2. ed. Jerusalem, 1947.

Chronological Listing

1947 - cont.

Arc 925.16.10	Rubinshtein, N.L. Arkheologicheskii sbornik. Moskva, 1947.
Arc 935.23F	St. Andrews. University. The great palace of the Byzantine emperors. London, 1947-58. 2v.
Arc 493.50	Sauvaget, J. Quatre décrets seldjoukides. Beyrouth, 1947.
Arc 925.13.115	Semenov-Zuser, Semen A. Opyt istoriografii skifov. Khar'kov, 1947.
Arc 543.45A	Shakur, M.A. A dash through the heart of Afghanistan. Peshawar, 1947.
Arc 537.10	Sjoeqvist, Erik. Reports on excavations in Cyprus. Stockholm, 1947. 2v.
Arc 953.26	Speck, F.G. Eastern Algonkian block stamp decoration. Trenton, New Jersey, 1947.
Arc 1076.3.103	Staercke, Alphonse E. de. Cloches et carillons. Bruxelles, 1947.
Arc 830.194	Toussaint, M. Répertoire archéologique du département de Meurthe-et-Moselle. Nancy, 1947.
Arc 936.40.16	Tsonchev, D. Contributions a l'histoire du stade antique de Philippopolis. Sofia, 1947.
Arc 936.14.515	Żaki, Andrzej. Archeologia Małopolski wczesnośredniowiecznej. Wrocław, 1947.

1948

Arc 383.87	An address presented to Marcus N. Tod. Oxford, 1948.
Arc 726.24.17	Aurigemma, S. La villa Adriana presso Tivoli. Tivoli, 1948.
Arc 895.42	Becker, C. Mosefund lerkar fra yngre stenalder. København, 1948.
Arc 925.8.37	Belov, G.D. Khersones tavricheskii. Leningrad, 1948.
Arc 815.25	Bicentenario degli scavi di Pompei. Napoli, 1948.
Arc 386.29	Brion, Marcel. La résurrection des villes mortes. v.1-2. Paris, 1948-49.
Arc 600.80F	Brunton, Guy. Matmar. London, 1948.
Arc 861.169F	Bulleid, Arthur. The Meare Lake village. v.1,3. Taunton, 1948- 2v.
Arc 608.17.11	Caputo, Giacomo. Lo scultore del grande bassorilievo. Roma, 1948.
Arc 785.22.15	Carettoni, G. A short guide to the Palatine. Bologna, 1948.
Arc 785.13.70	Carettoni, G. A short guide to the Roman Forum. Bologna, 1948.
Arc 600.6.20F	Carlier, A. Thèbes. Paris, 1948.
Arc 505.72	Carlsbergfondet, Copenhagen. Hama. v.2,4. København, 1948. 2v.
Arc 505.61.10F	Chicago. Oriental Institute. Megiddo Expedition. Megiddo II. Chicago, 1948. 2v.
Arc 743.20	Cles-Reden, S. Das versunkene Volk. Innsbruck, 1948.
Arc 1208.11F	Committee of Ancient Near Eastern Seals. Corpus of ancient Near Eastern seals in North American collections. pt.1-2. N.Y., 1948-
Arc 388.6	Daux, Georges. Les étapes de l'archéologie. 2. éd. Paris, 1948.
Arc 635.217.10	Deonna, W. La vie privée des Déliens. Paris, 1948.
Arc 513.34	Duyuran, Rüstem. Bati Anoidolu'da eski şehirler. Istanbul, 1948.
Arc 66.1.163	Effenterre, Henri van. La Crète et le monde grec. Paris, 1948.
Arc 608.23	Emery, Walter B. Nubian treasure. London, 1948.
Arc 543.3.55F	Field, Henry. Recent excavations at Khawazm. Ann Arbor, 1948.
Arc 915.20	Forrer, Robert. Die helvetishen und helvetarömischen Votivbeilchen der Schweiz. Basel, 1948.
Arc 895.7.30	Gabrielsen, S.V. De forhistoriske tider i Danmark. København, 1948.
Arc 843.90	García y Bellido, Antonio. Hispania graeca. v.1-2, atlas. Barcelona, 1948. 3v.
Arc 1276.20F	Grandjean. P.B. Danske gilders segl fra middelaldesen. København, 1948.
Arc 482.202.6F	Herzfeld, Ernst E. Geschichte der Stadt Samarra. Hamburg, 1948.
Arc 861.18.16.10	Home, Gordon. Roman London. London, 1948.
Arc 520.19	Kähler, Heinz. Der grosse Fries von Pergamon. Berlin, 1948.
Arc 672.5.20F	Kosmopoulos, L.W. The prehistoric inhabitation of Corinth. Munich, 1948.
Arc 395.13	Kraft, G. Der Urmensch als Schöpfer. 2. Aufl. Tübingen, 1948.
Arc 684.1.48	Kunze, Emil. Neue Meisterwerke griechischer Kunst aus Olympia. München, 1948.
Arc 530.54	Landsberger, Benno. Samial. Ankara, 1948.
Arc 530.54.5	Landsberger, Benno. Samial. Photoreproduction. Ankara, 1948.
Arc 595.40	Lauer, J.P. Le problème des pyramides d'Égypte. Paris, 1948.
Arc 915.4.11	Laur-Belart, Rudolf. Führer durch Augusta Raurica. 2. Aufl. Basel, 1948.
Arc 858.57	Lethbridge, Thomas C. Merlin's Island. London, 1948.
Arc 600.21.5	Lucas, Alfred. Ancient Egyptian materials and industries. 3. ed. London, 1948.
Arc 448.1.2	Mackay, Ernest. Early Indus civilization. 2. ed. London, 1948.
Arc 870.4.20	Margary, Ivan D. Roman ways in the Weald. London, 1948.
Arc 497.76.2	Markovski, Ivan S. Bibleiska arkheologiia. 2. izd. Sofiia, 1948.
Arc 895.41	Mathiassen, T. Studier over Vestjyllands oldtidsbebyggelse. København, 1948.
Arc 461.2	Mathur, J.C. Homage to Vaiṣali. Vaisali, 1948.
Arc 1578.5F	Miller zu Aichholz, V. von. Österreichische Münzprägungen. 2. Aufl. Wien, 1948. 2v.
Arc 1470.45	Milne, J.G. Finds of Greek coins in the British Isles. London, 1948.
Arc 530.52	Özgüc, T. Ön tarih'te Qnadolu'da dü Gomme Adetleri. Basimevi, 1948.
Arc 600.90F	Paujade, J. Trois flottilles de la VIIème dynastie des pharaons. Djibouti, 1948.
Arc 432.14	Punja, P.R.R. India's legacy. Mangalore, 1948.
Arc 416.17F	Rozanthal, A. Arts antiques de l'Asie occidentale. Nice, 1948.
Arc 843.115	Ruig y Cadafalch, José. Noves des cobertes a la catedral d'Égara. Barcelona, 1948.
Arc 885.7.5	Rutter, Joseph G. Prehistoric Gower; early archaeology of West Glamorgan. Swansea, 1948.
Arc 843.50.10	Schulter, Adolf. Tarraco. Barcelona, 1948.
Arc 383.42	Schwarz, K. Strana praehistorica...Martin John. Halle, 1948.

1948 - cont.

Arc 600.85F	Schweitzer, U. Löwe und Sphinx im alten Ägypten. Glückstadt, 1948.
Arc 925.12.6	Shevchenko, V. Sokrovishcha ischeznuvshikh gorodov. Moskva, 1948.
Arc 66.1.166	Simon, Marcel. Verus Israel. Paris, 1948.
Arc 441.10	Subbarao, B. Stone age cultures of Bellary. 1. ed. Poona, 1948.
Arc 1538.21	Sutherland, Carol Humphrey Vivian. Anglo-Saxon gold coinage in the light of the Crondall hoard. London, 1948.
Arc 392.11	A tribute to Sir George Hill on his 80th birthday. Oxford, 1948.
Arc 915.11F	Vogt, Emil. Der Lindenhof in Zürich. Zürich, 1948.

1949

Arc 608.25F	Addison, F. Jebel Moya. London, 1949. 2v.
Arc 493.6.10	Baku. Muzei Istorii Azerbaidzhana. Material'naia kultura Azerbaidzhana. v.2. Baku, 1949-
Arc 858.54.5	Beaumont, Comyns. Britain, the key to world history. London, 1949.
Arc 1285.30.5	Beneš, František. Pečeti v českých zemích a jejich cena jako dějepisného pramene. Praha, 1949.
Arc 1588.8	Bosch, E. Turkizenin ankils deviedeke meskukatina. Ankara, 1949.
Arc 885.18	Cambrian Archaeological Association. A hundred years of Welsh archaeology. Gloucester, 1949.
Arc 1153.12.20	Cappelli, A. Lexicon abbreviaturarum. 4. ed. Milano, 1949.
Arc 461.4	Casal, Jean Marie. Fouilles de Virampatnam Arikamedu. Paris, 1949.
Arc 600.110F	Černý, Jaroslav. Répertoire onomastique de Deir et Médineh. Le Caire, 1949.
Arc 1166.7	Cramer, Maria. Koptische Inschriften im Kaiser-Friedrich Museum zu Berlin. Le Caire, 1949.
Arc 1138.55	Dain, A. Les manuscrits. Paris, 1949.
Arc 505.71	Dussaud, René. L'art phénicien du IIe millenaire. Paris, 1949.
Arc 1163.19	Eis, Gerhard. Altdeutsche Handschriften. München, 1949.
Arc 584.3F	Emery, W.B. Great tombs of the First Dynasty. Cairo, 1949. 3v.
Arc 1163.17.5	Essex, England. Record Office. Some examples of English handwriting. Chelmsford, 1949.
Arc 66.1.167	Fabre, P. Saint Paulin de Nole. Paris, 1949.
Arc 383.90	Festschrift 50. Jahre Lehrkanzel für Urgeschichte. Wien, 1949.
Arc 390.9	Fett, Harry. Pa kulturvernets veier. Oslo, 1949.
Arc 925.12.7	Gaidukevich, V.F. Bosporskoe tsarstvo. Moskva, 1949.
Arc 391.9	Garrood, J.R. Archaeological remains. London, 1949.
Arc 1348.52	Gebhart, H. Numismatik und Geldgeschichte. Heidelberg, 1949.
Arc 493.25.5	Godard, André. Le trésor de Ziwiyè. Teheran, 1949.
Arc 858.47.10	Great Britain. Ministry of Works. Illustrated regional guides to ancient monuments. v.2-6. 2. ed. London, 1949- 5v.
Arc 630.11F	Herbig, R. Ganymed; Heidelberger Beiträge zur antiken Kunstgeschichte. Heidelberg, 1949.
Arc 1076.16	Heuven, Englebert W. van. Accoustical measurements on church-bells and carillons. 's-Gravenhage, 1949.
Arc 547.6.20F	Hickmann, Hans. Instruments de musique. Le Caire, 1949.
Arc 609.1.27	Jones, Neville. The prehistory of southern Rhodesia. Cambridge, Eng., 1949.
Arc 520.19.5	Kähler, Heinz. Pergamon. Berlin, 1949.
Arc 537.12	Karageorghis, Basos. Cyprus. London, 1949.
Arc 969.15.5	Kidd, Kenneth E. The excavations of Sainte-Marie I. Toronto, 1949.
Arc 925.20	Knipovich, Tatiana N. Tanais. Moskva, 1949.
Arc 925.8.20	Knipovick, T.N. Tamaie. Moskva, 1949.
Arc 716.7.20	Kontoleon, N.M. To Erehtheion ōs iokodomema chthonias latreias. Athénai, 1949.
Arc 936.75	Kostrzewski, J. Les origines de la civilisation polonaise. Paris, 1949.
Arc 936.14.149	Kostrzewski, Józef. Pradzieje Polski. Poznań, 1949.
Arc 1460.4	Lacroix, L. Les reproductions des statues. Liège, 1949.
Arc 1663.31	Lange, Kurt. Charakterkopfe der Weltgeschichte. München, 1949.
Arc 66.1.169	Launey, Marcel. Recherches sur les armées hellénistiques. Paris, 1949. 2v.
Arc 870.12.10	Leeds, E.T. The corpus of early Anglo-Saxon great square-headed broaches. Oxford, 1949.
Arc 726.112	Levi, Doro. L'ipogeo di San Salvatore di Cabras in Sardegna. Roma, 1949.
Arc 600.53F	MacAdam, M.F.L. The temples of Kawa. v.1-2; plates. London, 1949- 4v.
Arc 880.25.8A	Macalister, R.A.S. The archaeology of Ireland. 2. ed. London, 1949.
Arc 1367.3	Magnaguti, A.G. Ex nummis historia. Roma, 1949-53. 12v.
Arc 441.3.10	Maitra, Akshay Kumar. The ancient monuments of Varendra (North Bengal). Rajshahi, 1949?
Arc 810.42.5	Maiuri, Amedeo. Introduzione alla studio di Pompei. Napoli, 1949.
Arc 530.51F	Mansel, A.M. Pergede kazilar ne arastumalar. Ankara, 1949.
Arc 870.20	Marples, M. White horses. London, 1949.
Arc 1018.44.17	Marucchi, O. Manuel of Christian archaeology. 4. Italian ed. Paterson, N.J., 1949.
Arc 943.14.9	N.Y. Museum of the American Indian. Heye Foundation. Indian notes. Index, v.1-7. N.Y., 1949.
Arc 497.48	Needler, W. Palestine, ancient and modern...guide to the Palestinian collection...Royal Ontario Museum. Toronto, 1949.
Arc 830.182	Peyrony, D. Le périgord préhistorique. Perigneux, 1949.
Arc 925.195	Piatysheva, N.V. Tamanskii sarkofag. Moskva, 1949.
Arc 858.58	Piggott, Stuart. British prehistory. London, 1949.
Arc 567.1.10	Pisa. Università. Studi in memoria di Ippolito Rosellini nel primo centerario della morte. Pisa, 1949. 2v.
Arc 612.31	Pittioni, Richard. Die urgeschichtlichen Grundlagen der europäischen Kultur. Wien, 1949.
Arc 1153.85	Politzer, R.L. A study of the language of eighth century Lombardic documents. N.Y., 1949.
Arc 936.195.80	Poulík, Josef. Průvodce po výzkumech na staroslovanskim hradisku staré zámky u Lišně. Praha, 1949.
Arc 18.1.5	Revue archéologique. Tables des années, 1900-1955. Paris, 1949- 2v.
Arc 830.175.10	Rolland, Henri. Glanum. Paris, 1949.
Arc 925.13.8	Rudenko, S.I. Iskusstvo. Moskva, 1949.

Chronological Listing

1949 - cont.

Arc 1588.6.20 Saglani, O.F. Simdiye kadar görülmiyen Cimri Sikkesi. n.p., 1949.

Arc 630.12 Schefold, Karl. Orient, Hellas und Rom in der archäologischen Forschungszeit 1939. Bern, 1949.

Arc 403.16.15 Schliemann, Heinrich. Heinrich Schliemann. Selbstbiographie. 7. Aufl. Leipzig, 1949.

Arc 1615.10 Sheldon, W.H. Early American cents, 1793-1814. 1. ed. N.Y., 1949.

Arc 925.175 Smipnov, A.P. Arkheologicheskie pamiatniki na territorii Mariiskoi ASSR. Kozmodem'iansk, 1949-

Arc 905.12.12 Swoboda, Erich. Carnuntum. Wien, 1949.

Arc 608.28 Thouvenat, R. Volubilis. Paris, 1949.

Arc 913.17.10 Tschumi, O. Urgeschichte der Schweiz. Frauenfeld, 1949-

Arc 1588.4.20F Turnwald, K. Česki a Moravské denary a brakteaty. Praha, 1949.

Arc 1490.32 Ulrich-Bansa, O. Monete mediolanensis. Venezia, 1949.

Arc 830.70.10 Wuilleumier, P. L'eglise et la nécropole Saint-Laurent dans le quartier lyonnais de Chaueand. Lyon, 1949.

195-

Arc 1300.1.5 American Numismatic Society. The American Numismatic Society. N.Y., 195-

Arc 889.8.5 Daniels, M.P.M. Noviomagus. Nijmegen, 195-.

Arc 513.28 Duyuran, Rüstem. The ancient cities of Western Anatolia. n.p., 195-?

Arc 935.24.5 Kosay, Hâmit Z. Alacahöyük. n.p., 195-?

Arc 830.270 Lelièvre, Léon. Menhirs et marches sacrées. Caen, 195-.

Arc 1478.24.15 Mattingly, Harold. Roman numismatics. London, 195-?

Arc 1480.54.5 Mattingly, Harold. Some new studies of the Roman republican coinage. London, 195-.

1950

Arc 848.48 Adama van Scheltema, Z. Die Kunst der Vorzeit. Stuttgart, 1950.

Arc 1020.136 Agnello, G. Gli studi di archeologia cristiana in Sicilia. Catania, 1950.

Arc 66.1.170 Amandry, P. La mantique Apollenienne a Delphes. Paris, 1950. 2v.

Arc 943.36F Appleton, LeRoy H. Indian art of the Americas. N.Y., 1950.

Arc 895.44F Bagge, A. Die Funde aus Dolman. v.1-2. Stockholm, 1950-52.

Arc 383.75 Behrens, Gustav. Reinecke Festschrift zum 75. Geburtstag von Paul Reinecke. Mainz, 1950.

Arc 1356.6 Beltrán Martinez, A. Curso de numismatica. 2. ed. Cartagena, 1950.

Arc 522.35F Blegen, Carl William. Troy. v.1-4, pt.1-2. Princeton, N.J., 1950-51. 8v.

Arc 1153.72 Boson, G.G. Paléographie valdôtaine. v.1-3. Aoste, 1950-52.

Arc 1538.18.10 Brooke, George C. English coins. 3. ed. London, 1950.

Arc 843.160 Carballo, Jesús. El descubrimiento de la cueva y pinturas de altamira por Marcelino S. de Sauteola. Santander, 1950.

Arc 1190.50 Cheney, C. English bishops' chanceries. Manchester, 1950.

Arc 503.7F Colt Archaeological Institute. Excavations at Nessana. Princeton, 1950. 3v.

Arc 387.13.5 Curtius, Ludwig. Deutsche und antike Welt. Stuttgart, 1950.

Arc 858.59 Daniel, G. The prehistoric chamber tombs. Cambridge, Eng., 1950.

Arc 388.5.5 Daniel, G.E. A hundred years of archaeology. London, 1950.

Arc 1080.10F Deutsches Archäologisches Institut. Die langobardischen Fibeln aus Italien. Berlin, 1950.

Arc 608.24F Dunham, D. The Royal cemeteries of Kush. Hambridge, 1950-63. 5v.

Arc 1269.30 Engel, W. Würzburger Zunftsiegel aus fünf Jahrhunderten. Würzburg, 1950.

Arc 853.101F Fremersdorf, F. Die Denkmäler des römischen Köln. v.1-8,22. Köln, 1950- 9v.

Arc 861.125 Fullbrook-Leggatt, Lawrence Edward Wells Outen. Roman Gloucester. Gloucester, 1950.

Arc 936.220.15 Garašanin, Milutin V. Pregled materijame kulture juznih slovena u ranom s rednem veku. Beograd, 1950.

X Cg Arc 888.17 Giffen, Albert Egges van. Inheemse en Romeinse terpen. Atlas and plates. Groningen, 1950. 2v.

Arc 485.202.5 Godard, André. Persepolis. Teheran, 1950.

Arc 493.25 Godard, André. Le trésor de Ziwiyè. Haarlem, 1950.

Arc 1276.5 Grandjean, P.B. Danske haandvaerkerlavs segl. København, 1950.

Arc 1480.48 Grant, Michael. Aspects of the principate of Tiberius. N.Y., 1950.

Arc 1478.40 Grant, Michael. Roman anniversary issues. Cambridge, Eng., 1950.

Arc 925.38.5 Griaznov, M.P. Pervyi pazyrykskii kurgan. Leningrad, 1950.

Arc 853.120 Hachmann, Rolf. Studien zur Geschichte Mitteldeutschlands während der älteren Latènezeit. Hamburg, 1950.

Arc 387.23 Hagen, Victor Wolfgang von. Frederick Catherwood. N.Y., 1950.

Arc 630.11.5 Herbig, R. Vermächtnis der antiken Kunst. Heidelberg, 1950.

Arc 1025.72 Hertling, Ludwig. Die römischen Katakomben und ihre Martyrer. Wien, 1950.

Arc 1025.72.5 Hertling, Ludwig. Die römischen Katakomben und ihre Martyrer. 2. Aufl. Wien, 1950.

Arc 393.5 International Institute of Intellectual Cooperation. Manuel de la technique des fouilles archéologiques. Paris, 1950.

Arc 493.6.25 Ismizade, O.S. Ialoilutepinskaia kul'tura. Baku, 1950.

Arc 726.24.13FA Kähler, H. Hadrian und seine Villa bei Tivoli. Berlin, 1950.

Arc 488.14.10 Karimi, B.M. Rapport résumé de quinze mai de voyage. Teheran, 1950?

Arc 395.12 Kaufmann, C.M. Allah ist gross! Freiburg, 1950.

Arc 383.92A Kirchner, H. Ur- und Frühgeschichte als historische Wissenschaft. Heidelberg, 1950.

Arc 1163.22 Kirchner, J. Germanistische Handschriftenpraxis. München, 1950.

Arc 383.79 Kleinasien und Byzanz. Berlin, 1950.

Arc 936.250.5 Kuftin, Boris A. Materialy k arkheologii kolkhidy. v.2. Tbilisi, 1950.

Arc 608.2.38 Lapeyre, Gabriel G. Carthage latine et chrétienne. Paris, 1950.

1950 - cont.

Arc 743.17.10 Lawrence, D.H. Etruscan places. Middlesex, 1950.

Arc 66.1.168 Lesage, G. Marseille Angevine. Paris, 1950.

Arc 875.75 Lethbridge, T. Herdsmen and hermits. Cambridge, Eng., 1950.

Arc 397.17.3 Marek, Kurt W. Götter. Hamburg, 1950.

Arc 925.16.15 Margulan, A.K. Iz istorii gorodov i stroitel'nogo isskustva drevnego Kazakhstana. Alma-Ata, 1950.

Arc 1470.50 May, J.M.F. Ainos. London, 1950.

Arc 1190.35.5 Meisner, H.O. Urkunden- und Aktenlehre der Neuzeit. Leipzig, 1950.

Arc 383.9 Mélanges d'archéologie, d'histoire, et d'histoire de l'art, offerts à Louis Bosset. Lausanne, 1950.

Arc 383.56 Morleyana. Santa Fe, New Mexico, 1950.

Arc 905.70 Mozsolics, Amália. Der Goldfund von Velem-Szentvid. Basel, 1950.

Arc 1613.22 Mumey, N. Clark, Gruber and Co. Denver, 1950.

Arc 905.80 Neumann, Alfred. Die römischen Ruinen unter dem Hohen Markt. Wien, 1950.

Arc 923.65 Obladnikov, A.P. Uspekhi sovetskoi arkheologii. Leningrad, 1950.

Arc 530.75 Özgüc, T. Türk Tarih kurumu tarafindan yapelan Kültepe kazisi raporu, 1948. Ankara, 1950.

NEDL Arc 672.1.28.10 Pendlebury, J.D.S. Hodēgos tōn minoikou anaktoro tēs knōsa. Hēraklei, 1950.

Arc 838.32 Pericat y Garcia, Luis. La España primiva. Barcelona, 1950.

Arc 600.120 Pesce, Gennaro. Il Palazzo delle calonne in Talemaide di Cirenaria. Roma, 1950.

Arc 403.19 Piggott, Stuart. William Stukely. Oxford, 1950.

Arc 810.56 Pompeiana. Napoli, 1950.

Arc 1623.5 Prudeau, A.F. Historia numismatica de Mexico desde la epoca precortesiana hasta 1823. Mexico, 1950.

Arc 497.49 Reifenberg, A. Ancient Hebrew arts. N.Y., 1950.

Arc 1423.18.5 Reifenberg, A. Ancient Hebrew seals. London, 1950.

Arc 772.14 Robathan, D. The monuments of ancient Rome. Rome, 1950.

Arc 961.1.25 Sears, William H. Excavations at Kolomoki. v.1-2. Athens, 1950?

Arc 1330.15 Singhal, C.R. Bibliography of Indian coins. v.1-2. Bombay, 1950-52.

Arc 915.30 Spahni, Jean Christian. Les megálithes de la Suisse. Basel, 1950.

Arc 540.8F Stewart, E.M. Vounous 1937-38. Lund, 1950.

Arc 1508.10 Suhle, Arthur. Die deutschen Renaissance-Medaille. Leipzig, 1950.

Arc 830.196 Toussaint, M. Répertoire archéologique du département de la Moselle. Nancy, 1950.

Arc 1088.7F Ucelli, Guido. Le navi di Nemi. 2. ed. Roma, 1950.

Arc 405.2F UNESCO. Monuments et sites d'art. Paris, 1950.

Arc 505.58 Vaux, R. de. Fouilles à Qaryet el-'Enab Abu-Gôch. Paris, 1950.

Arc 455.3 Wheeler, R.E. Five thousand years of Pakistan. London, 1950.

Arc 446.10 Zluner, F.E. Stone age and Pleistocene chronology in Gujarat. 1. ed. Poona, 1950.

1951

Arc 530.65 Akademiia nauk Armianskoi SSR, Erevan. Institut Istorii. Garni. Erevan, 1951- 4v.

Arc 608.6.18 Algeria. Directoire de l'Intérieur et de Beaux-Arts. Villes d'or. Alger, 1951.

Arc 925.305 Andreev, N.V. O chëm rasskazyvaiut kurgany. Smolensk, 1951.

Arc 1540.37 Askew, Gilbert. The coinage of Roman Britain. London, 1951.

Arc 66.1.171 Aymard, Jacques. Essai sur les chasses romaines. Paris, 1951. 2v.

Arc 1500.55 Babelon, Jean. Histoire de Paris d'après les médailles de la Renaissance au XX. siècle. Paris, 1951.

Arc 1510.45 Badische Gesellschaft für Münzkunde. Münzkunde und Münzkabinette am Oberrheim. Karlsruhe am Rhein, 1951.

Arc 608.6.50 Berthier, A. Tiddis. Alger, 1951.

Arc 1348.81 Bosch, Enin. Eski sikkeler rehberi. Istanbul, 1951.

Arc 785.39.50 Broedner, Erika. Untersuchungen an der Caracallathermen. Berlin, 1951.

Arc 861.100.2 Bruce-Mitford, Rupert Leo. The Sutton-Hoo ship burial. London, 1951.

Arc 493.6 Burton Brown, T. Excavations in Azerbaijan. 1. ed. London, 1951.

Arc 608.6.55 Christople, M. Le tombeau de la Chrétienne. Paris, 1951.

Arc 488.18 Coon, Carleton Stevens. Cave explorations in Iran, 1949. Philadelphia, 1951.

Arc 861.110 Corder, Philip. The Roman town and villa at Great Casterton. Nottingham, 1951.

Arc 726.11.9 Corte, M. della. Cleopatra, M. Antonio e Ottaviano nelle allegorie storico-umoristiche delle argenterie del tesoro di Boscoreale. Pompei, 1951.

Arc 793.15 Corti, E.C. The destruction and resurection of Pompeii and Herculaneum. London, 1951.

Arc 552.4 Cottrell, L. The lost Pharaohs. N.Y., 1951.

Arc 608.6.4 Courtois, C. Timgad. Alger, 1951.

Arc 608.26F Crawfard, O.G.S. Abu Geili. London, 1951.

Arc 674.3.3 Crome, J.F. Die Skulpturen des Asklepiostempels von Epidauros. Berlin, 1951.

Arc 505.100.2 Damascus. Musée National Syrien. Catalogue illustré du Departement des antiquités gréco-romaines. Damas, 1951.

Arc 553.1 Dawson, W.R. Who was who in Egyptology. London, 1951.

Arc 518.10 Duyuran, Rüstem. Ephèse. Ankara, 1951.

Arc 785.74F Esplorazioni sotto la confessione di San Pietro in Vaticano. Città del Vaticano, 1951. 2v.

Arc 830.47.10 Fabre, Gabrielle. Inventaire des découvertes prohistoriques. Thèse. Paris, 1951.

Arc 843.5.30 Fletcher y Valls, D. Repertorio de bibliografía arqueológica. v.1-2, 4-6. Valencia, 1951. 4v.

Arc 66.1.173 François, M. Le cardinal François de Tournon. Paris, 1951. 2v.

Arc 1468.40 Gabrici, E. Tecnica e cronologia delle monete greche. Roma, 1951.

Arc 936.220F Garašanin, Milutin V. Arheološka nalazišta u Srbiji. Beograd, 1951.

Arc 861.40.15 Gilyard-Beer, R. The Romano-British baths at Well. Leeds, 1951.

Arc 388.7 Goessler, F.P. Wilhelm Dörpfeld. Stuttgart, 1951.

Arc 925.115 Golubtsova, E.S. Severnoe Prichernomor'e i Rim. Moskva, 1951.

Chronological Listing

1951 - cont.

Arc 1276.10F Grandjean, P.B. Danske konggelige segl fra Frederik ILS. København, 1951.
Arc 383.14 Grimes, W.F. Aspects of archaeology in Britain and beyond; essays presented to O.G.S. Crawford. London, 1951.
Arc 885.20 Grimes, W.F. The prehistory of Wales. 2. ed. Cardiff, 1951.
Arc 426.10 Groot, G.J. The prehistory of Japan. N.Y., 1951.
Arc 915.15 Guyan, Walter Ulrich. Das Grabhügelfeld im Sankert bei Hemishofen. Basel, 1951.
Arc 1033.3.42A Hanfmann, G.M. The season sarcophagus in Dumbarton Oakes. Cambridge, 1951. 2v.
Arc 830.184 Hatt, Jean J. La tombe gallo-romaine. Thèse. Paris, 1951.
Arc 858.60 Hawkes, Jacquette. A guide to the prehistoric and Roman monuments in England and Wales. London, 1951.
Arc 943.32 Hibben, F.C. Treasure in the dust. 1. ed. Philadelphia, 1951.
Arc 1163.3.50 Horodyski, Bogden. Podrecznik paleografii ruskiej. Kraków, 1951.
Arc 543.60F Iakhry, A. Anarchaeological journey to Yemen. v.1-3. Cairo, 1951-52. 2v.
Arc 1508.15 Jaeger, Kurt. Die neuren Münzprägungen der deutschen Staaten. pt.1-2,3-4,8,9,10,11,12. Stuttgart, 1951-72. 12v.
Arc 905.75 Jandaurek, H. Die Strassen der Römer. Wels, 1951.
Arc 383.79.10 Kersten, Karl. Festschrift für Gustav Schwante. Neumünster, 1951.
Arc 1498.15 Lafaurie, Jean. Les monnaies des rois de France. Paris, 1951. 2v.
Arc 612.34 Laming, A. L'art préhistorique. Paris, 1951.
Arc 386.28 A list of the published writings of John Davidson Beazley. Oxford, 1951.
Arc 397.17.5A Marek, Kurt W. Gods, graves, and scholars. 1. American ed. N.Y., 1951.
Arc 459.3.20 Marshall, John. Taxila. Cambridge, 1951. 3v.
Arc 66.1.174 Martin, R. Recherches sur l'agora grecque. Paris, 1951.
Arc 672.1.67 Matz, F. Forschungen auf Kreta 1942. Berlin, 1951.
Arc 66.1.172 Metzger, H. Les représentations dans la céramique attique du IV siècle. Paris, 1951. 3v.
Arc 1348.51 Milne, J.G. Coin collecting. London, 1951.
Arc 905.120.5 Miltner, Franz. Lavant und Aguntum. Lienz, 1951.
Arc 383.77 Mylonas, G.C. Studies presented to David Moore Robinson. St. Louis, 1951-53. 2v.
Arc 1448.10 Naville, Lucien. Les monnaies d'or de la Cyrenaïque de 450 à 250 avant J.C. Genève, 1951.
Arc 905.80.5 Neumann, Alfred. Ausgrabungen und Funde. v.1-3. Wien, 1951.
Arc 682.8 Papachatzēs, N. Mykēnes kai Tiryntha. Athēnai, 1951.
Arc 723.25.5 Patroni, G. La preistoria. Milano, 1951. 2v.
Arc 880.44 Raftery, J. Prehistoric Ireland. London, 1951.
Arc 1468.34 Robert, Louis. Études de numismatique grecque. Paris, 1951.
Arc 600.35.15 Roeder, Günther. Ein Jahrzehnt deutscher Ausgrabungen in einer ägyptischen Stadtruine. Hildesheim, 1951.
Arc 671.10 Rōmaios, K.A. Ho Makedonikoi taros tēs Berginas. Athēnai, 1951.
Arc 853.267 Roth, H. Wetterauer Fundberichte, 1941-49. Friedberg, 1951
Arc 543.50 Rudenko, Sergei I. Der zweite Kurgen von Pasyryk. Berlin, 1951.
Arc 505.2.10 Schlumberger, D. La Palmyrène du Nord-Ouest. Thèse. Paris, 1951.
Arc 520.20 Schober, A. Die Kunst von Pergamon. Wien, 1951.
Arc 1330.11 Sigler, Phares O. Numismatic bibliography. Dearborn, Mich., 1951.
Arc 1335.115 Signorelli, A. Collezione del Prof. Angelo Signorelli. pt.1-2. Roma, 1951-52.
Arc 936.70 Spomenitse kulture. Beograd, 1951.
Arc 383.39 Studia archaeologica Gerardo Van Hoorn Oblata. Leiden, 1951.
Arc 1478.42 Sutherland, C.H.V. Coinage in Roman imperial policy. London, 1951.
Arc 712.28 Syriopoulos, K.T. Ho stereobatēs toy Parthenonos. Athēnai, 1951.
Arc 830.26.20 Toussaint, M. Répertoire archéologique du département de Seine-et-Oise. Paris, 1951.
Arc 853.20.12 Treves. Rheinisches Landesmuseum. Aus der Schatzkammer des antiken Trier. Trier, 1951.
Arc 402.12 Vernadskii, G.V. M.I. Rostovtsev. Praga, 1951.
Arc 407.15 Wegner, Max. Altertumskunde. Freiburg, 1951.
Arc 726.97F Zancani Montuoro, P. Heraion. v.1-2, atlases. Roma, 1951. 4v.
Arc 612.32 Zatz, L.F. Altsteinzeitkunde Mitteleuropas. Stuttgart, 1951.

1952

Arc 1208.12 Academia...Bucharest. Documents de sigillographie byzantine. Paris, 1952.
Arc 395.6.10 Andrae, W. Babylon, die versunkene Weltstadt und ihr Ausgräber Robert Koldewey. Berlin, 1952.
Arc 80.1.7.5F Archaiologikē Hetairia, Athens. Leukōma tēs hekatontaeteridos. Athēnai, 1952.
Arc 608.16.15 Baradez, J.L. Tipasa. Alger, 1952.
Arc 1053.22 Bianchi Bandinelli, Ranuccio. Il problema del ritratto greco. Firenze, 1952.
Arc 925.13.70 Blavatskaia, T.V. Zapadnopontiiskie gopoda. Moskva, 1952.
Arc 673.1.20F Bousquet, Jean. Le trésor de Cyrène à Delphes. Thèse. Paris, 1952.
Arc 1478.45 Breglia, L. La prima fase della coniozione romana dell'argento. Roma, 1952.
Arc 889.10 Brom, Leo H.M. The Stevensweert Kantharos. The Hague, 1952.
Arc 1020.135 Camprubi Alemany, Francisco. El monumento paleocristiano de Centcelles. Barcelona, 1952.
Arc 447.5 Chand, Amar. Hastinăpura. Banoras, 1952.
Arc 612.33 Clark, John Desmond. Prehistoric Europe. London, 1952.
Arc 1086.5 Coimbra. Museu Machado de Castro. Catálogo de lucernas romanas. Coimbra, 1952.
Arc 3.3 Congresso Internazionale di Preistoria. Atti. Firenze, 1952.
Arc 67.5 Congresso Nazionale di Archealogia Cristiana. Atti del 1 congresso nazionale di archealogia cristiana. Roma, 1952.
Arc 387.30A Cooper, Gordon. Dead cities and forgotten tribes. N.Y., 1952.
Arc 1353.12 Copenhagen. National Museet. Orientalske, graeske og romerske. Kjøbenhavn, 1952.

1952 - cont.

Arc 609.7 Davies, Oliver. Natal archaeological studies. Pietermaritzburg, 1952.
Arc 1613.23 Del Monte, J. Fell's United States coin books. N.Y., 1952.
Arc 388.8 Diolé, P. Promenades d'archéologie sous-marine. Paris, 1952.
Arc 67.6 Durham, England. University. King's College, Newcastle upon Tyne. The congress of Roman frontier studies. Durham, 1952.
Arc 513.28.5 Duyuran, Rüstem. Carte archeologique de l'Anatolie occidentale. Izmir, 1952.
Arc 830.47 Fabre, Gabrielle. Les civilisations protohistoriques de l'Aquitaine. Paris, 1952.
Arc 383.22A Festschrfit für Rudolf Egge. Klagenfurt, 1952-53. 3v.
Arc 390.10 Fletcher y Valls, D. Nocines de prehistoria. Valencia, 1952.
Arc 723.20.12F Forma Italiae. Sardinia. v.1-2. Roma, 1952-54.
Arc 1500.62 Gamberini, Cesare. Prontuario. Bologna, 1952.
Arc 1264.15 Gardilhon, R. Sigillographie des universités de France. Paris, 1952.
Arc 646.2 Gerhard, E. Archäologischer Nachlass aus Rom. Berlin, 1952.
Arc 858.24.25 Great Britain. Commissions. Ancient and Historical Monuments and Constructions of England. An inventory of the historical monuments in Dorset. v.1,3. London, 1952- 3v.
Arc 953.28F Griffin, James. Archaeology of eastern United States. Chicago, 1952.
Arc 736.1.15 Griffo, Pietro. Sulla collocazione dei Telamoni nel Tempio. Agrigento, 1952.
Arc 608.6.24 Gsell, Stéphane. Cherchel. Alger, 1952.
Arc 1588.1.20 Gumowski, Marian. Zarys numizmatyki Polskiej. Łódź, 1952.
Arc 858.60.5 Hawkes, Jacquette. History in earth and stone. Cambridge, Mass., 1952.
Arc 925.332F Ivanov, Petr P. Materialy po istorii Mordvy VIII-IX vv. Moskva, 1952.
Arc 1510.50 Jesse, Wilhelm. Münz- und Geldgeschichte Niedersachsens. Braunschweig, 1952.
Arc 925.23 Kallistov, D.P. Sev. Prichernomor'e v antich. epolu. Moskva, 1952.
Arc 395.15.2 Kenyon, Kathleen Mary. Beginning in archaeology. London, 1952.
Arc 1269.35 Korn, Otto. Rheinisches Siegel- und Urkundenbuch. Brühl, 1952.
Arc 612.36 Kühn, Herbert. Die Felsbilder Europas. Zürich, 1952.
Arc 396.22 Laming, Annette. La découverte du passe. Paris, 1952.
Arc 66.1.176 Lerat, Lucien. Les Locriens de l'ouest. v. 1-2. Paris, 1952.
Arc 608.6.45 Leschi, Louis. Algérie antique. Paris, 1952.
Arc 716.2.20 Maass, Michael. Die Prohedrie des Dionysostheaters in Athen. München, 1952.
Arc 861.100.5 Magoren, F.P. The Sutton-Hoo ship burial. Cambridge, Mass., 1952.
Arc 383.53.5 Mainz. Römisch Germanisches Zentralmuseum. Festschrift des Römisch germanischen Zentralmuseums in Mainz. Mainz, 1952-53. 3v.
Arc 889.22 Mariën, M.E. Oud-België. Antwerpen, 1952.
Arc 1190.35.7 Meisner, H.O. Urkunden- und Aktenlehre der Neuzeit. 2. Aufl. Leipzig, 1952.
Arc 608.2.45 Meunié, Jacques. Recherches archéologiques à Marrakech. Paris, 1952.
Arc 416.21 Miles, G.C. Archaeologica orientalia in memoriam Ernst Herzfeld. Locust Valles, N.Y., 1952.
Arc 875.80 Miller, S.N. The Roman occupation of southwestern Scotland. Glasgow, 1952.
Arc 505.73.5 Mouterde, René. Beyrouth, ville romaine. Beyrouth, 1952.
Arc 736.12 Naselli, S. L'inesplorato Monte Albura o Albuchia. Castelbuono, 1952.
Arc 1030.59 Nunn, H.P.V. Christian inscriptions. N.Y., 1952.
Arc 895.45F Oldeberg, A. Studien über die schwedische Bootaxtkultur. Stockholm, 1952.
Arc 1163.3.40 Orlov, A.S. Bibliografiia russkikh nadpisei XI-XV vv. Moskva, 1952.
Arc 1163.5.20 Pandey, R.B. Indian palaeography. Banaras, 1952.
Arc 416.23 Parrot, A. Découverte des mondes ensevelés. Neuchâtel, 1952.
Arc 588.64F Petrie, W.M.F. City of shepherd kings. London, 1952.
Arc 588.65F Petrie, W.M.F. Seven Memphite tomb chapels. London, 1952.
Arc 888.25 Popping, H.J. Onze voorhistorie. Zutphen, 1952.
Arc 401.2.10 Quennell, Marjorie (Courtney). Everyday life in prehistoric times. 4. ed. London, 1952.
Arc 608.32 Reyniers, F.L.M. Port à Utique. Alger, 1952.
Arc 843.110 Rileas i Bertran, Marià. El poblament d'Ilduro. Barcelona, 1952.
Arc 925.13.8.10 Rudenko, S.I. Gornoaltaiskie nachadki iskify. Moskva, 1952.
Arc 1500.52 Rybat, N.V.L. Armorican art. Jersey, 1952.
Arc 925.136.10 Sal'nikov, Konstantin V. Drevnieshie pamiatniki istorii Urala. Sverdlovsk, 1952.
Arc 450.5 Sankalia, Hasmukh Dhirajlal. Excavations at Brahmapuri, 1945-46. Poona, 1952.
Arc 935.33 Sartiaux, Felix. Eski foca, foca taukin koker. Izmir, 1952.
Arc 540.7 Schaeffer, C.F.A. Enkomè-Alasia. Paris, 1952.
Arc 815.26 Schefold, Karl. Pompejanische Malerei. Basel, 1952.
Arc 1468.29.10 Seltman, C.T. A book of Greek coins. London, 1952.
Arc 608.38 Sérée de Roch. Tebessa. Alger, 1952.
Arc 505.5.120 Simons, Jan Jozef. Jerusalem in the Old Testament; researches and theories. Leiden, 1952.
Arc 432.15 Sivaramamurto, C. Indian epigraphy and south Indian scripts. Madra, 1952.
Arc 600.105F Stefanski, E. Coptic ostraca from Medinet Habu. Chicago, 1952.
Arc 853.130F Stroh, Armin. Katalog Günzburg. Kallmünz, 1952.
Arc 383.43F Svenska arkeologiska samfundet. Arkeologiska forskningar och fynd. Stockholm, 1952.
Arc 1480.19.10 Sydenham, E.A. The coinage of the Roman republic. London, 1952.
Arc 571.5 Vandier, Jacques. Manuel d'archéologie égyptienne. v.1-5; atlases. Paris, 1952. 10v.
Arc 1138.90 Velazquez de Velasco, L.J. Ensayo sobre los alphabetos de las letras des conocidas. Madrid, 1952.
Arc 830.186 Wuilleumier, P. Les médaillons d'applique gallo-romain. Paris, 1952.

Chronological Listing

1953

Arc 543.66 — Akademiia nauk Uzbek SSSR, Tashkend. Institut Istorii i Arkheologii. Istoriia material'noi kul'tury uzbekistana. Taskhend, 1953- 12v.
Arc 600.46.5F — Abd el Monem, Joussef Abubakr. Excavations at Giza, 1945-50. Cairo, 1953.
Arc 385.4 — Akademiia Nauk SSR. Institut Arkheologii. Protiv vyl'garizatsii marksisma v arkheologii. Moskva, 1953.
Arc 505.75 — Altheim, F. Das erste Auftreten der Hunnen das Alter der Jesaja-Rolle. Baden-Baden, 1953.
Arc 673.1.22F — Amandry, P. La colonne des Naxiens et le partique des Athéneéns. Thèse. Paris, 1953.
Arc 530.135.10 — Arik, Remri Ogur. Turk muzeciliéine bir bakis. Istanbul, 1953.
Arc 923.125 — Arkheologicheskii sbornik. Photoreproduction. Moskva, 1953.
Arc 726.24.20 — Aurigemma, S. La villa Adriana. 2a ed. Tivoli, 1953.
Arc 925.90.5 — Blavatskii, V.D. Zemdsd v antichnikh gorodov severnogo Prichernomor'ia. Moskva, 1953.
Arc 66.1.175 — Bruhl, A. Liber pater. Paris, 1953.
Arc 1588.4.25 — Castelin, K.O. Česka drobna mince v doly predhus, a husitske, 1300-1471. Praha, 1953.
Arc 800.15 — Catalano, V. Storia di Ercolano. Napoli, 1953.
Arc 66.1.177 — Chamoux, F. Cyrène sous la monarchie des Battiades. Paris, 1953.
Arc 642.8 — Cottrell, Leonard. The bull of Minos. London, 1953.
Arc 387.5.10 — Crawford, Osbert Guy S. Archaeology in the field. London, 1953.
Arc 387.5.12 — Crawford, Osbert Guy S. Archaeology in the field. N.Y., 1953.
Arc 726.105 — Cressedi, G. Velitrae. Roma, 1953.
Arc 1348.80 — Del Monte, Jacques. Fell's international coin book. N.Y., 1953.
Arc 450.10 — Dhama, B.L. Khajuraho. Delhi, 1953.
Arc 540.6.5 — Dikaios, P. Khirakitia. London, 1953.
Arc 513.17.20 — Dussaud, René. Prélydiens Hittites et Achéens. Paris, 1953.
Arc 935.45 — Duyaran, Rüstem. 1952 yilinda arkeolojik. Istanbul, 1953.
Arc 1190.86 — Elker, Salâhaddin. Divan rakamlari. Ankara, 1953.
Arc 530.60 — Garstang, John. Prehistoric Mersin. Oxford, 1953.
Arc 726.155 — Giorgi, Gello. Suasa senonum. Parma, 1953.
Arc 761.8F — Gjerstadt, E. Early Rome. v.1-6. Lund, 1953. 5v.
Arc 1276.15F — Grandjean, P.B. Slesvigske kobstaeders og herreders segl indtil 1660. København, 1953.
Arc 1480.54 — Grant, Michael. The six main AES coinages of Augustus. Edinburgh, 1953.
Arc 853.103F — Grohne, E. Mohndorf. Bremen, 1953.
Arc 1285.10 — Haisig, Marian. Studia nad legendą pieczęci miejskiej. Wrocław, 1953.
Arc 830.205 — Hatt, Jean J. Strasbourg au temps des Romaims. Strasbourg, 1953.
Arc 557.4 — Hayes, William Christopher. The scepter of Egypt. N.Y., 1953. 2v.
Arc 708.30.2A — Hill, I.C.T. The ancient city of Athens. Cambridge, 1953.
Arc 708.30 — Hill, I.C.T. The ancient city of Athens. London, 1953.
Arc 447.1.5 — Hyderabad, India (State). Archaeological Department. Antiquarian remains in Hyderabad State. Hyderabad, 1953.
Arc 1308.7 — International Numismatic Congress. Congrès international de numismatique. Paris, 1953-57. 2v.
Arc 925.92 — Iranova, A.P. Iskusstvo antichnikh gorodov severnogo Prichernomoria. Petrograd, 1953.
Arc 1413.5 — Jacobs, N.G. Japanese coinage. N.Y., 1953.
Arc 587.11 — James, Thomas Garnet H. The mastaba of Khentika called Ikhekhi. London, 1953.
Arc 673.1.25F — Jannosay, J. Le gymnase de Delphes. Thèse. Paris, 1953.
Arc 395.15 — Kenyon, Kathleen Mary. Beginning in archaeology. 2. ed. London, 1953.
Arc 925.95 — Kolchin, B.A. Tekhnika obra botki metala v drev. ruhssi. Moskva, 1953.
Arc 750.206.10 — Kraus, Theodor. Die Ranken der Ara Pacis. Berlin, 1953.
Arc 608.6.30 — Leschi, Louis. Djemila. Alger, 1953.
Arc 843.120 — López Cuevillas, Florentino. La civilización céltica en Galicia. Santiago, 1953.
Arc 766.4.15 — Lugli, Giuseppe. Fontes ad topographism veteris urbis Romae pertinentes. v.1-4; v.6, pt.1-2; v.8, pt.1. Roma, 1953. 7v.
Arc 397.18A — Macaulay, Rose. Pleasure of ruins. London, 1953.
Arc 1538.20 — Mack, R.P. The coinage of ancient Britain. London, 1953.
Arc 543.5.16 — Malleret, L. Le cinquantenaire de l'École française d'Extrême-Orient. Paris, 1953.
Arc 543.66.10 — Masson, M.E. Akhangeran. Tashkend, 1953.
Arc 905.18.10 — Morton, F. Hallstatt. Hallstatt, 1953. 2v.
Arc 682.6 — The Mycenae tablets. v.4. Phildelphia, 1953.
Arc 1138.85 — Navascués y de Juan, Joaquin Maria de. El concepto de la epigrafia consideraciones sobre la necesidad de su ampliación. Madrid, 1953.
Arc 880.46 — O'Riordain, Sean P. Antiquities of the Irish countryside. 3. ed. London, 1953.
Arc 530.76F — Özgüc, T. Türk Tarih kurumu tarafindan yapelan Kültepe kazisi raporu, 1949. Ankara, 1953.
Arc 1488.25 — Pagani, Antonio. Monete italiane moderne a sistema decimale da Napoleone console alla Repubblica Italiana. 2. ed. Milano, 1953.
Arc 387.13.10 — Pasquali, G. Storia dello spirito tedesco. Firenze, 1953.
Arc 895.46 — Paulsen, P. Schwertartbänder der Wikingerzeit. Stuttgart, 1953.
Arc 608.30F — Pesce, G. Il tempio d'Iside in Sabratha. Roma, 1953.
Arc 588.66F — Petrie, W.M.F. Flinders Petrie centenary...ceremonial slate palettes. London, 1953.
Arc 726.107 — Pietrangeli, Carlo. Mevania. Roma, 1953.
Arc 843.65.4 — Pla y Cargol, J. Ampurios y rosas. 4. ed. Gerona, 1953.
Arc 1200.25 — Purvis, J.S. An introduction to ecclesiastical records. London, 1953.
Arc 543.70.5F — Rathjens, Carl. Sabaeica. Hamburg, 1953.
Arc 1423.18.10 — Reifenberg, A. Israel's history in coins from the Maccabees to the Roman conquest. London, 1953.
Arc 1148.27 — Rémondon, R. Papyrus grecs d'Apollônos anô. Le Caire, 1953.
Arc 925.38.15 — Rudenko, Sergei Ivanovich. Kul'tura naseleniia Gornogo Altaia v skifskoe vremiia. Moskva, 1953.
Arc 402.18 — Rumpf, A. Archäologie. Berlin, 1953-56. 2v.
Arc 730.6.5 — Santangelo, M. Selinunte. Roma, 1953.
Arc 403.16.20 — Schliemann, Heinrich. Briefwechsel. Berlin, 1953. 2v.
Arc 1468.38 — Schlumberger, P. L'argent grec l'empire achémenide. Thèse. Paris, 1953.
Arc 493.2.10F — Schmidt, E.F. Persepolis. Chicago, 1953-70. 3v.

1953 - cont.

Arc 1530.10 — Scholten, C. The coins of the Dutch overseas territories, 1601-1948. Amsterdam, 1953.
Arc 925.85 — Shul'ts, P. Maveolei neapole skifskogo. Moskva, 1953.
Arc 925.97 — Smirnov, K.F. Severskii kurgan. Moskva, 1953.
Arc 830.200 — Société Nationale des Antiquaires de France. Mémorial d'un voyage d'études. Paris, 1953.
Arc 1433.70 — Sourdel, D. Inventaire des monnaies musulmanes anciennes du musée de Caboul. Damas, 1953.
Arc 810.57F — Spinazzola, Vittorio. Pompei alla luce degli scavi novi di Via dell'Abondanza (anni 1910-1923). Roma, 1953. 2v.
Arc 936.105 — Srpska Akademia Nauka Belgrade. Arkheol. Institut. Arkheologika slomenichi i malazishta u Srbiji. v.1-2. Beograd, 1953.
Arc 441.15 — Subbarao, B. Baroda through the ages. Baroda, 1953.
Arc 905.12.20 — Swoboda, Erich. Carnuntum. Wien, 1953.
Arc 608.31 — Tarradell, M. Guia arqueológica del Marruecos Español. Tetuán, 1953.
Arc 830.185 — Toussaint, M. Répertoire archéologique du département de la Seine. Paris, 1953.
Arc 830.190 — Toussaint, M. Répertoire archéologique du département de la Seine-et-Marne. Paris, 1953.
Arc 530.80A — Trever, K.V. Ocherki po istorii kultur' Erevnei Armenii. Moskva, 1953.
Arc 936.140.55 — Vasiliev, Asen. Ivanovskite stenopisi. Sofiia, 1953.
Arc 943.34 — Verrill, A.H. America's ancient civilizations. N.Y., 1953.
Arc 785.13.75 — Welin, Erik. Studien zur Topographie des Forum Romanum. Lund, 1953.
Arc 1033.34.50 — Wenzel, P. Die Ausgrabbungen unter der Peterskirche in Rom. Leipzig, 1953.
Arc 530.70 — Woolley, C.L. A forgotten kingdom. Baltimore, 1953.
Arc 407.10.11 — Woolley, Charles L. Spadework. London, 1953.
Arc 407.10.10 — Woolley, Charles L. Spadework in archaeology. N.Y., 1953.
Arc 925.8.45 — Zhebelev, S.A. Severnoe prichernomor. Moskva, 1953.

1954

Arc 848.50 — Akademie der Wissenschaften, Berlin. Frühe Burger und Städte. Berlin, 1954.
Arc 543.55A — Akademiia nauk SSSR. Institut Istorii Materialii Kul'tura. Zhivopis drevnogo Piandzhikenta. Moskva, 1954. 2v.
Arc 925.100 — Akademiia Nauk SSSR. Institut Istorii Materialy Kul'tury. Voprosy skifo-sarmatskoi arkheologicheskoi. Moskva, 1954.
Arc 497.30.3 — Albright, William Foxwell. The archaeology of Palestine. London, 1954.
Arc 1418.15 — Altekar, A.S. Catalogue of the Gupta gold coins in the Bayana Hoard. Bombay, 1954.
Arc 923.37 — Artsikhovskii, A.V. Osnovy arkheologii. Moskva, 1954.
Arc 340.30 — Banner, János. A Közép-Dunamedence régészeti bibliográfiája a legrégibb időktöl a XI. századig. Budapest, 1954.
Arc 746.22 — Bastianelli, S. Centumcellae (Civitavecchia). Roma, 1954.
Arc 1148.25 — Bataille, A. Pour une terminologie en paléographie grecque. Paris, 1954.
Arc 726.135 — Battisti, C. La Venezia Tridentina nella preistoria. Firenze, 1954.
Arc 1490.65F — Bernareggi, E. Monete d'oro con ritratto del rinascimento italiano. Milano, 1954.
Arc 925.140 — Bers, E.M. Arkheologicheskie pamiatniki Sverdlovska i ego obrestnostei. Sverdlovsk, 1954.
Arc 1030.60 — Beyer, Oskar. Fruhchristliche Sinnbilder und Inschriften. Kassel, 1954.
Arc 1251.26 — Biesantz, Hagen. Kretisch-mykenische Siegelbilder. Marburg, 1954.
Arc 925.90A — Blavatskii, V.D. Ocherki voen. dela. v antich. gosud. seleriogo Prichernomord. Moskva, 1954.
Arc 1020.137 — Bovini, G. Sarcofagi paleocristiani della Spagna. Roma, 1954.
Arc 386.30 — Brayda, C. Norme per il restauro dei monumenti. Torino, 1954.
Arc 853.110 — Brunn, W.A. von. Steinpockungsgräber von Köthen. Berlin, 1954.
Arc 700.30 — Burton-Brown, T. The coming of iron to Greece. Wincle, 1954.
Arc 838.30 — Camon Aznar, J. Los artes y los pueblos de la España primitiva. Madrid, 1954.
Arc 1077.2.44 — Cecchelli, Carlo. Il trionfo della croce. Roma, 1954.
Arc 936.115.5 — Cercetari privind istoria veche ARPR. Bucureşti, 1954.
Arc 600.165 — Chubb, Mary. Nefertiti lived here. N.Y., 1954.
Arc 861.120 — Clark, J.G.D. Excavations at Star Caer. Cambridge, Eng., 1954.
Arc 609.13 — Cole, Sonia Mary. The prehistory of east Africa. Harmondsworth, 1954.
Arc 1153.82 — Colloque International de Paléographie Latine, 1st, Paris, 1953. Nomenclature des écritures livresques du IXe au XVIe siècle. Photoreproduction. Paris, 1954.
Arc 307.3.35 — Comas, Juan. La congresos internacionales de Americanistas. Mexico, 1954.
Arc 810.54.5 — Corte, Matteo della. Case ed abitanti di Pompei. 2. ed. Pompei, 1954.
Arc 943.38 — Covarrubias, M. The eagle. 1. ed. N.Y., 1954.
Arc 387.13.7 — Curtius, Ludwig. Humanistisches und Humanes. Basel, 1954.
Arc 925.165 — Datsiak, B.D. Pervobytnoe obshchestvo na territorii nashei strang. Moskva, 1954.
Arc 448.1.20 — Deshmukh, P.R. The Indus civilization in the Rgveda. Yeotmal, 1954.
Arc 388.8.2 — Diolé, P. 4,000 years under the sea. N.Y., 1954.
Arc 853.155F — Dohn, Wolfgang. Die Steinzeit im kieslische Katalog der steinzeitlichen Altertümer. Kallmünz, 1954.
Arc 595.59 — Edwards, L.E.S. The pyramids of Egypt. London, 1954.
Arc 389.5 — Ehrich, R.W. Relative chronologies in old world archaeology. Chicago, 1954.
Arc 1163.17.7 — Essex, England. Record Office. Examples of English handwriting. Essex? 1954.
Arc 925.107 — Fedorov, G.B. Po sledam drevnik kul'tur. Moskva, 1954.
Arc 726.180 — Forno, Federico dal. Il teatro romano di Verona. Verona, 1954.
Arc 671.15 — Fraser, F.M. Boeotian and west Greek tombstones. Lund, 1954.
Arc 1138.65 — Friedrich, Johannes. Entzifferung verschollener Schriften und Sprachen. Berlin, 1954.
Arc 1478.40.2 — Grant, Michael. Roman imperial money. London, 1954.
Arc 858.47.12 — Great Britain. Ministry of Works. Illustrated regional guides to ancient monuments. v.1-2,4,6. London, 1954. 4v.
Arc 830.220 — Guérin, Gérard. Découverte du Baptistère de Sanctus Martinus de Joulle. Fontenay-le-Comte, 1954.

Chronological Listing

1954 - cont.

Arc 1143.12	Hanger, H. Studien zur griechischen Paläographie. Wien, 1954.
Arc 936.115	Histria monografie archeologică. București, 1954. 3v.
Arc 1349.60F	Hujer, L. Mein Leben und Streben. Wien, 1954.
Arc 936.42F	Ivanov, T. Rimska mozaika ot Ulpiia Eskus. Sofiia, 1954.
Arc 969.15.10	Jury, Wilfrid. Sainte-Marie among the Hurons. Toronto, 1954.
Arc 1411.13	Kann, Eduard. Illustrated catalog of Chinese coins, gold, silver, nickel and aluminum. Los Angeles, 1954.
Arc 843.95	Karst, Josef. Essai sur l'origine des Basques Ibères et peuples apparentés. Strasbourg, 1954.
Arc 1033.34.55	Kioschbaum, Engelbert. La tumba de San Pedro y las catacumbas romanas. Madrid, 1954.
Arc 609.8	Kirkman, James Spedding. The Arab city of Gedi. London, 1954.
Arc 923.111F	Korzukhina, G.F. Russkie klady IX-XIII vv. Moskva, 1954.
Arc 853.112	Kramert, K. Ausgrabungen unter der St. Jakobskirche Dokumertieren. n.p., 1954.
Arc 875.85	Lacaille, A.D. The Stone Age in Scotland. London, 1954.
Arc 396.10	Laet, Siegfried J. de. L'archélogie et ses problèmes. Berchem, 1954.
Arc 612.40	Laviosa, Zambotti. Il mediterraneo. Torino, 1954.
Arc 925.107.5	Lebende Vergangenheit; deutsche Übertragen von Alexander Becker und Ruth Kalinowski. 1. Aufl. Berlin, 1954.
Arc 66.1.180	Lefèvre, Yves. L'elucidarium et les lucidaires. Paris, 1954.
Arc 1500.53F	Lengyel, L. L'art gaulais dans les médailles. Montrange-Seine, 1954.
Arc 726.110	Lenotti, T. L'arena di Verona. Verona, 1954.
Arc 383.79.25	Lullies, R. Neue Beiträge zur klassischen Altertumswissenschaft. Stuttgart, 1954.
Arc 726.120	Maiuri, Amedeo. Saggi di varia antichità. Venezia, 1954.
Arc 608.2.50	Marec, Erwan. Hippone la Royale. Alger, 1954.
Arc 530.82	Martirosian, A. Raskopki v golovino. Erevan, 1954.
Arc 1330.20.2	Mayer, Leo Ary. Bibliography of Moslem numismatics, India excepted. 2. ed. London, 1954.
Arc 608.6.65	Mercier, Maurice. Prière sur le Tombeau de la Chrétienne. Paris, 1954.
Arc 936.80.5F	Mikov, Vasil. Antichnata grobnitsa pri Kazanlak. Sofiia, 1954.
Arc 936.80F	Mikov, Vasil. Le tombeau antique près de Kazanlak. Sofia, 1954.
Arc 923.55	Miller, M.A. Arkheologiia v SSSR. Miunchen, 1954.
Arc 1153.81	Moschetti, G. Primordi esegetici sulla legislazione longobardo. Spoleto, 1954.
Arc 853.140F	Müller-Karpe, H. Das Arnenfeld von Kelheim. Kallmünz, 1954.
Arc 885.19.5	Nash-Williams, Victor Erle. The Roman frontier in Wales. Cardiff, 1954.
Arc 726.115	Orsi, Libero d'. Gli scavi di Stabia a cura del Comitato per gli scavi di Stabia. Napoli, 1954.
Arc 1584.4	Pakhomov, Evgenii A. Monetnye klady Azerbaidzhana. pt.6,8. Baku, 1954.
Arc 505.5.35	Parrat, André. Le Temple de Jérusalem. Neuchâtel, 1954.
Arc 858.58.5	Piggott, Stuart. The neolithic cultures of the British Isles. Cambridge, Eng., 1954.
Arc 66.1.179	Pouillaux, Jean. La Forteresse de Rhamnonte. Paris, 1954.
Arc 1578.6	Probszt, Günther. Quellenkunde der Münz- und Geldgeschichte. Graz, 1954.
Arc 505.80	Saadé, Gabriel. Ras-Shamra. Beyrouth, 1954.
Arc 493.2.20	Sami, A. Persepolis. Shiraz, 1954.
Arc 66.1.178	Schilling, R. La religion romaine de Venias depuis les origines jusqu'au temps d'Auguste. Paris, 1954.
Arc 875.90	Simpson, William D. Dundarg Castle. Edinburgh, 1954.
Arc 875.95	Simpson, William D. The Viking congress. Edinburgh, 1954.
Arc 383.95	Società Archeologia Comense. Raccolta di scritti. Como, 1954.
Arc 1053.25	Stommel, Edward. Beiträge zur Ikonographie der konstantinischen Sarkophagplastik. Bonn, 1954.
Arc 853.135F	Stroh, Armin. Die Reihengräber der karolingisch-ottonischen Zeit. Kallmünz, 1954. 2 pam.
Arc 830.215	Toussaint, M. Répertoire archéologique du département de l'Aube. Paris, 1954.
Arc 785.34.25	Toynbee, Jocelyn M.C. The Ara Pacia reconsidered and historical art in Roman Italy. London, 1954.
Arc 383.34	Tübingen. Universität. Vor- und Frühgeschichtliches Institut. Festschrift für Peter Goessler. Stuttgart, 1954.
Arc 505.5.66	Vincent, Louis H. Jérusalem de l'Ancien Testament. Pt.1-3. Paris, 1954. 3v.
Arc 407.16	Wheeler, Robert Eric Mortimer. Archaeology from the earth. Oxford, 1954.
Arc 407.18	Wheeler, Robert Eric Mortimer. Rome beyond the imperial frontiers. London, 1954.

1955

Arc 530.65.5	Akademiia nauk Armianskoi SSR, Erevan. Institut Istorii. Karmir-blur. Erevan, 1955- 4v.
Arc 530.95F	Akademiia nauk Gruz SSR, Tiflis. Institut Istorii. Mtskheta; itogi arkheologicheskikh issledovanii. Tbilisi, 1955.
Arc 925.113	Akademiia Nauk SSSR. Institut Istorii Materialy Kul'tury. Antichnye goroda severnogo Prichernomoria. Moskva, 1955.
Arc 905.17.10F	Alzinger, Wilhelm. Kleinfunde von Aguntum aus den Jahren 1850 bis 1952. Wien, 1955.
Arc 383.3	Anthemon. Firenze, 1955.
Arc 923.37.5	Artsikhovskii, A.V. Osnovy arkheologii. Izd. 2. Moskva, 1955.
Arc 726.24.22	Aurigemma, S. Die Hadriansvilla bei Tivoli. Tivoli, 1955.
Arc 1148.25.5	Bataille, A. Les papyrus. 1. éd. Paris, 1955.
Arc 830.310	Blouet, L. Le chrismale de Mortain. Coutances, 1955.
Arc 889.17	Bogaers, J.E.A.T. De Gallo-Romeinse tempels te Elst in de Over Betuive. 's-Gravenhage, 1955.
Arc 543.2.10	Boisselier, Jean. La statuaire khmère son évolution. Saigon, 1955. 2v.
Arc 125.4.2	British Archaeological Association. Archaeological journal. General index, v.26-75 (1869-1918). London, 1955-73. 2v.
Arc 383.93	Bruns, G. Festschrift für Carl Weickert. Berlin, 1955.
Arc 1588.6.30	Butak, Bekzad. Cumhuriyet devrinde madeni para bois. Istanbul, 1955.
Arc 736.15	Canale, C.G. Engyon. Catania, 1955.
Arc 1033.10.10	Carcopino, Jérome. Le mystère d'un symbole chrétien. Paris, 1955.

1955 - cont.

Arc 383.79.12	Československá Ademie věd. Sekoe Jazyka a Literatury. Studie z antiky; Antonínu Salsčovi. Praha, 1955.
Arc 390.11	Childe, Vere Gordon. Henri Frankfort, 1897-1954. London, 1955?
Arc 726.145	Convegno di Studi Plorici e Archeologici Veleiati, 1st, Piacenza. Studi veleiati. Piacenza, 1955.
Arc 387.35	Crawford, Osbert Guy S. Said and done. London, 1955.
Arc 830.11.25	Daniel, G.E. Lascaux and Carnac. London, 1955.
Arc 600.185F	Daumot, F. Les mammisis de Dendara, le mammisi de Nectanébo. Le Caire, 1955.
Arc 905.24.14	Egger, Rudolf. Teurnia. 4. Aufl. Klagenfurt, 1955.
Arc 530.120	Egiazarian, O. Pamiatniki kul'tury...raiona. Erevan, 1955.
Arc 1190.80	Fekete, Lajos. Die Siyâquat-Schrift in der türkischen Finanzverwaltung. Budapest, 1955.
Arc 905.90	Folteny, Stephan. Zur Cronologie der Bronzezeit des Karpatenbeckens. Bonn, 1955.
Arc 853.101.10F	Fremersdorf, F. Das fränkische Reichengräberfeld Köln-Mungersdorf. Text and plates. Berlin, 1955. 2v.
Arc 66.1.182	Gagé, Jean. Apollon romain. Paris, 1955.
Arc 1530.5	Gelder, Hendrik Enno van. De Nederlandse noodmunten van de tachtigjarige vorlog. 's-Gravenhage, 1955.
Arc 726.150	Gentili, Gino Vinicio. Auximum (Osimo) regio V. Picenum. Roma, 1955.
Arc 870.10.9.5	Grinsell, L.V. The ancient burial-mounds of England. 2. ed. London, 1955.
Arc 1148.20.2	Groningen, B.A. Short manual of Greek palaeography. 2. ed. Leiden, 1955.
Arc 1522.3	Harpes, Jean. Médailles et jetons du pays de Luxembourg. Luxembourg, 1955.
Arc 387.13.30	Herbig, Reinhard. Ludwig Curtius, 1874-1954, zum Gedachtnis. Heidelberg, 1955.
Arc 612.45	Holmqvist, Wilhelm. Germanic art during the first millenium. Stockholm, 1955.
Arc 889.15	Hondius-Crone, Ada. The temple of Nehalennia at Domburg. Amsterdam, 1955.
Arc 936.195.285.5	Hrubý, Vilém. Staré Město-Veligrad. Gottwaldov, 1955.
Arc 66.1.181	Jannoray, Jean. Enserune. Paris, 1955.
Arc 936.195.60	Janšak, Stefan. Základy archeolog. vyskumu v teréne. Bratislava, 1955.
Arc 700.33	Jantzen, Ulf. Griechische Greifenkessel. Berlin, 1955.
Arc 74.5.2	Journal of Roman studies. Consolidated index, v.21-60. London, 1955-75. 2v.
Arc 1584.1.4	Kapanadze, D.G. Gruzinskia numizmatika. Moskva, 1955.
Arc 518.8.5	Keil, Josef. Ephesos. Wien, 1955.
Arc 1153.73	Kirchner, J. Scriptura latina libraria. Monachii, 1955.
Arc 650.10	Kirsten, Ernst. Griechenlandkunde. Heidelberg, 1955.
Arc 936.6.10	Kostrzewski, Józef. Wielkopolska w pradziejach. 3. wyd. Warszawa, 1955.
Arc 925.105	Kotsevalov, A.S. Antichnikh istoria i kul'tura severi Prichernomor'ia. Miunkhon, 1955.
Arc 395.20.5	Kühn, Herbert. Der Aufstieg der Menschheit. Frankfurt, 1955.
Arc 530.164	Labraunda; Swedish excavations and researches. v.1, pt.1-2; v.2, pt.1; v.3, pt.1. Lund, 1955- 4v.
Arc 688.6	Lehmann, Karl. Samothrace. N.Y., 1955.
Arc 843.100	Leisner, G.K. Antas nas herdades da Casa de Braganca no concelho de Estremoz. Lisboa, 1955.
Arc 861.130	Lincoln Archaeological Research Committee. Ten seasons digging, 1945-1954. Lincoln, 1955.
Arc 530.96	Lomatidze, C.A. Arkheologicheskie raskopki v srevnegruziiskoi storitse Mtskheta. Tbilisi, 1955.
Arc 608.6.60	Luiks, A.G. Cathedra en mensa. Franeker, 1955.
Arc 530.12.40	Marek, Kurt W. Enge Schlucht und Schwarzer Berg. Hamburg, 1955.
Arc 736.17	Margani, M.N. Casmene ritrovata? Comiso, 1955.
Arc 870.4.21	Margary, Ivan D. Roman roads in Britain. London, 1955. 2v.
Arc 458.1.12	Marshall, John. A guide to Sanchi. 3. ed. Delhi, 1955.
Arc 672.1.73	Matton, Raymond. La Crète antique. Athènes, 1955.
Arc 1448.5	Mazard, Jean. Corpus nummorum Nunudiae nauretaniaeque. Paris, 1955.
Arc 861.147	Meates, Geoffrey W. Lullingstone Roman villa. London, 1955.
Arc 935.23.5F	Miranda, S. El Gran Palacio Sagrado de Bizancio. Mexico, 1955.
Arc 925.110	Mongait, A.L. Arkheologiia v SSSR. Moskva, 1955.
Arc 608.33	Neukom, Tolantha T. Pitture rupestri del Tasili degli Azger. Firenze, 1955.
Arc 1588.4.17	Nohejlova, Eman. Nálezi minci v Cechacle na Morave a ve slezsku. Praha, 1955. 4v.
Arc 1588.4.30	Nohejlová, Emanuela. Krasa česke mince. Praha, 1955.
Arc 388.10	Paris. Université. Institut de Civilisation. Pierre Dupont. Paris, 1955.
Arc 416.23.5	Parrot, A. Discovering buried worlds. 1. ed. N.Y., 1955.
Arc 505.39.10	Parrot, André. Samarie. Neuchatel, 1955.
Arc 925.93	Popova, Tat'iana B. Plemena katakombnoi kul'tury. Photoreproduction. Moskva, 1955.
Arc 1138.70	Raalte, James van. De schrijfkunst in de Bijbellanden. Baarn, 1955.
Arc 1148.30	Roberts, C.H. Greek literary hands. Oxford, 1955.
Arc 402.19	Romaios, K.A. Mikra meletēmata. Thessalonikē, 1955.
Arc 493.2.5	Sami, A. Persepolis. 2. ed. Shiraz, 1955.
Arc 453.15	Sankalia, Hasmukh Dhirajlal. Report on the excavations at Nasik and Jorve. 1. ed. Poona, 1955.
Arc 936.225	Šašel, Jaro. Vodnik po Emoni. Ljubljana, 1955.
Arc 773.7	Scherer, M.R. Marvels of ancient Rome. N.Y., 1955.
Arc 403.16.17	Schliemann, Heinrich. Heinrich Schliemann. 8. Aufl. Wiesbaden, 1955.
Arc 386.31	Schreiber, Hermann. Versunkene Städte. Wien, 1955.
Arc 853.115	Schuldt, E. Pritzier. Berlin, 1955.
Arc 853.150F	Schwarz, Klaus. Die vor- und frühgeschichtlichen Gebäudedenkmäler Oberfrankens. Kallmünz, 1955. 2v.
Arc 1488.20	Secchi, Alberto. Le monete decimali sabaude. Milano, 1955.
Arc 630.13	Stevens, G.P. Restorations of classical buildings. Princeton, N.J., 1955.
Arc 1540.17.15	Stewart, Ian Halley. The Scottish coinage. London, 1955.
Arc 1390.15	Stockvis, Albert. Effective research on unknown mediaeval coinage. 1. ed. Cleveland, 1955.
Arc 1508.11	Suhle, Arthur. Deutsche Münz- und Geldgeschichte von den Anfanger bis zum 15. Jahrhundert. Berlin, 1955.
Arc 1348.55	Sutherland, C.H.V. Art in coinage. London, 1955.
Arc 936.4	Szafrański, W. Skarby brązowe z epoki wspólnoty. Warszawa, 1955.

1955 - cont.

Arc 830.199 Toussaint, M. Répertoire archéologique du département des Ardennes. Paris, 1955.
Arc 976.8 United States. National Park Service. Excavations at Green Spring Plantation. Yorktown, 1955.
Arc 603.5 Vaufrey, Raymond. Prehistoire de l'Afrigue. Paris, 1955.
Arc 853.160F Werner, Joachim. Das alamannische Gräberfeld von Mindelheim. Kallmünz, 1955.
Arc 407.17 Wheeler, Robert Eric Mortimer. Still digging. London, 1955.
Arc 66.1.183 Will, Ernest. Le relief culturel greco-romain. Paris, 1955.
Arc 497.52 Yeivin, Samuel. Archaeological activities in Israel. Jerusalem, 1955.
Arc 1493.15 Yriarte, José de. Catalogo de los reales de a ocho espanoles. Madrid, 1955.
Arc 1190.60 Zajączkowski, Anan. Zarys dyplomatyki osmánsko-tureckiej. Warszawa, 1955.
Arc 1353.15 Zeno, Apostalo. Sonder Münzenouktion. v.1-2,3. Wien, 1955. 2v.

1956

Arc 493.6.15 Akademiia Nauk Azerbaidzhanskoi SSR, Baku. Ockerki po drevnei istorii Azerbaidzhana SSR. Baku, 1956.
Arc 543.65 Akademiia nauk Tadzhikskoi SSSR, Stalinabad. Institut Istorii, Arkheologii i Etnografii. Arkheologicheskie i numzmaticheskie kollektsii. Stalinabad, 1956.
Arc 1433.80 Allouche-Le Page, M.T. L'art monétaire des royaumes bactriens. Paris, 1956.
Arc 843.105 Almeida, Fernando de. Egitânia. Lisboa, 1956.
Arc 530.135F Arik, Remri Ogur. Ankara-Konya. Ankara, 1956.
Arc 865.22 Atkinson, R.J.C. Stonehenge. London, 1956.
Arc 1143.14F Bassi, Stelio. Monumenta Italiae graphica. Cremona, 1956-57.
Arc 1033.53.24 Berchem, D. van. Le martyre de la Légion Thébaine. Basel, 1956.
Arc 726.165 Berti, Leo. Scoperte paletnologiche e archeologiche nella provincia di Treviso. 1. ed. Firenze, 1956.
Arc 858.63 Bruce-Mitford, R.L.S. Recent archaeological excavations in Britain. London, 1956.
Arc 547.35F Brunner-Traut, Emma. Die altägyptischen Scherbenbilder. Wiesbaden, 1956.
Arc 1643.4F Burzio, Humberto F. Diccionario de la moneda hispano-americana. Santiago, 1956-58. 2v.
Arc 853.220 Cämmerer, Erich. Vor- und Frühgeschichte Arnstadts und seiner weiteren Umgebung. Jena, 1956.
Arc 1025.74 Carcopino, J. De Pythagore aux apôtres. Paris, 1956.
Arc 1478.55 Carson, R.A.G. Essays in Roman coinage. Oxford, 1956.
Arc 455.5 Casal, Jean Marie. Site urbain et sites funéraires des environs de Pondichéry. Paris, 1956.
Arc 1163.3.55 Cherepnin, L.V. Russkaia paleografiia. Moskva, 1956.
Arc 497.50 Corswant, Willy. Dictionnaire d'archéologie biblique. Neuchâtel, 1956.
Arc 1494.25 Costa Couvreur, Raul de. Uma reproducão em cabre de moeda de retrato datado de 1630. Lisboa, 1956.
Arc 595.55 Cottrell, Leonard. The mountains of Pharaoh. N.Y., 1956.
Arc 905.85 Csallány, Dezsö. Archäologische Denkmäler der Awarenzeit in Mitteleuropa. Budapest, 1956.
Arc 1088.5 Dionisi, Francesco. Le navi sacre di Claudio nel lago di Nemi. Roma, 1956.
Arc 1190.65 Doelger, Franz. Byzantinische Diplomatik. Ettal, 1956.
Arc 905.24.13 Egger, Rudolf. Führer druch die Ausgrabungen und das Museum auf dem Magdalensberg. 3. Aufl. Klagenfurt, 1956.
Arc 1478.60 Elmer, Georg. Verzeichnis der römischen Reichsprägungen von Augustus bis Anastasius. 2. Aufl. Graz, 1956.
Arc 136.1.80 Evans, Joan. A history of the Society of Antiquaries. Oxford, 1956.
Arc 1588.7.5F Floca, Ochaviau. Coutributic la cunoasterea Syauselar de arguil doeice. Bucureşti, 1956.
Arc 853.101.5 Fremersdorf, F. Das römische Hans mit dem Dionysos-Mosaik vor dem Sudportal des Kölner Domes. Berlin, 1956.
Arc 340.7 French Bibliographical Digest. Archaeology, 1945-1955. N.Y., 1956- 2v.
Arc 936.235 Gabrovec, S. Najstarejša zgodovina Dolenjske. Novo Mesto, 1956.
Arc 1510.65.5 Gaettens, R. Münzporträts im 11. Jahrhundert? Heidelberg, 1956.
Arc 905.12.25 Gollob, Hedwig. Karnuntums Wiederaufbau. Wien, 1956.
Arc 595.45 Goneim, M. The buried pyramid. London, 1956.
Arc 875.52 Great Britain. Commissions. Ancient and Historical Monuments of Scotland. An inventory of the ancient and historical monuments of Roxburghshire. Edinburgh, 1956. 2v.
Arc 875.53 Great Britain. Commissions. Ancient and Historical Monuments of Scotland. An inventory of the ancient and historical monuments of Selkirkshire. Edinburgh, 1956.
Arc 853.185 Hahn, Heinrich. Die Ausgrabungen am Fuldaer Donaplatz. Fulda, 1956.
Arc 875.105 Hamilton, J.R.C. Excavations at Jarlshof. Edinburgh, 1956.
Arc 383.49 Harden, D.B. Dark-age Britain. London, 1956.
Arc 608.37 Haynes, D.E.L. An archaeological and historical guide to the pre-Islamic antiquities of Tripolitania. Tripoli, 1956.
Arc 1335.120F Hollschek, Karl. Sammlung Hollschek. v.1-3. Wien, 1956? 2v.
Arc 1335.120 Hollschek, Karl. Sammlung Hollschek. v.4-20. Wien, 1956? 4v.
Arc 936.12 Hołowińska, Z. Wczesnośredniowieczne grodziska w Bonikowie. Poznań, 1956.
Arc 483.7.2 Iraq. Department of Antiquities. Some works on the antiquities in the Abbasid Palace. 2. ed. Baghdad, 1956.
Arc 1508.15.5 Jaeger, Kurt. Die deutschen Reichsmünzen seit 1871. Basel, 1956.
Arc 493.35 Jaenichen, H. Bildzeichen der königlichen Hoheit bei den iranischen Völkern. Bonn, 1956.
Arc 497.51 Jirku, Anton. Der Ausgrabungen in Palästina und Syrien. Halle, 1956.
Arc 650.10.5 Kirsten, Ernst. Griechenlandkunde; ein Führer zu klassischen Stätten. Heidelberg, 1956.
Arc 383.48F Kleemann, Otto. Documento archaeologica. Bonn, 1956.
Arc 457.10 Kuraishi, M.M.H. Rājgir. 4. ed. Delhi, 1956.
Arc 843.100.5F Leisner, G.K. Die Negalithgräber der Iberischen Halbinsel. v.1-3; atlas. Berlin, 1956. 4v.
Arc 530.105 Lloyd, Seton. Early Anatolia. Harmondsworth, 1956.

1956 - cont.

Arc 543.70 Lysjsms, Philippe. Expédition en Arabie centrale. Paris, 1956. 3v.
Arc 652.7F Majewski, K. Kultura materialna starozytnej Grecji. Warszawa, 1956.
Arc 530.145F Mansel, A.M. Side agorasi ve civarindaki binalar. Ankara, 1956.
Arc 530.12.35 Marek, Kurt W. The secret of the Hittites. N.Y., 1956.
Arc 830.250 Meroc, L. Cougnac, grotte peinte. Stuttgart, 1956.
Arc 923.60 Miller, M.A. Archaeology in the U.S.S.R. N.Y., 1956.
Arc 562.7 Montet, Pierre. Isis; ou, À la recherche de l'Egypte ensevelie. Paris, 1956.
Arc 608.33.5 Neukom, Tolantha T. Les peintures rupestres du Tassili-n-Ajjer. Neuchâtel, 1956.
Arc 895.22.27F Nylén, Erik. Die jungere vorrömische Eisenzeit Gotlands. Stockholm, 1956.
Arc 383.90.10 Oviedo (Province). Diputacion Provincial. Servicio de Investigaciones Arqueologicas. Libro homenaje la Conde de la Vega del Sella. Oviedo, 1956.
Arc 493.40F Paris. Musée National du Louvre. Fouilles de Chapour. v.2. Paris, 1956.
Arc 400.11.30 Peake, Harold J.E. Times and places. Oxford, 1956.
Arc 925.50.15 Piatysheva, Natalia V. Iuvelirnye izdeliia Khersonesa. Moskva, 1956.
Arc 936.110F Poulék, J. Pravěké umení. Praha, 1956.
Arc 400.22F Poulik, Josef. Prehistoric art. London, 1956.
Arc 925.267 Raushenbakh, V.M. Srednee Zaural'e v epokhu neolita i bronzy. Moskva, 1956.
Arc 1500.57 Rolland, Henri. Monnaies des comtés de Provence, XII-XV siècles. Paris, 1956.
Arc 608.17.21 Rowe, Alan. Cyrenaican expedition of the University of Manchester. Manchester, Eng., 1956.
Arc 785.80 Salomonson, Jan Willem. Chair, sceptre and wreath. Amsterdam, 1956.
Arc 493.30 Sami, A. Pasargadae. Shiraz, 1956.
Arc 925.125 Shelov, D.B. Antichnyi mir v severnom Prichernomor'e. Moskva, 1956.
Arc 925.120 Shelov, D.B. Monetnoe delo Bospora. Moskva, 1956.
Arc 323.4 Society for American Archaeology. Seminars in archaeology: 1955. Salt Lake City, 1956.
Arc 543.75 Stutterheim, W.F. Studies in Indonesian archaeology. The Hague, 1956.
Arc 1348.55.2 Sutherland, C.H.V. Art in coinage. N.Y., 1956.
Arc 503.8F Svenske Syrien expeditionem, 1952-1953. Lund, 1956.
Arc 905.95F Szilágyi, János. Aquencum. Budapest, 1956.
Arc 905.100F Thomas, Baja. Archäologische Funde in Ungarn. Budapest, 1956.
Arc 1433.99 Tosun, Mebrure. Mejopotamya silindir muhurlerinder hurri mitanni usulü. Ankara, 1956.
Arc 785.77 Toynbee, J.M. The shrine of St. Peter. London, 1956.
Arc 936.40.5 Vuzharova, Z. Slaviano-bulgarskato selishte brai selo Popina. Sofiia, 1956.
Arc 936.140.40 Vuzharova, Zhivka N. O proiskhczhdenii bolgarskikh pakhotnykh orudii. Moskva, 1956.
Arc 385.5 Walker, John. John Allen. London, 1956?
Arc 383.34.5 Weinberg, S.S. The Aegean and the Near East. N.Y., 1956.
Arc 838.35 Wiseman, F.J. Roman Spain. London, 1956.
Arc 407.10.7 Woolley, Charles L. Digging up the past. Harmondsworth, 1956.
Arc 383.42.5 Zylmann, Peter. Zur Ur- und Frühgeschichte Nordwestdeutschlands. Hildesheim, 1956.

1957

Arc 540.9F Aastroem, Paul. The Middle Cypriote Bronze Age. Lund, 1957.
Arc 925.150 Akademiia Nauk BSSR, Minsk. Institut Historyi. Materialy po arkheologii BSSR. Minsk, 1957.
Arc 925.50.30 Akademiia Nauk URSR, Kiev. Kryms'kyi Filologicheskii. Istoriia i arkheologiia drev. Kryma. Kiev, 1957.
Arc 603.6.5 Alimen, Henriette. The prehistory of Africa. London, 1957.
Arc 1033.35.147.2 Almeida, R.V. d'. A cruz de vila Viçosa. 2. ed. Lisboa, 1957.
Arc 936.140.45 Arkheologicheski otkritiia v Bulgariia. Sofiia, 1957.
Arc 387.40 Ashmole, Bernhard. Cyriac of Ancona. London, 1957.
Arc 1208.13F Aulock, Hans von. Altorientalische Siegelsteine der Sammlung Hans Silvius von Aulock. Uppsala, 1957.
Arc 1138.108F Awad, G. Report in search of the condition of manuscripts in Egypt. n.p., 1957?
Arc 612.38 Behn, Friedrich. Aus europäischer Vorzeit. Stuttgart, 1957.
Arc 830.275 Benoît, Fernand. Entremont, capitale celto-ligure des Salyens de Provence. Aix-en-Provence, 1957.
Arc 1675.75 Bibliothèque Nationale, Paris. Exposition: Effigies et portraits. Paris? 1957.
Arc 823.11.3F Blážej, Benadík. Keltské pohrebiská na juhozápadnom Slovensku. Bratislava, 1957.
Arc 830.300 Bolnat, Georges. La nécropole protohistorique de La Colombine à Champlay-Yonne. Paris, 1957.
Arc 861.11.10 Boon, George Counsell. Roman Silchester. London, 1957.
Arc 386.32 Bradford, John. Ancient landscapes. London, 1957.
Arc 1093.2.19 Brjussow, A. Geschichte der neolithischen Stämme im europäischen Teil der Ud SSR. Berlin, 1957.
Arc 700.40A Brock, James K. Fortetsa. Cambridge, Eng., 1957.
Arc 895.7.25.2F Brøndsted, J. Danmarks oldtid. Kjøbenhavn, 1957- 3v.
Arc 1053.23 Budde, Ludwig. Der Ertstehung des antiken Repräsentationsbildes. Berlin, 1957.
Arc 853.145F Cambodunumforschungen, 1953- Kallmünz, 1957- 2v.
Arc 785.20.15F Castagnoli, F. Appia antica. Milano, 1957.
Arc 785.13.80F Castagnoli, F. Foro romano. Milano, 1957.
Arc 726.2.30 Caterino, Antonio. Bibliografia sulle catacombe napoletane. Firenze, 1957.
Arc 530.97 Chubinishvili, T.N. Drevneiskie arkheologicheskie...Mtskheta. Tbilisi, 1957.
Arc 387.21.5A Clark, John Grahame Douglas. Archaeology and society. Cambridge, Mass., 1957.
Arc 1033.34.60 Corte, Nicola. San Pietro e sepolto in Vaticano? Roma, 1957.
Arc 387.33 Cottrell, Leonard. Lost cities. N.Y., 1957.
Arc 830.260 Couture, Claude Paul. À l'assaut de la carrière du Puits. Le Havre, 1957.
Arc 1166.7.10 Cramer, Maria. Archäologische und epigrapische Klassifikation koptischer Denkmäler des Metropolitan Museum of Art, N.Y. und des Museum of Fine Arts, Boston, Mass. Wiesbaden, 1957.

Chronological Listing

1957 - cont.

Arc 830.290	Croix, Charles. Les anciennes fortifications d'Avesnes. Cholet, 1957.
Arc 875.110	Cruden, Stewart. The early Christian and Pictish monuments of Scotland. Edinburgh, 1957.
Arc 757.9F	Curtius, Ludwig. Das antike Rom. 3. Aufl. Wien, 1957.
Arc 1433.75	Czapkicwicz, A. Skarb dirhemov arabskich z Czechowa. Warszawa, 1957.
Arc 66.1.184	Delumeau, Jean. Vie economique et sociale de Rome. Paris, 1957. 2v.
Arc 66.1.186	Dessenore, André. Le sphinx. Paris, 1957.
Arc 1138.75	Doblhofer, Ernst. Zeichen und Wunder. Wien, 1957.
Arc 726.310	Fellmann, Rudolf. Das Grab des Lucius Munatius Plancus bei Gaeta. Basel, 1957.
Arc 726.185	Franciscis, Alfonso de. Mausolei romani di Campania. Napoli, 1957.
Arc 861.150	Frere, Sheppard. The city of Durovernum. Canterbury, 1957.
Arc 1138.65.5	Friedrich, Johannes. Extinct languages. N.Y., 1957.
Arc 1510.65F	Gaettens, R. Das Geld- und Münzwesen der Abtei Fulda im Hoch. Fulda, 1957.
Arc 936.13	Gardanski, A. Archeologia i pradzieje Polski. Warszawa, 1957.
Arc 340.11	Georgieva, Sonia. Bibliografiia na bulgarskata arkheologiia, 1879-1955. Sofiia, 1957.
Arc 1478.75	Goebl, Robert. Einführung in die Münzprägung der römischen Kaiserzeit. Wien, 1957.
Arc 905.12.26	Gollob, Helwig. Gäbber in Karnuntum. Wien, 1957.
Arc 608.35	Golvin, Lucien. Le Magrib central à l'époque des Zerides. Paris, 1957.
Arc 1473.8.2	Goodacre, H.G. A handbook of the coinage of the Byzantine empire. London, 1957.
Arc 391.10	Gordon, C.H. Adventures in the Nearest East. Fair Lawn, N.J., 1957.
Arc 600.140	Goyon, Georges. Nouvelles inscriptions rupestres du Wadi Hammamat. Paris, 1957.
Arc 543.2.5	Groslier, Bernard P. The arts and civilization of Angkor. N.Y., 1957.
Arc 1675.65	Grotemeyer, Paul. Da ich het die gestalt. München, 1957.
Arc 1588.1.30	Gutten Czapskii, E.K. Catalogue de la collection des medailles et monnaies polonaises. Graz, 1957. 5v.
Arc 383.51	Homaxe a Florentino A.L. Cuevillas. Vigo, 1957.
Arc 383.17	Hommages à Waldemar Deonna. Hommages à Waldemar Deonna. Bruxelles, 1957.
Arc 1490.68	Horzfelder, Hubert. Les monnaies d'argent de Rhegion frappées entre 461 et le milieu du IVe siècle avant J.-C. Paris, 1957.
Arc 432.17	India. Department of Archaeology. Ancient monuments. Delhi, 1957. 6 pam.
Arc 915.40.3	International Congress of Roman Frontier Studies, 3d, Rheinfelden, Switzerland. Limes-Studien; Vorträge des 3. Internationalen Limes-Kongresses in Rheinfelden. Basel, 1957.
Arc 1508.15.10	Jaeger, Kurt. Berwertungstablellen der deutschen Reichsmünzen seit 1871. Basel, 1957.
Arc 893.27F	Jankuhn, H. Denkmaler der Vorzeit zwischen Nord- und Ostsee. Schleswig, 1957.
Arc 1364.2	Janssen, A.J. Het antieke tropaion. Ledeberg, 1957.
Arc 1510.39	Jesse, Wilhelm. Der zweite Brakteatenfund von Mödesse und die Kunst der Brakteaten zur Zeit Heinrichs des Löwen. Braunschweig, 1957.
Arc 843.199F	Jordá Cerdá, F. Las murias de Beloño. Oviedo, 1957.
Arc 103.5	Journées Archéologiques d'Avignon, Avignon, 1956. Journées archéologiques d'Avignon. Avignon, 1957.
Arc 518.8.7	Keil, Josef. Ephesos. 4. Aufl. Wien, 1957.
Arc 505.66.5	Kenyon, K.M. Digging up Jericho. N.Y., 1957.
Arc 925.60	Khakovskii, V.F. Pamiatniki material'noi kul'tury Chuvashskoi ASSR. Cheboksary, 1957.
Arc 1027.32.10	Kirschbaum, E. Die Graeber der Apostelfürsten. Frankfurt, 1957.
Arc 650.10.7	Kirsten, Ernst. Griechenlandkunde. 3. Aufl. Heidelberg, 1957.
Arc 895.7.35	Klindt-Jensen, Ole. Denmark before the Vikings. London, 1957.
Arc 530.140F	Kosay, H.Z. Büyük Güllücek karisi. Ankara, 1957.
Arc 395.7.5	Kraus, Franz Xaver. Tagebücher. Köln, 1957.
Arc 395.20	Kühn, Herbert. Der Aufstieg der Menschheit. Frankfurt, 1957.
Arc 608.6.46	Leschi, Louis. Études d'épigraphie. Paris, 1957.
Arc 830.235	Lestocquoy, Jean. Nécropoles et civilisation en Artois et Boulounais. Arras, 1957.
Arc 1082.10	Lethbridge, T.C. Gogmagog. London, 1957.
Arc 66.1.185	Leveque, Pierre. Pyrrhos. Paris, 1957.
Arc 600.105.5F	Lichtheim, M. Demotic ostraca from Medinet Habu. Chicago, 1957.
Arc 830.245	Lille. Palais des Beaux-Arts. Baoai, cité gallo-romaine. Lille, 1957.
Arc 505.82	Mader, Andreas E. Mambre. v.1, text; v.2, plates. Freiburg im Breisgau, 1957. 2v.
Arc 672.1.85	Maltezos, G.P. Das alte Kreta. Kaiserslautern, 1957.
Arc 1494.40	Mateu y Llopis, Felipe. El ius monetae en el condado de Ampurias. Perelada, 1957.
Arc 608.2.45.5	Meunié, Jacques. Nouvelles recherches archéologiques à Marrakech. Paris, 1957.
Arc 843.130	Monteagudo, Luis. Galicia legendaria y arqueologica. Madrid, 1957.
Arc 830.230	Morlet, Antonin. Vichy gallo-romain. Macon, 1957.
Arc 848.52	Mueller, Adriaan von. Formenkreise der älteren römischen Kaiserzeit im Raum zwischen Havelseinplatte und Ostsee. Berlin, 1957.
Arc 843.153	Museo, Canario. El Museo Canario. Las Palmas de Gran Canaria, 1957.
Arc 682.30	Mylonas, George E. Ancient Mycenae. Princeton, 1957.
Arc 674.1.13F	Mylonas, George E. Ho prōtoattikos amphoreni tēs Eleusinos. Athēnai, 1957.
Arc 1138.27.5	Natale, Alfio Rosario. Ludwig Traube e la nuova metodologia paleografica. Milano, 1957.
Arc 905.80.3	Neumann, Alfred. Die römischen Ruinen unter dem Hohen Markt. 2. Aufl. Wien, 1957.
Arc 885.23	North, F.J. Sunken cities. Cardiff, 1957.
Arc 1418.15.5	Numismatic Society of India. Corpus of Indian coins. Banaras, 1957.
Arc 688.8.5	Oikonomides, A.N. Eounion. Athēnai, 1957.
Arc 936.150	Ondrouch, Vojtech. Bohaté hroby z doby rímskej na Slovensku. Bratislava, 1957.
Arc 893.26	Oxenstierna, E.C.G. Die Nordgermanen. Stuttgart, 1957.
Arc 1093.6.12	Paegle, Eduard. Salktis, Progenitor der Svastika. Würzburg, 1957.
Arc 1500.59	Paris. Musée Monétaire et des Médailles. Entente cordiale. v.1-2. Paris, 1957.
Arc 1493.20	Perelada, Spain. Castillo de los Condes de Perelada. Museo. Monetario. Perelada, 1957.
Arc 726.195	Pesce, Gennaro. Sarcafagi romani di Sardegna. Roma, 1957.
Arc 66.1.187	Picard, Gilbert. Les trophées romains. Paris, 1957.
Arc 1635.5	Prober, Kurt. Historia numismática de Guatemala. Guatemala, 1957.
Arc 1190.75	Purvis, John Stanley. Notarial signs from the York archiepescopal records. London, 1957.
Arc 925.50.5	Ratych, O.O. Drevnorus'ki arkheologii pam'iatky na teryt. Kyïv, 1957.
Arc 688.7F	Reuther, Oskar. Der Heratempel von Samos. Berlin, 1957.
Arc 772.16	Richmond, Ian A. The archaeology of the Roman empire. Oxford, 1957.
Arc 875.100	Robertson, Anne. An Antonine fort. Edinburgh, 1957.
Arc 710.14.2	Rodenwaldt, Gerhart. The acropolis. 2. ed. Oxford, 1957.
Arc 823.50	Sandars, Nancy K. Bronze Age cultures in France. Cambridge, Eng., 1957.
Arc 448.1.30	Sastri, K.N. New light on the Indus civilization. Delhi, 1957-65. 2v.
Arc 726.25.30	Schaal, Hans. Ostia, der Welthafen Roms. Bremen, 1957.
Arc 815.26.5	Schefold, Karl. Die Wände Pompejis. Berlin, 1957.
Arc 853.10.20	Schoeberger, H. Führer durch das Römerkastell Saalburg. Bad Homburg, 1957.
Arc 600.184	Schott, Siegfried. Wall scenes from the mortuary chapel of the Mayor Poser at Medinet Habu. Chicago, 1957.
Arc 386.31.5	Schreiber, Hermann. Vanished cities. N.Y., 1957.
Arc 600.135	Schwaller de Lubicz, R.A. Le Temple de l'homme. Paris, 1957. 3v.
Arc 925.50.25	Shovkoplias, Ivan H. Arkheolohichni doslidzheniia na Ukraini 1917-1957. Kyïv, 1957.
Arc 925.135	Smirnov, A.P. Novaia nakhodka vostochnogo serebra v Priural'e. Moskva, 1957.
Arc 925.50.10	Sorokina, N.P. Tuzlinskii nekropol'. Moskva, 1957.
Arc 915.25	Stehlin, Karl. Die spätrömischen Wachthürme am Rhein von Basel bis zum Bodensee. Basel, 1957.
Arc 403.16.25	Stoll, Heinrich A. Die Traum von Troja. Berlin, 1957.
Arc 1033.175	Stuiber, Alfred. Refrigerium interim. Bonn, 1957.
Arc 1468.28.5F	Sylloge nummorum Graecorum. pt.1-18. Berlin, 1957- 13v.
Arc 540.10F	Taylor, Joan. Myrton-Pigadhes. Oxford, 1957.
Arc 1478.65F	Thomsen, Rudi. Early Roman coinage. København, 1957. 3v.
Arc 936.195.55	Tinelka, Karel. Cezavy u Bluciny ve svetle archeologickych vyskumů a nalezů. Brno, 1957.
Arc 1500.61	Tricou, Jean. Numismatique des corporations. Paris, 1957.
Arc 925.130	Tsvetkova, I.K. Volosovskii klad. Moskva, 1957.
Arc 936.165	Vulpe, Radu. Le vallum de la Moldavie inférieure et le mur d'Athanaric. 's-Gravenhage, 1957.
Arc 543.85	Zuniatov, T.A. Zemledelie i skotovodstvo u Azerbaidzhane v epokhu bronzy. Baku, 1957.

1958

Arc 1.14.30	Accademia...Rome. Accademia Romana di S. Tommaso di Aquina. Triplice omaggio a sua santita Pio XII. Città de Vaticano, 1958. 2v.
Arc 1300.30	Adelson, Howard L. The American Numismatic Society. N.Y., 1958.
Arc 1663.34	African Museum. Commemorative medals of the Z.A.R. Johannesburg, 1958.
Arc 530.95.2F	Akademiia nauk Gruz SSR, Tiflis. Institut Istorii. Mtskheta; itogi arkheologicheskikh issledovanii. Tbilisi, 1958.
Arc 905.17.12	Alzinger, Wilhelm. Aguntum. Wien, 1958.
Arc 1300.1.8	American Numismatic Society. Centennial celebration. N.Y., 1958.
Arc 1300.1.7	American Numismatic Society. Centennial publication. N.Y., 1958.
Arc 550.10F	Angioletti, Giovanni B. Testimane in Egittto. Firenze, 1958.
Arc 861.145	Anthony, I.E. The Iron Age camp at Poston. Hereford, 1958.
Arc 925.170	Bader, Otto N. Nazare istorii Piskam'ia. Perm', 1958.
Arc 547.40	Bankes, Ralph. Egyptian Stelae in the Bankes collection. Oxford, 1958.
Arc 830.225	Baurés, Jacques. L'aventure souterraine. Paris, 1958.
Arc 830.330F	Bégouën, Henri. Les cavernes du Volp. Paris, 1958.
Arc 520.25	Belov, G.D. Altar' Zevsa v Pergame. Leningrad, 1958.
Arc 925.50.40	Belov, G.D. Khersones Tavricheskii. Simferopol', 1958.
Arc 830.240	Besançon, France. Musée des Beaux-Arts. Exposition. Besançon, 1958.
Arc 853.180F	Billig, Gerhard. Die Aunjebitzer Kultur in Sachsen. Leipzig, 1958.
Arc 382.9	Birley, Eric. Archaeology in the north of England. Durham, Eng., 1958. 6 pam.
Arc 853.20.32	Böhner, Kurt. Die fränkischen Altertümer des trierer Landes. v.1-2. Berlin, 1958.
Arc 796.5	Bogaerts, T. Kunst der illusie; antieke wandschilderungen uit Campanie. Den Haag, 1958.
Arc 66.1.190	Bompaire, J. Lucien écrivain. Paris, 1958.
Arc 547.29	Botti, Giuseppe. Le casse di mummie e i sarcofagi da el Hibeh. Fienze, 1958.
Arc 830.265	Boudon-Fashermes, Albert. Le Velay gallo-grec. Rodez, 1958.
Arc 543.80	Bowen, R. Archaeological discoveries in South Arabia. Baltimore, 1958.
Arc 1190.1.3	Bresslau, H. Handbuch der Urkundenlehre. 3. Aufl. Berlin, 1958. 2v.
Arc 383.50	Catania. Università. Scritti in onore di Guido Libertini. Firenze, 1958.
Arc 1033.177	Cecchelli, Carlo. Lezioni di archeologia cristiana; liturgia ed archeologia. Roma, 1958.
Arc 1500.54	Chevallier, Guy. Les trésors de monnaies romaines découverts dans le départément du Loiret. Gien, 1958.
Arc 925.160	Chilashvili, L.A. Gorod Rustavi. Tbilisi, 1958.
Arc 612.19.5	Childe, Vere G. The prehistory of European society. Harmondsworth, 1958.
Arc 609.13.5	Cole, Sonia Mary. Early man in east Africa. London, 1958.
Arc 976.5	Cotter, J.L. Archaeological excavations at Jamestown. Washington, 1958.
Arc 861.135	Cotton, M. Aylwin. Excavations at Clausentum (Southampton). London, 1958.
Arc 387.13.15	Curtius, Ludwig. Torso. Stuttgart, 1958.

Chronological Listing

1958 - cont.

Arc 889.24	Damme, Daniel van. Promenades archéologiques à Anderlecht. Bruxelles, 1958.
Arc 848.54	Deutsches Archäologisches Institut. Neue Ausgrabungen im Deutschland. Berlin, 1958.
Arc 925.240	Divov, N.N. Bronzovyi vek Zabaikal'ia. Ulan-Ude, 1958.
Arc 1584.1.5	Dzhalaganiia, I.L. Iz istorii monetnogo dela v gruzii XIII veha. Tbilisi, 1958.
Arc 905.24.15	Egger, Rudolf. Führer durch die Ausgrabungen und das Museum auf dem Magdalensberg. 5. Aufl. Klagenfurt, 1958.
Arc 66.1.191	Etienne, Robert. La culte imperial dans la peninsule iberique d'Auguste à Dioclétien. Paris, 1958.
Arc 915.34	Fellmann, Rudolf. Die Principia des Legionslageos Vindonissa und das Zentralgeläude der römischen Lager und Kastelle. Brugg, 1958.
Arc 895.50F	Flarin, Sten. Vråkulturen. Stockholm, 1958.
Arc 618.10	Fox, Cyril. Pattern and purpose. Cardiff, 1958.
Arc 853.101.2F	Fremersdorf, F. Die Denkmäler des römischen Köln. 2. Aufl. Köln, 1958-63. 2v.
Arc 66.1.192	Gallet de Santerre, Hubert. Délos primitive et archaique. Paris, 1958.
Arc 925.290	Gening, V.F. Arkheologicheskie pamiatniki Udmurtii. Izhevsk, 1958.
Arc 391.12	Gherardo Ghirardini nel centenario della nascità. Padova, 1958.
Arc 1490.5.10	Gian, M.L. dal. Il Leone di S. Marco. Venezia, 1958.
Arc 843.151	Gimenez, Reyna. La Cueva de la Pileta. Málaga, 1958.
Arc 307.3.50	Girard, Rafael. Guatemala en el XXXIII Congreso internacional de Americanistas. Guatemala, 1958.
Arc 1153.87F	Gordon, Arthur Ernest. Album of dated Latin inscriptions. v.1-4. Berkeley, 1958- 6v.
Arc 432.20	Gordon, Douglas Hamilton. The pre-historic background of Indian culture. Bombay, 1958.
Arc 1075.2	Grabar, André. Ampoules de Terre Sainte. Paris, 1958.
Arc 1478.40.5	Grant, Michael. Roman history from coins. Cambridge, Eng., 1958.
Arc 853.71.5F	Grimm, Paul. Die vor- und frühgeschichtlichen Burgwälle der Bezirke Halle und Magdeburg. Berlin, 1958. 2v.
Arc 861.140	Grinsell, L.V. The archaeology of Wessex. London, 1958.
Arc 1153.84	Guarducci, M. I graffiti sotto la confessione di San Petro in Vaticano. Città del Vaticano, 1958. 3v.
Arc 1163.30PF	Guboglu, Mihail. Paleografia si diplomatica Turco-Osmană. Bucureşti, 1958.
Arc 936.100.20	Gunjaca, S. Novi naucni rezultati u hrvatskoj arheologiji. Zagreb, 1958.
Arc 915.44	Guyan, Walter Ulrich. Das alamannische Gräberfeld von Beggingen-Löbern. Basel, 1958.
Arc 1163.17.35	Hector, Leonard C. The handwriting of English documents. London, 1958.
Arc 936.14	Hensel, Witold. Archäologische Forschungen in Polen. Warschau, 1958.
Arc 600.112	Hoelsche, Uvo. Die Wiedergewinnung von Medinet Habu im westlichen Theben. Tübingen, 1958.
Arc 853.230F	Hundt, Hans Jürgen. Katalog Stromling. Kallmünz, 1958. 2v.
Arc 1588.10.12	Huszár, Lajos. A budai pénzverés története a középkorban. Budapest, 1958.
Arc 1423.21	Israel Numismatic Society. The dating and meaning of ancient Jewish coins and symbols. Tel-Aviv, 1958.
Arc 726.210	Jacopi, Giulio. I ritrovamenti dell'antro cosiddetto "di Tiberio" a Sperlongo. Roma, 1958.
Arc 505.84F	Jerusalem. Hebrew Community. Hazor. v.1-4. Jerusalem, 1958. 3v.
Arc 600.145F	Junker, Hermann. Der Grosse Pylon des Tempels der Isis in Philä. Wien, 1958.
Arc 765.5	Kaehler, Heinz. Rom und seine Welt. München, 1958.
Arc 700.52	Kallipolites, B.G. Chronologikē katataxis. Athēnai, 1958.
Arc 736.19	Kayser, Hans. Paestum. Heidelburg, 1958.
Arc 943.40	Kinzhalov, R.V. Pamiatniki kul'tury i iskusstva drevnei Ameriki. Leningrad, 1958.
Arc 505.86	Kleemann, Ilse. Der Satrapen-Sarkophag aus Sidon. Berlin, 1958.
Arc 1588.6.5	Kolerkilic, Eksen. Osmarli inpatatorlugurda pava. Ankara, 1958.
Arc 684.1.50	Kontes, I.D. To Hieron tēs Olympias. Athēnai, 1958.
Arc 395.18	Kosidowski, Z. Gdy słońce było bogiem. Warszawa, 1958.
Arc 936.6.15	Kostrzewski, Józef. Kultura łużycka na Pomorzu. Poznań, 1958.
Arc 936.6.3	Kostrzewski, Józef. Z dziejów badań archeologja w Wielkopolsce. Wrocław, 1958.
Arc 936.140.50	Krusteva-Nozharova, Gina. Ukazatel na predmeti izobrazeni vurkhu antichni pametnitsi ot Bulgariia. Sofiia, 1958.
Arc 612.36.5	Kühn, Herbert. Die Kunst Alteuropas. Stuttgart, 1958.
Arc 1076.8	Kybalová, L. Pražské zvony. Praha, 1958.
Arc 888.45	Laet, Siegfried J. de. The Low Countries. London, 1958.
Arc 925.134.10	Lashuk, L. P. Ocherk etnicheskoi istorii Pechorskogo kraia. Syktyvkar, 1958.
Arc 1470.70	Lauckoranski, Leo Maria. Mythen und Münzen. 1. Aufl. München, 1958.
Arc 66.1.188	Laumonier, Alfred. Les cultes indigenes en Carie. Paris, 1958.
Arc 689.9	Lazarides, D.I. Hē Thasos. Thessalonikē, 1958.
Arc 853.195	Lehmann, F. Aus der Frühgeschichte der Oberlausitz. Berlin, 1958.
Arc 925.38.10	Leningrad. Ermitazh. Drevnee iskusstov Altaia. Leningrad, 1958.
Arc 800.9.8F	Maiuri, Amedeo. Ercolano. Roma, 1958.
Arc 673.1.6	Malteros, G.T. Delphi. Kaiserslautern, 1958.
Arc 608.2.52	Marec, Erwan. Monuments chrétiens d'Hippone. Paris, 1958.
Arc 397.17.10	Marek, Kurt W. The march of archaeology. 1. American ed. N.Y., 1958.
Arc 397.17.15	Marek, Kurt W. A picture history of archaeology. London, 1958.
Arc 66.1.145	Marrou, Henri-Irénée. Saint Augustin et la fin de la culture antique. v.1-2. Paris, 1958.
Arc 843.170	Mascaró i Pasarius, J. Els monuments megalitics a l'illa de Menorca. Barcelona, 1958.
Arc 925.50.45	Miller, Mykhailo O. Don i Priazov'e u drevnosti. v.1,3. Moskva, 1958- 2v.
Arc 518.11	Miltner, Franz. Ephesos, Stadt der Artemis. Wien, 1958.
Arc 1590.20	Mirchev, M. Amfornite pechati ot Muzeia vuv Varna. Sofiia, 1958.
Arc 945.8	Nantes. Trésors d'archéologie américaine et océanienne. Nantes, 1958?
Arc 1558.5	Nathorst-Böös, E. Atto samla numismatica. Stockholm, 1958.
Arc 743.21	Neppi Modona, Aldo. Guide des antiquités éstrusques. Florence, 1958.
Arc 938.60F	Nerman, Burger. Grobin-Seeburg. Stockholm, 1958.
Arc 843.125	Nieto Gallo, Gratiniano. El oppedum de Iruña. Victória, 1958.
Arc 138.10	North Munster Archaeologcial Society. Index to journal 1897-1919. Nenagh, 1958.
Arc 936.150.10	Novotný, B. Počiatky výtvarnéreo prejavu na Slovensku. Bratislava, 1958.
Arc 936.195.65	Novotný, B. Slovensko v mladšij dobe kaminej. Bratislava, 1958.
Arc 746.9.20F	Olfieri, Nereo. Spina. München, 1958.
Arc 1454.205	Ondrouch, V. Keltské mince typu Biatec z Bratislavy. Bratislava, 1958.
Arc 895.52	Oxenstierna, E.C.G. Die altere Eisenzeit im Ostergötland. Lidingö, 1958.
Arc 505.39.12	Parrot, André. Samaria. N.Y., 1958.
Arc 726.108	Pietrangeli, Carlo. Scavi e scoperte di antichità il pontificato di Pio VI. 2. ed. Roma, 1958.
Arc 823.60F	Pobé, Marcel. Kelten-Römer. Olten, 1958. 2v.
Arc 608.36	Poinssot, Claude. Les ruines de Dougga. Tunis, 1958.
Arc 1530.15	Polak, Arthur. Joodse penningen in de Nederlanden. Amsterdam, 1958.
Arc 936.195.275	Prague. Národní Muzeum. Prehistorické Oddeleni. The prehistory of Czechoslovakia; exhibition, 1958. Prague, 1958.
Arc 830.336	Prévost, R. Répertoire bibliographique. Arras, 1958.
Arc 1588.10.5	Rethy, Landislaus. Corpus nummorum Hungariae. Graz, 1958.
Arc 853.125	Reusch, Wilhelm. Augusta Treverorum. Trier, 1958.
Arc 600.130	Reuterswaerd, Patrick. Studien zur Polychromie der Plaskik. Stockholm, 1958- 2v.
Arc 843.135	Rico García, Manuel. Memoria relativa a los nuevos descubrimientos de la antigua Lucantum, 1892. Aicante, 1958.
Arc 391.15	Rome. Istituto di Studi Romani. Giulio Quirino Giglioli. Roma, 1958.
Arc 609.12F	Rosenkranz, Ingrid. Rock paintings and petroglyphs of south and central Africa. Capetown, 1958.
Arc 1348.60	Roubier, Jean. Dauernder als Erz. Wien, 1958.
Arc 858.24.30F	Royal Institute of British Architects, London. Library. Royal Commission on Historical Monuments. London, 1958.
Arc 452.10	Sankalia, Hasmukh Dhirajlal. The excavations at Maheshwar and Navdatoli. Baroda, 1958.
Arc 630.15	Schefold, Karl. Basler Antiken im Bild. Basel, 1958.
Arc 853.165	Schindler, Reinhard. Ausgrabungen in alt Hamburg. Hamburg, 1958.
Arc 925.50.35	Smirnov, A.P. Istoriia ii arkheologiia srednevek. Kryma. Moskva, 1958.
Arc 1285.35	Solovjev, A.V. Istorija srpskog grba. Melburn, 1958.
Arc 936.30	Stanchev, S. Neuropolüt do novi pazar. Sofiia, 1958.
Arc 861.141	Stone, J.F.S. Wessex before the Celts. London, 1958.
Arc 785.13.85	Stucchi, S. I monumenti della parte meridionale del Foro Romano. Roma, 1958.
Arc 1373.11	Sutherland, Carol H.V. Ancient numismatics. N.Y., 1958.
Arc 905.12.23	Swoboda, Erich. Carnuntum. 3. Aufl. Graz, 1958.
Arc 1538.23	Sylloge of coins of the British Isles. Series A. London, 1958- 23v.
Arc 936.7.10	Szymański, W. Kontakty handlowe Wielkopolski w IX-XI wieku. Poznań, 1958.
Arc 1018.55	Testini, P. Archeologia cristiana. Roma, 1958.
Arc 530.95.5	Tkeshelashvili, G. Mtskheta; putevaditel'. Tbilisi, 1958.
Arc 726.175	Toti, Odoardo. La città medioevale di Centocelle. Allumicre, 1958.
Arc 1500.60F	Tricou, Jean. Médailles lyonnaises du XVe au XVIIIe siècle. Paris, 1958.
Arc 983.15	United States. Inter-Agency Archaeological Salvage Program. River basin surveys papers. Washington, 1958.
Arc 1163.4.20F	Vajda, Georges. Album de paléographie arabe. Paris, 1958.
Arc 66.1.189	Vallet, Georges. Rhégion et Zanale. Paris, 1958.
Arc 1082.15	Verbrugge, A.R. Le symbole de la main. Couraucès, 1958.
Arc 497.77	Views of the Biblical world. Jerusalem, 1958- 4v.
Arc 938.65	Volkerite-Kulikauskiené, R. Lietuvos archeologiniai pominklai ir jų tyrinejimai. Vil'nius, 1958.
Arc 426.15	Vorob'ev, M.V. Drevniaia Iaponiia. Moskva, 1958.
Arc 1143.3.4	Wattenbach, W. Das Schriftwesen in Mittelalter. 4. Aufl. Graz, 1958.
Arc 861.38.10	Wedlake, William. Excavations at Camerton, Somerset. Camerton, 1958.
Arc 1663.15.10	Więcek, Adam. Medale Piastów Śląskich. Wyd. 1. Warszawa, 1958.
Arc 1232.5	Wisemar, D.J. Gotter und Menschen im Rollsiegel. Prague, 1958.
Arc 407.10.15	Woolley, Charles L. History unearthed. London, 1958.

1959

Arc 1584.1.10	Abramishvili, T.I. Zapadno-gruzinskie monety XIII-XIV vv. Tbilisi, 1959.
Arc 530.81	Akademiia nauk Armianskoi SSR, Erevan. Institut Istorii. Dzhrvezh. Erevan, 1959. 2v.
Arc 543.95	Akademiia nauk Tazhikskoi SSSR, Stalinabad. Institut Istorii, Arkheologii i Etnografii. Sektor Arkheologi i Numizmatiki. Arkheologi rasskazy-vaiut. Stalinabad, 1959.
Arc 1428.32	Akarca, A. Les monnaies grecques de Mylasa. Paris, 1959.
Arc 450.30	Altekar, Anant L. Report on Humrahar excavations. Patna, 1959.
Arc 385.9	Amal'rikh, Aleksei S. V poiskakh ischeznuvshikh tsivilizatsii. Moskva, 1959.
Arc 530.95.10	Apakidze, A.M. Mtskheta. Tbilisi, 1959.
Arc 385.6	Ardusin, D.A. Arkheologicheskie razvedki i rashopki. Moskva, 1959.
Arc 726.341	Arrigo, Agatino d'. Premessa geofisica alla ricerca di Sibari. Napoli, 1959.
Arc 493.6.35F	Aslanov, G.M. Drevnii Mingechaur. Baku, 1959.
Arc 520.25.2	Belov, G.D. Altar' Zevsa v Pergame. Leningrad, 1959.
Arc 905.65	Beninger, E. Die Wasserburg Neydharting. Linz, 1959.
Arc 712.30	Berger, Ernst. Parthenon-Ostgiebel. Bonn, 1959.
Arc 936.175	Bešlagić, S. Stećci na Blidinju. Zagreb, 1959.
Arc 723.30	Blake, Marion E. Roman construction in Italy from Tiberius through the Flavians. Washington, 1959.
Arc 925.37	Blavatskaia, T.V. Ocherki politicheskii istorii Vospora v V-IV vv. do n.e. Moskva, 1959.
Arc 925.50.65	Bondar, M.M. Pam'iatky starodavnoho Prydniprov'ia. Kyïv, 1959.
Arc 1584.15	Braichevs'kyi, M.I. Ryms'ka moneta naterytorii Ukraïny. Kyïv, 1959.

Chronological Listing

1959 - cont.

Arc 386.40 Breccia, E. Uomini e libri. Pisa, 1959.
Arc 612.42 Briard, Jacques. L'Age du Bronze. Paris, 1959.
Arc 712.36 Brommer, F. Die Giebel des Parthenon. Mainz, 1959.
Arc 853.210F Brunn, Wilhelm Albert von. Bronzezeitliche Hortfunde. Berlin, 1959.
Arc 1470.80 Brussels. Bibliothèque Royale. La collection Lucien de Hirsch. v.1-2. Bruxelles, 1959.
Arc 1588.10 Budapest. Magyor Eremmuveszet Nemzeti Galeria. Medailles hongroises aux XIXe et XXe siècles. Budapest, 1959.
Arc 936.195.40F Budinsky-Krička, V. Slovanské mohyly v Skalici. Bratislava, 1959.
Arc 590.16F Buhl, Marie Louise. The late Egyptian anthropoid stone sarcophagi. København, 1959.
Arc 416.25 Burton-Brown, Theodore. Early Mediterranean migration; an essay in archaeological interpretation. Manchester, 1959.
Arc 726.25.35 Calza, Raissa. Ostia. Firenze, 1959.
Arc 608.30.5 Caputa, Giacomo. Il teatro di Sabatha e l'architettura teatrale africana. Roma, 1959.
Arc 925.50.100 Chachkovs'kyi, L. Kniazhii galich. 2. vyd. Chikago, 1959.
Arc 421.22 Chêng, Tê-k'un. Archaeology in China. v.1-3. Cambridge, Eng., 1959-
Arc 925.50.60 Chernysh, K.K. Rannotrypil's'ke poselennia lenkivtsi seredn'omu Dnistri. Kyïv, 1959.
Arc 810.62 Ciprotti, Pio. Conoscere Pompei. Roma, 1959.
Arc 1490.98.15 Cirami, Giacomo. La monetazione greca della Sicilia antica. Bologna, 1959. 2v.
Arc 609.9 Clark, John Desmond. The prehistory of southern Africa. Harmondsworth, Middlesex, Eng., 1959.
Arc 1138.100 Cleator, Philip. Lost languages. London, 1959.
Arc 830.130.20 Côle, Léon. Glozel, trente ans après. St.-Etienne, 1959.
Arc 712.32 Corbett, Peter Edgar. The sculpture of the Parthenon. Harmondsworth, 1959.
Arc 609.10 Davidson, Basil. Old Africa rediscovered. London, 1959.
Arc 726.225F Degani, Mario. Il tesoro romano barbarico di Reggio Emilia. Firenze, 1959.
Arc 672.1.92 Deshayes, J. Les quatier Z à Mallia. Paris, 1959.
Arc 1348.65 Deutscher Numismatikertag, Göttingen. Wissenschaftliche Abhandlunger des deutschen Numismatikertages. Göttingen, 1959.
Arc 513.25 Deutsches Archäologisches Institut. Neue deutsche Ausgrabungen im Mittelmeergebiet. Berlin, 1959.
Arc 543.135 Dupont, P. L'archéologie moue de Dváravati. Paris, 1959. 2v.
Arc 1655.5 Dutton, M.K. The case of the elusive hubs and dies. Honolulu, 1959.
Arc 726.59.30 Evans, John D. Malta. London, 1959.
Arc 66.1.194 Festugière, Andre. Antioche paienne et chrétienne. Paris, 1959.
Arc 936.120.10 Florescu, Florea B. Monumentul de la Adamklissi Tropaeum Traiani. Bucureşti, 1959.
Arc 608.40 Forde-Johnston. Neolithic culture of North Africa. Liverpool, 1959.
Arc 805.2 Forti, Lidia. Le danzatrici di Ercolano. Napoli, 1959.
Arc 858.66 Fox, Cyril. Life and death in the bronze age. London, 1959.
Arc 1663.52F Frede, Lothar. Das klassische Weimar in Medaillen. Leipzig, 1959.
Arc 609.23 Galloway, Alexander. The skeletal remains of Bambandyanalo. Johannesburg, 1959.
Arc 1550.8.5 Galster, Georg. Coins and history. Kopenhagen, 1959.
Arc 925.185 Gaprindashvili, Givi M. Kldis sakhli skal'nye doma selishcha Pia. Tbilisi, 1959.
Arc 608.48 Goodchild, Richard G. Cyrene and Apollonia. Tripoli? 1959.
Arc 1076.10 Grundmann, Günther. Deutschen Glockenatlas. München, 1959- 3v.
Arc 1285.10.5 Gumowski, M. Pieczęcie i herby miejscowosci wojew lubelskiego. Lublin, 1959.
Arc 505.90F Hamilton, R.W. Khirbat al Mafjar. Oxford, 1959.
Arc 785.92 Hanson, John A. Roman theater-temples. Princeton, 1959.
Arc 505.68.5 Harding, Gerald. The antiquities of Jordan. London, 1959.
Arc 392.16 Heizer, Robert F. The archaeologist at work. N.Y., 1959.
Arc 1510.128F Hess, Adolph. Münzen der Hohenstauffenzeit. Zürich, 1959?
Arc 1584.10 Hrbas, M. Antike Münzen aus Olbia und Pantikapaum. Prag, 1959.
Arc 520.30 Humann, Karl. Der Pergamon Altar. Dortmund, 1959.
Arc 925.13.75 Iatsenko, I.V. Skifiia VII-V vekov do nashei ery. Moskva, 1959.
Arc 497.53 Ilton, Paul. Digging in the Holy Land. London, 1959.
Arc 609.15 Johnson, Townley. Rock painting of the southwest Cape. Capetown, 1959.
Arc 1613.24 Judd, T. Hewitt. United States pattern. Racine, 1959.
Arc 672.1.72F Karo, G.H. Greifen am Thron. Baden-Baden, 1959.
Arc 395.22 Karo, Georg H. Fünfzig Jahre aus dem Leben. Baden-Baden, 1959.
Arc 1588.11 Karys, Jonas K. Senoues lietuviu pinigai. Bridgeport, Conn., 1959.
Arc 426.12 Kidder, J.E. Japan before Buddhism. London, 1959.
Arc 1027.32.12 Kirschbaum, E. Die Graeber der Apostelfürsten. 2. Aufl. Frankfurt, 1959.
Arc 1468.42 Klawans, Zander H. An outline of ancient Greek coins. Racine, Wis. , 1959.
Arc 853.200 Konik, E. Śląsk starożytny a Imperium Rzymskie. Warszawa, 1959.
Arc 936.155.5 Kozhemiako, P.N. Radnesrednevekovye goroda i pos. Chuiskoi doliny. Frunze, 1959.
Arc 493.26 Laessøe, Jørgen. The Shemshāra tablets. København, 1959.
Arc 888.45.5 Laet, Siegfried J. de. De voorgeschiedenis der Lage Landen. Groningen, 1959.
Arc 785.45.5 Lafontaine, Jacqueline. Peintures médiévales dans le temple de la Fortune Virile à Rome. Bruxelles, 1959.
Arc 925.75.5 Lapin, V.V. Ol'viia. Kiev, 1959.
Arc 1443.6 Launois, Aimée. Estampilles et poids musulmans en verre du cabinet des médailles. Caire, 1959.
Arc 915.32 Laur-Belart, Rudolf. Uber die Colonia Raurica und den Ursprung von Basel. 2. Aufl. Basel, 1959.
Arc 688.6.5F Lehmann, Karl. Samothrace. v.1-4,6. N.Y., 1959-64. 5v.
Arc 547.46 Leyden. Rijksmuseum van Oudheden. Inleiding lot de oud-Egyptische beschaving. 's-Gravenhage, 1959.
Arc 608.39 Lhote, Henri. The search for the Tassili frescoes. London, 1959.
Arc 936.150.5 Limes Romanus Konferenz, Nitra, Slovakia, 1957. Limes Romanus Konferenz. Bratislava, 1959.
Arc 936.43 Litsov, Khristo. Rimskiiat grad Abritus pri Razgrad. Razgrad, 1959.
Arc 853.205 Łosiński, Władysław. Z badań nad rzemiostem we wczesnośredniowiecznym Kotobrzegu. Poznań, 1959.
Arc 815.28 Maiuri, Amedeo. Pompejanische Wandgemälde. Bern, 1959.
Arc 726.122 Maiuri, Amedeo. Vita d'archeologo. Napoli, 1959.
Arc 543.131 Malleret, Louis. L'archéologie du Delta du Nékoug. v.1-4. Paris, 1959- 7v.
Arc 936.220.115 Mano-Zisi, Djordje. Sliri i Grci, njihcvi kulturni odnosi u prošlosti naše zemlje na osnovu arheološkog materijala. Beograd, 1959.
Arc 672.1.75F Marinatos, Spyridon. Kreta und das mykenische Hellas. München, 1959.
Arc 386.33 Mayes, Stanley. The great Belzoni. London, 1959.
Arc 673.1.12 Michałowski, K. Delfy. Warszawa, 1959.
Arc 853.190 Mildenberger, Gerhard. Mitteldentschlands Ur- und Frühgeschichte. Leipzig, 1959.
Arc 505.123F Missione Archeologica. Caesarea Maritima (Israele). Milano, 1959.
Arc 432.12.5 Mode, Heinz. Das frühe Indien. Stuttgart, 1959.
Arc 925.110.5 Mongait, A.L. Archaeology in USSR. Moscow, 1959.
Arc 530.130 Moraux, Paul. Une imprécation funéraire a néocésarée. Paris, 1959.
Arc 1578.15 Mort, Selwyn R. Coins of the Hapsburg emperors and related issues. Melbourne, 1959.
Arc 383.31F Müller, Adrian von. Gandert-Festschrift zum sechzigsten Geburtstag. Berlin, 1959.
Arc 677.5F Mylonas, George E. Aghios Kosmas. Princeton, 1959.
Arc 1510.100 Neu, Heinrich. Die Münzen und Medaillen des Herrogstums und des herroglichen Hauses Arenberg. Bonn, 1959.
Arc 853.234F Nierhaus, Rolf. Das römische Brand- und Körpergräberfeld. Stuttgart, 1959.
Arc 925.180 Okladnikov, Aleksei Pavlovich. Dalekoe proshloe Primor'ia. Vladivostok, 1959-
Arc 1584.4.5 Pakhomov, Evgenii A. Monety Azerbaidzhana. Baku, 1959- 2v.
Arc 726.215 Pallottino, Massimo. Turquinia. Milano, 1959.
Arc 608.45F Paribeni, Enrico. Catalogo delle sculture di Cirene. Roma, 1959.
Arc 403.16.30 Payne, R. The gold of Troy. N.Y., 1959.
Arc 400.25 Piggott, Stuart. Approach to archaeology. Cambridge, 1959.
Arc 530.22.10 Piotrovskii, Boris Borisovich. Vanskoe tsarstvo (Urartu). 2. Izd. Moskva, 1959.
Arc 936.195.165.5 Poulík, Josef. Velkomoravské hradiště Mikulčice. 1. vyd. Gottwaldov, 1959.
Arc 505.88 Pritchard, James B. Hebrew inscriptions and stamps from Gibeon. Philadelphia, 1959.
Arc 1580.30 Probszt, Günther. Die Münzen Salzburgs. Bâle, 1959.
Arc 936.14.10 Rajewski, Z. Biskupin. Varsovie, 1959.
Arc 1590.9.5 Rengjeo, Ivan. Corpus der mittelalterlichen Münzen von Kroatien, Slavozien, Dalmatien und Bosnien. Graz, 1959.
Arc 457.15 Rydh, Hanna. Rang Mahal. Lund, 1959.
Arc 600.156F Sauneron, Serge. Catalogue des ostraca hiératiques littéraires de Deir el Médineh. Le Caire, 1959- 2v.
Arc 600.188 Sauneron, Serge. Esna. Le Caire, 1959- 5v.
Arc 853.170 Schleiermacher, Wilhelm. Der römische Limes in Deutschland. Berlin, 1959.
Arc 853.215 Schoppa, Helmut. Die fränkischen Friedhöfe von Weilbach Maintaunuskreis. Weisbaden, 1959.
Arc 630.22 Simon, Erika. Die Geburt der Aphrodite. Berlin, 1959.
Arc 925.50.50 Smirniv, A.P. Problemy istorii Sever. Prichernomor'ia. Moskva, 1959.
Arc 925.126 Solomonik, E.I. Sarmatskie znaki severnogo Prichernomor'ia. Kiev, 1959.
Arc 1490.80 Spahr, Rodolfo. Le monete siciliane dagli Aragonisi ai Borboni. Palermo, 1959.
Arc 925.16.5 Tavadze, F. Bronzy drevnei Gruzii. Tbilisi, 1959.
Arc 630.20 Thieman, Eugen. Hellenistische Vatergottheiten. Münster, 1959.
Arc 66.1.193 Thiriet, Freddy. La Romanie vénitienne au Moyen Age. Paris, 1959.
Arc 1077.10 Thoby, Paul. Le crucifix. Nantes, 1959.
Arc 861.155 Thompson, F.D. Deva: Roman Chester. Chester, Eng., 1959.
Arc 925.4.18 Tomsk, Siberia. Oblastnoi Kraevedcheskii Muzei. Nekotorye voprosy drevnei istorii Zapadnoi Sibiri. Tomsk, 1959.
Arc 905.115F Töräh, Gyula. Die Bewohner vor Halimbacseres noch. Leipzig, 1959.
Arc 853.225F Torbruegge, Walter. Die Bronzezeit in der Oberpfalz. Kallmünz, 1959.
Arc 608.52F Traversari, Gustavo. L'altorilievo di Afrodite a Cirene. Roma, 1959.
Arc 493.6.20 Trever, K.V. Ocherki po istorii i kul'ture Kavkozskoi Albanii. Moskva, 1959.
Arc 853.20.12.5 Treves. Rheinisches Landesmuseum. Aus der Schatzkammer des antiken Trier. 2. Aufl. Trier, 1959.
Arc 943.42 Trimborn, Hermann. Das alte Amerika. Stuttgart, 1959.
Arc 600.155F Vaudier, Jacques. Catalogue des ostraca figurés de Deir el Médineh. Pt. 4. Le Caire, 1959.
Arc 672.1.140 Vaughan, Agnes C. The house of the Double Axe; the palace at Knossos. Garden City, 1959.
Arc 936.65.5 Velkov, V.I. Gradût v Trakiia i Dakiia prez kûsnata antichnost. Sofiia, 1959.
Arc 600.35.20F Wace, Alan John. Hermopolis Magna. Alexandria, 1959.
Arc 1504.15 Wielandt, Friedrich. Schaffhausen Münz- und Geldgeschichte. Schaffhausen, 1959?
Arc 726.200 Willemsen, C.A. Apulia, imperial splendor in southern Italy. N.Y., 1959.
Arc 1540.26 Wright, L.V.W. Colonial and commonwealth coins. London, 1959.
Arc 830.285F Zervos, Christian. L'art de l'époque du Renne en France. Paris, 1959.
Arc 936.170 Zontschew, Dimiter. Der Goldschatz von Panagjurischte. Berlin, 1959.

196-

Arc 889.30.5 Faider-Feytmans, Germaine. Le site sacré de Fontaine-Valmont. Morlanwelz? 196-.
Arc 600.193 Haykal, Fa'iza. Tombeau de Pannout à Aniba. Le Caire, 196-.
Arc 875.120 Taylor, B. Archaeology of Tayside. Dundee, 196-?
Arc 600.195 United Arab Republic. Ministry of Culture and National Guidance. The salvation of the Nubian monuments. Cairo, 196-

Chronological Listing

1960

Arc 383.16 — Academia...Bucharest. Academia Republicii Populare Romîne. Amagiu lui Constantin Daicoviciu cu prilejne. București, 1960.
Arc 893.28 — Aeve, Astrid. I stider och märmiskor i Norden. Uppsala, 1960.
Arc 385.11 — L'âge de pierre. Paris, 1960.
Arc 543.66.5 — Al'baum, L.I. Balalyk-tepe. Tashkend, 1960.
Arc 925.310 — Alekseeva, Evgeniia P. O chem rasskazyvaiut arkheologicheskie pamiatniki Karachaevo-Cherkesii. Cherkessk, 1960.
Arc 383.30F — Analecta archaeologica. Köln, 1960.
Arc 923.70 — Arkheologicheskii sbornik. Moskva, 1960.
Arc 870.10.15 — Ashbee, Paul. The bronze age round barrow in Britain. London, 1960.
Arc 385.10 — Atkinson, R.J.C. Archaeology. Cardiff, 1960.
Arc 386.35 — Bacon, Edward. Digging for history. London, 1960.
Arc 1033.34.65 — Bagatti, Bellarmino. San Pietro nei monumenti di Palestina. Cairo, 1960.
Arc 936.220.5 — Bajalović-Biztašević, Marya. Srednjevekovna nekropola w Mirijevu. Beograd, 1960.
Arc 936.195.95 — Balaša, Gejza. Praveké osídlenie stredného Slovenska. Bratislava, 1960.
Arc 825.3.25 — Balty, J.C. Études sur la Maison Carrée de Nîmes. Bruxelles, 1960.
Arc 551.1.5 — Belzoni, G.B. G.B. Belzoni. Padova, 1960.
Arc 497.55 — Bentwich, Norman de Mattos. The new-old land of Israel. London, 1960.
Arc 543.25.10 — Bernet Kempers, A. Borobudur, mysteriegebeuren in steen. Den Haag, 1960.
Arc 936.190 — Beshevliev, V. Antike und Mittelalter in Bulgarien. Berlin, 1960.
Arc 1433.85 — Bibliothèque Nationale, Paris. Département des Médailles et Antiques. Catalogue des étalons monétaires. Paris, 1960.
Arc 1510.85 — Blaschke, Karlheinz. Siegel und Wappen in Sachsen. Leipzig, 1960.
Arc 543.115F — Braidwood, Robert John. Prehistoric investigations in Iraqi Kurdistan. Chicago, 1960.
Arc 1538.2.20 — British Museum. Department of Coins and Medals. English copper, tin, and bronze coins in the British Museum. London, 1960.
Arc 895.47.5F — Broholm, Hans Christian. Kulturforbindelser mellem Danmark og syden i aeldre. København, 1960.
Arc 710.2.4 — Buschor, Ernst. Winke für Akropolis-Pilger. München, 1960.
Arc 1130.10 — Cairo, Egypt. National Library. A bibliography of works about papyrology. Cairo, 1960.
Arc 628.30 — Calderini, A. Dizionario di antichità greche e romane. Milano, 1960.
Arc 1480.58 — Callu, Jean Pierre. Genio populi romani, 295-316. Paris, 1960.
Arc 440.7 — Centro scavi e ricerche archeologiche in Asia. Altinità archeologica italiana in Asia. Roma, 1960.
Arc 936.195.5 — Ceskoslovenska Academie Ved. Archeologichy Ustav. Nouvelles fouilles archéologiques en Tchécoslovaque. Prague, 1960.
Arc 1510.90 — Christ, Karl. Antike Münzfunde Südwestdeutschlands. pt.1-5. Heidelberg, 1960.
Arc 936.195.37F — Chropovský, Bohuslav. Pohrebiská zo staršej doby bronzovej na Slovensku. Bratislava, 1960.
Arc 387.21.10 — Clark, John Grahame Douglas. Archaeology and society. 3. ed. London, 1960.
Arc 861.167 — Clarke, R. East Anglia. London, 1960.
Arc 375.15 — The concise encyclopedia of archaeology. 1. ed. N.Y., 1960.
Arc 497.50.5 — Corswant, Willy. A dictionary of life in Bible times. N.Y., 1960.
Arc 843.175 — Costa, J.M. da. Novos elementos para a lócalização de Cetóbriga.Setúbal, 1960.
Arc 815.15.2 — Curtius, Ludwig. Die Wandmalerei Pompejis. Darmstadt, 1960.
Arc 1588.1.38 — Czapkiewicz, Maria. Skarb monet arabskich z okolic Drohiczyna nad Bugiem. Kraków, 1960.
Arc 936.185 — Daicovicui, C. Sarmizegetusa. București, 1960.
Arc 432.22 — Dani, A.H. Prehistory and protohistory of east India. Calcutta, 1960.
Arc 66.1.196 — Delorme, Jean. Gymnasion; étude sur les monuments consacrés à l'éducation en Grèce des origines à l'Empire romain. Paris, 1960.
Arc 700.55 — Delorme, Jean. Gymnasion. Paris, 1960.
Arc 505.105F — Delougaz, Pinhas. A Byzantine church at Khirbat al-Karak. Chicago, 1960.
Arc 1480.56 — Deutsches Archäologisches Institut. Die Fundmünzen der römischen Zeit in Deutschland. Berlin, 1960- 17v.
Arc 880.48 — Dublin. National Museum of Ireland. A brief guide to the collection of Irish antiquities. Dublin, 1960.
Arc 497.30.5 — Du Buit, Michel. Archéologie du peuple d'Israël. Paris, 1960.
Arc 608.24.5F — Dunham, D. Second cataract forts. Boston, 1960-67. 2v.
Arc 543.100 — École Française d'Extrême-Orient, Hanoi. Indochina Musée. Louis Premier. Paris, 1960.
Arc 584.5F — Egypt. Antiquities Department. The cheops boats. Cairo, 1960-
Arc 925.220 — Erdniev, U.E. Gorodishche maiak. Kemerovo, 1960.
Arc 1480.62 — Es, W.A. van. De romeinse muntvondsten uit de drie noordelijke provincies. Groningen, 1960.
Arc 608.50 — Etienne, Robert. Le guarbier nord-est de Volubilis. Paris, 1960. 2v.
Arc 505.102F — Excavations in the Plain of Antioch. Chicago, 1960- 2v.
Arc 823.65 — Eydoux, Henri Paul. Lumières sur la Gaule. Paris, 1960.
Arc 674.2.5 — Falcon-Barker, T. 1600 years under the sea. London, 1960.
Arc 1645.5 — Ferrari, Jorge N. La revolución de Mayo en la medalla. Buenos Aires, 1960.
Arc 1663.45 — Fuld, George. Patriotic Civil War tokens. Racine, 1960.
Arc 853.242F — Funk, A. Bilder aus der Vor- und Frühgeschichte des Hegaus. Singen, 1960.
Arc 1490.75 — Gamberini, Cesare. Prontuario pezzario delle monete. Bologna, 1960.
Arc 925.187 — Gaprindashvili, Givi M. Peshchernyi ansambl' Vardzia, 1156-1213 gg. Tbilisi, 1960.
Arc 843.77.5 — García y Bellido, Antonio. Colonia Aelia Augusta Halica. Madrid, 1960.
Arc 1020.138 — Gavrilova, A. Sviatyni Egipta; zemlia egipet kak sad gospoden. Buenos Aires, 1960.

1960 - cont.

Arc 1530.5.5 — Gelder, Hendrik Enno van. Les monnaies des Pays-Bas bourguignons et espagnols. Amsterdam, 1960.
Arc 73.20.6 — Germania. Gesamtinhaltsverzeichnis, v. 1-36 (1917-58). Berlin, 1960. 2v.
Arc 830.280 — Giot, Pierre Roland. Brittany. London, 1960.
Arc 432.20.2 — Gordon, Douglas Hamilton. The pre-historic background of Indian culture. 2. ed. Bombay, 1960.
Arc 858.92 — Great Britain. Commissions. Ancient and Historical Monuments and Constructions of England. A matter of time; an archaeological survey of the river gravels of England. London, 1960-61.
Arc 858.72 — Grimes, W.F. Excavations on defence sites. London, 1960.
Arc 1027.12.20 — Guarducci, Margherita. The tomb of Saint Peter. N.Y., 1960.
Arc 1285.10.6 — Gumowski, M. Herby miast polskich. Warszawa, 1960.
Arc 1510.110 — Gumowski, M. Pieniądz gdański. Gdańsk, 1960.
Arc 1285.10.7 — Gumowski, M. Sfragistyka. Warszawa, 1960.
Arc 1588.1.24 — Gumowski, Marian. Handbuch der polnischen Numismatik. Graz, 1960.
Arc 895.54 — Hallström, Gustaf. Monumental art of Northern Sweden from the Stone Age. Stockholm, 1960.
Arc 557.4.5 — Hayes, William Christopher. The scepter of Egypt. Cambridge, 1960.
Arc 936.14.20 — Hensel, Witold. Najdawniejsje stolice Polski. Warszawa, 1960.
Arc 936.200 — Hilczerowna, Z. Wczesnosredniowieczne grodzisko w Daleszynie (st. 2) w pow. gostynskim. Poznań, 1960.
Arc 762.7 — Huelsen, Hans von. Römische Funde. Göttingen, 1960.
Arc 1227.5 — India. National Archives. Indian seals; problems and prospects. New Delhi? 1960.
Arc 455.10 — Istituto Italiano per il Medio ed Estremo Oriente, Rome. Italian archaeological researches in Asia...Pakistan and Afghanistan, 1956-1959.. Turin, 1960.
Arc 493.9 — Ivanov, V.A. Alamut and Lamasar. Teheran, 1960.
Arc 726.220 — Jacopi, Giulio. L. Munazio Planco e il suo mausoleo a Gaeta. Milano, 1960.
Arc 505.66.10 — Joint Expedition of the British School of Archaeology. Excavations at Jerico. London, 1960. 2v.
Arc 1418.22 — Karim, A. Corpus of the Muslim coins of Bengal. Decca, 1960.
Arc 1251.10F — Kenna, V.E.G. Cretan seals. Oxford, 1960.
Arc 497.60 — Kenyon, Kathleen Mary. Archaeology in the Holy Land. N.Y., 1960.
Arc 925.215 — Khalikov, A.K. Materialy k drevnei istorii Povetluzh'ia. Gor'kii, 1960.
Arc 395.24 — Kir'ianov, A.V. Restavratsiia arkheologicheskikh predmetov. Moskva, 1960.
Arc 609.8.5 — Kirkman, James Spedding. The tomb of the dated inscription at Gedi. London, 1960.
Arc 895.7.35.2 — Klindt-Jensen, Ole. Le Danemark avant les Vikings. Grenoble, 1960.
Arc 936.215 — Kovačević, J. Arheologija i istorija varvarske kolonizacije juzroslov. oblasti. Novi Sad, 1960.
Arc 925.285 — Kozyreva, Rimma V. Drevneishee proshloe Sakhalina. Iuzhno, 1960.
Arc 925.9.15 — Krupnov, E.T. Drevniaia istoriia Severnogo Kavkaza. Moskva, 1960.
Arc 800.16 — Kusch, Eugen. Herculaneum. Nürnberg, 1960.
Arc 1348.76 — Lagerqvist, Lars. Myntoch medaljer. Stockholm, 1960.
Arc 1480.63 — Late Roman bronze coinage, A.D. 324-498. London, 1960.
Arc 889.28 — Leblois, C. Le cimetière merovingien de Cuesmes. Cuesmes, 1960.
Arc 925.190 — Leningrad. Ermitazh. New archaeological material relating to the history of the Soviet East. Leningrad, 1960.
Arc 743.23 — Lerici, C.M. Nuove testimonianze dell'arte e della civiltà etrusca. Milano, 1960.
Arc 393.15 — Libellus Richardo Indrelso sexagenario oblatuo. Stockholm, 1960.
Arc 810.60 — Lindsay, J. The writing on the wall. London, 1960.
Arc 785.22.20 — Lugli, G. Regio urbis decima. Roma, 1960.
Arc 608.42 — McBurney, Charles. The stone age of Northern Africa. Harmondsworth, 1960.
Arc 936.14.15F — Majewski, K. Importy rzymskie w Polsce. Warszawa, 1960.
Arc 925.200 — Maksimenkov, G.A. Verkhne-metliaevskii klad. Irkutsk, 1960.
Arc 810.58 — Man, Ivonne de. Dag faun. Amsterdam, 1960.
Arc 925.175.5 — Mariiskaia Arkheologicheskaia Ekspeditsiia, 1956-59. Materialy k arkheologicheskoi karte Mariiskoi ASSR. Ioshkar-Ola, 1960.
Arc 672.1.80F — Marinatos, Spyridon. Crete and Mycenae. N.Y., 1960.
Arc 459.3.19 — Marshall, John. A guide to Taxila. 4. ed. Cambridge, 1960.
Arc 936.165.5 — Materialy i issledovaniia po arkheologii Jugo-Zapada SSSR i Rumynskoi narodniki Respubliki. Kishinev, 1960.
Arc 1478.24.7.2 — Mattingly, Harold. Roman coins from the earliest times to the fall of the Western Empire. 2. ed. London, 1960.
Arc 905.120 — Meysels, T.F. Auf Römerstrassen durch Osterreich von Aguntum nach Carnuntum. Wien, 1960.
Arc 505.110 — Michalowski, Kazimierz. Palmyre. Warszawa, 1960. 6v.
Arc 936.40 — Mikov, Vasil. Devetashkata peshtera. Sofiia, 1960.
Arc 1478.82F — Milano. Gabinetto Numismatico. Le monete romane dell'età republicana. Milano, 1960.
Arc 1433.92F — Miles, George Carpenter. Trésor de dirhems du IXe siècle. Paris, 1960.
Arc 505.115 — Moortgat, Anton. Tell Chuēra in Nordost-Syrien. Köln, 1960.
Arc 936.195.300 — Neustupný, Jiří. Pravěk Československa. 1. vyd. Praha, 1960.
Arc 700.50 — Niemeyer, Hans G. Promachos. Waldsassen, 1960.
Arc 1538.25 — North, J.J. English hammered coinage. London, 1960-63. 2v.
Arc 875.115F — O'Dell, Andrew. St. Ninian's isle treasure. Edinburgh, 1960.
Arc 628.28 — Onofrio, Cesare d'. Quando il cielo stava quaggiù. Roma, 1960.
Arc 936.205F — Pašalić, E. Antička naselja i komunikacije u Bosni i Hercegovini. Sarajevo, 1960.
Arc 936.15.20 — Pelikan, 'Old. Slovensko a rémske impérium. Bratislava, 1960.
Arc 936.195.200 — Poláček, Josef. Divčé kámen. České Budějovice, 1960.
Arc 925.210 — Polesskikh, M.R. Pamiatniki material'noi kul'tury Penzenskoi oblasti. Penza, 1960.
Arc 853.65.20 — Polskie Towarzystwo Archeologiczne. Z przesztości Sląska. Wrocław, 1960.

Chronological Listing

1960 - cont.

Arc 548.5.10A Porter, Bertha. Topographical bibliography of ancient Egyptian hieroglyphic texts. v.1, pt.1-2; v.2; v.3, pt.1. 2. ed. Oxford, 1960- 4v.

Arc 673.1.40F Pouilloux, Jean. La région nord du sanctuaire de l'époque archaïque à la fin du sanctuaire. Paris, 1960. 2v.

Arc 936.195.35 Poulík, Josef. Staří Moravané budiyí svůj stát. Gottwaldov, 1960.

Arc 1645.1.10 Prober, Kurt. Catalogo das moedas brasileiras. Rio de Janeiro, 1960.

Arc 1675.90 Probszt, Günther. Ludwig Neufahrer. Wien, 1960.

Arc 112.5.5 Revue archéologique de l'est et du centre-est. Tables décennales, v.1-10, 1950-1959. Dijon, 1960.

Arc 853.240 Röder, J. Toutonenstein und Heinesäulen bei Mildenburg. Kallmünz, 1960.

Arc 830.315 Rolland, Henri. Glanum. Paris, 1960.

Arc 505.124.5F Rome (City). Università. Missione Archeologica. Il colle de Rachele. Roma, 1960.

Arc 488.16 Sanadi, H.A. Les découvertes fortuites. n.p., 1960.

Arc 453.16 Sankalia, Hasmukh Dhirajlal. From history to pre-history at Nevasa. Poona, 1960.

Arc 396.11 Sardi, Jorge. Obras completas. San Salvador, 1960.

Arc 746.9.25F Scavi di Spina. v.1, pt.1-2. Roma, 1960- 2v.

Arc 658.3.7 Schliemann, Heinrich. Abenteuer meines Lebens. Leipzig, 1960.

Arc 403.16.35 Schliemann, Heinrich. Kein Troja ohne Homer. Nürnberg, 1960.

Arc 903.5 Schreiber, Georg. Den Funden nach zu Schliessen. Wien, 1960.

Arc 674.20 Schroeder, Johan. Epidauros en Kreta. Amsterdam, 1960.

Arc 1190.1.12 Schulze, H. Handbuch der Urkundenlehre für Deutschland und Italien. 2. und 3. Aufl. Berlin, 1960.

Arc 493.6.30 Selimkhanov, I.S. Istoriko-khimicheskie i analiticheskie issledovaniia drevnikh predmetov iz mednykh splavov. Baku, 1960.

Arc 450.32 Sharma, G.R. The excavations at Kauśāmbī (1957-59). Allahabad, 1960.

Arc 925.50.55 Smishko, M.I. Karpats'ki kurhany pershoi polov. I tysiacholettia nash. ery. Kyïv, 1960.

Arc 543.110 Solá Solé, J.M. Las dos grandes inscripciones sudarabigas del dique de Marib. Barcelona, 1960.

Arc 1584.20 Spasskii, Ivan G. Talery v russkom denezhnom obrashchenii 1654-59 godov. Leningrad, 1960.

Arc 1390.15.5 Stockvis, Albert. Critical survey of mediaeval Teutonic and Spanish coinage. Cleveland, 1960.

Arc 726.261 Stoop, Maria W. Floral figurines from south Italy. Assen, 1960.

Arc 1190.84 Strennon, Jacques. L'écriture diplomatique dans le diocèse de Liège. Paris, 1960.

Arc 785.15.20 Stucchi, S. Contributo alla conoscenza della topografia dell'arte e della storia nella Colonna Traiana. Udine, 1960.

Arc 48.3.2 Sumer; a journal of archaeology in Iraq. Index, v.1-21, 1945-1965. Baghdad, 1960-1968.

Arc 1588.1.32 Terlecki, W. The catalogue of Polish coins. Warsaw, 1960.

Arc 1588.1.34 Terlecki, W. Katalog monet polskich. Warszawa, 1960.

Arc 858.80 Thomas, Nicholas. A guide to prehistoric England. London, 1960.

Arc 1153.53.5 Ullmann, B.L. The origin and development of humanistic script. Rome, 1960.

Arc 66.1.195 Villard, Francois. La ceramique grecque de Marseilles. Paris, 1960.

Arc 925.328 Vitkov, Z.A. Pervobytnye liudi na Kol'skom poluostrove. Murmansk, 1960.

Arc 936.140.60 Vuzharova, Zhivka N. Ruskite ucheni i bulgarskite starini. Sofiia, 1960.

Arc 421.24 Watson, William. Archaeology in China. London, 1960.

Arc 858.70A Wilson, David McKenzie. The Anglo-Saxons. London, 1960.

Arc 1588.1.36 Wojtulewicz, H. Moneta polska od X-XX wieku. Lublin, 1960.

Arc 1163.17.25 Wright, Cyril Ernest. English vernacular hands from the twelfth to the fifteenth centuries. Oxford, 1960.

Arc 497.65 Yeivin, Samuel. A decade of archaeology in Israel, 1948-1958. Istanbul, 1960.

Arc 300.5 Zadneprovskii, I.A. Arkheologicheskie pamiatniki iuzhnykh raionov osnskoi oblasti. Frunze, 1960.

1961

Arc 810.63.2 Aafjes, B. Dag van gramschap in Pompeji. 2. druk. Amsterdam, 1961.

Arc 936.195.10F Adámek, F. Pravěké Hradisko u Obřan. Brno, 1961.

Arc 1335.112PF American Numismatic Society. Sylloge nummoium Graecorum. v.1, pt.2. N.Y., 1961.

Arc 383.33 Amsterdam. Universiteit. Institut voor Prae- en Protohistorie. In het voetspoor van A.E. van Giffen. Groningen, 1961.

Arc 385.12 Andrae, Walter. Lebenserinnerungen eins Ausgräbers. Berlin, 1961.

Arc 530.65.20 Arin-berd. Erevan, 1961.

Arc 726.24.24F Aurigemma, S. Villa Adriana. Roma, 1961.

Arc 853.65.30 Badura-Simonides, D. Baśń i podanie górno-śląskie. Katowice, 1961. 4 pam.

Arc 340.30.3 Banner, János. A Közép-Dunamedence régészeti bibliográfiája, 1954-1959. Budapest, 1961.

Arc 843.197 Barandiaran, J.M. Excavaciones en Atxeta. Bilbao, 1961.

Arc 386.42 Behn, Friedrich. Ausgrabungen und Ausgräber. Stuttgart, 1961.

Arc 497.72 Biblical Archaeologist. The Biblical archaeologist reader. Chicago, 1961.

Arc 497.72.1 Biblical Archaeologist. The Biblical archaeologist reader. Garden City, 1961-70. 3v.

Arc 925.13.80 Blavatskii, V.D. Antichnaia arkheologiia Severnogo Prichernomor'ia. Moskva, 1961.

Arc 1025.71.2 Bock, Emil. Die Katakomben. 2. Aufl. Stuttgart, 1961.

Arc 925.13.105 Boriskovskii, P.I. Pamiatniki drevneishei chelovesheskoi kul'tury Severo-Zapadnogo Prichernomor'ia. Odessa, 1961.

Arc 543.75.5 Bosch, Frederick D.K. Selected studies in Indonesian archaeology. The Hague, 1961.

Arc 1540.28 Boundy, W.S. Bushell and Harman of Lundy. Bideford, 1961.

Arc 793.17 Brion, Marcel. Pompeii and Herculaneum. N.Y., 1961.

Arc 1478.80 Bruck, Guide. Die spatrömische Kupferprägung. Graz, 1961.

Arc 1500.40.10 Buisson, Honoré. Monnaies féodales bretonnes de Charles le Chauve a Anne de Bretagne. Perigueux, 1961.

Arc 383.81 Bulgarska Akademiia na Naukite, Sofia. Arkheologicheski Institut. Izsledvaniia v pamet na Karel Shkorpil. Sofiia, 1961.

1961 - cont.

Arc 1480.85 Burzio, Humberto F. La marina en la moneda romana. Buenos Aires, 1961.

Arc 936.14.35 Burzyński, R. Polska na więcej niz 1000 lat. Wrocław, 1961.

Arc 712.34 Buschor, E. Der Parthenonfries. München, 1961.

Arc 547.6.15 Cairo. Musée des Antiquités Égyptiennes. A brief description of the principal monuments. Cairo, 1961.

Arc 1190.77 Chhabra, Bahadur C. Diplomatic of Sanskrit copper-plate grants. Delhi? 1961?

Arc 936.14.50 Chmielewski, W. Civilisation de Jerzmanowice. Wrocław, 1961.

Arc 1330.35 Ciferri, Raffaello. Saggio di bibliografia numismata medioevale italiana. Pavia, 1961.

Arc 608.1.50 Cintas, Pierre. Éléments d'étude pour une protohistoire de la Tunisie. Paris, 1961.

Arc 1093.2.30 Cles-Reden, Sibylle. The realm of the great goddess; the story of the megalith builders. London, 1961.

Arc 3.1.27 Congrès Internatonal d'Archéologie Classique, 7th, Rome and Naples, 1958. Atti del settimo Congresso internazionale di archeologia classica. Roma, 1961. 3v.

Arc 642.10 Cook, R.M. The Greeks till Alexander. London, 1961.

Arc 925.50.295 Cynkałowski, Aleksandr. Materiały do pradziejów Wołynia i Polesia Wołyńskiego. Warszawa, 1961.

Arc 1453.8 Davenport, J.S. European crowns, 1700-1800. Galenburg, Ill., 1961.

Arc 609.40 Davies, Oliver. Archaeology in Ghana. Edinburgh, 1961.

Arc 416.24 Deuel, Leo. The treasures of time. 1. ed. Cleveland, 1961.

Arc 688.7.5F Deutsches Archäologisches Institut. Samos. v.1,5-8,12,14. Bonn, 1961- 7v.

Arc 1030.47.5 Diehl, Ernst. Inscriptiones latinae christianae veteres. Berolini, 1961- 4v.

Arc 936.38 Dimitrov, D. Bulgaria. Sofiia, 1961.

Arc 1138.75.5 Doblhofer, Ernst. Voices in stone. N.Y., 1961.

Arc 1540.27 Dolley, Reginald Hugh Michael. Anglo-Saxon coins. London, 1961.

Arc 1033.53.23 Dupraz, Louis. Les passions de S. Maurice d'Agaune. Fribourg, 1961.

Arc 830.325 Duval, Paul M. Paris antique des origines au troisième siécle. Paris, 1961.

Arc 595.60 Edwards, L.E.S. The pyramids of Egypt. London, 1961.

Arc 584.1.5 Egypt. Antiquities Department. Catalogue des publications du Service des Antiquités, mars 1961. Le Caire, 1961.

Arc 853.175 Endrich, Peter. Vor- und Frühgeschichts des bayerischen Untermaingebietes. Aschaffenburg, 1961.

Arc 554.7.2 Engelbach, Reginald. Introduation to Egyptian archaeology. 2. ed. Cairo, 1961.

Arc 823.70 Eydoux, Henri Paul. Hommes et dieux de la Gaule. Paris, 1961.

Arc 823.75 Eydoux, Henri Paul. Rescurrection de la Gaule. Paris, 1961.

Arc 595.62 Fakhry, A. The pyramids. Chicago, 1961.

Arc 1348.74 Ferreira Barros, A. Numismática. Porto, 1961.

Arc 923.75 Formozov, A.A. Ocherki po istorii russkoi arkheologii. Moskva, 1961.

Arc 1470.82 Franke, P.R. Die antiken Münzen von Epirus. v.1-2. Wiesbaden, 1961.

Arc 1480.66 Franke, Peter. Römische Kaiserporträts in Münzbild. München, 1961.

Arc 1033.35.160 Frolow, Anatole. La relique de la Vraie Croix. Paris, 1961.

Arc 1163.39 Garcés G, Jorge A. Cómo han de traducirse los documentos paleográficos de Hispanoámerica. Quinto, 1961.

Arc 936.6.20 Gedl, Marek. Uwagi v gospodarce i strukturze społecznej ludności kultury łuzyckiej. Kraków, 1961.

Arc 674.3.8F Gerhan, Armen. Das Theater von Epidauros. Stuttgart, 1961.

Arc 1163.3.65F Goskev, Ivan. Starobulgarski glayolicheski i kirilski nadpisi ot IX i X v. Sofiia, 1961.

Arc 925.225 Grach, A.D. Drevnetiurkskie izvaianiia Tuvy. Moskva, 1961.

Arc 938.17.5 Graudonis, J. Senatnes pēdās. Riga, 1961.

Arc 858.47.14 Great Britain. Ministry of Works. Illustrated guide to ancient monuments. Edinburgh, 1961.

Arc 383.69F Greifswalder Antiken. Berlin, 1961.

Arc 66.1.197 Grenade, P. Essai sur les origines du principat. Paris, 1961.

Arc 853.254F Grenz, Rudolf. Die slawischen Funde aus dem hanoverschen Wendland. Neumünster, 1961.

Arc 1580.45 Hans, Josef. Maria-Theresien-Taler. 2. Aufl. Leiden, 1961.

Arc 830.305 Harmand, Jacques. Les origines des recherches françaises sur l'habitat rural gallo-romain. Bruxelles, 1961.

Arc 853.65.25 Heckowa, K.W. Pod znakiem świętego słońca. Wrocław, 1961.

Arc 936.14.40 Hensel, Witold. Starodawna kruszwica. Wrocław, 1961.

Arc 785.34.20 Herman, Werner. Römische Götteraltaere. Kallmuerz, 1961.

Arc 383.53.20 Homenaje a Pablo Martinez del Rio en el vigesimoquento aniversario. Mexico, 1961.

Arc 672.1.90 Honour, Alan. Secrets of Minos. 1. ed. N.Y., 1961.

Arc 600.15.20 Hooper, Finley A. Funerary stelae from Kom Abour Billow. Ann Arbor, 1961.

Arc 936.195.125 Hrubý, Vilém. Velkomoravské hradisko sv. Klimenta u Osvětiman. Brno, 1961.

Arc 66.1.198 Hus, A. Recherches sur la statuaire en pierre étrusque archaique. Paris, 1961.

Arc 1308.7.6 International Numismatic Congress, 6th, Rome, 1961. Congresso internazionale di numismatica, Roma, 11-16 sett., 1961. Roma, 1961-65. 2v.

Arc 923.110 Iskhizov, M.D. Zagadki drevnikh Kurganov. Saratov, 1961.

Arc 925.12.15 Ivanova, A.P. Skul'ptura i zhivopis' Bospora. Kiev, 1961.

Arc 925.255 Kartsov, V.G. O chem govoriat kurgany Eniseia. Abakhan, 1961.

Arc 395.15.5 Kenyon, Kathleen Mary. Beginning in archaeology. N.Y., 1961.

Arc 1423.20 Kindler, A. The coins of Tiberias. Tiberias, 1961.

Arc 1163.32 Kirkham, E. Kay. How to read the handwriting and records of early America. Salt Lake City, 1961.

Arc 938.85 Kivikoski, Ella. Suomen esihistoria. Helsinki, 1961.

Arc 936.230 Klemenc, J. Rimske izkopanine v Šempetru. Ljubljana, 1961.

Arc 708.35 Kolobova, K.M. Drevnii gorod Afiny i ego pamiatniki. Leningrad, 1961.

Arc 936.14.5 Kostrzewski, Józef. Zagadnienie ciągłosci zaludnienia ziem polskich co pradziejach. Poznań, 1961.

Chronological Listing

1961 - cont.

Arc 612.44 Koztowski, J.K. Próba klasyfikacji górnopaleolitycznych przemysłów z płoszczami lesciowatymi w Europie. Krakow, 1961.

Arc 905.125 Kratzschmer, F. Die Entwicklungsgeschichte des antiken Bades und das Bad auf dem Maydalensberg. Düsseldorf, 1961.

Arc 1480.64F Kropotkin, V.V. Klady rimskikh monet na teriitorii SSSR. Moskva, 1961.

Arc 853.256F Krueger, Heinrich. Die Jastorf Kultur in der Kreisen. Neumünster, 1961.

Arc 936.14.60 Krzak, Zygmunt. Materiały doznajomości kyltury złockiej. Wrocław, 1961.

Arc 938.70 Kulikauskar, P. Lietuvos archeologijos bruočai. Vil'nius, 1961.

Arc 936.14.65 Kurnatowski, S. Z przeszłosci międzyrzecza. Poznań, 1961.

Arc 595.66 Lauer, Jean Philippe. Les pyramides de Sakkarah. Le Caire, 1961.

Arc 1550.8.10 Lauring, P. Regis Daniae. København, 1961.

Arc 853.205.5 Leciyewicz, Leah. Kołobrzeg we wczesnymsredniowieczu. Wrocław, 1961.

Arc 608.70 Leglay, Marcel. Saturne africain; monuments. Paris, 1961. 2v.

Arc 923.134 Leningrad. Universitet. Issledovaniia po arkheologii SSSR. Leningrad, 1961.

Arc 853.244F Linder, H. Die altsteinzeitlichen Kulturen der Räuberhöhle am Schelmeengraben bei Sinzing. Kallmünz, 1961.

Arc 943.44 Lothrop, S.K. Essays in pre-Columbian art and archaeology. Cambridge, Mass., 1961.

Arc 925.295.5 Maikop. Adygeiskogo Nauchno-Issledovatel'skogo Instituta Iazyka, Literatury, Istorii i Ekonomiki. Sbornik materialov po arkheologii adygei. Maikop, 1961.

Arc 793.19 Maiuri, Amedeo. Pompei, Ercolano e Stabia. Novara, 1961.

Arc 530.65.10 Martirosian, A. Gorod Teishenbaini po raskopkam 1947-1958 gg. Erevan, 1961.

Arc 543.142 Matheson, S. Time off to dig. London, 1961.

Arc 505.107 Mayerson, Philip. The ancient agricultural regime of Nessana and the Central Negeb. London, 1961.

Arc 608.64 Meanié, Djinn. Cités anciennes de Mauritanie. Paris, 1961.

Arc 1510.136 Metcalf, D. The coinage of South Germany in the thirteenth century. London, 1961.

Arc 390.12 Mitchell, Charles. Felice Feliciano antiquarius. London, 1961?

Arc 447.6 Mode, Heinz Adolph. The Harappa culture and the West. Calcutta, 1961.

Arc 925.205 Mongait, A.L. Riazanskaia zemlia. Moskva, 1961.

Arc 853.269F Müller-Karpe, H. Die spätneolithische Siedlung. Kallmünz, 1961.

Arc 768.6F Nash, Ernest. Pictorial dictionary of ancient Rome. London, 1961-62. 2v.

Arc 398.5 Nau, Karl J. Urgeschichte der Kultur. Stuttgart, 1961.

Arc 936.195 Neustupny, E. Czechoslovakia before the Slavs. London, 1961.

Arc 830.332 Nouel, André. La civilisation néolithique. Orléans, 1961.

Arc 399.4 Odobescu, Alexandru Ionescu. Istoria archeologiei. București, 1961.

Arc 1540.30 O'Sullivan, W. The earliest Irish coinage. Dublin, 1961.

Arc 936.14.45 Paris. Université. Les origines de l'etat polonais. Paris, 1961.

Arc 925.50.80 Pasternak, I. Arkheolohiia Ukraïny. Toronto, 1961.

Arc 865.27 Peach, Wystan A. Stonehenge; a new theory. Cardiff, 1961.

Arc 543.4.25F Pelliot, Paul. Toumchoug. v.2. Paris, 1961-1964.

Arc 726.246 Pesce, Gennaro. Sardegna punica. Cagliari, 1961.

Arc 1148.34 Polites, L.N. Odēgos katalogoy cheirographōn. Athēnia, 1961.

Arc 936.14.55 Polska Akademia Nauk. Oddział w Krakowie. Prace Komisji Archeologicznej. Igołomia. Wrocław, 1961.

Arc 936.14.95 Posen (City). Museum Archeologicznej Oddział w Gnieznie. Ziemia gnieźnieńska w okresie powstawania państwa polskiego. Poznań, 1961.

Arc 923.50 Preidel, Helmut. Slawische Altertumskunde das östlichen Mitteleuropa im 9. und 10. Jahrhundert. v.1-3. Grafeling bei München, 1961-

Arc 923.85 Rabinovich, M.G. Arkheologicheskie materialy v ekspozitsii kraevedcheskikh muzeev. v.2. Moskva, 1961.

Arc 938.80F Racz, István. Kivikirves ja hapearisti. Helsingissä, 1961.

Arc 1390.12 Rasmusson, Nils L. Commentationes de nummis saeculorum IX-XI in suecia repertis. Stockholm, 1961- 2v.

Arc 936.165.10 Rikman, Emmanuil A. Pamiatniki drevnego iskusstva Moldavii. Kishinev, 1961.

Arc 520.35 Rohde, Elisabeth. Pergamon: Burgberg und Altar. 2. Aufl. Berlin, 1961.

Arc 66.1.199 Roux, Georges. L'architecture de l'Argolide aux IV et IIIe siècles avant J.-C. Paris, 1961. 2v.

Arc 432.29 Roy, Sourindranath. The story of Indian archaeology, 1784-1947. New Delhi, 1961.

Arc 925.50.75 Rudyns'kyi, M.I. Kam'iana Mohyla. Kyïv, 1961.

Arc 936.14.115 Rzeszow, Poland. Muzeum. Rzeszowskie w zaraniu dziejów. Rzeszów, 1961.

Arc 1668.3.2 Schlickeysen, F.W.A. Erklärung der Abkürzungen auf Münzen der neueren Zeit. Graz, 1961.

Arc 658.3.8 Schliemann, Heinrich. Schliemann in Indianapolis. Indianapolis, 1961.

Arc 543.130 Schlumberger, D. The excavations at Surkh Kotal and the problem of Hellenism in Bactria and India. London, 1961.

Arc 853.246F Schuldt, Ewald. Hohen Viecheln. Berlin, 1961.

Arc 1468.55 Schwarz, Dietrich Wallo Horman. Aus einer Sammlung griechischer Münzen. Zürich, 1961.

Arc 609.17F Shaw, Thurstan. Excavation at Dawu. Edinburgh, 1961.

Arc 543.25.15 Sivaramamenti, C. Le stupa du Barabudur. Paris? 1961.

Arc 1584.27 Spasskii, Ivan G. Denezhnoe khoziaistvo Russkogo gosudarstva. Leningrad, 1961.

Arc 895.56 Strömberg, Märta. Untersuchungen zur jüngeren Eisenzeit in Schonen. Bonn, 1961.

Arc 1138.105F Strubbe, Egied I. Groudbegrippen van de paleografie. 3. druk. Gent, 1961. 2v.

Arc 726.235F Studi storici; topografici ed archeologici sul Portus Augusti di Ravenna e sul territorio classicano. Firenze, 1961.

Arc 925.50.130 Surov, E.G. Khersones Tavricheskii. Sverdlovsk, 1961.

Arc 612.46 Symposium Consacre aux Problèmes du Neolithique Européen. L'Europe à la fin de l'âge de la pierre. Praha, 1961.

Arc 936.14.30 Tasienica, P. Sławianski rodowod. Warszawa, 1961.

Arc 935.50 Taslikliogiu, Zafer. Trokya'da epigrafya arastirmalari. Istanbul, 1961-71. 2v.

1961 - cont.

Arc 925.50.90 Terenozhkin, A.I. Predskifskii period na Dneprovskom Pravoberezh'e. Kiev, 1961.

Arc 830.354 Thevenon, Urbain. La nécropole du monastier à Vagnas. Saint-Etienne, 1961.

Arc 936.220.10 Todorović, Jovan. Banjica, naselje vinčanske kulture. Beograd, 1961.

Arc 595.64 United Arab Republic. Ministry of Culture and National Guidance. Nocturnal magic of the pyramids. Paris, 1961.

Arc 925.265 Ural'skoe Arkheologicheskogo Soveshchanie. 2d, Sverdlovsk, 1961. Materialy. Sverdlovsk, 1961.

Arc 1185.26 Valenti, Filippo. Il documento medioevale. Modena, 1961.

Arc 936.172F Venechikov, Ivan. The Panagynoishte gold treasure. Sofia, 1961.

Arc 853.250 Vollrath, Friedrich. Die Hunbirg. Nürnberg, 1961.

Arc 925.230 Vologda, Russia (City). Ablastnoi Kraevedcheskii Muzei. Sbornik po arkheologii Vologodskoi oblasti. Vologda, 1961.

Arc 428.10 Vorob'ev, M.V. Drevniaia Korea. Moskva, 1961.

Arc 421.23 Watson, William. China before the Han dynasty. London, 1961.

Arc 1076.14 Weidenbaeck, A. Tönendes Erz. Graz, 1961.

Arc 1490.85 Weiss, Roberto. The medals of Pope Sixtus IV, 1471-1484. Rome, 1961.

Arc 1675.51.25 Wichura-Zajdel, E. Sląski medalier Jan Wysocki. Katowia, 1961.

Arc 936.14.25 Woźnicka, Z. Wyroby bednarskie i tokarskie średniowiécznego Medzurzecza. Poznań, 1961.

Arc 543.116.1 Zehren, Erich. Die biblischen Hügel. Berlin, 1961.

Arc 543.105 Ziablin, L.L. Vtoroi buddiiskii khram Ak-Beshimskogo gorodishcha. Frunze, 1961.

Arc 700.60 Zlatkovskaia, Tat'iana D. U istokov evropeiskoi kul'tury. Moskva, 1961.

1962

Arc 493.6.22 Akademiia Nauk Azerbaidzhanskoi SSR, Baku. Institut Istorii. Voprosy istorii Kavkazskoi Albanii; sbornik statei. Baku, 1962.

Arc 543.120 Akademiia nauk SSSR. Mongol'skii arkheologicheskii sbornik. Moskva, 1962.

Arc 923.80 Akademiia Nauk SSSR. Institut Arkheologii. Arkheologicheskie ekspechtsii gosudarstvennoi akademii istorii material'noi kul'tury instituta arkheologii Akademii nauk SSSR. Moskva, 1962.

Arc 843.210 Almagro Basch, Martin. El ajuar del 'Dolmen de la pastora' de Valentina del Alcor (Sevilla). Madrid, 1962.

Arc 518.12 Alzinger, Wilhelm. Die Stadt des siebenten Weltwunders. Wien, 1962.

Arc 1330.5F American Numismatic Society. Auction catalogue. Boston, 1962.

Arc 1330.6F American Numismatic Society. Dictionary catalogue. Boston, 1962. 6v.

Arc 716.4.20 American School of Classical Studies at Athens. The Athenian Agora. 2. ed. Athens, 1962.

Arc 497.71 Anati, E. Palestine before the Hebrews. 1. ed. N.Y., 1962.

Arc 375.12 Archäologische Encyclopedie. Zeist, 1962.

Arc 505.97 Bagatti, Bellarmino. L'archeologia cristiana in Palestina. Firenze, 1962.

Arc 600.55.5 Barguet, Paul. Le temple d'Amon-Rê à Karnak. Le Caire, 1962.

Arc 936.155.10 Baruzdin, J.D. Arkheologicheskie pamiatniki Batkena i Liailiaka, Jugo-Zapadnaia Kirgiziia. Frunze, 1962.

Arc 505.2.15F Bibliothèque Nationale. Département des Médailles et Antiques. Les tessères et les monnaies de Palmyre, 1944. Paris, 1962. 2v.

Arc 608.68 Birebent, Jean. Aquae Romanae. Alger, 1962.

Arc 935.34 Boysal, Yusuf. Uzuncaburç ve Ura kilavuzu. Istanbul, 1962.

Arc 861.166 British Museum. Department of British and Mediaeval Antiquities. Hox Hill. London, 1962.

Arc 1208.14F British Museum. Department of Western Asiatic Antiquities. Catalogue of the Western Asiatic seals in the British Museum. London, 1962.

Arc 547.43 Cairo, Egypt. Coptic Museum. The Coptic Museum and the fortress of Babylon at old Cairo. Cairo, 1962.

Arc 1348.78 Carson, Robert. Coins of the world. N.Y., 1962.

Arc 726.242 Cassani, Lino. Repertorio di antichità. Novara, 1962.

Arc 642.8.5 Cottrell, Leonard. The bull of Minos. London, 1962.

Arc 388.12 Daniel, G.E. The idea of prehistory. London, 1962.

Arc 853.262F Dannheimer, H. Die germanischen Funde der späten Kaiserzeit und des frühen Mittelalters in Mittelfranken. Text and atlas. Berlin, 1962. 2v.

Arc 905.132 Denk, Stefan. Das Erlaufgebiet im ur- und frühgeschichtlicher Zeit. Wien, 1962.

Arc 676.5F Die deutschen Ausgrabungen auf der Argissa-Magula in Thessalien. Bonn, 1962.

Arc 983.17 Dewdney, Selwya. Indian rock paintings of the Great Lakes. Toronto, 1962.

Arc 513.30 Diez, E. Die Sprache der Ruinen. Wien, 1962.

Arc 505.132 Dunand, Maurice. Oumm el-'Amed. Text and atlas. Paris, 1962. 2v.

Arc 830.337 Dupont, J. Le site et les lampes votives du Chasterland de Lardiers. Cavaillon, 1962?

Arc 1540.29 Duveen, G.E. The history of the gold sovereign. London, 1962.

Arc 759.2 Egger, Rudolf. Römische Antike und frühes Christentum. Klagenfurt, 1962-63. 2v.

Arc 547.6.27 Egypt. State Tourists. Egyptian museum. Cairo, 1962.

Arc 587.89 Egypt Exploration Society. Preliminary reports of the Egypt Exploration Society's Nubian Survey. Cairo, 1962.

Arc 600.15.25 Emery, Walter Bryan. A funerary repast in an Egyptian tomb of the archaic period. Leiden, 1962.

Arc 853.266 Engel, Carl. Typen ostpreussischer Hügelgräber. Neumünster, 1962.

Arc 543.70.10 Expédition Philhy-Ryckmans-Lippens en Arabie. Expédition Philhy-Ryskmane-Lippens en Arabie. v.3. Louvain, 1962- 3v.

Arc 823.80 Eydoux, Henri Paul. Monuments et trésors de la Gaule. Paris, 1962.

Arc 905.140 Fehér, Géza. A Közép-Duna-medence magyar honfoglalás. Budapest, 1962.

Arc 853.265F Fiedler, R. Katalog Kirchheim unter Teck. Stuttgart, 1962.

Arc 612.53 Filip, Jan. Evropský pravěk. Praha, 1962.

Chronological Listing

1962 - cont.

Arc 390.14 Ford, J.A. Método cuantitativo para establecer cronologias culturas. Washington, 1962.
Arc 861.153 Frere, Sheppard. The city of Durovernum. Canterbury, 1962.
Arc 925.75.10 Gansiniec, Z. Olbia. Kraków, 1962.
Arc 66.1.200 Ginouvès, René. Balaneutikè; recherches sur le bain dans l'antiquité grecque. Paris, 1962.
Arc 547.41F Goedicke, Hans. Ostraka Michaeliders. Wiesbaden, 1962.
Arc 391.13 Gordon, William J. Nelson Glueck: a bibliography. Cincinnati? 1962.
Arc 1033.178 Gotsmick, A. Proserpina - virgo sacrata Dei; ein fruhchristlichen Antithese. München, 1962.
Arc 672.1.94 Graham, J.W. The palace of Crete. Princeton, N.J., 1962.
Arc 861.160 Great Britain. Commissions. Ancient and Historical Monuments and Constructions of England. An inventory of the historical monuments in the city of York. London, 1962. 3v.
Arc 609.18 Green, L.G. Something rich and strange. Capetown, 1962.
Arc 497.73 Gryglewicz, F. Archeologiczne odkrycia w egzegezie Nowego Testamentu. Lublin, 1962.
Arc 895.58 Gudnitz, F. Broncealderens monumentalkunst. København, 1962.
Arc 66.1.201 Guillemain, B. La cour pontificale d'Avignon, 1309-1376. Paris, 1962.
Arc 925.150.5 Gurevich, F.D. Drevnosti Belorusskogo ponemania. Leningrad, 1962.
Arc 383.53.15 Himmelmann-Wildschütz, N. Festschrift für Friedrich Matz. Mainz, 1962.
Arc 726.241 Huelsen, Hans von. Funde in der Magna Graecia. Gottingen, 1962.
Arc 710.24 Iakōbidēs, S.E. E Mykēnaikē Akropolis tōn Athēnōn. Athēnai, 1962.
Arc 9.2.6 International Congress of Prehistoric and protohistoric Sciences, 6th, Rome, 1962. Atti del Congresso internazionale. Firenze, 1962.
Arc 923.133 Istoriko-arkheologicheskii sbornik. Moskva, 1962.
Arc 1510.133 Jesse, W. Die Münzen der Stadt Braunschweig von 1499 bis 1680. Braunschweig, 1962.
Arc 830.346 Joffroy, René. Le trésor de Vix; histoire et portée d'une grande découverte. Paris, 1962.
Arc 505.124F Joint Expedition of the University of Rome and the Hebrew University. Excavations at Ramat Rahel, seasons 1959 and 1960. Rome, 1962.
Arc 925.260 Kazan, Russia (City). Universitet. Arkheologicheskie pamiatniki u sela Rozhdestveno. Kazan, 1962.
Arc 925.4.7 Khlobystina, M.D. Bronzovye nozhi minusinskogo kraia i nekotorye voprosy razvitiia karasukskoi kul'tury. Leningrad, 1962.
Arc 925.245 Khudiak, M.M. Iz istorii Nimfeia VI-III vekov. Leningrad, 1962.
Arc 1588.1.42 Kiersnowski, R. Początki pieniadza polskiego. Warszawa, 1962.
Arc 1588.1.40 Kmietowicz, A. Skarb srebrny z miejscowosci Ochle. Wrocław, 1962.
Arc 395.18.2 Kosidowski, Z. Gdy słońce było bogiem. Warszawa, 1962.
Arc 936.14.75 Kostrzewski, B. Z najdawniejszych dziejow Giecza. Wrocław, 1962.
Arc 936.14.90F Kostrzewski, Józef. Odkrycia archeologja na ziemiach zachodnich i północnych Polski. Warszawa, 1962.
Arc 1480.42.10F Kraay, C.W. Die Münzfunde von Vindonissa bis Trafar. Basel, 1962.
Arc 1470.86 Kraay, Colin M. The composition of Greek silver coins. Oxford, 1962.
Arc 608.17.25F Kraeling, C.H. Ptolemais, city of the Libyan Pentapolis. Chicago, 1962.
Arc 933.2F Kruegar, Bruno. Die Kietzsiedlungen im nordlichen Mitteleuropa. Berlin, 1962.
Arc 608.33.10 Lajoux, Jean D. Merveilles du Tassili n'Ajjer. Paris, 1962.
Arc 612.34.5 Laming, A. La signification de l'art rupestre paléolithique. Paris, 1962.
Arc 688.6.7 Lehmann, Phyllis. The pedimental sculpture of the Hieron. N.Y., 1962.
Arc 600.21.6 Lucas, Alfred. Ancient Egyptian materials. London, 1962.
Arc 652.8 MacKendrick, P.L. The Greek stories speak. N.Y., 1962.
Arc 1540.31 Mathias, Peter. The English trade tokens. London, 1962.
Arc 454.1.5 Mohapatra, Gopal Chandra. The stone age cultures of Orissa. 1. ed. Poona, 1962.
Arc 505.115.2 Moortgat, Anton. Tell Chuēra in Nordost-Syrien. Köln, 1962.
Arc 830.130.23 Morlet, Antonin. Glozel. v.2. Macon, 1962.
Arc 853.268F Müller, A. von. Fohrde und Hohenferchesar; zwei germanische Gräberfelder der frühen römischen Kaiserzeit aus der Mark Brandenburg. Berlin, 1962.
Arc 1433.28.5 Mushegian, K. Denezhnoe obrashchenie Dvina po numizmaticheskim dannym. Erevan, 1962.
Arc 925.50.95 Nabodovs'ka, O.F. Mykhailivs'ke poselennia. Kyïv, 1962.
Arc 1615.14 Newman, Eric. The fantastic 1804 dollar. Racine, 1962.
Arc 593.6 Noakes, Aubrey. Cleopatra's needles. London, 1962.
Arc 936.195.25 Novotný, B. Luzianska skukina a pociatky malovanej keramiky na Slovensku. Bratislava, 1962.
Arc 925.250 Nowicka, M. Ad Fanagorii do Apollonii. Warszawa, 1962.
Arc 925.13.100F Ozols, Jekabs. Ursprung und Herkunft der zentralrussischen Fatjanowo Kultur. Berlin, 1962.
Arc 936.223 Pavlovič, L. Neki spomenici kulture; osvrti i Zapožanja. v.1-2. Smedrevo, 1962- 3v.
Arc 830.119.10 Pellerin, Pierre. En ressuscitant Vaison-la-Romaine. Paris, 1962.
Arc 861.165 Piggot, Stuart. The west Kennet long barrow. London, 1962.
Arc 875.127 Piggott, Stuart. The prehistoric peoples of Scotland. London, 1962.
Arc 936.195.30F Polla, B. Stredoveká zaniknuta osada na Spiši. Bratislava, 1962.
Arc 936.14.130 Polskie Towarzystwo Archeologiczne. Z przeszlósci Pomorza Wschodniego. Wrocław, 1962.
Arc 488.23 Porada, Edith. Alt-Iran. Baden-Baden, 1962.
Arc 1588.4.75 Pošvář, Jaroslav. Měna v českých zemích od 10. do poč 20. století. Opava, 1962.
Arc 936.195.15 Poulík, Josef. Zivot a umenie doby železnej na Slovensku. Bratislava, 1962.
Arc 608.69 Precleur-Canonge, Thérèse. La vie rurale en Afrique romaine d'après les mosaiques. Paris, 1962.
Arc 505.121 Pritchard, James. Gibeon, where the sun stood still. Princeton, 1962.

1962 - cont.

Arc 923.106 Les rapports et les informations des archéologues de l'URSS. Moscou, 1962.
Arc 383.34.10 Renard, M. Hommages à Albert Grenier. Bruxelles, 1962. 3v.
Arc 513.22.2 Robert, L. Villes d'Asie Mineure. 2. éd. Paris, 1962.
Arc 925.50.47 Rostov on the Don (Province). Muzei Kraevedeniia. Arkheologicheskie raskopki na Donu. v.2, photoreproduction. Rostov na Donu, 1962- 2v.
Arc 543.52 Rudenko, Sergei I. Kul'tura khunnov i Noinulinskie kurzany. Moskva, 1962.
Arc 1603.3.6 Sandham, Alfred. Coins, tokens and medals of the Dominion of Canada. Montreal, 1962.
Arc 432.24 Sankalis, Hasmukh Dhirajlal. Prehistory and protohistory in India and Pakistan. Bombay, 1962.
Arc 815.26.10 Schefold, Karl. Vergessene Pompeji. Bern, 1962.
Arc 568.2 Schenkel, W. Frühmittelägyptische Studien. Bonn, 1962.
Arc 1510.166 Schwalbach, Carl. Die neueren deutschen Taler. Lübeck, 1962.
Arc 925.50.42 Sebastopol. Khersoneskii Gosudarstvennyi Istoriko-Arkheologicheskii Muzei. Khersones Tavricheskii. Simferopol', 1962.
Arc 925.280 Shramko, B.A. Drevnosti Severskogo Dontsa. Khar'kov, 1962.
Arc 895.62 Sjoevold, T. The iron age settlement of Arctic Norway. v.1-2. Tromsö, 1962-74.
Arc 936.220.95 Srpska Akademija Nauka i Umetnosti, Belgrade. Arheološki Institut. Caričin Grad, 1912-62. Beograd, 1962.
Arc 726.251 Susini, Giancarlo. Fonti per la storia greca e romana del Salento. Bologna, 1962.
Arc 843.198 Tarradell, M. Les arrels de Catalunya. Barcelona, 1962.
Arc 1185.30.2 Tessier, Georges. La diplomatique. 2. éd. Paris, 1962.
Arc 1190.87 Tessier, Georges. Diplomatique royale française. Paris, 1962.
Arc 925.13.95 Trapsh, M.M. Pamiatniki kolkhidskoi i skifskoi kul'tur v sele kulanurkhva abkhazskoi ASSR. Sukhumi, 1962.
Arc 530.160 Tuchelt, Klaus Franz. Tiergefässe in Kopf- und Protomengestalt. Berlin, 1962.
Arc 923.100 Uspenskii, L.V.P. Za sem'iu pechatiami. Izd. 2. Moskva, 1962.
Arc 600.3.15 Vercoutter, J. Textes biographiques du Sérapéum de Memphis. Paris, 1962.
Arc 406.6 Viana, Abel. Algumas noções elementares do arqueologia pratica. Beja, 1962.
Arc 925.13.85 Viaz'mitina, M.I. Zalsta balka. Kyiv, 1962.
Arc 726.237 Visscher, Fernand de. Héraclès Epitrapezios. Paris, 1962.
Arc 936.195.90 Volovek, V. Pravek vychodnich a severovychodnich Cech. Hradec Králové, 1962.
Arc 848.23.3 Wahle, Ernst. Deutsche Vorzeit. 3. Aufl. Bad Homburg, 1962.
Arc 875.122 Wainwright, Frederick Threlfall. The northern isles. Edinburgh, 1962.
Arc 662.6 Warner, R. Eternal Greece. N.Y., 1962.
Arc 936.14.134 Warsaw. Uniwersytet. Zespoł Badan nad Polskim Srezniowieczem. I konferencja naukowa w Warszawie...1968. Warszawa, 1962.
Arc 1540.32 Watson, J.H. Ancient trial plates, a description of the ancient gold and silver. London, 1962.
Arc 442.2 Wheeler, Robert. Chārsada. London, 1962.
Arc 493.2.25 Wheeler, Robert E. Flames over Persepolis: turning point in history. London, 1962.
Arc 1349.65 Więcek, A. Sebastian Dadler. Gdańsk, 1962.
Arc 407.10.20 Woolley, Charles L. As I seem to remember. London, 1962.
Arc 407.10.18 Woolley, Charles L. History unearthed. N.Y., 1962.
Arc 497.31.5 Wright, G.E. Biblical archaeology. Philadelphia, 1962.
Arc 936.14.85 Wystawa Objazdowa Kielecczyzna w Swietle Wykopolisk. Przewodnik. Kielce, 1962.
Arc 861.160.10 Yorkshire Architectural and Archaeological Society. A short guide to Roman York. York, 1962.
Arc 547.45 Zayid, Abd al-Hamid. Egyptian antiquities. Cairo, 1962.
Arc 543.116 Zehren, Erich. The cresent and the bull; a survey. N.Y., 1962.
Arc 936.241 Zemun. Narodni Muzej. Seoba naroda. Zemun, 1962.
Arc 925.5.10 Zuikov, B.B. Pod volnami Issyk-Kuha. Moskva, 1962.

1963

Arc 936.155.15 Akademiia Nauk Kirgizskoi SSR, Frunze. Institut Istorii. Arkheologicheskie pamiatniki Talasskoi dolny. Frunze, 1963.
Arc 925.9.25 Akademiia nauk SSSR. Institut Arkheologii. Drevnosti checheno-ingushetii. Moskva, 1963.
Arc 385.14 Akademiia Nauk SSSR. Institut Arkheologii. Novye metody v arkheologicheskikh issledovaniiakh. Leningrad, 1963.
Arc 416.26 Akishev, K.A. Drevniaia kul'tura sakov i usunei doliny reki Ili. Alma Ata, 1963.
Arc 885.24 Alcock, L. Dinas Powys. Cardiff, 1963.
Arc 925.310.5 Alekseeva, Evgeniia P. Karachaevtsy i balkartsy, drevnii narod Kavkaza. Cherkessk, 1963.
Arc 443.5 Allchin, F.R. Neolithic cattle-keepers of south India; a study of the Deccan ashmounds. Cambridge, Eng., 1963.
Arc 925.322 Ataev, Dibir M. Nagornyi Dagestan v rannem srednevekove. Makhachkala, 1963.
Arc 726.249 Aurigemma, Salvatore. I monumenti della necropoli romana di Sarsina. Roma, 1963.
Arc 925.300 Autlev, P.U. Abadzekhskaia nizhnepaleoliticheskaia stoianka. Maikop, 1963.
Arc 1478.17.5 Babelon, Ernest. Description historique et chronologique des monnaies de la République romaine vulgairement appelées monnaies consulaires. Bologna, 1963. 2v.
Arc 925.172 Bader, Otto N. Baranovskii nogil'nik. Moskva, 1963.
Arc 1448.6 Becklake, J.T. From real to rand. South Africa, 1963?
Arc 681.5 Benson, Jack L. Ancient Leros. Durham, 1963.
Arc 915.35 Berger, L. Die Ausgrabungen am Petersberg in Basel. Basel, 1963.
Arc 870.24 Berry, B. A lost Roman road. London, 1963.
Arc 925.140.2 Bers, E.M. Arkheologicheskie pamiatniki Sverdlovska i ego obrestnostei. 2. izd. Sverdlovsk, 1963.
Arc 386.43 Blavatskii, V.D. Otkrytie zatonuvshezo mira. Moskva, 1963.
Arc 522.36 Blegen, Carl William. Troy and the Trojans. London, 1963.
Arc 1208.15 Borisov, Andrei Ivan Iakovlevich. Sasanidskie gemmy. Leningrad, 1963.
Arc 870.25 Bowen, H.C. Ancient fields. London, 1963.
Arc 1493.23 Brazão, Arnaldo. Numismatalogos contemporaneas. Lisboa, 1963.

1963 - cont.

Arc 861.168 — Brewster, Thomas. Excavation of Staple Howe. Wentringham, 1963.

Arc 1077.12 — Brockpaehler,W. Steinkreuze in Westfalen. Münster, 1963.

Arc 1138.112.2 — Brouwer, Hans. Geschreven verleden. 2. druk. 's-Gravenhage, 1963.

Arc 340.8.5 — Brünn. Universita. Knihovna. Minulost jižní Moravy. Brno, 1963.

Arc 936.40.10 — Bulgarska Akademiia na Naukite, Sofia. Arkheologicheskikh Institut. Apoloniía. Sofiia, 1963.

Arc 587.12F — Caminos, Ricardo A. Gebel es-Silsilah. London, 1963.

Arc 1480.67 — Cappelli, R. Profili imperiali romani. Milano, 1963.

Arc 1478.86 — Carney, Thomas Francis. A catalogue of the Roman and related foreign coins in the collections of Sir Stephen Courtland at the University College of Rhodesia and Nyasaland. Salisbury, 1963.

Arc 1027.12.26 — Carsopino, Jérôme. Les fouilles de Saint Pierre et la tradition. Paris, 1963.

Arc 1675.93 — Chamberlain, G.S. American medals and medalists. Annandale, Va., 1963.

Arc 421.28 — Chaung, K. The archaeology of ancient China. New Haven, 1963.

Arc 1488.27 — Ciferra, Raffaello. Repertorio alfabetico di numismatica medioevale e moderna. Pavia, 1963. 2v.

Arc 609.13.2 — Cole, Sonia Mary. The prehistory of east Africa. N.Y., 1963.

Arc 302.51.6 — Conference International d'Études Classiques des Pays Socialistes, 6th, Plovdiv, 1962. Acta antiqua Philippapolitana. Serdicae, 1963.

Arc 384.15 — Congrès International d'Archéologie Classique, 8th, Paris, 1963. VIIIe Congrès international d'archéologie classique. Photoreproduction. Paris, 1963.

Arc 421.26 — Crump, J. Dragon bones in the yellow earth. N.Y., 1963.

Arc 1163.5.25 — Dani, A.H. Indian palaeography. Oxford, 1963.

Arc 830.335 — Daniel, G.E. The hungry archaeologist in France. London, 1963.

Arc 462.5 — Das Gupta, Paresh Chandra. Archaeological discovery in West Bengal. Alipore, 1963.

Arc 543.7.30 — Delvert, Jean. Recherches sur l'érosin des gres des monuments d'Angkor. Paris, 1963.

Arc 935.29 — Dörner, Friedrich K. Arsameia am Nymphaios. Berlin, 1963.

Arc 543.136 — Dupree, Louis Benjamin. Deh Morasi Ghunelai: a cholcolithic site in south-central Afghanistan. N.Y., 1963.

Arc 554.6 — Emery, Walter. Archaic Egypt. Baltimore, 1963.

Arc 1588.13.5 — Erel, Serafeddin. Nadir hirkaç sikke. Istanbul, 1963.

Arc 608.1.37.5 — Fandri, Muhammed. Découverte archéologigue dans la région de Sfax: mosaique des océans. Tunis, 1963.

Arc 600.200F — Farid, Shafik. Exavations at Ballana, 1958-1959. Cairo, 1963.

Arc 875.126 — Feachem, R. A guide to prehistoric Scotland. London, 1963.

Arc 1583.24 — Fedorov-Davydov, German A. Monety rasskazy-vaiut. Moskva, 1963.

Arc 1153.92 — Foerster, H. Abriss der lateinische Paläographie. 2. Aufl. Stuttgart, 1963.

Arc 390.13 — Foster, I.L. Culture and environment. London, 1963.

Arc 608.1.43 — Foucher, Louis. La maison de la procession dionysiaque à el Jem. Paris, 1963.

Arc 830.48 — Fraysse, Jean. Les troglodytes en Anjou à travers les âges. Cholet, 1963.

Arc 612.47 — Frost, H. Under the Mediterranean. London, 1963.

Arc 726.270 — Giordano, Nicola. Civiltà millenarie in terra di Bari. Bari, 1963.

Arc 875.54 — Great Britain. Commissions. Ancient and Historical Monuments of Scotland. Ancient and historical monuments of Stirlingshire. Edinburgh, 1963. 2v.

Arc 861.100.10 — Green, C. Sutton-Hoo. London, 1963.

Arc 1148.20.3 — Groningen, B.A. Short manual of Greek palaeography. 3. ed. Leyden, 1963.

Arc 726.245 — Guido, M. Sardinia. London, 1963.

Arc 505.11.10 — Harding, G.L. Baalbek. Khayats, 1963.

Arc 392.14 — Hawkes, Jacquetta. The world of the past. 1. ed. N.Y., 1963. 2v.

Arc 875.131 — Henshall, Audrey Shore. The chambered tombs of Scotland. Edinburgh, 1963-72. 2v.

Arc 608.66 — Hugot, Henri J. Recherches préhistoriques dans l'Ahazzar nord-occidental. Paris, 1963.

Arc 1588.10.10 — Huszár, Lajos. Munzkunst in Ungarn. Budapest, 1963.

Arc 1580.46 — Innsbruck, F. Der Tiroler Taler. Innsbruck, 1963.

Arc 505.125 — Israel Exploration. The expedition to the Judean desert, 1960-1961. Jerusalem, 1963.

Arc 723.34 — Istituto Italiano di Preistoria e Protostoria. Atti della VII riunione scientifica. Firenze, 1963.

Arc 936.40.20 — Ivanova-Mavrodinova, Vera. Preslav. Sofiia, 1963.

Arc 1504.20.5 — Jaeger, Kurt. Die Münzprägungen der letzten Monarchien des teutschen Bundes von 1815. Fürstentum Liechtenstein. Basel, 1963.

Arc 936.14.80 — Jamka, Rudolf. Kraków w pradziejach. Wrocław, 1963.

Arc 1335.151 — Jewish Theological Seminary. Great Jewish portraits in metal. N.Y., 1963.

Arc 925.295 — Kafoev, A.Z. Adygskie pamiatniki. Nal'chik, 1963.

Arc 1588.1.44F — Kałkowski, Tadeusz. Tysiac lat monety polskiej. Kraków, 1963.

Arc 1282.10 — Kamentseva, Elena I. Russkaia spagistika i geral'dika. Moskva, 1963.

Arc 530.80.5 — Khachatrian, T.S. Materialnaia Kul'tura drevnego Artika. Erevan, 1963.

Arc 938.96F — Kivikoski, Ella. Kvaonbacken. Helsinki, 1963.

Arc 1478.85 — Klawans, Zander H. Reading and dating Roman imperial coins. 3. ed. Racine, Wis., 1963.

Arc 925.255.5F — Krasnoiarsk, Siberia (City). Kraevoi Kraevedcheskii Muzei. Materialy i issledovaniia po arkheologii etnografii i istorii Krasnoiarskogo kraia. Krasnoiarsk, 1963.

Arc 830.158.10 — Le Gall, J. Alésia. Paris, 1963.

Arc 1470.83 — Le Rider, Georges. Deux trésors de monnaies. Paris, 1963.

Arc 416.44 — Lloyd, Seton Howard Frederick. Mounds of the Near East. Edinburgh, 1963.

Arc 895.63 — Malmer, M.P. Metodproblem inom järnålderns konsthistoria. Bonn, 1963.

Arc 595.67F — Maragioglio, Vito. L'archittura delle piramidi menfite. v.2-7; plates. Torino, 1963- 9v.

Arc 843.225 — Martín Aguado, Máximo. El yacimiento prehistórico de Pinedo, Toledo, y su industria triedrica. Toledo, 1963.

Arc 530.165 — Matthiae, Paolo. Studi sui rilie vi di Karatepe. Roma, 1963.

Arc 595.6.5 — Mencken, A. Designing and building the Great Pyramid. Baltimore, 1963.

Arc 1367.2.2 — Miller, Max. Die Münzen des Altertums. 2. Aufl. Braunschweig, 1963.

Arc 397.22 — Mongait, A.L. Arkheologiia i sovremennost'. Moskva, 1963.

Arc 1163.3.80 — Mortero y Simón, C. Apuntes de iniciacion a la paleografia española de los siglos XII a XVII. Madrid, 1963.

Arc 925.320 — Moscow. Gosudarstvennyi Istoricheskii Muzei. Iaroslavskoe Povolzh'e X-XI vv. po materialam Timerevskogo Mikhailovskogo i Petrovskogo mogil'nikov. Moskva, 1963.

Arc 397.20 — Murray, M.A. My first hundred years. London, 1963.

Arc 653.2 — Neue Ausgrabungen in Griechenland. Olten, 1963.

Arc 976.7 — Noël Hume, Ivor. Here lies Virginia. N.Y., 1963.

Arc 1493.22 — Ortega Galindo, Julio. La España firmitiva a través de las monedas ibéricas. Bilbao, 1963.

Arc 848.55 — Paertner, Rudolf. Mit dem Fahrstuhl in die Römerzeit. Düsseldorf, 1963.

Arc 400.27 — Pallottino, Massimo. Che cos'è l'archeologia. Firenze, 1963.

Arc 672.1.110 — Palmer, Leonard R. On the Knossos tablets. Oxford, 1963.

Arc 441.22 — Patil, Devendrakumar Rajaram. The antiquarian remains in Bihar. Patna, 1963.

Arc 672.1.28.6 — Pendlebury, J.D.S. The archaeology of Crete. N.Y., 1963.

Arc 936.14.140 — Polskie Towarzystwo Archeologiczne. Pradzieje Rzeszowszczyzny. Rzeszów, 1963.

Arc 925.300.5 — Popova, T.B. Dol'meny stanitsy Novosvobodnoi. Moskva, 1963.

Arc 936.14.175 — Potemski, Gzesław. Pradzieje Bydgoszczy i powiatu bydgoskiego. Bydgoszcz, 1963.

Arc 673.1.35F — Pouilloux, Jean. Énigmes à Delphes. Paris, 1963.

Arc 1185.29 — Pratesi, A. Elementi di diplomatica generale. Bari, 1963?

Arc 505.121.10 — Pritchard, James. The Bronze Age Cemetery at Gibeon. Philadelphia, 1963.

Arc 383.46 — Przyjaciół Nauk. Poznańskie Tow. Munera archaeologica Iosepho Kostrzewski. Poznań, 1963.

Arc 1663.33 — Quinot, Henri. Recueil illustré des ordres de chevalerie et decorations belges de 1830 à 1963. 5. éd. Bruxelles, 1963.

Arc 815.27 — Ragghianti, C.L. Pittori di Pompei. Milano, 1963.

Arc 402.20 — Rapport, S.B. Archaeology. N.Y., 1963.

Arc 853.264F — Reinbacker, E. Börnicke. Berlin, 1963.

Arc 1500.56 — Richebé, C. Les monnaies féodales d'artois. Paris, 1963.

Arc 723.40 — Rodmilli, Antonio M. La preistoria d'Italia alla luce delle ultime scoperte. Firenze, 1963.

Arc 520.36 — Schulte, Eduard. Chronik der Ausgrabung von Pergamon. Dortmund, 1963.

Arc 403.20 — Schweitzer, B. Zur Kunst der Antike. Tübingen, 1963. 2v.

Arc 938.95 — Selirand, J. Läbi aastatuhandete. Tallinn, 1963.

Arc 925.9.30 — Semenov, L.P. Arkheologicheskie i etnograficheskie razyskaniia v Ingushetii v 1925-32 gg. Groznyi, 1963.

Arc 1433.91 — Smirnova, O.I. Katalog monet s gorodischa Pendzhikent...1949-1956 gg. Moskva, 1963.

Arc 936.12.5 — Sobociński, M. Materiał kostny zwierzecy z wykopalisk wczesnośredniowiecznego grodziska w Bonikowie. Poznań, 1963.

Arc 612.49 — Stacul, Giorgio. La grande madre. Roma, 1963.

Arc 609.1.45 — Summers, Roger. Zimbabwe. Johannesburg, 1963.

Arc 1033.112.5 — Swoboda, Franz. Die liturgischen Kämme. Thesis. n.p., 1963?

Arc 935.60 — Tasliklioglu, Zafer. Anadolu'da Apollon kültu ile ilgili kaynaklar. Istanbul, 1963.

Arc 925.9.35 — Tekhov, Bagrat V. K istorii izucheniia pamiatnikov epokhi eneolita i bronzy v nizhnem. Tbilisi, 1963.

Arc 1077.10.2 — Thoby, Paul. Le crucifix. Supplément. Nantes, 1963.

Arc 608.67 — Tixier, Jacques. Typologie de l'épipaléolithique du Maghreb. Paris, 1963.

Arc 936.220.20 — Todorović, Jovan. Stare kulture i narodi na tlu Beograd. Beograd, 1963.

Arc 925.301 — Tret'iakov, P.N. Drevnii gorodishcha Smolenshchiny. Leningrad, 1963.

Arc 1480.75 — Turcan, Robert. Le trésor de Guelma. Thèse. Paris, 1963.

Arc 936.195.45 — Turek, R. Čechy na úsvitě dějin. Praha, 1963.

Arc 923.107 — Vsesoiuznaia Arkheologicheskaia Studencheskaia Konferentsiia, 6th, Moscw, 1960. Sbornik dokladov na VI i VII vsesoiuznykh arkheologicheskikh studencheskikh konferentsiiakh. Moskva, 1963.

Arc 1153.93 — Wagner, L. Proba centum scripturarum. Leipzig, 1963. 2v.

Arc 875.124 — Wainwright, Fredrick Threlfall. The souterrains of southern Pictland. London, 1963.

Arc 1033.12.9.10 — Walsh, J.E. The shroud. N.Y., 1963.

Arc 936.14.125 — Warsaw. Uniwersytet. Zespoł Badan nad Polskim Sredniowieczem. Badania archeologiczne w okolicy wislicy. Warszawa, 1963-64.

Arc 936.14.135 — Warsaw. Uniwersytet. Zespoł Badan nad Polskim Sredniowieczem. II konferencja naukowa w Warszawie...1961. Warszawa, 1963.

Arc 936.14.120 — Warsaw. Uniwersytet. Zespoł Badan nad Polskim Sredniowieczem. Odrycia w wiślecy. Warszawa, 1963-64.

Arc 936.6.30 — Wiklak, Henryk. Początki kultury łuzyckiej w Polsce Środkowej. Łodź, 1963.

Arc 1200.26 — William of Hoo, S. The letter-book of William of Hoo. Ipswich, 1963.

Arc 785.103 — Winslow, E.M. A libation to the gods. London, 1963.

Arc 1480.65 — Wosnik, Bernhard. Untersuchungen zur Geschichte Sullas. Inaug. Diss. Würzburg, 1963.

Arc 936.14.70 — Zak, Jan. Importy skandynawskie na ziemiach zachodnioslowianskich. Poznań, 1963. 3v.

Arc 1163.3.70 — Zhukovskaia, L.P. Razvitie slaviano-russkoi paleografii v dosrevoluitsionnoi Rossii. Moskva, 1963.

Arc 853.271F — Ziegart, Helmut. Zur Chronologie und Gruppengliederung des westlichen Hügelgräberkultur. Berlin, 1963.

1964

Arc 936.165.15 — Akademiia Nauk Moldavskoi SSSR, Kishinev. Institut Istorii. Materialy i issledovanii po arkheologii i ethnografii Moldavskoi SSR. Kishinev, 1964.

Arc 608.23.5 — Akademiia Nauk SSSR. Institut Arkheologii. Drevniaia Nubiia. Leningrad, 1964.

Arc 612.48 — Akademiia Nauk SSSR. Institut Arkheologii. Pamiatniki kamennogo i bronz. vekov Evrazii. Moskva, 1964.

Arc 432.23 — Akademiia Nauk SSSR. Institut Narodov Azii. Indiia v drevnosti; sbornik statei. Moskva, 1964.

Chronological Listing

1964 - cont.

Arc 843.105.5 Almeida, Fernando de. Ruinas de Mirobriga dos Célticos. Lisboa, 1964.
Arc 700.56 Alsop, J. From the silent earth. N.Y., 1964.
Arc 416.27 Andrae, Walter. Alte Feststrassen im Nahen Orient. Stuttgart, 1964.
Arc 938.5.5 Archäologischer Kongress, 10th, Riga, 1896. Klusie liecinieki; senlietu albums. Lincoln, Nebraska, 1964.
Arc 608.17.30F Arkell, A.J. Wanyanga. London, 1964.
Arc 530.22.15 Arutiunian, Nikolai V. Zemledelic i skotovodstvo Urartu. Erevan, 1964.
Arc 935.31 Arutiunian, Varazdat. Gorod Ani. Erevan, 1964.
Arc 600.190 Bachatly, C. Le monastère de Phoebammon. Le Caire, 1964- 2v.
Arc 925.136 Bader, Otto N. Drevneishie metallurgi Priural'ia. Moskva, 1964.
Arc 936.195.96 Balaša, Gejza. Zvolen v období lužickej kultúry. Banská Bystrica, 1964.
Arc 843.205 Balil, Alberto. Colonia Iblia Augusta Paterna Farentia Barcino. Madrid, 1964.
Arc 383.9.10 Barcelona (Province). Instituto de Prehistoria y Arqueología. Miscelánea en homenaje al abate Hescri Breuil, 1877-1961. Barcelona, 1964-65. 2v.
Arc 936.251 Benae, Alojz. Studije o kamenom i bakarnom dobu u sjeverozapadnom Balkanu. Sarajevo, 1964.
Arc 936.205.10 Bešlagić, Šefik. Grborezi srednjovjckovna nekropola. Sarajevo, 1964.
Arc 488.25 Bittal, Kurt. Vorderasiatische Archäologie. Berlin, 1964.
Arc 925.8.50 Blavatskii, Vladimir D. Pantikapei; Ocherki istorii stolitsy Bospora. Moskva, 1964.
Arc 700.58 Boardman, J. The Greeks overseas. Harmondsworth, 1964.
Arc 915.36 Bocksberger, Olivier Jean. Age du Bronze en Valais et dans le chablais vaudois. Lausanne, 1964.
Arc 1468.50 Boston. Museum of Fine Arts. Greek coins, 1950-1963. Boston, 1964.
Arc 547.44 Botti, Giuseppe. I cimeli egizi del Museo. Firenze, 1964.
Arc 681.7F Brae, Luigi Bernabo. Poliochni. v.1-2. Roma, 1964.
Arc 925.50.110 Braichevs'kyi, Mykhailo I. Bilia dzherel plov'ians'koi derzhevnosti. Kyïv, 1964.
Arc 858.78 British Museum. Guide to the antiquities of Roman Britain. 3. ed. London, 1964.
Arc 1538.2.22 British Museum. Department of Coins and Medals. English copper, tin and bronze coins in the British Museum. 2. ed. London, 1964.
Arc 547.26 British Museum. Department of Egyptian and Assyrian Antiquities. A general introductory guide to the Egyptian collections in the British Museum. London, 1964.
Arc 302.2.14 Bulgarska Akademiia na Naukite, Sofia. Arkheolgicheski Institut. Serdika; arkheologicheski materiali. Sofiia, 1964.
Arc 608.72 Camps, Gabriel. La nécropole mégalithique du Djebel Mazela à Bou Nouara. Paris, 1964.
Arc 440.8 Casal, Jean Marie. Fouilles d'Amri. Paris, 1964. 2v.
Arc 540.12 Catling, H.W. Cypriot bronzework in the Mycenaean world. Oxford, 1964.
Arc 3.4 Colloque International d'Archéologie Aérienne. Colloque international d'archéologie aérienne. Paris, 1964.
Arc 1490.8.15 Consolo Langher, S. Contributo alla storia della...moneta. Milano, 1964.
Arc 700.57 Cook, R.M. Niobe and her children. Cambridge, 1964.
Arc 1166.7.15F Cramer, Maria. Koptische Paläographie. Wiesbaden, 1964.
Arc 936.14.155 Dabrowski, Krzysztof. Przymierze z archeologią. Warszawa, 1964.
Arc 1138.55.2 Dain, A. Les manuscrits. Paris, 1964.
Arc 1433.90 Davidovich, Elena A. Istoriia monetnogo dela Srednei Azii XVII-XVIII vv. Dushanbe, 1964.
Arc 609.41 Davies, Oliver. The quarternary in the coastlands of Guinea. Glasgow, 1964.
Arc 746.45 Decouflé, Pierre. La notion d'ex-voto anatomique chez les Etrusco Romains. Bruxelles, 1964.
Arc 682.31F Desborough, V.R. d'. The last Mycenaeans and their successors. Oxford, 1964.
Arc 1675.97 Dresden. Historisches Museum. Order und Ehrenzeichen der Deutschen Demokratischen Republik. Dresden, 1964.
Arc 530.163 Dupont-Sommer, André. La déesse de Hiérapolis Castabala (Cilicie). Paris, 1964.
Arc 1138.110 Ekschmitt, Werner. Das Gedächtnis der Völker. Berlin, 1964.
Arc 672.1.130 Evans, Arthur John. The palace of Minos. N.Y., 1964. 6v.
Arc 672.1.131 Evans, Arthur John. The palace of Minos. Index. N.Y., 1964.
Arc 389.6.2 Eydoux, Henri Paul. Realités et énigmes de l'archéologie. 2. éd. Paris, 1964.
Arc 672.1.105 Faure, Paul. Fonctions des cavernes crétoises. Paris, 1964.
Arc 66.1.202 Fevrier, Paul Albert. Le developpement urbain en Provence. Paris, 1964.
Arc 340.25.5 Field, Henry. Bibliography of Soviet archaeology and physical anthropology, 1936-1964. Miami? 1964.
Arc 935.30 Firatli, Nezih. Les stiles funéraires de Byzance gréco-romaine. Paris, 1964.
Arc 726.264 Fois, Foiso. I ponti romani in Sardegna. Sassari, 1964.
Arc 608.65 Foncher, L. Hodrumetum. Paris, 1964.
Arc 858.74 Fox, Aileen H. South west England. London, 1964.
Arc 1237.5.2 Frankfort, Henri. Stratified cylinder seals from the Diyala region. Chicago, 1964.
Arc 1077.2.65 Füglister, Robert L. Das Lebende Kreuz. Einsiedeln, 1964.
Arc 905.142 Gabori, Miklos. Akésöi paleolitikum Magyarországon. Budapest, 1964.
Arc 885.25 Gardner, Willoughby. Dinorben. Cardiff, 1964.
Arc 726.262 Gasperini, Lidio. Aletrium. Roma, 1964.
Arc 925.323.5 Gening, Vladimir F. Rannie bolgary na Volge. Moskva, 1964.
Arc 726.250 Gierow, Pär Göran. The iron age culture of Latium. v.2, pt.1. Lund, 1964.
Arc 830.339 Gilbert, Max. Menhirs et dolmens dans le nord-est de la Bretagne. Guernsey, 1964.
Arc 66.1.203 Glenisson, Jean. Correspondance des légats et vicaires-généraux. Paris, 1964.
Arc 1584.1.15 Golenko, Konstantin V. Denizhnoe obrashchenie kolkhidy v rimskoe vremia. Leningrad, 1964.
Arc 726.140.10 Grancelli, Umberto. Il piano di fondazione di Verona romana. Verona, 1964.
Arc 723.33 Grimal, Pierre. In search of Ancient Italy. 1st American ed. N.Y., 1964.

1964 - cont.

Arc 383.89F Grimm, Paul. Varia archaeologica. Berlin, 1964.
Arc 853.83.5 Gsaenger, Hans. Die Externsteine. Freiburg, 1964.
Arc 543.66.15 Gudkova, A.V. Tok-kala. Tashkend, 1964.
Arc 936.250 Gzelishvili, Iosif. Zhelezoplavil'noe proizvodstvo v drevnei Gruzii. Tbilisi, 1964.
Arc 1460.5 Haak, A.C. Gold coins of the Royal Netherlands Academy. Amsterdam, 1964.
Arc 543.81 Harding, Gerald Lankester. Archaeology in the Aden Protectorates. London, 1964.
Arc 1548.2F Hede, Holger. Danmarks og Norges mønter, 1541-1814-1963. Udgivet of Dansk numisatisk forening. Kjøbenhavn, 1964.
Arc 540.11F Hennessy, J.B. Stephania; a middle and late bronze-age cemetery in Cyprus. London, 1964.
Arc 1480.71 Hill, Philip V. The coinage of Septimius Severus and his family of the mint of Rome, A.D. 193-217. London, 1964.
Arc 383.9.25 Hiranyagarbha; a series of articles on the archaeological work and studies of Prof. Dr. F.D.K. Bosch. The Hague, 1964.
Arc 522.37 Holden, B.M. The metopes of the Temple of Athena at Ilion. Northampton, 1964.
Arc 936.195.285 Hrubý, Vilém. Staré Město-Velehrad. 1. vyd. Praha, 1964.
Arc 925.50.105 Iakobson, A.L. Srednevekovyi Krym. Leningrad, 1964.
Arc 435.26 India. Archaeological Survey. Archaeological remains. v.1-2. New Delhi, 1964.
Arc 938.104 Indreko, Richard. Mesolithische und frühneolithische Kulturen in Osteuropa und Westsebirien. Stockholm, 1964.
Arc 858.88 Jessup, Ronald Frederick. The story of archaeology in Britain. London, 1964.
Arc 1675.96F Johns Hopkins University. Medals relating to medicine and allied sciences in the numismatic collection. Baltimore, 1964.
Arc 505.124.2F Joint Expedition of the University of Rome and the Hebrew University. Excavations at Ramat Rahel, seasons 1961 and 1962. Rome, 1964.
Arc 936.14.145 Kaminska, Janina. Z dziejów prednowiecz sieradza. Wrocław, 1964.
Arc 925.134.5 Kanivets, Viacheslav I. Kaninskaia peshchera. Moskva, 1964.
Arc 925.9.45 Karakashly, K.T. Material'naia kul'tura azerbaidzhantsev severo-vostochnoi i Tsentral'noi zon Malogo Kavkaza. Balzu, 1964.
Arc 448.1.25 Khan, F.A. The Indus Valley and early Iran. Karachi, 1964.
Arc 543.146.15 Khlopin, Igor N. Geoksiurskaia gruppa poselenii epokhi eneolita. Leningrad, 1964.
Arc 1588.1.55 Kiersnowski, Ryszard. Wstęp do numizmatyki polskiej wieków średnich. Warszawa, 1964.
Arc 560.2 Kink, Khil'da A. Egipet do faraonov. Moskva, 1964.
Arc 936.15.25 Kongres archeologa Jugoslavije, 6th, Ljubljana, 1963. Kongrresni materijali VI Kongresa Jugoslovinskih arheoloya. Beograd, 1964. 2v.
Arc 935.70 Kosay, Hâmit Zübeyr. Pulur kazisi; 1960 mersimi çalişmalari raporu. Ankara, 1964.
Arc 936.14.160 Koszalin, Poland (City). Muzeum. Pradzieje pomorza srodkowego. Koszalin, 1964.
Arc 925.322.10 Kotovich, Vladimir G. Kamennyi vek Dagestana. Makhachkala, 1964.
Arc 936.14.210 Kozłowski, Janusz K. Paleolit na Gónnym Śląsku. Wrocław, 1964.
Arc 905.126 Kromer, Karl. Von frühen Eisen und reichen Salzherren die Hallstattkultur in Osterreich. Wien, 1964.
Arc 432.27 Lal, Braj Basi. Indian archaeology since independence. 1. ed. Delhi, 1964.
Arc 823.81 Laming, Annette. Origines de l'archéologie préhistorique en France. Paris, 1964.
Arc 925.50.48 Liberov, Petr D. Plemena srednego Dona v epokhu bronzy. Moskva, 1964.
Arc 397.18.10F Macaulay, Rose. Roloff Beny interprets in photographs Pleasure of ruins. London, 1964.
Arc 1190.25.12 Maffei, Scipione. Istoria diplomatica che serve d'introduzione all'arte critica in tal materia. Roma, 1964.
Arc 1550.10 Mansfeld-Bûllner, H.V. Afbildninger af panstlege indtil kjendte danske mønter. 2. Opl. Kjøbenhavn, 1964.
Arc 843.218 Martinez Hombre, Eduardo. Vindius; el lado septentrional clasico de Hispania. Madrid, 1964.
Arc 530.65.15 Martirosian, A. Armeniia v epokhu bronzy i rannego zheleza. Erevan, 1964.
Arc 416.28 Masson, V.M. Sredniaia Aziia i drevnii Vostok. Leningrad, 1964.
Arc 1153.95 Mazzoleni, Jole. Lezioni di paleografia latina e diplomatica. Napoli, 1964?
Arc 858.59.50 Meaney, A. A gazetteer of early Anglo-Saxon burial sites. London, 1964.
Arc 488.20 Mellink, M.J. Dark ages and nomads c.1000 B.C. Istanbul, 1964.
Arc 736.20 Missione Archeologica della Soprintendenza alle Antichità della Sicilia Occidentale e dell'Università di Roma. Mozia. Roma, 1964- 8v.
Arc 505.126F Missione archeologica italiana in Siria. Roma, 1964- 3v.
Arc 895.64 Moberg, Carl Axel. Innan Sverige blev Sverige. Stockholm, 1964.
Arc 1518.6 Morin, Francois. Monnaies de Belgique de 1832 à 1963. Boom, 1964.
Arc 936.14.142 Moskwa, Kazimierz. Pradzieje powiatu rzeszowskiego. Lublin, 1964.
Arc 853.273.5 Müller, Adriaan. Berlins Urgeschichte. Berlin, 1964.
Arc 853.273F Müller, Adriaan. Die jungbronzezeitliche Siedlung von Berlin-Lichterfelde. Berlin, 1964.
Arc 853.272F Müller, Hanns H. Die Haustiere der mitteldeutschen Bandkiramiker. Berlin, 1964.
Arc 1438.2 Mueller, L. Numismatique de l'ancienne Afrique. v.1-3. Bologne, 1964. 2v.
Arc 590.18 Muhammad, Ahmad Rajab. Lights on the royal mummies in the Egyptian Museum. Cairo, 1964.
Arc 1588.4.60 Nemeškal, Lubomir. Jáchymovská mincovna v první polovině 16. století, 1519/20-1561. Praha, 1964.
Arc 853.236.5F Nickel, Ernest. Der alte Markt in Magdeburg. Berlin, 1964.
Arc 1588.4.35 Nohejlová, Emanuela. Kratký přehled českého mincovnictví a tabulky cen a mezd. Praha, 1964.
Arc 853.270F Nowothnig, Walter. Brandgräber des Völkeswandernugszeit im siedlichen Niedersachsen. Neumünster, 1964.
Arc 398.6 Nylander, Carl. Den dijupa brunnen. Stockholm, 1964.
Arc 925.4.20 Okladnikov, A.P. Olen' zolotye goda. Leningrad, 1964.

Chronological Listing

1964 - cont.

Arc 925.75.4 Ol'viiskaia Ekspeditsiia, 1946. Ol'viia; temenos i agora. Leningrad, 1964.
Arc 1588.4.55 Ondrouch, Vojtech. Nálezy keltských, antických a byzantských mincí na Slovensku. Bratislava, 1964.
Arc 880.46.5 O'Riordain, Sean P. New Grange and the bend of the Boyne. London, 1964.
Arc 925.9.40 Pachulia, Vianor P. V kraiu zolotogo runa. Moskva, 1964.
Arc 503.6.5 Palestine. Department of Antiquities. Quarterly. Index, v.1-14 (1931-1950). Jerusalem, 1964.
Arc 925.321.5 Pankrushev, Grigorii A. Plemena Karelii v epokhu neolita i rannego metalla. Leningrad, 1964.
Arc 1153.94 Pelzer, Auguste. Abréviations latines médiévales. Louvain, 1964.
Arc 726.265 Pennucci, Umberto. Bisenzo e le antiche civiltà intorno al lago di Bolsena. Grotte di Castro, 1964.
Arc 925.50.18 Piatysheva, Natalia V. Zheleznaia maska iz Khersonesa. Moskva, 1964.
Arc 936.14.100 Polska Akademia Nauk. Oddział w Krakowie. Prace Komisja Archeologicznej. Studia i materiały do badań nad Neolitem Małopolski. Wrocław, 1964.
Arc 1588.1.50 Polskiej Akademja Nauk. Instytut Historyjka Kultury Materialnej. Skarb monet arabskich z klukowicz powiat siemiatycze. Wrocław, 1964.
Arc 1675.92 Probszt, Günther. Die Kärntner Medaillen. Klagenfurt, 1964.
Arc 708.36 Prokopiou, Angelos G. Athens, city of the Gods. N.Y., 1964.
Arc 936.14.170 Przeworska, Janina. Tradycje celtyckie w obrzędowości Protosłowian. Wrocław, 1964.
Arc 400.26 Pyddoke, E. The scientist and archaeology. N.Y., 1964.
Arc 1588.4.80 Radoměřský, Pavel. Nález přemyslovských denárů iz století v Hodkově u Kutné Hory. Kutná Hora, 1964.
Arc 1027.19.40F Reekmans, Louis. La tombe du Pape Corneille et su région cimetriale. Città del Vaticano, 1964.
Arc 935.33.5 Resit Mazhar Ertüzün. Kapidagi Yariniadasi ve Cevresindeki Adalar. Ankara, 1964.
Arc 1675.94 Respublička Izložba Hrvatskih Medalja i Plaketa. 1st, Zagreb, 1964-65. Medalja u hrvatskoj. Zagreb, 1964?
Arc 943.45 Rice University. Prehistoric man in the new world. Chicago, 1964.
Arc 746.50 Rilli, Nicola. Gli estruschi a Sesto Fiorentino. Firenze, 1964.
Arc 530.162 Robert, Louis. Nouvelles inscriptions de Sardes. Paris, 1964.
Arc 875.100.5 Robertson, Anne. The Roman fort at Castledykes. Edinburgh, 1964.
Arc 726.247 Rome. Università. Monte Sirai. Roma, 1964. 4v.
Arc 726.260 Rome (City). Università. Istituto di Topografia Antica. Saggio di fotointerpretazione archeologica. Roma, 1964.
Arc 1645.6F Salazar Bondy, Sebastian. Lima, su moneda y su ceca. v.1-2. Lima, 1964.
Arc 1093.9 Sankalia, Hasmukh Dhirajlal. Stone age tools. 1. ed. Poona, 1964.
Arc 530.14.26 Schede, Martin. Die Ruinen von Priene. 2. Aufl. Berlin, 1964.
Arc 682.1.5 Schliemann, Heinrich. Mykenae; Bericht über meine Forschungen und Entdeckungen in Mykenae und Tiryns. Faksimile. Darmstadt, 1964.
VArc 925.50.135 Shovkoplias, Ivan H. Osnovy arkheolohii. Kyïv, 1964.
Arc 403.21 Silverberg, R. Great adventures in archaeology. N.Y., 1964.
Arc 925.13.110 Smirnov, K.F. Savromaty. Moskva, 1964.
Arc 1584.26 Spasskii, Ivan G. Po sledam odnoi redkoi monety. Leningrad, 1964.
Arc 543.3.20 Stein, Mark Aurel. On ancient Central-Asian tracks. N.Y., 1964.
Arc 1340.2.2 Stevenson, Seth William. A dictionary of Roman coins, republican and imperial. London, 1964.
Arc 672.1.112 Stibbe, C.M. Kreta en Mykene. Zeist, 1964.
Arc 853.270.10 Sudholz, Gisela. Die ältere Bronzezeit zwischen Niederrhein und Mittelwesen. Hildesheim, 1964.
Arc 685.5 Syriopoulos, K. Hē proistoria...Peloponnēsou. Athēnai, 1964.
Arc 543.66.20 Termezskaia Arkheologicheskaia Kompleksnaia Ekspeditsiia, 1937, 1961-1962. Kara-tepe. Moskva, 1964.
Arc 1675.95 Todorović, Nada. Jugoslovenske i inostrane medalje. Beograd, 1964.
Arc 1088.1.7 Torr, Cecil. Ancient ships. Chicago, 1964.
Arc 936.195.50F Tučik, Añton. Opevnina osada z doby bronzovej vo Veselom. Bratislava, 1964.
Arc 421.27 Tung, Tso-pin. Fifty years of studies in oracle inscriptions. Tokyo, 1964.
Arc 865.23 Twist, Richard Marsden. Stonehenge. Truro, 1964.
Arc 936.14.110 Urbańska, A. Wytwórczość włokiennicza predniowiecznego międzyrzeeza. Poznań, 1964.
Arc 736.22 Vallet, Georges. Megara Hyblaca. v.2,4. Text and atlas. Paris, 1964- 4v.
Arc 968.2.85 Vivian, G. Gran Quivira. Washington, 1964.
Arc 923.108 Vsesoiuznaia Arkheologicheskaia Studencheskaia Konferentsiia, 8th, Leningrad, 1962. Arkheologicheskii sbornik trudy. Leningrad, 1964.
Arc 1097.5 Waals, Johannes D. van der. Prehistoric disc wheels in the Netherlands. Proefschrift. Groningen, 1964.
Arc 936.14.136 Warsaw. Uniwersytet. Zespoł Badan nad Polskim Sredniowieczem. III konferencja naukowa w Warszawie. Warszawa, 1964.
Arc 1504.25 Wielandt, Friedrich. Münz- und Geldgeschichte des Standes Schuyz. Schuyz, 1964.
Arc 777.4 Wiesel, Julius Maxim. Das alte Rom zur konstantinischen Zeit undHeute. Mainz, 1964.
Arc 572.2 Wilson, John Albert. Signs and wonders upon Pharaoh. Chicago, 1964.
Arc 861.171 Winchester, England. Winchester excavations, 1949-1960. Winchester, Hants, 1964.
Arc 858.73 Wood, E.S. Collins field guide to archaeology. London, 1964.

1965

Arc 493.6.40 Akademiia Nauk Azerbaidzhanskoi SSR, Baku. Institut Istorii. Arkheologicheskie issledoveniia v Azerbaidzhane. Baku, 1965.
Arc 375.13 Aken, Andreas Rudolphus Antonius van. Elseviers encyclopedie van de archeologie. Amsterdam, 1965.
Arc 943.46 Alcina Franch, José. Manual de arqueologia americana. Madrid, 1965.

1965 - cont.

Arc 1400.8 Altz, Charles G. Foreign coins struck at United States mints. Racine, Wis., 1965.
Arc 925.325 Bader, Otto N. Kapovaia peshchera. Moskva, 1965.
Arc 432.28 Banerjee, N.R. The iron age in India. Delhi, 1965.
Arc 936.20.75 Barbu, V. Adamclisi. Bucuresti, 1965.
Arc 1077.2.53.2 Baus, Karl. Der Kranz in Antike und Christentum. Bonn, 1965.
Arc 733.6 Belgiorno, Franco Libero. I Siciliani di 15 mila anni fa. Catania, 1965.
Arc 1390.17 Berghaus, Peter. Dona numismatica. Hamburg, 1965.
Arc 1552.1 Bjoerkman, S. Myntic Islands, 1836-1922-1963. Stockholm, 1965.
Arc 936.195.85 Borkovský, Ivan. Levý Hradec. Praha, 1965.
Arc 66.1.204 Boucher, Jean-Paul. Études sur Properce; problèmes d'inspiration et d'art. Paris, 1965.
Arc 340.8.10 Brünn. Universita. Knihovna. Přehled bibliografií a pokusů o soupisy moravské archeologické literatury. Brno, 1965.
Arc 1520.15 Brussels. Bibliothèque Royale. Mille ans de monnayage Bruxellois, 1965. Bruxelles, 1965.
Arc 609.1.40 Bruwer, Andries Johannes. Zimbabwe; Rhodesia's ancient greatness. Johannesburg, 1965.
Arc 925.331 Burov, Grigorii M. Vychegodskii krai. Moskva, 1965.
Arc 726.206F Capua preromana; le antichita etrusche di Santa Maria Capua Vetere. v.1, pt.7. v.2, pt.1,2. Firenze, 1965- 3v.
Arc 936.195.210 Castelin, Karel O. Die Goldprägung der Kelten in den böhmischen Ländern. Graz, 1965.
Arc 723.36 Centro Studi Ciociaria. Gli archeologi italiani in onore di Amedeo Maiuri. Cava dei Tirreni, 1965.
Arc 925.170.5 Charnoluskii, Vladimir V. Legenda ob olene-chelovcke. Moskva, 1965.
Arc 432.30 Chattopadhyay, Kshitis Prasad. Ancient Indian culture contacts and migration. Calcutta, 1965.
Arc 925.16.20 Chernikov, Sergei. Zagadka zolotogo kurgana. Moskva, 1965.
Arc 432.25 Chhabra, Bahadur Chand. Expansion of Indo-Aryan culture during Pallava rule as evidenced by inscriptions. Delhi, 1965.
Arc 736.24 Ciancio, Salvatore. Leontinoi: anni di ricerche archeologiche. Lentini, 1965.
Arc 1330.7 Clain-Stepanelli, Elvira Eliza. Select numismatic bibliography. N.Y., 1965.
Arc 543.82 Cleveland, Ray L. An ancient South Arabian necropolis. Baltimore, 1965.
Arc 497.78 Cohen, Lenore. Biblical treasure in Bible lands. Los Angeles, 1965.
Arc 853.277 Cologne. Römisch-Germanisches Museum. Frühchristliches Köln. Köln, 1965.
Arc 3.1.28 Congrès International d'Archéologie Classique, 8th, Paris, 1963. Le rayonnement des civilizations grecque et romaine sur les cultures périphériques. Paris, 1965. 2v.
Arc 595.65 Cormack, Maribelle. Imhotep, builder in stone. N.Y., 1965.
Arc 810.54.7 Corte, Matteo della. Case ed abitanti di Pompei. 3. ed. Napoli, 1965.
Arc 746.47 Cristofani, Mauro. La tomba delle iscrizioni a Cerveteri. Firenze, 1965.
Arc 488.24 Culican, William. The Medes and Persians. London, 1965.
Arc 936.14.200 Danzig (City). Muzeum Archeologiczne. Pomerania antiqua. Gdynia, 1965- 6v.
Arc 440.10 Das Gupta, Kalyan Kumar. The Audumbaras. Calcutta, 1965.
Arc 1025.75 Denis-Boulet, Noële M. Rome souterraine. Paris, 1965.
Arc 442.5 Deo, Shantavam Bhalchandra. Chalcolithic Chandoli. Poona, 1965.
Arc 388.14 Deuel, Leo. Testaments of time. 1. ed. N.Y., 1965.
Arc 612.52F Dieck, Alfred. Die europäischen Moorleichenfunde. Neumünster, 1965.
Arc 1504.20 Divo, Jean-Paul. Die neueren Münzen der Schweiz und des Fürstentums Liechtenstein, 1850-1963. Freiburg, 1965.
Arc 870.29 Evison, Vera I. The fifth-century invasions south of the Thames. London, 1965.
Arc 889.30 Faider-Feytmans, Germaine. La nécropole gallo-romaine de Thuin. Morlanwelz, 1965.
Arc 746.48F Falchi, Isidoro. Vetulonia e la sua necropoli antichissima ed anastatica. Roma, 1965.
Arc 861.170 Feachem, Richard. The North Britons. London, 1965.
Arc 385.16 Felgueiros, Francisco. Pequena história de uma vida gloriosa [Francisco M. Aloes]. Bragança, 1965.
Arc 1077.2.60 Foerster, Else. Das irische Hochkreuz. Inaug. Diss. München, 1965.
Arc 1494.50 Fontecha y Sanchez, Ramon de. La reforma monetaria de 1868; catalogo de monedas. Madrid, 1965.
Arc 830.360 Foramitti, Hans. Wiederbelebung historischer Stadtviertel; die Lösing in Frankreich als mögliches Vorbild. Graz, 1965.
Arc 925.300.10 Formozov, Aleksandr A. Kamennyi vek i eneolit Prikubania. Moskva, 1965.
Arc 885.26 Foster, Idris L. Prehistoric and early Wales. London, 1965.
Arc 1010.25 Fox, Robert B. The Calatagan excavations. Manila, 1965.
Arc 903.4 Franz, Leonhard. Lexikon ur- und frühgeschichtlicher Fundstätten Österreichs. Wien, 1965.
Arc 1335.157.2 Friedberg, Robert. Gold coins of the world, complete from 600 A.D. to the present. N.Y., 1965.
Arc 1033.35.161 Frolow, Anatole. Les reliquaires de la Vraie Croix. Paris, 1965.
Arc 390.15 Furtwängler, Adolf. Briefe aus dem Bonner Privatdozentenjahr 1879/80. Stuttgart, 1965.
Arc 609.19 Gabd, Creighton. Stone age hunters of the Kafue. Boston, 1965.
Arc 1468.52 Gardner, Percy. Archaeology and the types of Greek coins. Chicago, 1965.
Arc 925.38.20 Gavrilova, Antonina. Mogil'nik kudyrge kak istochnik po istorii altaiskikh plemen. Leningrad, 1965.
Arc 612.55F Gimbutas, Marija Alseikaites. Bronze age kultures in central and eastern Europe. The Hague, 1965.
Arc 1076.3.120 Glade, Heinz. Erdentiefe-Turmeshöhe; von Glocken und Glockengiessern. Berlin, 1965.
Arc 608.35.5 Golvin, Lucien. Recherches archéologiques à la Qal'a des Banû Hammâd. Paris, 1965.
Arc 1615.16 Gould, Maurice M. Alaska's coinage through the years. 2. ed. Racine, 1965.
Arc 726.285 Grillo, Francesco. Antichità storiche e monumentali di Corigliano Calabro. Cosenza, 1965.
Arc 1330.56.1 Gromachevskii, Semen G. Bibliograficheskii ukajatel' literatury po russkoi numizmatike. Ann Arbor, Mich., 1965.

Chronological Listing

1965 - cont.

Arc 609.30 Guide to the rock paintings of Tanzania. Dar es Salaam, 1965.

Arc 925.121 Haavio Martti, Henrikki. Bjarmien vallan kukoistur ja tuho. Porvoo, 1965.

Arc 505.92.5 Hammond, Philip C. The excavation of the main theater at Petra, 1961-1962, final report. London, 1965.

Arc 865.24 Hawkins, Gerald Stanley. Stonehenge decoded. 1. ed. Garden City, N.Y., 1965.

Arc 557.5 Hayes, William Christopher. Most ancient Egypt. Chicago, 1965.

Arc 853.302F Heiligendorff, Wolfgang. Das latènezeitliche Gräberfeld von Berlin-Blankenfelde. Berlin, 1965.

Arc 1093.2.35 Hirsch, Friedrich. Der Sonnwendbogen. Lahr, 1965.

Arc 1490.8.20 Holm, Adolf. Storia della moneta siciliana. Bologna, 1965.

Arc 682.32 Hope Simpson, Richard. A gazetteer and atlas of Mycenaean sites. London, 1965.

Arc 1588.4.65F Horák, Jan. Kremnická mincovňa. Banska Bystrica, 1965.

Arc 609.39 Inskeep, R.R. Preliminary investigation of a proto-historic cemetery at Nkudzi Bay, Malawi. Livingstone, 1965.

Arc 1433.67.2 Istanbul. Asari Atika Müzeleri. Catalogue des monnaies turcomanes. Bologne, 1965.

Arc 1588.1.31 Jabłoński, Tadeusz. Katalog monet polskich, 1765-1864. Warszawa, 1965.

Arc 609.20 Jaeger, Otto. Antiquities of north Ethiopia. Brockhaus, 1965.

Arc 936.14.185 Jamka, Rudolf. Pierwsi mieszkancy Gornego Slaska w swietle badan archeologicznych. Katowice, 1965.

Arc 936.195.130 Jansová, Libuše. Hrazany, Keltské oppidum na Sedlčansku. Praha, 1965.

Arc 810.64 Jashemski, Stanley A. Pompeii and the region destroyed by Vesuvius in A.D. 79. Garden City, 1965.

Arc 936.14.165A Jazdzewski, Konrad. Poland. London, 1965.

Arc 861.192 Joint Excavation Committee of the Wakefield Corporation and the Wakefield Historical Society. Sandal Castle; a short account of the history of the site and the 1964 excavations. Wakefield, Eng., 1965.

Arc 386.45 Kenawell, William W. The quest at Glastonbury, a biographical study of Frederick Bligh Bond. N.Y., 1965.

Arc 543.120.5 Kiselev, Sergei. Drevnemongol'skie goroda. Moskva, 1965.

Arc 385.15 Kolchin, B.A. Arkheologiia i estestvennye nauki. Moskva, 1965.

Arc 936.14.230 Kołodziejski, Adam. Rozwój archeologii województwa zielonogórskiego w dwudziestoleciu Polski Ludowej. Zielona Góra, 1965.

Arc 1480.68 Konik, Eugeniusz. Znaleziska monet rzymskich na Śląsku. Wrocław, 1965.

Arc 936.14.150 Kostrzewski, Józef. Pradzieje Polski. wyd. 2. Wrocław, 1965.

Arc 936.14.8 Kostrzewski, Józef. Zur Frage der Siedlungsstetigkeit in der Geschichte Polens. Wrocław, 1965.

Arc 925.322.20 Kotovich, Valentina M. Verkhnegunibskoe poselenie-pamiatnik epokhi bronzy gornogo Dagestana. Makhachkala, 1965.

Arc 497.75 Kryvelev, Iosif A. Raskopki v bibleiskikh stranakh. Moskva, 1965.

Arc 853.278 Kühn, Herbert. Die germanischen Bügelfibeln der Völkerwanderungszeit. v.1-2. Graz, 1965- 3v.

Arc 936.35.5 Lahtov, Vasil. Problem trebeniške kulture. Ohrid, 1965.

Arc 600.6.30 Leclant, Jean. Recherches sur les monuments thébains de la XXVe dynastie dite éthiopienne. Le Caire, 1965. 2v.

Arc 925.50.120 Leskov, Aleksandr M. Gornyi Krym v I tysicacheletii do nashei coy. Kiev, 1965.

Arc 766.4.20 Lugli, Giuseppe. Studi minori di topografia antica. Roma, 1965.

Arc 612.51 Lukan, Karl. Alpenwanderungen in die Vorzeit zu Drachenhöhlen und Druidensteinen. Wien, 1965.

Arc 953.29 McGregor, John Charles. Southwestern archaeology. 2. ed. Urbana, 1965.

Arc 384.2.10 Marek, Kurt W. Götter, Gräber und Gelehrte in Dokumenten. Reinbek bei Hamburg, 1965.

Arc 870.4.22 Margary, Ivan D. Roman ways in the Weald. London, 1965.

Arc 925.9.50 Markovin, Vladimir I. V ushchel'iakh Arguna i Fortangi. Moskva, 1965.

Arc 384.5 Matson, Frederick R. Ceramics and man. Chicago, 1965.

Arc 1480.15.1 Maurice, Jules. Numismatique constantinienne. Bruxelles, 1965. 3v.

Arc 505.116 Mécérian, Jean. Expedition archéologique dans l'Antiochène occidentale. Beyrouth, 1965.

Arc 416.36 Mellaart, James. Earliest civilizations of the Near East. N.Y., 1965.

Arc 861.18.16.15 Merrifield, Ralph. The Roman city of London. London, 1965.

Arc 726.253 Mertens, Jozef. Ordona. Bruxelles, 1965. 4v.

Arc 1588.5.5 Metcalf, David Michael. Coinage in the Balkans. Thessaloniki, 1965.

Arc 925.324 Mezentseva, Galina G. Kanivs'ke poselennia polian. Kyïv, 1965.

Arc 925.50.93 Miller, Mykhailo O. Pervobytnyi period v istorii Nizhego Dnepra. Miunkhen, 1965.

Arc 681.10 Milojčić, Vladmir. Paläolithikum um Larissa in Thessalien. Bonn, 1965.

Arc 925.327 Minaeva, Tat'iana M. Ocherki po arkheologii Stavropol'ia. Stavropol', 1965.

Arc 608.90 Mission Michela Schiff Giorgini. Soleb. Firenze, 1965- 2v.

Arc 505.115.3 Moortgat, Anton. Tell Chuēra in Nordost-Syrien. Köln, 1965.

Arc 1625.5 Moreno, Alvaro. El signo de pesos. México, 1965.

Arc 459.5 Nagaraja Rao, M.S. The stone age hill dwellers of Tekkalakota. Poona, 1965.

Arc 875.128 Newall, Frank. Excavation of prehistoric and mediaeval homesteads at Knapps, Renfrewshire. Paisley, 1965.

Arc 1033.182 Nussbaum, Otto. Der Standort des Liturgen am christlichen Altar vor dem Jahre 1000. Diss. Bonn, 1965.

Arc 925.180.10 Okladnikov, Aleksei Pavlovich. The Soviet Far East in antiquity. Toronto, 1965.

Arc 1153.102 Orlandelli, Gainfranco. Rinascimento giuridico e scrittura carolina a Bologna nel secolo XII. Bologna, 1965.

Arc 1488.32 Pagani, Antonio. Monete italiane dall'invasione napoleonica ai giorni nostri, 1796-1963. 2. ed. Milano, 1965.

Arc 497.79 Palestine Exploration Fund. World of the Bible. South Kensington, 1965?

Arc 655.5 Pannati, Ulrico. L'archeologia in Grecia. Napoli, 1965.

1965 - cont.

Arc 726.248 Pesce, Gennaro. Le statuette puniche di Bithia. Roma, 1965.

Arc 612.50 Piggott, Stuart. Ancient Europe from the beginings of agriculture to classical antiquity. Edinburgh, 1965.

Arc 936.14.360 Polska Akademia Nauk. Instytut Historii Kultury Materialnej. Badania archeologiczne w Polsce w latach 1944-64. Wrocław, 1965.

Arc 505.146 Queen Elizabeth of Belgium Institute of Archaeology, Hebrew University, Jerusalem. Livre d'or de l'Institute d'archéologie. Bruxelles, 1965.

Arc 726.255 Radmilli, Antonio Mario. Abruzzo preistorico. Firenze, 1965.

Arc 543.65.5 Ranov, V.A. Kamennye rek Tadzhikistana. Dushambe, 1965.

Arc 1423.18.4 Reifenberg, A. Ancient Jewish coins. Jerusalem, 1965.

Arc 1335.156 Reinfeld, Fred. Catalogue of the world's most popular coins. Garden City, 1965.

Arc 1590.25 Resch, Adolf. Siebenbürgishe Münzen und Medaillen von 1538 bis zur Gegenwart. Montreal, 1965.

Arc 843.220 Ribeiro, Fernando Nunes. O bronze meridional português. Beja, 1965.

Arc 925.4.50 Rizhskii, Mikhail I. Iz glubiny vekov. Irkutsk, 1965.

Arc 746.47.5 Roncalli, Francesco. Le lastre dipinte da Cerveteri. Firenze, 1965.

Arc 450.38 Roy, Sita Ram. Karian excavations, 1955. Patna, 1965.

Arc 451.3 Sankalia, Hasmukh Dhirajlal. Excavations at Langhnaj, 1944-63. 1. ed. v.1-2. Poona, 1965.

Arc 1470.84 Schoenert-Geiss, E. Griechisches Münzwerk. Berlin, 1965. 2v.

Arc 903.5.1 Schreiber, Georg. Den Funden nach zu schliessen. 2. Aufl. Wien, 1965.

Arc 1540.35 Schreier, Ulrich. Die Münzen der Kanal-Inseln. Dortmund, 1965?

Arc 853.274 Schuldt, Ewald. Behren-Lübchin. Berlin, 1965.

Arc 853.346 Seitz, Hermann Josf. Die Steinzeit im Donaumoos. Augsburg, 1965.

Arc 1588.4.70 Sejbal, Jiří. Moravská mince doby husitské. Brno, 1965.

Arc 432.32 Seminar on Indian Prehistory and Protohistory, Deccan College Post Graduate and Research Institute, 1964. Indian prehistory. 1. ed. Poona, 1965.

Arc 925.50.27 Shovkoplias, Ivan H. Mezinskaia stoianka. Kiev, 1965.

Arc 1488.18 Simonetti, Luigi. Manuale di numismatica ialiana medioevale e moderna dalla caduta dell'impero romano alla rivoluzione francese. v.1, pt. 1. Firenze, 1965.

Arc 435.86 Sircar, Dineschandra. Indian epigraphy. 1. ed. Delhi, 1965.

Arc 936.195.105 Slovenská Akademia Vied. Archeologický Ústav, Nitra. Pravek Slovenska. Bratislava, 1965- 2v.

Arc 925.50.115F Smilenko, Alla T. Hlodos'ki skarby. Kyïv, 1965.

Arc 861.31.25 Smith, Isobel F. Windmill Hill and Avebury. Oxford, 1965.

Arc 853.276F Sprockhoff, Ernst. Atlas der Megalithgräber Deutschlands. Text and atlas. Bonn, 1965-75. 4v.

Arc 936.195.110 Štěpánek, Miroslav. Opevněná sídliště 8.-12. století ve střední Ezvropě. Praha, 1965.

Arc 608.17.35 Stucchi, Sandro. L'Agorà di Cirene. Roma, 1965.

Arc 412.2 Taylor, Joan du Plat. Marine archaeology. London, 1965.

Arc 1588.1.33 Terlecki, W. Ilustrowany katalog monet polskich bitych w okresie 1916-1965. 2. wyd. Warszawa, 1965.

Arc 608.73 Thamurida, fouilles du Service des antiquités du Maroc. v.1-2. Paris, 1965. 3v.

Arc 858.96 Thomas, Stanley E. Pre-Roman Britain. London, 1965.

Arc 853.136 Torbruegge, Walter. Die Hallstattzeit in der Oberpfalz. v.2. Kallmünz, 1965.

Arc 936.20.40 Tudor, D. Sucidara; une cité daco-romaine en Dacie. Bruxelles, 1965.

Arc 936.40.35 Vŭzharova, Zhivka N. Slavianski i slavianobulgarski selishta v bulgarskite semi. Sofiia, 1965.

Arc 936.14.137 Warsaw. Uniwersytet. Zespol Badan nad Polskim Sredniowieczem. IV konferencja w kielcach, 5 kwietnia 1963. Warszawa, 1965.

Arc 936.14.215 Warsaw. Uniwersytet. Zespól Badań nad Polskim Średniowieczem. Kolegiata wislicka. Kielce, 1965.

Arc 497.74 Williams, Walter George. Archaeology in Biblical research. N.Y., 1965.

Arc 925.150.10 Zagorul'ski, Edward M. Arkheologiia Belorussii. Minsk, 1965.

Arc 1675.98 Zaretti, Vincenzo. Della medaglie di Murano. Bologna, 1965.

Arc 853.290 Zuern, Hartwig. Das jungsteinzeitliche Dorf Ehrenstein. Stuttgart, 1965. 3v.

1966

Arc 612.56 Abramova, Zoia. Izobrasheniia cheloveka v paleoliticheskom iskusstve Evrazii. Leningrad, 1966.

Arc 432.34 Abu, Imam. Sir Alexander Cunningham and...Indian archaeology. Dacca, 1966.

Arc 1680.20 Africana Museum, Johannesburg. Tokens of South Africa. Johannesburg, 1966.

Arc 543.3.65 Akademiia nauk SSSR. Institut Arkheologod. Sredniaia Aziia v epokhu Kamnia i bronzy. Leningrad, 1966.

Arc 543.3.70 Akademiia nauk SSSR. Institut Etnografii. Material'naia Kul'tura narodov Srednei Azii i Kazakustana. Moskva, 1966.

Arc 416.33 Akademiia nauk SSSR. Institut narodov Azii. Deshifrovka i interpretatsiia pis'mennostei drevnego Vostoka. Moskva, 1966.

Arc 925.321 Akademiia Nauk SSSR. Karel'skii Filial, Petrozavedsk. Instituta Iazyka, Literatury i Istorii. Novye pamiatniki istorii drevnei Karelii. Leningrad, 1966.

Arc 608.75 Aksha. Paris, 1966- 3v.

Arc 497.31.10 Albright, William Foxwell. New horizons in Biblical research. London, 1966.

Arc 936.180.10 Aleksova, Blaga. Prosek-Demir Kapija. Skopje, 1966.

Arc 385.9.5 Amal'rikh, Aleksei S. Chto tahoe arkheologiia. Izd. 3. Moskva, 1966.

Arc 385.9.2 Amal'rikh, Aleksei S. V poiskakh ischeznuvshikh tsivilizatsii. Izd. 2. Moskva, 1966.

Arc 383.33.2 Amsterdam. Universiteit. Institut voor Prae- en Protohistorie. In het voetspoor van A.E. van Giffen. 2. druk. Groningen, 1966.

Arc 443.2 Ansari, Zainuddin. Excavations at Dwarka. 1. ed. Poona, 1966.

Arc 385.22 Anti, Carlo. Propedeutica archeologica. Padova, 1966.

Arc 936.185.5 Antonescu, T. Cetatea Sarmizegetusa reconstitutiă. Iasi, 1966.

Arc 612.70 Archaeologia urbiom. Warszawa, 1966. 2v.

Arc 925.50.3 Arkheolochichni pam"iatky Ukrains'koi RSR. Kyïv, 1966.

Chronological Listing

1966 - cont.

Arc 923.115 Arkheologicheskii sbornik. Moskva, 1966.

Arc 384.3 Arkheologiia starogo i novogo sveta. Moskva, 1966.

Arc 1433.73 Artuk, S. Demýhoci definesi. Ankara, 1966.

Arc 953.30 Baldwin, Gordon Cortis. Race against time. N.Y., 1966.

Arc 905.134 Bamberger, Anton. Tergolape. Linz, 1966.

Arc 412.1 Bass, George Fletcher. Archaeology under water. London, 1966.

Arc 861.38.8 Bath and Camerton Archaeological Society. A north Somerset miscellany. Bath, 1966.

Arc 936.180.15 Batović, Šime. Stariji neolit u Dalmaciji. Zadar, 1966.

Arc 1663.58 Belden, Bauman Lowe. Indian peace medals issued in the United States. New Milford, Conn., 1966.

Arc 1680.18 Bell, Robert Charles. Tradesmen's tickets and private tokens: 1785-1819. Newcastle-upon-Tyne, 1966.

Arc 936.20.50 Berciu, Dumitru. Neue Forschungsergebnisse zur Vorgeschichte Rumäniens. Bonn, 1966.

Arc 923.113 Beregovaia, Nina Aleksandrovna. Contributions to the archaeology of the Soviet Union. Cambridge, 1966.

Arc 340.10 Berlin. Universität. Institut für Ur- und Frühgeschichte. Bibliographie zur archäologischen Germanenforschung. Deutschsprachige Literatur 1941-1953. Berlin, 1966.

Arc 861.10.22 Bersu, Gerhard. Three Viking graves in the Isle of Man. London, 1966.

Arc 543.132 Boriskovskii, Pavel Io. Pervobytnoe proshloe B'etnama. Leningrad, 1966.

Arc 1588.1.60 Breslau. Zakład Narodowy im Ossalińskikh. Biblioteka. Tysiąc lat monety na ziemiach poliskich. Wrocław, 1966.

Arc 1478.21.2 British Museum. Department of Coins and Medals. Coins of the Roman Empire. v.1-3; v.4, pt.1-2; v.6. London, 1966. 6v.

Arc 609.21 Brokensha, David W. Applied anthropology in English speaking Africa. Lexington, Ky., 1966.

Arc 1349.75 Brunetti, Lodovico. Opus monetale cigoi. Bologna, 1966.

Arc 600.210F Bruyère, Bernard. Fouilles de Clysma-Qolzoum (Suez) 1930-1932. Le Caire, 1966.

Arc 1020.142 Cagiano de Azevedo, Michelangelo. Testimonianze archaeologiche della tradizione paolina a Malta. Roma, 1966.

Arc 861.188 Calkin, John Bernard. Discovering prehistoric Bournemouth and Christchurch: a record of local finds in the twentieth century. Christchurch, Hants, 1966.

Arc 608.76 Camps-Fabrer, Henriette. Matière et art mobilier dans la préhistoire nord-africaine. Thèse. Paris, 1966.

Arc 66.1.206 Cèbe, Jean Pierre. La caricature et la parodie dans le monde romain, antique des origines a Juvenal. Paris, 1966.

Arc 612.57 Chernych, Evgenii N. Istoriia drevneishei metallurgii Vostochnoi Evropy. Moskva, 1966.

Arc 383.70 Chevallier, Raymond. Mélanges d'archéologie et d'histoire. Paris, 1966. 3v.

Arc 853.282 Christlein, Rainer. Das alamannische Reihengräberfeld von Marktoberdorf im Allgäu. Kallmünz, 1966.

Arc 936.195.215 Čilinská, Zlata. Slawisch-awarisches Gräberfeld in Nové Zámky. Bratislava, 1966.

Arc 830.341 Clébert, Jean Paul. Provence antique. Paris, 1966. 2v.

Arc 936.14.190 Cnotliwy, Eugeniusz. Powiat kamicński w starozytności. Szczecin, 1966.

Arc 858.77 Conference on Romano-British Cantonal Capitals, University of Leicester, 1963. The civitas capitals of Roman Britain. Leicester, 1966.

Arc 383.83 Corolla memoriae Erich Swoboda dedicata. Graz, 1966.

Arc 66.1.208 Courbin, Paul. La céramique géométrique de l'Argolide. Paris, 1966. 2v.

Arc 913.18 Degen, Rudolf. Helvetia antiqua. Uitikon, 1966.

Arc 1508.25 Deutsche Bundesbank. Deutsche Taler von den Anfängen der Talerprägung bis zum Dreissigjährigen Krieg aus der Münzensammlung der Deutschen Bundesbank. Frankfurt, 1966?-67? 2v.

Arc 933.10 Deutsche Historiker Gesellschaft. Fachgruppe Ur- und Frühgeschichte. Problem des frühen Mittelalters in archäologischer und historischer Sicht. Berlin, 1966.

Arc 936.220.40 Djuhnić, Milena. Ilirska kneževska nekropola u atenici. Cačak, 1966.

Arc 1540.27.5 Dolley, Reginald Hugh Michael. The Norman conquest and the English coinage. London, 1966.

Arc 936.195.100F Dostál, Bořivoj. Slovanská pohřebiště za střední doby hradištní na Moravě. Praha, 1966.

Arc 925.50.145 Dovzhenok, Vasyl' I. Drevn'orus'ke misto Voin. Kyïv, 1966.

Arc 66.1.209 Ducat, Jean. Les vases plastiques rhodiens. Paris, 1966.

Arc 1510.150 Dudik, Beda. Des hahen deutschen Ritterordens Münz-Sammlung in Wien. Bonn, 1966.

Arc 1473.19 Dumbarton Oaks. Catalogue of the Byzantine coins in the Dumbarton Oaks collection and in the Whittemore collection. v. 1-3. Washington, 1966- 5v.

Arc 936.195.115F Dušek, Mikuláš. Thrakisches Gräberfeld der Hallstattzeit in Chotín. Bratislava, 1966.

Arc 1510.154 Duve, Gebhard. History of the redeemable, multiple and mining talers of Brunswick-Luneburg. 1. ed. Johannesburg, 1966.

Arc 609.13.10 East African Vocation School in Pre-European African History and Archaeology. Prelude to East African history: a collection of papers given at the first East African Vocation School in Pre-European History and Archaeology, in December, 1962. London, 1966.

Arc 938.97 Eesti NSV Teaduste Akadeemia. Ajaloo Institut. Pronksiajast varase feodalisimini. Tallinn, 1966.

Arc 810.65 Etienne, Robert. La vie quotidienne à Pompéi. Paris, 1966.

Arc 880.32 Evans, Emyr Estyn. Prehistoric and early Christian Ireland. London, 1966.

Arc 66.1.211 Favier, Jean. Les finances pontificales à l'époque du grand schisme d'Occident, 1378-1409. Paris, 1966.

Arc 1588.5.10 Fedorov, Dimitrii I. Monety pribaltiki XIII-XVIII stoletii. Tallin, 1966.

VArc 1583.24.5 Fedorov-Davydov, German A. Monety opowiadają o historii. Warszawa, 1966.

Arc 612.53.5 Filip, Jan. Enzyklopädisches Handbuch zur Ur- und Frühgeschichte Europas. Stuttgart, 1966. 2v.

Arc 936.195.140 Filip, Jan. Recent archaeological finds in Czechoslavakia. Prague, 1966.

Arc 390.16 Frantov, Grigoriis. Geofizika v arkheologii. Leningrad, 1966.

Arc 1138.65.2 Friedrich, Johannes. Entzifferung verschollener Schriften und Sprachen. 2. Aufl. Berlin, 1966.

1966 - cont.

Arc 1510.152.5 Funck, Walter. Die Notmünzen der deutschen Städt, Gemeinden, Kreise, Länder. 5. Aufl. Münster, 1966.

Arc 936.14.220 Gabałówna, Lidia. Zé studiów nad grupą brzesko-kujawską kultury lendzielskiej. Łódź, 1966.

Arc 936.220.3 Garašanin, Milutin V. Arheološki nalazi u Jugoslaviji. Beograd, 1966.

Arc 412.8 García y Bellido, Antonio. Urbanistica de las grandes ciudades del mundo antiguo. Madrid, 1966.

Arc 1494.57 Gil Farres, Octavia. La moneda hispanica en la edad antigua. Madrid, 1966.

Arc 556.5 Greener, Leslie. The discovery of Egypt. London, 1966.

Arc 543.2.6 Groslier, Bernard P. Angkor: art and civilization. N.Y., 1966.

Arc 543.66.30 Guliamov, Iukliia G. Pervobytnaia kul'tura i vorniknovenie oroshaemogo zemledeliia v mizov'iakh Zara Fsbana. Tashkend, 1966.

Arc 1285.10.8 Gumowski, M. Handbuch der polnischen Siegelkunde. Graz, 1966.

Arc 1349.73 Gumowski, Marian. Wspomnienia numizmatyka. Kraków, 1966.

Arc 505.140 Hachmann, Rolf. Bericht über die Ergebnisse der Ausgrabungen in Kamid el-Loz (Libanon) in den Jahren 1963 und 1964. Bonn, 1966.

Arc 1138.80.6 Hector, Leonard Charles. The handwriting of English documents. 2. ed. London, 1966.

Arc 416.32 Hierche, Henri. Manuel d'archéologie d'Extrême-Orient. Paris, 1966- 2v.

Arc 861.25.5 Hill-Forts Study Group. Hill-forts in Dorset. Bristol, 1966.

Arc 1588.10.20 Hlinka, Jozef. Bratislavské korunovačné medaily a žetóny. Vyd. 1. Bratislava, 1966.

Arc 340.13 Holm, S.E. Bibliography of South African pre- and proto-historic archaeology. Pretoria, 1966.

Arc 435.1.1 India. Archaeological Survey. Reports. Varanasi, 1966-72. 24v.

Arc 923.112 International Congress of Prehistoric and Protohistoric Sciences. 7th, Moscow, 1966. Doklady i soobshcheniia arkheologov SSSR. Moskva, 1966.

Arc 936.195.150 International Congress of Prehistoric and Protohistoric Sciences, 7th, Prague. Investigations archéologiques en Tchécoslovaquie. Prague, 1966.

Arc 925.322.5 Isakov, Magomed I. Arkheologicheskie pamiatniki Dagestana. Makhachkala, 1966.

VArc 412.11 Jażdżewski, Konrad. Ochrona zabytków archeologicznych. Warszawa, 1966.

Arc 497.51.5 Jirku, Anton. Von Jerusalem nach Ugarit. Graz, 1966.

Arc 1588.1.65 Kamiński, Czesław. Katalog banknotów i monet Polskiej Rzeczy pospolitej Ludowej. pt.1-2. Warszawa, 1966-68.

Arc 848.57 Kellermann, Volkmar. Germanische Altertumskunde. Berlin, 1966.

Arc 938.85.10 Kivikoski, Ella. Suomen kiinteät muinaisjäännökset. Helsinki, 1966.

Arc 925.150.23 Konferentsiia no Arkheologii Belorussii i Smezhnykh Territorii, Minsk, 1966. Drevnosti Belorussii. Minsk, 1966.

Arc 936.14.92 Kostrzewski, Józef. Pradzieje Pomorza. Wrocław, 1966.

Arc 925.13.125 Lapin, Vladimir V. Grecheskaia kolonizatsiia Severnogo Prichernomor'ia. Kiev, 1966.

Arc 612.60 Laplace, Georges. Recherches sur l'origine et l'évolution des complexes leptolithiques. Paris, 1966.

Arc 925.180.25 Larichev, Vitalii E. Taina kamennoi cherepakhi. Novosibirsk, 1966.

Arc 915.4.14 Laur-Belart, Rudolf. Führer durch Augusta Raurica. 4. Aufl. Basel, 1966.

Arc 925.9.55 Lavrov, L.I. Epigraficheskie pamiatniki severnogo Kavkaza. Moskva, 1966- 2v.

Arc 66.1.205 Leglay, Marcel. Saturne africain; histoire. Paris, 1966.

Arc 815.30 Leppmann, Wolfgang. Pompeji. Eine Stadt in Literatur und Leben. München, 1966.

Arc 1470.26.5 Le Rider, Georges. Monnaies crétoises du Ve au Ier siècle avant J.C. Thèse. Paris, 1966.

VArc 396.21 Lesicjewicz, Anna. 500 zagadek archeologicznych. Warszawa, 1966.

Arc 1588.1.37 Lublin (City). Museum Lubelskie. Tysiąc lat monety polskiej. Lublin, 1966.

Arc 936.14.195 Łuka, Leon J. Kultura wschodniopomorska na Pomorzu Odańskim. Wrocław, 1966.

Arc 397.18.2 Macaulay, Rose. Pleasure of ruins. London, 1966.

Arc 936.14.225 Machnik, Jan. Studia nad kulturą ceramiki sznurowej w Małopolsce. Wrocław, 1966.

Arc 1542.2 Malmer, Brita. Nordiska mynt före år 1000. Bonn, 1966.

Arc 530.12.42 Marek, Kurt W. Enge Schlucht und Schwarzer Berg. Reinbek, 1966.

Arc 384.2.5 Marek, Kurt W. Hands on the past. 1. American ed. N.Y., 1966.

Arc 384.2 Marek, Kurt W. The world of archaeology. London, 1966.

Arc 925.16.17 Margulan, A.K. Drevniaia kul'tura Tsentral'nogo Kazakhstana. Alma-Ata, 1966.

Arc 843.235 Martinez i Hualde, Angel. El poblat ibèric de Puig Castellar. Barcelona, 1966.

Arc 925.4.25 Martynov, Anatolii O. Lodki, v strany predkov. Kemerovo, 1966.

Arc 1330.18 Mayer, Leo Ary. A bibliography of Jewish numismatics. Jerusalem, 1966.

Arc 383.55.5 Mélanges offerts à Kazimierz Michałowski. Warszawa, 1966.

Arc 513.32A Mellaart, James. The Chaleolithic and early Bronze Ages in the Near East and Anatolia. Beirut, 1966.

Arc 397.24 Mellersh, Harold Edward Leslie. Archaeology: science and romance. Exeter, 1966.

Arc 1588.5.6 Metcalf, David Michael. Coinage in the Balkans, 820-1355. Chicago, 1966.

Arc 936.180.5 Mikulčić, Ivan. Pelagonija u svetlosti arheoloških nalaza. Beograd, 1966.

Arc 895.67 Moberg, Carl Axel. Spår från tusentals år. Stockholm, 1966.

Arc 1274.9 Morgan, Frederick Charles. A concise list of seals belonging to the Dean and Chapter of Hereford Cathedral. Hereford, 1966.

Arc 1423.22 Muehsam, Alice. Coin and temple; a study of the architectural representation on ancient Jewish coins. Leeds, 1966.

Arc 397.26 Müller-Karpe, Hermann. Handbuch der Vorgeschichte. v.1-3. München, 1966- 6v.

Arc 450.34 Mujumdar, Ganesh. Ashmound excavations at Kupgal. 1. ed. Poona, 1966.

Arc 1190.86.5 Nedkov, Boris K. Osmanotwiska diplomatika: paleografiia. Sofiia, 1966-72. 2v.

Chronological Listing

1966 - cont.

Arc 505.129 Negev, Avraham. Cities of the desert. Tel-Aviv, 1966.

Arc 543.145 Negmatov, Numan. Srednevekovyi Shakhristan. Dushambe, 1966.

Arc 543.3.57 Nerazik, Elena E. Sel'skie poseleniia afriyid skogo Khorezma. Moskva, 1966.

Arc 853.294 Neuffer-Müller, Christiane. Ein Reihengräberfriedhof in Sontheim an der Brenz. Stuttgart, 1966.

Arc 66.1.207 Nicolet, Claude. L'ordre équestre. Paris, 1966-74. 2v.

Arc 1078.3 Niel, Fernand. Dolmens et menhirs. 3. éd. Paris, 1966.

Arc 880.43 Northern Ireland. Ministry of Finance. Ancient monuments of Northern Ireland. v.1-2. Belfast, 1966-69.

Arc 830.342 Nouel, André. Manuel de préhistoire par le sud du Bassin parisien. Orléans, 1966.

Arc 925.180.5F Okladnikov, Aleksei Pavlovich. Petroglify Angary. Leningrad, 1966.

Arc 1588.6.2.10 Ölçer, Cüneyt. San alti osmanli padişahi zamaninda Istanbulda basilan gümuç paralor. Istanbul, 1966.

Arc 936.14.180 Olczak, Jerzy. Zrodła archeologiczne do studiow nad wczesnosredniowiecznym osadnictwem grodowym na terenie wojewodztwa. Poznań, 1966- 4v.

Arc 726.36.10 Otto, prince of Hesse. Die langobardenzeitlichen Grabfunde aus Fiesole bei Florenz. München, 1966.

Arc 412.5 Pannell, John Percival Masterman. The technology of industrial archaeology. Newton Abbot, 1966.

Arc 843.208 Pavón Maldonado, Basilio. Memoria de la excavación de la Mezquita de Medinat al-Zahra. Madrid, 1966.

Arc 726.290 Pesce, Gennaro. Tharros. Cagliari, 1966.

Arc 853.286 Pirling, Renate. Das römisch-fränkische Gräberfeld vor Krefeld-Gellep. Berlin, 1966. 2v.

Arc 403.16.40 Poole, Lynn. One passion, two loves; the story of Heinrich and Sophia Schliemann. N.Y., 1966.

Arc 1076.20 Potratz, Johannes Albert Heinrich. Die Pferdetrensen des alten Orient. Roma, 1966.

Arc 1163.38F Poulle, Emmanuel. Paléographie des écritures cursives en France du 15e au 17e siècle. Genève, 1966.

Arc 936.195.135 Pravek východného Slovenska. Košice, 1966.

Arc 543.66.25 Puga-Chenkova, Galina A. Khalchaian. Tashkent, 1966.

Arc 853.275F Rempel, Heinrich. Reihengräberfriedhofe des 8. bis 11. Jahrhunderts. Berlin, 1966.

Arc 726.295 Rittatore Vonwiller, Ferrante. La necropoli preromana della Ca'Morta, Scavi 1955-1965. Como, 1966.

Arc 870.26 Rural settlement in Roman Britain. London, 1966.

Arc 672.10 Rutkowski, Bogdan. Larnaksy egejskie. Wrocław, 1966.

Arc 543.146 Sarianidi, Viktor I. Za barkhanami, proshloe. Moskva, 1966.

Arc 608.33.15 Savary, Jean Pierre. Monuments en pierres séches du Fadnoun, Tassili n'Ajjer. Paris, 1966.

Arc 848.56 Schrickel, Waldtraut. Westeuropäische Elemente im neolithischen Grabbau Mitteldeutschlands und die Galeriegräber Westdeutschlands und ihre Inventare. Bonn, 1966. 2v.

Arc 810.68 Seedorff Pedersen, Hans H.O. Pompeji. København, 1966.

Arc 383.29 Sen, D. Studies in prehistory; robert Bruce Foote memorial volume. Calcutta, 1966.

Arc 925.16.25 Sher, Iakov A. Kamennye iz vaianiia Semirech'ia. Leningrad, 1966.

Arc 458.12 Sircar, Dineschandra. Indian epigraphical glossary. 1. ed. Delhi, 1966.

Arc 1568.5 Skaare, Kolbjørn. Moneta Norwei. Oslo, 1966.

Arc 925.13.120 Smirnov, Aleksei P. Skify. Moskva, 1966.

Arc 1518.10 Société Royale de Numismatique de Belgique. Exposition numismatique, Bruxelles, Bibliothèque Albert I., 30 avril-24 mai, 1966. Bruxelles, 1966.

Arc 936.195.120 Soudský, Bohumil. Bylany. Praha, 1966.

Arc 889.35 Stadskernonderzoek in Amsterdam (1954-1962). Groningen, 1966.

Arc 543.3.60 Staviskii, Boris Ia. Mezhdu Pamirom i Kaspiem. Moskva, 1966.

Arc 340.9 Sviridova, I.N. Po sledam drevnikh kul'tur. Moskva, 1966.

Arc 1538.23.2 Sylloge of coins of the British Isles. Series B. London, 1966.

Arc 659.10 Terzaghi, Nicola. Prometeo; scritti di archeologia e filologia. Torino, 1966.

Arc 935.32.10 Tezcan, Burhan. 1964 kaçumbeli kazese. Ankara, 1966.

Arc 935.32.5 Tezcan, Burhan. 1964 yalencak köyü çaleşmalare. Ankara, 1966.

Arc 1163.3.85 Tikhomlrov, Mikhail N. Russkaia paleografiia. Moskva, 1966.

Arc 672.1.114 Tiré, Claire. Guide des fouilles françaises en Crète. Athènes, 1966.

Arc 726.254 Trump, David H. Central and suthern Italy before Rome. London, 1966.

Arc 66.1.210 Turcan, Robert. Les sarcophages romains à representations dionysiaques. Paris, 1966.

Arc 726.275 Usai, Angelino. Il villaggio nuragico di Seleni, Lanusei. Cagliari, 1966.

Arc 936.100.35 Vinkovci. Gradski Muzej. 20 godina Muzeja Vinkovci 1946-66. Vinkovci, 1966.

Arc 936.195.93 Volovek, V. Pohřebiště a súdliště lidu popelnicóvych poń v Třebešově. Hradec Králové, 1966.

Arc 700.59 Wąsowicz, Aleksandra. Obróbka drewna w Starożytnej Grecji. Wrocław, 1966.

Arc 407.20 Wheeler, Robert Eric Mortimer. Alms for oblivion: an antiquary's scrapbook. London, 1966.

Arc 432.26 Wheeler, Robert Eric Mortimer. Civilizations of the Indus Valley and beyond. London, 1966.

Arc 572.11 Wolf, Walther. Funde in Ägypten. Göttingen, 1966.

Arc 861.172 Workers' Educational Association. Slough and Eton Branch. The Middle Thames in antiquity. Slough, Bucks, 1966.

Arc 1251.2 Xenakē-Sakellariou, Agnē. Mykēnaike Zphragidoglyphia. Athēnai, 1966.

Arc 505.128 Yadin, Yigael. Masada; Herod's fortress and the Zealot's last stand. N.Y., 1966.

Arc 505.128.1 Yadin, Yigael. Masada: Herod's fortress and the Zealot's last stand. London, 1966.

Arc 530.167 Yesaian, Stepan. Oruzhie i voennoe delo drevnei Armenii. Greoan, 1966.

Arc 936.14.205 Zoll-Adamikowa, Helena. Wczesnośredniowieczne cmentarzyska szkieltowe Małopolski. Wrocław, 1966-71. 2v.

1967

Arc 384.12.3 Das Abenteuer Archäologie. 3. Aufl. München, 1967.

Arc 936.155.20 Akademiia Nauk Kirgizskoi SSR, Frunze. Institut Istorii. Drevniaia i rannesrednevekovaia kul'tura Kirgizstana. Frunze, 1967.

Arc 530.6.5F Alfoldi-Rosenbaum, Elizabeth. A survey of coastal cities in Western Cilicia. Ankara, 1967.

Arc 1330.6.2F American Numismatic Society. Library. Dictionary and auction catalogues of the Library of the American Numismatic Society. First and second supplement. Boston, 1967. 2v.

Arc 497.85 Applebaum, Shimon. Israel and her vicinity in the Roman and Byzantine periods. Tel-Aviv, 1967.

Arc 497.80 Archaeological discoveries in the Holy Land. N.Y., 1967.

Arc 612.72 L'archéologie du village médiéval. Louvain, 1967.

Arc 385.20 Arias, Paolo Enrico. Storia dell'archeologia. Milano, 1967.

Arc 1163.5.30 Arif, Aida S. Arabic lapidary Kūfic in Africa. London, 1967.

Arc 923.116 Avdusin, Daniil A. Arkheologiia SSSR. Moskva, 1967.

Arc 1033.12.9.15 Bachinger, Rudolf. Das Leichentuch von Turin. Stein am Rhein, 1967.

Arc 853.370 Bayer, Heinrich. Die ländliche Besiedlung Rheinhessens. Inaug. Diss. Mainz, 1967?

Arc 612.65 Behn, Friedrich. Die Bronzezeit in Nordeuropa. Bildnis einer prähistorischen Hochkultur. Stuttgart, 1967.

Arc 340.16 Beilekchi, V.S. Bibliografiia po arkheologii Moldavii, 1946-1966. Kishinev, 1967.

Arc 936.220.30 Belgrade. Narodni Muzej. Lepenski vir. Beograd, 1967.

Arc 936.24 Berciu, Dumitru. Romania. N.Y., 1967.

Arc 672.11 Boardman, John. Excavations in Chios, 1952-1955. London, 1967.

Arc 830.343 Bourdier, Franck. Préhistoire de France. Paris, 1967.

Arc 853.356 Brandt, Karl Heinz. Studien über steinerne Äxte und Beile der jüngeren Steinzeit und der Stein-Kupferzeit Nordwestdeutschlands. Hildesheim, 1967.

Arc 925.13.130 Brashinskii, I. Sokrovishcha skifskikh tsarei. Moskva, 1967.

Arc 551.20 Bratton, Fred Gladstone. A history of Egyptian archaeology. London, 1967.

Arc 386.29.10 Brion, Marcel. De Pompéi a l'île de Pâques. Paris, 1967.

Arc 925.331.5 Burov, Grigorii M. Arkheologicheskie pamiatniki Vychegodskoi doliny. Syktyvkar, 1967.

Arc 925.331.10 Burov, Grigorii M. Drevnii Sindar. Moskva, 1967.

Arc 1418.24 Chattopadhyay, Bhaskar. The age of the Kushānas; a numismatic study. 1. ed. Calcutta, 1967.

Arc 925.330 Chlenova, Natalia L. Proiskhozhdenie i ranniaia istoriia plemen Tagarskoi kul'tury. Moskva, 1967.

Arc 936.14.245 Chmtelewski, Waldemar. Materiały do prahistorii plejstocenu i wczesnego holocenu Polski. Wrocław, 1967.

Arc 1357.5 Christ, Karl. Antike Numismatik. Darmstadt, 1967.

Arc 889.36 Clason, Antje Trientje. Animal and man in Holland's past. v.1-2. Groningen, 1967.

Arc 861.175 Colchester, England. Museum and Muniment Committee. Colonia-Claudia Victricensis: the story of Roman Colchester. Colchester, 1967.

Arc 1411.14 Coole, Arthur Braddan. An encyclopedia of Chinese coins. 1. ed. Denver, 1967.

Arc 726.235.10 Cortesi, Giuseppe. Il porto e la città di classe. Alfonsine, 1967.

Arc 858.82 Council for British Archaeology, London. Iron Age and Roman Research Committees. The Iron Age in Northern Britain. Edinbrugh, 1967.

Arc 1520.20 Crab, Jan. De munt to Leuven tot het einde der XVe eeuw. Leuven, 1967.

Arc 865.26 Crampton, Patrick. Stonehenge of the kings: a people appear. London, 1967.

Arc 1503.7 Divo, Jean-Paul. Die Münzen der Schweiz im 19. und 20. Jahrhundert. Zürich, 1967.

Arc 1163.40.2 Duelfer, Kurt. Schrifttafeln zur deutschen Paläographie. v.1-2. 2. Aufl. Marburg, 1967.

Arc 853.315 Engels, Heinz-Josef. Die Hallstatt und Latènekultur in der Pfalz. Diss. n.p., 1967.

Arc 1185.9.5 Erben, Wilhelm. Die Kaiser- und Königsurkunden des Mittelalters in Deutschland, Frankreich und Italien. München, 1967.

Arc 513.38 Erder, Cevat. Hellenistik devir Anadolu nimorisinde kyma. Ankara, 1967.

Arc 1588.13 Ered, Serafeddin. Nadir hirkaç sikke. Ankara? 1967.

Arc 889.32 Es, William Albertus van. Wijster; a native village beyond the imperial frontier, 150-425 A.D. Text and atlas. Groningen, 1967. 2v.

Arc 609.24 Fagan, Brian. Iron Age cultures in Zambia. London, 1967- 2v.

Arc 1076.3.90 Fehrmann, Christiaan Nathanaël. De Kamper klokgieters. Kampen, 1967.

Arc 340.25.7 Field, Henry. Bibliography of Soviet archaeology and physical anthropology, 1936-1967. n.p., 1967.

Arc 497.67 Franken, Hedricus J. Van aartsvaders tot prafeten. Amsterdam, 1967.

Arc 600.222 Gamer-Wallert, Ingrid. Der verziete Löffel; seine Formgeschichte und Verwendung im alten Ägypten. Wiesbaden, 1967.

Arc 936.6.35 Gediga, Bogusław. Plemiona kultury łuzyckiej w epoce brazu na śląsku środkowym. Text and atlas. Wrocław, 1967.

Arc 543.83 Gerlach, Eva. Sand über den Tempeln Arabiens. 2. Aufl. Leipzig, 1967.

Arc 1433.96 Goebl, Robert. Dokumente zur Geschichte der iranischen Hunnen in Baktrien und Indien. v.1,2,3-4. Wiesbaden, 1967. 3v.

Arc 1550.8.15 Golster, Georg. Flensborg mønt, 14. og 16. århundrede. Udg. af numismatisk forening for nord-og sydslesvig. Sønderborg, 1967.

Arc 838.36 Gómez Tabanera, José Manuel. Las raices de España. Madrid, 1967.

Arc 938.17.10 Graudonis, Jánis. Latviia v epokhu pozdnei bronzy i rannego sheleza. Riga, 1967.

Arc 875.56 Great Britain. Commissions. Ancient and Historical Monuments of Scotland. Peeblesshire: an inventory of the ancient monuments. Edinburgh, 1967. 2v.

Arc 858.47.16.5 Great Britain. Ministry of Works. Illustrated guide to ancient monuments. Edinburgh, 1967.

Arc 1423.25 Haffner, Sylvia. The history of modern Israel's money, 1917 to 1967, including state medals and Palestine mandate. 1st ed. La Mesa? 1967.

Arc 895.70 Hagberg, Ulf Eric. The archaeology of Skedemosse. Stockholm, 1967. 3v.

Chronological Listing

1967 - cont.

Arc 785.83 Hagen, Victor Wolfgang von. The roads that led to Rome. London, 1967.

Arc 1433.5.15 Hamidi, Hakim. A catalog of modern coins of Afghanistan. 1. English ed. Kabal, 1967.

Arc 1570.8 Hansen, Per. Norsk numismatisk forenings historie: 1927-1967. Oslo, 1967.

Arc 505.68.6 Harding, Gerald. The antiquities of Jordan. London, 1967.

Arc 497.81F Hennessy, John Basil. The foreign relations of Palestine during the early bronze age. London, 1967.

Arc 421.30 Hentze, Carl. Funde in Alt-China. Göttingen, 1967.

Arc 936.14.260 Hilczerówna, Zofia. Dorzecze górnej i środkowej Obry od VI do początków XI wieku. Wrocław, 1967.

Arc 557.8 Hornung, Erik. Einführung in die Ägyptologie. Darmstadt, 1967.

Arc 936.195.190 Huml, Václav. Zaniklá turz Semonice. Hradec Králové, 1967.

Arc 1423.26 International Numismatic Convention, Jerusalem, 1963. The patterns of monetary development in Phoenicia and Palestine in antiquity. Tel-Aviv, 1967.

Arc 1010.17 Jacob, Teuku. Some problems pertaining to the racial history of the Indonesian region. Utrecht, 1967.

Arc 1508.15.20 Jaeger, Kurt. Die deutschen Münzen seit 1871. 6. Aufl. Basel, 1967.

Arc 1508.15.15 Jaeger, Kurt. Die Münzprägungen der deutschen Staaten von Einführung des Reichswährung. v.3. Basel, 1967.

Arc 1330.9 Janovský, Hubert. Katalog knihovny. Numismatické společnosti československé v Praze. vyd. 1. Praha, 1967.

Arc 858.86 Jessup, Ronald Frederick. Age by age. London, 1967.

Arc 861.192.5 Joint Excavation Committee of the Wakefield Corporation and the Wakefield Historical Society. Sandal Castle excavations, 1967. Wakefield, Eng., 1967?

Arc 1309.1.5 Journal international d'archéologie numismatique. Analytical index. 1898-1927. N.Y., 1967.

Arc 925.50.160 Kam'iana Mohyla. Kyïv, 1967. 2 pam.

Arc 505.5.105 Kenyon, Kathleen M. Jerusalem: excavating 3000 years of history. London, 1967.

Arc 595.68 Kink, Khil'da A. Kak stroilis' egipetskte piramidy. Moskva, 1967.

Arc 938.85.5 Kivikoski, Ella. Finland. London, 1967.

Arc 895.76 Knuth, Eigil. Archaeology of the musk-ox way. Paris, 1967.

Arc 1588.6.25 Kocaer, Remje. Osmanli altinlari. Istanbul, 1967.

Arc 853.284F Koch, Robert. Bodenfunde der Völkerwanderungszeit aus dem Main-Tauber-Gebiet. Diss. Berlin, 1967. 2v.

Arc 853.280F Koerber-Grohne, Udelgard. Geobotanische Untersuchungen auf der Feddersen Wierde. Wiesbaden, 1967. 2v.

Arc 925.150.25 Konferentsiia po Arkheologii Belorussii, Minsk, 1968. Belorusskie drevnosti. Minsk, 1967.

Arc 925.269 Konstantinov, Ivan V. Material'naia kul'tura Iakutov XVIII veka. Photoreproduction. Novosibirsk, 1967.

Arc 530.141F Kosay, H.Z. Guzelova karisi. Ankara, 1967.

Arc 925.50.140 Kovpanenko, Halyna T. Plemena skifs'koho chasu na Vorskli. Kyïv, 1967.

Arc 925.285.5 Kozyreva, Rimma V. Drevnii Sakhalin. Leningrad, 1967.

Arc 853.298 Krämer, Wolfgang. Neue Beiträge zur Vor- und Frühgeschichte von Gauting. München, 1967.

Arc 933.5 Kropotkin, Vladislav V. Ekonomicheskie sviazi Vostochnoi Evropy v I tysiacheletii neshei ery. Moskva, 1967.

Arc 853.325 Krueger, Bruno. Dessau-Mosigkau. Berlin, 1967.

Arc 853.287 La Baume, Peter. Das fränkische Gräberfeld von Junkersdorf bei Köln. Berlin, 1967.

Arc 505.130 Lafontaine-Dosogne, Jacqueline. Itinéraires archéologiques dans la région d'Antioche. Bruxelles, 1967.

Arc 766.1.9.1 Lanciani, R. The destruction of ancient Rome. N.Y., 1967.

Arc 608.78 Lefebvre, Gillette. Corpus des gravures et des peintures rupestres de la région de Constantine. Paris, 1967.

Arc 885.30 Lewis, Ewart Thomas. Mynachlogddu: a guide to its antiquities. Clunderwen, 1967.

Arc 853.26.5 Lindemann, Kurt. Der Hildesheimer Silberfund. Hildesheim, 1967.

Arc 416.35 Loofs, Helmut Hermann Ernst. Elements of the megalithic complex in Southeast Asia. Canberra, 1967.

Arc 608.42.5 McBurney, Charles. The Hana Fteah (Cyrenaica) and the Stone Age of the South-East Mediterranean. London, 1967.

Arc 1423.9.6 Madden, Frederic W. History of Jewish coinage, and of money. San Diego, 1967.

Arc 1423.9.7 Madden, Frederic W. History of Jewish coinage. N.Y., 1967.

Arc 853.20.35F Mahr, Gustav. Die jüngere Latènekultur des trierer Landes. Berlin, 1967.

Arc 870.4.21.2 Margary, Ivan D. Roman roads in Britain. London, 1967.

Arc 830.352 Maury, Jean. Les étapes du peuplement sur les grands causses des origines à l'époque gallo-romaine. Millau, 1967.

Arc 925.150.15 Mel'nikovskaia, Ol'ga N. Plemena Iuzhnoi Belorussii v rannem zheleznom veke. Moskva, 1967.

Arc 1423.23 Meshorer, Va'akov. Jewish coins of the second temple period. Tel-Aviv, 1967.

Arc 1588.5.8 Metcalf, David Michael. Classification of Byzantine stamena in the light of a hoard found in southern Serbia. Ljubljana, 1967.

Arc 936.14.255 Metodyka naukowo-techniczna badań archeologicznych i antropologicznych. Warszawa, 1967.

Arc 936.220.35 Mijović, Pavle. Monodija o kamenu. Kruševac, 1967.

Arc 441.23 Misra, Virendra Nath. Pre- and proto-history of the Berach Basin, South Rajasthan. 1. ed. Poona, 1967.

Arc 600.220F Missione Archeologica in Egitto. Tamit, 1964. Roma, 1967.

Arc 530.181 Mollaart, James. Çatal Hüyük. N.Y., 1967.

Arc 1408.7 Moshniagin, D.I. Monety stran zarubezhnoi Azii i Afriki XIX-XX veka. Moskva, 1967.

Arc 905.128 Mozsolics, Anália. Bronzefunde des Karpatenbeckens. Budapest, 1967.

Arc 936.14.235 Nadolski, Andrzej. Sciezki archeologów. Łódź, 1967.

Arc 1330.25 Noble, Fiona Virginia. South African numismatics, 1652-1965; a bibliography. Capetown, 1967.

Arc 936.14.240 Nosek, Stefan. Kultura amfor kulistych. Wrocław, 1967.

Arc 936.14.105 Nosek, Stefan. Zarys historii badań archeologicznych w Małopolsce. Wrocław, 1967.

Arc 905.12.35 Obermayr, August. Römerstadt Carnuntum. Wien, 1967.

Arc 726.258 Östenberg, Carl Eric. Luni sul Mignone e problemi della preistoria d'Italia. Lund, 1967.

Arc 530.169 Orthmann, Winfried. Das Gräberfeld bei Ilica. Wiesbaden, 1967.

Arc 1163.3.90 Paleografiia. Moskva, 1967.

Arc 925.322.15 Pikul', Milifsa I. Epokha rannego zheleza v Dagestane. Makhachkala, 1967.

Arc 925.41 Pomiatniki epokhi bronzy inga Evropeiskoi chasti SSSR. Kiev, 1967.

Arc 1010.15 Ponosov, V.V. Results of an archaeological survey of the southern region of Moreten Bay and of Moreten Island, 1963-64. St. Lucian, Brisbane, 1967.

Arc 936.195.165 Poulík, Josef. Pevnost v lužním lese. 1. vyd. Praha, 1967.

Arc 530.166 Przeworski, Stefan. Opera selecta. Wrocław, 1967.

Arc 66.1.63.5 Radet, Georges. La Lydie et le monde grec au temps des Mesmnades, 687-546. Roma, 1967.

Arc 726.341.5 Rainey, Froelich G. The search for Sybaris, 1960-1965. Roma, 1967.

Arc 1076.4.10 Rausing, Gad. The bow; some notes on its origin and development. Bonn, 1967.

Arc 1185.10.15 Redlich, Oswald. Der Privaturkunden des Mittelalters. München, 1967.

Arc 412.12 Rieth, Adolf. Vorzeit gefälscht. Tübingen, 1967.

Arc 1490.96 Rinaldi, Alfio. Catalogo delle medaglie papali annuali da Pio VII a Paolo VI. Verona, 1967.

Arc 1570.5 . Rønning, Bjørn R. Norges mynter i 150 år, 1816-1966. Oslo, 1967.

Arc 925.136.5 Sal'nikov, Konstantin V. Ocherki drevnei istorii Iuzhnogo Urala. Moskva, 1967.

Arc 505.35.10 Sapir, Baruch. Capernaum (Kfar-Nochum). Tel Aviv, 1967.

Arc 543.146.5 Sarianidi, Viktor I. Tainy ischeznuvshego iskusstva Karakumov. Moskva, 1967.

Arc 726.280 Sarsina: la cita romana, il museo archeologico. Faenza, 1967.

Arc 925.39 Savvateev, Iurii A. Risunki na skalakh. Petrozavodsk, 1967.

Arc 726.318 Schumacher, Erich. Die Protovillanova-Fundgruppe. Bonn, 1967.

Arc 1163.3.4 Shchepkin, Viacheslav N. Russkaia paleografiia. Moskva, 1967.

Arc 925.20.5 Shelov, Dmitrii B. Tanais, poteriannyi i naidennyi gorod. Moskva, 1967.

Arc 1548.5 Soemod, Jørgen. Danmarks og Norges mønter, 1448-1540. Kjøbenhavn, 1967.

Arc 726.300 Sommella, Paolo. Antichi campi di battaglia in Italia. Roma, 1967.

Arc 843.212 Sousa Gomes, A. A citânia de briteiros através dos séculos. Lisboa, 1967.

Arc 853.359 Stein, Frauke. Adelsgräber des achten Jahrhunderts in Deutschland. Berlin, 1967. 2v.

Arc 925.332.5 Stepanov, Pavel D. Osh Paudo. Saransk, 1967.

Arc 1077.13 Stjernqvist, Berta. Cesta a cordoni (Rippenzisten); Produktion-Funktion-Diffusion. v.1-2. Bonn, 1967.

Arc 658.10 Styrenius, Carl Gustaf. Submycenaean studies. Lund, 1967.

Arc 1330.10 A survey of numismatic research 1960-1965. v.1-3. Copenhagen, 1967.

Arc 612.69 Sympozjum Paleolityczne, 3d, Kraków, 1967. III. sympozjum paleolityczne, Kraków 30 XI-2 XII, 1967. v.1-2. Kraków, 1967.

Arc 936.14.250 Szymański, Wojciech. Szeligi pod Płockiem na początku wczesnego średniowiecza. Wrocław, 1967.

Arc 659.15 Tagung das Problem der Klassik im Alten Orient und in der Antike, Halle, 1966. Das Problem der klassik im Alten Orient und in der Antike. Berlin, 1967.

Arc 936.180.20 Tasić, Nikola. Badenski i vučedolski kulturni kompleks u Jugoslaviji. Beograd, 1967.

Arc 858.84 Thom, Alexander. Megalithic sites in Britain. Oxford, 1967.

Arc 861.174 Thomas, Charles. Christian antiquities of Camborne. St. Austell, Cornwall, 1967.

Arc 497.86 Thomas, David Winton. Archaeology and Old Testament study. Oxford, 1967.

Arc 925.329 Thompson, Michael W. Novgorod the Great. London, 1967.

Arc 1448.8 Vaccaro, Francesco. Le monete di Aksum. Casteldario, 1967.

Arc 925.237 Vadetskaia, El'ga B. Drevnie idoly Eniseia. Leningrad, 1967.

Arc 726.305 Venetia. Padova, 1967- 2v.

Arc 923.114 Vsesoiuznaia Sessiia, Posviashchennaia Itogam Arkheologicheskikh i Etnograficheskikh Issledovanii 1966 goda. Tezisy dokladov. Kishinev, 1967.

Arc 885.28 Wainwright, G. Coygan Camp; a prehistoric Romano-British and Dark Age settlemant in Carmarthenshire. Cwmgwyn, 1967.

Arc 609.28 Willett, Frank. Ife in the history of west African sculpture. N.Y., 1967.

Arc 1148.28F Wittek, Martin. Album de paléographie grecque. Gand, 1967.

Arc 969.15 Wright, James V. The laurel tradition and the middle woodland period. Ottawa, 1967.

1968

Arc 1018.60 Aebischer, Paul. Linguistique romane et histoire religieuse. Abadía de San Cugat del Valles, 1968.

Arc 1510.160 Alexander, Prince of Messe and of the Rhine, 1823-1888. Mainzisches Münzcabinet des Prinzen Alexander von Hessen. Faksimile. Münster, 1968.

Arc 609.17.15 Allison, Philip. Cross River monoliths. Laejos, 1968.

Arc 1232.10 Alp, Sedat. Zylinder- und Stempelsiegel aus Karahöyük bei Konya. Ankara, 1968.

Arc 1335.159 American University of Beirut. Archaeological Museum. The coins exhibited in the Archaeological Museum of the American University of Beirut. Beirut, 1968.

Arc 925.13.150 Antichnaia istoriia i kul'tura Sredizemnomor'ia i Prichernomor'ia. Leningrad, 1968.

Arc 1153.100 Apianus, Petrus. Abbrevationes vetustorum monumentorum, in ordinem alphabeticum digestae. München, 1968.

Arc 925.150.35 Arkheologicheskaia karta Belorussii. Minsk, 1968- 2v.

Arc 925.50.155 Arkheologicheskie issledovaniia srednevekovogo Kryma. Kiev, 1968.

Arc 936.165.20 Arkheologiia, etnografiia i iskusstvovedenie Moldavii. Kishinev, 1968.

Arc 861.31.30 Atkinson, Richard J.C. Silbury Hill: background information on the Silbury dig. London, 1968.

Arc 603.7A Background to evolution in Africa. Chicago, 1968.

Arc 936.195.195 Bánesz, Ladislav. Barca bei Košice - paläolithische Fundstelle. Bratislava, 1968.

Arc 340.30.5 Banner, János. A Közép-Dunamedence régészeti bibliográfiája, 1960-1966. Budapest, 1968.

Arc 936.251.5 Belgrade. Narodni Muzej. Neolit centralnog Balkana. Beograd, 1968.

Chronological Listing

1968 - cont.

Arc 1423.30 Bertram, Fred. Israel's 20-year catalog of coins and currency. N.Y., 1968.

Arc 416.38 Brentjes, Burchard. Von Schanidar bis Akkad. 1. Aufl. Leipzig, 1968.

Arc 547.50F British Museum. Department of Egyptian Antiquities. Catalogue of Egyptian antiquities in the British Museum. London, 1968- 2v.

Arc 861.180 Brodribb, Arthur Charles Conant. Excavations at Shakenoak Farm. v.1-4. Oxford, Eng., 1968- 3v.

Arc 861.100.15 Bruce-Mitford, Rupert Leo. The Sutton-Hoo ship burial. London, 1968.

Arc 936.220.50 Brukner, Bogdan. Neolit n Vojvodini. Beograd, 1968.

Arc 895.65 Brunius, Carl Georg. Försök till förklaringar öfver hällristningar. Lund, 1968.

Arc 587.13 Caminos, Ricardo A. The shrines and rock-inscriptions of Ibrim. London, 1968.

Arc 82.1.8 Carcopino, Jérome. Souvenirs romains. Paris, 1968.

Arc 925.13.155 Chernenko, Evgenii V. Skifskii dospekh. Kiev, 1968.

Arc 830.160.5 Chevalier, Alexandre. Altonum, fille d'Aeria, origines gallo-romaines de Montbrison. Valence, 1968.

Arc 830.160.10 Chevalier, Alexandre. Le site d'Aeria. Valence, 1968.

Arc 609.16F Clark, John Desmond. Further paleo-anthropological studies in northern Lunda. Lisboa, 1968.

Arc 387.45 Clarke, David Leonard. Analytical archaeology. London, 1968.

Arc 1540.36 Cleveland. Museum of Art. English gold coins. Cleveland, 1968.

Arc 609.36 Cole-King, P.A. Mwalawolemba on Mikolongwe Hill. Zomba, 1968.

Arc 552.5 Combined Pre-Historic Expedition to Egyptian and Sudanese Nubia. The prehistory of Nubia. Taos, N.M., 1968. 2v.

Arc 743.13.5 Comitato Permanente per l'Etruria. Studi etruschi. Indici, v.1-40, 1927-1972. Firenze, 1968- 2v.

Arc 612.66 Congrès International d'Archéologie Slave, 1st, Warsaw, 1965. I międzynarodoury kongres Archeologii Słowianskiej. Wrocław, 1968. 7v.

Arc 530.172 Contributions to the archaeology of Armenia. Cambridge, 1968.

Arc 726.235.5 Convegno internazionale di studi sulle antichità di classe. Atti del Convegno internazionale di studi sulle antichità di classe. Ravenna, 1968.

Arc 1153.110 Costamagna, Giorgio. Tachigrafia notarile e scritture segrete medioevali in Italia. Roma, 1968.

Arc 895.72 Cullberg, Carl. On artifact analysis. Bonn, 1968.

Arc 943.50 Cusack, Betty Bugbee. Collector's luck: giant steps into prehistory. 1. ed. Stoneham, Mass., 1968.

Arc 936.6.45 Dąbrowski, Jan. Zabytki metalowe epoki brązu między dolną wisłą a Niemnem. Wrocław, 1968.

Arc 938.68 Daugudis, V. Stakliškių lobis. Vil'nius, 1968.

Arc 936.100.50 Dimitrijevic, Stojan. Sopotsko-lendjelska kultura. Zagreb, 1968.

Arc 590.13.1 Drerup, Heinrich. Die Datierung der Mumienporträts. Paderborn, 1968.

Arc 925.16.35 Drevnosti chandary. Alma-Ata, 1968.

Arc 388.16 Driehaus, Jürgen. Archäologische Radiographie. Düsseldorf, 1968.

Arc 1498.20 Ernst, Barbara. Les monnaies françaises depuis 1848. Braunschweig, 1968.

Arc 1468.58 Essays in Greek coinage. Oxford, 1968.

Arc 682.35 Evans, John Davies. Excavations at Saliagos near Antiparos. London, 1968.

Arc 923.117 Fedorov-Davydov, German A. Kurgany, idoly, monety. Moskva, 1968.

Arc 925.333 Fedoseeva, Svetlana A. Drevnie kul'tury verkhnego Viliuia. Moskva, 1968.

Arc 830.356 Fixot, Michel. Les fortifications de terre et les origines féodales le Cinglais. Caen, 1968.

Arc 726.326 Franciosa, Nicola. La villa romana di Minori. Minori, 1968.

Arc 1428.33 Franke, Peter R. Kleinasien zur Römerzeit; griechisches Leben im Spiegel der Münzen. München, 1968.

Arc 861.126 Fullbrook-Leggatt, Lawrence Edward Wells Outen. Roman Gloucester. Lansdown, 1968.

Arc 905.130 Gábori-Csánk, V. La station du paléolithique moyen d'Erd-Hongrie. Budapest, 1968.

Arc 1558.6.14 Glück, Harry. Artalsförtecknia over soenskamynt med varderingspriser. Stockholm, 1968.

Arc 1478.15.10 Gnecchi, F. I medaglioni romani. Bologna, 1968. 3v.

Arc 1508.30 Göetz, Christian Jacob. Deutschlands Kayser-Münzen des Mittel-Alters. Leipzig, 1968.

Arc 412.14 Goguey, René. De l'aviation à l'archéologie. Paris, 1968.

Arc 1138.115 Gordon, Cyrus Herzl. Forgotten scripts. N.Y., 1968.

Arc 612.67 Grigor'ev, Gennadii P. Machalo verkhnego paleolita i proiskhozhdenie Homo Sapiens. Leningrad, 1968.

Arc 861.109 Grimes, William F. The excavation of Roman and mediaeval London. London, 1968.

Arc 943.51 Guliaev, Valerii I. Amerika i Staryi svet v dokolumbovu epokhu. Moskva, 1968.

Arc 830.348 Haensch, Wolf. Die paläolithischen Menschendarstellungen. Bonn, 1968.

Arc 905.90.5 Haensel, Bernhard. Beiträge zur Chronologie der Mittleren Bronzezeit im Karpatenbecken. Bonn, 1968. 2v.

Arc 387.23.6 Hagen, Victor Wolfgang von. F. Catherwood, architect-explorer of two worlds. Barre, Mass, 1968.

Arc 875.130 Hamilton, John. Excavations at Clicknimin, Shetland. Edinburgh, 1968.

Arc 726.215.5 Hencken, Hugh O'Neill. Tarquinia and Etruscan origins. London, 1968.

Arc 936.215.5 Hoeckmann, Olaf. Die menschengestaltige Figuralplastik der südosteuropäischen Jungsteinzeit und Steinkupferzeit. v.1-2. Hildesheim, 1968.

Arc 1588.4.85 Horák, Ján. Kremnické dukáty. Vyd. 1. Bratislava, 1968.

Arc 1418.26 Hussain, M.K. Catalogue of coins of the Mughal emperors. Bombay, 1968.

Arc 925.13.140 Il'inskaia, Vervara A. Skify dneprovskogo lesostepnogo Levoberezh'ia. Kiev, 1968.

Arc 925.339 Inadze, Meri P. Prichernomorskie goroda drevnei Kolkhidy. Tbilisi, 1968.

Arc 543.3.1 International Conference on the History, Archaeology and Culture of Central Asia in the Kushan Period, Dushanbe, 1968. Sovetskaiia arkheologiia frednei Azii i Kushanskaia problema. v.1-2. Moskva, 1968.

Arc 723.34.5 Istituto Italiano di Preistoria e Protostoria. Atti della XI e XII riunione scientifica. Firenze, 1968.

1968 - cont.

Arc 543.148 Istoriia, arkheologiia i etnografiia srednei Azii. Moskva, 1968.

Arc 383.46.5 Jażdżewski, Konrad. Liber Iosepho Kostrzewski octogenario a veneratoribus dicatur. Wrocław, 1968.

Arc 505.77.5 Jidejian, Nina. Byblos through the ages. Beirut, 1968.

Arc 407.30.10 Johann Joachim Winckelmann, 1768-1968. Bad Godesberg, 1968.

Arc 943.54 Judd, Neil Morton. Men met along the trail. 1. ed. Norman, 1968.

Arc 1583.28 Kaim, Reinhold. Russische Numismatik. Braunschweig, 1968.

Arc 853.65.35 Kaletyn, Marta. Grodziska wczesnośredniowieczne województwa wrocławskiego. Wrocław, 1968.

Arc 543.146.10 Karakumskie drevnosti. Photoreproduction. Ashkhabad, 1968- 4v.

Arc 1480.80 Kellner, Wendelin. Libertas und Christogramm. Thesis. Karlsruhe, 1968.

Arc 936.14.275 Kmieciński, Jerzy. Odry. Wrocław, 1968.

Arc 853.360 Koch, Ursula. Die Grabfunde der Merowingerzeit aus dem Donautal um Regensberg. Berlin, 1968. 2v.

Arc 853.300 Koester, Hans. Die mittlere Bronzezeit im nördlichen Rheingraben. Bonn, 1968.

Arc 1348.82.5 Kroha, Tyll. Münzen sammeln. 5. Aufl. Braunschweig, 1968.

Arc 66.1.212 Labrousse, Michel. Toulouse antique des origines à l'établissement des Wisigoths. Paris, 1968.

Arc 1473.50.5 Lampros, Paulos. Coins and medals of the Ionian Islands. Amsterdam, 1968.

Arc 543.147 Larichev, Vitalii E. Aziia dalekaia i tainstvennaia. Novosibirsk, 1968.

Arc 399.3 Larichev, Vitalii E. Bibliografiia nauchnykh trudov po arkheologii i istorii chlena-korrespondenta AN SSSR A.P. Okladnikova. Novosibirsk, 1968.

Arc 925.4.30 Larichev, Vitalii E. Okhotniki za mamontanii. Novosibirsk, 1968.

Arc 340.20.2 Lehmann, Herbert. Bibliographie zur Vor- und Frühgeschichte von Gross-Berlin. 2. Aufl. Berlin, 1968.

Arc 815.35 Leppmann, Wolfgang. Pompeii in fact and fiction. London, 1968.

Arc 421.31.2 Li, Chi. The beginnings of Chinese civilization. Seatle, 1968.

Arc 936.195.185 Lichardus, Jan. Taskjňa Domica, najuyznačnejšie sidlisko i udu bukovohorskej kultúry. 1. vyd. Bratislava, 1968.

Arc 938.99 Lietuvos archeologikiai paminklai. Vil'nius, 1968.

Arc 938.98 Lietuvos BR Mokslų Akademije, Vilna. Istorijas Institutas. Zo let. Vil'nius, 1968.

Arc 543.3.75 Litvinskii, Boris A. Kangiuisko-sarmatskii farn. Dushanbe, 1968.

Arc 936.14.270 Łomnicki, Jerzy. Ostrów Lednicki. Wyd 1. Poznań, 1968.

Arc 1130.15F London. University. Library. The palaeography collection. Boston, 1968. 2v.

Arc 543.120.10 Lubo-Lesnichenko, Evgenii. Mertvyi gorod Khara-Khoto. Moskva, 1968.

Arc 1542.2.5 Malmer, Brita. Mynt och människor. Stockholm, 1968.

Arc 893.29 Malmer, Mats P. Jungneolithische Studien. Habelt, 1968.

Arc 1330.30 Malter, Joel L. Byzantine numismatic bibliography, 1950-1965. Chicago, 1968.

Arc 1018.62 Mancini, Ignazio. Le scoperte archeologiche sui giudeo-cristiani. Assisi, 1968.

Arc 543.65.15 Mandel'shtam, Anatolii M. Pamiatniki epokhi bronzy v Iuzhnom Tadzhikistane. Leningrad, 1968.

Arc 397.17.6 Marek, Kurt W. Gods, graves, and scholars. 2. ed. N.Y., 1968.

Arc 1613.28 Massey, Joseph Earl. America's money. N.Y., 1968.

Arc 925.325.5 Mazhitov, Niiaz A. Bakhmutinskaia kul'tura. Moskva, 1968.

Arc 1423.28 Meyshan, Josef. Essays in Jewish numismatics. Jerusalem, 1968.

Arc 925.50.165 Mezentseva, Galina G. Drevn'orus'ke misto Roden', Kniazha hora. Kyïv, 1968.

Arc 600.5.20 Missione di Scavo a Medinet Madi. Rapporto preliminare delle campagine di Scavo 1966-1967. Milano, 1968.

Arc 1518.6.5 Morin, Francois. Monnaies de Belgique de 1832 à 1967. Anvers, 1968.

Arc 682.30.5 Mylonas, George E. Mycenae's last century of greatness. Sydney, 1968.

Arc 383.42.10 Na granicach archeologii. Łódź, 1968.

Arc 888.55 Narr, Karl J. Studien zur älteren und mittleren Steinzeit der Niederen Lande. Habilitationsschrift. Bonn, 1968.

Arc 925.334 Nikitin, Andrei L. Golubye doragi vekov. Moskva, 1968.

Arc 936.50.10 Nin. Zadar, 1968.

Arc 925.16.30 Novoe v arkheologii Kazakhstana. Alma-Ata, 1968.

Arc 1588.15 Numismatika. Rigā, 1968.

Arc 925.180.20 Okladnikov, Aleksei Pavlovich. Liki drevnego Amura. Novosibirsk, 1968.

Arc 726.202 Oliver, Andrew. The reconstruction of two Apulian tomb groups. Bern, 1968.

Arc 925.9.41 Pachulia, Vianor P. V kraiu zolotogo runa. Izd. 2. Moskva, 1968.

Arc 726.27.10 Paget, Robert F. In the footsteps of Orpheus. N.Y., 1968.

Arc 1163.3.95 Paleograficheskii al'bom. Leningrad, 1968.

Arc 785.83.5 Pekáry, Thomas. Untersuchungen zu den römischer Reichsstrassen. Bonn, 1968.

Arc 1588.14 Pere, Nuri. Osmanhlarda madeni paralar. Istanbul, 1968.

Arc 530.173 Person, Kenneth. The Dorak affair. N.Y., 1968.

Arc 925.13.160 Petrov, Viktor P. Skifi. Kyiv, 1968.

Arc 340.12 Phillipson, David W. An annotated bibliography of the archaeology of Zambia. Lusaka, 1968.

Arc 672.1.116 Pini, Ingo. Beiträge zur minoischen Gräberkunde. Wiesbaden, 1968.

Arc 936.225.5 Pirković, Ivo. Crucium. Ljubljana, 1968.

Arc 1560.4 Platbarzdis, Aleksander. Die königlich schwedische Münze in Livland. Stockholm, 1968.

Arc 925.150.20 Polikarpovich, Konstantin M. Paleolit verkhego podneptovia. Minsk, 1968.

Arc 1580.51.2 Polívka, Eduard. Mince Františka Josefa I., 1848-1916. 2. vyd. Praha, 1968.

Arc 936.14.265 Polska Akademia Nauk. Oddział w Krakowie. Prace Komisja Archeologicznej. Zagadnienia okresu lateńskiego w Polsce. Wrocław, 1968.

Arc 681.20 Popham, Mervyn R. Excavations at Lefkandi, Euboea, 1964-66. London, 1968.

Arc 1583.26 Potin, Vsevolod M. Drevniaia Rus' i evropeiskie gosudarstva. Leningrad, 1968.

Arc 400.28.2 La préhistoire par André Leroi-Gourhan. 2. éd. Paris, 1968.

Arc 936.195.170 Preidel, Helmut. Das grossmährische Reich im Spiegel der Bodenfunde. Gräfelfing, 1968.

1968 - cont.

Arc 915.4.20 Provincialia; Festschrift für Rudolf Laur-Belart. Basel, 1968.

Arc 848.4.2 Reallexikon der germanischen Altertumskunde. v.1-2, pt.1-5. 2. Aufl. Berlin, 1968-

Arc 1190.86.10 Reychman, Jan. Handbook of Ottoman-Turkish diplomatics. The Hague, 1968.

Arc 1423.32 Rosen, Josef. Münzen aus biblischer Zeit. Basel, 1968.

Arc 609.38 Sandelowsky, B.H. Fingira; preliminary report. Zomba, 1968.

Arc 1185.33.3 Santifaller, Leo. Urkundenforschung. 3. Aufl. Darmstadt, 1968.

Arc 407.30.5 Schadewaldt, Wolfgang. Winckelmann und Rilke: zwei Beschreibungen des Apollon. Pfullingen, 1968.

Arc 853.165.5 Schindler, Reinhard. Studien zum vorgeschichtlichen Siedlungs- und Befestigungswesen des Saarlandes. Trier, 1968.

Arc 1480.25.1 Schulz, Otto Theodor. Die Rechtstitel und Regierungsprogramme auf römischen Kaisermünzen. N.Y., 1968.

Arc 936.14.320 Sckice z najdawniejszej przesstosci Mazausza. Wrocław, 1968.

Arc 1538.27.3 Seaby, Herbert Allen. The English silver coinage from 1649. 3. ed. London, 1968.

Arc 1390.18 Seifedolini, M.A. Monety il'khakov XIV veka. Baku, 1968.

Arc 925.180.15 Shavkunov, Ernst V. Gosudarstvo bokhai i pamiatniki ego kul'tury v Primor'e. Leningrad, 1968.

Arc 443.6 Shchetenko, Anatolii I. Drevneishie zemledel'cheskie kul'tury Dekana. Leningrad, 1968.

Arc 925.13.145 Shtambok, Anatoii A. Iz tsarstva Ateia v Neapol' Skifskii. Moskva, 1968.

Arc 923.118 Slaviane i Rus'. Moskva, 1968.

Arc 973.10 Smith, Carl S. The two Teeth site [South Dakota]. Lincoln, 1968.

Arc 746.56 Staccioli, Romolo Augusto. Modelli di edifici etrusco-italici. Firenze, 1968.

Arc 853.373 Stolberg, Friedrich. Befastigungsanlagen im und am Harz von der Frühgeschichte bis zur Neuzeit. Ein Handbuch. Hildesheim, 1968.

Arc 895.74 Strömberg, Märta. Der Dolmen Trollasten in St. Köpinge, Schonen. Bonn, 1968.

Arc 612.74 Studien zur europäischen Vor- und Frühgeschichte. Neumünster, 1968.

Arc 612.68 Studies in ancient Europe. Leicester, 1968.

Arc 1468.60F Sylloge numorum Graecorum. v.1-3. Berlin, 1968.

Arc 1538.23.6 Sylloge of coins of the British Isles. London, 1968.

Arc 925.50.170 Telehin, Dmytro I. Dnipro-donets'ka kul'tura. Kyïv, 1968.

Arc 1237.10 Thailand. Ministry of Interior. Changwat seals. Bangkok, 1968.

Arc 1558.8.2 Tingström, Bertel. Svensk numismatisk uppslagsbok. 2. upp. Stockholm, 1968.

Arc 936.195.155 Točík, Anton. Altmagyarische Gräberfelder in der Südwestslowakei. Bratislava, 1968.

Arc 936.195.160 Točík, Anton. Slawisch-awarisches Gräberfeld in Šturovo. 1. Aufl. Bratislava, 1968.

Arc 936.220.45 Todorović, Jovan. Kelti na tlu Beograda. Beograd, 1968.

Arc 618.11 Todorovic, Jovan. Kelti u jugoistočnoj Evropi. Beograd, 1968.

Arc 853.24.7 Torbruegge, Walter. Bilder zur Vorgeschichte Bayerns. Konstanz, 1968.

Arc 936.220.65 Trbuhović, Vojislav B. Problemi porekla i datovanja bronzanog doba u Srbiji. Beograd, 1968.

Arc 925.13.165 Tsvetaeva, Galina A. Sokrovishcha prichernomorskikh kurganov. Moskva, 1968.

Arc 936.65.10 Tudor, D. Oltenia română. București, 1968.

Arc 923.109 Vsesoiuznaia Arkheologicheskaia Studencheskaia Konferentsiia, 11th, Erevan, 1965. Doklady, prochitannye na XI Vesesoiuznoi studencheskoi arkheologicheskoi konferentsii 1965 g. v Erevane. Erevan, 1968.

Arc 923.124 Vsesoiuznaia Arkheologicheskaia Studencheskaia Konferentsiia, 9th, Moscow, 1963. Sbornik dokladov na IX i X vsesoiuznykh arkheologicheskikh studencheskikh konferentsiiakh. Moskva, 1968.

Arc 915.42 Wandeler, Max. LuzernStadt und Land in römischer Zeit. Luzern, 1968.

Arc 936.14.138 Warsaw. Uniwersytet. Zespoł Badan nad Polskim Sredniowieczem. V konferencja naukowa w Busknzdroju i w Wislicy, 19-20 maja, 1966. Vyd. 1. Warszawa, 1968.

Arc 853.292 Wegewitz, Willi. Reihengräberfriedhöfe. Neumünster, 1968.

Arc 861.160.20 Wenham, Leslie. The Romano-British cemetery at Trentholm Drive. London, 1968.

Arc 1510.156 Wielandt, Friedrich. Münze und Geld in Pforzheim. Pforzheim, 1968.

Arc 543.83.5 Wissmann, Hermann. Zur Archäologie und antiken Geographie von Südarabien. Istanbul, 1968.

Arc 936.14.290 Wojtasik, Jerzy. Cmentarzysko wczesnośredniowieczne na wzgárzu "Młynówka" w Wolinie. Szczecin, 1968.

Arc 1663.62 Wojtulewicz, Henryk. Medale polskie XVI-XX w. Lublin, 1968.

Arc 936.14.285 Z badań nad kulturą ceramiki promienistej. Kraków, 1968.

Arc 1433.71F Zambaur, Edward K.M. von. Die Münzprägungen des Islams. Wiesbaden, 1968.

1969

Arc 543.66.35 Afrasiabskaia Kompleksnaia Arkheologicheskaia Ekspeditsiia. Afrasiab. Tashkent, 1969- 3v.

Arc 726.237.5 Alba fucens. Rapports et études présentes par J. Mercens. Bruxelles, 1969. 2v.

Arc 681.15 American School of Classical Studies at Athens. Lerna, a preclassical site in the Argolid. Princeton, N.J., 1969. 2v.

Arc 925.345 Andrianov, Boris V. Drevnie orositel'nye sistemy Priaral'ia. Moskva, 1969.

Arc 458.14 Ansari, Z.D. Excavations at Sanganakallu and Songaon. Poona, 1969. 3 pam.

Arc 936.165.35 Antropogen Moldavii. Kishinev, 1969.

Arc 920.4 Armtiunov, Sergei A. Drevnie kul'tury aziatskikh eskimosov. Moskva, 1969.

Arc 1460.8 Baldus, Hans Roland. Mor(eta) urb(is)-Antiona. Frankfurt am Main, 1969.

Arc 936.195.205 Barth, Fritz Eckart. Die hallstattzeitlichen Grabhügel im Bereiche der Kutscher bei Podsemel (Slowenien). Bonn, 1969.

Arc 543.138 Belenitskii, Aleksandr Markovich. Central Asia. London, 1969.

1969 - cont.

Arc 830.275.10 Benoît, Fernand. Entremont, capitale celto-ligure des Salyens de Provence. Gap, 1969.

Arc 976.9 Benthall, Joseph L. Archaeological investigation of the Shannon site, Montgomery County, Virginia. Richmond, 1969.

Arc 543.146.25 Berdyev, Ovliabuli. Drevneishie zemledel'tsy Iuzhnogo Turkmenistana. Ashkhabad, 1969.

Arc 1053.3.1 Bernoulli, J.J. Römische Ikonographie. v.1-2. Hildesheim, 1969. 4v.

Arc 543.88 Bibby, Geoffrey. Looking for Dilmun. 1st ed. N.Y., 1969.

Arc 340.15 Bibliografia d'archeologia classica. 1. ed. Roma, 1969.

Arc 66.1.213 Bon, Antoine. La morée franque. Paris, 1969. 2v.

Arc 726.335 Bonghi Jovino, Maria. La necropoli di Nola preromana. Napoli, 1969.

Arc 641.4A Bouzek, Jan. Homerisches Griechenland im Lichte der archäologischen Quellen. Praha, 1969.

Arc 853.335 Die Bremer Hanse-Kogge. Bremen, 1969.

Arc 412.5.5 Brolin, Per Erik. Gamla fynd och glömda folk. Göteborg, 1969.

Arc 505.131 Buhl, Marie Louise. Shiloh; the Danish excavations at Tall Sailūn, Palestine, in 1926, 1929, 1932, and 1963. Copenhagen, 1969.

Arc 936.6.40 Bukowski, Zbigniew. Studia nad południowym i południowowschodnim pograniczem kultury łuzyckiej. Wrocław, 1969.

Arc 936.260 Bŭlgarska Akademiia na Naukite, Sofia. Arkheologicheski Institut. Nessébre. Sofia, 1969.

Arc 674.3.15 Burford, Alison. The Greek temple builders at Epidauros. Liverpool, 1969.

Arc 1411.15 Bykov, Aleksei A. Monety Kitaia. Leningrad, 1969.

Arc 66.1.214 Callu, Jean Pierre. La politique monétaire des empereurs romains de 238 à 311. Paris, 1969.

Arc 746.54 Camporeale, Giovannangelo. I commerci di Vetulonia in età orientalizzante. Firenze, 1969.

Arc 448.1.35 Casal, Jean Marie. La civilisation de l'Indus et ses énigmes. Paris, 1969.

Arc 726.315 Cecchini, Serena Maria. I ritrovamenti fenici e punici in Sardegna. Roma, 1969.

Arc 1470.88 Centro Internazionale di Studi Numismatici. La circolazione della moneta ateniese in Sicilia e in Magna Grecia. Roma, 1969.

Arc 936.221 Čerškov, Emil. Rimljani na kosovu i Metohiji. Beograd, 1969.

Arc 1010.20 Chêng, Tê-k'un. Archaeology in Sarawak. Cambridge, 1969.

Arc 387.9.7.1 Childe, Vere Gordon. Piecing together the past. N.Y., 1969.

Arc 726.336 Chiostri, Frido. Le tombe a Tholos di Quinto nel comune di Sesto Fiorentino. n.p., 1969.

Arc 858.42.1 Collingwood, Robin George. The archaeology of Roman Britain. London, 1969.

Arc 726.328 Convegno su Archeologia e Storia nella Lombardia Pedemontana Occidentale. Archeologia e storia nella Lombardia pedemontana occidentale. Como, 1969.

Arc 1033.34.70 Corbo, Virgilio. Ricordi di San Pietro sul lago di Tiberiade. Jerusalem, 1969.

Arc 936.165.25 Dalekoe proshloe Moldavii. Kishinev, 1969.

Arc 925.50.185 Danilenko, Valentin N. Eneolit Ukrainy. Kiev, 1969.

Arc 600.230F Daumas, François. Kellia I. Le Caire, 1969- 2v.

Arc 1680.6.1 Davis, William John. The nineteenth century token coinage of Great Britain. London, 1969.

Arc 412.18 Devel, Leo. Flights into yesterday. N.Y., 1969.

Arc 925.346 Dikov, Nikolai N. Drevnie kostry Kamchatki i Chukotki. Magadan, 1969.

Arc 938.100 Dolukhanov, Pavel M. Istoriia Baltiki. Moskva, 1969.

Arc 590.20 Donadoni Roveri, Anna Maria. I sarcofagi egizi dalle origini alla fine dell'antico regno. Roma, 1969.

Arc 936.195.255 Dušek, Mikuláš. Bronzezeitliche Gräberfelder in der Südwestslowakei. Bratislava, 1969.

Arc 853.13.40 Field guide to prehistoric sites in Württemberg and Bavaria. Wiesbaden, 1969.

Arc 726.59.40 Frost, Honor. The mortar wreck in Mellieha Bay. London, 1969.

Arc 925.322.25 Gadzhiev, Magomed G. Iz istorii kul'tury Dagestana v epokhu bronzy. Makhachkala, 1969.

Arc 726.324 Garoffolo, Francesco. Ipponion; saggio storico-archeologico e nuove osservazioni. Reggio Calabria, 1969.

Arc 391.16 Gąsiorowski, Stanisław J. Pisma wybrane. Wrocław, 1969.

Arc 853.65.40 Godłowski, Kazimierz. Kultura przeworska na Górnym Śląsku. Wyd. 1. Katowice, 1969.

Arc 1480.40.1 Grant, Michael. From imperium to auctoritas. 1. ed. London, 1969.

Arc 861.190 Great Britain. Commissions. Ancient and Historical Monuments and Constructions of England. Peterborough New town. London, 1969.

Arc 736.26 Grotta Regina. Roma, 1969.

Arc 1493.24 Guadan, Antonio M. de. Numismatica iberica e iberoromana. Madrid, 1969.

Arc 505.136 Hachmann, Rolf. Vademecum der Grabung Kamid-el-Loz. Bonn, 1969.

Arc 392.15 Handbuch der Archäologie im Rahnen des Handbuchs der Altertumswissenschaft. München, 1969-

Arc 689.12 Hauptmann, Harald. Die Funde der früher Dimini-Zeit aus der Arapi-Magula. Diss. Bonn, 1969.

Arc 557.10 Helck, Hans Wolfgang. Ägyptologie an deutschen Universitäten. Wiesbaden, 1969.

Arc 1473.14 Hendy, Michael. Coinage and money in the Byzantine empire, 1081-1261. Washington, 1969.

Arc 936.14.330 Hensel, Witold. Ziemie polskie w pradziejach. wyd. 1. Warszawa, 1969.

Arc 700.62 Heres, Gerald. Die punischen und griechischen Tonlampen der Staatlichen Museen zu Berlin. Amsterdam, 1969.

Arc 853.296 Hinz, Hermann. Das fränkische Gräberfeld von Eick. Berlin, 1969.

Arc 488.28 Hinz, Walther. Altiranische Funde und Forschungen. Berlin, 1969.

Arc 936.14.310 Jaskanis, Danuta. Pradzieje Białostocczyzny. wyd. 1. Warszawa, 1969.

Arc 925.9.75 Kakhetskaia arkheologicheskaia ekspeditniia, 1965. Trudy. Tbilisi, 1969.

Arc 1335.165 Kapossy, Balázs. Münzen und Medaillen aus dem Bernischen Historischen Museum. Bern, 1969.

Arc 540.14 Karageōrgēs, Basos. Salamis; recent discoveries in Cyprus. N.Y., 1969.

Arc 1190.65.5 Karagiannopoulos, Iōannēs E. Byzantinē diplomatikē. Thessalonikē, 1969.

Chronological Listing

1969 - cont.

Arc 560.4 Kayser, Hans. Ägyptisches Kunstlandwerk. Braunschweig, 1969.

Arc 1365.5 Kazamanova, Liudmila N. Vvedenie v antichnaia numizmatiku. Moskva, 1969.

Arc 925.338 Khalikov, Al'fred K. Drevniaia istoriia Srednego Povolzhia. Moskva, 1969.

Arc 888.50 Klok, R.H.J. Archeologie en monument. Bussum, 1969.

Arc 1390.19 Kmietowicz, Anna. Wczesnośredniowieczny skarb srebrny z zalesia powiat słupca. Wrocław, 1969-74. 2v.

Arc 925.150.30 Konferentsiia po Arkheologii Belorussii, Minsk, 1969. Drevnosti Belorussii. Minsk, 1969.

Arc 1365.4 Kraft, Konrad. Der goldene Kranz Caesars und der Kampf um die Entlassung des "Tyrannen". 2. Aufl. Darmstadt, 1969.

Arc 853.65.50 Kramarek, Janusz. Wczesnośredniowieczne grodziska nyczyńskie na Śląsku. Wrocław, 1969.

Arc 936.14.340 Kramarkowa, Irena. Stosunki społeczno-gospodarcze i polityczne. Opole, 1969.

Arc 936.14.305 Kukharenko, I.V. Arkheologiia Pol'ski. Moskva, 1969.

Arc 925.16.40 Kul'tura drevnikh skotovodov i zemledel'tsev Kazakhstana. Alma-Ata, 1969.

Arc 1588.1.66 Kunisz, A. Chronologia naptywu pieniądza vzymskiegs na ziemie Matspoblei. Wyd. 1. Wrocław, 1969.

Arc 1473.1.3.5 Lampros, Paulos. Anekdota nomismata kopenta en Glarentsa kata mimēsin tōn Henetikōn. Oak Park, 1969.

Arc 530.180 Laodicée du Lycos; le nymphée; campagnes 1961-1963. Québec, 1969.

Arc 416.42 Laricheo, Vitalii E. Paleolit Severnoi, Tsentral'noi i Vostochnoi Azii. Novosibirsk, 1969- 2v.

Arc 403.16.36 Lavater-Sloman, Mary. Das Gold von Troja. Zürich, 1969.

Arc 1153.104.2 Lazzarini, Vittorio. Scritti di paleografia e diplomatica. 2. ed. Padova, 1969.

Arc 609.17.20 Lectures on Nigerian prehistory and archaeology. Ibadan, 1969.

Arc 608.2.65 Lézine, Alexandre. Les thermes d'Antonin à Carthage. Tunis, 1969.

Arc 853.338 Lindenschmit, Wilhelm. Das germanische Todtenlager bei Selzen. Faksimile. Mainz an Rhein, 1969.

Arc 1138.122 Lowe, Elias Avery. Handwriting. Our medieval legacy. Rome, 1969.

Arc 726.258.5 Luni sul Mignone. Lund, 1969.

Arc 936.140.20 Majewski, Kazimierz. Kultura rzymska w Bułgarii. Wrocław, 1969.

Arc 936.14.395 Malinowski, Tadeusz. Prasłowiańskie osadnictur w słupcy. Poznań, 1969.

Arc 936.14.203 Malinowski, Tadewsz. Obrzadek pogrzebowy ludności kultury pomorskiej. Wrocław, 1969.

Arc 936.220.60 Mano-Zisi, Djordje. Novi Pazar. Beograd, 1969.

Arc 66.1.215 Marcadé, Jean. Au musée de Délos. Paris, 1969.

Arc 925.9.52 Markovin, Vladimir I. V strane vainakhor. Moskva, 1969.

Arc 843.226 Martínez Fernandez, Jesus. Ensayo biologico sobre los hombres y los pueblos de la Asturias primativa. Oviedo, 1969.

Arc 925.332.10 Material'naia kul'tura sredne-tsninskoi Mordvy VIII-XIVV. Saransk, 1969.

Arc 853.330 Mauser-Goller, Katharina. Die relative Chronologie des Neolithikums in Südwestdeutschland und der Schweiz. Diss. Basel, 1969.

Arc 858.94 Megalithic enquiries in the West of Britain: a Liverpool symposium. Liverpool, 1969.

Arc 936.252 Melitauri, Konstantin N. Kreposti dofeodal'noi i rannefeodal'noi Gruzii. Tbilisi, 1969- 2v.

Arc 905.136 Menghin, Osmund. Beiträge zur Urgeschichte Tirols. Innsbruck, 1969.

Arc 905.138 Merhart, Gero von. Hallstatt und Italien. Bonn, 1969.

Arc 1153.96 Merkelbach, Reinhold. Lateinisches Leseheft zur Einführung in Paläographie und Textkritik. Göttingen, 1969.

Arc 1473.12 Metcalf, David Michael. The origins of the Anastasian currency reforms. Amsterdam, 1969.

Arc 658.3.22 Meyer, Ernst. Heinrich Schliemann: Kaufmann und Forscher. Göttingen, 1969.

Arc 505.2.20 Mission Archeologique Suisse en Syrie. Le sanctuaire de Baalshamin à Palmyre. Rome, 1969- 4v.

Arc 925.336 Mochanov, I.A. Mnogosloinaia stoianka Bel'kachi I. i periodizatsiia kamennogo veka Iakutii. Moskva, 1969.

Arc 1163.3.100 Mongait, Aleksandr L. Nadpis'na kamne. Moskva, 1969.

Arc 885.19.7 Nash-Williams, Victor Erle. The Roman frontier in Wales. Cardiff, 1969.

Arc 1493.26 Navascués y de Juan, Joaquin Maria de. Las monedas hispanicas del Museo arqueologico nacional de Madrid. Barcelona, 1969. 2v.

Arc 1588.4.62 Nemeškal, Lubomir. Českobudějovická mincovina v letech 1569-1611. Vyd. 1. Česke Budějovice, 1969.

Arc 497.88 New direction in Biblical archaeology. 1. ed. Garden City, N.Y., 1969.

Arc 843.230 Nicolini, Gerard. Les bronzes figurés des sanctuaires ibériques. 1. éd. Paris, 1969.

Arc 843.214 Niemeyer, Hans G. Toscanos, die altpunische Faktorei an der Mündung des Rio de Vélez. Berlin, 1969.

Arc 398.8 Noël Hume, Ivor. Historical archaeology. 1. ed. N.Y., 1969.

Arc 880.50 Norman, Edward R. The early development of Irish society: the evidence of aerial photography. Cambridge, Eng., 1969.

Arc 925.341 Okladnikov, Aleksei P. Petroglify zabaikal'ia. Leningrad, 1969- 2v.

Arc 672.1.135 Palmer, Leonard R. A new guide to the palace of Knossos. London, 1969.

Arc 1185.32.2 Paoli, Cesare. Diplomatica. Firenze, 1969.

Arc 1163.17.30 Parkes, Malcolm Beckwith. English cursive book hands, 1250-1500. Oxford, 1969.

Arc 1540.33 Petersson, H. Bertil A. Anglo-Saxon currency: King Edgar's reform to the Norman conquest. Lund, 1969.

Arc 936.195.180 Pichlerová, Magda. Nové košariská. 1. vyd. Bratislava, 1969.

Arc 925.50.175 Pidoplichko, Ivan G. Pozdnepaleoliticheskie zhilizhcha iz kostei mamontz na Ukraine. Kiev, 1969.

Arc 530.22.11 Piotrovskii, Boris Borisovich. Urartu. London, 1969.

Arc 925.152 Pobol', Leonid D. Drevnosti Turovshching. Minsk, 1969.

Arc 936.165.30 Polevoi, Lazar' L'. Gorodskoe goncharstvo Pruto-Dnestrov'ja v XIV v. Kishinev, 1969.

Arc 1588.4.95 Polivka, Eduard. Československé mince 1918-1968. Vyd. 1. Hradec Králové, 1969.

Arc 838.38F Raddatz, Klaus. Die Schaftzfunde der Iberischen Halbinsel. Berlin, 1969. 2v.

Arc 861.194 Rahtz, Philip. Excavations at King John's hunting lodge, Writtle, Essex, 1955-57. London, 1969.

1969 - cont.

Arc 925.340 Ranshenbakh, Vera M. Novye nakhodki na chetyrekhstolbovom ostrove. Moskva, 1969.

Arc 936.165.12 Rikman, Emmanuil A. Khudozhestvennye sokrovishcha drevnei Moldavii. Kishinev, 1969.

Arc 870.34 Rivet, Albert L.F. The Roman villa in Britain. London, 1969.

Arc 609.37 Robinson, Keith Radcliffe. The early Iron Age in Malawi: an appraisal. Zomba, 1969.

Arc 1423.32.1 Rosen, Josef. Münzen aus biblischer Zeit. n.p., 1969.

Arc 543.52.1 Rudenko, Sergei I. Die Kultur der Hsiung-nu und die Hügelgräber von Noin Ula. Bonn, 1969.

Arc 600.225 Saad, Zaki Yusef. The excavations at Helwan. 1st ed. Norman, 1969.

Arc 440.11 Sankalia, Hasmukh Dhirajlal. Excavations at Ahar (Tambavati) [1961-62]. 1. ed. Poona, 1969.

Arc 936.14.335 Sarnowska, Wanda. Kultura unietycka w Polsce. Wrocław, 1969-1975. 2v.

Arc 853.340 Schach-Dörges, Helga. Das jungkaiserzeitliche Gräberfeld von Wilhelmsaue in Brandenburg. Berlin, 1969.

Arc 1500.66 Scheers, Simone. Les monnaies de la Gaule inspirées de celles de la republique romaine. Leuven, 1969.

Arc 1200.28 Schiaparelli, Luigi. Raccolta di documenti latini. Torino, 1969.

Arc 853.344 Schrickel, Waldtraut. Die Funde vom Wartberg in Hessen. Marburg, 1969.

Arc 843.222 Schuele, Wilhelm. Die Meseta-Kulturen der iberischen Halbinsel. Berlin, 1969. 2v.

Arc 1528.12.1 Schulman, Jacques. Handboek van de Nederlandsche munten van 1795 tot 1969. 4. druk. Amsterdam, 1969.

Arc 609.17.10 Shaw, Thurstan. A bibliography of Nigerian archaeology. Ibadan, 1969.

Arc 925.50.33 Shchepinskii, Askold A. Severnoe prisivash'e v V-I tysiacheleliiakh do nashei ery. Simferopol', 1969.

Arc 925.322.30 Shikhsaidov, Amri Rzaevich. Nadpisi rasskazyvaiut. Dagknigoizdat, 1969.

Arc 925.50.1 Shovkoplias, Ivan H. Rozvitok radians'koi arkheolohii na Ukraini. Kyiv, 1969.

Arc 723.38 Simposia Internazionale di Protostoria Italiana. Atti. Roma, 1969.

Arc 936.14.295 Siuchniński, Kazimierz. Klasyfikacja czasowo-przestrzenna kultur neolitycznych na Pomorzu zachodnim. wyd. 1. Szczecin, 1969.

Arc 925.50.180 Slov'iano-rus'ki starozhytnosti. Kyïv, 1969.

Arc 1138.127 Sparrow, John. Visible words. London, 1969.

Arc 936.14.425 Sprawozdania z badań archeologicznych prowadzonych na terenie województwa koszolińskiego w Labach 1967-1968. Koszolin, 1969.

Arc 936.220.32 Srejović, Dragoslav. Lepenski vir. Beograd, 1969.

Arc 936.220.55 Srpska Akademija Nauka i Umetnosti, Belgrade, Galerije. Stare kul'ture u Djerdapu. Beograd, 1969.

Arc 543.3.80 Staviskii, Boris Ia. Arkheologicheskie raboty muzeia v Srednei Azii. Moskva, 1969.

Arc 505.133 Stékélis, Moshé. Archaeological excavations at Ubeidiya, 1964-1966. Jerusalem, 1969.

Arc 895.78 Stjernquist, Berta. Beiträge zum Studium von bronzeitlichen Siedlungen. Bonn, 1969.

Arc 936.180.25 Tasić, Nikola. Crnokalačka bara. Kruševac, 1969.

Arc 543.66.23 Termezskaia Arkheologicheskaia Kompleksnaia Ekspeditsiia, 1937, 1961-1962. Buddiiskie peshchery Kara-tepe v starom Termeze. Moskva, 1969.

Arc 1153.98F Thomson, Samuel Harrison. Latin bookhands of the later Middle Ages, 1110-1500. Cambridge, Eng., 1969.

Arc 659.12 Titov, Valerii S. Neolit Gretsii. Moskva, 1969.

Arc 688.7.10 Tölle-Kastenbein, Renate. Die antike Stadt Samos. Mainz am Rhein, 1969.

Arc 404.3 Trapsh, M.M. Trudy. v.2. Sukhumi, 1969.

Arc 1615.4.10 United States Mint. Medals of the United States Mint. Washington, 1969.

Arc 936.100.40 Valentic, Mirko. Kameni spomenici hrvatsko XIII-XIX stoljeća. Zagreb, 1969.

Arc 543.150 Van Beek, Gus Willard. Hajar Cin Humeid. Baltimore, 1969.

Arc 1494.60 Vaz, Joaquin Ferraro. Livro das moedas de Portugal. Book of the coins of Portugal. Braga, 1969-70. 2v.

Arc 843.71.2 Vives, José. Inscripciones cristianas de la España romana y visigoda. 2. ed. Barcelona, 1969.

Arc 672.1.118 Warren, Peter. Minoan stone vases. Cambridge, Eng., 1969.

Arc 723.42 Weiss, Robert. The Renaissance discovery of classical antiquity. Oxford, 1969.

Arc 1480.86 Weissgerber, Clemens. Der Fröndenberger Münzschatzfund römischer Denare. Dortmund, 1969?

Arc 1229.10 Welfen, Peter. Die Königs-Stempel. Wiesbaden, 1969.

Arc 853.354 Wetzel, Robert. Die Bocksteinschmiede im Lonetal (Markung Ramminger, Kreis Ulm). Stuttgart, 1969. 2v.

Arc 1504.30 Wielandt, Friedrich. Münz- und Geldgeschichte des Standes Luzern. Luzern, 1969.

Arc 493.2.30 Wilber, Donald Newton. Persepolis, the archaelogy of Parsa. N.Y., 1969.

Arc 936.14.300 Wiślański, Tadeusz. Podstawy gospodarcze plemion neolitycznych w Polsce połnocno-zachodniej. Wrocław, 1969.

Arc 530.174 Yesaian, Stepan. Erevan. Erevan, 1969.

Arc 1588.1.91 Zagórski, Ignacy. Monety dawnej Polski. Warszawa, 1969.

Arc 608.84 Ziegert, Helmut. Gebel Ben Ghnema und Nord-Tibesti; Habilitationsschrift. Wiesbaden, 1969.

197-

Arc 38.5.5 Gabriel, Albert. İstanbul Türk kaleleri. İstanbul, 197-.

1970

Arc 936.222 Adriatica praehistorica et antigua. Zagreb, 1970.

Arc 861.207 Alcock, Leslie. By South Cadbury is that Camelot. London, 1970.

Arc 497.98 Archaeologie und Altes Testament. Festschrift für Kurt Galling 28. Jan. 1970. Tübingen, 1970.

Arc 830.370 Archéologie du village déserté. Paris, 1970.

Arc 1433.73.5 Artuk, S. Istanbul arkeoloji murelen teşhirdeki islami sikkeler kotalogu. Istanbul, 1970. 2v.

Arc 870.10.20 Ashbee, Paul. The earthen long barrow in Britain. Toronto, 1970.

Arc 755.3.2 Ashby, Thomas. The Roman campagna in classical times. London, 1970.

Arc 612.71 Bachelot de la Pylaie, Auguste Jean Marie. Études archéologiques et géographiques. Quimper, 1970.

Arc 925.342 Bader, Otto N. Bassein Oki v epokhu bronzy. Moskva, 1970.

Chronological Listing

1970 - cont.

Arc 853.65.60	Bagniewski, Zbigniew. Dzieje zierni wydarte. Wrocław, 1970.
Arc 861.202	Barker, P.A. The mediaeval pottery of Shropshire from the conquest to 1400. Shropshire, 1970.
Arc 600.240F	Baumgaertel, Elise J. Petrie's Nagada excavation; a supplement. London, 1970.
Arc 853.342	Bergmann, Joseph. Die altere Bronzezeit Nordwestdeutschlands. Marburg, 1970. 2v.
Arc 1473.16	Bibliothèque Nationale, Paris. Département des Médailles et Antiques. Catalogue des monnaies byzantines de la Bibliothèque Nationale. Paris, 1970. 2v.
Arc 843.228	Blanco, A. Excavaciones arqueológicas en el cerro Salomón. Madrid, 1970.
Arc 861.204	Blank, Elizabeth. A guide to Leicestershire archaeology. Leicester, 1970.
Arc 785.83.15	Bosio, Luciano. Itinerari e strade della Venetia Romana. Padova, 1970.
Arc 1356.7	Brabich, Vladimir M. Puteshestire s drevnei monetoi. Leningrad, 1970.
Arc 392.18	Brandt, Karl. Otto Hauser. Witten-Ruhr, 1970.
Arc 672.1.120	Branigan, Keith. The tombs of Mesara; a study of funerary architecture and ritual in southern Crete, 2800-1700 B.C. London, 1970.
Arc 1538.7.2	British Museum. Department of Coins and Medals. Handbook of the coins of Great Britain and Ireland in the British Museum. 2. ed. London, 1970.
Arc 537.13.1PF	British Museum. Department of Greek and Roman Antiquities. Excavations in Cyprus. 1. ed. London, 1970.
Arc 66.1.217	Bruneau, Philippe. Recherches sur les cultes de Délos à l'époque hellénistique et à l'époque impériale. Paris, 1970.
Arc 505.5.110	Busink, T.A. Der Tempel von Jerusalem von Salomo bis Herodes. Leiden, 1970.
Arc 1494.62	Calbató de Grau, Gabriel. Compendio de las piezas de ocho reales. San Juan, 1970. 2v.
Arc 858.98	Cambrian Archaeological Association, London. The Irish Sea province in archaeology and history. Cardiff, 1970.
Arc 936.221.5	Čerškov, Emil. Municipium DD kod Sočanice. Priština, 1970.
Arc 936.140.25	Chichikova, Mariia. Sevtopolis. Sofiia, 1970.
Arc 936.195.37.5	Chropovský, Bohuslav. Slovensko na úsvite dejím. 1. vyd. Bratislava, 1970.
Arc 726.338	Colonna di Paolo, Elena. Castel d'Asso. Roma, 1970. 2v.
Arc 612.66.5	Congrès International d'Archéologie Slave, 2d. Berichte. Berlin, 1970. 3v.
Arc 925.151	Dal'nevostochnaia Arkheologicheskaia Ekspeditsiia. Materialy polevykh izsledovanii Dal'nevostochnoi arkheologicheskoi ekspeditsii. Novosibirsk, 1970- 2v.
Arc 600.215.5	Daumas, François. La ouabet de Kalabcha. Le Caire, 1970.
Arc 1180.5	Demundt, Karl Ernst. Lateinisch-deutsche Interpretationshilfen für spätmittelalterliche und frühneuzeitliche Archivalien. Marburg, 1970.
Arc 925.347.5	Derevianko, Anatolii P. Novopetrovskaia kul'tura Srednego Amura. Novosibirsk, 1970.
Arc 925.347	Derevianko, Anatolii P. V strane srekh solnts. Khabarovsk, 1970.
Arc 925.4.35	Drevnie pis'mena khakarii. Abakan, 1970.
Arc 925.325.10	Drevnosti Bashkirii. Moskva, 1970.
Arc 925.50.195	Drevnosti vostochnogo kryma. Kiev, 1970.
Arc 600.205	Edel, Elmar. Die Felsengräber der Qubbet el Hawa bei Assuan. Wiesbaden, 1970- 2v.
Arc 853.357	Findeisen, Jürgen. Spuren römerzeitlicher Siedlungsvorgänger im Dorfund Stadtbild Südeutschlands und seiner Nachbargebiete. Bonn, 1970.
Arc 1020.150	Fink, Josef. Der Mars Camulus-Stein in der Pfarrkirche zu Rindern. Kevelaer, 1970.
Arc 925.356.1	Fisenko, Vladimir A. Plemena iamnoi kul'tury Iugo-Vostoka. Photoreproduction. Saratov, 1970.
Arc 1510.169	Friedrich, Karl. Ein Beitrag zur Geschichte des Kontermarkenwesens. Münster, 1970.
Arc 843.233	García Guinea, Miguel Angel. El asentamiento cántabra de Celada Marlantes. Santander, 1970.
Arc 861.200	Garlick, Tom. Romans in the Lake counties. Clapham, 1970.
Arc 853.41.15	Garscha, Friedrich. Die Alamannen in Sudbaden. Berlin, 1970. 2v.
Arc 936.14.375	Gąsgowski, Jerzy. Z dziejów polskiej archeologii. wyd. 1. Warszawa, 1970.
Arc 936.6.36	Gediza, Boguslaw. Motyiwj tiguralne w sztuce ludnosci kultury luzyckiej. Wrocław, 1970.
Arc 936.14.380	Głosek, Marian. Miecze średniowieczne z ziem polskich. Łódź, 1970.
Arc 785.13.95	Grant, Michael. The Roman Forum. London, 1970.
Arc 861.100.20	Grohskoph, Bernice. The treasure of Sutton-Hoo. 1. ed. N.Y., 1970.
Arc 1077.2.47.2	Guénon, René. Le symbolisme de la croix. Paris, 1970.
Arc 505.140.5	Hachmann, Rolf. Bericht über die Ergebnisse der Ausgrabungen in Kamid el-Loz (Libanon) in den Jahren 1966 und 1967. Bonn, 1970.
Arc 1675.102	Hauek, Karl. Goldbrakteaten aus Sievern. München, 1970.
Arc 853.348	Hennig, Hilke. Die Grab- und Hortfunde der Urnenfelderkultur aus Ober- und Mittelfranken. Kallmünz, 1970.
Arc 1578.20	Herinek, Ludwig. Österreichische Münzprägungen von Ergänzungen, 1740-1969. Wien, 1970.
Arc 1480.72	Hill, Philip V. The dating and arrangement of the undated coins of Rome, A.D. 98-148. London, 1970.
Arc 736.11.5	Himera I. Campagne di scavo 1963-1965. Roma, 1970.
Arc 1588.4.90	Hlinka, Jozef. Vývgpeňazi a medailí na Slovensku. Bratislava, 1970.
Arc 1520.25	Hoc, Marcel. Histoire monétaire de Tournai. Bruxelles, 1970.
Arc 726.337	Holloway, Robert Ross. Satrianum. Providence, 1970.
Arc 853.308	Hoof, Dieter. Die Steinbeile und Steinarte im Gebiet der Niederrheins und der Maas. Bonn, 1970.
Arc 1086.10	Hula, Franz. Mittelalterliche Kultmale. Wien, 1970.
Arc 543.66.40	Iagadin, V.N. Nekropol' drevnego Mizdakhana. Tashkent, 1970.
Arc 1282.12	Ianin, Valentin L. Aktovye pechati drevnei Rusi X-XV vv. Moskva, 1970. 2v.
Arc 9.2.7	International Congress of Prehistoric and Protohistoric Sciences. Actes du VIIe Congrès international des sciences préhistoriques et protohistoriques. Prague, 1970-71. 2v.
Arc 1510.168	Isenbeck, Julius. Das nassauische Münzwesen. Münster, 1970.

1970 - cont.

Arc 543.66.50	Iuzhno-Turkmenistanskaia Arkheologicheskaia Ekspeditsiia, 1946-. Perechen' opublikovannykh rabot i materialov po tematike Iuzhno-Turkmenistanskoi Arkheologicheskoi Kompleksnoi Ekspeditsii. Ashkhabad, 1970.
VArc 682.25.19	Ivanov, Iordan. Bulgarski starini iz Makedoniia. 2. izd. Sofiia, 1970.
Arc 861.198	Jessup, Ronald-Ferederick. South east England. London, 1970.
Arc 838.40	Jornadas Arqueológicas. Actas. Lisboa, 1970. 2v.
Arc 74.5.2.5	Journal of Roman studies. Numismatic index, 1911-65. Cambridge, Eng., 1970.
Arc 505.136.5	Kamid el-Loz-Kumidi. Bonn, 1970.
Arc 608.82	Katsnel'son, Isidor S. Napata i meroe-drevnie tsarstva sudzna. Moskva, 1970.
Arc 1163.14.6	Keller, Wolfgang. Angelsächsiche Palaeographie. N.Y., 1970-71. 2v.
Arc 497.60.3	Kenyon, Kathleen Mary. Archaeology in the Holy Land. 3. ed. N.Y., 1970.
Arc 925.4.55	Khamzina, Evgeniia A. Arkheologicheskie pamiatniki zapadnogo zabaikal'ia. Ulan-Ude, 1970.
Arc 936.14.296	Kiersnowska, Teresa. Zycie codzienne na Pomorzu wczesnósredniowiecznym, wiek X-XII. Warszawa, 1970.
Arc 870.28	King, Alan. Early Pennine settlement: a field study. Lancaster, 1970.
Arc 513.40	Kink, Khilida A. Vostochnoe sredizemnamor'e v drevneishuiu epokhu. Moskva, 1970.
Arc 1020.146	Kollautz, Arnulf. Denkmäler byzantinischen Christentums aus der Awarenzeit der Donauländer. Amsterdam, 1970.
Arc 1138.120	Kondratov, Aleksandr Mikhailovich. Kogda molchat pis'mena. Moskva, 1970.
Arc 853.317	Kossack, Georg. Gräberfelder dur Hallstattzeit an Main und Fränkischer Saale. Kallmünz, 1970.
Arc 853.65.45	Kostrzewski, Józef. Pradzieje Sląska. Wrocław, 1970.
Arc 395.25	Kostrzewski, Józef. Z mego życia. Wrocław, 1970.
Arc 853.362	Krämer, Werner. Die Ausgrabungen in Manching 1955-1961. Wiesbaden, 1970.
Arc 925.344	Kropotkin, Vladislav V. Rinskie importnye izdeliia v Vostochnoi Evrope. Moskva, 1970.
Arc 936.14.61	Krzak, Zygmunt. Cmentarzysko kultury słockiej "nad Wawrem" w Złotej. Wrocław, 1970.
Arc 1588.1.75	Kubiak, Stanisława. Monety pierwszych Jagiellonów 1386-1444. Wyd. 1. Wrocław, 1970.
Arc 925.50.260	Kurinnyi, Petro. Istoriia arkheolohichnoho znannia pro Ukrainu. Miunkhen, 1970.
Arc 925.9.70	Kushmareva, Karinek. Drevnie kultury Izhnogo Kavkaza. Leningrad, 1970.
Arc 399.3.5	Larichev, Vitalii E. Sorok let sredi sibirskikh drevnostei. Novosibirsk, 1970.
Arc 1223.2	Ledderhose, Lothar. Die Siegelschrift (Chuan-shu) in der Ch'ing-Zeit. Wiesbaden, 1970.
Arc 923.122	Leninskie idei v izuchenii istorii pervobytnogo obshchestva, rabovladeniia i feodalizma. Moskva, 1970.
Arc 407.30	Leppmann, Wolfgang. Winckelmann. 1. ed. N.Y., 1970.
Arc 608.32.5	Lézine, Alexandre. Utique. Tunis, 1970.
Arc 136.1.4	London Society of Antiquaries. Index to Archaeologia. v.51-100 (1888-1966). London, 1970.
Arc 925.9.115	Lordkipanidze, Guram A. K istorii drevnei Kolkhidy. Tbilisi, 1970.
Arc 766.4.25	Lugli, Giuseppe. Itinerario di Roma antica. Milano, 1970.
Arc 889.34	Madderman, Pieter Jan Remees. Linearbandkeramik aus Elsloo und Stein. v.1-2. 's-Gravenhage, 1970.
Arc 936.14.390	Malinowska, Marie. Wczesnósredniowieczne skarby srebrne z Wielkopolski. Poznań, 1970.
Arc 925.225.5	Mannai-ool, Mongush. Tuva v skifskoe vremia. Moskva, 1970.
Arc 925.9.65	Materia'ly no arkheologii abkhazii. Tbilisi, 1970.
Arc 1153.95.1	Mazzoleni, Jole. Paleografia e diplomatica e scienze ausiliarie. Napoli, 1970.
Arc 861.196	Meany, Audrey. Two Anglo-Saxon cemeteries at Winnall, Winchester, Hampshire. London, 1970.
Arc 838.41	Mendes, Maria Teresa Pinto. Bibliografia arqueológica portuguesa 1960-1969. Coimbra, 1970.
Arc 936.220.38	Mijović, Pavle. Tragam drevnih kultura Crme Gore. Titograd, 1970.
Arc 853.320	Mildenberger, Gerhard. Die thuringischen Brandgräber der spätrömischen Zeit. Köln, 1970.
Arc 967.6	Miller, J. Jefferson. Eighteenth-century ceramics from Fort Michilimackinac, Michigan. Washington, 1970.
Arc 505.138	Mittmann, Siegfried. Beiträge zur Siedlungs- und Territorialgeschichte des nördlichen Ostjordanlandes. Wiesbaden, 1970.
Arc 925.10.5	Miziev, Ismail M. Srednevekovye bashni i sklepy Balkarii i Karachaia (XIII-XVIII vv). Nal'chik, 1970.
Arc 830.130.25	Morlet, Antonin. Petit historique de l'affaire de Glozel. Marsat, 1970.
Arc 726.246.5	Moscati, Sabatino. Le stele puniche di Nora nel museo nazionale di Cagliari. Roma, 1970.
Arc 743.27	Mostra del restauro archeologico. Grosseto, 1970.
Arc 612.80	Murray, Jacqueline. The first European agriculture. Edinburgh, 1970.
Arc 497.94	Near Eastern archaeology in the twentieth century. 1. ed. Garden City, N.Y., 1970.
Arc 936.14.315	The neolithic in Poland. Ossolinskich, 1970.
Arc 746.58	Neppi Modona, Aldo. I: Gli alfabeti etruschi; II: La scultura etrusca. Genova, 1970.
Arc 953.32	Nöel Hume, Ivor. A guide to artifacts of colonial America. 1. ed. N.Y., 1970.
Arc 830.358	Nouvelles recherches sur les origines de Clermont-Ferrand. Clermont-Ferrand, 1970.
Arc 543.3.85	Novgorodova, Eleonora A. Tsentral'naia Aziia i karasukskaia problema. Moskva, 1970.
Arc 936.195.225	Novotná, Mária. Die Bronzehortfunde in der Slowakei. 1. vyd. Bratislava, 1970.
Arc 925.150.40	Ocherki po arkheologii Belorussii. Minsk, 1970- 2v.
Arc 925.342.5	Okskii bassein v epokhu kamnia i bronzy. Moskva, 1970.
Arc 936.14.370	Okulicz, Łucja. Kultura kushanów zachodniobałtyjskich we wezesnej epoce zelasa. Wrocław, 1970.
Arc 1588.6.2.5	Ölçer, Cüneyt. Sultan Mohmut II zamomuda darpedilen osmanli madeni porolori. Istanbul, 1970.
Arc 925.50.215	Onaiko, Nadezhda A. Antichnyi import v Pridneprov'e i pobuzh'e v IV-II vv. do n.e. Moskva, 1970.
Arc 1460.6	Orlov, Georgije. Vimi nacijum. Beograd, 1970.
Arc 543.66.13	Ovezov, D.M. Akadenik Akademii nauk Turkmenskoi SSR Mikhail Evgen'evich Masson. Ashkhabad, 1970.
Arc 938.108	Pagirienė, L. Lietuvos TSR archeologija 1940-1967. Vil'nius, 1970.

Chronological Listing

1970 - cont.

Arc 1584.1.20 Pakhomov, Evgenii A. Monety Gruzii. Tbilisi, 1970.
Arc 682.40 Papastamos, Dēmētrios. Melische amphoren. Münster, 1970.
Arc 400.30 Philip Phillips: lower Mississippi survey, 1940-1970. Cambridge, Mass., 1970.
Arc 925.16.45 Po sledam drevnikh kul'tur Kazakhstana. Alma-Ata, 1970.
Arc 746.52 Poggio civitate (Murlo, Siena), il santuario arcaico. Firenze, 1970.
Arc 936.14.355 Polskie Towarzystwo Archeologiczne. Polskie towarzystwo archeologiczne społeczeństwu. Wrocław, 1970.
Arc 608.88.5 Ponsich, Michel. Recherches archéologiques à Tanger et dans sa région. Paris, 1970.
Arc 1510.3.10 Posern-Klett, Karl Friedrich von. Sachens Münzen im Mittelalter. Leipzig, 1970.
Arc 1588.4.73 Pŏsvář, Jaroslav. Moravské mincovny. Vyd. 1. Brno, 1970.
Arc 1590.30 Pošvář, Jaroslav. Die Währung in der Ländern der böhmischen Krone. Graz, 1970.
Arc 505.148 Prausnitz, Moshe W. Studies in the lithic industries of Israel and adjacent countries. Jerusalem, 1970.
Arc 936.14.345 Rajewski, Zolzisław. Biskupin. wyd. 1. Warszawa, 1970.
Arc 384.10 Recherches d'archéologie et d'histoire de l'art (antiquité). Louvain, 1970.
Arc 726.320 Ricerche puniche nel Mediterraneo centrale. Roma, 1970.
Arc 1212.6 Rittel, Erich. Siegel. Braunschweig, 1970.
Arc 609.35 Robinson, Keith Radcliffe. The Iron Age of the southern lake area of Malawi. Zomba, 1970.
Arc 925.38.16 Rudenko, Sergei Ivanovich. Frozen tombs of Siberia. 1. English ed. Berkeley, 1970.
Arc 938.101 Sauvateev, Iurii A. Zalavruga. Leningrad, 1970.
Arc 1190.85 Schwarz, Klaus. Osmanische Sultansurkunden des Sinai-Klosters in türkischer Sprache. Freiburg, 1970.
Arc 403.24 Scientific methods in medieval archaeology. Berkeley, 1970.
Arc 925.348 Sedov, Valentin V. Novgorodskie sopki. Moskva, 1970.
Arc 925.9.80 Shamba, G.K. Akhachcharkhu-drevnii mogil'nik nagornoi Abkhazii. Sukhumi, 1970.
Arc 1675.19.15 Shaten, Anatolii V. Sovetskaia memorial'naia medal', 1917-1967. Moskva, 1970.
Arc 925.20.10 Shelov, Dmitrii B. Tanais i Nizhnii Don v III-I vv. do n.e. Moskva, 1970.
Arc 936.100.45 Škobalj, Ante. Obredne gomile. Sveti Križ na Čiovu, 1970.
Arc 853.65.55 Śląsk w pradziejach Polski. Wrocław, 1970.
Arc 672.2.10 Sordinas, Augustus John. Stone implements from northwestern Corfu, Greece. Memphis, 1970.
Arc 9.5 Sources archeologiques de la civilisation européenne. International Association of South-East European Studies. Bucarest, 1970.
Arc 925.4.40 Soveshchanie po Problemam Khronologii i Kul'turnoi Prinadlezhnosti Arkheologicheskikh Pamiatnikov Zapadnoi Sibiri. Tomsk, 1970. Problemy khronologii i kul'turnoi prinadlezhnosti arkheologicheskikh pamiatnikov Zapadnoi Sibiri. Tomsk, 1970.
Arc 853.358 Spätkaiserzeitliche Funde in Westfalen. Münster, 1970.
Arc 1470.8.5 Starr, Chester. Athenian coinage, 480-449 B.C. Oxford, 1970.
Arc 403.22 Statistiko-kombinatornye metody v arkheologii. Moskva, 1970.
Arc 938.102 Studia archaelogica in memoriam Harri Moora. Tallinn, 1970.
Arc 416.40 Studia z archeologii Azji Przedniej i Starożytnego Wschodu. Wyd. 1. Kraków, 1970.
Arc 938.106 Šturms, Edward. Die steinzeitlichen Kulturen des Baltikums. Bonn, 1970.
Arc 1348.84.2 Suhle, Arthur. Die Münze von der Anfängen bis zur europäischen Neuzeit. 2. Aufl. Leipzig, 1970.
Arc 923.120 Sulimirski, Tadeusz. Prehistoric Russia; an outline. N.Y., 1970.
Arc 925.13.170 Sulimirski, Tadeusz. The Sarmatians. London, 1970.
Arc 1468.66F Sylloge nummorum Graecorum Grèce. Athènes, 1970- 2v.
Arc 612.73 Tabaczyński, Stanisław. Neolit środkowoeuropejski. Wrocław, 1970.
Arc 1588.1.70 Terlecki, W. Mennica warszawska 1765-1965. Wrocław, 1970.
Arc 785.115 Testaguzza, Otello. Portus. Roma, 1970.
Arc 412.16 Throckmorton, Peter. Shipwrecks and archaeology: the unharvested sea. 1. ed. Boston, 1970.
Arc 853.31.15 Timpel, Wolfgang. Burgen, Gräber, alte Kreuze. Weimar, 1970.
Arc 905.86 Tot, Tibor A. Antropologicheskie dannye k voprosu o velikom peseselenii narodov. Leningrad, 1970.
Arc 936.220.70 Trbuhović, Vojislav B. Donja toponica. Prokuplje, 1970.
Arc 938.17.15 Vankina, Lutsiia V. Tortianikovaia stoiankor Sarnate. Riga, 1970.
Arc 608.23.10 Vantini, Giovanni. The exavations at Faras. Thesis. Bologna, 1970.
Arc 925.9.100 Vinogradov, Vitalii B. Cherez khrebty vekov. Grozny, 1970.
Arc 936.14.139 Warsaw. Uniwersytet. Zespoł Badan nad Polskim Sredniowieczem. VI konferencja naukowa w Warszawie 10-11 styczhia 1969. Warszawa, 1970.
Arc 785.110 Wielowiejski, Jerzy. Kontakty Noricum i Pannonii z ludami połnochymi. Wrocław, 1970.
Arc 853.304 Wightman, Edith Mary. Roman Trier and the Treveri. London, 1970.
Arc 861.205 Woolf, Charles William. An introduction to the archaeology of Cornwall. Truro, 1970.
Arc 936.14.325 Woyda, Stefan. Bibliografia archeologiczna Mazowsza. wyd. 1. Warszawa, 1970.
Arc 936.14.365 Woźniak, Zenon. Osadnictwo celtyckie w Pobie. Wrocław, 1970.
Arc 936.14.286 Z badań nad kulturą ceramiki nytej. Wyd. 1. Kraków, 1970.
Arc 936.14.350 Z dziejsw regionu koninskiego. Wrocław, 1970.
Arc 853.13.35 Zuern, Hartwig. Hallstattforschungen in Nordwürttemberg. Stuttgart, 1970.

1971

Arc 1163.41.5 Aaberg, Alf. Läsning av gamla handstilar. 5. uppl. Stockholm, 1971.
Arc 608.2.60 Acquaro, Enrico. I rasoi punici. Roma, 1971.
Arc 925.310.10 Alekseeva, Evgeniia P. Drevniaia i srednevekovaia istoriia Karachaevo-Cherkesii. Moskva, 1971.
Arc 530.6.10F Alfoldi-Rosenbaum, Elizabeth. Anamur nekropolu. The necropolis Anemurium. Ankara, 1971.
Arc 681.15.5 Angel, John Lawrence. The people of Lerna. Princeton, N.J., 1971.

1971 - cont.

Arc 384.14 Anglo-Romanian Conference on Mathematics in the Archaeological and Historical Sciences. Mathematics in the archaeological and historical sciences; proceedings. Edinburgh, 1971.
Arc 925.50.230 Arkheolohiia Ukrains'koi RSR. Kyïv, 1971. 2v.
Arc 925.13.186 Bakay, Kornél. Scythian rattles in the Carpathian Basin and their eastern connections. Amsterdam, 1971.
Arc 1423.27 Baldus, Hans Roland. Uranius Antoninius. Bonn, 1971.
Arc 830.357 Ballet, Pierre. Le Haute-Marne antique. Chaumont, 1971.
Arc 723.46 Barfield, Lawrence. Northern Italy before Rome. London, 1971.
Arc 530.176 Bean, George Ewart. Turkey beyond the Maeander, an archaeological guide. London, 1971.
Arc 925.50.205 Bidzilia, Vasyl' I. Istoriia kul'tury Zakarpattia na rubezhi nashoi ery. Kyïv, 1971.
Arc 936.38.5 Böttger, Burkhard. Bulgarien; eine Reise zu antiken Kulturstätten. 1. Aufl. Berlin, 1971.
Arc 416.46 Borisovskii, Pavel I. Drevnii kamennyi vek Iuzhnoi i Iuga-Vostochnoi Azii. Leningrad, 1971.
Arc 716.14.2 Brunnsaaker, Sture. The tyrant slayers of Kritios and Nesiotes: a critical study of the sources and restorations. 2. ed. Stockholm, 1971.
Arc 658.3.25 Brusti, Franz Georg. Heinrich Schliemann. München, 1971.
Arc 861.21.30 Butler, Ronald Morley. Soldier and civilian in Roman Yorkshire; essay to commemorate the nineteenth century of the foundation of York. Leicester, 1971.
Arc 600.243 Cabra, Sami. Chez les derniers adorateurs du Trismegiste. Cairo, 1971.
Arc 1488.34 Cainola, Aldo. Le antiche zecche d'Italia. Roma, 1971.
Arc 853.96.10 Capelle, Torsten. Studien über elbgermanische Gräber felder im der ausgehenden Latènezeit und der alteren Kaiserzeit. Habilitationsschrift. Hildesheim, 1971.
Arc 1088.1.11 Casson, Lionel. Ships and seamanship in the ancient world. Princeton, N.J., 1971.
Arc 609.1.57 Caton-Thompson, Gertrude. The Zimbabwe culture: ruins and reactions. 2. ed. London, 1971.
Arc 1560.3.1 Cavalli, Gustaf. Gustaf Cavallis samlung av svenska kopparmynt. Facsimile. Stockholm, 1971.
Arc 1470.87 Centro Internazionale di Studi Numismatici. Atti del IIo Convegno del Centro internazionale di studi numismatici. Roma, 1971.
Arc 936.14.400 Chmielowska, Aldona. Grebienie starozytne i sredniowieczne z ziem polskich. Łódź, 1971.
Arc 853.350 Christlein, Rainer. Das alamannische Gräberfeld von Dirlewang bei Minchelheim. Kallmünz, 1971.
Arc 925.9.105 Chubinishvili, Taniel. K drevnei istorii Iuzhnogo Kavkaza. Tbilisi, 1971.
Arc 915.51 Colloque International sur les Cols des Alpes (Antiquité et Moyen-Age), Bourg-en-Bresse, France, 1969. Actes du Colloque International sur les Cols des Alpes, Antiquité et Moyen-Age, Bourg-en-Bresse, 1969. Orléans, 1971.
Arc 936.24.5 Condurachi, Emil. Romania. London, 1971.
Arc 642.8.1 Cottrell, Leonard. The bull of Minos. London, 1971.
Arc 861.40.20 Cunliffe, Barry W. Roman Bath discovered. London, 1971.
Arc 412.20 Dating techniques for the archaeologist. Cambridge, 1971.
Arc 936.195.230 Davidek, Vácalv. Co bylo préd Prahon. 1. vyd. Praha, 1971.
Arc 823.45.5 Déchelette, Joseph. Manuel d'archéologie préhistorique, celtique et gallo-romaine. v.1-2, pt.1-3. Westmead, Eng., 1971. 5v.
Arc 726.263.5 Découvertes archéologiques fortuites en Corse. v.1-2. Bastia, 1971-
Arc 710.28 Des Gagniers, Jean. L'acropole d'Athènes. Québec, 1971.
Arc 384.18 Deutsche Historiker Gesellschaft. Fachgruppe Ur- und Frühgeschichte. Evolution und Revolution in alten Orient und in Europa. Das Neolithikum als historische Erscheinung. Berlin, 1971.
Arc 681.10.5 Die deutschen Ausgrabungen auf der Otzaki-Magula in Thessalien. Bonn, 1971- 2v.
Arc 1588.3.5 Dimitrijević, Sergije. Novac kneza Lasara. Kruševac, 1971.
Arc 1503.8 Divo, Jean-Paul. Die neueren Münzen der Schweiz und des Fürstentums Leichtenstein. 1850-1970. 4. Aufl. Freiburg, 1971.
Arc 543.83.10 Doe, Brian. Southern Arabia. London, 1971.
Arc 388.18 Donnell, Robert C. Systematics in prehistory. N.Y., 1971.
Arc 861.210 Down, Alec. Chichester excavations. Chichester, 1971- 2v.
Arc 66.1.219 Ducat, Jean. Les kouroi du Ptoion. Paris, 1971.
Arc 1500.69 Dumas-Dubourg, Françoise. Le trésor de Fécamp et la monnayage en Francie occidentale pendant la seconde moitié du Xe siècle. Paris, 1971.
Arc 875.134 Dundee, Scotland. Museum and Art Gallery. Tayside before history. Dundee, 1971.
Arc 66.1.218 Duval, Noël. Les églises africaines à deux absides. Paris, 1971- 2v.
Arc 1190.90 Dyplomatyka wieków średnich. Wyd. 1. Warszawa, 1971.
Arc 383.36 The European community in later prehistory: studies in honour of C.F.C. Hawkes. London, 1971.
Arc 843.192 Ewert, Christian. Islamische Funde in Balaguer und die Aljaferia in Zaragoza. Berlin, 1971.
Arc 389.4.1 Eydoux, Henri Paul. In search of lost worlds. 1. American ed. N.Y., 1971.
Arc 853.361 Fingerlin, Gerhard. Die alamannischen Gräberfelder von Guttingen und Merdingen in Südbaden. Berlin, 1971. 2v.
Arc 915.53 Fischer, Franz. Die fruhbronzezeitliche Ansiedlung in der Bleiche bei Arbon T.G. Basel, 1971.
Arc 853.372 Fischer, Ulrich. Aus Frankfurts Vorgeschichte. Frankfurt am Main, 1971.
Arc 412.1.10 Flemming, Nicholas C. Cities in the sea. 1. ed. Garden City, N.Y., 1971.
Arc 726.342 Franciscis, Alfonso. Ricerche sulla topografia e i monumenti di Locri. Napoli, 1971-
Arc 925.12.7.2 Gaidukevich, V.F. Das bosporanische Reich. 2. Aufl. Berlin, 1971.
Arc 726.331 Galliazzo, Vittorio. I ponti di Padova romana. Padova, 1971.
Arc 861.21.35 Garlick, Tom. Roman sites in Yorkshire. Lancaster, 1971.
Arc 936.220.80 Girić, Milorad. Mokim. Washington, 1971-72. 2v.
Arc 391.18 Goodyear, Frank Haigh. Archaeological site science. N.Y., 1971.
Arc 1138.115.2 Gordon, Cyrus Herzl. Forgotten scripts. Harmondsworth, 1971.
Arc 925.13.175 Grakov, Boris N. Skify. Moskva, 1971.

1971 - cont.

Arc 793.22 Grant, Michael. Cities of Vesuvius: Pompeii and Herculaneum. London, 1971.
Arc 848.61.5 Hachmann, Rolf. Die Germanen. München, 1971.
Arc 848.61 Hachmann, Rolf. The Germanic peoples. London, 1971.
Arc 1510.11.20 Hahn, Wolfgang Reinhard Otto. Typenkatalog der Münzer der bayerischen Herzöge und Kurfürsten, 1506-1805. Braunschweig, 1971.
Arc 853.83.15 Hamkens, F.H. Der Externstein. Tübingen, 1971.
Arc 943.10.1 Hamy, Jules. Mémoires d'archéologie et d'ethnographié americaines. Graz, 1971.
RRC Arc 1583.30 Harris, Robert P. A guidebook of Russian coins, 1725 to 1970. 1. ed. Santa Cruz, California, 1971.
Arc 530.151 Haspels, Caroline H.E. The highlands of Phrygia: sites and monuments. Princeton, 1971. 2v.
Arc 936.14.333 Hensel, Witold. Archeologia i prahistoria. Wrocław, 1971.
Arc 710.26 Hopper, Robert John. The acropolis. London, 1971.
Arc 936.24.10 Horedt, Kurt. Die prähistorische Ansiedlung auf dem Wietenberg bei Sighisoara-Schässburg. Bonn, 1971.
Arc 925.50.200 Humenna, Dokiia. Rodynnyi al'bom. Niu-Iork, 1971.
Arc 746.60 Hus, Alain. Vulci étrusque et étrusco-romaine. Paris, 1971.
Arc 936.215.10 Les Illyriens et la genèse des Albanais; travaux de la session du 3-4 mars, 1969. Tirana, 1971.
Arc 9.2.8 International Congress of Prehistoric and Protohistoric Sciences, 8th, Belgrad, 1971. Actes du VIIIe Congrès international des sciences préhistoriques et protohistoriques. Beograd, 1971- 3v.
Arc 936.20.5 Ionitǎ, Ian. Das Gräberfeld von Independenta. Bonn, 1971.
Arc 858.83 The Iron Age and its hill-forts. Southampton, 1971.
Arc 678.5 Isthmia; excavations by the University of Chicago. Princeton, N.J., 1971. 2v.
Arc 933.7 Istoriia i kul'tura Vostochnoi Evropy po arkheologicheskim dannym. Moskva, 1971.
Arc 726.333 Italy. Soprintendenza alle Antichità della Basilicata. Popoli anellenici in Basilicata. Napoli, 1971.
Arc 865.9.11 Jones, Inigo. The most notable antiquity of Great Britain called Stone-Heng. Farnborough, 1971.
Arc 936.251.10 Jovanović, Borislav. Metalurgija eneolitskog perioda Yugoslavije. Beograd, 1971.
Arc 843.232 Julia, Dolorès. Étude épigraphique et iconographique des stèles funéraires de Vigo. Heidelberg, 1971.
Arc 1584.30 Kairn, Reinhold. Russische Münzstätten, Münzzeichen, Münzmeisterzeichen. Braunschweig, 1971.
Arc 1453.11 Kargel, Adolf. Münzen erzählen. Bielefeld, 1971.
Arc 497.96 Kenyon, Kathleen Mary. Royal cities of the Old Testament. N.Y., 1971.
Arc 925.13.180 Khazanov, Anatolii M. Ocherki noennogo dela sarmatov. Moskva, 1971.
Arc 853.364 Kleemann, Otto. Vor- und Frühgeschichte des Kreises Ahrweiler. Bonn, 1971.
Arc 925.50.225 Knyzhitskii, Sergei D. Zhilye ansambli drevnei Ol'vii IV-II vv. do n.e. Kiev, 1971.
Arc 853.368 Körner, Gerhard. Vorgeschichte im Landkreis Lüneburg. Lüneburg, 1971.
Arc 853.349 Kolling, Alfons. Funde aus der Römerstadt Schwarzenacke und ihrer nahen Ungebung. Homburg-Saar, 1971.
Arc 412.22 Kondratov, Aleksandr M. Tainy tsekh okeanov. Leningrad, 1971.
Arc 925.268 Konstantinov, Ivan V. Material'naia kul'tura iakutov XVIII veka. Iakutsk, 1971.
Arc 1390.20 Kotliar, Mykola F. Hroskovyi sbih na terytorii Ukrainy doby teodalizma. Kyïv, 1971.
Arc 612.78 Kowalczyk, Jan. Zmierzch epoki kamicnia. Wrocław, 1971.
Arc 612.82 Kozłowski, Janusz. Munj cyklopów. Wrocław, 1971.
Arc 612.76 Krueger, Karl Heinrich. Königsgrabkirchen der Franken. München, 1971.
Arc 925.9.120 Krupnov, Evgenii I. Srednovekoraia Ingushetiia. Moskva, 1971.
Arc 925.9.135 Kuznetsov, Vladimir A. Alaniia v X-XIII vv. Ordzhonikidze, 1971.
Arc 766.1.9.5 Lanciani, R. La distruzione di Roma antica. Milano, 1971.
Arc 497.100 Landay, Jerry M. Silent cities, sacred stones: archaeological discovery in the land of the Bible. London, 1971.
Arc 612.87 Lange, Elsbeth. Botanisch Beiträge zur mitteleuropäischen Siedlungsgeschichte. Berlin, 1971.
Arc 905.24.25 Leber, Paul Siegfried. Aus Kärntens römischer Vergangenheit. v.1-5. Wolfsberg, 1971-
Arc 608.93 Lézine, Alexandre. Deux villes d'Ifriqiya: Sousse, Tunis. Paris, 1971.
Arc 1580.50 Luschin von Ebengreath, Arnold. Steirische Münzfunde. Graz, 1971.
Arc 397.25 McDaniel, Walton B. Riding a hobby in the classical lands. Cambridge, 1971.
Arc 936.220.75 McPherron, Alan. Early farming cultures in Central Serbia (Eastern Yugoslavia). Krazujevać, 1971.
Arc 853.165.10 Maisant, Hermann. Der Kreis Saarlouis in vor- und frühgeschichtlichen Zeit. Bonn, 1971. 2v.
Arc 1190.90.5 Maleczyński, Karol. Studia nad dokumentem polskim. Wrocław, 1971.
Arc 953.34 Marek, Kurt W. The first American. 1. ed. N.Y., 1971.
Arc 925.4.29 Martynov, Anatolii I. Shestakovskie kurgany. Kemerovo, 1971.
Arc 505.147.1 Mazar, Benjamin. The excavations in the old city of Jerusalem near the Temple Mount. Jerusalem, 1971.
Arc 505.149 Meyers, Eric Mark. Jewish ossuaries: reburial and rebirth. Rome, 1971.
Arc 925.335 Mezolit Verkhnego Priangar'ia. Irkutsk, 1971-
Arc 925.353 Minaeva, Tat'iana M. K istorii alan Verkhnego Prikuban'ia po arkheologicheskim dannym. Staviopol', 1971.
Arc 493.62 Minasian, Caro Owen. Shah Diz of Isma'ili fame. London, 1971.
Arc 925.12.20F Minns, Ellis Hovell. Scythians and Greeks. N.Y., 1971.
Arc 505.144 Miroschedji, Pierre R. de. L'époque que pré-urbaine en Palestine. Paris, 1971.
Arc 913.25 Moosbrugger, Leu Rudolf. Die Schweiz zur Merowingerzeit. Bern, 1971. 2v.
Arc 608.92 Moscati, Sabatino. Tra Cartagine e Roma. Milano, 1971.
Arc 1583.32 Moscow. Gosudarstvennyi Istoricheskii Muzei. Monety SSSR. Moskva, 1971.
Arc 925.16.50 Musabaev, Gainetdin G. Epigrafika Kazakhstana. Alma-Ata, 1971.
Arc 925.296F Nat, Daniel. Éléments de préhistoire et d'archéologie nord-sibériennes. Paris, 1971-
Arc 543.146.20 Neoliticheskie poseleniia i srednevekovye goroda. Ashkhabad, 1971.

1971 - cont.

Arc 391.17 Niggl, Reto. Giacomo Grimaldi (1568-1623). Inaug. Diss. München, 1971.
Arc 925.95.5 Nikitin, Arkadii. Russkoe kwznechmoe remeslo XVI-XVII vv. Moskva, 1971.
Arc 1163.3.105 Nikolaeva, Tat'iana V. Proizvedeniia russkogo prikladnogo iskusstvo s nadpisiami XV- pervoi chetverti XVI v. Mosvka, 1971.
Arc 1675.106 Nikolić, Desanka. Naša odlikovanja do 1941. Beograd, 1971.
Arc 1588.4.38 Nohejlová, Emanuela. Dvě stoleti vědecké numismatiky v českých Zemich. 1771-1971. Praha, 1971.
Arc 936.238.5 Novo Mesto, Yugoslavia. Dolenjski Muzej. Prazgodovina Novego Mesta. Novo Mesto, 1971.
Arc 905.24.20 Obermayr, August. Kelten und Römer am Magdalensberg. Wien, 1971.
Arc 936.14.440 Ogólnopolska Konferencja Konserwatorów Zabytkow Archeologicznych. Wspolpraca z Przemyslem w Dziedzinie Ochrony Zabytkow Archeologicznych, Poznań, 1969. Przemysl a archeologia. Poznań, 1971.
Arc 956.2 Okladnikov, Aleksei P. Drevnie poseleniia Baranova mysa. Novosibirsk, 1971.
Arc 925.347.10 Okladnikov, Aleksei P. Petroglify Nizhnego Amura. Leningrad, 1971.
Arc 726.322 Otto, prince of Hesse. Primo contributo alla archeologia longobarda in Toscana: Le necropoli. Firenze, 1971.
Arc 1480.42.15 Pekary, Thomas. Die Fundmünzen von Vindonissa von Hadrian bis zum Ausgang der Römerherrschaft. Brugg, 1971.
Arc 723.44 Peroni, Renato. L'età del bronzo nella penisola italiana. Firenze, 1971-
Arc 936.225.10 Petru, Peter. Hišaste źare Latobikov. Ljubljana, 1971.
Arc 672.1.122 Platon, Nikolaos Eleutheriou. Zakros: the discovery of a lost places of ancient Crete. N.Y., 1971.
Arc 925.150.45 Pobol', Leonid D. Slavianskie drevnosti Belorussii. Minsk, 1971.
Arc 936.195.220 Polla, Belo. Kežmarok. 1. vyd. Bratislava, 1971.
Arc 925.337 Priakhin, Anatolii D. Abashevskaia kul'tura v Podon'e. Voronezh, 1971.
Arc 830.371 Pruvot, Georges. Épave antique étrusco-punique? Antibes, 1971.
Arc 402.22 Rehork, Joachim. Faszinierende Funde; Archäologie heute. Bergisch Gladbach, 1971.
Arc 936.165.40 Rikman, Emmanuil A. Ocherki istorii kul'tury Moldavii (II-XIV vv). Kishinev, 1971.
Arc 1568.6 Rønning, Bjørn R. Norges mynter. Oslo, 1971.
Arc 612.37 Rust, Alfred. Werkzeuge des Frühmenschen in Europa. Neumünster, 1971.
Arc 612.57.5 Ryndina, Nataliia Vadimovna. Drevneishee metalloobrabatyvainshchee proiznodstno Vostochnoi Evropy. Moskva, 1971.
Arc 493.6.45 Sadykhzade, S.G. Drevnie ukrashcheniia Azerbaidzhana. Baku, 1971.
Arc 453.18 Sankalia, Hasmukh Dhirajlal. Chalcolithic Navdatoli; the excavations at Navdatoli, 1957-59. 1. ed. Poona, 1971.
Arc 403.23 Santos Rocha, Antonio dos. Memórias e exploraçoes arquelógicas. Coimbra, 1971-
Arc 885.25.5 Savory, Hubert Newman. Excavations at Dinorben, 1965-69. Cardiff, 1971.
Arc 726.330 Scarani, Renato. Civiltà preromane del territorio parmense. Parma, 1971.
Arc 488.31 Schippmann, Klaus. Die iranischen Feuerheiligtümer. Habilitationsschrift. Berlin, 1971.
Arc 612.93 Schneider, Renate-Ursula. Zur Südabgrenzung des Bereichs der nordischen jüngeren Bronzezeit in Periode IV nach Montelius. Hamburg, 1971.
Arc 520.18.10 Schulte, Eduard. Carl Humann. Dortmund, 1971.
Arc 915.52 Schwab, Hanni. Jungsteinzeitliche Fundstellen im Kanton Freiburg. Basel, 1971.
Arc 1153.106 Scriptorum opus: Schreiber-Mönche am Werk. Wiesbaden, 1971.
Arc 925.50.210 Seredni viky na Ukraini. Kyïv, 1971.
Arc 609.32 Shinnie, Peter L. The African Iron Age. Oxford, 1971.
Arc 936.3.10F Shqiperia arkeologjike - Archaeological Albania. Tiranë, 1971.
Arc 700.64 Sinos, Stefan. Die vorklassischen Hausformen in der Ägäis. Mainz, 1971.
Arc 936.220.120 Sirmium. Beograd, 1971- 3v.
Arc 700.68A Snodgrass, Anthony M. The dark age of Greece: an archaeological survey of the eleventh to the eighth centuries B.C. Edinburgh, 1971.
Arc 74.4.1.5 Society for the Promotion of Hellenic Studies. Journal. Numismatic index, 1880-1969. Cambridge, Eng., 1971.
Arc 925.9.151 Solov'ev, L.N. Pervobytnoe obshchestvo na territorii Abkhazii. Photoreproduction. Sukhumi, 1971.
Arc 853.259 Spindler, Konrad. Magdalenenberg. Villingen, 1971. 3v.
Arc 895.56.6 Strömberg, Märta. Die Megalithgräber von Hagestad. Lund, 1971.
Arc 1453.10 Suchodolski, Stanisław. Początki mennictwa w Europie Środkowej, Wschodniej i Połnocnej. Wrocław, 1971.
Arc 609.34 Summers, Roger. Ancient ruins and vanished civilizations of southern Africa. Capetown, 1971.
Arc 412.7 Symposium on Archaeological Chemistry. Science and archaeology. Cambridge, Mass., 1971.
Arc 925.9.125 Tekhov, Bagrat V. Ocherki drevnei istorii i arkheologii Iugo-Osetri. Tbilisi, 1971.
Arc 830.201 Thévenot, Emile. Le Beaunois gallo-romain; ouvrage présenté et complété. Bruxelles, 1971.
Arc 858.105 Thomas, Charles. The early Christian archaeology of Northern Britain. London, 1971.
Arc 936.220.22 Todorović, Jovan. Katalog praistorijskih metalmih predmeta. Beograd, 1971.
Arc 925.9.110 Turchaninov, Georgii F. Pamiatniki pis'nu i iazyka narodov Kavkaza i vostochnoi Evropy. Leningrad, 1971.
Arc 1148.36 Turner, Eric Gardiner. Greek manuscripts of the ancient world. Oxford, 1971.
Arc 865.28 Twist, Richard Marsden. Stonehenge: a classical interpretation. St. Anthony, 1971.
Arc 861.208 Uhthoff-Kaufmann, Raymond R. The archaeology of Jodrell Hall (Terra Nova), Cheshire. Wilmslow, 1971.
Arc 746.40.5F Vagnetti, Lucia. Il deposito votivo di Competti a Veio. Firenze, 1971.
Arc 830.369 Veillard, Jean Yves. Celtes et Armorique. Rennes, 1971.
Arc 936.40.41 Venedikov, Ivan. Nessebre. Sofia, 1971.
Arc 1613.30 Vermeule, Cornelius Clarkson. Numismatic art in America. Cambridge, 1971.

Chronological Listing

1971 - cont.

Arc 609.24.5 Vogel, Joseph O. Kamanejoza: an introduction to the Iron Age cultures of the Victoria Falls region. London, 1971.

Arc 938.110 Volkaitė-Kulikauskienė, Regina. Lietuvio kario žirgas. Vil'nius, 1971.

Arc 421.32 Watson, William. Cultural frontiers in ancient east Asia. Edinburgh, 1971.

Arc 1510.164 Welter, Gerhard. Die Münzen der Welfen seit Heinrich dem Löwen. Braunschweig, 1971-73. 2v.

Arc 1680.16.5 Whiting, John Roger Scott. Trade tokens; a social and economic history. Newton Abbot, 1971.

Arc 870.30 Wildman, Samuel Gerald. The black horsemen: English inns and King Arthur. London, 1971.

Arc 700.19.10 Winter, F.E. Greek fortifications. London, 1971.

Arc 700.19.11 Winter, F.E. Greek fortifications. Toronto, 1971.

Arc 609.22.5 Woodhouse, Herbert Charles. Archaelogy in southern Africa. Capetown, 1971.

Arc 572.10.5 Wortham, John David. British Egyptology, 1549-1906. Newton Abbot, 1971.

Arc 572.10 Wortham, John David. The genesis of British Egyptology, 1549-1906. 1st ed. Norman, 1971.

Arc 915.48.2 Wyss, René. Die Egolzwiler Kultur. 2. Aufl. Bern, 1971.

Arc 384.13 Z polskich badań nad epokş kamienia. Wrocław, 1971.

Arc 695.2 Zagora I; excavation season 1967. Sydney, 1971.

Arc 726.216 Zecchini, Michelangelo. L'archeologia nell'Arcipelago toscano. Pisa, 1971.

Arc 936.14.385 25 lat archeologii na Dolnym Śląsku, 1945-70. Wrocław, 1971.

1972

Arc 925.16.60 Akishev, Kemal' A. Drevnii Otrar. Alma-Ata, 1972.

Arc 612.86 Albrecht, Gerd. Merkmalanalyse von Geschossspitzen des mittleren Jungpleistozäns im Mittel- und Osteuropa. Stuttgart, 1972.

Arc 936.220.90 Alexander, John. Jugoslavia before the Roman conquest. London, 1972.

Arc 936.220.91 Alexander, John. Yugoslavia before the Roman conquest. N.Y., 1972.

Arc 412.24 Animals in archaeology. N.Y., 1972.

Arc 726.325 Archeologia e storia nella Lombardia padana. Bedriacum nel XIX centenario delle Battaglie. Como, 1972.

Arc 895.79 Arkaeologisk ABC. Handbog i dansk forhistorie. København, 1972.

Arc 925.321.15 Arkheologicheskie issledovaniia v Karelii. Leningrad, 1972.

Arc 1588.6.1 Artuk, Ibrah. Konuni Sultan Suleymon adena basilon sikkeler. Ankara, 1972.

Arc 925.50.255 Aulikh, Vitold V. Zymnivs'ke horodyshche-slov'ians'ka pam'iatka. Kyïv, 1972.

Arc 923.127 Avdusin, Daniil A. Polevaia arkheologiia SSSR. Moskva, 1972.

Arc 1478.88.1F Bahrfeldt, Max von. Sammlung römischer Münzen der Republik und des West-Kaiserreichs. Aalen, 1972.

Arc 853.365 Bantelmann, Niels. Die Urgeschichte des Kreises Kusel. Speyer, 1972.

Arc 1478.89 Banti, Alberto. Corpus nummorum romanorum. Firenze, 1972- 8v.

Arc 925.50.265 Baran, Volodymyr D. Ranni slov'iany mizh Dnistrom i pnypiatkii. Kyïv, 1972.

Arc 412.1.5 Bass, George Fletcher. A history of seafaring based on underwater archaeology. London, 1972.

Arc 925.75.20 Belinde Ballu, Eugéne. Olbia. Leiden, 1972.

Arc 540.16F Benson, Jack L. Bamboula at Kourion. Philadelphia, 1972.

Arc 386.46 Berlitz, Charles F. Mysteries from forgotten worlds. Garden City, 1972.

Arc 925.50.245 Bevezans'ka, Sofiia S. Srednii period bronzovogo veka v Severnoi Ukraine. Kiev, 1972.

Arc 386.44 Binford, Lewis Roberts. An archaeological perspective. N.Y., 1972.

Arc 66.1.220 Bloch, Raymond. Recherches archéologique en territoire Volsinien. Paris, 1972.

Arc 726.296 Bondi, Sandro Filippo. Le stele di Monte Sirai. Roma, 1972.

Arc 885.15.8 Boon, George C. Isca, the Roman legionaryfortress at Caerleon. 3. ed. Cardiff, 1972.

Arc 830.368 Bordes, François. A tale of two caves. N.Y., 1972.

Arc 858.100 Bowen, Emrys George. Britain and the western seaways. London, 1972.

Arc 608.6.70 Brahime, Claude. Initiation à la préhistoire de l'Algérie. Alger, 1972.

Arc 861.209 Brixworth excavations. Northampton, Eng., 1972?

Arc 543.3.100 Bulatova, Vera A. Drevnaia kuvą. Tashkent, 1972.

Arc 905.146 Burgstaller, Ernst. Felsbilder in Österreich. Linz, 1972.

Arc 505.155F Callaway, Joseph A. The early bronze age sanctuary at Ai (et-Tell). London, 1972.

Arc 726.329 Cannas, Vincenzo Mario. I nuraghi Aleri e Nastasi e le nuove scoperte archeologiche nel territorio di Tertenia. Cagliari, 1972.

Arc 1470.43.5 Ceka, Hasan. Questions de numismatique illyrie. Tirana, 1972.

Arc 936.195.265 Celostátní Seminář o Problematice Zaniklých Středověkých Vesnic, 3rd, Uherské Hradiště, Czechoslovak Republic, 1971. Zaniklé středověké vesnice v ČSSR ve svetle archeologických výzkumů. Uherské Hradiště, 1972.

Arc 936.140.30 Changova, Iordanka. Srednovekovnoto selishte nad trakiiskiia grad Sevtopolis. Sofiia, 1972.

Arc 1087.5 Chernykh, Evgenii N. Metall-chelovsk-vremia. Moskva, 1972.

Arc 609.9.6 Clark, John Desmond. The prehistoric cultures of the Horn of Africa. N.Y., 1972.

Arc 412.9 Clarke, David L. Models in archaeology. London, 1972.

Arc 1153.112PF Codices latini antiquiores. pt.2. 2. ed. Oxford, 1972.

Arc 1493.27 Coelho, Antonio D.S. Numária da Lusitânia. Lisboa, 1972.

Arc 858.104 Coles, John M. Field archaeology in Britain. London, 1972.

Arc 830.275.15 Cornet, Jean M. Entremont et l'impérium arverne. Romans, 1972- 2v.

Arc 505.5.115 Cornfeld, Gaalyahu. The mystery of the Temple Mount. Tel Aviv, 1972.

Arc 843.231 Correia, Vergilio. Estudos arqueologicos. Coimbra, 1972.

Arc 1153.114 Costamagna, Giorgio. Studi di paleografia e diplomatica. Roma, 1972.

Arc 858.101 Cunliffe, Barry W. Cradle of England: an introduction through archaeology to the early history of England and a brief guide to selected sites in the South. London, 1972.

1972 - cont.

Arc 936.14.420 Dąbrowski, Jan. Powiązanie ziem polskich z terenami uschodnimi w epoce brązu. Wrocław, 1972.

Arc 1433.101 Davidovich, Elena A. Denezhnoe khoziaistvo Srednei Azii posle mongol'skaia zavoevaniia i reforma Mas'ud-beka. Moskva, 1972.

Arc 726.323 Davison, Jean M. Seven Italic tomb-groups from Narce. Firenze, 1972.

Arc 925.151.5 Derevianko, Anatolii P. Pannii zheleznyi vek Dal'nego Vostoka. v.2- Novosibirsk, 1972-

Arc 925.50.305 Doslidzhennia starodavn'oï istoriï Zakarpattia. Uzhhorod, 1972.

Arc 726.263 Les églises piévanes de Corse, de l'époque romaine au Moyen Age. Bastia, 1972-

Arc 493.60.5 Ellis, Richard Stephens. A bibliography of Mesopotamian archaeological sites. Wiesbaden, 1972.

Arc 1138.126 Epigrafika Vostochnoi i Iuzhnoi Azii. Moskva, 1972.

Arc 1248.2 Ewe, Herbert. Schiffe auf Siegeln. 1. Aufl. Rostock, 1972.

Arc 488.32 Excavations in Iran: the British contribution. Oxford, 1972.

Arc 853.363 Fehr, Horst. Die vor- und frühgeschichtliche Besiedlung der Kreise. Speyer, 1972.

Arc 861.200.5 Fell, Clare. Early settlement in the Lake counties. Clapham, 1972.

Arc 383.20 Festschrfit Luitpold Dussler: 28 Studien zur Archäologie und Kunstgeschichte. München, 1972.

Arc 340.25.9 Field, Henry. Bibliography of Soviet archaeology and physical anthropology, 1936-1972. no. 1-189. Coconut Grove, Fla., 1972.

Arc 905.29.5 Fitz, Jeno. Les Syriens à Intercisa. Bruxelles, 1972.

Arc 723.20.14F Forma Italiae. Serie II documenti. Firenze, 1972-

Arc 726.342.5 Franciscis, Alfonso. Stato e società in Loori. Napoli, 1972.

Arc 1542.3F Galster, Georg. Unionstidens udmøntninger. København, 1972.

Arc 1010.26 Garanger, José. Archéologie des Nouvelles Hébrides. Paris, 1972.

Arc 1528.8.5 Gelder, Hendrik Enno van. De Nederlandse munten. 5. druk. Utrecht, 1972.

Arc 543.3.105 Ginzburg, Vul'f V. Paleoantropologiia Srednei Azii. Moskva, 1972.

Arc 925.60.5 Gorodishche Khulash i pamiatniki srednevekov'ia chuvashskogo Povolzh'ia. Cheboksary, 1972.

Arc 432.19 Gupta, Swarajya Prakash. Disposal of the dead and physical types in ancient India. 1. ed. Delhi, 1972.

Arc 1093.11 Hald, Margrethe. Primitive shoes. København, 1972.

Arc 530.2.10 Hanfmann, George M.A. Letters from Sardis. Cambridge, 1972.

Arc 861.172.5 Harding, Derek William. The Iron Age in the Upper Thames basin. Oxford, 1972.

Arc 497.103 Harker, Ronald. Digging up the Bible lands. London, 1972.

Arc 1588.4.100 Hásková, Jarmila. Chebské mince z 12. a 13. století. Cheb, 1972.

Arc 861.211 Hassall, Tom Grafton. Oxford, the city beneath your feet. Oxford, 1972.

Arc 1578.20.1 Herinek, Ludwig. Österreichische Münzprägungen von Ergänzungen, 1740-1969. Wien, 1972.

Arc 1578.20.5 Herinek, Ludwig. Österreichische Münzprägungen von 1657-1740. Wien, 1972.

Arc 1340.9 Holtz, Walter. Abkürzungen auf Münzen. Braunschweig, 1972.

Arc 1460.7.1 Imhoof-Blumer, Friedrich. Tier- und Pflanzenbilder auf Münzen und Gemmen des klassischen Altertums. Hildesheim, 1972.

Arc 543.157 Iz istorii iskusstva velikogo goroda. Tashkent, 1972.

Arc 559.4 James, Thomas Garnet Henry. The archaeology of ancient Egypt. London, 1972.

Arc 1468.63 Jenkins, G. Kenneth. Ancient Greek coins. London, 1972.

Arc 443.4 Joseph, P. The Dravidian problem in the south Indian culture complex. Bombay, 1972.

Arc 936.3.5 Jubani, Bep. Bibliographi arkeologjisë dhe historisë së lashtë të Shqipërisë, 1945-71. Tiranë, 1972.

Arc 1508.31 Kahl, Hans Dietrich. Hauptlinien der deutschen Münzgeschichte vom Ende des 18. Jahrhunderts bis 1878. Frankfurt, 1972.

Arc 395.28 Kahlke, Hans Dietrich. Ausgrabungen in aller Welt. 1. Aufl. Leipzig, 1972.

Arc 543.3.110 Kasymov, M.R. Kremneobrabatyvaiushchie masterskie i shakhty Kamennogo veka Srednii Azii. Tashkent, 1972.

Arc 853.24.22 Kellner, Hans-Jörg. Die Römer in Bayern. 2. Aufl. München, 1972.

Arc 925.337.10 Kiiashko, Vladimir I. Legenda i byl' donskikh kurganov. Rostov-na-Donu, 1972.

Arc 935.31.5 Kipshidze, David A. Peshckery Ani. Erevan, 1972.

Arc 628.24 Knell, Heiner. Archäologie. Darmstadt, 1972.

Arc 936.238 Knez, Tone. Novo Mesto v davnini. Maribar, 1972.

Arc 1508.29 Knigge, Wilhelm. Münz- und Medaillen-Kabinet des Freiherrn Wilhelm Knigge. Bielefeld, 1972.

Arc 543.96 Knobloch, Edgar. Beyond the Oxus; archaeology, art and architecture of Central Asia. London, 1972.

Arc 925.50.240 Kolosov, Iurii H. Shaitan-Koba - mustievs'ka stoianka Knymii. Kyïv, 1972.

Arc 925.150.50 Konferentsiia po Arkheologii Belorussii i Smezhnykh Territorii, Minsk, 1972. Belorusskiia starazhytnastsi. Minsk, 1972.

Arc 416.49 Korfmann, Manfred. Schleuder und Bogen in Südwestasien; von der frühesten Belagen bis zum Beginn der historischen Stadtstaaten. Bonn, 1972.

Arc 395.26 Kozłowski, Janusz K. Archeologia prahistoryczna. Wyd. 1. Kraków, 1972- 2v.

Arc 936.14.405 Kozłowski, Stefan. Pradzieje ziem polskich od IX do V tysiąclecia. wyd. 1. Warszawa, 1972.

Arc 925.338.5 Krainov, Dmitrii A. Drevneishaia istoriia Volgo-Okskogo mezhdurech'ia. Moskva, 1972.

Arc 395.27 Kramarkowa, Irena. U źródeł archeologii. Wrocław, 1972.

Arc 936.195.280 Kraskovská, L'udmila. Slovansko-avarské pohrebisko pri Z'ahoiskej Bystrici. 1. vyd. Bratislava, 1972.

Arc 1033.181 Kriss-Rettenbeck, Lenz. Ex voto. Zürich, 1972.

Arc 1251.27 Kroll, John Hennig. Athenian bronze allotment plates. Thesis. Cambridge, 1972.

Arc 1163.4.32 Kühnel, Ernst. Islamische Schriftkunst. 2. Aufl. Graz, 1972.

Arc 680.1 Kythera - excavations and studies. London, 1972.

Arc 595.66.4 Lauer, Jean Philippe. Les pyramides de Sakkarah. 4. éd. Le Caire, 1972.

Chronological Listing

1972 - cont.

Arc 889.37 Laurent, René. L'habitat rural à l'époque romaine. Bruxelles, 1972.

Arc 396.13 Leone, Mark P. Comptemporary archaeology. Carbondale, 1972.

Arc 905.145 Lippert, Andreas. Das Gräberfeld von Welzelach. Bonn, 1972.

Arc 815.36 Little, Alan. A Roman bridal drama at the Villa of the Mysteries. Wheaton, Md., 1972.

Arc 543.3.95 Litvinskii, Boris A. Drevnie kochevniki "Kryshi mira". Moskva, 1972.

Arc 838.39 Llobregat Conesa, Enrique. Contestanía Ibérica. Alicante, 1972.

Arc 936.14.455 Lodowski, Jerzy. Sądowel we wczesnym średniowieczu. Wrocław, 1972.

Arc 505.35.5 Loffreda, Stanislao. A visit to Capharnaum. Jerusalem, 1972.

Arc 853.205.10 Łosinski, Władysław. Pouzọtki wczesnośredniowiecznego. Wrocław, 1972.

Arc 1138.122.5 Lowe, Elias Avery. Palaeographical papers, 1907-1965. Oxford, 1972. 2v.

Arc 925.350 Luzgin, Valerii E. Drevnie kul'tury Izhmy. Moskva, 1972.

Arc 830.362 MacKendrick, Paul Lachlan. Roman France. N.Y., 1972.

Arc 925.50.350 Maksimov, Evgenii V. Srednes Podneprov's na rubezhe nashei ery. Kiev, 1972.

Arc 953.34.1 Marek, Kurt W. Der erste Amerikaner. Reinbek bei Hamburg, 1972.

Arc 397.17.7 Marek, Kurt W. Götter, Gräber und Gelehrt. Reinbeck, 1972.

Arc 375.14 Marois, Roger. English-French, French-English vocabulary of prehistoric archaeology. Montreal, 1972.

Arc 540.15 Masson, Oliviér. Recherches sur les pheniciens a Chypre. Genève, 1972.

Arc 543.146.30 Masson, Vadim M. Karakumyi zavia tsivilizatsii. Moskva, 1972.

Arc 543.3.90 Masson, Vadim Mikhailovich. Central Asia. London, 1972.

Arc 488.30 Matheson, Sylvia A. Persia; an archaeological guide. London, 1972.

Arc 1153.108F Mazzoleni, Jole. Esempi di scritture cancelleresche. Napoli, 1972.

Arc 853.366 Mildenberger, Berhard. Römerzeitliche Siedlungen in Nordhessen. Marburg, 1972.

Arc 853.355 Müller, Adriaan von. Gesicherte Spuren. 1. Aufl. Berlin, 1972.

Arc 673.1.29 Mylonas, George Emmanuel. Eleusis and the Eleusinian mysteries. Princeton, 1972.

Arc 1348.85 Nau, Elisabeth. Epochen der Geldgeschichte. Stuttgart, 1972.

Arc 497.102 Negev, Avraham. Archaeological encyclopedia of the Holy Land. N.Y., 1972.

Arc 628.32 Nemirovskii, Aleksandr I. Nit' Ariadny. Voronesh, 1972.

Arc 853.294.5 Neuffer-Müller, Christiane. Das fränkische Gräberfeld von Iversheim, Kreis Euskirchen. Berlin, 1972.

Arc 905.76 Neumann, Alfred. Vindobona. Die römische Vergangenheit Wiens. Wien, 1972.

Arc 936.14.435 Niewęgłowski, Andrej. Mazowsze na przełomie er. Wrocław, 1972.

Arc 925.170.11 Nizhnekamskaia Arkheologicheskaia Ekspeditsiia, 1968-1969? Otchety Nizhnekamskoi arkheologicheskoi ekspeditsii. Photoreproduction. Moskva, 1972.

Arc 923.128 Novoe v arkheologii. Moskva, 1972.

Arc 936.14.430 Nowakowski, Andrej. Gorne Pobuze w wiskach VIII-XI. Łódź, 1972.

Arc 925.341.5 Okladnikov, Aleksei P. Petroglify srednei Leny. Leningrad, 1972.

Arc 1588.6.2 Ölçer, Cüneyt. Sovyet Rusya Müzelerindeki, Moskova ve Leningrad, Nardir Osmanli raralon. Istanbul, 1972.

Arc 936.225.20F Pahić, Stanka. Pobrežje. Lujbljana, 1972.

Arc 936.20.65 Pârvan, Vasile. Dacia. București, 1972.

Arc 971.5 Pendergast, James F. Cartier's Hochelaga and the Dawson site. Montreal, 1972.

Arc 843.234.4 Pericot Garcia, Luis. The Balearic Islands. London, 1972.

Arc 936.195.235 Peškař, Ivan. Fibeln aus der römischen Kaiserzeit in Mähren. Prag, 1972.

Arc 936.225.15F Petru, Sonja. Emonske nekropole. Ljubljana, 1972.

Arc 925.50.325 Pislarii, Ivan A. Tainy stepnykh kurganov. Donetsk, 1972.

Arc 1588.1.101 Plage, Karol. Monety bite dla Królestwa Polskiego w latach 1815-1864 i monety bite dla miasta Krakowa w roku 1835. Warszawa, 1972.

Arc 936.225.25F Plesničar-Gec, Ljudmila. Severno emonsko grobišče. Ljubljana, 1972.

Arc 726.332 Pohl, Ingrid. The iron age necropolis of Sorbo at Cerveteri. Lund, 1972.

Arc 925.16.55 Poiski i raskopki v Kazakhstane. Alma-Ata, 1972.

Arc 600.156.5F Posener, Georges. Catalogue des ostraca hiératiques littéraires de Deir el Médineh. Le Caire, 1972-

Arc 885.32 Prehistoric man in Wales and the west. Bath, 1972.

Arc 412.25 Problemy absoliutnogo datirovaniia v arkheologii. Moskva, 1972.

Arc 923.129 Problemy arkheologii i drevnei istorii ugrov. Moskva, 1972.

Arc 936.14.415 Pyrgała, Jerzy. Mikroregion osadniczy między wisłą a Dolną Wkrą w obresie rzymskini. Wrocław, 1972.

Arc 1148.37 Rainò, Beniamino. Giovanni Onorio da Maglie, trascrittore di codici greci. Bari, 1972.

Arc 893.30F Randsborg, Klavs. From period III to period IV. Copenhagen, 1972.

Arc 936.165.45 Ratalovich, Isak A. Slaviane VI-IX wkov v Moldavii. Kishinev, 1972.

Arc 853.341 Rau, Hermann Gunther. Das urnenfelderzeitliche Gräberfeld von Aschaffenburg-Streitwald. Kallmünz, 1972.

Arc 785.76 Recherches sur les amphores romains. Rome, 1972.

Arc 1522.6 Reding, Lucien. Les monnaies gauloises du Tetelbierg. Luxembourg, 1972.

Arc 497.101 Rehork, Joachim. Archäologie und biblisches Leben. Bergish Gladbach, 1972.

Arc 407.30.15 Rein, Ulrike G.M. Winckelmanns Begriff der Schönheit. Bonn, 1972.

Arc 1675.19.20 Rikhter, Vladimir G. Sobranie trudov po russkoi voennoi medalistike i istorii. v.1-2. Parizh, 1972.

Arc 938.109 Rimantienė, Rimutė Jablonskytė. Pirmieji Lietuvos gyventojai. Vil'ius, 1972.

Arc 875.132 Ritchie, James Neil Graham. Edinburgh and southeast Scotland. London, 1972.

Arc 1568.7 Rønning, Bjørn R. Norges mynter og pengesedler etter 1874. Oslo, 1972.

1972 - cont.

Arc 726.339 Rome, Italy. Università. Istituto di Topografia Antica. Lavinium. Roma, 1972- 2v.

Arc 670.8 Rutkowski, Bogdan. Cult places in the Aegean world. Wrocław, 1972.

Arc 726.340 San Giovenale. Results of excavations conducted by the Swedish Institute of Classical Studies. Stockholm, 1972-

Arc 543.153 Sarianidi, Viktor I. Raskopki Tillia-tepe v Severnom Afganistane. Moskva, 1972.

Arc 443.3 Sarkar, Sasanka Sekhar. Ancient races of the Deccan. New Delhi, 1972.

Arc 600.188.5 Sauneron, Serge. Les ermitages chrétiens du désert d'Esna. Le Caire, 1972.

Arc 1468.21.6 Sborōnos, Ioannēs N. Numismatique de la Crète ancienne. Bonn, 1972.

Arc 815.26.2 Schefold, Karl. La peinture pompéienne; essai sur l'évolution de sa signification. Bruxelles, 1972.

Arc 853.353 Schleier, Wilhelm. Cambodunum-Kempten. Bonn, 1972.

Arc 853.283 Schmid, Armin. Die Römer am Rein und Main. Frankfurt, 1972.

Arc 853.367 Seidel, Martin Fredrich. Thesaurus Orcivus Marchicus. Faksimile. Berlin, 1972.

Arc 1433.100 Selcuklulonn nadir paralarendon borilom. Istanbul, 1972.

Arc 830.158.15F Sénéchal, Robert. Contribution à l'étude de la céramique à reflects métalliques recueillie à Alésia. Dijon, 1972.

Arc 925.16.65 Senigova, Taisiia N. Srednevekovyi taraz. Alma-Ata, 1972.

Arc 936.14.410 Sesja naukowa Zorzanizowana Zokazji 50- Lecia Katedry Archeologii Pradziejavej i Wczesnoś Redniowiecznej UAM, Poznań, 1969. Problemy badań archeologicznych Polski połnocnozachodniej. 1. wyd. Poznań, 1972.

Arc 1588.1.105 Sesja Numizmatyczna, 3rd, Nowa Sól, 1970. III Sesja Numizmatyczna w Nowej Soli poświęcona monecie i mennicom Wielkopolski, 10-11 listopada 1970 r. Nowa Sól, 1972.

Arc 925.20.15 Shelov, Dmitrii B. Tanais i Nizhnyi Don v peroye veka nashei erg. Moskva, 1972.

Arc 925.50.137 Shovkoplias, Ivan H. Osnovy arkheolohii. 2. vyd. Kyïv, 1972.

Arc 875.45 Small, Alan. Craig Phadrig; interim report on 1971 excavation. Dundee, 1972.

Arc 1623.6 Sobrino, Jose Manuel. La moneda mexicana. Mexico, 1972.

Arc 1076.23 Spiritza, Juraj. Spišské zvony. Vyd. 1. Bratislava, 1972.

Arc 830.367 Stahl-Weber, Martine. Dix ans de recherches archéologiques région de Mulhouse. Mulhouse, 1972.

Arc 936.220.100 Stalio, Blaženka. Gradac. Beograd, 1972.

Arc 505.151 Stékélis, Moshé. The Yarmukian culture of the Neolithic period. Jerusalem, 1972.

Arc 1138.124 Stipišić, Jakov. Pomoćne povijesne znanosti u teoriji i praksi. Zagreb, 1972.

Arc 936.115.10 Stoian, Iorgu. Etudes histriennes. Bruxelles, 1972.

Arc 925.136.15 Stokolos, Vladimir S. Kul'tura naseleniia bronzovogo veka Iuzhnogo Zaural'ia. Moskva, 1972.

Arc 658.15 Stubbings, Frank Henry. Prehistoric Greece. London, 1972.

Arc 543.66.45 Suleimanov, R.K. Statisticheskoe izuchenie kul'tury grota Obi-Rakhmat. Tashkent, 1972.

Arc 936.195.305 Svoboda, Bedřich. Neuerworbene römische Metallgefässe aus Stáže bei Pieštany. 1. Aufl. Bratislava, 1972.

Arc 925.155.5 Sztetyłło, Zofia. Rola Mirmekionu w zyciu gospoelarczym panśtwa bosforskiego. 1. wyd. Warszawa, 1972.

Arc 543.66.24 Termezskaia Arkheologicheskaia Kompleksnaia Ekspeditsiia, 1937, 1961-1962. Buddiiskii kul'tovyi tsentr Kara-tepe v starom Termeze. Moskva, 1972.

Arc 1153.111 Thiel, Helmut van. Mittellateinische Texte: ein Handschriften-Lesebuch. Göttingen, 1972.

Arc 936.220.85 Todorović, Jovan. Praistorijska Karaburma. Beograd, 1972.

Arc 1433.102 Tolunogullan ve povalan. Istanbul, 1972.

Arc 404.4 Touchard, Michel C. L'archéologie mystérieuse. Paris, 1972.

Arc 925.351 Tret'iakov, Viktor P. Kul'tura iamochno-grebenchatoi keramiki v lesnoi polose evropeiskoi chasti SSSR. Leningrad, 1972.

Arc 726.59.45 Trump, David H. Malta: an archaeological guide. London, 1972.

Arc 1615.4.11 United States Mint. Medals of the United States Mint. Washington, 1972.

Arc 600.156.10F Valbelle, Dominique. Ouchebtis de Deir el-Médineh. Le Caire, 1972.

Arc 925.50.280 Viaz'mitina, Mariia I. Zolotobalkovskii mogil'nik. Kiev, 1972.

Arc 925.9.130 Vinogradov, Vitalii B. Tsentral'nyi i severo-vostochnyi Kavkaz v skitskoe vremia. Groznyi, 1972.

Arc 853.24.25 Vor- und frühgeschichtliche Archäologie in Bayern: Beiträge. München, 1972.

Arc 853.377 Vorgeschichte und römische Zeit zwischen Main und Lahn. Beiträge. Bonn, 1972.

Arc 925.50.250 Vynokur, Ion S. Istoriia da kul'tura cherniakhivs'kykh veemen dnistro-din'provs'koho mezhyrichchia. Kyïv, 1972.

Arc 925.50.275 Vysotskaia, Tat'iana N. Pozdnie skify viugo-zapadnom Kryma. Kiev, 1972.

Arc 682.42 Warren, Peter. Myrtos: an early Bronze Age settlement in Crete. London, 1972.

Arc 936.14.445 Węgzynowicz, Teresa. Wędrowki po wjkopaliskach. wyd. 1. Warszawa, 1972.

Arc 1522.5 Weiller, Raymond. Monnaies antiques découvertes au Grand-Duché de Luxembourg. Berlin, 1972.

Arc 746.61 Wetter, Erik. Med kungen på Acquarossa. Malmö, 1972.

Arc 1663.6.20 Whiting, John Roger Scott. Commemorative medals. Newton Abbot, 1972.

Arc 407.6.10 Wilson, John Albert. Thousands of years. N.Y., 1972.

Arc 672.1.150 Wunderlich, Hans-Georg. Wohin der Stier Europa trug. Reinbek bei Hamburg, 1972.

Arc 505.84.5 Yadin, Yigael. Hazor; the head of all those kingdoms. London, 1972.

Arc 1340.10 Zvarych, Volodymyr V. Numizmatychnyi slovnyk. L'viv, 1972.

Arc 684.1.55 100 Jahre deutsche Ausgrabung in Olympia. München, 1972.

1973

Arc 483.11 al-'Amid, Tahir Mudhaffar. The 'Abbasid architecture of Samarra in the reign of both al-Mu'tasim and al-Mutawakkil. Baghdad, 1973.

Arc 936.205.15 Andjelić, Pavao. Bobovac i Kraljeva Sutjeska. Sarajevo, 1973.

Arc 543.146.40 Arazov, O. Arkheologicheskie i arkhitekturnye pamiatniki Serakhskogo oazisa. Ashkhabad, 1973.

Arc 383.34.15 Archaeological theory and practice. Festschrift: Wm. F. Grimes. London, 1973.

Chronological Listing

1973 - cont.

Arc 936.165.50 Arkheologicheskaia karta Moldavskoi SSR. Kishinev, 1973- 5v.
Arc 925.175.10 Arkhipov, Gennadii A. Mariitsy IX-XI vv. Ioshkar-Ola, 1973.
Arc 543.66.60 Askarov, A.A. Sapallitepa. Tashkent, 1973.
Arc 543.146.45 Atagarryev, Egen. Material'naia kul'tura Shekhr-Islama. Ashkhabad, 1973.
Arc 543.3.115 Babaev, Aktam D. Kreposti drevnego Vakhana. Dushanbe, 1973.
Arc 612.83 Background to archaeology; Britain in its European setting. Cambridge, 1973.
Arc 1093.2.40 Bar, Henry. Les pierres levées. Paris, 1973.
Arc 935.75 Başar, Zeki. Evrurumda eski merorliklarve resimli mezar taşlari. Ankara, 1973.
Arc 853.343F Behm-Blancke, Günter. Gesellschaft und Kunst der Germanen. Dresden, 1973.
Arc 543.138.5 Belenitskii, Aleksandr Markovich. Srednevekovyi gorod Srednei Azii. Leningrad, 1973.
Arc 1356.8.3 Bernareggi, Ernesto. Istituzioni di numismatica antica. 3. ed. Milano, 1973.
Arc 505.150.1 Beth She'arim; report on the excavations during 1936-1940. Jerusalem, 1973.
Arc 505.150 Beth She'arim; report on the excavations during 1936-1940. New Brunswick, 1973-76. 3v.
Arc 1588.1.96 Beyer, Karol. Skorowidz monet polskich od 1506 do 1825. Warszawa, 1973.
Arc 785.118 Biernacka-Lukańska, Małgorzata. Wodociągi rzymskie i wczesnobizantyjskie z obszaru Mezji Dolnej i Północnej Tracji. Wrocław, 1973.
Arc 723.30.5 Blake, Marion E. Roman construction in Italy from Nerva through the Antonines. Philadelphia, 1973.
Arc 700.58.2 Boardman, J. The Greeks overseas. 2. ed. Harmondsworth, 1973.
Arc 936.195.240 Bolecek, B.V. Ancient Slovakia. n.p., 1973.
Arc 505.152 Boraas, Roger S. Heshbon 1971: the second campaign at Tell Hesbân. Berrien Spring, Mich., 1973.
Arc 726.327 Bovini, Giuseppe. Antichità cristiane di San Canzian d'Isonzo. Bologna, 1973.
Arc 861.195 Branigan, Keith. Town and country. Bourne End, 1973.
Arc 641.5 Buchholz, Hans-Günter. Prehistoric Greece and Cyprus: an archaeological handbook. London, 1973.
Arc 936.195.250 Budinsky-Kricka, Vojtech. Das altungarische Fürstengral von Zemplén. Bratislava, 1973.
Arc 1540.38 Cardiff, Wales. National Museum of Wales. Welsh tokens of the seventeenth century. Cardiff, 1973.
Arc 936.165.55 Chebotarenko, Georgii T. Kal'fa-gorodishche vos'mogo-desiatego v.v. na Dnestre. Kishinev, 1973.
Arc 936.195.245 Čilinská, Zlata. Frühmittelalterliches Gräberfeld in Želovce. Bratislava, 1973.
Arc 412.26 Cleator, Philip. Underwater archaeology. London, 1973.
Arc 936.14.297 Cnotliwy, Eugeniusz. Rzemiosło rogounicze na Pomorzu wczesnośredniowiecznym. Wrocław, 1973.
Arc 853.7.1 Cohausen, August. Der römische Grenzwall in Deutschland. Text, atlas. Faksimile. Walluf bei Weisbaden, 1973 2v.
Arc 672.1.125 Coldstream, John Nicolas. Knossos. London, 1973.
Arc 505.153 College of Wooster Expedition to Pella. Pella of the Decapolis. Wooster, 1973-
Arc 642.11 Colloquium on Bronze Age Migrations in the Aegean Region, Sheffield, Eng., 1970. Bronze Age migrations in the Aegean. London, 1973.
Arc 522.41 Cook, John Manuel. The Troad; an archaeological and topographical study. Oxford, 1973.
Arc 848.58 Corpus archäologischer Quellen zur Frühgeschichte auf dem Gebiet der Deutschen Demokratischen Republik (7. bis 12. Jahrhundert). Berlin, 1973- 2v.
Arc 936.14.500 Dąbrowska, Elżbieta. Wielkie grody dorzecza góinej Wisły. Wrocław, 1973.
Arc 1470.89 Davis, Norman. The Hellenistic kingdoms. London, 1973.
Arc 1540.20.1 Davis, William John. Tickets and passes of Great Britain and Ireland. N.Y., 1973.
Arc 1163.21.5F De la Mare, Albinia Cathérine. The handwriting of Italian humanists. Oxford, 1973-
Arc 925.50.335 Dombrovskii, Oleg I. Stolitsa feodoritov. Simferopol', 1973.
Arc 416.48 Drevnii Vostok. Erevan, 1973.
Arc 493.6.50 Dzhafarzade, Iskhak M. Gobustan. Baku, 1973.
Arc 925.9.145 Dzhavakhishvili, Aleksandr I. Stroitel'noe delo i arkhitektura poselenii Iuzhnogo Kavkaza. Tbilisi, 1973.
Arc 923.15.2 Ebert, Max. Südrussland im Altertum. Aalen, 1973.
Arc 915.54F Ettlinger, Elisabeth. Die römischen Fibeln in der Schweiz. Bern, 1973.
Arc 936.20.60 Fedorov, Georgii B. Arkheologiia Rumynii. Moskva, 1973.
Arc 853.4.20 Fischer, Ulrich. Grabungen im romischen Steinkastell von Heddernheim 1957-1959. Frankfurt am Main, 1973.
Arc 861.206 Fox, Aileen Mary Henderson. Exeter in Roman times. Exeter, 1973.
Arc 1433.60.5 Frye, Richard N. Sasanian remains from Qasr-i Abu Nasr; seals, sealings, and coins. Cambridge, 1973.
Arc 1285.10.10 Fudalej, Aleksander. Pieczęcie krięstw głogowskigeo [sic] i Żagańskiego. Nova Sól, 1973.
Arc 1510.152.7 Funck, Walter. Die Notmünzen der deutschen Städt, Gemeinden, Kreise, Länder. 2. Aufl. Münster, 1973.
Arc 936.220.105 Garašanin, Milutin V. Praistorija na thu SR Srbije. Beograd, 1973. 2v.
Arc 853.65.65 Gardawski, Aleksander. Z pradzisjćw zieme dolnosląskiej lod około. Wrocław, 1973.
Arc 1153.113 Gasparri, Françoise. L'écriture des actes de Louis VI, Louis VII et Philippe Auguste. Genève, 1973.
Arc 858.102 Gąssowski, Jerzy. Irlandia i Brytania w początkach średniowiecza w świetle badań archeologicznych. Warszawa, 1973.
Arc 936.14.485 Gąssowski, Jerzy. Przewodnik archeologiczny po Polsce. Wrocław, 1973.
Arc 936.14.460 Gedl, Marek. Cmentarzysko halsztackie w kietrzue. Wrocław, 1973.
Arc 1583.19.1 Georgii Mikhailovich, Grand Duke of Russia. Monnaies de l'empire de Russie, 1725-1894. Boston, 1973.
Arc 1153.109F Gilissen, Léon. L'expertise des écritures médiévales. Gand, 1973.
Arc 936.14.380.5 Głosek, Marian. Znaki i napisy na mieczach średniowiecznych w Polsce. Wrocław, 1973.
Arc 936.14.522 Godłowski, Kazimierz. Historia starożytna ziem polskich. 2. wyd. Kraków, 1973.
Arc 1454.210F Göbl, Robert. Ostkeltischer Typenatlas. Braunschweig, 1973.

1973 - cont.

Arc 925.230.5 Golubeva, Leonilla A. Ves' i Slaviane na Belom ozere X-XIII vv. Moskva, 1973.
Arc 556.4 Grapow, Hermann. Meine Begegnung mit einigen Agyptologen. Berlin, 1973.
Arc 853.347 Grenz, Rudolf. Die Anfänge der Stadt Münden nach den Ausgrabungen in der St. Blasius-Kirche. Hannoversch Münden, 1973.
Arc 810.66 Guerdan, René. Pompei. Paris, 1973.
Arc 843.229 Guerra y Gómez, Manuel. Constantes religiosas europeas y sotocuevenses (Ojo Guareña, cuna de Castilla). Burgos, 1973.
Arc 743.26 Guzzo, Piero G. Le fibule in Etruria dal VI al I secolo. Firenze, 1973.
Arc 590.22 Harris, James E. X-raying the pharaohs. N.Y., 1973.
Arc 421.33 Hay, John. Ancient China. London, 1973.
Arc 393.10 Hensel, Witold. Archeologia żywa. Wyd. 1. Warszawa, 1973.
Arc 936.14.334 Hensel, Witold. Polska starozytna. Wrocław, 1973.
Arc 853.309 Herrmann, Joachim. Der germanischen und slawischen Siedlungen und das mittelalterliche Dorf von Tornow. Berlin, 1973.
Arc 853.376F Huebener, Wolfgang. Die römischen Metallfunde von Augsburg-Oberhausen. Kallmünz, 1973.
Arc 1010.28 Hutterer, Karl. An archaeological picture of a pre-Spanish Cebuano community. Cebu City, 1973.
Arc 432.35 Indologische Arbeitstagung, Museum für Indische Kunst, Berlin, 1971. Indologen-Tagung 1971. Weisbaden, 1973.
Arc 612.88 International Archaeological Symposium on the Mesolithic in Europe. The mesolithic in Europe. Wyd. 1. Warsaw, 1973.
Arc 543.66.55 Iz istorii antichnoi kul'tury Uzbekistana. Tashkent, 1973.
Arc 1364.3 Jeločnik, Aleksander. Čenturska zakladna najdba folisov maksencija in tetrarhije. Ljubljana, 1973.
Arc 843.227 Jimenez Cisneros, Maria Josefa. Historia de Cadiz en la antigüedad. Cadiz, 1973.
Arc 838.40.2 Jornadas Arqueológicas, 2nd, Lisbon, 1972. Actas. Lisboa, 1973.
Arc 936.14.450 Kaletyn, Marta. Pierwsze lokacje miast w dorzeczu orli w XIII wieku. Wrocław, 1973.
Arc 1588.1.65.7 Kamiński, Czesław. Ilustrowany katakog monet polskich, 1916-1972. wyd. 2. Warszawa, 1973.
Arc 600.242 Kaplony, Peter. Beschriftete Kleinfunde in der Sammlung Georges Michailidis. Istanbul, 1973.
Arc 925.9.140 Kashkai, Mir-Ali. Iz istorii drevnei metallurgii Kavkaza. Baku, 1973.
Arc 936.165.65 Ketraru, Nikolai A. Sokrovishcha pyrkolaba Gangura. Kishinev, 1973.
Arc 936.165.60 Khynku, Ivan G. Kepreriia-pamiatnik kul'tury X-XII vv. Kishinev, 1973.
Arc 923.130 Kirpicknikov, Anatolii N. Snariazhenie vsadnika i verkhovogo konia na Rusi IX-XIII vv. Leningrad, 1973.
Arc 925.321.20 Kochkurkina, Svetlana I. Iugo-Vostochnoe Priladozh'e v desiatomtrinadtsatom vekakh. Leningrad, 1973.
Arc 1138.121 König, Marie E.P. Am Anfang der Kultur. Berlin, 1973.
Arc 936.261 Korošec, Paola. Predistariska naselba Barutnica kaj anzibegovo vo Makedonija. Prilep, 1973.
Arc 935.24.10 Kosay, Hâmit Z. Türk Tarih Kurumu tarafindan yapilan Alaca Höyük karisi. Ankara, 1973.
Arc 936.14.465 Kruk, Janusz. Studia osadnicze nad neolitem wyżym lessowych. Wrocław, 1973.
Arc 853.369 La Baume, Peter. Die Römer am Rhein. Bonn, 1973.
Arc 936.14.505 Lachowicz, Franciszek J. Dorobek archeologii koszalińskiej w latach 1945-70. Koszalin, 1973.
Arc 584.100.15 Lackany, Rudames Sany. La Société archéologique d'Alexandrie à 80 ans. Alexandrie, 1973.
Arc 915.50 Lambert, André. Führer durch die römische Schweiz. Zürich, 1973.
Arc 823.55 Laubenheimer-Leenhardt, F. Recherches sur les lingots de cuivre et de plomb d'époque romaine dans les régions de Languedoc-Roussillon et de Provence-Corse. Paris, 1973.
Arc 561.6 Leemans, Conrad. L'égyptologue Conrad Leemans et sa correspondance. Leiden, 1973.
Arc 861.21.40 Le Patourel, John Herbert. The moated sites of Yorkshire. London, 1973.
Arc 609.2.20 Leroy, Jules. L'Éthiopie. Paris, 1973.
Arc 936.180.30 Letića, Zagorka. Antropomorfne figurine bronzanog doba u Jugoslaviji. Beograd, 1973.
Arc 505.35.7 Loffreda, Stanislao. A visit to Capharnaum. 2d ed. Jerusalem, 1973.
Arc 726.135.5 Lunz, Reimo. Ur- und Frühgeschichte Südtirols. Bozen, 1973.
Arc 936.14.470 Malinowski, Tadeusz. Wielkopolska wdobie Prasłowian. wyd. 1. Poznań, 1973.
Arc 870.4.21.3 Margary, Ivan D. Roman roads in Britain. 3. ed. London, 1973.
Arc 923.131 Martynov, Anatolii I. Arkheologiia SSSR. Moskva, 1973.
Arc 810.11.11 Mau, August. Pompeii, its life and art. Washington, D.C., 1973.
Arc 1590.10 Mihailović, Vojislav. Katalog novca Srbije i Crne Gore 1868-1918. Beograd, 1973.
Arc 1138.125 Millares Carlo, Agustín. Consideraciones sobre la escritura visigótica cursiva. León, 1973.
Arc 1148.38 Mioni, Elpidio. Introduzione alla paleografia greca. Padova, 1973.
Arc 543.66.65 Mirsaatov, T. Drevnie shakhty Uchtuta. Tashkent, 1973.
Arc 612.90 Mongait, Aleksandr L. Arkheologiia Zapadnoi Evropy. Moskva, 1973- 2v.
Arc 1468.65.1 Münsterberg, Rudolf. Die Beamtennamen auf den griechischen Münzen. Hildesheim, 1973.
Arc 448.1.40 Mughal, M. Rafique. Present state of research on the Indus Valley civilization. Karachi, 1973.
Arc 936.14.545 Muzeum Ziemi Przemyskiej w Przemyślu. Historia badań archeologicznych i zbiorów Muzeum Ziemi Przemyskiej. Przemyśl, 1973.
Arc 853.371 Neuffer-Müller, Christiane. Das fränkische Gräberfeld von Rübenach. Berlin, 1973.
Arc 1166.8 Norlén, Saga-Marianne. Alt datera manuskript. Stockholm, 1973.
Arc 936.140.35 Novae-sektor zachodni 1970. Poznań, 1973.
Arc 925.180.30 Okladnikov, Aleksei Pavlovich. Dalekoe proshloe Primor'ia i Priamur'ia. Vladivostok, 1973.
Arc 936.14.480 Okulicz, Jerzy. Pradzieje ziem pruskich od późnego paleolitu do VII w.n.e. Wrocław, 1973.
Arc 513.41 Orient and Occident. Kevelaer, 1973.
Arc 712.37 Orlandos, Anastasios K. Ta charagmata tou Parthenōuos. Athēnai, 1973.
Arc 497.104 Paul, Sholom. Biblical archaeology. Jerusalem, 1973.

Chronological Listing

1973 - cont.

Arc 861.199.1	Pearson, Frederick Richard. Roman Yorkshire. 1. ed. Wakefield, 1973.
Arc 530.171	Pekmon, A. Son kari ve arasturmalann i syei altinda Penge tanhi. Ankara, 1973.
Arc 925.357	Pitskhelauri, Konstantin. Osnovnye problemy istorii plemen Vostochnoi Gruzii v XV-VII vv. do n.e. Tbilisi, 1973.
Arc 925.50.300	Pletneva, Svetlana A. Drevnosh Chernykh Klobukov. Moskva, 1973.
Arc 925.150.46	Pobol', Leonid D. Slavianskie drevnosti Belorussii. Minsk, 1973.
Arc 1138.129	Polák, Stanislav. Studium novověkého písma. Příbram, 1973.
Arc 543.146.35	Poliakov, Sergei P. Etnicheskaia istoriia Severo-Zapadnoi Turkmenii v srednie veka. Moskva, 1973.
Arc 140.5.2	Post-medieval archaeology. Index. v.1-5 (1967-71). London, 1973.
Arc 673.1.35	Poulsen, Frederik. Delphi. Washington, 1973.
Arc 925.354	Priakhin, Anatolii D. Drevnes naselenie Peschanki. Voronezh, 1973.
Arc 925.4.45	Problemy arkheologii Urala i Sibiri. Moskva, 1973.
Arc 1578.6.10	Probszt, Günther. Österreichische Münz- und Geldgeschichte. Wien, 1973.
Arc 451.5	Rao, Shikaripur R. Lothal and the Indus civilization. N.Y., 1973.
Arc 384.16	Redman, Charles L. Research and theory in current archeology. N.Y., 1973.
Arc 612.89	Renfrew, Colin. Before civilization; the radiocarbon revolution and prehistoric Europe. London, 1973.
Arc 830.345	Richard, Jean-Claude M. La région montpelliévaine à l'époque préromaine (750-121 avant J.-C.). Bruxelles, 1973.
Arc 905.148	Die Römer an der Donau. Wien, 1973.
Arc 772.11	Roma medio republicana. Aspetti culturali di Roma e del Lazio. Roma, 1973.
Arc 936.14.475	Romanow, Jerzy. Tomice, pow. Wrocław, 1973.
Arc 726.343	Roth, Helmut. Die Ornamentik der Langobarden in Italien. Bonn, 1973.
Arc 925.50.310	Rusanova, Irina P. Slavianskie drevnosti VI-IX vv. mezhdu Dneprom i Zapadnym Bugom. Moskva, 1973.
Arc 1453.13	Schlumberger, Hans. Goldmünzen Europas seit 1800. 3. Aufl. München, 1973.
Arc 861.212	Shotter, David Colin Arthur. Romans in Lancashire. Yorkshire, 1973.
Arc 925.13.195	Skifskie drevnosti. Kiev, 1973.
Arc 875.133	Small, Alan. St. Ninian's Isle and its treasure. London, 1973. 2v.
Arc 925.50.320	Smyrnov, Stanislav V. Paleolit Dniprovs'koho Nadporizhzhia. Kyïv, 1973.
Arc 416.47	South Asian archaeology; papers. 1. U.S. ed. Park Ridge, N.Y., 1973.
Arc 1153.115	Stiennon, Jacques. Paléographie du Moyen Age. Paris, 1973.
Arc 1588.1.85	Suchodolski, Stanisław. Mennictwo polskie w XI-XII wieku. Wrocław, 1973.
Arc 1538.21.5	Sutherland, Carol Humphrey Vivian. English coinage, 600-1900. London, 1973.
Arc 612.92	Symposium über die Entstehung und Chronologie der Badener Kultur, Archäologisches Institut der Slowakischen Akademie der Wissenschaften, 1969. Symposium über die Entstehung und Chronologie der Badener Kultur. Bratislava, 1973.
Arc 925.50.290	Telehin, Dnytro I. Seredn'ostohivs'ka kul'tura epokhy midi. Kyïv, 1973.
Arc 659.20F	Theocharēs, Dēmētrios R. Neolithikē Hellas. Athēnai, 1973.
Arc 1143.2.3	Thompson, Edward Maunde. Handbook of Greek and Latin palaeography. Ann Arbor, 1973.
Arc 1468.64	Thompson, Margaret. An inventory of Greek coin hoards. N.Y., 1973.
Arc 595.63	Tompkins, Peter. Secrets of the great pyramid. London, 1973.
Arc 1588.10.25	Tözen, Ibrahim. Türkiye cumhuriyeti madeni ponohr. Istanbul, 1973.
Arc 936.40.45	Tsarevgrad Turnov. Dvoretsutna bulgarskite tsare prez Utorata bulgarska durzhava. Sofiia, 1973-74. 2v.
Arc 513.1.10	Ugarit-Bibliographie/Manfried Dietrich. Neukirchen, 1973. 4v.
Arc 936.220.110	Vasić, Rastko. Kulturne grupe starijeg grozdenog doba u Jugoslaviji. Beograd, 1973.
Arc 1010.27	Vasil'evskii, Ruslan S. Drevnie kul'tury Tikhookeanskogo Severa. Novosibirsk, 1973.
Arc 1584.31	Veksler, Aleksandr G. Moskovskie klady. Moskva, 1973.
Arc 1493.25	Vicenti, Jose A. España, 1869-1973: la peseta. 8. ed. Madrid, 1973.
Arc 936.195.260	Vladár, Josef. Pohrebiská zo staršej doby bronzovej v Branči. 1. vyd. Bratislava, 1973.
Arc 1473.18	Whitting, Philip David. Byzantine coins. London, 1973.
Arc 936.180.35	Wisaman, James. Stobi; a guide to the excavations. Beograd, 1973.
Arc 915.48.5	Wyss, René. Wirtschaft und Gesellschaft in der Jungsteinzeit. Bern, 1973.
Arc 936.14.103	Z badań nad neolotem i wczesną epoką brącu w Małopolsce. Wrocław, 1973.
Arc 936.220.125	Zotovič, Ljubica. Mitraizam na thu Jugoslavije. Beograd, 1973.
Arc 853.375	Zotz, Lothar F. Die mittelpaläolithische Geröllgeräteindustrie aus der Umgebung von Kronach in Oberfranken. Kallmünz, 1973.

1974

Arc 600.241	Abitz, Friedrich. Die religiöse Bedeutung der sogenannten Grabräuberschächte in den ägyptischen Königsgräbern der 18. bis 20. Dynastie. Wiesbaden, 1974.
Arc 936.14.495	Abramowicz, Andrzej. Dalecy i bliscy. Łódź, 1974.
Arc 600.244.1F	Adams, Barbara. Ancien Hierakonpolis. Supplement. Warminster, 1974.
Arc 600.244F	Adams, Barbara. Ancient Hierakonpolis. Warminster, 1974.
Arc 432.31	Agrawal, Dharma Pal. Prehistoric chronology and radiocarbon dating in India. New Delhi, 1974.
Arc 1480.84	Alföldi, András. Caesar in 44 v. Chr. Bonn, 1974.
Arc 518.12.5F	Alzinger, Wilhelm. Augusteische Architektur in Ephesos. v.1-2. Wien, 1974.
Arc 1335.164F	American University of Beirut. Museum of Archaeology. The coin collection. Beirut, 1974.
Arc 1.18.2	Archaeology. Index, v.11-26, 1958-1973. N.Y., 1974.

1974 - cont.

Arc 923.123.1	Arkheologicheskie issledovaniia na iuge Vostochnoi Evropy. Photoreproduction. Moskva, 1974.
Arc 861.203	Ashbee, Paul. Ancient Scilly from the first farmers to the early Christians. Newton Abbot, 1974.
Arc 385.21	Aston, Michael. Landscape archaeology. Newton Abbot, Eng., 1974.
Arc 608.1.55	Baratte, François. Recherches archéologiques à Haïdra. Paris, 1974.
Arc 865.29	Bergström, Theo. Stonehenge. London, 1974.
Arc 1143.4.1	Birt, Theodor. Das antike Buchwesen in seinem Verhältnis zur Literatur. Aalen, 1974.
Arc 936.14.35.5	Blaszczyk, Włodzimierz. Die Anfänge der polnischen Städt im Lichte der Bodenforschung. Poznań, 1974.
Arc 1148.35	Boge, Herbert. Griechische Tachygraphie und tironische Noten. Hildesheim, 1974.
Arc 925.50.380	Bondar', Mykola M. Poseleniia srednego podneprov'ia epokhi rannei bronzy. Kiev, 1974.
Arc 861.11.11	Boon, George Counsell. Silchester, the Roman town of Calleva. Newton Abbot, 1974.
Arc 700.69	Bouzek, Jan. Graeco-Macedonian bronzes. Praha, 1974.
Arc 670.9	Branigan, Keith. Aegean metalwork of the early and middle Bronze Age. Oxford, 1974.
Arc 861.100.25	Bruce-Mitford, Rupert Leo. Aspects of Anglo-Saxon archaeology. London, 1974.
Arc 543.154	Brykina, Galina A. Karabulak. Moskva, 1974.
Arc 590.1.4	Budge, E.A.W. The mummy. 2. ed. N.Y., 1974.
Arc 543.156	Buriakov, Iurii F. Gornoe delo i metallurgia srednevekovogo Ilaka, V-nachalo XIII v. Moskva, 1974.
Arc 585.28F	Caminos, Ricardo A. The New Kingdom temples of Buhen. London, 1974. 2v.
Arc 608.2.75	Carthage: Cirque, Colline dite de Junon, Douar Chott. Wrocław, 1974.
Arc 925.349	Chernetsov, Valerii Nikolaevich. Prehistory of western Siberia. Montreal, 1974.
Arc 936.14.490	Chudziakowa, Jadwiga. Kultura łużycka na terenie międzyrzecza Wisły, Drwęcy i Osy. wyd. 1. Warszawa, 1974.
Arc 936.14.525	Chudziakowa, Jadwiga. Źródła archeologiczne zterenu zamku krzyżackiego w Towniu. 1. wyd. Warszawa, 1974.
Arc 1348.83F	Coins and the archaeologist. Oxford, 1974.
Arc 1163.37	Colloque International sur la Paléographie Hébraïque Médiévale, Paris, 1972. La paléographie hébraïque médiévale, Paris, 11-13 septembre 1972. Paris, 1974.
Arc 1138.123	Cope, Emma Elizabeth T. How to decipher and study old documents. Chicago, 1974.
Arc 726.319	Coradazzi, Giovanni. Le rete stradale romana fra Brescia, Bergamo e Milano. Brescia, 1974.
Arc 1478.3.10	Crawford, Michael H. Roman Republican coinage. N.Y., 1974. 2v.
Arc 1610.2.1	Crosby, S.S. The early coins of America. Lawrence, 1974.
Arc 858.103	Cunliffe, Barry W. Iron Age communities in Britain. London, 1974.
Arc 925.50.185.5	Danilenko, Valentin N. Eneolit Ukrainy. Kiev, 1974.
Arc 600.54.5	Deir el-Bahari. Varsovic, 1974-
Arc 861.197	Dickinson, Tania M. Cuddesdon and Dorcester-on-Thames, Oxfordshire. Oxford, 1974.
Arc 687.1.10	Dietz, Søren. Arkaelogens Rhodos. København, 1974.
Arc 1510.154.5	Duve, Gebhard. Dicktaler-Prägungen, 1544-1679. v.2. Frankfurt am Main, 1974-
Arc 388.9	Dymond, David Percy. Archaeology and history. London8 1974.
Arc 412.3	Dzhus, Vsevolod E. My-gedronavty. Leningrad, 1974.
Arc 925.50.360	Feodal'naia Tavrika. Kiev, 1974.
Arc 923.75.5	Formazov, Aleksandr A. Arkheologicheskie puteshestviia. Moskva, 1974.
Arc 843.223F	Fouilles de Conimbriga. Paris, 1974- 3v.
Arc 936.20.71	Gajewska, Halina. Topographie des fortifications romaines en Dobroudja. Wrocław, 1974.
Arc 1163.34F	Garcia Villada, Zacarias. Paleografía española. Album. Barcelona, 1974. 2v.
Arc 340.11.2	Georgieva, Sonia. Bibliografiia na bulgarskata arkheologiia, 1879-1966. 2. izd. Sofiia, 1974.
Arc 612.55.5	Gimbutas, Marija Alseikaites. The gods and goddesses of old Europe, 7000 to 3500 B.C. London, 1974.
Arc 600.46.10F	Giza mastabas. Boston, 1974- 2v.
Arc 1558.6.15	Glück, Harry. Årtalsförteckning över svenska mynt. Stockholm, 1974.
Arc 1510.172	Haas, Rudolf. Die Prägungen der Mannheimer Münzstätten. Mannheim, 1974.
Arc 858.97	Harbison, Peter. Some Iron Age Mediterranean imports in England. Oxford, 1974.
Arc 1079.2	Hardaker, Ron. A corpus of early Bronze Age dagger pommels from Great Britain and Ireland. Oxford, 1974.
Arc 870.33	Harding, Derek William. The Iron Age in lowland Britain. London, 1974.
Arc 1453.1.1	Hazlitt, William Carew. The coinage of the European continent. Chicago, 1974.
Arc 870.27	Henig, Martin. A corpus of Roman engraved gemstones from British sites. v.1-2. Oxford, 1974.
Arc 936.14.332	Hensel, Witold. Ur- und Frühgeschichte Polens. Berlin, 1974.
Arc 880.47F	Herity, Michael. Irish passage graves. Dublin, 1974.
Arc 1510.170	Hoffmeister, Jacob Christoph Carl. Historisch-kritische Beschreibung aller bis jetzt bekannt gewordenen nessischen Münzen. v.1-4. Leipzig, 1974. 3v.
Arc 925.50.315	Iakavenko, Ieleonora V. Skify skhidnego Krymu v V-III st. do n.e. Kyïv, 1974.
Arc 543.3.1.5	International Conference on the History, Archeology and Culture of Central Asia in the Kushan Period, Dushanbe, 1968. Tsentral'naia Aziia v kushanskuiu spokhu. Moskva, 1974- 2v.
Arc 736.6.10	Isserlin, B.S.J. Motya, a Phoenician and Carthaginian city in Sicily. Leiden, 1974.
Arc 1588.1.44.2	Kałkowski, Tadeusz. Tysiac lat monety polskiej. Wyd. 2. Kraków, 1974.
Arc 1588.1.65.8	Kamiński, Czesław. Ilustrowany katalog monet polskich, 1916-1974. Wyd. 3. Warszawa, 1974.
Arc 673.1.50	Karouzos, Chrēstos Iōannou. Delphoi. Athēnai, 1974.
Arc 710.27F	Kawerau, Georg. The excavation of the Athenian Acropolis 1882-1890. v.1-2. Copenhagen, 1974.
Arc 505.154	Kenyon, Kathleen Mary. Digging up Jerusalem. London, 1974.
Arc 925.50.330	Kezub, Iuliia I. Nekropol' Ol'viï V-VI st. do n.e. Kyïv, 1974.
Arc 302.9.15	Kiss, Zsolt. Les publications du Centre d'archéologie méditerranéenne. Warszawa, 1974.

Chronological Listing

1974 - cont.

Arc 412.22.1 Kondratov, Aleksandr M. The riddles of three oceans. Moscow, 1974.

Arc 1588.1.110 Kopicki, Edmund. Katalog podstawowych typów monet i banknotów Polski oraz ziem historycznie z Polską związanych. v.1, pt.1-2. Warszawa, 1974- 2v.

Arc 925.4.60 Kosarev, Mikhail F. Drevnie kul'tury Tomsko-Narymskogo Priob'ia. Moskva, 1974.

Arc 395.18.5.5 Kosidowski, Zenon. Rumaki Lizypa i inne opowiadania. 2. wyd. Warszawa, 1974.

Arc 1584.32.1 Kotliar, Mykola F. Kladoiskatel'stvo i numizmatika. Kiev, 1974.

Arc 395.7.10 Kraus, Franz Xaver. Liberal und integral: der Briefwechsel zwischen Franz Xaver Kraus und A. Stöck. Mainz, 1974.

Arc 1468.61 Lacroix, Léon. Études d'archéologie numismatique. Paris, 1974.

Arc 938.112 Latvijas PSR arheologija. Riga, 1974.

Arc 595.41 Lauer, J.P. Le mystère des pyramides. Paris, 1974.

Arc 905.147 Lichardus, Ján. Studien zur Bükker Kultur. Bonn, 1974.

Arc 938.111 Lietuvos TSR archeologijos atlasas. Vil'nius, 1974- 3v.

Arc 861.21.45 Manby, Terence George. Grooved ware sites in Yorkshire and the north of England. Oxford, 1974.

Arc 870.35 Marsden, Barry M. The early barrow-diggers. Park Ridge, N.J., 1974.

Arc 587.8.5F Martin, Geoffrey Torndike. The royal tomb at El-Amana. London, 1974.

Arc 853.316 Materialhefte zur Vor- und Frühgeschichte der Pfalz. Speyer, 1974.

Arc 925.332.15 Materialy po arkheologii i etnografii Mordevii. Saransk, 1974.

Arc 1190.65.10 Mazal, Otto. Die Prooimien der byzantinischen Patriarchenurkunden. Wien, 1974.

Arc 612.77 Medieval pottery from excavations. London, 1974.

Arc 595.69 Mendelssohn, Kurt. The riddle of the pyramids. London, 1974.

Arc 925.338.10 Merpert, Nikolai I. Drevneishie skotovody Volzhsko-Uraliskogo mezhdurech'ia. Moskva, 1974.

Arc 925.13.200 Moshkova, Marina G. Proiskhazhdenie rannesarmatskoi (prokhorovskoi) kul'tury. Moskva, 1974.

Arc 895.80 Munksgaard, Elisabeth. Oldtidsdragter. København, 1974.

Arc 1433.46F Near Eastern numismatics, iconography, epigraphy and history. Beirut, 1974.

Arc 340.38 Ödekan, Ayla. Türkiyede 50 yılda yayımlanmış Arkeoloji, sanat tarihi...bibliyografyası. Istanbul, 1974.

Arc 925.341.10 Okladnikov, Aleksei P. Petroglify Baikala - pamiatniki drevnei kul'tury narodov Sibiri. Novosibirsk, 1974.

Arc 895.66 Oldeberg, Andreas. Die ältere Metallzeit in Schweden. Stockholm, 1974.

Arc 383.43.5 Opuscula Iosepho Kastelíc sexagenario dicata. Ljubljana, 1974.

Arc 936.262 Pachkova, Svitlana P. Hospodarstvo skhidnoslov'ians'kykh plemen na rubezhi nashoï ery. Kyïv, 1974.

Arc 1163.3.110 Panaskenko, Vira V. Paleohrafiia ukraïns'koho skoiopysii durkoï polovyny XVII st. Kyïv, 1974.

Arc 925.50.355 Parovich-Peshikan, Maia. Nekropol' Ol'vii ellinisticheskogo vremeni. Kiev, 1974.

Arc 655.6 Perowne, Stewart. The archaeology of Greece and the Aegean. London, 1974.

Arc 861.101 Pettit, Paul. Prehistoric Dartmoor. Newton Abbot, 1974.

Arc 925.50.375 Pletneva, Svetlana A. Polovetskie kamennye izvaianiia. Moskva, 1974.

Arc 925.150.47 Pobol', Leonid D. Slavianskie drevnosti Belorussii. Minsk, 1974.

Arc 1185.5.1 Posse, Otto. Die Lehre von der Privaturkunden. Berlin, 1974.

Arc 1138.128 Problemy paleografii i kodikologii v SSSR. Moskva, 1974.

Arc 936.14.535 Przewoźna, Krystyna. Struktura i rozwój zasiedlenia południowowschedniej strefy nadbałtyckiej u schyłku starożytnosći. 1. wyd. Warszawa, 1974.

Arc 1076.24 Pukhnachev, Iurii V. Zagadki zvuchashchego metalla. Moskva, 1974.

Arc 889.33 Raepsuet, Georges. La céramique en terre sigillée de la ville belgo-romaine de Robelmont, campagnes 1968-1971. Bruxelles, 1974.

Arc 861.201 Rahtz, Philip. Beckery Chapel, Glastonbury, 1967-68. Glastonbury, 1974.

Arc 1010.29F The recent archaeology of the Sydney district: excavations, 1964-1967. Canberra, 1974.

Arc 830.175.11 Rolland, Henri. Glanum. Saint-Remy-de-Provence, 1974.

Arc 700.70 Schoder, Raymond Victor. Ancient Greece from the air. London, 1974.

Arc 925.355 Sedov, Valentin V. Dlinnye kurgany krivichei. Moskva, 1974.

Arc 938.95.5 Selirand, Jüri. Estlaste matmiskombed varafeodaalsete suhete tärkamise perioodil (11.-13. sajand). Tallinn, 1974.

Arc 1465.80.1 Seltman, Charles Theodore. Athens; its history and coinage before the Persian invasion. Chicago, 1974.

Arc 1261.3.15 Spain. Archivo Histórico Nacional, Madrid. Sección de Sigilografía. Catálogo de sellos de la Sección de Sigilografía del Archivo Histórico Nacional. Madrid, 1974- 3v.

Arc 1478.87 Sutherland, Carol H.V. Roman coins. London, 1974.

Arc 925.50.345 Svieshnikov, Ihor K. Istoriia naselennia Peredkarpattia, Podillia i Volyni v kintsi III-na pochatku II tysiacholittia do nashoï ery. Kyïv, 1974.

Arc 858.95 Swanton, M.J. A corpus of pagan Anglo-Saxon spear-types. Oxford, 1974.

Arc 1468.67F Sylloge nummorum Graecorum, Sweden. Stockholm, 1974-

Arc 936.253 Symposium zu Problemen der Jüngeren Hallstattzeit in Mitteleuropa, Smolenice, 1970. Symposium zu Problemen der jüngeren Hallstattzeit. Bratislava, 1974.

Arc 520.37 Szczepański, Jan A. Ołtarz i miasto. Wyd. 1. Kraków, 1974.

Arc 1510.171.1 Tergast, Pefrus. Die Münzen Ostfrieslands. Leer, 1974.

Arc 925.13.190 Terrakotovye statuetki. v.3- Moskva, 1974- 2v.

Arc 1588.6.35 Tesla-Zarić, Dobrila. Katalog novca Osmanske imperije sakupljenog- na području SFR Jugoslavije. Beograd, 1974.

Arc 938.107 Tönisson, Evald. Die Gauja-Liven und ihre materielle Kultur. Tallinn, 1974.

Arc 1163.3.115F Tomović, Gordana. Morfologija ćiriličkih natpisa na Balkanu. Beograd, 1974.

Arc 935.80 Türk Tarih Kurumu. Mansel'e armagan. Melanges mansel. Ankara, 1974. 3v.

Arc 936.14.530 Tyszkiewicz, Jan. Mozowsze północno-wschodnie we wczesnym średniowieczu. 1. wyd. Warszawa, 1974.

1974 - cont.

Arc 1613.29 United States. Domestic and foreign coins manufactured by mints of the United States, 1793-1973. Washington, 1974.

Arc 925.16.70 V glub' vekov. Alma-Ata, 1974.

Arc 399.3.2 Vasilevskii, Ruslan S. Annotirovannaia bibliografiia nauchnykh trudov akademika A.P. Okladnikova (1968-1973 gg). Ulan-Ude, 1974.

Arc 1185.34 Vittani, Giovanni. Scritti di diplomatica e archivistica. Milano, 1974-

Arc 938.65.5 Volkaitė-Kulikauskienė, Regina. Punios piliakalnis. Vilnius, 1974.

Arc 923.135 Voprosy okhrany, klassifikatsii i ispol'zovaniia arkheologicheskikh pamiatnikov. Moskva, 1974.

Arc 861.3.10 Watkin, W.T. Roman Cheshire. Wakefield, Eng., 1974.

Arc 400.25.5.2 Webster, Graham. Practical archaeology. 2. ed. London, 1974.

Arc 609.20.5 Wendorf, Fred. A Middle Stone Age sequence from the Central Riff Valley, Ethiopia. Wrocław, 1974.

Arc 407.31 Wilkinson, Edward M. Technische und naturwissensachaftliche Beiträge zur Feldarchäologie. Köln, 1974.

Arc 384.17 Willey, Gordon Randolph. Archaeological researches in retrospect. Cambridge, Mass., 1974.

Arc 612.91 Woźniak, Zenon. Wschodnie pogranicze kultury lateńskiej. Wrocław, 1974.

Arc 1190.3.6 Wright, Andrew. Court-hand restored, or The student's assistant in reading old deeds. London, 1974.

Arc 672.1.146 Wunderlich, Hans-Georg. The secret of Crete. N.Y., 1974.

Arc 936.14.510 Żaki, Andrzej. Wędrówki Sącza. Kraków, 1974.

Arc 403.25 Zenner, Klaus. Gang durch versunkene Städte; ein Ausflug ins Reich der Archäologie. Leipzig, 1974.

1975

Arc 412.28 Alpözen, Oğuz. Türkuiye'de sualt, arkeolojisi. İstanbul, 1975.

Arc 785.33.1 Altmann, W. Die römischen Grabaltäre der Kaiserzeit. N.Y., 1975.

Arc 936.225.30 Arheološka najdišča Slovenije. Ljubljana, 1975.

Arc 513.11.1 Arundell, F.V.J. Discoveries in Asia Minor. v.1-2. Hildesheim, 1975.

Arc 1076.21 Avent, Richard. Anglo-Saxon garnet inlaid and composite brooches. v.1-2. Oxford, 1975.

Arc 412.1.15 Bass, George Fletcher. Archaeology beneath the sea. N.Y., 1975.

Arc 435.2.32.1 Burgess, James. The architectural antiquities of northern Gujarat. 1. Indian ed. Varanasi, 1975.

Arc 543.7.25F Cohen, Joan Lebold. Angkor monuments of the god-kings. London, 1975.

Arc 943.53 Comas, Juan. Origen de las culturas precolombinas. 1. ed. México, 1975.

Arc 340.39 Coulson, William D.E. An annotated bibliography of Greek and Roman art. N.Y., 1975.

Arc 925.13.205 Drachuk, Viktor S. Sistemy znakov Severnogo Prichernomoria. Kiev, 1975.

Arc 853.351F Elisenhof: die Ergebnisse der Ausgrabung der frühgeschichtlichen Marschersiedlung beim Elisenhof in Eiderstedt 1957/58 und 1961/64. Bern, 1975-

Arc 870.31F Elsdon, Sheila M. Stamp and roulette decorated pottery of the La Tème period in Eastern England. Oxford, 1975.

Arc 497.99 Encyclopedia of archaeological excavations in the Holy Land. Englewood Cliffs, N.J., 1975- 2v.

Arc 861.135.5 Excavations in medieval Southampton 1953-1969. Leicester, Eng., 1975. 2v.

Arc 555.2 Fagan, Brian M. The rape of the Nile. N.Y., 1975.

Arc 513.4.6 Fellows, C. Travels and researches in Asia Minor. Hildesheim, 1975.

Arc 936.14.460.5 Gedl, Marek. Kultura przedłużycka. Wrocław, 1975.

Arc 936.14.550 Gierlach, Bogusław. Studia nad archeologią średniewiecznego Mazowsza. Wyd. 1. Warszawa, 1975.

Arc 1348.77 Grierson, Philip. Numismatics. London, 1975.

Arc 530.182 Khach'atryan, Telemak S. Drevnaia kul'tura Shiraka. Erevan, 1975.

Arc 893.31 Klindt-Jensen, Ole. A history of Scandinavian archaeology. London, 1975.

Arc 936.242F Köhler, Ralf. Untersuchungen zu Grabkomplexam der älteren römischen Kaiserzeit in Böhmen unter Aspekten der religiösen und sozialen Gliederung. Neumünster, 1975.

Arc 530.183 Korucutepe; final report on the excavations of the Universities of Chicago, California (Los Angeles). Amsterdam, 1975.

Arc 793.10F Kraus, Theodor. Pompeii and Herculaneum: the living cities of the dead. N.Y., 1975.

Arc 650.11 Kultura materialna starożytnej Grecji. Wrocław, 1975.

Arc 858.99 Laing, Lloyd Robert. The archaeology of late Celtic Britain and Ireland, c. 400-1200. London, 1975.

Arc 875.129 Laing, Lloyd Robert. Settlement types in post-Roman Scotland. Oxford, 1975.

Arc 1458.23 McGill University, Montreal. The McGill University collection of Greek and Roman coins. v.1-2. Amsterdam, 1975-

Arc 936.14.540 Materiały do studiów nad osadnictwem bnińskim. Poznań, 1975.

Arc 416.20 Mellaart, James. The Neolithic of the Near East. London, 1975.

Arc 861.18.16.20 Merrifield, Ralph. The archaeology of London. Park Ridge, 1975.

Arc 600.236 Michelucci, Maurizio. La collezione di lucerne del Museo egizio di Firenze. Firenze, 1975.

Arc 398.8.1 Noël Hume, Ivor. Historical archaeology. N.Y., 1975.

Arc 1138.130 Norman, James. Ancestral voices. N.Y., 1975.

Arc 936.140.35.5 Novae-sektor zachodni 1972. Wyd. 1. Poznań, 1975.

Arc 1588.6.2.20 Olçer, Cüneyt. Nakışlı Osmanlı mangırları. İstanbul, 1975.

Arc 925.50.365 Ol'viia. Kiev, 1975.

Arc 1090.6F Oswald, Adrian. Clay pipes for the archaeologists. Oxford, 1975.

Arc 1478.81F Oxford. University. Ashmolean Museum. Catalogue of coins of the Roman Empire in the Ashmolean Museum. Oxford, 1975

Arc 543.155 Pulatov, Uktam P. Chil'khudzhra. Dushanbe, 1975.

Arc 612.79 Recent archaeological excavations in Europe. London, 1975.

Arc 1030.48.5 Recueil des inscriptions de la Gaule antérieures à la Renaissance carolingienne. Paris, 1975-

Arc 875.13.10 Robertson, Anne S. Bar Will. Oxford, 1975.

Arc 785.119.1F Rostovtsev, Milchail Ivanovich. Tesserarum urbis Romae et suburbi plumbearum sylloge. Text and atlas. Leipzig, 1975. 2v.

1975 - cont.

Arc 925.50.370	Savych, Volodymyr P. Pizn'opaleolitychne naselennia pivdenno-zakhidnoï Volyni. Kyïv, 1975.
Arc 858.93F	Sedgley, Jeffrey. The Roman milestones of Britain. Oxford, 1975.
Arc 412.27	Selhus, Wilhelm. Und sie waren doch da: wissenschaftliche Beweise für den Besuch aus dem All. München, 1975.
Arc 858.91	The small towns of Roman Britain. Oxford, 1975.
Arc 925.50.385	Smilenko, Alla T. Slov'iany ta ïkh susidy v stepovomu Podniprov'ï II-XIII st. Kyïv, 1975.
Arc 925.50.390	Sukhobokov, Oleg V. Slaviane Dneprovskogo Levoberezh'ia. Kiev, 1975.
Arc 1285.25.5	Tomczyk, Damian. Pieczęcie górnośląskich cechów rzemieslniczych z XV-XVIII wisku i ich znaczenie historyczne. Wyd. 1. Opolu, 1975.
Arc 967.7	Voices from the rapids: an underwater search for fur trade artifacts, 1960-73 (Minnesota). St. Paul, 1975.
Arc 936.14.555	Wachowski, Krzysztof. Cmentarzyska doby wczesnopiastowskiej na Śląsku. Wrocław, 1975.
Arc 595.70.1	Wake, Charles Staniland. The origin and significance of the great pyramid. Minneapolis, 1975.
Arc 1163.3.120	Zapisi i letopisi. Skopje, 1975.

1976

Arc 861.193F	Froom, F.R. Wawcott II, a stratified Mesolithic succession. Oxford, 1976.
Arc 861.189F	Matthews, C.L. Occupation sites on a Chiltern ridge. Oxford, 1976.
Arc 1075.5F	Tyler, Alan. Neolithic flint axes from the Cotswold Hills. Oxford, 1976.
Arc 861.191F	Woodhouse, Jayne. Barrow Mead, Bath, 1964: excavation of a medieval peasant house. Oxford, 1976.

WIDENER LIBRARY SHELFLIST, 56

ARCHAEOLOGY

AUTHOR AND TITLE LISTING

Author and Title Listing

Arc 923.4 A.V. Tishchenko. (Tishchenko, Andrei V.) Petrograd, 1916.

Arc 830.260 A l'assaut de la carrière du Puits. (Couture, Claude Paul.) Le Havre, 1957.

Arc 1588.3 A' szerb zsupánok királyok es ezárok. (Luczenbacher, J.) Budán, 1843.

Arc 561.5 A travers la Haute Égypte. (Lagier, Camille.) Bruxelles, 1921.

Arc 1163.41.5 Aaberg, Alf. Läsning av gamla handstilar. 5. uppl. Stockholm, 1971.

Arc 612.21.7F Åberg, Nils. Bronzezeitliche und früheisenzeitliche Chronologie. v.4-5. Stockholm, 1933-35. 2v.

Arc 838.11 Åberg, Nils. La civilisation énéolithique dans la péninsule ibérique. Uppsala, 1921.

Arc 612.16 Åberg, Nils. Die Franken und Westgoten in der Volkewanderungszeit. Uppsala, 1922.

Arc 726.47 Åberg, Nils. Die Gothen und Langobarden in Italien. Uppsala, 1923.

Arc 895.32 Åberg, Nils. Nordische Ornamentik in vorgeschichtlicher Zeit. Leipzig, 1931.

Arc 893.15F Åberg, Nils. Den nordiska folkvandringstidens kronologi. Stockholm, 1924.

Arc 853.46 Åberg, Nils. Ostpreussen in der Völkerwanderungszeit. Uppsala, 1919.

Arc 888.1 Åberg, Nils. Die Steinzeit in der Niederlanden. Uppsala, 1916.

Arc 612.21 Åberg, Nils. Studier öfver den yngre stenildern i Norden och Vosteuropa. Norrköping, 1912.

Arc 895.37.5 Åberg, Nils. Die Typologie der nordischen Streitäxte. Würzburg, 1918.

Arc 810.63.2 Aafjes, B. Dag van gramschap in Pompeji. 2. druk. Amsterdam, 1961.

Arc 746.7.9F Åkerström, Åke. Studien über die etruskischen Gräber. Uppsala, 1934.

Arc 1558.6.15 Årtalsförteckning över svenska mynt. (Glück, Harry.) Stockholm, 1974.

Arc 540.9F Aastroem, Paul. The Middle Cypriote Bronze Age. Lund, 1957.

Arc 543.66 Academiia nauk Uzbek SSSR, Tashkend. Institut Istorii i Arkheologii. Istoriia material'noi kul'tury uzbekistana. Taskhend, 1953- 12v.

Arc 925.300 Abadzekhskaia nizhnepaleoliticheskaia stoianka. (Autlev, P.U.) Maikop, 1963.

Arc 505.68.15 Abalmelck-Lazarev, Semen S. Dzherash (Gerasa). Sankt Peterburg, 1897.

Arc 925.337 Abashevskaia kul'tura v Podon'e. (Priakhin, Anatolii D.) Voronezh, 1971.

Arc 483.11 The 'Abbasid architecture of Samarra in the reign of both al-Mu'tasim and al-Mutawakkil. (al-'Amid, Tahir Mudhaffar.) Baghdad, 1973.

Arc 1033.47.8 Abbatescianni, G. Primi Christiani e Nerone aproposito dell'opuscolo di Carlo Pascal. Bari, 1901.

Arc 1033.37.3 Abbati Olivieri Giordani, Annibale degli. Di alcune altre antichità cristiane. Pesaro, 1784.

Arc 1033.37 Abbati Olivieri Giordani, Annibale degli. Di alcune antichità cristiane...in Pesaro nel Museo Olivieri. Pesaro, 1781.

Arc 861.12.3 Abbatt, Richard. History of the Picts or Roman British wall. London, 1849.

Arc 830.149 L'abbaye royale du Lieu-Notre-Dame-les-Romorantin. (Plat, Ernest.) Romorantin, 1886.

Arc 853.24.12F Abbildungen zu dem I. u II. Heft der Römischen Alterthümer in Baiern. n.p., n.d.

Arc 628.13 Abbildungen zur Alten Geschichte der Oberen Klassen. (Luckenbach, H.) München, 1898.

Arc 953.1 Abbott, C.C. Primitive industry. Salem, 1881.

Arc 958.1.8 Abbott, C.C. Ten years' diggings in Lenâpè Sand, Delaware. Trenton, New Jersey, 1912.

Arc 968.4 Abbott, Charles C. Archaeologia nova caesarea, 1907-09. Trenton, New Jersey, 1907-08.

Arc 958.1 Abbott, Charles C. Recent archaeological explorations in the Valley of the Delaware. Boston, 1892.

Arc 958.1.3 Abbott, Charles C. Researches upon antiquities of man, Delaware Valley. Boston, 1897.

Arc 968.4.5 Abbott, Charles C. Stone age in New Jersey. Washington, 1877.

Arc 1348.26 Pamphlet box. Abbott, G.H. Numismatics.

Arc 547.1 Abbott, H. Catalogue of a collection of Egyptian antiquities. N.Y., 1853.

Arc 1163.4.25F Abbott, N. The rise of the north Arabic script and its Kur'ānic development. Chicago, 1939.

Arc 1153.100 Abbrevationes vetustorum monumentorum, in ordinem alphabeticum digestae. (Apianus, Petrus.) München, 1968.

Arc 1153.2.5 Le abbreviatore nella paleografia latina del Medio Evo. (Paoli, Cesare.) Firenze, 1891.

Arc 1153.31 Abbreviaturae vocabulorum. (Hulákovsky, J.M.) Pragae, 1913.

Arc 600.46.5F Abd el Monem, Joussef Abubakr. Excavations at Giza, 1945-50. Cairo, 1953.

Arc 657.2 Abdruck seiner italienischer Beschreibung des griechisches Archipelagus. (Pasch van Krienen.) Halle, 1860.

Arc 723.1 Abeken, W. Mittelitalien. Stuttgart, 1843.

Arc 384.12.3 Das Abenteuer Archäologie. 3. Aufl. München, 1967.

Arc 658.3.7 Abenteuer meines Lebens. (Schliemann, Heinrich.) Leipzig, 1960.

Arc 1025.68 Abgebildetes unterirdisches Rom. (Bosio, Antonio.) Arnheim, 1668.

Arc 1153.32 Die abgeleiteten Verba in den tironischen Noten. Inaug. Ddiss. (Söldner, Georg.) Borna, 1916.

Arc 1221.1 Abhandlung über die Siegel der Araber, Perser. (Hammer-Purgstall.) n.p., n.d.

Htn Arc 1093.3* Abhandlung von den Sonnenuhren der Alten. (Martini, G.H.) Leipzig, 1877.

Arc 33.3F Abhandlungen. (Deutsches Archäologisches Institut. Abteilung Kairo.) Hamburg. 5-6 2v.

Arc 86.1 Abhandlungen des archaeologisches-epigrammisches Seminars. (Vienna.) Wien. 1-15,1880-1913 5v.

Arc 446.12 Abid Ali Khan, M. Memoirs of Gaur and Pandua. Calcutta, 1931.

Arc 501.15.4 Abila of the Decapolis. (Schumacher, G.) London, 1889. 3 pam.

Arc 905.5.9 Abitati preistorici e romani nell'agro di Capodistria. (Degrassi, A.) Parenzo, 1933.

Arc 720.209 Le abitazioni Lacustri di Fimon. (Livy, P.) Venezia, 1876.

Arc 726.8 Le abitazioni Palustri di Fontanellato. (Pigorini, L.) Parma, 1865.

Arc 600.241 Abitz, Friedrich. Die religiöse Bedeutung der sogenannten Grabräuberschächte in den ägyptischen Königsgräbern der 18. bis 20. Dynastie. Wiesbaden, 1974.

Arc 1340.9 Abkürzungen auf Münzen. (Holtz, Walter.) Braunschweig, 1972.

Arc 545.223 Abney, W. de W. Thebes and its five greater temples. London, 1876.

Arc 945.4 Aboriginal American harpoons. (Mason, Otis J.) Washington, 1900.

Arc 950.202.38F Aboriginal sites on Tennessee River. (Moore, C.B.) Philadelphia, 1915.

Arc 961.1 Aboriginal structures in Georgia. (Jones, C.C.) Washington, 1878. 2 pam.

Arc 983.9 Aboriginal urn-burial in the United States. (Moore, C.B.) Lancaster, 1904.

Arc 550.5 Aboudi, M. Guide book to the antiquities of upper Egypt and Nubia. 4. ed. Cairo, 1946.

Arc 386.1 About monuments. (Bartlett, T.H.) Boston, 1878?

Arc 936.240 Abramič, M. Poetovio. Ptuj, 1925.

Arc 1584.1.10 Abramishvili, T.I. Zapadno-gruzinskie monety XIII-XIV vv. Tbilisi, 1959.

Arc 612.56 Abramova, Zoia. Izobrasheniia cheloveka v paleoliticheskom iskusstve Evrazii. Leningrad, 1966.

Arc 936.14.495 Abramowicz, Andrzej. Dalecy i bliscy. Łódź, 1974.

Arc 1153.94 Abréviations latines médiévales. (Pelzer, Auguste.) Louvain, 1964.

Arc 1413.2 Abridged history of copper coins in Japan. (Polder, L.) n.p., 1891.

Arc 1185.8 Abriss der Diplomatik. (Gatterer, J.C.) Göttingen, 1798.

Arc 1153.92 Abriss der lateinische Paläographie. 2. Aufl. (Foerster, H.) Stuttgart, 1963.

Arc 726.255 Abruzzo preistorico. (Radmilli, Antonio Mario.) Firenze, 1965.

Arc 547.2.15 Abtheilung der Aegyptischen Alterthümer - Die Wandgemaelde. (Berlin. Staatliche Museen.) Berlin, 1855.

Arc 547.2.16 Abtheilung der Aegyptischen Alterthümer - Die Wandgemaelde. (Berlin. Staatliche Museen.) Berlin, 1870.

Arc 432.34 Abu, Imam. Sir Alexander Cunningham and...Indian archaeology. Dacca, 1966.

Arc 608.26F Abu Geili. (Crawfard, O.G.S.) London, 1951.

Arc 585.20A Abydos. Pt.1-3. (Petrie, W.M.F.) London, 1902-04. 3v.

Arc 1208.12 Academia...Bucharest. Documents de sigillographie byzantine. Paris, 1952.

Arc 1300.5 Academia...Bucharest. Academia Republicii Populare Romêne, Bucharest. Studii si certcetari de numismatica. 1-5 5v.

Arc 383.16 Academia...Bucharest. Academia Republicii Populare Romîne. Amagiu lui Constantin Daicoviciu cu prilejne. București, 1960.

Arc 303.40F Academia...Bucharest. Academia Republicii Socialiste România. Institutul de Arheologie. Materiale si cercetări arheologice. București. 2,1956+ 9v.

Arc 303.35 Academia...Bucharest. Academia Republicii Socialiste România. Muzeul National de Antichitati. Studii si cercetări de istorie veche. București. 5,1954+ 15v.

Arc 303.67 Academia...Bucharest. Academie Republicii Socialiste România. Arheologie Moldovei. București. 2,1964+ 4v.

Arc 30.9 Académie...Bona. Académie d'Hippone. Bulletin. Bona. 1-37,1865-1921 10v.

Arc 30.9F Académie...Bona. Académie d'Hippone. Bulletin. Bona. 11,1873

Arc 30.9.10 Pamphlet vol. Académie d'Hippone. Bona, Algeria.

Arc 273.2.3F Académie Royale d'Archéologie de Belgique. Annales. Anvers. 1-3,1843-1900 2v.

Arc 273.2 Académie Royale d'Archéologie de Belgique. Annales. Anvers. 1-77 69v.

Arc 273.1 Académie Royale d'Archéologie de Belgique. Bulletin. Anvers. 1863-1929 18v.

Arc 273.2.10 Académie Royale d'Archéologie de Belgique. Minor publications.

Arc 273.2.5 Académie Royale d'Archéologie de Belgique. Table des publications de l'Académie Royale d'Archéologie de Belgique, 1843 à 1900. Anvers? n.d.

Arc 93.30 Accademia...Naples. Accademia dell'Archeologia, Lettere e Belle Arti. Memorie. Napoli. 1,1951+ 3v.

Arc 1.14.20 Accademia...Rome. Accademia Romana di Archeologia. Annuario. 1,1951+ 2v.

Arc 1.14F Accademia...Rome. Accademia Romana di Archeologia. Dissertazione. Roma. 1820-1921 32v.

Arc 1.14.2 Accademia...Rome. Accademia Romana di Archeologia. Indice delle dissertazioni e communicazioni. Roma, 1900.

Arc 1.14.15F Accademia...Rome. Accademia Romana di Archeologia. Memorie. 4,1934+ 6v.

Arc 1.14.10 Accademia...Rome. Accademia Romana di Archeologia. Rendiconti. 1,1921+ 31v.

Arc 1.14.30 Accademia...Rome. Accademia Romana di S. Tommaso di Aquina. Triplice omaggio a sua santita Pio XII. Città de Vaticano, 1958. 2v.

Arc 93.15 Accademia Etrusca, Cortona. Saggi di dissertazioni accademiche. Roma. 1-9,1742-1791 9v.

Arc 618.3 Account of a chemical examination of the Celtic antiquities. (Mallet, J.W.) Dublin, 1852.

Arc 875.25 An account of some remarkable ancient ruins. (Williams, J.) Edinburgh, 1777.

Htn Arc 861.18.17* Account of some urns. (Woodward, J.) London, 1713. 2 pam.

Arc 880.42 An account of the ancient monuments in state charge. (Northern Ireland. Ministry of Finance.) Belfast, 1947.

Arc 435.11.12 An account of the caves at Nadsur and Karsambla. (Cousens, Henry.) Bombay, 1891.

Arc 875.11.7 Account of the excavation of the Roman station at Ardoch. (Christison, D.) Edinburgh, 1898.

Arc 1540.7 An account of the hoard of Anglo-Saxon coins found at Chancton farm, Sussex. (Head, B.V.) n.p., n.d.

Arc 143.2.5 Account of the institution and progress of the society. (Society of Antiquaries of Scotland.) Edinburgh. 2,1784

Arc 757.10 An account of the Roman antiquities. 2. ed. (Chester, England. Museum.) London, 1907.

Arc 1076.16 Accoustical measurements on church-bells and carillons. (Heuven, Englebert W. van.) 's-Gravenhage, 1949.

Arc 776.1.3 Accurata e succinta descrizione topografica delle antichità di Roma. (Venuti, R.) Roma, 1824. 2v.

Htn Arc 776.1.2* Accurata e succinta descrizione topografica delle antichità di Roma. 2. ed. (Venuti, R.) Roma, 1803. 2v.

Author and Title Listing

Arc 776.1.7 Accurata e succinta descrizione topografica delle antichità di Roma moderna. (Venuti, R.) Roma, 1767. 4v.
Arc 1027.90 Achelis, H. Römische Katakombenbilder in Catania. Berlin, 1932.
Arc 1027.22 Achelis, H. Das Symbol des Fisches...Fischi der Römische Katakombe. Marburg, 1888.
Htn Arc 1027.24.25F* Achelis, Hans. Die Katakomben von Neapel. Leipzig, 1935-36.
Arc 1020.133 Acht Studien zur christlichen Altertumswissenschaft und zur Kirchengeschichte. (Schnyder, William.) Luzern, 1937.
Arc 1355.2 Ackerman, J.Y. Ancient coins of cities and princes. London, 1846.
Arc 1478.1 Ackerman, J.Y. A descriptive catalogue of rare Roman coins. London, 1834. 2v.
VArc 497.90 Ackermann, Peter Fourier. Bibliai régiségtan. Eger, 1889.
Arc 608.2.60 Acquaro, Enrico. I rasoi punici. Roma, 1971.
Arc 726.170 Acquedotti romani e medioevali. (Schiavo, Armando.) Napoli, 1935.
Arc 1033.122 Acquisito conservazione, ristaurato degli arredi sacri. (Sanna Solaro, G.) Torino, 1886.
Arc 710.16 L'acropole. (Thibaudet, A.) Paris, 1929.
Arc 710.1 L'acropole d'Athènes. (Beulé, E.) Paris, 1853-54. 2v.
Arc 710.28 L'acropole d'Athènes. (Des Gagniers, Jean.) Québec, 1971.
Arc 485.201 L'acropole de Suse. (Dieulafoy, M.) Paris, 1890-92. 4v.
Arc 710.13 The acropolis, from the Russian of Merejkowski. (Merezhkovskii, D.S.) London, 1909.
Arc 710.26 The acropolis. (Hopper, Robert John.) London, 1971.
Arc 710.14.2 The acropolis. 2. ed. (Rodenwaldt, Gerhart.) Oxford, 1957.
Arc 710.22 La acrópolis de Atenas en la época catalana. (Rubió y Lluch, Antonio.) Barcelona, 1908.
X Cg Arc 710.10 The acropolis of Athens. (D'Ooge, M.L.) N.Y., 1908.
Arc 710.12.5 The acropolis of Athens. (Schede, Martin.) Berlin, 1924.
Arc 705.7 The acropolis of Athens. (Stillman, W.J.) London, 1870.
Arc 501.15 Across the Jordan. (Schumacher, G.) London, 1886.
Arc 501.15.2 Across the Jordan. (Schumacher, G.) London, 1889.
Arc 1033.35.149 Acruz Manoelina do covento de Cristo. (Garces Teixeira, F.A.) Lisboa, 1922.
Arc 1033.104 Acta...de identitate SS. Corporum Ambrosii Episcopatum...et...Cristi martyrum Gervasii et Protasii. Romae, 1873.
Arc 302.51.6 Acta antiqua Philippapolitana. (Conference International d'Études Classiques des Pays Socialistes, 6th, Plovdiv, 1962.) Serdicae, 1963.
Arc 245.2 Acta archaeologica. København. 1,1930+ 34v.
Arc 225.3F Acta archeologica. Budapest. 1,1951+ 21v.
Arc 94.40F Acta arqueologica hispanica. Madrid. 1-5,1943-1950 3v.
Arc 1016.230 Acta congregationis praeparatoriae habitae die 4 iulii 1901. De authenticitate S. Sindonis Taurinensis. (Catholic Church. Congregatio Indulgentiarum et Sacrarum Reliquiarum.) Roma, 1901.
Arc 1033.172 Acta iberica...Speusippi, Eleusippi. Sankt Peterburg, 1906.
Arc 1033.164 Acta martyris Anastasii Persae. (Usener, H.K.) Bonnae, 1894.
Arc 265.1 Acta Musei antiquitatum septrionalium. (Upsala. Universitet. Museum för Nordiska Fornsaker.) Uppsala. 1-3,1942-1945 3v.
Arc 1300.34 Acta numismática. Barcelona. 1,1971+ 5v.
Arc 1016.228 Acta passionis SS. Crescii et S. Martyrum. (Laderchi, J.) Florentiae, 1707.
Arc 1033.171 Acta S. Timothei. (Usener, H.K.) Bonn, 1877.
Htn Arc 1027.34* Acta S. Victorini episcopi amiterni et martyres. (Marangoni, J.) Rome, 1740.
NEDL Arc 307.3.25F Actas. (International Congress of Americanists, 27th, Mexico and Lima, 1939.) México, 1942-47.
Arc 838.40.2 Actas. (Jornadas Arqueológicas, 2nd, Lisbon, 1972.) Lisboa, 1973.
Arc 838.40 Actas. (Jornadas Arqueológicas.) Lisboa, 1970. 2v.
Arc 3.1.5 Actes. (Congrès International pour la Reproduction des Manuscrits.) Bruxelles. 1905
Arc 915.51 Actes du Colloque International sur les Cols des Alpes, Antiquité et Moyen-Age, Bourg-en-Bresse, 1969. (Colloque International sur les Cols des Alpes (Antiquité et Moyen-Age), Bourg-en-Bresse, France, 1969.) Orléans, 1971.
Arc 100.5 Actes du Congrès national des sociétés savantes. (France. Comité des Travaux Historiques et Scientifiques. Section d'Archéologie.) 85,1960+
Arc 9.2.7 Actes du VIIe Congrès international des sciences préhistoriques et protohistoriques. (International Congress of Prehistoric and Protohistoric Sciences.) Prague, 1970-71. 2v.
Arc 9.2.8 Actes du VIIIe Congrès international des sciences préhistoriques et protohistoriques. (International Congress of Prehistoric and Protohistoric Sciences, 8th, Belgrad, 1971.) Beograd, 1971- 3v.
Arc 843.13F El acueducto y otras antiqüedades de Segovia. (Gomez de Somorrostro y Martin, A.) Madrid, 1820.
Arc 843.13.2 El acueducto y otras antiqüedades de Segovia. 2. ed. (Gomez de Somorrostro y Martin, A.) Segovia, 1861.
Arc 1033.12.35 Ad carolum...de Sindone Taurinensi. (Vigo, G.B.) Augustae Taurinorum, 1768.
Arc 925.250 Ad Fanagorii do Apollonii. (Nowicka, M.) Warszawa, 1962.
Arc 1360.2.7 Ad numismata regum veterum anecdota. (Froelich, E.) Viennae, 1756. 2 pam.
Arc 1480.5 Ad nummos consulares III viri M. Antonii. (Paciandi, P.M.) Rome, 1757.
Arc 893.13 Adama van Scheltema, F. Die altnordische Kunst. Berlin, 1923.
Arc 893.13.5 Adama van Scheltema, F. Die altnordische Kunst. 2. Aufl. Leipzig, 1923.
Arc 893.13.15 Adama van Scheltema, F. Die Kunst unserer Vorzeit. Leipzig, 1936.
Arc 848.48 Adama van Scheltema, Z. Die Kunst der Vorzeit. Stuttgart, 1950.
Arc 936.20.75 Adamclisi. (Barbu, V.) Bucuresti, 1965.
Arc 936.195.10F Adámek, F. Pravěké Hradisko u Obřan. Brno, 1961.
Arc 1030.13 Adami, L. Dell culto, A.S.S.M.M., cemeteriali e dell'antichita. Roma, 1815.
Arc 600.244.1F Adams, Barbara. Ancien Hierakonpolis. Supplement. Warminster, 1974.
Arc 600.244F Adams, Barbara. Ancient Hierakonpolis. Warminster, 1974.
Arc 1613.7 Adams, E.H. Adams' official premium list. United States gold coins. N.Y., 1909.
Arc 1615.5 Adams, E.H. Private gold coinage of California, 1849-55, its history and issues. Brooklyn, 1913.
Arc 1613.7.5 Adams, E.H. United States pattern, trial, and experimental pieces. N.Y., 1913.
Arc 793.2.5 Adams, W.H.D. The buried cities of Campania. London, 1870.
Arc 793.2 Adams, W.H.D. Pompeii and Herculaneum. London, n.d.
Arc 1613.7 Adams' official premium list. United States gold coins. (Adams, E.H.) N.Y., 1909.
Arc 936.195.310 Adámsk, František. Důkaz pravosti metodějských nálezů z "Hrobů" u Osvětiman. Brno, 1934.
Arc 608.25F Addison, F. Jebel Moya. London, 1949. 2v.
Htn Arc 1355.1* Addison, J. Dialogue upon the usefulness of ancient medals. Glasgow, 1751.
Arc 1355.1.5 Addison, J. Dialogue upon the usefulness of ancient medals. Glasgow, 1769.
Arc 950.202.2 Additional mounds of Duval and of Clay Counties, Florida. (Moore, C.B.) n.p., 1896.
Arc 1301.2.5 Address...on resigning the presidency of the Boston Numismatic Society, January 5, 1865. (Lewis, Winslow.) N.Y., 1866.
Arc 383.87 An address presented to Marcus N. Tod. Oxford, 1948.
Arc 861.58 Addy, S.O. The hall of Waltheof...Hallamshire. London, 1893.
Arc 853.359 Adelsgräber des achten Jahrhunderts in Deutschland. (Stein, Frauke.) Berlin, 1967. 2v.
Arc 1300.30 Adelson, Howard L. The American Numismatic Society. N.Y., 1958.
Arc 493.2 Adler, C. Two Persepolitan casts in the U.S. National Museum. Washington, 1893.
Arc 505.5.100F Adler, Cyrus. Memorandum on the Western Wall. Jerusalem, 1930.
Arc 87.1.31 Adler, F. Das Pantheon zu Rom. Berlin, 1871.
NEDL Arc 87.1.34 Adler, F. Stoa der Koenigs Attalos. Berlin, 1874.
Htn Arc 1433.6* Adler, I.G.C. Collectio nova numorum cuficum. Hafniae, 1782-92. 2v.
Arc 66.1.95 L'administration financiere du sanctuaire pythique. (Bourquet, E.) Paris, 1905.
Arc 700.25F Adriani, A. Le gobelet en argent des amours vendangeurs du musée d'Alexandrie. n.p., 1939.
Arc 1016.231 Adriano I. Lettera...sul culto delle sacre immagini. Roma, 1885.
Arc 936.222 Adriatica praehistorica et antigua. Zagreb, 1970.
Arc 1027.25.17 Adunanza della Pontificia accademia romana d'archeologia dedicata alla memoria di G.B. de Rossi. Roma, 1894.
Arc 1030.5.50 Adunanze solenne in commemorazione di Guglielmo Henzen. (Rossi, G.B. de.) Roma, 1887.
Arc 391.10 Adventures in the Nearest East. (Gordon, C.H.) Fair Lawn, N.J., 1957.
Arc 925.295 Adygskie pamiatniki. (Kafoev, A.Z.) Nal'chik, 1963.
Arc 1018.60 Aebischer, Paul. Linguistique romane et histoire religieuse. Abadía de San Cugat del Valles, 1968.
Arc 651.3 Die ägäische Kultur. (Lichtenberg, R.F.) Leipzig, 1911.
Arc 651.3.2 Die ägäische Kultur. 2. Aufl. (Lichtenberg, R.F.) Leipzig, 1918.
Arc 383.34.5 The Aegean and the Near East. (Weinberg, S.S.) N.Y., 1956.
Arc 416.30 The Aegean and the Orient in the second millennium B.C. (Kantor, H.J.) Bloomington, 1947.
Arc 647.3.2A Aegean archaeology. (Hall, H.R.) London, 1915.
Arc 647.3A Aegean archaeology. (Hall, H.R.) London, 1915.
Arc 670.9 Aegean metalwork of the early and middle Bronze Age. (Branigan, Keith.) Oxford, 1974.
Arc 635.207.5 Ägena, das Heiligtum der Aphaia. Text and atlas. (Furtwängler, A.) München, 1906. 2v.
Arc 670.2.3 Die Ägineten der Glypotothek König Ludwigs I. (Furtwängler, A.) München, 1906.
Arc 670.2.5 Ägineten und Archäologen. (Groote, M. von.) Strassburg, 1912.
Arc 545.224 Aegyptens vormetallische Zeit. (Mook, F.) Wuerzburg, 1880.
Arc 557.2 Aegyptiaca. (Hamilton, W.) London, 1809.
Arc 565.3 Aegyptiaca. (Pendlebury, J.D.S.) Cambridge, Eng., 1930.
Arc 545.237 Aegyptische Grabsteine und Denksteine aus Athen und Konstantinople. (Pörtner, B.) Strassburg, 1908.
Arc 547.15 Aegyptische Gräber. v.2. Strassburg, 1904.
Arc 600.13 Die ägyptische Pflanzensäule der Spätzeit. (Köster, A.) Paris, 1903.
Arc 600.45F Ägyptische Tempel mit Umgang. (Borchardt, Ludwig.) Kairo, 1938.
Arc 1135.201.3 Aegyptische Urkunden. Arabische Urkunden. (Berlin. Staatliche Museum.) Berlin. 1896-1900//
Arc 1135.201.2 Aegyptische Urkunden. Koptische Urkunden. (Berlin. Staatliche Museum.) Berlin. 1,1904+ 3v.
Arc 561.4 Die aegyptischen Denkmäler. (Lieblein, J.) Christiania, 1873.
Arc 560.4 Ägyptisches Kunstlandwerk. (Kayser, Hans.) Braunschweig, 1969.
Arc 547.16 Den aegyptiske samlung. (Schmidt, V.) Copenhagen, 1899.
Arc 557.10 Ägyptologie an deutschen Universitäten. (Helck, Hans Wolfgang.) Wiesbaden, 1969.
Arc 893.18 Den äldre jernåldern i Norrland. (Hildebrand, H.) Stockholm, 1869.
Arc 853.270.10 Die ältere Bronzezeit zwischen Niederrhein und Mittelwesen. (Sudholz, Gisela.) Hildesheim, 1964.
Arc 895.22.10F Die ältere Eisenzeit Gotlands. pt.1-2. (Almgren, Oscar.) Stockholm, 1914-23.
Arc 938.30 Die ältere Eisenzeit in Finnland. (Hackman, A.) Helsingfors, 1905.
Arc 895.66 Die ältere Metallzeit in Schweden. (Oldeberg, Andreas.) Stockholm, 1974.
Arc 684.1.2 Die Ältere von Olympia. (Curtius, E.) Berlin, 1882.
Arc 1080.5 Die älteren italischen Fibeln. (Sundwall, J.) Berlin, 1943.
Arc 1200.22 Die älteren Papsturkunden des Erzbistums Hamburg. (Curschmann, Fritz.) Hamburg, 1909.
Arc 853.79 Die älteste Erzgewinnung im nordischgermanischen Lehenskreis. (Witter, W.) Leipzig, 1938. 2v.
Arc 1570.1.9 Das älteste Münzwesen Norwegens. (Holmboe, C.A.) Berlin, 1846.
Arc 1411.2 Die ältesten chinesischen Staatsmünzen. (Kainz, C.) Berlin, 1894.
Arc 830.160 Aeria. Recherches sur son emplacement. (Saurel, Ferdinand.) Paris, 1885.
Arc 1480.26 Aes grave; a study of the cast coinage of Rome and Central Italy. (Sydenham, E.A.) London, 1926.
Arc 1480.4 L'aes grave del Museo Kircheriano. Text and atlas. (Rome. Museo Kircheriano.) Roma, 1839. 2v.

Author and Title Listing

Arc 1475.11 Aes grove das Schwergeld Roms und Mittelitaliens. v. 1, Text; v. 2, Plates. (Häberlin, J.E.J.) Frankfurt, 1910. 2v.

Arc 662.3 Aetolia, its geography and antiquities. (Woodhouse, W.J.) Oxford, 1897.

Arc 893.28 Aeve, Astrid. I stider och märmiskor i Norden. Uppsala, 1960.

Arc 1550.3 Afbildninger af danske mønter, 1241-1377. (Mansfeld-Bûllner, H.V.) Kjøbenhavn, 1887.

Arc 1550.10 Afbildninger af panstlege indtil kjendte danske mønter. 2. Opl. (Mansfeld-Bûllner, H.V.) Kjøbenhavn, 1964.

Arc 893.16F Affaldsdynger faa stenalderen i Denmark undersögte for Nationalmuseet. (Copenhagen. Nationalmuseet.) Paris, 1900.

Arc 543.66.35 Afrasiab. (Afrasiabskaia Kompleksnaia Arkheologicheskaia Ekspeditsiia.) Tashkent, 1969- 3v.

Arc 543.66.35 Afrasiabskaia Kompleksnaia Arkheologicheskaia Ekspeditsiia. Afrasiab. Tashkent, 1969- 3v.

Arc 30.30 Africa. Tunis. 1,1966+

Arc 609.32 The African Iron Age. (Shinnie, Peter L.) Oxford, 1971.

Arc 1663.34 African Museum. Commemorative medals of the Z.A.R. Johannesburg, 1958.

Arc 1680.20 Africana Museum, Johannesburg. Tokens of South Africa. Johannesburg, 1966.

Arc 608.13 L'Afrique chrétienne...ruines antiques. (Mesnege, P.J.) Paris, 1912.

Arc 1027.2 Agapea Michaëleia. (Morcelli, S.A.) Bononiae, 1822.

Arc 858.86 Age by age. (Jessup, Ronald Frederick.) London, 1967.

Arc 385.11 L'âge de pierre. Paris, 1960.

Arc 612.42 L'Age du Bronze. (Briard, Jacques.) Paris, 1959.

Arc 915.36 Age du Bronze en Valais et dans le chablais vaudois. (Bocksberger, Olivier Jean.) Lausanne, 1964.

Arc 400.15 L'âge du renne. (Paniagua, A. de.) Paris, 1926.

Arc 457.5 The age of the imperial Guptas. (Banerji, R.D.) Banares, 1933.

Arc 1418.24 The age of the Kushânas; a numismatic study. 1. ed. (Chattopadhyay, Bhaskar.) Calcutta, 1967.

Arc 838.1 Les âges préhistoriques de l'Espagne et du Portugal. (Cartailhac, É.) Paris, 1886.

Arc 900.201 Az aggteleki Barlang mint orkori temetö. (Nyáry, Jenö.) Budapest, 1881.

Arc 677.5F Aghios Kosmas. (Mylonas, George E.) Princeton, 1959.

Arc 1025.36 Agincourt, G.B.L.G. d'. Viaggio nelle catacombe di Roma. Milano, 1835.

Arc 1020.136 Agnello, G. Gli studi di archeologia cristiana in Sicilia. Catania, 1950.

Arc 700.9 Agonistische Studien I, Der Diskoswurf bei der Grechen. (Kietz, G.) München, 1892.

Arc 608.17.35 L'Agorà di Cirene. (Stucchi, Sandro.) Roma, 1965.

Arc 1.5.4.15 Agora excavations. Weekly report. (American School of Classical Studies at Athens.)

Arc 1033.17.107 Agostinho de Santa Maria. Santuario Mariano e historia das imagēs milagrosas de Nossa Senhora. Lisboa, 1707-23. 10v.

Htn Arc 1350.2* Agostini, A. Dialoghi - intorno alle medaglie...altre antichità. Rome, 1592.

Arc 432.31 Agrawal, Dharma Pal. Prehistoric chronology and radiocarbon dating in India. New Delhi, 1974.

Arc 858.49 Agricola in Britain. (Macdonald, George.) London, 1932.

Arc 870.15.7 Agricola's road into Scotland. (Mothersole, Jessie.) London, 1927.

Arc 736.1.9F Agrigento. (Marconi, Pirro.) Firenze, 1929.

Arc 736.1.12 Agrigento. (Marconi, Pirro.) Roma, 1933.

Arc 843.9 Aguilera y Gamboa, E. El alto Jalón. Madrid, 1909.

Arc 843.9.5 Aguilera y Gamboa, E. Las necropolis ibéricas. Madrid, 1916.

Arc 905.17.12 Aguntum. (Alzinger, Wilhelm.) Wien, 1958.

Htn Arc 1348.28* Agustin, Antonius. Dialogos de medallas, inscriciones y otras antiquedades. Madrid, 1744.

Arc 585.11A Ahnas el Medinek. (Naville, E.H.) London, 1894.

Arc 1030.46 De aid-christelijke monumenten van Ephesus. (Bakhuizen van den Brink, J.N.) Haag, 1923.

Arc 670.2.9 Aigina. (Weeter, G.) Berlin, 1938.

Arc 905.18 Aigner, A. Hallstatt. München, n.d.

Arc 1030.38 Aigrain, R. Manuel d'épigraphie chrétienne. Paris, 1912.

Arc 503.5.10F Ain Shems excavations (Palestine), 1933. Pt.3. (Grant, Elihu.) Haverford, 1934.

Arc 830.93 Ainay; son autel, son amphithéatre, ses martyrs. (Boissieu, A. de.) Lyon, 1864.

Arc 1470.50 Ainos. (May, J.M.F.) London, 1950.

Arc 870.18F Air survey and archaeology. (Crawford, O.G.S.) Southampton, 1924.

Arc 66.1.143 Les Aitoliens a Dalphes. (Flacelière, Robert.) Paris, 1937.

Arc 830.141F Aix. Commission d'Archéologie. Rapport sur les fouilles d'antiquités. pts.1-3. Aix, 1841-44.

Arc 830.97 Aix ancien et moderne. 2e éd. (Porte, J.F.) Aix, 1833.

Arc 843.210 El ajuar del 'Dolmen de la pastora' de Valentina del Alcor (Sevilla). (Almagro Basch, Martin.) Madrid, 1962.

Arc 302.15 Akademia nauk URSR, Kiev. Vseukrainha Akademia Nauk. Vseukrainshau Arkheologichnu Komitet, Kiev. Korotke zvidompennia. Kiev. 1926+

Arc 1528.5PF Akademie...Amsterdam. Akademie von Wetenschappen, Amsterdam. Beschrijving van Nederlandsche historie-penningen. v.1-4,6-10. Amsterdam, 1821-69. 6v.

Arc 1428.15 Akademie der Wissenschaften, Berlin. Die antiken Münzen Mysiens. Berlin, 1913.

Arc 848.50 Akademie der Wissenschaften, Berlin. Frühe Burger und Städte. Berlin, 1954.

Arc 930.205F Akademie der Wissenschaften in Wien. Schriften der Balkancommission. Antiquarische Abtheilung. v.1-7,9-10,13. Wien, 1900-39. 10v.

Arc 925.70 Akademii Nauk URSR, Kyïv. Vseukrains'kii arkheologichnii komitet. Zapiski. Kyïv, n.d.

Arc 925.65 Akademii Nauk URSR, Kyïv. Vseukrains'kii arkheologichnii komitet Tripil'ska kul'tura na Ukraini. Kyïv, n.d.

Arc 530.81 Akademiia nauk Armianskoi SSR, Erevan. Institut Istorii. Dzhrvezh. Erevan, 1959. 2v.

Arc 530.65 Akademiia nauk Armianskoi SSR, Erevan. Institut Istorii. Garni. Erevan, 1951- 4v.

Arc 530.65.5 Akademiia nauk Armianskoi SSR, Erevan. Institut Istorii. Karmir-blur. Erevan, 1955- 4v.

Arc 493.6.15 Akademiia Nauk Azerbaidzhanskoi SSR, Baku. Ockerki po drevnei istorii Azerbaidzhana SSR. Baku, 1956.

Arc 493.6.40 Akademiia Nauk Azerbaidzhanskoi SSR, Baku. Institut Istorii. Arkheologicheskie issledoveniia v Azerbaidzhane. Baku, 1965.

Arc 493.6.22 Akademiia Nauk Azerbaidzhanskoi SSR, Baku. Institut Istorii. Voprosy istorii Kavkazskoi Albanii; sbornik statei. Baku, 1962.

Arc 925.150 Akademiia Nauk BSSR, Minsk. Institut Historyi. Materialy po arkheologii BSSR. Minsk, 1957.

Arc 530.95F Akademiia nauk Gruz SSR, Tiflis. Institut Istorii. Mtskheta; itogi arkheologicheskikh issledovanii. Tbilisi, 1955.

Arc 530.95.2F Akademiia nauk Gruz SSR, Tiflis. Institut Istorii. Mtskheta; itogi arkheologicheskikh issledovanii. Tbilisi, 1958.

Arc 936.155.15 Akademiia Nauk Kirgizskoi SSR, Frunze. Institut Istorii. Arkheologicheskie pamiatniki Talasskoi dolny. Frunze, 1963.

Arc 936.155.20 Akademiia Nauk Kirgizskoi SSR, Frunze. Institut Istorii. Drevniaia i rannesrednevekovaia kul'tura Kirgizstana. Frunze, 1967.

Arc 936.165.15 Akademiia Nauk Moldavskoi SSSR, Kishinev. Institut Istorii. Materialy i issledovanii po arkheologii i ethnografii Moldavskoi SSR. Kishinev, 1964.

Arc 385.4 Akademiia Nauk SSR. Institut Arkheologii. Protiv vyl'garizatsii marksisma v arkheologii. Moskva, 1953.

Arc 543.120 Akademiia Nauk SSSR. Mongol'skii arkheologicheskii sbornik. Moskva, 1962.

Arc 923.80 Akademiia Nauk SSSR. Institut Arkheologii. Arkheologicheskie ekspechtsii gosudarstvennoi akademii istorii material'noi kul'tury instituta arkheologii Akademii nauk SSSR. Moskva, 1962.

Arc 608.23.5 Akademiia Nauk SSSR. Institut Arkheologii. Drevniaia Nubiia. Leningrad, 1964.

Arc 925.9.25 Akademiia Nauk SSSR. Institut Arkheologii. Drevnosti checheno-ingushetii. Moskva, 1963.

Arc 385.14 Akademiia Nauk SSSR. Institut Arkheologii. Novye metody v arkheologicheskikh issledovaniiakh. Leningrad, 1963.

Arc 612.48 Akademiia Nauk SSSR. Institut Arkheologii. Pamiatniki kamennogo i bronz. vekov Evrazii. Moskva, 1964.

Arc 923.132 Akademiia nauk SSSR. Institut Arkheologii. Stogi i perspektivy razvitiia sovetskoi arkheologii. Moskva, 1945.

Arc 543.3.65 Akademiia nauk SSSR. Institut Arkheologod. Sredniaia Aziia v epokhu Kamnia i bronzy. Leningrad, 1966.

Arc 543.3.70 Akademiia nauk SSSR. Institut Etnografii. Material'naia Kul'tura narodov Srednei Azii i Kazakustana. Moskva, 1966.

Arc 543.55A Akademiia nauk SSSR. Institut Istorii Materialii Kul'tura. Zhivopis drevnogo Piandzhikenta. Moskva, 1954. 2v.

Arc 925.113 Akademiia Nauk SSSR. Institut Istorii Materialy Kul'tury. Antichnye goroda severnogo Prichernomoria. Moskva, 1955.

Arc 925.100 Akademiia Nauk SSSR. Institut Istorii Materialy Kul'tury. Voprosy skifo-sarmatskoi arkheologicheskoi. Moskva, 1954.

Arc 416.33 Akademiia Nauk SSSR. Institut narodov Azii. Deshifrovka i interpretatsiia pis'mennostei drevnego Vostoka. Moskva, 1966.

Arc 432.23 Akademiia Nauk SSSR. Institut Narodov Azii. Indiia v drevnosti; sbornik statei. Moskva, 1964.

Arc 925.321 Akademiia Nauk SSSR. Karel'skii Filial, Petrozavedsk. Instituta Iazyka, Literatury i Istorii. Novye pamiatniki istorii drevnei Karelii. Leningrad, 1966.

Arc 543.65.20 Akademiia nauk Tadzhikskoi SSSR, Dushambe. Institut Istorii, Arkheologii i Etnografii. Arkheologicheskie raboty v Tadzhikistane. Stalinabad. 10,1970+

Arc 543.65 Akademiia nauk Tadzhikskoi SSSR, Stalinabad. Institut Istorii, Arkheologii i Etnografii. Arkheologicheskie i numzmaticheskie kollektsii. Stalinabad, 1956.

Arc 543.95 Akademiia nauk Tazhikskoi SSSR, Stalinabad. Institut Istorii, Arkheologii i Etnografii. Sektor Arkheologi i Numizmatiki. Arkheologi rasskazy-vaiut. Stalinabad, 1959.

Arc 925.75.3FA Akademiia Nauk URSR, Kiev. Institut Arkheologicheskaia. Ol'viia. Kiev, 1940.

Arc 925.50.30 Akademiia Nauk URSR, Kiev. Kryms'kyi Filologicheskii. Istoriia i arkheologiia drev. Kryma. Kiev, 1957.

Arc 925.55 Akademiia Nauk URSR, Kyïv. Khronyka arkheolohyi ta mystetstva. Kyïv, 1930.

Arc 853.18 Die akademische Kommission. (Ranke, Johannes.) München, 1900.

Arc 543.66.13 Akadenik Akademii nauk Turkmenskoi SSR Mikhail Evgen'evich Masson. (Ovezov, D.M.) Ashkhabad, 1970.

Arc 1428.32 Akarca, A. Les monnaies grecques de Mylasa. Paris, 1959.

Arc 435.2.35F Akbar's tomb, Sikandarah, near Agra. (Smith, E.W.) Allahabad, 1909.

Arc 375.13 Aken, Andreas Rudolphus Antonius van. Elseviers encyclopedie van de archeologie. Amsterdam, 1965.

Arc 858.1.5 Akerman, J.Y. An archaeological index. London, 1847.

Arc 1480.13 Akerman, J.Y. Coins of the Romans relative to Britain. London, 1844.

Arc 1348.1.5 Akerman, J.Y. Introductory study of ancient and modern coins. London, 1848.

Arc 1348.1 Akerman, J.Y. Numismatic manual. London, 1840.

Arc 858.1 Akerman, J.Y. Remains of Pagan Saxondom. London, 1855.

Arc 726.130 Akerstrom, A. Der geometrische Stil in Italien. Lund, 1943.

Arc 905.142 Akésöi paleolitikum Magyarországon. (Gabori, Miklos.) Budapest, 1964.

Arc 925.9.80 Akhachcharkhu-drevnii mogil'nik nagornoi Abkhazii. (Shamba, G.K.) Sukhumi, 1970.

Arc 543.66.10 Akhangeran. (Masson, M.E.) Tashkend, 1953.

Arc 416.26 Akishev, K.A. Drevniaia kul'tura sakov i usunei doliny reki Ili. Alma Ata, 1963.

Arc 925.16.60 Akishev, Kemal' A. Drevnii Otrar. Alma-Ata, 1972.

Arc 710.14F Die Akropolis. (Rodenwaldt, Gerhart.) Berlin, 1930.

Arc 710.2.2 Die Akropolis von Athen. (Boetticher, C.) Berlin, 1888.

Arc 710.3 Die Akropolis von Athen. (Curtius, E.) Berlin, 1844.

Arc 710.5 Die Akropolis von Athen. (Luckenbach, H.) München, 1896.

Arc 710.5.2 Die Akropolis von Athen. (Luckenbach, H.) München, 1905.

Arc 710.8 Akropolis von Athen im Zeitalter des Perikles. (Hachtmann, K.) Gütersloh, 1903.

Arc 608.75 Aksha. Paris, 1966- 3v.

Arc 1190.35 Aktenkunde. (Meisner, H.O.) Berlin, 1935.

Arc 1282.12 Aktovye pechati drevnei Rusi X-XV vv. (Ianin, Valentin L.) Moskva, 1970. 2v.

Arc 513.26 Akurgal, E. Arkeoloji arastirmalari. Ankara, 1945.

Arc 530.53 Akurgal, E. Remarques stylistiques sur les reliefs de Malatya. Istanbul, 1946.

Arc 590.4.2 Alabaster sarcophagus of Oimenepthah. (Sharpe, S.) London, 1864.

Arc 935.24.5 Alacahöyük. (Kosay, Hâmit Z.) n.p., 195-?

Arc 853.41.15 Die Alamannen in Sudbaden. (Garscha, Friedrich.) Berlin, 1970. 2v.

Arc 853.13.30F Die Alamannen in Württemberg. (Veeck, Walther.) Berlin, 1931. 2v.

Arc 853.99F Die Alamannen zwischen iller und lech. (Franken, M.) Berlin, 1944.
Arc 853.345.1 Die Alamannengräber von Hailfingen. Photoreproduction. (Stoll, Hermann.) Berlin, 1939.
Arc 915.44 Das alamannische Gräberfeld von Beggingen-Löbern. (Guyan, Walter Ulrich.) Basel, 1958.
Arc 853.350 Das alamannische Gräberfeld von Dirlewang bei Minchelheim. (Christlein, Rainer.) Kallmünz, 1971.
Arc 853.160F Das alamannische Gräberfeld von Mindelheim. (Werner, Joachim.) Kallmünz, 1955.
Arc 853.282 Das alamannische Reihengräberfeld von Marktoberdorf im Allgäu. (Christlein, Rainer.) Kallmünz, 1966.
Arc 853.361 Die alamannischen Gräberfelder von Guttingen und Merdingen in Südbaden. (Fingerlin, Gerhard.) Berlin, 1971. 2v.
Arc 493.9 Alamut and Lamasar. (Ivanov, V.A.) Teheran, 1960.
Arc 925.9.135 Alaniia v X-XIII vv. (Kuznetsov, Vladimir A.) Ordzhonikidze, 1971.
Arc 1615.16 Alaska's coinage through the years. 2. ed. (Gould, Maurice M.) Racine, 1965.
Arc 830.18.3 Alaunium Catuiaca. (Arbaud, Damase.) n.p., 1868.
Arc 726.237.5 Alba fucens. Rapports et études présentes par J. Mercens. Bruxelles, 1969. 2v.
Arc 936.3F Albania antica. (Ugalini, L.U.) Roma, 1927-42. 3v.
Arc 1033.173 Albarellio, G. Il cimitero "In clivum cucumeris". Aquila, 1909.
Arc 543.66.5 Al'baum, L.I. Balalyk-tepe. Tashkend, 1960.
Arc 66.1.31 Albert, M. Culte de castor et pollux en Italie. Paris, 1883.
Arc 726.56 Albert, Maurice. De villis Tiburtinis, principe Augusto Thesim proponebat. Parisios, 1883.
Arc 66.1.127 Albertini, E. La composition dans les ouvrages philosophiques de Sévèque. n.p., n.d.
Htn Arc 772.3* Albertini, F. De Roma prisca et nova varii auctores. Romae, 1523?
Htn Arc 1020.9.114* Albertini, F. Mirabilia Roma. Firenze, 1520.
Arc 1020.9.117 Albertini, F. Mirabilibus...Romae. Heilbron, 1886.
Arc 1027.25.9 Albo dei sottoscrittori...medaglio d'oro. (Rossi, J.B. de.) Roma, 1882.
Arc 1027.25.15 Albo dei sottoscrittori pel busto marmoreo. (Rossi, G.B. de.) Roma, 1892.
Arc 853.17.15F Albrecht, C. Frühgeschichtliche Funde aus Westfalen im städtischen Kunst- und Gewerbemuseum Dortmund. Dortmund, 1936.
Arc 853.27.10F Albrecht, C. Das Römerlager in Oberaden. Dortmund, 1938. 2v.
Arc 612.86 Albrecht, Gerd. Merkmalanalyse von Geschossspitzen des mittleren Jungpleistozäns im Mittel- und Osteuropa. Stuttgart, 1972.
Arc 1269.15F Albrecht, J. Die hohenlohischen Siegel des Mittelalters. Oehringen, 1859.
Arc 1510.139 Albrecht, J. Mittheilungen zur Geschichte der Reichs-Münzstaetten. Heilbronn, 1835.
Arc 497.30.3 Albright, William Foxwell. The archaeology of Palestine. London, 1954.
Arc 497.30 Albright, William Foxwell. The archaeology of Palestine and the Bible. N.Y., 1932.
Arc 497.31.10 Albright, William Foxwell. New horizons in Biblical research. London, 1966.
Arc 625.13 Album...Antike-Sammlung. (Schneider, R. von.) Wien, 1895.
Arc 1163.16F Album de paleografie românească. (Bianu, I.) București, 1929.
Arc 1163.4.20F Album de paléographie arabe. (Vajda, Georges.) Paris, 1958.
Arc 1148.28F Album de paléographie grecque. (Wittek, Martin.) Gand, 1967.
Arc 628.6 Album des klassischen Alterthums. (Rheinhard, H.) Stuttgart, 1882.
Arc 1153.87F Album of dated Latin inscriptions. v.1-4. (Gordon, Arthur Ernest.) Berkeley, 1958- 6v.
Arc 953.19.5 An album of prehistoric Canadian art. (Smith, Harlan I.) Ottawa, 1923.
Arc 855.214 Albury. Temple of the British Druids. (Stukeley, William.) London, 1743.
Arc 943.46 Alcina Franch, José. Manual de arqueologia americana. Madrid, 1965.
Arc 885.24 Alcock, L. Dinas Powys. Cardiff, 1963.
Arc 861.207 Alcock, Leslie. By South Cadbury is that Camelot. London, 1970.
Arc 1033.12.137 Alcune memorie sull'imagine acheropita del SS. Salvatore di Sancta Santorum. (Mencacci, P.) Roma, 1863.
Arc 1027.21.9 Alcuni recenti scavi nelle catacombe di San Gennaro. (Stornaiolo, C.) Roma, 1879.
Arc 87.2.75 Aldenkirchen, J. Mittelalterliche Kunst in Soest. Bonn, 1875.
Arc 888.35 De aldste kultuer yn de sânen feankriten fen Frysplân. (Boeles, P.C.J.A.) Boalsert, 1930.
Arc 925.310.10 Alekseeva, Evgeniia P. Drevniaia i srednevekovaia istoriia Karachaevo-Cherkesii. Moskva, 1971.
Arc 925.310.5 Alekseeva, Evgeniia P. Karachaevtsy i balkartsy, drevnii narod Kavkaza. Cherkessk, 1963.
Arc 925.310 Alekseeva, Evgeniia P. O chem rasskazyvaiut arkheologicheskie pamiatniki Karachaevo-Cherkesii. Cherkessk, 1960.
Arc 936.180.10 Aleksova, Blaga. Prosek-Demir Kapija. Skopje, 1966.
Arc 830.158.10 Alésia. (Le Gall, J.) Paris, 1963.
Arc 402.14 Alessandro Ricci e il suo giornale dei viaggi. v.2. (Sammarco, Angelo.) Cairo, 1930.
Arc 1033.160 Alēthēs ekthesis...thaymatourchou...touachiouspyridōnos. (Boulgaris, N.T.) Benetia, 1880.
Arc 726.262 Aletrium. (Gasperini, Lidio.) Roma, 1964.
Arc 936.220.90 Alexander, John. Jugoslavia before the Roman conquest. London, 1972.
Arc 936.220.91 Alexander, John. Yugoslavia before the Roman conquest. N.Y., 1972.
Arc 1510.160 Alexander, Prince of Messe and of the Rhine, 1823-1888. Mainzisches Münzcabinet des Prinzen Alexander von Hessen. Faksimile. Münster, 1968.
Arc 1084.7 Alexander, R. Jade; its philosophy. N.Y., 1928.
Arc 1335.45.9 Alexander and Company, Boston. Alexander and Company's Hub coin book. Boston, 1910.
Arc 1335.45.9 Alexander and Company's Hub coin book. (Alexander and Company, Boston.) Boston, 1910.
Arc 1468.32 Alexander Loards. v.3. (Newell, E.T.) N.Y., 1921-23.
Arc 600.1.15 Alexandrea ad Aegyptum. (Breccia, E.) Bergamo, 1914.
Arc 547.24.12F Alexandria. Musée Gréco-Romain. Annuaire. 1932-1950 3v.
Arc 547.24.10F Alexandria. Musée Gréco-Romain. Le Musée Gréco-Romain, 1925-1931. Bergamo, 1932.
Arc 547.24F Alexandria. Musée Gréco-Romain. Le Musée Gréco-Romain du cours de l'année 1922-23. Alexandrie, 1924.
X Cg Arc 1470.29 Die alexandrinischen Münzen. v.1-2. (Vogt, Joseph.) Stuttgart, 1924. (Changed to XP 9970)
Arc 1480.84 Alföldi, András. Caesar in 44 v. Chr. Bonn, 1974.
Arc 530.6.10F Alfoldi-Rosenbaum, Elizabeth. Anamur nekropolu. The necropolis Anemurium. Ankara, 1971.
Arc 530.6.5F Alfoldi-Rosenbaum, Elizabeth. A survey of coastal cities in Western Cilicia. Ankara, 1967.
Arc 1020.31 Alger, C. L'antica chiesa S. Anna...Gerusalemma. Gerusalemma, 1863.
Arc 608.6.18 Algeria. Directoire de l'Intérieur et de Beaux-Arts. Villes d'or. Alger, 1951.
Arc 30.10 Algeria. Services des Monuments Historiques. Rapport sur les travaux de fouilles et consalidations. Algeria. 2v.
Arc 608.6.45 Algérie antique. (Leschi, Louis.) Paris, 1952.
Arc 608.16.10 L'Algérie romaine; forums et basiliques. (Douël, M.) Paris, 1930.
Arc 406.6 Algumas noções elementares do arqueologia pratica. (Viana, Abel.) Beja, 1962.
Arc 1163.13 Algunas siglas e abreviaturas usadas. (Cordeiro de Sausa, J.M.) Lisboa, 1926.
Arc 889.2 Les alhuions de l'escault et les tourbières...d'Audenarde. (Delvaux, Emile.) Liége, 1885.
Arc 603.6.5 Alimen, Henriette. The prehistory of Africa. London, 1957.
Arc 530.35F The Alishar Hüyük, seasons of 1930-32. (Osten, H.H. von der.) Chicago, 1937.
Arc 853.27 Aliso...Ausgrabungen bei Haltern. (Schuchhardt, C.) Haltern, 1906.
Arc 853.27.5 Aliso bei Oberaden und Vernusschlacht. (Prein, Otto.) Münster, 1930.
Arc 726.48.2 Alla dissertazione epistolare sulle antiche città picene Falera e Tignio. Appendice. (Colucci, G.) Macerata, 1778.
Arc 395.12 Allah ist gross! (Kaufmann, C.M.) Freiburg, 1950.
Arc 1153.59 Allamoda, H. Beiträge zur Geschichte der äusseren Merkmale des ältesten Breslauer Bischofsurkunden bis zum Jahre 1319. Inaug. Diss. Oblau, 1924.
Arc 380.206 Allan, J.H. Pictorial tour in the Mediterranean. London, 1843.
Arc 443.5 Allchin, F.R. Neolithic cattle-keepers of south India; a study of the Deccan ashmounds. Cambridge, Eng., 1963.
Arc 870.9.10 Allcroft, A.H. The circle and the cross. London, 1927-30. 2v.
Arc 870.9 Allcroft, A.H. Earthwork of England. London, 1908.
Arc 1030.16 Allegrantia, J. De sepulcris christianis. Mediolani, 1773.
Htn Arc 1020.32* Allegranza, G. Spiegazione...sacri monumenti antichi di Milano. Milano, 1757.
Arc 1033.44.33 Allegranza, J. De monogrammate D.N. Jesu Christe. Milano, 1773.
Arc 1493.3 Allen, E.A. Monnaies d'or suévo-lusitaniennes. Paris, 1865.
Arc 618.6A Allen, J. Romilly. Celtic art in pagan and Christian times. London, 1904.
NEDL Arc 855.206 Allen, J.R. The early Christian monuments of Scotland. Edinburgh, 1903.
NEDL Arc 142.2 Allen, J.R. The reliquary...archaeological journal. London. 1860-1909 49v.
Arc 1148.1.5 Allen, T.W. Greek abbreviation in the 15th century. London, n.d.
Arc 551.10 Allerhand Kleinigkeiten. (Borchardt, L.) Leipzig, 1933?
Arc 1348.17 Allgemeine Münzkunde. (Luschin von Elengreuth, A.) München, 1904.
Arc 1348.17.2 Allgemeine Münzkunde und Geldgeschichte. 2. Aufl. (Luschin von Elengreuth, A.) München, 1926.
Arc 305.10 Alliance for the Preservation of Florida Antiquities. Papers. Jacksonville Beach.
Arc 861.9 Allies, J. The British, Roman, and Saxon antiquities and folklore of Worcestershire. London, 1856.
Arc 609.17.15 Allison, Philip. Cross River monoliths. Laejos, 1968.
Arc 830.60 Allmer, Auguste. Trion. Lyon, 1888.
Arc 307.3.12 Allocution fait à la Société de Géographie...sur la 2e session des Congrés international de Americanistes. (Grairer, Gabriel.) Rouen, 1877.
Arc 1468.45 Allotte de la Fuğe, F.M. Monnaies grecques. Paris, 1925.
Arc 830.71 Allou, Charles N. Descriptions des monumens des differeus âges observés dans le département de la Haute-Vienne. Paris, 1821.
Arc 1433.80 Allouche-Le Page, M.T. L'art monétaire des royaumes bactriens. Paris, 1956.
Arc 1033.11 Alma Mater. (Gaborel de Rossillon, J.) Paris, 1877.
Arc 843.210 Almagro Basch, Martin. El ajuar del 'Dolmen de la pastora' de Valentina del Alcor (Sevilla). Madrid, 1962.
Arc 843.5.25 Almarche, V.F. La antigua civilización ibérica en el reino de Valencia. Valencia, 1918.
Arc 843.105 Almeida, Fernando de. Egitânia. Lisboa, 1956.
Arc 843.105.5 Almeida, Fernando de. Ruinas de Mirobriga dos Célticos. Lisboa, 1964.
Arc 1033.35.147 Almeida, R.V. d'. A cruz de vila Viçosa. Lisboa, 1908.
Arc 1033.35.147.2 Almeida, R.V. d'. A cruz de vila Viçosa. 2. ed. Lisboa, 1957.
Arc 895.22.10F Almgren, Oscar. Die ältere Eisenzeit Gotlands. pt.1-2. Stockholm, 1914-23.
Arc 407.20 Alms for oblivion: an antiquary's scrapbook. (Wheeler, Robert Eric Mortimer.) London, 1966.
Arc 32.2F Almstead, A.T. Travels and studies in...nearer East. Ithaca, N.Y., 1911.
Arc 810.1 Aloe, Stanislas d'. Les ruines de Poméi. Naples, 1852.
Arc 810.1.3 Aloe, Stanislas d'. Les ruines de Pompéi. Naples, 1850-51. 3 pam.
Arc 810.1.2 Aloe, Stanislas d'. Les ruines de Pompéi. Naples, 1851.
Arc 292.30.2F Al'oom risunkov...v otchetakh. (Russia. Arkheologicheskaia Kommissiia.) Sankt Peterburg. 1882-1906
Arc 1232.10 Alp, Sedat. Zylinder- und Stempelsiegel aus Karahöyük bei Konya. Ankara, 1968.
Arc 743.3 Die Alpen-Etrusker. (Koch, M.) Leipzig, 1853.
Arc 612.51 Alpenwanderungen in die Vorzeit zu Drachenhöhlen und Druidensteinen. (Lukan, Karl.) Wien, 1965.
Arc 412.28 Alpözen, Oğuz. Türkuiye'de sualt, arkeolojisi. Istanbul, 1975.
Arc 830.162 L'Alsace romaine. (Forrer, Robert.) Paris, 1935.
Arc 700.56 Alsop, J. From the silent earth. N.Y., 1964.
Arc 716.4.5 Alt-Athen und seine Agora. (Dörpfeld, W.) Berlin, 1937-39. 2v.

Author and Title Listing

Arc 1166.8 Alt datera manuskript. (Norlén, Saga-Marianne.) Stockholm, 1973.
Arc 522.10.2 Alt-Ilion im Dumbrekthal. (Brentano, E.) Heilbronn, 1877?
Arc 488.23 Alt-Iran. (Porada, Edith.) Baden-Baden, 1962.
X Cg Arc 672.1.33 Alt Kreta. (Bossert, H.T.) Berlin, 1921.
Arc 672.1.34 Alt Kreta. 3. Aufl. (Bossert, H.T.) Berlin, 1937.
Arc 684.1.37 Alt-Olympia. (Dörpfeld, Wilhelm.) Berlin, 1935. 2v.
Arc 684.1.38 Alt-Olympia. Beiheft. (Dörpfeld, Wilhelm.) Berlin, 1935.
Arc 547.35F Die altägyptischen Scherbenbilder. (Brunner-Traut, Emma.) Wiesbaden, 1956.
Arc 530.10.15 Der Altar des Artemis-Tempels in Magnesia am Mäander. (Gerkan, Armin von.) Berlin, 1929.
Arc 785.34.9 Der Altar des Kaiserfriedens Ara Pacis Augustae. (Gardthausen, V.) Leipzig, 1908.
Arc 1033.123 Altar und Altargrab der christlichen Kirchen...Mensa und Confessio. v.1-2. (Wieland, F.) München, 1906-12.
Arc 520.17 Das Altar von Pergamon. (Napp, A.E.) München, 1936.
Arc 520.12 Der Altar von Pergamon. (Salis, A. von.) Berlin, 1912.
Arc 520.25 Altar' Zevsa v Pergame. (Belov, G.D.) Leningrad, 1958.
Arc 520.25.2 Altar' Zevsa v Pergame. (Belov, G.D.) Leningrad, 1959.
Arc 1020.9.28 Altarium et reliquarum...basilicae vaticanae. (Sindone, R.) Romae, 1744.
Arc 505.29 The altars of the Old Testament. (Wiener, H.M.) Leipzig, 1927.
Arc 890.203 Altas de l'archéologie du nord. (Copenhagen. Kongeligi Nordiske Oldskrift-Selskab.) Copenhagen, 1857.
X Cg Arc 510.10 Altas des antiquités troyennes. (Schliemann, H.) Leipzig, 1874.
Arc 1020.34 Altchristliche Basiliken und Lokaltraditionen in Südjudäa. (Mader, Andreas E.) Paderborn, 1918.
Arc 1033.28 Altchristliche Ehredenkmäler. (Pelka, O.) Strassburg, 1901.
Arc 1025.62 Die altchristliche Grabeskunst. (Styger, Paul.) München, 1927.
Arc 1025.55 Der altchristliche Gräberschmuck. (Hasenclever, A.) Braunschweig, 1886.
Arc 1027.23.9 Altchristliche Malerei...römischen Katacomben. (Hennecke, E.) Leipzig, 1896.
Arc 1033.20.13 Die altchristlichen Basiliken Roms. (Hessel, C.) Weslau, 1873.
Arc 1027.23.17 Die altchristlichen Bildwerke. (Schulke, V.) Erlangen, 1889.
Arc 1016.204 Die altchristlichen Inschriften der Rheinlande. (Kraus, F.X.) Freiburg, 1890.
Arc 1016.12 Die altchristlichen Skulpturen...deutschen Nationalstiftung am Campo Santo. (Wittig, Joseph.) Rom, 1906.
Arc 1020.14 Ein altchristliches Pompeji. (Kaufmann, C.M.) Mainz, 1902.
Arc 1163.19 Altdeutsche Handschriften. (Eis, Gerhard.) München, 1949.
Arc 943.42 Das alte Amerika. (Trimborn, Hermann.) Stuttgart, 1959.
Arc 628.8 Alte Denkmäler. v.1-5. (Welcker, F.G.) Göttingen, 1849-64. 4v.
Arc 416.27 Alte Feststrassen im Nahen Orient. (Andrae, Walter.) Stuttgart, 1964.
Arc 672.1.85 Das alte Kreta. (Maltezos, G.P.) Kaiserslautern, 1957.
Arc 396.6 Alte Kulturstätten. 2. Aufl. (Linde, Richard.) Bielefeld, 1924.
Arc 853.236.5F Der alte Markt in Magdeburg. (Nickel, Ernest.) Berlin, 1964.
Arc 415.1 Alte Metalltrommeln aus Südost-Asien. (Heger, Franz.) Leipzig, 1902. 2v.
Arc 30.1 Der alte Orient. Leipzig. 1-43,1899-1945 24v.
Arc 30.1.2 Der alte Orient. Ergänzungsband. Leipzig, n.d. 2v.
Arc 780.1 Das alte Rom. (Ziegler, C.) Stuttgart, 1882.
Arc 759.1 Das alte Rom im Mittelalter. (Elter, A.) Bonn, 1904.
Arc 756.13 Das alte Rom mit dem Triumphzuge Kaiser Constantins im Jahre 312 n. Chr. (Bühlmann, J.) München, 1892.
Arc 758.4 Das alte Rom sein Werden. (Diehl, Ernst.) Leipzig, 1909.
Arc 777.4 Das alte Rom zur konstantinischen Zeit undHeute. (Wiesel, Julius Maxim.) Mainz, 1964.
Arc 853.31.5 Die Alteburg bei Armstadt. (Cämmerer, E.) Leipzig, 1924.
Arc 1418.15 Altekar, A.S. Catalogue of the Gupta gold coins in the Bayana Hoard. Bombay, 1954.
Arc 450.30 Altekar, Anant L. Report on Humrahar excavations. Patna, 1959.
Arc 537.4 Die alten Kyprier in Kunst und Cultur. (Holwerda, A.E.J.) Leiden, 1885.
Arc 1200.18 Alter, Franz K. Beitrag zur praktischen Diplomatik für Slaven. Wien, 1801.
Arc 1348.5 Alter und neuer Münz-Schlüssel. (Hoffmann, L.W.) Nuremberg, 1692.
Arc 853.342 Die altere Bronzezeit Nordwestdeutschlands. (Bergmann, Joseph.) Marburg, 1970. 2v.
Arc 895.52 Die altere Eisenzeit im Ostergötland. (Oxenstierna, E.C.G.) Lidingö, 1958.
Arc 936.27 Die Alterthümer Daciens in dem heutigen Siebenbürgen. (Hachhausen und Hachlaus, S.J.) Wien, 1775.
Arc 853.21.5 Alterthümer der Bronzezeit in Westpreussen. (Lissauer, A.) Danzig, 1891.
Arc 905.31 Alterthümer des frühen Mittelalters in Ungarn. (Hampel, J.) Braunschweig, 1905. 3v.
Arc 853.98 Die Alterthümer des Oberamts Heidenheims. (Hertlein, F.) Eszlingen, 1912.
Arc 708.15 Die Alterthuemer von Athen. (Stuart, J.) Darmstadt, 1829-31. 2v.
Arc 853.10 Die Alterthümer vovon Hallstätter Salzberg. (Simony, F.) Wien, 1851.
Arc 848.24F Die Altertümer unserer heidnischen Vorzeit. v.5. (Mainz. Römisch-germanische Zentralmuseum.) Mainz, 1911.
Arc 510.2 Altertümer von Pergamon. (Deutsches Archäologisches Institut.) Berlin. 1,1912+ 18v.
Arc 510.2PF Altertümer von Pergamon. Atlases. (Deutches Archäologisches Institut.) 9v.
Arc 407.15 Altertumskunde. (Wegner, Max.) Freiburg, 1951.
Arc 612.11.2 Alteruopa; eine Vorgeschichte unseres Erdteils. 2. Aufl. (Schuchhardt, Carl.) Leipzig, 1926.
Arc 746.46 Altetruskische Plastik. (Hanfmann, George Maxim Anossov.) Würzburg, 1936.
Arc 612.11.4 Alteuropa. (Schuchhardt, Carl.) Berlin, 1941.
Arc 612.11 Alteuropa. (Schuchhardt, Carl.) Strassburg, 1919.
Arc 848.31 Altgermanische Kultur. (Behn, Friedrich.) Leipzig, 1935.
Arc 848.30.4 Altgermanische Kultur in Wort und Bild. 3. Aufl. (Schultz, W.) München, 1935.
Arc 848.30.5 Altgermanische Kultur in Wort und Bild. 4. Aufl. (Schultz, W.) München, 1937.
Arc 848.8.9 Altgermanische Kulturhöhe. (Kossinna, Gustaf.) München, 1927.
Arc 848.8.10 Altgermanische Kulturhöhe. 8. Aufl. (Kossinna, Gustaf.) Leipzig, 1942.
Arc 848.40 Altgermanische Kunst. 2. Aufl. (Behn, Friedrich.) München, 1930.
Arc 1468.8 Altgriechischen Münzorten. (Grunauer, E.) Basel, 1877.
Arc 87.1.59 Altgriechisches Bronzebecken aus Leontini. (Winnefeld, H.) Berlin, 1899.
Arc 635.10 Das Altgriechisches Theatergebäude. (Strack, J.H.) Potsdam, 1843.
Arc 505.75 Altheim, F. Das erste Auftreten der Hunnen das Alter der Jesaja-Rolle. Baden-Baden, 1953.
Arc 440.7 Altinità archeologica italiana in Asia. (Centro scavi e ricerche archeologiche in Asia.) Roma, 1960.
Arc 65.10 Altino romana. Venezia. 1,1956
Arc 488.28 Altiranische Funde und Forschungen. (Hinz, Walther.) Berlin, 1969.
Arc 700.12 Die altischen Gräber der Bluethezeit. (Holwerda, J.H.) Leiden, 1899.
Arc 520.16 Eine Altisdarstellung am grossen Fries von Pergamon. Inaug. Diss. (Dopp, W.) Rostock, 1934.
Arc 853.82 Die altmärkisch-osthannöverschen Schalenurnenfelder der spätrömischen Zeit. Inaug. Diss. (Kuchenbuch, F.) Halle an der Saale, 1938.
Arc 936.195.155 Altmagyarische Gräberfelder in der Südwestslowakei. (Točík, Anton.) Bratislava, 1968.
Arc 1093.4 Altmann, W. Architectur und Ornamentik der antiken Sarkophage. Berlin, 1902.
Arc 726.28 Altmann, W. Die italischen Rundbauten. Berlin, 1906.
Arc 785.33 Altmann, W. Die römischen Grabaltäre der Kaiserzeit. Berlin, 1905.
Arc 785.33.1 Altmann, W. Die römischen Grabaltäre der Kaiserzeit. N.Y., 1975.
Arc 848.31.5 Altmordisches Leben vor 3000 Jahren. (Behn, Friedrich.) München, 1935.
Arc 893.13 Die altnordische Kunst. (Adama van Scheltema, F.) Berlin, 1923.
Arc 893.13.5 Die altnordische Kunst. 2. Aufl. (Adama van Scheltema, F.) Leipzig, 1923.
Arc 843.9 El alto Jalón. (Aguilera y Gamboa, E.) Madrid, 1909.
Arc 830.160.5 Altonum, fille d'Aeria, origines gallo-romaines de Montbrison. (Chevalier, Alexandre.) Valence, 1968.
Arc 1208.13F Altorientalische Siegelsteine der Sammlung Hans Silvius von Aulock. (Aulock, Hans von.) Uppsala, 1957.
Arc 608.52F L'altorilievo di Afrodite a Cirene. (Traversari, Gustavo.) Roma, 1959.
Arc 185.3 Altpreussen. Königsburg. 1-8,1935-1943 3v.
Arc 185.2 Altschlesien. Breslau. 1-8,1922-1939 8v.
Arc 853.65.15 Die Altsteinzeit in Niederschlesien. (Zatz, Lothar.) Leipzig, 1939.
Arc 612.32 Altsteinzeitkunde Mitteleuropas. (Zatz, L.F.) Stuttgart, 1951.
Arc 513.42 Die altsteinzeitlichen Kulturen Anatoliens. (Pfannenstiel, Max.) Berlin, 1941.
Arc 853.244F Die altsteinzeitlichen Kulturen der Räuberhöhle am Schelmeengraben bei Sinzing. (Linder, H.) Kallmünz, 1961.
Arc 853.68F Die altthüringischen Funde von Weimar (5.-7. Jahrhundert nach Christus.) (Gätze, A.) Berlin, 1912.
Arc 1400.8 Altz, Charles G. Foreign coins struck at United States mints. Racine, Wis., 1965.
Arc 843.190 Alvarez-Ossori, F. Bronces ibericas o hispancion del Mueso Arquelogico Nacional. Madrid, 1935.
Arc 1160.202 Alvera Delgras, A. Compendio de paleografia española. Madrid, 1857.
Arc 720.16PF Alvino, Francesco. Amfiteatro campano illustrato. Napoli, 1842. 2v.
Arc 905.17.12 Alzinger, Wilhelm. Aguntum. Wien, 1958.
Arc 518.12.5F Alzinger, Wilhelm. Augusteische Architektur in Ephesos. v.1-2. Wien, 1974.
Arc 905.17.10F Alzinger, Wilhelm. Kleinfunde von Aguntum aus den Jahren 1850 bis 1952. Wien, 1955.
Arc 518.12 Alzinger, Wilhelm. Die Stadt des siebenten Weltwunders. Wien, 1962.
Arc 1138.121 Am Anfang der Kultur. (König, Marie E.P.) Berlin, 1973.
Arc 488.5F Am Tor von Asien. (Herzfeld, Ernst E.) Berlin, 1920.
Arc 843.77.15 Amador de los Ríos, Rodrigo. El anfiteatro de Italica. Madrid, 1916.
Arc 383.16 Amagiu lui Constantin Daicoviciu cu prilejne. (Academia...Bucharest. Academia Republicii Populare Romîne.) București, 1960.
Arc 385.9.5 Amal'rikh, Aleksei S. Chto tahoe arkheologiia. Izd. 3. Moskva, 1966.
Arc 385.9 Amal'rikh, Aleksei S. V poiskakh ischeznuvshikh tsivilizatsii. Moskva, 1959.
Arc 385.9.2 Amal'rikh, Aleksei S. V poiskakh ischeznuvshikh tsivilizatsii. Izd. 2. Moskva, 1966.
Arc 386.5.6 Amalthea. v.1-3. (Böttiger, Carl August.) Leipzig, 1820-25. 2v.
Arc 673.1.22F Amandry, P. La colonne des Naxiens et le partique des Athéneéns. Thèse. Paris, 1953.
Arc 66.1.170 Amandry, P. La mantique Apollenienne a Delphes. Paris, 1950. 2v.
Arc 1033.3.3 Amati, G. Emblemi sepolcrali degli antichi cristiani. Roma, 1825.
Arc 1030.23 Amati, G. Monumenti gentileschi e cristiani...Lorio nell'Aurelia. Roma, 1824.
Arc 520.7 Die Amazonengruppe die attalischen Weihgeschenks. (Habich, G.) Berlin, 1896.
Arc 708.21 Ambrosoli, G. Atene. Brevi cenni sulla città antica e moderna. Milano, 1901.
Arc 1348.29.3 Ambrosoli, S. Manuale di numismatica. 3. ed. Milano, 1904.
Arc 1317.4 Ambrosoli, S. Revista italiana di numismatica. Milano. 1,1888+ 43v.
Arc 1317.4F Ambrosoli, S. Revista italiana di numismatica. Milano. 37,1924
Arc 1488.7 Ambrosoli, Solone. Atlante numismatico italiano. Milano, 1906.
Arc 600.11 Amélineau, E. Les nouvelles fouilles d'Abydos, seconde campagne 1896-1897. Paris, 1902.
Arc 600.11.2 Amélineau, E. Les nouvelles fouilles d'Abydos 1897-1898. Paris, 1904-05. 2v.
Arc 772.6.2 Amelung, W. Die antiken Sammlungen. 2. Aufl. Stuttgart, 1913.
Arc 943.4 America for Columbus. (Kabell, S.K.) Roenne, 1892.
Arc 1.13.6F American Academy, Rome. The American Academy in Rome, 1894-1914. N.Y., 1914.
Arc 1.13 American Academy, Rome. Annual report. Rome? 1913-1942 6v.

Author and Title Listing

	Call number	Entry
	Arc 1.13.5F	American Academy, Rome. Memoirs. Bergamo. 1,1917+ 26v.
	Arc 1.13.10F	American Academy, Rome. Papers and monographs. Rome.
	Arc 1.13.10	American Academy, Rome. Papers and monographs. Rome. 1,1919+ 25v.
	Arc 1.13.3	American Academy, Rome. Report of executive committee. Rome? 1913
	Arc 1.13.7F	American Academy, Rome. Twenty fifth anniversary. N.Y.? 1920?
	Arc 1.13.6F	The American Academy in Rome, 1894-1914. (American Academy, Rome.) N.Y., 1914.
	Arc 340.5	American Academy in Rome. Library. A bibliographical guide to Latium and southern Eturia. Rome, 1916.
	Arc 340.5.2	American Academy in Rome. Library. A bibliographical guide to Latium and southern Eturia. 2. ed. Rome, 1925.
	Arc 340.5.3	American Academy in Rome. Library. A bibliographical guide to Latium and southern Eturia. 3. ed. Rome, 1933.
NEDL	Arc 305.1	American antiquarian. Cleveland. 1-36 35v.
	Arc 942.6	Pamphlet vol. American antiquities and archaeology. 26 pam.
X Cg	Arc 510.8	American Archaeological Institute. Investigations at Assos. v.1-2. Cambridge, 1902-21.
	Arc 1663.2	American colonial history illustrated by contemporary medals. (Betts, C.W.) N.Y., 1894.
	Arc 30.12.3F	American Institute for Iranian Art and Archaeology. Reprint [of the] American Institute. N.Y.
	Arc 30.12	American Institute for Persian Art and Archaeology. Bulletin. N.Y. 1-5,1931-1942 2v.
	Arc 30.12.5	American Institute of Persian Art and Archaeology. What it is, etc. N.Y., 1932.
	Arc 1.6	American journal of archaeology. Baltimore. 1-11 11v.
	Arc 1.6.15	American journal of archaeology. Index to I-X and appendix to XI. Princeton, n.d.
	Arc 1.6.16	American journal of archaeology. Index to 2nd series. v.1-10, (1897-1906); v.11-70 (1907-66). N.Y., n.d. 2v.
	Arc 1.6.2	American journal of archaeology. 2nd series. 1897+ 74v.
	Arc 1300.1	American journal of numismatics. (American Numismatic Society.) N.Y. 1-53,1866-1919 28v.
	Arc 1675.93	American medals and medalists. (Chamberlain, G.S.) Annandale, Va., 1963.
	Arc 1300.01	Pamphlet box. American Numismatic and Archaeological Society. Miscellaneous pamphlets.
	Arc 1610.1	The American numismatic manual. 2. ed. (Dickeson, M.W.) Philadelphia, 1860.
	Arc 1613.13	American Numismatic Society, N.Y. Exhibition of United States and colonial coins, Jan. 17 to Feb. 18, 1914. Catalogue. N.Y., 1914.
	Arc 1300.1	American Numismatic Society. American journal of numismatics. N.Y. 1-53,1866-1919 28v.
	Arc 1300.1.5	American Numismatic Society. The American Numismatic Society. N.Y., 195-
	Arc 1300.1.11	American Numismatic Society. Annual report. N.Y. 1962+ 2v.
	Arc 1330.5F	American Numismatic Society. Auction catalogue. Boston, 1962.
	Arc 1675.22F	American Numismatic Society. Catalogue of international exhibition of contemporary medals. N.Y., 1911.
	Arc 1329.2	AmericanNumismatic Society. Catalogue of numismatic books in the library. N.Y., 1883.
	Arc 1300.1.8	American Numismatic Society. Centennial celebration. N.Y., 1958.
	Arc 1300.1.7	American Numismatic Society. Centennial publication. N.Y., 1958.
	Arc 1330.6F	American Numismatic Society. Dictionary catalogue. Boston, 1962. 6v.
	Arc 1335.110	American Numismatic Society. International medallic exhibition. N.Y., 1910.
	Arc 1675.22.5	American Numismatic Society. International medallic exhibition of the American Numismatic Society. N.Y., 1910.
	Arc 1675.22.10	American Numismatic Society. International medallic exhibition of the American Numismatic Society. Catalogue. N.Y., 1910.
	Arc 1300.2	American Numismatic Society. Membership list. N.Y. 1930
	Arc 1300.1.17	American Numismatic Society. Museum notes. N.Y. 1-15 8v.
	Arc 1300.1.12	American Numismatic Society. Numismatic notes and monographs. N.Y. 1-157 40v.
	Arc 1300.1.15	American Numismatic Society. Numismatic studies. N.Y. 1-12 5v.
NEDL	Arc 1300.1.10	American Numismatic Society. Proceedings.
	Arc 1300.1.9	American Numismatic Society. Proceedings of annual meetings. 20-104,1878-1962 11v.
	Arc 1335.112PF	American Numismatic Society. Sylloge nummoium Graecorum. v.1, pt.2. N.Y., 1961.
	Arc 1300.30	The American Numismatic Society. (Adelson, Howard L.) N.Y., 1958.
	Arc 1300.1.5	The American Numismatic Society. (American Numismatic Society.) N.Y., 195-
	Arc 1330.6.2F	American Numismatic Society. Library. Dictionary and auction catalogues of the Library of the American Numismatic Society. First and second supplement. Boston, 1967. 2v.
	Arc 1613.10F	The American numismatical manual of the currency or money of the aborigines. (Dickeson, M.W.) Philadelphia, 1859.
	Arc 497.1	American Palestine Exploration Society. Catalogue of photographs. N.Y., 1876.
	Arc 30.11	American Research Center in Egypt. Newsletter. Boston. 13,1954+ 23v.
	Arc 1.5.4.15	American School of Classical Studies at Athens. Agora excavations. Weekly report.
	Arc 672.5.5	American School of Classical Studies at Athens. Ancient Corinth. Macon, 1928.
	Arc 672.5.25	American School of Classical Studies at Athens. Ancient Corinth. 4. ed. Athens, 1947.
	Arc 1.5.6	American School of Classical Studies at Athens. Annual report, 1-3. Reprint ed. Cambridge, 1886.
	Arc 1.5.2	American School of Classical Studies at Athens. Annual report. Cambridge, Mass. 1,1882+ 7v.
	Arc 716.4.10	American School of Classical Studies at Athens. The Athenian Agora. Princeton, n.d. 18v.
	Arc 716.4.20	American School of Classical Studies at Athens. The Athenian Agora. 2. ed. Athens, 1962.
	Arc 1.5	American School of Classical Studies at Athens. Bulletin. Boston. 1-5,1883-1902 3v.
	Arc 1.5F	American School of Classical Studies at Athens. Bulletin. Boston. 3
	Arc 672.5.7PF	American School of Classical Studies at Athens. Corinth. 1-6,1952-1964 4v.
	Arc 672.5.7F	American School of Classical Studies at Athens. Corinth. 2-16,1932-1957 26v.
	Arc 1.5.4.5	American School of Classical Studies at Athens. Corinth excavations. Weekly report.
	Arc 1.5.12	American School of Classical Studies at Athens. Directory of trustees, managing committee, faculty. 1882-1942
	Arc 716.4.12	American School of Classical Studies at Athens. Excavations of the Athenian Agora. Princeton. 1-9
	Arc 1.5.4.10	American School of Classical Studies at Athens. Excavations on the slopes of the Acropolis. Report. 7-20
	Arc 681.15	American School of Classical Studies at Athens. Lerna, a preclassical site in the Argolid. Princeton, N.J., 1969. 2v.
	Arc 1.5.4A	American School of Classical Studies at Athens. Papers. Boston. 1-6,1882-1897 6v.
	Arc 1.5.4.20	American School of Classical Studies at Athens. Report of excavations at Gözlü Kule.
	Arc 1.5.11	American School of Classical Studies at Athens. Alumni Association. Report. 1942
	Arc 1.5.3	Pamphlet box. American School of Classical Studies at Athens. Washington.
	Arc 1.5.15A	American School of Classical Studies in Rome. Supplementary papers. N.Y. 1-2,1905-1908 2v.
	Arc 726.70F	American School of Classical Studies in Rome. The triumphal arch of Trajan at Beneventum. Rome, 1896.
	Arc 726.70.5	American School of Classical Studies in Rome. The triumphal arch of Trajan at Beneventum. Rome, 19- ?
	Arc 1.5.17	American School of Classical Studies in Rome. Chairman of Managing Committee. Reports. Princeton, N.J.
	Arc 1.5.21	American School of Oriental Research, Jerusalem. Annual. New Haven. 1-40 27v.
	Arc 1.5.20	American School of Oriental Research, Jerusalem. Annual report of managing committee. Norwood, Mass.?
	Arc 1.5.22	American School of Oriental Research, Jerusalem. Bulletin. Philadelphia? 1,1919+ 11v.
	Arc 1.5.23	American School of Oriental Research, Jerusalem. Handbook. Philadelphia?
	Arc 1.5.27	American School of Oriental Research, Jerusalem. Newsletter. Jerusalem. 1939-1958 5v.
	Arc 1.5.25	American School of Oriental Research, Jerusalem. Papers.
	Arc 1.5.28	Pamphlet vol. American School of Oriental Research, Jerusalem.
	Arc 1.5.19	Pamphlet vol. American School of Oriental Research, Jerusalem. Bagdad.
	Arc 1.5.31F	American School of Oriental Reserach, Bagdad. Publications. Excavations. Philadelphia. 1935-1950 2v.
	Arc 1.1.15	American School of Prehistoric Research. Bulletin. Washington. 1-28 11v.
	Arc 1.5.24	American Schools of Oriental Research, Jerusalem. Catalogue. New Haven. 1935-1948 3v.
	Arc 983.14	American Society of Naturalists. Early man in America with particular reference to the southwestern United States. n.p., 1936.
	Arc 1335.159	American University of Beirut. Archaeological Museum. The coins exhibited in the Archaeological Museum of the American University of Beirut. Beirut, 1968.
	Arc 1335.164F	American University of Beirut. Museum of Archaeology. The coin collection. Beirut, 1974.
	Arc 943.34	America's ancient civilizations. (Verrill, A.H.) N.Y., 1953.
	Arc 1613.28	America's money. (Massey, Joseph Earl.) N.Y., 1968.
	Arc 945.7	America's rune stone of A.D. 1362 gains favor. (Peterson, Clarence S.) N.Y., 1946.
	Arc 945.6	Las Americas son un nuevo mundo. (Posnansky, Arthur.) La Paz, Bolivia, 1943.
	Arc 943.28	America's yesterday. (Brown, F.M.) Philadelphia, 1937.
	Arc 943.51	Amerika i Staryi svet v dokolumbovu epokhu. (Guliaev, Valerii I.) Moskva, 1968.
	Arc 1018.19.10	Amerika und Urchristentum. (Haufmann, C.M.) München, 1924.
	Arc 943.7	L'Amérique préhistorique. (Pouget, J.F.A. du Nadaillac.) Paris, 1883.
	Arc 720.16PF	Amfiteatro campano illustrato. (Alvino, Francesco.) Napoli, 1842. 2v.
	Arc 1590.20	Amfornite pechati ot Muzeia vuv Varna. (Mirchev, M.) Sofiia, 1958.
	Arc 483.11	al-'Amid, Tahir Mudhaffar. The 'Abbasid architecture of Samarra in the reign of both al-Mu'tasim and al-Mutawakkil. Baghdad, 1973.
	Arc 93.25	L'amministrazione delle antichità e belle arti in Italia. (Italy. Ministero dell'Istruzione Pubblica.) Roma, 1902.
	Arc 1148.16	Amphilochii, A. Snimki ne" Kondakaria XII-XIII. Moskva, 1869.
	Arc 830.70.7	Amphithéatre de Fourvière. (Lafon, M.A.) Lyon, 1896.
	Arc 785.7	The amphitheatres of ancient Rome. (Wells, C.L.) Boston, 1884.
	Arc 1070.208	Ampoules de pèlerinages en plomb...Bourgogne. (Marchant, Louis.) Dijon, 1873.
	Arc 1075.2	Ampoules de Terre Sainte. (Grabar, André.) Paris, 1958.
	Arc 94.20	Ampurias. Barcelona. 3,1941+ 14v.
	Arc 843.65.4	Ampurios y rosas. 4. ed. (Pla y Cargol, J.) Gerona, 1953.
	Arc 585.21	Amrah and Abydos. 1899-1901. (Randall-MacIver, D.) London, 1902.
	Arc 383.33	Amsterdam. Universiteit. Institut voor Prae- en Protohistorie. In het voetspoor van A.E. van Giffen. Groningen, 1961.
	Arc 383.33.2	Amsterdam. Universiteit. Institut voor Prae- en Protohistorie. In het voetspoor van A.E. van Giffen. 2. druk. Groningen, 1966.
	Arc 608.2.55	Amulettes puniques. (Cintas, Pierre.) Tunis, 1946.
	Arc 30.13	Anadolu. Séries 1: Prehistoire antiquité Byzance. Paris.
	Arc 30.13.5	Anadolu. Séries 2: Turquie medievale et moderne. Paris.
	Arc 39.4	Anadolu araştirmalari. Istanbul. 1,1955+ 3v.
	Arc 935.60	Anadolu'da Apollon kültu ile ilgili kaynaklar. (Taslikliogiu, Zafer.) Istanbul, 1963.
	Arc 382.5	Anaglyphi vaticani explicatio. (Michaelis, A.) Tubingae, 1865. 15 pam.
	Arc 1470.37	Anagraphē tōn nomismatōn tēs kypies Hellados. (Lampros, Paulos.) Athēnai, 1891.
	Arc 87.1.64	Anakabypteria. (Brueckner, A.) Berlin, 1904.
Htn	Arc 1033.20*	Analdi, E. Delle basiliche antiche. Vincenza, 1767.
	Arc 383.30F	Analecta archaeologica. Köln, 1960.
	Arc 1033.17.53	Analecta mensae reginalis seu historia imaginis...virginis...Claromontanae. (Nieszporkowicz, A.) Cracoviae, 1681.
	Arc 777.3	Analecta Romana topographica. (Wissowa, G.) Halis, 1897.

Arc 768.3 Analisi della carta de' dentorni di Roma. (Nibby, Antonio.) Roma, 1848. 3v.
Arc 1163.12 Analisi paleografia di...codici...secoli XIV e XV...in Cagliari. (Pillito, I.) Cagliari, 1879.
Arc 768.2.15 Analisi storico...dentorni di Roma. (Nibby, Antonio.) Roam, 1837. 3v.
Arc 768.2.16 Analisi storico...dentorni di Roma. (Nibby, Antonio.) Roma, 1837. 4v.
Arc 1015.205.15 Analsi geologica ed archilettonica de Cemet de Callisto. (Rossi, M.S. de.) Roma, 1867.
Arc 387.45 Analytical archaeology. (Clarke, David Leonard.) London, 1968.
Arc 530.6.10F Anamur nekropolu. The necropolis Anemurium. (Alfoldi-Rosenbaum, Elizabeth.) Ankara, 1971.
Arc 543.60F Anarchaeological journey to Yemen. v.1-3. (Iakhry, A.) Cairo, 1951-52. 2v.
Arc 710.20F He anaskaphē tēs Akropoleós apo tou 1885 mechri tou 1890. (Kakkadin, P.) Athēnai, 1906.
Arc 497.71 Anati, E. Palestine before the Hebrews. 1. ed. N.Y., 1962.
Arc 30.22 Anatolia; revue annuelle d'archéologie. Ankara. 1,1956+ 3v.
Arc 30.24 Anatolian studies. London. 15,1965+ 25v.
Arc 30.26 Anatolica; annuaire international pour les civilisations de l'Asie anterieure. Leiden. 1,1967+ 2v.
Arc 1033.118 Ancessi, V. Atlas géographique et archéologique...Testament. Paris, 1876.
Arc 1138.130 Ancestral voices. (Norman, James.) N.Y., 1975.
Arc 600.244.1F Ancien Hierakonpolis. Supplement. (Adams, Barbara.) Warminster, 1974.
Arc 1016.208 L'ancien trésor de l'Abbaye de Silos. (Roulin, E.) Paris, 1901.
Arc 600.1.2 L'ancienne Alexandrie. (Néroutsos-Bey, T.D.) Paris, 1888.
Arc 708.14 L'ancienne Athènes. (Pittakys, K.S.) Athens, 1835.
Arc 938.17 L'ancienne frontiére slavo-latvienne. (Balodis, F.) n.p., 192-.
Arc 825.11 L'ancienne inscription de la Maison Carrée. (Seguin, J.F.) Paris, 1759. 4 pam.
Arc 758.6 L'ancienne Rome. v.1-4. (Deseine, F.) Leide, 1713. 2v.
Arc 1264.11.5F Les anciennes abbayes de Normandie. (Mancel, G.) Caen, 1834.
Arc 830.290 Les anciennes fortifications d'Avesnes. (Croix, Charles.) Cholet, 1957.
Arc 612.13 Les anciens peuples de l'Europe. (Dottin, Georges.) Paris, 1916. 2v.
Arc 1020.83 Les anciens pupitres de Rheims. (Jadart, H.) n.p., n.d.
Arc 853.23.5 Les anciens tombeaux germaniques. (Wilhelmi, K.) Heidelberg, 1831.
Arc 505.107 The ancient agricultural regime of Nessana and the Central Negeb. (Mayerson, Philip.) London, 1961.
Arc 943.3.5 Ancient America. (Baldwin, J.D.) N.Y., 1872.
Arc 943.3 Ancient America. (Baldwin, J.D.) N.Y., 1878.
Arc 875.54 Ancient and historical monuments of Stirlingshire. (Great Britain. Commissions. Ancient and Historical Monuments of Scotland.) Edinburgh, 1963. 2v.
Arc 708.5 Ancient Athens. (Dyer, T.H.) London, 1873.
Arc 708.22.3 Ancient Athens. (Gardner, E.A.) London, 1902.
Arc 708.22.5 Ancient Athens. (Gardner, E.A.) London, 1907.
Arc 708.22A Ancient Athens. (Gardner, E.A.) N.Y., 1902.
Arc 861.71 The ancient British sculptured rocks of Northumberland. (Tate, George.) Alnwick, 1865.
Arc 870.1.3 The ancient bronze implements, weapons and ornaments of Great Britain. (Evans, J.) N.Y., 1881.
Arc 870.1.2 The ancient bronze implements, weapons and ornaments of Great Britain. (Evans, J.) London, 1881.
Arc 870.10.9 The ancient burial-mounds of England. (Grinsell, L.V.) London, 1936.
Arc 870.10.9.5 The ancient burial-mounds of England. 2. ed. (Grinsell, L.V.) London, 1955.
Arc 426.8 The ancient burial mounds of Japan. (Hitchcoke, R.) Washington, 1893.
Arc 30.32 Ancient Ceylon. Colombo. 1,1971+ 2v.
Arc 421.33 Ancient China. (Hay, John.) London, 1973.
Arc 1084.15F Ancient Chinese jade. (Wu, Henry H.) n.p., 1933.
Arc 1411.6 Ancient Chinese paper money. (Davis, Andrew.) Boston, 1918.
Htn Arc 1076.3.5* Ancient church bells in England. (Downman, E.A.) London, 1899.
Arc 513.28 The ancient cities of Western Anatolia. (Duyuran, Rüstem.) n.p., 195-?
Arc 708.30.2A The ancient city of Athens. (Hill, I.C.T.) Cambridge, 1953.
Arc 708.30 The ancient city of Athens. (Hill, I.C.T.) London, 1953.
Arc 1355.2 Ancient coins of cities and princes. (Ackerman, J.Y.) London, 1846.
Arc 672.5.5 Ancient Corinth. (American School of Classical Studies at Athens.) Macon, 1928.
Arc 672.5.10 Ancient Corinth. Photoreproduction. (O'Neill, J.G.) Baltimore, 1930.
Arc 672.5.25 Ancient Corinth. 4. ed. (American School of Classical Studies at Athens.) Athens, 1947.
Arc 875.31.5F Ancient cross shafts at Bewcastle and Ruthwell. (Brown, G.F.) Cambridge, 1916.
Arc 861.5.5 Ancient crosses and antiquities east of Cornwall. (Blight, J.T.) London, 1858.
Arc 861.49.5 Ancient crosses and holy wells of Lancashire. (Taylor, H.) Manchester, 1906.
Arc 861.13.5 The ancient crosses at Gosforth, Cumberland. (Parker, C.A.) London, 1896.
Arc 861.52 The ancient crosses of Stortford. (Glasscock, J.L.) Bishops, 1905.
Arc 975.1 The ancient culture of the Fremont River in Utah. (Morss, Noel.) Cambridge, Mass., 1931.
Arc 537.8A Ancient Cyprus; its art and archaeology. (Casson, S.) London, 1937.
Arc 855.218 Ancient Dorset. (Warne, Charles.) Bournemouth, 1872.
Arc 875.14.7 Ancient dwellings at Skara Brae. (Childe, V.G.) Edinburgh, 1933.
Arc 861.38.7 Ancient earthworks and camps of Somerset. (Burrow, E.J.) Cheltenham, 1924.
Arc 861.66 The ancient earthworks of New Forest. (Sumner, H.) London, 1917.
Arc 30.2 The ancient east. London. 2,1901
Arc 547.28 Ancient Egypt as represented in the Museum of Fine Arts. (Smith, W.S.) Boston, 1942.
Arc 600.21.6 Ancient Egyptian materials. (Lucas, Alfred.) London, 1962.
Arc 600.21 Ancient Egyptian materials. (Lucas, Alfred.) N.Y., 1926.
Arc 600.21.5 Ancient Egyptian materials and industries. 3. ed. (Lucas, Alfred.) London, 1948.
Arc 572.1.20 Ancient Egyptian works of art. (Weigall, Arthur Edward Pearse Brome.) London, 1924.
Htn Arc 861.30.5* The ancient entrenchments and camps of Gloucester. (Burrow, E.J.) Cheltenham, 1919.
Arc 612.50 Ancient Europe from the beginings of agriculture to classical antiquity. (Piggott, Stuart.) Edinburgh, 1965.
Arc 870.25 Ancient fields. (Bowen, H.C.) London, 1963.
Arc 588.53F Ancient Gaza. (Petrie, W.M.F.) London, 1931-34. 4v.
Arc 700.70 Ancient Greece from the air. (Schoder, Raymond Victor.) London, 1974.
Arc 1468.63 Ancient Greek coins. (Jenkins, G. Kenneth.) London, 1972.
Arc 1082.5F Ancient harvesting implements. (Steensberg, Axel.) København, 1943.
Arc 497.49 Ancient Hebrew arts. (Reifenberg, A.) N.Y., 1950.
Arc 1423.18.5 Ancient Hebrew seals. (Reifenberg, A.) London, 1950.
Arc 600.244F Ancient Hierakonpolis. (Adams, Barbara.) Warminster, 1974.
Arc 30.2.5 Ancient India; bulletin of the archaeological survey of India. Delhi. 1,1946+ 9v.
Arc 432.30 Ancient Indian culture contacts and migration. (Chattopadhyay, Kshitis Prasad.) Calcutta, 1965.
Arc 880.25.9A Ancient Ireland. (Macalister, R.A.S.) London, 1935.
Arc 1423.18.4 Ancient Jewish coins. (Reifenberg, A.) Jerusalem, 1965.
Arc 1423.18 Ancient Jewish coins. 2. ed. (Reifenberg, A.) Jerusalem, 1947.
Arc 543.3.5A Ancient Khotan. (Stein, Mark Aurel.) Oxford, 1907. 2v.
Arc 386.32 Ancient landscapes. (Bradford, John.) London, 1957.
Arc 681.5 Ancient Leros. (Benson, Jack L.) Durham, 1963.
Arc 943.5 Ancient man in America. (Larkin, F.) n.p., 1880.
Arc 858.35 Ancient man in Britain. (Mackenzie, D.A.) London, 1922.
Arc 969.1.17 Ancient man in northern Ohio. (Vietzen, R.C.) Lorain, Ohio, 1941.
Arc 861.76 The ancient mark-stones of East Anglia. (Dutt, W.A.) Lowestoft, 1926.
Arc 861.3 Ancient meols, or Some account of the antiquities found near Dove Point. (Hume, A.) London, 1863.
Arc 858.47 Ancient monuments. (Great Britain. Office of Works.) London. 1932-1958 7v.
Arc 432.17 Ancient monuments. (India. Department of Archaeology.) Delhi, 1957. 6 pam.
Arc 880.40 Ancient Monuments Advisory Council for Northern Ireland. A preliminary survey of the ancient monuments of Northern Ireland. Belfast, 1940.
Arc 950.212F Ancient monuments of...Mississippi Valley. Prospectus. N.Y., 1848.
Arc 440.4 Ancient monuments of India. Bombay. 1-4,1957-1958
Arc 450.2A Ancient monuments of Kashmir. (Kak, Ram C.) London, 1933.
Arc 880.43 Ancient monuments of Northern Ireland. v.1-2. (Northern Ireland. Ministry of Finance.) Belfast, 1966-69.
Arc 441.3.10 The ancient monuments of Varendra (North Bengal). (Maitra, Akshay Kumar.) Rajshahi, 1949?
Arc 125.8.5 Ancient Monuments Society. Transactions. London. 1,1953+ 20v.
Arc 125.8 Ancient Monuments Society. Year book. Manchester. 1926
Arc 682.30 Ancient Mycenae. (Mylonas, George E.) Princeton, 1957.
Arc 1373.11 Ancient numismatics. (Sutherland, Carol H.V.) N.Y., 1958.
Arc 1221.6 Ancient oriental cylinder and other seals with a description of the collection of Mrs. William H. Moore. (Moore, Ada S.) Chicago, 1940.
Arc 1221.5F Ancient oriental seals in the collection of Mr. E.T. Newell. (Newell, E.T.) Chicago, 1934.
Arc 1221.4F Ancient oriental seals in the collection of Mrs. Agnes Baldwin Brett. (Brett, Agnes B.) Chicago, 1936.
Arc 1015.221 Ancient pagan tombs and Christian cemeteries in Malta. (Caruana, A.A.) Malta, 1898.
Arc 30.27 Ancient Pakistan. Peshawar. 1,1964+ 2v.
Arc 443.3 Ancient races of the Deccan. (Sarkar, Sasanka Sekhar.) New Delhi, 1972.
Arc 855.226F The ancient remains at Stanton Drew. (Dymond, Charles W.) Bristol, 1896.
Arc 861.59 Ancient remains near Buxton. (Turner, William.) Buxton, 1899.
Arc 723.28F Ancient Roman construction in Italy from the pre-historica period to Augustus. (Blake, Marion E.) Washington, 1947.
Arc 758.1 Ancient Rome. (Dyer, T.H.) London, 1864.
Arc 756.5.3 Ancient Rome and its neighborhood. (Burn, R.) London, 1895.
Arc 776.2A Ancient Rome as revealed by recent discoveries. (Van Buren, A.W.) London, 1936.
Arc 766.1.2.8 Ancient Rome in the light of recent discoveries. (Lanciani, R.) Boston, 1888.
Arc 766.1.2.10 Ancient Rome in the light of recent discoveries. (Lanciani, R.) London, 1888.
Arc 766.1.2.11 Ancient Rome in the light of recent discoveries. (Lanciani, R.) London, 1888.
Arc 766.1.2.12 Ancient Rome in the light of recent discoveries. 5. ed. (Lanciani, R.) Boston, 1889.
Htn Arc 766.1.2.7* Ancient Rome in the light of recent discoveries. 7. ed. (Lanciani, R.) Boston, 1888.
Arc 766.1.2.15 Ancient Rome in the light of recent discoveries. 10. ed. (Lanciani, R.) Boston, 1894.
Arc 766.1.2A Ancient Rome in the light of recent excavations. (Lanciani, R.) Boston, 1888.
Arc 767.4 Ancient Rome in 1885. (Middleton, J.H.) Edinburgh, 1885.
Arc 609.34 Ancient ruins and vanished civilizations of southern Africa. (Summers, Roger.) Capetown, 1971.
Arc 609.1.9 The ancient ruins of Rhodesia. (Hall, R.N.) London, 1902.
Arc 609.1.10 The ancient ruins of Rhodesia. (Hall, R.N.) London, 1904.
Arc 861.203 Ancient Scilly from the first farmers to the early Christians. (Ashbee, Paul.) Newton Abbot, 1974.
X Cg Arc 875.5 Ancient Scottish lake-dwellings. (Munro, R.) Edinburgh, 1882.
Arc 1088.1.8 Ancient ships. (Torr, Cecil.) Cambridge, 1894.
Arc 1088.1.9A Ancient ships. (Torr, Cecil.) Cambridge, 1895.
Arc 1088.1.7 Ancient ships. (Torr, Cecil.) Chicago, 1964.
Arc 936.195.240 Ancient Slovakia. (Bolecek, B.V.) n.p., 1973.
Arc 543.82 An ancient South Arabian necropolis. (Cleveland, Ray L.) Baltimore, 1965.
Arc 861.19 The ancient stone crosses of Dartmoor. (Crossing, W.) Exeter, 1902.
Arc 858.22 Ancient stone crosses of England. (Rimmer, Alfred.) London, 1875.

Author and Title Listing

Arc 870.1 The ancient stone implements, weapons and ornaments of Great Britain. (Evans, J.) N.Y., 1872.

Arc 870.1.1 The ancient stone implements, weapons and ornaments of Great Britain. (Evans, J.) London, 1897.

Htn Arc 885.2* An ancient survey of Pen Maen Maur. (Halliwell, J.O.) London, 1859.

Arc 505.49F The ancient synagogue of Beth Alpha. (Iukenik, Eleazar L.) Jeruselem, 1932.

Arc 1540.32 Ancient trial plates, a description of the ancient gold and silver. (Watson, J.H.) London, 1962.

Arc 380.205 Ancient unedited monuments. (Millingen, J.) London, 1822.

Arc 983.4 Ancient village architecture in America. (Peet, S.D.) n.p., n.d.

Arc 588.39F Ancient weights and measures. (Petrie, W.M.F.) London, 1926.

Arc 1153.53 Ancient writing and its influence. (Ullmann, B.L.) N.Y., 1932.

Arc 1027.75 Ancora del sepolero originario di San Domnio. (Pietro, A.C.) Zara, 1906.

Arc 1175.11 Anderson, J. Selectus diplomatum et numismatum Scotiae Thesaurus. Edinburgi, 1739.

Arc 530.9 Anderson, J.G.C. Journey of exploration in Pontus. v.1. Bruxelles, 1903.

Arc 530.9.2 Anderson, J.G.C. Journey of exploration in Pontus. v.2. Bruxelles, 1903.

Arc 530.9.3 Anderson, J.G.C. Journey of exploration in Pontus. v.3. Bruxelles, 1903.

Arc 875.3 Anderson, Joseph. Scotland in early Christian times. Edinburgh, 1881.

Arc 875.3.2 Anderson, Joseph. Scotland in early Christian times. 2. series. Edinburgh, 1881.

Arc 875.4.2 Anderson, Joseph. Scotland in Pagan times. The Bronze and Stone Ages. Edinburgh, 1886.

Arc 875.4 Anderson, Joseph. Scotland in Pagan times. The Iron Age. Edinburgh, 1883.

Arc 421.10.15 Andersson, J. Children of the yellow earth. London, 1934.

Arc 421.10 Andersson, J. Preliminary report on archaeological research in Kansu. Pekin, 1925.

Arc 936.205.15 Andjelić, Pavao. Bobovac i Kraljeva Sutjeska. Sarajevo, 1973.

Arc 1675.27.5F Andorfer, Karl. Musica in nummis. Wien, 1901.

Arc 1675.27 Andorfer, Karl. Musica in nummis. Wien, 1907.

Arc 395.6.10 Andrae, W. Babylon, die versunkene Weltstadt und ihr Ausgräber Robert Koldewey. Berlin, 1952.

Arc 416.27 Andrae, Walter. Alte Feststrassen im Nahen Orient. Stuttgart, 1964.

Arc 385.12 Andrae, Walter. Lebenserinnerungen eins Ausgräbers. Berlin, 1961.

Arc 1335.62 André, Leon. Importante collection de monnaies et médailles. Paris, 1926.

Arc 1033.17.443 Andrea, G.A. Breve istoria della miracolosa immagine di Maria Sma...di Montenero. Livorno, 1774.

Arc 853.64 Andree, Julius. Beiträge zur Kenntnis des norddeutschen Paläolithikums und Mesolithikums. Leipzig, 1932.

Arc 853.56.7 Andree, Julius. Das Paläolithikum der Höhlen des Hönnetales in Westfalen. Leipzig, 1928.

Arc 925.305 Andreev, N.V. O chëm rasskazyvaiut kurgany. Smolensk, 1951.

Arc 746.25F Andrèn, A.Architectural terracottas from Etrusco-Italic temples. Leipzig, 1939-40. 2v.

Arc 1033.75 Andreucci, A.G. Notizie...SS. Valentino Prete ed Flario Diacono. Roma, 1740.

Arc 861.21.17 Andrew, S. Excavation of the Roman forts at Castleshaw. Manchester, 1911.

Arc 1540.12.5 Andrew, W.J. Notes on numismatic history of the reign of Henry I. v.1-2. London, 1903.

Arc 1540.12 Andrew, W.J. A numismatic history of the reign of Henry I. v.1-2. London, 1901.

Arc 1076.3.99 Andrews, H.C. A Hertfordshire worthy, John Briant. St. Albans, 1930.

Arc 925.345 Andrianov, Boris V. Drevnie orositel'nye sistemy Priaral'ia. Moskva, 1969.

Arc 1473.1.3 Anekdota nomismata en Glarentsa. (Lampros, Paulos.) Athēnai, 1876.

Arc 1473.1.3.5 Anekdota nomismata kopenta en Glarentsa kata mimēsin tōn Henetikōn. (Lampros, Paulos.) Oak Park, 1969.

Arc 1473.1.5 Anekdota nomismata tēs Hellados. (Lampros, Paulos.) Athēnai, 1880.

Arc 1473.1 Anekdota nomismata tēs kuprhoy. (Lampros, Paulos.) Athēnai, 1876.

Arc 1473.1.10 Anekdoton nomisma Saroykchan Emiry tēs Iōnias. (Lampros, Paulos.) n.p., n.d.

Arc 848.26 Die Anfänge der deutschen Vorgeschichtsforschung. Inaug. Diss. (Stemmermann, P.H.) Quakenbrück, 1934

Arc 936.14.35.5 Die Anfänge der polnischen Städt im Lichte der Bodenforschung. (Blaszczyk, Włodzimierz.) Poznań, 1974.

Arc 853.347 Die Anfänge der Stadt Münden nach den Ausgrabungen in der St. Blasius-Kirche. (Grenz, Rudolf.) Hannoversch Münden, 1973.

Arc 1020.130 Die Anfänge des Christentums im Rheinlande. 2. Aufl. (Neuss, Wilhelm.) Bonn, 1933.

Arc 673.1.9 Die Anfangsstreke der heiligen Strasse in Delphi. (Trendelenburg, A.) Berlin, 1908.

Arc 843.77.15 El anfiteatro de Italica. (Amador de los Ríos, Rodrigo.) Madrid, 1916.

Arc 785.8.7F L'anfiteatro Flavio nei suoi venti secoli di storia. (Colgrossi, P.) Firenze, 1913.

Arc 1016.9.15 L'anfiteatro Flavio rivendicato ai martiri. (Lugari, G.B.) Roma, 1899.

Arc 726.101 L'anfiteatro romano. (Calderini, A.) Milano, 1940.

Arc 830.18.23 Die Angaben der römischen Itinerare über die Heerstrasse Köln-Eifel-Reims. (Müller, Reiner.) Münstereifel, 1933.

Arc 1096.2 Angeiologie. (Krause, J.H.) Halle, 1854.

Arc 681.15.5 Angel, John Lawrence. The people of Lerna. Princeton, N.J., 1971.

Arc 1025.23 Angelini, A. Genni sopra i primi cimiteri...Roma christiana. Roma, 1840.

Arc 1033.51 Angelini, N. Brevi notizie intorno San Rufino. Frascati, 1885.

Arc 1033.51.3 Angelini, N. Brevi notizie intorno San Rufino ves e Martire. Roma, 1862.

Arc 1033.52 Angelini, N. Vita, martiro e culto di S. Ambrogio. Frascati, 1884.

Arc 1020.102.3 Angelis, L. de. Osservazioni critici...Siena...sopra croce di rame intagliata...1129. Siena, 1814.

Arc 1163.14.6 Angelsächsiche Palaeographie. (Keller, Wolfgang.) N.Y., 1970-71. 2v.

Arc 726.19 Angelucci, A. I cannoni veneti di Famagosta. Venezia, n.d.

Arc 550.10F Angioletti, Giovanni B. Testimane in Egittto. Firenze, 1958.

Arc 543.7.5 Angkor; ruins in Cambodia. (Beerski, A. (Mrs.).) London, 1923.

Arc 543.7.9 Angkor. (Groslier, G.) Paris, 1924.

Arc 543.7.21F Angkor. Paris, 1931.

Arc 543.2.6 Angkor: art and civilization. (Groslier, Bernard P.) N.Y., 1966.

Arc 543.7.25F Angkor monuments of the god-kings. (Cohen, Joan Lebold.) London, 1975.

Arc 543.7.7A Angkor the magnificent. (Candee, H.C.) N.Y., 1924.

Arc 384.14 Anglo-Romanian Conference on Mathematics in the Archaeological and Historical Sciences. Mathematics in the archaeological and historical sciences; proceedings. Edinburgh, 1971.

Arc 870.12.19 The Anglo-Saxon cemetery at Abingdon, Berkshire. (Leeds, E.T.) Oxford, 1936. 2v.

Arc 1540.27 Anglo-Saxon coins. (Dolley, Reginald Hugh Michael.) London, 1961.

Arc 1540.33 Anglo-Saxon currency: King Edgar's reform to the Norman conquest. (Petersson, H. Bertil A.) Lund, 1969.

Arc 1076.21 Anglo-Saxon garnet inlaid and composite brooches. v.1-2. (Avent, Richard.) Oxford, 1975.

Arc 1538.21 Anglo-Saxon gold coinage in the light of the Crondall hoard. (Sutherland, Carol Humphrey Vivian.) London, 1948.

Arc 858.70A The Anglo-Saxons. (Wilson, David McKenzie.) London, 1960.

Arc 1558.2 Anglosachisiska mynt i svenska kongliga myntkabinette funna i sveriges jord. (Stockholm. Statens Historiske Museum och Myntkabinett.) Stockholm, 1881.

Arc 726.334 Angrisani, Mario. La Villa Augustea in Somma Vesuviana. Aversa, 1936.

Arc 1033.12.55 Anguissola, G.B. Stromenti che servirono alla Passione...nostro signori. Piacenza, 1812.

Arc 889.36 Animal and man in Holland's past. v.1-2. (Clason, Antje Trientje.) Groningen, 1967.

Arc 983.3.5 Animal carvings from mounds of the Mississippi Valley. (Henshaw, H.W.) Washington, 1881?

Arc 925.13.55 The animal style in south Russia and China. (Rostovtsev, M.I.) Princeton, 1929.

Arc 412.24 Animals in archaeology. N.Y., 1972.

Arc 672.1.45 Les animaux dans la peinture de la Crete préhellénique. Thèse. (Oulié, Marthe.) Paris, 1926.

Arc 513.20.5 Anitlaria koranmasi ve onarilmasi. (Ülgen, Ali Saim.) Ankara, 1943.

Arc 830.68 L'Anjou aux âges de la pierre...bronze. (Bousrez, Louis.) Paris, 1897.

Arc 530.168 Ankara. Universite Enstitusu. Arkeoloji arasturmalari. Istanbul, 1941.

Arc 530.135F Ankara-Konya. (Arik, Remri Ogur.) Ankara, 1956.

Arc 530.37 Ankara und Augustus. (Schede, Martin.) Berlin, 1937.

Arc 1153.7 Anleitung zur lateinischen Palaeographie. (Wattenbach, W.) Leipzig, 1869.

Arc 1153.7.4 Anleitung zur lateinischen Palaeographie. 4. Aufl. (Wattenbach, W.) Leipzig, 1886.

Arc 273.2.3F Annales. (Académie Royale d'Archéologie de Belgique.) Anvers. 1-3,1843-1900 2v.

Arc 273.2 Annales. (Académie Royale d'Archéologie de Belgique.) Anvers. 1-77 69v.

Arc 273.6 Annales. (Belgium. Federation archéologique et historique.) Anvers. 16-35 12v.

Arc 273.10 Annales. (Société Royale d'Archéologie de Bruxelles.) Bruxelles. 1-50,1887-1961 38v.

Arc 1.7 Annales archéologiques. (Didron, A.N.) Paris, 1844-1870. 27v.

Arc 1.7.2 Annales archéologiques. Index, v.28. (Barbier de Montault.) Paris, 1881.

Arc 30.23F Les annales archéologiques de Syrie. Damas. 1,1951+ 17v.

Arc 1420.1.5F Annales compendiarii regum et rerum Syriae. (Froelich, E.) Vienna, 1744.

Htn Arc 1420.1* Annales compendiarii regum et rerum Syriae. 2. ed. (Froelich, E.) Vienna, 1754.

Arc 30.1.10 Annales d'Ethiopie. Paris. 3-6 3v.

Arc 30.3 Annales du service des antiquités de l'Égypte. Le Caire. 1,1900+ 44v.

Arc 30.3.2 Annales du service des antiquités de l'Égypte. Index, 1-30. Le Caire, n.d. 3v.

Arc 30.3.3 Annales du service des antiquités de l'Égypte. Supplement. Le Caire. 1-22 10v.

Arc 73.1 Annali, bulletino, and tavole. (Rome. Istituto.) Rome. 1829-1883 65v.

Arc 1033.43 Annali...degli Apostoli Pietro e Paolo. v.1-3. Torino, 1883. 2v.

Arc 1308.3 Annali. (Istituto Italiano di Numismatica, Rome.) 1-24 10v.

Arc 1490.21 Annali della zecca di Roma. v.1-11,12-16,17-24. (Martinori, Edoardo.) Roma, 1917-20. 3v.

Arc 1033.15 Annali delli scienze religiose. (De Lucca, A.A.) Roma, 1841.

Arc 125.6 Annals of archaeology and anthropology. (Liverpool. University. Institute of Archaeology.) Liverpool. 1-28,1908-1948 21v.

Arc 1535.4 Annals of the coinage of Great Britain. (Ruding, R.) London, 1817. 4v.

Arc 1535.4.2 Annals of the coinage of Great Britain. 3. ed. (Ruding, R.) London, 1840. 3v.

Arc 1433.52 Annam; études numismatiques. Text et atlas. (Schroeder, Albert.) Paris, 1905. 2v.

Arc 875.8 Annandale, C. A history of the Scottish people from the earliest times. London, 1892.

Arc 18.1.9 L'année épigraphique. Paris. 1964+ 2v.

Arc 1020.9.127 L'année liturgique à Rome. (Barbier de Montault, X.) Paris, 1857.

Arc 1020.9.130 L'année liturgique à Rome. (Barbier de Montault, X.) Rome, 1870.

Arc 1020.9.131 L'année liturgique à Rome. (Barbier de Montault, X.) Rome, 1902.

Arc 1020.9.128 L'année liturgique à Rome. 2. éd. (Barbier de Montault, X.) Rome, 1862.

Arc 1020.9.90 Anni storici intorno ad una basilica di S. Pietro in Campo di Mirlo. (Pellegrini, A.) Roma, 1860.

Htn Arc 1033.12.101* Anno domini 1512. Reliquie plurimorū. n.p., n.d.

Arc 340.39 An annotated bibliography of Greek and Roman art. (Coulson, William D.E.) N.Y., 1975.

Arc 340.12 An annotated bibliography of the archaeology of Zambia. (Phillipson, David W.) Lusaka, 1968.

Arc 760.6.11 Annotazioni alla memoria sui diritti del principato. (Fea, Carlo.) Roma, 1806.
Arc 399.3.2 Annotirovannaia bibliografiia nauchnykh trudov akademika A.P. Okladnikova (1968-1973 gg). (Vasilevskii, Ruslan S.) Ulan-Ude, 1974.
Arc 30.12.10 Announcement and outline of program. (Iranian Institute of America.) N.Y., 1930.
Arc 547.24.12F Annuaire. (Alexandria. Musée Gréco-Romain.) 1932-1950 3v.
Arc 65.6.10 Annuaire. (Association Internationale d'Archéologie Classique.) Rome. 2,1956 3v.
Arc 1315.1 Annuaire. (Société Francaise de Numismatique.) Paris. 1-20,1866-1896 20v.
Arc 100.1.10 Annuaire. (Société Nationale des Antiquaires de France.) Paris. 1848-1855 4v.
Arc 273.10.5 Annuaire. (Société Royale d'Archéologie de Bruxelles.) Bruxelles. 16-26,1905-1925 5v.
Arc 1.7.5 Annuaire de l'archéoloque du numismate et de l'antiquaire. Paris. 1,1862
Arc 1.24 Annuaire des sciences historiques. Paris. 1877
Arc 1.5.21 Annual. (American School of Oriental Research, Jerusalem.) New Haven. 1-40 27v.
Arc 37.5 Annual. (Hebrew Union College Biblical and Archaeological School in Jerusalem.) Jerusalem. 1,1970+ 2v.
Arc 505.74 Annual. (Jordan. Department of Antiquities.) 1-9 2v.
Arc 501.1.12 Annual. (Palestine Exploration Fund.) London. 1-6,1911-1953 6v.
Arc 432.07F Annual bibliography of Indian archaeology. Leyden. 1-17 17v.
Arc 435.60F Annual progress report. (India. Archaeological Survey. Central Circle.) Patna. 1920-1921
Arc 435.53.2F Annual progress report of the superintendent, Hindu and Buddhist monuments. (India. Archaeological Survey. Northern Circle, Punjab.) 1911-1921
Arc 435.53.3F Annual progress report of the superintendent, Muhammadan and British monuments. (India. Archaeological Survey. Northern Circle, Punjab.) Allahabad. 1910-1921// 5v.
Arc 435.53F Annual progress report of the superintendent. (India. Archaeological Survey. Northern Circle, Punjab.) 1906-1916
Arc 1.5.6 Annual report, 1-3. Reprint ed. (American School of Classical Studies at Athens.) Cambridge, 1886.
Arc 435.70.2F Annual report, 1903. Preliminary proof. (Ceylon. Archaeological Survey.) n.p., 1903.
Arc 1.13 Annual report. (American Academy, Rome.) Rome? 1913-1942 6v.
Arc 1300.1.11 Annual report. (American Numismatic Society.) N.Y. 1962+ 2v.
Arc 1.5.2 Annual report. (American School of Classical Studies at Athens.) Cambridge, Mass. 1,1882+ 7v.
Arc 1.1.2 Annual report. (Archaeological Institute of America.) Cambridge. 1-17,1879-1896 3v.
Arc 1.1.12 Annual report. (Archaeological Institute of America. Schools of American Research.) Santa Fe? 1934-1947 2v.
Arc 441.9.10F Annual report. (Baroda (State). Archaeological Department.) Baroda. 1935-1939 4v.
Arc 435.70.3F Annual report. (Ceylon. Archaeological Survey.) Colombo. 1892-1912 3v.
Arc 435.70F Annual report. (Ceylon. Archaeological Survey.) Colombo. 1904-1947 6v.
Arc 447.1F Annual report. (Hyderabad, India (State). Archaeological Department.) Calcutta. 1323-1349,1914-1940 11v.
Arc 435.3F Annual report. (India. Archaeological Survey.) Calcutta. 1902-1916// 14v.
Arc 435.52 Annual report. (India. Archaeological Survey. Eastern Circle, Bengal.) Calcutta. 1888-1921 2v.
Arc 435.59F Annual report. (India. Archaeological Survey. Frontier Circle, Peshawar.) Peshawar. 1904-1921 3v.
Arc 435.54F Annual report. (India. Archaeological Survey. Southern Circle, Madras.) Madras. 1858-1921 7v.
Arc 136.10 Annual report. (London. University. Institute of Archaeology.) London.
Arc 435.55F Annual report. (Mysore. Archaeological Survey.) Bangalore. 1909-1946 22v.
Arc 48.10 Annual report. (Society for Libyan Studies.) London. 1,1969+
Arc 1324.2 Annual report. (Yorkshire Numismatic Fellowship.) Hull. 1,1909
Arc 435.3.5F Annual report. Index, 1902-1916. (India. Archaeological Survey.) Calcutta, 1924.
Arc 501.1.7 Annual report and accounts with list of subscriptions. (Palestine Exploration Fund.) 1910-1923
Arc 459.2F Annual report for M.E. 1085 (1909-1910). (Travancore. Archaeological Survey.) n.p., 191-?
Arc 953.22 Annual report of department archaeologist. (United States. Department of the Interior.) Washington. 1928-1931
Arc 1.5.20 Annual report of managing committee. (American School of Oriental Research, Jerusalem.) Norwood, Mass.?
Arc 435.4.25F Annual report of the Archaeological Survey of India. (India. Archaeological Survey.) Calcutta. 1916-1936 18v.
Arc 435.54.3F Annual report of the assistant superintendent for epigraphy. (India. Archaeological Survey. Southern Circle, Madras.) Madras. 1881-1945 9v.
Arc 320.1.27 Annual report of the curator. (Pennsylvania. University. Museum of American Archaeology.) Philadelphia. 1,1890
Arc 535.4 Annual report of the director. (Cyprus. Department of Antiquities.) Nicosia. 1949+
Arc 435.4F Annual report of the director-general of archaeology. pt.1. (India. Archaeological Survey.) Calcutta. 1902-1921// 11v.
Arc 435.54.10F Annual report on Indian epigraphy. (India. Department of Archaeology.) Delhi. 1945-1964 2v.
NEDL Arc 66.10 Annual reports. (British School at Rome.) London.
Arc 1.14.20 Annuario. (Accademia...Rome. Accademia Romana di Archeologia.) 1,1951+ 2v.
Arc 65.7F Annuario. (Athens. R. Scuola Archeologica Italiana.) Bergamo. 1,1914+ 18v.
Arc 340.2.10 Annuario bibliografico di archeologia; opere e periodici. (Istituto Nazionale d'Archeologia e Storia dell'Arte, Roma. Biblioteca.) Modena. 1,1952+ 5v.
Arc 530.4 Anonymi Byzantini. (Preger, T.) München, 1898.
Arc 1027.61.5 Ansaldi, P.C. De caussis inopiae veterum monument. pro copia Martyrum. Medina, 1740.
Arc 458.14 Ansari, Z.D. Excavations at Sanganakallu and Songaon. Poona, 1969. 3 pam.
Arc 443.2 Ansari, Zainuddin. Excavations at Dwarka. 1. ed. Poona, 1966.
Arc 1510.122 Ansehnlichen Vorrath von Thalern und Schaustücken des langraflich-hessischen Gesamthauses. (Schwarzenau, J.L.) n.p., 1776.
Arc 843.40 Ansoleaga, F. de. El cementerio franco de Pamplona (Navarra). Pamplona, 1914.
Arc 1465.78 Anson, L. Numismata Graeca. pt.1-6. Londoni, 1910-16. 2v.
Arc 861.56 An answer to...Dr. Stukeley's Origines Roystonianae. (Parkin, Charles.) London, 1744. 2 pam.
Arc 1077.2.23 An answer to John Martiall's Treatise of the cross. (Calfhill, J.) Cambridge, Eng., 1846.
Arc 537.3.2 Answer to L.P. di Cesnola. (Feuardent, G.L.) N.Y., 1881.
Arc 588.51F Antaeopolis. (Petrie, W.M.F.) London, 1930.
Arc 843.100 Antas nas herdades da Casa de Braganca no concelho de Estremoz. (Leisner, G.K.) Lisboa, 1955.
Arc 588.58F Anthedon. (Petrie, W.M.F.) London, 1937.
Arc 383.3 Anthemon. Firenze, 1955.
Arc 861.145 Anthony, I.E. The Iron Age camp at Poston. Hereford, 1958.
Arc 340.36 An anthropological bibliography of the eastern seaboard. New Haven, 1947-63. 2v.
Arc 957.2 Anthropological studies in California. (Holmes, William H.) n.p., n.d.
Arc 385.22 Anti, Carlo. Propedeutica archeologica. Padova, 1966.
Arc 1033.20.9 Antica basilicografia. (Sarnelli, Pompeo.) Napoli, 1686.
Arc 1020.31 L'antica chiesa S. Anna...Gerusalemma. (Alger, C.) Gerusalemma, 1863.
Arc 746.40F L'antica città di Veil. (Canina, Luigi.) Roma, 1847.
Arc 1070.202.3 Le antiche lucerne. (Bartoli, P.S.) Roma, 1691.
Arc 1070.203 Le antiche lucerne. (Bartoli, P.S.) Roma, 1729.
Arc 1488.34 Le antiche zecche d'Italia. (Cainola, Aldo.) Roma, 1971.
Arc 726.300 Antichi campi di battaglia in Italia. (Sommella, Paolo.) Roma, 1967.
Arc 1025.30 Gli antichi cimiteri cristiani di Roma e d'Italia. (Armellini, M.) Roma, 1893.
Arc 726.1 Antichi monumenti della Pianosa. (Chienci, G.) Reggio, 1875.
Arc 1020.12 Antichi monumenti di religioni cristiani in Toscanella. (Lorenzo, Giuseppe di.) Rocca, 1883.
Arc 628.9 Antichi monumenti illustrati. (Lovatelli-Caetani, E.) Roma, 1889.
Arc 720.9.2.5F Antichi monumenti per servire all'opera...l'Italia. (Micali, G.) Firenze, 1810.
Arc 740.8 Antichi monumenti sepolcrali nel ducato di Ceri. (Visconti, C.P.E.) Roma, 1836.
Arc 1033.67 Antichi Mulini in Roma e nel Lazio. (Rossi, G.B. de.) Roma, 1857.
Arc 547.23 Gli antichi oggetti egiziani. (Marucchi, O.) Roma, 1901.
Arc 1070.201.9F Gli antichi sepolcri. (Bartoli, P.S.) Roma, 1697.
Arc 1070.202 Gli antichi sepolcri. (Bartoli, P.S.) Roma, 1727.
Arc 1027.4.17 L'antichissima imagine della B. Vergine nel cimitero di Priscilla. (Bonavenia, G.) Siena, 1897.
Arc 1030.21 Antichissima lapida cristiana. (Manni, D.M.) Firenze, 1763.
Arc 303.72 Antichità altoadriatiche. Trieste. 1,1972+ 4v.
Arc 1016.10 Antichita cristiane di Brescia. (Odorici, F.) Brescia, 1845.
Arc 726.327 Antichità cristiane di San Canzian d'Isonzo. (Bovini, Giuseppe.) Bologna, 1973.
Htn Arc 900.203* Le antichità d'Aquileja. (Bertoli, G.) Venice, 1739.
Htn Arc 761.4* Le antichita della città di Roma. (Gamucci, B.) Venetia, 1565.
Htn Arc 761.4.5* Le antichita della città di Roma. (Gamucci, B.) Vinegia, 1580.
Htn Arc 761.4.9* Le antichita della città di Roma. (Gamucci, B.) Vinegia, 1588. 2 pam.
Arc 767.10 Le antichità della città di Roma. (Mauro, L.) Venetia, 1562.
Htn Arc 761.4.3* Le antichita della città di Roma. 2. ed. (Gamucci, B.) Vinegia, 1569.
Arc 730.201 Le antichita della Sicilia. (Serradifalco.) Palermo, 1834. 5v.
Arc 720.18PF Le antichità di Aosta. (Promis, Carlo.) Torino, 1862. 2v.
Arc 537.3 Le antichita di Cipro. (Regaldi, G.) Roma, 1879.
Htn Arc 760.4.8* L'antichita di Roma. (Fulvio, A.) Venetia, 1588.
Htn Arc 767.2* L'antichita di Roma. (Marliani, B.) Roma, 1622.
Arc 770.5 L'antichita di Roma. (Pinarolo, G.) Roma, 1703. 2v.
Arc 730.200 Antichita siciliane spiegate. (Pancrazi, G.M.) Naples, 1751. 2v.
Arc 726.285 Antichità storiche e monumentali di Corigliano Calabro. (Grillo, Francesco.) Cosenza, 1965.
Arc 936.140 Antichna kultura v Bulgariia. (Todorov, Ianko.) Sofiia, 1942?
Arc 925.13.80 Antichnaia arkheologiia Severnogo Prichernomor'ia. (Blavatskii, V.D.) Moskva, 1961.
Arc 925.13.150 Antichnaia istoriia i kul'tura Sredizemnomor'ia i Prichernomor'ia. Leningrad, 1968.
Arc 936.80.5F Antichnata grobnitsa pri Kazanlak. (Mikov, Vasil.) Sofiia, 1954.
Arc 925.105 Antichnikh istoria i kul'tura severi Prichernomor'ia. (Kotsevalov, A.S.) Miunkhon, 1955.
Arc 1588.2.11 Antichnite moneti na Balkanskiia polustrov i monetite. (Mushmov, N.A.) Sofiia, 1912.
Arc 925.113 Antichnye goroda severnogo Prichernomoria. (Akademiia Nauk SSSR. Institut Istorii Materialy Kul'tury.) Moskva, 1955.
Arc 925.50.215 Antichnyi import v Pridneprov'e i pobuzh'e v IV-II vv. do n.e. (Onaiko, Nadezhda A.) Moskva, 1970.
Arc 1.32 Antichnyi mir i arkheologiia. Saratov. 1,1972+
Arc 925.125 Antichnyi mir v severnom Prichernomor'e. (Shelov, D.B.) Moskva, 1956.
Arc 936.205F Antička naselja i komunikacije u Bosni i Hercegovini. (Pašalić, E.) Sarajevo, 1960.
Arc 720.202 L'antico cassino e il primitivo monasterio. (Bartolini, D.) Montecassino, 1880.
Arc 1033.70.19 L'antico oratorio di S. Agnese. (Nardoni, L.) Roma, 1870.
Arc 1364.2 Het antieke tropaion. (Janssen, A.J.) Ledeberg, 1957.
Arc 843.5.25 La antigua civilización ibérica en el reino de Valencia. (Almarche, V.F.) Valencia, 1918.
Arc 843.30 Antigüedades del partido oficial de Arcos de la Frontera. (Mancheño y Olivares, Miguel.) Arcos de la Frontera, 1901.
Arc 843.195 Antigüedades ebusitanas. (Román, Carlos.) Barcelona, 1913.
Arc 1033.17.504 Antiguidade da sagrada imagem de Nossa S. de Nazareth...Pederneira. (Brito Alão, M. de.) Lisboa, 1628.
Arc 1360.4 Antik érmészet. (Farkas, Sandor.) Aiud, 1932.

Arc 65.5 Die Antike. Berlin. 1-20,1925-1944 18v.
Arc 1053.6 Antike. Portraits. (Ebers, G.) Leipzig, 1893.
Arc 625.4 Antike Bildwerke. Text. (Gerhard, E.) München, 1828.
Arc 1143.4.1 Das antike Buchwesen in seinem Verhältnis zur Literatur. (Birt, Theodor.) Aalen, 1974.
Arc 1087.4F Antike Gesichtshelme und Sepulcralmasken. (Benndorf, Otto.) Wien, 1878.
Arc 1070.206 Antike Himmelsbilder. (Thiele, G.) Berlin, 1898.
Arc 628.17 Antike Kunstwerke im klassischen Unterricht. (Luckenbach, H.) München, 1901.
Arc 1478.11 Antike Münzbilder. (Pfeiffer, A.) Winterthur, 1895.
Arc 1372.3 Die antike Münze als Kunstwerk. 1. Aufl. (Regling, Kurt.) Berlin, 1924.
Arc 1584.10 Antike Münzen aus Olbia und Pantikapaum. (Hrbas, M.) Prag, 1959.
Arc 1300.9 Antike Münzen und Geschnittere Steine. Berlin. 1,1969+ 9v.
Arc 1510.90 Antike Münzfunde Südwestdeutschlands. pt.1-5. (Christ, Karl.) Heidelberg, 1960.
Arc 1357.5 Antike Numismatik. (Christ, Karl.) Darmstadt, 1967.
Arc 757.9F Das antike Rom. 3. Aufl. (Curtius, Ludwig.) Wien, 1957.
Arc 1088.1.25 Das antike Seewesen. 1. Aufl. (Köster, August.) Berlin, 1923.
Arc 688.7.10 Die antike Stadt Samos. (Tölle-Kastenbein, Renate.) Mainz am Rhein, 1969.
Arc 87.1.45 Antike Steinmetzzeichen. (Richter, O.) Berlin, 1885.
Arc 936.190 Antike und Mittelalter in Bulgarien. (Beshevliev, V.) Berlin, 1960.
Arc 688.2 Die antiken Kunstwerke aus Sparta und Umgebung. (Dressel, H.) Athen, 1878.
Arc 1087.2 Die antiken Mühlen. (Engelmann, R.) Berlin, 1904.
Arc 1490.7 Die antiken Münzen...Malta. (Mayr, A.) München, 1895.
Arc 1353.1.5 Die antiken Münzen. (Berlin. Staatliche Museen.) Berlin, 1851.
Arc 1428.15 Die antiken Münzen Mysiens. (Akademie der Wissenschaften, Berlin.) Berlin, 1913.
Arc 1468.12 Die antiken Münzen von Dacien. (Pick, Bekrendt.) Berlin, 1898-1910. 2v.
Arc 1470.82 Die antiken Münzen von Epirus. v.1-2. (Franke, P.R.) Wiesbaden, 1961.
Arc 1468.12.3 Die antiken Münzen von Makedonia. (Gaebler, Hugo.) Berlin, 1906-35. 2v.
Arc 1468.12.2 Die antiken Münzen von Thrakien. (Münzer, Friedrich.) Berlin, 1912.
Arc 1053.6.6F Die antiken Porträtgemälde aus den Grabstätten des Fayum. (Graul, Richard.) Leipzig, 1888.
Arc 772.6.2 Die antiken Sammlungen. 2. Aufl. (Amelung, W.) Stuttgart, 1913.
Arc 87.1.5 Antikenkranz. (Panofka, T.S.) Berlin, 1845-
Arc 1361.4 Antikes Geldwesen. (Giesecke, W.) Leipzig, 1938.
Arc 600.48 Antinoë and its papyri; excavations by the Graeco-Roman branch, 1913-14. (Johnson, J. de M.) London, 1914.
Arc 1053.5 Antinoos. (Dietrichson, L.) Christiania, 1884.
Arc 505.1.9F Antioch-on-the-Orontes. v.1-4. Princeton, 1934-48. 5v.
Arc 66.1.194 Antioche paienne et chrétienne. (Festugière, Andre.) Paris, 1959.
Arc 1.12 Antiqua. Zürich. 1882-1891 2v.
Arc 861.42 Antiqua explorata. Chesterford. (Neville, R.C.) Walden Saffron, 1847.
Arc 1333.1 Antiqua numismata. v.1-2. (Venuti, R.) Rome, 1739-44.
Arc 823.19.45 Antiquaires 1880. (Thédenat, H.) Paris, 1880.
Arc 823.19.60 Antiquaires 1881. (Thédenat, H.) Paris, 1881.
Arc 125.9 Antiquarian Association of the British Isles. Journal. London. 1-3,1930-1932
Arc 441.1.3 Antiquarian remains at Sopârâ and Padana, being an account of the Buddhist Stüpa and Asoka edict. (Indraje, B.) Bombay, 1882.
Arc 441.22 The antiquarian remains in Bihar. (Patil, Devendrakumar Rajaram.) Patna, 1963.
Arc 447.1.5 Antiquarian remains in Hyderabad State. (Hyderabad, India (State). Archaeological Department.) Hyderabad, 1953.
Arc 885.7 An antiquarian survey of East Gower, Glamorganshire. (Morgan, W.D.) London, 1899.
Arc 136.2.5 The antiquaries journal. London. 1,1921+ 46v.
Arc 136.2.5.3 Antiquaries journal. General index. v.1-10. London, 1934.
Arc 930.205F Antiquarische Abtheilung. v.1-7,9-10,13. (Akademie der Wissenschaften in Wien. Schriften der Balkancommission.) Wien, 1900-39. 10v.
Arc 180.1.501 Antiquarische Gesellschaft in Zürich-Bibliothek. Liederchronik der Antiquarischen Gesellschaft in Zürich. Frauenfeld, 1880.
Arc 380.202 Antiquarischer Atlas. (Steinbüchel, A. von.) Wien, 1833.
NEDL Arc 125.1 The antiquary. London. 1-51 51v.
Arc 843.5 Antiquedades de Valencia. (Teixidor, J.) Valencia, 1895. 2v.
Arc 396.9 Antiques, their restoration and preservation. (Lucas, A.) London, 1924.
Arc 396.9.5 Antiques, their restoration and preservation. 2. ed. (Lucas, A.) London, 1932.
Arc 1490.25 Antiqui romanorum pontificum denarii a Benedicto XI ad Paulum III. (Benedictus Floravantensis.) Romae, 1738.
Arc 835.203FA Antiquidades de Mafra. (Veiga, Estacio da.) Lisboa, 1879.
Arc 835.202F Antiquidades prehistoricas do conselho da Figueira. v.1-4. (Santos Rocha, A. dos.) Coimbra, 1888-1900. 2v.
Arc 1490.9 Antiquiores pontificum romanorum denarii. (Vignoli, Giovanni.) Romae, 1709.
Htn Arc 618.4* Antiquitas...septentrionales et celticae. (Keysler, J.G.) Hannover, 1720.
Arc 215.10 Antiquitas hungarica. Budapest. 1947-1949
Arc 505.1 Antiquitates Antiochenae. (Mueller, K.O.) Goettingen, 1839.
Arc 861.33.3 Antiquitates Bremetonacenses, or Roman antiquitites of Overborough. (Rauthmell, R.) Kirkby Lonsdale, 1824.
Arc 861.33 Antiquitates Bremetonacenses. (Rauthmell, R.) London, 1746.
Arc 1510.137 Antiquitates nummariae, oder Historische Beschreibung vieleralten. (Leuckfeld, J.G.) Leipzig, 1721.
Arc 861.8.5 Antiquitates rutupinae. (Battely, J.) Oxoniae, 1811.
Arc 861.8.6 Antiquitates rutupinae. 2. ed. (Battely, J.) Oxoniae, 1745. 2 pam.
Htn Arc 760.4* Antiquitates urbis. (Fulvio, A.) Roma, 1527.
Arc 1048.1 Antiquitatis Muhammedanae monumenta varia. pt.1-2. (Fraehn, C.M.) Petropoli, 1820-22.
Arc 1018.17 Antiquitatum christianarum institutiones. (Selvaggio, J.L.) Vercellis, 1778. 3v.
Arc 1478.26F Antiquitatum romanorum Hispanarumque in nummis veterum dialogi XI. (Augustin, A.) Antverpiae, 1617.
Htn Arc 720.204* Antiquitatum veronensium libri VIII. (Panvini, O.) Padua, 1648.
Arc 380.200.2 L'antiquité expliquée. Supplément. (Montfaucon, B. de.) Paris, 1724. 5v.
Arc 380.200 L'antiquité expliquée. 2. éd. v.1-5. (Montfaucon, B. de.) Paris, 1722. 10v.
Arc 30.29 Antiquités africaines. Paris. 1,1967+
Arc 1027.4.5 Les antiquités chrétiennes...Cappella greca. (Davin, V.) Paris, 1892.
Arc 635.24 Antiquités crétoises. (Maraghiannio, G.) Vienne, n.d.
Arc 635.24.5 Antiquités crétoises. 2. série. (Maraghiannio, G.) Athène, 1911.
Arc 830.15.7 Les antiquités d'Arles. (Seguin, J.) Avignon, 1877.
Arc 830.128 Les antiquités de Castres. (Borel, Pierre.) Paris, 1868.
Arc 820.210F Antiquités de Grenoble. (Champollion-Figeac, Jacques J.) Grenoble, 1807.
Arc 830.1 Antiquités de la Bretagne. (Freminville.) Brest, 1834.
Arc 822.5 Pamphlet vol. Antiquités de la Gaule. v.1. 6 pam.
Arc 822.6 Pamphlet vol. Antiquités de la Gaule. v.2. 12 pam.
Arc 920.203F Antiquités de la Russie méridionale. (Kondakov, N.) Paris, 1891.
Arc 925.4 Antiquités de la Sibérie Occidentale. (Heikel, A.) Helsingfors, 1894.
Arc 522.3 Les antiquités de la Troade. (Lenormant, F.) Paris, 1876.
Arc 830.58 Antiquités de la vallée de l'Arc en Provence. (Gerin-Ricard, H. de.) Aix, 1907.
Arc 767.5 Les antiquités de la ville de Rome. (Muentz, E.) Paris, 1886.
Arc 830.5.15 Antiquités de l'arrondissement de Castellanne. 2e éd. (Gras-Bourguet.) Digne, 1842.
Arc 853.24.15F Antiquités de Rheinzabern. (Schweighauser, J.G.) Strasbourg, 181-.
Arc 830.49.15F Antiquités de Vésone. (Taillefer, W.) Périgneux, 1826. 2v.
Arc 830.103 Antiquités des eaux minérales de Vichy. (Beaulieu, J.L.D.) Paris, 1851.
Arc 726.2.19 Antiquités des environs de Naples. Naples, 1913.
Arc 800.2 Antiquités d'Herculanum. (Maréchal, P.S.) Paris, 1780-1803. 12v.
Arc 800.2.5 Antiquités d'Herculanum. (Maréchal, P.S.) Paris, 1871. 8v.
Arc 925.1 Antiquités du Bosphore Cimmérien. (Bibliotheque des Monuments Figurés.) Paris, 1892.
Arc 938.15F Antiquités du Nord-Finno-Ougrien. v.1-5. (Aspelin, J.R.) St. Pétersbourg, 1877.
Arc 830.90 Antiquités et inscriptions des villes de Die, d'Orange. (Martin, Jean C.) Orange, 1818.
Arc 830.99 Antiquités gauloises et gallo-romaines de l'arrondissement de Mantes. (Cassan, A.) Mantes, 1835.
Arc 830.22.14F Antiquités gauloises et romaines. Atlas. (Grivaud de la Vincelle, C.M.) Paris, 1807.
Arc 830.22.14 Antiquités gauloises et romaines. Texte. (Grivaud de la Vincelle, C.M.) Paris, 1807.
Arc 830.74 Antiquités générales de l'Ain. (Sirand, Alexandre.) Bourg-en-Bresse, 1855.
Arc 625.11 Antiquités grecques et romaines. Paris, 1904.
Arc 820.217F Antiquités Mandeure. (Morel-Macler, F.) Montbéliard, 1847.
Arc 723.9 Antiquités romaines...mémoires de comte de B. La Haye, 1750.
Arc 853.97 Les antiquités romaines de la Rhenanie. (Colin, Jean.) Paris, 1927.
Arc 823.19.90 Antiquités romaines trouvées aux Lilas-Romainville. (Thédenat, H.) Paris, 1881.
Arc 1020.89 Antiquités sacrées...S. Servais et de Notre Dame à Maestricht. (Bock.) Maestricht, 1873.
Arc 885.3 Antiquities...Kirrier and Penwith, West Cornwall. (Blight, J.C.) Truro, 1862.
Arc 943.26 Antiquities of America explained. (Hill, Ira.) Hagerstown, 1831.
Htn Arc 705.5* Antiquities of Athens. (Stuart, J.) London, 1762-1816. 4v.
Htn Arc 705.6* Antiquities of Athens and other places in Greece and Sicily. (Cockerell, C.R.) London, 1830.
Htn Arc 861.2* The antiquities of Canterbury. (Somner, W.) London, 1640.
Arc 967.2 Antiquities of central and southeastern Missouri. (Folvke, G.) Washington, 1910.
Arc 435.2.36F Antiquities of Chamba state. (Vogel, J.P.) Calcutta, 1911.
Arc 435.2.38F Antiquities of Indian Tibet. (Francke, A.H.) Calcutta, 1914-26. 2v.
Arc 875.39 Antiquities of Iona. (Graham, H.D.) London, 1850.
Arc 720.201 The antiquities of Italy. 2. ed. (Montfaucon, B. de.) London, 1725.
Arc 505.68.5 The antiquities of Jordan. (Harding, Gerald.) London, 1959.
Arc 505.68.6 The antiquities of Jordan. (Harding, Gerald.) London, 1967.
Arc 925.45F Antiquities of Kertch. (McPherson, Duncan.) London, 1857.
Htn Arc 861.6.5* The antiquities of Lyme. (Marriott, William.) Stockport, 1810.
Arc 609.20 Antiquities of north Ethiopia. (Jaeger, Otto.) Brockhaus, 1965.
Arc 430.2F Antiquities of Orissa. (Rájendralála Mitra.) Calcutta, 1875-80. 2v.
Arc 861.8 The antiquities of Richborough, Reculver, and Lyme. (Smith, C.R.) London, 1850.
Arc 861.8.9 The antiquities of Richborough and Reculver. (Battely, J.) London, 1774.
Arc 974.1 The antiquities of Tennessee. (Thruston, G.P.) Cincinnati, 1890.
Arc 861.62 Antiquities of the borough of Leeds. (Wardell, James.) London, 1853.
Arc 1018.25.25 Antiquities of the Christian church. (Coleman, Lyman.) Andover, 1841.
Arc 880.46 Antiquities of the Irish countryside. 3. ed. (O'Riordain, Sean P.) London, 1953.
Arc 968.2.10 Antiquities of the Jemez Plateau, New Mexico. (Hewett, E.L.) Washington, 1906.
Arc 957.1 Antiquities of the Mesa Verde National Park Cliff Palace (Colorado). (Fewkes, J.W.) Washington, 1911.
Arc 957.1.5 Antiquities of the Mesa Verde National Park Spruce Tree House. (Fewkes, J.W.) Washington, 1909.
Arc 950.202.25 Antiquities of the Onachita Valley. (Moore, C.B.) Philadelphia, 1909.
Arc 497.19 Antiquities of the Orient unveiled. (Redding, M.W.) N.Y., 1872.

Author and Title Listing

Arc 961.1.5 Antiquities of the southern Indians. (Jones, C.C.) N.Y., 1873.

Arc 950.202.29 Antiquities of the St. Francis, White and Black rivers, Arkansas. (Moore, C.B.) Philadelphia, 1910.

Arc 968.1 Antiquities of the state of New York. (Squier, E.G.) Buffalo, 1851.

Arc 955.2 Antiquities of the Upper Gila...(Arizona). (Hough, W.) Washington, 1907.

Arc 950.203 The antiquities of Wisconsin. (Lapham, I.A.) Washington, 1855?

Arc 1.16 Antiquity. Gloucester, Eng. 1,1927+ 32v.

Arc 1.16.5 Antiquity. General index, v.1-25, 1927-1951. Gloucester, Eng., n.d.

Arc 380.201 Antiquity explained. (Montfaucon, B. de.) London, 1721. 7v.

Arc 630.10 Antiquorum monimentorum, sylloge altera. (Martini, G.H.) Lipsiae, 1787.

Arc 1335.30 Antoine-Feill. Münzen- und Medaillen-Sammlung. Frankfurt, 1908.

Arc 726.20.7PF Antolini, G. Le rovine di Veleia misurate e disegnate. Pt.1-2. Milano, 1819-22.

Arc 1349.72 Anton Scharff, K. und K. Kammer-Medaillen. (Domanig, K.) Wien, 1895.

Arc 936.185.5 Antonescu, T. Cetatea Sarmizegetusa reconstitutiă. Iasi, 1966.

Arc 936.120 Antonescu, Teohari. Le trophée d'Adamclissi. Jarsy, 1905.

Arc 726.87 Antonielli, U. La prima nave imperiale del lago di Nemi. Roma, 1930.

Arc 875.100 An Antonine fort. (Robertson, Anne.) Edinburgh, 1957.

Arc 875.10 The Antonine wall report. (Glasgow, Scotland. Archaeological Society.) Glasgow, 1899.

Arc 925.50.285F Antonovich, V.B. Arkheologicheskaia karta Kievskoi gubernii. Moskva, 1895.

Arc 936.165.35 Antropogen Moldavii. Kishinev, 1969.

Arc 905.86 Antropologicheskie dannye k voprosu o velikom peseselenii narodov. (Tot, Tibor A.) Leningrad, 1970.

Arc 936.180.30 Antropomorfne figurine bronzanog doba u Jugoslaviji. (Letića, Zagorka.) Beograd, 1973.

Arc 94.1 Anuari. (Institut d'Estudis Catalans.) Barcelona. 1907-1931 11v.

Arc 923.45F Anuchin, D.N. K' voprosu o sostavlenii legendy dlia arkheologicheskoi karty Rossii. Moskva, 1885.

Arc 185.1 Anzeiger für Kunde des deutschen Mittelalters. Nürnberg. 1-8,1832-1839 6v.

Arc 185.1.2 Anzeiger für Kunde des deutschen Mittelalters. Nürnberg. 1-30,1853-1883 15v.

Arc 155.1 Anzeiger für Schweizerische Altertumskunde. Zürich. 1-40,1872-1938 28v.

Arc 530.95.10 Apakidze, A.M. Mtskheta. Tbilisi, 1959.

Arc 1493.7F Apendice á la crónica nuevamente impressa del señor rey don Juan el II. (Saez, Liciniano.) Madrid, 1786.

Arc 1025.29.5 Aperçu général sur les catacombes de Rome. (Rossi, G.B. de.) Paris, 1867.

Arc 1583.2 Aperçu sur les monnaies russes. (Fraehn, C.M.J.) n.p., n.d. 2 pam.

Arc 1583.22 Aperçu sur les monnaies russes et sur les monnaies étrangères. v.1-3. (Chaudoir, S.) St. Petersbourg, 1836. 2v.

Arc 650.1 Aphoristische Bemerkungen gesammelt...Reise nach Griechenland. (Klenze, L. von.) Berlin, 1838.

Htn Arc 1016.240* Apianus, P. Inscriptiones sacrosanctae vetustatis...Romanae. Ingolstadii, 1534.

Arc 1153.100 Apianus, Petrus. Abbrevationes vetustorum monumentorum, in ordinem alphabeticum digestae. München, 1968.

Arc 710.17 The apisthodomus on the acropolis at Athens. (White, John W.) Boston, 1895.

Arc 635.218 Apollon - Gavlgruppen fra Zeustemp. Olympia. (Skovgaard, N.K.) København, 1905.

Arc 87.1.21 Apollon mit den Lamm. (Friederichs, K.) Berlin, 1861.

Arc 66.1.182 Apollon romain. (Gagé, Jean.) Paris, 1955.

Arc 746.5 Apollon's Ankunft in Delphi. (Forchhammer, P.W.) Kiel, 1840.

Arc 1033.17.97.5 Apología de la aparición de Nuestra Señora de Guadalupe de Méjico. (Guridi, José M.) Méjico, 1820.

Arc 1033.12.158 Apologia del Volto santo di Lucca. (Serantoni, G.M.) Lucca, 1765.

Arc 1033.41 Apologia di protomartiri...Tolomeo e Romano. (Bobone, G.) Roma, 1865.

Arc 936.40.10 Apoloniía. (Bulgarska Akademiia na Naukite, Sofia. Arkheologicheskikh Institut.) Sofiia, 1963.

Arc 1030.49.5 Apontamentos de epigrafia portuguesa. 2a ed. (Cordeiro de Sousa, J.M.) Lisboa, 1937.

Arc 1027.12 Die Apostelgruft ad Catacumbas S. Peter und S. Paul. (DeWaal, A.) Rom, 1894.

Arc 1033.17.25 Apparitione della Madonna Santissima di Misericordia di Savona. (Zocca, I.M.) Modena, 1632.

Arc 1033.17.622 Apparitionum et celebriorum imaginum...Mariae...Venetiis. Venetia, 1760.

Arc 1033.12.135 Apparizione del santo volto. Napoli, 1849.

Arc 1027.33 Appell, J.W. Monuments of early Christian art. London, 1872.

Arc 1015.205.2 Appendice...al tomo terzo della Roma sotterranea. (Rossi, M.S. de.) Roma, 1877.

Arc 730.2.2 Appendice. Topografia archaeologica. Siracusa. (Cavallari, F.S.) Torino, 1891.

Arc 785.20.15F Appia antica. (Castagnoli, F.) Milano, 1957.

Arc 497.85 Applebaum, Shimon. Israel and her vicinity in the Roman and Byzantine periods. Tel-Aviv, 1967.

Arc 943.36F Appleton, LeRoy H. Indian art of the Americas. N.Y., 1950.

Arc 1613.3 Appleton, W.S. Description of a selection of coins and medals relating to America. Cambridge, 1870-76. 2 pam.

Arc 609.21 Applied anthropology in English speaking Africa. (Brokensha, David W.) Lexington, Ky., 1966.

Arc 400.25 Approach to archaeology. (Piggott, Stuart.) Cambridge, 1959.

Arc 1645.1 Apreciação do medalheiro da casa da Moeda. (Azeredo, C. de.) Rio de Janeiro, 1862.

Arc 726.200 Apulia, imperial splendor in southern Italy. (Willemsen, C.A.) N.Y., 1959.

Arc 726.37F Apulien vor und während der Hellenisirung. (Maye, M.) Leipzig, 1914.

Arc 835.201F Apuntes arqueologicos. (Mastorelly Peña, F.) Barcelona, 1879.

Arc 1163.3.80 Apuntes de iniciacion a la paleografia española de los siglos XII a XVII. (Mortero y Simón, C.) Madrid, 1963.

Arc 843.81F Apuntes sobre la villa de Tossa de Mar. (Masriera y Manovens, J.) Barcelona, 1923.

Arc 785.62F The Aqua Traiana and the mills on the Janiculum. (Van Buren, A.W.) Bergamo, 1917.

Arc 608.68 Aquae Romanae. (Birebent, Jean.) Alger, 1962.

Arc 861.40 Aquae solis...Roman Bath. (Scarth, H.M.) London, 1864.

Arc 830.6.17 Les aqueducs antiques de Lyon. (Germain de Montauzen, C.) Paris, 1908.

Arc 785.6.10 Aqueducts fountains of ancient Rome. (Forbes, S.R.) Rome, 1899.

Arc 785.6.19 The aqueducts of ancient Rome. (Ashby, T.) Oxford, 1935.

Arc 905.95F Aquencum. (Szilágyi, János.) Budapest, 1956.

Arc 726.95F Aquileia. (Brusin, G.) n.p., n.d.

Arc 1033.12.71 Aquilini, H. De pretiosissimo Jesu Christi Sanguine Mantuae asservato. Venezia, 1782.

Arc 905.40 Aquincum; Ausgrabungen und Funde. (Kuzsinszky, V.) Budapest, 1934.

Arc 785.32 L'ara massima ed il tempio d'Ercole. (Rossi, G.B. de.) Roma, 1854.

Arc 785.34.25 The Ara Pacia reconsidered and historical art in Roman Italy. (Toynbee, Jocelyn M.C.) London, 1954.

Arc 785.34 Ara Pacis Augustae. (Cannizzaro, M.E.) Roma, 1907.

Arc 785.34.13 Ara Pacis Augustae. (Paribeni, R.) Roma, 1932.

Arc 750.206 Ara Pacis Augustae. (Petersen, E.) Wien, 1902. 2v.

Arc 609.8 The Arab city of Gedi. (Kirkman, James Spedding.) London, 1954.

Arc 497.12 Arabia Petraca. v.1-3. (Musil, A.) Wien, 1907. 4v.

Arc 500.3 Arabic and English name lists. (Conder, C.R.) London, 1881.

Arc 1163.5.30 Arabic lapidary Kūfic in Africa. (Arif, Aida S.) London, 1967.

Arc 1493.2 Aragão, A.C. de. Descripção...das moedas cunhadas en home dos reis. Lisboa, 1874-80. 3v.

Arc 1018.53 Aragón Fernández, A. Tratado de arqueología eclesiástica. Barcelona, 1935.

Arc 426.4 Arai, Hakuseki. The sword book, in Honiko Gunkiko. Reading, 1913. 2 pam.

Arc 843.59 Aranzadi, T. Exploración de calorce dolmenes del Aralar. Pamplona, 1918.

Arc 843.57 Aranzadi, T. de. Exploraciones prehistóricas en Guepiezcoa los años 1924-1927. San Sebastian, 1928.

Arc 543.146.40 Arazov, O. Arkheologicheskie i arkhitekturnye pamiatniki Serakhskogo oazisa. Ashkhabad, 1973.

Arc 691.5F Arbanitopoulos, A.S. Graptai stēlai Dēmetriidos-Palasōn. Athēnai, 1928.

Arc 830.18.3 Arbaud, Damase. Alaunium Catuiaca. n.p., 1868.

Arc 853.117 Arbeits- und Forschungsberichte zur sächsischen Bodendenkmalspflege. Dresden. 2,1950+ 11v.

Arc 853.117.5 Arbeits- und Forschungsberichte zur sächsischen Bodendenkmalspflege. Beiheft, 1-9, 1956-1971. n.p., n.d.

Htn Arc 1350.4* Arbuthnot, J. Tables of ancient coins, weights and measures. London, 1727.

NEDL Arc 720.208 L'arc d'Auguste à Suse. (Ferrero, E.) Turin, 1901.

Arc 635.210 L'Arc de Triomphe de Salonique. (Kinch, K.F.) Paris, 1890.

Arc 1033.69 Arcangeli, P. Della interpretazione del Monogramma. Roma, 1879.

Arc 785.42.5 The arch of Titus. (Knight, William.) London, 1896.

Arc 936.35F Die archäische Nekropole von Trebenischte am Ochrida-See. (Filov, B.) Leipzig, 1927.

Arc 609.22.5 Archaelogy in southern Africa. (Woodhouse, Herbert Charles.) Capetown, 1971.

Arc 273.12 Archaeologia traiectina. Groningen. 1-6 3v.

Arc 136.1 Archaeologia. (London Society of Antiquaries.) London. 1-104 123v.

X Cg Arc 136.1 Archaeologia. (London Society of Antiquaries.) London. 41-60

Arc 136.1.1 Archaeologia. Table of contents. (London Society of Antiquaries.) London. 1-88,1804-1938

Arc 136.1.10 Archaeologia. 2. ed., 3. ed. (London Society of Antiquaries.) London. 1773-1809 2v.

Arc 861.21.12 Archaeologia Adelensis...West Riding of Yorkshire. (Simpson, H.T.) London, 1879.

Arc 1.20F Archaeologia geographica. Hamburg. 1-5,1950-1956

Arc 880.4.8 Archaeologia Hibernica. (Wakeman, W.F.) Dublin, 1848.

Arc 905.29F Archaeologia Hungarica. Budapest. 1,1926+ 25v.

Arc 302.35 Archaeologia Iugoslavica. Beograd. 1-5,1954-1961 2v.

Arc 968.4 Archaeologia nova caesarea, 1907-09. (Abbott, Charles C.) Trenton, New Jersey, 1907-08.

Arc 855.222F Archaeologia scotica; sculptured monuments in Iona. (Drummond, James.) Edinbrugh, 1881.

Arc 143.2 Archaeologia Scotica. (Society of Antiquaries of Scotland.) Edinburgh, 1792- 5v.

Arc 612.70 Archaeologia urbiom. Warszawa, 1966. 2v.

Arc 227.2 Archaeologiai értesito. 1882-1938 43v.

Arc 858.52 Archaeologic and historic fragments. (Wright, G.R.) London, 1887.

Arc 416.21 Archaeologica orientalia in memoriam Ernst Herzfeld. (Miles, G.C.) Locust Valles, N.Y., 1952.

Arc 497.52 Archaeological activities in Israel. (Yeivin, Samuel.) Jerusalem, 1955.

Arc 858.12 The archaeological album; or Museum of National Antiquities. (Wright, T.) London, 1845.

Arc 608.37 An archaeological and historical guide to the pre-Islamic antiquities of Tripolitania. (Haynes, D.E.L.) Tripoli, 1956.

Arc 340.1 Archaeological book lists. n.p., 1884-1891.

Arc 127.6 Archaeological bulletin for Great Britain and Ireland. 1940+ 7v.

Arc 956.1 Archaeological collection from the southern interior of British Columbia. Museum of Geological Survey, Canada. (Smith, Harlan I.) Ottawa, 1913.

Arc 635.224F An archaeological cruise in the Levant. (Schwab, G.H.) N.Y.? 1904.

Arc 543.80 Archaeological discoveries in South Arabia. (Bowen, R.) Baltimore, 1958.

Arc 497.80 Archaeological discoveries in the Holy Land. N.Y., 1967.

Arc 462.5 Archaeological discovery in West Bengal. (Das Gupta, Paresh Chandra.) Alipore, 1963.

Arc 497.102 Archaeological encyclopedia of the Holy Land. (Negev, Avraham.) N.Y., 1972.

Arc 403.8 Archaeological essays. (Simpson, J.Y.) Edinburgh, 1872. 2v.

Arc 388.2 Archaeological excavation. (Droop, J.P.) Cambridge, Eng., 1915.

Arc 131.4 Archaeological excavations. (Great Britain. Department of the Environment.) London. 1973+

Arc 976.5 Archaeological excavations at Jamestown. (Cotter, J.L.) Washington, 1958.

Arc 505.133 Archaeological excavations at Ubeidiya, 1964-1966. (Stékélis, Moshé.) Jerusalem, 1969.

Arc 843.8.5F The archaeological expedition along the Guadalquivir, 1889-1901. (Bonson, J.E.) N.Y., 1931. 2v.

Arc 968.1.15 Archaeological exploration of Fishers Island, New York. (Ferguson, Henry L.) N.Y., 1935.

Arc 530.2.6 Archaeological Exploration of Sardis. Monograph. Cambridge. 1,1971+ 4v.

Arc 488.15 Archaeological history of Iran. (Herzfeld, Ernst E.) London, 1935.

Arc 858.1.5 An archaeological index. (Akerman, J.Y.) London, 1847.

Arc 1.1.2 Archaeological Institute of America. Annual report. Cambridge. 1-17,1879-1896 3v.

Arc 1.1 Archaeological Institute of America. Bulletin. Boston. 1,1883

Arc 1.1.7 Archaeological Institute of America. Bulletin. Norwood, Mass. 1,1909+ 14v.

Arc 1.1.5 Archaeological Institute of America. Index to publications, 1879-89. Cambridge, 1891.

Arc 1.4 Archaeological Institute of America. Papers. Boston. 1-3,1882-1890 4v.

Arc 1.2 Archaeological Institute of America. Papers. Boston. 1-5,1881-1890 5v.

Arc 1.2.5 Archaeological Institute of America. Papers. 2nd ed. Boston. 1,1883

Arc 1.1.6 Archaeological Institute of America. Report of the fellow in American archaeology. N.Y., 1907.

Arc 1.1.4 Pamphlet box. Archaeological Institute of America.

Arc 1.5.50 Pamphlet vol. Archaeological Institute of America.

Arc 1.3.9 Pamphlet box. Archaeological Institute of America. Boston Society.

Arc 1.1.11 Archaeological Institute of America. School of American Archaeology. Papers. Santa Fé. 1-43,1908-1919 3v.

Arc 1.1.12 Archaeological Institute of America. Schools of American Research. Annual report. Santa Fe? 1934-1947 2v.

Arc 305.3 Archaeological Institute of America. Southwest Society, Los Angeles. Bulletin. Los Angeles. 1-8 2v.

Arc 305.3.5 Archaeological Institute of America. Southwest Society, Los Angeles. Two great gifts. The Lummies Library and collections; the Munk Library. Los Angeles, 1910.

Arc 1.3 Archaeological Institute of America. Wisconsin Society. Reports of annual meeting. Madison.

Arc 125.5.9 Archaeological Institute of Great Britain. Proceedings. London.

Arc 125.5 Archaeological Institute of Great Britain. Proceedings. London. 1845

Arc 125.5.2 Archaeological Institute of Great Britain. Proceedings. London. 1846

Arc 125.5.3 Archaeological Institute of Great Britain. Proceedings. London. 1847

NEDL Arc 125.5.4 Archaeological Institute of Great Britain. Proceedings. London. 1848

Arc 125.5.5 Archaeological Institute of Great Britain. Proceedings. London. 1849

X Cg Arc 125.5.6 Archaeological Institute of Great Britain. Proceedings. London. 1850

Arc 125.5.7 Archaeological Institute of Great Britain. Proceedings. London. 1851

Arc 125.5.8 Archaeological Institute of Great Britain. Proceedings. London. 1852 2v.

Arc 976.9 Archaeological investigation of the Shannon site, Montgomery County, Virginia. (Benthall, Joseph L.) Richmond, 1969.

Arc 953.21 Archaeological investigations. (Fowke, G.) Washington, 1922.

Arc 543.3.50F Archaeological investigations in Central Asia, 1917-37. (Field, Henry.) n.p., 1938.

Arc 975.5 Archaeological investigations in central Utah. (Gillin, John.) Cambridge, 1941.

Arc 925.4.13F Archaeological investigations in Kamchatka. (Jochelsen, W.) Washington, 1928.

Arc 968.2.15 Archaeological investigations in New Mexico, Colorado, and Utah. (Fewkes, J.W.) Washington, 1917.

Arc 975.2 Archaeological investigations in Nine Mile Canyon, Utah, during the year 1936. (Gillin, John.) Salt Lake City, 1938?

Arc 125.4 Archaeological journal. (British Archaeological Association.) London. 1+ 119v.

Arc 125.4.2 Archaeological journal. General index, v.26-75 (1869-1918). (British Archaeological Association.) London, 1955-73. 2v.

Arc 861.48 Archaeological memoirs...district of the Severn and the Wye. (Ormerod, George.) London, 1861.

Arc 1.38 Archaeological news. Tallahassee. 1,1972+

Arc 125.10 The archaeological news letter. London. 1-7,1948-1965// 2v.

Arc 1.1.13 Archaeological newsletter. N.Y. 1-25,1946-1956

Arc 325.2 Archaeological number. (Utah. University.) 1,1910

Arc 975.12 Archaeological observations north of the Rio Colorado, Utah. (Judd, Neil M.) Washington, 1926.

Arc 386.44 An archaeological perspective. (Binford, Lewis Roberts.) N.Y., 1972.

Arc 1010.28 An archaeological picture of a pre-Spanish Cebuano community. (Hutterer, Karl.) Cebu City, 1973.

Arc 430.10F Archaeological reconnaissances in north-western India and south-eastern Iran. (Stein, Mark A.) London, 1937.

Arc 488.13 Archaeological reconnaissances in southern Persia. (Stein, Mark A.) London, 1934.

Arc 772.12 An archaeological record of Rome from the seventh to the second century B.C. v.1-2. (Ryberg, Inez.) Philadelphia, 1940.

Arc 391.9 Archaeological remains. (Garrood, J.R.) London, 1949.

Arc 435.26 Archaeological remains. v.1-2. (India. Archaeological Survey.) New Delhi, 1964.

Arc 586.2 Archaeological reports. (Egypt Exploration Society.) London. 1890-1912 5v.

Arc 65.11 Archaeological reports. London. 1957-1964

Arc 543.78F Archaeological research in Indo-China. (Janse, Olov R.T.) Cambridge, 1947- 2v.

Arc 957.1.15 Archaeological research in the northeast San Juan basin of Colorado. (Jeancon, J.A.) Denver, 1922.

Arc 500.6 Archaeological researches in Palestine. (Clermont-Ganneau, C.) London, 1896. 2v.

Arc 384.17 Archaeological researches in retrospect. (Willey, Gordon Randolph.) Cambridge, Mass., 1974.

Arc 969.9 Archaeological researches in the northern great basin. (Cressman, L.S.) Washington, 1942.

Arc 391.18 Archaeological site science. (Goodyear, Frank Haigh.) N.Y., 1971.

Arc 843.19.15FA An archaeological sketch-book of the Roman necropolis at Carmona. (Bonson, J.E.) N.Y., 1931.

Arc 80.10 Archaeological Society, Athens. Praktika. Athēnai. 1,1837+ 40v.

Arc 69.1F Archaeological Society of Athens. Epheneriz Archaiologikē. Athēnai. 1837+ 54v.

Arc 968.2.70 Archaeological studies in the La Plata district, southwestern Colorado and northwestern New Mexico. (Morris, E.H.) Washington, 1939.

Arc 977.2 Archaeological survey of eastern Wyoming, summer 1931. (Renaud, E.B.) Denver, 1932.

Arc 587.87F Archaeological survey of Nubia; report. (Egypt. Ministry of Finance.) Cairo. 1907-1911 8v.

Arc 587.85 Archaeological survey of Nubia. v.1-7. (Egypt. Ministry of Finance.) Cairo, 1908.

Arc 974.1.5 An archaeological survey of the Norris Basen in eastern Tennessee. (Webb, William S.) Washington, 1938.

Arc 858.6 An archaeological survey of the United Kingdom. (Murray, D.) Glasgow, 1896.

Arc 383.34.15 Archaeological theory and practice. Festschrift: Wm. F. Grimes. London, 1973.

Arc 493.20 An archaeological tour in the ancient Persis. (Stein, Mark A.) Oxford, 1936.

Arc 900.215F Archaeologický výzhum. pt.1-3. (Pič, Josef L.) Praha, 1893-97.

Arc 1018.35 Archäologie...Christliche Archäologie, 1880-86. (Kraus, F.X.) Stuttgart, 1882. 2v.

Arc 386.5 Archäologie. (Böttiger, Carl August.) Dresden, 1806.

Arc 628.24 Archäologie. (Knell, Heiner.) Darmstadt, 1972.

Arc 402.18 Archäologie. (Rumpf, A.) Berlin, 1953-56. 2v.

Arc 395.4 Archäologie. 2. Aufl. v.2,4. (Koepp, Friedrich.) Berlin, 1920. 2v.

Arc 1018.5 Archäologie der altchristlichen Kunst. (Schultze, Victor.) München, 1895.

Arc 497.98 Archaeologie und Altes Testament. Festschrift für Kurt Galling 28. Jan. 1970. Tübingen, 1970.

Arc 386.23 Archäologie und Anschauung. (Brunn, H. von.) München, 1885.

Arc 497.101 Archäologie und biblisches Leben. (Rehork, Joachim.) Bergish Gladbach, 1972.

Arc 395.3 Archäologie und Geschichts Wissenschaft. (Körte, G.) Göttingen, 1911.

Arc 386.5.2 Archäologie und Kunst. (Böttiger, Carl August.) Breslau, 1828.

Arc 705.14 Archäologisch-artische Mittheilungen...über die Ausgrabungen auf der Akropolis zu Athen. (Heller, B.R.) Nuremberg, 1852.

Arc 402.4 Archaeologische Aufsaetze. (Ross, L.) Leipzig, 1855. 2v.

Arc 73.11.3 Archäologische Bibliographie; Beilage zum Jahrbuch des Deutsches Archäologisches Institut. (Archäologisches Institut des Deutschen Reichs.) Berlin. 1942+ 13v.

Arc 905.85 Archäologische Denkmäler der Awarenzeit in Mitteleuropa. (Csallány, Dezsö.) Budapest, 1956.

Arc 1027.25.41 Archäologische Ehren-Gabe zur 70. Geburtstage De Rossi. Rom, 1892.

Arc 375.12 Archäologische Encyclopedie. Zeist, 1962.

Arc 65.2.3 Archaeologische-Epigraphische Mittheilungen am Österreich. Vienna. 1-20,1877-1897

Arc 65.2 Archaeologische-Epigraphische Mittheilungen am Österreich. Vienna. 1-20,1877-1897 8v.

Arc 930.206F Archäologische Forschungen in Albanien und Montenegro. (Praschniker, C.) Wien, 1919.

Arc 936.14 Archäologische Forschungen in Polen. (Hensel, Witold.) Warschau, 1958.

Arc 215.5 Archaeologische Forschungen in Tirol. Innsbruck. 1-2

Arc 155.5 Archaeologische Führer der Schweiz. Zürich. 1,1969+

Arc 185.4 Archaeologische für Pilzkunde. Frankfurt. 1-2

Arc 905.100F Archäologische Funde in Ungarn. (Thomas, Baja.) Budapest, 1956.

Arc 853.232 Archaeologische Funde und Denkmäler des Rheinlandes. Köln. 1,1960+ 3v.

Arc 87.1.78 Archäologische Gesellschaft zu Berlin. Winckelmannsprogramm. Berlin. 77,1921+ 29v.

Arc 1.37 Archäologische Informationen. Köln. 1,1972+

Arc 936.180 Archäologische Karte von Jugoslavien. (Klemenc, J.) Beograd, 1938.

Arc 513.14 Archäologische Karte von Kleinasien. (Maps. Asia Minor (1899).) Halle, 1899.

Arc 30.15 Archaeologische Mitteilungen aus Iran. Berlin. 1,1929+ 10v.

Arc 30.15.5 Archaeologische Mitteilungen aus Iran. Ergänzungsband. Berlin. 1,1938

Arc 275.25F Archäologische Mitteilungen aus russischen Sammlungen. Berlin. 1-5,1928-1936 5v.

Arc 388.16 Archäologische Radiographie. (Driehaus, Jürgen.) Düsseldorf, 1968.

Arc 482.201F Archäologische Reise im Euphrat. (Sarre, Friedrich.) Berlin, 1911-20. 4v.

Arc 391.1 Archäologische Schriften. (Gurlitt, J.) Altona, 1831.

Arc 380.203 Archäologische Schriften. (Rathgeber, D.G.) Gotha, 1851-57.

Arc 853.20.19 Archäologische Siedlungskunde des trierer Landes. (Steinhausen, J.) Trier, 1936.

Arc 635.207 Archäologische Studien...Heinrich Brunn...dargebracht. (Furtwängler, A.) Berlin, 1893.

Arc 641.1 Archäologische Studien. (Blenkenberg, C.) Leipzig, 1904.

Arc 1018.5.5 Archäologische Studien über altchristliche Monumente. (Schultze, Victor.) Wien, 1880.

Arc 1.15 Archaeologische Studien zum Christlichen Altertum. Freiburg, 1895.

Arc 1166.7.10 Archäologische und epigrapische Klassifikation koptischer Denkmäler des Metropolitan Museum of Art, N.Y. und des Museum of Fine Arts, Boston, Mass. (Cramer, Maria.) Wiesbaden, 1957.

Arc 635.200 Archäologische Untersuchungen auf Samothrake. (Conze, A.) Wien, 1875-80. 2v.

Arc 65.1 Archaeologische Zeitung. Berlin. 1-43,1843-1885 28v.

Arc 397.7 Die archäologischen Entdeckungen des 19. Jahrhunderts. (Michaelis, A.) Leipzig, 1906.

Arc 73.11.2 Archäologischer Anzeiger. (Archäologisches Institut des Deutschen Reichs.) Berlin. 78,1963+ 9v.

Arc 938.5 Archäologischer Kongress, 10th, Riga, 1896. Katalog der Ausstellung. Riga, 1896.

Arc 938.5.5 Archäologischer Kongress, 10th, Riga, 1896. Klusie liecinieki; senlietu albums. Lincoln, Nebraska, 1964.

Author and Title Listing

Arc 938.9 Archäologischer Kongress. Baltischen...Komitee. Baltische Studien zur Archäologie und Geschichte. Berlin, 1914.
Arc 646.2 Archäologischer Nachlass aus Rom. (Gerhard, E.) Berlin, 1952.
Arc 73.11.3 Archäologisches Institut des Deutschen Reichs. Archäologische Bibliographie; Beilage zum Jahrbuch des Deutsches Archäologisches Institut. Berlin. 1942+ 13v.
Arc 73.11.2 Archäologisches Institut des Deutschen Reichs. Archäologischer Anzeiger. Berlin. 78,1963+ 9v.
Arc 73.8F Archäologisches Institut des Deutschen Reichs. Denkmäler antiker Architektur. Berlin. 1-10 11v.
Arc 73.11 Archäologisches Institut des Deutschen Reichs. Jahrbuch. Berlin. 1,1886+ 23v.
Arc 73.11.10 Archäologisches Institut des Deutschen Reichs. Jahrbuch. Bibliographie, Register, 1-50. Berlin, 1904-21. 4v.
Arc 73.12 Archäologisches Institut des Deutschen Reichs. Jahrbuch. Ergänzungsheft. Berlin. 1,1888+ 22v.
Arc 73.20.20 Archäologisches Institut des Deutschen Reichs. Mitteilungen. München. 1-6,1948-1953 3v.
Arc 73.17 Pamphlet box. Archäologisches Institut des Deutschen Reichs.
Arc 73.20.15F Archäologisches Institut des Deutschen Reichs. Funfundzwanzig Jahre Römisch-Germanische Kommission. Römische-germanische Kommission. Berlin, 1930.
Arc 73.20 Archäologisches Institut des Deutschen Reichs. Römisch-Germanische Kommission. Bericht. Frankfurt. 1904+ 27v.
Arc 65.3.10F Archäologisches Institut des Deutschen Reichs-Athenische Zweiganstalt. Argolis. Athens.
Arc 682.14F Archäologisches Institut des Deutschen Reichs-Athenische Zweigeanstalt. Das Kuppelgrab bei Menidi. Athen, 1880.
Arc 1.30 Archäologisches Korrespondenzblatt. Mainz am Rhein. 1,1971+
Arc 375.1 Archäologisches Wörterbuch. (Müller, H.A.) Leipzig, 1877-78. 2v.
Arc 375.4 Archäologisches Wörterbuch. (Otte, H.) Leipzig, 1857.
Arc 375.4.2 Archäologisches Wörterbuch. (Otte, H.) Leipzig, 1883.
Arc 1.9 Archaeologist. London. 1-10
Arc 392.16 The archaeologist at work. (Heizer, Robert F.) N.Y., 1959.
Arc 1.40 The archaeologists' year book. Christchurch. 1973+ 2v.
Arc 1.18 Archaeology; a magazine dealing with the antiquity of the world. Cambridge, Mass. 1,1948+ 18v.
Arc 340.7 Archaeology, 1945-1955. (French Bibliographical Digest.) N.Y., 1956- 2v.
Arc 1018.41 The archaeology...Christian altar...western Europe. (Heales, Alfred.) London, 1881.
Arc 385.10 Archaeology. (Atkinson, R.J.C.) Cardiff, 1960.
Arc 402.20 Archaeology. (Rapport, S.B.) N.Y., 1963.
Arc 662.5 Archaeology. (Wheeler, J.R.) N.Y., 1908.
Arc 942.7 Pamphlet vol. Archaeology. Aboriginal America. 31 pam.
Arc 942.2 Pamphlet vol. Archaeology. American. 5 pam.
Arc 942.3 Pamphlet vol. Archaeology. American. 7 pam.
Arc 942.5 Pamphlet vol. Archaeology. American. 17 pam.
Arc 942.8 Pamphlet box. Archaeology. American. Miscellaneous pamphlets.
Arc 942.1 Pamphlet vol. Archaeology. American. 1880- 32 pam.
Arc 513.02 Pamphlet vol. Archaeology. Asia Minor. General works. 10 pam.
Arc 513.01 Pamphlet box. Archaeology. Asia Minor. General works.
Arc 902.05F Pamphlet box. Archaeology. Austrian Empire.
Arc 902.01 Pamphlet box. Archaeology. Austrian Empire.
Arc 1033.02 Pamphlet box. Archaeology. Christian.
Arc 1033.01 Pamphlet box. Archaeology. Christian.
Arc 935.01 Pamphlet box. Archaeology. Constantinople.
Arc 549 Pamphlet box. Archaeology. Egypt.
Arc 549.1 Pamphlet box. Archaeology. Egypt.
Arc 847.2 Pamphlet box. Archaeology. German dissertations.
Arc 847.1 Pamphlet box. Archaeology. Germany. Miscellaneous pamphlets.
Arc 847 Pamphlet box. Archaeology. Germany. Miscellaneous pamphlets.
Arc 125.01 Pamphlet box. Archaeology. Great Britain.
Arc 857.1 Pamphlet box. Archaeology. Great Britain.
Arc 857 Pamphlet box. Archaeology. Great Britain.
Arc 857.15 Pamphlet box. Archaeology. Great Britain. Miscellaneous pamphlets by T. McKenny Hughes.
Arc 632.4 Pamphlet box. Archaeology. Greece and Rome. 7 pam.
Arc 632 Pamphlet box. Archaeology. Greece and Rome. 39 pam.
Arc 1053 Pamphlet box. Archaeology. Iconography.
Arc 1.18.2 Archaeology. Index, v.11-26, 1958-1973. N.Y., 1974.
Htn Arc 985.01PF* Pamphlet box. Archaeology. Mexico and Central America.
Arc 382 Pamphlet box. Archaeology. Miscellaneous pamphlets. 38 pam.
Arc 382.8 Pamphlet box. Archaeology. Miscellaneous pamphlets.
Htn Arc 380.05PF* Pamphlet box. Archaeology. Miscellaneous plates.
Arc 543.01 Pamphlet box. Archaeology. Other Asiatic. General and special.
Arc 487.1 Pamphlet box. Archaeology. Persia. Tracts.
Arc 754.5 Pamphlet box. Archaeology. Rome.
Arc 754 Pamphlet box. Archaeology. Rome.
Arc 923 Pamphlet box. Archaeology. Russia.
Arc 925.50.01 Pamphlet vol. Archaeology. Russia. Ukraine. 4 pam.
Arc 923.1 Pamphlet box. Archaeology. Russia and Slavic.
Arc 891 Pamphlet box. Archaeology. Scandinavia.
Arc 397.24 Archaeology: science and romance. (Mellersh, Harold Edward Leslie.) Exeter, 1966.
Arc 1210.01 Pamphlet box. Archaeology. Sigillography.
Arc 837.1 Pamphlet box. Archaeology. Spain and Portugal.
Arc 837 Pamphlet box. Archaeology. Spain and Portugal.
Arc 496.1 Pamphlet box. Archaeology. Syria and Palestine.
Arc 496 Pamphlet box. Archaeology. Syria and Palestine.
Arc 953.17 Pamphlet vol. Archaeology. United States. 15 pam.
Arc 953.01 Pamphlet box. Archaeology. United States and Canada.
Arc 955.01 Pamphlet box. Archaeology. United States and Canada. Miscellaneous pamphlets.
Arc 1.27 Archaeology abroad. London. 1,1972+
Arc 875.12 Archaeology and false antiquities. (Munro, Robert.) London, 1905.
Arc 875.12.2 Archaeology and false antiquities. (Munro, Robert.) Philadelphia, 1906.
Arc 388.9 Archaeology and history. (Dymond, David Percy.) London8 1974.
Arc 497.86 Archaeology and Old Testament study. (Thomas, David Winton.) Oxford, 1967.
Arc 875.6 The archaeology and prehistoric annals of Scotland. (Wilson, D.) Edinburgh, 1851.
Arc 387.21.5A Archaeology and society. (Clark, John Grahame Douglas.) Cambridge, Mass., 1957.
Arc 387.21A Archaeology and society. 2. ed. (Clark, John Grahame Douglas.) London, 1947.
Arc 387.21.10 Archaeology and society. 3. ed. (Clark, John Grahame Douglas.) London, 1960.
Arc 1468.52 Archaeology and the types of Greek coins. (Gardner, Percy.) Chicago, 1965.
Arc 412.1.15 Archaeology beneath the sea. (Bass, George Fletcher.) N.Y., 1975.
Arc 407.16 Archaeology from the earth. (Wheeler, Robert Eric Mortimer.) Oxford, 1954.
Arc 441.9.5 Archaeology in Baroda, 1934-1947. (Gadre, A.S.) Baroda, 1947.
Arc 497.74 Archaeology in Biblical research. (Williams, Walter George.) N.Y., 1965.
Arc 421.24 Archaeology in China. (Watson, William.) London, 1960.
Arc 421.22 Archaeology in China. v.1-3. (Chêng, Tê-k'un.) Cambridge, Eng., 1959-
Arc 858.46 Archaeology in England and Wales, 1914-1931. (Kendrick, T.D.) London, 1932.
Arc 609.40 Archaeology in Ghana. (Davies, Oliver.) Edinburgh, 1961.
Arc 446.5 Archaeology in Gwalior. 2. ed. (Garde, M.B.) Gwalior, 1934.
Arc 432.1.5 Archaeology in India. (Fergusson, J.) London, 1884.
Arc 1010.20 Archaeology in Sarawak. (Chêng, Tê-k'un.) Cambridge, 1969.
Arc 543.81 Archaeology in the Aden Protectorates. (Harding, Gerald Lankester.) London, 1964.
Arc 387.5.10 Archaeology in the field. (Crawford, Osbert Guy S.) London, 1953.
Arc 387.5.12 Archaeology in the field. (Crawford, Osbert Guy S.) N.Y., 1953.
Arc 497.60 Archaeology in the Holy Land. (Kenyon, Kathleen Mary.) N.Y., 1960.
Arc 497.60.3 Archaeology in the Holy Land. 3. ed. (Kenyon, Kathleen Mary.) N.Y., 1970.
Arc 382.9 Archaeology in the north of England. (Birley, Eric.) Durham, Eng., 1958. 6 pam.
Arc 923.60 Archaeology in the U.S.S.R. (Miller, M.A.) N.Y., 1956.
Arc 925.110.5 Archaeology in USSR. (Mongait, A.L.) Moscow, 1959.
Arc 1.33 Archaeology into history. London. 1,1973+
Arc 421.28 The archaeology of ancient China. (Chaung, K.) New Haven, 1963.
Arc 559.4 The archaeology of ancient Egypt. (James, Thomas Garnet Henry.) London, 1972.
Arc 861.91 The archaeology of Berkshire. (Peake, Harold.) London, 1931.
Arc 861.5.15 The archaeology of Cornwall and Scilly. (Hencken, H.O.) London, 1932.
Arc 672.1.28.5 The archaeology of Crete. (Pendlebury, J.D.S.) London, 1939.
Arc 672.1.28.6 The archaeology of Crete. (Pendlebury, J.D.S.) N.Y., 1963.
Arc 975.10 The archaeology of Deadman Cave, Utah. (Smith, E.R.) Salt Lake City, 1941.
Arc 953.28F Archaeology of eastern United States. (Griffin, James.) Chicago, 1952.
Arc 655.6 The archaeology of Greece and the Aegean. (Perowne, Stewart.) London, 1974.
Arc 880.25.7 The archaeology of Ireland. (Macalister, R.A.S.) London, 1928.
Arc 880.25.8A The archaeology of Ireland. 2. ed. (Macalister, R.A.S.) London, 1949.
Arc 861.208 The archaeology of Jodrell Hall (Terra Nova), Cheshire. (Uhthoff-Kaufmann, Raymond R.) Wilmslow, 1971.
Arc 861.89 Archaeology of Kent. (Jessup, Ronald F.) London, 1930.
Arc 428.5PF Archaeology of Korea. Plates and maps. Tokyo, 1913. 7v.
Arc 858.99 The archaeology of late Celtic Britain and Ireland, c. 400-1200. (Laing, Lloyd Robert.) London, 1975.
Arc 861.18.16.20 The archaeology of London. (Merrifield, Ralph.) Park Ridge, 1975.
Arc 861.7.5 The archaeology of Middlesex and London. (Vulliamy, Colwyn E.) London, 1930.
Arc 967.1.13 Archaeology of Mississippi. (Brown, C.S.) University, 1926.
Arc 969.1 Archaeology of Ohio. (Read, M.C.) Cleveland, 1888.
Arc 497.30.3 The archaeology of Palestine. (Albright, William Foxwell.) London, 1954.
Arc 497.30 The archaeology of Palestine and the Bible. (Albright, William Foxwell.) N.Y., 1932.
Arc 963.3 The archaeology of Porter County, Indiana. (McAllister, J.G.) Indianapolis, 1932.
Arc 858.42.1 The archaeology of Roman Britain. (Collingwood, Robin George.) London, 1969.
Arc 858.42 The archaeology of Roman Britain. (Collingwood, Robin George.) N.Y., 1930.
Arc 770.1 The archaeology of Rome. v.1-2, 4-11. (Parker, J.H.) Oxford, 1874. 12v.
Arc 895.70 The archaeology of Skedemosse. (Hagberg, Ulf Eric.) Stockholm, 1967. 3v.
Arc 861.38.9 The archaeology of Somerset. (Dobson, Dina P.) London, 1931.
Arc 861.23.9 The archaeology of Surrey. (Whimster, D.C.) London, 1931.
Arc 861.41.25 The archaeology of Sussex. (Curwen, E. Cecil.) London, 1937.
Arc 875.120 Archaeology of Tayside. (Taylor, B.) Dundee, 196-?
Arc 870.12 The archaeology of the Anglo-Saxon settlements. (Leeds, E.T.) Oxford, 1913.
Arc 861.16.5 The archaeology of the Cambridge region. (Fox, Cyril.) Cambridge, Eng., 1923.
Arc 861.83 The archaeology of the Channel Islands. (Kendrick, T.D.) London, 1928.
Arc 958.1.5 The archaeology of the Delaware Valley. (Volk, E.) Cambridge, 1911.
Arc 497.18 Archaeology of the Holy Land. (Handcock, P.S.P.) London, 1916.
Arc 968.2.20 Archaeology of the lower Mimbres Valley, New Mexico. (Fewkes, J.W.) Washington, 1914.
Arc 895.76 Archaeology of the musk-ox way. (Knuth, Eigil.) Paris, 1967.
Arc 772.16 The archaeology of the Roman empire. (Richmond, Ian A.) Oxford, 1957.
Arc 953.20F Archaeology of the United States. (Haven, S.F.) Washington, 1856.
Arc 861.140 The archaeology of Wessex. (Grinsell, L.V.) London, 1958.

Arc 861.21.21 The archaeology of Yorkshire. (Elgee, Frank.) London, 1933.
Arc 324.5 Archaeology series. (Texas. University. Department of Anthropology.) Austin.
Arc 412.1 Archaeology under water. (Bass, George Fletcher.) London, 1966.
Arc 1.22 Archaeometry. Oxford. 4v.
Arc 700.35 Archaic attic gravestones. (Richter, G.M.A.) Cambridge, 1944.
Arc 1084.12 Archaic Chinese jades collections in China. (Field Museum of Natural History, Chicago.) N.Y., 1927.
Arc 554.6 Archaic Egypt. (Emery, Walter.) Baltimore, 1963.
Arc 858.32 Archaic England. (Bayley, Harold.) London, 1919.
Arc 1077.4 Archaic rock inscriptions...cup and ring markings. London, 1891.
Arc 870.7 Archaic sculpturings of cups, circles. (Simpson, J.Y.) Edinbrugh, 1867.
Arc 861.16.10 Archaic tracks round Cambridge. (Watkins, A.) London, 1932.
Arc 68.5F Archailogikon deltion. (Greece. Hypourgeion tōn ekklesiasticon.) Athēnai. 1,1915+ 29v.
Arc 688.1 Archaiologia tēs Nesou Sikinou. (Schinas, D.) Athēnai, 1837.
Arc 65.14 Archaiologika analekta ex Athenon. Athēnai. 1,1968+
Arc 80.1.8 Archaiologikē Hetairia, Athens. To ergon tēs Archaiologikēs Hetaireias. Athēnai. 1954+ 9v.
Arc 80.1.6 Archaiologikē Hetairia, Athens. To ergon tēs en Athēnais, Archaiologikēs Hetairias kata ten prōten autēs hekatontaetias. Athēnai, 1938.
Arc 80.1.7.5F Archaiologikē Hetairia, Athens. Leukōma tēs hekatontaeteridos. Athēnai, 1952.
Arc 80.8 Archaiologikē Hetairia, Athens. Organismos. Athēnai, 1876.
Arc 935.8 Archaiologikos chartēs. (Constantinople, Turkey. Hellēnikos Philologikos Syllogos. Archaiologikē Epitropē.) Konstantinople, 1884.
Arc 746.12 Die archaischen etruskischen Terracottasarkophage aus Caere. Diss. (Sauer, Hertha.) Rendsburg, 1930.
Arc 65.8 Archeion tōn Byzantinōn mnēmeiōn tēs Hellados. Athēnai. 1-9,1935-1961 5v.
Arc 396.10 L'archélogie et ses problèmes. (Laet, Siegfried J. de.) Berchem, 1954.
Arc 723.36 Gli archeologi italiani in onore di Amedeo Maiuri. (Centro Studi Ciociaria.) Cava dei Tirreni, 1965.
Arc 1.21 Archeologia; rocznik Polskiego Towarzystwa Archeologicgnego. Warszawa. 1,1947+ 10v.
VArc 1.25 Archeologia. Paris. 9,1966+ 5v.
VArc 1.25.5 Archeologia. Document Archéologie aérienne. Paris. 1,1973+
Arc 1.19 Archeologia classica. Roma. 1,1949+ 30v.
Arc 1018.55 Archeologia cristiana. (Testini, P.) Roma, 1958.
Arc 505.97 L'archeologia cristiana in Palestina. (Bagatti, Bellarmino.) Firenze, 1962.
Arc 726.325 Archeologia e storia nella Lombardia padana. Bedriacum nel XIX centenario delle Battaglie. Como, 1972.
Arc 726.328 Archeologia e storia nella Lombardia pedemontana occidentale. (Convegno su Archeologia e Storia nella Lombardia Pedemontana Occidentale.) Como, 1969.
Arc 936.13 Archeologia i pradzieje Polski. (Gardanski, A.) Warszawa, 1957.
Arc 936.14.333 Archeologia i prahistoria. (Hensel, Witold.) Wrocław, 1971.
Arc 655.5 L'archeologia in Grecia. (Pannati, Ulrico.) Napoli, 1965.
Arc 936.14.515 Archeologia Małopolski wczesnośredniowiecznej. (Żaki, Andrzej.) Wrocław, 1947.
Arc 93.54 Archeologia medievale. Firenze. 1,1974+
Arc 726.216 L'archeologia nell'Arcipelago toscano. (Zecchini, Michelangelo.) Pisa, 1971.
Arc 395.26 Archeologia prahistoryczna. Wyd. 1. (Kozłowski, Janusz K.) Kraków, 1972- 2v.
Arc 1027.24.13 Archeologia sacra: Catacombe napolitane. (Scherillo, G.) Napoli, 1875.
Arc 1025.21 Archeologia sacra. v.1-2. (Scherillo, G.) Napoli, 1875.
Arc 393.10 Archeologia żywa. Wyd. 1. (Hensel, Witold.) Warszawa, 1973.
Arc 1.1.10 Archeological Institute of America. School of American Archaeology. Bulletin. Washington.
Arc 628.23 Archeological papers. v.1-5, 6-10. (Elderkin, G.W.) Springfield, Mass., 1941- 2v.
Arc 1.8 Archeological review. London, 1888-90. 4v.
Arc 302.12 Archeologické studijné materiály. Praha. 1,1964+ 2v.
Arc 497.73 Archeologiczne odkrycia w egzegezie Nowego Testamentu. (Gryglewicz, F.) Lublin, 1962.
Arc 388.3 L'archéologie, son domaine, son but. (Deonna, Waldemar.) Paris, 1922.
Arc 925.9 L'archéologie au Caucase. (Mourier, J.) Paris, 1887.
Arc 823.1.5 Archéologie celtique et gaulois. (Bertrand, A.) Paris, 1889.
Arc 820.220F Archéologie celto-romaine de l'arrondissement de Chatillon-sur-Seine. pt.1-2. (Leclere, J.B.) Paris, 1840-1843.
Arc 1018.1 Archéologie chrétienne. (Bourassé, J.J.) Tours, 1878.
Arc 1018.3 L'archéologie chrétienne. (Pératé, A.) Paris, 1892.
Arc 1020.35 Archéologie chrétienne de Carthage. (Delattre, R.P.) Lyon, 1886.
NEDL Arc 823.12 Archéologie de la Gaule. (Molin, Jean.) Paris, 1908.
Arc 830.334F Archéologie de la Meuse. v.1-3, texte. v.4-6, carte. (Liénard, F.) Verdun, 1881-85. 6v.
Arc 608.1.3 L'archéologie de la Tunisie. (Gauckler, Paul.) Paris, 1896.
Arc 340.2.15 Archéologie de l'Afrique antique. Aix en Provence. 1970+
Arc 830.142 Archéologie de Mons Seleucus. (Lebreton, J.) Gap, 1806.
Arc 1010.26 Archéologie des Nouvelles Hébrides. (Garanger, José.) Paris, 1972.
Arc 543.131 L'archéologie du Delta du Nékoug. v.1-4. (Malleret, Louis.) Paris, 1959- 7v.
Arc 497.30.5 Archéologie du peuple d'Israël. (Du Buit, Michel.) Paris, 1960.
Arc 830.370 Archéologie du village déserté. Paris, 1970.
Arc 612.72 L'archéologie du village médiéval. Louvain, 1967.
Arc 562.2 L'archéologie égyptienne (in Bibliothèque de l'Enseignement des Beaux-Arts). (Maspero, Gaston.) Paris, 1887.
Arc 936.50 L'archéologie en Dalmatie du Xe siècle. (Bulić, France.) n.p., 1924-25.
Arc 888.50 Archeologie en monument. (Klok, R.H.J.) Bussum, 1969.
Arc 1.23 Archéologie et civilisation. Paris. 1,1963
Arc 513.18.5 L'archéologie française en Asie Mineure et l'expansion allemande. (Sartiaux, Félix.) Paris, 1918.
Arc 830.40.5 Archéologie gauloise, gallo-romaine, franque et carolingienne. v.1-2, 3-5. (Coutil, Léon.) Paris, 1895-1925. 2v.
Arc 822.3 Pamphlet vol. Archéologie Gauloise. 17 pam.
Arc 822.4 Pamphlet vol. Archéologie Gauloise. 21 pam.
Arc 642.2.15 L'archéologie grecque. (Collignon, Maxime.) Paris, n.d.
Arc 830.6.8 Archéologie lyonnaise. (Niepce, L.) Lyon, n.d.
Arc 543.135 L'archéologie moue de Dváravati. (Dupont, P.) Paris, 1959. 2v.
Arc 404.4 L'archéologie mystérieuse. (Touchard, Michel C.) Paris, 1972.
Arc 1088.1.6 Archéologie navale. (Jal, A.) Paris, 1840. 2v.
Arc 386.2 L'archéologie préhistorique. (Baye, J. de.) Paris, 1888.
Arc 1018.38 Archéologie religieuse. v.1-2. (Bruyn, H. de.) Bruxelles, 1869.
Arc 273.20 Archeologische monumenten in Nederland. Bussum. 1,1971+
Arc 822.01 Pamphlet box. Archeology. France.
Arc 822 Pamphlet box. Archeology. France.
Arc 722.5 Pamphlet box. Archeology. Italy.
Arc 1093.4 Architectur und Ornamentik der antiken Sarkophage. (Altmann, W.) Berlin, 1902.
NEDL Arc 1668.1 Architectura numismatica. (Donaldson, T.L.) London, 1859.
Arc 125.12 Architectural and Archaeological Society of Durham and Northumberland. Transactions. Gateshead on Tyne. 1-10,1862-1953 9v.
X Cg Arc 435.2.32F The architectural antiquities of northern Gujarat. (Burgess, James.) London, 1903.
Arc 435.2.32.1 The architectural antiquities of northern Gujarat. 1. Indian ed. (Burgess, James.) Varanasi, 1975.
Arc 855.6 Architectural sketches in Scotland - Kintyre. (White, T.P.) Edinburgh, 1873.
Arc 855.6.2 Architectural sketches in Scotland - Knapdale. (White, T.P.) Edinburgh, 1875.
Arc 855.203 Architectural survey of Herefordshire. (Bevan, J.O.) Westminster, 1896. 2 pam.
Arc 746.25F Architectural terracottas from Etrusco-Italic temples. (Andrèn, A.) Leipzig, 1939-40. 2v.
Arc 495.204.2 Architecture and other arts. (Butler, H.C.) N.Y., 1903.
Arc 435.22 Architecture and sculpture in Mysore. v.2. (Narasimhachar, R.) Bangalore, 1919.
Arc 66.1.199 L'architecture de l'Argolide aux IV et IIIe siècles avant J.-C. (Roux, Georges.) Paris, 1961. 2v.
Arc 66.1.157 L'architecture hellénique et hellenistique a Délos. (Vallois, René.) Paris, 1944-53. 2v.
Arc 845.211F Architekten und Ingenieur-Verein für Niederrhein und Westfalen, Cologne. Cölner Thorburgen und Befestigungen, 1180-1882. Cöln, 1883.
Arc 625.2PF Architektonische Studien. (Ivanoff, S.A.) Berlin, 1892-95. 4v.
Arc 625.2 Architektonische Studien. (Ivanoff, S.A.) Berlin, 1892-95. 3v.
Arc 726.59.5 Architettura dei templi magalitici di Malta. (Ceschi, Carlo.) Roma, 1939.
Arc 595.67F L'architturra delle piramidi menfite. v.2-7; plates. (Maragioglio, Vito.) Torino, 1963- 9v.
Arc 30.18 Archiv für ägyptische Archäologie. Wien. 1,1938
Arc 1185.1.5 Archiv für Diplomatik, Schriftgeschichte, Siegel- und Wappenkunde. Münster. 1,1955+ 14v.
Arc 1300.4 Archiv für Medaillen- und Plaketten-Kunde. Halle an der Saale. 1-5,1913-1926 3v.
Arc 1125.5 Archiv für Urkundenforschung. Leipzig. 1-18,1907-1944 14v.
Arc 1125.3 Archivalische Zeitschrift. Stuttgart. 1876+ 47v.
Arc 1125.3.10 Archivalische Zeitschrift. Beiheft. Stuttgart. 1-4,1925-1932 4v.
Arc 66.1.32 Les archives...à Malte. (Delaville Le Roulx, J.) Paris, 1883.
Arc 66.1.46 Archives angevines de Naples. (Durrieu, P.) Paris, 1886-1887. 2v.
Arc 66.1.80 Les archives de la chambre apostolique XIVe siècle. (Loye, J. de.) Paris, 1899.
Arc 66.1.49 Archives de l'intendance sacrée à Délos. (Homolle, T.) Paris, 1887.
Arc 1.10 Archives des missions scientifiques. (France. Ministre de l'Instruction Publique et des Beaux Arts.) Paris. 1-31 30v.
Arc 1185.30 L'archiviste françois. 2. éd. (Battheney.) Paris, 1775.
Arc 94.18 Archivo español de arqueología. Madrid. 14,1940+ 18v.
Arc 720.207 L'arco antico di Susa. (Massazza, P.A.) Torino, 1750.
Arc 1027.30.19 Arcosolio dipinto del cimitero di Ciriaca. (Rossi, G.B. de.) Roma, 1876.
Arc 1033.12.243 The Ardagh chalice. (Gogan, L.S.) Dublin, 1932.
Arc 405.1.40F Ardashev, Nikolai N. Grat A.S. Uvarov, kak teoretik arkheologii. Moskva, 1911.
Arc 385.6 Ardusin, D.A. Arkheologicheskie razvedki i rashopki. Moskva, 1959.
Arc 1027.41.15 L'area di Lucina sulla via Ostiense. (Stevenson, H.) Roma, 1898.
Arc 785.68 L'"area sacra" ed i templi repubblicani del Largo Argentina. (Marchetti-Longhi, G.) Roma, 1930.
Arc 606.1 Areika. (Randall-MacIver, David.) Oxford, 1909.
Arc 726.110 L'arena di Verona. (Lenotti, T.) Verona, 1954.
Arc 830.22.5 Les arènes de Lutèce. (Bournon, Fernand.) Paris, 1908.
Arc 830.22 Les arènes de Lutèce. (Du Seigneur, M.) Paris, 1886.
Arc 830.180 Les Arenes de Saints en 1882. (Letelié, J.A.) Pons, 1883.
Arc 830.21 Les arènes de Vesontio. (Castan, Auguste.) Besançon, 1886.
Arc 1200.24 Die Arengen der Papsturkunden nach ihrer Bedeutung und Verwendung bis zu Gregor VII. Inaug. Diss. (Kopczynski, M.) Bottrop, 1936.
Arc 1163.18 Arens, Fritz V. Mainzer Inschriften. Stuttgart, 1945.
Arc 95.3 Arethuse. Paris. 1-8,1923-1931 5v.
Arc 1485.8 Argelati, P. De monetis italiae variorum illustrium virorum. Mediolani, 1750. 6v.
Arc 1468.38 L'argent grec l'empire achémenide. Thèse. (Schlumberger, P.) Paris, 1953.
Arc 726.11.5 L'argenterie et les bijoux d'or du trésor de Boscoreale. (Héron de Villefosse, Antoine.) Paris, 1903.
Arc 670.4.5F The Argive Heraeum. (Walston, Charles.) Boston, 1902-05. 2v.
Arc 302.28 Argo; informativno glasilo za antiko. Ljubljana. 4,1965+
Arc 65.3.10F Argolis. (Archäologisches Institut des Deutschen Reichs-Athenische Zweiganstalt.) Athens.

Author and Title Listing

Arc 303.67 Arheologie Moldovei. (Academia...Bucharest. Academie Republicii Socialiste România.) Bucureşti. 2,1964+ 4v.
Arc 936.215 Arheologija i istorija varvarske kolonizacije juzroslov. oblasti. (Kovačević, J.) Novi Sad, 1960.
Arc 936.225.30 Arheološka najdišča Slovenije. Ljubljana, 1975.
Arc 936.220F Arheološka nalazišta u Srbiji. (Garašanin, Milutin V.) Beograd, 1951.
Arc 302.36 Arheoloski muzej zbornik. (Skopje, Yugoslavia.) 1955+ 2v.
Arc 936.220.3 Arheološki nalazi u Jugoslaviji. (Garašanin, Milutin V.) Beograd, 1966.
Arc 302.32 Arheološki pregled. Beograd. 7,1965+ 4v.
Arc 302.30 Arheološki vestnik. Ljubljana. 2+ 15v.
Arc 302.33 Arheološko Društvo Jugoslaviji. Materijali. Beograd. 3,1966+ 2v.
Arc 385.20 Arias, Paolo Enrico. Storia dell'archeologia. Milano, 1967.
Arc 1163.5.30 Arif, Aida S. Arabic lapidary Kūfic in Africa. London, 1967.
Arc 530.135F Arik, Remri Ogur. Ankara-Konya. Ankara, 1956.
Arc 530.135.10 Arik, Remri Ogur. Turk muzeciliéine bir bakis. Istanbul, 1953.
Arc 530.178F Arik, Remri Ogur. Türk Tarih kurumu tarafindan yapilan Alaca noyük nafriyoti. Ankara, 1937.
Arc 530.135.5 Arik, Remri Ogur. Turkiye de 1936 yelendaki arkeoloji isleri. Istanbul, 1938.
Arc 530.65.20 Arin-berd. Erevan, 1961.
Arc 687.1.10 Arkaelogens Rhodos. (Dietz, Søren.) København, 1974.
Arc 895.79 Arkaeologisk ABC. Handbog i dansk forhistorie. København, 1972.
Arc 608.17.30F Arkell, A.J. Wanyanga. London, 1964.
Arc 383.43F Arkeologiska forskningar och fynd. (Svenska arkeologiska samfundet.) Stockholm, 1952.
Arc 895.40 Arkeologiska studier tillägnade H.K.H. kronprins Gustaf Adrolf. (Swenska Farnminnesföreningen.) Stockholm, 1932.
Arc 513.26 Arkeoloji arastirmalari. (Akurgal, E.) Ankara, 1945.
Arc 530.168 Arkeoloji arasturmalari. (Ankara. Universite Enstitusu.) Istanbul, 1941.
Arc 275.30 Arkheograficheskii ezhegodnik. Moskva. 1957+ 17v.
Arc 925.50.3 Arkheolochichni pam"iatky Ukrains'koi RSR. Kyïv, 1966.
Arc 543.95 Arkheologi rasskazy-vaiut. (Akademiia nauk Tazhikskoi SSSR, Stalinabad. Institut Istorii, Arkheologii i Etnografii. Sektor Arkheologi i Numizmatiki.) Stalinabad, 1959.
Arc 289.10.5 Arkheologicheshie issledovaniia na Ukraine; informatsionnye soobshcheniia. Kiev. 1,1965+ 2v.
Arc 925.150.35 Arkheologicheskaia karta Belorussii. Minsk, 1968- 2v.
Arc 925.50.285F Arkheologicheskaia karta Kievskoi gubernii. (Antonovich, V.B.) Moskva, 1895.
Arc 936.165.50 Arkheologicheskaia karta Moldavskoi SSR. Kishinev, 1973- 5v.
Arc 925.12.10 Arkheologicheskaia tipografiia tapanskago poluostrova. pts. 1-9. (Gerts, K.K.) Sankt Peterburg, 1898-1901. 8v.
Arc 936.140.45 Arkheologicheski otkritiia v Bulgariia. Sofiia, 1957.
Arc 923.80 Arkheologicheskie ekspechtsii gosudarstvennoi akademii istorii material'noi kul'tury instituta arkheologii Akademii nauk SSSR. (Akademiia Nauk SSSR. Institut Arkheologii.) Moskva, 1962.
Arc 543.146.40 Arkheologicheskie i arkhitekturnye pamiatniki Serakhskogo oazisa. (Arazov, O.) Ashkhabad, 1973.
Arc 925.9.30 Arkheologicheskie i etnograficheskie razyskaniia v Ingushetii v 1925-32 gg. (Semenov, L.P.) Groznyi, 1963.
Arc 543.65 Arkheologicheskie i numzmaticheskie kollektsii. (Akademiia nauk Tadzhikskoi SSSR, Stalinabad. Institut Istorii, Arkheologii i Etnografii.) Stalinabad, 1956.
Arc 923.123.1 Arkheologicheskie issledovaniia na iuge Vostochnoi Evropy. Photoreproduction. Moskva, 1974.
Arc 925.50.155 Arkheologicheskie issledovaniia srednevekovogo Kryma. Kiev, 1968.
Arc 925.321.15 Arkheologicheskie issledovaniia v Karelii. Leningrad, 1972.
Arc 303.70 Arkheologicheskie issledovaniia v Moldavii. Kishinev. 1968+
Arc 493.6.40 Arkheologicheskie issledoveniia v Azerbaidzhane. (Akademiia Nauk Azerbaidzhanskoi SSR, Baku. Institut Istorii.) Baku, 1965.
Arc 923.85 Arkheologicheskie materialy v ekspozitsii kraevedcheskikh muzeev. v.2. (Rabinovich, M.G.) Moskva, 1961.
Arc 275.50 Arkheologicheskie otkrytiia. Moskva. 1965+ 6v.
Arc 403.17 Arkheologicheskie pamiatniki. (Sukhov, P.A.) Moskva, 1941.
Arc 936.155.10 Arkheologicheskie pamiatniki Batkena i Liailiaka, Jugo-Zapadnaia Kirgiziia. (Baruzdin, J.D.) Frunze, 1962.
Arc 925.322.5 Arkheologicheskie pamiatniki Dagestana. (Isakov, Magomed I.) Makhachkala, 1966.
Arc 300.5 Arkheologicheskie pamiatniki iuzhnykh raionov osnskoi oblasti. (Zadneprovskii, I.A.) Frunze, 1960.
Arc 303.65 Arkheologicheskie pamiatniki Moldavii. Kishinev. 1,1967+
Arc 925.175 Arkheologicheskie pamiatniki na territorii Mariiskoi ASSR. (Smipnov, A.P.) Kozmodem'iansk, 1949-
Arc 925.337.15 Arkheologicheskie pamiatniki Nizhnego Podon'ia. Moskva. 1,1974+
Arc 925.140 Arkheologicheskie pamiatniki Sverdlovska i ego obrestnostei. (Bers, E.M.) Sverdlovsk, 1954.
Arc 925.140.2 Arkheologicheskie pamiatniki Sverdlovska i ego obrestnostei. 2. izd. (Bers, E.M.) Sverdlovsk, 1963.
Arc 936.155.15 Arkheologicheskie pamiatniki Talasskoi dolny. (Akademiia Nauk Kirgizskoi SSR, Frunze. Institut Istorii.) Frunze, 1963.
Arc 925.260 Arkheologicheskie pamiatniki u sela Rozhdestveno. (Kazan, Russia (City). Universitet.) Kazan, 1962.
Arc 925.290 Arkheologicheskie pamiatniki Udmurtii. (Gening, V.F.) Izhevsk, 1958.
Arc 925.331.5 Arkheologicheskie pamiatniki Vychegodskoi doliny. (Burov, Grigorii M.) Syktyvkar, 1967.
Arc 925.4.55 Arkheologicheskie pamiatniki zapadnogo zabaikal'ia. (Khamzina, Evgeniia A.) Ulan-Ude, 1970.
Arc 923.75.5 Arkheologicheskie puteshestviia. (Formazov, Aleksandr A.) Moskva, 1974.
Arc 543.3.80 Arkheologicheskie raboty muzeia v Srednei Azii. (Staviskii, Boris Ia.) Moskva, 1969.
Arc 543.65.20 Arkheologicheskie raboty v Tadzhikistane. (Akademiia nauk Tadzhikskoi SSSR, Dushambe. Institut Istorii, Arkheologii i Etnografii.) Stalinabad. 10,1970+
Arc 925.50.47 Arkheologicheskie raskopki na Donu. v.2, photoreproduction. (Rostov on the Don (Province). Muzei Kraevedeniia.) Rostov na Donu, 1962- 2v.
Arc 530.96 Arkheologicheskie raskopki v srevnegruziiskoi storitse Mtskheta. (Lomatidze, C.A.) Tbilisi, 1955.
Arc 385.6 Arkheologicheskie razvedki i rashopki. (Ardusin, D.A.) Moskva, 1959.
Arc 628.19 Arkheologicheskie trudy. v.1-3. (Olenin', A.N.) Sankt Peterburg, 1877-82.
Arc 543.125 Arkheologicheskii dnevnik poezdki v Sredniuiu Mongoliiu v 1891 godu. (Klements, D.A.) Sankt Peterburg, 1895.
Arc 925.25 Arkheologicheskii razvedki. (Spitsyn, A.) St. Peterburg, 1908.
Arc 925.16.10 Arkheologicheskii sbornik. (Rubinshtein, N.L.) Moskva, 1947.
Arc 275.35 Arkheologicheskii sbornik. Leningrad. 4-8 2v.
Arc 923.70 Arkheologicheskii sbornik. Moskva, 1960.
Arc 923.115 Arkheologicheskii sbornik. Moskva, 1966.
Arc 275.40 Arkheologicheskii sbornik. Ulan-Ude.
Arc 923.125 Arkheologicheskii sbornik. Photoreproduction. Moskva, 1953.
Arc 923.108 Arkheologicheskii sbornik trudy. (Vsesoiuznaia Arkheologicheskaia Studencheskaia Konferentsiia, 8th, Leningrad, 1962.) Leningrad, 1964.
Arc 275.16 Arkheologicheskii s"ezd, 8th, Moscow, 1890. Katalog vystavki VIII Arkheologicheskago s"ezda v Moskve, 1890 g. Pt.1-10. Moskva, 1890.
Arc 275.17 Arkheologicheskii s"ezd, 16th, Pskov, 1915. Katalog vystaki. Pskov, 1915.
Arc 275.10F Arkheologicheskii s"ezd. Trud'y. 1869-1911 28v.
Arc 275.20 Pamphlet box. Arkheologicheskii s"ezd. Russian archeological congresses.
Arc 530.22F Arkheologicheskiia ekspeditsiia 1916 g. (Marr, H.) Sankt Peterburg, 1922.
Arc 287.5 Arkheologicheskiia izvestiia i zametki. (Moskovskoe Arkheologicheskoe Obshchestvo.) Moskva. 2-7,1894-1900 7v.
Arc 302.21 Arkheologichesko Druzhestvo, Sofia. Izvestiia.
Arc 495.206F Arkheologicheskoe puteshestvie in Sirii. (Kondakov, N.P.) Sankt Peterburg, 1904.
Arc 936.165.20 Arkheologiia, etnografiia i iskusstvovedenie Moldavii. Kishinev, 1968.
Arc 925.150.10 Arkheologiia Belorussii. (Zagorul'ski, Edward M.) Minsk, 1965.
Arc 385.15 Arkheologiia i estestvennye nauki. (Kolchin, B.A.) Moskva, 1965.
Arc 275.45 Arkheologiia i ethnografiia Bashkirii. Ufa. 1,1962+ 5v.
Arc 275.65 Arkheologiia i etnografiia Tatarii. Kazan. 1,1971+
Arc 397.22 Arkheologiia i sovremennost'. (Mongait, A.L.) Moskva, 1963.
Arc 936.14.305 Arkheologiia Pol'ski. (Kukharenko, I.V.) Moskva, 1969.
Arc 923.25F Arkheologiia Rossii. (Uvarob, A.S.) Moskva, 1881. 2v.
Arc 936.20.60 Arkheologiia Rumynii. (Fedorov, Georgii B.) Moskva, 1973.
Arc 923.116 Arkheologiia SSSR. (Avdusin, Daniil A.) Moskva, 1967.
Arc 923.131 Arkheologiia SSSR. (Martynov, Anatolii I.) Moskva, 1973.
Arc 384.3 Arkheologiia starogo i novogo sveta. Moskva, 1966.
Arc 923.55 Arkheologiia v SSSR. (Miller, M.A.) Miunchen, 1954.
Arc 925.110 Arkheologiia v SSSR. (Mongait, A.L.) Moskva, 1955.
Arc 612.90 Arkheologiia Zapadnoi Evropy. (Mongait, Aleksandr L.) Moskva, 1973- 2v.
Arc 936.105 Arkheologika slomenichi i malazishta u Srbiji. v.1-2. (Srpska Akademia Nauka Belgrade. Arkheol. Institut.) Beograd, 1953.
Arc 275.55 Arkheologo-ethnograficheskii sbornik. Groznyi. 3,1969+
Arc 925.50.25 Arkheolohichni doslidzheniia na Ukraini 1917-1957. (Shovkoplias, Ivan H.) Kyïv, 1957.
Arc 275.60 Arkheolohiia. Kyiv. 1971+
Arc 925.50.230 Arkheolohiia Ukrains'koi RSR. Kyïv, 1971. 2v.
Arc 925.50.80 Arkheolohiia Ukraïny. (Pasternak, I.) Toronto, 1961.
Arc 925.175.10 Arkhipov, Gennadii A. Mariitsy IX-XI vv. Ioshkar-Ola, 1973.
Arc 923.7 Arkhivnye kursy. pt.1-3. Sankt Petersburg, 1920.
Arc 830.15.13 Arles. (Constans, L.A.) Paris, 1928.
Arc 66.1.119 Arles antique. (Constans, L.A.) Paris, 1921.
Arc 830.15.15 Arles antique. (Véran, Auguste.) Tours, 1876.
Arc 830.15.9 Arles antique. Thèse. (Constans, L.A.) Paris, 1921.
Arc 830.15.5 Arles gallo-romain. Guide du touriste archéologue. (Bazin, H.) Paris, 1896.
Arc 595.33.5 Armageddon has come; the climax of the ages is near. 2. ed. (Haberman, F.) St. Petersburg, 1940.
Arc 1020.9.153 Armailhacq. L'eglise nationale de Saint Louis des Français à Rome. Rome, 1894.
Arc 1675.2 Armand, A. Les médailleurs italiens. Paris, 1879.
Arc 1675.3 Armand, A. Les médailleurs italiens. v.1-2. 2. éd. Paris, 1883.
Arc 1025.30 Armellini, M. Gli antichi cimiteri cristiani di Roma e d'Italia. Roma, 1893.
Arc 1027.9 Armellini, M. Le catacombe e il protestantesimo. Roma, 1875.
Arc 1025.30.5 Armellini, M. Le catacombe romane. Roma, 1880.
Arc 1027.37 Armellini, M. I cemeteri cristiano della via latina. Roma, 1874.
Arc 1027.35 Armellini, M. Il cimiterio di S. Agnese sulla via nomentana. Roma, 1880.
Arc 1027.12.17 Armellini, M. D'una transl...SS. Pietro e Paolo in...le catacombe. Roma, 1874.
Arc 1018.6 Armellini, M. Lezioni di archaeologici cristiana. Roma, 1898.
Arc 1018.6.3 Armellini, M. Lezioni popolari di archaeologici cristiana. Roma, 1903.
Arc 1020.9.35 Armellini, M. Notizie istoriche...Domine Quo Vadis. Roma, 1874.
Arc 1027.40 Armellini, M. Scoperta...cripta S. Emerenziana...cimiteri Ostriano. Roma, 1877.
Arc 1027.39 Armellini, M. Scoperta d'un graffito storico...cimiteri di Pretestato. Roma, 1874.
Arc 1033.70 Armellini, M. Scoperta d'una pittura nel Laterno. Roma, 1880.
Arc 1015.216 Armellini, M.J. Vetri cristiani della collezione di Campo-Santo. n.p., n.d.
Arc 1033.30 Armellini, Mariano. Scoperta della cripta di Santa Emerenziana e di una memoria relativa alla cattedra di San Pietro. Roma, 1877.
Arc 66.1.117 L'arménie entre Byzance et l'Islam. (Laurent, J.) Paris, 1919.
Arc 530.65.15 Armeniia v epokhu bronzy i rannego zheleza. (Martirosian, A.) Erevan, 1964.
Arc 858.8 Armitage, E.S. Key to English antiquities. Sheffield, 1897.

Arc 1500.23 Armorial du jetonophile. (Florange, J.) Paris, 1907. 2v.

Arc 1500.52 Armorican art. (Rybat, N.V.L.) Jersey, 1952.

Arc 920.4 Armtiunov, Sergei A. Drevnie kul'tury aziatskikh eskimosov. Moskva, 1969.

Arc 1033.12.87 Arnason, H. The history of the chalice of Antioch. n.p., 1941.

Arc 895.23.10F Arne, T.J. Das Bootgräberfeld von Tuna in Alsike, Uppland. Stockholm, 1934.

Arc 1033.21 Arnellini, M. Scoperta oratorio presso Via Appia. Roma, 1875.

Arc 853.140F Das Arnenfeld von Kelheim. (Müller-Karpe, H.) Kallmünz, 1954.

Arc 1468.3 Arneth, J. Synopsis numorum Graecorum. Vienna, 1837.

Arc 1663.11 Arnold, H.P. The evolution of the Boston medal. Boston, 1901.

Arc 1190.2 Aronius, J. Diplomatische Studien über die älteren angelsächischen Urkunden. Inaug. Diss. Königsberg, 1883.

Arc 838.2 La arqueologia de España. (Hübner, E.) Barcelona, 1888.

Arc 843.60 Arqueología romana y visigotica de extremadura. (Monsalad, M.C.S.G.) Madrid, 1900.

Arc 838.9.10 Arqueológica española. 2. ed. (Mélida, José R.) Barcelona, 1942.

Arc 1663.22 An arrangement of medals and tokens struck in honor of the presidents of the United States. (Satterlee, Alfred H.) N.Y., 1862.

Arc 1538.13 An arrangement of provincial coins...Great Britain, Ireland. (Conder, James.) Ipswich, 1799.

Arc 1680.2 An arrangement of tradesmen's cards, political tokens; also election medals. (Bushnell, C.I.) N.Y., 1858.

Arc 726.341 Arrigo, Agatino d'. Premessa geofisica alla ricerca di Sibari. Napoli, 1959.

Arc 830.114 L'arrondissement d'Uzès avant l'histoire. (Raymond, Paul.) Paris, 1900.

Arc 1458.21.5 Ars Classica, Geneva. Monnaies antiques grecques, romaines, byzantines. Genève, 1930.

Arc 1458.21 Ars Classica, Geneva. Monnaies antiques grecques et romaines. Genève, 1933.

Arc 1468.53 Ars Classica, Geneva. Monnaies grecques. Genève, 1929.

Arc 1428.30 Arsaciden-Münzen. (Petrowicz, A. von.) Wien, 1904.

Arc 935.29 Arsameia am Nymphaios. (Dörner, Friedrich K.) Berlin, 1963.

Arc 1.1.8 Art and archaeology. Baltimore. 1-35,1914-1934 20v.

Arc 485.200 L'art antique de la Perse. (Dieulafoy, M.) Paris, 1884-89. 5v.

Arc 830.285F L'art de l'époque du Renne en France. (Zervos, Christian.) Paris, 1959.

Arc 672.1.63 L'art égéen. (Charbonneaux, J.) Paris, 1929.

Arc 823.35 Art gallo-romain et sculpture romane. (Durand-Lefebvre, M.) Paris, 1937.

Arc 823.35.5 Art gallo-romain et sculpture romane. Thèse. (Durand-Lefebvre, M.) Paris, 1937.

Arc 1500.53F L'art gaulais dans les médailles. (Lengyel, L.) Montrange-Seine, 1954.

Arc 1348.55 Art in coinage. (Sutherland, C.H.V.) London, 1955.

Arc 1348.55.2 Art in coinage. (Sutherland, C.H.V.) N.Y., 1956.

Arc 953.14 Art in shell of ancient Americans. (Holmes, William H.) Washington, 1880-81.

Arc 543.7.50 L'art khmèr primitif. (Parmentier, H.) Paris, 1927. 2v.

Arc 1433.80 L'art monétaire des royaumes bactriens. (Allouche-Le Page, M.T.) Paris, 1956.

Arc 552.2 L'art monumental des Égyptiens et des Assyriens. (Cloquet, L.) n.p., n.d.

Arc 432.3 L'art munumental des Indous et des Perses. (Cloquet, L.) Bruxelles, 1896.

NEDL Arc 1088.1.10 L'art nautique dans l'antiquité. (Vars, J.) Paris, 1887.

Arc 545.231 The art of ancient Egypt. (Burlington Five Arts Club, London.) London, 1895.

Arc 1675.58 The art of the medal. (Brenner, V.D.) N.Y., 1910.

Arc 925.12.3 The art of the northern nomads. (Minns, E.H.) London, 1942.

Arc 830.122F L'art pendant l'âge du Renne. (Piette, Édouard.) Paris, 1907.

Arc 505.71 L'art phénicien du IIe millenaire. (Dussaud, René.) Paris, 1949.

X Cg Arc 823.30 L'art pré-roman. (Hubert, J.) Paris, 1938.

Arc 612.34 L'art préhistorique. (Laming, A.) Paris, 1951.

Arc 303.18.20F Arta si arheologia; revistă. Bucureşti. 1-12,1927-1936

Arc 1558.6.14 Artalsförtecknia over soenskamynt med varderingspriser. (Glück, Harry.) Stockholm, 1968.

Arc 925.337.5 Artamonov, Mikhail I. Srednevekovye poseleniia na Nizhnem Donu. Leningrad, 1935.

Arc 1480.31F Artaud, F. Discours sur les médailles d'Auguste et de Tibère. Lyon, 1818.

Arc 1025.59 Artaud de Montor, A.F. Voyages dans les catacombes de Rome. Paris, 1810.

Arc 1033.25 L'arte cristiana nello studio della storia della chiesa. (Taglialatela, G.) Napoli, 1901.

Arc 1300.8 Arte e moneta. Roma. 3

Arc 843.147 El arte rupestre en España. (Cabre-Aguilo, Juan.) Madrid, 1915.

Arc 838.30 Los artes y los pueblos de la España primitiva. (Camon Aznar, J.) Madrid, 1954.

Arc 1348.30 Articles on numismatics. (Sbōronos, I.N.) Athenes, 1898-1903. 16 pam.

Arc 900.2.5F Articles on the palace of Diocletian in Spalato. (Austria. Zentral Kommission für Enforschung und Erhaltung der Kunst- und Historischen Denkmäle in Wien.) Wien? 1903.

Arc 1033.12.185 Articolo sulla corona ferrea...dal Geornale. Venezia, 1821.

Arc 968.2.50 The artifacts of Pecas. (Kidder, Alfred V.) New Haven, 1932.

Arc 785.13.51 Artioli, Romolo. The Roman Forum. Rome, 19- .

Arc 855.3 Artis, E.T. The Durobrivae of Antoninus. London, 1828.

Arc 397.13 Les artistes préhistoriques. (Morin, Jean.) Paris, 1933.

Arc 66.1.4 Arts à la cour des papes. (Muentz, E.) Paris, 1878-82. 3v.

Arc 543.2.5 The arts and civilization of Angkor. (Groslier, Bernard P.) N.Y., 1957.

Arc 848.19 The arts and crafts of our Teutonic forefathers. (Brown, Gerard Baldwin.) London, 1910.

Arc 416.17F Arts antiques de l'Asie occidentale. (Rozanthal, A.) Nice, 1948.

Arc 820.204 Les arts industriels. (Barrière-Flavy, Casimir.) Paris, 1901. 3v.

Arc 600.191 The arts of ancient Egypt. (Petrie, W.M.F.) London, 1884.

Arc 385.3.5 Artsikhovshii, A.V. Vvedenie v arkheologiiu. 3. izd. Moskva, 1947.

Arc 923.37 Artsikhovskii, A.V. Osnovy arkheologii. Moskva, 1954.

Arc 923.37.5 Artsikhovskii, A.V. Osnovy arkheologii. Izd. 2. Moskva, 1955.

Arc 1588.6 Artuk, Ibrah. Fatik sikke re madalyalari. Istanbul, 1946.

Arc 1588.6.1 Artuk, Ibrah. Konuni Sultan Suleymon adena basilon sikkeler. Ankara, 1972.

Arc 1433.73 Artuk, S. Demýhoci definesi. Ankara, 1966.

Arc 1433.73.5 Artuk, S. Istanbul arkeoloji murelen teşhirdeki islami sikkeler kotalogu. Istanbul, 1970. 2v.

Arc 513.11.1 Arundell, F.V.J. Discoveries in Asia Minor. v.1-2. Hildesheim, 1975.

Arc 513.11 Arundell, F.V.J. Discoveries in Asia Minor. v.2, photoreproduction. London, 1834. 2v.

Arc 530.22.15 Arutiunian, Nikolai V. Zemledelic i skotovodstvo Urartu. Erevan, 1964.

Arc 935.31 Arutiunian, Varazdat. Gorod Ani. Erevan, 1964.

Arc 689.3 Arvanitopoulas, A.S. Thessalika Mnēmeia. Athēnai, 1909.

Arc 407.10.20 As I seem to remember. (Woolley, Charles L.) London, 1962.

Arc 960.2.15F As to Cooper from the mounds of the St. John's River, Florida. (Moore, C.B.) Philadelphia, 1894.

Arc 66.1.23 L'asclépicion d'Athènes. (Girard, P.) Paris, 1881.

Arc 843.233 El asentamiento cántabra de Celada Marlantes. (García Guinea, Miguel Angel.) Santander, 1970.

Arc 861.203 Ashbee, Paul. Ancient Scilly from the first farmers to the early Christians. Newton Abbot, 1974.

Arc 870.10.15 Ashbee, Paul. The bronze age round barrow in Britain. London, 1960.

Arc 870.10.20 Ashbee, Paul. The earthen long barrow in Britain. Toronto, 1970.

Arc 785.6.19 Ashby, T. The aqueducts of ancient Rome. Oxford, 1935.

Arc 855.224F Ashby, Thomas. Excavations at Caerwent, Monmouthshire 1901-1903. London, 1902-1904.

Arc 755.3.2 Ashby, Thomas. The Roman campagna in classical times. London, 1970.

Arc 925.12.5 Ashik, Anton. Vosporskoe tsarstvo. Odessa, 1848.

Arc 387.40 Ashmole, Bernhard. Cyriac of Ancona. London, 1957.

Arc 450.34 Ashmound excavations at Kupgal. 1. ed. (Mujumdar, Ganesh.) Poona, 1966.

Arc 513.4 Asia Minor. (Fellows, C.) London, 1839.

Arc 513.19.5 Asia Minor in ruins. (Ximinez, S.) N.Y., 1925.

Arc 416.5 Asie centrale et Tibet. Missions Pelliot et Bacot, documens exposés au Musée Guimet. Paris, 1921.

Arc 513.16 Asie-Mineure et Syrie. (Gallois, E.) Paris, n.d.

Arc 670.5F Asine; results of the Swedish excavations 1922-1930. (Frödin, Otto.) Stockholm, 1938.

Arc 543.66.60 Askarov, A.A. Sapallitepa. Tashkent, 1973.

Arc 1540.37 Askew, Gilbert. The coinage of Roman Britain. London, 1951.

Arc 493.6.35F Aslanov, G.M. Drevnii Mingechaur. Baku, 1959.

Arc 94.11 Asociación Artistico-Arqueológica Barcelona. Boletin. Barcelona. 1-35,1891-1894

Arc 94.10 Asociación Artistico-Arqueológica Barcelona. Revista. Barcelona. 1-5,1896-1908 5v.

Arc 861.100.25 Aspects of Anglo-Saxon archaeology. (Bruce-Mitford, Rupert Leo.) London, 1974.

Arc 383.14 Aspects of archaeology in Britain and beyond; essays presented to O.G.S. Crawford. (Grimes, W.F.) London, 1951.

Arc 1480.48 Aspects of the principate of Tiberius. (Grant, Michael.) N.Y., 1950.

Arc 938.15F Aspelin, J.R. Antiquités du Nord-Finno-Ougrien. v.1-5. St. Pétersbourg, 1877.

Arc 938.27 Aspelin, Johan R. Suomalais-Ugrilaisen muinaistutkinnon alkeita. Helsingissä, 1875.

Arc 938.27.5 Aspelin, Johan R. Suomen asukkaat pakanuuden aikana. Helsingissä, 1885.

Arc 1663.25 Les assemblées du clergé de France avant 1789. (Florange, Charles.) Paris, 1927.

Arc 94.50 Associação dos Arqueologos Portugueses. Trabalhos. Lisboa. 1-6,1934-1942 6v.

Arc 65.6.10 Association Internationale d'Archéologie Classique. Annuaire. Rome. 2,1956 3v.

Arc 635.208 Association pour l'Encouragement des Études Grècques en France, Paris. Monuments grècs. Paris, 1882-97. 2v.

Arc 93.18 Associazione Archeologica Romana. Bullettino. Roma. 1-7,1911-1917 3v.

Arc 755.4 Associazione artistica fra i cultori di architecttura. La zona monumentale di Roma. Roma, 1910.

Arc 65.6F Associazione Internazionale degli Studi Mediterranei. Bolletino. Roma. 1-6,1930-1936 2v.

Arc 421.6 Astasiatiska bulletin. v.1-30,35-42. (Stockholm.) Stockholm, 1929-58.

Arc 385.2 Astle, Thomas. Observations on stone pillars. London, 1800.

Arc 1138.18 Astle, Thomas. Origin and progress of writing. London, 1803.

Arc 1033.17.101 Astolfi, G.F. Historia universale delle imagini miracolose...Madre di Dio...tutte le parti del Mondo. Venezia, 1623.

Arc 385.21 Aston, Michael. Landscape archaeology. Newton Abbot, Eng., 1974.

Arc 435.2.40F The astronomical observatories of Jai Singh. (Kaye, G.R.) Calcutta, 1918.

Arc 843.181 Astucias. v.1-4. (Vega de la Sella, Ricardo.) Madrid, 1916.

Arc 30.21 Asutosh Museum memoir. (Calcutta. University. Asutosh Museum of Indian Art and Archaeology.)

Arc 925.322 Ataev, Dibir M. Nagornyi Dagestan v rannem srednevekove. Makhachkala, 1963.

Arc 543.146.45 Atagarryev, Egen. Material'naia kul'tura Shekhr-Islama. Ashkhabad, 1973.

Arc 766.3 Les ateliers de sculpture chez les premiers chrétiens. (Le Blant, Edmond.) Rome, 1884.

Arc 708.21 Atene. Brevi cenni sulla città antica e moderna. (Ambrosoli, G.) Milano, 1901.

Arc 30.20 Athar-e-Iran. Paris. 1-4,1936-1949 4v.

Arc 710.15A Athen, Akropolis. (Walter, Otto.) Wien, 1929.

Arc 708.25 Athen. (Petersen, E.) Leipzig, 1908.

Arc 708.20 Athen mit Umgebung (1877). (Maps, Athens.) Berlin, 1881.

Arc 87.1.32 Athena und Marsyas. (Hirschfeld, G.) Berlin, 1872.

Arc 708.11 Athenae Christianae. (Mommsen, A.) Leipzig, 1868.

Arc 708.23.7 Athènes. (Fougères, G.) Paris, 1914.

Arc 708.23.9 Athènes. 4e éd. (Gougères, G.) Paris, 1923.

Arc 705.211F Athènes antique. (Maurras, Charles.) Paris, 1918.

Arc 708.8 Athènes aux XVe, XVIe et XVIIe siècles. (Laborde, L.E.S.J.) Paris, 1854. 2v.
Arc 708.9.9 Athènes d'après le colonel Leake. (Leake, W.M.) Paris, 1876.
Arc 708.23 Athènes et ses environs. (Fougères, G.) Paris, 1906.
Arc 716.4.10 The Athenian Agora. (American School of Classical Studies at Athens.) Princeton, n.d. 18v.
Arc 716.4.20 The Athenian Agora. 2. ed. (American School of Classical Studies at Athens.) Athens, 1962.
Arc 1251.27 Athenian bronze allotment plates. Thesis. (Kroll, John Hennig.) Cambridge, 1972.
Arc 1470.8.5 Athenian coinage, 480-449 B.C. (Starr, Chester.) Oxford, 1970.
Arc 708.18 Atheniensia, or Remarks on the topography and buildings of Athens. (Wilkins, W.) London, 1816.
Arc 708.36 Athens, city of the Gods. (Prokopiou, Angelos G.) N.Y., 1964.
Arc 1465.80F Athens, its history and coinage before the Persian invasion. (Seltman, Charles Theodore.) Cambridge, 1924.
Arc 1465.80.1 Athens; its history and coinage before the Persian invasion. (Seltman, Charles Theodore.) Chicago, 1974.
Arc 66.3 Athens. Bulletin de correspondance hellénique. Paris. 1,1877+ 92v.
Arc 66.3.2 Athens. Bulletin de correspondance hellénique. Table générale. Paris. 1877-1886
Arc 710.01 Pamphlet box. Athens. Acropolis.
Arc 66.3.5 Athens. École française. Bulletin. Athènes. 1-12,1868-1871
Arc 65.12 Athens. École Française. Études chypriotes. Paris. 1-2,1961-1962 2v.
Arc 672.1.55 Athens. École Française. Études crétoises. Paris. 1-19 16v.
Arc 65.9 Athens. École Française. Études péloponnésiennes. Paris. 1-5 5v.
Arc 69.4 Athens. École Française. Études thasiennes. Paris. 1-8 8v.
Arc 1335.76.5 Athens. Ethnikon Nomismatikon Mouseion. Ekthesis • ŏerileōtikē. Athēnai, 1857.
Arc 1335.76.14 Athens. Ethnikon Nomismatikon Mouseion. Karmatia symbolika. Athēnai, 1880.
Arc 1335.76.10F Athens. Ethnikon Nomismatikon Mouseion. Katalogos. Athēnai, 1868.
Arc 1335.76.11F Athens. Ethnikon Nomismatikon Mouseion. Katalogos. Athēnai, 1872.
Arc 1335.76.3 Athens. Ethnikon Nomismatikon Mouseion. Katalogos. Athēnai, 1910.
Arc 1335.76.16 Athens. Ethnikon Nomismatikon Mouseion. Nomismata. Athēnai, 1885.
Arc 1335.76.13F Athens. Ethnikon Nomismatikon Mouseion. Synopsis numorum veterum. Athenes, 1878.
Arc 65.7F Athens. R. Scuola Archeologica Italiana. Annuario. Bergamo. 1,1914+ 18v.
Arc 662.2 Athens and Attica. Journal of a residence there. (Wordsworth, C.) London, 1837.
Arc 708.27 Athens and its monuments. (Weller, C.H.) N.Y., 1913.
Arc 708.27.5 Athens and its monuments. (Weller, C.H.) N.Y., 1924.
Arc 588.19 Athribis. (Petrie, W.M.F.) London, 1908.
Arc 30.16 Atiqot; journal of the Israel Department of Antiquities. Jerusalem. 1+ 4v.
Arc 1540.18 Atkins, James. The coins and tokens of the possessions and colonies of the British empire. London, 1889.
Arc 1680.14 Atkins, James. The tradesmen's tokens of the eighteenth century. London, 1892.
Arc 861.118 Atkinson, Donald. Report on excavations at Wroxeter...1923-1927. Oxford, 1942.
Arc 861.60 Atkinson, Donald. The Romano-British site on Lowbury Hill in Berkshire. Reading, 1916.
Arc 385.10 Atkinson, R.J.C. Archaeology. Cardiff, 1960.
Arc 865.22 Atkinson, R.J.C. Stonehenge. London, 1956.
Arc 861.31.30 Atkinson, Richard J.C. Silbury Hill: background information on the Silbury dig. London, 1968.
Arc 730.2 Atlante. Topografia archaeologica. Siracusa. (Cavallari, F.S.) Palermo, 1883. 2v.
Arc 1488.7 Atlante numismatico italiano. Milano, 1906 (Ambrosoli, Solone.)
Arc 853.276F Atlas der Megalithgräber Deutschlands. Text and atlas. (Sprockhoff, Ernst.) Bonn, 1965-75. 4v.
Arc 1160.12 Atlas der Nederlandsche palaeographie. (Brugmans, H.) 's Gravenhage, 1910.
Arc 1033.118 Atlas géographique et archéologique...Testament. (Ancessi, V.) Paris, 1876.
Arc 925.35.5F Atlas gochevskikh drevnostei. (Samoksavov, D.I.) Moskva, 1915.
Arc 925.9.95PF Atlas k puteshestviiu po Kavkazu i iuzknomu poberezh'iu kaspiskago moria. (Dorn, Boris A.) Sankt Petersburg, 1895. 2v.
Arc 1033.17.102.2 Atlas Marianus sive de imaginibus deiparae. v.1-2. (Gumppenberg, G.) Ingaldeladii, 1657.
Arc 1033.17.102 Atlas Marianus sive de imaginibus deiparae per orbem. (Gumppenberg, G.) Monachii, 1657. 2v.
Arc 820.222F Atlas monumental de la France. (Roussel, Jules.) Paris, 1922.
Arc 628.5 Atlas of classical antiquities. (Schreiber, T.) London, 1895.
Arc 705.201A Atlas von Athen. (Maps, Athens.) Berlin, 1878.
Arc 545.240F Atlas zur altaegyptischen Kulturgeschichte. (Wreszinski, Walter.) Leipzig, 1914. 4v.
Arc 545.240PF Atlas zur altaegyptischen Kulturgeschichte. v.2. (Wreszinski, Walter.) Leipzig, 1939.
Arc 785.13.39 The Atrium Vestae. (Van Deman, E.B.) Washington, 1909.
Arc 1027.14.5 Atti...S. Alessandro I...memorie del suo sepolcro. Roma, 1858.
Arc 93.46F Atti. (Centro Studi e Documentazione sull'Italia Romana.) Milano. 1,1967+ 6v.
Arc 3.3 Atti. (Congresso Internazionale di Preistoria.) Firenze, 1952.
Arc 743.16 Atti. (Congresso Internazionale Etrusco.) Firenze. 1,1928
Arc 743.14 Atti. (Covegno Nazionale Etrusco.) Firenze. 1-2
Arc 723.38 Atti. (Simposia Internazionale di Protostoria Italiana.) Roma, 1969.
Arc 93.7 Atti. (Società Piemontese di Archeologia e Belle Arti.) Torino. 1875-1958 15v.
Arc 1033.16 Atti dei tre santi martiri Sarace, Probo e Andronico. (Cavedoni, C.) Modena, 1839.
Arc 1027.42 Atti del collegium cultorum martyrum. Romae, 1888.
Arc 9.2.6 Atti del Congresso internazionale. (International Congress of Prehistoric and protohistoric Sciences, 6th, Rome, 1962.) Firenze, 1962.
Arc 726.235.5 Atti del Convegno internazionale di studi sulle antichità di classe. (Convegno internazionale di studi sulle antichità di classe.) Ravenna, 1968.
Arc 73.100.5 Atti del II Congresso internazionale...tenuto in Roma nell'aprile 1900. (International Congress of Christian Archaeology, 2nd, Rome, 1900.) Roma, 1902.
Arc 1470.87 Atti del IIo Convegno del Centro internazionale di studi numismatici. (Centro Internazionale di Studi Numismatici.) Roma, 1971.
Arc 1033.40 Gli atti del martirio...S. Cecilia. (Bartolini, D.) Roma, 1867.
Arc 1016.223 Atti del martiro della S. Agnese. (Bartolini, D.) Roma, 1858.
Arc 3.1.27 Atti del settimo Congresso internazionale di archeologia classica. (Congrès Internatonal d'Archéologie Classique, 7th, Rome and Naples, 1958.) Roma, 1961. 3v.
Arc 67.5 Atti del 1 congresso nazionale di archealogia cristiana. (Congresso Nazionale di Archealogia Cristiana.) Roma, 1952.
Arc 1033.18.5 Gli atti della Passione degli ss. Abdon e Sennen. (Bartolini, A.) Roma, 1859.
Arc 723.34 Atti della VII riunione scientifica. (Istituto Italiano di Preistoria e Protostoria.) Firenze, 1963.
Arc 723.34.5 Atti della XI e XII riunione scientifica. (Istituto Italiano di Preistoria e Protostoria.) Firenze, 1968.
Arc 1308.2 Atti e memorie. (Istituto Italiano di Numismatica, Rome.) Roma. 1-4,1913-1921 2v.
Arc 1033.107 Gli atti più antichi del martirio di S. Felice. (Fratini, G.) Foligno, 1881.
Arc 716.12A An Attic cemetery. (Karo, G.H.) Philadelphia, 1943.
Arc 670.3.10 Attika. (Wrede, W.) Athens, 1934.
Arc 830.13.10 Die Attika an römischen Triumphbogen...Bogens von Orange. (Grube, G.) Karlsruhe-Baden, 1931.
Arc 87.1.55 Eine attische Lekythos. (Winter, F.) Berlin, 1895.
Arc 1468.18 Attischen Münzen des neueren Stiles. (Sundwall, J.) Helsingfors, 1907.
Arc 1558.5 Atto samla numismatica. (Nathorst-Böös, E.) Stockholm, 1958.
Arc 1018.64 Die Attribute der Heiligen, alphabetisch Geordnet. Hannover, 1843.
Arc 66.1.215 Au musée de Délos. (Marcadé, Jean.) Paris, 1969.
Arc 66.1.138 Au musée de Delphes. (La Coste-Messelière, P. de.) Paris, 1936.
Arc 673.1.15 Au musée de Delphes. Thèse. (Frotier de la Coste Messelière, P.) Paris, 1936.
Arc 712.3 Au Parthénon. (Ronchaud, L. de.) Paris, 1886.
Arc 823.25 Au seuil de notre histoire. (Jullian, C.) Paris, 1930-1931. 3v.
Arc 1033.165 Aubé, Benjamin. Polyeucte dans l'histoire. Paris, 1882.
Arc 396.8 Aubert, M. Notice nécrologique sur le comte Robert de Lesteyrie du Saillant, 1849-1919. Paris, 1926.
Arc 755.6 Aucler, Paul. Rome; restauration archéologique. Paris, 1899.
Arc 1330.5F Auction catalogue. (American Numismatic Society.) Boston, 1962.
Arc 1613.20 Auction prices: "United States coins." 3. ed. (Johnson, J.B.) Cincinnati, 1944.
Arc 1335.101 Auctions-Catalog der bedeutenden Sammlung römischer und byzantinischer Münzen. (Hirsch, Jacob.) München, 1907.
Arc 1468.16.2 Auctions-Catalog XIV, XV. Greek and Roman coins. (Hirsch, F.) München, 1905-06.
Arc 1468.16 Auctions-Katalog XIII. (Hirsch, F.) München, 1905.
Arc 830.181.2 Audiat, L. Le capitole de Saintes. Paris, 1881.
Arc 830.364 Audiat, Louis. Fouilles dans les remparts gallo-romains de saintes. Paris, 1887.
Arc 830.88 Audollent, A. Clermont gallo-romain. Clermont-Ferrand, 19- .
Arc 830.88.5 Audollent, A. Les tombes à l'incinération du Musée de Clermont-Ferrand. Paris, 1911. 3 pam.
Arc 440.10 The Audumbaras. (Das Gupta, Kalyan Kumar.) Calcutta, 1965.
Arc 1640.7F Die auf das Kaiserreich Brasilien...1822 bis 1889. (Meili, Julius.) Zürich, 1890.
Arc 543.4.13 Auf Hellas spuren in Ostturkistan. (LeCoq, Albert.) Leipzig, 1926.
Arc 905.120 Auf Römerstrassen durch Osterreich von Aguntum nach Carnuntum. (Meysels, T.F.) Wien, 1960.
Arc 1512.2F Aufbau der niederländischen Kunstgeschichte und Museologie...Niederländischen Münzen und Medaillen dis Herzoglichen Museums zu Gotha. (Rathgeber, Georg.) Weissensee, 1839.
Arc 853.77 Auffindung eines römischen Bades in Augsburg. (Scheuermayer.) n.p., 1867?
Arc 407.11 Der Aufgang der Menschheit. (Wirth, Herman.) Jena, 1928.
Arc 400.21 Aufsätze zur Numismatik und Archäologie. (Pick, Behrendt.) Jena, 1931.
Arc 395.20.5 Der Aufstieg der Menschheit. (Kühn, Herbert.) Frankfurt, 1955.
Arc 395.20 Der Aufstieg der Menschheit. (Kühn, Herbert.) Frankfurt, 1957.
Arc 785.13.50 Augé de Lassus, L. Le Forum. Paris, 1892.
Arc 830.108 Augey, Edmond. Suite de recherches archéologiques relatives à la préhistoire du département de la Gironde. 7e série. Bordeaux, 1910.
Arc 853.125 Augusta Treverorum. (Reusch, Wilhelm.) Trier, 1958.
Arc 518.12.5F Augusteische Architektur in Ephesos. v.1-2. (Alzinger, Wilhelm.) Wien, 1974.
Arc 1018.25 Augusti, J.C.W. Denkwürdigkeiten und der christlichen Archäologie. Leipzig, 1817-26. 12v.
Arc 1018.25.5 Augusti, J.C.W. Handbuch der christlichen Archäologie. Leipzig, 1838. 3v.
Arc 1478.26F Augustin, A. Antiquitatum romanorum Hispanarumque in nummis veterum dialogi XI. Antverpiae, 1617.
Arc 1500.50 Augustin Dupré: ofèvre, médailleur et graveur général des monnaies. (Saunier, Charles.) Paris, 1894.
Arc 830.16.11 Augustoduni amplissimae civitatis. (Ladonne, E.) Augustoduni, 1640.
Arc 87.1.28 Augustus. (Huebner, E.) Berlin, 1868.
Arc 1335.48 Auktions-Katalog. (Helbing, Otto.) München, 1910.
Arc 1335.87 Auktions-Katalog enthaltend die Münzen- und Medaillen-Bestände der aufgelösten Firma zschiesche und Köder. (Helbing, Otto.) München, 1913.
Arc 1020.9.169 L'aula del senato romano e la chiesa di S. Adriano. (Dattoli, M.) Roma, 1921.

Author and Title Listing

Arc 925.50.255	Aulikh, Vitold V. Zymnivs'ke horodyshche-slov'ians'ka pam'iatka. Kyïv, 1972.
Arc 1208.13F	Aulock, Hans von. Altorientalische Siegelsteine der Sammlung Hans Silvius von Aulock. Uppsala, 1957.
Arc 858.33	Ault, Norman. Life in ancient Britain. London, 1920.
Arc 1020.84	Les aumonières du trésor...cathedrale de Troyes. (Le Brun Dalbaune.) Troyes, 1864.
Arc 853.180F	Die Aunjebitzer Kultur in Sachsen. (Billig, Gerhard.) Leipzig, 1958.
Arc 757.6.5	Aurea Roma. (Caetani Lovatelli, E.) Roma, 1915.
Arc 830.101	Aurès, Auguste. Monographie des bornes milliaires du département du Gard. Nîmes, 1877.
Arc 1300.6	Aureus; Zeitschrift für Numismatik und Geldwesen. München. 3-16,1960-1971//
Arc 1480.8	L'aureus romain se divisait en six-millièmes. v.1-2. (Blancard, Louis.) Marseille, n.d.
Arc 673.1.4	L'aurige de Delphes. (Bourguet, E.) Paris, 1912.
Arc 726.24.22	Aurigemma, S. Die Hadriansvilla bei Tivoli. Tivoli, 1955.
Arc 726.24.24F	Aurigemma, S. Villa Adriana. Roma, 1961.
Arc 726.24.20	Aurigemma, S. La villa Adriana. 2a ed. Tivoli, 1953.
Arc 726.24.17	Aurigemma, S. La villa Adriana presso Tivoli. Tivoli, 1948.
Arc 726.249	Aurigemma, Salvatore. I monumenti della necropoli romana di Sarsina. Roma, 1963.
Arc 394.1	Aus der Alterthumswissenschaft. (Jahn, Otto.) Bonn, 1868.
Arc 385.1	Aus der Anomia; archaeologische Beitraege. Berlin, 1890.
Arc 853.195	Aus der Frühgeschichte der Oberlausitz. (Lehmann, F.) Berlin, 1958.
Arc 1020.18	Aus der mittelalterlichen Sammlung desMuseums in Bergen. (Bendixen, B.E.) Bergen, 1889-
Arc 853.20.12	Aus der Schatzkammer des antiken Trier. (Treves. Rheinisches Landesmuseum.) Trier, 1951.
Arc 853.20.12.5	Aus der Schatzkammer des antiken Trier. 2. Aufl. (Treves. Rheinisches Landesmuseum.) Trier, 1959.
Arc 853.5	Aus der Verzeit Reuthingens. 2. Aufl. (Rupp, T.) Stuttgart, 1869.
Arc 520.15A	Aus der Welt des Pergamonaltars. (Stier, Hans Erich.) Berlin, 1932.
Arc 848.9.3	Aus Deutschlands Urgeschichts. 3. Aufl. (Schwantes, G.) Leipzig, 1921.
Arc 1468.55	Aus einer Sammlung griechischer Münzen. (Schwarz, Dietrich Wallo Horman.) Zürich, 1961.
Arc 612.38	Aus europäischer Vorzeit. (Behn, Friedrich.) Stuttgart, 1957.
Arc 853.372	Aus Frankfurts Vorgeschichte. (Fischer, Ulrich.) Frankfurt am Main, 1971.
Arc 905.24.25	Aus Kärntens römischer Vergangenheit. v.1-5. (Leber, Paul Siegfried.) Wolfsberg, 1971-
Arc 403.18	Aus Leben und Arbeit. (Schuckhartt, C.) Berlin, 1944.
Arc 810.15	Aus Pompeji. (Ziegeler, E.) Guetersloh, 1895.
Arc 1453.5	Auserlesenes und hochstansehnliches Ducatenkabinett. (Soothe, J.C. von.) Hamburg, 1784.
Arc 547.2.2	Ausführliches Verzeichniss der Aegyptischen Altertuemer, Gipsabguesse und Papyrus. (Berlin. Staatliche Museen.) Berlin, 1894.
Arc 545.244F	Ausgewählte Denkmäler aus ägyptischen Sammlungen in Schweden. (Lugn, Pehr.) Leipzig, 1922.
Arc 1033.34.50	Die Ausgrabbungen unter der Peterskirche in Rom. (Wenzel, P.) Leipzig, 1953.
Arc 700.2	Ausgrabung beim Tempel der Hera Unweit Argos. (Rangabé, A.R.) Halle, 1855.
Arc 853.21.20	Die Ausgrabung des bronzezeitlichen Dorfes Buch bei Berlin. (Kiekebusch, A.) Berlin, 1923.
Arc 600.14	Die Ausgrabung des Menas-Heiligtümes. v.1-3. (Kaufmann, C.M.) Cairo, 1906.
Arc 853.76.5	Die Ausgrabung des steinzeitlichen Dorfes von Berlin-Britz. Inaug. Diss. (Umbreit, Carl.) Leipzig, 1936.
Arc 853.185	Die Ausgrabungen am Fuldaer Donaplatz. (Hahn, Heinrich.) Fulda, 1956.
Arc 915.35	Die Ausgrabungen am Petersberg in Basel. (Berger, L.) Basel, 1963.
Arc 785.13.20	Die Ausgrabungen auf dem Forum Romanum. v.1-2. (Huelsen, Christian.) Roma, 1902-05.
Arc 685.1	Ausgrabungen auf Kalaureia. (Wide, S.) n.p., n.d.
Arc 530.47	Die Ausgrabungen der zweiten Ktesiphon-Expedition. (Berlin. Staatliche Museen.) Berlin, 1933.
Arc 395.28	Ausgrabungen in aller Welt. 1. Aufl. (Kahlke, Hans Dietrich.) Leipzig, 1972.
Arc 853.165	Ausgrabungen in alt Hamburg. (Schindler, Reinhard.) Hamburg, 1958.
Arc 155.10	Ausgrabungen in Augst. Basel. 2-4,1962-1974
Arc 185.5	Ausgrabungen in Berlin; Forschungen und Funde zür Ur- und Frühgeschichte. Berlin. 1,1970+
Arc 853.252F	Die Ausgrabungen in Haithabu. Neumünster. 2,1959+ 4v.
Arc 853.362	Die Ausgrabungen in Manching 1955-1961. (Krämer, Werner.) Wiesbaden, 1970.
Arc 497.51	Der Ausgrabungen in Palästina und Syrien. (Jirku, Anton.) Halle, 1956.
Arc 386.42	Ausgrabungen und Ausgräber. (Behn, Friedrich.) Stuttgart, 1961.
Arc 905.80.5	Ausgrabungen und Funde. v.1-3. (Neumann, Alfred.) Wien, 1951.
Arc 853.112	Ausgrabungen unter der St. Jakobskirche Dokumertieren. (Kramert, K.) n.p., 1954.
Arc 93.1	Ausonia; rivista della Società italiana di archeologia. Roma. 1-10 6v.
Arc 1033.12.103	Ausstellung des heiligen Roches in die Domkirche zur Trier. (Marx, J.) Trier, 1845.
Arc 518.7	Ausstellung von Fundstücken aus Ephesos im unteren Belvedere. (Vienna. Kaiserhaus.) Wien, 1905.
Arc 30.31	The Australian journal of Biblical archaeology. Sydney. 1,1968+
Arc 1.39	Australian studies in archaeology. Sydney. 1,1973+
Arc 1578.10	Austria. Haupt Münzamt in Wien. Katalog der Münzen- und Medaillen-Stampel. Wien, 1901-06. 4v.
Arc 900.205	Austria. K.K. Central Commission. Kunst historischer Atlas. Wien. 1-10,1889-1894 2v.
Arc 900.2.5F	Austria. Zentral Kommission für Enforschung und Erhaltung der Kunst- und Historischen Denkmäle in Wien. Articles on the palace of Diocletian in Spalato. Wien? 1903.
Arc 900.211F	Austria exarchivis mellicensilus. (Hueber, P.) Lipsiae, 1722.
Arc 1020.72.15	L'autel de Sainte-Sixte et ses reliques. (La Croix, C. de.) Poitiers, 1907.
Arc 830.27	L'autel de saintes et les triades gauloises. (Bertrand, Alexandre.) Paris, 1880.
Arc 505.3.12	L'authenticité du Saint-Sépulcre. (Clermont-Ganneau, Charles.) Paris, 1877.
Arc 1020.77	Authentiques de reliques...decouvertes à Vergy. (Delisle, Léopold.) Rome, 1884.
Arc 392.3	Authority and archaeology. (Hogarth, David George.) N.Y., 1899.
Arc 925.300	Autlev, P.U. Abadzekhskaia nizhnepaleoliticheskaia stoianka. Maikop, 1963.
Arc 830.130	Autour des inscriptions de Glozel. (Dussaud, René.) Paris, 1927.
Arc 830.16.5	Autun archéologique. (Société Eduenne.) Autun, 1848.
Arc 66.1.56	Auvray, L. Manuscrits de Dante des Bibliothèques de France. Paris, 1892.
Arc 726.150	Auximum (Osimo) regio V. Picenum. (Gentili, Gino Vinicio.) Roma, 1955.
Arc 843.149	Avance al estudio de las pinturas. (Cabre-Aguilo, Juan.) Madrid, 1915.
Arc 1033.70.5	Avanzi di pitture del secolo IX in una cripta. (Taeggi, O.P.) n.p., 1885.
Arc 923.116	Avdusin, Daniil A. Arkheologiia SSSR. Moskva, 1967.
Arc 923.127	Avdusin, Daniil A. Polevaia arkheologiia SSSR. Moskva, 1972.
Arc 1033.17.250	Ave Maria. La milagrosa imagen de Nuestra Señora del Rosario. (Castellano, U.) Córdoba, 1891.
Arc 861.31.10	Avebury; a guide. (Cunnington, M.E. (Mrs.)) Devizes, 19-
Arc 861.31	Avebury in Wiltshire. (Twining, T.) London, 1723.
Arc 790.200	Avellino, F.M. Descrizione di una lasa disotterrata in Pompeii. Naples, 1837. 2 pam.
Arc 1076.21	Avent, Richard. Anglo-Saxon garnet inlaid and composite brooches. v.1-2. Oxford, 1975.
Arc 915.8.5	Aventicum. (Secretan, Eugène.) Lausanne, 1896.
Arc 915.8	Aventicum. (Secretan, Eugène.) Lausanne, 1905.
Arc 66.1.97	L'aventin dans l'antiquité. (Merlin, A.) Paris, 1906.
Arc 1016.9.5	L'aventino e le origine pagane e Christian di Roma. (Lugari, G.B.) Roma, 1886.
Arc 830.225	L'aventure souterraine. (Baurés, Jacques.) Paris, 1958.
Arc 843.3	Averignaciones de las antiguedades de Cantabria. (Henao, G. de.) Salamanca, 1689-91. 2v.
Arc 1153.43.7	Avviamento allo studio delle abbreviature latine nel medievo. (Schiaparelli, L.) Firenze, 1926.
Arc 1138.108F	Awad, G. Report in search of the condition of manuscripts in Egypt. n.p., 1957?
Arc 66.1.171	Aymard, Jacques. Essai sur les chasses romaines. Paris, 1951. 2v.
Arc 585.26F	Ayrton, Edward R. Pre-dynastic cemetery at El Mahasna. London, 1911.
Arc 609.2.7F	Azaïs, R.P. Cinq années de recherches archéologiques en Ethiopie. Paris, 1931. 2v.
Arc 30.25	Azania. Nairobi. 1,1966+ 2v.
Arc 1584.28	Azbabskii klad'. (Chizhov, Sergei I.) Moskva, 1911. 2 pam.
Arc 1163.3.25	Azbuka i skoropis' XVII. Moskva, 1875.
Arc 275.70	Azebardzhanskii Arkheologicheskii Komitet. Izvestiia. Baku. 2,1926
Arc 1645.1	Azeredo, C. de. Apreciação do medalheiro da casa da Moeda. Rio de Janeiro, 1862.
Arc 543.147	Aziia dalekaia i tainstvennaia. (Larichev, Vitalii E.) Novosibirsk, 1968.
Arc 1349.55.5	Azzurri, Francesco. Cenni biografici di Bennedetto Pistrucci. Roma, 1887.
Arc 505.11.10	Baalbek. (Harding, G.L.) Khayats, 1963.
Arc 495.5.5F	Baalbek. v.1-3; atlas. (Wiegand, Theodor.) Berlin, 1921-25. 4v.
Arc 543.3.115	Babaev, Aktam D. Kreposti drevnego Vakhana. Dushanbe, 1973.
Arc 608.2.15	Babelon, E. Carthage. Paris, 1896.
Arc 1356.2	Babelon, E. Les collections de monnaies anciennes. Paris, 1897.
Arc 1335.14.4	Babelon, E. Guide illustré au cabinet des médailles. Paris, 1900.
Arc 1480.24	Babelon, E. L'iconographie monetaire de Julien l'Apostat. Paris, 1903.
Arc 416.1.2	Babelon, E. Manual of Oriental antiquities. N.Y., 1889.
Arc 416.1.3A	Babelon, E. Manual of Oriental antiquities. N.Y., 1906.
Arc 416.1	Babelon, E. Manuel d'archéologie orientale. Paris, 1888.
Arc 1348.19	Babelon, E. Mélanges numismatiques. Paris, 1892-1912. 5v.
Arc 1468.22	Babelon, E. Les monnaies grecques. Paris, 1921.
X Cg Arc 1433.33	Babelon, E. Perses achemenides les satrapes. Paris, 1893.
Arc 1458.13	Babelon, E. Traite des monnaies grecques et romaines. Paris, 1901-33. 8v.
Arc 1478.17	Babelon, Ernest. Description historique et chronologique des monnaies de la République romaine vulgairement appelées monnaies consulaires. Paris, 1885-86. 2v.
Arc 1478.17.5	Babelon, Ernest. Description historique et chronologique des monnaies de la République romaine vulgairement appelées monnaies consulaires. Bologna, 1963. 2v.
Arc 1665.4F	Babelon, Ernest. Les medailles historique...Napoléon le Grand. Paris, 1912.
Arc 1500.55	Babelon, Jean. Histoire de Paris d'après les médailles de la Renaissance au XX. siècle. Paris, 1951.
Arc 1356.5	Babelon, Jean. Le portrait dans l'antiquité d'apres les monnaies. Paris, 1942.
Arc 1348.53F	Babelon, Jean. Portraits en médaille. Paris, 1946.
Arc 395.6.10	Babylon, die versunkene Weltstadt und ihr Ausgräber Robert Koldewey. (Andrae, W.) Berlin, 1952.
Arc 1033.12.183	Bacci, G. Corona di ferro. Ferrara, 1884.
Arc 600.190	Bachatly, C. Le monastère de Phoebammon. Le Caire, 1964- 2v.
Arc 595.31	Bache, R.M. The latest phase of the Great Pyramid discussion. Philadelphia, 1885.
Arc 612.71	Bachelot de la Pylaie, Auguste Jean Marie. Études archéologiques et géographiques. Quimper, 1970.
Arc 1033.12.9.15	Bachinger, Rudolf. Das Leichentuch von Turin. Stein am Rhein, 1967.
Arc 1086.2	Bachofen, J.J. Römische Grablampen. Basel, 1890.
Arc 612.83	Background to archaeology; Britain in its European setting. Cambridge, 1973.
Arc 603.7A	Background to evolution in Africa. Chicago, 1968.
Arc 386.35	Bacon, Edward. Digging for history. London, 1960.
Arc 87.2.61	Bad der roemische Villa bei Allenz. (Weerth, E.) Bonn, 1861-1870.
Arc 302.53	Badania archeologiczne. (Muzeum Żup Krakowskich, Wieliczka.) Wieliczka. 1968+
Arc 936.14.125	Badania archeologiczne w okolicy wislicy. (Warsaw. Uniwersytet. Zespoł Badan nad Polskim Sredniowieczem.) Warszawa, 1963-64.

Arc 936.14.360 Badania archeologiczne w Polsce w latach 1944-64. (Polska Akademia Nauk. Instytut Historii Kultury Materialnej.) Wrocław, 1965.
Arc 588.46F The Badarian civilization. (Brunton, Guy.) London, 1928.
Arc 1458.19 Badeigts de Laborde. Description des médailles grecques. Paris, 1869.
Arc 853.41 Baden-Baden. Städtischen historischen Sammlungen. Baden-Baden. 1908-1910
Arc 936.180.20 Badenski i vučedolski kulturni kompleks u Jugoslaviji. (Tasić, Nikola.) Beograd, 1967.
Arc 925.172 Bader, Otto N. Baranovskii nogil'nik. Moskva, 1963.
Arc 925.342 Bader, Otto N. Bassein Oki v epokhu bronzy. Moskva, 1970.
Arc 925.136 Bader, Otto N. Drevneishie metallurgi Priural'ia. Moskva, 1964.
Arc 925.325 Bader, Otto N. Kapovaia peshchera. Moskva, 1965.
Arc 925.170 Bader, Otto N. Nazare istorii Piskam'ia. Perm', 1958.
Arc 1510.45 Badische Gesellschaft für Münzkunde. Münzkunde und Münzkabinette am Oberrheim. Karlsruhe am Rhein, 1951.
Arc 853.65.30 Badura-Simonides, D. Baśń i podanie górno-śląskie. Katowice, 1961. 4 pam.
Arc 1033.12.22 Baffico, G.F. Istoria del Santo Sudario. Genova, n.d.
Htn Arc 1020.96* Bagatas, R. SS. episcoparum...antiqua monumenta. Venetiis, 1576.
Arc 1027.41.3F Bagatti, B. Il cimitero di Commodilla. Città del Vaticano, 1936.
Arc 505.97 Bagatti, Bellarmino. L'archeologia cristiana in Palestina. Firenze, 1962.
Arc 1033.34.65 Bagatti, Bellarmino. San Pietro nei monumenti di Palestina. Cairo, 1960.
Arc 895.44F Bagge, A. Die Funde aus Dolman. v.1-2. Stockholm, 1950-52.
Arc 895.15.25 Bagge, A. Stenåldersboplatserna vid Siretorp i Blekinge. Stockholm, 1939.
Arc 493.55 Baghdaden Mitteilungen. Berlin. 1,1960+ 4v.
Arc 1033.17.543 Bagnari, P. Divozioni..in onore di Nostra Signora del Carmine. Roma, 1728.
Arc 853.65.60 Bagniewski, Zbigniew. Dzieje zierni wydarte. Wrocław, 1970.
Arc 600.194F Bahgat, Aly. Fouilles d'al Foustât. Paris, 1921.
Arc 938.25F Bahr, Johann K. Die Gräber der Liven. Dresden, 1850.
Arc 588.47F Bahrein and Hemamieh. (MacKay, Ernest.) London, 1929.
Arc 1333.16F Bahrfeldt, Emil. Die Münzen- und Medaillen-Sammlung. Danzig, 1901-10. 6v.
Arc 1510.174F Bahrfeldt, Emil. Das Münzwesen der Mark Brandenburg. Berlin, 1889- 2v.
Arc 1478.13 Bahrfeldt, M. Nachträge und Bericht zur Münzkunde. Wien, 1897.
Arc 1675.80 Bahrfeldt, Max. Die Schaumünzen der Universität Halle-Wittenberg. Halle, 1926.
Arc 1510.29 Bahrfeldt, Max von. Das Geprägte amtliche Notgeld der Provinz Schlesien, 1917-1921. Breslau, 1935.
Arc 1510.10 Bahrfeldt, Max von. Die Münzen der Stadt Stade. Wien, 1879.
Arc 1510.10.5F Bahrfeldt, Max von. Niedersachsisches Münzarchiv. Halle, 1927. 4v.
Arc 1478.88.1F Bahrfeldt, Max von. Sammlung römischer Münzen der Republik und des West-Kaiserreichs. Aalen, 1972.
Arc 726.27.3 Baiae, das erste luxusbad der Römer. (Schmatz, Joseph.) Regensburg, 1905-06.
Arc 551.6.5 Baikie, James. A century of excavation in the land of the Pharaohs. London, 1924.
Arc 551.6 Baikie, James. Egyptian antiquities in the Nile Valley. London, 1932.
Arc 672.1.19A Baikie, James. The sea-kings of Crete. London, 1910.
Arc 672.1.21 Baikie, James. The sea-kings of Crete. 3. ed. London, 1920.
Arc 672.1.22 Baikie, James. The sea-kings of Crete. 4. ed. London, 1926.
Arc 441.7 Les bains dans l'Inde antique; monuments et textes médicaux. (Doreau, Jean Louis.) Paris, 1936.
Arc 815.21 Baizini, G.B. Due lettere sopra il musaico di Pompei. Bergamo, 1836.
Arc 936.220.5 Bajalović-Biztašević, Marya. Srednjevekovna nekropola w Mirijevu. Beograd, 1960.
Arc 925.13.186 Bakay, Kornél. Scythian rattles in the Carpathian Basin and their eastern connections. Amsterdam, 1971.
Arc 963.2 Baker, Frank C. The Cahokia mounds. [Illinois]. Urbana, 1923.
Arc 925.325.5 Bakhmutinskaia kul'tura. (Mazhitov, Niiaz A.) Moskva, 1968.
Arc 435.2.43F Bakhshali manuscript. pt.1-3. (Kaye, G.R.) Calcutta, 1927-33. 2v.
Arc 1025.69 Bakhuitzen van den Brink, J.N. De romeinsche catacomben en haar frescos. 's-Gravenhage, 1933.
Arc 1030.46 Bakhuizen van den Brink, J.N. De aid-christelijke monumenten van Ephesus. Haag, 1923.
Arc 493.6.10 Baku. Muzei Istorii Azerbaidzhana. Material'naia kultura Azerbaidzhana. v.2. Baku, 1949-
Arc 585.29F Balabish. (Wainwright, G.A.) London, 1920.
Arc 543.66.5 Balalyk-tepe. (Al'baum, L.I.) Tashkend, 1960.
Arc 66.1.200 Balaneutikè; recherches sur le bain dans l'antiquité grecque. (Ginouvès, René.) Paris, 1962.
Arc 710.18F Balanos, N. Les monuments de l'acropole. Paris, 1936.
Arc 936.195.95 Balaša, Gejza. Praveké osídlenie stredného Slovenska. Bratislava, 1960.
Arc 936.195.96 Balaša, Gejza. Zvolen v období lužickej kultúry. Banská Bystrica, 1964.
Arc 444.2.10 Balasaheb, Pant Pratinidhi. Ellora; a handbook of Verul (Ellora caves). Bombay, 1929.
Arc 1016.243 Balasko, F. Majesticus...Delatio...S. Stephani Manus Dexterae. Budae, n.d.
Arc 505.12.10.5 Balazs, György. Egy feltárt bibliai város. Budapest, 1940.
Arc 302.31 Balcanoslavica. Beograd. 1,1972+
Arc 848.27 Balch, E.S. Roman and pre-historic remains in central Germany. Philadelphia, 1903.
Arc 861.57F Balch, H.E. Wookey Hole; its caves and cave dwellers. London, 1914.
Arc 1460.8 Baldus, Hans Roland. Mor(eta) urb(is)-Antiona. Frankfurt am Main, 1969.
Arc 1423.27 Baldus, Hans Roland. Uranius Antoninius. Bonn, 1971.
Arc 1470.24 Baldwin, Agnes. Symbolism on Greek coins. N.Y., 1916.
Arc 953.30 Baldwin, Gordon Cortis. Race against time. N.Y., 1966.
Arc 943.3.5 Baldwin, J.D. Ancient America. N.Y., 1872.
Arc 943.3 Baldwin, J.D. Ancient America. N.Y., 1878.
Arc 843.234.4 The Balearic Islands. (Pericot Garcia, Luis.) London, 1972.
Arc 875.22 Balfour, J.A. Book of Arran - archaeology. Glasgow, 1910. 2v.
Arc 843.205 Balil, Alberto. Colonia Iblia Augusta Paterna Farentia Barcino. Madrid, 1964.
Arc 936.02 Pamphlet vol. Balkan states. Archaeology.
Arc 936.01 Pamphlet box. Balkan states. Archaeology.
Arc 595.1 Ballard, R. The solution of the Pyramid problem. N.Y., 1882.
Arc 830.357 Ballet, Pierre. Le Haute-Marne antique. Chaumont, 1971.
Arc 1033.12.38 Balliani, C. Ragionamenti della sacra sindone. Torino, 1610.
Arc 900.206 Ballif, P. Römische Strasen in Bosnien. Wien, 1893.
Arc 925.21 Ballod, F.V. Privolzhskie Pompei. Moskva, 1923.
Arc 608.6.6 Ballu, Albert. Guide illustré de Timgad (antique Thamrigadi). 2. éd. Paris, 1910.
Arc 608.6.5 Ballu, Albert. Les ruines de Timgad. Paris, 1897.
Arc 608.6.7 Ballu, Albert. Les ruines de Timgad. Paris, 1911.
Arc 1510.144F Bally, Otto. Beschreibung von Münzen und Medaillen des Fürsten-Hauses und Landes Baden in chronologischer Folge. Aarau, 1896- 2v.
Arc 938.17 Balodis, F. L'ancienne frontiére slavo-latvienne. n.p., 192-.
Arc 938.13 Eine baltische Halsringform der Volkerwanderungszeit. Inaug. Diss. (Lincke, B.) Berlin, 1937.
Arc 938.9 Baltische Studien zur Archäologie und Geschichte. (Archäologischer Kongress. Baltischen...Komitee.) Berlin, 1914.
Arc 825.3.25 Balty, J.C. Études sur la Maison Carrée de Nîmes. Bruxelles, 1960.
Arc 716.3.2 Die Balustrade des Templs der Athena-Nike. (Kekulé, R.) Leipzig, 1869.
Arc 608.1.35 Balut, Georges. Tunisie. Tunis, 1903.
Arc 1033.17.36 Bambacari, C. La città di refugio panegirico...greca imagine di Maria da Constantinopoli. Forli, 1678.
Arc 905.134 Bamberger, Anton. Tergolape. Linz, 1966.
Arc 540.16F Bamboula at Kourion. (Benson, Jack L.) Philadelphia, 1972.
Arc 913.8 Bandi, Hans. Die Schweiz zur Rentierzeit. Frauenfeld, 1947.
Arc 1588.1.14 Bandtki, K.W.S. Numismatyka Krajowa. Warszawa, 1839. 2v.
Arc 1330.1 Banduri, A. Bibliotheca nummaria. Hamburg, 1719.
Htn Arc 1475.2* Banduri, A. Numismata imperatorum romanorum. Paris, 1718. 2v.
Arc 432.28 Banerjee, N.R. The iron age in India. Delhi, 1965.
Arc 457.5 Banerji, R.D. The age of the imperial Guptas. Banares, 1933.
Arc 936.195.195 Bánesz, Ladislav. Barca bei Košice - paläolithische Fundstelle. Bratislava, 1968.
Arc 545.205 Bangeschichte des Denderatempels. (Duemichen, J.) Strassburg, 1877.
Arc 1610.3 Bangs, Merwin C. Catalogue of coins and medals. Roxbury, 1863.
Arc 936.220.10 Banjica, naselje vinčanske kulture. (Todorović, Jovan.) Beograd, 1961.
Arc 547.40 Bankes, Ralph. Egyptian Stelae in the Bankes collection. Oxford, 1958.
Arc 340.30.3 Banner, János. A Közép-Dunamedence régészeti bibliográfiája, 1954-1959. Budapest, 1961.
Arc 340.30.5 Banner, János. A Közép-Dunamedence régészeti bibliográfiája, 1960-1966. Budapest, 1968.
Arc 340.30 Banner, János. A Közép-Dunamedence régészeti bibliográfiája a legrégibb idöktöl a XI. századig. Budapest, 1954.
Arc 905.60 Banner, János. Népvándorlás koté sérok Nagykamaráson. Szeged, 1927.
Arc 853.365 Bantelmann, Niels. Die Urgeschichte des Kreises Kusel. Speyer, 1972.
Arc 1478.89 Banti, Alberto. Corpus nummorum romanorum. Firenze, 1972- 8v.
Arc 746.30F Banti, Luisa. Luni. Firenze, 1937.
Arc 830.245 Baoai, cité gallo-romaine. (Lille. Palais des Beaux-Arts.) Lille, 1957.
Arc 925.9.10 Bapst, Y. Souvenirs de deux missions an Caucase. Paris, 1886.
Arc 1093.2.40 Bar, Henry. Les pierres levées. Paris, 1973.
Arc 875.13.10 Bar Will. (Robertson, Anne S.) Oxford, 1975.
Arc 1264.9 Barabé, A. Recherches historiques sur le tabellionage royal. Rouen, 1863.
Arc 543.27.5 Barabudur. (Krom, N.J.) The Hague, 1927. 2v.
Arc 542.200.5 Barabudur. v.1, pt.1-2; v.2. (Mus, Paul.) Hanoi, 1935. 3v.
Arc 1020.9.13 Baracconi, G. Il panteon e la tomba reale monografia. Roma, 1878. 3 pam.
Arc 608.16.15 Baradez, J.L. Tipasa. Alger, 1952.
Arc 386.24 Baraldi, Giuseppe. Notizia biografica sul cardinale S. Borgia. Modena, 1830.
Arc 925.50.265 Baran, Volodymyr D. Ranni slov'iany mizh Dnistrom i pnypiatkii. Kyïv, 1972.
Arc 843.197 Barandiaran, J.M. Excavaciones en Atxeta. Bilbao, 1961.
Arc 925.172 Baranovskii nogil'nik. (Bader, Otto N.) Moskva, 1963.
Arc 608.1.55 Baratte, François. Recherches archéologiques à Haïdra. Paris, 1974.
Arc 726.59.25 Barbaro, C.A. Degli avanzi d'alcuni antichissimi edifizi, scoperti in Malta l'anno 1768. Malta, 1794.
Arc 830.64 Barbe, Henri. Jublains, Mayenne. Mayenne, 1865.
Arc 830.56 Barbey, A. Les grottes préhistoriques du village de Jouaignes. v.1-3. Chateau-Thierry, 1870-75.
Arc 1020.9.127 Barbier de Montault, X. L'année liturgique à Rome. Paris, 1857.
Arc 1020.9.130 Barbier de Montault, X. L'année liturgique à Rome. Rome, 1870.
Arc 1020.9.131 Barbier de Montault, X. L'année liturgique à Rome. Rome, 1902.
Arc 1020.9.128 Barbier de Montault, X. L'année liturgique à Rome. 2. éd. Rome, 1862.
Arc 1020.9.32 Barbier de Montault, X. La bibliothèque vaticane et ses annexes. Rome, 1867.
Arc 1033.35.47 Barbier de Montault, X. Croix-reliquiare de l'eglise de S. Florent-les-Saumur. Angers, n.d.
Arc 1016.3 Barbier de Montault, X. Étude archéologique sur le reliquaire du chef de S. Laurent. Rome, 1864.
Arc 1020.9.135 Barbier de Montault, X. Exposition religieuse de Rome 1870. Antiquités chrétiennes. Rome, 1870.
Arc 1020.9.137 Barbier de Montault, X. Exposition religieuse de Rome 1870. L'archéologie et l'art chrétien. Arras, 1877.
Arc 1264.4 Barbier de Montault, X. Le grand sceau de Raoul du Fou. Reims, n.d.

Author and Title Listing

Arc 1020.9.33 — Barbier de Montault, X. Inventaire de la chapelle papale sous Paul III en 1547. Tours, 1878.
Arc 1020.88 — Barbier de Montault, X. Inventaires de la Basilique Royale de Monza. Paris, 1886. 3 pam.
Arc 1033.35.45 — Barbier de Montault, X. Lettres testimoniales...portant donation d'un morceau de la vrai croix...Angers. Tours, n.d.
Arc 1020.26.5 — Barbier de Montault, X. Les manuscrits du trésor de Bari. Toulouse, 1876.
Arc 1020.72 — Barbier de Montault, X. Le martyrium de Poitiers. Poitiers, 1885.
Arc 1020.68.9 — Barbier de Montault, X. Notes archéologiques sur Moutiers et la Tarentaise. Montiers, 1877.
Arc 1020.9.120 — Barbier de Montault, X. Observations archéologique...les églises de Rome. Arras, 1878.
Arc 1033.12.166 — Barbier de Montault, X. Saint Clou à la cathédrale de Toul. Nancy, 1885.
Arc 1053.16 — Barbier de Montault, X. Solution d'un problème iconographique. Poitiers, 1877.
Arc 1020.9.103 — Barbier de Montault, X. Les souterrains et le tresor...St. Pierre à Rome. Rome, 1866.
Arc 1020.50 — Barbier de Montault, X. Le trésor de la cathédrale de Bénévent. Arras, 1879.
Arc 1020.68 — Barbier de Montault, X. Le trésor de la cathédrale de Moutiers. Tours, n.d.
Arc 1020.72.5 — Barbier de Montault, X. Le trésor de l'abbaye de Ste. Croix de Poitiers. Poitiers, 1883.
Arc 1020.49 — Barbier de Montault, X. Le trésor du dame d'Aix-La-Chapelle. Tours, 1877.
Arc 1016.246F — Barbier de Montault, X. La trésor liturgique de Cherves en Angoumois. Angoulême, 1897.
Arc 1020.55 — Barbier de Montault, X. La visite de la Cathédrale St. Bertrand de Comminges. Montpélier, 1877.
Arc 1.7.2 — Barbier de Montault. Annales archéologiques. Index, v.28. Paris, 1881.
Arc 936.20.75 — Barbu, V. Adamclisi. Bucuresti, 1965.
Arc 936.195.195 — Barca bei Košice - paläolithische Fundstelle. (Bánesz, Ladislav.) Bratislava, 1968.
Arc 383.9.10 — Barcelona (Province). Instituto de Prehistoria y Arqueología. Miscelánea en homenaje al abate Hescri Breuil, 1877-1961. Barcelona, 1964-65. 2v.
Arc 875.19 — Barclay, A. Perthia Romana: line or chain of forts erected by Agricola. Perth, 1883.
Arc 865.1.10 — Barclay, E. The ruined temple Stonehenge. London, 1911.
X Cg Arc 865.1 — Barclay, E. Stonehenge and its earth works. London, 1895.
Arc 843.11 — Bardavíu Ponz, V. Estaciones prehistoricas...desiertos. Zaragoza, 1918.
Arc 726.24.8 — Bardi, Giovanni de'. Della imp. villa Adriana. Firenze, 1825.
Arc 723.46 — Barfield, Lawrence. Northern Italy before Rome. London, 1971.
Arc 1033.124 — Bargès, Jean. Notice sur quelques antels chrétiens. Paris, 1890.
Arc 600.55.5 — Barguet, Paul. Le temple d'Amon-Rê à Karnak. Le Caire, 1962.
Arc 1185.10 — Baring, D.E. Clavis diplomatica. Hanoverae, 1737.
Arc 1185.10.5 — Baring, D.E. Clavis diplomatica. Hanoverae, 1754.
Arc 612.7 — Baring-Gould, S. Cliff castles and cave dwellings of Europe. London, 1911.
Arc 800.7 — Barker, E.R. Buried Herculaneum. London, 1908.
Arc 708.1 — Barker, H.A. Description of the view of Athens. n.p., n.d.
Arc 861.202 — Barker, P.A. The mediaeval pottery of Shropshire from the conquest to 1400. Shropshire, 1970.
Htn Arc 522.8* — Barker-Webb, P. Topographie de la Troade. Paris, 1844.
Arc 505.19.5 — Barnabas. Deux questions d'archéologie palestinienne. Jérusalem, 1902. 2v.
Arc 790.208 — Barnabei, F. La villa pompeiana. Roma, 1901.
Arc 1670.54F — Barnard, F.P. The casting-counter and the counting board...numismatics. Oxford, 1916.
Arc 1663.26 — Barnard, F.P. Saterical and controversial medals of the reformation. Oxford, 1927.
Arc 1033.12.27 — Barnate, C. Il furto del "Santo Sudario" nel 1507. Genova, 1915.
Arc 1018.37 — Barnes, A.S. The early church in the light of monuments. London, 1913.
Arc 441.9.10F — Baroda (State). Archaeological Department. Annual report. Baroda. 1935-1939 4v.
Arc 441.15 — Baroda through the ages. (Subbarao, B.) Baroda, 1953.
Arc 1185.19.3F — Barone, N. Paleografia latina diplomatica. Atlas. 3. ed. Napoli, 1923.
Arc 1185.19.3 — Barone, N. Paleografia latina diplomatica. 3. ed. Napoli, 1923.
Arc 830.26 — Barranger, A. Étude d'archéologie celtique...Seine-et-Oise. Paris, 1864.
Arc 1033.35.3 — Barrau, J.B. Notice historique sur la vraie croix de Baugé. Angers, 1874.
Arc 793.5 — Barré, L. Herculanum et Pompéi. Paris, 1840. 7v.
Arc 793.5.5 — Barré, L. Herculanum et Pompéi. Paris, 1863-72. 7v.
Htn Arc 793.5* — Barré, L. Herculanum et Pompéi. v.8. Paris, 1840.
Htn Arc 793.5.5* — Barré, L. Herculanum et Pompéi. v.8. Paris, 1872.
Arc 1033.101 — Barreca, C. Santa Lucia di Siracusa. Roma, 1902.
Arc 830.49.25 — Barrière, P. Vesunna Petrucoriorum. Périgueux, 1930.
Arc 820.204 — Barrière-Flavy, Casimir. Les arts industriels. Paris, 1901. 3v.
Arc 820.207F — Barrière-Flavy, Casimir. Étude sur les sépultures barbares du midi et de l'ouest de la France. Toulouse, 1892.
Arc 870.10 — Barrow diggers. (Woolls, C.) London, 1839.
Arc 861.191F — Barrow Mead, Bath, 1964: excavation of a medieval peasant house. (Woodhouse, Jayne.) Oxford, 1976.
Arc 785.54 — Barsari, Luigi. Del Pons Agruppae sul Tevere tra le regioni IX e XIII. Roma, 1888.
Arc 595.18 — Bart, J.Y.S. On some points in certain theories...of the great Pyramid of Jeeseh. Glasgow, 1868.
Arc 853.47 — Bartelt, Wilhelm. Die Burgwälle des Ruppiner Kreises. Würzburg, 1910.
Arc 936.195.205 — Barth, Fritz Eckart. Die hallstattzeitlichen Grabhügel im Bereiche der Kutscher bei Podsemel (Slowenien). Bonn, 1969.
Arc 608.5 — Barth, H. Wanderungen...Kuestenlaender...Mittelmeeres. Berlin, 1849.
Arc 1498.4 — Barthélemy, A. de. Numatisque de la France. Paris, 1891.
Arc 1390.1 — Barthélemy, A.J.B.A. Nouveau manuel complet de numismatique du moyen age et moderne. Text et atlas. Paris, n.d. 2v.
Arc 1390.1.3 — Barthélemy, A.J.B.A. Nouveau manuel complet de numismatique du moyen age et moderne. Text et atlas. Paris, 1874. 2v.
Arc 1356.1.3 — Barthélemy, A.J.B.A. Nouveau manuel complete de numismatique ancienne. Paris, 1866.
Arc 1356.1 — Barthélemy, A.J.B.A. Nouveau manuel complete de numismatique ancienne. Text and atlas. Paris, 1866. 2v.
Arc 1500.16 — Barthélemy, Anatole de. Liste des noms d'hommes gravés sur les monnaies. Paris, 1881.
Arc 1500.15 — Barthélemy, Anatole de. Monnaie gauloise inédite de Luctérius, chef Cadurque. n.p., 1880.
Arc 1500.14 — Barthélemy, Anatole de. Note sur les monnaies trouvées au Mont César. Paris, 1881.
Arc 726.10.4 — Barthélemy, J.J. Explication de la mosaique de Palestrine. Paris, 1760.
Arc 723.14 — Barthélemy, J.J. Voyage en Italie. Paris, 1801.
Htn Arc 1033.12.211* — Bartholini, T. De latere Christi aperto. Lugdunum Batavorum, 1646.
Arc 1540.22.7 — Bartlet, B. The episcopal coins of Durham. Newcastle, 1817.
Arc 386.1 — Bartlett, T.H. About monuments. Boston, 1878?
Arc 608.12.15 — Bartoccini, R. Guida di Sabratha. Roma, 1927.
Arc 608.18.5F — Bartoccini, R. Le terme di Lepcis (Leptis Magna). Bergamo, 1929.
Arc 1020.103 — Bartoletti, T. Privato santuario atessano...de'santi, beati. Napoli, 1835.
Arc 785.13.55 — Bartoli, Alfonso. Il Foro Romano, il Palatino. Milano, 1924.
Arc 785.13.57 — Bartoli, Alfonso. The Roman Forum; the Palatine. Milan, 1924.
Arc 1070.202.3 — Bartoli, P.S. Le antiche lucerne. Roma, 1691.
Arc 1070.203 — Bartoli, P.S. Le antiche lucerne. Roma, 1729.
Arc 1070.201.9F — Bartoli, P.S. Gli antichi sepolcri. Roma, 1697.
Arc 1070.202 — Bartoli, P.S. Gli antichi sepolcri. Roma, 1727.
Arc 785.15.15 — Bartoli, P.S. Die Traianssäule. Voorburg, 1941.
Arc 1086.2.9F — Bartoli, Pietro. Veterum lucernae sepulcrales. Lugduni Batavorum, 1723. 2 pam.
Arc 1033.18.5 — Bartolini, A. Gli atti della Passione degli ss. Abdon e Sennen. Roma, 1859.
Arc 1018.6.21 — Bartolini, A. Elogio del cavalier professore Mariano Armellini. Roma, 1896.
Arc 720.202 — Bartolini, D. L'antico cassino e il primitivo monasterio. Montecassino, 1880.
Arc 1033.40 — Bartolini, D. Gli atti del martirio...S. Cecilia. Roma, 1867.
Arc 1016.223 — Bartolini, D. Atti del martiro della S. Agnese. Roma, 1858.
Arc 1027.26 — Bartolini, D. Le catacombe di Siracusa. Roma, 1847.
Arc 1033.46 — Bartolini, D. Cenni biografici di S. Giacomo apostolo il maggiore. Roma, 1885.
Arc 1027.74 — Bartolini, D. Il cimitero d'Aproniano di anche della S. Eugenia. Roma, 1840.
Arc 1027.30.15 — Bartolini, D. Inscrizione S. Martire Fortissima nel cimitero...Ciriaca. Roma, 1842.
Arc 1033.40.5 — Bartolini, D. Istoria del Martirio di S. Cecilia. Roma, 1759.
Arc 1027.27 — Bartolini, D. Le nuove catacombe di Chiusi. Roma, 1852.
Arc 1027.27.2 — Bartolini, D. Le nuove catacombe di Chiusi. Roma, 1853.
Arc 1027.1.17 — Bartolini, D. Relazione severamente i vasi...sangue dei martiri. Roma, 1863.
Arc 1033.13.13 — Bartolini, D. Sopra l'anno LXII dell'era...Pietro e Paolo. 2. ed. Roma, 1867.
Arc 1020.9.142 — Bartolini, D. Sopra l'antichissimo altare di legno...Lateranense. Roma, 1852.
Arc 1027.60 — Bartolini, D. Sopra l'antico oratorio...regione de Marsi. Roma, 1855.
Arc 1033.27.5 — Bartolini, D. La sotterranea confessoni...di San Marco. Roma, 1844.
Arc 1020.26 — Bartolini, D. Su l'antica basilica di S. Nicola in Bari. Roma, 1882.
Arc 505.5.25 — Bartolini, D. Sull'antico Tempio Salomone. Roma, 1868.
Arc 1020.9.15 — Bartolomei, L. Memorie autentiche sulla chiesa di S. Paolo alla Regola. Roma, 1858.
Arc 1033.106 — Bartolomei. Della scuola di S. Paolo. Roma, 1850.
Arc 386.4.25 — Bartolomeo Borghesi. (Borghesi, Bartolomeo.) Firenze, 1905.
Arc 441.1.7 — Barua, B.M. Gaya and Buddha-Gaya. Calcutta, 1931-34. 2v.
Arc 1033.88 — Baruffaldi, G. Del Colpo di Spada...la morte a i Martiri. Venezia, 1759.
Arc 1027.39.5 — Baruffaldi, G. Dissertazione intorno...sepolcro...cimitero di Prestato. Venezia? 1747?
Arc 936.155.10 — Baruzdin, J.D. Arkheologicheskie pamiatniki Batkena i Liailiaka, Jugo-Zapadnaia Kirgiziia. Frunze, 1962.
Arc 66.1.81 — Le Bas-Relief Romain a représentations historiques. (Courbaud, E.) Paris, 1899.
Arc 543.7.23 — Les bas-reliefs d'Angkor-Vat. (Coedès, George.) Paris, 1911.
Arc 1345.1.3 — Bas-reliefs du Parthénon. Paris, 1858.
Arc 935.75 — Başar, Zeki. Evrurumda eski merorliklarve resimli mezar taşlari. Ankara, 1973.
Arc 1500.28 — Bascle de Lagrèze, G. Essai sur l'histoire monetaire...de Béarn. Toulouse, 1855.
Arc 1027.12.9 — La basilica apostolorum e la critta apostolica. (Bufalieré, P.) Roma, 1891.
Arc 1020.20.5 — La Basilica di Costantino. (Fea, C.) Roma, 1819.
Arc 815.16F — La Basilica di Pompei. (Sogliano, A.) Napoli, 1911. 6 pam.
Arc 1027.30.9 — La basilica di S. Lorenzo fuor delle mura. (Salvatore da Morrovalle, P.) Bologna, 1861.
Arc 1016.206.9 — Basilica di S. Maria Maggiore. (Iozzi, Oliviero.) Roma, 1903.
Arc 1027.4.35 — La basilica di S. Silvestro nel cimitero di Priscilla. (Rossi, G.B. de.) Roma, 1890.
Arc 1033.40.15 — Basilica e Casa Romana di S. Cecilia in Trastevere. (Picarelli, T.) Roma, 1904.
Arc 1020.9.43 — La basilica esquilina di Santa Maria ed il palazzo apostolico. (Biasiotti, G.) Roma, 1911.
Arc 1033.20.28 — The Basilica of Saint Clemente in Rome. (Nolan, Louis.) Rome, 1910.
Arc 1033.20.29 — The Basilica of Saint Clemente in Rome. 2. ed. (Nolan, Louis.) Rome, 1914.
Arc 1033.20.26 — Basilica of St. Clement in Rome. (Brownlow.) London, 1900.
Arc 1027.4.40 — La basilica papale del cimitero di Priscilla. (Marucchi, O.) Roma, 1908.
Arc 1033.20.5 — Le basiliche cristiane. (Carini, I.) Roma, 1893.

Author and Title Listing

Arc 785.47 La basilique pythagoricienne de la Porte Majeure. (Carcopino, J.) Paris, 1927.

Arc 955.2.11 Basket-maker, caves of northeastern Arizona. (Fewkes, J.W.) Cambridge, 1921.

Arc 630.15 Basler Antiken im Bild. (Schefold, Karl.) Basel, 1958.

Arc 853.65.30 Baśń i podanie górno-śląskie. (Badura-Simonides, D.) Katowice, 1961. 4 pam.

Arc 412.1.15 Bass, George Fletcher. Archaeology beneath the sea. N.Y., 1975.

Arc 412.1 Bass, George Fletcher. Archaeology under water. London, 1966.

Arc 412.1.5 Bass, George Fletcher. A history of seafaring based on underwater archaeology. London, 1972.

Arc 925.342 Bassein Oki v epokhu bronzy. (Bader, Otto N.) Moskva, 1970.

Arc 1027.79 Bassi, A. Della torre Antonia d'una stupenda galleria...in Gerusalemme. Gerusalemme, 1860.

Arc 1143.14F Bassi, Stelio. Monumenta Italiae graphica. Cremona, 1956-57.

Arc 1033.89 Bassich, A. Della vita e del martirio di San Trifone. Vienna, 1845.

Arc 887.1F Bast, M.J. de. Recueeil d'antiquités romaines et gauloises trouvées dans la Flandre. Gand, 1808.

Arc 1033.35.41 Bastelaer, D.A. Etude sur les précieux reliquaire phylactère du XIIe siècle. Anvers, 1880.

Arc 746.22 Bastianelli, S. Centumcellae (Civitavecchia). Roma, 1954.

Arc 936.100.10 Baština djedova. (Karaman, L.) Zagreb, 1944.

Arc 1148.25.5 Bataille, A. Les papyrus. 1. éd. Paris, 1955.

Arc 1148.25 Bataille, A. Pour une terminologie in paléographie grecque. Paris, 1954.

Arc 1411.7 Batairaasch Genootschap van Kunsten in Wetenschappen. Catalogus der munten en amuletten van China. Batavia, 1904.

Arc 1494.6 Batalha Reis, Pedro. Moedas de Toro. Lisboa, 1933.

Arc 1335.56.2 Bataviaasch Genootschap van Kunsten en Wetenschappen. Museum. Catalogus der numismatische afdeeling. 2. druk. Batavia, 1877.

Arc 1335.56.3 Bataviaasch Genootschap van Kunsten en Wetenschappen. Museum. Catalogus der numismatische versameling. 3. druk. Batavia, 1886.

Arc 858.11 Bateman, T. Ten years' diggings in Celtic and Saxon grave hills. London, 1861.

Arc 861.27 Bateman, T. Vestiges of the antiquities of Derbyshire. London, 1848.

Arc 861.38.8 Bath and Camerton Archaeological Society. A north Somerset miscellany. Bath, 1966.

Arc 861.28 Bathurst, W.H. Roman antiquities at Lyndney Park. London, 1879.

Arc 513.34 Bati Anoidolu'da eski şehirler. (Duyuran, Rüstem.) Istanbul, 1948.

Arc 936.180.15 Batović, Šime. Stariji neolit u Dalmaciji. Zadar, 1966.

Arc 1027.12.5 Battandier, A. La Platonia...sepulcre des Sts. Pierre et Paul. Paris, 1896.

Arc 861.8.5 Battely, J. Antiquitates rutupinae. Oxoniae, 1811.

Arc 861.8.6 Battely, J. Antiquitates rutupinae. 2. ed. Oxoniae, 1745. 2 pam.

Arc 861.8.9 Battely, J. The antiquities of Richborough and Reculver. London, 1774.

Arc 1185.30 Battheney. L'archiviste françois. 2. éd. Paris, 1775.

Arc 726.135 Battisti, C. La Venezia Tridentina nella preistoria. Firenze, 1954.

Arc 1538.4 Batty, D.T. Catalogue of the copper coinage of Great Britain. Manchester, 1868-98. 4v.

Arc 889.5 Die Bauart der Einzelgräber. Text and atlas. (Giffen, Albert Egges van.) Leipzig, 1930. 2v.

Arc 1138.25 Bauckner, A. Einführung in das mittelalterliche Schriftum. München, 1923.

Arc 386.14 Baudelot de Dairval, C.C. De l'utilité des voyages...la recherche des antiquitéz. Paris, 1686. 2v.

Arc 386.14.5 Baudelot de Dairval, C.C. De l'utilité des voyages...la recherche des antiquitéz. Rouen, 1727. 2v.

Arc 1093.2.11 Baudon, T. Des silex perforés naturellement. Paris, 1909.

Arc 830.331 Baudot, L.B. Observations sur la passage de M. Millin à Dijon. Dijon, 1808.

Arc 830.178 Baudouin, M. Le Rocher aux pieds du mas d'île à Lessac. Paris, 1915.

Arc 66.1.68 Baudrillart, A. Divinités de la victoire en Grèce et en Italie. Paris, 1894.

Arc 822.1 Baudry, F. Recherches archéologiques à Pareds. La-Roche-sur-Yon, 1874. 21 pam.

Arc 830.65 Baudry, Ferdinand. Puits funéraires gallo-romains. La Roche-sur-Yon, 1873.

Arc 830.124.5 Bauernfarmen der Steinzeit. (Forrer, Robert.) Strassburg, 1903.

Arc 505.5.3 Baugeschichte des Jüdischen Heiligthums...Tempel Salomons. (Prestel, J.) Strassburg, 1902.

Arc 403.7.3 Die Baukunst der Armenier und Europa. (Strzygowski, J.) Wien, 1918. 2v.

Htn Arc 968.2.75* Baumann, G. Frijoles Canyon pictographs. Santa Fe, 1939.

Arc 600.240F Baumgaertel, Elise J. Petrie's Nagada excavation; a supplement. London, 1970.

Arc 551.9F Baumgartel, Elise J. The cultures of prehistoric Egypt. London, 1947.

Arc 708.2.3 Baumgarten, Fritz. Ein Rundgang durch die Ruinen Athens. Leipzig, 1888.

Arc 708.2 Baumgarten, Fritz. Ein Rundgang durch die Ruinen Athens. Wertheim, 1887.

Arc 1027.25.19 Baumgarten, P.M. Giovanni Battista de Rossi. Köln, 1892.

Arc 1027.25.20 Baumgarten, P.M. Giovanni Battista de Rossi. Roma, 1892.

Arc 1020.31.17 Baumstark, Anton. Die Modestianischen...zu Jerusalem. Paderborn, 1915.

Arc 1663.55 Bauquier, Henri. Histoire numismatique du comte de Chanbord. Paris, 1911-40.

Arc 505.45A Baur, P.V.C. The excavations at Dura-Europas. pt.1-9. New Haven, 1929-1946. 9v.

Arc 830.225 Baurés, Jacques. L'aventure souterraine. Paris, 1958.

Arc 1077.2.53.2 Baus, Karl. Der Kranz in Antike und Christentum. Bonn, 1965.

Arc 545.205.2 Bauurkunde der Tempelanlagen von Dendera. (Duemichen, J.) Leipzig, 1865.

Arc 386.2 Baye, J. de. L'archéologie préhistorique. Paris, 1888.

Arc 855.202 Baye, J. de. The industrial arts of the Anglo-Saxons. London, 1893.

Arc 1093.2.6 Baye, J. de. Les instruments en pierre à l'epoque de métaux. Paris, 1881.

Arc 612.22F Baye, Joseph. De l'influence de l'art des Goths en Occident. Paris, 1891.

Arc 853.370 Bayer, Heinrich. Die ländliche Besiedlung Rheinhessens. Inaug. Diss. Mainz, 1967?

Arc 785.16 Bayer, J. Stuck-Reliefs...Casa Farnesina in Rom. Wien, 1897.

Arc 1510.11.10 Bayerische Münzkataloge. Günwald. 1,1957 4v.

Arc 1301.6 Bayerische Numismatische Gesellschaft. Mitteilungen. München. 1-52,1882-1934

Arc 1301.6.2 Bayerische Numismatische Gesellschaft. Mitteilungen. Register. München. 1-48,1882-1930

Arc 1510.126 Bayerns Ehrenbuch. (Kraemer, Georg.) Nürnberg, 1834.

Arc 1030.6 Bayet, C. De titulis atticae christianis. Paris, 1878.

Arc 66.1.10 Bayet, C. Peinture et sculpture chrétiennes en Orient. Paris, 1879.

Arc 66.1.132.5 Bayet, J. Herclé, étude critique. Paris, 1926.

Arc 66.1.132 Bayet, J. Les origines de l'Hercule Romain. Paris, 1926.

Arc 858.32 Bayley, Harold. Archaic England. London, 1919.

Arc 861.18.19 Bayley, Harold. The lost language of London. London, 1935.

Arc 542.205 Bayon d'Angkor Thom. (Mission Henri Dufour.) Paris, 1910.

Arc 830.15.5 Bazin, H. Arles gallo-romain. Guide du touriste archéologue. Paris, 1896.

Arc 825.6 Bazin, H. Nîmes gallo-romain. Paris, 1892.

Arc 830.6 Bazin, H. Villes antiques - Vienne et Lyon gallo-romain. Paris, 1891.

Arc 1468.65.1 Die Beamtennamen auf den griechischen Münzen. (Münsterberg, Rudolf.) Hildesheim, 1973.

Arc 530.176 Bean, George Ewart. Turkey beyond the Maeander, an archaeological guide. London, 1971.

Arc 968.1.5 Beauchamp, W.M. Metallic ornaments of the New York Indians. n.p., n.d.

Arc 968.1.5.5 Beauchamp, W.M. Wampum and shell articles used by the New York Indians. Albany, 1901. 2 pam.

Arc 66.1.36 Beaudoin, M. Étude du dialecte chypriote. Paris, 1884.

Htn Arc 513.2* Beaufort, F. Karamania. London, 1817.

Arc 830.103 Beaulieu, J.L.D. Antiquités des eaux minérales de Vichy. Paris, 1851.

Arc 858.54.5 Beaumont, Comyns. Britain, the key to world history. London, 1949.

Arc 858.54 Beaumont, Comyns. The riddle of prehistoric Britain. London, 1946.

Arc 830.201 Le Beaunois gallo-romain; ouvrage présenté et complété. (Thévenot, Emile.) Bruxelles, 1971.

Arc 810.33 Beccarini, Paolo. Un decennio di nuovi scavi in Pompei. Milano, 1922.

Htn Arc 1033.17.96.3* Becerra Tanco, Luis. Felicidad de México...Nuestra Señora de Guadalupe. México, 1780.

Arc 1033.17.96.6 Becerra Tanco, Luis. Nuestra Señora de Guadalupe y origen. 6. ed. México, 1883.

Arc 888.5F Die Becherkultur in den Niederlanden. Inaug. Diss. (Bursch, F.C.) Leiden, 1933.

Arc 853.21 Becherstatuen in Ostpreussen. (Hartmann, A.) Braunschweig, 1892.

Arc 505.11 Bechstein, O. 30 Ansichten der deutschen Ausgraben Baalbek. Berlin, 1905.

Arc 853.95 Beck, F. Der Karlsgraben. Nürnberg, 1911.

Arc 895.42 Becker, C. Mosefund lerkar fra yngre stenalder. København, 1948.

Arc 1027.45.5 Becker, Erich. Malta Sotterranea...Sepulkralkunst. Strassburg, 1913.

Arc 1027.23 Becker, F. Die Darstellung Jesu Christi...Bilde des Fisches. Gero, 1876.

Arc 1033.69.20 Becker, F. Die Heidnische Weiheformel Diis Manibus. Gera, 1881.

Arc 1030.33 Becker, F. Inschriften der römischen Coemeterien. Gera, 1878.

Arc 1027.23.5 Becker, F. Die Waud- und Decken-Gernälde Römischen Katakomben. Düsseldorf, 1874.

Arc 853.4.13 Becker, J. Castellum Mattiacorum. Wiesbaden, 1863. 6 pam.

Arc 853.4 Becker, J. Drei römische Votivhaende aus den Rheinlanden. Frankfurt am Main, 1862.

Arc 853.4.2 Becker, J. Die Heddernheimer Votivhand. Frankfurt am Main, 1861.

Arc 1025.53 Becker, T. Rom's altchristliche Coemeterien. Düsseldorf, 1874.

Arc 756.1 Becker, W.A. Die römische Topographie in Rom. Leipzig, 1844.

Arc 756.1.2 Becker, W.A. Zur römischen Topographie. Leipzig, 1845.

Arc 889.26 Beckers, H.J. Voorgeschiedenis van Zuid Limburg. Maastricht, 1940.

Arc 861.201 Beckery Chapel, Glastonbury, 1967-68. (Rahtz, Philip.) Glastonbury, 1974.

Arc 1448.6 Becklake, J.T. From real to rand. South Africa, 1963?

Arc 400.9 Bedenken zur Vorgeschichts-Forschung. (Piper, Otto.) München, 1913.

Arc 1200.12 Bedeutung der Salutatio...14. Jahrhundert. (Krüger, P.) Greifswald, 1912.

Arc 853.20.27 Bedeutung und Gefährdung der grossen Tempelgrabung in Trier. (Loeschcke, S.) Trier, 1930.

Arc 126.5 Bedfordshire archaeological journal. Luton, England.

Arc 1033.17.136 Bédouet, Z. Pélérinage de la sainte ceinture au Puy-Notre Dame. Paris, n.d.

Arc 543.7.5 Beerski, A. (Mrs.). Angkor; ruins in Cambodia. London, 1923.

Arc 853.373 Befastigungsanlagen im und am Harz von der Frühgeschichte bis zur Neuzeit. Ein Handbuch. (Stolberg, Friedrich.) Hildesheim, 1968.

Arc 612.89 Before civilization; the radiocarbon revolution and prehistoric Europe. (Renfrew, Colin.) London, 1973.

Arc 87.1.42 Befreining des Prometheus. (Milchhoefer, A.) Berlin, 1882.

Arc 1485.2 Beger, L. Numismata...Brandenburgici sectio prima. Brandenburgi, 1704.

Htn Arc 380.208* Beger, L. Spicilgium antiquitates. Coloniae Brandenburgicae, 1692.

Htn Arc 1455.1* Beger, L. Thesaurus Brandenburgicus. Colonia Marchica, 1696. 3v.

Arc 395.15.2 Beginning in archaeology. (Kenyon, Kathleen Mary.) London, 1952.

Arc 395.15.5 Beginning in archaeology. (Kenyon, Kathleen Mary.) N.Y., 1961.

Arc 395.15 Beginning in archaeology. 2. ed. (Kenyon, Kathleen Mary.) London, 1953.

Arc 421.31.2 The beginnings of Chinese civilization. (Li, Chi.) Seatle, 1968.

Arc 830.330F Bégouën, Henri. Les cavernes du Volp. Paris, 1958.

Arc 1033.120 Beheim, J.C. Dissertatio...de archeiois sive tabulariis sacris. Norimburgi, n.d.

Author and Title Listing

Arc 1090.1 Behlen, H. Der Pflug und der Pflügen. Dillenburg, 1904.
Arc 853.343F Behm-Blancke, Günter. Gesellschaft und Kunst der Germanen. Dresden, 1973.
Arc 853.93F Behmer, E. Das zweischneidige Schwert der germanischen völkerwanderungszeit. Stockholm, 1939.
Arc 726.10.10 Behn, F. Die ficoronische Cista. Leipzig, 1907.
Arc 726.10.9 Behn, F. Die ficoronische Cista. Diss. Rostock, 1907.
Arc 848.31 Behn, Friedrich. Altgermanische Kultur. Leipzig, 1935.
Arc 848.40 Behn, Friedrich. Altgermanische Kunst. 2. Aufl. München, 1930.
Arc 848.31.5 Behn, Friedrich. Altmordisches Leben vor 3000 Jahren. München, 1935.
Arc 612.38 Behn, Friedrich. Aus europäischer Vorzeit. Stuttgart, 1957.
Arc 386.42 Behn, Friedrich. Ausgrabungen und Ausgräber. Stuttgart, 1961.
Arc 612.65 Behn, Friedrich. Die Bronzezeit in Nordeuropa. Bildnis einer prähistorischen Hochkultur. Stuttgart, 1967.
Arc 853.57 Behn, Friedrich. Führer durch die römische Granitindustrie auf dem Felsberg im Odenwald. Mainz, 1925.
Arc 853.274 Behren-Lübchin. (Schuldt, Ewald.) Berlin, 1965.
Arc 383.75 Behrens, Gustav. Reinecke Festschrift zum 75. Geburtstag von Paul Reinecke. Mainz, 1950.
Arc 1510.80 Behrens, Heinrich. Münzen und Medaillen der Stadt und des Bisthums Siebeck. Berlin, 1905.
Arc 853.94 Die beidnischen Alterthümer Ostfrieslands. (Tergast.) Emden, 1879.
Arc 913.5.5 Beilage zur archäologischen Karte den Ostschweiz. 2. Aufl. (Keller, F.) Frauenfeld, 1873.
Arc 340.16 Beilekchi, V.S. Bibliografiia po arkheologii Moldavii, 1946-1966. Kishinev, 1967.
Arc 31.11 Beirut. Musée National Libanais. Bulletin du musée de Beyrouth. Paris. 1,1937+ 9v.
Arc 186.10 Beitraage zur Oberpfalzforschung. Kallmünz. 1,1965+
Arc 895.78 Beiträge zum Studium von bronzeitlichen Siedlungen. (Stjernquist, Berta.) Bonn, 1969.
Arc 1200.8 Beiträge zum Urkundenwesen der ältern Bischöfe. (Schillmann, F.) Leipzig, 1908.
Arc 2.3F Beiträge zur ägyptischen Bauforschung und Altertumskunde. Kairo. 1-9 6v.
Arc 1370.3 Beiträge zur älteren Münzkunde. (Pinder, M.) Berlin, 1851.
Arc 905.24 Beiträge zur alten Geschichte des Obergailthales in Kärnten. (Schlechter, Max.) Wien, 1885.
Arc 723.5A Beiträge zur altitalischen Kultur und Kunstgeschichte. (Helbig, W.) Leipzig, 1879.
Arc 2.8 Beitraege zur Archäologie. Würzburg. 1,1970+
Arc 31.16 Beitraege zur Archäologie und Geologie des Zendan-I. Wiesbaden. 1,1968+
Arc 905.90.5 Beiträge zur Chronologie der Mittleren Bronzezeit im Karpatenbecken. (Haensel, Bernhard.) Bonn, 1968. 2v.
Arc 1200.3 Beiträge zur Diplomatik der ältern Bischoefe von Hildesheim. Inaug. Diss. (Heinemann, O.) Marburg, 1895.
Arc 1175.7 Beiträge zur Diplomatik der langodardischen Fürsten. (Voigt, Karl.) Göttingen, 1902.
Arc 662.4 Beiträge zur Erklärung...griechische Kunstwerke. (Weissmann, K.) Schweinfurt, 1903.
Arc 1153.59 Beiträge zur Geschichte der äusseren Merkmale des ältesten Breslauer Bischofsurkunden bis zum Jahre 1319. Inaug. Diss. (Allamoda, H.) Oblau, 1924.
Arc 1200.21 Beiträge zur Geschichte der Staatskanzlei im islamischen Ägypten. (Björkman, Walther.) Hamburg, 1928.
Arc 672.5 Beiträge zur Geschichte des alten Korinth. (Wilisch, E.) Zittau, 1901.
Arc 630.8 Beiträge zur Geschichte des Tropaions. (Woelcke, Karl.) Bonn, 1911.
Arc 925.8.30 Beiträge zur Geschichte und Archäologie von Cherronesos in Taurien. (Koehne, B.) St. Petersburg, 1850.
Arc 1470.11 Beiträge zur Geschichte und Numismatik...des Pontus. (Sallet, A. von.) Berlin, 1866.
Arc 1053.25 Beiträge zur Ikonographie der konstantinischen Sarkophagplastik. (Stommel, Edward.) Bonn, 1954.
Arc 700.3 Beiträge zur Kenntnis der Griechischen Kuppelgraeber. (Belger, C.) Berlin, 1887.
Arc 915.37 Beiträge zur Kenntnis der Haustiere der romischkeltischen Ansiedlung auf der Engehalbinsel bei Bern. (Traininas, Davidas.) Bern, 1933.
Arc 853.64 Beiträge zur Kenntnis des norddeutschen Paläolithikums und Mesolithikums. (Andree, Julius.) Leipzig, 1932.
Arc 383.9.5 Beiträge zur Kulturgeschichte; Festschrfit Reinhold Bosch. (Drack, Walter.) Aarau, 1947.
Arc 628.11 Beiträge zur Kunstgeschichte. (Urlichs, L. von.) Leipzig, n.d.
Arc 522.6 Beitraege zur Landeskunde der Troas. (Virchow, R.) Berlin, 1879.
Arc 672.1.116 Beiträge zur minoischen Gräberkunde. (Pini, Ingo.) Wiesbaden, 1968.
Arc 1433.10 Beiträge zur Muhammedanischen Münzkunde. (Fraehn, C.M.J.) Berlin, n.d.
Arc 785.19 Beiträge zur römischen Topographie. v.1-2,3. (Richter, O.) Berlin, 1903. 2v.
Arc 1510.143 Beiträge zur schwäbisch-fränkischen Münzkunde des späteren Mittelalters. (Buchenau, H.) n.p., 19- .
Arc 505.138 Beiträge zur Siedlungs- und Territorialgeschichte des nördlichen Ostjordanlandes. (Mittmann, Siegfried.) Wiesbaden, 1970.
Arc 1279.5 Beiträge zur Siegelkunde des Mittelalters. (Melly, Edward.) Wien, 1850. 2v.
Arc 1279.5F Beiträge zur Siegelkunde des Mittelalters. Supplement. (Melly, Edward.) Wien, 1850.
Arc 1510.5.5 Beiträge zur süddeutschen Münzgeschichte. (Goessler, Peter.) Stuttgart, 1927.
Arc 673.1 Beiträge zur Topographie von Delphi. (Pomtow, H.) Berlin, 1889.
Arc 905.136 Beiträge zur Urgeschichte Tirols. (Menghin, Osmund.) Innsbruck, 1969.
Arc 1185.6 Beitraege zur Urkundenlehre. (Ficker, J.) Innsbruck, 1877-78. 2v.
Arc 1510.169 Ein Beitrag zur Geschichte des Kontermarkenwesens. (Friedrich, Karl.) Münster, 1970.
Arc 87.1.37 Beitrag zur griechischen Gewichtskunde. (Schillbach, D.) Berlin, 1877.
Arc 1033.62.9 Ein Beitrag zur Lösung zer Felicitas-Frage. (Führer, Joseph.) Leipzig, 1890.
Arc 1200.18 Beitrag zur praktischen Diplomatik für Slaven. (Alter, Franz K.) Wien, 1801.
Arc 1675.19.5 Beitrag zur russischen Medaillenkunde. (Iversen, I.) St. Petersburg, 1870.

Arc 1613.25 Belden, Bauman. United States war medals. N.Y., 1916.
Arc 1663.58 Belden, Bauman Lowe. Indian peace medals issued in the United States. New Milford, Conn., 1966.
Arc 543.138 Belenitskii, Aleksandr Markovich. Central Asia. London, 1969.
Arc 543.138.5 Belenitskii, Aleksandr Markovich. Srednevekovyi gorod Srednei Azii. Leningrad, 1973.
Arc 1478.36 Belfort, A. Recherches des monnaies impériales romaines non décrites dans l'ouvrage de H. Cohen. Macon, 1884.
Arc 700.3 Belger, C. Beiträge zur Kenntnis der Griechischen Kuppelgraeber. Berlin, 1887.
Htn Arc 700.4* Belger, C. Die Mykenische Lokalsage von den Gräbern Agamemnons und der Seinen. Berlin, 1893.
Arc 889.12 Les Belges avant César. (Tourneur, V.) Bruxelles, 1944.
Arc 733.6 Belgiorno, Franco Libero. I Siciliani di 15 mila anni fa. Catania, 1965.
Arc 273.6 Belgium. Federation archéologique et historique. Annales. Anvers. 16-35 12v.
Arc 936.220.30 Belgrade. Narodni Muzej. Lepenski vir. Beograd, 1967.
Arc 936.251.5 Belgrade. Narodni Muzej. Neolit centralnog Balkana. Beograd, 1968.
Arc 302.37 Belgrade. Zavod za zoš title i naučno proučavanje e spomenika kulture NR Srbije. Saopštenja. 2+ 3v.
Arc 1163.3.3 Beliaev, Ivan S. Prakticheskii kurs izucheniia drevnei russkoi skoropisi dlia chteniia rukopisei XV-XVIII stoletii. 2. izd. Reproduction. Moskva, 1911.
Arc 925.75.20 Belinde Ballu, Eugéne. Olbia. Leiden, 1972.
Arc 968.11 Bell, Earl Hoyt. Chapters in Nebraska archaeology. Lincoln, Nebraska, 1936.
Arc 672.1.37 Bell, Edward. Prehellenic architecture in the Aegean. London, 1926.
Arc 1425.4F Bell, H.W. Sardis, coins. v.11. Leiden, 1916.
Arc 1680.18 Bell, Robert Charles. Tradesmen's tickets and private tokens: 1785-1819. Newcastle-upon-Tyne, 1966.
Arc 1020.9.179 Bella congregazione illirica e de' nuovi affreschi. (Gerardi, F.M.) Roma, 1853.
Arc 600.5.2 Bellefonds, L. de. Mémoire sur le Lac Moeris. Alexandrie, 1843.
Arc 1027.24 Bellermann, C.F. Über die ältesten christlichen Begrabnifsstätten. Hamburg, 1839.
Arc 1027.25.65 Bellesheim, A. Der heilige Johannes Baptista de Rossi. Mainz, 1882.
X Cg Arc 672.1.11 Belli, Onorio. A description of some theatres in Crete. London, 1854.
Arc 800.1 Bellicard, J.C. Observations on the antiques of the town of Herculaneum. London, 1753.
Arc 1453.2F Bellinger, A.R. Catalogue of the coins found at Corinth, 1925. New Haven, 1930.
Htn Arc 1488.6* Bellini, V. De monetis Italiae medii aeirhactenus. Ferrariae, 1755.
Htn Arc 1490.17* Bellini, Y. Delle monete di Ferrara. Ferrara, 1761.
Arc 1335.51 Bellissima, G.B. Riordinamento del museo numismatico. v.1-2. Siena, 1914.
Arc 750.218F Pamphlet box. Bellissima, G.B.
Arc 1018.14 Belloc, J.T. de. Ste. Agnès et son siècle. Lille, 1893.
Arc 1016.238 Bellomo, G. La pala d'oro dell...basilica di San Marco. Venezia, 1847.
Arc 1016.218 Belloni, P. Sulla grandezza della primitiva basilica ostiense. Roma, 1853.
Htn Arc 750.25* Bellori, G.A. Veteres Arcus Augustorum. Roma, 1690.
Htn Arc 750.220F* Bellori, G.P. Fragmenta vestigii veteris Romae. Colophon, 1673.
Arc 1076.3.95 Bells; their history, legends, making, and uses. (Coleman, Satis N. (Barton).) Chicago, 1928.
Arc 1076.3.50 Pamphlet box. Bells. Miscellaneous pamphlets.
Arc 1076.3.31 The bells of England. (Raven, J.J.) London, 1906.
Arc 1076.3.77F Bells of the church. (Ellacombe, H.T.) Exeter, 1872.
Arc 1076.3.93 Bells thro' the ages. (Nichols, J.R.) London, 1928.
Arc 746.8 Bellucci, G. L'ipoge della famiglia etrusca "Rufia". Perugia, 1911.
Arc 1033.12.66 Bellum de sanguine Christi. (Quiroga, M.P. de.) Valladolid, 1721.
Arc 925.150.25 Belorusskie drevnosti. (Konferentsiia po Arkheologii Belorussii, Minsk, 1968.) Minsk, 1967.
Arc 925.150.50 Belorusskiia starazhytnastsi. (Konferentsiia po Arkheologii Belorussii i Smezhnykh Territorii, Minsk, 1972.) Minsk, 1972.
Arc 520.25 Belov, G.D. Altar' Zevsa v Pergame. Leningrad, 1958.
Arc 520.25.2 Belov, G.D. Altar' Zevsa v Pergame. Leningrad, 1959.
Arc 925.8.37 Belov, G.D. Khersones tavricheskii. Leningrad, 1948.
Arc 925.50.40 Belov, G.D. Khersones Tavricheskii. Simferopol', 1958.
Arc 925.8.35 Belov, G.D. Muzei i raskopki khersonesa. Simferopol, 1936.
Arc 925.50.340 Belov, Grigorii D. Otchet o raskopkakh v Khersonese za 1935-36 gg. Sevastopol', 1938.
Arc 1356.6 Beltrán Martinez, A. Curso de numismatica. 2. ed. Cartagena, 1950.
Arc 1663.14 Belts, Benjamin. Descriptive list of medals relating to John Law. n.p., 1907.
Arc 750.205 Beltzami, L. Il pantheon. Milano, 1898.
Arc 551.1.5 Belzoni, G.B. G.B. Belzoni. Padova, 1960.
Arc 545.14 Belzoni, G.B. Narrative of the operations...in Egypt and Nubia. 3. ed. London, 1822. 2v.
Arc 545.14PF Belzoni, G.B. Narrative of the operations...in Egypt and Nubia. 3. ed. Atlas. London, 1822.
Arc 551.1 Belzoni, G.B. Narrative of the operations in Egypt and Nubia. Brussels, 1835.
Arc 684.1.4 Bemerkungen über den olympischen Tempel und seine Bildwerke. (Urlichs, K.L.) Würzburg, 1877.
Arc 936.251 Benae, Alojz. Studije o kamenom i bakarnom dobu u sjeverozapadnom Balkanu. Sarajevo, 1964.
Arc 453.1 Bendall, C. Journey in Nepal and northern India. Cambridge, 1886.
VArc 543.152 Bendefy, Lásylo. Syallam tolmács kűldetése Naagy Sändor folokog. Budapest, 1941.
Arc 1020.18 Bendixen, B.E. Aus der mittelalterlichen Sammlung des Museums in Bergen. Bergen, 1889-
Arc 453.10 Bendrey, F. A study of Muslim inscriptions. Bombay, 1944?
Arc 1349.55 Benedetto Pistrucci. (Ciampi, Ignazio.) n.p., n.d.
Arc 1490.25 Benedictus Floravantensis. Antiqui romanorum pontificum denarii a Benedicto XI ad Paulum III. Romae, 1738.
Arc 1033.169.5 Benedictus XIII. Discorso nel quale si prova...S. Bartholomeo. Benevento, 1695.
Arc 1285.30.5 Beneš, František. Pečeti v českých zemích a jejich cena jako dějepisného pramene. Praha, 1949.
Arc 1153.27 The Benevetan script. (Lowe, E.A.) Oxford, 1914.
Arc 441.3.2F Bengal. Public Works Department. List of ancient monuments in Bengal. Calcutta, 1896.

Author and Title Listing

Arc 441.3F Bengal. Public Works Department. Revised list of ancient monuments in Bengal, 1886. Calcutta, 1887.

Arc 587.1A Beni Hasan. (Newberry, P.E.) London, 1893. 4v.

Arc 1027.54 Benigni, U. Le madonne delle catacombe. Roma, 1904.

Arc 905.65 Beninger, E. Die Wasserburg Neydharting. Linz, 1959.

Arc 382.4 Benndorf, O. De anthologiae Graecae epigrammatis. Bonn, 1862. 20 pam.

Arc 510.6 Benndorf, O. Das Heroon von Gjoelbaschi-Trysa. Vienna, 1889. 2v.

Arc 635.205 Benndorf, O. Die Metopen von Selinunt. Berlin, 1873.

Arc 510.201 Benndorf, O. Reisen in Lykien und Karien. Vienna, 1884.

Arc 86.2.2PF Benndorf, O. Vorlegeblätter für archaeologische Uebungen. Wien. 1888-1891 3v.

Arc 1087.4F Benndorf, Otto. Antike Gesichtshelme und Sepulcralmasken. Wien, 1878.

Arc 830.275 Benoît, Fernand. Entremont, capitale celto-ligure des Salyens de Provence. Aix-en-Provence, 1957.

Arc 830.275.10 Benoît, Fernand. Entremont, capitale celto-ligure des Salyens de Provence. Gap, 1969.

Arc 1077.2.43 Benson, G.W. The cross, its history and symbolism. Buffalo, 1934.

Arc 681.5 Benson, Jack L. Ancient Leros. Durham, 1963.

Arc 540.16F Benson, Jack L. Bamboula at Kourion. Philadelphia, 1972.

Arc 600.30 Benson, Margaret. The temple of Mut in Asher. London, 1899.

Arc 609.1 Bent, J.T. The ruined cities of Mashonaland. London, 1892.

Arc 976.9 Benthall, Joseph L. Archaeological investigation of the Shannon site, Montgomery County, Virginia. Richmond, 1969.

Arc 1675.51.5 Bentkowski, F. Spis medalów poliskich lub z dziejami krainy polskiej stycznych. Warszawa, 1830.

Arc 497.55 Bentwich, Norman de Mattos. The new-old land of Israel. London, 1960.

Arc 689.3.15 Béquignon, Y. Recherches archéologiques à Phères de Thessalie. Paris, 1937.

Arc 689.3.17 Bequignon, Y. Recherches archéologiques à Phères de Thessalie. Thèse. Strasbourg, 1937.

Arc 688.5 Béquignon, Y. La vallée du Spercheios des origines au IVe siècle. Thèse. Paris, 1937.

Arc 66.1.144 Béquignon, Yves. La Vallée du spercheios. Paris, 1937.

Arc 66.1.150 Bérard, Jean. La colonisation grecque de l'Italie meridionale et de la Sicilie. Paris, 1941.

Arc 66.1.67 Bérard, V. Origine des cultes arcadiens. Paris, 1894.

Arc 1027.76 Berbrugger, M. Le tombeau de la chrétienne. Alger, 1867.

Arc 1033.53.24 Berchem, D. van. Le martyre de la Légion Thébaine. Basel, 1956.

Arc 1269.22.3 Berchem, E.F. von. Siegel. 2. Aufl. Berlin, 1923.

Arc 936.20.50 Berciu, Dumitru. Neue Forschungsergebnisse zur Vorgeschichte Rumäniens. Bonn, 1966.

Arc 936.24 Berciu, Dumitru. Romania. N.Y., 1967.

Arc 543.146.25 Berdyev, Ovliabuli. Drevneishie zemledel'tsy Iuzhnogo Turkmenistana. Ashkhabad, 1969.

Arc 923.113 Beregovaia, Nina Aleksandrovna. Contributions to the archaeology of the Soviet Union. Cambridge, 1966.

Arc 583.1 Berend, W.B. Principaux monuments du Musée Egyptienne de Florence. no.51. Paris, 1882.

Arc 66.1.70 Berger, E. Histoire de Blanche de Castile. Paris, 1895.

Arc 66.1.6 Berger, E. Notice sur des manuscrits de la Bibliothèque Vaticane. Paris, 1879.

Arc 712.30 Berger, Ernst. Parthenon-Ostgiebel. Bonn, 1959.

Arc 915.35 Berger, L. Die Ausgrabungen am Petersberg in Basel. Basel, 1963.

Arc 608.1.41F Berger, P. Stèles trouvées à Hadrumète. Paris, 1884.

Arc 830.31.5 Berger de Xivrey, Jules. Lettre à Monsieur Hase sur une inscription latine du second siècle. Paris, 1833.

Arc 1390.17 Berghaus, Peter. Dona numismatica. Hamburg, 1965.

Arc 1077.2.42 Bergmann, Alois. Die Schmiedkreuze Westböhmens. Elbogen, 1926.

Arc 547.11 Bergmann, E. Uebersichtung der Sammlung Aegyptischen Alterthuemer des Allerhöchsten Kaiserhauses. Vienna, 1880.

Arc 853.342 Bergmann, Joseph. Die altere Bronzezeit Nordwestdeutschlands. Marburg, 1970. 2v.

Arc 1076.3 Bergner, H.H. Zur Glockenkunde Thürigens. Jena, 1896.

Arc 865.29 Bergström, Theo. Stonehenge. London, 1974.

Arc 1470.32.7 Beribe-Delagart, A.L. Popravki obshchagi kataloga monet. P.O. Burachkov'. Moskva, 1907.

Arc 73.20 Bericht. (Archäologisches Institut des Deutschen Reichs. Römisch-Germanische Kommission.) Frankfurt. 1904+ 27v.

Arc 853.238 Bericht der Staatlichen Denkmalpflege im Saarland. (Saarland. Staatliches Konservatoramt.) Saarbrücken. 6,1953+ 5v.

Arc 900.210 Bericht des Vereins Carnuntum. Wien. 1887-1911 11v.

Arc 3.1.26.5 Bericht über den VI. Internationalen Kongress für Archäologie, Berlin, 21.-26. August, 1939. (Congrès International d'Archéologie Classique, 6th, Berlin, 1939.) Berlin, 1940.

Arc 522.4.7 Bericht ueber der Ausgrabungen in Troja im Jahre 1890. (Schliemann, H.) Leipzig, 1891.

Arc 845.3 Bericht ueber die...Ausgrabungen. v.1-4. (Kempten. Allgaüer Alterthumsverein.) Kempten, 1888. 2v.

Arc 68.10 Bericht über die Ausgrabungen in Olympia. (Deutsches Archäologisches Institut.) Berlin. 4,1940+ 5v.

Arc 505.140 Bericht über die Ergebnisse der Ausgrabungen in Kamid el-Loz (Libanon) in den Jahren 1963 und 1964. (Hachmann, Rolf.) Bonn, 1966.

Arc 505.140.5 Bericht über die Ergebnisse der Ausgrabungen in Kamid el-Loz (Libanon) in den Jahren 1966 und 1967. (Hachmann, Rolf.) Bonn, 1970.

Arc 545.242F Bericht über die Grabungen der Akademie des Wissenschaften in Wien. (Junker, Hermann.) Wien, 1919.

Arc 1076.3.47 Bericht über die Sammlung der Glockensprüche, Glockensagen und Glockenbräuche. (Verband Deutscher Vereine für Volkskunde.) Freiburg, 1918.

Arc 710.2 Bericht über die Untersuchungen auf der Akropolis von Athen. (Boetticher, C.) n.p., n.d.

Arc 562.5 Bericht über eine Expedition nach Ägypten zur Erforschung der Darstellungen der Fremdvolker. (Meyer, Eduard.) Berlin, 1913. 9v.

Arc 612.66.5 Berichte. (Congrès International d'Archéologie Slave, 2d.) Berlin, 1970. 3v.

Arc 520.10.5 Berlin. Königliches Museum. Beschreibung der Skulpturen aus Pergamon. Berlin, 1895.

Arc 520.10 Berlin. Königliches Museum. Beschreibung der Skulpturen aus Pergamon. Berlin, 1904.

Arc 520.11.5 Berlin. Königliches Museum. Führer durch das Pergamon Museum. Berlin, 1904.

Arc 520.6 Berlin. Königliches Museum. Führer durch die Ruinen von Pergamon. Berlin, 1887.

Arc 520.6.5 Berlin. Königliches Museum. Führer durch die Ruinen von Pergamon. 5. Aufl. Berlin, 1911.

Arc 520.11.6 Berlin. Königliches Museum. Führer durch die Ruinen von Pergamon. 6. Aufl. Berlin, 1922.

Arc 520.11 Berlin. Königliches Museum. Guide to the Pergamon Museum. Berlin, 1904. 2v.

Arc 522.4.9 Berlin. Königliches Museum. Heinrich Schliemanns Sammlung Trojanischer Altertümer. Berlin, 1902.

Arc 547.2.15 Berlin. Staatliche Museen. Abtheilung der Aegyptischen Alterthümer - Die Wandgemaelde. Berlin, 1855.

Arc 547.2.16 Berlin. Staatliche Museen. Abtheilung der Aegyptischen Alterthümer - Die Wandgemaelde. Berlin, 1870.

Arc 1353.1.5 Berlin. Staatliche Museen. Die antiken Münzen. Berlin, 1851.

Arc 547.2.2 Berlin. Staatliche Museen. Ausführliches Verzeichniss der Aegyptischen Altertuemer, Gipsabguesse und Papyrus. Berlin, 1894.

Arc 530.47 Berlin. Staatliche Museen. Die Ausgrabungen der zweiten Ktesiphon-Expedition. Berlin, 1933.

Arc 1510.16.2 Berlin. Staatliche Museen. Die Münzen Friedrich Wilhelms des Grossen Kurfürsten und Friedrichs III. Berlin, 1922.

Arc 1428.11F Berlin. Staatliche Museen. Die Münzen von Priene. Berlin, 1927.

Arc 1138.50 Berlin. Staatliche Museen. Zur Einführung in die Papyrusausstellung. Berlin, 1908.

Arc 1135.201.3 Berlin. Staatliche Museum. Aegyptische Urkunden. Arabische Urkunden. Berlin. 1896-1900//

Arc 1135.201.2 Berlin. Staatliche Museum. Aegyptische Urkunden. Koptische Urkunden. Berlin. 1,1904+ 3v.

Arc 1335.65 Berlin. Staatliche Museum. Kaiser Friedrich Museum. Die Schausammlung des Münzkabinetts im Kaiser Friedrich Museum Berlin, 1919.

Arc 530.45 Berlin. Tell Halaf Museum. Führer durch das Tell Halaf Maueum. Berlin, 1934.

Arc 340.10 Berlin. Universität. Institut für Ur- und Frühgeschichte. Bibliographie zur archäologischen Germanenforschung. Deutschsprachige Literatur 1941-1953. Berlin, 1966.

Arc 545.207F Berlin Museum. Mitteilungen aus der Aegyptischen Sammlung. Berlin, 1910- 6v.

Arc 186.5 Berliner Blatter für Vor- und Frühgeschichte. Berlin. 1-12,1952-1972// 5v.

Arc 2.5 Berliner Jahrbuch für Vor- und Frühgeschichte. Berlin. 1,1961+ 8v.

Arc 2.6 Berliner Jahrbuch für Vor- und Frühgeschichte. Ergänzungsbände. Berlin. 1,1964+

Arc 853.273.5 Berlins Urgeschichte. (Müller, Adriaan.) Berlin, 1964.

Arc 386.46 Berlitz, Charles F. Mysteries from forgotten worlds. Garden City, 1972.

Arc 1018.33 Bermischte Schriften über christliche Kunst. (Reichensperger.) Leipzig, 1856.

Arc 543.6 The Bernadou collection in the United States National Museum. (Hough, W.) n.p., n.d.

Arc 820.201 Bernard, A. Le temple d'Auguste et la nationalité. Lyon, 1863.

Arc 830.70.5 Bernard, Auguste. Description du pays des Ségusiaves. Paris, 1858. 11 pam.

Arc 830.22.16 Bernard, Eugene. Découverte d'une statue de Bacchus dans la rue de Fossés Saint Jacques. Paris, 1883.

Arc 1490.65F Bernareggi, E. Monete d'oro con ritratto del rinascimento italiano. Milano, 1954.

Arc 1356.8.3 Bernareggi, Ernesto. Istituzioni di numismatica antica. 3. ed. Milano, 1973.

Arc 1504.5 Die Berner Schulpfennige und die Tischlivierer. (Fluri, Adolf.) Bern, 1910.

Arc 543.25.10 Bernet Kempers, A. Borobudur, mysteriegebeuren in steen. Den Haag, 1960.

Arc 1460.3 Bernhard, O. Griechische und römische Münzbilder. Zürich, 1926.

Arc 395.1.5 Bernhardi, K. Textbuch zu Th. Schreibers Kulturhistorischem Bilderatlas des klassischen Altertums. Leipzig, 1888.

Arc 1675.13 Bernhart, M. Medaillen und Plaketten. Berlin, 1911.

Arc 1478.23.5 Bernhart, Max. Handbuch zur Münzkunde der römischen Kaiserzeit. Halle an der Saale, 1926. 2v.

Arc 1510.125 Bernhart, Max. Die Münzen und Medaillen der Stadt Kaufbeureh nebst einer münzgeschichtlichen Einleitung. n.p., 1923.

Arc 1580.48 Bernhart, Max. Die Münzen und Medaillen des Erzstiftes Salzburg. München, 1929-30.

Arc 1478.23 Bernhart, Max. Münzkunde der römischen Kaiserzeit. Genève, 1922.

Arc 1163.36 Bernheimer, K. Paleografia ebraica. Firenze, 1924.

Arc 1053.2.2 Bernoulli, J.J. Die erhaltenen Bildnisse berühmter Griechen. Basel, 1877.

Arc 1053.2.5 Bernoulli, J.J. Griechische Ikonographie. München, 1901. 2v.

Arc 1053.3.1 Bernoulli, J.J. Römische Ikonographie. v.1-2. Hildesheim, 1969. 4v.

X Cg Arc 1053.3 Bernoulli, J.J. Römische Ikonographie. v.2, pt.1. Stuttgart, 1882-94.

Arc 936.155 Bernshtam, A.N. Istoriko-kul'turnoe proshloe severnoi Kirgizii. Frunze, 1943.

Arc 870.24 Berry, B. A lost Roman road. London, 1963.

Arc 925.140 Bers, E.M. Arkheologicheskie pamiatniki Sverdlovska i ego obrestnostei. Sverdlovsk, 1954.

Arc 925.140.2 Bers, E.M. Arkheologicheskie pamiatniki Sverdlovska i ego obrestnostei. 2. izd. Sverdlovsk, 1963.

Arc 1490.82 I bersaglieri nelle medaglie 1836-1936. (Pagani, Antonio.) Milano, 1937.

Arc 1510.22 Berstett, A. Versuch einer Münzgeschichte des Elsasses. Freiburg, 1840. 2 pam.

Arc 861.10.22 Bersu, Gerhard. Three Viking graves in the Isle of Man. London, 1966.

Arc 1033.12.33 Berta, G. Della sacra sindone di Nostro Signor. Torino, 1826?

Arc 1020.10.29 Bertaux, E. Rome. Paris, 1905.

Arc 756.11.2 Bertaux, Emile. Rome, l'antiquité. Paris, 1904.

Arc 756.11 Bertaux, Emile. Rome; l'antiquité. 2. éd. Paris, 1907.

Arc 756.11.3 Bertaux, Emile. Rome, l'antiquité. 3. éd. Paris, 1913.

Arc 756.11.4 Bertaux, Emile. Rome, l'antiquité. 4. éd. Paris, 1924.

Arc 1076.3.39 Berthele, J. La famille Cavillier et les fonderies de cloches de Carrepuits. Caen, 1901. 2 pam.

Arc 1076.3.38 Berthele, J. Mélanges. Montpellier, 1906.

Arc 608.6.50 Berthier, A. Tiddis. Alger, 1951.

Arc 726.165 Berti, Leo. Scoperte paletnologiche e archeologiche nella provincia di Treviso. 1. ed. Firenze, 1956.

Author and Title Listing

Htn Arc 900.203* Bertoli, G. Le antichità d'Aquileja. Venice, 1739.

Arc 505.4.2 Berton, J. de. Essai sur la topographie de Tyr. Paris, 1843.

Arc 505.4 Berton, J. de. La topographie de Tyr. Paris, 1881.

Arc 726.91 Bertoni, G. La cattedrale modenese. Modena, 1914.

Arc 785.40.15 Bertotti Scamozzi, Ottavio. Les thermes des Romains. v.5. Vicenza, 1797.

Arc 1423.30 Bertram, Fred. Israel's 20-year catalog of coins and currency. N.Y., 1968.

Arc 823.1.5 Bertrand, A. Archéologie celtique et gaulois. Paris, 1889.

Arc 386.11 Bertrand, A. De la valeur historique des documents archéologiques. Chartres, 1879.

Arc 823.1 Bertrand, A. Nos origines - La Gaule avant les Gaulois. Paris, 1891.

Arc 823.1.3 Bertrand, A. Nos origines - La religion des Gaulois. Paris, 1897.

Arc 386.10 Bertrand, A. Rapport sur les questions archéologiques...Congrès de Stockholm. Paris, 1875.

Arc 726.21 Bertrand, A. Sepultures à l'incinération de Poggio Renzo. n.p., 1874.

Arc 830.27 Bertrand, Alexandre. L'autel de saintes et les triades gauloises. Paris, 1880.

Arc 830.30 Bertrand, Alexandre. Les bijoux de Jouy-le-Comte. Paris, 1879.

Arc 830.18 Bertrand, Alexandre. Les voies romaines en Gaule. Paris, 1864.

Arc 1508.15.10 Berwertungstablellen der deutschen Reichsmünzen seit 1871. (Jaeger, Kurt.) Basel, 1957.

Arc 31.4 Berytus. Beirut. 1,1934+ 9v.

Arc 920.8 Berzhe, A. Zapiski...knigai. Tiflis, 1875.

Arc 1020.60 Besançon, B. Description des monuments de l'Abbaye de Rosières. n.p., 1714.

Arc 830.240 Besançon, France. Musée des Beaux-Arts. Exposition. Besançon, 1958.

Arc 501.5.2 Besant, W. Palestine Exploration Fund. Thirty years' work in the Holy Land, 1865-1895. London, 1895.

Arc 501.5A Besant, W. Twenty-one years' work in the Holy Land. London, 1886.

Arc 1433.17 Le besant d'or sarrazinas pendant les croisades. (Blancard, Louis.) Marseille, 1880.

Arc 1588.4.50 Beschreibung. (Vereine für Numismatik.) Prag, 1852-70.

Arc 1335.34 Beschreibung der Bekanntesten. v.1,2,3-4,5,6. (Neumann, J.) Prag, 1858-72. 5v.

Arc 1580.7 Beschreibung der bisher bekaunten böhmischen Münzen. v.1-2,3-4. (Voigt, A.) Prag, 1771-87. 2v.

Arc 1470.20 Beschreibung der Griechischen Autonomen Münzen. (Königliche Academie der Wissenschaft zu Amsterdam.) Amsterdam, 1912.

Arc 1335.75 Beschreibung der köllnischen Munzsammlung des domherrn und kurfürstlich-weltlichen Hofgerichts Präsidenten von Merle. (Wallraf, F.F.) Kölln am Rhein, 1792.

Arc 1510.138 Beschreibung der Münzen und Medaillen. (Rueppell, E.) Frankfurt am Main, 1857.

Arc 1580.5 Beschreibung der Sammlung böhmischer Münzen. pt.1-2. (Donebauer, Max.) Prag, 1889-90.

Arc 520.10.5 Beschreibung der Skulpturen aus Pergamon. (Berlin. Königliches Museum.) Berlin, 1895.

Arc 520.10 Beschreibung der Skulpturen aus Pergamon. (Berlin. Königliches Museum.) Berlin, 1904.

Arc 853.43 Beschreibung der vaterländischen Alterthümer. (Kasiski, F.W.) Danzig, 1881.

Arc 853.23 Beschreibung der 14alten deutschen Todtenhügel. (Wilhelmi, K.) Heidelberg, 1830.

Arc 1510.33 Beschreibung des Mainzer Münzen des Mittelalters. (Cappe, H.P.) Dresden, 1856.

Arc 1510.144F Beschreibung von Münzen und Medaillen des Fürsten-Hauses und Landes Baden in chronologischer Folge. (Bally, Otto.) Aarau, 1896- 2v.

Arc 600.242 Beschriftete Kleinfunde in der Sammlung Georges Michailidis. (Kaplony, Peter.) Istanbul, 1973.

Arc 1528.5.5PF Beschrijving der Nederlandsche historie-penningen. (Loon, Gerard van.) 's-Gravenhage, 1723-31. 4v.

Arc 1528.5PF Beschrijving van Nederlandsche historie-penningen. v.1-4,6-10. (Akademie...Amsterdam. Akademie von Wetenschappen, Amsterdam.) Amsterdam, 1821-69. 6v.

Arc 936.190 Beshevliev, V. Antike und Mittelalter in Bulgarien. Berlin, 1960.

Arc 853.8.5F Die Besiedlungschlesiens in vor- und frühgeschichtlicher Zeit. 2. Aufl. (Hellmich, Max.) Breslau, 1923.

X Cg Arc 66.1.87 Besiner, M. L'ile tiberine dans l'antiquité. Paris, 1902.

Arc 1550.11F Beskrivelse of danske og norske mønter. (Schou, Hans Henrich.) Kjøbenhavn, 1926.

Arc 936.175 Bešlagić, Š. Stećci na Blidinju. Zagreb, 1959.

Arc 936.205.10 Bešlagié, Šefik. Grborezi srednjovjckovna nekropola. Sarajevo, 1964.

Arc 1025.48 Besnier, M. Les catacombes de Rome. Paris, 1904.

Arc 1025.48.3 Besnier, M. Les catacombes de Rome. Paris, 1909.

Arc 1663.56 Besondere Münzen. (Lesser, Friedrich Christian.) Frankfurt, 1739.

Arc 1020.31.15 Besozzi, R. La storia della Basilica di Santa Croce in Gerusalemma. Roma, 1750.

Arc 1027.19.33 Ein Besuch in der römischen Katakomben...S. Kallisto. (Huthmacher, L.) Mainz, 1861.

Arc 555.1 Besuch in El-Achmem. Reisebriefe aus Aegypten. (Forrer, R.) Strassburg, 1895.

Arc 588.48F Beth-Pelet. (Petrie, W.M.F.) London, 1930-32. 2v.

Arc 505.150.1 Beth She'arim; report on the excavations during 1936-1940. Jerusalem, 1973.

Arc 505.150 Beth She'arim; report on the excavations during 1936-1940. New Brunswick, 1973-76. 3v.

Arc 503.5 Beth Shemesh (Palestine). (Grant, Elihu.) Haverford, Pa., 1929.

Arc 1663.2 Betts, C.W. American colonial history illustrated by contemporary medals. N.Y., 1894.

Arc 943.12 Beuchat, H. Manuel d'archéologie americaine. Paris, 1912.

Arc 793.3 Beulé, C.E. Le drame du Vésuve. Paris, 1872.

Arc 386.3 Beulé, C.E. Fouilles et découvertes. Paris, 1873. 2v.

Arc 736.2 Beulé, C.E. Les temples de Syracuse. n.p., n.d.

Arc 710.1 Beulé, E. L'acropole d'Athènes. Paris, 1853-54. 2v.

Arc 1465.4 Beulé, E. Les monnaies d'Athènes. Paris, 1858.

Arc 1020.9.175 Bevan, Gladys M. Early Christians of Rome. London, 1927.

Arc 855.203 Bevan, J.O. Architectural survey of Herefordshire. Westminster, 1896. 2 pam.

Arc 858.34 Bevan, J.O. The towns of Roman Britain. London, 1917.

Arc 875.24 Beveridge, E. Coll and Tiree - their prehistoric forts. Edinburgh, 1903.

Arc 925.50.245 Bevezans'ka, Sofiia S. Srednii period bronzovogo veka v Severnoi Ukraine. Kiev, 1972.

Arc 1190.88F Beveztés a hodoltśag török diplomatikájála. (Fekete, Lajos.) Budapest, 1926.

Arc 905.115F Die Bewohner vor Halimbacseres noch. (Töräh, Gyula.) Leipzig, 1959.

Arc 796.2.10F Beyen, Hendrik G. Die pompejanischen Wanddekoration. v.1-2. Haag, 1938. 4v.

Arc 796.2F Beyen, Hendrik G. Über Stilleben aus Pompeji und Herculaneum. 's-Gravenhage, 1928.

Arc 1027.18.15 Beyer, Hermann W. Die jüdische Katakombe der Villa Torlonia in Rom. Berlin, 1930.

Arc 1588.1.96 Beyer, Karol. Skorowidz monet polskich od 1506 do 1825. Warszawa, 1973.

Arc 1030.60 Beyer, Oskar. Fruhchristliche Sinnbilder und Inschriften. Kassel, 1954.

Arc 1025.63 Beyer, Oskar. Die Katakombenwelt. Tübingen, 1927.

Arc 386.16 Beyermann, Erich. Das Recht an Denkmälern. Inaug. Diss. Halle, 1917.

Arc 608.15 Béylié, Leon. La Kaloa des Beni-Hammad. Paris, 1909.

Arc 416.10 Beylié, Léon de. Prome et Samara; voyage archéologique en Birmanie et en Mesopotamie. Paris, 1907.

Arc 543.96 Beyond the Oxus; archaeology, art and architecture of Central Asia. (Knobloch, Edgar.) London, 1972.

Arc 505.73.5 Beyrouth, ville romaine. (Mouterde, René.) Beyrouth, 1952.

Arc 1510.146 Beyschlag, Daniel Eberhardt. Versuch einer Münzgeschichte Augsburgs in dem Mittelalter. Stuttgart, 1835.

Arc 1335.145 Beyträge zum Groschen-Cabinet. (Götz, Christian.) Dresden, 1810. 3v.

Arc 530.25 Bezobrazov, P.V. Trapezunt', ego sviatyni i drevnosti. Petrograd, 1916.

Arc 1418.10 Bhandarkar, D.R. Lectures on ancient Indian numismatics. Calcutta, 1921.

Arc 441.2.9 Bhavanagar pracina sodh a samgraha. (Kathiawar. Department for an Archaeological and Antiquarian Survey.) Bhavanagar, 1885.

Arc 628.7 Biagi, C. Monumenta Graeca ex Museo Jacobi Nanni. Monumenta Graeca et Latina Jacobi Nanni. Roma, 1785-87. 2v.

Arc 746.13 Bianchi-Bandinelli, R. Sovana, topografia ed arte. Firenze, 1929.

Arc 1053.22 Bianchi Bandinelli, Ranuccio. Il problema del ritratto greco. Firenze, 1952.

Arc 1033.40.9 Bianchi-Cagliesi. Santa Cecilia et La Sua Basilica nel Trastevere. Roma, 1902. 2 pam.

Arc 1033.12.184 Bianconi, A. Memoria intorno la corona di ferro longobardo. Milano, 1860.

Arc 1163.16F Bianu, I. Album de paleografie românească. București, 1929.

Arc 1020.9.43 Biasiotti, G. La basilica esquilina di Santa Maria ed il palazzo apostolico. Roma, 1911.

Arc 1020.9.187 Biasiotti, G. Le diaconie cardinatizie e la diaconia "S. Vite in Macello". Roma, 1911.

Arc 543.88 Bibby, Geoffrey. Looking for Dilmun. 1st ed. N.Y., 1969.

Arc 497.44 The Bible and archaeology. (Kenyon, F.G.) London, 1940.

Arc 497.20.5 The Bible and modern discoveries. 4. ed. (Harper, H.A.) London, 1891.

Arc 497.40A Bible and spade. (Caiger, S.L.) London, 1938.

Arc 497.23 Bible and spade. (Peters, John B.) N.Y., 1922.

Arc 1356.4 Bible coins...facsimile of coins in...scripture. London, n.d.

Arc 497.76.2 Bibleiska arkheologiia. 2. izd. (Markovski, Ivan S.) Sofiia, 1948.

Arc 31.1 Biblia. Meriden. 4-18,1891-1905 15v.

VArc 497.90 Bibliai régiségtan. (Ackermann, Peter Fourier.) Eger, 1889.

Arc 497.92 A bibliai régiségtudomány kézikönyve. (Szekrényi, Lajos.) Szeged, 1894.

Arc 497.72 Biblical Archaeologist. The Biblical archaeologist reader. Chicago, 1961.

Arc 497.72.1 Biblical Archaeologist. The Biblical archaeologist reader. Garden City, 1961-70. 3v.

Arc 31.1.35 The Biblical archaeologist. New Haven. 1,1938+ 9v.

Arc 497.72 The Biblical archaeologist reader. (Biblical Archaeologist.) Chicago, 1961.

Arc 497.72.1 The Biblical archaeologist reader. (Biblical Archaeologist.) Garden City, 1961-70. 3v.

Arc 497.41 Biblical archaeology, its use and abuse. (Richardson, George H.) London, 1938.

Arc 497.104 Biblical archaeology. (Paul, Sholom.) Jerusalem, 1973.

Arc 497.31.5 Biblical archaeology. (Wright, G.E.) Philadelphia, 1962.

Arc 497.78 Biblical treasure in Bible lands. (Cohen, Lenore.) Los Angeles, 1965.

Arc 936.14.325 Bibliografia archeologiczna Mazowsza. wyd. 1. (Woyda, Stefan.) Warszawa, 1970.

Arc 838.41 Bibliografia arqueológica portuguesa 1960-1969. (Mendes, Maria Teresa Pinto.) Coimbra, 1970.

Arc 340.15 Bibliografia d'archeologia classica. 1. ed. Roma, 1969.

Arc 793.1.2 Bibliografia di Pompei, Ercolano e Stabia. (Furchheim, F.) Napoli, 1891.

Arc 1488.3 Bibliografia numismatica. (Società Numismatica Italiana.) Milano, 1918-20.

Arc 1330.40 Bibliografia numismatica española. (Roda y Delgada, Juan de Dios de la.) Madrid, 1886.

Arc 726.2.30 Bibliografia sulle catacombe napoletane. (Caterino, Antonio.) Firenze, 1957.

Arc 1330.56.1 Bibliograficheskii ukajatel' literatury po russkoi numizmatike. (Gromachevskii, Semen G.) Ann Arbor, Mich., 1965.

Arc 340.11 Bibliografiia na bulgarskata arkheologiia, 1879-1955. (Georgieva, Sonia.) Sofiia, 1957.

Arc 340.11.2 Bibliografiia na bulgarskata arkheologiia, 1879-1966. 2. izd. (Georgieva, Sonia.) Sofiia, 1974.

Arc 399.3 Bibliografiia nauchnykh trudov po arkheologii i istorii chlena-korrespondenta AN SSSR A.P. Okladnikova. (Larichev, Vitalii E.) Novosibirsk, 1968.

Arc 292.155 Bibliografiia obozrenie trydov. (Polenov, D.) Sankt Peterburg, 1871.

Arc 340.16 Bibliografiia po arkheologii Moldavii, 1946-1966. (Beilekchi, V.S.) Kishinev, 1967.

Arc 1163.3.38 Bibliografiia russkikh nadpisei XI-XV vv. (Orlov, A.S.) Moskva, 1936.

Arc 1163.3.40 Bibliografiia russkikh nadpisei XI-XV vv. (Orlov, A.S.) Moskva, 1952.

Arc 936.3.5 Bibliographi arkeologjisë dhe historisë së lashtë të Shqipërisë, 1945-71. (Jubani, Bep.) Tiranë, 1972.

Arc 545.8.3 Bibliographical account...of La description de l'Egypt. (London. Institution Library.) London, 1838.

Arc 340.5 A bibliographical guide to Latium and southern Eturia. (American Academy in Rome. Library.) Rome, 1916.

Arc 340.5.2 A bibliographical guide to Latium and southern Eturia. 2. ed. (American Academy in Rome. Library.) Rome, 1925.

Arc 340.5.3 A bibliographical guide to Latium and southern Eturia. 3. ed. (American Academy in Rome. Library.) Rome, 1933.

Arc 340.17 A bibliographical list descriptive of Romano-British architectural remains in Great Britain. (Lyell, Arthur H.) Cambridge, 1912.

Arc 895.5.5 Bibliographie de l'archéologie préhistorique de la Suède. (Montelius, Oscar.) Stockholm, 1875.

Arc 402.2.25 Bibliographie de S. Reinach. (Reinach, S.) Paris, 1936.

Arc 403.14 Bibliographie der geschriften van Jhr. Dr. Jan Six. (Oudheidkundig Genootschap, Amsterdam.) Amsterdam, 1933.

Arc 562.2.10 Bibliographie des oeuvres de Gaston Maspero. (Cordier, Henri.) Paris, 1922.

Arc 1205.5 Bibliographie générale de la sigillographie. (Tourneur-Nicodème, Mariette.) Besançon, 1933.

Arc 1330.45 Bibliographie générale et raisonnée de la numismatique belge. (Camont, Georges.) Bruxelles, 1883.

Arc 340.10 Bibliographie zur archäologischen Germanenforschung. Deutschsprachige Literatur 1941-1953. (Berlin. Universität. Institut für Ur- und Frühgeschichte.) Berlin, 1966.

Arc 340.20.2 Bibliographie zur Vor- und Frühgeschichte von Gross-Berlin. 2. Aufl. (Lehmann, Herbert.) Berlin, 1968.

Arc 386.17.5 A bibliography of Howard Crosby Butler, 1872-1922. (Leach, H.S.) Princeton, 1924.

Arc 1330.15 Bibliography of Indian coins. v.1-2. (Singhal, C.R.) Bombay, 1950-52.

Arc 1330.18 A bibliography of Jewish numismatics. (Mayer, Leo Ary.) Jerusalem, 1966.

Arc 493.60.5 A bibliography of Mesopotamian archaeological sites. (Ellis, Richard Stephens.) Wiesbaden, 1972.

Arc 1330.20 Bibliography of Moslem numismatics, India excepted. (Mayer, Leo Ary.) London, 1939.

Arc 1330.20.2 Bibliography of Moslem numismatics, India excepted. 2. ed. (Mayer, Leo Ary.) London, 1954.

Arc 609.17.10 A bibliography of Nigerian archaeology. (Shaw, Thurstan.) Ibadan, 1969.

Arc 969.1.05 Bibliography of Ohio archaeology. (Morgan, Richard G.) Columbus, 1947.

Arc 340.13 Bibliography of South African pre- and proto-historic archaeology. (Holm, S.E.) Pretoria, 1966.

Arc 340.25.5 Bibliography of Soviet archaeology and physical anthropology, 1936-1964. (Field, Henry.) Miami? 1964.

Arc 340.25.7 Bibliography of Soviet archaeology and physical anthropology, 1936-1967. (Field, Henry.) n.p., 1967.

Arc 340.25.9 Bibliography of Soviet archaeology and physical anthropology, 1936-1972. no. 1-189. (Field, Henry.) Coconut Grove, Fla., 1972.

Arc 404.1.30 A bibliography of the published writings of Sir William St. John Hope. (Thompson, Alexander Hamilton.) Leeds, 1929.

Arc 793.1 Bibliography of Vesuvius, Pompeii, Herculaneum. (Hoepli, U.) Milan, 1883.

Arc 1130.10 A bibliography of works about papyrology. (Cairo, Egypt. National Library.) Cairo, 1960.

Arc 303.50 Biblioteca de arheologie. București. 1,1957+ 16v.

Arc 303.50.5 Biblioteca de arheologie. Seria complementară. București. 1,1972+

Arc 1330.3 Bibliotheca numaria. (Leitzmann, J.) Weissensee, 1867.

Arc 1330.2 Bibliotheca numaria. (Lipsius, J.G.) Leipzig, 1801. 2v.

Arc 1329.1 Bibliotheca numismatica. (Hirsch, J.C.) Nuremberg, 1760.

Arc 1330.1 Bibliotheca nummaria. (Banduri, A.) Hamburg, 1719.

Arc 94.54F Bibliotheca praehistorica Hispana. Madrid. 1,1958+ 12v.

Arc 608.10 Bibliothèque d'archéologie africaine. Paris, 1897-1906. 7v.

Arc 830.13.5 Bibliothéque d'école des hautes études. Monuments romains d'Orange. (Chatelain, L.) Paris, 1908.

Arc 925.1 Bibliotheque des Monuments Figurés. Antiquités du Bosphore Cimmérien. Paris, 1892.

Arc 582.2 Bibliothèque d'étude. (Institut Français d'Archéologie Orientale du Caire.) Le Caire. 1+ 53v.

Arc 66.1.48 Bibliothèque du Vatican au XVe siècle. (Muentz, E.) Paris, 1887.

Arc 1433.1 Bibliothèque Nationale, Paris. Catalogue des monnaies musulmanes. Paris, 1887-96. 3v.

Arc 1675.75 Bibliothèque Nationale, Paris. Exposition: Effigies et portraits. Paris? 1957.

Arc 1680.17 Bibliothèque Nationale, Paris. Département des Médailles et Antiques. Collection Rouyer. Catalogue de la collection Rouyer. Paris, 1899-1910. 2v.

X Cg Arc 1468.5.5 Bibliothèque Nationale, Paris. Département des Médailles et Antiques. Catalogue de la collection de Luynes. v.1-3 and plates. Paris, 1924. 6v.

Arc 1468.5.6 Bibliothèque Nationale, Paris. Département des Médailles et Antiques. Catalogue de la collection de Luynes. pt.2-3 and plates. Paris, 1925-30. 2v.

Arc 1433.85 Bibliothèque Nationale, Paris. Département des Médailles et Antiques. Catalogue des étalons monétaires. Paris, 1960.

Arc 1500.45 Bibliothèque Nationale, Paris. Département des Médailles et Antiques. Catalogue des jetons. Paris, 1897.

Arc 1473.16 Bibliothèque Nationale, Paris. Département des Médailles et Antiques. Catalogue des monnaies byzantines de la Bibliothèque Nationale. Paris, 1970. 2v.

Arc 1468.5 Bibliothèque Nationale, Paris. Département des Médailles et Antiques. Catalogue des monnaies grecques. Les rois de Syrie, d'Arménie et de Commagène. Paris, 1890.

Arc 1510.22.10 Bibliothèque Nationale, Paris. Département des Médailles et Antiques. Collection de monnaies et médailles d'Alsace. Paris, 1902.

Arc 1458.18 Bibliothèque Nationale, Paris. Département des Médailles et Antiques. Collections Armand-Valton. Paris, 1912.

Arc 1470.14.13 Bibliothèque Nationale, Paris. Département des Médailles et Antiques. Inventaire sommaire de la collection Waddington...1897. Paris, 1897.

Arc 1470.14.15 Bibliothèque Nationale, Paris. Département des Médailles et Antiques. Inventaire sommaire de la collection Waddington...1897. Paris, 1898.

Arc 1500.5.35 Bibliothèque Nationale, Paris. Département des Médailles et Antiques. Inventaire sommaire des monnaies mérovingiennes de la collection d'Amécourt. Paris, 1890.

Arc 1335.27.25 Bibliothèque Nationale, Paris. Département des Médailles et Antiques. Les monnaies. Paris, 1929.

Arc 820.6PF Bibliotheque Nationale, Paris. Département des Médailles et Antiques. Le trésor d'argenterie de Berthouville, près Bernay. Paris, 1916.

Arc 505.2.15F Bibliothèque Nationale. Département des Médailles et Antiques. Les tessères et les monnaies de Palmyre, 1944. Paris, 1962. 2v.

Arc 1020.9.32 La bibliothèque vaticane et ses annexes. (Barbier de Montault, X.) Rome, 1867.

Arc 1423.12.5 Biblische Numismatik. (Cavedoni, C.) Hannover, 1855-56. 2v.

Arc 543.116.1 Die biblischen Hügel. (Zehren, Erich.) Berlin, 1961.

Arc 830.17.5 Bibracte. (Bircher, H.) Aarau, 1904.

Arc 815.25 Bicentenario degli scavi di Pompei. Napoli, 1948.

Arc 853.72 Bicker, F.K. Dünenmesolithikum aus dem Fiener Bruch. Inaug. Diss. Halle an der Saale, 1934.

Arc 895.39.5 Ett bidrag till frågan om suöroornamentiken på stenålders boplatsernas lerkärl. (Rydh, Hanna.) Lund, 1937.

Arc 925.50.205 Bidzilia, Vasyl' I. Istoriia kul'tury Zakarpattia na rubezhi nashoi ery. Kyïv, 1971.

Arc 938.55 Bielenstein, A. Die Holzbauten und Holzgeräte der Litten. pt.1-2. n.p., 1907-18.

Arc 746.9 Bienkowski, P. De speculis Etruscis et cista in museo. Cracoviae, 1912.

Arc 705.209 Bienkowski, P. von. Die Darstellungen der Gallier in der Hellenistischen Kunst. Wien, 1908.

Arc 785.118 Biernacka-Lukańska, Małgorzata. Wodociągi rzymskie i wczesnobizantyjskie z obszaru Mezji Dolnej i Północnej Tracji. Wrocław, 1973.

Arc 1251.26 Biesantz, Hagen. Kretisch-mykenische Siegelbilder. Marburg, 1954.

Arc 1500.43 Bigot, A. Essai sur les monnaies du royaume. Paris, 1857.

Arc 756.10 Bigot, P. Rome imperiale. Rome, 1911.

Arc 785.50 Bigot, Paul. Recherche des limites du Grand Arque. Rome, 1909.

Arc 858.31 Bigsley, R. Old places revisited. London, 1851. 3v.

Arc 858.31.5 Bigsley, R. Visions of the times of old. London, 1848. 3v.

Arc 888.6 Een bijdrage tot de kennis der vóór-Romeinsche urnenvelden in Nederland. Proefschrift. (Willems, W.J.A.) Maastricht, 1935.

Arc 1528.10.5 Bijdragen tot de numismatiek van Gelderland. (Voogt, W.J. de.) Arnhem, 1869.

Arc 830.30 Les bijoux de Jouy-le-Comte. (Bertrand, Alexandre.) Paris, 1879.

Arc 848.12 Bilder aus dem römisch-germanischen Kulturleben. 2. Aufl. (Blümlein, Carl.) München, 1926.

Arc 853.53.3 Bilder aus der märkischen Vorzeit. 3. Aufl. (Kiekebusch, A.) Berlin, 1921.

Arc 853.242F Bilder aus der Vor- und Frühgeschichte des Hegaus. (Funk, A.) Singen, 1960.

Arc 1510.5 Die Bilder der Süddeutschen. (Bürkel, L. von.) München, 1903.

Arc 853.24.7 Bilder zur Vorgeschichte Bayerns. (Torbruegge, Walter.) Konstanz, 1968.

Arc 73.6.15 Bilderhefte. (Deutsches Archäologisches Institut. Römische Abteilung.) Tübingen. 1,1962+ 4v.

Arc 1025.52 Die bildischen Darstellungen in die römischen Katakomben. (Grillwitzer, A.) Graz, 1876.

Arc 87.1.52 Das Bildnis Alexanders des Grossen. (Koepp, F.) Berlin, 1892.

Arc 1053.5.7 Das Bildnis des Antinous. Inaug. Diss. (Holm, Erich.) Würzburg, 1933.

Arc 87.1.33 Bildniss einer Roemerin. (Huebner, E.) Berlin, 1873.

Arc 1675.9 Bildt. Les médailles romaines de Christine de Suède. Rome, 1908.

Arc 493.35 Bildzeichen der königlichen Hoheit bei den iranischen Völkern. (Jaenichen, H.) Bonn, 1956.

Arc 447.2 Bilgrami, S.A.A. Landmarks of the Deccan; a comprehensive guide to the archaeological remains of the city and suburbs of Hyderabad. Hyderabad, 1927.

Arc 925.50.110 Bilia dzherel plov'ians'koi derzhevnosti. (Braichevs'kyi, Mykhailo I.) Kyïv, 1964.

Arc 1027.14 Billaud, Pelissier B. Pelerinage au cauc du Pape S. Alexandre I. Rome, 1856.

Arc 853.80 Die Billendorfer Kultur auf Grund der Grabfunde. (Kropf, W.) Leipzig, 1938.

Arc 853.180F Billig, Gerhard. Die Aunjebitzer Kultur in Sachsen. Leipzig, 1958.

Arc 1668.4 Biltnusse der Rhömischen Keyseren. (Keller, D.) Zürich, 1558.

Arc 1510.55 Binder, C. Württembergische Münz- und Medaillen-Kunde. Stuttgart, 1846.

Arc 726.252 Bindi, Vincenzo. Castel S. Flaviano. Napoli, 1879-82. 4v.

Arc 386.44 Binford, Lewis Roberts. An archaeological perspective. N.Y., 1972.

Arc 387.10 Biografia del generale americano e console in Cipro, Luigi Palma di Cesnola. (Gallo, Francesco.) Vercelli, 1869.

Arc 1349.5 Biographical dictionary of medallists. (Forrer, L.) London, 1904-30. 8v.

Arc 1020.32.12 Biraghi, L. I tre sepolcri santambrisiani scoperti...1864. Milano, 1864.

Arc 1020.19 Biragus, A. Datiana historica ecclesiastica Mediolanensis. Mediolani, 1848.

Arc 590.11 Birch, Samuel. Remarks upon the cover of the granite sarcophagus of Rameses III in the Fitzwilliam Museum. Cambridge, Eng., 1876.

X Cg Arc 1212.3 Birch, William de Gray. Seals. London, 1907?

Arc 1274.4 Birch de Gray, W. History of Scottish seals. London, 1905. 2v.

Arc 830.17.5 Bircher, H. Bibracte. Aarau, 1904.

Arc 430.202 Bird, James. Historical researches...caves of western India. Bombay, 1847.

Arc 608.68 Birebent, Jean. Aquae Romanae. Alger, 1962.

Arc 895.20.15F Birka. Stockholm.

Arc 895.20.10F Birka. Stockholm. 1,1913 2v.

Arc 382.9 Birley, Eric. Archaeology in the north of England. Durham, Eng., 1958. 6 pam.

Arc 1143.4.1 Birt, Theodor. Das antike Buchwesen in seinem Verhältnis zur Literatur. Aalen, 1974.

Arc 1143.4.5 Birt, Theodor. Die Buchrolle in der Kunst. Leipzig, 1907.

Arc 843.64 Biscay, Sain. Disputación Provincial. Junta de Cultura. Exploraciones de la caverna de Santimamiñe. Basondo: Cortezubi. Memoria 2-3. Bilbao, 1931-35. 2v.

Arc 726.265 Bisenzo e le antiche civiltà intorno al lago di Bolsena. (Pennucci, Umberto.) Grotte di Castro, 1964.

Htn Arc 1084.3PF* The Bishop collections. (New York (City). Metropolitan Museum of Art.) N.Y., 1906. 2v.
Arc 936.14.10 Biskupin. (Rajewski, Z.) Varsovie, 1959.
Arc 936.14.345 Biskupin. wyd. 1. (Rajewski, Zolzisław.) Warszawa, 1970.
Arc 1588.1.80 Biskupstwo kniszwickie w XI wieku. (Gumowski, Marian.) Poznań, 1921.
Arc 551.4 Bissing, F.W. Die Kunst der alten Ägypter. Leipzig, 1911.
Arc 545.236 Bissing, F.W. Die Mastaba des Gem-Ni-Kai. Berlin, 1905- 2v.
Arc 545.236.5F Bissing, F.W. Das Re-Heiligtum des Ne-Woser-Re. Berlin, 1905-23. 2v.
Arc 600.172 Bisson de la Roque, Fernand. Tôd, 1934 à 1936. Le Caire, 1937.
Arc 488.25 Bittal, Kurt. Vorderasiatische Archäologie. Berlin, 1964.
Arc 530.12.25 Bittel, Kurt. Die Felsbilder von Yazilikaya. Bamberg, 1934.
Arc 513.21.10 Bittel, Kurt. Kleinasiatische Studien. Istanbul, 1942.
Arc 513.21 Bittel, Kurt. Prähistorische Forschung in Kleinasien. Istanbul, 1934.
Arc 530.12.30 Bittel, Kurt. Die Ruinen von Boğazköy, der Hauptstadt des Hethiterreiches. Berlin, 1937.
Arc 1301.10 Biuletyn numizmatyczny. Warszawa. 2,1965+ 2v.
Arc 830.1.4 Pamphlet vol. Bizeul, de Blain. Géographie ancienne de la Bretagne. 7 pam.
Arc 1528.1 Bizot, P. Histoire metallique de la Republique de Hollande. Amsterdam, 1688. 2v.
Arc 1528.1.5 Bizot, P. Histoire metallique de la Republique de Hollande. Amsterdam, 1688. 2v.
Arc 1528.1.7 Bizot, P. Histoire metallique de la Republique de Hollande. Supplément. Amsterdam, 1690.
Arc 925.121 Bjarmien vallan kukoistur ja tuho. (Haavio Martti, Henrikki.) Porvoo, 1965.
Arc 1552.1 Bjoerkman, S. Myntic Islands, 1836-1922-1963. Stockholm, 1965.
Arc 1200.21 Björkman, Walther. Beiträge zur Geschichte der Staatskanzlei im islamischen Ägypten. Hamburg, 1928.
Arc 875.38 Black, George F. Descriptive catalogue of antiquities in Ayrshire. n.p., n.d.
Arc 875.29 Black, William G. Glasgow cross. Glasgow, 1913.
Arc 875.29.7 Black, William G. The Scots mercat "cross"; an inquiry as to its history and meaning. Glasgow, 1928.
Arc 870.30 The black horsemen: English inns and King Arthur. (Wildman, Samuel Gerald.) London, 1971.
Arc 587.10F Blackman, A.M. The rock tombs of Meir. London, 1914-24. 6v.
Arc 545.227.33 Blackman, A.M. Temple of Dendûr. Le Caire, 1911.
Arc 545.227.40 Blackman, A.M. The temple of Derr. Le Caire, 1913.
Arc 1279.6 Blaetter für altere Sphragiotik. (Lind, Karl.) Wien, 1878.
Arc 1301.8 Blätter für Münzfreunde und Münzforschung. Lübeck. 1,1865+ 19v.
Arc 1313.5 Blätter für Münzkunde. Leipzig. 1-4,1834-1844 2v.
Arc 406.5 Blaise de Vigenère, archéologue et critique d'art, 1523-1596. Thèse. (Métral, D.) Paris, 1839.
Arc 723.28F Blake, Marion E. Ancient Roman construction in Italy from the pre-historica period to Augustus. Washington, 1947.
Arc 723.30.5 Blake, Marion E. Roman construction in Italy from Nerva through the Antonines. Philadelphia, 1973.
Arc 723.30 Blake, Marion E. Roman construction in Italy from Tiberius through the Flavians. Washington, 1959.
Arc 551.2 Blanc, C. Voyage de la Haute Egypte. Paris, 1876.
Arc 1480.8 Blancard, Louis. L'aureus romain se divisait en six-millièmes. v.1-2. Marseille, n.d.
Arc 1433.17 Blancard, Louis. Le besant d'or sarrazinas pendant les croisades. Marseille, 1880.
Arc 1500.11 Blancard, Louis. Des monogrammes...deniers capétiens. Marseille, n.d.
Arc 1494.2 Blancard, Louis. Essai d'interpretation des lettres B.N.M...dinars. Marseille, n.d.
Arc 1500.4 Blancard, Louis. Essai sur les monnaies de Charles Ier, comté de Provence. Paris, 1868.
Arc 1500.19 Blancard, Louis. Le gros tournois est imite du sarrazinas Chrétien d'Acre. n.p., n.d.
Arc 1500.7 Blancard, Louis. Les marcs de la ville et de la cour romaine d'Avignon. Tours, n.d. 2 pam.
Arc 1500.13 Blancard, Louis. La médaille d'argent de Fauquembergue...dame au faucon. Marseille, 1883.
Arc 1500.8.5 Blancard, Louis. Monnaies féodales françaises par M.E. Caron. Résumé. Draguignan, 1885.
Arc 1500.10 Blancard, Louis. Nouveau classement des monnaies bretonnes. Marseille, 1888-89.
Arc 1390.4 Blancard, Louis. L'origine du marc. Macon, 1888.
Arc 1390.5 Blancard, Louis. Rapport...concernant le trésor de Vallon. Marseille, n.d.
Arc 1390.3 Blancard, Louis. Le saiga mérovingien dérive de la silique byzantine. v.1-2. Marseille, 1883.
Arc 1480.10 Blancard, Louis. Sur les chiffres romaines ou grecs...des monnaies impériales. Marseille, n.d.
Arc 1433.16 Blancard, Louis. Sur l'origine du monnayage musulman. Paris, n.d.
Arc 1500.12 Blancard, Louis. Sur quelques points obscurs de la numismatique de Charles VIII. Paris, n.d.
Arc 1356.3 Blancard, Louis. Le trésor d'Auriol et les dieux nègres de la Grèce. Marseille, n.d.
Arc 823.10.15 Blanchet, A. Carte archéologique de la Gaule romaine. pts.1-3,5-8,10-11,14. Paris, 1931- 10v.
Arc 823.10.15PF Blanchet, A. Carte archéologique de la Gaule romaine. pts.8-9. Paris, n.d.
Arc 823.10 Blanchet, A. Cronique archéologique de la France. Paris, 1902.
Arc 823.10.2 Blanchet, A. Cronique archéologique de la France. Paris, 1903.
Arc 1264.7.5 Blanchet, A. Les drapiers de Beauvais et leurs plombs de contrôle. Beauvais, 1927.
Arc 823.10.5 Blanchet, A. Les enceintes Romaines de la Gaule. Paris, 1907.
Arc 386.12 Blanchet, A. Guide pratique de l'antiquaire. Paris, 1899.
Arc 1498.7 Blanchet, A. Manuel de numismatique francaise. Paris, 1912-36. 4v.
Arc 1348.23 Blanchet, A. Mémoires et notes de numismatique. Paris, 1909.
Arc 1478.12 Blanchet, A. Les monnaies romaines. Paris, 1896.
Arc 830.44 Blanchet, A. Recherches sur les aqueducs et cloaques de la Gaule. Paris, 1908.
Arc 1264.7 Blanchet, A. Sigillographie française. Paris, 1902.
Arc 1500.21 Blanchet, A. Traité des monnaies gauloises. v.1-2. Paris, 1905.
Arc 823.2.7 Pamphlet box. Blanchet, A. Miscellaneous pamphlets.
Arc 1348.23.5 Pamphlet box. Blanchet, A. Numismatics.
Arc 1500.28.5 Blanchet, J.A. Histoire monetaire du Béarn et description des monnaies...Béarn. v.1-2. Paris, 1893.
Arc 823.2 Blanchet, J.A. Mélanges d'archéologie gallo-romaine. fasc.1-2. Paris, 1893. 2v.
Arc 1390.1.5 Blanchet, J.A. Nouveau manuel de numismatique du moyen age et moderne. Text et atlas. Paris, 1890. 3v.
Arc 608.6.25 Blanchet, P. La porte de Sidi Oqba. Paris, 1900.
Arc 843.228 Blanco, A. Excavaciones arqueológicas en el cerro Salomón. Madrid, 1970.
Arc 861.204 Blank, Elizabeth. A guide to Leicestershire archaeology. Leicester, 1970.
Arc 1510.85 Blaschke, Karlheinz. Siegel und Wappen in Sachsen. Leipzig, 1960.
Arc 1264.1.3 Blasons et chevaliers du Moyen Âge. (Forgeais, Arthur.) Paris, 1877.
Arc 936.14.35.5 Blaszczyk, Włodzimierz. Die Anfänge der polnischen Städt im Lichte der Bodenforschung. Poznań, 1974.
Arc 925.37 Blavatskaia, T.V. Ocherki politicheskii istorii Vospora v V-IV vv. do n.e. Moskva, 1959.
Arc 925.13.70 Blavatskaia, T.V. Zapadnopontiiskie gopoda. Moskva, 1952.
Arc 925.13.80 Blavatskii, V.D. Antichnaia arkheologiia Severnogo Prichernomor'ia. Moskva, 1961.
Arc 925.13.6 Blavatskii, V.D. Iskusstvo severnogo Prichernomor'ia. Moskva, 1947.
Arc 925.90A Blavatskii, V.D. Ocherki voen. dela. v antich. gosud. seleriogo Prichernomord. Moskva, 1954.
Arc 386.43 Blavatskii, V.D. Otkrytie zatonuvshezo mira. Moskva, 1963.
Arc 925.90.5 Blavatskii, V.D. Zemdsd v antichnikh gorodov severnogo Prichernomor'ia. Moskva, 1953.
Arc 925.8.40 Blavatskii, Vladimir D. Iskusstvo severnoi prichernomoriia. Moskva, 1946.
Arc 925.8.50 Blavatskii, Vladimir D. Pantikapei; Ocherki istorii stolitsy Bospora. Moskva, 1964.
Arc 1076.3.27 Blavignac, J.D. La cloche, études. Genève, 1877.
Arc 823.11.3F Blážej, Benadík. Keltské pohrebiská na juhozápadnom Slovensku. Bratislava, 1957.
Arc 1020.106 Bled, O. Livre d'or de Notre Dame des miracles à Saint Omer. St. Omer, 1913.
Arc 685.2FA Blegen, C.W. Prosymna; the Helladic settlement preceding the Argive Heraeum. Cambridge, Eng., 1937. 2v.
Arc 635.226F Blegen, Carl W. Korakou, a prehistoric settlement near Corinth. Boston, 1921.
Arc 695.1F Blegen, Carl W. Zygouries. Cambridge, 1928.
Arc 522.35F Blegen, Carl William. Troy. v.1-4, pt.1-2. Princeton, N.J., 1950-51. 8v.
Arc 522.36 Blegen, Carl William. Troy and the Trojans. London, 1963.
Arc 823.22 Bleicher, G. Guide pour les recherches archéologiques. Nancy, 1896.
Arc 895.15 Blekingske mindemaerker fra hedenold. (Worsaae, J.J.A.) Kjøbenhavn, 1846.
Arc 641.1 Blenkenberg, C. Archäologische Studien. Leipzig, 1904.
Arc 1025.3 Ein Blick in die römischen Katakomben. (Ludwig, C.) Bern, 1876.
Arc 885.3 Blight, J.C. Antiquities...Kirrier and Penwith, West Cornwall. Truro, 1862.
Arc 861.5.5 Blight, J.T. Ancient crosses and antiquities east of Cornwall. London, 1858.
Arc 687.1.5 Blinkenberg, C. Exploration archéologique de Rhodes. v.1-6. København, 1903-12.
Arc 687.1F Blinkenberg, C. Lindos; fouilles et recherches, 1902-1914. Berlin, 1931. 4v.
Arc 497.11 Bliss, F.J. The development of Palestine exploration. N.Y., 1906.
X Cg Arc 501.17.5A Bliss, F.J. Excavations at Jerusalem 1894-1897. London, 1898.
X Cg Arc 500.7 Bliss, F.J. Excavations in Palestine, 1895-1900. London, 1902.
Arc 501.17 Bliss, F.J. A mound of many cities. London, 1894.
Arc 66.1.29 Bloch, G. Origines du sénat romain. Paris, 1883.
Arc 66.1.220 Bloch, Raymond. Recherches archéologique en territoire Volsinien. Paris, 1972.
Arc 1274.5 Blood, J.H. English seals. London, n.d.
Arc 1033.17.448 Blot, F. Notre Dame du Mont Carmel. Paris, 1878.
Arc 830.310 Blouet, L. Le chrismale de Mortain. Coutances, 1955.
Arc 858.20 Bloxam, M.H. Fragmenta sepulchralia. Sepulchral and early monumental remains of Great Britain. n.p., n.d.
Arc 705.200.5F Blümel, Carl. Der Fries des Tempels der Athena Nike. Berlin, 1923.
Arc 848.12 Blümlein, Carl. Bilder aus dem römisch-germanischen Kulturleben. 2. Aufl. München, 1926.
Arc 853.44 Blume, Erich. Die germanischen Stämme und die Kulturen. Würzburg, 1912-15. 2v.
Arc 853.26 Blume, T. The treasure-trove of Hildesheim. Hildesheim, n.d.
Arc 785.6.5 Blumenstihl, B. Brevi notizie sull'acqua pia (antica Marcia). Roma, 1872.
Arc 1027.1 Die Blutampullen der römischen Katakomben. (Kaus, F.X.) Frankfurt, 1868.
Arc 600.36 Boak, A.E.R. Karanis. Ann Arbor, 1931.
Arc 600.36.5 Boak, A.E.R. Karanis. Ann Arbor, 1933.
Arc 600.40 Boak, A.E.R. Soknopaiou Nesos. Ann Arbor, 1935.
Arc 700.58 Boardman, J. The Greeks overseas. Harmondsworth, 1964.
Arc 700.58.2 Boardman, J. The Greeks overseas. 2. ed. Harmondsworth, 1973.
Arc 672.11 Boardman, John. Excavations in Chios, 1952-1955. London, 1967.
Arc 1033.41 Bobone, G. Apologia di protomartiri...Tolomeo e Romano. Roma, 1865.
Arc 936.205.15 Bobovac i Kraljeva Sutjeska. (Andjelić, Pavao.) Sarajevo, 1973.
Arc 920.206F Bobrinskii, A. Kurgany i sluchainyia arkheologicheskiia nakhodki. Sankt Petersburg, 1887.
Arc 1027.58 La bocca della verita. (De Feis, L.) Roma, 1885.
Arc 1033.17.59 Bocchi, M.F. Opera sopra l'imagine. Fiorenza, 1592.
Arc 1025.71.2 Bock, Emil. Die Katakomben. 2. Aufl. Stuttgart, 1961.
Arc 1020.1 Bock, F. Das Heiligthum zu Aachen. Köln, 1867.
Arc 1020.1.3 Bock, F. Der Reliquienschatz des Leibfrauen-Münsters zu Aachen in seinen Kunstreichen Behältern. Aachen, 1860.
Arc 1020.51 Bock, Franz. Les trésors sacrés de Cologne. Paris, 1862.
Arc 1020.89 Bock. Antiquités sacrées...S. Servais et de Notre Dame à Maestricht. Maestricht, 1873.
Arc 915.36 Bocksberger, Olivier Jean. Age du Bronze en Valais et dans le chablais vaudois. Lausanne, 1964.
Arc 853.354 Die Bocksteinschmiede im Lonetal (Markung Ramminger, Kreis Ulm). (Wetzel, Robert.) Stuttgart, 1969. 2v.

Author and Title Listing

Arc 853.284F Bodenfunde der Völkerwanderungszeit aus dem Main-Tauber-Gebiet. Diss. (Koch, Robert.) Berlin, 1967. 2v.

Arc 905.21 Böhmens...Opferplätz, Gräber und Alterthümer. (Kalina, M.) Prag, 1836.

Arc 1018.30 Böhmer, W. Die socialen Verhältnisse. Breslau, 1836.

Arc 936.195.70 Boehn, Jároslav. Kronika objeveného véku. Praha, 1941.

Arc 853.20.32 Böhner, Kurt. Die fränkischen Altertümer des trierer Landes. v.1-2. Berlin, 1958.

Arc 510.2.9F Boehringer, C. Das Temenos für den Herrscher Kult. Berlin, 1937.

Htn Arc 1053.18* Boehringer, E. Der Caesar von Acireale. Stuttgart, 1933.

Arc 888.35 Boeles, P.C.J.A. De aldste kultuer yn de sânen feankriten fen Frysplân. Boalsert, 1930.

Arc 671.15 Boeotian and west Greek tombstones. (Fraser, F.M.) Lund, 1954.

Arc 1468.26 Börger, Hans. Griechische Münzen. Leipzig, 1922.

Arc 641.2 Börger, Hans. Griechische Reisetage. Hamburg, 1925.

Arc 853.264F Börnicke. (Reinbacker, E.) Berlin, 1963.

Arc 605.205 Boeswillwald, E. Timgad, une cité africaine. Londres, 1892-

Arc 1153.9 Boethii fragmentum notis Tironianis descript. (Vries, S.G. de.) Lugduni Batavorum, 1893.

Arc 936.38.5 Böttger, Burkhard. Bulgarien; eine Reise zu antiken Kulturstätten. 1. Aufl. Berlin, 1971.

Arc 684.1.5 Boetticher, A. Olympia. Berlin, 1886.

X Cg Arc 684.1 Boetticher, A. Olympia - das Fest und seine Stätte. Berlin, 1883. (Changed to XP 9960)

Arc 710.2.2 Boetticher, C. Die Akropolis von Athen. Berlin, 1888.

Arc 710.2 Boetticher, C. Bericht über die Untersuchungen auf der Akropolis von Athen. n.p., n.d.

Arc 87.1.24 Boetticher, C. Dirke. Berlin, 1864.

Arc 87.1.18 Boetticher, C. Grab des Dionysos. Berlin, 1858.

Arc 87.1.19 Boetticher, C. Omphalos der Zeus zu Delphi. Berlin, 1859.

Arc 522.4.15 Boetticher, E. Hissarlik wie es ist. Berlin, 1890.

Arc 522.4.18 Boetticher, E. Der Trojanische Humbug. Berlin, 1911.

Arc 712.1 Boetticher, K. Der Zophorus am Parthenon. Berlin, 1875.

Arc 716.7.5A Bötticher, Karl. Das Poliastempel als Wohnhaus des Königs Erechtheus. Berlin, 1851.

Arc 716.3 Bötticher, Karl. Die Thymele der Athena Nike. Berlin, 1880.

Arc 386.5.6 Böttiger, Carl August. Amalthea. v.1-3. Leipzig, 1820-25. 2v.

Arc 386.5 Böttiger, Carl August. Archäologie. Dresden, 1806.

Arc 386.5.2 Böttiger, Carl August. Archäologie und Kunst. Breslau, 1828.

Arc 386.5.4A Böttiger, Carl August. Kleine Schriften. Dresden, 1837-38. 3v.

Arc 386.5.3 Böttiger, Carl August. Kleine Schriften. 2. Aufl. Leipzig, 1850. 3v.

Arc 386.5.18 Böttiger, Carl Wilhelm. Karl August Böttiger. Leipzig, 1837.

Arc 889.17 Bogaers, J.E.A.T. De Gallo-Romeinse tempels te Elst in de Over Betuive. 's-Gravenhage, 1955.

Arc 796.5 Bogaerts, T. Kunst der illusie; antieke wandschilderungen uit Campanie. Den Haag, 1958.

Arc 925.68 Bogaevskii, B.L. Druzhiia proiz. i dom. zhivotn. tripol'ia. Leningrad, 1937.

Arc 530.12.32 Boğazköy. (Krause, K.) Berlin, 1940.

Arc 530.12.28F Boğazköy. v.3-5. Berlin, 1935- 3v.

Arc 1148.35 Boge, Herbert. Griechische Tachygraphie und tironische Noten. Hildesheim, 1974.

Arc 853.236 Bogen, Alfred. Die Vorgeschichte des magdeburger Landes. Magdeburg, 1937.

Arc 936.150 Bohaté hroby z doby rímskej na Slovensku. (Ondrouch, Vojtech.) Bratislava, 1957.

Arc 936.195.270 La Bohême préhistorique. (Stocký, Albin.) Prague, 1929.

Arc 1433.27 Bohlen, P. von. Über die wissenschaftlichen Werth...Arabischen Münzen. n.p., 1835.

Arc 520.1 Bohn, R. Tempel des Athena Polias zu Pergamon. Berlin, 1881.

Arc 853.306 Bohnsack, Dietrich. Die Burgunden in Ostdeutschland und Palen während des letzten Jahrhunderts vor Christus. Inaug. Diss. Leipzig, 1938.

Arc 895.36.5 Bohulänska hällristningar. (Montelius, Oscar.) Stockholm, 1876.

Arc 1088.1.23 Boisacq, E. La trière antique et la guerre navale. Bruxelles, 1905.

Htn Arc 756.2* Boissard, J.J. Topographia Romae. pt.1-6. Frankfort, 1627. 2v.

Arc 543.2.10 Boisselier, Jean. La statuaire khmère son évolution. Saigon, 1955. 2v.

Arc 756.7 Boissier, Gaston. Promenades archéologiques, Rome et Pompéi. Paris, 1880.

Arc 756.7.1 Boissier, Gaston. Promenades archéologiques, Rome et Pompéi. 2. éd. Paris, 1881.

Arc 756.7.3 Boissier, Gaston. Promenades archéologiques, Rome et Pompéi. 3. éd. Paris, 1887.

Arc 756.7.8 Boissier, Gaston. Promenades archéologiques, Rome et Pompéi. 8. éd. Paris, 1904.

Arc 756.7.2A Boissier, Gaston. Rome and Pompeii. N.Y., 1896.

Arc 830.93 Boissieu, A. de. Ainay; son autel, son amphithéatre, ses martyrs. Lyon, 1864.

Arc 1020.4.5 Boissoudy, A. de. La sainte-chapelle de Bourges. n.p., 1884.

Arc 843.56 Boix, Vicente. Memorias de Sagunto. Valencia, 1865.

Arc 1015.207 Boldetti, M.A. Osservazioni sopra i cimitery. Roma, 1720.

Arc 936.195.240 Bolecek, B.V. Ancient Slovakia. n.p., 1973.

Arc 1588.4.40 Bolesław Chrobry v Czechach. (Gumowski, Marian.) Poznań, 1934.

Arc 94.11 Boletin. (Asociación Artistico-Arqueológica Barcelona.) Barcelona. 1-35,1891-1894

Arc 1304.5 Boletin. (Exposición Iberoamericana de Numismatica y Medallistica.) Barcelona. 1,1958

Arc 307.3.20 Boletin. (International Congress of Americanists, 27th, Mexico, 1939.) México.

Arc 94.25 Boletin. (Orense, Spain. Museo Arqueológico Provincial.) 1-4,1943-1948 2v.

Arc 94.15 Boletín. (Sociedad Cordobesa de Arqueología y Excursiones.) Córdoba. 1928

Arc 94.43 Boletin arqueologico. Tarragona. 1,1921+ 12v.

Arc 1260.4.5 Bolle dei dogi di Venezia. (Cecchetti, B.) Venezia, 1865.

Arc 1260.4 Bolle dei dogi di Venezia. (Cecchetti, B.) Venezia, 1888.

Arc 1208.8 Le bolle d'oro dell'archivio vaticano. (Vatican. Biblioteca Vaticana.) Città del Vaticano, 1934.

Arc 65.6F Bolletino. (Associazione Internazionale degli Studi Mediterranei.) Roma. 1-6,1930-1936 2v.

Arc 3.1.23 Bolletino riassuntivo. (Congrès International d'Archéologie Classique, 3d, Rome, 1912.) Roma, 1912.

Arc 830.300 Bolnat, Georges. La nécropole protohistorique de La Colombine à Champlay-Yonne. Paris, 1957.

Arc 785.57 Bologna. Università. Per un centro di studi di archeologia dell'Impero Romano. Bologna, 1932.

Arc 66.1.106 Bologne villanovienne et etrusque. (Grenier, A.) Paris, 1912.

Arc 1668.2 Bolton, H.C. Contribution of alchemy to numismatics. N.Y., 1890.

Arc 1033.12.186 Bombelli, R. Storia della corona ferrea dei re d'Italia. Firenze, 1870.

Arc 66.1.190 Bompaire, J. Lucien écrivain. Paris, 1958.

Arc 1470.28.5 Bompois, H.F. Médailles grecques autonomes. Paris, 1869.

Arc 1470.28 Bompois, H.F. Les médailles restitutées par M.F. Lenormant à Lyncus ou Héraclée de Lyncestide. Paris, 1867-76. 3 pam.

Arc 1500.37 Bompois, H.F. Notice sur un dèpot de monnaies carlovingiennes. Paris, 1871.

Arc 1490.23 Bompois, H.F. Les types monétaires de la guerre sociale. Paris, 1873.

Arc 66.1.213 Bon, Antoine. La morée franque. Paris, 1969. 2v.

Arc 1027.4.17 Bonavenia, G. L'antichissima imagine della B. Vergine nel cimitero di Priscilla. Siena, 1897.

Arc 1027.4.21 Bonavenia, G. La cuestione...controversia filumeniana. Roma, 1907.

Arc 1027.4.19 Bonavenia, G. Soluzione di un problema...cimitero di Priscilla. Roma, 1903.

Arc 1018.20 Bonavenia. Una pittura di basilica di Antiochia. Roma, 1888.

Arc 925.50.65 Bondar, M.M. Pam'iatky starodavnoho Prydniprov'ia. Kyïv, 1959.

Arc 925.50.380 Bondar', Mykola M. Poseleniia srednego podneprov'ia epokhi rannei bronzy. Kiev, 1974.

Arc 800.10 Bondaroy, F. de. Recherches sur les ruines d'Herculanum. Paris, 1770.

Arc 726.296 Bondi, Sandro Filippo. Le stele di Monte Sirai. Roma, 1972.

Arc 1020.20 Bonelli, G.A. Memorie storiche della Basilica Costantiniana. Roma, 1879.

Arc 1033.66 Bonet, F.R. Breve notizia...d'alcuni Santi del Colosseo. Roma, 1796.

Arc 1033.66.5 Bonet, F.R. Breve notizia...di alcuni Santi del Colosseo. Roma, 1759.

Arc 736.1.5 Bonfiglio, S. Su l'akropoli Akragantina. Girgenti, 1897.

Arc 726.335 Bonghi Jovino, Maria. La necropoli di Nola preromana. Napoli, 1969.

Arc 785.15.9 Boni, G. Trajan's column. (The British Academy). London, n.d.

Arc 830.66.9 Bonnard, Louis. La Gaule thermale. Paris, 1908.

Arc 2.10 Bonner Hefte zur Vorgeschichte. Bonn. 2,1974+

Arc 830.168 Bonnet, E. Périodes wisigothique, carolingienne et romane. Montpellier, 1938.

Arc 1335.46 Bonnet, Emile. Médaillier de la Société archéologique de Montpellier. Montpellier, 1896.

Arc 1348.33F Bonneville, P.F. Traité des monnaies d'or et d'argent qui circulent chez les différens peuples. Paris, 1806.

Arc 843.75 Bonser, J.E. El coto de Doña Ana. Madrid, 1922.

Arc 843.8.5F Bonson, J.E. The archaeological expedition along the Guadalquivir, 1889-1901. N.Y., 1931. 2v.

Arc 843.19.15FA Bonson, J.E. An archaeological sketch-book of the Roman necropolis at Carmona. N.Y., 1931.

Arc 830.174 Bonsor, G. Les colonies agricoles pré-romaines de la vallée du betes. Paris, 1899.

Arc 910.9F Bonstetten, W. Carte archeologique du canton de Fribourg. Genève, 1878.

Arc 820.221F Bonstetten, W. Carte archéologique du départment du Var. Toulon, 1873. 2 pam.

Arc 1020.9.11 Bonties, G.B. Brevi notitie archeologici sull'origine delle chiese di Roma. Roma, 1825.

Arc 810.2 Bonucci, Carlo. Pompéi. Naples, 1828.

Arc 810.2.5 Bonucci, Carlo. Pompéi. 2. éd. Naples, 1830.

Arc 1076.3.14 A book about bells. (Tyack, G.S.) London, 1898.

Arc 875.22 Book of Arran - archaeology. (Balfour, J.A.) Glasgow, 1910. 2v.

Arc 1468.29.10 A book of Greek coins. (Seltman, C.T.) London, 1952.

Arc 1138.15 Books in manuscript. (Madan, F.) London, 1893.

Arc 547.6 Boolak Museum. Guide du visiteur au Musée de Boulaq. Boolak, 1883.

Arc 885.15.8 Boon, George C. Isca, the Roman legionaryfortress at Caerleon. 3. ed. Cardiff, 1972.

Arc 861.11.10 Boon, George Counsell. Roman Silchester. London, 1957.

Arc 861.11.11 Boon, George Counsell. Silchester, the Roman town of Calleva. Newton Abbot, 1974.

Arc 895.23.10F Das Bootgräberfeld von Tuna in Alsike, Uppland. (Arne, T.J.) Stockholm, 1934.

Arc 505.152 Boraas, Roger S. Heshbon 1971: the second campaign at Tell Hesbân. Berrien Spring, Mich., 1973.

Arc 551.10 Borchardt, L. Allerhand Kleinigkeiten. Leipzig, 1933?

Arc 600.45F Borchardt, Ludwig. Ägyptische Tempel mit Umgang. Kairo, 1938.

Arc 547.6.35F Borchardt, Ludwig. Denkmäler des alten Reiches. Berlin, 1937-1964. 2v.

Arc 595.51 Borchardt, Ludwig. Einiges zur dritten Bauperiode der grossen Pyramide bei Gise. Berlin, 1932.

Arc 595.50 Borchardt, Ludwig. Die Entstehung der Pyramide an der Baugeschichte. Berlin, 1928.

Arc 595.16 Borchardt, Ludwig. Gegen die Zahlenmystik an der grossen Pyramide bei Gise. Berlin, 1922.

Arc 595.16.10 Borchardt, Ludwig. Längen und Richtungen der vier Grandkanten der grossen Pyramide bei Gise. Berlin, 1926.

Arc 830.368 Bordes, François. A tale of two caves. N.Y., 1972.

Arc 31.18 Boreas. Uppsala. 1,1970+

Arc 830.128 Borel, Pierre. Les antiquités de Castres. Paris, 1868.

Arc 386.4.25 Borghesi, Bartolomeo. Bartolomeo Borghesi. Firenze, 1905.

Arc 386.4 Borghesi, Bartolomeo. Oeuvres complètes. Paris, 1862-72. 10v.

Arc 726.26 Borgia, S. Breve i storia dell'antica città di Tadino. Roma, 1751.

Htn Arc 1033.35.13F* Borgia, S. De cruce vaticana...commentarius. Roma, 1779.

Htn Arc 1033.35.15F* Borgia, S. De cruce veliterna. Roma, 1780.

Arc 785.6.13 Borgnana, C. Dell'acqua di Q. Marcio Ré e del suo acquedotto. Roma, 1861.

Arc 1335.44 Borioni, T. Collana di medaglie antiche e moderne. Loreto, 1835.

Arc 925.13.105 Boriskovskii, P.I. Pamiatniki drevneishei chelovesheskoi kul'tury Severo-Zapadnogo Prichernomor'ia. Odessa, 1961.

	Arc 543.132	Boriskovskii, Pavel Io. Pervobytnoe proshloe B'etnama. Leningrad, 1966.
	Arc 1208.15	Borisov, Andrei Ivan Iakovlevich. Sasanidskie gemmy. Leningrad, 1963.
	Arc 416.46	Borisovskii, Pavel I. Drevnii kamennyi vek Iuzhnoi i Iuga-Vostochnoi Azii. Leningrad, 1971.
	Arc 936.195.85	Borkovský, Ivan. Levý Hradec. Praha, 1965.
	Arc 880.2	Borlase, W.C. The dolmens of Ireland. London, 1897. 3v.
	Arc 861.5	Borlase, W.C. Naema Cornubiae. London, 1872.
	Arc 890.208	Bornholms oldtidsminder og oldsager. (Vedel, E.) Kjøbenhavn, 1886.
	Arc 542.2	Boro-Boudour dans l'Isle de Jara. (Leemans, C.) Leyden, 1874. 5v.
	Arc 543.25.10	Borobudur, mysteriegebeuren in steen. (Bernet Kempers, A.) Den Haag, 1960.
	Arc 1274.3.5	Borough seals of the Gothic period. (Pedrick, G.) London, 1904.
	Arc 925.13.50	Borovka, Grigorii I. Scythian art. London, 1927.
	Arc 925.13.52	Borovka, Grigorii I. Scythian art. London, 1928.
	Arc 820.5	Borrel, E.L. Les monuments anciens de la Tarentaise (Savoie). Paris, 1884. 2v.
	Arc 1335.43	Borrell, H.P. Catalogue of...Greek, Roman, Byzantine and Mediterranean coins. v.1-2. London? 1852?
	Arc 815.19.5	Borrelli, L. Le tombe di Pompei a schola semicircolare. Napoli, 1937.
	Arc 756.8	Borsari, L. Topografia di Roma antica. Milano, 1897.
	Arc 785.13.15	Borsari, Luigi. Le Forum Romain selon les dernières fouilles. Rome, 1900.
	Arc 1033.12.127	Bortolan, D. S. spina di Vicenza. Vicenza, 1887.
	Arc 685.4	Bosanquet, Robert. The unpublished objects from the Palaikastro excavations, 1902-06. London, 1923.
	Arc 375.10	Bosc, E. Dictionnaire général de l'archéologie. Paris, 1881.
	Arc 1428.13F	Bosch, C. Die kleinasiatischen Münzen der römischen Kaiserzeit. Stuttgart, 1935.
	Arc 1588.8	Bosch, E. Turkizenin ankils deviedeke meskukatina. Ankara, 1949.
	Arc 1348.81	Bosch, Enin. Eski sikkeler rehberi. Istanbul, 1951.
	Arc 543.75.5	Bosch, Frederick D.K. Selected studies in Indonesian archaeology. The Hague, 1961.
	Arc 843.15.9	Bosch Gimpera, P. Prehistoria catalana. Barcelona, 1919.
	Arc 843.62	Bosch-Gimpera, P. La prehistoria de las Iberas y la etnologia vasca. San Sebastian, 1926.
	Arc 843.62.10	Bosch-Gimpera, P. Two Celtic waves in Spain. London, 1939.
	Arc 1015.202.5	Bosio, A. Roma scotterranea. Paris, 1658.
	Arc 1015.202	Bosio, A. Roma scotterranea. Roma, 1651. 2v.
	Arc 1025.35	Bosio, A. Roma subterranea novissima. Arnhemi, 1671.
	Arc 1025.68	Bosio, Antonio. Abgebildetes unterirdisches Rom. Arnheim, 1668.
Htn	Arc 1033.35.21F*	Bosio, I. Trionfante e gloriosa croce trattato. Roma, 1610.
	Arc 785.83.15	Bosio, Luciano. Itinerari e strade della Venetia Romana. Padova, 1970.
	Arc 905.19	Bosnien und Herzegowina in Römischer Zeit. (Patsch, Carl.) Sarajevo, 1911.
	Arc 1153.72	Boson, G.G. Paléographie valdôtaine. v.1-3. Aoste, 1950-52.
	Arc 925.12.7.2	Das bosporanische Reich. 2. Aufl. (Gaidukevich, V.F.) Berlin, 1971.
	Arc 925.12.7	Bosporskoe tsarstvo. (Gaidukevich, V.F.) Moskva, 1949.
	Arc 1263.3	Bosredon, P. de. Sigillographie du Périgord. Perigneux, 1880.
	Arc 1153.35	Bosseboeuf, L.A. École de calligraphie et de miniature de Tours. Tours, 1891.
X Cg	Arc 672.1.33	Bossert, H.T. Alt Kreta. Berlin, 1921.
	Arc 672.1.34	Bossert, H.T. Alt Kreta. 3. Aufl. Berlin, 1937.
	Arc 1229.5	Bossert, H.T. Die hethitisches Königssiegel. Berlin, 1944.
	Arc 1020.9.30	Bossi, G. La chiesa di Santa Marta al Vaticano. Roma, 1883.
	Arc 1468.50	Boston. Museum of Fine Arts. Greek coins, 1950-1963. Boston, 1964.
	Arc 1458.10	Boston. Museum of Fine Arts. Guide to the C.P. Perkins collection of Greek and Roman coins. Boston, 1902.
	Arc 1301.2	Pamphlet box. The Boston Numismatic Society. Miscellaneous pamphlets.
	Arc 953.15	Boston Society of Natural History. Palaeolithic implements of...Delaware. v.1-3. Cambridge, 1881.
	Arc 925.2	Bostor Kimmeriiskii sego drevnostiami i dostopamiasnostiami. (Spasskii, Grigorii I.) Moskva, 1846.
	Arc 612.87	Botanisch Beiträge zur mitteleuropäischen Siedlungsgeschichte. (Lange, Elsbeth.) Berlin, 1971.
	Arc 843.14	Botet y Sisó, J. Monumento sepulcral romano de Lloret de Mar. Gerona, 1892.
	Arc 1494.4.9	Botet y Sisó, Joaquim. Les monedes Catalanes. Barcelona, 1908-11. 3v.
	Arc 1015.203	Bottari, G.G. Sculture e pitture sagre estratte dai cimitery de Roma. Roma, 1737-54. 3v.
	Arc 1033.3	Bottazzi, G.A. Emblemi...del...sarcofago...di Tortona. Tortona, 1824.
	Arc 600.1.5	Botti, G. Plan du Quartier "Rhacotis" dans l'Alexandrie. Alexandrie, 1897.
	Arc 547.29	Botti, Giuseppe. Le casse di mummie e i sarcofagi da el Hibeh. Fienze, 1958.
	Arc 547.44	Botti, Giuseppe. I cimeli egizi del Museo. Firenze, 1964.
	Arc 830.146	Bottin, S. Mélangés d'archéologie. Paris, 1831.
	Arc 1200.9	Boüard, A. de. Etudes de diplomatique sur les actes, des iquenotaires de Paris. Paris, 1910.
	Arc 1190.30	Boüard, Alain de. Manuel de diplomatique française et pontificale. Paris, 1929-52. 2v.
	Arc 1190.30F	Boüard, Alain de. Manuel de diplomatique française et pontificale. Atlas. Paris, 1929-52. 2v.
	Arc 66.1.139	Boüard, Michel de. La France et l'Italie au temps du Grand Schisme d'Occident. Paris, 1936.
	Arc 66.1.204	Boucher, Jean-Paul. Études sur Properce; problèmes d'inspiration et d'art. Paris, 1965.
	Arc 830.20	Boucher de Molandon. Le tumulus de Reuilly. Orléans, 1887.
	Arc 1264.22F	Bouches-du-Rhone. Archives. Iconographie des sceaux et bulles conservés dans la partie antérieure à 1790 des archives départementales des Bouches-du-Rhone. Marseille, 1860.
	Arc 825.4	Boucoiran, L. Guide...dans Nîmes et les environs. Nîmes, 1863.
	Arc 825.4.4	Boucoiran, L. Guide aux monuments de Nîmes et au Pont du Gard. Nîmes, 1863.
	Arc 1335.31	Boudeau, E. Catalogue général illustré de monnaies antiques. 2. ed. Paris, n.d.
	Arc 1335.31.3	Boudeau, E. Catalogue général illustré de monnaies françaises. Paris, n.d.
	Arc 830.265	Boudon-Fashermes, Albert. Le Velay gallo-grec. Rodez, 1958.
	Arc 66.1.126	Boulanger, André. Relius Aristide. n.p., n.d.
	Arc 66.1.156	Boulet, Marquerite. Questiones Johannes Galli. Paris, 1944.
	Arc 1033.160	Boulgaris, N.T. Alēthēs ekthesis...thaymatourchou...touachiouspyridōnos. Benetia, 1880.
	Arc 1540.28	Boundy, W.S. Bushell and Harman of Lundy. Bideford, 1961.
	Arc 1018.1	Bourassé, J.J. Archéologie chrétienne. Tours, 1878.
	Arc 830.343	Bourdier, Franck. Préhistoire de France. Paris, 1967.
	Arc 1076.3.85	Le Bourdon de Notre-Dame de Reims. (Jadart, Henri.) Reims, 1884.
	Arc 66.1.102	Bourgin, G. La France et Rome de 1788 à 1797. Paris, 1909.
	Arc 673.1.4	Bourguet, E. L'aurige de Delphes. Paris, 1912.
	Arc 673.1.3	Bourguet, E. Les ruines de Delphes. Paris, 1914.
	Arc 726.41	Bourguet, Louis. Spiegazione di alcuni monumenti degli antichi Palasgi. Pesaro, 1735.
	Arc 830.22.5	Bournon, Fernand. Les arènes de Lutèce. Paris, 1908.
	Arc 935.7	Bourquelot, Félix. La colonne serpentine à Constantinople. Paris, n.d.
	Arc 1030.11	Bourquelot, M.F. Inscriptions chrétiennes trouvées en Italie. n.p., n.d.
	Arc 505.16	Bourquenond, A. Mémoire sur les ruines de Séleucie de Piérie. Paris, 1860.
	Arc 66.1.95	Bourquet, E. L'administration financiere du sanctuaire pythique. Paris, 1905.
	Arc 673.1.20F	Bousquet, Jean. Le trésor de Cyrène à Delphes. Thèse. Paris, 1952.
	Arc 830.68	Bousrez, Louis. L'Anjou aux âges de la pierre...bronze. Paris, 1897.
	Arc 830.63	Bousrez, Louis. Les monuments mégalithiques. Tours, 1894.
	Arc 1340.4	Boutkowski, Alex. Dictionnaire numismatique. Leipzig, 1877.
	Arc 838.23	Boutroue, A. Rapport...sur une mission archéologique en Portugal et dans le sud de l'Espagne. Paris, 1893.
	Arc 700.69	Bouzek, Jan. Graeco-Macedonian bronzes. Praha, 1974.
	Arc 641.4A	Bouzek, Jan. Homerisches Griechenland im Lichte der archäologischen Quellen. Praha, 1969.
	Arc 1020.137	Bovini, G. Sarcofagi paleocristiani della Spagna. Roma, 1954.
	Arc 726.327	Bovini, Giuseppe. Antichità cristiane di San Canzian d'Isonzo. Bologna, 1973.
	Arc 1076.4.10	The bow; some notes on its origin and development. (Rausing, Gad.) Bonn, 1967.
	Arc 858.100	Bowen, Emrys George. Britain and the western seaways. London, 1972.
	Arc 870.25	Bowen, H.C. Ancient fields. London, 1963.
	Arc 543.80	Bowen, R. Archaeological discoveries in South Arabia. Baltimore, 1958.
	Arc 435.2.22F	The Bower manuscript. (Hoernle, A.F.R.) Calcutta, 1893-1912.
	Arc 785.34.14	Bowerman, H.C. Roman sacrificial altars. Lancaster, Pa., 1913.
	Arc 66.1.141	Boyancé, Pierre. Le culte des muses. Paris, 1937.
	Arc 830.150	Boyer, H. Noviodunum Biturigum et ses graffiti. Bourges, 1861.
	Arc 1680.9	Boyne, William. Tokens issued in seventeenth century England...by corporations. London, 1858.
	Arc 1680.9.3	Boyne, William. Trade tokens...seventeenth century...England, Wales and Ireland. London, 1889. 2v.
	Arc 935.34	Boysal, Yusuf. Uzuncaburç ve Ura kilavuzu. Istanbul, 1962.
	Arc 1190.55	Bozner Schreibschriften der Neuzeit. (Santifaller, Leo.) Jena, 1930.
	Arc 1356.7	Brabich, Vladimir M. Puteshestire s drevnei monetoi. Leningrad, 1970.
	Arc 843.28	Os braceletes d'ouro de arnozella. (Severo, Ricardo.) Porto, 1905. 2 pam.
	Arc 1505.203	Der Bracteatenfund von Seega. (Buchenau, H.) Marburg, 1905.
	Arc 785.13.17.5	Braddeley, S.C. Recent discoveries in the Forum, 1898-1904. London, 1904.
	Arc 785.13.17	Braddeley, S.C. Recent discoveries in the Forum. N.Y., 1904.
	Arc 968.2.23	Bradfield, W. Cameron Creek village...New Mexico. Santa Fé, 1931.
	Arc 386.32	Bradford, John. Ancient landscapes. London, 1957.
	Arc 681.7F	Brae, Luigi Bernabo. Poliochni. v.1-2. Roma, 1964.
	Arc 608.6.70	Brahime, Claude. Initiation à la préhistoire de l'Algérie. Alger, 1972.
	Arc 1584.15	Braichevs'kyi, M.I. Ryms'ka moneta naterytorii Ukraïny. Kyïv, 1959.
	Arc 925.50.110	Braichevs'kyi, Mykhailo I. Bilia dzherel plov'ians'koi derzhevnosti. Kyïv, 1964.
	Arc 543.115F	Braidwood, Robert John. Prehistoric investigations in Iraqi Kurdistan. Chicago, 1960.
	Arc 1490.35	Brambilla, C. Monete di Pavia. Pavia, 1883.
	Arc 1412.1	Bramsen, W. The coins of Japan. pt.1. Yokohama, 1880.
	Arc 1510.140	Die Brandenburg Frankischen Kippermünzstätten, 1620-1622. (Gebert, Carl Friedrich.) München, 1901.
	Arc 1510.148	Die Brandenburger Denare von Heinrich König der Wenden bis auf Friedrich I. Kurfürst aus dem Hause Hohenzollern. (Weidhas, J.F.) Berlin, 1855.
	Arc 1200.4	Die Brandenburgische Kanzlei und die Urkundenwesen. Inaug. Diss. (Lewinski, L.) Strassburg, 1893.
	Arc 853.270F	Brandgräber des Völkeswandernugszeit im siedlichen Niedersachsen. (Nowothnig, Walter.) Neumünster, 1964.
	Arc 1185.16	Brandi, Karl. Urkunden und Akten. Leipzig, 1913.
	Arc 1408.1	Brandis, J. Das Münz-, Mass- und Gewichtswesen in Vorderasien. Berlin, 1866.
	Arc 387.12.25	Brandoli, Placido. Monsignor Celestino Cavedoni. Modena, 1870.
	Arc 392.18	Brandt, Karl. Otto Hauser. Witten-Ruhr, 1970.
	Arc 853.356	Brandt, Karl Heinz. Studien über steinerne Äxte und Beile der jüngeren Steinzeit und der Stein-Kupferzeit Nordwestdeutschlands. Hildesheim, 1967.
	Arc 670.9	Branigan, Keith. Aegean metalwork of the early and middle Bronze Age. Oxford, 1974.

Author and Title Listing

Arc 672.1.120 Branigan, Keith. The tombs of Mesara; a study of funerary architecture and ritual in southern Crete, 2800-1700 B.C. London, 1970.
Arc 861.195 Branigan, Keith. Town and country. Bourne End, 1973.
Arc 925.13.130 Brashinskii, I. Sokrovishcha skifskikh tsarei. Moskva, 1967.
Arc 1645.1.15 Das brasilianische Geldwesen. (Meili, Julius.) Zürich, 1897-1905. 2v.
Arc 1588.10.20 Bratislavské korunovačné medaily a žetóny. Vyd. 1. (Hlinka, Jozef.) Bratislava, 1966.
Arc 551.20 Bratton, Fred Gladstone. A history of Egyptian archaeology. London, 1967.
Arc 756.3.5 Braun, Emil. Handbook...ruins and museums of Rome. London, 1855.
Arc 756.3 Braun, Emil. Die Ruinen und Museen Roms. Braunschweig, 1854.
Arc 756.3.4 Braun, Emil. The ruins and museums of Rome. Brunswick, 1854.
Arc 689.6 Braun, I. De theraeorum rebus sacris. Inaug. Diss. Halis Saxonum, 1932.
Arc 1033.35.155 Braun, J. Die Reliquiare des christlichen Kultes und ihre Entwicklung. Freiburg, 1940.
Arc 386.6 Braun, J. Studien und Skizzen. Mannheim, 1854.
Arc 87.2.49 Braun, J.W.J. Die Kapitole. Bonn, 1849-
Arc 1510.162 Braun von Stumm, Gustaf. Die Münzen der Abtei Hornbach nebst Beiträgen zur Münzkunde von Speyergau und Elsass im 12-14. Halle an der Saale, 1926.
Arc 386.30 Brayda, C. Norme per il restauro dei monumenti. Torino, 1954.
Arc 1493.23 Brazão, Arnaldo. Numismatalogos contemporaneas. Lisboa, 1963.
Arc 386.26 Breasted, C. Pioneer to the past. N.Y., 1943.
Arc 495.208F Breasted, J.H. Oriental forerunners of Byzantine painting...wall-paintings from the fortress of Dura. Chicago, 1924.
Arc 600.1.15 Breccia, E. Alexandrea ad Aegyptum. Bergamo, 1914.
Arc 1148.22 Breccia, E. Note epigrafiche. Alexandria, 1931.
Arc 600.95 Breccia, E. Nuovi scari nelle necropoli di Hadra. Alexandria, 1930.
Arc 547.24.15 Breccia, E. Sculture inedite del Museo Greco-Romano. Alexandrie, 1931.
Arc 600.1.17 Breccia, E. Una statuetta del Buon Pastore da Marsa Matruh. Alexandria, 1931.
Arc 590.10.5 Breccia, E. La tomba di Alessandro Magno. Alexandria, 1930.
Arc 386.40 Breccia, E. Uomini e libri. Pisa, 1959.
Arc 1478.45 Breglia, L. La prima fase della coniozione romana dell'argento. Roma, 1952.
Arc 1033.12.89 Bréhier, L. The treasures of Syrian silverwar. Paris, 1921.
Arc 1053.21F Bréhier, L. Les visions apocalyptiques dans l'art byzantin. Bucarest, 1930?
Arc 1153.4.5 Breidenbach, H. Zwei Abhandlungen...tironischen Noten. Darmstadt, 1900.
Arc 880.36 Bremer, Walther. Ireland's place in prehistoric and early historic Europe. Dublin, 1928.
Arc 2.12 Bremer archäologische Blätter. Bremen. 2,1961+
Arc 853.335 Die Bremer Hanse-Kogge. Bremen, 1969.
Arc 1510.9 Die bremischen Münzen. (Jungk, H.) Bremen, 1875.
Arc 843.25 Brenha, José. Dolmens ou antas de ville ponco d'Aguir. (Traz-os-montes). Porto, 1903.
Arc 1675.58 Brenner, V.D. The art of the medal. N.Y., 1910.
Arc 905.10 Die Brennerstrasse im Alterthum und Mittelalter. (Rodlow, O.W. von.) Prag, 1900.
Arc 1076.22 Brensztejn, Michał E. Zarys dziejów lvdwisarstwa na ziemiach b. Wielkiego Księstwa Litewskiego. Wilno, 1924.
Arc 522.10.2 Brentano, E. Alt-Ilion im Dumbrekthal. Heilbronn, 1877?
Arc 522.10.3 Brentano, E. Troia und Neu-Ilion. Heilbronn, 1882.
Arc 522.10 Brentano, E. Zur Loesung der Troianischen Frage. Heilbronn, 1881.
Arc 416.38 Brentjes, Burchard. Von Schanidar bis Akkad. 1. Aufl. Leipzig, 1968.
Arc 726.68.5 Brescia antica. (Nazari, G.B.) Brescia, 1658.
Arc 1588.1.60 Breslau. Zakład Narodowy im Ossalińskikh. Biblioteka. Tysiąc lat monety na ziemiach poliskich. Wrocław, 1966.
Arc 1033.38.9 Bresnicio, C.B. Historia de Insigni Martyrio...Laurentii. Leipzig, 1572.
Htn Arc 726.68* Bressa anticha. (Nazari, G.B.) Bressa, 1562.
Arc 1190.1.2 Bresslau, H. Diplomata centum. Berlin, 1872.
Arc 1190.1.3 Bresslau, H. Handbuch der Urkundenlehre. 3. Aufl. Berlin, 1958. 2v.
Arc 1190.1 Bresslau, H. Handbuch der Urkundenlehre fuer Deutschland und Italien. Leipzig, 1889.
Arc 830.1.5 La Bretagne. (Jéhan, L.F.) Tours, 1863.
Arc 1153.23 Bretholtz, B. Lateinische Paläographie. 2. Aufl. Leipzig, 1912.
Arc 793.9.2 Breton, Ernest. Pompeia. 3. éd. Paris, 1869.
Arc 793.9 Breton, Ernest. Pompeia. 3. éd. Paris, 1870.
Arc 1603.1 Breton, P.N. Le collectionneur...des monnaies canadiennes. Montreal, 1890.
Arc 1603.1.5 Breton, P.N. Popular illustrated guide to Canadian coins. Montreal, 1912.
Arc 1428.27 Brett, A. The electrum coinage of Lampakos. N.Y., 1914.
Arc 1221.4F Brett, Agnes B. Ancient oriental seals in the collection of Mrs. Agnes Baldwin Brett. Chicago, 1936.
Arc 1088.1 Breusing, A. Die Nautik der Alten. Bremen, 1886.
Arc 1020.6.5 Breve descrittione del sacro thesoro...San Marco. Milano, 1617.
Arc 1020.102 Breve distinta relazione...sacre relique... S. Maria...città di Siena. Siena, 1750.
Arc 726.26 Breve i storia dell'antica città di Tadino. (Borgia, S.) Roma, 1751.
Arc 1020.113 Breve istoria del santuario di Belmonte presso Valperga. (Furno, A.) Torino, 1788.
Arc 1033.17.443 Breve istoria della miracolosa immagine di Maria Sma...di Montenero. (Andrea, G.A.) Livorno, 1774.
Arc 1033.66 Breve notizia...d'alcuni Santi del Colosseo. (Bonet, F.R.) Roma, 1796.
Arc 1033.66.5 Breve notizia...di alcuni Santi del Colosseo. (Bonet, F.R.) Roma, 1759.
Arc 1033.43.9 Breve Notizia dell'Orato in Memoria Abitazione. Roma, 1770.
Arc 785.4 Breve notizie delle antiche pitture. (Mullooly, J.) Roma, 1866.
Arc 1033.12.4 Breve racconta del SS. Prepuzio di Gesu Christi. Roma, 1728.
Arc 1027.46 Brevi cenni...scoprimento...martire...S. Stefano. (Fortunati, L.) Roma, 1858.
Arc 1590.7 Brevi cenni storici...una medaglià di Ugone III. (Schweitzer, F.) Trieste, 1846.
Arc 1033.87 Brevi compendio di memorie...martire S. Agapito. (Marucchi, O.) Roma, 1898.
Arc 1020.9.11 Brevi notitie archeologici sull'origine delle chiese di Roma. (Bonties, G.B.) Roma, 1825.
Arc 1033.51 Brevi notizie intorno San Rufino. (Angelini, N.) Frascati, 1885.
Arc 1033.51.3 Brevi notizie intorno San Rufino ves e Martire. (Angelini, N.) Roma, 1862.
Arc 1033.17.242 Brevi notizie sul celebre santuario di Maria sma. nel Sacro Monte di Novi. (Ronzini, D.) Napoli, 1853.
Arc 785.6.5 Brevi notizie sull'acqua pia (antica Marcia). (Blumenstihl, B.) Roma, 1872.
Arc 1033.58.9 Brevi racconto sopra immagini S. Sebastiano. Roma, 1830.
Arc 861.168 Brewster, Thomas. Excavation of Staple Howe. Wentringham, 1963.
Arc 612.42 Briard, Jacques. L'Age du Bronze. Paris, 1959.
Arc 1353.3 A brief account of the collection of coins belonging to the mint of the United States. (DuBois, W.E.) Philadelphia, 1846.
Htn Arc 950.5* Brief account of the discovery of the brass plates...Kinderbrook, Illinois. (Harris, W.P.) Nauvoo, Illinois, 1843.
Arc 943.2 A brief account of the more important public collections of American archaeology in the United States. (Phillips, H.) n.p., n.d.
Arc 547.6.10 A brief description of the principal monuments. (Cairo. Musée des Antiquités Égyptiennes.) Cairo, 1927.
Arc 547.6.15 A brief description of the principal monuments. (Cairo. Musée des Antiquités Égyptiennes.) Cairo, 1961.
Arc 710.4.2 A brief explanation of the ground plan of the akropolis of Athens. (Michaelis, A.) Cambridge, 1882.
Arc 501.2 Brief geographical account of the survey of Western Palestine. (Saunders, T.) London, 1882.
Arc 880.48 A brief guide to the collection of Irish antiquities. (Dublin. National Museum of Ireland.) Dublin, 1960.
Arc 1033.70.9 Brief notice of the ancient paintings...Rome. (Mullooly, J.) Rome, 1866.
Arc 1680.8 Brief particulars...eighteenth century tokens...county of Middlesex. n.p., 1914?
Arc 1675.59 A brief word on medals. (De Kay, Charles.) N.Y., 1910.
Arc 561.1.2 Briefe aus Aegypten. (Lepsius, R.) Berlin, 1852.
Arc 390.15 Briefe aus dem Bonner Privatdozentenjahr 1879/80. (Furtwängler, Adolf.) Stuttgart, 1965.
Arc 658.3.1 Briefe von Heinrich Schliemann. (Schliemann, H.) Berlin, 1936.
Arc 403.16.20 Briefwechsel. (Schliemann, Heinrich.) Berlin, 1953. 2v.
Arc 861.50 Brighton and Hove Archaeological Club. Brighton and Hove archaeologist, 1914. Hove, 1914.
Arc 861.50 Brighton and Hove archaeologist, 1914. (Brighton and Hove Archaeological Club.) Hove, 1914.
Arc 1166.3 Brigiuti, R. La paleografia ed i Raggi di Röntgen. Roma, 1899.
Arc 1180.1 Brinckmeier, E. Glossarium diplomaticum. Gotha, 1856-63. 2v.
Arc 658.3.11 Brinckmeier. Heinrich Schliemann und die Ausgrabungen auf Hissarlik. Burg, 1901.
Arc 983.10 Brinton, D.G. The Taki, the Swastika, and the Cross in America. Philadelphia, 1889.
Arc 386.29.10 Brion, Marcel. De Pompéi a l'île de Pâques. Paris, 1967.
Arc 793.17 Brion, Marcel. Pompeii and Herculaneum. N.Y., 1961.
Arc 386.29 Brion, Marcel. La résurrection des villes mortes. v.1-2. Paris, 1948-49.
Arc 1076.3.97 Briscoe, J.P. Curiosities of the belfry. London, 1883.
Arc 870.19 Bristol. University. Spelaeological Society. Proceedings. Bristol, Eng. 1,1919+ 6v.
Arc 858.54.5 Britain, the key to world history. (Beaumont, Comyns.) London, 1949.
Arc 858.100 Britain and the western seaways. (Bowen, Emrys George.) London, 1972.
Arc 858.62 Britain B.C. (Winbolt, S.E.) Harmondsworth, Eng., 1945.
Htn Arc 870.6* Britannia Romana, or Romans in Britain. (Pointer, J.) Oxford, 1724. 4 pam.
Arc 855.200 Britannia Romana, or The Roman antiquities of Britain. (Horsley, J.) London, 1732.
Arc 861.9 The British, Roman, and Saxon antiquities and folklore of Worcestershire. (Allies, J.) London, 1856.
Arc 935.9.25 British Academy. Report upon the excavations carried out in and near the hippodrome of Constantinople. London. 1-2,1927-1928
Arc 1468.28F British Academy. Sylloge nummorum Graecorum. London, 1931-51. 4v.
Arc 66.11 British and American Archaeological Society of Rome. Journal. Rome.
Arc 66.11.5 British and American Archaeological Society of Rome. Proceedings. Rome.
Arc 861.32 British and Roman remains in Axminster. (Davidson, J.) London, 1833.
Arc 335.5 British archaeological abstracts. London. 1967+ 4v.
Arc 125.4 British Archaeological Association. Archaeological journal. London. 1+ 119v.
Arc 125.4.2 British Archaeological Association. Archaeological journal. General index, v.26-75 (1869-1918). London, 1955-73. 2v.
Arc 125.4.8 British Archaeological Association. Communications made to the association. London, 1862. 2v.
Arc 125.4.3 British Archaeological Association. Journal. London. 1+ 96v.
Arc 125.4.5 British Archaeological Association. Transactions at its 2nd Congress, 1845. London, 1846.
Arc 125.4.10 Pamphlet box. British Archaeological Association.
Arc 858.10 British barrows. (Greenwell, G.) Oxford, 1877.
Arc 572.10.5 British Egyptology, 1549-1906. (Wortham, John David.) Newton Abbot, 1971.
Arc 31.9 British Institute of Archaeology in Ankara. Occasional publications. London. 1,1949+ 10v.
Arc 861.14 British lake-village near Glastonbury. (Glastonbury, England. Antiquarian Society.) Taunton, 1899.
Arc 630.6 British Museum. Catalogue of Greek and Roman lamps in the British Museum. London, 1914.
Arc 1208.1 British Museum. Catalogue of seals in the department of manuscripts. London, 1887-1900. 6v.
Arc 858.78 British Museum. Guide to the antiquities of Roman Britain. 3. ed. London, 1964.
Arc 547.13 British Museum. A guide to the Egyptian collections. London, 1909.

Arc 547.12 British Museum. A guide to the 1st and 2nd Egyptian rooms. London, n.d.
Arc 547.12.2 British Museum. A guide to the 3rd and 4th Egyptian rooms. London, 1904.
Arc 547.17 British Museum. Hieroglyphic Texts from Egyptian Stelae. Pt.1-7, 9. London, 1911-25. 8v.
Arc 386.15.5 British Museum. How to observe in archaeology. 2. ed. London, 1929.
Arc 1333.3 British Museum. Nummi veteres - in Museo R.P. Knight asservati. London, 1830.
Arc 712.12 British Museum. Sculpures...Parthenon. London, 1900.
Arc 1333.4 British Museum. Veteres pop. et reg. numi. London, 1814.
Arc 861.166 British Museum. Department of British and Mediaeval Antiquities. Hox Hill. London, 1962.
Arc 861.100 British Museum. Department of British and Mediaeval Antiquities. The Sutton-Hoo ship burial. 1. ed. London, 1947.
Arc 1473.6.5 British Museum. Department of Coins and Medals. Catalogue of coins of vandals, ostrogoths. London, 1911.
Arc 1538.2.15 British Museum. Department of Coins and Medals. A catalogue of English coins in the British Museum. Anglo-Saxon series. London, 1887-93. 2v.
Arc 1538.2 British Museum. Department of Coins and Medals. Catalogue of English coins in the British Museum. London, 1916. 2v.
Arc 1418.1 British Museum. Department of Coins and Medals. Catalogue of Indian coins. v.1-5,7. London, 1884-1936. 6v.
X Cg Arc 1408.5 British Museum. Department of Coins and Medals. Catalogue of Oriental coins. London, 1875-90. 10v.
Arc 1418.2.7 British Museum. Department of Coins and Medals. Catalogue of the coins of the Gupta dynasties and of Sásánka. London, 1914.
Arc 1468.1 British Museum. Department of Coins and Medals. A catalogue of the Greek coins. London, 1873-94. 29v.
Arc 1433.43 British Museum. Department of Coins and Medals. A catalogue of the Muhammadan coins in the British Museum. London, 1941. 2v.
Arc 1478.21.2 British Museum. Department of Coins and Medals. Coins of the Roman Empire. v.1-3; v.4, pt.1-2; v.6. London, 1966. 6v.
Arc 1478.21 British Museum. Department of Coins and Medals. Coins of the Roman Empire in the British Museum. v.1-4,6. London, 1923-40. 5v.
Arc 1535.2 British Museum. Department of Coins and Medals. Description of the Anglo-Gallic coins. London, 1826.
Arc 1538.2.20 British Museum. Department of Coins and Medals. English copper, tin, and bronze coins in the British Museum. London, 1960.
Arc 1538.2.22 British Museum. Department of Coins and Medals. English copper, tin and bronze coins in the British Museum. 2. ed. London, 1964.
Arc 1353.2.15 British Museum. Department of Coins and Medals. Greek coins acquired by the British Museum. London. 1887-1896
Arc 1335.63.3 British Museum. Department of Coins and Medals. A guide to the department of coins and medals. London, 1922.
Arc 1478.21.5 British Museum. Department of Coins and Medals. A guide to the exhibition of Roman coins in the British Museum. London, 1927.
Arc 1353.2.5 British Museum. Department of Coins and Medals. A guide to the gold and silver coins of the ancients. 4. ed. London, 1895.
Arc 1353.2.10 British Museum. Department of Coins and Medals. A guide to the gold and silver coins of the ancients. 5. ed. London, 1909.
Arc 1468.2.10 British Museum. Department of Coins and Medals. A guide to the principal coins of Greeks from circa 700 B.C. to A.D. 270. London, 1932.
Arc 1353.2.3 British Museum. Department of Coins and Medals. A guide to the principal gold and silver coins of the ancients. London, 1881.
Arc 1353.2.2 British Museum. Department of Coins and Medals. A guide to the principal gold and silver coins of the ancients. London, 1886.
Arc 1468.2 British Museum. Department of Coins and Medals. A guide to the select Greek coins. London, 1872.
Arc 1538.7.2 British Museum. Department of Coins and Medals. Handbook of the coins of Great Britain and Ireland in the British Museum. 2. ed. London, 1970.
Arc 1675.20F British Museum. Department of Coins and Medals. Select Italian medals of the Renaissance. London, 1915.
Arc 1675.55 British Museum. Department of Coins and Medals. Synopsis of the contents of the British Museum. London, 1881.
Arc 547.25F British Museum. Department of Egyptian and Assyrian Antiquities. Egyptian sculptures in the British Museum. London, 1914.
Arc 547.25.5 British Museum. Department of Egyptian and Assyrian Antiquities. Gallery of antiquities. London, 1842.
Arc 547.26 British Museum. Department of Egyptian and Assyrian Antiquities. A general introductory guide to the Egyptian collections in the British Museum. London, 1964.
Arc 547.50F British Museum. Department of Egyptian Antiquities. Catalogue of Egyptian antiquities in the British Museum. London, 1968- 2v.
Arc 537.13.1PF British Museum. Department of Greek and Roman Antiquities. Excavations in Cyprus. 1. ed. London, 1970.
Arc 1208.14F British Museum. Department of Western Asiatic Antiquities. Catalogue of the Western Asiatic seals in the British Museum. London, 1962.
Arc 561.3 British Museum. Egyptian antiquities. (Long, G.) London, 1832. 2v.
Arc 1535.200F British naval medals. (Milford Haven, L.) London, 1919.
Arc 1301.1 British numismatic journal. (British Numismatic Society.) London. 1,1905+ 39v.
Arc 1301.1 British Numismatic Society. British numismatic journal. London. 1,1905+ 39v.
Arc 1301.1.15 Pamphlet box. The British Numismatic Society. Miscellaneous pamphlets.
Arc 858.58 British prehistory. (Piggott, Stuart.) London, 1949.
Arc 66.8 British School at Athens. British School at Athens...annual. Rome. 1,1894+ 68v.
Arc 66.8.2 British School at Athens. British School at Athens...index, 1-32. London, n.d. 2v.
Arc 66.8 British School at Athens...annual. (British School at Athens.) Rome. 1,1894+ 68v.
Arc 66.8.2 British School at Athens...index, 1-32. (British School at Athens.) London, n.d. 2v.
Arc 66.8.15 Pamphlet box. British School at Athens.
NEDL Arc 66.10 British School at Rome. Annual reports. London.
Arc 66.9 British School at Rome. Papers. London. 1,1902+ 41v.
Arc 589.5 British School of Archaeology in Egypt. Report. London. 13-20,1907-1914
Arc 31.12 British School of Archaeology in Jerusalem. Bulletin. 1-7,1922-1925 2v.
Arc 31.7F British School of Archaeology in Jerusalem. Supplementary papers. London.
Arc 1033.17.504 Brito Alão, M. de. Antiguidade da sagrada imagem de Nossa S. de Nazareth...Pederneira. Lisboa, 1628.
Arc 830.280 Brittany. (Giot, Pierre Roland.) London, 1960.
Arc 925.321.10 Briusov, Aleksandr I. Istoriia drevnei Karelii. Moskva, 1940.
Arc 861.209 Brixworth excavations. Northampton, Eng., 1972?
Arc 785.3 Brizio, E. Pitture e sipolcri scoperti sull'Esquilino. Roma, 1876.
Arc 746.14 Brizio, E. Una Pompei etrusca a Marzabotto nel Bolognese. Bologna, 1928.
Arc 1093.2.19 Brjussow, A. Geschichte der neolithischen Stämme im europäischen Teil der Ud SSR. Berlin, 1957.
Arc 1020.87 Brocchi, G.M. Descrizione delle reliquare di Santi...Rocca di Lutiano. Firenze, 1744.
Arc 700.40A Brock, James K. Fortetsa. Cambridge, Eng., 1957.
Arc 1077.12 Brockpaehler,W. Steinkreuze in Westfalen. Münster, 1963.
Arc 785.63 Broderick, B.F. The so-called Altar of Calvinus on the Palatine hill, in Rome. N.Y., 1930. 3 pam.
Arc 861.180 Brodribb, Arthur Charles Conant. Excavations at Shakenoak Farm. v.1-4. Oxford, Eng., 1968- 3v.
Arc 551.3 Brodrick, M. A concise dictionary of Egyptian archaeology. London, 1902.
Arc 785.39.50 Broedner, Erika. Untersuchungen an der Caracallathermen. Berlin, 1951.
Arc 895.17 Brøgger, A.W. Studier over Norges stenalder. Christiania, 1906.
Arc 893.14 Brøgger, A.W. Universitetets oldsakamlings skrifter. Oslo, 1929.
Arc 895.7.25F Brøndsted, J. Danmarks oldtid. Kjøbenhavn, 1938-40. 3v.
Arc 895.7.25.2F Brøndsted, J. Danmarks oldtid. Kjøbenhavn, 1957- 3v.
Arc 895.7.26 Brøndsted, J. Danmarks stengrave og gravhøge i forhold til landets jordbund. Kjøbenhavn, 1939.
Arc 635.203 Bröndsted, P.O. Voyages dans la Gréce. Paris, 1826.
Arc 895.47.5F Broholm, Hans Christian. Kulturforbindelser mellem Danmark og syden i aeldre. København, 1960.
Arc 895.47 Broholm, Hans Christian. Studier over den yngre Bronzealder Danmark. København, 1933.
Arc 609.21 Brokensha, David W. Applied anthropology in English speaking Africa. Lexington, Ky., 1966.
Arc 412.5.5 Brolin, Per Erik. Gamla fynd och glömda folk. Göteborg, 1969.
Arc 889.10 Brom, Leo H.M. The Stevensweert Kantharos. The Hague, 1952.
Arc 712.36 Brommer, F. Die Giebel des Parthenon. Mainz, 1959.
Arc 895.58 Broncealderens monumentalkunst. (Gudnitz, F.) København, 1962.
Arc 843.7.5 Los bronces de Osuna. (Rodriquez de Berlanga, M.) Malaga, 1873.
Arc 843.190 Bronces ibericas o hispancion del Mueso Arquelogico Nacional. (Alvarez-Ossori, F.) Madrid, 1935.
Arc 670.6 Broneer, O. The lion monument at Amphipolis. Cambridge, Mass., 1941.
Arc 895.22.20F Bronsaldersmanteln fran Gerumsberget i Vastergötland. (Post, Linnart.) Stockholm, 1924-25.
Arc 1033.17.249 Bronte, G. da. Santuario di Maria Sma. di Gibilmanna. Catania, 1856.
Arc 387.9 Bronze age. (Childe, Vere Gordon.) Cambridge, Eng., 1930.
Arc 505.121.10 The Bronze Age Cemetery at Gibeon. (Pritchard, James.) Philadelphia, 1963.
Arc 823.50 Bronze Age cultures in France. (Sandars, Nancy K.) Cambridge, Eng., 1957.
Arc 880.10 The bronze age in Ireland. (Coffey, George.) Dublin, 1913.
Arc 612.55F Bronze age kultures in central and eastern Europe. (Gimbutas, Marija Alseikaites.) The Hague, 1965.
Arc 642.11 Bronze Age migrations in the Aegean. (Colloquium on Bronze Age Migrations in the Aegean Region, Sheffield, Eng., 1970.) London, 1973.
Arc 870.10.15 The bronze age round barrow in Britain. (Ashbee, Paul.) London, 1960.
Arc 830.52 Le bronze dans le Finistère. (Du Chatellier, Paul.) Quimper, 1899.
Arc 843.220 O bronze meridional português. (Ribeiro, Fernando Nunes.) Beja, 1965.
Arc 421.4 A bronze table with accompanying vessels. (Ferguson, J.C.) Peking, 1924.
Arc 87.1.73 Bronzefigur einer Spinnerin. (Wiegand, Theodore.) Berlin, 1913.
Arc 905.128 Bronzefunde des Karpatenbeckens. (Mozsolics, Anália.) Budapest, 1967.
Arc 936.195.225 Die Bronzehortfunde in der Slowakei. 1. vyd. (Novotná, Mária.) Bratislava, 1970.
Arc 87.1.69 Bronzes. (Kekule, R.) Berlin, 1909.
Arc 843.7 Les bronzes d'Osuna. (Giraud, C.) Paris, 1874.
Arc 843.230 Les bronzes figurés des sanctuaires ibériques. 1. éd. (Nicolini, Gerard.) Paris, 1969.
Arc 746.11F Die Bronzeschnabelkannen. (Jacobsthal, Paul.) Berlin, 1929.
Arc 87.1.49 Bronzestatue des sogenannten Idolino. (Kekule, R.) Berlin, 1889.
Arc 925.4.9 Bronzezeit am Janissei. (Merhard, Gero von.) Wien, 1926.
Arc 853.225F Die Bronzezeit in der Oberpfalz. (Torbruegge, Walter.) Kallmünz, 1959.
Arc 612.65 Die Bronzezeit in Nordeuropa. Bildnis einer prähistorischen Hochkultur. (Behn, Friedrich.) Stuttgart, 1967.
Arc 723.22 Bronzezeit und frühe Eisenzeit in Italien. (Messerschmidt, Franz.) Berlin, 1935.
Arc 936.195.255 Bronzezeitliche Gräberfelder in der Südwestslowakei. (Dušek, Mikuláš.) Bratislava, 1969.
Arc 853.210F Bronzezeitliche Hortfunde. (Brunn, Wilhelm Albert von.) Berlin, 1959.
Arc 612.21.7F Bronzezeitliche und früheisenzeitliche Chronologie. v.4-5. (Aberg, Nils.) Stockholm, 1933-35. 2v.
Arc 905.41 A Bronzkor emlékei magyarhonban. (Hampel, J.) Budapest, 1886. 3v.
Arc 925.4.7 Bronzovye nozhi minusinskogo kraia i nekotorye voprosy razvitiia karasukskoi kul'tury. (Khlobystina, M.D.) Leningrad, 1962.

Arc 925.240 Bronzovyi vek Zabaikal'ia. (Divov, N.N.) Ulan-Ude, 1958.
Arc 925.16.5 Bronzy drevnei Gruzii. (Tavadze, F.) Tbilisi, 1959.
Arc 1680.10.5 Brook, A.J.S. Communion tokens of the established Church of Scotland. Edinburgh, 1907.
Arc 1538.18.10 Brooke, George C. English coins. 3. ed. London, 1950.
Arc 1538.18 Brooke, George C. English coins from the seventh century to the present day. London, 1932.
Arc 505.69 Broome, E.C. The dolmens of Palestine and Transjordania. Philadelphia, 1940.
Arc 800.11 Brosses, Charles de. Lettres sur l'état actuel de la ville souterraine d'Herculée. Dijon, 1750.
Arc 1584.1.6 Brosset, M.F. Rapport sur l'ouvrage intitulé. St. Petersbourg, 1847.
Arc 510.215 Brosset. Les ruines d'Ani, capitale de l'Arménie. Text and atlas. St. Petersbourg, 1860. 2v.
Arc 762.4.2 Broughton, J.C.H. Historical illustrations of 4th canto of Childe Harold. 2. ed. London, 1818.
Arc 708.19 Broughton, V. Delves (Mrs.). Handbook to antiquities of Athens. Athens, 1896.
Arc 1020.110 Brouillet, A. Description des reliquaires...abboye de Charroux. Poitiers, 1856.
Arc 830.67.5 Brouillet, A. Epoques antédiluvienne et celtique du Poitu. pt.1-2. Poitiers, 1865.
Arc 830.67.10 Brouillet, A. Mémoire sur l'enceinte gallo-romaine de Poitiers. Poitiers, 1872.
Arc 1138.112.2 Brouwer, Hans. Geschreven verleden. 2. druk. 's-Gravenhage, 1963.
Arc 950.207 Brower, J.V. Memoirs of explorations...basin...Mississippi. v.1-3,4-5,6-7,8. St. Paul, Minn., 1898. 7v.
Arc 943.29 Brown, A. Indian relics and their values. Chicago, 1942.
Arc 1418.6.5 Brown, C.J. The coins of India. Calcutta, 1922.
Arc 967.1.13 Brown, C.S. Archaeology of Mississippi. University, 1926.
Arc 1478.38 Brown, D.F. Temples of Rome as coin types. N.Y., 1940.
Arc 943.28 Brown, F.M. America's yesterday. Philadelphia, 1937.
Arc 386.13 Brown, G.B. The care of ancient monuments. Cambridge, 1905.
Arc 875.31.5F Brown, G.F. Ancient cross shafts at Bewcastle and Ruthwell. Cambridge, 1916.
Arc 848.19 Brown, Gerard Baldwin. The arts and crafts of our Teutonic forefathers. London, 1910.
Arc 861.7 Brown, J.A. Paleolithic man in northwest Middlesex. London, 1887.
Arc 870.14.15 Brown, Paul. The great wall of Hadrian in Roman times. London, 1932.
Arc 600.5 Brown, R.H. The Fayûm and Lake Moeris. London, 1892.
Arc 452.3 Brown, William N. A pillared hall from a temple at Madura, India. Philadelphia, 1940.
Arc 865.14.5 Brown and Company, Salisbury, publishers. The illustrated guide to Old Sarum and Stonehenge. Salisbury, 1877.
Arc 865.14 Brown and Company, Salisbury, publishers. Illustrated guide to Old Sarum and Stonehenge. London, 1888.
Arc 865.3 Browne, H. An illustration of Stonehenge and Abury. 4. ed. Salisbury, 1854.
Arc 1033.20.26 Brownlow. Basilica of St. Clement in Rome. London, 1900.
Arc 756.12 Brtnický, L. Topografie starověkého Říma. Praha, 1925.
Arc 861.12 Bruce, J.C. The handbook to the Roman wall. 4. ed. London, 1895.
Arc 861.12.2 Bruce, J.C. The handbook to the Roman wall. 9. ed. Newcastle-upon-Tyne, 1933.
Arc 861.12.2.5 Bruce, J.C. Handbook to the Roman wall. 10. ed. Newcastle-upon-Tyne, 1947.
Htn Arc 1480.16* Bruce, J.C. The story...of the Thorngrafton "Find". n.p., 1871.
Arc 861.18.9 Bruce, J.C. The wall of Hadrian. Newcastle-upon-Tyne, 1874.
Arc 870.14.3 Bruce, John C. Hadrian, the builder of the Roman wall. London, 1853.
Arc 870.14F Bruce, John C. The Roman wall. 3. ed. London, 1867.
Arc 858.63 Bruce-Mitford, R.L.S. Recent archaeological excavations in Britain. London, 1956.
Arc 861.100.25 Bruce-Mitford, Rupert Leo. Aspects of Anglo-Saxon archaeology. London, 1974.
Arc 861.100.2 Bruce-Mitford, Rupert Leo. The Sutton-Hoo ship burial. London, 1951.
Arc 861.100.15 Bruce-Mitford, Rupert Leo. The Sutton-Hoo ship burial. London, 1968.
Arc 1478.80 Bruck, Guide. Die spatrömische Kupferprägung. Graz, 1961.
Arc 87.1.64 Brueckner, A. Anakabypteria. Berlin, 1904.
Arc 705.210 Brueckner, A. Der Friedhof am Eridanos...zu Athen. Berlin, 1909.
Arc 87.1.62 Brueckner, A. Lebensregeln auf Athens. Hochzeitsgeschenken. Berlin, 1907.
Arc 700.10 Brueckner, A. Ornament und Form der altischen Grabstelen. Weimar, 1886.
Arc 340.8.5 Brünn. Universita. Knihovna. Minulost jižní Moravy. Brno, 1963.
Arc 340.8.10 Brünn. Universita. Knihovna. Přehled bibliografií a pokusů o soupisy moravské archeologické literatury. Brno, 1965.
Arc 495.205 Brünnow, R.E. Die Provincia Arabia. Strassburg, 1904. 3v.
Arc 1020.3 Bruges, Belgium. Commission Provinciale. Inventaire des objets d'art et d'antique...Bruges. Bruges, 1848.
Arc 1160.12 Brugmans, H. Atlas der Nederlandsche palaeographie. 's Gravenhage, 1910.
Arc 545.222 Brugsch, E. La trouvaille de Deir-el-Bahari. Cairo, 1881.
Arc 547.2 Brugsch, H. Uebersichtliche Erklaerung Aegyptischer Denkmaeler des Koenigliche Neuen Museum zu Berlin. Berlin, 1850.
Arc 600.2 Brugsch-Bey, H. Reise nach der grossen Oase El-Khargeh. Leipzig, 1878.
Arc 66.1.175 Bruhl, A. Liber patér. Paris, 1953.
Arc 432.9 Bruhl, O. Indian temples. Calcutta, 1937.
Arc 936.220.50 Brukner, Bogdan. Neolit n Vojvodini. Beograd, 1968.
Arc 925.8 Brun. Chernomorek. Gotyieledy dolgago ikh prebyv. Sankt Petersburg, 1874. 2 pam.
Arc 1033.35.9 Brunati. Di un antica stauroteca istoriata...Brescia. Roma, 1839.
Arc 1033.42 Brunatio, J. De Christianorum veterum monumentorum im rem biblicam utilitate. Diss. Mediolani, 1838.
Arc 1030.2 Brunatius, J. Musei kircheriani inscript. ethnicae et christianae. Mediolani, 1837.
Arc 66.1.217 Bruneau, Philippe. Recherches sur les cultes de Délos à l'époque hellénistique et à l'époque impériale. Paris, 1970.
Arc 935.3 Brunet de Presle. Extrait d'un notice sur les tombeaux des empereurs de Constantinople. Paris, 1856.
Arc 1077.2.9 Brunet y Bellet, J. La creu els monuments megalitics. Barcelona, 1892.
Arc 830.86.5 Brunette, N. Notice sur les antiquités de Reims. Reims, 1861.
Arc 1349.75 Brunetti, Lodovico. Opus monetale cigoi. Bologna, 1966.
Arc 895.65 Brunius, Carl Georg. Försök till förklaringar öfver hällristningar. Lund, 1968.
Arc 726.10.2 Brunn, H. Cista prenestina. Roma, 1864.
Arc 628.12 Brunn, H. Kleine Schriften. Leipzig, 1898. 3v.
Arc 740.202 Brunn, H. I relievi delle urne etrusche. Rome, 1870-1916. 3v.
Arc 746.1 Brunn, H. Über die Ausgrabungen der Certosa von Bologna. München, 1887.
Arc 386.23 Brunn, H. von. Archäologie und Anschauung. München, 1885.
Arc 853.110 Brunn, W.A. von. Steinpockungsgräber von Köthen. Berlin, 1954.
Arc 853.210F Brunn, Wilhelm Albert von. Bronzezeitliche Hortfunde. Berlin, 1959.
Arc 547.35F Brunner-Traut, Emma. Die altägyptischen Scherbenbilder. Wiesbaden, 1956.
Arc 716.14.2 Brunnsaaker, Sture. The tyrant slayers of Kritios and Nesiotes: a critical study of the sources and restorations. 2. ed. Stockholm, 1971.
Arc 383.93 Bruns, G. Festschrift für Carl Weickert. Berlin, 1955.
Arc 935.9.30 Bruns, G. Der Obelisk und seine Basis auf dem Hippodrom zu Konstantinopel. Istanbul, 1935.
Arc 889.8 Brunsting, H. Het grafveld onder hees bij Nijmegen. Amsterdam, 1937.
Arc 588.46F Brunton, Guy. The Badarian civilization. London, 1928.
Arc 588.41F Brunton, Guy. Gurob. London, 1927.
Arc 588.28 Brunton, Guy. Lahun I, II; the treasure. London, 1920. 2v.
Arc 600.80F Brunton, Guy. Matmar. London, 1948.
Arc 588.44F Brunton, Guy. Qau and Badari. London, 1927-30. 3v.
Arc 726.95F Brusin, G. Aquileia. n.p., n.d.
Arc 905.35 Brusin, G. Gli scavi di Aquileia. Udine, 1934.
Arc 1470.80 Brussels. Bibliothèque Royale. La collection Lucien de Hirsch. v.1-2. Bruxelles, 1959.
Arc 1520.15 Brussels. Bibliothèque Royale. Mille ans de monnayage Bruxellois, 1965. Bruxelles, 1965.
Arc 547.42 Brussels. Musées Coyaux d'Art et d'Histoire. Fondation Egyptologique Reine Elisabeth. Département égyptien; album. Bruxelles, 1934.
Arc 658.3.25 Brusti, Franz Georg. Heinrich Schliemann. München, 1971.
Arc 861.4.9 Brutton, F.A. Classical Association...Roman fort at Manchester. Manchester, 1909.
Arc 810.46 Bruun, Carl. Pompeji, dets historie og mindesmärker. Kjøbenhavn, 1881.
Arc 609.1.40 Bruwer, Andries Johannes. Zimbabwe; Rhodesia's ancient greatness. Johannesburg, 1965.
Arc 600.210F Bruyère, Bernard. Fouilles de Clysma-Qolzoum (Suez) 1930-1932. Le Caire, 1966.
Arc 1018.38 Bruyn, H. de. Archéologie religieuse. v.1-2. Bruxelles, 1869.
Arc 895.36.9 Bruzelius, N.G. Sur des rochers sculptés decouverts en Scanie. Stockholm, 1875.
Arc 1033.69.5 Bruzza, L. Della interpretazione del Monogramma. Roma, 1877.
Arc 1030.14.5 Bruzza, L. Fistula plumbea acquaria di Porto. Roma, 1878.
Arc 1030.15 Bruzza, L. Iscrizione antiche vercellesi. Roma, 1874.
Arc 1030.14 Bruzza, L. Iscrizione in onore di Iallia Bassia. Roma, 1883.
Arc 1027.64 Bruzza, L. Oggetti ritrovati in un sepolcro della via Prinistina. Roma, 1882.
Arc 726.22.5A Bryan, W.R. Italic hut urns and hut urn cemeteries. Rome, 1925.
Htn Arc 522.2.3* Bryant, Jacob. Observations upon a treatise: Description of plain of Troy. Eton, 1795.
Arc 522.2 Bryant, Jacob. Observations upon a treatise entitled A description of the plain of Troy. Eton, 1795.
Arc 875.21 Brydall, R. The monumental effigies of Scotland. Glasgow, 1895.
Arc 543.154 Brykina, Galina A. Karabulak. Moskva, 1974.
Arc 585.8 Bubastis. (Naville, E.H.) London, 1891.
Arc 590.12 Buberl, Paul. Die griechisch-ägyptischen Mumienbildnisse der Sammlung T. Graf. Wien, 1922.
Arc 1033.4 Bucci, P. Sulla comunione christiana nei primi secoli. Roma, 1862.
Arc 726.71 Bucciolotti, A. Della origine e delle antiche città de' Sabini. Roma, 1825.
Arc 726.160 Buccolini, Geralberto. Il problema archeologico di Orvieto antica. Orvieto, 1935.
Arc 303.18.25 Bucharest. Muzeul de Istorie a Orasului. Cercetări arheologice ên Bucureşti. Bucureşti. 2,1965+
Arc 1510.143 Buchenau, H. Beiträge zur schwäbisch-fränkischen Münzkunde des späteren Mittelalters. n.p., 19- .
Arc 1505.203 Buchenau, H. Der Bracteatenfund von Seega. Marburg, 1905.
Arc 585.32F The Bucheum. (Mond, Robert.) London, 1934. 3v.
Arc 641.5 Buchholz, Hans-Günter. Prehistoric Greece and Cyprus: an archaeological handbook. London, 1973.
Arc 1143.4.5 Die Buchrolle in der Kunst. (Birt, Theodor.) Leipzig, 1907.
Arc 1510.134F Buck, H. Die Münzen der Stadt Einbeck. Hildesheim, 1939.
Arc 1510.30F Buck, H. Die Münzen der Stadt Hannover. Hannover, 1935.
Arc 1027.25.55 Buck, V. de. M. de Rossi ets ses récents travaux...catacombes. v.1-2. Paris, 1865.
Arc 386.7 Bucke, C. Ruins of ancient cities. London, 1840. 2v.
Arc 861.81 Buckler, Geroge. Colchester castle, a Roman building. Colchester, 1876.
Arc 386.8 Buckley, T.A. Great cities of the ancient world. London, 1852.
Arc 1588.12 A Budai penzverde muveszett orterenete a kesoi kozepkorban. (Horvath, Henrik.) Budapest, 1932.
Arc 1588.10.12 A budai pénzverés története a középkorban. (Huszár, Lajos.) Budapest, 1958.
Arc 1588.10 Budapest. Magyor Eremmuveszet Nemzeti Galeria. Medailles hongroises aux XIXe et XXe siècles. Budapest, 1959.
Arc 1588.10.15 Budapest. Orszagos Széchenyi-Könyvtár. Catalogus numorum Hungariae ac Transiwaniae Instituti Nationalis Széchényrani. Pestini, 1807. 2v.
Arc 225.10 Budapest. Tudomany Egyetem-Régészeti Intézet. Régészeti dolgozatok. 3,1959+ 4v.
Arc 227.10 Budapest régiségei; régészeti es történeti évkönyv. Budapest. 1-18,1889-1959 14v.
Arc 1053.23 Budde, Ludwig. Der Ertstehung des antiken Reprasentationsbildes. Berlin, 1957.
Arc 441.1F Buddha Gayá. (Rájendralála Mitra.) Calcutta, 1878.
Arc 542.200 Die Buddha-Legende. (Pleyte, C.M.) Amsterdam, 1901.

Author and Title Listing

Arc 543.27A Die Buddha-Legende auf den Flachreliefs der ersten Galerie des Stupa von Boro-Budur, Java. (Nelsen, F.C.) Leipzig, 1923.

Arc 442.10 Buddhist cave temples of India. (Wauchope, Robert S.) Calcutta, 1933.

Arc 440.3 Buddhist remains in Andhra. (Subramanian, K.) Madras, 1932.

Arc 435.2.6F The Buddhist stupas of Amarayati and Jaggayyapeta. (Burgess, James.) London, 1887.

Arc 430.5 Buddhistische Studien. (Gruenwedel, A.) Berlin, 1897.

Arc 543.66.23 Buddiiskie peshchery Kara-tepe v starom Termeze. (Termezskaia Arkheologicheskaia Kompleksnaia Ekspeditsiia, 1937, 1961-1962.) Moskva, 1969.

Arc 543.66.24 Buddiiskii kul'tovyi tsentr Kara-tepe v starom Termeze. (Termezskaia Arkheologicheskaia Kompleksnaia Ekspeditsiia, 1937, 1961-1962.) Moskva, 1972.

Arc 593.4 Budge, E.A.W. Cleopatra's needles and other Egyptian obelisks. London, 1926.

Arc 590.1A Budge, E.A.W. The mummy. Chapters on Egyptian funereal archaeology. Cambridge, 1893.

Arc 590.1.5 Budge, E.A.W. The mummy. 2. ed. Cambridge, 1925.

Arc 590.1.4 Budge, E.A.W. The mummy. 2. ed. N.Y., 1974.

Arc 551.5 Budge, Ernest A. By Nile and Tigris. London, 1920. 2v.

Arc 545.241F Budge, Ernest A. The Rosetta stone. London, 1913.

Arc 936.195.40F Budinsky-Krička, V. Slovanské mohyly v Skalici. Bratislava, 1959.

Arc 936.195.250 Budinsky-Kricka, Vojtech. Das altungarische Fürstengral von Zemplén. Bratislava, 1973.

NEDL Arc 1163.5.15 Bühler, G. Indian paleography. Bombay, 1904.

Arc 1163.5.10 Bühler, G. Indische Palaeographie von Arca. Strassburg, 1896.

Arc 756.13 Bühlmann, J. Das alte Rom mit dem Triumphzuge Kaiser Constantins im Jahre 312 n. Chr. München, 1892.

Arc 756.13.5 Bühlmann, J. Rom mit dem Triumphzuge Constantins im Jahre 312. 4. Aufl. München, 1894.

Arc 1033.17.133 Buenchini, G.M. Notizie istoriche intorno alla sma. Cintola. Prato, 1795.

Arc 1076.3.37 Die bündner Glocken. (Caminada, Christian.) Zürich, 1915.

Arc 1510.5 Bürkel, L. von. Die Bilder der Süddeutschen. München, 1903.

Arc 1027.12.9 Bufalieré, P. La basilica apostolorum e la critta apostolica. Roma, 1891.

Arc 1027.47 Bufalieri da Montécelio, P. Ricersa...tomba S. Cecilia. Roma, 1891.

Arc 606.7 Buhen. (Randall-MacIver, David.) Philadelphia, 1911. 2v.

Arc 590.16F Buhl, Marie Louise. The late Egyptian anthropoid stone sarcophagi. København, 1959.

Arc 505.131 Buhl, Marie Louise. Shiloh; the Danish excavations at Tall Sailūn, Palestine, in 1926, 1929, 1932, and 1963. Copenhagen, 1969.

Arc 785.6.17F The building of the Roman aqueducts. (Van Deman, E.B.) Washington, 1934.

Arc 1500.40.10 Buisson, Honoré. Monnaies féodales bretonnes de Charles le Chauve a Anne de Bretagne. Perigueux, 1961.

Arc 936.6.40 Bukowski, Zbigniew. Studia nad południowym i południowowschodnim pograniczem kultury łuzyckiej. Wrocław, 1969.

Arc 1163.3.30 Bukvitsa na 77 listakh. (Moskovskii Arkheologicheskii Institut.) Moskva, 1909.

Arc 66.1.131 Bulard, M. La religion domestique. Paris, 1926.

Arc 543.3.100 Bulatova, Vera A. Drevnaia kuva. Tashkent, 1972.

Arc 303.18.5 Buletiuul. (Rumania. Comisune Monumentelar Istoriće.) 1-38,1908-1945 13v.

Arc 936.38 Bulgaria. (Dimitrov, D.) Sofiia, 1961.

Arc 936.140.01 Pamphlet vol. Bulgaria. Antiquities. 4 pam.

Arc 936.38.5 Bulgarien; eine Reise zu antiken Kulturstätten. 1. Aufl. (Böttger, Burkhard.) Berlin, 1971.

Arc 302.2.14 Bulgarska Akademiia na Naukite, Sofia. Arkheolgicheski Institut. Serdika; arkheologicheski materiali. Sofiia, 1964.

Arc 383.81 Bulgarska Akademiia na Naukite, Sofia. Arkheologicheski Institut. Izsledvaniia v pamet na Karel Shkorpil. Sofiia, 1961.

Arc 302.2.6 Bulgarska Akademiia na Naukite, Sofia. Arkheologicheski Institut. Izvestiia. Sofiia. 1,1921+ 28v.

Arc 936.260 Bŭlgarska Akademiia na Naukite, Sofia. Arkheologicheski Institut. Nessébre. Sofia, 1969.

Arc 302.2.4 Bulgarska Akademiia na Naukite, Sofia. Arkheologicheski institut. Trudove na sektsiata za slavianska arkheologiia. Sofiia. 1-2,1947-1948

Arc 936.40.10 Bulgarska Akademiia na Naukite, Sofia. Arkheologicheskikh Institut. Apoloniía. Sofiia, 1963.

Arc 302.2.5 Bulgarski ArkheologicheSki Institut, Sofia. Bulletin. Sophia. 1-7,1910-1920 7v.

Arc 682.25.15 Bulgarski starini iz Makedoniia. (Ivanov, Iordan.) Sofiia, 1908.

VArc 682.25.17 Bulgarski starini iz Makedoniia. 2. izd. (Ivanov, Iordan.) Sofiia, 1931.

VArc 682.25.19 Bulgarski starini iz Makedoniia. 2. izd. (Ivanov, Iordan.) Sofiia, 1970.

Arc 1033.39 Bulic, F. Frammento di pettine son reppresentanze cristiane. Roma, 1902.

Arc 1027.43 Bulic, F. Necropoli antica cristiana a Slano di Ragusa. Roma, 1901.

Arc 936.50 Bulić, France. L'archéologie en Dalmatie du Xe siècle. n.p., 1924-25.

Arc 936.50.5 Bulić, France. Povodom pedestgod jubileja "Vjesnika za arh. hist. Dalmatinsku". Split, 1931.

Arc 905.4.10 Bulić, Frane. Po ruševinama staroga Salina. Zagreb, 1900.

Arc 642.8 The bull of Minos. (Cottrell, Leonard.) London, 1953.

Arc 642.8.5 The bull of Minos. (Cottrell, Leonard.) London, 1962.

Arc 642.8.1 The bull of Minos. (Cottrell, Leonard.) London, 1971.

Arc 855.217F Bulleid, A. The Glastonbury Lake village. n.p., 1911. 2v.

Arc 861.169F Bulleid, Arthur. The Meare Lake village. v.1,3. Taunton, 1948- 2v.

Arc 861.80 Bullen, R.A. Harlyn Bay and the discoveries of its prehistoric remains. 3. ed. Harlyn Padstow, 1912.

Arc 1200.6 Bullen der Päpste. (Pflugh-Harttung, J.) Gotha, 1901.

Arc 1254.3 Bulles byzantines de la collection de M...de Köhne. (Miller, E.) Paris, 1867.

Arc 1259.2 Les bulles de plomb des lettres pontificales. (Chamard, François.) Paris, 1883.

Arc 1254.15 Les bulles métriques dans la sigillographie byzantine. (Taurent, Vitalieu.) Eetjia, 1932.

Arc 30.9 Bulletin. (Académie...Bona. Académie d'Hippone.) Bona. 1-37,1865-1921 10v.

Arc 30.9F Bulletin. (Académie...Bona. Académie d'Hippone.) Bona. 11,1873

Arc 273.1 Bulletin. (Académie Royale d'Archéologie de Belgique.) Anvers. 1863-1929 18v.

Arc 30.12 Bulletin. (American Institute for Persian Art and Archaeology.) N.Y. 1-5,1931-1942 2v.

Arc 1.5 Bulletin. (American School of Classical Studies at Athens.) Boston. 1-5,1883-1902 3v.

Arc 1.5F Bulletin. (American School of Classical Studies at Athens.) Boston. 3

Arc 1.5.22 Bulletin. (American School of Oriental Research, Jerusalem.) Philadelphia? 1,1919+ 11v.

Arc 1.1.15 Bulletin. (American School of Prehistoric Research.) Washington. 1-28 11v.

Arc 1.1 Bulletin. (Archaeological Institute of America.) Boston. 1,1883

Arc 1.1.7 Bulletin. (Archaeological Institute of America.) Norwood, Mass. 1,1909+ 14v.

Arc 305.3 Bulletin. (Archaeological Institute of America. Southwest Society, Los Angeles.) Los Angeles. 1-8 2v.

Arc 1.1.10 Bulletin. (Archeological Institute of America. School of American Archaeology.) Washington.

Arc 66.3.5 Bulletin. (Athens. École française.) Athènes. 1-12,1868-1871

Arc 31.12 Bulletin. (British School of Archaeology in Jerusalem.) 1-7,1922-1925 2v.

Arc 302.2.5 Bulletin. (Bulgarski ArkheologicheSki Institut, Sofia.) Sophia. 1-7,1910-1920 7v.

Arc 1302.7 Bulletin. (Cercle d'Études Numismatiques.) Bruxelles. 1,1964+

Arc 302.14 Bulletin. (Československá Akademie Ved. Archeologický Ustav. Záchranné Oddělení.) Praha. 2,1964+

Arc 32.5.3 Bulletin. (Chicago. University. Oriental Institute.) Chicago.

Arc 35.1 Bulletin. (France. Commission Archéologique de l'Indochine.) Paris. 1908-1934 3v.

Arc 131.2 Bulletin. (Group for the Study of Irish Historic Settlement.) Belfast, Ire.? 1,1970+

Arc 582.1 Bulletin. (Institut Français d'Archéologie Orientale du Caire.) Le Caire. 1,1901+ 48v.

Arc 42.25 Bulletin. (Medelhavsmuseet.) Stockholm. 2,1962+

Arc 317.2 Bulletin. (Missouri. Historical Society. Department of Archaeology.) St. Louis. 1,1913

Arc 45.5 Bulletin. (Pahlari University. Asia Institute.) Shiraz. 1,1969+

Arc 320.1.21 Bulletin. (Pennsylvania. University. University Museum.) Philadelphia. 1-3 2v.

Arc 293.2 Bulletin. (Russkoe Arkheologicheskoe Obshchestvo, Leningrad.) St. Pétersbourg. 21-25

Arc 113.3.20 Bulletin. (Société Archéologique du Midi de la France.) Toulouse. 1869-1945 19v.

Arc 584.2 Bulletin. (Société d'Archéologie Copte, Cairo.) 4,1938+ 10v.

Arc 113.5 Bulletin. (Société d'Archéologie de Saint-Jean-d'Angély et de sa Région.) Saint-Jean-d'Angély. 2,1924+

Arc 101.5 Bulletin. (Société d'Histoire et d'Archéologie de Nimes et du Gard.) Nimes. 1933-1939

Arc 19.4 Bulletin. (Société Française des Fouilles Archéologiques.) Paris. 1-5,1904-1924 2v.

Arc 100.1.8 Bulletin. (Société Nationale des Antiquaires de France.) 1901+ 36v.

Arc 584.100 Bulletin. (Société Royale d'Archéologie d'Alexandrie.) Alexandrie. 1-41,1898-1956 11v.

Arc 273.10.12 Bulletin. (Société Royale d'Archéologie de Bruxelles.) Bruxelles.

Arc 1318.3 Bulletin. (Société Suisse de Numismatique.) Fribourg. 1-11,1882-1892 4v.

Arc 273.8 Bulletin. (Vereeniging tot Bevordering der Kennis van de Antieke Beschaving.) 's Gravenhage. 1,1926+

Arc 273.9 Bulletin. Index, v.1-40, 1926-1965. (Vereeniging tot Bevordering der Kennis van de Antieke Beschaving.) Leiden, n.d.

Arc 584.2.2 Bulletin. Index, 1-10, 1935-44. (Société d'Archéologie Copte, Cairo.) Le Caire, n.d.

Arc 584.100.3 Bulletin. Index analytique, 1-41 (1898-1956). (Société Royale d'Archéologie d'Alexandrie.) Alexandrie, 1937-63. 2v.

Arc 273.9.3 Bulletin antieke beschaving. Supplement. Leiden. 1,1975+

Arc 2.1.2 Bulletin archéologique. (France. Comité des Travaux Historiques et Scientifiques.) Paris. 1897+ 45v.

Arc 2.1.2.5 Bulletin archéologique. (France. Comité des Travaux Historiques et Scientifiques.) Paris. 1883-1915

Arc 31.3 Bulletin archéologique. (Paris. Musée Guimet.) Paris. 1,1921

Arc 96.1 Bulletin archéologique. Paris. 1-4,1843-1848 4v.

Arc 116.5 Bulletin archéologique du Vexin français. Guiry-en-Vexin. 2,1966+

Arc 1125.11 Bulletin codiocologique; bibliographie courante des études relatives aux manuscrits. Bruxelles. 1959-1960

Arc 2.1 Bulletin de Comité des travaux historiques et scientifiques. Section historique et archéologique. (France. Ministère de l'Instruction.) Paris. 1882-1896 15v.

Arc 673.5 Bulletin de Correspondance Hellénique. Fouilles de Délos exécutées de M. de Loubat 1904-1907. Paris, n.d.

Arc 66.3 Bulletin de correspondance hellénique. (Athens.) Paris. 1,1877+ 92v.

Arc 66.3.2 Bulletin de correspondance hellénique. Table générale. (Athens.) Paris. 1877-1886

Arc 1301.3 Bulletin de numisnatique. v.1-3,4-7,8-13. Paris, 1891-1906. 3v.

Arc 96.1.2 Bulletin du Comité Historique-Archéologie. Paris. 1-4,1849-1853 2v.

Arc 31.11 Bulletin du musée de Beyrouth. (Beirut. Musée National Libanais.) Paris. 1,1937+ 9v.

Arc 103.1 Bulletin et memoires. (Institut des Fouilles de Préhistoire et d'Archéologie des Alpes, Mautimes.) Nice. 2-7 4v.

Arc 2.1.3 Bulletin historique et philologique. (France. Comité des Travaux Historiques et Scientifiques.) Paris. 1897+ 44v.

Arc 2.1.3.5 Bulletin historique et philologique. (France. Comité des Travaux Historiques et Scientifiques.) Paris. 1882-1915

Arc 15.5 Bulletin périodique. (Office des Instituts d'Archéologie et d'Histoire de l'Art.) Paris. 2-3,1935-1937

Author and Title Listing

Arc 968.2.40F Bulletin survey series. (New Mexico. University.) Albuquerque. 1,1931

Arc 66.6.2 Bulletino archeologico italiano. Naples. 1-2,1861-1862

Arc 66.6 Bulletino archeologico napoletano. Naples. 1-8,1843-1863 14v.

Arc 66.4F Bulletino di archeologia cristiana. Roma. 1863-1869

Arc 66.4 Bulletino di archeologia cristiana. Roma. 1870-1894 11v.

Arc 66.4.1 Bulletino di archeologia cristiana. Indici generali, 1882-1889. 4. serie. Roma, n.d.

Arc 66.7 Bulletino di commissione archeologico municipale. Roma. 1,1872+ 56v.

Arc 66.7.2 Bulletino di commissione archeologico municipale. Indici, 1872-1885. Roma, n.d. 3v.

Arc 66.7.3 Bulletino di commissione archeologico municipale. Indici generali dal 1922-1938. Roma, 1942.

Arc 83.1 Bulletino di commissione di antichita in Sicilia. Palermo, 1864.

Arc 93.18 Bullettino. (Associazione Archeologica Romana.) Roma. 1-7,1911-1917 3v.

Arc 1301.4 Bullettino di numismatica e sfragistica per la storia d'Italia. Camerino. 1-3,1882-1887 5v.

Arc 830.17 Bulliot, J.G. Fouilles du Mont Beuvray. Autun, 1899. 3v.

Arc 1584.5F Bulychev, N.I. Imennye serebrian. kop. i denezhki Ivana IV. Sankt Peterburg, 1906.

Arc 925.19F Bulychov, N. Kourgans et Gorodietz. Moskva, 1900. 3 pam.

Arc 925.173F Bulychov, Nikolai I. Raskopki po chasti vodorazdela verkhnikh pritokov Dnepra i Volgi, 1903 g. Moskva, 1903.

Arc 925.173.5F Bulychov, Nikolai I. Zhurnal raskopok po chasti vodorazdela verkhnikh pritokov Volgi i Dnepra. Moskva, 1899.

Arc 612.30 Bumüller, J. Leitfaden der Vorgeschichte Europas. Augsburg, 1925. 2v.

Arc 421.16 Bunakov, I.V. Tadatel'nie kosti iz Khznani. Moskva, 1935.

Arc 1077.2.35 Bunsen, E. von. Das Symbol des Kreuzes. Berlin, 1876.

Arc 1033.12.31 Buonafede, G. Panegirici sacri a i misterii della S. Sindone. Asti, 1654.

Arc 1033.12.167 Buonafede, G. Sacro chiodo del redentore. Siena, 1653.

Arc 1485.1 Buonanni, P. Numismata pontificum romanorum. Rome, 1699. 2v.

Arc 1485.1.2 Buonanni, P. Numismata summorum pontificum. Rome, 1715.

Htn Arc 1033.1* Buonarroti, F. Osservazioni sopra alcune frammenti di vasi antichi. Firenze, 1716.

Arc 1470.32F Burachkov', P. Obshchagi katalog' monety. Odessa, 1884.

Arc 880.33F Burchell, J.P.T. The early Mousterian implements of Sligo, Ireland. Ipswich, 1928.

Arc 674.3.15 Burford, Alison. The Greek temple builders at Epidauros. Liverpool, 1969.

Arc 87.2.69 Burg-Kapelle zu Iben. (Peters, F.) Bonn, 1869.

Arc 710.12 Die Burg von Athen. (Schede, Martin.) Berlin, 1922.

Arc 853.31.15 Burgen, Gräber, alte Kreuze. (Timpel, Wolfgang.) Weimar, 1970.

Arc 1348.27 Burgess, F.W. Chats on old coins. London, 1913.

Arc 432.11 Burgess, J. Indian architecture. Oxford, 1907.

X Cg Arc 435.2.32F Burgess, James. The architectural antiquities of northern Gujarat. London, 1903.

Arc 435.2.32.1 Burgess, James. The architectural antiquities of northern Gujarat. 1. Indian ed. Varanasi, 1975.

Arc 435.2.6F Burgess, James. The Buddhist stupas of Amarayati and Jaggayyapeta. London, 1887.

Arc 435.25.6 Burgess, James. Descriptive account of the rock temples of western India. Bombay, 187-?

Arc 435.11.10 Burgess, James. Inscriptions from cave-temples of western India. Bombay, 1881.

Arc 435.11.11 Burgess, James. Lists of antiquarian remains in the Bombay presidency. Bombay, 1885.

Arc 435.12.4F Burgess, James. Memorandum on the survey of architecture and other archaeological remians...Sindh, Berar. Bombay, 1870. 2 pam.

Arc 435.2.33F Burgess, James. The Muhammadan architecture. pt.2. London, 1905.

Arc 435.2.24F Burgess, James. The Muhammadan architecture of Ahmadabad. London, 1900.

Arc 435.9.5 Burgess, James. Notes on the Amarâvati stûpa. Madras, 1882. 2 pam.

Arc 435.9.3 Burgess, James. Notes on the Amarâvati stûpa. Madras, 1882.

Arc 435.2.23F Burgess, James. On the Muhammadan architecture of Bharoch, Cambay. London, 1896.

Arc 435.2.16F Burgess, James. Revised lists of antiquarian remains in the Bombay presidency. Bombay, 1897.

Arc 444.1 Burgess, James. Rock-temples of Elephanta. Bombay, 1871.

Arc 444.2 Burgess, James. Rock temples of Elurâ or Verul. Bombay, 1877.

Arc 444.2.5 Burgess, James. Rock temples of Elurâ or Verul. Bombay, 1877.

Arc 756.4 Burgess, R. The topography and antiquities of Rome. London, 1831. 2v.

Arc 386.25 Burgess, Thomas. An essay on the study of antiquities. Oxford, 1781.

Arc 905.146 Burgstaller, Ernst. Felsbilder in Österreich. Linz, 1972.

Arc 710.9.5 Die Burgtempel der Athenaia. (Petersen, E.) Berlin, 1907.

Arc 853.306 Die Burgunden in Ostdeutschland und Palen während des letzten Jahrhunderts vor Christus. Inaug. Diss. (Bohnsack, Dietrich.) Leipzig, 1938.

Arc 853.47 Die Burgwälle des Ruppiner Kreises. (Bartelt, Wilhelm.) Würzburg, 1910.

Arc 543.156 Buriakov, Iurii F. Gornoe delo i metallurgia srednevekovogo Ilaka, V-nachalo XIII v. Moskva, 1974.

Arc 600.51F The burial chamber of the treasurer Sobk-Mosĕ from Er Rizeikät. (Hayes, William C.) N.Y., 1939.

Arc 600.15 The burial customs of ancient Egypt. (Garstang, J.) London, 1907.

Arc 983.12 Burial mounds of the northern sections of the United States. (Thomas, C.) Washington? 1884?

Arc 793.2.5 The buried cities of Campania. (Adams, W.H.D.) London, 1870.

Arc 416.9 Buried empires; the earliest civilizations of the Middle East. (Carleton, P.) London, 1939.

Arc 800.7 Buried Herculaneum. (Barker, E.R.) London, 1908.

Arc 31.14 Buried history. Melbourne. 1,1964+

Arc 595.45 The buried pyramid. (Goneim, M.) London, 1956.

Arc 543.4.14 Buried treasures of Chinese Turkestan. (LeCoq, Albert.) London, 1928.

Arc 386.20.10 Burkitt, M.C. The old stone age. Cambrige, 1933.

Arc 386.20A Burkitt, M.C. Our early ancestors. Cambridge, 1926.

Arc 545.231 Burlington Five Arts Club, London. The art of ancient Egypt. London, 1895.

Arc 545.231.7F Burlington Five Arts Club, London. Catalogue of an exhibition of ancient Egyptian art. London, 1922.

Arc 435.51F Burma. Archaeological Survey. Report of the superintendent. Rangoon. 1901-1939 5v.

Arc 672.1.57A Burn, A.R. Minoans, Philistines, and Greeks, B.C. 1400-900. N.Y., 1930.

Arc 1680.1 Burn, J.H. A descriptive catalogue of the London traders, tavern and coffee-house tokens. London, 1855.

Arc 756.5.3 Burn, R. Ancient Rome and its neighborhood. London, 1895.

Arc 756.5.2 Burn, R. Old Rome. London, 1880.

Arc 756.5 Burn, R. Rome and the campagna. Cambridge, 1871.

Arc 1163.5.6 Burnell, A.C. Elements of south-Indian palaeography. 2. ed. London, 1878.

Arc 1163.5.5 Burnell, A.C. Elements of south-Indian palaeography. 2. ed. London, 1878.

Arc 386.9 Burnouf, E. Mémoires sur l'antiquité. Paris, 1879.

Arc 708.3 Burnouf, E. La ville et l'acropole d'Athènes. Paris, 1877.

Arc 1535.10F Burns, Edward. The coinage of Scotland. Edinburgh, 1837. 3v.

Arc 955.1 Burns, Frank. The Crump burial cave (Blount County, Alabama). n.p., 1892.

Arc 925.331.5 Burov, Grigorii M. Arkheologicheskie pamiatniki Vychegodskoi doliny. Syktyvkar, 1967.

Arc 925.331.10 Burov, Grigorii M. Drevnii Sindar. Moskva, 1967.

Arc 925.331 Burov, Grigorii M. Vychegodskii krai. Moskva, 1965.

Arc 815.20 Burrascano, N. I misteri orfici nell'antica Pompei. Roma, 1928.

Arc 861.38.7 Burrow, E.J. Ancient earthworks and camps of Somerset. Cheltenham, 1924.

Htn Arc 861.30.5* Burrow, E.J. The ancient entrenchments and camps of Gloucester. Cheltenham, 1919.

Arc 497.47 Burrows, M. What mean these stones? New Haven, 1941.

Arc 672.1.15 Burrows, R.M. The discoveries in Crete; with addenda. London, 1908.

Arc 672.1.13 Burrows, R.M. The discoveries in Crete. London, 1907.

Arc 672.1.16A Burrows, R.M. The discoveries in Crete and their bearing. N.Y., 1907.

Arc 888.5F Bursch, F.C. Die Becherkultur in den Niederlanden. Inaug. Diss. Leiden, 1933.

Arc 716.4 Bursian, C. De Foro Atheniensium Disputatio. Zürich, 1865.

Arc 756.6.3 Burton, Edward. A description of the antiquities and other curiosities of Rome. v.1-2. Florence, 1830.

Arc 756.6 Burton, Edward. A description of the antiquities and other curiosities of Rome. 2. ed. London, 1828. 2v.

Arc 746.1.2 Burton, R.F. Etruscan Bologna. London, 1876.

Arc 905.5 Burton, R.F. Notes on the castellieri or prehistoric ruins of the Istrian Peninsula. Trieste, n.d.

Arc 785.13.11 Burton Brown, E. Recent excavations in the Roman Forum. N.Y., 1905.

Arc 785.13.9 Burton Brown, E. Recent excavations in the Roman Forum. 1898-1904. N.Y., 1904.

Arc 700.30 Burton-Brown, T. The coming of iron to Greece. Wincle, 1954.

Arc 493.6 Burton Brown, T. Excavations in Azerbaijan. 1. ed. London, 1951.

Arc 416.25 Burton-Brown, Theodore. Early Mediterranean migration; an essay in archaeological interpretation. Manchester, 1959.

Arc 1643.4F Burzio, Humberto F. Diccionario de la moneda hispano-americana. Santiago, 1956-58. 2v.

Arc 1480.85 Burzio, Humberto F. La marina en la moneda romana. Buenos Aires, 1961.

Arc 936.14.35 Burzyński, R. Polska na więcej niz 1000 lat. Wrocław, 1961.

Arc 712.34 Buschor, E. Der Parthenonfries. München, 1961.

Arc 684.1.25 Buschor, E. Die Skulpturen des Zeustempels zu Olympia. Giessen, 1924. 2v.

Arc 710.2.4 Buschor, Ernst. Winke für Akropolis-Pilger. München, 1960.

Arc 1411.1 Bushell, S.W. Coins of the present dynesty in China. n.p., 1880.

Arc 1540.28 Bushell and Harman of Lundy. (Boundy, W.S.) Bideford, 1961.

Arc 1680.2 Bushnell, C.I. An arrangement of tradesmen's cards, political tokens; also election medals. N.Y., 1858.

Arc 1613.11F Bushnell, C.I. Catalogue of...American coins and medals of C.I. Bushnell. Philadelphia, 1882.

Arc 1680.3 Bushnell, C.I. An historical account of the first three business tokens issued in N.Y. N.Y., 1859.

Arc 505.5.110 Busink, T.A. Der Tempel von Jerusalem von Salomo bis Herodes. Leiden, 1970.

Arc 1016.4 Busiri Vici, A. La colonna santa. Tempio de Gerusalemme. Roma, 1888.

Arc 830.163 Busset, Maurice. Gergovia, capitale des Gaules. Paris, 1933.

Arc 1588.6.30 Butak, Bekzad. Cumhuriyet devrinde madeni para bois. Istanbul, 1955.

Arc 1588.6.15 Butak, Bekzad. Resimli Turk paralari. Istanbul, 1947.

Arc 1348.31 Butkovskii. Numismatika ili istoriia monet'. Moskva, 1861.

Arc 495.204.2 Butler, H.C. Architecture and other arts. N.Y., 1903.

Arc 861.21.30 Butler, Ronald Morley. Soldier and civilian in Roman Yorkshire; essay to commemorate the nineteenth century of the foundation of York. Leicester, 1971.

Arc 588.38F Buttons and design scarabs. (Petrie, W.M.F.) London, 1925.

Arc 530.140F Büyük Güllücek karisi. (Kosay, H.Z.) Ankara, 1957.

Arc 551.5 By Nile and Tigris. (Budge, Ernest A.) London, 1920. 2v.

Arc 861.207 By South Cadbury is that Camelot. (Alcock, Leslie.) London, 1970.

Arc 870.14.5 By the Roman wall. (Hoyer, M.A.) London, 1908.

Arc 505.77.5 Byblos through the ages. (Jidejian, Nina.) Beirut, 1968.

Arc 1411.15 Bykov, Aleksei A. Monety Kitaia. Leningrad, 1969.

Arc 936.195.120 Bylany. (Soudský, Bohumil.) Praha, 1966.

Arc 1347.2 Bytemeister, H.J. Delineatio rei numismaticae. Helmstadt, 1738? 3 pam.

Arc 923.90 Bytovaia arkheologiia. (Gorodtsov, V.A.) Moskva, 1910.

Arc 888.10 Byvonck, A.W. De voorgeschiedenis nou Nederland. Leiden, 1944.

Arc 935.5 Byzantinai meletai topographikai kai istorikai. (Paspati, A.G.) Konstantinople, 1877.

Arc 505.105F A Byzantine church at Khirbat al-Karak. (Delougaz, Pinhas.) Chicago, 1960.

Arc 1473.18 Byzantine coins. (Whitting, Philip David.) London, 1973.

Arc 1190.65.5 Byzantinē diplomatikē. (Karagiannopoulos, Iōannēs E.) Thessalonikē, 1969.
Arc 1330.30 Byzantine numismatic bibliography, 1950-1965. (Malter, Joel L.) Chicago, 1968.
Arc 1190.65 Byzantinische Diplomatik. (Doelger, Franz.) Ettal, 1956.
Arc 1148.32 Byzantinoi sēmeiographoi. (Plagiannēs, D.I.) Athēnia, 1940.
Arc 935.20 Byzanz; Vorarbeiten zur Topographie und Archäologie der Stadt. (Schneider, A.M.) Berlin, 1936.
Arc 943.8 Cabinet d'antiquités americaines. (Rafn, K.C.) Copenhagen, 1858.
Htn Arc 343.225F* Le cabinet de la bibliothèque de Sainte Geneviève. (Du Molinet, Claude.) Paris, 1692.
Arc 1528.2 Cabinet de monnaies, J.W. Stephanik. (Muller, F.) Amsterdam, 1904.
Arc 1335.52 Cabinet de monnaies. (Stephanik, J.W.) Amsterdam, 1904.
Arc 600.243 Cabra, Sami. Chez les derniers adorateurs du Trismegiste. Cairo, 1971.
Arc 726.5 Cabral, S. Delle ville e de' più notabili monumenti. Roma, 1779.
Arc 843.147 Cabre-Aguilo, Juan. El arte rupestre en España. Madrid, 1915.
Arc 843.149 Cabre-Aguilo, Juan. Avance al estudio de las pinturas. Madrid, 1915.
Arc 843.186 Cabré-Aguiló, Juan. El paleolítico inferior de Puento Mochs. Madrid, 1916.
Arc 635.211 Cabrol, E. Voyage en Grèce. Paris, 1890.
Arc 1020.92.3 Caccia, Franciscus. Mater dolorosa et gratiosa. Wienn, 1703.
Arc 823.19.10 Cachet d'oculiste. (Thédenat, H.) Paris, 1879.
Arc 823.19.40 Cachet du médecin Feror. (Thédenat, H.) Paris, 1880.
Arc 830.110 Cachette d'objets en bronze découverte à Vénat. (George, J.) Angoulême, 1895.
Arc 66.1.59 Cadier, L. Essai sur l'administration du Royaume de Sicile. Paris, 1891.
Arc 843.150 Cadiz; primeros pobladores. (Quintero y de Atuuci, Pelayo.) Cadiz, 1917.
Arc 970.2.5 Cadzow, D.A. Petroglyphs (rock carvings) in the Susquehanna River near Safe Harbor, Pennsylvania. Harrisburg, 1934.
Arc 853.31.5 Cämmerer, E. Die Alteburg bei Armstadt. Leipzig, 1924.
Arc 853.220 Cämmerer, Erich. Vor- und Frühgeschichte Arnstadts und seiner weiteren Umgebung. Jena, 1956.
Arc 861.20 Caer Pensauelcoit. (Kerslake, T.) London, 1882.
Arc 1480.84 Caesar in 44 v. Chr. (Alföldi, András.) Bonn, 1974.
Htn Arc 1053.18* Der Caesar von Acireale. (Boehringer, E.) Stuttgart, 1933.
Arc 505.123F Caesarea Maritima (Israele). (Missione Archeologica.) Milano, 1959.
Arc 757.6.5 Caetani Lovatelli, E. Aurea Roma. Roma, 1915.
Arc 757.6 Caetani Lovatelli, E. Passeggiate nella Roma antica. Roma, 1909.
Arc 1020.32.8 Caffi, M. Della chiesa di Sant'Eustorgio in Milano. Milano, 1841.
Arc 1020.142 Cagiano de Azevedo, Michelangelo. Testimonianze archaeologiche della tradizione paolina a Malta. Roma, 1966.
Arc 1488.9 Cagiati, Memmo. Manuale per il raccoglitore di monete del regno d'Italia. Napoli, 1918.
Arc 1490.24 Cagiati, Memmo. Le monete del reame delle Due Sicilie da Carlo I d'Angio a Vittorio Emanuele II. Napoli, 1911-16.
Arc 608.1.5 Cagnat, R. Explorations épigraphiques et archéologiques en Tunise. v.1-3. Paris, 1883-6.
Arc 608.6 Cagnat, R. Guides en Algérie...Lambèse. Paris, 1893.
Arc 605.204 Cagnet, R. Les monuments historiques de la Tunise. Paris, 1898-99. 2v.
Arc 608.11 Cagnot, R. Carthage, Timgad Febessa. Paris, 1909.
Arc 66.1.134 Cahen, Emile. Callimaque. Paris, 1929.
Arc 66.1.134.5 Cahen, Emile. Les hymes de Callimaque. Paris, 1930.
Arc 880.38A Cahercomnaun, a stone fort in county Clare. (Hencken, H.O.) Dublin, 1938.
Arc 97.4 Cahien d'archéologie du Nord-Est. Laon. 1-8,1958-1965 3v.
Arc 1163.4.5 Cahier d'écritures arabes. (Combarel, E.) Paris, 1848.
Arc 38.40 Cahiers. (Institut Ethiopien d'Archéologie.) Addis-Ababa. 1,1965+
Arc 95.4 Cahiers alsaciens d'archéologie, d'art et d'histoire. Strasbourg. 1,1957+
Arc 605.204.5F Cahiers d'archéologie tunisienne. v.1-4. (Renault, Jules.) Tunis, 1908-11.
Arc 608.2.41 Cahiérs de Byrsa. Paris. 1-10,1951-1965// 6v.
Arc 1302.8 Cahiers numismatiques. Paris. 1,1964+
Arc 1335.59 Cahn, A.E. Versteigerungskatalog nr. 57. Frankfurt, 1926.
Arc 1335.59.5 Cahn, A.E. Versteigerungskatalog nr. 63. v.2. Frankfurt am Main, 1929.
Arc 1335.59.10 Cahn, A.E. Versteigerungskatalog nr. 71. v.2. Frankfurt am Main, 1931.
Arc 1510.36 Cahn, Julius. Der Rappenmünzbund. Heidelberg, 1901.
Arc 963.2 The Cahokia mounds. [Illinois]. (Baker, Frank C.) Urbana, 1923.
Arc 497.40A Caiger, S.L. Bible and spade. London, 1938.
Arc 545.16 Cailliand, F. Voyage à l'Oasis de Thèbes. pt.1-2. Paris, 1821.
Arc 1488.34 Cainola, Aldo. Le antiche zecche d'Italia. Roma, 1971.
Arc 1125.30 Cairo, Egypt. Ayn Shams University. Ibrahim University studies in papyrology.
Arc 547.43 Cairo, Egypt. Coptic Museum. The Coptic Museum and the fortress of Babylon at old Cairo. Cairo, 1962.
Arc 1130.10 Cairo, Egypt. National Library. A bibliography of works about papyrology. Cairo, 1960.
Arc 1428.25 Cairo. Egyptian Library. Catalogue of the collection of Arabic coins...in the Khedivial Library at Cairo. London, 1897.
Arc 547.6.10 Cairo. Musée des Antiquités Égyptiennes. A brief description of the principal monuments. Cairo, 1927.
Arc 547.6.15 Cairo. Musée des Antiquités Égyptiennes. A brief description of the principal monuments. Cairo, 1961.
Arc 545.227F Cairo. Musée des Antiquités Égyptiennes. Catalogue général des antiquités égyptiennes Ostraca. Le Caire. 1-100,1901-1937 77v.
X Cg Arc 545.227F Cairo. Musée des Antiquités Égyptiennes. Catalogue général des antiquités égyptiennes Ostraca. Le Caire. 10
Arc 547.6.12 Cairo. Musée des Antiquités Égyptiennes. Guide du visiteur au Musée du Caire. Caire, 1902.
Arc 547.6.13 Cairo. Musée des Antiquités Égyptiennes. Guide du visiteur au Musée du Caire. 2. éd. Caire, 1912.
Arc 547.6.25 Cairo. Musée des Antiquités Égyptiennes. Guide to the Cairo Museum. 4. ed. Cairo, 1908.
Arc 547.6.5 Cairo. Musée des Antiquités Égyptiennes. Notice des principaux monuments...à Boulaq. Alexandrie, 1864.
Arc 547.6.7 Cairo. Musée des Antiquités Égyptiennes. Notice des principaux monuments...du Musée d'Antiquités Égyptiennes à Boulaq. 3. éd. Paris, 1869.
Arc 1349.35F Calabi, A. Matteo dei Pasti. Milano, 1926.
Arc 1675.10.7 Calabi, A. Pisanello. Milano, 1928.
Arc 1010.25 The Calatagan excavations. (Fox, Robert B.) Manila, 1965.
Arc 1494.62 Calbató de Grau, Gabriel. Compendio de las piezas de ocho reales. San Juan, 1970. 2v.
Arc 1033.12.23 Calcagnino, A. Dell'imagine Edessena. Genova, 1639.
Arc 1033.130 Calcagnino, A. Historia del glorioso precursore di N.S.S. G. Battista. Genova, 1648.
Arc 785.15.50 Calcografia di Roma. v.6-7. Roma, 1779.
Arc 1138.28 The calculus of variants, an essay on textual criticism. (Greg, Walter W.) Oxford, 1927.
Arc 30.21 Calcutta. University. Asutosh Museum of Indian Art and Archaeology. Asutosh Museum memoir.
Arc 513.20 Calder, W.M. Monumenta Asiae Minoris antiqua. London, 1928-39. 8v.
Arc 726.101 Calderini, A. L'anfiteatro romano. Milano, 1940.
Arc 700.14 Calderini, A. Di un'ara greca. Milano, 1907.
Arc 628.30 Calderini, A. Dizionario di antichità greche e romane. Milano, 1960.
Arc 785.75 Calderini, A. La zona di piazza S. Sepolcro. Milano, 1940.
Arc 961.1.20 Caldwell, Joseph. Irene Mound site, Chatham County, Georgia. Athens, 1941.
Arc 875.26.2 Caledonia Romana...Roman antiquities of Scotland. (Stuart, Robert.) Edinburgh, 1852.
Arc 875.26 Caledonia romana. (Stuart, Robert.) Edinburgh, 1845.
Arc 1470.47 Caley, Earle R. The composition of ancient Greek bronze coins. Philadelphia, 1939.
Arc 1077.2.23 Calfhill, J. An answer to John Martiall's Treatise of the cross. Cambridge, Eng., 1846.
Arc 1033.12.239 Le calice d'Antioche. (Jerphanion, G. de.) Rome, 1926.
Arc 307.2 California. University. Publications. Berkeley. 1-50,1904-1964 48v.
Arc 67.4 California. University. Publications in classical archaeology. Berkeley. 1-3,1929-1957 5v.
Arc 861.188 Calkin, John Bernard. Discovering prehistoric Bournemouth and Christchurch: a record of local finds in the twentieth century. Christchurch, Hants, 1966.
Arc 505.155F Callaway, Joseph A. The early bronze age sanctuary at Ai (et-Tell). London, 1972.
Arc 853.41.9 Calliano, G. Prähistorische Funde in der Umgebung von Baden. Wein, 1894.
Arc 1145.206 Calligraphia Graeca et poecilographia Graeca. (Hodgkin, J.) Londini, 1794.
Arc 66.1.134 Callimaque. (Cahen, Emile.) Paris, 1929.
Arc 1480.58 Callu, Jean Pierre. Genio populi romani, 295-316. Paris, 1960.
Arc 66.1.214 Callu, Jean Pierre. La politique monétaire des empereurs romains de 238 à 311. Paris, 1969.
Arc 1033.60 Calo, Luigi. S. Beatrice vergine e martire. Napoli, 1894.
Arc 1027.22.13 Calori Cesis, F. Un insigne monumento cristiano del secolo III. Bologna, 1873.
Arc 830.171 Les calvaires bretons. (Gruyer, Paul.) Paris, 1920.
Arc 861.13 Calverley, W.S. Notes on the early sculptured crosses...present diocese of Carlisle. Kendal, 1899.
Arc 1033.17.241 Calvi, D. Delle grandezze della Madonna di Carvaggio. v.3. Napoli, 1749.
Arc 726.25.15F Calza, Guido. La necropoli del porto di Roma nell'isola sacra. Roma, 1940.
Arc 726.25.17 Calza, Guido. Ostia, guida storico monumentale. Milano, 1925?
Arc 726.25.18 Calza, Guido. Ostia; historical guide to the monuments. Milano, 1926.
Arc 726.25.13 Calza, Guido. Il teatro romano di Ostia. Roma, 1927.
Arc 726.25.35 Calza, Raissa. Ostia. Firenze, 1959.
Arc 853.353 Cambodunum-Kempten. (Schleier, Wilhelm.) Bonn, 1972.
Arc 853.145F Cambodunumforschungen, 1953- Kallmünz, 1957- 2v.
Arc 858.98 Cambrian Archaeological Association, London. The Irish Sea province in archaeology and history. Cardiff, 1970.
Arc 885.18 Cambrian Archaeological Association. A hundred years of Welsh archaeology. Gloucester, 1949.
Arc 1468.24 Cambridge, Eng. University. Fitzwilliam Museum. Catalogue of the McClean collection of Greek coins. Cambridge, 1923-29. 3v.
Arc 547.30 Cambridge. University. Fitzwilliam Museum. A catalogue of the Egyptian collection. Cambridge, Eng., 1893.
Arc 843.2.5 Cambridge evcavations in Minorca. (Murray, M.A.) London, 1932- 2v.
Arc 1490.12 Camera, Matteo. Importante scoperta del famoso Tarèno di Amalfi. Napoli, 1872.
Arc 743.10 Cameron, M.L. Old Etruria and modern Tuscany. London, 1909.
Arc 968.2.23 Cameron Creek village...New Mexico. (Bradfield, W.) Santa Fé, 1931.
Arc 1033.35.25 Camers, A.R. De particula ex pretioso...crucis...commentarius. Roma, 1609.
Arc 389.1 Camille, Enlart, 1862-1927. Paris, 1929.
Arc 1076.3.37 Caminada, Christian. Die bündner Glocken. Zürich, 1915.
Arc 587.12F Caminos, Ricardo A. Gebel es-Silsilah. London, 1963.
Arc 585.28F Caminos, Ricardo A. The New Kingdom temples of Buhen. London, 1974. 2v.
Arc 587.13 Caminos, Ricardo A. The shrines and rock-inscriptions of Ibrim. London, 1968.
Arc 838.30 Camon Aznar, J. Los artes y los pueblos de la España primitiva. Madrid, 1954.
Arc 1330.45 Camont, Georges. Bibliographie générale et raisonnée de la numismatique belge. Bruxelles, 1883.
Arc 1663.7.5F Camozzi Vertova, G. Dissertazione sul medagliere relativo alla storia mederna d'Italia. Bergamo, 1879.
Arc 1663.7.7F Camozzi Vertova, G. Dissertazione sul medagliere relativo alla storia moderna d'Italia. Bergamo, 1880.
Arc 1663.28 Camozzi Vertova, G. Medaglie coniate in onore del generale Giuseppe Garibaldi. Bergamo, 1885.
Arc 1663.28.2 Camozzi Vertova, G. Medaglie coniate in onore del generale Giuseppe Garibaldi. Bergamo, 1885.
Arc 774.1 La campagna romana. (Tomassetti, G.) Roma, 1910. 4v.
Arc 1494.59 Campaner y Fuertes, Álvaro. Numismática balear. Palma de Mallorca, 1879.
Arc 772.10 Campania romana. (Rome (City). Istituto di studi romani.) Napoli, 1938.
Arc 600.6.5 Campbell, C. Two Theben queens. London, 1909.
Arc 1033.3.45 Campenhausen, Hans von. Die Passionssarkophage. Marburg, 1929.

Arc 392.10.5 Campfire and trail. (Hewett, Edgar Lee.) Albuquerque, 1943.

Arc 746.54 Camporeale, Giovannangelo. I commerci di Vetulonia in età orientalizzante. Firenze, 1969.

Arc 1418.7 Campos, M.J. da C. Numismatica indo-portuguesa. Lisboa, 1901.

Htn Arc 1020.120* Campos, Manoel de. Relaçam do solenne recebimento que se fez em Lisboa. Lisboa, 1588.

Arc 1020.135 Camprubi Alemany, Francisco. El monumento paleocristiano de Centcelles. Barcelona, 1952.

Arc 608.72 Camps, Gabriel. La nécropole mégalithique du Djebel Mazela à Bou Nouara. Paris, 1964.

Arc 608.76 Camps-Fabrer, Henriette. Matière et art mobilier dans la préhistoire nord-africaine. Thèse. Paris, 1966.

Htn Arc 750.5* Campus Martius. (Pianesi, G.B.) Roma, 1762.

Htn Arc 1605.1* Canadian blacksmith coppers. (Wood, H.) Philadelphia, 1910.

Arc 1330.55 Canadian numismatic bibliography. A review of R.W. McLachlan's Canadian numismatics and other books and pamphlets describing Canadian coins and medals. Montreal, 1866.

Arc 736.15 Canale, C.G. Engyon. Catania, 1955.

Arc 1033.49 Canallotti, G.B. Vita di S. Severino e di S. Vittorio. Pariso, 1643.

Arc 1025.39 Cancellieri, F. Dissertazione epistolare. Roma, 1819.

Arc 1016.217 Cancellieri, F. Memorie storiche delle sacre teste. 2. ed. Roma, 1852.

Arc 785.40.5 Cancellieri, F. Notizie del carcere Tulliano. Roma, 1788.

Arc 785.40 Cancellieri, F. Notizie del carcere Tulliano. Roma, 1855.

Arc 1020.9.25 Cancellieri, F. Sagrestica vaticana eretta...Pio Sesto. Roma, 1784.

Arc 543.7.7A Candee, H.C. Angkor the magnificent. N.Y., 1924.

Arc 746.40F Canina, Luigi. L'antica città di Veil. Roma, 1847.

Arc 785.13.40 Canina, Luigi. Descrizione storica del Foro Romano. Roma, 1834.

Arc 750.39F Canina, Luigi. Esposizione storica e topografica del foro romano. 2a ed. Roma, 1845.

Arc 757.1 Canina, Luigi. Indicazione topografica di Roma antica. 3. ed. Roma, 1841.

Arc 757.2 Canina, Luigi. Pianta topografica di Roma antica. Roma? 1844?

Arc 757.2.2 Canina, Luigi. Pianta topografica di Roma antica. Roma? 1851?

Arc 750.202 Canina, Luigi. La prima parte della Via Appia. Roma, 1853. 2v.

Arc 750.222F Canina, Luigi. Sugli antichi edifizj. Roma, 1840.

Arc 750.39PF Canina, Luigi. Tavole...foro romano. Atlas. Roma, 1845.

Htn Arc 1050.201* Canini, G.A. Iconografia. Romae, 1669.

Arc 1053.1 Canini, G.A. Images des héros et des grandes hommes de l'antiquité. Amsterdam, 1731.

Arc 726.329 Cannas, Vincenzo Mario. I nuraghi Aleri e Nastasi e le nuove scoperte archeologiche nel territorio di Tertenia. Cagliari, 1972.

Arc 785.34 Cannizzaro, M.E. Ara Pacis Augustae. Roma, 1907.

Arc 726.19 I cannoni veneti di Famagosta. (Angelucci, A.) Venezia, n.d.

Arc 845.208F Cannstatt zur Römerzeit. (Wurttembergisches Landesamt für Denkmalpflege.) Stuttgart, 1921.

Arc 1030.31 Cantarelli, L. Un frammento epigrafico cristiano dell'isola Portuense. Roma, 1896.

Arc 1030.52 Cantini, Giuseppe. Inscriptiones. Colle, 1844.

Arc 545.233 Capart, J. Recueil de monuments egyptiens. Bruxelles, 1902-05. 2v.

Arc 545.233.5FA Capart, J. Une rue de tombeaux a Saqqarah. Bruxelles, 1907. 2v.

Arc 600.6.15F Capart, Jean. Thèbes. Bruxelles, 1925.

Arc 726.2.5 Capasso, B. Napoli greca-romana. Topografia. Napoli, 1905.

Arc 726.2.4 Capasso, B. Sull'antico sito di Napoli e Palepoli dubbie e conghietture. Napoli, 1855.

Arc 1020.105 Capece, G. Dissertazione...intorno alle due campane della chiesa parochiale di S. Giovanni. Napoli, 1750.

Arc 853.96.10 Capelle, Torsten. Studien über elbgermanische Gräber felder im der ausgehenden Latènezeit und der alteren Kaiserzeit. Habilitationsschrift. Hildesheim, 1971.

Arc 505.35.10 Capernaum (Kfar-Nochum). (Sapir, Baruch.) Tel Aviv, 1967.

Arc 505.35 Capharnaüm et Bethsaïde, suivi d'une étude sur l'âge de la synagogue de Tell Houm. (Meistermann, Barnabé.) Paris, 1921.

Arc 945.5F Capitan, Louis. Décades américaines. Levallois-Perret, 1907.

Arc 387.6 Capitan, Louis. La préhistoire. Paris, 1922.

Arc 785.14 Capitol, Forum und Sacra Via in Rom. (Jordan, Henri.) Berlin, 1881.

Arc 830.181.2 Le capitole de Saintes. (Audiat, L.) Paris, 1881.

Arc 830.21.3 Le capitole de Vesontio et les capitoles provinciaux du monde romain. (Castan, Auguste.) Paris, 1869.

Arc 750.207 Le capitole romain. (Rodocanachi, E.) Paris, 1904.

Arc 630.2 Les capitoles provinciaux du monde romain. (Castan, Auguste.) Besançon, 1886.

Arc 785.12 Der capitolinische Plan der Stadt Rom. (Jordan, Henri.) Berlin, 1867.

Arc 750.213 Das Capitolium von Signia. (Delbrück, R.) Rom, 1903.

Arc 1510.33 Cappe, H.P. Beschreibung des Mainzer Münzen des Mittelalters. Dresden, 1856.

Arc 1510.8.10 Cappe, H.P. Die Mittelalter-Münzen von Münster. Dresden, n.d.

Arc 1510.8 Cappe, H.P. Münzen der deutschen Kaiser des Mittelalters. v.1,3. Dresden, 1848-57.

Arc 1510.8.5 Cappe, H.P. Münzen der Herzöge von Baiern. Dresden, 1850.

Arc 387.12.30 Cappeli, A. Monsignor Celestino Cavedoni. Firenze, 1866.

Arc 726.72 La cappella degli Scrovigni e l'arena di Padova. (Tolomei, Antonio.) Padova, 1881.

Arc 1020.6.12 Cappelletti, G. La chiesa di S. Simone profeta. Venezia, 1860.

Arc 1153.12 Cappelli, A. Dizionario di abbreviature latine ed italiane. Milano, 1899.

Arc 1153.12.3 Cappelli, A. Lexicon abbreviaturarum. Leipzig, 1901.

Arc 1153.12.10A Cappelli, A. Lexicon abbreviaturarum. 2. Aufl. Leipzig, 1928.

Arc 1153.12.15 Cappelli, A. Lexicon abbreviaturarum. 3. ed. Milano, 1929.

Arc 1153.12.20 Cappelli, A. Lexicon abbreviaturarum. 4. ed. Milano, 1949.

Arc 387.12.31 Cappelli, A. Necrologia di Mons. Celestino Cavedoni. 2. ed. Modena, 1866.

Arc 1480.67 Cappelli, R. Profili imperiali romani. Milano, 1963.

Arc 1033.34.5 Caprara, C. Venuta di San Pietro in Roma. Roma, 1872.

Arc 1033.71 La capsella d'argent africaine. (Rossi, J.B. de.) Caen, 1890.

Arc 726.206F Capua preromana; le antichita etrusche di Santa Maria Capua Vetere. v.1, pt.7. v.2, pt.1,2. Firenze, 1965- 3v.

Arc 608.30.5 Caputa, Giacomo. Il teatro di Sabatha e l'architettura teatrale africana. Roma, 1959.

Arc 608.17.11 Caputo, Giacomo. Lo scultore del grande bassorilievo. Roma, 1948.

Arc 1503.2F Caraggioni, L. Münzgeschichte der Schweiz. Geneve, 1896.

Arc 635.212 Carapanos, C. Dodone et ses ruines. Paris, 1878. 2v.

Arc 858.53 Caravan essays. no.1-12. (Harris, James R.) Cambridge, 1929.

Arc 843.160 Carballo, Jesús. El descubrimiento de la cueva y pinturas de altamira por Marcelino S. de Sauteola. Santander, 1950.

Arc 785.47 Carcopino, J. La basilique pythagoricienne de la Porte Majeure. Paris, 1927.

Arc 1025.74 Carcopino, J. De Pythagore aux apôtres. Paris, 1956.

Arc 726.25.25A Carcopino, J. Ostie. Paris, 1929.

Arc 1033.10.10 Carcopino, Jérome. Le mystère d'un symbole chrétien. Paris, 1955.

Arc 82.1.8 Carcopino, Jérome. Souvenirs romains. Paris, 1968.

Htn Arc 1033.47.28* Cardani, H. Neronis encomium. Amstelodami, 1640.

Arc 1540.38 Cardiff, Wales. National Museum of Wales. Welsh tokens of the seventeenth century. Cardiff, 1973.

Arc 66.1.173 Le cardinal François de Tournon. (François, M.) Paris, 1951. 2v.

Arc 1251.3 Cardoni, B. De siglis veterum graecorum. v.1-3. Romae, 1757.

Arc 1540.19 Cardonnel-Lawson, Adam. Numismata Scotiae. Edinburgi, 1786.

Arc 1458.7 Cardwell, E. Lectures on the coinage of the Greeks and Romans. Oxford, 1832.

Arc 386.13 The care of ancient monuments. (Brown, G.B.) Cambridge, 1905.

Arc 785.22.15 Carettoni, G. A short guide to the Palatine. Bologna, 1948.

Arc 785.13.70 Carettoni, G. A short guide to the Roman Forum. Bologna, 1948.

Arc 66.1.206 La caricature et la parodie dans le monde romain, antique des origines a Juvenal. (Cèbe, Jean Pierre.) Paris, 1966.

Arc 936.220.95 Caričin Grad, 1912-62. (Srpska Akademija Nauka i Umetnosti, Belgrade. Arheološki Institut.) Beograd, 1962.

Arc 1033.20.5 Carini, I. Le basiliche cristiane. Roma, 1893.

Arc 1015.226 Carini, I. Catacombe di S. Giovanni in Siracusa. Roma, 1890.

Arc 1027.3.5 Carini, I. Il crocifesso negli antichi monumenti. Roma, 1889.

Arc 1030.24 Carini, I. Dell'utilità che la teologia può trarre dall'epigrafia. Roma, 1891.

Arc 1027.26.15 Carini, I. Rassegna archeologica. Iscrizioni cristiana dei catacombe di Siracusa. Palermo, 1876.

Arc 1033.99 Carini, Isidoro. La passione di Cristo. Milano, 1894.

Arc 1033.100 Carini, Isidoro. Simbolismo dei primi secoli. Romae, 1890.

Arc 1018.43 Pamphlet vol. Carini, Isidoro. Writings. 6 pam.

Arc 1018.42 Pamphlet vol. Carini, Isidoro. Writings. 23 pam.

Arc 790.212F Carini, P.B. Pompei principali monumenti e nuovissimi scavi. Milano, 1921.

Arc 520.18.10 Carl Humann. (Schulte, Eduard.) Dortmund, 1971.

Arc 1033.12.10 Carles, A. Histoire du Saint Suaire de Cadouin. Perigueux, 1868.

Arc 1033.12.11 Carles, A. Histoire du Saint Suaire de Notre Seigneur. Paris, 1875. 2 pam.

Arc 416.9 Carleton, P. Buried empires; the earliest civilizations of the Middle East. London, 1939.

Arc 1490.4.7 Carli, G.R. Delle monete e dell'istituzione delle Zecche d'Italia. L'Aja, 1754-57. 2v.

Arc 1490.4.5 Carli, G.R. Delle monete e dell'istituzione delle Zecche d'Italia. Mantova, 1754. 3v.

Arc 600.6.20F Carlier, A. Thèbes. Paris, 1948.

Arc 505.72 Carlsbergfondet, Copenhagen. Hama. v.2,4. København, 1948. 2v.

Arc 1027.52 Carmelo, D. Guida delle catacombe e dei monumenti. Roma, 1900.

Arc 830.11.9 Carnac; fouilles faites dans la région. (Le Rouzic, Z.) Vannes. 1897-1902

Arc 830.11.9.10 Carnac; fouilles faites dans la région. Campagne 1922. (Le Rouzic, Z.) Paris, 1931.

Arc 830.11.8 Carnac; menhirs, statues. (Le Rouzic, Z.) Nantes, 1931.

Arc 830.11.7 Carnac; restaurations faites dans la région. (Le Rouzic, Z.) Vannes, 1930.

Arc 830.11.9.9 Carnac. (Le Rouzic, Z.) Nancy, 1922.

Arc 830.11.9.5 Carnac. (Le Rouzic, Z.) Vannes, 1932.

Arc 830.11 Carnac et ses monuments. (Le Rouzic, Z.) Morlaix, 1897.

Arc 875.32 Carnegie, J. Origins of Pictish symbolism. Edinburgh, 1893.

Arc 757.5 Carnevale, C.G. Roma nel III secolo - era volgare. Roma, 1896.

Arc 1478.86 Carney, Thomas Francis. A catalogue of the Roman and related foreign coins in the collections of Sir Stephen Courtland at the University College of Rhodesia and Nyasaland. Salisbury, 1963.

Arc 905.12.12 Carnuntum. (Swoboda, Erich.) Wien, 1949.

Arc 905.12.20 Carnuntum. (Swoboda, Erich.) Wien, 1953.

Arc 905.12.23 Carnuntum. 3. Aufl. (Swoboda, Erich.) Graz, 1958.

Arc 217.5 Carnuntum Jahrbuch. Wien. 1955-1960 2v.

Arc 905.12.9 Carnuntum 1885-1910. (Verein Carnuntum, Wien.) Wien, 1911.

Arc 905.12.9.5 Carnuntum 1885-1910. (Verein Carnuntum, Wien.) Wien, 1935.

Arc 1498.6 Caron, E. Monnaies féodales françaises. fasc. 1-3. Paris, 1882.

Arc 543.7 Carpeaux, C. Les ruines d'Angkor. Paris, 1908.

Arc 838.18 Carpenter, Rhys. The Greeks in Spain. Bryn Mawr, 1925.

Arc 642.9 Carpenter, Rhys. The humanistic value of archaeology. Cambridge, Mass., 1933.

Arc 716.3.5 Carpenter, Rhys. The sculpture of the Nike temple parapet. Cambridge, 1929.

Arc 1033.102 Carpini, J. Sacro-historica disquisitio emblematibus in Cimelio. Roma, 1691.

Arc 967.1.3 Carr, L. The mounds of the Mississippi Valley. Cambridge, 188-?

Arc 967.1.5 Carr, L. The mounds of the Mississippi Valley. Frankfort, 1883.

Arc 967.1.4 Carr, L. The mounds of the Mississippi Valley. Washington, 1893.

Author and Title Listing

Arc 458.4 Carr, Mark William. Descriptive and historical papers...the seven pagodas on the Coromandel coast. Madras, 1869.
Arc 905.4.5 Carrara, F. Di scavi di Salona nel 1850. Memoria. Praga, 1852.
Arc 1254.1 Carrara, F. Teodora Ducaina Paleologhina. Vienna, 1840.
Arc 905.4 Carrara, F. Topografia e scavi di Salona. Trieste, 1850.
Arc 1030.36 Carrière, A. Inscriptions d'un reliquare arménien. Paris, 1883.
Arc 810.50A Carrington, R.C. Pompeii. Oxford, 1936.
Arc 843.72 Carro, Jesús. Otesouro de Toxados. Santiago, 1933.
Arc 1478.55 Carson, R.A.G. Essays in Roman coinage. Oxford, 1956.
Arc 1348.78 Carson, Robert. Coins of the world. N.Y., 1962.
Arc 1027.12.26 Carsopino, Jérôme. Les fouilles de Saint Pierre et la tradition. Paris, 1963.
Arc 1166.2 Carta di cotone e carta di lino. (Paoli, Cesare.) Firenze, 1885.
Arc 838.1 Cartailhac, É. Les âges préhistoriques de l'Espagne et du Portugal. Paris, 1886.
Arc 843.63F Cartailhac, Émile. La caverne d'Altamira à Santillane près Santander (Espagne). Monaco, 1906.
Arc 66.1.20 Cartault, A. La trière athénienne. Paris, 1881.
Arc 823.10.15 Carte archéologique de la Gaule romaine. pts.1-3,5-8,10-11,14. (Blanchet, A.) Paris, 1931- 10v.
Arc 823.10.15PF Carte archéologique de la Gaule romaine. pts.8-9. (Blanchet, A.) Paris, n.d.
Arc 513.28.5 Carte archeologique de l'Anatolie occidentale. (Duyuran, Rüstem.) Izmir, 1952.
Arc 910.9F Carte archeologique du canton de Fribourg. (Bonstetten, W.) Genève, 1878.
Arc 915.9 Carte archéologique du Canton de Vaud des origines à l'époque de Charlemagne. (Viollier, David.) Lausanne, 1927.
Arc 820.221F Carte archéologique du départment du Var. (Bonstetten, W.) Toulon, 1873. 2 pam.
Arc 600.180F Carte de la nécropole memphite. (Morzan, J. de.) n.p., 1897.
Arc 820.213F Carte des voies romaines du départment de l'Allier. (Tudot, Edmond.) Paris, 1859.
Htn Arc 1520.1* Carte ou liste contenant le pris de chascun marcq. Anvers, 1621. 5 pam.
Arc 1520.3 Carte ou liste contenant le pris de chascun marcq. Anvers, 1627.
Arc 545.238 Carter, H. Five years' explorations at Thebes. London, 1912.
Arc 600.6.25F Carter, H. The tomb of Thoutmôsis. Westminster, 1904.
Arc 830.130.15 Cartereau, E. Glozel et sa signification. Paris, 1928.
Arc 830.130.10 Cartereau, E. La mise au point de Glozel. Paris, 1928.
Arc 608.11 Carthage, Timgad Febessa. (Cagnot, R.) Paris, 1909.
Arc 608.86 Pamphlet vol. Carthage. 3 pam.
Arc 608.2.15 Carthage. (Babelon, E.) Paris, 1896.
Arc 608.2.70 Carthage. (Carton, Louis B.C.) Strasbourg, 1926.
X Cg Arc 608.2.27 Carthage. Carthage, 19- .
Arc 608.2.75 Carthage: Cirque, Colline dite de Junon, Douar Chott. Wrocław, 1974.
Arc 608.2.2 Carthage and her remains. (Davis, N.) London, 1861.
Arc 608.2.38 Carthage latine et chrétienne. (Lapeyre, Gabriel G.) Paris, 1950.
Arc 608.2.8 Carthage of the Phoenicians. (Moore, M.) London, 1905.
Arc 608.2.37 Carthage punique. (Lapeyre, Gabriel G.) Paris, 1942.
Arc 830.36 Les Carthaginois en France. (Ollier de Marichard, J.) Montpellier, 1870.
Arc 971.5 Cartier's Hochelaga and the Dawson site. (Pendergast, James F.) Montreal, 1972.
Arc 608.2.70 Carton, Louis B.C. Carthage. Strasbourg, 1926.
Arc 1027.72.3 Carton, Louis B.C. Les catacombes d'Hadrumète. Sousse, 1905.
Arc 608.1.30 Carton, Louis B.C. La colonisation romaine dans le pays de Dougga. Tunis, 1904.
Arc 608.1 Carton, Louis B.C. Découvertes épigraphiques et archéologiques faites en Tunisie. Paris, 1895.
Arc 608.1.28 Carton, Louis B.C. Le sanctuaire de Base-Saturne à Dougga. Paris, 1896.
Arc 608.1.29 Carton, Louis B.C. Le théâtre de Dougga. Paris, 1902.
Arc 1015.221 Caruana, A.A. Ancient pagan tombs and Christian cemeteries in Malta. Malta, 1898.
Arc 726.51F Caruana, A.A. Report on the Phoenician and Roman antiquities in the group of the islands of Malta. Malta, 1882.
Arc 382.6 Carus, K.G. Ueber die typisch gewordenen Abbildungen menschlichen Kopfformen. Jena, 1863. 15 pam.
Arc 1030.8.14 Carus, P. The Nestorian monument; an ancient record of Christianity in China. Chicago, 1909.
Arc 843.24 Carvalho, M. O dolmen da Barroza. Porto, 1898.
Arc 875.28 The carved stones of Islay. (Graham, R.C.) Glasgow, 1895.
Arc 1033.6 La casa celimontana...Giovanni e Paolo. (Germano, Stanislao P.) Roma, 1894.
Arc 1033.6.25 La casa celimontana dei Valerii e il Monastero di S. Erasmo. (Gatti, Giuseppe.) Roma, 1902.
Arc 815.24F La casa del Menandro e il suo tesoro di Argenteria. (Maiuri, Amedeo.) Roma, 1933. 2v.
Arc 955.2.9 Casa Grande, Arizona (28th report of the Bureau of American Ethnology). (Fewkes, J.W.) Washington, 1913.
Arc 1033.6.10 La casa pagano cristiana del Celio (Titulus Byzantis sive Pammachii). (Gasdia, U.E.) Roma, 1937.
Arc 448.1.35 Casal, Jean Marie. La civilisation de l'Indus et ses énigmes. Paris, 1969.
Arc 440.8 Casal, Jean Marie. Fouilles d'Amri. Paris, 1964. 2v.
Arc 461.4 Casal, Jean Marie. Fouilles de Virampatnam Arikamedu. Paris, 1949.
Arc 455.5 Casal, Jean Marie. Site urbain et sites funéraires des environs de Pondichéry. Paris, 1956.
Arc 1668.7 Casali, J. De nummulis Peioesa inscriptis. Romae, 1796.
Arc 1016.202 Casano, A. Del sotterraneo della chiesa cattedrale di Palermo. Palermo, 1849.
Arc 1433.34 Casanova, Paul. Inventaire sommaire des monnaies musulmanes. Paris, 1896.
Arc 1027.51 Cascioli, C.G. S. Damaso poeta insigne di martiri. Roma, 1898.
Arc 1033.34.21 Cascioli, J. De aeneo simulacro divi Petri apostoli. Roma, 1895.
Arc 810.54.5 Case ed abitanti di Pompei. 2. ed. (Corte, Matteo della.) Pompei, 1954.
Arc 810.54.7 Case ed abitanti di Pompei. 3. ed. (Corte, Matteo della.) Napoli, 1965.
Arc 1655.5 The case of the elusive hubs and dies. (Dutton, M.K.) Honolulu, 1959.
Arc 543.7.17A Casey, R.J. Four faces of Siva. Indianapolis, 1929.
Arc 830.161 Casimir, Philippe. Le trophée d'Auguste a la Turbie. Marseille, 1932.
Arc 736.17 Casmene ritrovata? (Margani, M.N.) Comiso, 1955.
Arc 830.99 Cassan, A. Antiquités gauloises et gallo-romaines de l'arrondissement de Mantes. Mantes, 1835.
Arc 726.242 Cassani, Lino. Repertorio di antichità. Novara, 1962.
Arc 547.29 Le casse di mummie e i sarcofagi da el Hibeh. (Botti, Giuseppe.) Fienze, 1958.
Arc 750.30 Cassini, G.M. Pitture antiche. Roma, 1783.
Arc 1027.38 Cassini da Perinaldo, F. Le veglie notturne al cimitero di Cimella. Genova, 1858.
Arc 1088.1.11 Casson, Lionel. Ships and seamanship in the ancient world. Princeton, N.J., 1971.
Arc 537.8A Casson, S. Ancient Cyprus; its art and archaeology. London, 1937.
Arc 642.6 Casson, S. Essays in Aegean archaeology. Oxford, 1927.
Arc 387.11 Casson, Stanley. Progress of archaeology. London, 1934.
Arc 543.4.50 Castagné, J. Les monuments funeraires de la steppe des Kirghizes. Orenburg, 1911.
Arc 785.20.15F Castagnoli, F. Appia antica. Milano, 1957.
Arc 785.13.80F Castagnoli, F. Foro romano. Milano, 1957.
Arc 830.21 Castan, Auguste. Les arènes de Vesontio. Besançon, 1886.
Arc 830.21.3 Castan, Auguste. Le capitole de Vesontio et les capitoles provinciaux du monde romain. Paris, 1869.
Arc 630.2 Castan, Auguste. Les capitoles provinciaux du monde romain. Besançon, 1886.
Arc 830.21.5 Castan, Auguste. Le théâtre de Vesontio. Besançon, 1873.
Arc 1494.15 Castejan, R. Medina Zahira. Cordoba, 1924.
Arc 726.338 Castel d'Asso. (Colonna di Paolo, Elena.) Roma, 1970. 2v.
Arc 726.252 Castel S. Flaviano. (Bindi, Vincenzo.) Napoli, 1879-82. 4v.
Arc 1588.4.25 Castelin, K.O. Česka drobna mince v doly predhus, a husitske, 1300-1471. Praha, 1953.
Arc 936.195.210 Castelin, Karel O. Die Goldprägung der Kelten in den böhmischen Ländern. Graz, 1965.
Arc 1033.17.250 Castellano, U. Ave Maria. La milagrosa imagen de Nuestra Señora del Rosario. Córdoba, 1891.
Arc 736.2.10F Il castello Eurialo. Syracuse. (Mauceri, L.) Roma, 1912.
Arc 608.6.40 Castellum Dimmidi. (Picard, G.C.) Paris, 1947.
Arc 853.4.13 Castellum Mattiacorum. (Becker, J.) Wiesbaden, 1863. 6 pam.
Arc 1030.56 Il castillo sforzesco in Milano. (Milan. Castillo Sforzesco.) Milano, 1915.
Arc 1670.54F The casting-counter and the counting board...numismatics. (Barnard, F.P.) Oxford, 1916.
Arc 1033.80 Castro, V. de. Difesa della causa di S. Marcellino. Roma, 1819.
Arc 736.7 Castrogiovanni...nebst einer Untersuchung. (Rossbach, Otto.) Leipzig, 1912.
Arc 1015.222 La catacomba e la basilica costantiniana. (Franconi, F.) Roma, 1877.
Arc 1025.46 Le catacombe. (Minoccheri, L.) Roma, 1897.
Arc 1025.44 Le catacombe. (Prina, B.) Firenze, 1894.
Arc 1027.18.5 Le catacombe degli ebrei...via Appia. (Müller, Nikolaus.) Roma, 1885?
Arc 1025.24 Le catacombe di Roma. (Martorelli, I.) Vercelli, 1881.
Arc 1025.7.11 Le catacombe di Roma. (Raoul-Rochette, D.) Milano, 1841.
Arc 1015.226 Catacombe di S. Giovanni in Siracusa. (Carini, I.) Roma, 1890.
Arc 1027.26 Le catacombe di Siracusa. (Bartolini, D.) Roma, 1847.
Arc 1027.27.9 Catacombe e antichità cristiana di Chiusi. (Liverani, F.) Siena, 1872.
Arc 1027.9 Le catacombe e il protestantesimo. (Armellini, M.) Roma, 1875.
Arc 1027.9.9 Le catacombe ed il protestantesimo. (Marucchi, O.) Roma, 1911.
Arc 1015.209 Le catacombe ossia il sepolcro. (Lugari, G.B.) Roma, 1888.
Arc 1025.30.5 Le catacombe romane. (Armellini, M.) Roma, 1880.
Arc 1025.54 Le catacombe romane. (Desimoni, C.) Firenze, 1870.
Arc 1025.28.50F Le catacombe romane. (Marucchi, O.) Roma, 1933.
Arc 1025.28.25 La catacombe romane a proposito della recente opera del Roller. (Marucchi, O.) Roma, 1883.
Arc 1027.78 Les catacombes africaines. (Leynaud, A.F.) Sousse, 1910.
Arc 1027.78.2 Les catacombes africaines. 2e éd. (Leynaud, A.F.) Alger, 1922.
Arc 1025.48 Les catacombes de Rome. (Besnier, M.) Paris, 1904.
Arc 1025.48.3 Les catacombes de Rome. (Besnier, M.) Paris, 1909.
Arc 1025.20 Les catacombes de Rome. (L'Epinovis, H. de.) Paris, 1875.
Arc 1025.47 Les catacombes de Rome. Conférence. Paris, n.d.
Arc 1027.19 Les catacombes de Saint Calixte. (Nortet.) Rome, 1887.
Arc 1027.72.3 Les catacombes d'Hadrumète. (Carton, Louis B.C.) Sousse, 1905.
Arc 1015.204 Les catacombes di Rome. (Roller, T.) Paris, 1881. 2v.
Arc 1025.73 The catacombs of Rome. (Kirsch, G.P.) Rome, 1946.
Arc 1025.58 The catacombs of Rome. (MacFarlane, Charles.) London, 1852.
Arc 1025.1 The catacombs of Rome. (Rip, W.I.) N.Y., 1854.
Arc 1025.50 The catacombs of Rome. (Treat, J.H.) Boston, 1907.
Arc 1025.33 The catacombs of Rome. (Treat, J.H.) n.p., n.d.
Arc 1025.11 Catacombs of Rome. (Withrow, W.H.) London, 1877.
Arc 530.181 Çatal Hüyük. (Mollaart, James.) N.Y., 1967.
Arc 1335.135 Catalago. (Madrid. Museo Argueológico Nacional.) Madrid, 1925.
Arc 1335.140 Catalago de las monedas y medallas de la biblioteca de San Lorenzo de el Escorial. (Escorial. Biblioteca.) Madrid, 1935.
Arc 800.15 Catalano, V. Storia di Ercolano. Napoli, 1953.
Arc 1433.5.15 A catalog of modern coins of Afghanistan. 1. English ed. (Hamidi, Hakim.) Kabal, 1967.
Arc 843.155 Catáloga de las antigüedades que se conservan en el Patio Arabe. (Madrid. Museo Archeologica.) Madrid, 1932.
Arc 720.200.5 Catalogi...ad thesauros antiquitatum. (Poleni, G.) Bononiae, 1853.
Arc 983.2.5 Catálogo...objetos...Estados Unidos de América. Madrid, 1892.
Arc 1261.3.5 Catálogo. (Spain. Archivo Historico Nacional, Madrid. Sección de Sigilografía.) Madrid, 1918.
Arc 1027.28 Catalogo cimiteriale romano. (Rampolla, M.) Roma, 1900.
Arc 1645.1.10 Catalogo das moedas brasileiras. (Prober, Kurt.) Rio de Janeiro, 1960.
Arc 1675.37.15 Catalogo das moedas portuguesas. (Oporto, Portugal. Museu Municipal.) Porto. 1-2,1929-1934
Arc 843.83 Catalogo de las exvatos de bronce. (Madrid. Museo Arqueologico Nacional.) Madrid, 1941. 2v.

Author and Title Listing

Arc 1494.35 Catalogo de las monedas previsigadas. (Madrid. Museo Arqueologico Nacional.) Madrid, 1936.

Arc 983.2 Catalogo de los objetos etnológicos y arqueológicos. (Hemenway, S.W.) Madrid, 1892.

Arc 1493.15 Catalogo de los reales de a ocho espanoles. (Yriarte, José de.) Madrid, 1955.

Arc 1086.5 Catálogo de lucernas romanas. (Coimbra. Museu Machado de Castro.) Coimbra, 1952.

Arc 1261.3.15 Catálogo de sellos de la Sección de Sigilografía del Archivo Histórico Nacional. (Spain. Archivo Histórico Nacional, Madrid. Sección de Sigilografía.) Madrid, 1974- 3v.

Arc 1335.83 Catalogo della collezione A. Ancona di Milano. (Pertusi, G., firm, auctioneer, Milan.) Milano, 1892.

Arc 1488.26F Catalogo della raccolta numismatica Papadopoli-Aldobandino. (Venice. Museo.) Venezia, 1925. 2v.

Arc 1675.52 Catalogo delle medaglie del rinascimento e moderne di uomini illustri. (Sambon, Giulio.) Roma, 1883.

Arc 1490.96 Catalogo delle medaglie papali annuali da Pio VII a Paolo VI. (Rinaldi, Alfio.) Verona, 1967.

Arc 1433.2 Catalogo delle monete arabe. (Palermo. Biblioteca Comunale.) Palermo, 1892.

Arc 1335.37 Catalogo delle monete italiane...collezione A. Cantoni di Milano. (Sambon, G.) Milano, 1887.

Arc 608.45F Catalogo delle sculture di Cirene. (Paribeni, Enrico.) Roma, 1959.

Arc 1493.10 Catalogo descriptivo das moedas portuguesas. Lisboa, 1903.

Arc 1480.3 Catalogo di antiche medaglie consolari e di famiglie romane. (Riccio, G.G.) Naples, 1855.

Arc 387.4.7 Catalogo di tutte le produzioni letterarie...dell'abate Francesco Girolamo Cancellieri. Roma, 1846. 2 pam.

Arc 1261.3 Catálogo i sellos españoles de la edad media por Juan Menéndez Pidal. (Spain. Archivo Historico Nacional, Madrid. Sección de Sigilografía.) Madrid, 1907.

Arc 547.19 Catalogo illustrato dei monumenti egizii. pt. 2. (Turin. R. Museo di Antichità.) Torino, 1855.

Arc 875.7 Catalogue...British Museum...sculptured stones...Scotland. (Maclagan, C.) Edinburgh, 1898.

Arc 1333.9 Catalogue...coins of the U.S. (Smith, Harlan P.) Philadelphia, 1906.

Arc 1.5.24 Catalogue. (American Schools of Oriental Research, Jerusalem.) New Haven. 1935-1948 3v.

Arc 448.1.10 Catalogue and hand-book of the archaeological collections in the Indian Museum. (Indian Museum, Calcutta.) Calcutta, 1883. 2v.

Arc 830.38 Catalogue de la collection Caranda. v.1-2. Supplément. (Moreau, Frédéric.) St. Quentin, 1895-96.

Arc 1468.5.6 Catalogue de la collection de Luynes. pt.2-3 and plates. (Bibliothèque Nationale, Paris. Département des Médailles et Antiques.) Paris, 1925-30. 2v.

X Cg Arc 1468.5.5 Catalogue de la collection de Luynes. v.1-3 and plates. (Bibliothèque Nationale, Paris. Département des Médailles et Antiques.) Paris, 1924. 6v.

Arc 1335.50 Catalogue de la collection de monnaies. v.1, pt.1-2; v.2, pt.1-3; v.3, pt.1-2. (Thomsen, C.J.) Copenhague, 1869-76. 7v.

Arc 1264.5 Catalogue de la collection de sceaux matrices. (Hucher, Eugène.) Paris, 1863.

Arc 1588.1.30 Catalogue de la collection des medailles et monnaies polonaises. (Gutten Czapskii, E.K.) Graz, 1957. 5v.

Arc 1680.17 Catalogue de la collection Rouyer. (Bibliothèque Nationale, Paris. Département des Médailles et Antiques. Collection Rouyer.) Paris, 1899-1910. 2v.

Arc 1020.63 Catalogue de l'exposition d'objets d'art...à Lille en 1874. 2. éd. (Van Drival.) Lille, 1874.

Arc 1498.10 Catalogue de monnaies françaises. pt.1-3. (Ciani, Louis.) Paris, 1927-29.

Arc 1334.6.10 Catalogue de monnaies royales francaise en or. Paris, 1864. 9 pam.

Arc 825.3.5 Catalogue de Musée de Nîmes. 6e éd. (Nîmes. Musée des Antiques et Cabinet des Médailles.) Nîmes, 1863.

Arc 825.3.8 Catalogue de Musée de Nîmes. 6e éd. (Nîmes. Musée des Antiques et Cabinet des Médailles.) Nîmes, 1863-75.

Arc 1208.2 Catalogue de sigillographie du Musée de Troyes. (Le Clert, Louis.) Troyes, 1887.

Arc 547.5 Catalogue des antiquités découvertes en Egypte. (Passalacqua, J.) Paris, 1826.

Arc 66.1.69 Catalogue des bronzes de la société archeologique d'Athènes. (Ridder, A. de.) Paris, 1894.

Arc 66.1.74 Catalogue des bronzes trouvés sur l'Acropole. (Ridder, A. de.) Paris, 1896. 2v.

Arc 1518.2 Catalogue des coins, poincons et matrices. 2. ed. (Piot, C.) Bruxelles, 1880.

Arc 830.167 Catalogue des collections lapidaires. (Société d'Histoire et d'Archéologie de Châlon-sur-Saône. Musée Denon.) Châlon-sur-Saône, 1936.

Arc 1500.5.25 Catalogue des deniers mérovingiens de la trouvaille de Bais (Ille et Vilaine). (Prou, Maurice.) Paris, 1908.

Arc 1433.85 Catalogue des étalons monétaires. (Bibliothèque Nationale, Paris. Département des Médailles et Antiques.) Paris, 1960.

Arc 66.1.16 Catalogue des figurines en terre cuite. (Martha, J.) Paris, 1880.

Arc 750.208.5F Catalogue des fresques de Boscoreale. (Sambon, Arthur.) Macon, 1903.

Arc 1500.45 Catalogue des jetons. (Bibliothèque Nationale, Paris. Département des Médailles et Antiques.) Paris, 1897.

Arc 1518.3 Catalogue des medailles du Royaume de Belgique. (Tourneur, Victor.) Bruxelles, 1911.

Arc 1473.16 Catalogue des monnaies byzantines de la Bibliothèque Nationale. (Bibliothèque Nationale, Paris. Département des Médailles et Antiques.) Paris, 1970. 2v.

Arc 1468.5 Catalogue des monnaies grecques. Les rois de Syrie, d'Arménie et de Commagène. (Bibliothèque Nationale, Paris. Département des Médailles et Antiques.) Paris, 1890.

Arc 1433.1 Catalogue des monnaies musulmanes. (Bibliothèque Nationale, Paris.) Paris, 1887-96. 3v.

Arc 1433.67.2 Catalogue des monnaies turcomanes. (Istanbul. Asari Atika Müzeleri.) Bologne, 1965.

Arc 545.228 Catalogue des monuments et inscriptions de l'Egypte antique. (Egypt. Antiquities Department.) Vienne, 1894-1909. 3v.

Arc 1020.65 Catalogue des objets d'art religieux...à l'Hotel Liederkerke à Malines. 2. éd. (Weale, W.H.J.) Bruxelles, 1864.

Arc 600.155F Catalogue des ostraca figurés de Deir el Médineh. Pt. 4. (Vaudier, Jacques.) Le Caire, 1959.

Arc 600.156.5F Catalogue des ostraca hiératiques littéraires de Deir el Médineh. (Posener, Georges.) Le Caire, 1972-

Arc 600.156F Catalogue des ostraca hiératiques littéraires de Deir el Médineh. (Sauneron, Serge.) Le Caire, 1959- 2v.

Arc 584.1.5 Catalogue des publications du Service des Antiquités, mars 1961. (Egypt. Antiquities Department.) Le Caire, 1961.

Arc 1020.52.5 Catalogue des reliques...Notre Dame de Chartres. (Merlet, L.) Chartres, 1885.

Arc 1254.14 Catalogue des sceaux byzantins. (Ebersolt, Jean.) Paris, 1922.

Arc 682.1.17 Catalogue des trésors de Mycènes au Musée d'Athènes. (Schliemann, Heinrich.) Leipzig, 1882.

Arc 682.1.16 Catalogue des trésors de Mycènes au Musée d'Athènes. (Schliemann, Heinrich.) Leipzig, 1882.

Arc 66.1.85 Catalogue des vases peints. (Collignon, M.) Paris, 1902. 4v.

Arc 66.1.3 Catalogue des vases peints du musée. (Collignon, M.) Paris, 1878.

Arc 1335.20 Catalogue descriptive des monnaies luxembourgeoises. (Werveke, N. van.) Luxembourg, 1880.

Arc 1433.67 Catalogue dis monnaies turcomanes. (Istanbul. Asari Atika Müzeleri.) Constantinople, 1894.

Arc 830.50 Catalogue du Musée. (Société Historique et Archéologique de Langres.) Langres, 1902.

Arc 830.155 Catalogue du Musée lapidaire de Bourges. (Société des Antiquaires du Centre, Bourges.) Bourges, 1873.

Arc 830.147F Catalogue du trésor de Chaource. Paris, 1888.

Arc 1478.30 Catalogue d'une collection de médailles romaines. pt.1-2,3. Paris, 18- . 2v.

Arc 1335.33 Catalogue général de monnaies, médailles et jetons. (D'Angers, D.) Paris, n.d.

Arc 545.227F Catalogue général des antiquités égyptiennes Ostraca. (Cairo. Musée des Antiquités Egyptiennes.) Le Caire. 1-100,1901-1937 77v.

X Cg Arc 545.227F Catalogue général des antiquités égyptiennes Ostraca. (Cairo. Musée des Antiquités Egyptiennes.) Le Caire. 10

Arc 545.226 Catalogue général des monuments d'Abydos. (Mariette, A.) Paris, 1880.

Arc 1335.31 Catalogue général illustré de monnaies antiques. 2. ed. (Boudeau, E.) Paris, n.d.

Arc 1335.31.3 Catalogue général illustré de monnaies françaises. (Boudeau, E.) Paris, n.d.

Arc 505.100.2 Catalogue illustré du Departement des antiquités gréco-romaines. (Damascus. Musée National Syrien.) Damas, 1951.

Arc 1613.11F Catalogue of...American coins and medals of C.I. Bushnell. (Bushnell, C.I.) Philadelphia, 1882.

Arc 1335.38 Catalogue of...coins and medals in gold, silver, and copper. pt.1. (Young, Matthew.) London, 1839.

Arc 1335.43 Catalogue of...Greek, Roman, Byzantine and Mediterranean coins. v.1-2. (Borrell, H.P.) London? 1852?

Arc 1053.6.4 Catalogue of...Theodor Graf collection. n.p., n.d.

Arc 1335.2 Catalogue of a collection of coins and medals. (Chadbourne, S.H.) Boston, 1867.

Arc 547.1 Catalogue of a collection of Egyptian antiquities. (Abbott, H.) N.Y., 1853.

Arc 770.2 Catalogue of a series of photographs illustrative of the archaeology of Rome. (Parker, J.H.) n.p., 1867.

Arc 983.1 Catalogue of a unique collection of cliff dweller relics. (Green, C.H.) Chicago? n.d.

Arc 1335.130 A catalogue of a valuable collection. (Landowne, William P.) London, 18- ?

Arc 1443.5F Catalogue of Alexandrian coins. (Oxford. University. Ashmolean Museum.) Oxford, 1933.

Arc 1613.6 Catalogue of American and foreign coins, medals, tokens. (Woodward, W.E.) Providence, 1866.

Arc 1613.6.2 Catalogue of American and foreign coins, medals, tokens. (Woodward, W.E.) Roxbury, 1867.

Arc 1335.18 Catalogue of American coins. (Leonard and Company.) Boston, 1860-70. 4 pam.

Arc 1335.7 Catalogue of an excellent choice and select collection of coins, medals, and autographs. (Leavitt, Strebeigh and Company.) n.p., 1870.

Arc 545.231.7F Catalogue of an exhibition of ancient Egyptian art. (Burlington Five Arts Club, London.) London, 1922.

Arc 858.48 Catalogue of an exhibition of recent archaeological discoveries in Great Britain. (London Museum.) London, 1932.

Arc 340.3F Catalogue of books on archaeology and art. (London. University. Library.) London, 1935-37. 2v.

Arc 340.3.5F Catalogue of books on archaeology and art. Index. (London. University. Library.) London, 1937.

Arc 340.3.2F Catalogue of books on archaeology and art. Supplement. (London. University. Library.) London, 1937.

Arc 1411.8 Catalogue of Chinese coins from the 7th century B.C. to A.D. 621. (Terrien de Lacouperie, A.E.J.B.) London, 1892.

Arc 1335.4 Catalogue of choice English, French, and American coins and medals. (Harzfeld, S.K.) Boston, 1878.

Arc 1623.1 Catalogue of coins, medals, and tokens of Mexico. (Fisher, A.) N.Y., 1891.

Arc 1615.4 Catalogue of coins, tokens, and medals. (United States Mint.) Washington, 1912.

Arc 1615.4.2 Catalogue of coins, tokens, and medals. 2. ed. (United States Mint.) Washington, 1913.

Arc 1615.4.3 Catalogue of coins, tokens, and medals. 3. ed. (United States Mint.) Washington, 1914.

Arc 1610.3 Catalogue of coins and medals. (Bangs, Merwin C.) Roxbury, 1863.

Arc 1335.77 Catalogue of coins in the Colombo Museum. (Colombo Museum. Colombo, Ceylon.) Hertford, 1914.

Arc 1418.5A Catalogue of coins in the Indian Museum, Calcutta. (Indian Museum.) Oxford, 1906-08. 3v.

Arc 1418.8F Catalogue of coins in the museum. (Phayre Provincial Museum, Rangoon.) Rangoon, 1924.

Arc 1418.6 Catalogue of coins in the Provincial Museum. (Lucknow, India. Provincial Museum.) Oxford, 1920. 2v.

Arc 1418.20 Catalogue of coins in the Punjab Museum. (Lahore Museum.) Oxford, 1914-34. 3v.

Arc 1470.10 Catalogue of coins of the Achaean League. (Clerk, M.G.) London, 1895.

Arc 1418.26 Catalogue of coins of the Mughal emperors. (Hussain, M.K.) Bombay, 1968.

Arc 1478.81F Catalogue of coins of the Roman Empire in the Ashmolean Museum. (Oxford. University. Ashmolean Museum.) Oxford, 1975-

Arc 1613.9 Catalogue of coins of the United States. (United States Mint.) Washington, 1928.

Arc 1473.6.5 Catalogue of coins of vandals, ostrogoths. (British Museum. Department of Coins and Medals.) London, 1911.
Arc 1333.10 Catalogue of collections of coins of M.A. Trickney. (Chapman, H.) Philadelphia, 1907.
Arc 1200.16 Catalogue of copper-plate grants. (Madras. Government Museum.) Madras, 1918.
Arc 545.227.44F Catalogue of demotic graffiti of the Dodecaschoenus. (Griffith, F.L.) Oxford, 1935.
Arc 545.227.44PF Catalogue of demotic graffiti of the Dodecaschoenus. v.2. (Griffith, F.L.) Oxford, 1937.
Arc 547.50F Catalogue of Egyptian antiquities in the British Museum. (British Museum. Department of Egyptian Antiquities.) London, 1968- 2v.
Arc 600.12.10F A catalogue of Egyptian scarabs by Alan Rowe. (Palestine. Archaeological Museum.) La Caire, 1936.
Arc 1538.2 Catalogue of English coins in the British Museum. (British Museum. Department of Coins and Medals.) London, 1916. 2v.
Arc 1538.2.15 A catalogue of English coins in the British Museum. Anglo-Saxon series. (British Museum. Department of Coins and Medals.) London, 1887-93. 2v.
Arc 653.1 Catalogue of Greece and Sicily. (Nebraska. University.) Lincoln, Neb., 1905.
Arc 630.6 Catalogue of Greek and Roman lamps in the British Museum. (British Museum.) London, 1914.
Arc 1465.6 Catalogue of Greek coins in the Hunterian collection. (MacDonald, G.) Glasgow, 1899. 3v.
Arc 1473.6A Catalogue of imperial Byzantine coins in the British Museum. (Wroth, W.) London, 1908. 2v.
Arc 1418.1 Catalogue of Indian coins. v.1-5,7. (British Museum. Department of Coins and Medals.) London, 1884-1936. 6v.
Arc 1675.22F Catalogue of international exhibition of contemporary medals. (American Numismatic Society.) N.Y., 1911.
Arc 1675.38 Catalogue of Italian placquettes. (Victoria and Albert Museum.) London, 1924.
Arc 1335.82F Catalogue of J.S. Jenks collection of coins. (Chapman, H.) Philadelphia, 1921.
Arc 1663.6.15 Catalogue of Jacobite medals and touch pieces. (Widdington, M.) Leeds, 1938.
Arc 1478.2 A catalogue of medals from Julius Caesar to Heraclius. London, 1716.
Arc 1329.2 Catalogue of numismatic books in the library. (American Numismatic Society.) N.Y., 1883.
X Cg Arc 1408.5 Catalogue of Oriental coins. (British Museum. Department of Coins and Medals.) London, 1875-90. 10v.
Arc 497.1 Catalogue of photographs. (American Palestine Exploration Society.) N.Y., 1876.
Arc 1588.1.32 The catalogue of Polish coins. (Terlecki, W.) Warsaw, 1960.
Arc 1535.207F A catalogue of provincial copper coins, tokens, tickets, medals issued in Great Britain, Ireland and the colonies...18th century. (Chetwynd, George.) London, 1834.
Arc 1480.7 Catalogue of Roman coins. (London, England. Society of Antiquaries.) London? 1852.
Arc 1208.1 Catalogue of seals in the department of manuscripts. (British Museum.) London, 1887-1900. 6v.
Arc 1473.19 Catalogue of the Byzantine coins in the Dumbarton Oaks collection and in the Whittemore collection. v. 1-3. (Dumbarton Oaks.) Washington, 1966- 5v.
Arc 1335.58 Catalogue of the cabinet of coins belonging to Yale College. (Yale College.) New Haven, 1863.
Arc 1453.2F Catalogue of the coins found at Corinth, 1925. (Bellinger, A.R.) New Haven, 1930.
Arc 1418.2.7 Catalogue of the coins of the Gupta dynasties and of Sásanka. (British Museum. Department of Coins and Medals.) London, 1914.
Arc 1335.32 Catalogue of the collection of American coins and medals. (Zabriskie, A.C.) N.Y., 1909.
Arc 1428.25 Catalogue of the collection of Arabic coins...in the Khedivial Library at Cairo. (Cairo. Egyptian Library.) London, 1897.
Arc 1335.60 A catalogue of the collection of curious...coins. (Hutchins.) London, 1790.
Arc 547.8 Catalogue of the collection of Egyptian antiquities belonging to the late Robert Hay, Esq. (Hay, J.) London, 1869.
Arc 1335.89 Catalogue of the collection of Greek coins in gold. (Sotheby, W.) London, 1894.
Arc 1433.55 Catalogue of the collection of oriental coins belonging to C. Sefan Guthrie. (Guthrie, C.S.) Hertford, 1874.
Arc 1680.16 Catalogue of the collection of Wiltshire trade tokens. (Wiltshire Archaeological and Natural History Society, Devizes. Museum.) Devizes, 1893.
Arc 1538.4 Catalogue of the copper coinage of Great Britain. (Batty, D.T.) Manchester, 1868-98. 4v.
Arc 547.30 A catalogue of the Egyptian collection. (Cambridge. University. Fitzwilliam Museum.) Cambridge, Eng., 1893.
Arc 1458.2 Catalogue of the Greek and Roman coins in the numismatic collection. (Yale College.) New Haven, 1880.
Arc 1468.1 A catalogue of the Greek coins. (British Museum. Department of Coins and Medals.) London, 1873-94. 29v.
Arc 1418.15 Catalogue of the Gupta gold coins in the Bayana Hoard. (Altekar, A.S.) Bombay, 1954.
Arc 861.10.9 Catalogue of the Manks crosses. (Kermode, P.M.) London, 1892.
Arc 1468.24 Catalogue of the McClean collection of Greek coins. (Cambridge, Eng. University. Fitzwilliam Museum.) Cambridge, 1923-29. 3v.
Arc 1540.17.10 Catalogue of the medals of Scotland. (Cochran-Patrick, R.W.) Edinburgh, 1884.
Arc 1433.43 A catalogue of the Muhammadan coins in the British Museum. (British Museum. Department of Coins and Medals.) London, 1941. 2v.
Arc 435.25.8F Catalogue of the Museum of Archaeology at Sanchi, Bhopal State. (Sanchi, Bhopal State. Museum of Archaeology.) Calcutta, 1922.
Arc 1335.6 Catalogue of the numismatic collection of F.S. Hoffman. (Woodward, W.E.) N.Y., 1866.
Arc 1478.86 A catalogue of the Roman and related foreign coins in the collections of Sir Stephen Courtland at the University College of Rhodesia and Nyasaland. (Carney, Thomas Francis.) Salisbury, 1963.
Arc 861.17 Catalogue of the Roman inscribed and sculptured stones...ms. of Tullie House. (Haverfield, F.) Kendal, 1899.

Arc 1208.14F Catalogue of the Western Asiatic seals in the British Museum. (British Museum. Department of Western Asiatic Antiquities.) London, 1962.
Arc 1335.156 Catalogue of the world's most popular coins. (Reinfeld, Fred.) Garden City, 1965.
Arc 1500.3 Catalogue raisonné de la collection de deniers merovingiens. (Morel-Fatio, A.) Paris, 1890.
Arc 1335.1 Catalogue raisonné d'une collection de médailles. Leipzig, 1774.
Arc 435.1.10 Catalogue raisonné of the prehistoric antiquities. (Indian Museum, Calcutta.) Simla, 1917.
Arc 1208.4 Catalogues des plombs antiques. (Dissard, Paul.) Paris, 1905.
Arc 1411.7 Catalogus der munten en amuletten van China. (Batairaasch Genootschap van Kunsten in Wetenschappen.) Batavia, 1904.
Arc 1335.56.2 Catalogus der numismatische afdeeling. 2. druk. (Bataviaasch Genootschap van Kunsten en Wetenschappen. Museum.) Batavia, 1877.
Arc 1335.56.3 Catalogus der numismatische versameling. 3. druk. (Bataviaasch Genootschap van Kunsten en Wetenschappen. Museum.) Batavia, 1886.
Htn Arc 1335.10* Catalogus numism. mus. Lefroyani. (Lefroy, A.) Livorno, 1763.
Arc 1588.10.15 Catalogus numorum Hungariae ac Transiwaniae Instituti Nationalis Szechényrani. (Budapest. Orszagos Széchenyi-Könyvtár.) Pestini, 1807. 2v.
NEDL Arc 1353.4 Catalogus numorum veterum graecorum et latinorum. pt. 1-2. (Ramus, Christian.) Hafniae, 1816.
Arc 1353.7.5 Catalogus numorum veterum graecorum et Latinorum musei. (Copenhagen. National Museet.) Hafniae, 1816. 3v.
Arc 383.50 Catania. Università. Scritti in onore di Guido Libertini. Firenze, 1958.
Arc 1033.12.168 Cateni, P.F. Notizie della reliquia...del sacro chiodo. Colle, 1821.
Arc 1020.9.20 Caterbi, G. La chiesa di S. Onofrio. Roma, 1858.
Arc 726.2.30 Caterino, Antonio. Bibliografia sulle catacombe napoletane. Firenze, 1957.
Arc 1033.12.188 Cathalogus authorum, qui de corona. Roma, 1715.
Arc 608.6.60 Cathedra en mensa. (Luiks, A.G.) Franeker, 1955.
Arc 1016.230 Catholic Church. Congregatio Indulgentiarum et Sacrarum Reliquiarum. Acta congregationis praeparatoriae habitae die 4 iulii 1901. De authenticitate S. Sindonis Taurinensis. Roma, 1901.
Arc 1016.230.2 Catholic Church. Congregatio Indulgentiarum et Sacrarum Reliquiarum. Excellentissimo ac revm̃o dño Aloisio Tripepi. De authenticitate S. Sindonis Taurinensis. Roma, 1901.
Arc 1153.47PF Catholic Church. Pope. Pontificum Romanorum diplomata. Romae, 1928.
Arc 1030.8.21 La catholicisme en Chine au VIIIe siècle de notre ère. (Dabry de Thiessaut.) Paris, 1877.
Arc 540.12 Catling, H.W. Cypriot bronzework in the Mycenaean world. Oxford, 1964.
Arc 600.5.15F Caton-Thompson, G. The desert Fayum. London, 1934. 2v.
Arc 609.1.57 Caton-Thompson, Gertrude. The Zimbabwe culture: ruins and reactions. 2. ed. London, 1971.
Arc 1016.237 La cattedra Alessandrina di San Marco Evangelista e Martire. (Secchi, P.G.) Venezia, 1853.
Arc 726.91 La cattedrale modenese. (Bertoni, G.) Modena, 1914.
Arc 830.57 Cauchemè, V. Description des fouilles archéologiques...Compiègne. pt.1-4. Compiègne, 1900-12.
Arc 588.13 Caulfield, A.S.G. Temple of the Kings at Abydos. London, 1902.
Arc 1274.7 Caulfield, R. Sigilla ecclesiae Hibernicae illustrata. pt.1-4. Dublin, 1853.
Arc 830.165.5 Caumont, Arcisse de. Les monuments historiques de l'Orne. Caen, 187-. 2v.
Arc 562.2.35 Causeries d'Égypte. 2. éd. (Maspero, Gaston.) Paris, 1907.
Arc 66.1.100 Cavaignac, E. Études sur l'histoire financière d'Athènes au Ve siècle. Paris, 1908.
Arc 1033.17.325 Cavalieri, M. Il Pellegrino al Gargano...di San Michele. Napoli, 1690.
Arc 66.1.47 Les cavaliers athéniens. (Martin, A.) Paris, 1886.
Arc 730.2.2 Cavallari, F.S. Appendice. Topografia archaeologica. Siracusa. Torino, 1891.
Arc 730.2 Cavallari, F.S. Atlante. Topografia archaeologica. Siracusa. Palermo, 1883. 2v.
Arc 730.2.3 Cavallari, F.S. Euryalos e le opere di difesa di Siracusa. Palermo, 1893.
Arc 733.1 Cavallari, F.S. Sulla topografia di Talune città greche. Palermo, 1879.
Arc 1077.3.2 Cavallari, S. Lettre sur la chape arabe de Chinon. Paris, 1857.
Arc 1027.26.9 Cavallari, S. Osservazioni sulle basiliche e le catacombe...Siracusa. Palermo, 1874.
Arc 1560.3.1 Cavalli, Gustaf. Gustaf Cavallis samlung av svenska kopparmynt. Facsimile. Stockholm, 1971.
Arc 1033.17.163 Cavallucci, V. Istoria critica del sagro anello...Perugia. Perugia, 1783.
Arc 543.1 Cave, H.W. The ruined cities of Ceylon. London, 1897.
Arc 543.1.4 Cave, H.W. The ruined cities of Ceylon. 4th ed. London, 1907.
Arc 691.2 The cave at Vari. (Weller.) n.p., n.d.
Arc 488.18 Cave explorations in Iran, 1949. (Coon, Carleton Stevens.) Philadelphia, 1951.
Arc 432.1 Cave temples of India. (Fergusson, J.) London, 1880.
Arc 1033.16 Cavedoni, C. Atti dei tre santi martiri Sarace, Probo e Andronico. Modena, 1839.
Arc 1423.12.5 Cavedoni, C. Biblische Numismatik. Hannover, 1855-56. 2v.
Arc 1033.53.9 Cavedoni, C. Cenni cronologica...rescritti di Traiano e di Adriano. Modena, 1855.
Arc 1030.3 Cavedoni, C. Cenni sopra alcume antiche iscrizioni cristiane. Modena, 1839.
Arc 1033.17.138 Cavedoni, C. Cenni storici e critici intorno alla S. Zona della...Vergine. Modena, 1842.
Arc 1033.4.5 Cavedoni, C. La credenza della primitiva chiesa del Sacramento dell'Eucaristia. Modena, 1869.
Arc 1033.44.9 Cavedoni, C. Dell'origine...IHS del SS. Nome de Gesú. Modena, n.d.
Arc 1077.2.13 Cavedoni, C. Di tre antiche stauroteche...cattedrale di Modena. Modena, 1847.
Arc 1033.35.55 Cavedoni, C. Dichiarazione de' tre antiche Stauroteche. Modena, 1847.
Arc 1030.3.13 Cavedoni, C. Dichiarazione dell'epetaffo di S. Georgio Martire. Modena, 1843.

Arc 1030.3.5 Cavedoni, C. Dichiarazione dell'iscrizione sepolcrale di San Decenzio Martire. Modena, 1839.

Arc 1030.3.11 Cavedoni, C. Dichiarazione di due antiche gemme incise. Modena, n.d.

Arc 1033.93 Cavedoni, C. Dichiarazione di 5 bassirilievi biblici...Modena. Modena, 1855.

Arc 1033.53.15 Cavedoni, C. L'era de' martiri osia di Diocleziano. Modena, 1848.

Arc 1033.85 Cavedoni, C. Osservazioni...sepolcro di Maria. Modena, 1865.

Arc 1033.1.9 Cavedoni, C. Osservazioni sopra alcuni frammenti di vasi. Modena, 1859.

Arc 1030.40 Cavedoni, C. Ragguaglio critico delle iscrizioni cristiane. Modena, 185-?

Arc 1027.27.13 Cavedoni, C. Ragguaglio di due antichi cimiteri. Modena, 1853.

Arc 1033.73 Cavedoni, C. Ricerche...del sacro pallio ecclesiastico. Modena, 1856.

Arc 1033.44.13 Cavedoni, C. Ricerche critiche...medaglie di Constantino. Modena, 1858.

Arc 1027.54.5 Cavedoni, C. Sacra imagine della beata Virgine Maria. Modena, 1855.

Arc 1033.3.23 Cavedoni, C. Sarcofago cristiano nel templo di Fermo. Roma, 1843.

Arc 1030.3.9 Cavedoni, C. Sopra l'iscrizione sepolcrale di S. Gemello. Modena, 1839.

Arc 1025.27 Cavedoni, Celestino. Ragguaglio critico dei monumenti delle arti cristiane. Modena, 1849.

Arc 843.67 La caverna de la Peña de Candamo (Asturias). (Hernández-Pecheco, E.) Madrid, 1919.

Arc 950.209 La caverne d'Aknanh, ile d'Ounga. (Pinart, A.L.) Paris, 1875.

Arc 843.63F La caverne d'Altamira à Santillane près Santander (Espagne). (Cartailhac, Emile.) Monaco, 1906.

Arc 830.330F Les cavernes du Volp. (Bégouën, Henri.) Paris, 1958.

Arc 635.13 Cavvadias, P. Fouilles d'Epidaure. Athène, 1893.

Arc 830.170 Le cayla de Mailhac, Aube. (Taffanel, O.) Carcassonne, 1938.

Arc 1480.30F Caylus, A.C.P. Numismata aurea imperatorum Romanorum. n.p., n.d.

Arc 387.1.2 Caylus, A.C.P. Recueil d'antiquités. Paris, 1761.

Arc 387.1 Caylus, A.C.P. Recueil d'antiquités égyptiennes. Paris, 1752. 7v.

Arc 835.200 Cean-Bermudez, J.A. Sumario de las antiqüedades Romanas que hay en España. Madrid, 1832.

Arc 66.1.206 Cèbe, Jean Pierre. La caricature et la parodie dans le monde romain, antique des origines a Juvenal. Paris, 1966.

Arc 1025.70 Cecchelli, C. La chiesa delle catacombe. Roma, 1943.

Arc 1018.58 Cecchelli, Carlo. Il cenacolo filippino e l'archeologia cristiana. Roma, 1938.

Arc 1033.177 Cecchelli, Carlo. Lezioni di archeologia cristiana; liturgia ed archeologia. Roma, 1958.

Arc 1077.2.44 Cecchelli, Carlo. Il trionfo della croce. Roma, 1954.

Arc 1260.4.5 Cecchetti, B. Bolle dei dogi di Venezia. Venezia, 1865.

Arc 1260.4 Cecchetti, B. Bolle dei dogi di Venezia. Venezia, 1888.

Arc 726.315 Cecchini, Serena Maria. I ritrovamenti fenici e punici in Sardegna. Roma, 1969.

Arc 936.195.45 Čechy na úsvitě dějin. (Turek, R.) Praha, 1963.

Arc 1580.35 Cejnek, Josef. Österreichische, ungarische, böhmische, und schlesische Münzen. v.2. Wien, 1936.

Arc 1470.43.5 Ceka, Hasan. Questions de numismatique illyrie. Tirana, 1972.

Arc 1.5.8 Pamphlet vol. The celebration of the seventy-fifth anniversary and dedication of the stoa of Attalus as the museum. 2 pam.

Arc 1033.50 La celebre contesa fra S. Stefano e S. Cipriano. (Tizzani, V.) Roma, 1862.

Arc 66.1.103 Celier, Léonce. Les dataires du XVe siècle et les origines de la daterie apostolique. Paris, 1910.

Arc 822.2 Cellerier. Notice relative à la découverte d'un tombeau. Paris, 1818. 25 pam.

Arc 1033.35.51 Cellier. La sainte vraie croix de Douchy. Valenciennes, 1863.

Arc 936.195.265 Celostátní Seminář o Problematice Zaniklých Středověkých Vesnic, 3rd, Uherské Hradiště, Czechoslovak Republic, 1971. Zaniklé středověké vesnice v ČSSR ve svetle archeologických výzkumů. Uherské Hradiště, 1972.

Arc 618.1 Les celtes dans les vallées du Po et du Danube. (Reinach, S.) Paris, 1894.

Arc 830.369 Celtes et Armorique. (Veillard, Jean Yves.) Rennes, 1971.

Arc 618.6A Celtic art in pagan and Christian times. (Allen, J. Romilly.) London, 1904.

Arc 618.7 The Celtic druids. (Higgins, G.) London, 1827.

Arc 618.7.3 The Celtic druids. (Higgins, G.) London, 1829.

Arc 1540.21 Celtic inscriptions on Gaulish and British coins. (Poste, Beale.) London, 1861.

Arc 855.216 The Celtic Tumuli of Dorset. (Warne, C.) London, 1866.

Arc 618.2 Celticism a myth. 2. ed. (Roger, J.C.) London, 1889.

Arc 843.40 El cementerio franco de Pamplona (Navarra). (Ansoleaga, F. de.) Pamplona, 1914.

Arc 1027.37 I cemeteri cristiano della via latina. (Armellini, M.) Roma, 1874.

Arc 585.27 The cemeteries of Abydos. (Peet, T.E.) London, 1913-14. 3v.

Arc 585.34F Cemeteries of Armant. (Mond, Robert.) London, 1937. 2v.

Arc 1015.228 Cemetero di S. Ipolisto in Atripalda. (Galante, G.A.) Napoli, 1893.

Arc 830.3 Cenac-Moncaut, J.E.M. Voyage archéologique et historique dans l'ancien Comté de Comminges. Tarbes, 1856.

Arc 1018.58 Il cenacolo filippino e l'archeologia cristiana. (Cecchelli, Carlo.) Roma, 1938.

Arc 1025.35.20 Cenni biografici di Antonio Bosio. (Valeri, A.) Roma, 1900.

Arc 1349.55.5 Cenni biografici di Bennedetto Pistrucci. (Azzurri, Francesco.) Roma, 1887.

Arc 390.3.25 Cenni biografici di Carlo Fea. Roma, n.d.

Arc 1033.46 Cenni biografici di S. Giacomo apostolo il maggiore. (Bartolini, D.) Roma, 1885.

Arc 1033.53.9 Cenni cronologica...rescritti di Traiano e di Adriano. (Cavedoni, C.) Modena, 1855.

Arc 1033.17.545 Cenni intorno la chiesa di S. Salvatore alle Coppelle. (Santelamazza, M.) Roma, 1863.

Arc 1030.3 Cenni sopra alcume antiche iscrizioni cristiane. (Cavedoni, C.) Modena, 1839.

Arc 1033.17.445 Cenni storici della taumaturga effigie di Santa Maria di Monserrato. Napoli, 1848.

Arc 1033.17.138 Cenni storici e critici intorno alla S. Zona della...Vergine. (Cavedoni, C.) Modena, 1842.

Arc 1033.12.70 Cenni storici intorno al Sangue Mirae...Ferrara. (Cimatti, E.) Ferrara, 1857.

Arc 1033.59.5 Cenni storici sul culto di S. Vittoria. (Pennesi, A.) S. Vittoria, 1893.

Arc 726.4.5 Cenni storici sulla distrutta città di Cuma. (Minieri Riccio, C.) Napoli, 1846.

Arc 1033.104.5 Cenni storici sulla sepoltura...Gervasi e Protasi. Milano, 1873.

Arc 1020.9.12 Cenni sulla forma primitiva del panteon di Roma. (Torres, C.A.) Roma, 1838.

Arc 1033.12.43 Cenni sulla Santissima Sindone. Torino, 1842?

Arc 1033.17.423 Cenno istorico sul duomo e sagra immagine di Santa Maria...in Lucera. (Nocelli.) Napoli, 1843.

Arc 1033.17.444 Cenno storico del culto di Santa Maria dell'abbondanza...Marzano. Napoli, 1855.

Arc 726.54 Cenno storico della antica Libarna. (Iozzi, Oliviero.) Pisa, 1890.

Arc 1033.17.441 Cenno storico della Taumaturga efficie di Santa Maria dell'Arco...Miano. (Portenico, E.) Napoli, 1851.

Arc 1033.17.421 Cenno storico dell'insigne di Santa Maria a Pareta. Napoli, 1857.

Arc 585.31F The cenotaph of Seti I at Abydos. (Frankfort, H.) London, 1933. 2v.

Arc 100.1.7 Centenaire (1804-1904). Compte-rendu de la journée du 11 avril 1904. (Société Nationale des Antiquaires de France.) Paris, 1904.

Arc 100.1.6 Centenaire 1804-1904. Recueil de mémoires. (Société Nationale des Antiquaires de France.) Paris, 1904.

Arc 1300.1.8 Centennial celebration. (American Numismatic Society.) N.Y., 1958.

Arc 1300.1.7 Centennial publication. (American Numismatic Society.) N.Y., 1958.

Arc 726.254 Central and suthern Italy before Rome. (Trump, David H.) London, 1966.

Arc 543.138 Central Asia. (Belenitskii, Aleksandr Markovich.) London, 1969.

Arc 543.3.90 Central Asia. (Masson, Vadim Mikhailovich.) London, 1972.

Arc 101.11 Centre de documentation. Circulaire d'information. (Société d'Histoire, d'Archéologie et de Tradition Gauloises.) Paris. 1,1964+

Arc 97.5 Centre d'Etudes Gallo-Romaines. Publications. Villeurbanne. 1,1968+

Arc 273.16 Centre National de Recherches Archéologiques en Belgique. Série A: Répertoires archéologigues. Brussel. 1,1960+ 4v.

Arc 273.16.3 Centre National de Recherches Archéologiques en Belgique. Série B: Collections. Bruxelles. 1,1965+

Arc 273.16.5 Centre National de Recherches Archéologiques en Belgique. Série C: Répertoires divers. Brussel. 1,1964+ 2v.

Arc 1470.87 Centro Internazionale di Studi Numismatici. Atti del IIo Convegno del Centro internazionale di studi numismatici. Roma, 1971.

Arc 1470.88 Centro Internazionale di Studi Numismatici. La circolazione della moneta ateniese in Sicilia e in Magna Grecia. Roma, 1969.

Arc 440.7 Centro scavi e ricerche archeologiche in Asia. Altinità archeologica italiana in Asia. Roma, 1960.

Arc 32.8F Centro Scavi e Ricerche Archeologiche in Asia dell'I.M.E.O. e di Torino. Reports and memoirs. Roma. 1,1962+ 13v.

Arc 723.36 Centro Studi Ciociaria. Gli archeologi italiani in onore di Amedeo Maiuri. Cava dei Tirreni, 1965.

Arc 93.46F Centro Studi e Documentazione sull'Italia Romana. Atti. Milano. 1,1967+ 6v.

Arc 93.46.3 Centro Studi e Documentazione sull'Italia Romana. Monografie a supplemento degli Atti. Milano. 1,1972+ 5v.

Arc 746.22 Centumcellae (Civitavecchia). (Bastianelli, S.) Roma, 1954.

Arc 726.34 Centurione, P.A.M. Studie recenti sopra i Nuraghi. Prato, 1886.

Arc 736.8F Çenturipe. (Libertini, Guido.) Catania, 1926.

Arc 1364.3 Centurska zakladna najdba folisov maksencija in tetrarhije. (Jeločnik, Aleksander.) Ljubljana, 1973.

Arc 397.8 A century of archaeological discoveries. (Michaelis, A.) London, 1908.

Arc 497.25 A century of excavation in Palestine. (Macalister, R.A.S.) London, 1925.

Arc 551.6.5 A century of excavation in the land of the Pharaohs. (Baikie, James.) London, 1924.

Arc 384.5 Ceramics and man. (Matson, Frederick R.) Chicago, 1965.

Arc 66.1.129 La céramique des cyclades. (Dugas, Charles.) Paris, 1925.

Arc 889.33 La céramique en terre sigillée de la ville belgo-romaine de Robelmont, campagnes 1968-1971. (Raepsuet, Georges.) Bruxelles, 1974.

Arc 66.1.208 La céramique géométrique de l'Argolide. (Courbin, Paul.) Paris, 1966. 2v.

Arc 66.1.195 La ceramique grecque de Marseilles. (Villard, Francois.) Paris, 1960.

Arc 1033.17.132 Cerbelli, D. Opuscoletti varii ovvero monografia di Mottafollone storia della sacra cinta. Napoli, 1857.

Arc 303.18.25 Cercetări arheologice ên Bucureşti. (Bucharest. Muzeul de Istorie a Orasului.) Bucureşti. 2,1965+

Arc 936.115.5 Cercetari privind istoria veche ARPR. Bucureşti, 1954.

Arc 1302.7 Cercle d'Études Numismatiques. Bulletin. Bruxelles. 1,1964+

Arc 1302.6 Cercle d'Études Numismatiques. Travaux. Bruxelles. 1,1964+

Arc 66.1.130 Les céréales dans l'antiquité grecque. (Jardé, A.) Paris, 1925.

Arc 1510.7 Cerexhe, M. Les monnaies de Charlemagne. Gand, 1887.

Arc 1033.17.151 Cerf. Notice sur la relique...Cathédrale de Reims. n.p., n.d.

Arc 1588.4.10 Cermák, K. Mince kralowstvi Českéko za panováné rodu Habsburskeho od voku 1526. n.p., 1891-1913. 3v.

Arc 600.110F Černý, Jaroslav. Répertoire onomastique de Deir et Médineh. Le Caire, 1949.

Arc 1033.12.144 Cerqueira Pinto, Antonio. Historia da prodigiosa imagem de Christo crucificado. Lisboa, 1737.

Arc 936.221.5 Čerškov, Emil. Municipium DD kod Sočanice. Priština, 1970.

Arc 936.221 Čerškov, Emil. Rimljani na kosovu i Metohiji. Beograd, 1969.

Arc 950.202.11 Certain aborginal remains of the northwestern Florida coast. pt.1-2. (Moore, C.B.) Philadelphia, 1901. 2v.

Arc 950.200.9 Certain aboriginal mounds. (Moore, C.B.) Philadelphia, 1898.

Arc 950.202.5 Certain aboriginal mounds of the Georgia coast. (Moore, C.B.) Philadelphia, 1897.

Arc 950.202.9 Certain aboriginal remains...Alabama River. (Moore, C.B.) Philadelphia, 1899.

Arc 950.202.15 Certain aboriginal remains...Florida coast. (Moore, C.B.) Philadelphia, 1903.

Arc 950.202.17 Certain aboriginal remains of the Black Warrior River. (Moore, C.B.) Philadelphia, 1905.

Arc 950.202.13 Certain antiquities of the Florida west coast. (Moore, C.B.) Philadelphia, 1900.

Arc 950.202.23 Certain mounds of Arkansas and Mississippi. (Moore, C.B.) Philadelphia, 1908.

Arc 967.3 Certain peculiar earthworks near Andover, Massachusetts. (Moorehead, W.K.) Andover, 1912.

Arc 950.202 Certain river mounds of Duval County, Florida. (Moore, C.B.) Philadelphia, 1895.

Arc 950.201A Certain sand mounds of the St. John's River. pt.1-2. (Moore, C.B.) Philadelphia, 1894.

Arc 1474.5 Cesano, Secondina L. Tipi monetali etruschi. Roma, 1926.

Htn Arc 1475.12F* I Cesari in oro. (Pedrusi, Paolo.) Parma, 1694-1727. 10v.

Arc 726.59.5 Ceschi, Carlo. Architettura dei templi magalitici di Malta. Roma, 1939.

Arc 1588.4.25 Česka drobna mince v doly predhus, a husitske, 1300-1471. (Castelin, K.O.) Praha, 1953.

Arc 1580.8 České denáry. (Fiala, E.) Praha, 1895-

Arc 1588.4.20F Česki a Moravské denary a brakteaty. (Turnwald, K.) Praha, 1949.

Arc 1588.4.62 Českobudějovická mincovina v letech 1569-1611. Vyd. 1. (Nemeškal, Lubomir.) Česke Budějovice, 1969.

Arc 936.195.5 Ceskoslovenska Academie Ved. Archeologichy Ustav. Nouvelles fouilles archéologiques en Tchécoslovaque. Prague, 1960.

Arc 383.79.12 Československá Adademie věd. Sekoe Jazyka a Literatury. Studie z antiky; Antonínu Salsčovi. Praha, 1955.

Arc 302.45.5 Československá Akademie Věd. Archeologický Ústav. Pobočka v Brně. Studie. Praha. 1,1972+

Arc 302.14 Československá Akademie Ved. Archeologický Ustav. Záchranné Oddělení. Bulletin. Praha. 2,1964+

Arc 1588.4.95 Československé mince 1918-1968. Vyd. 1. (Polivka, Eduard.) Hradec Králové, 1969.

Arc 537.2 Cesnola, L.P. Cyprus. London, 1877.

Arc 537.2.3A Cesnola, L.P. Cyprus. N.Y., 1878.

Arc 540.1.12 Cesnola, L.P. Extraits de l'histoire générale des hommes vivants. Genève, 1869.

Arc 540.1.5 Cesnola, L.P. Gaston L. Feuardent vs. L.P. Cesnola - testimony of the defendant. N.Y., 1884.

Arc 540.2 Cesnola, L.P. Salaminia. London, 1882.

Arc 540.1 Cesnola, L.P. Scoperta del tempio di Venere a Golgos. Turin, 1871.

Arc 1663.9 Cessac. Un trésor de monnaies des comtes de la Marche. v.1-2. Paris, 1882.

Arc 1077.13 Cesta a cordoni (Rippenzisten); Produktion-Funktion-Diffusion. v.1-2. (Stjernqvist, Berta.) Bonn, 1967.

Arc 936.28F Cetalea Sucerii. (Romstorfer, K.A.) București, 1913.

Arc 936.185.5 Cetatea Sarmizegetusa reconstituiă. (Antonescu, T.) Iasi, 1966.

Arc 1033.35.61 Ceva Grimaldi, F. Su la vera forma delle croce di N. Signore. Medina, n.d.

Arc 435.70.2F Ceylon. Archaeological Survey. Annual report, 1903. Preliminary proof. n.p., 1903.

Arc 435.70.3F Ceylon. Archaeological Survey. Annual report. Colombo. 1892-1912 3v.

Arc 435.70F Ceylon. Archaeological Survey. Annual report. Colombo. 1904-1947 6v.

Arc 435.70.5F Ceylon. Archaeological Survey. Memoirs. Colombo. 1-6,1924-1953 7v.

Arc 435.71F Ceylon. Archaeological Survey. Progress report. Colombo. 1-7

Arc 435.70.9F Pamphlet box. Ceylon. Archaeological Survey.

Arc 936.195.55 Cezavy u Bluciny ve svetle archeologickych vyskumů a nalezů. (Tinelka, Karel.) Brno, 1957.

Arc 387.2 Chabas, F. Études sur l'antiquité historique. Paris, 1873.

Arc 830.31 Chabouillet, A. Notice sur dea inscriptions...Bourbonne-les-Bains. Paris, 1881.

Arc 113.2.5 Chabouillet. Discours et compte rendu des lectures...section d'archéologie. Réunion annuelle des délégués de société savantes à la Sorbonne. Paris, 1878-81. 3v.

Arc 925.50.100 Chachkovs'kyi, L. Kniazhii galich. 2. vyd. Chikago, 1959.

Arc 1335.2 Chadbourne, S.H. Catalogue of a collection of coins and medals. Boston, 1867.

Arc 1163.3.45 Chaev, N.S. Russkaia paleografiia. Moskva, 1946.

Arc 1033.34 Les chaines de Saint Pierre. (Merracci P.) Rome, 1877.

Arc 785.80 Chair, sceptre and wreath. (Salomonson, Jan Willem.) Amsterdam, 1956.

Arc 1418.11 Chakrabortty, S.K. A study of ancient Indian numismatics. Calcutta, 1931.

Arc 442.5 Chalcolithic Chandoli. (Deo, Shantavam Bhalchandra.) Poona, 1965.

Arc 453.18 Chalcolithic Navdatoli; the excavations at Navdatoli, 1957-59. 1. ed. (Sankalia, Hasmukh Dhirajlal.) Poona, 1971.

Arc 513.32A The Chaleolithic and early Bronze Ages in the Near East and Anatolia. (Mellaart, James.) Beirut, 1966.

Arc 830.129 Chalieu, Alexis. Mémoires sur diverses antiquités du département de la Drôme. Valence, 1811.

Arc 1540.6A Chalmers, R. History of currency in the British colonies. London, n.d.

Arc 1335.155 Chalon, Renier. Collection de feu M. Renier Chalon. v.2. Bruxelles, 1889.

Arc 1500.51 Chalon, Rénier. Recherches sur les monnaies de Wallincourt en Cambrésis. Bruxelles, 1847.

Arc 1520.12 Chalon, Renier. Recherches sur les monnaies des Comtes de Hainout. Supplement. Bruxelles, 1848-54. 2v.

Arc 853.73 Die Chalten. (Hofmeister, Hans.) Frankfurt am Main, 1930.

Arc 435.2.42F Chalukyan architecture. (Cousens, Henry.) Calcutta, 1926.

Arc 435.2.21F Châlukyan architecture. (Rea, Alexander.) Madras, 1898.

Arc 1020.72.9 Chamard, F. L'hypogée des dunes à Poitiers. Paris, 1884.

Arc 1259.2 Chamard, François. Les bulles de plomb des lettres pontificales. Paris, 1883.

Arc 875.131 The chambered tombs of Scotland. (Henshall, Audrey Shore.) Edinburgh, 1963-72. 2v.

Arc 1675.93 Chamberlain, G.S. American medals and medalists. Annandale, Va., 1963.

Arc 861.63 Chambers, J. The stone age and Lake Lothing. Norwich, 1911.

Arc 66.1.177 Chamoux, F. Cyrène sous la monarchie des Battiades. Paris, 1953.

Arc 387.7 Champollion, J.F. Champollion inconnu. Paris, 1897.

Arc 552.1.2 Champollion, J.F. Lettres à M. le Duc de Blacas d'Aulps. Paris, 1824.

Arc 552.1 Champollion, J.F. Lettres écrites d'Egypte et de Nubie. Paris, 1833.

Arc 552.1.4 Champollion, J.F. Lettres écrites d'Égypte et de Nubie en 1828 et 1829. Paris, 1868.

Arc 545.2 Champollion, J.F. Monuments de l'Égypte et de la Nubie. Paris, 1835-45.

Arc 547.9 Champollion, J.F. Notice descriptive des monumens égyptiens du Musée Charles X. Paris, 1827.

Arc 590.6 Champollion, J.F. Notice sur le papyrus hiératique et les peintures du cercueil de Pétaménoph. Paris, 1827.

Arc 552.1.6 Champollion-Figeac, J.J. Les deux Champollion, leur vie. Grenoble, 1887.

Arc 820.210F Champollion-Figeac, Jacques J. Antiquités de Grenoble. Grenoble, 1807.

Arc 387.7 Champollion inconnu. (Champollion, J.F.) Paris, 1897.

Arc 447.5 Chand, Amar. Hastināpura. Banoras, 1952.

Arc 1500.39 Changarnier, A. Monnaies des Boïens de la Germanie. Dijon, 1914.

Arc 936.140.30 Changova, Iordanka. Srednovekovnoto selishte nad trakiiskiia grad Sevtopolis. Sofiia, 1972.

Arc 1237.10 Changwat seals. (Thailand. Ministry of Interior.) Bangkok, 1968.

Arc 97.6 Chantiers d'études médiévales. Strasbourg. 2,1966+

Arc 530.16F Chantre, E. Mission en Cappadoce. Paris, 1898.

Arc 820.2 Chantre, Ernest. Études paléoethnologiques dans le bassin du Rhône. Âge du bronze. Paris, 1875-76. 4v.

Arc 1033.17.152 Chapelle dans la Cathédrale de Reims. (Paris, L.) Epernay, 1885.

Arc 1020.54 La Chapelle des Comtes de Flandre à Courtrai. (Van de Putte, F.) Bruges, 1875.

Arc 1333.10 Chapman, H. Catalogue of collections of coins of M.A. Trickney. Philadelphia, 1907.

Arc 1335.82F Chapman, H. Catalogue of J.S. Jenks collection of coins. Philadelphia, 1921.

Arc 66.1.99 Chapot, V. La frontière de l'Euphrate de Pompée à la Conquête Arabe. Paris, 1907.

Arc 66.1.137 Chapouthier, F. Les dioscures au service d'une déesse. Paris, 1935.

Arc 673.12F Chapouthier, F. Exploration archéologique de Délos. Paris, 1935.

Arc 968.11 Chapters in Nebraska archaeology. (Bell, Earl Hoyt.) Lincoln, Nebraska, 1936.

Arc 712.37 Ta charagmata tou Parthenōuos. (Orlandos, Anastasios K.) Athēnai, 1973.

Arc 1663.31 Charakterkopfe der Weltgeschichte. (Lange, Kurt.) München, 1949.

Arc 672.1.63 Charbonneaux, J. L'art égéen. Paris, 1929.

Arc 830.62 La Charente-Inferieure avant l'histoire. (Musset, Georges.) La Rochelle, 1885.

Arc 1033.119 Charles, archbishop of Alger. Sainte Anne de Jérusalem et Sainte Anne d'Auray. Alger, 1879.

Htn Arc 865.6* Charleton, W. Chorea gigantum, or...Stone-Heng restored to the Danes. London, 1663.

Arc 925.170.5 Charnoluskii, Vladimir V. Legenda ob olene-chelovcke. Moskva, 1965.

Arc 1033.17.424 Charpentier, L.F. Nouveau histoire de l'image miraculeux de Notre-Dame-de-Liesse. Soissons, 1888.

Arc 1448.1 Charrier, Louis. Description des monnaies de la Numidie et de la Maurétanie. Macon, 1912.

Arc 442.2 Chārsada. (Wheeler, Robert.) London, 1962.

Arc 66.1.19 Chartes de terre sainte. (Delaborde, H.F.) Paris, 1880.

Arc 830.18.27 Charvet, G. Les voies romaines chez les Volkes-Arécomiques. Alais, 1874.

Arc 1335.19 Charvet, Jules. Collection Charvet. Paris, 1883.

Arc 387.16.5 Pamphlet box. Chase, G.H. Collected papers.

Arc 658.3.2 Chase, T. Dr. Schliemann and the archaeological value of his discoveries. Worcester, 1891.

Arc 642.1 Chase, T. Hellas. Cambridge, 1863.

Arc 1348.44 The Chase architrave. (Chase National Bank, N.Y.) N.Y., 19- .

Arc 1348.44 Chase National Bank, N.Y. The Chase architrave. N.Y., 19-

Arc 1153.29.2 Chassant, A. Dictionnaire des abréviations latines et françaises. 2. éd. Paris, 1862.

Arc 1153.29.3 Chassant, A. Dictionnaire des abréviations latines et françaises. 3. éd. Paris, 1866.

Arc 1153.29.4 Chassant, A. Dictionnaire des abréviations latines et françaises. 4. éd. Paris, 1876.

Arc 1153.29.5 Chassant, A. Dictionnaire des abréviations latines et françaises. 5. éd. Paris, 1884.

Arc 1209.1 Chassant, A.A.L. Dictionnaire de sigillographie pratique. Paris, 1860.

Arc 1138.5.4 Chassant, Alphonse. Paléographie des chartes. 4. éd. Paris, 1854.

Arc 1138.5.3 Chassant, Alphonse. Paléographie des chartes. 5. éd. Paris, 1862.

Arc 1138.5 Chassant, Alphonse. Paléographie des chartes. 7. éd. Paris, 1876.

Arc 1138.5.2 Chassant, Alphonse. Paléographie des chartes. 8. éd. Paris, 1885.

Arc 66.1.14 Chatelain, E. Manuscrits des poesies de S. Paulin de Nole. Paris, 1880.

Arc 830.13.5 Chatelain, L. Bibliothéque d'école des hautes études. Monuments romains d'Orange. Paris, 1908.

Arc 66.1.160 Chatelain, Louis. Le Maroc des romains. Paris, 1944. 2v.

Arc 1348.27 Chats on old coins. (Burgess, F.W.) London, 1913.

Arc 1418.24 Chattopadhyay, Bhaskar. The age of the Kushānas; a numismatic study. 1. ed. Calcutta, 1967.

Arc 432.30 Chattopadhyay, Kshitis Prasad. Ancient Indian culture contacts and migration. Calcutta, 1965.

Arc 672.1.29.5 Chatzidakēs, I. Istoria tou Krētikou Monseiou kai tōn archaiologikōn ereynōn en Krēte. Athēnai, 1931.

Arc 1583.22 Chaudoir, S. Aperçu sur les monnaies russes et sur les monnaies étrangères. v.1-3. St. Petersbourg, 1836. 2v.

Arc 1077.2.45 Chauncey Ross, M. La croix Gaillard de la Dionnerie au Musée metropolitan. Poitiers, 1934.

Author and Title Listing

Arc 421.28 Chaung, K. The archaeology of ancient China. New Haven, 1963.
Arc 1588.4.15 Chaura, K. Die Wahrheit übes den St. Wenzel-Denar. Praha, 1929.
Htn Arc 750.221F* Chausse, M.A. de la. Le grand cabinet romain. Amsterdam, 1706.
Arc 830.103.5 Chauvet, J.M. Notice...des antiquités de Vichy-les-Bains. Cusset, 1851.
Arc 420.5F Chavannes, E. Mission archéologique dans la Chine septentrionale. v.1-2; planches, pt.3. Paris, 1909-15. 4v.
Arc 1020.61 Chavannes, E. Le trésor de l'église cathédrale de Lausanne. Lausanne, 1873.
Arc 1583.8 Chdel'n. velikokn. idsarsk. den'gi drevn. Rusi. (Gutten'-Chalskii, F.K.) Sankt Peterburg, 1875.
Arc 400.27 Che cos'è l'archeologia. (Pallottino, Massimo.) Firenze, 1963.
Arc 936.165.55 Chebotarenko, Georgii T. Kal'fa-gorodishche vos'mogo-desiatego v.v. na Dnestre. Kishinev, 1973.
Arc 1588.4.100 Chebské mince z 12. a 13. století. (Hásková, Jarmila.) Cheb, 1972.
Arc 402.3 Chefs-d'oeuvre de l'art antique. 1st ser., 1-3; 2d ser., 1-4. (Robiou, F.) Paris, 1867. 7v.
Arc 562.1.3 Chèlu, Alfred Jacques. Mariette Pacha. Le Caire, 1911.
Arc 830.18.5 Les chemins gaulois et romains. 2e éd. (Lievre, A.F.) Niort, 1893.
Arc 853.8 Chemische Untersuchung an Vorgeschichts Bronzen Schleswig-Holsteins. (Kröhnke, O.) Kiel, 1897.
Arc 1033.17.181 Chemises de la Vierge. (Mély, F. de.) Chartres, n.d.
Arc 1190.50 Cheney, C. English bishops' chanceries. Manchester, 1950.
Arc 421.22 Chêng, Tê-k'un. Archaeology in China. v.1-3. Cambridge, Eng., 1959-
Arc 1010.20 Chêng, Tê-k'un. Archaeology in Sarawak. Cambridge, 1969.
Arc 600.6.9 Chenillon, A. Terres mortes. Paris, 1897.
Arc 584.5F The cheops boats. (Egypt. Antiquities Department.) Cairo, 1960-
Arc 1027.8.13 Chéramy, H. Saint-Sébastien hors les murs. Paris, 1925.
Arc 1163.4 Cherbonneau, A. Exercises pour la lecture des manuscrits arabes. Paris, 1853.
Arc 608.6.24 Cherchel. (Gsell, Stéphane.) Alger, 1952.
Arc 1163.3.55 Cherepnin, L.V. Russkaia paleografiia. Moskva, 1956.
Arc 925.9.100 Cherez khrebty vekov. (Vinogradov, Vitalii B.) Grozny, 1970.
Arc 925.13.155 Chernenko, Evgenii V. Skifskii dospekh. Kiev, 1968.
Arc 925.349 Chernetsov, Valerii Nikolaevich. Prehistory of western Siberia. Montreal, 1974.
Arc 925.16.20 Chernikov, Sergei. Zagadka zolotogo kurgana. Moskva, 1965.
Arc 925.8 Chernomorek. Gotyieledy dolgago ikh prebyv. (Brun.) Sankt Petersburg, 1874. 2 pam.
Arc 612.57 Chernych, Evgenii N. Istoriia drevneishei metallurgii Vostochnoi Evropy. Moskva, 1966.
Arc 1087.5 Chernykh, Evgenii N. Metall-chelovsk-vremia. Moskva, 1972.
Arc 925.50.60 Chernysh, K.K. Rannotrypil's'ke poselennia lenkivtsi seredn'omu Dnistri. Kyïv, 1959.
Arc 1583.5 Chertkov, A. Opisanie drevnikh Russkik' monet'. Moskva, 1834.
Arc 1583.5.2 Chertkov, A. Pribavlenie. Moskva, 1837-42. 3v.
Arc 757.10 Chester, England. Museum. An account of the Roman antiquities. 2. ed. London, 1907.
Arc 1535.207F Chetwynd, George. A catalogue of provincial copper coins, tokens, tickets, medals issued in Great Britain, Ireland and the colonies...18th century. London, 1834.
Arc 830.160.5 Chevalier, Alexandre. Altonum, fille d'Aeria, origines gallo-romaines de Montbrison. Valence, 1968.
Arc 830.160.10 Chevalier, Alexandre. Le site d'Aeria. Valence, 1968.
Arc 380.207 Chevalier, N. Recherche curieuse d'antiquité. Utrecht, n.d.
Arc 785.61 Chevalier, N. Remarques sur la pièce antique de bronze. Amsterdam, 1694.
Arc 830.78.20PF Chevalier, Pierre. Nantes et la Loire-Inférieure. Nantes, 1850.
Arc 1500.54 Chevallier, Guy. Les trésors de monnaies romaines découverts dans le département du Loiret. Gien, 1958.
Arc 383.70 Chevallier, Raymond. Mélanges d'archéologie et d'histoire. Paris, 1966. 3v.
Arc 394.2 Cheynier, A. Jovannet, grand-père de la préhistoire. Brive, 1936.
Arc 600.243 Chez les derniers adorateurs du Trismegiste. (Cabra, Sami.) Cairo, 1971.
Arc 1190.77 Chhabra, Bahadur C. Diplomatic of Sanskrit copper-plate grants. Delhi? 1961?
Arc 432.25 Chhabra, Bahadur Chand. Expansion of Indo-Aryan culture during Pallava rule as evidenced by inscriptions. Delhi, 1965.
Arc 1033.5.5 Le chiavi di S. Pietro. (Luzi, G.C.) Roma, 1884.
Arc 505.61.10F Chicago. Oriental Institute. Megiddo Expedition. Megiddo II. Chicago, 1948. 2v.
Arc 32.5.3 Chicago. University. Oriental Institute. Bulletin. Chicago.
Arc 32.5 Chicago. University. Oriental Institute. Communications. Chicago. 2-18 5v.
Arc 861.210 Chichester excavations. (Down, Alec.) Chichester, 1971- 2v.
Arc 936.140.25 Chichikova, Mariia. Sevtopolis. Sofiia, 1970.
Arc 1018.39 Chiefletius, J.J. De linteis sepulchralibus. Antverpiae, 1688. 4 pam.
Arc 726.1 Chienci, G. Antichi monumenti della Pianosa. Reggio, 1875.
Arc 1020.24 Chiesa...Pietro e Paolo...Cancelli. (Pulignani, M.F.) Foligno, 1882.
Arc 1025.70 La chiesa delle catacombe. (Cecchelli, C.) Roma, 1943.
Arc 1020.9.20 La chiesa di S. Onofrio. (Caterbi, G.) Roma, 1858.
Arc 1020.6.12 La chiesa di S. Simone profeta. (Cappelletti, G.) Venezia, 1860.
Arc 1020.9.40 La chiesa di Santa Maria di Loreto IV. Sacre notizio V. (Gianuizzi, P.) Roma, 1884.
Arc 1020.9.30 La chiesa di Santa Marta al Vaticano. (Bossi, G.) Roma, 1883.
Arc 1020.9.60 Le chiese di Roma...nel secolo XIX. (Iozzi, Oliviero.) Roma, 1900. 4 pam.
Arc 1020.9.163 Le chiese di Roma. (Tani, A.D.) Torino, 1922.
Arc 1033.12.30 Chifflet, J.J. De linteis sepulchralibus Cristi servatoris crisis historica. Antverpiae, 1624.
Htn Arc 1033.17.247* Chifflet, J.J. De sacris inscriptionibus, quibus tabella D. Viginis Cameracensis. Antverp, 1749.

Arc 1190.80.5 Les chiffres siyâk et la comptabilitié persane. (Irānshahr Husayn, Kazimz ādah.) Paris, 1915.
Arc 1033.17.88 Chigi, A. La città diletta di Maria...miracolosa immagine di Nostra Donna. Roma, 1716.
Arc 1528.7 Chijs, P.O. van der. De munten. Haarlem, 1851-66. 9v.
Arc 925.160 Chilashvili, L.A. Gorod Rustavi. Tbilisi, 1958.
Arc 875.14.7 Childe, V.G. Ancient dwellings at Skara Brae. Edinburgh, 1933.
Arc 858.50A Childe, V.G. Prehistoric communities of the British Isles. London, 1940.
Arc 858.50.5 Childe, V.G. Prehistoric communities of the British Isles. 2. ed. London, 1947.
Arc 875.14.15 Childe, V.G. The prehistory of Scotland. London, 1935.
Arc 875.14.20 Childe, V.G. Scotland before the Scots. London, 1946.
Arc 875.14.10 Childe, V.G. Skara Brae. London, 1931.
Arc 612.19 Childe, Vere G. The Danube in prehistory. Oxford, 1929.
Arc 612.19.5 Childe, Vere G. The prehistory of European society. Harmondsworth, 1958.
Arc 387.9 Childe, Vere Gordon. Bronze age. Cambridge, Eng., 1930.
Arc 390.11 Childe, Vere Gordon. Henri Frankfort, 1897-1954. London, 1955?
Arc 387.9.7.1 Childe, Vere Gordon. Piecing together the past. N.Y., 1969.
Arc 387.9.5A Childe, Vere Gordon. Progress and archaeology. London, 1944.
Arc 421.10.15 Children of the yellow earth. (Andersson, J.) London, 1934.
Arc 543.155 Chil'khudzhra. (Pulatov, Uktam P.) Dushanbe, 1975.
Htn Arc 1093.1* Chimentelli, V. Marmor pisanum. Bononiae, 1666.
Arc 419.1 Pamphlet box. China. Miscellaneous pamphlets.
Arc 421.23 China before the Han dynasty. (Watson, William.) London, 1961.
Arc 1084.17F Chinese jades in the S.C. Nott collection. (Nott, S.C.) St. Augustine, 1942.
Arc 1411.11 The Chinese numismatic riddle. (Higgins, F.C.) N.Y., 1910.
Arc 543.4.20F Die chinesischen Handschriften..Sven Hedins in Lou-lan. (Conrady, A.) Stockholm, 1920.
Arc 830.143 Chinon et ses monuments. 3. éd. (Cougny, G. de.) Chinon, 1889.
Arc 726.336 Chiostri, Frido. Le tombe a Tholos di Quinto nel comune di Sesto Fiorentino. n.p., 1969.
Arc 875.37.5 Chips from old stones. (Maclagan, Christian.) Edinburgh, 1881.
Arc 642.7F Chisholm, H.J. Hellas. N.Y., 1943.
Arc 1584.28 Chizhov, Sergei I. Azbabskii klad'. Moskva, 1911. 2 pam.
Arc 925.330 Chlenova, Natalia L. Proiskhozhdenie i ranniaia istoriia plemen Tagarskoi kul'tury. Moskva, 1967.
Arc 845.1 Chlingesnsperg-Berg, M. von. Das Graeberfeld von Reichenhall. Reichenhall, 1890.
Arc 845.1.5 Chlingesnsperg-Berg, M. von. Die Römischen Brandgräber. Braunsch, 1896.
Arc 936.14.50 Chmielewski, W. Civilisation de Jerzmanowice. Wrocław, 1961.
Arc 936.14.400 Chmielowska, Aldona. Grebienie starozytne i sredniowieczne z ziem polskich. Łódź, 1971.
Arc 936.14.245 Chmtelewski, Waldemar. Materiały do prahistorii plejstocenu i wczesnego holocenu Polski. Wrocław, 1967.
Arc 865.13 Choir Gaur...Orrery of Druids...Stonehenge. 2. ed. (Smith, John.) Salisbury, 1771. 2 pam.
Arc 865.13.2 Choir Gaur...Orrery of Druids...Stonehenge. 2. ed. (Smith, John.) Salisbury, 1771.
Arc 865.18 Choir Gaure, vulgarly called Stonehenge. (Wood, John.) Oxford, 1747.
Arc 712.4 Choisy, A. Note sur la courbure dissymétrique des degrés qui limitent au couchant la plate-forme du Parthénon. Paris, 1865.
Arc 1465.1 Choix de monnaies grecques. 2. ed. (Imhoof-Blumer, Friedrich.) Paris, 1883.
Arc 600.3 Choix de monuments et de dessins...Sérapéum de Memphis. (Mariette, A.) Paris, 1856.
Arc 1345.1.6 Choix histoires des médailles des papes. Paris, 1858.
Htn Arc 865.6* Chorea gigantum, or...Stone-Heng restored to the Danes. (Charleton, W.) London, 1663.
Arc 830.310 Le chrismale de Mortain. (Blouet, L.) Coutances, 1955.
Arc 1510.90 Christ, Karl. Antike Münzfunde Südwestdeutschlands. pt.1-5. Heidelberg, 1960.
Arc 1357.5 Christ, Karl. Antike Numismatik. Darmstadt, 1967.
Arc 1015F Pamphlet box. Christian. Folios. Catacombs.
Arc 861.174 Christian antiquities of Camborne. (Thomas, Charles.) St. Austell, Cornwall, 1967.
Arc 1020.9.01 Pamphlet vol. Christian archaeology of Rome.
Arc 1027.01 Pamphlet box. Christian catacombs.
Arc 1027 Pamphlet box. Christian catacombs.
Arc 1025.01 Pamphlet box. Christian catacombs.
Arc 505.45.25 Christian church at Dura-Europas. New Haven, 1934.
Arc 1020.10.19 A Christian corner in Roman Forum. Rome, 1901.
Arc 785.13.42 A Christian corner in the Roman Forum. Rome, 1901.
Arc 1030.4.30 Christian epigraphy. (Marucchi, O.) Cambridge, 1912.
Arc 1030.17 Christian epitaphs. (McCaul, J.) Toronto, 1869.
Arc 1030.59 Christian inscriptions. (Nunn, H.P.V.) N.Y., 1952.
Arc 1020.10.37 Christian Rome. (Cruickshank, J.W.) London, 1906.
Arc 1020.10.9 Christian Rome. (La Gournerie, E. de.) London, 1898. 2v.
Arc 1020.10.38 Christian Rome. 2. ed. (Cruickshank, J.W.) London, 1911.
Arc 67.3 Christianekē Archaiologikē Hetaireia, Athens. Katastatikon Psēphisthen yvo tēs Genikēs synelenseus. Athēnai. 1903
Arc 67.3.5 Christianekē Archaiologikē Hetaireia, Athens. Praktika. Athēnai. 1,1892+ 6v.
Arc 1020.22 Christianichē archaiologia. (Lampake, G.) Athēnai, 1889.
Arc 689.3.20F Ai Christianikai Thebai tēs Thessalias kai at palaiochristianikai basilikai tēs Ellados. (Soteriou, G.A.) Athēnai, 1931.
Arc 1025.37 Christianikē gechnē...katakombai. (Lampake, G.) Athēnai, 1900.
Arc 875.11.7 Christison, D. Account of the excavation of the Roman station at Ardoch. Edinburgh, 1898.
Arc 875.11 Christison, D. Early fortifications in Scotland. London, 1898.
Arc 853.350 Christlein, Rainer. Das alamannische Gräberfeld von Dirlewang bei Minchelheim. Kallmünz, 1971.
Arc 853.282 Christlein, Rainer. Das alamannische Reihengräberfeld von Marktoberdorf im Allgäu. Kallmünz, 1966.
Arc 1016.242 Der Christliche Altar. (Heideloff, C.) Nürnberg, 1838.
Arc 1018.23 Christliche Antike. (Sybel, L. von.) Marburg, 1906. 2v.

Author and Title Listing

	Arc 1027.22.17	Das Christliche Fischsymbol. Freiburg, 1905.
	Arc 1018.32.7	Die christliche Kunst in ihren frühesten Anfängen. (Kraus, F.X.) Leipzig, 1872.
	Arc 1020.45	Christliche Römerfunde in Carnuntum. (Deirnel, T.) Wien, 1911.
	Arc 1020.48	Die christlichen Altertümer der Dobrogia. (Nitzhammer, R.) Bukarest, 1906.
	Arc 608.6.55	Christople, M. Le tombeau de la Chrétienne. Paris, 1951.
	Arc 936.25	Chronik der Archäologischenfund Siebenbürgens. (Gooss, Carl.) Hermanstadt, 1876.
	Arc 520.36	Chronik der Ausgrabung von Pergamon. (Schulte, Eduard.) Dortmund, 1963.
	Arc 402.2	Chroniques d'Orient. (Reinach, S.) Paris, 1891. 2v.
	Arc 1588.1.66	Chronologia naptywu pieniądza vzymskiegs na ziemie Matspoblei. Wyd. 1. (Kunisz, A.) Wrocław, 1969.
	Arc 1470.30	A chronological arrangement of the coins of Chios. pt.1-5. (Mavrogordato, J.) London, 1915-18.
	Arc 1027.24.9	Chronologie des peintures des catacombes de Naples. (Lefort, L.) Rome, 1883.
	Arc 1025.32	Chronologie des peintures des catacombes romaines. (Lefort, Louis.) Paris, 1881.
	Arc 510.212	Chronologie du Royaume de Bosphore. (Sabatier, J.) St. Petersbourg, 1849.
	Arc 700.52	Chronologikē katataxis. (Kallipolites, B.G.) Athēnai, 1958.
	Arc 700.19.5	The chronology of Greek walls. Thesis. (Scranton, R.L.) Chicago, 1941.
	Arc 773.6F	Chronology of the building operations in Rome from the death of Caesar. (Shipley, F.W.) n.p., 1931.
	Arc 936.195.37F	Chropovský, Bohuslav. Pohrebiská zo staršej doby bronzovej na Slovensku. Bratislava, 1960.
	Arc 936.195.37.5	Chropovský, Bohuslav. Slovensko na úsvite dejím. 1. vyd. Bratislava, 1970.
	Arc 385.9.5	Chto tahoe arkheologiia. Izd. 3. (Amal'rikh, Aleksei S.) Moskva, 1966.
	Arc 600.165	Chubb, Mary. Nefertiti lived here. N.Y., 1954.
	Arc 1033.12.24	Chubinashvili, G.N. Siriiskaia chasha v Ushgule. n.p., 1941.
	Arc 530.97	Chubinishvili, T.N. Drevneiskie arkheologicheskie...Mtskheta. Tbilisi, 1957.
	Arc 925.9.105	Chubinishvili, Taniel. K drevnei istorii Iuzhnogo Kavkaza. Tbilisi, 1971.
	Arc 861.73	Chudleigh, J. Devonshire antiquities. 2. ed. Exeter, 1893.
	Arc 936.14.490	Chudziakowa, Jadwiga. Kultura łużycka na terenie międzyrzecza Wisły, Drwęcy i Osy. wyd. 1. Warszawa, 1974.
	Arc 936.14.525	Chudziakowa, Jadwiga. Źródła archeologiczne zterenu zamku krzyżackiego w Towniu. 1. wyd. Warszawa, 1974.
	Arc 485.4F	Churasaniche Baudenkmäler. (Diez, Ernst.) Berlin, 1918.
Htn	Arc 880.14*	Church and shrine of St. Manchan. (Graves, James.) Dublin, 1875.
	Arc 1076.3.17	Church bells. (Walters, Henry Beauchamp.) London, 1908.
	Arc 1076.3.70	The church bells of Buckinghamshire. (Cocks, A.H.) London, 1897.
	Arc 1076.3.18	Church bells of England. (Walters, Henry Beauchamp.) London, 1912.
	Arc 1076.3.79F	The church bells of Gloucestershire. (Ellacombe, H.T.) Exeter, 1881.
	Arc 1076.3.13.5	The church bells of Kent. (Stahlschmidt, J.C.L.) London, 1887.
	Arc 1076.3.53	The church bells of Norfolk. (L'Estrange, John.) Norwich, 1874.
	Arc 1076.3.65	The church bells of Rutland. (North, Thomas.) Leicester, 1880.
	Arc 1076.3.18.15	The church bells of Shropshire. (Walter, Henry Beauchamp.) Oswestry, 1915.
	Arc 1076.3.78	The church bells of Somerset. (Ellacombe, H.T.) Exeter, 1875.
	Arc 1076.3.55	The church bells of Suffolk. (Raven, John J.) London, 1890.
	Arc 1076.3.60	The church bells of Sussex. (Tyssen, A.D.) Lewes, 1915.
	Arc 1076.3.67F	The church bells of the county of Stafford. (Lyman, Charles.) London, 1889.
	Arc 1076.3.75	The church bells of Warwickshire. (Tilley, H.T.) Birmingham, 1910.
	Arc 1076.3.18.10	Church bells of Wiltshire. (Walters, Henry Beauchamp.) Devizes, 1927-29.
	Arc 1025.10	Church in the catacombs. (Maitland, C.) London, 1847.
	Arc 606.2	Churches in lower Nubia. (Mileham, G.S.) Philadelphia, 1910.
	Arc 1033.17.302	Ciabilli, G. Notizie risguardanti lo stato antico e moderno del sacro eratorio....miracolosa immagine di Maria. Firenze, 1802.
	Arc 1349.55	Ciampi, Ignazio. Benedetto Pistrucci. n.p., n.d.
	Arc 1033.35.101	Ciampini, G.G. De cruce stationale investigatio historica. Roma, 1737.
	Arc 1033.72	Ciampini, J. Explicatio 2 sarcophagorum...baptismatis. Roma, 1597.
	Arc 930.202	Ciampinus, Joan. De sacris aêdificiis a Constantino Magno constr. Romae, 1693.
	Arc 736.24	Ciancio, Salvatore. Leontinoi: anni di ricerche archeologiche. Lentini, 1965.
	Arc 1498.10	Ciani, Louis. Catalogue de monnaies françaises. pt.1-3. Paris, 1927-29.
	Arc 1033.17.321	Ciappolini, D. Divoto compendio della storia...s. immagine di Maria...Scutari. Napoli, 1810.
	Arc 750.1.5	Cichorius, C. Die Reliefs der Trajanssäule. v.1,2, plates. v.2,3, text. Berlin, 1896-1900. 4v.
	Arc 1488.27	Ciferra, Raffaello. Repertorio alfabetico di numismatica medioevale e moderna. Pavia, 1963. 2v.
	Arc 1330.35	Ciferri, Raffaello. Saggio di bibliografia numismata medioevale italiana. Pavia, 1961.
	Arc 936.195.245	Čilinská, Zlata. Frühmittelalterliches Gräberfeld in Želovce. Bratislava, 1973.
	Arc 936.195.215	Čilinská, Zlata. Slawisch-awarisches Gräberfeld in Nové Zámky. Bratislava, 1966.
	Arc 1033.12.70	Cimatti, E. Cenni storici intorno al Sangue Mirae...Ferrara. Ferrara, 1857.
	Arc 547.44	I cimeli egizi del Museo. (Botti, Giuseppe.) Firenze, 1964.
	Arc 830.107	Le cimetière barbare de Lezéville. (Salin, Édouard.) Nancy, 1922.
	Arc 1027.19.2	Cimetière de Saint Calixte. 3e éd. (Nortet.) Rome, 1888.
	Arc 1027.19.3	Cimetière de Saint Calixte. 3e éd. (Nortet.) Rome, 1899.
	Arc 1027.19.5	Cimetière de Saint Calixte. 3e éd. (Nortet.) Rome, 1900.
	Arc 915.3	Le cimetiere Gallo-Helvète de Vevey. (Naef, A.) n.p., 1903.
	Arc 830.123	Le cimetière gallo-romain de Strasbourg. (Straub, A.) Strasbourg, 1881.
	Arc 889.28	Le cimetière merovingien de Cuesmes. (Leblois, C.) Cuesmes, 1960.
	Arc 1027.35	Il cimiterio di S. Agnese sulla via nomentana. (Armellini, M.) Roma, 1880.
	Arc 1027.74	Il cimitero d'Aproniano di anche della S. Eugenia. (Bartolini, D.) Roma, 1840.
	Arc 1027.18	Cimitero degli antichi ebrei. (Garruci, R.) Roma, 1862.
	Arc 1027.41.3F	Il cimitero di Commodilla. (Bagatti, B.) Città del Vaticano, 1936.
	Arc 1027.41	Il cimitero di Commodilla. (Marucchi, O.) Roma, 1904.
	Arc 1027.71	Il cimitero di S. Ippolito presso la via Tiburtina. (Rossi, G.B. de.) Roma, 1882.
	Arc 1027.20	Il cimitero di Zotico. Dec miglio...Labicana. (Stevenson, E.) Modena, 1876.
X Cg	Arc 1027.15	Il cimitero e la Basilica di San Valentino. (Marucchi, O.) Roma, 1890.
	Arc 1033.173	Il cimitero "In clivum cucumeris". (Albarellio, G.) Aquila, 1909.
	Arc 1485.4	Cinagli, Angelo. Le monete de' papi. Fermo, 1848.
	Arc 609.2.7F	Cinq années de recherches archéologiques en Ethiopie. (Azaïs, R.P.) Paris, 1931. 2v.
	Arc 1254.9	Cinq sceaux de l'époque byzantine. (Schlumberger, G.) Paris, 1883.
	Arc 543.5.16	Le cinquantenaire de l'École française d'Extrême-Orient. (Malleret, L.) Paris, 1953.
	Arc 3.1.25	Cinquième Congrès international d'archéologie, Alger, 14-16 avril 1930. (Congrès International d'Archéologie Classique, 5th, Algiers, 1930.) Alger, 1933.
	Arc 608.2.55	Cintas, Pierre. Amulettes puniques. Tunis, 1946.
	Arc 608.1.50	Cintas, Pierre. Éléments d'étude pour une protohistoire de la Tunisie. Paris, 1961.
	Arc 1030.27	Ciofi, A. Lectio inscriptionum...sulpicii maximi. Roma, 1872.
	Arc 1020.58	Cionacci, T. Relazione delle Sante Relique...della città di Firenze. Bologna, 1685.
	Arc 1433.15	Cipelli, Luigi. Di una moneta Turca coniata nella zecca di Parma. Parma, 1868.
	Arc 1033.12.59	Ciprian, E.S. Diss. eccl. pentas. De sudore Christi. Jenae, n.d.
	Arc 810.62	Ciprotti, Pio. Conoscere Pompei. Roma, 1959.
	Arc 1490.98.15	Cirami, Giacomo. La monetazione greca della Sicilia antica. Bologna, 1959. 2v.
	Arc 870.9.10	The circle and the cross. (Allcroft, A.H.) London, 1927-30. 2v.
	Arc 1470.88	La circolazione della moneta ateniese in Sicilia e in Magna Grecia. (Centro Internazionale di Studi Numismatici.) Roma, 1969.
	Arc 608.17.13	Cirene. (Wilamowitz-Moellendorff, U.) Bergamo, 1930.
	Arc 642.5	Ciriacus, Pizzicolli. Itinerarium. Florentiae, 1742.
	Arc 726.10.2	Cista prenestina. (Brunn, H.) Roma, 1864.
	Arc 505.120	The citadel of Beth-Zur. (Presbyterian Theological Seminary, Chicago, Illinois.) Philadelphia, 1933.
	Arc 843.22	Citania. (Hübner, E.) Porto, 1879.
	Arc 843.212	A citânia de briteiros através dos séculos. (Sousa Gomes, A.) Lisboa, 1967.
	Arc 810.28	La cité antique de Pompéi. (Monod, Jules.) Paris, 1911.
	Arc 505.25	La cité de David. Plans and atlas. (Weill, Raymond.) Paris, 1920. 2v.
	Arc 936.1.7	La cité pontique de Dionysopolis. (Tafrali, O.) Paris, 1927.
	Arc 608.64	Cités anciennes de Mauritanie. (Meanié, Djinn.) Paris, 1961.
	Arc 743.1.9	The cities and cemeteries of Etruria. (Dennis, G.) London, 19- . 2v.
	Arc 743.1	The cities and cemeteries of Etruria. (Dennis, G.) London, 1848. 2v.
	Arc 743.1.2	The cities and cemeteries of Etruria. (Dennis, G.) London, 1878. 2v.
	Arc 743.1.5	The cities and cemeteries of Etruria. (Dennis, G.) London, 1906. 2v.
	Arc 743.1.3	The cities and cemeteries of Etruria. 3. ed. (Dennis, G.) London, 1883. 2v.
	Arc 412.1.10	Cities in the sea. 1. ed. (Flemming, Nicholas C.) Garden City, N.Y., 1971.
	Arc 505.129	Cities of the desert. (Negev, Avraham.) Tel-Aviv, 1966.
	Arc 793.22	Cities of Vesuvius: Pompeii and Herculaneum. (Grant, Michael.) London, 1971.
	Arc 1033.17.36	La città di refugio panegirico...greca imagine di Maria da Constantinopoli. (Bambacari, C.) Forli, 1678.
	Arc 750.200	La città di Roma. (Magnan, D.) Roma, 1779. 2v.
	Arc 1033.17.88	La città diletta di Maria...miracolosa immagine di Nostra Donna. (Chigi, A.) Roma, 1716.
	Arc 720.217	La città d'Umbria. (Pallastrelli, B.) Piacenza, 1864.
	Arc 726.175	La città medioevale di Centocelle. (Toti, Odoardo.) Allumicre, 1958.
	Arc 687.2	La città sacra (Lindo). (Montesanto, M.) Roma, 1930.
	Arc 501.6.3	The city and the land. Seven lectures. London, 1894.
	Arc 585.30F	The city of Akhenaten. v.1-3. London, 1923-33. 4v.
	Arc 861.150	The city of Durovernum. (Frere, Sheppard.) Canterbury, 1957.
	Arc 861.153	The city of Durovernum. (Frere, Sheppard.) Canterbury, 1962.
	Arc 588.64F	City of shepherd kings. (Petrie, W.M.F.) London, 1952.
	Arc 785.29.10	The city wall of imperial Rome. (Richmond, Ian A.) Oxford, 1930.
	Arc 936.14.50	Civilisation de Jerzmanowice. (Chmielewski, W.) Wrocław, 1961.
	Arc 448.1.35	La civilisation de l'Indus et ses énigmes. (Casal, Jean Marie.) Paris, 1969.
	Arc 452.1.15	La civilisation de Mohen-Jo-Daro. Thèse. (Puri, K.N.) Paris? 1938.
	Arc 838.11	La civilisation énéolithique dans la péninsule ibérique. (Åberg, Nils.) Uppsala, 1921.
	Arc 823.3	Civilisation et art des Romains...Gaule-Belgique. (Fleury, E.) Paris, 1860-1861.
	Arc 830.332	La civilisation néolithique. (Nouel, André.) Orléans, 1961.
	Arc 513.17	Les civilisations prehelléniques. (Dussaud, René.) Paris, 1910.
	Arc 513.17.2	Les civilisations prehelléniques. 2. éd. (Dussaud, René.) Paris, 1914.
	Arc 830.47	Les civilisations protohistoriques de l'Aquitaine. (Fabre, Gabrielle.) Paris, 1952.
	Arc 843.120	La civilización céltica en Galicia. (López Cuevillas, Florentino.) Santiago, 1953.

Author and Title Listing

Arc 647.3.5 The civilization of Greece in the bronze age. (Hall, H.R.) London, 1928.
Arc 720.212 La civilization primitive en Italie. pt.1-2; plates. (Monteluis, O.) Stockholm, 1895. 5v.
Arc 432.26 Civilizations of the Indus Valley and beyond. (Wheeler, Robert Eric Mortimer.) London, 1966.
Arc 726.270 Civiltà millenarie in terra di Bari. (Giordano, Nicola.) Bari, 1963.
Arc 726.330 Civiltà preromane del territorio parmense. (Scarani, Renato.) Parma, 1971.
Arc 858.77 The civitas capitals of Roman Britain. (Conference on Romano-British Cantonal Capitals, University of Leicester, 1963.) Leicester, 1966.
Arc 1330.7 Clain-Stepanelli, Elvira Eliza. Select numismatic bibliography. N.Y., 1965.
Arc 861.108F Clapham, A.W. On the topography of the Cistercian Abbey of Tower Hill. Oxford, 1915.
Arc 861.106F Clapham, A.W. On the topography of the Dominican Priory of London. Oxford, 1912.
Arc 861.104 Clapham, A.W. St. John of Jerusalem, Clerkenwell. London, 1912.
Arc 865.4 Clapperton, W. Stonehenge handbook. Salisbury, n.d.
Arc 810.49 Clarac, Frédéric. Fouille faite a Pompéi en présence de S.M. la reine des deux Siciles. n.p., 1813.
Arc 590.10 Clark, Edward. The tomb of Alexander. Cambridge, 1805.
Arc 552.3 Clark, Edward L. Daleth; or The homestead of the nations. Boston, 1864.
Arc 1613.22 Clark, Gruber and Co. (Mumey, N.) Denver, 1950.
Arc 861.120 Clark, J.G.D. Excavations at Star Caer. Cambridge, Eng., 1954.
Arc 609.16F Clark, John Desmond. Further paleo-anthropological studies in northern Lunda. Lisboa, 1968.
Arc 612.23 Clark, John Desmond. The mesolithic settlement of northern Europe. Cambridge, Eng., 1936.
Arc 609.9.6 Clark, John Desmond. The prehistoric cultures of the Horn of Africa. N.Y., 1972.
Arc 612.33 Clark, John Desmond. Prehistoric Europe. London, 1952.
Arc 609.9 Clark, John Desmond. The prehistory of southern Africa. Harmondsworth, Middlesex, Eng., 1959.
Arc 387.21.5A Clark, John Grahame Douglas. Archaeology and society. Cambridge, Mass., 1957.
Arc 387.21A Clark, John Grahame Douglas. Archaeology and society. 2. ed. London, 1947.
Arc 387.21.10 Clark, John Grahame Douglas. Archaeology and society. 3. ed. London, 1960.
Arc 858.51 Clark, John Grahame Douglas. Prehistoric England. London, 1940.
Arc 858.51.2 Clark, John Grahame Douglas. Prehistoric England. 2. ed. London, 1941.
Arc 412.9 Clarke, David L. Models in archaeology. London, 1972.
Arc 387.45 Clarke, David Leonard. Analytical archaeology. London, 1968.
Arc 1663.8 Clarke, H. The early history of the Mediterranean populations. London, 1882.
Arc 518.5 Clarke, Hyde. Ephesus. Smyrna, 1863.
Arc 875.10.13 Clarke, John. The Roman fort at Cadder near Glasgow. Glasgow, 1933.
Arc 861.167 Clarke, R. East Anglia. London, 1960.
Arc 969.1.6 Clarke, R. The pre-historic remains...of the city of Cincinnati, Ohio. Cincinnati, 1876.
Arc 1033.12.106 Clarke, R.F. A pilgrimage to the Holy Coat of Treves. London, 1892.
Htn Arc 1538.1* Clarke, W. The connexion of the Roman, Saxon, and English coins. London, 1767.
Arc 810.3 Clarke, W. Pompeii (in library of entertaining knowledge). London, 1831-32. 2v.
Arc 858.41 Clarke, W.G. Our homeland prehistoric antiquities and how to study them. London, 1924.
Arc 889.36 Clason, Antje Trientje. Animal and man in Holland's past. v.1-2. Groningen, 1967.
Arc 1500.27 Classement des monnaies épiscopales. (Roman, J.) Paris, 1886.
Arc 1373.10 Classes generales seu moneta vetus urbium populorum et regum ordine. (Sestini, Domenico.) Florentiae, 1821.
Arc 643.2 A classical and topographical tour through Greece. (Dodwell, E.) London, 1819. 2v.
Arc 625.9 Classical archaeology on the shores of the Mediterranean. (Sturgis, R.) Rochester, n.d.
Arc 861.4.5 Classical Association. Melandra Castle. Manchester, 1906.
Arc 861.4.9 Classical Association...Roman fort at Manchester. (Brutton, F.A.) Manchester, 1909.
Arc 723.12 Classical excursion from Rome to Arpino. (Kelsall, Charles.) Geneva, 1820.
Arc 723.2 A classical tour through Italy. (Eustace, J.C.) London, 1841. 3v.
Arc 723.3 A classical tour through Italy and Sicily. (Hoare, R.C.) London, 1819. 2v.
Arc 953.25 Classification and description of Indian stone artifacts. (Renaud, E.B.) Gunnison, 1941.
Arc 1588.5.8 Classification of Byzantine stamena in the light of a hoard found in southern Serbia. (Metcalf, David Michael.) Ljubljana, 1967.
Arc 1615.3 A classification of early half-dimes in the United States. (Newlin, H.P.) Philadelphia, 1883.
Arc 74.4.15 A classified catalogue of the books, pamphlets and maps in the library. (Society for the Promotion of Hellenic Studies.) London, 1924.
Arc 435.1.18 Classified catalogue of the library of the director general of archaeology. (India. Archaeological Survey. Library.) Calcutta, 1908.
Arc 1670.50F Claude de Héry, médailleur du roi Henri III. (Mazerolle, Fernand.) Paris, 18- ?
Arc 1185.10 Clavis diplomatica. (Baring, D.E.) Hanoverae, 1737.
Arc 1185.10.5 Clavis diplomatica. (Baring, D.E.) Hanoverae, 1754.
Arc 1090.6F Clay pipes for the archaeologists. (Oswald, Adrian.) Oxford, 1975.
Arc 861.12.15 Clayton, J. Observations on centurial stones found on the Roman wall in Northumberland and Cumberland. Newcastle-on-Tyne, 1880.
Arc 1138.100 Cleator, Philip. Lost languages. London, 1959.
Arc 412.26 Cleator, Philip. Underwater archaeology. London, 1973.
Arc 830.341 Clébert, Jean Paul. Provence antique. Paris, 1966. 2v.
Arc 66.1.7 Clédat, L. Role historique de Bertrand de Born. Paris, 1879.
Arc 387.8A Cleland, H.F. Our prehistoric ancestors. N.Y., 1928.
Htn Arc 1160.206* Clemen, O. Handschriftenproben aus der Reformationzeit. Zwickau, 1911.
Arc 757.7 Clementi, F. Roma imperiale nelle XIV regioni Agustee secondo. Roma, 1935. 2v.
Arc 726.11.9 Cleopatra, M. Antonio e Ottaviano nelle allegorie storico-umoristiche delle argenterie del tesoro di Boscoreale. (Corte, M. della.) Pompei, 1951.
Arc 593.5 Cleopatra's needle. (Wilson, E.) London, 1878.
Arc 593.6 Cleopatra's needles. (Noakes, Aubrey.) London, 1962.
Arc 593.4 Cleopatra's needles and other Egyptian obelisks. (Budge, E.A.W.) London, 1926.
Arc 830.111 Clerc, E. La Franche-Comté à l'époque romaine. Besançon, 1847.
Arc 66.1.64 Clerc, M. Les meteques atheniens. Paris, 1893.
Arc 830.183 Clerc, Michele. Découvertes archéologiques à Marseille. Marseille, 1904.
Arc 1470.10 Clerk, M.G. Catalogue of coins of the Achaean League. London, 1895.
Arc 830.88 Clermont gallo-romain. (Audollent, A.) Clermont-Ferrand, 19- .
Arc 500.6 Clermont-Ganneau, C. Archaeological researches in Palestine. London, 1896. 2v.
Arc 505.3.12 Clermont-Ganneau, Charles. L'authenticité du Saint-Sépulcre. Paris, 1877.
Arc 416.2.2 Clermont-Ganneau, Charles. Études d'archéologie orientale. Paris, 1880. 2v.
Arc 505.6 Clermont-Ganneau, Charles. Fraudes archeologiques en Palestine. (Bibliothéque Orientale Elzevirienne). Paris, 1885.
Arc 505.8 Clermont-Ganneau, Charles. La pierre de Bethphagé. Paris, 1877.
Arc 497.2 Clermont-Ganneau, Charles. Premiers rapports sur une mission en Palestine et en Phénicie. Paris, 1882.
Arc 505.7 Clermont-Ganneau, Charles. La présentation du Christ au Temple. Paris, 1877.
VArc 416.2 Clermont-Ganneau, Charles. Recueil d'archéologie orientale. Paris, 1888-1924. 8v.
Arc 505.7.5 Clermont-Ganneau, Charles. Resultats...archéologies des fouilles entreprises à Jérusalem. n.p., 1872.
Arc 743.20 Cles-Reden, S. Das versunkene Volk. Innsbruck, 1948.
Arc 1093.2.30 Cles-Reden, Sibylle. The realm of the great goddess; the story of the megalith builders. London, 1961.
Arc 543.82 Cleveland, Ray L. An ancient South Arabian necropolis. Baltimore, 1965.
Arc 1540.36 Cleveland. Museum of Art. English gold coins. Cleveland, 1968.
Arc 612.7 Cliff castles and cave dwellings of Europe. (Baring-Gould, S.) London, 1911.
Arc 983.1.2 The cliff dwellers. (Henderson, P.) St. Paul, 1893.
Arc 950.200 The cliff dwellers of the Mesa Verde. (Nordenskiold, G.) Stockholm, 1893.
Arc 858.17 Clinch, George. Handbook of English antiquities. London, 1905.
Arc 1076.3.27 La cloche, études. (Blavignac, J.D.) Genève, 1877.
Arc 1076.3.103 Cloches et carillons. (Staercke, Alphonse E. de.) Bruxelles, 1947.
Arc 1093.2.5 Clodd, E. The later stone age in Europe. London, 1880.
Arc 552.2 Cloquet, L. L'art monumental des Égyptiens et des Assyriens. n.p., n.d.
Arc 432.3 Cloquet, L. L'art munumental des Indous et des Perses. Bruxelles, 1896.
Arc 880.25.10 Cluain Maccu Nois [Clonmacmois]. (Macalister, R.A.S.) Dublin, 1911.
Arc 225.1 Cluj, Rumania. Erdelye nemzeti. Dolgozatok. Erem-es régiségtárából. Kolozsvár. 2-7,1911-1916 3v.
Arc 875.33 The Clyde mystery. (Lang, Andrew.) Glasgow, 1905.
Arc 936.14.555 Cmentarzyska doby wczesnopiastowskiej na Śląsku. (Wachowski, Krzysztof.) Wrocław, 1975.
Arc 936.14.460 Cmentarzysko halsztackie w kietrzue. (Gedl, Marek.) Wrocław, 1973.
Arc 936.14.61 Cmentarzysko kultury słockiej "nad Wawrem" w Złotej. (Krzak, Zygmunt.) Wrocław, 1970.
Arc 936.14.290 Cmentarzysko wczesnośredniowieczne na wzgárzu "Młynówka" w Wolinie. (Wojtasik, Jerzy.) Szczecin, 1968.
Arc 936.14.190 Cnotliwy, Eugeniusz. Powiat kamicński w starozytności. Szczecin, 1966.
Arc 936.14.297 Cnotliwy, Eugeniusz. Rzemiosło rogounicze na Pomorzu wczesnośredniowiecznym. Wrocław, 1973.
Arc 936.195.230 Co bylo préd Prahon. 1. vyd. (Davidek, Vácalv.) Praha, 1971.
Arc 1018.49 Cobern, C.M. The new archaeological discoveries and their bearing upon the New Testament. N.Y., 1917.
Arc 1018.49.5 Cobern, C.M. The new archaeological discoveries and their bearing upon the New Testament. 3. ed. N.Y., 1918.
Arc 790.207 Cocchia, E. La forma del Vesuvio nelle pitture...antiche. n.p., n.d.
Arc 830.29.4 Cochet, J.B.D. La Normandie souterraine. Rouen, 1854.
Arc 830.32 Cochet, J.B.D. Notice sur une sépulture gauloise. Rouen, 1866.
Arc 823.4.6 Cochet, J.B.D. Répertoire archéologique du département de la Seine-Inférieure. Paris, 1871.
Arc 830.32.8 Cochet, J.B.D. La Seine-Inférieure historique et archéologique. 2e éd. Paris, 1866.
Arc 830.29.5 Cochet, J.B.D. Sépultures gauloises, romaines. Paris, 1857.
Arc 830.32.5 Cochet, J.B.D. Le tombeau de Childéric. Paris, 1859.
Arc 800.8.2 Cochin, Charles N. Observations sur les antiquités d'Herculanum. 2e éd. Paris, 1755.
Arc 800.8.3 Cochin, Charles N. Observations sur les antiquités d'Herculanum. 2e éd. Paris, 1757.
Arc 1540.17.10 Cochran-Patrick, R.W. Catalogue of the medals of Scotland. Edinburgh, 1884.
Arc 1535.8 Cochran-Patrick, R.W. Records of the coinage of Scotland. Edinburgh, 1876. 2v.
Arc 880.22 Cochrane, Robert. List of ancient and national monuments in county of Cork. Cork, 1913.
Htn Arc 705.6* Cockerell, C.R. Antiquities of Athens and other places in Greece and Sicily. London, 1830.
Arc 1076.3.70 Cocks, A.H. The church bells of Buckinghamshire. London, 1897.
Arc 1494.8 Codera y Zaiden, F. Tratado de numismática. Madrid, 1879.
Arc 1433.37 Codera y Zaidin, F. Titulos y nombres propios monedas arábigo-españolas. Madrid, 1878.
Arc 775.1.2 Codex urbis Romae topographicus. (Urlichs, K.L.) Wirceburg, 1871.
Arc 1163.35 Codices Hungarici. Budapest. 4-7 4v.
Arc 1153.112PF Codices latini antiquiores. pt.2. 2. ed. Oxford, 1972.
Arc 1433.31 Codrington, O. Manuel of Musalman numismatics. London, 1904.
Arc 870.4 Codrington, Thomas. Roman roads in Britain. London, 1903.

Arc 870.4.2 Codrington, Thomas. Roman roads in Britain. 2. ed. London, 1905.

Arc 870.4.3 Codrington, Thomas. Roman roads in Britain. 3. ed. London, 1918.

Arc 870.4.4 Codrington, Thomas. Roman roads in Britain. 3. ed. N.Y., 1919.

Arc 543.7.23 Coedès, George. Les bas-reliefs d'Angkor-Vat. Paris, 1911.

Arc 1493.27 Coelho, Antonio D.S. Numária da Lusitânia. Lisboa, 1972.

Arc 1138.30 Coellen, Ludwig. Die Stilentwicklung der Schrift im christlichen Abendlande. Darmstadt, 1922.

Arc 87.2.45 Das coelner Mosaik. (Lersch, J.H.L.) Bonn, 1846.

Arc 845.211F Cölner Thorburgen und Befestigungen, 1180-1882. (Architekten und Ingenieur-Verein für Niederrhein und Westfalen, Cologne.) Cöln, 1883.

Arc 1033.47.21 Coen, J.A. La persecuzione neroniana dei Cristiani. Firenze, 1900.

Arc 1027.17 Das Coerneterium de H. Christina zu Bolsena. (Stevenson, H.) n.p., n.d.

Arc 880.10 Coffey, George. The bronze age in Ireland. Dublin, 1913.

X Cg Arc 880.8 Coffey, George. New Grange and other incised tumuli. Dublin, 1912.

Arc 1613.17 Coffin, J. Our American money. N.Y., 1940.

Arc 1020.84.9 Coffinet, L'Abbé. Trésor de St. Etienne...collegiale de Troyes. Paris, 1860.

Arc 736.6 Coglitore, I. Mozia, studi storico-archeologico. Catania, 1894.

Arc 823.19.4F Cognitio cognitionibus. (Thédenat, H.) Parisiis, 1873.

Arc 853.10.15 Cohausen, August. Das Römerkastell Saalburg. 4. Aufl. Homburg vor der Höhe, 1893.

Arc 853.7.1 Cohausen, August. Der römische Grenzwall in Deutschland. Text, atlas. Faksimile. Walluf bei Weisbaden, 1973 2v.

Arc 1478.3 Cohen, H. Description générale des monnaies de la Republique Romaine. Paris, 1857.

Arc 1478.3.2 Cohen, H. Description historique des monnaies frappées sons l'Empire Romain. Paris, 1859. 7v.

Arc 1478.3.3 Cohen, H. Description historique des monnaies frappées sons l'Empire Romain. Paris, 1880-92. 8v.

Arc 543.7.25F Cohen, Joan Lebold. Angkor monuments of the god-kings. London, 1975.

Arc 497.78 Cohen, Lenore. Biblical treasure in Bible lands. Los Angeles, 1965.

Arc 66.1.146 Les cohortes prétoriennes. (Durry, Marcel.) Paris, 1938.

Arc 1086.5 Coimbra. Museu Machado de Castro. Catálogo de lucernas romanas. Coimbra, 1952.

Arc 1478.25 Coimbra. Universidade. Biblioteca. Moedas romanas da Biblioteca da Universidade de Coimbra. Coimbra, 1905.

Arc 1423.22 Coin and temple; a study of the architectural representation on ancient Jewish coins. (Muehsam, Alice.) Leeds, 1966.

Arc 1334.02 Pamphlet vol. Coin catalogue. A-Z, by collector.

Arc 1334.04 Pamphlet vol. Coin catalogue. A-Z, by dealer.

Arc 1334.06 Pamphlet vol. Coin catalogue of miscellaneous dealers and special collectors, A-Z. 12 pam.

Arc 1348.36 The coin chart manual. St. Louis, 1848?

Arc 1348.51 Coin collecting. (Milne, J.G.) London, 1951.

Arc 1335.164F The coin collection. (American University of Beirut. Museum of Archaeology.) Beirut, 1974.

Arc 1348.4A The coin collector. (Hazlitt, W.C.) N.Y., 1896.

Arc 1302.1 The coin collector's journal 1876-1882. N.Y. 1876-1888 10v.

NEDL Arc 1348.6 The coin collector's manual. (Humphreys, H.N.) London, 1875. 2v.

Arc 1302.10 Coin hoards. London. 1,1975+

Arc 1348.20 Coin types, their origin and development. (McDonald, George.) Glasgow, 1905.

Arc 1540.23 Coinage and currency in Roman Britain. (Sutherland, Carol Humphrey Vivian.) London, 1937.

Arc 1473.14 Coinage and money in the Byzantine empire, 1081-1261. (Hendy, Michael.) Washington, 1969.

Arc 1478.42 Coinage in Roman imperial policy. (Sutherland, C.H.V.) London, 1951.

Arc 1588.5.6 Coinage in the Balkans, 820-1355. (Metcalf, David Michael.) Chicago, 1966.

Arc 1588.5.5 Coinage in the Balkans. (Metcalf, David Michael.) Thessaloniki, 1965.

Arc 1538.20 The coinage of ancient Britain. (Mack, R.P.) London, 1953.

Arc 1428.23 The coinage of Caesarea in Cappadocia. (Sydenham, E.A.) London, 1933.

Arc 1470.43 The coinage of Damastion and the lesser coinages of the Illyra-Paeonian region. (May, J.M.F.) London, 1939.

Arc 1470.31 The coinage of Demetrius Poliorcetes. (Newell, E.T.) London, 1927.

Arc 1538.17 The coinage of England. (Oman, C.W.C.) Oxford, 1931.

Arc 1540.37 The coinage of Roman Britain. (Askew, Gilbert.) London, 1951.

Arc 1535.10F The coinage of Scotland. (Burns, Edward.) Edinburgh, 1837. 3v.

Arc 1480.71 The coinage of Septimius Severus and his family of the mint of Rome, A.D. 193-217. (Hill, Philip V.) London, 1964.

Arc 1433.50 The coinage of Siam. (Le May, R.S.) Bangkok, 1932.

Arc 1510.136 The coinage of South Germany in the thirteenth century. (Metcalf, D.) London, 1961.

Arc 1540.25 The coinage of Suffolk. (Golding, Charles.) London, 1868.

Arc 1538.3 The coinage of the British empire. (Humphreys, H.N.) London, 1854.

Htn Arc 1538.3.2* The coinage of the British empire. (Humphreys, H.N.) London, 1855.

Arc 1453.1.1 The coinage of the European continent. (Hazlitt, William Carew.) Chicago, 1974.

Arc 1453.1 The coinage of the European continent. (Hazlitt, William Carew.) London, 1893.

Arc 1480.19.10 The coinage of the Roman republic. (Sydenham, E.A.) London, 1952.

Arc 1613.4 The coinage of the United States of America. (Phillips, H.) Philadelphia, 1883.

X Cg Arc 1390.9 Coinage of western Europe. (Keary, C.F.) London, 1879.

Arc 1348.39 The coinages of the world. (Mathews, George D.) N.Y., 1876.

Arc 1433.60 Coins, medals, and seals of the shâhs of Irân. (Rabino, Hyacinth L.) Hertford, 1945.

Arc 1348.12 Coins, medals and seals. (Prime, W.C.) N.Y., 1861. 4 pam.

Arc 1603.3.5 Coins, tokens and medals of the Dominion of Canada. (Sandham, Alfred.) Montreal, 1869.

Arc 1603.3.6 Coins, tokens and medals of the Dominion of Canada. (Sandham, Alfred.) Montreal, 1962.

Arc 1613.12 Coins and coinage. The United States Mint, Philadelphia. (Smith, A.M.) Philadelphia, 1884.

Arc 1550.8.5 Coins and history. (Galster, Georg.) Kopenhagen, 1959.

Arc 1348.21 Coins and how to know them. (Rawlings, G.B.) N.Y., n.d.

Htn Arc 1334.5* Pamphlet vol. Coins and medals, 1749-1756.

Htn Arc 1334.6* Pamphlet vol. Coins and medals, 1860-1865. 4 pam.

Arc 1348.8 Coins and medals. (Poole, S. Lane.) London, 1885.

Arc 1490.16 Coins and medals of knights of Malta. (Schembri, H.C.) London, 1908.

Arc 1473.50.5 Coins and medals of the Ionian Islands. (Lampros, Paulos.) Amsterdam, 1968.

Arc 1348.83F Coins and the archaeologist. Oxford, 1974.

Arc 1335.47 Coins and their values. London, 1917.

Arc 1540.18 The coins and tokens of the possessions and colonies of the British empire. (Atkins, James.) London, 1889.

Arc 1335.159 The coins exhibited in the Archaeological Museum of the American University of Beirut. (American University of Beirut. Archaeological Museum.) Beirut, 1968.

Arc 1433.65.5 Coins from Seleucia on the Tigris. (McDowell, Robert H.) Ann Arbor, 1935.

Htn Arc 1418.2.4* Coins of Alexander's succesors in the East. (Cunningham, A.) London, 1884?

Arc 1418.2 Coins of ancient India. (Cunningham, A.) London, 1891.

Arc 1428.21 Coins of ancient Lycia before the reign of Alexander. (Fellows, Charles.) London, 1855.

Arc 1490.8.5 Coins of ancient Sicily. (Hill, G.F.) Westminster, 1903.

Arc 1418.6.5 The coins of India. (Brown, C.J.) Calcutta, 1922.

Arc 1413.1 Coins of Japan. (Munro, N.G.) London, 1905.

Arc 1412.1 The coins of Japan. pt.1. (Bramsen, W.) Yokohama, 1880.

X Cg Arc 1413.09 Coins of Japan. 1. ed. (Munro, N.G.) Yokohama, 1904.

Arc 1470.3.5 Coins of Magna Graecia. (Hands, A.W.) London, 1909.

Arc 1418.2.2 Coins of mediaeval India. (Cunningham, A.) London, 1894.

Arc 1625.3 The coins of Mexico in silver and copper, 1536-1939. (Raymond, W.) N.Y., 1940.

Arc 1645.2 The coins of South America; silver and copper. British Guiana, Dutch Guiana, French Guiana. (Raymond, Wayte.) N.Y., 1942.

Arc 1433.62F Coins of Tabaristân and some Sassenian coins from Susa. (Unvala, Jamshedji M.) Paris, 1938.

Arc 1538.11 Coins of the ancient Britons. v.1 and supplement. (Evans, J.) London, 1864-90. 2v.

Arc 1530.10 The coins of the Dutch overseas territories, 1601-1948. (Scholten, C.) Amsterdam, 1953.

Arc 1578.15 Coins of the Hapsburg emperors and related issues. (Mort, Selwyn R.) Melbourne, 1959.

Arc 1433.4 Coins of the Indo-Scythians. pt.1-2. (Cunningham, A.) London, 1888.

Arc 1423.9.5F Coins of the Jews. (Madden, Frederic W.) Boston, 1881.

Arc 1405.1.2 Coins of the Jews. v.2. (Madden, F.W.) London, 1881.

Arc 1400.6 Coins of the modern world, 1870-1936. (Comencini, M.) London, 1937.

Arc 1411.1 Coins of the present dynesty in China. (Bushell, S.W.) n.p., 1880.

Arc 1478.21.2 Coins of the Roman Empire. v.1-3; v.4, pt.1-2; v.6. (British Museum. Department of Coins and Medals.) London, 1966. 6v.

Arc 1478.21 Coins of the Roman Empire in the British Museum. v.1-4,6. (British Museum. Department of Coins and Medals.) London, 1923-40. 5v.

Arc 1478.20 Coins of the Roman Republic in the British Museum. v.1-3,5; pt.1-2. (Grueber, H.A.) London, 1910. 5v.

Arc 1480.13 Coins of the Romans relative to Britain. (Akerman, J.Y.) London, 1844.

Arc 1411.3 Coins of the Ta-ts'ing dynasty. (Wylie, A.) Shanghai, 1858.

Arc 1400.7 Coins of the world; the standard catalogue of twentieth century issues. 1. ed. N.Y., 1938.

Arc 1400.7.2 Coins of the world, twentieth century issues. 2. ed. (Raymond, Wayte.) N.Y., 1945.

Arc 1348.78 Coins of the world. (Carson, Robert.) N.Y., 1962.

Arc 1423.20 The coins of Tiberias. (Kindler, A.) Tiberias, 1961.

Arc 1033.35.17 Colá, C. Memorie historiche dell'apparitione delle croci. Napoli, 1661.

Arc 543.5.25 Colani, M. Mégalithes du Haut-Laos. Paris, 1935. 2v.

Arc 1027.57 Colasanti, A. Le stagione nell'antichità...arte christiano. Roma, 1901.

Arc 861.175 Colchester, England. Museum and Muniment Committee. Colonia-Claudia Victricensis: the story of Roman Colchester. Colchester, 1967.

Arc 861.81 Colchester castle, a Roman building. (Buckler, Geroge.) Colchester, 1876.

Arc 672.1.125 Coldstream, John Nicolas. Knossos. London, 1973.

Arc 963.2.20 Cole, Fay C. Rediscovering Illinois. Chicago, 1937.

Arc 435.25 Cole, H.H. Mixed Hindu-Mahamedan style. London, 1873.

Arc 830.130.20 Côle, Léon. Glozel, trente ans après. St.-Etienne, 1959.

Arc 609.13.5 Cole, Sonia Mary. Early man in east Africa. London, 1958.

Arc 609.13 Cole, Sonia Mary. The prehistory of east Africa. Harmondsworth, 1954.

Arc 609.13.2 Cole, Sonia Mary. The prehistory of east Africa. N.Y., 1963.

Arc 609.36 Cole-King, P.A. Mwalawolemba on Mikolongwe Hill. Zomba, 1968.

Arc 1675.14 Coleccion de leyes, decretos. (Rosa, A.) Buenos Aires, 1891.

Arc 1018.25.25 Coleman, Lyman. Antiquities of the Christian church. Andover, 1841.

Arc 1076.3.95 Coleman, Satis N. (Barton). Bells; their history, legends, making, and uses. Chicago, 1928.

Arc 858.104 Coles, John M. Field archaeology in Britain. London, 1972.

Arc 785.8.7F Colgrossi, P. L'anfiteatro Flavio nei suoi venti secoli di storia. Firenze, 1913.

Arc 66.1.93 Colin, G. Le culte d'Apollon Pythien à Athènes. Paris, 1905.

Arc 66.1.94 Colin, G. Rome et la Grèce de 200 a 146 avant Jésus-Christ. Paris, 1905.

Arc 853.97 Colin, Jean. Les antiquités romaines de la Rhenanie. Paris, 1927.

Arc 726.58 Colini, Giuseppe A. Necropoli de Pianello presso Genza (Ancona). Parma, 1913.

Arc 726.44 Colini, Giuseppe A. Il sepolcreto de Remedello-Sotto. Parma, 1899-1902.

Arc 875.24 Coll and Tiree - their prehistoric forts. (Beveridge, E.) Edinburgh, 1903.

Arc 1335.44 Collana di medaglie antiche e moderne. (Borioni, T.) Loreto, 1835.

Author and Title Listing

Arc 67.7 Collana di quaderni di antichità ravennati cristiane e bizantine. Ravenna. 1,1963+ 12v.

Arc 785.23.5 Collare di servo fuggitivo novo Scoperto. (Rossi, M.S. de.) Roma, 1892.

Arc 505.124.5F Il colle de Rachele. (Rome (City). Università. Missione Archeologica.) Roma, 1960.

Arc 403.2 Collectanea antiqua. (Smith, C.R.) London, 1848-80. 7v.

Arc 861.65 Collectanea cantiana. (Payne, George.) London, 1893.

Arc 861.19.5 Collectanea curiosa antiqua Dunmonia. (Shortt, W.T.P.) Londinium, n.d.

Arc 1200.5 Der collectarus perpeturom formorum des Johann von Gelnhausen. (Kaiser, H.) Strassburg, 1898.

Htn Arc 1433.6* Collectio nova numorum cuficum. (Adler, I.G.C.) Hafniae, 1782-92. 2v.

Arc 1433.11 Collectio nummorum cuficorum. (Hallenberg, Jonas.) Stockholm, 1800.

Arc 1335.28 Collection. pt.1,3. (Judice dos Santos, J.J.) Amsterdam, 1906. 2v.

Arc 608.2.80F Collection cahiers de Byrsa. Série monographies. Paris. 1,1974+ 2v.

Arc 820.202 Collection Caranda. (Moreau, F.) St. Quentin, 1877. 4v.

Arc 1335.19 Collection Charvet. (Charvet, Jules.) Paris, 1883.

Arc 625.12 Collection d'antiquités, grecques et romaines. (Delestre, M.) Paris, 1901.

Arc 1335.155 Collection de feu M. Renier Chalon. v.2. (Chalon, Renier.) Bruxelles, 1889.

Arc 497.35 Collection de Louis Courtin. (Courtin, Louis.) Paris, 189-.

Arc 1335.42 Collection de M. le Vicomte de...monnaies. (Quelen, E. de.) Paris, 1883.

Arc 1510.22.10 Collection de monnaies et médailles d'Alsace. (Bibliothèque Nationale, Paris. Département des Médailles et Antiques.) Paris, 1902.

Arc 1613.5 Collection de monnaies et médailles de l'Amérique. (Vattemare, A.) Paris, 1861.

Arc 1468.48 Collection de monnaies grecques. (Nanteuil, H. de.) Paris, 1925. 2v.

Arc 750.30.5 Collection de peintures antiques...Rome. Rome, 1781.

Arc 1033.12.172 Collection de pièces sur le saint clou veneri à Tours. n.p., n.d.

Arc 1264.1 Collection de plombs historiés trouvés dans la Seine. v.1-3. (Forgeais, Arthur.) Paris, 1858-66. 2v.

Arc 1263.1 Collection de sceaux. (Douët d'Arcq, L.C.) Paris, 1863-67. 2v.

Arc 1455.6F Collection du vicomte de Sartiges. (Sartiges.) Paris, 19-?

Arc 1335.54 Collection Ernest Prinz zu Windisch Gratz. (Fiala, Eduard.) Prag, 1895-99. 7v.

Arc 1470.80 La collection Lucien de Hirsch. v.1-2. (Brussels. Bibliothèque Royale.) Bruxelles, 1959.

Arc 823.15 La collection Millon. (Millon, Henry E.) Paris, 1913.

Arc 857.5 A collection of archaeological pamphlets on Roman remains...Great Britain. (Windle, Bertram.) n.p., n.d. 12v.

Arc 530.155 Collection of cuttings from Turkish archeological periodicals. (Ülgen, Ali Saim.) n.p., n.d.

Arc 1458.15 Collection of monnaies grecques et romaines. v.1-2. (Jameson, R.) Paris, 1913. 3v.

Htn Arc 1268.5* A collection of seals - mostly German. n.p., n.d.

Htn Arc 1208.9PF* Pamphlet box. Collection of the seals of various individuals, cities and institutions mounted on sheets.

Arc 1538.14 Collection of 28 plates illustrating ancient coins of Great Britain. (Leigh, Sotheby, and Son.) London, 1803.

Arc 1200.5.5 Collection perpetuorum formorum. (Kaiser, H.) Innsbruck, 1900.

Arc 1458.16 Collection Strozzi. Médailles grecques et romaines aes grave. (Strozzi.) Paris, 1907.

Arc 1603.1 Le collectionneur...des monnaies canadiennes. (Breton, P.N.) Montreal, 1890.

Arc 1458.18 Collections Armand-Valton. (Bibliothèque Nationale, Paris. Département des Médailles et Antiques.) Paris, 1912.

Arc 1356.2 Les collections de monnaies anciennes. (Babelon, E.) Paris, 1897.

Arc 1335.53 Collections numismatiques. (Stroehlin, P.C.) Genève, 1909.

Arc 1208.6 Collections sigillographiques de G. Schlumberger. (Schlumberger, G.) Paris, 1914.

Arc 943.50 Collector's luck: giant steps into prehistory. 1. ed. (Cusack, Betty Bugbee.) Stoneham, Mass., 1968.

Arc 505.153 College of Wooster Expedition to Pella. Pella of the Decapolis. Wooster, 1973-

Arc 1033.35.7F Collégiale de S. Walburge à Furnes. Relique de la croix. (Van de Putte, F.) Bruges, 1864. 3 pam.

Arc 1025.67 Collezione "Amici della catacombe". Roma. 1-25,1933-1956 13v.

Arc 1335.115 Collezione del Prof. Angelo Signorelli. pt.1-2. (Signorelli, A.) Roma, 1951-52.

Arc 600.236 La collezione di lucerne del Museo egizio di Firenze. (Michelucci, Maurizio.) Firenze, 1975.

Arc 93.29 Collezione di monografie preistoriche ed archeologicho. Bordighera. 1-2,1946-1956 2v.

Arc 1348.42PF Collezione di tavole monetarie. Venezia, 1796.

Arc 66.1.85 Collignon, M. Catalogue des vases peints. Paris, 1902. 4v.

Arc 66.1.3 Collignon, M. Catalogue des vases peints du musée. Paris, 1878.

Arc 66.1.2 Collignon, M. Essai sur les monuments grecs et romains relatifs au mythe de psyché. Paris, 1877.

Arc 510.214 Collignon, M. Pergame restauration des monuments de l'Aropole. Paris, 1900.

Arc 642.2.15 Collignon, Maxime. L'archéologie grecque. Paris, n.d.

Arc 642.2.5A Collignon, Maxime. A manual of Greek archaeology. London, 1886.

Arc 642.2.6 Collignon, Maxime. A manual of Greek archaeology. N.Y., 1886.

Arc 642.2.3 Collignon, Maxime. Manuel d'archéologie grecque. Paris, 188-.

Arc 642.2A Collignon, Maxime. Manuel d'archéologie grecque. Paris, 1881.

Arc 1033.116 Collin de Plancy, J.A.S. Dictionnaire des reliques. Paris, 1821-1822. 3v.

Arc 858.42.1 Collingwood, Robin George. The archaeology of Roman Britain. London, 1969.

Arc 858.42 Collingwood, Robin George. The archaeology of Roman Britain. N.Y., 1930.

Arc 861.71.5F Collingwood, W.G. Northumbrian crosses of the pre-Norman age. London, 1927.

Arc 861.13.9 Collingwood, W.G. On some ancient sculptures of the devil bound. Kendal, 1903.

Arc 858.73 Collins field guide to archaeology. (Wood, E.S.) London, 1964.

Arc 1138.33 Collomp, Paul. La critique des textes. Paris, 1931.

Arc 3.4 Colloque International d'Archéologie Aérienne. Colloque international d'archéologie aérienne. Paris, 1964.

Arc 3.4 Colloque international d'archéologie aérienne. (Colloque International d'Archéologie Aérienne.) Paris, 1964.

Arc 1153.82 Colloque International de Paléographie Latine, 1st, Paris, 1953. Nomenclature des écritures livresques du IXe au XVIe siècle. Photoreproduction. Paris, 1954.

Arc 1163.37 Colloque International sur la Paléographie Hébraïque Médiévale, Paris, 1972. La paléographie hébraïque médiévale, Paris, 11-13 septembre 1972. Paris, 1974.

Arc 915.51 Colloque International sur les Cols des Alpes (Antiquité et Moyen-Age), Bourg-en-Bresse, France, 1969. Actes du Colloque International sur les Cols des Alpes, Antiquité et Moyen-Age, Bourg-en-Bresse, 1969. Orléans, 1971.

Arc 642.11 Colloquium on Bronze Age Migrations in the Aegean Region, Sheffield, Eng., 1970. Bronze Age migrations in the Aegean. London, 1973.

Arc 861.21.5 Colls, J.M.N. Letters upon some early remains discovered in Yorkshire. v.1-2. n.p., n.d.

Arc 1510.31F Cologne. Die Münzen und Medaillen von Köln. Köln, 1913-35. 4v.

Arc 853.277 Cologne. Römisch-Germanisches Museum. Frühchristliches Köln. Köln, 1965.

Arc 1335.77 Colombo Museum. Colombo, Ceylon. Catalogue of coins in the Colombo Museum. Hertford, 1914.

Arc 1160.202.9F Colomera y Rodriguez, V. Paleografía castellana. Valladolid, 1862.

Arc 830.6.19 Colonia, Dominique de. Dissertation sur un monument antique decouvert a Lyon. Lyon, 1705.

Arc 843.77.5 Colonia Aelia Augusta Halica. (García y Bellido, Antonio.) Madrid, 1960.

Arc 861.175 Colonia-Claudia Victricensis: the story of Roman Colchester. (Colchester, England. Museum and Muniment Committee.) Colchester, 1967.

Arc 843.205 Colonia Iblia Augusta Paterna Farentia Barcino. (Balil, Alberto.) Madrid, 1964.

Arc 853.2 Colonia Sumlocenne-Rottenburg am Neckar unter die Roemern. (Jaumann, V.) Stuttgart, 1840.

Arc 1540.26 Colonial and commonwealth coins. (Wright, L.V.W.) London, 1959.

Arc 830.174 Les colonies agricoles pré-romaines de la vallée du betes. (Bonsor, G.) Paris, 1899.

Arc 66.1.150 La colonisation grecque de l'Italie meridionale et de la Sicilie. (Bérard, Jean.) Paris, 1941.

Arc 608.1.30 La colonisation romaine dans le pays de Dougga. (Carton, Louis B.C.) Tunis, 1904.

Arc 726.338 Colonna di Paolo, Elena. Castel d'Asso. Roma, 1970. 2v.

Arc 1016.4 La colonna santa. Tempio de Gerusalemme. (Busiri Vici, A.) Roma, 1888.

Arc 673.1.22F La colonne des Naxiens et le partique des Athéneéns. Thèse. (Amandry, P.) Paris, 1953.

Arc 935.7 La colonne serpentine à Constantinople. (Bourquelot, Félix.) Paris, n.d.

Arc 785.15 La colonne trajane. (Froehner, W.) Paris, 1865.

Arc 785.15.13 La colonne trajane au Musee de Saint-Germain. (Reinach, S.) Paris, 1886.

Arc 785.43 Le colosse de Néron. (Préchac, F.) Paris, 1920.

Arc 785.8 The Colosseum at Rome. (Parker, J.H.) London, 1882.

Arc 1500.35 Colson, Achille. Recherches sur les monnaiss qui ont en cours en Roussillon. Perpignan, 1853.

Arc 503.7F Colt Archaeological Institute. Excavations at Nessana. Princeton, 1950. 3v.

Arc 32.10F Colt Archaeological Institute. Monograph series. London. 1-5

Arc 1153.62 Coltura e attività calligrafica nel secolo XII a Verona. (Giuliano, M.L.) Padova, 1933.

Arc 726.48.2 Colucci, G. Alla dissertazione epistolare sulle antiche città picene Falera e Tignio. Appendice. Macerata, 1778.

Arc 726.48 Colucci, G. Sulle antiche città picene Falera e Tignio. Fermo, 1777.

Arc 830.144F Comarmond, A. Description de l'écrin d'une dame romaine. Paris, 1844.

Arc 307.3.35 Comas, Juan. La congresos internacionales de Americanistas. Mexico, 1954.

Arc 943.53 Comas, Juan. Origen de las culturas precolombinas. 1. ed. México, 1975.

Arc 1163.4.5 Combarel, E. Cahier d'écritures arabes. Paris, 1848.

Arc 458.2.10 Combaz, Gisbert. L'évolution du Stūpa en Asie. Bruxelles, 1933. 3 pam.

Arc 432.18 Combaz, Gisbert. L'Inde et l'Orient classique. Paris, 1937. 2v.

Arc 1033.35.5 Combes, L. de. Finding of the Cross. London, 1907.

Arc 552.5 Combined Pre-Historic Expedition to Egyptian and Sudanese Nubia. The prehistory of Nubia. Taos, N.M., 1968. 2v.

Arc 1025.28.19 Come lo studio dell'archeologia cristiana. (Marucchi, O.) Roma, 1900.

Arc 1025.28.8 Come lo studio dell'archeologia cristiana giovi grandemente. (Marucchi, O.) Roma, 1903.

Arc 1400.6 Comencini, M. Coins of the modern world, 1870-1936. London, 1937.

Arc 1027.2.5 Comento sull'iscrizione sepolcrale. (Morcelli, S.A.) Modena, 1824.

Arc 815.5 Comes, O. Illustrazione delle piante rappresentativa nei diputi Pompeiani. Napoli, 1879.

Arc 700.30 The coming of iron to Greece. (Burton-Brown, T.) Wincle, 1954.

Arc 723.26 Comitato esecutivo per le fete del 1911, Rome. Per una esposizione di etnografia italiana in Roma nel 1911. 2a ed. Firenze, 1909.

Arc 743.13 Comitato Permanente per l'Etruria. Studi etruschi. Firenze. 1,1927+ 41v.

Arc 743.13.5 Comitato Permanente per l'Etruria. Studi etruschi. Indici, v.1-40, 1927-1972. Firenze, 1968- 2v.

Arc 785.30 Comitium, rostra, Grab des Romulus. (Petersen, Eugen.) Rom, 1904.

Arc 785.30.5 Il comizio romano...ed i suoi monumenti. (Pinza, G.) Roma, 1905.

Arc 1663.6.20 Commemorative medals. (Whiting, John Roger Scott.) Newton Abbot, 1972.

Author and Title Listing

Arc 1663.34 Commemorative medals of the Z.A.R. (African Museum.) Johannesburg, 1958.

Arc 1033.92 Commemorazione del P. Luigi Bruzza. (Rossi, G.B. de.) Roma, 1883.

Arc 1018.18.18 Commemorazione di P. Raffaele Garucci. (Montescaglioro, F.) Napoli, 1885.

Arc 387.10.15 Commemoriazione del generale Luigi Palma di Cesnola. (Toesca di Castellazzo, G.) Torino, 1905.

Arc 823.19.5F Commentariensis a commentarus commentarius. (Thédenat, H.) Parisiis, 1873.

Arc 1033.12.34F Commentarii critico archeologici sopra la SS. Sindone. (Piano, L.G.) Torino, 1833. 2v.

Arc 1150.202 Commentarii notarum tironianarum. (Schmitz, W.) Lipsiae, 1893. 2v.

Arc 73.100 Commentarius authenticus. v.1-6. (International Congress of Christian Archaeology, 2nd, Rome, 1900.) Rome, 1900.

Arc 1423.3 Commentatio de numis punicis sextorum. (Lindberg, J.C.) Havniae, 1824.

Arc 1390.12 Commentationes de nummis saeculorum IX-XI in suecia repertis. (Rasmusson, Nils L.) Stockholm, 1961- 2v.

X Cg Arc 66.1.88 Le commerce et les marchands. (Yver, G.) Paris, 1903.

Arc 746.54 I commerci di Vetulonia in età orientalizzante. (Camporeale, Giovannangelo.) Firenze, 1969.

Arc 830.3.20 Le Comminges et le Censeraus avant la domination romaine. Thèse. (Lizop, Raymond.) Toulouse, 1931.

Arc 830.338 Commission Historique du Département du Nord. Statistique archéologique du département du Nord. Lille, 1867. 2v.

Arc 1027.10 Commissione de archeologia sagrada...Basilica di San Clemente. (Tizzani, V.) Roma, 1886.

Arc 1208.11F Committee of Ancient Near Eastern Seals. Corpus of ancient Near Eastern seals in North American collections. pt.1-2. N.Y., 1948-

Arc 501.4 Committee of the Fund. Our work in Palestine. London, 1873.

Arc 1468.15 Common Greek coins. (Hands, A.W.) London, 1907.

Arc 950.10F Les communautés anciennes dans le désert américain. (Hewett, E.L.) Genève, 1908.

Arc 32.5 Communications. (Chicago. University. Oriental Institute.) Chicago. 2-18 5v.

Arc 830.177 Communications. (Cousset, A.) Le Mans, 1913.

Arc 104.5 Communications. (Journées Archéologiques Internationales.) Paris. 1,1964+

Arc 125.4.8 Communications made to the association. (British Archaeological Association.) London, 1862. 2v.

Arc 1680.10.9 Communion tokens. (Tenney, M.M.) Grand Rapids, 1936.

Arc 1680.10.5 Communion tokens of the established Church of Scotland. (Brook, A.J.S.) Edinburgh, 1907.

Arc 1163.39 Cómo han de traducirse los documentos paleográficos de Hispanoámerica. (Garcés G, Jorge A.) Quinto, 1961.

Arc 810.41 A companion to Pompeian studies. (Van Buren, A.W.) Rome, 1927.

Arc 793.13 A companion to the study of Pompeii and Herculaneum. (Van Buren, Albert W.) Rome, 1933.

Arc 488.19F The comparative stratigraphy of early Iran. (McCown, D.E.) Chicago, 1942.

Arc 458.3 Comparative view of antient monuments of India...island of Salset. (Gough, Richard.) London, 1785.

Arc 790.35 Comparette, D. Villa ercolanese dei Pisoni i suoi monumenti. Torino, 1888.

Arc 815.9F Comparetti, D. Le nozze di Bacco et Arianna. Firenze, 1921.

Arc 387.4 Compendio completo di archeologia. Milano, 1834. 2v.

Arc 1494.62 Compendio de las piezas de ocho reales. (Calbató de Grau, Gabriel.) San Juan, 1970. 2v.

Arc 1160.202 Compendio de paleografia española. (Alvera Delgras, A.) Madrid, 1857.

Arc 505.5.40 Compendio del Rico Aparato, y Hermosa del templo de Salomon. (Estevan, M.) Alcala, 1615.

Arc 1138.6 Compendio delle lezioni teorico-pratiche di paleografia e diplomatica. (Gloria, A.) Padova, 1870.

Arc 1138.6F Compendio delle lezioni teorico-pratiche di paleografia e diplomatica. Atlas. (Gloria, A.) Padova, 1870.

Arc 1033.17.131 Compendio dell'origine...della sacra cintura. Verona, 1642.

Arc 1033.55.6 Compendio istorico cronologico delle cose più cospicul concernenti la Scala Santa. (Soresini, G.M.) Roma, 1674.

Arc 1025.28.40 Compendio storico e topografico delle catacombe romane. (Marucchi, O.) Albano Laziale, 1928.

Arc 830.4 Compiègne, France. Société Historique. Excursions archéologiques dans les environs de Compiègne. 1869-74, 1875-1900. Compiègne, 1875. 2v.

Arc 66.1.127 La composition dans les ouvrages philosophiques de Sévèque. (Albertini, E.) n.p., n.d.

Arc 1470.47 The composition of ancient Greek bronze coins. (Caley, Earle R.) Philadelphia, 1939.

Arc 1470.86 The composition of Greek silver coins. (Kraay, Colin M.) Oxford, 1962.

Arc 307.3 Compte-rendu. (International Congress of Americanists.) 1875+ 60v.

Arc 292.40PF Compte rendu. (Russia. Arkheologicheskaia Kommissiia.) St. Petersbourg, n.d.

Arc 292.40F Compte rendu. (Russia. Arkheologicheskaia Kommissiia.) St. Petersbourg. 1-21,1859-1888 9v.

Arc 608.1.15 Compte rendu de la marche du service. (Tunis.) Tunis, 1898.

Arc 396.13 Comptemporary archaeology. (Leone, Mark P.) Carbondale, 1972.

Arc 1315.1.5 Comptes rendu. (Société Francaise de Numismatique.) Paris, 1869-75. 7v.

Arc 3.1.22 Comptes rendus. (Congrès International d'Archéologie Classique, 2d, Cairo, 1909.) Le Caire, 1909.

Arc 3.1.21 Comptes rendus du Congrès International d'Archéologie Ire Session, Athènes, 1905. (Congrès International d'Archéologie Classique, 1st, Athens, 1905.) Athènes, 1905.

Arc 967.1.9 Conant, Alban J. Foot-prints of vanished races in the Mississippi Valley. St. Louis, 1879.

Arc 1138.85 El concepto de la epigrafia consideraciones sobre la necesidad de su ampliación. (Navascués y de Juan, Joaquin Maria de.) Madrid, 1953.

Arc 551.3 A concise dictionary of Egyptian archaeology. (Brodrick, M.) London, 1902.

Arc 375.15 The concise encyclopedia of archaeology. 1. ed. N.Y., 1960.

Arc 1274.9 A concise list of seals belonging to the Dean and Chapter of Hereford Cathedral. (Morgan, Frederick Charles.) Hereford, 1966.

Arc 1020.9.7 Conclusione per l'integrita del panteon. (Fea, Carlo.) Roma, 1807.

Htn Arc 402.13* Conde de Raczynski (Athanasius). (Vasconcellos, Joaquim de.) Porto, 1875.

Arc 1033.17.98.5 Conde y Oquendo, F. Dissertación histórica sobre la aparición de Nuestra Señora de Guadalupe. México, 1852. 2v.

Arc 500.3 Conder, C.R. Arabic and English name lists. London, 1881.

Arc 501.16 Conder, C.R. Heth and Moab. London, 1885.

Arc 501.16.2 Conder, C.R. Heth and Moab. London, 1892.

Arc 500.4 Conder, C.R. Memoirs of the topography. London, 1881-83. 3v.

Arc 500.5 Conder, C.R. Memoirs of the topography. London, 1889.

Arc 497.5 Conder, C.R. Palestine. London, 1889.

Arc 497.5.3 Conder, C.R. Palestine. N.Y., 1889.

Arc 501.16.8 Conder, C.R. Syrian stone-lore. N.Y., 1887.

Arc 501.16.12 Conder, C.R. The Tell Amarna tablets. London, 1893.

Arc 501.16.11 Conder, C.R. The Tell Amarna tablets. London, 1893.

Arc 501.16.13A Conder, C.R. The Tell Amarna tablets. 2. ed. London, 1894.

Arc 501.16.5 Conder, C.R. Tent work in Palestine. London, 1878. 2v.

Arc 501.16.7 Conder, C.R. Tent work in Palestine. London, 1887.

Arc 1538.13 Conder, James. An arrangement of provincial coins...Great Britain, Ireland. Ipswich, 1799.

Arc 936.24.5 Condurachi, Emil. Romania. London, 1971.

Arc 406.3F Conestabile, G. Della vita degli studî, e delle opere di Giambattista Vermiglioli discorso. Perugia, 1855.

Arc 726.83 Conestabile, Giancarlo. Sopra un cista in bronzo con rapparesentanze a graffito. Firenze, 1866.

Arc 435.25.4F The conference...including museums and archaeological conference...Simla, 1911. (Conference of Orientalists, Simla.) Simla, 1911.

Arc 584.100.5 Conférence. (Société Royale d'Archéologie d'Alexandrie.) Alexandrie. 1,1964+

Arc 302.51.6 Conference International d'Études Classiques des Pays Socialistes, 6th, Plovdiv, 1962. Acta antiqua Philippapolitana. Serdicae, 1963.

Arc 435.25.4F Conference of Orientalists, Simla. The conference...including museums and archaeological conference...Simla, 1911. Simla, 1911.

Arc 967.1.11 Conference on Midwestern Archaeology, St. Louis. Report. Washington, 1929.

Arc 858.77 Conference on Romano-British Cantonal Capitals, University of Leicester, 1963. The civitas capitals of Roman Britain. Leicester, 1966.

Arc 396.16 Conference on the Future of Archaeology, University of London, 1943. Conference on the future of archaeology held at the University of London. London, 1943?

Arc 396.16 Conference on the future of archaeology held at the University of London. (Conference on the Future of Archaeology, University of London, 1943.) London, 1943?

Arc 38.30 Conférences. (Institut Français d'Archéologie Orientale du Caire.) 3 2v.

Arc 1020.9.65 Conferenze della società di cultura della cristianità archeologia. (Marucchi, O.) Roma, 1877.

Arc 66.1.128 Confession a l'Allemagne. (Constant, G.) n.p., n.d. 2v.

Arc 1033.12.17 Confrérie du Saint Suaire. (Eberlé, L.) Besançon, 1886.

Arc 1494.1 Congeturae sobre las medallos. (Velazquez, L.J.) Malaga, 1759.

Arc 1675.21 Congeturas sobre las medallas de los reyes godos y suevos de España. (Velazquez, L.J.) Malaga, 1759. 2 pam.

Arc 3.1.21 Congrès International d'Archéologie Classique, 1st, Athens, 1905. Comptes rendus du Congrès International d'Archéologie Ire Session, Athènes, 1905. Athènes, 1905.

Arc 3.1.22 Congrès International d'Archéologie Classique, 2d, Cairo, 1909. Comptes rendus. Le Caire, 1909.

Arc 3.1.23 Congrès International d'Archéologie Classique, 3d, Rome, 1912. Bolletino riassuntivo. Roma, 1912.

Arc 3.1.24 Congrès International d'Archéologie Classique, 4th, Barcelona, 1929. IV Congresso internazionale d'archéologia; 23-29 settembre 1929. Barcelona? 1929.

Arc 3.1.25 Congrès International d'Archéologie Classique, 5th, Algiers, 1930. Cinquième Congrès international d'archéologie, Alger, 14-16 avril 1930. Alger, 1933.

Arc 3.1.26.5 Congrès International d'Archéologie Classique, 6th, Berlin, 1939. Bericht über den VI. Internationalen Kongress für Archäologie, Berlin, 21.-26. August, 1939. Berlin, 1940.

Arc 3.1.26 Congrès International d'Archéologie Classique, 6th, Berlin, 1939. Vorläufiges Programm. Berlin? 1939?

Arc 3.1.28 Congrès International d'Archéologie Classique, 8th, Paris, 1963. Le rayonnement des civilizations grecque et romaine sur les cultures périphériques. Paris, 1965. 2v.

Arc 384.15 Congrès International d'Archéologie Classique, 8th, Paris, 1963. VIIIe Congrès international d'archéologie classique. Photoreproduction. Paris, 1963.

Arc 388.1 Le congrès international d'archéologie préhistorique de Copenhague en 1869. (Demarsy, A.) Arras, 1870.

Arc 3.2 Congrès International d'Archéologie Prehistorique et d'Anthropologie, 11th, Moscow, 1892. Congrès internationational d'archéologie préhistorique et d'anthropologie. v.1-2. Moscou, 1892-93.

Arc 612.66 Congrès International d'Archéologie Slave, 1st, Warsaw, 1965. I międzynarodoury kongres Archeologii Słowianskiej. Wrocław, 1968. 7v.

Arc 612.66.5 Congrès International d'Archéologie Slave, 2d. Berichte. Berlin, 1970. 3v.

Arc 1308.7 Congrès international de numismatique. (International Numismatic Congress.) Paris, 1953-57. 2v.

Arc 3.1.5 Congrès International pour la Reproduction des Manuscrits. Actes. Bruxelles. 1905

Arc 3.2 Congrès internationational d'archéologie préhistorique et d'anthropologie. v.1-2. (Congrès International d'Archéologie Prehistorique et d'Anthropologie, 11th, Moscow, 1892.) Moscou, 1892-93.

Arc 3.1.27 Congrès Internatonal d'Archéologie Classique, 7th, Rome and Naples, 1958. Atti del settimo Congresso internazionale di archeologia classica. Roma, 1961. 3v.

Arc 94.30 Congreso Arqueológico del Sudeste Español. Cronica. Cartageno.

Arc 307.3.7 Congreso de Americanistas. Reunion en Mexico. (International Congress of Americanists, 11th, Mexico, 1895.) México, 1895.

Arc 307.3.6 Congreso internacional de Americanistas. (International Congress of Americanists, 9th, Madrid, 1892.) Madrid, 1891.

Arc 307.3.2 Congreso international de Americanistas. (International Congress of Americanists, 4th, Madrid, 1881.) Madrid, 1881.

Arc 307.3.35 La congresos internacionales de Americanistas. (Comas, Juan.) Mexico, 1954.

Arc 127.3.10 Pamphlet box. Congress of Archaeological Societies.

Arc 127.3.2 Congress of Archaeological Societies in Union with the Society of Antiquaries. Report of proceedings. London. 1901-1913

Arc 127.3 Congress of Archaeological Societies in Union with the Society of Antiquaries. Report of the committee on ancient earthworks. London? 1905-1920

Arc 127.3.4 Congress of Archaeological Societies in Union with the Society of Antiquaries. Report of the earthworks committee. 1921-1939

Arc 67.6 The congress of Roman frontier studies. (Durham, England. University. King's College, Newcastle upon Tyne.) Durham, 1952.

Arc 1308.7.6 Congresso internazionale di numismatica, Roma, 11-16 sett., 1961. (International Numismatic Congress, 6th, Rome, 1961.) Roma, 1961-65. 2v.

Arc 3.3 Congresso Internazionale di Preistoria. Atti. Firenze, 1952.

Arc 743.16 Congresso Internazionale Etrusco. Atti. Firenze. 1,1928

Arc 743.15 Congresso Internazionale Etrusco. Miscellaneous pamphlets. 1,1928+ 2v.

Arc 67.5 Congresso Nazionale di Archealogia Cristiana. Atti del 1 congresso nazionale di archealogia cristiana. Roma, 1952.

Arc 303.25 Congressus secundus archaeologorum balticorum. (Kongress Baltischer Archäologen, 2d, Riga, 1930.) Riga, 1931.

Arc 1675.30 Conjecturas sobre huma medallia de bronze. (Salgado, Vicente.) Lisboa, 1784.

Htn Arc 1538.1* The connexion of the Roman, Saxon, and English coins. (Clarke, W.) London, 1767.

Arc 810.62 Conoscere Pompei. (Ciprotti, Pio.) Roma, 1959.

Arc 968.1.2 Conover, G.S. Reasons why the state should acquire the famous burial mound of the Seneca Indians. n.p., n.d.

Arc 612.24 La conquête du massif alpin et de ses abords. Thèse. (Dellenbach, M.E.) Grenoble, 1935.

Arc 400.12.25 Conrad Peutinger in seinem Verhältnisse zum Kaiser Maximilian I. (Herberger, T.) Augsburg, 1851.

Arc 543.4.20F Conrady, A. Die chinesischen Handschriften..Sven Hedins in Lou-lan. Stockholm, 1920.

Arc 657.1 Conseils aux voyageurs archéologues en Grèce. (Reinach, S.) Paris, 1886.

Arc 397.11 Conservation manual. (Marshall, John.) Calcutta, 1923.

Arc 1138.125 Consideraciones sobre la escritura visigótica cursiva. (Millares Carlo, Agustín.) León, 1973.

Arc 1458.4 Considerations générales sur l'évaluation des monnaies grecques et romaines. (Letronne, J.A.) Paris, 1817.

Arc 1498.11 Considérations historiques et artistiques sur les monnaies de France. (Fillon, B.) Fontenay, 1850.

Arc 726.4.15A Consoli Fiego, G. Cumae and the Phlegraean fields. Naples, 1927.

Arc 435.1.20 Consolidated catalogue. (India. Archaeological Survey. Library.) New Delhi, 1940.

Arc 1490.8.15 Consolo Langher, S. Contributo alla storia della...moneta. Milano, 1964.

Arc 726.99 Consortini, L. Volterra nell'antichità. Volterra, 1940.

Arc 746.19 Consortini, P.L. Le necropoli etrusche di Volterra. Lucca, 1933.

Arc 830.15.13 Constans, L.A. Arles. Paris, 1928.

Arc 66.1.119 Constans, L.A. Arles antique. Paris, 1921.

Arc 830.15.9 Constans, L.A. Arles antique. Thèse. Paris, 1921.

Arc 66.1.128 Constant, G. Confession a l'Allemagne. n.p., n.d. 2v.

Arc 843.229 Constantes religiosas europeas y sotocuevenses (Ojo Guareña, cuna de Castilla). (Guerra y Gómez, Manuel.) Burgos, 1973.

Arc 935.2.5 Constantiniade, ou Description de Constantinople. Constantinople, 1861.

Arc 935.8 Constantinople, Turkey. Hellēnikos Philologikos Syllogos. Archaiologikē Epitropē. Archaiologikos chartēs. Konstantinople, 1884.

Arc 830.63.5 Contades, G. Les monuments mégalithiques. Paris, 1886.

Arc 1020.9.55 Contarino, F.L. Dell antiquita sito, chiese...di Roma. Napoli, 1678.

Arc 387.10.5 Il conte L. Palma di Cesnola e il Museo metropolitano di Nuova York. (Vedova, Giuseppe.) Roma, 1899.

Arc 493.45F Conténau, G. Fouilles du Tépé-Giyan. Paris, 1935.

Arc 416.6 Contenau, Georges. Manuel d'archéologie orientale depuis les origines jusqu'a l'époque d'Alexandre. Paris, 1927-47. 4v.

Arc 1229.1 Conteneau, G. La glyptique syro-hittite. Thèse. Paris, 1922.

Arc 1025.17 Contents...catacombs of Rome. (Scott, B.) London, 1873.

Arc 838.39 Contestanía Ibérica. (Llobregat Conesa, Enrique.) Alicante, 1972.

Arc 1033.12.160 Conti, G.B. Dell'origine invenzione...del...simulacro di...Gesu Crocifisso...volto santo. Lucca, 1834.

Arc 1033.12.159 Conti, G.B. Dell'origine invenzione...simulacro di Gesu Crocifisso...Volto santo. Lucca, n.d.

Arc 1153.8.5 Contractions in early Latin miniscule MSS. (Lindsay, W.M.) Oxford, 1908.

Arc 1163.2.32 Contribución al "corpus" de códices visigoticos. (Millares Carlo, A.) Madrid, 1931.

Arc 13.10 Contributi. (Milan. Università Cattolica del Sacro Cuore. Istituto di Archeologia.) Milano. 1,1967+ 2v.

Arc 608.17.5 Contributi di Cirene alla storia della religione greca. (Ferri, Silvio.) Roma, 1923.

Arc 1660.19F Contribution à la documentation du temps de guerre. (Lefebure, Charles.) Bruxelles, 1923.

Arc 830.158.15F Contribution à l'étude de la céramique à reflects métalliques recueillie à Alésia. (Sénéchal, Robert.) Dijon, 1972.

Arc 1433.38 Contribution à l'étude des ateliers monétaires...rois Sassanides. (Morgan, J. de.) Paris, 1913.

Arc 1668.2 Contribution of alchemy to numismatics. (Bolton, H.C.) N.Y., 1890.

Arc 943.14 Contributions. (N.Y. Museum of the American Indian. Heye Foundation.) N.Y. 1-18 13v.

Arc 936.40.16 Contributions a l'histoire du stade antique de Philippopolis. (Tsonchev, D.) Sofia, 1947.

Arc 726.2.9 Contributions to a study of earth movements in the Bay of Naples. (Günther, R.T.) Oxford, 1903.

Arc 530.172 Contributions to the archaeology of Armenia. Cambridge, 1968.

Arc 958.2 Contributions to the archaeology of the District of Columbia. (Kengla, L.A.) Washington, 1883.

Arc 923.113 Contributions to the archaeology of the Soviet Union. (Beregovaia, Nina Aleksandrovna.) Cambridge, 1966.

Arc 785.15.20 Contributo alla conoscenza della topografia dell'arte e della storia nella Colonna Traiana. (Stucchi, S.) Udine, 1960.

Arc 1490.8.15 Contributo alla storia della...moneta. (Consolo Langher, S.) Milano, 1964.

Arc 97.3 La controverse de Glozel. Paris.

Arc 522.19.10 Controverses autour de Troie. (Vellay, Charles.) Paris, 1936.

Htn Arc 1033.12.58* Controversia de excellentia instrumentorum passionis. (Vigerius, M.) Roma, 1512.

Arc 1033.14 Una controversia famosa di archeologia cristiana. n.p., 1872.

Arc 93.38F Il Convegno archeologico en Sardegna. 2. ed. (Convegno Archeologico in Sardegna.) Reggio nell'Emilia, 1929.

Arc 93.38F Convegno Archeologico in Sardegna. Il Convegno archeologico en Sardegna. 2. ed. Reggio nell'Emilia, 1929.

Arc 726.145 Convegno di Studi Plorici e Archeologici Veleiati, 1st, Piacenza. Studi veleiati. Piacenza, 1955.

Arc 726.235.5 Convegno internazionale di studi sulle antichità di classe. Atti del Convegno internazionale di studi sulle antichità di classe. Ravenna, 1968.

Arc 726.328 Convegno su Archeologia e Storia nella Lombardia Pedemontana Occidentale. Archeologia e storia nella Lombardia pedemontana occidentale. Como, 1969.

Arc 830.3.15 Les convenae et les consoranni. Thèse. (Lizop, Raymond.) Toulouse, 1931.

Arc 880.13 Conwell, E.A. Discovery of tomb of Ollamh Fodhla. Dublin, 1873.

Arc 635.200 Conze, A. Archäologische Untersuchungen auf Samothrake. Wien, 1875-80. 2v.

Arc 510.208.2 Conze, A. Die Ergebnisse der Ausgrabungen zu Pergamon, 1880-1881. Berlin, 1882.

Arc 510.208 Conze, A. Die Ergebnisse der Ausgrabungen zu Pergamon. Berlin, 1880.

Arc 520.3 Conze, A. Pergamon. Berlin, 1880.

Arc 642.3 Conze, A. Rapporto d'un viaggio fatto nella Grecia nel 1860. Roma, 1861.

Arc 681.1 Conze, A. Reise auf der Insel Lesbos. Hannover, 1865.

Arc 642.3.2 Conze, A. Reise auf Inseln des Thrak. Meeres. Hannover, 1860.

Arc 87.1.38 Conze, Alexander. Thesens und Minotauros. Berlin, 1878.

Arc 861.13.15 Cook, A.S. Some accounts of the Bewcastle Cross. N.Y., 1914.

Arc 630.9 Cook, Arthur B. Rise and progress of classical archaeology. Cambridge, Eng., 1931.

Arc 537.3.3 Cook, C. Transformations and migrations of certain statues in the Cesnola collection. N.Y., 1882.

Arc 522.41 Cook, John Manuel. The Troad; an archaeological and topographical study. Oxford, 1973.

Arc 642.10 Cook, R.M. The Greeks till Alexander. London, 1961.

Arc 700.57 Cook, R.M. Niobe and her children. Cambridge, 1964.

Arc 757.3 Cookesley, W.G. Explanatory index to the map of ancient Rome. Eton, 1851.

Arc 1411.14 Coole, Arthur Braddan. An encyclopedia of Chinese coins. 1. ed. Denver, 1967.

Arc 488.18 Coon, Carleton Stevens. Cave explorations in Iran, 1949. Philadelphia, 1951.

Arc 387.30A Cooper, Gordon. Dead cities and forgotten tribes. N.Y., 1952.

Arc 1138.123 Cope, Emma Elizabeth T. How to decipher and study old documents. Chicago, 1974.

Arc 247.4.2 Copenhagen. Mémoires de la Société Royale des Antiquaires du Nord (1840-44). Copenhagen, n.d.

Arc 893.3.2 Copenhagen. Kongelige Nordiske Oldskrift-Selskab. Guide to northern archaeology. London, 1848.

Arc 893.3 Copenhagen. Kongelige Nordiske Oldskrift-Selskab. Guide to northern archaeology. v.1-10. London, 1848.

Arc 893.3.3 Copenhagen. Kongelige Nordiske Oldskrift-Selskab. Ledetraad til nordisk oldkyndighed. Kjøbenhavn, 1836.

Arc 893.2 Copenhagen. Kongelige Nordiske Oldskrift-Selskab. Report addressed by the Royal Society of Northern Antiquaries ot its British and American members. Copenhagen, 1836.

Arc 890.203 Copenhagen. Kongeligi Nordiske Oldskrift-Selskab. Altas de l'archéologie du nord. Copenhagen, 1857.

Arc 1353.7.5 Copenhagen. National Museet. Catalogus numorum veterum graecorum et Latinorum musei. Hafniae, 1816. 3v.

Arc 1353.12 Copenhagen. National Museet. Orientalske, graeske og romerske. Kjøbenhavn, 1952.

Arc 1353.7F Copenhagen. National Museet. Sylloge nummorum Graecorum. v.1-30,41-42. Copenhagen, 1942- 20v.

Arc 893.16F Copenhagen. Nationalmuseet. Affaldsdynger faa stenalderen i Denmark undersögte for Nationalmuseet. Paris, 1900.

Arc 720.215 La coppa tarantina di argento dorato. (Mayer, M.) Bari, 1910.

Arc 1540.2 The copper coinage of the Earl of Stirling. (Shafter, E.F.) Boston, 1874.

Arc 1538.12 Copper coins of England. (Montagu, H.) London, 1893.

Arc 1033.105 Coppola, G. Relazione dello scoprimento del corpo del...martire S. Eusanio. Roma, 1749.

Arc 547.43 The Coptic Museum and the fortress of Babylon at old Cairo. (Cairo, Egypt. Coptic Museum.) Cairo, 1962.

Arc 585.22 Coptic Ostraca. (Crum, W.E.) London, 1902.

Arc 600.105F Coptic ostraca from Medinet Habu. (Stefanski, E.) Chicago, 1952.

Arc 136.1.50 A copy of the royal charter and statutes. (London Society of Antiquaries.) London, 1800.

Arc 396.7F Pamphlet box. Le Coq, A. von. Reprinted articles.

Arc 726.319 Coradazzi, Giovanni. Le rete stradale romana fra Brescia, Bergamo e Milano. Brescia, 1974.

Arc 712.32 Corbett, Peter Edgar. The sculpture of the Parthenon. Harmondsworth, 1959.

Arc 1033.34.70 Corbo, Virgilio. Ricordi di San Pietro sul lago di Tiberiade. Jerusalem, 1969.

Arc 1163.13 Cordeiro de Sausa, J.M. Algunas siglas e abreviaturas usadas. Lisboa, 1926.

Arc 1030.49.5 Cordeiro de Sousa, J.M. Apontamentos de epigrafía portuguesa. 2a ed. Lisboa, 1937.

Arc 1030.49 Cordeiro de Sousa, J.M. Inscrições sepulcrais da sé de Lisboa. Lisboa, 1927.

Arc 861.93 Corder, Philip. Excavations at the Roman fort at Brough-on-Humber. Hull, 1934.

Arc 861.93.5 Corder, Philip. Excavations at the Roman town at Brough-Petuaria, 1937. Hull, 1938.

Arc 861.110 Corder, Philip. The Roman town and villa at Great Casterton. Nottingham, 1951.

Author and Title Listing

Arc 562.2.10 Cordier, Henri. Bibliographie des oeuvres de Gaston Maspero. Paris, 1922.

Arc 875.40 Cordiner, Charles. Remarkable ruins and romantic prospects of North Britain. London, 1788-95.

Arc 1413.25 Corean coin charms and amulets. (Ramsden, H.A.) Yokohama, 1910.

Arc 672.5.7PF Corinth. (American School of Classical Studies at Athens.) 1-6,1952-1964 4v.

Arc 672.5.7F Corinth. (American School of Classical Studies at Athens.) 2-16,1932-1957 26v.

Arc 1.5.4.5 Corinth excavations. Weekly report. (American School of Classical Studies at Athens.)

Arc 595.65 Cormack, Maribelle. Imhotep, builder in stone. N.Y., 1965.

Arc 1033.17.85 Cornaro, F. Notizie...delle apparizioni e delle immagini di Maria...di Bergamo. Bergamo, 1868.

Arc 830.275.15 Cornet, Jean M. Entremont et l'impérium arverne. Romans, 1972- 2v.

Arc 505.5.115 Cornfeld, Gaalyahu. The mystery of the Temple Mount. Tel Aviv, 1972.

Arc 127.7 Cornish archaeology. St. Austell. 1,1962+ 2v.

Arc 1033.34.13 Cornoldi, G.M. San Pietro a Roma. Roma, 1872.

Arc 608.20 Corò, Francesco. Vestigia di colonie agricole romane Gebel Nefusa. Roma, 1928.

Arc 387.13F Corolia Ludwig Curtius zum sechzigsten Geburtstag dargebracht. Stuttgart, 1937. 2v.

Arc 628.25F Corolla archaeologica principi hereditario regni sueciae Gustavo Adolpho dedicata. Lund, 1932.

Arc 383.83 Corolla memoriae Erich Swoboda dedicata. Graz, 1966.

Arc 1458.11 Corolla numismatica...in honour of B.V. Head. London, 1906.

Arc 838.27 Corona de estudios. (Sociedad Española de Antropología, Etnografía y Prehistoria.) Madrid, 1941.

Arc 1033.12.183 Corona di ferro. (Bacci, G.) Ferrara, 1884.

Arc 1033.12.187 Corona ferrea al funebri nazionali di Vittorio Emanuele. (Zerbi, L.) Monza, 1878.

Arc 1033.17.461 Coronella in onore della G. Madre di Dio....Santa Maria di Caravaggio...Porta Reale. Napoli, 1748.

Arc 1033.77 Il corpo di S. Leonzio Martire. (Navarro, G.) Napoli, 1846.

Arc 1020.116 Les corps saints de l'insigne Basilique Saint Saturnin de Toulouse. Toulouse, n.d.

Arc 848.58 Corpus archäologischer Quellen zur Frühgeschichte auf dem Gebiet der Deutschen Demokratischen Republik (7. bis 12. Jahrhundert). Berlin, 1973- 2v.

Arc 1030.54F Corpus der griechisch-christlichen Inschriften von Hellas. (Lietzmann, Hans.) Athen, 1941.

Arc 1251.12 Corpus der minoischen und mykenischen Siegel. Berlin. 1,1964+ 10v.

Arc 1590.9.5 Corpus der mittelalterlichen Münzen von Kroatien, Slavozien, Dalmatien und Bosnien. (Rengjeo, Ivan.) Graz, 1959.

Arc 608.78 Corpus des gravures et des peintures rupestres de la région de Constantine. (Lefebvre, Gillette.) Paris, 1967.

Arc 635.201 Corpus des monuments grecs. Livre II: Lycosoura. (Normand, C.) Paris, n.d.

Arc 435.20.1F Corpus inscriptionum Indicarum. Calcutta, 1877.

Arc 435.20.5 Corpus inscriptionum Indicarum. Oxford, 1925.

Arc 435.20.2F Corpus inscriptionum Indicarum. v.1-4. Calcutta, 1879-1929. 5v.

Arc 1588.10.5 Corpus nummorum Hungariae. (Rethy, Landislaus.) Graz, 1958.

Arc 1485.7F Corpus nummorum italicorum. Roma, 1910-29. 15v.

Arc 1448.5 Corpus nummorum Nunudiae nauretaniaeque. (Mazard, Jean.) Paris, 1955.

Arc 1423.19 Corpus nummorum Palaestinensium; publications of the Israel Numismatic Society. Jerusalem. 1-4,1956-1961 4v.

Arc 1478.89 Corpus nummorum romanorum. (Banti, Alberto.) Firenze, 1972- 8v.

Arc 1588.1.22 Corpus numniorum Poloniae. (Gumowski, Marian.) Kraków, 1939.

Arc 1208.11F Corpus of ancient Near Eastern seals in North American collections. pt.1-2. (Committee of Ancient Near Eastern Seals.) N.Y., 1948-

Arc 588.49F Corpus of dated Palestinian pottery. (Duncan, J.G.) London, 1930.

Arc 870.12.10 The corpus of early Anglo-Saxon great square-headed broaches. (Leeds, E.T.) Oxford, 1949.

Arc 1079.2 A corpo of early Bronze Age dagger pommels from Great Britain and Ireland. (Hardaker, Ron.) Oxford, 1974.

Arc 1418.15.5 Corpus of Indian coins. (Numismatic Society of India.) Banaras, 1957.

Arc 858.95 A corpus of pagan Anglo-Saxon spear-types. (Swanton, M.J.) Oxford, 1974.

Arc 870.27 A corpus of Roman engraved gemstones from British sites. v.1-2. (Henig, Martin.) Oxford, 1974.

Arc 1418.22 Corpus of the Muslim coins of Bengal. (Karim, A.) Decca, 1960.

Arc 843.231 Correia, Vergilio. Estudos arqueologicos. Coimbra, 1972.

Arc 66.2.85 Correspondance d'Emmanuel Roux. (Radet, G.) Bordeaux, 1898.

Arc 66.1.203 Correspondance des légats et vicaires-généraux. (Glenisson, Jean.) Paris, 1964.

Arc 1018.22 Correspondenza di L.A. Muratori. (Tacchi-Venturi, P.) Roma, 1901.

Arc 1033.12.56 Corrieris, L. de. De sessorianis praecepuis passionis...reliquiis commentariis. Romae, 1830.

Arc 785.28 Corsi, F. Delle pietre antiche. Roma, 1845.

Arc 785.28.5 Corsi, F. Delle pietre antiche. 2. ed. Roma, 1833.

Arc 726.61 Das corsinische Silbergefäss. (Michaelis, Adolf.) Leipzig, 1859.

Arc 497.50.5 Corswant, Willy. A dictionary of life in Bible times. N.Y., 1960.

Arc 497.50 Corswant, Willy. Dictionnaire d'archéologie biblique. Neuchâtel, 1956.

Arc 726.11.9 Corte, M. della. Cleopatra, M. Antonio e Ottaviano nelle allegorie storico-umoristiche delle argenterie del tesoro di Boscoreale. Pompei, 1951.

Arc 810.54.5 Corte, Matteo della. Case ed abitanti di Pompei. 2. ed. Pompei, 1954.

Arc 810.54.7 Corte, Matteo della. Case ed abitanti di Pompei. 3. ed. Napoli, 1965.

Arc 815.10 Corte, Matteo della. Inventus. Arpino, 1924.

Arc 810.54 Corte, Matteo della. Piccola guida di Pompei. Pompei, 1939.

Arc 810.40.10 Corte, Matteo della. Pompei; i nuovi scavi e l'anfiteatro. Pompei, 1930.

Arc 810.40 Corte, Matteo della. Pompéi; les nouvelles fouilles. Pompéi, 1926.

Arc 810.40.3 Corte, Matteo della. Pompéi. Pompéi, 1935.

Arc 810.40.5 Corte, Matteo della. Pompeji. Pompeji, 1926.

Arc 1033.34.60 Corte, Nicola. San Pietro e sepolto in Vaticano? Roma, 1957.

Arc 726.235.10 Cortesi, Giuseppe. Il porto e la città di classe. Alfonsine, 1967.

Arc 793.15 Corti, E.C. The destruction and resurection of Pompeii and Herculaneum. London, 1951.

Arc 793.14.5A Corti, Egon C. Untergang und Auferstehung von Pompeji und Herculaneum. 3. Aufl. München, 1941.

Arc 726.53 Cortona etrusca e romana. (Neppi Modona, A.) Firenze, 1925.

Arc 1033.17.463 Corvino, R. Tesoro nascosto minifestato per la miracolosa invenzione di Santa Maria...Napoli. Napoli, 1831.

Arc 968.2.25 Cosgrove, H.S. The Swarts ruin...New Mexico. Cambridge, 1932.

Arc 843.175 Costa, J.M. da. Novos elementos para a lócalização de Cetóbriga.Setúbal, 1960.

Arc 1675.37 Costa, Luiz X. da. Domingos Antonio de Sequeira e Francesco Vieira Lusitano. Lisboa, 1923. 2 pam.

Arc 1494.25 Costa Couvreur, Raul de. Uma reproducão em cabre de moeda de retrato datado de 1630. Lisboa, 1956.

Arc 1153.114 Costamagna, Giorgio. Studi di paleografia e diplomatica. Roma, 1972.

Arc 1153.110 Costamagna, Giorgio. Tachigrafia notarile e scritture segrete medioevali in Italia. Roma, 1968.

Arc 1020.9.110 Costanzi, G. Le instituzioni di Pieta...in Roma. v.1-2. Roma, 1825.

Arc 820.214F Côte-d'Or. Commission des Antiquités. Voies romaines...de la Côte-d'Or. Dijon, 1872.

Arc 843.75 El coto de Doña Ana. (Bonser, J.E.) Madrid, 1922.

Arc 612.8 Cotteau, G.H. Le préhistorique en Europe. Paris, 1889.

Arc 976.5 Cotter, J.L. Archaeological excavations at Jamestown. Washington, 1958.

Arc 861.135 Cotton, M. Aylwin. Excavations at Clausentum (Southampton). London, 1958.

Arc 552.4 Cottrell, L. The lost Pharaohs. N.Y., 1951.

Arc 642.8 Cottrell, Leonard. The bull of Minos. London, 1953.

Arc 642.8.5 Cottrell, Leonard. The bull of Minos. London, 1962.

Arc 642.8.1 Cottrell, Leonard. The bull of Minos. London, 1971.

Arc 387.33 Cottrell, Leonard. Lost cities. N.Y., 1957.

Arc 595.55 Cottrell, Leonard. The mountains of Pharaoh. N.Y., 1956.

Arc 628.20.5 Couch, Herbert N. Treasure of the Greeks and Romans. Thesis. Menasha, 1929.

Arc 628.20 Couch, Herbert N. The treasuries of the Greeks and Romans. Menasha, 1929.

Arc 830.250 Cougnac, grotte peinte. (Meroc, L.) Stuttgart, 1956.

Arc 830.143 Cougny, G. de. Chinon et ses monuments. 3. éd. Chinon, 1889.

Arc 340.39 Coulson, William D.E. An annotated bibliography of Greek and Roman art. N.Y., 1975.

Arc 858.82 Council for British Archaeology, London. Iron Age and Roman Research Committees. The Iron Age in Northern Britain. Edinbrugh, 1967.

Arc 127.5 Council for British Archaeology. London.

Arc 935.4 Les coupes du palais des empereurs byzantins. (Montucci, Henry.) Paris, 1877.

Arc 66.1.201 La cour pontificale d'Avignon, 1309-1376. (Guillemain, B.) Paris, 1962.

Arc 66.1.81 Courbaud, E. Le Bas-Relief Romain a représentations historiques. Paris, 1899.

Arc 66.1.208 Courbin, Paul. La céramique géométrique de l'Argolide. Paris, 1966. 2v.

Arc 688.3F Courby, F. Recherches archéologiques à Stratos d'Acarnanie. Paris, 1924.

Arc 66.1.125 Courby, Fernand. Les vases grecs à reliefs. n.p., n.d.

Arc 823.14 Courcelle-Seneuil, Jean L. Les dieux gaulois d'après les monuments figurés. Paris, 1910.

Arc 1033.17.222 Couronnement de Notre-Dame de Boulogne. (Haigneré, D.) Boulogne, 1885.

Arc 1190.3.6 Court-hand restored, or The student's assistant in reading old deeds. (Wright, Andrew.) London, 1974.

Arc 1190.3 Court hand restored. 2. ed. (Wright, Andrew.) London, 1778.

Arc 1190.3.2 Court hand restored. 8. ed. (Wright, Andrew.) London, 1867.

Arc 1190.3.3 Court hand restored. 9. ed. (Wright, Andrew.) London, 1879.

NEDL Arc 1190.3.5 Court hand restored. 10. ed. (Wright, Andrew.) London, 1912.

Arc 497.35 Courtin, Louis. Collection de Louis Courtin. Paris, 189-.

Arc 608.6.4 Courtois, C. Timgad. Alger, 1951.

Arc 435.11.12 Cousens, Henry. An account of the caves at Nadsur and Karsambla. Bombay, 1891.

Arc 435.2.42F Cousens, Henry. Chalukyan architecture. Calcutta, 1926.

Arc 435.2.19F Cousens, Henry. Lists of antiquarian remains in the central provinces and Berâr. Calcutta, 1897.

Arc 642.4 Cousinéry, E.M. Voyage dans la Macédoine. Paris, 1831. 2v.

Arc 830.177 Cousset, A. Communications. Le Mans, 1913.

Arc 830.176 Cousset, A. Découverte de gravures de sabots d'équides sur Rocher. Paris, 1911.

Arc 830.40.5 Coutil, Léon. Archéologie gauloise, gallo-romaine, franque et carolingienne. v.1-2, 3-5. Paris, 1895-1925. 2v.

Arc 830.40 Coutil, Léon. Inventaire des menhirs et dolmens de France. Eure. Louviers, 1897.

Arc 830.39 Coutil, Léon. Inventaire des monuments megalithiques du Calvados. Caen, 1902.

Arc 830.40.9 Coutil, Léon. Les ruines romaines de Noyers-sur-Andelys (Eure); villa rustica et théatre. Évreux, 1928. 2 pam.

Arc 1588.7.5F Coutributic la cunoasterea Syauselar de arguil doeice. (Floca, Ochaviau.) București, 1956.

Arc 830.260 Couture, Claude Paul. À l'assaut de la carrière du Puits. Le Havre, 1957.

Arc 943.38 Covarrubias, M. The eagle. 1. ed. N.Y., 1954.

Arc 743.14 Covegno Nazionale Etrusco. Atti. Firenze. 1-2

Arc 608.12 Cowper, H.S. The hill of the Graces...Tripoli. London, 1897.

Arc 858.23 Cox, R.H. The green roads of England. London, 1914.

Arc 885.28 Coygan Camp; a prehistoric Romano-British and Dark Age settlemant in Carmarthenshire. (Wainwright, G.) Cwmgwyn, 1967.

Arc 1027.25.13 Cozza, Luzi G. Per un busto...G.B. de Rossi. Roma, 1883- 3 pam.

Author and Title Listing

Arc 1033.57 Cozza-Luzi, G. Di un antico filiatterio christiano. Napoli, 1887.
Arc 1033.12 Cozza-Luzi. Le memorie...dell'infanzia di Gesù Cristo. Roma, 1894.
Arc 757.8 Cozzo, G. Il luogo primitivo di Roma. Roma, 1935.
Arc 1520.20 Crab, Jan. De munt to Leuven tot het einde der XVe eeuw. Leuven, 1967.
Arc 858.101 Cradle of England: an introduction through archaeology to the early history of England and a brief guide to selected sites in the South. (Cunliffe, Barry W.) London, 1972.
Arc 543.4.15 The cradle of humanity. (Tai, Tse tsan.) n.p., 1926.
Arc 875.45 Craig Phadrig; interim report on 1971 excavation. (Small, Alan.) Dundee, 1972.
Arc 505.21 Cramer, F. Scythische Denkmahlen in Palästina. Kiel, 1777.
Arc 1166.7.10 Cramer, Maria. Archäologische und epigrapische Klassifikation koptischer Denkmäler des Metropolitan Museum of Art, N.Y. und des Museum of Fine Arts, Boston, Mass. Wiesbaden, 1957.
Arc 1166.7 Cramer, Maria. Koptische Inschriften im Kaiser-Friedrich Museum zu Berlin. Le Caire, 1949.
Arc 1166.7.15F Cramer, Maria. Koptische Paläographie. Wiesbaden, 1964.
Arc 865.26 Crampton, Patrick. Stonehenge of the kings: a people appear. London, 1967.
Arc 608.26F Crawfard, O.G.S. Abu Geili. London, 1951.
Arc 1478.3.10 Crawford, Michael H. Roman Republican coinage. N.Y., 1974. 2v.
Arc 870.18F Crawford, O.G.S. Air survey and archaeology. Southampton, 1924.
Arc 870.10.5 Crawford, O.G.S. The long barrows of Cotswolds. Gloucester, Eng., 1925.
Arc 861.82F Crawford, O.G.S. Wessex from the air. Oxford, 1928.
Arc 387.5.10 Crawford, Osbert Guy S. Archaeology in the field. London, 1953.
Arc 387.5.12 Crawford, Osbert Guy S. Archaeology in the field. N.Y., 1953.
Arc 387.5 Crawford, Osbert Guy S. Man and his past. London, 1921.
Arc 387.35 Crawford, Osbert Guy S. Said and done. London, 1955.
Arc 440.2F Crawley-Boevey, A.W. A scheme for the protection and conservation of antient buildings...city of Ahmedabad. Bombay, 1886.
Arc 1033.4.5 La credenza della primitiva chiesa del Sacramento dell'Eucaristia. (Cavedoni, C.) Modena, 1869.
Arc 421.12 Creel, H.G. Studies in early Chinese culture. London, 1938.
Arc 853.90 Crefeld, Germany. Städtischen Kulturamt Schriftenreihe. Krefeld. 1-2,1937-1938 2v.
Arc 785.44 Crellius, C. Priteal libonis ex antquus erutis. Wittenberg, 1729.
Arc 936.205.5 Čremošnik, Gregor. Nalazi iz rimskog doba na stupu kod. Sarajeva. Sarajevo, 1930.
Arc 543.116 The cresent and the bull; a survey. (Zehren, Erich.) N.Y., 1962.
Arc 726.74F Crespellani, A. Del sepolcreto e degli altri monumenti antichi scoperti presso Bazzano. Modena, 1875.
Arc 726.105 Cressedi, G. Velitrae. Roma, 1953.
Arc 969.9 Cressman, L.S. Archaeological researches in the northern great basin. Washington, 1942.
Arc 505.5.95 Creswell, K.A. La mosquée Al Aqsa et la Néa de Justinien. Liege, 1929.
Arc 1251.10F Cretan seals. (Kenna, V.E.G.) Oxford, 1960.
Arc 672.1.51F A Cretan statuette in the Fitzwilliam Museum. (Wace, A.J.B.) Cambridge, Eng., 1927.
Arc 672.1.9.5 Crete, the forerunner of Greece. (Hawes, C.H.) London, 1922.
Arc 672.1.8 La Crete ancienne. (Lagrange, M.J.) Paris, 1908.
Arc 672.1.80F Crete and Mycenae. (Marinatos, Spyridon.) N.Y., 1960.
Arc 672.1.73 La Crète antique. (Matton, Raymond.) Athènes, 1955.
Arc 672.1.96 La Crète dédalique. (Demargne, P.) Paris, 1947.
Arc 66.1.164 La Crète dédalique. (Demargne, Pierre.) Paris, 1947. 2v.
Arc 66.1.163 La Crète et le monde grec. (Effenterre, Henri van.) Paris, 1948.
Arc 1077.2.9 La creu els monuments megalitics. (Brunet y Bellet, J.) Barcelona, 1892.
Arc 1077.2.39F Les creus d'Argenteria a Catalunya. (Gudiol y Cunill, José.) Barcelona, 1920.
Arc 432.6 Crinwasa Aiyangar, P.T. The stone age in India. Madras, 1926.
Arc 1015.213.12 La cripta dei Papi et la capella di Santa Cecilia. (Wilpert, J.) Roma, 1910.
Arc 1027.31 La cripta di S. Angelo de Profoglio...Camerino. (Santoni, M.) Camerino, 1892.
Arc 1020.9.125 Cripta di S. Gennaro nel cimeterio. (Scognamiglio, A.) Roma, 1863.
Arc 1027.15.5 La cripta sepolceale di San Valentio sulla Flaminia. (Marucchi, O.) Roma, 1878.
Arc 1033.17.58 Crispi, L. Dissertazione anti-critica...S. Luca evangelista fosse pittore. Faenza, 1776.
Arc 746.47 Cristofani, Mauro. La tomba delle iscrizioni a Cerveteri. Firenze, 1965.
Arc 800.3.13 Critical account of the situation and destruction by the first eruptions of Mount Vesuvius. (Winckelmann, J.) London, 1771.
Arc 1390.15.5 Critical survey of mediaeval Teutonic and Spanish coinage. (Stockvis, Albert.) Cleveland, 1960.
Arc 823.19.95 Critique, 1881. (Thédenat, H.) Paris, 1881.
Arc 823.19.110 Critique, 1882. (Thédenat, H.) Paris, 1882.
Arc 1138.33 La critique des textes. (Collomp, Paul.) Paris, 1931.
Arc 823.19.25 Critique 1880. (Thédenat, H.) Paris, 1880.
Arc 936.180.25 Crnokalačka bara. (Tasić, Nikola.) Kruševac, 1969.
Arc 1027.3 La croce sui monumenti delle catacombe. (Wilpert, G.) Roma, 1902.
Arc 1027.3.5 Il crocifesso negli antichi monumenti. (Carini, I.) Roma, 1889.
Arc 1033.34.41 La crocifisione di San Pietro nel Vaticano. (Marucchi, O.) Roma, 1905.
Arc 1030.5.62 Il crocifisso graffito. (Garruci, P.R.) Roma, 1857.
Arc 830.290 Croix, Charles. Les anciennes fortifications d'Avesnes. Cholet, 1957.
Arc 1077.2.45 La croix Gaillard de la Dionnerie au Musée metropolitan. (Chauncey Ross, M.) Poitiers, 1934.
Arc 1033.35.47 Croix-reliquiare de l'eglise de S. Florent-les-Saumur. (Barbier de Montault, X.) Angers, n.d.
Arc 495.3.5F Croly, George. The Holy Land, Syria, Idumea, Arabia, Egypt and Nubia. London, 1855-56. 3v.
Arc 674.3.3 Crome, J.F. Die Skulpturen des Asklepiostempels von Epidauros. Berlin, 1951.
Arc 880.21 The cromlechs of county Dublin. (Poe, J.W.) Dublin, 1918?
Arc 94.30 Cronica. (Congreso Arqueológico del Sudeste Español.) Cartageno.
Arc 67.1 Cronichetta mensuale. Rome. 1-26,1867-1894 11v.
Arc 823.10 Cronique archéologique de la France. (Blanchet, A.) Paris, 1902.
Arc 823.10.2 Cronique archéologique de la France. (Blanchet, A.) Paris, 1903.
Arc 963.2.15 Crook, A.R. The origin of the Cahokia mounds. Springfield, 1922.
Htn Arc 1020.111* Croques reliques. Poéme burlesque. Paris, 1876.
Arc 1610.2 Crosby, S.S. The early coins of America. Boston, 1875.
Arc 1610.2.1 Crosby, S.S. The early coins of America. Lawrence, 1974.
Arc 1615.2 Crosby, S.S. United States coinage of 1793, cents and half cents. Boston, 1897.
Arc 1077.2.43 The cross, its history and symbolism. (Benson, G.W.) Buffalo, 1934.
Arc 1077.2.5 The cross. (Seymour, W.W.) N.Y., 1898.
Arc 1077.2.33 The cross in ritual architecture and art. 2. ed. (Tyack, G.S.) London, 1900.
Arc 1033.35.146 The cross of Christ. (Zöckler, Otto.) London, 1877.
Arc 609.17.15 Cross River monoliths. (Allison, Philip.) Laejos, 1968.
Arc 880.37A The crosses and culture of Ireland. (Porter, Arthur Kingsley.) New Haven, 1931.
Arc 861.92 The crosses of Monmouthshire. (Mitchell, E.H.) Newport, 1893.
Arc 861.19 Crossing, W. The ancient stone crosses of Dartmoor. Exeter, 1902.
Arc 1025.43 Crostarosa, P. Notizie sullo stato delle catacombe romane. Roma, 1901.
Arc 1033.2 Crostarosa, P. Osservazioni sul musaico di S. Pudenziana. Roma, 1895.
Arc 505.5.90 Crowfoot, J.W. Excavations...Tyropoeon Valley, Jerusalem, 1927. London, 1929.
Htn Arc 1480.35F* Croy, Charles. Regum et imperatorum Romanorum numismata. Antverpiae, 1654.
Arc 823.4.4 Croyes, H. Répertoire archéologique du département du Tarn. Paris, 1865.
Arc 1077.10 Le crucifix. (Thoby, Paul.) Nantes, 1959.
Arc 1077.10.2 Le crucifix. Supplément. (Thoby, Paul.) Nantes, 1963.
Arc 936.225.5 Crucium. (Pirković, Ivo.) Ljubljana, 1968.
Arc 875.110 Cruden, Stewart. The early Christian and Pictish monuments of Scotland. Edinburgh, 1957.
Arc 1020.10.37 Cruickshank, J.W. Christian Rome. London, 1906.
Arc 1020.10.38 Cruickshank, J.W. Christian Rome. 2. ed. London, 1911.
Arc 585.22 Crum, W.E. Coptic Ostraca. London, 1902.
Arc 421.26 Crump, J. Dragon bones in the yellow earth. N.Y., 1963.
Arc 955.1 The Crump burial cave (Blount County, Alabama). (Burns, Frank.) n.p., 1892.
Arc 505.55 A crusaders' fortress in Palestine. (New York. Metropolitan Museum of Art.) N.Y., 1927.
Htn Arc 1077.2.25* Crux dominica adorabile christianae religionis vexillum observationibus. (Gori, A.F.) Florentiae, 1749.
Htn Arc 1016.244* Crux triumphans et gloriosa. Antwerp, 1617.
Arc 1033.35.147 A cruz de vila Viçosa. (Almeida, R.V. d'.) Lisboa, 1908.
Arc 1033.35.147.2 A cruz de vila Viçosa. 2. ed. (Almeida, R.V. d'.) Lisboa, 1957.
Arc 1015.206.9 Cryptae Carciliae trans Tiberim descriptio. 2. ed. (Iozzi, Oliviero.) Romae, 1902.
Arc 1027.32 Les cryptes vaticanes. (Dufresne, D.) Paris, 1902.
Arc 905.85 Csallány, Dezsö. Archäologische Denkmäler der Awarenzeit in Mitteleuropa. Budapest, 1956.
Arc 530.115 Ctesiphon and Hatra. (Iraq. Department of Antiquities.) Baghdad, 1943.
Arc 82.3 Cuadernos de trabajos. (Rome. Escuela Espagnola de Arqueologia é Historia.) Madrid. 3-11 6v.
Arc 815.5.5 Cube, G. von. Die römische "Scenae Frons". Berlin, 1906.
Arc 1027.5.4 Il cubicolo di Ampliato nel cimitero di Domitilla. (Rossi, G.B. de.) Roma, 1900.
Arc 861.197 Cuddesdon and Dorcester-on-Thames, Oxfordshire. (Dickinson, Tania M.) Oxford, 1974.
Arc 1348.14 Cueilloir numismatique. (Marsy, Arthur.) n.p., 1887.
Arc 1027.4.21 La cuestione...controversia filumeniana. (Bonavenia, G.) Roma, 1907.
Arc 843.151 La Cueva de la Pileta. (Gimenez, Reyna.) Málaga, 1958.
Arc 843.182 La cueva del Buar. (Obermaier, Hugo.) Madrid, 1918.
Arc 1033.17.100 Cuevas, J. de J. La santissima virgen de Guadalupe. México, 1887.
Arc 488.24 Culican, William. The Medes and Persians. London, 1965.
Arc 895.72 Cullberg, Carl. On artifact analysis. Bonn, 1968.
Arc 1077.6 The cult of the circle-builders. (Nelson, E.M.) London, 1909.
Arc 670.8 Cult places in the Aegean world. (Rutkowski, Bogdan.) Wrocław, 1972.
Arc 66.1.93 Le culte d'Apollon Pythien à Athènes. (Colin, G.) Paris, 1905.
Arc 66.1.31 Culte de castor et pollux en Italie. (Albert, M.) Paris, 1883.
Arc 1033.12.133 Culte de la sainte-face à S. Pierre du Vatican. (Janvier.) Tours, 1883.
Arc 1033.17.105 Le culte de la Sainte Vierge en Afrique. (Delattre, A.L.) Paris, 1907.
Arc 66.1.141 Le culte des muses. (Boyancé, Pierre.) Paris, 1937.
Arc 66.1.191 La culte imperial dans la peninsule iberique d'Auguste à Dioclétien. (Etienne, Robert.) Paris, 1958.
Arc 66.1.188 Les cultes indigenes en Carie. (Laumonier, Alfred.) Paris, 1958.
Arc 1033.34.11F Il culto di San Pietro sul Gianicolo. (Lugari, J.B.) Roma, 1907.
Arc 421.32 Cultural frontiers in ancient east Asia. (Watson, William.) Edinburgh, 1971.
Arc 390.13 Culture and environment. (Foster, I.L.) London, 1963.
Arc 551.9F The cultures of prehistoric Egypt. (Baumgartel, Elise J.) London, 1947.
Arc 726.4.15A Cumae and the Phlegraean fields. (Consoli Fiego, G.) Naples, 1927.
Arc 755.1 Cumelung, W. Museums and ruins of Rome. London, 1906. 2v.
Arc 1588.6.30 Cumhuriyet devrinde madeni para bois. (Butak, Bekzad.) Istanbul, 1955.
Arc 861.10.5 Cumming, J.G. Runic and other monumental remains...Isle of Man. London, 1857.
Arc 432.8 Cumming, John. Revealing India's past. London, 1939.
Arc 955.5 Cummings, B. Kinishba. Phoenix, Arizona, 1940.
Arc 497.24 Cumont, Franz. Études syriennes. Paris, 1917.
Arc 830.172 Cumont, Franz. La stèle du danseur d'Antibes et son decor végétal. Paris, 1942.

Arc 1663.23 Cunha, Xavier. A medalha de Casimiro José de Lima em homenagem a Sousa Martins. Coimbra, 1903.

Arc 1663.24 Cunha, Xavier. A medalha escolar do coll. do Corpo-Santo noticia numismatic. Coimbra, 1907.

Arc 1030.44 Cunha de Almeida, Jeronymo. Quizo historico sobre o letreiro que se achon em hua pedra que estaua no celeiro do Monst. de Vayrão. Pôrto, 1918.

Arc 858.101 Cunliffe, Barry W. Cradle of England: an introduction through archaeology to the early history of England and a brief guide to selected sites in the South. London, 1972.

Arc 858.103 Cunliffe, Barry W. Iron Age communities in Britain. London, 1974.

Arc 861.40.20 Cunliffe, Barry W. Roman Bath discovered. London, 1971.

Htn Arc 1418.2.4* Cunningham, A. Coins of Alexander's succesors in the East. London, 1884?

Arc 1418.2 Cunningham, A. Coins of ancient India. London, 1891.

Arc 1418.2.2 Cunningham, A. Coins of mediaeval India. London, 1894.

Arc 1433.4 Cunningham, A. Coins of the Indo-Scythians. pt.1-2. London, 1888.

Arc 441.6F Cunningham, Alexander. The stûpa of Bharhut. London, 1879.

Arc 861.31.10 Cunnington, M.E. (Mrs.) Avebury; a guide. Devizes, 19- .

Arc 855.227F Cunnington, M.E. (Mrs.) The early iron age inhabited site at All Cannings Cross farm, Wiltshire. Devizes, 1923.

Arc 861.86F Cunnington, M.E. (Mrs.) Woodhenge. Devizes, 1929.

Arc 861.31.20 Cunnington, M.E. (Mrs.). Introduction to the archaeology of Wiltshire. Devizes, 1933.

Arc 865.21 Cunnington, R.H. Stonehenge and its date. London, 1935.

Arc 1302.9 Cunobelin; the yearbook of the British Association of Numismatic Societies. Leeds. 3-14,1956-1968//

Arc 66.1.21 Cuq, E. Études d'epigraphie juridique. Paris, 1881.

Arc 391.5 Un curieuse figure d'artiste, Girault de Prangey, 1802-1892. (Simony, C. de.) Dijon, 1937.

Arc 1076.3.97 Curiosities of the belfry. (Briscoe, J.P.) London, 1883.

Arc 397.15 Curle, Alexander O. Sir George Macdonald, 1862-1940. London, 1941?

Arc 855.9 Curle, James. A Roman frontier post and its people. Glasgow, 1911.

Arc 1418.9 The currencies of Hindu states of Réjputána. (Webb, W.W.) Westminster, 1893.

Arc 1411.10F The currency of the Far East. (Schjöth, F.) London, 1929.

X Cg Arc 1408.3 Currency of the Farther East from earliest times up to 1895. (Lockhart, James H.S.) Hong Kong, 1895-1907. 3v.

Arc 1400.5 The current gold and silver coins of all countries. (Martin, Leopold Charles.) London, 1863?

Arc 307.3.8 Currier, C.W. Seventeenth international congress of Americanists. Washington, 1910?

Arc 1200.22 Curschmann, Fritz. Die älteren Papsturkunden des Erzbistums Hamburg. Hamburg, 1909.

Arc 1356.6 Curso de numismatica. 2. ed. (Beltrán Martinez, A.) Cartagena, 1950.

Arc 1138.60 Curso general de paleografia y diplomatica españolas. v.1-2. (Floriano, A.C.) Oviedo, 1946.

Arc 810.34 Curti, Pier A. Pompei e le sue rovine. Milano, 1872-74. 3v.

Arc 1335.3 Curtis, J.K. Priced catalogue of coins, medals and numismatic works. v.1-2. N.Y., 1858-59.

Arc 1033.12.51.3 Curtius, C. De clavis Dominicis liber. Antverpiae, 1634.

Arc 1033.12.51 Curtius, C. De clavis Dominicis liber. Antverpiae, 1670.

Arc 684.1.2 Curtius, E. Die Altere von Olympia. Berlin, 1882.

Arc 710.3 Curtius, E. Die Akropolis von Athen. Berlin, 1844.

Arc 518.2 Curtius, E. Ephesos. Berlin, 1874.

Arc 387.3 Curtius, E. Festrede. Göttingen, 1862.

Arc 635.4 Curtius, E. Die Funde von Olympia. Berlin, 1882.

Arc 87.1.12 Curtius, E. Herakles der Satyr und Dreifussränber. Berlin, 1852.

Arc 87.1.29 Curtius, E. Die knieenden Figuren der altgriechische Kunst. Berlin, 1870.

Arc 684.1.3 Curtius, E. Olympia und Umgegend. Berlin, 1882.

Arc 705.11 Curtius, E. Sieben Karten zur Topographie von Athen. Gotha, 1868.

Arc 705.11PF Curtius, E. Sieben Karten zur Topographie von Athen. Atlas. Gotha, 1868.

Arc 635.216 Curtius, E. Zur Geschichte des Wegebaus bei den Griechen. Berlin, 1855.

Arc 684.5.10F Curtius, Ernst. Olympia: die Ergebnisse. v.5. Berlin, 1896.

Arc 757.9F Curtius, Ludwig. Das antike Rom. 3. Aufl. Wien, 1957.

Arc 387.13.5 Curtius, Ludwig. Deutsche und antike Welt. Stuttgart, 1950.

Arc 387.13.7 Curtius, Ludwig. Humanistisches und Humanes. Basel, 1954.

Arc 387.13.15 Curtius, Ludwig. Torso. Stuttgart, 1958.

Arc 815.15.2 Curtius, Ludwig. Die Wandmalerei Pompejis. Darmstadt, 1960.

Arc 815.15 Curtius, Ludwig. Die Wandmalerei Pompejis. Leipzig, 1929.

Arc 861.41.25 Curwen, E. Cecil. The archaeology of Sussex. London, 1937.

Arc 861.41.20 Curwen, E. Cecil. Prehistoric Sussex. London, 1929.

Arc 943.50 Cusack, Betty Bugbee. Collector's luck: giant steps into prehistory. 1. ed. Stoneham, Mass., 1968.

Arc 1077.2.28 Cutts, E.L. Manuel...sepulchral slabs and crosses of the Middle Ages. London, 1849.

Arc 530.13 Cybébé. (Radet, G.) Paris, 1909.

Arc 865.5 Cyclops Christianus; disprove...Stonehenge. (Herbert, A.) London, 1849.

Arc 1015.232F Ein Cyclus christologischer Gemälde. (Wilpert, J.) Freiburg, 1891.

Arc 925.50.295 Cynkałowski, Aleksandr. Materiały do pradziejów Wołynia i Polesia Wołyńskiego. Warszawa, 1961.

Arc 1025.34 Cyprian, E.S. De ecclesia subterranea liber. Helmstedt, 1699. 8 pam.

Arc 1033.12.25 Cyprian, E.S. Facias Christi. Helmestad, n.d.

Arc 505.3.9 Cyprien. Le vraie forme primitive...du Saint Sépulcre. Paris, 1879.

Arc 540.12 Cypriot bronzework in the Mycenaean world. (Catling, H.W.) Oxford, 1964.

Arc 537.2 Cyprus. (Cesnola, L.P.) London, 1877.

Arc 537.2.3A Cyprus. (Cesnola, L.P.) N.Y., 1878.

Arc 537.12 Cyprus. (Karageorghis, Basos.) London, 1949.

Arc 535.4 Cyprus. Department of Antiquities. Annual report of the director. Nicosia. 1949+

Arc 535.3 Cyprus. Department of Antiquities. Report. Nicosia. 1936+ 6v.

Arc 608.17.21 Cyrenaican expedition of the University of Manchester. (Rowe, Alan.) Manchester, Eng., 1956.

Arc 608.48 Cyrene and Apollonia. (Goodchild, Richard G.) Tripoli? 1959.

Arc 66.1.177 Cyrène sous la monarchie des Battiades. (Chamoux, F.) Paris, 1953.

Arc 387.40 Cyriac of Ancona. (Ashmole, Bernhard.) London, 1957.

Arc 757.4 Cyriacus. Anconitanus. La Roma antica...desegnii inedite. Roma, 1907.

Arc 1433.75 Czapkicwicz, A. Skarb dirhemov arabskich z Czechowa. Warszawa, 1957.

Arc 1588.1.38 Czapkiewicz, Maria. Skarb monet arabskich z okolic Drohiczyna nad Bugiem. Kraków, 1960.

Arc 936.8 Czarnowski, S.J. Siedziba paleolityczna. Warszawa, 1910-14. 4 pam.

Arc 936.195 Czechoslovakia before the Slavs. (Neustupny, E.) London, 1961.

Arc 815.6 Czechowski, D. Die Hausgötter in Pompeji. Peremyal, 1900.

Arc 1020.144 Czober, Béla. Egyházi emlékek a törtenelmi kiállitison. Budapest, 1898.

Arc 1279.10 Czobor, Béla. Magyarország világi és egyházi hatóságai kiadott pecseteinek jegyzeke. Pest, 1872.

Arc 1675.65 Da ich het die gestalt. (Grotemeyer, Paul.) München, 1957.

Arc 1493.9 Da numismatica em Portugal. (Leite de Vasconcellos, J.) Lisboa, 1923.

Arc 936.14.500 Dąbrowska, Elżbieta. Wielkie grody dorzecza góinej Wisły. Wrocław, 1973.

Arc 936.14.420 Dąbrowski, Jan. Powięzanie ziem polskich z terenami uschodnimi w epoce brązu. Wrocław, 1972.

Arc 936.6.45 Dąbrowski, Jan. Zabytki metalowe epoki brązu między dolną wisłą a Niemnem. Wrocław, 1968.

Arc 936.14.155 Dabrowski, Krzysztof. Przymierze z archeologią. Warszawa, 1964.

Arc 1030.8.21 Dabry de Thiessaut. La catholicisme en Chine au VIIIe siècle de notre ère. Paris, 1877.

Arc 936.20.65 Dacia. (Pârvan, Vasile.) București, 1972.

Arc 936.20 Dacia. (Pârvan, Vasile.) Cambridge, 1928.

Arc 303.18.10F Dacia. București. 1,1924+ 15v.

Arc 810.58 Dag faun. (Man, Ivonne de.) Amsterdam, 1960.

Arc 810.63.2 Dag van gramschap in Pompeji. 2. druk. (Aafjes, B.) Amsterdam, 1961.

Arc 936.185 Daicovicui, C. Sarmizegetusa. București, 1960.

Arc 1138.55 Dain, A. Les manuscrits. Paris, 1949.

Arc 1138.55.2 Dain, A. Les manuscrits. Paris, 1964.

Arc 936.14.495 Dalecy i bliscy. (Abramowicz, Andrzej.) Łódź, 1974.

Arc 936.165.25 Dalekoe proshloe Moldavii. Kishinev, 1969.

Arc 925.180 Dalekoe proshloe Primor'ia. (Okladnikov, Aleksei Pavlovich.) Vladivostok, 1959-

Arc 925.180.30 Dalekoe proshloe Primor'ia i Priamur'ia. (Okladnikov, Aleksei Pavlovich.) Vladivostok, 1973.

Arc 1453.7 Daler. (Wilcke, Julius.) Kjøbenhavn, 1931.

Arc 552.3 Daleth; or The homestead of the nations. (Clark, Edward L.) Boston, 1864.

Arc 983.7 Dall, William H. On masks, labrets and certain aboriginal customs. Washington, 1881-82.

Arc 530.90.5 Dalla Paflagonia alla Commagene. (Jacopi, G.) Roma, 1936.

Arc 830.78.100F Dallas tumulaires et pierres tombales du département d'Eure-et-Loire. (Société Archéologique d'Eure-et-Loire.) Chartres, 1895-1930. 2v.

Arc 1020.122 Une dalle mérovingienne trouvée à Challans (Vendée). (La Croix, C. de.) Poitiers, 1909.

Arc 925.151 Dal'nevostochnaia Arkheologicheskaia Ekspeditsiia. Materialy polevykh izsledovanii Dal'nevostochnoi arkheologicheskoi ekspeditsii. Novosibirsk, 1970- 2v.

Arc 402.11 Dalton, O.M. Sir Hercules Read. London, 1936.

X Cg Arc 1680.7 Dalton, R. The provincial token - coinage of the eighteenth century. 1-9 2v.

Arc 838.28 La dama de Elche. (Garcia y Bellido, A.) Madrid, 1943.

Arc 505.100.2 Damascus. Musée National Syrien. Catalogue illustré du Departement des antiquités gréco-romaines. Damas, 1951.

Arc 505.100 Damascus. Musée National Syrien. Etat de Syree. Damas, 1931.

Arc 1033.38.15 Damascus et Laurentius. (Pérez Báyes, F.) Rome, 1756.

Arc 889.24 Damme, Daniel van. Promenades archéologiques à Anderlecht. Bruxelles, 1958.

Arc 87.1.14 Danae. (Gerhard, E.) Berlin, 1854.

Arc 1500.63 Dancoisne, Louis. Recueil de monnaies...de Douai. Douai, 1836.

Arc 1020.10.15 Dandolo, C.J. Roma christiana nei primi secoli. Asisi, 1865-67. 3v.

Arc 895.7.35.2 Le Danemark avant les Vikings. (Klindt-Jensen, Ole.) Grenoble, 1960.

Arc 1335.33 D'Angers, D. Catalogue général de monnaies, médailles et jetons. Paris, n.d.

Arc 1163.5.25 Dani, A.H. Indian palaeography. Oxford, 1963.

Arc 432.22 Dani, A.H. Prehistory and protohistory of east India. Calcutta, 1960.

Arc 830.94 Danicourt, A. Étude sur quelques antiquités trouvées en Picardie. Paris, 1886.

Arc 858.59 Daniel, G. The prehistoric chamber tombs. Cambridge, Eng., 1950.

Arc 388.5.5 Daniel, G.E. A hundred years of archaeology. London, 1950.

Arc 830.335 Daniel, G.E. The hungry archaeologist in France. London, 1963.

Arc 388.12 Daniel, G.E. The idea of prehistory. London, 1962.

Arc 830.11.25 Daniel, G.E. Lascaux and Carnac. London, 1955.

Arc 889.8.5 Daniels, M.P.M. Noviomagus. Nijmegen, 195-.

Arc 925.50.185 Danilenko, Valentin N. Eneolit Ukrainy. Kiev, 1969.

Arc 925.50.185.5 Danilenko, Valentin N. Eneolit Ukrainy. Kiev, 1974.

Arc 600.15.5 Daninos, A. Les monuments funéraires de l'Egypte ancienne. Paris, 1899.

Arc 1548.5 Danmarks og Norges mønter, 1448-1540. (Soemod, Jørgen.) Kjøbenhavn, 1967.

Arc 1548.2F Danmarks og Norges mønter, 1541-1814-1963. Udgivet of Dansk numisatisk forening. (Hede, Holger.) Kjøbenhavn, 1964.

Arc 895.7.25F Danmarks oldtid. (Brøndsted, J.) Kjøbenhavn, 1938-40. 3v.

Arc 895.7.25.2F Danmarks oldtid. (Brøndsted, J.) Kjøbenhavn, 1957- 3v.

Arc 895.7.5 Danmarks oldtid oplyst ved oldsager og gravhøie. (Worsaae, J.J.A.) Kjøbenhavn, 1843.

Arc 895.7.26 Danmarks stengrave og gravhøge i forhold til landets jordbund. (Brøndsted, J.) Kjøbenhavn, 1939.

Arc 1505.1 Dannenberg, H. Die deutschen Münzender Saeschischen und Frankischen Kaiserzeit. Text und Plates. Berlin, 1876. 2v.

Arc 1505.2 Dannenberg, H. Pommerns Münzen im Mittelalter. Berlin, 1864.

Arc 853.262F Dannheimer, H. Die germanischen Funde der späten Kaiserzeit und des frühen Mittelalters in Mittelfranken. Text and atlas. Berlin, 1962. 2v.

Arc 1276.31F Danske adelige sigiller. (Petersen, H.) København, 1897.

Arc 1276.20F Danske gilders segl fra middelaldesen. (Grandjean. P.B.) København, 1948.

Arc 1276.5 Danske haandvaerkerlavs segl. (Grandjean, P.B.) København, 1950.

Arc 1276.25F Danske herreders segl indtil 1660. (Grandjean, P.B.) København, 1946.

Arc 1276.30F Danske kobstaeders segl indtil 1660. (Grandjean, P.B.) København, 1937.

Arc 1276.10F Danske konggelige segl fra Frederik ILS. (Grandjean, P.B.) København, 1951.

Arc 1550.8 Danske og norske medailler og jetons. (Galster, Georg.) Kjøbenhavn, 1936.

Arc 248.3F Danske Oldsager. 1-4 2v.

Arc 612.19 The Danube in prehistory. (Childe, Vere G.) Oxford, 1929.

Arc 805.2 Le danzatrici di Ercolano. (Forti, Lidia.) Napoli, 1959.

Arc 936.14.200 Danzig (City). Muzeum Archeologiczne. Pomerania antiqua. Gdynia, 1965- 6v.

Arc 736.1.10 Dara, G. Sulla topografia d'Agrigento del F.S. Cavallari. Girgenti, 1883.

Arc 823.4 D'Arbois de Jubainville. Répertoire archéologique du département de l'Aube. Paris, 1861.

Arc 1020.125 Darcel, Alfred. Trésor de l'église de conques. Paris, 1861.

Arc 830.127 D'Ardé, J. Musée lapidaire, l'histoire de Béziers. Béziers, 1912.

Arc 1348.43 Darier, Hugues. Tableau du titre. Geneve, 1807.

Arc 383.49 Dark-age Britain. (Harden, D.B.) London, 1956.

Arc 700.68A The dark age of Greece: an archaeological survey of the eleventh to the eighth centuries B.C. (Snodgrass, Anthony M.) Edinburgh, 1971.

Arc 488.20 Dark ages and nomads c.1000 B.C. (Mellink, M.J.) Istanbul, 1964.

Arc 188.5 Darmstadt, Germany. Amt für Badenlenkmalpflege im Regierungsbezirk. Inventar der Bodendenkmäler. 1,1959+

Arc 1027.23 Die Darstellung Jesu Christi...Bilde des Fisches. (Becker, F.) Gero, 1876.

Arc 1025.13 Die Darstellungen...Maria...Katakomben. (Liell, H.F.J.) Freiburg, 1887.

Arc 705.209 Die Darstellungen der Gallier in der Hellenistischen Kunst. (Bienkowski, P. von.) Wien, 1908.

Arc 936.195.250 Das altungarische Fürstengral von Zemplén. (Budinsky-Kricka, Vojtech.) Bratislava, 1973.

Arc 440.10 Das Gupta, Kalyan Kumar. The Audumbaras. Calcutta, 1965.

Arc 462.5 Das Gupta, Paresh Chandra. Archaeological discovery in West Bengal. Alipore, 1963.

Arc 672.7 Das heroon von Kalydon. (Dyggve, E.) København, 1934.

Arc 543.45A A dash through the heart of Afghanistan. (Shakur, M.A.) Peshawar, 1947.

Arc 746.6 Dasti, L. Notizie storiche archeologiche di Tarquinia e Corneto. Roma, 1878.

Arc 66.1.103 Les dataires du XVe siècle et les origines de la daterie apostolique. (Celier, Léonce.) Paris, 1910.

Arc 1077.2.46F The date and provenance of a bronze reliquary cross in the Museo Cristiano. (King, E.S.) Rome, 1928.

Arc 1478.24.13 The date of the Roman denarius. (Mattingly, Harold.) London, 1933.

Arc 1020.19 Datiana historica ecclesiastica Mediolanensis. (Biragus, A.) Mediolani, 1848.

Arc 590.13.1 Die Datierung der Mumienporträts. (Drerup, Heinrich.) Paderborn, 1968.

Arc 1163.8.10 Datierung und Lokalisierung nach den Schreibformen von K und Z im Althochdeutschen. Inaug. Diss. (Ziemer, Meline.) Breslau, 1933.

Arc 1480.72 The dating and arrangement of the undated coins of Rome, A.D. 98-148. (Hill, Philip V.) London, 1970.

Arc 1423.21 The dating and meaning of ancient Jewish coins and symbols. (Israel Numismatic Society.) Tel-Aviv, 1958.

Arc 412.20 Dating techniques for the archaeologist. Cambridge, 1971.

Arc 1493.12 Datos epigráficos y numismáticos de España. (Martin Minquez, Bernardino.) Valladolid, 1883.

Arc 925.165 Datsiak, B.D. Pervobytnoe obshchestvo na territorii nashei strang. Moskva, 1954.

Arc 1020.9.169 Dattoli, M. L'aula del senato romano e la chiesa di S. Adriano. Roma, 1921.

Arc 543.8 Daubrée, Auguste. Rapport sur une collection d'instrument en pierre. Paris, 1868.

Arc 1348.60 Dauernder als Erz. (Roubier, Jean.) Wien, 1958.

Arc 1260.1 Daugnon, F.F. La vera arma della città di Crema. v.1-2. Fermo, 1874.

Arc 938.68 Daugudis, V. Stakliškių lobis. Vil'nius, 1968.

Arc 600.230F Daumas, François. Kellia I. Le Caire, 1969- 2v.

Arc 600.215.5 Daumas, François. La ouabet de Kalabcha. Le Caire, 1970.

Arc 600.185F Daumot, F. Les mammisis de Dendara, le mammisi de Nectanébo. Le Caire, 1955.

Arc 66.1.140 Daux, Georges. Delphes au IIe et au Ier siècle. Paris, 1936.

Arc 388.6 Daux, Georges. Les étapes de l'archéologie. 2. éd. Paris, 1948.

Arc 1453.8 Davenport, J.S. European crowns, 1700-1800. Galenburg, Ill., 1961.

Arc 1016.13.5 David, J. Sainte Marie antigue. Roma, 1911.

Arc 392.3.25 David George Hogarth, 1862-1927. (Sayce, A.H.) London, 1928.

Arc 936.195.230 Davidek, Vácalv. Co bylo préd Prahon. 1. vyd. Praha, 1971.

Arc 1433.101 Davidovich, Elena A. Denezhnoe khoziaistvo Srednei Azii posle mongol'skaia zavoevaniia i reforma Mas'ud-beka. Moskva, 1972.

Arc 1433.90 Davidovich, Elena A. Istoriia monetnogo dela Srednei Azii XVII-XVIII vv. Dushanbe, 1964.

Arc 609.10 Davidson, Basil. Old Africa rediscovered. London, 1959.

Arc 595.32.15 Davidson, D. The Great Pyramid; its divine message. 8th ed. London, 1940.

Arc 861.32 Davidson, J. British and Roman remains in Axminster. London, 1833.

Arc 712.8 Davidson, T. The Parthenon frieze and other essays. London, 1882.

Arc 595.28 Davie, John G. Phythagoras takes the second step, and other works on the pyramids. Griffin, 1935.

Arc 861.78 Davies, J.A. Early life in the West. Clifton, 1927.

Arc 587.9.15 Davies, N. de Garis. Five Theban tombs. London, 1913.

Arc 587.7 Davies, N. de Garis. The rock tombs of Deir el Gebrâevi. London, 1902. 2v.

Arc 587.8 Davies, N. de Garis. The rock tombs of El Amarna. London, 1903. 6v.

Arc 587.6 Davies, N. de Garis. The rock tombs of Sheikh Said. London, 1901.

Arc 609.40 Davies, Oliver. Archaeology in Ghana. Edinburgh, 1961.

Arc 609.7 Davies, Oliver. Natal archaeological studies. Pietermaritzburg, 1952.

Arc 609.41 Davies, Oliver. The quarternary in the coastlands of Guinea. Glasgow, 1964.

Arc 1027.4.5 Davin, V. Les antiquités chrétiennes...Cappella greca. Paris, 1892.

Arc 1033.12.113 Davin, V. Sainte tunique. Discours...Argeteuil...1865. Paris, n.d.

Arc 1025.60 Davin, V. Les sanctuaires primitifs de Rome et des Gaules. Paris, 1873?

Arc 1411.6 Davis, Andrew. Ancient Chinese paper money. Boston, 1918.

Arc 861.11.5 Davis, F. The Romano-British city of Silchester. London, 1898.

Arc 608.2.2 Davis, N. Carthage and her remains. London, 1861.

Arc 1470.89 Davis, Norman. The Hellenistic kingdoms. London, 1973.

Arc 545.232.5 Davis, T.M. The tomb of Iouiya and Touiyou. London, 1907.

Arc 545.232.9 Davis, T.M. The tomb of Queen Tiyi. London, 1910.

Arc 545.232.13 Davis, T.M. The tomb of Siptah. London, 1908.

Arc 1535.9 Davis, W.J. Old Warwickshire coins, tokens and medals. n.p., 1896.

Arc 1680.6 Davis, William John. The nineteenth century token coinage. London, 1904.

Arc 1680.6.1 Davis, William John. The nineteenth century token coinage of Great Britain. London, 1969.

Arc 1540.20.1 Davis, William John. Tickets and passes of Great Britain and Ireland. N.Y., 1973.

Arc 1540.20 Davis, William John. Tickets and passes of Great Britain and Ireland struck or engraved on metal, ivory. Leamington Spa, 1922.

NEDL Arc 1680.6.5 Davis, William John. The token coinage of Warwickshire. Birmingham, 1895.

Arc 726.323 Davison, Jean M. Seven Italic tomb-groups from Narce. Firenze, 1972.

Arc 858.2 Dawkins, W.B. Early man in Britain. London, 1880.

Arc 672.1.7 Dawn of Mediterranean civilization. (Mosso, Angelo.) London, 1910.

Arc 672.1.7.5 Dawn of Mediterranean civilization. (Mosso, Angelo.) N.Y., 1911.

Arc 1588.1.18 Dawne monety Polskie dynastyi Piasłow Jagiełłonow. Piotrkow, 1883-85. 3v.

Arc 497.17 Dawson, J.W. Modern science in Bible lands. N.Y., 1889.

Arc 553.5 Dawson, John W. Notes on prehistoric man in Egypt and Lebanon. London, 1884.

Arc 553.1 Dawson, W.R. Who was who in Egyptology. London, 1951.

Arc 762.1.20 Days near Rome. v.1-2. (Hare, A.J.C.) Philadelphia, 1875.

Arc 762.1.25 Days near Rome. 3. ed. (Hare, A.J.C.) N.Y., 1902.

Arc 762.1.30 Days near Rome. 4. ed. (Hare, A.J.C.) London, 1906.

Arc 762.1.35 Days near Rome. 5. ed. (Hare, A.J.C.) London, 1907.

Arc 1163.20 De abbreviationibus et signis scripturae gothicae. (Laurent, M.) Romae, 1939.

Arc 1033.34.21 De aeneo simulacro divi Petri apostoli. (Cascioli, J.) Roma, 1895.

Arc 1433.9.3 De aliquot numis Kuficis. (Fraehn, C.M.J.) n.p., 1824.

Arc 1033.17.162 De annulo proniebo...virginis...Perusiae. (Lauro, G.B.) Colonia Agrippina, 1626.

Arc 1033.17.161 De annulo pronubo...virginis...Perusiae. (Lauro, G.B.) Roma, 1622.

Arc 382.4 De anthologiae Graecae epigrammatis. (Benndorf, O.) Bonn, 1862. 20 pam.

Arc 1087.1.2 De antiquis marmoribus. 2. ed. (Garofalo, Biagio.) Oxonii, 1828.

Arc 1087.1 De antiquis marmoribus opuculum. (Garofalo, Biagio.) Ad Rhenum, 1743.

Arc 1423.1 De antiquis numis. (Waserus, C.) Zürich, 1605.

Arc 925.5 De antiquis quibusdam sculptures. (Spasskii, Grigorii I.) Petropoli, 1822.

Arc 746.16 De antiquitatibus Hortae coloniae etruscorum. 3a ed. (Fontani, Giusto.) Roma, 1723.

Htn Arc 760.1.5* De antiquitiae Romae. (Faunus, L.) Venetiis, 1549.

Arc 785.6 De aquis et aquaeductis veteris Romae. (Fabretti, R.) Romae, 1680.

Arc 1540.4 De argento runis siu lit. (Keder, N.) Lipsiae, 1703-08. 4 pam.

Arc 1470.35 De Aristotle in nummo aureo. (Koch, Cornelius D.) Helmestadi, 1703.

Arc 1016.222 De basilica et patriarchio Lateranensi. (Rasponi, C.) Roma, 1656.

Arc 1033.20.19 De Basilica S. Paneratii M. Christi. (Paulinus a S. Barthol.) Roma, 1703.

Arc 608.16.7 De Caesareae monumentis quae supersunt. (Waille, Victor.) Alger, 1891.

Htn Arc 1076.3.110* De campanis commentarius. (Rocca, Angelo.) Romae, 1612.

Arc 396.5 De Campolide a Melrose. (Leite de Vasconcellos, J.) Lisboa, 1915.

Arc 1033.43.13 De capitibus S. apostolorum Petri et Pauli in Lateran. (Soresinas, I.M.) Roma, 1673.

Arc 1033.34.3 De catenis San Petri dissertatio. (Monsacrati, M.A.) Roma, 1828.

Arc 1016.219 De cathedra romana B. Petri. (Rampolla, M.) Roma, 1868.

Arc 1027.61.5 De caussis inopiae veterum monument. pro copia Martyrum. (Ansaldi, P.C.) Medina, 1740.

Arc 1027.22.5 De christianis monumentes Ichthys. (Rossi, J.B. de.) Paris, 1855.

Arc 1033.42 De Christianorum veterum monumentorum im rem biblicam utilitate. Diss. (Brunatio, J.) Mediolani, 1838.

Arc 1025.56 De christianorum viterum rebus sepulchralibus. (Schultze, M.V.) Gothae, 1879.

Arc 853.19 De cipporum germaniae romanorum ornamentis. (Weynand, R.) Bonnae, 1902.

Arc 1033.12.51.3 De clavis Dominicis liber. (Curtius, C.) Antverpiae, 1634.

Arc 1033.12.51 De clavis Dominicis liber. (Curtius, C.) Antverpiae, 1670.

Arc 66.1.13 De codd. mss. graecis Pü II in Biblioteca Vaticana. (Duchesne, L.) Paris, 1880.

Htn Arc 750.212* De columna traiani syntaqua. (Fabretti, R.) Roma, 1683.

Arc 1033.12.181 De corona ferrea...commentarius. (Muratori, L.A.) Mediolani, 1719.

Arc 1018.15 De' costumi de' primitivi cristiani. (Mamachi, T.M.) Venezia, 1757. 3v.

Arc 1018.15.3 De' costumi de' primitivi cristiani. v.1-2. (Mamachi, T.M.) Firenze, 1853.

Author and Title Listing

Htn Arc 1033.35.141* De cruce Christi. (Gretser, J.) Inglodstadii, 1600. 3v.
Arc 1033.35.27 De cruce cortonensi dissertatio. (Venuti, F.) Florenzia, 1781.
Htn Arc 1077.2.1* De cruce libri tres...cum notis. 3. ed. (Lipsius, J.) Antverpiae, 1597.
Htn Arc 1077.2* De cruce libri tres. (Lipsius, J.) Antverpiae, 1594.
Htn Arc 1077.2.2* De cruce libri tres. (Lipsius, J.) Parisiis, 1598.
Arc 1033.35.101 De cruce stationale investigatio historica. (Ciampini, G.G.) Roma, 1737.
Htn Arc 1033.35.13F* De cruce vaticana...commentarius. (Borgia, S.) Roma, 1779.
Htn Arc 1033.35.15F* De cruce veliterna. (Borgia, S.) Roma, 1780.
Htn Arc 1033.137* De cultu S. J. Baptistae...commentarius. (Paciandi, P.) Roma, 1755.
Arc 1025.34 De ecclesia subterranea liber. (Cyprian, E.S.) Helmstedt, 1699. 8 pam.
Arc 1665.2 De elephantis in numis obviis exercitationes duae. (Knifer, Gijsbert.) Hagae, 1719. 2 pam.
Htn Arc 740.203* De Etruria regali libri VII. (Dempster, T.) Florence, 1723-24. 2v.
Arc 1018.16 De falea veterum christianorum rituum. (Rinaldi, P.) Romae, 1777.
Arc 764.1.2 De formae urbis Romae...novo disputatio. (Jordan, Henri.) Roma, 1883.
Arc 716.4 De Foro Atheniensium Disputatio. (Bursian, C.) Zürich, 1865.
Arc 1053.11 De historia variisque generibus statuarum iconicarum. (Stenersen, L.B.) Christianiae, 1877.
Arc 1033.12.136 De imagine SS. Salvatoris...ad Sancta Sanctorum. (Soresinus, J.M.) Roma, 1675.
Arc 1473.9 De imperatorum constantinopalitanorum. (Du Cange, C. du F.) Romae, 1755.
Arc 1020.9.102 De indentitate cathedral...Sanct. Petrus Romae. (Phoebeus, F.) Romae, 1666.
Arc 1033.64 De invicta veritate anni, mensis, et diei. (Levera, F.) Roma, 1668.
Arc 830.40.15 De la découverte d'un prétendu cimitière mérovingien a la Chapelle-Saint-Eloi (Eure). (Lenormant, François.) Evreux, 1855. 2 pam.
Arc 1500.6.3 De la monnaie Mahométane atribuée à um évêque. (Germain, A.) Montpellier, 1854.
Arc 1478.8 De la rareté et du prix des médailles romaines. (Mionnet, T.E.) Paris, 1858. 2v.
Arc 386.11 De la valeur historique des documents archéologiques. (Bertrand, A.) Chartres, 1879.
Arc 1033.12.122 De lancea qua perfossum latus...Christi. (Lange, P.) Jena, 1673.
Htn Arc 1033.12.211* De latere Christi aperto. (Bartholini, T.) Lugdunum Batavorum, 1646.
Arc 830.40.17 De l'authenticité des monuments découverts a la Chapelle-Saint-Eloi. (Lenormant, François.) Paris, 1855.
Arc 412.14 De l'aviation à l'archéologie. (Goguey, René.) Paris, 1968.
Arc 1143.1 De libris palimpsestis. (Mone, F.) Carlsruhae, 1855.
Arc 1033.96 De Liminibus Apostolorum. (Salomoni, P.) Romae, 1775.
Arc 612.22F De l'influence de l'art des Goths en Occident. (Baye, Joseph.) Paris, 1891.
Arc 1018.39 De linteis sepulchralibus. (Chiefletius, J.J.) Antverpiae, 1688. 4 pam.
Arc 1033.12.30 De linteis sepulchralibus Cristi servatoris crisis historica. (Chifflet, J.J.) Antverpiae, 1624.
Htn Arc 1200.10* De l'origine de la signature...au Moyen Âge. (Guigue, M.C.) Paris, 1863.
Htn Arc 1070.201* De lucernis antiquorum reconditis libb. sex. (Liceti, F.) Utini, 1653.
Arc 1033.25.7 De lucernis veterum christianorum sepulcralibus. (Troppanneger, C.) Vitembergae, 1710?
Arc 1025.57 De luctie christianorum. (Nicolai, Joannis.) Lugdnum Batavorum, 1739.
Arc 386.14 De l'utilité des voyages...la recherche des antiquitéz. (Baudelot de Dairval, C.C.) Paris, 1686. 2v.
Arc 386.14.5 De l'utilité des voyages...la recherche des antiquitéz. (Baudelot de Dairval, C.C.) Rouen, 1727. 2v.
Arc 608.2.17 De l'utilité d'une mission archéologique permanente à Carthage. (Lavigerie, C.M.A.) Alger, 1881.
Arc 726.66 De marmoreo sepulcrali cinerario. (Passeri, G.B.) Romae, 1773.
Arc 1670.57F De Medaillon der italienischen Renaissance. (Habich, Georg.) Stuttgart, 1924.
Arc 843.15.14 De mental-lurgia prehistorica a Catalunya. (Serra-Vilars, J.) Solsona, 1924.
Arc 1540.9 De moneta Anglo-Saxonica. (Schröder, J.H.) Upsaliae, 1849.
Htn Arc 1488.6* De monetis Italiae medii aeirhactenus. (Bellini, V.) Ferrariae, 1755.
Arc 1485.8 De monetis italiae variorum illustrium virorum. (Argelati, P.) Mediolani, 1750. 6v.
Arc 1033.44 De monogrammate Christi Domini. Diss. (Georgius, D.) Roma, 1738.
Arc 1033.44.33 De monogrammate D.N. Jesu Christe. (Allegranza, J.) Milano, 1773.
Arc 1033.44.19 De monogrammate D.N. Jesu Christe. n.p., n.d.
Arc 1033.44.5 De monogrammate sanetissimi nominis Jesu. Roma, 1747.
Arc 1433.9.4 De Musei Sprewitziani Mosquae numis Kuficis. (Fraehn, C.M.J.) Petropoli, 1825.
Arc 1335.25 De numis cuficis in biblio. regia Gottingense. (Tychsen, T.C.) n.p., n.d.
Arc 1423.4 De numis Hasmonaeorum paralipomena. (Tychsen, T.C.) n.p., 1792.
Arc 1540.3 De numis MD medii aevi in Norvegia nuper repertis. (Holmboe, C.A.) Christiania, 1837.
Arc 1433.25 De numis Muhammadanis in Numophylacio regio Dresdensi. (Dresden. K. Münzkabinett.) Lipsiae, 1856.
Arc 1433.20 De numis Orientalibus in numophylacio Gothano. (Moeller, J.H.) Erford, 1826-31. 2v.
Htn Arc 1480.18* De nummis aliquot...epistola. (Zelada, F.X. de.) Romae, 1778.
Arc 1668.6 De nummorum bracteatorum et cavorum. (Sperling, Otto.) Lubecae, 1700.
Arc 1668.7 De nummulis Peioesa inscriptis. (Casali, J.) Romae, 1796.
Arc 1588.2 De numorum Bulgharicorum forte antiguissimo. (Fraehn, C.M.J.) Casani, 1816.
Arc 545.20 De origine et usu obeliscorum. (Zoega, G.) Rome, 1797.
Arc 1033.35.25 De particula ex pretioso...crucis...commentarius. (Camers, A.R.) Roma, 1609.
Arc 1027.25 De phiala cruenta...Christo martyrii. (Scognamiglio, A.) Paris, 1867.
Arc 700.13 De plumbeis apud graecos tesseris. (Dumont, Albert.) Paris, 1870.
Arc 386.29.10 De Pompéi a l'île de Pâques. (Brion, Marcel.) Paris, 1967.
Arc 1020.21 De portuensi S. Hippolyti. (Ruggieri, C.) Romae, 1771.
Arc 1020.19.5 De praeclaris Mediolani aedificiciis. (Gratiolio, P.) Mediolani, 1735.
Arc 1033.12.71 De pretiosissimo Jesu Christi Sanguine Mantuae asservato. (Aquilini, H.) Venezia, 1782.
Arc 1568.1.3 De prisca re monetaria Norvegiae. (Holmboe, C.A.) Christiania, 1841.
Arc 1568.1 De prisca re monetaria Norvegiae. 2. ed. (Holmboe, C.A.) Christiania, 1854.
Arc 1033.48 De Priscorum Christianorum Synaxibus. (Sandellius, D.) Venetiis, 1770.
Arc 630.17 De profusionum receptaeulis sepulchalilus. (Oikonomes, Georgios P.) Athenis, 1921.
Arc 1025.74 De Pythagore aux apôtres. (Carcopino, J.) Paris, 1956.
Arc 1070.204 De quelques mors de cheval italiques et de l'épée de Ronzano en bronze. (Gozzadini, G.) Bologne, 1875.
Arc 843.79 De re arqueologica. (Vielva, M.) Valencia, 1924.
Arc 1175.5F De re diplomatica libri VI. (Mabillon, J.) Luteciae Parisiorum, 1681.
Htn Arc 1455.3F* De re nummaria antiqua opera. (Goltzius, H.) Antwerp, 1708. 5v.
Arc 1096.1 De re vehiculari veterum libri duo. (Scheffer, J.) Francofurti, 1671.
Htn Arc 772.3* De Roma prisca et nova varii auctores. (Albertini, F.) Romae, 1523?
Arc 930.202 De sacris aêdificiis a Constantino Magno constr. (Ciampinus, Joan.) Romae, 1693.
Arc 1027.7.13 De sacris Basilicis S. Martyrum. (Laderchu, J.) Roma, 1705.
Htn Arc 1033.17.247* De sacris inscriptionibus, quibus tabella D. Viginis Cameracensis. (Chifflet, J.J.) Antverp, 1749.
Arc 1033.35 De sacrosancta...cruce...quae in S. Crucis osservantur. (Regazzi, A.) Roma, 1777.
Htn Arc 1033.12.65* De sanguine Christi tractatus. (Domenechi, D.) Venetiis, 1557.
Arc 530.11 De sarcophagis Clazomeniis. (Joubin, André.) Paris, 1901.
Arc 1033.55.5 De scala sancta ante S. Sanctorum in Lateran. (Soresini, I.M.) Roma, 1672.
Arc 1015.5 De S'Callisto pp. etm ejusque Basilica. (Moretto, P.) Romae, 1767.
Arc 1030.16 De sepulcris christianis. (Allegrantia, J.) Mediolani, 1773.
Arc 1033.12.56 De sessorianis praecepuis passionis...reliquiis commentariis. (Corrieris, L. de.) Romae, 1830.
Arc 1460.1 De sestertüs. (Gronovius, J.F.) Leyden, 1691.
Arc 1251.3 De siglis veterum graecorum. v.1-3. (Cardoni, B.) Romae, 1757.
Arc 746.9 De speculis Etruscis et cista in museo. (Bienkowski, P.) Cracoviae, 1912.
Arc 505.5.8 De spoliis templi Hierosolymitani. (Reeland, Adriaan.) Utrecht, 1716.
Arc 505.5.70 De tabernaculo foederis...Jerusalem. (Lanvy, B.) Paris, 1720.
Arc 843.69 De Talabriga a Lancobriga pela via militar romano. (Oliveira, M.) Coimbra, 1943.
Arc 505.5.37 De templo Hierosolymitano. (Jehuda Leon, J.) Helmaestadi, 1665.
Arc 838.3.13 De terra em terra. v.1-2. (Leite de Vasconcellos, J.) Lisboa, 1927.
Arc 1020.115 De terra iheroslimitana...allate sunt relique. (Poquet, A.E.) n.p., n.d.
Arc 689.6 De theraeorum rebus sacris. Inaug. Diss. (Braun, I.) Halis Saxonum, 1932.
Htn Arc 1033.63* De Tintinnabulis. (Magi, H.) Amstelodami, 1664. 2 pam.
Arc 1076.3.19 De tintinnalbulis. (Maggi, G.) Hanoviae, 1608.
Arc 608.16 De Tipasa, Mauretaniae Caesariensis urbe. Diss. (Gsell, Stéphane.) Algerii, 1894.
Arc 1030.6 De titulis atticae christianis. (Bayet, C.) Paris, 1878.
Htn Arc 760.4.5* De urbis antiquitatibus. (Fulvio, A.) Roma, 1545.
Arc 770.2.5 De variis structurarum generibus penes romanos veteres. (Parker, J.H.) Romae, 1868.
Arc 830.83.5 De vetere Massilia disquisitiones. (Mery, Louis.) Massillae, 1849.
Arc 1088.1.3 De veterum re navali. (Graser, B.) Berolini, 1864.
Arc 1088.1.4 De veterum trirenium fabrica. (Graser, B.) Berolini, 1864.
Arc 823.19.85 De Villefosse. Inscription de Gordien. (Thédenat, H.) Vienne, 1881.
Arc 726.56 De villis Tiburtinis, principe Augusto Thesim proponebat. (Albert, Maurice.) Parisios, 1883.
Arc 853.11.15 De vis militaribus romanorum in vetiri Germania. (Steger, Adrian.) Lipsiae, 1738.
Arc 1033.162 De vita et Lipsanis S. Marci Evangelistae. (Molini, A.M.) Romae, 1864.
Arc 387.30A Dead cities and forgotten tribes. (Cooper, Gordon.) N.Y., 1952.
Arc 733.2 The dead cities of Sicily. (Rivela, A.) Palermo, 1905.
Arc 407.10 Dead towns and living men. (Woolley, Charles L.) London, 1920.
Arc 820.206F Deane, John Bathurst. Dracontia. London, 1834.
Arc 1020.69 Deblaye, L.F. Reliques de l'église de Moyenmoutier. Nancy, 1856.
Arc 545.227.31 Debod bis Bal Kalabach. (Roeder, G.) Le Caire, 1911. 3v.
Arc 66.1.118 De Boüard, A. Le régime politique et les institutions de Rome au Moyen-Age, 1252-1347. Paris, 1920.
Arc 497.65 A decade of archaeology in Israel, 1948-1958. (Yeivin, Samuel.) Istanbul, 1960.
Arc 945.5F Décades américaines. (Capitan, Louis.) Levallois-Perret, 1907.
Arc 810.33 Un decennio di nuovi scavi in Pompei. (Beccarini, Paolo.) Milano, 1922.
Arc 1428.3 Dechant, Norbert. Kreuzfahrer-Münzen. Wien, 1868.
Arc 830.17.3 Déchelette, J. Fouilles du Mont Beuvray 1897-1901. Paris, 1904.
Arc 823.11 Déchelette, Joseph. Manuel d'archéologie. v.1-2. Paris, 1908-14. 5v.
Arc 823.11.5 Déchelette, Joseph. Manuel d'archéologie préhistorique, celtique et gallo-romaine. v.1-2. Paris, 1913-1924. 4v.
Arc 823.45 Déchelette, Joseph. Manuel d'archéologie prêhistorique, celtique et gallo-romaine. v.1-6; v.1-4, 2. éd. Paris, 1924-34. 7v.

Arc 823.45.5 — Déchelette, Joseph. Manuel d'archéologie préhistorique, celtique et gallo-romaine. v.1-2, pt.1-3. Westmead, Eng., 1971. 5v.
Arc 1020.57 — Dechristé, Louis. Les tableaux...appartenant aux églises...de Douai. Douai, 1877.
Htn Arc 672.1.47F* — Decoration égéenne. (Oulié, Marthe.) Paris, 1927.
Arc 746.45 — Decouflé, Pierre. La notion d'ex-voto anatomique chez les Etrusco Romains. Bruxelles, 1964.
Arc 1588.1.9 — Decouverte à Gtebokie de monnaies polonaises. (Polkowski, J.) Gnesen, 1876.
Arc 608.1.37.5 — Découverte archéologigue dans la région de Sfax: mosaique des océans. (Fandri, Muhammed.) Tunis, 1963.
Arc 830.176 — Découverte de gravures de sabots d'équides sur Rocher. (Cousset, A.) Paris, 1911.
Arc 830.173 — Découverte de trois sarcophages merovingiens du VIIe siècle aux Sables-d'Olonne. (Ydier, F.) La Roche-sur-Yon, 1925.
Arc 416.23 — Découverte des mondes ensevelés. (Parrot, A.) Neuchâtel, 1952.
Arc 600.14.5 — La découverte des sanctuaires. (Kaufmann, C.M.) Alexandrie, 1908.
Arc 830.220 — Découverte du Baptistère de Sanctus Martinus de Joulle. (Guérin, Gérard.) Fontenay-le-Comte, 1954.
Arc 396.22 — La découverte du passe. (Laming, Annette.) Paris, 1952.
Arc 1033.53.22 — La découverte du tombeau du tombeau de St. Maurice. (Peissard, N.) St. Maurice, 1922.
Arc 830.22.16 — Découverte d'une statue de Bacchus dans la rue de Fossés Saint Jacques. (Bernard, Eugene.) Paris, 1883.
Arc 830.183 — Découvertes archéologiques à Marseille. (Clerc, Michele.) Marseille, 1904.
Arc 825.8 — Découvertes archéologiques faites à Nîmes, 1870-72. (Germer-Durand, E.) Nîmes, 1871-73.
Arc 825.8.5 — Découvertes archéologiques faites a Nîmes. 1873. (Germer-Durand, E.) Nîmes, 1876.
Arc 726.263.5 — Découvertes archéologiques fortuites en Corse. v.1-2. Bastia, 1971-
Arc 1027.63 — Decouvertes dans l'arenaire situé...sur la voie Salaria. (Rossi, G.B. de.) Rome, 1873.
Arc 1020.28 — Découvertes de divers monuments chrétiens en Sardaigne. (Rossi, G.B. de.) Rome, 1873.
Arc 608.1 — Découvertes épigraphiques et archéologiques faites en Tunisie. (Carton, Louis B.C.) Paris, 1895.
Arc 488.16 — Les découvertes fortuites. (Sanadi, H.A.) n.p., 1960.
Arc 1433.12.3 — Découvertes récentes de monnaies koufiques. (Tornberg, Carl Johan.) Bruxelles, n.d.
Arc 497.14 — Découvertes récentes en Terre-Sainte. (St. Aignan, L. de.) n.p., 1874.
Arc 530.163 — La déesse de Hiérapolis Castabala (Cilicie). (Dupont-Sommer, André.) Paris, 1964.
Arc 1027.58 — De Feis, L. La bocca della verita. Roma, 1885.
Arc 1033.17.98.3 — Defensa de la aparición de Nuestra Señora de Guadalupe. (Rosa, Agustin de.) Guadalajara, 1896.
Arc 830.16.9 — De Fontenay, H. Notice des tableaux, Dessins. Autun, n.d.
Arc 726.225F — Degani, Mario. Il tesoro romano barbarico di Reggio Emilia. Firenze, 1959.
Arc 913.18 — Degen, Rudolf. Helvetia antiqua. Uitikon, 1966.
Arc 785.41 — Degli antichi templi di Vespasiano e della concordia. (Piale, Stefano.) Roma, 1821. 2 pam.
Arc 1185.13 — Degli archivii, ricerche archaeologiche, storiche, critiche, diplomatiche. (Lustro, G.N. di.) Napoli, 1880.
Arc 726.59.25 — Degli avanzi d'alcuni antichissimi edifizi, scoperti in Malta l'anno 1768. (Barbaro, C.A.) Malta, 1794.
Arc 769.1 — Degli avanzi dell'antica Roma. (Rolli, P.) Londra, 1739.
Arc 905.5.9 — Degrassi, A. Abitati preistorici e romani nell'agro di Capodistria. Parenzo, 1933.
Arc 543.136 — Deh Morasi Ghunelai: a cholcolithic site in south-central Afghanistan. (Dupree, Louis Benjamin.) N.Y., 1963.
Arc 1027.2.15 — Dei conviti effigiati a simbolo ne' monumenti cristiani. (Polidori, L.) Milano, 1844.
Arc 1020.9.5.25 — Dei diritti del principato. (Fea, Carlo.) Roma, 1806.
Arc 712.18 — Dei due figure alate sul fregio del Partenone. (Michaelis, A.) Lipsia, 1865.
Arc 720.11.5 — Dei monumenti di Perugia etrusca e romana. Pt.1. (Vermiglioli, G.B.) Perugia, 1855.
Arc 720.11 — Dei monumenti di Perugia etrusca e romana. pts.1-4. (Vermiglioli, G.B.) Perugia, 1855-70. 2v.
Arc 720.11PF — Dei monumenti di Perugia etrusca e romana. Table. (Vermiglioli, G.B.) Perugia, 1870.
Arc 1033.28.15 — Dei riti nuziali degli antichi cristiani. (Tori, G.) Perugia, 1793.
Arc 1033.109 — Dei santi martiri Domno, Domnione ed Eusebia. (Uccelli, P.A.) Bergamo, 1874.
Arc 1163.25F — Deimel, Anton. Keilschrift-Palaeographie. Roma, 1929.
Arc 375.7 — Deinard, S.N. Descriptive charts of ancient monuments. no.1-5. Minneapolis, 1912.
Arc 600.54.5 — Deir el-Bahari. Varsovic, 1974-
Arc 1020.45 — Deirnel, T. Christliche Römerfunde in Carnuntum. Wien, 1911.
Arc 1675.59 — De Kay, Charles. A brief word on medals. N.Y., 1910.
Arc 1030.5.43 — Del arco fabiano nel foro. (Rossi, G.B. de.) Roma, 1859.
Arc 1033.88 — Del Colpo di Spada...la morte a i Martiri. (Baruffaldi, G.) Venezia, 1759.
Arc 1020.10.33 — Del Foro Romano e de' luoghi adjacenti. (Nibby, A.) Roma, 1819.
Arc 1025.29 — Del luogo appellato ad Caprean. (Rossi, G.B. de.) Roma, 1888.
Htn Arc 720.14* — Del modo tenuto...liobelisco vaticano. (Fontana, D.) Roma, 1590.
Arc 726.65F — Del monumento sepolcrale detto volgarmente degli Orazii e Curiazii; discurso. (Nibby, Antonio.) Roma, 1834.
Arc 1033.12.1 — Del nome di S. Maria ad Praesepe. (Liverani, F.) Roma, 1854.
Arc 785.54 — Del Pons Agruppae sul Tevere tra le regioni IX e XIII. (Barsari, Luigi.) Roma, 1888.
Arc 1033.45 — Del pontificato di S. Sisto I. (Persus, L. de.) Alatri, 1884.
Arc 1033.34.45 — Del primato e della residenza in Roma dell'apostolo Pietro. (Mancini, Pietro.) Roma, 1898.
Arc 1033.79 — Del primo vescovo di Napoli Sant'Aspreno. (Taglialatela, G.) Napoli, 1879.
Arc 726.74F — Del sepolcreto e degli altri monumenti antichi scoperti presso Bazzano. (Crespellani, A.) Modena, 1875.
Arc 1016.202 — Del sotterraneo della chiesa cattedrale di Palermo. (Casano, A.) Palermo, 1849.
Arc 1020.9.9 — Del tempio della pace e della basiilica di Costantino. (Nibby, A.) Roma, 1819.
Arc 785.1.5 — Del tempio volgarmente detto di Vesta. (Piale, Stefano.) Roma, 1817.

Arc 1458.5 — Del tesoro britannico. (Haym, N.F.) London, 1719-20. 2v.
Arc 66.1.19 — Delaborde, H.F. Chartes de terre sainte. Paris, 1880.
Arc 66.1.22 — Delaborde, H.F. Étude sur la chronique de Guillaume le Breton. Paris, 1881.
Arc 1163.21.5F — De la Mare, Albinia Cathérine. The handwriting of Italian humanists. Oxford, 1973-
Arc 830.2 — Delandre, M.C. Le Morbihan son histoire et ses monuments. Paris, 1847. 2v.
Arc 1675.16 — De La Tour, H. Jean de Candida. Paris, 1895.
Arc 1033.17.105 — Delattre, A.L. Le culte de la Sainte Vierge en Afrique. Paris, 1907.
Arc 608.2.3 — Delattre, A.L. Souvenir de la Croisade de Saint-Louis trouvé à Carthage. Lyon, 1888.
Arc 1033.25.8 — Delattré, Alfred Louis. Lampes chrétiennes de Carthage. Lyon, 1880.
Arc 1020.35 — Delattre, R.P. Archéologie chrétienne de Carthage. Lyon, 1886.
Arc 1030.12 — Delattre, R.P. Inscriptions chrétiennes. Constantine, 1887.
Arc 608.2.5 — Delattre, R.P. Notice sur les plombs chrétiens trouvés à Carthage. Lyon, 1887.
Arc 608.2.10 — Delattre, R.P. Un pélerinage aux ruines de Carthage. Lyon, 1906.
Arc 66.1.32 — Delaville Le Roulx, J. Les archives...à Malte. Paris, 1883.
Arc 1285.2 — Delaville Le Roulx, J. Des sceaux des prieurs anglais de l'ordre de l'hôpital. Rome, 1881.
Arc 1285.2.3 — Delaville Le Roulx, J. Des sceaux des prieurs anglais de l'ordre de l'hôpital. Rome, 1881. 2 pam.
Arc 66.1.44 — Delaville Le Roulx, J. La France en Orient au XIVe siècle. Paris, 1886. 2v.
Arc 1285.1 — Delaville Le Roulx, J. Note sur les sceaux de l'ordre de Saint Jean de Jérusalem. Paris, 1881.
Arc 958.1.15 — Delaware's buried past. (Weslager, Clinton Alfred.) Philadelphia, 1944.
Arc 750.213 — Delbrück, R. Das Capitolium von Signia. Rom, 1903.
Arc 785.18 — Delbrück, R. Die drei Tempel am Forum Holitorium in Rom. Rom, 1903.
Arc 750.211 — Delbrück, R. Hellenistische Bauten in Latium. Strassburg, 1907.
Arc 1053.6.25 — Delbrück, R. Spätantike Kaiserporträts. Berlin, 1933.
Arc 1663.30 — Delbrueck, Richard. Die Münzbildnisse von Maximinus bis Carenus. Berlin, 1940.
Arc 493.3 — Le délégation en Perse. (Morgan, J. de.) Paris, 1902.
Arc 625.12 — Delestre, M. Collection d'antiquités, grecques et romaines. Paris, 1901.
Arc 673.1.12 — Delfy. (Michałowski, K.) Warszawa, 1959.
Arc 1493.6 — Delgado, Antonio. Nuevo método de clasificacion de las medallas autonomas de España. Sevilla, 1871-76. 3v.
Arc 1163.4.13F — Delhi. Museum of Archaeology. Specimens of calligraphy in the Delhi Museum of Archaeology. Calcutta, 1926.
Arc 1347.2 — Delineatio rei numismaticae. (Bytemeister, H.J.) Helmstadt, 1738? 3 pam.
Arc 861.67F — Delineations of Roman antiquities...at Caerleon. (Lee, John Edward.) London, 1845.
Arc 861.38.5 — Delineations of the northwest division of the county of Somerset. (Rutter, John.) London, 1829.
Arc 861.38.6 — Delineations of the northwest division of the county of Somerset. (Rutter, John.) London, 1829.
Arc 1150.208.9F — Delisle, L. L'evangeliaire de Saint-Vaast d'Arras. Paris, 1888.
Arc 1153.1 — Delisle, L. Forme des abréviations et des liaisons dans les lettres des papes. Paris, 1887.
Arc 1153.1.5 — Delisle, L. Mémoire sur l'école calligraphique de Tours au IXe siècle. Paris, 1885.
Arc 1150.208 — Delisle, L. Notice sur un manuscript Mérovingun. Paris, 1875.
Arc 1150.208.5 — Delisle, L. Notice sur un manuscript Mérovingun. Paris, 1878.
Arc 1020.77 — Delisle, Léopold. Authentiques de reliques...decouvertes à Vergy. Rome, 1884.
Arc 1020.9.55 — Dell antiquita sito, chiese...di Roma. (Contarino, F.L.) Napoli, 1678.
Arc 1030.13 — Dell culto, A.S.S.M.M., cemeteriali e dell'antichita. (Adami, L.) Roma, 1815.
Arc 774.3 — Della campagna romana. (Tomassetti, G.) Roma, 1885.
Arc 774.3.5 — Della campagna romana. (Tomassetti, G.) Roma, 1907.
Arc 1033.47.25 — Della Casa Aurea di Nerone. (Fea, C.) Roma, 1832.
Arc 1020.32.8 — Della chiesa di Sant'Eustorgio in Milano. (Caffi, M.) Milano, 1841.
Arc 1027.36.5 — Della città di Preconi nominata negli atti di SS. MM. fermo e rustico. (Dionisi, G.J.) Vinegia, 1782.
Arc 1016.213 — Della forma degli antichi templi cristiani. (Nibby, A.) Roma, 1825.
Arc 726.24.8 — Della imp. villa Adriana. (Bardi, Giovanni de'.) Firenze, 1825.
Arc 1020.78 — Della insigne di S. Stefano di Bologna. (Petracchi, C.) Bologna, 1747.
Arc 1033.69 — Della interpretazione del Monogramma. (Arcangeli, P.) Roma, 1879.
Arc 1033.69.5 — Della interpretazione del Monogramma. (Bruzza, L.) Roma, 1877.
Arc 1033.12.161 — Della lampada d'oro offerta dai Lucchssi al volto santo. (Pera, P.) Lucca, 1836. 2 pam.
Arc 1675.98 — Della medaglie di Murano. (Zaretti, Vincenzo.) Bologna, 1965.
Arc 1490.2 — Della moneta antica di Genova. v.1-2. (Gandolfi, G.C.) Genova, 1841-42.
Arc 726.71 — Della origine e delle antiche città de' Sabini. (Bucciolotti, A.) Roma, 1825.
Arc 1027.30.5 — Della porta e basilica di S. Lorenzo dell catacombe. (Gori, F.) Roma, 1862.
Arc 1030.5.17 — Della praepositus della via flaminia. (Rossi, G.B. de.) n.p., 1888.
Arc 1373.3 — Della rarità delle medaglie antiche. (Scotti, V.N.) Florence, 1809.
Arc 1373.3.3 — Della rarità delle medaglie antiche. (Scotti, V.N.) Roma, 1838.
Arc 1033.12.33 — Della sacra sindone di Nostro Signor. (Berta, G.) Torino, 1826?
Arc 1027.12.11 — Della sacrosanta basilica di S. Pietro. (Sindone.) Roma, 1750.
Arc 1033.12.42 — Della Santissima Sindone e la vanda dei piedi. (Talamini, G.) Torino, n.d.
Arc 1033.106 — Della scuola di S. Paolo. (Bartolomei.) Roma, 1850.
Arc 1033.34.35 — Della statua di bronzo di San Pietro. (Grissar, H.) Roma, 1898.

Arc 1027.79 Della torre Antonia d'una stupenda galleria...in Gerusalemme. (Bassi, A.) Gerusalemme, 1860.
Arc 726.64 Della via portuense. (Nibby, Antonio.) Roma, 1827.
Arc 406.3F Della vita degli studî, e delle opere di Giambattista Vermiglioli discorso. (Conestabile, G.) Perugia, 1855.
Arc 1033.89 Della vita e del martirio di San Trifone. (Bassich, A.) Vienna, 1845.
Arc 1490.40F Della zecca e delle monete perugine. (Vermiglioli, G.B.) Perugia, 1816.
Arc 785.6.13 Dell'acqua di Q. Marcio Ré e del suo acquedotto. (Borgnana, C.) Roma, 1861.
Arc 1027.29 Dell'ampiezza. Romane catacombe macchina. (Rossi, M.S.) Roma, 1860.
Arc 1027.53 Dell'antica basilica e della catacomba di Prata. (Taglialatela, G.) n.p., n.d.
Arc 1027.46.5 Dell'antica chiesa di S. Stefano sulla via Cassia. (Nardoni, L.) Roma, 1859.
Arc 1033.17.623 Dell'antica immagine di Maria...S. Marco in Venezia. (Molin, A.) Venezia, 1821.
Arc 1016.215 Dell'antichissimo codice della Bibbia Graeca. (Rossi, G.B. de.) Roma, 1860.
Arc 726.2 Dell'antico ginnasio napoletano. (Lasena, P.) n.p., n.d.
Arc 726.2.2 Dell'antico ginnasio napoletano. (Lasena, P.) n.p., n.d.
Arc 750.223F Dell'antico pago Lemonio in oggi Roma Vecchia. (Riccy, G.A.) Roma, 1802.
Arc 900.202 Dell'antico Palazzo di Dioclez in Spalato. (Lanza, F.) Trieste, 1855.
Arc 1033.43.5 Dell'antico Pellegrinaggio XVIII centenario Martirio Pietro e Paolo. (Ruggieri, E.) Roma, 1867.
Arc 1030.37 Dell'arte...le iscrizione lapidarie. (Romano, C.C.) Roma, 1846.
Htn Arc 760.1* Delle antichità della città di Roma. (Faunus, L.) Venice? 1548.
Htn Arc 1033.20* Delle basiliche antiche. (Analdi, E.) Vincenza, 1767.
Arc 1033.17.241 Delle grandezze della Madonna di Carvaggio. v.3. (Calvi, D.) Napoli, 1749.
Arc 1016.212 Delle iscrizioni cristiani del Piemonte. (Gazzera, C.) Torino, 1847.
Arc 1016.212.3 Delle iscrizioni cristiani del Piemonte. (Gazzera, C.) Torino, 1849.
Arc 1390.6 Delle monete battute da Carlo Magno in Italia. (Morbio, Carlo.) Milano, 1866.
Htn Arc 1490.17* Delle monete di Ferrara. (Bellini, Y.) Ferrara, 1761.
Arc 1490.4.7 Delle monete e dell'istituzione delle Zecche d'Italia. (Carli, G.R.) L'Aja, 1754-57. 2v.
Arc 1490.4.5 Delle monete e dell'istituzione delle Zecche d'Italia. (Carli, G.R.) Mantova, 1754. 3v.
Arc 785.28 Delle pietre antiche. (Corsi, F.) Roma, 1845.
Arc 785.28.5 Delle pietre antiche. 2. ed. (Corsi, F.) Roma, 1833.
Arc 770.9 Delle porte del recinto di servio Tullio nella parte orientale di Roma. (Piale, Stefano.) Roma, 1833. 13 pam.
Arc 1020.100 Delle reliquie insigni...chiesa di Bergamo. (Mutio, Mario.) Bergamo, 1616.
Arc 1030.5.25 Delle sillogi epigrafiche di Smezio e di Panvinio. (Rossi, G.B. de.) Roma, 1862.
Arc 726.5 Delle ville e de' più notabili monumenti. (Cabral, S.) Roma, 1779.
Arc 612.24 Dellenbach, M.E. La conquête du massif alpin et de ses abords. Thèse. Grenoble, 1935.
Arc 1033.8 Dell'errore che persiste...al Santo Evangelista. (Manni, D.M.) Firenze, 1766.
Arc 1033.12.23 Dell'imagine Edessena. (Calcagnino, A.) Genova, 1639.
Arc 1030.4.15 Dell'importanza dell'epigrafia romana. (Marucchi, O.) Roma, 1898.
Arc 1027.36 Dell'indentila dei S. Corpi dei S. Fermo Rustico, e Procolo. (Volpi, A.T.) Milano, 1761.
Arc 905.3 Dello anfiteatro di Pola. (Stancovick, P.) Venice, 1822.
Arc 1033.44.9 Dell'origine...IHS del SS. Nome de Gesú. (Cavedoni, C.) Modena, n.d.
Arc 1033.12.160 Dell'origine invenzione...del...simulacro di...Gesu Crocifisso...volto santo. (Conti, G.B.) Lucca, 1834.
Arc 1033.12.159 Dell'origine invenzione...simulacro di Gesu Crocifisso...Volto santo. (Conti, G.B.) Lucca, n.d.
Arc 1033.63.5 Dell'uso...dei monumenti cristiani cronologici. (Visconti, C.L.) Roma, 1856.
Arc 1030.24 Dell'utilità che la teologia può trarre dall'epigrafia. (Carini, I.) Roma, 1891.
Arc 1613.23 Del Monte, J. Fell's United States coin books. N.Y., 1952.
Arc 1348.80 Del Monte, Jacques. Fell's international coin book. N.Y., 1953.
Arc 66.1.196 Delorme, Jean. Gymnasion; étude sur les monuments consacrés à l'éducation en Grèce des origines à l'Empire romain. Paris, 1960.
Arc 700.55 Delorme, Jean. Gymnasion. Paris, 1960.
Arc 820.208F Delort, J.B. Dix années de fouilles en Auvergne. Lyon, 1901.
Arc 66.1.111 Délos; colonie athénienne. (Roussel, Pierre.) Paris, 1916.
Arc 673.7 Delos, die Insel des Apolon. (Fritsch, O.) Gütersloh, 1908.
Arc 673.10 Pamphlet box. Delos.
Arc 66.1.192 Délos primitive et archaique. (Gallet de Santerre, Hubert.) Paris, 1958.
Arc 505.105F Delougaz, Pinhas. A Byzantine church at Khirbat al-Karak. Chicago, 1960.
Arc 66.1.140 Delphes au IIe et au Ier siècle. (Daux, Georges.) Paris, 1936.
Arc 673.1.17 Delphes et son oracle. (Graindor, P.) Le Caire, 1930.
Arc 673.1.6 Delphi. (Malteros, G.T.) Kaiserslautern, 1958.
Arc 673.1.35 Delphi. (Poulsen, Frederik.) Washington, 1973.
X Cg Arc 673.1.13 Delphi. (Poulson, F.) London, 1920.
Arc 673.1.7 Ein Delphische Weihgeschenk. (Preuner, E.) Bonn, 1899.
Arc 673.1.8 Ein Delphische Weihgeschenk. (Preuner, E.) Leipzig, 1900.
Arc 673.1.50 Delphoi. (Karouzos, Chrēstos Iōannou.) Athēnai, 1974.
Arc 68.1 Deltion archaiologikon. (Greece. Genikē ephoreia tōn archaiotētōn kai mouseiōn.) Athēnai. 1888-1892 4v.
Arc 1033.15 De Lucca, A.A. Annali delli scienze religiose. Roma, 1841.
Arc 66.1.184 Delumeau, Jean. Vie economique et sociale de Rome. Paris, 1957. 2v.
Arc 889.2 Delvaux, Emile. Les alhuions de l'escault et les tourbières...d'Audenarde. Liége, 1885.
Arc 543.7.30 Delvert, Jean. Recherches sur l'érosin des gres des monuments d'Angkor. Paris, 1963.
Arc 66.1.136 Demangel, R. La frise ionique. Paris, 1932.
Arc 935.9.40F Demangel, Robert. Le quartier des Manganes et la première région de Constantinople. Paris, 1939.
Arc 4.1 Demareteion. Paris. 1-2,1935-1936
Arc 672.1.96 Demargne, P. La Crète dédalique. Paris, 1947.
Arc 66.1.164 Demargne, Pierre. La Crète dédalique. Paris, 1947. 2v.
Arc 388.1 Demarsy, A. Le congrès international d'archéologie préhistorique de Copenhague en 1869. Arras, 1870.
Arc 1247.2 Demay, G. Inventaire des sceaux de la Flandre. v.1-2. Paris, 1873.
Arc 1263.2 Demay, G. Inventaire des sceaux de l'Artois et de la Picardie. v.1-2. Paris, 1877-81.
Arc 1583.6 Demmeni, M. Sbornik' ukazov' po monetnomu delu. Sankt Peterburg, 1887. 3v.
Arc 1492.203F Demonstración histórica del verdadero valor detodas las monedas que corrian en Castilla. (Saez, Liciniano.) Madrid, 1796.
Arc 1493.8 Demostración histórica del verdadero valor de todas las monedas que corrián en Castilla. (Saez, Liciniano.) Madrid, 1805.
Arc 600.105.5F Demotic ostraca from Medinet Habu. (Lichtheim, M.) Chicago, 1957.
Htn Arc 740.203* Dempster, T. De Etruria regali libri VII. Florence, 1723-24. 2v.
Arc 1180.5 Demundt, Karl Ernst. Lateinisch-deutsche Interpretationshilfen für spätmittelalterliche und frühneuzeitliche Archivalien. Marburg, 1970.
Arc 1433.73 Demýhoci definesi. (Artuk, S.) Ankara, 1966.
Arc 903.5 Den Funden nach zu Schliessen. (Schreiber, Georg.) Wien, 1960.
Arc 903.5.1 Den Funden nach zu schliessen. 2. Aufl. (Schreiber, Georg.) Wien, 1965.
Htn Arc 1033.17.362* Denaise, Pierre. Dissertatio deidolo hallensi. n.p., 1605.
Arc 1588.4 Denár knizete Vaclava Svatého a. (Skalsky, G.) Praha, 1929.
Arc 585.17A Dendereh. 1898. (Petrie, W.M.F.) London, 1900.
Arc 1584.27 Denezhnoe khoziaistvo Russkogo gosudarstva. (Spasskii, Ivan G.) Leningrad, 1961.
Arc 1433.101 Denezhnoe khoziaistvo Srednei Azii posle mongol'skaia zavoevaniia i reforma Mas'ud-beka. (Davidovich, Elena A.) Moskva, 1972.
Arc 1433.28.5 Denezhnoe obrashchenie Dvina po numizmaticheskim dannym. (Mushegian, K.) Erevan, 1962.
Arc 1583.14 Denezhnye znaki domongol'. Rusi. (Oreshnikov, A.V.) Moskva, 1936.
Arc 1025.75 Denis-Boulet, Noële M. Rome souterraine. Paris, 1965.
Arc 1584.1.15 Denizhnoe obrashchenie kolkhidy v rimskoe vremia. (Golenko, Konstantin V.) Leningrad, 1964.
Arc 905.132 Denk, Stefan. Das Erlaufgebiet im ur- und frühgeschichtlicher Zeit. Wien, 1962.
Arc 73.8F Denkmäler antiker Architektur. (Archäologisches Institut des Deutschen Reichs.) Berlin. 1-10 11v.
Arc 910.1 Denkmäler aus der Feudalzeit im Lande Uri. (Zeller-Werdmüller, H.) Zürich, 1884.
Arc 530.39F Denkmäler aus Lykaonien, Pamphylien und Isaurien. (Swoboda, H.) Brunn, 1935.
Arc 1020.146 Denkmäler byzantinischen Christentums aus der Awarenzeit der Donauländer. (Kollautz, Arnulf.) Amsterdam, 1970.
Arc 628.4 Denkmäler der alten Kunst. (Müller, K.O.) Göttingen, 1854-81. 2v.
Arc 628.4.2 Denkmäler der alten Kunst. v.1-2. (Müller, K.O.) Göttingen, 1832.
Arc 547.6.35F Denkmäler des alten Reiches. (Borchardt, Ludwig.) Berlin, 1937-1964. 2v.
Arc 853.101F Die Denkmäler des römischen Köln. v.1-8,22. (Fremersdorf, F.) Köln, 1950- 9v.
Arc 853.101.2F Die Denkmäler des römischen Köln. 2. Aufl. (Fremersdorf, F.) Köln, 1958-63. 2v.
Arc 497.36 Denkmäler Palästinas. v.1-2. (Watzinger, Carl.) Leipzig, 1933-35.
Arc 845.209F Denkmaeler von Castra Vetera. (Houben, P.) Xanten, 1839.
Arc 87.2.62 Denkmal der Hercules Saxanus. (Frendenberg, J.) Bonn, 1862.
Arc 935.6 Das Denkmal des Porphyrius. (Mordtmann, J.) Athen, 1880.
Arc 380.214 Der Denkmal und Heimatschutz...der Gegenwart. (Wieland, C.A.) Basel, 1905.
Arc 893.27F Denkmaler der Vorzeit zwischen Nord- und Ostsee. (Jankuhn, H.) Schleswig, 1957.
Arc 188.1.5F Die Denkmalpflege. Inhattsverzeichnis der Jahrg, 1899-1913. Berlin, 1914.
Arc 188.1F Die Denkmalpflegen. Berlin. 1899-1922
Arc 188.1 Die Denkmalpflegen. Berlin. 1923+ 37v.
NEDL Arc 180.1.2 Denkschrift zu fuenfzigjaehrigen Stiftungsfeier. (Zürich. Antiquarische Gesellschaft.) Zürich, 1882?
Arc 1018.25 Denkwürdigkeiten und der christlichen Archäologie. (Augusti, J.C.W.) Leipzig, 1817-26. 12v.
Arc 895.7.35 Denmark before the Vikings. (Klindt-Jensen, Ole.) London, 1957.
Arc 758.5 Dennie, John. Rome of to-day and yesterday. Boston, 1894.
Arc 758.5.5 Dennie, John. Rome of to-day and yesterday. 5. ed. N.Y., 1910.
Arc 743.1.9 Dennis, G. The cities and cemeteries of Etruria. London, 19- . 2v.
Arc 743.1 Dennis, G. The cities and cemeteries of Etruria. London, 1848. 2v.
Arc 743.1.2 Dennis, G. The cities and cemeteries of Etruria. London, 1878. 2v.
Arc 743.1.5 Dennis, G. The cities and cemeteries of Etruria. London, 1906. 2v.
Arc 743.1.3 Dennis, G. The cities and cemeteries of Etruria. 3. ed. London, 1883. 2v.
Arc 545.15F Denon, V. Voyages dans la Basse et la Haute Égypte. London, 1807.
Arc 545.15PF Denon, V. Voyages dans la Basse et la Haute Égypte. Atlas. London, 1807.
Arc 595.17 Denslow, Van Buren. The pyramid of Gizeh. N.Y., 18- .
Arc 442.5 Deo, Shantavam Bhalchandra. Chalcolithic Chandoli. Poona, 1965.
Arc 635.217.10 Deonna, W. La vie privée des Déliens. Paris, 1948.
Arc 388.3 Deonna, Waldemar. L'archéologie, son domaine, son but. Paris, 1922.
Arc 547.42 Département égyptien; album. (Brussels. Musées Coyaux d'Art et d'Histoire. Fondation Égyptologique Reine Elisabeth.) Bruxelles, 1934.
Arc 746.40.5F Il deposito votivo di Competti a Veio. (Vagnetti, Lucia.) Firenze, 1971.

Author and Title Listing

Arc 830.124.15 Un dépôt d'outils et un trésor de bronzes...à Seltz. (Schaeffer, F.A.) Haguenau, 1927.
Arc 66.1.86 Déprez, E. Les préliminaires de la guerre de cents ans. Paris, 1902.
Arc 830.2.13 Le déput de l'age du bronze dans le Morbihan. (Marsille, Louis.) Vannes, 1913.
Arc 712.14 Der...Kopf und die Giebelgruppen der Parthenon. (Sauer, B.) Berlin, 1903.
Arc 925.347.5 Derevianko, Anatolii P. Novopetrovskaia kul'tura Srednego Amura. Novosibirsk, 1970.
Arc 925.151.5 Derevianko, Anatolii P. Pannii zheleznyi vek Dal'nego Vostoka. v.2- Novosibirsk, 1972-
Arc 925.347 Derevianko, Anatolii P. V strane srekh solnts. Khabarovsk, 1970.
Arc 726.10.11 Dernan Mugoffin, R. Study of the topography of Preneste. Baltimore, 1908.
Arc 1027.4 De Rossi, G.B. Fouilles et découverts...cimetière de Priscille. Rome, 1880.
Arc 128.5 Derwent Archaeological Society. Research report. Matlock, Derbyshire, Eng. 1,1973+
Arc 825.1 Des antiquités de la ville de Nismes. (Deyron, J.) Nîmes, 1663.
Arc 1510.150 Des hahen deutschen Ritterordens Münz-Sammlung in Wien. (Dudik, Beda.) Bonn, 1966.
Arc 1333.8 Des hohen deutschen Ritter-Ordens Münz-Sammlung in Wien. (Dudik, Beda.) Wien, 1858.
Arc 785.26 Des Marcus Vitruvius Pollio Basilika zu Fanum Fortunae. (Prestel, J.) Strassburg, 1900.
Arc 1500.11 Des monogrammes...deniers capétiens. (Blancard, Louis.) Marseille, n.d.
Arc 925.3 Des monuments de la Russie connus sous le nom de Tumulus Tchoudes. (Maury, A.) Paris, n.d.
Arc 1092.1.2 Des rouelles et des anneaux antiques. (Longpérier, H.) Paris, 1867.
Arc 1285.2 Des sceaux des prieurs anglais de l'ordre de l'hôpital. (Delaville Le Roulx, J.) Rome, 1881.
Arc 1285.2.3 Des sceaux des prieurs anglais de l'ordre de l'hôpital. (Delaville Le Roulx, J.) Rome, 1881. 2 pam.
Arc 1093.2.11 Des silex perforés naturellement. (Baudon, T.) Paris, 1909.
Arc 1027.25.51 Des travaux de M. de Rossi. Arras, n.d.
Arc 1033.97 Des voies d'exception...contre les martyrs. (Le Blant, E.) Rome, 1884.
Arc 1495.2 De Sauley, F. Recherches sur les monnaies. Paris, 1843.
Arc 1025.25 Desbassayns de Richemont, M.C. Les nouvelles études...catacombes romaines. Paris, 1870.
Arc 682.31F Desborough, V.R. d'. The last Mycenaeans and their successors. Oxford, 1964.
Arc 66.1.15 Descemet, C. Inscriptions doliaires latines. Paris, 1880.
Arc 1030.57 Deschamps, P. Étude sur la paléographie des inscriptions lapidaires de la fin de l'époque mérovingienne aux dernières années du XIIe siècle. Paris, 1929.
Arc 1493.2 Descripção...das moedas cunhadas en home dos reis. (Aragão, A.C. de.) Lisboa, 1874-80. 3v.
Arc 1478.27 Descripção historica das moedas romanas existentes no gabinete numismatico de S.M. el Rei o Senhor Dom Luiz I. (Teixeira de Aragão, Augusto.) Lisboa, 1870.
Arc 1492.200 Descripcion generale de las monedas hispanicas cristianas. (Heiss, Aloiss.) Madrid, 1865. 3v.
Arc 513.6 Descripitive catalogue to accompany a series of photographs of Asia Minor. (Haynes, J.H.) N.Y., 1892.
Arc 1020.8 Description...de l'église des Saints Apotres de Constantinople. (Legrand, E.) Paris, 1896.
Arc 825.7.2 Description...des antiquités. 2. éd. Nismes, 1786.
Arc 1333.6 Description. Musée...Prince Basile Kotschoubey. (Koehne.) St. Petersbourg, 1857. 2v.
Arc 805.3 Description de deux monumens antiques. (Koehler, H.K.E. von.) St. Petersbourg, 1810.
Arc 497.9 Description de la Palestine. pt.1-3. (Guérin, V.) Paris, 1868-80. 7v.
Arc 1033.12.76 Déscription de la relique...du...sang...Bruges. Bruges, 1782.
Arc 825.3 Description de l'amphithéâtre de Nîmes. (Pelet, Auguste.) Nîmes, 1853.
Arc 825.3.1 Description de l'amphithéâtre de Nîmes. 2e éd. (Pelet, Auguste.) Nîmes, 1859. 9 pam.
Arc 825.3.2 Description de l'amphithéâtre de Nîmes. 3e éd. (Pelet, Auguste.) Nîmes, 1866.
Arc 510.4 Description de l'Asie Mineure. (Texier, Charles.) Paris, 1839-1849. 3v.
Arc 830.144F Description de l'écrin d'une dame romaine. (Comarmond, A.) Paris, 1844.
Arc 1458.1 Description de médailles antiques. (Mionnet, T.E.) Paris, 1806-08. 7v.
Arc 1458.1.2 Description de médailles antiques. Supplément. (Mionnet, T.E.) Paris, 1819-37. 10v.
Arc 1443.1 Description de quelques monnaies nouveaux des nomes d'Égypte. (Rougé, Jacques de.) Paris, 1882.
Arc 1208.10 Description des collections de sceaux matrices. (Dongé, E.) Paris, 1872.
Arc 830.57 Description des fouilles archéologiques...Compiègne. pt.1-4. (Cauchemè, V.) Compiègne, 1900-12.
Arc 800.4 Description des fouilles d'Herculanum. (Pagano, N.) Naples, 1871.
Arc 1468.30 Description des médailles antiques du cabinet de feu M. Allier de Hauteroche. (Dumersan, T.M.) Paris, 1829.
Arc 1411.9F Description des médailles chinoises du cabinet imperial de France. (Hager, Joseph.) Paris, 1805.
Arc 1500.2 Description des médailles gauloises...de la Bibliothèque Royale. (Duchalais, A.) Paris, 1846.
Arc 1458.19 Description des médailles grecques. (Badeigts de Laborde.) Paris, 1869.
Arc 1558.1 Description des monnaies de Cuivre...Suedois. (Stiernstedt, A.V.) Stockholm, 1871-72.
Arc 1448.1 Description des monnaies de la Numidie et de la Maurétanie. (Charrier, Louis.) Macon, 1912.
Arc 1020.60 Description des monuments de l'Abbaye de Rosières. (Besançon, B.) n.p., 1714.
Arc 595.2 Description des pyramides de Ghizé. (Grobert, J.) Paris, 1801.
Arc 1020.110 Description des reliquaires...abboye de Charroux. (Brouillet, A.) Poitiers, 1856.
Arc 815.19 Description des tombeaux qui ont été découverts à Pompéi dans l'année 1812. (Millin, A.L.) Naples, 1813.
Arc 785.13.28 Description du Forum Romain et guide pour le visiteur. (Marucchi, O.) Rome, 1885.
Arc 530.18 Description du palais de al-Montasim. (Viollet, H.) Paris, 1909.
Arc 830.70.5 Description du pays des Ségusiaves. (Bernard, Auguste.) Paris, 1858. 11 pam.
Arc 785.58F Description du théâtre de Marcellus à Rome. (Vaudoyer.) Paris, 1812.
Arc 746.15 Description d'une collection de vases peints et bronzes. (DeWitte, J.) Paris, 1837.
Arc 830.6.13 Description d'une voie romaine. (Martin-Daussigny, E.C.) Lyon, 1855. 12 pam.
Arc 545.17 Description générale de Memphis et des Pyramides. (Jomard, E.F.) Paris, 1829.
Arc 1492.201 Description générale des monnaies antiques de l'Espagne. (Heiss, Aloiss.) Paris, 1870.
Arc 1478.4 Description générale des monnaies byzantines. Text and plates. (Sabatier, J.) Paris, 1862. 2v.
Arc 1478.3 Description générale des monnaies de la Republique Romaine. (Cohen, H.) Paris, 1857.
Arc 1492.202 Description générale des monnaies des rois wisigoths. (Heiss, Aloiss.) Paris, 1872.
Arc 1478.3.3 Description historique des monnaies frappées sons l'Empire Romain. (Cohen, H.) Paris, 1880-92. 8v.
Arc 1478.3.2 Description historique des monnaies frappées sons l'Empire Romain. (Cohen, H.) Paris, 1859. 7v.
Arc 825.12 Description historique et abrégée des antiquités de Nismes. (Maucomble, Jean François Dieudonné.) Nismes, 1789.
Arc 1478.17 Description historique et chronologique des monnaies de la République romaine vulgairement appelées monnaies consulaires. (Babelon, Ernest.) Paris, 1885-86. 2v.
Arc 1478.17.5 Description historique et chronologique des monnaies de la République romaine vulgairement appelées monnaies consulaires. (Babelon, Ernest.) Bologna, 1963. 2v.
Arc 885.14 Description of a Roman building and other remains...at Caerleon. (Lee, J.E.) London, 1850. 5 pam.
Arc 1613.3 Description of a selection of coins and medals relating to America. (Appleton, W.S.) Cambridge, 1870-76. 2 pam.
Htn Arc 875.36* Description of an ancient cross at Kilmory. (Wilson, Wilson D.) Edinburgh, 1839.
Arc 861.22 Description of an ancient font in Bridekirk. (Lyttelton.) n.p., 1767.
Arc 590.2 Description of an Egyptian mummy. (Warren, J.C.) Boston, n.d.
Arc 1335.16 A description of ancient and modern coins. (United States Mint, Philadelphia.) Philadelphia, 1860.
X Cg Arc 672.1.11 A description of some theatres in Crete. (Belli, Onorio.) London, 1854.
Arc 1535.2 Description of the Anglo-Gallic coins. (British Museum. Department of Coins and Medals.) London, 1826.
Arc 756.6.3 A description of the antiquities and other curiosities of Rome. v.1-2. (Burton, Edward.) Florence, 1830.
Arc 756.6 A description of the antiquities and other curiosities of Rome. 2. ed. (Burton, Edward.) London, 1828. 2v.
Arc 861.54 A description of the deverel barrow. (Miles, William A.) London, 1826.
Arc 547.7 Description of the Egyptian court erected in the Crystal Palace. (Jones, O.) London, 1854.
Arc 800.5.10 A description of the first discoveries of...ancient city of Heraclea. (Venuti, N.M. de.) London, 1750.
Arc 1660.8 A description of the medals of Washington. (Snowden, J.R.) Philadelphia, 1861.
Arc 1663.1 A description of the national medals of America. (Wyatt, T.) N.Y., 1854. 2 pam.
Arc 522.1 Description of the plain of Troy. (Lechevalier, Jean Baptiste.) Edinburgh, 1791.
Arc 770.1.5 Description of the plan of Rome. (Parker, J.H.) Oxford, 1878.
Arc 1663.27 A description of the series of medals struck at the national medal mint by...Napoleon Bonaparte. (Laskey, John C.) London, 1818.
Arc 861.37.3 Description of the Tumulus. 3. ed. (Williamson, W.C.) Scarborough, 1872.
Arc 708.1 Description of the view of Athens. (Barker, H.A.) n.p., n.d.
Arc 1500.5.3 Description raisonnée des monnaies mérovingiennes de Châlon-sur-Saône. (Ponton d'Amécourt, G. de.) Paris, 1874-83. 3 pam.
Arc 830.71 Descriptions des monumens des differeus âges observés dans le département de la Haute-Vienne. (Allou, Charles N.) Paris, 1821.
Arc 1433.5 A descriptive account of antiquity and coins of Afghanistan. (Wilson, H.) London, 1841.
Arc 435.25.6 Descriptive account of the rock temples of western India. (Burgess, James.) Bombay, 187-?
Arc 458.4 Descriptive and historical papers...the seven pagodas on the Coromandel coast. (Carr, Mark William.) Madras, 1869.
Arc 1480.36F Descriptive catalogue of a cabinet of Roman family coins belonging to...the Duke of Northumberland. (Northumberland, A.P.) London, 1856.
Arc 1335.17 Descriptive catalogue of a collection of current coins of all countries. (Yates, J.) London, 1862.
Arc 861.17.9 Descriptive catalogue of antiquities...Roman London. (Tite, William.) London, 1848.
Arc 875.38 Descriptive catalogue of antiquities in Ayrshire. (Black, George F.) n.p., n.d.
Arc 1680.5 Descriptive catalogue of Australian tradesmen's tokens. (Stainsfield, C.W.) London, 1883.
Arc 1335.8 Descriptive catalogue of coins belonging to the Historical Society of Maryland. (Groux, D.E.) n.p., n.d.
Arc 1675.7.5 A descriptive catalogue of papal medals. (Lincoln, W.S. and Son, firm, auctioneers, London.) London, 1898.
Arc 1478.1 A descriptive catalogue of rare Roman coins. (Ackerman, J.Y.) London, 1834. 2v.
Arc 880.49 A descriptive catalogue of the antiquities. (Royal Irish Academy, Dublin. Museum.) Dublin, 1857.
Arc 1680.1 A descriptive catalogue of the London traders, tavern and coffee-house tokens. (Burn, J.H.) London, 1855.
Arc 375.7 Descriptive charts of ancient monuments. no.1-5. (Deinard, S.N.) Minneapolis, 1912.
Arc 1663.14 Descriptive list of medals relating to John Law. (Belts, Benjamin.) n.p., 1907.
Arc 870.1.9 Descriptive lists of flint implements. St. Mary Bourne. (Stevens, J.) London, 1867.
Arc 435.13 Descriptive lists of inscriptions in the central provinces and Berar. (Hīrālāl, Rai Bahādur.) Nagpur, 1916.
Arc 950.210 Descriptive notes on certain implements...Graham Island. (Mackenzie, A.) n.p., 1891.
Arc 758.3 Descrittione di Roma antica e moderna. Roma, 1650.
Arc 1468.19 Descrizione d'alcune medaglie greche. (Sestini, D.) Firenze, 1821.

Arc 1470.9 Descrizione degli stateri antichi. (Sestini, D.) Florence, 1817.

Arc 726.24.9 Descrizione della villa Adriana. (Nibby, Antonio.) Roma, 1827.

Arc 800.5.2 Descrizione delle prime scoperte dell'antica città d'Ercolano. (Venuti, N.M. de.) Roma, 1748.

Htn Arc 800.5* Descrizione delle prime scoperte dell'antica città d'Ercolano. (Venuti, N.M. de.) Venezia, 1749.

Arc 1020.87 Descrizione delle reliquare di Santi...Rocca di Lutiano. (Brocchi, G.M.) Firenze, 1744.

Arc 1430.2 Descrizione di alcune monete cufiche del Museo. (Mainoni, S. de.) Milano, 1820.

Arc 810.5.2A Descrizione di Pompei. (Fiorelli, G.) Naples, 1875.

Arc 767.2.5 Descrizione di Roma antica. (Marliani, B.) Roma, 1697.

Arc 767.2.7 Descrizione di Roma antica. (Marliani, B.) Roma, 1708. 2v.

Arc 767.2.10 Descrizione di Roma antica. (Marliani, B.) Roma, 1739.

Arc 790.200 Descrizione di una lasa disotterrata in Pompeii. (Avellino, F.M.) Naples, 1837. 2 pam.

Arc 785.13.40 Descrizione storica del Foro Romano. (Canina, Luigi.) Roma, 1834.

Arc 1033.9.5 Descrizioni dei vetri ornati di figure in oro. (Garrucci, R.) n.p., n.d.

Arc 843.160 El descubrimiento de la cueva y pinturas de altamira por Marcelino S. de Sauteola. (Carballo, Jesús.) Santander, 1950.

Arc 758.6 Deseine, F. L'ancienne Rome. v.1-4. Leide, 1713. 2v.

Arc 600.5.15F The desert Fayum. (Caton-Thompson, G.) London, 1934. 2v.

Arc 710.28 Des Gagniers, Jean. L'acropole d'Athènes. Québec, 1971.

Arc 585.15A Deshashek. 1897. (Petrie, W.M.F.) London, 1898.

Arc 672.1.92 Deshayes, J. Les quatier Z à Mallia. Paris, 1959.

Arc 416.33 Deshifrovka i interpretatsiia pis'mennostei drevnego Vostoka. (Akademiia nauk SSSR. Institut narodov Azii.) Moskva, 1966.

Arc 448.1.20 Deshmukh, P.R. The Indus civilization in the Rgveda. Yeotmal, 1954.

Arc 595.6.5 Designing and building the Great Pyramid. (Mencken, A.) Baltimore, 1963.

Arc 1025.54 Desimoni, C. Le catacombe romane. Firenze, 1870.

Arc 853.325 Dessau-Mosigkau. (Krueger, Bruno.) Berlin, 1967.

Arc 889.3 Dessel, Camille. Topographie des voies romaines de la Belgique. Bruxelles, 1877.

Arc 66.1.186 Dessenore, André. Le sphinx. Paris, 1957.

Arc 793.15 The destruction and resurection of Pompeii and Herculaneum. (Corti, E.C.) London, 1951.

Arc 766.1.9 The destruction of ancient Rome. (Lanciani, R.) N.Y., 1899.

Arc 766.1.9.1 The destruction of ancient Rome. (Lanciani, R.) N.Y., 1967.

Arc 441.5 Detailed report of an archaeological tour with the Buner Field Force. (Stein, Mark A.) Lahore, 1898.

Arc 930.203 Dethier. Nouvelles découvertes archéologiques à Constantinople. Constantinople, 1867.

Arc 388.14 Deuel, Leo. Testaments of time. 1. ed. N.Y., 1965.

Arc 416.24 Deuel, Leo. The treasures of time. 1. ed. Cleveland, 1961.

Arc 510.2PF Deutches Archäologisches Institut. Altertümer von Pergamon. Atlases. 9v.

Arc 503.3F Deutsch-Turkischer Denkmalschutz-Kommando. Wissenschaftliche Veröffentlichungen. v.1-6. Berlin, 1920-

Arc 609.2F Deutsche Aksum-Expedition. v.1-4. (Littmann, Enno.) Berlin, 1913.

Arc 848.6 Deutsche Altertumskunde. (Kauffmann, F.) München, 1913-23. 2v.

Arc 1508.25 Deutsche Bundesbank. Deutsche Taler von den Anfängen der Talerprägung bis zum Dreissigjährigen Krieg aus der Münzensammlung der Deutschen Bundesbank. Frankfurt, 1966?-67? 2v.

Arc 384.18 Deutsche Historiker Gesellschaft. Fachgruppe Ur- und Frühgeschichte. Evolution und Revolution in alten Orient und in Europa. Das Neolithikum als historische Erscheinung. Berlin, 1971.

Arc 933.10 Deutsche Historiker Gesellschaft. Fachgruppe Ur- und Frühgeschichte. Problem des frühen Mittelalters in archäologischer und historischer Sicht. Berlin, 1966.

Arc 1505.201 Die deutsche Medaille in Kunst oc Hinsicht. (Domanig, K.) Wien, 1907.

Arc 1510.41 Deutsche Medailleure des sechzehnten und siebzehnten Jahrhunderts. (Erman, Adolf.) Berlin, 1884.

Arc 1508.11 Deutsche Münz- und Geldgeschichte von den Anfanger bis zum 15. Jahrhundert. (Suhle, Arthur.) Berlin, 1955.

Arc 1303.3 Deutsche Münzblätter. Berlin. 26-62,1905-1943 14v.

Arc 1510.6 Deutsche Münzgeschichte biz zu der Ottonenzeit. (Müller, J.H.) Leipzig, 1860.

Arc 1508.25 Deutsche Taler von den Anfängen der Talerprägung bis zum Dreissigjährigen Krieg aus der Münzensammlung der Deutschen Bundesbank. (Deutsche Bundesbank.) Frankfurt, 1966?-67? 2v.

Arc 387.13.5 Deutsche und antike Welt. (Curtius, Ludwig.) Stuttgart, 1950.

Arc 848.25 Deutsche Ur- und Vorgeschichtswissenschaft der Gegenwart. (Neckel, Gustav.) Berlin, 1934.

Arc 848.15.10 Deutsche Vor- und Frühgeschichte in Bildern. (Schuchhardt, C.) München, 1936.

Arc 848.8.2 Die deutsche Vorgeschichte. 2. Aufl. (Kossinna, Gustaf.) Würzburg, 1914.

Arc 848.8.4 Die deutsche Vorgeschichte. 7. Aufl. (Kossinna, Gustaf.) Leipzig, 1936.

Arc 848.23 Deutsche Vorzeit. (Wahle, Ernst.) Leipzig, 1932.

Arc 848.16.2 Deutsche Vorzeit. 2. Aufl. (Wilser, Ludwig.) Steglitz, 1918.

Arc 848.23.3 Deutsche Vorzeit. 3. Aufl. (Wahle, Ernst.) Bad Homburg, 1962.

Arc 848.28.5 Deutsche Vorzeit. 6. Aufl. (Hohne, Hans.) Bielefeld, 1937.

Arc 676.5F Die deutschen Ausgrabungen auf der Argissa-Magula in Thessalien. Bonn, 1962.

Arc 681.10.5 Die deutschen Ausgrabungen auf der Otzaki-Magula in Thessalien. Bonn, 1971- 2v.

Arc 1076.10 Deutschen Glockenatlas. (Grundmann, Günther.) München, 1959- 3v.

Arc 1247.1 Die deutschen Kaiser- und Königs-Siegel. (Heffner, Carl.) Würzburg, 1875.

Arc 1508.8 Die deutschen Medailleure des XVI. Jahrhunderts. (Habich, Georg.) Halle an der Saale, 1916.

Arc 1508.7 Die deutschen Münzen des Mittelalters. 4. Aufl. (Gebhart, H.) Berlin, 1929.

Arc 1508.15.20 Die deutschen Münzen seit 1871. 6. Aufl. (Jaeger, Kurt.) Basel, 1967.

Arc 1505.1 Die deutschen Münzender Saeschischen und Frankischen Kaiserzeit. Text und Plates. (Dannenberg, H.) Berlin, 1876. 2v.

Arc 188.2 Deutschen Orient Gesellschaft. Sendschriften. Leipzig. 1-6,1901-1938 7v.

Arc 55.1.4 Deutschen Palästine Verein. Mitteilungen und Nachrichten-Register. Leipzig. 1895-1912 2v.

Arc 1508.15.5 Die deutschen Reichsmünzen seit 1871. (Jaeger, Kurt.) Basel, 1956.

Arc 1508.10 Die deutschen Renaissance-Medaille. (Suhle, Arthur.) Leipzig, 1950.

Arc 1348.65 Deutscher Numismatikertag, Göttingen. Wissenschaftliche Abhandlunger des deutschen Numismatikertages. Göttingen, 1959.

Arc 510.2 Deutsches Archäologisches Institut. Altertümer von Pergamon. Berlin. 1,1912+ 18v.

Arc 68.10 Deutsches Archäologisches Institut. Bericht über die Ausgrabungen in Olympia. Berlin. 4,1940+ 5v.

Arc 1480.56 Deutsches Archäologisches Institut. Die Fundmünzen der römischen Zeit in Deutschland. Berlin, 1960- 17v.

Arc 848.14F Deutsches Archäologisches Institut. Germania romana. Bamberg, 1922.

Arc 1080.10F Deutsches Archäologisches Institut. Die langobardischen Fibeln aus Italien. Berlin, 1950.

Arc 848.54 Deutsches Archäologisches Institut. Neue Ausgrabungen im Deutschland. Berlin, 1958.

Arc 513.25 Deutsches Archäologisches Institut. Neue deutsche Ausgrabungen im Mittelmeergebiet. Berlin, 1959.

Arc 688.7.5F Deutsches Archäologisches Institut. Samos. v.1,5-8,12,14. Bonn, 1961- 7v.

Arc 33.3F Deutsches Archäologisches Institut. Abteilung Kairo. Abhandlungen. Hamburg. 5-6 2v.

Arc 65.3.6 Deutsches Archäologisches Institut. Athenische Abteilung. Mitteilungen. Beiheft. Berlin. 1,1971+

Arc 853.55F Deutsches Archaeologisches Institut. Römisch-Germanische Kommission. Römische Grabmäler des Mosellandes. Trier. 1-2,1924-1932 3v.

Arc 73.6.15 Deutsches Archäologisches Institut. Römische Abteilung. Bilderhefte. Tübingen. 1,1962+ 4v.

Arc 73.6 Deutsches Archäologisches Institut. Römische Abteilung. Mittheilungen. Rom. 1,1886+ 60v.

Arc 73.6.10 Deutsches Archäologisches Institut. Römische Abteilung. Mittheilungen. Ergänzungsheft. München. 1,1931+ 19v.

Arc 73.6.2 Deutsches Archäologisches Institut. Römische Abteilung. Mittheilungen. Register, Bd. I-X. Rom, 1902.

Arc 340.2 Deutsches Archäologisches Institut. Römische Abteilung. Bibliothek. Katalog der Bibliothek. Rom, 1900-02. 2v.

Arc 340.2.5 Deutsches Archäologisches Institut. Römische Abteilung. Bibliothek. Katalog der Bibliothek. v.1-2. Rom, 1913-32. 4v.

Arc 340.2.7 Deutsches Archäologisches Institut. Römische Abteilung. Bibliothek. Katalog der Bibliothek. Supplement. Berlin, 1930.

Arc 33.2 Deutsches Institut für ägyptische Altertumskunde in Kairo. Mitteilungen. Augsburg. 1,1930+ 17v.

Arc 1303.2 Deutsches Jahrbuch für Numismatik. München. 1-4,1938-1941 3v.

Arc 1508.30 Deutschlands Kayser-Münzen des Mittel-Alters. (Göetz, Christian Jacob.) Leipzig, 1968.

Arc 785.13.25 Deux actes de Domitien. (Visconti, C.L.) Rome, 1873.

Arc 552.1.6 Les deux Champollion, leur vie. (Champollion-Figeac, J.J.) Grenoble, 1887.

Arc 1254.7 Deux chefs normands des armées byzantines. (Schlumberger, G.) Paris, 1881.

Arc 1254.12 Deux epagia...sceau d'un capitaine arménien. (Schlumberger, G.) Paris, 1884.

Arc 823.19.155 Deux masques d'enfants. (Thédenat, H.) Paris, 1886.

Arc 1033.44.27 Deux monuments des premiers siècles. (Garrucci, R.) Rome, 1862.

Arc 1033.113 Deux mosaiques chrétiennes du IVe siècle. (Leport, L.) Paris, 1894.

Arc 1590.4 Deux plombs satiriques. (Schlumberger, G.) Paris, 1878. 3 pam.

Arc 505.19.5 Deux questions d'archéologie palestinienne. (Barnabas.) Jérusalem, 1902. 2v.

Arc 1470.83 Deux trésors de monnaies. (Le Rider, Georges.) Paris, 1963.

Arc 608.93 Deux villes d'Ifriqiya: Sousse, Tunis. (Lézine, Alexandre.) Paris, 1971.

Arc 861.155 Deva: Roman Chester. (Thompson, F.D.) Chester, Eng., 1959.

Arc 1335.105 Devegge, Ole. Ole Devegge's mynt-og medaille-samling. Kjøbenhavn, 1851.

Arc 412.18 Devel, Leo. Flights into yesterday. N.Y., 1969.

Arc 497.11 The development of Palestine exploration. (Bliss, F.J.) N.Y., 1906.

Arc 1478.33A The development of Roman coinage. (Milne, J.G.) Oxford, 1937.

Arc 600.41FA The development of the Egyptian tomb down to the accession of Cheops. (Reisner, George A.) Cambridge, 1936.

Arc 66.1.202 Le developpement urbain en Provence. (Fevrier, Paul Albert.) Paris, 1964.

Arc 936.40 Devetashkata peshtera. (Mikov, Vasil.) Sofiia, 1960.

Arc 537.1 Devia Cypria. (Hogarth, D.G.) London, 1889.

Arc 1274.1 Deville, J. Achille. Dissertation sur les sceaux de Richard-Coeur-de-Lion. Rouen, 1828.

Arc 861.73 Devonshire antiquities. 2. ed. (Chudleigh, J.) Exeter, 1893.

Arc 870.5.5 Dew-ponds; history, observation and experiment. (Martin, E. A.) London, 1915.

Arc 870.5.7 Dew-ponds in fable and fact. (Pugsley, A.J.) London, 1939.

Arc 1027.12 DeWaal, A. Die Apostelgruft ad Catacumbas S. Peter und S. Paul. Rom, 1894.

Arc 983.17 Dewdney, Selwya. Indian rock paintings of the Great Lakes. Toronto, 1962.

Arc 1510.107 Dewerdeck, G. Silesia numismatica. Jauer, 1711.

Arc 746.15 DeWitte, J. Description d'une collection de vases peints et bronzes. Paris, 1837.

Arc 825.1 Deyron, J. Des antiquités de la ville de Nismes. Nîmes, 1663.

Arc 450.10 Dhama, B.L. Khajuraho. Delhi, 1953.

Arc 1027.13 Di alcunce cripte nell'agro di Brindisi. (Tarantini, G.) Napoli, 1878.

Arc 1033.37.3 Di alcune altre antichità cristiane. (Abbati Olivieri Giordani, Annibale degli.) Pesaro, 1784.

Arc 1033.37 Di alcune antichità cristiane...in Pesaro nel Museo Olivieri. (Abbati Olivieri Giordani, Annibale degli.) Pesaro, 1781.

Arc 1027.44 Di alcune iscrizioni...Basilia de S. Petronella. (Marucchi, O.) Roma, n.d.

Arc 815.14 Di alcune memorie bibliche scaperte a Pompei. (Feis, Leopoldo.) Firenze, 1906.

Arc 1033.27 Di alcune sotterrance confessoni...Basiliche di Roma. (Nardoni.) Roma, 1881.

Arc 1030.4.25 Di alcuni antiche monumenti. (Marucchi, O.) Roma, 1899-1900.

Arc 1433.32 Di alcuni conii osmani della museo di Modena. (Ghiron, I.) Firenze, 1870.

Arc 905.4.5 Di scavi di Salona nel 1850. Memoria. (Carrara, F.) Praga, 1852.

Arc 1077.2.13 Di tre antiche stauroteche...cattedrale di Modena. (Cavedoni, C.) Modena, 1847.

Arc 1033.35.9 Di un antica stauroteca istoriata...Brescia. (Brunati.) Roma, 1839.

Arc 1033.57 Di un antico filiatterio christiano. (Cozza-Luzi, G.) Napoli, 1887.

Arc 1016.225 Di un antico sarcofago cristiano...Mantova. (Odorici, F.) Brescia, 1855.

Arc 1027.4.13 Di un battistero scoperto nel cimitero di Priscilla. (Marucchi, O.) Roma, 1901.

Arc 1027.7.9 Di un cielo di rappresent cristianità...SS. Pietro ed Marcelino. (Wilpert, J.) Roma, 1892.

Arc 1027.5.15 Di un gruppo di antiche iscrizioni...Domitilla. (Marucchi, O.) Roma, 1902.

Arc 1027.8.9 Di un ipogeo scoperto nel cimitero di S. Sebastian. (Marucchi, O.) Roma, 1879.

Arc 1027.18.9 Di un nuovo cimitero giudaico. (Marucchi, O.) Roma, 1884.

Arc 1015.225.5 Di un nuovo cimitero giudaico. (Marucchi, O.) Roma, 1884.

Arc 1020.9.70 Di un nuovo cippo del pomerio urbano. (Marucchi, O.) Roma, 1900.

Arc 1027.28.5 Di un nuovo insigne esemplare...indice dei cimiteri cristiani di Roma. (Stevenson, Enrico.) Roma, 1897.

Arc 1027.7.5 Di un nuovo tratto catacombe San Marcellino Pietro. (Visconti, P.E.) Roma, 1839.

Arc 1490.20 Di un quadrante unico ed inedito. (Vermiglioli, G.B.) Perugia, 1825.

Arc 1033.3.17 Di un sarcofago cristiano del palazzo torlonia. (Torlonia, L.) Roma, 1897.

Arc 1030.4 Di una...iscrizione cristiana. (Marucchi, O.) Roma, 1883.

Arc 1259.1 Di una bolla plumbea papale. (Rossi, G.B. de.) Roma, 1882.

Arc 1027.24.5 Di una imagine de S. Protasio, nella catacombe severiana. (Taglialatela, G.) Napoli, 1874.

Arc 1027.66 Di una iscrizione monumentale al cimitero di Generosa. (Huelsen, C.) Roma, 1900.

Arc 1433.15 Di una moneta Turca coniata nella zecca di Parma. (Cipelli, Luigi.) Parma, 1868.

Arc 1030.4.5 Di una rarissima epigrafe cristiana. (Marucchi, O.) Roma, 1878.

Arc 700.14 Di un'ara greca. (Calderini, A.) Milano, 1907.

Arc 875.32.10 Diack, F.C. The inscription of Pictland. Aberdeen, 1944.

Arc 875.32.5 Diack, F.C. The Newton stone and other Pictish inscriptions. Paisley, 1922.

Arc 1020.23 Diaconia S. Agathae in subura. (Martinelli, F.) Roma, 1638.

Arc 1020.9.187 Le diaconie cardinatizie e la diaconia "S. Vite in Macello". (Biasiotti, G.) Roma, 1911.

Htn Arc 1350.2* Dialoghi - intorno alle medaglie...altre antichità. (Agostini, A.) Rome, 1592.

Arc 68.15 Dialoghi di archeologia. Milano. 1,1967+ 4v.

Htn Arc 1348.28* Dialogos de medallas, inscriciones y otras antiquedades. (Agustin, Antonius.) Madrid, 1744.

Htn Arc 1355.1* Dialogue upon the usefulness of ancient medals. (Addison, J.) Glasgow, 1751.

Arc 1355.1.5 Dialogue upon the usefulness of ancient medals. (Addison, J.) Glasgow, 1769.

Arc 1027.62 Diamilla. I monumenti degli antichi cristiani in relazione col progresso. Roma, 1850.

Arc 1020.9.5 Diario sacro. 2. ed. (Mazzolari, G.M.) Roma, 1805-06. 4v.

Arc 1020.9 Diario sacro le sacre vie, le sacre basilicho. (Mazzolari, G.M.) Roma, 1779-81. 5v.

Arc 726.9 Diarium italicum. (Montfaucon, B. de.) Paris, 1702.

Htn Arc 726.9.15* Diarium italicum. (Montjaucon, B. de.) London, 1711.

Arc 861.31.5 Diary of a dean. (Merewether, J.) London, 1851.

Arc 1033.24 Di Carlo. Risposta al P. Grisar...contre il sacro tesoro. Tivoli, 1896. 3 pam.

Arc 1643.4F Diccionario de la moneda hispano-americana. (Burzio, Humberto F.) Santiago, 1956-58. 2v.

Arc 1033.35.55 Dichiarazione de' tre antiche Stauroteche. (Cavedoni, C.) Modena, 1847.

Arc 1030.3.13 Dichiarazione dell'epetaffo di S. Georgio Martire. (Cavedoni, C.) Modena, 1843.

Arc 1030.3.5 Dichiarazione dell'iscrizione sepolcrale di San Decenzio Martire. (Cavedoni, C.) Modena, 1839.

Arc 1030.3.11 Dichiarazione di due antiche gemme incise. (Cavedoni, C.) Modena, n.d.

Arc 1020.6.9 Dichiarazione di un monumento sepolcrale cristiano. (Veludo, G.) Venezia, 1877.

Arc 1033.3.27 Dichiarazione di un sarcofago cristiano ostiense. (Visconti, C.L.) Roma, 1859.

Arc 1033.93 Dichiarazione di 5 bassirilievi biblici...Modena. (Cavedoni, C.) Modena, 1855.

Arc 736.2.9 Dichiarazioni della pianta dell'antiche Siracuse. (Mirabella a Alagona, V.) Napoli, 1625.

Arc 1610.1 Dickeson, M.W. The American numismatic manual. 2. ed. Philadelphia, 1860.

Arc 1613.10F Dickeson, M.W. The American numismatical manual of the currency or money of the aborigines. Philadelphia, 1859.

Arc 861.197 Dickinson, Tania M. Cuddesdon and Dorcester-on-Thames, Oxfordshire. Oxford, 1974.

Arc 1335.161 Dickmann-Secherau, Johanna N. Dickmann's Münzsammlung in Wien. Wien, 1836.

Arc 1335.161 Dickmann's Münzsammlung in Wien. (Dickmann-Secherau, Johanna N.) Wien, 1836.

Arc 530.8 Dickson, W.K. The life of Major General Sir R.M. Smith. Edinburgh, 1901.

Arc 1510.154.5 Dicktaler-Prägungen, 1544-1679. v.2. (Duve, Gebhard.) Frankfurt am Main, 1974-

Arc 1518.4 Dictionaire géographique de l'histoire monétaire belge. (Serrure, Raymond.) Bruxelles, 1880.

Arc 1330.6.2F Dictionary and auction catalogues of the Library of the American Numismatic Society. First and second supplement. (American Numismatic Society. Library.) Boston, 1967. 2v.

Arc 1330.6F Dictionary catalogue. (American Numismatic Society.) Boston, 1962. 6v.

Arc 497.50.5 A dictionary of life in Bible times. (Corswant, Willy.) N.Y., 1960.

Arc 1340.2.2 A dictionary of Roman coins, republican and imperial. (Stevenson, Seth William.) London, 1964.

Arc 1340.2 A dictionary of Roman coins. (Stevenson, Seth William.) London, 1889.

Arc 820.203 Dictionnaire archéologique de la Gaule. (France. Ministère de l'Instruction.) Paris, 1875-1923. 2v.

Arc 830.78 Dictionnaire archéologique de la Loire-Inférieure. (Lisle, Pitre de.) Nantes, 1882.

Arc 497.50 Dictionnaire d'archéologie biblique. (Corswant, Willy.) Neuchâtel, 1956.

Arc 1018.01 Dictionnaire d'archéologie chrétienne et littérature. v.1-15. Paris, 1903-52. 28v.

Arc 565.2 Dictionnaire d'archéologie égyptienne. (Pierret, Paul.) Paris, 1875.

Arc 1209.1 Dictionnaire de sigillographie pratique. (Chassant, A.A.L.) Paris, 1860.

Arc 1153.29.2 Dictionnaire des abréviations latines et françaises. 2. éd. (Chassant, A.) Paris, 1862.

Arc 1153.29.3 Dictionnaire des abréviations latines et françaises. 3. éd. (Chassant, A.) Paris, 1866.

Arc 1153.29.4 Dictionnaire des abréviations latines et françaises. 4. éd. (Chassant, A.) Paris, 1876.

Arc 1153.29.5 Dictionnaire des abréviations latines et françaises. 5. éd. (Chassant, A.) Paris, 1884.

Arc 1018.02 Dictionnaire des antiquités chrétiennes. (Martigny, J.A.) Paris, 1877.

Arc 1033.116 Dictionnaire des reliques. (Collin de Plancy, J.A.S.) Paris, 1821-1822. 3v.

Arc 375.10 Dictionnaire général de l'archéologie. (Bosc, E.) Paris, 1881.

Arc 1340.4 Dictionnaire numismatique. (Boutkowski, Alex.) Leipzig, 1877.

Arc 1180.2 Dictionnaire raisonnè de diploéatique. (Vaines, J. de.) Paris, 1774. 2v.

Arc 1340.6 Dictionnaire spécial et classique des monnaies. (Girod, Joseph.) Paris, 1827.

Arc 1.7 Didron, A.N. Annales archéologiques. Paris, 1844-1870. 27v.

Arc 530.19F Didymes fouilles de 1895 et 1896. (Pontrenioli, E.) Paris, 1904.

Arc 1020.91 Die St. Matthias-Kirche bei Trier. (Diehl, P.) Trier, 1881.

Arc 612.52F Dieck, Alfred. Die europäischen Moorleichenfunde. Neumünster, 1965.

Arc 66.1.55 Diehl, C. L'église...du Couvent de Saint-Luc en Procide. Paris, 1889.

X Cg Arc 66.1.53 Diehl, C. Études sur l'administration Byzantine. Paris, 1888.

Arc 643.1 Diehl, C. Excursions archéologiques en Grèce. Paris, 1890.

Arc 643.1.4 Diehl, C. Excursions archéologiques en Grèce. 5. éd. Paris, 1903.

Arc 643.1.5A Diehl, C. Excursions in Greece. London, 1893.

Arc 1033.12.83 Diehl, C. Un nouveau trésor d'argenterie syrienne. Paris, 1926.

Arc 1020.30.5 Diehl, Charles. Ravenne. Paris, 1907.

Arc 758.4 Diehl, Ernst. Das alte Rom sein Werden. Leipzig, 1909.

Arc 1030.47 Diehl, Ernst. Inscriptiones latinae christianae veteres. Berolini, 1924-31. 3v.

Arc 1030.47.5 Diehl, Ernst. Inscriptiones latinae christianae veteres. Berolini, 1961- 4v.

Arc 1020.91 Diehl, P. Die St. Matthias-Kirche bei Trier. Trier, 1881.

Arc 848.37 Diekmann, H. Steinzeitseidlungen im Teutoburger Walde. Bielefeld, 1931.

Arc 1053.5 Dietrichson, L. Antinoos. Christiania, 1884.

Arc 875.14 Dietrichson, L. Monumenta orcadica. Kristiania, 1906.

Arc 687.1.10 Dietz, Søren. Arkaelogens Rhodos. København, 1974.

Arc 1498.9 Dieudonné, A. Les monnaies françaises. Paris, 1923.

Arc 1317.1.5 Dieudonné, A. Table de la revue numismatique. Paris. 1836-1915 2v.

Arc 485.201 Dieulafoy, M. L'acropole de Suse. Paris, 1890-92. 4v.

Arc 485.200 Dieulafoy, M. L'art antique de la Perse. Paris, 1884-89. 5v.

Arc 823.14 Les dieux gaulois d'après les monuments figurés. (Courcelle-Seneuil, Jean L.) Paris, 1910.

Arc 513.30 Diez, E. Die Sprache der Ruinen. Wien, 1962.

Arc 485.4F Diez, Ernst. Churasaniche Baudenkmäler. Berlin, 1918.

Arc 1033.80 Difesa della causa di S. Marcellino. (Castro, V. de.) Roma, 1819.

Arc 823.19.130 Diffusion du droit latin. (Thédenat, H.) Paris, 1885.

Arc 386.35 Digging for history. (Bacon, Edward.) London, 1960.

Arc 608.19 Digging for lost African gods. (Khun de Prorok, Byron.) N.Y., 1926.

Arc 497.53 Digging in the Holy Land. (Ilton, Paul.) London, 1959.

Arc 497.31 Digging up Biblical history. (Duncan, J.G.) N.Y., 1931- 2v.

Arc 505.66.5 Digging up Jericho. (Kenyon, K.M.) N.Y., 1957.

Arc 505.154 Digging up Jerusalem. (Kenyon, Kathleen Mary.) London, 1974.

Arc 497.103 Digging up the Bible lands. (Harker, Ronald.) London, 1972.

Arc 407.10.5 Digging up the past. (Woolley, Charles L.) Harmondsworth, 1937.

Arc 407.10.7 Digging up the past. (Woolley, Charles L.) Harmondsworth, 1956.

Arc 398.6 Den dijupa brunnen. (Nylander, Carl.) Stockholm, 1964.

Arc 540.6 Dikaios, P. The excavations at Vounous-Bellapais in Cyprus. London, 1940.

Arc 540.6.5 Dikaios, P. Khirakitia. London, 1953.

Arc 925.346 Dikov, Nikolai N. Drevnie kostry Kamchatki i Chukotki. Magadan, 1969.

Arc 432.10 Dikshit, K.N. Prehistoric civilization of the Indus Valley. Madras, 1939.

Arc 609.1.4 Dillmann, A. Über die geschichtlichen Ergebnisse der Th. Bent'schen Reisen in Ostafrica. Berlin, 1894.

Arc 1588.3.5 Dimitrijević, Sergije. Novac kneza Lasara. Kruševac, 1971.

Arc 936.100.50 Dimitrijevic, Stojan. Sopotsko-lendjelska kultura. Zagreb, 1968.

Arc 936.38 Dimitrov, D. Bulgaria. Sofiia, 1961.

Arc 936.140.15 Dimitrov, Dimitur P. Nadgrobnite plochi ot rimsko vreme. Sofiia, 1942.

Arc 885.24 Dinas Powys. (Alcock, L.) Cardiff, 1963.

Arc 1528.3 Dingniolle, J.F. Le jeton historique des dix-sept provinces des Pays-Bas. Bruxelles, 1876-77. 2v.

Arc 1033.169 Dini, F. Dissertatio...de translatio...S. Bartholomaei. Venetiis, 1700.

Arc 885.25 Dinorben. (Gardner, Willoughby.) Cardiff, 1964.

Arc 875.31.10 Dinwiddie, J. The Ruthwell cross and its story. Dumfries, 1927.

Arc 66.1.162 Dioclétien et la tétrarchie. (Seston, William.) Paris, 1946. 2v.

Arc 1490.18 Diodati, D. Illustrazione delle monete. 2. ed. Napoli, 1849.

Arc 388.8 Diolé, P. Promenades d'archéologie sous-marine. Paris, 1952.

Arc 388.8.2 Diolé, P. 4,000 years under the sea. N.Y., 1954.

Arc 750.201 Dionisi, F.L. Sacr. Vat. Basilicae. Roma, 1773.

Arc 1088.5 Dionisi, Francesco. Le navi sacre di Claudio nel lago di Nemi. Roma, 1956.

Arc 1027.36.5 Dionisi, G.J. Della città di Preconi nominata negli atti di SS. MM. fermo e rustico. Vinegia, 1782.

Arc 785.72A Dionysiac sarcophagi in Baltimore. (Lehmann-Hartleben, K.) Baltimore, 1942.

Arc 1015.230 Dionysius, P.L. Sacrarum vaticanae...cryptarum. Romae, 1773.

Arc 716.2.10F Das Dionysos Theater in Athen. v.1-3,4. Stuttgart, 1935-50. 2v.

Arc 746.4 Dionysos und Semele. v.1. (Gerhard, E.) Berlin, 1833. 2 pam.

Arc 66.1.137 Les dioscures au service d'une déesse. (Chapouthier, F.) Paris, 1935.

Arc 585.19 Diospolis Parva...1898-99. (Petrie, W.M.F.) London, 1901.

Arc 1033.17.544 Diotallevi, D. Notizie della prodigiosa immagine di Maria Sma. della Grazie a Pta Angelica in Roma. Roma, 1887.

Arc 1190.1.2 Diplomata centum. (Bresslau, H.) Berlin, 1872.

Arc 1190.1.9 Diplomata quadraginta. (Jaffé, P.) Berlin, 1863.

Arc 1190.77 Diplomatic of Sanskrit copper-plate grants. (Chhabra, Bahadur C.) Delhi? 1961?

Arc 1185.32.2 Diplomatica. (Paoli, Cesare.) Firenze, 1969.

Arc 1178.2 Pamphlet box. Diplomatics. Miscellaneous pamphlets.

Arc 1178 Pamphlet box. Diplomatics. Miscellaneous pamphlets.

Arc 1185.20 Diplomatika. (Likhachev, N.P.) Sankt Peterburg, 1901.

Arc 1185.30.2 La diplomatique. 2. éd. (Tessier, Georges.) Paris, 1962.

Arc 1185.23 Diplomatique-pratique. (Lemoine, P.C.) Metz, 1765.

Arc 1190.87 Diplomatique royale française. (Tessier, Georges.) Paris, 1962.

Arc 1190.2 Diplomatische Studien über die älteren angelsächischen Urkunden. Inaug. Diss. (Aronius, J.) Königsberg, 1883.

Arc 1190.4.15 Diplomatische und rechtsgeschichtliche Untersuchungen über Immunität und Königsschutz in Deutschland seit dem 12. Jahrhundert. Inaug. Diss. (Sprenger, G.) Breslau, 1936.

Arc 1078.1 Das Diptychon Quirinianum zu Brescia. (Wieseler, F.) Göttingen, 1868.

Arc 1.5.12 Directory of trustees, managing committee, faculty. (American School of Classical Studies at Athens.) 1882-1942

Arc 87.1.24 Dirke. (Boetticher, C.) Berlin, 1864.

Arc 1433.18 Dirks, J. Souveniers numismatiques des croisades. Photoreproduction. Bruxelles, 1861.

Arc 1530.20 Dirks, Jacob. De noord-Nederlandsche gildepenningen. Haarlem, 1878. 2v.

Arc 843.73.5F El disco de Teodosio. (Mélida, José R.) Madrid, 1930.

Htn Arc 785.2* Discorsa sopra l'antico Monte Citabrio. (Fontana, C.) Roma, 1708.

Arc 1033.169.5 Discorso nel quale si prova...S. Bartholomeo. (Benedictus XIII.) Benevento, 1695.

Arc 790.210.5F Discorso pronunziato in Pompei. (Ruggiero, Michele.) Napoli, 1879.

Arc 1033.12.40F Discorso sopra la sacra sindone...Torino. (Vassalli, M.) Parma, n.d.

Htn Arc 1359.2* Discorso sopra le medaglie de gli antichi. (Erizzo, S.) Venice, 1568.

Arc 113.2.5 Discours et compte rendu des lectures...section d'archéologie. Réunion annuelle des délégués de société savantes à la Sorbonne. (Chabouillet.) Paris, 1878-81. 3v.

Htn Arc 825.10F* Discours historial de l'antique et illustrie cité de Nismes. (Poldo d'Albenas, J.) Lyon, 1560.

Htn Arc 1373.2* Discours sur les médailles antiques. (Savot, L.) Paris, 1627.

Arc 1480.31F Discours sur les médailles d'Auguste et de Tibère. (Artaud, F.) Lyon, 1818.

Arc 380.212 Discours sur les monumens publics. (Lubersac, M.) Paris, 1775.

Arc 518.1.3 Discoveries at Ephesus. (Wood, J.T.) Boston, 1877.

Arc 518.1 Discoveries at Ephesus. (Wood, J.T.) London, 1877.

Arc 513.11.1 Discoveries in Asia Minor. v.1-2. (Arundell, F.V.J.) Hildesheim, 1975.

Arc 513.11 Discoveries in Asia Minor. v.2, photoreproduction. (Arundell, F.V.J.) London, 1834. 2v.

Arc 672.1.15 The discoveries in Crete; with addenda. (Burrows, R.M.) London, 1908.

Arc 672.1.13 The discoveries in Crete. (Burrows, R.M.) London, 1907.

Arc 672.1.16A The discoveries in Crete and their bearing. (Burrows, R.M.) N.Y., 1907.

Arc 561.1 Discoveries in Egypt, Ethiopia and the Peninsula of Sinai. (Lepsius, R.) London, 1853.

Arc 513.4.2 Discoveries in Lycia. (Fellows, C.) London, 1841.

Arc 33.4 Discoveries in the Judean Desert of Jordan. Oxford. 1,1955+ 7v.

Arc 416.23.5 Discovering buried worlds. 1. ed. (Parrot, A.) N.Y., 1955.

Arc 861.188 Discovering prehistoric Bournemouth and Christchurch: a record of local finds in the twentieth century. (Calkin, John Bernard.) Christchurch, Hants, 1966.

Arc 8.2 Discovery; peoples, civilization. Philadelphia.

Arc 128.10 Discovery and excavation in Scotland. Edinburgh. 1974+

Arc 652.4 Discovery in Greek lands. (Marshall, Fred H.) Cambridge, 1920.

Arc 556.5 The discovery of Egypt. (Greener, Leslie.) London, 1966.

Arc 455.1 Discovery of Pātaliputra. (Waddell, L.A.) Calcutta, 1892.

Arc 861.36 Discovery of Roman-British remains. (Michell-Whitley, H.) n.p., 1890.

Arc 880.13 Discovery of tomb of Ollamh Fodhla. (Conwell, E.A.) Dublin, 1873.

Htn Arc 1020.126* Discursos de la certidumbre de las reliquias descubiertas en Granada. (López Madera, G.) Madrid, 1601.

Arc 1675.47 Discursos de medallas y antiguedades. (Ribagarza, Martin de Gurrea y Aragon.) Madrid, 1903.

Arc 843.21F Discursos leidos ante la Academia de la Historia. (Rada y Delgado, Juan de Dios de la.) Madrid, 1875.

Arc 1033.17.455 Disertación crítico-theo-filosófica sobre la conservación de la santa imagen de Nuestra Señora de los Angeles. (Patiño, P.P.) México, 1801.

Arc 432.19 Disposal of the dead and physical types in ancient India. 1. ed. (Gupta, Swarajya Prakash.) Delhi, 1972.

Arc 1033.12.210 Disputatio theologica de Vulneribus Christi. (Jacob, J.N.) Wittenbergae, 1663.

Htn Arc 1373.5* Diss. de praestantia et usu numismata antiqua. (Spanheim, E.) Rome, 1664.

Arc 1033.12.59 Diss. eccl. pentas. De sudore Christi. (Ciprian, E.S.) Jenae, n.d.

Arc 1208.4 Dissard, Paul. Catalogues des plombs antiques. Paris, 1905.

Arc 785.34.5 Dissel, Karl. Der Opferzug der Ara Pacis Augustae. Hamburg, 1907.

Arc 1033.17.98.5 Dissertación histórica sobre la aparición de Nuestra Señora de Guadalupe. (Conde y Oquendo, F.) México, 1852. 2v.

Arc 1033.120 Dissertatio...de archeiois sive tabulariis sacris. (Beheim, J.C.) Norimburgi, n.d.

Arc 1033.169 Dissertatio...de translatio...S. Bartholomaei. (Dini, F.) Venetiis, 1700.

Arc 1016.232.2 Dissertatio...severae martyris epitaphium. (Lupi, A.M.) Panormi, 1734.

Arc 1016.232 Dissertatio...severae martyris epitaphium. (Lupi, A.M.) Panormi, 1734.

Arc 1033.12.52 Dissertatio de corona ferrea Langobardoum. (Fontanini, J.) Romae, 1717.

Arc 1433.14 Dissertatio de recentioribus numis Arabicis. (Winbom, Jonas A.) Upsaliae, 1815.

Htn Arc 1033.17.362* Dissertatio deidolo hallensi. (Denaise, Pierre.) n.p., 1605.

Arc 1033.17.98 Dissertatio historico-theologica de apparitione B.M.V. de Guadalupe. (Rosa, Agustin de.) Guadalaxarae, 1887.

Arc 505.5.42 Dissertatio historico-theologica de templi Hierosolymitani Iuliani. (Holtzfuss, V.S.) Halae Magdeburgicae, 1751. 2 pam.

Arc 1030.30 Dissertatio philologica qua nonnulla monimenta sacrae vetera ex museo Vict. (Vettori, P.) Roma, 1751.

Arc 1033.145 Dissertatio storico-critico-dogmatico...mano destra di S. Giovanni Battista...Repagnano. (Odvardo a S. Francisco Xaverio.) Roma, 1738.

Htn Arc 1350.1* Dissertation de praestantia et usu numismatum. (Spanheim, E.) Londoni, 1706-17. 2v.

Arc 595.3 Dissertation of the antiquity...of the principal pyramids of Egypt. London, 1833.

Arc 830.140 Dissertation sur Genabum-Gien. (Petit, Ange.) Orléans, 1863.

Arc 1033.12.191 Dissertation sur la sainte larme de Vendome. (Thiers, J.B.) Amsterdam, 1751.

Arc 1274.1 Dissertation sur les sceaux de Richard-Coeur-de-Lion. (Deville, J. Achille.) Rouen, 1828.

Arc 830.6.19 Dissertation sur un monument antique decouvert a Lyon. (Colonia, Dominique de.) Lyon, 1705.

Arc 4.6 Dissertationes archaeologicae gandenses. Brugge. 1-10 3v.

Arc 905.30 Dissertationes Pannonicae. Ser. 1. Budapest. 1-14,1932-1944 12v.

Arc 905.30F Dissertationes Pannonicae. Ser. 2. Budapest. 1-23

Arc 823.7 Dissertations et mémoires sur differens sujets d'antiquité et d'histoire. (Pasumot, Francois.) Paris, 1810-1813.

Arc 823.6 Dissertations historiques sur divers sujets. (L'Empereur, J.) Paris, 1706.

Arc 830.81 Dissertations sur les anciens monumens de la ville de Bordeaux. (Venuti, Niccolo M.) Bordeaux, 1754.

Arc 830.79.5 Dissertations sur l'origine de la ville de Dijon. (Le Goux de Gerland.) Dijon, 1771.

Arc 1016.226 Dissertazione...cristianita di Costantino Magno. (Visconti, A.) Roma, 1835.

Arc 1020.105 Dissertazione...intorno alle due campane della chiesa parochiale di S. Giovanni. (Capece, G.) Napoli, 1750.

Arc 1016.227 Dissertazione...iscrizione cristiana. (Visconti, P.E.) Roma, 1833.

Arc 726.35 Dissertazione...monumento etrusco...di Volterra. (Giorgi, Antonio.) Firenze, 1752.

Arc 1.14F Dissertazione. (Accademia...Rome. Accademia Romana di Archeologia.) Roma. 1820-1921 32v.

Arc 1033.17.58 Dissertazione anti-critica...S. Luca evangelista fosse pittore. (Crispi, L.) Faenza, 1776.

Arc 1025.39 Dissertazione epistolare. (Cancellieri, F.) Roma, 1819.

Arc 1027.39.5 Dissertazione intorno...sepolcro...cimitero di Prestato. (Baruffaldi, G.) Venezia? 1747?

Arc 1033.26 Dissertazione postume del P. Luigi Bruzza. (Rossi, G.B. de.) Roma, 1889.

Arc 1663.7.5F Dissertazione sul medagliere relativo alla storia mederna d'Italia. (Camozzi Vertova, G.) Bergamo, 1879.

Arc 1663.7.7F Dissertazione sul medagliere relativo alla storia moderna d'Italia. (Camozzi Vertova, G.) Bergamo, 1880.

Arc 1033.54 Dissertazioni...di S. Giuseppe. (Gori, A.F.) Modena, 1865.

Arc 726.24.7 Dissertazioni...la villa d'Orazio, il mausoleo di Plauzj in Tivoli. (Sanctis, D. de.) Ravenna, 1784.

Arc 1015.208.5 Dissertazioni archaeologiche di vario argomento. v.1-2. (Garrucci, R.) Roma, 1864.

Arc 93.48 Dissertazioni di etruscologia e antichità italiche. Firenze. 1,1972+

Arc 766.1.9.5 La distruzione di Roma antica. (Lanciani, R.) Milano, 1971.

Arc 848.33 Dittmann, K.H. Untersuchungen zur Geschichte der ältern Bronzezeit im Nordwestdeutschland. Inaug. Diss. Hamburg, 1938.

Arc 1033.17.248 Diva Virgo de Cortenbosch, eius miracula. (Lambert, R.) Leodii, 1656.

Htn Arc 1033.17.361* Diva virgo hallensis. (Lipsius, I.) Antverp, 1604.

Arc 1190.86 Divan rakamlari. (Elker, Salâhaddin.) Ankara, 1953.

Arc 936.195.200 Divčé kámen. (Poláček, Josef.) České Budějovice, 1960.

Arc 608.17.9F Divinità ignate. (Ferri, Silvio.) Firenze, 1929.

Arc 66.1.68 Divinités de la victoire en Grèce et en Italie. (Baudrillart, A.) Paris, 1894.

Arc 1503.7 Divo, Jean-Paul. Die Münzen der Schweiz im 19. und 20. Jahrhundert. Zürich, 1967.
Arc 1503.8 Divo, Jean-Paul. Die neueren Münzen der Schweiz und des Fürstentums Leichtenstein. 1850-1970. 4. Aufl. Freiburg, 1971.
Arc 1504.20 Divo, Jean-Paul. Die neueren Münzen der Schweiz und des Fürstentums Liechtenstein, 1850-1963. Freiburg, 1965.
Arc 1033.17.321 Divoto compendio della storia...s. immagine di Maria...Scutari. (Ciappolini, D.) Napoli, 1810.
Arc 925.240 Divov, N.N. Bronzovyi vek Zabaikal'ia. Ulan-Ude, 1958.
Arc 1033.17.543 Divozioni..in onore di Nostra Signora del Carmine. (Bagnari, P.) Roma, 1728.
Arc 820.208F Dix années de fouilles en Auvergne. (Delort, J.B.) Lyon, 1901.
Arc 830.367 Dix ans de recherches archéologiques région de Mulhouse. (Stahl-Weber, Martine.) Mulhouse, 1972.
Arc 838.25 Dixon, P. The Iberians of Spain. London, 1940.
Arc 1153.12 Dizionario di abbreviature latine ed italiane. (Cappelli, A.) Milano, 1899.
Arc 628.30 Dizionario di antichità greche e romane. (Calderini, A.) Milano, 1960.
Arc 608.6.30 Djemila. (Leschi, Louis.) Alger, 1953.
Arc 608.6.29 Djemila Cuicul de Numidie. (Leschi, Louis.) Alger, 1938.
Arc 936.220.40 Djuhnić, Milena. Ilirska kneževsha nekropola u atenici. Čačak, 1966.
Arc 925.355 Dlinnye kurgany krivichei. (Sedov, Valentin V.) Moskva, 1974.
Arc 925.50.170 Dnipro-donets'ka kul'tura. (Telehin, Dmytro I.) Kyïv, 1968.
Arc 1138.37 Dobiaš-Rozhdestvenskaia, O.A. Istoriia pis'ma v srednie veka. Moskva, 1936.
Arc 1138.75.5 Doblhofer, Ernst. Voices in stone. N.Y., 1961.
Arc 1138.75 Doblhofer, Ernst. Zeichen und Wunder. Wien, 1957.
Arc 861.38.9 Dobson, Dina P. The archaeology of Somerset. London, 1931.
Arc 1359.1 Doctrina numorum veterum. (Eckhel, J.H.) Viennae, 1792-98. 8v.
Arc 726.20 Documenti inediti...scoperta di Velleia. (Tononi, A.G.) Modena, 1881.
Arc 383.48F Documento archaeologica. (Kleemann, Otto.) Bonn, 1956.
Arc 1185.26 Il documento medioevale. (Valenti, Filippo.) Modena, 1961.
Arc 1200.17.5 Documentos pontificios en papiro de archivos. (Millares Carlo, A.) Madrid, 1918.
Arc 1200.17 Documentos pontificios en papiro de archivos. pt.1. (Millares Carlo, A.) Madrid, 1918.
Arc 545.227.35 Documents. (Maspero, Gaston.) Le Caire, 1912.
Arc 42.5F Documents archéologiques. (Mission Paul Pelliot.) Paris. 1-3 2v.
Arc 1208.12 Documents de sigillographie byzantine. (Academia...Bucharest.) Paris, 1952.
Arc 1254.10 Documents pour servir à l'histoire des thémes byzantines. (Schlumberger, G.) Paris, 1883.
Arc 673.2 Dodona. (Gerlach, F.D.) Basel, 1859.
Arc 635.212 Dodone et ses ruines. (Carapanos, C.) Paris, 1878. 2v.
Arc 643.2 Dodwell, E. A classical and topographical tour through Greece. London, 1819. 2v.
Arc 543.83.10 Doe, Brian. Southern Arabia. London, 1971.
Arc 1190.65 Doelger, Franz. Byzantinische Diplomatik. Ettal, 1956.
Arc 1033.180 Doelger, Franz J. Ichthys. v.2-5. Münster, 1910-43. 4v.
Arc 535.201 Doell, J. Die Sammlung Cesnola. St. Petersburg, 1873.
Arc 1033.17.650 Dörffel, F. St. Maria Culm das ist Bremdliche Historia. n.p., 1721.
Arc 1093.6.9 Doering, J.F. The swastika. Kitchner, Ontario, 1936.
Arc 530.85 Doerner, F.K. Inschriften und Denkmäler aus Bithynien. Berlin, 1941.
Arc 935.29 Dörner, Friedrich K. Arsameia am Nymphaios. Berlin, 1963.
Arc 716.4.5 Dörpfeld, W. Alt-Athen und seine Agora. Berlin, 1937-39. 2v.
Arc 716.7.15F Dörpfeld, W. Erechtheion. Berlin, 1942.
Arc 700.6 Dörpfeld, W. Das Griechische Theater. Athen, 1896.
Arc 522.15 Dörpfeld, W. Troja und Ilion. Athen, 1902. 2v.
Arc 522.12 Dörpfeld, W. Troja 1893. Leipzig, 1894.
Arc 87.1.41 Doerpfeld, W. Die Verwendung von Terrakotten. Berlin, 1881.
Arc 684.1.37 Dörpfeld, Wilhelm. Alt-Olympia. Berlin, 1935. 2v.
Arc 684.1.38 Dörpfeld, Wilhelm. Alt-Olympia. Beiheft. Berlin, 1935.
Arc 66.1.83 Dofourco, A. Etudes sur les gesta martyrum. Paris, 1900.
Arc 726.81F Dohan, Edith H. Italic tomb-groups in the University Museum. Philadelphia, 1942.
Arc 955.2.20 The Doheny scientific expedition to the Hava Supai Canyon, northern Arizona...1924. (Oakland, California. Museum.) San Francisco, 1925.
Arc 880.11 Doherty, W.J. Round towers of Ireland. Dublin, 1881.
Arc 853.155F Dohn, Wolfgang. Die Steinzeit im kieslische Katalog der steinzeitlichen Altertümer. Kallmünz, 1954.
Arc 843.70 Dois estudos: "Manis Pallas"; "Giral Cabrom". (Mattos, A. de.) Porto, 1943.
Arc 923.109 Doklady, prochitannye na XI Vsesoiuznoi studencheskoi arkheologicheskoi konferentsii 1965 g. v Erevane. (Vsesoiuznaia Arkheologicheskaia Studencheskaia Konferentsiia, 11th, Erevan, 1965.) Erevan, 1968.
Arc 923.112 Doklady i soobshchenia arkheologov SSSR. (International Congress of Prehistoric and Protohistoric Sciences. 7th, Moscow, 1966.) Moskva, 1966.
Arc 1433.96 Dokumente zur Geschichte der iranischen Hunnen in Baktrien und Indien. v.1,2,3-4. (Goebl, Robert.) Wiesbaden, 1967. 3v.
Arc 225.1 Dolgozatok. Erem-es régiségtárából. (Cluj, Rumania. Erdelye nemzeti.) Kolozsvár. 2-7,1911-1916 3v.
Arc 1540.27 Dolley, Reginald Hugh Michael. Anglo-Saxon coins. London, 1961.
Arc 1540.27.5 Dolley, Reginald Hugh Michael. The Norman conquest and the English coinage. London, 1966.
Arc 1505.3 Dollinger, F. Furstenbergischen Münzen und Medaillen. Donaueschingen, 1903.
Arc 843.24 O dolmen da Barroza. (Carvalho, M.) Porto, 1898.
Arc 843.180 El dolmen de la capilla de Santa Cruz. (Vega de la Sella, Ricardo.) Madrid, 1919.
Arc 889.6 Le dolmen de Solwaster. (Loë, Alfred de.) Bruxelles, 1889.
Arc 830.2.6 Le dolmen royal de Gavrénis près d'Auray. (Hirmenech, H.P.) Le Mans, 1908.
Arc 895.74 Der Dolmen Trollasten in St. Köpinge, Schonen. (Strömberg, Märta.) Bonn, 1968.
Arc 426.7F The dolmens and burial mounds in Japan. (Gowland, William.) London, 1897.
Arc 1078.3 Dolmens et menhirs. 3. éd. (Niel, Fernand.) Paris, 1966.
Arc 880.2 The dolmens of Ireland. (Borlase, W.C.) London, 1897. 3v.
Arc 505.69 The dolmens of Palestine and Transjordania. (Broome, E.C.) Philadelphia, 1940.
Arc 843.25 Dolmens ou antas de ville ponco d'Aguir. (Traz-os-montes). (Brenha, José.) Porto, 1903.
Arc 925.300.5 Dol'meny stanitsy Novosvobodnoi. (Popova, T.B.) Moskva, 1963.
Arc 1027.41.39 Il "Dolocenum" della XIII regione. (Lugari, G.B.) Roma, 1893.
Arc 938.100 Dolukhanov, Pavel M. Istoriia Baltiki. Moskva, 1969.
Arc 1349.72 Domanig, K. Anton Scharff, K. und K. Kammer-Medaillen. Wien, 1895.
Arc 1505.201 Domanig, K. Die deutsche Medaille in Kunst oc Hinsicht. Wien, 1907.
Arc 925.13.65 Domanovszky, G. Steppenvölker und Germanen. Budapest, 1939.
Arc 925.50.335 Dombrovskii, Oleg I. Stolitsa feodoritov. Simferopol', 1973.
Htn Arc 1033.12.65* Domenechi, D. De sanguine Christi tractatus. Venetiis, 1557.
Arc 1613.29 Domestic and foreign coins manufactured by mints of the United States, 1793-1973. (United States.) Washington, 1974.
Arc 1675.37 Domingos Antonio de Sequeira e Francesco Vieira Lusitano. (Costa, Luiz X. da.) Lisboa, 1923. 2 pam.
Arc 1468.9 Dominicis, F. de. Repertorio numismatico. v.1-2. Naples, 1826.
Arc 1510.1 Domus Wittelbachensis numismatica. (Widmer, M.J. von.) Munich, 1784-85.
Arc 925.50.45 Don i Priazov'e u drevnosti. v.1,3. (Miller, Mykhailo O.) Moskva, 1958- 2v.
Arc 1390.17 Dona numismatica. (Berghaus, Peter.) Hamburg, 1965.
Arc 590.20 Donadoni Roveri, Anna Maria. I sarcofagi egizi dalle origini alla fine dell'antico regno. Roma, 1969.
NEDL Arc 1668.1 Donaldson, T.L. Architectura numismatica. London, 1859.
Arc 1580.5 Donebauer, Max. Beschreibung der Sammlung böhmischer Münzen. pt.1-2. Prag, 1889-90.
Arc 1208.10 Dongé, E. Description des collections de sceaux matrices. Paris, 1872.
Arc 936.220.70 Donja toponica. (Trbuhović, Vojislav B.) Prokuplje, 1970.
Arc 830.126.3 Donnadieu, A. Fréjus le port militaire du Forum Julii. Paris, 1935.
Arc 830.126 Donnadieu, A. La Pompéi de la Provence, Fréjus. Paris, 1927.
Arc 388.18 Donnell, Robert C. Systematics in prehistory. N.Y., 1971.
X Cg Arc 710.10 D'Ooge, M.L. The acropolis of Athens. N.Y., 1908.
Arc 520.16 Dopp, W. Eine Altisdarstellung am grossen Fries von Pergamon. Inaug. Diss. Rostock, 1934.
Arc 530.173 The Dorak affair. (Person, Kenneth.) N.Y., 1968.
Arc 861.95 Dorchester antiquities. (Moule, H.J.) Dorchester, 1906.
Arc 441.7 Doreau, Jean Louis. Les bains dans l'Inde antique; monuments et textes médicaux. Paris, 1936.
Arc 682.25.40 The Dorians in archaeology. (Skeat, T.C.) London, 1932?
Arc 612.14 Die dorische Wanderung in ihren europaischen Zusammenhängen. (Neubert, Max.) Stuttgart, 1920.
Arc 1033.17.547 La dormitio B. Mariae. (Grossi-Gondi, F.) Roma, 1910.
Arc 1510.1.2 Dormus Wittelbachensis numismatica. (Widmer, M.J. von.) Munich, 1784.
Arc 925.9.95PF Dorn, Boris A. Atlas k puteshestviiu po Kavkazu i iuzknomu poberezh'iu kaspiskago moria. Sankt Petersburg, 1895. 2v.
Arc 936.14.505 Dorobek archeologii koszalińskiej w latach 1945-70. (Lachowicz, Franciszek J.) Koszalin, 1973.
Arc 1190.25 Dorsualkonzept und Imbreviatur in Italien. (Kern, Fritz.) Stuttgart, 1906.
Arc 936.14.260 Dorzecze górnej i środkowej Obry od VI do początków XI wieku. (Hilczerówna, Zofia.) Wrocław, 1967.
Arc 543.110 Las dos grandes inscripciones sudarabigas del dique de Marib. (Solá Solé, J.M.) Barcelona, 1960.
Arc 758.2.5F Dosio, G.A. Das Skizzenbuch des G. Dosio im staatlichen Kupferstichkabinett zu Berlin. Berlin, 1933.
Htn Arc 758.2* Dosio, G.A. Urbis Romae aedificae illustrae quae supersunt reliquiae. n.p., n.d.
Arc 925.50.305 Doslidzhennia starodavn'oï istoriï Zakarpattia. Uzhhorod, 1972.
Arc 936.195.100F Dostál, Bořivoj. Slovanská pohřebiště za střední doby hradištní na Moravě. Praha, 1966.
Arc 1485.7.5 Dotti, E. Tariffa di monete medioevale e moderne italiane. Milano, 1913.
Arc 612.13 Dottin, Georges. Les anciens peuples de l'Europe. Paris, 1916. 2v.
Arc 608.16.10 Douël, M. L'Algérie romaine; forums et basiliques. Paris, 1930.
Arc 1020.73.15 Douet d'Arco, L.C. Inventaire des reliques de la Sainte-Chapelle. Paris, 1848.
Arc 1263.1 Douët d'Arcq, L.C. Collection de sceaux. Paris, 1863-67. 2v.
Arc 953.24A Douglas, F.H. Indian art of the United States. N.Y., 1941.
Htn Arc 855.14F* Douglas, J. Nenia Britannica, or Sepulchral history of Great Britain. London, 1793.
Htn Arc 726.73.15* Douglas, N. Some antiquarian notes. Napoli, 1907.
Arc 600.70 Douze ans de fouilles dans la nécropole memphite, 1924-1936. (Jéquier, Gustave.) Neuchâtel, 1940.
Arc 925.50.145 Dovzhenok, Vasyl' I. Drevn'orus'ke misto Voin. Kyïv, 1966.
Arc 861.210 Down, Alec. Chichester excavations. Chichester, 1971- 2v.
Arc 858.37.2 Downland man. (Massingham, H.J.) London, 1927.
Htn Arc 1076.3.5* Downman, E.A. Ancient church bells in England. London, 1899.
Arc 658.3.2 Dr. Schliemann and the archaeological value of his discoveries. (Chase, T.) Worcester, 1891.
Arc 1033.35.49 Drach, P.L.B. Inscription hébräique du titre de S. Croix. 2e éd. Rome, 1831.
Arc 925.13.205 Drachuk, Viktor S. Sistemy znakov Severnogo Prichernomoria. Kiev, 1975.
Arc 383.9.5 Drack, Walter. Beiträge zur Kulturgeschichte; Festschrfit Reinhold Bosch. Aarau, 1947.
Arc 820.206F Dracontia. (Deane, John Bathurst.) London, 1834.
Arc 853.30.5 Dragendorff, Hans. II. Ausgrabungen bei Haltern. n.p., 1902.
Arc 421.26 Dragon bones in the yellow earth. (Crump, J.) N.Y., 1963.

Arc 1016.239 Dragoni, A. Sul dittico eburneo de santi martiri Teodoro ed Acacio. Parma, 1810.

Arc 793.3 Le drame du Vésuve. (Beulé, C.E.) Paris, 1872.

Arc 1264.7.5 Les drapiers de Beauvais et leurs plombs de contrôle. (Blanchet, A.) Beauvais, 1927.

Arc 443.4 The Dravidian problem in the south Indian culture complex. (Joseph, P.) Bombay, 1972.

Arc 1433.2.2 Drei Abhandlungen von der Geschichte der Araber. (Murr, C.G. von.) Nüremberg, 1770.

Arc 710.9 Die drei Athenetempel der Akropolis. (Freericks, H.) Münster, 1905.

Arc 853.4 Drei römische Votivhaende aus den Rheinlanden. (Becker, J.) Frankfurt am Main, 1862.

Arc 785.18 Die drei Tempel am Forum Holitorium in Rom. (Delbrück, R.) Rom, 1903.

Arc 87.2.46 Dreizehn Gemmen. (Urlichs, K.L.) Bonn, 1846.

Arc 1282.5 Drenieishiia bully i nechati shiriully. (Likhachen, N.I.) Sankt Peterburg, 1907.

Arc 590.13.1 Drerup, Heinrich. Die Datierung der Mumienporträts. Paderborn, 1968.

Arc 1675.97 Dresden. Historisches Museum. Order und Ehrenzeichen der Deutschen Demokratischen Republik. Dresden, 1964.

Arc 1433.25 Dresden. K. Münzkabinett. De numis Muhammadanis in Numophylacio regio Dresdensi. Lipsiae, 1856.

Arc 688.2 Dressel, H. Die antiken Kunstwerke aus Sparta und Umgebung. Athen, 1878.

Arc 785.27 Dressel, H. Untersuchungen über Ziegelstempel des Geno Domitia. Berlin, 1886.

Arc 530.182 Drevnaia kul'tura Shiraka. (Khach'atryan, Telemak S.) Erevan, 1975.

Arc 543.3.100 Drevnaia kuva. (Bulatova, Vera A.) Tashkent, 1972.

Arc 925.38.10 Drevnee iskusstov Altaia. (Leningrad. Ermitazh.) Leningrad, 1958.

Arc 925.338.5 Drevneishaia istoriia Volgo-Okskogo mezhdurech'ia. (Krainov, Dmitrii A.) Moskva, 1972.

Arc 612.57.5 Drevneishee metalloobrabatyvainshchee proiznodstno Vostochnoi Evropy. (Ryndina, Nataliia Vadimovna.) Moskva, 1971.

Arc 925.285 Drevneishee proshloe Sakhalina. (Kozyreva, Rimma V.) Iuzhno, 1960.

Arc 925.136 Drevneishie metallurgi Priural'ia. (Bader, Otto N.) Moskva, 1964.

Arc 925.338.10 Drevneishie skotovody Volzhsko-Uraliskogo mezhdurech'ia. (Merpert, Nikolai I.) Moskva, 1974.

Arc 443.6 Drevneishie zemledel'cheskie kul'tury Dekana. (Shchetenko, Anatolii I.) Leningrad, 1968.

Arc 543.146.25 Drevneishie zemledel'tsy Iuzhnogo Turkmenistana. (Berdyev, Ovliabuli.) Ashkhabad, 1969.

Arc 530.97 Drevneiskie arkheologicheskie...Mtskheta. (Chubinishvili, T.N.) Tbilisi, 1957.

Arc 543.120.5 Drevnemongol'skie goroda. (Kiselev, Sergei.) Moskva, 1965.

Arc 925.354 Drevnes naselenie Peschanki. (Priakhin, Anatolii D.) Voronezh, 1973.

Arc 925.225 Drevnetiurkskie izvaianiia Tuvy. (Grach, A.D.) Moskva, 1961.

Arc 936.155.20 Drevniaia i rannesrednevekovaia kul'tura Kirgizstana. (Akademiia Nauk Kirgizskoi SSR, Frunze. Institut Istorii.) Frunze, 1967.

Arc 925.310.10 Drevniaia i srednevekovaia istoriia Karachaevo-Cherkesii. (Alekseeva, Evgeniia P.) Moskva, 1971.

Arc 426.15 Drevniaia Iaponiia. (Vorob'ev, M.V.) Moskva, 1958.

Arc 33.5 Drevniaia istoriia iuga Vostochnoi Sibiri. Irkutsk. 1,1974+

Arc 925.9.15 Drevniaia istoriia Severnogo Kavkaza. (Krupnov, E.T.) Moskva, 1960.

Arc 925.338 Drevniaia istoriia Srednego Povolzhia. (Khalikov, Al'fred K.) Moskva, 1969.

Arc 428.10 Drevniaia Korea. (Vorob'ev, M.V.) Moskva, 1961.

Arc 416.26 Drevniaia kul'tura sakov i usunei doliny reki Ili. (Akishev, K.A.) Alma Ata, 1963.

Arc 925.16.17 Drevniaia kul'tura Tsentral'nogo Kazakhstana. (Margulan, A.K.) Alma-Ata, 1966.

Arc 608.23.5 Drevniaia Nubiia. (Akademiia Nauk SSSR. Institut Arkheologii.) Leningrad, 1964.

Arc 1583.26 Drevniaia Rus' i evropeiskie gosudarstva. (Potin, Vsevolod M.) Leningrad, 1968.

Arc 925.237 Drevnie idoly Eniseia. (Vadetskaia, El'ga B.) Leningrad, 1967.

Arc 543.3.95 Drevnie kochevniki "Kryshi mira". (Litvinskii, Boris A.) Moskva, 1972.

Arc 925.346 Drevnie kostry Kamchatki i Chukotki. (Dikov, Nikolai N.) Magadan, 1969.

Arc 920.4 Drevnie kul'tury aziatskikh eskimosov. (Armtiunov, Sergei A.) Moskva, 1969.

Arc 925.350 Drevnie kul'tury Izhmy. (Luzgin, Valerii E.) Moskva, 1972.

Arc 925.9.70 Drevnie kultury Izhnogo Kavkaza. (Kushmareva, Karinek.) Leningrad, 1970.

Arc 1010.27 Drevnie kul'tury Tikhookeanskogo Severa. (Vasil'evskii, Ruslan S.) Novosibirsk, 1973.

Arc 925.4.60 Drevnie kul'tury Tomsko-Narymskogo Priob'ia. (Kosarev, Mikhail F.) Moskva, 1974.

Arc 925.333 Drevnie kul'tury verkhnego Viliuia. (Fedoseeva, Svetlana A.) Moskva, 1968.

Arc 925.50.125 Drevnie obitateli Sredniago Pridneprov'ia. (Khvoika, V.V.) Kiev, 1913.

Arc 925.345 Drevnie orositel'nye sistemy Priaral'ia. (Andrianov, Boris V.) Moskva, 1969.

Arc 925.4.35 Drevnie pis'mena khakarii. Abakan, 1970.

Arc 956.2 Drevnie poseleniia Baranova mysa. (Okladnikov, Aleksei P.) Novosibirsk, 1971.

Arc 543.66.65 Drevnie shakhty Uchtuta. (Mirsaatov, T.) Tashkent, 1973.

Arc 493.6.45 Drevnie ukrashcheniia Azerbaidzhana. (Sadykhzade, S.G.) Baku, 1971.

Arc 925.136.10 Drevnieshie pamiatniki istorii Urala. (Sal'nikov, Konstantin V.) Sverdlovsk, 1952.

Arc 708.35 Drevnii gorod Afiny i ego pamiatniki. (Kolobova, K.M.) Leningrad, 1961.

Arc 925.301 Drevnii gorodishcha Smolenshchiny. (Tret'iakov, P.N.) Leningrad, 1963.

Arc 459.3.30 Drevnii indiiskii gorod Taksila. (Il'in, G.F.) Moskva, 1918.

Arc 416.46 Drevnii kamennyi vek Iuzhnoi i Iuga-Vostochnoi Azii. (Borisovskii, Pavel I.) Leningrad, 1971.

Arc 493.6.35F Drevnii Mingechaur. (Aslanov, G.M.) Baku, 1959.

Arc 923.5 Drevnii mir' na Iug' Rossii. (Turaeb, B.A.) Moskva, 1918.

Arc 925.16.60 Drevnii Otrar. (Akishev, Kemal' A.) Alma-Ata, 1972.

Arc 925.285.5 Drevnii Sakhalin. (Kozyreva, Rimma V.) Leningrad, 1967.

Arc 925.331.10 Drevnii Sindar. (Burov, Grigorii M.) Moskva, 1967.

Arc 416.48 Drevnii Vostok. Erevan, 1973.

Arc 925.50.165 Drevn'orus'ke misto Roden', Kniazha hora. (Mezentseva, Galina G.) Kyiv, 1968.

Arc 925.50.145 Drevn'orus'ke misto Voin. (Dovzhenok, Vasyl' I.) Kyïv, 1966.

Arc 925.50.5 Drevnorus'ki arkheologii pam'iatky na teryt. (Ratych, O.O.) Kyïv, 1957.

Arc 925.50.300 Drevnosh Chernykh Klobukov. (Pletneva, Svetlana A.) Moskva, 1973.

Arc 287.3F Drevnosti. Arkheologicheskii vestnike. (Moskovskoe Arkheologicheskoe Obshchestvo.) Moskva. 1867-1868//

Arc 925.325.10 Drevnosti Bashkirii. Moskva, 1970.

Arc 925.150.23 Drevnosti Belorussii. (Konferentsiia no Arkheologii Belorussii i Smezhnykh Territorii, Minsk, 1966.) Minsk, 1966.

Arc 925.150.30 Drevnosti Belorussii. (Konferentsiia po Arkheologii Belorussii, Minsk, 1969.) Minsk, 1969.

Arc 925.150.5 Drevnosti Belorusskogo ponemania. (Gurevich, F.D.) Leningrad, 1962.

Arc 925.16.35 Drevnosti chandary. Alma-Ata, 1968.

Arc 925.9.25 Drevnosti checheno-ingushetii. (Akademiia nauk SSSR. Institut Arkheologii.) Moskva, 1963.

Arc 925.9.7 Drevnosti chernomorskia poberezh'ia kavkaza. (Vladimirova, N.) Sankt Petersburg, 1900.

Arc 925.280 Drevnosti Severskogo Dontsa. (Shramko, B.A.) Khar'kov, 1962.

Arc 925.152 Drevnosti Turovshching. (Pobol', Leonid D.) Minsk, 1969.

Arc 416.7F Drevnosti vostoch'iia trudi vostochnoi kommissii. (Moskovskoe Arkheologicheskoe Obshchestvo.) Moskva, 1889-1915. 5v.

Arc 925.50.195 Drevnosti vostochnogo kryma. Kiev, 1970.

Arc 388.16 Driehaus, Jürgen. Archäologische Radiographie. Düsseldorf, 1968.

Arc 600.115 Drioton, E. Sakkarah. Le Caire, 1939.

Arc 853.248 Die dritte Hallstattstufe im Gebeit. (Haermann, S.) Nürnberg, 1925.

Arc 815.8 Der dritte pompejanische Stil. (Ippel, Albert.) Berlin, 1910.

Arc 404.2 Driver, Godfrey Rolles. Reginald Cambell Thompson. London, 1944.

Arc 497.13A Driver, S.R. Modern research as illustrating the Bible. London, 1909.

Arc 823.19.30 Droit latin de O. Hirschfeld. (Thédenat, H.) Paris, 1880.

Arc 388.2 Droop, J.P. Archaeological excavation. Cambridge, Eng., 1915.

Arc 875.60 The Drostin stone at St. Vigeans and its inscription. Aberdeen, 1928.

Arc 870.8 The druidical temples of the county of Wilts. (Duke, E.) London, 1846.

Arc 858.26 Druidism exhumed. (Rust, J.) Edinburgh, 1871.

Arc 855.222F Drummond, James. Archaeologia scotica; sculptured monuments in Iona. Edinbrugh, 1881.

Arc 853.14 Die Drusenverschanzungen bei Deisenhofen. (Seyler, E.) München, 1900.

Arc 925.68 Druzhiia proiz. i dom. zhivotn. tripol'ia. (Bogaevskii, B.L.) Leningrad, 1937.

Arc 1163.3.7 Druzhinin, V.G. Pomorskie paleografy 18 stol. Petrograd, 1921.

Arc 1015.227 Duale metodo tecnico per dirigere l'escavazione. (Rossi, M.S. de.) Roma, 1880.

Arc 880.48 Dublin. National Museum of Ireland. A brief guide to the collection of Irish antiquities. Dublin, 1960.

Arc 66.1.98 Dubois, C. Pouzzoles antique. Paris, 1907.

Arc 66.1.40 Dubois, M. Les ligues étolienne et achéenne. Paris, 1885.

Arc 1348.2 Dubois, P. Moneta: a study. n.p., 1884.

Arc 1353.3 DuBois, W.E. A brief account of the collection of coins belonging to the mint of the United States. Philadelphia, 1846.

Arc 830.109 Dubreuil-Chambardel, Louis. La Touraine préhistorique. Paris, 1923.

Arc 497.30.5 Du Buit, Michel. Archéologie du peuple d'Israël. Paris, 1960.

Arc 1660.15F Duby, P.A.T. Recueil général des pieces obsidionales. Paris, 1786.

Arc 1660.15.5F Duby, P.A.T. Trauté des monnaies des barons. Paris, 1790. 2v.

Arc 396.3.18 Le duc de Loubat, 1831-1894. Paris, 1894.

Arc 396.3.20 Le duc de Loubat, 1894-1912. Paris, 1912.

Arc 1033.19 Du Camp, M. Iconographie chrétienne. n.p., n.d.

Arc 1473.9 Du Cange, C. du F. De imperatorum constantinopalitanorum. Romae, 1755.

Htn Arc 1033.131* Du Cange, C. du F. Traite historique du chef de S. Jean Baptiste. Paris, 1665.

Arc 66.1.219 Ducat, Jean. Les kouroi du Ptoion. Paris, 1971.

Arc 66.1.209 Ducat, Jean. Les vases plastiques rhodiens. Paris, 1966.

Arc 1500.2 Duchalais, A. Description des médailles gauloises...de la Bibliothèque Royale. Paris, 1846.

Arc 830.52 Du Chatellier, Paul. Le bronze dans le Finistère. Quimper, 1899.

Arc 830.53 Du Chatellier, Paul. Époques préhistoriques...dans le Finistère. 2e éd. Rennes, 1907.

Arc 66.1.13 Duchesne, L. De codd. mss. graecis Pü II in Biblioteca Vaticana. Paris, 1880.

Arc 66.1 Duchesne, L. Étude sur le liber pontificalis. Paris, 1877.

Arc 1020.10.23 Duchesne, L. Le forum chrétien. Rome, 1899.

Arc 1033.53.20 Ducis, C.A. Saint Maurice et le Légion Thébéenne. Annecy, 1882.

Arc 830.5.3 Ducis, Claude A. Mémoire sur les voies romaines de la Savoie. Annecy, 1863.

Arc 1500.31 Ducrocq, T. Les nouveaux types monétaires de la France. Poitiers, 1900.

Arc 1510.150 Dudik, Beda. Des hahen deutschen Ritterordens Münz-Sammlung in Wien. Bonn, 1966.

Arc 1333.8 Dudik, Beda. Des hohen deutschen Ritter-Ordens Münz-Sammlung in Wien. Wien, 1858.

Arc 815.21 Due lettere sopra il musaico di Pompei. (Baizini, G.B.) Bergamo, 1836.

Arc 1163.40.2 Duelfer, Kurt. Schrifttafeln zur deutschen Paläographie. v.1-2. 2. Aulf. Marburg, 1967.

Arc 545.205 Duemichen, J. Bangeschichte des Denderatempels. Strassburg, 1877.

Arc 545.205.2 Duemichen, J. Bauurkunde der Tempelanlagen von Dendera. Leipzig, 1865.

Arc 382.3 Dümichen, J. Über die Tempel und Gräber im alten Ägypten. Strassburg, 1872. 7 pam.

Arc 853.72 Dünenmesolithikum aus dem Fiener Bruch. Inaug. Diss. (Bicker, F.K.) Halle an der Saale, 1934.

Arc 66.1.57 Duerrbach, F. L'orateur Lycurgue. Paris, 1890.

Arc 1020.30 Dütschke, H. Ravennatische Studien. Leipzig, 1909.

Arc 1027.32 Dufresne, D. Les cryptes vaticanes. Paris, 1902.

Arc 689.5F Dugas, C. Le sanctuaire d'Aléa Athéna à Tégée au IVe siècle. Text and atlas. Paris, 1924. 2v.

Arc 66.1.129 Dugas, Charles. La céramique des cyclades. Paris, 1925.

Arc 726.22.9 Duhn, F. von. Italische Gräberkunde. Heidelberg, 1924-39. 2v.

Arc 810.23 Duhn, F. von. Pompeii, eine hellenistische Stadt in Italien. Leipzig, 1906.

Arc 1081.1.5 Duhn, F. von. Ein Rückblick auf die Gräberforschung. Heidelberg, 1911.

Arc 830.148 Dujardin, A. Estampes mythologiques des Celtes. Étampes, 1904.

Arc 936.195.310 Důkaz pravosti metodějských nálezů z "Hrobů" u Osvětiman. (Adámsk, František.) Brno, 1934.

Arc 870.8 Duke, E. The druidical temples of the county of Wilts. London, 1846.

Arc 1500.69 Dumas-Dubourg, Françoise. Le trésor de Fécamp et la monnayage en Francie occidentale pendant la seconde moitié du Xe siècle. Paris, 1971.

Arc 1473.19 Dumbarton Oaks. Catalogue of the Byzantine coins in the Dumbarton Oaks collection and in the Whittemore collection. v. 1-3. Washington, 1966- 5v.

Arc 1468.30 Dumersan, T.M. Description des médailles antiques du cabinet de feu M. Allier de Hauteroche. Paris, 1829.

Arc 1335.14.2 Du Mersan, T.M. Histoire du cabinet des médailles. Paris, 1838.

Arc 1335.14.3 Du Mersan, T.M. Notice des monuments exposés dans le cabinet des médailles. Paris, 1840.

Arc 1335.14 Du Mersan, T.M. Notice sur la bibliothèque royale...sur le cabinet des médailles. Paris, 1836.

Arc 726.60 Dumitrescu, V. L'età del ferro nel Piceno. Tesi. Bucarest, 1929.

Htn Arc 343.225F* Du Molinet, Claude. Le cabinet de la bibliothèque de Sainte Geneviève. Paris, 1692.

Arc 635.206 Dumon, K. Le théâtre de Polyclète. Paris, 1889.

Arc 388.4 Dumont, A. Mélanges d'archéologie et d'épigraphie. Paris, 1892.

Arc 700.13 Dumont, Albert. De plumbeis apud graecos tesseris. Paris, 1870.

Arc 421.1 Dumontier, G. Le grand-Bouddha de Hanoi. Hanoi, 1888.

Arc 1033.95 D'un nouveau monument...Sainte Félicité. (Le Blant, E.) Rome, 1888.

Htn Arc 726.30* D'una antica villa. (Zuzzeri, G.L.) Venezia, 1746.

Arc 1030.5.13 D'una mutila epigrafe...nel torrione della porta flaminia. (Rossi, G.B. de.) Roma, 1877.

Arc 1027.12.17 D'una transl...SS. Pietro e Paolo in...le catacombe. (Armellini, M.) Roma, 1874.

Arc 505.77F Dunand, Maurice. Fouilles de Byblos. Paris, 1937- 3v.

Arc 505.132 Dunand, Maurice. Oumm el-'Amed. Text and atlas. Paris, 1962. 2v.

Arc 915.7 Dunant, Émile. Guide illustrative du Musée d'Avenches. Genève, 1900.

Arc 584.4F Dunbar, J.H. The rock-picutres of Lower Nubia. Cairo, 1941.

Arc 588.49F Duncan, J.G. Corpus of dated Palestinian pottery. London, 1930.

Arc 497.31 Duncan, J.G. Digging up Biblical history. N.Y., 1931- 2v.

Arc 875.90 Dundarg Castle. (Simpson, William D.) Edinburgh, 1954.

Arc 875.134 Dundee, Scotland. Museum and Art Gallery. Tayside before history. Dundee, 1971.

Arc 608.24F Dunham, D. The Royal cemeteries of Kush. Hambridge, 1950-63. 5v.

Arc 608.24.5F Dunham, D. Second cataract forts. Boston, 1960-67. 2v.

Arc 870.15.11 Dunning, J.E. The Roman road to Portslade. London, 1925.

Arc 1480.1 Duodenorum nomismatum antehac ineditorum brevis expositio. (Venutis, P. de.) Leghorn, 1760.

Htn Arc 750.31* DuPerac, E. I vestigi dell'antichità di Roma. Roma, 1575.

Arc 889.4.2 Dupont, Édouard. Les temps préhistoriques en Belgique. 2. éd. Bruxelles, 1872.

Arc 830.337 Dupont, J. Le site et les lampes votives du Chasterland de Lardiers. Cavaillon, 1962?

Arc 543.135 Dupont, P. L'archéologie moue de Dváravati. Paris, 1959. 2v.

Arc 530.163 Dupont-Sommer, André. La déesse de Hiérapolis Castabala (Cilicie). Paris, 1964.

Arc 1033.53.23 Dupraz, Louis. Les passions de S. Maurice d'Agaune. Fribourg, 1961.

Arc 543.136 Dupree, Louis Benjamin. Deh Morasi Ghunelai: a cholcolithic site in south-central Afghanistan. N.Y., 1963.

Arc 1335.61 Dupriez, C. La grande guerre. Bruxelles, 19- ?

Arc 505.45.15 Dura-Europas and its art. (Rostovtsen, M.I.) Oxford, 1938.

Arc 505.45.5 Dura studies. (Johnson, J.) Philadelphia, 1932.

Arc 1670.4 Durand, Anthony. Médailles et jetons des numismates. Genève, 1865.

Arc 1020.6 Durand, J. Trésor de l'église Saint-Marc à Venise. Paris, 1862.

Arc 1033.19.9 Durand, Paul. Étude sur l'étimacia symbole du jugement dernier dans l'iconographie grecque chrétienne. Chartres, 1867.

Arc 823.35 Durand-Lefebvre, M. Art gallo-romain et sculpture romane. Paris, 1937.

Arc 823.35.5 Durand-Lefebvre, M. Art gallo-romain et sculpture romane. Thèse. Paris, 1937.

Arc 608.2.12 Dureau de la Malle, Adolphe. Recherches sur la topographie de Carthage. Paris, 1835.

Arc 67.6 Durham, England. University. King's College, Newcastle upon Tyne. The congress of Roman frontier studies. Durham, 1952.

Arc 705.202 Durm, J. Der Zustand der Antiken Athenischen Bauwerke. Berlin, 1895.

Arc 1494.20F El duro. (Herrera y Chiesanova, A.) Madrid, 1914. 2v.

Arc 855.3 The Durobrivae of Antoninus. (Artis, E.T.) London, 1828.

Arc 66.1.46 Durrieu, P. Archives angevines de Naples. Paris, 1886-1887. 2v.

Arc 66.1.146 Durry, Marcel. Les cohortes prétoriennes. Paris, 1938.

Arc 830.22 Du Seigneur, M. Les arènes de Lutèce. Paris, 1886.

Arc 936.195.255 Dušek, Mikuláš. Bronzezeitliche Gräberfelder in der Südwestslowakei. Bratislava, 1969.

Arc 936.195.115F Dušek, Mikuláš. Thrakisches Gräberfeld der Hallstattzeit in Chotín. Bratislava, 1966.

Arc 1020.53 Dusevel, M.H. Histoire...du trésor...de Saint Pierre de Corbie. Amiens, 1861.

Arc 505.71 Dussaud, René. L'art phénicien du IIe millenaire. Paris, 1949.

Arc 830.130 Dussaud, René. Autour des inscriptions de Glozel. Paris, 1927.

Arc 513.17 Dussaud, René. Les civilisations prehelléniques. Paris, 1910.

Arc 513.17.2 Dussaud, René. Les civilisations prehelléniques. 2. éd. Paris, 1914.

Arc 513.17.15 Dussaud, René. La Lydie et ses voisins aus hautes époques. Paris, 1930.

Arc 513.17.20 Dussaud, René. Prélydiens Hittites et Achéens. Paris, 1953.

Arc 505.9 Dussaud, René. Voyage archéologique au Safâ. Paris, 1901.

Arc 853.52 Dutschmann, G. Literatur zur Vor- und Frühgeschichte Sachsens. Leipzig, 1921.

Arc 861.76 Dutt, W.A. The ancient mark-stones of East Anglia. Lowestoft, 1926.

Arc 1655.5 Dutton, M.K. The case of the elusive hubs and dies. Honolulu, 1959.

Arc 66.1.218 Duval, Noël. Les églises africaines à deux absides. Paris, 1971- 2v.

Arc 830.325 Duval, Paul M. Paris antique des origines au troisième siécle. Paris, 1961.

Arc 1510.154.5 Duve, Gebhard. Dicktaler-Prägungen, 1544-1679. v.2. Frankfurt am Main, 1974-

Arc 1510.154 Duve, Gebhard. History of the redeemable, multiple and mining talers of Brunswick-Luneburg. 1. ed. Johannesburg, 1966.

Arc 1540.29 Duveen, G.E. The history of the gold sovereign. London, 1962.

Arc 830.75 Duvernoy, Clement. Notice sur le pays de Montbéliard. Montbéliard, 1869.

Arc 1675.25 Les Duvivier. (Nocz, Henry.) Paris, 1911.

Arc 935.45 Duyaran, Rüstem. 1952 yilinda arkeolojik. Istanbul, 1953.

Arc 513.28 Duyuran, Rüstem. The ancient cities of Western Anatolia. n.p., 195-?

Arc 513.34 Duyuran, Rüstem. Bati Anoidolu'da eski şehirler. Istanbul, 1948.

Arc 513.28.5 Duyuran, Rüstem. Carte archeologique de l'Anatolie occidentale. Izmir, 1952.

Arc 518.10 Duyuran, Rüstem. Ephèse. Ankara, 1951.

Arc 1588.4.38 Dvě stoleti vědecké numismatiky v českých Zemich. 1771-1971. (Nohejlová, Emanuela.) Praha, 1971.

Arc 1348.46 Dye, John S. Dye's coin encyclopaedia. Philadelphia, 1883.

Arc 708.5 Dyer, T.H. Ancient Athens. London, 1873.

Arc 758.1 Dyer, T.H. Ancient Rome. London, 1864.

Arc 810.4 Dyer, T.H. Pompeii: its history, buildings and antiquities. London, 1867.

Arc 1348.46 Dye's coin encyclopaedia. (Dye, John S.) Philadelphia, 1883.

Arc 672.7 Dyggve, E. Das heroon von Kalydon. København, 1934.

Arc 855.209.2F Dymond, C.W. Worlebury - an ancient stronghold. Bristol, 1886.

Arc 855.209F Dymond, C.W. Worlebury - an ancient stronghold. Bristol, 1902.

Arc 855.226F Dymond, Charles W. The ancient remains at Stanton Drew. Bristol, 1896.

Arc 388.9 Dymond, David Percy. Archaeology and history. London8 1974.

Arc 1190.90 Dyplomatyka wieków średnich. Wyd. 1. Warszawa, 1971.

Arc 493.6.50 Dzhafarzade, Iskhak M. Gobustan. Baku, 1973.

Arc 1584.1.5 Dzhalaganiia, I.L. Iz istorii monetnogo dela v gruzii XIII veha. Tbilisi, 1958.

Arc 925.9.145 Dzhavakhishvili, Aleksandr I. Stroitel'noe delo i arkhitektura poselenii Iuzhnogo Kavkaza. Tbilisi, 1973.

Arc 505.68.15 Dzherash (Gerasa). (Abalmelck-Lazarev, Semen S.) Sankt Peterburg, 1897.

Arc 530.81 Dzhrvezh. (Akademiia nauk Armianskoi SSR, Erevan. Institut Istorii.) Erevan, 1959. 2v.

Arc 412.3 Dzhus, Vsevolod E. My-gedronavty. Leningrad, 1974.

Arc 1143.10 Dziatzko, K. Untersuchungen...antiken Buchwesens. Leipzig, 1900.

Arc 853.65.60 Dzieje zierni wydarte. (Bagniewski, Zbigniew.) Wrocław, 1970.

Arc 710.24 E Mykēnaikē Akropolis tōn Athēnōn. (Iakōbidēs, S.E.) Athēnai, 1962.

Arc 943.38 The eagle. 1. ed. (Covarrubias, M.) N.Y., 1954.

Arc 1153.44.5F The earliest book of Tours. (Rand, Edward K.) Cambridge, Mass., 1934.

Arc 416.36 Earliest civilizations of the Near East. (Mellaart, James.) N.Y., 1965.

Arc 1540.30 The earliest Irish coinage. (O'Sullivan, W.) Dublin, 1961.

Arc 1615.10 Early American cents, 1793-1814. 1. ed. (Sheldon, W.H.) N.Y., 1949.

Arc 530.105 Early Anatolia. (Lloyd, Seton.) Harmondsworth, 1956.

Arc 777.2 Early and imperial Rome. (Westropp, H.M.) London, 1884.

Arc 870.12.15A Early Anglo-Saxon art and archaeology. (Leeds, E.T.) Oxford, 1936.

Arc 870.35 The early barrow-diggers. (Marsden, Barry M.) Park Ridge, N.J., 1974.

Arc 858.55.3 Early Britain. (Hawkes, Jacquette.) London, 1946.

Arc 505.155F The early bronze age sanctuary at Ai (et-Tell). (Callaway, Joseph A.) London, 1972.

Arc 1084.10 Early Chinese jades. (Pope-Hennessy, U. (Mrs.).) London, 1923.

Arc 875.110 The early Christian and Pictish monuments of Scotland. (Cruden, Stewart.) Edinburgh, 1957.

Arc 858.105 The early Christian archaeology of Northern Britain. (Thomas, Charles.) London, 1971.

Arc 1030.53 Early Christian inscriptions in the Bennett Museum of Christian archaeology. (Patten, A.W.) Evanston, 1915.

Arc 880.31 Early Christian Ireland. (Power, P.) Dublin, 1925.

NEDL Arc 855.206 The early Christian monuments of Scotland. (Allen, J.R.) Edinburgh, 1903.

Arc 1365.2 Early Christian numismatics. (King, Charles W.) London, 1873.

Arc 1020.9.175 Early Christians of Rome. (Bevan, Gladys M.) London, 1927.

Arc 1018.37 The early church in the light of monuments. (Barnes, A.S.) London, 1913.

Arc 689.3.10 Early civilization in Thessaly. (Hansen, H.D.) Baltimore, 1933.

Author and Title Listing

Arc 1610.2 The early coins of America. (Crosby, S.S.) Boston, 1875.
Arc 1610.2.1 The early coins of America. (Crosby, S.S.) Lawrence, 1974.
Arc 880.50 The early development of Irish society: the evidence of aerial photography. (Norman, Edward R.) Cambridge, Eng., 1969.
Arc 936.220.75 Early farming cultures in Central Serbia (Eastern Yugoslavia). (McPherron, Alan.) Krazujevać, 1971.
Arc 875.11 Early fortifications in Scotland. (Christison, D.) London, 1898.
Arc 309.10 Early Georgia. Athens, Ga.
Arc 1663.8 The early history of the Mediterranean populations. (Clarke, H.) London, 1882.
Arc 448.1.2 Early Indus civilization. 2. ed. (Mackay, Ernest.) London, 1948.
Arc 1163.6 Early Irish minuscule script. (Lindsay, W.M.) Oxford, 1910.
Arc 609.37 The early Iron Age in Malawi: an appraisal. (Robinson, Keith Radcliffe.) Zomba, 1969.
Arc 855.227F The early iron age inhabited site at All Cannings Cross farm, Wiltshire. (Cunnington, M.E. (Mrs.)) Devizes, 1923.
Arc 861.78 Early life in the West. (Davies, J.A.) Clifton, 1927.
Arc 407.3 Early man. (Wright, G.F.) Cleveland, 1883.
Arc 983.14 Early man in America with particular reference to the southwestern United States. (American Society of Naturalists.) n.p., 1936.
Arc 858.2 Early man in Britain. (Dawkins, W.B.) London, 1880.
Arc 609.13.5 Early man in east Africa. (Cole, Sonia Mary.) London, 1958.
Arc 861.21.19 Early man in north east Yorkshire. (Elgee, Frank.) Gloucester, 1930.
Arc 416.25 Early Mediterranean migration; an essay in archaeological interpretation. (Burton-Brown, Theodore.) Manchester, 1959.
Arc 880.33F The early Mousterian implements of Sligo, Ireland. (Burchell, J.P.T.) Ipswich, 1928.
Arc 672.1.26 Early Nilotic, Libyan, and Egyptian relations with Minoan Crete. (Evans, Arthur John.) London, 1925.
Arc 870.28 Early Pennine settlement: a field study. (King, Alan.) Lancaster, 1970.
Arc 505.134 Early pottery of the Jebeleh region. (Ehrich, Ann M.) Philadelphia, 1939.
Arc 957.1.25 Early pueblo in the Piedra district. (Roberts, Frank H.H.) Washington, 1930.
Arc 875.15 The early races of Scotland and their monuments. (Leslie, Forbes.) Edinburgh, 1866. 2v.
Arc 1478.65F Early Roman coinage. (Thomsen, Rudi.) København, 1957. 3v.
Arc 761.8F Early Rome. v.1-6. (Gjerstadt, E.) Lund, 1953. 5v.
Arc 861.200.5 Early settlement in the Lake counties. (Fell, Clare.) Clapham, 1972.
Arc 1163.9 Early Welsh script. (Lindsay, W.M.) Oxford, 1912.
Arc 870.10.20 The earthen long barrow in Britain. (Ashbee, Paul.) Toronto, 1970.
Arc 870.9 Earthwork of England. (Allcroft, A.H.) London, 1908.
Arc 861.4 Earwaker, J.P. The recent discoveries of Roman remains found in the...City of Chester. Manchester, 1888.
Arc 861.102F The Easby cross. (Longhurst, M.H.) Oxford, 1931.
Arc 609.13.10 East African Vocation School in Pre-European African History and Archaeology. Prelude to East African history: a collection of papers given at the first East African Vocation School in Pre-European History and Archaeology, in December, 1962. London, 1966.
Arc 861.167 East Anglia. (Clarke, R.) London, 1960.
Arc 149.5 East Riding archaeologist. Hull, Eng. 1,1968+
Arc 953.26 Eastern Algonkian block stamp decoration. (Speck, F.G.) Trenton, New Jersey, 1947.
Arc 505.22.2 Eastern exploration past and future. (Petrie, W.M.F.) London, 1918.
Arc 493.1 Easton, M.W. Observations on the platform at Persepolis. Philadelphia, 1892.
Arc 522.11 Die Ebene von Troja. (Lenz, C.G.) Neu-Strelitz, 1798.
Arc 1033.12.17 Eberlé, L. Confrérie du Saint Suaire. Besançon, 1886.
Arc 1053.6 Ebers, G. Antike. Portraits. Leipzig, 1893.
Arc 1053.6.2 Ebers, G. The Hellenic portraits from the Fayum. N.Y., 1893.
Arc 1033.10 Ebers, G. Sinnbildliches die koptische Kunst. Leipzig, 1892.
Arc 561.1.10 Ebers, George. Richard Lepsius. N.Y., 1887.
Arc 1254.14 Ebersolt, Jean. Catalogue des sceaux byzantins. Paris, 1922.
Arc 935.10.3 Ebersolt, Jean. Mission archéologique de Constantinople. Paris, 1921.
Arc 1138.17 Ebert, F.A. Zur Handschriftenkunde. v.1-2. Leipzig, 1825.
Arc 375.8 Ebert, Max. Reallexikon der Vorgeschichte. v.1-15. Berlin, 1924-32. 16v.
Arc 923.15.2 Ebert, Max. Südrussland im Altertum. Aalen, 1973.
Arc 861.21 Eburacum, or York under the Romans. (Wellbeloved, C.) York, 1842.
Arc 159.5 Eburodunum. Yverdon. 2,1975+
Arc 760.6.17 Eccellentissima congregazione diputata da sua Santità Papa Leone XII. (Fea, Carlo.) Roma, 1827.
Arc 87.1.65 Echelos und Basile. (Kekule, R.) Berlin, 1905.
Arc 1400.1.2 Eckfeldt, J.R. A manual of gold and silver coins. Philadelphia, 1851.
Arc 1400.1 Eckfeldt, J.R. New varieties of gold and silver coins. N.Y., 1851.
Arc 1353.5 Eckhel, J. Thesauro Caesarum...Numorun Gemmarumque. Budae, 1799.
Arc 1359.1 Eckhel, J.H. Doctrina numorum veterum. Viennae, 1792-98. 8v.
Arc 1033.17.55 Ecloga historia qua fabula pontificia de Luca Pictore exploditur. (Schlichter, C.L.) Halae, 1734.
Arc 1153.35 École de calligraphie et de miniature de Tours. (Bosseboeuf, L.A.) Tours, 1891.
Arc 82.1.5 L'école française de Rome. (Geffroy, M.A.) Paris, 1884.
Arc 543.5.15 École Française d'Extrême-Orient, Hanoi, Indo-China. L'École française d'Extrême Orient. Hanoi, 1930.
Arc 34.2F École Française d'Extreme Orient, Hanoi, Indo-China. Mémoires archéologiques. Paris. 1926-1932 10v.
Arc 543.7.19F École Française d'Extrême-Orient, Hanoi, Indo-China. Le temple d'Angkor Vat. pt.2. Paris, 1930. 2v.
Arc 543.100 École Française d'Extrême-Orient, Hanoi. Indochina Musée. Louis Premier. Paris, 1960.
Arc 543.5.15 L'École française d'Extrême Orient. (École Française d'Extrême-Orient, Hanoi, Indo-China.) Hanoi, 1930.
Arc 1153.113 L'écriture des actes de Louis VI, Louis VII et Philippe Auguste. (Gasparri, Françoise.) Genève, 1973.
Arc 1190.84 L'écriture diplomatique dans le diocèse de Liège. (Strennon, Jacques.) Paris, 1960.
Arc 600.205 Edel, Elmar. Die Felsengräber der Qubbet el Hawa bei Assuan. Wiesbaden, 1970- 2v.
Arc 1076.3.89 Edel, Friederich W. Von den Glocken. pt.1-2. Strassburg, 1862-63.
Arc 600.47F Edgar, C.A. Der Isistempel von Behbet. pt.2. Rom, 1913.
Arc 770.8 Gli edifici antichi di Roma. (Piroli, T.) Roma, 1800?
Arc 875.132 Edinburgh and southeast Scotland. (Ritchie, James Neil Graham.) London, 1972.
Arc 1020.128F Un édit de l'empereur Justinien II. (Pappageorgios, P.) Leipzig, 1900.
Arc 391.2.17 Eduard Gerhard. (Jahn, Otto.) Berlin, 1868.
Arc 554.1.3 Edwards, A.B. Pharaohs, fellahs and explorers. N.Y., 1891.
Arc 554.1 Edwards, A.B. Pharaohs, fellahs and explorers. N.Y., 1891.
Arc 554.1.5 Edwards, A.B. Pharaohs, fellahs and explorers. N.Y., 1892.
Arc 1660.18F Edwards, Edward. The Napoleon medals. London, 1837.
Arc 595.59 Edwards, L.E.S. The pyramids of Egypt. London, 1954.
Arc 595.60 Edwards, L.E.S. The pyramids of Egypt. London, 1961.
Arc 1125.35 The Edwards lectures. Glasgow. 2,1966+
Arc 938.97 Eesti NSV Teaduste Akademia. Ajaloo Institut. Pronksiajast varase feodalisimini. Tallinn, 1966.
Arc 518.9 Efeso; studj. (Lauria, G.A.) Napoli, 1874.
Arc 1390.15 Effective research on unknown mediaeval coinage. 1. ed. (Stockvis, Albert.) Cleveland, 1955.
Arc 66.1.163 Effenterre, Henri van. La Crète et le monde grec. Paris, 1948.
Htn Arc 969.1.8* Effigy, or Symbolic mound in Licking County, Ohio. (Manuscripts. English.) n.p., n.d.
Arc 890.208.2 Efterskrift oldtidsminder og oldsager. (Vedel, E.) Kjøbenhavn, 1897.
Arc 905.24.13 Egger, Rudolf. Führer druch die Ausgrabungen und das Museum auf dem Magdalensberg. 3. Aufl. Klagenfurt, 1956.
Arc 905.24.15 Egger, Rudolf. Führer durch die Ausgrabungen und das Museum auf dem Magdalensberg. 5. Aufl. Klagenfurt, 1958.
Arc 759.2 Egger, Rudolf. Römische Antike und frühes Christentum. Klagenfurt, 1962-63. 2v.
Arc 905.24.5 Egger, Rudolf. Teurnia; die römischen und frühchristlichen Altertümer Oberkärntens. Wien, 1924.
Arc 905.24.6 Egger, Rudolf. Teurnia. 2. Aufl. Wien, 1926.
Arc 905.24.14 Egger, Rudolf. Teurnia. 4. Aufl. Klagenfurt, 1955.
Arc 935.16 Eggraphoi liphoi kai keramia. (Gedeon, M.J.) Konstantinople, 1892.
Arc 530.120 Egiazarian, O. Pamiatniki kul'tury...raiona. Erevan, 1955.
Arc 560.2 Egipet do faraonov. (Kink, Khil'da A.) Moskva, 1964.
Arc 843.105 Egitânia. (Almeida, Fernando de.) Lisboa, 1956.
Arc 66.1.55 L'église...du Couvent de Saint-Luc en Procide. (Diehl, C.) Paris, 1889.
Arc 1020.7 L'église cathedrale de Sienne...trésor. (Lebarte, J.) Paris, 1868.
Arc 830.70.10 L'eglise et la nécropole Saint-Laurent dans le quartier lyonnais de Chaueand. (Wuilleumier, P.) Lyon, 1949.
Arc 1020.9.153 L'eglise nationale de Saint Louis des Français à Rome. (Armailhacq.) Rome, 1894.
Arc 66.1.218 Les églises africaines à deux absides. (Duval, Noël.) Paris, 1971- 2v.
Arc 726.263 Les églises piévanes de Corse, de l'époque romaine au Moyen Age. Bastia, 1972-
Arc 915.48.2 Die Egolzwiler Kultur. 2. Aufl. (Wyss, René.) Bern, 1971.
Arc 1020.144 Egyházi emlékek a törtenelmi kiállitison. (Czober, Béla.) Budapest, 1898.
Arc 562.2.40 Egypt: ancient sites and modern scenes. (Maspero, Gaston.) N.Y., 1911.
Arc 545.228 Egypt. Antiquities Department. Catalogue des monuments et inscriptions de l'Egypte antique. Vienne, 1894-1909. 3v.
Arc 584.1.5 Egypt. Antiquities Department. Catalogue des publications du Service des Antiquités, mars 1961. Le Caire, 1961.
Arc 584.5F Egypt. Antiquities Department. The cheops boats. Cairo, 1960-
Arc 584.1 Egypt. Antiquities Department. Rapports sur la Marche, 1899-1910. Le Caire, 1912.
Arc 587.87F Egypt. Ministry of Finance. Archaeological survey of Nubia; report. Cairo. 1907-1911 8v.
Arc 587.85 Egypt. Ministry of Finance. Archaeological survey of Nubia. v.1-7. Cairo, 1908.
Arc 547.6.27 Egypt. State Tourists. Egyptian museum. Cairo, 1962.
Arc 557.3 Egypt and its monuments. (Hichens, Robert.) London, 1908.
Arc 557.3.2A Egypt and its monuments. (Hichens, Robert.) N.Y., 1908.
Arc 557.3.2.5 Egypt and its monuments. (Hichens, Robert.) N.Y., 1909.
Arc 565.5 Egypt and the Old Testament. (Put, Thomas C.) Liverpool, 1924.
Arc 560.1 Egypt and Western Asia. (King, L.W.) London, 1907.
Arc 586.2 Egypt Exploration Society. Archaeological reports. London. 1890-1912 5v.
Arc 586.7 Egypt Exploration Society. Guide to the temple of Deir el Bahari. London? 1895?
Arc 587.89 Egypt Exploration Society. Preliminary reports of the Egypt Exploration Society's Nubian Survey. Cairo, 1962.
Arc 586.5 Egypt Exploration Society. The proposed excavations at Tell-el-Amarna. n.p., n.d.
Arc 586.1 Egypt Exploration Society. Reports of annual meetings. London. 1884-1937 6v.
Arc 585.40F Egypt Exploration Society. Studies presented to F.L. Griffith. London, 1932.
Arc 586.40 Pamphlet box. Egypt Exploration Society.
Arc 561.5.5 L'Egypte monumentale et pittoresque. 2. éd. (Lagier, Camille.) Paris, 1922.
Arc 561.4.5 Egypten i dess minnesmärken o chi dess färhållande till Palestine och Grekland. (Lieblein, J.) Stockholm, 1877.
Arc 547.45 Egyptian antiquities. (Zayid, Abd al-Hamid.) Cairo, 1962.
Arc 600.10 Egyptian antiquities for our museums. (Winslow, W.C.) n.p., 1900.
Arc 561.3.3 Egyptian antiquities in British Museum. (Long, G.) London, 1846. 2v.
Arc 551.6 Egyptian antiquities in the Nile Valley. (Baikie, James.) London, 1932.
Arc 549.5 Egyptian archaeology. (Fuscaldo, Perla.) n.p., n.d. 3 pam.
Arc 562.2.7 Egyptian archaeology. (Maspero, Gaston.) London, 1893.
Arc 562.2.5 Egyptian archaeology. (Maspero, Gaston.) N.Y., 1887.
Arc 545.229 Egyptian archaeology. (University of California. Hearst Egyptian Expedition.) Leipzig. 1-7 6v.
Arc 562.2.6 Egyptian archaeology. 2. ed. (Maspero, Gaston.) N.Y., 1892.

Author and Title Listing

Arc 588.60 Egyptian architecture. (Petrie, W.M.F.) London, 1938.
Arc 585.37F Egyptian letters to the dead. (Gardiner, Alan H.) London, 1928.
Arc 590.01 Pamphlet box. Egyptian mummies and sarcophagi.
Arc 547.6.27 Egyptian museum. (Egypt. State Tourists.) Cairo, 1962.
Arc 545.202FA Egyptian obelisks. (Gorringe, H.H.) N.Y., 1882.
Arc 545.225 Egyptian Palaeolithic implements. (Haynes, H.W.) Cambridge, 1882.
Arc 595.29 The Egyptian pyramids. (Fish, E.W.) Chicago, 1880.
Arc 595.35 Egyptian pyramids. (Grinsell, Leslie V.) Gloucester, 1947.
Arc 547.25F Egyptian sculptures in the British Museum. (British Museum. Department of Egyptian and Assyrian Antiquities.) London, 1914.
Arc 547.40 Egyptian Stelae in the Bankes collection. (Bankes, Ralph.) Oxford, 1958.
Arc 600.37A Egyptian temples. (Murray, M.A.) London, 1931.
Arc 545.230 Egyptological researches. Results, 1904. (Müller, W.M.) Washington, 1906. 3v.
Arc 561.6 L'égyptologue Conrad Leemans et sa correspondance. (Leemans, Conrad.) Leiden, 1973.
Arc 585.23A Ehnasya. 1904. (Petrie, W.M.F.) London, 1905.
Arc 505.45.10 Ehrenstein, Theodor. Über die Fresken der Synagoge von Dura Europas. Wien, 1937.
Arc 505.134 Ehrich, Ann M. Early pottery of the Jebeleh region. Philadelphia, 1939.
Arc 389.5 Ehrich, R.W. Relative chronologies in old world archaeology. Chicago, 1954.
Arc 1153.24.2F Ehrle, Franz. Specimina codicum latinorum Vaticanorum. Berolini, 1932.
Arc 853.60 Eichhorn, G. Der Urnenfriedhof auf der Schanze bei Grossromstedt. Leipzig, 1927.
Arc 967.6 Eighteenth-century ceramics from Fort Michilimackinac, Michigan. (Miller, J. Jefferson.) Washington, 1970.
Arc 853.28 Einfluss der Römischen Kultur. (Kickebunde, A.) Berlin, 1908.
Arc 1138.25 Einführung in das mittelalterliche Schriftum. (Bauckner, A.) München, 1923.
Arc 905.15.5 Einführung in der Urgeschichte Böhmens und Mährens. (Menghin, Oswald.) Reichenberg, 1926.
Arc 557.8 Einführung in die Ägyptologie. (Hornung, Erik.) Darmstadt, 1967.
Arc 1138.32 Einführung in die Handschriftenkunde. (Löffler, Karl.) Leipzig, 1929.
Arc 1478.75 Einführung in die Münzprägung der römischen Kaiserzeit. (Goebl, Robert.) Wien, 1957.
Arc 1138.23 Einführung in die Textkritik. (Kantorowicz, Hermann.) Leipzig, 1921.
Arc 913.23 Einführung in die Vorgeschichte der Schweiz. 2. Aufl. (Tschumi, O.) Bern, 1918.
Arc 595.51 Einiges zur dritten Bauperiode der grossen Pyramide bei Gise. (Borchardt, Ludwig.) Berlin, 1932.
Arc 853.22 Eining die Dortigen Römerausgrabungen. (Schreiner, P.W.) Landsbut, 1882. 2v.
Arc 1348.16 Einleitung in das Studium des Numismatik. (Halke, H.) Berlin, 1889.
Arc 1348.16.2 Einleitung in das Studium des Numismatik. 3. Aufl. (Halke, H.) Berlin, 1905.
Arc 1018.27 Einleitung in die Monumentale Theologie. (Piper, F.) Gotha, 1867.
Arc 845.203 Einzelforschungen über Kunst- undAltertumsgegenstände zu Frankfurt am Main. (Frankfurt am Main. Historisches Museum.) Frankfurt, 1908.
Arc 1163.19 Eis, Gerhard. Altdeutsche Handschriften. München, 1949.
Arc 905.126.1 Die Eisentechnik der Hallstattzeit. Photoreproduction. (Rieth, Adolf.) Leipzig, 1942.
Arc 1298.2 Eitel, Anton. Über Blei- und Goldbullen. Freiburg, 1912.
Arc 1215.2 Eitel, Anton. Ueber Blei- und Goldbullen im Mittelalter. Freiburg, 1912.
Arc 895.23 Ekholm, Gunnar. Studier i Upplands bebyggelse-historia. Uppsala, 1915.
Arc 933.5 Ekonomicheskie sviazi Vostochnoi Evropy v I tysiacheletii neshei ery. (Kropotkin, Vladislav V.) Moskva, 1967.
Arc 1138.110 Ekschmitt, Werner. Das Gedächtnis der Völker. Berlin, 1964.
Arc 1335.76.5 Ekthesis ōerilēotikē. (Athens. Ethnikon Nomismatikon Mouseion.) Athēnai, 1857.
Arc 925.13.60 Ekufika. (Seminar Kondakovianum, Prague.) Praha. 1-4,1929-1931 2v.
Arc 588.11 El Arábah. (Garstang, John.) London, 1901.
Arc 600.60F El Bersheh. (Mewberry, P.E.) London, 1894-95. 2v.
Arc 587.3 El Bersheh. Pt.1-2. (Newberry, P.E.) London, 1894-95. 2v.
Arc 588.8 El Kab. 1897. (Quibell, J.E.) London, 1898.
Arc 66.1.60 Élatée. (Paris, P.) Paris, 1892.
Arc 1335.39 Elder, Thomas L. Rare coins and medals of William S. Appleton. N.Y., 1913.
Arc 628.23 Elderkin, G.W. Archeological papers. v.1-5, 6-10. Springfield, Mass., 1941- 2v.
Htn Arc 1458.8* Electa rei numariae. (Woltereck, C.) Hamburgi, 1709.
Arc 1458.8.5 Electa rei numariae. (Woltereck, C.) Hamburgi, 1709.
Arc 1428.27 The electrum coinage of Lampakos. (Brett, A.) N.Y., 1914.
Arc 403.1 Element of archaeology. (Seabird, H.) n.p., 1878.
Arc 1185.21 Elementi di diplomatica. (Lodolini, A.) Milano, 1926.
Arc 1185.29 Elementi di diplomatica generale. (Pratesi, A.) Bari, 1963?
Arc 1025.28.3 Eléments d'archélogie chrétienne. v.1-2. (Marucchi, O.) Paris, 1899. 3v.
Arc 1025.28.4 Eléments d'archéologie chrétienne. (Marucchi, O.) Paris, 1903. 2v.
Arc 1018.4 Eléments d'archéologie chrétienne. (Reusens, E.) Louvain, 1871-75. 2v.
Arc 1200.15 Les éléments de la diplomatique pontificale. (MasLatrie, L.) Paris, 1886.
Arc 1518.5 Elements de l'histoire monétaire de Flandre. (Serrure, Raymond.) Gand, 1879.
Arc 400.19 Éléments de préhistoire. (Peyrony, D.) Ussel, 1923.
Arc 925.296F Éléments de préhistoire et d'archéologie nord-sibériennes. (Nat, Daniel.) Paris, 1971-
Arc 608.1.50 Éléments d'étude pour une protohistoire de la Tunisie. (Cintas, Pierre.) Paris, 1961.
Arc 1163.5.5 Elements of south-Indian palaeography. 2. ed. (Burnell, A.C.) London, 1878.
Arc 1163.5.6 Elements of south-Indian palaeography. 2. ed. (Burnell, A.C.) London, 1878.
Arc 416.35 Elements of the megalithic complex in Southeast Asia. (Loofs, Helmut Hermann Ernst.) Canberra, 1967.
Arc 983.3.2 Elephant pipes and inscribed tablets. (Putnam, C.E.) Davenport, 1885.
Arc 983.3 Elephant pipes and inscribed tablets in the Museum of the Academy of Natural Sciences. (Putnam, C.E.) Davenport, 1886.
Arc 674.1.9F Eleusiniaka. (Kourouniotos, K.) Athēnai, 1932.
Arc 674.1.25 Pamphlet box. Eleusis.
Arc 674.1.10 Eleusis. (Kourouniotos, K.) Athēnai, 1934.
Arc 674.1.12 Eleusis. (Kourouniotos, K.) Athens, 1936.
Arc 674.1.5F Eleusis. Text and plates. (Noack, F.) Berlin, 1927. 2v.
Arc 673.1.29 Eleusis and the Eleusinian mysteries. (Mylonas, George Emmanuel.) Princeton, 1972.
Arc 1033.167 Eleuterio. I martirii di S. Teodoto e di S. Ariadne. Roma, 1901.
Arc 861.21.21 Elgee, Frank. The archaeology of Yorkshire. London, 1933.
Arc 861.21.19 Elgee, Frank. Early man in north east Yorkshire. Gloucester, 1930.
Arc 861.72 Elgee, Frank. The Romans in Cleveland. Middlesbrough, 1923.
Arc 853.351F Elisenhof: die Ergebnisse der Ausgrabung der frühgeschichtlichen Marschersiedlung beim Elisenhof in Eiderstedt 1957/58 und 1961/64. Bern, 1975-
Arc 600.26 Elkab. Bruxelles. 1,1971+
Arc 1190.86 Elker, Salâhaddin. Divan rakamlari. Ankara, 1953.
Arc 793.12 Ellaby, Christopher G. Pompeii and Herculaneum. London, 1930.
Arc 1076.3.77F Ellacombe, H.T. Bells of the church. Exeter, 1872.
Arc 1076.3.79F Ellacombe, H.T. The church bells of Gloucestershire. Exeter, 1881.
Arc 1076.3.78 Ellacombe, H.T. The church bells of Somerset. Exeter, 1875.
Arc 390.5 Elliger, W. Forschungen zur Kirchengeschichte...Johannes Ficker als Festgabe. Leipzig, 1931.
Arc 925.13 Ellinstvo i iranstvo na iuge Rossii. (Rostovtsev, M.I.) Petrograd, 1918.
Arc 493.60.5 Ellis, Richard Stephens. A bibliography of Mesopotamian archaeological sites. Wiesbaden, 1972.
Arc 444.2.10 Ellora; a handbook of Verul (Ellora caves). (Balasaheb, Pant Pratinidhi.) Bombay, 1929.
Arc 1478.60 Elmer, Georg. Verzeichnis der römischen Reichsprägungen von Augustus bis Anastasius. 2. Aufl. Graz, 1956.
Arc 1018.6.21 Elogio del cavalier professore Mariano Armellini. (Bartolini, A.) Roma, 1896.
Arc 1030.5.21 L'elogio funebre di Turia...Q. Lucrezio Vespillone. (Rossi, G.B. de.) Roma, 1880.
Arc 843.170 Els monuments megalitics a l'illa de Menorca. (Mascaró i Pasarius, J.) Barcelona, 1958.
Arc 870.31F Elsdon, Sheila M. Stamp and roulette decorated pottery of the La Tème period in Eastern England. Oxford, 1975.
Arc 375.13 Elseviers encyclopedie van de archeologie. (Aken, Andreas Rudolphus Antonius van.) Amsterdam, 1965.
Arc 759.1 Elter, A. Das alte Rom im Mittelalter. Bonn, 1904.
Arc 66.1.180 L'elucidarium et les lucidaires. (Lefèvre, Yves.) Paris, 1954.
Arc 389.2 Ely, Talfourd. Manual of archaeology. N.Y., 1890.
Arc 861.35 Ely, Talfourd. Roman Hayling. London, 1914.
Arc 861.35.5 Ely, Talfourd. Roman Hayling. 2. ed. London, 1908.
Arc 977.1 The emblematic mounds of Wisconsin. (Peet, S.D.) n.p., n.d.
Arc 1033.3 Emblemi...del...sarcofago...di Tortona. (Bottazzi, G.A.) Tortona, 1824.
Arc 1033.3.3 Emblemi sepolcrali degli antichi cristiani. (Amati, G.) Roma, 1825.
Arc 1033.115 Emerton, E. The religious environment of early Christianity. Cambridge, 1910.
Arc 584.3.10 Emery, W.B. Excavations at Saqqara, 1937-1938. Cairo, 1939.
Arc 584.3.5F Emery, W.B. Excavations at Saqqara. Cairo, 1938.
Arc 584.3F Emery, W.B. Great tombs of the First Dynasty. Cairo, 1949. 3v.
Arc 554.6 Emery, Walter. Archaic Egypt. Baltimore, 1963.
Arc 608.23 Emery, Walter B. Nubian treasure. London, 1948.
Arc 600.15.25 Emery, Walter Bryan. A funerary repast in an Egyptian tomb of the archaic period. Leiden, 1962.
Arc 1025.42 Emiliani, A. Ricordi di viaggio ad catacumbas. Livorno, 1883.
Arc 225.1.5 Emlékkünyv az Erdélyi Muzeum-Egyesületjélszázados ünnepére, 1859-1909. (Erdélyi Muzéum-Egyesület, Cluj.) Kolozsvár, 1942.
Arc 905.22 Emona; archaeologischen Studien aus Krain. (Müllner, Alfons.) Laibach, 1879.
Arc 936.225.15F Emonske nekropole. (Petru, Sonja.) Ljubljana, 1972.
Arc 843.65.2 Empúries i roses. 2. ed. (Pla y Cargol, J.) Girona, 1934.
Arc 830.119.10 En ressuscitant Vaison-la-Romaine. (Pellerin, Pierre.) Paris, 1962.
Arc 823.21.5F L'enceinte d'Haulzy et sa nécropole. (Goury, Georges.) Nancy, 1911.
Arc 823.10.5 Les enceintes Romaines de la Gaule. (Blanchet, A.) Paris, 1907.
Arc 825.8.6 Enceintes successives de Nîmes depuis les Romains. 2e éd. (Germer-Durand, E.) Nîmes, 1877.
Arc 968.2.5 The enchanted Mesa. v.1-2. (Hodge, F.W.) Washington, 1897.
Arc 375.2 Encyclopaedia of Antiquities. (Fosbroke, T.D.) London, 1825. 2v.
Arc 497.99 Encyclopedia of archaeological excavations in the Holy Land. Englewood Cliffs, N.J., 1975- 2v.
Arc 1411.14 An encyclopedia of Chinese coins. 1. ed. (Coole, Arthur Braddan.) Denver, 1967.
Arc 853.175 Endrich, Peter. Vor- und Frühgeschichts des bayerischen Untermaingebietes. Aschaffenburg, 1961.
Arc 925.50.185 Eneolit Ukrainy. (Danilenko, Valentin N.) Kiev, 1969.
Arc 925.50.185.5 Eneolit Ukrainy. (Danilenko, Valentin N.) Kiev, 1974.
Arc 530.12.40 Enge Schlucht und Schwarzer Berg. (Marek, Kurt W.) Hamburg, 1955.
Arc 530.12.42 Enge Schlucht und Schwarzer Berg. (Marek, Kurt W.) Reinbek, 1966.
Arc 843.4 Engel, A. Une forteresse ibérique...de 1903. Paris, 1906.
Arc 1490.15 Engel, A. Recherches sur la numismatique...des nomands de Sicile. Paris, 1882.
Arc 1498.1 Engel, A. Répertoire...de la numismatique française. Paris, 1887-89. 2v.
Arc 1498.1.2 Engel, A. Répertoire...de la numismatique française. Supplément et table. Paris, 1889.
Arc 1390.8 Engel, A. Traite de numismatique en moyen age. Paris, 1891. 3v.
Arc 1505.6 Engel, Arthur. Numismatique de l'Alsace. Paris, 1887.

Author and Title Listing

Arc 853.266 Engel, Carl. Typen ostpreussischer Hügelgräber. Neumünster, 1962.
Arc 1269.30 Engel, W. Würzburger Zunftsiegel aus fünf Jahrhunderten. Würzburg, 1950.
Arc 588.29F Engelbach, R. Harageh. London, 1923.
Arc 593.3 Engelbach, R. The problem of the obelisks. London, 1923.
Arc 554.7.2 Engelbach, Reginald. Introduation to Egyptian archaeology. 2. ed. Cairo, 1961.
Arc 893.17 Engelhardt, C. Influence classique sur le nord pendant l'antiquité. Copenhagen, 1876.
Arc 1148.19 Engelhes, W. Het Griehsche boek in voor. Amsterdam, 1926.
Arc 1087.2 Engelmann, R. Die antiken Mühlen. Berlin, 1904.
Arc 810.21 Engelmann, R. Pompeii. London, 1904.
Arc 810.38 Engelmann, W. Neuer Führer durch Pompeji. Leipzig, 1925.
Arc 810.38.5 Engelmann, W. New guide to Pompeii. Leipzig, 1925.
Arc 853.315 Engels, Heinz-Josef. Die Hallstatt und Latènekultur in der Pfalz. Diss. n.p., 1967.
Arc 895.17.15F Engelstad, E.S. Ostnorske ristninger og malinger av den arktiske gruppe. Oslo, 1934.
Arc 1027.18.12 Engeström, Adolf von. Om Judarne i Rom...och deras...katakomber. Upsala, 1876.
Htn Arc 1025.66* Englefield, T.B. Some of the notes...on various subjects, especially the catacombs. n.p., n.d.
Arc 855.01F Pamphlet box. English antiquities.
Arc 858.3 The English archaeologist's hand-book. (Godwin, H.) Oxford, 1867.
Arc 1190.50 English bishops' chanceries. (Cheney, C.) Manchester, 1950.
Arc 1538.21.5 English coinage, 600-1900. (Sutherland, Carol Humphrey Vivian.) London, 1973.
Arc 1538.18.10 English coins. 3. ed. (Brooke, George C.) London, 1950.
Arc 1538.18 English coins from the seventh century to the present day. (Brooke, George C.) London, 1932.
Arc 1538.2.20 English copper, tin, and bronze coins in the British Museum. (British Museum. Department of Coins and Medals.) London, 1960.
Arc 1538.2.22 English copper, tin and bronze coins in the British Museum. 2. ed. (British Museum. Department of Coins and Medals.) London, 1964.
Arc 1163.17.30 English cursive book hands, 1250-1500. (Parkes, Malcolm Beckwith.) Oxford, 1969.
Arc 375.14 English-French, French-English vocabulary of prehistoric archaeology. (Marois, Roger.) Montreal, 1972.
Arc 1540.36 English gold coins. (Cleveland. Museum of Art.) Cleveland, 1968.
Arc 1538.25 English hammered coinage. (North, J.J.) London, 1960-63. 2v.
Arc 1274.5 English seals. (Blood, J.H.) London, n.d.
Arc 1538.27.3 The English silver coinage from 1649. 3. ed. (Seaby, Herbert Allen.) London, 1968.
Arc 1540.31 The English trade tokens. (Mathias, Peter.) London, 1962.
Arc 1163.17.25 English vernacular hands from the twelfth to the fifteenth centuries. (Wright, Cyril Ernest.) Oxford, 1960.
Arc 1207.1PF Engravings from ancient seals attached to deeds. (Hare, Thomas.) Stowe-Bardolph, 1847.
Arc 736.15 Engyon. (Canale, C.G.) Catania, 1955.
Arc 673.1.35F Énigmes à Delphes. (Pouilloux, Jean.) Paris, 1963.
Arc 540.7 Enkomè-Alasia. (Schaeffer, C.F.A.) Paris, 1952.
Arc 823.9A Enlart, C. Manuel d'archéologie française. Paris, 1902-1904. 3v.
Arc 823.9.2 Enlart, C. Manuel d'archéologie française. v.1, pts.1-3. Paris, 1919-1920. 3v.
Arc 823.9.3 Enlart, C. Manuel d'archéologie française. 3e éd. pt.2. Paris, 1929.
Arc 66.1.66 Enlart, C. Origines françaises de l'architecture gothique en Italie. Paris, 1894.
Arc 406.2 Ennio Quirion Visconti Giacobino. (Sforza, G.) n.p., n.d. 2 pam.
Arc 608.1.25 Enquête sur les installations hydrologiques romaines en Tunisie. (Gauckler, Paul.) Tunis, 1897-
Arc 895.25 Enquist, Arvid. Stenaldersbebyggeken på Arnst och Tjöm. Uppsala, 1922.
Arc 1349.80 Enrique Peña. (Quesada, Ernesto.) Buenos Aires, 1924.
Arc 843.226 Ensayo biologico sobre los hombres y los pueblos de la Asturias primativa. (Martínez Fernandez, Jesus.) Oviedo, 1969.
Arc 1668.8 Ensayo de un catalogo...de las medallas. (Perez Varela, H.) Habana, 1863.
Arc 1138.90 Ensayo sobre los alphabetos de las letras des conocidas. (Velazquez de Velasco, L.J.) Madrid, 1952.
Arc 66.1.181 Enserune. (Jannoray, Jean.) Paris, 1955.
Arc 520.18 Der Entdecker von Pergamon. (Humann, K.) Berlin, 1930.
Arc 522.9 Die Entdeckung Ilions zu Hissarlik. (Keller, O.) Freiburg in Baden, 1875.
Arc 1500.59 Entente cordiale. v.1-2. (Paris. Musée Monétaire et des Médailles.) Paris, 1957.
Arc 830.275 Entremont, capitale celto-ligure des Salyens de Provence. (Benoît, Fernand.) Aix-en-Provence, 1957.
Arc 830.275.10 Entremont, capitale celto-ligure des Salyens de Provence. (Benoît, Fernand.) Gap, 1969.
Arc 830.275.15 Entremont et l'impérium arverne. (Cornet, Jean M.) Romans, 1972- 2v.
Arc 595.50 Die Entstehung der Pyramide an der Baugeschichte. (Borchardt, Ludwig.) Berlin, 1928.
Arc 905.125 Die Entwicklungsgeschichte des antiken Bades und das Bad auf dem Maydalensberg. (Kratzschmer, F.) Düsseldorf, 1961.
Arc 1138.65 Entzifferung verschollener Schriften und Sprachen. (Friedrich, Johannes.) Berlin, 1954.
Arc 1138.65.2 Entzifferung verschollener Schriften und Sprachen. 2. Aufl. (Friedrich, Johannes.) Berlin, 1966.
Arc 391.7 Environment, tools and man. (Garrod, Dorothy A.E.) Cambridge, 1946.
Arc 1335.125 Enzenberg, Arthur. Katalog der Münzensammlung Arthur Graf Enzenberg. Luzern, 1935.
Arc 612.53.5 Enzyklopädisches Handbuch zur Ur- und Frühgeschichte Europas. (Filip, Jan.) Stuttgart, 1966. 2v.
Arc 1033.17.33 Eoniade della translazione...miracolosa immagine di Santa Maria...Constantinopoli. (Garruba, M.) Napoli, 1834.
Arc 688.8.5 Eounion. (Oikonomides, A.N.) Athēnai, 1957.
Arc 688.8 To Eounion. (Staés, B.) Athēnai, 1920.
Arc 830.371 Épave antique étrusco-punique? (Pruvot, Georges.) Antibes, 1971.
Arc 1076.3.52 Ephemeris campanographica. Montpellier.
Arc 69.1F Epheneriz Archaiologikē. (Archaeological Society of Athens.) Athēnai. 1837+ 54v.
Arc 518.10 Éphèse. (Duyuran, Rüstem.) Ankara, 1951.
Arc 66.1.123 Éphèse et Claros. (Picard, Charles.) Paris, 1922.
Arc 518.11 Ephesos, Stadt der Artemis. (Miltner, Franz.) Wien, 1958.
Arc 518.2 Ephesos. (Curtius, E.) Berlin, 1874.
Arc 518.8 Ephesos. (Keil, Josef.) Wien, 1915.
Arc 518.8.5 Ephesos. (Keil, Josef.) Wien, 1955.
Arc 518.8.7 Ephesos. 4. Aufl. (Keil, Josef.) Wien, 1957.
Arc 518.5 Ephesus. (Clarke, Hyde.) Smyrna, 1863.
Arc 518.3 Ephesus and the Temple of Diana. (Falkener, E.) London, 1862.
Arc 674.20 Epidauros en Kreta. (Schroeder, Johan.) Amsterdam, 1960.
Arc 674.3 Epidaurus, eine antike Heilstätte. (Herrlich, S.) Berlin, 1898.
Arc 1027.69.5 Epigrafi rinvenute nell'arenaria tra i cimiteri di Trasone e dei Giordani sulla via Salaria. (Rossi, G.B. de.) Roma, 1873.
Arc 1030.4.29 Epigrafia christiana. (Marucchi, O.) Milano, 1910.
Arc 93.50F Epigrafia e antichità. Faenza. 1,1969+
Arc 1190.45 Epigrafia giuridica greca e romana. (Luzzatto, G.I.) Milano, 1942.
Arc 925.9.55 Epigraficheskie pamiatniki severnogo Kavkaza. (Lavrov, L.I.) Moskva, 1966- 2v.
Arc 925.16.50 Epigrafika Kazakhstana. (Musabaev, Gainetdin G.) Alma-Ata, 1971.
Arc 34.6 Epigrafika Kirgizii. Fruze.
Arc 1138.126 Epigrafika Vostochnoi i Iuzhnoi Azii. Moskva, 1972.
Arc 34.5 Epigrafika Vostoka. Moskva. 1-18 5v.
Arc 1030.22 Epigramma greco christiano...Autun. (Secchi, G.) Roma, 1840.
Arc 441.2.3 Epigraphia Birmanica. Rangoon. 2-4,1921-1936 3v.
Arc 435.2.39F Epigraphia caratica. (Rice, B.S.) Madras, 1914.
Arc 435.21.5F Epigraphia carnatica. (Rice, B.L.) Bangalore, 1923.
Arc 435.21 Epigraphia carnatica. v.1-2. (Rice, B.L.) Bangalore, 1889- 15v.
Arc 435.20 Epigraphia Indica. (India. Archaeological Survey.) 1,1888+ 35v.
Arc 435.20.3 Epigraphia Indo-Moslemica. Arabic and Persian supplement. (India. Archaeological Survey.) 1927+ 7v.
Arc 435.72F Epigraphia zeylanica. London. 1-4,1904-1941 5v.
Arc 1030.9 L'épigraphie chrétienne en Gaule. (Le Blant, E.) n.p., 1890.
Arc 823.19.15 L'epigraphie romaine en France. (Thédenat, H.) Paris, 1879.
Arc 1163.11 Epigraphische Denkmäler aus China. (Franke, O.) Berlin, 1914. 2v.
Arc 1540.22.7 The episcopal coins of Durham. (Bartlet, B.) Newcastle, 1817.
Arc 1030.61 Die Epitaphien der Päpste und andere stadtrömische Inschriften des Mittelalters. (Schneider, Fedor.) Rom, 1933.
Htn Arc 1373.7* Epitome du thresor des antiquitez. (Strada, J. de.) Lyon, 1553.
Arc 1348.85 Epochen der Geldgeschichte. (Nau, Elisabeth.) Stuttgart, 1972.
Arc 925.322.15 Epokha rannego zheleza v Dagestane. (Pikul', Milifsa I.) Makhachkala, 1967.
Arc 830.34 L'époque gauloise dans...la Marne. (Nicaise, Auguste.) Paris, 1884.
Arc 505.144 L'époque que pré-urbaine en Palestine. (Miroschedji, Pierre R. de.) Paris, 1971.
Arc 830.67.5 Époques antédiluvienne et celtique du Poitu. pt.1-2. (Brouillet, A.) Poitiers, 1865.
Arc 915.1 Epoques antéhistoriques an Mont Salève. (Thioly, F.) Genève, 1867.
Arc 830.53 Époques préhistoriques...dans le Finistère. 2e éd. (Du Chatellier, Paul.) Rennes, 1907.
Arc 1033.53.15 L'era de' martiri osia di Diocleziano. (Cavedoni, C.) Modena, 1848.
Arc 1185.9.5 Erben, Wilhelm. Die Kaiser- und Königsurkunden des Mittelalters in Deutschland, Frankreich und Italien. München, 1967.
Arc 1185.9 Erben, Wilhelm. Urkundenlehre. v.1,3. München, 1907. 2v.
Arc 1510.95 Erbstein, H.A. Der Münzfund von Trebitz bei Wittenberg. Halle an der Saale, 1924.
Arc 1335.40 Erbstein, J. Die Schellhass'sche Münzsammlung. Dresden, 1870.
Arc 1510.158 Erbstein, Julius. Zur mittelalterlichen Münzgeschichte der Grafen von Mansfeld und der Edlen Hessen von Querfurt. Dresden, 1876.
Arc 1510.145 Erbstein, Karl Friedrich Wilhelm. Numismatische Bruchstücke in Bezug auf sächsische Geschichte. v.1-3. Dresden, 1816.
Arc 848.11 Erbt, Wilhelm. Germanische Kultur im Bronzezeitalter (2200-800 v. Chr.) Leipzig, 1926.
Arc 800.9F Ercolano. (Maiuri, Amedeo.) Roma, 1932.
Arc 800.9.8F Ercolano. (Maiuri, Amedeo.) Roma, 1958.
Arc 800.9.5 Ercolano. 2. ed. (Maiuri, Amedeo.) Roma, 1937.
Arc 1590.8 Az erdélyi érmek müvészete. (Farkas, Sandor.) Aiud, 1936.
Arc 225.1.5 Erdélyi Múzeum-Egyesület, Cluj. Emlékkönyv az Erdélyi Muzeum-Egyesületjélszázados ünnepére, 1859-1909. Kolozsvár, 1942.
Arc 936.26.10 Az Erdelyi Múzeum-Egyesület. (György, L.) Kolozsvár, 1937.
Arc 1076.3.120 Erdentiefe-Turmeshöhe; von Glocken und Glockengiessern. (Glade, Heinz.) Berlin, 1965.
Arc 513.38 Erder, Cevat. Hellenistik devir Anadolu nimorisinde kyma. Ankara, 1967.
Arc 1333.7 Erdmann, F. Numi asiatici musei univ. caes. liter. Casanensis. Casani, 1834.
Arc 1433.23 Erdmann, F. von. Zur Muhammedanischen Münzkunde. St. Petersburg, 1856.
Arc 925.220 Erdniev, U.E. Gorodishche maiak. Kemerovo, 1960.
Arc 554.5 Erdöse, K. Mumiäk es minarétek. Budapest, 1937.
Arc 716.7.15F Erechtheion. (Dörpfeld, W.) Berlin, 1942.
Arc 716.7 Das Erechtheion. (Forchhammer, P.W.) Kiel, 1879.
Arc 1588.13 Ered, Serafeddin. Nadir hirkaç sikke. Ankara? 1967.
Arc 716.7.20 To Erehtheion ōs iokodomema chthonias latreias. (Kontoleon, N.M.) Athēnai, 1949.
Arc 1588.13.5 Erel, Serafeddin. Nadir hirkaç sikke. Istanbul, 1963.
Arc 1300.32 Az érem. Budapest. 1922+
Arc 530.174 Erevan. (Yesaian, Stepan.) Erevan, 1969.
Arc 853.20.29 Die Erforschung des Tempelbezirkes im Altbachtale zu Trier. (Loeschcke, S.) Berlin, 1928.
Arc 1033.12.80 Erfreulicher Ursprung...am Semmering. Neustadt, 1738.
Arc 1510.14.3 Ergänzungen und Berichtigungen. (Rudolph, E.) Dresden, 1908.
Arc 510.208.2 Die Ergebnisse der Ausgrabungen zu Pergamon, 1880-1881. (Conze, A.) Berlin, 1882.

Author and Title Listing

Arc 510.208 Die Ergebnisse der Ausgrabungen zu Pergamon. (Conze, A.) Berlin, 1880.

Arc 80.1.8 To ergon tēs Archaiologikēs Hetaireias. (Archaiologikē Hetairia, Athens.) Athēnai. 1954+ 9v.

Arc 80.1.6 To ergon tēs en Athēnais, Archaiologikēs Hetairias kata ten prōten autēs hekatontaetias. (Archaiologikē Hetairia, Athens.) Athēnai, 1938.

Arc 1053.2.2 Die erhaltenen Bildnisse berühmter Griechen. (Bernoulli, J.J.) Basel, 1877.

Arc 407.5.2 Die Erhaltung der Denkmäler. (Wussow, A. von.) Berlin, 1885.

Arc 407.5 Der Erhaltung der Denkmäler. (Wussow, A. von.) Berlin, 1885.

Arc 853.40 Die Erhaltung der Römerstrassen. (Hauptmann, Carl.) Bonn, 1912.

Htn Arc 1359.2* Erizzo, S. Discorso sopra le medaglie de gli antichi. Venice, 1568.

Arc 1668.3 Erklärung der Abkürzungen auf Münzen der neueren Zeit. (Schlickeysen, F.W.A.) Berlin, 1882.

Arc 1668.3.2 Erklärung der Abkürzungen auf Münzen der neueren Zeit. (Schlickeysen, F.W.A.) Graz, 1961.

Arc 625.5.2 Erklaren der Text. v.1-2. 2. Aufl. Leipzig, 1901.

Arc 705.207 Erläuterungen...Rekonstruktion des östlichen Parthenongiebels. (Schwerzek, Karl.) Wien, 1904.

Arc 705.208 Erläuterungen...Rekonstruktion Westgiebels des Parthenongiebels. (Schwerzek, Karl.) Wien, 1896.

Arc 1335.153 Erlangen. Universität. Bibliothek. Die Voit von Salzburg'sche Münz. München, 1933.

Arc 1510.70 Erlangen in Spiegel der Münze. (Wintz, Hermann.) Erlangen, 1936.

Arc 905.132 Das Erlaufgebiet im ur- und frühgeschichtlicher Zeit. (Denk, Stefan.) Wien, 1962.

Arc 1025.65 Erlebnisse und Ergebnisse im Dienste der christlichen Archäologie. (Wilpert, Josef.) Freiburg, 1930.

Arc 1510.41 Erman, Adolf. Deutsche Medailleure des sechzehnten und siebzehnten Jahrhunderts. Berlin, 1884.

Arc 600.188.5 Les ermitages chrétiens du désert d'Esna. (Sauneron, Serge.) Le Caire, 1972.

Arc 1498.20 Ernst, Barbara. Les monnaies françaises depuis 1848. Braunschweig, 1968.

Arc 684.1.15 Die Ernst Curtius-Büste. Berlin, 1895.

Arc 392.15F Ernst Justus Haeberlin, sein Wirken. (Haeberlin, Ernst Justus.) München, 1929. 2v.

Arc 589.75F Ernst von Sieglin Expedition in Ägypten. Veröffentlichungen. Leipzig. 1-6,1912-1936 6v.

Arc 1033.17.481 Eroli, G. Narrazione storica sopra il santuario della madonna del Ponte. Roma, 1856.

Arc 1020.9.8 Eroli, Giovanni. Raccolta generale delle iscrizioni pagne e cristiane...nel panteon di Roma. Narni, 1895.

Arc 1033.17.22 Erra, C.A. Storia dell'imagine...Santa Maria in portico di Campitelli. Roma, 1750.

Arc 1027.9.5 Gli errori della scuola protestante. (Marucchi, O.) n.p., 1884.

Arc 953.34.1 Der erste Amerikaner. (Marek, Kurt W.) Reinbek bei Hamburg, 1972.

Arc 505.75 Das erste Auftreten der Hunnen das Alter der Jesaja-Rolle. (Altheim, F.) Baden-Baden, 1953.

Arc 1083.1 Das erste Auftreten des Eisens in Nord-Europa. (Undset, I.) Hamburg, 1882.

Arc 1053.23 Der Ertstehung des antiken Reprasentationsbildes. (Budde, Ludwig.) Berlin, 1957.

Arc 1675.85 Die erzgebirgische Prägmedaille des XVI. Jahrhundert. (Katz, Viktor.) Praha, 1932.

Arc 1033.72.5 Die Erztaufen Norddeutschlands. (Mundt, A.) Leipzig, 1908.

Arc 1480.62 Es, W.A. van. De romeinse muntvondsten uit de drie noordelijke provincies. Groningen, 1960.

Arc 889.32 Es, William Albertus van. Wijster; a native village beyond the imperial frontier, 150-425 A.D. Text and atlas. Groningen, 1967. 2v.

Arc 1033.68 Esame...dell'Immagine di Urbano II. (Rossi, G.B. de.) Roma, 1881.

Arc 1016.224 Esame della numismatica costantiniana. (Garrucci, R.) Roma, 1858.

Arc 1025.28.35 Esame di un opuscolo di Mons. G. Wilpert. (Marucchi, O.) Roma, 1909.

Arc 1027.70 Escavazione di un antico diverticolo della via Tiburtina. (Stevenson, H.) Roma, 1878.

Arc 1015.229 Escavazioni in un ipogeo cristiano de Bolsena. (Stevenson, H.) Roma, 1881.

Arc 1027.7.17 Escavazioni nel cimitero dei SS. Pietro e Marcellino. (Rossi, G.B. de.) Roma, 1882.

Arc 1348.24 Escher, A. Schweizerische Münz- und Geldgeschichte. Bern, 1881.

Arc 1335.140 Escorial. Biblioteca. Catalago de las monedas y medallas de la biblioteca de San Lorenzo de el Escorial. Madrid, 1935.

Arc 843.35 Escornalbou prehistòrich. (Serra-Viláró, J.) Castell de Sant Miquel d'Escornalbou, 1925.

Arc 838.12 Escriptos diversos. (Simões, A.F.) Coimbra, 1888.

Arc 1163.2.22 Escritura y lenguaje de España. (Paluzie y Cantelozella, Esteban.) Barcelona, 1935.

Arc 1261.4 Escudero de la Penna, José Marie. Sigilografía española. Madrid, 1875.

Htn Arc 1160.202.5* Escuela paleographica...letras antiguas. (Merino, Andres.) Madrid, 1780.

Arc 1153.19 Esempi di corsiva antico del secolo I...al IV. (Federici, V.) Roma, 1908.

Arc 1153.108F Esempi di scritture cancelleresche. (Mazzoleni, Jole.) Napoli, 1972.

Arc 1153.13 Esempj di scrittura latina. (Monaci, E.) Roma, 1898.

Arc 1261.50 Esfragistica medieval portuguesa. (Tovar.) Lisboa, 1937.

Arc 935.33 Eski foca, foca taukin koker. (Sartiaux, Felix.) Izmir, 1952.

Arc 1348.81 Eski sikkeler rehberi. (Bosch, Enin.) Istanbul, 1951.

Arc 1190.82.5 Eski yazilari okuma anahtari. (Yazir, Mahmud.) Istanbul, 1942.

Arc 830.84.5 Esmonnot, L. Néris. Vicus Neriomagus. Recherches sur ses monuments. Moulins, 1885.

Arc 600.188 Esna. (Sauneron, Serge.) Le Caire, 1959- 5v.

Arc 1493.25 España, 1869-1973: la peseta. 8. ed. (Vicenti, Jose A.) Madrid, 1973.

Arc 1493.22 La España firmitiva a través de las monedas ibéricas. (Ortega Galindo, Julio.) Bilbao, 1963.

Arc 838.32 La España primiva. (Pericat y Garcia, Luis.) Barcelona, 1950.

Arc 848.14.35 Espérandieu, Émile. Recueil général des bas-reliefs. Paris, 1931.

Arc 825.3.15 Espéraudieu, E. La maison carrée a Nîmes. Paris, 1929.

Htn Arc 1033.12.49*A Esplicatione del sacro lenzvolo ove fu involto il Signore. (Paleotti, A.) Bologna, 1599.

Arc 530.90 Esplorazioni e studi in Paflagonia e Cappadocia. (Jacopi, G.) Roma, 1937.

Arc 1015.223 Esplorazioni nelle catacombe. Siracusa. (Orsi, P.) Roma, 1893.

Arc 785.74F Esplorazioni sotto la confessione di San Pietro in Vaticano. Città del Vaticano, 1951. 2v.

Arc 750.39F Esposizione storica e topografica del foro romano. 2a ed. (Canina, Luigi.) Roma, 1845.

Arc 1020.10.46 Esquisse de Rome chrétienne. (Gerbet, O.P.) Paris, 1889. 3v.

Arc 935.10 Esquisse topographique de Constantinople. (Mordtmann, J.) Lille, 1892.

Arc 402.2.2 Esquisses archéologiques. (Reinach, S.) Paris, 1888.

Arc 736.2.3 Essai critique sur la topographie de Syracuse. (Letronne, A.) Paris, 1812.

Arc 1520.5 Essai de numismatique yproise. (Vandenpeereboom, A.) Bruxelles, 1877.

Arc 1500.1 Essai d'interpretation...médailles...celtes-gaulois. (Jeuffrain, A.) Tours, 1846.

Arc 1494.2 Essai d'interpretation des lettres B.N.M...dinars. (Blancard, Louis.) Marseille, n.d.

Arc 66.1.65 Essai sur Domitien. (Gsell, S.) Paris, 1894.

Arc 505.4.2 Essai sur la topographie de Tyr. (Berton, J. de.) Paris, 1843.

Arc 66.1.59 Essai sur l'administration du Royaume de Sicile. (Cadier, L.) Paris, 1891.

Arc 838.4 Essai sur l'art et l'industrie de l'Espagne primitive. (Paris, Pierre.) Paris, 1903. 2v.

Arc 387.1.25 Essai sur le comte de Caylus. (Rocheblave, S.) Paris, 1889.

Arc 66.1.149 Essai sur le province romaine de Béteque. (Thouvenot, R.) Paris, 1940.

Arc 66.1.89 Essai sur le regne de l'empereur Aurélien. (Homo, Leon.) Paris, 1904.

Arc 823.21.10F Essai sur l'époque barbare dans la Marne. (Goury, Georges.) Nancy, 1908.

Arc 830.76 Essai sur les antiquités du département de Lot-et-Garonne. (Saint-Amans, J.F.B.) Agen, 1859.

Arc 1473.2 Essai sur les arpres comnénats...de Trébisonde. (Pfaffenhoffen, F.) Paris, 1847.

Arc 66.1.171 Essai sur les chasses romaines. (Aymard, Jacques.) Paris, 1951. 2v.

Arc 590.3 Essai sur les momies. (Perrot, J.F.A.) Nimes, 1844.

Arc 1500.4 Essai sur les monnaies de Charles Ier, comté de Provence. (Blancard, Louis.) Paris, 1868.

Arc 1495.4F Essai sur les monnaies du Comte de Bourgogne. (Plantet, L.) Paris, 1865.

Arc 1500.43 Essai sur les monnaies du royaume. (Bigot, A.) Paris, 1857.

Arc 66.1.2 Essai sur les monuments grecs et romains relatifs au mythe de psyché. (Collignon, M.) Paris, 1877.

Arc 66.1.197 Essai sur les origines du principat. (Grenade, P.) Paris, 1961.

Arc 913.16 Essai sur les rites funéraires en Suisse des origines à la conquête romaine. (Viollier, David.) Paris, 1911.

Arc 1371.1 Essai sur les systèmes métriques et monétaires. v.1-2, tables. (Queipo, V.V.) Paris, 1859. 3v.

Arc 1166.4 Essai sur l'histoire du parchemin. (Peignot, G.) Paris, 1812.

Arc 1500.28 Essai sur l'histoire monetaire...de Béarn. (Bascle de Lagrèze, G.) Toulouse, 1855.

Arc 843.95 Essai sur l'origine des Basques Ibères et peuples apparentés. (Karst, Josef.) Strasbourg, 1954.

Arc 66.1.82 Essai sur Suétone. (Macé, A.) Paris, 1900.

Arc 1138.29 Essais de critique textuelle. (Quentin, Henri.) Paris, 1926.

Arc 830.78.15A Essais historiques sur les antiquités du département de la Haute-Loire. (Mangou de la Lande, C.F.J.) Saint-Quentin, 1826.

Arc 1377.1 An essay on ancient coins, medals, and gems. 2. ed. (Walsh, R.) London, 1828.

Arc 1470.6 An essay on Greek federal coinage. (Warren, J.L.) London, 1863.

Arc 1348.10 An essay on medals. (Pinkerton, John.) London, 1784.

Arc 1348.10.3 An essay on medals. (Pinkerton, John.) London, 1808. 2v.

Arc 1540.11 Essay on the numismatic history of the East Angles. (Haigh, D.H.) Leeds, 1845.

Arc 386.25 An essay on the study of antiquities. (Burgess, Thomas.) Oxford, 1781.

Arc 642.6 Essays in Aegean archaeology. (Casson, S.) Oxford, 1927.

Arc 1468.58 Essays in Greek coinage. Oxford, 1968.

Arc 1423.28 Essays in Jewish numismatics. (Meyshan, Josef.) Jerusalem, 1968.

Arc 943.44 Essays in pre-Columbian art and archaeology. (Lothrop, S.K.) Cambridge, Mass., 1961.

Arc 1478.55 Essays in Roman coinage. (Carson, R.A.G.) Oxford, 1956.

Arc 407.4A Essays on archaeological subjects. v.1-2. (Wright, T.) London, 1861.

Arc 398.2 Essays on art and archaeology. (Newton C.T.) London, 1880.

Arc 1418.3 Essays on Indian antiquities. (Prinsep, J.) London, 1858. 2v.

Arc 1163.17.7 Essex, England. Record Office. Examples of English handwriting. Essex? 1954.

Arc 1163.17.5 Essex, England. Record Office. Some examples of English handwriting. Chelmsford, 1949.

Arc 843.17 Estacio da Veiga, S.P.M. Memoria da antiquidades de Mertola. Lisboa, 1880.

Arc 843.11 Estaciones prehistoricas...desiertos. (Bardavíu Ponz, V.) Zaragoza, 1918.

Arc 843.27 Estações pre-romanas da idade do ferre nas visinhanças da figueira. (Santos Rocha, A. dos.) Porto, 1908.

Arc 830.148 Estampes mythologiques des Celtes. (Dujardin, A.) Étampes, 1904.

Arc 1443.6 Estampilles et poids musulmans en verre du cabinet des médailles. (Launois, Aimée.) Caire, 1959.

Arc 843.165 Estelas discoideas de la Peninsula Iberica. (Frankowski, Eugeniusz.) Madrid, 1920.

Arc 505.5.40 Estevan, M. Compendio del Rico Aparato, y Hermosa del templo de Salomon. Alcala, 1615.

Arc 938.95.5 Estlaste matmiskombed varafeodaalsete suhete tärkamise perioodil (11.-13. sajand). (Selirand, Jüri.) Tallinn, 1974.

Author and Title Listing

Arc 830.15 Estrangin, J.J. Études archéologiques, histoire et statistique sur Arles. Zix, 1838.
Arc 1033.17.253 Estratto di una lettera di Ancona di 27 giugno 1796. n.p., 1796.
Arc 746.50 Gli estruschi a Sesto Fiorentino. (Rilli, Nicola.) Firenze, 1964.
Arc 608.2.19 Estudio de arqueología cartaginesa. (Vives y Escudero, Antonio.) Madrid, 1917.
Arc 1493.4 Estudio de la moneda antigua española. (Zobel de Zangroniz, J.) Madrid, 1878. 2v.
Arc 94.32 Estudios ibéricos. Valencia. 1-4,1953-1956
Arc 1660.12 Estudios numismaticos. (Rosa, A.) Buenos Aires, n.d.
Arc 1153.33 Estudios paleográficos. (Millares Carlo, A.) Madrid, 1918.
Arc 943.6 Estudios sobre la historia de America. (Larrainzar, M.) Mexico, 1875-78. 5v.
Arc 843.231 Estudos arqueologicos. (Correia, Vergilio.) Coimbra, 1972.
Arc 723.44 L'età del bronzo nella penisola italiana. (Peroni, Renato.) Firenze, 1971-
Arc 726.60 L'età del ferro nel Piceno. Tesi. (Dumitrescu, V.) Bucarest, 1929.
Arc 830.96 Les établissements gallo-romaines de la plaine de Martres-Tolosanes. (Joulin, Léon.) Paris, 1901.
Arc 388.6 Les étapes de l'archéologie. 2. éd. (Daux, Georges.) Paris, 1948.
Arc 830.352 Les étapes du peuplement sur les grands causses des origines à l'époque gallo-romaine. (Maury, Jean.) Millau, 1967.
Arc 505.100 Etat de Syree. (Damascus. Musée National Syrien.) Damas, 1931.
Arc 66.1.73 L'état pontificale après le grand schisme. (Guiraud, J.) Paris, 1896.
Arc 858.7 Etchings of ancient remains. (Smith, C.R.) London, 1852.
Arc 861.10.7 Etchings of the Runic monuments in Isle of Man. (Kinnebrook, William.) London, 1841.
Arc 662.6 Eternal Greece. (Warner, R.) N.Y., 1962.
Arc 609.2.20 L'Éthiopie. (Leroy, Jules.) Paris, 1973.
Arc 5.5 Ethnographisch-archäologische Forschungen. Berlin. 1-6,1953-1959 2v.
Arc 5.10 Ethnographisch-archäologische Zeitschrift. Berlin. 1,1960+ 7v.
Arc 66.1.191 Etienne, Robert. La culte imperial dans la peninsule iberique d'Auguste à Dioclétien. Paris, 1958.
Arc 608.50 Etienne, Robert. Le guarbier nord-est de Volubilis. Paris, 1960. 2v.
Arc 810.65 Etienne, Robert. La vie quotidienne à Pompéi. Paris, 1966.
Arc 936.20.10 Etiopienii in Dacia preistorica. (Tonescu, G.M.) București, 1926.
Arc 543.146.35 Etnicheskaia istoriia Severo-Zapadnoi Turkmenii v srednie veka. (Poliakov, Sergei P.) Moskva, 1973.
Arc 742.01 Pamphlet box. Etruscan antiquities.
Arc 746.1.2 Etruscan Bologna. (Burton, R.F.) London, 1876.
Arc 746.20 Etruscan Perugia. (Shaw, C.) Baltimore, 1939.
X Cg Arc 743.17 Etruscan places. (Lawrence, D.H.) London, 1932.
Arc 743.17.10 Etruscan places. (Lawrence, D.H.) Middlesex, 1950.
Arc 743.11 The Etruscans. (Randall-MacIver, D.) Oxford, 1927.
Arc 743.18 The Etruscans and their art. (Hanfmann, G.M.A.) n.p., 1940.
Arc 740.201 Etruskische Spiegel. v.1-2,3,4,5. (Gerhard, E.) Berlin, 1843- 4v.
Arc 743.19 Les Etrusques et leur civilisation. (Nogara, B.) Paris, 1936.
Arc 915.54F Ettlinger, Elisabeth. Die römischen Fibeln in der Schweiz. Bern, 1973.
Arc 1016.3 Étude archéologique sur le reliquaire du chef de S. Laurent. (Barbier de Montault, X.) Rome, 1864.
Arc 830.26 Étude d'archéologie celtique...Seine-et-Oise. (Barranger, A.) Paris, 1864.
Arc 672.1.29 Étude de préhistorie crétoise. (Hazzidakis, J.) Paris, 1921.
Arc 66.1.36 Étude du dialecte chypriote. (Beaudoin, M.) Paris, 1884.
Arc 843.232 Étude épigraphique et iconographique des stèles funéraires de Vigo. (Julia, Dolorès.) Heidelberg, 1971.
Arc 1500.40.5 Étude historique sur la numismatique bretonne. (Lecoq-Kerneven, J.) Rennes, 1868.
Arc 1590.5 Étude historique sur les monnaies...de l'ordre de Saint Jean de Jérusalem. (Laugier.) Marseille, 1868.
Arc 820.200 Etude préhistorique sur la Savoie. (Perrin, A.) Paris, 1870.
Arc 830.95 Étude sur la basilique de Saint-Just. (Fiancette d'Agos, L. de.) Saint-Gaudens, 1856.
Arc 66.1.22 Étude sur la chronique de Guillaume le Breton. (Delaborde, H.F.) Paris, 1881.
Arc 1030.57 Étude sur la paléographie des inscriptions lapidaires de la fin de l'époque mérovingienne aux dernières années du XIIe siècle. (Deschamps, P.) Paris, 1929.
Arc 830.18.15 Étude sur la viabilité romaine dans le département de Vauclus. (Rochetin, L.) Avignon, 1883.
Arc 823.19.125 Étude sur Lambèse par Wilmanns. (Thédenat, H.) Paris, 1884.
Arc 66.1.62 Étude sur le liber censuum. (Fabre, P.) Paris, 1892.
Arc 66.1 Étude sur le liber pontificalis. (Duchesne, L.) Paris, 1877.
Arc 1076.3.23 Étude sur l'emploi de clochettes. (Morillot, L.) Dijon, 1888.
Arc 66.1.30 Étude sur les lécythes blancs attiques. (Pottier, E.) Paris, 1883.
Arc 1500.36 Étude sur les messageries et les postes. (Florange, C.) Paris, 1925.
Arc 1033.35.41 Étude sur les précieux reliquaire phylactère du XIIe siècle. (Bastelaer, D.A.) Anvers, 1880.
Arc 820.207F Étude sur les sépultures barbares du midi et de l'ouest de la France. (Barrière-Flavy, Casimir.) Toulouse, 1892.
Arc 1033.19.9 Étude sur l'étimacia symbole du jugement dernier dans l'iconographie grecque chrétienne. (Durand, Paul.) Chartres, 1867.
Arc 66.1.42 Étude sur l'histoire des sarcophages chrétiens. (Grousset, R.) Paris, 1885.
Arc 66.1.17 Étude sur préneste. (Fernique, E.) Paris, 1880.
Arc 830.94 Étude sur quelques antiquités trouvées en Picardie. (Danicourt, A.) Paris, 1886.
Arc 66.1.79 Étude sur Théocrite. (Legrand, P.E.) Paris, 1898.
Arc 830.15 Études archéologiques, histoire et statistique sur Arles. (Estrangin, J.J.) Zix, 1838.
Arc 380.213 Études archéologiques, linguistiques. (Leemans, C.) Leide, 1885.
Arc 612.71 Études archéologiques et géographiques. (Bachelot de la Pylaie, Auguste Jean Marie.) Quimper, 1970.
Arc 830.66 Études archéologiques sur les Eaux Thermalès. (Greppo, J.G.H.) Paris, 1846.
Arc 65.12 Études chypriotes. (Athens. École Française.) Paris. 1-2,1961-1962 2v.
Arc 672.1.55 Études crétoises. (Athens. École Française.) Paris. 1-19 16v.
Arc 618.5 Études d'archéologie celtique. (Martin, Henri.) Paris, 1872.
Arc 402.1 Études d'archéologie et d'art. (Rayet, O.) Paris, 1888.
Arc 1468.61 Études d'archéologie numismatique. (Lacroix, Léon.) Paris, 1974.
Arc 416.2.2 Études d'archéologie orientale. (Clermont-Ganneau, Charles.) Paris, 1880. 2v.
Arc 853.3.15 Études d'archéologie rhénane. (Grenier, Albert.) Paris, 1925.
Arc 1200.9 Etudes de diplomatique sur les actes, des iquenotaires de Paris. (Boüard, A. de.) Paris, 1910.
Arc 1468.34 Études de numismatique grecque. (Robert, Louis.) Paris, 1951.
Arc 608.6.46 Études d'épigraphie. (Leschi, Louis.) Paris, 1957.
Arc 66.1.21 Études d'epigraphie juridique. (Cuq, E.) Paris, 1881.
Arc 400.16 Études d'ethnographie préhistorique. (Pietto, E.) Paris, 189-. 9 pam.
Arc 936.115.10 Études histriennes. (Stoian, Iorgu.) Bruxelles, 1972.
Arc 397.4 Études iconographiques et archéologiques. (Müntz, Eugène.) Paris, 1887.
Arc 1304.10 Études numismatiques. Bruxelles. 1-4,1960-1967//
Arc 820.2 Études paléoethnologiques dans le bassin du Rhône. Âge du bronze. (Chantre, Ernest.) Paris, 1875-76. 4v.
Arc 65.9 Études péloponnésiennes. (Athens. École Française.) Paris. 1-5 5v.
Arc 112.10 Études Roussillonnaises. Perpignan. 1-5,1951-1956 6v.
Arc 34.10 Études sud-arabiques. Le Caire.
Arc 830.91.10 Études sur d'anciens lieux de sépultre dans l'Aisne. (Pilloy, Jules.) Saint-Quentin, 1880-99. 3v.
Arc 66.1.11 Études sur la langue de Yite-Live. (Riemann, O.) Paris, 1879.
Arc 825.3.25 Études sur la Maison Carrée de Nîmes. (Balty, J.C.) Bruxelles, 1960.
X Cg Arc 66.1.53 Études sur l'administration Byzantine. (Diehl, C.) Paris, 1888.
Arc 903.1 Etudes sur l'age de bronze...Hongrie. (Undset, F.) Christiana, 1880.
Arc 600.1.13 Études sur l'ancienne Alexandrie. (Togheb, A.M. de.) Paris, 1909.
Arc 387.2 Études sur l'antiquité historique. (Chabas, F.) Paris, 1873.
Arc 66.1.83 Etudes sur les gesta martyrum. (Dofourco, A.) Paris, 1900.
Arc 1018.2 Études sur les monuments primitifs. (Lefort, L.) Paris, 1885.
Arc 66.1.100 Études sur l'histoire financière d'Athènes au Ve siècle. (Cavaignac, E.) Paris, 1908.
Arc 66.1.204 Études sur Properce; problèmes d'inspiration et d'art. (Boucher, Jean-Paul.) Paris, 1965.
Arc 497.24 Études syriennes. (Cumont, Franz.) Paris, 1917.
Arc 69.4 Études thasiennes. (Athens. École Française.) Paris. 1-8 8v.
Arc 823.19.70 Etvi à collyre égyptien. (Thédenat, H.) Paris, 1881.
Arc 1033.12.175 Eufrasio. Memorie storico-critiche...lagrime di...Dongo. Lugano, 1808.
Arc 279.2 Eurasia septentrionalis antiqua. Helsinki. 1-3
Arc 612.52F Die europäischen Moorleichenfunde. (Dieck, Alfred.) Neumünster, 1965.
Arc 612.46 L'Europe à la fin de l'âge de la pierre. (Symposium Consacre aux Problèmes du Neolithique Européen.) Praha, 1961.
Arc 612.5 L'Europe préhistorique. (Müller, S.) Paris, 1907.
Arc 383.36 The European community in later prehistory: studies in honour of C.F.C. Hawkes. London, 1971.
Arc 1453.8 European crowns, 1700-1800. (Davenport, J.S.) Galenburg, Ill., 1961.
Arc 730.2.3 Euryalos e le opere di difesa di Siracusa. (Cavallari, F.S.) Palermo, 1893.
Arc 723.2 Eustace, J.C. A classical tour through Italy. London, 1841. 3v.
Arc 1150.208.9F L'evangeliaire de Saint-Vaast d'Arras. (Delisle, L.) Paris, 1888.
Arc 1470.40 Evans, A.J. The "Horsemen" of Tarentum. London, 1889.
Arc 1470.4.15 Evans, A.J. Syracusan "medallions" and their engravers in the light of recent finds. London, 1892.
Arc 682.11 Evans, Arthur. The shaft graves and bee-hive tombs of Mycenae and their interrelation. London, 1929.
Arc 672.1.26 Evans, Arthur John. Early Nilotic, Libyan, and Egyptian relations with Minoan Crete. London, 1925.
Arc 672.1.27.5 Evans, Arthur John. Index to the palace of Minos. London, 1936.
Arc 672.1.130 Evans, Arthur John. The palace of Minos. N.Y., 1964. 6v.
Arc 672.1.131 Evans, Arthur John. The palace of Minos. Index. N.Y., 1964.
Arc 672.1.27 Evans, Arthur John. The palace of Minos. v.1; v.2, pt.1-2; v.3; v.4, pt.1-2. London, 1921-35. 6v.
Arc 880.32 Evans, Emyr Estyn. Prehistoric and early Christian Ireland. London, 1966.
Arc 1613.2.3 Evans, G.G. Illustrated history of the United States mint. Philadelphia, 1889.
Arc 1613.2 Evans, G.G. Illustrated history of the United States mint. Philadelphia, 1890.
Arc 1613.2.4 Evans, G.G. Illustrated history of the United States mint. Philadelphia, 1891.
Arc 1613.2.2 Evans, G.G. Illustrated history of the United States mint. Philadelphia, 1892.
Arc 1613.2.5 Evans, G.G. Illustrated history of the United States mint. Philadelphia, 1893.
Arc 543.29 Evans, Ivor H.N. Papers on the ethnology and archaeology of the Malay Peninsula. Cambridge, Eng., 1927.
Arc 870.1.2 Evans, J. The ancient bronze implements, weapons and ornaments of Great Britain. London, 1881.
Arc 870.1.3 Evans, J. The ancient bronze implements, weapons and ornaments of Great Britain. N.Y., 1881.
Arc 870.1.1 Evans, J. The ancient stone implements, weapons and ornaments of Great Britain. London, 1897.
Arc 870.1 Evans, J. The ancient stone implements, weapons and ornaments of Great Britain. N.Y., 1872.

Arc 1538.11 Evans, J. Coins of the ancient Britons. v.1 and supplement. London, 1864-90. 2v.

Arc 136.1.80 Evans, Joan. A history of the Society of Antiquaries. Oxford, 1956.

Arc 389.3 Evans, Joan. Time and chance; story of Arthur Evans and his forebears. London, 1943.

Arc 726.59.30 Evans, John D. Malta. London, 1959.

Arc 682.35 Evans, John Davies. Excavations at Saliagos near Antiparos. London, 1968.

Arc 885.10 Evans, William. The Meini Hirion and Sarns of Anglesey. Llangefni, 1927.

Htn Arc 1670.2* Evelyn, J. Numismata. A discourse of medals. London, 1697.

Arc 401.2.10 Everyday life in prehistoric times. 4. ed. (Quennell, Marjorie (Courtney).) London, 1952.

Arc 858.36 Everyday life in Roman Britain. (Quennell, M. (Mrs.)) London, 1924.

Arc 401.2.5 Everyday life in the new stone, bronze, and early iron ages. 2. ed. (Quennell, Marjorie (Courtney).) London, 1931.

Arc 1025.28.45 The evidencce of the catacombs for the doctrines and organization of the primitive church. (Marucchi, O.) London, 1929.

Arc 968.2.55 Evidence of early man in North America...archaeological work in New Mexico. (Howard, E.B.) Philadelphia, 1935.

Arc 870.29 Evison, Vera I. The fifth-century invasions south of the Thames. London, 1965.

Arc 226.2 Evkönyve. (Orsjágos Magyar Régészeti Jársulat.) Budapest. 1-2,1920-1926

Arc 458.2.10 L'évolution du Stûpa en Asie. (Combaz, Gisbert.) Bruxelles, 1933. 3 pam.

Arc 1348.25 Evolution of coinage. (McDonald, George.) Cambridge, 1916.

Arc 1663.11 The evolution of the Boston medal. (Arnold, H.P.) Boston, 1901.

Arc 384.18 Evolution und Revolution in alten Orient und in Europa. Das Neolithikum als historische Erscheinung. (Deutsche Historiker Gesellschaft. Fachgruppe Ur- und Frühgeschichte.) Berlin, 1971.

Arc 612.53 Evropský pravěk. (Filip, Jan.) Praha, 1962.

Arc 935.75 Evrurumda eski merorliklarve resimli mezar taşlari. (Başar, Zeki.) Ankara, 1973.

Arc 1212.4 Ewald, W. Siegelkunde. München, 1914.

Arc 1248.2 Ewe, Herbert. Schiffe auf Siegeln. 1. Aufl. Rostock, 1972.

Arc 953.23A Ewers, J.C. Plains Indian painting. Stanford, 1939.

Arc 843.192 Ewert, Christian. Islamische Funde in Balaguer und die Aljaferia in Zaragoza. Berlin, 1971.

Arc 1367.3 Ex nummis historia. (Magnaguti, A.G.) Roma, 1949-53. 12v.

Arc 1033.181 Ex voto. (Kriss-Rettenbeck, Lenz.) Zürich, 1972.

Arc 1200.14 Examen des chartes de l'eglise romaine. (Huillard-Bréholles.) Paris, 1865.

Arc 397.6 An examination of the tithe. (March, H.C.) Rochdale, 1887. 5 pam.

Arc 1163.17.7 Examples of English handwriting. (Essex, England. Record Office.) Essex? 1954.

Arc 600.200F Exavations at Ballana, 1958-1959. (Farid, Shafik.) Cairo, 1963.

Arc 608.23.10 The exavations at Faras. Thesis. (Vantini, Giovanni.) Bologna, 1970.

Arc 843.228 Excavaciones arqueológicas en el cerro Salomón. (Blanco, A.) Madrid, 1970.

Arc 843.32F Excavaciones de Numancia. (Spain. Comisión ejecutiva de las excavaciones de Numancia.) Madrid, 1912.

Arc 843.197 Excavaciones en Atxeta. (Barandiaran, J.M.) Bilbao, 1961.

Arc 843.77 Excavaciones en Italica. (Fernandez, L.M.) Sevilla, 1904.

Arc 843.85 Excavaciones en Navarra. (Institución Principe de Viana Pamplona.) Pamplona, 1947. 7v.

Arc 609.17F Excavation at Dawu. (Shaw, Thurstan.) Edinburgh, 1961.

Arc 136.4.5 Excavation Committee. Report for 1909. Oxford, 1910.

X Cg Arc 505.14 Excavation of Gezer, 1902-1905, 1907-1909. (Macalister, R.A.S.) London, 1912. 3v.

Arc 875.128 Excavation of prehistoric and mediaeval homesteads at Knapps, Renfrewshire. (Newall, Frank.) Paisley, 1965.

Arc 861.109 The excavation of Roman and mediaeval London. (Grimes, William F.) London, 1968.

Arc 861.168 Excavation of Staple Howe. (Brewster, Thomas.) Wentringham, 1963.

Arc 710.27F The excavation of the Athenian Acropolis 1882-1890. v.1-2. (Kawerau, Georg.) Copenhagen, 1974.

Arc 861.178 The excavation of the Iron Age camp on Bredon Hill. (Hencken, Thalassa Cruso.) London, 1939.

Arc 505.92.5 The excavation of the main theater at Petra, 1961-1962, final report. (Hammond, Philip C.) London, 1965.

Arc 861.21.17 Excavation of the Roman forts at Castleshaw. (Andrew, S.) Manchester, 1911.

Arc 505.5.85 Excavations...Ophel, Jerusalem, 1923-1925. (Macalister, R.A.S.) London, 1926.

Arc 861.11.3 Excavations...Roman city at Silchester, Hants in 1890. (Fox, G.E.) Westminster, 1891.

Arc 861.11 Excavations...Roman city at Silchester, Hants in 1895. (Hope, W.H. St. J.) Westminster, 1896.

Arc 505.5.90 Excavations...Tyropoeon Valley, Jerusalem, 1927. (Crowfoot, J.W.) London, 1929.

Arc 440.11 Excavations at Ahar (Tambavati) [1961-62]. 1. ed. (Sankalia, Hasmukh Dhirajlal.) Poona, 1969.

Arc 450.5 Excavations at Brahmapuri, 1945-46. (Sankalia, Hasmukh Dhirajlal.) Poona, 1952.

Arc 855.224F Excavations at Caerwent, Monmouthshire 1901-1903. (Ashby, Thomas.) London, 1902-1904.

Arc 861.38.10 Excavations at Camerton, Somerset. (Wedlake, William.) Camerton, 1958.

Arc 830.11.15 Excavations at Carnac. (Miln, James.) Edinburgh, 1877.

Arc 830.11.19 Excavations at Carnac. (Miln, James.) Edinburgh, 1881.

Arc 608.2.23 Excavations at Carthage 1925. (Kelsey, Francis W.) N.Y., 1926.

Arc 955.2.4 Excavations at Casa Grande, Arizona in 1906-07. v.1-2. (Fewkes, J.W.) Washington, 1907.

Arc 442.15 Excavations at Chanhu-Daro...1935-36. (Mackay, Ernest J.H.) Washington, 1938.

Arc 861.135 Excavations at Clausentum (Southampton). (Cotton, M. Aylwin.) London, 1958.

Arc 875.130 Excavations at Clicknimin, Shetland. (Hamilton, John.) Edinburgh, 1968.

Arc 608.17 The excavations at Cyrene. (Norton, Richard.) N.Y., 1911.

Arc 600.54 Excavations at Deir el Bahri, 1911-1931. (Winlock, H.E.) N.Y., 1942.

Arc 885.25.5 Excavations at Dinorben, 1965-69. (Savory, Hubert Newman.) Cardiff, 1971.

Arc 505.45.20 The excavations at Dura-Europas. (Yale University.) New Haven, 1943-1949. 13v.

Arc 505.45A The excavations at Dura-Europas. pt.1-9. (Baur, P.V.C.) New Haven, 1929-1946. 9v.

Arc 443.2 Excavations at Dwarka. 1. ed. (Ansari, Zainuddin.) Poona, 1966.

Arc 674.15F Excavations at Eutresis in Boeotia. (Goldman, Hetty.) Cambridge, Mass., 1931.

Arc 885.5 Excavations at Gelli Gaer camp. (James, C.H.) Cardiff, 1899?

Arc 600.46F Excavations at Giza, 1929-1930. v.1-10. (Hassan, S.) Oxford, 1932. 13v.

Arc 600.46.5F Excavations at Giza, 1945-50. (Abd el Monem, Joussef Abubakr.) Cairo, 1953.

Arc 976.8 Excavations at Green Spring Plantation. (United States. National Park Service.) Yorktown, 1955.

Arc 447.6.5F Excavations at Harappa. (Vats, Madho Sarup.) Delhi, 1940. 2v.

Arc 600.225 The excavations at Helwan. 1st ed. (Saad, Zaki Yusef.) Norman, 1969.

Arc 875.105 Excavations at Jarlshof. (Hamilton, J.R.C.) Edinburgh, 1956.

Arc 505.66.10 Excavations at Jerico. (Joint Expedition of the British School of Archaeology.) London, 1960. 2v.

X Cg Arc 501.17.5A Excavations at Jerusalem 1894-1897. (Bliss, F.J.) London, 1898.

Arc 450.32 The excavations at Kauśāmbī (1957-59). (Sharma, G.R.) Allahabad, 1960.

Arc 861.194 Excavations at King John's hunting lodge, Writtle, Essex, 1955-57. (Rahtz, Philip.) London, 1969.

Arc 961.1.25 Excavations at Kolomoki. v.1-2. (Sears, William H.) Athens, 1950?

Arc 451.3 Excavations at Langhnaj, 1944-63. 1. ed. v.1-2. (Sankalia, Hasmukh Dhirajlal.) Poona, 1965.

Arc 681.20 Excavations at Lefkandi, Euboea, 1964-66. (Popham, Mervyn R.) London, 1968.

Arc 452.10 The excavations at Maheshwar and Navdatoli. (Sankalia, Hasmukh Dhirajlal.) Baroda, 1958.

Arc 726.69F Excavations at Minturnae. (Pennsylvania. University. University Museum.) Rome, 1933-35. 2v.

Arc 503.7F Excavations at Nessana. (Colt Archaeological Institute.) Princeton, 1950. 3v.

Arc 684.9 Excavations at Olynthus. (John Hopkins University.) Baltimore, 1929-52. 14v.

Arc 505.124F Excavations at Ramat Rahel, seasons 1959 and 1960. (Joint Expedition of the University of Rome and the Hebrew University.) Rome, 1962.

Arc 505.124.2F Excavations at Ramat Rahel, seasons 1961 and 1962. (Joint Expedition of the University of Rome and the Hebrew University.) Rome, 1964.

Arc 682.35 Excavations at Saliagos near Antiparos. (Evans, John Davies.) London, 1968.

Arc 483.10 Excavations at Samarra, 1936-1939. (Iraq. Department of Antiquities.) Baghdad, 1940.

Arc 458.14 Excavations at Sanganakallu and Songaon. (Ansari, Z.D.) Poona, 1969. 3 pam.

Arc 584.3.10 Excavations at Saqqara, 1937-1938. (Emery, W.B.) Cairo, 1939.

Arc 584.3.5F Excavations at Saqqara. (Emery, W.B.) Cairo, 1938.

Arc 600.175 Excavations at Saqqara. (Firth, Cecil M.) Le Caire, 1926. 2v.

Arc 861.180 Excavations at Shakenoak Farm. v.1-4. (Brodribb, Arthur Charles Conant.) Oxford, Eng., 1968- 3v.

Arc 861.120 Excavations at Star Caer. (Clark, J.G.D.) Cambridge, Eng., 1954.

Arc 543.130 The excavations at Surkh Kotal and the problem of Hellenism in Bactria and India. (Schlumberger, D.) London, 1961.

Arc 670.4F Excavations at the Heraion of Argos. 1892. (Walston, Charles.) Boston, 1892.

Arc 861.93 Excavations at the Roman fort at Brough-on-Humber. (Corder, Philip.) Hull, 1934.

Arc 861.93.5 Excavations at the Roman town at Brough-Petuaria, 1937. (Corder, Philip.) Hull, 1938.

Arc 681.1.5 Excavations at Thermi in Lesbos. (Lamb, Winifred.) Cambridge, Eng., 1936.

Arc 861.29.20 Excavations at Virsconium (Wroxeter), 1937. (Kenyon, K.M.) Shrewsbury, 1937.

Arc 540.6 The excavations at Vounous-Bellapais in Cyprus. (Dikaios, P.) London, 1940.

Arc 861.29.15 Excavations at Wroxeter, 1936. (Kenyon, K.M.) Shrewsbury, 1936.

Arc 968.1.9 Excavations in an Erie Indian village. (Parker, A.C.) n.p., 1907.

Arc 493.6 Excavations in Azerbaijan. 1. ed. (Burton Brown, T.) London, 1951.

Arc 672.11 Excavations in Chios, 1952-1955. (Boardman, John.) London, 1967.

Arc 855.219.5F Excavations in Cranbone Chase. (Fox-Pitt-Rivers.) London, 1887-1905. 5v.

Arc 537.13.1PF Excavations in Cyprus. 1. ed. (British Museum. Department of Greek and Roman Antiquities.) London, 1970.

Arc 488.32 Excavations in Iran: the British contribution. Oxford, 1972.

Arc 861.135.5 Excavations in medieval Southampton 1953-1969. Leicester, Eng., 1975. 2v.

X Cg Arc 500.7 Excavations in Palestine, 1895-1900. (Bliss, F.J.) London, 1902.

Arc 505.147.1 The excavations in the old city of Jerusalem near the Temple Mount. (Mazar, Benjamin.) Jerusalem, 1971.

Arc 505.102F Excavations in the Plain of Antioch. Chicago, 1960- 2v.

Arc 969.15.5 The excavations of Sainte-Marie I. (Kidd, Kenneth E.) Toronto, 1949.

Arc 716.4.12 Excavations of the Athenian Agora. (American School of Classical Studies at Athens.) Princeton. 1-9

Arc 600.49 The excavations of the Egyptian university in the neolithic site at Maadi. (Menghin, O.) Cairo, 1932.

Arc 858.72 Excavations on defence sites. (Grimes, W.F.) London, 1960.

Arc 861.55 Excavations on Rockbourne Downs, Hampshire. (Summer, H.) London, 1914.

Arc 885.22 Excavations on the site of the Roman fort of Kanovium at Caerhun. (Reynolds, P.K.B.) Cardiff, 1938.

Arc 861.61 Excavations on the site of the Romano-British town of Magna, Kenchester. (Jack, G.H.) Hereford, 1916.

Author and Title Listing

Arc 1.5.4.10 — Excavations on the slopes of the Acropolis. Report. (American School of Classical Studies at Athens.) 7-20

Arc 309.15 — Excavators' Club. Papers. Cambridge, Mass. 1-2,1940-1945

Arc 1016.230.2 — Excellentissimo ac revm̃o dño Aloisio Tripepi. De authenticitate S. Sindonis Taurinensis. (Catholic Church. Congregatio Indulgentiarum et Sacrarum Reliquiarum.) Roma, 1901.

Arc 785.13.65 — Excerpta ex antiquis scriptoribus quae ad Forum Romanum spectant. (Owen, A.S.) Oxonii, 1930.

Arc 810.19 — Une excursion à Pompéi. (Guillaume, Paul.) Paris, 1880.

Arc 662.1 — An excursion in the Peloponnesus. (Wyse, T.) London, 1865- 2v.

Arc 830.4 — Excursions archéologiques dans les environs de Compiègne. 1869-74, 1875-1900. (Compiègne, France. Société Historique.) Compiègne, 1875. 2v.

Arc 643.1 — Excursions archéologiques en Grèce. (Diehl, C.) Paris, 1890.

Arc 643.1.4 — Excursions archéologiques en Grèce. 5. éd. (Diehl, C.) Paris, 1903.

Arc 843.15 — Excursions arqueológicas. Ciutats focenses del litoral coseta. (Gibert y Olivé, A.M.) Barcelona, 1900.

Arc 643.1.5A — Excursions in Greece. (Diehl, C.) London, 1893.

Arc 1163.4 — Exercises pour la lecture des manuscrits arabes. (Cherbonneau, A.) Paris, 1853.

Arc 1510.17 — Exercitatio historica de Joh. Uratislaviensibus. (Rhon, G.) Uratslaviae, 1693.

Arc 861.206 — Exeter in Roman times. (Fox, Aileen Mary Henderson.) Exeter, 1973.

Arc 421.20 — An exhibition of Chinese antiquities from Ch'ang Sha. (Yale University. Gallery of Fine Arts.) New Haven, 1939.

Arc 1613.13 — Exhibition of United States and colonial coins, Jan. 17 to Feb. 18, 1914. Catalogue. (American Numismatic Society, N.Y.) N.Y., 1914.

Arc 432.25 — Expansion of Indo-Aryan culture during Pallava rule as evidenced by inscriptions. (Chhabra, Bahadur Chand.) Delhi, 1965.

Arc 505.116 — Expedition archéologique dans l'Antiochène occidentale. (Mécérian, Jean.) Beyrouth, 1965.

Arc 543.70 — Expédition en Arabie centrale. (Lysjsms, Philippe.) Paris, 1956. 3v.

Arc 543.70.10 — Expédition Philhy-Ryckmans-Lippens en Arabie. Expédition Philhy-Ryskmane-Lippens en Arabie. v.3. Louvain, 1962- 3v.

Arc 543.70.10 — Expédition Philhy-Ryskmane-Lippens en Arabie. v.3. (Expédition Philhy-Ryckmans-Lippens en Arabie.) Louvain, 1962- 3v.

Arc 505.125 — The expedition to the Judean desert, 1960-1961. (Israel Exploration.) Jerusalem, 1963.

Arc 1153.109F — L'expertise des éscritures médiévales. (Gilissen, Léon.) Gand, 1973.

Arc 757.3 — Explanatory index to the map of ancient Rome. (Cookesley, W.G.) Eton, 1851.

Arc 1033.72 — Explicatio 2 sarcophagorum...baptismatis. (Ciampini, J.) Roma, 1597.

Arc 1418.4 — Explication de cinq médailles...du Bengale. (Reinaud, J.T.) Paris, 1823.

Arc 1582.1 — Explication de la figure problématique. (Tilesius von Tilenau, Adolf.) St. Petersbourg, 1864.

Arc 726.10.4 — Explication de la mosaique de Palestrine. (Barthélemy, J.J.) Paris, 1760.

Arc 561.1.5 — Explication des monuments de l'Égypte et de l'Ethiopie. (Pierret, Paul.) Paris, 1885.

Arc 1480.11 — Explication d'une marque monétaire du tempe de Constantin. (Mowat, Robert.) Paris, 1886.

Htn Arc 1670.56.5F* — Explication historique et critique des médailles de l'oeuvre du Chevalier Hedlinger. (Hedlinger, J.K.) Basle, 1778.

Arc 843.59 — Exploración de calorce dolmenes del Aralar. (Aranzadi, T.) Pamplona, 1918.

Arc 843.64 — Exploraciones de la caverna de Santimamiñe. Basondo: Cortezubi. Memoria 2-3. (Biscay, Sain. Disputación Provincial. Junta de Cultura.) Bilbao, 1931-35. 2v.

Arc 843.57 — Exploraciones prehistóricas en Guepiezcoa los años 1924-1927. (Aranzadi, T. de.) San Sebastian, 1928.

Arc 673.12F — Exploration archéologique de Délos. (Chapouthier, F.) Paris, 1935.

Arc 687.1.5 — Exploration archéologique de Rhodes. v.1-6. (Blinkenberg, C.) København, 1903-12.

Arc 543.4FA — Exploration in Turkestan. Expedition of 1904. (Pumpelly, R.) Washington, 1908. 2v.

Arc 967.4 — The exploration of Bushey Cavern near Cavetown, Maryland. (Peabody, Charles.) Andover, 1908.

Arc 967.2.5 — The exploration of Jacobs Cavern, McDonald County, Missouri. (Peabody, Charles.) Norwood, 1904.

Arc 608.6.22 — Exploration scientifique de l'Algérie. Paris, 1912. 2v.

Arc 608.1.5 — Explorations épigraphiques et archéologiques en Tunise. v.1-3. (Cagnat, R.) Paris, 1883-6.

Arc 530.12.10 — Explorations in Hittite Asia Minor, 1927-28. (Osten, H.H. von der.) Chicago, 1929.

Arc 530.12.5 — Explorations in Hittite Asia Minor. (Osten, H.H. von der.) Chicago, 1927.

Arc 955.2.12 — Explorations in northeastern Arizona. (Guernsey, S.J.) Cambridge, Mass., 1931.

Arc 682.15A — Explorations in the island of Mochlos. (Seager, R.B.) Boston, 1912.

Arc 635.217.5F — Exploratoire archéologique de Délos. (Homolle, T.) Paris. 1-30 7v.

Arc 785.21 — Exposé Diene découverte...le Chévalier de Freden. (Oberlin, J.J.) Strasbourg, 1796.

Arc 1033.35.66 — Exposé historique de l'honneur...du culte...au bois de la vraie croix. Bruxelles, 1790. 2 pam.

Arc 838.16F — Exposición de arte prehistórico español. (Sociedad Española de Amigos del Arte.) Madrid, 1921.

Arc 1304.5 — Exposición Iberoamericana de Numismatica y Medallistica. Boletin. Barcelona. 1,1958

Arc 830.240 — Exposition. (Besançon, France. Musée des Beaux-Arts.) Besançon, 1958.

Arc 1675.75 — Exposition: Effigies et portraits. (Bibliothèque Nationale, Paris.) Paris? 1957.

Arc 823.19.75 — Exposition d'Utique. (Thédenat, H.) Paris, 1881.

Arc 1518.10 — Exposition numismatique, Bruxelles, Bibliothèque Albert I., 30 avril-24 mai, 1966. (Société Royale de Numismatique de Belgique.) Bruxelles, 1966.

Arc 1020.9.135 — Exposition religieuse de Rome 1870. Antiquités chrétiennes. (Barbier de Montault, X.) Rome, 1870.

Arc 1020.9.137 — Exposition religieuse de Rome 1870. L'archéologie et l'art chrétien. (Barbier de Montault, X.) Arras, 1877.

Arc 853.83.15 — Der Externstein. (Hamkens, F.H.) Tübingen, 1971.

Arc 853.17 — Der Externstein aus Zeit des Heithenthums in Westfalen. Detmold, 1879.

Arc 853.83.5 — Die Externsteine. (Gsaenger, Hans.) Freiburg, 1964.

Arc 853.83.10 — Die Externsteine im Fürstenthum Lippe-Detmold. (Giefers, Wilhelm.) Paderborn, 1851.

Arc 1138.65.5 — Extinct languages. (Friedrich, Johannes.) N.Y., 1957.

Arc 953.7 — Extinct races of America - the mound builders. Review. (Morris, C.) n.p., n.d.

Arc 823.19.100 — Extrait des procès-verbaux. (Thédenat, H.) Nogent-le-Rotrou, 1881.

Arc 935.3 — Extrait d'un notice sur les tombeaux des empereurs de Constantinople. (Brunet de Presle.) Paris, 1856.

Arc 540.1.12 — Extraits de l'histoire générale des hommes vivants. (Cesnola, L.P.) Genève, 1869.

Arc 823.70 — Eydoux, Henri Paul. Hommes et dieux de la Gaule. Paris, 1961.

Arc 389.4.1 — Eydoux, Henri Paul. In search of lost worlds. 1. American ed. N.Y., 1971.

Arc 823.65 — Eydoux, Henri Paul. Lumières sur la Gaule. Paris, 1960.

Arc 823.80 — Eydoux, Henri Paul. Monuments et trésors de la Gaule. Paris, 1962.

Arc 389.6.2 — Eydoux, Henri Paul. Realités et énigmes de l'archéologie. 2. éd. Paris, 1964.

Arc 823.75 — Eydoux, Henri Paul. Rescurrection de la Gaule. Paris, 1961.

Arc 1264.12 — Eygun, F. Sigillographie du Poitou jusqu'en 1515. Poitiers, 1938.

Arc 1264.12.5 — Eygun, F. Sigillographie du Poitou jusqu'en 1515. Thèse. Macon, 1938.

Arc 672.4 — Ta ez antikythēren eyrēmata. (Staïs,V.) Athēnai, 1905.

Arc 387.23.6 — F. Catherwood, architect-explorer of two worlds. (Hagen, Victor Wolfgang von.) Barre, Mass, 1968.

Arc 392.7.80 — F. Haverfield, 1860-1919. (MacDonald, G.) London, 1921.

Htn Arc 1420.2F* — F. Perezii Bayerii. De numis hebraeo-samaritanis. (Pérez Báyer, F.) Valentia, 1781.

Htn Arc 1053.4* — Faber, Johannes. Illustrium imagines ex...Fuliri Ursini. Antwerpiae, 1606.

Arc 1020.95 — Fabiani, G. Sulla Cattedra Alessandria di S. Marco. Modena, 1869.

Arc 1020.108 — Fabre, A. Trésor de la ste. chapelle des ducs de Savoie. Lyon, 1875.

Arc 830.47 — Fabre, Gabrielle. Les civilisations protohistoriques de l'Aquitaine. Paris, 1952.

Arc 830.47.10 — Fabre, Gabrielle. Inventaire des découvertes prohistoriques. Thèse. Paris, 1951.

Arc 66.1.62 — Fabre, P. Etude sur le liber censuum. Paris, 1892.

Arc 66.1.167 — Fabre, P. Saint Paulin de Nole. Paris, 1949.

Arc 785.6 — Fabretti, R. De aquis et aquaeductis veteris Romae. Romae, 1680.

Htn Arc 750.212* — Fabretti, R. De columna traiani syntaqua. Roma, 1683.

Arc 1675.3.7 — Fabriczy, C. von. Italian medal. London, 1904.

Arc 1033.12.25 — Facias Christi. (Cyprian, E.S.) Helmestad, n.d.

Arc 1145.1 — Facsimiles de manuscrits grecs d'Espagne. (Graux, C.) Paris, 1897. 2v.

Arc 1145.3 — Facsimiles des manuscrits grecs datés de la Bibliothèque Nationale. (Omont, H.) Paris, 1891.

Arc 1125.28PF — Facsimiles in collotype of Irish manuscripts. (Ireland. Manuscripts Commission.) Dublin. 1-6,1931-1954 6v.

Arc 810.16 — Facts about Pompeii. (Marriott, H.P.F.) London, 1895.

Arc 746.24 — Faesulae (Fiesole) Regio VII Etruria. (Lombardi, M.) Roma, 1941.

Arc 609.24 — Fagan, Brian. Iron Age cultures in Zambia. London, 1967- 2v.

Arc 555.2 — Fagan, Brian M. The rape of the Nile. N.Y., 1975.

Arc 1020.73.5 — Fagniez, G. Inventaires du trésor de Notre Dame de Paris. Paris, 1874.

Arc 889.30 — Faider-Feytmans, Germaine. La nécropole gallo-romaine de Thuin. Morlanwelz, 1965.

Arc 889.30.5 — Faider-Feytmans, Germaine. Le site sacré de Fontaine-Valmont. Morlanwelz? 196-.

Arc 861.34 — Fairford graves. (Wylie, W.M.) Oxford, 1852.

Arc 595.62 — Fakhry, A. The pyramids. Chicago, 1961.

Arc 838.22F — Falcata iberica. (Madrid. Museo Arqueológico Nacional.) N.Y., 1916.

Arc 746.48F — Falchi, Isidoro. Vetulonia e la sua necropoli antichissima ed anastatica. Roma, 1965.

Arc 674.2.5 — Falcon-Barker, T. 1600 years under the sea. London, 1960.

Arc 726.52 — The Faliscans in prehistoric times. (Holland, Louise.) Rome, 1925.

Arc 1020.66 — Falk, V.A.F. Heiliges Mainz...Heiligenthümer. Mainz, 1877.

Arc 1020.129F — Falke, Otto von. Der Welfenschatz. Frankfurt, 1930.

Arc 518.3 — Falkener, E. Ephesus and the Temple of Diana. London, 1862.

Arc 390.1 — Falkener, E. Museum of classical antiquities. London, 1860.

Arc 830.158 — Fallue, Léon. Sur les mouvements stratégiques de César...avant le siége d'Alise. n.p., 1856. 12 pam.

Arc 1478.29 — False and imitation Roman coins. (Robinson, A.E.) n.p., 1932.

Htn Arc 1475.5* — Familiae Romanae. (Orsini, F.) Rome, 1577.

Htn Arc 1475.4* — Familiae Romanae. (Patin, C.) Paris, 1663.

Arc 1076.3.39 — La famille Cavillier et les fonderies de cloches de Carrepuits. (Berthele, J.) Caen, 1901. 2 pam.

Arc 430.3 — Famous monuments of central India. (Griffin, L.) London, 1886.

Arc 1033.62.2 — Fanchi de' Cavalieri, P. La Passio SS. Perpetuae et Felicitatis. Roma, 1896.

Arc 608.1.37.5 — Fandri, Muhammed. Découverte archéologigue dans la région de Sfax: mosaique des océans. Tunis, 1963.

Arc 1615.14 — The fantastic 1804 dollar. (Newman, Eric.) Racine, 1962.

Arc 1264.11 — Farcy, Paul de. Sigillographie de la Normandie. Caen, 1875.

Arc 600.200F — Farid, Shafik. Exavations at Ballana, 1958-1959. Cairo, 1963.

Arc 547.19.5 — Farina, G. Il R. Museo di Antichità di Torino. 2. ed. Roma, 1938.

Arc 1360.4 — Farkas, Sandor. Antik érmészet. Aiud, 1932.

Arc 1590.8 — Farkas, Sandor. Az erdélyi érmek müvészete. Aiud, 1936.

Arc 1433.64 — Farkas, Sándor. Die Ikonographie der Partherkönige. Aiud, 1933.

Htn Arc 1590.8.5* — Farkas, Sandor. Die Kunst und der Wert...Münzen. Aiud, 1938.

Htn Arc 1020.90* — Farnese. Il santoario di Parma. Parma, 1593.

Arc 6.2 — Fasti archaeologici. Firenze. 1,1946+ 20v.

Arc 93.16 — I fasti dell'Accademia Etrusca di Cortona. (Neppi Modona, Aldo.) Cortona, 1928.

Author and Title Listing

Htn Arc 1490.5.5* Fasti ducales ab Anafesto I. (Palati, J.) Venetiis, 1696.
Arc 402.22 Faszinierende Funde; Archäologie heute. (Rehork, Joachim.) Bergisch Gladbach, 1971.
Arc 1588.6 Fatik sikke re madalyalari. (Artuk, Ibrah.) Istanbul, 1946.
Arc 66.1.43 Faucon, M. Libraire des papes d'Avignon. Paris, 1886. 2v.
NEDL Arc 1480.20 The fauna and flora on the coin-types of...Rome. (Gnecchi, Francesco.) London, 1919.
Htn Arc 760.1.5* Faunus, L. De antiquitiae Romae. Venetiis, 1549.
Htn Arc 760.1* Faunus, L. Delle antichità della città di Roma. Venice? 1548.
Arc 672.1.105 Faure, Paul. Fonctions des cavernes crétoises. Paris, 1964.
Arc 855.211 Faussett, B. Inventorium sepulchrale. London, 1856.
Arc 66.1.211 Favier, Jean. Les finances pontificales à l'époque du grand schisme d'Occident, 1378-1409. Paris, 1966.
Arc 1033.150 Favilli, A. Relazione dell'origine...Firenze...Bastone del S.P. Giuseppe. Lucca, 1721.
Arc 630.7 Favissae utriusque antiqtam Romanae quam Graecae. (Spoor, Henricus.) Ultrajecti, 1707.
Arc 1020.10.39 Favshingham, A.L. The monuments of Christian Rome. N.Y., 1908.
Arc 66.1.121 Fawtier, Robert. Sainte Catherine de Sienne. Paris, 1921.
Arc 66.1.135 Fawtier, Robert. Sainte Catherine de Sienne. Paris, 1930.
Arc 1053.6.7F Faymskii portret. (Strelkov, A.) Moskva, 1936.
Arc 1349.45 Fayolle, A. Evrard. Recherches sur Bertrand Andrieu de Bordeau. Chalon-sur-Saone, 1902.
Arc 600.5 The Fayûm and Lake Moeris. (Brown, R.H.) London, 1892.
Arc 1020.20.5 Fea, C. La Basilica di Costantino. Roma, 1819.
Arc 1033.47.25 Fea, C. Della Casa Aurea di Nerone. Roma, 1832.
Arc 760.6.11 Fea, Carlo. Annotazioni alla memoria sui diritti del principato. Roma, 1806.
Arc 1020.9.7 Fea, Carlo. Conclusione per l'integrita del panteon. Roma, 1807.
Arc 1020.9.5.25 Fea, Carlo. Dei diritti del principato. Roma, 1806.
Arc 760.6.17 Fea, Carlo. Eccellentissima congregazione diputata da sua Santità Papa Leone XII. Roma, 1827.
Arc 785.48 Fea, Carlo. La Fossa Trajana confermata al Ludovico Linotte. Roma, 1824.
Arc 1020.9.6 Fea, Carlo. L'integrita del panteon di M. Agrippa. Roma, 1807.
Arc 1020.9.6.2 Fea, Carlo. L'integrita del panteon rivendicata a Marco Agrippo. 2a ed. Roma, 1820.
Arc 760.6.5 Fea, Carlo. Miscellanea filologica critica e antiquaria. Roma, 1790-1836. 2v.
Arc 760.6.7 Fea, Carlo. Nuova descrizione de' monumenti antichi. Roma, 1819.
Arc 760.6.15 Fea, Carlo. Ossequiosissimo rapporto alla Santità. Roma, 1826. 2 pam.
Arc 785.20.13 Fea, Carlo. Osservazioni suo ristabilimento della Via Appia da Roma a Brindisi. Roma, 1833.
Arc 785.49 Fea, Carlo. I reclami del Foro Trajano esposti al pubblico e giustificati. Roma, 1832.
Arc 726.25 Fea, Carlo. Relazione di un viaggio ad Ostia. Roma, 1802.
Arc 760.6 Fea, Carlo. Varieta di notizie economiche fisiche antiquarie. Rome, 1820.
Arc 760.6.2 Pamphlet vol. Fea, Carlo. Opuscoli. 10 pam.
Arc 875.126 Feachem, R. A guide to prehistoric Scotland. London, 1963.
Arc 861.170 Feachem, Richard. The North Britons. London, 1965.
Arc 1153.19 Federici, V. Esempi di corsiva antico del secolo I...al IV. Roma, 1908.
Arc 1588.5.10 Fedorov, Dimitrii I. Monety pribaltiki XIII-XVIII stoletii. Tallin, 1966.
Arc 925.107 Fedorov, G.B. Po sledam drevnik kul'tur. Moskva, 1954.
Arc 936.20.60 Fedorov, Georgii B. Arkheologiia Rumynii. Moskva, 1973.
Arc 923.117 Fedorov-Davydov, German A. Kurgany, idoly, monety. Moskva, 1968.
VArc 1583.24.5 Fedorov-Davydov, German A. Monety opowiadają o historii. Warszawa, 1966.
Arc 1583.24 Fedorov-Davydov, German A. Monety rasskazy-vaiut. Moskva, 1963.
Arc 925.333 Fedoseeva, Svetlana A. Drevnie kul'tury verkhnego Viliuia. Moskva, 1968.
Arc 858.37.5 Fee, fi, fo, fum, or, The giants in England. (Massingham, H.J.) London, 1926.
Arc 905.140 Fehér, Géza. A Közép-Duna-medence magyar honfoglalás. Budapest, 1962.
Arc 936.40.50 Féher, Géza. Roliata i kulturata na prabulgarite. Sofiia, 1940.
Arc 853.363 Fehr, Horst. Die vor- und frühgeschichtliche Besiedlung der Kreise. Speyer, 1972.
Arc 1076.3.90 Fehrmann, Christiaan Nathanaël. De Kamper klokgieters. Kampen, 1967.
Arc 815.13.20 Feiler, Leopold. Mysterion Gedanken vor den dionysischen Fresken der Mysterienvilla in Pompeji. Wien, 1946.
Arc 1458.12 Der Feingehalt die griechischen und römischen Münzen. (Hammer, J.) Berlin, 1906.
Arc 815.14 Feis, Leopoldo. Di alcune memorie bibliche scaperte a Pompei. Firenze, 1906.
Arc 1190.88F Fekete, Lajos. Beveztés a hodoltság török diplomatikájála. Budapest, 1926.
Arc 1190.80 Fekete, Lajos. Die Siyāquat-Schrift in der türkischen Finanzverwaltung. Budapest, 1955.
Arc 385.16 Felgueiros, Francisco. Pequena história de uma vida gloriosa [Francisco M. Aloes]. Bragança, 1965.
Arc 390.12 Felice Feliciano antiquarius. (Mitchell, Charles.) London, 1961?
Htn Arc 1033.17.96.3* Felicidad de México...Nuestra Señora de Guadalupe. (Becerra Tanco, Luis.) México, 1780.
Arc 861.200.5 Fell, Clare. Early settlement in the Lake counties. Clapham, 1972.
Arc 726.310 Fellmann, Rudolf. Das Grab des Lucius Munatius Plancus bei Gaeta. Basel, 1957.
Arc 915.34 Fellmann, Rudolf. Die Principia des Legionslageos Vindonissa und das Zentralgeläude der römischen Lager und Kastelle. Brugg, 1958.
Arc 513.4 Fellows, C. Asia Minor. London, 1839.
Arc 513.4.2 Fellows, C. Discoveries in Lycia. London, 1841.
Arc 513.4.6 Fellows, C. Travels and researches in Asia Minor. Hildesheim, 1975.
Arc 513.4.5 Fellows, C. Travels and researches in Asia Minor. London, 1852.
Arc 530.3 Fellows, C. The Xanthian marbles. London, 1843.
Arc 1428.21 Fellows, Charles. Coins of ancient Lycia before the reign of Alexander. London, 1855.
Arc 1348.80 Fell's international coin book. (Del Monte, Jacques.) N.Y., 1953.
Arc 1613.23 Fell's United States coin books. (Del Monte, J.) N.Y., 1952.
Arc 716.1 Der Felsaltar des Höchsten Zens oder das Pelasgikon zu Athen. (Welcker, F.G.) Berlin, 1852.
Arc 612.36 Die Felsbilder Europas. (Kühn, Herbert.) Zürich, 1952.
Arc 905.146 Felsbilder in Österreich. (Burgstaller, Ernst.) Linz, 1972.
Arc 530.12.25 Die Felsbilder von Yazilikaya. (Bittel, Kurt.) Bamberg, 1934.
Arc 600.205 Die Felsengräber der Qubbet el Hawa bei Assuan. (Edel, Elmar.) Wiesbaden, 1970- 2v.
Arc 530.1.5 Felsenreliefs in Kleinasien und die Volk der Hitteter. (Hirschfeld, G.) Berlin, 1887.
Arc 505.12.10.5 Egy feltárt bibliai város. (Balazs, György.) Budapest, 1940.
Arc 136.1.60 Fenn, John. Three...tables...exhibiting a state of...Society of Antiquaries. London, 1784. 2 pam.
Arc 726.240 I fenomeni fra disisneici del Serapeo di pozzuoli. (Paroscandola, A.) Napoli, 1947.
Arc 925.50.360 Feodal'naia Tavrika. Kiev, 1974.
Arc 1033.17.323 Fera di Plati, D. Sul santuario di Polsi sito...Gerace memorie. Napoli, 1851.
Arc 1020.67 Feraud, J.J.M. Les saintes reliques...chateau de Manosque. Digne, 1885.
Arc 968.1.15 Ferguson, Henry L. Archaeological exploration of Fishers Island, New York. N.Y., 1935.
Arc 421.4 Ferguson, J.C. A bronze table with accompanying vessels. Peking, 1924.
Arc 421.4.5 Ferguson, J.C. The four bronze vessels of the Marquis. Peking, 1928.
Arc 421.4.10 Ferguson, J.C. Two bronze drums. Peking, 1932.
Arc 432.1.2 Fergusson, F. Rock-cut temples of India. London, 1864.
Arc 432.1.5 Fergusson, J. Archaeology in India. London, 1884.
Arc 432.1 Fergusson, J. Cave temples of India. London, 1880.
Arc 505.3.5 Fergusson, J. The Holy Sepulchre and Temple at Jerusalem. London, 1865.
Arc 505.3 Fergusson, J. Notes on the site of the Holy Sepulchre. London, 1861.
Arc 712.19 Fergusson, J. The Parthenon. London, 1883.
Arc 432.1.3 Fergusson, J. Rock-cut temples of India. London, 1864.
Arc 1093.2 Fergusson, J. Rude stone monuments. London, 1872.
Arc 518.4 Fergusson, J. The Temple of Diana at Ephesus. London, 1883.
Arc 505.5 Fergusson, J. The temples of the Jews. London, 1878.
Arc 875.35 Fergusson, James. Short essay on age and uses of brochs...Orkeney Islands. London, 1877.
Arc 843.77 Fernandez, L.M. Excavaciones en Italica. Sevilla, 1904.
Arc 608.54 Fernandez de Castro y Pedrera, R. Historia y exploración de las ruinas de Cazaza. Larache, 1943.
Arc 1494.10 Fernandez Lopez, M. El tesoro visigotico de la Capilla. Sevilla, 1895.
Arc 66.1.17 Fernique, E. Étude sur préneste. Paris, 1880.
Arc 66.1.5 Fernique, E. Inscriptions du pays des marses. Paris, 1879.
Arc 390.8 Feron, R. La préhistoire. Paris, 1928.
Arc 1493.14 Ferrandis Torres, J. Les monnaies hispaniques. Barcelona, 1929.
Arc 726.89 Ferrare, F. Relazione sulle antichita prehistoriche rinvenute nella contrado comino presso Guardeagrele. Guardeagrele, 1913.
Arc 1033.59 Ferrari, G. de. Panegirico di S. Vittoria. Roma, 1850.
Arc 1645.5 Ferrari, Jorge N. La revolución de Mayo en la medalla. Buenos Aires, 1960.
Arc 1033.65 Ferrari, L.F. dei. Sul valore storico dell'atti S.S. Flavia Domitilla, Nereo, Achilleo. Roma, 1880.
Arc 843.23 Ferraz de Macedo, F. Luzitanos e romanos en Villa Franca de Xira. Lisboa, 1893.
Arc 1494.7 Ferreira Barros, A. Moedas portuguesas dos reinados de D. Carlos I. e de D. Manuel II. Pôrto, 1943.
Arc 1348.74 Ferreira Barros, A. Numismática. Porto, 1961.
NEDL Arc 720.208 Ferrero, E. L'arc d'Auguste à Suse. Turin, 1901.
Arc 1018.50 Ferretto, Giuseppe. Note storico-bibliografiche di archeologia cristiana. Città del Vaticano, 1942.
Arc 608.17.5 Ferri, Silvio. Contributi di Cirene alla storia della religione greca. Roma, 1923.
Arc 608.17.9F Ferri, Silvio. Divinità ignate. Firenze, 1929.
Arc 830.113F Ferry, H. de. Le Maconnais préhistorique. Macon, 1870.
Arc 712.2 Die Feste der Pallas Athene in Athen. (Petersen, C.) Hamburg, 1855.
Arc 585.10A Festival-Hall of Osorkon II in the Great Temple of Bubastis. (Naville, E.H.) London, 1892.
Arc 387.3 Festrede. (Curtius, E.) Göttingen, 1862.
Arc 383.22A Festschrfit für Rudolf Egge. Klagenfurt, 1952-53. 3v.
Arc 383.20 Festschrfit Luitpold Dussler: 28 Studien zur Archäologie und Kunstgeschichte. München, 1972.
Arc 383.53.5 Festschrift des Römisch germanischen Zentralmuseums in Mainz. (Mainz. Römisch Germanisches Zentralmuseum.) Mainz, 1952-53. 3v.
Arc 383.67 Festschrift für August Oxé. Darmstadt, 1938.
Arc 383.93 Festschrift für Carl Weickert. (Bruns, G.) Berlin, 1955.
Arc 383.53.15 Festschrift für Friedrich Matz. (Himmelmann-Wildschütz, N.) Mainz, 1962.
Arc 383.79.10 Festschrift für Gustav Schwante. (Kersten, Karl.) Neumünster, 1951.
Arc 625.8 Festschrift für Johannes Overbeck. Leipzig, 1893.
Arc 625.10 Festschrift für Otto Benndorf. Wien, 1898.
Arc 383.34 Festschrift für Peter Goessler. (Tübingen. Universität. Vor- und Frühgeschichtliches Institut.) Stuttgart, 1954.
Arc 196.2 Festschrift zum 50 Jährigen Jubiläum des Lahnsteiner Altertumsvereins. (Schoenenberg, J.) Oberlahnstein, 1930.
Arc 845.201 Festschrift zur Begrüssung des XVIII. Kongresses der Gesellschaft. (Nürnberg. Deutschen Anthropologischen Gesellschaft.) Nürnberg, 1887.
Arc 383.53.10F Festschrift zur Feier des fünfundsiebzigjährigen Bestehens. (Mainz. Römisch Germanisches Zentralmuseum.) Mainz, 1927.
Arc 383.90 Festschrift 50. Jahre Lehrkanzel für Urgeschichte. Wien, 1949.
Arc 66.1.194 Festugière, Andre. Antioche paienne et chrétienne. Paris, 1959.
Arc 1027.25.11 Une fête archéologique à Rome. (Geffroy, A.) Paris, 1883.
Arc 390.9 Fett, Harry. Pa kulturvernets veier. Oslo, 1949.
Arc 1670.51 Feuardent, F. Jetons et méreaux depuis Louis IX...consulat. Paris, 1904. 2v.
Arc 1670.51.2 Feuardent, F. Jetons et méreaux depuis Louis IX...plandres. London, 1907.

Author and Title Listing

Arc 537.3.2 Feuardent, G.L. Answer to L.P. di Cesnola. N.Y., 1881.
Arc 853.91 Die Feuersteingeröte der Pfahlbaukultur. (Ströbel, R.) Leipzig, 1939.
Arc 66.1.202 Fevrier, Paul Albert. Le developpement urbain en Provence. Paris, 1964.
Arc 957.1 Fewkes, J.W. Antiquities of the Mesa Verde National Park Cliff Palace (Colorado). Washington, 1911.
Arc 957.1.5 Fewkes, J.W. Antiquities of the Mesa Verde National Park Spruce Tree House. Washington, 1909.
Arc 968.2.15 Fewkes, J.W. Archaeological investigations in New Mexico, Colorado, and Utah. Washington, 1917.
Arc 968.2.20 Fewkes, J.W. Archaeology of the lower Mimbres Valley, New Mexico. Washington, 1914.
Arc 955.2.11 Fewkes, J.W. Basket-maker, caves of northeastern Arizona. Cambridge, 1921.
Arc 955.2.9 Fewkes, J.W. Casa Grande, Arizona (28th report of the Bureau of American Ethnology). Washington, 1913.
Arc 955.2.4 Fewkes, J.W. Excavations at Casa Grande, Arizona in 1906-07. v.1-2. Washington, 1907.
Arc 957.1.8A Fewkes, J.W. Prehistoric villages, castles, and towers of southwestern Colorado. Washington, 1919.
Arc 955.2.7 Fewkes, J.W. A preliminary account of archaeological field work in Arizona in 1897. Washington, 1898.
Arc 960.2.5 Fewkes, J.W. Preliminary archaeological explorations at Weeden Island, Florida. Washington, 1924.
Arc 955.2.5 Fewkes, J.W. Preliminary report on a visit to Navaha national monument Arizona. Washington, 1911.
Arc 961.1.15 Fewkes, J.W. W.P.A. excavations at Irene Mound, Savannah, Georgia, May 4, 1938. Savannah, 1938.
Arc 943.18 Pamphlet box. Fewkes, J.W. American archaeology.
Arc 936.15.5 Fewkes, V.J. Neolithic sites in the Mozavo-Danubian area. n.p., 1936.
Arc 936.15.10 Fewkes, V.J. Neolithic sites in the Yugoslavian portion of the lower Danube valley. Lancaster, 1937?
Arc 936.15 Pamphlet vol. Fewkes, V.J. Archaeology. 6 pam.
Arc 66.1.152 Feyel, Michel. Palybe et l'histoire de Biotre. Paris, 1942.
Arc 880.9 Ffrench, J.F.M. Prehistoric faith and worship. London, 1912.
Arc 1580.8 Fiala, E. České denáry. Praha, 1895-
Arc 1335.54 Fiala, Eduard. Collection Ernest Prinz zu Windisch Gratz. Prag, 1895-99. 7v.
Arc 830.95 Fiancette d'Agos, L. de. Étude sur la basilique de Saint-Just. Saint-Gaudens, 1856.
Arc 936.195.235 Fibeln aus der römischen Kaiserzeit in Mähren. (Peškař, Ivan.) Prag, 1972.
Arc 1027.15.19 Fibula d'oro aquiliforme. (Rossi, G.B. de.) Roma, 1894.
Arc 743.26 Le fibule in Etruria dal VI al I secolo. (Guzzo, Piero G.) Firenze, 1973.
Arc 1153.65 Fichtenau, Heinrich. Mensch und Schrift im Mittelalter. Wien, 1946.
Arc 1185.6 Ficker, J. Beitraege zur Urkundenlehre. Innsbruck, 1877-78. 2v.
Arc 1018.9 Ficker, J. Studien über christliche Denkmäler. Leipzig. 1-24,1902-1937 19v.
Htn Arc 726.46* Ficorini, Francesco de. Le memorie ritrovate...de Labrico. Roma, 1745.
Htn Arc 1360.3* Ficoroni, F. de. I piombi antichi. Roma, 1740.
Htn Arc 760.2* Ficoroni, F. de. Le vestigia e rarità di Roma antica. Rome, 1744.
Arc 726.10.10 Die ficoronische Cista. (Behn, F.) Leipzig, 1907.
Arc 726.10.9 Die ficoronische Cista. Diss. (Behn, F.) Rostock, 1907.
Arc 635.207.9 Fiechter, E.R. Der Tempel der Aphaia auf Aegena. München, 1906.
Arc 87.2.63 Fiedler, F. Gripswalder Matronen- und Mereurius-Statuen. Bonn, 1863.
Arc 853.265F Fiedler, R. Katalog Kirchheim unter Teck. Stuttgart, 1962.
Arc 543.3.50F Field, Henry. Archaeological investigations in Central Asia, 1917-37. n.p., 1938.
Arc 340.25.5 Field, Henry. Bibliography of Soviet archaeology and physical anthropology, 1936-1964. Miami? 1964.
Arc 340.25.7 Field, Henry. Bibliography of Soviet archaeology and physical anthropology, 1936-1967. n.p., 1967.
Arc 340.25.9 Field, Henry. Bibliography of Soviet archaeology and physical anthropology, 1936-1972. no. 1-189. Coconut Grove, Fla., 1972.
Arc 543.3.55F Field, Henry. Recent excavations at Khawazm. Ann Arbor, 1948.
Arc 858.104 Field archaeology in Britain. (Coles, John M.) London, 1972.
Arc 853.13.40 Field guide to prehistoric sites in Württemberg and Bavaria. Wiesbaden, 1969.
Arc 1084.12 Field Museum of Natural History, Chicago. Archaic Chinese jades collections in China. N.Y., 1927.
Arc 861.97 Fieldhouse, William J. A Romano-British industrial settlement near Tiddington, Stratford-upon-Avon. Birmingham, 1931.
Arc 712.9 Fielitz, W. Der Parthenon. Ein Vortag. Stralsund, 1871.
Arc 726.36.5 Fiesole. Gli scair, il museo civico. (Galli, Edoardo.) Milano, 1914.
Arc 870.29 The fifth-century invasions south of the Thames. (Evison, Vera I.) London, 1965.
Arc 421.27 Fifty years of studies in oracle inscriptions. (Tung, Tso-pin.) Tokyo, 1964.
Arc 501.7 Fifty years' work in the Holy Land, 1924-1948. (Watson, C.M.) London, 1915. 2v.
Arc 746.9.15 Figure mitologiche degli specchi "Etruschi". pt.1-7. (Ulisse (pseud.).) Roma, 1929-37.
Arc 600.15.15 Les figurines funéraires égyptiennes. (Speleers, L.) Bruxelles, 1923.
Arc 612.53.5 Filip, Jan. Enzyklopädisches Handbuch zur Ur- und Frühgeschichte Europas. Stuttgart, 1966. 2v.
Arc 612.53 Filip, Jan. Evropský pravěk. Praha, 1962.
Arc 936.6.25 Filip, Jan. Pocatkij slovanskeho osidlene. Praha, 1946.
Arc 936.195.140 Filip, Jan. Recent archaeological finds in Czechoslavakia. Prague, 1966.
Arc 936.195.20 Filip, Jan. Umělecký řemeslo v pravěku. Praha, 1941.
Arc 830.14 Fillion, B. Lettre à M.J. Quicherat...sur une decouverte...dans l'etang de Nesmy. La Roche-sur-Yon, 1879.
Arc 1500.47.5 Fillioux, A. Nouvel essai d'interprétation et de classification des monnaies de la Gaule. 2. éd. Paris, 1867.
Arc 1498.11 Fillon, B. Considérations historiques et artistiques sur les monnaies de France. Fontenay, 1850.
Arc 628.27 Filologia classica. (Paribeni, R.) Milano, 1945.
Arc 936.35F Filov, B. Die archäische Nekropole von Trebenischte am Ochrida-See. Leipzig, 1927.
Arc 936.39F Filov, Bogdan. Die Grabhügelnekropole bei Duvanlij in Südbulgarien. Sofiia, 1934.
Arc 936.39.5 Filov, Bogdan. Nadgrobnité mogili pri Duvanlii v Plovdivsko. Sofiia, 1934.
Arc 1033.12.85 Filson, F.V. Who are the figures on the chalice of Antioch? n.p., 1942.
Arc 682.9 Fimmen, Diedrich. Die kritisch-mykenische Kultur. Leipzig, 1921.
Arc 66.1.211 Les finances pontificales à l'époque du grand schisme d'Occident, 1378-1409. (Favier, Jean.) Paris, 1966.
Arc 1510.11 Finauer, P.P. Münzreihe der Herzoge in Baiern. München, 1777.
Arc 853.357 Findeisen, Jürgen. Spuren römerzeitlicher Siedlungsvorgänger im Dorfund Stadtbild Südeutschlands und seiner Nachbargebiete. Bonn, 1970.
Arc 1033.35.5 Finding of the Cross. (Combes, L. de.) London, 1907.
Arc 1470.45 Finds of Greek coins in the British Isles. (Milne, J.G.) London, 1948.
Arc 880.5 Fine arts and civilization of ancient Ireland. (O'Neill, Henry.) London, 1863.
Arc 853.361 Fingerlin, Gerhard. Die alamannischen Gräberfelder von Guttingen und Merdingen in Südbaden. Berlin, 1971. 2v.
Arc 609.38 Fingira; preliminary report. (Sandelowsky, B.H.) Zomba, 1968.
Arc 830.53.25 Le Finistère préhistorique. (Le Pontois, B.) Paris, 1929.
Arc 630.1 Fink, J. Der Verschluss bei den Griechen und Römern. Regensburg, 1890.
Arc 1020.150 Fink, Josef. Der Mars Camulus-Stein in der Pfarrkirche zu Rindern. Kevelaer, 1970.
Arc 938.85.5 Finland. (Kivikoski, Ella.) London, 1967.
Arc 684.4 Finlay, G. Remarks on the topography of Oropia and Diacria. Athens, 1838. 2 pam.
Arc 282.1 Finska fornminnesföreningens tidskrift. (Suomen Muinaimuistoyhdestys, Helsinki.) 16,1896+ 24v.
Arc 1166.5 Finzi, A.M. La fotografia quale mezzo di scoperta della falsità in documenti. Firenze, 1911.
Arc 1505.205 Fiola, Eduard. Münzen und Medaillen der Wellischenlande. v.1-8. Prag, 1916. 6v.
Arc 1020.9.51 Fioravanti, G.A. Visita...delle sette chiese. Fermo, 1763.
Arc 810.5.2A Fiorelli, G. Descrizione di Pompei. Naples, 1875.
Arc 810.25 Fiorelli, G. Guida di Pompei. Roma, 1877.
Arc 720.216 Fiorelli, G. Monumenti cumani. Napoli, 1853.
Arc 810.5 Fiorelli, G. Pompeianarum antiquitatum historia. Naples, 1860-62. 3v.
Arc 790.201 Fiorelli, G. Gli scavi di Pompei dal 1861 al 1872. Napoli, 1873.
Arc 1508.20 Fiorino, Alexander. Sammlung des Herrn Alexander Fiorino in Cassel. Frankfurt am Main, 1917.
Arc 1490.10 Il fiorino d'oro antico illustrato. (Vettori, Francesco.) Firenze, 1738.
Arc 935.30 Firatli, Nezih. Les stiles funéraires de Byzance gréco-romaine. Paris, 1964.
Arc 953.34 The first American. 1. ed. (Marek, Kurt W.) N.Y., 1971.
Arc 612.80 The first European agriculture. (Murray, Jacqueline.) Edinburgh, 1970.
Arc 1340.5 Pamphlet box. First part of a German numismatic dictionary.
Arc 1468.27.5 The first stages in the development of Greek coinage. (Milne, Joseph G.) Oxford, 1934.
Arc 74.4.17 First supplementary catalogue of lantern slides. (Society for the Promotion of Hellenic Studies.) London, 1914.
Arc 545.227.10F Firth, C.M. The step pyramid. Le Caire, 1935-36. 2v.
Arc 600.175 Firth, Cecil M. Excavations at Saqqara. Le Caire, 1926. 2v.
Arc 66.1.96 La fiscalité pontificale en France XIVe siècle. (Samarin, C.M.D.) Paris, 1905.
Arc 905.9 Fischbach, O. Römische Lampen aus Poetovio. Graz, 1896.
Arc 915.53 Fischer, Franz. Die fruhbronzezeitliche Ansiedlung in der Bleiche bei Arbon T.G. Basel, 1971.
Arc 416.3 Fischer, H. Stone implements in Asia. Worcester, 1884.
Arc 853.372 Fischer, Ulrich. Aus Frankfurts Vorgeschichte. Frankfurt am Main, 1971.
Arc 853.4.20 Fischer, Ulrich. Grabungen im romischen Steinkastell von Heddernheim 1957-1959. Frankfurt am Main, 1973.
Arc 790.211F Fischetti, Luigi. Pompei com'era e com'è. Milano, 19- ? 2v.
Arc 925.356.1 Fisenko, Vladimir A. Plemena iamnoi kul'tury Iugo-Vostoka. Photoreproduction. Saratov, 1970.
Arc 595.29 Fish, E.W. The Egyptian pyramids. Chicago, 1880.
Arc 1623.1 Fisher, A. Catalogue of coins, medals, and tokens of Mexico. N.Y., 1891.
Arc 1030.14.5 Fistula plumbea acquaria di Porto. (Bruzza, L.) Roma, 1878.
Arc 1033.7 Fita y Colomé, Fidel. Recuerdos de un viaje a Santiago de Galicia. Madrid, 1880.
Arc 905.29.5 Fitz, Jeno. Les Syriens à Intercisa. Bruxelles, 1972.
Arc 505.65F Fitzgerald, G.M. A sixth century monastery at Beth-Shan (Scythopolis). Philadelphia, 1939.
Arc 587.9.15 Five Theban tombs. (Davies, N. de Garis.) London, 1913.
Arc 455.3 Five thousand years of Pakistan. (Wheeler, R.E.) London, 1950.
Arc 545.238 Five years' explorations at Thebes. (Carter, H.) London, 1912.
Arc 830.356 Fixot, Michel. Les fortifications de terre et les origines féodales dans le Cinglais. Caen, 1968.
Arc 66.1.143 Flacelière, Robert. Les Aitoliens a Dalphes. Paris, 1937.
Arc 493.2.25 Flames over Persepolis: turning point in history. (Wheeler, Robert E.) London, 1962.
Arc 895.50F Flarin, Sten. Vråkulturen. Stockholm, 1958.
Arc 712.6 Flasch, A. Zum Parthenonfries. Wuerzburg, 1877.
Arc 905.25 Flavia Solva. 2. Aufl. (Schmid, Walter.) Graz, 1917.
Arc 453.5 Fleet, J.F. Indian epigraphy. Oxford, 1907.
Arc 435.12F Fleet, J.F. Pâli, Sanskrit and old Canarese inscriptions. London, 1878.
Arc 1675.24 Fleming, J.W. Medals, clasps, and crosses, military and naval in the collection of J.W. Fleming. Brighton, 1871.
Arc 412.1.10 Flemming, Nicholas C. Cities in the sea. 1. ed. Garden City, N.Y., 1971.
Arc 1550.8.15 Flensborg mønt, 14. og 16. århundrede. Udg. af numismatisk forening for nord-og sydslesvig. (Golster, Georg.) Sønderborg, 1967.
Arc 609.1.50 Fletcher, Harold Clarkson. Psychic episodes of Great Zimbabwe. Johannesburg, 1941.

Author and Title Listing

Arc 390.10 Fletcher y Valls, D. Nocines de prehistoria. Valencia, 1952.

Arc 843.5.30 Fletcher y Valls, D. Repertorio de bibliografía arqueológica. v.1-2, 4-6. Valencia, 1951. 4v.

Htn Arc 1660.6* Fleurimont, G.R. Médailles du règne de Louis XV. n.p., n.d.

Arc 823.3 Fleury, E. Civilisation et art des Romains...Gaule-Belgique. Paris, 1860-1861.

Arc 1020.112 Fleury, E. Trésor de Notre-Dame-de-Liesse...de 1655 à 1790. Paris, 1854.

Arc 1348.70 Fliessbach, Ferdinand. Münzsammlung, Enthaltend. Leipzig, 1853. 2v.

Arc 412.18 Flights into yesterday. (Devel, Leo.) N.Y., 1969.

Arc 488.17F Flights over ancient cities of Iran. (Schmidt, E.F.) Chicago, 1940.

Arc 588.66F Flinders Petrie centenary...ceremonial slate palettes. (Petrie, W.M.F.) London, 1953.

Arc 403.5 Flint chips. A guide to pre-historical archaeology. (Stevens, E.T.) London, 1870.

Arc 1588.7.5F Floca, Ochaviau. Coutributic la cunoasterea Syauselar de arguil doeice. București, 1956.

Arc 726.261 Floral figurines from south Italy. (Stoop, Maria W.) Assen, 1960.

Arc 1500.36 Florange, C. Étude sur les messageries et les postes. Paris, 1925.

Arc 1663.25 Florange, Charles. Les assemblées du clergé de France avant 1789. Paris, 1927.

Arc 1500.23 Florange, J. Armorial du jetonophile. Paris, 1907. 2v.

Arc 547.10 Florence, Italy. Guida del Museo Archeologico I. Antichita Egiziane. Florence, 1880.

Arc 567.1.15F Florence. Università. Scritti dedicati alla memoria di Ippolito Rosellini. Firenze, 1945.

Arc 726.103 Florentia (Firenze). (Maetzke, G.) Rome, 1941.

Arc 1033.91 Florentinio, M. Hetruscae...Pietates...de Prima Thusciae Christianae. Lucae, 1701.

Arc 936.120.10 Florescu, Florea B. Monumentul de la Adamklissi Tropaeum Traiani. București, 1959.

Htn Arc 1675.26* Florez, Enrique. Medallas de la colonias, municipios y pueblos antiguos de España. Madrid, 1757-73. 3v.

Arc 1138.60 Floriano, A.C. Curso general de paleografia y diplomatica españolas. v.1-2. Oviedo, 1946.

Arc 820.216F Flouest, E. Notice archéologique sur le camp de Chassey. Chalon-sur-Saône, 1869.

Arc 861.23 Flower, J.W. Notices of an Anglo-Saxon cemetery...Surrey. London, 1872.

Arc 1504.5 Fluri, Adolf. Die Berner Schulpfennige und die Tischlivierer. Bern, 1910.

Arc 612.26 Fock, G. Die steinzeitlichen Keulen Mitteleuropas. Inaug. Diss. Düsseldorf, 1937.

Arc 1388.1 Fölhagen-fyndet. (Tornberg, C.J.) Stockholm, 1870.

Arc 895.19 Förhistoriska flintgrufvor och kulturlager vid kvarn. (Schnittger, Bror.) Stockholm, 1910.

Arc 895.39F Förhistoriska undersökningar på Adelso. (Rydh, Hanna.) Stockholm, 1936.

Arc 895.65 Försök till förklaringar öfver hällristningar. (Brunius, Carl Georg.) Lund, 1968.

Arc 1077.2.60 Foerster, Else. Das irische Hochkreuz. Inaug. Diss. München, 1965.

Arc 1153.92 Foerster, H. Abriss der lateinische Paläographie. 2. Aufl. Stuttgart, 1963.

Arc 700.17 Foerster, R. Die Hochzeit des Zeus und der Hera; Relief der Schaubert'schen Sammlung. Breslau, 1867.

Arc 1160.204 Foerster, W. Sulla questione...codice di Arborea. Torino, 1905.

Arc 1560.2 Förteckning öfver C.P. Humbles. (Humbles, C.P.) Stockholm, 1852.

Arc 853.268F Fohrde und Hohenferchesar; zwei germanische Gräberfelder der frühen römischen Kaiserzeit aus der Mark Brandenburg. (Müller, A. von.) Berlin, 1962.

Arc 726.264 Fois, Foiso. I ponti romani in Sardegna. Sassari, 1964.

Arc 220.10F Folia archaeologica. Budapest. 1-5,1939-1945// 10v.

Arc 220.10 Folia archaeologica. Budapest. 6,1954+ 15v.

Arc 858.14 Folk-memory. (Johnson, W.) Oxford, 1908.

Arc 387.14.5 Folkers, T. Liste des publications de Jean Capart. Leiden, 1938.

Htn Arc 1535.3* Folkes, M. Tables of English silver and gold coins. London, 1763. 2v.

Arc 905.90 Folteny, Stephan. Zur Cronologie der Bronzezeit des Karpatenbeckens. Bonn, 1955.

Arc 967.2 Folvke, G. Antiquities of central and southeastern Missouri. Washington, 1910.

Arc 1412.5 Fonahn, Adolf. Japanische Bildermünze. Leipzig, 1934.

Arc 608.65 Foncher, L. Hodrumetum. Paris, 1964.

Arc 672.1.105 Fonctions des cavernes crétoises. (Faure, Paul.) Paris, 1964.

Arc 830.152 Une fondation du connétable Henri de Montmorency. (Macon, Gustave.) Senlis, 1908.

Arc 625.7 Fongères, G. La vie...des Grecs et des Romains. Paris, 1894.

Htn Arc 785.2* Fontana, C. Discorsa sopra l'antico Monte Citabrio. Roma, 1708.

Htn Arc 720.14* Fontana, D. Del modo tenuto...liobelisco vaticano. Roma, 1590.

Arc 1025.40 Fontana, G. Le notti cristiane. Colle, 1829.

Arc 746.16 Fontani, Giusto. De antiquitatibus Hortae coloniae etruscorum. 3a ed. Roma, 1723.

Arc 1033.12.52 Fontanini, J. Dissertatio de corona ferrea Langobardoum. Romae, 1717.

Arc 785.37 Fonteanive, R. Sui munimenti ed altre costruzione poligonie...provincia romana. Roma, 1887.

Arc 1494.50 Fontecha y Sanchez, Ramon de. La reforma monetaria de 1868; catalogo de monedas. Madrid, 1965.

Arc 1500.26 Fontenay, J. de. Nouvelle étude de jetons. Autun, 1850.

Arc 766.4.15 Fontes ad topographism veteris urbis Romae pertinentes. v.1-4; v.6, pt.1-2; v.8, pt.1. (Lugli, Giuseppe.) Roma, 1953. 7v.

Arc 302.45 Fontes archeologicae Moraviae. Brno. 1965+

Arc 608.17.15 Fonti per la storia della religione cyrenaica. (Vitali, L.) Padova, 1932.

Arc 726.251 Fonti per la storia greca e romana del Salento. (Susini, Giancarlo.) Bologna, 1962.

Arc 967.1.9 Foot-prints of vanished races in the Mississippi Valley. (Conant, Alban J.) St. Louis, 1879.

Arc 830.360 Foramitti, Hans. Wiederbelebung historischer Stadtviertel; die Lösing in Frankreich als mögliches Vorbild. Graz, 1965.

Arc 760.7 Forbes, S. Russell. Rambles in Rome. London, 1882.

Arc 785.6.10 Forbes, S.R. Aqueducts fountains of ancient Rome. Rome, 1899.

Arc 969.1.10 Force, M.F. Indians of Ohio. Cincinnati, 1879.

Arc 708.6.2 Forchhammer, P. Zur Topographie Athens. Göttingen, 1833. 2 pam.

Arc 708.6 Forchhammer, P. Zur Topographie von Athen. Göttingen, 1873.

Arc 746:5 Forchhammer, P.W. Apollon's Ankunft in Delphi. Kiel, 1840.

Arc 716.7 Forchhammer, P.W. Das Erechtheion. Kiel, 1879.

Arc 677.1 Forchhammer, P.W. Halkyoma. Berlin, 1857.

Arc 645.1 Forchhammer, P.W. Hellenika. Berlin, 1837.

Arc 510.210 Forchhammer, P.W. Das homerische Troja. n.p., 1874.

Arc 390.14 Ford, J.A. Método cuantitativo para establecer cronologias culturas. Washington, 1962.

Arc 608.40 Forde-Johnston. Neolithic culture of North Africa. Liverpool, 1959.

Arc 800.14 Fordyce, W. Memoirs concerning Herculaneum. London, 1750.

Arc 1400.8 Foreign coins struck at United States mints. (Altz, Charles G.) Racine, Wis., 1965.

Arc 497.81F The foreign relations of Palestine during the early bronze age. (Hennessy, John Basil.) London, 1967.

Arc 375.2.2 Foreign topography. Encyclopaedia of antiquites. v.3. (Fosbroke, T.D.) London, 1828.

Arc 726.2.25 Il forestiere alle antichità e curiosità nationali Pozzuoli. (Panvini, P.) Napoli, 1818.

Arc 1264.1.3 Forgeais, Arthur. Blasons et chevaliers du Moyen Âge. Paris, 1877.

Arc 1264.1 Forgeais, Arthur. Collection de plombs historiés trouvés dans la Seine. v.1-3. Paris, 1858-66. 2v.

Arc 530.70 A forgotten kingdom. (Woolley, C.L.) Baltimore, 1953.

Arc 543.40.15 Forgotten kingdoms in Sumatra. (Schnitger, F.M.) Leiden, 1939.

Arc 1138.115.2 Forgotten scripts. (Gordon, Cyrus Herzl.) Harmondsworth, 1971.

Arc 1138.115 Forgotten scripts. (Gordon, Cyrus Herzl.) N.Y., 1968.

Arc 895.7.30 De forhistoriske tider i Danmark. (Gabrielsen, S.V.) København, 1948.

Arc 612.17 De forhistoriske tider i Europa. (Johansen, K. Friis.) København, 1927. 2v.

Arc 785.13.205 I fori imperiali. (Paribeni, R.) Roma, 1930.

Arc 790.207 La forma del Vesuvio nelle pitture...antiche. (Cocchia, E.) n.p., n.d.

Arc 723.20.10F Forma Italiae. Roma, 1926- 17v.

Arc 723.20.12F Forma Italiae. Sardinia. v.1-2. Roma, 1952-54.

Arc 723.20.14F Forma Italiae. Serie II documenti. Firenze, 1972-

Arc 750.29 Forma urbis Romae. (Jordan, Henri.) Berolino, 1874.

Arc 767.1.5 Formae urbis Romae antiquae. (Maps, Rome. Ancient (1896).) Berolino, 1896.

Arc 767.1.7A Formae urbis Romae antiquae. (Maps, Rome. Ancient (1912).) Berolino, 1912.

Arc 589.1.3 The formation of the alphabet. (Petrie, W.M.F.) London, 1912.

Arc 923.75.5 Formazov, Aleksandr A. Arkheologicheskie puteshestviia. Moskva, 1974.

Arc 1153.1 Forme des abréviations et des liaisons dans les lettres des papes. (Delisle, L.) Paris, 1887.

Arc 848.52 Formenkreise der älteren römischen Kaiserzeit im Raum zwischen Havelseinplatte und Ostsee. (Mueller, Adriaan von.) Berlin, 1957.

Arc 923.75 Formozov, A.A. Ocherki po istorii russkoi arkheologii. Moskva, 1961.

Arc 925.300.10 Formozov, Aleksandr A. Kamennyi vek i eneolit Prikubania. Moskva, 1965.

Arc 1190.5 A formula book of English historical documents. (Hall, Hubert.) Cambridge, 1908. 2v.

Arc 726.180 Forno, Federico dal. Il teatro romano di Verona. Verona, 1954.

Arc 785.13.55 Il Foro Romano, il Palatino. (Bartoli, Alfonso.) Milano, 1924.

Arc 785.13.24.7 Il Foro Romano; storia e monumenti. (Huelsen, Christian.) Roma, 1905.

Arc 785.13.80F Foro romano. (Castagnoli, F.) Milano, 1957.

Arc 785.13.48 Il Foro Romano. (Ruggiero, E. de.) Roma, 1913.

Arc 1349.5 Forrer, L. Biographical dictionary of medallists. London, 1904-30. 8v.

Arc 555.1 Forrer, R. Besuch in El-Achmem. Reisebriefe aus Aegypten. Strassburg, 1895.

Arc 545.217 Forrer, R. Die fruehchristliche Alterthuemer aus....Achmim Panopolis. Strassburg, 1893.

Arc 545.215 Forrer, R. Die Graeber- und Textilfunde von Achmim-Panopolis. Strassburg, 1891.

Arc 375.6 Forrer, R. Reallexikon der prähistorischen, klassischen...Altertümer. Berlin, 1907.

X Cg Arc 545.216 Forrer, R. Roemische und Byzantinische Seiden-Textilien aus.....Achmim-Panopolis. Strassburg, 1891.

Arc 830.162 Forrer, Robert. L'Alsace romaine. Paris, 1935.

Arc 830.124.5 Forrer, Robert. Bauernfarmen der Steinzeit. Strassburg, 1903.

Arc 915.20 Forrer, Robert. Die helvetishen und helvetarömischen Votivbeilchen der Schweiz. Basel, 1948.

Arc 1454.200 Forrer, Robert. Keltische Numismatik der Rhein. Strassburg, 1908.

Arc 830.210 Forrer, Robert. Das römische Zabern. Strassburg, 1918.

Arc 830.166 Forrer, Robert. Strasbourg-Argentorate. Strausbourg, 1927. 2v.

Arc 672.1.67 Forschungen auf Kreta 1942. (Matz, F.) Berlin, 1951.

Arc 155.11 Forschungen in Augst. Basel. 2,1975+

Arc 510.219F Forschungen in Ephesop. v.1-4, pt.1-3; v.5. (Österreichisches Archäologisches Institut.) Wien, 1906-51. 8v.

Arc 905.55 Forschungen in Lauriacum. Linz. 1,1953+ 7v.

Arc 853.20.2 Forschungen über die römischen Alterthümer. 2. Aufl. (Wyttenback, J.H.) Trier, 1844.

Arc 190.11 Forschungen und Berichte der Archäologie des Mittelalters in Baden-Württemberg. Stuttgart. 1,1972+ 4v.

Arc 190.10 Forschungen und Berichte zür Vor- und Frühgeschichte in Baden-Württemberg. Stuttgart. 1,1972+ 8v.

Arc 390.5 Forschungen zur Kirchengeschichte...Johannes Ficker als Festgabe. (Elliger, W.) Leipzig, 1931.

Arc 1027.26.25 Forschungen zur Sicilia sotterranea. (Führer, J.) München, 1897.

Arc 848.34 Forschungsgeschichte in Deutschland. (Gummel, H.) Berlin, 1938.

Arc 672.1.59 Forsdyke, E.J. Minoan art. London, 1931.

Arc 893.20 Forssander, J.E. Der Ostskandinavische Norden während der ältesten Metallzeit Europas. Lund, 1936.

Author and Title Listing

Arc 853.101.10F — Das fränkische Reichengräberfeld Köln-Mungersdorf. Text and plates. (Fremersdorf, F.) Berlin, 1955. 2v.
Arc 853.20.32 — Die fränkischen Altertümer des trierer Landes. v.1-2. (Böhner, Kurt.) Berlin, 1958.
Arc 1093.5 — Die fränkischen Epitaphen im 4. und 5. Jahrhundert. Inaug. Diss. (Redslob, E.) Nürnberg, 1907.
Arc 853.215 — Die fränkischen Friedhöfe von Weilbach Maintaunuskreis. (Schoppa, Helmut.) Weisbaden, 1959.
Arc 853.59 — Fränkisches Mesolithikum. (Gumpert, Carl.) Leipzig, 1927.
Arc 830.89 — Fragment d'un voyage dans les Basses-Alpes. (Villeneuve-Bargemon, Christophe.) Agen, 1811. 3 pam.
Arc 858.20 — Fragmenta sepulchralia. Sepulchral and early monumental remains of Great Britain. (Bloxam, M.H.) n.p., n.d.
Htn Arc 750.220F* — Fragmenta vestigii veteris Romae. (Bellori, G.P.) Colophon, 1673.
Arc 915.5 — Fragments d'archeologie genevoise. (Mayor, J.) Genève, 1892.
Arc 1020.73.9 — Fragments d'un inventaire du trésor de l'abbaye de Saint Victor de Paris. (Molinier, E.) Paris, 1882.
Arc 497.7 — Fragments d'un journal de voyage en Orient. (Vogüé, M. de.) Paris, 1855.
Arc 1030.5.9 — Frammenti di fasti di Ludi Capenati. (Rossi, G.B. de.) Roma, 1884.
Arc 1033.1.5 — Frammento di Becchiere Vitreo. (Rossi, G.B. de.) Roma, 1885.
Arc 1033.39 — Frammento di pettine son reppresentanze cristiane. (Bulic, F.) Roma, 1902.
Arc 1033.3.13 — Un frammento di sarcofago cristiano. (Marucchi, O.) Roma, 1897.
Arc 1033.3.37 — Un frammento di sarcofago cristiano. (Stuhlfauth, G.) Roma, 1897.
Arc 1033.3.9 — Un frammento di sarcofago cristiano del Museo Laterano. (Marucchi, O.) Roma, 1896.
Arc 1030.31 — Un frammento epigrafico cristiano dell'isola Portuense. (Cantarelli, L.) Roma, 1896.
Arc 113.3 — France. Mémoires de la Société archéologique du midi de la France. Toulouse. 1-24 21v.
Arc 113.3.5 — France. Mémoires de la Société archéologique du midi de la France. Tables générales. Toulouse. 1831-1871
Arc 113.3.7 — France. Memoires de la Société archéologique du midi de la France. Tables générales. 1.-2. séries. Toulouse.
Arc 113.2 — France. Mémoires lus à la Sorbonne. Archéologie, 1861, 63-68. Paris, 1863-69. 7v.
Arc 1.11F — France. Academie des Inscriptions. Monuments et memoirs. Paris. 1-55 45v.
Arc 1208.7 — France. Archives Nationales. Le service sigillographique et les collections d'empreintes de sceaux des archives. Paris, 1916.
Arc 823.40 — France. Centre National de la Recherche Scientifique. Gallia. Paris. 1,1943+ 28v.
Arc 2.1.2.5 — France. Comité des Travaux Historiques et Scientifiques. Bulletin archéologique. Paris. 1883-1915
Arc 2.1.2 — France. Comité des Travaux Historiques et Scientifiques. Bulletin archéologique. Paris. 1897+ 45v.
Arc 2.1.3.5 — France. Comité des Travaux Historiques et Scientifiques. Bulletin historique et philologique. Paris. 1882-1915
Arc 2.1.3 — France. Comité des Travaux Historiques et Scientifiques. Bulletin historique et philologique. Paris. 1897+ 44v.
Arc 100.5 — France. Comité des Travaux Historiques et Scientifiques. Section d'Archéologie. Actes du Congrès national des sociétés savantes. 85,1960+
Arc 35.1 — France. Commission Archéologique de l'Indochine. Bulletin. Paris. 1908-1934 3v.
Arc 488.9F — France. Délégation Archéologique en Iran. Mémoires. Paris. 1,1900+ 35v.
Arc 543.12F — France. Délégation Archéologique Française en Afghanistan. Mémoires. Paris. 1-19 14v.
Arc 1263.4 — France. Direction des Archives. Inventaire des sceaux de la Bourgogné. Paris, 1912.
Htn Arc 1660.5.2* — France. Institut. Médailles sur les principaux evenements du règne de Louis le Grand. Baden, 1705.
Arc 66.2 — France. Institutes. Rapports de la commission des écoles d'Athènes et de Rome. Paris. 1878-1889 2v.
Arc 2.1 — France. Ministère de l'Instruction. Bulletin de Comité des travaux historiques et scientifiques. Section historique et archéologique. Paris. 1882-1896 15v.
Arc 820.203 — France. Ministère de l'Instruction. Dictionnaire archéologique de la Gaule. Paris, 1875-1923. 2v.
Arc 605.202 — France. Ministère de l'Instruction Publique. Musées de l'Algérie. Paris. 1-21,1890-1928 24v.
Arc 1.10 — France. Ministre de l'Instruction Publique et des Beaux Arts. Archives des missions scientifiques. Paris. 1-31 30v.
Arc 1.10.2 — France. Ministre de l'Instruction Publique et des Beaux Arts. Nouvelles archives des missions scientifiques. Paris. 1-18 31v.
Arc 580.1 — France. Mission Archéologique Française au Caire. Mémoires. Paris. 1-31,1889-1934 25v.
Arc 66.1.44 — La France en Orient au XIVe siècle. (Delaville Le Roulx, J.) Paris, 1886. 2v.
Arc 66.1.139 — La France et l'Italie au temps du Grand Schisme d'Occident. (Boüard, Michel de.) Paris, 1936.
Arc 66.1.102 — La France et Rome de 1788 à 1797. (Bourgin, G.) Paris, 1909.
Arc 66.1.35 — Francesco da Barberino. (Thomas, A.) Paris, 1883.
Arc 830.111 — La Franche-Comté à l'époque romaine. (Clerc, E.) Besançon, 1847.
Arc 1033.62 — Franchi de' Cavalieri, P. La Passio SS. Perpetuae et Felicitatis. Roma, 1896.
Arc 1033.61 — Franchi de Cavalieri, P. S. Agnese nella tradizione e nella leggenda. Roma, 1899.
Arc 1148.14.5 — Franchi de' Cavalieri, P. Specimina codicum graecorum vaticanorum. Berolini, 1929.
Arc 1148.14 — Franchi de' Cavalieri, P. Specimina codicum graecorum vaticanorum. Bonniae, 1910.
Arc 726.326 — Franciosa, Nicola. La villa romana di Minori. Minori, 1968.
Arc 1020.47 — Franciotti, C. Historia delle Miracolose Imagni...città di Lucca. Lucca, 1613.
Arc 726.342 — Franciscis, Alfonso. Ricerche sulla topografia e i monumenti di Locri. Napoli, 1971-
Arc 726.342.5 — Franciscis, Alfonso. Stato e società in Loori. Napoli, 1972.
Arc 726.185 — Franciscis, Alfonso de. Mausolei romani di Campania. Napoli, 1957.
Arc 1033.17.95 — Francisco de San Joseph. Historia universal...Nuestra Señora de Guadalupe. Madrid, 1743.
Arc 1033.17.95.2F — Francisco de San Joseph. Historia universal...Nuestra Señora de Guadalupe. Madrid, 1743.
Arc 435.2.38F — Francke, A.H. Antiquities of Indian Tibet. Calcutta, 1914-26. 2v.
Arc 66.1.173 — François, M. Le cardinal François de Tournon. Paris, 1951. 2v.
Arc 1015.222 — Franconi, F. La catacomba e la basilica costantiniana. Roma, 1877.
Arc 1305.2 — Frank Caucey Wilson's monthly rare coin bulletin. Chicago. 63,1943
Arc 1163.11 — Franke, O. Epigraphische Denkmäler aus China. Berlin, 1914. 2v.
Arc 1470.82 — Franke, P.R. Die antiken Münzen von Epirus. v.1-2. Wiesbaden, 1961.
Arc 1480.66 — Franke, Peter. Römische Kaiserporträts in Münzbild. München, 1961.
Arc 1428.33 — Franke, Peter R. Kleinasien zur Römerzeit; griechisches Leben im Spiegel der Münzen. München, 1968.
Arc 497.67 — Franken, Hedricus J. Van aartsvaders tot prafeten. Amsterdam, 1967.
Arc 853.99F — Franken, M. Die Alamannen zwischen iller und lech. Berlin, 1944.
Arc 612.16 — Die Franken und Westgoten in der Volkewanderungszeit. (Åberg, Nils.) Uppsala, 1922.
Arc 585.31F — Frankfort, H. The cenotaph of Seti I at Abydos. London, 1933. 2v.
Htn Arc 585.38F* — Frankfort, H. The mural painting of El-Amarneh. London, 1929.
Arc 1237.5.2 — Frankfort, Henri. Stratified cylinder seals from the Diyala region. Chicago, 1964.
Arc 845.203 — Frankfurt am Main. Historisches Museum. Einzelforschungen über Kunst- undAltertumsgegenstände zu Frankfurt am Main. Frankfurt, 1908.
Arc 845.2 — Frankfurt am Main. Verein für Geschichte und Alterthumskunde. Mittheilungen über Römische Funde in Heddernheim. Frankfurt, 1894. 6v.
Arc 1428.4 — Frankische im Orient geprägte Münzen. (Friedländer, J.) n.p., n.d.
Arc 843.165 — Frankowski, Eugeniusz. Estelas discoideas de la Peninsula Iberica. Madrid, 1920.
Arc 830.350 — Frantin, Jean Marie. Notice sur les origines de Dijon et sur les fragments romains découverts dans les substructions de l'ancien palais ducal de Dijon. Dijon, 1854?
Arc 390.16 — Frantov, Grigoriis. Geofizika v arkheologii. Leningrad, 1966.
Arc 513.8 — Franz, J. Fuenf Inschriften und fuenf Staedte in Kleinasien. Berlin, 1840.
Arc 913.21 — Franz, L. Vorgeschichtliches Leben in den Alpen. Wien, 1929.
Arc 903.4 — Franz, Leonhard. Lexikon ur- und frühgeschichtlicher Fundstätten Österreichs. Wien, 1965.
Arc 395.7.2 — Franz Xaver Kraus. (Hauviller, E.) München, 1905.
Arc 1570.1 — Et frar fund af norske mynter. (Holmboe, C.A.) Kjøbenhavn, 1866.
Arc 671.15 — Fraser, F.M. Boeotian and west Greek tombstones. Lund, 1954.
Arc 1033.107 — Fratini, G. Gli atti più antichi del martirio di S. Felice. Foligno, 1881.
Arc 505.6 — Fraudes archeologiques en Palestine. (Bibliothéque Orientale Elzevirienne). (Clermont-Ganneau, Charles.) Paris, 1885.
Arc 830.48 — Fraysse, Jean. Les troglodytes en Anjou à travers les âges. Cholet, 1963.
Arc 1185.14 — Frazer, P. Manual of the study of documents. Philadelphia, 1894.
Arc 1663.52F — Frede, Lothar. Das klassische Weimar in Medaillen. Leipzig, 1959.
Arc 387.23 — Frederick Catherwood. (Hagen, Victor Wolfgang von.) N.Y., 1950.
Arc 1093.2.3.5 — Frederik VII, king of Denmark. Om bygningsmaaden af oldtidens jaettestuer. 2. udg. København, 1862.
Arc 1093.2.3 — Frederik VII, king of Denmark. Sur la construction des ralles dites des géants. Copenhague, 1857.
Arc 1093.2.3.7 — Frederik VII, king of Denmark. Über den Bau des Riesenbetten der Vorzeit. Kopenhagen, 1863.
Arc 1528.14 — Frederiks, J.W. Penningen. Amsterdam, 1947.
Arc 1076.12 — Frederiksborg amts kirkekloffer. (Gribsoe, Erland.) Hillerød, 1934.
Arc 853.36 — Fredrich. Die in Ostdeutschland gefundenen römischen Bronzestatuellen. Cüstrin, 1912. 3 pam.
Arc 710.9 — Freericks, H. Die drei Athenetempel der Akropolis. Münster, 1905.
Arc 830.126.5 — Fréjus et les carrières...de l'Esterel. (Pottier, Raimond.) Draguignan, 1885.
Arc 830.126.3 — Fréjus le port militaire du Forum Julii. (Donnadieu, A.) Paris, 1935.
Arc 853.101F — Fremersdorf, F. Die Denkmäler des römischen Köln. v.1-8,22. Köln, 1950- 9v.
Arc 853.101.2F — Fremersdorf, F. Die Denkmäler des römischen Köln. 2. Aufl. Köln, 1958-63. 2v.
Arc 853.101.10F — Fremersdorf, F. Das fränkische Reichengräberfeld Köln-Mungersdorf. Text and plates. Berlin, 1955. 2v.
Arc 853.101.5 — Fremersdorf, F. Das römische Hans mit dem Dionysos-Mosaik vor dem Sudportal des Kölner Domes. Berlin, 1956.
Arc 830.1 — Freminville. Antiquités de la Bretagne. Brest, 1834.
Arc 340.7 — French Bibliographical Digest. Archaeology, 1945-1955. N.Y., 1956- 2v.
Arc 87.2.62 — Frendenberg, J. Denkmal der Hercules Saxanus. Bonn, 1862.
Arc 848.32 — Frenzel, W. Grundzüge der Vorgeschichte Deutschlands. Stuttgart, 1935.
Arc 861.150 — Frere, Sheppard. The city of Durovernum. Canterbury, 1957.
Arc 861.153 — Frere, Sheppard. The city of Durovernum. Canterbury, 1962.
Arc 960.2 — Fresh-water shell mounds...St. John's River, Florida. (Wyman, J.) Salem, 1875.
Arc 750.208 — Les fresques de Boscoreale. (Sambon, Arthur.) Paris, 1903.
Arc 1033.35.11 — Freuz und die Kreuzigung. (Fulda, H.) Breslau, 1878.
Arc 915.4 — Frey, F. Führer durch die Ruinen vor Augusta Raurica. Liestal, 1907.
Arc 1027.18.20 — Frey, J.B. Nouvelles inscriptions inedites de la cata-combe juive de la via Appia. n.p., 193-.
Arc 87.1.72 — Frickenhaus, A. Lenäenvasen. Berlin, 1912.
Arc 635.223F — Frickenhaus, A. Tiryns. v.1-8. Athēnai, 1912- 9v.
Arc 1335.157.2 — Friedberg, Robert. Gold coins of the world, complete from 600 A.D. to the present. N.Y., 1965.

Author and Title Listing

Arc 1348.22 Friedensburg, F. Die Münze in der Kulturgeschichte. Berlin, 1909.
Arc 1390.10 Friedensburg, F. Münzkunde und Geldgeschichte der Einzelstaaten des Mittelalters und der neuer Zeit. München, 1926.
Arc 1510.105F Friedensburg, F. Die schlesischen Münzen des Mittelalters. Breslau, 1931.
Arc 1668.10 Friedensburg, F. Die Symbolik der Mittlaltermünzen. v.1,2-3. Berlin, 1913-22. 2v.
Arc 87.1.21 Friederichs, K. Apollon mit den Lamm. Berlin, 1861.
Arc 705.210 Der Friedhof am Eridanos...zu Athen. (Brueckner, A.) Berlin, 1909.
Arc 1428.4 Friedländer, J. Frankische im Orient geprägte Münzen. n.p., n.d.
Arc 1590.3 Friedlaender, J. Recherches sur les monnaies frappées dans l'île de Rhodes. Paris, 1855.
Arc 1360.1 Friedlaender, J. Repertorium zur antiken Numismatik. Berlin, 1885.
Arc 1485.5 Friedländer, Julius. Die italienischen Schaumünzen der fünfzehnten Jahrhundert. Berlin, 1882.
Arc 1490.37 Friedländer, Julius. Die Münzen der Ostgothen. Berlin, 1844.
Arc 1490.3 Friedländer, Julius. Die Oskischen Münzen. Leipzig, 1850.
Arc 1335.11.5 Friedlander. Das königliche Münzkabinet. 2. Aufl. Berlin, 1877.
Arc 1153.18 Friedrich, G. Učebna kniha palaeografie latinskě. Praha, 1898.
Arc 1138.65 Friedrich, Johannes. Entzifferung verschollener Schriften und Sprachen. Berlin, 1954.
Arc 1138.65.2 Friedrich, Johannes. Entzifferung verschollener Schriften und Sprachen. 2. Aufl. Berlin, 1966.
Arc 1138.65.5 Friedrich, Johannes. Extinct languages. N.Y., 1957.
Arc 1510.169 Friedrich, Karl. Ein Beitrag zur Geschichte des Kontermarkenwesens. Münster, 1970.
Arc 482.206 Friedrich Sarre Schriften. (Schmidt, J.H.) Berlin, 1935.
Arc 1033.17.330 Fries, Felix. Histoire de Notre Dame de Foy. Namur, 1909.
Arc 530.10 Der Fries des Artemisions von Magnesia. (Herkenrath, E.) Berlin, 1902.
Arc 530.29 Der Fries des Hekateions von Lagina. (Shober, Arnold.) Baden, 1933.
Arc 682.10F Der Fries des Megarons von Mykenai. (Rodenwaldt, G.) Halle an der Saale, 1921.
Arc 705.200.5F Der Fries des Tempels der Athena Nike. (Blümel, Carl.) Berlin, 1923.
Arc 889.20F Friesch Genootschap van Geschied-Oudheid en Taalkunde te Leeuwarden. Friesche oudheden. Leeuwarden, 1875.
Arc 889.20F Friesche oudheden. (Friesch Genootschap van Geschied-Oudheid en Taalkunde te Leeuwarden.) Leeuwarden, 1875.
Htn Arc 968.2.75* Frijoles Canyon pictographs. (Baumann, G.) Santa Fe, 1939.
Arc 1020.140 Friken, A. Rimskaia katakomby i pamiatniki pervonachal'nago Khristianskago iskusstva. Moskva, 1872-
Arc 66.1.136 La frise ionique. (Demangel, R.) Paris, 1932.
Arc 673.7 Fritsch, O. Delos, die Insel des Apolon. Gütersloh, 1908.
Arc 1465.77 Fritze. Nomisma, Untersuchungen auf dem gebiete. Berlin, 1907-12. 12v.
Arc 1468.4 Frochner, W. Monnaies grecques de la collection Photiadès Pacha. Paris, 1890.
Arc 670.5F Frödin, Otto. Asine; results of the Swedish excavations 1922-1930. Stockholm, 1938.
Arc 1675.23 Froehner, Vilhelm. Les medaillons de l'Empire romain depuis le règne d'Auguste jusqu'à Priscus Attale. Paris, 1878.
Arc 785.15 Froehner, W. La colonne trajane. Paris, 1865.
Arc 1360.2.7 Froelich, E. Ad numismata regum veterum anecdota. Viennae, 1756. 2 pam.
Arc 1420.1.5F Froelich, E. Annales compendiarii regum et rerum Syriae. Vienna, 1744.
Htn Arc 1420.1* Froelich, E. Annales compendiarii regum et rerum Syriae. 2. ed. Vienna, 1754.
Arc 1360.2.5 Froelich, E. Quatuor tentamina in re. numaria vetere. Viennae, 1737.
Arc 1360.2 Froelich, E. Utilitas rei numariae veteris. Viennae, 1733.
Arc 1480.86 Der Fröndenberger Münzschatzfund römischer Denare. (Weissgerber, Clemens.) Dortmund, 1969?
Arc 1033.35.161 Frolow, Anatole. Les reliquaires de la Vraie Croix. Paris, 1965.
Arc 1033.35.160 Frolow, Anatole. La relique de la Vraie Croix. Paris, 1961.
Arc 608.17.3 From Bengazi to Cyrene. (Norton, Richard.) n.p., 1911.
Arc 453.16 From history to pre-history at Nevasa. (Sankalia, Hasmukh Dhirajlal.) Poona, 1960.
Arc 1480.40 From imperium to auctoritas. (Grant, Michael.) Cambridge, 1946.
Arc 1480.40.1 From imperium to auctoritas. 1. ed. (Grant, Michael.) London, 1969.
Arc 893.30F From period III to period IV. (Randsborg, Klavs.) Copenhagen, 1972.
Arc 1448.6 From real to rand. (Becklake, J.T.) South Africa, 1963?
Arc 700.56 From the silent earth. (Alsop, J.) N.Y., 1964.
Arc 712.15 Le frontal orientale du Parthenon. (Mot, J. de.) Bruxelles, 1906.
Arc 340.37 Frontier Forts and Trails Survey. A partial bibliography of the archaeology of Pennsylvania and adjacent states. Harrisburg, 1941.
Arc 66.1.99 La frontière de l'Euphrate de Pompée à la Conquête Arabe. (Chapot, V.) Paris, 1907.
Arc 66.1.165 Le fronton sculpté en Grèce. (Lapalus, Etienne.) Paris, 1947. 2v.
Arc 861.193F Froom, F.R. Wawcott II, a stratified Mesolithic succession. Oxford, 1976.
Arc 1615.7 Frossard, E. Monograph of United States cents and half cents issued between the years 1793 and 1857. Irvington, 1879.
Arc 612.47 Frost, H. Under the Mediterranean. London, 1963.
Arc 726.59.40 Frost, Honor. The mortar wreck in Mellieha Bay. London, 1969.
Arc 723.11 Frothingham, Arthur L. Roman cities in Italy and Dalmatia. N.Y., 1910.
Arc 723.11.5 Frothingham, Arthur L. Roman cities in Northern Italy and Dalmatia. London, 1910.
Arc 673.1.15 Frotier de la Coste Messelière, P. Au musée de Delphes. Thèse. Paris, 1936.
Arc 925.38.16 Frozen tombs of Siberia. 1. English ed. (Rudenko, Sergei Ivanovich.) Berkeley, 1970.
Arc 545.217 Die fruehchristliche Alterthuemer aus....Achmim Panopolis. (Forrer, R.) Strassburg, 1893.
Arc 303.30 Fruehchristliche Türkei. Basel.
Arc 853.277 Frühchristliches Köln. (Cologne. Römisch-Germanisches Museum.) Köln, 1965.
Arc 853.85 Die frühe Altsteinzeit am der Weser. (Meier-Böke, A.) Leipzig, 1940.
Arc 848.50 Frühe Burger und Städte. (Akademie der Wissenschaften, Berlin.) Berlin, 1954.
Arc 432.12.5 Das frühe Indien. (Mode, Heinz.) Stuttgart, 1959.
Arc 848.46 Die frühgermanische Landnahme im mitteldeutsch-sächsisch-nordböhmischen Gebiet. (Mähling, W.) Prag, 1944.
Arc 853.17.15F Frühgeschichtliche Funde aus Westfalen im städtischen Kunst- und Gewerbemuseum Dortmund. (Albrecht, C.) Dortmund, 1936.
Arc 1251.25 Die frühkretischen Siegel. (Matz, F.) Berlin, 1928.
Arc 568.2 Frühmitteläg yptische Studien. (Schenkel, W.) Bonn, 1962.
Arc 905.105 Der frühmittelalterliche Gräberfund von Köttloch. (Pittioni, Richard.) Brun, 1943.
Arc 936.195.245 Frühmittelalterliches Gräberfeld in Želovce. (Čilinská, Zlata.) Bratislava, 1973.
Arc 915.53 Die fruhbronzezeitliche Ansiedlung in der Bleiche bei Arbon T.G. (Fischer, Franz.) Basel, 1971.
Arc 1030.60 Fruhchristliche Sinnbilder und Inschriften. (Beyer, Oskar.) Kassel, 1954.
Arc 1433.60.5 Frye, Richard N. Sasanian remains from Qasr-i Abu Nasr; seals, sealings, and coins. Cambridge, 1973.
Arc 853.83 Fuchs, Alois. Im Streit um die Externsteine. Paderborn, 1934.
Arc 645.3 Fuchs, Siegfried. Die griechischen Fundgruppen der frühen Bronzezeit und ihre auswärtigen Beziehungen. Berlin, 1937.
Arc 1285.10.10 Fudalej, Aleksander. Pieczęcie kięstw glogowskigeo [sic] i Żagańskiego. Nova Sól, 1973.
Arc 1077.2.65 Füglister, Robert L. Das Lebende Kreuz. Einsiedeln, 1964.
Htn Arc 435.8.6* Führer, A.A. Monograph on Buddha Sâkyamuni's birth-place in the Nepalese Tarâi. Allahabad, 1897.
Arc 435.2.12F Führer, A.A. Monumental antiquities and inscriptions. Allahabad, 1891.
Arc 435.2.11F Führer, A.A. The Sharqi architecture of Jaunpur. Calcutta, 1889.
Arc 1027.26.25 Führer, J. Forschungen zur Sicilia sotterranea. München, 1897.
Arc 1033.62.9 Führer, Joseph. Ein Beitrag zur Lösung zer Felicitas-Frage. Leipzig, 1890.
Arc 905.24.13 Führer druch die Ausgrabungen und das Museum auf dem Magdalensberg. 3. Aufl. (Egger, Rudolf.) Klagenfurt, 1956.
Arc 905.17.5 Führer durch Aguntum. (Swoboda, Erich.) Baden, 1935.
Arc 915.4.10 Führer durch Augusta Raurica. (Laur-Belart, Rudolf.) Basel, 1937.
Arc 915.4.11 Führer durch Augusta Raurica. 2. Aufl. (Laur-Belart, Rudolf.) Basel, 1948.
Arc 915.4.14 Führer durch Augusta Raurica. 4. Aufl. (Laur-Belart, Rudolf.) Basel, 1966.
Arc 905.12.5 Führer durch Carnuntum. (Kubitschek, W.) Wien, 1904.
Arc 905.20 Führer durch das K.K. Staatsmuseum in S. Donato in Zara. (Österreichisches Archäologisches Institut.) Wien, 1912.
Arc 520.11.5 Führer durch das Pergamon Museum. (Berlin. Königliches Museum.) Berlin, 1904.
Arc 853.10.20 Führer durch das Römerkastell Saalburg. (Schoeberger, H.) Bad Homburg, 1957.
Arc 853.10.5 Führer durch das Römerkastell Saalburg. 4. Aufl. (Jacobi, H.) Homburg, 1908.
Arc 530.45 Führer durch das Tell Halaf Maueum. (Berlin. Tell Halaf Museum.) Berlin, 1934.
Arc 600.3.10 Führer durch die Altertümer von Memphis und Sakkara. (Hermann, A.) Berlin, 1938.
Arc 905.24.15 Führer durch die Ausgrabungen und das Museum auf dem Magdalensberg. 5. Aufl. (Egger, Rudolf.) Klagenfurt, 1958.
Arc 853.57 Führer durch die römische Granitindustrie auf dem Felsberg im Odenwald. (Behn, Friedrich.) Mainz, 1925.
Arc 915.50 Führer durch die römische Schweiz. (Lambert, André.) Zürich, 1973.
Arc 505.11.5 Führer durch die Ruinen von Baalbek. (Puchstein, O.) Berlin, 1905.
Arc 520.6 Führer durch die Ruinen von Pergamon. (Berlin. Königliches Museum.) Berlin, 1887.
Arc 520.6.5 Führer durch die Ruinen von Pergamon. 5. Aufl. (Berlin. Königliches Museum.) Berlin, 1911.
Arc 520.11.6 Führer durch die Ruinen von Pergamon. 6. Aufl. (Berlin. Königliches Museum.) Berlin, 1922.
Arc 915.4 Führer durch die Ruinen vor Augusta Raurica. (Frey, F.) Liestal, 1907.
Arc 810.11.2 Fuehrer durch Pompeji. (Mau, August.) Naples, 1893.
Arc 810.11.3 Fuehrer durch Pompeji. 2. Aufl. (Mau, August.) Leipzig, 1896.
Arc 810.11.4 Fuehrer durch Pompeji. 3. Aufl. (Mau, August.) Leipzig, 1898.
Arc 810.11.4.5 Fuehrer durch Pompeji. 4e Aufl. (Mau, August.) Leipzig, 1903.
Arc 810.11.5 Fuehrer durch Pompeji. 6. Aufl. (Mau, August.) Leipzig, 1928.
Arc 190.7 Fuehrer zu archäologischen Denkmalen in Bayern. Bayern. 1,1971+
Arc 190.5 Fuehrer zu Vor- und Frühgeschichten Denkmälern. Mainz am Rhein. 2,1965+ 16v.
Arc 848.18 Führer zur Urgeschichte. Augsburg. 1,1928
Arc 204.5 Führungsblätter. (Treves. Rheinisches Landesmuseum.)
Arc 513.8 Fuenf Inschriften und fuenf Staedte in Kleinasien. (Franz, J.) Berlin, 1840.
Arc 925.255.10 Fünf Sulfekinschriften. (Toettermann, A.) Helsingfors, 1891.
Arc 395.22 Fünfzig Jahre aus dem Leben. (Karo, Georg H.) Baden-Baden, 1959.
Arc 689.7.5 Fürhrer durch Tiryns. 2. Aufl. (Karo, G.) Athen, 1934.
Arc 1663.45 Fuld, George. Patriotic Civil War tokens. Racine, 1960.
Arc 1033.35.11 Fulda, H. Freuz und die Kreuzigung. Breslau, 1878.
Arc 861.125 Fullbrook-Leggatt, Lawrence Edward Wells Outen. Roman Gloucester. Gloucester, 1950.
Arc 861.126 Fullbrook-Leggatt, Lawrence Edward Wells Outen. Roman Gloucester. Lansdown, 1968.
Htn Arc 760.4.8* Fulvio, A. L'antichita di Roma. Venetia, 1588.
Htn Arc 760.4* Fulvio, A. Antiquitates urbis. Roma, 1527.
Htn Arc 760.4.5* Fulvio, A. De urbis antiquitatibus. Roma, 1545.
Arc 1510.152.7 Funck, Walter. Die Notmünzen der deutschen Städt, Gemeinden, Kreise, Länder. 2. Aufl. Münster, 1973.

Arc 1510.152.5 Funck, Walter. Die Notmünzen der deutschen Städt, Gemeinden, Kreise, Länder. 5. Aufl. Münster, 1966.
Arc 830.192 Der Fund von Ittenheim. (Werner, J.) Strassburg, 1943.
Arc 845.202 Der Fund von Sackrau. pts.1-3. (Grempler, Wilhelm.) Berlin, 1887-88.
Arc 220.5 Fundberichte aus Österreich. Wien. 1-5,1930-1952
Arc 1368.1 Funde antiker Münzen im königrieche Württemberg. (Nestle, W.) Stuttgart, 1893.
Arc 853.349 Funde aus der Römerstadt Schwarzenacke und ihrer nahen Ungebung. (Kolling, Alfons.) Homburg-Saar, 1971.
Arc 895.44F Die Funde aus Dolman. v.1-2. (Bagge, A.) Stockholm, 1950-52.
Arc 600.4.5 Funde aus Naukratis. (Prinz, H.) Leipzig, 1906.
Arc 689.12 Die Funde der früher Dimini-Zeit aus der Arapi-Magula. Diss. (Hauptmann, Harald.) Bonn, 1969.
Arc 572.11 Funde in Ägypten. (Wolf, Walther.) Göttingen, 1966.
Arc 421.30 Funde in Alt-China. (Hentze, Carl.) Göttingen, 1967.
Arc 726.241 Funde in der Magna Graecia. (Huelsen, Hans von.) Gottingen, 1962.
Arc 1490.92 Funde venezianischer Münzen des 13. Jahrhundert in der Ostukraine als geschichtliche Quelle. (Shuhaievs'kyi, Valentyn.) Berlin, 1944.
Arc 853.344 Die Funde vom Wartberg in Hessen. (Schrickel, Waldtraut.) Marburg, 1969.
Arc 635.4 Die Funde von Olympia. (Curtius, E.) Berlin, 1882.
Arc 1480.56 Die Fundmünzen der römischen Zeit in Deutschland. (Deutsches Archäologisches Institut.) Berlin, 1960- 17v.
Arc 1305.3 Die Fundmünzen der römischen Zeit in Österreich. Burgenland. Eisenstadt. 1,1970+
Arc 1480.42.15 Die Fundmünzen von Vindonissa von Hadrian bis zum Ausgang der Römerherrschaft. (Pekary, Thomas.) Brugg, 1971.
Arc 588.59F The funeral furniture of Egypt. (Petrie, W.M.F.) London, 1937.
X Cg Arc 568.1.2 The funeral tent of an Egyptian queen. (Stuart, V.) London, 1882.
Arc 600.15.25 A funerary repast in an Egyptian tomb of the archaic period. (Emery, Walter Bryan.) Leiden, 1962.
Arc 600.15.20 Funerary stelae from Kom Abour Billow. (Hooper, Finley A.) Ann Arbor, 1961.
Arc 853.242F Funk, A. Bilder aus der Vor- und Frühgeschichte des Hegaus. Singen, 1960.
Arc 793.1.2 Furchheim, F. Bibliografia di Pompei, Ercolano e Stabia. Napoli, 1891.
Arc 1020.113 Furno, A. Breve istoria del santuario di Belmonte presso Valperga. Torino, 1788.
Arc 1428.8 Furse, E.H. Mémories numismatiques de l'ordre...St. Jean de Jerusalem. Rome, 1889.
Arc 1505.3 Furstenbergischen Münzen und Medaillen. (Dollinger, F.) Donaueschingen, 1903.
Arc 452.1.25F Further excavations at Mohenjo-daro. (Mackay, Ernest.) Delhi, 1938. 2v.
Arc 609.16F Further paleo-anthropological studies in northern Lunda. (Clark, John Desmond.) Lisboa, 1968.
Arc 1033.12.27 Il furto del "Santo Sudario" nel 1507. (Barnate, C.) Genova, 1915.
Arc 635.207.5 Furtwängler, A. Ägena, das Heiligtum der Aphaia. Text and atlas. München, 1906. 2v.
Arc 670.2.3 Furtwängler, A. Die Ägineten der Glypothothek König Ludwigs I. München, 1906.
Arc 635.207 Furtwängler, A. Archäologische Studien...Heinrich Brunn...dargebracht. Berlin, 1893.
Arc 87.1.43 Furtwaengler, A. Goldfund von Vettersfelde. Berlin, 1883.
Arc 1070.207 Furtwängler, A. Neuere Faelschungen von Antiken. Berlin, 1899.
Arc 87.1.40 Furtwaengler, A. Der Satyr aus Pergamon. Berlin, 1880.
Arc 390.15 Furtwängler, Adolf. Briefe aus dem Bonner Privatdozentenjahr 1879/80. Stuttgart, 1965.
Arc 390.2.12 Furtwängler, Adolf. Kleine Schriften. München, 1912. 2v.
Arc 549.5 Fuscaldo, Perla. Egyptian archaeology. n.p., n.d. 3 pam.
Arc 1490.50F Fusco, G.V. Intorno alle zecche ed alle monete battute nel reame di Napoli da Re Carlo VIII di Francia. Napoli, 1846.
Arc 522.13 Fynden i Troas och Homeroe' Troja. (Hildebrand, H.H.) Stockholm, 1878.
Arc 551.1.5 G.B. Belzoni. (Belzoni, G.B.) Padova, 1960.
Arc 936.14.220 Gabałówna, Lidia. Zé studiów nad grupą brzesko-kujawską kultury lendzielskiej. Łódź, 1966.
Arc 609.19 Gabd, Creighton. Stone age hunters of the Kafue. Boston, 1965.
Arc 1033.11 Gaborel de Rossillon, J. Alma Mater. Paris, 1877.
Arc 905.142 Gabori, Miklos. Akésöi paleolitikum Magyarországon. Budapest, 1964.
Arc 905.130 Gábori-Csánk, V. La station du paléolithique moyen d'Erd-Hongrie. Budapest, 1968.
Arc 1468.40 Gabrici, E. Tecnica e cronologia delle monete greche. Roma, 1951.
Arc 1465.76 Gabrici, E. Topografia e numismatica dell'antica Imera, Sicily. Napoli, 1893.
Arc 761.7 Gabrici, Ettore. Il problema delle origini di Roma secondo le recenti scoperti archeologiche. Padova, 1906.
Arc 38.5.5 Gabriel, Albert. İstanbul Türk kaleleri. İstanbul, 197-.
Arc 513.24F Gabriel, Albert. Voyages archeologiques dans la Turquie orientale. Paris, 1940. 2v.
Arc 1027.89 Gabrieli, Giuseppe. Inventario topografico e bibliografico delle cripte eremitiche basiliane di Puglia. Roma, 1936.
Arc 895.7.30 Gabrielsen, S.V. De forhistoriske tider i Danmark. København, 1948.
Arc 936.235 Gabrovec, S. Najstarejša zgodovina Dolenjske. Novo Mesto, 1956.
Arc 441.9.5 Gadre, A.S. Archaeology in Baroda, 1934-1947. Baroda, 1947.
Arc 441.9 Gadre, A.S. Important inscriptions from the Baroda state. Baroda, 1943.
Arc 925.322.25 Gadzhiev, Magomed G. Iz istorii kul'tury Dagestana v epokhu bronzy. Makhachkala, 1969.
Arc 905.12.26 Gäbber in Karnuntum. (Gollob, Helwig.) Wien, 1957.
Arc 1468.12.3 Gaebler, Hugo. Die antiken Münzen von Makedonia. Berlin, 1906-35. 2v.
Arc 87.2.74 Gaedechens, R. Medusenhaupt von Blariacum. Bonn, 1874.
Arc 380.204 Gaedechens, R. Unedirte antike Bildwerke. Jena, 1873.
Arc 87.1.71 Gaertringen, F.H. Hira und Andania...zum Winckelmannsfeste. Berlin, 1911.
Arc 1027.1.13 Gaetani, V. Trina comunicazione...vasello col sangui. Palermo, 1895.
Arc 1510.65F Gaettens, R. Das Geld- und Münzwesen der Abtei Fulda im Hoch. Fulda, 1957.
Arc 1510.131 Gaettens, R. Die Münzen der Grafschaft Lüchow. Halle, 1937.
Arc 1510.65.5 Gaettens, R. Münzporträts im 11. Jahrhundert? Heidelberg, 1956.
Arc 853.68F Gätze, A. Die altthüringischen Funde von Weimar (5.-7. Jahrhundert nach Christus.) Berlin, 1912.
Arc 66.1.182 Gagé, Jean. Apollon romain. Paris, 1955.
Arc 905.50 Gaheis, Alexander. Lauriacum; Führer durch die Altertümer von Enns. Linz, 1937.
Arc 925.12.7.2 Gaidukevich, V.F. Das bosporanische Reich. 2. Aufl. Berlin, 1971.
Arc 925.12.7 Gaidukevich, V.F. Bosporskoe tsarstvo. Moskva, 1949.
Arc 936.20.71 Gajewska, Halina. Topographie des fortifications romaines en Dobroudja. Wrocław, 1974.
Arc 1015.228 Galante, G.A. Cemetero di S. Ipolisto in Atripalda. Napoli, 1893.
Arc 1027.25.45 Galante, G.A. Giovanni Battista de Rossi e l'archeologia cristiana. Napoli, 1900.
Arc 1030.1 Galante, G.A. Lapida sepolcrale di Teofilatto. Napoli, 1867.
Arc 1016.220A Galante, G.A. Memorie dell'antico cenobio di S. Severino. Napoli, 1869.
Arc 556.3 Galassi, G. Tehena. Roma, 1942.
Arc 1020.81 Galeron, F. Sur un reliquare...monastère de St. Évroult. n.p., n.d.
Arc 843.82 Galia y Sarañana, José. Prehistoria de Aragón. Zaragoza, 1945.
Arc 843.130 Galicia legendaria y arqueologica. (Monteagudo, Luis.) Madrid, 1957.
Arc 1033.17.601 Galizia, C.M. Rapporto cronistorico della formazione...del simolacro...Vergine Maria di Trapani. Palermo, 1733.
Arc 1470.4.5F Gallatin, A.E. Syracusan dekadrachmas. Cambridge, 1930.
Arc 547.25.5 Gallery of antiquities. (British Museum. Department of Egyptian and Assyrian Antiquities.) London, 1842.
Arc 830.33 Galles, René. Manné-er-H'roëk; dolmen découvert. Vannes, 1863.
Arc 66.1.192 Gallet de Santerre, Hubert. Délos primitive et archaique. Paris, 1958.
Arc 1030.41 Galletthio, P.A. Inscriptiones Bononienses. Roma, 1759.
Arc 726.36.5 Galli, Edoardo. Fiesole. Gli scair, il museo civico. Milano, 1914.
Arc 823.40 Gallia. (France. Centre National de la Recherche Scientifique.) Paris. 1,1943+ 28v.
Arc 823.41 Gallia. Supplément. Paris. 1+ 18v.
Arc 823.42 Gallia préhistoire. Paris. 1,1958+ 22v.
Arc 823.42.5 Gallia préhistoire. Supplément. Paris. 1,1963+ 8v.
Arc 823.17 Galliae antiguitates quaedam selectae atque in plures epistolas distributaes. (Maffei, Scipione.) Parisiis, 1733.
Arc 726.331 Galliazzo, Vittorio. I ponti di Padova romana. Padova, 1971.
Arc 547.14 Der Gallier. (Schreiber, T.) Leipzig, 1896.
Arc 823.8 Gallische Studien. (Hirshfeld, O.) Wien, 1883-1884.
Arc 387.10 Gallo, Francesco. Biografia del generale americano e console in Cipro, Luigi Palma di Cesnola. Vercelli, 1869.
Arc 889.17 De Gallo-Romeinse tempels te Elst in de Over Betuive. (Bogaers, J.E.A.T.) 's-Gravenhage, 1955.
Arc 513.16 Gallois, E. Asie-Mineure et Syrie. Paris, n.d.
Arc 1033.63.9 Gallonio, A. Traité des instruments de martyre. Paris, 1904.
Arc 609.23 Galloway, Alexander. The skeletal remains of Bambandyanalo. Johannesburg, 1959.
Arc 1550.8.5 Galster, Georg. Coins and history. Kopenhagen, 1959.
Arc 1550.8 Galster, Georg. Danske og norske medailler og jetons. Kjøbenhavn, 1936.
Arc 1542.3F Galster, Georg. Unionstidens udmøntninger. København, 1972.
Arc 1027.45 Galt Said, G. Grotta di San Paolo a Malta. Malta, 1863.
Arc 1500.62 Gamberini, Cesare. Prontuario. Bologna, 1952.
Arc 1490.75 Gamberini, Cesare. Prontuario pezzario delle monete. Bologna, 1960.
Arc 600.222 Gamer-Wallert, Ingrid. Der verziete Löffel; seine Formgeschichte und Verwendung im alten Ägypten. Wiesbaden, 1967.
Arc 412.5.5 Gamla fynd och glömda folk. (Brolin, Per Erik.) Göteborg, 1969.
Htn Arc 761.4* Gamucci, B. Le antichita della città di Roma. Venetia, 1565.
Htn Arc 761.4.5* Gamucci, B. Le antichita della città di Roma. Vinegia, 1580.
Htn Arc 761.4.9* Gamucci, B. Le antichita della città di Roma. Vinegia, 1588. 2 pam.
Htn Arc 761.4.3* Gamucci, B. Le antichita della città di Roma. 2. ed. Vinegia, 1569.
Arc 383.31F Gandert-Festschrift zum sechzigsten Geburtstag. (Müller, Adrian von.) Berlin, 1959.
Arc 1490.2 Gandolfi, G.C. Della moneta antica di Genova. v.1-2. Genova, 1841-42.
Arc 403.25 Gang durch versunkene Städte; ein Ausflug ins Reich der Archäologie. (Zenner, Klaus.) Leipzig, 1974.
Arc 454.1 Ganguly, M.M. Orissa and her remains. Calcutta, 1912.
Arc 925.75.10 Gansiniec, Z. Olbia. Kraków, 1962.
Arc 630.11F Ganymed; Heidelberger Beiträge zur antiken Kunstgeschichte. (Herbig, R.) Heidelberg, 1949.
Arc 925.185 Gaprindashvili, Givi M. Kldis sakhli skal'nye doma selishcha Pia. Tbilisi, 1959.
Arc 925.187 Gaprindashvili, Givi M. Peshchernyi ansambl' Vardzia, 1156-1213 gg. Tbilisi, 1960.
Arc 736.5 Garafalo, F.B. Le vie romane in Sicilia. Napoli, 1901.
Arc 1010.26 Garanger, José. Archéologie des Nouvelles Hébrides. Paris, 1972.
Arc 936.220F Garašanin, Milutin V. Arheološka nalazišta u Srbiji. Beograd, 1951.
Arc 936.220.3 Garašanin, Milutin V. Arheološki nalazi u Jugoslaviji. Beograd, 1966.
Arc 936.220.105 Garašanin, Milutin V. Praistorija na thu SR Srbije. Beograd, 1973. 2v.
Arc 936.220.15 Garašanin, Milutin V. Pregled materijame kulture juznih slovena u ranom s rednem veku. Beograd, 1950.
Arc 1163.39 Garcés G, Jorge A. Cómo han de traducirse los documentos paleográficos de Hispanoámerica. Quinto, 1961.
Arc 1033.35.149 Garces Teixeira, F.A. Acruz Manoelina do convento de Cristo. Lisboa, 1922.
Arc 1033.17.98.7 García, Juan C. Rasgo histórico acerca de nuestra Señora de la antigua de Guadalajara. Guadalajara, 1884.
Arc 1494.55 Garcia de la Fuente, Arturo. La numismática española en el reinado de Felipe II. Escorial, 1927.

Arc 843.233 García Guinea, Miguel Angel. El asentamiento cántabra de Celada Marlantes. Santander, 1970.
Arc 1163.34F Garcia Villada, Zacarias. Paleografía española. Album. Barcelona, 1974. 2v.
Arc 838.28 Garcia y Bellido, A. La dama de Elche. Madrid, 1943.
Arc 843.77.5 García y Bellido, Antonio. Colonia Aelia Augusta Halica. Madrid, 1960.
Arc 843.90 García y Bellido, Antonio. Hispania graeca. v.1-2, atlas. Barcelona, 1948. 3v.
Arc 412.8 García y Bellido, Antonio. Urbanistica de las grandes ciudades del mundo antiguo. Madrid, 1966.
Arc 936.13 Gardanski, A. Archeologia i pradzieje Polski. Warszawa, 1957.
Arc 853.65.65 Gardawski, Aleksander. Z pradzisjćw zieme dolnoslązkiej lod okolo. Wroclaw, 1973.
Arc 446.5 Garde, M.B. Archaeology in Gwalior. 2. ed. Gwalior, 1934.
Arc 1264.15 Gardilhon, R. Sigillographie des universités de France. Paris, 1952.
Arc 585.37F Gardiner, Alan H. Egyptian letters to the dead. London, 1928.
Arc 684.1.19 Gardiner, E.N. Olympia; its history and remains. Oxford, 1925.
Arc 708.22.3 Gardner, E.A. Ancient Athens. London, 1902.
Arc 708.22.5 Gardner, E.A. Ancient Athens. London, 1907.
Arc 708.22A Gardner, E.A. Ancient Athens. N.Y., 1902.
Arc 700.7 Gardner, P. Sculptured tombs of Hellas. London, 1896.
Arc 1465.2 Gardner, P. The types of Greek coins. Cambridge, Eng., 1883.
Arc 1468.52 Gardner, Percy. Archaeology and the types of Greek coins. Chicago, 1965.
Arc 1433.35 Gardner, Percy. Gold coinage of Asia before Alexander the Great. London, 1908.
Arc 1361.3 Gardner, Percy. A history of ancient coinage. 700-300 B.C. Oxford, 1918.
Arc 1348.50 Gardner, Percy. Macedonian and Greek coins of the Seleucidae. London, 1878.
Arc 1470.42 Gardner, Percy. Samos and Samian coins. London, 1882.
Arc 885.25 Gardner, Willoughby. Dinorben. Cardiff, 1964.
Arc 785.34.9 Gardthausen, V. Der Altar des Kaiserfriedens Ara Pacis Augustae. Leipzig, 1908.
Arc 1148.5.5 Gardthausen, V. Geschichte der griechischen Tachygraphie. Berlin, 1906.
NEDL Arc 1148.5 Gardthausen, V. Griechische Palaeographie. v.1-2. Leipzig, 1879.
Arc 1148.5.2 Gardthausen, V. Griechische Palaeographie. 2. Aufl. Leipzig, 1911. 2v.
Arc 726.70.10F Garger, E. Der Trajansbogen in Benevent. Berlin, 1943.
Arc 1663.28.10 Garibaldi nelle medaglie del Museo del Risorgimento in Milano. (Romussi, Carlo.) Milano, 1905.
Arc 861.21.35 Garlick, Tom. Roman sites in Yorkshire. Lancaster, 1971.
Arc 861.200 Garlick, Tom. Romans in the Lake counties. Clapham, 1970.
Arc 530.65 Garni. (Akademiia nauk Armianskoi SSR, Erevan. Institut Istorii.) Erevan, 1951- 4v.
Arc 1500.48 Garnier, Alphonse. La monnaie de Troyes de 1422 à 1434. n.p., n.d.
Arc 1087.1.2 Garofalo, Biagio. De antiquis marmoribus. 2. ed. Oxonii, 1828.
Arc 1087.1 Garofalo, Biagio. De antiquis marmoribus opusculum. Ad Rhenum, 1743.
Arc 726.324 Garoffolo, Francesco. Ipponion; saggio storico-archeologico e nuove osservazioni. Reggio Calabria, 1969.
Arc 495.204 Garrett, Robert. Topography and itinerary (American archaeological exedition to Syria). N.Y., 1914.
Arc 858.38 Garrod, D.A.E. The upper palaeolithic age in Britain. Oxford, 1926.
Arc 391.7 Garrod, Dorothy A.E. Environment, tools and man. Cambridge, 1946.
Arc 391.9 Garrood, J.R. Archaeological remains. London, 1949.
Arc 1033.17.33 Garruba, M. Eoniade della translazione...miracolosa immagine di Santa Maria...Constantinopoli. Napoli, 1834.
Arc 1033.9.5 Garrucci, R. Descrizioni dei vetri ornati di figure in oro. n.p., n.d.
Arc 1033.44.27 Garrucci, R. Deux monuments des premiers siècles. Rome, 1862.
Arc 1015.208.5 Garrucci, R. Dissertazioni archaeologiche di vario argomento. v.1-2. Roma, 1864.
Arc 1016.224 Garrucci, R. Esame della numismatica costantiniana. Roma, 1858.
Arc 1033.9 Garrucci, R. Nuova interpretazione di un vetro cimiteriale. n.p., n.d.
Arc 1018.18 Garrucci, R. Opuscoli archeologici profana e cristiana. Roma, 1860-77.
Arc 1018.18.2 Garrucci, R. Opuscoli di archeologia christiana e profana. Roma, n.d.
Arc 1207.200F Garrucci, R. I piombi antichi. Roma, 1847.
Arc 1015.208.13 Garrucci, R. Relazione generale degli scavi e scoperte...via Satina. Roma, 1859.
Arc 1015.208.8 Garrucci, R. Tre sepolcri con pitture ed iscrizione. Napoli, 1852.
Arc 1015.208 Garrucci, R. Vetri ornati di figura in oro. Roma, 1858.
Arc 1015.208.2 Garrucci, R. Vetri ornati di figure in oro. Roma, 1864.
Arc 810.31 Garrucci, Räffaele. Questioni Pompeiane. Napoli, 1853.
Arc 1030.5.62 Garruci, P.R. Il crocifisso graffito. Roma, 1857.
Arc 1027.18 Garruci, R. Cimitero degli antichi ebrei. Roma, 1862.
Arc 853.41.15 Garscha, Friedrich. Die Alamannen in Sudbaden. Berlin, 1970. 2v.
Arc 600.15 Garstang, J. The burial customs of ancient Egypt. London, 1907.
Arc 589.7 Garstang, J. The third Egyptian dynasty. Westminster, 1904.
Arc 588.11 Garstang, John. El Arábah. London, 1901.
Arc 530.12 Garstang, John. The land of the Hittites. London, 1910.
Arc 588.12 Garstang, John. Mahâsna and Bêt Khalfâf. London, 1902.
Arc 609.2.15 Garstang, John. Meroë, the city of the Ethiopians. Oxford, 1911.
Arc 530.60 Garstang, John. Prehistoric Mersin. Oxford, 1953.
Arc 505.66 Garstang, John. The story of Jericho. London, 1940.
Arc 1588.1.27 Gartman, V.G. Pol'skiia i litobskiia star. monety. Syzran, 1901.
Arc 1490.8 Garufi, C.A. Monete econii nella storia del diritto siculo. Palermo, 1898.
Arc 1033.6.10 Gasdia, U.E. La casa pagano cristiana del Celio (Titulus Byzantis sive Pammachii). Roma, 1937.
Arc 936.14.375 Gąsgowski, Jerzy. Z dziejów polskiej archeologii. wyd. 1. Warszawa, 1970.
Arc 391.16 Gąsiorowski, Stanislaw J. Pisma wybrane. Wroclaw, 1969.
Arc 1153.113 Gasparri, Françoise. L'écriture des actes de Louis VI, Louis VII et Philippe Auguste. Genève, 1973.
Arc 726.262 Gasperini, Lidio. Aletrium. Roma, 1964.
Arc 830.100 Gasser, A. Recherches archéologiques sur le térritoire de Mantoche. Gray, 1901.
Arc 858.102 Gąssowski, Jerzy. Irlandia i Brytania w początkach średniowiecza w świetle badań archeologicznych. Warszawa, 1973.
Arc 936.14.485 Gąssowski, Jerzy. Przewodnik archeologiczny po Polsce. Wroclaw, 1973.
Arc 720.220F Gastaldi, B. Nuovi cenni sugli oggetti di alta antichità. Torino, 1862.
Arc 540.1.5 Gaston L. Feuardent vs. L.P. Cesnola - testimony of the defendant. (Cesnola, L.P.) N.Y., 1884.
Arc 1185.8 Gatterer, J.C. Abriss der Diplomatik. Göttingen, 1798.
Arc 1185.8.2 Gatterer, J.C. Praktische Diplomatik. Göttingen, 1799.
Arc 761.6F Gatteschi, Giuseppe. Restauri della Roma imperiale. Roma, 1924.
Arc 1033.6.25 Gatti, Giuseppe. La casa celimontana dei Valerii e il Monastero di S. Erasmo. Roma, 1902.
Arc 785.46 Gauckler, P. Le sanctuaire syrien du Janicule. Paris, 1912.
Arc 608.1.3 Gauckler, Paul. L'archéologie de la Tunisie. Paris, 1896.
Arc 608.1.25 Gauckler, Paul. Enquête sur les installations hydrologiques romaines en Tunisie. Tunis, 1897-
Arc 608.2.9 Gauckler, Paul. Nécropoles puniques de Carthage. pt.1-2. Paris, 1915. 2v.
Arc 938.107 Die Gauja-Liven und ihre materielle Kultur. (Tönisson, Evald.) Tallinn, 1974.
Arc 101.10 Gaule. (Société d'Histoire, d'Archéologie et de Tradition Gauloises.) Paris. 2-24,1956-1963 2v.
Arc 830.66.9 La Gaule thermale. (Bonnard, Louis.) Paris, 1908.
Arc 1025.31 Gaume, J. Histoire des catacombes. Paris, 1848.
Arc 1025.31.3 Gaume, J. Histoire des catacombes de Rome. Paris, n.d.
Arc 545.227.38 Gauthier, H. Le temple d'Amada. Le Caire, 1913.
Arc 545.227.36 Gauthier, H. Temple de Ouadi Es-Seboua. Le Caire, 1912.
Arc 1033.12.16 Gauthier, J. Notes iconographique sur le Saint Suaire de Besançon. Besançon, 1884.
Arc 1264.6 Gauthier, Jules. L'origine des armoiries de l'église de Besançon. n.p., 1880.
Arc 545.227.29 Gauthier, M.H. Le temple de Kalabach. Le Caire, 1911. 2v.
Arc 1138.13 Gautier, Léon. Quelques mots sur l'étude de la paléographie. Paris, 1864.
Htn Arc 815.4* Gautier, T. Le palais pompéien. Paris, 1866.
Arc 1020.138 Gavrilova, A. Sviatyni Egipta; zemlia egipet kak sad gospoden. Buenos Aires, 1960.
Arc 925.38.20 Gavrilova, Antonina. Mogil'nik kudyrge kak istochnik po istorii altaiskikh plemen. Leningrad, 1965.
Arc 375.3F Gay, V. Glossaire archéologique. Paris, 1887-1928. 2v.
Arc 441.1.7 Gaya and Buddha-Gaya. (Barua, B.M.) Calcutta, 1931-34. 2v.
Arc 583.2F Gayet, E. Musée du Louvre - Stèles de la XIIe Dynastie. pt.1-2. no.68. Paris, 1886.
Arc 830.151 Gazan, A. Notice sur une pierre tumulaire découverte aux environs de Solliès-Pont. Antibes, 1873.
Arc 7.1 Gazette archéologique. Paris, n.d. 14v.
Arc 7.1.2 Gazette archéologique. v.7. Paris, n.d.
Arc 1306.3 La gazette numismatique. Bruxelles.
Arc 1306.4 Gazette numismatique française. Paris. 1897
Arc 682.32 A gazetteer and atlas of Mycenaean sites. (Hope Simpson, Richard.) London, 1965.
Arc 858.59.50 A gazetteer of early Anglo-Saxon burial sites. (Meaney, A.) London, 1964.
Arc 1033.17.223 Gazulla, F.D. La patrona de Barcelona y su santuario. Barcelona, 1918.
Arc 1016.212 Gazzera, C. Delle iscrizioni cristiani del Piemonte. Torino, 1847.
Arc 1016.212.3 Gazzera, C. Delle iscrizioni cristiani del Piemonte. Torino, 1849.
Arc 1030.29 Gazzera, C. Ragguaglio critico del discorso sopra le iscrizioni cristiane. Modena, 1851.
Arc 925.343F Gdovskie kurgany v raskopkakh U.N. Glazova. (Spitsyn, Aleksandr A.) Sankt Petersburg, 1903.
Arc 395.18 Gdy slońce bylo bogiem. (Kosidowski, Z.) Warszawa, 1958.
Arc 395.18.2 Gdy slońce bylo bogiem. (Kosidowski, Z.) Warszawa, 1962.
Arc 684.5 Eine Gebäudegruppe in Olympia. (Schwarzstein, A.) Strassburg, 1909.
Arc 608.84 Gebel Ben Ghnema und Nord-Tibesti; Habilitationsschrift. (Ziegert, Helmut.) Wiesbaden, 1969.
Arc 587.12F Gebel es-Silsilah. (Caminos, Ricardo A.) London, 1963.
Arc 1510.140 Gebert, Carl Friedrich. Die Brandenburg Frankischen Kippermünzstätten, 1620-1622. München, 1901.
Arc 1508.7 Gebhart, H. Die deutschen Münzen des Mittelalters. 4. Aufl. Berlin, 1929.
Arc 1348.52 Gebhart, H. Numismatik und Geldgeschichte. Heidelberg, 1949.
Arc 630.22 Die Geburt der Aphrodite. (Simon, Erika.) Berlin, 1959.
Arc 1138.110 Das Gedächtnis der Völker. (Ekschmitt, Werner.) Berlin, 1964.
Arc 545.227.42F Der Gedächtnistempel Sethos' Izu Abydos. (Zippert, Erwin.) Berlin, 1931.
Arc 935.16 Gedeon, M.J. Eggraphoi liphoi kai keramia. Konstantinople, 1892.
Arc 936.6.35 Gediga, Boguslaw. Plemiona kultury Iuzyckiej w epoce brazu na śląsku środkowym. Text and atlas. Wroclaw, 1967.
Arc 936.6.36 Gediza, Boguslaw. Motyiwj tiguralne w sztuce ludnosci kultury luzyckiej. Wroclaw, 1970.
Arc 936.14.460 Gedl, Marek. Cmentarzysko halsztackie w kietrzue. Wroclaw, 1973.
Arc 936.14.460.5 Gedl, Marek. Kultura przedlużycka. Wroclaw, 1975.
Arc 936.6.20 Gedl, Marek. Uwagi v gospodarce i strukturze spolecznej ludności kultury Iuzyckiej. Kraków, 1961.
Arc 1027.25.11 Geffroy, A. Une fête archéologique à Rome. Paris, 1883.
Arc 82.1.5 Geffroy, M.A. L'école française de Rome. Paris, 1884.
Arc 595.16 Gegen die Zahlenmystik an der grossen Pyramide bei Gise. (Borchardt, Ludwig.) Berlin, 1922.
Arc 853.108 Geidel, H. Münchens Vorzeit. München, 1930.
Arc 1510.65F Das Geld- und Münzwesen der Abtei Fulda im Hoch. (Gaettens, R.) Fulda, 1957.
Arc 1530.5.5 Gelder, Hendrik Enno van. Les monnaies des Pays-Bas bourguigons et espagnols. Amsterdam, 1960.
Arc 1528.8.5 Gelder, Hendrik Enno van. De Nederlandse munten. 5. druk. Utrecht, 1972.
Arc 1530.5 Gelder, Hendrik Enno van. De Nederlandse noodmunten van de tachtigjarige vorlog. 's-Gravenhage, 1955.

Arc 1306.6 Geldgeschichtliche Nachrichten. Frankfurt am Main. 1,1966+

Arc 646.1 Gell, W. The itinerary of Greece: the geography of Ithaca. v.1-2. London, 1810.

Arc 700.1 Gell, W. Probestuecke von Städtemanern des Alten Griechenlands. München, 1831.

Arc 761.1.2 Gell, W. The topography of Rome and its vicinity. London, 1834. 3v.

Arc 761.1 Gell, W. The topography of RomeAnd its vicinity. London, 1846. 2v.

Arc 510.203 Gell, W. The topography of Troy. London, 1804.

Arc 810.6.7 Gell, William. Pompeiana; the topography, edifices, and ornaments of Pompeii. London, 1835. 2v.

Arc 810.6 Gell, William. Pompeiana. London, 1817-19.

Arc 810.6.5 Gell, William. Pompeiana. London, 1832. 2v.

Arc 810.6.2 Gell, William. Pompeiana. London, 1837. 2v.

Arc 810.6.3A Gell, William. Pompeiana. London, 1852.

Arc 1053.5.2 Der Gemüthsansdruck des Antinous. (Laban, F.) Berlin, 1891.

Arc 547.26 A general introductory guide to the Egyptian collections in the British Museum. (British Museum. Department of Egyptian and Assyrian Antiquities.) London, 1964.

Arc 635.221 La genesi dello Scorcio nell'arte greca. (Seta, A.D.) Roma, 1907.

Arc 572.10 The genesis of British Egyptology, 1549-1906. 1st ed. (Wortham, John David.) Norman, 1971.

Arc 915.10 Genève et la colonie de Vienne sous les Romains. pt.1. (Morel, C.) Genève, 1879? 2 pam.

Arc 925.290 Gening, V.F. Arkheologicheskie pamiatniki Udmurtii. Izhevsk, 1958.

Arc 925.323.5 Gening, Vladimir F. Rannie bolgary na Volge. Moskva, 1964.

Arc 1480.58 Genio populi romani, 295-316. (Callu, Jean Pierre.) Paris, 1960.

Arc 646.4 Gennadios, I. O Lordoz Elgin. Athēnai, 1930.

Arc 1488.15F Gennarelli, Achille. La moneta primitiva e i monumenti dell'Italia antica. Diss. Roma, 1843.

Arc 1025.23 Genni sopra i primi cimiteri...Roma christiana. (Angelini, A.) Roma, 1840.

Arc 723.8 Gentile, I. Trattato di archeologia e storia dell'arte italiano. Milano, 1901. 2v.

Arc 726.150 Gentili, Gino Vinicio. Auximum (Osimo) regio V. Picenum. Roma, 1955.

Arc 858.16 The gentleman's magazine library - Romano-British remains. London, 1887. 2v.

Arc 131.1 The Gentlemen's Society at Spalding. (Moore, William.) Cambridge, 1909. 2 pam.

Arc 853.280F Geobotanische Untersuchungen auf der Feddersen Wierde. (Koerber-Grohne, Udelgard.) Wiesbaden, 1967. 2v.

Arc 1020.80.7 Geoffroy de Couleron. Livre des reliques de l'abbaye de St. Pierre-le-Vif de Sens. Sens, 1887.

Arc 547.5.25 Geoffroy Saint Hillaire, E. Rapport fait à l'Académie royale des sciences. Paris, 1826.

Arc 390.16 Geofizika v arkheologii. (Frantov, Grigoriis.) Leningrad, 1966.

Arc 830.78.5 Geographie historique et descriptive de la Loire-Inférieure. (Maitre, Léon.) Nantes, 1893.

Arc 772.5 Geographie und Geschichte des Römischen Altertums. (Richter, O.) Nordlingen, 1889.

Arc 609.5 Die geographischen und geopolitischen Grundlagen der sudafrikanischen Ruinenkultur. (Seekirchner, A.) Memmingen, 1933.

Arc 543.146.15 Geoksiurskaia gruppa poselenii epokhi eneolita. (Khlopin, Igor N.) Leningrad, 1964.

Arc 726.130 Der geometrische Stil in Italien. (Akerstrom, A.) Lund, 1943.

Arc 392.12.80 Georg Habich zum 60. Geburtstag. München, 1928.

Arc 830.110 George, J. Cachette d'objets en bronze découverte à Vénat. Angoulême, 1895.

Arc 861.43 George, W. On an inscribed stone at Orchard Wyndham, Somerset. Bristol, 1879.

Arc 340.11 Georgieva, Sonia. Bibliografiia na bulgarskata arkheologiia, 1879-1955. Sofiia, 1957.

Arc 340.11.2 Georgieva, Sonia. Bibliografiia na bulgarskata arkheologiia, 1879-1966. 2. izd. Sofiia, 1974.

Arc 1583.19.1 Georgii Mikhailovich, Grand Duke of Russia. Monnaies de l'empire de Russie, 1725-1894. Boston, 1973.

Arc 1033.44 Georgius, D. De monogrammate Christi Domini. Diss. Roma, 1738.

Arc 1510.29 Das Geprägte amtliche Notgeld der Provinz Schlesien, 1917-1921. (Bahrfeldt, Max von.) Breslau, 1935.

Arc 1675.104 Die geprägten Schaumünzen Innerösterreichs; Steinmark, Kärnten, Krain. (Probszt, Günther.) Zürich, 1928.

Arc 670.3.5 Gerando, A. de. Gróf teleki Emma Görögorszagi a Rége Attikanak. Pest, 1873.

Arc 588.43F Gerar. (Petrie, W.M.F.) London, 1928.

Arc 1020.9.179 Gerardi, F.M. Bella congregazione illirica e de' nuovi affreschi. Roma, 1853.

Arc 505.68 Gerasa, city of the Decapolis. (Kraeling, C.H.) New Haven, Conn., 1938.

Arc 302.2.7 Gerasimov, T. Ukaz, kumuizv na bulgarekoto archeologichesko. Sofiia, 1934.

Arc 1033.12.111 Gerberon, G. Histoire de la robe sans couture de...J.-C....Argenteuil. Paris, 1677.

Arc 1020.10.46 Gerbet, O.P. Esquisse de Rome chrétienne. Paris, 1889. 3v.

Arc 830.163 Gergovia, capitale des Gaules. (Busset, Maurice.) Paris, 1933.

Arc 674.3.8F Gerhan, Armen. Das Theater von Epidauros. Stuttgart, 1961.

Arc 625.4 Gerhard, E. Antike Bildwerke. Text. München, 1828.

Arc 646.2 Gerhard, E. Archäologischer Nachlass aus Rom. Berlin, 1952.

Arc 87.1.14 Gerhard, E. Danae. Berlin, 1854.

Arc 746.4 Gerhard, E. Dionysos und Semele. v.1. Berlin, 1833. 2 pam.

Arc 740.201 Gerhard, E. Etruskische Spiegel. v.1-2,3,4,5. Berlin, 1843- 4v.

Arc 87.1.3 Gerhard, E. Die Heilung des Telephos. Berlin, 1843-

Arc 87.1 Gerhard, E. Kunstgeschichtliche Vasenbilder. Berlin, 1841.

Arc 87.1.6 Gerhard, E. Das Orakel der Themis. Berlin, 1846.

Arc 87.1.2 Gerhard, E. Phrixos der Herold. Berlin, 1842.

Arc 746.2 Gerhard, E. Über die Metallspiegel der Etrusker. Berlin, 1838.

Arc 391.2.5 Gerhard, Eduard. Über archäologische Sammlungen und Studien. Berlin, 1860.

Arc 391.2 Gerhard, Eduard. Über die Metallspiegel der Etrusker. Berlin, 1836. 11 pam.

Arc 830.58 Gerin-Ricard, H. de. Antiquités de la vallée de l'Arc en Provence. Aix, 1907.

Arc 530.10.15 Gerkan, Armin von. Der Altar des Artemis-Tempels in Magnesia am Mäander. Berlin, 1929.

Arc 530.14.15F Gerkan, Armin von. Das Theater von Priene. München, 1921.

Arc 1016.211.5F Gerke, F. Der Sarkophag des Iunius Bassus. Berlin, 1936.

Arc 543.83 Gerlach, Eva. Sand über den Tempeln Arabiens. 2. Aufl. Leipzig, 1967.

Arc 673.2 Gerlach, F.D. Dodona. Basel, 1859.

Arc 1500.6.3 Germain, A. De la monnaie Mahométane atribuée à um évêque. Montpellier, 1854.

Arc 1500.6 Germain, A. Mémoire sur les anciennes monnaies seigneuriales. Montpellier, 1852.

Arc 830.6.17 Germain de Montauzen, C. Les aqueducs antiques de Lyon. Paris, 1908.

Arc 848.61.5 Die Germanen. (Hachmann, Rolf.) München, 1971.

Arc 853.63.7 Die Germanen in der Prignitz zur Zeit der Völkerwanderung. (Matthes, W.) Leipzig, 1931.

Arc 853.15.5 Die Germanen in Mecklenburg im 2. Jahrtausend vor Christus. (Lütjen-Janssen, Hans.) Leipzig, 1935.

Arc 848.36 Germanenkunde. (Hofmeister, H.) Frankfurt am Main, 1936.

Arc 73.20.6 Germania. Gesamtinhaltsverzeichnis, v. 1-36 (1917-58). Berlin, 1960. 2v.

Arc 73.20.5 Germania: Korrespondenzblatt der Römisch-germanische Kommission. Berlin. 1,1917+ 41v.

Arc 848.14F Germania romana. (Deutsches Archäologisches Institut.) Bamberg, 1922.

Arc 612.45 Germanic art during the first millenium. (Holmqvist, Wilhelm.) Stockholm, 1955.

Arc 848.61 The Germanic peoples. (Hachmann, Rolf.) London, 1971.

Arc 848.57 Germanische Altertumskunde. (Kellermann, Volkmar.) Berlin, 1966.

Arc 848.20 Die germanische Familie in der Vorzeit. (Schulz, Walther.) Leipzig, 1925.

Arc 848.17 Germanische Heiligtümer. (Teudt, Wilhelm.) Jena, 1929.

Arc 848.17.5 Germanische Heiligtümer. 4. Aufl. (Teudt, Wilhelm.) Jena, 1936.

Arc 848.11 Germanische Kultur im Bronzezeitalter (2200-800 v. Chr.) (Erbt, Wilhelm.) Leipzig, 1926.

Arc 848.8.11 Germanische Kultur im letzten Jahrtausend nach Christus. (Kossinna, Gustaf.) Leipzig, 1932.

Arc 853.338 Das germanische Todtenlager bei Selzen. Faksimile. (Lindenschmit, Wilhelm.) Mainz an Rhein, 1969.

Arc 848.13 Die germanische Vorzeit. (Wels, K.H.) Leipzig, 1923.

Arc 853.278 Die germanischen Bügelfibeln der Völkerwanderungszeit. v.1-2. (Kühn, Herbert.) Graz, 1965- 3v.

Arc 853.262F Die germanischen Funde der späten Kaiserzeit und des frühen Mittelalters in Mittelfranken. Text and atlas. (Dannheimer, H.) Berlin, 1962. 2v.

Arc 853.44 Die germanischen Stämme und die Kulturen. (Blume, Erich.) Würzburg, 1912-15. 2v.

Arc 853.309 Der germanischen und slawischen Siedlungen und das mittelalterliche Dorf von Tornow. (Herrmann, Joachim.) Berlin, 1973.

Arc 848.29.5 Germanischer Lebensraum. 4. Aufl. (Radig, Werner.) Stuttgart, 1934.

Arc 1163.22 Germanistische Handschriftenpraxis. (Kirchner, J.) München, 1950.

Arc 1033.6 Germano, Stanislao P. La casa celimontana...Giovanni e Paolo. Roma, 1894.

Arc 1027.48 Germano di S. Stanislalo, P. Memorie archeologico...il cimitero S. Eutizio di Ferento. Roma, 1886.

Arc 845.5 Germany. Reichskommission. Limes. Der obergermanisch-raetische Limes. Abteilung A und B. Heidelberg. 1894-1910 14v.

Arc 825.8 Germer-Durand, E. Découvertes archéologiques faites à Nîmes, 1870-72. Nîmes, 1871-73.

Arc 825.8.5 Germer-Durand, E. Découvertes archéologiques faites a Nîmes. 1873. Nîmes, 1876.

Arc 825.8.6 Germer-Durand, E. Enceintes successives de Nîmes depuis les Romains. 2e éd. Nîmes, 1877.

Arc 825.8.3 Germer-Durand, E. Notes épigraphiques. Nîmes, 1869. 6 pam.

Arc 672.1.49F Gerola, G. Monumenti veneti nell'isola di Creta. v.1, pt.1-2, v.2-4. Venezia, 1905-32. 5v.

Arc 1153.45 Gerrard, John. Siglarium romanum. Londini, 1792.

Arc 925.12.10 Gerts, K.K. Arkheologicheskaia tipografiia tapanskago poluostrova. pts. 1-9. Sankt Peterburg, 1898-1901. 8v.

Arc 1033.17.134 Gervasi, F.A. Sorte invidiabile di Prato...della sagra Cintola. Firenze, 1742.

Arc 1148.13 Geschichte...der griechischen Tachygraphie. (Mentz, A.) Berlin, 1907.

Arc 1478.16 Geschichte älteren römischen Münzwesens...200 B.C. (Samer, K.) Wien, 1883.

Arc 1153.34 Geschichte der griechisch-römischen Schrift. (Mentz, Arthur.) Leipzig, 1920.

Arc 1148.5.5 Geschichte der griechischen Tachygraphie. (Gardthausen, V.) Berlin, 1906.

Arc 1423.15 Geschichte der jüdischen Münzen. (Levy, Moritz Abraham.) Breslau, 1862.

Arc 1423.15.1 Geschichte der jüdischen Münzen. (Levy, Moritz Abraham.) Leipzig, 1862.

Arc 1093.2.19 Geschichte der neolithischen Stämme im europäischen Teil der Ud SSR. (Brjussow, A.) Berlin, 1957.

Arc 1480.14 Geschichte der römischen Kupferprägung. (Willers, H.) Leipzig, 1909.

Arc 1200.20 Die Geschichte der Schriftsprache im ehemaligen Amt und in der Stadt Heusburg bis 1650. (Schütt, Otto.) Heusburg, 1919.

Arc 1212.2 Geschichte der Siegel. (Seyler, Gustav A.) Leipzig, 1894.

Arc 482.202.6F Geschichte der Stadt Samarra. (Herzfeld, Ernst E.) Hamburg, 1948.

Arc 1153.4.7 Die Geschichte der tironischen Noten. (Traube, L.) Berlin, 1901.

Arc 73.15 Geschichte des deutschen archäologisches Institut. (Michaelis, A.) Berlin, 1879.

Arc 1033.12.102 Geschichte des heiligen Rockes...Trier. v.1-2. (Hommer, J. von.) Bonn, 1844.

Arc 1033.163 Die Geschichte des Mâr Abhdiso und seines Jüngers Mâr Quardagh. (Kardag.) Kiel, 1889.

Arc 1478.10 Geschichte des römisches Münzwesens. (Mommsen, T.) Berlin, 1860.

Arc 1373.8 Die Geschichte im Lichte der Münzen. (Steuer.) Luckenwalde, 1911.

Arc 773.1 Geschichte und Beschreibung der alten Stadt Rom. (Sachse, K.) Hannover, 1824.

Author and Title Listing

Arc 1020.9.95 Geschichtsbilder aus alt christlicher Zeit. Roms. (Wolff.) Berlin, 1907.

Arc 1138.112.2 Geschreven verleden. 2. druk. (Brouwer, Hans.) 's-Gravenhage, 1963.

Arc 853.65 Geschwendt, F. Die steinurnen Streitäxte und Keulen Schlesiens. Inaug. Diss. Breslau, 1931.

Arc 1335.150F Gesellschaft der Freunde. Die Siegelsammlung des Mannheimer. Manheim, 1897.

Arc 191.2 Gesellschaft für Österreichische Frühmittelalterforschung. Veröffentlichungen. Linz.

Arc 503.4 Gesellschaft für Palästina. Forschung. Veröffentlichung. Wien. 1,1910

Arc 156.1.5 Gesellschaft für Vaterländische Alterthümer in Basel. Mittheilungen. Basel. 1-10,1843-1867

Arc 853.343F Gesellschaft und Kunst der Germanen. (Behm-Blancke, Günter.) Dresden, 1973.

Arc 1470.34 Ein Gesetz der Stadt Olbia zum Schulze ihres Silbergeldes. (Schmitz, Hermann.) Freiburg, 1925.

Arc 853.355 Gesicherte Spuren. 1. Aufl. (Müller, Adriaan von.) Berlin, 1972.

Arc 1027.59 Gesù Cristo nelle catacombe di Roma. (Labanca, B.) Roma, 1902.

Htn Arc 1020.9.75* Gesualdo, E. Osservazione...storia via Appia di Pratelle. Napoli, 1754.

Arc 1084.5 Getz, John. The Woodward collection of jades and other hard stones. n.p., 1913.

Arc 1033.112 Die Gewandung der Christen in den ersten Jahrhunderten. (Wilpert, J.) Köln, 1898.

Arc 391.12 Gherardo Ghirardini nel centenario della nascità. Padova, 1958.

Arc 1027.23.13 Ghignoni, A. Le pitture della catacombe romane. Firenze, 1905.

Arc 726.31 Ghirardini, G. Il museo nazionale atestino. Padova, 1903.

Arc 1433.32 Ghiron, I. Di alcuni conii osmani della museo di Modena. Firenze, 1870.

Arc 1430.10 Ghiron, I. Monete arabiche del gabinetto numismatico di Milano. Milano, 1878.

Arc 495.210F Ghirshman, Roman. Fouilles de Sialk près de Kashan. Paris, 1938-39. 2v.

Arc 386.22 Giacomo Boni nella vita del suo tempo. (Tea, Eva.) Milano, 1932. 2v.

Arc 391.17 Giacomo Grimaldi (1568-1623). Inaug. Diss. (Niggl, Reto.) München, 1971.

Arc 1490.5.10 Gian, M.L. dal. Il Leone di S. Marco. Venezia, 1958.

Arc 386.27 Gian Domenico Bertoli. (Vale, Giuseppe.) Aquileia, 1946.

Arc 1020.9.40 Gianuizzi, P. La chiesa di Santa Maria di Loreto IV. Sacre notizio V. Roma, 1884.

Arc 830.97.5 Gibelin, Antoine. Lettre sur les tours antiques qu'on a démoliés à Aix en Provence et sur les antiquités qu'elles renfermoient. Aix, 1787.

Arc 505.121 Gibeon, where the sun stood still. (Pritchard, James.) Princeton, 1962.

Arc 843.50 Gibert, Auguste M. Tarragona prehistòrica i protohistòrica. Barcelona, 1909.

Arc 843.15 Gibert y Olivé, A.M. Excursions arqueológicas. Ciutats focenses del litoral coseta. Barcelona, 1900.

Arc 865.11 Gidley, L. Stonehenge...by the light of ancient history. London, 1873.

Arc 712.36 Die Giebel des Parthenon. (Brommer, F.) Mainz, 1959.

Arc 670.2 Die Giebelgruppen von Aegina. (Schildt, A.) Leipzig, 1895.

Arc 853.83.10 Giefers, Wilhelm. Die Externsteine im Fürstenthum Lippe-Detmold. Paderborn, 1851.

Arc 608.2.25 Gielly, Paul. Quelques lueurs nouvelles sur l'emplacement de la Carthage punique et de ses ports. Casablanca, 1927.

Arc 936.14.550 Gierlach, Bogusław. Studia nad archeologią średniewiecznego Mazowsza. Wyd. 1. Warszawa, 1975.

Arc 726.250 Gierow, Pär Göran. The iron age culture of Latium. v.2, pt.1. Lund, 1964.

Arc 1361.4 Giesecke, W. Antikes Geldwesen. Leipzig, 1938.

Arc 1488.8F Giesecke, Walther. Italia numismatica. Leipzig, 1928.

Arc 1443.4 Giesecke, Walther. Das Ptalemäergeld. Leipzig, 1930.

Arc 1490.98.10F Giesecke, Walther. Sicilia numismata. Leipzig, 1923.

Arc 889.5 Giffen, Albert Egges van. Die Bauart der Einzelgräber. Text and atlas. Leipzig, 1930. 2v.

X Cg Arc 888.17 Giffen, Albert Egges van. Inheemse en Romeinse terpen. Atlas and plates. Groningen, 1950. 2v.

Arc 888.15 Giffen, Albert Egges van. Oudheidkundige perspectieven in het bijzonder ten aanzien van de vaderlandsche Prae en protohistorie. Groningen, 1947.

Arc 895.28 Gihl, Gunnar. Sigtunna och Norrsunda. Uppsala, 1925.

Arc 1494.57 Gil Farres, Octavia. La moneda hispanica en la edad antigua. Madrid, 1966.

Arc 1615.6 Gilbert, Ebenezer. The United States half cents. N.Y., 1916.

Arc 830.339 Gilbert, Max. Menhirs et dolmens dans le nord-est de la Bretagne. Guernsey, 1964.

Arc 1033.12.104 Gildemeister, J. Heilige Rock zu Trier. Düsseldorf, 1845.

Arc 1153.109F Gilissen, Léon. L'expertise des éscritures médiévales. Gand, 1973.

Arc 1584.3 Gille, F. Lettre...sur une monnaie attribuée à Oleg. Paris, 1861.

Arc 830.46 Gilles, Isidore. Précis historique et chronique des monuments triomphaux. Paris, 1873.

Arc 830.18.11 Gilles, Isidore. Saint Gens, ermite et Boèce. Supplément. v.1-2. Avignon, 1885.

Arc 830.18.10 Gilles, Isidore. Les voies romaines et massiliennes. Avignon, 1884.

Arc 975.5 Gillin, John. Archaeological investigations in central Utah. Cambridge, 1941.

Arc 975.2 Gillin, John. Archaeological investigations in Nine Mile Canyon, Utah, during the year 1936. Salt Lake City, 1938?

Arc 861.40.15 Gilyard-Beer, R. The Romano-British baths at Well. Leeds, 1951.

Arc 612.55F Gimbutas, Marija Alseikaites. Bronze age kultures in central and eastern Europe. The Hague, 1965.

Arc 612.55.5 Gimbutas, Marija Alseikaites. The gods and goddesses of old Europe, 7000 to 3500 B.C. London, 1974.

Arc 843.151 Gimenez, Reyna. La Cueva de la Pileta. Málaga, 1958.

Arc 66.1.200 Ginouvès, René. Balaneutikè; recherches sur le bain dans l'antiquité grecque. Paris, 1962.

Arc 543.3.105 Ginzburg, Vul'f V. Paleoantropologiia Srednei Azii. Moskva, 1972.

Arc 726.270 Giordano, Nicola. Civiltà millenarie in terra di Bari. Bari, 1963.

Arc 726.35 Giorgi, Antonio. Dissertazione...monumento etrusco...di Volterra. Firenze, 1752.

Arc 1033.38 Giorgi, Calisto. Sull'autenticità del capo di S. Lorenzo. Roma, 1864.

Arc 726.155 Giorgi, Gello. Suasa senonum. Parma, 1953.

Arc 71.1.2F Giornale degli Scavi di Pompei. Napoli. 1-4 2v.

Arc 71.1 Giornale degli Scavi di Pompei. Napoli. 1861-1865

Arc 830.280 Giot, Pierre Roland. Brittany. London, 1960.

Arc 1015.215 Giovanni, V. di. Palermo sotterranea. Palermo, n.d.

Arc 1033.34.25 Giovanni, V. di. San Pietro in Roma. Monumenti e testimoni. Palermo, 1895.

Arc 1027.25.37 Giovanni Battista de Rossi, archeologo romano. (Grossi-Gondi, A.) Roma, 1894.

Arc 1027.25.19 Giovanni Battista de Rossi. (Baumgarten, P.M.) Köln, 1892.

Arc 1027.25.20 Giovanni Battista de Rossi. (Baumgarten, P.M.) Roma, 1892.

Arc 1027.25.29 Giovanni Battista de Rossi. (Marucchi, O.) Roma, 1895.

Arc 1027.25.31 Giovanni Battista de Rossi. (Marucchi, O.) Roma, 1901.

Arc 1027.25.33 Giovanni Battista de Rossi. (Stevensen, H.) Roma, 1895.

Arc 1027.25.45 Giovanni Battista de Rossi e l'archeologia cristiana. (Galante, G.A.) Napoli, 1900.

Arc 1148.37 Giovanni Onorio da Maglie, trascrittore di codici greci. (Rainò, Beniamino.) Bari, 1972.

Arc 391.8 Giovannoni, G. Il restauro dei monumenti. Roma, 1941?

Arc 66.1.23 Girard, P. L'asclépicion d'Athènes. Paris, 1881.

Arc 307.3.50 Girard, Rafael. Guatemala en el XXXIII Congreso internacional de Americanistas. Guatemala, 1958.

Arc 1020.4 Girardot. Histoire et inventaire du trésor Bourges. Paris, 1859.

Arc 843.7 Giraud, C. Les bronzes d'Osuna. Paris, 1874.

Arc 936.220.80 Girić, Milorad. Mokim. Washington, 1971-72. 2v.

Arc 1340.6 Girod, Joseph. Dictionnaire spécial et classique des monnaies. Paris, 1827.

Arc 1504.10 Girtamner-Solchli, H. Das Münzwesen im Kanton St. Gallen. Genf, 1923.

Arc 1185.4A Giry, Arthur. Manuel de diplomatique. Paris, 1894.

Arc 1185.4.5 Giry, Arthur. Manuel de diplomatique. Paris, 1925. 2v.

Arc 1148.12 Gitlbauer, M. Studien zur griechischen Tachygraphie. Berlin, 1903.

Arc 1153.62 Giuliano, M.L. Coltura e attività calligrafica nel secolo XII a Verona. Padova, 1933.

Arc 391.15 Giulio Quirino Giglioli. (Rome. Istituto di Studi Romani.) Roma, 1958.

Arc 600.18.15F Gîza. (Junker, H.) Leipzig, 1929-38. 3v.

Arc 600.46.10F Giza mastabas. Boston, 1974- 2v.

Arc 588.18 Gizeh and Rifeh. (Petrie, W.M.F.) London, 1907.

Arc 537.6 Gjerstad, Einar. Studies on prehistoric Cyprus. Inaug. Diss. Uppsala, 1926.

Arc 537.7F Gjerstad, Einar. The Swedish Cyprus expedition...1927-1931. v.1-4. Stockholm, 1934-48. 8v.

Arc 761.8F Gjerstadt, E. Early Rome. v.1-6. Lund, 1953. 5v.

Arc 895.35 Gjessing, H.J. Rogalands stenalder. Stavanger, 1920.

Arc 1076.3.120 Glade, Heinz. Erdentiefe-Turmeshöhe; von Glocken und Glockengiessern. Berlin, 1965.

Arc 830.175.10 Glanum. (Rolland, Henri.) Paris, 1949.

Arc 830.315 Glanum. (Rolland, Henri.) Paris, 1960.

Arc 830.175.11 Glanum. (Rolland, Henri.) Saint-Remy-de-Provence, 1974.

Arc 556.2 Glanville, Stephen A.K. The growth and nature of Egyptology. Cambridge, 1947.

Arc 482.202.4F Das Glas von Samarra. (Lamm, C.J.) Berlin, 1928.

Arc 672.1.53 Glasgow, George. The Minoans. London, 1923.

Arc 875.10 Glasgow, Scotland. Archaeological Society. The Antonine wall report. Glasgow, 1899.

Arc 131.3 Glasgow archaeological journal. Glasgow. 1,1969+

Arc 875.29 Glasgow cross. (Black, William G.) Glasgow, 1913.

Arc 588.40F Glass stamps and weights. (Petrie, W.M.F.) London, 1926.

Arc 861.52 Glasscock, J.L. The ancient crosses of Stortford. Bishops, 1905.

Arc 861.14 Glastonbury, England. Antiquarian Society. British lake-village near Glastonbury. Taunton, 1899.

Arc 855.217F The Glastonbury Lake village. (Bulleid, A.) n.p., 1911. 2v.

Arc 1348.13 Gleichius, J. Historia numismatum succincta. Lipsiae, 1698.

Arc 66.1.203 Glenisson, Jean. Correspondance des légats et vicaires-généraux. Paris, 1964.

Arc 545.204 The Gliddon mummy-case. (Pickering, C.) Washington, 1869.

Arc 1033.20.17 Globočnik, G.N. Le sette basiliche di Roma. Venesia, 1877.

Arc 1076.3.48 Die Glocken im Friedländischen. (Metzger, O.H.) Friedland, 1912.

Arc 1076.3.41 Die Glocken in herzogtum Anhalt. (Schubart, F.W.) Dessau, 1896.

Arc 1076.3.9 Glockenkunde. (Otte, H.) Leipzig, 1884.

Arc 1076.3.115 Glockenkunde. (Walter, Karl.) Regensburg, 1913.

Arc 1076.3.49 Glockensagen im pommerschen Volksmunde. (Haas, A.) Stettin, 1919.

Arc 1138.6 Gloria, A. Compendio delle lezioni teorico-pratiche di paleografia e diplomatica. Padova, 1870.

Arc 1138.6F Gloria, A. Compendio delle lezioni teorico-pratiche di paleografia e diplomatica. Atlas. Padova, 1870.

Arc 572.1.5A The glory of the Pharaohs. (Weigall, Arthur Edward Pearse Brome.) N.Y., 1923.

Arc 1494.9 Glosario hispanico de numismatica. (Mateu y Llopis, Felipe.) Barcelona, 1946.

Arc 936.14.380 Głosek, Marian. Miecze średniowieczne z ziem polskich. Łódź, 1970.

Arc 936.14.380.5 Głosek, Marian. Znaki i napisy na mieczach średniowiecznych w Polsce. Wrocław, 1973.

Arc 375.3F Glossaire archéologique. (Gay, V.) Paris, 1887-1928. 2v.

Arc 1180.1 Glossarium diplomaticum. (Brinckmeier, E.) Gotha, 1856-63. 2v.

Arc 858.27 Glossary of archaeology. (Norman, A.) London, 1915. 2v.

Arc 830.130.20 Glozel, trente ans après. (Côle, Léon.) St.-Etienne, 1959.

Arc 830.130.30 Glozel, und die Einwanderung von Semiten im heutigen französischen Departement. (Veelter, Daniel.) Strassburg, 1929.

Arc 830.130.23 Glozel. v.2. (Morlet, Antonin.) Macon, 1962.

Arc 830.130.15 Glozel et sa signification. (Cartereau, E.) Paris, 1928.

Arc 1558.6.15 Glück, Harry. Artalsförteckning över svenska mynt. Stockholm, 1974.

Arc 1558.6.14 Glück, Harry. Artalsförtecknia over soenskamynt med varderingspriser. Stockholm, 1968.

Arc 505.67 Glueck, N. The other side of the Jordan. New Haven, Conn., 1940.

Arc 1229.1 — La glyptique syro-hittite. Thèse. (Conteneau, G.) Paris, 1922.
Arc 1335.84.5 — Gnecchi, F. Guida numismatica universale. 4. ed. Milano, 1903.
Arc 1478.15.10 — Gnecchi, F. I medaglioni romani. Bologna, 1968. 3v.
Arc 1478.15.4 — Gnecchi, F. Monetazione romana. Genève, 1897.
Arc 1478.15.2 — Gnecchi, F. Monete romane. Milano, 1896.
Arc 1478.15 — Gnecchi, F. Monete romane. Milano, 1900.
Arc 1478.15.5 — Gnecchi, F. Roman coins. London, 1903.
NEDL Arc 1480.20 — Gnecchi, Francesco. The fauna and flora on the coin-types of...Rome. London, 1919.
Arc 1490.94.1 — Gnecchi, Francesco. Monete di Milano; inedite supplemento all'opera: Le monete di Milano da Carlo Magno a Vittorio Emanuele II. Milano, 1894.
Arc 1660.17F — Gnechi, Francesco. Le monete dei Trivulzio. Milano, 1887.
Arc 905.5.7 — Gnirs, Anton. Istria praeromana. Karlsbad, 1925.
Arc 905.15.9 — Gnirs, Anton. Die römischen Schutzbezirke an der Oberen Donau. Augsburg, 1929.
Arc 700.25F — Le gobelet en argent des amours vendangeurs du musée d'Alexandrie. (Adriani, A.) n.p., 1939.
Arc 830.18.19 — Gobin, Léon. Viae, apud arvenos Romanae. Thesis. Augustonemeti, 1896.
Arc 493.6.50 — Gobustan. (Dzhafarzade, Iskhak M.) Baku, 1973.
Arc 485.202.5 — Godard, André. Persepolis. Teheran, 1950.
Arc 493.25 — Godard, André. Le trésor de Ziwiyè. Haarlem, 1950.
Arc 493.25.5 — Godard, André. Le trésor de Ziwiyè. Teheran, 1949.
Arc 421.5 — Godfrey, E.F. Die Kaiserspräher der Tsing Dynastie in China. Berlin, 1930.
Arc 936.14.522 — Godłowski, Kazimierz. Historia starożytna ziem polskich. 2. wyd. Kraków, 1973.
Arc 853.65.40 — Godłowski, Kazimierz. Kultura przeworska na Górnym Śląsku. Wyd. 1. Katowice, 1969.
Arc 397.17.5A — Gods, graves, and scholars. 1. American ed. (Marek, Kurt W.) N.Y., 1951.
Arc 397.17.6 — Gods, graves, and scholars. 2. ed. (Marek, Kurt W.) N.Y., 1968.
Arc 612.55.5 — The gods and goddesses of old Europe, 7000 to 3500 B.C. (Gimbutas, Marija Alseikaites.) London, 1974.
Arc 858.3 — Godwin, H. The English archaeologist's hand-book. Oxford, 1867.
Arc 1433.96 — Goebl, Robert. Dokumente zur Geschichte der iranischen Hunnen in Baktrien und Indien. v.1,2,3-4. Wiesbaden, 1967. 3v.
Arc 1478.75 — Goebl, Robert. Einführung in die Münzprägung der römischen Kaiserzeit. Wien, 1957.
Arc 1454.210F — Göbl, Robert. Ostkeltischer Typenatlas. Braunschweig, 1973.
Arc 547.41F — Goedicke, Hans. Ostraka Michaeliders. Wiesbaden, 1962.
Arc 1508.30 — Göetz, Christian Jacob. Deutschlands Kayser-Münzen des Mittel-Alters. Leipzig, 1968.
Arc 388.7 — Goessler, F.P. Wilhelm Dörpfeld. Stuttgart, 1951.
Arc 1510.5.5 — Goessler, Peter. Beiträge zur süddeutschen Münzgeschichte. Stuttgart, 1927.
Arc 1084.19 — Goette, J.A. Jade lore. N.Y., 1937.
Arc 397.17.7 — Götter, Gräber und Gelehrt. (Marek, Kurt W.) Reinbeck, 1972.
Arc 384.2.10 — Götter, Gräber und Gelehrte in Dokumenten. (Marek, Kurt W.) Reinbek bei Hamburg, 1965.
Arc 397.17.3 — Götter. (Marek, Kurt W.) Hamburg, 1950.
Arc 1470.44 — Götter Griechenlands. (Lange, Kurt.) Berlin, 1941.
Arc 1335.145 — Götz, Christian. Beyträge zum Groschen-Cabinet. Dresden, 1810. 3v.
Arc 853.31 — Götze. Die vor- und frühgeschichtlichen altertümer Thüringens. Würzburg, 1902.
Arc 1033.12.243 — Gogan, L.S. The Ardagh chalice. Dublin, 1932.
Arc 1082.10 — Gogmagog. (Lethbridge, T.C.) London, 1957.
Arc 412.14 — Goguey, René. De l'aviation à l'archéologie. Paris, 1968.
Arc 1335.57F — Gohl, Ödön. Gróf Dessewffy Miklos barbár pénzei. pt.1-2. Budapest, 1910-11.
Arc 1538.3.5 — The gold, silver, and copper coins of England. 6. ed. (Humphreys, H.N.) London, 1849.
Arc 1335.5 — Gold and silver coin chart manual. (Hodges, D.M.) N.Y., n.d.
Arc 1400.2 — Gold and silver coin examiner. (Taylor, S.) N.Y., 1846-57. 3 pam.
Arc 1478.50 — Gold and silver coin standards in the Roman empire. (West, Louis.) N.Y., 1941.
Arc 960.1 — Gold and silver ornaments from mounds of Florida. (Kunz, G.F.) Chicago, 1887.
Arc 1433.35 — Gold coinage of Asia before Alexander the Great. (Gardner, Percy.) London, 1908.
X Cg Arc 1538.9 — Gold coins of England, sequel to the silver coins of England. (Kenyon, R.L.) London, 1884.
Arc 1460.5 — Gold coins of the Royal Netherlands Academy. (Haak, A.C.) Amsterdam, 1964.
Arc 1335.157.2 — Gold coins of the world, complete from 600 A.D. to the present. (Friedberg, Robert.) N.Y., 1965.
Arc 403.16.30 — The gold of Troy. (Payne, R.) N.Y., 1959.
Arc 403.16.36 — Das Gold von Troja. (Lavater-Sloman, Mary.) Zürich, 1969.
Arc 1675.102 — Goldbrakteaten aus Sievern. (Hauek, Karl.) München, 1970.
Arc 1016.210 — The golden age of classic Christian art. (Richter, J.P.) London, 1904.
Arc 1365.4 — Der goldene Kranz Caesars und der Kampf um die Entlassung des "Tyrannen". 2. Aufl. (Kraft, Konrad.) Darmstadt, 1969.
Arc 905.26 — Der Goldfund von Nagy-Szent-Miklos. (Hampel, J.) Budapest, 1885.
Arc 905.70 — Der Goldfund von Velem-Szentvid. (Mozsolics, Anália.) Basel, 1950.
Arc 87.1.43 — Goldfund von Vettersfelde. (Furtwaengler, A.) Berlin, 1883.
Arc 1540.25 — Golding, Charles. The coinage of Suffolk. London, 1868.
Arc 674.15F — Goldman, Hetty. Excavations at Eutresis in Boeotia. Cambridge, Mass., 1931.
Arc 1033.3.41 — Goldmann, K. Die ravennatischen Sarkophage. Strassburg, 1906.
Arc 1453.13 — Goldmünzen Europas seit 1800. 3. Aufl. (Schlumberger, Hans.) München, 1973.
Arc 1033.17.54 — Goldonowski, A. Historia...B.V. Maria Claromontanae s. imaginis origine Jerosolymis Constantinopolim. n.p., n.d.
Arc 936.195.210 — Die Goldprägung der Kelten in den böhmischen Ländern. (Castelin, Karel O.) Graz, 1965.
Arc 936.170 — Der Goldschatz von Panagjurischte. (Zontschew, Dimiter.) Berlin, 1959.
Arc 1584.1.15 — Golenko, Konstantin V. Denizhnoe obrashchenie kolkhidy v rimskoe vremia. Leningrad, 1964.
Arc 543.10 — Golgatha, seine Kirchen und Kloster. (Tobler, T.) St. Gallen, 1851.
Arc 905.12.25 — Gollob, Hedwig. Karnuntums Wiederaufbau. Wien, 1956.
Arc 905.12.26 — Gollob, Helwig. Gäbber in Karnuntum. Wien, 1957.
Arc 923.35F — Golomshtok, E.A. The old stone age in European Russia. Diss. Philadelphia, 1938.
Arc 1550.8.15 — Golster, Georg. Flensborg mønt, 14. og 16. århundrede. Udg. af numismatisk forening for nord-og sydslesvig. Sønderborg, 1967.
Htn Arc 1455.3F* — Goltzius, H. De re nummaria antiqua opera. Antwerp, 1708. 5v.
Arc 925.230.5 — Golubeva, Leonilla A. Ves' i Slaviane na Belom ozere X-XIII vv. Moskva, 1973.
Arc 925.115 — Golubtsova, E.S. Severnoe Prichernomor'e i Rim. Moskva, 1951.
Arc 925.334 — Golubye doragi vekov. (Nikitin, Andrei L.) Moskva, 1968.
Arc 608.35 — Golvin, Lucien. Le Magrib central à l'époque des Zerides. Paris, 1957.
Arc 608.35.5 — Golvin, Lucien. Recherches archéologiques à la Qal'a des Banû Hammâd. Paris, 1965.
Arc 838.6 — Gomes-Moreno, M. Materiales de arqueologia española. Madrid, 1912.
Arc 843.13F — Gomez de Somorrostro y Martin, A. El acueducto y otras antiqüedades de Segovia. Madrid, 1820.
Arc 843.13.2 — Gomez de Somorrostro y Martin, A. El acueducto y otras antiqüedades de Segovia. 2. ed. Segovia, 1861.
Arc 838.36 — Gómez Tabanera, José Manuel. Las raices de España. Madrid, 1967.
Arc 335.2 — Gomme, G.L. Index of archaeological papers, 1665-1890. London, 1907.
Arc 1148.4 — Gomperz, T. Ueber eine bisher Unbekanntes griechisches Schriftsystem. Wien, 1884.
Arc 843.56.5 — Gomzalez Simancos, M. Sagunto. 1. ed. Sagunto? n.d.
Arc 595.45 — Goneim, M. The buried pyramid. London, 1956.
Htn Arc 1033.17.583* — Gonzalez de Mendoza, P. Historia del Monte Celia de Nuestra Señora de la Salceda. Granada, 1616.
Arc 1020.71 — Gonzati, B. Il santuario delle relique...di Padova. Padova, 1851.
Arc 1033.12.128 — Gonzati, L. Sopra un patrio monumento di antica oreficeria. Vicenza, 1871.
Arc 1473.8.2 — Goodacre, H.G. A handbook of the coinage of the Byzantine empire. London, 1957.
Arc 1473.8 — Goodacre, H.G. A handbook of the coinage of the Byzantine empire. pt.1-3. London, 1928-33.
Arc 608.48 — Goodchild, Richard G. Cyrene and Apollonia. Tripoli? 1959.
Arc 968.12A — Goodwin, William B. The ruins of Great Ireland in New England. Boston, 1946.
Arc 391.18 — Goodyear, Frank Haigh. Archaeological site science. N.Y., 1971.
Arc 936.25 — Gooss, Carl. Chronik der Archäologischenfund Siebenbürgens. Hermanstadt, 1876.
Arc 1153.87F — Gordon, Arthur Ernest. Album of dated Latin inscriptions. v.1-4. Berkeley, 1958- 6v.
Arc 391.10 — Gordon, C.H. Adventures in the Nearest East. Fair Lawn, N.J., 1957.
Arc 497.45 — Gordon, Cyrus H. The living past. N.Y., 1941.
Arc 1138.115.2 — Gordon, Cyrus Herzl. Forgotten scripts. Harmondsworth, 1971.
Arc 1138.115 — Gordon, Cyrus Herzl. Forgotten scripts. N.Y., 1968.
Arc 432.20 — Gordon, Douglas Hamilton. The pre-historic background of Indian culture. Bombay, 1958.
Arc 432.20.2 — Gordon, Douglas Hamilton. The pre-historic background of Indian culture. 2. ed. Bombay, 1960.
Arc 861.18.15 — Gordon, E.O. Prehistoric London; its mounds. London, 1914.
Arc 391.13 — Gordon, William J. Nelson Glueck: a bibliography. Cincinnati? 1962.
Htn Arc 1077.2.25* — Gori, A.F. Crux dominica adorabile christianae religionis vexillum observationibus. Florentiae, 1749.
Arc 1033.54 — Gori, A.F. Dissertazioni...di S. Giuseppe. Modena, 1865.
Arc 743.5 — Gori, A.F. Risposta. Firenze, 1739.
Arc 391.3 — Gori, A.F. Symbolia litterariae. Decas I. Florentiae, 1748-53. 10v.
Arc 391.3.5 — Gori, A.F. Symbolia litterariae. Decas II. v.1-10. Romae, 1751-54. 5v.
Arc 1027.30.5 — Gori, F. Della porta e basilica di S. Lorenzo dell catacombe. Roma, 1862.
Arc 1033.22 — Gori, F. Sul tesoro di antiche suppellettili sacre. Spoleto, 1891.
Arc 785.22.8 — Gori, Fabio. Sugli edifizi palatini. Roma, 1867.
Arc 785.53 — Gori, Fabio. La torre del Monzone presso il Ponte Ratto. Roma, 1872.
Htn Arc 740.200* — Gorio, A.F. Museum Etruscum. Florence, 1737. 3v.
Arc 936.14.430 — Gorne Pobuze w wiskach VIII-XI. (Nowakowski, Andrej.) Łódź, 1972.
Arc 925.13.8.10 — Gornoaltaiskie nachadki iskify. (Rudenko, S.I.) Moskva, 1952.
Arc 543.156 — Gornoe delo i metallurgia srednevekovogo Ilaka, V-nachalo XIII v. (Buriakov, Iurii F.) Moskva, 1974.
Arc 925.50.120 — Gornyi Krym v I tysicacheletii do nashei coy. (Leskov, Aleksandr M.) Kiev, 1965.
Arc 935.31 — Gorod Ani. (Arutiunian, Varazdat.) Erevan, 1964.
Arc 925.160 — Gorod Rustavi. (Chilashvili, L.A.) Tbilisi, 1958.
Arc 530.65.10 — Gorod Teishenbaini po raskopkam 1947-1958 gg. (Martirosian, A.) Erevan, 1961.
Arc 925.60.5 — Gorodishche Khulash i pamiatniki srednevekov'ia chuvashskogo Povolzh'ia. Cheboksary, 1972.
Arc 925.220 — Gorodishche maiak. (Erdniev, U.E.) Kemerovo, 1960.
Arc 936.165.30 — Gorodskoe goncharstvo Pruto-Dnestrov'ia v XIV v. (Polevoi, Lazar' L.) Kishinev, 1969.
Arc 923.90 — Gorodtsov, V.A. Bytovaia arkheologiia. Moskva, 1910.
Arc 545.202FA — Gorringe, H.H. Egyptian obelisks. N.Y., 1882.
Arc 861.77.5 — The Gosforth district. (Parker, C.A.) Kendal, 1926.
Arc 1163.3.65F — Goskev, Ivan. Starobulgarski glayolicheski i kirilski nadpisi ot IX i X v. Sofiia, 1961.
Arc 588.36 — The gospel of St. John. (Thompson, H.) London, 1924.
Arc 1020.73.6 — Gosselin, J.E.A. Notice historique et critique sur le sainte couronne d'épines...l'église metropolitaine de Paris. Paris, 1828.
Arc 925.180.15 — Gosudarstvo bokhai i pamiatniki ego kul'tury v Primor'e. (Shavkunov, Ernst V.) Leningrad, 1968.
Arc 612.18 — Gotbe, I.V. Ocherki po istorii...Evropy. Leningrad, 1925.
Arc 726.47 — Die Gothen und Langobarden in Italien. (Åberg, Nils.) Uppsala, 1923.
Arc 895.22 — Gotlands stenalder. (Lithberg, Nils.) Stockholm, 1914.
Arc 1033.178 — Gotsmick, A. Proserpina - virgo sacrata Dei; ein fruhchristlichen Antithese. München, 1962.
Arc 1232.5 — Gotter und Menschen im Rollsiegel. (Wisemar, D.J.) Prague, 1958.

Author and Title Listing

Arc 1016.209 Die Gottgeweihten Jungfrauen. (Wilpert, J.) Freiburg, 1892.
Arc 1335.13 Die Gotthard mimus'sche Thaler und Medaillensammlung. (Wesener, F.J.) Wien, 1874.
Arc 708.23.9 Gougères, G. Athènes. 4e éd. Paris, 1923.
Arc 458.3 Gough, Richard. Comparative view of antient monuments of India...island of Salset. London, 1785.
Arc 1615.16 Gould, Maurice M. Alaska's coinage through the years. 2. ed. Racine, 1965.
Arc 1033.12.8 Gourgues, A. de. Le Saint Suaire. Perigueux, 1868.
Arc 823.21.5F Goury, Georges. L'enceinte d'Haulzy et sa nécropole. Nancy, 1911.
Arc 823.21.10F Goury, Georges. Essai sur l'époque barbare dans la Marne. Nancy, 1908.
Arc 426.7F Gowland, William. The dolmens and burial mounds in Japan. London, 1897.
Arc 1020.10.50F Goyau, Georges. Le visage de Rome chrétienne. Genève, 1926.
Arc 600.140 Goyon, Georges. Nouvelles inscriptions rupestres du Wadi Hammamat. Paris, 1957.
Arc 1070.204 Gozzadini, G. De quelques mors de cheval italiques et de l'épée de Ronzano en bronze. Bologne, 1875.
Arc 853.348 Die Grab- und Hortfunde der Urnenfelderkultur aus Ober- und Mittelfranken. (Hennig, Hilke.) Kallmünz, 1970.
Arc 87.1.18 Grab des Dionysos. (Boetticher, C.) Berlin, 1858.
Arc 726.310 Das Grab des Lucius Munatius Plancus bei Gaeta. (Fellmann, Rudolf.) Basel, 1957.
Arc 700.12.15 Grab und Jenseits. (Wiesner, J.) Berlin, 1938.
Arc 1075.2 Grabar, André. Ampoules de Terre Sainte. Paris, 1958.
Arc 900.214 Das Grabfeld von Hallstatt. (Sacken, E. von.) Wien, 1868.
Arc 895.22.3 Das Grabfeld von Västerbjers auf Gotland. (Stenberger, M.) Stockholm, 1943.
Arc 838.24F Die Grabfunde aus dem spanischen Westgotenreich. (Zeiss, Hans.) Berlin, 1934.
Arc 853.360 Die Grabfunde der Merowingerzeit aus dem Donautal um Regensberg. (Koch, Ursula.) Berlin, 1968. 2v.
Arc 746.11.10F Die Grabfunde mit Bronzeschnabelkannen. Inaug. Diss. (Langsdorff, A.) Berlin, 1929.
Arc 915.15 Das Grabhügelfeld im Sankert bei Hemishofen. (Guyan, Walter Ulrich.) Basel, 1951.
Arc 936.39F Die Grabhügelnekropole bei Duvanlij in Südbulgarien. (Filov, Bogdan.) Sofiia, 1934.
Arc 726.42 Das Grabmal des Theoderich zu Ravenna. (Schulz, Bruno.) Würzburg, 1911.
Arc 925.50.70 Grabowski, M. Ukraina davna i terazniejsza. Kijów, 1850.
Arc 1027.41.35 Die Grabplatte des H. Paulus. (Grisar, H.) Rom, 1892.
Arc 716.8 Die Grabsteine der alten Griechen. (Pervanoglu, P.) Leipzig, 1863.
Arc 936.85 Die Grabung in Westhofler Sophienkirche zu Istanbul. (Schneider, A.M.) Berlin, 1941.
Arc 65.2.7F Grabungen. (Oesterreichisches Archäologisches Institut, Vienna.) Wien. 1965
Arc 853.4.20 Grabungen im romischen Steinkastell von Heddernheim 1957-1959. (Fischer, Ulrich.) Frankfurt am Main, 1973.
Arc 1033.17.100.5 The grace of Guadalupe. (Keyer, F.P.W. (Mrs.).) N.Y., 1941.
Arc 925.225 Grach, A.D. Drevnetiurkskie izvaianiia Tuvy. Moskva, 1961.
Arc 1493.17 Gracia de la Fuente, Arturo. Resumen historico. Madrid, 1934.
Arc 936.220.100 Gradac. (Stalio, Blaženka.) Beograd, 1972.
Arc 936.65.5 Gradŭt v Trakiia i Dakiia prez kŭsnata antichnost. (Velkov, V.I.) Sofiia, 1959.
Arc 520.2 Graeber, F. Die Wasserleitungen von Pergamon. / Berlin, 1888.
Arc 545.215 Die Graeber- und Textilfunde von Achmim-Panopolis. (Forrer, R.) Strassburg, 1891.
Arc 1027.32.10 Die Graeber der Apostelfürsten. (Kirschbaum, E.) Frankfurt, 1957.
Arc 1027.32.12 Die Graeber der Apostelfürsten. 2. Aufl. (Kirschbaum, E.) Frankfurt, 1959.
Arc 938.25F Die Gräber der Liven. (Bahr, Johann K.) Dresden, 1850.
Arc 700.11 Die Gräber von Attika. (Gropengiesser, H.) Athen, 1907.
Arc 530.169 Das Gräberfeld bei Ilica. (Orthmann, Winfried.) Wiesbaden, 1967.
Arc 936.20.5 Das Gräberfeld von Independenta. (Ionitā, Ian.) Bonn, 1971.
Arc 920.7 Das Gräberfeld von Koban. Text und Atlas. (Virchow, R.) Berlin, 1883. 2v.
Arc 87.1.48 Graeberfeld von Marion. (Herrmann, P.) Berlin, 1888.
Arc 845.1 Das Graeberfeld von Reichenhall. (Chlingensperg-Berg, M. von.) Reichenhall, 1890.
Arc 905.145 Das Gräberfeld von Welzelach. (Lippert, Andreas.) Bonn, 1972.
Arc 853.317 Gräberfelder dur Hallstattzeit an Main und Fränkischer Saale. (Kossack, Georg.) Kallmünz, 1970.
Arc 700.69 Graeco-Macedonian bronzes. (Bouzek, Jan.) Praha, 1974.
Arc 1361.1 Grässe, J.G.T. Handbuch der alten Numismatik. Leipzig, 1854.
NEDL Arc 720.200.2 Graevius, J.G. Thesaurus antiquitatum et historiarum Siciliae. v.1-15. Lugdunum Batavorum, 1723-25. 8v.
NEDL Arc 720.200 Graevuis, J.G. Thesaurus antiquitatum et historiarum Italiae. Lugdunum Batavorum, 1704-23. 16v.
Arc 895.30F Graffältet oid Vendel. (Stolpe, Hjalmar.) Stockholm, 1912.
Arc 1153.84 I graffiti sotto la confessione di San Petro in Vaticano. (Guarducci, M.) Città del Vaticano, 1958. 3v.
Arc 889.8 Het grafveld onder hees bij Nijmegen. (Brunsting, H.) Amsterdam, 1937.
Arc 875.39 Graham, H.D. Antiquities of Iona. London, 1850.
Arc 672.1.94 Graham, J.W. The palace of Crete. Princeton, N.J., 1962.
Arc 875.28 Graham, R.C. The carved stones of Islay. Glasgow, 1895.
Arc 673.1.17 Graindor, P. Delphes et son oracle. Le Caire, 1930.
Arc 307.3.12 Grairer, Gabriel. Allocution fait à la Société de Géographie...sur la 2e session des Congrés international de Americanistes. Rouen, 1877.
Arc 925.13.175 Grakov, Boris N. Skify. Moskva, 1971.
Arc 66.1.122 Grammaire descriptive du Roméique littéraire. (Roussel, Louis.) Paris, n.d.
Arc 1153.4.25 Grammatica tironiana. (Molina, E.) Padova, 1933.
Arc 935.23.5F El Gran Palacio Sagrado de Bizancio. (Miranda, S.) Mexico, 1955.
Arc 968.2.85 Gran Quivira. (Vivian, G.) Washington, 1964.
Arc 726.140.10 Grancelli, Umberto. Il piano di fondazione di Verona romana. Verona, 1964.
Arc 1138.3 Grand, E. Daniel. Leçon d'ouverture du cours de paléographie. Montpellier, 1890.
Arc 830.1.7 Grand, Roger. Mélanges d'archéologie bretonne. Série I. Nantes, 1921.
Arc 421.1 Le grand-Bouddha de Hanoi. (Dumontier, G.) Hanoi, 1888.
Htn Arc 750.221F* Le grand cabinet romain. (Chausse, M.A. de la.) Amsterdam, 1706.
Arc 590.5 Le grand sarcophage du Musée civique de Bologne. (Szedlo, G.) Bologne, 1876.
Arc 1264.4 Le grand sceau de Raoul du Fou. (Barbier de Montault, X.) Reims, n.d.
Arc 1335.61 La grande guerre. (Dupriez, C.) Bruxelles, 19- ?
Arc 612.49 La grande madre. (Stacul, Giorgio.) Roma, 1963.
Arc 1663.7 Grande museo rivoluzionario. Roma, 1850.
Arc 843.55 Grandezas y antiguedades de la isla y ciudad de Cadiz. (Suarez de Salazar, Juan B.) Cadiz, 1610.
Arc 1276.5 Grandjean, P.B. Danske haandvaerkerlavs segl. København, 1950.
Arc 1276.25F Grandjean, P.B. Danske herreders segl indtil 1660. København, 1946.
Arc 1276.30F Grandjean, P.B. Danske kobstaeders segl indtil 1660. København, 1937.
Arc 1276.10F Grandjean, P.B. Danske konggelige segl fra Frederik ILS. København, 1951.
Arc 1276.15F Grandjean, P.B. Slesvigske kobstaeders og herreders segl indtil 1660. København, 1953.
Arc 1276.20F Grandjean. P.B. Danske gilders segl fra middelaldesen. København, 1948.
Arc 689.2 Granidor, P. Les fouilles de Tēnos. Louvain, 1906.
Arc 503.5.10F Grant, Elihu. Ain Shems excavations (Palestine), 1933. Pt.3. Haverford, 1934.
Arc 503.5 Grant, Elihu. Beth Shemesh (Palestine). Haverford, Pa., 1929.
Arc 1480.48 Grant, Michael. Aspects of the principate of Tiberius. N.Y., 1950.
Arc 793.22 Grant, Michael. Cities of Vesuvius: Pompeii and Herculaneum. London, 1971.
Arc 1480.40 Grant, Michael. From imperium to auctoritas. Cambridge, 1946.
Arc 1480.40.1 Grant, Michael. From imperium to auctoritas. 1. ed. London, 1969.
Arc 1478.40 Grant, Michael. Roman anniversary issues. Cambridge, Eng., 1950.
Arc 785.13.95 Grant, Michael. The Roman Forum. London, 1970.
Arc 1478.40.5 Grant, Michael. Roman history from coins. Cambridge, Eng., 1958.
Arc 1478.40.2 Grant, Michael. Roman imperial money. London, 1954.
Arc 1480.54 Grant, Michael. The six main AES coinages of Augustus. Edinburgh, 1953.
Arc 556.4 Grapow, Hermann. Meine Begegnung mit einigen Agyptologen. Berlin, 1973.
Arc 1500.30 Grappin, Pierre-Philippe. Recherches sur les anciennes monnaies du comté de Bourgogne. Paris, 1782.
Arc 691.5F Graptai stēlai Dēmetriidos-Palasōn. (Arbanitopoulos, A.S.) Athēnai, 1928.
Arc 830.5.15 Gras-Bourguet. Antiquités de l'arrondissement de Castellanne. 2e éd. Digne, 1842.
Arc 1088.1.3 Graser, B. De veterum re navali. Berolini, 1864.
Arc 1088.1.4 Graser, B. De veterum trirenium fabrica. Berolini, 1864.
Arc 1070.200 Graser, B. Das Model eines athenischen Fuenfreihenschiffs Pentere. Berlin, 1866.
Arc 1088.1.2 Graser, B. Untersuchungen und das Seewesen des Alterthums. Göttingen, 1867.
Arc 720.214F Grassi. Rappresentazione...edifizi...di Piza. Piza, 1839.
Arc 405.1.40F Grat A.S. Uvarov, kak teoretik arkheologii. (Ardashev, Nikolai N.) Moskva, 1911.
Arc 1020.19.5 Gratiolio, P. De praeclaris Mediolani aedificiciis. Mediolani, 1735.
Arc 938.17.5 Graudonis, J. Senatnes pédás. Riga, 1961.
Arc 938.17.10 Graudonis, Jánis. Latviia v epokhu pozdnei bronzy i rannego sheleza. Riga, 1967.
Arc 1053.6.6F Graul, Richard. Die antiken Porträtgemälde aus den Grabstätten des Fayum. Leipzig, 1888.
Arc 1145.1 Graux, C. Facsimiles de manuscrits grecs d'Espagne. Paris, 1897. 2v.
Arc 1081.1 Grave mounds and their contents. (Jewett, L.) London, 1870.
Arc 967.2.10 Graves, H.B. The pre-Cambrian structure of Missouri. Diss. St. Louis, 1938.
Htn Arc 880.14* Graves, James. Church and shrine of St. Manchan. Dublin, 1875.
Arc 743.2 Gray, H. (Mrs.). Tour to the sepulchres of Etruria. London, 1840.
Arc 861.68 Gray, Harold St. George. Maumbury Rings excavations. Interim report. Dorchester, 1913.
Arc 1675.56 Gray, J.M. James and William Tassie. Edinburgh, 1894.
Arc 936.205.10 Grborezi srednjovjckovna nekropola. (Bešlagié, Šefik.) Sarajevo, 1964.
Arc 403.21 Great adventures in archaeology. (Silverberg, R.) N.Y., 1964.
Arc 386.33 The great Belzoni. (Mayes, Stanley.) London, 1959.
Arc 858.24.5F Great Britain. Ancient Monuments Advisory Committee. Report of the committee. London, n.d.
Arc 861.190 Great Britain. Commissions. Ancient and Historical Monuments and Constructions of England. Peterborough New town. London, 1969.
Arc 858.24.10 Great Britain. Commissions. Ancient and Historical Monuments and Constructions of England. An inventory of the historical monuments in Hertfordshire. London, 1910.
Arc 858.24.9 Great Britain. Commissions. Ancient and Historical Monuments and Constructions of England. An inventory of the historical monuments in Hertfordshire. London, 1911.
Arc 858.24.11 Great Britain. Commissions. Ancient and Historical Monuments and Constructions of England. An inventory of the historical monuments in Buckinghamshire. London, 1912-13. 2v.
Arc 858.24.13 Great Britain. Commissions. Ancient and Historical Monuments and Constructions of England. An inventory of the historical monuments in Essex. London, 1916-23. 4v.
Arc 858.24.15 Great Britain. Commissions. Ancient and Historical Monuments and Constructions of England. An inventory of the historical monuments in Huntingdonshire. London, 1926.
Arc 858.24.17 Great Britain. Commissions. Ancient and Historical Monuments and Constructions of England. An inventory of the historical monuments in Herefordshire. London, 1931-34. 3v.
Arc 858.24.19 Great Britain. Commissions. Ancient and Historical Monuments and Constructions of England. An inventory of the historical monuments in Westmorland. London, 1936.

Arc 858.24.21 Great Britain. Commissions. Ancient and Historical Monuments and Constructions of England. An inventory of the historical monuments in Middlesex. London, 1937.
Arc 858.24.23 Great Britain. Commissions. Ancient and Historical Monuments and Constructions of England. An inventory of the historical monuments in the city of Oxford. London, 1939.
Arc 858.24.25 Great Britain. Commissions. Ancient and Historical Monuments and Constructions of England. An inventory of the historical monuments in Dorset. v.1,3. London, 1952- 3v.
Arc 861.160 Great Britain. Commissions. Ancient and Historical Monuments and Constructions of England. An inventory of the historical monuments in the city of York. London, 1962. 3v.
Arc 858.92 Great Britain. Commissions. Ancient and Historical Monuments and Constructions of England. A matter of time; an archaeological survey of the river gravels of England. London, 1960-61.
Arc 885.17 Great Britain. Commissions. Ancient and Historical Monuments and Constructions of Wales and Monmouthshire. Interim report. London. 9-11,1920-1956
Arc 855.225F Great Britain. Commissions. Ancient and Historical Monuments and Constructions in Wales and Monmouthshire. A inventory of the ancient monuments in Wales and Monmouthshire. v.1-5,7-8. London, 1911-37. 4v.
Arc 875.54 Great Britain. Commissions. Ancient and Historical Monuments of Scotland. Ancient and historical monuments of Stirlingshire. Edinburgh, 1963. 2v.
Arc 875.53 Great Britain. Commissions. Ancient and Historical Monuments of Scotland. An inventory of the ancient and historical monuments of Selkirkshire. Edinburgh, 1956.
Arc 875.52 Great Britain. Commissions. Ancient and Historical Monuments of Scotland. An inventory of the ancient and historical monuments of Roxburghshire. Edinburgh, 1956. 2v.
Arc 875.56 Great Britain. Commissions. Ancient and Historical Monuments of Scotland. Peeblesshire: an inventory of the ancient monuments. Edinburgh, 1967. 2v.
Arc 875.50 Great Britain. Commissions. Ancient and Historical Monuments of Scotland. Report and inventory of monuments and constructions. Edinburgh. 1-13,1909-1957 11v.
Arc 131.4 Great Britain. Department of the Environment. Archaeological excavations. London. 1973+
Arc 858.47.14 Great Britain. Ministry of Works. Illustrated guide to ancient monuments. Edinburgh, 1961.
Arc 858.47.16.5 Great Britain. Ministry of Works. Illustrated guide to ancient monuments. Edinburgh, 1967.
Arc 858.47.5A Great Britain. Ministry of Works. Illustrated regional guides to ancient monuments. London, 1936-48. 5v.
Arc 858.47.10 Great Britain. Ministry of Works. Illustrated regional guides to ancient monuments. v.2-6. 2. ed. London, 1949- 5v.
Arc 858.47.12 Great Britain. Ministry of Works. Illustrated regional guides to ancient monuments. v.1-2,4,6. London, 1954. 4v.
Arc 858.47 Great Britain. Office of Works. Ancient monuments. London. 1932-1958 7v.
Arc 858.24F Great Britain. Royal Commission on Ancient and Historical Monuments. Interim report. London. 1-22 2v.
Arc 386.8 Great cities of the ancient world. (Buckley, T.A.) London, 1852.
Arc 855.228F The great flint implements of Cromer, Norfolk. (Moir, J. Reid.) Ipswich, 1923?
Arc 861.11.7F A great free city; the book of Silchester. (Thomson, James.) London, 1924. 2v.
Arc 1335.151 Great Jewish portraits in metal. (Jewish Theological Seminary.) N.Y., 1963.
Arc 595.20 The great law, told simply in seven visits. v.2. (MacHuisdean, Hamish.) Glasgow, 1928.
Arc 935.23F The great palace of the Byzantine emperors. (St. Andrews. University.) London, 1947-58. 2v.
Arc 595.32.15 The Great Pyramid; its divine message. 8th ed. (Davidson, D.) London, 1940.
Arc 595.6 The Great Pyramid. (Proctor, R.A.) London, 1883.
Arc 595.6.2 The Great Pyramid. (Proctor, R.A.) N.Y., 1883.
Arc 595.34.5 The Great Pyramid. 2. ed. (Marks, T.S.) London, 1879?
Arc 595.27 The Great Pyramid in fact and in theory. (Kingsland, William.) London, 1932-35. 2v.
Arc 595.8 The Great Pyramid of Jizeh. (Skinner, J.R.) Cincinnati, 1871. 2 pam.
Arc 1273.1 The great seals of England. (Wyon, A.) London, 1887.
Arc 584.3F Great tombs of the First Dynasty. (Emery, W.B.) Cairo, 1949. 3v.
Arc 870.14.15 The great wall of Hadrian in Roman times. (Brown, Paul.) London, 1932.
Arc 609.1.13 Great Zimbabwe. (Hall, R.N.) London, 1905.
Arc 609.1.25 The great Zimbabwe ruins. (Rhodesia (Southern). Bureau of Publicity.) Bulawayo, 1930.
Arc 595.13 Greaves, John. Pyramidographia. London, 1646.
Arc 936.14.400 Grebienie starozytne i sredniowieczne z ziem polskich. (Chmielowska, Aldona.) Łódź, 1971.
Arc 652.5F La Grèce préclassique. (Montelius, Oscar.) Stockholm, 1924-28. 2v.
Arc 925.13.125 Grecheskaia kolonizatsiia Severnogo Prichernomor'ia. (Lapin, Vladimir V.) Kiev, 1966.
Htn Arc 720.12* Grecian remains in Italy. (Middleton, J.) London, 1812.
Arc 68.1 Greece. Genikē ephoreia tōn archaiotētōn kai mouseiōn. Deltion archaiologikon. Athēnai. 1888-1892 4v.
Arc 68.5F Greece. Hypourgeion tōn ekklesiasticon. Archailogikon deltion. Athēnai. 1,1915+ 29v.
Arc 1148.1.5 Greek abbreviation in the 15th century. (Allen, T.W.) London, n.d.
Arc 495.204.3 Greek and Latin inscriptions. (Prentice, William K.) N.Y., 1908.
Arc 1458.22 Greek and Roman coins and the study of history. (Milne, Joseph G.) London, 1939.
Htn Arc 1460.2* The Greek and Roman history illustrated by coins and medals. (Walker, O.) London, 1692.
Arc 638.5 Pamphlet vol. Greek Archaeology. 36 pam.
Arc 638.5.2 Pamphlet vol. Greek archaeology. 7 pam.
Arc 638.7 Pamphlet vol. Greek archaeology. Furtwängler pamphlets. 8 pam.
Arc 638.7.3 Pamphlet vol. Greek archaeology. Furtwängler pamphlets. 11 pam.
Arc 638.7.2 Pamphlet vol. Greek archaeology. Furtwängler pamphlets. 20 pam.
Arc 638.8 Pamphlet box. Greek archaeology. Miscellaneous pamphlets.
Arc 651.2 Greek buildings. (Lethaby, W.R.) London, 1908.
Arc 1468.27 Greek coinage. (Milne, Joseph G.) Oxford, 1931.
Arc 1468.50 Greek coins, 1950-1963. (Boston. Museum of Fine Arts.) Boston, 1964.
Arc 1353.2.15 Greek coins acquired by the British Museum. (British Museum. Department of Coins and Medals.) London. 1887-1896
Arc 1468.11 Greek coins and their parent cities. (Ward, J.) London, 1902.
Arc 1468.62 Greek coins in North American collections. N.Y. 1,1969+
Arc 700.19.10 Greek fortifications. (Winter, F.E.) London, 1971.
Arc 700.19.11 Greek fortifications. (Winter, F.E.) Toronto, 1971.
Arc 1148.30 Greek literary hands. (Roberts, C.H.) Oxford, 1955.
Arc 1148.36 Greek manuscripts of the ancient world. (Turner, Eric Gardiner.) Oxford, 1971.
Arc 652.8 The Greek stories speak. (MacKendrick, P.L.) N.Y., 1962.
Arc 674.3.15 The Greek temple builders at Epidauros. (Burford, Alison.) Liverpool, 1969.
Arc 700.19 Greek walls. (Scranton, R.L.) Cambridge, 1941.
Arc 838.18 The Greeks in Spain. (Carpenter, Rhys.) Bryn Mawr, 1925.
Arc 700.58 The Greeks overseas. (Boardman, J.) Harmondsworth, 1964.
Arc 700.58.2 The Greeks overseas. 2. ed. (Boardman, J.) Harmondsworth, 1973.
Arc 642.10 The Greeks till Alexander. (Cook, R.M.) London, 1961.
Arc 1361.2 Green, B.R. A lecture on the study of ancient coins. London, 1829.
Arc 861.100.10 Green, C. Sutton-Hoo. London, 1963.
Arc 983.1 Green, C.H. Catalogue of a unique collection of cliff dweller relics. Chicago? n.d.
Arc 609.18 Green, L.G. Something rich and strange. Capetown, 1962.
Arc 858.23 The green roads of England. (Cox, R.H.) London, 1914.
Arc 556.5 Greener, Leslie. The discovery of Egypt. London, 1966.
Arc 858.10 Greenwell, G. British barrows. Oxford, 1877.
Arc 1468.25 Greenwell, W. Rare Greek coins. London, 1893.
Arc 1138.28 Greg, Walter W. The calculus of variants, an essay on textual criticism. Oxford, 1927.
Arc 830.80 Gregoire d'Essigny, L.A.J. Mémoire sur la question des voies romaines. Paris, 1811. 2 pam.
Arc 1033.17.34 Gregorio. Storia della translazione...immagine di Santa Maria di Constantinopoli. 2a ed. Napoli, 1813.
Arc 1033.17.35 Gregorio. Storia della translazione...immagine di Santa Maria di Constantinopoli. 2a ed. Napoli, 1824.
Arc 672.1.72F Greifen am Thron. (Karo, G.H.) Baden-Baden, 1959.
Arc 383.69F Greifswalder Antiken. Berlin, 1961.
Arc 845.202 Grempler, Wilhelm. Der Fund von Sackrau. pts.1-3. Berlin, 1887-88.
Arc 66.1.197 Grenade, P. Essai sur les origines du principat. Paris, 1961.
Arc 66.1.106 Grenier, A. Bologne villanovienne et etrusque. Paris, 1912.
Arc 830.42 Grenier, A. Habitations gauloises et villas latines. Paris, 1906.
Arc 853.3.15 Grenier, Albert. Etudes d'archéologie rhénane. Paris, 1925.
Arc 823.11.9 Grenier, Albert. Manuel d'archéologie gallo-romaine. v.1-4. Paris, 1931-1934. 6v.
Arc 853.347 Grenz, Rudolf. Die Anfänge der Stadt Münden nach den Ausgrabungen in der St. Blasius-Kirche. Hannoversch Münden, 1973.
Arc 853.254F Grenz, Rudolf. Die slawischen Funde aus dem hanoverschen Wendland. Nęumünster, 1961.
Arc 830.66 Greppo, J.G.H. Études archéologiques sur les Eaux Thermalès. Paris, 1846.
Arc 1663.20 Greppo, J.G.H. Mémoire sur les voyages de...Hadrien et sur les médailles. Paris, 1842.
Htn Arc 1033.35.141* Gretser, J. De cruce Christi. Inglodstadii, 1600. 3v.
Arc 1033.35.85 Gretser, J. Hortus S. Crucis. Ingolstadii, 1610.
Arc 925.38 Griaznov, M.P. Pazyrykskii kurgan. Moskva, 1937.
Arc 925.38.5 Griaznov, M.P. Pervyi pazyrykskii kurgan. Leningrad, 1950.
Arc 1076.12 Gribsoe, Erland. Frederiksborg amts kirkekloffer. Hillerød, 1934.
Arc 650.10.5 Griechenlandkunde; ein Führer zu klassischen Stätten. (Kirsten, Ernst.) Heidelberg, 1956.
Arc 650.10 Griechenlandkunde. (Kirsten, Ernst.) Heidelberg, 1955.
Arc 650.10.7 Griechenlandkunde. 3. Aufl. (Kirsten, Ernst.) Heidelberg, 1957.
Arc 590.12 Die griechisch-ägyptischen Mumienbildnisse der Sammlung T. Graf. (Buberl, Paul.) Wien, 1922.
Arc 1335.101.51 Griechische, römische, byzantinische Münzen. (Hirsch, Jacob.) München, 1914.
Arc 1335.101.25 Griechische, römische und byzantinische Münzen aus dem Besitze von Friedrich von Schennis. (Hirsch, Jacob.) München, 1913.
Arc 635.225F Griechische Alterthümer südrussischen Fundorts. (Vogell, A.) Cassel, 1908.
Arc 87.1.74 Griechische Bronzeeimer im berlinen Antiquarium. (Schröder, Bruno.) Berlin, 1914.
Arc 920.9 Griechische Grabreliefs aus Südrussland. (Kieseritzky, G. von.) Berlin, 1909.
Arc 700.33 Griechische Greifenkessel. (Jantzen, Ulf.) Berlin, 1955.
Arc 1053.2.5 Griechische Ikonographie. (Bernoulli, J.J.) München, 1901. 2v.
Arc 1468.26 Griechische Münzen. (Börger, Hans.) Leipzig, 1922.
Arc 1465.79 Griechische Münzen. (Imhoof-Blumer, Friedrich.) München, 1890.
Arc 1468.20 Griechische Münzen. (Lambros, J.P.) München, 1910.
NEDL Arc 1148.5 Griechische Palaeographie. v.1-2. (Gardthausen, V.) Leipzig, 1879.
Arc 1148.5.2 Griechische Palaeographie. 2. Aufl. (Gardthausen, V.) Leipzig, 1911. 2v.
Arc 87.1.76 Griechische Porträts aus dem Ausgang der Antike. (Rodenwaldt, Gerhart.) Berlin, 1919.
Arc 641.2 Griechische Reisetage. (Börger, Hans.) Hamburg, 1925.
Arc 1148.35 Griechische Tachygraphie und tironische Noten. (Boge, Herbert.) Hildesheim, 1974.
Arc 700.6 Das Griechische Theater. (Dörpfeld, W.) Athen, 1896.
Arc 1460.3 Griechische und römische Münzbilder. (Bernhard, O.) Zürich, 1926.
Arc 700.16 Griechische Urkunden. (Kairo. Ägyptischen Museums.) Strassburg, 1911.
Arc 645.3 Die griechischen Fundgruppen der frühen Bronzezeit und ihre auswärtigen Beziehungen. (Fuchs, Siegfried.) Berlin, 1937.
Arc 1468.14 Griechischen Münzen der Sammlung Warren. Text and plates. (Regling, H.) Berlin, 1906. 2v.
Arc 1470.84 Griechisches Münzwerk. (Schoenert-Geiss, E.) Berlin, 1965. 2v.

Author and Title Listing

Arc 87.1.56 Griechisches Pferdegeschirr...Königlichen Museum. (Pernice, E.) Berlin, 1896.
Arc 1148.19 Het Griehsche boek in voor. (Engelhes, W.) Amsterdam, 1926.
Arc 1348.77 Grierson, Philip. Numismatics. London, 1975.
Arc 953.28F Griffin, James. Archaeology of eastern United States. Chicago, 1952.
Arc 969.1.3.7 Griffin, James B. The Fort Ancient aspect. Ann Arbor, 1943.
Arc 430.3 Griffin, L. Famous monuments of central India. London, 1886.
Arc 545.227.44F Griffith, F.L. Catalogue of demotic graffiti of the Dodecaschoenus. Oxford, 1935.
Arc 545.227.44PF Griffith, F.L. Catalogue of demotic graffiti of the Dodecaschoenus. v.2. Oxford, 1937.
Arc 587.4 Griffith, F.L. Hieroglyphs. London, 1898.
Arc 606.6 Griffith, F.L. Karanòg, the Meroitic inscriptions. Philadelphia, 1911.
Arc 587.5 Griffith, F.L. The Mastabo of Ptalshetep and Alsbrethetep. London, 1900. 2v.
Arc 587.9 Griffith, F.L. Meroitic inscriptions. London, 1911. 2 pam.
Arc 585.9 Griffith, F.L. Two hieroglyphic papyri from Tanis. London, 1889.
Arc 556.1 Griffith, Francis L. The study of Egyptology. Oxford, 1901.
Arc 855.220 Griffith, J.E. Portfolio of photographs of Cromlechs of Anglesey and Carnarvonshire. Derby, 1900.
Arc 736.1.15 Griffo, Pietro. Sulla collocazione dei Telamoni nel Tempio. Agrigento, 1952.
Arc 746.12.10F Grifi, L. Monumenti di cere antica. Roma, 1841.
Arc 1433.24 Grigorbev, V.V. Opisanie kuficheskikh monet' X veka. Sankt Peterburg, 1841.
Arc 612.67 Grigor'ev, Gennadii P. Machalo verkhnego paleolita i proiskhozhdenie Homo Sapiens. Leningrad, 1968.
Arc 1349.70 Grigor'ev, V.V. Zhizn' i trudy P.S. Savel'eva. Sankt Peterburg, 1861.
Arc 726.285 Grillo, Francesco. Antichità storiche e monumentali di Corigliano Calabro. Cosenza, 1965.
Arc 1025.52 Grillwitzer, A. Die bildischen Darstellungen in die römischen Katakomben. Graz, 1876.
Arc 723.33 Grimal, Pierre. In search of Ancient Italy. 1st American ed. N.Y., 1964.
Arc 66.1.155 Grimal, Pierre. Las jardins romains. Paris, 1943.
Arc 383.14 Grimes, W.F. Aspects of archaeology in Britain and beyond; essays presented to O.G.S. Crawford. London, 1951.
Arc 858.72 Grimes, W.F. Excavations on defence sites. London, 1960.
Arc 885.20 Grimes, W.F. The prehistory of Wales. 2. ed. Cardiff, 1951.
Arc 861.109 Grimes, William F. The excavation of Roman and mediaeval London. London, 1968.
Arc 1510.15 Grimm, E. Münzen und Medaillen der Stadt Wismar. Berlin, 1897.
Arc 383.89F Grimm, Paul. Varia archaeologica. Berlin, 1964.
Arc 853.66 Grimm, Paul. Die vor- und frühgeschichtliche Besiedlung des Unterharzes und seines Vorlandes auf Grund der Bodenfunde. Inaug. Diss. Halle an der Saale, 1931.
Arc 853.71.5F Grimm, Paul. Die vor- und frühgeschichtlichen Burgwälle der Bezirke Halle und Magdeburg. Berlin, 1958. 2v.
Arc 870.10.9 Grinsell, L.V. The ancient burial-mounds of England. London, 1936.
Arc 870.10.9.5 Grinsell, L.V. The ancient burial-mounds of England. 2. ed. London, 1955.
Arc 861.140 Grinsell, L.V. The archaeology of Wessex. London, 1958.
Arc 595.35 Grinsell, Leslie V. Egyptian pyramids. Gloucester, 1947.
Arc 87.2.63 Gripswalder Matronen- und Mereurius-Statuen. (Fiedler, F.) Bonn, 1863.
Arc 1027.41.35 Grisar, H. Die Grabplatte des H. Paulus. Rom, 1892.
Arc 1027.8 Grisar, H. Die römische Sebastianuskirche. Rom, 1895.
Arc 1033.23 Grisar, H. Il sancta sanctorum...tesoro sacro. Roma, 1907.
Arc 1015.224 Grisar, H. Tombe apostoliche di Roma. Roma, 1892.
Arc 1033.17.5 Griscembeni, G.M. Memorie istoriche della miracolosa immagine di S. Maria in Portico. Roma, 1716.
Arc 1033.34.35 Grissar, H. Della statua di bronzo di San Pietro. Roma, 1898.
Arc 830.22.14F Grivaud de la Vincelle, C.M. Antiquités gauloises et romaines. Atlas. Paris, 1807.
Arc 830.22.14 Grivaud de la Vincelle, C.M. Antiquités gauloises et romaines. Texte. Paris, 1807.
Arc 823.16 Grivaud de la Vincelle, C.M. Recueil de monumens antiques. v.1-2. Paris, 1817.
Arc 595.2 Grobert, J. Description des pyramides de Ghizé. Paris, 1801.
Arc 938.60F Grobin-Seeburg. (Nerman, Burger.) Stockholm, 1958.
Arc 853.65.35 Grodziska wczesnośredniowieczne województwa wrocławskiego. (Kaletyn, Marta.) Wrocław, 1968.
Arc 1335.57F Gróf Dessewffy Miklos barbár pénzei. pt.1-2. (Gohl, Ödön.) Budapest, 1910-11.
Arc 670.3.5 Gróf teleki Emma Görögorszagi a Rége Attikanak. (Gerando, A. de.) Pest, 1873.
Arc 853.103F Grohne, E. Mohndorf. Bremen, 1953.
Arc 861.100.20 Grohskoph, Bernice. The treasure of Sutton-Hoo. 1. ed. N.Y., 1970.
Arc 1330.56.1 Gromachevskii, Semen G. Bibliograficheskii ukajatel' literatury po russkoi numizmatike. Ann Arbor, Mich., 1965.
Arc 543.25 Groneman, I. The Tyandi-Barabudur in Central Java. Samarang, 1901.
Arc 543.25.5 Groneman, I. The Tyandi-Barabudur in Central Java. 2. ed. Samarang, 1906.
Arc 1148.20 Groningen, B.A. Short manual of Greek palaeography. Leiden, 1940.
Arc 1148.20.2 Groningen, B.A. Short manual of Greek palaeography. 2. ed. Leiden, 1955.
Arc 1148.20.3 Groningen, B.A. Short manual of Greek palaeography. 3. ed. Leyden, 1963.
Arc 1460.1 Gronovius, J.F. De sestertüs. Leyden, 1691.
Arc 426.10 Groot, G.J. The prehistory of Japan. N.Y., 1951.
Arc 505.15 Groot, J. de. Palestijnsche masseben (Opgerichte Steenen). Groningen, 1913.
Arc 670.2.5 Groote, M. von. Ägineten und Archäologen. Strassburg, 1912.
Arc 861.21.45 Grooved ware sites in Yorkshire and the north of England. (Manby, Terence George.) Oxford, 1974.
Arc 700.11 Gropengiesser, H. Die Gräber von Attika. Athen, 1907.
Arc 1500.19 Le gros tournois est imite du sarrazinas Chrétien d'Acre. (Blancard, Louis.) n.p., n.d.
Arc 543.2.6 Groslier, Bernard P. Angkor: art and civilization. N.Y., 1966.
Arc 543.2.5 Groslier, Bernard P. The arts and civilization of Angkor. N.Y., 1957.
Arc 543.7.9 Groslier, G. Angkor. Paris, 1924.
Arc 910.4 Gross, V. Les protohelvètes. Paris, 1883.
Arc 520.19 Der grosse Fries von Pergamon. (Kähler, Heinz.) Berlin, 1948.
Arc 600.145F Der Grosse Pylon des Tempels der Isis in Philä. (Junker, Hermann.) Wien, 1958.
Arc 87.1.35 Grosse Thongefaesse in Statuetten- und Buestenform. (Tren, G.) Berlin, 1875.
Arc 830.83 Grossen, J.B.B. Recueil des antiquités et monumens marseillos. Marseille, 1773.
Arc 1335.22 Die grossherzogliche morgenländische Münzsammlung in Jena. (Stickel, J.G.) Jena, 1846.
Arc 595.12 Grossi, V. Le leggende delle piramidi. Genova, 1890.
Arc 945.2 Grossi, V. Teocalli e piramidi. Torino, 1888.
Arc 1027.25.37 Grossi-Gondi, A. Giovanni Battista de Rossi, archeologo romano. Roma, 1894.
Arc 1033.17.547 Grossi-Gondi, F. La dormitio B. Mariae. Roma, 1910.
Arc 1018.52 Grossi-Gondi, F. I monumenti cristiani. Roma, 1920-23. 2v.
Arc 936.195.170 Das grossmährische Reich im Spiegel der Bodenfunde. (Preidel, Helmut.) Gräfelfing, 1968.
Arc 1503.9 Grossmann, Theodor. Sammlung Schweizer Münzen und Medaillen des Herrn Theodor Grossmann. Frankfurt, 1926?
Arc 935.9 Grosvenor, E.A. The hippodrome of Constantinople. London, 1889.
Arc 1348.48 Grote, Hermann. Münzstudien. v.1-2. Leipzig, 1857-62.
Arc 1675.65 Grotemeyer, Paul. Da ich het die gestalt. München, 1957.
Arc 612.27 Grott-människornas årtusenden. (Rydh, H.) Stockholm, 1926.
Arc 1027.45 Grotta di San Paolo a Malta. (Galt Said, G.) Malta, 1863.
Arc 736.26 Grotta Regina. Roma, 1969.
Arc 608.7.25 Les grottes préhistoriques d'"El Khenzira" (région de Mazagan). Thèse. (Ruhlmann, A.) Nogent-le-Rotrou, 1936.
Arc 830.56 Les grottes préhistoriques du village de Jouaignes. v.1-3. (Barbey, A.) Chateau-Thierry, 1870-75.
Arc 1138.105F Groudbegrippen van de paleografie. 3. druk. (Strubbe, Egied I.) Gent, 1961. 2v.
Arc 131.2 Group for the Study of Irish Historic Settlement. Bulletin. Belfast, Ire.? 1,1970+
Arc 543.7.15 Le groupe d'Angkor vu par les ecrivains et les étrangers. (Naudin, G.) Saigon, 1928.
Arc 66.1.42 Grousset, R. Étude sur l'histoire des sarcophages chrétiens. Paris, 1885.
Arc 1335.8 Groux, D.E. Descriptive catalogue of coins belonging to the Historical Society of Maryland. n.p., n.d.
Arc 865.19 Grover, Henry M. A voice from Stonehenge. pt.1. London, 1847.
Arc 556.2 The growth and nature of Egyptology. (Glanville, Stephen A.K.) Cambridge, 1947.
Arc 830.13.10 Grube, G. Die Attika an römischen Triumphbogen...Bogens von Orange. Karlsruhe-Baden, 1931.
Arc 1478.20 Grueber, H.A. Coins of the Roman Republic in the British Museum. v.1-3,5; pt.1-2. London, 1910. 5v.
Arc 430.5 Gruenwedel, A. Buddhistische Studien. Berlin, 1897.
Arc 1478.14 Gruman, G. Inschriften und Darstellungen Römus. Biel, 1899.
Arc 1163.23 Grun, Paul A. Leseschlüssel zu unserer alten Schrift. Görlitz, 1935.
Arc 1468.8 Grunauer, E. Altgriechischen Münzorten. Basel, 1877.
Arc 1076.10 Grundmann, Günther. Deutschen Glockenatlas. München, 1959- 3v.
Arc 1153.2.9 Grundriss - lateinische Palaeographie. (Paoli, Cesare.) Innsbruck, 1889-95.
Arc 1153.2.15 Grundriss - lateinische Palaeographie. (Paoli, Cesare.) Innsbruck, 1902.
Arc 1018.5.9 Grundriss der christlichen Archäologie. (Schultze, Victor.) München, 1919.
Arc 1153.2.3 Grundriss der lateinischen Palaeographie und der Urkundenlehre. (Paoli, Cesare.) Innsbruck, 1885.
Arc 785.36 Die Grundrissentwicklung der römischen Thermen. (Pfretzschner, E.) Strassburg, 1909.
Arc 396.2 Grundsätze der modernen Denkmalpflege. (Lange, Konrad.) Tübingen, 1906.
Arc 905.15 Grundzüge der böhmischen Alterthumskunde. (Wocel, J.E.) Prag, 1845.
Arc 848.32 Grundzüge der Vorgeschichte Deutschlands. (Frenzel, W.) Stuttgart, 1935.
Arc 853.24.9 Grundzüge der vorrömischen Besiedelung Bayerns. Inaug. Diss. (Hülle, Werner.) Augsburg, 1932.
Arc 1480.42F Grunwald, Michael. Die römischen Bronze- und Kupfermünzen mit schlagmarken um legionslager Vindonissa. Basel, 1946.
Arc 87.2.67 Die Gruppe des Pasquino. (Urlichs, L.) Bonn, 1867.
Arc 830.171 Gruyer, Paul. Les calvaires bretons. Paris, 1920.
Arc 1584.1.4 Gruzinskia numizmatika. (Kapanadze, D.G.) Moskva, 1955.
Arc 497.73 Gryglewicz, F. Archeologiczne odkrycia w egzegezie Nowego Testamentu. Lublin, 1962.
Arc 853.83.5 Gsaenger, Hans. Die Externsteine. Freiburg, 1964.
Arc 66.1.65 Gsell, S. Essai sur Domitien. Paris, 1894.
Arc 740.205 Gsell, S. Fouilles...nécropole de Vulci. Paris, 1891.
Arc 608.6.24 Gsell, Stéphane. Cherchel. Alger, 1952.
Arc 608.16 Gsell, Stéphane. De Tipasa, Mauretaniae Caesariensis urbe. Diss. Algerii, 1894.
Arc 608.6.13 Gsell, Stéphane. Fouilles de Gouraya. Paris, 1903.
Arc 608.6.31 Gsell, Stéphane. Guide archéologique des environs d'Alger. Alger, 1896.
Arc 608.6.21F Gsell, Stéphane. Khamissa, Mdaourouch, Announa. Alger, 1914-22.
Arc 608.6.23 Gsell, Stéphane. Promenades archéologiques aux environs d'Alger. Paris, 1926.
Arc 608.6.35 Gsell, Stéphane. Recherches archéologiques en Algérie. Paris, 1893.
Arc 761.2 Gsell-Fels, T. Roemische Ausgrabungen. Hildburghausen, 1870.
Arc 1493.24 Guadan, Antonio M. de. Numismatica iberica e iberoromana. Madrid, 1969.
Arc 1033.35.153 Gualzetti, G.B. Pel giorno dell'invenzione di S. Croce, 1848. Milano, 1848.
Arc 608.50 Le guarbier nord-est de Volubilis. (Etienne, Robert.) Paris, 1960. 2v.
Arc 1153.84 Guarducci, M. I graffiti sotto la confessione di San Petro in Vaticano. Città del Vaticano, 1958. 3v.
Arc 1027.12.20 Guarducci, Margherita. The tomb of Saint Peter. N.Y., 1960.

Arc 726.49 Guarini, R. Ricerche sull'antica città di Eclano. 2a ed. Appendice. Napoli, 1814-15.
Arc 307.3.50 Guatemala en el XXXIII Congreso internacional de Americanistas. (Girard, Rafael.) Guatemala, 1958.
Arc 726.71.10 Guattani, G.A. Monumenti Sabini. Roma, 1827-28. 3v.
tn Arc 761.5.2* Guattani, G.A. Roma descritta ed illustrata. 2. ed. v.1-2. Roma, 1805.
Arc 1033.108 Guazzugli, M. Notizie riguardanti il culto di S. Irene. Osimo, 1783.
Arc 1163.30PF Guboglu, Mihail. Paleografia si diplomatica Turco-Osmană. București, 1958.
Arc 684.9.10 Gude, Mabel. A history of Olynthus. Baltimore, 1933.
Arc 1020.119 Gudiol y Cunill, J. Nocions d'arqueologia sagrada catalana. Vich, 1911.
Arc 1020.119.5 Gudiol y Cunill, J. Nocions d'arqueologia sagrada catalana. 2a ed. Vich, 1931-33. 2v.
Arc 1077.2.39F Gudiol y Cunill, José. Les creus d'Argenteria a Catalunya. Barcelona, 1920.
Arc 543.66.15 Gudkova, A.V. Tok-kala. Tashkend, 1964.
Arc 895.58 Gudnitz, F. Broncealderens monumentalkunst. København, 1962.
Arc 1033.17.305 Guelfone. Orazione...Foggia...dell'icona...Santa Maria. Foggia, 1669.
Arc 1020.85 Guélou, P.F. Un reliquare romano Byzantin (Auverogne). Clermont-Ferrand, 1883.
Arc 1153.21 Guénin, L.P. Histoire de la sténographie...notes tironiennes. Paris, 1908.
Arc 1077.2.47 Guénon, René. Le symbolisme de la croix. Paris, 1931.
Arc 1077.2.47.2 Guénon, René. Le symbolisme de la croix. Paris, 1970.
Arc 1298.1 Guenther, M. Ins sigillorum mediiaevi. Lipsiae, 1813.
Arc 1298.1.5 Guenther, M. Das Siegelrecht des Mittelalters. Stuttgart, 1870.
Arc 726.2.9 Günther, R.T. Contributions to a study of earth movements in the Bay of Naples. Oxford, 1903.
Arc 726.2.15 Günther, R.T. Pausilypon...imperial villa near Naples. Oxford, 1913.
Arc 1675.70 Günzburger, Julius. Medaillen badischer Klöster. Nürnberg, 1930.
Arc 810.66 Guerdan, René. Pompei. Paris, 1973.
Arc 1018.29 Guericke, H. Lehrbuch der christlich kirchlichen Archäologie. Berlin, 1859.
Arc 1018.29.7 Guericke, H. Manual of the antiquities of the church. London, 1851.
Arc 830.220 Guérin, Gérard. Découverte du Baptistère de Sanctus Martinus de Joulle. Fontenay-le-Comte, 1954.
Arc 1033.12.114 Guérin, L.F. Notice abrégée sur la sainte tunique de...Christ. Paris, 1864.
Arc 497.9 Guérin, V. Description de la Palestine. pt.1-3. Paris, 1868-80. 7v.
Arc 505.17 Guérin, V. Tombeau de Josué. Note sur le Khirbet-Tibneh. Paris, 1865.
Arc 955.2.12 Guernsey, S.J. Explorations in northeastern Arizona. Cambridge, Mass., 1931.
Arc 843.229 Guerra y Gómez, Manuel. Constantes religiosas europeas y sotocuevenses (Ojo Guareña, cuna de Castilla). Burgos, 1973.
Arc 1264.13 Guesnon, A. Sigillographie de la ville d'Arras. Arras, 1865.
Arc 608.31 Guia arqueológica del Marruecos Español. (Tarradell, M.) Tetuán, 1953.
Arc 726.10.14 Guida archeologica della città di Palestrina. (Marucchi, Orazio.) Roma, 1912.
Arc 726.10.5 Guida archeologica dell'antica Preneste. (Marucchi, Orazio.) Roma, 1885.
Arc 672.1.70 Guida degli scavi italiani in Creta. (Pernier, Luigi.) Roma, 1947.
Arc 1027.19.17 Guida del cimitero di Callisto. (Marucchi, O.) Paris, 1902.
Arc 1027.5.13 Guida del cimitero di Domitilla. (Marucchi, O.) Paris, 1902.
Arc 1027.4.15 Guida del cimitero di Priscilla. (Marucchi, O.) Paris, 1903.
Arc 547.10 Guida del Museo Archeologico I. Antichita Egiziane. (Florence, Italy.) Florence, 1880.
Arc 1033.56 Guida del Museo Christiano Christiano Lateranense. (Marucchi, O.) Roma, 1898.
Arc 785.22.5 Guida del Palatino. (Lanciani, Visconti de.) Roma, 1873.
Arc 1027.56 Guida delle catacombe di Albano. (Marucchi, O.) Roma, 1903.
Arc 1027.52 Guida delle catacombe e dei monumenti. (Carmelo, D.) Roma, 1900.
Arc 810.25 Guida di Pompei. (Fiorelli, G.) Roma, 1877.
Arc 810.48.10 Guida di Pompei. (Jorio, Andrea.) Napoli, 1836.
Arc 608.12.15 Guida di Sabratha. (Bartoccini, R.) Roma, 1927.
Arc 1335.84.5 Guida numismatica universale. 4. ed. (Gnecchi, F.) Milano, 1903.
Arc 777.1.5 Guida per la campagna di Roma. (Westphal, Enrico.) Roma, 1854.
Arc 825.4 Guide...dans Nîmes et les environs. (Boucoiran, L.) Nîmes, 1863.
Arc 1335.16.5 Guide. (United States Mint, Philadelphia.) Washington, 1913.
Arc 543.7.13 Guide archéologique aux temples d'Angkor. (Marchal, H.) Paris, 1928.
Arc 608.6.31 Guide archéologique des environs d'Alger. (Gsell, Stéphane.) Alger, 1896.
Arc 825.4.4 Guide aux monuments de Nîmes et au Pont du Gard. (Boucoiran, L.) Nîmes, 1863.
Arc 550.5 Guide book to the antiquities of upper Egypt and Nubia. 4. ed. (Aboudi, M.) Cairo, 1946.
Arc 1588.1.13 Guide de l'amateur de monnaies polonaises. (Tyszkiewicz, J.) Posen, 1890.
Arc 810.7 Guide de Pompéi. Naples, 1866.
Arc 810.47.5 Guide de Pompéi. 5. éd. (Pagano, N.) Naples, 1875.
Arc 810.47.7 Guide de Pompéi. 17. éd. (Pagano, N.) Scafati, 1886.
Arc 810.47 Guide de Pompéi tirée de toutes les ouvrages les plus intéressantes. 4. éd. (Pagano, N.) Naples, 1874.
Arc 743.21 Guide des antiquités éstrusques. (Neppi Modona, Aldo.) Florence, 1958.
Arc 1025.28.27 Guide des catacombes romaines. 2. éd. (Marucchi, O.) Paris, 1903.
Arc 672.1.114 Guide des fouilles françaises en Crète. (Tiré, Claire.) Athènes, 1966.
Arc 547.6 Guide du visiteur au Musée de Boulaq. (Boolak Museum.) Boolak, 1883.
Arc 547.6.12 Guide du visiteur au Musée du Caire. (Cairo. Musée des Antiquités Égyptiennes.) Caire, 1902.
Arc 547.6.13 Guide du visiteur au Musée du Caire. 2. éd. (Cairo. Musée des Antiquités Égyptiennes.) Caire, 1912.
Arc 915.7 Guide illustrative du Musée d'Avenches. (Dunant, Émile.) Genève, 1900.
Arc 1335.14.4 Guide illustré au cabinet des médailles. (Babelon, E.) Paris, 1900.
Arc 608.6.6 Guide illustré de Timgad (antique Thamrigadi). 2. éd. (Ballu, Albert.) Paris, 1910.
Arc 823.22 Guide pour les recherches archéologiques. (Bleicher, G.) Nancy, 1896.
Arc 386.12 Guide pratique de l'antiquaire. (Blanchet, A.) Paris, 1899.
Arc 953.32 A guide to artifacts of colonial America. 1. ed. (Nöel Hume, Ivor.) N.Y., 1970.
X Cg Arc 855.8 Guide to British and Roman antiquities in north Wiltshire. (Smith, A.C.) n.p., 1884. 2v.
Arc 444.1.15 A guide to Elephanta. (Hiranandа, Sastri.) Delhi, 1934.
Arc 861.204 A guide to Leicestershire archaeology. (Blank, Elizabeth.) Leicester, 1970.
Arc 893.3.2 Guide to northern archaeology. (Copenhagen. Kongelige Nordiske Oldskrift-Selskab.) London, 1848.
Arc 893.3 Guide to northern archaeology. v.1-10. (Copenhagen. Kongelige Nordiske Oldskrift-Selskab.) London, 1848.
Arc 810.53 Guide to Pompei illustrated. (Morlicchio, F.) Pompei, 1901.
Arc 858.80 A guide to prehistoric England. (Thomas, Nicholas.) London, 1960.
Arc 875.126 A guide to prehistoric Scotland. (Feachem, R.) London, 1963.
Arc 458.1.9 A guide to Sanchi. (Marshall, John.) Calcutta, 1918.
Arc 458.1.10 A guide to Sanchi. 2. ed. (Marshall, John.) Delhi, 1936.
Arc 458.1.12 A guide to Sanchi. 3. ed. (Marshall, John.) Delhi, 1955.
Arc 459.3 A guide to Taxila. (Marshall, John.) Calcutta, 1918.
Arc 459.3.15 A guide to Taxila. 3. ed. (Marshall, John.) Delhi, 1936.
Arc 459.3.19 A guide to Taxila. 4. ed. (Marshall, John.) Cambridge, 1960.
Arc 858.78 Guide to the antiquities of Roman Britain. 3. ed. (British Museum.) London, 1964.
Arc 572.1 Guide to the antiquities of upper Egypt. (Weigall, Arthur Edward Pearse Brome.) London, 1910.
Arc 572.1.2 A guide to the antiquities of upper Egypt from Abydos to the Sudan frontier. (Weigall, Arthur Edward Pearse Brome.) N.Y., 1910.
Arc 861.31.15F Guide to the British and Roman antiquities of the North Wiltshire downs. 2. ed. (Smith, Alfred Charles.) Devizes, 1885.
Arc 458.9 Guide to the Buddhist ruins of Sarnath. 5. ed. (Sahni, Daya Ram.) Delhi, 1933.
Arc 1458.10 Guide to the C.P. Perkins collection of Greek and Roman coins. (Boston. Museum of Fine Arts.) Boston, 1902.
Arc 547.6.25 Guide to the Cairo Museum. 4. ed. (Cairo. Musée des Antiquités Égyptiennes.) Cairo, 1908.
Arc 537.2.7 Guide to the Cesnola collection...Island of Cyprus. (New York (City). Metropolitan Museum of Art. Cesnola Collection.) N.Y., 1876.
Arc 1335.63.3 A guide to the department of coins and medals. (British Museum. Department of Coins and Medals.) London, 1922.
Arc 547.13 A guide to the Egyptian collections. (British Museum.) London, 1909.
Arc 1478.21.5 A guide to the exhibition of Roman coins in the British Museum. (British Museum. Department of Coins and Medals.) London, 1927.
Arc 1353.2.5 A guide to the gold and silver coins of the ancients. 4. ed. (British Museum. Department of Coins and Medals.) London, 1895.
Arc 1353.2.10 A guide to the gold and silver coins of the ancients. 5. ed. (British Museum. Department of Coins and Medals.) London, 1909.
Arc 520.11 Guide to the Pergamon Museum. (Berlin. Königliches Museum.) Berlin, 1904. 2v.
Arc 858.60 A guide to the prehistoric and Roman monuments in England and Wales. (Hawkes, Jacquette.) London, 1951.
Arc 1468.2.10 A guide to the principal coins of Greeks from circa 700 B.C. to A.D. 270. (British Museum. Department of Coins and Medals.) London, 1932.
Arc 1353.2.3 A guide to the principal gold and silver coins of the ancients. (British Museum. Department of Coins and Medals.) London, 1881.
Arc 1353.2.2 A guide to the principal gold and silver coins of the ancients. (British Museum. Department of Coins and Medals.) London, 1886.
Arc 609.30 Guide to the rock paintings of Tanzania. Dar es Salaam, 1965.
Arc 1468.2 A guide to the select Greek coins. (British Museum. Department of Coins and Medals.) London, 1872.
Arc 586.7 Guide to the temple of Deir el Bahari. (Egypt Exploration Society.) London? 1895?
Arc 547.12 A guide to the 1st and 2nd Egyptian rooms. (British Museum.) London, n.d.
Arc 547.12.2 A guide to the 3rd and 4th Egyptian rooms. (British Museum.) London, 1904.
RRC Arc 1583.30 A guidebook of Russian coins, 1725 to 1970. 1. ed. (Harris, Robert P.) Santa Cruz, California, 1971.
Arc 608.6 Guides en Algérie...Lambèse. (Cagnat, R.) Paris, 1893.
Arc 726.245 Guido, M. Sardinia. London, 1963.
Arc 726.4.10 Guidobaldi, D. de. Intorno ad una imagine cerea. Napoli, 1853.
Htn Arc 1200.10* Guigue, M.C. De l'origine de la signature...au Moyen Âge. Paris, 1863.
Arc 1033.121 Guillaume, P. Le navi cavensi nel Mediterraneo...vita di S. Costabile de Lucania. Napoli, 1876.
Arc 810.19 Guillaume, Paul. Une excursion à Pompéi. Paris, 1880.
Arc 830.73 Guillaume, Paul. La station préhistorique de Panacelle. Gap, 1878.
Arc 66.1.201 Guillemain, B. La cour pontificale d'Avignon, 1309-1376. Paris, 1962.
Arc 646.3 Guillet de St.-George, George. Lettres écrites sur une dissertation d'un voyage de Grèce. Paris, 1679.
Arc 66.1.153 Guillon, P. Les trépieds du Ptoion. Paris, 1943.
Arc 830.340F Guimet, Emile. Les isiaques de la Gaule. Paris, 1900.
Arc 66.1.73 Guiraud, J. L'état pontificale après le grand schisme. Paris, 1896.
Arc 1550.1 Et guldbracteat-praeg som ofte forekommer. (Holmboe, C.A.) Kjøbenhavn, 1869.
Arc 943.51 Guliaev, Valerii I. Amerika i Staryi svet v dokolumbovu epokhu. Moskva, 1968.

Arc 543.66.30 Guliamov, Iukliia G. Pervobytnaia kul'tura i vorniknovenie oroshaemogo zemledeliia v mizov'iakh Zara Fsbana. Tashkend, 1966.

Arc 848.34 Gummel, H. Forschungsgeschichte in Deutschland. Berlin, 1938.

Arc 1285.10.8 Gumowski, M. Handbuch der polnischen Siegelkunde. Graz, 1966.

Arc 1285.10.6 Gumowski, M. Herby miast polskich. Warszawa, 1960.

Arc 1285.10.5 Gumowski, M. Pieczęcie i herby miejscowosci wojew lubelskiego. Lublin, 1959.

Arc 1510.110 Gumowski, M. Pieniądz gdański. Gdańsk, 1960.

Arc 1285.10.7 Gumowski, M. Sfragistyka. Warszawa, 1960.

Arc 1588.1.80 Gumowski, Marian. Biskupstwo kniszwickie w XI wieku. Poznań, 1921.

Arc 1588.4.40 Gumowski, Marian. Bolesław Chrobry v Czechach. Poznań, 1934.

Arc 1588.1.22 Gumowski, Marian. Corpus numniorum Poloniae. Kraków, 1939.

Arc 1588.1.24 Gumowski, Marian. Handbuch der polnischen Numismatik. Graz, 1960.

Arc 1663.60 Gumowski, Marian. Medale polskie. Warszawa, 1925.

Arc 1663.61 Gumowski, Marian. Medale Tagiellonów. Kraków, 1906.

Arc 1663.63 Gumowski, Marian. Medale Zygmunta III. Kraków, 1924.

Arc 1588.11.5 Gumowski, Marian. Mennica wileńska w XVI i XVII wieku. Warszawa, 1921.

Arc 1588.1.23 Gumowski, Marian. Monety polskie. Warszawa, 1924.

Arc 1588.1.21 Gumowski, Marian. Numizmatyczno-historyczne z wieku. Poznań, 1924.

Arc 1588.1.19 Gumowski, Marian. Podrecznik numiznatyki Polskiej. Kraków, 1914.

Arc 1349.73 Gumowski, Marian. Wspomnienia numizmatyka. Kraków, 1966.

Arc 1588.1.20 Gumowski, Marian. Zarys numizmatyki Polskiej. Łódź, 1952.

Arc 853.59 Gumpert, Carl. Fränkisches Mesolithikum. Leipzig, 1927.

Arc 1033.17.102.2 Gumppenberg, G. Atlas Marianus sive de imaginibus deiparae. v.1-2. Ingaldeladii, 1657.

Arc 1033.17.102 Gumppenberg, G. Atlas Marianus sive de imaginibus deiparae per orbem. Monachii, 1657. 2v.

Arc 936.100.20 Gunjaca, S. Novi naucni rezultati u hrvatskoj arheologiji. Zagreb, 1958.

Arc 432.19 Gupta, Swarajya Prakash. Disposal of the dead and physical types in ancient India. 1. ed. Delhi, 1972.

Arc 925.150.5 Gurevich, F.D. Drevnosti Belorusskogo ponemania. Leningrad, 1962.

Arc 1033.17.97.5 Guridi, José M. Apología de la aparición de Nuestra Señora de Guadalupe de Méjico. Méjico, 1820.

Arc 391.1 Gurlitt, J. Archäologische Schriften. Altona, 1831.

Arc 588.41F Gurob. (Brunton, Guy.) London, 1927.

Arc 790.206.3 Gusman, P. Pompei; la ville, les moeurs, les arts. Paris, 1906.

Arc 790.206.5 Gusman, P. Pompei; the city, its life and art. London, 1900.

Arc 790.206 Gusman, P. Pompei. Paris, n.d.

Arc 720.213 Gusmann, P. La villa imperiale de Tibur. Paris, 1904.

Arc 1560.3.1 Gustaf Cavallis samlung av svenska kopparmynt. Facsimile. (Cavalli, Gustaf.) Stockholm, 1971.

Arc 890.214 Gustafson, G. Norges oldtid. Mindesmärker og oldsager. Kristiania, 1906.

Arc 395.11.5 Gustav Kossinna. (Stampfuss, Rudolf.) Leipzig, 1935.

Arc 853.78 Guthjahr, R. Die Semnonen im Havelland zur frühen Kaiserzeit. Diss. Greifswald, 1934.

Arc 1433.55 Guthrie, C.S. Catalogue of the collection of oriental coins belonging to C. Sefan Guthrie. Hertford, 1874.

Arc 1583.8 Gutten'-Chalskii, F.K. Chdel'n. velikokn. idsarsk. den'gi drevn. Rusi. Sankt Peterburg, 1875.

Arc 1588.1.30 Gutten Czapskii, E.K. Catalogue de la collection des medailles et monnaies polonaises. Graz, 1957. 5v.

Arc 505.61.5 Guy, P.L.O. Megiddo tombs. Chicago, 1938.

Arc 915.44 Guyan, Walter Ulrich. Das alamannische Gräberfeld von Beggingen-Löbern. Basel, 1958.

Arc 915.15 Guyan, Walter Ulrich. Das Grabhügelfeld im Sankert bei Hemishofen. Basel, 1951.

Arc 530.141F Guzelova karisi. (Kosay, H.Z.) Ankara, 1967.

Arc 743.26 Guzzo, Piero G. Le fibule in Etruria dal VI al I secolo. Firenze, 1973.

Arc 673.1.25F Le gymnase de Delphes. Thèse. (Jannosay, J.) Paris, 1953.

Arc 66.1.196 Gymnasion; étude sur les monuments consacrés à l'éducation en Grèce des origines à l'Empire romain. (Delorme, Jean.) Paris, 1960.

Arc 700.55 Gymnasion. (Delorme, Jean.) Paris, 1960.

Arc 905.144 Gyor története a tizenharmadik század közepéig. Györ, 1942.

Arc 936.26.10 György, L. Az Erdelyi Múzeum-Egyesület. Kolozsvár, 1937.

Arc 936.250 Gzelishvili, Iosif. Zhelezoplavil'noe proizvodstvo v drevnei Gruzii. Tbilisi, 1964.

Arc 1084.1 H.R. Bishop and his jade collection. (Kunz, G.F.) Lancaster, 1903.

Arc 1460.5 Haak, A.C. Gold coins of the Royal Netherlands Academy. Amsterdam, 1964.

Arc 1076.3.49 Haas, A. Glockensagen im pommerschen Volksmunde. Stettin, 1919.

Arc 1510.172 Haas, Rudolf. Die Prägungen der Mannheimer Münzstätten. Mannheim, 1974.

Arc 925.121 Haavio Martti, Henrikki. Bjarmien vallan kukoistur ja tuho. Porvoo, 1965.

Arc 595.33.5 Haberman, F. Armageddon has come; the climax of the ages is near. 2. ed. St. Petersburg, 1940.

Arc 520.7 Habich, G. Die Amazonengruppe die attalischen Weihgeschenks. Berlin, 1896.

Arc 1670.57F Habich, Georg. De Medaillon der italienischen Renaissance. Stuttgart, 1924.

Arc 1508.8 Habich, Georg. Die deutschen Medailleure des XVI. Jahrhunderts. Halle an der Saale, 1916.

Arc 889.37 L'habitat rural à l'époque romaine. (Laurent, René.) Bruxelles, 1972.

Arc 830.42 Habitations gauloises et villas latines. (Grenier, A.) Paris, 1906.

Arc 936.27 Hachhausen und Hachlaus, S.J. Die Alterthümer Daciens in dem heutigen Siebenbürgen. Wien, 1775.

Arc 505.140 Hachmann, Rolf. Bericht über die Ergebnisse der Ausgrabungen in Kamid el-Loz (Libanon) in den Jahren 1963 und 1964. Bonn, 1966.

Arc 505.140.5 Hachmann, Rolf. Bericht über die Ergebnisse der Ausgrabungen in Kamid el-Loz (Libanon) in den Jahren 1966 und 1967. Bonn, 1970.

Arc 848.61.5 Hachmann, Rolf. Die Germanen. München, 1971.

Arc 848.61 Hachmann, Rolf. The Germanic peoples. London, 1971.

Arc 853.120 Hachmann, Rolf. Studien zur Geschichte Mitteldeutschlands während der älteren Latènezeit. Hamburg, 1950.

Arc 505.136 Hachmann, Rolf. Vademecum der Grabung Kamid-el-Loz. Bonn, 1969.

Arc 710.8 Hachtmann, K. Akropolis von Athen im Zeitalter des Perikles. Gütersloh, 1903.

Arc 520.8 Hachtmann, K. Pergamon. Pflanzstätte Hellenisches Kunst. Gütersloh, 1900.

Arc 416.8 Hackin, J. Recherches archéologiques en Asie centrale (1931). Paris, 1936.

Arc 543.12.5 Hackin, Joseph. L'oeuvre de la délégation archéologique française en Afghanistan, 1922-1932. Tokyo, 1933.

Arc 938.30 Hackman, A. Die ältere Eisenzeit in Finnland. Helsingfors, 1905.

Arc 726.73.5 Hadrawa, N. Ragguagli di varii scavi. Dresda, 1794.

Arc 726.73 Hadrawa, N. Ragguagli di varii scavi. Napoli, 1793.

Arc 870.14.3 Hadrian, the builder of the Roman wall. (Bruce, John C.) London, 1853.

Arc 726.24.13FA Hadrian und seine Villa bei Tivoli. (Kähler, H.) Berlin, 1950.

Arc 870.14.9 Hadrian's wall. (Mothersole, Jessie.) London, 1922.

Arc 726.24.22 Die Hadriansvilla bei Tivoli. (Aurigemma, S.) Tivoli, 1955.

Arc 1510.40 Haeberle, Adolf. Ulmer Münz- und Geldgeschichte des Mittelalters. n.p., 1935.

Arc 1480.12 Haeberlin, E.J. Zum corpus numorum aeris gravis. Berlin, 1905.

Arc 392.15F Haeberlin, Ernst Justus. Ernst Justus Haeberlin, sein Wirken. München, 1929. 2v.

Arc 1475.11 Häberlin, J.E.J. Aes grove das Schwergeld Roms und Mittelitaliens. v. 1, Text; v. 2, Plates. Frankfurt, 1910. 2v.

Arc 895.60 Hällgröpningstudier i arsbetring till nya sydsverska fynd. (Lidén, Oskar L.) Lund, 1938.

Arc 830.348 Haensch, Wolf. Die paläolithischen Menschendarstellungen. Bonn, 1968.

Arc 905.90.5 Haensel, Bernhard. Beiträge zur Chronologie der Mittleren Bronzezeit im Karpatenbecken. Bonn, 1968. 2v.

Arc 853.248 Haermann, S. Die dritte Hallstattstufe im Gebeit. Nürnberg, 1925.

Arc 1423.25 Haffner, Sylvia. The history of modern Israel's money, 1917 to 1967, including state medals and Palestine mandate. 1st ed. La Mesa? 1967.

Arc 723.24 Haftmann, W. Das italienische Säulenmonument. Leipzig, 1939.

Arc 895.70 Hagberg, Ulf Eric. The archaeology of Skedemosse. Stockholm, 1967. 3v.

Arc 1510.142 Hagen, Johann Georg Friedrich von. Münzbeschreibung des gräflich und fürstlichen Hauses Mansfeld. Nürnberg, 1778.

Arc 387.23.6 Hagen, Victor Wolfgang von. F. Catherwood, architect-explorer of two worlds. Barre, Mass, 1968.

Arc 387.23 Hagen, Victor Wolfgang von. Frederick Catherwood. N.Y., 1950.

Arc 785.83 Hagen, Victor Wolfgang von. The roads that led to Rome. London, 1967.

Arc 1411.9F Hager, Joseph. Description des médailles chinoises du cabinet imperial de France. Paris, 1805.

Arc 1016.8 Hager, Joseph. Monument de Yu, ou La plus ancienne inscription de la Chine. Paris, 1802.

Arc 936.1.15 Die Hagia Sophia von Thessalonike. Inaug. Diss. (Kalliga, M.) Würzburg, 1935.

Arc 1670.6F Hague. Koninklijk Kabinet van Munten. Les médailles et plaquettes modernes. v.1-6. Haarlem, 1899-1900.

Arc 830.25 Hahn, Alexandre. Monuments celtiques des environs de Luzarches. Paris, 1867.

Arc 853.185 Hahn, Heinrich. Die Ausgrabungen am Fuldaer Donaplatz. Fulda, 1956.

Arc 1510.11.20 Hahn, Wolfgang Reinhard Otto. Typenkatalog der Münzer der bayerischen Herzöge und Kurfürsten, 1506-1805. Braunschweig, 1971.

Arc 612.25 Hahne, Hans. Totenehre im alten Norden. Jena, 1929.

Arc 612.6 Hahne, Hans. Das vorgeschichtliche Europa. Bielefeld, 1910.

Arc 845.207F Hahne, Hans. Vorzeitfunde aus Niedersachsen. Hannover, 1915-25.

Arc 612.6.5 Hahne, Hans. 25 Jahre Siedlungsarchäologie. Leipzig, 1922.

Arc 1540.11 Haigh, D.H. Essay on the numismatic history of the East Angles. Leeds, 1845.

Arc 1033.17.222 Haigneré, D. Couronnement de Notre-Dame de Boulogne. Boulogne, 1885.

Arc 1033.12.73 Haignere, D. Notre-Dame de Saint-Sang. 2e éd. Paris, 1884.

Arc 1285.10 Haisig, Marian. Studia nad legendą pieczęci miejskiej. Wrocław, 1953.

Arc 543.150 Hajar Cin Humeid. (Van Beek, Gus Willard.) Baltimore, 1969.

Arc 1190.9 Hajnal, Istvan. Írástörtenet az írásbeliség felujulása korából. Budapest, 1921.

Arc 1093.6.15 Das Hakenkreuz nach Ursprung, Vorkommen und Bedeutung. 5. Aufl. (Wilser, L.) Leipzig, 1922.

Arc 672.1.31F Halbherr, F. Relazione sugli scavi...in Gortyna. Roma, 1889.

Arc 1093.11 Hald, Margrethe. Primitive shoes. København, 1972.

Arc 950.205 Haldeman, S.S. On the contents of a rock retreat in Southeast Pennsylvania. n.p., n.d.

Arc 858.43 Half-hours among some English antiquities. (Jewitt, L.) London, 1877.

Arc 510.5 Halicarnassus, Cnidas and Branchidae. v.1; v.2, pt.1-2. (Newton, C.T.) London, 1862-1863. 3v.

Arc 1348.16 Halke, H. Einleitung in das Studium des Numismatik. Berlin, 1889.

Arc 1348.16.2 Halke, H. Einleitung in das Studium des Numismatik. 3. Aufl. Berlin, 1905.

Arc 677.1 Halkyoma. (Forchhammer, P.W.) Berlin, 1857.

Arc 700.21 Hall, Elise von. Over den oorsprong van de grieksche grafstele. Proefschrift. Amsterdam, 1941.

Arc 647.3A Hall, H.R. Aegean archaeology. London, 1915.

Arc 647.3.2A Hall, H.R. Aegean archaeology. London, 1915.

Arc 647.3.5 Hall, H.R. The civilization of Greece in the bronze age. London, 1928.

Arc 682.4 Hall, H.R. The oldest civilization of Greece. London, 1901. 2v.

Arc 1190.5 Hall, Hubert. A formula book of English historical documents. Cambridge, 1908. 2v.

Arc 609.1.9 Hall, R.N. The ancient ruins of Rhodesia. London, 1902.

Arc 609.1.10 Hall, R.N. The ancient ruins of Rhodesia. London, 1904.

Arc 609.1.13 Hall, R.N. Great Zimbabwe. London, 1905.

Arc 609.1.15 Hall, R.N. Pre-historic Rhodesia. Philadelphia, 1910.

Author and Title Listing

Arc 861.58 The hall of Waltheof...Hallamshire. (Addy, S.O.) London, 1893.
Arc 895.21.15 Hallenberg, J. Quatuor monumenta aenea e terra i Suecia eruta. Stockholm, 1802.
Arc 1433.11 Hallenberg, Jonas. Collectio nummorum cuficorum. Stockholm, 1800.
Arc 1433.11.3 Hallenberg, Jonas. Numismata orientalia aere expressa. pt. 1-2. Upsaliae, 1822.
Arc 1503.1 Haller, G.E. von. Schweizerisches Münz- und Medaillenkabinet. v.1-2. Bern, 1780-81.
Arc 1020.134F Das hallesche Heiltum. Berlin, 1931.
Arc 853.71 Die Hallesche Kultur der frühen Eisenzeit. Inaug. Diss. (Holter, F.) Halle, 1934.
Arc 87.3 Hallisches Winckelmann's Program. Halle. 1-28 4v.
Arc 87.3F Hallisches Winckelmann's Program. Halle. 15,1891
Htn Arc 885.2* Halliwell, J.O. An ancient survey of Pen Maen Maur. London, 1859.
Arc 861.10 Halliwell, J.O. Round about notes...Isle of Man. London, 1863.
Arc 905.18 Hallstatt. (Aigner, A.) München, n.d.
Arc 905.18.10 Hallstatt. (Morton, F.) Hallstatt, 1953. 2v.
Arc 905.138 Hallstatt und Italien. (Merhart, Gero von.) Bonn, 1969.
Arc 853.315 Die Hallstatt und Latènekultur in der Pfalz. Diss. (Engels, Heinz-Josef.) n.p., 1967.
Arc 853.13.35 Hallstattforschungen in Nordwürttemberg. (Zuern, Hartwig.) Stuttgart, 1970.
Arc 853.136 Die Hallstattzeit in der Oberpfalz. v.2. (Torbruegge, Walter.) Kallmünz, 1965.
Arc 936.195.205 Die hallstattzeitlichen Grabhügel im Bereiche der Kutscher bei Podsemel (Slowenien). (Barth, Fritz Eckart.) Bonn, 1969.
Arc 895.17.20 Hallström, Gustaf. Monumental art of Northern Europe from the Stone Age. Stockholm, 1938. 2v.
Arc 895.54 Hallström, Gustaf. Monumental art of Northern Sweden from the Stone Age. Stockholm, 1960.
Arc 505.72 Hama. v.2,4. (Carlsbergfondet, Copenhagen.) København, 1948. 2v.
Arc 712.21A Hambidge, Jay. The Parthenon and other Greek temples. New Haven, 1924.
Arc 1490.13.10 Hamburger, L. Katalog alte Sammlung päpstlicher Münzen. Frankfurt, 1921.
Arc 1510.35 Hamburger, L. Sammlung Pfalzischer. Frankfurt am Main, 1929.
Arc 8.3 Hamburger Beiträge zur Archäologie. Hamburg. 1,1971+
Arc 8.3.3 Hamburger Beiträge zur Archäologie. Beiheft. Hamburg. 1,1974+
Arc 1307.7 Hamburger Beiträge zur Numismatik. Hamburg. 6,1947+ 9v.
Arc 510.211 Hamdy Bey, O. Le Tumulus de Nemroud-Dagh. Constantinople, 1883.
Arc 830.16 Hamerton, P.G. The mount. Boston, 1897.
Arc 1433.5.15 Hamidi, Hakim. A catalog of modern coins of Afghanistan. 1. English ed. Kabal, 1967.
Arc 875.105 Hamilton, J.R.C. Excavations at Jarlshof. Edinburgh, 1956.
Arc 875.130 Hamilton, John. Excavations at Clicknimin, Shetland. Edinburgh, 1968.
Arc 505.90F Hamilton, R.W. Khirbat al Mafjar. Oxford, 1959.
Arc 557.2 Hamilton, W. Aegyptiaca. London, 1809.
Arc 513.5 Hamilton, W.J. Researches in Asia Minor, Pontus and Armenia. London, 1842. 2v.
Arc 853.83.15 Hamkens, F.H. Der Externstein. Tübingen, 1971.
Arc 1458.12 Hammer, J. Der Feingehalt die griechischen und römischen Münzen. Berlin, 1906.
Arc 1221.1 Hammer-Purgstall. Abhandlung über die Siegel der Araber, Perser. n.p., n.d.
Arc 392.5 Hammerton, J.A. Wonders of the past; the romance of antiquity and its splendours. N.Y., 1925-26. 4v.
Arc 392.5.7 Hammerton, J.A. Wonders of the past. N.Y., 1937. 2v.
Arc 505.92.5 Hammond, Philip C. The excavation of the main theater at Petra, 1961-1962, final report. London, 1965.
Arc 905.31 Hampel, J. Alterthümer des frühen Mittelalters in Ungarn. Braunschweig, 1905. 3v.
Arc 905.41 Hampel, J. A Bronzkor emlékei magyarhonban. Budapest, 1886. 3v.
Arc 905.26 Hampel, J. Der Goldfund von Nagy-Szent-Miklos. Budapest, 1885.
Arc 905.42 Hampel, J. Ujabb tanulmányok a honfoglalasi kor emlékeiral. Budapest, 1907.
Arc 870.3 Hamper, William. Observations on certain ancient pillars of memoir called Hoar-Stones. Birmingham, 1820.
Arc 943.10.1 Hamy, Jules. Mémoires d'archéologie et d'ethnographié americaines. Graz, 1971.
Arc 985.210F Hamy, M.E.T. Recherches historiques et archéologiques. Paris, 1885.
Arc 608.42.5 The Hana Fteah (Cyrenaica) and the Stone Age of the South-East Mediterranean. (McBurney, Charles.) London, 1967.
Arc 925.9.12 Hancăr, Franz. Urgeschichte Kaukasuns. Wien, 1937.
Arc 1528.12.1 Handboek van de Nederlandsche munten van 1795 tot 1969. 4. druk. (Schulman, Jacques.) Amsterdam, 1969.
Arc 1528.12 Handboek van de Nederlandsche munten van 1795-1945. (Schulman, Jacques.) Amsterdam, 1946.
Arc 895.79 Handbog i dansk forhistorie. (Arkaeologisk ABC.) København, 1972.
Arc 756.3.5 Handbook...ruins and museums of Rome. (Braun, Emil.) London, 1855.
Arc 1.5.23 Handbook. (American School of Oriental Research, Jerusalem.) Philadelphia?
Arc 861.10.24 Handbook and guide to the replicas and casts of Manx crosses on exhibition in the Free Public Museums. 2. ed. (Liverpool. Public Libraries, Museum and Art Gallery.) Liverpool, 1920.
Arc 407.9.2 Handbook of archaeology. 2. ed. (Westropp, Hodder Michael.) London, 1878.
Arc 547.20 A handbook of Egyptian rooms. (New York (City). Metropolitan Museum of Art.) N.Y., 1920.
Arc 858.17 Handbook of English antiquities. (Clinch, George.) London, 1905.
Arc 1538.19 Handbook of English coins. (Jewitt, L.) London, 1879.
Arc 1143.2.3 Handbook of Greek and Latin palaeography. (Thompson, Edward Maunde.) Ann Arbor, 1973.
Arc 1143.2 Handbook of Greek and Latin palaeography. (Thompson, Edward Maunde.) N.Y., 1893.
Arc 1458.9 A handbook of Greek and Roman coins. (Hill, G.F.) London, 1899.
Arc 645.2.2A Handbook of Greek archaeology. (Fowler, H.N.) N.Y., 1909.
Arc 1190.86.10 Handbook of Ottoman-Turkish diplomatics. (Reychman, Jan.) The Hague, 1968.
Arc 1478.7 The handbook of Roman numismatics. (Madden, F.W.) London, 1861.
Arc 537.2.12 Handbook of th Cesnola collection of antiquities from Cyprus. (Metropolitan Museum of Art.) N.Y., 1914.
Arc 1473.8.2 A handbook of the coinage of the Byzantine empire. (Goodacre, H.G.) London, 1957.
Arc 1473.8 A handbook of the coinage of the Byzantine empire. pt.1-3. (Goodacre, H.G.) London, 1928-33.
Arc 1538.7.2 Handbook of the coins of Great Britain and Ireland in the British Museum. 2. ed. (British Museum. Department of Coins and Medals.) London, 1970.
Arc 1307.5 Handbook of United States coins. Racine, Wis. 2,1943
Arc 708.19 Handbook to antiquities of Athens. (Broughton, V. Delves (Mrs.).) Athens, 1896.
Arc 1540.17 Handbook to coinage of Scotland. (Robertson, John D.) London, 1878.
Arc 432.16 A handbook to the Inscription Gallery in the Peshhawar Museum. (Shakur, M.A.) Peshawar, 1946.
Arc 672.1.28 Handbook to the palace of Minos at Knossos. (Pendlebury, J.D.S.) London, 1933.
Arc 861.12 The handbook to the Roman wall. 4. ed. (Bruce, J.C.) London, 1895.
Arc 861.12.2 The handbook to the Roman wall. 9. ed. (Bruce, J.C.) Newcastle-upon-Tyne, 1933.
Arc 861.12.2.5 Handbook to the Roman wall. 10. ed. (Bruce, J.C.) Newcastle-upon-Tyne, 1947.
Arc 785.24 Handbooks of ancient Rome. (Pullen, H.W.) London, 1894.
Arc 497.27F Handbuch der altarabischen Altertumskunde. (Nielsen, D.) Kopenhagen, 1927.
Arc 1030.39 Handbuch der altchristlichen Epigraphik im Breisgau. (Kaufmann, Carl M.) Freiburg, 1917.
Arc 1361.1 Handbuch der alten Numismatik. (Grässe, J.G.T.) Leipzig, 1854.
Arc 403.3 Handbuch der Archäologie der Kunst. (Stark, K.B.) Leipzig, 1880.
Arc 392.15 Handbuch der Archäologie im Rahnen des Handbuchs der Altertumswissenschaft. München, 1969-
Arc 1018.26 Handbuch der christlich-kirchlichen Alterthümer. (Siegel, C.C.F.) Leipzig, 1836-38. 4v.
Arc 1018.25.5 Handbuch der christlichen Archäologie. (Augusti, J.C.W.) Leipzig, 1838. 3v.
Arc 1018.19 Handbuch der christlichen Archäologie. (Haufmann, C.M.) Paderborn, 1905.
Arc 1025.28.6 Handbuch der christlichen Archäologie. (Marucchi, O.) N.Y., 1912.
Arc 1018.19.2 Handbuch der christlichen Archäologie. 2. Aufl. (Haufmann, C.M.) Paderborn, 1913.
Arc 1018.19.3 Handbuch der christlichen Archäologie. 3. Aufl. (Kaufmann, C.M.) Paderborn, 1922.
Arc 848.1 Handbuch der Deutsche Alterthumskunde. (Lindenschmit, L.) Braunschweig, 1880.
Arc 570.1A Handbuch der gesammten aegyptischen Alterthumskunde. v.1-4. (Uhlemann, M.) Leipzig, 1857. 2v.
Arc 1588.1.11 Handbuch der polnischen Münzkunde. (Kirmis, M.) Posen, 1892.
Arc 1588.1.24 Handbuch der polnischen Numismatik. (Gumowski, Marian.) Graz, 1960.
Arc 1285.10.8 Handbuch der polnischen Siegelkunde. (Gumowski, M.) Graz, 1966.
Arc 830.124 Handbuch der staatlichen Denkmalpflege in Elsass-Lothringen. (Wolff, F.) Strassburg, 1903.
Arc 1190.1.3 Handbuch der Urkundenlehre. 3. Aufl. (Bresslau, H.) Berlin, 1958. 2v.
Arc 1190.1 Handbuch der Urkundenlehre fuer Deutschland und Italien. (Bresslau, H.) Leipzig, 1889.
Arc 1190.1.12 Handbuch der Urkundenlehre für Deutschland und Italien. 2. und 3. Aufl. (Schulze, H.) Berlin, 1960.
Arc 1185.11 Handbuch der Urkundwissen. (Rietsch, K.F.) Berlin, 1904.
Arc 397.26 Handbuch der Vorgeschichte. v.1-3. (Müller-Karpe, Hermann.) München, 1966- 6v.
Arc 1185.15 Handbuch für angehende Archivare und Registratoren. (Zinkernagel, K.F.B.) Nördlingen, 1800.
Arc 1478.23.5 Handbuch zur Münzkunde der römischen Kaiserzeit. (Bernhart, Max.) Halle an der Saale, 1926. 2v.
Arc 1307.15 Handbuecker der mittelasiatischen Numismatik. Braunschweig. 1-4,1968-1973// 5v.
Arc 497.18 Handcock, P.S.P. Archaeology of the Holy Land. London, 1916.
Arc 1528.11 Handleiding tot de kennis der Nederlandsche munten. Amsterdam, 1850.
Arc 1470.3.5 Hands, A.W. Coins of Magna Graecia. London, 1909.
Arc 1468.15 Hands, A.W. Common Greek coins. London, 1907.
Arc 384.2.5 Hands on the past. 1. American ed. (Marek, Kurt W.) N.Y., 1966.
Arc 1163.8 Handschriften der Reformationszeit. (Mentz, G.) Bonn, 1912.
Htn Arc 1160.206* Handschriftenproben aus der Reformationzeit. (Clemen, O.) Zwickau, 1911.
Arc 1138.122 Handwriting. Our medieval legacy. (Lowe, Elias Avery.) Rome, 1969.
Arc 1163.17.35 The handwriting of English documents. (Hector, Leonard C.) London, 1958.
Arc 1138.80.6 The handwriting of English documents. 2. ed. (Hector, Leonard Charles.) London, 1966.
Arc 1163.21.5F The handwriting of Italian humanists. (De la Mare, Albinia Cathérine.) Oxford, 1973-
Arc 1163.17.15A The handwriting of the Renaissance. (Tannenbaum, S.A.) N.Y., 1930.
Arc 1423.16 A handy guide to Jewish coins. (Rogers, Edgar.) London, 1914.
Arc 1033.3.42A Hanfmann, G.M. The season sarcophagus in Dumbarton Oakes. Cambridge, 1951. 2v.
Arc 743.18 Hanfmann, G.M.A. The Etruscans and their art. n.p., 1940.
Arc 530.2.10 Hanfmann, George M.A. Letters from Sardis. Cambridge, 1972.
Arc 746.46 Hanfmann, George Maxim Anossov. Altetruskische Plastik. Würzburg, 1936.
Arc 853.13 Hang, F. Die römischen Inschriften und Bildwerke Württembergs. v.1-2. Stuttgart, 1898-1900.
Arc 853.13.2 Hang, F. Die römischen Inschriften und Bildwerke Württembergs. v.1-3. Stuttgart, 1913.
Arc 853.13.3 Hang, F. Die römischen Inschriften und Bildwerke Württembergs. 2. Aufl. Stuttgart, 1914-15.
Arc 1143.12 Hanger, H. Studien zur griechischen Paläographie. Wien, 1954.
Arc 392.6 Hanno, Georges. Les villes retrouvées. Paris, 1881.

Arc 1580.45 Hans, Josef. Maria-Theresien-Taler. 2. Aufl. Leiden, 1961.
Arc 689.3.10 Hansen, H.D. Early civilization in Thessaly. Baltimore, 1933.
Arc 1570.8 Hansen, Per. Norsk numismatisk forenings historie: 1927-1967. Oslo, 1967.
Arc 1335.9 Hansen von Ehrencron, F.A. Numophylacium Ehrencronianum. n.p., 1730.
Arc 785.92 Hanson, John A. Roman theater-temples. Princeton, 1959.
Arc 1580.10 Hanthaler, C. Verzeichnung...wiennerischer...Müntzen. Lintz, 1745.
Arc 588.29F Harageh. (Engelbach, R.) London, 1923.
Arc 447.6 The Harappa culture and the West. (Mode, Heinz Adolph.) Calcutta, 1961.
Arc 483.5 Harba bridge. (Iraq. Department of Antiquities.) Baghdad, 1935.
Arc 858.97 Harbison, Peter. Some Iron Age Mediterranean imports in England. Oxford, 1974.
Arc 1079.2 Hardaker, Ron. A corpus of early Bronze Age dagger pommels from Great Britain and Ireland. Oxford, 1974.
Arc 383.49 Harden, D.B. Dark-age Britain. London, 1956.
Arc 870.33 Harding, Derek William. The Iron Age in lowland Britain. London, 1974.
Arc 861.172.5 Harding, Derek William. The Iron Age in the Upper Thames basin. Oxford, 1972.
Arc 505.11.10 Harding, G.L. Baalbek. Khayats, 1963.
Arc 505.68.5 Harding, Gerald. The antiquities of Jordan. London, 1959.
Arc 505.68.6 Harding, Gerald. The antiquities of Jordan. London, 1967.
Arc 543.81 Harding, Gerald Lankester. Archaeology in the Aden Protectorates. London, 1964.
Arc 1362.1 Harduin, J. Nummi antiqui pop. et urb. illustrati. Parisii, 1684.
Arc 861.12.18 Hardy, James. On urns and other antiquities found round the southern skirts of the Cheviot Hills. n.p., 1886.
Arc 762.1.20 Hare, A.J.C. Days near Rome. v.1-2. Philadelphia, 1875.
Arc 762.1.25 Hare, A.J.C. Days near Rome. 3. ed. N.Y., 1902.
Arc 762.1.30 Hare, A.J.C. Days near Rome. 4. ed. London, 1906.
Arc 762.1.35 Hare, A.J.C. Days near Rome. 5. ed. London, 1907.
Arc 762.1 Hare, A.J.C. Walks in Rome. London, 1871. 2v.
Arc 762.1.4 Hare, A.J.C. Walks in Rome. London, 1878. 2v.
Arc 762.1.3 Hare, A.J.C. Walks in Rome. N.Y., 1875.
Arc 762.1.2.5 Hare, A.J.C. Walks in Rome. 4. American ed. N.Y., 1874.
Arc 762.1.2 Hare, A.J.C. Walks in Rome. 4. ed. London, 1874. 2v.
Arc 762.1.3.5 Hare, A.J.C. Walks in Rome. 6. American ed. N.Y., 1877.
Arc 762.1.3.7 Hare, A.J.C. Walks in Rome. 7. American ed. N.Y., 187-.
Arc 762.1.3.9 Hare, A.J.C. Walks in Rome. 8. American ed. N.Y., 1882.
Arc 762.1.4.5 Hare, A.J.C. Walks in Rome. 13th ed. London, 1893. 2v.
Arc 762.1.5 Hare, A.J.C. Walks in Rome. 14th ed. N.Y., 1899. 2v.
Arc 762.1.5.5 Hare, A.J.C. Walks in Rome. 15th ed. N.Y., 190-?
Arc 762.1.6 Hare, A.J.C. Walks in Rome. 16th ed. London, 1903. 2v.
Arc 762.1.9 Hare, A.J.C. Walks in Rome. 20th ed. London, 1913.
Arc 762.1.10 Hare, A.J.C. Walks in Rome. 21st ed. London, 1923.
Arc 1207.1PF Hare, Thomas. Engravings from ancient seals attached to deeds. Stowe-Bardolph, 1847.
Arc 497.103 Harker, Ronald. Digging up the Bible lands. London, 1972.
Arc 670.2.7 Harland, J.P. Prehistoric Aigina. Diss. Paris, 1925.
Arc 861.80 Harlyn Bay and the discoveries of its prehistoric remains. 3. ed. (Bullen, R.A.) Harlyn Padstow, 1912.
Arc 830.305 Harmand, Jacques. Les origines des recherches françaises sur l'habitat rural gallo-romain. Bruxelles, 1961.
Arc 505.5.19 Das Harom von Jerusalem und Tempelplatz des Maria. (Rosen, G.) Gotha, 1866.
Arc 497.20.5 Harper, H.A. The Bible and modern discoveries. 4. ed. London, 1891.
Arc 1522.3 Harpes, Jean. Médailles et jetons du pays de Luxembourg. Luxembourg, 1955.
Arc 1166.1 Harris, J.R. Stichometry. Baltimore, 1883.
Arc 590.22 Harris, James E. X-raying the pharaohs. N.Y., 1973.
Arc 858.53 Harris, James R. Caravan essays. no.1-12. Cambridge, 1929.
RRC Arc 1583.30 Harris, Robert P. A guidebook of Russian coins, 1725 to 1970. 1. ed. Santa Cruz, California, 1971.
Htn Arc 950.5* Harris, W.P. Brief account of the discovery of the brass plates...Kinderbrook, Illinois. Nauvoo, Illinois, 1843.
Arc 392.8.80 Harrison, E.R. Harrison of Ightham. London, 1928.
Arc 392.8.80 Harrison of Ightham. (Harrison, E.R.) London, 1928.
Arc 392.9.80 Harry R.H. Hall, 1873-1930. (Thompson, R.C.) London, 1930.
Arc 1613.8 Hart, C.H. A historical sketch of the national medals. Philadelphia, 1867.
Arc 853.21 Hartmann, A. Becherstatuen in Ostpreussen. Braunschweig, 1892.
Arc 1086.1 Hartmann, A. Zur Hochächerfrage. München, 1876.
Arc 1458.3 Hartmann, H.L. Tabellarische Übersicht der gewoehnlichsten Altrömische Münzen. Leipzig, 1828.
Arc 495.13FA Harvard excavations at Samaria 1908-1910. (Reisner, George A.) Cambridge, 1924. 2v.
Arc 320.2.5 Harvard University. Peabody Museum. Memoirs. Cambridge. 1-12 12v.
Arc 320.2.9 Harvard University. Peabody Museum. Papers. Cambridge. 1,1888+ 66v.
Arc 320.2 Harvard University. Peabody Museum. Reports. Cambridge. 1-3 3v.
Arc 1335.4 Harzfeld, S.K. Catalogue of choice English, French, and American coins and medals. Boston, 1878.
Arc 1025.55 Hasenclever, A. Der altchristliche Gräberschmuck. Braunschweig, 1886.
Arc 1588.4.100 Hásková, Jarmila. Chebské mince z 12. a 13. století. Cheb, 1972.
Arc 870.16 Haslam, William. Perran-zabuloe. London, 1844.
Arc 530.151 Haspels, Caroline H.E. The highlands of Phrygia: sites and monuments. Princeton, 1971. 2v.
Arc 861.211 Hassall, Tom Grafton. Oxford, the city beneath your feet. Oxford, 1972.
Arc 600.46F Hassan, S. Excavations at Giza, 1929-1930. v.1-10. Oxford, 1932. 13v.
Arc 447.5 Hastinâpura. (Chand, Amar.) Banoras, 1952.
Arc 670.3 Hastings, H.R. Relations between inscriptions and sculptured representations on Attica tombstones. Madison, 1912.
Arc 132.5 Hastings area archaeological papers. Robertsbridge. 1,1973+
Arc 830.205 Hatt, Jean J. Strasbourg au temps des Romaims. Strasbourg, 1953.
Arc 830.184 Hatt, Jean J. La tombe gallo-romaine. Thèse. Paris, 1951.
Arc 1550.4 Hauberg, Peter C. Myntforhold og utmyntninger i Danmark indtil 1146. Kjøbenhavn, 1900.
Arc 1675.102 Hauek, Karl. Goldbrakteaten aus Sievern. München, 1970.
Arc 1018.19.10 Haufmann, C.M. Amerika und Urchristentum. München, 1924.
Arc 1018.19 Haufmann, C.M. Handbuch der christlichen Archäologie. Paderborn, 1905.
Arc 1018.19.2 Haufmann, C.M. Handbuch der christlichen Archäologie. 2. Aufl. Paderborn, 1913.
Arc 785.22.2 Haugwitz, E. Der Palatin. Rom, 1901.
Arc 785.22 Haugwitz, E. Der Palatin seine Geschichte und seine Ruinen. Rom, 1901.
Arc 1508.31 Hauptlinien der deutschen Münzgeschichte vom Ende des 18. Jahrhunderts bis 1878. (Kahl, Hans Dietrich.) Frankfurt, 1972.
Arc 853.40 Hauptmann, Carl. Die Erhaltung der Römerstrassen. Bonn, 1912.
Arc 853.38 Hauptmann, Carl. Die strategischen Rheinübergange der Römer bei Bonn. Bonn, 1912.
Arc 689.12 Hauptmann, Harald. Die Funde der früher Dimini-Zeit aus der Arapi-Magula. Diss. Bonn, 1969.
Arc 905.6 Hauser, A. Spalato und die römischen Monumente Dalmatiens. Wien, 1883.
Arc 1510.28 Hauser, Josef. Die Münzen und Medaillen der im Jahre 1156 gegründeten (seit 1255). München, 1905.
Arc 830.69 Hauser, Otto. La Micoque; die Kultur einer neuen Diluvialrasse. Leipzig, 1916.
Arc 815.6 Die Hausgötter in Pompeji. (Czechowski, D.) Peremyal, 1900.
Arc 700.5 Haussoullier, B. Quomodo sepulera Tanagraei decoravirent. Paris, 1884.
Arc 66.1.38 Haussoullier, B. La vie municipale en Attique. Paris, 1884.
Arc 853.272F Die Haustiere der mitteldeutschen Bandkiramiker. (Müller, Hanns H.) Berlin, 1964.
Arc 830.357 Le Haute-Marne antique. (Ballet, Pierre.) Chaumont, 1971.
Arc 830.5 La Haute-Savoie avant les Romains. (Revon, L.) Paris, 1878.
Arc 66.1.105 Hautecoeur, L. Rome et la Renaissance de l'antiquite. Photoreproduction. Paris, 1912.
Arc 1307.11 Hautes études numismatiques. Paris. 1,1966+ 4v.
Arc 66.1.41 Hauvette-Besnault, A. Les stratèges athéniens. Paris, 1885.
Arc 395.7.2 Hauviller, E. Franz Xaver Kraus. München, 1905.
Arc 953.20F Haven, S.F. Archaeology of the United States. Washington, 1856.
Htn Arc 1455.2* Havercamp, S. Nummophylacium Reginae Christinae. The Hague, 1742.
Arc 861.17 Haverfield, F. Catalogue of the Roman inscribed and sculptured stones...ms. of Tullie House. Kendal, 1899.
Arc 858.25 Haverfield, F. Roman Britain in 1913- v.1-2. Oxford, 1914- 5v.
Arc 1335.85F Haverkamp, S. Nummophylacium reginae Christinae. Comitum Hagae, 1742.
Arc 545.208FA Hawara, Biahmu and Arsinoe. (Petrie, William M.F.) London, 1889.
Arc 588.25A Hawara portfolio; paintings. (Petrie, W.M.F.) London, 1913.
Arc 672.1.9.5 Hawes, C.H. Crete, the forerunner of Greece. London, 1922.
Arc 612.28 Hawkes, C.F.C. The prehistoric foundations of Europe to the Mycenean age. London, 1940.
Arc 392.14 Hawkes, Jacquetta. The world of the past. 1. ed. N.Y., 1963. 2v.
Arc 858.55.3 Hawkes, Jacquette. Early Britain. London, 1946.
Arc 858.60 Hawkes, Jacquette. A guide to the prehistoric and Roman monuments in England and Wales. London, 1951.
Arc 858.60.5 Hawkes, Jacquette. History in earth and stone. Cambridge, Mass., 1952.
Arc 1663.3 Hawkins, E. Medallic illustrations of the history of Great Britain and Ireland. London, 1885. 2v.
Arc 1538.8 Hawkins, E. The silver coins of England. London, 1887.
Arc 865.24 Hawkins, Gerald Stanley. Stonehenge decoded. 1. ed. Garden City, N.Y., 1965.
Arc 557.1 Hawks, F.L. The monuments of Egypt. N.Y., 1850.
Arc 547.8 Hay, J. Catalogue of the collection of Egyptian antiquities belonging to the late Robert Hay, Esq. London, 1869.
Arc 421.33 Hay, John. Ancient China. London, 1973.
Arc 600.51F Hayes, William C. The burial chamber of the treasurer Sobk-Mosĕ from Er Rizeikât. N.Y., 1939.
Arc 590.14 Hayes, William C. Royal sarcophagi of the XVIII Dynasty. Princeton, 1935.
Arc 557.5 Hayes, William Christopher. Most ancient Egypt. Chicago, 1965.
Arc 557.4.5 Hayes, William Christopher. The scepter of Egypt. Cambridge, 1960.
Arc 557.4 Hayes, William Christopher. The scepter of Egypt. N.Y., 1953. 2v.
Arc 600.193 Haykal, Fa'iza. Tombeau de Pannout à Aniba. Le Caire, 196-.
Arc 1458.5 Haym, N.F. Del tesoro britannico. London, 1719-20. 2v.
Arc 608.37 Haynes, D.E.L. An archaeological and historical guide to the pre-Islamic antiquities of Tripolitania. Tripoli, 1956.
Arc 785.70F Haynes, D.E.L. Porta Argentoriorum. London, 1939.
Arc 545.225 Haynes, H.W. Egyptian Palaeolithic implements. Cambridge, 1882.
Arc 953.3 Haynes, H.W. The prehistoric archaeology of North America. Boston, 1889.
Arc 513.6 Haynes, J.H. Descripitive catalogue to accompany a series of photographs of Asia Minor. N.Y., 1892.
Arc 1348.4A Hazlitt, W.C. The coin collector. N.Y., 1896.
Arc 1453.1.1 Hazlitt, William Carew. The coinage of the European continent. Chicago, 1974.
Arc 1453.1 Hazlitt, William Carew. The coinage of the European continent. London, 1893.
Arc 505.84.5 Hazor; the head of all those kingdoms. (Yadin, Yigael.) London, 1972.
Arc 505.84F Hazor. v.1-4. (Jerusalem. Hebrew Community.) Jerusalem, 1958. 3v.
Arc 672.1.29 Hazzidakis, J. Étude de préhistorie crétoise. Paris, 1921.
Arc 1540.7 Head, B.V. An account of the hoard of Anglo-Saxon coins found at Chancton farm, Sussex. n.p., n.d.
Arc 1468.6 Head, B.V. Historia numorum. Oxford, 1887.
Arc 1468.6.5A Head, B.V. Historia numorum. Oxford, 1911.

Author and Title Listing

Arc 1470.39 Head, B.V. On the chronological sequence of the coins of Boeotia. London, 1881.

Arc 1470.38 Head, B.V. On the chronological sequence of the coins of Ephesus. London, 1880.

Arc 1470.4 Head, B.V. On the chronological sequence of the coins of Syracuse. London, 1874.

Arc 1018.41 Heales, Alfred. The archaeology...Christian altar...western Europe. London, 1881.

Arc 505.88 Hebrew inscriptions and stamps from Gibeon. (Pritchard, James B.) Philadelphia, 1959.

Arc 37.5 Hebrew Union College Biblical and Archaeological School in Jerusalem. Annual. Jerusalem. 1,1970+ 2v.

Arc 495.207F Hebron le haram el-Khalîl, sépulture des patriachs. (Vincent L.H.) Paris, 1923. 2v.

Arc 853.65.25 Heckowa, K.W. Pod znakiem świętego słońca. Wrocław, 1961.

Arc 1163.17.35 Hector, Leonard C. The handwriting of English documents. London, 1958.

Arc 1138.80.6 Hector, Leonard Charles. The handwriting of English documents. 2. ed. London, 1966.

Arc 853.4.2 Die Heddernheimer Votivhand. (Becker, J.) Frankfurt am Main, 1861.

Arc 1548.2F Hede, Holger. Danmarks og Norges mønter, 1541-1814-1963. Udgivet of Dansk numisatisk forening. Kjøbenhavn, 1964.

Htn Arc 1670.56.5F* Hedlinger, J.K. Explication historique et critique des médailles de l'oeuvre du Chevalier Hedlinger. Basle, 1778.

Htn Arc 1670.56F* Hedlinger, J.K. Oeuvre du chevalier Hedlinger. Basle, 1776.

Arc 888.20 Heemskerck Düker, W.F. van. Wat aarde bewaarde. Den Haag, 1942?

Arc 1247.1 Heffner, Carl. Die deutschen Kaiser- und Königs-Siegel. Würzburg, 1875.

Arc 853.24 Hefner, J. von. Das römische Bayern, in antiquarischer Hinsicht. München, 1842.

Arc 415.1 Heger, Franz. Alte Metalltrommeln aus Südost-Asien. Leipzig, 1902. 2v.

Arc 1016.242 Heideloff, C. Der Christliche Altar. Nürnberg, 1838.

Arc 1033.69.20 Die Heidnische Weiheformel Diis Manibus. (Becker, F.) Gera, 1881.

Arc 913.19 Heierli, J. Urgeschichte der Schweiz. Zürich, 1901.

Arc 925.4 Heikel, A. Antiquités de la Sibérie Occidentale. Helsingfors, 1894.

Arc 1153.4.23 Der heilige Cassian. (Wikenhauser, A.) Berlin, 1906.

Arc 1027.25.65 Der heilige Johannes Baptista de Rossi. (Bellesheim, A.) Mainz, 1882.

Arc 1033.170 Der heilige Märtyrer - Apollonius von Rom. Mainz, 1903.

Arc 1033.12.169 Heilige Nagel...zu Trier. (Kraus, F.X.) Trier, 1868.

Arc 1033.12.105 Heilige Rock; eine archäologische Prüfung...Trier. (Wilmowsky, J.N. von.) Trier, 1876.

Arc 1033.12.104 Heilige Rock zu Trier. (Gildemeister, J.) Düsseldorf, 1845.

Arc 1020.99.9 Die heilige Stadt der Wüste. 2.-3. Aufl. (Kaufmann, C.M.) Kempten, 1921.

Arc 1020.99.10 Die heilige Stadt der Wüste. 4e Aufl. (Kaufmann, C.M.) Kempten, 1921.

Arc 853.302F Heiligendorff, Wolfgang. Das latènezeitliche Gräberfeld von Berlin-Blankenfelde. Berlin, 1965.

Arc 1020.66 Heiliges Mainz...Heiligenthümer. (Falk, V.A.F.) Mainz, 1877.

Arc 1020.1 Das Heiligthum zu Aachen. (Bock, F.) Köln, 1867.

Arc 87.1.3 Die Heilung des Telephos. (Gerhard, E.) Berlin, 1843-

Arc 1200.3 Heinemann, O. Beiträge zur Diplomatik der ältern Bischoefe von Hildesheim. Inaug. Diss. Marburg, 1895.

Arc 1588.9 Heinrich Jochumsen. Verzeichnis aller bisher nachweisbaren boltischen Münzen und der Desiderata der Sammlung Anton Buchholtz. (Sengbusch, R. von.) Riga, 1928.

Arc 658.3.25 Heinrich Schliemann. (Brusti, Franz Georg.) München, 1971.

Arc 658.3.22 Heinrich Schliemann: Kaufmann und Forscher. (Meyer, Ernst.) Göttingen, 1969.

Arc 403.16.15 Heinrich Schliemann. Selbstbiographie. 7. Aufl. (Schliemann, Heinrich.) Leipzig, 1949.

Arc 403.16.10 Heinrich Schliemann. 3. Aufl. (Schliemann, Heinrich.) Leipzig, 1939.

Arc 403.16.17 Heinrich Schliemann. 8. Aufl. (Schliemann, Heinrich.) Wiesbaden, 1955.

Arc 658.3.11 Heinrich Schliemann und die Ausgrabungen auf Hissarlik. (Brinckmeier.) Burg, 1901.

Arc 658.3.9 Heinrich Schliemann und die Homersche Welt. (Nelson, J.) Leipzig, 1900.

Arc 522.4.9 Heinrich Schliemanns Sammlung Trojanischer Altertümer. (Berlin. Königliches Museum.) Berlin, 1902.

Arc 1670.1 Heiss, A. Les médailleurs de la Renaissance. v.3,8. Paris, 1883. 2v.

Arc 1492.200 Heiss, Aloiss. Descripcion generale de las monedas hispanicas cristianas. Madrid, 1865. 3v.

Arc 1492.201 Heiss, Aloiss. Description générale des monnaies antiques de l'Espagne. Paris, 1870.

Arc 1492.202 Heiss, Aloiss. Description générale des monnaies des rois wisigoths. Paris, 1872.

Arc 395.6 Heitere und ernst Briefe aus einem deutschen Archäologenleben. (Koldewey, Robert.) Berlin, 1920.

Arc 392.16 Heizer, Robert F. The archaeologist at work. N.Y., 1959.

Arc 80.1.7F Ta hekaton etē tēs en Athēnais Archaiologikēs Hetaireias. (Oikonomos, G.P.) Athēnai, 1938.

Arc 1020.94 Helbig, Jules. Reliques...données par St. Louis, roi de France, au couvent des Dominicains de Liége. Bruxelles, 1881.

Arc 723.5A Helbig, W. Beiträge zur altitalischen Kultur und Kunstgeschichte. Leipzig, 1879.

Arc 796.1 Helbig, W. Untersuchungen über die campanische Wandmalerei. Leipzig, 1873.

Arc 790.203 Helbig, W. Wandgemaelde der...Staedte Campaniens. Leipzig, 1868. 2v.

Arc 1335.48 Helbing, Otto. Auktions-Katalog. München, 1910.

Arc 1335.87 Helbing, Otto. Auktions-Katalog enthaltend die Münzen- und Medaillen-Bestände der aufgelösten Firma zschiesche und Köder. München, 1913.

Arc 557.10 Helck, Hans Wolfgang. Ägyptologie an deutschen Universitäten. Wiesbaden, 1969.

Arc 830.333 Helena, T. Les origines de Narbonne. Toulouse, 1937.

Arc 895.43 Den helige Eskils buskopsdöme. (Lindqvist, Sune.) Stockholm, 1924.

Arc 273.14 Helinium. Wettern. 1,1961+ 8v.

Arc 588.26 Heliopolis. (Petrie, W.M.F.) London, 1915.

Arc 588.27 Heliopolis. (Petrie, W.M.F.) London, 1915.

Arc 642.1 Hellas. (Chase, T.) Cambridge, 1863.

Arc 642.7F Hellas. (Chisholm, H.J.) N.Y., 1943.

Arc 1053.6.2 The Hellenic portraits from the Fayum. (Ebers, G.) N.Y., 1893.

Arc 72.5 Hellenic Travellers' Club. Proceedings. London? 1925-1930 7v.

Arc 72.7 Pamphlet vol. Hellenic Travellers' Club.

Arc 72.10 Hellenica. Limoges. 1-13 5v.

Arc 645.1 Hellenika. (Forchhammer, P.W.) Berlin, 1837.

Arc 1470.89 The Hellenistic kingdoms. (Davis, Norman.) London, 1973.

Arc 513.38 Hellenistik devir Anadolu nimorisinde kyma. (Erder, Cevat.) Ankara, 1967.

Arc 750.211 Hellenistische Bauten in Latium. (Delbrück, R.) Strassburg, 1907.

Arc 810.36F Die hellenistische Kunst in Pompeji. Berlin. 4-6,1925-1938 3v.

Arc 87.1.58 Hellenistische Silbergefässe...Königlichen Museum. (Pernice, E.) Berlin, 1898.

Arc 1213.1 Hellenistische Silberreliefs. (Winnefeld, H.) Berlin, 1908.

Arc 600.1.9 Hellenistische und koptische Kunst in Alexandria. (Strzygowski, J.) Wien, 1902.

Arc 630.20 Hellenistische Vatergottheiten. (Thieman, Eugen.) Münster, 1959.

Arc 510.2.10F Die hellenistischen Arsenale. (Szalay, Akos.) Berlin, 1937.

Arc 705.14 Heller, B.R. Archäologisch-artische Mittheilungen...über die Ausgrabungen auf der Akropolis zu Athen. Nuremberg, 1852.

Arc 853.8.5F Hellmich, Max. Die Besiedlungschlesiens in vor- und frühgeschichtlicher Zeit. 2. Aufl. Breslau, 1923.

Arc 853.58.5 Helmke, Paul. Hügelgräber im Vorderwald von Muschenheim. Giessen, 1919. 2v.

Arc 913.18 Helvetia antiqua. (Degen, Rudolf.) Uitikon, 1966.

Arc 162.5 Helvetia archaeologica; Mittheilungsblatt der schweizerischen Gesellschaft für Ur- und Frühgeschichte. Basel. 1,1970+

Arc 915.20 Die helvetishen und helvetarömischen Votivbeilchen der Schweiz. (Forrer, Robert.) Basel, 1948.

Arc 983.2 Hemenway, S.W. Catalogo de los objetos etnológicos y arqueológicos. Madrid, 1892.

Arc 843.3 Henao, G. de. Averignaciones de las antiguedades de Cantabria. Salamanca, 1689-91. 2v.

Arc 1143.2.11 Hencheiridion Hellēnikēs. (Thompson, Edward Maunde.) Athēnai, 1903.

Arc 861.5.15 Hencken, H.O. The archaeology of Cornwall and Scilly. London, 1932.

Arc 880.38A Hencken, H.O. Cahercomnaun, a stone fort in county Clare. Dublin, 1938.

Arc 880.38.15 Hencken, H.O. A tumulus at Carrowlesdooaun, County Mayo. n.p., 1935. 2 pam.

Arc 726.215.5 Hencken, Hugh O'Neill. Tarquinia and Etruscan origins. London, 1968.

Arc 861.178 Hencken, Thalassa Cruso. The excavation of the Iron Age camp on Bredon Hill. London, 1939.

Arc 1025.61 Henderson, Alexander. The lesson of the catacombs. London, 1920.

Arc 983.1.2 Henderson, P. The cliff dwellers. St. Paul, 1893.

Arc 1020.9.164F Hendrichs, F. La voce delle chiese antichissime di Roma. Roma, 1933.

Arc 968.2.80 Hendron, J.W. Prehistory of El Rito de los Frijoles, Bandelier national monument. Phoenix, 1940.

Arc 1473.14 Hendy, Michael. Coinage and money in the Byzantine empire, 1081-1261. Washington, 1969.

Arc 1540.14 Henfrey, H.W. Numismata Cromwelliana. Londini, 1877.

Arc 1663.4 Henfrey, H.W. Numismata Cromwelliana. London, 1873.

Arc 870.27 Henig, Martin. A corpus of Roman engraved gemstones from British sites. v.1-2. Oxford, 1974.

Arc 845.205F Henkel, F. Die Römischen Fingerringe der Rheinlande. Berlin, 1913. 2v.

Arc 1027.23.9 Hennecke, E. Altchristliche Malerei...römischen Katacomben. Leipzig, 1896.

Arc 540.11F Hennessy, J.B. Stephania; a middle and late bronze-age cemetery in Cyprus. London, 1964.

Arc 497.81F Hennessy, John Basil. The foreign relations of Palestine during the early bronze age. London, 1967.

Arc 853.348 Hennig, Hilke. Die Grab- und Hortfunde der Urnenfelderkultur aus Ober- und Mittelfranken. Kallmünz, 1970.

Arc 1362.2 Hennin, M. Manuel de numismatique ancienne. Paris, 1830-69. 3v.

Arc 390.11 Henri Frankfort, 1897-1954. (Childe, Vere Gordon.) London, 1955?

Arc 830.89.7 Henry, Dominique M.J. Recherches sur la géographie ancienne et les antiquités du département des Basses-Alpes. 2e éd. Digne, 1842.

Arc 830.138 Henry, Françoise. Les tumulus du département de la Côte-d'Or. Thèse. Paris, 1932.

Arc 936.14 Hensel, Witold. Archäologische Forschungen in Polen. Warschau, 1958.

Arc 936.14.333 Hensel, Witold. Archeologia i prahistoria. Wrocław, 1971.

Arc 393.10 Hensel, Witold. Archeologia żywa. Wyd. 1. Warszawa, 1973.

Arc 936.14.20 Hensel, Witold. Najdawniejsje stolice Polski. Warszawa, 1960.

Arc 936.14.334 Hensel, Witold. Polska starozytna. Wrocław, 1973.

Arc 936.14.40 Hensel, Witold. Starodawna kruszwica. Wrocław, 1961.

Arc 936.14.332 Hensel, Witold. Ur- und Frühgeschichte Polens. Berlin, 1974.

Arc 936.14.330 Hensel, Witold. Ziemie polskie w pradziejach. wyd. 1. Warszawa, 1969.

Arc 875.131 Henshall, Audrey Shore. The chambered tombs of Scotland. Edinburgh, 1963-72. 2v.

Arc 983.3.5 Henshaw, H.W. Animal carvings from mounds of the Mississippi Valley. Washington, 1881?

Arc 421.30 Hentze, Carl. Funde in Alt-China. Göttingen, 1967.

Arc 726.237 Héraclès Epitrapezios. (Visscher, Fernand de.) Paris, 1962.

Arc 726.97F Heraion. v.1-2, atlases. (Zancani Montuoro, P.) Roma, 1951. 4v.

Arc 302.8.10 Herakleja. Bitola. 2,1965+

Arc 87.1.12 Herakles der Satyr und Dreifussränber. (Curtius, E.) Berlin, 1852.

Arc 853.30 Heranìesche Funde in Haltern. (Loeschcke, S.) Münster, 1909.

Arc 688.7F Der Heratempel von Samos. (Reuther, Oskar.) Berlin, 1957.

Arc 400.12.25 Herberger, T. Conrad Peutinger in seinem Verhältnisse zum Kaiser Maximilian I. Augsburg, 1851.

Arc 865.5 Herbert, A. Cyclops Christianus; disprove...Stonehenge. London, 1849.

Htn Arc 1333.5* Herbert, T. Numismata antiqua. n.p., 1746.

Author and Title Listing

Arc 630.11F Herbig, R. Ganymed; Heidelberger Beiträge zur antiken Kunstgeschichte. Heidelberg, 1949.
Arc 630.11.5 Herbig, R. Vermächtnis der antiken Kunst. Heidelberg, 1950.
Arc 387.13.30 Herbig, Reinhard. Ludwig Curtius, 1874-1954, zum Gedachtnis. Heidelberg, 1955.
Arc 1285.10.6 Herby miast polskich. (Gumowski, M.) Warszawa, 1960.
Arc 66.1.132.5 Herclé, étude critique. (Bayet, J.) Paris, 1926.
Arc 800.6A Herculaneum, past, present and future. (Waldstein, C.) London, 1908.
Arc 800.16 Herculaneum. (Kusch, Eugen.) Nürnberg, 1960.
Arc 793.5 Herculanum et Pompéi. (Barré, L.) Paris, 1840. 7v.
Arc 793.5.5 Herculanum et Pompéi. (Barré, L.) Paris, 1863-72. 7v.
Htn Arc 793.5* Herculanum et Pompéi. v.8. (Barré, L.) Paris, 1840.
Htn Arc 793.5.5* Herculanum et Pompéi. v.8. (Barré, L.) Paris, 1872.
Arc 875.75 Herdsmen and hermits. (Lethbridge, T.) Cambridge, Eng., 1950.
Arc 976.7 Here lies Virginia. (Noël Hume, Ivor.) N.Y., 1963.
Arc 1033.90 Heredia del Rio, P.M. Historia Sanctorum Martyrum...Ruderici, et Salomonis. Romae, 1838.
Arc 700.62 Heres, Gerald. Die punischen und griechischen Tonlampen der Staatlichen Museen zu Berlin. Amsterdam, 1969.
Arc 1020.124.5 Hergueta y Martin, Domingo. Santa María la mayor de la catedral de Burgos y su culto. Lérida, 1922.
Arc 1578.20 Herinek, Ludwig. Österreichische Münzprägungen von Ergänzungen, 1740-1969. Wien, 1970.
Arc 1578.20.1 Herinek, Ludwig. Österreichische Münzprägungen von Ergänzungen, 1740-1969. Wien, 1972.
Arc 1578.20.5 Herinek, Ludwig. Österreichische Münzprägungen von 1657-1740. Wien, 1972.
Arc 608.1.39 Hérisson, M. d'. Relation d'une mission archéologique en Tunisie. Paris, 1881.
Arc 880.47F Herity, Michael. Irish passage graves. Dublin, 1974.
Arc 530.10 Herkenrath, E. Der Fries des Artemisions von Magnesia. Berlin, 1902.
Arc 848.8.5 Die Herkunft der Germanen. (Kossinna, Gustaf.) Würzburg, 1911.
Arc 785.34.20 Herman, Werner. Römische Götteraltaere. Kallmuerz, 1961.
Arc 1264.10 Hermand, A. Histoire sigillaire de la ville de Saint-Omer. Paris, 1860.
Arc 600.3.10 Hermann, A. Führer durch die Altertümer von Memphis und Sakkara. Berlin, 1938.
Arc 830.13 Hermann, M.J. Le Théâtre d'Orange. Paris, 1897.
Arc 600.35.20F Hermopolis Magna. (Wace, Alan John.) Alexandria, 1959.
Arc 843.3.5 Hernandez Morales, Angel. Juliobriga, ciudad romana en Cantabria. Santander, 1946.
Arc 843.185 Hernández-Pacheco, E. La vida de nuestros antecesores paleolíticos. Madrid, 1923.
Arc 843.140 Hernandez-Pacheco, Eduardo. Las pinturas prehistoricas de las cuevas de la Araña (Valencia). Madrid, 1924.
Arc 843.145 Hernandez-Pacheco, Eduardo. Las pinturas prehistoricas de Peña Tú. Madrid, 1914.
Arc 843.67 Hernández-Pecheco, E. La caverna de la Peña de Candamo (Asturias). Madrid, 1919.
Arc 497.15 Héron de Villefosse, A. Notice des monuments de la Palestine conservés au Musée du Louvre. 2. éd. Paris, 1879.
Arc 726.11.5 Héron de Villefosse, Antoine. L'argenterie et les bijoux d'or du trésor de Boscoreale. Paris, 1903.
Arc 726.11.7 Héron de Villefosse, Antoine. Le trésor d'argenterie de Boscoreale. Paris, 189-.
Arc 1033.25.5 Héron de Villefosse. Lampes chrétiennes inédites. Paris, 1875.
Arc 510.6 Das Heroon von Gjoelbaschi-Trysa. (Benndorf, O.) Vienna, 1889. 2v.
Arc 448.1.15 Heros, Henry. Studies in proto-Indo-Mediterranean culture. Bombay, 1933.
Arc 1033.43.11 Der Herr der Seligkeit. Archäologische Studie. (Sybel, L. von.) Marburg, 1913.
Arc 1494.20F Herrera y Chiesanova, A. El duro. Madrid, 1914. 2v.
Arc 1663.19 Herrera y Chiesanova, A. Medallos de los gobernadores. Madrid, 1901.
Arc 674.3 Herrlich, S. Epidaurus, eine antike Heilstätte. Berlin, 1898.
Arc 543.4.17 Herrmann, A. Lou-lan. Leipzig, 1931.
Arc 505.5.50 Herrmann, J. Temple de Jérusalem. Valenciennes, 1882.
Arc 853.309 Herrmann, Joachim. Der germanischen und slawischen Siedlungen und das mittelalterliche Dorf von Tornow. Berlin, 1973.
Arc 87.1.48 Herrmann, P. Graeberfeld von Marion. Berlin, 1888.
Arc 1076.3.99 A Hertfordshire worthy, John Briant. (Andrews, H.C.) St. Albans, 1930.
Arc 853.98 Hertlein, F. Die Alterthümer des Oberamts Heidenheims. Eszlingen, 1912.
Arc 853.37 Hertlein, F. Die Juppitergigantensäulen. Stuttgart, 1910.
Arc 853.13.25 Hertlein, F. Die Römer in Württemberg. pt.1-3. Stuttgart, 1928-32. 3v.
Arc 1025.72 Hertling, Ludwig. Die römischen Katakomben und ihre Martyrer. Wien, 1950.
Arc 1025.72.5 Hertling, Ludwig. Die römischen Katakomben und ihre Martyrer. 2. Aufl. Wien, 1950.
Arc 712.16 Hertz, A.P. Parthenons Kvindefigurer. n.p., 1905.
Arc 1010.10 The Hervey Islands adzes in the Peabody Museum of Salem. (Peabody Museum of Salem, Salem, Massachusetts.) Salem, 1937.
Arc 488.5F Herzfeld, Ernst E. Am Tor von Asien. Berlin, 1920.
Arc 488.15 Herzfeld, Ernst E. Archaeological history of Iran. London, 1935.
Arc 482.202.6F Herzfeld, Ernst E. Geschichte der Stadt Samarra. Hamburg, 1948.
Arc 488.10F Herzfeld, Ernst E. Iran in the ancient East. London, 1941.
Arc 488.21F Herzfeld, Ernst E. Iranische Denkmäler. v.1-4. Berlin, 1932-
Arc 482.202.3F Herzfeld, Ernst E. Die Malereien von Samarra. Berlin, 1927.
Arc 493.2.15 Herzfeld, Ernst E. Rapport sur l'état actuel des ruines de Persépole. Berlin, 1928.
Arc 482.202.5F Herzfeld, Ernst E. Die vorgeschichtlichen Töpfereien von Samarra. Berlin, 1930.
Arc 482.202F Herzfeld, Ernst E. Der Wandschmuck der Bauten. Berlin, 1923.
Arc 482.203PF Herzfled, Ernst E. Paikuli. Berlin, 1924. 2v.
Arc 647.2 Herzog, A. Studien zur Geschichte der griechischen Kunst. Leipzig, 1888.
Arc 505.152 Heshbon 1971: the second campaign at Tell Hesbân. (Boraas, Roger S.) Berrien Spring, Mich., 1973.
Arc 1.5.7 Hesperia. Cambridge. 1,1932+ 40v.
Arc 1.5.10 Hesperia. Index 1-10, supplements 1-6. Baltimore, Md., 1946.
Arc 1.5.9 Hesperia. The American excavations in the Athenian Agora. Supplement. Athens. 1-13 6v.
Arc 1580.20 Hess, A. Die Siebenbürgischen Münzen des furstlich Montenuoro'schen Münzcabinets. Frankfurt, 1880.
Arc 1510.128F Hess, Adolph. Münzen der Hohenstauffenzeit. Zürich, 1959?
Arc 1663.15.5 Hesse, Waldemar E. Die tragbaren Ehrenzeichen des Deutschen Reiches. Berlin, 1940.
Arc 1033.20.13 Hessel, C. Die altchristlichen Basiliken Roms. Weslau, 1873.
Arc 638.1 Hesselmeyer, E. Die Urspruenge der Stadt Pergamos in Kleinasien. Tübingen, 1884-85. 7 pam.
Arc 501.16 Heth and Moab. (Conder, C.R.) London, 1885.
Arc 501.16.2 Heth and Moab. (Conder, C.R.) London, 1892.
Arc 1229.5 Die hethitisches Königssiegel. (Bossert, H.T.) Berlin, 1944.
Arc 1033.91 Hetruscae...Pietates...de Prima Thusciae Christianae. (Florentinio, M.) Lucae, 1701.
Arc 853.20.5 Hettner, F. Illustrierter Führer...Provinzialmuseum in Trier. Trier, 1903.
Arc 848.2 Hettner, Felix. Die römischen Steindenkmäler der Provinzialmuseum zu Trier. Trier, 1893.
Arc 853.20.10 Hetzrodt, J.B.M. Notices sur les anciens Trévirois. Trèves, 1809.
Arc 66.1.154 Heurgon, J. Recherches sur l'histoire, la religion et la civilisation. Paris, 1942.
Arc 682.25.35F Heurtley, W.A. Prehistoric Macedonia. Cambridge, Eng., 1939.
Arc 1200.19 Heusburgen Akten- und Urkundensprache im 14., 15., und 16. Jahrhundert. (Schütt, Otto.) Heusburg, 1919.
Arc 600.3.5 Heuser, G. Die Katochëim Sarapieion bei Memphis. Inaug. Diss. Marburg, 1935.
Arc 1510.12 Heusinger, F. Versuch einer Abhandlung von den Nutzen der teutschen Münzwissenschaft. Nürnberg, 1750.
Arc 1076.16 Heuven, Englebert W. van. Accoustical measurements on church-bells and carillons. 's-Gravenhage, 1949.
Arc 635.204 Heuzey, L. Mission archéologique de Macédoine. Paris, 1876.
Arc 647.1 Heuzey, L. Le Mont Olympe et l'Acarnanie. Paris, 1860.
Arc 1076.1 Heuzey, Léon. Recherches sur les lits antiques. Paris, 1873.
Arc 935.15 Heuzy, Leon. Panthéon des rochers de Philippes. Paris, n.d.
Arc 935.12 Heuzy, Leon. Reconnaissance archéologique...cours de l'Érigon et des ruines de Stobi. Paris, 1873.
Arc 968.2.10 Hewett, E.L. Antiquities of the Jemez Plateau, New Mexico. Washington, 1906.
Arc 950.10F Hewett, E.L. Les communautés anciennes dans le désert américain. Genève, 1908.
Arc 968.2.12 Hewett, E.L. Pajarito Plateau and its ancient people. Albuquerque, 1938.
Arc 392.10.5 Hewett, Edgar Lee. Campfire and trail. Albuquerque, 1943.
Arc 875.31.7 Hewison, J.K. The romance of Bewcastle cross. Glasgow, 1923.
Arc 875.31 Hewison, J.K. Runic roods of Ruthwell and Bewcastle. Glasgow, 1914.
Arc 87.1.30 Heydemann, H. Humoristische Vasenbilder. Berlin, 1870.
Arc 943.32 Hibben, F.C. Treasure in the dust. 1. ed. Philadelphia, 1951.
Arc 557.3 Hichens, Robert. Egypt and its monuments. London, 1908.
Arc 557.3.2A Hichens, Robert. Egypt and its monuments. N.Y., 1908.
Arc 557.3.2.5 Hichens, Robert. Egypt and its monuments. N.Y., 1909.
Arc 557.3.5 Hichens, Robert. The spell of Egypt. Leipzig, 1910.
Arc 557.3.3 Hichens, Robert. The spell of Egypt. London, 1910.
Arc 1613.1 Hickcox, J.H. An historical account of American coinage. Albany, 1858.
Arc 547.6.20F Hickmann, Hans. Instruments de musique. Le Caire, 1949.
NEDL Arc 588.10 Hierakonpolis. Pt.1-2. (Quibell, J.E.) London, 1900-1902.
Arc 588.10 Hierakonpolis. Pt.1-2. (Quibell, J.E.) London, 1900-1902.
Arc 416.32 Hierche, Henri. Manuel d'archéologie d'Extrême-Orient. Paris, 1966- 2v.
Arc 547.17 Hieroglyphic Texts from Egyptian Stelae. Pt.1-7, 9. (British Museum.) London, 1911-25. 8v.
Arc 587.4 Hieroglyphs. (Griffith, F.L.) London, 1898.
Arc 684.1.50 To Hieron tēs Olympias. (Kontes, I.D.) Athēnai, 1958.
Arc 1411.11 Higgins, F.C. The Chinese numismatic riddle. N.Y., 1910.
Arc 618.7 Higgins, G. The Celtic druids. London, 1827.
Arc 618.7.3 Higgins, G. The Celtic druids. London, 1829.
Arc 530.151 The highlands of Phrygia: sites and monuments. (Haspels, Caroline H.E.) Princeton, 1971. 2v.
Arc 1033.17.57 Hilaire. Madone de Saint Luc. Paris, 1886.
Arc 936.200 Hilczerowna, Z. Wczesnosredniowieczne grodzisko w Daleszynie (st. 2) w pow. gostynskim. Poznań, 1960.
Arc 936.14.260 Hilczerówna, Zofia. Dorzecze górnej i środkowej Obry od VI do początków XI wieku. Wrocław, 1967.
Arc 1675.8 Hildebrand, B.E. Minnespenningar öfver svenska män och qvinnor. Stockholm, 1860.
Arc 1663.12 Hildebrand, B.E. Sveriges konungahusets minnespenningar. Stockholm, 1874. 2v.
Arc 893.18 Hildebrand, H. Den äldre jernåldern i Norrland. Stockholm, 1869.
Arc 1560.1 Hildebrand, H. Sveriges mynt under medeltiden. Stockholm, 1887.
Arc 522.13 Hildebrand, H.H. Fynden i Troas och Homeroe' Troja. Stockholm, 1878.
Arc 853.26.5 Der Hildesheimer Silberfund. (Lindemann, Kurt.) Hildesheim, 1967.
Arc 87.2.68 Hildesheimer Silberfund. (Wieseler, F.) Bonn, 1868.
Arc 1490.8.5 Hill, G.F. Coins of ancient Sicily. Westminster, 1903.
Arc 1458.9 Hill, G.F. A handbook of Greek and Roman coins. London, 1899.
Arc 1468.13A Hill, G.F. Historical Greek coins. London, 1906.
Arc 1468.13.2 Hill, G.F. Historical Greek coins. N.Y., 1906.
Arc 1478.18 Hill, G.F. Historical Roman coins. London, 1909.
Arc 1675.10.5 Hill, G.F. Pisanello. London, 1905.
Arc 1468.13.5F Hill, G.F. Select Greek coins. Paris, 1927.
Arc 391.6 Hill, George. Percy Gardner, 1846-1937. London, 1937.
Arc 1660.16F Hill, George F. Medals of the renaissance. Oxford, 1920.
Arc 1675.20.10 Hill, George F. Portrait medals of Italian artists of the Renaissance. London, 1912.
Arc 708.30.2A Hill, I.C.T. The ancient city of Athens. Cambridge, 1953.
Arc 708.30 Hill, I.C.T. The ancient city of Athens. London, 1953.
Arc 762.6 Hill, Ida T. Rome of the kings. N.Y., 1925.

Arc 943.26 — Hill, Ira. Antiquities of America explained. Hagerstown, 1831.
Arc 1480.71 — Hill, Philip V. The coinage of Septimius Severus and his family of the mint of Rome, A.D. 193-217. London, 1964.
Arc 1480.72 — Hill, Philip V. The dating and arrangement of the undated coins of Rome, A.D. 98-148. London, 1970.
Arc 855.204 — Hill forts, stone circles...Scotland. (MacLagan, C.) Edinburgh, 1875.
Arc 861.25.5 — Hill-forts in Dorset. (Hill-Forts Study Group.) Bristol, 1966.
Arc 861.25.5 — Hill-Forts Study Group. Hill-forts in Dorset. Bristol, 1966.
Arc 608.12 — The hill of the Graces...Tripoli. (Cowper, H.S.) London, 1897.
Arc 635.20F — Hiller von Gärtringen. Thera 1895-. Berlin, 1899- 4v.
Arc 736.11 — Himera; lo scavo del Tempio della Vittoria e del temenos. (Marconi, P.) Roma, 1931.
Arc 736.11.5 — Himera I. Campagne di scavo 1963-1965. Roma, 1970.
Arc 383.53.15 — Himmelmann-Wildschütz, N. Festschrift für Friedrich Matz. Mainz, 1962.
Arc 861.5.9 — Hingston, F.C. Specimens of ancient Cornish crosses, fonts. London, 1850.
Arc 853.296 — Hinz, Hermann. Das fränkische Gräberfeld von Eick. Berlin, 1969.
Arc 488.28 — Hinz, Walther. Altiranische Funde und Forschungen. Berlin, 1969.
Arc 935.9 — The hippodrome of Constantinople. (Grosvenor, E.A.) London, 1889.
Arc 608.2.50 — Hippone la Royale. (Marec, Erwan.) Alger, 1954.
Arc 87.1.71 — Hira und Andania...zum Winckelmannsfeste. (Gaertringen, F.H.) Berlin, 1911.
Arc 435.13 — Hirālāl, Rai Bahādur. Descriptive lists of inscriptions in the central provinces and Berar. Nagpur, 1916.
Arc 444.1.15 — Hirananda, Sastri. A guide to Elephanta. Delhi, 1934.
Arc 383.9.25 — Hiranyagarbha; a series of articles on the archaeological work and studies of Prof. Dr. F.D.K. Bosch. The Hague, 1964.
Arc 830.2.6 — Hirmenech, H.P. Le dolmen royal de Gavrénis près d'Auray. Le Mans, 1908.
Arc 830.2.7 — Hirmenech, H.P. Le Men-letonniec de Locmariaquer, Morbihan. Paris? 1911.
Arc 830.2.5 — Hirmenech, H.P. Morbihan antiquités. Paris, n.d. 5 pam.
Arc 1010.5 — Hirmenech, H.P. Une tablette de l'ile de Pâques. Paris, 1912.
Arc 1478.39 — Hirmer, Max. Römische Kaisermünzen. Leipzig, 1941.
Arc 1468.16.2 — Hirsch, F. Auctions-Catalog XIV, XV. Greek and Roman coins. München, 1905-06.
Arc 1468.16 — Hirsch, F. Auctions-Katalog XIII. München, 1905.
Arc 1093.2.35 — Hirsch, Friedrich. Der Sonnwendbogen. Lahr, 1965.
Arc 1335.49 — Hirsch, J. Sammlung Gustav Philipsen. München, 1909.
Arc 1329.1 — Hirsch, J.C. Bibliotheca numismatica. Nuremberg, 1760.
Arc 1335.101 — Hirsch, Jacob. Auctions-Catalog der bedeutenden Sammlung römischer und byzantinischer Münzen. München, 1907.
Arc 1335.101.51 — Hirsch, Jacob. Griechische, römische, byzantinische Münzen. München, 1914.
Arc 1335.101.25 — Hirsch, Jacob. Griechische, römische und byzantinische Münzen aus dem Besitze von Friedrich von Schennis. München, 1913.
Arc 1670.52 — Hirsch, Jacob. Kunstmedaillen und Plaketten des XV. bis XVII. Jahrhunderts. München, 1908.
Arc 1335.101.71 — Hirsch, Jacob. Sammlung Consul Eduard Friedrich Weber, Hamburg. München, 1908-09. 2v.
Arc 66.1.120 — Hirschauer, C. La politique de St. Pie V en France. Paris, n.d.
Arc 87.1.32 — Hirschfeld, G. Athena und Marsyas. Berlin, 1872.
Arc 530.1.5 — Hirschfeld, G. Felsenreliefs in Kleinasien und die Volk der Hitteter. Berlin, 1887.
Arc 530.1 — Hirschfeld, G. Paphlagonische Felsengraeber. Berlin, 1885.
Arc 823.8 — Hirshfeld, O. Gallische Studien. Wien, 1883-1884.
Arc 936.225.10 — Hišaste žare Latobikov. (Petru, Peter.) Ljubljana, 1971.
Arc 94.17 — Hispania antiqua epigraphica. Madrid. 1-5,1950-1954
Arc 843.90 — Hispania graeca. v.1-2, atlas. (García y Bellido, Antonio.) Barcelona, 1948. 3v.
Arc 1307.9 — Hispanic numismatic series. N.Y. 3v.
Arc 522.4.15 — Hissarlik wie es ist. (Boetticher, E.) Berlin, 1890.
Arc 1020.53 — Histoire...du trésor...de Saint Pierre de Corbie. (Dusevel, M.H.) Amiens, 1861.
Arc 830.139 — Histoire ancienne de Luchon. (Sacaze, Julien.) Saint-Gaudens, 1887.
Arc 830.61 — Histoire archéologique de l'époque gallo-romaine de la ville de Rennes. (Toulmoudre, Adolphe.) Rennes, 1847.
Arc 66.1.70 — Histoire de Blanche de Castile. (Berger, E.) Paris, 1895.
Arc 830.159 — Histoire de différents cultes. (Mignard, T.J.A.P.) Dijon, 1851.
Arc 1345.1.13 — Histoire de France par médailles: Charles VII-Louis XVI. Paris, 1858. 3v.
Arc 1345.1.15 — Histoire de France par médailles: Empire français. Paris, 1858.
Arc 1345.1.14 — Histoire de France par médailles: Révolution française. Paris, 1858.
Arc 1033.12.197 — Histoire de la larme sainte...Selincourt. (Le Mercier, J.) Amiens, 1707.
Arc 1478.10.5 — Histoire de la monnaie romaine. (Mommsen, T.) Paris, 1865. 4v.
Arc 1033.12.111 — Histoire de la robe sans couture de...J.-C....Argenteuil. (Gerberon, G.) Paris, 1677.
Arc 1033.12.112 — Histoire de la robe sans couture de...Jésus Christ. 4e éd. Paris, 1838.
Arc 1033.12.142 — Histoire de la sainte-face de...Christ. Laon, 1884.
Arc 1153.21 — Histoire de la sténographie...notes tironiennes. (Guénin, L.P.) Paris, 1908.
Arc 830.16.7 — Histoire de l'antique cité d'Autun. (Thomas, Edme.) Autun, 1846.
Arc 1345.1.5 — Histoire de l'art monétaires...modernes. Paris, 1858.
Arc 66.1.71 — Histoire de l'Opera en Europe. (Rolland, R.) Paris, 1895.
Arc 600.9 — Histoire de l'Ordre Lotiforme. (Foucart, G.) Paris, 1897.
Arc 1033.17.221 — Histoire de Notre-Dame de Boulogne. (Le Roy, A.) Boulogne, 1704.
Arc 1033.17.330 — Histoire de Notre Dame de Foy. (Fries, Felix.) Namur, 1909.
Arc 1020.74 — Histoire de Notre Dame de France. (Nampoon, P.) Puy, 1868.
Arc 1033.17.425 — Histoire de Notre-Dame de Liesse. (Villette, E.N.) Laon, 1708?

Arc 1500.55 — Histoire de Paris d'après les médailles de la Renaissance au XX. siècle. (Babelon, Jean.) Paris, 1951.
Arc 825.2.11 — Histoire des antiquités de la ville de Nîmes. 11e éd. (Ménard, L.) Nîmes, 1856.
Arc 825.2 — Histoire des antiquités de la ville de Nismes. (Ménard, L.) Nîmes, 1803.
Arc 825.2.2 — Histoire des antiquités de la ville de Nismes. (Ménard, L.) Nîmes, 1814.
Arc 825.2.5 — Histoire des antiquités de la ville de Nismes. (Ménard, L.) Nîmes, 1832.
Arc 825.2.9 — Histoire des antiquités de la ville de Nismes. 7e éd. (Ménard, L.) Nismes, 1838.
Arc 825.2.10 — Histoire des antiquités de la ville de Nismes. 9e éd. (Ménard, L.) Nismes, 1842. 3 pam.
Arc 1025.31 — Histoire des catacombes. (Gaume, J.) Paris, 1848.
Arc 1025.31.3 — Histoire des catacombes de Rome. (Gaume, J.) Paris, n.d.
Arc 1185.28 — Histoire des contestations sur la diplomatique. (Mabillon, Jean.) Naples, 1767.
Arc 1033.17.255 — Histoire des images miraculeuses. Paris, 1850.
Arc 1335.14.2 — Histoire du cabinet des médailles. (Du Mersan, T.M.) Paris, 1838.
Arc 1033.143 — Histoire du chef de S. J.-Baptiste...Amiens. (Salmon, C.) Amiens, 1876.
X Cg Arc 66.1.33 — Histoire du culte des divinités d'Alexandre. (Lafaye, G.) Paris, 1884. (Changed to XP 9785)
Arc 66.1.33 — Histoire du culte des divinités d'Alexandre. Photoreproduction. (Lafaye, G.) Paris, 1884.
Arc 1033.12.72 — Histoire du précieux sang de Jésus-Christ...à Fécamp. Fécamp, 1874.
Htn Arc 1660.5* — Histoire du Roy Louis le Grand. (Menestrier, C.F.) Paris, 1691.
Arc 1033.12.10 — Histoire du Saint Suaire de Cadouin. (Carles, A.) Perigueux, 1868.
Arc 1033.12.11 — Histoire du Saint Suaire de Notre Seigneur. (Carles, A.) Paris, 1875. 2 pam.
Arc 1016.241 — L'histoire ecclesiastico...les antiquitez...de la chapelle et oratoire du Roy de France. (Peyrat, G. du.) Paris, 1645.
Arc 830.157 — Pamphlet vol. Histoire et inscriptions de Vence. 2 pam.
Arc 1020.4 — Histoire et inventaire du trésor Bourges. (Girardot.) Paris, 1859.
Arc 66.2.80 — L'histoire et l'oeuvre de l'école française d'Athènes. (Radet, G.) Paris, 1901.
Arc 1528.1 — Histoire metallique de la Republique de Hollande. (Bizot, P.) Amsterdam, 1688. 2v.
Arc 1528.1.5 — Histoire metallique de la Republique de Hollande. (Bizot, P.) Amsterdam, 1688. 2v.
Arc 1528.1.7 — Histoire metallique de la Republique de Hollande. Supplément. (Bizot, P.) Amsterdam, 1690.
Arc 1335.103 — Histoire métallique de l'Europe, ou Catalogue des médailles modernes. (Poulhariez, P.N.) Lyon, 1767.
Arc 1525.1 — Histoire metallique des XVII provinces des Pays-Bas. (Loon, Gerard van.) La Haye, 1732-37. 5v.
Arc 1520.25 — Histoire monétaire de Tournai. (Hoc, Marcel.) Bruxelles, 1970.
Arc 1500.28.5 — Histoire monetaire du Béarn et description des monnaies...Béarn. v.1-2. (Blanchet, J.A.) Paris, 1893.
Arc 1660.3 — Histoire numismatique de la révolution de 1848. (Liesville, A.R. de.) Paris, 1877-83.
Arc 1663.55 — Histoire numismatique du comte de Chanbord. (Bauquier, Henri.) Paris, 1911-40.
NEDL Arc 1372.1 — L'histoire par les monnaies. (Reinach, T.) Paris, 1902.
Arc 1264.10 — Histoire sigillaire de la ville de Saint-Omer. (Hermand, A.) Paris, 1860.
Arc 72.6 — Historia; studi storici per l'antichità classica. Milano. 1-9,1927-1935 9v.
Arc 1307.13 — Historia; the journal of the Historical Medal Society of Australia and New Zealand. Sydney. 1,1968+
Arc 1033.17.54 — Historia...B.V. Maria Claromontanae s. imaginis origine Jerosolymis Constantinopolim. (Goldonowski, A.) n.p., n.d.
Arc 936.14.545 — Historia badań archeologicznych i zbiorów Muzeum Ziemi Przemyskiej. (Muzeum Ziemi Przemyskiej w Przemyślu.) Przemyśl, 1973.
Arc 1033.17.20 — Historia breve della miracolosa imagine della Madre di Dio. Napoli, 1638.
Arc 838.26 — Historia da arquitectura primitiva em Portugal. (Montey, P.) Lisboa, 1943.
Arc 1033.12.144 — Historia da prodigiosa imagem de Christo crucificado. (Cerqueira Pinto, Antonio.) Lisboa, 1737.
Arc 843.227 — Historia de Cadiz en la antigüedad. (Jimenez Cisneros, Maria Josefa.) Cadiz, 1973.
Htn Arc 1033.12.143* — Historia de como fue hallada la ymage del Sancto Crucifixo. Burgos? 1554?
Arc 1033.38.9 — Historia de Insigni Martyrio...Laurentii. (Bresnicio, C.B.) Leipzig, 1572.
Arc 843.77.10 — Historia de Italica. (Yali Lassaletta, Aurelio.) Sevilla, 1892.
Arc 1033.12.57 — Historia de Jesu Christi stigmatibus. (Paleotti, A.) Antverpiae, 1616.
Arc 1033.35.53 — Historia de la milagrosa renovación. (Velasco, Alfonso A.) México, 1845.
Arc 1033.17.106 — Historia de Nuestra Señora de Lujan. Buenos Aires, 1885. 2v.
Arc 1033.17.531 — Historia de Queralt. (Pla, José.) Barcelona, 1893.
Arc 1033.130 — Historia del glorioso precursore di N.S.S. G. Battista. (Calcagnino, A.) Genova, 1648.
Htn Arc 1033.17.583* — Historia del Monte Celia de Nuestra Señora de la Salceda. (Gonzalez de Mendoza, P.) Granada, 1616.
Htn Arc 1033.12.156* — Historia del santissimo Volto di S. Croce di Lucca. Lucca, 1582.
Arc 1033.12.182 — Historia della corona ferrea...Monza descritta. (Zucchi, B.) Milano, 1707.
Arc 1020.47 — Historia delle Miracolose Imagni...città di Lucca. (Franciotti, C.) Lucca, 1613.
Arc 1033.17.109 — Historia do insigne aparecimento de N. Senhora da Luz. (Soveral, Roque do.) Lisboa, 1610.
Arc 838.3.7 — Historia do museu etnologico português (1893-1914). (Leite de Vasconcellos, J.) Lisboa, 1915.
Htn Arc 785.13.60* — Historia Fori Romani restituto et aucta per Philippum Broidaeum Ariensem. (Palletus, F.) Buaci, 1576.
Arc 1635.5 — Historia numismática de Guatemala. (Prober, Kurt.) Guatemala, 1957.
Arc 1623.5 — Historia numismatica de Mexico desde la epoca precortesiana hasta 1823. (Prudeau, A.F.) Mexico, 1950.
Arc 1348.13 — Historia numismatum succincta. (Gleichius, J.) Lipsiae, 1698.
Arc 1468.6 — Historia numorum. (Head, B.V.) Oxford, 1887.

Author and Title Listing

Arc 1468.6.5A Historia numorum. (Head, B.V.) Oxford, 1911.

Arc 1668.12 Historia numorum contumeliosorum. (Klotz, C.A.) Altenburgi, 1765. 2 pam.

Arc 1033.98 Historia sacra. (Mauro, G.D.) Roma, 1682.

Arc 1033.90 Historia Sanctorum Martyrum...Ruderici, et Salomonis. (Heredia del Rio, P.M.) Romae, 1838.

Arc 936.14.522 Historia starożytna ziem polskich. 2. wyd. (Godłowski, Kazimierz.) Kraków, 1973.

Arc 80.1.5 Historia tēs Archaiologikēs Hetairias. (Kabbadias, P.) Athēnai, 1900.

Arc 1033.17.95 Historia universal...Nuestra Señora de Guadalupe. (Francisco de San Joseph.) Madrid, 1743.

Arc 1033.17.95.2F Historia universal...Nuestra Señora de Guadalupe. (Francisco de San Joseph.) Madrid, 1743.

Arc 1033.17.101 Historia universale delle imagini miracolose...Madre di Dio...tutte le parti del Mondo. (Astolfi, G.F.) Venezia, 1623.

Htn Arc 1033.12.64* Historia von der Erfindung, Wunderwerken und Zerstörung der vermeinten Heiligenbluts zur Wilssnagk. (Ludecus, M.) Wittenberg, 1586.

Arc 1020.126.5 Historia y discursos de la certidumbre de las reliquias, láminas. (López Madera, G.) Granada, 1602.

Arc 608.54 Historia y exploración de las ruinas de Cazaza. (Fernandez de Castro y Pedrera, R.) Larache, 1943.

Arc 1663.5.5 Historic medals of Canada. (Sandham, Alfred.) Quebec, 1873.

Arc 1468.17 Historic notices of coins in Greece. (Weston, S.) London, 1826.

Arc 1613.1 An historical account of American coinage. (Hickcox, J.H.) Albany, 1858.

Htn Arc 1538.5* Historical account of English money from the conquest. (Leake, S.M.) London, 1745.

Arc 1680.3 An historical account of the first three business tokens issued in N.Y. (Bushnell, C.I.) N.Y., 1859.

Arc 1535.205F An historical and critical account...medals. (Mudie, James.) London, 1820.

Arc 880.17 A historical and critical inquiry into the origin and primitive use of the Irish pillar-tower. (Morres, Hervey Montmorency.) London, 1821.

Arc 861.38 An historical and descriptive account of the old stone crosses of Somerset. (Pooley, C.) London, 1877.

Arc 398.8.1 Historical archaeology. (Noël Hume, Ivor.) N.Y., 1975.

Arc 398.8 Historical archaeology. 1. ed. (Noël Hume, Ivor.) N.Y., 1969.

Arc 1615.8 Historical arrangement of United States commemorative coins. (Foster, Charles W.) Rochester, 1936.

X Cg Arc 513.13 The historical geography of Asia Minor. v.1-2. (Ramsay, W.M.) London, 1890.

Arc 513.13 The historical geography of Asia Minor. v.1-2. Photoreproduction. (Ramsay, W.M.) London, 1890.

Arc 1468.13A Historical Greek coins. (Hill, G.F.) London, 1906.

Arc 1468.13.2 Historical Greek coins. (Hill, G.F.) N.Y., 1906.

Htn Arc 762.4* Historical illustrations of 4th canto of Childe Harold. (Hobhouse, J.) London, 1818.

Arc 762.4.2 Historical illustrations of 4th canto of Childe Harold. 2. ed. (Broughton, J.C.H.) London, 1818.

Htn Arc 861.62.10* Historical notices of Ilkley, Rombald's Moor, Baildon Common. 2. ed. (Wardell, James.) Leeds, 1881.

Arc 1480.19 Historical references on coins of the Roman empire. (Sydenham, E.A.) London, 1917.

Arc 430.202 Historical researches...caves of western India. (Bird, James.) Bombay, 1847.

Arc 1478.18 Historical Roman coins. (Hill, G.F.) London, 1909.

Arc 1613.8 A historical sketch of the national medals. (Hart, C.H.) Philadelphia, 1867.

Arc 588.23 Historical studies. (Petrie, W.M.F.) London, 1911.

Arc 80.1 Historikē ekthesis tōn praxeon tēs Archaiologikēs Hetairias. (Kastorkes, E.) Athēnai, 1879.

Arc 1269.20 Historisch-diplomatische Beschreibung der Nürnbergischen Kloster-Siegel. (Kiefhaber, J.K.S.) Nürnberg, 1797.

Arc 1510.170 Historisch-kritische Beschreibung aller bis jetzt bekannt gewordenen nessischen Münzen. v.1-4. (Hoffmeister, Jacob Christoph Carl.) Leipzig, 1974. 3v.

Arc 1510.127 Historische Nachricht von bayerischen Münzen. (Obermayr, J.) Frankfurt, 1763.

Arc 736.1 Historische Topographie von Akragas in Sicilien. (Sehnbring, J.) Leipzig, 1870.

Arc 905.14 Historischer Verein für Innerösterreich. Schriften. Graz, 1848.

Arc 858.60.5 History in earth and stone. (Hawkes, Jacquette.) Cambridge, Mass., 1952.

Arc 1361.3 A history of ancient coinage. 700-300 B.C. (Gardner, Percy.) Oxford, 1918.

Arc 1540.6A History of currency in the British colonies. (Chalmers, R.) London, n.d.

Arc 551.20 A history of Egyptian archaeology. (Bratton, Fred Gladstone.) London, 1967.

Arc 1423.9.6 History of Jewish coinage, and of money. (Madden, Frederic W.) San Diego, 1967.

Arc 1423.9 History of Jewish coinage. (Madden, Frederic W.) London, 1864.

Arc 1423.9.7 History of Jewish coinage. (Madden, Frederic W.) N.Y., 1967.

Arc 1423.25 The history of modern Israel's money, 1917 to 1967, including state medals and Palestine mandate. 1st ed. (Haffner, Sylvia.) La Mesa? 1967.

Arc 684.9.10 A history of Olynthus. (Gude, Mabel.) Baltimore, 1933.

Arc 893.31 A history of Scandinavian archaeology. (Klindt-Jensen, Ole.) London, 1975.

Arc 1274.4 History of Scottish seals. (Birch de Gray, W.) London, 1905. 2v.

Arc 412.1.5 A history of seafaring based on underwater archaeology. (Bass, George Fletcher.) London, 1972.

Arc 1.13.15 History of the American Academy in Rome. (La Farge, C.G.) N.Y., 1915.

Arc 1033.12.87 The history of the chalice of Antioch. (Arnason, H.) n.p., 1941.

Arc 595.23.5F A history of the Giza mecropolis. (Reisner, G.A.) Cambridge, Mass., 1942- 2v.

Arc 1540.29 The history of the gold sovereign. (Duveen, G.E.) London, 1962.

Arc 861.12.3 History of the Picts or Roman British wall. (Abbatt, Richard.) London, 1849.

Htn Arc 861.69* A history of the public crosses of old Nottingham. (Stapleton, A.) Nottingham, 1893.

Arc 605.201 History of the recent discovery at Cyrene. (Smith, R.M.) London, 1864.

Arc 1510.154 History of the redeemable, multiple and mining talers of Brunswick-Luneburg. 1. ed. (Duve, Gebhard.) Johannesburg, 1966.

Arc 861.12.12 History of the Roman wall. (Hutton, W.) London, 1802.

Arc 875.8 A history of the Scottish people from the earliest times. (Annandale, C.) London, 1892.

Arc 74.4.25 History of the Society for the promotion of Hellenic studies. (MacMillan, G.A.) n.p., n.d.

Arc 136.1.80 A history of the Society of Antiquaries. (Evans, Joan.) Oxford, 1956.

Arc 407.10.15 History unearthed. (Woolley, Charles L.) London, 1958.

Arc 407.10.18 History unearthed. (Woolley, Charles L.) N.Y., 1962.

Arc 303.60.5 Histria archaeologica. Pula. 1,1970+ 5v.

Arc 936.115 Histria monografie archeologică. București, 1954. 3v.

Arc 426.8 Hitchcoke, R. The ancient burial mounds of Japan. Washington, 1893.

Arc 1220.5F Hittite seals. (Hogarth, D.G.) Oxford, 1920.

Arc 974.3 Hiwassee Island: an archaeological account of 4 Tennessee Indian peoples. (Lewis, Thomas M.) Knoxville, 1946.

Arc 1588.10.20 Hlinka, Jozef. Bratislavské korunovačné medaily a žetóny. Vyd. 1. Bratislava, 1966.

Arc 1588.4.90 Hlinka, Jozef. Vývgpeňazi a medailí na Slovensku. Bratislava, 1970.

Arc 925.50.115F Hlodos'ki skarby. (Smilenko, Alla T.) Kyïv, 1965.

Arc 1480.46 A hoard of Roman folles from Diocletian's reform. (Leeds, Edward T.) Oxford, 1946.

Arc 723.3 Hoare, R.C. A classical tour through Italy and Sicily. London, 1819. 2v.

Htn Arc 762.4* Hobhouse, J. Historical illustrations of 4th canto of Childe Harold. London, 1818.

Arc 1475.7.2 Hobler, F. Records of Roman history. n.p., n.d. 2v.

Arc 1475.7 Hobler, F. Records of Roman history. Westminster, 1860. 2v.

Arc 1520.25 Hoc, Marcel. Histoire monétaire de Tournai. Bruxelles, 1970.

Arc 700.17 Die Hochzeit des Zeus und der Hera; Relief der Schaubert'schen Sammlung. (Foerster, R.) Breslau, 1867.

Arc 684.7 Hodēgos tēs Olympias. (Kourouniotos, K.) Athēnai, 1904.

NEDL Arc 672.1.28.10 Hodēgos tōn minoikou anaktoro tēs knōsa. (Pendlebury, J.D.S.) Hērakleí, 1950.

Arc 968.2.5 Hodge, F.W. The enchanted Mesa. v.1-2. Washington, 1897.

Arc 1335.5 Hodges, D.M. Gold and silver coin chart manual. N.Y., n.d.

Arc 858.4 Hodgetts, J.F. Older England. London, 1884.

Arc 858.4.2 Hodgetts, J.F. Older England. 2. series. London, 1884.

Arc 1145.206 Hodgkin, J. Calligraphia Graeca et poecilographia Graeca. Londini, 1794.

Arc 608.65 Hodrumetum. (Foncher, L.) Paris, 1964.

Arc 936.215.5 Hoeckmann, Olaf. Die menschengestaltige Figuralplastik der südosteuropäischen Jungsteinzeit und Steinkupferzeit. v.1-2. Hildesheim, 1968.

Arc 1033.17.104 Hoedoporicum Mariana Benedictinum seu historia de imaginibus. (Stengel, K.) Augsbourg, 1659.

Arc 1580.15 Höfken, Rudolf von. Numismatische Denkmale...in Österreich. Wien, 1904.

Arc 600.112 Hoelsche, Uvo. Die Wiedergewinnung von Medinet Habu im westlichen Theben. Tübingen, 1958.

Arc 793.1 Hoepli, U. Bibliography of Vesuvius, Pompeii, Herculaneum. Milan, 1883.

Arc 612.2 Hoernes, M. Urgeschichte der bildenden Kunst in Europa. Wien, 1898.

Arc 612.2.2 Hoernes, M. Urgeschichte der bildenden Kunst in Europa. 2. Aufl. Wien, 1915.

Arc 435.2.22F Hoernle, A.F.R. The Bower manuscript. Calcutta, 1893-1912.

Arc 1027.73 Hoferdt, E. Ursprung und Entwickelung der Chorkrypta. Breslau, 1905.

Arc 1348.5 Hoffmann, L.W. Alter und neuer Münz-Schlüssel. Nuremberg, 1692.

Arc 1510.170 Hoffmeister, Jacob Christoph Carl. Historisch-kritische Beschreibung aller bis jetzt bekannt gewordenen nessischen Münzen. v.1-4. Leipzig, 1974. 3v.

Arc 853.4.15 Hofmann, H. Römische Militärgrabsteine der Donauländer. Wien, 1905.

Arc 848.36 Hofmeister, H. Germanenkunde. Frankfurt am Main, 1936.

Arc 853.8.10 Hofmeister, H. Urholstein. Glückstadt, 1932.

Arc 853.73 Hofmeister, Hans. Die Chalten. Frankfurt am Main, 1930.

Arc 537.1 Hogarth, D.G. Devia Cypria. London, 1889.

Arc 1220.5F Hogarth, D.G. Hittite seals. Oxford, 1920.

Arc 600.1.3 Hogarth, D.G. Report on prospects of research in Alexandria. London, 1895.

Arc 392.3 Hogarth, David George. Authority and archaeology. N.Y., 1899.

Arc 853.246F Hohen Viecheln. (Schuldt, Ewald.) Berlin, 1961.

Arc 1510.75 Hohenlohe Waldenburg, Friedrich. Sphragistische Aphorismen. Heilbronn, 1882.

Arc 1269.15F Die hohenlohischen Siegel des Mittelalters. (Albrecht, J.) Oehringen, 1859.

Arc 848.28.5 Hohne, Hans. Deutsche Vorzeit. 6. Aufl. Bielefeld, 1937.

Arc 1020.118 Holahan, J. Notes on the antiquities of united parishes of Ballycollan, Kilmaugh and Killaloe. Kilkenny, 1875.

Arc 522.37 Holden, B.M. The metopes of the Temple of Athena at Ilion. Northampton, 1964.

Arc 726.52 Holland, Louise. The Faliscans in prehistoric times. Rome, 1925.

Arc 66.1.124 Holleaux, Maurice. Rome, la Grèce, et les monarchies hellénistiques. Paris, 1921.

Arc 66.1.113 Holleaux, Maurice. Stratēgos Ypatos. Paris, 1918.

Arc 726.337 Holloway, Robert Ross. Satrianum. Providence, 1970.

Arc 1335.120F Hollschek, Karl. Sammlung Hollschek. v.1-3. Wien, 1956? 2v.

Arc 1335.120 Hollschek, Karl. Sammlung Hollschek. v.4-20. Wien, 1956? 4v.

Arc 1490.8.20 Holm, Adolf. Storia della moneta siciliana. Bologna, 1965.

Arc 1053.5.7 Holm, Erich. Das Bildnis des Antinous. Inaug. Diss. Würzburg, 1933.

Arc 1030.8.15 Holm, F.W. My Nestorian adventure in China. N.Y., 1923.

Arc 340.13 Holm, S.E. Bibliography of South African pre- and proto-historic archaeology. Pretoria, 1966.

Arc 890.209 Holmberg, A.E. Skandinairens hällristningar. Stockholm, 1848.

Arc 670.7F Holmberg, E.J. The Swedish excavations at sea in Arcadia. Lund, 1944.

Arc 1570.1.9 Holmboe, C.A. Das älteste Münzwesen Norwegens. Berlin, 1846.

Author and Title Listing

Arc 1540.3 Holmboe, C.A. De numis MD medii aevi in Norvegia nuper repertis. Christiania, 1837.
Arc 1568.1.3 Holmboe, C.A. De prisca re monetaria Norvegiae. Christiania, 1841.
Arc 1568.1 Holmboe, C.A. De prisca re monetaria Norvegiae. 2. ed. Christiania, 1854.
Arc 1570.1 Holmboe, C.A. Et frar fund af norske mynter. Kjøbenhavn, 1866.
Arc 1550.1 Holmboe, C.A. Et guldbracteat-praeg som ofte forekommer. Kjøbenhavn, 1869.
Arc 1500.20 Holmboe, C.A. Im vildsvintypen fraa galliske mynter. Kjøbenhavn, 1868.
Arc 1550.2 Holmboe, C.A. Et lidet fund af mynter fra 11. aaehundrede. Kjøbenhavn, 1871.
Arc 1570.1.5 Holmboe, C.A. Om nogle norske pengeten. Kjøbenhavn, 1868.
Arc 970.1 Holmes, W.H. Stone implements; Potomac-Chesapeake Province. Washington, 1893-94.
Arc 943.17 Pamphlet box. Holmes, W.H. American archaeology.
Arc 957.2 Holmes, William H. Anthropological studies in California. n.p., n.d.
Arc 953.14 Holmes, William H. Art in shell of ancient Americans. Washington, 1880-81.
Arc 612.45 Holmqvist, Wilhelm. Germanic art during the first millenium. Stockholm, 1955.
Arc 936.12 Hołowińska, Z. Wczesnośredniowieczne grodziska w Bonikowie. Poznań, 1956.
Arc 853.71 Holter, F. Die Hallesche Kultur der frühen Eisenzeit. Inaug. Diss. Halle, 1934.
Arc 1340.9 Holtz, Walter. Abkürzungen auf Münzen. Braunschweig, 1972.
Arc 505.5.42 Holtzfuss, V.S. Dissertatio historico-theologica de templi Hierosolymitani Iuliani. Halae Magdeburgicae, 1751. 2 pam.
Arc 772.6 Holtzinger, H. Die Ruinen Roms. 2. Aufl. Stuttgart, 1912.
Arc 605.205.5 Holtzinger, H. Timgad und die römische Provinzial-Architektur. Berlin, 1906.
Arc 537.4 Holwerda, A.E.J. Die alten Kyprier in Kunst und Cultur. Leiden, 1885.
Arc 700.12 Holwerda, J.H. Die altischen Gräber der Bluethezeit. Leiden, 1899.
Arc 1033.35.151 Holy Cross. (Prime, W.C.) London, 1877.
Arc 495.3.5F The Holy Land, Syria, Idumea, Arabia, Egypt and Nubia. (Croly, George.) London, 1855-56. 3v.
Arc 505.3.5 The Holy Sepulchre and Temple at Jerusalem. (Fergusson, J.) London, 1865.
Arc 938.55 Die Holzbauten und Holzgeräte der Litten. pt.1-2. (Bielenstein, A.) n.p., 1907-18.
Arc 461.2 Homage to Vaisali. (Mathur, J.C.) Vaisali, 1948.
Arc 1588.10.30 Hóman, Bálint. Magyar pénztörténet, 1000-1325. Budapest, 1916.
Arc 383.51 Homaxe a Florentino A.L. Cuevillas. Vigo, 1957.
Arc 861.18.16 Home, Gordon. Roman London. London, 1926.
Arc 861.18.16.10 Home, Gordon. Roman London. London, 1948.
Arc 861.18.16.5 Home, Gordon. Roman London. N.Y., 1926.
Arc 861.21.15 Home, Gordon. Roman York. London, 1924.
Arc 383.53.20 Homenaje a Pablo Martinez del Rio en el vigesimoquento aniversario. Mexico, 1961.
Arc 87.1.50 Homerische Becher. (Robert, C.) Berlin, 1890.
Arc 510.210 Das homerische Troja. (Forchhammer, P.W.) n.p., 1874.
Arc 641.4A Homerisches Griechenland im Lichte der archäologischen Quellen. (Bouzek, Jan.) Praha, 1969.
Arc 830.45 Hommage à Boucher de Perthes. (Thiellen, A.) Paris, 1904.
Arc 383.34.10 Hommages à Albert Grenier. (Renard, M.) Bruxelles, 1962. 3v.
Arc 383.17 Hommages à Waldemar Deonna. Hommages à Waldemar Deonna. Bruxelles, 1957.
Arc 383.17 Hommages à Waldemar Deonna. (Hommages à Waldemar Deonna Bruxelles, 1957.
Arc 830.43 L'homme de la Barma-Grande. 2e éd. (Verneau, R.) Baoussé-Roussé, 1908.
Arc 1033.12.102 Hommer, J. von. Geschichte des heiligen Rockes...Trier. v.1-2. Bonn, 1844.
Arc 823.70 Hommes et dieux de la Gaule. (Eydoux, Henri Paul.) Paris, 1961.
Arc 762.2 Homo, L. Lexique de topographie romaine. Paris, 1900.
Arc 66.1.89 Homo, Leon. Essai sur le regne de l'empereur Aurélien. Paris, 1904.
Arc 66.1.49 Homolle, T. Archives de l'intendance sacrée à Délos. Paris, 1887.
Arc 635.217.5F Homolle, T. Exploratoire archéologique de Délos. Paris. 1-30 7v.
Arc 635.217 Homolle, T. Fouilles de Delphes. 1902+ 19v.
Arc 889.15 Hondius-Crone, Ada. The temple of Nehalennia at Domburg. Amsterdam, 1955.
Arc 905.110 A honfoglaló magyar nép élete. 2. biadás. (László, Gyula.) Budapest, 1944.
Arc 672.1.90 Honour, Alan. Secrets of Minos. 1. ed. N.Y., 1961.
Arc 853.308 Hoof, Dieter. Die Steinbeile und Steinarte im Gebiet der Niederrheins und der Maas. Bonn, 1970.
Arc 600.15.20 Hooper, Finley A. Funerary stelae from Kom Abour Billow. Ann Arbor, 1961.
Arc 861.45 Hooppell, R.E. On the discovery...of Roman remains at South Shields. London, 1878.
Arc 848.4 Hoops, J. Reallexikon der germanischen Altertumskunde. Strassburg, 1911. 4v.
Arc 861.11 Hope, W.H. St. J. Excavations...Roman city at Silchester, Hants in 1895. Westminster, 1896.
Arc 682.32 Hope Simpson, Richard. A gazetteer and atlas of Mycenaean sites. London, 1965.
Arc 1411.4 Hopkins, L.C. Origin and earlier history of Chinese coinage. n.p., n.d.
Arc 861.84 Hopkinson, J.H. The Roman fort at Ribchester. 3. ed. Manchester, 1928.
Arc 710.26 Hopper, Robert John. The acropolis. London, 1971.
Arc 610.5F Horae ferales. (Kemble, John M.) London, 1863.
Arc 1588.4.65F Horák, Jan. Kremnická mincovňa. Banska Bystrica, 1965.
Arc 1588.4.85 Horák, Ján. Kremnické dukáty. Vyd. 1. Bratislava, 1968.
Arc 936.24.10 Horedt, Kurt. Die prähistorische Ansiedlung auf dem Wietenberg bei Sighisoara-Schässburg. Bonn, 1971.
Arc 1510.115F Horn, Otto. Die Münzen und Medaillen. Leipzig, 1923.
Arc 793.7 Horne, J.F. The mirage of two buried cities. London, 1900.
Arc 557.8 Hornung, Erik. Einführung in die Ägyptologie. Darmstadt, 1967.
Arc 1163.3.50 Horodyski, Bogden. Podrecznik paleografii ruskiej. Kraków, 1951.
Arc 1027.65 Le horrea sotto l'aventino. (Rossi, G.B. de.) Roma, 1885.
Arc 400.11.20 The horse and the sword. (Peake, Harold J.E.) New Haven, 1933.
Arc 1470.40 The "Horsemen" of Tarentum. (Evans, A.J.) London, 1889.
Arc 855.200 Horsley, J. Britannia Romana, or The Roman antiquities of Britain. London, 1732.
Arc 1033.35.85 Hortus S. Crucis. (Gretser, J.) Ingolstadii, 1610.
Arc 936.100.25 Horvat, L.A. Konzervatorski rad kod Hrvata. Zagreb, 1944.
Arc 1588.12 Horvath, Henrik. A Budai penzverde muveszett orterenete a kesoi kozepkorban. Budapest, 1932.
Arc 1490.68 Horzfelder, Hubert. Les monnaies d'argent de Rhegion frappées entre 461 et le milieu du IVe siècle avant J.-C. Paris, 1957.
Arc 895.21.30 Hos stenåldersfolket. (Rydh, Hanna.) Stockholm, 1933.
Arc 936.262 Hospodarstvo skhidnoslov'ians'kykh plemen na rubezhi nashoï ery. (Pachkova, Svitlana P.) Kyïv, 1974.
Arc 845.209F Houben, P. Denkmaeler von Castra Vetera. Xanten, 1839.
Arc 955.2 Hough, W. Antiquities of the Upper Gila...(Arizona). Washington, 1907.
Arc 543.6 Hough, W. The Bernadou collection in the United States National Museum. n.p., n.d.
Arc 945.1 Hough, W. The lamp of the Eskimo. Washington, 1898.
Arc 421.9F Houo-Ming-Tse, P. Preuves des antiquités. Pekin, 1930.
Arc 672.1.140 The house of the Double Axe; the palace at Knossos. (Vaughan, Agnes C.) Garden City, 1959.
Arc 1025.14 Housse, L. Die Katakomben über das Unterirdische. Lurenburg, 1867.
Arc 1138.123 How to decipher and study old documents. (Cope, Emma Elizabeth T.) Chicago, 1974.
Arc 1138.1 How to decipher and study old documents. (Thoyts, E.E.) London, 1893.
Arc 386.15.5 How to observe in archaeology. 2. ed. (British Museum.) London, 1929.
Arc 1163.32 How to read the handwriting and records of early America. (Kirkham, E. Kay.) Salt Lake City, 1961.
Arc 968.2.55 Howard, E.B. Evidence of early man in North America...archaeological work in New Mexico. Philadelphia, 1935.
Arc 386.17 Howard Crosby Butler, 1872-1922. Princeton, 1923.
Arc 861.166 Hox Hill. (British Museum. Department of British and Mediaeval Antiquities.) London, 1962.
Arc 870.14.5 Hoyer, M.A. By the Roman wall. London, 1908.
Arc 900.215.5 Le Hradischt de Stradonitz en Bohême. (Pič, Josef L.) Leipzig, 1906.
Arc 936.195.130 Hrazany, Keltské oppidum na Sedlčansku. (Jansová, Libuše.) Praha, 1965.
Arc 1584.10 Hrbas, M. Antike Münzen aus Olbia und Pantikapaum. Prag, 1959.
Arc 1390.20 Hroskovyi sbih na terytorii Ukrainy doby teodalizma. (Kotliar, Mykola F.) Kyïv, 1971.
Arc 936.195.285 Hrubý, Vilém. Staré Město-Velehrad. 1. vyd. Praha, 1964.
Arc 936.195.285.5 Hrubý, Vilém. Staré Město-Veligrad. Gottwaldov, 1955.
Arc 936.195.125 Hrubý, Vilém. Velkomoravské hradisko sv. Klimenta u Osvětiman. Brno, 1961.
Arc 302.8.9 Hrvatsko arheološko društvo u Zagrebu. Izvješće. Zagreb. 1880-1886
Arc 302.7 Hrvatsko Arheološko Društvo u Zagrebu. Viestnik. Zagreb. 1-14 4v.
Arc 302.7.5 Hrvatsko Arheološko Društvo u Zagrebu. Viestnik. New series. Zagreb. 1-23,1895-1942 17v.
Arc 1223.3 Hsiang, Huai-shu. Recueil de cachets sur la Montagne jeune. Saigon, 1932?
Arc 870.5 Hubbard, A.J. Neolithic dew-ponds and cattle ways. London, 1905.
Arc 870.5.3 Hubbard, A.J. Neolithic dew-ponds and cattle ways. 3. ed. London, 1916.
Arc 820.11PF Huber, Émile. La ville de Rouhling. Texte et atlas. Metz, 1905.
X Cg Arc 823.30 Hubert, J. L'art pré-roman. Paris, 1938.
Arc 810.18 Hubik, J. Pompeji im Gymnasialunterricht. Wien, 1900.
Arc 1030.58F Hubner, E. Inscriptiones Britanniae christianae. Berolini, 1876.
Arc 1264.5 Hucher, Eugène. Catalogue de la collection de sceaux matrices. Paris, 1863.
Arc 943.27 Hudlicka, A. Recent discoveries attributed to early man in America. Washington, 1918.
Arc 853.376F Huebener, Wolfgang. Die römischen Metallfunde von Augsburg-Oberhausen. Kallmünz, 1973.
Arc 900.211F Hueber, P. Austria exarchivis mellicensilus. Lipsiae, 1722.
Arc 1016.205 Hübner, A. Inscritione hispaniae christianae. Berlolini, 1871.
Arc 1016.205.5 Hübner, A. Inscritione hispaniae christianarum. Supplement. Berolini, 1900.
Arc 838.2 Hübner, E. La arqueologia de España. Barcelona, 1888.
Arc 87.1.28 Huebner, E. Augustus. Berlin, 1868.
Arc 87.1.33 Huebner, E. Bildniss einer Roemerin. Berlin, 1873.
Arc 843.22 Hübner, E. Citania. Porto, 1879.
Arc 87.1.26 Huebner, E. Relief eines roemischen Kriegers. Berlin, 1866.
Arc 837.2 Pamphlet vol. Hübner, E. Géographie et archéologie anciennes de l'Espagne. 5 pam.
Arc 628.22 Pamphlet vol. Hübner, E. Opuscules. 16 pam.
Arc 853.58.5 Hügelgräber im Vorderwald von Muschenheim. (Helmke, Paul.) Giessen, 1919. 2v.
Arc 853.41.5F Hügelgräber und Urnen-Friedhöfe. (Wagner, E.) Karlsruhe, 1885.
Arc 853.24.9 Hülle, Werner. Grundzüge der vorrömischen Besiedelung Bayerns. Inaug. Diss. Augsburg, 1932.
Arc 1027.66 Huelsen, C. Di una iscrizione monumentale al cimitero di Generosa. Roma, 1900.
Arc 762.5 Huelsen, C. La pianta di Roma dell'anonimo einsidlense. Roma, 1907.
Arc 87.1.46 Huelsen, C. Septizonim des Septimius Severus. Berlin, 1886.
Arc 785.38 Huelsen, C. Die Thermen des Agrippa. Rom, 1910.
Arc 785.13.20 Huelsen, Christian. Die Ausgrabungen auf dem Forum Romanum. v.1-2. Roma, 1902-05.
Arc 785.13.24.7 Huelsen, Christian. Il Foro Romano; storia e monumenti. Roma, 1905.
Arc 785.13.24.13 Huelsen, Christian. The Forum and the Palatine. N.Y., 1928.
Arc 785.13.22.15 Huelsen, Christian. Le Forum Romain, son histoire et ses monuments. Rome, 1906.
Arc 785.13.21 Huelsen, Christian. Das Forum Romanum. Rom, 1904.
Arc 785.13.22 Huelsen, Christian. Das Forum Romanum. Rom, 1905.
Arc 785.13.24.9 Huelsen, Christian. Forum und Palatin. München, 1926.
Arc 785.13.22.5 Huelsen, Christian. Die neuesten Ausgrabungen...Nachtrag. Rom, 1910.

Arc 785.13.24 Huelsen, Christian. The Roman Forum. Rome, 1906.
Arc 785.13.23 Huelsen, Christian. The Roman Forum. Rome, 1906.
Arc 785.13.24.5 Huelsen, Christian. The Roman Forum. Rome, 1909.
Arc 726.241 Huelsen, Hans von. Funde in der Magna Graecia. Gottingen, 1962.
Arc 762.7 Huelsen, Hans von. Römische Funde. Göttingen, 1960.
Arc 870.4.15 Hughes, G.M. Roman roads in south-east Britain. London, 1936.
Arc 885.11 Hughes, I.T. Out of the dark. Wrexham, 1930.
Arc 608.66 Hugot, Henri J. Recherches préhistoriques dans l'Ahazzar nord-occidental. Paris, 1963.
Arc 830.181 Huguenotte, A. Les mosaïques de Clervae. Besançon, 1925.
Arc 1020.124 Huidobro Serna, Luciano. Nuestra Señora del Espino en Santa Gadea del Cid Burgos. Lérida, 1922. 3 pam.
Arc 1200.14 Huillard-Bréholles. Examen des chartes de l'eglise romaine. Paris, 1865.
Arc 1349.60F Hujer, L. Mein Leben und Streben. Wien, 1954.
Arc 762.3 Hula, E. Römische Altertümer. Leipzig, 1901.
Arc 1086.10 Hula, Franz. Mittelalterliche Kultmale. Wien, 1970.
Arc 1153.31 Hulákovsky, J.M. Abbreviaturae vocabulorum. Pragae, 1913.
Arc 501.18 Hull, E. Mount Seir. London, 1885.
Arc 500.5.5 Hull, E. The survey of Western Palestine. Adelphi, 1886.
Arc 730.6 Hulot, J. Sélimonte. Paris, 1910.
Htn Arc 1478.5* Hulsius, L. Impp. Romanorum numismatum series. Frankfort, 1603.
Arc 642.9 The humanistic value of archaeology. (Carpenter, Rhys.) Cambridge, Mass., 1933.
Arc 387.13.7 Humanistisches und Humanes. (Curtius, Ludwig.) Basel, 1954.
X Cg Arc 510.217 Humann, Carl. Magnesia am Maeander. Berlin, 1904.
Arc 520.18 Humann, K. Der Entdecker von Pergamon. Berlin, 1930.
X Cg Arc 510.202 Humann, K. Reisen in Kleinasien und Nordsyrien. Text and atlas. Berlin, 1890. (Changed to XP 9867) 2v.
Arc 520.30 Humann, Karl. Der Pergamon Altar. Dortmund, 1959.
Arc 1560.2 Humbles, C.P. Förteckning öfver C.P. Humbles. Stockholm, 1852.
Arc 861.3 Hume, A. Ancient meols, or Some account of the antiquities found near Dove Point. London, 1863.
Arc 925.50.200 Humenna, Dokiia. Rodynnyi al'bom. Niu-Iork, 1971.
Arc 936.195.190 Huml, Václav. Zaniklá turz Semonice. Hradec Králové, 1967.
Arc 87.1.30 Humoristische Vasenbilder. (Heydemann, H.) Berlin, 1870.
NEDL Arc 1348.6 Humphreys, H.N. The coin collector's manual. London, 1875. 2v.
Arc 1538.3 Humphreys, H.N. The coinage of the British empire. London, 1854.
Htn Arc 1538.3.2* Humphreys, H.N. The coinage of the British empire. London, 1855.
Arc 1538.3.5 Humphreys, H.N. The gold, silver, and copper coins of England. 6. ed. London, 1849.
Arc 853.250 Die Hunbirg. (Vollrath, Friedrich.) Nürnberg, 1961.
Arc 180.1.25 Hundert Jahre Antiquarische Gesellschaft in Zürich, 1832-1932. (Largiader, Anton.) Zürich, 1932.
Arc 388.5.5 A hundred years of archaeology. (Daniel, G.E.) London, 1950.
Arc 885.18 A hundred years of Welsh archaeology. (Cambrian Archaeological Association.) Gloucester, 1949.
Arc 853.230F Hundt, Hans Jürgen. Katalog Stromling. Kallmünz, 1958. 2v.
Arc 1279.2 Hungary. K. Orszagos Leveltar. A Magy. Kiral. Orszagos Leveltar diplom. osztalyaban orzalt. Budapest, 1909.
Arc 830.335 The hungry archaeologist in France. (Daniel, G.E.) London, 1963.
Arc 392.4 Hunter, R. Preservation of places of interest or beauty. Manchester, 1907.
Arc 392.1 Hunter-Duvar, J. Stone, bronze and iron ages. London, 1892.
Arc 1335.81 The Hunterian coin cabinet. (MacDonald, G.) Glasgow, 1933.
Arc 1335.55 The Hunterian Museum in the old college of Glasgow. (Murray, David.) Glasgow, 1925.
Arc 400.11 Hunters and artists. (Peake, Harold J.E.) New Haven, 1927.
Arc 861.96 Hurd, Howard. Some notes on recent archaeological discoveries at Broadstairs. Broadstairs, 1913.
Arc 830.92 Hure, Auguste. Le sénonais préhistorique. Sens, 1921.
Arc 66.1.198 Hus, A. Recherches sur la statuaire en pierre étrusque archaique. Paris, 1961.
Arc 746.60 Hus, Alain. Vulci étrusque et étrusco-romaine. Paris, 1971.
Arc 1418.26 Hussain, M.K. Catalogue of coins of the Mughal emperors. Bombay, 1968.
Arc 1588.10.12 Huszár, Lajos. A budai pénzverés története a középkorban. Budapest, 1958.
Arc 1588.10.10 Huszár, Lajos. Munzkunst in Ungarn. Budapest, 1963.
Arc 875.43 Hutcheson, Alexander. Old stories in stones and other papers. Dundee, 1927.
Arc 1335.60 Hutchins. A catalogue of the collection of curious...coins. London, 1790.
Arc 392.2 Hutchinson, H.N. Prehistoric man and beast. N.Y., 1897.
Arc 1027.19.33 Huthmacher, L. Ein Besuch in der römischen Katakomben...S. Kallisto. Mainz, 1861.
Arc 830.70 Hutinel, F. La préhistoire dans la région lyonnaise. Lyon, 1913.
Arc 1010.28 Hutterer, Karl. An archaeological picture of a pre-Spanish Cebuano community. Cebu City, 1973.
Arc 861.12.12 Hutton, W. History of the Roman wall. London, 1802.
Arc 785.83.10 Hyde, Walter Woodburn. Roman Alpine routes (with map showing chief Roman passes). Philadelphia, 1935.
Arc 447.1F Hyderabad, India (State). Archaeological Department. Annual report. Calcutta. 1323-1349,1914-1940 11v.
Arc 447.1.5 Hyderabad, India (State). Archaeological Department. Antiquarian remains in Hyderabad State. Hyderabad, 1953.
Arc 588.17 Hyksos and Graelite cities. (Petrie, W.M.F.) London, 1906.
Arc 66.1.134.5 Les hymes de Callimaque. (Cahen, Emile.) Paris, 1930.
Arc 1020.72.9 L'hypogée des dunes à Poitiers. (Chamard, F.) Paris, 1884.
Arc 746.58 I: Gli alfabeti etruschi; II: La scultura etrusca. (Neppi Modona, Aldo.) Genova, 1970.
Arc 936.14.134 I konferencja naukowa w Warszawie...1968. (Warsaw. Uniwersytet. Zespol Badan nad Polskim Srezniowieczem.) Warszawa, 1962.
Arc 612.66 I międzynarodoury kongres Archeologii Słowianskiej. (Congrès International d'Archéologie Slave, 1st, Warsaw, 1965.) Wrocław, 1968. 7v.
Arc 893.28 I stider och märmiskor i Norden. (Aeve, Astrid.) Uppsala, 1960.

Arc 543.66.40 Iagadin, V.N. Nekropol' drevnego Mizdakhana. Tashkent, 1970.
Arc 925.50.315 Iakavenko, Ieleonora V. Skify skhidnego Krymu v V-III st. do n.e. Kyïv, 1974.
Arc 543.60F Iakhry, A. Anarchaeological journey to Yemen. v.1-3. Cairo, 1951-52. 2v.
Arc 710.24 Iakōbidēs, S.E. E Mykēnaikē Akropolis tōn Athēnōn. Athēnai, 1962.
Arc 925.50.105 Iakobson, A.L. Srednevekovyi Krym. Leningrad, 1964.
Arc 493.6.25 Ialoilutepinskaia kul'tura. (Ismizade, O.S.) Baku, 1950.
Arc 1282.12 Ianin, Valentin L. Aktovye pechati drevnei Rusi X-XV vv. Moskva, 1970. 2v.
Arc 1584.25 Iaroslavskaia Uchenaia Arkhivnaia Kommissii. Opisanie russikh monet muzeia Iaroslavskoi uchenoi arkkivnoi kommissii. Iaroslav, 1898.
Arc 925.320 Iaroslavskoe Povolzh'e X-XI vv. po materialam Timerevskogo Mikhailovskogo i Petrovskogo mogil'nikov. (Moscow. Gosudarstvennyi Istoricheskii Muzei.) Moskva, 1963.
Arc 925.13.75 Iatsenko, I.V. Skifiia VII-V vekov do nashei ery. Moskva, 1959.
Arc 838.9 Iberia arqueológica ante-romana, discursos. (Mélida, José R.) Madrid, 1906.
Arc 838.25 The Iberians of Spain. (Dixon, P.) London, 1940.
Arc 1125.30 Ibrahim University studies in papyrology. (Cairo, Egypt. Ayn Shams University.)
Arc 1348.32 Icard, Séverin. Identification des monnaies. Paris, 1927.
Arc 1033.180 Ichthys. v.2-5. (Doelger, Franz J.) Münster, 1910-43. 4v.
Arc 1027.22.9 L'Ichthys eucaristico nei monumenti. (Majocchi, R.) Milano, 1895.
Htn Arc 1050.204* Icones, vitae et elogia...Romanorum. Antwerp, 1645.
Htn Arc 1050.201* Iconografia. (Canini, G.A.) Romae, 1669.
Arc 1053.20 Iconografia greca. (Visconti, E.Q.) Milano, 1923-25. 3v.
Arc 1033.19 Iconographie chrétienne. (Du Camp, M.) n.p., n.d.
Arc 1345.1.4 Iconographie des empereurs romains. Paris, 1858.
Arc 1264.22F Iconographie des sceaux et bulles conservés dans la partie antérieure à 1790 des archives départementales des Bouches-du-Rhone. (Bouches-du-Rhone. Archives.) Marseille, 1860.
Arc 1480.24 L'iconographie monetaire de Julien l'Apostat. (Babelon, E.) Paris, 1903.
Arc 388.12 The idea of prehistory. (Daniel, G.E.) London, 1962.
Arc 1348.32 Identification des monnaies. (Icard, Séverin.) Paris, 1927.
Arc 1163.1 Idioma y escritura de España. (Muñoz y Rivero, J.) Madrid, 1888.
Arc 193.1 Idunna und Hermode. Breslan. 1812-1816 2v.
Arc 925.9.60 Iessen, Aleksandr A. Mozdokskii mogil'nik. Leningrad, 1940.
Arc 609.28 Ife in the history of west African sculpture. (Willett, Frank.) N.Y., 1967.
Arc 936.14.55 Igołomia. (Polska Akademia Nauk. Oddział w Krakowie. Prace Komisji Archeologicznej.) Wrocław, 1961.
Arc 853.30.5 II. Ausgrabungen bei Haltern. (Dragendorff, Hans.) n.p., 1902.
Arc 936.14.135 II konferencja naukowa w Warszawie...1961. (Warsaw. Uniwersytet. Zespol Badan nad Polskim Sredniowieczem.) Warszawa, 1963.
Arc 612.69 III. sympozjum paleolityczne, Kraków 30 XI-2 XII, 1967. v.1-2. (Sympozjum Paleolityczne, 3d, Kraków, 1967.) Kraków, 1967.
Arc 936.14.136 III konferencja naukowa w Warszawie. (Warsaw. Uniwersytet. Zespol Badan nad Polskim Sredniowieczem.) Warszawa, 1964.
Arc 1588.1.105 III Sesja Numizmatyczna w Nowej Soli poświęcona monecie i mennicom Wielkopolski, 10-11 listopada 1970 r. (Sesja Numizmatyczna, 3rd, Nowa Sól, 1970.) Nowa Sól, 1972.
Arc 1433.64 Die Ikonographie der Partherkönige. (Farkas, Sándor.) Aiud, 1933.
Arc 923.105 Ilarionov, V.T. Opyt istoriografii paleolita SSSR. Gor'kei, 1947.
X Cg Arc 66.1.87 L'ile tiberine dans l'antiquité. (Besiner, M.) Paris, 1902.
Arc 66.1.8 Les îles ioniennes. (Riemann, O.) Paris, 1879-80. 3v.
Arc 459.3.30 Il'in, G.F. Drevnii indiiskii gorod Taksila. Moskva, 1918.
Arc 925.13.140 Il'inskaia, Vervara A. Skify dneprovskogo lesostepnogo Levoberezh'ia. Kiev, 1968.
Arc 522.4.5 Ilios. (Schliemann, H.) Leipzig, 1881.
Arc 522.4.5.3 Ilios. (Schliemann, H.) London, 1880.
Arc 522.4.6 Ilios. (Schliemann, H.) N.Y., 1881.
Arc 936.220.40 Ilirska kneževsha nekropola u atenici. (Djuhnić, Milena.) Čačak, 1966.
Arc 1590.9 Illustr. katal. nov. srpekhikh tsareva, 700-1710 g. (Rajić, N.P.) Beograd, 1940.
Arc 1411.13 Illustrated catalog of Chinese coins, gold, silver, nickel and aluminum. (Kann, Eduard.) Los Angeles, 1954.
Arc 720.210 Illustrated catalogue of classical antiquities. (Nottingham. Museum.) Nottingham, n.d.
Arc 843.8 Illustrated descriptive account of the museum of Andalucian pottery and lace. (Whishaw, B.) Seville, 1912.
Arc 1340.7 Illustrated encyclopedia of gold and silver coins of the world. (Smith, Alfred M.) Philadelphia, 1886.
Arc 858.47.14 Illustrated guide to ancient monuments. (Great Britain. Ministry of Works.) Edinburgh, 1961.
Arc 858.47.16.5 Illustrated guide to ancient monuments. (Great Britain. Ministry of Works.) Edinburgh, 1967.
Arc 865.14.5 The illustrated guide to Old Sarum and Stonehenge. (Brown and Company, Salisbury, publishers.) Salisbury, 1877.
Arc 865.14 Illustrated guide to Old Sarum and Stonehenge. (Brown and Company, Salisbury, publishers.) London, 1888.
Arc 1613.2.3 Illustrated history of the United States mint. (Evans, G.G.) Philadelphia, 1889.
Arc 1613.2 Illustrated history of the United States mint. (Evans, G.G.) Philadelphia, 1890.
Arc 1613.2.4 Illustrated history of the United States mint. (Evans, G.G.) Philadelphia, 1891.
Arc 1613.2.2 Illustrated history of the United States mint. (Evans, G.G.) Philadelphia, 1892.
Arc 1613.2.5 Illustrated history of the United States mint. (Evans, G.G.) Philadelphia, 1893.
Arc 858.47.5A Illustrated regional guides to ancient monuments. (Great Britain. Ministry of Works.) London, 1936-48. 5v.
Arc 858.47.12 Illustrated regional guides to ancient monuments. v.1-2,4,6. (Great Britain. Ministry of Works.) London, 1954. 4v.

Arc 858.47.10 Illustrated regional guides to ancient monuments. v.2-6. 2. ed. (Great Britain. Ministry of Works.) London, 1949- 5v.

Arc 865.3 An illustration of Stonehenge and Abury. 4. ed. (Browne, H.) Salisbury, 1854.

Arc 861.40.5 An illustration of the Roman antiquities discovered at Bath. (Warner, Richard.) Bath, 1797.

Arc 435.25.5F Illustrations of ancient buildings of Kashmir. (India. Archaeological Survey.) London, 1869.

Arc 1540.15 Illustrations of coinage of Scotland. (Wingate, James.) Glasgow, 1868.

Arc 861.18 Illustrations of Roman London. (Smith, C.R.) London, 1858.

Arc 1535.5 Illustrations of the Anglo French coinage. London, 1830.

Arc 861.16 Illustrations of the traces...Romans and Saxons. (Miller, S.H.) n.p., 1871.

Arc 1490.18 Illustrazione delle monete. 2. ed. (Diodati, D.) Napoli, 1849.

Arc 815.5 Illustrazione delle piante rappresentativa nei diputi Pompeiani. (Comes, O.) Napoli, 1879.

Arc 1033.32 Illustrazione di due monumenti cristiani. (Polidori, L.) Verona, 1843.

Arc 1015.211 Illustrazione di un antico monumento cristiano. (Settele, G.) Roma, 1829.

Arc 853.20.5 Illustrierter Führer...Provinzialmuseum in Trier. (Hettner, F.) Trier, 1903.

Htn Arc 1053.4* Illustrium imagines ex...Fuliri Ursini. (Faber, Johannes.) Antwerpiae, 1606.

Arc 936.215.10 Les Illyriens et la genèse des Albanais; travaux de la session du 3-4 mars, 1969. Tirana, 1971.

Arc 497.53 Ilton, Paul. Digging in the Holy Land. London, 1959.

Arc 1480.50 Ilustrovani katalog novaca rimskih i vizantiskih vladaoca. (Rajic, H.P.) Beograd, 1939?

Arc 1588.1.65.7 Ilustrowany katakog monet polskich, 1916-1972. wyd. 2. (Kamiński, Czesław.) Warszawa, 1973.

Arc 1588.1.65.8 Ilustrowany katalog monet polskich, 1916-1974. Wyd. 3. (Kamiński, Czesław.) Warszawa, 1974.

Arc 1588.1.33 Ilustrowany katalog monet polskich bitych w okresie 1916-1965. 2. wyd. (Terlecki, W.) Warszawa, 1965.

Arc 1570.2 Im et fund af norske mynter fraa Sando. (Schive, C.) Kjøbenhavn, 1866.

Arc 853.83 Im Streit um die Externsteine. (Fuchs, Alois.) Paderborn, 1934.

Arc 1500.20 Im vildsvintypen fraa galliske mynter. (Holmboe, C.A.) Kjøbenhavn, 1868.

Htn Arc 1033.17.97* Imagen de la virgen Maria...de Guadalupe. (Sánchez, Miguel.) México, 1648.

Arc 618.8 Imagery in early Celtic art. (Jacobsthal, P.) London, 1941.

Arc 1053.1 Images des héros et des grandes hommes de l'antiquité. (Canini, G.A.) Amsterdam, 1731.

Arc 1584.5F Imennye serebrian. kop. i denezhki Ivana IV. (Bulychev, N.I.) Sankt Peterburg, 1906.

X Cg Arc 1665.1 Imhoof-Blumer, F. Tier- und Pflanzenbilder auf Münzen und Gemmen. Leipzig, 1889.

Arc 1465.1 Imhoof-Blumer, Friedrich. Choix de monnaies grecques. 2. ed. Paris, 1883.

Arc 1465.79 Imhoof-Blumer, Friedrich. Griechische Münzen. München, 1890.

Arc 1430.200 Imhoof-Blumer, Friedrich. Kleinasiatische Münzen. Wien, 1901-02. 2v.

Arc 1428.14 Imhoof-Blumer, Friedrich. Lydische Stadtmünzen. Genf, 1897.

Arc 1468.7 Imhoof-Blumer, Friedrich. Monnaies grecques. Amsterdam, 1883.

Arc 1468.7.5 Imhoof-Blumer, Friedrich. Monnaies grecques. Paris, 1883.

Arc 1465.3 Imhoof-Blumer, Friedrich. Porträtköpfe auf antiken Münzen. Leipzig, 1885.

Arc 1475.9 Imhoof-Blumer, Friedrich. Porträtköpfe auf Römischen Münzen. Leipzig, 1892.

Arc 1460.7.1 Imhoof-Blumer, Friedrich. Tier- und Pflanzenbilder auf Münzen und Gemmen des klassischen Altertums. Hildesheim, 1972.

Arc 1458.14 Imhoof-Blumer, Friedrich. Zur griechischen und römischen Münzkunde. Genf, 1908.

Arc 1470.3 Imhoof-Blumer, Friedrich. Zur Münzkunde Grossgriechenlands. Wien, 1887.

Arc 595.65 Imhotep, builder in stone. (Cormack, Maribelle.) N.Y., 1965.

Htn Arc 1475.1.2F* Imperatorum romanorum numismata. (Occo, A.) Milan, n.d.

Htn Arc 1475.1F* Imperatorum romanorum numismata. (Occo, A.) Milan, 1730.

Arc 1475.4.5 Imperatorum romanorum numismata. (Patin, C.) Paris, 1697.

Arc 441.9 Important inscriptions from the Baroda state. (Gadre, A.S.) Baroda, 1943.

Arc 1335.62 Importante collection de monnaies et médailles. (André, Leon.) Paris, 1926.

Arc 1490.12 Importante scoperta del famoso Tarèno di Amalfi. (Camera, Matteo.) Napoli, 1872.

Arc 1027.5 Importantes decouvertes...cimetiere de Domitille. (Rossi, G.B. de.) Paris, 1875.

Arc 936.14.15F Importy rzymskie w Polsce. (Majewski, K.) Warszawa, 1960.

Arc 936.14.70 Importy skandynawskie na ziemiach zachodnioslowianskich. (Zak, Jan.) Poznań, 1963. 3v.

Htn Arc 1478.5* Impp. Romanorum numismatum series. (Hulsius, L.) Frankfort, 1603.

Arc 530.130 Une imprécation funéraire a néocésarée. (Moraux, Paul.) Paris, 1959.

Arc 1033.17.49 Les impressions d'un pelerinou l'ecole de Marie à Pontmain. (Vandel, R.P.) Issoudun, 1872.

Arc 383.33 In het voetspoor van A.E. van Giffen. (Amsterdam. Universiteit. Institut voor Prae- en Protohistorie.) Groningen, 1961.

Arc 383.33.2 In het voetspoor van A.E. van Giffen. 2. druk. (Amsterdam. Universiteit. Institut voor Prae- en Protohistorie.) Groningen, 1966.

Htn Arc 785.10* In Marmor Isiacum...exercitationes. (Oliva, G.) Rome, 1719.

Arc 400.17 In onore di Luigi Pigorini, Roma, 11 gennaio 1914. Roma, 1914.

Arc 853.36 Die in Ostdeutschland gefundenen römischen Bronzestatuellen. (Fredrich.) Cüstrin, 1912. 3 pam.

Htn Arc 1020.6.15* In perantiquam sacram tabulam...S. Mariae Caritatis. (Schioppalalba, I.B.) Venetiis, 1767.

Arc 1025.41 In Roma i cristianai...soterranei cimiteri. (Scognamiglio, A.) Roma, 1863.

Arc 875.41 In Roman Scotland. (Mothersole, Jessie.) London, 1927.

Arc 723.33 In search of Ancient Italy. 1st American ed. (Grimal, Pierre.) N.Y., 1964.

Arc 389.4.1 In search of lost worlds. 1. American ed. (Eydoux, Henri Paul.) N.Y., 1971.

Arc 726.27.10 In the footsteps of Orpheus. (Paget, Robert F.) N.Y., 1968.

Arc 925.339 Inadze, Meri P. Prichernomorskie goroda drevnei Kolkhidy. Tbilisi, 1968.

Arc 1033.47.17 L'incendio di Roma e i primi Cristiani. (Mapelli, L.) Milano, 1900.

Arc 1033.47 L'incendio neroniano ed i Cristiani. (Profumo, A.) Roma, 1903.

Arc 1020.9.80 Incrementi del museo sacro della Biblioteca Vaticana di Leone XIII. (Rossi, G.B. di.) Roma, n.d.

Arc 77.8 Incunabula Graeca. (Rome. Università. Centro di Studi Micenei.) 1,1961+ 56v.

Arc 1077.2.21 Indagini archeologiche del "Signum Christi". (Strazzulla, V.) Palermo, 1899.

Arc 432.18 L'Inde et l'Orient classique. (Combaz, Gisbert.) Paris, 1937. 2v.

NEDL Arc 136.2.15 Index. v.1-20. 2d series. (London Society of Antiquaries.) London, 1908.

Arc 335.2 Index of archaeological papers, 1665-1890. (Gomme, G.L.) London, 1907.

Arc 335.3 Index of archaeological papers, 1891-1908. London, 1892- 2v.

Arc 589.1 Index of names and titles of the old kingdoms. (Murray, M.A.) London, 1908.

NEDL Arc 136.2.3 Index Society. Index to engravings in proceedings of Society of Antiquaries. London, 1885.

Arc 136.1.2 Index to Archaeologia. v.1-30. (London Society of Antiquaries.) London, 1809-44. 2v.

Arc 136.1.3 Index to Archaeologia. v.1-50. (London Society of Antiquaries.) London, 1889.

Arc 136.1.4 Index to Archaeologia. v.51-100 (1888-1966). (London Society of Antiquaries.) London, 1970.

NEDL Arc 136.2.3 Index to engravings in proceedings of Society of Antiquaries. (Index Society.) London, 1885.

Arc 138.10 Index to journal 1897-1919. (North Munster Archaeologcial Society.) Nenagh, 1958.

Arc 1.1.5 Index to publications, 1879-89. (Archaeological Institute of America.) Cambridge, 1891.

Arc 435.55.2F Index to the annual reports of the Mysore Archaeological Department for the years 1906-1922. (Mysore. Archaeological Survey.) Bangalore, 1929.

Arc 672.1.27.5 Index to the palace of Minos. (Evans, Arthur John.) London, 1936.

Arc 340.4 An indexed bibliography of the writings of W.F. Albright. (Orlinsky, H.M.) New Haven, 1941.

Arc 435.3F India. Archaeological Survey. Annual report. Calcutta. 1902-1916// 14v.

Arc 435.3.5F India. Archaeological Survey. Annual report. Index, 1902-1916. Calcutta, 1924.

Arc 435.4.25F India. Archaeological Survey. Annual report of the Archaeological Survey of India. Calcutta. 1916-1936 18v.

Arc 435.4F India. Archaeological Survey. Annual report of the director-general of archaeology. pt.1. Calcutta. 1902-1921// 11v.

Arc 435.26 India. Archaeological Survey. Archaeological remains. v.1-2. New Delhi, 1964.

Arc 435.20 India. Archaeological Survey. Epigraphia Indica. 1,1888+ 35v.

Arc 435.20.3 India. Archaeological Survey. Epigraphia Indo-Moslemica. Arabic and Persian supplement. 1927+ 7v.

Arc 435.25.5F India. Archaeological Survey. Illustrations of ancient buildings of Kashmir. London, 1869.

Arc 435.25.7F India. Archaeological Survey. Loan exhibition of antiquities, Coronation Durbar, 1911. Calcutta, 1912.

Arc 435.1.15F India. Archaeological Survey. Memoirs. Calcutta. 1-73,1919-1955 14v.

Arc 435.2 India. Archaeological Survey. Report. London. 1-5,1874-1883// 4v.

X Cg Arc 435.2 India. Archaeological Survey. Report. London. 3

Arc 435.1.1 India. Archaeological Survey. Reports. Varanasi, 1966-72. 24v.

Arc 435.60F India. Archaeological Survey. Central Circle. Annual progress report. Patna. 1920-1921

Arc 435.52 India. Archaeological Survey. Eastern Circle, Bengal. Annual report. Calcutta. 1888-1921 2v.

Arc 435.59F India. Archaeological Survey. Frontier Circle, Peshawar. Annual report. Peshawar. 1904-1921 3v.

Arc 435.1.18 India. Archaeological Survey. Library. Classified catalogue of the library of the director general of archaeology. Calcutta, 1908.

Arc 435.1.20 India. Archaeological Survey. Library. Consolidated catalogue. New Delhi, 1940.

Arc 435.53F India. Archaeological Survey. Northern Circle, Punjab. Annual progress report of the superintendent. 1906-1916

Arc 435.53.3F India. Archaeological Survey. Northern Circle, Punjab. Annual progress report of the superintendent, Muhammadan and British monuments. Allahabad. 1910-1921// 5v.

Arc 435.53.2F India. Archaeological Survey. Northern Circle, Punjab. Annual progress report of the superintendent, Hindu and Buddhist monuments. 1911-1921

Arc 435.57 India. Archaeological Survey. Punjab Circle. Report. Calcutta. 1888-1889

Arc 435.54F India. Archaeological Survey. Southern Circle, Madras. Annual report. Madras. 1858-1921 7v.

Arc 435.54.3F India. Archaeological Survey. Southern Circle, Madras. Annual report of the assistant superintendent for epigraphy. Madras. 1881-1945 9v.

Arc 435.56F India. Archaeological Survey. Uttar Pradesh. Progress reports of the epigraphical and architectural branches. Allahabad. 1887-1905 2v.

Arc 435.58F India. Archaeological Survey. Western Circle, Bombay. Progress report. 1889-1921 3v.

Arc 435.16.2F India. Curator of Ancient Monuments. Plan of Delhi. v.1-15. n.p., 1881.

NEDL Arc 435.16 India. Curator of Ancient Monuments. Preservation of national monuments. v.1-3. Simla, 1882-84.

Arc 432.17 India. Department of Archaeology. Ancient monuments. Delhi, 1957. 6 pam.

Arc 435.54.10F India. Department of Archaeology. Annual report on Indian epigraphy. Delhi. 1945-1964 2v.

Arc 435.2.9F India. Department of Archaeology. South-Indian inscriptions. Madras. 1890-1949 16v.

Arc 432.01 Pamphlet box. India. Miscellaneous pamphlets.

Arc 1227.5 India. National Archives. Indian seals; problems and prospects. New Delhi? 1960.

Arc 416.11 India and the Pacific world. (Nag, K.) Calcutta, 1941.
Arc 1163.4.10 India Office Library. Specimens of Arabic and Persian palaeography. London, 1939.
Arc 432.4 India prehistorica. (Pinto, Christoram.) Lisboa, 1909.
Arc 943.13 The Indian and antiquities of America. (Shipp, B.) Philadelphia, 1897.
Arc 432.2A Indian antiquities. (Maurice, G.) London, 1800. 7v.
Arc 38.20 Indian archaeology; a review. Delhi. 1953+ 7v.
Arc 965.1 Indian archaeology in Saline County, Kansas. (Whiteford, Guy L.) Salina, 1941.
Arc 432.27 Indian archaeology since independence. 1. ed. (Lal, Braj Basi.) Delhi, 1964.
Arc 432.11 Indian architecture. (Burgess, J.) Oxford, 1907.
Arc 943.36F Indian art of the Americas. (Appleton, LeRoy H.) N.Y., 1950.
Arc 953.24A Indian art of the United States. (Douglas, F.H.) N.Y., 1941.
Arc 1418.12 Indian coins. (Rapson, E.J.) Strassburg, 1897.
Arc 458.12 Indian epigraphical glossary. 1. ed. (Sircar, Dineschandra.) Delhi, 1966.
Arc 453.5 Indian epigraphy. (Fleet, J.F.) Oxford, 1907.
Arc 435.86 Indian epigraphy. 1. ed. (Sircar, Dineschandra.) Delhi, 1965.
Arc 432.15 Indian epigraphy and south Indian scripts. (Sivaramamurto, C.) Madra, 1952.
Arc 543.35.15 Indian influences in old Balinese art. (Stutterheim, W.F.) London, 1935.
Arc 435.1.5 Pamphlet box. Indian inscriptions.
Arc 448.1.10 Indian Museum, Calcutta. Catalogue and hand-book of the archaeological collections in the Indian Museum. Calcutta, 1883. 2v.
Arc 435.1.10 Indian Museum, Calcutta. Catalogue raisonné of the prehistoric antiquities. Simla, 1917.
Arc 435.25.3F Indian Museum, Calcutta. A list of the photographic negatives of Indian antiquities. Calcutta, 1900.
Arc 1418.5A Indian Museum. Catalogue of coins in the Indian Museum, Calcutta. Oxford, 1906-08. 3v.
Arc 943.14.8 Indian notes. (N.Y. Museum of the American Indian. Heye Foundation.) N.Y. 1-7,1924-1930 6v.
Arc 943.14.9 Indian notes. Index, v.1-7. (N.Y. Museum of the American Indian. Heye Foundation.) N.Y., 1949.
Arc 943.14.4 Indian notes and monographs. (N.Y. Museum of the American Indian. Heye Foundation.) N.Y. 1-53,1920-1943 20v.
Arc 943.14.3 Indian notes and monographs. (N.Y. Museum of the American Indian. Heye Foundation.) N.Y. 1-10,1919-1928 9v.
Arc 1163.5.25 Indian palaeography. (Dani, A.H.) Oxford, 1963.
Arc 1163.5.20 Indian palaeography. (Pandey, R.B.) Banaras, 1952.
NEDL Arc 1163.5.15 Indian paleography. (Bühler, G.) Bombay, 1904.
Arc 1663.58 Indian peace medals issued in the United States. (Belden, Bauman Lowe.) New Milford, Conn., 1966.
Arc 432.32 Indian prehistory. 1. ed. (Seminar on Indian Prehistory and Protohistory, Deccan College Post Graduate and Research Institute, 1964.) Poona, 1965.
Arc 943.29 Indian relics and their values. (Brown, A.) Chicago, 1942.
Arc 961.1.3 Indian remains in southern Georgia. (Jones, C.C.) Savannah, 1859.
Arc 983.17 Indian rock paintings of the Great Lakes. (Dewdney, Selwya.) Toronto, 1962.
Arc 1227.5 Indian seals; problems and prospects. (India. National Archives.) New Delhi? 1960.
Arc 458.7 Indian serpent-lore. (Vogel, J.P.) London, 1926.
Arc 432.9 Indian temples. (Bruhl, O.) Calcutta, 1937.
Arc 313.1 Indiana. Historical Society, Indianapolis. Prehistory research series. Indianapolis. 1-3,1937-1955 3v.
Arc 943.25 Indianer-Kunst. (Utzinger, Rudolf.) München, 1921.
Arc 969.1.10 Indians of Ohio. (Force, M.F.) Cincinnati, 1879.
Arc 432.14 India's legacy. (Punja, P.R.R.) Mangalore, 1948.
Arc 1027.41.25 Indicazione dei dipinti a buon presco dell'Apostolo S. Paolo. (Moreschi, L.) Roma, 1867.
Arc 757.1 Indicazione topografica di Roma antica. 3. ed. (Canina, Luigi.) Roma, 1841.
Arc 1.14.2 Indice delle dissertazioni e communicazioni. (Accademia...Rome. Accademia Romana di Archeologia.) Roma, 1900.
Arc 1490.4 Indice delle Zecche d'Italia. (Schweitzer, F.) Trieste, 1857.
Arc 740.204.2 Indici dei monumenti etruschi. (Inghirami, F.) Badia, 1826.
Arc 432.23 Indiia v drevnosti; sbornik statei. (Akademiia Nauk SSSR. Institut Narodov Azii.) Moskva, 1964.
Arc 432.12 Indische Frühkulturen und ihre Beziehungen zum Westen. (Mode, Heinz.) Basel, 1944.
Arc 1163.5.10 Indische Palaeographie von Arca. (Bühler, G.) Strassburg, 1896.
Arc 432.35 Indologen-Tagung 1971. (Indologische Arbeitstagung, Museum für Indische Kunst, Berlin, 1971.) Weisbaden, 1973.
Arc 432.35 Indologische Arbeitstagung, Museum für Indische Kunst, Berlin, 1971. Indologen-Tagung 1971. Weisbaden, 1973.
Arc 441.1.3 Indraje, B. Antiquarian remains at Sopârâ and Padana, being an account of the Buddhist Stüpa and Asoka edict. Bombay, 1882.
Arc 938.104 Indreko, Richard. Mesolithische und frühneolithische Kulturen in Osteuropa und Westsebirien. Stockholm, 1964.
Arc 448.1 The Indus civilization. (Mackay, Ernest.) London, 1935.
Arc 448.1.20 The Indus civilization in the Rgveda. (Deshmukh, P.R.) Yeotmal, 1954.
Arc 448.1.25 The Indus Valley and early Iran. (Khan, F.A.) Karachi, 1964.
Arc 895.7 The industrial arts of Denmark. (Worsaae, J.J.A.) London, 1882.
Arc 855.202 The industrial arts of the Anglo-Saxons. (Baye, J. de.) London, 1893.
Arc 736.12 L'inesplorato Monte Albura o Albuchia. (Naselli, S.) Castelbuono, 1952.
Arc 893.17 Influence classique sur le nord pendant l'antiquité. (Engelhardt, C.) Copenhagen, 1876.
Arc 1033.17.99 Informaciones sobre la milagrosa aparición de la virgen de Guadalupe. (Vera, Fortino Hipólito.) Amecameca, 1889.
Arc 302.48 Informator archeologiczny; badania. Warszawa. 1967+ 2v.
Arc 302.52 Informator konserwatora zabytków archeologicznych na Województwo Wrocławskie. Wrocław. 1964+
Arc 740.204.2 Inghirami, F. Indici dei monumenti etruschi. Badia, 1826.
Arc 743.7 Inghirami, F. Lettere di Etrusca erudizione. Poligrafia, 1828.
Arc 740.204 Inghirami, F. Monumenti etruschi. Badia, 1821-25. 9v.
X Cg Arc 888.17 Inheemse en Romeinse terpen. Atlas and plates. (Giffen, Albert Egges van.) Groningen, 1950. 2v.

Arc 1348.79 Initiation à la numismatique. (Tourneur, Victor.) Bruxelles, 1945.
Arc 608.6.70 Initiation à la préhistoire de l'Algérie. (Brahime, Claude.) Alger, 1972.
Arc 547.46 Inleiding lot de oud-Egyptische beschaving. (Leyden. Rijksmuseum van Oudheden.) 's-Gravenhage, 1959.
Arc 889.9 Inleiding tot de Gallo-Romeinsche archeologie der Nederlanden. (Weerd, H. van de.) Antwerpen, 1944.
Arc 895.64 Innan Sverige blev Sverige. (Moberg, Carl Axel.) Stockholm, 1964.
Htn Arc 543.3.15F* Innermost Asia. (Stein, Mark Aurel.) Oxford, 1928. 4v.
Arc 543.3.17F Innermost Asia. (Stein, Mark Aurel.) Oxford, 1928. 4v.
Arc 1580.46 Innsbruck, F. Der Tiroler Taler. Innsbruck, 1963.
Arc 1458.6 An inquiry into the value of the ancient Greek and Roman money. (Raper, M.) London, 1772.
Arc 1298.1 Ins sigillorum mediiaevi. (Guenther, M.) Lipsiae, 1813.
Arc 421.25 Inschrift des Yu. (Yu.) Halle, 1811.
Arc 1027.18.6 Die Inschriften der jüdischen Katakombe. (Müller, Nikolaus.) Leipzig, 1919.
Arc 1030.33 Inschriften der römischen Coemeterien. (Becker, F.) Gera, 1878.
Arc 1478.14 Inschriften und Darstellungen Römus. (Gruman, G.) Biel, 1899.
Arc 530.85 Inschriften und Denkmäler aus Bithynien. (Doerner, F.K.) Berlin, 1941.
Arc 1030.49 Inscrições sepulcrais da sé de Lisboa. (Cordeiro de Sousa, J.M.) Lisboa, 1927.
Arc 843.71 Inscripciones cristianas de la España romana y visigoda. (Vives, José.) Barcelona, 1942.
Arc 843.71.2 Inscripciones cristianas de la España romana y visigoda. 2. ed. (Vives, José.) Barcelona, 1969.
Arc 843.2 Inscripciones romanas que existen en Menorca. (Ramis y Ramis, J.) Mahon, 1817.
Arc 830.156 Pamphlet vol. Inscription d'Auch. 4 pam.
Arc 823.19.170 Inscription de la caserne des Vigiles à Ostie. (Thédenat, H.) Paris, 1904.
Arc 1030.5.31 L'inscription du tombeau d'Hadrien I. (Rossi, G.B. de.) Rome, 1888.
Arc 1033.35.49 Inscription hébräique du titre de S. Croix. 2e éd. (Drach, P.L.B.) Rome, 1831.
Arc 875.32.10 The inscription of Pictland. (Diack, F.C.) Aberdeen, 1944.
Arc 1030.8.17 L'inscription syro-chinois de Si-Ngan-Fou. (Pauthier, G.) Paris, 1858. 2 pam.
Arc 1016.6F Inscriptionae christianae urbis Romae. (Rossi, J. de.) Romae. 1-3 7v.
Arc 1016.6.3F Inscriptionae christianae urbis Romae. Supplement. (Rossi, J. de.) Romae. 1,1925
Arc 1030.52 Inscriptiones. (Cantini, Giuseppe.) Colle, 1844.
Arc 1030.41 Inscriptiones Bononienses. (Galletthio, P.A.) Roma, 1759.
Arc 1030.58F Inscriptiones Britanniae christianae. (Hubner, E.) Berolini, 1876.
Arc 1030.32 Inscriptiones christianae urbis Romae. (Reumont, A.) n.p., 1862.
Arc 1030.51 Inscriptiones graecae christianae veteres occidentes. Diss. inaug. (Wessel, C.) Halae Saxonum, 1936.
Arc 1030.47 Inscriptiones latinae christianae veteres. (Diehl, Ernst.) Berolini, 1924-31. 3v.
Arc 1030.47.5 Inscriptiones latinae christianae veteres. (Diehl, Ernst.) Berolini, 1961- 4v.
Htn Arc 1016.240* Inscriptiones sacrosanctae vetustatis...Romanae. (Apianus, P.) Ingolstadii, 1534.
Arc 822.7 Pamphlet vol. Inscriptions antiques. 15 pam.
Arc 1030.7 Inscriptions byzantines de Mistra. (Millet, G.) Athènes, 1899.
Arc 1030.12 Inscriptions chrétiennes. (Delattre, R.P.) Constantine, 1887.
Arc 1030.48 Inscriptions chrétiennes de la Gaule antérieure au VIIIe siècle. (Le Blant, E.) Paris, 1856-65. 2v.
Arc 1030.11 Inscriptions chrétiennes trouvées en Italie. (Bourquelot, M.F.) n.p., n.d.
Arc 830.117 Inscriptions da la ville de Saint-Maixent du Xe au XIXe siècle. (Lévesque, L.) n.p., n.d.
Arc 1027.25.5 Inscriptions des...Rome chretienne. (Pitra, J.B.) Paris, 1862-92. 3 pam.
Arc 66.1.15 Inscriptions doliaires latines. (Descemet, C.) Paris, 1880.
Arc 66.1.5 Inscriptions du pays des marses. (Fernique, E.) Paris, 1879.
Arc 1030.36 Inscriptions d'un reliquare arménien. (Carrière, A.) Paris, 1883.
Arc 435.11.10 Inscriptions from cave-temples of western India. (Burgess, James.) Bombay, 1881.
Arc 547.27 Inscriptions hiéroglyphiques du Musée national de Copenhague. (Mogensen, M.) Copenhague, 1918.
Arc 823.19.115 Inscriptions latines des fouilles d'Utique. (Thédenat, H.) Vienne, 1882.
Arc 1016.205 Inscritione hispaniae christianae. (Hübner, A.) Berlolini, 1871.
Arc 1016.205.5 Inscritione hispaniae christianarum. Supplement. (Hübner, A.) Berolini, 1900.
Arc 1027.30.15 Inscrizione S. Martire Fortissima nel cimitero...Ciriaca. (Bartolini, D.) Roma, 1842.
Arc 936.20.30 Inseputurite vietii romane. (Pârvan, Vasile.) București, 1923.
Arc 1033.1.4 Insigne...Battesimo d'una fanciulla. (Rossi, G.B. de.) Roma, 1872.
Arc 1027.22.13 Un insigne monumento cristiano del secolo III. (Calori Cesis, F.) Bologna, 1873.
Arc 609.39 Inskeep, R.R. Preliminary investigation of a proto-historic cemetery at Nkudzi Bay, Malawi. Livingstone, 1965.
Arc 843.85 Institución Principe de Viana Pamplona. Excavaciones en Navarra. Pamplona, 1947. 7v.
Arc 94.35 Institucione Fennando el Catolico Seminario de Arqueología y Numismatico Aragonesas. Publicaciones. Zaragoza. 1,1951+ 6v.
Arc 103.1 Institut des Fouilles de Préhistoire et d'Archéologie des Alpes, Mautimes. Bulletin et memoires. Nice. 2-7 4v.
Arc 94.1 Institut d'Estudis Catalans. Anuari. Barcelona. 1907-1931 11v.
Arc 38.40 Institut Ethiopien d'Archéologie. Cahiers. Addis-Ababa. 1,1965+
Arc 530.150 Institut Français d'Archéologie, Istanbul. Phrygie, exploration archéologique. v.1-3. Paris, 1941- 2v.

Author and Title Listing

Arc 38.5F Institut Français d'Archéologie de Stamboul. Mémoires. Paris. 2-7 6v.

Arc 582.2 Institut Français d'Archéologie Orientale du Caire. Bibliothèque d'étude. Le Caire. 1+ 53v.

Arc 582.1 Institut Français d'Archéologie Orientale du Caire. Bulletin. Le Caire. 1,1901+ 48v.

Arc 38.30 Institut Français d'Archéologie Orientale du Caire. Conférences. 3 2v.

Arc 582.9 Institut Français d'Archéologie Orientale du Caire. Fouilles franco-suisses. Rapports. 1-2 2v.

Arc 580.1.2 Institut Français d'Archéologie Orientale du Caire. Mémoires. Le Caire. 1,1902+ 92v.

Arc 582.4F Institut Français d'Archéologie Orientale du Caire. Rapport sur les fouilles d'Abou-Roarch. Le Caire. 1922-1924

Arc 582.5F Institut Français d'Archéologie Orientale du Caire. Rapport sur les fouilles de Dair el Médineh. Le Caire. 1922-1951 10v.

Arc 582.6F Institut Français d'Archéologie Orientale du Caire. Rapport sur les fouilles de Médamoud. Le Caire. 1925-1932 7v.

Arc 582.7F Institut Français d'Archéologie Orientale du Caire. Rapport sur les fouilles de Tell Edfou. La Caire. 1921-1933 2v.

Arc 9.1 Institute Français d'Archeologie Orientale du Caire. Publications. Recherches d'archeologie. Le Caire. 1,1930+ 20v.

Arc 720.211 Instituto archeologica centrum semertria. (Rome. Istituto di Archeologia.) Roma, 1879.

Arc 608.7.9 Instituts pour les recherches préhistoriques. (Pallary, P.) Alger, 1909.

Arc 1020.9.110 Le instituzioni di Pieta...in Roma. v.1-2. (Costanzi, G.) Roma, 1825.

Arc 547.6.20F Instruments de musique. (Hickmann, Hans.) Le Caire, 1949.

Arc 1093.2.6 Les instruments en pierre à l'epoque de métaux. (Baye, J. de.) Paris, 1881.

Arc 1020.9.6 L'integrita del panteon di M. Agrippa. (Fea, Carlo.) Roma, 1807.

Arc 1020.9.6.2 L'integrita del panteon rivendicata a Marco Agrippo. 2a ed. (Fea, Carlo.) Roma, 1820.

Arc 875.2 Interesting Roman antiquities recently discovered in Fife. (Small, A.) Edinbrugh, 1823.

Arc 885.17 Interim report. (Great Britain. Commissions. Ancient and Historical Monuments and Constructions of Wales and Monmouthshire.) London. 9-11,1920-1956

Arc 858.24F Interim report. (Great Britain. Royal Commission on Ancient and Historical Monuments.) London. 1-22 2v.

Arc 612.88 International Archaeological Symposium on the Mesolithic in Europe. The mesolithic in Europe. Wyd. 1. Warsaw, 1973.

Arc 543.3.1 International Conference on the History, Archaeology and Culture of Central Asia in the Kushan Period, Dushanbe, 1968. Sovetskaiia arkheologiia frednei Azii i Kushanskaia problema. v.1-2. Moskva, 1968.

Arc 543.3.1.5 International Conference on the History, Archeology and Culture of Central Asia in the Kushan Period, Dushanbe, 1968. Tsentral'naia Aziia v kushanskuiu spokhu. Moskva, 1974- 2v.

Arc 307.3.2 International Congress of Americanists, 4th, Madrid, 1881. Congreso international de Americanistas. Madrid, 1881.

Arc 307.3.6 International Congress of Americanists, 9th, Madrid, 1892. Congreso internacional de Americanistas. Madrid, 1891.

Arc 307.3.7 International Congress of Americanists, 11th, Mexico, 1895. Congreso de Americanistas. Reunion en Mexico. México, 1895.

Arc 307.3.4 International Congress of Americanists, 17th, Buenos Aires, 1910. Sumarios de la conferencias y memorias presentadas al congreso. Buenos Aires, 1910.

Arc 307.3.9 International Congress of Americanists, 17th, May 1910 (2d meeting, Mexico, Sept. 1910). Reseña de la segunda sesion del XVII Congresso...de Americanistes. México, 1912.

Arc 307.3.10 International Congress of Americanists, 24th, Hamburg, 1930. Internationale Amerikanisten Kongress. Vorläufiges Program. n.p., 1930.

Arc 307.3.15 International Congress of Americanists, 26th, Seville, 1935. Programa. Madrid, 1935.

Arc 307.3.20 International Congress of Americanists, 27th, Mexico, 1939. Boletin. México.

NEDL Arc 307.3.25F International Congress of Americanists, 27th, Mexico and Lima, 1939. Actas. México, 1942-47.

Arc 307.3 International Congress of Americanists. Compte-rendu. 1875+ 60v.

Arc 307.3.5F Pamphlet box. International Congress of Americanists. Miscellaneous pamphlets.

Arc 73.100.5 International Congress of Christian Archaeology, 2nd, Rome, 1900. Atti del II Congresso internazionale...tenuto in Roma nell'aprile 1900. Roma, 1902.

Arc 73.100 International Congress of Christian Archaeology, 2nd, Rome, 1900. Commentarius authenticus. v.1-6. Rome, 1900.

Arc 9.2.1 International Congress of Prehistoric and Protohistoric Sciences, 1st, London, 1932. Proceedings. London, 1934.

Arc 9.2.8 International Congress of Prehistoric and Protohistoric Sciences, 8th, Belgrad, 1971. Actes du VIIIe Congrès international des sciences préhistoriques et protohistoriques. Beograd, 1971- 3v.

Arc 9.2.7 International Congress of Prehistoric and Protohistoric Sciences. Actes du VIIe Congrès international des sciences préhistoriques et protohistoriques. Prague, 1970-71. 2v.

Arc 9.2.6 International Congress of Prehistoric and protohistoric Sciences, 6th, Rome, 1962. Atti del Congresso internazionale. Firenze, 1962.

Arc 923.112 International Congress of Prehistoric and Protohistoric Sciences. 7th, Moscow, 1966. Doklady i soobshchenia arkheologov SSSR. Moskva, 1966.

Arc 936.195.150 International Congress of Prehistoric and Protohistoric Sciences, 7th, Prague. Investigations archéologiques en Tchécoslovaquie. Prague, 1966.

Arc 915.40.3 International Congress of Roman Frontier Studies, 3d, Rheinfelden, Switzerland. Limes-Studien; Vorträge des 3. Internationalen Limes-Kongresses in Rheinfelden. Basel, 1957.

Arc 393.5 International Institute of Intellectural Cooperation. Manuel de la technique des fouilles archéologiques. Paris, 1950.

Arc 1335.110 International medallic exhibition. (American Numismatic Society.) N.Y., 1910.

Arc 1675.22.5 International medallic exhibition of the American Numismatic Society. (American Numismatic Society.) N.Y., 1910.

Arc 1675.22.10 International medallic exhibition of the American Numismatic Society. Catalogue. (American Numismatic Society.) N.Y., 1910.

Arc 93.27 International Mediterranean Research Association. The International Mediterranean Research Association of Rome, Villa Celeniontana. Roma, 1930.

Arc 93.27 The International Mediterranean Research Association of Rome, Villa Celeniontana. (International Mediterranean Research Association.) Roma, 1930.

Arc 1308.7.6 International Numismatic Congress, 6th, Rome, 1961. Congresso internazionale di numismatica, Roma, 11-16 sett., 1961. Roma, 1961-65. 2v.

Arc 1308.7 International Numismatic Congress. Congrès international de numismatique. Paris, 1953-57. 2v.

Arc 1423.26 International Numismatic Convention, Jerusalem, 1963. The patterns of monetary development in Phoenicia and Palestine in antiquity. Tel-Aviv, 1967.

Arc 307.3.10 Internationale Amerikanisten Kongress. Vorläufiges Program. (International Congress of Americanists, 24th, Hamburg, 1930.) n.p., 1930.

Arc 1016.9 Intorno ad alcuni monumenti antichi. (Lugari, G.B.) Roma, 1882.

Arc 726.4.10 Intorno ad una imagine cerea. (Guidobaldi, D. de.) Napoli, 1853.

Arc 1490.50F Intorno alle zecche ed alle monete battute nel reame di Napoli da Re Carlo VIII di Francia. (Fusco, G.V.) Napoli, 1846.

Arc 726.75F Intorno un antico specchio metallico epistola...Cavaaliere Odoardo Gerhard in occasion di sue nozze...Emilia de Riess. (Lanci, Fortunato.) Roma, 1842.

Arc 554.7.2 Introduation to Egyptian archaeology. 2. ed. (Engelbach, Reginald.) Cairo, 1961.

Arc 838.13 Introducção à archeologia da Peninsula Iberica. pt.1. (Simões, A.F.) Lisboa, 1878.

Arc 1433.3 Introductio in rem numariam Muhammedanorum. (Tychsen, O.G.) Rostock, 1794. 2 pam.

Arc 943.9.5 Introduction...study North American archaeology. (Thomas, C.) Cincinnati, 1903.

Arc 1345.5F Introduction a la science des médailles. (Mangeart, Thomas.) Paris, 1763.

Arc 1675.45 Introduction à l'histoire par la connoissance des medailles. (Patin, Charles.) Paris, 1665.

Arc 1200.25 An introduction to ecclesiastical records. (Purvis, J.S.) London, 1953.

Arc 861.51 Introduction to field archaeology...Hampshire. (Williams-Freeman, J.P.) London, 1915.

Arc 1143.2.5A Introduction to Greek and Latin palaeography. (Thompson, Edward Maunde.) Oxford, 1912.

Arc 1190.40 A introduction to James Anderson's Diplomata Scotiae. (Ruddiman, T.) Edinburgh, 1773.

Arc 1138.36 An introduction to palaeography for librarians. (Stieg, Lewis.) Chicago, 1938.

Arc 861.205 An introduction to the archaeology of Cornwall. (Woolf, Charles William.) Truro, 1970.

Arc 861.31.20 Introduction to the archaeology of Wiltshire. (Cunnington, M.E. (Mrs.).) Devizes, 1933.

Htn Arc 1364.1* An introduction to the knowledge of medals. (Jennings, D.) London, 1764.

Htn Arc 1364.1.2* An introduction to the knowledge of medals. 2. ed. (Jennings, D.) Birmingham, 1775.

Arc 400.7 An introduction to the study of prehistoric art. (Parkyn, E.A.) London, 1915.

Arc 968.2.45 An introduction to the study of southwestern archaeology. (Kidder, Alfred V.) New Haven, 1924.

Arc 501.3 Introduction to the survey of Western Palestine. (Saunders, T.) London, 1881.

Arc 1348.1.5 Introductory study of ancient and modern coins. (Akerman, J.Y.) London, 1848.

Arc 1148.38 Introduzione alla paleografia greca. (Mioni, Elpidio.) Padova, 1973.

Arc 810.42.5 Introduzione alla studio di Pompei. (Maiuri, Amedeo.) Napoli, 1949.

Arc 1020.9.33 Inventaire de la chapelle papale sous Paul III en 1547. (Barbier de Montault, X.) Tours, 1878.

Arc 830.47.10 Inventaire des découvertes prohistoriques. Thèse. (Fabre, Gabrielle.) Paris, 1951.

Arc 830.40 Inventaire des menhirs et dolmens de France. Eure. (Coutil, Léon.) Louviers, 1897.

Arc 1433.70 Inventaire des monnaies musulmanes anciennes du musée de Caboul. (Sourdel, D.) Damas, 1953.

Arc 830.39 Inventaire des monuments megalithiques du Calvados. (Coutil, Léon.) Caen, 1902.

Arc 1020.3 Inventaire des objets d'art et d'antique...Bruges. (Bruges, Belgium. Commission Provinciale.) Bruges, 1848.

Arc 1020.80 Inventaire des reliques...l'église metropolitaine de Sens. (Julliot, M.G.) Sens, 1877.

Arc 1020.73.15 Inventaire des reliques de la Sainte-Chapelle. (Douet d'Arco, L.C.) Paris, 1848.

Arc 1020.80.5 Inventaire des sainctes reliques...de St. Pierre-le-Vif de Sens. (Julliot, M.G.) Sens, 1877.

Arc 1263.4 Inventaire des sceaux de la Bourgogné. (France. Direction des Archives.) Paris, 1912.

Arc 1247.2 Inventaire des sceaux de la Flandre. v.1-2. (Demay, G.) Paris, 1873.

Arc 1263.2 Inventaire des sceaux de l'Artois et de la Picardie. v.1-2. (Demay, G.) Paris, 1877-81.

Arc 1269.40 Inventaire des sceaux des archives de la ville de Strasbourg de 1050 à 1300. (Wittmer, C.) Strasbourg, 1946.

Arc 543.2 Inventaire descriptif des monuments du Cambodge. v.1-3 and map. (Lunet de Lagonquiere, E.) Paris, 1902. 4v.

Arc 1020.73.12 Inventaire du trésor...de Saint-Sépulchre de Paris. (Molinier, E.) Paris, 1883.

Arc 1020.13 Inventaire du trésor du Saint Siège. (Molinier, E.) Paris, 1888.

Arc 1470.14.13 Inventaire sommaire de la collection Waddington...1897. (Bibliothèque Nationale, Paris. Département des Médailles et Antiques.) Paris, 1897.

Arc 1470.14.15 Inventaire sommaire de la collection Waddington...1897. (Bibliothèque Nationale, Paris. Département des Médailles et Antiques.) Paris, 1898.

Arc 1500.5.35 Inventaire sommaire des monnaies mérovingiennes de la collection d'Amécourt. (Bibliothèque Nationale, Paris. Département des Médailles et Antiques.) Paris, 1890.

Author and Title Listing

Arc 1433.34 Inventaire sommaire des monnaies musulmanes. (Casanova, Paul.) Paris, 1896.

Arc 1020.88 Inventaires de la Basilique Royale de Monza. (Barbier de Montault, X.) Paris, 1886. 3 pam.

Arc 1020.52.9 Les inventaires de l'Abbaye Saint Pére en Vallés de Chartres. (Mély, F. de.) Paris, 1887.

Arc 543.5 Inventaires des monuments Cams de l'Annam. (Parmentier, H.) Paris, 1909. 2v.

Arc 1020.64.5 Inventaires du trésor de l'église de Lyon. (Valouse, V. de.) Lyon, 1877.

Arc 1020.73.5 Inventaires du trésor de Notre Dame de Paris. (Fagniez, G.) Paris, 1874.

Arc 188.5 Inventar der Bodendenkmäler. (Darmstadt, Germany. Amt für Badenlenkmalpflege im Regierungsbezirk.) 1,1959+

Arc 1027.89 Inventario topografico e bibliografico delle cripte eremitiche basiliane di Puglia. (Gabrieli, Giuseppe.) Roma, 1936.

Arc 1433.45F Inventarnyi katalog musulbmanskikh monet. (Leningrad. Ermitazh.) Sankt Peterburg, 1896.

Arc 505.72.5F Inventoire archéologique de la région au nord-est de Hama. v.1-2. (Lassus, Jean.) Damas, 1935-1936.

Arc 855.211 Inventorium sepulchrale. (Faussett, B.) London, 1856.

Arc 1468.64 An inventory of Greek coin hoards. (Thompson, Margaret.) N.Y., 1973.

Arc 875.52 An inventory of the ancient and historical monuments of Roxburghshire. (Great Britain. Commissions. Ancient and Historical Monuments of Scotland.) Edinburgh, 1956. 2v.

Arc 875.53 An inventory of the ancient and historical monuments of Selkirkshire. (Great Britain. Commissions. Ancient and Historical Monuments of Scotland.) Edinburgh, 1956.

Arc 855.225F An inventory of the ancient monuments in Wales and Monmouthshire. v.1-5,7-8. (Great Britain. Commissions. Ancient and Historical Monuments and Constructions in Wales and Monmouthshire.) London, 1911-37. 4v.

Arc 858.24.11 An inventory of the historical monuments in Buckinghamshire. (Great Britain. Commissions. Ancient and Historical Monuments and Constructions of England.) London, 1912-13. 2v.

Arc 858.24.25 An inventory of the historical monuments in Dorset. v.1,3. (Great Britain. Commissions. Ancient and Historical Monuments and Constructions of England.) London, 1952- 3v.

Arc 858.24.13 An inventory of the historical monuments in Essex. (Great Britain. Commissions. Ancient and Historical Monuments and Constructions of England.) London, 1916-23. 4v.

Arc 858.24.17 An inventory of the historical monuments in Herefordshire. (Great Britain. Commissions. Ancient and Historical Monuments and Constructions of England.) London, 1931-34. 3v.

Arc 858.24.10 An inventory of the historical monuments in Hertfordshire. (Great Britain. Commissions. Ancient and Historical Monuments and Constructions of England.) London, 1910.

Arc 858.24.9 An inventory of the historical monuments in Hertfordshire. (Great Britain. Commissions. Ancient and Historical Monuments and Constructions of England.) London, 1911.

Arc 858.24.15 An inventory of the historical monuments in Huntingdonshire. (Great Britain. Commissions. Ancient and Historical Monuments and Constructions of England.) London, 1926.

Arc 858.24.21 An inventory of the historical monuments in Middlesex. (Great Britain. Commissions. Ancient and Historical Monuments and Constructions of England.) London, 1937.

Arc 858.24.23 An inventory of the historical monuments in the city of Oxford. (Great Britain. Commissions. Ancient and Historical Monuments and Constructions of England.) London, 1939.

Arc 861.160 An inventory of the historical monuments in the city of York. (Great Britain. Commissions. Ancient and Historical Monuments and Constructions of England.) London, 1962. 3v.

Arc 858.24.19 An inventory of the historical monuments in Westmorland. (Great Britain. Commissions. Ancient and Historical Monuments and Constructions of England.) London, 1936.

Arc 815.10 Inventus. (Corte, Matteo della.) Arpino, 1924.

Arc 843.12 Investigaciones acerca de arqueologia y prehistoria de la region salamantina. (Morán Bardon, C.) Salamanca, 1919.

Arc 936.195.150 Investigations archéologiques en Tchécoslovaquie. (International Congress of Prehistoric and Protohistoric Sciences, 7th, Prague.) Prague, 1966.

X Cg Arc 510.8 Investigations at Assos. v.1-2. (American Archaeological Institute.) Cambridge, 1902-21.

Arc 87.1.47 Das ionische Capitell. (Puchstein, O.) Berlin, 1887.

Arc 936.20.5 Ionitä, Ian. Das Gräberfeld von Independenta. Bonn, 1971.

Arc 1016.206.9 Iozzi, Oliviero. Basilica di S. Maria Maggiore. Roma, 1903.

Arc 726.54 Iozzi, Oliviero. Cenno storico della antica Libarna. Pisa, 1890.

Arc 1020.9.60 Iozzi, Oliviero. Le chiese di Roma...nel secolo XIX. Roma, 1900. 4 pam.

Arc 1015.206.9 Iozzi, Oliviero. Cryptae Carciliae trans Tiberim descriptio. 2. ed. Romae, 1902.

Arc 1020.9.64 Iozzi, Oliviero. La reale chiesa del SS. Sudario in Roma. Roma, 1910.

Arc 1015.206.5 Iozzi, Oliviero. Roma sotterranea; il cimitero di S. Castolo M. Roma, 1904.

Arc 1015.206 Iozzi, Oliviero. Supplementa alla Roma sotterranea cristiana. Roma, 1898.

Arc 1020.9.63 Iozzi, Oliviero. La veneranda antica chiesa di S. Andrea e Gregoria. Roma, 1902.

Arc 1016.206 Iozzi, Oliviero. Vetri cimiteriali con figure in oro conservati nell Museo Britannico. Roma, 1900.

Arc 1016.206.3 Iozzi, Oliviero. Vetri cimiteriali con figure in oro conservati nell Museo Sacro Vaticano. Roma, 1900.

Arc 746.8 L'ipoge della famiglia etrusca "Rufia". (Bellucci, G.) Perugia, 1911.

Arc 726.112 L'ipogeo di San Salvatore di Cabras in Sardegna. (Levi, Doro.) Roma, 1949.

Arc 815.8 Ippel, Albert. Der dritte pompejanische Stil. Berlin, 1910.

Arc 810.37 Ippel, Albert. Pompeji. Leipzig, 1925.

Arc 567.1.5 Ippolito Rosellini e il suo giornale della spedizione letteraria toscana in Egitto. (Rosellini, Ippolito.) Roma, 1925.

Arc 726.324 Ipponion; saggio storico-archeologico e nuove osservazioni. (Garoffolo, Francesco.) Reggio Calabria, 1969.

Arc 530.115 Irag. Department of Antiquities. Ctesiphon and Hatra. Baghdad, 1943.

Arc 488.10F Iran in the ancient East. (Herzfeld, Ernst E.) London, 1941.

Arc 30.12.10 Iranian Institute of America. Announcement and outline of program. N.Y., 1930.

Arc 925.13.5 Iranians and Greeks in south Russia. (Rostovtsev, M.I.) Oxford, 1922.

Arc 38.25 Iranica antiqua. Leiden. 1-6 5v.

Arc 38.25.5 Iranica antiqua. Supplements. Leiden. 1,1962

Arc 488.21F Iranische Denkmäler. v.1-4. (Herzfeld, Ernst E.) Berlin, 1932-

Arc 488.31 Die iranischen Feuerheiligtümer. Habilitationsschrift. (Schippmann, Klaus.) Berlin, 1971.

Arc 925.92 Iranova, A.P. Iskusstvo antichnikh gorodov severnogo Prichernomoria. Petrograd, 1953.

Arc 1190.80.5 Irānshahr Husayn, Kazimz ādah. Les chiffres siyâk et la comptabilitié persane. Paris, 1915.

Arc 483.10 Iraq. Department of Antiquities. Excavations at Samarra, 1936-1939. Baghdad, 1940.

Arc 483.5 Iraq. Department of Antiquities. Harba bridge. Baghdad, 1935.

Arc 483.7.2 Iraq. Department of Antiquities. Some works on the antiquities in the Abbasid Palace. 2. ed. Baghdad, 1956.

Arc 1190.9 Írástörténet az írásbeliség felujulása korából. (Hajnal, Istvan.) Budapest, 1921.

Arc 865.7 Ireland, A.J. Stonehenge: story of its building and its legends. London, 1903.

Arc 1125.28PF Ireland. Manuscripts Commission. Facsimiles in collotype of Irish manuscripts. Dublin. 1-6,1931-1954 6v.

Arc 880.24 Ireland in pre-Celtic times. (Macalister, R.A.S.) Dublin, 1921.

Arc 880.36 Ireland's place in prehistoric and early historic Europe. (Bremer, Walther.) Dublin, 1928.

Arc 961.1.20 Irene Mound site, Chatham County, Georgia. (Caldwell, Joseph.) Athens, 1941.

Arc 1077.2.60 Das irische Hochkreuz. Inaug. Diss. (Foerster, Else.) München, 1965.

Arc 880.47F Irish passage graves. (Herity, Michael.) Dublin, 1974.

Arc 858.98 The Irish Sea province in archaeology and history. (Cambrian Archaeological Association, London.) Cardiff, 1970.

Arc 880.39.5A The Irish Stone Age. (Movius, H.L.) Cambridge, Eng., 1942.

Arc 595.19 Irish wisdom preserved in bibles and pyramids. (MacDari, C.) Boston, 1923.

Arc 858.102 Irlandia i Brytania w początkach średniowiecza w świetle badań archeologicznych. (Gąssowski, Jerzy.) Warszawa, 1973.

Arc 858.83 The Iron Age and its hill-forts. Southampton, 1971.

Arc 861.145 The Iron Age camp at Poston. (Anthony, I.E.) Hereford, 1958.

Arc 858.103 Iron Age communities in Britain. (Cunliffe, Barry W.) London, 1974.

Arc 726.250 The iron age culture of Latium. v.2, pt.1. (Gierow, Pär Göran.) Lund, 1964.

Arc 609.24 Iron Age cultures in Zambia. (Fagan, Brian.) London, 1967- 2v.

Arc 432.28 The iron age in India. (Banerjee, N.R.) Delhi, 1965.

Arc 723.15.7 The iron age in Italy. (Randall-McIver, David.) Oxford, 1927.

Arc 870.33 The Iron Age in lowland Britain. (Harding, Derek William.) London, 1974.

Arc 858.82 The Iron Age in Northern Britain. (Council for British Archaeology, London. Iron Age and Roman Research Committees.) Edinbrugh, 1967.

Arc 861.172.5 The Iron Age in the Upper Thames basin. (Harding, Derek William.) Oxford, 1972.

Arc 726.332 The iron age necropolis of Sorbo at Cerveteri. (Pohl, Ingrid.) Lund, 1972.

Arc 609.35 The Iron Age of the southern lake area of Malawi. (Robinson, Keith Radcliffe.) Zomba, 1970.

Arc 895.62 The iron age settlement of Arctic Norway. v.1-2. (Sjoevold, T.) Tromsö, 1962-74.

Arc 969.1.7 Iron from the Ohio mounds. v.2. (Putnam, F.W.) n.p., n.d.

Arc 925.322.5 Isakov, Magomed I. Arkheologicheskie pamiatniki Dagestana. Makhachkala, 1966.

Arc 505.5.54 Isambert, E. Visite au temple de Jerusalem et à la Mosquée d'Omar. Paris, 1860.

Arc 885.15.8 Isca, the Roman legionaryfortress at Caerleon. 3. ed. (Boon, George C.) Cardiff, 1972.

Arc 1030.15 Iscrizione antiche vercellesi. (Bruzza, L.) Roma, 1874.

Arc 1030.5.59 Iscrizione cristiana di Tropea in Calabria. (Rossi, G.B. de.) Roma, 1857. 2v.

Arc 1030.5.40 Iscrizione della statua...di Nicomaco Flaviano Seniore. (Rossi, G.B. de.) Roma, 1849.

Arc 1030.19 L'iscrizione di Abercio. (Zaccheri, G.) Roma, 1898.

Arc 1030.4.19 L'iscrizione di Quirinio. (Marucchi, O.) Siena, 1897.

Arc 1030.14 Iscrizione in onore di Iallia Bassia. (Bruzza, L.) Roma, 1883.

Arc 1016.215.5 Iscrizione in scritta e lingua Nabatea...Madaba. (Rossi, G.B. de.) Roma, 1893.

Arc 1030.5.35 Iscrizione in un spillo d'oso, trovato a Bolsena. (Rossi, G.B. de.) Roma, 1890.

Arc 1016.235 Iscrizioni antiche doliari. (Marini, G.) Roma, 1884.

Arc 1510.168 Isenbeck, Julius. Das nassauische Münzwesen. Münster, 1970.

Arc 830.340F Les isiaques de la Gaule. (Guimet, Émile.) Paris, 1900.

Arc 1027.5.2 Isigni scoperte nel cimitero di Domitilla. (Rossi, G.B. de.) Roma, n.d.

Arc 562.7 Isis; ou, A la recherche de l'Egypte ensevelie. (Montet, Pierre.) Paris, 1956.

Arc 600.47F Der Isistempel von Behbet. pt.2. (Edgar, C.A.) Rom, 1913.

Arc 923.110 Iskhizov, M.D. Zagadki drevnikh Kurganov. Saratov, 1961.

Arc 925.13.8 Iskusstvo. (Rudenko, S.I.) Moskva, 1949.

Arc 925.92 Iskusstvo antichnikh gorodov severnogo Prichernomoria. (Iranova, A.P.) Petrograd, 1953.

Arc 925.13.6 Iskusstvo severnogo Prichernomor'ia. (Blavatskii, V.D.) Moskva, 1947.

Arc 925.8.40 Iskusstvo severnoi prichernomoriia. (Blavatskii, Vladimir D.) Moskva, 1946.

Arc 843.192 Islamische Funde in Balaguer und die Aljaferia in Zaragoza. (Ewert, Christian.) Berlin, 1971.

Arc 530.100 Das Islamische Iznik. (Otto-Dorn, K.) Berlin, 1941.

Arc 1163.4.32 Islamische Schriftkunst. 2. Aufl. (Kühnel, Ernst.) Graz, 1972.

Arc 861.10.20F Isle of Man. Natural History and Antiquarian Society. The Manx archaeological survey; reports. pt.1-6. Douglas, 1909-35.

Arc 493.6.25 Ismizade, O.S. Ialoilutepinskaia kul'tura. Baku, 1950.

Author and Title Listing

Arc 785.73 L'isolamento del Colle Capitolino. (Munoz, A.) Roma, 1943.

Arc 497.85 Israel and her vicinity in the Roman and Byzantine periods. (Applebaum, Shimon.) Tel-Aviv, 1967.

Arc 505.125 Israel Exploration. The expedition to the Judean desert, 1960-1961. Jerusalem, 1963.

Arc 1308.10 Israel numismatic journal. Tel-Aviv. 1,1963

Arc 1423.21 Israel Numismatic Society. The dating and meaning of ancient Jewish coins and symbols. Tel-Aviv, 1958.

Arc 1423.18.10 Israel's history in coins from the Maccabees to the Roman conquest. (Reifenberg, A.) London, 1953.

Arc 1423.30 Israel's 20-year catalog of coins and currency. (Bertram, Fred.) N.Y., 1968.

Arc 736.6.10 Isserlin, B.S.J. Motya, a Phoenician and Carthaginian city in Sicily. Leiden, 1974.

Arc 923.134 Issledovaniia po arkheologii SSSR. (Leningrad. Universitet.) Leningrad, 1961.

Htn Arc 1033.12.54* Ista sunt queda notabilia de passione Christi...de biblia hebreorum. Venetiis, 1506.

Arc 1433.67.2 Istanbul. Asari Atika Müzeleri. Catalogue des monnaies turcomanes. Bologne, 1965.

Arc 1433.67 Istanbul. Asari Atika Müzeleri. Catalogue dis monnaies turcomanes. Constantinople, 1894.

Arc 293.3 Istanbul. Russkii Arkheologicheskii Institut. Izvestiia. Sofiia. 1-9 6v.

Arc 293.3F Istanbul. Russkii Arkheologicheskii Institut. Izvestiia. Sofiia. 10-16// 5v.

Arc 293.3PF Istanbul. Russkii Arkheologicheskii Institut. Izvestiia. Atlas. Sofiia, n.d.

Arc 1433.73.5 Istanbul arkeoloji murelen teşhirdeki islami sikkeler kotalogu. (Artuk, S.) Istanbul, 1970. 2v.

Arc 38.5.5 İstanbul Türk kaleleri. (Gabriel, Albert.) İstanbul, 197-.

Arc 38.35 Istanbuler Mitteilungen. Tübingen. 1,1933+ 8v.

Arc 38.36 Istanbuler Mitteilungen. Beiheft. Tübingen. 1,1966+ 3v.

Arc 678.5 Isthmia; excavations by the University of Chicago. Princeton, N.J., 1971. 2v.

Arc 93.28F Istituto di Archeologia e Storia dell'Arte. Rivista. Roma. 1,1929+ 22v.

Arc 93.40 Istituto di Studi Etruschi e Italici. Quaderni di studi etruschi. Serie 1: Ricerche preistoriche in Etruria. Firenze.

Arc 1308.3 Istituto Italiano di Numismatica, Rome. Annali. 1-24 10v.

Arc 1308.2 Istituto Italiano di Numismatica, Rome. Atti e memorie. Roma. 1-4,1913-1921 2v.

Arc 723.34 Istituto Italiano di Preistoria e Protostoria. Atti della VII riunione scientifica. Firenze, 1963.

Arc 723.34.5 Istituto Italiano di Preistoria e Protostoria. Atti della XI e XII riunione scientifica. Firenze, 1968.

Arc 455.10 Istituto Italiano per il Medio ed Estremo Oriente, Rome. Italian archaeological researches in Asia...Pakistan and Afghanistan, 1956-1959.. Turin, 1960.

Arc 340.2.10 Istituto Nazionale d'Archeologia e Storia dell'Arte, Roma. Biblioteca. Annuario bibliografico di archeologia; opere e periodici. Modena. 1,1952+ 5v.

Arc 1356.8.3 Istituzioni di numismatica antica. 3. ed. (Bernareggi, Ernesto.) Milano, 1973.

Arc 399.4 Istoria archeologiei. (Odobescu, Alexandru Ionescu.) București, 1961.

Arc 1033.17.163 Istoria critica del sagro anello...Perugia. (Cavallucci, V.) Perugia, 1783.

Arc 1033.40.5 Istoria del Martirio di S. Cecilia. (Bartolini, D.) Roma, 1759.

Arc 1033.12.22 Istoria del Santo Sudario. (Baffico, G.F.) Genova, n.d.

Arc 1020.31.9 Istoria del tempio della resurrezione. (Mariti, Giovanni.) Livorno, 1784.

Arc 1033.55.3 Istoria dell'...oratorio...Lateran...Sancta Sanctorum. (Marangoni, G.) Roma, 1798.

Arc 1033.17.71 Istoria della miracolosa immagine...della...vergine di S. Luca. Bologna, 1783.

Arc 1033.17.464 Istoria della miracolosa immagine della...Maria del Carmine...Napoli. Napoli, 1788.

Arc 1033.17.442 Istoria della miracolosa immagine di Nostra Signora di Montenero. (Oberhausen, G.) Lucca, 1745.

Arc 1033.17.245 Istoria dell'immagine di S. Maria di Pozzano. (Ruggieri, S.) Napoli, 1743.

Arc 1190.25.10 Istoria diplomatica che serve d'introduzione all'arte critica in tal materia. (Maffei, Scipione.) Mantova, 1727.

Arc 1190.25.12 Istoria diplomatica che serve d'introduzione all'arte critica in tal materia. (Maffei, Scipione.) Roma, 1964.

Arc 659.5 Istoria tēs archaias Hellēnikēs technēs. (Tsountas, Chrēstos.) Athēnai, 1928.

Arc 672.1.29.5 Istoria tou Krētikou Monseiou kai tōn archaiologikōn ereynōn en Krēte. (Chatzidakēs, I.) Athēnai, 1931.

Arc 1033.17.322 Istoriche notizie...dell'immagine di Maria...di Genazzano. 3. ed. (Orgio.) Roma, 1790.

Arc 292.150 Istorii. (Veselovskii, H.I.) Sankt Peterburg, 1900.

Arc 543.148 Istoriia, arkheologiia i etnografiia srednei Azii. Moskva, 1968.

Arc 925.50.260 Istoriia arkheolohichnoho znannia pro Ukrainu. (Kurinnyi, Petro.) Miunkhen, 1970.

Arc 938.100 Istoriia Baltiki. (Dolukhanov, Pavel M.) Moskva, 1969.

Arc 925.50.250 Istoriia da kul'tura cherniakhivs'kykh veemen dnistro-din'provs'koho mezhyrichchia. (Vynokur, Ion S.) Kyïv, 1972.

Arc 925.321.10 Istoriia drevnei Karelii. (Briusov, Aleksandr I.) Moskva, 1940.

Arc 612.57 Istoriia drevneishei metallurgii Vostochnoi Evropy. (Chernych, Evgenii N.) Moskva, 1966.

Arc 925.50.30 Istoriia i arkheologiia drev. Kryma. (Akademiia Nauk URSR, Kiev. Kryms'kyi Filologicheskii.) Kiev, 1957.

Arc 933.7 Istoriia i kul'tura Vostochnoi Evropy po arkheologicheskim dannym. Moskva, 1971.

Arc 925.50.35 Istoriia ii arkheologiia srednevek. Kryma. (Smirnov, A.P.) Moskva, 1958.

Arc 1076.3.43 Istoriia kolokolov i kolokitenoe iskusstvo. (Olovianishnikov, N.) Moskva, 1912.

Arc 925.50.205 Istoriia kul'tury Zakarpattia na rubezhi nashoi ery. (Bidzilia, Vasyl' I.) Kyïv, 1971.

Arc 543.66 Istoriia material'noi kul'tury uzbekistana. (Abademiia nauk Uzbek SSSR, Tashkend. Institut Istorii i Arkheologii.) Taskhend, 1953- 12v.

Arc 1433.90 Istoriia monetnogo dela Srednei Azii XVII-XVIII vv. (Davidovich, Elena A.) Dushanbe, 1964.

Arc 925.50.345 Istoriia naselennia Peredkarpattia, Podillia i Volyni v kintsi III-na pochatku II tysiacholittia do nashoï ery. (Svieshnikov, Ihor K.) Kyïv, 1974.

Arc 1138.37 Istoriia pis'ma v srednie veka. (Dobiaš-Rozhdestvenskaia, O.A.) Moskva, 1936.

Arc 1285.35 Istorija srpskog grba. (Solovjev, A.V.) Melburn, 1958.

Arc 923.133 Istoriko-arkheologicheskii sbornik. Moskva, 1962.

Arc 493.6.30 Istoriko-khimicheskie i analiticheskie issledovaniia drevnikh predmetov iz mednykh splavov. (Selimkhanov, I.S.) Baku, 1960.

Arc 936.155 Istoriko-kul'turnoe proshloe severnoi Kirgizii. (Bernshtam, A.N.) Frunze, 1943.

Arc 905.5.7 Istria praeromana. (Gnirs, Anton.) Karlsbad, 1925.

Arc 723.17 Italia, le origini. (Sergi, Giuseppi.) Torino, 1919.

Arc 723.19.2 Italia antica. 2a ed. (Seta, Alessandro.) Bergamo, 1928.

Arc 93.21 L'Italia antichissima. Reggio. 1-12,1929-1938

Arc 1488.8F Italia numismatica. (Giesecke, Walther.) Leipzig, 1928.

Arc 455.10 Italian archaeological researches in Asia...Pakistan and Afghanistan, 1956-1959.. (Istituto Italiano per il Medio ed Estremo Oriente, Rome.) Turin, 1960.

Arc 1675.3.7 Italian medal. (Fabriczy, C. von.) London, 1904.

Arc 1486.2 Pamphlet vol. Italian medals. 16 pam.

Arc 726.22.5A Italic hut urns and hut urn cemeteries. (Bryan, W.R.) Rome, 1925.

Arc 726.81F Italic tomb-groups in the University Museum. (Dohan, Edith H.) Philadelphia, 1942.

Arc 723.24 Das italienische Säulenmonument. (Haftmann, W.) Leipzig, 1939.

Arc 1485.5 Die italienischen Schaumünzen der fünfzehnten Jahrhundert. (Friedländer, Julius.) Berlin, 1882.

Arc 726.22.9 Italische Gräberkunde. (Duhn, F. von.) Heidelberg, 1924-39. 2v.

Arc 726.28 Die italischen Rundbauten. (Altmann, W.) Berlin, 1906.

Arc 722.1 Pamphlet box. Italy. Archeology.

Arc 772.9F Italy. Commissione reale per la zona monumentale di Roma. La zona monumentale di Roma e l'opera commissione reale. Roma, 1910.

Arc 750.224F Italy. Commissione reale per la zona monumentale di Roma. La zona monumentale di Roma e l'opera della Commissione reale. Roma, 1914.

Arc 93.25F Italy. Direzione generale della antichità e belle arti. Sull'ordinamento del servizio archeologico. Roma, 1885.

Arc 1675.20.25F Italy. Esercito Corpo di Stato Maggiore. Ufficio Storico. Nel I. centenario della istituzione delle medaglie al valore. Roma, 1933.

Arc 93.5F Italy. Ministero delle Colonie. Notizie archeologico. Roma. 1-3,1916-1922 3v.

Arc 93.25 Italy. Ministero dell'Istruzione Pubblica. L'amministrazione delle antichità e belle arti in Italia. Roma, 1902.

Arc 726.333 Italy. Soprintendenza alle Antichità della Basilicata. Popoli anellenici in Basilicata. Napoli, 1971.

Arc 790.213F Italy. Ufficio Tecnico degli Scavi delle Province Meridionale. Pompei e la regione sotterrata dal Vesuvio nell'anno LXXXIX. Napoli, 1879.

Arc 723.15.15 Italy before the Romans. (Randall-McIver, David.) Oxford, 1928.

Arc 658.3 Ithaka, der Peleponnes und Troja. (Schliemann, H.) Leipzig, 1869.

Arc 785.107 Itinera Romana; Beitrage zur Strassengeschichte des römischen Reiches. Bern. 1-3,1967-1970// 2v.

Arc 562.1 Itinéraire de la Haute-Égypte. (Mariette, A.) Paris, 1880.

Arc 505.130 Itinéraires archéologiques dans la région d'Antioche. (Lafontaine-Dosogne, Jacqueline.) Bruxelles, 1967.

Arc 830.91 Itinéraires gallo-romains dans le département de l'Aisne. (Piette, Amédée.) Léon, 1856-62.

Arc 785.83.15 Itinerari e strade della Venetia Romana. (Bosio, Luciano.) Padova, 1970.

Arc 785.20 Itinerario. Descrizione dei monumenti...Via Appia. Roma, 1854.

Arc 750.204 L'itinerario di Einsiedeln. (Lanciani, R.) Roma, 1891.

Arc 766.4.25 Itinerario di Roma antica. (Lugli, Giuseppe.) Milano, 1970.

Arc 642.5 Itinerarium. (Ciriacus, Pizzicolli.) Florentiae, 1742.

Arc 646.1 The itinerary of Greece: the geography of Ithaca. v.1-2. (Gell, W.) London, 1810.

Arc 925.321.20 Iugo-Vostochnoe Priladozh'e v desiatomtrinadtsatom vekakh. (Kochkurkina, Svetlana I.) Leningrad, 1973.

Arc 505.49F Iukenik, Eleazar L. The ancient synagogue of Beth Alpha. Jeruselem, 1932.

Arc 1494.40 El ius monetae en el condado de Ampurias. (Mateu y Llopis, Felipe.) Perelada, 1957.

Arc 925.50.15 Iuvelirnye izdeliia Khersonesa. (Piatysheva, Natalia V.) Moskva, 1956.

Arc 543.66.50 Iuzhno-Turkmenistanskaia Arkheologicheskaia Ekspeditsiia, 1946-. Perechen' opublikovannykh rabot i materialov po tematike Iuzhno-Turkmenistanskoi Arkheologicheskoi Kompleksnoi Ekspeditsii. Ashkhabad, 1970.

Arc 3.1.24 IV Congresso internazionale d'archéologia; 23-29 settembre 1929. (Congrès International d'Archéologie Classique, 4th, Barcelona, 1929.) Barcelona? 1929.

Arc 936.14.137 IV konferencja w kielcach, 5 kwietnia 1963. (Warsaw. Uniwersytet. Zespol Badan nad Polskim Sredniowieczem.) Warszawa, 1965.

Arc 625.2PF Ivanoff, S.A. Architektonische Studien. Berlin, 1892-95. 4v.

Arc 625.2 Ivanoff, S.A. Architektonische Studien. Berlin, 1892-95. 3v.

Arc 1282.9F Ivanov, I. Sbornik' snimkov's' drevnikh' pechatei. Moskva, 1858.

Arc 682.25.15 Ivanov, Iordan. Bulgarski starini iz Makedoniia. Sofiia, 1908.

VArc 682.25.17 Ivanov, Iordan. Bulgarski starini iz Makedoniia. 2. izd. Sofiia, 1931.

VArc 682.25.19 Ivanov, Iordan. Bulgarski starini iz Makedoniia. 2. izd. Sofiia, 1970.

Arc 1163.3.35 Ivanov, P.I. Sbornik paleograficheskikh snimkov. Moskva, 1844.

Arc 925.332F Ivanov, Petr P. Materialy po istorii Mordvy VIII-IX vv. Moskva, 1952.

Arc 936.42F Ivanov, T. Rimska mozaika ot Ulpiia Eskus. Sofiia, 1954.

Arc 493.9 Ivanov, V.A. Alamut and Lamasar. Teheran, 1960.

Arc 925.12.15 Ivanova, A.P. Skul'ptura i zhivopis' Bospora. Kiev, 1961.

Arc 936.40.20 Ivanova-Mavrodinova, Vera. Preslav. Sofiia, 1963.

Arc 936.140.55 Ivanovskite stenopisi. (Vasiliev, Asen.) Sofiia, 1953.

Arc 1675.19.5 Iversen, I. Beitrag zur russischen Medaillenkunde. St. Petersburg, 1870.

Arc 1675.19.10F Iversen, I. Medaillen auf die Thaten Peter des Grossen. St. Petersburg, 1872.
Arc 1670.3 Iversen, J. Unedited and rare Russian medals. St. Petersburg, 1874.
Arc 861.15.5 Ives, J. Remarks on the Garianorum...Romans. 2. ed. London, 1774.
Arc 861.15 Ives, J. Remarks on the Garianorum...Romans. 2. ed. Yarmouth, 1803.
Arc 1285.35.5 Ivić, Aleksa. Stari srpski pečati i grbovi. Novi Sad, 1910.
Arc 925.4.50 Iz glubiny vekov. (Rizhskii, Mikhail I.) Irkutsk, 1965.
Arc 543.66.55 Iz istorii antichnoi kul'tury Uzbekistana. Tashkent, 1973.
Arc 925.9.140 Iz istorii drevnei metallurgii Kavkaza. (Kashkai, Mir-Ali.) Baku, 1973.
Arc 925.16.15 Iz istorii gorodov i stroitel'nogo isskustva drevnego Kazakhstana. (Margulan, A.K.) Alma-Ata, 1950.
Arc 543.157 Iz istorii iskusstva velikogo goroda. Tashkent, 1972.
Arc 925.322.25 Iz istorii kul'tury Dagestana v epokhu bronzy. (Gadzhiev, Magomed G.) Makhachkala, 1969.
Arc 1584.1.5 Iz istorii monetnogo dela v gruzii XIII veha. (Dzhalaganiia, I.L.) Tbilisi, 1958.
Arc 925.245 Iz istorii Nimfeia VI-III vekov. (Khudiak, M.M.) Leningrad, 1962.
Arc 936.100.15 Iz kdijerke hrvatsbe prostosti. (Karaman, L.) Zagreb, 1930.
Arc 925.13.145 Iz tsarstva Ateia v Neapol' Skifskii. (Shtambok, Anatoii A.) Moskva, 1968.
Arc 612.56 Izobrasheniia cheloveka v paleoliticheskom iskusstve Evrazii. (Abramova, Zoia.) Leningrad, 1966.
Arc 925.13.7 Izobrazheniia raznykh' pamiashchnikov drevnosti. (Vaksel, H.C.L.) Sankt Petersburg, 1801.
Arc 383.81 Izsledvaniia v pamet na Karel Shkorpil. (Bulgarska Akademiia na Naukite, Sofia. Arkheologicheski Institut.) Sofiia, 1961.
Arc 302.21 Izvestiia. (Arkheologichesko Druzhestvo, Sofia.)
Arc 275.70 Izvestiia. (Azebardzhanskii Arkheologicheskii Komitet.) Baku. 2,1926
Arc 302.2.6 Izvestiia. (Bulgarska Akademiia na Naukite, Sofia. Arkheologicheski Institut.) Sofiia. 1,1921+ 28v.
Arc 293.3 Izvestiia. (Istanbul. Russkii Arkheologicheskii Institut.) Sofiia. 1-9 6v.
Arc 293.3F Izvestiia. (Istanbul. Russkii Arkheologicheskii Institut.) Sofiia. 10-16// 5v.
Arc 285.5 Izvestiia. (Kemerovo. Pedagogicheskii Institut. Laboratoriia Arkheologicheskikh Issledovanii.) Kemerovo. 1,1967+ 2v.
NEDL Arc 292.10 Izvestiia. (Russia. Arkheologicheskaia Kommissiia.) Sankt Peterburg. 1-66,1901-1918 21v.
Arc 292.120F Izvestiia. (Russkoe Arkheologicheskoe Obshchestov, Leningrad.) Sankt Peterburg. 1-10,1859-1881// 6v.
Arc 302.2.9.5 Izvestiia. (Varna, Bulgaria. Naroden Muzei.) 1,1965+ 4v.
Arc 302.2.9 Izvestiia. (Varnensko Arkheologichesko Druzhestvo, Stalin.) Stalin. 3-13 10v.
Arc 293.3PF Izvestiia. Atlas. (Istanbul. Russkii Arkheologicheskii Institut.) Sofiia, n.d.
Arc 925.16 Izviestiia Kavkazskago otdieleniia. Vyp. 6 (1921). (Moskovskoe Arkheologicheskoe Obshchestvo.) Tifilis, n.d.
Arc 302.8.9 Izvješće. (Hrvatsko arheološko društvo u Zagrebu.) Zagreb. 1880-1886
Arc 1319.2 Jaarboek. (K. Nederlandsch Genootschap voor Munt en Penningkunde.) Amsterdam. 1-26,1914-1939 9v.
Arc 1588.1.31 Jabłoński, Tadeusz. Katalog monet polskich, 1765-1864. Warszawa, 1965.
Arc 900.204 Jabornegg-Altenfels. Kärnten's römischen Alterthümer. Klagenfurt, 1870.
Arc 1588.4.60 Jáchymovská mincovna v první polovině 16. století, 1519/20-1561. (Nemeškal, Lubomir.) Praha, 1964.
Arc 861.61 Jack, G.H. Excavations on the site of the Romano-British town of Magna, Kenchester. Hereford, 1916.
Arc 505.39A Jack, J.M. Samaria in Ahab's time. Edinburgh, 1929.
Arc 1033.12.210 Jacob, J.N. Disputatio theologica de Vulneribus Christi. Wittenbergae, 1663.
Arc 845.206F Jacob, Karl H. Zur Prähistorie Nordwest-Sachsens. Halle an der Saale, 1911.
Arc 1010.17 Jacob, Teuku. Some problems pertaining to the racial history of the Indonesian region. Utrecht, 1967.
Arc 915.4.5 Jacob-Kolb, G. Recherches historiques sur les antiquités d'Augst. Rheims, 1823.
Arc 853.10.5 Jacobi, H. Führer durch das Römerkastell Saalburg. 4. Aufl. Homburg, 1908.
Arc 853.11 Jacobi, L. Das Römerkastell Saalburg. Text und plates. Homburg vor der Höhe, 1897 2v.
Arc 1413.5 Jacobs, N.G. Japanese coinage. N.Y., 1953.
Arc 618.8 Jacobsthal, P. Imagery in early Celtic art. London, 1941.
Arc 746.11F Jacobsthal, Paul. Die Bronzeschnabelkannen. Berlin, 1929.
Arc 530.90.5 Jacopi, G. Dalla Paflagonia alla Commagene. Roma, 1936.
Arc 530.90 Jacopi, G. Esplorazioni e studi in Paflagonia e Cappadocia. Roma, 1937.
Arc 726.220 Jacopi, Giulio. L. Munazio Planco e il suo mausoleo a Gaeta. Milano, 1960.
Arc 726.210 Jacopi, Giulio. I ritrovamenti dell'antro cosiddetto "di Tiberio" a Sperlongo. Roma, 1958.
Arc 1020.83 Jadart, H. Les anciens pupitres de Rheims. n.p., n.d.
Arc 1076.3.85 Jadart, Henri. Le Bourdon de Notre-Dame de Reims. Reims, 1884.
Arc 1084.7 Jade; its philosophy. (Alexander, R.) N.Y., 1928.
Arc 1084.19 Jade lore. (Goette, J.A.) N.Y., 1937.
Arc 1508.15.10 Jaeger, Kurt. Berwertungstablellen der deutschen Reichsmünzen seit 1871. Basel, 1957.
Arc 1508.15.20 Jaeger, Kurt. Die deutschen Münzen seit 1871. 6. Aufl. Basel, 1967.
Arc 1508.15.5 Jaeger, Kurt. Die deutschen Reichsmünzen seit 1871. Basel, 1956.
Arc 1508.15.15 Jaeger, Kurt. Die Münzprägungen der deutschen Staaten von Einführung des Reichswährung. v.3. Basel, 1967.
Arc 1504.20.5 Jaeger, Kurt. Die Münzprägungen der letzten Monarchien des teutschen Bundes von 1815. Fürstentum Liechtenstein. Basel, 1963.
Arc 1508.15 Jaeger, Kurt. Die neuren Münzprägungen der deutschen Staaten. pt.1-2,3-4,8,9,10,11,12. Stuttgart, 1951-72. 12v.
Arc 609.20 Jaeger, Otto. Antiquities of north Ethiopia. Brockhaus, 1965.
Arc 493.35 Jaenichen, H. Bildzeichen der königlichen Hoheit bei den iranischen Völkern. Bonn, 1956.
Arc 1190.1.9 Jaffé, P. Diplomata quadraginta. Berlin, 1863.
Arc 628.2 Jahn, O. Socrate et Diotime. Greifswald, 1846. 9 pam.
Arc 394.1 Jahn, Otto. Aus der Alterthumswissenschaft. Bonn, 1868.
Arc 391.2.17 Jahn, Otto. Eduard Gerhard. Berlin, 1868.
Arc 394.1.6 Pamphlet vol. Jahn, Otto. Collection of articles on art and archaeology. 16 pam.
Arc 394.1.5 Pamphlet vol. Jahn, Otto. Collection of articles on art and archaeology. 17 pam.
Arc 73.11 Jahrbuch. (Archäologisches Institut des Deutschen Reichs.) Berlin. 1,1886+ 23v.
Arc 77.5 Jahrbuch. (Munz. Römisch-Germanisches Zentralmuseum.) 1,1954+ 99v.
Arc 73.11.10 Jahrbuch. Bibliographie, Register, 1-50. (Archäologisches Institut des Deutschen Reichs.) Berlin, 1904-21. 4v.
Arc 73.12 Jahrbuch. Ergänzungsheft. (Archäologisches Institut des Deutschen Reichs.) Berlin. 1,1888+ 22v.
Arc 39.2 Jahrbuch für kleinasiatische Forschung. Heidelberg. 1-3 3v.
Arc 1309.5 Jahrbuch für Numismatik und Geldgeschichte. München. 1,1949+ 8v.
Arc 173.1 Jahresbericht. (Schweizerische Gesellschaft für Urgeschichte, Zürich.) Zürich. 1,1909+ 23v.
Arc 52.4 Jahresbericht. (Vooraziatisch-Egyptische Gezelschap "Ex Oriente Lux".) Leiden. 3,1935+ 10v.
Arc 203.5 Jahresgabe. (Stendal, Germany. Altmarkisches Museum.) 2v.
Arc 65.2.5 Jahreshefte. (Oesterreich-Archäologisches Institut, Wien.) Vienna. 1,1898+ 37v.
Arc 1200.23 Die Jahresmerkmale in den Datierungen der Papsturkunden bis zum Ausgang des 11. Jahrhundert. Inaug. Diss. (Menzer, Anne.) Berlin, 1932.
Arc 194.1 Jahresschrift für die Vorgeschichte der sächsisch-thüringischen Länder. Halle. 1,1902+ 39v.
Arc 194.1.2 Jahresschrift für die Vorgeschichte der sächsisch-thüringischen Länder. Register. v.1-32, 1954. Halle, n.d.
Arc 600.35.15 Ein Jahrzehnt deutscher Ausgrabungen in einer ägyptischen Stadtruine. (Roeder, Günther.) Hildesheim, 1951.
X Cg Arc 435.2.20F The Jain stûpa and other antiquities of Mathûra. (Smith, V.A.) Allahabad, 1901.
Arc 1088.1.6 Jal, A. Archéologie navale. Paris, 1840. 2v.
Arc 885.5 James, C.H. Excavations at Gelli Gaer camp. Cardiff, 1899?
Arc 595.4 James, H. Notes on the Great Pyramid of Egypt. Southampton, 1869. 2 pam.
Arc 855.212 James, H. Plans and photographs of Stonehenge. n.p., 1867.
Arc 587.11 James, Thomas Garnet H. The mastaba of Khentika called Ikhekhi. London, 1953.
Arc 559.4 James, Thomas Garnet Henry. The archaeology of ancient Egypt. London, 1972.
Arc 1675.56 James and William Tassie. (Gray, J.M.) Edinburgh, 1894.
Arc 1458.15 Jameson, R. Collection of monnaies grecques et romaines. v.1-2. Paris, 1913. 3v.
Arc 936.14.80 Jamka, Rudolf. Kraków w pradziejach. Wrocław, 1963.
Arc 936.14.185 Jamka, Rudolf. Pierwsi mieszkancy Gornego Slaska w swietle badan archeologicznych. Katowice, 1965.
Arc 402.10.25 Jamot, Paul. Theodore Reinach, (1860-1928). Paris, 1928.
Arc 905.75 Jandaurek, H. Die Strassen der Römer. Wels, 1951.
Arc 1335.64 Jandolo et Lavazzi, Rome, auctioneers. Vente aux enchères publiques de la collection de médailles grecques. Roma, 1908.
Arc 893.27F Jankuhn, H. Denkmaler der Vorzeit zwischen Nord- und Ostsee. Schleswig, 1957.
Arc 66.1.181 Jannoray, Jean. Enserune. Paris, 1955.
Arc 673.1.25F Jannosay, J. Le gymnase de Delphes. Thèse. Paris, 1953.
Arc 1330.9 Janovský, Hubert. Katalog knihovny. Numismatické společnosti československé v Praze. vyd. 1. Praha, 1967.
Arc 936.195.60 Janšak, Stefan. Základy archeolog. vyskumu v teréne. Bratislava, 1955.
Arc 543.78F Janse, Olov R.T. Archaeological research in Indo-China. Cambridge, 1947- 2v.
Arc 895.26 Janse, Olov Robert. Le travail de l'or en Suède à l'époque mérovingienne. Orléans, 1922.
Arc 936.195.130 Jansová, Libuše. Hrazany, Keltské oppidum na Sedlčansku. Praha, 1965.
Arc 1364.2 Janssen, A.J. Het antieke tropaion. Ledeberg, 1957.
Arc 1025.22 Janssen, L.J.F. Over de catacomben van Rome. Utrecht, 1854.
Arc 700.33 Jantzen, Ulf. Griechische Greifenkessel. Berlin, 1955.
Arc 1033.12.133 Janvier. Culte de la sainte-face à S. Pierre du Vatican. Tours, 1883.
Arc 424.01 Pamphlet box. Japan. Miscellaneous pamphlets.
Arc 426.12 Japan before Buddhism. (Kidder, J.E.) London, 1959.
Arc 421.14 Japanese archaeological work on the Asiatic continent. (Reischauer, E.O.) Baltimore, 1940.
Arc 1413.5 Japanese coinage. (Jacobs, N.G.) N.Y., 1953.
Arc 1412.5 Japanische Bildermünze. (Fonahn, Adolf.) Leipzig, 1934.
Arc 66.1.130 Jardé, A. Les céréales dans l'antiquité grecque. Paris, 1925.
Arc 810.64 Jashemski, Stanley A. Pompeii and the region destroyed by Vesuvius in A.D. 79. Garden City, 1965.
Arc 936.14.310 Jaskanis, Danuta. Pradzieje Białostocczyzny. wyd. 1. Warszawa, 1969.
Arc 853.256F Die Jastorf Kultur in der Kreisen. (Krueger, Heinrich.) Neumünster, 1961.
Arc 501.15.8 The Jaulân. (Schumacher, G.) London, 1888.
Arc 853.2 Jaumann, V. Colonia Sumlocenne-Rottenburg am Neckar unter die Roemern. Stuttgart, 1840.
Arc 497.21 Jaussen, Antonin J. Mission archéologique en Arabie. v.1-3 et Atlas. Paris, 1909-22. 4v.
Arc 1663.64 Jaworski, Franciszek. Medalionej polskie. Lwow, 1911.
Arc 383.46.5 Jażdżewski, Konrad. Liber Iosepho Kostrzewski octogenario a veneratoribus dicatur. Wrocław, 1968.
VArc 412.11 Jażdżewski, Konrad. Ochrona zabytków archeologicznych. Warszawa, 1966.
Arc 936.14.165A Jazdzewski, Konrad. Poland. London, 1965.
Arc 1027.25.61 Jean-Baptiste de Rossi. (LeBlant, E.) Paris, 1894.
Arc 1675.57 Jean-Baptiste Nini. (Storelli, A.) Tours, 1896.
Arc 1675.16 Jean de Candida. (De La Tour, H.) Paris, 1895.
Arc 957.1.15 Jeancon, J.A. Archaeological research in the northeast San Juan basin of Colorado. Denver, 1922.
Arc 608.25F Jebel Moya. (Addison, F.) London, 1949. 2v.
Arc 830.1.5 Jéhan, L.F. La Bretagne. Tours, 1863.
Arc 505.5.37 Jehuda Leon, J. De templo Hierosolymitano. Helmaestadi, 1665.

Author and Title Listing

Arc 905.4.15 Jelić, Luka. Raccolta di documenti relativi ai monumenti artistici di Spalato e Salona. Spalato, 1894.
Arc 1364.3 Jeločnik, Aleksander. Čenturska zakladna najdba folisov maksencija in tetrarhije. Ljubljana, 1973.
Arc 1468.63 Jenkins, G. Kenneth. Ancient Greek coins. London, 1972.
Arc 1190.10F Jenkinson, H. The later court hands in England. Test and atlas. Cambridge, 1927. 2v.
Arc 1175.12FA Jenkinson, H. Palaeography and...study of court hand. Cambridge, 1915.
Htn Arc 1364.1* Jennings, D. An introduction to the knowledge of medals. London, 1764.
Htn Arc 1364.1.2* Jennings, D. An introduction to the knowledge of medals. 2. ed. Birmingham, 1775.
Arc 900.208 Jenny, S. Die römische Begräbnisstätte von Bugant. Wien, 1898.
Arc 559.1 Jéquier, G. Manuele d'archéologie egyptienne. Paris, 1924.
Arc 600.70 Jéquier, Gustave. Douze ans de fouilles dans la nécropole memphite, 1924-1936. Neuchâtel, 1940.
Arc 600.72F Jéquier, Gustave. Fouilles à Saqqarah. La Caire, 1928.
Arc 600.71F Jéquier, Gustave. Fouilles à Saqqarah. Le Caire, 1928.
Arc 612.1 Jernalderens Begyndelse i nord Europa. (Undset, F.) Kristiania, 1881.
Arc 1033.12.239 Jerphanion, G. de. Le calice d'Antioche. Rome, 1926.
Arc 1018.46 Jerphanion, G. de. La voix des monuments. Paris, 1930.
Arc 1018.46.5 Jerphanion, G. de. La voix des monuments. Rome, 1938.
Arc 500.1 Jerusalem. (Warren, C.) London, 1884.
Arc 505.5.105 Jerusalem: excavating 3000 years of history. (Kenyon, Kathleen M.) London, 1967.
Arc 505.84F Jerusalem. Hebrew Community. Hazor. v.1-4. Jerusalem, 1958. 3v.
Arc 505.5.66 Jérusalem de l'Ancien Testament. Pt.1-3. (Vincent, Louis H.) Paris, 1954. 3v.
Arc 495.201 Jerusalem explored. (Pierotti, E.) London, 1864. 2v.
Arc 505.5.60 Jerusalem in Bible times. (Paton, Lewis B.) Chicago, 1913.
Arc 505.5.120 Jerusalem in the Old Testament; researches and theories. (Simons, Jan Jozef.) Leiden, 1952.
Arc 505.5.65F Jérusalem sous terre. (Vincent, Louis H.) Londres, 1911.
Arc 1510.133 Jesse, W. Die Münzen der Stadt Braunschweig von 1499 bis 1680. Braunschweig, 1962.
Arc 1510.50 Jesse, Wilhelm. Münz- und Geldgeschichte Niedersachsens. Braunschweig, 1952.
Arc 1510.39 Jesse, Wilhelm. Der zweite Brakteatenfund von Mödesse und die Kunst der Brakteaten zur Zeit Heinrichs des Löwen. Braunschweig, 1957.
Arc 390.4 Jesse Walter Fewkes. (Swanton, J.R.) Washington, 1931.
Arc 861.89 Jessup, Ronald F. Archaeology of Kent. London, 1930.
Arc 861.198 Jessup, Ronald-Ferederick. South east England. London, 1970.
Arc 858.86 Jessup, Ronald Frederick. Age by age. London, 1967.
Arc 858.88 Jessup, Ronald Frederick. The story of archaeology in Britain. London, 1964.
Arc 1033.12.126 Jesu...coronam spineam. (Schreck, J.A.) Lipsiae, n.d.
Arc 1033.12.6 Jesus Christ. Narrazione critico storica della reliquia...Santissimo Prepuzio. Roma, 1802.
Arc 1528.3 Le jeton historique des dix-sept provinces des Pays-Bas. (Dingniolle, J.F.) Bruxelles, 1876-77. 2v.
Arc 1670.5 Les jetons des Doyens...de Paris. (Fournie, H.) Chalon-sur-Saone, 1907.
Arc 1500.25 Jetons des états de Bourgogne. (Rossignol.) Autun, 1851.
Arc 1670.51 Jetons et méreaux depuis Louis IX...consulat. (Feuardent, F.) Paris, 1904. 2v.
Arc 1670.51.2 Jetons et méreaux depuis Louis IX...plandres. (Feuardent, F.) London, 1907.
Arc 1500.1 Jeuffrain, A. Essai d'interpretation...médailles...celtes-gaulois. Tours, 1846.
Arc 1081.1 Jewett, L. Grave mounds and their contents. London, 1870.
Arc 1423.10.5 Jewish coins. (Reinach, Théodore.) London, 1903.
Arc 1423.23 Jewish coins of the second temple period. (Meshorer, Va'akov.) Tel-Aviv, 1967.
Arc 505.149 Jewish ossuaries: reburial and rebirth. (Meyers, Eric Mark.) Rome, 1971.
Arc 1423.17 Jewish symbols on ancient Jewish coins. (Romanoff, P.) Philadelphia, 1944.
Arc 1335.151 Jewish Theological Seminary. Great Jewish portraits in metal. N.Y., 1963.
Arc 858.43 Jewitt, L. Half-hours among some English antiquities. London, 1877.
Arc 1538.19 Jewitt, L. Handbook of English coins. London, 1879.
Arc 505.77.5 Jidejian, Nina. Byblos through the ages. Beirut, 1968.
Arc 843.227 Jimenez Cisneros, Maria Josefa. Historia de Cadiz en la antigüedad. Cadiz, 1973.
Arc 497.51 Jirku, Anton. Der Ausgrabungen in Palästina und Syrien. Halle, 1956.
Arc 497.51.5 Jirku, Anton. Von Jerusalem nach Ugarit. Graz, 1966.
Arc 1348.18 Joachim, J.F. Unterricht von dem Münzwesen. Halle, 1754.
Arc 1348.7.2 Jobert, L. The knowledge of medals. London, 1697.
Arc 1348.7.3 Jobert, L. Notitia rei nummariae. Leipzig, 1695.
Arc 1348.7 Jobert, L. La science des médailles. Paris, 1715.
Arc 1348.7.1 Jobert, L. La scienza delle medaglie. Venezia, 1756. 2v.
Arc 1675.53F Jocelyn, Arthur. The orders, decorations and medals of the world. London, 1934.
Arc 925.4.13F Jochelsen, W. Archaeological investigations in Kamchatka. Washington, 1928.
Arc 830.346 Joffroy, René. Le trésor de Vix; histoire et portée d'une grande découverte. Paris, 1962.
Arc 407.30.10 Johann Joachim Winckelmann, 1768-1968. Bad Godesberg, 1968.
Arc 726.17 Johanneau, E. Lettre...sur l'inscription...du Lion de Venise. n.p., 1808.
Arc 390.5.5 Johannes Ficker. (Thulin, Oskar.) Halle, 1936.
Arc 612.17 Johansen, K. Friis. De forhistoriske tider i Europa. København, 1927. 2v.
Arc 385.5 John Allen. (Walker, John.) London, 1956?
Arc 684.9 John Hopkins University. Excavations at Olynthus. Baltimore, 1929-52. 14v.
Arc 1077.5 Johns, C.H.W. Ur-Engur. Treatise on canephorous statues. N.Y., 1908.
Arc 1675.96F Johns Hopkins University. Medals relating to medicine and allied sciences in the numismatic collection. Baltimore, 1964.
Arc 505.45.5 Johnson, J. Dura studies. Philadelphia, 1932.
Arc 600.48 Johnson, J. de M. Antinoë and its papyri; excavations by the Graeco-Roman branch, 1913-14. London, 1914.
Arc 1613.20 Johnson, J.B. Auction prices: "United States coins." 3. ed. Cincinnati, 1944.
Arc 609.1.20 Johnson, J.P. The pre-historic period in South Africa. London, 1912.
Arc 1675.3.9 Johnson, Stephen C. Le rivendicazioni italiane del Trentino...nelle medaglie. Milano, 1919-20.
Arc 609.15 Johnson, Townley. Rock painting of the southwest Cape. Capetown, 1959.
Arc 858.14 Johnson, W. Folk-memory. Oxford, 1908.
Arc 861.23.7 Johnson, Walter. Neolithic man in northeast Surrey. London, 1903.
Arc 861.23.5 Johnston, P.M. Schedule of antiquities in the county of Surrey. London, 1913.
Arc 861.192 Joint Excavation Committee of the Wakefield Corporation and the Wakefield Historical Society. Sandal Castle; a short account of the history of the site and the 1964 excavations. Wakefield, Eng., 1965.
Arc 861.192.5 Joint Excavation Committee of the Wakefield Corporation and the Wakefield Historical Society. Sandal Castle excavations, 1967. Wakefield, Eng., 1967?
Arc 505.66.10 Joint Expedition of the British School of Archaeology. Excavations at Jerico. London, 1960. 2v.
Arc 505.57 Joint Expedition of the British School of Archaeology in Jerusalem. The stone age of Mount Carmel. Oxford, 1937-1939. 2v.
Arc 505.124F Joint Expedition of the University of Rome and the Hebrew University. Excavations at Ramat Rahel, seasons 1959 and 1960. Rome, 1962.
Arc 505.124.2F Joint Expedition of the University of Rome and the Hebrew University. Excavations at Ramat Rahel, seasons 1961 and 1962. Rome, 1964.
Arc 820.212.5F Jollois, J.B.P. Mémoire sur guelques antiquités...des Vosges. Paris, 1843.
Arc 820.212F Jollois, J.B.P. Mémoire sur les antiquités du département du Loiret. Paris, 1836.
Arc 545.17 Jomard, E.F. Description générale de Memphis et des Pyramides. Paris, 1829.
Arc 961.1 Jones, C.C. Aboriginal structures in Georgia. Washington, 1878. 2 pam.
Arc 961.1.5 Jones, C.C. Antiquities of the southern Indians. N.Y., 1873.
Arc 961.1.3 Jones, C.C. Indian remains in southern Georgia. Savannah, 1859.
Arc 961.1.4 Jones, C.C. Monumental remains of Georgia. Savannah, 1861.
Arc 855.215 Jones, I. Most notable antiquity of Great Britain called Stone-Heng. London, 1725.
Htn Arc 865.9* Jones, Inigo. The most notable antiquity of Great Britain. London, 1655. 2 pam.
Htn Arc 865.9.5* Jones, Inigo. The most notable antiquity of Great Britain. London, 1655.
Arc 865.9.11 Jones, Inigo. The most notable antiquity of Great Britain called Stone-Heng. Farnborough, 1971.
Htn Arc 865.9.10F* Jones, Inigo. The most notable antiquity of Great Britain called Stone-Heng. London, 1725.
Arc 609.1.27 Jones, Neville. The prehistory of southern Rhodesia. Cambridge, Eng., 1949.
Arc 547.7 Jones, O. Description of the Egyptian court erected in the Crystal Palace. London, 1854.
Arc 600.4.9 Jong, E.F.P. Scherben aus Naukratis. Proefschrift. n.p., 1925.
Arc 1353.6 Jonge, J.C. de. Notice sur le cabinet des médailles et des pierres gravées de...roi des Pays-Bas. La Haye, 1824.
Arc 1530.15 Joodse penningen in de Nederlanden. (Polak, Arthur.) Amsterdam, 1958.
Arc 843.199F Jordá Cerdá, F. Las murias de Beloño. Oviedo, 1957.
Arc 785.14 Jordan, Henri. Capitol, Forum und Sacra Via in Rom. Berlin, 1881.
Arc 785.12 Jordan, Henri. Der capitolinische Plan der Stadt Rom. Berlin, 1867.
Arc 764.1.2 Jordan, Henri. De formae urbis Romae...novo disputatio. Roma, 1883.
Arc 750.29 Jordan, Henri. Forma urbis Romae. Berolino, 1874.
Arc 785.1 Jordan, Henri. Tempel der Vesta und das Haus der Vestalinnen. Berlin, 1886.
Arc 764.1 Jordan, Henri. Topographie der Stadt Rom in Alterthum. v.1-2. Berlin, 1878. 4v.
Arc 87.1.25 Jordan, Henri. Vesta und die Laren auf einem pompischen Wandgemälde. Berlin, 1865.
Arc 505.74 Jordan. Department of Antiquities. Annual. 1-9 2v.
Arc 505.68.10 Jordan. Department of Antiquities. Official guide to Jerash. Jerusalem, 194-?
Arc 630.3 Jordt, H. Untersuch über Silikat und Carbenatbiblung in antiken Morteln. Leipzig, 1906.
Arc 1411.12 Jorgensen, Holgar. Old coins of China. n.p., 19- .
Arc 1027.21.5 Jorio, A. de. Notzie sulle crepte...San Gennaro di Poveri. v.1-2. Napoli, 1833-39.
Arc 726.4 Jorio, A. de. Scheletri cumani. Napoli, 1810.
Arc 810.48.10 Jorio, Andrea. Guida di Pompei. Napoli, 1836.
Arc 810.48 Jorio, Andrea. Plan de Pompéi. Naples, 1828.
Arc 838.40.2 Jornadas Arqueológicas, 2nd, Lisbon, 1972. Actas. Lisboa, 1973.
Arc 838.40 Jornadas Arqueológicas. Actas. Lisboa, 1970. 2v.
Arc 443.4 Joseph, P. The Dravidian problem in the south Indian culture complex. Bombay, 1972.
Arc 1510.23.5 Joseph, Paul. Die Medaillen und Münzen der Wild- und Rheingrafen Fürsten zu Salm. Frankfurt am Main, 1914.
Arc 1510.23 Joseph, Paul. Die Münzen von Worms. Darmstadt, 1906.
Arc 865.16 Jottings on some of the objects of interest in the Stonehenge excursion. (Stevens, E.T.) Salisbury, 1882.
Arc 1500.49 Joubert, André. Les monnaies anglo-françaises. Mamers, 1886.
Arc 530.11 Joubin, André. De sarcophagis Clazomeniis. Paris, 1901.
Arc 66.1.104 Jouguet, P. La vie municipale dans l'Égypte Romaine. Paris, 1911.
Arc 830.96 Joulin, Léon. Les établissements gallo-romaines de la plaine de Martres-Tolosanes. Paris, 1901.
Arc 125.9 Journal. (Antiquarian Association of the British Isles.) London. 1-3,1930-1932
Arc 66.11 Journal. (British and American Archaeological Society of Rome.) Rome.
Arc 125.4.3 Journal. (British Archaeological Association.) London. 1+ 96v.
Arc 1311.1 Journal. (Liverpool Numismatic Society.) Liverpool. 1-2,1873-1877
Arc 1308.5 Journal. (Numismatic Society of India.) Calcutta. 1,1939+ 12v.

Author and Title Listing

	Arc 74.4.1	Journal. Index. v.9-42. (Society for the Promotion of Hellenic Studies.) London, 1898-1923. 3v.
	Arc 74.4.1.5	Journal. Numismatic index, 1880-1969. (Society for the Promotion of Hellenic Studies.) Cambridge, Eng., 1971.
	Arc 74.4.2F	Journal. Plates 1-83. v.1-8. (Society for the Promotion of Hellenic Studies.) London, 1888?
	Arc 1309.1	Journal international d'archéologie numismatique. Athenes. 1-21,1898-1927// 12v.
	Arc 1309.1.5	Journal international d'archéologie numismatique. Analytical index. 1898-1927. N.Y., 1967.
	Arc 513.12	Journal of a tour in Asia Minor. (Leake, William M.) London, 1824.
	Arc 652.1	Journal of a tour in Greece. (Mure, W.) Edinburgh, 1842. 2v.
	Arc 39.1	Journal of Egyptian archaeology. London. 17,1931+ 38v.
	Arc 74.4	Journal of Hellenic studies. (Society for the Promotion of Hellenic Studies.) London. 1,1880+ 60v.
	Arc 74.5	Journal of Roman studies. London. 1,1911+ 47v.
	Arc 74.5.3	Journal of Roman studies. London. 13-28,1923-1938 16v.
	Arc 74.5.2	Journal of Roman studies. Consolidated index, v.21-60. London, 1955-75. 2v.
	Arc 74.5.2.5	Journal of Roman studies. Numismatic index, 1911-65. Cambridge, Eng., 1970.
	Arc 488.1.5	Journal of the British embassy to Persia. (Price, W.) London, 1832.
	Arc 488.1	Journal of the British embassy to Persia. v.1-2. (Price, W.) London, 1832.
	Arc 103.5	Journées Archéologiques d'Avignon, Avignon, 1956. Journées archéologiques d'Avignon. Avignon, 1957.
	Arc 103.5	Journées archéologiques d'Avignon. (Journées Archéologiques d'Avignon, Avignon, 1956.) Avignon, 1957.
	Arc 104.5	Journées Archéologiques Internationales. Communications. Paris. 1,1964+
	Arc 453.1	Journey in Nepal and northern India. (Bendall, C.) Cambridge, 1886.
Htn	Arc 635.215*	A journey into Greece. (Wheler, G.) London, 1682.
	Arc 530.9	Journey of exploration in Pontus. v.1. (Anderson, J.G.C.) Bruxelles, 1903.
	Arc 530.9.2	Journey of exploration in Pontus. v.2. (Anderson, J.G.C.) Bruxelles, 1903.
	Arc 530.9.3	Journey of exploration in Pontus. v.3. (Anderson, J.G.C.) Bruxelles, 1903.
	Arc 432.7	Jouveau-Dubreuil, D. Vedic antiquities. London, 1922.
	Arc 455.2	Jouveau-Dubreuil, G. Pallava antiquites. v.1-2. Pondicherry, 1916-18.
	Arc 394.2	Jovannet, grand-père de la préhistoire. (Cheynier, A.) Brive, 1936.
	Arc 936.251.10	Jovanović, Borislav. Metalurgija eneolitskog perioda Yugoslavije. Beograd, 1971.
	Arc 936.3.5	Jubani, Bep. Bibliographi arkeologjisë dhe historisë së lashtë të Shqipërisë, 1945-71. Tiranë, 1972.
	Arc 830.64	Jublains, Mayenne. (Barbe, Henri.) Mayenne, 1865.
	Arc 975.12	Judd, Neil M. Archaeological observations north of the Rio Colorado, Utah. Washington, 1926.
	Arc 943.54	Judd, Neil Morton. Men met along the trail. 1. ed. Norman, 1968.
	Arc 1613.24	Judd, T. Hewitt. United States pattern. Racine, 1959.
	Arc 224.5	Judenburger Museumsschriften. Judenburg.
	Arc 1163.17.20FA	Judge, C.B. Specimens of sixteenth-century English handwriting. Cambridge, 1925.
	Arc 1335.28	Judice dos Santos, J.J. Collection. pt.1,3. Amsterdam, 1906. 2v.
	Arc 1027.18.7	Die jüdische Katakombe am Monteverde zu Rom. (Müller, Nikolaus.) Leipzig, 1912.
	Arc 1027.18.15	Die jüdische Katakombe der Villa Torlonia in Rom. (Beyer, Hermann W.) Berlin, 1930.
	Arc 853.20.35F	Die jüngere Latènekultur des trierer Landes. (Mahr, Gustav.) Berlin, 1967.
	Arc 513.15	Jüthner, J. Vorläufiger Bericht...Expeditionen Kleinasien. Prag, 1903.
	Arc 936.220.90	Jugoslavia before the Roman conquest. (Alexander, John.) London, 1972.
	Arc 1675.95	Jugoslovenske i inostrane medalje. (Todorović, Nada.) Beograd, 1964.
	Arc 401.1.8	Jules Quicherat, 1814-1882. (Quicherat, Jules.) Paris, 1882.
	Arc 843.232	Julia, Dolorès. Étude épigraphique et iconographique des stèles funéraires de Vigo. Heidelberg, 1971.
	Arc 593.2	Julien, A.A. Notes of research on the New York obelisk. N.Y., 1893.
	Arc 400.13	Julien Poinssot; souvenirs 1844-1900. (Pallu de Lessert, A.C.) Paris, 1905.
	Arc 843.3.5	Juliobriga, ciudad romana en Cantabria. (Hernandez Morales, Angel.) Santander, 1946.
	Arc 823.25	Jullian, C. Au seuil de notre histoire. Paris, 1930-1931. 3v.
	Arc 66.1.37	Jullian, C. Transformations politiques de l'Italie. Paris, 1884.
	Arc 830.44.5	Julliot, Gustave. Notice sur l'aqueduc romain de Sens. Paris, 1875.
	Arc 1020.80	Julliot, M.G. Inventaire des reliques...l'église metropolitaine de Sens. Sens, 1877.
	Arc 1020.80.5	Julliot, M.G. Inventaire des sainctes reliques...de St. Pierre-le-Vif de Sens. Sens, 1877.
	Arc 853.273F	Die jungbronzezeitliche Siedlung von Berlin-Lichterfelde. (Müller, Adriaan.) Berlin, 1964.
	Arc 895.22.27F	Die jungere vorrömische Eisenzeit Gotlands. (Nylén, Erik.) Stockholm, 1956.
	Arc 1510.9	Jungk, H. Die bremischen Münzen. Bremen, 1875.
	Arc 853.340	Das jungkaiserzeitliche Gräberfeld von Wilhelmsaue in Brandenburg. (Schach-Dörges, Helga.) Berlin, 1969.
	Arc 853.62	Jungklaus, Ernst. Römische Funde in Pommein. Greifswald, 1924.
	Arc 893.29	Jungneolithische Studien. (Malmer, Mats P.) Habelt, 1968.
	Arc 853.75F	Jungsteinzeit-Siedlungen im Federseemoor. (Schmidt, R.R.) Augsburg, 1930-37.
	Arc 853.290	Das jungsteinzeitliche Dorf Ehrenstein. (Zuern, Hartwig.) Stuttgart, 1965. 3v.
	Arc 915.52	Jungsteinzeitliche Fundstellen im Kanton Freiburg. (Schwab, Hanni.) Basel, 1971.
	Arc 847.10	Pamphlet vol. Die jungsteinzeitlichen Felsgeräte des Landes Braun und der Nachbargebiete. 7 pam.
	Arc 1033.3.47	Junius Bassus sarkofag och dess datering. (Roosval, J.) Stockholm, 1932.
	Arc 600.18.15F	Junker, H. Gîza. Leipzig, 1929-38. 3v.
	Arc 545.242F	Junker, Hermann. Bericht über die Grabungen der Akademie des Wissenschaften in Wien. Wien, 1919.
	Arc 600.145F	Junker, Hermann. Der Grosse Pylon des Tempels der Isis in Philä. Wien, 1958.
	Arc 853.37	Die Juppitergigantensäulen. (Hertlein, F.) Stuttgart, 1910.
	Arc 969.15.10	Jury, Wilfrid. Sainte-Marie among the Hurons. Toronto, 1954.
	Arc 1319.1.5	K. Nederlandsch Genootschap voor Munt en Penningknude. Tijdschrift van het (Koninklyk) genootschap. Index, 1-20, 1893-1912. Amsterdam, 1903.
	Arc 1319.2	K. Nederlandsch Genootschap voor Munt en Penningkunde. Jaarboek. Amsterdam. 1-26,1914-1939 9v.
	Arc 1319.1	K. Nederlandsch Genootschap voor Munt en Penningkunde. Tijdschrift van het (Koninklyk) genootschap. Amsterdam. 1-21,1893-1913 14v.
	Arc 925.9.105	K drevnei istorii Iuzhnogo Kavkaza. (Chubinishvili, Taniel.) Tbilisi, 1971.
	Arc 925.353	K istorii alan Verkhnego Prikuban'ia po arkheologicheskim dannym. (Minaeva, Tat'iana M.) Staviopol', 1971.
	Arc 925.9.115	K istorii drevnei Kolkhidy. (Lordkipanidze, Guram A.) Tbilisi, 1970.
	Arc 925.9.35	K istorii izucheniia pamiatnikov epokhi eneolita i bronzy v nizhnem. (Tekhov, Bagrat V.) Tbilisi, 1963.
	Arc 925.11	K voproscho proiskhozhdenii gotskago stilia. (Shchtern, E. von.) Odessa, 1897.
	Arc 923.45F	K' voprosu o sostavlenii legendy dlia arkheologicheskoi karty Rossii. (Anuchin, D.N.) Moskva, 1885.
	Arc 635.209	Kabbadias, P. Fouilles de Lycosoura. Série 1. Athène, 1893.
	Arc 80.1.5	Kabbadias, P. Historia tēs Archaiologikēs Hetairias. Athēnai, 1900.
	Arc 395.5	Kabbadias, P. Proistorikē archaiologia. Athēnai, 1914.
	Arc 674.3.5	Kabbaria. Toieron toy asklēpioy. Athēnai, 1900.
	Arc 943.4	Kabell, S.K. America for Columbus. Roenne, 1892.
	Arc 689.8	Das Kabirenheiligtum bei Theben. (Nolters, P.) Berlin, 1940.
	Arc 848.21	Kadig, Werner. Der Wohnbau im jungsteinzeitlichen Deutschland. pt.1-2. Inaug. Diss. Leipzig, 1930.
	Arc 726.24.13FA	Kähler, H. Hadrian und seine Villa bei Tivoli. Berlin, 1950.
	Arc 520.19	Kähler, Heinz. Der grosse Fries von Pergamon. Berlin, 1948.
	Arc 520.19.5	Kähler, Heinz. Pergamon. Berlin, 1949.
	Arc 765.5	Kaehler, Heinz. Rom und seine Welt. München, 1958.
	Arc 900.204	Kärnten's römischen Alterthümer. (Jabornegg-Altenfels.) Klagenfurt, 1870.
	Arc 1675.92	Die Kärntner Medaillen. (Probszt, Günther.) Klagenfurt, 1964.
	Arc 925.295	Kafoev, A.Z. Adygskie pamiatniki. Nal'chik, 1963.
	Arc 1508.31	Kahl, Hans Dietrich. Hauptlinien der deutschen Münzgeschichte vom Ende des 18. Jahrhunderts bis 1878. Frankfurt, 1972.
	Arc 395.28	Kahlke, Hans Dietrich. Ausgrabungen in aller Welt. 1. Aufl. Leipzig, 1972.
	Arc 588.2	Kahum, Gurob, and Hawara. (Petrie, W.M.F.) London, 1890.
	Arc 1583.28	Kaim, Reinhold. Russische Numismatik. Braunschweig, 1968.
	Arc 858.5	Kains-Jackson, C.P. Our ancient monuments and the land around them. London, 1880.
	Arc 1411.2	Kainz, C. Die ältesten chinesischen Staatsmünzen. Berlin, 1894.
	Arc 1584.30	Kairn, Reinhold. Russische Münzstätten, Münzzeichen, Münzmeisterzeichen. Braunschweig, 1971.
	Arc 700.16	Kairo. Ägyptischen Museums. Griechische Urkunden. Strassburg, 1911.
	Arc 1200.5	Kaiser, H. Der collectarus perpeturom formorum des Johann von Gelnhausen. Strassburg, 1898.
	Arc 1200.5.5	Kaiser, H. Collection perpetuorum formorum. Innsbruck, 1900.
	Arc 1185.9.5	Die Kaiser- und Königsurkunden des Mittelalters in Deutschland, Frankreich und Italien. (Erben, Wilhelm.) München, 1967.
	Arc 785.5	Das kaiserliches Stadium auf dem Palatin. (Sturm, J.) Würzburg, 1888.
	Arc 935.19F	Die Kaiserpaläste von Konstantinopel zwischen Hippodrom und Marmara-Meer. (Mamboury, Ernest.) Berlin, 1934.
	Arc 421.5	Die Kaiserspräher der Tsing Dynastie in China. (Godfrey, E.F.) Berlin, 1930.
	Arc 1175.1	Kaiserurkunden in Abbildungen. v.1-11 and atlas. (Sybel, H. von.) Berlin, 1880-91. 12v.
	Arc 450.2A	Kak, Ram C. Ancient monuments of Kashmir. London, 1933.
	Arc 595.68	Kak stroilis' egipetskte piramidy. (Kink, Khil'da A.) Moskva, 1967.
	Arc 925.9.75	Kakhetskaia arkheologicheskaia ekspeditniia, 1965. Trudy. Tbilisi, 1969.
	Arc 710.20F	Kakkadin, P. He anaskaphē tēs Akropoleōs apo tou 1885 mechri tou 1890. Athēnai, 1906.
	Arc 600.215	Kalabsha. (United Arab Republic. Centre of Documentation and Studies on Ancient Egypt.) Cairo, n.d.
	Arc 853.65.35	Kaletyn, Marta. Grodziska wczesnośredniowieczne województwa wrocławskiego. Wrocław, 1968.
	Arc 936.14.450	Kaletyn, Marta. Pierwsze lokacje miast w dorzeczu orli w XIII wieku. Wrocław, 1973.
	Arc 936.165.55	Kal'fa-gorodishche vos'mogo-desiatego v.v. na Dnestre. (Chebotarenko, Georgii T.) Kishinev, 1973.
	Arc 905.21	Kalina, M. Böhmens...Opferplätz, Gräber und Alterthümer. Prag, 1836.
	Arc 87.1.53	Kalkmann, A. Proportionen des Gesichts in der Grosse Kunst. Berlin, 1893.
	Arc 1588.1.44F	Kałkowski, Tadeusz. Tysiac lat monety polskiej. Kraków, 1963.
	Arc 1588.1.44.2	Kałkowski, Tadeusz. Tysiac lat monety polskiej. Wyd. 2. Kraków, 1974.
	Arc 936.1.15	Kalliga, M. Die Hagia Sophia von Thessalonike. Inaug. Diss. Würzburg, 1935.
	Arc 700.52	Kallipolites, B.G. Chronologikē katataxis. Athēnai, 1958.
	Arc 925.23	Kallistov, D.P. Sev. Prichernomor'e v antich. epolu. Moskva, 1952.
	Arc 608.15	La Kaloa des Beni-Hammad. (Béylié, Leon.) Paris, 1909.
	Arc 545.227.15	Kamal, A.B. Livre des perles enfoneio. Leipzig, 1907. 2v.
	Arc 609.24.5	Kamanejoza: an introduction to the Iron Age cultures of the Victoria Falls region. (Vogel, Joseph O.) London, 1971.
	Arc 936.100.40	Kameni spomenici hrvatsko XIII-XIX stoljeća. (Valentic, Mirko.) Zagreb, 1969.
	Arc 925.16.25	Kamennye iz vaianiia Semirech'ia. (Sher, Iakov A.) Leningrad, 1966.
	Arc 543.65.5	Kamennye rek Tadzhikistana. (Ranov, V.A.) Dushambe, 1965.
	Arc 925.322.10	Kamennyi vek Dagestana. (Kotovich, Vladimir G.) Makhachkala, 1964.

Arc 925.300.10 Kamennyi vek i eneolit Prikubania. (Formozov, Aleksandr A.) Moskva, 1965.

Arc 1282.10 Kamentseva, Elena I. Russkaia spagistika i geral'dika. Moskva, 1963.

Arc 925.50.75 Kam'iana Mohyla. (Rudyns'kyi, M.I.) Kyïv, 1961.

Arc 925.50.160 Kam'iana Mohyla. Kyïv, 1967. 2 pam.

Arc 505.136.5 Kamid el-Loz-Kumidi. Bonn, 1970.

Arc 936.14.145 Kaminska, Janina. Z dziejów prednowiecz sieradza. Wrocław, 1964.

Arc 1588.1.65.7 Kamiński, Czesław. Ilustrowany katakog monet polskich, 1916-1972. wyd. 2. Warszawa, 1973.

Arc 1588.1.65.8 Kamiński, Czesław. Ilustrowany katalog monet polskich, 1916-1974. Wyd. 3. Warszawa, 1974.

Arc 1588.1.65 Kamiński, Czesław. Katalog banknotów i monet Polskiej Rzeczy pospolitej Ludowej. pt.1-2. Warszawa, 1966-68.

Arc 1076.3.90 De Kamper klokgieters. (Fehrmann, Christiaan Nathanaël.) Kampen, 1967.

Arc 1027.23.23 Kampffmeyer, K. Die Landschaft in der altchristlichen Katakombenmalerei. Greifswald, 1933.

Arc 426.2A Kanda, T. Notes on ancient stone implements...of Japan. Tokio, 1884.

Arc 522.40 Kandemir, Selâhattin. Tarova harabesi. 2. basi. Istanbul, 1938.

Arc 522.40.5 Kandemir, Selâhattin. Turova harabeleri ve skalor. Izmir, 1933.

Arc 543.3.75 Kangiuisko-sarmatskii farn. (Litvinskii, Boris A.) Dushanbe, 1968.

Arc 925.134.5 Kaninskaia peshchera. (Kanivets, Viacheslav I.) Moskva, 1964.

Arc 925.134.5 Kanivets, Viacheslav I. Kaninskaia peshchera. Moskva, 1964.

Arc 925.324 Kanivs'ke poselennia polian. (Mezentseva, Galina G.) Kyïv, 1965.

Arc 1411.13 Kann, Eduard. Illustrated catalog of Chinese coins, gold, silver, nickel and aluminum. Los Angeles, 1954.

Arc 935.28F Kansu, S. Türk Tarih Kurumu tarafindan yapilan Etiyrkusu kafiryati raporu. Ankara, 1940.

Arc 416.30 Kantor, H.J. The Aegean and the Orient in the second millennium B.C. Bloomington, 1947.

Arc 1138.23 Kantorowicz, Hermann. Einführung in die Textkritik. Leipzig, 1921.

Arc 1584.1.4 Kapanadze, D.G. Gruzinskia numizmatika. Moskva, 1955.

Arc 935.33.5 Kapidagi Yariniadasi ve Cevresindeki Adalar. (Resit Mazhar Ertüzün.) Ankara, 1964.

Arc 87.2.49 Die Kapitole. (Braun, J.W.J.) Bonn, 1849-

Arc 600.242 Kaplony, Peter. Beschriftete Kleinfunde in der Sammlung Georges Michailidis. Istanbul, 1973.

Arc 1335.165 Kapossy, Balázs. Münzen und Medaillen aus dem Bernischen Historischen Museum. Bern, 1969.

Arc 925.325 Kapovaia peshchera. (Bader, Otto N.) Moskva, 1965.

Arc 543.66.20 Kara-tepe. (Termezskaia Arkheologicheskaia Kompleksnaia Ekspeditsiia, 1937, 1961-1962.) Moskva, 1964.

Arc 600.7 Karabaček. Die Theodor Graf'schen Funde in Aegypten. Wien, 1883.

Arc 543.154 Karabulak. (Brykina, Galina A.) Moskva, 1974.

Arc 925.310.5 Karachaevtsy i balkartsy, drevnii narod Kavkaza. (Alekseeva, Evgeniia P.) Cherkessk, 1963.

Arc 540.14 Karageōrgēs, Basos. Salamis; recent discoveries in Cyprus. N.Y., 1969.

Arc 537.12 Karageorghis, Basos. Cyprus. London, 1949.

Arc 1190.65.5 Karagiannopoulos, Iōannēs E. Byzantinē diplomatikē. Thessalonikē, 1969.

Arc 925.9.45 Karakashly, K.T. Material'naia kul'tura azerbaidzhantsev severo-vostochnoi i Tsentral'noi zon Malogo Kavkaza. Balzu, 1964.

Arc 543.146.10 Karakumskie drevnosti. Photoreproduction. Ashkhabad, 1968- 4v.

Arc 543.146.30 Karakumyi zavia tsivilizatsii. (Masson, Vadim M.) Moskva, 1972.

Arc 936.100.10 Karaman, L. Baština djedova. Zagreb, 1944.

Arc 936.100.15 Karaman, L. Iz kdijerke hrvatsbe prostosti. Zagreb, 1930.

Arc 936.100 Karaman, L. Živa stariua. Zagreb, 1943.

Htn Arc 513.2* Karamania. (Beaufort, F.) London, 1817.

Arc 600.36 Karanis. (Boak, A.E.R.) Ann Arbor, 1931.

Arc 600.36.5 Karanis. (Boak, A.E.R.) Ann Arbor, 1933.

Arc 606.6 Karanòg, the Meroitic inscriptions. (Griffith, F.L.) Philadelphia, 1911.

Arc 606.3 Karanòg, the Romano-Nubian cemetery. (Woolley, C.L.) Philadelphia, 1910. 2v.

Arc 606.5 Karanòg, the town. (Woolley, C.L.) Philadelphia, 1911.

Arc 1033.163 Kardag. Die Geschichte des Mâr Abhdiso und seines Jüngers Mâr Quardagh. Kiel, 1889.

Arc 1453.11 Kargel, Adolf. Münzen erzählen. Bielefeld, 1971.

Arc 450.38 Karian excavations, 1955. (Roy, Sita Ram.) Patna, 1965.

Arc 1418.22 Karim, A. Corpus of the Muslim coins of Bengal. Decca, 1960.

Arc 488.14.10 Karimi, B.M. Rapport résumé de quinze mai de voyage. Teheran, 1950?

Htn Arc 1163.3.20PF* Karinskii, N.M. Obraztsy pis'ma brevneishego perioda istorii russkoi knigi. Leningrad, 1925.

Arc 386.5.18 Karl August Böttiger. (Böttiger, Carl Wilhelm.) Leipzig, 1837.

Arc 853.33 Die Karl Knorrsche Sammlung von Benin-Altertümern. (Luschan, F. von.) Stuttgart, 1901.

Arc 853.95 Der Karlsgraben. (Beck, F.) Nürnberg, 1911.

Arc 1335.76.14 Karmatia symbolika. (Athens. Ethnikon Nomismatikon Mouseion.) Athēnai, 1880.

Arc 530.65.5 Karmir-blur. (Akademiia nauk Armianskoi SSR, Erevan. Institut Istorii.) Erevan, 1955- 4v.

Arc 600.55F Karnak. v.1,3-4. (Varille, Alexandre.) Le Caire, 1943-51. 4v.

Arc 905.12.25 Karnuntums Wiederaufbau. (Gollob, Hedwig.) Wien, 1956.

Arc 689.7.5 Karo, G. Fürhrer durch Tiryns. 2. Aufl. Athen, 1934.

Arc 716.12A Karo, G.H. An Attic cemetery. Philadelphia, 1943.

Arc 672.1.72F Karo, G.H. Greifen am Thron. Baden-Baden, 1959.

Arc 682.12F Karo, Georg. Die Schachtgräber von Mykenai. Text and plates. München, 1930-33. 2v.

Arc 395.22 Karo, Georg H. Fünfzig Jahre aus dem Leben. Baden-Baden, 1959.

Arc 673.1.50 Karouzos, Chrēstos Iōannou. Delphoi. Athēnai, 1974.

Arc 925.50.55 Karpats'ki kurhany pershoi polov. I tysiacholettia nash. ery. (Smishko, M.I.) Kyïv, 1960.

Arc 936.14.280 Karpińska, Aleksandra. Kurhany, zokresw rzymskiego w Polsce ze szczegolnem uwzględnieniem typu siedlemińskiego. Poznań, 1926.

Arc 1163.3.10 Karskii, E.F. Obraztsy slavianskago kirillovskago pis'ma. Varshava, 1902.

Arc 1163.3.15 Karskii, E.F. Slavianskaia kirillovskaia paleografiia. Leningrad, 1928.

Arc 1584.1.9 Karst, J. Précis de numismatique géorgienne. Paris, 1938.

Arc 843.95 Karst, Josef. Essai sur l'origine des Basques Ibères et peuples apparentés. Strasbourg, 1954.

Arc 40.2 Karthago; revue trimestrielle l'archeologie africaine. Paris. 1-14 8v.

Arc 925.255 Kartsov, V.G. O chem govoriat kurgany Eniseia. Abakhan, 1961.

Arc 1588.11 Karys, Jonas K. Senoues lietuviu pinigai. Bridgeport, Conn., 1959.

Arc 925.9.140 Kashkai, Mir-Ali. Iz istorii drevnei metallurgii Kavkaza. Baku, 1973.

Arc 435.85 Kashmir. Archaeological Survey. Memoirs. Mysore City. 1-2 2v.

Arc 853.43 Kasiski, F.W. Beschreibung der vaterländischen Alterthümer. Danzig, 1881.

Arc 80.1 Kastorkes, E. Historikē ekthesis tōn praxeon tēs Archaiologikēs Hetairias. Athēnai, 1879.

Arc 543.3.110 Kasymov, M.R. Kremneobrabatyvaiushchie masterskie i shakhty Kamennogo veka Srednii Azii. Tashkent, 1972.

Arc 1433.44 Katakog' dzhelairidskiu' monety Sost. A. Markov'. (Leningrad. Ermitazh.) Sankt Peterburg, 1897.

Arc 1025.8 Die Katakomben. Photoreproduction. (Schultze, V.) Leipzig, 1882.

Arc 1025.71.2 Die Katakomben. 2. Aufl. (Bock, Emil.) Stuttgart, 1961.

Arc 1025.14 Die Katakomben über das Unterirdische. (Housse, L.) Lurenburg, 1867.

Htn Arc 1027.24.25F* Die Katakomben von Neapel. (Achelis, Hans.) Leipzig, 1935-36.

Arc 1027.21 Die Katakomben von San Gennaro die Poveri. (Schultze, V.) Jena, 1877.

Arc 1015.213 Die Katakombengemalde. Ihre alten Copiers. (Wilpert, J.) Freiburg, 1891.

Arc 1027.80 Die Katakombenheiligen der Schweiz. (Stückelberg, E.A.) Kempten, 1907.

Arc 1025.63 Die Katakombenwelt. (Beyer, Oskar.) Tübingen, 1927.

Arc 1490.13.10 Katalog alte Sammlung päpstlicher Münzen. (Hamburger, L.) Frankfurt, 1921.

Arc 1588.1.65 Katalog banknotów i monet Polskiej Rzeczy pospolitej Ludowej. pt.1-2. (Kamiński, Czesław.) Warszawa, 1966-68.

Arc 938.5 Katalog der Ausstellung. (Archäologischer Kongress, 10th, Riga, 1896.) Riga, 1896.

Arc 340.2 Katalog der Bibliothek. (Deutsches Archäologisches Institut. Römische Abteilung. Bibliothek.) Rom, 1900-02. 2v.

Arc 340.2.7 Katalog der Bibliothek. Supplement. (Deutsches Archäologisches Institut. Römische Abteilung. Bibliothek.) Berlin, 1930.

Arc 340.2.5 Katalog der Bibliothek. v.1-2. (Deutsches Archäologisches Institut. Römische Abteilung. Bibliothek.) Rom, 1913-32. 4v.

Arc 1093.8 Katalog der Bleisarkophage. (Müfid, Arif.) Istanbul, 1932.

Arc 1578.10 Katalog der Münzen- und Medaillen-Stampel. (Austria. Haupt Münzamt in Wien.) Wien, 1901-06. 4v.

Arc 1335.125 Katalog der Münzensammlung Arthur Graf Enzenberg. (Enzenberg, Arthur.) Luzern, 1935.

Arc 708.24 Katalog der Sculpturen zu Athen. (Sybel, L. von.) Marburg, 1881.

Arc 1335.154 Katalog des grossen Freiherrlich von Wambolt'schen Münzkabinets in Heidelberg. v.1-2. (Wambolt, F. von.) Heidelberg, 1833.

Arc 1335.11 Katalog des Münzkabinets. (Leipzig. Stadtbibliothek.) Leipzig, 1853.

Arc 1453.9 Katalog evropeiskikh medalei i monet. (Russkoe Arkheologischeskoe Obshchestvo, Leningrad. Muzei.) Sankt Peterburg, 1864.

Arc 853.130F Katalog Günzburg. (Stroh, Armin.) Kallmünz, 1952.

Arc 853.265F Katalog Kirchheim unter Teck. (Fiedler, R.) Stuttgart, 1962.

Arc 1330.9 Katalog knihovny. Numismatické společnosti československé v Praze. vyd. 1. (Janovský, Hubert.) Praha, 1967.

Arc 925.50.270 Katalog kolleztni drevnostei A.N. Pol', v Ekaterinoslave. (Pol', Aleksandr N.) Kiev, 1893.

Arc 1583.7 Katalog' monet' chekannyk' v' Rossii. (Shrapeznikov', A.N.) Sankt Peterburg, 1909.

Arc 1588.1.31 Katalog monet polskich, 1765-1864. (Jabłoński, Tadeusz.) Warszawa, 1965.

Arc 1588.1.34 Katalog monet polskich. (Terlecki, W.) Warszawa, 1960.

Arc 1433.91 Katalog monet s gorodischa Pendzhikent...1949-1956 gg. (Smirnova, O.I.) Moskva, 1963.

Arc 1588.6.35 Katalog novca Osmanske imperije sakupljenog- na području SFR Jugoslavije. (Tesla-Zarić, Dobrila.) Beograd, 1974.

Arc 1590.10 Katalog novca Srbije i Crne Gore 1868-1918. (Mihailović, Vojislav.) Beograd, 1973.

Arc 1588.1.110 Katalog podstawowych typów monet i banknotów Polski oraz ziem historycznie z Polską związanych. v.1, pt.1-2. (Kopicki, Edmund.) Warszawa, 1974- 2v.

Arc 936.220.22 Katalog praistorijskih metalmih predmeta. (Todorović, Jovan.) Beograd, 1971.

Arc 405.1.30 Katalog sobraniia drevnostei. v.1,3-11. (Uvarov, Aleksei S.) Moskva, 1887- 10v.

Arc 853.230F Katalog Stromling. (Hundt, Hans Jürgen.) Kallmünz, 1958. 2v.

Arc 275.17 Katalog vystaki. (Arkheologicheskii s"ezd, 16th, Pskov, 1915.) Pskov, 1915.

Arc 275.16 Katalog vystavki VIII Arkheologicheskago s"ezda v Moskve, 1890 g. Pt.1-10. (Arkheologicheskii s"ezd, 8th, Moscow, 1890.) Moskva, 1890.

Arc 1675.51 Katalog wejborów. (Poland. Mennica Panstwowa.) Warszawa, 19- ?

Arc 848.10 Kataloge west- und süddeutscher Altertumssammlungen. Frankfurt am Main. 1-6,1911-1926 5v.

Arc 1335.76.10F Katalogos. (Athens. Ethnikon Nomismatikon Mouseion.) Athēnai, 1868.

Arc 1335.76.11F Katalogos. (Athens. Ethnikon Nomismatikon Mouseion.) Athēnai, 1872.

Arc 1335.76.3 Katalogos. (Athens. Ethnikon Nomismatikon Mouseion.) Athēnai, 1910.

Arc 684.7.5 Katalogos tōn mouseiou Lukosouras. (Kourouniotos, K.) Athēnai, 1911.

Arc 67.3 Katastatikon Psēphisthen yvo tēs Genikēs synelenseus. (Christianekē Archaiologikē Hetaireia, Athens.) Athēnai. 1903

Arc 441.2.9 Kathiawar. Department for an Archaeological and Antiquarian Survey. Bhavanagar pracina sodh a samgraha. Bhavanagar, 1885.

Author and Title Listing

	Arc 600.3.5	Die Katochëim Sarapieion bei Memphis. Inaug. Diss. (Heuser, G.) Marburg, 1935.
	Arc 608.82	Katsnel'son, Isidor S. Napata i meroe-drevnie tsarstva sudzna. Moskva, 1970.
	Arc 1675.85	Katz, Viktor. Die erzgebirgische Prägmedaille des XVI. Jahrhundert. Praha, 1932.
	Arc 1590.31	Katz, Viktor. Kontramarky na pražských groších. Praha, 1927.
	Arc 1675.86	Katz, Viktor. Medaile na přátelstir a při buzné památky. Praha, 1938.
	Arc 1588.4.45	Katz, Viktor. Ocuronolozu denaru Boleslava I a II. Praha, 1935.
	Arc 1588.4.45.5	Katz, Viktor. Tisíc let české vládní mince (929-1929). Praha, 1929.
	Arc 848.6	Kauffmann, F. Deutsche Altertumskunde. München, 1913-23. 2v.
	Arc 1016.200	Kaufmann, C.I. Die sepulcralen Jenseits Denkmäler. Mainz, 1900.
	Arc 395.12	Kaufmann, C.M. Allah ist gross! Freiburg, 1950.
	Arc 1020.14	Kaufmann, C.M. Ein altchristliches Pompeji. Mainz, 1902.
	Arc 600.14	Kaufmann, C.M. Die Ausgrabung des Menas-Heiligtümes. v.1-3. Cairo, 1906.
	Arc 600.14.5	Kaufmann, C.M. La découverte des sanctuaires. Alexandrie, 1908.
	Arc 1018.19.3	Kaufmann, C.M. Handbuch der christlichen Archäologie. 3. Aufl. Paderborn, 1922.
	Arc 1020.99.9	Kaufmann, C.M. Die heilige Stadt der Wüste. 2.-3. Aufl. Kempten, 1921.
	Arc 1020.99.10	Kaufmann, C.M. Die heilige Stadt der Wüste. 4e Aufl. Kempten, 1921.
	Arc 1020.99	Kaufmann, C.M. Der Menastempel und die Heiligtümer von Karm Abu Mina. Frankfurt, 1909.
	Arc 1020.99.15	Kaufmann, C.M. Zur Ikonographie des Menas-Ampullen. Cairo, 1910.
	Arc 1030.39	Kaufmann, Carl M. Handbuch der altchristlichen Epigraphik im Breisgau. Freiburg, 1917.
	Arc 1269.27	Kaufmann, E. Studien über Amtssiegel des 13. und 14. Jahrhunderts vornehmlich in Hessen. Inaug. Diss. Marburg, 1937.
	Arc 1016.236	Kaufmann, K.W. Die Menasstadt. Leipzig, 1910.
	Arc 1160.11	Kaulek, J. Recueil de fac-simile...paléographie moderne. Paris, 1889.
	Arc 1027.1	Kaus, F.X. Die Blutampullen der römischen Katakomben. Frankfurt, 1868.
	Arc 710.27F	Kawerau, Georg. The excavation of the Athenian Acropolis 1882-1890. v.1-2. Copenhagen, 1974.
	Arc 435.2.40F	Kaye, G.R. The astronomical observatories of Jai Singh. Calcutta, 1918.
	Arc 435.2.43F	Kaye, G.R. Bakhshali manuscript. pt.1-3. Calcutta, 1927-33. 2v.
	Arc 560.4	Kayser, Hans. Ägyptisches Kunstlandwerk. Braunschweig, 1969.
	Arc 736.19	Kayser, Hans. Paestum. Heidelburg, 1958.
	Arc 1365.5	Kazamanova, Liudmila N. Vvedenie v antichnaia numizmatiku. Moskva, 1969.
	Arc 925.260	Kazan, Russia (City). Universitet. Arkheologicheskie pamiatniki u sela Rozhdestveno. Kazan, 1962.
	Arc 880.7	Keane, Marcus. Towers and temples of ancient Ireland. Dublin, 1867.
X Cg	Arc 1390.9	Keary, C.F. Coinage of western Europe. London, 1879.
	Arc 1540.4	Keder, N. De argento runis siu lit. Lipsiae, 1703-08. 4 pam.
	Arc 1433.21	Kehr, G. Jacob. Monarchiae Asiatico-Saracenicae status. Lipsiae, 1724.
	Arc 518.8	Keil, Josef. Ephesos. Wien, 1915.
	Arc 518.8.5	Keil, Josef. Ephesos. Wien, 1955.
	Arc 518.8.7	Keil, Josef. Ephesos. 4. Aufl. Wien, 1957.
	Arc 1163.25F	Keilschrift-Palaeographie. (Deimel, Anton.) Roma, 1929.
	Arc 403.16.35	Kein Troja ohne Homer. (Schliemann, Heinrich.) Nürnberg, 1960.
	Arc 716.3.2	Kekulé, R. Die Balustrade des Templs der Athena-Nike. Leipzig, 1869.
	Arc 87.1.69	Kekule, R. Bronzes. Berlin, 1909.
	Arc 87.1.49	Kekule, R. Bronzestatue des sogenannten Idolino. Berlin, 1889.
	Arc 87.1.65	Kekule, R. Echelos und Basile. Berlin, 1905.
	Arc 705.200	Kekulé, R. Die Reliefs an der Balustrade der Athena Nike. Stuttgart, 1881.
	Arc 87.1.57	Kekule, R. Ueber Copien einer Frauenstatue. Berlin, 1897.
	Arc 87.1.61	Kekule, R. Über ein Bildnis des Perikles in den Königlichen Museum. Berlin, 1901.
	Arc 87.1.54	Kekule, R. Ueber einen bisher Marcellus genannten Kopf. Berlin, 1894.
	Arc 493.5	Kelianshchin, stela u Topuzava. (Minorekii, V.) Petrograd, 1917.
	Arc 1668.4	Keller, D. Biltnusse der Rhömischen Keyseren. Zürich, 1558.
	Arc 913.5.5	Keller, F. Beilage zur archäologischen Karte den Ostschweiz. 2. Aufl. Frauenfeld, 1873.
	Arc 913.5	Keller, F. Lake dwellings of Switzerland and other parts of Europe. London, 1878. 2v.
	Arc 522.9	Keller, O. Die Entdeckung Ilions zu Hissarlik. Freiburg in Baden, 1875.
	Arc 87.2.71	Keller, O. Vicus Aurelii. Bonn, 1871.
	Arc 1163.14.6	Keller, Wolfgang. Angelsächsiche Palaeographie. N.Y., 1970-71. 2v.
	Arc 915.46	Keller-Tarnuzzer, Karl. Urgeschichte des Thurgaus. Frauenfeld, 1925.
	Arc 848.57	Kellermann, Volkmar. Germanische Altertumskunde. Berlin, 1966.
	Arc 600.230F	Kellia I. (Daumas, François.) Le Caire, 1969- 2v.
	Arc 853.24.22	Kellner, Hans-Jörg. Die Römer in Bayern. 2. Aufl. München, 1972.
	Arc 1480.80	Kellner, Wendelin. Libertas und Christogramm. Thesis. Karlsruhe, 1968.
	Arc 1076.4.5	Kellot temppelin. (Kuuliala, Vilji K.) Sortavala, 1943.
	Arc 723.12	Kelsall, Charles. Classical excursion from Rome to Arpino. Geneva, 1820.
	Arc 608.2.23	Kelsey, Francis W. Excavations at Carthage 1925. N.Y., 1926.
	Arc 823.60F	Kelten-Römer. (Pobé, Marcel.) Olten, 1958. 2v.
	Arc 905.24.20	Kelten und Römer am Magdalensberg. (Obermayr, August.) Wien, 1971.
	Arc 936.220.45	Kelti na tlu Beograda. (Todorović, Jovan.) Beograd, 1968.
	Arc 618.11	Kelti u jugoistočnoj Evropi. (Todorovic, Jovan.) Beograd, 1968.
	Arc 618.9	Keltische Kunst. (Verworm, M.) Berlin, 1919.
	Arc 1454.200	Keltische Numismatik der Rhein. (Forrer, Robert.) Strassburg, 1908.
	Arc 1454.205	Keltské mince typu Biatec z Bratislavy. (Ondrouch, V.) Bratislava, 1958.
	Arc 823.11.3F	Keltské pohrebiská na juhozápadnom Slovensku. (Blăzej, Benadík.) Bratislava, 1957.
	Arc 610.5F	Kemble, John M. Horae ferales. London, 1863.
	Arc 285.5	Kemerovo. Pedagogicheskii Institut. Laboratoriia Arkheologicheskikh Issledovanii. Izvestiia. Kemerovo. 1,1967+ 2v.
	Arc 845.3	Kempten. Allgaüer Alterthumsverein. Bericht ueber die...Ausgrabungen. v.1-4. Kempten, 1888. 2v.
	Arc 386.45	Kenawell, William W. The quest at Glastonbury, a biographical study of Frederick Bligh Bond. N.Y., 1965.
	Arc 858.46	Kendrick, T.D. Archaeology in England and Wales, 1914-1931. London, 1932.
	Arc 861.83	Kendrick, T.D. The archaeology of the Channel Islands. London, 1928.
	Arc 958.2	Kengla, L.A. Contributions to the archaeology of the District of Columbia. Washington, 1883.
	Arc 1251.10F	Kenna, V.E.G. Cretan seals. Oxford, 1960.
	Arc 497.26F	Kennedy, A.B. William. Petra; its history and monuments. London, 1925.
	Arc 1510.38	Kennepohl, K. Die Münzen von Osnabrück. München, 1938.
	Arc 135.5	Kent Archaeological Research Groups' Council. Research report. Bromley. 1,1968+ 2v.
	Arc 395.1	Kenward, J. Place of archaeology in science. Birmingham, 1877.
	Arc 497.44	Kenyon, F.G. The Bible and archaeology. London, 1940.
	Arc 505.66.5	Kenyon, K.M. Digging up Jericho. N.Y., 1957.
	Arc 861.29.20	Kenyon, K.M. Excavations at Virsconium (Wroxeter), 1937. Shrewsbury, 1937.
	Arc 861.29.15	Kenyon, K.M. Excavations at Wroxeter, 1936. Shrewsbury, 1936.
	Arc 505.5.105	Kenyon, Kathleen M. Jerusalem: excavating 3000 years of history. London, 1967.
	Arc 497.60	Kenyon, Kathleen Mary. Archaeology in the Holy Land. N.Y., 1960.
	Arc 497.60.3	Kenyon, Kathleen Mary. Archaeology in the Holy Land. 3. ed. N.Y., 1970.
	Arc 395.15.2	Kenyon, Kathleen Mary. Beginning in archaeology. London, 1952.
	Arc 395.15.5	Kenyon, Kathleen Mary. Beginning in archaeology. N.Y., 1961.
	Arc 395.15	Kenyon, Kathleen Mary. Beginning in archaeology. 2. ed. London, 1953.
	Arc 505.154	Kenyon, Kathleen Mary. Digging up Jerusalem. London, 1974.
	Arc 497.96	Kenyon, Kathleen Mary. Royal cities of the Old Testament. N.Y., 1971.
X Cg	Arc 1538.9	Kenyon, R.L. Gold coins of England, sequel to the silver coins of England. London, 1884.
	Arc 936.165.60	Kepreriia-pamiatnik kul'tury X-XII vv. (Khynku, Ivan G.) Kishinev, 1973.
	Arc 482.202.2F	Die Keramik von Samarra. (Sarre, Friedrich.) Berlin, 1925.
	Arc 673.1.30	Keramopoullos, A.D. Topographia tōn Delphōn. Athēnai, 1917.
	Arc 1470.55	Kerényi, K. Der Mythos der Hellenen. Amsterdam, 1941.
	Arc 861.10.9	Kermode, P.M. Catalogue of the Manks crosses. London, 1892.
	Arc 1190.25	Kern, Fritz. Dorsualkonzept und Imbreviatur in Italien. Stuttgart, 1906.
	Arc 861.20	Kerslake, T. Caer Pensauelcoit. London, 1882.
	Arc 383.79.10	Kersten, Karl. Festschrift für Gustav Schwante. Neumünster, 1951.
	Arc 936.165.65	Ketraru, Nikolai A. Sokrovishcha pyrkolaba Gangura. Kishinev, 1973.
	Arc 590.7	Kettner, F.G. Moymia tōn Aigyptian. 2. ed. Lipsiae, 1703. 3 pam.
	Arc 858.8	Key to English antiquities. (Armitage, E.S.) Sheffield, 1897.
	Arc 1033.17.100.5	Keyer, F.P.W. (Mrs.). The grace of Guadalupe. N.Y., 1941.
Htn	Arc 618.4*	Keysler, J.G. Antiquitas...septentrionales et celticae. Hannover, 1720.
	Arc 936.195.220	Kežmarok. 1. vyd. (Polla, Belo.) Bratislava, 1971.
	Arc 925.50.330	Kezub, Iuliia I. Nekropol' Ol'vii V-VI st. do n.e. Kyïv, 1974.
	Arc 530.80.5	Khachatrian, T.S. Materialnaia Kul'tura drevnego Artika. Erevan, 1963.
	Arc 530.182	Khach'atryan, Telemak S. Drevnaia kul'tura Shiraka. Erevan, 1975.
	Arc 450.10	Khajuraho. (Dhama, B.L.) Delhi, 1953.
	Arc 925.60	Khakovskii, V.F. Pamiatniki material'noi kul'tury Chuvashskoi ASSR. Cheboksary, 1957.
	Arc 543.66.25	Khalchaian. (Puga-Chenkova, Galina A.) Tashkent, 1966.
	Arc 925.215	Khalikov, A.K. Materialy k drevnei istorii Povetluzh'ia. Gor'kii, 1960.
	Arc 925.338	Khalikov, Al'fred K. Drevniaia istoriia Srednego Povolzhia. Moskva, 1969.
	Arc 608.6.21F	Khamissa, Mdaourouch, Announa. (Gsell, Stéphane.) Alger, 1914-22.
	Arc 925.4.55	Khamzina, Evgeniia A. Arkheologicheskie pamiatniki zapadnogo zabaikal'ia. Ulan-Ude, 1970.
	Arc 448.1.25	Khan, F.A. The Indus Valley and early Iran. Karachi, 1964.
	Arc 925.13.180	Khazanov, Anatolii M. Ocherki noennogo dela sarmatov. Moskva, 1971.
	Arc 925.8.37	Khersones tavricheskii. (Belov, G.D.) Leningrad, 1948.
	Arc 925.50.40	Khersones Tavricheskii. (Belov, G.D.) Simferopol', 1958.
	Arc 925.50.42	Khersones Tavricheskii. (Sebastopol. Khersoneskii Gosudarstvennyi Istoriko-Arkheologicheskii Muzei.) Simferopol', 1962.
	Arc 925.50.130	Khersones Tavricheskii. (Surov, E.G.) Sverdlovsk, 1961.
	Arc 925.8.15F	Khersonesskii sbornik. Sevastopol. 1,1926+ 4v.
	Arc 1365.1	Khevenhueller, F.A. Regum veterum numismata. v.1-2. Vienna, 17- .
	Arc 540.6.5	Khirakitia. (Dikaios, P.) London, 1953.
	Arc 505.90F	Khirbat al Mafjar. (Hamilton, R.W.) Oxford, 1959.
	Arc 925.4.7	Khlobystina, M.D. Bronzovye nozhi minusinskogo kraia i nekotorye voprosy razvitiia karasukskoi kul'tury. Leningrad, 1962.
	Arc 543.146.15	Khlopin, Igor N. Geoksiurskaia gruppa poselenii epokhi eneolita. Leningrad, 1964.
	Arc 925.55	Khronyka arkheolohyi ta mystetstva. (Akademiia Nauk URSR, Kyïv.) Kyïv, 1930.
	Arc 925.245	Khudiak, M.M. Iz istorii Nimfeia VI-III vekov. Leningrad, 1962.

Author and Title Listing

Arc 936.165.12 Khudozhestvennye sokrovishcha drevnei Moldavii. (Rikman, Emmanuil A.) Kishinev, 1969.

Arc 608.19 Khun de Prorok, Byron. Digging for lost African gods. N.Y., 1926.

Arc 608.2.39 Khun de Prorot, Byron. Fouilles à Carthage. Paris, 1923.

Arc 925.50.125 Khvoika, V.V. Drevnie obitateli Sredniago Pridneprov'ia. Kiev, 1913.

Arc 936.165.60 Khynku, Ivan G. Kepreriia-pamiatnik kul'tury X-XII vv. Kishinev, 1973.

Arc 225.20 Kiadványok. (Szeged, Hungary. Móra Ferenc Múzeum.) 3v.

Arc 225.20F Kiadványok. (Szeged, Hungary. Móra Ferenc Múzeum.) 2

Arc 853.28 Kickebunde, A. Einfluss der Römischen Kultur. Berlin, 1908.

Arc 969.15.5 Kidd, Kenneth E. The excavations of Sainte-Marie I. Toronto, 1949.

Arc 968.2.50 Kidder, Alfred V. The artifacts of Pecas. New Haven, 1932.

Arc 968.2.45 Kidder, Alfred V. An introduction to the study of southwestern archaeology. New Haven, 1924.

Arc 426.12 Kidder, J.E. Japan before Buddhism. London, 1959.

Arc 1033.17.50 Kiedrzynski, A. Mensa nazaraea...seu historia imagine divae Claromontanae. Claromontanae, 1763.

Arc 1033.17.51 Kiedrzynski, A. Mensa nazaraea...seu historia imagine divae Claromontanae. Cracoviae, 1760.

Arc 1269.20 Kiefhaber, J.K.S. Historisch-diplomatische Beschreibung der Nürnbergischen Kloster-Siegel. Nürnberg, 1797.

Arc 853.21.20 Kiekebusch, A. Die Ausgrabung des bronzezeitlichen Dorfes Buch bei Berlin. Berlin, 1923.

Arc 853.53.3 Kiekebusch, A. Bilder aus der märkischen Vorzeit. 3. Aufl. Berlin, 1921.

Arc 1335.158 Kiel. Universität. Museum für Vor- und Frühgeschichte. Kieler Münzkatalog. Verzeichniss der Münzsammlung des Schleswig-Holsteinischen Museum Vaterländischer Alterthümer. 1863-1887//

Arc 195.3F Kiel. Universität. Schleswig-Holsteinisches Museum Vorgeschichtlicher Altertümer. Vor- und frühgeschichtliche Untersuchungen. Neumünster. 1,1933+ 27v.

Arc 1335.158 Kieler Münzkatalog. Verzeichniss der Münzsammlung des Schleswig-Holsteinischen Museum Vaterländischer Alterthümer. (Kiel. Universität. Museum für Vor- und Frühgeschichte.) 1863-1887//

Arc 600.1 Kiepert, H. Zur Topographie des alten Alexandria. Berlin, n.d.

Arc 936.14.296 Kiersnowska, Teresa. Zycie codzienne na Pomorzu wczesnósredniowiecznym, wiek X-XII. Warszawa, 1970.

Arc 1588.1.42 Kiersnowski, R. Początki pieniadza polskiego. Warszawa, 1962.

Arc 1588.1.55 Kiersnowski, Ryszard. Wstęp do numizmatyki polskiej wieków średnich. Warszawa, 1964.

Arc 920.9 Kieseritzky, G. von. Griechische Grabreliefs aus Südrussland. Berlin, 1909.

Arc 700.9 Kietz, G. Agonistische Studien I, Der Diskoswurf bei der Grechen. München, 1892.

Arc 933.2F Die Kietzsiedlungen im nordlichen Mitteleuropa. (Kruegar, Bruno.) Berlin, 1962.

Arc 925.337.10 Kiiashko, Vladimir I. Legenda i byl' donskikh kurganov. Rostov-na-Donu, 1972.

Arc 935.32.15 Kilavuzlar. v.1,4,6. (Turkey. Maarif Vekaleli Antikiteler ve Muzeler Direktorlügü. Aniflari Koruma Kurulu.) Ankara, 1935- 7v.

Arc 880.39 Kilgreany cove, county Waterford. (Movius, H.L.) Dublin? 1935.

Arc 612.10 Kimakowicz-Winnicki, M. Spinn und Webewerkzeuge. Würzburg, 1910.

Arc 635.210 Kinch, K.F. L'Arc de Triomphe de Salonique. Paris, 1890.

Arc 510.220F Kinch, K.F. Vroulia [Rhodes]. Berlin, 1914.

Arc 1423.20 Kindler, A. The coins of Tiberias. Tiberias, 1961.

Arc 870.28 King, Alan. Early Pennine settlement: a field study. Lancaster, 1970.

Arc 1365.2 King, Charles W. Early Christian numismatics. London, 1873.

Arc 1077.2.46F King, E.S. The date and provenance of a bronze reliquary cross in the Museo Cristiano. Rome, 1928.

Arc 136.1.63 King, Edward. A speech...23rd April 1784. London, 1784.

Arc 505.5.81 King, J. Recent discoveries on the Temple Hill at Jerusalem. 2. ed. London, 1885.

Arc 560.1 King, L.W. Egypt and Western Asia. London, 1907.

Arc 855.219 King John's house, Tollard Royal, Wilts. (Fox-Pitt-Rivers.) n.p., 1890.

Arc 595.27 Kingsland, William. The Great Pyramid in fact and in theory. London, 1932-35. 2v.

Arc 955.5 Kinishba. (Cummings, B.) Phoenix, Arizona, 1940.

Arc 560.2 Kink, Khil'da A. Egipet do faraonov. Moskva, 1964.

Arc 595.68 Kink, Khil'da A. Kak stroilis' egipetskte piramidy. Moskva, 1967.

Arc 513.40 Kink, Khilida A. Vostochnoe sredizemnamor'e v drevneishuiu epokhu. Moskva, 1970.

Arc 861.10.7 Kinnebrook, William. Etchings of the Runic monuments in Isle of Man. London, 1841.

Arc 861.10.15 Kinnebrook, William. List of Manx antiquities. Douglas, 1930.

Arc 861.10.17 Kinnebrook, William. Manks antiquities. 2. ed. Liverpool, 1914.

Arc 861.10.11 Kinnebrook, William. Manx crosses...monuments...Isle of Man. London, 1907.

Arc 861.10.13 Kinnebrook, William. Traces of the Norse mythology. London, 1904.

Arc 943.40 Kinzhalov, R.V. Pamiatniki kul'tury i iskusstva drevnei Ameriki. Leningrad, 1958.

Arc 1033.34.55 Kioschbaum, Engelbert. La tumba de San Pedro y las catacumbas romanas. Madrid, 1954.

Arc 935.31.5 Kipshidze, David A. Peshckery Ani. Erevan, 1972.

Htn Arc 545.200* Kircher, A. Oedipus Aegyptiacus. v.1-3. Romae, 1652-54. 4v.

Arc 716.2.2 Kirchhoff, F.C. Neue Messungen der Überreste vom Theater des Dionysus zu Athen. Altona, 1883.

Arc 716.2 Kirchhoff, F.C. Vergleichung der Überreste vom Theater des Dionysuszu Athen. Altona, 1882.

Arc 383.92A Kirchner, H. Ur- und Frühgeschichte als historische Wissenschaft. Heidelberg, 1950.

Arc 1163.22 Kirchner, J. Germanistische Handschriftenpraxis. München, 1950.

Arc 1153.73 Kirchner, J. Scriptura latina libraria. Monachii, 1955.

Arc 638.4 Kirckhoff, C. Der Rhombus in der Orchestra des Dionysustheaters zu Athen. Altona, 1885. 3 pam.

Arc 395.24 Kir'ianov, A.V. Restavratsiia arkheologicheskikh predmetov. Moskva, 1960.

Arc 1163.32 Kirkham, E. Kay. How to read the handwriting and records of early America. Salt Lake City, 1961.

Arc 609.8 Kirkman, James Spedding. The Arab city of Gedi. London, 1954.

Arc 609.8.5 Kirkman, James Spedding. The tomb of the dated inscription at Gedi. London, 1960.

Arc 1588.1.11 Kirmis, M. Handbuch der polnischen Münzkunde. Posen, 1892.

Arc 923.130 Kirpicknikov, Anatolii N. Snariazhenie vsadnika i verkhovogo konia na Rusi IX-XIII vv. Leningrad, 1973.

Arc 1025.73 Kirsch, G.P. The catacombs of Rome. Rome, 1946.

Arc 1020.9.97 Kirsch, Johann P. Die römischen Titelkirchen im Altertum. Paderborn, 1918.

Arc 1027.32.10 Kirschbaum, E. Die Graeber der Apostelfürsten. Frankfurt, 1957.

Arc 1027.32.12 Kirschbaum, E. Die Graeber der Apostelfürsten. 2. Aufl. Frankfurt, 1959.

Arc 650.10.5 Kirsten, Ernst. Griechenlandkunde; ein Führer zu klassischen Stätten. Heidelberg, 1956.

Arc 650.10 Kirsten, Ernst. Griechenlandkunde. Heidelberg, 1955.

Arc 650.10.7 Kirsten, Ernst. Griechenlandkunde. 3. Aufl. Heidelberg, 1957.

Arc 543.120.5 Kiselev, Sergei. Drevnemongol'skie goroda. Moskva, 1965.

Arc 302.9.15 Kiss, Zsolt. Les publications du Centre d'archéologie méditerranéenne. Warszawa, 1974.

Arc 505.13 Kittel, D.R. Schlaugenstein im Kidrontal bei Jerusalem. Leipzig, 1907.

Arc 938.80F Kivikirves ja hapearisti. (Racz, István.) Helsingissä, 1961.

Arc 938.85.5 Kivikoski, Ella. Finland. London, 1967.

Arc 938.96F Kivikoski, Ella. Kvaonbacken. Helsinki, 1963.

Arc 938.85 Kivikoski, Ella. Suomen esihistoria. Helsinki, 1961.

Arc 938.85.10 Kivikoski, Ella. Suomen kiinteät muinaisjäännökset. Helsinki, 1966.

Arc 938.75F Kivikoski, Ella. Suomen rantakauden kuoasto. Helsinki, 1947-51. 2v.

Arc 1433.39 Klad' serebianykh' monet' s" vodianskago gorodishcha. (Krotkov', A.A.) Saragov', 1913.

Arc 1584.32.1 Kladoiskatel'stvo i numizmatika. (Kotliar, Mykola F.) Kiev, 1974.

Arc 1480.64F Klady rimskikh monet na teriitorii SSSR. (Kropotkin, V.V.) Moskva, 1961.

Arc 630.4 Die klassische Archäologie und die altchristliche Kunst. (Sybel, L. von.) Marburg, 1906.

Arc 1663.52F Das klassische Weimar in Medaillen. (Frede, Lothar.) Leipzig, 1959.

Arc 628.3 Klassisches Bilderbuch. (Oehler, R.) n.p., 1892?

Arc 936.14.295 Klasyfikacja czasowo-przestrzenna kultur neolitycznych na Pomorzu zachodnim. wyd. 1. (Siuchniński, Kazimierz.) Szczecin, 1969.

Arc 1468.42 Klawans, Zander H. An outline of ancient Greek coins. Racine, Wis. , 1959.

Arc 1478.85 Klawans, Zander H. Reading and dating Roman imperial coins. 3. ed. Racine, Wis., 1963.

Arc 925.185 Kldis sakhli skal'nye doma selishcha Pia. (Gaprindashvili, Givi M.) Tbilisi, 1959.

Arc 505.86 Kleemann, Ilse. Der Satrapen-Sarkophag aus Sidon. Berlin, 1958.

Arc 383.48F Kleemann, Otto. Documento archaeologica. Bonn, 1956.

Arc 853.364 Kleemann, Otto. Vor- und Frühgeschichte des Kreises Ahrweiler. Bonn, 1971.

Arc 853.3 Klein, C. Die römischen Denkmäler in und bei Mainz. Mainz, 1861.

Arc 1033.17.60 Klein, Dorothee. St. Lukas als Maler der Maria. Berlin, 1933.

Arc 1430.200 Kleinasiatische Münzen. (Imhoof-Blumer, Friedrich.) Wien, 1901-02. 2v.

Arc 513.21.10 Kleinasiatische Studien. (Bittel, Kurt.) Istanbul, 1942.

Arc 1428.13F Die kleinasiatischen Münzen der römischen Kaiserzeit. (Bosch, C.) Stuttgart, 1935.

Arc 383.79 Kleinasien und Byzanz. Berlin, 1950.

Arc 1428.33 Kleinasien zur Römerzeit; griechisches Leben im Spiegel der Münzen. (Franke, Peter R.) München, 1968.

Arc 386.5.4A Kleine Schriften. (Böttiger, Carl August.) Dresden, 1837-38. 3v.

Arc 628.12 Kleine Schriften. (Brunn, H.) Leipzig, 1898. 3v.

Arc 390.2.12 Kleine Schriften. (Furtwängler, Adolf.) München, 1912. 2v.

Arc 386.5.3 Kleine Schriften. 2. Aufl. (Böttiger, Carl August.) Leipzig, 1850. 3v.

Arc 905.17.10F Kleinfunde von Aguntum aus den Jahren 1850 bis 1952. (Alzinger, Wilhelm.) Wien, 1955.

Arc 936.180 Klemenc, J. Archäologische Karte von Jugoslavien. Beograd, 1938.

Arc 936.230 Klemenc, J. Rimske izkopanine v Šempetru. Ljubljana, 1961.

Arc 543.125 Klements, D.A. Arkheologicheskii dnevnik poezdki v Sredniuiu Mongoliiu v 1891 godu. Sankt Peterburg, 1895.

Arc 650.1 Klenze, L. von. Aphoristische Bemerkungen gesammelt...Reise nach Griechenland. Berlin, 1838.

Arc 895.7.35.2 Klindt-Jensen, Ole. Le Danemark avant les Vikings. Grenoble, 1960.

Arc 895.7.35 Klindt-Jensen, Ole. Denmark before the Vikings. London, 1957.

Arc 893.31 Klindt-Jensen, Ole. A history of Scandinavian archaeology. London, 1975.

Arc 888.50 Klok, R.H.J. Archeologie en monument. Bussum, 1969.

Arc 900.213 Klose, O. Die römischen Meilensteine in Salzberg. Wien, 1902.

Arc 1668.12 Klotz, C.A. Historia numorum contumeliosorum. Altenburgi, 1765. 2 pam.

Arc 395.10 Klotz, C.A. Ueber das Studium des Alterthums. Halle, 1766.

Arc 1510.147 Klotzsch, Johann Friedrich. Versuch einer chur-sächsischen Münzgeschichte von den Ältesten, bis auf jetzige Zeiten. v.1-2. Chemnitz, 1779-80.

Arc 726.76F Klumbach, H. Tarentiner Grabkunst. Reuttingen, 1937.

Arc 938.5.5 Klusie liecinieki; senlietu albums. (Archäologischer Kongress, 10th, Riga, 1896.) Lincoln, Nebraska, 1964.

Arc 936.14.275 Kmieciński, Jerzy. Odry. Wrocław, 1968.

Arc 1588.1.40 Kmietowicz, A. Skarb srebrny z miejscowosci Ochle. Wrocław, 1962.

Arc 1390.19 Kmietowicz, Anna. Wczesnośredniowieczny skarb srebrny z zalesia powiat słupca. Wrocław, 1969-74. 2v.

Arc 905.2 Knabl, R. Wo stand das "Flavium Solvense?" n.p., n.d.

Arc 853.31.10 Knack, H. Die Latènekulter in Thüringen. Inaug. Diss. Stettin, 1929?

Arc 628.24 Knell, Heiner. Archäologie. Darmstadt, 1972.

Author and Title Listing

Arc 936.238 Knez, Tone. Novo Mesto v davnini. Maribar, 1972.

Arc 925.50.100 Kniazhii galich. 2. vyd. (Chachkovs'kyi, L.) Chikago, 1959.

Arc 87.1.29 Die knieenden Figuren der altgriechische Kunst. (Curtius, E.) Berlin, 1870.

Arc 1665.2 Knifer, Gijsbert. De elephantis in numis obviis exercitationes duae. Hagae, 1719. 2 pam.

Arc 1508.29 Knigge, Wilhelm. Münz- und Medaillen-Kabinet des Freiherrn Wilhelm Knigge. Bielefeld, 1972.

Arc 785.42.5 Knight, William. The arch of Titus. London, 1896.

Arc 925.20 Knipovich, Tatiana N. Tanais. Moskva, 1949.

Arc 925.8.20 Knipovick, T.N. Tamaie. Moskva, 1949.

Arc 543.96 Knobloch, Edgar. Beyond the Oxus; archaeology, art and architecture of Central Asia. London, 1972.

Arc 672.1.125 Knossos. (Coldstream, John Nicolas.) London, 1973.

Arc 1348.7.2 The knowledge of medals. (Jobert, L.) London, 1697.

Arc 895.76 Knuth, Eigil. Archaeology of the musk-ox way. Paris, 1967.

Arc 925.50.225 Knyzhitskii, Sergei D. Zhilye ansambli drevnei Ol'vii IV-II vv. do n.e. Kiev, 1971.

Arc 1588.6.25 Kocaer, Remje. Osmanli altinlari. Istanbul, 1967.

Arc 1470.35 Koch, Cornelius D. De Aristotle in nummo aureo. Helmestadi, 1703.

Arc 743.3 Koch, M. Die Alpen-Etrusker. Leipzig, 1853.

Arc 853.284F Koch, Robert. Bodenfunde der Völkerwanderungszeit aus dem Main-Tauber-Gebiet. Diss. Berlin, 1967. 2v.

Arc 1093.7.2 Koch, Rudolf. Das Zeichenbuch. 2. Aufl. Offenbach am Main, 1926.

Arc 853.360 Koch, Ursula. Die Grabfunde der Merowingerzeit aus dem Donautal um Regensberg. Berlin, 1968. 2v.

Arc 925.321.20 Kochkurkina, Svetlana I. Iugo-Vostochnoe Priladozh'e v desiatomtrinadtsatom vekakh. Leningrad, 1973.

Arc 805.3 Koehler, H.K.E. von. Description de deux monumens antiques. St. Petersbourg, 1810.

Arc 936.242F Köhler, Ralf. Untersuchungen zu Grabkomplexam der älteren römischen Kaiserzeit in Böhmen unter Aspekten der religiösen und sozialen Gliederung. Neumünster, 1975.

Arc 925.8.30 Koehne, B. Beiträge zur Geschichte und Archäologie von Cherronesos in Taurien. St. Petersburg, 1850.

Arc 1333.6 Koehne. Description. Musée...Prince Basile Kotschoubey. St. Petersbourg, 1857. 2v.

Arc 1325.2 Kölme, B. Zeitschrift für Münz, Siegel und Wappenkunde. Berlin. 1-6 3v.

Arc 1138.121 König, Marie E.P. Am Anfang der Kultur. Berlin, 1973.

Arc 1560.4 Die königlich schwedische Münze in Livland. (Platbarzdis, Aleksander.) Stockholm, 1968.

Arc 1470.20 Königliche Academie der Wissenschaft zu Amsterdam. Beschreibung der Griechischen Autonomen Münzen. Amsterdam, 1912.

Arc 1335.11.5 Das königliche Münzkabinet. 2. Aufl. (Friedlander.) Berlin, 1877.

Arc 1229.10 Die Königs-Stempel. (Welfen, Peter.) Wiesbaden, 1969.

Arc 510.204 Die Koenigsburg von Pergamon. (Thiersch, F.) Stuttgart, 1883.

Arc 612.76 Königsgrabkirchen der Franken. (Krueger, Karl Heinrich.) München, 1971.

Arc 87.1.52 Koepp, F. Das Bildnis Alexanders des Grossen. Berlin, 1892.

Arc 848.5 Koepp, F. Die Römer in Deutschland. Bielefeld, 1912.

Arc 395.4 Koepp, Friedrich. Archäologie. 2. Aufl. v.2,4. Berlin, 1920. 2v.

Arc 497.34 Köppel, Robert. Untersuchungen über die Steinzeit Palästina-Syriens. Inaug. Diss. Rom, 1933.

Arc 853.280F Koerber-Grohne, Udelgard. Geobotanische Untersuchungen auf der Feddersen Wierde. Wiesbaden, 1967. 2v.

Arc 853.368 Körner, Gerhard. Vorgeschichte im Landkreis Lüneburg. Lüneburg, 1971.

Arc 1663.57 Koernlein, Melchior. Thesaurus numismatum modernorum huius seculi, sive numismata mnemonica et iconica qui bus praecipui eventus et res gestae ab anno MDCC illustrantur. Norimbergae, 1711-17?

Arc 395.3 Körte, G. Archäologie und Geschichts Wissenschaft. Göttingen, 1911.

Arc 600.13 Köster, A. Die ägyptische Pflanzensäule der Spätzeit. Paris, 1903.

Arc 710.11 Köster, A. Das Pelargikon. Strasburg, 1909.

Arc 716.9 Köster, A. Das Stadion von Athen. Berlin, n.d.

Arc 1088.1.25 Köster, August. Das antike Seewesen. 1. Aufl. Berlin, 1923.

Arc 853.300 Koester, Hans. Die mittlere Bronzezeit im nördlichen Rheingraben. Bonn, 1968.

Arc 1138.120 Kogda molchat pis'mena. (Kondratov, Aleksandr Mikhailovich.) Moskva, 1970.

Arc 1033.35.37 Kohler, C. Réfugié à Jérusalem au VIe siècle. Nogent-le-Rotrou, n.d.

Arc 1033.33 Koimeterien die altchristlichen Begrabnis. (Müller, N.) Leipzig, 1901.

Arc 1578.3 Kolb, J. von. Die Münzen, Medaillen und Jetone. Linz, 1882.

Arc 385.15 Kolchin, B.A. Arkheologiia i estestvennye nauki. Moskva, 1965.

Arc 925.95 Kolchin, B.A. Tekhnika obra botki metala v drev. ruhssi. Moskva, 1953.

Arc 87.1.51 Koldewery, R. Neandrid. Berlin, 1891.

Arc 395.6 Koldewey, Robert. Heitere und ernst Briefe aus einem deutschen Archäologenleben. Berlin, 1920.

Arc 936.14.215 Kolegiata wiślicka. (Warsaw. Uniwersytet. Zespól Badań nad Polskim Średniowieczem.) Kielce, 1965.

Arc 1588.6.5 Kolerkilic, Eksen. Osmarli inpatatorlugurda pava. Ankara, 1958.

Arc 1020.146 Kollautz, Arnulf. Denkmäler byzantinischen Christentums aus der Awarenzeit der Donauländer. Amsterdam, 1970.

Arc 853.349 Kolling, Alfons. Funde aus der Römerstadt Schwarzenacke und ihrer nahen Ungebung. Homburg-Saar, 1971.

Arc 1020.131 Kollwitz, J. Die Lipsanothek von Brescia. Berlin, 1933.

Arc 1020.131PF Kollwitz, J. Die Lipsanothek von Brescia. Atlas. Berlin, 1933.

Arc 708.35 Kolobova, K.M. Drevnii gorod Afiny i ego pamiatniki. Leningrad, 1961.

Arc 853.205.5 Kołobrzeg we wczesnymsredniowieczu. (Leciyewicz, Leah.) Wrocław, 1961.

Arc 936.14.230 Kołodziejski, Adam. Rozwój archeologii województwa zielonogórskiego w dwudziestoleciu Polski Ludowej. Zielona Góra, 1965.

Arc 925.50.240 Kolosov, Iurii H. Shaitan-Koba - mustievs'ka stoianka Knymii. Kyiv, 1972.

Arc 785.8.5 Das Kolosseum. (Viola, Joseph.) Rom, 1913.

Arc 815.7 Komposition der Pompejanischen Wandgewälde. (Rodenwaldt, G.) Berlin, 1909.

Arc 450.1 Konarka. (Swarup, B.) Bengal, 1910.

Arc 920.203F Kondakov, N. Antiquités de la Russie méridionale. Paris, 1891.

Arc 923.20F Kondakov, N. Russkie klady. Sankt Petersburg, 1896.

Arc 495.206F Kondakov, N.P. Arkheologicheskoe puteshestvie in Sirii. Sankt Peterburg, 1904.

Arc 682.25 Kondakov, N.P. Makedoniia arkheologiia putesh. Sankt Peterburg, 1909.

Arc 543.11F Kondakov, N.P. Opic' pamiatnikov' drevnosti. Sankt Peterburg, 1890.

Arc 543.9 Kondakov, N.P. Puteshestvie na Cinai. Odessa, 1882.

Arc 395.8 Kondakov, N.P. Vospominaniia i dumy. Praga, 1927.

Arc 412.22.1 Kondratov, Aleksandr M. The riddles of three oceans. Moscow, 1974.

Arc 412.22 Kondratov, Aleksandr M. Tainy tsekh okeanov. Leningrad, 1971.

Arc 1138.120 Kondratov, Aleksandr Mikhailovich. Kogda molchat pis'mena. Moskva, 1970.

Arc 925.150.23 Konferentsiia no Arkheologii Belorussii i Smezhnykh Territorii, Minsk, 1966. Drevnosti Belorussii. Minsk, 1966.

Arc 925.150.25 Konferentsiia po Arkheologii Belorussii, Minsk, 1968. Belorusskie drevnosti. Minsk, 1967.

Arc 925.150.30 Konferentsiia po Arkheologii Belorussii, Minsk, 1969. Drevnosti Belorussii. Minsk, 1969.

Arc 925.150.50 Konferentsiia po Arkheologii Belorussii i Smezhnykh Territorii, Minsk, 1972. Belorusskiia starazhytnastsi. Minsk, 1972.

Arc 936.15.25 Kongres archeologa Jugoslavije, 6th, Ljubljana, 1963. Kongrresni materijali VI Kongresa Jugoslovinskih arheoloya. Beograd, 1964. 2v.

Arc 303.25 Kongress Baltischer Archäologen, 2d, Riga, 1930. Congressus secundus archaeologorum balticorum. Riga, 1931.

Arc 936.15.25 Kongrresni materijali VI Kongresa Jugoslovinskih arheoloya. (Kongres archeologa Jugoslavije, 6th, Ljubljana, 1963.) Beograd, 1964. 2v.

Arc 853.200 Konik, E. Ślask starożytny a Imperium Rzymskie. Warszawa, 1959.

Arc 1480.68 Konik, Eugeniusz. Znaleziska monet rzymskich na Śląsku. Wrocław, 1965.

Arc 925.268 Konstantinov, Ivan V. Material'naia kul'tura iakutov XVIII veka. Iakutsk, 1971.

Arc 925.269 Konstantinov, Ivan V. Material'naia kul'tura Iakutov XVIII veka. Photoreproduction. Novosibirsk, 1967.

Arc 936.7.10 Kontakty handlowe Wielkopolski w IX-XI wieku. (Szymański, W.) Poznań, 1958.

Arc 785.110 Kontakty Noricum i Pannonii z ludami polnochymi. (Wielowiejski, Jerzy.) Wrocław, 1970.

Arc 684.1.50 Kontes, I.D. To Hieron tēs Olympias. Athēnai, 1958.

Arc 716.7.20 Kontoleon, N.M. To Erehtheion ōs iokodomema chthonias latreias. Athēnai, 1949.

Arc 1590.31 Kontramarky na pražských groších. (Katz, Viktor.) Praha, 1927.

Arc 1588.6.1 Konuni Sultan Suleymon adena basilon sikkeler. (Artuk, Ibrah.) Ankara, 1972.

Arc 936.100.25 Konzervatorski rad kod Hrvata. (Horvat, L.A.) Zagreb, 1944.

Arc 1200.24 Kopczynski, M. Die Arengen der Papsturkunden nach ihrer Bedeutung und Verwendung bis zu Gregor VII. Inaug. Diss. Bottrop, 1936.

Arc 1588.1.110 Kopicki, Edmund. Katalog podstawowych typów monet i banknotów Polski oraz ziem historycznie z Polską związanych. v.1, pt.1-2. Warszawa, 1974- 2v.

Arc 1138.9 Kopp, U.F. Palaeographia critica. Mannheim, 1817-29. 4v.

Arc 1163.3.75 Koppen, P.I. Spisok. russkim pamiatnikam, sluzhashchim k postavleniiu istorii khudozhestv i otechestvennoi paleografii. Moskva, 1822.

Arc 600.160F Koptische Friedhöfe bei Karâra und der Amontempel Schesehonks I bei El Hibe. (Ranke, Hermann.) Berlin, 1926.

Arc 1166.7 Koptische Inschriften im Kaiser-Friedrich Museum zu Berlin. (Cramer, Maria.) Le Caire, 1949.

Arc 1166.7.15F Koptische Paläographie. (Cramer, Maria.) Wiesbaden, 1964.

Arc 588.5 Koptos. (Petrie, W.M.F.) London, 1896.

Arc 635.226F Korakou, a prehistoric settlement near Corinth. (Blegen, Carl W.) Boston, 1921.

Htn Arc 1033.17.52* Kordecki, A. Nova gigantomachia contra...imagine...virgine...Lucea depictam. Czestochovia, n.d.

Arc 416.49 Korfmann, Manfred. Schleuder und Bogen in Südwestasien; von der frühesten Belagen bis zum Beginn der historischen Stadtstaaten. Bonn, 1972.

Arc 853.35 Korhl, C. Neue prähistorische Funde aus Worms und Augsburg. n.p., n.d.

Arc 672.2.5F Korkya. Berlin. 1-2,1939-1940

Arc 672.2 Korkyraeische Studien. (Schmidt, B.) Leipzig, 1890. 2v.

Arc 1269.35 Korn, Otto. Rheinisches Siegel- und Urkundenbuch. Brühl, 1952.

Arc 936.261 Korošec, Paola. Predistariska naselba Barutnica kaj anzibegovo vo Makedonija. Prilep, 1973.

Arc 302.15 Korotke zvidompennia. (Akademia nauk URSR, Kiev. Vseukrainha Akademia Nauk. Vseukrainshau Arkheologichnu Komitet, Kiev.) Kiev. 1926+

Arc 893.19 Kort udsigt over Nordens oldtidsminder. (Winkel Horn, F.) Kjøbenhavn, 1883.

Arc 530.183 Korucutepe; final report on the excavations of the Universities of Chicago, California (Los Angeles). Amsterdam, 1975.

Arc 923.111F Korzukhina, G.F. Russkie klady IX-XIII vv. Moskva, 1954.

Arc 672.6F Kos. Berlin. 1,1932

Arc 925.4.60 Kosarev, Mikhail F. Drevnie kul'tury Tomsko-Narymskogo Priob'ia. Moskva, 1974.

Arc 530.140F Kosay, H.Z. Büyük Güllücek karisi. Ankara, 1957.

Arc 530.141F Kosay, H.Z. Guzelova karisi. Ankara, 1967.

Arc 522.20 Kosay, Hamit. "Troad" da dört yerleş me yeri. Istanbul, 1936.

Arc 935.24.5 Kosay, Hâmit Z. Alacahöyük. n.p., 195-?

Arc 935.26F Kosay, Hâmit Z. Türk Tarih Kurumu tarafindan apilan Pazarli kafreyati raporu. Ankara, 1941.

Arc 935.24F Kosay, Hâmit Z. Türk Tarih Kurumu tarafindan yapilan Alaca Höyük kafriyati. Ankara, 1938.

Arc 935.24.10 Kosay, Hâmit Z. Türk Tarih Kurumu tarafindan yapilan Alaca Höyük karisi. Ankara, 1973.

Author and Title Listing

Arc 935.70 Kosay, Hâmit Zübeyr. Pulur kazisi; 1960 mersimi çalişmalari raporu. Ankara, 1964.
Arc 395.18 Kosidowski, Z. Gdy słońce było bogiem. Warszawa, 1958.
Arc 395.18.2 Kosidowski, Z. Gdy słońce było bogiem. Warszawa, 1962.
Arc 395.18.5.5 Kosidowski, Zenon. Rumaki Lizypa i inne opowiadania. 2. wyd. Warszawa, 1974.
Arc 672.5.20F Kosmopoulos, L.W. The prehistoric inhabitation of Corinth. Munich, 1948.
Arc 853.317 Kossack, Georg. Gräberfelder dur Hallstattzeit an Main und Fränkischer Saale. Kallmünz, 1970.
Arc 848.8.9 Kossinna, Gustaf. Altgermanische Kulturhöhe. München, 1927.
Arc 848.8.10 Kossinna, Gustaf. Altgermanische Kulturhöhe. 8. Aufl. Leipzig, 1942.
Arc 848.8.2 Kossinna, Gustaf. Die deutsche Vorgeschichte. 2. Aufl. Würzburg, 1914.
Arc 848.8.4 Kossinna, Gustaf. Die deutsche Vorgeschichte. 7. Aufl. Leipzig, 1936.
Arc 848.8.11 Kossinna, Gustaf. Germanische Kultur im letzten Jahrtausend nach Christus. Leipzig, 1932.
Arc 848.8.5 Kossinna, Gustaf. Die Herkunft der Germanen. Würzburg, 1911.
Arc 848.8.13 Kossinna, Gustaf. Ursprung und Verbreitung der Germanen in vor-und frühgeschichtlicher Zeit. Leipzig, 1928.
Arc 936.14.75 Kostrzewski, B. Z najdawniejszych dziejow Giecza. Wrocław, 1962.
Arc 936.75 Kostrzewski, J. Les origines de la civilisation polonaise. Paris, 1949.
Arc 853.50 Kostrzewski, J. Die ostgermanische Kultur. Leipzig, 1919. 2v.
Arc 936.6.15 Kostrzewski, Józef. Kultura łużycka na Pomorzu. Poznań, 1958.
Arc 936.14.90F Kostrzewski, Józef. Odkrycia archeologja na ziemaich zachodnich i północnych Polski. Warszawa, 1962.
Arc 936.14.149 Kostrzewski, Józef. Pradzieje Polski. Poznań, 1949.
Arc 936.14.150 Kostrzewski, Józef. Pradzieje Polski. wyd. 2. Wrocław, 1965.
Arc 936.14.92 Kostrzewski, Józef. Pradzieje Pomorza. Wrocław, 1966.
Arc 853.65.45 Kostrzewski, Józef. Pradzieje Śląska. Wrocław, 1970.
Arc 936.6 Kostrzewski, Józef. Wielkopolska w czasach. Poznań, 1914.
Arc 936.6.5 Kostrzewski, Józef. Wielkopolska w czasach. Poznań, 1923.
Arc 936.6.10 Kostrzewski, Józef. Wielkopolska w pradziejach. 3. wyd. Warszawa, 1955.
Arc 936.6.3 Kostrzewski, Józef. Z dziejów badań archeologja w Wielkopolsce. Wrocław, 1958.
Arc 395.25 Kostrzewski, Józef. Z mego życia. Wrocław, 1970.
Arc 936.14.5 Kostrzewski, Józef. Zagadnienie ciągłosci zaludnienia ziem polskich co pradziejach. Poznań, 1961.
Arc 936.14.8 Kostrzewski, Józef. Zur Frage der Siedlungsstetigkeit in der Geschichte Polens. Wrocław, 1965.
Arc 936.14.160 Koszalin, Poland (City). Muzeum. Pradzieje pomorza srodkowego. Koszalin, 1964.
Arc 302.17 Koszalinskie zeszyty muzealne. Koszalin. 1,1971+
Arc 1390.20 Kotliar, Mykola F. Hroskovyi sbih na terytorii Ukrainy doby teodalizma. Kyïv, 1971.
Arc 1584.32.1 Kotliar, Mykola F. Kladoiskatel'stvo i numizmatika. Kiev, 1974.
Arc 925.322.20 Kotovich, Valentina M. Verkhnegunibskoe poselenie-pamiatnik epokhi bronzy gornogo Dagestana. Makhachkala, 1965.
Arc 925.322.10 Kotovich, Vladimir G. Kamennyi vek Dagestana. Makhachkala, 1964.
Arc 925.105 Kotsevalov, A.S. Antichnikh istoria i kul'tura severi Prichernomor'ia. Miunkhon, 1955.
Arc 925.19F Kourgans et Gorodietz. (Bulychov, N.) Moskva, 1900. 3 pam.
Arc 66.1.219 Les kouroi du Ptoion. (Ducat, Jean.) Paris, 1971.
Arc 674.1.9F Kourouniotos, K. Eleusiniaka. Athēnai, 1932.
Arc 674.1.10 Kourouniotos, K. Eleusis. Athēnai, 1934.
Arc 674.1.12 Kourouniotos, K. Eleusis. Athens, 1936.
Arc 684.7 Kourouniotos, K. Hodēgos tēs Olympias. Athēnai, 1904.
Arc 684.7.5 Kourouniotos, K. Katalogos tōn mouseiou Lukosouras. Athēnai, 1911.
Arc 936.215 Kovačević, J. Arheologija i istorija varvarske kolonizacije juzroslov. oblasti. Novi Sad, 1960.
Arc 925.50.140 Kovpanenko, Halyna T. Plemena skifs'koho chasu na Vorskli. Kyïv, 1967.
Arc 612.78 Kowalczyk, Jan. Zmierzch epoki kamicnia. Wrocław, 1971.
Arc 905.140 A Közép-Duna-medence magyar honfoglalás. (Fehér, Géza.) Budapest, 1962.
Arc 340.30.3 A Közép-Dunamedence régészeti bibliográfiája, 1954-1959. (Banner, János.) Budapest, 1961.
Arc 340.30.5 A Közép-Dunamedence régészeti bibliográfiája, 1960-1966. (Banner, János.) Budapest, 1968.
Arc 340.30 A Közép-Dunamedence régészeti bibliográfiája a legrégibb időktöl a XI. századig. (Banner, János.) Budapest, 1954.
Arc 936.155.5 Kozhemiako, P.N. Radnesrednevekovye goroda i pos. Chuiskoi doliny. Frunze, 1959.
Arc 612.82 Kozłowski, Janusz. Munj cyklopów. Wrocław, 1971.
Arc 395.26 Kozłowski, Janusz K. Archeologia prahistoryczna. Wyd. 1. Kraków, 1972- 2v.
Arc 936.14.210 Kozłowski, Janusz K. Paleolit na Gónnym Śląsku. Wrocław, 1964.
Arc 936.14.405 Kozłowski, Stefan. Pradzieje ziem polskich od IX do V tysiąclecia. wyd. 1. Warszawa, 1972.
Arc 612.44 Koztowski, J.K. Próba klasyfikacji górnopaleolitycznych przemysłów z płoszczami leściowatymi w Europie. Krakow, 1961.
Arc 925.285 Kozyreva, Rimma V. Drevneishee proshloe Sakhalina. Iuzhno, 1960.
Arc 925.285.5 Kozyreva, Rimma V. Drevnii Sakhalin. Leningrad, 1967.
Arc 1480.42.10F Kraay, C.W. Die Münzfunde von Vindonissa bis Trafar. Basel, 1962.
Arc 1470.86 Kraay, Colin M. The composition of Greek silver coins. Oxford, 1962.
Arc 505.68 Kraeling, C.H. Gerasa, city of the Decapolis. New Haven, Conn., 1938.
Arc 608.17.25F Kraeling, C.H. Ptolemais, city of the Libyan Pentapolis. Chicago, 1962.
Arc 1510.126 Kraemer, Georg. Bayerns Ehrenbuch. Nürnberg, 1834.
Arc 853.362 Krämer, Werner. Die Ausgrabungen in Manching 1955-1961. Wiesbaden, 1970.
Arc 853.298 Krämer, Wolfgang. Neue Beiträge zur Vor- und Frühgeschichte von Gauting. München, 1967.
Arc 395.13 Kraft, G. Der Urmensch als Schöpfer. 2. Aufl. Tübingen, 1948.
Arc 853.21.25 Kraft, Georg. Die Kultur der Bronzezeit in Süddeutschland auf Grund der Funde in Württemberg. Augsburg, 1926.
Arc 1365.4 Kraft, Konrad. Der goldene Kranz Caesars und der Kampf um die Entlassung des "Tyrannen". 2. Aufl. Darmstadt, 1969.
Arc 925.338.5 Krainov, Dmitrii A. Drevneishaia istoriia Volgo-Okskogo mezhdurech'ia. Moskva, 1972.
Arc 936.14.80 Kraków w pradziejach. (Jamka, Rudolf.) Wrocław, 1963.
Arc 853.65.50 Kramarek, Janusz. Wczesnośredniowieczne grodziska nyczyńskie na Śląsku. Wrocław, 1969.
Arc 936.14.340 Kramarkowa, Irena. Stosunki społeczno-gospodarcze i polityczne. Opole, 1969.
Arc 395.27 Kramarkowa, Irena. U źródeł archeologii. Wrocław, 1972.
Arc 853.112 Kramert, K. Ausgrabungen unter der St. Jakobskirche Dokumertieren. n.p., 1954.
Arc 1077.2.53.2 Der Kranz in Antike und Christentum. (Baus, Karl.) Bonn, 1965.
Arc 1588.4.30 Krasa česke mince. (Nohejlová, Emanuela.) Praha, 1955.
Arc 936.195.280 Kraskovská, L'udmila. Slovansko-avarské pohrebisko pri Z'ahoiskej Bystrici. 1. vyd. Bratislava, 1972.
Arc 925.255.5F Krasnoiarsk, Siberia (City). Kraevoi Kraevedcheskii Muzei. Materialy i issledovaniia po arkheologii etnografii i istorii Krasnoiarskogo kraia. Krasnoiarsk, 1963.
Arc 289.10 Kratkie soobshcheniia o polevykh arkheologicheskikh issledovaniiskh. (Odessa. Derzhavnyi Arkheolohichnye Muzei.) 1961-1963 3v.
Arc 925.10 Kratkii ocherk arkheologii kabardinskoi ASSR. (Krupnov, Evgenii I.) Nal'chik, 1946.
Arc 925.50.235 Kratkii putevoditel' po antichnomu otdelu i vaskopkam khersonesa. (Lisin, V.) Sevastopol', 1939.
Arc 923.11.5F Kratkoe opisanie novago vladaniia imperatopskago rossiiskago istoricheskago muzeia. (Shchukinym, P.I.) Moskva, 1906.
Arc 1588.4.35 Kratký přehled českého mincovnictví a tabulky cen a mezd. (Nohejlová, Emanuela.) Praha, 1964.
Arc 905.125 Kratzschmer, F. Die Entwicklungsgeschichte des antiken Bades und das Bad auf dem Maydalensberg. Düsseldorf, 1961.
Arc 1025.2 Kraus, F.K. Roma Sotterranea, die römischen Katakomben. Freiburg, 1879.
Arc 1016.204 Kraus, F.X. Die altchristlichen Inschriften der Rheinlande. Freiburg, 1890.
Arc 1018.35 Kraus, F.X. Archäologie...Christliche Archäologie, 1880-86. Stuttgart, 1882. 2v.
Arc 1018.32.7 Kraus, F.X. Die christliche Kunst in ihren frühesten Anfängen. Leipzig, 1872.
Arc 1033.12.169 Kraus, F.X. Heilige Nagel...zu Trier. Trier, 1868.
Arc 1018.32 Kraus, F.X. Über Begriff...christlichen Archäologie. Freiburg, 1879.
Arc 1027.1.5 Kraus, F.X. Über den gegenwärtigenStand der Frage. Freiburg, 1872.
Arc 1018.05 Kraus, Franz X. Real-Encyclopädie der Christlichen Alterthümer. Freiburg, 1882-86. 2v.
Arc 395.7.10 Kraus, Franz Xaver. Liberal und integral: der Briefwechsel zwischen Franz Xaver Kraus und A. Stöck. Mainz, 1974.
Arc 395.7.5 Kraus, Franz Xaver. Tagebücher. Köln, 1957.
Arc 793.10F Kraus, Theodor. Pompeii and Herculaneum: the living cities of the dead. N.Y., 1975.
Arc 750.206.10 Kraus, Theodor. Die Ranken der Ara Pacis. Berlin, 1953.
Arc 1096.2 Krause, J.H. Angeiologie. Halle, 1854.
Arc 530.12.32 Krause, K. Boğazköy. Berlin, 1940.
Arc 853.9 Krause E. Die megalithischen Gräber...Deutschlands. Berlin, 1893.
Arc 853.56 Krebs, Albert. Die vorrömische Metallzeit im östlichen Westfalen. Leipzig, 1925.
Arc 853.165.10 Der Kreis Saarlouis in vor- und frühgeschichtlichen Zeit. (Maisant, Hermann.) Bonn, 1971. 2v.
Arc 543.3.110 Kremneobrabatyvaiushchie masterskie i shakhty Kamennogo veka Srednii Azii. (Kasymov, M.R.) Tashkent, 1972.
Arc 1588.4.65F Kremnická mincovňa. (Horák, Jan.) Banska Bystrica, 1965.
Arc 1588.4.85 Kremnické dukáty. Vyd. 1. (Horák, Ján.) Bratislava, 1968.
Arc 853.20.7 Krencher, D. Das römische Trier. Berlin, 1923.
Arc 936.252 Kreposti dofeodal'noi i rannefeodal'noi Gruzii. (Melitauri, Konstantin N.) Tbilisi, 1969- 2v.
Arc 543.3.115 Kreposti drevnego Vakhana. (Babaev, Aktam D.) Dushanbe, 1973.
Arc 40.10 Kresh; journal of the Sudan Antiquities Service. Khartoum. 1,1953+ 9v.
Arc 672.1.112 Kreta en Mykene. (Stibbe, C.M.) Zeist, 1964.
Arc 672.1.75F Kreta und das mykenische Hellas. (Marinatos, Spyridon.) München, 1959.
Arc 1251.26 Kretisch-mykenische Siegelbilder. (Biesantz, Hagen.) Marburg, 1954.
Arc 672.1.52F Kretische Bonzereliefs. Text and plates. (Kunze, Emil.) Stuttgart, 1931. 2v.
Arc 672.1.61 Kretische Kunst. (Snijder, G.A.S.) Berlin, 1936.
Arc 905.78 Kreuz, Trans. Rätsel um Carnuntum. Wien, 1939.
Arc 1033.35.145 Das Kreuz Christi. (Zöckler, Otto.) Gütersloh, 1875.
Arc 1428.3 Kreuzfahrer-Münzen. (Dechant, Norbert.) Wien, 1868.
Arc 1033.181 Kriss-Rettenbeck, Lenz. Ex voto. Zürich, 1972.
Arc 785.102 Kristensen, W.B. De Romeinsche fascas. Amsterdam, 1932.
Arc 682.9 Die kritisch-mykenische Kultur. (Fimmen, Diedrich.) Leipzig, 1921.
Arc 682.7 Die kritisch-mykenische Kultur. (Seunig, Vingenz.) Graz, 1921.
Arc 853.8 Kröhnke, O. Chemische Untersuchung an Vorgeschichts Bronzen Schleswig-Holsteins. Kiel, 1897.
Arc 1348.82.5 Kroha, Tyll. Münzen sammeln. 5. Aufl. Braunschweig, 1968.
Arc 1251.27 Kroll, John Hennig. Athenian bronze allotment plates. Thesis. Cambridge, 1972.
Arc 936.195.315 Krolmus, Wácslaw. Poslední bčiště Černoboha s runami na Skalsku, v kraji Boleslavském, v Čechach, na své archaeologické cestě vypátral Václeslav Krolmus. Praha, 1857.
Arc 543.27.5 Krom, N.J. Barabudur. The Hague, 1927. 2v.
Arc 543.27.15 Krom, N.J. De levensgeschiedenis van den Buddha op Barabudur. 's Gravenhage, 1926.
Arc 905.126 Kromer, Karl. Von frühen Eisen und reichen Salzherren die Hallstattkultur in Osterreich. Wien, 1964.
Arc 936.195.70 Kronika objeveného věku. (Boehn, Jároslav.) Praha, 1941.
Arc 853.80 Kropf, W. Die Billendorfer Kultur auf Grund der Grabfunde. Leipzig, 1938.
Arc 1480.64F Kropotkin, V.V. Klady rimskikh monet na teriitorii SSSR. Moskva, 1961.
Arc 933.5 Kropotkin, Vladislav V. Ekonomicheskie sviazi Vostochnoi Evropy v I tysiacheletii neshei ery. Moskva, 1967.
Arc 925.344 Kropotkin, Vladislav V. Rinskie importnye izdeliia v Vostochnoi Evrope. Moskva, 1970.
Arc 853.48 Kropp, Philipp. Latenezeitliche Funde an der keltischgermanischen Völkergrenze. Würzburg, 1911.
Arc 1433.39 Krotkov', A.A. Klad' serebianykh' monet' s" vodianskago gorodishcha. Saragov', 1913.

Arc 933.2F Kruegar, Bruno. Die Kietzsiedlungen im nordlichen Mitteleuropa. Berlin, 1962.
Arc 853.325 Krueger, Bruno. Dessau-Mosigkau. Berlin, 1967.
Arc 853.256F Krueger, Heinrich. Die Jastorf Kultur in der Kreisen. Neumünster, 1961.
Arc 612.76 Krueger, Karl Heinrich. Königsgrabkirchen der Franken. München, 1971.
Arc 1200.12 Krüger, P. Bedeutung der Salutatio...14. Jahrhundert. Greifswald, 1912.
Arc 1583.9 Krug, A.L. Zur Münzkunde Russlands. St. Petersburg, 1805.
Arc 936.14.465 Kruk, Janusz. Studia osadnicze nad neolitem wyżym lessowych. Wrocław, 1973.
Arc 925.9.15 Krupnov, E.T. Drevniaia istoriia Severnogo Kavkaza. Moskva, 1960.
Arc 925.10 Krupnov, Evgenii I. Kratkii ocherk arkheologii kabardinskoi ASSR. Nal'chik, 1946.
Arc 925.9.120 Krupnov, Evgenii I. Srednovekoraia Ingushetiia. Moskva, 1971.
Arc 290.1 Kruse, F. Russische Alterthümer 1844. Dorpat, 1844.
Arc 938.19F Kruse, F.K.H. Necrolivonica. Dorpat, 1842.
Arc 936.140.50 Krusteva-Nozharova, Gina. Ukazatel na predmeti izobrazeni vurkhu antichni pametnitsi ot Bulgariia. Sofiia, 1958.
Arc 497.75 Kryvelev, Iosif A. Raskopki v bibleiskikh stranakh. Moskva, 1965.
Arc 936.14.61 Krzak, Zygmunt. Cmentarzysko kultury złockiej "nad Wawrem" w Złotej. Wrocław, 1970.
Arc 936.14.60 Krzak, Zygmunt. Materiały doznajomości kyltury złockiej. Wrocław, 1961.
Arc 1588.1.75 Kubiak, Stanisława. Monety pierwszych Jagiellonów 1386-1444. Wyd. 1. Wrocław, 1970.
Arc 905.27F Kubinyi, August von. Szekszár der Alterthümer. Pest, 1857.
Arc 905.12.5 Kubitschek, W. Führer durch Carnuntum. Wien, 1904.
Arc 1480.22 Kubitschek, Wilhelm. Zur Geschichte von Städten des römischen Kaiserreiches. Wien, 1916.
Arc 853.82 Kuchenbuch, F. Die altmärkisch-osthannöverschen Schalenurnenfelder der spätrömischen Zeit. Inaug. Diss. Halle an der Saale, 1938.
Arc 395.20.5 Kühn, Herbert. Der Aufstieg der Menschheit. Frankfurt, 1955.
Arc 395.20 Kühn, Herbert. Der Aufstieg der Menschheit. Frankfurt, 1957.
Arc 612.36 Kühn, Herbert. Die Felsbilder Europas. Zürich, 1952.
Arc 853.278 Kühn, Herbert. Die germanischen Bügelfibeln der Völkerwanderungszeit. v.1-2. Graz, 1965- 3v.
Arc 612.36.5 Kühn, Herbert. Die Kunst Alteuropas. Stuttgart, 1958.
Arc 1163.4.32 Kühnel, Ernst. Islamische Schriftkunst. 2. Aufl. Graz, 1972.
Arc 1335.91 Kündig, W. Monnaies grecques antiques provenant des collection de S.A.I. le grand-duc Alexandra Michäilouit. Genève, 1922.
Arc 1335.91.25 Kündig, W. Monnaies grecques antiques provenant des doubles du British Museum des collections de feu le Gen. A.L. Bertier. Genève, 1923.
Arc 1335.90 Kündig, W. Monnaies romaines impériales provenant des collections de Paul Vautier. Genève, 1922.
Arc 1470.5 Die Künstlerinschriften auf Griechischen Münzen. (Sallet, A. von.) Berlin, 1871.
Arc 87.1.44 Kuenstlerinschriften der sicilienischen Muenzen. (Weil, R.) Berlin, 1884.
Arc 936.250.5 Kuftin, Boris A. Materialy k arkheologii kolkhidy. v.2. Tbilisi, 1950.
Arc 1087.3 Kugnezow, S. Die Sepulkralmasken, ihre Gebrauch und Bedeutung. Kasan, 1906.
Arc 936.14.305 Kukharenko, I.V. Arkheologiia Pol'ski. Moskva, 1969.
Arc 936.100.30 Kukuljevic-Sakcinski, I. Nadpisi sredovječni i novovjeki na crkvah. Zagreb, 1891.
Arc 938.70 Kulikauskar, P. Lietuvos archeologijos bruočai. Vil'nius, 1961.
Arc 1510.11.5 Kull, J.V. Repertorium zur Münzkunde Bayerns und Forzetz. v.1-3. München, 1894. 2v.
Arc 853.21.25 Die Kultur der Bronzezeit in Süddeutschland auf Grund der Funde in Württemberg. (Kraft, Georg.) Augsburg, 1926.
Arc 543.52.1 Die Kultur der Hsiung-nu und die Hügelgräber von Noin Ula. (Rudenko, Sergei I.) Bonn, 1969.
Arc 936.14.240 Kultura amfor kulistych. (Nosek, Stefan.) Wrocław, 1967.
Arc 925.16.40 Kul'tura drevnikh skotovodov i zemledel'tsev Kazakhstana. Alma-Ata, 1969.
Arc 925.351 Kul'tura iamochno-grebenchatoi keramiki v lesnoi polose evropeiskoi chasti SSSR. (Tret'iakov, Viktor P.) Leningrad, 1972.
Arc 543.52 Kul'tura khunnov i Noinulinskie kurzany. (Rudenko, Sergei I.) Moskva, 1962.
Arc 936.14.370 Kultura kushanów zachodniobałtyjskich we wezesnej epoce zelasa. (Okulicz, Łucja.) Wrocław, 1970.
Arc 936.6.15 Kultura łużycka na Pomorzu. (Kostrzewski, Józef.) Poznań, 1958.
Arc 936.14.490 Kultura lużycka na terenie nięedzyrzecza Wisły, Drwęcy i Osy. wyd. 1. (Chudziakowa, Jadwiga.) Warszawa, 1974.
Arc 652.7F Kultura materialna starozytnej Grecji. (Majewski, K.) Warszawa, 1956.
Arc 650.11 Kultura materialna starożytnej Grecji. Wrocław, 1975.
Arc 925.136.15 Kul'tura naseleniia bronzovogo veka Iuzhnogo Zaural'ia. (Stokolos, Vladimir S.) Moskva, 1972.
Arc 925.38.15 Kul'tura naseleniia Gornogo Altaia v skifskoe vremiia. (Rudenko, Sergei Ivanovich.) Moskva, 1953.
Arc 936.5 Kultura przedhistoryczne podola. (Tanusz, Bohdan.) Lwów, 1919.
Arc 936.14.460.5 Kultura przedłużycka. (Gedl, Marek.) Wrocław, 1975.
Arc 853.65.40 Kultura przeworska na Górnym Śląsku. Wyd. 1. (Godłowski, Kazimierz.) Katowice, 1969.
Arc 936.140.20 Kultura rzymska w Bułgarii. (Majewski, Kazimierz.) Wrocław, 1969.
Arc 936.14.335 Kultura unietycka w Polsce. (Sarnowska, Wanda.) Wrocław, 1969-1975. 2v.
Arc 936.14.195 Kultura wschodniopomorska na Pomorzu Odańskim. (Łuka, Leon J.) Wrocław, 1966.
Arc 665.1 Kulturbilder aus griechischen Städten. (Ziebarth, E.) Leipzig, 1907.
Arc 895.47.5F Kulturforbindelser mellem Danmark og syden i aeldre. (Broholm, Hans Christian.) København, 1960.
Arc 893.12 Kulturgeschichte Schwedens von den ältesten Zeiten bis zum elften Jahrhundert nach Christus. (Montelius, Oscar.) Leipzig, 1906.
Arc 395.1.2 Kulturhistorischer Bilder-Atlas. Leipzig, 1883-85. 2v.
Arc 936.220.110 Kulturne grupe starijeg grozdenog doba u Jugoslaviji. (Vasić, Rastko.) Beograd, 1973.
Arc 303.60 Kulturno-povijesni spomenici Istre. Pula. 1,1963+ 2v.

Arc 1510.130 Kundmann, J.C. Numuni jubilaei, oder Jubel Schau-Stücke. Bresslau, 1735.
Arc 1510.135 Kundmann, J.C. Silesii in nummis, oder Berühmte Schlesier in Müntzen. Bresslau, 1738.
Arc 1584.29 Kunik, Anst A. O russko-vizantiiskikh monetakh Iaroslava I Vladiminovicha. Sankt Peterburg, 1860.
Arc 1588.1.66 Kunisz, A. Chronologia naptywu pieniądza vzymskiegs na ziemie Matspoblei. Wyd. 1. Wrocław, 1969.
Arc 853.58 Kunkel, Otto. Oberhessens vorgeschichtliche Altertümer. Marburg, 1926.
Arc 853.62.7 Kunkel, Otto. Pommersche Urgeschichte in Bildern. Stettin, 1931. 2v.
Arc 853.58.10 Kunkel, Otto. Vorgeschichtliches aus dem Lumdstale. Giessen, 1919.
Arc 612.36.5 Die Kunst Alteuropas. (Kühn, Herbert.) Stuttgart, 1958.
Arc 551.4 Die Kunst der alten Ägypter. (Bissing, F.W.) Leipzig, 1911.
Arc 796.5 Kunst der illusie; antieke wandschilderungen uit Campanie. (Bogaerts, T.) Den Haag, 1958.
Arc 848.48 Die Kunst der Vorzeit. (Adama van Scheltema, Z.) Stuttgart, 1950.
Arc 900.205 Kunst historischer Atlas. (Austria. K.K. Central Commission.) Wien. 1-10,1889-1894 2v.
Htn Arc 1590.8.5* Die Kunst und der Wert...Münzen. (Farkas, Sandor.) Aiud, 1938.
Arc 628.13.5 Kunst und Geschichte. (Luckenbach, H.) München, 1902-03. 3v.
Arc 628.13.7 Kunst und Geschichte. (Luckenbach, H.) München, 1904.
Arc 628.13.8 Kunst und Geschichte. 6. Aufl. (Luckenbach, H.) München, 1906.
Arc 893.13.15 Die Kunst unserer Vorzeit. (Adama van Scheltema, F.) Leipzig, 1936.
Arc 520.20 Die Kunst von Pergamon. (Schober, A.) Wien, 1951.
Arc 397.3 Kunstarchaeologische Werke. v.1-5. (Müller, K.O.) Berlin, 1873. 2v.
Arc 1077.2.30 Kunstgeschichte des Kreuzes. (Stockbauer, J.) Schaffhausen, 1870.
Arc 87.1 Kunstgeschichtliche Vasenbilder. (Gerhard, E.) Berlin, 1841.
Arc 1670.52 Kunstmedaillen und Plaketten des XV. bis XVII. Jahrhunderts. (Hirsch, Jacob.) München, 1908.
Arc 708.17 Die Kunstwerke Athens. (Warsberg, A. von.) Wien, 1892.
Arc 960.1 Kunz, G.F. Gold and silver ornaments from mounds of Florida. Chicago, 1887.
Arc 1084.1 Kunz, G.F. H.R. Bishop and his jade collection. Lancaster, 1903.
Arc 672.1.52F Kunze, Emil. Kretische Bonzereliefs. Text and plates. Stuttgart, 1931. 2v.
Arc 684.1.48 Kunze, Emil. Neue Meisterwerke griechischer Kunst aus Olympia. München, 1948.
Arc 654.1 Kunze, Emil. Olympische Forschungen. Berlin, 1944- 8v.
Arc 1077.1 Die Kupferzeit in Europa. (Much, M.) Jena, 1893.
Arc 682.14F Das Kuppelgrab bei Menidi. (Archäologisches Institut des Deutschen Reichs-Athenische Zweigeanstalt.) Athen, 1880.
Arc 435.2.51F Ḳuraishi, M.M.Ḥ. List of ancient monuments protected in Bihar and Orissa. Calcutta, 1931.
Arc 457.10 Ḳuraishi, M.M.Ḥ. Rājgir. 4. ed. Delhi, 1956.
Arc 1550.6 Kurantmønten. (Wilcke, Julius.) Kjøbenhavn, 1927.
Arc 923.117 Kurgany, idoly, monety. (Fedorov-Davydov, German A.) Moskva, 1968.
Arc 920.206F Kurgany i sluchainyia arkheologicheskiia nakhodki. (Bobrinskii, A.) Sankt Petersburg, 1887.
Arc 936.14.280 Kurhany, zokresw rzymskiego w Polsce ze szczegolnem uwzględnieniem typu siedlemińskiego. (Karpińska, Aleksandra.) Poznań, 1926.
Arc 195.5 Kurhessische Bodenaltertümer. Marburg. 1-4,1951-1964// 2v.
Arc 925.50.260 Kurinnyi, Petro. Istoriia arkheolohichnoho znannia pro Ukrainu. Miunkhen, 1970.
Arc 936.14.65 Kurnatowski, S. Z przeszłosci międzyrzecza. Poznań, 1961.
Arc 800.16 Kusch, Eugen. Herculaneum. Nürnberg, 1960.
Arc 505.95PF Kusejr 'Amra. (Musil, Alois.) Wien, 1907.
Arc 925.9.70 Kushmareva, Karinek. Drevnie kultury Izhnogo Kavkaza. Leningrad, 1970.
Arc 1076.4.5 Kuuliala, Vilji K. Kellot temppelin. Sortavala, 1943.
Arc 925.9.135 Kuznetsov, Vladimir A. Alaniia v X-XIII vv. Ordzhonikidze, 1971.
Arc 905.40 Kuzsinszky, V. Aquincum; Ausgrabungen und Funde. Budapest, 1934.
Arc 938.96F Kvaonbacken. (Kivikoski, Ella.) Helsinki, 1963.
Arc 888.30 Een kwart eeun. Meppal, 1947.
Arc 1076.8 Kybalová, L. Pražské zvony. Praha, 1958.
Arc 497.29 Kyle, M.G. Moses and the monuments. London, 1920.
Arc 426.5 Kyoto. University. Archaeological Institute. Report upon archaeological research. Tokyo. 3-10,1919-1927 4v.
Arc 535.200 Kypros, the Bible and Homer. (Ohnefalsch-Richter, M.) London, 1893. 2v.
Arc 680.1 Kythera - excavations and studies. London, 1972.
Arc 726.220 L. Munazio Planco e il suo mausoleo a Gaeta. (Jacopi, Giulio.) Milano, 1960.
Arc 830.69 La Micoque; die Kultur einer neuen Diluvialrasse. (Hauser, Otto.) Leipzig, 1916.
Arc 1033.62.2 La Passio SS. Perpetuae et Felicitatis. (Fanchi de' Cavalieri, P.) Roma, 1896.
Arc 1033.62 La Passio SS. Perpetuae et Felicitatis. (Franchi de' Cavalieri, P.) Roma, 1896.
Arc 830.51 La Scava...excavation of a Roman town on the hill of Chatelet. London, 1818.
Arc 785.20.5 La Via Appia en ruine et en reconstruction. (Ripostelli, Giuseppe.) Rome, 1904.
Arc 1053.5.2 Laban, F. Der Gemüthsansdruck des Antinous. Berlin, 1891.
Arc 1027.59 Labanca, B. Gesù Cristo nelle catacombe di Roma. Roma, 1902.
Arc 1077.2.41 Das Labarum und der Sonnen-Cultus. (Rapp, Edward.) Bonn, 1865.
Arc 853.287 La Baume, Peter. Das fränkische Gräberfeld von Junkersdorf bei Köln. Berlin, 1967.
Arc 853.369 La Baume, Peter. Die Römer am Rhein. Bonn, 1973.
Arc 853.21.15 LaBaume, W. Vorgeschichte von Westpreussen in ihren Grundzügen allgemeinverstandlich dargestellt. Danzig, 1920.
Arc 66.1.34 La Blanchere, M.R. de. Terracine. Paris, 1884.
Arc 608.21 La Blanchère, R. du C. Voyage d'étude dans une partie de la Maurétanie césarienne. Paris, 1883.
Arc 510.3 Laborde, L. de. Voyate de l'Asie Mineure. Paris, 1838.
Arc 708.8 Laborde, L.E.S.J. Athènes aux XVe, XVIe et XVIIe siècles. Paris, 1854. 2v.

Author and Title Listing

Arc 530.164 Labraunda; Swedish excavations and researches. v.1, pt.1-2; v.2, pt.1; v.3, pt.1. Lund, 1955- 4v.

Arc 66.1.212 Labrousse, Michel. Toulouse antique des origines à l'établissement des Wisigoths. Paris, 1968.

Arc 588.24 Labyrinth Gerzeh and Mazghumeh. (Petrie, W.M.F.) London, 1912.

Arc 875.85 Lacaille, A.D. The Stone Age in Scotland. London, 1954.

Arc 505.12.10F Lachish I (Tell Ed Durveir). v.1-4. (Torczyner, H.) London, 1938-1940. 6v.

Arc 936.14.505 Lachowicz, Franciszek J. Dorobek archeologii koszalińskiej w latach 1945-70. Koszalin, 1973.

Arc 584.100.15 Lackany, Rudames Sany. La Société archéologique d'Alexandrie à 80 ans. Alexandrie, 1973.

Arc 830.77 Lacoste, Pierre F. Observations sur les travaux qui doivent être faits pour la recherche des objets d'antiquité. Clermont, 1824.

Arc 66.1.138 La Coste-Messelière, P. de. Au musée de Delphes. Paris, 1936.

Arc 820.211F Lacour, Pierre. Tombeaux antiques. Bordeaux, 1806.

Arc 1020.72.15 La Croix, C. de. L'autel de Sainte-Sixte et ses reliques. Poitiers, 1907.

Arc 1020.122 La Croix, C. de. Une dalle mérovingienne trouvée à Challans (Vendée). Poitiers, 1909.

Arc 830.82.5 La Croix, C. de. Mémoire archéologique sur les découvertes d'Herbord dites de Sanxay. Niort, 1883.

Arc 830.118 La Croix, C. de. Notes archéologiques sur Nouaillé. Poitiers, 1910.

Arc 1027.85F LaCroix, Camille. Monographie de l'hypogée-martyrium. Paris, 1883. 2v.

Arc 830.67 La Croix, Camille. Les origines des anciens monuments...de Poitiers. Poitiers, 1906.

Arc 1433.30 Lacroix, D. Numismatique annamite. Text and atlas. Saigon, 1900. 2v.

Arc 1460.4 Lacroix, L. Les reproductions des statues. Liège, 1949.

Arc 1468.61 Lacroix, Léon. Études d'archéologie numismatique. Paris, 1974.

Arc 497.46 The ladder of progress in Palestine. (McGown, J.C.) N.Y., 1943.

Arc 1016.228 Laderchi, J. Acta passionis SS. Crescii et S. Martyrum. Florentiae, 1707.

Arc 1027.7.13 Laderchu, J. De sacris Basilicis S. Martyrum. Roma, 1705.

Arc 830.16.11 Ladonne, E. Augustoduni amplissimae civitatis. Augustoduni, 1640.

Arc 938.95 Läbi aastatuhandete. (Selirand, J.) Tallinn, 1963.

Arc 853.370 Die ländliche Besiedlung Rheinhessens. Inaug. Diss. (Bayer, Heinrich.) Mainz, 1967?

Arc 595.16.10 Längen und Richtungen der vier Grandkanten der grossen Pyramide bei Gise. (Borchardt, Ludwig.) Berlin, 1926.

Arc 1163.41.5 Läsning av gamla handstilar. 5. uppl. (Aaberg, Alf.) Stockholm, 1971.

Arc 493.26 Laessøe, Jørgen. The Shemshāra tablets. København, 1959.

Arc 396.10 Laet, Siegfried J. de. L'archélogie et ses problèmes. Berchem, 1954.

Arc 888.45 Laet, Siegfried J. de. The Low Countries. London, 1958.

Arc 888.45.5 Laet, Siegfried J. de. De voorgeschiedenis der Lage Landen. Groningen, 1959.

Arc 1.13.15 La Farge, C.G. History of the American Academy in Rome. N.Y., 1915.

Arc 1498.15 Lafaurie, Jean. Les monnaies des rois de France. Paris, 1951. 2v.

X Cg Arc 66.1.33 Lafaye, G. Histoire du culte des divinités d'Alexandre. Paris, 1884. (Changed to XP 9785)

Arc 66.1.33 Lafaye, G. Histoire du culte des divinités d'Alexandre. Photoreproduction. Paris, 1884.

Arc 830.70.7 Lafon, M.A. Amphithéatre de Fourvière. Lyon, 1896.

Arc 785.45.5 Lafontaine, Jacqueline. Peintures médiévales dans le temple de la Fortune Virile à Rome. Bruxelles, 1959.

Arc 505.130 Lafontaine-Dosogne, Jacqueline. Itinéraires archéologiques dans la région d'Antioche. Bruxelles, 1967.

Arc 838.20 Lagar de Mouros. (Fortes, José.) Porto, 1901-08. 6 pam.

Arc 1348.76 Lagerqvist, Lars. Myntoch medaljer. Stockholm, 1960.

Arc 561.5 Lagier, Camille. A travers la Haute Égypte. Bruxelles, 1921.

Arc 561.5.5 Lagier, Camille. L'Égypte monumentale et pittoresque. 2. éd. Paris, 1922.

Arc 1020.10.9 La Gournerie, E. de. Christian Rome. London, 1898. 2v.

Arc 1020.10.5 La Gournerie, E. de. Rome chrétienne. Paris, 1843. 2v.

Arc 830.165 La Grange, E. de. Notice sur des antiquités romaines découvertes en 1834 à Chandai (Orne). Caen, 1835.

Arc 672.1.8 Lagrange, M.J. La Crete ancienne. Paris, 1908.

Arc 1020.31.23 Lagrange, Marie. Saint Étienne et son sanctuaire à Jérusalem. Paris, 1894.

Arc 810.8 Lagrèze, G.B. de. Pompéi, les catacombes, l'Alhambra. Paris, 1889.

Arc 1418.20 Lahore Museum. Catalogue of coins in the Punjab Museum. Oxford, 1914-34. 3v.

Arc 936.35.5 Lahtov, Vasil. Problem trebeniške kulture. Ohrid, 1965.

Arc 588.28 Lahun I, II; the treasure. (Brunton, Guy.) London, 1920. 2v.

Arc 1274.2.3 Laing, Henry. Supplemental descriptive catalogue of ancient Scottish seals. Edinburgh, 1866.

Arc 858.99 Laing, Lloyd Robert. The archaeology of late Celtic Britain and Ireland, c. 400-1200. London, 1975.

Arc 875.129 Laing, Lloyd Robert. Settlement types in post-Roman Scotland. Oxford, 1975.

Arc 875.23 Laing, S. Prehistoric remains of Caithness. Edinburgh, 1866.

Arc 1033.65.5 Lais, G. Memoire del titolo di Fasciola. Roma, 1880.

Arc 608.33.10 Lajoux, Jean D. Merveilles du Tassili n'Ajjer. Paris, 1962.

Arc 612.3 The lake-dwellings of Europe. (Munro, Robert.) London, 1890.

Arc 880.20A The lake-dwellings of Ireland. (Wood-Martin, W.G.) Dublin, 1886.

Arc 913.5 Lake dwellings of Switzerland and other parts of Europe. (Keller, F.) London, 1878. 2v.

Arc 600.5.3 Lake Moeris and the pyramids. (Whitehouse, F.C.) n.p., 1884?

Arc 432.27 Lal, Braj Basi. Indian archaeology since independence. 1. ed. Delhi, 1964.

Arc 830.104 Lalande P. Ruines romaines de Tintignac (Corrèze). Brive, 1885.

Arc 1264.2 Lalore, C. Le sceau et les armoiries...Saint Pierre de Troyes. Troyes, 1887.

Arc 1675.36 Lamas, A. Portuguese medals. Lisbon, 1905-10. 12 pam.

Arc 1493.11 Lamas, Arthur. Medalhas portuguesas e estrangeiras referentes a Portugal. Lisboa, 1916.

Arc 726.85 Lamb, Carl. Die Tempel von Paestum. Leipzig, 1944.

Arc 681.1.5 Lamb, Winifred. Excavations at Thermi in Lesbos. Cambridge, Eng., 1936.

Arc 915.50 Lambert, André. Führer durch die römische Schweiz. Zürich, 1973.

Arc 1033.17.248 Lambert, R. Diva Virgo de Cortenbosch, eius miracula. Leodii, 1656.

Arc 1027.23.20 Lamberton, C.D. Themes from St. John's gospel in early Roman catacomb painting. Princeton, 1905.

Arc 1468.20 Lambros, J.P. Griechische Münzen. München, 1910.

Arc 1590.2 Lambros, P. Monete inedite dei gran maestri...in Rodi. Venezia, 1865.

Arc 1590.2.3 Lambros, P. Monete inedite dei gran maestri. Primo supplemento. Venezia, 1866.

Arc 1590.2.5 Lambros, P. Monnaies inédites de Raimond Zacosta. Athènes, 1877.

Arc 1590.6 Lambros, Paulos. Monnaies de Chypre et de Salona. n.p., 1866.

Arc 612.34 Laming, A. L'art préhistorique. Paris, 1951.

Arc 612.34.5 Laming, A. La signification de l'art rupestre paléolithique. Paris, 1962.

Arc 396.22 Laming, Annette. La découverte du passe. Paris, 1952.

Arc 823.81 Laming, Annette. Origines de l'archéologie préhistorique en France. Paris, 1964.

Arc 482.202.4F Lamm, C.J. Das Glas von Samarra. Berlin, 1928.

Arc 482.205F Lamm, C.J. Mittelalterliche Gläser und Steinschnittarbeiten aus dem Nahen Osten. Berlin, 1930. 2v.

Arc 505.61F Lamon, R.S. Megiddo I. Chicago, 1939.

Arc 945.1 The lamp of the Eskimo. (Hough, W.) Washington, 1898.

Arc 1020.22 Lampake, G. Christianichē archaiologia. Athēnai, 1889.

Arc 1025.37 Lampake, G. Christianikē gechnē...katakombai. Athēnai, 1900.

X Cg Arc 1020.22.5 Lampake, G. Hē monē daphnioy. Athēnai, 1889.

Arc 910.8F Lampen aus Vindonissa. (Loeschcke, Siegfried.) Zürich, 1919.

Arc 1033.25.8 Lampes chrétiennes de Carthage. (Delattré, Alfred Louis.) Lyon, 1880.

Arc 1033.25.5 Lampes chrétiennes inédites. (Héron de Villefosse.) Paris, 1875.

Arc 1470.37 Lampros, Paulos. Anagraphē tōn nomismatōn tēs kypies Hellados. Athēnai, 1891.

Arc 1473.1.3 Lampros, Paulos. Anekdota nomismata en Glarentsa. Athēnai, 1876.

Arc 1473.1.3.5 Lampros, Paulos. Anekdota nomismata kopenta en Glarentsa kata mimēsin tōn Henetikōn. Oak Park, 1969.

Arc 1473.1.5 Lampros, Paulos. Anekdota nomismata tēs Hellados. Athēnai, 1880.

Arc 1473.1 Lampros, Paulos. Anekdota nomismata tēs kuprhoy. Athēnai, 1876.

Arc 1473.1.10 Lampros, Paulos. Anekdoton nomisma Saroykchan Emiry tēs Iōnias. n.p., n.d.

Arc 1473.50.5 Lampros, Paulos. Coins and medals of the Ionian Islands. Amsterdam, 1968.

Arc 1473.1.9 Lampros, Paulos. Mesaiōnika nomismara tēs Chiny. Athēnai, 1886.

Arc 1473.50 Lampros, Paulos. Nomismata tēs Hepianēdon politeias. Athēnai, 1884.

Arc 1470.13 Lampros, Paulos. Nomismata tēs nēsoy Amorgy. Athēnai, 1870.

Arc 1473.1.8 Lampros, Paulos. Nomismata tōn ademiōn Zachariōn. Athēnai, 1884.

Arc 726.75F Lanci, Fortunato. Intorno un antico specchio metallico epistola...Cavaaliere Odoardo Gerhard in occasion di sue nozze...Emilia de Riess. Roma, 1842.

Arc 766.1.2.8 Lanciani, R. Ancient Rome in the light of recent discoveries. Boston, 1888.

Arc 766.1.2.11 Lanciani, R. Ancient Rome in the light of recent discoveries. London, 1888.

Arc 766.1.2.10 Lanciani, R. Ancient Rome in the light of recent discoveries. London, 1888.

Arc 766.1.2.12 Lanciani, R. Ancient Rome in the light of recent discoveries. 5. ed. Boston, 1889.

Htn Arc 766.1.2.7* Lanciani, R. Ancient Rome in the light of recent discoveries. 7. ed. Boston, 1888.

Arc 766.1.2.15 Lanciani, R. Ancient Rome in the light of recent discoveries. 10. ed. Boston, 1894.

Arc 766.1.2A Lanciani, R. Ancient Rome in the light of recent excavations. Boston, 1888.

Arc 766.1.9 Lanciani, R. The destruction of ancient Rome. N.Y., 1899.

Arc 766.1.9.1 Lanciani, R. The destruction of ancient Rome. N.Y., 1967.

Arc 766.1.9.5 Lanciani, R. La distruzione di Roma antica. Milano, 1971.

Arc 750.204 Lanciani, R. L'itinerario di Einsiedeln. Roma, 1891.

Arc 766.1.13A Lanciani, R. New tales of old Rome. Boston, 1901.

Arc 766.1.14 Lanciani, R. New tales of old Rome. Boston, 1902.

Arc 766.1.15 Lanciani, R. New tales of old Rome. London, 1901.

Arc 766.1.2.30 Lanciani, R. Pagan and Christian Rome. Boston, 1892.

Arc 766.1.3 Lanciani, R. Pagan and Christian Rome. Boston, 1893.

Htn Arc 766.1.4* Lanciani, R. Pagan and Christian Rome. Boston, 1893.

Arc 766.1.3.5 Lanciani, R. Pagan and Christian Rome. London, 1893.

Arc 785.9 Lanciani, R. Ricerche sulle XIV regioni urbane. Roma, 1890.

Arc 766.1.5A Lanciani, R. Ruins and excavations of ancient Rome. Boston, 1897.

Arc 766.1.10 Lanciani, R. The ruins and excavations of ancient Rome. Boston, 1900.

Arc 766.1.6 Lanciani, R. The ruins and excavations of ancient Rome. London, 1897.

Arc 766.1.17A Lanciani, R. Storia degli scavi di Roma. v.1-4. Roma, 1902. 5v.

Arc 766.1 Lanciani, R. Topografia di Roma antica. Roma, 1880.

Arc 726.24.11 Lanciani, R. La villa Adriana; guida e descrizione. Roma, 1906.

Arc 766.1.19 Lanciani, R. Wanderings in the Roman campagns. Boston, 1909.

Arc 1020.9.147 Lanciani, R. Wanderings through ancient Roman churches. Boston, 1924.

Arc 785.22.5 Lanciani, Visconti de. Guida del Palatino. Roma, 1873.

Arc 1480.44 Lanckorónski, L.M. Das römische Bildnis in Meisterwerken der Münzkunst. Amsterdam, 1944.

Arc 497.6 The land of Moab. (Tristram, H.B.) London, 1873.

Arc 530.12 The land of the Hittites. (Garstang, John.) London, 1910.

Arc 497.100 Landay, Jerry M. Silent cities, sacred stones: archaeological discovery in the land of the Bible. London, 1971.

Author and Title Listing

Arc 1478.6 Landi, C. Selectiorum numismatum, praecipue Romanorum expositiones. Leyden, 1695.
Arc 447.2 Landmarks of the Deccan; a comprehensive guide to the archaeological remains of the city and suburbs of Hyderabad. (Bilgrami, S.A.A.) Hyderabad, 1927.
Arc 1470.25 Landon, Charles P. Numismatique du voyage du jeune Anacharsis. Paris, 1846. 2v.
Arc 1335.130 Landowne, William P. A catalogue of a valuable collection. London, 18- ?
Arc 530.54 Landsberger, Benno. Samial. Ankara, 1948.
Arc 530.54.5 Landsberger, Benno. Samial. Photoreproduction. Ankara, 1948.
Arc 385.21 Landscape archaeology. (Aston, Michael.) Newton Abbot, Eng., 1974.
Arc 1027.23.23 Die Landschaft in der altchristlichen Katakombenmalerei. (Kampffmeyer, K.) Greifswald, 1933.
Arc 1020.9.99 Landucci, A. Origine del tempio. Roma, 1646.
Arc 875.33 Lang, Andrew. The Clyde mystery. Glasgow, 1905.
Arc 628.16 Lang, G. Von Rom nach Sardes. Stuttgart, 1900.
Arc 885.1 Langdon, A.G. Old Cornish crosses. Truro, 1896.
Arc 1510.32F Lange, C.C.A. Sammlung schleswig-holsteinischer Münzen und Medaillen. Berlin, 1908-12. 2v.
Arc 612.87 Lange, Elsbeth. Botanisch Beiträge zur mitteleuropäischen Siedlungsgeschichte. Berlin, 1971.
Arc 396.2 Lange, Konrad. Grundsätze der modernen Denkmalpflege. Tübingen, 1906.
Arc 1663.31 Lange, Kurt. Charakterkopfe der Weltgeschichte. München, 1949.
Arc 1470.44 Lange, Kurt. Götter Griechenlands. Berlin, 1941.
Arc 1390.11 Lange, Kurt. Münzkunst des Mittelalters. Leipzig, 1942.
Arc 1033.12.122 Lange, P. De lancea qua perfossum latus...Christi. Jena, 1673.
Arc 1510.4 Langermann, J.P. Die neuren Hamburgischen Münzen und Medaillen. Hamburg, 1843.
Arc 66.1.58 Langlois, E. Origines et sources du Roman de la Rose. Paris, 1891.
Arc 1443.3 Langlois, V. Numismatique des nomes d'Égypte. Paris, 1852.
Arc 1428.1 Langlois, Victor. Monnaies inédites, ou Peu connues de la Cilicie. Paris, 1854.
Arc 1584.1.3 Langlois, Victor. Numismatique de la Géorgie au moyen âge. Paris, 1852.
Arc 1433.28.2 Langlois, Victor. Numismatique général. v.2. Paris, 1855.
Arc 1433.28 Langlois, Victor. Numismatique général de l'Armenie. v.1-2. Paris, 1855-59.
Arc 530.6 Langlois, Victor. Rapport...de la Cilicie et de la Petite-Arménie. Paris, 1854.
Arc 726.36.10 Die langobardenzeitlichen Grabfunde aus Fiesole bei Florenz. (Otto, prince of Hesse.) München, 1966.
Arc 1080.10F Die langobardischen Fibeln aus Italien. (Deutsches Archäologisches Institut.) Berlin, 1950.
Arc 746.11.10F Langsdorff, A. Die Grabfunde mit Bronzeschnabelkannen. Inaug. Diss. Berlin, 1929.
Arc 493.15F Langsdorff, A. Tall-i-Bakun A, season of 1932. Chicago, 1942.
Arc 1350.4.2 Langwith, B. Observations on Doctor Arbuthnot's dissertation. London, 1754.
Arc 785.13.53A Lansiani, Rodolfo. The Roman forum. Rome, 1910.
Arc 505.5.70 Lanvy, B. De tabernaculo foederis...Jerusalem. Paris, 1720.
Arc 900.202 Lanza, F. Dell'antico Palazzo di Dioclez in Spalato. Trieste, 1855.
Arc 530.180 Laodicée du Lycos; le nymphée; campagnes 1961-1963. Québec, 1969.
Arc 66.1.165 Lapalus, Etienne. Le fronton sculpté en Grèce. Paris, 1947. 2v.
Arc 608.2.38 Lapeyre, Gabriel G. Carthage latine et chrétienne. Paris, 1950.
Arc 608.2.37 Lapeyre, Gabriel G. Carthage punique. Paris, 1942.
Arc 950.203 Lapham, I.A. The antiquities of Wisconsin. Washington, 1855?
Arc 1027.12.19 La Piana, George. The tombs of Peter and Paul ad catacumbas. Cambridge, 1920.
Arc 1030.1 Lapida sepolcrale di Teofilatto. (Galante, G.A.) Napoli, 1867.
Arc 855.7 Lapidarium Septentrionale, or A description of the monument of Roman rule. London, 1875.
Arc 855.208 Lapidarium Walliae. (Westwood, J.O.) Oxford, 1876-79.
Arc 925.75.5 Lapin, V.V. Ol'viia. Kiev, 1959.
Arc 925.13.125 Lapin, Vladimir V. Grecheskaia kolonizatsiia Severnogo Prichernomor'ia. Kiev, 1966.
Arc 612.60 Laplace, Georges. Recherches sur l'origine et l'évolution des complexes leptolithiques. Paris, 1966.
Arc 843.224 L'aqueducte Romà de Pineda. (Prat Puig, Francisco.) Barcelona, 1936.
Arc 1613.21 Large United States cents. (Venn, T.J.) Chicago, 1915.
Arc 180.1.25 Largiader, Anton. Hundert Jahre Antiquarische Gesellschaft in Zürich, 1832-1932. Zürich, 1932.
Arc 416.42 Laricheo, Vitalii E. Paleolit Severnoi, Tsentral'noi i Vostochnoi Azii. Novosibirsk, 1969- 2v.
Arc 543.147 Larichev, Vitalii E. Aziia dalekaia i tainstvennaia. Novosibirsk, 1968.
Arc 399.3 Larichev, Vitalii E. Bibliografiia nauchnykh trudov po arkheologii i istorii chlena-korrespondenta AN SSSR A.P. Okladnikova. Novosibirsk, 1968.
Arc 925.4.30 Larichev, Vitalii E. Okhotniki za mamontanii. Novosibirsk, 1968.
Arc 399.3.5 Larichev, Vitalii E. Sorok let sredi sibirskikh drevnostei. Novosibirsk, 1970.
Arc 925.180.25 Larichev, Vitalii E. Taina kamennoi cherepakhi. Novosibirsk, 1966.
Arc 943.5 Larkin, F. Ancient man in America. n.p., 1880.
Arc 672.10 Larnaksy egejskie. (Rutkowski, Bogdan.) Wrocław, 1966.
Arc 943.6 Larrainzar, M. Estudios sobre la historia de America. Mexico, 1875-78. 5v.
Arc 66.1.155 Las jardins romains. (Grimal, Pierre.) Paris, 1943.
Arc 830.105 La Sauvagère, F. Recherches sur la nature et l'etendue d'un ancien ouvrage des Romains. Paris, 1740.
Arc 823.18 La Sauvagère, F. Recueil d'antiquités dans les Gaules. Paris, 1770.
Arc 830.11.25 Lascaux and Carnac. (Daniel, G.E.) London, 1955.
Arc 726.2.2 Lasena, P. Dell'antico ginnasio napoletano. n.p., n.d.
Arc 726.2 Lasena, P. Dell'antico ginnasio napoletano. n.p., n.d.
Arc 925.134.10 Lashuk, L. P. Ocherk etnicheskoi istorii Pechorskogo kraia. Syktyvkar, 1958.
Arc 1663.27 Laskey, John C. A description of the series of medals struck at the national medal mint by...Napoleon Bonaparte. London, 1818.
Arc 505.72.5F Lassus, Jean. Inventoire archéologique de la région au nord-est de Hama. v.1-2. Damas, 1935-1936.
Arc 682.31F The last Mycenaeans and their successors. (Desborough, V.R. d'.) Oxford, 1964.
Arc 1494.45 Lastanosa, V.J. de. Tratado de la moneda jaquesa y otras de oro. Zaragozana, 1681.
Arc 746.47.5 Le lastre dipinte da Cerveteri. (Roncalli, Francesco.) Firenze, 1965.
Arc 905.110 László, Gyula. A honfoglaló magyar nép élete. 2. biadás. Budapest, 1944.
Arc 590.16F The late Egyptian anthropoid stone sarcophagi. (Buhl, Marie Louise.) København, 1959.
Arc 1480.63 Late Roman bronze coinage, A.D. 324-498. London, 1960.
Arc 1180.5 Lateinisch-deutsche Interpretationshilfen für spätmittelalterliche und frühneuzeitliche Archivalien. (Demundt, Karl Ernst.) Marburg, 1970.
Arc 1153.23 Lateinische Paläographie. 2. Aufl. (Bretholtz, B.) Leipzig, 1912.
Arc 1153.25 Lateinische Stenographie...Wilhelm Stolze. (Voss, Ulrich.) Berlin, 1907.
Arc 1153.96 Lateinisches Leseheft zur Einführung in Paläographie und Textkritik. (Merkelbach, Reinhold.) Göttingen, 1969.
Arc 853.31.10 Die Latènekulter in Thüringen. Inaug. Diss. (Knack, H.) Stettin, 1929?
Arc 853.48 Latenezeitliche Funde an der keltischgermanischen Völkergrenze. (Kropp, Philipp.) Würzburg, 1911.
Arc 853.302F Das latènezeitliche Gräberfeld von Berlin-Blankenfelde. (Heiligendorff, Wolfgang.) Berlin, 1965.
Arc 1190.10F The later court hands in England. Test and atlas. (Jenkinson, H.) Cambridge, 1927. 2v.
Arc 1093.2.5 The later stone age in Europe. (Clodd, E.) London, 1880.
Arc 595.31 The latest phase of the Great Pyramid discussion. (Bache, R.M.) Philadelphia, 1885.
Arc 1153.98F Latin bookhands of the later Middle Ages, 1110-1500. (Thomson, Samuel Harrison.) Cambridge, Eng., 1969.
Arc 938.17.10 Latviia v epokhu pozdnei bronzy i rannego sheleza. (Graudonis, Jánis.) Riga, 1967.
Arc 938.112 Latvijas PSR arheologija. Riga, 1974.
Arc 1030.50 Latyshchev', B.B. Sbornik' grech. nadlisei Chrisi bre.-men'. Sankt Peterburg, 1896.
Arc 925.13.15 Latyshev, V.V. Pontika...skifiia, Kavkaz. Sankt Petersburg, 1909.
Arc 823.55 Laubenheimer-Leenhardt, F. Recherches sur les lingots de cuivre et de plomb d'époque romaine dans les régions de Languedoc-Roussillon et de Provence-Corse. Paris, 1973.
Arc 1470.70 Lauckoranski, Leo Maria. Mythen und Münzen. 1. Aufl. München, 1958.
Arc 545.227.11A Lauer, J.P. Fouilles à Saqqarah, la pyramide à degrés. v.1-2, 4-5. La Caire, 1936. 4v.
Arc 595.41 Lauer, J.P. Le mystère des pyramides. Paris, 1974.
Arc 595.40 Lauer, J.P. Le problème des pyramides d'Égypte. Paris, 1948.
Arc 595.66.4 Lauer, Jean Philippe. Les pyramides de Sakkarah. 4. éd. Le Caire, 1972.
Arc 595.66 Lauer, Jean Philippe. Les pyramides de Sakkarah. Le Caire, 1961.
Arc 1033.17.549F Lauer, Philippe. Le trésor du Sancta Sanctorum. Paris, 1906.
Arc 1590.5 Laugier. Étude historique sur les monnaies...de l'ordre de Saint Jean de Jérusalem. Marseille, 1868.
Arc 66.1.188 Laumonier, Alfred. Les cultes indigenes en Carie. Paris, 1958.
Arc 66.1.169 Launey, Marcel. Recherches sur les armées hellénistiques. Paris, 1949. 2v.
Arc 1443.6 Launois, Aimée. Estampilles et poids musulmans en verre du cabinet des médailles. Caire, 1959.
Arc 915.4.10 Laur-Belart, Rudolf. Führer durch Augusta Raurica. Basel, 1937.
Arc 915.4.11 Laur-Belart, Rudolf. Führer durch Augusta Raurica. 2. Aufl. Basel, 1948.
Arc 915.4.14 Laur-Belart, Rudolf. Führer durch Augusta Raurica. 4. Aufl. Basel, 1966.
Arc 915.32 Laur-Belart, Rudolf. Uber die Colonia Raurica und den Ursprung von Basel. 2. Aufl. Basel, 1959.
Arc 969.15 The laurel tradition and the middle woodland period. (Wright, James V.) Ottawa, 1967.
Arc 66.1.117 Laurent, J. L'arménie entre Byzance et l'Islam. Paris, 1919.
Arc 1163.20 Laurent, M. De abbreviationibus et signis scripturae gothicae. Romae, 1939.
Arc 889.37 Laurent, René. L'habitat rural à l'époque romaine. Bruxelles, 1972.
Arc 1033.94 Laurenti, V. Vita SS. Apostoli Filippo et Giacono Minore. Roma, 1873.
Arc 518.9 Lauria, G.A. Efeso; studj. Napoli, 1874.
Arc 905.50 Lauriacum; Führer durch die Altertümer von Enns. (Gaheis, Alexander.) Linz, 1937.
Arc 1550.8.10 Lauring, P. Regis Daniae. København, 1961.
Arc 1033.17.162 Lauro, G.B. De annulo proniebo...virginis...Perusiae. Colonia Agrippina, 1626.
Arc 1033.17.161 Lauro, G.B. De annulo pronubo...virginis...Perusiae. Roma, 1622.
Arc 905.120.5 Lavant und Aguntum. (Miltner, Franz.) Lienz, 1951.
Arc 403.16.36 Lavater-Sloman, Mary. Das Gold von Troja. Zürich, 1969.
Arc 1663.15 Laverrenz, C. Die Medaillen und Gedachtniszeichen der deutschen Hochschulen. Berlin, 1887. 2v.
Arc 608.2.17 Lavigerie, C.M.A. De l'utilité d'une mission archéologique permanente à Carthage. Alger, 1881.
Arc 726.339 Lavinium. (Rome, Italy. Università. Istituto di Topografia Antica.) Roma, 1972- 2v.
Arc 612.40 Laviosa, Zambotti. Il mediterraneo. Torino, 1954.
Arc 1423.7 Lavoix, Henri. Monnaies à légendes arabes frappées en Syrie. Paris, 1877.
Arc 925.9.55 Lavrov, L.I. Epigraficheskie pamiatniki severnogo Kavkaza. Moskva, 1966- 2v.
Arc 1160.209F Lavrov, P.A. Paleograficheskie snimki. Sankt Peterburg, n.d.
Arc 880.29 Lawlor, H.C. The monastery of St. Mochaoi of Nendrum. Belfast, 1925.
Arc 880.35 Lawlor, H.C. Ulster. Belfast, 1928.
X Cg Arc 743.17 Lawrence, D.H. Etruscan places. London, 1932.
Arc 743.17.10 Lawrence, D.H. Etruscan places. Middlesex, 1950.
Arc 1675.1 Lawrence, R.H. Medals by Giovanni Carino. N.Y., 1883.
Arc 1613.14 Laws authorizing issuance of medals. (Lewis, E.A.) Washington, 1936.
Arc 1613.14.5 Laws authorizing issuance of medals and commerative coins. (Lewis, E.A.) Washington, 1936.

Author and Title Listing

Arc 861.4.3 Lawson, P.H. Schedule of the Roman remains of Chester. Chester, 1928.

Arc 1490.5 Lazari, V. Le monete dei possedimenti veneziani. Venezia, 1851.

Arc 689.9 Lazarides, D.I. Hē Thasos. Thessalonikē, 1958.

Arc 1153.104.2 Lazzarini, Vittorio. Scritti di paleografia e diplomatica. 2. ed. Padova, 1969.

Arc 608.6.55 Le tombeau de la Chrétienne. (Christople, M.) Paris, 1951.

Arc 386.17.5 Leach, H.S. A bibliography of Howard Crosby Butler, 1872-1922. Princeton, 1924.

Arc 943.14.5F Leaflets. (N.Y. Museum of the American Indian. Heye Foundation.) N.Y. 1-5,1919-1926

Arc 513.1 Leaflets from the notebook of an archaeological traveller in Asia Minor. (Sterrett, J.R.S.) Austin, 1889.

Htn Arc 1538.5* Leake, S.M. Historical account of English money from the conquest. London, 1745.

Arc 708.9.9 Leake, W.M. Athènes d'après le colonel Leake. Paris, 1876.

Arc 1465.5 Leake, W.M. Numismata Hellenica. London, 1854.

Arc 708.9 Leake, W.M. Topographie von Athen. Halle, 1829.

Arc 708.9.2 Leake, W.M. The topography of Athens. London, 1821.

Arc 708.9.3 Leake, W.M. The topography of Athens. London, 1841. 2v.

Arc 513.12 Leake, William M. Journal of a tour in Asia Minor. London, 1824.

Arc 1335.7 Leavitt, Strebeigh and Company. Catalogue of an excellent choice and select collection of coins, medals, and autographs. n.p., 1870.

Arc 1020.7 Lebarte, J. L'église cathedrale de Sienne...trésor. Paris, 1868.

Arc 635.17 Lebas, P. Voyage archéologique en Grèce et en Asie Mineure. Paris, 1847-77. 5v.

X Cg Arc 651.1 Le Bas, P. Voyage archéologique en Grèce et en Asie Mineure. Paris, 1888.

Arc 673.3 Lebègue, J.A. Recherches sur Délos. Paris, 1876.

Arc 1077.2.65 Das Lebende Kreuz. (Füglister, Robert L.) Einsiedeln, 1964.

Arc 925.107.5 Lebende Vergangenheit; deutsche Übertragen von Alexander Becker und Ruth Kalinowski. 1. Aufl. Berlin, 1954.

Arc 385.12 Lebenserinnerungen eins Ausgräbers. (Andrae, Walter.) Berlin, 1961.

Arc 87.1.62 Lebensregeln auf Athens. Hochzeitsgeschenken. (Brueckner, A.) Berlin, 1907.

Arc 905.24.25 Leber, Paul Siegfried. Aus Kärntens römischer Vergangenheit. v.1-5. Wolfsberg, 1971-

Arc 830.145 Lebeuf, Jean. Mémoire sur quelques antiquités du diocese de Bayeux. n.p., 1747.

Arc 1498.2 Leblanc, F. Traité historique des monnayes de France. Amsterdam, 1692.

Arc 1498.2.5 Leblanc, F. Traité historique des monnayes de France. Paris, 1690.

Arc 1033.97 Le Blant, E. Des voies d'exception...contre les martyrs. Rome, 1884.

Arc 1033.95 Le Blant, E. D'un nouveau monument...Sainte Félicité. Rome, 1888.

Arc 1030.9 Le Blant, E. L'épigraphie chrétienne en Gaule. n.p., 1890.

Arc 1030.48 Le Blant, E. Inscriptions chrétiennes de la Gaule antérieure au VIIIe siècle. Paris, 1856-65. 2v.

Arc 1027.25.61 LeBlant, E. Jean-Baptiste de Rossi. Paris, 1894.

Arc 1030.34 Le Blant, E. Manuel d'épigraphie chrétienne. Paris, 1869.

Arc 1033.110 Le Blant, E. Les premiers Chrétiens et le Démon. Rome, 1888.

Arc 1033.111 Le Blant, E. Les songes et les visions des martyrs. Rome, 1892.

Arc 1030.9.5 Le Blant, E. Sur une pierre tumulaire. Arras, 1877.

Arc 766.3 Le Blant, Edmond. Les ateliers de sculpture chez les premiers chrétiens. Rome, 1884.

Arc 889.28 Leblois, C. Le cimetière merovingien de Cuesmes. Cuesmes, 1960.

Arc 1500.24 Leblond, V. Le pays des Bellovaques. Essai...numismatique. Caen, 1906.

Arc 430.201 Lebon, G. Les monuments de l'Inde. Paris, 1893.

Arc 830.142 Lebreton, J. Archéologie de Mons Seleucus. Gap, 1806.

Arc 1020.84 Le Brun Dalbaune. Les aumonières du trésor...cathedrale de Troyes. Troyes, 1864.

Arc 1020.84.5 Le Brun Dalbaune. Recherches...emaux du trésor de la Cathedrale de Troyes. Troyes, 1862.

Arc 609.3F Lebzelter, Viktor. Die Vorgeschichte von Süd- und Südwestafrica. Leipzig, 1930-34. 2v.

Arc 66.1.92 Lechat, Henri. La sculpture attique avant Phidias. Paris, 1904.

Arc 1093.6.20 Lecher, Jörg. Vom Hakenkreuz. Leipzig, 1921.

Arc 1093.6.22 Lecher, Jörg. Vom Hakenkreuz. 2. Aufl. Leipzig, 1934.

Arc 522.1 Lechevalier, Jean Baptiste. Description of the plain of Troy. Edinburgh, 1791.

Arc 522.1.2.3 Lechevalier, Jean Baptiste. Voyage dans la Troade. 2. éd. Paris, 1799.

Arc 522.1.2 Lechevalier, Jean Baptiste. Voyage de la Troade. Paris, 1802. 3v.

Arc 853.205.5 Leciyewicz, Leah. Kołobrzeg we wczesnymsredniowieczu. Wrocław, 1961.

Arc 600.6.30 Leclant, Jean. Recherches sur les monuments thébains de la XXVe dynastie dite éthiopienne. Le Caire, 1965. 2v.

Arc 1018.24 LeClercq, H. Manuel d'archéologie chrétienne. Paris, 1907. 2v.

Arc 820.220F Leclere, J.B. Archéologie celto-romaine de l'arrondissement de Chatillon-sur-Seine. pt.1-2. Paris, 1840-1843.

Arc 1208.2 Le Clert, Louis. Catalogue de sigillographie du Musée de Troyes. Troyes, 1887.

Arc 1408.10 L'Ecluse, Charles de. Monnaies orientales. Paris, 1888.

Arc 1020.82 Lecocq, G. Notice sur un reliquare de St. Quentin. St. Quentin, 1875.

Arc 1033.12.132 Lecomte, A. Sainte-face de la cathédrale de Laon. Laon, 1885.

Arc 1138.3 Leçon d'ouverture du cours de paléographie. (Grand, E. Daniel.) Montpellier, 1890.

Arc 543.4.13 LeCoq, Albert. Auf Hellas spuren in Ostturkistan. Leipzig, 1926.

Arc 543.4.14 LeCoq, Albert. Buried treasures of Chinese Turkestan. London, 1928.

Arc 1500.40.5 Lecoq-Kerneven, J. Étude historique sur la numismatique bretonne. Rennes, 1868.

Arc 1500.40 Lecoq-Kerneven, J. Monnaies du moyen-age (Gaule). Rennes, 1870.

Arc 1212.1 Lecoy de la Marche, A. Les sceaux. Paris, 1889.

Arc 66.1.52 Lécrivain, C. Le Sénat Romain depuis Dioclétien. Paris, 1888.

Arc 1030.27 Lectio inscriptionum...sulpicii maximi. (Ciofi, A.) Roma, 1872.

Arc 861.89.5 A lecture on the antiquities of the Anglo-Saxon cemeteries of the ages of paganism. (Wright, Thomas.) Liverpool, 1854.

Arc 1361.2 A lecture on the study of ancient coins. (Green, B.R.) London, 1829.

Arc 1418.10 Lectures on ancient Indian numismatics. (Bhandarkar, D.R.) Calcutta, 1921.

Arc 609.17.20 Lectures on Nigerian prehistory and archaeology. Ibadan, 1969.

Arc 1458.7 Lectures on the coinage of the Greeks and Romans. (Cardwell, E.) Oxford, 1832.

Htn Arc 823.13* Ledain, A. Lettres et notices d'archéologie. Metz, 1869.

Arc 1223.2 Ledderhose, Lothar. Die Siegelschrift (Chuan-shu) in der Ch'ing-Zeit. Wiesbaden, 1970.

Arc 1366.2 Lederer, Philipp. Neue Beiträge zur antike Münzkunde. Bern, 1943.

Arc 1490.8.9 Lederer, Philipp. Die Tetrodrachmenprägung von Segesta. München, 1910.

Arc 893.3.3 Ledetraad til nordisk oldkyndighed. (Copenhagen. Kongelige Nordiske Oldskrift-Selskab.) Kjøbenhavn, 1836.

Arc 885.14 Lee, J.E. Description of a Roman building and other remains...at Caerleon. London, 1850. 5 pam.

Arc 861.67F Lee, John Edward. Delineations of Roman antiquities...at Caerleon. London, 1845.

Arc 583.3 Leedrain, E. Monumens égyptiens de la Bibliothèque Nationale. pt.1-3. no.38. Paris, 1879-81.

Arc 870.12.19 Leeds, E.T. The Anglo-Saxon cemetery at Abingdon, Berkshire. Oxford, 1936. 2v.

Arc 870.12 Leeds, E.T. The archaeology of the Anglo-Saxon settlements. Oxford, 1913.

Arc 870.12.10 Leeds, E.T. The corpus of early Anglo-Saxon great square-headed broaches. Oxford, 1949.

Arc 870.12.15A Leeds, E.T. Early Anglo-Saxon art and archaeology. Oxford, 1936.

Arc 1480.46 Leeds, Edward T. A hoard of Roman folles from Diocletian's reform. Oxford, 1946.

Arc 542.2 Leemans, C. Boro-Boudour dans l'Isle de Jara. Leyden, 1874. 5v.

Arc 380.213 Leemans, C. Études archéologiques, linguistiques. Leide, 1885.

Arc 561.6 Leemans, Conrad. L'égyptologue Conrad Leemans et sa correspondance. Leiden, 1973.

Arc 1660.19F Lefebure, Charles. Contribution à la documentation du temps de guerre. Bruxelles, 1923.

Arc 545.227.13 Lefebvre, G. Recueil des inscriptions grecques. Le Caire, 1907.

Arc 545.227.21F Lefebvre, G. Le tombeau de Petosiris. v.1-3. Le Caire, 1923-1924.

Arc 608.78 Lefebvre, Gillette. Corpus des gravures et des peintures rupestres de la région de Constantine. Paris, 1967.

Arc 66.1.180 Lefêvre, Yves. L'elucidarium et les lucidaires. Paris, 1954.

Arc 1027.24.9 Lefort, L. Chronologie des peintures des catacombes de Naples. Rome, 1883.

Arc 1018.2 Lefort, L. Études sur les monuments primitifs. Paris, 1885.

Arc 1033.70.13 Lefort, L. Peintures inédites de L'Église St. Nicolas. Paris, 1879.

Arc 1027.2.19 Lefort, L. Les scènes de banquets. Paris, 1883.

Arc 1025.32 Lefort, Louis. Chronologie des peintures des catacombes romaines. Paris, 1881.

Htn Arc 1335.10* Lefroy, A. Catalogus numism. mus. Lefroyani. Livorno, 1763.

Arc 830.158.10 Le Gall, J. Alésia. Paris, 1963.

Arc 1016.229 Legati, L. Museo Cospiano. Bologna, 1677.

Arc 1033.5.9 The legend of Saint Peter's chair. (Rich, Anthony.) London, 1851.

Arc 925.337.10 Legenda i byl' donskikh kurganov. (Kiiashko, Vladimir I.) Rostov-na-Donu, 1972.

Arc 925.170.5 Legenda ob olene-chelovcke. (Charnoluskii, Vladimir V.) Moskva, 1965.

Arc 1076.3.105 Legends o' the bells. (Morris, E.) London, 1935.

Arc 1500.64 Le Gentilhomme, P. Melanges de numismatique merovingienne. Paris, 1940.

Arc 595.12 Le leggende delle piramidi. (Grossi, V.) Genova, 1890.

Arc 66.1.205 Leglay, Marcel. Saturne africain; histoire. Paris, 1966.

Arc 608.70 Leglay, Marcel. Saturne africain; monuments. Paris, 1961. 2v.

Arc 830.79.5 Le Goux de Gerland. Dissertations sur l'origine de la ville de Dijon. Dijon, 1771.

Arc 545.227.19 Legrain, G. Repertoire genealogique et onomastique. Genève, 1908.

Arc 1020.8 Legrand, E. Description...de l'église des Saints Apotres de Constantinople. Paris, 1896.

Arc 66.1.79 Legrand, P.E. Étude sur Théocrite. Paris, 1898.

Arc 853.195 Lehmann, F. Aus der Frühgeschichte der Oberlausitz. Berlin, 1958.

Arc 340.20.2 Lehmann, Herbert. Bibliographie zur Vor- und Frühgeschichte von Gross-Berlin. 2. Aufl. Berlin, 1968.

Arc 688.6 Lehmann, Karl. Samothrace. N.Y., 1955.

Arc 688.6.5F Lehmann, Karl. Samothrace. v.1-4,6. N.Y., 1959-64. 5v.

Arc 1148.2 Lehmann, O. Die Tachygraphischen Abkürzungen der griechischen Handschriften. Leipzig, 1880.

Arc 688.6.7 Lehmann, Phyllis. The pedimental sculpture of the Hieron. N.Y., 1962.

Arc 785.72A Lehmann-Hartleben, K. Dionysiac sarcophagi in Baltimore. Baltimore, 1942.

Arc 785.15.11FA Lehmann-Hartleben, Karl. Die Trajanssaule. Text and Atlas. Berlin, 1926. 2v.

Arc 853.74 Lehner, Hans. Das Römerlager Vetera bei Hauten. Bonn, 1926.

Arc 1510.22.5 Lehr, Ernest. Les monnaies des landgraves autrichiens de la Haute Alsace. Supplement. Mulhouse, 1896. 2 pam.

Arc 1018.29 Lehrbuch der christlich kirchlichen Archäologie. (Guericke, H.) Berlin, 1859.

Arc 1185.7 Lehre von dem Urkundenbeweise. (Spangenberg, E.) Heidelberg, 1827. 2v.

Arc 1185.5.1 Die Lehre von der Privaturkunden. (Posse, Otto.) Berlin, 1974.

Arc 1033.12.9.15 Das Leichentuch von Turin. (Bachinger, Rudolf.) Stein am Rhein, 1967.

Arc 1538.14 Leigh, Sotheby, and Son. Collection of 28 plates illustrating ancient coins of Great Britain. London, 1803.

Author and Title Listing

Arc 1335.11 Leipzig. Stadtbibliothek. Katalog des Münzkabinets. Leipzig, 1853.
Arc 843.100 Leisner, G.K. Antas nas herdades da Casa de Braganca no concelho de Estremoz. Lisboa, 1955.
Arc 843.100.5F Leisner, G.K. Die Negalithgräber der Iberischen Halbinsel. v.1-3; atlas. Berlin, 1956. 4v.
Arc 1297.5 Leist, F. Die Notariats-Signete. Leipzig, n.d.
Arc 1185.3 Leist, F. Urkundenlehre. Leipzig, 1882.
Arc 1185.3.2 Leist, F. Urkundenlehre. 2. Aufl. Leipzig, 1893.
Arc 1493.9 Leite de Vasconcellos, J. Da numismatica em Portugal. Lisboa, 1923.
Arc 396.5 Leite de Vasconcellos, J. De Campolide a Melrose. Lisboa, 1915.
Arc 838.3.13 Leite de Vasconcellos, J. De terra em terra. v.1-2. Lisboa, 1927.
Arc 838.3.7 Leite de Vasconcellos, J. Historia do museu etnologico português (1893-1914). Lisboa, 1915.
Arc 838.3 Leite de Vasconcellos, J. Portugal pre-historico. Lisboa, 1885.
Arc 838.3.5 Leite de Vasconcellos, J. Religiões da Lusitania. Lisboa, 1897. 3v.
Arc 612.30 Leitfaden der Vorgeschichte Europas. (Bumüller, J.) Augsburg, 1925. 2v.
Arc 612.9 Leitfaden zur Kunde des heidnischen Alterthümes. (Sacken, Eduard.) Wien, 1865.
Arc 893.3.5 Leitfaden zur Nordischen Alterthumskunde. (Nordiske Oldskrift-Selskab.) Copenhagen, 1837.
Arc 1020.9.145 Leitzmann, Hans. Petrus und Paulus in Rom. Bonn, 1915.
Arc 1020.9.146 Leitzmann, Hans. Petrus und Paulus in Rom. 2. Aufl. Berlin, 1927.
Arc 1330.3 Leitzmann, J. Bibliotheca numaria. Weissensee, 1867.
Arc 1588.1 Lelewel, J. Notice sur la monnaie de Pologne. Bruxelles, 1842.
Arc 1500.41 Lelewel, Joachim. Réapparitions du type gaulois dans le coin du moyen age. Bruxelles, 1841.
Arc 830.270 Lelièvre, Léon. Menhirs et marches sacrées. Caen, 195-.
Arc 396.12 Lemaire, Raymond. La restauration des monuments anciens. Anvers, 1935.
Arc 1433.50 Le May, R.S. The coinage of Siam. Bangkok, 1932.
Arc 1033.12.197 Le Mercier, J. Histoire de la larme sainte...Selincourt. Amiens, 1707.
Arc 1185.23 Lemoine, P.C. Diplomatique-pratique. Metz, 1765.
Arc 823.6 L'Empereur, J. Dissertations historiques sur divers sujets. Paris, 1706.
Arc 87.1.72 Lenäenvasen. (Frickenhaus, A.) Berlin, 1912.
Arc 983.11 The Lenape stone. (Mercer, H.C.) N.Y., 1885.
Arc 1500.53F Lengyel, L. L'art gaulais dans les médailles. Montrange-Seine, 1954.
Arc 925.38.10 Leningrad. Ermitazh. Drevnee iskusstov Altaia. Leningrad, 1958.
Arc 1433.45F Leningrad. Ermitazh. Inventarnyi katalog musulbmanskikh monet. Sankt Peterburg, 1896.
Arc 1433.44 Leningrad. Ermitazh. Katakog' dzhelairidskiu' monety Sost. A. Markov'. Sankt Peterburg, 1897.
Arc 925.190 Leningrad. Ermitazh. New archaeological material relating to the history of the Soviet East. Leningrad, 1960.
Arc 1311.2 Leningrad. Ermitazh. Trutsy otts. numizmatiki. Leningrad. 1,1945 4v.
Arc 923.134 Leningrad. Universitet. Issledovaniia po arkheologii SSSR. Leningrad, 1961.
Arc 923.122 Leninskie idei v izuchenii istorii pervobytnogo obshchestva, rabovladeniia i feodalizma. Moskva, 1970.
Arc 522.3 Lenormant, F. Les antiquités de la Troade. Paris, 1876.
Arc 1366.1A Lenormant, F. La monnaie dans l'antiquité. Paris, 1878-79. 3v.
Arc 1348.9 Lenormant, F. Monnaies et médailles. Paris, 1883.
Arc 700.8 Lenormant, F. Monographie de la voie sacrée éleusinienne. Paris, 1884.
Arc 830.40.15 Lenormant, François. De la découverte d'un prétendu cimitière mérovingien a la Chapelle-Saint-Eloi (Eure). Evreux, 1855. 2 pam.
Arc 830.40.17 Lenormant, François. De l'authenticité des monuments découverts a la Chapelle-Saint-Eloi. Paris, 1855.
Arc 726.110 Lenotti, T. L'arena di Verona. Verona, 1954.
Arc 522.11 Lenz, C.G. Die Ebene von Troja. Neu-Strelitz, 1798.
Arc 609.1.7 Lenz, Oskar. Ophir und die Ruinen von Zimbabye. Prag, 1896.
Htn Arc 1020.9.116* Léon, François. Les merveilles de la ville de Rome. Rome, 1646.
Arc 1020.9.118 Léon, François. Les merveilles de la ville de Rome. Rome, 1750.
Arc 830.63.9 Léon des Ormeaux, A. La Roche aux Feés. Laval, 188-?
Arc 1335.18 Leonard and Company. Catalogue of American coins. Boston, 1860-70. 4 pam.
Arc 684.1.7 Leonardos, B. Hē Olympia. Athēnai, 1901.
Arc 396.13 Leone, Mark P. Comptemporary archaeology. Carbondale, 1972.
Arc 1490.5.10 Il Leone di S. Marco. (Gian, M.L. dal.) Venezia, 1958.
Arc 638.3 Il Leone Nemeo. (Michaelis, A.T.F.) Roma, 1859. 7 pam.
Arc 785.20.9A Leoni, N. On the Appian Way. Florence, 1907.
Arc 736.24 Leontinoi: anni di ricerche archeologiche. (Ciancio, Salvatore.) Lentini, 1965.
Arc 396.20 Leopold, Hendrik M.R. Uit de school van de spade. Zutphen, 1928-34. 6v.
Arc 861.21.40 Le Patourel, John Herbert. The moated sites of Yorkshire. London, 1973.
Arc 936.220.30 Lepenski vir. (Belgrade. Narodni Muzej.) Beograd, 1967.
Arc 936.220.32 Lepenski vir. (Srejović, Dragoslav.) Beograd, 1969.
Arc 1025.20 L'Epinovis, H. de. Les catacombes de Rome. Paris, 1875.
Arc 900.207 Lepkowski, J. Monumenta epigraphica Cracoviensia. Krakow, 1883.
Arc 830.53.25 Le Pontois, B. Le Finistère préhistorique. Paris, 1929.
Arc 1033.113 Leport, L. Deux mosaiques chrétiennes du IVe siècle. Paris, 1894.
Arc 1033.113.3 Leport, L. Nouvelles observations sur la Mosaique de S. Pudentienne. Rome, 1896.
Arc 815.35 Leppmann, Wolfgang. Pompeii in fact and fiction. London, 1968.
Arc 815.30 Leppmann, Wolfgang. Pompeji. Eine Stadt in Literatur und Leben. München, 1966.
Arc 407.30 Leppmann, Wolfgang. Winckelmann. 1. ed. N.Y., 1970.
Arc 1020.132 Le Prevost, A. Notice sur la châsse de Saint Taurin d'Évreux. Évreux, 1838.
Arc 561.1.2 Lepsius, R. Briefe aus Aegypten. Berlin, 1852.
Arc 561.1 Lepsius, R. Discoveries in Egypt, Ethiopia and the Peninsula of Sinai. London, 1853.
Arc 608.18F Leptis Magna. (Romanelli, P.) Roma, 1925.
Arc 66.1.176 Lerat, Lucien. Les Locriens de l'ouest. v. 1-2. Paris, 1952.
Arc 743.23 Lerici, C.M. Nuove testimonianze dell'arte e della civiltà etrusca. Milano, 1960.
Arc 1470.83 Le Rider, Georges. Deux trésors de monnaies. Paris, 1963.
Arc 1470.26.5 Le Rider, Georges. Monnaies crétoises du Ve au Ier siècle avant J.C. Thèse. Paris, 1966.
Arc 681.15 Lerna, a preclassical site in the Argolid. (American School of Classical Studies at Athens.) Princeton, N.J., 1969. 2v.
X Cg Arc 1603.4 Lerouv, J. Le médaillier du Canada. Montreal, 1888.
Arc 66.1.108 Leroux, Gabriel. Les origines de l'édifice hypostyle. Paris, 1913.
Arc 830.11.9 Le Rouzic, Z. Carnac; fouilles faites dans la région. Vannes. 1897-1902
Arc 830.11.9.10 Le Rouzic, Z. Carnac; fouilles faites dans la région. Campagne 1922. Paris, 1931.
Arc 830.11.8 Le Rouzic, Z. Carnac; menhirs, statues. Nantes, 1931.
Arc 830.11.7 Le Rouzic, Z. Carnac; restaurations faites dans la région. Vannes, 1930.
Arc 830.11.9.9 Le Rouzic, Z. Carnac. Nancy, 1922.
Arc 830.11.9.5 Le Rouzic, Z. Carnac. Vannes, 1932.
Arc 830.11 Le Rouzic, Z. Carnac et ses monuments. Morlaix, 1897.
Arc 830.2.19 Le Rouzic, Z. Locmariaquer. La table des marchands. 2e ed. Vannes, 1923.
Arc 830.11.5 Le Rouzic, Z. Les monuments mégalithiques de Carnac et de Locmariaquer. n.p., 1901?
Arc 1033.17.221 Le Roy, A. Histoire de Notre-Dame de Boulogne. Boulogne, 1704.
Arc 609.2.20 Leroy, Jules. L'Éthiopie. Paris, 1973.
Arc 87.2.45 Lersch, J.H.L. Das coelner Mosaik. Bonn, 1846.
Arc 87.2.48 Lersch, J.H.L. Schwert des Giberins. Bonn, 1849.
Arc 843.198 Les arrels de Catalunya. (Tarradell, M.) Barcelona, 1962.
Arc 1025.4.9 Les catacombes romaines. (Northcote, J.S.) Rome, 1859.
Arc 595.66.4 Les pyramides de Sakkarah. 4. éd. (Lauer, Jean Philippe.) Le Caire, 1972.
Arc 66.1.168 Lesage, G. Marseille Angevine. Paris, 1950.
Arc 681.1.10 Das lesbische Kymation. (Weickert, Carl.) Leipzig, 1913.
Arc 608.6.45 Leschi, Louis. Algérie antique. Paris, 1952.
Arc 608.6.30 Leschi, Louis. Djemila. Alger, 1953.
Arc 608.6.29 Leschi, Louis. Djemila Cuicul de Numidie. Alger, 1938.
Arc 608.6.46 Leschi, Louis. Études d'épigraphie. Paris, 1957.
Arc 1163.23 Leseschlüssel zu unserer alten Schrift. (Grun, Paul A.) Görlitz, 1935.
VArc 396.21 Lesicjewicz, Anna. 500 zagadek archeologicznych. Warszawa, 1966.
Arc 925.50.120 Leskov, Aleksandr M. Gornyi Krym v I tysicacheletii do nashei coy. Kiev, 1965.
Arc 875.15 Leslie, Forbes. The early races of Scotland and their monuments. Edinburgh, 1866. 2v.
Arc 1663.56 Lesser, Friedrich Christian. Besondere Münzen. Frankfurt, 1739.
Arc 1025.61 The lesson of the catacombs. (Henderson, Alexander.) London, 1920.
Arc 830.235 Lestocquoy, Jean. Nécropoles et civilisation en Artois et Boulounais. Arras, 1957.
Arc 1076.3.53 L'Estrange, John. The church bells of Norfolk. Norwich, 1874.
Arc 830.180 Letelié, J.A. Les Arenes de Saints en 1882. Pons, 1883.
Arc 651.2 Lethaby, W.R. Greek buildings. London, 1908.
Arc 875.75 Lethbridge, T. Herdsmen and hermits. Cambridge, Eng., 1950.
Arc 1082.10 Lethbridge, T.C. Gogmagog. London, 1957.
Arc 858.57 Lethbridge, Thomas C. Merlin's Island. London, 1948.
Arc 936.180.30 Letića, Zagorka. Antropomorfne figurine bronzanog doba u Jugoslaviji. Beograd, 1973.
Arc 736.2.3 Letronne, A. Essai critique sur la topographie de Syracuse. Paris, 1812.
Arc 1458.4 Letronne, J.A. Considerations générales sur l'évaluation des monnaies grecques et romaines. Paris, 1817.
Arc 561.2 Letronne, J.A. Recherches pour servir à l'histoire de l'Égypte. Paris, 1823.
Arc 1200.26 The letter-book of William of Hoo. (William of Hoo, S.) Ipswich, 1963.
Htn Arc 407.2* Letter to Dr. Mead. (Wise, F.) Oxford, 1738-64. 4 pam.
Arc 875.18 A letter to Sir Walter Scott, Baronet. (Mackenzie, G.S.) Edinburgh, 1824.
Arc 1016.231 Lettera...sul culto delle sacre immagini. (Adriano I.) Roma, 1885.
Arc 726.22 Lettera al signor Giuseppe Carnevali di Albano. (Visconti, A.) Roma, 1817.
Arc 730.5.3 Lettera di...Grove-Olympico in Agrigento. (Politi, R.) Palermo, 1819.
Arc 1018.6.18 Lettera intorno...premessa all...Armellini. (Stevenson, E.) Roma, 1898.
Arc 743.7 Lettere di Etrusca erudizione. (Inghirami, F.) Poligrafia, 1828.
Arc 397.14 Lettere inedite. v.1-3. (Marini, G.) Roma, 1916-40. 2v.
Arc 380.199 Lettere sopra vari punti di erudizione. (Noris, Enrico.) n.p., 1720.
Arc 530.2.10 Letters from Sardis. (Hanfmann, George M.A.) Cambridge, 1972.
Arc 861.21.5 Letters upon some early remains discovered in Yorkshire. v.1-2. (Colls, J.M.N.) n.p., n.d.
Arc 726.17 Lettre...sur l'inscription...du Lion de Venise. (Johanneau, E.) n.p., 1808.
Arc 1473.4 Lettre...sur quelques monnaies byzantines. (Pfaffenhoffen, F.) Paris, 1865.
Arc 1584.3 Lettre...sur une monnaie attribuée à Oleg. (Gille, F.) Paris, 1861.
Arc 1033.35.71 Lettre à...Piolin sur la legende hébraïque du titre de la viaie croix. (Sionnet, A.) n.p., n.d.
Arc 823.19.80 Lettre a M. Ernest Desjardins. (Thédenat, H.) Paris, 1881.
Arc 830.14 Lettre à M.J. Quicherat...sur une decouverte...dans l'etang de Nesmy. (Fillion, B.) La Roche-sur-Yon, 1879.
Arc 1443.2 Lettre à M.P. Charles Robert sur les monnaies égyptiennes. (Revillout, Eugène.) Macon, 1884.
Arc 82.1.10 Lettre à Mollien le directeur de la Revue archéologique. (Ravaisson-Mollien, F.) Paris, 1876.
Arc 830.31.5 Lettre à Monsieur Hase sur une inscription latine du second siècle. (Berger de Xivrey, Jules.) Paris, 1833.
Arc 800.3.7 Lettre à Monsieur le Comte de Brühl. (Winckelmann, J.) Dresde, 1764.
Arc 1033.135 Lettre circulaire de M....d'Amiens...de la reception de la face de S. Jean Baptiste. Amiens, 1879.

Author and Title Listing

Arc 1033.12.193 Lettre d'un Benedictin...touchant le discernement. Diss. Paris, 1700.

Arc 1077.3.2 Lettre sur la chape arabe de Chinon. (Cavallari, S.) Paris, 1857.

Arc 800.12 Lettre sur les peintures d'Herculanum. Bruxelles, 1751.

Arc 830.97.5 Lettre sur les tours antiques qu'on a démoliés à Aix en Provence et sur les antiquités qu'elles renfermoient. (Gibelin, Antoine.) Aix, 1787.

Arc 505.10 Lettre sur un plan du Haram El-Khalil. (Raint.) Paris, 1886.

Arc 552.1.2 Lettres à M. le Duc de Blacas d'Aulps. (Champollion, J.F.) Paris, 1824.

Htn Arc 1153.60* Lettres à M.C.N. Amanton sur deux manuscrits précieux des temps de Charlemagne. (Peignot, G.) Dijon, 1829.

Arc 708.12 Lettres athéniennes. (Moüy, Charles.) Paris, 1887.

Arc 400.23 Lettres au comte de Caylus. (Paciaudi, Paolo M.) Paris, 1802.

Arc 552.1 Lettres écrites d'Egypte et de Nubie. (Champollion, J.F.) Paris, 1833.

Arc 552.1.4 Lettres écrites d'Égypte et de Nubie en 1828 et 1829. (Champollion, J.F.) Paris, 1868.

Arc 646.3 Lettres écrites sur une dissertation d'un voyage de Grèce. (Guillet de St.-George, George.) Paris, 1679.

Htn Arc 823.13* Lettres et notices d'archéologie. (Ledain, A.) Metz, 1869.

Arc 66.1.54 Lettres inedites de Michel Apostolis. (Noiret, H.) Paris, 1889.

Arc 800.11 Lettres sur l'état actuel de la ville souterraine d'Herculée. (Brosses, Charles de.) Dijon, 1750.

Arc 825.9 Lettres sur Nismes et le Midi. (Perrot, J.F.A.) Nismes, 1840. 2v.

Arc 1433.19 Lettres sur quelques points de la numismatique arabe. Lettres 4,5, et 6. (Saulcy, L.F.J.C. de.) Paris, 1841.

Arc 1033.35.45 Lettres testimoniales...portant donation d'un morceau de la vrai croix...Angers. (Barbier de Montault, X.) Tours, n.d.

Arc 1510.137 Leuckfeld, J.G. Antiquitates nummariae, oder Historische Beschreibung vieleralten. Leipzig, 1721.

Arc 80.1.7.5F Leukōma tēs hekatontaeteridos. (Archaiologikē Hetairia, Athens.) Athēnai, 1952.

Arc 41.5 Levant; journal of the British School of Archaeology in Jerusalem. London. 1,1969+ 2v.

Arc 543.27.15 De levensgeschiedenis van den Buddha op Barabudur. (Krom, N.J.) 's Gravenhage, 1926.

Arc 66.1.185 Leveque, Pierre. Pyrrhos. Paris, 1957.

Arc 1033.64 Levera, F. De invicta veritate anni, mensis, et diei. Roma, 1668.

Arc 830.117 Lévesque, L. Inscriptions da la ville de Saint-Maixent du Xe au XIXe siècle. n.p., n.d.

Arc 1470.12 Levezow, J.A.K. Über mehrere im...Posen...griechische Münzen. n.p., 1833.

Arc 1053.5.3 Levezow, R. Ueber den Antinous. Berlin, 1808.

Arc 1088.1.21 Levi, C.A. Navi venete. Venezia, 1892.

Arc 726.112 Levi, Doro. L'ipogeo di San Salvatore di Cabras in Sardegna. Roma, 1949.

Arc 785.13.3 Levy, L. Das Forum Romanum der Kaiser Zeit. München, 1895.

Arc 1423.15 Levy, Moritz Abraham. Geschichte der jüdischen Münzen. Breslau, 1862.

Arc 1423.15.1 Levy, Moritz Abraham. Geschichte der jüdischen Münzen. Leipzig, 1862.

Arc 936.195.85 Levý Hradec. (Borkovský, Ivan.) Praha, 1965.

Arc 1200.4 Lewinski, L. Die Brandenburgische Kanzlei und die Urkundenwesen. Inaug. Diss. Strassburg, 1893.

Arc 1613.14 Lewis, E.A. Laws authorizing issuance of medals. Washington, 1936.

Arc 1613.14.5 Lewis, E.A. Laws authorizing issuance of medals and commerative coins. Washington, 1936.

Arc 885.30 Lewis, Ewart Thomas. Mynachlogddu: a guide to its antiquities. Clunderwen, 1967.

Arc 963.1 Lewis, T.H. Stone monuments in northwestern Iowa and southwestern Minnesota. n.p., 1890?

NEDL Arc 953.4 Lewis, T.H. Tracts for archaeologists. First series, 1880-91. St. Paul, 1892.

Arc 974.3 Lewis, Thomas M. Hiwassee Island: an archaeological account of 4 Tennessee Indian peoples. Knoxville, 1946.

Arc 1301.2.5 Lewis, Winslow. Address...on resigning the presidency of the Boston Numismatic Society, January 5, 1865. N.Y., 1866.

Arc 1340.1.2 Lex. univ. rei numariae veterum. Supplement. (Rasche, J.C.) Leipzig, 1802-05. 3v.

Arc 1340.1 Lex. univ. rei nummariae. v.1-5, pt.1-2; v.6, pt.1. (Rasche, J.C.) Leipzig, 1785-95. 11v.

Arc 1153.12.3 Lexicon abbreviaturarum. (Cappelli, A.) Leipzig, 1901.

Arc 1153.12.10A Lexicon abbreviaturarum. 2. Aufl. (Cappelli, A.) Leipzig, 1928.

Arc 1153.12.15 Lexicon abbreviaturarum. 3. ed. (Cappelli, A.) Milano, 1929.

Arc 1153.12.20 Lexicon abbreviaturarum. 4. ed. (Cappelli, A.) Milano, 1949.

Arc 903.4 Lexikon ur- und frühgeschichtlicher Fundstätten Österreichs. (Franz, Leonhard.) Wien, 1965.

Arc 762.2 Lexique de topographie romaine. (Homo, L.) Paris, 1900.

Arc 273.2.15F Leyden. Rigksmuseum van Oudheden. Oudheidkundige mededeelingen. 29-50 17v.

Arc 547.46 Leyden. Rijksmuseum van Oudheden. Inleiding lot de oud-Egyptische beschaving. 's-Gravenhage, 1959.

Arc 1027.78 Leynaud, A.F. Les catacombes africaines. Sousse, 1910.

Arc 1027.78.2 Leynaud, A.F. Les catacombes africaines. 2e éd. Alger, 1922.

Arc 1027.72 Leynaud, A.F. Rapports sur les fouilles des catacombes d'Hadrumète. Paris, 1905.

Arc 608.93 Lézine, Alexandre. Deux villes d'Ifriqiya: Sousse, Tunis. Paris, 1971.

Arc 608.2.65 Lézine, Alexandre. Les thermes d'Antonin à Carthage. Tunis, 1969.

Arc 608.32.5 Lézine, Alexandre. Utique. Tunis, 1970.

Arc 1018.6 Lezioni di archaeologici cristiana. (Armellini, M.) Roma, 1898.

Arc 1033.177 Lezioni di archeologia cristiana; liturgia ed archeologia. (Cecchelli, Carlo.) Roma, 1958.

Arc 1153.95 Lezioni di paleografia latina e diplomatica. (Mazzoleni, Jole.) Napoli, 1964?

Arc 1018.6.3 Lezioni popolari di archaeologici cristiana. (Armellini, M.) Roma, 1903.

Arc 608.39 Lhote, Henri. The search for the Tassili frescoes. London, 1959.

Arc 421.31.2 Li, Chi. The beginnings of Chinese civilization. Seatle, 1968.

Arc 785.103 A libation to the gods. (Winslow, E.M.) London, 1963.

Arc 1153.5 Libellus aurarius sivi tabulae ceratae. (Massmann, H.P.) Lipsaie, 1840.

Arc 393.15 Libellus Richardo Indrelso sexagenario oblatuo. Stockholm, 1960.

Htn Arc 767.6* Liber de vilitate coditionis humane Mirabilia Romae. Paris, 1509.

Arc 383.46.5 Liber Iosepho Kostrzewski octogenario a veneratoribus dicatur. (Jażdżewski, Konrad.) Wrocław, 1968.

Arc 66.1.175 Liber patér. (Bruhl, A.) Paris, 1953.

Arc 1076.2 Liber singularis de Bysso antiquorum. (Foster, J.R.) Londini, 1776.

Arc 395.7.10 Liberal und integral: der Briefwechsel zwischen Franz Xaver Kraus und A. Stöck. (Kraus, Franz Xaver.) Mainz, 1974.

Arc 1033.103 Liberati, D.P. Processo belle reliquie false. Roma, 1871.

Arc 925.50.48 Liberov, Petr D. Plemena srednego Dona v epokhu bronzy. Moskva, 1964.

Arc 1480.80 Libertas und Christogramm. Thesis. (Kellner, Wendelin.) Karlsruhe, 1968.

Arc 736.8F Libertini, Guido. Centuripe. Catania, 1926.

Arc 66.1.43 Libraire des papes d'Avignon. (Faucon, M.) Paris, 1886. 2v.

Htn Arc 600.16*A The library of Rameses the Great. (Nichols, C.L.) Boston, 1909.

Arc 1033.17.466 Libretto che contiene l'istoria...di Santa Maria...Nocera-Pagani. Napoli, 1834.

Arc 383.90.10 Libro homenaje la Conde de la Vega del Sella. (Oviedo (Province). Diputacion Provincial. Servicio de Investigaciones Arqueologicas.) Oviedo, 1956.

Arc 41.4 Libyca; série archéologie-epigraphie. Alger. 1-7,1953-1959 9v.

Htn Arc 1070.201* Liceti, F. De lucernis antiquorum reconditis libb. sex. Utini, 1653.

Arc 905.147 Lichardus, Ján. Studien zur Bükker Kultur. Bonn, 1974.

Arc 936.195.185 Lichardus, Jan. Taskjňa Domica, najuyznačnejšie sidlisko i udu bukovohorskej kultúry. 1. vyd. Bratislava, 1968.

Arc 651.3 Lichtenberg, R.F. Die ägäische Kultur. Leipzig, 1911.

Arc 651.3.2 Lichtenberg, R.F. Die ägäische Kultur. 2. Aufl. Leipzig, 1918.

Arc 1053.10 Lichteuber, G.R. von. Das Porträt an Grabdenkmalen. Strassburg, 1902.

Arc 600.105.5F Lichtheim, M. Demotic ostraca from Medinet Habu. Chicago, 1957.

Arc 895.60 Lidén, Oskar L. Hällgröpningstudier i arsbetring till nya sydsverska fynd. Lund, 1938.

Arc 1550.2 Et lidet fund af mynter fra 11. aaehundrede. (Holmboe, C.A.) Kjøbenhavn, 1871.

Arc 561.4 Lieblein, J. Die aegyptischen Denkmäler. Christiania, 1873.

Arc 561.4.5 Lieblein, J. Egypten i dess minnesmärken o chi dess färhållande till Palestine och Grekland. Stockholm, 1877.

Arc 180.1.501 Liederchronik der Antiquarischen Gesellschaft in Zürich. (Antiquarische Gesellschaft in Zürich-Bibliothek.) Frauenfeld, 1880.

Arc 1025.13 Liell, H.F.J. Die Darstellungen...Maria...Katakomben. Freiburg, 1887.

Arc 830.334F Liénard, F. Archéologie de la Meuse. v.1-3, texte. v.4-6, carte. Verdun, 1881-85. 6v.

Arc 853.45 Lienau, M.M. Über Megalithgräber und sonstige Grabformen der Lüneburger Gegend. Würzburg, 1914.

Arc 1660.3 Liesville, A.R. de. Histoire numismatique de la révolution de 1848. Paris, 1877-83.

Arc 938.110 Lietuvio kario žirgas. (Volkaitė-Kulikauskienė, Regina.) Vil'nius, 1971.

Arc 938.70 Lietuvos archeologijos bruočai. (Kulikauskar, P.) Vil'nius, 1961.

Arc 938.99 Lietuvos archeologikiai paminklai. Vil'nius, 1968.

Arc 938.65 Lietuvos archeologiniai pominklai ir jų tyrinejimai. (Volkerite-Kulikauskiené, R.) Vil'nius, 1958.

Arc 938.98 Lietuvos BR Mokslų Akademije, Vilna. Istorijas Institutas. Zo let. Vil'nius, 1968.

Arc 938.108 Lietuvos TSR archeologija 1940-1967. (Pagirienė, L.) Vil'nius, 1970.

Arc 938.111 Lietuvos TSR archeologijos atlasas. Vil'nius, 1974- 3v.

Arc 1030.54F Lietzmann, Hans. Corpus der griechisch-christlichen Inschriften von Hellas. Athen, 1941.

Arc 1033.34.9 Lieu du crucifiement de Saint Pierre. (Lugari, J.B.) Tours, 1898.

Arc 830.18.5 Lievre, A.F. Les chemins gaulois et romains. 2e éd. Niort, 1893.

Arc 858.66 Life and death in the bronze age. (Fox, Cyril.) London, 1959.

NEDL Arc 880.19 The life and labors in art and archaeology of George Petrie. (Stokes, William.) London, 1868.

Arc 595.9.5 Life and work at the Great Pyramid. (Smyth, C.P.) Edinburgh, 1867. 3v.

Arc 858.33 Life in ancient Britain. (Ault, Norman.) London, 1920.

Arc 858.9 Life in early Britain. (Windle, B.C.A.) London, 1897.

Arc 858.9.3 Life in early Britain. (Windle, B.C.A.) N.Y., 1897.

Arc 530.8 The life of Major General Sir R.M. Smith. (Dickson, W.K.) Edinburgh, 1901.

Arc 587.50 The life of Rekhmara. (Newberry, P.E.) Westminster, 1900.

Htn Arc 505.5.5* Lightfoot, J. The temple. London, 1650.

Arc 590.18 Lights on the royal mummies in the Egyptian Museum. (Muhammad, Ahmad Rajab.) Cairo, 1964.

Arc 66.1.40 Les ligues étolienne et achéenne. (Dubois, M.) Paris, 1885.

Arc 1282.5 Likhachen, N.I. Drenieishiia bully i nechati shiriully. Sankt Peterburg, 1907.

Arc 1282.7 Likhachen, N.I. Zemskaia nechat' Moskovskago gosudarstva. Moskva, 1914.

Arc 1185.20 Likhachev, N.P. Diplomatika. Sankt Peterburg, 1901.

Arc 925.180.20 Liki drevnego Amura. (Okladnikov, Aleksei Pavlovich.) Novosibirsk, 1968.

Arc 870.22F Lilienthal-Gesellschaft für Luft. Lufthild und Vorgeschichte. Berlin, 1938.

Arc 830.245 Lille. Palais des Beaux-Arts. Baoai, cité gallo-romaine. Lille, 1957.

Arc 963.3.5 Lilly, Eli. Prehistoric antiquities of Indiana. Indianapolis, 1937.

Arc 1645.6F Lima, su moneda y su ceca. v.1-2. (Salazar Bondy, Sebastian.) Lima, 1964.

Arc 936.150.5 Limes Romanus Konferenz, Nitra, Slovakia, 1957. Limes Romanus Konferenz. Bratislava, 1959.

Arc 936.150.5 Limes Romanus Konferenz. (Limes Romanus Konferenz, Nitra, Slovakia, 1957.) Bratislava, 1959.

Arc 936.195.75 Limes Romanus na Slovensku. (Ondrouch, Vojtěch.) Bratislava, 1938.

Arc 915.40.3 Limes-Studien; Vorträge des 3. Internationalen Limes-Kongresses in Rheinfelden. (International Congress of Roman Frontier Studies, 3d, Rheinfelden, Switzerland.) Basel, 1957.

Arc 196.1 Limesblatt, 1892-1903. Trien, 1892.

Arc 76.2F Limesforschungen. Berlin. 1,1959+ 12v.

Arc 938.13 Lincke, B. Eine baltische Halsringform der Volkerwanderungszeit. Inaug. Diss. Berlin, 1937.

Arc 830.121 Linckenheld, E. Les stèles funéraires enforme de maison chez les médiomatriques et en Gaule. Paris, 1927.

Arc 1675.7.5 Lincoln, W.S. and Son, firm, auctioneers, London. A descriptive catalogue of papal medals. London, 1898.

Arc 861.130 Lincoln Archaeological Research Committee. Ten seasons digging, 1945-1954. Lincoln, 1955.

Arc 1279.6 Lind, Karl. Blaetter für altere Sphragiotik. Wien, 1878.

Arc 1423.3 Lindberg, J.C. Commentatio de numis punicis sextorum. Havniae, 1824.

Arc 505.5.30 Lindberg, N. Templet i Jerusalem. Kolding, 1880.

Arc 505.5.32 Lindberg, N. Templet i Jerusalem. Stockholm, 1881.

Arc 396.6 Linde, Richard. Alte Kulturstätten. 2. Aufl. Bielefeld, 1924.

Arc 853.26.5 Lindemann, Kurt. Der Hildesheimer Silberfund. Hildesheim, 1967.

Arc 915.11F Der Lindenhof in Zürich. (Vogt, Emil.) Zürich, 1948.

Arc 848.1 Lindenschmit, L. Handbuch der Deutsche Alterthumskunde. Braunschweig, 1880.

Arc 853.338 Lindenschmit, Wilhelm. Das germanische Todtenlager bei Selzen. Faksimile. Mainz an Rhein, 1969.

Arc 853.244F Linder, H. Die altsteinzeitlichen Kulturen der Räuberhöhle am Schelmeengraben bei Sinzing. Kallmünz, 1961.

Arc 687.1F Lindos; fouilles et recherches, 1902-1914. (Blinkenberg, C.) Berlin, 1931. 4v.

Arc 1033.12.100 Lindovius, J. Rubram Jesu Christi chlamydem...exponent...respondens. Jenae, 1772?

Arc 895.43 Lindqvist, Sune. Den helige Eskils buskopsdöme. Stockholm, 1924.

Arc 1538.6 Lindsay, J. View of the coinage of Ireland. Cork, 1839.

Arc 810.60 Lindsay, J. The writing on the wall. London, 1960.

Arc 1540.16 Lindsay, John. View of coinage of Scotland, tables. Cork, 1845.

Arc 1153.8.5 Lindsay, W.M. Contractions in early Latin miniscule MSS. Oxford, 1908.

Arc 1163.6 Lindsay, W.M. Early Irish minuscule script. Oxford, 1910.

Arc 1163.9 Lindsay, W.M. Early Welsh script. Oxford, 1912.

Arc 1153.8.7A Lindsay, W.M. Notae Latinae...abbreviation in Latin MSS...miniscule period. Cambridge, 1915.

Arc 889.34 Linearbandkeramik aus Elsloo und Stein. v.1-2. (Madderman, Pieter Jan Remees.) 's-Gravenhage, 1970.

Arc 925.40 Linevskii, A.M. Petroglify Karelii. Petrozavodsk, 1939.

Arc 1018.60 Linguistique romane et histoire religieuse. (Aebischer, Paul.) Abadía de San Cugat del Valles, 1968.

Arc 235.5 Linzer archäologische Forschungen. Linz. 1,1962+

Arc 235.6 Linzer archäologische Forschungen. Sonderheft. Linz. 1,1964+

Arc 830.18.9 Lion, J. Les voies romaines après la table Théodosienne. Amiens, 1907.

Arc 670.6 The lion monument at Amphipolis. (Broneer, O.) Cambridge, Mass., 1941.

Arc 905.145 Lippert, Andreas. Das Gräberfeld von Welzelach. Bonn, 1972.

Arc 1020.131 Die Lipsanothek von Brescia. (Kollwitz, J.) Berlin, 1933.

Arc 1020.131PF Die Lipsanothek von Brescia. Atlas. (Kollwitz, J.) Berlin, 1933.

Htn Arc 1033.17.361* Lipsius, I. Diva virgo hallensis. Antverp, 1604.

Htn Arc 1077.2.1* Lipsius, J. De cruce libri tres...cum notis. 3. ed. Antverpiae, 1597.

Htn Arc 1077.2* Lipsius, J. De cruce libri tres. Antverpiae, 1594.

Htn Arc 1077.2.2* Lipsius, J. De cruce libri tres. Parisiis, 1598.

Arc 1330.2 Lipsius, J.G. Bibliotheca numaria. Leipzig, 1801. 2v.

Arc 1033.161 Liquefaction of the blood of St. Januarius. N.Y., 1872.

Arc 853.15 Lisch, G. Pfahlbauten in Mechlenberg. Schwerin, 1865.

Arc 925.50.235 Lisin, V. Kratkii putevoditel' po antichnomu otdelu i vaskopkam khersonesa. Sevastopol', 1939.

Arc 830.78 Lisle, Pitre de. Dictionnaire archéologique de la Loire-Inférieure. Nantes, 1882.

Arc 853.21.5 Lissauer, A. Alterthümer der Bronzezeit in Westpreussen. Danzig, 1891.

Arc 905.12 List, G. Der Wiederauflau von Carnuntum. Wien, 1900.

Arc 880.22 List of ancient and national monuments in county of Cork. (Cochrane, Robert.) Cork, 1913.

Arc 441.3.2F List of ancient monuments in Bengal. (Bengal. Public Works Department.) Calcutta, 1896.

Arc 435.2.51F List of ancient monuments protected in Bihar and Orissa. (Kuraishi, M.M.H.) Calcutta, 1931.

Arc 435.2.17F List of architectural and archaeological remains in Coorg. (Rea, Alexander.) Madras, 1894.

Arc 861.10.15 List of Manx antiquities. (Kinnebrook, William.) Douglas, 1930.

Arc 1680.13 List of the Lincolnshire series of tradesmen's tokens. (Simpson, Justin.) London, 1880.

Arc 435.25.3F A list of the photographic negatives of Indian antiquities. (Indian Museum, Calcutta.) Calcutta, 1900.

Arc 386.28 A list of the published writings of John Davidson Beazley. Oxford, 1951.

Arc 1330.4 List of works relating to numismatics. (New York Public Library.) N.Y., 1914.

Arc 1500.16 Liste des noms d'hommes gravés sur les monnaies. (Barthélemy, Anatole de.) Paris, 1881.

Arc 387.14.5 Liste des publications de Jean Capart. (Folkers, T.) Leiden, 1938.

Arc 435.11.11 Lists of antiquarian remains in the Bombay presidency. (Burgess, James.) Bombay, 1885.

Arc 435.2.19F Lists of antiquarian remains in the central provinces and Berâr. (Cousens, Henry.) Calcutta, 1897.

Arc 435.2.8F Lists of inscriptions and sketch...dynasties of southern India. (Sewell, Robert.) Madras, 1884.

Arc 435.2.7F Lists of the antiquarian remains in the presidency of Madras. (Sewell, Robert.) Madras, 1882.

Arc 1373.9 Literae de re nummaria. (Smith, W.) Newcastle-upon-Tyne, 1729.

Arc 853.52 Literatur zur Vor- und Frühgeschichte Sachsens. (Dutschmann, G.) Leipzig, 1921.

Arc 895.22 Lithberg, Nils. Gotlands stenalder. Stockholm, 1914.

Arc 505.5.67 Le Lithostrotos d'après des fouilles récentes. Paris, 1933.

Arc 936.43 Litsov, Khristo. Rimskiiat grad Abritus pri Razgrad. Razgrad, 1959.

Arc 815.36 Little, Alan. A Roman bridal drama at the Villa of the Mysteries. Wheaton, Md., 1972.

Arc 861.16.2 Little, W.C. Roman fen road in Cambridgeshire. n.p., n.d.

Arc 495.204.4 Littman, Enno. Semitic inscriptions. N.Y., 1904.

Arc 609.2F Littmann, Enno. Deutsche Aksum-Expedition. v.1-4. Berlin, 1913.

Arc 1033.112.5 Die liturgischen Kämme. Thesis. (Swoboda, Franz.) n.p., 1963?

Arc 543.3.95 Litvinskii, Boris A. Drevnie kochevniki "Kryshi mira". Moskva, 1972.

Arc 543.3.75 Litvinskii, Boris A. Kangiuisko-sarmatskii farn. Dushanbe, 1968.

Arc 938.11 Litzka, J. Verzeichnis archäologischer Fundorte in Liv-, Est- und Kurland. Jurjew, 1896.

Arc 1027.27.9 Liverani, F. Catacombe e antichità cristiana di Chiusi. Siena, 1872.

Arc 1033.12.1 Liverani, F. Del nome di S. Maria ad Praesepe. Roma, 1854.

Arc 861.10.24 Liverpool. Public Libraries, Museum and Art Gallery. Handbook and guide to the replicas and casts of Manx crosses on exhibition in the Free Public Museums. 2. ed. Liverpool, 1920.

Arc 125.6 Liverpool. University. Institute of Archaeology. Annals of archaeology and anthropology. Liverpool. 1-28,1908-1948 21v.

Arc 1311.1 Liverpool Numismatic Society. Journal. Liverpool. 1-2,1873-1877

Arc 1312.1 Liverpool Numismatic Society. Melanges numismatique. Le Mens. 1-3,1874-1882 3v.

Arc 1311.1.3 Liverpool Numismatic Society. Report, proceedings. Liverpool. 1,1871

Arc 855.223F Lives of topographers and antiquaries. (Malcolm, J.P.) London, 1815.

Arc 497.45 The living past. (Gordon, Cyrus H.) N.Y., 1941.

Arc 545.227.15 Livre des perles enfoneio. (Kamal, A.B.) Leipzig, 1907. 2v.

Arc 1020.80.7 Livre des reliques de l'abbaye de St. Pierre-le-Vif de Sens. (Geoffroy de Couleron.) Sens, 1887.

Arc 505.146 Livre d'or de l'Institute d'archéologie. (Queen Elizabeth of Belgium Institute of Archaeology, Hebrew University, Jerusalem.) Bruxelles, 1965.

Arc 1020.106 Livre d'or de Notre Dame des miracles à Saint Omer. (Bled, O.) St. Omer, 1913.

Arc 1494.60 Livro das moedas de Portugal. Book of the coins of Portugal. (Vaz, Joaquin Ferraro.) Braga, 1969-70. 2v.

Arc 1033.17.503 Livro do romeiro ao sumptuoso sanctuario da Senhora do Porto Ava. (Oliveira Lemos, F.J. de.) n.p., 1875.

Arc 720.209 Livy, P. Le abitazioni Lacustri di Fimon. Venezia, 1876.

Arc 830.3.20 Lizop, Raymond. Le Comminges et le Censeraus avant la domination romaine. Thèse. Toulouse, 1931.

Arc 830.3.15 Lizop, Raymond. Les convenae et les consoranni. Thèse. Toulouse, 1931.

Arc 838.39 Llobregat Conesa, Enrique. Contestanía Ibérica. Alicante, 1972.

Arc 530.105 Lloyd, Seton. Early Anatolia. Harmondsworth, 1956.

Arc 416.44 Lloyd, Seton Howard Frederick. Mounds of the Near East. Edinburgh, 1963.

Arc 712.22 Lloyd, W.W. On the general theory of proportion in archaeological design and its exemplification in detail in the Parthenon. London, 1863.

Arc 530.3.5 Lloyd, W.W. The Xanthian marbles. Londdon, 1845.

Arc 435.25.7F Loan exhibition of antiquities, Coronation Durbar, 1911. (India. Archaeological Survey.) Calcutta, 1912.

Arc 858.44 Local papers. (Sumner, H.) London, 1931.

Arc 1333.13F Lockhart, J.H.S. The S. Lockhart collection of Chinese copper coins. Shanghai, 1915.

X Cg Arc 1408.3 Lockhart, James H.S. Currency of the Farther East from earliest times up to 1895. Hong Kong, 1895-1907. 3v.

Arc 865.8 Lockyer, N. Stonehenge and other British stone monuments. London, 1906.

Arc 830.2.19 Locmariaquer. La table des marchands. 2e ed. (Le Rouzic, Z.) Vannes, 1923.

Arc 66.1.176 Les Locriens de l'ouest. v. 1-2. (Lerat, Lucien.) Paris, 1952.

Arc 925.4.25 Lodki, v strany predkov. (Martynov, Anatolii O.) Kemerovo, 1966.

Arc 1185.21 Lodolini, A. Elementi di diplomatica. Milano, 1926.

Arc 936.14.455 Lodowski, Jerzy. Sądowel we wczesnym średniowieczu. Wrocław, 1972.

Arc 889.6 Loë, Alfred de. Le dolmen de Solwaster. Bruxelles, 1889.

Arc 889.7 Loë, Alfred de. Les roches-polissoirs du "Bruzel" à Saint-Mard, province de Luxembourg. Bruxelles, 1896.

Arc 1138.32 Löffler, Karl. Einführung in die Handschriftenkunde. Leipzig, 1929.

Arc 1528.9 Loehr, August. Die niederlandische Medaille des 17. Wien, 1921.

Htn Arc 1660.4F* Loehr, August. Wiener Medailleure, 1899. Wien, 1899.

Arc 1660.4.2F Loehr, August. Wiener Medailleure. Nachtrag, 1901. Wien, 1902.

Arc 1433.26 Loerve, L. Observations on a unique Cufic gold coin. London, 1849.

Arc 853.20.27 Loeschcke, S. Bedeutung und Gefährdung der grossen Tempelgrabung in Trier. Trier, 1930.

Arc 853.20.29 Loeschcke, S. Die Erforschung des Tempelbezirkes im Altbachtale zu Trier. Berlin, 1928.

Arc 853.30 Loeschcke, S. Heranieche Funde in Haltern. Münster, 1909.

Arc 853.20.25F Loeschcke, S. Der Tempelbezirk im Altbachtale zu Trier. Berlin, 1938-42.

Arc 910.8F Loeschcke, Siegfried. Lampen aus Vindonissa. Zürich, 1919.

Arc 1088.1.5 Die Lösung der Frierenrätsels. (Weber, L.) Danzig, 1896.

Arc 600.85F Löwe und Sphinx im alten Ägypten. (Schweitzer, U.) Glückstadt, 1948.

Arc 505.35.5 Loffreda, Stanislao. A visit to Capharnaum. Jerusalem, 1972.

Arc 505.35.7 Loffreda, Stanislao. A visit to Capharnaum. 2d ed. Jerusalem, 1973.

Arc 87.1.20 Lohde, L. Die Skene der Alten. Berlin, 1860.

Arc 895.36.7F Lohse, E. Versuch einer Typologie der Felszeichnungen von Bohuslän. Inaug. Diss. Dresden, 1934.

Arc 530.96 Lomatidze, C.A. Arkheologicheskie raskopki v srevnegruziiskoi storitse Mtskheta. Tbilisi, 1955.

Author and Title Listing

Arc 746.24 Lombardi, M. Faesulae (Fiesole) Regio VII Etruria. Roma, 1941.
Arc 1033.12.44 Lombardo, V.G. Panegirico della Sacra Sindone. Torino, 1884.
Arc 936.14.270 Łomnicki, Jerzy. Ostrów Lednicki. Wyd 1. Poznań, 1968.
Arc 1033.17.243 Lomonaco, V. Monografia sul santuario di Nostra Donna della Grotta nella Praja della Schiavi. 3a ed. Napoli, 1858.
Arc 1480.7 London, England. Society of Antiquaries. Catalogue of Roman coins. London? 1852.
Arc 545.8.3 London. Institution Library. Bibliographical account...of La description de l'Egypt. London, 1838.
Arc 136.10 London. University. Institute of Archaeology. Annual report. London.
Arc 340.3F London. University. Library. Catalogue of books on archaeology and art. London, 1935-37. 2v.
Arc 340.3.5F London. University. Library. Catalogue of books on archaeology and art. Index. London, 1937.
Arc 340.3.2F London. University. Library. Catalogue of books on archaeology and art. Supplement. London, 1937.
Arc 1130.15F London. University. Library. The palaeography collection. Boston, 1968. 2v.
Arc 136.9.6 London and Middlesex Archaeological Society. Report of the council.
Arc 136.9 London and Middlesex Archaeological Society. Transactions. London. 1,1860+ 25v.
Arc 136.9.5 Pamphlet box. London and Middlesex Archaeological Society. 2 pam.
Arc 858.48 London Museum. Catalogue of an exhibition of recent archaeological discoveries in Great Britain. London, 1932.
Arc 136.1 London Society of Antiquaries. Archaeologia. London. 1-104 123v.
Cg Arc 136.1 London Society of Antiquaries. Archaeologia. London. 41-60
Arc 136.1.1 London Society of Antiquaries. Archaeologia. Table of contents. London. 1-88,1804-1938
Arc 136.1.10 London Society of Antiquaries. Archaeologia. 2. ed., 3. ed. London. 1773-1809 2v.
Arc 136.1.50 London Society of Antiquaries. A copy of the royal charter and statutes. London, 1800.
EDL Arc 136.2.15 London Society of Antiquaries. Index. v.1-20. 2d series. London, 1908.
Arc 136.1.2 London Society of Antiquaries. Index to Archaeologia. v.1-30. London, 1809-44. 2v.
Arc 136.1.3 London Society of Antiquaries. Index to Archaeologia. v.1-50. London, 1889.
Arc 136.1.4 London Society of Antiquaries. Index to Archaeologia. v.51-100 (1888-1966). London, 1970.
EDL Arc 136.2 London Society of Antiquaries. Proceedings. London. 1-32,1843-1920 34v.
Arc 136.4 London Society of Antiquaries. Report for 1909-1911. Old Sarum Excavation fund. Oxford, 1912.
Arc 136.5 London Society of Antiquaries. Report of research committee. Oxford. 1-30 26v.
Arc 136.1.11 London Society of Antiquaries. Review of Archaeologia. London, 1881.
Arc 136.1.75 Pamphlet box. London Society of Antiquaries.
Arc 561.3 Long, G. British Museum. Egyptian antiquities. London, 1832. 2v.
Arc 561.3.3 Long, G. Egyptian antiquities in British Museum. London, 1846. 2v.
Arc 865.10 Long, william. Stonehenge and its barrows. Devizes, 1876.
Arc 12.5 Long ago. London. 1,1873
Arc 870.10.5 The long barrows of Cotswolds. (Crawford, O.G.S.) Gloucester, Eng., 1925.
Arc 861.102F Longhurst, M.H. The Easby cross. Oxford, 1931.
Arc 1680.12 Longman, W. Tokens of the eighteenth century connected with booksellers. London, 1916.
Arc 1675.15 Longpérier, A. de. Médailles de rois Perses de la Dynastie Sassanide. Paris, 1840.
Arc 1053.13 Longpérier, A. de. Mémoires sur la chronologie et l'iconographie des rois parthes arsacides. Paris, 1853-82.
Arc 396.1 Longpérier, A. de. Oeuvres. Paris, 1883-87. 7v.
Arc 1480.29 Longpérier, Adrien. Recherches sur les insignes de la questure et sur les récipients monétaires. Paris, 1868.
Arc 1092.1.2 Longpérier, H. Des rouelles et des anneaux antiques. Paris, 1867.
Arc 1092.1 Longpérier, H. Note sur les rouelles antiques de bronze. Paris, 1867.
Arc 416.35 Loofs, Helmut Hermann Ernst. Elements of the megalithic complex in Southeast Asia. Canberra, 1967.
Arc 543.88 Looking for Dilmun. 1st ed. (Bibby, Geoffrey.) N.Y., 1969.
Arc 1528.5.5PF Loon, Gerard van. Beschrijving der Nederlandsche historie-penningen. 's-Gravenhage, 1723-31. 4v.
Arc 1525.1 Loon, Gerard van. Histoire metallique des XVII provinces des Pays-Bas. La Haye, 1732-37. 5v.
Arc 1493.5 Lopes Fernandes, M.B. Memoria das moedas correntes em Portugal. Lisboa, 1856.
Arc 1675.31 Lopes Fernandes, Manuel Bernardo. Memoria das medallias e condecorações port. Lisboa, 1861.
Arc 843.120 López Cuevillas, Florentino. La civilización céltica en Galicia. Santiago, 1953.
Htn Arc 1020.126* López Madera, G. Discursos de la certidumbre de las reliquias descubiertas en Granada. Madrid, 1601.
Arc 1020.126.5 López Madera, G. Historia y discursos de la certidumbre de las reliquias, láminas. Granada, 1602.
Arc 843.66 Lopez Martí, L. Santa Eulalia de Bóveda. Lugo, 1934.
Arc 785.52.5PF L'Orange, N.P. Der spätantike Bildschmuch. Tafeln. Berlin. 10,1939
Arc 785.52.5 L'Orange, N.P. Der spätantike Bildschmuch. Berlin, 1939.
Arc 925.9.115 Lordkipanidze, Guram A. K istorii drevnei Kolkhidy. Tbilisi, 1970.
Arc 1020.12 Lorenzo, Giuseppe di. Antichi monumenti di religioni cristiani in Toscanella. Rocca, 1883.
Arc 1670.53 Lorichs, G.D. de. Recherches numismatiques...les médailles celtiberiennes. Paris, 1852.
Arc 830.86 Loriquet, Charles. Reims pendant la domination romaine. Reims, 1860.
Arc 853.205.10 Łosinski, Władysław. Pouzọtki wczesnośredniowiecznego. Wrocław, 1972.
Arc 853.205 Łosiński, Władysław. Z badań nad rzemiostem we wczesnośredniowiecznym Kotobrzegu. Poznań, 1959.
Arc 387.33 Lost cities. (Cottrell, Leonard.) N.Y., 1957.
Arc 861.18.19 The lost language of London. (Bayley, Harold.) London, 1935.
Arc 1138.100 Lost languages. (Cleator, Philip.) London, 1959.
Arc 552.4 The lost Pharaohs. (Cottrell, L.) N.Y., 1951.
Arc 870.24 A lost Roman road. (Berry, B.) London, 1963.
Arc 407.19 Lost worlds; the romance of archaeology. (White, Anne Terry.) N.Y., 1941.
Arc 451.5 Lothal and the Indus civilization. (Rao, Shikaripur R.) N.Y., 1973.
Arc 943.44 Lothrop, S.K. Essays in pre-Columbian art and archaeology. Cambridge, Mass., 1961.
Arc 543.4.17 Lou-lan. (Herrmann, A.) Leipzig, 1931.
Arc 1660.1 Loubat, J.F. The medallic history of the United States of America, 1776-1876. Text and plates. N.Y., 1878. 2v.
Arc 830.101.7 Louis, Maurice. Le néolithique dans le Gard. Thèse. Nîmes, 1932.
Arc 543.100 Louis Premier. (École Française d'Extrême-Orient, Hanoi. Indochina Musée.) Paris, 1960.
Arc 66.1.75 Louis XII et Ludovic Sforza. (Pélissier, L.G.) Paris, 1896. 3v.
Arc 1018.7.2 Lourie, W. Monuments of the early church. N.Y., 1901.
Arc 1018.7.5 Lourie, W. Monuments of the early church. N.Y., 1906.
Arc 880.12.2 Louthiana, or Introduction to antiquities of Ireland. (Wright, Thomas.) London, 1758.
Arc 628.9 Lovatelli-Caetani, E. Antichi monumenti illustrati. Roma, 1889.
Arc 1625.1 Low, Lyman H. Sketch of coinage of Mexican revolutionary General Morelos. N.Y., 1886.
Arc 888.45 The Low Countries. (Laet, Siegfried J. de.) London, 1958.
Arc 1153.27 Lowe, E.A. The Benevetan script. Oxford, 1914.
Arc 1138.122 Lowe, Elias Avery. Handwriting. Our medieval legacy. Rome, 1969.
Arc 1138.122.5 Lowe, Elias Avery. Palaeographical papers, 1907-1965. Oxford, 1972. 2v.
Arc 66.1.80 Loye, J. de. Les archives de la chambre apostolique XIVe siècle. Paris, 1899.
Arc 380.212 Lubersac, M. Discours sur les monumens publics. Paris, 1775.
Arc 1588.1.37 Lublin (City). Museum Lubelskie. Tysiąc lat monety polskiej. Lublin, 1966.
Arc 543.120.10 Lubo-Lesnichenko, Evgenii. Mertvyi gorod Khara-Khoto. Moskva, 1968.
Arc 302.9.10 Lubuskie Towarzystwo Naukowe. Komisja Archeologiczna. Materiały. Zielona Góra. 1,1965+
Arc 1490.14 Lucania numismatica. (Maguan, A.P.D.) Roma, 1775.
Arc 396.9 Lucas, A. Antiques, their restoration and preservation. London, 1924.
Arc 396.9.5 Lucas, A. Antiques, their restoration and preservation. 2. ed. London, 1932.
Arc 600.21.6 Lucas, Alfred. Ancient Egyptian materials. London, 1962.
Arc 600.21 Lucas, Alfred. Ancient Egyptian materials. N.Y., 1926.
Arc 600.21.5 Lucas, Alfred. Ancient Egyptian materials and industries. 3. ed. London, 1948.
Arc 1033.58.5 Lucatelli, G. Notizie istoriche...la testa di S. Sebastiano. Roma, 1757.
Arc 843.5.15 Lucentum, oy La ciudad de Alicante. (Valcarcel, A.) Valencia, 1780.
Arc 1070.205 Lucernae futiles Musei Passerii. (Passeri, J.B.) Pisauri, 1739-51. 3v.
Arc 66.1.190 Lucien écrivain. (Bompaire, J.) Paris, 1958.
Arc 628.13 Luckenbach, H. Abbildungen zur Alten Geschichte der Oberen Klassen. München, 1898.
Arc 710.5 Luckenbach, H. Die Akropolis von Athen. München, 1896.
Arc 710.5.2 Luckenbach, H. Die Akropolis von Athen. München, 1905.
Arc 628.17 Luckenbach, H. Antike Kunstwerke im klassischen Unterricht. München, 1901.
Arc 628.13.5 Luckenbach, H. Kunst und Geschichte. München, 1902-03. 3v.
Arc 628.13.7 Luckenbach, H. Kunst und Geschichte. München, 1904.
Arc 628.13.8 Luckenbach, H. Kunst und Geschichte. 6. Aufl. München, 1906.
Arc 684.1.11 Luckerrbach, H. Olympia und Delphi. München, 1904.
Arc 1660.11 Luckius, J.J. Sylloge numismatum elegantiorum. Argentina, 1620.
Arc 1418.6 Lucknow, India. Provincial Museum. Catalogue of coins in the Provincial Museum. Oxford, 1920. 2v.
Arc 451.1F Lucknow Exhibit. A memorandum of suggestions for use of contributors to the Loan Collection Department of the Exhibit. Lucknow, 1885.
Arc 1588.3 Luczenbacher, J. A' szerb zsupánok királyok es ezárok. Budán, 1843.
Htn Arc 1033.12.64* Ludecus, M. Historia von der Erfindung, Wunderwerken und Zerstörung der vermeinten Heiligenbluts zur Wilssnagk. Wittenberg, 1586.
Arc 1025.3 Ludwig, C. Ein Blick in die römischen Katakomben. Bern, 1876.
Arc 658.3.14 Ludwig, Emil. Schliemann. Berlin, 1932.
Arc 658.3.16 Ludwig, Emil. Schliemann. Boston, 1931.
Arc 658.3.15A Ludwig, Emil. Schliemann. Boston, 1932.
Arc 658.3.17 Ludwig, Emil. Schliemann of Troy. London, 1931.
Arc 387.13.30 Ludwig Curtius, 1874-1954, zum Gedachtnis. (Herbig, Reinhard.) Heidelberg, 1955.
Arc 1663.13 Ludwig I. von Bayern und sein Wirken. Leipzig, 1853.
Arc 1675.90 Ludwig Neufahrer. (Probszt, Günther.) Wien, 1960.
Arc 1138.27.5 Ludwig Traube e la nuova metodologia paleografica. (Natale, Alfio Rosario.) Milano, 1957.
Arc 853.15.5 Lütjen-Janssen, Hans. Die Germanen in Mecklenburg im 2. Jahrtausend vor Christus. Leipzig, 1935.
Arc 870.22F Lufthild und Vorgeschichte. (Lilienthal-Gesellschaft für Luft.) Berlin, 1938.
Arc 1016.9.15 Lugari, G.B. L'anfiteatro Flavio rivendicato ai martiri. Roma, 1899.
Arc 1016.9.5 Lugari, G.B. L'aventino e le origine pagane e Christian di Roma. Roma, 1886.
Arc 1015.209 Lugari, G.B. Le catacombe ossia il sepolcro. Roma, 1888.
Arc 1027.41.39 Lugari, G.B. Il "Dolocenum" della XIII regione. Roma, 1893.
Arc 1016.9 Lugari, G.B. Intorno ad alcuni monumenti antichi. Roma, 1882.
Arc 1016.221 Lugari, G.B. La pontificia accademia romana di archeologia. Roma, 1900.
Arc 1016.9.9 Lugari, G.B. S. Bonifazio e S. Alessio sull'aventino. Roma, 1894.
Arc 1033.58 Lugari, G.B. S. Sebastiano; memorie. Roma, 1889.
Arc 1033.114 Lugari, G.B. Sopra l'età di alcuni Bolli di figuline. Roma, 1895.
Arc 1027.12.15 Lugari, G.B. I varii seppellimenti...Pietro e Paolo. Roma, 1898.
Arc 1033.34.11F Lugari, J.B. Il culto di San Pietro sul Gianicolo. Roma, 1907.
Arc 1033.34.9 Lugari, J.B. Lieu du crucifiement de Saint Pierre. Tours, 1898.

Arc 726.25.16F Lugli, G. Il porto di Roma imperiale e l'agro portuense. Roma, 1935.
Arc 785.22.20 Lugli, G. Regio urbis decima. Roma, 1960.
Arc 766.4.15 Lugli, Giuseppe. Fontes ad topographism veteris urbis Romae pertinentes. v.1-4; v.6, pt.1-2; v.8, pt.1. Roma, 1953. 7v.
Arc 766.4.25 Lugli, Giuseppe. Itinerario di Roma antica. Milano, 1970.
Arc 766.4.5 Lugli, Giuseppe. I monumenti antichi di Roma e suburbio. Roma, 1930-40. 4v.
Arc 766.4.10 Lugli, Giuseppe. Roma antica. Roma, 1946.
Arc 396.15F Lugli, Giuseppe. Saggi di explorazione archeologica. Roma, 1939.
Arc 766.4.20 Lugli, Giuseppe. Studi minori di topografia antica. Roma, 1965.
Arc 766.4 Lugli, Giuseppe. La zona archeologica di Roma. Roma, 1924.
Arc 545.244F Lugn, Pehr. Ausgewählte Denkmäler aus ägyptischen Sammlungen in Schweden. Leipzig, 1922.
Arc 608.6.60 Luiks, A.G. Cathedra en mensa. Franeker, 1955.
Arc 936.14.195 Łuka, Leon J. Kultura wschodniopomorska na Pomorzu Odańskim. Wrocław, 1966.
Arc 612.51 Lukan, Karl. Alpenwanderungen in die Vorzeit zu Drachenhöhlen und Druidensteinen. Wien, 1965.
Arc 855.201 Lukis, W.C. The prehistoric stone monuments of the British Isles - Cornwall. London, 1885.
Arc 383.79.25 Lullies, R. Neue Beiträge zur klassischen Altertumswissenschaft. Stuttgart, 1954.
Arc 861.147 Lullingstone Roman villa. (Meates, Geoffrey W.) London, 1955.
Arc 823.65 Lumières sur la Gaule. (Eydoux, Henri Paul.) Paris, 1960.
Arc 766.2 Lumisden, A. Remarks on the antiquities of Rome and its environs. London, 1797.
Arc 830.115 Lunet, B. La ville de Rodez à l'époque romaine. Rodez, 1888.
Arc 543.2 Lunet de Lagonquiere, E. Inventaire descriptif des monuments du Cambodge. v.1-3 and map. Paris, 1902. 4v.
Arc 416.4 Lunet de Lajonquière, É.E. Rapport...mission archéologique (Cambodge, Siam, presqu'île Malaise, Inde). Paris, 1907-08.
Arc 746.30F Luni. (Banti, Luisa.) Firenze, 1937.
Arc 726.258.5 Luni sul Mignone. Lund, 1969.
Arc 726.258 Luni sul Mignone e problemi della preistoria d'Italia. (Östenberg, Carl Eric.) Lund, 1967.
Arc 726.135.5 Lunz, Reimo. Ur- und Frühgeschichte Südtirols. Bozen, 1973.
Arc 757.8 Il luogo primitivo di Roma. (Cozzo, G.) Roma, 1935.
Arc 1016.232.2 Lupi, A.M. Dissertatio...severae martyris epitaphium. Panormi, 1734.
Arc 1016.232 Lupi, A.M. Dissertatio...severae martyris epitaphium. Panormi, 1734.
Arc 1153.11 Lupi, C. Manuale di paleografia delle carte. Firenze, 1875.
Arc 726.45 Lupi, Clemente. Nuovi studi sulle antiche terme pisane. Pisa, 1885.
Arc 736.2.4 Lupus, B. Die Stadt Skyrakus im Alterthum. Strassburg, 1887.
Arc 853.33 Luschan, F. von. Die Karl Knorrsche Sammlung von Benin-Altertümern. Stuttgart, 1901.
Arc 1580.50 Luschin von Ebengreath, Arnold. Steirische Münzfunde. Graz, 1971.
Arc 1348.17 Luschin von Elengreuth, A. Allgemeine Münzkunde. München, 1904.
Arc 1348.17.2 Luschin von Elengreuth, A. Allgemeine Münzkunde und Geldgeschichte. 2. Aufl. München, 1926.
Arc 1185.13 Lustro, G.N. di. Degli archivii, ricerche archaeologiche, storiche , critiche, diplomatiche. Napoli, 1880.
Arc 1425.1 Luynes, H.T.P.J. Numismatique et inscription Cypriotes. Paris, 1852.
Arc 495.200 Luynes, H.T.P.J. d'Albert de. Voyage d'exploration à la Mer Morte. Paris, 1874. 3v.
Arc 915.42 LuzernStadt und Land in römischer Zeit. (Wandeler, Max.) Luzern, 1968.
Arc 925.350 Luzgin, Valerii E. Drevnie kul'tury Izhmy. Moskva, 1972.
Arc 1033.5.5 Luzi, G.C. Le chiavi di S. Pietro. Roma, 1884.
Arc 936.195.25 Luzianska skukina a pociatky malovanej keramiky na Slovensku. (Novotný, B.) Bratislava, 1962.
Arc 843.23 Luzitanos e romanos en Villa Franca de Xira. (Ferraz de Macedo, F.) Lisboa, 1893.
Arc 1190.45 Luzzatto, G.I. Epigrafia giuridica greca e romana. Milano, 1942.
Arc 66.1.63 La Lydie et le monde grec. (Radet, Georges.) Paris, 1893.
Arc 66.1.63.5 La Lydie et le monde grec au temps des Mesmnades, 687-546. (Radet, Georges.) Roma, 1967.
Arc 513.17.15 La Lydie et ses voisins aus hautes époques. (Dussaud, René.) Paris, 1930.
Arc 530.2 Lydische Koenigsgraeber bei Sardes. (Olfers, J.F.M.) Berlin, 1859.
Arc 1428.14 Lydische Stadtmünzen. (Imhoof-Blumer, Friedrich.) Genf, 1897.
Arc 340.17 Lyell, Arthur H. A bibliographical list descriptive of Romano-British architectural remains in Great Britain. Cambridge, 1912.
Arc 1076.3.67F Lyman, Charles. The church bells of the county of Stafford. London, 1889.
Arc 785.71 Lyngby, H. Die Tempel der Fortuna und der Mater Matuta am Forum Boarium in Rom. Berlin, 1939.
Arc 545.210 Lyons, H.G. Report on the island and temples of Philae. Cairo, 1896.
Arc 545.210.5 Lyons, H.G. Report on the temples of Philae. Cairo, 1908.
Arc 543.70 Lysjsms, Philippe. Expédition en Arabie centrale. Paris, 1956. 3v.
Arc 861.22 Lyttelton. Description of an ancient font in Bridekirk. n.p., 1767.
Arc 1027.25.55 M. de Rossi ets ses récents travaux...catacombes. v.1-2. (Buck, V. de.) Paris, 1865.
Arc 823.19.168 M. Henri Thélier et Mlle Henriette Filhos. (Thédenat, H.) Paris, 1903.
Arc 402.12 M.I. Rostovtsev. (Vernadskii, G.V.) Praga, 1951.
Arc 716.2.20 Maass, Michael. Die Prohedrie des Dionysostheaters in Athen. München, 1952.
Arc 853.40.5 Maassen, F. Die römische Staatsstrasse. Bonn, 1881.
Arc 1480.32 Mabbott, T.O. A small bronze of Nero. Rome, 1936.
Arc 1175.5F Mabillon, J. De re diplomatica libri VI. Luteciae Parisiorum, 1681.
Arc 1185.28 Mabillon, Jean. Histoire des contestations sur la diplomatique. Naples, 1767.
Arc 600.53F MacAdam, M.F.L. The temples of Kawa. v.1-2; plates. London, 1949- 4v.
Arc 967.1.2 McAdams, William. Records of ancient races. St. Louis, 1887.
Arc 880.25.9A Macalister, R.A.S. Ancient Ireland. London, 1935.
Arc 880.25.7 Macalister, R.A.S. The archaeology of Ireland. London, 1928.
Arc 880.25.8A Macalister, R.A.S. The archaeology of Ireland. 2. ed. London, 1949.
Arc 497.25 Macalister, R.A.S. A century of excavation in Palestine. London, 1925.
Arc 880.25.10 Macalister, R.A.S. Cluain Maccu Nois [Clonmacmois]. Dublin, 1911.
X Cg Arc 505.14 Macalister, R.A.S. Excavation of Gezer, 1902-1905, 1907-1909. London, 1912. 3v.
Arc 505.5.85 Macalister, R.A.S. Excavations...Ophel, Jerusalem, 1923-1925. London, 1926.
Arc 880.24 Macalister, R.A.S. Ireland in pre-Celtic times. Dublin, 1921.
Arc 880.23 Macalister, R.A.S. The memorial slabs of Clonmacnois, King's County. Dublin, 1909.
Arc 880.25 Macalister, R.A.S. The present and future of archaeology in Ireland. Dublin, 1925.
Arc 612.15 Macalister, R.A.S. A text-book of European archaeology. Cambridge, Eng., 1921.
Arc 963.3 McAllister, J.G. The archaeology of Porter County, Indiana. Indianapolis, 1932.
Arc 397.18A Macaulay, Rose. Pleasure of ruins. London, 1953.
Arc 397.18.2 Macaulay, Rose. Pleasure of ruins. London, 1966.
Arc 397.18.10F Macaulay, Rose. Roloff Beny interprets in photographs Pleasure of ruins. London, 1964.
Arc 608.42.5 McBurney, Charles. The Hana Fteah (Cyrenaica) and the Stone Age of the South-East Mediterranean. London, 1967.
Arc 608.42 McBurney, Charles. The stone age of Northern Africa. Harmondsworth, 1960.
Arc 1030.17 McCaul, J. Christian epitaphs. Toronto, 1869.
NEDL Arc 815.13 Macchiaro, V. Die Villa des Mysterien in Pompei. Neapel, 1926?
Arc 93.4 Macchioro, V. Neapolis, revista di archeologia, epigrafia e numio. Napoli. 1-2,1913-1915 2v.
Arc 488.19F McCown, D.E. The comparative stratigraphy of early Iran. Chicago, 1942.
Arc 943.11 Pamphlet box. MacCurdy, G.G. American archaeology pamphlets.
Arc 397.25 McDaniel, Walton B. Riding a hobby in the classical lands. Cambridge, 1971.
Arc 595.19 MacDari, C. Irish wisdom preserved in bibles and pyramids. Boston, 1923.
Arc 1465.6 MacDonald, G. Catalogue of Greek coins in the Hunterian collection. Glasgow, 1899. 3v.
Arc 392.7.80 MacDonald, G. F. Haverfield, 1860-1919. London, 1921.
Arc 1335.81 MacDonald, G. The Hunterian coin cabinet. Glasgow, 1933.
Arc 875.13 Macdonald, G. The Roman forts on the Bar Hill, Dumbartonshire. Glasgow, 1906.
Arc 875.13.5 Macdonald, G. The Roman wall in Scotland. Glasgow, 1911.
Arc 875.13.7 Macdonald, G. The Roman wall in Scotland. 2. ed. Oxford, 1934.
Arc 858.49 Macdonald, George. Agricola in Britain. London, 1932.
Arc 1348.20 McDonald, George. Coin types, their origin and development. Glasgow, 1905.
Arc 1348.25 McDonald, George. Evolution of coinage. Cambridge, 1916.
Arc 858.45 Macdonald, George. Roman Britain, 1914-1928. London, 1931.
Arc 1470.26 MacDonald, George. The silver coinage of Crete. London, 1919?
Arc 875.9 Macdonald, J. Tituli Hunteriani, an account of the Roman stones in the Hunterian Museum. Glasgow, 1897.
Arc 700.20 McDonald, W.A. The political meeting places of the Greeks. Baltimore, 1943.
Arc 1433.65.5 McDowell, Robert H. Coins from Seleucia on the Tigris. Ann Arbor, 1935.
Arc 66.1.82 Macé, A. Essai sur Suétone. Paris, 1900.
Arc 1348.50 Macedonian and Greek coins of the Seleucidae. (Gardner, Percy.) London, 1878.
Arc 875.30 McFarlan, J. The Ruthwell cross. Dumfries, 1896.
Arc 1025.58 MacFarlane, Charles. The catacombs of Rome. London, 1852.
Arc 1458.23 McGill University, Montreal. The McGill University collection of Greek and Roman coins. v.1-2. Amsterdam, 1975-
Arc 497.46 McGown, J.C. The ladder of progress in Palestine. N.Y., 1943.
Arc 953.29 McGregor, John Charles. Southwestern archaeology. 2. ed. Urbana, 1965.
Arc 1093.2.4 McGuire, J.D. The stone hammer and its various uses. Washington, 1891.
Arc 612.67 Machalo verkhnego paleolita i proiskhozhdenie Homo Sapiens. (Grigor'ev, Gennadii P.) Leningrad, 1968.
Arc 936.14.225 Machnik, Jan. Studia nad kulturą ceramiki sznurowej w Małopolsce. Wrocław, 1966.
Arc 595.20 MacHuisdean, Hamish. The great law, told simply in seven visits. v.2. Glasgow, 1928.
Arc 609.1.17F Maciver, D.R. Mediaeval Rhodesia. London, 1906.
Arc 1538.20 Mack, R.P. The coinage of ancient Britain. London, 1953.
Arc 588.47F MacKay, Ernest. Bahrein and Hemamieh. London, 1929.
Arc 448.1.2 Mackay, Ernest. Early Indus civilization. 2. ed. London, 1948.
Arc 452.1.25F Mackay, Ernest. Further excavations at Mohenjo-daro. Delhi, 1938. 2v.
Arc 448.1 Mackay, Ernest. The Indus civilization. London, 1935.
Arc 442.15 Mackay, Ernest J.H. Excavations at Chanhu-Daro...1935-36. Washington, 1938.
Arc 652.8 MacKendrick, P.L. The Greek stories speak. N.Y., 1962.
Arc 830.362 MacKendrick, Paul Lachlan. Roman France. N.Y., 1972.
Arc 950.210 Mackenzie, A. Descriptive notes on certain implements...Graham Island. n.p., 1891.
Arc 858.35 Mackenzie, D.A. Ancient man in Britain. London, 1922.
Arc 875.18 Mackenzie, G.S. A letter to Sir Walter Scott, Baronet. Edinburgh, 1824.
Arc 810.26 Mackenzie, W.M. Pompeii. London, 1910.
Arc 875.7 Maclagan, C. Catalogue...British Museum...sculptured stones...Scotland. Edinburgh, 1898.
Arc 855.204 MacLagan, C. Hill forts, stone circles...Scotland. Edinbrugh, 1875.
Arc 875.37.5 Maclagan, Christian. Chips from old stones. Edinburgh, 1881.
Arc 875.37 Maclagan, Christian. What means these stones? Edinburgh, 1894.
Arc 855.11 MacLauchlan, H. Memoir...survey of eastern branch of Watling Street. London, 1864. 2v.

Arc 870.15.5 MacLauchlan, H. Memoir written during a survey of the Watling Street. London, 1852.
Arc 953.5 MacLean, J.P. The mound builders. Cincinnati, 1879.
Arc 74.4.25 MacMillan, G.A. History of the Society for the promotion of Hellenic studies. n.p., n.d.
Arc 830.152 Macon, Gustave. Une fondation du connétable Henri de Montmorency. Senlis, 1908.
Arc 830.113F Le Maconnais préhistorique. (Ferry, H. de.) Macon, 1870.
Arc 505.20 Macpela, ou Tombeau des patriarches à Hebron. (Pierotti, E.) Lausanne, 1869.
Arc 936.220.75 McPherron, Alan. Early farming cultures in Central Serbia (Eastern Yugoslavia). Krazujevać, 1971.
Arc 925.45F McPherson, Duncan. Antiquities of Kertch. London, 1857.
Arc 600.170 Maczamallah, R. Fouilles à Saqqarah. Le Caire, 1935.
Arc 1138.15 Madan, F. Books in manuscript. London, 1893.
Arc 936.40.30F Madara. (Sofia. Naroden Arkheologicheski Muzei.) Sofiia, 1934.
Arc 1405.1.2 Madden, F.W. Coins of the Jews. v.2. London, 1881.
Arc 1478.7 Madden, F.W. The handbook of Roman numismatics. London, 1861.
Arc 1423.9.5F Madden, Frederic W. Coins of the Jews. Boston, 1881.
Arc 1423.9.6 Madden, Frederic W. History of Jewish coinage, and of money. San Diego, 1967.
Arc 1423.9 Madden, Frederic W. History of Jewish coinage. London, 1864.
Arc 1423.9.7 Madden, Frederic W. History of Jewish coinage. N.Y., 1967.
Arc 889.34 Madderman, Pieter Jan Remees. Linearbandkeramik aus Elsloo und Stein. v.1-2. 's-Gravenhage, 1970.
Arc 1020.34 Mader, Andreas E. Altchristliche Basiliken und Lokaltraditionen in Südjudäa. Paderborn, 1918.
Arc 505.82 Mader, Andreas E. Mambre. v.1, text; v.2, plates. Freiburg im Breisgau, 1957. 2v.
Arc 1510.37 Mader, Joseph. Versuch über die Brakteaten. v.2. Prag, 1808.
Arc 1033.17.57 Madone de Saint Luc. (Hilaire.) Paris, 1886.
Arc 1027.54.9 Le madonne antiche delle catacombe. (Montenovesi, O.) Roma, 1904.
Arc 1027.54 Le madonne delle catacombe. (Benigni, U.) Roma, 1904.
Arc 1200.16 Madras. Government Museum. Catalogue of copper-plate grants. Madras, 1918.
Arc 94.58 Madrid, Spain. Casa de Velasquez. Publications de la Casa de Velasquez. Série archéologie. Paris. 1,1973+
Arc 843.155 Madrid. Museo Archeologica. Catáloga de las antigüedades que se conservan en el Patio Arabe. Madrid, 1932.
Arc 1335.135 Madrid. Museo Argueológico Nacional. Catalago. Madrid, 1925.
Arc 843.83 Madrid. Museo Arqueologico Nacional. Catalogo de las exvatos de bronce. Madrid, 1941. 2v.
Arc 1494.35 Madrid. Museo Arqueologico Nacional. Catalogo de las monedas previsigadas. Madrid, 1936.
Arc 838.22F Madrid. Museo Arqueológico Nacional. Falcata iberica. N.Y., 1916.
Arc 1663.18 Madrid. Real Biblioteca. Medallas de la casa de Borbón. Madrid, 1916.
Arc 94.56 Madrider Mitteilungen. Heidelberg. 1,1960+ 14v.
Arc 848.46 Mähling, W. Die frühgermanische Landnahme im mitteldeutsch-sächsisch-nordböhmischen Gebiet. Prag, 1944.
Arc 785.13.13 Maes, C. Primo trofeo della croce nel Foro Romano. Roma, 1901.
Arc 785.1.8 Maes, C. Vesta e vestali. 2. ed. Roma, 1884.
Arc 1088.1.20F Maes, Constantino. La nave di Tiberio sommersa nel lago di Nemi. Roma, 1895. 2 pam.
Arc 785.38.7 Maes, Constantino. Le terme di Agrippa. Roma, 1882.
Arc 1088.1.20.5 Maes, Constantino. Trionfo navale ovvero prassima estrazione. Roma, 1899.
Arc 785.14.9 Maes, Costantino. Tutte le rovine, le memorie storiche. Roma, 1900.
Arc 726.103 Maetzke, G. Florentia (Firenze). Rome, 1941.
Arc 889.4.15 Maeyer, R. de. De overblijfselev der Romainsche villa's in België. Antwerpen, 1940.
Arc 889.4.10 Maeyer, R. de. De Romeinsche villa's in België. Antwerpen, 1937.
Arc 823.17 Maffei, Scipione. Galliae antiguitates quaedam selectae atque in plures epistolas distributaes. Parisiis, 1733.
Arc 1190.25.10 Maffei, Scipione. Istoria diplomatica che serve d'introduzione all'arte critica in tal materia. Mantova, 1727.
Arc 1190.25.12 Maffei, Scipione. Istoria diplomatica che serve d'introduzione all'arte critica in tal materia. Roma, 1964.
Arc 853.259 Magdalenenberg. (Spindler, Konrad.) Villingen, 1971. 3v.
Arc 1076.3.19 Maggi, G. De tintinnalbulis. Hanoviae, 1608.
Htn Arc 1033.63* Magi, H. De Tintinnabulis. Amstelodami, 1664. 2 pam.
Arc 397.16 Magic spades. (Magoffin, Rolf V.D.) N.Y., 1929.
Arc 1367.3 Magnaguti, A.G. Ex nummis historia. Roma, 1949-53. 12v.
Arc 750.200 Magnan, D. La città di Roma. Roma, 1779. 2v.
Arc 1348.40 Magnan, D. Miscellanea numismatica. Romae, 1772-74. 3v.
Arc 712.11 Magne, L. Le Parthénon. Paris, 1895.
X Cg Arc 510.217 Magnesia am Maeander. (Humann, Carl.) Berlin, 1904.
Arc 397.16 Magoffin, Rolf V.D. Magic spades. N.Y., 1929.
Arc 397.12 Magoffin, Rolf V.D. Romance of archaeology. London, 1930.
Arc 861.100.5 Magoren, F.P. The Sutton-Hoo ship burial. Cambridge, Mass., 1952.
Arc 608.35 Le Magrib central à l'époque des Zerides. (Golvin, Lucien.) Paris, 1957.
Arc 1033.35.31 Magrini, A. Sopra la insigne reliquia della S. Croce. Thiene, 1860.
Arc 1490.14 Maguan, A.P.D. Lucania numismatica. Roma, 1775.
Arc 1279.2 A Magy. Kiral. Orszagos Leveltar diplom. osztalyaban orzalt. (Hungary. K. Orszagos Leveltar.) Budapest, 1909.
Arc 900.200 Magyar, Yudo. Monumenta Hungariae archaeologica. Pesth, 1869-79. 4v.
Arc 1190.70 Magyar oklevéltan. (Szentpetery, Imre.) Budapest, 1930.
Arc 1588.10.30 Magyar pénztörténet, 1000-1325. (Hóman, Bálint.) Budapest, 1916.
Arc 225.30 A Magyar régészet kézikönyve. Budapest. 1,1965+
Arc 1588.10.35 Magyarorszag ekkorig ismeretes pénzei. (Rupp, Jakab.) Budan, 1841.
Arc 227.4 Magyarország régészeti topografiája. Budapest. 1,1966+ 4v.
Arc 1279.10 Magyarország világi és egyházi hatóságai kiadott pecseteinek jegyzeke. (Czobor, Béla.) Pest, 1872.
Arc 652.2 Mahaffy, J.P. Rambles and studies in Greece. London, 1876.
Arc 588.12 Mahâsna and Bêt Khalfâf. (Garstang, John.) London, 1902.
Arc 66.1.161 Mahor, J.B. L'ordre cistercien et son gouvernement. Paris, 1945.
Arc 905.18.5 Mahr, Adolf. Das vorgeschichtliche Hallstatt. Wien, 1925.
Arc 853.20.35F Mahr, Gustav. Die jüngere Latènekultur des trierer Landes. Berlin, 1967.
Arc 925.295.5 Maikop. Adygeiskogo Nauchno-Issledovatel'skogo Instituta Iazyka, Literatury, Istorii i Ekonomiki. Sbornik materialov po arkheologii adygei. Maikop, 1961.
Arc 1430.2 Mainoni, S. de. Descrizione di alcune monete cufiche del Museo. Milano, 1820.
Arc 845.4 Mainz, Germany. Römisch-Germanische Centralmuseum. Das Römisch-Germanische Centralmuseum. Mainz, 1889.
Arc 848.24F Mainz. Römisch-germanische Zentralmuseum. Die Altertümer unserer heidnischen Vorzeit. v.5. Mainz, 1911.
Arc 383.53.5 Mainz. Römisch Germanisches Zentralmuseum. Festschrift des Römisch germanischen Zentralmuseums in Mainz. Mainz, 1952-53. 3v.
Arc 383.53.10F Mainz. Römisch Germanisches Zentralmuseum. Festschrift zur Feier des fünfundsiebzigjährigen Bestehens. Mainz, 1927.
Arc 13.5 Mainz. Römisch-Germanisches Zentralmuseum. Technische Beiträge Archäologie. 1,1959+ 2v.
Arc 1163.18 Mainzer Inschriften. (Arens, Fritz V.) Stuttgart, 1945.
Arc 1510.160 Mainzisches Münzcabinet des Prinzen Alexander von Hessen. Faksimile. (Alexander, Prince of Messe and of the Rhine, 1823-1888.) Münster, 1968.
Arc 853.165.10 Maisant, Hermann. Der Kreis Saarlouis in vor- und frühgeschichtlichen Zeit. Bonn, 1971. 2v.
Arc 458.1 Maisey, F.C. Sanchi and its remains. London, 1892.
Arc 825.3.15 La maison carrée a Nîmes. (Espéraudieu, E.) Paris, 1929.
Arc 608.1.43 La maison de la procession dionysiaque à el Jem. (Foucher, Louis.) Paris, 1963.
Arc 830.179 Une maison d'époque romaine à Blesle. (Segret, Gabriel.) Clermont-Ferrand, 1925.
Arc 1025.10 Maitland, C. Church in the catacombs. London, 1847.
Arc 441.3.10 Maitra, Akshay Kumar. The ancient monuments of Varendra (North Bengal). Rajshahi, 1949?
Arc 830.78.5 Maitre, Léon. Geographie historique et descriptive de la Loire-Inférieure. Nantes, 1893.
Arc 815.24F Maiuri, Amedeo. La casa del Menandro e il suo tesoro di Argenteria. Roma, 1933. 2v.
Arc 800.9F Maiuri, Amedeo. Ercolano. Roma, 1932.
Arc 800.9.8F Maiuri, Amedeo. Ercolano. Roma, 1958.
Arc 800.9.5 Maiuri, Amedeo. Ercolano. 2. ed. Roma, 1937.
Arc 810.42.5 Maiuri, Amedeo. Introduzione alla studio di Pompei. Napoli, 1949.
Arc 726.4.20 Maiuri, Amedeo. The Phlegraean fields, from Virgil's tomb to the grotto of the Cumaean Sibyl. Rome, 1937.
Arc 793.19 Maiuri, Amedeo. Pompei, Ercolano e Stabia. Novara, 1961.
Arc 810.42F Maiuri, Amedeo. Pompeii. Roma, 1929.
Arc 815.28 Maiuri, Amedeo. Pompejanische Wandgemälde. Bern, 1959.
Arc 726.120 Maiuri, Amedeo. Saggi di varia antichità. Venezia, 1954.
Arc 810.42.10 Maiuri, Amedeo. L'ultima fase edilizia di Pompei. Roma, 1942.
Htn Arc 815.13.15F* Maiuri, Amedeo. La villa dei misteri. Roma, 1931.
Htn Arc 815.13.15PF* Maiuri, Amedeo. La villa dei misteri. Plates. Roma, 1931.
Arc 726.122 Maiuri, Amedeo. Vita d'archeologo. Napoli, 1959.
Arc 1016.243 Majesticus...Delatio...S. Stephani Manus Dexterae. (Balasko, F.) Budae, n.d.
Arc 936.14.15F Majewski, K. Importy rzymskie w Polsce. Warszawa, 1960.
Arc 652.7F Majewski, K. Kultura materialna starozytnej Grecji. Warszawa, 1956.
Arc 936.140.20 Majewski, Kazimierz. Kultura rzymska w Bułgarii. Wrocław, 1969.
Arc 1027.22.9 Majocchi, R. L'Ichthys eucaristico nei monumenti. Milano, 1895.
Arc 870.17F Major, Albany F. The mystery of Wansdyke. Cheltenham, 1926.
Htn Arc 720.7.5* Major, T. Les ruines de Paestum. Londres, 1769.
Arc 1663.16.10 Majorca Mortillaro, L.M. Ventitre medaglie borboniche napoletane. Pitigliano, 1889.
Arc 682.25 Makedoniia arkheologiia putesh. (Kondakov, N.P.) Sankt Peterburg, 1909.
Arc 671.10 Ho Makedonikoi taros tēs Berginas. (Rōmaios, K.A.) Athēnai, 1951.
Arc 925.200 Maksimenkov, G.A. Verkhne-metliaevskii klad. Irkutsk, 1960.
Arc 925.50.350 Maksimov, Evgenii V. Srednes Podneprov's na rubezhe nashei ery. Kiev, 1972.
Arc 843.215 Pamphlet vol. Málaga. Antigüedad. 4 pam.
Arc 855.223F Malcolm, J.P. Lives of topographers and antiquaries. London, 1815.
Arc 1190.90.5 Maleczyński, Karol. Studia nad dokumentem polskim. Wrocław, 1971.
Arc 482.202.3F Die Malereien von Samarra. (Herzfeld, Ernst E.) Berlin, 1927.
Arc 1027.19.29 Die Malerein der Sacramentskapellen in der Katakombe des honorable Callistus. (Wilpert, J.) Freiburg, 1897.
Arc 1088.1.19 Malfatti, V. Le navi romane del lago di Nemi. Roma, 1896.
Arc 936.14.390 Malinowska, Marie. Wczesnósredniowieczne skarby srebrne z Wielkopolski. Poznań, 1970.
Arc 936.14.395 Malinowski, Tadeusz. Prasłowiańskie osadnictur w słupcy. Poznań, 1969.
Arc 936.14.470 Malinowski, Tadeusz. Wielkopolska wdobie Prasłowian. wyd. 1. Poznań, 1973.
Arc 936.14.203 Malinowski, Tadewsz. Obrzadek pogrzebowy ludności kultury pomorskiej. Wrocław, 1969.
Arc 543.5.16 Malleret, L. Le cinquantenaire de l'École française d'Extrême-Orient. Paris, 1953.
Arc 543.131 Malleret, Louis. L'archéologie du Delta du Nékoug. v.1-4. Paris, 1959- 7v.
Arc 618.3 Mallet, J.W. Account of a chemical examination of the Celtic antiquities. Dublin, 1852.
Arc 1542.2.5 Malmer, Brita. Mynt och människor. Stockholm, 1968.
Arc 1542.2 Malmer, Brita. Nordiska mynt före år 1000. Bonn, 1966.
Arc 895.63 Malmer, M.P. Metodproblem inom järnålderns konsthistoria. Bonn, 1963.
Arc 893.29 Malmer, Mats P. Jungneolithische Studien. Habelt, 1968.
Arc 726.59.15 Malta; origini della civiltà mediterranea. (Ugolini, L.M.) Roma, 1934.
Arc 726.59.30 Malta. (Evans, John D.) London, 1959.
Arc 726.59.45 Malta: an archaeological guide. (Trump, David H.) London, 1972.
Arc 1027.45.5 Malta Sotterranea...Sepulkralkunst. (Becker, Erich.) Strassburg, 1913.
Arc 1330.30 Malter, Joel L. Byzantine numismatic bibliography, 1950-1965. Chicago, 1968.
Arc 673.1.6 Malteros, G.T. Delphi. Kaiserslautern, 1958.

Arc 672.1.85 Maltezos, G.P. Das alte Kreta. Kaiserslautern, 1957.

Arc 1033.17.70 Malvasia, D. Venuta, et i progressi miracolosi della S. Madonna...S. Luca...1160-1617. Bononia, 1617.

Arc 1018.15 Mamachi, T.M. De' costumi de' primitivi cristiani. Venezia, 1757. 3v.

Arc 1018.15.3 Mamachi, T.M. De' costumi de' primitivi cristiani. v.1-2. Firenze, 1853.

Arc 935.19F Mamboury, Ernest. Die Kaiserpaläste von Konstantinopel zwischen Hippodrom und Marmara-Meer. Berlin, 1934.

Arc 505.82 Mambre. v.1, text; v.2, plates. (Mader, Andreas E.) Freiburg im Breisgau, 1957. 2v.

Arc 600.185F Les mammisis de Dendara, le mammisi de Nectanébo. (Daumot, F.) Le Caire, 1955.

Arc 810.58 Man, Ivonne de. Dag faun. Amsterdam, 1960.

Arc 387.5 Man and his past. (Crawford, Osbert Guy S.) London, 1921.

Arc 861.21.45 Manby, Terence George. Grooved ware sites in Yorkshire and the north of England. Oxford, 1974.

Arc 1264.11.5F Mancel, G. Les anciennes abbayes de Normandie. Caen, 1834.

Arc 843.30 Mancheño y Olivares, Miguel. Antigüedades del partido oficial de Arcos de la Frontera. Arcos de la Frontera, 1901.

Arc 1312.2 Manchester Numismatic Society. Proceedings. Manchester.

Arc 1018.62 Mancini, Ignazio. Le scoperte archeologiche sui giudeo-cristiani. Assisi, 1968.

Arc 1033.34.45 Mancini, Pietro. Del primato e della residenza in Roma dell'apostolo Pietro. Roma, 1898.

Arc 968.10 The Mandans. [North Dakota]. (Will, G.F.) Cambridge, 1906.

Arc 543.65.15 Mandel'shtam, Anatolii M. Pamiatniki epokhi bronzy v Iuzhnom Tadzhikistane. Leningrad, 1968.

Arc 1345.5F Mangeart, Thomas. Introduction a la science des médailles. Paris, 1763.

Arc 830.78.15A Mangou de la Lande, C.F.J. Essais historiques sur les antiquités du département de la Haute-Loire. Saint-Quentin, 1826.

Htn Arc 362.1.20* Manilli, Jacomo. Villa Borghese. Roma, 1650.

Arc 1033.162.5F Manin, Leonardo. Memorie storico-critiche...di S. Marco. Venezia, 1835.

Arc 838.19.2 Manjarrés, J. de. Nociones de arqueologia españolas. 2. ed. Barcelona, 1874.

Arc 861.10.17 Manks antiquities. 2. ed. (Kinnebrook, William.) Liverpool, 1914.

Arc 875.17 Mann, L.M. Prehistoric pile-structures in pits. Edinburgh, 1904.

Arc 925.225.5 Mannai-ool, Mongush. Tuva v skifskoe vremia. Moskva, 1970.

Arc 830.33 Manné-er-H'roëk; dolmen découvert. (Galles, René.) Vannes, 1863.

Arc 1033.83 Mannerini, L. Memorie del Martiro, S. Vitale e Valeria. Roma, 1848.

Arc 1030.21 Manni, D.M. Antichissima lapida cristiana. Firenze, 1763.

Arc 1033.8 Manni, D.M. Dell'errore che persiste...al Santo Evangelista. Firenze, 1766.

Arc 1260.3 Manno, Antonio. Sopra alcuni piombi sardi. Torino, 1878.

Arc 1480.34 Manns, F. Münzkundliche und historische Unterschungen über die Zeit der Illyrerkaiser. Inaug. Diss. Würzburg, 1939.

Arc 936.220.60 Mano-Zisi, Djordje. Novi Pazar. Beograd, 1969.

Arc 936.220.115 Mano-Zisi, Djordje. Sliri i Grci, njihcvi kulturni odnosi u prošlosti naše zemlje na osnovu arheološkog materijala. Beograd, 1959.

Arc 530.51F Mansel, A.M. Pergede kazilar ne arastumalar. Ankara, 1949.

Arc 530.145F Mansel, A.M. Side agorasi ve civarindaki binalar. Ankara, 1956.

Arc 936.65F Mansel, A.M. Trakya-Kirklareli. Ankara, 1943.

Arc 935.80 Mansel'e armagan. Melanges mansel. (Türk Tarih Kurumu.) Ankara, 1974. 3v.

Arc 1550.3 Mansfeld-Bûllner, H.V. Afbildninger af danske mønter, 1241-1377. Kjøbenhavn, 1887.

Arc 1550.10 Mansfeld-Bûllner, H.V. Afbildninger af panstlege indtil kjendte danske mønter. 2. Opl. Kjøbenhavn, 1964.

Arc 820.205 Mantellier, P. Mémoire sur les bronzes antiques. Paris, 1865.

Arc 830.41 Manteyer, G. de. Le nom et les 2 premières encientes de Gap. Gap, 1905.

Arc 66.1.78 Mantinée et l'arcadie orientale. (Fougères, G.) Paris, 1898.

Arc 66.1.170 La mantique Apollenienne a Delphes. (Amandry, P.) Paris, 1950. 2v.

Arc 943.46 Manual de arqueologia americana. (Alcina Franch, José.) Madrid, 1965.

Arc 1163.2.14 Manual de paleografía diplomática española. (Muñoz y Rivero, J.) Madrid, 1880.

Arc 1163.2.15 Manual de paleografía diplomática española. (Muñoz y Rivero, J.) Madrid, 1889.

Arc 1163.2.17.1 Manual de paleografía diplomática española. 2. ed. (Muñoz y Rivero, J.) Madrid, 1917.

Arc 1163.2.17 Manual de paleografía diplomática española. 2. ed. (Muñoz y Rivero, J.) Madrid, 1917.

Arc 1645.3 Manual ilustrado de numismatica chilena. (Medina, J.T.) Santiago, 1919.

Arc 389.2 Manual of archaeology. (Ely, Talfourd.) N.Y., 1890.

Arc 562.2.9 Manual of Egyptian archaeology. (Maspero, Gaston.) London, 1895.

Arc 562.2.13 Manual of Egyptian archaeology. (Maspero, Gaston.) London, 1902.

Arc 562.2.14 Manual of Egyptian archaeology. (Maspero, Gaston.) London, 1902.

Arc 562.2.8 Manual of Egyptian archaeology. (Maspero, Gaston.) N.Y., 1895.

Arc 562.2.16A Manual of Egyptian archaeology. 6. ed. (Maspero, Gaston.) N.Y., 1914.

Arc 562.2.20A Manual of Egyptian archaeology. 6th English ed. (Maspero, Gaston.) N.Y., 1926.

Arc 1400.1.2 A manual of gold and silver coins. (Eckfeldt, J.R.) Philadelphia, 1851.

Arc 642.2.5A A manual of Greek archaeology. (Collignon, Maxime.) London, 1886.

Arc 642.2.6 A manual of Greek archaeology. (Collignon, Maxime.) N.Y., 1886.

Arc 416.1.2 Manual of Oriental antiquities. (Babelon, E.) N.Y., 1889.

Arc 416.1.3A Manual of Oriental antiquities. (Babelon, E.) N.Y., 1906.

Arc 1018.29.7 Manual of the antiquities of the church. (Guericke, H.) London, 1851.

Arc 1185.14 Manual of the study of documents. (Frazer, P.) Philadelphia, 1894.

Arc 1018.31 Manuale di archeologia cristiana. (Scaglia, P.S.) Roma, 1911.

Arc 1018.44 Manuale di archeologia cristiana. 3. ed. (Marucchi, O.) Roma, 1923.

Arc 1348.29.3 Manuale di numismatica. 3. ed. (Ambrosoli, S.) Milano, 1904.

Arc 1488.18 Manuale di numismatica ialiana medioevale e moderna dalla caduta dell'impero romano alla rivoluzione francese. v.1, pt. 1. (Simonetti, Luigi.) Firenze, 1965.

Arc 1153.11 Manuale di paleografia delle carte. (Lupi, C.) Firenze, 1875.

Arc 1488.9 Manuale per il raccoglitore di monete del regno d'Italia. (Cagiati, Memmo.) Napoli, 1918.

Arc 1411.5 Manuals of Far Eastern numismatics. Yokohama, 1911.

Arc 1077.2.28 Manuel...sepulchral slabs and crosses of the Middle Ages. (Cutts, E.L.) London, 1849.

Arc 823.11 Manuel d'archéologie. v.1-2. (Déchelette, Joseph.) Paris, 1908-14. 5v.

Arc 943.12 Manuel d'archéologie americaine. (Beuchat, H.) Paris, 1912.

Arc 1018.24 Manuel d'archéologie chrétienne. (LeClercq, H.) Paris, 1907. 2v.

Arc 1018.31.3 Manuel d'archéologie chrétienne. (Scaglia, P.S.) Turin, 1916.

Arc 416.32 Manuel d'archéologie d'Extrême-Orient. (Hierche, Henri.) Paris, 1966- 2v.

Arc 571.5 Manuel d'archéologie égyptienne. v.1-5; atlases. (Vandier, Jacques.) Paris, 1952. 10v.

Arc 723.6 Manuel d'archéologie étrusque et romaine. (Martha, Jules.) Paris, 1884.

Arc 823.9A Manuel d'archéologie française. (Enlart, C.) Paris, 1902-1904. 3v.

Arc 823.9.2 Manuel d'archéologie française. v.1, pts.1-3. (Enlart, C.) Paris, 1919-1920. 3v.

Arc 823.9.3 Manuel d'archéologie française. 3e éd. pt.2. (Enlart, C.) Paris, 1929.

Arc 823.11.9 Manuel d'archéologie gallo-romaine. v.1-4. (Grenier, Albert.) Paris, 1931-1934. 6v.

Arc 642.2.3 Manuel d'archéologie grecque. (Collignon, Maxime.) Paris, 188-.

Arc 642.2A Manuel d'archéologie grecque. (Collignon, Maxime.) Paris, 1881.

Arc 416.1 Manuel d'archéologie orientale. (Babelon, E.) Paris, 1888.

Arc 416.6 Manuel d'archéologie orientale depuis les origines jusqu'a l'époque d'Alexandre. (Contenau, Georges.) Paris, 1927-47. 4v.

Arc 823.45.5 Manuel d'archéologie préhistorique, celtique et gallo-romaine. v.1-2, pt.1-3. (Déchelette, Joseph.) Westmead, Eng., 1971. 5v.

Arc 823.11.5 Manuel d'archéologie préhistorique, celtique et gallo-romaine. v.1-2. (Déchelette, Joseph.) Paris, 1913-1924. 4v.

Arc 823.45 Manuel d'archéologie prêhistorique, celtique et gallo-romaine. v.1-6; v.1-4, 2. éd. (Déchelette, Joseph.) Paris, 1924-34. 7v.

Arc 1185.4A Manuel de diplomatique. (Giry, Arthur.) Paris, 1894.

Arc 1185.4.5 Manuel de diplomatique. (Giry, Arthur.) Paris, 1925. 2v.

Arc 1190.30 Manuel de diplomatique française et pontificale. (Boüard, Alain de.) Paris, 1929-52. 2v.

Arc 1190.30F Manuel de diplomatique française et pontificale. Atlas. (Boüard, Alain de.) Paris, 1929-52. 2v.

Arc 393.5 Manuel de la technique des fouilles archéologiques. (International Institute of Intellectural Cooperation.) Paris, 1950.

Arc 1362.2 Manuel de numismatique ancienne. (Hennin, M.) Paris, 1830-69. 3v.

Arc 1498.7 Manuel de numismatique francaise. (Blanchet, A.) Paris, 1912-36. 4v.

Arc 1408.4 Manuel de numismatique orientale de l'antiquité et du moyen-age. (Morgan, J. de.) Paris, 1923-36.

Arc 1135.206FA Manuel de paléographie. (Prou, Maurice.) Paris, 1904.

Arc 1138.4.4A Manuel de paléographie latine et française. 3. éd. (Prou, Maurice.) Paris, 1910.

Arc 1138.4.5 Manuel de paléographie latine et française avec atlas. 4. éd. (Prou, Maurice.) Paris, 1924. 2v.

Arc 830.342 Manuel de préhistoire par le sud du Bassin parisien. (Nouel, André.) Orléans, 1966.

Arc 403.12.2 Manuel de recherches préhistoriques. 2. éd. (Société Préhistorique de France.) Paris, 1929.

Arc 1264.8A Manuel de sigillographie française. (Roman, J.) Paris, 1912.

Arc 1030.38 Manuel d'épigraphie chrétienne. (Aigrain, R.) Paris, 1912.

Arc 1030.34 Manuel d'épigraphie chrétienne. (Le Blant, E.) Paris, 1869.

Arc 830.107.5 Manuel des fouilles archéologiques. 1e éd. (Salin, Édouard.) Paris, 1946.

Arc 1018.44.15 Manuel of Christian archaeology. 4. Italian ed. (Marucchi, O.) Paterson, N.J., 1935.

Arc 1018.44.17 Manuel of Christian archaeology. 4. Italian ed. (Marucchi, O.) Paterson, N.J., 1949.

Arc 1433.31 Manuel of Musalman numismatics. (Codrington, O.) London, 1904.

Arc 559.1 Manuele d'archéologie egyptienne. (Jéquier, G.) Paris, 1924.

Htn Arc 969.1.8* Manuscripts. English. Effigy, or Symbolic mound in Licking County, Ohio. n.p., n.d.

Arc 66.1.24 Manuscrit d'Isocrate, Urbinas CXI. (Martin, A.) Paris, 1881.

Arc 1138.55 Les manuscrits. (Dain, A.) Paris, 1949.

Arc 1138.55.2 Les manuscrits. (Dain, A.) Paris, 1964.

Arc 66.1.56 Manuscrits de Dante des Bibliothèques de France. (Auvray, L.) Paris, 1892.

Arc 66.1.14 Manuscrits des poesies de S. Paulin de Nole. (Chatelain, E.) Paris, 1880.

Arc 1020.26.5 Les manuscrits du trésor de Bari. (Barbier de Montault, X.) Toulouse, 1876.

Arc 861.10.20F The Manx archaeological survey; reports. pt.1-6. (Isle of Man. Natural History and Antiquarian Society.) Douglas, 1909-35.

Arc 861.10.11 Manx crosses...monuments...Isle of Man. (Kinnebrook, William.) London, 1907.

Arc 1033.47.17 Mapelli, L. L'incendio di Roma e i primi Cristiani. Milano, 1900.

Arc 708.20 Maps, Athens. Athen mit Umgebung (1877). Berlin, 1881.

Arc 705.201A Maps, Athens. Atlas von Athen. Berlin, 1878.

Arc 767.1.5 Maps, Rome. Ancient (1896). Formae urbis Romae antiquae. Berolino, 1896.
Arc 767.1.7A Maps, Rome. Ancient (1912). Formae urbis Romae antiquae. Berolino, 1912.
Arc 513.14 Maps. Asia Minor (1899). Archäologische Karte von Kleinasien. Halle, 1899.
Arc 720.206 Maps. Pozzuoli. Pozzuoli e contorni. Napoli, 1810.
Arc 609.6F Mapungubwe, ancient Bantu civilization on the Limpopo. (Fouché, Leo.) Cambridge, Eng., 1937. 2v.
Arc 635.24 Maraghiannio, G. Antiquités crétoises. Vienne, n.d.
Arc 635.24.5 Maraghiannio, G. Antiquités crétoises. 2. série. Athène, 1911.
Arc 595.67F Maragioglio, Vito. L'architura delle piramidi menfite. v.2-7; plates. Torino, 1963- 9v.
Arc 1033.55.3 Marangoni, G. Istoria dell'...oratorio...Lateran...Sancta Sanctorum. Roma, 1798.
Htn Arc 1027.34* Marangoni, J. Acta S. Victorini episcopi amiterni et martyres. Rome, 1740.
Arc 77.4 Marberger Winckelmann-Program. Marburg. 1956+ 4v.
Arc 66.1.215 Marcadé, Jean. Au musée de Délos. Paris, 1969.
X Cg Arc 1045.5 Marçais, W. Les monumens arabes. Paris, 1903.
Arc 397.6 March, H.C. An examination of the tithe. Rochdale, 1887. 5 pam.
Arc 397.17.10 The march of archaeology. 1. American ed. (Marek, Kurt W.) N.Y., 1958.
Arc 543.7.13 Marchal, H. Guide archéologique aux temples d'Angkor. Paris, 1928.
Arc 712.7 Marchal. Le Parthénon. Paris, 1864.
Arc 1070.208 Marchant, Louis. Ampoules de pèlerinages en plomb...Bourgogne. Dijon, 1873.
Arc 1390.7 Marchant, N.D. Mélanges de numismatique et d'histoire. Paris, 1818.
Arc 785.68 Marchetti-Longhi, G. L'"area sacra" ed i templi repubblicani del Largo Argentina. Roma, 1930.
Arc 726.67F Marchi, G. La stipe tributata alle divinità delle acque Apollinari. Roma, 1852.
Arc 1015.210 Marchi, Giuseppe. Monumenti delle arti cristiane primitive nella metropoli del cristianismo. Roma, 1844.
Arc 1015.210.5 Marchi, Giuseppe. Il sepolcro dei ss martiri Proto e Giacinta. Roma, 1845.
Arc 726.38 Marchisio, A.F. Per l'archeologia del territorio albese. Alba, 1913.
Arc 682.5 Marcks, F. Die mykenische Zeit. Cöln, 1902.
Arc 736.11 Marconi, P. Himera; lo scavo del Tempio della Vittoria e del temenos. Roma, 1931.
Arc 736.1.9F Marconi, Pirro. Agrigento. Firenze, 1929.
Arc 736.1.12 Marconi, Pirro. Agrigento. Roma, 1933.
Arc 726.140 Marconi, Pirro. Verona romana. Bergamo, 1937.
Arc 1500.7 Les marcs de la ville et de la cour romaine d'Avignon. (Blancard, Louis.) Tours, n.d. 2 pam.
Arc 608.2.50 Marec, Erwan. Hippone la Royale. Alger, 1954.
Arc 608.2.52 Marec, Erwan. Monuments chrétiens d'Hippone. Paris, 1958.
Arc 800.2 Maréchal, P.S. Antiquités d'Herculanum. Paris, 1780-1803. 12v.
Arc 800.2.5 Maréchal, P.S. Antiquités d'Herculanum. Paris, 1871. 8v.
Arc 530.12.40 Marek, Kurt W. Enge Schlucht und Schwarzer Berg. Hamburg, 1955.
Arc 530.12.42 Marek, Kurt W. Enge Schlucht und Schwarzer Berg. Reinbek, 1966.
Arc 953.34.1 Marek, Kurt W. Der erste Amerikaner. Reinbek bei Hamburg, 1972.
Arc 953.34 Marek, Kurt W. The first American. 1. ed. N.Y., 1971.
Arc 397.17.5A Marek, Kurt W. Gods, graves, and scholars. 1. American ed. N.Y., 1951.
Arc 397.17.6 Marek, Kurt W. Gods, graves, and scholars. 2. ed. N.Y., 1968.
Arc 397.17.7 Marek, Kurt W. Götter, Gräber und Gelehrt. Reinbeck, 1972.
Arc 384.2.10 Marek, Kurt W. Götter, Gräber und Gelehrte in Dokumenten. Reinbek bei Hamburg, 1965.
Arc 397.17.3 Marek, Kurt W. Götter. Hamburg, 1950.
Arc 384.2.5 Marek, Kurt W. Hands on the past. 1. American ed. N.Y., 1966.
Arc 397.17.10 Marek, Kurt W. The march of archaeology. 1. American ed. N.Y., 1958.
Arc 397.17.15 Marek, Kurt W. A picture history of archaeology. London, 1958.
Arc 530.12.35 Marek, Kurt W. The secret of the Hittites. N.Y., 1956.
Arc 384.2 Marek, Kurt W. The world of archaeology. London, 1966.
Arc 726.77F Marescalchi, A. Storia della vite e del vino in Italia. Milano, 1931-37. 3v.
Arc 736.17 Margani, M.N. Casmene ritrovata? Comiso, 1955.
Arc 870.4.21 Margary, Ivan D. Roman roads in Britain. London, 1955. 2v.
Arc 870.4.21.2 Margary, Ivan D. Roman roads in Britain. London, 1967.
Arc 870.4.21.3 Margary, Ivan D. Roman roads in Britain. 3. ed. London, 1973.
Arc 870.4.20 Margary, Ivan D. Roman ways in the Weald. London, 1948.
Arc 870.4.22 Margary, Ivan D. Roman ways in the Weald. London, 1965.
Arc 925.16.17 Margulan, A.K. Drevniaia kul'tura Tsentral'nogo Kazakhstana. Alma-Ata, 1966.
Arc 925.16.15 Margulan, A.K. Iz istorii gorodov i stroitel'nogo isskustva drevnego Kazakhstana. Alma-Ata, 1950.
Arc 505.59 Mari, une ville perdue...et retrouvée par l'archéologie française. (Parrot, André.) Paris, 1936.
Arc 1580.45 Maria-Theresien-Taler. 2. Aufl. (Hans, Josef.) Leiden, 1961.
Arc 1088.4 Mariani, Lucilla. Le nave di Nemi nella bibliografia. Roma, 1942.
Arc 1033.17.542.5 Mariano, Filoteo. La miracolosa imagine della B.V. Maria del Mont'Allegro in Rapello. Venezia, 1688.
Arc 889.22 Mariën, M.E. Oud-België. Antwerpen, 1952.
Arc 545.226 Mariette, A. Catalogue général des monuments d'Abydos. Paris, 1880.
Arc 600.3 Mariette, A. Choix de monuments et de dessins...Sérapéum de Memphis. Paris, 1856.
Arc 562.1 Mariette, A. Itinéraire de la Haute-Égypte. Paris, 1880.
Arc 545.226.5F Mariette, A. Les mastabas de l'ancien empire. Paris, 1884.
Arc 545.28.3 Mariette, A. Monuments divers..en Égypte et en Nubie. Paris, 1872-1889. 2v.
Arc 562.1.6 Mariette, A. The monuments of upper Egypt. Alexandria, 1877.
Arc 562.1.5 Mariette, A. The monuments of upper Egypt. Boston, 1890.
Arc 870.14.12 Mariette, E. The Roman walls. 2. ed. Paris, 1906.
Arc 562.1.3 Mariette Pacha. (Chèlu, Alfred Jacques.) Le Caire, 1911.
Arc 925.175.5 Mariiskaia Arkheologicheskaia Ekspeditsiia, 1956-59. Materialy k arkheologicheskoi karte Mariiskoi ASSR. Ioshkar-Ola, 1960.
Arc 925.175.10 Mariitsy IX-XI vv. (Arkhipov, Gennadii A.) Ioshkar-Ola, 1973.
Arc 1480.85 La marina en la moneda romana. (Burzio, Humberto F.) Buenos Aires, 1961.
Arc 672.1.80F Marinatos, Spyridon. Crete and Mycenae. N.Y., 1960.
Arc 672.1.75F Marinatos, Spyridon. Kreta und das mykenische Hellas. München, 1959.
Arc 412.2 Marine archaeology. (Taylor, Joan du Plat.) London, 1965.
Arc 1088.1.17 Les marines de guerre. (Serre, Paul.) Paris, 1885.
Arc 1016.235 Marini, G. Iscrizioni antiche doliari. Roma, 1884.
Arc 397.14 Marini, G. Lettere inedite. v.1-3. Roma, 1916-40. 2v.
Arc 1175.10 Marini, G.L. I papiri diplomatici. Roma, 1805.
Arc 1020.31.9 Mariti, Giovanni. Istoria del tempio della resurrezione. Livorno, 1784.
Arc 545.234 Marius of Northampton. Report on some excavations...Theban necropolis. London, 1908.
Arc 861.47.5 Markham, C.A. Stone crosses of county of Northampton. London, 1901.
Arc 1494.3 Markl, M. Die Münzen, Medaillen, und Prägungen. Prag, 1896. 2v.
Arc 1348.37 Markov', A.K. O chistk' drevnikh' monet'. Sankt Peterburg, 1908.
Arc 925.9.52 Markovin, Vladimir I. V strane vainakhor. Moskva, 1969.
Arc 925.9.50 Markovin, Vladimir I. V ushchel'iakh Arguna i Fortangi. Moskva, 1965.
Arc 497.76.2 Markovski, Ivan S. Bibleiska arkheologiia. 2. izd. Sofiia, 1948.
Arc 595.34.5 Marks, T.S. The Great Pyramid. 2. ed. London, 1879?
Arc 1490.11 Marks von Marksfeld, J. Vierzig Münzen der Normannen Hohenstaufen. Mailand, 1858.
Htn Arc 767.2* Marliani, B. L'antichità di Roma. Roma, 1622.
Arc 767.2.5 Marliani, B. Descrizione di Roma antica. Roma, 1697.
Arc 767.2.7 Marliani, B. Descrizione di Roma antica. Roma, 1708. 2v.
Arc 767.2.10 Marliani, B. Descrizione di Roma antica. Roma, 1739.
Htn Arc 767.2.2* Marliani, B. Urbis Romae topographia. Colophon, 1544.
Arc 861.47 Marmor Estonianum...in agro Northamptoniensi. (Nixon, J.) Londinium, 1744.
Htn Arc 1093.1* Marmor pisanum. (Chimentelli, V.) Bononiae, 1666.
Arc 66.1.160 Le Maroc des romains. (Chatelain, Louis.) Paris, 1944. 2v.
Arc 375.14 Marois, Roger. English-French, French-English vocabulary of prehistoric archaeology. Montreal, 1972.
Arc 870.20 Marples, M. White horses. London, 1949.
Arc 530.22F Marr, H. Arkheologicheskiia ekspeditsiia 1916 g. Sankt Peterburg, 1922.
Arc 510.215.5 Marr, N. Raskopki...1904 godu. Sankt Peterburg, 1906.
Arc 1033.17.10 Marracci, L. Memorie di Santa Maria in Portico di Roma. Roma, 1675.
Arc 1033.17.92 Marracci, Lodovico. Memorie di Santa Maria in Portico. Roma, 1871.
Arc 810.16 Marriott, H.P.F. Facts about Pompeii. London, 1895.
Arc 1025.12 Marriott, W.B. Testimony of the catacombs. London, 1870.
Htn Arc 861.6.5* Marriott, William. The antiquities of Lyme. Stockport, 1810.
Arc 66.1.145 Marrou, Henri-Irénée. Saint Augustin et la fin de la culture antique. v.1-2. Paris, 1958.
Arc 1020.150 Der Mars Camulus-Stein in der Pfarrkirche zu Rindern. (Fink, Josef.) Kevelaer, 1970.
Arc 870.35 Marsden, Barry M. The early barrow-diggers. Park Ridge, N.J., 1974.
Arc 1405.1 Marsden's Numismata orientalia. v.1. (Thomas, E.) London, 1874.
Arc 66.1.168 Marseille Angevine. (Lesage, G.) Paris, 1950.
Arc 652.4 Marshall, Fred H. Discovery in Greek lands. Cambridge, 1920.
Arc 397.11 Marshall, John. Conservation manual. Calcutta, 1923.
Arc 458.1.9 Marshall, John. A guide to Sanchi. Calcutta, 1918.
Arc 458.1.10 Marshall, John. A guide to Sanchi. 2. ed. Delhi, 1936.
Arc 458.1.12 Marshall, John. A guide to Sanchi. 3. ed. Delhi, 1955.
Arc 459.3 Marshall, John. A guide to Taxila. Calcutta, 1918.
Arc 459.3.15 Marshall, John. A guide to Taxila. 3. ed. Delhi, 1936.
Arc 459.3.19 Marshall, John. A guide to Taxila. 4. ed. Cambridge, 1960.
Arc 452.1F Marshall, John. Mohenjo-daro and the Indus civilization. London, 1931. 3v.
Arc 459.3.20 Marshall, John. Taxila. Cambridge, 1951. 3v.
Arc 720.218F Marsiliana d'Albegna. (Minto, Antonio.) Firenze, 1921.
Arc 830.2.13 Marsille, Louis. Le déput de l'age du bronze dans le Morbihan. Vannes, 1913.
Arc 830.2.15 Marsille, Louis. Le tumulus de cote-er-garf, en elven et les sépulture de l'age du bronze dans le Morbihan. Vannes, 1913.
Arc 1348.14 Marsy, Arthur. Cueilloir numismatique. n.p., 1887.
Arc 66.1.16 Martha, J. Catalogue des figurines en terre cuite. Paris, 1880.
Arc 66.1.26 Martha, J. Sacerdoces anthéniens. Paris, 1882.
Arc 723.6 Martha, Jules. Manuel d'archéologie étrusque et romaine. Paris, 1884.
Arc 540.4 Marti, I.I. Raskopki goradishcha kiteia v 1928 g. Simferopol, 1929.
Arc 925.8.25 Marti, Iu.Iu. Problema raskopok drevnego pantikapeia. n.p., 1928?
Arc 1018.02 Martigny, J.A. Dictionnaire des antiquités chrétiennes. Paris, 1877.
Arc 66.1.47 Martin, A. Les cavaliers athéniens. Paris, 1886.
Arc 66.1.24 Martin, A. Manuscrit d'Isocrate, Urbinas CXI. Paris, 1881.
Arc 66.1.27 Martin, A. Scolies du ms. d'Aristophane à Ravenne. Paris, 1882.
Arc 870.5.5 Martin, E. A. Dew-ponds; history, observation and experiment. London, 1915.
Arc 587.8.5F Martin, Geoffrey Torndike. The royal tomb at El-Amana. London, 1974.
Arc 618.5 Martin, Henri. Études d'archéologie celtique. Paris, 1872.
Arc 830.90 Martin, Jean C. Antiquités et inscriptions des villes de Die, d'Orange. Orange, 1818.
Arc 1400.5 Martin, Leopold Charles. The current gold and silver coins of all countries. London, 1863?
Arc 66.1.174 Martin, R. Recherches sur l'agora grecque. Paris, 1951.
Arc 843.225 Martín Aguado, Máximo. El yacimiento prehistórico de Pinedo, Toledo, y su industria triedrica. Toledo, 1963.
Arc 830.6.13 Martin-Daussigny, E.C. Description d'une voie romaine. Lyon, 1855. 12 pam.

Arc 1493.12 Martin Minquez, Bernardino. Datos epigráficos y numismáticos de España. Valladolid, 1883.
Arc 1020.23 Martinelli, F. Diaconia S. Agathae in subura. Roma, 1638.
Arc 843.226 Martínez Fernandez, Jesus. Ensayo biologico sobre los hombres y los pueblos de la Asturias primativa. Oviedo, 1969.
Arc 843.218 Martinez Hombre, Eduardo. Vindius; el lado septentrional clasico de Hispania. Madrid, 1964.
Arc 843.235 Martinez i Hualde, Angel. El poblat ibèric de Puig Castellar. Barcelona, 1966.
Htn Arc 1093.3* Martini, G.H. Abhandlung von den Sonnenuhren der Alten. Leipzig, 1877.
Arc 630.10 Martini, G.H. Antiquorum monimentorum, sylloge altera. Lipsiae, 1787.
Arc 1340.3F Martinori, E. Moneta; vocabolario. Roma, 1915.
Arc 785.55 Martinori, E. Via Cassia. Roma, 1930.
Arc 1490.21 Martinori, Edoardo. Annali della zecca di Roma. v.1-11,12-16,17-24. Roma, 1917-20. 3v.
Arc 1020.59 Martinov, J. Le trésor de la cathédrale de Gran. Arras, 1881.
Arc 1053.15 Martinov, Jean. Un tétraptique russe. Arras, 1877.
Arc 1033.167 I martirii di S. Teodoto e di S. Ariadne. (Eleuterio.) Roma, 1901.
Arc 530.65.15 Martirosian, A. Armeniia v epokhu bronzy i rannego zheleza. Erevan, 1964.
Arc 530.65.10 Martirosian, A. Gorod Teishenbaini po raskopkam 1947-1958 gg. Erevan, 1961.
Arc 530.82 Martirosian, A. Raskopki v golovino. Erevan, 1954.
Arc 843.50.5 Martorell, Jeroni. Tarragona i els seus antics monuments. Barcelona, 1920.
Arc 1025.24 Martorelli, I. Le catacombe di Roma. Vercelli, 1881.
Arc 923.131 Martynov, Anatolii I. Arkheologiia SSSR. Moskva, 1973.
Arc 925.4.29 Martynov, Anatolii I. Shestakovskie kurgany. Kemerovo, 1971.
Arc 925.4.25 Martynov, Anatolii O. Lodki, v strany predkov. Kemerovo, 1966.
Arc 1033.53.24 Le martyre de la Légion Thébaine. (Berchem, D. van.) Basel, 1956.
Arc 1020.72 Le martyrium de Poitiers. (Barbier de Montault, X.) Poitiers, 1885.
Arc 547.23 Marucchi, O. Gli antichi oggetti egiziani. Roma, 1901.
Arc 1027.4.40 Marucchi, O. La basilica papale del cimitero di Priscilla. Roma, 1908.
Arc 1033.87 Marucchi, O. Brevi compendio di memorie...martire S. Agapito. Roma, 1898.
Arc 1027.9.9 Marucchi, O. Le catacombe ed il protestantesimo. Roma, 1911.
Arc 1025.28.50F Marucchi, O. Le catacombe romane. Roma, 1933.
Arc 1025.28.25 Marucchi, O. La catacombe romane a proposito della recente opera del Roller. Roma, 1883.
Arc 1030.4.30 Marucchi, O. Christian epigraphy. Cambridge, 1912.
Arc 1027.41 Marucchi, O. Il cimitero di Commodilla. Roma, 1904.
X Cg Arc 1027.15 Marucchi, O. Il cimitero e la Basilica di San Valentino. Roma, 1890.
Arc 1025.28.19 Marucchi, O. Come lo studio dell'archeologia cristiana. Roma, 1900.
Arc 1025.28.8 Marucchi, O. Come lo studio dell'archeologia cristiana giovi grandemente. Roma, 1903.
Arc 1025.28.40 Marucchi, O. Compendio storico e topografico delle catacombe romane. Albano Laziale, 1928.
Arc 1020.9.65 Marucchi, O. Conferenze della società di cultura della cristianità archeologia. Roma, 1877.
Arc 1027.15.5 Marucchi, O. La cripta sepolceale di San Valentio sulla Flaminia. Roma, 1878.
Arc 1033.34.41 Marucchi, O. La crocifisione di San Pietro nel Vaticano. Roma, 1905.
Arc 1030.4.15 Marucchi, O. Dell'importanza dell'epigrafia romana. Roma, 1898.
Arc 785.13.28 Marucchi, O. Description du Forum Romain et guide pour le visiteur. Rome, 1885.
Arc 1027.44 Marucchi, O. Di alcune iscrizioni...Basilia de S. Petronella. Roma, n.d.
Arc 1030.4.25 Marucchi, O. Di alcuni antiche monumenti. Roma, 1899-1900.
Arc 1027.4.13 Marucchi, O. Di un battistero scoperto nel cimitero di Priscilla. Roma, 1901.
Arc 1027.5.15 Marucchi, O. Di un gruppo di antiche iscrizioni...Domitilla. Roma, 1902.
Arc 1027.8.9 Marucchi, O. Di un ipogeo scoperto nel cimitero di S. Sebastian. Roma, 1879.
Arc 1027.18.9 Marucchi, O. Di un nuovo cimitero giudaico. Roma, 1884.
Arc 1015.225.5 Marucchi, O. Di un nuovo cimitero giudaico. Roma, 1884.
Arc 1020.9.70 Marucchi, O. Di un nuovo cippo del pomerio urbano. Roma, 1900.
Arc 1030.4 Marucchi, O. Di una...iscrizione cristiana. Roma, 1883.
Arc 1030.4.5 Marucchi, O. Di una rarissima epigrafe cristiana. Roma, 1878.
Arc 1025.28.3 Marucchi, O. Eléments d'archélogie chrétienne. v.1-2. Paris, 1899. 3v.
Arc 1025.28.4 Marucchi, O. Eléments d'archéologie chrétienne. Paris, 1903. 2v.
Arc 1030.4.29 Marucchi, O. Epigrafia christiana. Milano, 1910.
Arc 1027.9.5 Marucchi, O. Gli errori della scuola protestante. n.p., 1884.
Arc 1025.28.35 Marucchi, O. Esame di un opuscolo di Mons. G. Wilpert. Roma, 1909.
Arc 1025.28.45 Marucchi, O. The evidencce of the catacombs for the doctrines and organization of the primitive church. London, 1929.
Arc 785.13.35 Marucchi, O. Le Forum Romain et le Palatin. Paris, 1902.
Arc 1033.3.13 Marucchi, O. Un frammento di sarcofago cristiano. Roma, 1897.
Arc 1033.3.9 Marucchi, O. Un frammento di sarcofago cristiano del Museo Laterano. Roma, 1896.
Arc 1027.25.29 Marucchi, O. Giovanni Battista de Rossi. Roma, 1895.
Arc 1027.25.31 Marucchi, O. Giovanni Battista de Rossi. Roma, 1901.
Arc 1027.19.17 Marucchi, O. Guida del cimitero di Callisto. Paris, 1902.
Arc 1027.5.13 Marucchi, O. Guida del cimitero di Domitilla. Paris, 1902.
Arc 1027.4.15 Marucchi, O. Guida del cimitero di Priscilla. Paris, 1903.
Arc 1033.56 Marucchi, O. Guida del Museo Christiano Christiano Lateranense. Roma, 1898.
Arc 1027.56 Marucchi, O. Guida delle catacombe di Albano. Roma, 1903.
Arc 1025.28.27 Marucchi, O. Guide des catacombes romaines. 2. éd. Paris, 1903.
Arc 1025.28.6 Marucchi, O. Handbuch der christlichen Archäologie. N.Y., 1912.
Arc 1030.4.19 Marucchi, O. L'iscrizione di Quirinio. Siena, 1897.
Arc 1018.44 Marucchi, O. Manuale di archeologia cristiana. 3. ed. Roma, 1923.
Arc 1018.44.15 Marucchi, O. Manuel of Christian archaeology. 4. Italian ed. Paterson, N.J., 1935.
Arc 1018.44.17 Marucchi, O. Manuel of Christian archaeology. 4. Italian ed. Paterson, N.J., 1949.
Arc 1033.28.5 Marucchi, O. Il matrimonio cristiano sopra antico monumento. Roma, 1882.
Arc 1027.5.18 Marucchi, O. La memoria dei santi...cimitero di Domitilla. n.p., n.d.
Arc 1033.13.5 Marucchi, O. Le memorie dei SS. apostoli Pietro e Paolo nella città di Roma. Roma, 1894.
Arc 785.13.29 Marucchi, O. Nova descrizione della casa dell Vestali. Roma, 1887.
Arc 785.13.31 Marucchi, O. Nova scoperte nella casa dell Vestali. Roma, 1884.
Arc 1027.4.11 Marucchi, O. Le nuove scoperte nelle catacombe di Priscilla. v.1-2. Roma, 1888.
Arc 1033.53 Marucchi, O. Un nuovo monumento della persecuzione diocleziana. Roma, 1893.
Arc 1027.49 Marucchi, O. Osservazioni intorno al cimitero delle catacombe. n.p., n.d.
Arc 1027.19.21 Marucchi, O. Osservazioni sulla iscrizione della madre del papa Damaso. Roma, 1903.
Arc 1030.4.32 Marucchi, O. Il pontificato del papa Damaso. Roma, 1905.
Arc 1027.40.5 Marucchi, O. La recente condroversia sul cimitero Ostriano. Roma, 1903.
Arc 785.31 Marucchi, O. Recenti scoperte dell'Iseo Compense. Roma, 1883.
Arc 1020.29 Marucchi, O. Le recenti scoperte nel Duomo di Parinzo. Roma, 1896.
Arc 1027.15.9 Marucchi, O. Le recenti scoperte presso il cimitero di San Valentino. Roma, 1888.
Arc 785.13.35.5 Marucchi, O. The Roman Forum and the Palatine. Rome, 1906.
Arc 1033.28.8 Marucchi, O. La santità del matrimonio. Roma, 1902.
Arc 1027.39.9 Marucchi, O. Scavi eseguiti nell'antica Basilica di S. Agapito. Roma, 1899.
Arc 1015.225.9 Marucchi, O. Scavi nella Platonia. Roma, 1892.
Arc 1025.28.30 Marucchi, O. Scavi nelle catacombe romane. Roma, 1899.
Arc 1027.6 Marucchi, O. Sepolcro apostolico delle catacombe. Roma, 1892.
Arc 1015.225 Marucchi, O. Il sepolcro gentilizio di Sant'Ambrogio. Milano, 1897.
Arc 1030.4.9 Marucchi, O. Silloge di alcune iscrizioni. Roma, 1881.
Arc 1027.25.27 Marucchi, O. Solenne festa in onore del Comm. G.B. de Rossi. Roma, 1883.
Arc 1027.4.29 Marucchi, O. Studio archaeologico...iscrizione di Filomena. Roma, 1907.
Arc 1033.5 Marucchi, O. La supremazia della sede romana considerata nei monumenti dei primi secoli. Roma, 1897.
Arc 726.10.14 Marucchi, Orazio. Guida archeologica della città di Palestrina. Roma, 1912.
Arc 726.10.5 Marucchi, Orazio. Guida archeologica dell'antica Preneste. Roma, 1885.
Arc 726.10.17 Marucchi, Orazio. Il tempio della fortuna prenestina. Roma, 1908.
Arc 773.7 Marvels of ancient Rome. (Scherer, M.R.) N.Y., 1955.
Arc 1675.100 Marvin, William Theophilus Rogers. Materials for a catalogue of masonic medals. Boston, 1877.
Arc 1033.12.103 Marx, J. Ausstellung des heiligen Roches in die Domkirche zur Trier. Trier, 1845.
Arc 1495.1 Marx, R. Les médailleurs français contemporains. Paris, 1898.
X Cg Arc 1675.29 Marx, Roger. Les medailleurs modernes, 1789-1900. Paris, 190-.
Arc 1033.17.541 Mary mother of Christ. Facsimile. London, 1878.
Arc 726.79 Marzulla, A. Tombe dipinte scoperte nel territorio Pestano. Salerno, 1935.
Arc 1033.17.560 Más, Joseph. Nota historica de la Mare de Deu de la Cisa. Barcelona, 1908.
Arc 1020.127 Más, Joseph. Les reliquies del Monastir de Sant Cugat del Vallès. Barcelona, 1908.
Arc 935.11 Mas Latrie. Rapport. Paris, 1846.
Arc 505.128 Masada; Herod's fortress and the Zealot's last stand. (Yadin, Yigael.) N.Y., 1966.
Arc 505.128.1 Masada: Herod's fortress and the Zealot's last stand. (Yadin, Yigael.) London, 1966.
Arc 843.170 Mascaró i Pasarius, J. Els monuments megalitics a l'illa de Menorca. Barcelona, 1958.
Arc 1020.9.183 Masetti, Pio. Memorie istoriche della chiesa di S. Maria. Roma, 1855.
Arc 1200.15 MasLatrie, L. Les éléments de la diplomatique pontificale. Paris, 1886.
Arc 953.6 Mason, O.T. Miscellaneous papers relating to anthropology. Washington, 1883.
Arc 945.4 Mason, Otis J. Aboriginal American harpoons. Washington, 1900.
Arc 1312.3 Mason's monthly illustrated coin collectors' magazine. Boston.
Arc 402.9.25 Maspero, G. Notice biographique du vicomte Emmanuel de Rouge. Paris, 1908.
Arc 562.2 Maspero, Gaston. L'archéologie égyptienne (in Bibliothèque de l'Enseignement des Beaux-Arts). Paris, 1887.
Arc 562.2.35 Maspero, Gaston. Causeries d'Égypte. 2. éd. Paris, 1907.
Arc 545.227.35 Maspero, Gaston. Documents. Le Caire, 1912.
Arc 562.2.40 Maspero, Gaston. Egypt: ancient sites and modern scenes. N.Y., 1911.
Arc 562.2.7 Maspero, Gaston. Egyptian archaeology. London, 1893.
Arc 562.2.5 Maspero, Gaston. Egyptian archaeology. N.Y., 1887.
Arc 562.2.6 Maspero, Gaston. Egyptian archaeology. 2. ed. N.Y., 1892.
Arc 562.2.9 Maspero, Gaston. Manual of Egyptian archaeology. London, 1895.
Arc 562.2.14 Maspero, Gaston. Manual of Egyptian archaeology. London, 1902.
Arc 562.2.13 Maspero, Gaston. Manual of Egyptian archaeology. London, 1902.
Arc 562.2.8 Maspero, Gaston. Manual of Egyptian archaeology. N.Y., 1895.
Arc 562.2.16A Maspero, Gaston. Manual of Egyptian archaeology. 6. ed. N.Y., 1914.
Arc 562.2.20A Maspero, Gaston. Manual of Egyptian archaeology. 6th English ed. N.Y., 1926.
Arc 562.2.26 Maspero, Gaston. New light on ancient Egypt. London, 1908.
Arc 562.2.27 Maspero, Gaston. New light on ancient Egypt. N.Y., 1909.

Arc 562.1.20 Maspero, Gaston. Notice biographique sur Auguste Mariette. Paris, 1904.
Arc 545.227.25 Maspero, Gaston. Rapports. Le Caire, 1909. 2v.
Arc 843.81F Masriera y Manovens, J. Apuntes sobre la villa de Tossa de Mar. Barcelona, 1923.
Arc 720.207 Massazza, P.A. L'arco antico di Susa. Torino, 1750.
Arc 1613.28 Massey, Joseph Earl. America's money. N.Y., 1968.
Arc 608.1.37F Massigli, T. Musée de Sfax. Paris, 1912.
Arc 858.37.2 Massingham, H.J. Downland man. London, 1927.
Arc 858.37.5 Massingham, H.J. Fee, fi, fo, fum, or, The giants in England. London, 1926.
Arc 1153.5 Massmann, H.P. Libellus aurarius sivi tabulae ceratae. Lipsaie, 1840.
Arc 543.66.10 Masson, M.E. Akhangeran. Tashkend, 1953.
Arc 540.15 Masson, Oliviér. Recherches sur les pheniciens a Chypre. Genève, 1972.
Arc 416.28 Masson, V.M. Sredniaia Aziia i drevnii Vostok. Leningrad, 1964.
Arc 543.146.30 Masson, Vadim M. Karakumyi zavia tsivilizatsii. Moskva, 1972.
Arc 543.3.90 Masson, Vadim Mikhailovich. Central Asia. London, 1972.
Arc 545.236 Die Mastaba des Gem-Ni-Kai. (Bissing, F.W.) Berlin, 1905- 2v.
Arc 600.18A Le mastaba égyptien de la glyphtothèque de Carlsberg. (Mogensen, Maria.) Copenhagen, 1921.
Arc 587.11 The mastaba of Khentika called Ikhekhi. (James, Thomas Garnet H.) London, 1953.
Arc 545.226.5F Les mastabas de l'ancien empire. (Mariette, A.) Paris, 1884.
Arc 587.5 The Mastabo of Ptalshetep and Alsbrethetep. (Griffith, F.L.) London, 1900. 2v.
Arc 1033.17.446 Mastelloni, A. Memorie istoriche della Madonna de' bagno di Magliano. Napoli, 1711.
Arc 562.6 Masters, D. The romance of excavation. N.Y., 1923.
Arc 835.201F Mastorelly Peña, F. Apuntes arqueologicos. Barcelona, 1879.
Arc 1020.92.3 Mater dolorosa et gratiosa. (Caccia, Françiscus.) Wienn, 1703.
Arc 1020.31.19 Mater ecclesiarum. (Schmaltz, Karl.) Strassburg, 1918.
Arc 936.12.5 Materiał kostny zwierzecy z wykopalisk wczesnośredniowiecznego grodziska w Bonikowie. (Sobociński, M.) Poznań, 1963.
Arc 303.40F Materiale si cercetări arheologice. (Academia...Bucharest. Academia Republicii Socialiste România. Institutul de Arheologie.) Bucureşti. 2,1956+ 9v.
Arc 838.6 Materiales de arqueologia española. (Gomes-Moreno, M.) Madrid, 1912.
Arc 853.316 Materialhefte zur Vor- und Frühgeschichte der Pfalz. Speyer, 1974.
Arc 740.10PF Materiali per la etnologia antica toscana laziale. (Pinza, G.) Milano, 1915.
Arc 302.2.8 Materiali za arkheologicheska karta na Bulgariia. Sofiia. 1-8,1914-1956
Arc 493.6.10 Material'naia kultura Azerbaidzhana. v.2. (Baku. Muzei Istorii Azerbaidzhana.) Baku, 1949-
Arc 925.9.45 Material'naia kul'tura azerbaidzhantsev severo-vostochnoi i Tsentral'noi zon Malogo Kavkaza. (Karakashly, K.T.) Balzu, 1964.
Arc 530.80.5 Materialnaia Kul'tura drevnego Artika. (Khachatrian, T.S.) Erevan, 1963.
Arc 925.268 Material'naia kul'tura iakutov XVIII veka. (Konstantinov, Ivan V.) Iakutsk, 1971.
Arc 925.269 Material'naia kul'tura Iakutov XVIII veka. Photoreproduction. (Konstantinov, Ivan V.) Novosibirsk, 1967.
Arc 543.3.70 Material'naia Kul'tura narodov Srednei Azii i Kazakustana. (Akademiia nauk SSSR. Institut Etnografii.) Moskva, 1966.
Arc 543.146.45 Material'naia kul'tura Shekhr-Islama. (Atagarryev, Egen.) Ashkhabad, 1973.
Arc 925.332.10 Material'naia kul'tura sredne-tsninskoi Mordvy VIII-XIVV. Saransk, 1969.
Arc 543.65.10 Material'naia kul'tura Tadzhikistana. Dushambe. 1,1968+
Arc 1675.100 Materials for a catalogue of masonic medals. (Marvin, William Theophilus Rogers.) Boston, 1877.
Arc 925.50 Materialy...stantsiia. Bila Hira pid Poltavoiu. (Rudins'kyi, M.) Kyïv, 1926.
Arc 302.9.10 Materiały. (Lubuskie Towarzystwo Naukowe. Komisja Archeologiczna.) Zielona Góra. 1,1965+
Arc 925.265 Materialy. (Ural'skoe Arkheologicheskogo Soveshchanie. 2d, Sverdlovsk, 1961.) Sverdlovsk, 1961.
Arc 302.47 Materiały archeologiczne. Nowej huły. Kraków. 1,1968+
Arc 925.50.295 Materiały do pradziejów Wołynia i Polesia Wołyńskiego. (Cynkałowski, Aleksandr.) Warszawa, 1961.
Arc 936.14.245 Materiały do prahistorii plejstocenu i wczesnego holocenu Polski. (Chmtelewski, Waldemar.) Wrocław, 1967.
Arc 936.14.540 Materiały do studiów nad osadnictwem bnińskim. Poznań, 1975.
Arc 936.14.60 Materiały doznajomości kyltury złockiej. (Krzak, Zygmunt.) Wrocław, 1961.
Arc 936.165.15 Materialy i issledovanii po arkheologii i ethnografii Moldavskoi SSR. (Akademiia Nauk Moldavskoi SSSR, Kishinev Institut Istorii.) Kishinev, 1964.
Arc 925.255.5F Materialy i issledovaniia po arkheologii etnografii i istorii Krasnoiarskogo kraia. (Krasnoiarsk, Siberia (City). Kraevoi Kraevedcheskii Muzei.) Krasnoiarsk, 1963.
Arc 936.165.5 Materialy i issledovaniia po arkheologii Jugo-Zapada SSSR i Rumynskoi narodniki Respubliki. Kishinev, 1960.
Arc 302.49 Materiały i sprawozdania. (Rzeszowski Ośrodek Archeologiczny.) Rzeszów. 1964+
Arc 925.175.5 Materialy k arkheologicheskoi karte Mariiskoi ASSR. (Mariiskaia Arkheologicheskaia Ekspeditsiia, 1956-59.) Ioshkar-Ola, 1960.
Arc 936.250.5 Materialy k arkheologii kolkhidy. v.2. (Kuftin, Boris A.) Tbilisi, 1950.
Arc 925.215 Materialy k drevnei istorii Povetluzh'ia. (Khalikov, A.K.) Gor'kii, 1960.
Arc 925.9.65 Materia'ly no arkheologii abkhazii. Tbilisi, 1970.
Arc 925.15F Materialy po...Rossii. (Moskovskoe Arkheologicheskoe Obshchestvo.) Moskva, 1893- 2v.
Arc 925.150 Materialy po arkheologii BSSR. (Akademiia Nauk BSSR, Minsk. Institut Historyi.) Minsk, 1957.
Arc 287.7 Materialy po arkheologii Dagestana. Makhachkala. 1,1959+ 2v.
Arc 287.6 Materialy po arkheologii i drevnei istoriia Severnoi Osetii. Ordzhonikidze. 1,1961+
Arc 925.332.15 Materialy po arkheologii i etnografii Mordevii. Saransk, 1974.
Arc 925.14F Materialy po arkheologii Kavkaza. Moskva. 1-13,1888-1916 5v.
Arc 292.20F Materialy po arkheologii Rossii. (Russia. Arkheologicheskaia Kommissiia.) Petrograd. 3-37,1888-1918 24v.
Arc 925.13.90 Materialy po arkheologii Severnago Prichernomor'ia. Odessa. 2,1959
Arc 293.6 Materialy po arkheologii Sibiri i Dal'nego Vostoka. Novosibirsk. 1,1972+ 2v.
Arc 925.332F Materialy po istorii Mordvy VIII-IX vv. (Ivanov, Petr P.) Moskva, 1952.
Arc 925.18F Materialy po istorii russkikh odezhd. (Prokhorov, V.) Sankt Petersburg, 1881-85. 3v.
Arc 925.151 Materialy polevykh izsledovanii Dal'nevostochnoi arkheologicheskoi ekspeditsii. (Dal'nevostochnaia Arkheologicheskaia Ekspeditsiia.) Novosibirsk, 1970- 2v.
Arc 302.54 Materiały starożytne i wczesnośredniowieczne. Wrocław. 1,1971+ 2v.
Arc 936.11F Materiały wczesnośredniowieczne (1949). Warszawa. 1,1951+ 4v.
Arc 925.50.85 Materialy z antropolohii Ukraïny. Kyïv. 1960-1964 5v.
Arc 302.33 Materijali. (Arheološko Društvo Jugoslaviji.) Beograd. 3,1966+ 2v.
Arc 1494.9 Mateu y Llopis, Felipe. Glosario hispanico de numismatica. Barcelona, 1946.
Arc 1494.40 Mateu y Llopis, Felipe. El ius monetae en el condado de Ampurias. Perelada, 1957.
Arc 384.14 Mathematics in the archaeological and historical sciences; proceedings. (Anglo-Romanian Conference on Mathematics in the Archaeological and Historical Sciences.) Edinburgh, 1971.
Arc 543.142 Matheson, S. Time off to dig. London, 1961.
Arc 488.30 Matheson, Sylvia A. Persia; an archaeological guide. London, 1972.
Arc 1348.39 Mathews, George D. The coinages of the world. N.Y., 1876.
Arc 1540.31 Mathias, Peter. The English trade tokens. London, 1962.
Arc 895.41 Mathiassen, T. Studier over Vestjyllands oldtidsbebyggelse. København, 1948.
Arc 830.87 Mathieu, P.P. Le Puy deDome. Clermont-Ferrand, 1876.
Arc 461.2 Mathur, J.C. Homage to Vaisali. Vaisali, 1948.
Arc 608.76 Matière et art mobilier dans la préhistoire nord-africaine. Thèse. (Camps-Fabrer, Henriette.) Paris, 1966.
Arc 600.80F Matmar. (Brunton, Guy.) London, 1948.
Arc 1033.28.5 Il matrimonio cristiano sopra antico monumento. (Marucchi, O.) Roma, 1882.
Arc 384.5 Matson, Frederick R. Ceramics and man. Chicago, 1965.
Arc 925.35 Matsulevich, L.A. Pogrebenie varvarskogo kniazia v vostochnoi Evrope. Moskva, 1934.
Arc 1349.35F Matteo dei Pasti. (Calabi, A.) Milano, 1926.
Arc 858.92 A matter of time; an archaeological survey of the river gravels of England. (Great Britain. Commissions. Ancient and Historical Monuments and Constructions of England.) London, 1960-61.
Arc 853.63.7 Matthes, W. Die Germanen in der Prignitz zur Zeit der Völkerwanderung. Leipzig, 1931.
Arc 853.63 Matthes, W. Die nördlichen Elbgermanen in spätrömischer Zeit. Leipzig, 1931.
Arc 861.189F Matthews, C.L. Occupation sites on a Chiltern ridge. Oxford, 1976.
Arc 530.165 Matthiae, Paolo. Studi sui rilie vi di Karatepe. Roma, 1963.
Arc 746.2.9 Matthies, S. Die Praenestinischen Spiegel. Strassburg, 1912.
Arc 1478.24.13 Mattingly, Harold. The date of the Roman denarius. London, 1933.
Arc 1478.24.7 Mattingly, Harold. Roman coins from the earliest times to the fall of the Western Empire. London, 1928.
Arc 1478.24.7.2 Mattingly, Harold. Roman coins from the earliest times to the fall of the Western Empire. 2. ed. London, 1960.
Arc 1478.24 Mattingly, Harold. The Roman imperial coinage. v.1-9. London, 1923-38. 10v.
Arc 1478.24.15 Mattingly, Harold. Roman numismatics. London, 195-?
Arc 1480.54.5 Mattingly, Harold. Some new studies of the Roman republican coinage. London, 195-.
Arc 672.1.73 Matton, Raymond. La Crète antique. Athènes, 1955.
Arc 843.70 Mattos, A. de. Dois estudos: "Manis Pallas"; "Giral Cabrom". Porto, 1943.
Arc 672.1.67 Matz, F. Forschungen auf Kreta 1942. Berlin, 1951.
Arc 1251.25 Matz, F. Die frühkretischen Siegel. Berlin, 1928.
Arc 810.11.2 Mau, August. Fuehrer durch Pompeji. Naples, 1893.
Arc 810.11.3 Mau, August. Fuehrer durch Pompeji. 2. Aufl. Leipzig, 1896.
Arc 810.11.4 Mau, August. Fuehrer durch Pompeji. 3. Aufl. Leipzig, 1898.
Arc 810.11.4.5 Mau, August. Fuehrer durch Pompeji. 4e Aufl. Leipzig, 1903.
Arc 810.11.5 Mau, August. Fuehrer durch Pompeji. 6. Aufl. Leipzig, 1928.
Arc 810.11.8 Mau, August. Pompeii, its life and art. N.Y., 1899.
Arc 810.11.9 Mau, August. Pompeii, its life and art. N.Y., 1902.
Arc 810.11.10 Mau, August. Pompeii, its life and art. N.Y., 1907.
Arc 810.11.11 Mau, August. Pompeii, its life and art. Washington, D.C., 1973.
Arc 810.11 Mau, August. Pompejanische Beitraege. Berlin, 1879.
Arc 810.11.6 Mau, August. Pompeji in Leben und Kunst. Leipzig, 1900.
Arc 810.11.7 Mau, August. Pompeji in Leben und Kunst. 2. Aufl. Leipzig, 1908.
Arc 810.11.7.2 Mau, August. Pompeji in Leben und Kunst. 2. Aufl. Leipzig, 1913.
Arc 736.2.10F Mauceri, L. Il castello Eurialo. Syracuse. Roma, 1912.
Arc 825.12 Maucomble, Jean François Dieudonné. Description historique et abrégée des antiquités de Nismes. Nismes, 1789.
Arc 861.68 Maumbury Rings excavations. Interim report. (Gray, Harold St. George.) Dorchester, 1913.
Arc 820.215F Maupercher. Paris ancien, Paris moderne. Paris, 1814.
Arc 432.2A Maurice, G. Indian antiquities. London, 1800. 7v.
Arc 1480.15.1 Maurice, Jules. Numismatique constantinienne. Bruxelles, 1965. 3v.
Arc 1033.98 Mauro, G.D. Historia sacra. Roma, 1682.
Arc 767.10 Mauro, L. Le antichità della città di Roma. Venetia, 1562.
Arc 1033.34.39 Mauro di Polvica, Francesco di. Storia di San Pietro apostolo. Bologna, 1872.
Arc 705.211F Maurras, Charles. Athènes antique. Paris, 1918.
Arc 925.3 Maury, A. Des monuments de la Russie connus sous le nom de Tumulus Tchoudes. Paris, n.d.

Author and Title Listing

Arc 830.352 Maury, Jean. Les étapes du peuplement sur les grands causses des origines à l'époque gallo-romaine. Millau, 1967.
Arc 853.330 Mauser-Goller, Katharina. Die relative Chronologie des Neolithikums in Südwestdeutschland und der Schweiz. Diss. Basel, 1969.
Arc 726.185 Mausolei romani di Campania. (Franciscis, Alfonso de.) Napoli, 1957.
Arc 925.85 Maveolei neapole skifskogo. (Shul'ts, P.) Moskva, 1953.
Arc 1470.30 Mavrogordato, J. A chronological arrangement of the coins of Chios. pt.1-5. London, 1915-18.
Arc 1335.26 Max Ritter von Wilmersdörfferische Münzen-Sammlung. (Wilmersdörffer, M. von.) Frankfurt am Main, 1905-07. 2v.
Arc 1500.18 Maxe-Werly, L. Note sur l'origine du gros tournois. Paris, 1880.
Arc 1470.50 May, J.M.F. Ainos. London, 1950.
Arc 1470.43 May, J.M.F. The coinage of Damastion and the lesser coinages of the Illyra-Paeonian region. London, 1939.
Arc 861.70 May, Thomas. The Roman forts of Templeborough near Rotherham. Rotherham, 1922.
Arc 726.37F Maye, M. Apulien vor und während der Hellenisirung. Leipzig, 1914.
Arc 853.16 Mayer, Anton. Ein paar Worte über ein paar Drudenbäume. Eichstatt, 1826.
Arc 810.20 Mayer, E. von. Pompeji in seiner Kunst. Berlin, n.d.
Arc 1330.18 Mayer, Leo Ary. A bibliography of Jewish numismatics. Jerusalem, 1966.
Arc 1330.20 Mayer, Leo Ary. Bibliography of Moslem numismatics, India excepted. London, 1939.
Arc 1330.20.2 Mayer, Leo Ary. Bibliography of Moslem numismatics, India excepted. 2. ed. London, 1954.
Arc 720.215 Mayer, M. La coppa tarantina di argento dorato. Bari, 1910.
Arc 726.12.5 Mayer, M. Molfetta und Matera. Leipzig, 1924.
Arc 767.3 Mayerhoefer, A. Studien über das alte Rom. München, 1887.
Arc 505.107 Mayerson, Philip. The ancient agricultural regime of Nessana and the Central Negeb. London, 1961.
Arc 386.33 Mayes, Stanley. The great Belzoni. London, 1959.
Arc 1540.5 Mayo, J. Medals and decorations of the army and navy. Westminster, 1897. 2v.
Arc 915.5 Mayor, J. Fragments d'archeologie genevoise. Genève, 1892.
Arc 1490.7 Mayr, A. Die antiken Münzen...Malta. München, 1895.
Arc 1190.65.10 Mazal, Otto. Die Prooimien der byzantinischen Patriarchenurkunden. Wien, 1974.
Arc 505.147.1 Mazar, Benjamin. The excavations in the old city of Jerusalem near the Temple Mount. Jerusalem, 1971.
Arc 1448.5 Mazard, Jean. Corpus nummorum Nunudiae nauretaniaeque. Paris, 1955.
Arc 1670.50F Mazerolle, Fernand. Claude de Héry, médailleur du roi Henri III. Paris, 18- ?
Arc 925.325.5 Mazhitov, Niiaz A. Bakhmutinskaia kul'tura. Moskva, 1968.
Arc 1018.11 Mazochuis, A.S. Mélanges de litterature et d'histoire religieuses. Paris, 1899. 3v.
Arc 785.11 Mazois, F. Le palais de Scaurus. Paris, 1822.
Arc 785.11.4 Mazois, F. Le palais de Scaurus. 4. éd. Paris, 1869.
Arc 785.11.5 Mazois, F. Il palazzo di Scauro. 2. ed. Milano, 1825.
Arc 936.14.435 Mazowsze na przełomie er. (Nieweglowski, Andrej.) Wrocław, 1972.
Htn Arc 726.55* Mazzella, S. Sito, et antichita della città di Pozzuolo e del sus amenissimo distretto. Napoli, 1606.
Arc 1020.9.5 Mazzolari, G.M. Diario sacro. 2. ed. Roma, 1805-06. 4v.
Arc 1020.9 Mazzolari, G.M. Diario sacro le sacre vie, le sacre basilicho. Roma, 1779-81. 5v.
Arc 1153.108F Mazzoleni, Jole. Esempi di scritture cancelleresche. Napoli, 1972.
Arc 1153.95 Mazzoleni, Jole. Lezioni di paleografia latina e diplomatica. Napoli, 1964?
Arc 1153.95.1 Mazzoleni, Jole. Paleografia e diplomatica e scienze ausiliarie. Napoli, 1970.
Arc 1033.55.7 Mazzucconi, L. Memorie storiche della scala santa...di Sancto Sanctorum. Roma, 1840.
Arc 1675.49F Mazzuchelli, G.M. Museum Mazzuchellianum. Venetiis, 1761-63. 2v.
Arc 1675.49.5F Mazzuchelli, G.M. Museum Mazzuchellianum. Venetiis, 1761-63. 2v.
Arc 1458.23 The McGill University collection of Greek and Roman coins. v.1-2. (McGill University, Montreal.) Amsterdam, 1975-
Htn Arc 1335.12* Mead, R. Museum Meadianum. London, n.d.
Htn Arc 1335.12.2* Mead, R. Museum Meadianum. London, n.d.
Htn Arc 1428.9* Mead, Richard. Oratio dissertio de nummis...a Symrnaeis. Londoni, 1724.
Htn Arc 1428.9.2* Mead, Richard. Oratio dissertio de nummis...a Symrnaeis. Londoni, 1724.
Arc 858.59.50 Meaney, A. A gazetteer of early Anglo-Saxon burial sites. London, 1964.
Arc 608.64 Meanié, Djinn. Cités anciennes de Mauritanie. Paris, 1961.
Arc 861.196 Meany, Audrey. Two Anglo-Saxon cemeteries at Winnall, Winchester, Hampshire. London, 1970.
Arc 861.169F The Meare Lake village. v.1,3. (Bulleid, Arthur.) Taunton, 1948- 2v.
Arc 861.147 Meates, Geoffrey W. Lullingstone Roman villa. London, 1955.
Arc 843.61 Meca. (Zuazo y Palacios, J.) Madrid, 1916.
Arc 1027.12.13 Mecchi, F.E. La tomba di San Pietro. Roma, 1893.
Arc 505.116 Mécérian, Jean. Expedition archéologique dans l'Antiochène occidentale. Beyrouth, 1965.
Arc 746.61 Med kungen på Acquarossa. (Wetter, Erik.) Malmö, 1972.
Arc 1663.28 Medaglie coniate in onore del generale Giuseppe Garibaldi. (Camozzi Vertova, G.) Bergamo, 1885.
Arc 1663.28.2 Medaglie coniate in onore del generale Giuseppe Garibaldi. (Camozzi Vertova, G.) Bergamo, 1885.
Arc 1663.16 Medaglie del Regno delle due Sicilie 1735-1861. (Ricciardi, E.) Napoli, 1900.
Arc 1663.16.5F Medaglie del Regno delle due Sicilie 1735-1861. 2. ed. (Ricciardi, E.) Napoli, 1930.
Arc 1675.99 Le medaglie di Leone XII, 1823-1829. (Patrignani, Antonio.) Catania, 1938.
Arc 1490.90 Le medaglie di Pio VII, 1829-1830. (Patrignani, Antonio.) Catania, 1933.
Arc 1475.10 Medagliere II. Monete Romane. pt.1-2. (Naples. Museo Nazionale.) Naples, 1870-71. 3v.
Arc 1478.15.10 I medaglioni romani. (Gnecchi, F.) Bologna, 1968. 3v.
Arc 1675.86 Medaile na přátelstir a při buzné památky. (Katz, Viktor.) Praha, 1938.
Arc 1500.13 La médaille d'argent de Fauquembergue...dame au faucon. (Blancard, Louis.) Marseille, 1883.
Arc 1675.19.10F Medaillen auf die Thaten Peter des Grossen. (Iversen, I.) St. Petersburg, 1872.
Arc 1675.11 Medaillen auf Privat-Personen. (Rosenberg, S.) Frankfurt, n.d.
Arc 1675.70 Medaillen badischer Klöster. (Günzburger, Julius.) Nürnberg, 1930.
Arc 1663.15 Die Medaillen und Gedachtniszeichen der deutschen Hochschulen. (Laverrenz, C.) Berlin, 1887. 2v.
Arc 1510.23.5 Die Medaillen und Münzen der Wild- und Rheingrafen Fürsten zu Salm. (Joseph, Paul.) Frankfurt am Main, 1914.
Arc 1510.1.5 Medaillen und Münzen des Gesammthauses Wittelsbach. v.1, pt.1-2. (Munich.) München, 1897. 2v.
Arc 1663.21 Medaillen und Münzen im Dienste der Religion. (Müller, Bernhard.) Berlin, 1915.
Arc 1675.13 Medaillen und Plaketten. (Bernhart, M.) Berlin, 1911.
Arc 1663.6 Les médailles de la Princesse Charlotte d'Angleterre. (Storer, H.R.) Bruxelles, 1888-91. 2 pam.
Arc 1675.15 Médailles de rois Perses de la Dynastie Sassanide. (Longpérier, A. de.) Paris, 1840.
Arc 1675.63 Les médailles décerniés aux Indien. (Morin, Victor.) Ottawa, 1916.
Htn Arc 1660.6* Médailles du règne de Louis XV. (Fleurimont, G.R.) n.p., n.d.
Arc 1670.4 Médailles et jetons des numismates. (Durand, Anthony.) Genève, 1865.
Arc 1522.3 Médailles et jetons du pays de Luxembourg. (Harpes, Jean.) Luxembourg, 1955.
Arc 1670.6F Les médailles et plaquettes modernes. v.1-6. (Hague. Koninklijk Kabinet van Munten.) Haarlem, 1899-1900.
Arc 1470.28.5 Médailles grecques autonomes. (Bompois, H.F.) Paris, 1869.
Arc 1665.4F Les medailles historique...Napoléon le Grand. (Babelon, Ernest.) Paris, 1912.
Arc 1588.10 Medailles hongroises aux XIXe et XXe siècles. (Budapest. Magyor Eremmuveszet Nemzeti Galeria.) Budapest, 1959.
Arc 1500.60F Médailles lyonnaises du XVe au XVIIIe siècle. (Tricou, Jean.) Paris, 1958.
Arc 1470.28 Les médailles restitutées par M.F. Lenormant à Lyncus ou Héraclée de Lyncestide. (Bompois, H.F.) Paris, 1867-76. 3 pam.
Arc 1675.9 Les médailles romaines de Christine de Suède. (Bildt.) Rome, 1908.
Htn Arc 1660.5.2* Médailles sur les principaux evenements du règne de Louis le Grand. (France. Institut.) Baden, 1705.
Arc 1675.51.10 Le médailleur de Pologne. (Raczynski, E.) Berlin, 1845. 4v.
Arc 1675.4 Les médailleurs de la Renaissance. (Robert, Charles.) Paris, 1882.
Arc 1670.1 Les médailleurs de la Renaissance. v.3,8. (Heiss, A.) Paris, 1883. 2v.
Arc 1675.12 Les médailleurs et l. graveurs de monnaies. (Rondot, N.) Paris, 1904.
Arc 1495.1 Les médailleurs français contemporains. (Marx, R.) Paris, 1898.
Arc 1675.2 Les médailleurs italiens. (Armand, A.) Paris, 1879.
Arc 1675.3 Les médailleurs italiens. v.1-2. 2. éd. (Armand, A.) Paris, 1883.
X Cg Arc 1675.29 Les medailleurs modernes, 1789-1900. (Marx, Roger.) Paris, 190-.
Arc 1335.46 Médaillier de la Société archéologique de Montpellier. (Bonnet, Emile.) Montpellier, 1896.
X Cg Arc 1603.4 Le médaillier du Canada. (Lerouv, J.) Montreal, 1888.
Arc 830.186 Les médaillons d'applique gallo-romain. (Wuilleumier, P.) Paris, 1952.
Arc 1675.23 Les medaillons de l'Empire romain depuis le règne d'Auguste jusqu'à Priscus Attale. (Froehner, Vilhelm.) Paris, 1878.
Arc 1663.15.10 Medale Piastów Śląskich. Wyd. 1. (Więcek, Adam.) Warszawa, 1958.
Arc 1663.60 Medale polskie. (Gumowski, Marian.) Warszawa, 1925.
Arc 1663.62 Medale polskie XVI-XX w. (Wojtulewicz, Henryk.) Lublin, 1968.
Arc 1663.61 Medale Tagiellonów. (Gumowski, Marian.) Kraków, 1906.
Arc 1663.63 Medale Zygmunta III. (Gumowski, Marian.) Kraków, 1924.
Arc 1663.23 A medalha de Casimiro José de Lima em homenagem a Sousa Martins. (Cunha, Xavier.) Coimbra, 1903.
Arc 1663.24 A medalha escolar do coll. do Corpo-Santo noticia numismatic. (Cunha, Xavier.) Coimbra, 1907.
Arc 1493.11 Medalhas portuguesas e estrangeiras referentes a Portugal. (Lamas, Arthur.) Lisboa, 1916.
Arc 1663.64 Medalionej polskie. (Jaworski, Franciszek.) Lwow, 1911.
Arc 1675.94 Medalja u hrvatskoj. (Respublička Izložba Hrvatskih Medalja i Plaketa. 1st, Zagreb, 1964-65.) Zagreb, 1964?
Arc 1660.13 Las medallas chilenas. (Medina, J.T.) Santiago, 1601.
Arc 1643.1.5 Medallas coloniales hispano-americanas. (Medina, J.T.) Santiago, 1900.
Arc 1663.18 Medallas de la casa de Borbón. (Madrid. Real Biblioteca.) Madrid, 1916.
Htn Arc 1675.26* Medallas de la colonias, municipios y pueblos antiguos de España. (Florez, Enrique.) Madrid, 1757-73. 3v.
Arc 1540.24F Las medallas del almirante Vernon. (Medina, J.T.) Santiago, 1919.
Arc 1660.2 The medallic history of England. (Pinkerton, J.) London, 1790.
Arc 1540.1 The medallic history of M.A.V. Carausins. (Stukeley, W.) London, 1757-89.
Arc 1660.1 The medallic history of the United States of America, 1776-1876. Text and plates. (Loubat, J.F.) N.Y., 1878. 2v.
Arc 1660.9 Medallic illustrations. History of Great Britain and Ireland. v.1-50,101-120. London, 1904. 7v.
Arc 1663.3 Medallic illustrations of the history of Great Britain and Ireland. (Hawkins, E.) London, 1885. 2v.
Arc 1663.19 Medallos de los gobernadores. (Herrera y Chiesanova, A.) Madrid, 1901.
Arc 1675.24 Medals, clasps, and crosses, military and naval in the collection of J.W. Fleming. (Fleming, J.W.) Brighton, 1871.
Htn Arc 1273.2F* Medals, coins, great seals, impressions from the elaborate works of Thomas Simon. (Vertue, G.) London, 1753.
Arc 1675.17.5 Medals, jetons and tokens illustrative of obstetrics and gynaecology. (Storer, H.R.) Bridgeport, Conn., 1887.
Arc 1540.5 Medals and decorations of the army and navy. (Mayo, J.) Westminster, 1897. 2v.
Arc 1453.3 Medals and plaquettes from the S. Morgenroth collection. (Morgenroth, Sigmund.) Chicago, 1944.

Author and Title Listing

Arc 1675.17 Medals and tokens of Rhode Island. (Storer, H.R.) Boston, 1895.
Arc 1675.1 Medals by Giovanni Carino. (Lawrence, R.H.) N.Y., 1883.
Arc 1663.5 Medals commemorative of the visit of H.R.H. the Prince of Wales to Montreal. (Sandham, Alfred.) Montreal, 1871.
Arc 1490.85 The medals of Pope Sixtus IV, 1471-1484. (Weiss, Roberto.) Rome, 1961.
Arc 1480.6 Medals of the Caesars. n.p., n.d.
Arc 1660.16F Medals of the renaissance. (Hill, George F.) Oxford, 1920.
Arc 1615.4.10 Medals of the United States Mint. (United States Mint.) Washington, 1969.
Arc 1615.4.11 Medals of the United States Mint. (United States Mint.) Washington, 1972.
Arc 1675.96F Medals relating to medicine and allied sciences in the numismatic collection. (Johns Hopkins University.) Baltimore, 1964.
Arc 1660.14F Medals struck by the corporation of London. (Welch, Charles.) London, 1894.
Arc 823.19.50 Les médecins Magillius et D. Gallius Sextus. (Thédenat, H.) Paris, 1880.
Arc 52.2 Mededeelingen en verhandelingen. (Vooraziatisch-Egyptische Gezelschap "Ex Oriente Lux".) Leiden. 1,1934+ 4v.
Arc 42.25 Medelhavsmuseet. Bulletin. Stockholm. 2,1962+
Arc 895.38F Den medeltida borgen i Skanör. (Rydbeck, Otto.) Lund, 1935.
Arc 488.24 The Medes and Persians. (Culican, William.) London, 1965.
Arc 137.5 Mediaeval archaeology. London. 1,1957+ 9v.
Arc 137.6 Mediaeval archaeology. Index. v.1-5, (1957-61). London, n.d.
Arc 861.202 The mediaeval pottery of Shropshire from the conquest to 1400. (Barker, P.A.) Shropshire, 1970.
Arc 609.1.17F Mediaeval Rhodesia. (Maciver, D.R.) London, 1906.
Arc 1675.17.10 Medicina in nummis. (Storer, H.R.) Boston, 1931.
Arc 1166.6 Medieval parchment-making. (Thompson, D.V.) London, 1935.
Arc 612.77 Medieval pottery from excavations. London, 1974.
Arc 1645.3 Medina, J.T. Manual ilustrado de numismatica chilena. Santiago, 1919.
Arc 1660.13 Medina, J.T. Las medallas chilenas. Santiago, 1601.
Arc 1643.1.5 Medina, J.T. Medallas coloniales hispano-americanas. Santiago, 1900.
Arc 1540.24F Medina, J.T. Las medallas del almirante Vernon. Santiago, 1919.
Arc 1640.5 Medina, J.T. Las monedas chilenas. Santiago, 1902.
Arc 1645.3.5F Medina, J.T. Las monedas coloniales de Chile. Santiago, 1919. 2 pam.
Arc 1643.1.10F Medina, J.T. Las monedas coloniales hispano-americanas. Santiago, 1919.
Arc 1643.1.15F Medina, J.T. Las monedas obsidionales hispano-americanas. Santiago, 1919.
Arc 1643.1 Medina, J.T. Monedas y medallas hispano-americanas. Santiago, 1891.
Arc 1494.15 Medina Zahira. (Castejan, R.) Cordoba, 1924.
Arc 612.40 Il mediterraneo. (Laviosa, Zambotti.) Torino, 1954.
Arc 406.1 Il Mediterraneo illustrato. (Vecchi, M.M.) Firenze, 1841.
Arc 588.3 Medum. (Petrie, W.M.F.) London, 1892.
Arc 87.2.74 Medusenhaupt von Blariacum. (Gaedechens, R.) Bonn, 1874.
Arc 505.4.8 Meerfahrt nach Tyrus zur Ausgrabung der Kathedrale mit Barbarossa's Grab. (Sepp, J.N.) Leipzig, 1879.
Arc 915.30 Les megálithes de la Suisse. (Spahni, Jean Christian.) Basel, 1950.
Arc 543.5.25 Mégalithes du Haut-Laos. (Colani, M.) Paris, 1935. 2v.
Arc 895.56.6 Die Megalithgräber von Hagestad. (Strömberg, Märta.) Lund, 1971.
Arc 543.32 The megalithic culture of Indonesia. (Perry, William J.) Manchester, 1918.
Arc 858.94 Megalithic enquiries in the West of Britain: a Liverpool symposium. Liverpool, 1969.
Arc 858.84 Megalithic sites in Britain. (Thom, Alexander.) Oxford, 1967.
Arc 543.40F Megalithische oudheden in Zuid-Sumatra. Proefschrift. (Thomassen à Thuessink van der Hoop, A.N.J.) Zutphen, 1932.
Arc 853.9 Die megalithischen Gräber...Deutschlands. (Krause E.) Berlin, 1893.
Arc 736.22 Megara Hyblaca. v.2,4. Text and atlas. (Vallet, Georges.) Paris, 1964- 4v.
Arc 505.61F Megiddo I. (Lamon, R.S.) Chicago, 1939.
Arc 505.61.10F Megiddo II. (Chicago. Oriental Institute. Megiddo Expedition.) Chicago, 1948. 2v.
Arc 505.61.5 Megiddo tombs. (Guy, P.L.O.) Chicago, 1938.
Arc 853.25 Mehlis, C. Studien zur ältesten Geschichte der Rheinlands. v.1-9. Leipzig, 1875-1886. 2v.
Arc 1312.4 Mehl's numismatic monthly. Fort Worth, Texas.
Arc 853.85 Meier-Böke, A. Die frühe Altsteinzeit am der Weser. Leipzig, 1940.
Arc 595.26 Meier-Graefe, J. Pyramid and temple. London, 1931.
Arc 1640.7F Meili, Julius. Die auf das Kaiserreich Brasilien...1822 bis 1889. Zürich, 1890.
Arc 1645.1.15 Meili, Julius. Das brasilianische Geldwesen. Zürich, 1897-1905. 2v.
Arc 1645.1.5 Meili, Julius. Die Münzen der Colonie Brasilien, 1645-1822. Zürich, 1895.
Arc 1645.1.7 Meili, Julius. Die Münzen des Kaiserreichs Brasilien, 1822-1889. Leipzig, 1890.
Arc 1675.35 Meili, Julius. Die Werke des Medailleur's Hans Frei in Basel, 1894-1906. Zürich, 1906.
Arc 1349.60F Mein Leben und Streben. (Hujer, L.) Wien, 1954.
Arc 556.4 Meine Begegnung mit einigen Agyptologen. (Grapow, Hermann.) Berlin, 1973.
Arc 885.10 The Meini Hirion and Sarns of Anglesey. (Evans, William.) Llangefni, 1927.
Arc 1190.35 Meisner, H.O. Aktenkunde. Berlin, 1935.
Arc 1190.35.5 Meisner, H.O. Urkunden- und Aktenlehre der Neuzeit. Leipzig, 1950.
Arc 1190.35.7 Meisner, H.O. Urkunden- und Aktenlehre der Neuzeit. 2. Aufl. Leipzig, 1952.
Arc 520.14F Die Meister des grossen Frieses von Pergamon. (Schuchhardt, W.H.) Berlin, 1925.
Arc 505.25.5 Meistermann, B. La ville de David. Paris, 1905.
Arc 505.35 Meistermann, Barnabé. Capharnaüm et Bethsaïde, suivi d'une étude sur l'âge de la synagogue de Tell Houm. Paris, 1921.
Arc 505.31 Meistermann, Barnabé. Questions de topographie palestinienne. Jerusalem, 1903.
Arc 1433.99 Mejopotamya silindir muhurlerinder hurri mitanni usulü. (Tosun, Mebrure.) Ankara, 1956.
Arc 861.4.5 Melandra Castle. (Classical Association.) Manchester, 1906.
Arc 1370.4.3 Mélange de diverses médailles. (Pellerin, J.) Paris, 1765. 2v.
Arc 1076.3.38 Mélanges. (Berthele, J.) Montpellier, 1906.
Arc 82.1.3 Mélanges. Antiquité. (Rome, Italy. École Française.) Rome. 83,1971+
Arc 407.7 Mélanges archéologiques. (Werveke, N. van.) Luxembourg, 1882.
Arc 397.10 Mélanges d'archéologie; antiquité romaine et moyen âge. (Mortel, Victor.) Paris, 1914-15. 2v.
Arc 383.9 Mélanges d'archéologie, d'histoire, et d'histoire de l'art, offerts à Louis Bosset. Lausanne, 1950.
Arc 830.146 Mélangés d'archéologie. (Bottin, S.) Paris, 1831.
Arc 402.7 Mélanges d'archéologie. (Robert, Charles.) Paris, 1875.
Arc 830.1.7 Mélanges d'archéologie bretonne. Série I. (Grand, Roger.) Nantes, 1921.
Arc 401.1.2 Mélanges d'archéologie du Moyen Age. (Quicherat, Jules.) Paris, 1886.
Arc 562.4 Mélanges d'archéologie égyptienne et assyrienne. v.1-3. Paris, 1873-78.
Arc 388.4 Mélanges d'archéologie et d'épigraphie. (Dumont, A.) Paris, 1892.
Arc 936.1 Mélanges d'archéologie et d'epigraphie byzantines. (Tafrali, O.) Paris, 1913.
Arc 383.70 Mélanges d'archéologie et d'histoire. (Chevallier, Raymond.) Paris, 1966. 3v.
Arc 401.1 Mélanges d'archéologie et d'histoire. (Quicherat, Jules.) Paris, 1885.
Arc 82.1 Mélanges d'archéologie et d'histoire. (Rome, Italy. École Française.) Paris. 1-82,1881-1970// 81v.
Arc 82.1.2 Mélanges d'archéologie et d'histoire. Tables des tomes 58-72, 1941-60. (Rome, Italy. École Française.) Paris, n.d.
Arc 823.2 Mélanges d'archéologie gallo-romaine. fasc.1-2. (Blanchet, J.A.) Paris, 1893. 2v.
Arc 822.9 Pamphlet vol. Mélanges d'archéologie nationale. 9 pam.
Arc 1018.11 Mélanges de litterature et d'histoire religieuses. (Mazochuis, A.S.) Paris, 1899. 3v.
Arc 1390.7 Mélanges de numismatique et d'histoire. (Marchant, N.D.) Paris, 1818.
Arc 1500.64 Melanges de numismatique merovingienne. (Le Gentilhomme, P.) Paris, 1940.
Arc 383.53 Mélanges en hommage à la mémoire de Fr. Martroye. (Société Nationale des Antiquaires de France.) Paris, 1940.
Arc 1027.25.24 Melanges G.B. Rossi. (Rossi, G.B. de.) Paris, 1892.
Arc 652.3 Mélanges Holleaux - recueil de memoires concernant l'antiquité grecque offert à Maurice Holleaux. Paris, 1913.
Arc 398.3 Mélanges Nicole...recueil de mémoires. (Nicole, J.) Genève, 1905.
Arc 1312.1 Melanges numismatique. (Liverpool Numismatic Society.) Le Mens. 1-3,1874-1882 3v.
Arc 1348.19 Mélanges numismatiques. (Babelon, E.) Paris, 1892-1912. 5v.
Arc 1150.1.9 Mélanges offert à M. Émile Chatelain. Paris, 1910.
Arc 383.55.5 Mélanges offerts à Kazimierz Michałowski. Warszawa, 1966.
Arc 628.18 Melanges Perrot; recueil de memoires. Paris, 1903.
Arc 537.11 Melbourne. University. Cyprus Expedition. Publication. 1-2,1957-1964// 2v.
Arc 838.9.10 Mélida, José R. Arqueológica española. 2. ed. Barcelona, 1942.
Arc 843.73.5F Mélida, José R. El disco de Teodosio. Madrid, 1930.
Arc 843.73 Mélida, José R. Les fouilles de Merida. n.p., 19- ?
Arc 838.9 Mélida, José R. Iberia arqueológica ante-romana, discursos. Madrid, 1906.
Arc 843.74 Mélida, José R. El teatro de Mérida. Madrid, 1915.
Arc 682.40 Melische amphoren. (Papastamos, Dēmētrios.) Münster, 1970.
Arc 936.252 Melitauri, Konstantin N. Kreposti dofeodal'noi i rannefeodal'noi Gruzii. Tbilisi, 1969- 2v.
Arc 513.32A Mellaart, James. The Chaleolithic and early Bronze Ages in the Near East and Anatolia. Beirut, 1966.
Arc 416.36 Mellaart, James. Earliest civilizations of the Near East. N.Y., 1965.
Arc 416.20 Mellaart, James. The Neolithic of the Near East. London, 1975.
Arc 1578.1 Melle, Jakob von. Sylloge nummorum ex arg. uncialium. v.1-3. Lubeck, 1697-98.
Arc 1578.2 Melle, Jakob von. Sylloge nummorum ex arg. uncialium. v.1-3. Lubeck, 1698-99.
Arc 397.24 Mellersh, Harold Edward Leslie. Archaeology: science and romance. Exeter, 1966.
Arc 488.20 Mellink, M.J. Dark ages and nomads c.1000 B.C. Istanbul, 1964.
Arc 1279.5 Melly, Edward. Beiträge zur Siegelkunde des Mittelalters. Wien, 1850. 2v.
Arc 1279.5F Melly, Edward. Beiträge zur Siegelkunde des Mittelalters. Supplement. Wien, 1850.
Arc 925.150.15 Mel'nikovskaia, Ol'ga N. Plemena Iuzhnoi Belorussii v rannem zheleznom veke. Moskva, 1967.
Arc 1033.17.181 Mély, F. de. Chemises de la Vierge. Chartres, n.d.
Arc 1020.52.9 Mély, F. de. Les inventaires de l'Abbaye Saint Pére en Vallés de Chartres. Paris, 1887.
Arc 1033.31 Mély, F. de. Le Saint Suaire de Turin. Paris, 1902?
Arc 1020.52 Mély, F. de. Le trésor de Chartres. Paris, 1886.
Arc 1300.2 Membership list. (American Numismatic Society.) N.Y. 1930
Arc 42.1 Memnon, Zeitschrift für den Kunst...alten Orients. Leipzig. 1-7 3v.
Arc 855.11 Memoir...survey of eastern branch of Watling Street. (MacLauchlan, H.) London, 1864. 2v.
Arc 870.15.5 Memoir written during a survey of the Watling Street. (MacLauchlan, H.) London, 1852.
Arc 830.82.5 Mémoire archéologique sur les découvertes d'Herbord dites de Sanxay. (La Croix, C. de.) Niort, 1883.
Arc 1033.65.5 Memoire del titolo di Fasciola. (Lais, G.) Roma, 1880.
Arc 505.18 Memoire sur...maçonnerii...du Haram-Ech-Cherif de Jerusalem. (Saulcy.) Paris, 1866.
Arc 820.212.5F Mémoire sur guelques antiquités...des Vosges. (Jollois, J.B.P.) Paris, 1843.
Arc 830.80 Mémoire sur la question des voies romaines. (Gregoire d'Essigny, L.A.J.) Paris, 1811. 2 pam.
Arc 800.13 Mémoire sur la ville. Paris, 1748. 3 pam.
Arc 600.5.2 Mémoire sur le Lac Moeris. (Bellefonds, L. de.) Alexandrie, 1843.

Author and Title Listing

Arc 1153.1.5 Mémoire sur l'école calligraphique de Tours au IXe siècle. (Delisle, L.) Paris, 1885.

Arc 830.67.10 Mémoire sur l'enceinte gallo-romaine de Poitiers. (Brouillet, A.) Poitiers, 1872.

Arc 1500.6 Mémoire sur les anciennes monnaies seigneuriales. (Germain, A.) Montpellier, 1852.

Arc 820.212F Mémoire sur les antiquités du départment du Loiret. (Jollois, J.B.P.) Paris, 1836.

Arc 820.205 Mémoire sur les bronzes antiques. (Mantellier, P.) Paris, 1865.

Arc 785.25 Mémoire sur les fouilles exécutées à Santa Sabina. 1855-1857

Arc 1033.12.53F Memoire sur les instruments de la Passion. (Rohault de Fleury, C.) Paris, 1870.

Arc 1480.23 Mémoire sur les médailles de Marinus. (Tochon D'Annecy, J.F.) Paris, 1817.

Arc 505.16 Mémoire sur les ruines de Séleucie de Piérie. (Bourquenond, A.) Paris, 1860.

Arc 830.85 Mémoire sur les ruines du Vieil-Évreux. (Rever, Marie F.) Évreux, 1827.

Arc 830.5.3 Mémoire sur les voies romaines de la Savoie. (Ducis, Claude A.) Annecy, 1863.

Arc 1663.20 Mémoire sur les voyages de...Hadrien et sur les médailles. (Greppo, J.G.H.) Paris, 1842.

Arc 830.145 Mémoire sur quelques antiquités du diocese de Bayeux. (Lebeuf, Jean.) n.p., 1747.

Arc 488.9F Mémoires. (France. Délégation Archéologique en Iran.) Paris. 1,1900+ 35v.

Arc 543.12F Mémoires. (France. Délégation Archéologique Française en Afghanistan.) Paris. 1-19 14v.

Arc 580.1 Mémoires. (France. Mission Archéologique Française au Caire.) Paris. 1-31,1889-1934 25v.

Arc 38.5F Mémoires. (Institut Français d'Archéologie de Stamboul.) Paris. 2-7 6v.

Arc 580.1.2 Mémoires. (Institut Français d'Archéologie Orientale du Caire.) Le Caire. 1,1902+ 92v.

Arc 293.1 Mémoires. (Russkoe Arkheologicheskoe Obshchestvo, Leningrad.) St. Pétersbourg. 1-6,1847-1852 6v.

Arc 100.1 Mémoires. (Société Nationale des Antiquaires de France.) Paris. 1-9 86v.

Arc 584.100.10 Mémoires. (Société Royale d'Archéologie d'Alexandrie.) Le Caire. 1-8,1922-1936 4v.

Arc 822.8 Pamphlet vol. Mémoires archéologiques. 13 pam.

Arc 34.2F Mémoires archéologiques. (École Française d'Extreme Orient, Hanoi, Indo-China.) Paris. 1926-1932 10v.

Arc 400.2 Mémoires d'archéologie. (Perrot, G.) Paris, 1875.

Arc 943.10.1 Mémoires d'archéologie et d'ethnographié americaines. (Hamy, Jules.) Graz, 1971.

Arc 113.3 Mémoires de la Société archéologique du midi de la France. (France.) Toulouse. 1-24 21v.

Arc 113.3.5 Mémoires de la Société archéologique du midi de la France. Tables générales. (France.) Toulouse. 1831-1871

Arc 113.3.7 Memoires de la Société archéologique du midi de la France. Tables générales. 1.-2. séries. (France.) Toulouse.

Arc 247.4 Mémoires de la Société Royale des Antiquaires du Nord. (Nordiske Oldskrift-Selskab.) Copenhagen. 1836-1933 15v.

Arc 247.4.2 Mémoires de la Société Royale des Antiquaires du Nord (1840-44). (Copenhagen.) Copenhagen, n.d.

Arc 95.1 Mémoires de l'Académie Celtique. Paris. 1-5,1807-1810 5v.

Arc 1348.23 Mémoires et notes de numismatique. (Blanchet, A.) Paris, 1909.

Arc 823.7.5 Mémoires géographiques sur quelques antiquités de la Gaule. (Pasumot, Francois.) Paris, 1765. 2 pam.

Arc 113.2 Mémoires lus à la Sorbonne. Archéologie, 1861, 63-68. (France.) Paris, 1863-69. 7v.

Arc 590.8F Mémoires présentés à l'Institut Égyptien. (Smith, G. Elliot.) Le Caire, 1906.

Arc 712.5 Mémoires sur des ouvrages de sculpture du Parthénon. (Visconti, E.Q.) Paris, 1818.

Arc 830.129 Mémoires sur diverses antiquités du département de la Drôme. (Chalieu, Alexis.) Valence, 1811.

Arc 1053.13 Mémoires sur la chronologie et l'iconographie des rois parthes arsacides. (Longpérier, A. de.) Paris, 1853-82.

Arc 386.9 Mémoires sur l'antiquité. (Burnouf, E.) Paris, 1879.

Arc 830.72 Mémoires sur les ruines de Lillebonne. (Reser, François.) Evreux, 1821.

Arc 1.13.5F Memoirs. (American Academy, Rome.) Bergamo. 1,1917+ 26v.

Arc 435.70.5F Memoirs. (Ceylon. Archaeological Survey.) Colombo. 1-6,1924-1953 7v.

Arc 320.2.5 Memoirs. (Harvard University. Peabody Museum.) Cambridge. 1-12 12v.

Arc 435.1.15F Memoirs. (India. Archaeological Survey.) Calcutta. 1-73,1919-1955 14v.

Arc 435.85 Memoirs. (Kashmir. Archaeological Survey.) Mysore City. 1-2 2v.

Arc 800.14 Memoirs concerning Herculaneum. (Fordyce, W.) London, 1750.

Arc 950.207 Memoirs of explorations...basin...Mississippi. v.1-3,4-5,6-7,8. (Brower, J.V.) St. Paul, Minn., 1898. 7v.

Arc 446.12 Memoirs of Gaur and Pandua. (Abid Ali Khan, M.) Calcutta, 1931.

Arc 500.4 Memoirs of the topography. (Conder, C.R.) London, 1881-83. 3v.

Arc 500.5 Memoirs of the topography. (Conder, C.R.) London, 1889.

Arc 885.13 Memoirs on remains of ancient dwellings in Holyhead Island. (Stanley, W.O.) London, 1871.

Arc 407.1 Memoirs relating to European and Asiatic Turkey. (Walpole, R.) London, 1817-20. 2v.

Arc 1033.12.121 Memorabilium...specimen sive de festo lanceae et clavorum. (Seelen, I.H.) Flensburgi, 1715.

Arc 451.1F A memorandum of suggestions for use of contributors to the Loan Collection Department of the Exhibit. (Lucknow Exhibit.) Lucknow, 1885.

Arc 435.12.4F Memorandum on the survey of architecture and other archaeological remians...Sindh, Berar. (Burgess, James.) Bombay, 1870. 2 pam.

Arc 505.5.100F Memorandum on the Western Wall. (Adler, Cyrus.) Jerusalem, 1930.

Arc 94.5 Memoria. (Spain. Junta Superior de Excavaciones y Antiguedades.) Madrid, 1915-1926. 7v.

Arc 1027.88F La memoria apostolorum in catacombas. (Prandi, A.) Città del Vaticano, 1936.

Arc 843.17 Memoria da antiquidades de Mertola. (Estacio da Veiga, S.P.M.) Lisboa, 1880.

Arc 1675.31 Memoria das medallias e condecorações port. (Lopes Fernandes, Manuel Bernardo.) Lisboa, 1861.

Arc 1493.5 Memoria das moedas correntes em Portugal. (Lopes Fernandes, M.B.) Lisboa, 1856.

Arc 843.208 Memoria de la excavación de la Mezquita de Medinat al-Zahra. (Pavón Maldonado, Basilio.) Madrid, 1966.

Arc 1027.5.18 La memoria dei santi...cimitero di Domitilla. (Marucchi, O.) n.p., n.d.

Arc 1033.12.184 Memoria intorno la corona di ferro longobardo. (Bianconi, A.) Milano, 1860.

Arc 843.135 Memoria relativa a los nuevos descubrimientos de la antigua Lucantum, 1892. (Rico García, Manuel.) Aicante, 1958.

Arc 843.16 Memoria sobre las notables escavaciones hechas en el Cerrode los Santos. Madrid, 1871.

Arc 830.200 Mémorial d'un voyage d'études. (Société Nationale des Antiquaires de France.) Paris, 1953.

Arc 1312.10 Memorial numismático español. Barcelona. 1-2,1866-1868

Arc 880.23 The memorial slabs of Clonmacnois, King's County. (Macalister, R.A.S.) Dublin, 1909.

Arc 42.10 Memorias. (Misión Arqueológica Española en Nubia.) Madrid. 1,1963+ 9v.

Arc 94.7 Memorias de la sociedad arqueologica de Carmona. (Sociedad Arqueologica de Carmona.) Carmona, 1887. 9v.

Arc 843.56 Memorias de Sagunto. (Boix, Vicente.) Valencia, 1865.

Arc 403.23 Memórias e exploraçoes arquelógicas. (Santos Rocha, Antonio dos.) Coimbra, 1971-

Arc 1033.12 Le memorie...dell'infanzia di Gesù Cristo. (Cozza-Luzi.) Roma, 1894.

Arc 1033.17.18 Memorie...miracolosa immagine della Madonna Ssma detta della Vittoria. (Teodoro di Santa Maria.) Roma, 1796.

Arc 1027.4.27 Memorie...S. Filomena e l'invenzione del suo corpo. (Povèda, G. de.) Foligno, 1834.

Arc 93.30 Memorie. (Accademia...Naples. Accademia dell'Archeologia, Lettere e Belle Arti.) Napoli. 1,1951+ 3v.

Arc 1.14.15F Memorie. (Accademia...Rome. Accademia Romana di Archeologia.) 4,1934+ 6v.

Arc 793.11 Memorie. v.1-9. (Reale Accademia Ercolanese di Archeologia, Naples.) Napoli, 1822-62. 10v.

Arc 1027.11 Memorie archeologica su di S. Aurelia Procope vergine e martire. (Michettoni, V.) Ripatransone, 1845.

Arc 1027.48 Memorie archeologico...il cimitero S. Eutizio di Ferento. (Germano di S. Stanislalo, P.) Roma, 1886.

Arc 1020.9.15 Memorie autentiche sulla chiesa di S. Paolo alla Regola. (Bartolomei, L.) Roma, 1858.

Arc 1030.5.15 Memorie degli apostoli Pietro e Paolo. (Rossi, G.B. de.) Roma, 1877.

Arc 1033.13.5 Le memorie dei SS. apostoli Pietro e Paolo nella città di Roma. (Marucchi, O.) Roma, 1894.

Arc 1033.83 Memorie del Martiro, S. Vitale e Valeria. (Mannerini, L.) Roma, 1848.

Arc 1033.17.301 Memorie del ritrovamento della santissima immagine della...annunziata. Firenze, 1733.

Arc 93.3 Memorie della Reale Academia. (Societa Reale di Napoli.) Napoli. 1-6,1911-1942 4v.

Arc 1033.38.5 Memorie della Vita del Martirio...S. Lorenzo. Roma, 1756.

Arc 1016.220A Memorie dell'antico cenobio di S. Severino. (Galante, G.A.) Napoli, 1869.

Arc 1033.17.92 Memorie di Santa Maria in Portico. (Marracci, Lodovico.) Roma, 1871.

Arc 1033.17.10 Memorie di Santa Maria in Portico di Roma. (Marracci, L.) Roma, 1675.

Arc 1033.35.17 Memorie historiche dell'apparitione delle croci. (Colá, C.) Napoli, 1661.

Arc 1033.12.138 Memorie istoriche...miracolosa crocifisso...Chiavari. Chiavari, 1856.

Arc 1020.9.183 Memorie istoriche della chiesa di S. Maria. (Masetti, Pio.) Roma, 1855.

Arc 1033.17.446 Memorie istoriche della Madonna de' bagno di Magliano. (Mastelloni, A.) Napoli, 1711.

Arc 1033.17.5 Memorie istoriche della miracolosa immagine di S. Maria in Portico. (Griscembeni, G.M.) Roma, 1716.

Htn Arc 726.46* Le memorie ritrovate...de Labrico. (Ficorini, Francesco de.) Roma, 1745.

Arc 1033.55 Memorie sacre della cappella...e di...la Scola Santa. (Romano, G.B.) Roma, 1798.

Arc 1020.9.50 Memorie sacre delle sette chiese di Roma. (Severano, G.) Roma, 1630.

Arc 1020.9.85 Memorie sacre Lateranensi. (Vannitelli, V.) Roma, 1900.

Arc 1020.20 Memorie storiche della Basilica Costantiniana. (Bonelli, G.A.) Roma, 1879.

Arc 1033.55.7 Memorie storiche della scala santa...di Sancto Sanctorum. (Mazzucconi, L.) Roma, 1840.

Arc 1016.217 Memorie storiche delle sacre teste. 2. ed. (Cancellieri, F.) Roma, 1852.

Arc 1033.17.90 Memorie storiche di S. Maria del Glorioso. (Ranaldi, Giuseppe.) Macerata, 1837.

Arc 1033.162.5F Memorie storico-critiche...di S. Marco. (Manin, Leonardo.) Venezia, 1835.

Arc 1033.12.175 Memorie storico-critiche...lagrime di...Dongo. (Eufrasio.) Lugano, 1808.

Arc 1468.10 Mémories de numismatique et d'antiquité. (Raoul-Rachette.) Paris, 1840.

Arc 1428.8 Mémories numismatiques de l'ordre...St. Jean de Jerusalem. (Furse, E.H.) Rome, 1889.

Arc 404.1.5A Memories of an old collector. (Tyskiewicz, M.) London, 1898.

Arc 588.20 Memphis. (Petrie, W.M.F.) London, 1909-1915. 7 pam.

Arc 830.2.7 Le Men-letonniec de Locmariaquer, Morbihan. (Hirmenech, H.P.) Paris? 1911.

Arc 943.54 Men met along the trail. 1. ed. (Judd, Neil Morton.) Norman, 1968.

Arc 1588.4.75 Měna v českých zemích od 10. do poč 20. století. (Pǒsvář, Jaroslav.) Opava, 1962.

Arc 825.2.11 Ménard, L. Histoire des antiquités de la ville de Nîmes. 11e éd. Nîmes, 1856.

Arc 825.2 Ménard, L. Histoire des antiquités de la ville de Nismes. Nîmes, 1803.

Arc 825.2.2 Ménard, L. Histoire des antiquités de la ville de Nismes. Nîmes, 1814.

Arc 825.2.5 Ménard, L. Histoire des antiquités de la ville de Nismes. Nîmes, 1832.

Arc 825.2.9 Ménard, L. Histoire des antiquités de la ville de Nismes. 7e éd. Nismes, 1838.

Arc 825.2.10 Ménard, L. Histoire des antiquités de la ville de Nismes. 9e éd. Nismes, 1842. 3 pam.

Arc 825.2.4 Ménard, L. Supplément à l'édition de 1829 de l'Histoire des antiquités de la ville de Nismes. Nîmes, 1830.

Arc 1016.236 Die Menasstadt. (Kaufmann, K.W.) Leipzig, 1910.

Author and Title Listing

Arc 1020.99 — Der Menastempel und die Heiligtümer von Karm Abu Mina. (Kaufmann, C.M.) Frankfurt, 1909.

Arc 1033.12.137 — Mencacci, P. Alcune memorie sull'imagine acheropita del SS. Salvatore di Sancta Santorum. Roma, 1863.

Arc 595.6.5 — Mencken, A. Designing and building the Great Pyramid. Baltimore, 1963.

Arc 595.69 — Mendelssohn, Kurt. The riddle of the pyramids. London, 1974.

Arc 838.41 — Mendes, Maria Teresa Pinto. Bibliografia arqueológica portuguesa 1960-1969. Coimbra, 1970.

Arc 838.17 — Mendes Corrêa, A.A. Os povos primitivos da Lusitânia. Porto, 1924.

Htn Arc 1660.5* — Menestrier, C.F. Histoire du Roy Louis le Grand. Paris, 1691.

Arc 518.13 — Menestrier, C.F. Symbolica Dianae Ephesiae statua a Claudio Menetreio exposita. Romae, 1657. 3 pam.

Arc 600.49 — Menghin, O. The excavations of the Egyptian university in the neolithic site at Maadi. Cairo, 1932.

Arc 1093.2.15 — Menghin, O. Weltgeschichte der Steinzeit. Wien, 1931.

Arc 905.136 — Menghin, Osmund. Beiträge zur Urgeschichte Tirols. Innsbruck, 1969.

Arc 905.15.5 — Menghin, Oswald. Einführung in der Urgeschichte Böhmens und Mährens. Reichenberg, 1926.

Arc 830.339 — Menhirs et dolmens dans le nord-est de la Bretagne. (Gilbert, Max.) Guernsey, 1964.

Arc 830.270 — Menhirs et marches sacrées. (Lelièvre, Léon.) Caen, 195-.

Arc 1588.1.70 — Mennica warszawska 1765-1965. (Terlecki, W.) Wrocław, 1970.

Arc 1588.11.5 — Mennica wileńska w XVI i XVII wieku. (Gumowski, Marian.) Warszawa, 1921.

Arc 1588.1.85 — Mennictwo polskie w XI-XII wieku. (Suchodolski, Stanisław.) Wrocław, 1973.

Arc 1033.17.51 — Mensa nazaraea...seu historia imagine divae Claromontanae. (Kiedrzynski, A.) Cracoviae, 1760.

Arc 1033.17.50 — Mensa nazaraea...seu historia imagine divae Claromontanae. (Kiedrzynski, A.) Claromontanae, 1763.

Arc 1153.65 — Mensch und Schrift im Mittelalter. (Fichtenau, Heinrich.) Wien, 1946.

Arc 936.215.5 — Die menschengestaltige Figuralplastik der südosteuropäischen Jungsteinzeit und Steinkupferzeit. v.1-2. (Hoeckmann, Olaf.) Hildesheim, 1968.

Arc 1148.13 — Mentz, A. Geschichte...der griechischen Tachygraphie. Berlin, 1907.

Arc 1153.34 — Mentz, Arthur. Geschichte der griechisch-römischen Schrift. Leipzig, 1920.

Arc 1163.8 — Mentz, G. Handschriften der Reformationszeit. Bonn, 1912.

Arc 1200.23 — Menzer, Anne. Die Jahresmerkmale in den Datierungen der Papsturkunden bis zum Ausgang des 11. Jahrhundert. Inaug. Diss. Berlin, 1932.

NEDL Arc 726.40 — Meomartini, A. I monumenti e le opere d'arte. Benevento, 1889.

Arc 983.11 — Mercer, H.C. The Lenape stone. N.Y., 1885.

Arc 400.11.10 — Merchant venturers in bronze. (Peake, Harold J.E.) New Haven, 1931.

Arc 608.6.65 — Mercier, Maurice. Prière sur le Tombeau de la Chrétienne. Paris, 1954.

Arc 1077.7 — Mercklin, E. von. Der Rennwagen in Griechenland. Leipzig, 1909.

Arc 861.31.5 — Merewether, J. Diary of a dean. London, 1851.

Arc 710.13 — Merezhkovskii, D.S. The acropolis, from the Russian of Merejkowski. London, 1909.

Arc 925.4.9 — Merhard, Gero von. Bronzezeit am Janissei. Wien, 1926.

Arc 905.138 — Merhart, Gero von. Hallstatt und Italien. Bonn, 1969.

Arc 925.4.5 — Merhart, Gero von. The palaeolithic period in Siberia contributions to the prehistory of the Yenisei region. n.p., 1923.

Htn Arc 830.7* — Mérimée, Prosper. Notes d'un voyage dans le midi de la France. Paris, 1835.

Arc 830.8.3A — Mérimée, Prosper. Notes d'un voyage dans l'ouest de la France. Bruxelles, 1837.

Arc 830.8 — Mérimée, Prosper. Notes d'un voyage dans l'ouest de la France. Paris, 1836.

Arc 830.9 — Mérimée, Prosper. Notes d'un voyage en Auvergne. Paris, 1838.

Arc 830.10 — Mérimée, Prosper. Notes d'un voyage en Corse. Paris, 1840.

Htn Arc 1160.202.5* — Merino, Andres. Escuela paleographica...letras antiguas. Madrid, 1780.

Arc 400.6 — Merkbuch. 2. Aufl. (Voss, Albert.) Berlin, 1894.

Arc 1153.96 — Merkelbach, Reinhold. Lateinisches Leseheft zur Einführung in Paläographie und Textkritik. Göttingen, 1969.

Arc 612.86 — Merkmalanalyse von Geschossspitzen des mittleren Jungpleistozäns im Mittel- und Osteuropa. (Albrecht, Gerd.) Stuttgart, 1972.

Arc 1020.52.5 — Merlet, L. Catalogue des reliques...Notre Dame de Chartres. Chartres, 1885.

Arc 66.1.97 — Merlin, A. L'aventin dans l'antiquité. Paris, 1906.

Arc 858.57 — Merlin's Island. (Lethbridge, Thomas C.) London, 1948.

Arc 830.250 — Meroc, L. Cougnac, grotte peinte. Stuttgart, 1956.

Arc 609.2.15 — Meroë, the city of the Ethiopians. (Garstang, John.) Oxford, 1911.

Arc 587.9 — Meroitic inscriptions. (Griffith, F.L.) London, 1911. 2 pam.

Arc 42.30 — Meroitica. Berlin. 1,1973+

Arc 925.338.10 — Merpert, Nikolai I. Drevneishie skotovody Volzhsko-Uraliskogo mezhdurech'ia. Moskva, 1974.

Arc 1033.34 — Merracci P. Les chaines de Saint Pierre. Rome, 1877.

Arc 861.18.16.20 — Merrifield, Ralph. The archaeology of London. Park Ridge, 1975.

Arc 861.18.16.15 — Merrifield, Ralph. The Roman city of London. London, 1965.

Arc 967.5 — The Merrimack archaeological survey. (Moorehead, W.K.) Salem, Mass., 1931.

Arc 1510.25 — Mertens, E. Münz- und Geldgeschichte der Stadt Northeim. Diss. Halle an der Saale, 1928.

Arc 726.253 — Mertens, Jozef. Ordona. Bruxelles, 1965. 4v.

Arc 543.120.10 — Mertvyi gorod Khara-Khoto. (Lubo-Lesnichenko, Evgenii.) Moskva, 1968.

Htn Arc 1020.9.116* — Les merveilles de la ville de Rome. (Léon, François.) Rome, 1646.

Arc 1020.9.118 — Les merveilles de la ville de Rome. (Léon, François.) Rome, 1750.

Htn Arc 1020.9.115* — Les merveilles de la ville de Rome. Rome, 1690.

Arc 608.33.10 — Merveilles du Tassili n'Ajjer. (Lajoux, Jean D.) Paris, 1962.

Arc 830.83.5 — Mery, Louis. De vetere Massilia disquisitiones. Massillae, 1849.

Arc 830.22.11 — Mes fouilles dans le sol du vieux Paris. (Toulouze, Eugène.) Dunkerque, 1888.

Arc 1473.1.9 — Mesaiōnika nomismara tēs Chiny. (Lampros, Paulos.) Athēnai, 1886.

Arc 785.1.3 — Meschler, M. Der Vestatempel und der Vestalenhof am römische Forum. Freiburg, 1898.

Arc 1033.12.139 — Mese di luglio ovvero esercizii divoti...giorni...miracolosa immagine di Gesu. Venezia, 1867.

Arc 843.222 — Die Meseta-Kulturen der iberischen Halbinsel. (Schuele, Wilhelm.) Berlin, 1969. 2v.

Arc 1423.23 — Meshorer, Va'akov. Jewish coins of the second temple period. Tel-Aviv, 1967.

Arc 608.13 — Mesnege, P.J. L'Afrique chrétienne...ruines antiques. Paris, 1912.

Arc 505.51 — Mesnil du Buisson, R. du. Le site archéologique de Mishrifé-Qatna. Thèse. Paris, 1935.

Arc 612.88 — The mesolithic in Europe. Wyd. 1. (International Archaeological Symposium on the Mesolithic in Europe.) Warsaw, 1973.

Arc 612.23 — The mesolithic settlement of northern Europe. (Clark, John Desmond.) Cambridge, Eng., 1936.

Arc 938.104 — Mesolithische und frühneolithische Kulturen in Osteuropa und Westsibirien. (Indreko, Richard.) Stockholm, 1964.

Arc 42.15 — Mesopotamia. Torino. 1,1966+ 5v.

Arc 1033.12.74 — Messe du précieux Sang...Fécamp. Fécamp, 1874.

X Cg Arc 1016.207 — La messe études archéologiques sur ses monuments. v.1-2,8. (Rohault de Fleury, C.) Paris, 1883- 3v.

Arc 1016.207 — La messe études archéologiques sur ses monuments. v.3-7. (Rohault de Fleury, C.) Paris, 1883- 5v.

Arc 723.22 — Messerschmidt, Franz. Bronzezeit und frühe Eisenzeit in Italien. Berlin, 1935.

Arc 910.10F — Messikommer, H. Die Pfahlbauten von Robenhausen. Zürich, 1913.

Arc 853.1 — Mestorf, J. Vorgeschichtliche Alterthuemer. Hamburg, 1885.

Arc 785.64 — La "Meta Romuli" e una lettera di Michele Ferno. (Peebles, Bernard M.) Roma, 1936.

Arc 1033.12.195 — Métais, C. Processions de la sainte-larme à Vendome. Orléans, 1886.

Arc 1087.5 — Metall-chelovsk-vremia. (Chernykh, Evgenii N.) Moskva, 1972.

Arc 968.1.5 — Metallic ornaments of the New York Indians. (Beauchamp, W.M.) n.p., n.d.

Arc 936.251.10 — Metalurgija eneolitskog perioda Yugoslavije. (Jovanović, Borislav.) Beograd, 1971.

Arc 1510.136 — Metcalf, D. The coinage of South Germany in the thirteenth century. London, 1961.

Arc 1588.5.8 — Metcalf, David Michael. Classification of Byzantine stamena in the light of a hoard found in southern Serbia. Ljubljana, 1967.

Arc 1588.5.6 — Metcalf, David Michael. Coinage in the Balkans, 820-1355. Chicago, 1966.

Arc 1588.5.5 — Metcalf, David Michael. Coinage in the Balkans. Thessaloniki, 1965.

Arc 1473.12 — Metcalf, David Michael. The origins of the Anastasian currency reforms. Amsterdam, 1969.

Arc 66.1.64 — Les meteques atheniens. (Clerc, M.) Paris, 1893.

Arc 400.24 — Methods and aims in archaeology. (Petrie, William M. Flinders.) London, 1904.

Htn Arc 1373.6* — Metilia: sive de quinario gentis metiliae. (Swinton, J.) Oxford, 1750.

Arc 390.14 — Método cuantitativo para establecer cronologias culturas. (Ford, J.A.) Washington, 1962.

Arc 895.63 — Metodproblem inom järnålderns konsthistoria. (Malmer, M.P.) Bonn, 1963.

Arc 936.14.255 — Metodyka naukowo-techniczna badań archeologicznych i antropologicznych. Warszawa, 1967.

Arc 635.205 — Die Metopen von Selinunt. (Benndorf, O.) Berlin, 1873.

Arc 522.37 — The metopes of the Temple of Athena at Ilion. (Holden, B.M.) Northampton, 1964.

Arc 406.5 — Métral, D. Blaise de Vigenère, archéologue et critique d'art, 1523-1596. Thèse. Paris, 1839.

Arc 595.10 — The metrology of the Great Pyramid. (Totten, C.A.L.) N.Y., 1884.

Arc 537.2.12 — Metropolitan Museum of Art. Handbook of th Cesnola collection of antiquities from Cyprus. N.Y., 1914.

Arc 66.1.172 — Metzger, H. Les représentations dans la céramique attique du IV siècle. Paris, 1951. 3v.

Arc 1076.3.48 — Metzger, O.H. Die Glocken im Friedländischen. Friedland, 1912.

Arc 608.2.45.5 — Meunié, Jacques. Nouvelles recherches archéologiques à Marrakech. Paris, 1957.

Arc 608.2.45 — Meunié, Jacques. Recherches archéologiques à Marrakech. Paris, 1952.

Arc 726.107 — Mevania. (Pietrangeli, Carlo.) Roma, 1953.

Arc 600.60F — Mewberry, P.E. El Bersheh. London, 1894-95. 2v.

Arc 522.25 — Mey, Oscar. Das Schlachtfeld vor Troja, eine Untersuchung. Berlin, 1926.

Arc 1510.167 — Meyer, Adolf. Prägungen Brandenburg-Preussens. Berlin, 1885.

Arc 562.5 — Meyer, Eduard. Bericht über eine Expedition nach Ägypten zur Erforschung der Darstellungen der Fremdvolker. Berlin, 1913. 9v.

Arc 658.3.22 — Meyer, Ernst. Heinrich Schliemann: Kaufmann und Forscher. Göttingen, 1969.

Arc 905.17 — Meyer. Die Römerstadt Agunt. Berlin, 1908.

Arc 505.149 — Meyers, Eric Mark. Jewish ossuaries: reburial and rebirth. Rome, 1971.

Arc 905.120 — Meysels, T.F. Auf Römerstrassen durch Osterreich von Aguntum nach Carnuntum. Wien, 1960.

Arc 1423.28 — Meyshan, Josef. Essays in Jewish numismatics. Jerusalem, 1968.

Arc 925.50.165 — Mezentseva, Galina G. Drevn'orus'ke misto Roden', Kniazha hora. Kyïv, 1968.

Arc 925.324 — Mezentseva, Galina G. Kanivs'ke poselennia polian. Kyïv, 1965.

Arc 543.3.60 — Mezhdu Pamirom i Kaspiem. (Staviskii, Boris Ia.) Moskva, 1966.

Arc 925.50.27 — Mezinskaia stoianka. (Shovkoplias, Ivan H.) Kiev, 1965.

Arc 925.335 — Mezolit Verkhnego Priangar'ia. Irkutsk, 1971-

Arc 720.9.2.5F — Micali, G. Antichi monumenti per servire all'opera...l'Italia. Firenze, 1810.

Arc 720.9 — Micali, G. Storia degli antichi popoli italiani. v.1-3; atlas. Firenze, 1832. 4v.

Arc 720.9.2 — Micali, G. Storia degli antichi popoli italiani. 2. ed. Firenze, 1833.

Arc 720.9.7 Micali, G. Storia degli antichi popoli italiani. 3. ed. v.1-4. Firenze, 1849. 2v.
Arc 726.63 Miceli, Salvatore. Vicovaro e la villa di Q. Orazio Flacco. Roma, 1929.
Arc 382.5 Michaelis, A. Anaglyphi vaticani explicatio. Tubingae, 1865. 15 pam.
Arc 397.7 Michaelis, A. Die archäologischen Entdeckungen des 19. Jahrhunderts. Leipzig, 1906.
Arc 710.4.2 Michaelis, A. A brief explanation of the ground plan of the akropolis of Athens. Cambridge, 1882.
Arc 397.8 Michaelis, A. A century of archaeological discoveries. London, 1908.
Arc 712.18 Michaelis, A. Dei due figure alate sul fregio del Partenone. Lipsia, 1865.
Arc 73.15 Michaelis, A. Geschichte des deutschen archäologisches Institut. Berlin, 1879.
Arc 394.1.20 Michaelis, A. Otto Jahn in seinen Briefen. Leipzig, 1913.
Arc 705.15A Michaelis, A. Der Parthenon. Text and atlas. Leipzig, 1871. 2v.
Arc 726.11 Michaelis, A. Der Silberschatz von Boscoreale. Berlin, 1896.
Arc 73.15.5 Michaelis, A. Storia dell'Instituto archeologico germanico, 1829-1879. Roma, 1879.
Arc 710.4 Michaelis, A. Über den jetzigen Zustand der Akropolis von Athen. Frankfurt, 1861.
Arc 712.10 Michaelis, A. Über die Composition der Giebelgruppen am Parthenon. Tübingen, 1870.
Arc 638.3 Michaelis, A.T.F. Il Leone Nemeo. Roma, 1859. 7 pam.
Arc 726.61 Michaelis, Adolf. Das corsinische Silbergefäss. Leipzig, 1859.
Arc 673.1.12 Michałowski, K. Delfy. Warszawa, 1959.
Arc 505.110 Michałowski, Kazimierz. Palmyre. Warszawa, 1960. 6v.
Arc 1033.35.19 Michele, I. de. Sopra un'antica croce nel duomo di Termini-Imerese. Palermo, 1859.
Arc 785.13 Michelet, C.L. Das Forum Romanum, oder Die...Region des alten Rom. Berlin, 1877.
Arc 861.36 Michell-Whitley, H. Discovery of Roman-British remains. n.p., 1890.
Arc 600.236 Michelucci, Maurizio. La collezione di lucerne del Museo egizio di Firenze. Firenze, 1975.
Arc 1027.11 Michettoni, V. Memorie archeologica su di S. Aurelia Procope vergine e martire. Ripatransone, 1845.
Arc 1478.34 Mickwitz, G. Die Systeme des römischen Silbergeldes. Helsingfors, 1933.
Arc 1163.7 Middeleeuwsche handschriften kunde. (Vries, S.G. de.) Leiden, 1909.
Arc 540.9F The Middle Cypriote Bronze Age. (Aastroem, Paul.) Lund, 1957.
Arc 609.20.5 A Middle Stone Age sequence from the Central Riff Valley, Ethiopia. (Wendorf, Fred.) Wrocław, 1974.
Arc 861.172 The Middle Thames in antiquity. (Workers' Educational Association. Slough and Eton Branch.) Slough, Bucks, 1966.
Htn Arc 720.12* Middleton, J. Grecian remains in Italy. London, 1812.
Arc 767.4 Middleton, J.H. Ancient Rome in 1885. Edinburgh, 1885.
Arc 767.4.2 Middleton, J.H. The remains of ancient Rome. London, 1892. 2v.
Arc 936.14.380 Miecze średniowieczne z ziem polskich. (Głosek, Marian.) Łódź, 1970.
Arc 815.12 Mifologicheskii peizazh 3-go pompeiaiskago stilia. (Rostovtsev, M.I.) n.p., n.d.
Arc 1215.1 Migieu. Recueil des sceaux du Moyen Âge dits sceaux gothiques. Paris, 1779.
Arc 830.159 Mignard, T.J.A.P. Histoire de différents cultes. Dijon, 1851.
Arc 1590.10 Mihailović, Vojislav. Katalog novca Srbije i Crne Gore 1868-1918. Beograd, 1973.
Arc 936.220.35 Mijović, Pavle. Monodija o kamenu. Kruševac, 1967.
Arc 936.220.38 Mijović, Pavle. Tragam drevnih kultura Crme Gore. Titograd, 1970.
Arc 1335.70 Mikocki, Leon. Verzeichniss einer grossen und sehr gewählten polnischen Münz- und Medaillen-Sammlung. Wien, 1850.
Arc 936.80.5F Mikov, Vasil. Antichnata grobnitsa pri Kazanlak. Sofiia, 1954.
Arc 936.40 Mikov, Vasil. Devetashkata peshtera. Sofiia, 1960.
Arc 936.80F Mikov, Vasil. Le tombeau antique près de Kazanlak. Sofia, 1954.
Arc 402.19 Mikra meletēmata. (Romaios, K.A.) Thessalonikē, 1955.
Arc 936.14.415 Mikroregion osadniczy między wisłą a Dolną Wkrą w obresie rzymskini. (Pyrgała, Jerzy.) Wrocław, 1972.
Arc 936.180.5 Mikulčić, Ivan. Pelagonija u svetlosti arheoloških nalaza. Beograd, 1966.
Arc 1030.56 Milan. Castillo Sforzesco. Il castillo sforzesco in Milano. Milano, 1915.
Arc 1445.5 Milan. I.R. Museo. Monete cufiche dell'I.R. Museo di Milano. Milano, 1819.
Arc 93.35 Milan. Università. Istituto di Archeologia. Tesi dl laurear. Roma. 1-2
Arc 13.10 Milan. Università Cattolica del Sacro Cuore. Istituto di Archeologia. Contributi. Milano. 1,1967+ 2v.
Arc 726.33 Milani, L.A. Le recenti scoperte di antichita in Verona. Verona, 1891.
Arc 19.1 Milani, L.A. Studi e materiali di archeologia e numismatica. v.1-3. Firenze, 1899. 4v.
Arc 1478.82F Milano. Gabinetto Numismatico. Le monete romane dell'età republicana. Milano, 1960.
Arc 87.1.42 Milchhoefer, A. Befreining des Prometheus. Berlin, 1882.
Arc 710.7 Milchhoefer, A. Rede zum Winckelmann-Zage. Kiel, 1898.
Arc 710.7.5 Milchhoefer, A. Über die alten Burgheiligthümer in Athen. Kiliae, 1899.
Arc 853.366 Mildenberger, Berhard. Römerzeitliche Siedlungen in Nordhessen. Marburg, 1972.
Arc 853.190 Mildenberger, Gerhard. Mitteldentschlands Ur- und Frühgeschichte. Leipzig, 1959.
Arc 853.320 Mildenberger, Gerhard. Die thuringischen Brandgräber der spätrömischen Zeit. Köln, 1970.
Arc 606.2 Mileham, G.S. Churches in lower Nubia. Philadelphia, 1910.
Arc 416.21 Miles, G.C. Archaeologica orientalia in memoriam Ernst Herzfeld. Locust Valles, N.Y., 1952.
Arc 1433.92F Miles, George Carpenter. Trésor de dirhems du IXe siècle. Paris, 1960.
Arc 861.54 Miles, William A. A description of the deverel barrow. London, 1826.
Arc 510.218PF Milet. Bd.1, Heft 5 (Tafeln); Bd.4, Atlas. Berlin, n.d. 3v.
Arc 510.218F Milet-Ergebnisse der Ausgrabungen. (Wiegand, Theodor.) Berlin, 1906- 18v.
Arc 510.7 Milet et le golfe latmique. (Rayet, O.) Paris, 1877-85.
Arc 1535.200F Milford Haven, L. British naval medals. London, 1919.
Arc 1670.7F Milford Haven, L.A.M. Naval medals. London, 1921-28. 2v.
Arc 275.101 Miliukov, P.N. VIII Arkheologicheskii s"ezd v Moskve. Moskva, 1890.
Arc 1163.2.32 Millares Carlo, A. Contribución al "corpus" de códices visigoticos. Madrid, 1931.
Arc 1200.17.5 Millares Carlo, A. Documentos pontificios en papiro de archivos. Madrid, 1918.
Arc 1200.17 Millares Carlo, A. Documentos pontificios en papiro de archivos. pt.1. Madrid, 1918.
Arc 1153.33 Millares Carlo, A. Estudios paleográficos. Madrid, 1918.
Arc 1163.2.29 Millares Carlo, A. Nuevos estudios de paleografía española. Mexico, 1941.
Arc 1163.2.25 Millares Carlo, A. Paleografía española. Barcelona, 1929. 2v.
Arc 1138.125 Millares Carlo, Agustín. Consideraciones sobre la escritura visigótica cursiva. León, 1973.
Arc 1520.15 Mille ans de monnayage Bruxellois, 1965. (Brussels. Bibliothèque Royale.) Bruxelles, 1965.
Arc 1254.3 Miller, E. Bulles byzantines de la collection de M...de Köhne. Paris, 1867.
Arc 967.6 Miller, J. Jefferson. Eighteenth-century ceramics from Fort Michilimackinac, Michigan. Washington, 1970.
Arc 1077.2.51 Miller, M. (Sweeney). My hobby of the cross. N.Y., 1939.
Arc 923.60 Miller, M.A. Archaeology in the U.S.S.R. N.Y., 1956.
Arc 923.55 Miller, M.A. Arkheologiia v SSSR. Miunchen, 1954.
Arc 1367.2 Miller, Max. Die Münzen des Altertums. Berlin, 1933.
Arc 1367.2.2 Miller, Max. Die Münzen des Altertums. 2. Aufl. Braunschweig, 1963.
Arc 925.50.45 Miller, Mykhailo O. Don i Priazov'e u drevnosti. v.1,3. Moskva, 1958- 2v.
Arc 925.50.93 Miller, Mykhailo O. Pervobytnyi period v istorii Nizhego Dnepra. Miunkhen, 1965.
Arc 861.16 Miller, S.H. Illustrations of the traces...Romans and Saxons. n.p., 1871.
Arc 875.10.7 Miller, S.N. The Roman fort at Balmuildy. Glasgow, 1922.
Arc 875.80 Miller, S.N. The Roman occupation of southwestern Scotland. Glasgow, 1952.
Arc 1578.5F Miller zu Aichholz, V. von. Österreichische Münzprägungen. 2. Aufl. Wien, 1948. 2v.
Arc 1578.4F Miller zu Aicholz, V. von. Österreichische Münzprägungen, 1519-1918. Wien, 1920.
Arc 1030.7 Millet, G. Inscriptions byzantines de Mistra. Athènes, 1899.
Arc 66.1.109 Millet, G. Recherches sur l'conographie de l'évangile aux XIV, XV et XVI siècles. Paris, 1916.
Arc 66.1.91 Millet, J. Recueil des inscriptiosn chrétiennes du Mont Athos. Paris, 1904.
Arc 823.19.150 Milliaires du Var. (Thédenat, H.) Paris, 1886.
Arc 815.19 Millin, A.L. Description des tombeaux qui ont été découverts à Pompéi dans l'année 1812. Naples, 1813.
Arc 397.1 Millin, A.L. Monumens antiques. Paris, 1802-06. 2v.
Arc 386.24.5 Millin, A.L. Notice sur la vie du Cardinal Borgia. n.p., n.d.
Arc 397.1.5 Pamphlet vol. Millin, A.L. Varia. 31 pam.
Arc 380.205 Millingen, J. Ancient unedited monuments. London, 1822.
Arc 823.15 Millon, Henry E. La collection Millon. Paris, 1913.
Arc 830.11.15 Miln, James. Excavations at Carnac. Edinburgh, 1877.
Arc 830.11.19 Miln, James. Excavations at Carnac. Edinburgh, 1881.
Arc 830.11.10 Miln, James. Fouilles faites a Carnac. Paris, 1877.
Arc 1348.51 Milne, J.G. Coin collecting. London, 1951.
Arc 1478.33A Milne, J.G. The development of Roman coinage. Oxford, 1937.
Arc 1470.45 Milne, J.G. Finds of Greek coins in the British Isles. London, 1948.
Arc 1468.27.5 Milne, Joseph G. The first stages in the development of Greek coinage. Oxford, 1934.
Arc 1458.22 Milne, Joseph G. Greek and Roman coins and the study of history. London, 1939.
Arc 1468.27 Milne, Joseph G. Greek coinage. Oxford, 1931.
Arc 1033.17.56 Milochau, A. Vierge de Saint Luc à S.-Marie Majeure. Paris, 1862.
Arc 681.10 Milojčić, Vladmir. Paläolithikum um Larissa in Thessalien. Bonn, 1965.
Arc 905.12.15 Miltner, F. Das zweite Amphitheater von Carnuntum. Wien, 1939.
Arc 518.11 Miltner, Franz. Ephesos, Stadt der Artemis. Wien, 1958.
Arc 905.120.5 Miltner, Franz. Lavant und Aguntum. Lienz, 1951.
Arc 925.353 Minaeva, Tat'iana M. K istorii alan Verkhnego Prikuban'ia po arkheologicheskim dannym. Staviopol', 1971.
Arc 925.327 Minaeva, Tat'iana M. Ocherki po arkheologii Stavropol'ia. Stavropol', 1965.
Arc 493.62 Minasian, Caro Owen. Shah Diz of Isma'ili fame. London, 1971.
Arc 1580.51.2 Mince Františka Josefa I., 1848-1916. 2. vyd. (Polívka, Eduard.) Praha, 1968.
Arc 1588.4.10 Mince kralowstvi Českéko za panováné rodu Habsburskeho od voku 1526. (Cermák, K.) n.p., 1891-1913. 3v.
Arc 955.2.13 Mindeleff, C. The repair of Casa Grande ruin, Arizona, in 1891. Washington, n.d. 2 pam.
Arc 1312.9 Minerva numismatic handbooks. Newcastle-upon-Tyne. 1,1967+
Arc 716.6 Minervae Poliadis Sacra et Aedem in Arce Athenarum. (Mueller, R.O.) Göttingen, 1820.
Arc 1033.3.21 Minicis, G. de. Sarcofago cristiano nel templo di Fermo. Roma, 1848.
Arc 1490.22 Minicis, Gaetano de. Numismatica ascolana...ascoli nel piceno. Fermo, 1853.
Arc 726.4.5 Minieri Riccio, C. Cenni storici sulla distrutta città di Cuma. Napoli, 1846.
Arc 895.21.25 Minnen från lapparnes stenålder i Sverige. (Montelius, Oscar.) Stockholm, 1875-76.
Arc 895.5.4F Minnen från vår forntide. (Montelius, Oscar.) Stockholm, 1917.
Arc 1675.8 Minnespenningar öfver svenska män och qvinnor. (Hildebrand, B.E.) Stockholm, 1860.
Arc 925.12.3 Minns, E.H. The art of the northern nomads. London, 1942.
Arc 925.12 Minns, E.H. Scythians and Greeks...ancient history and archaeology. Cambridge, 1913.
Arc 925.12.20F Minns, Ellis Hovell. Scythians and Greeks. N.Y., 1971.
Arc 672.1.59 Minoan art. (Forsdyke, E.J.) London, 1931.
Arc 672.1.118 Minoan stone vases. (Warren, Peter.) Cambridge, Eng., 1969.

Arc 672.1.57A Minoans, Philistines, and Greeks, B.C. 1400-900. (Burn, A.R.) N.Y., 1930.
Arc 672.1.53 The Minoans. (Glasgow, George.) London, 1923.
Arc 1025.46 Minoccheri, L. Le catacombe. Roma, 1897.
Arc 273.2.10 Minor publications. (Académie Royale d'Archéologie de Belgique.)
Arc 140.1.10 Minor publications. (Prehistoric Society of East Anglia.) n.p., n.d.
Arc 493.5 Minorekii, V. Kelianshchin, stela u Topuzava. Petrograd, 1917.
Arc 720.218F Minto, Antonio. Marsiliana d'Albegna. Firenze, 1921.
Arc 746.10 Minto, Antonio. Populonia; la necropoli arcaica. Firenze, 1922.
Arc 340.8.5 Minulost jižní Moravy. (Brünn. Universita. Knihovna.) Brno, 1963.
Arc 458.5 Minute stone implements from India. (Wilson, Thomas.) n.p., 1892.
Arc 793.3.8 Miola, Alfonso. Ricordi Vesuviani. n.p., 1879.
Arc 1148.38 Mioni, Elpidio. Introduzione alla paleografia greca. Padova, 1973.
Arc 1478.8 Mionnet, T.E. De la rareté et du prix des médailles romaines. Paris, 1858. 2v.
Arc 1458.1 Mionnet, T.E. Description de médailles antiques. Paris, 1806-08. 7v.
Arc 1458.1.2 Mionnet, T.E. Description de médailles antiques. Supplément. Paris, 1819-37. 10v.
Arc 736.2.9 Mirabella a Alagona, V. Dichiarazioni della pianta dell'antiche Siracuse. Napoli, 1625.
Htn Arc 1020.9.114* Mirabilia Roma. (Albertini, F.) Firenze, 1520.
Arc 767.6.3 Mirabilia Romae. Berlin, 1869.
Arc 767.6.5 Mirabilia urbis Romae. London, 1889.
Htn Arc 767.6.2* Mirabilia urbis Romae nova. Roma, 1550.
Arc 1020.9.117 Mirabilibus...Romae. (Albertini, F.) Heilbron, 1886.
Arc 595.7 A miracle in stone, or The Great Pyramid of Egypt. (Seiss, J.A.) Philadelphia, 1877?
Arc 595.7.4 A miracle in stone, or The Great Pyramid of Egypt. 4th ed. (Seiss, J.A.) Philadelphia, 1877.
Arc 1033.29 Miracles et bien-faits obtenus...invocation du...T. Xavier en ses reliques. Malines, 1661.
Arc 1033.17.31 Miracolo...Maria...Ancona. n.p., n.d. 2 pam.
Arc 1033.17.542.5 La miracolosa imagine della B.V. Maria del Mont'Allegro in Rapello. (Mariano, Filoteo.) Venezia, 1688.
Arc 1033.12.77 The miraculous host tortured by the Jew. 3. ed. London, 1822.
Arc 793.7 The mirage of two buried cities. (Horne, J.F.) London, 1900.
Arc 402.2.9 Le mirage oriental. (Reinach, S.) Paris, 1893.
Arc 935.23.5F Miranda, S. El Gran Palacio Sagrado de Bizancio. Mexico, 1955.
Arc 1590.20 Mirchev, M. Amfornite pechati ot Muzeia vuv Varna. Sofiia, 1958.
Arc 505.144 Miroschedji, Pierre R. de. L'époque que pré-urbaine en Palestine. Paris, 1971.
Arc 543.66.65 Mirsaatov, T. Drevnie shakhty Uchtuta. Tashkent, 1973.
Arc 383.9.10 Miscelánea en homenaje al abate Hescri Breuil, 1877-1961. (Barcelona (Province). Instituto de Prehistoria y Arqueología.) Barcelona, 1964-65. 2v.
Arc 403.6 Miscellanea di archaeologia, storia, e filologia. (Salinas, A.) Palermo, 1907.
Arc 383.66 Miscellanea di studi sicelioti ed italioti in onore di Paolo Orsi. Catania, 1921.
Arc 760.6.5 Miscellanea filologica critica e antiquaria. (Fea, Carlo.) Roma, 1790-1836. 2v.
Arc 562.2.45F Miscellanea gregoriana. Roma, 1941.
Arc 1033.53.19 Miscellanea in onore di S. Maurizio. Roma, 1847.
Arc 1348.40 Miscellanea numismatica. (Magnan, D.) Romae, 1772-74. 3v.
Arc 743.15 Miscellaneous pamphlets. (Congresso Internazionale Etrusco.) 1,1928+ 2v.
Arc 953.6 Miscellaneous papers relating to anthropology. (Mason, O.T.) Washington, 1883.
Arc 1020.9.45 Miscellania...la topografia...dei monumenti de Roma. (Rossi, G.B. di.) Roma, 1889.
Arc 830.130.10 La mise au point de Glozel. (Cartereau, E.) Paris, 1928.
Arc 42.10 Misión Arqueológica Española en Nubia. Memorias. Madrid. 1,1963+ 9v.
Arc 441.23 Misra, Virendra Nath. Pre- and proto-history of the Berach Basin, South Rajasthan. 1. ed. Poona, 1967.
Arc 608.2 Mission à Carthage. (Sainte-Marie, E. de.) Paris, 1884.
Arc 537.14 Mission Archéologique d'Alasia. Mission archéologique d'Alasia. Paris, 19- .
Arc 537.14 Mission archéologique d'Alasia. (Mission Archéologique d'Alasia.) Paris, 19- .
Arc 420.5F Mission archéologique dans la Chine septentrionale. v.1-2; planches, pt.3. (Chavannes, E.) Paris, 1909-15. 4v.
Arc 935.10.3 Mission archéologique de Constantinople. (Ebersolt, Jean.) Paris, 1921.
Arc 635.204 Mission archéologique de Macédoine. (Heuzey, L.) Paris, 1876.
Arc 497.21 Mission archéologique en Arabie. v.1-3 et Atlas. (Jaussen, Antonin J.) Paris, 1909-22. 4v.
Arc 421.8 Mission archéologique en Chine (1914). (Ségalen, V.) Paris, 1935.
Arc 420.8F Mission archéologique en Chine (1914 et 1917). Atlas. (Segalen, V.) Paris, 1923-24. 2v.
Arc 505.2.20 Mission Archeologique Suisse en Syrie. Le sanctuaire de Baalshamin à Palmyre. Rome, 1969- 4v.
Arc 495.7 Mission de Phénicie. (Renan, E.) Paris, 1864. 2v.
Arc 530.16F Mission en Cappadoce. (Chantre, E.) Paris, 1898.
Arc 542.205 Mission Henri Dufour. Bayon d'Angkor Thom. Paris, 1910.
Arc 608.90 Mission Michela Schiff Giorgini. Soleb. Firenze, 1965- 2v.
Arc 42.5F Mission Paul Pelliot. Documents archéologiques. Paris. 1-3 2v.
Arc 505.123F Missione Archeologica. Caesarea Maritima (Israele). Milano, 1959.
Arc 736.20 Missione Archeologica della Soprintendenza alle Antichità della Sicilia Occidentale e dell'Università di Roma. Mozia. Roma, 1964- 8v.
Arc 600.220F Missione Archeologica in Egitto. Tamit, 1964. Roma, 1967.
Arc 726.59.35 Missione archeologica italiana a Malta. Rapporto preliminare della campagna. Roma. 1963+ 6v.
Arc 505.126F Missione archeologica italiana in Siria. Roma, 1964- 3v.
Arc 600.5.20 Missione di Scavo a Medinet Madi. Rapporto preliminare delle campagine di Scavo 1966-1967. Milano, 1968.
Arc 537.9 Missions en Chypre, 1932-1935. (Schaeffer, C.F.A.) Paris, 1936.
Arc 317.2 Missouri. Historical Society. Department of Archaeology. Bulletin. St. Louis. 1,1913
Arc 815.20 I misteri orfici nell'antica Pompei. (Burrascano, N.) Roma, 1928.
Arc 848.55 Mit dem Fahrstuhl in die Römerzeit. (Paertner, Rudolf.) Düsseldorf, 1963.
Arc 397.2 Mitchell, A. The past in the present. Edinburgh, 1880.
Arc 390.12 Mitchell, Charles. Felice Feliciano antiquarius. London, 1961?
Arc 861.92 Mitchell, E.H. The crosses of Monmouthshire. Newport, 1893.
Arc 520.4 Mitchell, L.M. (Mrs.). Sculptures of the Great Pergamon Altar. N.Y., 1882.
Arc 432.5.2 Mitra, Panchanan. Prehistoric India. 2. ed. Calcutta, 1927.
Arc 936.220.125 Mitraizam na thu Jugoslavije. (Zotovič, Ljubica.) Beograd, 1973.
Arc 73.20.20 Mitteilungen. (Archäologisches Institut des Deutschen Reichs.) München. 1-6,1948-1953 3v.
Arc 1301.6 Mitteilungen. (Bayerische Numismatische Gesellschaft.) München. 1-52,1882-1934
Arc 33.2 Mitteilungen. (Deutsches Institut für ägyptische Altertumskunde in Kairo.) Augsburg. 1,1930+ 17v.
Arc 1302.5 Mitteilungen. (Österreich Gesellschaft für Münz und Medaillenkunde.) Wien. 1890-1905 3v.
Arc 1313.40 Mitteilungen. (Österreichische Numismatische Gesellschaft.) Wien. 1,1937+ 6v.
Arc 206.6 Mitteilungen. (Verein für Geschichte und Altertumskunde Westfalens. Altertums-Kommission.) Münster. 1-7,1899-1922// 4v.
Arc 65.3.6 Mitteilungen. Beiheft. (Deutsches Archäologisches Institut. Athenische Abteilung.) Berlin. 1,1971+
Arc 1301.6.2 Mitteilungen. Register. (Bayerische Numismatische Gesellschaft.) München. 1-48,1882-1930
Arc 545.207F Mitteilungen aus der Aegyptischen Sammlung. (Berlin Museum.) Berlin, 1910- 6v.
Arc 55.1.4 Mitteilungen und Nachrichten-Register. (Deutschen Palästine Verein.) Leipzig. 1895-1912 2v.
Arc 1510.8.10 Die Mittelalter-Münzen von Münster. (Cappe, H.P.) Dresden, n.d.
Arc 482.205F Mittelalterliche Gläser und Steinschnittarbeiten aus dem Nahen Osten. (Lamm, C.J.) Berlin, 1930. 2v.
Arc 1086.10 Mittelalterliche Kultmale. (Hula, Franz.) Wien, 1970.
Arc 87.2.75 Mittelalterliche Kunst in Soest. (Aldenkirchen, J.) Bonn, 1875.
Arc 853.190 Mitteldentschlands Ur- und Frühgeschichte. (Mildenberger, Gerhard.) Leipzig, 1959.
Arc 723.1 Mittelitalien. (Abeken, W.) Stuttgart, 1843.
Arc 1153.111 Mittellateinische Texte: ein Handschriften-Lesebuch. (Thiel, Helmut van.) Göttingen, 1972.
Arc 853.375 Die mittelpaläolithische Geröllgeräteindustrie aus der Umgebung von Kronach in Oberfranken. (Zotz, Lothar F.) Kallmünz, 1973.
Arc 73.6 Mittheilungen. (Deutsches Archäologisches Institut. Römische Abteilung.) Rom. 1,1886+ 60v.
Arc 156.1.5 Mittheilungen. (Gesellschaft für Vaterländische Alterthümer in Basel.) Basel. 1-10,1843-1867
Arc 73.6.10 Mittheilungen. Ergänzungsheft. (Deutsches Archäologisches Institut. Römische Abteilung.) München. 1,1931+ 19v.
Arc 73.6.2 Mittheilungen. Register, Bd. I-X. (Deutsches Archäologisches Institut. Römische Abteilung.) Rom, 1902.
NEDL Arc 180.1 Mittheilungen der Antiquarischen Gesellschaft. (Zürich. Antiquarische Gesellschaft.) Zürich. 1-30,1841-1931
Arc 180.1 Mittheilungen der Antiquarischen Gesellschaft. (Zürich. Antiquarische Gesellschaft.) Zürich. 31-43 26v.
Arc 65.3 Mittheilungen des deutsches archäologisches Institut in Athen. Athens. 1,1876+ 69v.
Arc 845.2 Mittheilungen über Römische Funde in Heddernheim. (Frankfurt am Main. Verein für Geschichte und Alterthumskunde.) Frankfurt, 1894. 6v.
Arc 1510.139 Mittheilungen zur Geschichte der Reichs-Münzstaetten. (Albrecht, J.) Heilbronn, 1835.
Arc 853.300 Die mittlere Bronzezeit im nördlichen Rheingraben. (Koester, Hans.) Bonn, 1968.
Arc 853.65.5 Die mittlere Steinzeit in Schlesien. (Rothert.) Leipzig, 1936.
Arc 505.138 Mittmann, Siegfried. Beiträge zur Siedlungs- und Territorialgeschichte des nördlichen Ostjordanlandes. Wiesbaden, 1970.
Arc 435.25 Mixed Hindu-Mahamedan style. (Cole, H.H.) London, 1873.
Arc 925.10.5 Miziev, Ismail M. Srednevekovye bashni i sklepy Balkarii i Karachaia (XIII-XVIII vv). Nal'chik, 1970.
Arc 635.219 Mnémeia. Tés Ellados. Athēnai, 1906.
Arc 383.94F Mnemosynon Theodor Wiegand. München, 1938.
Arc 925.336 Mnogosloinaia stoianka Bel'kachi I. i periodizatsiia kamennogo veka Iakutii. (Mochanov, I.A.) Moskva, 1969.
Arc 13.15 Moated Site Research Group. Report - Moated Site Research Group. Kirkleavington. 1,1973+
Arc 861.21.40 The moated sites of Yorkshire. (Le Patourel, John Herbert.) London, 1973.
Arc 895.64 Moberg, Carl Axel. Innan Sverige blev Sverige. Stockholm, 1964.
Arc 895.67 Moberg, Carl Axel. Spår från tusentals år. Stockholm, 1966.
Arc 925.336 Mochanov, I.A. Mnogosloinaia stoianka Bel'kachi I. i periodizatsiia kamennogo veka Iakutii. Moskva, 1969.
Arc 432.12.5 Mode, Heinz. Das frühe Indien. Stuttgart, 1959.
Arc 432.12 Mode, Heinz. Indische Frühkulturen und ihre Beziehungen zum Westen. Basel, 1944.
Arc 447.6 Mode, Heinz Adolph. The Harappa culture and the West. Calcutta, 1961.
Arc 1070.200 Das Model eines athenischen Fuenfreihenschiffs Pentere. (Graser, B.) Berlin, 1866.
Arc 746.56 Modelli di edifici etrusco-italici. (Staccioli, Romolo Augusto.) Firenze, 1968.
Arc 412.9 Models in archaeology. (Clarke, David L.) London, 1972.
Arc 1433.36 Modern copper coins of the Muhammadan states. (Valentine, W.H.) London, 1911.
Arc 518.1.5 Modern discoveries on the site of ancient Ephesus. (Wood, J.T.) London, 1890.
Arc 497.13A Modern research as illustrating the Bible. (Driver, S.R.) London, 1909.
Arc 497.17 Modern science in Bible lands. (Dawson, J.W.) N.Y., 1889.
Arc 1020.31.17 Die Modestianischen...zu Jerusalem. (Baumstark, Anton.) Paderborn, 1915.
Arc 700.10.15F Moebius, Hans. Die Ornamente der griechischen Grabstelen. Berlin, 1929.

Author and Title Listing

Arc 505.5.75 Möblenbrinck, K. Studien zum Salomonischen Tempel. Inaug. Diss. Stuttgart, 1931.

Arc 1494.6 Moedas de Toro. (Batalha Reis, Pedro.) Lisboa, 1933.

Arc 1494.7 Moedas portuguesas dos reinados de D. Carlos I. e de D. Manuel II. (Ferreira Barros, A.) Põrto, 1943.

Arc 1478.25 Moedas romanas da Biblioteca da Universidade de Coimbra. (Coimbra. Universidade. Biblioteca.) Coimbra, 1905.

Arc 1433.20 Moeller, J.H. De numis Orientalibus in numophylacio Gothano. Erford, 1826-31. 2v.

Arc 547.27 Mogensen, M. Inscriptions hiéroglyphiques du Musée national de Copenhague. Copenhague, 1918.

Arc 600.18A Mogensen, Maria. Le mastaba égyptien de la glyphtothèque de Carlsberg. Copenhagen, 1921.

Arc 435.2.30F Moghul colour decoration of Agra. (Smith, E.W.) Allahabad, 1901.

Arc 936.140.10 Mogili Ot. Kh. i K. Shkorpil. (Škorpil, Hermeneyild.) Plovdiv, 1898.

Arc 925.38.20 Mogil'nik kudyrge kak istochnik po istorii altaiskikh plemen. (Gavrilova, Antonina.) Leningrad, 1965.

Arc 280.2 Mogil'niki Zapadnoi Fergany. Moskva. 1,1972+

Arc 454.1.5 Mohapatra, Gopal Chandra. The stone age cultures of Orissa. 1. ed. Poona, 1962.

Arc 452.1F Mohenjo-daro and the Indus civilization. (Marshall, John.) London, 1931. 3v.

Arc 853.103F Mohndorf. (Grohne, E.) Bremen, 1953.

Arc 855.228F Moir, J. Reid. The great flint implements of Cromer, Norfolk. Ipswich, 1923?

Arc 936.220.80 Mokim. (Girić, Milorad.) Washington, 1971-72. 2v.

Arc 593.1.2 Moldenke, C.E. The New York obelisk. N.Y., 1891.

Arc 593.1 Moldenke, C.E. The New York obelisk. N.Y., 1891.

Arc 726.12.5 Molfetta und Matera. (Mayer, M.) Leipzig, 1924.

Arc 1033.17.623 Molin, A. Dell'antica immagine di Maria...S. Marco in Venezia. Venezia, 1821.

NEDL Arc 823.12 Molin, Jean. Archéologie de la Gaule. Paris, 1908.

Arc 1153.4.25 Molina, E. Grammatica tironiana. Padova, 1933.

Arc 1033.162 Molini, A.M. De vita et Lipsanis S. Marci Evangelistae. Romae, 1864.

Arc 1020.73.9 Molinier, E. Fragments d'un inventaire du trésor de l'abbaye de Saint Victor de Paris. Paris, 1882.

Arc 1020.73.12 Molinier, E. Inventaire du trésor...de Saint-Sépulchre de Paris. Paris, 1883.

Arc 1020.13 Molinier, E. Inventaire du trésor du Saint Siège. Paris, 1888.

Arc 1016.1 Molinier, E. Le trésor de la cathédrale de Coire. Paris, 1895.

Arc 530.181 Mollaart, James. Çatal Hüyük. N.Y., 1967.

Arc 136.1.6 Momentores minutes of the meeting. (Society of Noviomagus.) London, 1845.

Arc 1020.31.25 Mommert, Carl. Saint Étienne et ses sanctuaires à Jérusalem. Jérusalem, 1912.

Arc 1025.45 Mommesen, T. The Roman catacombs. Londin, 1871.

Arc 708.11 Mommsen, A. Athenae Christianae. Leipzig, 1868.

Arc 1478.10 Mommsen, T. Geschichte des römisches Münzwesens. Berlin, 1860.

Arc 1478.10.5 Mommsen, T. Histoire de la monnaie romaine. Paris, 1865. 4v.

Arc 1478.9 Mommsen, T. Über das römische Münzwesen. Leipzig, 1850.

Arc 505.12.15F Momumenta Sinaitica. pt.1- Leningrad, 1912-1925. 2v.

Arc 861.1.3 Mona antiqua restaurata. (Rowlands, Henry.) Dublin, 1723.

Arc 861.1.6 Mona antiqua restaurata. 2. ed. (Rowlands, Henry.) London, 1766.

Arc 785.52F Monaci, Alfredo. Nuovi studi sull'arco di Constantino. Roma, 1904.

Arc 1153.13 Monaci, E. Esempj di scrittura latina. Roma, 1898.

Arc 1433.21 Monarchiae Asiatico-Saracenicae status. (Kehr, G. Jacob.) Lipsiae, 1724.

Arc 600.190 Le monastère de Phoebammon. (Bachatly, C.) Le Caire, 1964- 2v.

Arc 880.29 The monastery of St. Mochaoi of Nendrum. (Lawlor, H.C.) Belfast, 1925.

Arc 1274.3 Monastic seals of the XIIIth century. (Pedrick, G.) London, 1902.

Arc 1313.7 Monatsblatt. (Numismatische Gesellschaft in Wien.) Wien. 69,1956

Arc 608.6.75 Monceaux, Paul. Tingad chrétien. Paris, 1911.

Arc 585.32F Mond, Robert. The Bucheum. London, 1934. 3v.

Arc 585.34F Mond, Robert. Cemeteries of Armant. London, 1937. 2v.

Arc 585.47 Mond, Robert. Temples of Armant. London, 1940. 2v.

Arc 943.31 Un monde était leur empire. (Panneton, P.) Montréal, 1943.

Arc 1675.50 Mondini, R. Spigolando tra medaglie e date, 1848-71. Livorno, 1913.

Arc 1143.1 Mone, F. De libris palimpsestis. Carlsruhae, 1855.

X Cg Arc 1020.22.5 Hē monē daphnioy. (Lampake, G.) Athēnai, 1889.

Arc 1493.13 La moneda hispánica. (Vives y Escudero, Antonio.) Madrid, 1926. 2v.

Arc 1494.57 La moneda hispanica en la edad antigua. (Gil Farres, Octavia.) Madrid, 1966.

Arc 1623.6 La moneda mexicana. (Sobrino, Jose Manuel.) Mexico, 1972.

Arc 1640.5 Las monedas chilenas. (Medina, J.T.) Santiago, 1902.

Arc 1645.3.5F Las monedas coloniales de Chile. (Medina, J.T.) Santiago, 1919. 2 pam.

Arc 1643.1.10F Las monedas coloniales hispano-americanas. (Medina, J.T.) Santiago, 1919.

Arc 1433.37.10 Monedas de las dinastiás arábigo-españolas. (Vives y Escudero, A.) Madrid, 1893.

Arc 1493.26 Las monedas hispanicas del Museo arqueologico nacional de Madrid. (Navascués y de Juan, Joaquin Maria de.) Barcelona, 1969. 2v.

Arc 1643.1.15F Las monedas obsidionales hispano-americanas. (Medina, J.T.) Santiago, 1919.

Arc 1643.1 Monedas y medallas hispano-americanas. (Medina, J.T.) Santiago, 1891.

Arc 1494.4.9 Les monedes Catalanes. (Botet y Sisó, Joaquim.) Barcelona, 1908-11. 3v.

Arc 1340.3F Moneta; vocabolario. (Martinori, E.) Roma, 1915.

Arc 1348.2 Moneta: a study. (Dubois, P.) n.p., 1884.

Arc 1470.22 La moneta di P. Ovidio Nasone. (Pansa, G.) Milano, 1912.

Arc 1583.10 Moneta i vec' v' Rossii do kontsa XVIII stoletiia. (Prozarovskii, D.I.) Sankt Peterburg, 1865.

Arc 1568.5 Moneta Norwei. (Skaare, Kolbjørn.) Oslo, 1966.

Arc 1588.1.36 Moneta polska od X-XX wieku. (Wojtulewicz, H.) Lublin, 1960.

Arc 1488.15F La moneta primitiva e i monumenti dell'Italia antica. Diss. (Gennarelli, Achille.) Roma, 1843.

Arc 1493.20 Monetario. (Perelada, Spain. Castillo de los Condes de Perelada. Museo.) Perelada, 1957.

Arc 1643.2 Monetario americano. (Rosa, A.) Buenos Aires, 1892.

Arc 1490.98.15 La monetazione greca della Sicilia antica. (Cirami, Giacomo.) Bologna, 1959. 2v.

Arc 1478.15.4 Monetazione romana. (Gnecchi, F.) Genève, 1897.

Arc 1430.10 Monete arabiche del gabinetto numismatico di Milano. (Ghiron, I.) Milano, 1878.

Arc 1445.5 Monete cufiche dell'I.R. Museo di Milano. (Milan. I.R. Museo.) Milano, 1819.

Arc 1485.4 Le monete de' papi. (Cinagli, Angelo.) Fermo, 1848.

Arc 1488.20 Le monete decimali sabaude. (Secchi, Alberto.) Milano, 1955.

Arc 1490.5 Le monete dei possedimenti veneziani. (Lazari, V.) Venezia, 1851.

Arc 1490.28F Monete dei reali di Savoia. (Promis, D.) Torino, 1841. 2v.

Arc 1490.13 Monete dei romani pontefici avanti il mille. (Promis, Domenico.) Torino, 1858.

Arc 1660.17F Le monete dei Trivulzio. (Gnechi, Francesco.) Milano, 1887.

Arc 1490.24 Le monete del reame delle Due Sicilie da Carlo I d'Angio a Vittorio Emanuele II. (Cagiati, Memmo.) Napoli, 1911-16.

Arc 1490.45 Monete del regno di Napoli da Roggiero. (Vergare, Cesare A.) Roma, 1715.

Arc 1490.98.5F Le monete dell'antiche città di Sicilia. (Salinas Gargotta, Antonino.) Palermo, 1867-72.

Arc 1480.2 Le monete delle antiche famiglie di Roma. 2. ed. (Riccio, G.G.) Naples, 1843.

Arc 1448.8 Le monete di Aksum. (Vaccaro, Francesco.) Casteldario, 1967.

Arc 1490.94.1 Monete di Milano; inedite supplemento all'opera: Le monete di Milano da Carlo Magno a Vittorio Emanuele II. (Gnecchi, Francesco.) Milano, 1894.

Arc 1490.35 Monete di Pavia. (Brambilla, C.) Pavia, 1883.

Arc 1490.5.7 Le monete di Venezia. pt.1-3. (Papadopoli, Nicolo.) Venezia, 1893-1919. 4v.

Arc 1490.27.5 Le monete di Verona. (Perini, Quintilio.) Rovereto, 1902.

Arc 1490.65F Monete d'oro con ritratto del rinascimento italiano. (Bernareggi, E.) Milano, 1954.

Arc 1333.11 Monete e bolle plumbee...del Medaghere Vaticano. (Serafini, C.) Milano, 1910. 4v.

Arc 1675.10.9 Monete e medaglie degli Spinola di Tassarolo. (Olivieri, A.) Genova, 1860.

Arc 1490.8 Monete econii nella storia del diritto siculo. (Garufi, C.A.) Palermo, 1898.

Arc 1400.3 Monete franco-italiche ossidionali. (Morbio, Carlo.) Asti, 1865.

Arc 1590.2 Monete inedite dei gran maestri...in Rodi. (Lambros, P.) Venezia, 1865.

Arc 1590.2.3 Monete inedite dei gran maestri. Primo supplemento. (Lambros, P.) Venezia, 1866.

Arc 1488.32 Monete italiane dall'invasione napoleonica ai giorni nostri, 1796-1963. 2. ed. (Pagani, Antonio.) Milano, 1965.

Arc 1488.25 Monete italiane moderne a sistema decimale da Napoleone console alla Repubblica Italiana. 2. ed. (Pagani, Antonio.) Milano, 1953.

Arc 1490.32 Monete mediolanensis. (Ulrich-Bansa, O.) Venezia, 1949.

Arc 1478.15.2 Monete romane. (Gnecchi, F.) Milano, 1896.

Arc 1478.15 Monete romane. (Gnecchi, F.) Milano, 1900.

Arc 1478.82F Le monete romane dell'età republicana. (Milano. Gabinetto Numismatico.) Milano, 1960.

Arc 1490.80 Le monete siciliane dagli Aragonisi ai Borboni. (Spahr, Rodolfo.) Palermo, 1959.

Arc 925.120 Monetnoe delo Bospora. (Shelov, D.B.) Moskva, 1956.

Arc 1584.4 Monetnye klady Azerbaidzhana. pt.6,8. (Pakhomov, Evgenii A.) Baku, 1954.

Arc 1584.4.5 Monety Azerbaidzhana. (Pakhomov, Evgenii A.) Baku, 1959- 2v.

Arc 1588.1.101 Monety bite dla Królestwa Polskiego w latach 1815-1864 i monety bite dla miasta Krakowa w roku 1835. (Plage, Karol.) Warszawa, 1972.

Arc 1433.42F Monety bostochnago khalifata. (Tizengauzen', V.) Sankt Peterburg, 1873.

Arc 1588.1.91 Monety dawnej Polski. (Zagórski, Ignacy.) Warszawa, 1969.

Arc 1433.40 Monety dzhuchidov' dzhagataidov", I.D.R. (Savelbev', P.) Sankt Peterburg, 1858.

Arc 1588.1.15 Monety fawney Polski jakotez prowincyj i nuast. (Zagorski, I.) Warszawa, 1845.

Arc 1584.1.20 Monety Gruzii. (Pakhomov, Evgenii A.) Tbilisi, 1970.

Arc 1588.2.10 Monety i pechatite na bolg. Acare. (Mushmov, N.A.) Sofiia, 1924.

Arc 1390.18 Monety il'khakov XIV veka. (Seifedolini, M.A.) Baku, 1968.

Arc 1433.41 Monety khanov' uluea dzhuchieva. (Fraehn, C.M.J.) Sankt Peterburg, 1832.

Arc 1411.15 Monety Kitaia. (Bykov, Aleksei A.) Leningrad, 1969.

VArc 1583.24.5 Monety opowiadają o historii. (Fedorov-Davydov, German A.) Warszawa, 1966.

Arc 1588.1.75 Monety pierwszych Jagiellonów 1386-1444. Wyd. 1. (Kubiak, Stanisława.) Wrocław, 1970.

Arc 1588.1.23 Monety polskie. (Gumowski, Marian.) Warszawa, 1924.

Arc 1588.5.10 Monety pribaltiki XIII-XVIII stoletii. (Fedorov, Dimitrii I.) Tallin, 1966.

Arc 1583.24 Monety rasskazy-vaiut. (Fedorov-Davydov, German A.) Moskva, 1963.

Arc 1583.32 Monety SSSR. (Moscow. Gosudarstvennyi Istoricheskii Muzei.) Moskva, 1971.

Arc 1408.7 Monety stran zarubezhnoi Azii i Afriki XIX-XX veka. (Moshniagin, D.I.) Moskva, 1967.

Arc 1582.9PF Monety vel. kniazhestva Kievskago. (Tolstoi, I.I.) Sankt Peterburg, 1882.

Arc 1423.14.5 The money of the Bible. (Williamson, G.C.) N.Y., 18- ?

Arc 1423.14 The money of the Bible illustrated by numerous woodcuts. (Williamson, G.C.) London, 1894.

Arc 925.110.5 Mongait, A.L. Archaeology in USSR. Moscow, 1959.

Arc 397.22 Mongait, A.L. Arkheologiia i sovremennost'. Moskva, 1963.

Arc 925.110 Mongait, A.L. Arkheologiia v SSSR. Moskva, 1955.

Arc 925.205 Mongait, A.L. Riazanskaia zemlia. Moskva, 1961.

Arc 612.90 Mongait, Aleksandr L. Arkheologiia Zapadnoi Evropy. Moskva, 1973- 2v.

Arc 1163.3.100 Mongait, Aleksandr L. Nadpis'na kamne. Moskva, 1969.

Arc 543.120 Mongol'skii arkheologicheskii sbornik. (Akademiia nauk SSSR.) Moskva, 1962.

Arc 1366.1A La monnaie dans l'antiquité. (Lenormant, F.) Paris, 1878-79. 3v.

Arc 1500.48 La monnaie de Troyes de 1422 à 1434. (Garnier, Alphonse.) n.p., n.d.

Arc 1500.15 Monnaie gauloise inédite de Luctérius, chef Cadurque. (Barthélemy, Anatole de.) n.p., 1880.

Arc 1423.6 Monnaie inédite des seigneurs du Toron, en Syrie. (Schlumberger, G.) Paris, 1875.

Arc 1335.27.25 Les monnaies. (Bibliothèque Nationale, Paris. Département des Médailles et Antiques.) Paris, 1929.

Arc 1423.7 Monnaies à légendes arabes frappées en Syrie. (Lavoix, Henri.) Paris, 1877.

Arc 1428.2 Les monnaies à légendes grecques. (Schlumberger, G.) Paris, 1880.

Arc 1500.49 Les monnaies anglo-françaises. (Joubert, André.) Mamers, 1886.

Arc 1488.5 Les monnaies antiques. (Sambon, Arthur.) Paris, 1903.

Arc 1522.5 Monnaies antiques découvertes au Grand-Duché de Luxembourg. (Weiller, Raymond.) Berlin, 1972.

Arc 1458.21.5 Monnaies antiques grecques, romaines, byzantines. (Ars Classica, Geneva.) Genève, 1930.

Arc 1458.21 Monnaies antiques grecques et romaines. (Ars Classica, Geneva.) Genève, 1933.

Arc 1473.7 Monnaies byzantines. v.1-4,8-9. (Tolstoi, Jean.) St. Petersbourg, 1912-14. 4v.

Arc 1470.26.5 Monnaies crétoises du Ve au Ier siècle avant J.C. Thèse. (Le Rider, Georges.) Paris, 1966.

Arc 1490.68 Les monnaies d'argent de Rhegion frappées entre 461 et le milieu du IVe siècle avant J.-C. (Horzfelder, Hubert.) Paris, 1957.

Arc 1465.4 Les monnaies d'Athènes. (Beulé, E.) Paris, 1858.

Arc 1518.6 Monnaies de Belgique de 1832 à 1963. (Morin, Francois.) Boom, 1964.

Arc 1518.6.5 Monnaies de Belgique de 1832 à 1967. (Morin, Francois.) Anvers, 1968.

Arc 1510.7 Les monnaies de Charlemagne. (Cerexhe, M.) Gand, 1887.

Arc 1590.6 Monnaies de Chypre et de Salona. (Lambros, Paulos.) n.p., 1866.

Arc 1500.66 Les monnaies de la Gaule inspirées de celles de la republique romaine. (Scheers, Simone.) Leuven, 1969.

Arc 1583.19.1 Monnaies de l'empire de Russie, 1725-1894. (Georgii Mikhailovich, Grand Duke of Russia.) Boston, 1973.

Arc 1500.39 Monnaies des Boïens de la Germanie. (Changarnier, A.) Dijon, 1914.

Arc 1500.57 Monnaies des comtés de Provence, XII-XV siècles. (Rolland, Henri.) Paris, 1956.

Arc 1510.22.5 Les monnaies des landgraves autrichiens de la Haute Alsace. Supplement. (Lehr, Ernest.) Mulhouse, 1896. 2 pam.

Arc 1530.5.5 Les monnaies des Pays-Bas bourguignons et espagnols. (Gelder, Hendrik Enno van.) Amsterdam, 1960.

Arc 1498.15 Les monnaies des rois de France. (Lafaurie, Jean.) Paris, 1951. 2v.

Arc 1433.65 Les monnaies des rois Parthes. (Prokesch-Osten, A.) Paris, 1874-75.

Arc 1448.10 Les monnaies d'or de la Cyrenaïque de 450 à 250 avant J.C. (Naville, Lucien.) Genève, 1951.

Arc 1335.88F Monnaies d'or romaines et byzantines. (Rollin et Teuardent, firm, Paris.) Paris, 1887.

Arc 1335.88.25F Monnaies d'or romaines et byzantines vente aux enchères publiques 20-28 avril, 1896. (Rollin et Teuardent, firm, Paris.) Paris, 1896.

Arc 1493.3 Monnaies d'or suévo-lusitaniennes. (Allen, E.A.) Paris, 1865.

Arc 1500.40 Monnaies du moyen-age (Gaule). (Lecoq-Kerneven, J.) Rennes, 1870.

Arc 1348.9 Monnaies et médailles. (Lenormant, F.) Paris, 1883.

Arc 1500.40.10 Monnaies féodales bretonnes de Charles le Chauve a Anne de Bretagne. (Buisson, Honoré.) Perigueux, 1961.

Arc 1500.56 Les monnaies féodales d'artois. (Richebé, C.) Paris, 1963.

Arc 1498.8 Monnaies féodales de France. (Poey d'Avant, F.) Paris, 1858. 4v.

Arc 1498.6 Monnaies féodales françaises. fasc. 1-3. (Caron, E.) Paris, 1882.

Arc 1500.8.5 Monnaies féodales françaises par M.E. Caron. Résumé. (Blancard, Louis.) Draguignan, 1885.

Arc 1498.9 Les monnaies françaises. (Dieudonné, A.) Paris, 1923.

Arc 1498.20 Les monnaies françaises depuis 1848. (Ernst, Barbara.) Braunschweig, 1968.

Arc 1500.17 Monnaies gauloises. (Robert, Charles.) Paris, 1880.

Arc 1522.6 Les monnaies gauloises du Tetelbierg. (Reding, Lucien.) Luxembourg, 1972.

Arc 1468.45 Monnaies grecques. (Allotte de la Fuÿe, F.M.) Paris, 1925.

Arc 1468.53 Monnaies grecques. (Ars Classica, Geneva.) Genève, 1929.

Arc 1468.22 Les monnaies grecques. (Babelon, E.) Paris, 1921.

Arc 1468.7 Monnaies grecques. (Imhoof-Blumer, Friedrich.) Amsterdam, 1883.

Arc 1468.7.5 Monnaies grecques. (Imhoof-Blumer, Friedrich.) Paris, 1883.

Arc 1468.54 Monnaies grecques antiques en or en argent. pt. 2. (Naville et Cie, Geneva.) Genève, 1924.

Arc 1335.91 Monnaies grecques antiques provenant des collection de S.A.I. le grand-duc Alexandra Michäilouit. (Kündig, W.) Genève, 1922.

Arc 1335.91.25 Monnaies grecques antiques provenant des doubles du British Museum des collections de feu le Gen. A.L. Bertier. (Kündig, W.) Genève, 1923.

Arc 1468.4 Monnaies grecques de la collection Photiadès Pacha. (Frochner, W.) Paris, 1890.

Arc 1428.32 Les monnaies grecques de Mylasa. (Akarca, A.) Paris, 1959.

Arc 1468.36 Les monnaies grecques du musée Saint Raymond de Toulouse. (Pierfitte, G.) Toulouse, 1939.

Arc 1458.20 Monnaies grecques et romaines. (Naville et Cie, Geneva.) Genève, 1925.

Arc 1493.14 Les monnaies hispaniques. (Ferrandis Torres, J.) Barcelona, 1929.

Arc 1500.22 Monnaies inconnues des évêques des innocens. (Rigollot, M.J.) Paris, 1857.

Arc 1428.1 Monnaies inédites, ou Peu connues de la Cilicie. (Langlois, Victor.) Paris, 1854.

Arc 1590.2.5 Monnaies inédites de Raimond Zacosta. (Lambros, P.) Athènes, 1877.

Arc 1428.7 Monnaies inédites des Croisades. (Vogué, C.J.) Paris, 1864.

Arc 1423.10 Les monnaies juives. (Reinach, Théodore.) Paris, 1887.

Arc 1500.5.5 Monnaies mérovingiennes de Saint-Denis. (Ponton d'Amécourt, G. de.) Macon, 1884.

Arc 1500.5 Monnaies mérovingiennes du palais et de l'ecole. (Ponton d'Amécourt, G. de.) Paris, 1862.

Arc 1408.10 Monnaies orientales. (L'Ecluse, Charles de.) Paris, 1888.

Arc 1478.12 Les monnaies romaines. (Blanchet, A.) Paris, 1896.

Arc 1500.46 Monnaies romaines. (Recamier, E.) Paris, 1925.

Arc 1478.83 Monnaies romaines antiques. (Naville et Cie, Geneva.) Genève, 1924.

Arc 1478.83.5 Monnaies romaines antiques. (Naville et Cie, Geneva.) Genève, 1925.

Arc 1335.90 Monnaies romaines impériales provenant des collections de Paul Vautier. (Kündig, W.) Genève, 1922.

Arc 1582.7 Monnayes russes, 1547-1855. (Shubert, Fedor F.) Leipsic, 1857.

Arc 1582.7.2PF Monnayes russes, 1547-1855. Atlas. (Shubert, Fedor F.) Leipsic, 1857.

Arc 810.10 Monnier, Marc. Pompéi et les Pompéiens. 3. éd. Paris, 1873.

Arc 810.10.5 Monnier, Marc. The wonders of Pompeii. N.Y., 1870.

Arc 810.28 Monod, Jules. La cité antique de Pompéi. Paris, 1911.

Arc 936.220.35 Monodija o kamenu. (Mijović, Pavle.) Kruševac, 1967.

Arc 1033.17.243 Monografia sul santuario di Nostra Donna della Grotta nella Praja della Schiavi. 3a ed. (Lomonaco, V.) Napoli, 1858.

Arc 93.46.3 Monografie a supplemento degli Atti. (Centro Studi e Documentazione sull'Italia Romana.) Milano. 1,1972+ 5v.

Arc 93.37F Monografie archeologiche della Sicilia. Series 3. (Società di Storia Patria per la Sicilia Orientale, Catania.) 1,1956

Arc 1033.44.15 Il monogramma del nome ss. di Gesú. (Sodo, G.) Napoli, 1885.

Arc 530.2.6 Monograph. (Archaeological Exploration of Sardis.) Cambridge. 1,1971+ 4v.

Arc 1598.15 A monograph of the silver dollar, good and bad. (Riddell, J.L.) New Orleans, 1845.

Arc 1615.7 Monograph of United States cents and half cents issued between the years 1793 and 1857. (Frossard, E.) Irvington, 1879.

Htn Arc 435.8.6* Monograph on Buddha Sâkyamuni's birth-place in the Nepalese Tarâi. (Führer, A.A.) Allahabad, 1897.

Arc 32.10F Monograph series. (Colt Archaeological Institute.) London. 1-5

Arc 700.8 Monographie de la voie sacrée éleusinienne. (Lenormant, F.) Paris, 1884.

Arc 1027.85F Monographie de l'hypogée-martyrium. (LaCroix, Camille.) Paris, 1883. 2v.

Arc 1020.86 Monographie de l'insigne Basilique de St. Saturnin. Paris, 1854.

Arc 830.101 Monographie des bornes milliaires du département du Gard. (Aurès, Auguste.) Nîmes, 1877.

Arc 1033.34.3 Monsacrati, M.A. De catenis San Petri dissertatio. Roma, 1828.

Arc 843.60 Monsalad, M.C.S.G. Arqueología romana y visigotica de extremadura. Madrid, 1900.

Arc 387.12.25 Monsignor Celestino Cavedoni. (Brandoli, Placido.) Modena, 1870.

Arc 387.12.30 Monsignor Celestino Cavedoni. (Cappeli, A.) Firenze, 1866.

Arc 647.1 Le Mont Olympe et l'Acarnanie. (Heuzey, L.) Paris, 1860.

Arc 830.35 La montagne d'Espiaup. (Piette, Edouard.) Paris, 1877.

Arc 1538.12 Montagu, H. Copper coins of England. London, 1893.

Arc 830.54 Montauzan, C. Germain de. Les fouilles de fourvière en 1911. Lyon, 1912.

Arc 726.247 Monte Sirai. (Rome. Università.) Roma, 1964. 4v.

Arc 843.130 Monteagudo, Luis. Galicia legendaria y arqueologica. Madrid, 1957.

Arc 1335.36 Montélhet, A. Musée crozatier - catalogue du médaillier. v.1-2. Paris, 1912.

Arc 895.5.5 Montelius, Oscar. Bibliographie de l'archéologie préhistorique de la Suède. Stockholm, 1875.

Arc 895.36.5 Montelius, Oscar. Bohulänska hällristningar. Stockholm, 1876.

Arc 893.23F Montelius, Oscar. Från jernåldern. Stockholm, 1869.

Arc 652.5F Montelius, Oscar. La Grèce préclassique. Stockholm, 1924-28. 2v.

Arc 893.12 Montelius, Oscar. Kulturgeschichte Schwedens von den ältesten Zeiten bis zum elften Jahrhundert nach Christus. Leipzig, 1906.

Arc 895.21.25 Montelius, Oscar. Minnen från lapparnes stenålder i Sverige. Stockholm, 1875-76.

Arc 895.5.4F Montelius, Oscar. Minnen från vår forntide. Stockholm, 1917.

Arc 895.5.25 Montelius, Oscar. Studier tillägnade Oscar Montelius. Stockholm, 1903.

Arc 895.5 Montelius, Oscar. La Suède préhistorique. Stockholm, n.d.

Arc 895.37 Montelius, Oscar. Sur les différents types des haches en Silex suédoise. Stockholm, 1875. 5 pam.

Arc 895.5.27F Montelius, Oscar. Swedish antiquities. Stockholm, 1922.

Arc 895.5.3 Montelius, Oscar. Les temps préhistoriques en Suède. Paris, 1895.

Arc 720.212 Monteluis, O. La civilization primitive en Italie. pt.1-2; plates. Stockholm, 1895. 5v.

Arc 726.16 Monteluis, O. Tombe ed antichità galliche in Italia. Roma, 1877.

Arc 720.212.5 Monteluis, O. Die vorklassiche Chronologie Italiens. Stockholm, 1912. 2v.

Arc 1027.54.9 Montenovesi, O. Le madonne antiche delle catacombe. Roma, 1904.

Arc 687.2 Montesanto, M. La città sacra (Lindo). Roma, 1930.

Arc 1018.18.18 Montescaglioro, F. Commemorazione di P. Raffaele Garucci. Napoli, 1885.

Arc 562.7 Montet, Pierre. Isis; ou, A la recherche de l'Egypte ensevelie. Paris, 1956.

Arc 600.75.5F Montet, Pierre. La nécropole royale de Tanis. Paris, 1947. 3v.

Arc 600.39 Montet, Pierre. Les nouvelles fouilles de Tanis (1929-32). Paris, 1933.

Arc 505.42 Montet, Pierre. Les reliques de l'art syrien dans l'Égypte du nouvel empire. Paris, 1937.

Arc 600.75 Montet, Pierre. Tanis, douze années de fouilles. Paris, 1942.

Arc 838.26 Montey, P. Historia da arquitectura primitiva em Portugal. Lisboa, 1943.

Arc 380.200.2 Montfaucon, B. de. L'antiquité expliquée. Supplément. Paris, 1724. 5v.

Arc 380.200 Montfaucon, B. de. L'antiquité expliquée. 2. éd. v.1-5. Paris, 1722. 10v.

Arc 720.201 Montfaucon, B. de. The antiquities of Italy. 2. ed. London, 1725.

Arc 380.201 Montfaucon, B. de. Antiquity explained. London, 1721. 7v.

Arc 726.9 Montfaucon, B. de. Diarium italicum. Paris, 1702.

Author and Title Listing

Htn	Arc 726.9.15*	Montjaucon, B. de. Diarium italicum. London, 1711.
	Arc 1033.17.462	Montorio, S. Zodiaco di Maria...Napoli. Napoli, 1715.
	Arc 935.4	Montucci, Henry. Les coupes du palais des empereurs byzantins. Paris, 1877.
	Arc 1550.7	Montvaesenet under Christian IV og Frederik III i tidsrummet, 1625-70. (Wilcke, Julius.) Kjøbenhavn, 1924.
	Arc 397.1	Monumens antiques. (Millin, A.L.) Paris, 1802-06. 2v.
X Cg	Arc 1045.5	Les monumens arabes. (Marçais, W.) Paris, 1903.
	Arc 673.1.2	Monumens de Delphes. (Witte, J. de Baron.) Roma, 1842.
	Arc 583.3	Monumens égyptiens de la Bibliothèque Nationale. pt.1-3. no.38. (Leedrain, E.) Paris, 1879-81.
	Arc 1016.8	Monument de Yu, ou La plus ancienne inscription de la Chine. (Hager, Joseph.) Paris, 1802.
	Arc 396.4.20	Monument érigé à la mémoire de R.P. de la Croix. (Société des Antiquaires de l'Ouest, Poitiers.) Poitiers, 1912.
	Arc 930.200	Das Monument von Adamklissi. (Tocilescou, G.G.) Wien, 1895.
	Arc 42.20	Monumenta Aegyptiaca. Bruxelles. 1,1968+
	Arc 302.35.2	Monumenta archaeologica. Novi Sad. 1,1974+ 2v.
	Arc 302.10F	Monumenta archaeologica. Pragae. 1,1948+ 18v.
	Arc 513.20	Monumenta Asiae Minoris antiqua. (Calder, W.M.) London, 1928-39. 8v.
	Arc 1030.55PF	Monumenta epigraphica christiana saeculo XIII. v.1-2. (Silvagni, Angelo.) Civitate Vaticana, 1943-
	Arc 900.207	Monumenta epigraphica Cracoviensia. (Lepkowski, J.) Krakow, 1883.
	Arc 628.7	Monumenta Graeca ex Museo Jacobi Nanni. Monumenta Graeca e Latina Jacobi Nanni. (Biagi, C.) Roma, 1785-87. 2v.
	Arc 900.200	Monumenta Hungariae archaeologica. (Magyar, Yudo.) Pesth, 1869-79. 4v.
	Arc 1143.14F	Monumenta Italiae graphica. (Bassi, Stelio.) Cremona, 1956-57.
	Arc 875.14	Monumenta orcadica. (Dietrichson, L.) Kristiania, 1906.
Htn	Arc 726.6*	Monumenta patavina. (Orsati, S.) Padova, 1652.
	Arc 1027.5.59	Monumenta subterranea selecta urbis Romae praesertim ex coemeterio Domitillae. Roma, n.d.
	Arc 1150.203	Monumenta tachygraphica codicus parisienis Latini. (Schmitz, W.) Hannoverae, 1882.
	Arc 435.2.12F	Monumental antiquities and inscriptions. (Führer, A.A.) Allahabad, 1891.
	Arc 895.17.20	Monumental art of Northern Europe from the Stone Age. (Hallström, Gustaf.) Stockholm, 1938. 2v.
	Arc 895.54	Monumental art of Northern Sweden from the Stone Age. (Hallström, Gustaf.) Stockholm, 1960.
	Arc 875.21	The monumental effigies of Scotland. (Brydall, R.) Glasgow, 1895.
	Arc 961.1.4	Monumental remains of Georgia. (Jones, C.C.) Savannah, 1861.
	Arc 435.2.25F	Monumental remains of the Dutch East India Company in the presidency of Madras. (Rea, Alexander.) Madras, 1897.
	Arc 73.2	Monumenti - annali - bulletini 1854-5 and Monumenti - annali 1856. (Rome. Istituto.) Rome.
	Arc 77.1.2	Monumenti antichi. Milan. 1-47 47v.
	Arc 766.4.5	I monumenti antichi di Roma e suburbio. (Lugli, Giuseppe.) Roma, 1930-40. 4v.
Htn	Arc 380.209*	Monumenti antichi inedite. v.1-2. (Winckelmann, J.) Roma, 1767.
	Arc 1018.52	I monumenti cristiani. (Grossi-Gondi, F.) Roma, 1920-23. 2v.
	Arc 1033.36	Monumenti cristiani. (Zardetti, C.) Milano, 1843.
	Arc 1020.10	Monumenti cristiani del Foro Romano. (Valeri, A.) Roma, 1900.
	Arc 1020.16	Monumenti cristiani del Trentino. (Orsi, P.) Roma, 1883.
	Arc 720.216	Monumenti cumani. (Fiorelli, G.) Napoli, 1853.
	Arc 1027.62	I monumenti degli antichi cristiani in relazione col progresso. (Diamilla.) Roma, 1850.
	Arc 726.249	I monumenti della necropoli romana di Sarsina. (Aurigemma, Salvatore.) Roma, 1963.
	Arc 785.13.85	I monumenti della parte meridionale del Foro Romano. (Stucchi, S.) Roma, 1958.
	Arc 1015.210	Monumenti delle arti cristiane primitive nella metropoli del cristianismo. (Marchi, Giuseppe.) Roma, 1844.
	Arc 746.12.10F	Monumenti di cere antica. (Grifi, L.) Roma, 1841.
NEDL	Arc 726.40	I monumenti e le opere d'arte. (Meomartini, A.) Benevento, 1889.
	Arc 740.204	Monumenti etruschi. (Inghirami, F.) Badia, 1821-25. 9v.
	Arc 93.44F	Monumenti etruschi. Firenze. 1,1967+ 3v.
	Arc 726.7	Monumenti gabini della Villa Pinciana. (Visconti, E.A.) Milano, 1835.
	Arc 726.7.5	Monumenti gabini della Villa Pinciana. (Visconti, E.A.) Roma, 1797.
	Arc 1030.23	Monumenti gentileschi e cristiani...Lorio nell'Aurelia. (Amati, G.) Roma, 1824.
	Arc 785.104	Monumenti romani scoperti negli anni 1938-XVI-1939-XVII nell'area del Palazzo della Cancelleria. (Nogara, Bartolomeo.) Roma, 1942.
	Arc 726.71.10	Monumenti Sabini. (Guattani, G.A.) Roma, 1827-28. 3v.
	Arc 672.1.49F	Monumenti veneti nell'isola di Creta. v.1, pt.1-2, v.2-4. (Gerola, G.) Venezia, 1905-32. 5v.
	Arc 1033.58.15	Il monumento apostolico a San Sebastiano sulla Via Appia. (Styger, Paolo.) Roma, 1925.
	Arc 1020.135	El monumento paleocristiano de Centcelles. (Camprubi Alemany, Francisco.) Barcelona, 1952.
	Arc 843.14	Monumento sepulcral romano de Lloret de Mar. (Botet y Sisó, J.) Gerona, 1892.
	Arc 94.45	Los monumentos arqueologicos y tesoro artistico de Tarragona y su provincia. 1936-1939
	Arc 820.5	Les monuments anciens de la Tarentaise (Savoie). (Borrel, E.L.) Paris, 1884. 2v.
	Arc 930.204	Monuments byzantins inédits. (Schlumberger, G.) Macon, 1884.
	Arc 830.25	Monuments celtiques des environs de Luzarches. (Hahn, Alexandre.) Paris, 1867.
	Arc 608.2.52	Monuments chrétiens d'Hippone. (Marec, Erwan.) Paris, 1958.
	Arc 1150.14	Monuments de l'abbaye celtique. (Staerk, Antonio.) Tournai, 1914.
	Arc 710.18F	Les monuments de l'acropole. (Balanos, N.) Paris, 1936.
	Arc 545.2	Monuments de l'Égypte et de la Nubie. (Champollion, J.F.) Paris, 1835-45.
	Arc 584.100.20F	Monuments de l'Egypte gréco-romaine. (Société Royale d'Archéologie d'Alexandrie.) Bergamo. 1-2,1926-1934 3v.
	Arc 430.201	Les monuments de l'Inde. (Lebon, G.) Paris, 1893.
	Arc 750.217F	Les monuments de Rome après la chute de l'empire. (Rodacanchi, E.) Paris, 1914.
	Arc 545.28.3	Monuments divers..en Égypte et en Nubie. (Mariette, A.) Paris, 1872-1889. 2v.
	Arc 608.33.15	Monuments en pierres séches du Fadnoun, Tassili n'Ajjer. (Savary, Jean Pierre.) Paris, 1966.
	Arc 1.11F	Monuments et memoirs. (France. Academie des Inscriptions.) Paris. 1-55 45v.
	Arc 380.210	Monuments et ouvrages d'art antiques. (Quatremère de Quincy, A.C.) Paris, 1829.
	Arc 405.2F	Monuments et sites d'art. (UNESCO.) Paris, 1950.
	Arc 823.80	Monuments et trésors de la Gaule. (Eydoux, Henri Paul.) Paris, 1962.
	Arc 543.4.50	Les monuments funeraires de la steppe des Kirghizes. (Castagné, J.) Orenburg, 1911.
	Arc 600.15.5	Les monuments funéraires de l'Egypte ancienne. (Daninos, A.) Paris, 1899.
	Arc 830.98	Monuments gallo-romains du département de l'Jndre. (Voisin, F.) Chateauroux, 1877.
	Arc 635.208	Monuments grècs. (Association pour l'Encouragement des Études Grècques en France, Paris.) Paris, 1882-97. 2v.
	Arc 605.204	Les monuments historiques de la Tunise. (Cagnet, R.) Paris, 1898-99. 2v.
	Arc 830.165.5	Les monuments historiques de l'Orne. (Caumont, Arcisse de.) Caen, 187-. 2v.
	Arc 830.63	Les monuments mégalithiques. (Bousrez, Louis.) Tours, 1894.
	Arc 830.63.5	Les monuments mégalithiques. (Contades, G.) Paris, 1886.
	Arc 1093.2.13	Les monuments mégalithiques. (Paniagua, A.) Paris, 1912.
	Arc 830.11.5	Les monuments mégalithiques de Carnac et de Locmariaquer. (Le Rouzic, Z.) n.p., 1901?
	Arc 497.39	Les monuments megalithiques de Palestine. Thèse. (Stekelis, M.) Paris, 1935.
	Arc 1473.3	Monuments numismatiques et sphragistiques...byzantin. (Schlumberger, G.) Paris, 1880.
	Arc 772.14	The monuments of ancient Rome. (Robathan, D.) Rome, 1950.
	Arc 1020.10.39	The monuments of Christian Rome. (Favshingham, A.L.) N.Y., 1908.
	Arc 1027.33	Monuments of early Christian art. (Appell, J.W.) London, 1872.
	Arc 557.1	The monuments of Egypt. (Hawks, F.L.) N.Y., 1850.
	Arc 1018.7.2	Monuments of the early church. (Lourie, W.) N.Y., 1901.
	Arc 1018.7.5	Monuments of the early church. (Lourie, W.) N.Y., 1906.
	Arc 562.1.6	The monuments of upper Egypt. (Mariette, A.) Alexandria, 1877.
	Arc 562.1.5	The monuments of upper Egypt. (Mariette, A.) Boston, 1890.
	Arc 936.120.10	Monumentul de la Adamklissi Tropaeum Traiani. (Florescu, Florea B.) București, 1959.
	Arc 545.224	Mook, F. Aegyptens vormetallische Zeit. Wuerzburg, 1880.
	Arc 1221.6	Moore, Ada S. Ancient oriental cylinder and other seals with a description of the collection of Mrs. William H. Moore. Chicago, 1940.
	Arc 950.202.38F	Moore, C.B. Aboriginal sites on Tennessee River. Philadelphia, 1915.
	Arc 983.9	Moore, C.B. Aboriginal urn-burial in the United States. Lancaster, 1904.
	Arc 950.202.2	Moore, C.B. Additional mounds of Duval and of Clay Counties, Florida. n.p., 1896.
	Arc 950.202.25	Moore, C.B. Antiquities of the Onachita Valley. Philadelphia, 1909.
	Arc 950.202.29	Moore, C.B. Antiquities of the St. Francis, White and Black rivers, Arkansas. Philadelphia, 1910.
	Arc 960.2.15F	Moore, C.B. As to Cooper from the mounds of the St. John's River, Florida. Philadelphia, 1894.
	Arc 950.202.11	Moore, C.B. Certain aboriginal remains of the northwestern Florida coast. pt.1-2. Philadelphia, 1901. 2v.
	Arc 950.200.9	Moore, C.B. Certain aboriginal mounds. Philadelphia, 1898.
	Arc 950.202.5	Moore, C.B. Certain aboriginal mounds of the Georgia coast. Philadelphia, 1897.
	Arc 950.202.9	Moore, C.B. Certain aboriginal remains...Alabama River. Philadelphia, 1899.
	Arc 950.202.15	Moore, C.B. Certain aboriginal remains...Florida coast. Philadelphia, 1903.
	Arc 950.202.17	Moore, C.B. Certain aboriginal remains of the Black Warrior River. Philadelphia, 1905.
	Arc 950.202.13	Moore, C.B. Certain antiquities of the Florida west coast. Philadelphia, 1900.
	Arc 950.202.23	Moore, C.B. Certain mounds of Arkansas and Mississippi. Philadelphia, 1908.
	Arc 950.202	Moore, C.B. Certain river mounds of Duval County, Florida. Philadelphia, 1895.
	Arc 950.201A	Moore, C.B. Certain sand mounds of the St. John's River. pt.1-2. Philadelphia, 1894.
	Arc 950.202.21	Moore, C.B. Moundville revisited. Philadelphia, 1907.
	Arc 950.202.12F	Moore, C.B. The northwestern Florida coast revisited. Philadelphia, 1918.
	Arc 1077.1.9	Moore, C.B. Sheet-copper from the mounds. Washington, 1903.
	Arc 950.202.35	Moore, C.B. Some aboriginal sites in Louisiana and Arkansas. Philadelphia, 1913.
	Arc 950.202.33	Moore, C.B. Some aboriginal sites on Mississippi River. Philadelphia, 1911.
	Arc 950.202.32	Moore, C.B. Some aboriginal sites on the Red River. Philadelphia, 1912.
	Arc 608.2.8	Moore, M. Carthage of the Phoenicians. London, 1905.
	Arc 1130.5	Moore, Margaret F. Two select bibliographies mediaeval historical study. London, 1912.
	Arc 131.1	Moore, William. The Gentlemen's Society at Spalding. Cambridge, 1909. 2 pam.
	Arc 967.3	Moorehead, W.K. Certain peculiar earthworks near Andover, Massachusetts. Andover, 1912.
	Arc 969.1.3	Moorehead, W.K. Fort Ancient. Cincinnati, 1890.
	Arc 967.5	Moorehead, W.K. The Merrimack archaeological survey. Salem, Mass., 1931.
	Arc 953.18.5	Moorehead, W.K. A narrative of explorations of New Mexico, Arizona, Indiana. Andover, 1906.
	Arc 969.1.2	Moorehead, W.K. Primitive man in Ohio. N.Y., 1892.
	Arc 953.18	Moorehead, W.K. The stone age in North America. Boston, 1910. 2v.
	Arc 505.115	Moortgat, Anton. Tell Chuēra in Nordost-Syrien. Köln, 1960.
	Arc 505.115.2	Moortgat, Anton. Tell Chuēra in Nordost-Syrien. Köln, 1962.
	Arc 505.115.3	Moortgat, Anton. Tell Chuēra in Nordost-Syrien. Köln, 1965.

Arc 913.25 Moosbrugger, Leu Rudolf. Die Schweiz zur Merowingerzeit. Bern, 1971. 2v.
Arc 1460.8 Mor(eta) urb(is)-Antiona. (Baldus, Hans Roland.) Frankfurt am Main, 1969.
Arc 1020.97 Morales, Ambrosio de. Viage...para reconocer las reliquias de santos, sepulcros reales. Madrid, 1765.
Arc 843.12 Morán Bardon, C. Investigaciones acerca de arqueologia y prehistoria de la region salamantina. Salamanca, 1919.
Arc 530.130 Moraux, Paul. Une imprécation funéraire a néocésarée. Paris, 1959.
Arc 1588.4.70 Moravská mince doby husitské. (Sejbal, Jiří.) Brno, 1965.
Arc 1588.4.73 Moravské mincovny. Vyd. 1. (Pŏsvář, Jaroslav.) Brno, 1970.
Arc 1312.12 Moravské numismatické zprávy. Brno. 1,1956+
Arc 830.2.5 Morbihan antiquités. (Hirmenech, H.P.) Paris, n.d. 5 pam.
Arc 830.2 Le Morbihan son histoire et ses monuments. (Delandre, M.C.) Paris, 1847. 2v.
Arc 1490.6 Morbio, C. Opere storico-numismatiche. Bologna, 1870.
Arc 1390.6 Morbio, Carlo. Delle monete battute da Carlo Magno in Italia. Milano, 1866.
Arc 1400.3 Morbio, Carlo. Monete franco-italiche ossidionali. Asti, 1865.
Arc 1335.21 Morbio, Carlo. VI catalogo dei duplicati delle raccolte. Milano, 1876.
Arc 1027.2 Morcelli, S.A. Agapea Michaëleia. Bononiae, 1822.
Arc 1027.2.5 Morcelli, S.A. Comento sull'iscrizione sepolcrale. Modena, 1824.
Arc 1254.5 Mordtmann, A.D. Peri byzantinōn molybdoboyllōn. n.p., n.d.
Arc 1254.4 Mordtmann, A.D. Sur les sceaux et plombs byzantins. Constantinople, 1873.
Arc 935.6 Mordtmann, J. Das Denkmal des Porphyrius. Athen, 1880.
Arc 935.10 Mordtmann, J. Esquisse topographique de Constantinople. Lille, 1892.
Arc 820.202 Moreau, F. Collection Caranda. St. Quentin, 1877. 4v.
Arc 830.38 Moreau, Frédéric. Catalogue de la collection Caranda. v.1-2. Supplément. St. Quentin, 1895-96.
Arc 830.38.2 Moreau, Frédéric. Petit album suite au Caranda. St. Quentin, 1896.
Arc 830.22.9 Moreau de Mantour, Philibert B. Observations sur des monuments d'antiquité trouvez dans l'eglise cathedrale de Paris. Paris, 1711.
Arc 830.84 Moreau de Néris, E. Néris, capitale des Gaules. Paris, 1902.
Arc 66.1.213 La morée franque. (Bon, Antoine.) Paris, 1969. 2v.
Arc 1367.1 Morel, André. Specimen universae rei nummariae antiquae. Paris, 1683.
Arc 915.10 Morel, C. Genève et la colonie de Vienne sous les Romains. pt.1. Genève, 1879? 2 pam.
Arc 1500.3 Morel-Fatio, A. Catalogue raisonné de la collection de deniers merovingiens. Paris, 1890.
Arc 820.217F Morel-Macler, F. Antiquités Mandeure. Montbéliard, 1847.
Htn Arc 1475.3* Morelli, A. Thesaurus Morellianus. Amsterdam, 1734. 2v.
Arc 1625.5 Moreno, Alvaro. El signo de pesos. México, 1965.
Arc 1027.41.25 Moreschi, L. Indicazione dei dipinti a buon presco dell'Apostolo S. Paolo. Roma, 1867.
Arc 1016.216.3 Moreschi, L. Sulla sedia pontificale della basilica di S. Paolo. n.p., n.d.
Arc 1016.216 Moreschi, L. Sulla sedia pontificale della basilica di S. Paolo. Roma, 1838.
Arc 1015.5 Moretto, P. De S'Callisto pp. etm ejusque Basilica. Romae, 1767.
Arc 530.2.4F Morey, Charles B. Roman and Christian sculpture. Princeton, 1924.
Arc 1163.3.115F Morfologija ćiriličkih natpisa na Balkanu. (Tomović, Gordana.) Beograd, 1974.
Arc 1274.9 Morgan, Frederick Charles. A concise list of seals belonging to the Dean and Chapter of Hereford Cathedral. Hereford, 1966.
Arc 545.203 Morgan, J. Fouilles à Dahchour. Vienna, 1895.
Arc 562.3 Morgan, J. Recherches sur les origines de l'Égypte. Paris, 1896-97.
Arc 1433.38 Morgan, J. de. Contribution à l'étude des ateliers monétaires...rois Sassanides. Paris, 1913.
Arc 493.3 Morgan, J. de. Le délégation en Perse. Paris, 1902.
Arc 1408.4 Morgan, J. de. Manuel de numismatique orientale de l'antiquité et du moyen-age. Paris, 1923-36.
Arc 968.2 Morgan, L.H. On the ruins of a stone pueblo on the Animas River in New Mexico. Salem, 1879.
Arc 885.15 Morgan, O. Notice of a tessellated pavement. Newport, 1866.
Arc 969.1.05 Morgan, Richard G. Bibliography of Ohio archaeology. Columbus, 1947.
Arc 885.7 Morgan, W.D. An antiquarian survey of East Gower, Glamorganshire. London, 1899.
Htn Arc 1675.23.5* Morganti, Bento. Nummismalogia, ou Breve recopilação de algunas medalhas dos emperadores romanos de ouro. Lisboa, 1737.
Arc 1453.3 Morgenroth, Sigmund. Medals and plaquettes from the S. Morgenroth collection. Chicago, 1944.
Arc 1163.2.23 Moriano, F. Ortografía general paleográfica-bibliográfica de la lengua castellana. Sevilla, 1866.
Htn Arc 1020.32.5* Morigi, P. Santuario della città e diocesi di Milano. Milano, 1603.
Arc 1076.3.23 Morillot, L. Étude sur l'emploi de clochettes. Dijon, 1888.
Arc 1518.6 Morin, Francois. Monnaies de Belgique de 1832 à 1963. Boom, 1964.
Arc 1518.6.5 Morin, Francois. Monnaies de Belgique de 1832 à 1967. Anvers, 1968.
Arc 397.13 Morin, Jean. Les artistes préhistoriques. Paris, 1933.
Arc 1675.63 Morin, Victor. Les médailles décerniés aux Indien. Ottawa, 1916.
Arc 830.59 Morin-Jean. La verrerie en Gaule à l'époque romaine. Le Mans, 1913.
Arc 830.59.2 Morin-Jean. La verrerie en Gaule sous l'empire romain. Paris, 1913.
Arc 830.59.5 Morin-Jean. La verrerie en Gaule sous l'empire romain. Paris, 1923.
Arc 830.130.23 Morlet, Antonin. Glozel. v.2. Macon, 1962.
Arc 830.130.25 Morlet, Antonin. Petit historique de l'affaire de Glozel. Marsat, 1970.
Arc 830.230 Morlet, Antonin. Vichy gallo-romain. Macon, 1957.
Arc 383.56 Morleyana. Santa Fe, New Mexico, 1950.
Arc 810.53 Morlicchio, F. Guide to Pompei illustrated. Pompei, 1901.
Arc 387.4.8 Moroni, A. Nuovo catalogo delle opere...dell'abate Francesco Cancellieri. Roma, 1881.
Arc 880.17 Morres, Hervey Montmorency. A historical and critical inquiry into the origin and primitive use of the Irish pillar-tower. London, 1821.
Arc 953.7 Morris, C. Extinct races of America - the mound builders. Review. n.p., n.d.
Arc 1076.3.105 Morris, E. Legends o' the bells. London, 1935.
Arc 968.2.70 Morris, E.H. Archaeological studies in the La Plata district, southwestern Colorado and northwestern New Mexico. Washington, 1939.
Arc 1475.8 Morris, R. The twelve Caesars. La Grange, Ky., 1877.
Arc 501.19 Morrison, W. The recovery of Jerusalem. London, 1871.
Arc 1076.4 Morse, E.S. On the so-called bow puller of antiquity. Salem, 1894.
Arc 426.1 Morse, E.S. Traces of an early race in Japan. N.Y., 1879.
Arc 975.1 Morss, Noel. The ancient culture of the Fremont River in Utah. Cambridge, Mass., 1931.
Arc 1578.15 Mort, Selwyn R. Coins of the Hapsburg emperors and related issues. Melbourne, 1959.
Arc 726.59.40 The mortar wreck in Mellieha Bay. (Frost, Honor.) London, 1969.
Arc 397.10 Mortel, Victor. Mélanges d'archéologie; antiquité romaine et moyen âge. Paris, 1914-15. 2v.
Arc 1163.3.80 Mortero y Simón, C. Apuntes de iniciacion a la paleografia española de los siglos XII a XVII. Madrid, 1963.
Arc 1077.2.3 Mortillet, G. de. Le signe de la croix avant de Christianité. Paris, 1866.
Arc 861.21.9 Mortimer, J.P. Forty years' research in British and Saxon burial grounds of East Yorkshire. London, 1879.
Arc 905.18.10 Morton, F. Hallstatt. Hallstatt, 1953. 2v.
Arc 600.180F Morzan, J. de. Carte de la nécropole memphite. n.p., 1897.
Arc 830.181 Les mosaïques de Clervae. (Huguenotte, A.) Besançon, 1925.
Arc 726.246.5 Moscati, Sabatino. Le stele puniche di Nora nel museo nazionale di Cagliari. Roma, 1970.
Arc 608.92 Moscati, Sabatino. Tra Cartagine e Roma. Milano, 1971.
Arc 1153.81 Moschetti, G. Primordi esegetici sulla legislazione longobardo. Spoleto, 1954.
Arc 925.320 Moscow. Gosudarstvennyi Istoricheskii Muzei. Iaroslavskoe Povolzh'e X-XI vv. po materialam Timerevskogo Mikhailovskogo i Petrovskogo mogil'nikov. Moskva, 1963.
Arc 1583.32 Moscow. Gosudarstvennyi Istoricheskii Muzei. Monety SSSR. Moskva, 1971.
Arc 923.126 Moscow. Gosudarstvennyi Istoricheskii Muzei. Raboty arhheologicheskikh ekspeditsii. Moskva, 1941. 2v.
Arc 1335.107 Moscow. Gosudarstvennyi Rumiantsovskii Muzei. Numizmaticheskii kabinet. Moskva, 1884.
Arc 895.42 Mosefund lerkar fra yngre stenalder. (Becker, C.) København, 1948.
Arc 497.29 Moses and the monuments. (Kyle, M.G.) London, 1920.
Arc 1615.9 Mosher, S. United States commemorative coins, 1892-1939. N.Y., 1940.
Arc 925.13.200 Moshkova, Marina G. Proiskhazhdenie rannesarmatskoi (prokhorovskoi) kul'tury. Moskva, 1974.
Arc 1408.7 Moshniagin, D.I. Monety stran zarubezhnoi Azii i Afriki XIX-XX veka. Moskva, 1967.
Arc 1584.31 Moskovskie klady. (Veksler, Aleksandr G.) Moskva, 1973.
Arc 1163.3.30 Moskovskii Arkheologicheskii Institut. Bukvitsa na 77 listakh. Moskva, 1909.
Arc 1160.210F Moskovskii Arkheologicheskii Institut. Sbornik snimkov s russkago pis'ma. Moskva, 1913. 2v.
Arc 1160.210.5F Moskovskii Arkheologicheskii Institut. Sbornik snimkov s russkago pis'ma XIII-XVIII vv. Moskva, 1908.
Arc 287.5 Moskovskoe Arkheologicheskoe Obshchestvo. Arkheologicheskiia izvestiia i zametki. Moskva. 2-7,1894-1900 7v.
Arc 287.3F Moskovskoe Arkheologicheskoe Obshchestvo. Drevnosti. Arkheologicheskii vestnike. Moskva. 1867-1868//
Arc 416.7F Moskovskoe Arkheologicheskoe Obshchestvo. Drevnosti vostoch'iia trudi vostochnoi kommissii. Moskva, 1889-1915. 5v.
Arc 925.16 Moskovskoe Arkheologicheskoe Obshchestvo. Izviestiia Kavkazskago otdieleniia. Vyp. 6 (1921). Tifilis, n.d.
Arc 925.15F Moskovskoe Arkheologicheskoe Obshchestvo. Materialy po...Rossii. Moskva, 1893- 2v.
Arc 287.2F Moskovskoe Arkheologicheskoe Obshchestvo. Slisok izdanii. Moskva, 1913.
Arc 1312.6 Moskovskoe Numizmaticheskoe Obshchestvo. Numizmaticheskii sbornik. Moskva. 3,1915
Arc 936.14.142 Moskwa, Kazimierz. Pradzieje powiatu rzeszowskiego. Lublin, 1964.
Arc 505.5.95 La mosquée Al Aqsa et la Néa de Justinien. (Creswell, K.A.) Liege, 1929.
Arc 672.1.7 Mosso, Angelo. Dawn of Mediterranean civilization. London, 1910.
Arc 672.1.7.5 Mosso, Angelo. Dawn of Mediterranean civilization. N.Y., 1911.
Arc 672.1.6 Mosso, Angelo. Le origini della civilta Mediterranea. Milano, 1910.
Arc 672.1.5 Mosso, Angelo. Palaces of Crete and their builders. London, 1907.
Arc 672.1.4 Mosso, Angelo. The palaces of Crete and their builders. N.Y., 1907.
Arc 557.5 Most ancient Egypt. (Hayes, William Christopher.) Chicago, 1965.
Htn Arc 865.9.5* The most notable antiquity of Great Britain. (Jones, Inigo.) London, 1655.
Htn Arc 865.9* The most notable antiquity of Great Britain. (Jones, Inigo.) London, 1655. 2 pam.
Arc 855.215 Most notable antiquity of Great Britain called Stone-Heng. (Jones, I.) London, 1725.
Arc 865.9.11 The most notable antiquity of Great Britain called Stone-Heng. (Jones, Inigo.) Farnborough, 1971.
Htn Arc 865.9.10F* The most notable antiquity of Great Britain called Stone-Heng. (Jones, Inigo.) London, 1725.
Arc 743.27 Mostra del restauro archeologico. Grosseto, 1970.
Arc 712.15 Mot, J. de. Le frontal orientale du Parthenon. Bruxelles, 1906.
Arc 870.15.7 Mothersole, Jessie. Agricola's road into Scotland. London, 1927.
Arc 870.14.9 Mothersole, Jessie. Hadrian's wall. London, 1922.
Arc 875.41 Mothersole, Jessie. In Roman Scotland. London, 1927.
Arc 736.6.10 Motya, a Phoenician and Carthaginian city in Sicily. (Isserlin, B.S.J.) Leiden, 1974.
Arc 736.6.5 Motya. (Whitaker, J.I.S.) London, 1921.

Arc 936.6.36 Motyiwj tiguralne w sztuce ludnosci kultury luzyckiej. (Gediza, Boguslaw.) Wrocław, 1970.
Arc 861.95 Moule, H.J. Dorchester antiquities. Dorchester, 1906.
Arc 1033.17.201 Mouls, X. Pélérinage de Notre-Dame d'Arcachon. Bordeaux, 1857.
Arc 953.5 The mound builders. (MacLean, J.P.) Cincinnati, 1879.
Arc 501.17 A mound of many cities. (Bliss, F.J.) London, 1894.
NEDL Arc 585.7 Mound of the Jew and City of Onias. (Naville, E.H.) London, 1890.
Arc 967.1.3 The mounds of the Mississippi Valley. (Carr, L.) Cambridge, 188-?
Arc 967.1.5 The mounds of the Mississippi Valley. (Carr, L.) Frankfort, 1883.
Arc 967.1.4 The mounds of the Mississippi Valley. (Carr, L.) Washington, 1893.
Arc 416.44 Mounds of the Near East. (Lloyd, Seton Howard Frederick.) Edinburgh, 1963.
Arc 950.202.21 Moundville revisited. (Moore, C.B.) Philadelphia, 1907.
Arc 830.16 The mount. (Hamerton, P.G.) Boston, 1897.
Arc 501.18 Mount Seir. (Hull, E.) London, 1885.
Arc 595.55 The mountains of Pharaoh. (Cottrell, Leonard.) N.Y., 1956.
Arc 925.9 Mourier, J. L'archéologie au Caucase. Paris, 1887.
Arc 505.73.5 Mouterde, René. Beyrouth, ville romaine. Beyrouth, 1952.
Arc 708.12 Moüy, Charles. Lettres athéniennes. Paris, 1887.
Arc 880.39.5A Movius, H.L. The Irish Stone Age. Cambridge, Eng., 1942.
Arc 880.39 Movius, H.L. Kilgreany cove, county Waterford. Dublin? 1935.
Arc 1480.11 Mowat, Robert. Explication d'une marque monétaire du tempe de Constantin. Paris, 1886.
Arc 590.7 Moymia tōn Aigyptian. 2. ed. (Kettner, F.G.) Lipsiae, 1703. 3 pam.
Arc 69.2 Moyseion kai Bibliothēkē. (Smyrna. Enaggelikēs Scholēs.) Smyrna. 1873-1886 3v.
Arc 925.9.60 Mozdokskii mogil'nik. (Iessen, Aleksandr A.) Leningrad, 1940.
Arc 736.6 Mozia, studi storico-archeologico. (Coglitore, I.) Catania, 1894.
Arc 736.20 Mozia. (Missione Archeologica della Soprintendenza alle Antichità della Sicilia Occidentale e dell'Università di Roma.) Roma, 1964- 8v.
Arc 936.14.530 Mozowsze pólnocno-wschodnie we wczesnym średniowieczu. 1. wyd. (Tyszkiewicz, Jan.) Warszawa, 1974.
Arc 905.128 Mozsolics, Anália. Bronzefunde des Karpatenbeckens. Budapest, 1967.
Arc 905.70 Mozsolics, Anália. Der Goldfund von Velem-Szentvid. Basel, 1950.
Arc 530.95F Mtskheta; itogi arkheologicheskikh issledovanii. (Akademiia nauk Gruz SSR, Tiflis. Institut Istorii.) Tbilisi, 1955.
Arc 530.95.2F Mtskheta; itogi arkheologicheskikh issledovanii. (Akademiia nauk Gruz SSR, Tiflis. Institut Istorii.) Tbilisi, 1958.
Arc 530.95.5 Mtskheta; putevaditel'. (Tkeshelashvili, G.) Tbilisi, 1958.
Arc 530.95.10 Mtskheta. (Apakidze, A.M.) Tbilisi, 1959.
Arc 1433.29 Mubarek, Ghalib Bey. Notices sur les monnaies turques. Bruxelles, 1899.
Arc 1077.1 Much, M. Die Kupferzeit in Europa. Jena, 1893.
Arc 612.20 Much, M. Die Trugspiegelung orientalischer Kultur in den vorgeschichtlichen Zeitaltern Nord- und Mitteleuropas. Jena, 1907.
Arc 1535.205F Mudie, James. An historical and critical account...medals. London, 1820.
Arc 1093.8 Müfid, Arif. Katalog der Bleisarkophage. Istanbul, 1932.
Arc 1423.22 Muehsam, Alice. Coin and temple; a study of the architectural representation on ancient Jewish coins. Leeds, 1966.
Arc 853.268F Müller, A. von. Fohrde und Hohenferchesar; zwei germanische Gräberfelder der frühen römischen Kaiserzeit aus der Mark Brandenburg. Berlin, 1962.
Arc 853.273.5 Müller, Adriaan. Berlins Urgeschichte. Berlin, 1964.
Arc 853.273F Müller, Adriaan. Die jungbronzezeitliche Siedlung von Berlin-Lichterfelde. Berlin, 1964.
Arc 848.52 Mueller, Adriaan von. Formenkreise der älteren römischen Kaiserzeit im Raum zwischen Havelseinplatte und Ostsee. Berlin, 1957.
Arc 853.355 Müller, Adriaan von. Gesicherte Spuren. 1. Aufl. Berlin, 1972.
Arc 383.31F Müller, Adrian von. Gandert-Festschrift zum sechzigsten Geburtstag. Berlin, 1959.
Arc 1663.21 Müller, Bernhard. Medaillen und Münzen im Dienste der Religion. Berlin, 1915.
Arc 726.24 Müller, G.A. Tempel zu Tivoli bei Rom. Leipzig, 1899.
Arc 375.1 Müller, H.A. Archäologisches Wörterbuch. Leipzig, 1877-78. 2v.
Arc 853.272F Müller, Hanns H. Die Haustiere der mitteldeutschen Bandkiramiker. Berlin, 1964.
Arc 1510.6 Müller, J.H. Deutsche Münzgeschichte biz zu der Ottonenzeit. Leipzig, 1860.
Arc 505.1 Mueller, K.O. Antiquitates Antiochenae. Goettingen, 1839.
Arc 628.4 Müller, K.O. Denkmäler der alten Kunst. Göttingen, 1854-81. 2v.
Arc 628.4.2 Müller, K.O. Denkmäler der alten Kunst. v.1-2. Göttingen, 1832.
Arc 397.3 Müller, K.O. Kunstarchaeologische Werke. v.1-5. Berlin, 1873. 2v.
Arc 397.3.2 Müller, K.O. Nouveau manuel d'archéologie. v.1-2 and atlas. Paris, 1841. 3v.
Arc 1190.4 Müller, Karl. Unsere Kanzleisprache. Dresden, 1926.
Arc 1470.21.5 Müller, L. Die Münzen des thracischen Königs Lysimachus. Kopenhagen, 1858.
Htn Arc 1470.21.6* Müller, L. Die Münzen des thracischen Königs Lysimachus. Kopenhagen, 1858.
Arc 1470.1 Mueller, L. Numismatique d'Alexander le Grand. Text and atlas. Copenhagen, 1855. 2v.
Arc 1435.1 Mueller, L. Numismatique de l'ancienne Afrique. v.1 and supplement. Copenhague, 1860-94. 2v.
Arc 1438.2 Mueller, L. Numismatique de l'ancienne Afrique. v.1-3. Bologne, 1964. 2v.
Arc 1435.1.5 Mueller, L. Numismatique de l'ancienne Afrique. v.1-3. Copenhague, 1860-62.
Arc 1470.21 Müller, L. Den thraciske konge Lysimachus's mynter. Kjøbenhavn, 1857.
Arc 1077.2.49 Müller, Ludvig. Det saakaldte Hagekors's Anvendelse og Betydning i Aldtiden. København, 1877.
Arc 1033.33 Müller, N. Koimeterien die altchristlichen Begrabnis. Leipzig, 1901.
Arc 1027.18.5 Müller, Nikolaus. Le catacombe degli ebrei...via Appia. Roma, 1885?
Arc 1027.18.6 Müller, Nikolaus. Die Inschriften der jüdischen Katakombe. Leipzig, 1919.
Arc 1027.18.7 Müller, Nikolaus. Die jüdische Katakombe am Monteverde zu Rom. Leipzig, 1912.
Arc 716.6 Mueller, R.O. Minervae Poliadis Sacra et Aedem in Arce Athenarum. Göttingen, 1820.
Arc 830.18.23 Müller, Reiner. Die Angaben der römischen Itinerare über die Heerstrasse Köln-Eifel-Reims. Münstereifel, 1933.
Arc 612.5 Müller, S. L'Europe préhistorique. Paris, 1907.
Arc 893.1A Mueller, S. Nordische Altertumskunde. Strassburg, 1896. 2v.
Arc 890.206 Mueller, S. Ordnung af Danmark's oldsager stenalderen. Paris, 1888. 2v.
Arc 612.4 Müller, S. Urgeschichte Europas. Strassburg, 1905.
X Cg Arc 893.1.5 Mueller, S. Vor oldtisminder Danmarks. Kjøbenhavn, 1897.
Arc 545.230 Müller, W.M. Egyptological researches. Results, 1904. Washington, 1906. 3v.
Arc 853.140F Müller-Karpe, H. Das Arnenfeld von Kelheim. Kallmünz, 1954.
Arc 853.269F Müller-Karpe, H. Die spätneolithische Siedlung. Kallmünz, 1961.
Arc 397.26 Müller-Karpe, Hermann. Handbuch der Vorgeschichte. v.1-3. München, 1966- 6v.
Arc 905.22 Müllner, Alfons. Emona; archaeologischen Studien aus Krain. Laibach, 1879.
Arc 390.2.8 Münchener archäologische Studien...A. Furtwängler. München, 1909.
Arc 853.108 Münchens Vorzeit. (Geidel, H.) München, 1930.
Arc 197.2F Münchner Beiträge zur Vor- und Frühgeschichte. München. 1,1950+ 18v.
Arc 197.2.5F Münchner Beiträge zur Vor- und Frühgeschichte. Ergänzungsband. München. 1,1974+ 2v.
Arc 1468.65.1 Münsterberg, Rudolf. Die Beamtennamen auf den griechischen Münzen. Hildesheim, 1973.
Arc 505.5.44 Münter, F. Om den Davidische families begravelse under Zions bierg. Kjobenhavn, 1804.
Arc 1428.5 Münter, F.C.K.H. Om Frankernes mynter i Orienten. v.1-2. n.p., n.d.
Arc 767.5 Muentz, E. Les antiquités de la ville de Rome. Paris, 1886.
Arc 66.1.4 Muentz, E. Arts à la cour des papes. Paris, 1878-82. 3v.
Arc 66.1.48 Muentz, E. Bibliothèque du Vatican au XVe siècle. Paris, 1887.
Arc 397.4 Müntz, Eugène. Études iconographiques et archéologiques. Paris, 1887.
Arc 397.5 Müntz, Eugène. Richerche intorno...Grimaldi. Firenze, 1881. 8 pam.
Arc 1408.1 Das Münz-, Mass- und Gewichtswesen in Vorderasien. (Brandis, J.) Berlin, 1866.
Arc 1510.26 Münz- und Geldgeschichte der Mark Meissen und Münzen. (Schwinkowski, Walter.) Frankfurt am Main, 1931.
Arc 1510.25 Münz- und Geldgeschichte der Stadt Northeim. Diss. (Mertens, E.) Halle an der Saale, 1928.
Arc 1504.30 Münz- und Geldgeschichte des Standes Luzern. (Wielandt, Friedrich.) Luzern, 1969.
Arc 1504.25 Münz- und Geldgeschichte des Standes Schuyz. (Wielandt, Friedrich.) Schuyz, 1964.
Arc 1510.50 Münz- und Geldgeschichte Niedersachsens. (Jesse, Wilhelm.) Braunschweig, 1952.
Arc 1508.29 Münz- und Medaillen-Kabinet des Freiherrn Wilhelm Knigge. (Knigge, Wilhelm.) Bielefeld, 1972.
Arc 1510.142 Münzbeschreibung des gräflich und fürstlichen Hauses Mansfeld. (Hagen, Johann Georg Friedrich von.) Nürnberg, 1778.
Arc 1663.30 Die Münzbildnisse von Maximinus bis Carenus. (Delbrueck, Richard.) Berlin, 1940.
Arc 1348.22 Die Münze in der Kulturgeschichte. (Friedensburg, F.) Berlin, 1909.
Arc 1510.156 Münze und Geld in Pforzheim. (Wielandt, Friedrich.) Pforzheim, 1968.
Arc 1348.84.2 Die Münze von der Anfängen bis zur europäischen Neuzeit. 2. Aufl. (Suhle, Arthur.) Leipzig, 1970.
Arc 1494.3 Die Münzen, Medaillen, und Prägungen. (Markl, M.) Prag, 1896. 2v.
Arc 1578.3 Die Münzen, Medaillen und Jetone. (Kolb, J. von.) Linz, 1882.
Arc 1335.30 Münzen- und Medaillen-Sammlung. (Antoine-Feill.) Frankfurt, 1908.
Arc 1333.16F Die Münzen- und Medaillen-Sammlung. (Bahrfeldt, Emil.) Danzig, 1901-10. 6v.
Arc 1312.8 Der Münzen- und Medaillensammler. Freiburg im Breisgau. 1,1961+ 3v.
Arc 1423.32 Münzen aus biblischer Zeit. (Rosen, Josef.) Basel, 1968.
Arc 1423.32.1 Münzen aus biblischer Zeit. (Rosen, Josef.) n.p., 1969.
Arc 1510.11.15 Münzen bayerischer Klöster, Kirchen. (Och, Friedrich.) München, 1897.
Arc 1510.162 Die Münzen der Abtei Hornbach nebst Beiträgen zur Münzkunde von Speyergau und Elsass im 12-14. (Braun von Stumm, Gustaf.) Halle an der Saale, 1926.
Arc 1645.1.5 Die Münzen der Colonie Brasilien, 1645-1822. (Meili, Julius.) Zürich, 1895.
Arc 1510.8 Münzen der deutschen Kaiser des Mittelalters. v.1,3. (Cappe, H.P.) Dresden, 1848-57.
Arc 1510.19F Die Münzen der Grafen von Hanau. (Suchier, Reinhard.) Hanau, 1897.
Arc 1510.131 Die Münzen der Grafschaft Lüchow. (Gaettens, R.) Halle, 1937.
Arc 1510.8.5 Münzen der Herzöge von Baiern. (Cappe, H.P.) Dresden, 1850.
Arc 1510.128F Münzen der Hohenstauffenzeit. (Hess, Adolph.) Zürich, 1959?
Arc 1540.35 Die Münzen der Kanal-Inseln. (Schreier, Ulrich.) Dortmund, 1965?
Arc 1490.37 Die Münzen der Ostgothen. (Friedländer, Julius.) Berlin, 1844.
Arc 1433.2.5 Münzen der Rasuliden. (Nützel, Heinrich.) Berlin, 1891.
Arc 1503.7 Die Münzen der Schweiz im 19. und 20. Jahrhundert. (Divo, Jean-Paul.) Zürich, 1967.
Arc 1510.133 Die Münzen der Stadt Braunschweig von 1499 bis 1680. (Jesse, W.) Braunschweig, 1962.
Arc 1510.134F Die Münzen der Stadt Einbeck. (Buck, H.) Hildesheim, 1939.
Arc 1510.30F Die Münzen der Stadt Hannover. (Buck, H.) Hannover, 1935.
Arc 1510.132 Die Münzen der Stadt Kaufbeuren. (Rehle, Q.) Kaufbeuren, 1880.

Author and Title Listing

Arc 1510.10 Die Münzen der Stadt Stade. (Bahrfeldt, Max von.) Wien, 1879.
Arc 1510.164 Die Münzen der Welfen seit Heinrich dem Löwen. (Welter, Gerhard.) Braunschweig, 1971-73. 2v.
Arc 1367.2 Die Münzen des Altertums. (Miller, Max.) Berlin, 1933.
Arc 1367.2.2 Die Münzen des Altertums. 2. Aufl. (Miller, Max.) Braunschweig, 1963.
Arc 1510.120F Die Münzen des Bistums und der Stadt Hildesheim. Hildesheim, 1937.
Arc 1433.41.5 Die Münzen des Chane vom Ulus. (Fraehn, C.M.J.) St. Petersburg, 1832.
Arc 1645.1.7 Die Münzen des Kaiserreichs Brasilien, 1822-1889. (Meili, Julius.) Leipzig, 1890.
Arc 1480.33 Die Münzen des Kaisers Aurelianus. v.1-2. (Rohde, T.) Miskoloz, 1881-82.
Arc 1470.21.5 Die Münzen des thracischen Königs Lysimachus. (Müller, L.) Kopenhagen, 1858.
Htn Arc 1470.21.6* Die Münzen des thracischen Königs Lysimachus. (Müller, L.) Kopenhagen, 1858.
Arc 1453.11 Münzen erzählen. (Kargel, Adolf.) Bielefeld, 1971.
Arc 1510.16 Die Münzen F. Wilhelms des Grossen Kurfürst und Friedrichs III von Brandenberg. (Schrötter, F.F. von.) Berlin, 1913.
Arc 1510.16.2 Die Münzen Friedrich Wilhelms des Grossen Kurfürsten und Friedrichs III. (Berlin. Staatliche Museen.) Berlin, 1922.
Arc 1480.21 Die Münzen Justinians. (Pinder, Moritz.) Berlin, 1843.
Arc 1510.171.1 Die Münzen Ostfrieslands. (Tergast, Pefrus.) Leer, 1974.
Arc 1580.30 Die Münzen Salzburgs. (Probszt, Günther.) Bâle, 1959.
Arc 1348.82.5 Münzen sammeln. 5. Aufl. (Kroha, Tyll.) Braunschweig, 1968.
Arc 1510.115F Die Münzen und Medaillen. (Horn, Otto.) Leipzig, 1923.
Arc 1335.165 Münzen und Medaillen aus dem Bernischen Historischen Museum. (Kapossy, Balázs.) Bern, 1969.
Arc 1510.28 Die Münzen und Medaillen der im Jahre 1156 gegründeten (seit 1255). (Hauser, Josef.) München, 1905.
Arc 1510.125 Die Münzen und Medaillen der Stadt Kaufbeureh nebst einer münzgeschichtlichen Einleitung. (Bernhart, Max.) n.p., 1923.
Arc 1510.80 Münzen und Medaillen der Stadt und des Bisthums Siebeck. (Behrens, Heinrich.) Berlin, 1905.
Arc 1510.15 Münzen und Medaillen der Stadt Wismar. (Grimm, E.) Berlin, 1897.
Arc 1505.205 Münzen und Medaillen der Wellischenlande. v.1-8. (Fiola, Eduard.) Prag, 1916. 6v.
Arc 1580.48 Die Münzen und Medaillen des Erzstiftes Salzburg. (Bernhart, Max.) München, 1929-30.
Arc 1510.100 Die Münzen und Medaillen des Herrogstums und des herroglichen Hauses Arenberg. (Neu, Heinrich.) Bonn, 1959.
Arc 1510.31F Die Münzen und Medaillen von Köln. (Cologne.) Köln, 1913-35. 4v.
Arc 1510.38 Die Münzen von Osnabrück. (Kennepohl, K.) München, 1938.
Arc 1428.11F Die Münzen von Priene. (Berlin. Staatliche Museen.) Berlin, 1927.
Arc 1510.23 Die Münzen von Worms. (Joseph, Paul.) Darmstadt, 1906.
Arc 1333.17F Die Münzensammlung des Stiftes Schotten in Wien. (Vienna. U.L.F. zu den Schotten. Benedictine Monastery.) Wien, 1910-20. 2v.
Arc 1468.12.2 Münzer, Friedrich. Die antiken Münzen von Thrakien. Berlin, 1912.
Arc 1510.95 Der Münzfund von Trebitz bei Wittenberg. (Erbstein, H.A.) Halle an der Saale, 1924.
Arc 1480.42.10F Die Münzfunde von Vindonissa bis Trafar. (Kraay, C.W.) Basel, 1962.
Arc 1503.2F Münzgeschichte der Schweiz. (Caraggioni, L.) Geneve, 1896.
Arc 1510.173F Münzgeschichte der Stadt Berlin. (Vossberg, Friedrich August.) Berlin, 1869.
Arc 1510.24 Die Münzgeschichte Regensburgs. Inaug. Diss. (Sperl, Karl.) Kallmünz, 1928.
Arc 1478.23 Münzkunde der römischen Kaiserzeit. (Bernhart, Max.) Genève, 1922.
Arc 1390.10 Münzkunde und Geldgeschichte der Einzelstaaten des Mittelalters und der neuer Zeit. (Friedensburg, F.) München, 1926.
Arc 1510.45 Münzkunde und Münzkabinette am Oberrheim. (Badische Gesellschaft für Münzkunde.) Karlsruhe am Rhein, 1951.
Arc 1480.34 Münzkundliche und historische Unterschungen über die Zeit der Illyrerkaiser. Inaug. Diss. (Manns, F.) Würzburg, 1939.
Arc 1390.11 Münzkunst des Mittelalters. (Lange, Kurt.) Leipzig, 1942.
Arc 1510.65.5 Münzporträts im 11. Jahrhundert? (Gaettens, R.) Heidelberg, 1956.
Arc 1508.15.15 Die Münzprägungen der deutschen Staaten von Einführung des Reichswährung. v.3. (Jaeger, Kurt.) Basel, 1967.
Arc 1504.20.5 Die Münzprägungen der letzten Monarchien des teutschen Bundes von 1815. Fürstentum Liechtenstein. (Jaeger, Kurt.) Basel, 1963.
Arc 1433.71F Die Münzprägungen des Islams. (Zambaur, Edward K.M. von.) Wiesbaden, 1968.
Arc 1510.11 Münzreihe der Herzoge in Baiern. (Finauer, P.P.) München, 1777.
Arc 1348.15 Der Münzsammler. (Stuckelburg, E.A.) Zürich, 1899.
Arc 1348.70 Münzsammlung, Enthaltend. (Fliessbach, Ferdinand.) Leipzig, 1853. 2v.
Arc 1333.15F Die Münzsammlung. (St. Florian, Austria.) Wien, 1871.
Arc 1312.5 Muenzstudien. Halle an der Saale. 1-7,1923-1929 4v.
Arc 1312.7 Münzstudien. Leipzig. 1-9,1857-1877 7v.
Arc 1348.48 Münzstudien. v.1-2. (Grote, Hermann.) Leipzig, 1857-62.
Arc 1510.174F Das Münzwesen der Mark Brandenburg. (Bahrfeldt, Emil.) Berlin, 1889- 2v.
Arc 1504.10 Das Münzwesen im Kanton St. Gallen. (Girtamner-Solchli, H.) Genf, 1923.
Arc 1510.60F Münzwesen und Münzen der Grafschaft Mansfeld von der Mitte. (Tornau, Otto.) Prag, 1937.
Arc 448.1.40 Mughal, M. Rafique. Present state of research on the Indus Valley civilization. Karachi, 1973.
Arc 590.18 Muhammad, Ahmad Rajab. Lights on the royal mummies in the Egyptian Museum. Cairo, 1964.
Arc 435.2.33F The Muhammadan architecture. pt.2. (Burgess, James.) London, 1905.
Arc 435.2.24F The Muhammadan architecture of Ahmadabad. (Burgess, James.) London, 1900.
Arc 1433.8.5 Das Muhammedanische Münzkabinet. (Fraehn, C.M.J.) St. Petersburg, 1821.
Arc 450.34 Mujumdar, Ganesh. Ashmound excavations at Kupgal. 1. ed. Poona, 1966.
Arc 682.2 Mukyrai. (Tsountas, C.) Athênai, 1893.
Arc 1528.2 Muller, F. Cabinet de monnaies, J.W. Stephanik. Amsterdam, 1904.
Arc 785.4 Mullooly, J. Breve notizie delle antiche pitture. Roma, 1866.
Arc 1033.70.9 Mullooly, J. Brief notice of the ancient paintings...Rome. Rome, 1866.
Arc 1033.20.25.2 Mullooly, Joseph. Saint Clement, pope and martyr. 2. ed. Rome, 1873.
Arc 1033.20.25. Mullooly, Joseph. Saint Clement, pope and martyr and his Basilica in Rome. Rome, 1869.
Arc 1613.22 Mumey, N. Clark, Gruber and Co. Denver, 1950.
Arc 554.5 Mumiák es minarétek. (Erdöse, K.) Budapest, 1937.
Arc 590.1A The mummy. Chapters on Egyptian funereal archaeology. (Budge, E.A.W.) Cambridge, 1893.
Arc 590.1.5 The mummy. 2. ed. (Budge, E.A.W.) Cambridge, 1925.
Arc 590.1.4 The mummy. 2. ed. (Budge, E.A.W.) N.Y., 1974.
Arc 1033.72.5 Mundt, A. Die Erztaufen Norddeutschlands. Leipzig, 1908.
Arc 383.46 Munera archaeologica Iosepho Kostrzewski. (Przyjaciól Nauk. Poznańskie Tow.) Poznań, 1963.
Arc 1510.1.5 Munich. Medaillen und Münzen des Gesammthauses Wittelsbach. v.1, pt.1-2. München, 1897. 2v.
Arc 936.221.5 Municipium DD kod Sočanice. (Čerškov, Emil.) Priština, 1970.
Arc 612.82 Munj cyklopów. (Kozlowski, Janusz.) Wroclaw, 1971.
Arc 895.80 Munksgaard, Elisabeth. Oldtidsdragter. København, 1974.
Arc 1020.25 Munorie della Chiesa S. Maria di Monte Granaro. (Olivieri, Abati.) Pesaro, 1777.
Arc 785.73 Munoz, A. L'isolamento del Colle Capitolino. Roma, 1943.
Arc 785.45 Munoz, A. Il restauro del tiempo della Fortuna Virile. Roma, 1925.
Arc 785.67F Munoz, A. I templi della Zona Argentina. Roma, 1929.
Arc 785.59F Munoz, A. Via dei trionfi isolamento del Campidoglio. 2a ed. Roma, 1933.
Arc 785.69.5F Munoz, A. La via del Circo Massimo. 2. ed. Roma, 1934.
Arc 785.69.10F Munoz, A. Il Parco di Traiano. Roma, 1936.
Arc 1163.1 Muñoz y Rivero, J. Idioma y escritura de España. Madrid, 1888.
Arc 1163.2.14 Muñoz y Rivero, J. Manual de paleografía diplomática española. Madrid, 1880.
Arc 1163.2.15 Muñoz y Rivero, J. Manual de paleografía diplomática española. Madrid, 1889.
Arc 1163.2.17.1 Muñoz y Rivero, J. Manual de paleografía diplomática española. 2. ed. Madrid, 1917.
Arc 1163.2.17 Muñoz y Rivero, J. Manual de paleografía diplomática española. 2. ed. Madrid, 1917.
Arc 1153.6 Muñoz y Rivero, J. Paleografía visigoda. Madrid, 1881.
Arc 1153.6.5 Muñoz y Rivero, J. Paleografía visigoda. Madrid, 1919.
Arc 1163.2 Muñoz y Rivero, J. Scripturae hispanae veteris. Matriti, 1890.
Arc 1413.1 Munro, N.G. Coins of Japan. London, 1905.
X Cg Arc 1413.09 Munro, N.G. Coins of Japan. 1. ed. Yokohama, 1904.
Arc 426.3 Munro, N.G. Prehistoric Japan. Yokohama, 1908.
Arc 426.3.5 Munro, N.G. Prehistoric Japan. Yokohama, 1911.
X Cg Arc 875.5 Munro, R. Ancient Scottish lake-dwellings. Edinburgh, 1882.
Arc 875.5.5 Munro, R. Prehistoric Scotland. Edinburgh, 1899.
Arc 875.12 Munro, Robert. Archaeology and false antiquities. London, 1905.
Arc 875.12.2 Munro, Robert. Archaeology and false antiquities. Philadelphia, 1906.
Arc 612.3 Munro, Robert. The lake-dwellings of Europe. London, 1890.
Arc 858.21 Munro, Robert. Prehistoric Britain. London, n.d.
Arc 905.1 Munro, Robert. Rambles and studies in Bosnia. Edinburgh, 1895.
Arc 905.1.5 Munro, Robert. Rambles and studies in Bosnia-Herzegovina and Dalmatia, with an account of the proceedings of the congress of archaeologists and anthropologists. 2. ed. Edinburgh, 1900.
Arc 1520.20 De munt to Leuven tot het einde der XVe eeuw. (Crab, Jan.) Leuven, 1967.
Arc 1528.7 De munten. (Chijs, P.O. van der.) Haarlem, 1851-66. 9v.
Arc 77.5 Munz. Römisch-Germanisches Zentralmuseum. Jahrbuch. 1,1954+ 99v.
Arc 1588.10.10 Munzkunst in Ungarn. (Huszár, Lajos.) Budapest, 1963.
Arc 785.29 Le mura di Roma. (Nibby, A.) Roma, 1820.
Arc 785.29.5 Le mura di Roma. (Quarenghi, G.) Roma, 1880.
Arc 785.29.15F Le mura di Roma republicana. (Säflund, G.) Uppsala, 1932.
Htn Arc 585.38F* The mural painting of El-Amarneh. (Frankfort, H.) London, 1929.
Arc 1033.12.181 Muratori, L.A. De corona ferrea...commentarius. Mediolani, 1719.
Arc 652.1 Mure, W. Journal of a tour in Greece. Edinburgh, 1842. 2v.
Arc 843.199F Las murias de Beloño. (Jordá Cerdá, F.) Oviedo, 1957.
Arc 1433.2.2 Murr, C.G. von. Drei Abhandlungen von der Geschichte der Araber. Nüremberg, 1770.
Arc 518.6 Murray, A.S. Sculptured columns...Temple of Diana at Ephesus. London, 1895-96.
Arc 858.6 Murray, D. An archaeological survey of the United Kingdom. Glasgow, 1896.
Arc 1033.12.234 Murray, D. A small brass cup...Rodil, Harris. Glasgow, 1898.
Arc 1335.55 Murray, David. The Hunterian Museum in the old college of Glasgow. Glasgow, 1925.
Arc 612.80 Murray, Jacqueline. The first European agriculture. Edinburgh, 1970.
Arc 588.14 Murray, M. The Osireron at Abydos. London, 1904.
Arc 588.15 Murray, M. Saqqara Mastabas. London, 1905-37. 2v.
Arc 843.2.5 Murray, M.A. Cambridge evcavations in Minorca. London, 1932- 2v.
Arc 600.37A Murray, M.A. Egyptian temples. London, 1931.
Arc 589.1 Murray, M.A. Index of names and titles of the old kingdoms. London, 1908.
Arc 397.20 Murray, M.A. My first hundred years. London, 1963.
Arc 588.62F Murray, M.A. A street in Petra. London, 1940.
Arc 505.92 Murray, Margaret A. Petra, the rock city of Edom. London, 1939.
Arc 1093.6.5 Murray-Aynsley, L.H.G.M. The swastika. Margate, 1891.
Arc 936.140.5 Murtvi gradove. (Velkov, Ivan.) Sofiia, 1933.
Arc 542.200.5 Mus, Paul. Barabudur. v.1, pt.1-2; v.2. Hanoi, 1935. 3v.
Arc 925.16.50 Musabaev, Gainetdin G. Epigrafika Kazakhstana. Alma-Ata, 1971.
Arc 1335.36 Musée crozatier - catalogue du médaillier. v.1-2. (Montélhet, A.) Paris, 1912.

Author and Title Listing

Arc 547.18 Musée de Gizeh. Notice des principaux monuments. Le Caire, 1897.
Arc 608.1.37F Musée de Sfax. (Massigli, T.) Paris, 1912.
Arc 608.1.27 La musée du Bardo à Tunis et les fouilles de M. Gauckler. (Perrot, G.) Paris, 1899.
Arc 583.2F Musée du Louvre - Stèles de la XIIe Dynastie. pt.1-2. no.68. (Gayet, E.) Paris, 1886.
Htn Arc 545.206* Le Musée Egyptien. v.1-4. Cairo, 1890-1924.
Arc 547.24.10F Le Musée Gréco-Romain, 1925-1931. (Alexandria. Musée Gréco-Romain.) Bergamo, 1932.
Arc 547.24F Le Musée Gréco-Romain du cours de l'année 1922-23. (Alexandria. Musée Gréco-Romain.) Alexandrie, 1924.
Arc 935.10.5 Pamphlet box. Musée Imperial Ottoman.
Arc 830.127 Musée lapidaire, l'histoire de Béziers. (D'Ardé, J.) Béziers, 1912.
Arc 605.202 Musées de l'Algérie. (France. Ministère de l'Instruction Publique.) Paris. 1-21,1890-1928 24v.
Arc 1030.2 Musei kircheriani inscript. ethnicae et christianae. (Brunatius, J.) Mediolani, 1837.
Arc 87.1.36 Der Musenchor. (Trendelenburg, A.) Berlin, 1876.
Arc 843.153 Museo, Canario. El Museo Canario. Las Palmas de Gran Canaria, 1957.
Arc 843.153 El Museo Canario. (Museo, Canario.) Las Palmas de Gran Canaria, 1957.
Arc 905.5.5 Il museo civico di antichita. (Trieste.) Trieste, 1879.
Arc 1016.229 Museo Cospiano. (Legati, L.) Bologna, 1677.
Arc 1015.205.13 Il museo epigrafico cristiano pio-sateranense. (Rossi, G.B. de.) Roma, 1877.
Arc 77.1 Museo Italiano di antichita classica. v.1-3 and atlas. Florence, 1884-90. 4v.
Arc 726.31 Il museo nazionale atestino. (Ghirardini, G.) Padova, 1903.
Arc 1025.26 Museum epigraphicum. (Strazzula, V.) Panormi, 1897.
Htn Arc 740.200* Museum Etruscum. (Gorio, A.F.) Florence, 1737. 3v.
Arc 1675.49F Museum Mazzuchellianum. (Mazzuchelli, G.M.) Venetiis, 1761-63. 2v.
Arc 1675.49.5F Museum Mazzuchellianum. (Mazzuchelli, G.M.) Venetiis, 1761-63. 2v.
Htn Arc 1335.12* Museum Meadianum. (Mead, R.) London, n.d.
Htn Arc 1335.12.2* Museum Meadianum. (Mead, R.) London, n.d.
Arc 1335.24 Museum Munterianum. v.1-3. Hauniae, n.d.
Arc 1300.1.17 Museum notes. (American Numismatic Society.) N.Y. 1-15 8v.
Arc 390.1 Museum of classical antiquities. (Falkener, E.) London, 1860.
Arc 48.6 Museum pamphlet. (Sudan. Antiquities Service.) Khartoum. 1,1953+
Arc 755.1 Museums and ruins of Rome. (Cumelung, W.) London, 1906. 2v.
Arc 1433.28.5 Mushegian, K. Denezhnoe obrashchenie Dvina po numizmaticheskim dannym. Erevan, 1962.
Arc 1588.2.11 Mushmov, N.A. Antichnite moneti na Balkanskiia polustrov i monetite. Sofiia, 1912.
Arc 1588.2.10 Mushmov, N.A. Monety i pechatite na bolg. Acare. Sofiia, 1924.
Arc 1675.27.5F Musica in nummis. (Andorfer, Karl.) Wien, 1901.
Arc 1675.27 Musica in nummis. (Andorfer, Karl.) Wien, 1907.
Arc 497.12 Musil, A. Arabia Petraca. v.1-3. Wien, 1907. 4v.
Arc 505.95PF Musil, Alois. Kusejr 'Amra. Wien, 1907.
Arc 830.62 Musset, Georges. La Charente-Inferieure avant l'histoire. La Rochelle, 1885.
Arc 1020.100 Mutio, Mario. Delle reliquie insigni...chiesa de Bergamo. Bergamo, 1616.
Arc 925.8.35 Muzei i raskopki khersonesa. (Belov, G.D.) Simferopol, 1936.
Arc 936.14.545 Muzeum Ziemi Przemyskiej w Przemyślu. Historia badań archeologicznych i zbiorów Muzeum Ziemi Przemyskiej. Przemyśl, 1973.
Arc 302.53 Muzeum Żup Krakowskich, Wieliczka. Badania archeologiczne. Wieliczka. 1968+
Arc 609.36 Mwalawolemba on Mikolongwe Hill. (Cole-King, P.A.) Zomba, 1968.
Arc 397.20 My first hundred years. (Murray, M.A.) London, 1963.
Arc 412.3 My-gedronavty. (Dzhus, Vsevolod E.) Leningrad, 1974.
Arc 1077.2.51 My hobby of the cross. (Miller, M. (Sweeney).) N.Y., 1939.
Arc 1030.8.15 My Nestorian adventure in China. (Holm, F.W.) N.Y., 1923.
Arc 682.1.3A Mycenae; a narrative. (Schliemann, Heinrich.) N.Y., 1878.
Arc 682.1.2 Mycenae; a narrative. (Schliemann, Heinrich.) N.Y., 1880.
Arc 682.1 Mycenae; a narrative of researches and discoveries at Mycenae and Tiryns. (Schliemann, Heinrich.) London, 1878.
Arc 682.6 The Mycenae tablets. v.4. Phildelphia, 1953.
Arc 659.3 The Mycenaean age. (Tsountas, Chrēstos.) London, 1897.
Arc 522.16A Mycenaean Troy. (Tolman, H.C.) N.Y., 1903.
Arc 682.30.5 Mycenae's last century of greatness. (Mylonas, George E.) Sydney, 1968.
Arc 595.23FA Mycerinus; the temples of the third pyramid at Giza. (Reisner, G.A.) Cambridge, 1931.
Arc 1660.7 Myer, I. The Waterloo medal. Philadelphia, 1885.
Arc 682.1.5 Mykenae; Bericht über meine Forschungen und Entdeckungen in Mykenae und Tiryns. Faksimile. (Schliemann, Heinrich.) Darmstadt, 1964.
Arc 682.1.15 Mykenai - eine kritische Untersuchung der Schliemannschen Alterthümer. (Schulze, E.) St. Petersburg, 1880.
Arc 1251.2 Mykēnaike Zphragidoglyphia. (Xenakē-Sakellariou, Agnē.) Athēnai, 1966.
Arc 682.8 Mykēnes kai Tiryntha. (Papachatzēs, N.) Athēnai, 1951.
Arc 638.6 Pamphlet vol. Mykenische Archäologie 1875-1903. 2 pam.
Htn Arc 700.4* Die Mykenische Lokalsage von den Gräbern Agamemnons und der Seinen. (Belger, C.) Berlin, 1893.
Arc 682.5 Die mykenische Zeit. (Marcks, F.) Cöln, 1902.
Arc 925.50.95 Mykhailivs'ke poselennia. (Nabodovs'ka, O.F.) Kyïv, 1962.
Arc 925.155F Mykopalicka polsko-radzi eckie w Mirmeki. Warszawa, n.d. 2v.
Arc 383.77 Mylonas, G.C. Studies presented to David Moore Robinson. St. Louis, 1951-53. 2v.
Arc 652.6 Mylonas, G.E. Hē neolithike epoche en Helladi. Athēnai, 1928.
Arc 677.5F Mylonas, George E. Aghios Kosmas. Princeton, 1959.
Arc 682.30 Mylonas, George E. Ancient Mycenae. Princeton, 1957.
Arc 682.30.5 Mylonas, George E. Mycenae's last century of greatness. Sydney, 1968.
Arc 684.9.5 Mylonas, George E. The neolithic settlement at Olynthus. Baltimore, 1929.
Arc 674.1.13F Mylonas, George E. Ho prōtoattikos amphoreni tēs Eleusinos. Athēnai, 1957.
Arc 673.1.29 Mylonas, George Emmanuel. Eleusis and the Eleusinian mysteries. Princeton, 1972.
Arc 885.30 Mynachlogddu: a guide to its antiquities. (Lewis, Ewart Thomas.) Clunderwen, 1967.
Arc 1542.2.5 Mynt och människor. (Malmer, Brita.) Stockholm, 1968.
Arc 1550.4 Myntforhold og utmyntninger i Danmark indtil 1146. (Hauberg, Peter C.) Kjøbenhavn, 1900.
Arc 1565.1 Myntfundet fra Graeslid i Thydalen. (Stenersen, L.B.) Christiania, 1881.
Arc 1552.1 Myntic Islands, 1836-1922-1963. (Bjoerkman, S.) Stockholm, 1965.
Arc 1348.76 Myntoch medaljer. (Lagerqvist, Lars.) Stockholm, 1960.
Arc 540.10F Myrton-Pigadhes. (Taylor, Joan.) Oxford, 1957.
Arc 682.42 Myrtos: an early Bronze Age settlement in Crete. (Warren, Peter.) London, 1972.
Arc 435.55F Mysore. Archaeological Survey. Annual report. Bangalore. 1909-1946 22v.
Arc 435.55.2F Mysore. Archaeological Survey. Index to the annual reports of the Mysore Archaeological Department for the years 1906-1922. Bangalore, 1929.
Arc 595.41 Le mystère des pyramides. (Lauer, J.P.) Paris, 1974.
Arc 1033.10.10 Le mystère d'un symbole chrétien. (Carcopino, Jérome.) Paris, 1955.
Arc 674.1 Die Mysterienheiligtuemer in Eleusis und Samothrake. (Rubensohn, O.) Berlin, 1892.
Arc 386.46 Mysteries from forgotten worlds. (Berlitz, Charles F.) Garden City, 1972.
Arc 815.13.20 Mysterion Gedanken vor den dionysischen Fresken der Mysterienvilla in Pompeji. (Feiler, Leopold.) Wien, 1946.
Arc 505.5.115 The mystery of the Temple Mount. (Cornfeld, Gaalyahu.) Tel Aviv, 1972.
Arc 870.17F The mystery of Wansdyke. (Major, Albany F.) Cheltenham, 1926.
Arc 1470.70 Mythen und Münzen. 1. Aufl. (Lauckoranski, Leo Maria.) München, 1958.
Arc 1470.55 Der Mythos der Hellenen. (Kerényi, K.) Amsterdam, 1941.
Arc 943.14 N.Y. Museum of the American Indian. Heye Foundation. Contributions. N.Y. 1-18 13v.
Arc 943.14.8 N.Y. Museum of the American Indian. Heye Foundation. Indian notes. N.Y. 1-7,1924-1930 6v.
Arc 943.14.9 N.Y. Museum of the American Indian. Heye Foundation. Indian notes. Index, v.1-7. N.Y., 1949.
Arc 943.14.4 N.Y. Museum of the American Indian. Heye Foundation. Indian notes and monographs. N.Y. 1-53,1920-1943 20v.
Arc 943.14.3 N.Y. Museum of the American Indian. Heye Foundation. Indian notes and monographs. N.Y. 1-10,1919-1928 9v.
Arc 943.14.5F N.Y. Museum of the American Indian. Heye Foundation. Leaflets. N.Y. 1-5,1919-1926
Arc 383.42.10 Na granicach archeologii. Łódź, 1968.
Arc 925.50.95 Nabodovs'ka, O.F. Mykhailivs'ke poselennia. Kyïv, 1962.
Arc 1470.2 Die Nachfolger Alexanders des Grossen. (Sallet, A. von.) Berlin, 1879.
Arc 1077.7.5 Nachod, H. Der Rennwagen bei ben Italikern. Leipzig, 1909.
Arc 853.374 Nachricht von den Alterthümern in der Gegend und auf dem Gebürge bey Homburg vor der Höhe. (Neuhof, Elias.) Homburg, 1780.
Arc 198.5 Nachrichten zur Niedersachsens Urgeschichte. Hildesheim. 38,1969+ 8v.
Arc 1478.13 Nachträge und Bericht zur Münzkunde. (Bahrfeldt, M.) Wien, 1897.
Arc 398.1.2 Nadaillac, J.F.A. du Pouget de. Prehistoric peoples. N.Y., 1892.
Arc 398.1 Nadaillac, J.F.A. du Pouget de. Les premiers hommes. Paris, 1881. 2v.
Arc 936.39.5 Nadgrobnité mogili pri Duvanlii v Plovdivsko. (Filov, Bogdan.) Sofiia, 1934.
Arc 936.140.15 Nadgrobnite plochi ot rimsko vreme. (Dimitrov, Dimitur P.) Sofiia, 1942.
Arc 1588.13 Nadir hirkaç sikke. (Ered, Serafeddin.) Ankara? 1967.
Arc 1588.13.5 Nadir hirkaç sikke. (Erel, Serafeddin.) Istanbul, 1963.
Arc 936.14.235 Nadolski, Andrzej. Sciezki archeologów. Łódź, 1967.
Arc 925.322.30 Nadpisi rasskazyvaiut. (Shikhsaidov, Amri Rzaevich.) Dagknigoizdat, 1969.
Arc 936.100.30 Nadpisi sredovječni i novovjeki na crkvah. (Kukuljevic-Sakcinski, I.) Zagreb, 1891.
Arc 1163.3.100 Nadpis'na kamne. (Mongait, Aleksandr L.) Moskva, 1969.
Arc 915.3 Naef, A. Le cimetiere Gallo-Helvète de Vevey. n.p., 1903.
Arc 853.12 Naelier, J. Die römischen Militarstrassen. Strassburg, 1887.
Arc 861.5 Naema Cornubiae. (Borlase, W.C.) London, 1872.
Arc 416.11 Nag, K. India and the Pacific world. Calcutta, 1941.
Arc 588.4 Nagada and Ballas. (Petrie, W.M.F.) London, 1895.
Arc 459.5 Nagaraja Rao, M.S. The stone age hill dwellers of Tekkalakota. Poona, 1965.
Arc 830.22.13 Nagne, Charles. Les voies romaines de l'antique Lutèce. Paris, 189-?
Arc 925.322 Nagornyi Dagestan v rannem srednevekove. (Ataev, Dibir M.) Makhachkala, 1963.
Arc 936.14.20 Najdawniejsje stolice Polski. (Hensel, Witold.) Warszawa, 1960.
Arc 936.235 Najstarejša zgodovina Dolenjske. (Gabrovec, S.) Novo Mesto, 1956.
Arc 1588.6.2.20 Nakışlı Osmanlı mangırları. (Olçer, Cüneyt.) Istanbul, 1975.
Arc 936.205.5 Nalazi iz rimskog doba na stupu kod. Sarajeva. (Čremošnik, Gregor.) Sarajevo, 1930.
Arc 1588.4.80 Nález přemyslovských denárů iz století v Hodkově u Kutné Hory. (Radoměřský, Pavel.) Kutná Hora, 1964.
Arc 1588.4.17 Nálezi minci v Cechacle na Morave a ve slezsku. (Nohejlova, Eman.) Praha, 1955. 4v.
Arc 1588.4.55 Nálezy keltských, antických a byzantských mincí na Slovensku. (Ondrouch, Vojtech.) Bratislava, 1964.
Arc 1313.36 Nálezy mincé na Slovensku. Bratislava. 2,1968+
Arc 1020.74 Nampoon, P. Histoire de Notre Dame de France. Puy, 1868.
Arc 945.8 Nantes. Trésors d'archéologie américaine et océanienne. Nantes, 1958?
Arc 830.78.20PF Nantes et la Loire-Inférieure. (Chevalier, Pierre.) Nantes, 1850.
Arc 1468.48 Nanteuil, H. de. Collection de monnaies grecques. Paris, 1925. 2v.
Arc 608.82 Napata i meroe-drevnie tsarstva sudzna. (Katsnel'son, Isidor S.) Moskva, 1970.
Arc 1475.10 Naples. Museo Nazionale. Medagliere II. Monete Romane. pt.1-2. Naples, 1870-71. 3v.
Arc 793.6.9F Naples. Museo Nazionale. Raccolta...pinture...musaici...Ercolano, di Pompei, e di Stabia. Napoli, 1854.

Arc 793.6 Naples. Museo Nazionale. Raccolta...pinture e di...musaici...di Ercolano, di Pompei, e di Stabia. Napoli, 183-.

Arc 793.6.5 Naples. Museo Nazionale. Raccolta...pinture e di...musaici...di Ercolano, di Pompei, e di Stabia. Napoli, 1843.

Arc 810.14 Naples and Pompeii. (Wall, J.W.) Burlington, 1856.

Arc 1660.18F The Napoleon medals. (Edwards, Edward.) London, 1837.

Arc 726.2.5 Napoli greca-romana. Topografia. (Capasso, B.) Napoli, 1905.

Arc 520.17 Napp, A.E. Das Altar von Pergamon. München, 1936.

Arc 435.22 Narasimhachar, R. Architecture and sculpture in Mysore. v.2. Bangalore, 1919.

Arc 768.1 Nardini, F. Roma antica. Roma, 1666.

Arc 768.1.25 Nardini, F. Roma antica. 4. ed. Roma, 1818-20. 4v.

Arc 1033.70.19 Nardoni, L. L'antico oratorio di S. Agnese. Roma, 1870.

Arc 1027.46.5 Nardoni, L. Dell'antica chiesa di S. Stefano sulla via Cassia. Roma, 1859.

Arc 1033.27 Nardoni. Di alcune sotterrance confessoni...Basiliche di Roma. Roma, 1881.

Arc 750.38 Narducci, P. Sulla fognatura della città di Roma. Roma, 1889. 2v.

Arc 888.55 Narr, Karl J. Studien zur älteren und mittleren Steinzeit der Niederen Lande. Habilitationsschrift. Bonn, 1968.

Arc 953.18.5 A narrative of explorations of New Mexico, Arizona, Indiana. (Moorehead, W.K.) Andover, 1906.

Arc 609.1.5 A narrative of further excavations at Zimbabye (Mashonaland). (Willoughby, J.C.) London, 1893.

Arc 545.14 Narrative of the operations...in Egypt and Nubia. 3. ed. (Belzoni, G.B.) London, 1822. 2v.

Arc 545.14PF Narrative of the operations...in Egypt and Nubia. 3. ed. Atlas. (Belzoni, G.B.) London, 1822.

Arc 551.1 Narrative of the operations in Egypt and Nubia. (Belzoni, G.B.) Brussels, 1835.

Arc 785.42 Narrazione artistica dell'operato finora nel ristauro dell'arco di Tito. (Valadier, G.) Roma, 1822.

Arc 1033.12.5 Narrazione critico storica...Prepuzio de Gesu. Roma, 1802.

Arc 1033.12.6 Narrazione critico storica della reliquia...Santissimo Prepuzio. (Jesus Christ.) Roma, 1802.

Arc 1033.12.39 Narrazione della solennita...Torino...SS. Sindone. Torino, n.d.

Arc 1033.17.481 Narrazione storica sopra il santuario della madonna del Ponte. (Eroli, G.) Roma, 1856.

Arc 1675.106 Naša odlikovanja do 1941. (Nikolić, Desanka.) Beograd, 1971.

Arc 736.12 Naselli, S. L'inesplorato Monte Albura o Albuchia. Castelbuono, 1952.

Arc 768.6F Nash, Ernest. Pictorial dictionary of ancient Rome. London, 1961-62. 2v.

Arc 885.19.5 Nash-Williams, Victor Erle. The Roman frontier in Wales. Cardiff, 1954.

Arc 885.19.7 Nash-Williams, Victor Erle. The Roman frontier in Wales. Cardiff, 1969.

Arc 1510.168 Das nassauische Münzwesen. (Isenbeck, Julius.) Münster, 1970.

Arc 925.296F Nat, Daniel. Éléments de préhistoire et d'archéologie nord-sibériennes. Paris, 1971-

Arc 609.7 Natal archaeological studies. (Davies, Oliver.) Pietermaritzburg, 1952.

Arc 1138.27.5 Natale, Alfio Rosario. Ludwig Traube e la nuova metodologia paleografica. Milano, 1957.

Arc 1558.5 Nathorst-Böös, E. Atto samla numismatica. Stockholm, 1958.

Arc 138.2 National ancient monuments yearbook. London. 1,1927

Arc 895.20 Naturhistoriska och arkaeologiska undersökninger pa Björkö i Mälaren. (Stolpe, H.) Stockholm, 1872.

Arc 1348.85 Nau, Elisabeth. Epochen der Geldgeschichte. Stuttgart, 1972.

Arc 398.5 Nau, Karl J. Urgeschichte der Kultur. Stuttgart, 1961.

Arc 288.1 Nauchnoe Obshchestvo po Izucheniiu Votskogo Kraia. Trudy. Moskva. 4,1928

Arc 543.7.15 Naudin, G. Le groupe d'Angkor vu par les ecrivains et les étrangers. Saigon, 1928.

Arc 845.200 Die Nauheimer Funde. (Quilling, F.) Frankfurt am Main, 1903.

Arc 600.4.13 Naukratis. Diss. (Smith, E.M.) Vienna, 1926.

Arc 585.3 Naukratis. Pt.1-2. (Petrie, W.M.F.) London, 1886-88. 2v.

Arc 600.4 Naukratis - a Greek city in Egypt. (Winslow, W.C.) Boston, 1887.

Arc 1088.1 Die Nautik der Alten. (Breusing, A.) Bremen, 1886.

Arc 1670.7F Naval medals. (Milford Haven, L.A.M.) London, 1921-28. 2v.

Arc 1033.77 Navarro, G. Il corpo di S. Leonzio Martire. Napoli, 1846.

Arc 1138.85 Navascués y de Juan, Joaquin Maria de. El concepto de la epigrafia consideraciones sobre la necesidad de su ampliación. Madrid, 1953.

Arc 1493.26 Navascués y de Juan, Joaquin Maria de. Las monedas hispanicas del Museo arqueologico nacional de Madrid. Barcelona, 1969. 2v.

Arc 1088.4 Le nave di Nemi nella bibliografia. (Mariani, Lucilla.) Roma, 1942.

Arc 1088.1.20F La nave di Tiberio sommersa nel lago di Nemi. (Maes, Constantino.) Roma, 1895. 2 pam.

Arc 1033.121 Le navi cavensi nel Mediterraneo...vita di S. Costabile de Lucania. (Guillaume, P.) Napoli, 1876.

Arc 1088.7F Le navi di Nemi. 2. ed. (Ucelli, Guido.) Roma, 1950.

Arc 1088.1.19 Le navi romane del lago di Nemi. (Malfatti, V.) Roma, 1896.

Arc 1088.5 Le navi sacre di Claudio nel lago di Nemi. (Dionisi, Francesco.) Roma, 1956.

Arc 1088.1.21 Navi venete. (Levi, C.A.) Venezia, 1892.

Arc 600.17 Naville, E. Les têtes de pierre...tombeaux égyptiens. Genève, 1909.

Arc 545.232 Naville, E. Tomb of Hâtshopsitu. Life and monuments of queen. London, 1906.

Arc 585.11A Naville, E.H. Ahnas el Medinek. London, 1894.

Arc 585.8 Naville, E.H. Bubastis. London, 1891.

Arc 585.10A Naville, E.H. Festival-Hall of Osorkon II in the Great Temple of Bubastis. London, 1892.

NEDL Arc 585.7 Naville, E.H. Mound of the Jew and City of Onias. London, 1890.

Arc 585.5F Naville, E.H. The shrine of Saft el Henneh. Malagny, 1887.

Arc 585.1 Naville, E.H. The store-city of Pithom. 3. ed. London, 1888.

Arc 585.12.2 Naville, E.H. The temple of Deir el Bahari. London, 1894.

Htn Arc 585.14F* Naville, E.H. The temple of Deir el Bahari. London, 1895-1908. 7v.

Arc 585.25 Naville, E.H. XI Dynasty temple at Deir El-Bahari. London, 1907-13. 3v.

Arc 1448.10 Naville, Lucien. Les monnaies d'or de la Cyrenaïque de 450 à 250 avant J.C. Genève, 1951.

Arc 1468.54 Naville et Cie, Geneva. Monnaies grecques antiques en or en argent. pt. 2. Genève, 1924.

Arc 1458.20 Naville et Cie, Geneva. Monnaies grecques et romaines. Genève, 1925.

Arc 1478.83 Naville et Cie, Geneva. Monnaies romaines antiques. Genève, 1924.

Arc 1478.83.5 Naville et Cie, Geneva. Monnaies romaines antiques. Genève, 1925.

Arc 925.170 Nazare istorii Piskam'ia. (Bader, Otto N.) Perm', 1958.

Arc 726.68.5 Nazari, G.B. Brescia antica. Brescia, 1658.

Htn Arc 726.68* Nazari, G.B. Bressa anticha. Bressa, 1562.

Arc 1033.53.5 Ne' primi tre secoli di persecuzione cristiane. (Scognamiglio, A.) Napoli, 1869.

Arc 87.1.51 Neandrid. (Koldewery, R.) Berlin, 1891.

Arc 93.4 Neapolis, revista di archeologia, epigrafia e numio. (Macchioro, V.) Napoli. 1-2,1913-1915 2v.

Arc 497.94 Near Eastern archaeology in the twentieth century. 1. ed. Garden City, N.Y., 1970.

Arc 1433.46F Near Eastern numismatics, iconography, epigraphy and history. Beirut, 1974.

Arc 653.1 Nebraska. University. Catalogue of Greece and Sicily. Lincoln, Neb., 1905.

Arc 848.25 Neckel, Gustav. Deutsche Ur- und Vorgeschichtswissenschaft der Gegenwart. Berlin, 1934.

Arc 938.19F Necrolivonica. (Kruse, F.K.H.) Dorpat, 1842.

Arc 387.12.31 Necrologia di Mons. Celestino Cavedoni. 2. ed. (Cappelli, A.) Modena, 1866.

Arc 320.1.2 Necrology. (Numismatic and Antiquarian Society of Philadelphia.) Philadelphia. 1882-1884

Arc 510.1 Nécropole de Camiros. (Salzmann, A.) Paris, 1875.

Arc 843.26 A necropole de condidello (Terrada-Maia). (Sousa Maia.) Porto, 1908.

Arc 510.207 La Nécropole de Myrina. (Pottier, E.) Paris, 1888. 2v.

Arc 830.354 La nécropole du monastier à Vagnas. (Thevenon, Urbain.) Saint-Etienne, 1961.

Arc 889.30 La nécropole gallo-romaine de Thuin. (Faider-Feytmans, Germaine.) Morlanwelz, 1965.

Arc 608.72 La nécropole mégalithique du Djebel Mazela à Bou Nouara. (Camps, Gabriel.) Paris, 1964.

Arc 830.300 La nécropole protohistorique de La Colombine à Champlay-Yonne. (Bolnat, Georges.) Paris, 1957.

Arc 600.75.5F La nécropole royale de Tanis. (Montet, Pierre.) Paris, 1947. 3v.

Arc 830.235 Nécropoles et civilisation en Artois et Boulounais. (Lestocquoy, Jean.) Arras, 1957.

Arc 608.2.9 Nécropoles puniques de Carthage. pt.1-2. (Gauckler, Paul.) Paris, 1915. 2v.

Arc 1027.43 Necropoli antica cristiana a Slano di Ragusa. (Bulic, F.) Roma, 1901.

Arc 726.58 Necropoli de Pianello presso Genza (Ancona). (Colini, Giuseppe A.) Parma, 1913.

Arc 726.25.15F La necropoli del porto di Roma nell'isola sacra. (Calza, Guido.) Roma, 1940.

Arc 726.335 La necropoli di Nola preromana. (Bonghi Jovino, Maria.) Napoli, 1969.

Arc 746.19 Le necropoli etrusche di Volterra. (Consortini, P.L.) Lucca, 1933.

Arc 726.295 La necropoli preromana della Ca'Morta, Scavi 1955-1965. (Rittatore Vonwiller, Ferrante.) Como, 1966.

Arc 843.55.10 Necropolis ante-romana de Cadiz. (Quintero, P.) Madrid, 1915.

Arc 843.19 Necropolis de Carmona; memoria. (Rada y Delgado, Juan de Dios de la.) Madrid, 1885.

Arc 843.9.5 Las necropolis ibéricas. (Aguilera y Gamboa, E.) Madrid, 1916.

Arc 1271.2 Nederlandsche kloosterzegels voor 1600. v.1-23. 's Gravenhage, 1935-52. 4v.

Arc 888.40F Nederlandsche oudheden van de vroegste tijden tot op Karel dan Groote. (Pleyte, Willem.) Leiden, 1902. 2v.

Arc 1528.8.5 De Nederlandse munten. 5. druk. (Gelder, Hendrik Enno van.) Utrecht, 1972.

Arc 1530.5 De Nederlandse noodmunten van de tachtigjarige vorlog. (Gelder, Hendrik Enno van.) 's-Gravenhage, 1955.

Arc 1190.86.5 Nedkov, Boris K. Osmanotwiska diplomatika: paleografiia. Sofiia, 1966-72. 2v.

Arc 497.48 Needler, W. Palestine, ancient and modern...guide to the Palestinian collection...Royal Ontario Museum. Toronto, 1949.

Arc 600.165 Nefertiti lived here. (Chubb, Mary.) N.Y., 1954.

Arc 843.100.5F Die Negalithgräber der Iberischen Halbinsel. v.1-3; atlas. (Leisner, G.K.) Berlin, 1956. 4v.

Arc 497.102 Negev, Avraham. Archaeological encyclopedia of the Holy Land. N.Y., 1972.

Arc 505.129 Negev, Avraham. Cities of the desert. Tel-Aviv, 1966.

Arc 543.145 Negmatov, Numan. Srednevekovyi Shakhristan. Dushambe, 1966.

Arc 1033.47.12 Negri, G. Nerone e il cristianesimo. Roma, 1899.

Arc 1285.25 Nehmiz, H. Untersuchungen über die Besiegelung der schlesichen Herzogsurkunden im 13. Jahrhundert. Inaug. Diss. Breslau, 1938.

Arc 936.223 Neki spomenici kulture; osvrti i Zapožanja. v.1-2. (Pavlovič, L.) Smedrevo, 1962- 3v.

Arc 925.4.18 Nekotorye voprosy drevnei istorii Zapadnoi Sibiri. (Tomsk, Siberia. Oblastnoi Kraevedcheskii Muzei.) Tomsk, 1959.

Arc 543.66.40 Nekropol' drevnego Mizdakhana. (Iagadin, V.N.) Tashkent, 1970.

Arc 925.50.355 Nekropol' Ol'vii ellinisticheskogo vremeni. (Parovich-Peshikan, Maia.) Kiev, 1974.

Arc 925.50.330 Nekropol' Ol'vii V-VI st. do n.e. (Kezub, Iuliia I.) Kyïv, 1974.

Arc 545.243F Nekropolis. (Pagenstrecher, R.) Leipzig, 1919.

Arc 1675.20.25F Nel I. centenario della istituzione delle medaglie al valore. (Italy. Esercito Corpo di Stato Maggiore. Ufficio Storico.) Roma, 1933.

Arc 1033.17.624 Nelli, A. Origine della Madonna della Quercia di Viterbo. n.p., n.d.

Arc 543.27A Nelsen, F.C. Die Buddha-Legende auf den Flachreliefs der ersten Galerie des Stupa von Boro-Budur, Java. Leipzig, 1923.

Arc 1077.6 Nelson, E.M. The cult of the circle-builders. London, 1909.

Arc 658.3.9 Nelson, J. Heinrich Schliemann und die Homersche Welt. Leipzig, 1900.
Arc 391.13 Nelson Glueck: a bibliography. (Gordon, William J.) Cincinnati? 1962.
Arc 1588.4.62 Nemeškal, Lubomir. Českobudějovická mincovina v letech 1569-1611. Vyd. 1. Česke Budějovice, 1969.
Arc 1588.4.60 Nemeškal, Lubomir. Jáchymovská mincovna v první polovině 16. století, 1519/20-1561. Praha, 1964.
Arc 628.32 Nemirovskii, Aleksandr I. Nit' Ariadny. Voronesh, 1972.
Htn Arc 855.14F* Nenia Britannica, or Sepulchral history of Great Britain. (Douglas, J.) London, 1793.
Arc 936.251.5 Neolit centralnog Balkana. (Belgrade. Narodni Muzej.) Beograd, 1968.
Arc 659.12 Neolit Gretsii. (Titov, Valerii S.) Moskva, 1969.
Arc 936.220.50 Neolit n Vojvodini. (Brukner, Bogdan.) Beograd, 1968.
Arc 612.73 Neolit środkowaeuropejski. (Tabaczyński, Stanisław.) Wrocław, 1970.
Arc 443.5 Neolithic cattle-keepers of south India; a study of the Deccan ashmounds. (Allchin, F.R.) Cambridge, Eng., 1963.
Arc 608.40 Neolithic culture of North Africa. (Forde-Johnston.) Liverpool, 1959.
Arc 858.58.5 The neolithic cultures of the British Isles. (Piggott, Stuart.) Cambridge, Eng., 1954.
Arc 870.5 Neolithic dew-ponds and cattle ways. (Hubbard, A.J.) London, 1905.
Arc 870.5.3 Neolithic dew-ponds and cattle ways. 3. ed. (Hubbard, A.J.) London, 1916.
Arc 1075.5F Neolithic flint axes from the Cotswold Hills. (Tyler, Alan.) Oxford, 1976.
Arc 936.14.315 The neolithic in Poland. Ossolinskich, 1970.
Arc 861.23.7 Neolithic man in northeast Surrey. (Johnson, Walter.) London, 1903.
Arc 416.20 The Neolithic of the Near East. (Mellaart, James.) London, 1975.
Arc 684.9.5 The neolithic settlement at Olynthus. (Mylonas, George E.) Baltimore, 1929.
Arc 936.15.5 Neolithic sites in the Mozavo-Danubian area. (Fewkes, V.J.) n.p., 1936.
Arc 936.15.10 Neolithic sites in the Yugoslavian portion of the lower Danube valley. (Fewkes, V.J.) Lancaster, 1937?
Arc 652.6 Hē neolithikē epoche en Helladi. (Mylonas, G.E.) Athēnai, 1928.
Arc 659.20F Neolithikē Hellas. (Theocharēs, Dēmētrios R.) Athēnai, 1973.
Arc 830.101.7 Le néolithique dans le Gard. Thèse. (Louis, Maurice.) Nîmes, 1932.
Arc 543.146.20 Neoliticheskie poseleniia i srednevekovye goroda. Ashkhabad, 1971.
Arc 726.53 Neppi Modona, A. Cortona etrusca e romana. Firenze, 1925.
Arc 93.16 Neppi Modona, Aldo. I fasti dell'Accademia Etrusca di Cortona. Cortona, 1928.
Arc 743.21 Neppi Modona, Aldo. Guide des antiquités éstrusques. Florence, 1958.
Arc 746.58 Neppi Modona, Aldo. I: Gli alfabeti etruschi; II: La scultura etrusca. Genova, 1970.
Arc 905.60 Népvándorlás koté sérok Nagykamaráson. (Banner, János.) Szeged, 1927.
Arc 543.3.57 Nerazik, Elena E. Sel'skie poseleniia afriyid skogo Khorezma. Moskva, 1966.
Arc 830.84 Néris, capitale des Gaules. (Moreau de Néris, E.) Paris, 1902.
Arc 830.84.5 Néris. Vicus Neriomagus. Recherches sur ses monuments. (Esmonnot, L.) Moulins, 1885.
Arc 938.60F Nerman, Burger. Grobin-Seeburg. Stockholm, 1958.
Arc 1033.47.12 Nerone e il cristianesimo. (Negri, G.) Roma, 1899.
Htn Arc 1033.47.28* Neronis encomium. (Cardani, H.) Amstelodami, 1640.
Arc 600.1.2 Néroutsos-Bey, T.D. L'ancienne Alexandrie. Paris, 1888.
Arc 968.2.65 Nesbitt, Paul H. Starkweather ruin: a Mogollon-Pueblo site in the Upper Gila area of New Mexico. Diss. Chicago, 1938.
Arc 936.260 Nessébre. (Bŭlgarska Akademiia na Naukite, Sofia. Arkheologicheski Institut.) Sofia, 1969.
Arc 936.40.41 Nessebre. (Venedikov, Ivan.) Sofia, 1971.
Arc 1335.23 Nesselmann, G.H.F. Die orientalischen Münzen...in Königsberg. Leipzig, 1858.
Htn Arc 773.5F* Nestigi della antichita di Roma. (Sadeler, Marco.) Roma, 1660.
Arc 1368.1 Nestle, W. Funde antiker Münzen im königrieche Württemberg. Stuttgart, 1893.
Arc 1030.8.14 The Nestorian monument; an ancient record of Christianity in China. (Carus, P.) Chicago, 1909.
Arc 1030.8.12 The Nestorian monument in China. (Saeki, P.Y.) London, 1916.
Arc 1030.8.13 The Nestorian monument of Hsian Fu in Shen-hsi, China, 7th and 8th centuries. (Nestorian Tablet of Sian-fu.) London, 1888.
Arc 1030.8.13 Nestorian Tablet of Sian-fu. The Nestorian monument of Hsian Fu in Shen-hsi, China, 7th and 8th centuries. London, 1888.
Arc 1510.100 Neu, Heinrich. Die Münzen und Medaillen des Herrogstums und des herroglichen Hauses Arenberg. Bonn, 1959.
Arc 612.14 Neubert, Max. Die dorische Wanderung in ihren europaischen Zusammenhängen. Stuttgart, 1920.
Arc 497.16 Neue architektonische Studien...Forschungen in Palästina. (Sepp, J.N.) Würzburg, 1867.
Arc 848.54 Neue Ausgrabungen im Deutschland. (Deutsches Archäologisches Institut.) Berlin, 1958.
Arc 653.2 Neue Ausgrabungen in Griechenland. Olten, 1963.
Arc 1366.2 Neue Beiträge zur antike Münzkunde. (Lederer, Philipp.) Bern, 1943.
Arc 383.79.25 Neue Beiträge zur klassischen Altertumswissenschaft. (Lullies, R.) Stuttgart, 1954.
Arc 853.298 Neue Beiträge zur Vor- und Frühgeschichte von Gauting. (Krämer, Wolfgang.) München, 1967.
Arc 513.25 Neue deutsche Ausgrabungen im Mittelmeergebiet. (Deutsches Archäologisches Institut.) Berlin, 1959.
Arc 14.1 Neue Dokumente zur Menschheitsgeschichte. Weimar. 1,1928
Arc 853.20 Neue Forschungen über Römischen architektonisch Alterhümer. (Wyttenback, J.H.) Trier, 1835.
Arc 853.76 Neue Forschungen zur ostdeutschen Steinzeit und frühen Bronzezeit. (Umbreit, Carl.) Leipzig, 1937.
Arc 936.20.50 Neue Forschungsergebnisse zur Vorgeschichte Rumäniens. (Berciu, Dumitru.) Bonn, 1966.
Arc 1020.123 Neue Funde aus dem altchristlichen Österreich. (Swoboda, H.) Wien, 1909.
Arc 684.1.48 Neue Meisterwerke griechischer Kunst aus Olympia. (Kunze, Emil.) München, 1948.
Arc 716.2.2 Neue Messungen der Überreste vom Theater des Dionysus zu Athen. (Kirchhoff, F.C.) Altona, 1883.
Arc 853.35 Neue prähistorische Funde aus Worms und Augsburg. (Korhl, C.) n.p., n.d.
Arc 810.38 Neuer Führer durch Pompeji. (Engelmann, W.) Leipzig, 1925.
Arc 1070.207 Neuere Faelschungen von Antiken. (Furtwängler, A.) Berlin, 1899.
Arc 1510.166 Die neueren deutschen Taler. (Schwalbach, Carl.) Lübeck, 1962.
Arc 1503.8 Die neueren Münzen der Schweiz und des Fürstentums Leichtenstein. 1850-1970. 4. Aufl. (Divo, Jean-Paul.) Freiburg, 1971.
Arc 1504.20 Die neueren Münzen der Schweiz und des Fürstentums Liechtenstein, 1850-1963. (Divo, Jean-Paul.) Freiburg, 1965.
Arc 936.195.305 Neuerworbene römische Metallgefässe aus Stáže bei Pieštany. 1. Aufl. (Svoboda, Bedřich.) Bratislava, 1972.
Arc 1400.4 Neueste Münzkunde. Leipzig, 1853. 2v.
Arc 785.13.22.5 Die neuesten Ausgrabungen...Nachtrag. (Huelsen, Christian.) Rom, 1910.
Arc 853.294.5 Neuffer-Müller, Christiane. Das fränkische Gräberfeld von Iversheim, Kreis Euskirchen. Berlin, 1972.
Arc 853.371 Neuffer-Müller, Christiane. Das fränkische Gräberfeld von Rübenach. Berlin, 1973.
Arc 853.294 Neuffer-Müller, Christiane. Ein Reihengräberfriedhof in Sontheim an der Brenz. Stuttgart, 1966.
Arc 853.374 Neuhof, Elias. Nachricht von den Alterthümern in der Gegend und auf dem Gebürge bey Homburg vor der Höhe. Homburg, 1780.
Arc 608.33.5 Neukom, Tolantha T. Les peintures rupestres du Tassili-n-Ajjer. Neuchâtel, 1956.
Arc 608.33 Neukom, Tolantha T. Pitture rupestri del Tasili degli Azger. Firenze, 1955.
Arc 905.80.5 Neumann, Alfred. Ausgrabungen und Funde. v.1-3. Wien, 1951.
Arc 905.80 Neumann, Alfred. Die römischen Ruinen unter dem Hohen Markt. Wien, 1950.
Arc 905.80.3 Neumann, Alfred. Die römischen Ruinen unter dem Hohen Markt. 2. Aufl. Wien, 1957.
Arc 905.76 Neumann, Alfred. Vindobona. Die römische Vergangenheit Wiens. Wien, 1972.
Arc 1335.34 Neumann, J. Beschreibung der Bekanntesten. v.1,2,3-4,5,6. Prag, 1858-72. 5v.
Arc 1470.8 Neumundneunzig Silberne Münzen der Athenaier. (Rathgeber, G.) Weissensee, 1858.
Arc 1510.4 Die neuren Hamburgischen Münzen und Medaillen. (Langermann, J.P.) Hamburg, 1843.
Arc 1508.15 Die neuren Münzprägungen der deutschen Staaten. pt.1-2,3-4,8,9,10,11,12. (Jaeger, Kurt.) Stuttgart, 1951-72. 12v.
Arc 936.30 Neuropolüt do novi pazar. (Stanchev, S.) Sofiia, 1958.
Arc 1020.130 Neuss, Wilhelm. Die Anfänge des Christentums im Rheinlande. 2. Aufl. Bonn, 1933.
Arc 936.195 Neustupny, E. Czechoslovakia before the Slavs. London, 1961.
Arc 936.195.300 Neustupný, Jiří. Pravěk Československa. 1. vyd. Praha, 1960.
Arc 861.42 Neville, R.C. Antiqua explorata. Chesterford. Walden Saffron, 1847.
Arc 861.87F Neville, R.C. Saxon obsequies illustrated by ornaments and weapons. London, 1851.
Arc 810.44 Neville-Rolfe, Eustace. Pompeii, popular and practical. Naples, 1888.
Arc 1018.49 The new archaeological discoveries and their bearing upon the New Testament. (Cobern, C.M.) N.Y., 1917.
Arc 1018.49.5 The new archaeological discoveries and their bearing upon the New Testament. 3. ed. (Cobern, C.M.) N.Y., 1918.
Arc 925.190 New archaeological material relating to the history of the Soviet East. (Leningrad. Ermitazh.) Leningrad, 1960.
Arc 497.88 New direction in Biblical archaeology. 1. ed. Garden City, N.Y., 1969.
Arc 790.6 New Entdeckte Wandgemälde in Pompeji. (Zahn, W.) München, 1828.
X Cg Arc 880.8 New Grange and other incised tumuli. (Coffey, George.) Dublin, 1912.
Arc 880.46.5 New Grange and the bend of the Boyne. (O'Riordain, Sean P.) London, 1964.
Arc 810.38.5 New guide to Pompeii. (Engelmann, W.) Leipzig, 1925.
Arc 672.1.135 A new guide to the palace of Knossos. (Palmer, Leonard R.) London, 1969.
Arc 497.31.10 New horizons in Biblical research. (Albright, William Foxwell.) London, 1966.
Arc 585.28F The New Kingdom temples of Buhen. (Caminos, Ricardo A.) London, 1974. 2v.
Arc 562.2.26 New light on ancient Egypt. (Maspero, Gaston.) London, 1908.
Arc 562.2.27 New light on ancient Egypt. (Maspero, Gaston.) N.Y., 1909.
Arc 448.1.30 New light on the Indus civilization. (Sastri, K.N.) Delhi, 1957-65. 2v.
Arc 968.2.40F New Mexico. University. Bulletin survey series. Albuquerque. 1,1931
Arc 497.55 The new-old land of Israel. (Bentwich, Norman de Mattos.) London, 1960.
Arc 861.18.3 New points in the history of Roman Britain, as illustrated by discoveries at Warwick Square. (Tylor, Alfred.) Westminster, 1884.
Arc 612.12A The new stone age in northern Europe. (Tyler, John Mason.) N.Y., 1921.
Arc 766.1.13A New tales of old Rome. (Lanciani, R.) Boston, 1901.
Arc 766.1.14 New tales of old Rome. (Lanciani, R.) Boston, 1902.
Arc 766.1.15 New tales of old Rome. (Lanciani, R.) London, 1901.
Arc 1400.1 New varieties of gold and silver coins. (Eckfeldt, J.R.) N.Y., 1851.
Arc 505.55 New York. Metropolitan Museum of Art. A crusaders' fortress in Palestine. N.Y., 1927.
Htn Arc 1084.3PF* New York (City). Metropolitan Museum of Art. The Bishop collections. N.Y., 1906. 2v.
Arc 547.20 New York (City). Metropolitan Museum of Art. A handbook of Egyptian rooms. N.Y., 1920.
Arc 600.38 New York (City). Metropolitan Museum of Art. The tomb of Perneb. N.Y., 1916.
Arc 537.2.7 New York (City). Metropolitan Museum of Art. Cesnola Collection. Guide to the Cesnola collection...Island of Cyprus. N.Y., 1876.
Arc 547.22.10F New York (City). Metropolitan Museum of Art. Department of Egyptian Art. Publication. N.Y. 1-5,1921-1936 3v.
Arc 547.21 Pamphlet box. New York (City). Metropolitan Museum of Art. Egyptian antiquities.

Author and Title Listing

Arc 547.22F New York (City). Metropolitan Museum of Art. Egyptian Expedition. Publications. N.Y. 1-18,1916-1955 14v.
Arc 1090.5A New York (City). Museum of Modern Art. Prehistoric rock pictures in Europe and Africa. N.Y., 1937.
Arc 593.1.2 The New York obelisk. (Moldenke, C.E.) N.Y., 1891.
Arc 593.1 The New York obelisk. (Moldenke, C.E.) N.Y., 1891.
Arc 1330.4 New York Public Library. List of works relating to numismatics. N.Y., 1914.
Arc 318.5 New York State Archaeological Association. Occasional papers. Albany. 1-2,1958-1959
Arc 875.128 Newall, Frank. Excavation of prehistoric and mediaeval homesteads at Knapps, Renfrewshire. Paisley, 1965.
Arc 587.1A Newberry, P.E. Beni Hasan. London, 1893. 4v.
Arc 587.3 Newberry, P.E. El Bersheh. Pt.1-2. London, 1894-95. 2v.
Arc 587.50 Newberry, P.E. The life of Rekhmara. Westminster, 1900.
Arc 600.12.5A Newberry, P.E. Scarabs. London, 1906.
Arc 1468.32 Newell, E.T. Alexander Loards. v.3. N.Y., 1921-23.
Arc 1221.5F Newell, E.T. Ancient oriental seals in the collection of Mr. E.T. Newell. Chicago, 1934.
Arc 1470.31 Newell, E.T. The coinage of Demetrius Poliorcetes. London, 1927.
Arc 1470.31.10 Newell, E.T. Royal Greek portrait coins. N.Y., 1937.
Arc 1423.11 Newell, E.T. The Seleucid mint of Antioch. N.Y., 1918.
Arc 1470.31.5 Newell, E.T. Tyrus rediviva. N.Y., 1923.
Arc 1615.3 Newlin, H.P. A classification of early half-dimes in the United States. Philadelphia, 1883.
Arc 895.22.17F Newman, B. Die Volkerwanderungszeit Gotlands. Stockholm, 1935.
Arc 1615.14 Newman, Eric. The fantastic 1804 dollar. Racine, 1962.
Arc 861.26 Newmarch, C.H. Remains of Roman art Corinum. London, n.d.
Arc 30.11 Newsletter. (American Research Center in Egypt.) Boston. 13,1954+ 23v.
Arc 1.5.27 Newsletter. (American School of Oriental Research, Jerusalem.) Jerusalem. 1939-1958 5v.
Arc 510.5 Newton, C.T. Halicarnassus, Cnidas and Branchidae. v.1; v.2, pt.1-2. London, 1862-1863. 3v.
Arc 513.7 Newton, C.T. Travels and discoveries in the Levant. London, 1865. 2v.
Arc 398.2 Newton C.T. Essays on art and archaeology. London, 1880.
Arc 875.32.5 The Newton stone and other Pictish inscriptions. (Diack, F.C.) Paisley, 1922.
Arc 405.1.35 Nezabvennoi pamiati grafa Alekseia Sergeevicha Uvarova. Moskva, 1885.
Arc 1020.10.33 Nibby, A. Del Foro Romano e de' luoghi adjacenti. Roma, 1819.
Arc 1020.9.9 Nibby, A. Del tempio della pace e della basiilica di Costantino. Roma, 1819.
Arc 1016.213 Nibby, A. Della forma degli antichi templi cristiani. Roma, 1825.
Arc 785.29 Nibby, A. Le mura di Roma. Roma, 1820.
Arc 768.3 Nibby, Antonio. Analisi della carta de' dentorni di Roma. Roma, 1848. 3v.
Arc 768.2.15 Nibby, Antonio. Analisi storico...dentorni di Roma. Roam, 1837. 3v.
Arc 768.2.16 Nibby, Antonio. Analisi storico...dentorni di Roma. Roma, 1837. 4v.
Arc 726.65F Nibby, Antonio. Del monumento sepolcrale detto volgarmente degli Orazii e Curiazii; discurso. Roma, 1834.
Arc 726.64 Nibby, Antonio. Della via portuense. Roma, 1827.
Arc 726.24.9 Nibby, Antonio. Descrizione della villa Adriana. Roma, 1827.
Arc 768.3.5 Nibby, Antonio. Roma nell'anno 1838. Roma, 1838-41. 4v.
Arc 720.219F Nibby, Antonio. Viaggio antiquario ad Ostia. Roma, 1829.
Arc 830.34 Nicaise, Auguste. L'époque gauloise dans...la Marne. Paris, 1884.
Htn Arc 600.16*A Nichols, C.L. The library of Rameses the Great. Boston, 1909.
Arc 785.13.63 Nichols, Francis M. A revised history of the column of Phocas in the Roman Forum. Westminster, 1890.
Arc 1076.3.93 Nichols, J.R. Bells thro' the ages. London, 1928.
Arc 853.92 Nickel, E. Die Steinwerkzeuge der jüngeren Steinzeit. Inaug. Diss. Würzburg, 1938.
Arc 853.236.5F Nickel, Ernest. Der alte Markt in Magdeburg. Berlin, 1964.
Arc 1025.57 Nicolai, Joannis. De luctie christianorum. Lugdnum Batavorum, 1739.
Arc 895.12 Nicolaysen, N. Norske fornlevninger. Hefte 1-5. Kristiania, 1862-65.
Arc 785.46.5 Nicole, Georges. Le sanctuaire des dieux orientaux au Janicule. Rome, 1909.
Arc 398.3 Nicole, J. Mélanges Nicole...recueil de mémoires. Genève, 1905.
Arc 66.1.207 Nicolet, Claude. L'ordre équestre. Paris, 1966-74. 2v.
Arc 843.230 Nicolini, Gerard. Les bronzes figurés des sanctuaires ibériques. 1. éd. Paris, 1969.
Arc 1528.9 Die niederlandische Medaille des 17. (Loehr, August.) Wien, 1921.
Arc 1510.10.5F Niedersachsisches Münzarchiv. (Bahrfeldt, Max von.) Halle, 1927. 4v.
Arc 1078.3 Niel, Fernand. Dolmens et menhirs. 3. éd. Paris, 1966.
Arc 497.27F Nielsen, D. Handbuch der altarabischen Altertumskunde. Kopenhagen, 1927.
X Cg Arc 510.206 Niemann, S. Les villes de la Pamphylie et de la Pisidie. Paris, 1890-1893. 2v.
Arc 700.50 Niemeyer, Hans G. Promachos. Waldsassen, 1960.
Arc 843.214 Niemeyer, Hans G. Toscanos, die altpunische Faktorei an der Mündung des Rio de Vélez. Berlin, 1969.
Arc 830.6.8 Niepce, L. Archéologie lyonnaise. Lyon, n.d.
Arc 853.234F Nierhaus, Rolf. Das römische Brand- und Körpergräberfeld. Stuttgart, 1959.
Arc 1033.17.53 Nieszporkowicz, A. Analecta mensae reginalis seu historia imaginis...virginis...Claromontanae. Cracoviae, 1681.
Arc 843.125 Nieto Gallo, Gratiniano. El oppedum de Iruña. Victória, 1958.
Arc 936.14.435 Niewęgłowski, Andrej. Mazowsze na przełomie er. Wrocław, 1972.
Arc 391.17 Niggl, Reto. Giacomo Grimaldi (1568-1623). Inaug. Diss. München, 1971.
Arc 925.334 Nikitin, Andrei L. Golubye doragi vekov. Moskva, 1968.
Arc 925.95.5 Nikitin, Arkadii. Russkoe kwznechmoe remeslo XVI-XVII vv. Moskva, 1971.
Arc 395.9 Nikodim Pavlovich Kondakov, 1844-1924. Praga, 1924.
Arc 1163.3.105 Nikolaeva, Tat'iana V. Proizvedeniia russkogo prikladnogo iskusstvo s nadpisiami XV- pervoi chetverți XVI v. Mosvka, 1971.
Arc 1675.106 Nikolić, Desanka. Naša odlikovanja do 1941. Beograd, 1971.
Arc 568.1 Nile gleanings. (Stuart, V.) London, 1879.
Arc 893.8 Nilsson, S. Skandinaviska nordens ur-invånare. Stockholm, 1862-66. 2v.
Arc 893.8.5 Nilsson, S. Die Ureinwohner des Scandinavischen Nordens. Hamburg, 1863-68. 2v.
Arc 893.8.6 Nilsson, S. Die Ureinwohner des Scandinavischen Nordens. pt.1-2. Hamburg, 1865-66.
Arc 825.3.5 Nîmes. Musée des Antiques et Cabinet des Médailles. Catalogue de Musée de Nîmes. 6e éd. Nîmes, 1863.
Arc 825.3.8 Nîmes. Musée des Antiques et Cabinet des Médailles. Catalogue de Musée de Nîmes. 6e éd. Nîmes, 1863-75.
Arc 825.6 Nîmes gallo-romain. (Bazin, H.) Paris, 1892.
Arc 936.50.10 Nin. Zadar, 1968.
Arc 1680.6 The nineteenth century token coinage. (Davis, William John.) London, 1904.
Arc 1680.6.1 The nineteenth century token coinage of Great Britain. (Davis, William John.) London, 1969.
Arc 700.57 Niobe and her children. (Cook, R.M.) Cambridge, 1964.
Arc 830.320 Niort, France. Bibliothèque Municipale. Répertoire des dessins archéologiques. Niort, 1915.
Arc 768.2 Nispi-Landi, Ciro. Roma monumentale dinanzi all'umanita. Roma, 1892.
Arc 810.12 Nissen, H. Pompeianische Studien zur Staedtekunde des Altertums. Leipzig, 1877.
Arc 628.1 Nissen, H. Pompeji. 2. Aufl. Berlin, 1827. 22 pam.
Arc 628.32 Nit' Ariadny. (Nemirovskii, Aleksandr I.) Voronesh, 1972.
Arc 1033.51.5 Nitizie dei Sante Rufino e Cesidio Martire. (Vincenti, D. de.) Avezzano, 1885.
Arc 1020.48 Nitzhammer, R. Die christlichen Altertümer der Dobrogia. Bukarest, 1906.
Arc 861.47 Nixon, J. Marmor Estonianum...in agro Northamptoniensi. Londinium, 1744.
Arc 925.170.11 Nizhnekamskaia Arkheologicheskaia Ekspeditsiia, 1968-1969? Otchety Nizhnekamskoi arkheologicheskoi ekspeditsii. Photoreproduction. Moskva, 1972.
Arc 674.1.5F Noack, F. Eleusis. Text and plates. Berlin, 1927. 2v.
Arc 672.1.25 Noack, F. Ovalhaus und Paläst in Kreta. Leipzig, 1908.
Arc 593.6 Noakes, Aubrey. Cleopatra's needles. London, 1962.
Arc 1330.25 Noble, Fiona Virginia. South African numismatics, 1652-1965; a bibliography. Capetown, 1967.
Arc 1540.22 Noble, Mark. Two dissertations upon the mint and coins of Durham. Birmingham, 1780.
Arc 1033.17.423 Nocelli. Cenno istorico sul duomo e sagra immagine di Santa Maria...in Lucera. Napoli, 1843.
Arc 1018.12.8 Nochmals Principienfragen. (Wilpert, J.) Rom, 1890.
Arc 390.10 Nocines de prehistoria. (Fletcher y Valls, D.) Valencia, 1952.
Arc 838.19.2 Nociones de arqueologia españolas. 2. ed. (Manjarrés, J. de.) Barcelona, 1874.
Arc 1020.119 Nocions d'arqueologia sagrada catalana. (Gudiol y Cunill, J.) Vich, 1911.
Arc 1020.119.5 Nocions d'arqueologia sagrada catalana. 2a ed. (Gudiol y Cunill, J.) Vich, 1931-33. 2v.
Arc 403.10 Noções elementares de archeologia. (Silva, J.P.N. da.) Lisboa, 1878.
Arc 835.205F Noções sobre o estado prehistorico de terra e do homein. (Pereira da Costa, Francisco.) Lisboa, 1868. 2v.
Arc 595.64 Nocturnal magic of the pyramids. (United Arab Republic. Ministry of Culture and National Guidance.) Paris, 1961.
Arc 1675.25 Nocz, Henry. Les Duvivier. Paris, 1911.
Arc 953.32 Nöel Hume, Ivor. A guide to artifacts of colonial America. 1. ed. N.Y., 1970.
Arc 976.7 Noël Hume, Ivor. Here lies Virginia. N.Y., 1963.
Arc 398.8.1 Noël Hume, Ivor. Historical archaeology. N.Y., 1975.
Arc 398.8 Noël Hume, Ivor. Historical archaeology. 1. ed. N.Y., 1969.
Arc 853.63 Die nördlichen Elbgermanen in spätrömischer Zeit. (Matthes, W.) Leipzig, 1931.
Arc 743.19 Nogara, B. Les Etrusques et leur civilisation. Paris, 1936.
Arc 785.104 Nogara, Bartolomeo. Monumenti romani scoperti negli anni 1938-XVI-1939-XVII nell'area del Palazzo della Cancelleria. Roma, 1942.
Arc 1588.4.17 Nohejlova, Eman. Nálezi minci v Cechacle na Morave a ve slezsku. Praha, 1955. 4v.
Arc 1588.4.38 Nohejlová, Emanuela. Dvě stoleti vědecké numismatiky v českých Zemich. 1771-1971. Praha, 1971.
Arc 1588.4.30 Nohejlová, Emanuela. Krasa česke mince. Praha, 1955.
Arc 1588.4.35 Nohejlová, Emanuela. Kratký přehled českého mincovnictví a tabulky cen a mezd. Praha, 1964.
Arc 66.1.54 Noiret, H. Lettres inedites de Michel Apostolis. Paris, 1889.
Arc 1033.20.28 Nolan, Louis. The Basilica of Saint Clemente in Rome. Rome, 1910.
Arc 1033.20.29 Nolan, Louis. The Basilica of Saint Clemente in Rome. 2. ed. Rome, 1914.
Arc 689.8 Nolters, P. Das Kabirenheiligtum bei Theben. Berlin, 1940.
Arc 830.41 Le nom et les 2 premières encientes de Gap. (Manteyer, G. de.) Gap, 1905.
Arc 1153.82 Nomenclature des écritures livresques du IXe au XVIe siècle. Photoreproduction. (Colloque International de Paléographie Latine, 1st, Paris, 1953.) Paris, 1954.
Arc 1440.200 Ta nomiomata toy kratoys tōn ptolemaiōn. (Sborōnos, I.N.) Athēnai, 1904. 2v.
Arc 1465.77 Nomisma, Untersuchungen auf dem gebiete. (Fritze.) Berlin, 1907-12. 12v.
Arc 1335.76.16 Nomismata. (Athens. Ethnikon Nomismatikon Mouseion.) Athēnai, 1885.
Arc 1473.50 Nomismata tēs Hepianēdon politeias. (Lampros, Paulos.) Athēnai, 1884.
Arc 1470.13 Nomismata tēs nēsoy Amorgy. (Lampros, Paulos.) Athēnai, 1870.
Arc 1473.1.8 Nomismata tōn ademiōn Zachariōn. (Lampros, Paulos.) Athēnai, 1884.
Arc 1313.46 Nomismatika chronika. Athēnai. 1,1972+
Arc 823.19.20 Les noms des deux premiers Gordiens par Sallet. (Thédenat, H.) Paris, 1883.
Arc 1530.20 De noord-Nederlandsche gildepenningen. (Dirks, Jacob.) Haarlem, 1878. 2v.
Arc 895.22.5F Nordén, Arthur. Östergötlands bronsälder. Linköping, 1925.
Arc 893.5.4 Nordene forhistorie. (Worsaae, J.J.A.) Kjøbenhavn, 1881.
Arc 950.200 Nordenskiold, G. The cliff dwellers of the Mesa Verde. Stockholm, 1893.

Author and Title Listing

Arc 893.26 Die Nordgermanen. (Oxenstierna, E.C.G.) Stuttgart, 1957.

Arc 853.96 Die Nordharzgruppe der Elbgermanen bis zur sächsischen Überlagerung. (Thärigen, Günter.) Berlin, 1939.

Arc 893.1A Nordische Altertumskunde. (Mueller, S.) Strassburg, 1896. 2v.

Arc 895.32 Nordische Ornamentik in vorgeschichtlicher Zeit. (Åberg, Nils.) Leipzig, 1931.

Arc 895.14 Nordisk archaelogi. (Zinck, L.) Kjøbenhavn, 1890.

Arc 1313.18 Nordisk numismatisk årsskrift. Stockholm. 1936+ 14v.

Arc 893.15F Den nordiska folkvandringstidens kronologi. (Åberg, Nils.) Stockholm, 1924.

Arc 1542.2 Nordiska mynt före år 1000. (Malmer, Brita.) Bonn, 1966.

Arc 893.3.5 Nordiske Oldskrift-Selskab. Leitfaden zur Nordischen Alterthumskunde. Copenhagen, 1837.

Arc 247.4 Nordiske Oldskrift-Selskab. Mémoires de la Société Royale des Antiquaires du Nord. Copenhagen. 1836-1933 15v.

Arc 247.4.3 Pamphlet box. Nordiske oldskrift selskab.

Arc 848.22 Nordwestdeutschland und die Frage des Germanenursprungs. (Schuchhardt, C.) n.p., 1928.

Arc 1568.6 Norges mynter. (Rønning, Bjørn R.) Oslo, 1971.

Arc 1565.2 Norges mynter i middetalderen. pt.1-6. (Schive, C.I.) Christiania, 1858-65.

Arc 1570.5 Norges mynter i 150 år, 1816-1966. (Rønning, Bjørn R.) Oslo, 1967.

Arc 1568.7 Norges mynter og pengesedler etter 1874. (Rønning, Bjørn R.) Oslo, 1972.

Arc 890.214 Norges oldtid. Mindesmärker og oldsager. (Gustafson, G.) Kristiania, 1906.

Arc 380.199 Noris, Enrico. Lettere sopra vari punti di erudizione. n.p., 1720.

Arc 1166.8 Norlén, Saga-Marianne. Alt datera manuskript. Stockholm, 1973.

Arc 858.27 Norman, A. Glossary of archaeology. London, 1915. 2v.

Arc 880.50 Norman, Edward R. The early development of Irish society: the evidence of aerial photography. Cambridge, Eng., 1969.

Arc 1138.130 Norman, James. Ancestral voices. N.Y., 1975.

Arc 1540.27.5 The Norman conquest and the English coinage. (Dolley, Reginald Hugh Michael.) London, 1966.

Arc 635.201 Normand, C. Corpus des monuments grecs. Livre II: Lycosoura. Paris, n.d.

Arc 830.22.3 Normand, Charles. Nouvelles antiquités gallo-romaines de Paris. Paris, 1894. 2v.

Arc 510.209 Normand, Charles. La Troie d'Homère. Paris, 1892.

Arc 830.29.4 La Normandie souterraine. (Cochet, J.B.D.) Rouen, 1854.

Arc 386.30 Norme per il restauro dei monumenti. (Brayda, C.) Torino, 1954.

Arc 875.14.25 Norse building customs in the Scottish isles. (Roussell, Aage.) Copenhagen, 1934.

Arc 1570.8 Norsk numismatisk forenings historie: 1927-1967. (Hansen, Per.) Oslo, 1967.

Arc 895.12 Norske fornlevninger. Hefte 1-5. (Nicolaysen, N.) Kristiania, 1862-65.

Arc 890.207 Norske oldsager. (Rygh, O.) Christiania, 1885.

Arc 893.4 Norske oldsager i fremmede museer. (Undset, I.M.) Christiania, 1878.

Arc 1027.19 Nortet. Les catacombes de Saint Calixte. Rome, 1887.

Arc 1027.19.2 Nortet. Cimetière de Saint Calixte. 3e éd. Rome, 1888.

Arc 1027.19.3 Nortet. Cimetière de Saint Calixte. 3e éd. Rome, 1899.

Arc 1027.19.5 Nortet. Cimetière de Saint Calixte. 3e éd. Rome, 1900.

Arc 885.23 North, F.J. Sunken cities. Cardiff, 1957.

Arc 1538.25 North, J.J. English hammered coinage. London, 1960-63. 2v.

Arc 1076.3.65 North, Thomas. The church bells of Rutland. Leicester, 1880.

Arc 953.11 The North Americans of antiquity. (Short, J.F.) N.Y., 1879-80.

Arc 861.170 The North Britons. (Feachem, Richard.) London, 1965.

Arc 138.3F North Munster antiquarian journal. Limerick. 1-2,1936-1941

Arc 138.3 North Munster antiquarian journal. Limerick. 3,1942+ 3v.

Arc 138.10 North Munster Archaeologcial Society. Index to journal 1897-1919. Nenagh, 1958.

Arc 861.38.8 A north Somerset miscellany. (Bath and Camerton Archaeological Society.) Bath, 1966.

Arc 1025.4.9 Northcote, J.S. Les catacombes romaines. Rome, 1859.

Arc 1025.5 Northcote, J.S. Roma sotterranea. pts.1-3. London, 1879. 2v.

Arc 1025.4 Northcote, J.S. The Roman catacombs. London, 1857.

Arc 1025.4.2 Northcote, J.S. The Roman catacombs. Philadelphia, 1857.

Arc 1025.6 Northcote, J.S. Rome souterraine. 2. éd. Paris, 1874.

Arc 1025.4.5 Northcote, J.S. A visit to the Roman catacombs. London, 1877.

Arc 1025.4.7 Northcote, J.S. Visite aux catacombes de Rome. Paris, 1878.

Arc 501.15.5 Northern Ajlûn. (Schumacher, G.) London, 1890.

Arc 880.42 Northern Ireland. Ministry of Finance. An account of the ancient monuments in state charge. Belfast, 1947.

Arc 880.43 Northern Ireland. Ministry of Finance. Ancient monuments of Northern Ireland. v.1-2. Belfast, 1966-69.

Arc 875.122 The northern isles. (Wainwright, Frederick Threlfall.) Edinburgh, 1962.

Arc 723.46 Northern Italy before Rome. (Barfield, Lawrence.) London, 1971.

Arc 1480.36F Northumberland, A.P. Descriptive catalogue of a cabinet of Roman family coins belonging to...the Duke of Northumberland. London, 1856.

Arc 861.71.5F Northumbrian crosses of the pre-Norman age. (Collingwood, W.G.) London, 1927.

Arc 950.202.12F The northwestern Florida coast revisited. (Moore, C.B.) Philadelphia, 1918.

Arc 608.17 Norton, Richard. The excavations at Cyrene. N.Y., 1911.

Arc 608.17.3 Norton, Richard. From Bengazi to Cyrene. n.p., 1911.

Arc 823.1 Nos origines - La Gaule avant les Gaulois. (Bertrand, A.) Paris, 1891.

Arc 823.1.3 Nos origines - La religion des Gaulois. (Bertrand, A.) Paris, 1897.

Arc 936.14.240 Nosek, Stefan. Kultura amfor kulistych. Wrocław, 1967.

Arc 936.14.243 Nosek, Stefan. Słowianie w pradziejach siem polskich. Kraków, 1946.

Arc 936.14.105 Nosek, Stefan. Zarys historii badań archeologicznych w Małopolsce. Wrocław, 1967.

Arc 1033.17.560 Nota historica de la Mare de Deu de la Cisa. (Más, Joseph.) Barcelona, 1908.

Arc 1153.8.7A Notae Latinae...abbreviation in Latin MSS...miniscule period. (Lindsay, W.M.) Cambridge, 1915.

Arc 1190.75 Notarial signs from the York archiepescopal records. (Purvis, John Stanley.) London, 1957.

Arc 1297.5 Die Notariats-Signete. (Leist, F.) Leipzig, n.d.

Arc 843.18 Notas d'archeologia. (Pereira, Gabriel.) Erora, 1879.

Arc 772.4.5 Note di Ruderi e monumenti antico di Roma. (Rossi, G.B. de.) Roma, 1883.

Arc 772.4 Note di topographia romana. (Rossi, G.B. de.) Roma, 1882.

Arc 1148.22 Note epigrafiche. (Breccia, E.) Alexandria, 1931.

Arc 1433.5.10 Note on the historical results deducible from recent discoveries in Afghanistan. (Prinsep, H.T.) London, 1844.

Arc 1018.50 Note storico-bibliografiche di archeologia cristiana. (Ferretto, Giuseppe.) Città del Vaticano, 1942.

Arc 712.4 Note sur la courbure dissymétrique des degrés qui limitent au couchant la plate-forme du Parthénon. (Choisy, A.) Paris, 1865.

Arc 505.5.23 Note sur le Temple de Jerusalem. (Vogüé.) n.p., n.d.

Arc 1500.14 Note sur les monnaies trouvées au Mont César. (Barthélemy, Anatole de.) Paris, 1881.

Arc 1423.2 Note sur les plus anciennes monnaies hébraiques. (Révillout, Eugène.) Macon, 1884.

Arc 1092.1 Note sur les rouelles antiques de bronze. (Longpérier, H.) Paris, 1867.

Arc 1285.1 Note sur les sceaux de l'ordre de Saint Jean de Jérusalem. (Delaville Le Roulx, J.) Paris, 1881.

Arc 830.23 Note sur les tumulus de Bartrès et d'Ossun. (Piette, Edouard.) Toulouse, 1881. 2 pam.

Arc 1500.18 Note sur l'origine du gros tournois. (Maxe-Werly, L.) Paris, 1880.

Arc 608.6.27 Note sur quelques villes romaines de l'Algérie. Paris, 1849?

Arc 830.344F Note sur un foyer de l'âge de la Pierre Polie découvert an camp de Chassey en septembre 1869. (Perrault, Ernest.) Chalons-sur-Saône, 1870.

Arc 1680.4 Notes...eighteenth century tokens. (Waters, A.W.) Leamington, 1906.

Arc 830.51.5 Notes archéologiques sur les fouilles et les monuments découverts sur la montagne du Chatêlet. (Phulpin, A.) Neufchateau, 1840.

Arc 1020.68.9 Notes archéologiques sur Moutiers et la Tarentaise. (Barbier de Montault, X.) Montiers, 1877.

Arc 830.118 Notes archéologiques sur Nouaillé. (La Croix, C. de.) Poitiers, 1910.

Arc 830.12 Notes d'archéologie gallo-romaine. (Sauvage, H.E.) Boulogne, n.d.

Arc 708.13 Notes descriptive of panoramic sketch of Athens. Coventry, 1836? 3 pam.

Htn Arc 830.7* Notes d'un voyage dans le midi de la France. (Mérimée, Prosper.) Paris, 1835.

Arc 830.8.3A Notes d'un voyage dans l'ouest de la France. (Mérimée, Prosper.) Bruxelles, 1837.

Arc 830.8 Notes d'un voyage dans l'ouest de la France. (Mérimée, Prosper.) Paris, 1836.

Arc 830.9 Notes d'un voyage en Auvergne. (Mérimée, Prosper.) Paris, 1838.

Arc 830.10 Notes d'un voyage en Corse. (Mérimée, Prosper.) Paris, 1840.

Arc 825.8.3 Notes épigraphiques. (Germer-Durand, E.) Nîmes, 1869. 6 pam.

Arc 608.1.31 Notes et documents. (Tunis. Direction des Antiquités et Arts.) Paris. 1,1908+ 9v.

Arc 1033.12.16 Notes iconographique sur le Saint Suaire de Besançon. (Gauthier, J.) Besançon, 1884.

Arc 593.2 Notes of research on the New York obelisk. (Julien, A.A.) N.Y., 1893.

Arc 426.2A Notes on ancient stone implements...of Japan. (Kanda, T.) Tokio, 1884.

Arc 457.20 Notes on antiquities in Ramannadesa. (Temple, Richard C.) Bombay, 1894.

Arc 1540.12.5 Notes on numismatic history of the reign of Henry I. v.1-2. (Andrew, W.J.) London, 1903.

Arc 810.52 Notes on Pompei. (Seymour-Browne, C.) Naples, 1913.

Arc 861.41 Notes on prehistoric burial in Sussex. (Smith, H.) n.p., n.d.

Arc 553.5 Notes on prehistoric man in Egypt and Lebanon. (Dawson, John W.) London, 1884.

Arc 855.205 Notes on Roman architectural remains. (Tite, Will.) London, 1867. 2 pam.

Arc 435.9.3 Notes on the Amarāvati stūpa. (Burgess, James.) Madras, 1882.

Arc 435.9.5 Notes on the Amarāvati stūpa. (Burgess, James.) Madras, 1882. 2 pam.

Arc 1020.118 Notes on the antiquities of united parishes of Ballycollan, Kilmaugh and Killaloe. (Holahan, J.) Kilkenny, 1875.

Arc 905.5 Notes on the castellieri or prehistoric ruins of the Istrian Peninsula. (Burton, R.F.) Trieste, n.d.

Arc 855.221 Notes on the Cross of Cong. (Stokes, Margaret.) Dublin, 1895.

Arc 861.13 Notes on the early sculptured crosses...present diocese of Carlisle. (Calverley, W.S.) Kendal, 1899.

Arc 595.4 Notes on the Great Pyramid of Egypt. (James, H.) Southampton, 1869. 2 pam.

Arc 861.30 Notes on the old crosses of Gloucester. (Pooley, C.) London, 1868.

Arc 458.4.5 Notes on the seven pagodas. (Temple, Richard C.) London, 1928-29.

Arc 505.3 Notes on the site of the Holy Sepulchre. (Fergusson, J.) London, 1861.

Arc 823.19.35 Notes sur deux inscriptions fausses. (Thédenat, H.) Paris, 1880.

Arc 830.103.5 Notice...des antiquités de Vichy-les-Bains. (Chauvet, J.M.) Cusset, 1851.

Arc 1033.12.114 Notice abrégée sur la sainte tunique de...Christ. (Guérin, L.F.) Paris, 1864.

Arc 820.216F Notice archéologique sur le camp de Chassey. (Flouest, E.) Chalon-sur-Saône, 1869.

Arc 830.26.15 Notice archéologique sur le département de l'Oise. Beauvais, 1839.

Arc 402.9.25 Notice biographique du vicomte Emmanuel de Rouge. (Maspero, G.) Paris, 1908.

Arc 562.1.20 Notice biographique sur Auguste Mariette. (Maspero, Gaston.) Paris, 1904.

Arc 497.15 Notice des monuments de la Palestine conservés au Musée du Louvre. 2. éd. (Héron de Villefosse, A.) Paris, 1879.

Arc 1335.14.3 Notice des monuments exposés dans le cabinet des médailles. (Du Mersan, T.M.) Paris, 1840.

Arc 547.6.5 Notice des principaux monuments...à Boulaq. (Cairo. Musée des Antiquités Egyptiennes.) Alexandrie, 1864.

Arc 547.6.7 Notice des principaux monuments...du Musée d'Antiquités Égyptiennes à Boulaq. 3. éd. (Cairo. Musée des Antiquités Égyptiennes.) Paris, 1869.

Author and Title Listing

Arc 547.18 Notice des principaux monuments. (Musée de Gizeh.) Le Caire, 1897.
Arc 830.16.9 Notice des tableaux, Dessins. (De Fontenay, H.) Autun, n.d.
Arc 547.9 Notice descriptive des monumens égyptiens du Musée Charles X. (Champollion, J.F.) Paris, 1827.
Arc 1033.12.21 Notice historique et critique de Saint Suaire. Poitiers, 1882.
Arc 1020.73.6 Notice historique et critique sur le sainte couronne d'épines...l'église metropolitaine de Paris. (Gosselin, J.E.A.) Paris, 1828.
Arc 505.19 Notice historique sur...sanctuaire d'Emmans. Paris, 1862.
Arc 1675.5 Notice historique sur la médaille...en souvenir de l'expulsion. (Vallet de Viriville, A.) Paris, n.d.
Arc 1033.35.3 Notice historique sur la vraie croix de Baugé. (Barrau, J.B.) Angers, 1874.
Arc 1020.73 Notice historique sur les saintes reliques...de S. Jacques-des-Hauts-Pas à Paris. Paris, 1835.
Arc 396.8 Notice nécrologique sur le comte Robert de Lesteyrie du Saillant, 1849-1919. (Aubert, M.) Paris, 1926.
Arc 885.15 Notice of a tessellated pavement. (Morgan, O.) Newport, 1866.
Arc 822.2 Notice relative à la découverte d'un tombeau. (Cellerier.) Paris, 1818. 25 pam.
Arc 547.4.10 Notice sommaire des monuments égyptiens. (Paris. Musée Nationale du Louvre. Départément des Antiquités Égyptiennes.) Paris, 1873.
Arc 547.4 Notice sommaire des monuments égyptiens du Musée du Louvre. (Rougé, E. de.) Paris, 1855.
Arc 830.31 Notice sur dea inscriptions...Bourbonne-les-Bains. (Chabouillet, A.) Paris, 1881.
Arc 830.165 Notice sur des antiquités romaines découvertes en 1834 à Chandai (Orne). (La Grange, E. de.) Caen, 1835.
Arc 66.1.6 Notice sur des manuscrits de la Bibliothèque Vaticane. (Berger, E.) Paris, 1879.
Arc 1015.212 Notice sur deux catacombs. (Scognamiglio, A.) Paris, 1863.
Arc 391.2.15 Notice sur Edouard Gerhard. (Witte, J.) Bruxelles, 1871.
Arc 390.7F Notice sur Jules-Francois-Paul Fauris Saint-Vincens. Aix, 1807.
Arc 1335.14 Notice sur la bibliothèque royale...sur le cabinet des médailles. (Du Mersan, T.M.) Paris, 1836.
Arc 1020.132 Notice sur la châsse de Saint Taurin d'Évreux. (Le Prevost, A.) Évreux, 1838.
Arc 1588.1 Notice sur la monnaie de Pologne. (Lelewel, J.) Bruxelles, 1842.
Arc 1033.17.151 Notice sur la relique...Cathédrale de Reims. (Cerf.) n.p., n.d.
Arc 386.24.5 Notice sur la vie du Cardinal Borgia. (Millin, A.L.) n.p., n.d.
Arc 1033.35.43 Notice sur la vraie croix de St. Guilhelm-du-Désert. (Sévérac, G.) Lodève, 1861.
Arc 830.44.5 Notice sur l'aqueduc romain de Sens. (Julliot, Gustave.) Paris, 1875.
Arc 1353.6 Notice sur le cabinet des médailles et des pierres gravées de...roi des Pays-Bas. (Jonge, J.C. de.) La Haye, 1824.
Arc 1020.83.5 Notice sur le mobilier de l'église cathedrale de Reims. Reims, 1856.
Arc 590.6 Notice sur le papyrus hiératique et les peintures du cercueil de Pétaménoph. (Champollion, J.F.) Paris, 1827.
Arc 830.75 Notice sur le pays de Montbéliard. (Duvernoy, Clement.) Montbéliard, 1869.
Arc 1033.35.39 Notice sur le reliquaire de la sainte croix...à Tongres. (Reinartz, J.L.) n.p., n.d.
Arc 1033.17.447 Notice sur le temple et l'hospice du Mont Carmel dédiés à la Vierge. Paris, 1843.
Arc 936.26 Notice sur les antiquités de la Roumanie. Paris, 1868.
Arc 830.86.5 Notice sur les antiquités de Reims. (Brunette, N.) Reims, 1861.
Arc 547.3 Notice sur les antiquités égyptiennes du Musée Britannique. (Prisse d'Avennes.) Paris, 1847.
Arc 830.350 Notice sur les origines de Dijon et sur les fragments romains découverts dans les substructions de l'ancien palais ducal de Dijon. (Frantin, Jean Marie.) Dijon, 1854?
Arc 608.2.5 Notice sur les plombs chrétiens trouvés à Carthage. (Delattre, R.P.) Lyon, 1887.
Arc 1020.64 Notice sur les reliques...l'église de lYon. Lyon, 1865.
Arc 1033.124 Notice sur quelques antels chrétiens. (Bargès, Jean.) Paris, 1890.
Arc 1500.37 Notice sur un dèpot de monnaies carlovingiennes. (Bompois, H.F.) Paris, 1871.
Arc 1150.208 Notice sur un manuscript Mérovingun. (Delisle, L.) Paris, 1875.
Arc 1150.208.5 Notice sur un manuscript Mérovingun. (Delisle, L.) Paris, 1878.
Arc 1020.82 Notice sur un reliquare de St. Quentin. (Lecocq, G.) St. Quentin, 1875.
Arc 1264.3 Notice sur un sceau de Landfriede du XIVe siècle. (Prost, A.) Paris, 1879.
Arc 830.151 Notice sur une pierre tumulaire découverte aux environs de Solliès-Pont. (Gazan, A.) Antibes, 1873.
Arc 830.32 Notice sur une sépulture gauloise. (Cochet, J.B.D.) Rouen, 1866.
Arc 830.112 Notices historiques sur les anciens cintrons. (Roche, J.J.) Moutiers, 1819.
Arc 861.23 Notices of an Anglo-Saxon cemetery...Surrey. (Flower, J.W.) London, 1872.
Arc 880.16 Notices of the round tower of Ulster. Belfast, 1854.
Arc 853.20.10 Notices sur les anciens Trévirois. (Hetzrodt, J.B.M.) Trèves, 1809.
Arc 1433.29 Notices sur les monnaies turques. (Mubarek, Ghalib Bey.) Bruxelles, 1899.
Arc 746.45 La notion d'ex-voto anatomique chez les Etrusco Romains. (Decouflé, Pierre.) Bruxelles, 1964.
Arc 1018.36 Notiones archaeologiae christianae. v.1-2. (Syxtus, P.) Romae, 1909-10. 4v.
Arc 1348.7.3 Notitia rei nummariae. (Jobert, L.) Leipzig, 1695.
Arc 386.24 Notizia biografica sul cardinale S. Borgia. (Baraldi, Giuseppe.) Modena, 1830.
Arc 1033.35.35 Notizia storica sulla croce del Carroccio. Milano, 1870.
Arc 1033.76 Notizie, regole...ss. Martire della ss. Basilica Vaticana. Roma, 1756.
Arc 1033.17.85 Notizie...delle apparizioni e delle immagini di Maria...di Bergamo. (Cornaro, F.) Bergamo, 1868.
Arc 1033.17.14 Notizie...miracolosa immagine Bma Vergine...di S. Maria in Cosmedin. Roma, 1835.
Arc 1027.4.9 Notizie...S. Feliciano...cimitero di Priscilla. (Paoli.) Roma, 1796.
Arc 1033.75 Notizie...SS. Valentino Prete ed Flario Diacono. (Andreucci, A.G.) Roma, 1740.
Arc 93.5F Notizie archeologico. (Italy. Ministero delle Colonie.) Roma. 1-3,1916-1922 3v.
Arc 393.1 Notizie biografiche del cavaliere Francesco Inghirami. (Vegni, V. de.) Volterra, 1849.
Arc 1020.10.43 Notizie compendiose delle sagre stazioni e chiese stazionali di Roma. Roma, 1833.
Arc 78.3 Notizie degli Scavi. (Rome. Accademia dei Lincei.) Rome. 1876+ 99v.
Arc 78.3.2 Notizie degli Scavi. Indici epigrafici. 1876-85. (Rome. Accademia dei Lincei.) Rome, 1886.
Arc 78.3.3 Notizie degli Scavi. Indici generali, 1876-1955. (Rome. Accademia dei Lincei.) Milano, 1904-1961. 3v.
Arc 387.15 Notizie degli studi conte Giancarlo Conestabile della Staffa. (Sclopis de Salerano, F.) Torino, 1877.
Arc 785.40.5 Notizie del carcere Tulliano. (Cancellieri, F.) Roma, 1788.
Arc 785.40 Notizie del carcere Tulliano. (Cancellieri, F.) Roma, 1855.
Arc 1033.17.544 Notizie della prodigiosa immagine di Maria Sma. della Grazie a Pta Angelica in Roma. (Diotallevi, D.) Roma, 1887.
Arc 1033.12.168 Notizie della reliquia...del sacro chiodo. (Cateni, P.F.) Colle, 1821.
Arc 1033.17.12 Notizie dell'origine e dell'antichità del Monastero di S. Ambrozio. Roma, 1755.
Arc 1033.12.2 Notizie intorno alla novena...di natale. Roma, 1788.
Arc 1033.17.502 Notizie istoriche...alla transformazione di una immagine della B.V...Palazzolo. Brescia, 1805.
Arc 1033.12.141 Notizie istoriche...della immagine del...Salvatore. Roma, 1798.
Arc 1020.9.35 Notizie istoriche...Domine Quo Vadis. (Armellini, M.) Roma, 1874.
Arc 1033.58.5 Notizie istoriche...la testa di S. Sebastiano. (Lucatelli, G.) Roma, 1757.
Arc 1033.34.1 Notizie istoriche delle sacre catene del principe degli apostoli. (Palmieri, N.) Orvieto, 1846.
Arc 1033.34.2 Notizie istoriche delle sacre catene del principe degli apostoli. (Palmieri, N.) n.p., n.d.
Arc 1033.17.582 Notizie istoriche intorno alla miracolosa immagine...Maria. (Sassi, G.A.) Milano, 1765.
Arc 1033.17.133 Notizie istoriche intorno alla sma. Cintola. (Buenchini, G.M.) Prato, 1795.
Arc 1033.108 Notizie riguardanti il culto di S. Irene. (Guazzugli, M.) Osimo, 1783.
Arc 1033.17.302 Notizie risguardanti lo stato antico e moderno del sacro eratorio....miracolosa immagine di Maria. (Ciabilli, G.) Firenze, 1802.
Arc 746.6 Notizie storiche archeologiche di Tarquinia e Corneto. (Dasti, L.) Roma, 1878.
Arc 1033.17.625 Notizie storiche intorno al santuario...Madonna della croce de Varazze. Varazze, 1875.
Arc 1033.12.140 Notizie storiche intorno al SS. Crocifisso...in Trastevere. Roma, 1801.
Arc 1033.17.501 Notizie storiche sulla...effigie di Maria...Paterno. (Rienzo, G. de.) Napoli, 1829.
Arc 1027.55 Notizie sul cimitero cristiano di Bonaria [Sardini]. (Pinza, G.) Roma, 1902.
Arc 1025.43 Notizie sullo stato delle catacombe romane. (Crostarosa, P.) Roma, 1901.
Arc 1510.152.7 Die Notmünzen der deutschen Städt, Gemeinden, Kreise, Länder. 2. Aufl. (Funck, Walter.) Münster, 1973.
Arc 1510.152.5 Die Notmünzen der deutschen Städt, Gemeinden, Kreise, Länder. 5. Aufl. (Funck, Walter.) Münster, 1966.
Arc 1033.17.137 Notre-Dame de Déliverance et la ceinture de la S. Vierge. Quintin, 1872.
Arc 1020.70 Notre Dame de Myans. Chambéry, 1856.
Arc 1033.12.73 Notre-Dame de Saint-Sang. 2e éd. (Haignere, D.) Paris, 1884.
Arc 1033.17.203 Notre-Dame du Joyel, ou Histoire légendaire et numismatique de la chandelle d'Arras. (Terninck, A.) Arras, 1853.
Arc 1033.17.448 Notre Dame du Mont Carmel. (Blot, F.) Paris, 1878.
Arc 1084.17F Nott, S.C. Chinese jades in the S.C. Nott collection. St. Augustine, 1942.
Arc 1025.40 Le notti cristiane. (Fontana, G.) Colle, 1829.
Arc 720.210 Nottingham. Museum. Illustrated catalogue of classical antiquities. Nottingham, n.d.
Arc 1027.21.5 Notzie sulle crepte...San Gennaro di Poveri. v.1-2. (Jorio, A. de.) Napoli, 1833-39.
Arc 830.332 Nouel, André. La civilisation néolithique. Orléans, 1961.
Arc 830.342 Nouel, André. Manuel de préhistoire par le sud du Bassin parisien. Orléans, 1966.
Arc 1500.10 Nouveau classement des monnaies bretonnes. (Blancard, Louis.) Marseille, 1888-89.
Arc 1033.17.424 Nouveau histoire de l'image miraculeux de Notre-Dame-de-Liesse. (Charpentier, L.F.) Soissons, 1888.
Arc 1390.1 Nouveau manuel complet de numismatique du moyen age et moderne. Text et atlas. (Barthélemy, A.J.B.A.) Paris, n.d. 2v.
Arc 1390.1.3 Nouveau manuel complet de numismatique du moyen age et moderne. Text et atlas. (Barthélemy, A.J.B.A.) Paris, 1874. 2v.
Arc 1356.1.3 Nouveau manuel complete de numismatique ancienne. (Barthélemy, A.J.B.A.) Paris, 1866.
Arc 1356.1 Nouveau manuel complete de numismatique ancienne. Text and atlas. (Barthélemy, A.J.B.A.) Paris, 1866. 2v.
Arc 397.3.2 Nouveau manuel d'archéologie. v.1-2 and atlas. (Müller, K.O.) Paris, 1841. 3v.
Arc 1390.1.5 Nouveau manuel de numismatique du moyen age et moderne. Text et atlas. (Blanchet, J.A.) Paris, 1890. 3v.
Arc 1185.1 Nouveau traité de diplomatique. (Tassin, R.P.) Paris, 1750-65. 6v.
Arc 1033.12.83 Un nouveau trésor d'argenterie syrienne. (Diehl, C.) Paris, 1926.
Arc 522.19.2 Les nouveaux aspects de la question de Troie. (Vellay, Charles.) Paris, 1930.
Arc 522.19 Les nouveaux aspects de la question de Troie. (Vellay, Charles.) Paris, 1930.
Arc 1500.31 Les nouveaux types monétaires de la France. (Ducrocq, T.) Poitiers, 1900.
Arc 1500.47.5 Nouvel essai d'interprétation et de classification des monnaies de la Gaule. 2. éd. (Fillioux, A.) Paris, 1867.
Arc 14.3 La nouvelle clio. Bruxelles. 1-12,1949-1962 23v.
Arc 1500.26 Nouvelle étude de jetons. (Fontenay, J. de.) Autun, 1850.

Arc 1480.38 Nouvelle explication d'une médaille d'or du cabinet du roy. (Vallemont, P.) Paris, 1699.

Arc 1345.1.2 Nouvelle galerie mythologique. Paris, 1858.

Arc 1590.1 Une nouvelle monnaie a legende grecque...de Cappadoce. (Schlumberger, G.) Paris, 1887.

Arc 830.116 Une nouvelle page ajoutèe à l'histoire de Rosny-sur-Seine. (Thomas, Henri.) Paris, 1893.

Arc 73.7 Nouvelles annales. (Rome. Institut Archéologique. La Section Française.) Paris. 1-2,1836-1839 2v.

Arc 830.22.3 Nouvelles antiquités gallo-romaines de Paris. (Normand, Charles.) Paris, 1894. 2v.

Arc 1.10.2 Nouvelles archives des missions scientifiques. (France. Ministre de l'Instruction Publique et des Beaux Arts.) Paris. 1-18 31v.

Arc 930.203 Nouvelles découvertes archéologiques à Constantinople. (Dethier.) Constantinople, 1867.

Arc 1025.25 Les nouvelles études...catacombes romaines. (Desbassayns de Richemont, M.C.) Paris, 1870.

Arc 936.195.5 Nouvelles fouilles archéologiques en Tchécoslovaque. (Ceskoslovenska Academie Ved. Archeologichy Ustav.) Prague, 1960.

Arc 600.11 Les nouvelles fouilles d'Abydos, seconde campagne 1896-1897. (Amélineau, E.) Paris, 1902.

Arc 600.11.2 Les nouvelles fouilles d'Abydos 1897-1898. (Amélineau, E.) Paris, 1904-05. 2v.

Arc 600.39 Les nouvelles fouilles de Tanis (1929-32). (Montet, Pierre.) Paris, 1933.

Arc 530.162 Nouvelles inscriptions de Sardes. (Robert, Louis.) Paris, 1964.

Arc 1027.18.20 Nouvelles inscriptions inedites de la cata-combe juive de la via Appia. (Frey, J.B.) n.p., 193-.

Arc 600.140 Nouvelles inscriptions rupestres du Wadi Hammamat. (Goyon, Georges.) Paris, 1957.

Arc 1033.113.3 Nouvelles observations sur la Mosaique de S. Pudentienne. (Leport, L.) Rome, 1896.

Arc 608.2.45.5 Nouvelles recherches archéologiques à Marrakech. (Meunié, Jacques.) Paris, 1957.

Arc 830.358 Nouvelles recherches sur les origines de Clermont-Ferrand. Clermont-Ferrand, 1970.

Arc 1027.16 Nouvi studi su alcuni elemente Pagani. (Strazzulla, V.) Messina, 1900.

Arc 1033.23.5 Nova circa thesaurum sacelli Palalini "sancta sanctorum". (Scaglia, Sisto.) Roma, 1909

Arc 785.13.29 Nova descrizione della casa dell Vestali. (Marucchi, O.) Roma, 1887.

Htn Arc 1033.17.52* Nova gigantomachia contra...imagine...virgine...Lucea depictam. (Kordecki, A.) Czestochovia, n.d.

Arc 785.13.31 Nova scoperte nella casa dell Vestali. (Marucchi, O.) Roma, 1884.

Arc 1433.8.3 Nova supplementa ad recesionem numorum Muhammedanum. (Fraehn, C.M.J.) Petropoli, 1855.

Arc 1588.3.5 Novac kneza Lasara. (Dimitrijević, Sergije.) Kruševac, 1971.

Arc 936.140.35 Novae-sektor zachodni 1970. Poznań, 1973.

Arc 936.140.35.5 Novae-sektor zachodni 1972. Wyd. 1. Poznań, 1975.

Arc 1433.9 Novae symbolae ad rem numariam Muhammedanorum. (Fraehn, C.M.J.) Petropoli, 1819.

Arc 925.135 Novaia nakhodka vostochnogo serebra v Priural'e. (Smirnov, A.P.) Moskva, 1957.

Arc 936.195.180 Nové košariská. 1. vyd. (Pichlerová, Magda.) Bratislava, 1969.

Arc 1033.17.542 Novena in preparazione alla...festa...in Rapallo Nostra Signora sue Montallegro. Rapallo, 1878.

Arc 843.115 Noves des cobertes a la catedral d'Egara. (Ruig y Cadafalch, José.) Barcelona, 1948.

Arc 925.329 Novgorod the Great. (Thompson, Michael W.) London, 1967.

Arc 543.3.85 Novgorodova, Eleonora A. Tsentral'naia Aziia i karasukskaia problema. Moskva, 1970.

Arc 925.348 Novgorodskie sopki. (Sedov, Valentin V.) Moskva, 1970.

Arc 936.100.20 Novi naucni rezultati u hrvatskoj arheologiji. (Gunjaca, S.) Zagreb, 1958.

Arc 936.220.60 Novi Pazar. (Mano-Zisi, Djordje.) Beograd, 1969.

Arc 830.150 Noviodunum Biturigum et ses graffiti. (Boyer, H.) Bourges, 1861.

Arc 889.8.5 Noviomagus. (Daniels, M.P.M.) Nijmegen, 195-.

Arc 936.238.5 Novo Mesto, Yugoslavia. Dolenjski Muzej. Prazgodovina Novega Mesta. Novo Mesto, 1971.

Arc 936.238 Novo Mesto v davnini. (Knez, Tone.) Maribar, 1972.

Arc 923.128 Novoe v arkheologii. Moskva, 1972.

Arc 925.16.30 Novoe v arkheologii Kazakhstana. Alma-Ata, 1968.

Arc 925.347.5 Novopetrovskaia kul'tura Srednego Amura. (Derevianko, Anatolii P.) Novosibirsk, 1970.

Arc 843.175 Novos elementos para a lócalização de Cetóbriga.%Costa, J.M. da.) Setúbal, 1960.

Arc 936.195.225 Novotná, Mária. Die Bronzehortfunde in der Slowakei. 1. vyd. Bratislava, 1970.

Arc 936.195.25 Novotný, B. Luzianska skukina a pociatky malovanej keramiky na Slovensku. Bratislava, 1962.

Arc 936.150.10 Novotný, B. Počiatky výtvarnéreo prejavu na Slovensku. Bratislava, 1958.

Arc 936.195.65 Novotný, B. Slovensko v mladšij dobe kaminej. Bratislava, 1958.

Htn Arc 720.203* Novus thesaurus antiquitatum romanorum. (Sallengre, A. de.) The Hague, 1716. 3v.

Arc 385.14 Novye metody v arkheologicheskikh issledovaniiakh. (Akademiia Nauk SSSR. Institut Arkheologii.) Leningrad, 1963.

Arc 925.340 Novye nakhodki na chetyrekhstolbovom ostrove. (Ranshenbakh, Vera M.) Moskva, 1969.

Arc 925.321 Novye pamiatniki istorii drevnei Karelii. (Akademiia Nauk SSSR. Karel'skii Filial, Petrozavedsk. Instituta Iazyka, Literatury i Istorii.) Leningrad, 1966.

Arc 1335.80 Novyia numizmaticheskiia priobreteniia N.P. Linevicha. (Tizengauzen', V.) Sankt Peterburg, 1896.

Arc 936.14.430 Nowakowski, Andrej. Gorne Pobuze w wiskach VIII-XI. Łódź, 1972.

Arc 925.250 Nowicka, M. Ad Fanagorii do Apollonii. Warszawa, 1962.

Arc 853.270F Nowothnig, Walter. Brandgräber des Völkeswandernugszeit im siedlichen Niedersachsen. Neumünster, 1964.

Arc 815.9F Le nozze di Bacco et Arianna. (Comparetti, D.) Firenze, 1921.

Arc 608.23 Nubian treasure. (Emery, Walter B.) London, 1948.

Arc 845.201 Nürnberg. Deutschen Anthropologischen Gesellschaft. Festschrift zur Begrüssung des XVIII. Kongresses der Gesellschaft. Nürnberg, 1887.

Arc 1033.17.96.6 Nuestra Señora de Guadalupe y origen. 6. ed. (Becerra Tanco, Luis.) México, 1883.

Arc 1020.124 Nuestra Señora del Espino en Santa Gadea del Cid Burgos. (Huidobro Serna, Luciano.) Lérida, 1922. 3 pam.

Arc 1433.2.5 Nützel, Heinrich. Münzen der Rasuliden. Berlin, 1891.

Arc 1493.6 Nuevo método de clasificacion de las medallas autonomas de España. (Delgado, Antonio.) Sevilla, 1871-76. 3v.

Arc 843.7.7 Los nuevos bronces de Osuna. (Rodriquez de Berlanga, M.) Malaga, 1876.

Arc 1163.2.29 Nuevos estudios de paleografía española. (Millares Carlo, A.) Mexico, 1941.

Arc 1493.27 Numária da Lusitânia. (Coelho, Antonio D.S.) Lisboa, 1972.

Arc 1318.7 Numario hispánico. (Spain. Consejo Superior de Investigaciones Cientificas. Instituto Antonio Agustin de Numismatica.) 1-10,1952-1961 5v.

Arc 1498.4 Numatisque de la France. (Barthélemy, A. de.) Paris, 1891.

Htn Arc 1475.6* Numi antiqui familiae romanarum. (Vaillant, J.) Amsterdam, 1703. 2v.

Arc 1333.7 Numi asiatici musei univ. caes. liter. Casanensis. (Erdmann, F.) Casani, 1834.

Arc 1433.12 Numi cufici regii numophylacii Holmiensis. (Tornberg, Carl Johan.) Upsaliae, 1848.

Arc 1433.22 Numi Mohammedani. (Pietraszewski, Ignatius.) Berolini, 1843.

Arc 1433.8 Numi Muhammedani...Museo Asiatico. (Fraehn, C.M.J.) Petropoli, 1826.

Arc 1313.9 Numisma. Irvington, N.Y.

Arc 1313.15 Numisma. Madrid. 1,1951+ 9v.

Arc 1485.2 Numismata...Brandenburgici sectio prima. (Beger, L.) Brandenburgi, 1704.

Htn Arc 1670.2* Numismata. A discourse of medals. (Evelyn, J.) London, 1697.

Arc 1540.9.5 Numismata Angliae vetusta. pt.1. (Schröder, J.H.) Upsaliae, 1833.

Htn Arc 1333.5* Numismata antiqua. (Herbert, T.) n.p., 1746.

Htn Arc 1350.5F* Numismata antiqua. (Pembroke, T.H.) London, 1746.

Arc 1333.2 Numismata antiqua. Scriniis bodleianis rec. catalogus. (Wise, F.) Oxford, 1750.

Arc 1480.30F Numismata aurea imperatorum Romanorum. (Caylus, A.C.P.) n.p., n.d.

Arc 1540.14 Numismata Cromwelliana. (Henfrey, H.W.) Londini, 1877.

Arc 1663.4 Numismata Cromwelliana. (Henfrey, H.W.) London, 1873.

Arc 1465.78 Numismata Graeca. pt.1-6. (Anson, L.) Londoni, 1910-16. 2v.

Arc 1465.5 Numismata Hellenica. (Leake, W.M.) London, 1854.

Htn Arc 1455.4* Numismata imperatorum. (Vaillant, J.) Amsterdam, 1700.

Arc 1478.19.5 Numismata imperatorum Augustarum et Caesarum. (Foy-Vaillant, J.) Amsterdami, 1700.

Htn Arc 1475.2* Numismata imperatorum romanorum. (Banduri, A.) Paris, 1718. 2v.

Arc 1478.19 Numismata imperatorum romanorum. (Foy-Vaillant, J.) Romae, 1743. 3v.

Arc 1478.19.2 Numismata imperatorum romanorum. Supplementum. (Susomni, J.B.) Vindobonae, 1767.

Arc 1405.1.3 Numismata orientalia. v.3. pt.1-3. (Phayre, A.P.) n.p., n.d.

Arc 1433.11.3 Numismata orientalia aere expressa. pt. 1-2. (Hallenberg, Jonas.) Upsaliae, 1822.

Arc 1485.1 Numismata pontificum romanorum. (Buonanni, P.) Rome, 1699. 2v.

Arc 1540.19 Numismata Scotiae. (Cardonnel-Lawson, Adam.) Edinburgi, 1786.

Arc 1485.1.2 Numismata summorum pontificum. (Buonanni, P.) Rome, 1715.

Htn Arc 1478.35F* Numismata vetera et inscriptiones ex voto. (Phillipps, Thomas.) Medio-Montana, 1855.

Arc 1493.23 Numismatalogos contemporaneas. (Brazão, Arnaldo.) Lisboa, 1963.

Arc 320.1.2 Numismatic and Antiquarian Society of Philadelphia. Necrology. Philadelphia. 1882-1884

Arc 320.1 Numismatic and Antiquarian Society of Philadelphia. Reports of proceedings. Philadelphia. 1865-1935 5v.

Arc 320.1.3 Pamphlet vol. Numismatic and Antiquarian Society of Philadelphia. Miscellaneous pamphlets. 4 pam.

Arc 320.1.4 Pamphlet vol. Numismatic and Antiquarian Society of Philadelphia. Miscellaneous pamphlets. 6 pam.

Arc 1313.11 Numismatic and philatelic journal of Japan. Yokohama. 1-4,1913-1914 4v.

Arc 1613.30 Numismatic art in America. (Vermeule, Cornelius Clarkson.) Cambridge, 1971.

Arc 1330.11 Numismatic bibliography. (Sigler, Phares O.) Dearborn, Mich., 1951.

Arc 1313.1 Numismatic chronicle. (Royal Numismatic Society.) London. 1,1894+ 105v.

Arc 1333.14F Numismatic circular. (Spink and Son, Ltd.) London. 1-72,1893-1964 36v.

Arc 1333.14.7 Numismatic circular of coins, medals, war medals, books, offered for sale. (Spink and Son, Ltd.) London. 1,1940+ 19v.

Arc 1333.01F Pamphlet box. Numismatic collections.

Arc 1313.12 Numismatic gallery monthly. California? 1-6,1948-1953

Arc 1540.12 A numismatic history of the reign of Henry I. v.1-2. (Andrew, W.J.) London, 1901.

Arc 1313.3 Numismatic journal. London. 1887

Arc 1300.3 Numismatic literature. N.Y. 1,1947+ 13v.

Arc 1348.1 Numismatic manual. (Akerman, J.Y.) London, 1840.

Arc 1300.1.12 Numismatic notes and monographs. (American Numismatic Society.) N.Y. 1-157 40v.

Arc 1418.13 Numismatic parallels of Kālidāsa. (Sivaramamurti, C.) Madras, 1945.

Arc 1313.10 Numismatic review. N.Y. 2-4,1944-1947 2v.

Arc 1418.15.5 Numismatic Society of India. Corpus of Indian coins. Banaras, 1957.

Arc 1308.5 Numismatic Society of India. Journal. Calcutta. 1,1939+ 12v.

Arc 1300.1.15 Numismatic studies. (American Numismatic Society.) N.Y. 1-12 5v.

Arc 1348.74 Numismática. (Ferreira Barros, A.) Porto, 1961.

Arc 1313.22 Numismática. Madrid. 2-3

Arc 1490.22 Numismatica ascolana...ascoli nel piceno. (Minicis, Gaetano de.) Fermo, 1853.

Arc 1494.59 Numismática balear. (Campaner y Fuertes, Álvaro.) Palma de Mallorca, 1879.

Arc 1643.5 Numismatica colombiana. (Posada, Eduardo.) Bogotá, 1937.

Arc 1494.55 La numismática española en el reinado de Felipe II. (Garcia de la Fuente, Arturo.) Escorial, 1927.

Arc 1493.24 Numismatica iberica e iberoromana. (Guadan, Antonio M. de.) Madrid, 1969.

Author and Title Listing

Arc 1418.7 Numismatica indo-portuguesa. (Campos, M.J. da C.) Lisboa, 1901.
Arc 1313.21 Numismatické listý. Praha. 1+ 8v.
Arc 1302.4 Numismatický časopis československý. Praha. 1-21 9v.
Arc 1313.20 Numismatický sbornik. Praha. 1-8,1953-1964 10v.
Arc 1347 Pamphlet box. Numismatics.
Arc 1348.77 Numismatics. (Grierson, Philip.) London, 1975.
Arc 1334.8 Numismatics. (Phillips, H.) Philadelphia, 1863-80. 12 pam.
Arc 1354 Pamphlet box. Numismatics. Ancient.
Arc 1406 Pamphlet box. Numismatics. Asia. 4 pam.
Arc 1576.01 Pamphlet box. Numismatics. Austria.
Arc 1349.01 Pamphlet box. Numismatics. Biography.
Arc 1588.2.5 Pamphlet vol. Numismatics. Bulgaria.
Arc 1601 Pamphlet box. Numismatics. Canada. 3 pam.
Arc 1496.01 Pamphlet box. Numismatics. France.
Arc 1506.01 Pamphlet box. Numismatics. Germany.
Arc 1506 Pamphlet box. Numismatics. Germany.
Arc 1536 Pamphlet box. Numismatics. Great Britain.
Arc 1536.01 Pamphlet box. Numismatics. Great Britain.
Arc 1456 Pamphlet box. Numismatics. Greek and Roman.
Arc 1456.1 Pamphlet box. Numismatics. Greek and Roman.
Arc 1418.01 Pamphlet box. Numismatics. India.
Arc 1486.1 Pamphlet box. Numismatics. Italy.
Arc 1413.01 Pamphlet box. Numismatics. Japan.
Arc 1671 Pamphlet box. Numismatics. Medals.
Arc 1671.01 Pamphlet box. Numismatics. Medals.
Arc 1583.01 Pamphlet box. Numismatics. Russia.
Arc 1631.01 Pamphlet box. Numismatics. South America.
Arc 1493 Pamphlet box. Numismatics. Spain and Portugal. 2 pam.
Arc 1661 Pamphlet box. Numismatics. Special.
Arc 1666 Pamphlet box. Numismatics. Special.
Arc 1611.1 Pamphlet box. Numismatics. United States. 5 pam.
Arc 1347.4 Pamphlet vol. Numismatik. 27 pam.
Arc 1348.52 Numismatik und Geldgeschichte. (Gebhart, H.) Heidelberg, 1949.
Arc 1588.15 Numismatika. Rigā, 1968.
Arc 1348.31 Numismatika ili istoriia monet'. (Butkovskii.) Moskva, 1861.
Arc 1433.30 Numismatique annamite. Text and atlas. (Lacroix, D.) Saigon, 1900. 2v.
Arc 1349.25 Numismatique beckerienne. (Pinder, Moritz.) Paris, 1853.
Arc 1480.15.1 Numismatique constantinienne. (Maurice, Jules.) Bruxelles, 1965. 3v.
Arc 1470.1 Numismatique d'Alexander le Grand. Text and atlas. (Mueller, L.) Copenhagen, 1855. 2v.
Arc 1425.3 Numismatique de Croisades. (Saulcy, L.F.J.C. de.) Paris, 1847.
Arc 1468.21.6 Numismatique de la Crète ancienne. (Sborōnos, Ioannēs N.) Bonn, 1972.
Arc 1584.1.3 Numismatique de la Géorgie au moyen âge. (Langlois, Victor.) Paris, 1852.
Arc 1423.5 Numismatique de la Terre-Sainte. (Saulcy, L.F.J.C. de.) Paris, 1877.
Arc 1505.6 Numismatique de l'Alsace. (Engel, Arthur.) Paris, 1887.
Arc 1435.1 Numismatique de l'ancienne Afrique. v.1 and supplement. (Mueller, L.) Copenhague, 1860-94. 2v.
Arc 1438.2 Numismatique de l'ancienne Afrique. v.1-3. (Mueller, L.) Bologne, 1964. 2v.
Arc 1435.1.5 Numismatique de l'ancienne Afrique. v.1-3. (Mueller, L.) Copenhague, 1860-62.
Arc 1425.2 Numismatique de l'Orient Latin. (Schlumberger, G.) Paris, 1878.
Arc 1425.2.2 Numismatique de l'Orient Latin. (Schlumberger, G.) Paris, 1882.
Arc 1500.61 Numismatique des corporations. (Tricou, Jean.) Paris, 1957.
Arc 1443.3 Numismatique des nomes d'Égypte. (Langlois, V.) Paris, 1852.
Arc 1428.29 Numismatique des Scythes et des Sarmates. (Vacquier, Polydore.) Paris, 1881.
Arc 1470.25 Numismatique du voyage du jeune Anacharsis. (Landon, Charles P.) Paris, 1846. 2v.
Arc 1425.1 Numismatique et inscription Cypriotes. (Luynes, H.T.P.J.) Paris, 1852.
Arc 1433.28.2 Numismatique général. v.2. (Langlois, Victor.) Paris, 1855.
Arc 1433.28 Numismatique général de l'Armenie. v.1-2. (Langlois, Victor.) Paris, 1855-59.
Arc 1313.44 Numismatique romaine. Wetteren. 1,1965+ 3v.
Arc 1313.5.6 Numismatisch-sphragistischer Anzeiger. Hannover. 1-29,1870-1898 5v.
Arc 1510.145 Numismatische Bruchstücke in Bezug auf sächsische Geschichte. v.1-3. (Erbstein, Karl Friedrich Wilhelm.) Dresden, 1816.
Arc 1580.15 Numismatische Denkmale...in Österreich. (Höfken, Rudolf von.) Wien, 1904.
Arc 1313.7 Numismatische Gesellschaft in Wien. Monatsblatt. Wien. 69,1956
Arc 1329.3 Numismatische Literatur. (Riechmann, A. and Co.) Halle am der Saale, 1926.
Arc 1330.8 Numismatische Literatur Osteuropas und des Balkans. Graz. 1,1960+
Arc 1313.14 Numismatische Studien. Hamburg. 1-7 3v.
Arc 1313.8 Numismatische Zeitschrift. Wien. 1-88 41v.
Arc 1313.5.3 Numismatischer Anzeiger. Hannover. 1-2,1868-1869
Arc 1668.5.3 Numismatisches Legenden-Lexicon. (Rentzmann, W.) Berlin, 1881.
Arc 1668.5 Numismatisches Legenden-Lexicon. v.1-2. (Rentzmann, W.) Berlin, 1865-66.
Arc 1313.19 Numismatisches Nachrichtenblatt; Organ des Verbandes der westdeutschen Münzvereine und der numismatischen Kommissio der Länder in der Bundesrepublik Deutschland. Hamburg. 6,1957+ 9v.
Arc 1665.3 Numismatisches Wappen-Lexicon. (Rentzmann, W.) Berlin, 1876.
Arc 1665.3.5 Numismatisches Wappen-Lexicon. Index. (Rentzmann, W.) Berlin, 1876.
Arc 1318.2 Numismatiska meddelanden. (Svenska Numismatika Föreningen.) Stockholm. 1-29,1874-1943 7v.
Arc 1313.4 The numismatist. Federalsburg. 1,1894+ 99v.
Arc 1458.17 Numismatum antiquorum sylloge populis Graecis. (Wren, C.) Londini, 1708.
Arc 1588.1.14 Numismatyka Krajowa. (Bandtki, K.W.S.) Warszawa, 1839. 2v.
Arc 1335.107 Numizmaticheskii kabinet. (Moscow. Gosudarstvennyi Rumiantsovskii Muzei.) Moskva, 1884.
Arc 1312.6 Numizmaticheskii sbornik. (Moskovskoe Numizmaticheskoe Obshchestvo.) Moskva. 3,1915
Arc 1313.25 Numizmaticheskii sbornik. Moskva. 1-2,1955-1957 2v.
Arc 1313.35 Numizmatičke vijesti. Zagreb. 15+ 2v.
Arc 1313.30 Numizmatika i epigrafika. Moskva. 1-4,1960-1963 11v.
Arc 1313.32 Numizmatika i sfragistika. Kiev. 1,1963 4v.
Arc 1340.10 Numizmatychnyi slovnyk. (Zvarych, Volodymyr V.) L'viv, 1972.
Arc 1588.1.21 Numizmatyczno-historyczne z wieku. (Gumowski, Marian.) Poznań, 1924.
Arc 1362.1 Nummi antiqui pop. et urb. illustrati. (Harduin, J.) Parisii, 1684.
Arc 1538.10 Nummi Britannici historia. London, 1626.
Arc 1333.3 Nummi veteres - in Museo R.P. Knight asservati. (British Museum.) London, 1830.
Htn Arc 1675.23.5* Nummismalogia, ou Breve recopilação de algunas medalhas dos emperadores romanos de ouro. (Morganti, Bento.) Lisboa, 1737.
Htn Arc 1455.2* Nummophylacium Reginae Christinae. (Havercamp, S.) The Hague, 1742.
Arc 1335.85F Nummophylacium reginae Christinae. (Haverkamp, S.) Comitum Hagae, 1742.
Arc 1313.3.5 Nummus; numismática - medalhística - arqueologia. Porto. 1,1952+ 7v.
Arc 1335.9 Numophylacium Ehrencronianum. (Hansen von Ehrencron, F.A.) n.p., 1730.
Arc 1433.7 Numophylacium orientale Pototianum. (Fraehn, C.M.J.) Casani, 1813.
Arc 1510.130 Numuni jubilaei, oder Jubel Schau-Stücke. (Kundmann, J.C.) Bresslau, 1735.
Arc 1030.59 Nunn, H.P.V. Christian inscriptions. N.Y., 1952.
Arc 760.6.7 Nuova descrizione de' monumenti antichi. (Fea, Carlo.) Roma, 1819.
Arc 1033.9 Nuova interpretazione di un vetro cimiteriale. (Garrucci, R.) n.p., n.d.
Arc 810.27 Nuova pianta degli scavi di Pompei. n.p., n.d.
Arc 768.5 Nuova raccolta...antiche e moderne...Roma. Roma, 18- .
Arc 1485.9F Nuova raccolta delle monete e zecche d'Italia. (Zanetti, G.A.) Bologna, 1775-89. 5v.
Arc 400.4 Nuova raccolta representante i costumi. (Pronti, D.) Roma, 1808.
Arc 1027.27 Le nuove catacombe di Chiusi. (Bartolini, D.) Roma, 1852.
Arc 1027.27.2 Le nuove catacombe di Chiusi. (Bartolini, D.) Roma, 1853.
Arc 1027.26.5 Nuove esplorazioni nelle catacombe di S. Giovanni Battista de Rossi nell 1894 in Siracusa. (Orsi, Paolo.) Roma, 1896.
Arc 73.4 Nuove memorie dell'instituto. (Rome. Istituto.) Leipzig, 1865. 2v.
Arc 730.207 Nuove metope arcaiche selinantine. (Salinas, A.) Roma, 1892.
Arc 1027.4.11 Le nuove scoperte nelle catacombe di Priscilla. v.1-2. (Marucchi, O.) Roma, 1888.
Arc 743.23 Nuove testimonianze dell'arte e della civiltà etrusca. (Lerici, C.M.) Milano, 1960.
Arc 720.220F Nuovi cenni sugli oggetti di alta antichità. (Gastaldi, B.) Torino, 1862.
Arc 600.95 Nuovi scari nelle necropoli di Hadra. (Breccia, E.) Alexandria, 1930.
Arc 785.52F Nuovi studi sull'arco di Constantino. (Monaci, Alfredo.) Roma, 1904.
Arc 726.45 Nuovi studi sulle antiche terme pisane. (Lupi, Clemente.) Pisa, 1885.
Arc 66.4.2 Nuovo bulletino de archeologia cristiana. Roma. 1-28,1895-1922 13v.
Arc 387.4.8 Nuovo catalogo delle opere...dell'abate Francesco Cancellieri. (Moroni, A.) Roma, 1881.
Arc 1033.53 Un nuovo monumento della persecuzione diocleziana. (Marucchi, O.) Roma, 1893.
Arc 726.329 I nuraghi Aleri e Nastasi e le nuove scoperte archeologiche nel territorio di Tertenia. (Cannas, Vincenzo Mario.) Cagliari, 1972.
Arc 1033.182 Nussbaum, Otto. Der Standort des Liturgen am christlichen Altar vor dem Jahre 1000. Diss. Bonn, 1965.
Arc 900.201 Nyáry, Jenö. Az aggteleki Barlang mint orkori temetö. Budapest, 1881.
Arc 398.6 Nylander, Carl. Den dijupa brunnen. Stockholm, 1964.
Arc 895.22.27F Nylén, Erik. Die jungere vorrömische Eisenzeit Gotlands. Stockholm, 1956.
Arc 925.255 O chem govoriat kurgany Eniseia. (Kartsov, V.G.) Abakhan, 1961.
Arc 925.310 O chem rasskazyvaiut arkheologicheskie pamiatniki Karachaevo-Cherkesii. (Alekseeva, Evgeniia P.) Cherkessk, 1960.
Arc 925.305 O chëm rasskazyvaiut kurgany. (Andreev, N.V.) Smolensk, 1951.
Arc 1348.37 O chistk' drevnikh' monet'. (Markov', A.K.) Sankt Peterburg, 1908.
Arc 925.4.3F O drevnikh pamiatnikakh na Enisev. (Savenkov, I.T.) Moskva, 1910.
Arc 646.4 O Lordoz Elgin. (Gennadios, I.) Athēnai, 1930.
Arc 712.17 O Parthenōn. (Pousopoulos, A.) Athēnai, 1895.
Arc 1285.30 O pečetech a erbech měst pražskych a jinych českych. (Vojtíšek, V.) Praha, 1928.
Arc 936.140.40 O proiskhozhdenii bolgarskikh pakhotnykh orudii. (Vuzharova, Zhivka N.) Moskva, 1956.
Arc 1584.29 O russko-vizantiiskikh monetakh Iaroslava I Vladiminovicha. (Kunik, Anst A.) Sankt Peterburg, 1860.
Arc 955.2.20 Oakland, California. Museum. The Doheny scientific expedition to the Hava Supai Canyon, northern Arizona...1924. San Francisco, 1925.
Arc 861.23.15 Oakley, K.P. A survey of the prehistory of the Farnham district, Surrey. Guildford, 1939.
Arc 925.352 Ob ostatkakh drevnosti i stariny v Tserskoi Gubernii. (Pletnev, V.A.) Tver', 1903.
Arc 935.9.30 Der Obelisk und seine Basis auf dem Hippodrom zu Konstantinopel. (Bruns, G.) Istanbul, 1935.
Arc 845.5 Der obergermanisch-raetische Limes. Abteilung A und B. (Germany. Reichskommission. Limes.) Heidelberg. 1894-1910 14v.
Arc 1033.17.442 Oberhausen, G. Istoria della miracolosa immagine di Nostra Signora di Montenero. Lucca, 1745.
Arc 853.58 Oberhessens vorgeschichtliche Altertümer. (Kunkel, Otto.) Marburg, 1926.
Arc 785.21 Oberlin, J.J. Exposé Diene découverte...le Chévalier de Freden. Strasbourg, 1796.
Arc 838.15 Obermaier, H. Fossil man in Spain. New Haven, 1924.
Arc 843.68 Obermaier, H. Las pinturas rupestres del Barranco de Valltorta (Castellón). Madrid, 1919.

Arc 843.182 Obermaier, Hugo. La cueva del Buar. Madrid, 1918.
Arc 1015.231 Obermann, H.T. De oud-christelijke sarkophagen. 's-Gravenhage, 1911.
Arc 905.24.20 Obermayr, August. Kelten und Römer am Magdalensberg. Wien, 1971.
Arc 905.12.35 Obermayr, August. Römerstadt Carnuntum. Wien, 1967.
Arc 1510.127 Obermayr, J. Historische Nachricht von bayerischen Münzen. Frankfurt, 1763.
Arc 588.42F Objects of daily use. (Petrie, W.M.F.) London, 1927.
Arc 889.1 Objets étrusques découvertes en Belgique. pt.1-5. (Schuermans, H.) Bruxelles, 1872.
Arc 923.65 Obladnikov, A.P. Uspekhi sovetskoi arkheologii. Leningrad, 1950.
Arc 396.11 Obras completas. (Sardi, Jorge.) San Salvador, 1960.
Htn Arc 1163.3.20PF* Obraztsy pis'ma brevneishego perioda istorii russkoi knigi. (Karinskii, N.M.) Leningrad, 1925.
Arc 1163.3.10 Obraztsy slavianskago kirillovskago pis'ma. (Karskii, E.F.) Varshava, 1902.
Arc 936.100.45 Obredne gomile. (Škobalj, Ante.) Sveti Križ na Čiovu, 1970.
Arc 880.1 O'Brien, H. The round towers of Ireland. London, 1834.
Arc 609.1.35 O'Brien, T.P. The prehistory of Uganda Protectorate. Cambridge, Eng., 1939.
Arc 700.59 Obróbka drewna w Starożytnej Grecji. (Wąsowicz, Aleksandra.) Wrocław, 1966.
Arc 936.14.203 Obrzadek pogrzebowy ludności kultury pomorskiej. (Malinowski, Tadewsz.) Wrocław, 1969.
Arc 1020.9.120 Observations archéologique...les églises de Rome. (Barbier de Montault, X.) Arras, 1878.
Arc 1433.26 Observations on a unique Cufic gold coin. (Loerve, L.) London, 1849.
Arc 861.12.15 Observations on centurial stones found on the Roman wall in Northumberland and Cumberland. (Clayton, J.) Newcastle-on-Tyne, 1880.
Arc 870.3 Observations on certain ancient pillars of memoir called Hoar-Stones. (Hamper, William.) Birmingham, 1820.
Arc 1350.4.2 Observations on Doctor Arbuthnot's dissertation. (Langwith, B.) London, 1754.
Arc 385.2 Observations on stone pillars. (Astle, Thomas.) London, 1800.
Arc 967.1 Observations on the aboriginal monuments of the Mississippi Valley. (Squier, E.G.) N.Y., 1847.
Arc 800.1 Observations on the antiques of the town of Herculaneum. (Bellicard, J.C.) London, 1753.
Arc 493.1 Observations on the platform at Persepolis. (Easton, M.W.) Philadelphia, 1892.
Arc 522.7 Observations on the topography of the plain of Troy. (Rennell, J.) London, 1814.
Arc 830.22.9 Observations sur des monuments d'antiquité trouvez dans l'eglise cathedrale de Paris. (Moreau de Mantour, Philibert B.) Paris, 1711.
Arc 830.331 Observations sur la passage de M. Millin à Dijon. (Baudot, L.B.) Dijon, 1808.
Arc 823.19.55 Observations sur l'èpigraphie des Alpes maritimes de M.E. Blanc. (Thédenat, H.) Paris, 1881.
Arc 800.8.2 Observations sur les antiquités d'Herculanum. 2e éd. (Cochin, Charles N.) Paris, 1755.
Arc 800.8.3 Observations sur les antiquités d'Herculanum. 2e éd. (Cochin, Charles N.) Paris, 1757.
Arc 682.25.25 Observations sur les premiers habitats de la Macédoine. (Rey, Léon.) Paris, 1921-22. 2v.
Arc 830.77 Observations sur les travaux qui doivent être faits pour la recherche des objets d'antiquité. (Lacoste, Pierre F.) Clermont, 1824.
Htn Arc 522.2.3* Observations upon a treatise: Description of plain of Troy. (Bryant, Jacob.) Eton, 1795.
Arc 522.2 Observations upon a treatise entitled A description of the plain of Troy. (Bryant, Jacob.) Eton, 1795.
Arc 1470.32F Obshchagi katalog' monety. (Burachkov', P.) Odessa, 1884.
Arc 140.1.20 Occasional paper. (Prehistoric Society of East Anglia.) Bayswater. 1,1929 2v.
Arc 318.5 Occasional papers. (New York State Archaeological Association.) Albany. 1-2,1958-1959
Arc 48.4 Occasional papers. (Sudan. Antiquities Service.) Khartoum. 1-5 3v.
Arc 31.9 Occasional publications. (British Institute of Archaeology in Ankara.) London. 1,1949+ 10v.
Htn Arc 1475.1.2F* Occo, A. Imperatorum romanorum numismata. Milan, n.d.
Htn Arc 1475.1F* Occo, A. Imperatorum romanorum numismata. Milan, 1730.
Arc 861.189F Occupation sites on a Chiltern ridge. (Matthews, C.L.) Oxford, 1976.
Arc 1510.11.15 Och, Friedrich. Münzen bayerischer Klöster, Kirchen. München, 1897.
Arc 925.134.10 Ocherk etnicheskoi istorii Pechorskogo kraia. (Lashuk, L. P.) Syktyvkar, 1958.
Arc 925.9.125 Ocherki drevnei istorii i arkheologii Iugo-Osetri. (Tekhov, Bagrat V.) Tbilisi, 1971.
Arc 925.136.5 Ocherki drevnei istorii Iuzhnogo Urala. (Sal'nikov, Konstantin V.) Moskva, 1967.
Arc 936.165.40 Ocherki istorii kul'tury Moldavii (II-XIV vv). (Rikman, Emmanuil A.) Kishinev, 1971.
Arc 925.13.180 Ocherki noennogo dela sarmatov. (Khazanov, Anatolii M.) Moskva, 1971.
Arc 925.150.40 Ocherki po arkheologii Belorussii. Minsk, 1970- 2v.
Arc 925.327 Ocherki po arkheologii Stavropol'ia. (Minaeva, Tat'iana M.) Stavropol', 1965.
Arc 612.18 Ocherki po istorii...Evropy. (Gotbe, I.V.) Leningrad, 1925.
Arc 493.6.20 Ocherki po istorii i kul'ture Kavkozskoi Albanii. (Trever, K.V.) Moskva, 1959.
Arc 530.80A Ocherki po istorii kultur' Erevnei Armenii. (Trever, K.V.) Moskva, 1953.
Arc 923.75 Ocherki po istorii russkoi arkheologii. (Formozov, A.A.) Moskva, 1961.
Arc 925.37 Ocherki politicheskii istorii Vospora v V-IV vv. do n.e. (Blavatskaia, T.V.) Moskva, 1959.
Arc 925.90A Ocherki voen. dela. v antich. gosud. seleriogo Prichernomord. (Blavatskii, V.D.) Moskva, 1954.
VArc 412.11 Ochrona zabytków archeologicznych. (Jażdżewski, Konrad.) Warszawa, 1966.
Arc 302.9 Ochrona zakytków. Warszawa. 5+ 11v.
Arc 493.6.15 Ockerki po drevnei istorii Azerbaidzhana SSR. (Akademiia Nauk Azerbaidzhanskoi SSR, Baku.) Baku, 1956.
Arc 1588.4.45 Ocuronolozu denaru Boleslava I a II. (Katz, Viktor.) Praha, 1935.
Arc 925.5.5 Odastoporimiechatel'ineishikh pamatnikakh sibirskikh drevnatei. (Spasskii, Grigorii I.) Sankt Petersburg, 1857.
Arc 1148.34 Odēgos katalogoy cheirographōn. (Polites, L.N.) Athēnia, 1961.
Arc 340.38 Ödekan, Ayla. Türkiyede 50 yılda yayımlanmış Arkeoloji, sanat tarihi...bibliyografyası. Istanbul, 1974.
Arc 875.115F O'Dell, Andrew. St. Ninian's isle treasure. Edinburgh, 1960.
Arc 289.10 Odessa. Derzhavnyi Arkheolohichnye Muzei. Kratkie soobshcheniia o polevykh arkheologicheskikh issledovaniiskh. 1961-1963 3v.
Arc 936.14.90F Odkrycia archeologja na ziemiach zachodnich i pólnocnych Polski. (Kostrzewski, Józef.) Warszawa, 1962.
Arc 399.4 Odobescu, Alexandru Ionescu. Istoria archeologiei. Bucureşti, 1961.
Arc 1016.10 Odorici, F. Antichita cristiane di Brescia. Brescia, 1845.
Arc 1016.225 Odorici, F. Di un antico sarcofago cristiano...Mantova. Brescia, 1855.
Arc 1025.29.18 Odorici, F. Sulla Roma sotterranea dal G.B. de Rossi. Milano, 1866.
Arc 936.14.275 Odry. (Kmieciński, Jerzy.) Wrocław, 1968.
Arc 936.14.120 Odrycia w wiślecy. (Warsaw. Uniwersytet. Zespol Badan nad Polskim Sredniowieczem.) Warszawa, 1963-64.
Arc 1033.145 Odvardo a S. Francisco Xaverio. Dissertatio storico-critico-dogmatico...mano destra di S. Giovanni Battista...Repagnano. Roma, 1738.
Arc 885.16 O'Dwyer, S. The Roman roads of Wales. Newtown, 1936.
Arc 870.23 O'Dwyer, Stanhope. The Roman roads of Cheshire. Newtown, 1935.
Htn Arc 545.200* Oedipus Aegyptiacus. v.1-3. (Kircher, A.) Romae, 1652-54. 4v.
Arc 628.3 Oehler, R. Klassisches Bilderbuch. n.p., 1892?
Arc 895.34F Öland under äldre järnaldern. (Stenberger, Mårten.) Stockholm, 1933.
Arc 895.34.5F Öland under äldre järnaldern. (Stenberger, Mårten.) Stockholm, 1933.
Arc 730.208 Oeri tou pelaryikon epiperikleous. (White, J.W.) Athēnai, 1894.
Arc 1369.1 Oesel, J. Thesaurus sel. numismata antiqua. Amsterdam, 1677.
Arc 726.258 Östenberg, Carl Eric. Luni sul Mignone e problemi della preistoria d'Italia. Lund, 1967.
Arc 895.22.5F Östergötlands bronsälder. (Nordén, Arthur.) Linköping, 1925.
Arc 65.2.5 Oesterreich-Archäologisches Institut, Wien. Jahreshefte. Vienna. 1,1898+ 37v.
Arc 1302.5 Österreich Gesellschaft für Münz und Medaillenkunde. Mitteilungen. Wien. 1890-1905 3v.
Arc 1580.35 Österreichische, ungarische, böhmische, und schlesische Münzen. v.2. (Cejnek, Josef.) Wien, 1936.
Arc 1578.6.10 Österreichische Münz- und Geldgeschichte. (Probszt, Günther.) Wien, 1973.
Arc 1578.4F Österreichische Münzprägungen, 1519-1918. (Miller zu Aicholz, V. von.) Wien, 1920.
Arc 1578.5F Österreichische Münzprägungen. 2. Aufl. (Miller zu Aichholz, V. von.) Wien, 1948. 2v.
Arc 1578.20 Österreichische Münzprägungen von Ergänzungen, 1740-1969. (Herinek, Ludwig.) Wien, 1970.
Arc 1578.20.1 Österreichische Münzprägungen von Ergänzungen, 1740-1969. (Herinek, Ludwig.) Wien, 1972.
Arc 1578.20.5 Österreichische Münzprägungen von 1657-1740. (Herinek, Ludwig.) Wien, 1972.
Arc 1313.40 Österreichische Numismatische Gesellschaft. Mitteilungen. Wien. 1,1937+ 6v.
Arc 65.2.7F Oesterreichisches Archäologisches Institut, Vienna. Grabungen. Wien. 1965
Arc 510.219F Österreichisches Archäologisches Institut. Forschungen in Ephesop. v.1-4, pt.1-3; v.5. Wien, 1906-51. 8v.
Arc 905.20 Österreichisches Archäologisches Institut. Führer durch das K.K. Staatsmuseum in S. Donato in Zara. Wien, 1912.
Arc 543.12.5 L'oeuvre de la délégation archéologique française en Afghanistan, 1922-1932. (Hackin, Joseph.) Tokyo, 1933.
Htn Arc 1670.56F* Oeuvre du chevalier Hedlinger. (Hedlinger, J.K.) Basle, 1776.
Arc 396.1 Oeuvres. (Longpérier, A. de.) Paris, 1883-87. 7v.
Arc 386.4 Oeuvres complètes. (Borghesi, Bartolomeo.) Paris, 1862-72. 10v.
Arc 15.5 Office des Instituts d'Archéologie et d'Histoire de l'Art. Bulletin périodique. Paris. 2-3,1935-1937
Arc 505.68.10 Official guide to Jerash. (Jordan. Department of Antiquities.) Jerusalem, 194-?
Arc 1033.17.450 Officium commemorationis solemnis beatae virginis Maria de Monte Carmelo. Ulysarpone, 1679.
Arc 1027.64 Oggetti ritrovati in un sepolcro della via Prinistina. (Bruzza, L.) Roma, 1882.
Arc 936.14.440 Ogólnopolska Konferencja Konserwatorów Zabytkow Archeologicznych. Wspolpraca z Przemyslem w Dziedzinie Ochrony Zabytkow Archeologicznych, Poznań, 1969. Przemysl a archeologia. Poznań, 1971.
Arc 875.65 Ogston, Alexander. The prehistoric antiquities of the Howe of Cromar. Aberdeen, 1931.
Arc 319.5 Ohio archaeologist. Columbus.
Arc 1166.1.5 Ohly, Kurt. Stichometrische Untersuchungen. Leipzig, 1928.
Arc 535.200 Ohnefalsch-Richter, M. Kypros, the Bible and Homer. London, 1893. 2v.
Arc 630.17 Oikonomes, Georgios P. De profusionum receptaeulis sepulchalilus. Athenis, 1921.
Arc 688.8.5 Oikonomides, A.N. Eounion. Athēnai, 1957.
Arc 80.1.7F Oikonomos, G.P. Ta hekaton etē tēs en Athēnais Archaiologikēs Hetaireias. Athēnai, 1938.
Arc 1163.5 Ojha, G.H. The palaeography of India (in Sansk). Oodeypore, 1894.
Arc 1160.13F Ojha, Gaurishankar. The palaeography of India. 2. ed. Ajmer, 1918.
Arc 925.4.30 Okhotniki za mamontanii. (Larichev, Vitalii E.) Novosibirsk, 1968.
Arc 925.4.20 Okladnikov, A.P. Olen' zolotye goda. Leningrad, 1964.
Arc 956.2 Okladnikov, Aleksei P. Drevnie poseleniia Baranova mysa. Novosibirsk, 1971.
Arc 925.341.10 Okladnikov, Aleksei P. Petroglify Baikala - pamiatniki drevnei kul'tury narodov Sibiri. Novosibirsk, 1974.
Arc 925.347.10 Okladnikov, Aleksei P. Petroglify Nizhnego Amura. Leningrad, 1971.
Arc 925.341.5 Okladnikov, Aleksei P. Petroglify srednei Leny. Leningrad, 1972.
Arc 925.341 Okladnikov, Aleksei P. Petroglify zabaikal'ia. Leningrad, 1969- 2v.

Author and Title Listing

Arc 925.180 Okladnikov, Aleksei Pavlovich. Dalekoe proshloe Primor'ia. Vladivostok, 1959-

Arc 925.180.30 Okladnikov, Aleksei Pavlovich. Dalekoe proshloe Primor'ia i Priamur'ia. Vladivostok, 1973.

Arc 925.180.20 Okladnikov, Aleksei Pavlovich. Liki drevnego Amura. Novosibirsk, 1968.

Arc 925.180.5F Okladnikov, Aleksei Pavlovich. Petroglify Angary. Leningrad, 1966.

Arc 925.180.10 Okladnikov, Aleksei Pavlovich. The Soviet Far East in antiquity. Toronto, 1965.

Arc 925.342.5 Okskii bassein v epokhu kamnia i bronzy. Moskva, 1970.

Arc 936.14.480 Okulicz, Jerzy. Pradzieje ziem pruskich od późnego paleolitu do VII w.n.e. Wrocław, 1973.

Arc 936.14.370 Okulicz, Łucja. Kultura kushanów zachodniobałtyjskich we wezesnej epoce zelasa. Wrocław, 1970.

Arc 925.75.20 Olbia. (Belinde Ballu, Eugéne.) Leiden, 1972.

Arc 925.75.10 Olbia. (Gansiniec, Z.) Kraków, 1962.

Arc 925.75 Olbia. (Ziebell, W.) Hamburg, 1937.

Arc 1588.6.2.20 Olçer, Cüneyt. Nakįslį Osmanlį mangįrlarį. İstanbul, 1975.

Arc 1588.6.2.10 Ölçer, Cüneyt. San alti osmanli padişahi zamaninda İstanbulda basilan gümuç paralor. Istanbul, 1966.

Arc 1588.6.2 Ölçer, Cüneyt. Sovyet Rusya Müzelerindeki, Moskova ve Leningrad, Nardir Osmanli raralon. Istanbul, 1972.

Arc 1588.6.2.5 Ölçer, Cüneyt. Sultan Mohmut II zamomuda darpedilen osmanli madeni porolori. Istanbul, 1970.

Arc 1588.6.2.15 Ölçer, Cüneyt. Yildivim Bayezid'in agullanu ait akçe ve mangirlav. Istanbul, n.d.

Arc 936.14.180 Olczak, Jerzy. Zrodła archeologiczne do studiow nad wczesnosredniowiecznym osadnictwem grodowym na terenie wojewodztwa. Poznań, 1966- 4v.

Arc 609.10 Old Africa rediscovered. (Davidson, Basil.) London, 1959.

Arc 1413.3 The old and new coins of Japan. (Tsukamoto, Toyojino.) Tokyo, 1930.

Arc 1411.12 Old coins of China. (Jorgensen, Holgar.) n.p., 19- .

Arc 885.1 Old Cornish crosses. (Langdon, A.G.) Truro, 1896.

Arc 858.22.5 Old crosses and lychgates. (Vallance, A.) London, 1920.

Arc 743.10 Old Etruria and modern Tuscany. (Cameron, M.L.) London, 1909.

Arc 858.31 Old places revisited. (Bigsley, R.) London, 1851. 3v.

Arc 756.5.2 Old Rome. (Burn, R.) London, 1880.

Arc 488.14A Old routes of western Iran. (Stein, Mark A.) London, 1940.

Arc 861.88 The old standing crosses of Herefordshire. (Watkins, Alfred.) London, 1930.

Arc 386.20.10 The old stone age. (Burkitt, M.C.) Cambrige, 1933.

Arc 923.35F The old stone age in European Russia. Diss. (Golomshtok, E.A.) Philadelphia, 1938.

Arc 885.4 Old stone crosses...ancient manners. (Owen, E.) London, 1886.

Arc 861.25 The old stone crosses of Dorset. (Pope, Alfred.) London, 1906.

Arc 875.43 Old stories in stones and other papers. (Hutcheson, Alexander.) Dundee, 1927.

Arc 858.40 The old straight track. (Watkins, A.) London, 1925.

Arc 1535.9 Old Warwickshire coins, tokens and medals. (Davis, W.J.) n.p., 1896.

Arc 895.45F Oldeberg, A. Studien über die schwedische Bootaxtkultur. Stockholm, 1952.

Arc 895.66 Oldeberg, Andreas. Die ältere Metallzeit in Schweden. Stockholm, 1974.

Arc 858.4 Older England. (Hodgetts, J.F.) London, 1884.

Arc 858.4.2 Older England. 2. series. (Hodgetts, J.F.) London, 1884.

Arc 682.4 The oldest civilization of Greece. (Hall, H.R.) London, 1901. 2v.

Arc 895.80 Oldtidsdragter. (Munksgaard, Elisabeth.) København, 1974.

Arc 1335.105 Ole Devegge's mynt-og medaille-samling. (Devegge, Ole.) Kjøbenhavn, 1851.

Arc 925.4.20 Olen' zolotye goda. (Okladnikov, A.P.) Leningrad, 1964.

Arc 628.19 Olenin', A.N. Arkheologicheskie trudy. v.1-3. Sankt Peterburg, 1877-82.

Arc 530.2 Olfers, J.F.M. Lydische Koenigsgraeber bei Sardes. Berlin, 1859.

Arc 746.9.20F Olfieri, Nereo. Spina. München, 1958.

Htn Arc 785.10* Oliva, G. In Marmor Isiacum...exercitationes. Rome, 1719.

Arc 843.69 Oliveira, M. De Talabriga a Lancobriga pela via militar romano. Coimbra, 1943.

Arc 1033.17.503 Oliveira Lemos, F.J. de. Livro do romeiro ao sumptuoso sanctuario da Senhora do Porto Ava. n.p., 1875.

Arc 726.202 Oliver, Andrew. The reconstruction of two Apulian tomb groups. Bern, 1968.

Arc 1675.10.9 Olivieri, A. Monete e medaglie degli Spinola di Tassarolo. Genova, 1860.

Arc 1020.25 Olivieri, Abati. Munorie della Chiesa S. Maria di Monte Granaro. Pesaro, 1777.

Arc 682.20 Olkonomlkes, S. Ta sōzomena Ithōmēs Messenes kai tōn Perix. Athēnai, 1879.

Arc 588.1 Ollahum, Kahun, and Gurob. 1889-90. (Petrie, W.M.F.) London, 1891.

Arc 830.36 Ollier de Marichard, J. Les Carthaginois en France. Montpellier, 1870.

Arc 1076.3.43 Olovianishnikov, N. Istoriia kolokolov i kolokitenoe iskusstvo. Moskva, 1912.

Arc 520.37 Ołtarz i miasto. Wyd. 1. (Szczepański, Jan A.) Kraków, 1974.

Arc 936.65.10 Oltenia română. (Tudor, D.) Bucureşti, 1968.

Arc 925.75.4 Ol'viia; temenos i agora. (Ol'viiskaia Ekspeditsiia, 1946.) Leningrad, 1964.

Arc 925.75.3FA Ol'viia. (Akademiia Nauk URSR, Kiev. Institut Arkheologicheskaia.) Kiev, 1940.

Arc 925.75.5 Ol'viia. (Lapin, V.V.) Kiev, 1959.

Arc 925.50.365 Ol'viia. Kiev, 1975.

Arc 925.75.4 Ol'viiskaia Ekspeditsiia, 1946. Ol'viia; temenos i agora. Leningrad, 1964.

Arc 684.1.19 Olympia; its history and remains. (Gardiner, E.N.) Oxford, 1925.

Arc 684.1.5 Olympia. (Boetticher, A.) Berlin, 1886.

Arc 684.1.7 Hē Olympia. (Leonardos, B.) Athēnai, 1901.

Arc 684.1.45F Olympia. (Rodenwaldt, G.) Berlin, 1926.

Arc 684.1.12 Olympia. (Wernick, F.) Leipzig, 1877.

Arc 684.5.10F Olympia: die Ergebnisse. v.5. (Curtius, Ernst.) Berlin, 1896.

X Cg Arc 684.1 Olympia - das Fest und seine Stätte. (Boetticher, A.) Berlin, 1883. (Changed to XP 9960)

Arc 684.1.11 Olympia und Delphi. (Luckerrbach, H.) München, 1904.

Arc 684.1.3 Olympia und Umgegend. (Curtius, E.) Berlin, 1882.

Arc 730.205 L'olympieion di Siracusa. (Orsi, P.) Roma, 1903.

Arc 654.1 Olympische Forschungen. (Kunze, Emil.) Berlin, 1944- 8v.

Arc 654.1PF Olympische Forschungen. Plates. Berlin, 1944-50.

Arc 1093.2.3.5 Om bygningsmaaden af oldtidens jaettestuer. 2. udg. (Frederik VII, king of Denmark.) København, 1862.

Arc 1433.12.5 Om de i Svensk jord funna Österländska mynt. (Tornberg, Carl Johan.) Stockholm, 1857.

Arc 505.5.44 Om den Davidische families begravelse under Zions bierg. (Münter, F.) Kjobenhavn, 1804.

Arc 1428.5 Om Frankernes mynter i Orienten. v.1-2. (Münter, F.C.K.H.) n.p., n.d.

Arc 895.7.9 Om jernålderen i Denmark. (Worsaae, J.J.A.) Kjøbenhavn, 1858.

Arc 1027.18.12 Om Judarne i Rom...och deras...katakomber. (Engeström, Adolf von.) Upsala, 1876.

Arc 1570.1.5 Om nogle norske pengeten. (Holmboe, C.A.) Kjøbenhavn, 1868.

Arc 895.29.15 Om Sleswigs eller Sønderjyllands oldtidsminder. (Worsaae, J.J.A.) Kjøbenhavn, 1865.

Arc 895.22.25 Om Våstergötlands stenålders bebyggelse. (Sahlström, K.E.) Stockholm, 1915.

Arc 1538.17 Oman, C.W.C. The coinage of England. Oxford, 1931.

Arc 1145.3 Omont, H. Facsimiles des manuscrits grecs datés de la Bibliothèque Nationale. Paris, 1891.

Arc 87.1.19 Omphalos der Zeus zu Delphi. (Boetticher, C.) Berlin, 1859.

Arc 861.18.5 On a bastion of London Wall. (Price, J.E.) Westminster, 1880.

Arc 861.18.13 On a palaeolithic floor at north east London. (Smith, Washington G.) London, 1884.

Arc 458.8A On Alexander's track to the Indus. (Stein, Mark A.) London, 1929.

Arc 861.43 On an inscribed stone at Orchard Wyndham, Somerset. (George, W.) Bristol, 1879.

Arc 543.3.20 On ancient Central-Asian tracks. (Stein, Mark Aurel.) N.Y., 1964.

Arc 895.72 On artifact analysis. (Cullberg, Carl.) Bonn, 1968.

Arc 382.2 On Carn Goch in Caermarthenshire. (Williams, John.) London, 1853. 17 pam.

Arc 543.3.19A On Central-Asian tracks. (Stein, Mark Aurel.) London, 1933.

Arc 983.7 On masks, labrets and certain aboriginal customs. (Dall, William H.) Washington, 1881-82.

Arc 861.44 On newly discovered Roman remains at Finkley near Andover. (Stevens, J.) London, n.d.

Arc 971.1 On some ancient mounds upon the shores of the Bay of Quinte. (Wallbridge, T.C.) Toronto, 1860.

Arc 861.13.9 On some ancient sculptures of the devil bound. (Collingwood, W.G.) Kendal, 1903.

Arc 595.18 On some points in certain theories...of the great Pyramid of Jeeseh. (Bart, J.Y.S.) Glasgow, 1868.

Arc 530.52 Ön tarih'te Qnadolu'da dü Gomme Adetleri. (Özgüc, T.) Basimevi, 1948.

Arc 785.20.9A On the Appian Way. (Leoni, N.) Florence, 1907.

Arc 1470.39 On the chronological sequence of the coins of Boeotia. (Head, B.V.) London, 1881.

Arc 1470.38 On the chronological sequence of the coins of Ephesus. (Head, B.V.) London, 1880.

Arc 1470.4 On the chronological sequence of the coins of Syracuse. (Head, B.V.) London, 1874.

Arc 1408.6 On the coins of the kings of Ghazni. (Thomas, E.) London, 1848.

Arc 950.205 On the contents of a rock retreat in Southeast Pennsylvania. (Haldeman, S.S.) n.p., n.d.

Arc 861.45 On the discovery...of Roman remains at South Shields. (Hooppell, R.E.) London, 1878.

Arc 712.22 On the general theory of proportion in archaeological design and its exemplification in detail in the Parthenon. (Lloyd, W.W.) London, 1863.

Arc 672.1.110 On the Knossos tablets. (Palmer, Leonard R.) Oxford, 1963.

Arc 435.2.23F On the Muhammadan architecture of Bharoch, Cambay. (Burgess, James.) London, 1896.

Arc 1347.3 On the Parthian coins. (Scott, W.H.) London, 1836-54. 28 pam.

Arc 968.2 On the ruins of a stone pueblo on the Animas River in New Mexico. (Morgan, L.H.) Salem, 1879.

Arc 1076.4 On the so-called bow puller of antiquity. (Morse, E.S.) Salem, 1894.

Arc 861.108F On the topography of the Cistercian Abbey of Tower Hill. (Clapham, A.W.) Oxford, 1915.

Arc 861.106F On the topography of the Dominican Priory of London. (Clapham, A.W.) Oxford, 1912.

Arc 635.214 On the track of Ulysses. (Stillman, W.J.) Boston, 1888.

Arc 861.12.18 On urns and other antiquities found round the southern skirts of the Cheviot Hills. (Hardy, James.) n.p., 1886.

Arc 925.50.215 Onaiko, Nadezhda A. Antichnyi import v Pridneprov'e i pobuzh'e v IV-II vv. do n.e. Moskva, 1970.

Arc 1454.205 Ondrouch, V. Keltské mince typu Biatec z Bratislavy. Bratislava, 1958.

Arc 1480.60 Ondrouch, V. Der römische Denarfund von Vyşkovce aus der Frühkaiserzeit. Bratislava, 1934.

Arc 936.150 Ondrouch, Vojtech. Bohaté hroby z doby rímskej na Slovensku. Bratislava, 1957.

Arc 936.195.75 Ondrouch, Vojtěch. Limes Romanus na Slovensku. Bratislava, 1938.

Arc 1588.4.55 Ondrouch, Vojtech. Nálezy keltských, antických a byzantských mincí na Slovensku. Bratislava, 1964.

Arc 403.16.40 One passion, two loves; the story of Heinrich and Sophia Schliemann. (Poole, Lynn.) N.Y., 1966.

Arc 880.5 O'Neill, Henry. Fine arts and civilization of ancient Ireland. London, 1863.

Arc 672.5.10 O'Neill, J.G. Ancient Corinth. Photoreproduction. Baltimore, 1930.

Arc 628.28 Onofrio, Cesare d'. Quando il cielo stava quaggiù. Roma, 1960.

Arc 888.25 Onze voorhistorie. (Popping, H.J.) Zutphen, 1952.

Arc 1494.5 Opataco apontamentos para a sua historia. (Reis de Sanches Ferreira, M.) Coimbra, 1911.

Arc 1349.30 L'opera numismatica di Solone Ambrosoli. (Ricci, Serafino.) Milano, 1908.

Arc 1053.7.5 Opera omnia. (Patarolo, Lorenzo.) Venetiis, 1743. 2v.

Arc 530.166 Opera selecta. (Przeworski, Stefan.) Wrocław, 1967.

Arc 1033.17.59 Opera sopra l'imagine. (Bocchi, M.F.) Fiorenza, 1592.

Arc 595.11 Operations carried on at the pyramids of Gizeh in 1837. (Vyse, H.) London, 1840. 2v.

Arc 1490.6 Opere storico-numismatiche. (Morbio, C.) Bologna, 1870.

Arc 1584.12 Opeshnikov, A.V. Russkiia monety do 1547 g. Moskva, 1896.

Author and Title Listing

Arc 936.195.110 Opeyněná sídliště 8.-12. století ve střední Ezvropě. (Štěpánek, Miroslav.) Praha, 1965.

Arc 936.195.50F Opevnina osada z doby bronzovej vo Veselom. (Tučik, Anton.) Bratislava, 1964.

Arc 785.34.5 Der Opferzug der Ara Pacis Augustae. (Dissel, Karl.) Hamburg, 1907.

Arc 497.38 Opgravingen in Palestina. (Simons, J.J.) Roermond-Maaseik, 1935.

Arc 609.1.7 Ophir und die Ruinen von Zimbabye. (Lenz, Oskar.) Prag, 1896.

Arc 543.11F Opic' pamiatnikov' drevnosti. (Kondakov, N.P.) Sankt Peterburg, 1890.

Arc 920.208F Opisanie arkheologicheskich raskopok. (Samokbasov, D.Ia.) Moskva, 1908.

Arc 1583.5 Opisanie drevnikh Russkik' monet'. (Chertkov, A.) Moskva, 1834.

Arc 1433.24 Opisanie kuficheskikh monet' X veka. (Grigorbev, V.V.) Sankt Peterburg, 1841.

Arc 1584.25 Opisanie russikh monet muzeia Iaroslavskoi uchenoi arkkivnoi kommissii. (Iaroslavskaia Uchenaia Arkhivnaia Kommissii.) Iaroslav, 1898.

Arc 1675.19 Opisanie russkikh medalei. (Russia. Monetnyi.) Sankt Peterburg, 1908.

Arc 1583.1 Opisanie Russkikh monet. (Shubert, Fedor F.) Sankt Peterburg, 1843.

Arc 925.30 Opisanie smolenskago klada. (Prozorovskii, D.I.) St. Peterburg, 1870.

Arc 716.5 The Opisthodomus on the Acropolis at Athens. (White, J.W.) n.p., 1894?

Arc 1675.37.15 Oporto, Portugal. Museu Municipal. Catalogo das moedas portuguesas. Porto. 1-2,1929-1934

Arc 843.125 El oppedum de Iruña. (Nieto Gallo, Gratiniano.) Victória, 1958.

Arc 1349.75 Opus monetale cigoi. (Brunetti, Lodovico.) Bologna, 1966.

Arc 1033.17.132 Opuscoletti varii ovvero monografia di Mottafollone storia della sacra cinta. (Cerbelli, D.) Napoli, 1857.

Arc 1018.18 Opuscoli archeologici profana e cristiana. (Garrucci, R.) Roma, 1860-77.

Arc 1018.18.2 Opuscoli di archeologia christiana e profana. (Garrucci, R.) Roma, n.d.

Arc 302.34 Opuscula archaeologia. (Zagreb. Univerzitet. Filozofski Fakultet. Odsjek za Arheologiju.) 1-5,1956-1961

Arc 79.2F Opuscula archaeologica; edidit Institutum Romanum regni Sueciae. Lund. 3-7,1944-1952 4v.

Arc 79.3F Opuscula Atheniensia. Lund. 1-6 4v.

Arc 383.43.5 Opuscula Iosepho Kastelíc sexagenario dicata. Ljubljana, 1974.

Arc 79.2.3F Opuscula Romana; edidit Institutum Romanum regni Sueciae. Lund. 1,1954+ 6v.

Arc 403.9 Opyt instruktsii po sostaleniiu arkheologicheskikh kart. (Smolin, V.F.) Kazan', 1921.

Arc 923.105 Opyt istoriografii paleolita SSSR. (Ilarionov, V.T.) Gor'kei, 1947.

Arc 925.13.115 Opyt istoriografii skifov. (Semenov-Zuser, Semen A.) Khar'kov, 1947.

Arc 87.1.6 Das Orakel der Themis. (Gerhard, E.) Berlin, 1846.

Arc 66.1.57 L'orateur Lycurgue. (Duerrbach, F.) Paris, 1890.

Htn Arc 1428.9.2* Oratio dissertio de nummis...a Symrnaeis. (Mead, Richard.) Londoni, 1724.

Htn Arc 1428.9* Oratio dissertio de nummis...a Symrnaeis. (Mead, Richard.) Londoni, 1724.

Arc 1033.86 Oratorio privato del secolo IV...nel Monte della Giustizia. (Rossi, G.B. de.) Roma, 1876.

Arc 1033.17.305 Orazione...Foggia...dell'icona...Santa Maria. (Guelfone.) Foggia, 1669.

Htn Arc 684.2* Orchomenos. (Schliemann, Heinrich.) Athēnai, 1883.

Arc 684.3 Orchomenos. (Schliemann, Heinrich.) Leipzig, 1881.

Arc 1675.97 Order und Ehrenzeichen der Deutschen Demokratischen Republik. (Dresden. Historisches Museum.) Dresden, 1964.

Arc 1675.53F The orders, decorations and medals of the world. (Jocelyn, Arthur.) London, 1934.

Arc 890.206 Ordnung af Danmark's oldsager stenalderen. (Mueller, S.) Paris, 1888. 2v.

Arc 726.253 Ordona. (Mertens, Jozef.) Bruxelles, 1965. 4v.

Arc 66.1.161 L'ordre cistercien et son gouvernement. (Mahor, J.B.) Paris, 1945.

Arc 66.1.207 L'ordre équestre. (Nicolet, Claude.) Paris, 1966-74. 2v.

Arc 94.25 Orense, Spain. Museo Arqueológico Provincial. Boletin. 1-4,1943-1948 2v.

Arc 1470.60 Oreshnikov, A. Zkskursy v oblast' drevnsi numizmatiki cherno morskago pobereniia. Moskva, 1914.

Arc 1583.14 Oreshnikov, A.V. Denezhnye znaki domongol'. Rusi. Moskva, 1936.

Arc 80.8 Organismos. (Archaiologikē Hetairia, Athens.) Athēnai, 1876.

Arc 1033.17.322 Orgio. Istoriche notizie...dell'immagine di Maria...di Genazzano. 3. ed. Roma, 1790.

Arc 630.12 Orient, Hellas und Rom in der archäologischen Forschungszeit 1939. (Schefold, Karl.) Bern, 1949.

Arc 513.41 Orient and Occident. Kevelaer, 1973.

Arc 495.208F Oriental forerunners of Byzantine painting...wall-paintings from the fortress of Dura. (Breasted, J.H.) Chicago, 1924.

Arc 1335.41.5 Oriental numismatics - catalogue of collections of books related to coinage of the east presented to Essex Institute, Salem. (Robinson, John.) Salem, 1913.

Arc 1335.23 Die orientalischen Münzen...in Königsberg. (Nesselmann, G.H.F.) Leipzig, 1858.

Arc 1353.12 Orientalske, graeske og romerske. (Copenhagen. National Museet.) Kjøbenhavn, 1952.

Arc 943.53 Origen de las culturas precolombinas. 1. ed. (Comas, Juan.) México, 1975.

Arc 1153.53.5 The origin and development of humanistic script. (Ullmann, B.L.) Rome, 1960.

Arc 1411.4 Origin and earlier history of Chinese coinage. (Hopkins, L.C.) n.p., n.d.

Arc 1138.18 Origin and progress of writing. (Astle, Thomas.) London, 1803.

Arc 595.70.1 The origin and significance of the great pyramid. (Wake, Charles Staniland.) Minneapolis, 1975.

Arc 1372.2 The origin of metallic currency and weight standards. (Ridgeway, W.) Cambridge, 1892.

Arc 963.2.15 The origin of the Cahokia mounds. (Crook, A.R.) Springfield, 1922.

Arc 820.219F L'origine de Marseille. (Vasseur, G.) Marseille, 1914.

Arc 1020.9.99 Origine del tempio. (Landucci, A.) Roma, 1646.

Arc 1033.17.624 Origine della Madonna della Quercia di Viterbo. (Nelli, A.) n.p., n.d.

Arc 1264.6 L'origine des armoiries de l'église de Besançon. (Gauthier, Jules.) n.p., 1880.

Arc 66.1.67 Origine des cultes arcadiens. (Bérard, V.) Paris, 1894.

Arc 1390.4 L'origine du marc. (Blancard, Louis.) Macon, 1888.

Arc 66.1.112 Les origines chrétiennes...provinces danubiennes. (Zeiller, Jacques.) Paris, 1918.

Arc 936.75 Les origines de la civilisation polonaise. (Kostrzewski, J.) Paris, 1949.

Arc 522.30 Les origines de la legende troyenne de Rome. Thèse. (Perret, J.) Paris, 1942.

Arc 823.81 Origines de l'archéologie préhistorique en France. (Laming, Annette.) Paris, 1964.

Arc 66.1.108 Les origines de l'édifice hypostyle. (Leroux, Gabriel.) Paris, 1913.

Arc 936.14.45 Les origines de l'etat polonais. (Paris. Université.) Paris, 1961.

Arc 66.1.132 Les origines de l'Hercule Romain. (Bayet, J.) Paris, 1926.

Arc 830.333 Les origines de Narbonne. (Helena, T.) Toulouse, 1937.

Arc 830.67 Les origines des anciens monuments...de Poitiers. (La Croix, Camille.) Poitiers, 1906.

Arc 830.305 Les origines des recherches françaises sur l'habitat rural gallo-romain. (Harmand, Jacques.) Bruxelles, 1961.

Arc 830.79 Origines dijonnaises. (Roget de Belloguet, Dominique F.L.) Dijon, 1851.

Arc 66.1.29 Origines du sénat romain. (Bloch, G.) Paris, 1883.

Arc 66.1.58 Origines et sources du Roman de la Rose. (Langlois, E.) Paris, 1891.

Arc 66.1.66 Origines françaises de l'architecture gothique en Italie. (Enlart, C.) Paris, 1894.

Arc 672.1.6 Le origini della civilta Mediterranea. (Mosso, Angelo.) Milano, 1910.

Arc 1163.21 Le origini della scriturra gotica padovana. (Pagnin, B.) Padova, 1933.

Arc 723.18 Le origini italiche. (Toscanelli, Nello.) Milano, 1914.

Arc 875.32 Origins of Pictish symbolism. (Carnegie, J.) Edinburgh, 1893.

Arc 1473.12 The origins of the Anastasian currency reforms. (Metcalf, David Michael.) Amsterdam, 1969.

Arc 880.46 O'Riordain, Sean P. Antiquities of the Irish countryside. 3. ed. London, 1953.

Arc 880.46.5 O'Riordain, Sean P. New Grange and the bend of the Boyne. London, 1964.

Arc 454.1 Orissa and her remains. (Ganguly, M.M.) Calcutta, 1912.

Arc 1153.102 Orlandelli, Gainfranco. Rinascimento giuridico e scrittura carolina a Bologna nel secolo XII. Bologna, 1965.

Arc 712.37 Orlandos, Anastasios K. Ta charagmata tou Parthenōuos. Athēnai, 1973.

Arc 340.4 Orlinsky, H.M. An indexed bibliography of the writings of W.F. Albright. New Haven, 1941.

Arc 1163.3.38 Orlov, A.S. Bibliografiia russkikh nadpisei XI-XV vv. Moskva, 1936.

Arc 1163.3.40 Orlov, A.S. Bibliografiia russkikh nadpisei XI-XV vv. Moskva, 1952.

Arc 1460.6 Orlov, Georgije. Vimi nacijum. Beograd, 1970.

Arc 861.48 Ormerod, George. Archaeological memoirs...district of the Severn and the Wye. London, 1861.

Arc 700.10 Ornament und Form der altischen Grabstelen. (Brueckner, A.) Weimar, 1886.

Arc 700.10.15F Die Ornamente der griechischen Grabstelen. (Moebius, Hans.) Berlin, 1929.

Arc 726.343 Die Ornamentik der Langobarden in Italien. (Roth, Helmut.) Bonn, 1973.

Htn Arc 1143.9.5* Ornamentis librorum. (Schwarz, M.C.G.) Lipsiae, 1756.

Arc 1143.9 Ornamentis librorum apud veteres usitatis. v.1-3. (Schwarz, M.C.G.) Lipsiae, 1705-

Htn Arc 726.6* Orsati, S. Monumenta patavina. Padova, 1652.

Arc 726.115 Orsi, Libero d'. Gli scavi di Stabia a cura del Comitato per gli scavi di Stabia. Napoli, 1954.

Arc 1015.223 Orsi, P. Esplorazioni nelle catacombe. Siracusa. Roma, 1893.

Arc 1020.16 Orsi, P. Monumenti cristiani del Trentino. Roma, 1883.

Arc 730.205 Orsi, P. L'olympieion di Siracusa. Roma, 1903.

Arc 1027.26.5 Orsi, Paolo. Nuove esplorazioni nelle catacombe di S. Giovanni Battista de Rossi nell 1894 in Siracusa. Roma, 1896.

Htn Arc 1475.5* Orsini, F. Familiae Romanae. Rome, 1577.

Arc 1033.17.45 Orsini, Mathieu. La Virgen. 4. ed. Barcelona, 1867. 2v.

Arc 226.2 Orsjágos Magyar Régészeti Jársulat. Evkönyve. Budapest. 1-2,1920-1926

Arc 1493.22 Ortega Galindo, Julio. La España firmitiva a través de las monedas ibéricas. Bilbao, 1963.

Arc 530.169 Orthmann, Winfried. Das Gräberfeld bei Ilica. Wiesbaden, 1967.

Arc 1163.2.23 Ortografía general paleográfica-bibliográfica de la lengua castellana. (Moriano, F.) Sevilla, 1866.

Arc 530.167 Oruzhie i voennoe delo drevnei Armenii. (Yesaian, Stepan.) Greoan, 1966.

Arc 746.18F Orvieto, Italy. Orvieto etrusca. Roma, 1928.

Arc 746.18F Orvieto etrusca. (Orvieto, Italy.) Roma, 1928.

Arc 730.202 Orville, J.P. d'. Sicula, guibus Sicilae veritis ruderd. Amsterdam, 1764.

Arc 1033.46.8 Os miragres de Santiago. Valladolid, 1918.

Arc 936.14.365 Osadnictwo celtyckie w Pobie. (Woźniak, Zenon.) Wrocław, 1970.

Arc 505.5.15 Osgood, P.E. The Temple of Solomon. Chicago, 1910.

Arc 925.332.5 Osh Paudo. (Stepanov, Pavel D.) Saransk, 1967.

Arc 588.14 The Osireron at Abydos. (Murray, M.) London, 1904.

Arc 1490.3 Die Oskischen Münzen. (Friedländer, Julius.) Leipzig, 1850.

Arc 1588.14 Osmanhlarda madeni paralar. (Pere, Nuri.) Istanbul, 1968.

Arc 1190.85 Osmanische Sultansurkunden des Siṅai-Klosters in türkischer Sprache. (Schwarz, Klaus.) Freiburg, 1970.

Arc 1588.6.25 Osmanli altinlari. (Kocaer, Remje.) Istanbul, 1967.

Arc 1190.86.5 Osmanotwiska diplomatika: paleografiia. (Nedkov, Boris K.) Sofiia, 1966-72. 2v.

Arc 1588.6.5 Osmarli inpatatorlugurda pava. (Kolerkilic, Eksen.) Ankara, 1958.

Arc 925.357 Osnovnye problemy istorii plemen Vostochnoi Gruzii v XV-VII vv. do n.e. (Pitskhelauri, Konstantin.) Tbilisi, 1973.

Arc 923.37 Osnovy arkheologii. (Artsikhovskii, A.V.) Moskva, 1954.

Arc 923.37.5 Osnovy arkheologii. Izd. 2. (Artsikhovskii, A.V.) Moskva, 1955.

VArc 925.50.135 Osnovy arkheolohii. (Shovkoplias, Ivan H.) Kyïv, 1964.

Author and Title Listing

Arc 925.50.137 Osnovy arkheolohii. 2. vyd. (Shovkoplias, Ivan H.) Kyïv, 1972.
Arc 1033.17.465 Ossequi e preghiere onde meritarsi...di Maria...Napoli. Napoli, 1839.
Arc 760.6.15 Ossequiosissimo rapporto alla Santità. (Fea, Carlo.) Roma, 1826. 2 pam.
Htn Arc 1020.9.75* Osservazione...storia via Appia di Pratelle. (Gesualdo, E.) Napoli, 1754.
Arc 1027.41.9 Osservazione sulla topografia della via Ostiense. (Stevenson, H.) Roma, 1897.
Arc 1033.85 Osservazioni...sepolcro di Maria. (Cavedoni, C.) Modena, 1865.
Arc 1020.102.3 Osservazioni critici...Siena...sopra croce di rame intagliata...1129. (Angelis, L. de.) Siena, 1814.
Arc 1027.49 Osservazioni intorno al cimitero delle catacombe. (Marucchi, O.) n.p., n.d.
Htn Arc 1033.1* Osservazioni sopra alcune frammenti di vasi antichi. (Buonarroti, F.) Firenze, 1716.
Arc 1033.1.9 Osservazioni sopra alcuni frammenti di vasi. (Cavedoni, C.) Modena, 1859.
Arc 1015.207 Osservazioni sopra i cimitery. (Boldetti, M.A.) Roma, 1720.
Arc 1027.87 Osservazioni sopra i recenti studi intorne ai cimiteri di Marco e Marcelliano. (Scaglia, Sisto.) Saronno, 1909. 3 pam.
Arc 726.39 Osservazioni sopra il fiume Clitunno. (Venuti, R.) Roma, 1753.
Arc 746.3 Osservazioni sopra un'Etrusco Lampadario. Montepulciano, 1844.
Arc 1033.2 Osservazioni sul musaico di S. Pudenziana. (Crostarosa, P.) Roma, 1895.
Arc 1027.19.21 Osservazioni sulla iscrizione della madre del papa Damaso. (Marucchi, O.) Roma, 1903.
Arc 1027.26.9 Osservazioni sulle basiliche e le catacombe...Siracusa. (Cavallari, S.) Palermo, 1874.
Arc 785.20.13 Osservazioni suo ristabilimento della Via Appia da Roma a Brindisi. (Fea, Carlo.) Roma, 1833.
Arc 930.201 Ossowski, G. Zabytki przedhistoryczne Ziem Polskich. Krakow, 1879-88.
Arc 530.35F Osten, H.H. von der. The Alishar Hüyük, seasons of 1930-32. Chicago, 1937.
Arc 530.12.10 Osten, H.H. von der. Explorations in Hittite Asia Minor, 1927-28. Chicago, 1929.
Arc 530.12.5 Osten, H.H. von der. Explorations in Hittite Asia Minor. Chicago, 1927.
Arc 853.50 Die ostgermanische Kultur. (Kostrzewski, J.) Leipzig, 1919. 2v.
Arc 726.25.7 Ostia; cenni storici e guida. (Vagliere, Dante.) Roma, 1914.
Arc 726.25.30 Ostia, der Welthafen Roms. (Schaal, Hans.) Bremen, 1957.
Arc 726.25.17 Ostia, guida storico monumentale. (Calza, Guido.) Milano, 1925?
Arc 726.25.18 Ostia; historical guide to the monuments. (Calza, Guido.) Milano, 1926.
Arc 726.25.35 Ostia. (Calza, Raissa.) Firenze, 1959.
Arc 726.25.25A Ostie. (Carcopino, J.) Paris, 1929.
Arc 1454.210F Ostkeltischer Typenatlas. (Göbl, Robert.) Braunschweig, 1973.
Arc 895.17.15F Ostnorske ristninger og malinger av den arktiske gruppe. (Engelstad, E.S.) Oslo, 1934.
Arc 853.46 Ostpreussen in der Völkerwanderungszeit. (Åberg, Nils.) Uppsala, 1919.
Arc 547.41F Ostraka Michaeliders. (Goedicke, Hans.) Wiesbaden, 1962.
Arc 936.14.270 Ostrów Lednicki. Wyd 1. (Łomnicki, Jerzy.) Poznań, 1968.
Arc 893.20 Der Ostskandinavische Norden während der ältesten Metallzeit Europas. (Forssander, J.E.) Lund, 1936.
Arc 1540.30 O'Sullivan, W. The earliest Irish coinage. Dublin, 1961.
Arc 1090.6F Oswald, Adrian. Clay pipes for the archaeologists. Oxford, 1975.
Arc 292.30F Otchet". (Russia. Arkheologicheskaia Kommissiia.) Petrograd. 1889-1915 8v.
Arc 925.50.340 Otchet o raskopkakh v Khersonese za 1935-36 gg. (Belov, Grigorii D.) Sevastopol', 1938.
Arc 289.20 Otchety arkheologicheskikh ekspeditsii. Irkutsk. 1963+
Arc 925.170.11 Otchety Nizhnekamskoi arkheologicheskoi ekspeditsii. Photoreproduction. (Nizhnekamskaia Arkheologicheskaia Ekspeditsiia, 1968-1969?) Moskva, 1972.
Arc 843.72 Otesouro de Toxados. (Carro, Jesús.) Santiago, 1933.
Arc 1160.201 Otfrid...Weissenburg. Schreiber XIX Jahrhundert. (Peper, P.) Frankfurt, 1899.
Arc 505.67 The other side of the Jordan. (Glueck, N.) New Haven, Conn., 1940.
Arc 386.43 Otkrytie zatonuvshezo mira. (Blavatskii, V.D.) Moskva, 1963.
Arc 386.18 Otkrytyia XIX i nachala XX v. (Touzeskul, V.) Sankt Peterburg, 1923.
Arc 375.4 Otte, H. Archäologisches Wörterbuch. Leipzig, 1857.
Arc 375.4.2 Otte, H. Archäologisches Wörterbuch. Leipzig, 1883.
Arc 1076.3.9 Otte, H. Glockenkunde. Leipzig, 1884.
Arc 726.36.10 Otto, prince of Hesse. Die langobardenzeitlichen Grabfunde aus Fiesole bei Florenz. München, 1966.
Arc 726.322 Otto, prince of Hesse. Primo contributo alla archeologia longobarda in Toscana: Le necropoli. Firenze, 1971.
Arc 530.100 Otto-Dorn, K. Das Islamische Iznik. Berlin, 1941.
Arc 392.18 Otto Hauser. (Brandt, Karl.) Witten-Ruhr, 1970.
Arc 394.1.20 Otto Jahn in seinen Briefen. (Michaelis, A.) Leipzig, 1913.
Arc 600.215.5 La ouabet de Kalabcha. (Daumas, François.) Le Caire, 1970.
Arc 600.156.10F Ouchebtis de Deir el-Médineh. (Valbelle, Dominique.) Le Caire, 1972.
Arc 889.22 Oud-België. (Mariën, M.E.) Antwerpen, 1952.
Arc 1030.42 De oud christelijke monumenten van Spanje. (Smit, E.L.) 's-Gravenhage, 1916.
Arc 1015.231 De oud-christelijke sarkophagen. (Obermann, H.T.) 's-Gravenhage, 1911.
Arc 543.35 Oudheden van Bali I. (Stutterheim, W.F.) Singaradja, 1930.
Arc 403.14 Oudheidkundig Genootschap, Amsterdam. Bibliographie der geschriften van Jhr. Dr. Jan Six. Amsterdam, 1933.
Arc 273.2.15F Oudheidkundige mededeelingen. (Leyden. Rigksmuseum van Oudheden.) 29-50 17v.
Arc 888.15 Oudheidkundige perspectieven in het bijzonder ten aanzien van de vaderlandsche Prae en protohistorie. (Giffen, Albert Egges van.) Groningen, 1947.
Arc 672.1.45 Oulié, Marthe. Les animaux dans la peinture de la Crete préhellénique. Thèse. Paris, 1926.
Htn Arc 672.1.47F* Oulié, Marthe. Decoration égéenne. Paris, 1927.
Arc 505.132 Oumm el-'Amed. Text and atlas. (Dunand, Maurice.) Paris, 1962. 2v.
Arc 1613.17 Our American money. (Coffin, J.) N.Y., 1940.
Arc 858.5 Our ancient monuments and the land around them. (Kains-Jackson, C.P.) London, 1880.
Arc 386.20A Our early ancestors. (Burkitt, M.C.) Cambridge, 1926.
Arc 858.41 Our homeland prehistoric antiquities and how to study them. (Clarke, W.G.) London, 1924.
Arc 595.9.2 Our inheritance in the Great Pyramid. (Smyth, C.P.) London, 1864.
Arc 595.9 Our inheritance in the Great Pyramid. (Smyth, C.P.) London, 1877.
Arc 595.9.3 Our inheritance in the Great Pyramid. 4. ed. (Smyth, C.P.) London, 1880.
Arc 387.8A Our prehistoric ancestors. (Cleland, H.F.) N.Y., 1928.
Arc 501.4 Our work in Palestine. (Committee of the Fund.) London, 1873.
Arc 885.11 Out of the dark. (Hughes, I.T.) Wrexham, 1930.
Arc 1468.42 An outline of ancient Greek coins. (Klawans, Zander H.) Racine, Wis. , 1959.
Arc 875.20 Outlines of Scottish archaeology. (Sutherland, G.) Edinburgh, 1870.
Arc 672.1.25 Ovalhaus und Paläst in Kreta. (Noack, F.) Leipzig, 1908.
Arc 1025.22 Over de catacomben van Rome. (Janssen, L.J.F.) Utrecht, 1854.
Arc 700.21 Over den oorsprong van de grieksche grafstele. Proefschrift. (Hall, Elise von.) Amsterdam, 1941.
Arc 810.13 Overbeck, J. Pompeji. Leipzig, 1856.
Arc 810.13.2A Overbeck, J. Pompeji. Leipzig, 1884.
Arc 810.13.5 Overbeck, J. Pompeji in seinen Gebäuden. 3. Aufl. Leipzig, 1875.
Arc 700.18 Overbeck, J. Über die Lade des Kypselos. Leipzig, 1865.
Arc 87.2.51 Overbeck, J.A. Roemische Villa bei Weingarten. Bonn, 1851.
Arc 889.4.15 De overblijfselev der Romainsche villa's in België. (Maeyer, R. de.) Antwerpen, 1940.
Arc 543.66.13 Ovezov, D.M. Akadenik Akademii nauk Turkmenskoi SSR Mikhail Evgen'evich Masson. Ashkhabad, 1970.
Arc 383.90.10 Oviedo (Province). Diputacion Provincial. Servicio de Investigaciones Arqueologicas. Libro homenaje la Conde de la Vega del Sella. Oviedo, 1956.
Arc 785.13.65 Owen, A.S. Excerpta ex antiquis scriptoribus quae ad Forum Romanum spectant. Oxonii, 1930.
Arc 885.4 Owen, E. Old stone crosses...ancient manners. London, 1886.
Arc 895.52 Oxenstierna, E.C.G. Die altere Eisenzeit im Ostergötland. Lidingö, 1958.
Arc 893.26 Oxenstierna, E.C.G. Die Nordgermanen. Stuttgart, 1957.
Arc 861.211 Oxford, the city beneath your feet. (Hassall, Tom Grafton.) Oxford, 1972.
Arc 1443.5F Oxford. University. Ashmolean Museum. Catalogue of Alexandrian coins. Oxford, 1933.
Arc 1478.81F Oxford. University. Ashmolean Museum. Catalogue of coins of the Roman Empire in the Ashmolean Museum. Oxford, 1975
Arc 1540.10 Oxford silver pennies, 925-1272. (Stainer, C.L.) Oxford, 1904.
Arc 530.52 Özgüc, T. Ön tarih'te Qnadolu'da dü Gomme Adetleri. Basimevi, 1948.
Arc 530.55F Özgüc, T. Türk Tarih kurumu tarafindan yapelan karakoyuk hafreyate raporu. Ankara, 1947.
Arc 530.75 Özgüc, T. Türk Tarih kurumu tarafindan yapelan Kültepe kazisi raporu, 1948. Ankara, 1950.
Arc 530.76F Özgüc, T. Türk Tarih kurumu tarafindan yapelan Kültepe kazisi raporu, 1949. Ankara, 1953.
Arc 925.13.100F Ozols, Jekabs. Ursprung und Herkunft der zentralrussischen Fatjanowo Kultur. Berlin, 1962.
Arc 1033.26.5 Pamphlet box. P.L. Bruzza.
Arc 390.9 Pa kulturvernets veier. (Fett, Harry.) Oslo, 1949.
Arc 853.16 Ein paar Worte über ein paar Drudenbäume. (Mayer, Anton.) Eichstatt, 1826.
Arc 1675.91 Pachinger, A.M. Wallfahrts-, Bruderschafts- und Weihe. Wien, 1908.
Arc 936.262 Pachkova, Svitlana P. Hospodarstvo skhidnoslov'ians'kykh plemen na rubezhi nashoï ery. Kyïv, 1974.
Arc 605.1 Pacho, J.R. Relation d'un voyage dans la Marmarique. Text, plates. Paris, 1827. 2v.
Arc 925.9.40 Pachulia, Vianor P. V kraiu zolotogo runa. Moskva, 1964.
Arc 925.9.41 Pachulia, Vianor P. V kraiu zolotogo runa. Izd. 2. Moskva, 1968.
Htn Arc 1033.137* Paciandi, P. De cultu S. J. Baptistae...commentarius. Roma, 1755.
Arc 1480.5 Paciandi, P.M. Ad nummos consulares III viri M. Antonii. Rome, 1757.
Arc 400.23 Paciaudi, Paolo M. Lettres au comte de Caylus. Paris, 1802.
Arc 1093.6.12 Paegle, Eduard. Salktis, Progenitor der Svastika. Würzburg, 1957.
Arc 848.55 Paertner, Rudolf. Mit dem Fahrstuhl in die Römerzeit. Düsseldorf, 1963.
Arc 736.19 Paestum. (Kayser, Hans.) Heidelburg, 1958.
Arc 766.1.2.30 Pagan and Christian Rome. (Lanciani, R.) Boston, 1892.
Htn Arc 766.1.4* Pagan and Christian Rome. (Lanciani, R.) Boston, 1893.
Arc 766.1.3 Pagan and Christian Rome. (Lanciani, R.) Boston, 1893.
Arc 766.1.3.5 Pagan and Christian Rome. (Lanciani, R.) London, 1893.
Arc 880.3 Pagan Ireland. An archaeological sketch. (Wood-Martin, W.G.) London, 1895.
Arc 1490.82 Pagani, Antonio. I bersaglieri nelle medaglie 1836-1936. Milano, 1937.
Arc 1488.32 Pagani, Antonio. Monete italiane dall'invasione napoleonica ai giorni nostri, 1796-1963. 2. ed. Milano, 1965.
Arc 1488.25 Pagani, Antonio. Monete italiane moderne a sistema decimale da Napoleone console alla Repubblica Italiana. 2. ed. Milano, 1953.
Arc 800.4 Pagano, N. Description des fouilles d'Herculanum. Naples, 1871.
Arc 810.47.5 Pagano, N. Guide de Pompéi. 5. éd. Naples, 1875.
Arc 810.47.7 Pagano, N. Guide de Pompéi. 17. éd. Scafati, 1886.
Arc 810.47 Pagano, N. Guide de Pompéi tirée de toutes les ouvrages les plus intéressantes. 4. éd. Naples, 1874.
Arc 726.32 Pagenstecher, R. Unteritalische Grabdenkmäler. Strassburg, 1912.
Arc 545.243F Pagenstrecher, R. Nekropolis. Leipzig, 1919.
Arc 885.12 Paget, Clara. Some ancient stone forts in Carnarvonshire. Cambridge, 1896.
Arc 726.27.10 Paget, Robert F. In the footsteps of Orpheus. N.Y., 1968.
Arc 938.108 Pagirienė, L. Lietuvos TSR archeologija 1940-1967. Vil'nius, 1970.

Author and Title Listing

Arc 1163.21 Pagnin, B. Le origini della scriturra gotica padovana. Padova, 1933.
Arc 936.225.20F Pahić, Stanka. Pobrežje. Lujbljana, 1972.
Arc 45.5 Pahlari University. Asia Institute. Bulletin. Shiraz. 1,1969+
Arc 482.203PF Paikuli. (Herzfled, Ernst E.) Berlin, 1924. 2v.
Arc 505.5.6 Paine, T.O. Solomon's temple. Boston, 1861.
Arc 495.203 Paine, T.O. Solomon's Temple. Boston, 1886.
Arc 500.8 Painted tombs in the necropolis of Marissa. (Peters, John P.) London, 1905.
Arc 968.2.12 Pajarito Plateau and its ancient people. (Hewett, E.L.) Albuquerque, 1938.
Arc 1584.4 Pakhomov, Evgenii A. Monetnye klady Azerbaidzhana. pt.6,8. Baku, 1954.
Arc 1584.4.5 Pakhomov, Evgenii A. Monety Azerbaidzhana. Baku, 1959- 2v.
Arc 1584.1.20 Pakhomov, Evgenii A. Monety Gruzii. Tbilisi, 1970.
Arc 45.3 Pakistan archaeology. Karachi. 1,1964+ 3v.
Arc 1016.238 La pala d'oro dell...basilica di San Marco. (Bellomo, G.) Venezia, 1847.
Arc 672.1.94 The palace of Crete. (Graham, J.W.) Princeton, N.J., 1962.
Arc 672.1.130 The palace of Minos. (Evans, Arthur John.) N.Y., 1964. 6v.
Arc 672.1.131 The palace of Minos. Index. (Evans, Arthur John.) N.Y., 1964.
Arc 672.1.27 The palace of Minos. v.1; v.2, pt.1-2; v.3; v.4, pt.1-2. (Evans, Arthur John.) London, 1921-35. 6v.
Arc 672.1.5 Palaces of Crete and their builders. (Mosso, Angelo.) London, 1907.
Arc 672.1.4 The palaces of Crete and their builders. (Mosso, Angelo.) N.Y., 1907.
Arc 318.2 El palacio. 11,1921+ 8v.
Arc 858.30 Palaeographia brittanica. (Stukely, William.) London, 1743. 2 pam.
Arc 1138.9 Palaeographia critica. (Kopp, U.F.) Mannheim, 1817-29. 4v.
Arc 1138.122.5 Palaeographical papers, 1907-1965. (Lowe, Elias Avery.) Oxford, 1972. 2v.
Arc 1153.58 Paläographie des mainfränkischen Monumentalinscriften. Inaug. Diss. (Rauh, Rudolf.) München, 1935.
Arc 1175.12FA Palaeography and...study of court hand. (Jenkinson, H.) Cambridge, 1915.
Arc 1130.15F The palaeography collection. (London. University. Library.) Boston, 1968. 2v.
Arc 1160.13F The palaeography of India. 2. ed. (Ojha, Gaurishankar.) Ajmer, 1918.
Arc 1163.5 The palaeography of India (in Sansk). (Ojha, G.H.) Oodeypore, 1894.
Arc 953.15 Palaeolithic implements of...Delaware. v.1-3. (Boston Society of Natural History.) Cambridge, 1881.
Arc 925.4.5 The palaeolithic period in Siberia contributions to the prehistory of the Yenisei region. (Merhart, Gero von.) n.p., 1923.
Arc 853.56.7 Das Paläolithikum der Höhlen des Hönnetales in Westfalen. (Andree, Julius.) Leipzig, 1928.
Arc 681.10 Paläolithikum um Larissa in Thessalien. (Milojčić, Vladmir.) Bonn, 1965.
Arc 830.348 Die paläolithischen Menschendarstellungen. (Haensch, Wolf.) Bonn, 1968.
Arc 497.3 Palaestina. (Reeland, Adriaan.) Utrecht, 1714. 2v.
Arc 45.1 Palästina Jährbuch. Berlin. 1-36,1905-1940 36v.
Arc 497.43 Palästina und seine Kultur in fünf Jahrtausenden. 2. Aufl. (Thomsen, P.) Leipzig, 1917.
Arc 1148.33 Palaiographikos eranos. (Sarros, D.M.) Konstantinoypolei, 1914.
Arc 493.4 Le palais de Darius. (Pillet, M.L.) Paris, 1914.
Arc 785.11 Le palais de Scaurus. (Mazois, F.) Paris, 1822.
Arc 785.11.4 Le palais de Scaurus. 4. éd. (Mazois, F.) Paris, 1869.
Htn Arc 815.4* Le palais pompéien. (Gautier, T.) Paris, 1866.
Htn Arc 1490.5.5* Palati, J. Fasti ducales ab Anafesto I. Venetiis, 1696.
Arc 785.22.2 Der Palatin. (Haugwitz, E.) Rom, 1901.
Arc 785.22 Der Palatin seine Geschichte und seine Ruinen. (Haugwitz, E.) Rom, 1901.
Arc 785.22.10F Il palazzo de' Cesari sul monte Palatino. (Thon, C.) Roma, 1828.
Arc 600.120 Il Palazzo delle calonne in Talemaide di Cirenaria. (Pesce, Gennaro.) Roma, 1950.
Arc 785.11.5 Il palazzo di Scauro. 2. ed. (Mazois, F.) Milano, 1825.
Arc 672.1.65F Il palazzo minoico di Festos. (Pernier, Luigi.) Roma, 1935-51. 3v.
Arc 543.3.105 Paleoantropologiia Srednei Azii. (Ginzburg, Vul'f V.) Moskva, 1972.
Arc 1160.202.9F Paleografía castellana. (Colomera y Rodriguez, V.) Valladolid, 1862.
Arc 1190.7 Paleografia e diplomatica...province napolitane. (Russi, M.) Napoli, 1883.
Arc 1153.95.1 Paleografia e diplomatica e scienze ausiliarie. (Mazzoleni, Jole.) Napoli, 1970.
Arc 1163.36 Paleografia ebraica. (Bernheimer, K.) Firenze, 1924.
Arc 1166.3 La paleografia ed i Raggi di Röntgen. (Brigiuti, R.) Roma, 1899.
Arc 1163.2.25 Paleografía española. (Millares Carlo, A.) Barcelona, 1929. 2v.
Arc 1163.2.21F Paleografía española. (Paluzie y Cantalozella, Esteban.) Barcelona, 1846.
Htn Arc 1163.2.3* Paleografía española. (Terreros y Pando, E.) Madrid, 1758.
Arc 1163.34F Paleografía española. Album. (Garcia Villada, Zacarias.) Barcelona, 1974. 2v.
Arc 1143.2.7 Paleografia greca e latina. (Thompson, Edward Maunde.) Milano, 1899.
Arc 1185.19.3F Paleografia latina diplomatica. Atlas. 3. ed. (Barone, N.) Napoli, 1923.
Arc 1185.19.3 Paleografia latina diplomatica. 3. ed. (Barone, N.) Napoli, 1923.
Arc 1153.69 Paleografia latina e diplomatica. 6. ed. (Zazo, Alfredo.) Napoli, 1946.
Arc 1163.2.9 Paleografía que para inteligencia de les manuscrites. (Tos, Joaquin.) Barcelona, 1820.
Arc 1163.30PF Paleografia si diplomatica Turco-Osmanӑ. (Guboglu, Mihail.) București, 1958.
Arc 1153.6 Paleografía visigoda. (Muñoz y Rivero, J.) Madrid, 1881.
Arc 1153.6.5 Paleografía visigoda. (Muñoz y Rivero, J.) Madrid, 1919.
Arc 1160.209F Paleograficheskie snimki. (Lavrov, P.A.) Sankt Peterburg, n.d.
Arc 1163.3.6 Paleograficheskie snimki. (Savva, archbishop of Tver.) Moskva, 1863.
Arc 1163.3.95 Paleograficheskii al'bom. Leningrad, 1968.
Arc 1148.17 Paleograficheskiia navliudeniia. v.1-2. (Sreznevski, I.I.) Sankt Peterburg, 1876.
Arc 1163.3.90 Paleografiia. Moskva, 1967.
Arc 1138.5.4 Paléographie des chartes. 4. éd. (Chassant, Alphonse.) Paris, 1854.
Arc 1138.5.3 Paléographie des chartes. 5. éd. (Chassant, Alphonse.) Paris, 1862.
Arc 1138.5 Paléographie des chartes. 7. éd. (Chassant, Alphonse.) Paris, 1876.
Arc 1138.5.2 Paléographie des chartes. 8. éd. (Chassant, Alphonse.) Paris, 1885.
Arc 1163.38F Paléographie des écritures cursives en France du 15e au 17e siècle. (Poulle, Emmanuel.) Genève, 1966.
Arc 1153.115 Paléographie du Moyen Age. (Stiennon, Jacques.) Paris, 1973.
Arc 1163.37 La paléographie hébraïque médiévale, Paris, 11-13 septembre 1972. (Colloque International sur la Paléographie Hébraïque Médiévale, Paris, 1972.) Paris, 1974.
Arc 1153.72 Paléographie valdôtaine. v.1-3. (Boson, G.G.) Aoste, 1950-52.
Arc 1163.3.110 Paleohrafiia ukraïns'koho skoiopysii durkoï polovyny XVII st. (Panaskenko, Vira V.) Kyïv, 1974.
Arc 925.50.320 Paleolit Dniprovs'koho Nadporizhzhia. (Smyrnov, Stanislav V.) Kyïv, 1973.
Arc 936.14.210 Paleolit na Gónnym Śląsku. (Kozlowski, Janusz K.) Wrocław, 1964.
Arc 416.42 Paleolit Severnoi, Tsentral'noi i Vostochnoi Azii. (Laricheo, Vitalii E.) Novosibirsk, 1969- 2v.
Arc 925.150.20 Paleolit verkhego podneptovia. (Polikarpovich, Konstantin M.) Minsk, 1968.
Arc 861.7 Paleolithic man in northwest Middlesex. (Brown, J.A.) London, 1887.
Arc 843.186 El paleolítico inferior de Puento Mochs. (Cabré-Aguiló, Juan.) Madrid, 1916.
Arc 770.7 Paléologue, M. Rome, notes d'histoire et d'art. 11. éd. Paris, 1921.
Arc 770.7.5 Paléologue, M. Rome, notes d'histoire et d'art. 22. éd. Paris, 1935.
Htn Arc 1033.12.49*A Paleotti, A. Esplicatione del sacro lenzvolo ove fu involto il Signore. Bologna, 1599.
Arc 1033.12.57 Paleotti, A. Historia de Jesu Christi stigmatibus. Antverpiae, 1616.
Arc 1033.12.50 Paleotti, A. Tableau de mortification...stigmates...Christ...S. Suaire. Paris, 1609.
Arc 1433.2 Palermo. Biblioteca Comunale. Catalogo delle monete arabe. Palermo, 1892.
Arc 1015.215 Palermo sotterranea. (Giovanni, V. di.) Palermo, n.d.
Arc 505.15 Palestijnsche masseben (Opgerichte Steenen). (Groot, J. de.) Groningen, 1913.
Arc 497.48 Palestine, ancient and modern...guide to the Palestinian collection...Royal Ontario Museum. (Needler, W.) Toronto, 1949.
Arc 497.5 Palestine. (Conder, C.R.) London, 1889.
Arc 497.5.3 Palestine. (Conder, C.R.) N.Y., 1889.
Arc 600.12.10F Palestine. Archaeological Museum. A catalogue of Egyptian scarabs by Alan Rowe. La Caire, 1936.
Arc 503.6 Palestine. Department of Antiquities. Quarterly. 1-14,1931-1950 10v.
Arc 503.6.5 Palestine. Department of Antiquities. Quarterly. Index, v.1-14 (1931-1950). Jerusalem, 1964.
Arc 497.71 Palestine before the Hebrews. 1. ed. (Anati, E.) N.Y., 1962.
Arc 501.1.12 Palestine Exploration Fund. Annual. London. 1-6,1911-1953 6v.
Arc 501.1.7 Palestine Exploration Fund. Annual report and accounts with list of subscriptions. 1910-1923
Arc 497.79 Palestine Exploration Fund. World of the Bible. South Kensington, 1965?
Arc 501.1.5 Pamphlet box. Palestine Exploration Fund.
Arc 501.5.2 Palestine Exploration Fund. Thirty years' work in the Holy Land, 1865-1895. (Besant, W.) London, 1895.
Arc 501.1 Palestine exploration quarterly. London. 1,1869+ 67v.
Arc 501.1.2 Palestine exploration quarterly. Index, 1869-1881. London, 1882.
Arc 501.1.3 Palestine exploration quarterly. Index, 1869-1892. London, n.d.
Arc 501.1.4 Palestine exploration quarterly. Index, 1911-1963. London, n.d.
Arc 502.1 Palestine Exploration Society, New York. Statements. N.Y. 1-4,1871-1877 4v.
Arc 502.1.5 Pamphlet box. Palestine Exploration Society, New York.
Arc 435.12F Pâli, Sanskrit and old Canarese inscriptions. (Fleet, J.F.) London, 1878.
Htn Arc 785.40.10* Palladio, A. Le terme dei Romani disegnate. Vicenza, 1797.
Arc 608.7.9 Pallary, P. Instituts pour les recherches préhistoriques. Alger, 1909.
Arc 720.217 Pallastrelli, B. La città d'Umbria. Piacenza, 1864.
Arc 455.2 Pallava antiquites. v.1-2. (Jouveau-Dubreuil, G.) Pondicherry, 1916-18.
Arc 435.2.34F Pallava architecture. (Rea, Alexander.) Madras, 1909.
Htn Arc 785.13.60* Palletus, F. Historia Fori Romani restituto et aucta per Philippum Broidaeum Ariensem. Buaci, 1576.
Arc 400.27 Pallottino, Massimo. Che cos'è l'archeologia. Firenze, 1963.
Arc 726.215 Pallottino, Massimo. Turquinia. Milano, 1959.
Arc 400.13 Pallu de Lessert, A.C. Julien Poinssot; souvenirs 1844-1900. Paris, 1905.
Arc 672.1.135 Palmer, Leonard R. A new guide to the palace of Knossos. London, 1969.
Arc 672.1.110 Palmer, Leonard R. On the Knossos tablets. Oxford, 1963.
Arc 1033.34.1 Palmieri, N. Notizie istoriche delle sacre catene del principe degli apostoli. Orvieto, 1846.
Arc 1033.34.2 Palmieri, N. Notizie istoriche delle sacre catene del principe degli apostoli. n.p., n.d.
Arc 505.2.5F Palmyra; Ergebnisse der Expeditionen von 1902 und 1917. Text and plates. (Wiegand, T.) Berlin, 1932. 2v.
Arc 505.110 Palmyre. (Michalowski, Kazimierz.) Warszawa, 1960. 6v.
Arc 505.2.10 La Palmyrène du Nord-Ouest. Thèse. (Schlumberger, D.) Paris, 1951.
Arc 1016.201 Palustre, L. Le trésor de Trèves. Paris, 1886.
Arc 1163.2.21F Paluzie y Cantalozella, Esteban. Paleografía española. Barcelona, 1846.
Arc 1163.2.22 Paluzie y Cantelozella, Esteban. Escritura y lenguaje de España. Barcelona, 1935.

Arc 66.1.152 Palybe et l'histoire de Biotre. (Feyel, Michel.) Paris, 1942.

Arc 16.5 Památky archeologické. Praha. 37,1953+ 41v.

Arc 405.1.25 Pamiati grafa Alekseia Sergeevicha Uvarova. Kazan, 1885.

Arc 925.50.65 Pam'iatky starodavnoho Prydniprov'ia. (Bondar, M.M.) Kyïv, 1959.

Arc 936.165.10 Pamiatniki drevnego iskusstva Moldavii. (Rikman, Emmanuil A.) Kishinev, 1961.

Arc 925.13.105 Pamiatniki drevneishei cheloveshekoi kul'tury Severo-Zapadnogo Prichernomor'ia. (Boriskovskii, P.I.) Odessa, 1961.

Arc 543.65.15 Pamiatniki epokhi bronzy v Iuzhnom Tadzhikistane. (Mandel'shtam, Anatolii M.) Leningrad, 1968.

Arc 612.48 Pamiatniki kamennogo i bronz. vekov Evrazii. (Akademiia Nauk SSSR. Institut Arkheologii.) Moskva, 1964.

Arc 45.7 Pamiatniki Kirgizstana. Frunze. 1,1970+

Arc 925.13.95 Pamiatniki kolkhidskoi i skifskoi kul'tur v sele kulanurkhva abkhazskoi ASSR. (Trapsh, M.M.) Sukhumi, 1962.

Arc 530.120 Pamiatniki kul'tury...raiona. (Egiazarian, O.) Erevan, 1955.

Arc 943.40 Pamiatniki kul'tury i iskusstva drevnei Ameriki. (Kinzhalov, R.V.) Leningrad, 1958.

Arc 925.60 Pamiatniki material'noi kul'tury Chuvashskoi ASSR. (Khakovskii, V.F.) Cheboksary, 1957.

Arc 925.210 Pamiatniki material'noi kul'tury Penzenskoi oblasti. (Polesskikh, M.R.) Penza, 1960.

Arc 925.9.110 Pamiatniki pis'nu i iazyka narodov Kavkaza i vostochnoi Evropy. (Turchaninov, Georgii F.) Leningrad, 1971.

Arc 936.195.145 Pamphlet vol. Pamphlets on antiquities of Slovakia. 10 pam.

Arc 1348.11 Pamphlets on numismatics. (Phillips, H.) Philadelphia, 1867-83. 4 pam.

Arc 936.172F The Panagynoishte gold treasure. (Venechikov, Ivan.) Sofia, 1961.

Arc 1163.3.110 Panaskenko, Vira V. Paleohrafiia ukraïns'koho skoiopysii durkoï polovyny XVII st. Kyïv, 1974.

Arc 730.200 Pancrazi, G.M. Antichita siciliane spiegate. Naples, 1751. 2v.

Arc 1163.5.20 Pandey, R.B. Indian palaeography. Banaras, 1952.

Arc 1033.12.31 Panegirici sacri a i misterii della S. Sindone. (Buonafede, G.) Asti, 1654.

Arc 1033.12.44 Panegirico della Sacra Sindone. (Lombardo, V.G.) Torino, 1884.

Arc 1033.59 Panegirico di S. Vittoria. (Ferrari, G. de.) Roma, 1850.

Arc 1093.2.13 Paniagua, A. Les monuments mégalithiques. Paris, 1912.

Arc 400.15 Paniagua, A. de. L'âge du renne. Paris, 1926.

Arc 925.321.5 Pankrushev, Grigorii A. Plemena Karelii v epokhu neolita i rannego metalla. Leningrad, 1964.

Arc 655.5 Pannati, Ulrico. L'archeologia in Grecia. Napoli, 1965.

Arc 412.5 Pannell, John Percival Masterman. The technology of industrial archaeology. Newton Abbot, 1966.

Arc 1020.17 Pannelli, D. Ragguaglio della univerzione...dei S.S. Martue. Pesaro, 1751.

Arc 943.31 Panneton, P. Un monde était leur empire. Montréal, 1943.

Arc 925.151.5 Pannii zheleznyi vek Dal'nego Vostoka. v.2- (Derevianko, Anatolii P.) Novosibirsk, 1972-

Arc 87.1.5 Panofka, T.S. Antikenkranz. Berlin, 1845-

Arc 87.1.17 Panofka, T.S. Poseidon Basileus und Athene Sthenias. Berlin, 1857.

Arc 87.1.13 Panofka, T.S. Zur Erklärung der Plinius. Berlin, 1853.

Arc 1020.9.47 Panorama circolari di Roma, deliniato nu 1534. (Rossi, G.B. di.) Roma, 1892.

Arc 1470.22 Pansa, G. La moneta di P. Ovidio Nasone. Milano, 1912.

Arc 1480.27 Pansa, Giovanni. Il tipo.di Roma dei denari consolari. Milano, 1911.

Arc 708.38 Pantazēs, Dēmētrios. Periēgētēs Athēnōn. Athēnai, 1868.

Arc 1020.9.13 Il panteon e la tomba reale monografia. (Baracconi, G.) Roma, 1878. 3 pam.

Arc 750.205 Il pantheon. (Beltzami, L.) Milano, 1898.

Arc 935.15 Panthéon des rochers de Philippes. (Heuzy, Leon.) Paris, n.d.

Arc 87.1.31 Das Pantheon zu Rom. (Adler, F.) Berlin, 1871.

Arc 925.8.50 Pantikapei; Ocherki istorii stolitsy Bospora. (Blavatskii, Vladimir D.) Moskva, 1964.

Htn Arc 720.204* Panvini, O. Antiquitatum veronensium libri VIII. Padua, 1648.

Arc 726.2.25 Panvini, P. Il forestiere alle antichità e curiosità nationali Pozzuoli. Napoli, 1818.

Htn Arc 1020.9.106* Panvinus, Onuphrus. Veronesia fatris...de praecipius urbis. Romae, 1570.

Arc 1153.2.5 Paoli, Cesare. Le abbreviatore nella paleografia latina del Medio Evo. Firenze, 1891.

Arc 1166.2 Paoli, Cesare. Carta di cotone e carta di lino. Firenze, 1885.

Arc 1185.32.2 Paoli, Cesare. Diplomatica. Firenze, 1969.

Arc 1153.2.9 Paoli, Cesare. Grundriss - lateinische Palaeographie. Innsbruck, 1889-95.

Arc 1153.2.15 Paoli, Cesare. Grundriss - lateinische Palaeographie. Innsbruck, 1902.

Arc 1153.2.3 Paoli, Cesare. Grundriss der lateinischen Palaeographie und der Urkundenlehre. Innsbruck, 1885.

Arc 1153.2 Paoli, Cesare. Programma scolastico di paleografia latina. Firenze, 1888.

Arc 1153.2.2 Paoli, Cesare. Programma scolastico di paleografia latina. 3. ed. Firenze, 1901.

Arc 1027.4.9 Paoli. Notizie...S. Feliciano...cimitero di Priscilla. Roma, 1796.

Arc 399.2 Paolo Orsi. (Zaratti-Bianco, Umberto.) n.p., n.d.

Arc 674.10F Papabasileios, G.A. Peri tōn en Euboia archaiōn taphōn. Athēnai, 1910.

Arc 682.8 Papachatzēs, N. Mykēnes kai Tiryntha. Athēnai, 1951.

Arc 1490.5.7 Papadopoli, Nicolo. Le monete di Venezia. pt.1-3. Venezia, 1893-1919. 4v.

Arc 682.40 Papastamos, Dēmētrios. Melische amphoren. Münster, 1970.

Arc 305.10 Papers. (Alliance for the Preservation of Florida Antiquities.) Jacksonville Beach.

Arc 1.5.4A Papers. (American School of Classical Studies at Athens.) Boston. 1-6,1882-1897 6v.

Arc 1.5.25 Papers. (American School of Oriental Research, Jerusalem.)

Arc 1.4 Papers. (Archaeological Institute of America.) Boston. 1-3,1882-1890 4v.

Arc 1.2 Papers. (Archaeological Institute of America.) Boston. 1-5,1881-1890 5v.

Arc 1.1.11 Papers. (Archaeological Institute of America. School of American Archaeology.) Santa Fé. 1-43,1908-1919 3v.

Arc 66.9 Papers. (British School at Rome.) London. 1,1902+ 41v.

Arc 309.15 Papers. (Excavators' Club.) Cambridge, Mass. 1-2,1940-1945

Arc 320.2.9 Papers. (Harvard University. Peabody Museum.) Cambridge. 1,1888+ 66v.

Arc 320.4 Papers. University extension series. (Point Loma, California. School of Antiquity.) Point Loma. 2-12,1915-1921

Arc 1.2.5 Papers. 2nd ed. (Archaeological Institute of America.) Boston. 1,1883

Arc 1.13.10F Papers and monographs. (American Academy, Rome.) Rome.

Arc 1.13.10 Papers and monographs. (American Academy, Rome.) Rome. 1,1919+ 25v.

Arc 543.29 Papers on the ethnology and archaeology of the Malay Peninsula. (Evans, Ivor H.N.) Cambridge, Eng., 1927.

Htn Arc 969.1.9* Papers relative to certain American antiquities. (Sargent, W.) Philadelphia, 1796.

Arc 66.1.133 Les papes et les ducs de Bretagne. (Pocquet, J. du Haut-Jusse.) Paris, 1928. 2v.

Arc 530.1 Paphlagonische Felsengraeber. (Hirschfeld, G.) Berlin, 1885.

Arc 1175.10 I papiri diplomatici. (Marini, G.L.) Roma, 1805.

Arc 530.5 Papodopoulos, A. Phōkaika. Smyrnē, 1899.

Arc 1251.1 Pappadopoulos, G.G. Perigraphē ektypōmatōn archaiōn sphragidolithōn. Athēnai, 1855.

Arc 1020.128F Pappageorgios, P. Un édit de l'empereur Justinien II. Leipzig, 1900.

Arc 1015.5.5 Die Papstgräber und di Cäciliengruf. (Wilpert, J.) Freiburg, 1909.

Arc 1148.25.5 Les papyrus. 1. éd. (Bataille, A.) Paris, 1955.

Arc 1135.200.5 Papyrus Erzherzog Rainer; Führer...Ausstellung. Wien, 1894.

Arc 1148.27 Papyrus grecs d'Apollônos anô. (Rémondon, R.) Le Caire, 1953.

Arc 635.213 Parerga zur alten Kunstgeschichte. (Sittl, C.) Würzburg, 1893.

Arc 608.45F Paribeni, Enrico. Catalogo delle sculture di Cirene. Roma, 1959.

Arc 785.34.13 Paribeni, R. Ara Pacis Augustae. Roma, 1932.

Arc 628.27 Paribeni, R. Filologia classica. Milano, 1945.

Arc 785.13.205 Paribeni, R. I fori imperiali. Roma, 1930.

Arc 815.18F Paribeni, R. Pompei. n.p., 1902.

Arc 1053.19F Paribeni, R. Il ritratto nell'arte antica. Milano, 1934.

Arc 726.24.15 Paribeni, R. The villa of the emperor Hadrian at Tivoli. Milan, 1930?

Arc 1033.17.152 Paris, L. Chapelle dans la Cathédrale de Reims. Epernay, 1885.

Arc 66.1.60 Paris, P. Elatée. Paris, 1892.

Arc 838.4 Paris, Pierre. Essai sur l'art et l'industrie de l'Espagne primitive. Paris, 1903. 2v.

Arc 843.58 Paris, Pierre. Fouilles dans la région d'Alcañis, province de Teruel. Bordeaux, 1926.

Arc 838.5 Paris, Pierre. Promenades archéologiques en Espagne. Paris, 1910-1921. 2v.

Arc 31.3 Paris. Musée Guimet. Bulletin archéologique. Paris. 1,1921

Arc 1500.59 Paris. Musée Monétaire et des Médailles. Entente cordiale. v.1-2. Paris, 1957.

Arc 493.40F Paris. Musée National du Louvre. Fouilles de Chapour. v.2. Paris, 1956.

Arc 547.4.10 Paris. Musée Nationale du Louvre. Département des Antiquités Égyptiennes. Notice sommaire des monuments égyptiens. Paris, 1873.

Arc 936.14.45 Paris. Université. Les origines de l'etat polonais. Paris, 1961.

Arc 388.10 Paris. Université. Institut de Civilisation. Pierre Dupont. Paris, 1955.

Arc 820.215F Paris ancien, Paris moderne. (Maupercher.) Paris, 1814.

Arc 830.325 Paris antique des origines au troisième siécle. (Duval, Paul M.) Paris, 1961.

Arc 1490.30 Parisio, Prospero. Rariora magnae Graeciae numismata...1592. n.p., 1683.

Arc 968.1.9 Parker, A.C. Excavations in an Erie Indian village. n.p., 1907.

Arc 861.13.5 Parker, C.A. The ancient crosses at Gosforth, Cumberland. London, 1896.

Arc 861.77.5 Parker, C.A. The Gosforth district. Kendal, 1926.

Arc 770.1 Parker, J.H. The archaeology of Rome. v.1-2, 4-11. Oxford, 1874. 12v.

Arc 770.2 Parker, J.H. Catalogue of a series of photographs illustrative of the archaeology of Rome. n.p., 1867.

Arc 785.8 Parker, J.H. The Colosseum at Rome. London, 1882.

Arc 770.2.5 Parker, J.H. De variis structurarum generibus penes romanos veteres. Romae, 1868.

Arc 770.1.5 Parker, J.H. Description of the plan of Rome. Oxford, 1878.

Arc 770.2.2 Pamphlet vol. Parker, J.H. Antiquities of Rome in danger. 6 pam.

Arc 1163.17.30 Parkes, Malcolm Beckwith. English cursive book hands, 1250-1500. Oxford, 1969.

Arc 861.56 Parkin, Charles. An answer to...Dr. Stukeley's Origines Roystonianae. London, 1744. 2 pam.

Arc 400.7 Parkyn, E.A. An introduction to the study of prehistoric art. London, 1915.

Arc 543.7.50 Parmentier, H. L'art khmèr primitif. Paris, 1927. 2v.

Arc 543.5 Parmentier, H. Inventaires des monuments Čams de l'Annam. Paris, 1909. 2v.

Arc 726.240 Paroscandola, A. I fenomeni fra disisneici del Serapeo di pozzuoli. Napoli, 1947.

Arc 925.50.355 Parovich-Peshikan, Maia. Nekropol' Ol'vii ellinisticheskogo vremeni. Kiev, 1974.

Arc 505.5.35 Parrat, André. Le Temple de Jérusalem. Neuchâtel, 1954.

Arc 416.23 Parrot, A. Découverte des mondes ensevelés. Neuchâtel, 1952.

Arc 416.23.5 Parrot, A. Discovering buried worlds. 1. ed. N.Y., 1955.

Arc 505.59 Parrot, André. Mari, une ville perdue...et retrouvée par l'archéologie française. Paris, 1936.

Arc 505.39.12 Parrot, André. Samaria. N.Y., 1958.

Arc 505.39.10 Parrot, André. Samarie. Neuchatel, 1955.

Arc 1025.38 Partenio, G.M. Vie sacre. 2a ed. Roma, 1806-07. 2v.

Arc 712.19 The Parthenon. (Fergusson, J.) London, 1883.

Arc 712.11 Le Parthénon. (Magne, L.) Paris, 1895.

Arc 712.7 Le Parthénon. (Marchal.) Paris, 1864.

Arc 712.9 Der Parthenon. Ein Vortag. (Fielitz, W.) Stralsund, 1871.

Arc 705.15A Der Parthenon. Text and atlas. (Michaelis, A.) Leipzig, 1871. 2v.

Arc 712.21A The Parthenon and other Greek temples. (Hambidge, Jay.) New Haven, 1924.

Arc 712.8 The Parthenon frieze and other essays. (Davidson, T.) London, 1882.

Arc 712.30 Parthenon-Ostgiebel. (Berger, Ernst.) Bonn, 1959.

Arc 712.34 Der Parthenonfries. (Buschor, E.) München, 1961.

Arc 712.16 Parthenons Kvindefigurer. (Hertz, A.P.) n.p., 1905.

Arc 712.23 Parthenonstudien. (Praschniker, C.) Augsburg, 1928.

Arc 340.37 A partial bibliography of the archaeology of Pennsylvania and adjacent states. (Frontier Forts and Trails Survey.) Harrisburg, 1941.

Arc 1433.38.10F Paruck, F.D.J. Sassanian coins. Bombay, 1924.

Arc 1485.6 Paruta, F. Sicilia numismatica. v.1-3. Lugdunum Batavorum, 1723. 2v.

Arc 936.20.65 Pârvan, Vasile. Dacia. București, 1972.

Arc 936.20 Pârvan, Vasile. Dacia. Cambridge, 1928.

Arc 936.20.30 Pârvan, Vasile. Inseputurite vietii romane. București, 1923.

Arc 936.205F Pašalić, E. Antička naselja i komunikacije u Bosni i Hercegovini. Sarajevo, 1960.

Arc 493.30 Pasargadae. (Sami, A.) Shiraz, 1956.

Arc 657.2 Pasch van Krienen. Abdruck seiner italienischer Beschreibung des griechisches Archipelagus. Halle, 1860.

Arc 672.1 Pashley, R. Travels in Crete. Cambridge, 1837. 2v.

Arc 1030.25 Pasini, P. Sovra un'antica lapida cristiana. n.p., 1843.

Arc 935.5 Paspati, A.G. Byzantinai meletai topographikai kai istorikai. Konstantinople, 1877.

Arc 387.13.10 Pasquali, G. Storia dello spirito tedesco. Firenze, 1953.

Arc 1027.27.5 Pasquini, G. Relazione...cimitero di cristiani. Montepulciano, 1833.

Arc 547.5 Passalacqua, J. Catalogue des antiquités découvertes en Egypte. Paris, 1826.

Arc 757.6 Passeggiate nella Roma antica. (Caetani Lovatelli, E.) Roma, 1909.

Arc 400.18 Passemard, L. (Mme). Les statuettes feminines paléolithiques dites venus stéatophyges. Thèse. Nimes, 1938.

Arc 726.66 Passeri, G.B. De marmoreo sepulcrali cinerario. Romae, 1773.

Arc 1070.205 Passeri, J.B. Lucernae futiles Musei Passerii. Pisauri, 1739-51. 3v.

Arc 1020.6.3 Passini, A. Sul frontale dell'altar maggiore in San Marco. Venezia, 1881.

Arc 1020.6.7 Passini, A. Il tesoro di San Marco in Venezia. Venezia, 1878.

Arc 1033.62.7 Passio Sanctarum Perpetuae et Felicitatis. (Perpetua, Saint Legend.) Noviomagi, 1936.

Arc 1033.166 La passio Ss. Mariani et Iacobi. Roma, 1900.

Arc 1033.99 La passione di Cristo. (Carini, Isidoro.) Milano, 1894.

Arc 1033.53.23 Les passions de S. Maurice d'Agaune. (Dupraz, Louis.) Fribourg, 1961.

Arc 1033.3.45 Die Passionssarkophage. (Campenhausen, Hans von.) Marburg, 1929.

Arc 397.2 The past in the present. (Mitchell, A.) Edinburgh, 1880.

Arc 925.50.80 Pasternak, I. Arkheolohiia Ukraïny. Toronto, 1961.

Arc 925.50.220 Pasternak, Iaroslav. Staryi Halych. Krakiv, 1944.

Arc 823.7 Pasumot, Francois. Dissertations et mémoires sur differens sujets d'antiquité et d'histoire. Paris, 1810-1813.

Arc 823.7.5 Pasumot, Francois. Mémoires géographiques sur quelques antiquités de la Gaule. Paris, 1765. 2 pam.

Arc 1053.7.5 Patarolo, Lorenzo. Opera omnia. Venetiis, 1743. 2v.

Htn Arc 1053.6.9* Patarolo, Lorenzo. Series Augustorum, Augustarum, Caesarum. Venetiis, 1702.

Arc 1053.6.12 Patarolo, Lorenzo. Series Augustorum, Augustarum, Caesarum. 3. ed. Venetiis, 1740.

Arc 1053.7 Patarolo, Lorenzo. Series Augustorum, Augustarum, Caesarum. 4. ed. Venetiis, 1743.

Arc 733.4.5 Paterno, I.V. Viaggio per tutte le antichita della Sicilia. 3a ed. Palermo, 1817.

Arc 830.137 Pathier, Edgard L.F. Les tumulus du plateau de Ger. Paris, 1900.

Arc 441.22 Patil, Devendrakumar Rajaram. The antiquarian remains in Bihar. Patna, 1963.

Htn Arc 1475.4* Patin, C. Familiae Romanae. Paris, 1663.

Arc 1475.4.5 Patin, C. Imperatorum romanorum numismata. Paris, 1697.

Arc 1370.1 Patin, C. Thesaurus numismatum. Amsterdam? 1672.

Htn Arc 1370.2* Patin, C. Thesaurus numismatum. v.1-2. Amsterdam? 1672.

Arc 1675.45 Patin, Charles. Introduction à l'histoire par la connoissance des medailles. Paris, 1665.

Arc 1033.17.455 Patiño, P.P. Disertación crítico-theo-filosófica sobre la conservación de la santa imagen de Nuestra Señora de los Angeles. México, 1801.

Arc 716.7.10F Paton, James M. The Erechtheum. Cambridge, 1927.

Arc 716.7.10PF Paton, James M. The Erechtheum. Atlas. Cambridge, 1927.

Arc 505.5.60 Paton, Lewis B. Jerusalem in Bible times. Chicago, 1913.

Arc 1675.99 Patrignani, Antonio. Le medaglie di Leone XII, 1823-1829. Catania, 1938.

Arc 1490.90 Patrignani, Antonio. Le medaglie di Pio VII, 1829-1830. Catania, 1933.

Arc 1663.45 Patriotic Civil War tokens. (Fuld, George.) Racine, 1960.

Arc 1033.17.223 La patrona de Barcelona y su santuario. (Gazulla, F.D.) Barcelona, 1918.

Arc 723.25.5 Patroni, G. La preistoria. Milano, 1951. 2v.

Arc 723.25 Patroni, G. Storia politica d'Italia. Milano, 1937. 2v.

Arc 905.19 Patsch, Carl. Bosnien und Herzegowina in Römischer Zeit. Sarajevo, 1911.

Arc 1030.53 Patten, A.W. Early Christian inscriptions in the Bennett Museum of Christian archaeology. Evanston, 1915.

Arc 618.10 Pattern and purpose. (Fox, Cyril.) Cardiff, 1958.

Arc 1423.26 The patterns of monetary development in Phoenicia and Palestine in antiquity. (International Numismatic Convention, Jerusalem, 1963.) Tel-Aviv, 1967.

Arc 600.90F Paujade, J. Trois flottilles de la VIIème dynastie des pharaons. Djibouti, 1948.

Arc 497.104 Paul, Sholom. Biblical archaeology. Jerusalem, 1973.

Arc 1033.20.19 Paulinus a S. Barthol. De Basilica S. Paneratii M. Christi. Roma, 1703.

Arc 895.46 Paulsen, P. Schwertartbänder der Wikingerzeit. Stuttgart, 1953.

Arc 726.2.15 Pausilypon...imperial villa near Naples. (Günther, R.T.) Oxford, 1913.

Arc 1030.8.17 Pauthier, G. L'inscription syro-chinois de Si-Ngan-Fou. Paris, 1858. 2 pam.

Arc 936.223 Pavlovič, L. Neki spomenici kulture; osvrti i Zapožanja. v.1-2. Smedrevo, 1962- 3v.

Arc 843.208 Pavón Maldonado, Basilio. Memoria de la excavación de la Mezquita de Medinat al-Zahra. Madrid, 1966.

Arc 861.65 Payne, George. Collectanea cantiana. London, 1893.

Arc 672.5.15F Payne, H. Perachora, the sanctuaries of Hera Akraia and Lemenia. Oxford, 1940. 2v.

Arc 1020.107 Payne, J.O. St. Paul's Cathedral...account of the treasures. London, 1893.

Arc 403.16.30 Payne, R. The gold of Troy. N.Y., 1959.

Arc 1500.24 Le pays des Bellovaques. Essai...numismatique. (Leblond, V.) Caen, 1906.

Arc 925.38 Pazyrykskii kurgan. (Griaznov, M.P.) Moskva, 1937.

Arc 967.4 Peabody, Charles. The exploration of Bushey Cavern near Cavetown, Maryland. Andover, 1908.

Arc 967.2.5 Peabody, Charles. The exploration of Jacobs Cavern, McDonald County, Missouri. Norwood, 1904.

Arc 983.8 Peabody, Charles. The so called "gorgets". Andover, 1906.

Arc 1010.10 Peabody Museum of Salem, Salem, Massachusetts. The Hervey Islands adzes in the Peabody Museum of Salem. Salem, 1937.

Arc 865.27 Peach, Wystan A. Stonehenge; a new theory. Cardiff, 1961.

Arc 861.91 Peake, Harold. The archaeology of Berkshire. London, 1931.

Arc 400.11.20 Peake, Harold J.E. The horse and the sword. New Haven, 1933.

Arc 400.11 Peake, Harold J.E. Hunters and artists. New Haven, 1927.

Arc 400.11.10 Peake, Harold J.E. Merchant venturers in bronze. New Haven, 1931.

Arc 400.11.30 Peake, Harold J.E. Times and places. Oxford, 1956.

Arc 974.2 Pearce, J.E. A prehistoric rock shelter in Val Verde County, Tennessee. Austin, Texas, 1933.

Arc 444.1.10 Pearse and Company, ltd. Pearse guide to Elephanta, or Gharapuri. Devonport, 1884.

Arc 444.1.10 Pearse guide to Elephanta, or Gharapuri. (Pearse and Company, ltd.) Devonport, 1884.

Arc 861.199.1 Pearson, Frederick Richard. Roman Yorkshire. 1. ed. Wakefield, 1973.

Arc 1285.30.10 Pamphlet vol. "Pečete". 2 pam.

Arc 1285.30.5 Pečeti v českých zemích a jejich cena jako dějepisného pramene. (Beneš, František.) Praha, 1949.

Arc 688.6.7 The pedimental sculpture of the Hieron. (Lehmann, Phyllis.) N.Y., 1962.

Arc 843.20 A pedra dos namorados. (Rocha Peixoto, A.A. da.) Porto, 1903. 4 pam.

Arc 1274.3.5 Pedrick, G. Borough seals of the Gothic period. London, 1904.

Arc 1274.3 Pedrick, G. Monastic seals of the XIIIth century. London, 1902.

Htn Arc 1475.12F* Pedrusi, Paolo. I Cesari in oro. Parma, 1694-1727. 10v.

Arc 785.64 Peebles, Bernard M. La "Meta Romuli" e una lettera di Michele Ferno. Roma, 1936.

Arc 875.56 Peeblesshire: an inventory of the ancient monuments. (Great Britain. Commissions. Ancient and Historical Monuments of Scotland.) Edinburgh, 1967. 2v.

Arc 983.4 Peet, S.D. Ancient village architecture in America. n.p., n.d.

Arc 977.1 Peet, S.D. The emblematic mounds of Wisconsin. n.p., n.d.

Arc 953.8 Peet, S.D. Prehistoric America. v.1, The mound builders. v.3, Cliff dwellers. v.4, Ancient monuments. v.5, Myths and symbols. Chicago, 1890-1905. 4v.

Arc 585.27 Peet, T.E. The cemeteries of Abydos. London, 1913-14. 3v.

Arc 723.10A Peet, T.E. Stone and bronze ages in Italy and Sicily. Oxford, 1909.

Arc 1093.2.17 Pei Wen Chung. Le rôle des phénomènes naturels dans l'éclatement. Thèse. Paris, 1936.

Arc 830.18.7 Peigné-Delacourt, A. Recherche sur divers lieux du pays des Silvanectes. Amiens, 1864.

Arc 830.37 Peigné-Delacourt, A. Recherches sur le lieu...bataille d'Attila en 451. Paris, 1860. 2v.

Arc 1093.2.9F Peigne-Delacourt, M. Un tranche-tête. Paris, 1866.

Arc 1166.4 Peignot, G. Essai sur l'histoire du parchemin. Paris, 1812.

Htn Arc 1153.60* Peignot, G. Lettres à M.C.N. Amanton sur deux manuscrits précieux des temps de Charlemagne. Dijon, 1829.

Arc 66.1.10 Peinture et sculpture chrétiennes en Orient. (Bayet, C.) Paris, 1879.

Arc 815.26.2 La peinture pompéienne; essai sur l'évolution de sa signification. (Schefold, Karl.) Bruxelles, 1972.

Arc 1033.70.13 Peintures inédites de L'Église St. Nicolas. (Lefort, L.) Paris, 1879.

Arc 785.45.5 Peintures médiévales dans le temple de la Fortune Virile à Rome. (Lafontaine, Jacqueline.) Bruxelles, 1959.

Arc 608.33.5 Les peintures rupestres du Tassili-n-Ajjer. (Neukom, Tolantha T.) Neuchâtel, 1956.

Arc 1033.53.22 Peissard, N. La découverte du tombeau du tombeau de St. Maurice. St. Maurice, 1922.

Arc 1480.42.15 Pekary, Thomas. Die Fundmünzen von Vindonissa von Hadrian bis zum Ausgang der Römerherrschaft. Brugg, 1971.

Arc 785.83.5 Pekáry, Thomas. Untersuchungen zu den römischer Reichsstrassen. Bonn, 1968.

Arc 530.171 Pekmon, A. Son kari ve arasturmalann i syei altinda Penge tanhi. Ankara, 1973.

Arc 1033.35.153 Pel giorno dell'invenzione di S. Croce, 1848. (Gualzetti, G.B.) Milano, 1848.

Arc 936.180.5 Pelagonija u svetlosti arheoloških nalaza. (Mikulčić, Ivan.) Beograd, 1966.

Arc 710.11 Das Pelargikon. (Köster, A.) Strasburg, 1909.

Arc 1027.14 Pelerinage au cauc du Pape S. Alexandre I. (Billaud, Pelissier B.) Rome, 1856.

Arc 608.2.10 Un pélerinage aux ruines de Carthage. (Delattre, R.P.) Lyon, 1906.

Arc 1033.17.136 Pélérinage de la sainte ceinture au Puy-Notre Dame. (Bédouet, Z.) Paris, n.d.

Arc 1033.17.201 Pélérinage de Notre-Dame d'Arcachon. (Mouls, X.) Bordeaux, 1857.

Arc 825.3 Pelet, Auguste. Description de l'amphithéâtre de Nîmes. Nîmes, 1853.

Arc 825.3.1 Pelet, Auguste. Description de l'amphithéâtre de Nîmes. 2e éd. Nîmes, 1859. 9 pam.

Arc 825.3.2 Pelet, Auguste. Description de l'amphithéâtre de Nîmes. 3e éd. Nîmes, 1866.

Arc 936.15.20 Pelikan, 'Old. Slovensko a rémske impérium. Bratislava, 1960.

Arc 66.1.75 Pélissier, L.G. Louis XII et Ludovic Sforza. Paris, 1896. 3v.

Arc 1033.28 Pelka, O. Altchristliche Ehredenkmäler. Strassburg, 1901.

Arc 505.153 Pella of the Decapolis. (College of Wooster Expedition to Pella.) Wooster, 1973-

Arc 1020.9.90 Pellegrini, A. Anni storici intorno ad una basilica di S. Pietro in Campo di Mirlo. Roma, 1860.

Author and Title Listing

Arc 785.39.45 Pellegrini, A. Scavi nelle terme di Novato ed in altri luoghi di Roma. Roma, 1870.

Arc 1027.50 Pellegrini, C. Il pensiero e il dogma cristiano. n.p., n.d.

Arc 1033.12.36 Pellegrini, C. Sermone sulla SS. Sindone di Torino. Torino, 1844.

Arc 1033.17.325 Il Pellegrino al Gargano...di San Michele. (Cavalieri, M.) Napoli, 1690.

Arc 1370.4.3 Pellerin, J. Mélange de diverses médailles. Paris, 1765. 2v.

Arc 1370.4.2 Pellerin, J. Recueil de médailles de peuples. Paris, 1763. 3v.

Arc 1370.4 Pellerin, J. Recueil de médailles de rois. Paris, 1762.

Arc 1370.4.4 Pellerin, J. Suppléments aux six volumes. Paris, 1767.

Arc 830.119.10 Pellerin, Pierre. En ressuscitant Vaison-la-Romaine. Paris, 1962.

Arc 1033.84 Pellino, G. Trattenimento...S. Igino Papa e Martire. Napoli, 1831.

Arc 543.4.25F Pelliot, Paul. Toumchoug. v.2. Paris, 1961-1964.

Arc 1153.94 Pelzer, Auguste. Abréviations latines médiévales. Louvain, 1964.

Htn Arc 1350.5F* Pembroke, T.H. Numismata antiqua. London, 1746.

Arc 971.5 Pendergast, James F. Cartier's Hochelaga and the Dawson site. Montreal, 1972.

Arc 565.3 Pendlebury, J.D.S. Aegyptiaca. Cambridge, Eng., 1930.

Arc 672.1.28.5 Pendlebury, J.D.S. The archaeology of Crete. London, 1939.

Arc 672.1.28.6 Pendlebury, J.D.S. The archaeology of Crete. N.Y., 1963.

Arc 672.1.28 Pendlebury, J.D.S. Handbook to the palace of Minos at Knossos. London, 1933.

NEDL Arc 672.1.28.10 Pendlebury, J.D.S. Hodēgos tōn minoikou anaktoro tēs knōsa. Hēraklei, 1950.

Arc 1033.59.5 Pennesi, A. Cenni storici sul culto di S. Vittoria. S. Vittoria, 1893.

Arc 1528.14 Penningen. (Frederiks, J.W.) Amsterdam, 1947.

Arc 1490.8.10 Pennisi, Agostino. Siciliae veteres nummi. Acireale, 1940.

Arc 320.1.27 Pennsylvania. University. Museum of American Archaeology. Annual report of the curator. Philadelphia. 1,1890

Arc 320.1.21 Pennsylvania. University. University Museum. Bulletin. Philadelphia. 1-3 2v.

Arc 726.69F Pennsylvania. University. University Museum. Excavations at Minturnae. Rome, 1933-35. 2v.

Arc 16.1 Pennsylvania. University. University Museum. Transactions. Paris. 1-2,1904-1907

Arc 584.6F Pennsylvania-Yale Expedition to Egypt. Publications. New Haven. 1,1963+ 4v.

Arc 726.265 Pennucci, Umberto. Bisenzo e le antiche civiltà intorno al lago di Bolsena. Grotte di Castro, 1964.

Arc 1027.50 Il pensiero e il dogma cristiano. (Pellegrini, C.) n.p., n.d.

Arc 681.15.5 The people of Lerna. (Angel, John Lawrence.) Princeton, N.J., 1971.

Arc 1160.201 Peper, P. Otfrid...Weissenburg. Schreiber XIX Jahrhundert. Frankfurt, 1899.

Arc 385.16 Pequena história de uma vida gloriosa [Francisco M. Aloes]. (Felgueiros, Francisco.) Bragança, 1965.

Arc 726.42.5 Per i monumenti e per la storia di Ravenna. (Savini, Gaetano.) Ravenna, 1914.

Arc 1033.17.303 Per la icona vetere di Maria sma. Venerata in Foggia. Napoli, 1850.

Arc 726.38 Per l'archeologia del territorio albese. (Marchisio, A.F.) Alba, 1913.

Arc 1027.25.13 Per un busto...G.B. de Rossi. (Cozza, Luzi G.) Roma, 1883- 3 pam.

Arc 785.57 Per un centro di studi di archeologia dell'Impero Romano. (Bologna. Università.) Bologna, 1932.

Arc 726.23 Per un ricordo al padre L. Bruzza. (Vercelli, C. di.) Vercelli, 1884.

Arc 723.26 Per una esposizione di etnografia italiana in Roma nel 1911. 2a ed. (Comitato esecutivo per le fete del 1911, Rome.) Firenze, 1909.

Arc 1033.12.161 Pera, P. Della lampada d'oro offerta dai Lucchssi al volto santo. Lucca, 1836. 2 pam.

Arc 672.5.15F Perachora, the sanctuaries of Hera Akraia and Lemenia. (Payne, H.) Oxford, 1940. 2v.

Arc 1018.3 Pératé, A. L'archéologie chrétienne. Paris, 1892.

Arc 391.6 Percy Gardner, 1846-1937. (Hill, George.) London, 1937.

Arc 66.1.101 Perdrizet, P. La vierge de miséricorde. Paris, 1908.

Arc 1588.14 Pere, Nuri. Osmanhlarda madeni paralar. Istanbul, 1968.

Arc 543.66.50 Perechen' opublikovannykh rabot i materialov po tematike Iuzhno-Turkmenistanskoi Arkheologicheskoi Kompleksnoi Ekspeditsii. (Iuzhno-Turkmenistanskaia Arkheologicheskaia Ekspeditsiia, 1946-.) Ashkhabad, 1970.

Arc 843.18 Pereira, Gabriel. Notas d'archeologia. Erora, 1879.

Arc 835.205F Pereira da Costa, Francisco. Noções sobre o estado prehistorico de terra e do homein. Lisboa, 1868. 2v.

Arc 1493.20 Perelada, Spain. Castillo de los Condes de Perelada. Museo. Monetario. Perelada, 1957.

Htn Arc 1420.2F* Pérez Báyer, F. F. Perezii Bayerii. De numis hebraeo-samaritanis. Valentia, 1781.

Arc 1033.38.15 Pérez Báyes, F. Damascus et Laurentius. Rome, 1756.

Arc 1668.8 Perez Varela, H. Ensayo de un catalogo...de las medallas. Habana, 1863.

Arc 510.214 Pergame restauration des monuments de l'Aropole. (Collignon, M.) Paris, 1900.

Arc 520.3 Pergamon. (Conze, A.) Berlin, 1880.

Arc 520.19.5 Pergamon. (Kähler, Heinz.) Berlin, 1949.

Arc 520.9 Pergamon. (Schmidt.) Lübeck, 1899.

Arc 520.35 Pergamon: Burgberg und Altar. 2. Aufl. (Rohde, Elisabeth.) Berlin, 1961.

Arc 520.8 Pergamon. Pflanzstätte Hellenisches Kunst. (Hachtmann, K.) Gütersloh, 1900.

Arc 520.5 Pergamon - Geschichte und Kunst. (Urlichs, L.) Leipzig, 1883.

Arc 520.30 Der Pergamon Altar. (Humann, Karl.) Dortmund, 1959.

Arc 520.13 Pergamon und seine Kunst. (Schwabe, L. von.) Tubingen, 1882.

Arc 510.213 Pergamos seine Geschichte und Monumente. (Ussing, J.L.) Berlin, 1899

Arc 530.51F Pergede kazilar'ne arastumalar. (Mansel, A.M.) Ankara, 1949.

Arc 1254.5 Peri byzantinōn molybdoboyllōn. (Mordtmann, A.D.) n.p., n.d.

Arc 674.10F Peri tōn en Euboia archaiōn taphōn. (Papabasileios, G.A.) Athēnai, 1910.

Arc 655.1 Peri tou pōs graphontai ta tōn araskaphōn. (Philios, Demetrios.) Athēnai, 1890.

Arc 838.32 Pericat y Garcia, Luis. La España primiva. Barcelona, 1950.

Arc 710.19FA The Periclean entrance court of the acropolis of Athens. (Stevens, G.P.) Cambridge, 1936.

Arc 843.234.4 Pericot Garcia, Luis. The Balearic Islands. London, 1972.

Arc 708.38 Periēgētēs Athēnōn. (Pantazēs, Dēmētrios.) Athēnai, 1868.

Arc 830.182 Le périgord préhistorique. (Peyrony, D.) Perigneux, 1949.

Arc 1251.1 Perigraphē ektypōmatōn archaiōn sphragidolithōn. (Pappadopoulos, G.G.) Athēnai, 1855.

Arc 1490.19 Perini, L. La repubblica di San Marino sue monete medaglie decorazioni. Roverto, 1900.

Arc 1490.27.5 Perini, Quintilio. Le monete di Verona. Rovereto, 1902.

Arc 1490.27 Perini, Quintilio. La repubblica romana del 1849 e le sue monete. Rovereto, 1903.

Arc 830.168 Périodes wisigothique, carolingienne et romane. (Bonnet, E.) Montpellier, 1938.

Arc 1315.5 Periodico di numismatica e sfragistica per la storia d'Italia. (Strozzi, Carlo.) Firenze, 1868-74. 6v.

Arc 1313.15.5 Periodico di numismatica e sfragistica per la storia d'Italia. Firenze. 1-6,1868-1874 3v.

Arc 708.26 Peritou Archaioterou Attikou Ergastēriou. (Sophoules, T.) Athēnai, 1887.

Arc 400.1 Perkins, F.B. Prehistoric man. San Francisco, 1883.

Arc 87.1.56 Pernice, E. Griechisches Pferdegeschirr...Königlichen Museum. Berlin, 1896.

Arc 87.1.58 Pernice, E. Hellenistische Silbergefässe...Königlichen Museum. Berlin, 1898.

Arc 810.32.5 Pernice, Erich. Pompeji. Leipzig, 1926.

Arc 810.32 Pernice, Erich. Pompejiforschung und Archäologie nach dem Kriege. Griefswald, 1920.

Arc 672.1.70 Pernier, Luigi. Guida degli scavi italiani in Creta. Roma, 1947.

Arc 672.1.65F Pernier, Luigi. Il palazzo minoico di Festos. Roma, 1935-51. 3v.

Arc 608.17.19F Pernier, Luigi. Il tempio e l'altare di Apollo a Cirene. Bergamo, 1935.

Arc 723.44 Peroni, Renato. L'età del bronzo nella penisola italiana. Firenze, 1971-

Arc 655.6 Perowne, Stewart. The archaeology of Greece and the Aegean. London, 1974.

Arc 1033.62.7 Perpetua, Saint Legend. Passio Sanctarum Perpetuae et Felicitatis. Noviomagi, 1936.

Arc 870.16 Perran-zabuloe. (Haslam, William.) London, 1844.

Arc 830.344F Perrault, Ernest. Note sur un foyer de l'âge de la Pierre Polie découvert an camp de Chassey en septembre 1869. Chalons-sur-Saône, 1870.

Arc 1663.10 Perreau, A. Recherches sur les comtes de Looz et sur leurs monnaies. Bruxelles, 1845.

Arc 522.30 Perret, J. Les origines de la legende troyenne de Rome. Thèse. Paris, 1942.

Arc 608.22 Perret, Robert. Recherches archéologiques et ethnographiques au Tassili des Ajjers (Sahara Central). Paris, 1936.

Arc 820.200 Perrin, A. Etude préhistorique sur la Savoie. Paris, 1870.

Arc 400.2 Perrot, G. Mémoires d'archéologie. Paris, 1875.

Arc 608.1.27 Perrot, G. La musée du Bardo à Tunis et les fouilles de M. Gauckler. Paris, 1899.

Arc 590.3 Perrot, J.F.A. Essai sur les momies. Nimes, 1844.

Arc 825.9 Perrot, J.F.A. Lettres sur Nismes et le Midi. Nismes, 1840. 2v.

Htn Arc 1540.13* Perry, Francis. Series of English medals. London, 1762.

Arc 543.32 Perry, William J. The megalithic culture of Indonesia. Manchester, 1918.

Arc 1033.47.21 La persecuzione neroniana dei Cristiani. (Coen, J.A.) Firenze, 1900.

Arc 493.2.30 Persepolis, the archaelogy of Parsa. (Wilber, Donald Newton.) N.Y., 1969.

Arc 485.202.5 Persepolis. (Godard, André.) Teheran, 1950.

Arc 493.2.20 Persepolis. (Sami, A.) Shiraz, 1954.

Arc 493.2.10F Persepolis. (Schmidt, E.F.) Chicago, 1953-70. 3v.

Arc 493.2.5 Persepolis. 2. ed. (Sami, A.) Shiraz, 1955.

Arc 485.202 Persepolis illustrata. London, 1739.

X Cg Arc 1433.33 Perses achemenides les satrapes. (Babelon, E.) Paris, 1893.

Arc 488.30 Persia; an archaeological guide. (Matheson, Sylvia A.) London, 1972.

Arc 726.3 Persichetti, N. Viaggio archeologico sulla Via Salaria. Roma, 1893.

Arc 530.173 Person, Kenneth. The Dorak affair. N.Y., 1968.

Arc 682.13F Persson, A.W. The royal tombs at Dendra near Midea. Lund, 1931.

Arc 790.204 Persuhn, E. Pompeji. Leipzig, 1878-82. 2v.

Arc 1033.45 Persus, L. de. Del pontificato di S. Sisto I. Alatri, 1884.

Arc 875.19 Perthia Romana: line or chain of forts erected by Agricola. (Barclay, A.) Perth, 1883.

Arc 1335.83 Pertusi, G., firm, auctioneer, Milan. Catalogo della collezione A. Ancona di Milano. Milano, 1892.

Arc 1175.3 Pertz, G.H. Schrifttafeln zum Gebrauch bei diplomatischen Vorlesungen. Hannover, 1844.

Arc 716.8 Pervanoglu, P. Die Grabsteine der alten Griechen. Leipzig, 1863.

Arc 543.66.30 Pervobytnaia kul'tura i vorniknovenie oroshaemogo zemledeliia v mizov'iakh Zara Fsbana. (Guliamov, Iukliia G.) Tashkend, 1966.

Arc 925.9.151 Pervobytnoe obshchestvo na territorii Abkhazii. Photoreproduction. (Solov'ev, L.N.) Sukhumi, 1971.

Arc 925.165 Pervobytnoe obshchestvo na territorii nashei strang. (Datsiak, B.D.) Moskva, 1954.

Arc 543.132 Pervobytnoe proshloe B'etnama. (Boriskovskii, Pavel Io.) Leningrad, 1966.

Arc 925.328 Pervobytnye liudi na Kol'skom poluostrove. (Vitkov, Z.A.) Murmansk, 1960.

Arc 925.50.93 Pervobytnyi period v istorii Nizhego Dnepra. (Miller, Mykhailo O.) Miunkhen, 1965.

Arc 925.17 Pervobytnyia drevnosti. (Veselovskii, N.I.) Tuapse, 1904.

Arc 925.38.5 Pervyi pazyrykskii kurgan. (Griaznov, M.P.) Leningrad, 1950.

Arc 608.30F Pesce, G. Il tempio d'Iside in Sabratha. Roma, 1953.

Arc 600.120 Pesce, Gennaro. Il Palazzo delle calonne in Talemaide di Cirenaria. Roma, 1950.

Arc 726.205F Pesce, Gennaro. I rilievi dell'anfiteatro Campano. Roma, 1941.

Arc 726.195 Pesce, Gennaro. Sarcafagi romani di Sardegna. Roma, 1957.

Arc 726.246 Pesce, Gennaro. Sardegna punica. Cagliari, 1961.

Arc 726.248 Pesce, Gennaro. Le statuette puniche di Bithia. Roma, 1965.

Arc 726.290 Pesce, Gennaro. Tharros. Cagliari, 1966.
Arc 925.187 Peshchernyi ansambl' Vardzia, 1156-1213 gg. (Gaprindashvili, Givi M.) Tbilisi, 1960.
Arc 935.31.5 Peshckery Ani. (Kipshidze, David A.) Erevan, 1972.
Arc 936.29.5F Peshterata Mirezlivka. (Popov, R.) Sofiia, 1933.
Arc 936.29 Peshterata Temnata dupka. (Popov, R.) Sofiia, 1936.
Arc 936.195.235 Peškař, Ivan. Fibeln aus der römischen Kaiserzeit in Mähren. Prag, 1972.
Arc 1510.34 Pestilantia in nummis. (Pfeiffer, L.) Tübingen, 1882.
Arc 861.190 Peterborough New town. (Great Britain. Commissions. Ancient and Historical Monuments and Constructions of England.) London, 1969.
Arc 87.2.69 Peters, F. Burg-Kapelle zu Iben. Bonn, 1869.
Arc 497.23 Peters, John B. Bible and spade. N.Y., 1922.
Arc 500.8 Peters, John P. Painted tombs in the necropolis of Marissa. London, 1905.
Arc 712.2 Petersen, C. Die Feste der Pallas Athene in Athen. Hamburg, 1855.
Arc 400.5 Petersen, C. Ueber dea Verhaltniss des Broncealters. Hamburg, 1868.
Arc 750.206 Petersen, E. Ara Pacis Augustae. Wien, 1902. 2v.
Arc 708.25 Petersen, E. Athen. Leipzig, 1908.
Arc 710.9.5 Petersen, E. Die Burgtempel der Athenaia. Berlin, 1907.
Arc 510.201.2 Petersen, E. Reiden in Lykien, Milyas und Kibyratis. Vienna, 1889.
Arc 785.15.5 Petersen, E. Trajans Dakische Kriege. Leipzig, 1899.
Arc 785.30 Petersen, Eugen. Comitium, rostra, Grab des Romulus. Rom, 1904.
Arc 770.6.2 Petersen, Eugen. Vom alten Rom. 2. Aufl. Leipzig, 1900.
Arc 770.6.5 Petersen, Eugen. Vom alten Rom. 3. Aufl. Leipzig, 1904.
Arc 1276.31F Petersen, H. Danske adelige sigiller. København, 1897.
Arc 945.7 Peterson, Clarence S. America's rune stone of A.D. 1362 gains favor. N.Y., 1946.
Arc 1540.33 Petersson, H. Bertil A. Anglo-Saxon currency: King Edgar's reform to the Norman conquest. Lund, 1969.
Arc 830.140 Petit, Ange. Dissertation sur Genabum-Gien. Orléans, 1863.
Arc 830.38.2 Petit album suite au Caranda. (Moreau, Frédéric.) St. Quentin, 1896.
Arc 1027.5.55 Petit guide du cimetière de Domitille. Rome, 1900.
Arc 830.130.25 Petit historique de l'affaire de Glozel. (Morlet, Antonin.) Marsat, 1970.
Arc 1093.2.2 Petit-Radel, L.C.F. Recherches sur les monuments cyclopéens. Paris, 1841.
Arc 815.23F Petra, Giulio de. Le tavolette cerate di Pompei. Roma, 1876.
Arc 497.26F Petra; its history and monuments. (Kennedy, A.B. William.) London, 1925.
Arc 505.92 Petra, the rock city of Edom. (Murray, Margaret A.) London, 1939.
Arc 1020.78 Petracchi, C. Della insigne di S. Stefano di Bologna. Bologna, 1747.
Arc 585.20A Petrie, W.M.F. Abydos. Pt.1-3. London, 1902-04. 3v.
Arc 588.53F Petrie, W.M.F. Ancient Gaza. London, 1931-34. 4v.
Arc 588.39F Petrie, W.M.F. Ancient weights and measures. London, 1926.
Arc 588.51F Petrie, W.M.F. Antaeopolis. London, 1930.
Arc 588.58F Petrie, W.M.F. Anthedon. London, 1937.
Arc 600.191 Petrie, W.M.F. The arts of ancient Egypt. London, 1884.
Arc 588.19 Petrie, W.M.F. Athribis. London, 1908.
Arc 588.48F Petrie, W.M.F. Beth-Pelet. London, 1930-32. 2v.
Arc 588.38F Petrie, W.M.F. Buttons and design scarabs. London, 1925.
Arc 588.64F Petrie, W.M.F. City of shepherd kings. London, 1952.
Arc 585.17A Petrie, W.M.F. Dendereh. 1898. London, 1900.
Arc 585.15A Petrie, W.M.F. Deshashek. 1897. London, 1898.
Arc 585.19 Petrie, W.M.F. Diospolis Parva...1898-99. London, 1901.
Arc 505.22.2 Petrie, W.M.F. Eastern exploration past and future. London, 1918.
Arc 588.60 Petrie, W.M.F. Egyptian architecture. London, 1938.
Arc 585.23A Petrie, W.M.F. Ehnasya. 1904. London, 1905.
Arc 588.66F Petrie, W.M.F. Flinders Petrie centenary...ceremonial slate palettes. London, 1953.
Arc 589.1.3 Petrie, W.M.F. The formation of the alphabet. London, 1912.
Arc 588.59F Petrie, W.M.F. The funeral furniture of Egypt. London, 1937.
Arc 588.43F Petrie, W.M.F. Gerar. London, 1928.
Arc 588.18 Petrie, W.M.F. Gizeh and Rifeh. London, 1907.
Arc 588.40F Petrie, W.M.F. Glass stamps and weights. London, 1926.
Arc 588.25A Petrie, W.M.F. Hawara portfolio; paintings. London, 1913.
Arc 588.27 Petrie, W.M.F. Heliopolis. London, 1915.
Arc 588.26 Petrie, W.M.F. Heliopolis. London, 1915.
Arc 588.23 Petrie, W.M.F. Historical studies. London, 1911.
Arc 588.17 Petrie, W.M.F. Hyksos and Graelite cities. London, 1906.
Arc 588.2 Petrie, W.M.F. Kahum, Gurob, and Hawara. London, 1890.
Arc 588.5 Petrie, W.M.F. Koptos. London, 1896.
Arc 588.24 Petrie, W.M.F. Labyrinth Gerzeh and Mazghumeh. London, 1912.
Arc 588.3 Petrie, W.M.F. Medum. London, 1892.
Arc 588.20 Petrie, W.M.F. Memphis. London, 1909-1915. 7 pam.
Arc 588.4 Petrie, W.M.F. Nagada and Ballas. London, 1895.
Arc 585.3 Petrie, W.M.F. Naukratis. Pt.1-2. London, 1886-88. 2v.
Arc 588.42F Petrie, W.M.F. Objects of daily use. London, 1927.
Arc 588.1 Petrie, W.M.F. Ollahum, Kahun, and Gurob. 1889-90. London, 1891.
Arc 588.31 Petrie, W.M.F. Prehistoric Egypt. London, 1920.
X Cg Arc 595.5 Petrie, W.M.F. Pyramids and temples of Gizeh. London, 1883.
Arc 588.21 Petrie, W.M.F. Qurneh. London, 1909.
Arc 505.12 Petrie, W.M.F. Researches in Sinai. London, 1906.
Arc 585.23.2 Petrie, W.M.F. Roman Ehnasya. 1904. Supplement. London, 1905.
Arc 585.18A Petrie, W.M.F. The royal tombs of the First Dynasty. v.1; v.2, pt.1-2. London, 1900. 3v.
X Cg Arc 545.235F Petrie, W.M.F. Scarabs and cylinders with names. London, 1917. (Changed to XP 9838 F)
Arc 588.34 Petrie, W.M.F. Sedment I, II. London, 1924. 2v.
Arc 588.65F Petrie, W.M.F. Seven Memphite tomb chapels. London, 1952.
Arc 565.1.5 Petrie, W.M.F. Seventy years in archaeology. London, 1931.
Arc 565.1.6A Petrie, W.M.F. Seventy years in archaeology. N.Y., 1932.
Arc 588.57F Petrie, W.M.F. Shabtis. London, 1935.
Arc 588.6 Petrie, W.M.F. Six temples at Thebes. 1896. London, 1897.
Arc 865.2 Petrie, W.M.F. Stonehenge; plans, descriptions and theories. London, 1880.
Arc 585.2.2F Petrie, W.M.F. Tanis. Pt.1. 2. ed. London, 1889.
Arc 585.2A Petrie, W.M.F. Tannis. Pt.1-2. London, 1885-88. 2v.
Arc 565.1 Petrie, W.M.F. Ten years' digging in Egypt. N.Y., 1892.
Arc 565.1.2 Petrie, W.M.F. Ten years' digging in Egypt. 2. ed. London, 1893.
Arc 505.12.5 Petrie, W.M.F. Till el Hesy (Lachish). London, 1891.
Arc 588.37 Petrie, W.M.F. Tombs of the courtiers and oxyrhynkhos. London, 1925.
Arc 588.30A Petrie, W.M.F. Tools and weapons. London, 1917.
Arc 588.63 Petrie, W.M.F. Wisdom of the Egyptians. London, 1940.
Arc 400.24 Petrie, William M. Flinders. Methods and aims in archaeology. London, 1904.
Arc 545.208FA Petrie, William M.F. Hawara, Biahmu and Arsinoe. London, 1889.
Arc 600.240F Petrie's Nagada excavation; a supplement. (Baumgaertel, Elise J.) London, 1970.
Arc 925.180.5F Petroglify Angary. (Okladnikov, Aleksei Pavlovich.) Leningrad, 1966.
Arc 925.341.10 Petroglify Baikala - pamiatniki drevnei kul'tury narodov Sibiri. (Okladnikov, Aleksei P.) Novosibirsk, 1974.
Arc 925.40 Petroglify Karelii. (Linevskii, A.M.) Petrozavodsk, 1939.
Arc 925.347.10 Petroglify Nizhnego Amura. (Okladnikov, Aleksei P.) Leningrad, 1971.
Arc 925.341.5 Petroglify srednei Leny. (Okladnikov, Aleksei P.) Leningrad, 1972.
Arc 925.341 Petroglify zabaikal'ia. (Okladnikov, Aleksei P.) Leningrad, 1969- 2v.
Arc 970.2.5 Petroglyphs (rock carvings) in the Susquehanna River near Safe Harbor, Pennsylvania. (Cadzow, D.A.) Harrisburg, 1934.
Arc 983.13 Petroglyphs of the United States. (Steward, J.H.) Washington, 1937.
Arc 925.13.160 Petrov, Viktor P. Skifi. Kyiv, 1968.
Arc 1428.30 Petrowicz, A. von. Arsaciden-Münzen. Wien, 1904.
Arc 936.225.10 Petru, Peter. Hišaste źare Latobikov. Ljubljana, 1971.
Arc 936.225.15F Petru, Sonja. Emonske nekropole. Ljubljana, 1972.
Arc 1033.3.46 Petrus- och Moses-gruppen bland Roms sarkofagy. (Roosval, J.) Stockholm, 1932.
Arc 1020.9.145 Petrus und Paulus in Rom. (Leitzmann, Hans.) Bonn, 1915.
Arc 1020.9.146 Petrus und Paulus in Rom. 2. Aufl. (Leitzmann, Hans.) Berlin, 1927.
Arc 861.101 Pettit, Paul. Prehistoric Dartmoor. Newton Abbot, 1974.
Arc 936.195.165 Pevnost v lužním lese. 1. vyd. (Poulík, Josef.) Praha, 1967.
Arc 1016.241 Peyrat, G. du. L'histoire ecclesiastico...les antiquitez...de la chapelle et oratoire du Roy de France. Paris, 1645.
Arc 400.19 Peyrony, D. Éléments de préhistoire. Ussel, 1923.
Arc 830.182 Peyrony, D. Le périgord préhistorique. Perigneux, 1949.
Arc 1473.2 Pfaffenhoffen, F. Essai sur les arpres comnénats...de Trébisonde. Paris, 1847.
Arc 1473.4 Pfaffenhoffen, F. Lettre...sur quelques monnaies byzantines. Paris, 1865.
Arc 1423.8 Pfaffenhoffen, F. von. Le prince croisé Baudouin. Paris, 1863.
Arc 915.2 Die Pfahlbauten des Bodensees. (Schnarrenberger.) Konstanz, 1891.
Arc 913.7 Die Pfahlbauten in den Schweizerseen bei Fluntern. (Staub, Johannes.) Zürich, 1864.
Arc 853.15 Pfahlbauten in Mechlenberg. (Lische, G.) Schwerin, 1865.
Arc 910.10F Die Pfahlbauten von Robenhausen. (Messikommer, H.) Zürich, 1913.
Arc 853.260 Die Pfalz unter den Römern. (Sprater, Friedrich.) Speier, 1929-30. 2v.
Arc 513.42 Pfannenstiel, Max. Die altsteinzeitlichen Kulturen Anatoliens. Berlin, 1941.
Arc 1478.11 Pfeiffer, A. Antike Münzbilder. Winterthur, 1895.
Arc 1138.8 Pfeiffer, A.F. Ueber Buecher-Handschriften. Erlangen, 1810.
Arc 1510.34 Pfeiffer, L. Pestilantia in nummis. Tübingen, 1882.
Arc 1076.20 Die Pferdetrensen des alten Orient. (Potratz, Johannes Albert Heinrich.) Roma, 1966.
Arc 1348.34 Pfister, J.G. Stray leaves from the journal of a traveler. London, 1857.
Arc 1090.1 Der Pflug und der Pflügen. (Behlen, H.) Dillenburg, 1904.
Arc 1200.6 Pflugh-Harttung, J. Bullen der Päpste. Gotha, 1901.
Arc 1285.27F Pfotenhauer, P. Die schlesischen Siegel von 1250 bis 1300 beziehentlich 1324. Breslau, 1879.
Arc 785.36 Pfretzschner, E. Die Grundrissentwicklung der römischen Thermen. Strassburg, 1909.
Arc 87.1.70 Phantasiai. (Trendelenburg, A.) Berlin, 1910.
Arc 554.1 Pharaohs, fellahs and explorers. (Edwards, A.B.) N.Y., 1891.
Arc 554.1.3 Pharaohs, fellahs and explorers. (Edwards, A.B.) N.Y., 1891.
Arc 554.1.5 Pharaohs, fellahs and explorers. (Edwards, A.B.) N.Y., 1892.
Arc 936.1.8 Pharsalos. (Stählin, F.) Nürnberg, 1914.
Arc 1405.1.3 Phayre, A.P. Numismata orientalia. v.3. pt.1-3. n.p., n.d.
Arc 1418.8F Phayre Provincial Museum, Rangoon. Catalogue of coins in the museum. Rangoon, 1924.
Arc 655.1 Philios, Demetrios. Peri tou pos graphontai ta tōn araskaphōn. Athēnai, 1890.
Arc 400.30 Philip Phillips: lower Mississippi survey, 1940-1970. Cambridge, Mass., 1970.
Arc 612.29 Philipp, H. Vor- und Frühgeschichte des Nordens und des Mittelmeerraumes. Berlin, 1937.
Htn Arc 1478.35F* Phillipps, Thomas. Numismata vetera et inscriptiones ex voto. Medio-Montana, 1855.
Arc 943.2 Phillips, H. A brief account of the more important public collections of American archaeology in the United States. n.p., n.d.
Arc 1613.4 Phillips, H. The coinage of the United States of America. Philadelphia, 1883.
Arc 1334.8 Phillips, H. Numismatics. Philadelphia, 1863-80. 12 pam.
Arc 1348.11 Phillips, H. Pamphlets on numismatics. Philadelphia, 1867-83. 4 pam.
Arc 1470.7 Phillips, H. Remarks upon a coin of Sicyon. Philadelphia, 1882.
Arc 340.12 Phillipson, David W. An annotated bibliography of the archaeology of Zambia. Lusaka, 1968.
Arc 726.4.20 The Phlegraean fields, from Virgil's tomb to the grotto of the Cumaean Sibyl. (Maiuri, Amedeo.) Rome, 1937.
Arc 1020.9.102 Phoebeus, F. De indentitate cathedral...Sanct. Petrus Romae. Romae, 1666.
Arc 16.3 Phoenix. Leiden. 9,1963+ 3v.

Arc 530.5 Phōkaika. (Papodopoulos, A.) Smyrnē, 1899.
Htn Arc 1163.17.10* Photographic slides of English manuscripts. (Sisson, C.J.) n.p., n.d.
Arc 1680.11 Photographs of merchant and political medals...of the United States...1825-1845. n.p., n.d.
Arc 87.1.2 Phrixos der Herold. (Gerhard, E.) Berlin, 1842.
Arc 530.150 Phrygie, exploration archéologique. v.1-3. (Institut Français d'Archéologie, Istanbul.) Paris, 1941- 2v.
Arc 830.51.5 Phulpin, A. Notes archéologiques sur les fouilles et les monuments découverts sur la montagne du Chatêlet. Neufchateau, 1840.
Arc 595.28 Phythagoras takes the second step, and other works on the pyramids. (Davie, John G.) Griffin, 1935.
Arc 754.6 Piale, S. Roman archaeology in the city of Rome. Diss. Rome, 1832-33. 12 pam.
Arc 785.41 Piale, Stefano. Degli antichi templi di Vespasiano e della concordia. Roma, 1821. 2 pam.
Arc 785.1.5 Piale, Stefano. Del tempio volgarmente detto di Vesta. Roma, 1817.
Arc 770.9 Piale, Stefano. Delle porte del recinto di servio Tullio nella parte orientale di Roma. Roma, 1833. 13 pam.
Htn Arc 750.5* Pianesi, G.B. Campus Martius. Roma, 1762.
Arc 1033.12.34F Piano, L.G. Commentarii critico archeologici sopra la SS. Sindone. Torino, 1833. 2v.
Arc 726.140.10 Il piano di fondazione di Verona romana. (Grancelli, Umberto.) Verona, 1964.
Arc 762.5 La pianta di Roma dell'anonimo einsidlense. (Huelsen, C.) Roma, 1907.
Arc 757.2 Pianta topografica di Roma antica. (Canina, Luigi.) Roma? 1844?
Arc 757.2.2 Pianta topografica di Roma antica. (Canina, Luigi.) Roma? 1851?
Arc 925.195 Piatysheva, N.V. Tamanskii sarkofag. Moskva, 1949.
Arc 925.50.15 Piatysheva, Natalia V. Iuvelirnye izdeliia Khersonesa. Moskva, 1956.
Arc 925.50.18 Piatysheva, Natalia V. Zheleznaia maska iz Khersonesa. Moskva, 1964.
Arc 900.215F Pič, Josef L. Archaeologický výzhum. pt.1-3. Praha, 1893-97.
Arc 900.215.5 Pič, Josef L. Le Hradischt de Stradonitz en Bohême. Leipzig, 1906.
Arc 66.1.123 Picard, Charles. Éphèse et Claros. Paris, 1922.
Arc 608.6.40 Picard, G.C. Castellum Dimmidi. Paris, 1947.
Arc 66.1.187 Picard, Gilbert. Les trophées romains. Paris, 1957.
Arc 1033.40.15 Picarelli, T. Basilica e Casa Romana di S. Cecilia in Trastevere. Roma, 1904.
Arc 726.25.5 Piccola giuda di Ostia. (Vagliere, Dante.) Roma, 1914.
Arc 810.54 Piccola guida di Pompei. (Corte, Matteo della.) Pompei, 1939.
Arc 726.60.5 Il Piceno dalle origini alla fine d'ogni sua autonomia sotto Augusto. v.1-2. (Speranza, G.) Ancona, 1934.
Arc 936.195.180 Pichlerová, Magda. Nové košariská. 1. vyd. Bratislava, 1969.
Arc 400.21 Pick, Behrendt. Aufsätze zur Numismatik und Archäologie. Jena, 1931.
Arc 1468.12 Pick, Bekrendt. Die antiken Münzen von Dacien. Berlin, 1898-1910. 2v.
Arc 716.2.15 Pickard-Cambridge, Arthur Wallace. The theater of Dionysus in Athens. Oxford, 1946.
Arc 545.204 Pickering, C. The Gliddon mummy-case. Washington, 1869.
Arc 785.56 Pickett, Cora Aileen. Temple of Quirinus. Thesis. Philadelphia, 1930.
Arc 768.6F Pictorial dictionary of ancient Rome. (Nash, Ernest.) London, 1961-62. 2v.
Arc 380.206 Pictorial tour in the Mediterranean. (Allan, J.H.) London, 1843.
Arc 397.17.15 A picture history of archaeology. (Marek, Kurt W.) London, 1958.
Arc 953.9 Pidgeon, W. Traditions of De-coo-dah and antiquarian researches. N.Y., 1858.
Arc 925.50.175 Pidoplichko, Ivan G. Pozdnepaleoliticheskie zhilizhcha iz kostei mamonta na Ukraine. Kiev, 1969.
Arc 387.9.7.1 Piecing together the past. (Childe, Vere Gordon.) N.Y., 1969.
Arc 1285.25.5 Pieczęcie górnośląskich cechów rzemieslniczych z XV-XVIII wisku i ich znaczenie historyczne. Wyd. 1. (Tomczyk, Damian.) Opolu, 1975.
Arc 1285.10.5 Pieczęcie i herby miejscowosci wojew lubelskiego. (Gumowski, M.) Lublin, 1959.
Arc 1285.10.10 Pieczęcie kręstw głogowskiego [sic] i Żagańskiego. (Fudalej, Aleksander.) Nova Sól, 1973.
Arc 1588.1.25F Pieczecie miast dawnej Polski. (Wittyg, W.) Kraków, 1905.
Arc 1510.110 Pieniądz gdański. (Gumowski, M.) Gdańsk, 1960.
Arc 1468.36 Pierfitte, G. Les monnaies grecques du musée Saint Raymond de Toulouse. Toulouse, 1939.
Arc 495.201 Pierotti, E. Jerusalem explored. London, 1864. 2v.
Arc 505.20 Pierotti, E. Macpela, ou Tombeau des patriarches à Hebron. Lausanne, 1869.
Arc 505.8 La pierre de Bethphagé. (Clermont-Ganneau, Charles.) Paris, 1877.
Arc 388.10 Pierre Dupont. (Paris. Université. Institut de Civilisation.) Paris, 1955.
Arc 608.94F Les pierres écrites de la Berbérie orientale. (Solignac, Marcel.) Tunis, 1928.
Arc 1093.2.40 Les pierres levées. (Bar, Henry.) Paris, 1973.
Arc 565.2 Pierret, Paul. Dictionnaire d'archéologie égyptienne. Paris, 1875.
Arc 561.1.5 Pierret, Paul. Explication des monuments de l'Égypte et de l'Ethiopie. Paris, 1885.
Arc 936.14.185 Pierwsi mieszkancy Gornego Slaska w swietle badan archeologicznych. (Jamka, Rudolf.) Katowice, 1965.
Arc 936.14.450 Pierwsze lokacje miast w dorzeczu orli w XIII wieku. (Kaletyn, Marta.) Wrocław, 1973.
Arc 853.70 Piesker, Hans. Vorneolithische Kulturen der südlichen Lüneburger Heide. Inaug. Diss. Hildesheim, 1932.
Arc 726.107 Pietrangeli, Carlo. Mevania. Roma, 1953.
Arc 726.108 Pietrangeli, Carlo. Scavi e scoperte di antichità il pontificato di Pio VI. 2. ed. Roma, 1958.
Arc 1433.22 Pietraszewski, Ignatius. Numi Mohammedani. Berolini, 1843.
Arc 1027.75 Pietro, A.C. Ancora del sepolero originario di San Domnio. Zara, 1906.
Arc 1033.12.37 Pietro, S. di. Santa sindone. Sermone. Torino, 1884.
Arc 830.91 Piette, Amédée. Itinéraires gallo-romains dans le département de l'Aisne. Léon, 1856-62.
Arc 830.122F Piette, Edouard. L'art pendant l'âge du Renne. Paris, 1907.
Arc 830.35 Piette, Edouard. La montagne d'Espiaup. Paris, 1877.
Arc 830.23 Piette, Edouard. Note sur les tumulus de Bartrès et d'Ossun. Toulouse, 1881. 2 pam.
Arc 400.16 Pietto, E. Études d'ethnographie préhistorique. Paris, 189-. 9 pam.
Arc 861.165 Piggot, Stuart. The west Kennet long barrow. London, 1962.
Arc 612.50 Piggott, Stuart. Ancient Europe from the beginings of agriculture to classical antiquity. Edinburgh, 1965.
Arc 400.25 Piggott, Stuart. Approach to archaeology. Cambridge, 1959.
Arc 858.58 Piggott, Stuart. British prehistory. London, 1949.
Arc 858.58.5 Piggott, Stuart. The neolithic cultures of the British Isles. Cambridge, Eng., 1954.
Arc 875.127 Piggott, Stuart. The prehistoric peoples of Scotland. London, 1962.
Arc 432.13 Piggott, Stuart. Some ancient cities of India. London, 1945.
Arc 403.19 Piggott, Stuart. William Stukely. Oxford, 1950.
Htn Arc 382.1* Pignoria, L. Vetustissimae tabulae aeneae. Venetiis, 1605.
Arc 726.8 Pigorini, L. Le abitazioni Palustri di Fontanellato. Parma, 1865.
Arc 925.322.15 Pikul', Milifsa I. Epokha rannego zheleza v Dagestane. Makhachkala, 1967.
Arc 726.18 I pilastri acritani. (Saccardo, G.) Venezia, 1887.
Arc 1033.12.107 Pilgerbuchlein zum heiligen Rock in Trier. (Sauren, J.) Köln, 1891. 2 pam.
Arc 1033.12.106 A pilgrimage to the Holy Coat of Treves. (Clarke, R.F.) London, 1892.
Arc 452.3 A pillared hall from a temple at Madura, India. (Brown, William N.) Philadelphia, 1940.
Arc 1027.19.13 Pillet, A. Souvenirs du cimetière de Saint Calliste. Arras, 1881.
Arc 493.4 Pillet, M.L. Le palais de Darius. Paris, 1914.
Arc 1163.12 Pillito, I. Analisi paleografia di...codici...secoli XIV e XV...in Cagliari. Cagliari, 1879.
Arc 820.202.2 Pilloy, J. Table générale de la Collection Caranda. Paris, 1908.
Arc 830.91.10 Pilloy, Jules. Études sur d'anciens lieux de sépultre dans l'Aisne. Saint-Quentin, 1880-99. 3v.
Arc 770.5 Pinarolo, G. L'antichita di Roma. Roma, 1703. 2v.
Arc 950.209 Pinart, A.L. La caverne d'Aknanh, ile d'Ounga. Paris, 1875.
Arc 1370.3 Pinder, M. Beiträge zur älteren Münzkunde. Berlin, 1851.
Arc 1480.21 Pinder, Moritz. Die Münzen Justinians. Berlin, 1843.
Arc 1349.25 Pinder, Moritz. Numismatique beckerienne. Paris, 1853.
Htn Arc 1033.12.32* Pingone, E.F. Sindon evangelica. Augustae Taurinorum, 1581.
Arc 1033.12.32.2 Pingone, E.F. Sindon evangelica. Augustae Taurinorum, 1777.
Arc 672.1.116 Pini, Ingo. Beiträge zur minoischen Gräberkunde. Wiesbaden, 1968.
Arc 1660.2 Pinkerton, J. The medallic history of England. London, 1790.
Arc 1348.10 Pinkerton, John. An essay on medals. London, 1784.
Arc 1348.10.3 Pinkerton, John. An essay on medals. London, 1808. 2v.
Arc 432.4 Pinto, Christoram. India prehistorica. Lisboa, 1909.
Arc 843.140 Las pinturas prehistoricas de las cuevas de la Araña (Valencia). (Hernandez-Pacheco, Eduardo.) Madrid, 1924.
Arc 843.145 Las pinturas prehistoricas de Peña Tú. (Hernandez-Pacheco, Eduardo.) Madrid, 1914.
Arc 843.68 Las pinturas rupestres del Barranco de Valltorta (Castellón). (Obermaier, H.) Madrid, 1919.
Arc 785.30.5 Pinza, G. Il comizio romano...ed i suoi monumenti. Roma, 1905.
Arc 740.10PF Pinza, G. Materiali per la etnologia antica toscana laziale. Milano, 1915.
Arc 1027.55 Pinza, G. Notizie sul cimitero cristiano di Bonaria [Sardini]. Roma, 1902.
Arc 723.16PF Pinza, Giovanni. Storia della civitá latina dalle origini al secolo V avante Christo. Roma, 1924.
Htn Arc 1360.3* I piombi antichi. (Ficoroni, F. de.) Roma, 1740.
Arc 1207.200F I piombi antichi. (Garrucci, R.) Roma, 1847.
Arc 386.26 Pioneer to the past. (Breasted, C.) N.Y., 1943.
Arc 1518.2 Piot, C. Catalogue des coins, poincons et matrices. 2. ed. Bruxelles, 1880.
Arc 530.22.11 Piotrovskii, Boris Borisovich. Urartu. London, 1969.
Arc 530.22.10 Piotrovskii, Boris Borisovich. Vanskoe tsarstvo (Urartu). 2. Izd. Moskva, 1959.
Arc 1018.27 Piper, F. Einleitung in die Monumentale Theologie. Gotha, 1867.
Arc 400.9 Piper, Otto. Bedenken zur Vorgeschichts-Forschung. München, 1913.
Arc 936.225.5 Pirković, Ivo. Crucium. Ljubljana, 1968.
Arc 853.286 Pirling, Renate. Das römisch-fränkische Gräberfeld vor Krefeld-Gellep. Berlin, 1966. 2v.
Arc 938.109 Pirmieji Lietuvos gyventojai. (Rimantienė, Rimutė Jablonskytė.) Vil'ius, 1972.
Arc 770.8 Piroli, T. Gli edifici antichi di Roma. Roma, 1800?
Arc 567.1.10 Pisa. Università. Studi in memoria di Ippolito Rosellini nel primo centerario della morte. Pisa, 1949. 2v.
Arc 726.45.15 Pisa nell'antichità dalle età preistoriche alla caduta dell'impero romano. (Toscanelli, N.) Pisa, 1933. 2v.
Arc 1675.10.7 Pisanello. (Calabi, A.) Milano, 1928.
Arc 1675.10.5 Pisanello. (Hill, G.F.) London, 1905.
Arc 1675.10 Pisanello et les médailleurs italiens. (Foville, J. de.) Paris, 1908.
Arc 925.50.325 Pislarii, Ivan A. Tainy stepnykh kurganov. Donetsk, 1972.
Arc 391.16 Pisma wybrane. (Gąsiorowski, Stanisław J.) Wrocław, 1969.
Arc 1027.25.5 Pitra, J.B. Inscriptions des...Rome chretienne. Paris, 1862-92. 3 pam.
Arc 925.357 Pitskhelauri, Konstantin. Osnovnye problemy istorii plemen Vostochnoi Gruzii v XV-VII vv. do n.e. Tbilisi, 1973.
Arc 708.14 Pittakys, K.S. L'ancienne Athènes. Athens, 1835.
Arc 967.3.5 Pitted stones. (Sheldon, J.M.A. (Mrs.).) Deerfield, 1925.
Arc 905.105 Pittioni, Richard. Der frühmittelalterliche Gräberfund von Köttloch. Brun, 1943.
Arc 612.31 Pittioni, Richard. Die urgeschichtlichen Grundlagen der europäischen Kultur. Wien, 1949.
Arc 815.27 Pittori di Pompei. (Ragghianti, C.L.) Milano, 1963.
Arc 1018.20 Una pittura di basilica di Antiochia. (Bonavenia.) Roma, 1888.
Arc 750.30 Pitture antiche. (Cassini, G.M.) Roma, 1783.
Arc 1033.70.23 Le pitture della Basilica primitiva di S. Clemente. (Wilpert, G.) Roma, 1906.

Author and Title Listing

Arc 1027.23.13 Le pitture della catacombe romane. (Ghignoni, A.) Firenze, 1905.
Arc 785.3 Pitture e sipolcri scoperti sull'Esquilino. (Brizio, E.) Roma, 1876.
Arc 790.214F Le pitture murali campane. (Sogliano, A.) Napoli, 1880.
Arc 608.33 Pitture rupestri del Tasili degli Azger. (Neukom, Tolantha T.) Firenze, 1955.
Arc 925.50.370 Pizn'opaleolitychne naselennia pivdenno-zakhidnoï Volyni. (Savych, Volodymyr P.) Kyïv, 1975.
Arc 1478.32F Pizzamiglio, Luigi. Saggio cronologico, ossia storia della moneta romana. Roma, 1867.
Arc 1033.17.531 Pla, José. Historia de Queralt. Barcelona, 1893.
Arc 843.65.4 Pla y Cargol, J. Ampurios y rosas. 4. ed. Gerona, 1953.
Arc 843.65.2 Pla y Cargol, J. Empúries i roses. 2. ed. Girona, 1934.
Arc 395.1 Place of archaeology in science. (Kenward, J.) Birmingham, 1877.
Arc 1588.1.101 Plage, Karol. Monety bite dla Królestwa Polskiego w latach 1815-1864 i monety bite dla miasta Krakowa w roku 1835. Warszawa, 1972.
Arc 1148.32 Plagiannēs, D.I. Byzantinoi sēmeiographoi. Athēnia, 1940.
Arc 953.23A Plains Indian painting. (Ewers, J.C.) Stanford, 1939.
Arc 810.48 Plan de Pompéi. (Jorio, Andrea.) Naples, 1828.
Arc 600.1.5 Plan du Quartier "Rhacotis" dans l'Alexandrie. (Botti, G.) Alexandrie, 1897.
Arc 435.16.2F Plan of Delhi. v.1-15. (India. Curator of Ancient Monuments.) n.p., 1881.
Arc 545.15.2PF Planches du Voyage dans la Basse et la Haute Égypte. Atlas. London, 18- ?
Arc 855.212 Plans and photographs of Stonehenge. (James, H.) n.p., 1867.
Arc 1495.4F Plantet, L. Essai sur les monnaies du Comte de Bourgogne. Paris, 1865.
Arc 673.11F Plassart, A. Les sanctuaires et les cultes du Mont Cynthe a Délos. Thèse. Paris, 1928.
Arc 830.149 Plat, Ernest. L'abbaye royale du Lieu-Notre-Dame-les-Romorantin. Romorantin, 1886.
Arc 1560.4 Platbarzdis, Aleksander. Die königlich schwedische Münze in Livland. Stockholm, 1968.
Arc 770.4.10 Platner, S.B. A topographical dictionary of ancient Rome. London, 1929.
Arc 770.4A Platner, S.B. Topography and monuments of ancient Rome. Boston, 1904.
Arc 770.4.2 Platner, S.B. Topography and monuments of ancient Rome. 2. ed. Boston, 1911.
Arc 672.1.122 Platon, Nikolaos Eleutheriou. Zakros: the discovery of a lost places of ancient Crete. N.Y., 1971.
Arc 1027.12.5 La Platonia...sepulcre des Sts. Pierre et Paul. (Battandier, A.) Paris, 1896.
Arc 1015.217 La platonia ossia il sepolcro apostolico della via Appia. (Waal, A. de.) Roma, 1892.
Arc 605.203 Playfair, R.L. Travels in the footsteps of Bruce in Algeria and Tunis. London, 1877.
Arc 513.1.5 A plea for research in Asia Minor. (Sterrett, J.R.S.) Ithaca, 1911.
Arc 397.18A Pleasure of ruins. (Macaulay, Rose.) London, 1953.
Arc 397.18.2 Pleasure of ruins. (Macaulay, Rose.) London, 1966.
Arc 925.356.1 Plemena iamnoi kul'tury Iugo-Vostoka. Photoreproduction. (Fisenko, Vladimir A.) Saratov, 1970.
Arc 925.150.15 Plemena Iuzhnoi Belorussii v rannem zheleznom veke. (Mel'nikovskaia, Ol'ga N.) Moskva, 1967.
Arc 925.321.5 Plemena Karelii v epokhu neolita i rannego metalla. (Pankrushev, Grigorii A.) Leningrad, 1964.
Arc 925.93 Plemena katakombnoi kul'tury. Photoreproduction. (Popova, Tat'iana B.) Moskva, 1955.
Arc 925.50.140 Plemena skifs'koho chasu na Vorskli. (Kovpanenko, Halyna T.) Kyïv, 1967.
Arc 925.50.48 Plemena srednego Dona v epokhu bronzy. (Liberov, Petr D.) Moskva, 1964.
Arc 936.6.35 Plemiona kultury łuzyckiej w epoce brazu na ślasku środkowym. Text and atlas. (Gediga, Bogusław.) Wrocław, 1967.
Arc 870.2 Plenderleath, W.C. The white horses of the west of England. London, 1886.
Arc 936.225.25F Plesničar-Gec, Ljudmila. Severno emonsko grobišče. Ljubljana, 1972.
Arc 925.352 Pletnev, V.A. Ob ostatkakh drevnosti i stariny v Tserskoi Gubernii. Tver', 1903.
Arc 925.50.300 Pletneva, Svetlana A. Drevnosh Chernykh Klobukov. Moskva, 1973.
Arc 925.50.375 Pletneva, Svetlana A. Polovetskie kamennye izvaianiia. Moskva, 1974.
Arc 542.200 Pleyte, C.M. Die Buddha-Legende. Amsterdam, 1901.
Arc 888.40F Pleyte, Willem. Nederlandsche oudheden van de vroegste tijden tot op Karel dan Groote. Leiden, 1902. 2v.
Arc 1254.2 Plombs, bulles et sceaux byzantins. (Sabatier, J.) Paris, 1858.
Arc 383.18 Plovdiv, Bulgaria. Durzhavna biblioteka "Ivan Vazov". Sbornik Boris Liabovich. Plovdiv, 1927.
Arc 905.4.10 Po ruševinama staroga Salina. (Bulić, Frane.) Zagreb, 1900.
Arc 925.107 Po sledam drevnik kul'tur. (Fedorov, G.B.) Moskva, 1954.
Arc 340.9 Po sledam drevnikh kul'tur. (Sviridova, I.N.) Moskva, 1966.
Arc 925.16.45 Po sledam drevnikh kul'tur Kazakhstana. Alma-Ata, 1970.
Arc 1584.26 Po sledam odnoi redkoi monety. (Spasskii, Ivan G.) Leningrad, 1964.
Arc 823.60F Pobé, Marcel. Kelten-Römer. Olten, 1958. 2v.
Arc 843.110 El poblament d'Ilduro. (Rileas i Bertran, Marià.) Barcelona, 1952.
Arc 843.235 El poblat ibèric de Puig Castellar. (Martinez i Hualde, Angel.) Barcelona, 1966.
Arc 925.152 Pobol', Leonid D. Drevnosti Turovshching. Minsk, 1969.
Arc 925.150.45 Pobol', Leonid D. Slavianskie drevnosti Belorussii. Minsk, 1971.
Arc 925.150.46 Pobol', Leonid D. Slavianskie drevnosti Belorussii. Minsk, 1973.
Arc 925.150.47 Pobol', Leonid D. Slavianskie drevnosti Belorussii. Minsk, 1974.
Arc 936.225.20F Pobrežje. (Pahić, Stanka.) Lujbljana, 1972.
Arc 936.6.25 Pocatkij slovanskeho osidlene. (Filip, Jan.) Praha, 1946.
Arc 936.150.10 Počiatky výtvarnéreo prejavu na Slovensku. (Novotný, B.) Bratislava, 1958.
Arc 66.1.133 Pocquet, J. du Haut-Jusse. Les papes et les ducs de Bretagne. Paris, 1928. 2v.
Arc 936.6.30 Początki kultury łuzyckiej w Polsce Środkowej. (Wiklak, Henryk.) Łodź, 1963.
Arc 1453.10 Początki mennictwa w Europie Środkowej, Wschodniej i Polnocnej. (Suchodolski, Stanisław.) Wrocław, 1971.
Arc 1588.1.42 Początki pieniadza polskiego. (Kiersnowski, R.) Warszawa, 1962.
Arc 925.5.10 Pod volnami Issyk-Kuha. (Zuikov, B.B.) Moskva, 1962.
Arc 853.65.25 Pod znakiem świętego słońca. (Heckowa, K.W.) Wrocław, 1961.
Arc 1588.1.19 Podrecznik numiznatyki Polskiej. (Gumowski, Marian.) Kraków, 1914.
Arc 1163.3.50 Podrecznik paleografii ruskiej. (Horodyski, Bogden.) Kraków, 1951.
Arc 936.14.300 Podstawy gospodarcze plemion neolitycznych w Polsce połnocno-zachodniej. (Wiślański, Tadeusz.) Wrocław, 1969.
Arc 880.21 Poe, J.W. The cromlechs of county Dublin. Dublin, 1918?
Arc 545.237 Pörtner, B. Aegyptische Grabsteine und Denksteine aus Athen und Konstantinople. Strassburg, 1908.
Arc 936.240 Poetovio. (Abramič, M.) Ptuj, 1925.
Arc 1498.8 Poey d'Avant, F. Monnaies féodales de France. Paris, 1858. 4v.
Arc 1255.1F Poggi, Vittorio. Sigilli antichi romani raccolti e publicati da Vittorio Poggi. Torino, 1876.
Arc 746.52 Poggio civitate (Murlo, Siena), il santuario arcaico. Firenze, 1970.
Arc 925.35 Pogrebenie varvarskogo kniazia v vostochnoi Evrope. (Matsulevich, L.A.) Moskva, 1934.
Arc 726.332 Pohl, Ingrid. The iron age necropolis of Sorbo at Cerveteri. Lund, 1972.
Arc 936.195.37F Pohrebiská zo staršej doby bronzovej na Slovensku. (Chropovský, Bohuslav.) Bratislava, 1960.
Arc 936.195.260 Pohrebiská zo staršej doby bronzovej v Branči. 1. vyd. (Vladár, Josef.) Bratislava, 1973.
Arc 936.195.93 Pohřebiště a súdliště lidu popelnicóvych poh v Třebešově. (Volovek, V.) Hradec Králové, 1966.
Arc 608.36 Poinssot, Claude. Les ruines de Dougga. Tunis, 1958.
Arc 320.4 Point Loma, California. School of Antiquity. Papers. University extension series. Point Loma. 2-12,1915-1921
Htn Arc 870.6* Pointer, J. Britannia Romana, or Romans in Britain. Oxford, 1724. 4 pam.
Arc 925.16.55 Poiski i raskopki v Kazakhstane. Alma-Ata, 1972.
Arc 925.50.270 Pol', Aleksandr N. Katalog kolleztni drevnostei A.N. Pol', v Ekaterinoslave. Kiev, 1893.
Arc 936.195.200 Poláček, Josef. Divčé kámen. České Budějovice, 1960.
Arc 1530.15 Polak, Arthur. Joodse penningen in de Nederlanden. Amsterdam, 1958.
Arc 1138.129 Polák, Stanislav. Studium novověkého písma. Přibram, 1973.
Arc 936.14.165A Poland. (Jazdzewski, Konrad.) London, 1965.
Arc 1675.51 Poland. Mennica Panstwowa. Katalog wejborów. Warszawa, 19- ?
Arc 936.14.04 Pamphlet vol. Poland - Antiquities. 4 pam.
Arc 1413.2 Polder, L. Abridged history of copper coins in Japan. n.p., 1891.
Htn Arc 825.10F* Poldo d'Albenas, J. Discours historial de l'antique et illustrie cité de Nismes. Lyon, 1560.
Arc 80.15 Polemōn archaiologikon periodikon syggramma. Athēnai. 1-6,1929-1957 3v.
Arc 720.200.5 Poleni, G. Catalogi...ad thesauros antiquitatum. Bononiae, 1853.
Arc 292.155 Polenov, D. Bibliografiia obozrenie trydov. Sankt Peterburg, 1871.
Arc 925.210 Polesskikh, M.R. Pamiatniki material'noi kul'tury Penzenskoi oblasti. Penza, 1960.
Arc 923.127 Polevaia arkheologiia SSSR. (Avdusin, Daniil A.) Moskva, 1972.
Arc 936.165.30 Polevoi, Lazar' L'. Gorodskoe goncharstvo Pruto-Dnestrov'ia v XIV v. Kishinev, 1969.
Arc 543.146.35 Poliakov, Sergei P. Etnicheskaia istoriia Severo-Zapadnoi Turkmenii v srednie veka. Moskva, 1973.
Arc 716.7.5A Das Poliastempel als Wohnhaus des Königs Erechtheus. (Bötticher, Karl.) Berlin, 1851.
Arc 1027.2.15 Polidori, L. Dei conviti effigiati a simbolo ne' monumenti cristiani. Milano, 1844.
Arc 1033.32 Polidori, L. Illustrazione di due monumenti cristiani. Verona, 1843.
Arc 925.150.20 Polikarpovich, Konstantin M. Paleolit verkhego podneptovia. Minsk, 1968.
Arc 681.7F Poliochni. v.1-2. (Brae, Luigi Bernabo.) Roma, 1964.
Arc 936.14.9 Polish archaeological abstracts. Wroclaw. 1,1972+
Arc 1148.34 Polites, L.N. Odēgos katalogoy cheirographōn. Athēnia, 1961.
Arc 705.205 Polites, N.G. To ranathēnaikon stadion. Athēnai, 1896.
Arc 736.2.2 Politi, G. Siracusa pei Viaggiatori. Siracusa, 1835.
Arc 730.5.3 Politi, R. Lettera di...Grove-Olympico in Agrigento. Palermo, 1819.
Arc 700.20 The political meeting places of the Greeks. (McDonald, W.A.) Baltimore, 1943.
Arc 66.1.120 La politique de St. Pie V en France. (Hirschauer, C.) Paris, n.d.
Arc 66.1.214 La politique monétaire des empereurs romains de 238 à 311. (Callu, Jean Pierre.) Paris, 1969.
Arc 1153.85 Politzer, R.L. A study of the language of eighth century Lombardic documents. N.Y., 1949.
Arc 1588.4.95 Polivka, Eduard. Československé mince 1918-1968. Vyd. 1. Hradec Králové, 1969.
Arc 1580.51.2 Polívka, Eduard. Mince Františka Josefa I., 1848-1916. 2. vyd. Praha, 1968.
Arc 1588.1.9 Polkowski, J. Decouverte à Gtebokie de monnaies polonaises. Gnesen, 1876.
Arc 936.195.30F Polla, B. Stredoveká zaniknuta osada na Spiši. Bratislava, 1962.
Arc 936.195.220 Polla, Belo. Kežmarok. 1. vyd. Bratislava, 1971.
Arc 1033.82 Pollidoro, J.B. Vita...S. Pardi...de SS. Primiano, Firmiano et Casto. Roma, 1741.
Arc 925.50.375 Polovetskie kamennye izvaianiia. (Pletneva, Svetlana A.) Moskva, 1974.
Arc 936.14.360 Polska Akademia Nauk. Instytut Historii Kultury Materialnej. Badania archeologiczne w Polsce w latach 1944-64. Wrocław, 1965.
Arc 936.14.100 Polska Akademia Nauk. Oddział w Krakowie. Prace Komisja Archeologicznej. Studia i materiały do badań nad Neolitem Małopolski. Wrocław, 1964.
Arc 936.14.265 Polska Akademia Nauk. Oddział w Krakowie. Prace Komisja Archeologicznej. Zagadnienia okresu lateńskiego w Polsce. Wrocław, 1968.
Arc 936.14.55 Polska Akademia Nauk. Oddział w Krakowie. Prace Komisji Archeologicznej. Igołomia. Wrocław, 1961.
Arc 302.9.5 Polska Akademia Nauk. Zaktad Archeologii Śródziemnomorskiej. Travaux. Warsaw. 1968+ 2v.
Arc 16.4 Polska Akademiia Nauk Zakład Archeologei Antycznej. Prace. Warszawa. 1-25 6v.

Author and Title Listing

Arc 936.14.35 Polska na więcej niz 1000 lat. (Burzyński, R.) Wrocław, 1961.

Arc 936.14.334 Polska starozytna. (Hensel, Witold.) Wrocław, 1973.

Arc 936.14.355 Polskie Towarzystwo Archeologiczne. Polskie towarzystwo archeologiczne społeczeństwu. Wrocław, 1970.

Arc 936.14.140 Polskie Towarzystwo Archeologiczne. Pradzieje Rzeszowszczyzny. Rzeszów, 1963.

Arc 936.14.130 Polskie Towarzystwo Archeologiczne. Z przeszłósci Pomorza Wschodniego. Wrocław, 1962.

Arc 853.65.20 Polskie Towarzystwo Archeologiczne. Z przesztośći Sląska. Wrocław, 1960.

Arc 936.14.355 Polskie towarzystwo archeologiczne społeczeństwu. (Polskie Towarzystwo Archeologiczne.) Wrocław, 1970.

Arc 1588.1.50 Polskiej Akademja Nauk. Instytut Historyjka Kultury Materialnej. Skarb monet arabskich z klukowicz powiat siemiatycze. Wrocław, 1964.

Arc 1588.1.27 Pol'skiia i litobskiia star. monety. (Gartman, V.G.) Syzran, 1901.

Arc 1033.165 Polyeucte dans l'histoire. (Aubé, Benjamin.) Paris, 1882.

Arc 936.14.200 Pomerania antiqua. (Danzig (City). Muzeum Archeologiczne.) Gdynia, 1965- 6v.

Arc 925.41 Pomiatniki epokhi bronzy inga Evropeiskoi chasti SSSR. Kiev, 1967.

Arc 1505.2 Pommerns Münzen im Mittelalter. (Dannenberg, H.) Berlin, 1864.

Arc 853.62.7 Pommersche Urgeschichte in Bildern. (Kunkel, Otto.) Stettin, 1931. 2v.

Arc 1138.124 Pomoćne povijesne znanosti u teoriji i praksi. (Stipišić, Jakov.) Zagreb, 1972.

Arc 1163.3.7 Pomorskie paleografy 18 stol. (Druzhinin, V.G.) Petrograd, 1921.

Arc 793.19 Pompei, Ercolano e Stabia. (Maiuri, Amedeo.) Novara, 1961.

Arc 810.40.10 Pompei; i nuovi scavi e l'anfiteatro. (Corte, Matteo della.) Pompei, 1930.

Arc 790.206.3 Pompei; la ville, les moeurs, les arts. (Gusman, P.) Paris, 1906.

Arc 810.8 Pompéi, les catacombes, l'Alhambra. (Lagrèze, G.B. de.) Paris, 1889.

Arc 810.40 Pompéi; les nouvelles fouilles. (Corte, Matteo della.) Pompéi, 1926.

Arc 790.206.5 Pompei; the city, its life and art. (Gusman, P.) London, 1900.

Arc 810.2 Pompéi. (Bonucci, Carlo.) Naples, 1828.

Arc 810.40.3 Pompéi. (Corte, Matteo della.) Pompéi, 1935.

Arc 810.66 Pompei. (Guerdan, René.) Paris, 1973.

Arc 790.206 Pompei. (Gusman, P.) Paris, n.d.

Arc 815.18F Pompei. (Paribeni, R.) n.p., 1902.

Arc 810.22 Pompéi. Vie privée. Histoire. (Thédenat, H.) Paris, 1906.

Arc 810.22.2 Pompéi. Vie publique. (Thédenat, H.) Paris, 1906.

Arc 810.22.5 Pompéi. Vie publique. (Thédenat, H.) Paris, 1910.

Arc 810.2.5 Pompéi. 2. éd. (Bonucci, Carlo.) Naples, 1830.

Arc 810.57F Pompei alla luce degli scavi novi di Via dell'Abondanza (anni 1910-1923). (Spinazzola, Vittorio.) Roma, 1953. 2v.

Arc 790.211F Pompei com'era e com'è. (Fischetti, Luigi.) Milano, 19- ? 2v.

Arc 830.126 La Pompéi de la Provence, Fréjus. (Donnadieu, A.) Paris, 1927.

Arc 790.213F Pompei e la regione sotterrata dal Vesuvio nell'anno LXXXIX. (Italy. Ufficio Tecnico degli Scavi delle Province Meridionale.) Napoli, 1879.

Arc 810.34 Pompei e le sue rovine. (Curti, Pier A.) Milano, 1872-74. 3v.

Arc 810.10 Pompéi et les Pompéiens. 3. éd. (Monnier, Marc.) Paris, 1873.

Arc 746.14 Una Pompei etrusca a Marzabotto nel Bolognese. (Brizio, E.) Bologna, 1928.

Arc 810.51 Pompei nel suo sviluppo storico. (Sogliano, A.) Roma, 1937.

Arc 790.212F Pompei principali monumenti e nuovissimi scavi. (Carini, P.B.) Milano, 1921.

Arc 810.17.13 Pompei vor der Zerstoerung. 3. Aufl. (Weichardt, C.) München, 1909.

Arc 815.2 The Pompeia. (Smith, F.W.) Saratoga, 1890.

Arc 793.9.2 Pompeia. 3. éd. (Breton, Ernest.) Paris, 1869.

Arc 793.9 Pompeia. 3. éd. (Breton, Ernest.) Paris, 1870.

Arc 815.3 The Pompeian court in the Crystal Palace. (Scharf, G.J.) London, 1854.

Arc 810.6.7 Pompeiana; the topography, edifices, and ornaments of Pompeii. (Gell, William.) London, 1835. 2v.

Arc 810.6 Pompeiana. (Gell, William.) London, 1817-19.

Arc 810.6.5 Pompeiana. (Gell, William.) London, 1832. 2v.

Arc 810.6.2 Pompeiana. (Gell, William.) London, 1837. 2v.

Arc 810.6.3A Pompeiana. (Gell, William.) London, 1852.

Arc 810.56 Pompeiana. Napoli, 1950.

Arc 810.5 Pompeianarum antiquitatum historia. (Fiorelli, G.) Naples, 1860-62. 3v.

Arc 810.12 Pompeianische Studien zur Staedtekunde des Altertums. (Nissen, H.) Leipzig, 1877.

Arc 810.23 Pompeii, eine hellenistische Stadt in Italien. (Duhn, F. von.) Leipzig, 1906.

Arc 810.11.8 Pompeii, its life and art. (Mau, August.) N.Y., 1899.

Arc 810.11.9 Pompeii, its life and art. (Mau, August.) N.Y., 1902.

Arc 810.11.10 Pompeii, its life and art. (Mau, August.) N.Y., 1907.

Arc 810.11.11 Pompeii, its life and art. (Mau, August.) Washington, D.C., 1973.

Arc 810.44 Pompeii, popular and practical. (Neville-Rolfe, Eustace.) Naples, 1888.

Arc 810.50A Pompeii. (Carrington, R.C.) Oxford, 1936.

Arc 810.21 Pompeii. (Engelmann, R.) London, 1904.

Arc 810.26 Pompeii. (Mackenzie, W.M.) London, 1910.

Arc 810.42F Pompeii. (Maiuri, Amedeo.) Roma, 1929.

Arc 810.30 Pompeii. N.Y., n.d.

Arc 810.24 Pompeii. Beschreibung der Stadt. (Schoener, R.) Stuttgart, n.d.

Arc 810.29 Pompeii: its destruction and re-discovery. London, 1853.

Arc 810.4 Pompeii: its history, buildings and antiquities. (Dyer, T.H.) London, 1867.

Arc 810.3 Pompeii (in library of entertaining knowledge). (Clarke, W.) London, 1831-32. 2v.

Arc 793.2 Pompeii and Herculaneum. (Adams, W.H.D.) London, n.d.

Arc 793.17 Pompeii and Herculaneum. (Brion, Marcel.) N.Y., 1961.

Arc 793.12 Pompeii and Herculaneum. (Ellaby, Christopher G.) London, 1930.

Arc 793.10F Pompeii and Herculaneum: the living cities of the dead. (Kraus, Theodor.) N.Y., 1975.

Arc 810.64 Pompeii and the region destroyed by Vesuvius in A.D. 79. (Jashemski, Stanley A.) Garden City, 1965.

Arc 810.17 Pompeii before its destruction. (Weichardt, C.) Leipzig, n.d.

Arc 815.35 Pompeii in fact and fiction. (Leppmann, Wolfgang.) London, 1968.

Arc 810.45 Pompeii in three hours. (Warsher, Tatiana.) Rome, 1930.

Arc 810.11 Pompejanische Beitraege. (Mau, August.) Berlin, 1879.

Arc 815.26 Pompejanische Malerei. (Schefold, Karl.) Basel, 1952.

Arc 815.28 Pompejanische Wandgemälde. (Maiuri, Amedeo.) Bern, 1959.

Arc 796.2.10F Die pompejanischen Wanddekoration. v.1-2. (Beyen, Hendrik G.) Haag, 1938. 4v.

Arc 810.46 Pompeji, dets historie og mindesmärker. (Bruun, Carl.) Kjøbenhavn, 1881.

Arc 810.39 Pompeji; ein Führer durch die Ruinen. (Warscher, Tatiana.) Berlin, 1925.

Arc 810.40.5 Pompeji. (Corte, Matteo della.) Pompeji, 1926.

Arc 810.37 Pompeji. (Ippel, Albert.) Leipzig, 1925.

Arc 810.13 Pompeji. (Overbeck, J.) Leipzig, 1856.

Arc 810.13.2A Pompeji. (Overbeck, J.) Leipzig, 1884.

Arc 810.32.5 Pompeji. (Pernice, Erich.) Leipzig, 1926.

Arc 790.204 Pompeji. (Persuhn, E.) Leipzig, 1878-82. 2v.

Arc 810.68 Pompeji. (Seedorff Pedersen, Hans H.O.) København, 1966.

Arc 815.30 Pompeji. Eine Stadt in Literatur und Leben. (Leppmann, Wolfgang.) München, 1966.

Arc 628.1 Pompeji. 2. Aufl. (Nissen, H.) Berlin, 1827. 22 pam.

Arc 810.18 Pompeji im Gymnasialunterricht. (Hubik, J.) Wien, 1900.

Arc 810.11.6 Pompeji in Leben und Kunst. (Mau, August.) Leipzig, 1900.

Arc 810.11.7 Pompeji in Leben und Kunst. 2. Aufl. (Mau, August.) Leipzig, 1908.

Arc 810.11.7.2 Pompeji in Leben und Kunst. 2. Aufl. (Mau, August.) Leipzig, 1913.

Arc 810.13.5 Pompeji in seinen Gebäuden. 3. Aufl. (Overbeck, J.) Leipzig, 1875.

Arc 810.20 Pompeji in seiner Kunst. (Mayer, E. von.) Berlin, n.d.

Arc 810.32 Pompejiforschung und Archäologie nach dem Kriege. (Pernice, Erich.) Griefswald, 1920.

Arc 673.1 Pomtow, H. Beiträge zur Topographie von Delphi. Berlin, 1889.

Arc 1010.15 Ponosov, V.V. Results of an archaeological survey of the southern region of Moreten Bay and of Moreten Island, 1963-64. St. Lucian, Brisbane, 1967.

Arc 861.53 Pons Aelii; the site of the Roman station. (Richardson, G.B.) Newcastle-upon-Tyne, 1852.

Arc 608.88.5 Ponsich, Michel. Recherches archéologiques à Tanger et dans sa région. Paris, 1970.

Arc 726.331 I ponti di Padova romana. (Galliazzo, Vittorio.) Padova, 1971.

Arc 726.264 I ponti romani in Sardegna. (Fois, Foiso.) Sassari, 1964.

Arc 1030.4.32 Il pontificato del papa Damaso. (Marucchi, O.) Roma, 1905.

Arc 1016.221 La pontificia accademia romana di archeologia. (Lugari, G.B.) Roma, 1900.

Arc 1153.47PF Pontificum Romanorum diplomata. (Catholic Church. Pope.) Romae, 1928.

Arc 925.13.15 Pontika...skifiia, Kavkaz. (Latyshev, V.V.) Sankt Petersburg, 1909.

Arc 1500.5.3 Ponton d'Amécourt, G. de. Description raisonnée des monnaies mérovingiennes de Châlon-sur-Saône. Paris, 1874-83. 3 pam.

Arc 1500.5.5 Ponton d'Amécourt, G. de. Monnaies mérovingiennes de Saint-Denis. Macon, 1884.

Arc 1500.5 Ponton d'Amécourt, G. de. Monnaies mérovingiennes du palais et de l'ecole. Paris, 1862.

Arc 530.19F Pontrenioli, E. Didymes fouilles de 1895 et 1896. Paris, 1904.

Arc 403.16.40 Poole, Lynn. One passion, two loves; the story of Heinrich and Sophia Schliemann. N.Y., 1966.

Arc 1212.5 Poole, Reginald Lane. Seals and documents. London, 1919?

Arc 1348.8 Poole, S. Lane. Coins and medals. London, 1885.

Arc 861.38 Pooley, C. An historical and descriptive account of the old stone crosses of Somerset. London, 1877.

Arc 861.30 Pooley, C. Notes on the old crosses of Gloucester. London, 1868.

Arc 861.25 Pope, Alfred. The old stone crosses of Dorset. London, 1906.

Arc 1084.10 Pope-Hennessy, U. (Mrs.). Early Chinese jades. London, 1923.

Arc 681.20 Popham, Mervyn R. Excavations at Lefkandi, Euboea, 1964-66. London, 1968.

Arc 726.333 Popoli anellenici in Basilicata. (Italy. Soprintendenza alle Antichità della Basilicata.) Napoli, 1971.

Arc 936.29.5F Popov, R. Peshterata Mirezlivka. Sofiia, 1933.

Arc 936.29 Popov, R. Peshterata Temnata dupka. Sofiia, 1936.

Arc 925.300.5 Popova, T.B. Dol'meny stanitsy Novosvobodnoi. Moskva, 1963.

Arc 925.93 Popova, Tat'iana B. Plemena katakombnoi kul'tury. Photoreproduction. Moskva, 1955.

Arc 888.25 Popping, H.J. Onze voorhistorie. Zutphen, 1952.

Arc 1470.32.7 Popravki obshchagi kataloga monet. P.O. Burachkov'. (Beribe-Delagart, A.L.) Moskva, 1907.

Arc 1603.1.5 Popular illustrated guide to Canadian coins. (Breton, P.N.) Montreal, 1912.

Arc 746.10 Populonia; la necropoli arcaica. (Minto, Antonio.) Firenze, 1922.

Arc 1020.115 Poquet, A.E. De terra iheroslimitana...allate sunt relique. n.p., n.d.

Arc 488.23 Porada, Edith. Alt-Iran. Baden-Baden, 1962.

Arc 608.32 Port à Utique. (Reyniers, F.L.M.) Alger, 1952.

Arc 730.204 La porta arabo-normanna. (Riolo, G.) Palermo, 1871.

Arc 785.70F Porta Argentoriorum. (Haynes, D.E.L.) London, 1939.

Arc 830.97 Porte, J.F. Aix ancien et moderne. 2e éd. Aix, 1833.

Arc 608.6.25 La porte de Sidi Oqba. (Blanchet, P.) Paris, 1900.

Arc 458.1.5 La porte orientale du stûpa de Sânchi. (Foucher, A.) Paris, 1910.

Arc 1033.17.441 Portenico, E. Cenno storico della Taumaturga efficie di Santa Maria dell'Arco...Miano. Napoli, 1851.

Arc 1274.6 Porteous, A. The town council seals. Edinburgh, 1906.

Arc 880.37A Porter, Arthur Kingsley. The crosses and culture of Ireland. New Haven, 1931.

Arc 548.5 Porter, Bertha. Topographical bibliography of ancient Egyptian hieroglyphic texts, reliefs. Oxford, 1927-39. 7v.

Arc 548.5.10A Porter, Bertha. Topographical bibliography of ancient Egyptian hieroglyphic texts. v.1, pt.1-2; v.2; v.3, pt.1. 2. ed. Oxford, 1960- 4v.

Arc 400.14.25 Porter, Lucy W. Kingsley. Writings of A. Kingsley Porter. Cambridge, 1934.

Author and Title Listing

Arc 785.35 — Porter, M.W. What Rome was built with. London, 1907.
Arc 400.3 — Porter, R.K. Travels in Georgia, Persia. London, 1821-22. 2v.
Arc 855.220 — Portfolio of photographs of Cromlechs of Anglesey and Carnarvonshire. (Griffith, J.E.) Derby, 1900.
Arc 726.27 — Porticus triumphi. (Rossi, G.B. de.) Roma, 1889.
Arc 726.25.16F — Il porto di Roma imperiale e l'agro portuense. (Lugli, G.) Roma, 1935.
Arc 726.235.10 — Il porto e la città di classe. (Cortesi, Giuseppe.) Alfonsine, 1967.
Arc 1053.10 — Das Porträt an Grabdenkmalen. (Lichteuber, G.R. von.) Strassburg, 1902.
Arc 1050.203 — Porträt-Munzen und Grafs...Porträt Gallerie. (Virchow, R.) Berlin, 1903.
Arc 1465.3 — Porträtköpfe auf antiken Münzen. (Imhoof-Blumer, Friedrich.) Leipzig, 1885.
Arc 1475.9 — Porträtköpfe auf Römischen Münzen. (Imhoof-Blumer, Friedrich.) Leipzig, 1892.
Arc 1356.5 — Le portrait dans l'antiquité d'apres les monnaies. (Babelon, Jean.) Paris, 1942.
Arc 1675.20.10 — Portrait medals of Italian artists of the Renaissance. (Hill, George F.) London, 1912.
Arc 1348.53F — Portraits en médaille. (Babelon, Jean.) Paris, 1946.
Arc 1050.202 — Portraits I. Roman emperors. n.p., n.d.
Arc 838.3 — Portugal pre-historico. (Leite de Vasconcellos, J.) Lisboa, 1885.
Arc 1675.36 — Portuguese medals. (Lamas, A.) Lisbon, 1905-10. 12 pam.
Arc 785.115 — Portus. (Testaguzza, Otello.) Roma, 1970.
Arc 1643.5 — Posada, Eduardo. Numismatica colombiana. Bogotá, 1937.
Arc 87.1.17 — Poseidon Basileus und Athene Sthenias. (Panofka, T.S.) Berlin, 1857.
Arc 925.50.380 — Poseleniia srednego podneprov'ia epokhi rannei bronzy. (Bondar', Mykola M.) Kiev, 1974.
Arc 936.14.95 — Posen (City). Museum Archeologicznej Oddział w Gnieznie. Ziemia gnieźnieńska w okresie powstawania państwa polskiego. Poznań, 1961.
Arc 600.52 — Posener, G. Princes et pays d'Asie et de Nubie. Bruxelles, 1940.
Arc 600.156.5F — Posener, Georges. Catalogue des ostraca hiératiques littéraires de Deir el Médineh. Le Caire, 1972-
Arc 1510.3.10 — Posern-Klett, Karl Friedrich von. Sachens Münzen im Mittelalter. Leipzig, 1970.
Arc 936.195.315 — Poslední bčiště Černoboha s runami na Skalsku, v kraji Boleslavském, v Čechach, na své archaeologické cestě vypátral Václeslav Krolmus. (Krolmus, Wácslaw.) Praha, 1857.
Arc 945.6 — Posnansky, Arthur. Las Americas son un nuevo mundo. La Paz, Bolivia, 1943.
Arc 1185.5.1 — Posse, Otto. Die Lehre von der Privaturkunden. Berlin, 1974.
Arc 1269.10F — Posse, Otto. Die Siegel der deutschen Kaiser und Könige von 751 bis 1913. Dresden, 1909-13. 5v.
Arc 895.22.20F — Post, Linnart. Bronsaldersmanteln fran Gerumsberget i Vastergötland. Stockholm, 1924-25.
Arc 140.5 — Post-medieval archaeology. London. 1,1967+ 3v.
Arc 140.5.2 — Post-medieval archaeology. Index. v.1-5 (1967-71). London, 1973.
Arc 920.204F — Pósta, Béla. Régészeti tanulmányok az Oroszföldon. v.3-4. Leipzig, 1905. 2v.
Arc 1540.21 — Poste, Beale. Celtic inscriptions on Gaulish and British coins. London, 1861.
Arc 1540.21.5 — Poste, Beale. A vindication of the Celtic inscription on Gaulish and British coins. London, 1862.
Arc 1588.4.75 — Pošvář, Jaroslav. Měna v českých zemích od 10. do poč 20. století. Opava, 1962.
Arc 1588.4.73 — Pošvář, Jaroslav. Moravské mincovny. Vyd. 1. Brno, 1970.
Arc 1590.30 — Pošvář, Jaroslav. Die Währung in der Ländern der böhmischen Krone. Graz, 1970.
Arc 936.14.175 — Potemski, Gzesław. Pradzieje Bydgoszczy i powiatu bydgoskiego. Bydgoszcz, 1963.
Arc 1583.26 — Potin, Vsevolod M. Drevniaia Rus' i evropeiskie gosudarstva. Leningrad, 1968.
Arc 1076.20 — Potratz, Johannes Albert Heinrich. Die Pferdetrensen des alten Orient. Roma, 1966.
Arc 66.1.30 — Pottier, E. Étude sur les lécythes blancs attiques. Paris, 1883.
Arc 510.207 — Pottier, E. La Nécropole de Myrina. Paris, 1888. 2v.
Arc 700.15 — Pottier, Edmond. Quam ab causam Graeci in sepulcris figlina na sigilla deposuerint. Parisiis, 1883.
Arc 830.126.5 — Pottier, Raimond. Fréjus et les carrières...de l'Esterel. Draguignan, 1885.
Arc 943.7 — Pouget, J.F.A. du Nadaillac. L'Amérique préhistorique. Paris, 1883.
Arc 943.7.5A — Pouget, J.F.A. du Nadaillac. Prehistoric America. N.Y., 1884.
Arc 66.1.179 — Pouillaux, Jean. La Forteresse de Rhamnonte. Paris, 1954.
Arc 673.1.35F — Pouilloux, Jean. Énigmes à Delphes. Paris, 1963.
Arc 673.1.40F — Pouilloux, Jean. La région nord du sanctuaire de l'épogue archaïque à la fin du sanctuaire. Paris, 1960. 2v.
Arc 1470.41 — Les "Poulains" de Corinthe; monographie des statères corinthiens. (Ravel, O.E.) Bâle, 1936-48. 2v.
Arc 936.110F — Poulék, J. Pravěké umení. Praha, 1956.
Arc 1335.103 — Poulhariez, P.N. Histoire métallique de l'Europe, ou Catalogue des médailles modernes. Lyon, 1767.
Arc 936.195.165 — Poulík, Josef. Pevnost v lužním lese. 1. vyd. Praha, 1967.
Arc 400.22F — Poulik, Josef. Prehistoric art. London, 1956.
Arc 936.195.80 — Poulík, Josef. Průvodce po výzkumech na staroslovanskim hradisku staré zámky u Líšně. Praha, 1949.
Arc 936.195.35 — Poulík, Josef. Staří Moravané budiyí svůj stát. Gottwaldov, 1960.
Arc 936.195.165.5 — Poulík, Josef. Velkomoravské hradiště Mikulčice. 1. vyd. Gottwaldov, 1959.
Arc 936.195.15 — Poulík, Josef. Zivot a umenie doby železnej na Slovensku. Bratislava, 1962.
Arc 1163.38F — Poulle, Emmanuel. Paléographie des écritures cursives en France du 15e au 17e siècle. Genève, 1966.
Arc 673.1.35 — Poulsen, Frederik. Delphi. Washington, 1973.
X Cg Arc 673.1.13 — Poulson, F. Delphi. London, 1920.
Arc 1148.25 — Pour une terminologie in paléographie grecque. (Bataille, A.) Paris, 1954.
Arc 712.17 — Pousopoulos, A. O Parthenōn. Athēnai, 1895.
Arc 853.205.10 — Pouzotki wczesnośredniowiecznego. (Łosinski, Władysław.) Wrocław, 1972.
Arc 66.1.98 — Pouzzoles antique. (Dubois, C.) Paris, 1907.

Arc 1027.4.27 — Povèda, G. de. Memorie...S. Filomena e l'invenzione del suo corpo. Foligno, 1834.
Arc 936.50.5 — Povodom pedestgod jubileja "Vjesnika za arh. hist. Dalmatinsku". (Bulić, France.) Split, 1931.
Arc 838.17 — Os povos primitivos da Lusitânia. (Mendes Corrêa, A.A.) Porto, 1924.
Arc 400.20 — Powell, D. The traveller's journey is done. London, 1943.
Arc 880.31 — Power, P. Early Christian Ireland. Dublin, 1925.
Arc 936.14.190 — Powiat kamicński w starozytności. (Cnotliwy, Eugeniusz.) Szczecin, 1966.
Arc 936.14.420 — Powiązanie ziem polskich z terenami uschodnimi w epoce brązu. (Dąbrowski, Jan.) Wrocław, 1972.
Arc 400.8 — Pownall, T. Treatise on the study of antiquities. London, 1782.
Arc 925.50.175 — Pozdnepaleoliticheskie zhilizhcha iz kostei mamontz na Ukraine. (Pidoplichko, Ivan G.) Kiev, 1969.
Arc 925.50.275 — Pozdnie skify viugo-zapadnom Kryma. (Vysotskaia, Tat'iana N.) Kiev, 1972.
Arc 720.206 — Pozzuoli e contorni. (Maps. Pozzuoli.) Napoli, 1810.
Arc 16.4 — Prace. (Polska Akademiia Nauk Zakład Archeologei Antycznej.) Warszawa. 1-25 6v.
Arc 400.25.5.2 — Practical archaeology. 2. ed. (Webster, Graham.) London, 1974.
Arc 936.14.310 — Pradzieje Białostocczyzny. wyd. 1. (Jaskanis, Danuta.) Warszawa, 1969.
Arc 936.14.175 — Pradzieje Bydgoszczy i powiatu bydgoskiego. (Potemski, Gzesław.) Bydgoszcz, 1963.
Arc 936.14.149 — Pradzieje Polski. (Kostrzewski, Józef.) Poznań, 1949.
Arc 936.14.150 — Pradzieje Polski. wyd. 2. (Kostrzewski, Józef.) Wrocław, 1965.
Arc 936.14.92 — Pradzieje Pomorza. (Kostrzewski, Józef.) Wrocław, 1966.
Arc 936.14.160 — Pradzieje pomorza srodkowego. (Koszalin, Poland (City). Muzeum.) Koszalin, 1964.
Arc 936.14.142 — Pradzieje powiatu rzeszowskiego. (Moskwa, Kazimierz.) Lublin, 1964.
Arc 936.14.140 — Pradzieje Rzeszowszczyzny. (Polskie Towarzystwo Archeologiczne.) Rzeszów, 1963.
Arc 853.65.45 — Pradzieje Śląska. (Kostrzewski, Józef.) Wrocław, 1970.
Arc 936.14.405 — Pradzieje ziem polskich od IX do V tysiąclecia. wyd. 1. (Kozłowski, Stefan.) Warszawa, 1972.
Arc 936.14.480 — Pradzieje ziem pruskich od późnego paleolitu do VII w.n.e. (Okulicz, Jerzy.) Wrocław, 1973.
Arc 1510.167 — Prägungen Brandenburg-Preussens. (Meyer, Adolf.) Berlin, 1885.
Arc 1510.172 — Die Prägungen der Mannheimer Münzstätten. (Haas, Rudolf.) Mannheim, 1974.
Arc 34.2.5 — Praehistorica Asiae Orientalis. Hanoi.
Arc 382.7 — Pamphlet vol. Prähistorie. 10 pam.
Arc 936.24.10 — Die prähistorische Ansiedlung auf dem Wietenberg bei Sighisoara-Schässburg. (Horedt, Kurt.) Bonn, 1971.
Arc 513.21 — Prähistorische Forschung in Kleinasien. (Bittel, Kurt.) Istanbul, 1934.
Arc 853.41.9 — Prähistorische Funde in der Umgebung von Baden. (Calliano, G.) Wein, 1894.
Arc 905.37 — Die prähistorische Jagd in Mähren. (Wankel, Jindřich.) Olmütz, 1892.
Arc 905.7 — Das prähistorische Schanzwerk von Lengyel. (Wosinsky, M.) Budapest, 1888.
Arc 726.10 — Eine Praenestinische Ciste. (Schumacher, K.) Heidelberg, 1891.
Arc 746.2.9 — Die Praenestinischen Spiegel. (Matthies, S.) Strassburg, 1912.
Arc 936.195.275 — Prague. Národní Muzeum. Prehistorické Oddeleni. The prehistory of Czechoslovakia; exhibition, 1958. Prague, 1958.
Arc 936.220.105 — Praistorija na thu SR Srbije. (Garašanin, Milutin V.) Beograd, 1973. 2v.
Arc 936.220.85 — Praistorijska Karaburma. (Todorović, Jovan.) Beograd, 1972.
Arc 1163.3.3 — Prakticheskii kurs izucheniia drevnei russkoi skoropisi dlia chteniia rukopisei XV-XVIII stoletii. 2. izd. Reproduction. (Beliaev, Ivan S.) Moskva, 1911.
Arc 80.10 — Praktika. (Archaeological Society, Athens.) Athēnai. 1,1837+ 40v.
Arc 67.3.5 — Praktika. (Christianekē Archaiologikē Hetaireia, Athens.) Athēnai. 1,1892+ 6v.
Arc 1185.8.2 — Praktische Diplomatik. (Gatterer, J.C.) Göttingen, 1799.
Arc 1027.88F — Prandi, A. La memoria apostolorum in catacombas. Città del Vaticano, 1936.
Arc 930.206F — Praschniker, C. Archäologische Forschungen in Albanien und Montenegro. Wien, 1919.
Arc 712.23 — Praschniker, C. Parthenonstudien. Augsburg, 1928.
Arc 936.14.395 — Prasłowiańskie osadnictur w słupcy. (Malinowski, Tadeusz.) Poznań, 1969.
Arc 843.224 — Prat Puig, Francisco. L'aqueducte Romà de Pineda. Barcelona, 1936.
Arc 1185.29 — Pratesi, A. Elementi di diplomatica generale. Bari, 1963?
Htn Arc 1033.12.48* — Pratique pour honorer le St. Suaire de...Jésus Crist. Cain, 1881.
Arc 505.148 — Prausnitz, Moshe W. Studies in the lithic industries of Israel and adjacent countries. Jerusalem, 1970.
Arc 936.195.300 — Pravěk Československa. 1. vyd. (Neustupný, Jiří.) Praha, 1960.
Arc 936.195.105 — Pravek Slovenska. (Slovenská Akademia Vied. Archeologický Ustav, Nitra.) Bratislava, 1965- 2v.
Arc 936.195.135 — Pravek východného Slovenska. Košice, 1966.
Arc 936.195.90 — Pravek vychodnich a severovychodnich Cech. (Volovek, V.) Hradec Králové, 1962.
Arc 936.195.295 — Pravěk země české. (Vocel, Jan E.) Praha, 1866-68.
Arc 936.195.10F — Pravěké Hradisko u Obřan. (Adámek, F.) Brno, 1961.
Arc 936.195.175 — Pravěké nálezy na Klobnoucku. (Skutil, Josef.) Klobuka, 1939.
Arc 936.195.95 — Praveké osídlenie stredného Slovenska. (Balaša, Gejza.) Bratislava, 1960.
Arc 936.110F — Pravěké umení. (Poulék, J.) Praha, 1956.
Arc 936.238.5 — Prazgodovina Novego Mesta. (Novo Mesto, Yugoslavia. Dolenjski Muzej.) Novo Mesto, 1971.
Arc 1076.8 — Pražské zvony. (Kybalová, L.) Praha, 1958.
Arc 441.23 — Pre- and proto-history of the Berach Basin, South Rajasthan. 1. ed. (Misra, Virendra Nath.) Poona, 1967.
Arc 967.2.10 — The pre-Cambrian structure of Missouri. Diss. (Graves, H.B.) St. Louis, 1938.
Arc 585.26F — Pre-dynastic cemetery at El Mahasna. (Ayrton, Edward R.) London, 1911.
Arc 432.20 — The pre-historic background of Indian culture. (Gordon, Douglas Hamilton.) Bombay, 1958.
Arc 432.20.2 — The pre-historic background of Indian culture. 2. ed. (Gordon, Douglas Hamilton.) Bombay, 1960.

Arc 609.1.20 The pre-historic period in South Africa. (Johnson, J.P.) London, 1912.

Arc 407.25 Pre-historic phases. (Westropp, Hodder Michael.) London, 1872.

Arc 969.1.6 The pre-historic remains...of the city of Cincinnati, Ohio. (Clarke, R.) Cincinnati, 1876.

Arc 609.1.15 Pre-historic Rhodesia. (Hall, R.N.) Philadelphia, 1910.

NEDL Arc 893.5.3 The pre-history of the North. (Worsaae, J.J.A.) London, 1886.

Arc 858.96 Pre-Roman Britain. (Thomas, Stanley E.) London, 1965.

Arc 785.43 Préchac, F. Le colosse de Néron. Paris, 1920.

Arc 830.29 Précis...monument arabe du moyen âge en Normandie. (Spencer-Smith, I.) Caen, n.d.

Arc 1584.1.9 Précis de numismatique géorgienne. (Karst, J.) Paris, 1938.

Arc 830.46 Précis historique et chronique des monuments triomphaux. (Gilles, Isidore.) Paris, 1873.

Arc 1027.61 Precis recitandae in recognitione, et extractione Corporum S. Martyrum. Romae, 1774.

Arc 608.69 Precleur-Canonge, Thérèse. La vie rurale en Afrique romaine d'après les mosaiques. Paris, 1962.

Arc 936.261 Predistariska naselba Barutnica kaj anzibegovo vo Makedonija. (Korošec, Paola.) Prilep, 1973.

Arc 925.9.5 Predmety drevnosti. (Vyrubov, V.) Tiflis, 1877.

Arc 925.50.90 Predskifskii period na Dneprovskom Pravoberezh'e. (Terenozhkin, A.I.) Kiev, 1961.

Arc 530.4 Preger, T. Anonymi Byzantini. München, 1898.

Arc 936.220.15 Pregled materijame kulture juznih slovena u ranom s rednem veku. (Garašanin, Milutin V.) Beograd, 1950.

Arc 672.1.37 Prehellenic architecture in the Aegean. (Bell, Edward.) London, 1926.

Arc 387.6 La préhistoire. (Capitan, Louis.) Paris, 1922.

Arc 390.8 La préhistoire. (Feron, R.) Paris, 1928.

Arc 406.4 La préhistoire. (Vayson de Pradenne, A.) Paris, 1938.

Arc 16.2 Préhistoire. Paris. 1-16 7v.

Arc 830.70 La préhistoire dans la région lyonnaise. (Hutinel, F.) Lyon, 1913.

Arc 830.343 Préhistoire de France. (Bourdier, Franck.) Paris, 1967.

Arc 895.17.12 Préhistoire de la Norvège. (Shetelig, Haakon.) Oslo, 1926.

Arc 603.5 Prehistoire de l'Afrigue. (Vaufrey, Raymond.) Paris, 1955.

Arc 830.164 La préhistoire du département de l'Avignon. Thèse. (Temple, P.) Nîmes, 1935.

Arc 400.28.2 La préhistoire par André Leroi-Gourhan. 2. éd. Paris, 1968.

Arc 843.15.9 Prehistoria catalana. (Bosch Gimpera, P.) Barcelona, 1919.

Arc 843.82 Prehistoria de Aragón. (Galia y Sarañana, José.) Zaragoza, 1945.

Arc 843.62 La prehistoria de las Iberas y la etnologia vasca. (Bosch-Gimpera, P.) San Sebastian, 1926.

Arc 670.2.7 Prehistoric Aigina. Diss. (Harland, J.P.) Paris, 1925.

Arc 943.7.5A Prehistoric America. (Pouget, J.F.A. du Nadaillac.) N.Y., 1884.

Arc 953.8 Prehistoric America. v.1, The mound builders. v.3, Cliff dwellers. v.4, Ancient monuments. v.5, Myths and symbols. (Peet, S.D.) Chicago, 1890-1905. 4v.

Arc 880.32 Prehistoric and early Christian Ireland. (Evans, Emyr Estyn.) London, 1966.

Arc 885.26 Prehistoric and early Wales. (Foster, Idris L.) London, 1965.

Arc 885.8 Prehistoric and Roman Wales. (Wheeler, R.E.M.) Oxford, 1925.

Arc 963.3.5 Prehistoric antiquities of Indiana. (Lilly, Eli.) Indianapolis, 1937.

Arc 875.65 The prehistoric antiquities of the Howe of Cromar. (Ogston, Alexander.) Aberdeen, 1931.

Arc 953.3 The prehistoric archaeology of North America. (Haynes, H.W.) Boston, 1889.

Arc 400.22F Prehistoric art. (Poulik, Josef.) London, 1956.

Arc 407.6 Prehistoric art. (Wilson, John Albert.) Washington, 1898.

Arc 858.21 Prehistoric Britain. (Munro, Robert.) London, n.d.

Arc 858.59 The prehistoric chamber tombs. (Daniel, G.) Cambridge, Eng., 1950.

Arc 432.31 Prehistoric chronology and radiocarbon dating in India. (Agrawal, Dharma Pal.) New Delhi, 1974.

Arc 432.10 Prehistoric civilization of the Indus Valley. (Dikshit, K.N.) Madras, 1939.

Arc 858.50A Prehistoric communities of the British Isles. (Childe, V.G.) London, 1940.

Arc 858.50.5 Prehistoric communities of the British Isles. 2. ed. (Childe, V.G.) London, 1947.

Arc 983.6 Prehistoric copper implements. (Slafter, E.F.) Boston, 1879.

Arc 609.9.6 The prehistoric cultures of the Horn of Africa. (Clark, John Desmond.) N.Y., 1972.

Arc 861.101 Prehistoric Dartmoor. (Pettit, Paul.) Newton Abbot, 1974.

Arc 1097.5 Prehistoric disc wheels in the Netherlands. Proefschrift. (Waals, Johannes D. van der.) Groningen, 1964.

Arc 588.31 Prehistoric Egypt. (Petrie, W.M.F.) London, 1920.

Arc 858.51 Prehistoric England. (Clark, John Grahame Douglas.) London, 1940.

Arc 858.51.2 Prehistoric England. 2. ed. (Clark, John Grahame Douglas.) London, 1941.

Arc 612.33 Prehistoric Europe. (Clark, John Desmond.) London, 1952.

Arc 880.9 Prehistoric faith and worship. (Ffrench, J.F.M.) London, 1912.

Arc 612.28 The prehistoric foundations of Europe to the Mycenean age. (Hawkes, C.F.C.) London, 1940.

Arc 885.7.5 Prehistoric Gower; early archaeology of West Glamorgan. (Rutter, Joseph G.) Swansea, 1948.

Arc 658.15 Prehistoric Greece. (Stubbings, Frank Henry.) London, 1972.

Arc 641.5 Prehistoric Greece and Cyprus: an archaeological handbook. (Buchholz, Hans-Günter.) London, 1973.

Arc 432.5.2 Prehistoric India. 2. ed. (Mitra, Panchanan.) Calcutta, 1927.

Arc 672.5.20F The prehistoric inhabitation of Corinth. (Kosmopoulos, L.W.) Munich, 1948.

Arc 543.115F Prehistoric investigations in Iraqi Kurdistan. (Braidwood, Robert John.) Chicago, 1960.

Arc 880.44 Prehistoric Ireland. (Raftery, J.) London, 1951.

Arc 426.3 Prehistoric Japan. (Munro, N.G.) Yokohama, 1908.

Arc 426.3.5 Prehistoric Japan. (Munro, N.G.) Yokohama, 1911.

Arc 861.18.15 Prehistoric London; its mounds. (Gordon, E.O.) London, 1914.

Arc 682.25.35F Prehistoric Macedonia. (Heurtley, W.A.) Cambridge, Eng., 1939.

Arc 726.59 Prehistoric Malta; the Tarxien temples. (Zammit, Themistocles.) London, 1930.

Arc 400.1 Prehistoric man. (Perkins, F.B.) San Francisco, 1883.

Arc 392.2 Prehistoric man and beast. (Hutchinson, H.N.) N.Y., 1897.

Arc 861.16.7 Prehistoric man and the Cambridge gravels. (Smith, F.) Cambridge, Eng., 1926.

Arc 943.45 Prehistoric man in the new world. (Rice University.) Chicago, 1964.

Arc 885.32 Prehistoric man in Wales and the west. Bath, 1972.

Arc 530.60 Prehistoric Mersin. (Garstang, John.) Oxford, 1953.

Arc 398.1.2 Prehistoric peoples. (Nadaillac, J.F.A. du Pouget de.) N.Y., 1892.

Arc 875.127 The prehistoric peoples of Scotland. (Piggott, Stuart.) London, 1962.

Arc 875.17 Prehistoric pile-structures in pits. (Mann, L.M.) Edinburgh, 1904.

Arc 953.2 Prehistoric races of the United States of America. 4. ed. (Foster, J.W.) Chicago, 1878.

Arc 953.2.3 Prehistoric races of the United States of America. 5. ed. (Foster, J.W.) Chicago, 1881.

Arc 953.1.50 Prehistoric races of U.S.A. (Foster, J.W.) Chicago, 1873.

Arc 875.23 Prehistoric remains of Caithness. (Laing, S.) Edinburgh, 1866.

Arc 1090.5A Prehistoric rock pictures in Europe and Africa. (New York (City). Museum of Modern Art.) N.Y., 1937.

Arc 974.2 A prehistoric rock shelter in Val Verde County, Tennessee. (Pearce, J.E.) Austin, Texas, 1933.

Arc 923.120 Prehistoric Russia; an outline. (Sulimirski, Tadeusz.) N.Y., 1970.

Arc 875.5.5 Prehistoric Scotland. (Munro, R.) Edinburgh, 1899.

Arc 140.1.10 Prehistoric Society of East Anglia. Minor publications. n.p., n.d.

Arc 140.1.20 Prehistoric Society of East Anglia. Occasional paper. Bayswater. 1,1929 2v.

Arc 140.1 Prehistoric Society of East Anglia. Proceedings. London. 1,1908+ 40v.

Arc 861.75 Prehistoric Society of East Anglia. Report on excavations at Grime's Graves, Weeting, Norfolk, March-May, 1914. London, 1915.

Arc 855.201 The prehistoric stone monuments of the British Isles - Cornwall. (Lukis, W.C.) London, 1885.

Arc 861.41.20 Prehistoric Sussex. (Curwen, E. Cecil.) London, 1929.

Arc 635.222 Prehistoric Thessaly. (Wace, A.J.B.) Cambridge, 1912.

Arc 957.1.8A Prehistoric villages, castles, and towers of southwestern Colorado. (Fewkes, J.W.) Washington, 1919.

Arc 612.8 Le préhistorique en Europe. (Cotteau, G.H.) Paris, 1889.

Arc 406.4.5 Prehistory. (Vayson de Pradenne, A.) London, 1940.

Arc 432.24 Prehistory and protohistory in India and Pakistan. (Sankalis, Hasmukh Dhirajlal.) Bombay, 1962.

Arc 432.22 Prehistory and protohistory of east India. (Dani, A.H.) Calcutta, 1960.

Arc 603.6.5 The prehistory of Africa. (Alimen, Henriette.) London, 1957.

Arc 936.195.275 The prehistory of Czechoslovakia; exhibition, 1958. (Prague. Národní Muzeum. Prehistorické Oddeleni.) Prague, 1958.

Arc 609.13 The prehistory of east Africa. (Cole, Sonia Mary.) Harmondsworth, 1954.

Arc 609.13.2 The prehistory of east Africa. (Cole, Sonia Mary.) N.Y., 1963.

Arc 968.2.80 Prehistory of El Rito de los Frijoles, Bandelier national monument. (Hendron, J.W.) Phoenix, 1940.

Arc 612.19.5 The prehistory of European society. (Childe, Vere G.) Harmondsworth, 1958.

Arc 426.10 The prehistory of Japan. (Groot, G.J.) N.Y., 1951.

Arc 552.5 The prehistory of Nubia. (Combined Pre-Historic Expedition to Egyptian and Sudanese Nubia.) Taos, N.M., 1968. 2v.

Arc 875.14.15 The prehistory of Scotland. (Childe, V.G.) London, 1935.

Arc 609.9 The prehistory of southern Africa. (Clark, John Desmond.) Harmondsworth, Middlesex, Eng., 1959.

Arc 609.1.27 The prehistory of southern Rhodesia. (Jones, Neville.) Cambridge, Eng., 1949.

Arc 609.1.35 The prehistory of Uganda Protectorate. (O'Brien, T.P.) Cambridge, Eng., 1939.

Arc 885.20 The prehistory of Wales. 2. ed. (Grimes, W.F.) Cardiff, 1951.

Arc 925.349 Prehistory of western Siberia. (Chernetsov, Valerii Nikolaevich.) Montreal, 1974.

Arc 313.1 Prehistory research series. (Indiana. Historical Society, Indianapolis.) Indianapolis. 1-3,1937-1955 3v.

Arc 340.8.10 Přehled bibliografií a pokusů o soupisy moravské archeologické literatury. (Brünn. Universita. Knihovna.) Brno, 1965.

Arc 936.195.170 Preidel, Helmut. Das grossmährische Reich im Spiegel der Bodenfunde. Gräfelfing, 1968.

Arc 923.50 Preidel, Helmut. Slawische Altertumskunde das östlichen Mitteleuropa im 9. und 10. Jahrhundert. v.1-3. Grafeling bei München, 1961-

Arc 853.27.5 Prein, Otto. Aliso bei Oberaden und Vernusschlacht. Münster, 1930.

Arc 723.25.5 La preistoria. (Patroni, G.) Milano, 1951. 2v.

Arc 723.40 La preistoria d'Italia alla luce delle ultime scoperte. (Rodmilli, Antonio M.) Firenze, 1963.

Arc 66.1.86 Les préliminaires de la guerre de cents ans. (Déprez, E.) Paris, 1902.

Arc 955.2.7 A preliminary account of archaeological field work in Arizona in 1897. (Fewkes, J.W.) Washington, 1898.

Arc 960.2.5 Preliminary archaeological explorations at Weeden Island, Florida. (Fewkes, J.W.) Washington, 1924.

Arc 609.39 Preliminary investigation of a proto-historic cemetery at Nkudzi Bay, Malawi. (Inskeep, R.R.) Livingstone, 1965.

Arc 505.53 Preliminary report of the University of Michigan excavations at Sepphoris, Palestine, in 1931. (Waterman, Leroy.) Ann Arbor, 1937.

Arc 543.3.3 Preliminary report on a journey of archaeological exploration...Turkestan. (Stein, Mark Aurel.) London, 1901.

Arc 955.2.5 Preliminary report on a visit to Navaha national monument Arizona. (Fewkes, J.W.) Washington, 1911.

Arc 421.10 Preliminary report on archaeological research in Kansu. (Andersson, J.) Pekin, 1925.

Arc 587.89 Preliminary reports of the Egypt Exploration Society's Nubian Survey. (Egypt Exploration Society.) Cairo, 1962.

Arc 1153.44.25 A preliminary study of Alcuin's Bible. (Rand, Edward K.) Cambridge, 1931.

Location	Call number	Entry
	Arc 125.5	Proceedings. (Archaeological Institute of Great Britain.) London. 1845
	Arc 125.5.2	Proceedings. (Archaeological Institute of Great Britain.) London. 1846
	Arc 125.5.3	Proceedings. (Archaeological Institute of Great Britain.) London. 1847
NEDL	Arc 125.5.4	Proceedings. (Archaeological Institute of Great Britain.) London. 1848
	Arc 125.5.5	Proceedings. (Archaeological Institute of Great Britain.) London. 1849
X Cg	Arc 125.5.6	Proceedings. (Archaeological Institute of Great Britain.) London. 1850
	Arc 125.5.7	Proceedings. (Archaeological Institute of Great Britain.) London. 1851
	Arc 125.5.8	Proceedings. (Archaeological Institute of Great Britain.) London. 1852 2v.
	Arc 870.19	Proceedings. (Bristol. University. Spelaeological Society.) Bristol, Eng. 1,1919+ 6v.
	Arc 66.11.5	Proceedings. (British and American Archaeological Society of Rome.) Rome.
	Arc 72.5	Proceedings. (Hellenic Travellers' Club.) London? 1925-1930 7v.
	Arc 9.2.1	Proceedings. (International Congress of Prehistoric and Protohistoric Sciences, 1st, London, 1932.) London, 1934.
NEDL	Arc 136.2	Proceedings. (London Society of Antiquaries.) London. 1-32,1843-1920 34v.
	Arc 1312.2	Proceedings. (Manchester Numismatic Society.) Manchester.
	Arc 140.1	Proceedings. (Prehistoric Society of East Anglia.) London. 1,1908+ 40v.
	Arc 1313.2	Proceedings. (Royal Numismatic Society.) London. 1836-1837
NEDL	Arc 143.1	Proceedings. (Society of Antiquaries of Scotland.) Edinburgh. 1-63,1851-1929
	Arc 143.1	Proceedings. (Society of Antiquaries of Scotland.) Edinburgh. 64,1929+ 32v.
	Arc 41.1	Proceedings. (Society of Biblical Archaeology.) London. 1-40 37v.
	Arc 41.1.5	Proceedings. Index, v.11-30. (Society of Biblical Archaeology.) London, n.d. 2v.
	Arc 143.1.5	Proceedings. Index. v.25-81. (Society of Antiquaries of Scotland.) Edinburgh, 1897-1968. 2v.
	Arc 1300.1.9	Proceedings of annual meetings. (American Numismatic Society.) 20-104,1878-1962 11v.
	Arc 1033.12.195	Processions de la sainte-larme à Vendome. (Métais, C.) Orléans, 1886.
	Arc 1033.103	Processo belle reliquie false. (Liberati, D.P.) Roma, 1871.
	Arc 595.6	Proctor, R.A. The Great Pyramid. London, 1883.
	Arc 595.6.2	Proctor, R.A. The Great Pyramid. N.Y., 1883.
	Arc 1373.1	Production de l'or, de l'argent et du cuivre. (Sabatier, P.J.) St. Petersbourg, 1850.
	Arc 1480.67	Profili imperiali romani. (Cappelli, R.) Milano, 1963.
	Arc 1033.47	Profumo, A. L'incendio neroniano ed i Cristiani. Roma, 1903.
	Arc 307.3.15	Programa. (International Congress of Americanists, 26th, Seville, 1935.) Madrid, 1935.
	Arc 1153.2	Programma scolastico di paleografia latina. (Paoli, Cesare.) Firenze, 1888.
	Arc 1153.2.2	Programma scolastico di paleografia latina. 3. ed. (Paoli, Cesare.) Firenze, 1901.
	Arc 387.9.5A	Progress and archaeology. (Childe, Vere Gordon.) London, 1944.
	Arc 387.11	Progress of archaeology. (Casson, Stanley.) London, 1934.
	Arc 435.71F	Progress report. (Ceylon. Archaeological Survey.) Colombo. 1-7
	Arc 435.58F	Progress report. (India. Archaeological Survey. Western Circle, Bombay.) 1889-1921 3v.
	Arc 435.56F	Progress reports of the epigraphical and architectural branches. (India. Archaeological Survey. Uttar Pradesh.) Allahabad. 1887-1905 2v.
	Arc 716.2.20	Die Prohedrie des Dionysostheaters in Athen. (Maass, Michael.) München, 1952.
	Arc 925.13.200	Proiskhazhdenie rannesarmatskoi (prokhorovskoi) kul'tury. (Moshkova, Marina G.) Moskva, 1974.
	Arc 925.330	Proiskhozhdenie i ranniaia istoriia plemen Tagarskoi kul'tury. (Chlenova, Natalia L.) Moskva, 1967.
	Arc 685.5	Hē proistoria...Peloponnēsou. (Syriopoulos, K.) Athēnai, 1964.
	Arc 635.220	Ai Proistorikai...diménioy kaiseskloy. (Tsoynta, C.) Athēnai, 1900.
	Arc 395.5	Proistorikē archaiologia. (Kabbadias, P.) Athēnai, 1914.
	Arc 1163.3.105	Proizvedeniia russkogo prikladnogo iskusstvo s nadpisiami XV- pervoi chetverti XVI v. (Nikolaeva, Tat'iana V.) Mosvka, 1971.
	Arc 1433.65	Prokesch-Osten, A. Les monnaies des rois Parthes. Paris, 1874-75.
	Arc 925.18F	Prokhorov, V. Materialy po istorii russkikh odezhd. Sankt Petersburg, 1881-85. 3v.
	Arc 708.36	Prokopiou, Angelos G. Athens, city of the Gods. N.Y., 1964.
	Arc 1153.46	Prolegomena ad tachygraphiam Romanam. (Sarpe, Gustav.) Rostochii, 1829.
	Arc 700.50	Promachos. (Niemeyer, Hans G.) Waldsassen, 1960.
	Arc 416.10	Prome et Samara; voyage archéologique en Birmanie et en Mesopotamie. (Beylié, Léon de.) Paris, 1907.
	Arc 773.3	La promenade archéologique. (Scaglia, S.) Rome, 1911.
	Arc 756.7	Promenades archéologiques, Rome et Pompéi. (Boissier, Gaston.) Paris, 1880.
	Arc 756.7.1	Promenades archéologiques, Rome et Pompéi. 2. éd. (Boissier, Gaston.) Paris, 1881.
	Arc 756.7.3	Promenades archéologiques, Rome et Pompéi. 3. éd. (Boissier, Gaston.) Paris, 1887.
	Arc 756.7.8	Promenades archéologiques, Rome et Pompéi. 8. éd. (Boissier, Gaston.) Paris, 1904.
	Arc 889.24	Promenades archéologiques à Anderlecht. (Damme, Daniel van.) Bruxelles, 1958.
	Arc 608.6.23	Promenades archéologiques aux environs d'Alger. (Gsell, Stéphane.) Paris, 1926.
	Arc 838.5	Promenades archéologiques en Espagne. (Paris, Pierre.) Paris, 1910-1921. 2v.
	Arc 388.8	Promenades d'archéologie sous-marine. (Diolé, P.) Paris, 1952.
	Arc 659.10	Prometeo; scritti di archeologia e filologia. (Terzaghi, Nicola.) Torino, 1966.
	Arc 720.18PF	Promis, Carlo. Le antichità di Aosta. Torino, 1862. 2v.
	Arc 1490.28F	Promis, D. Monete dei reali di Savoia. Torino, 1841. 2v.
	Arc 1490.13	Promis, Domenico. Monete dei romani pontefici avanti il mille. Torino, 1858.
	Arc 1020.79	Promis, V. Reliquiario armeno...convento...Alessandria in Piemonte. Torino, 1883.
Htn	Arc 1675.6.5*	Promtuarii iconum insigniorum a secule homenum. pt.1-2. 2. ed. (Roville, G.) Lugduni, 1581.
	Arc 938.97	Pronksiajast varase feodalisimini. (Eesti NSV Teaduste Akademia. Ajaloo Institut.) Tallinn, 1966.
	Arc 400.4	Pronti, D. Nuova raccolta representante i costumi. Roma, 1808.
	Arc 1500.62	Prontuario. (Gamberini, Cesare.) Bologna, 1952.
	Arc 1490.75	Prontuario pezzario delle monete. (Gamberini, Cesare.) Bologna, 1960.
	Arc 1190.65.10	Die Prooimien der byzantinischen Patriarchenurkunden. (Mazal, Otto.) Wien, 1974.
	Arc 385.22	Propedeutica archeologica. (Anti, Carlo.) Padova, 1966.
	Arc 87.1.53	Proportionen des Gesichts in der Grosse Kunst. (Kalkmann, A.) Berlin, 1893.
	Arc 586.5	The proposed excavations at Tell-el-Amarna. (Egypt Exploration Society.) n.p., n.d.
	Arc 936.180.10	Prosek-Demir Kapija. (Aleksova, Blaga.) Skopje, 1966.
	Arc 1033.178	Proserpina - virgo sacrata Dei; ein fruhchristlichen Antithese. (Gotsmick, A.) München, 1962.
	Arc 1033.17.72	Prospetto storico dell'imagine di Maria vergine...S.Luca. Bologna, 1812.
	Arc 1033.17.73	Prospetto storico dell'immagine di Maria vergine dipinta dall'evangelista S. Luca. Bologna, 1826.
	Arc 1264.3	Prost, A. Notice sur un sceau de Landfriede du XIVe siècle. Paris, 1879.
Htn	Arc 1020.2*	Prost, B. Le trésor de l'Abbaye St. Bénique de Dijon. Dijon, 1894.
	Arc 685.2FA	Prosymna; the Helladic settlement preceding the Argive Heraeum. (Blegen, C.W.) Cambridge, Eng., 1937. 2v.
	Arc 385.4	Protiv vyl'garizatsii marksisma v arkheologii. (Akademiia Nauk SSR. Institut Arkheologii.) Moskva, 1953.
	Arc 674.1.13F	Ho prōtoattikos amphoreni tēs Eleusinos. (Mylonas, George E.) Athēnai, 1957.
	Arc 910.4	Les protohelvètes. (Gross, V.) Paris, 1883.
	Arc 292.125	Protokoly obshchikhe sobraniia. (Russkoe Arkheologicheskoe Obshchestvo, Leningrad.) Petrograd. 1899-1908
	Arc 292.127	Protokoly zasedaniia. (Russkoe Arkheologicheskoe Obshchestvo, Leningrad.) Sankt Peterburg. 1897-1898
	Arc 726.318	Die Protovillanova-Fundgruppe. (Schumacher, Erich.) Bonn, 1967.
	Arc 1500.5.25	Prou, Maurice. Catalogue des deniers mérovingiens de la trouvaille de Bais (Ille et Vilaine). Paris, 1908.
	Arc 1135.206FA	Prou, Maurice. Manuel de paléographie. Paris, 1904.
	Arc 1138.4.4A	Prou, Maurice. Manuel de paléographie latine et française. 3. éd. Paris, 1910.
	Arc 1138.4.5	Prou, Maurice. Manuel de paléographie latine et française avec atlas. 4. éd. Paris, 1924. 2v.
	Arc 1135.202	Prou, Maurice. Recueil de facsimiles d'écritures du XIIe au XVIIe siècle. Paris, 1892.
	Arc 1135.202.5	Prou, Maurice. Recueil de facsimiles d'écritures du XIIe au XVIIe siècle. Paris, 1896.
	Arc 830.341	Provence antique. (Clébert, Jean Paul.) Paris, 1966. 2v.
	Arc 875.44	The province of Mar. (Simpson, William D.) Aberdeen, 1943.
	Arc 495.205	Die Provincia Arabia. (Brünnow, R.E.) Strassburg, 1904. 3v.
	Arc 1535.7.2	Provincial copper coins, tokens of trade...1787-1801. 2. ed. (Pye, Charles.) London, 1801.
	Arc 1535.7	Provincial copper coins or tokens, 1787-1796. (Pye, Charles.) London, 1795.
	Arc 754.3	Pamphlet vol. Provincial Römisches, 1847-1899. 6 pam.
X Cg	Arc 1680.7	The provincial token - coinage of the eighteenth century. (Dalton, R.) 1-9 2v.
	Arc 915.4.20	Provincialia; Festschrift für Rudolf Laur-Belart. Basel, 1968.
	Arc 100.1.25	Prow, M. Table alphabétique...l'Académie Celtique...Antiquaires de France. Paris, 1894. 2v.
	Arc 1583.10	Prozarovskii, D.I. Moneta i vec' v' Rossii do kontsa XVIII stoletiia. Sankt Peterburg, 1865.
	Arc 925.30	Prozorovskii, D.I. Opisanie smolenskago klada. St. Peterburg, 1870.
	Arc 1623.5	Prudeau, A.F. Historia numismatica de Mexico desde la epoca precortesiana hasta 1823. Mexico, 1950.
	Arc 936.195.80	Průvodce po výzkumech na staroslovanskim hradisku staré zámky u Lišně. (Poulík, Josef.) Praha, 1949.
	Arc 830.371	Pruvot, Georges. Épave antique étrusco-punique? Antibes, 1971.
	Arc 936.14.440	Przemysl a archeologia. (Ogólnopolska Konferencja Konserwatorów Zabytkow Archeologicznych. Wspolpraca z Przemyslem w Dziedzinie Ochrony Zabytkow Archeologicznych Poznań, 1969.) Poznań, 1971.
	Arc 936.14.85	Przewodnik. (Wystawa Objazdowa Kielecczyzna w Swietle Wykopolisk.) Kielce, 1962.
	Arc 936.14.485	Przewodnik archeologiczny po Polsce. (Gąssowski, Jerzy.) Wrocław, 1973.
	Arc 936.14.170	Przeworska, Janina. Tradycje celtyckie w obrzędowości Protosłowian. Wrocław, 1964.
	Arc 925.80	Przeworski, S. Zagadnienie wpływów Bl. wschodnie. Warszawa, 1933.
	Arc 530.166	Przeworski, Stefan. Opera selecta. Wrocław, 1967.
	Arc 936.14.535	Przewoźna, Krystyna. Struktura i rozwój zasiedlenia południowowschedniej strefy nadbałtyckiej u sckyłku starożytności. 1. wyd. Warszawa, 1974.
	Arc 905.8	Przyborowski, J. Wycieczki archeologizne po...Wisly. Warszawa, 1874.
	Arc 383.46	Przyjaciół Nauk. Poznańskie Tow. Munera archaeologica Iosepho Kostrzewski. Poznań, 1963.
	Arc 936.14.155	Przymierze z archeologią. (Dabrowski, Krzysztof.) Warszawa, 1964.
	Arc 609.1.50	Psychic episodes of Great Zimbabwe. (Fletcher, Harold Clarkson.) Johannesburg, 1941.
	Arc 1443.4	Das Ptalemäergeld. (Giesecke, Walther.) Leipzig, 1930.
	Arc 608.17.25F	Ptolemais, city of the Libyan Pentapolis. (Kraeling, C.H.) Chicago, 1962.
	Arc 94.35	Publicaciones. (Institucione Fennando el Catolico Seminario de Arqueologia y Numismatico Aragonesas.) Zaragoza. 1,1951+ 6v.
	Arc 273.18	Publicaties. (Tongres, Belgium. Musée Provincial Gallo-Romains.) 1,1964+
	Arc 537.11	Publication. (Melbourne. University. Cyprus Expedition.) 1-2,1957-1964// 2v.

Arc 547.22.10F Publication. (New York (City). Metropolitan Museum of Art. Department of Egyptian Art.) N.Y. 1-5,1921-1936 3v.
Arc 143.7 Publication. (Somersetshire, England. Museum.) 2v.
Arc 307.2 Publications. (California. University.) Berkeley. 1-50,1904-1964 48v.
Arc 97.5 Publications. (Centre d'Études Gallo-Romaines.) Villeurbanne. 1,1968+
Arc 547.22F Publications. (New York (City). Metropolitan Museum of Art. Egyptian Expedition.) N.Y. 1-18,1916-1955 14v.
Arc 584.6F Publications. (Pennsylvania-Yale Expedition to Egypt.) New Haven. 1,1963+ 4v.
Arc 503.2.2F Publications. (Princeton University Archaeological Expeditions to Syria in 1904-1905 and 1909.) Leyden, 1907-1934. 18v.
Arc 970.2 Publications. (Society for Pennsylvania Archaeology.) Athens. 1,1931
Arc 1.5.31F Publications. Excavations. (American School of Oriental Reserach, Bagdad.) Philadelphia. 1935-1950 2v.
Arc 9.1 Publications. Recherches d'archeologie. (Institute Français d'Archeologie Orientale du Caire.) Le Caire. 1,1930+ 20v.
Arc 94.58 Publications de la Casa de Velasquez. Série archéologie. (Madrid, Spain. Casa de Velasquez.) Paris. 1,1973+
Arc 302.9.15 Les publications du Centre d'archéologie méditerranéenne. (Kiss, Zsolt.) Warszawa, 1974.
Arc 67.4 Publications in classical archaeology. (California. University.) Berkeley. 1-3,1929-1957 5v.
Arc 505.11.5 Puchstein, O. Führer durch die Ruinen von Baalbek. Berlin, 1905.
Arc 87.1.47 Puchstein, O. Das ionische Capitell. Berlin, 1887.
Arc 853.6 Der 'Puestrich' zu Sondershausen. (Suettich, S.) Naumburg an der Saale, 1894.
Arc 543.66.25 Puga-Chenkova, Galina A. Khalchaian. Tashkent, 1966.
Arc 746.18.5 Puglisi, S. Studi e ricerche su Orvieto etrusca. Catania, 1934.
Arc 870.5.7 Pugsley, A.J. Dew-ponds in fable and fact. London, 1939.
Arc 830.65 Puits funéraires gallo-romains. (Baudry, Ferdinand.) La Roche-sur-Yon, 1873.
Arc 1076.24 Pukhnachev, Iurii V. Zagadki zvuchashchego metalla. Moskva, 1974.
Arc 543.155 Pulatov, Uktam P. Chil'khudzhra. Dushanbe, 1975.
Arc 1020.24 Pulignani, M.F. Chiesa...Pietro e Paolo...Cancelli. Foligno, 1882.
Arc 785.24 Pullen, H.W. Handbooks of ancient Rome. London, 1894.
Arc 935.70 Pulur kazisi; 1960 mersimi çalişmalari raporu. (Kosay, Hâmit Zübeyr.) Ankara, 1964.
Arc 543.4FA Pumpelly, R. Exploration in Turkestan. Expedition of 1904. Washington, 1908. 2v.
Arc 938.65.5 Punios piliakalnis. (Volkaitė-Kulikauskienė, Regina.) Vilnius, 1974.
Arc 700.62 Die punischen und griechischen Tonlampen der Staatlichen Museen zu Berlin. (Heres, Gerald.) Amsterdam, 1969.
Arc 432.14 Punja, P.R.R. India's legacy. Mangalore, 1948.
Arc 452.1.15 Puri, K.N. La civilisation de Mohen-Jo-Daro. Thèse. Paris? 1938.
Arc 435.2.26F Purna Chandra, Mukhopādhyāya. Report of a tour of exploration of the antiquities in the Tarai, Nepal. Calcutta, 1901.
Arc 1200.25 Purvis, J.S. An introduction to ecclesiastical records. London, 1953.
Arc 1190.75 Purvis, John Stanley. Notarial signs from the York archiepescopal records. London, 1957.
Arc 565.5 Put, Thomas C. Egypt and the Old Testament. Liverpool, 1924.
Arc 1356.7 Puteshestire s drevnei monetoi. (Brabich, Vladimir M.) Leningrad, 1970.
Arc 543.9 Puteshestvie na Cinai. (Kondakov, N.P.) Odessa, 1882.
Arc 983.3.2 Putnam, C.E. Elephant pipes and inscribed tablets. Davenport, 1885.
Arc 983.3 Putnam, C.E. Elephant pipes and inscribed tablets in the Museum of the Academy of Natural Sciences. Davenport, 1886.
Arc 969.1.7 Putnam, F.W. Iron from the Ohio mounds. v.2. n.p., n.d.
Arc 983.5 Putnam, F.W. Remarks upon chipped stone implements. Salem, 1885.
Arc 943.15 Pamphlet box. Putnam, F.W. American archaeology.
Arc 950.211 Putnam anniversary volume. N.Y., 1909. 2v.
Arc 830.87 Le Puy deDome. (Mathieu, P.P.) Clermont-Ferrand, 1876.
Arc 1020.75 Le Puy et Rome. Souvenirs et monuments. Paris, 1877.
Arc 938.50 Puzinas, Jonas. Vorgeschichtsforschung und Nationalbewusstsein in Litauen. Inaug. Diss. Kaunas, 1935.
Arc 400.26 Pyddoke, E. The scientist and archaeology. N.Y., 1964.
Arc 1535.7.2 Pye, Charles. Provincial copper coins, tokens of trade...1787-1801. 2. ed. London, 1801.
Arc 1535.7 Pye, Charles. Provincial copper coins or tokens, 1787-1796. London, 1795.
Arc 595.26 Pyramid and temple. (Meier-Graefe, J.) London, 1931.
Arc 595.17 The pyramid of Gizeh. (Denslow, Van Buren.) N.Y., 18- .
Arc 545.201 Das Pyramidenfeld von Abusir. n.p., n.d.
Arc 595.66 Les pyramides de Sakkarah. (Lauer, Jean Philippe.) Le Caire, 1961.
Arc 595.13 Pyramidographia. (Greaves, John.) London, 1646.
Arc 595.62 The pyramids. (Fakhry, A.) Chicago, 1961.
Arc 595.01F Pyramids. Haverhill, 1943.
X Cg Arc 595.5 Pyramids and temples of Gizeh. (Petrie, W.M.F.) London, 1883.
Arc 595.59 The pyramids of Egypt. (Edwards, L.E.S.) London, 1954.
Arc 595.60 The pyramids of Egypt. (Edwards, L.E.S.) London, 1961.
Arc 936.14.415 Pyrgała, Jerzy. Mikroregion osadniczy między wisłą a Dolną Wkrą w obresie rzymskini. Wrocław, 1972.
Arc 66.1.185 Pyrrhos. (Leveque, Pierre.) Paris, 1957.
Arc 588.44F Qau and Badari. (Brunton, Guy.) London, 1927-30. 3v.
Arc 684.6 Quaatz, H. Wie sind die Figuren im Ostgiebel des Zeustempels zu Olympia anzuordnen. Berlin, 1908.
Arc 785.29.20 Quaderni dellimpero. Al linies romano. Romano. 1-10
Arc 785.82 Quaderni dell'impero. Le grandi strade del mondo romano. Roma. 1-15
Arc 1478.70 Quaderni dell'impero. L'impero di Roma nella sua moneta. Roma. 1,1939.
Arc 46.5 Quaderni di archeologia della Libia. Roma. 1,1950+ 6v.
Arc 93.40 Quaderni di studi etruschi. Serie 1: Ricerche preistoriche in Etruria. (Istituto di Studi Etruschi e Italici.) Firenze.
Arc 81.11 Quaderni di studi romani; a cura della Sezione lombarda dell'Istituto di studi romani. Milano. 1-6,1948-1955 2v.
Arc 81.10 Quaderni e guide di archeologia. Roma. 1,1958+ 3v.
Arc 81.9 Quaderni per lo studeo dell'archeologia. Firenze. 1-6,1938-1943
Arc 1348.41 Quadro di geografia numismatica da servire. (Strozzi, Carlo.) Firenze, 1836.
Arc 700.15 Quam ab causam Graeci in sepulcris figlina na sigilla deposuerint. (Pottier, Edmond.) Parisiis, 1883.
Arc 628.28 Quando il cielo stava quaggiù. (Onofrio, Cesare d'.) Roma, 1960.
Arc 823.4.5 Quantin, M. Répertoire archéologique du département de l'Yonne. Paris, 1868.
Arc 785.29.5 Quarenghi, G. Le mura di Roma. Roma, 1880.
Arc 503.6 Quarterly. (Palestine. Department of Antiquities.) 1-14,1931-1950 10v.
Arc 503.6.5 Quarterly. Index, v.1-14 (1931-1950). (Palestine. Department of Antiquities.) Jerusalem, 1964.
Arc 609.41 The quarternary in the coastlands of Guinea. (Davies, Oliver.) Glasgow, 1964.
Arc 935.9.40F Le quartier des Manganes et la première région de Constantinople. (Demangel, Robert.) Paris, 1939.
Arc 672.1.92 Les quatier Z à Mallia. (Deshayes, J.) Paris, 1959.
Arc 493.50 Quatre décrets seldjoukides. (Sauvaget, J.) Beyrouth, 1947.
Arc 380.210 Quatremère de Quincy, A.C. Monuments et ouvrages d'art antiques. Paris, 1829.
Arc 895.21.15 Quatuor monumenta aenea e terra i Suecia eruta. (Hallenberg, J.) Stockholm, 1802.
Arc 1360.2.5 Quatuor tentamina in re. numaria vetere. (Froelich, E.) Viennae, 1737.
Arc 505.146 Queen Elizabeth of Belgium Institute of Archaeology, Hebrew University, Jerusalem. Livre d'or de l'Institute d'archéologie. Bruxelles, 1965.
Arc 554.1.15 The queen of Egyptology. (Winslow, William C.) n.p., 1892.
Arc 1371.1 Queipo, V.V. Essai sur les systèmes métriques et monétaires. v.1-2, tables. Paris, 1859. 3v.
Arc 1335.42 Quelen, E. de. Collection de M. le Vicomte de...monnaies. Paris, 1883.
Arc 81.5 Quellen und Studien zur Geschichte und Kultur des Altertums, etc. Reihe A. Heidelberg.
Arc 81.6 Quellen und Studien zur Geschichte und Kultur des Altertums, etc. Reihe B. Heidelberg. 2 2v.
Arc 81.7 Quellen und Studien zur Geschichte und Kultur des Altertums, etc. Reihe C. Heidelberg.
Arc 81.7PF Quellen und Studien zur Geschichte und Kultur des Altertums, etc. Reihe C. Heidelberg. 1
Arc 81.8 Quellen und Studien zur Geschichte und Kultur des Altertums, etc. Reihe D. Heidelberg. 1-10,1934-1939
Arc 1578.6 Quellenkunde der Münz- und Geldgeschichte. (Probszt, Günther.) Graz, 1954.
Arc 1578.6.5 Quellenkunde der Münz- und Geldgeschichte. Nachtrag. (Probszt, Günther.) Graz. 1,1960+
Arc 201.5 Quellenschriften zür westdeutschen Vor- und Frühgeschichte. Bonn. 1,1939+ 3v.
Arc 608.2.25 Quelques lueurs nouvelles sur l'emplacement de la Carthage punique et de ses ports. (Gielly, Paul.) Casablanca, 1927.
Arc 1138.13 Quelques mots sur l'étude de la paléographie. (Gautier, Léon.) Paris, 1864.
Arc 830.169 Quelques notes sur Noviodurum Biturigum. Bourges, n.d.
Arc 600.235 Quelques observations sur l'épisode d'Aristée; à propos d'un monument égyptien. Paris, 1889. (Virey, Philippe.) Paris, 1889.
Arc 858.36 Quennell, M. (Mrs.) Everyday life in Roman Britain. London, 1924.
Arc 401.2.10 Quennell, Marjorie (Courtney). Everyday life in prehistoric times. 4. ed. London, 1952.
Arc 401.2.5 Quennell, Marjorie (Courtney). Everyday life in the new stone, bronze, and early iron ages. 2. ed. London, 1931.
Arc 1138.29 Quentin, Henri. Essais de critique textuelle. Paris, 1926.
Arc 1349.80 Quesada, Ernesto. Enrique Peña. Buenos Aires, 1924.
Arc 386.45 The quest at Glastonbury, a biographical study of Frederick Bligh Bond. (Kenawell, William W.) N.Y., 1965.
Arc 522.19.5 La question de Troie. (Vellay, Charles.) Chartres, 1931. 4 pam.
Arc 66.1.156 Questiones Johannes Galli. (Boulet, Marquerite.) Paris, 1944.
Arc 810.31 Questioni Pompeiane. (Garrucci, Räffaele.) Napoli, 1853.
Arc 830.49 Questionnaire. (Société Historique et Archéologique du Périgord.) Périgueux, 1874.
Arc 1470.43.5 Questions de numismatique illyrie. (Ceka, Hasan.) Tirana, 1972.
Arc 505.31 Questions de topographie palestinienne. (Meistermann, Barnabé.) Jerusalem, 1903.
Arc 588.8 Quibell, J.E. El Kab. 1897. London, 1898.
NEDL Arc 588.10 Quibell, J.E. Hierakonpolis. Pt.1-2. London, 1900-1902.
Arc 588.10 Quibell, J.E. Hierakonpolis. Pt.1-2. London, 1900-1902.
Arc 588.7 Quibell, J.E. Teh Rainesseum. 1896. London, 1898.
Arc 401.1.8 Quicherat, Jules. Jules Quicherat, 1814-1882. Paris, 1882.
Arc 401.1.2 Quicherat, Jules. Mélanges d'archéologie du Moyen Age. Paris, 1886.
Arc 401.1 Quicherat, Jules. Mélanges d'archéologie et d'histoire. Paris, 1885.
Arc 845.200 Quilling, F. Die Nauheimer Funde. Frankfurt am Main, 1903.
Arc 1663.33 Quinot, Henri. Recueil illustré des ordres de chevalerie et decorations belges de 1830 à 1963. 5. éd. Bruxelles, 1963.
Arc 843.55.10 Quintero, P. Necropolis ante-romana de Cadiz. Madrid, 1915.
Arc 843.150 Quintero y de Atuuci, Pelayo. Cadiz; primeros pobladores. Cadiz, 1917.
Arc 1033.12.66 Quiroga, M.P. de. Bellum de sanguine Christi. Valladolid, 1721.
Arc 1030.44 Quizo historico sobre o letreiro que se achon em hua pedra que estaua no celeiro do Monst. de Vayrão. (Cunha de Almeida, Jeronymo.) Pôrto, 1918.
Arc 700.5 Quomodo sepulera Tanagraei decoravirent. (Haussoullier, B.) Paris, 1884.
Arc 588.21 Qurneh. (Petrie, W.M.F.) London, 1909.
Arc 547.19.5 Il R. Museo di Antichità di Torino. 2. ed. (Farina, G.) Roma, 1938.
Arc 1138.70 Raalte, James van. De schrijfkunst in de Bijbellanden. Baarn, 1955.
Arc 1433.60 Rabino, Hyacinth L. Coins, medals, and seals of the shâhs of Irân. Hertford, 1945.

Author and Title Listing

Arc 923.85 Rabinovich, M.G. Arkheologicheskie materialy v ekspozitsii kraevedcheskikh muzeev. v.2. Moskva, 1961.

Arc 923.126 Raboty arhheologicheskikh ekspeditsii. (Moscow. Gosudarstvennyi Istoricheskii Muzei.) Moskva, 1941. 2v.

Arc 1153.14 Raccolta...abbreviazioni e frasi abbreviate. (Vianini, G.) Roma, 1898.

Arc 793.6.9F Raccolta...pinture...musaici...Ercolano, di Pompei, e di Stabia. (Naples. Museo Nazionale.) Napoli, 1854.

Arc 793.6 Raccolta...pinture e di...musaici...di Ercolano, di Pompei, e di Stabia. (Naples. Museo Nazionale.) Napoli, 183-.

Arc 793.6.5 Raccolta...pinture e di...musaici...di Ercolano, di Pompei, e di Stabia. (Naples. Museo Nazionale.) Napoli, 1843.

Arc 1200.28 Raccolta di documenti latini. (Schiaparelli, Luigi.) Torino, 1969.

Arc 905.4.15 Raccolta di documenti relativi ai monumenti artistici di Spalato e Salona. (Jelić, Luka.) Spalato, 1894.

Arc 383.95 Raccolta di scritti. (Società Archeologia Comense.) Como, 1954.

Arc 1033.17.30 Raccolta di varie lettere...relique ed immagine...Santissima Vergine Maria Cattedrale...Ancona. Roma, 1796.

Arc 1020.9.8 Raccolta generale delle iscrizioni pagne e cristiane...nel panteon di Roma. (Eroli, Giovanni.) Narni, 1895.

Arc 1033.12.69 Racconto dell'apparato...espositione del Sangue Venetia...1617. (Vergaro, G.C.) Venezia, 1617.

Arc 953.30 Race against time. (Baldwin, Gordon Cortis.) N.Y., 1966.

Arc 938.80F Racz, István. Kivikirves ja hapearisti. Helsingissä, 1961.

Arc 1675.51.10 Raczynski, E. Le médailleur de Pologne. Berlin, 1845. 4v.

Arc 843.21F Rada y Delgado, Juan de Dios de la. Discursos leidos ante la Academia de la Historia. Madrid, 1875.

Arc 843.19 Rada y Delgado, Juan de Dios de la. Necropolis de Carmona; memoria. Madrid, 1885.

Arc 838.38F Raddatz, Klaus. Die Schaftzfunde der Iberischen Halbinsel. Berlin, 1969. 2v.

Arc 853.51 Rademacher, C. Die vorgeschichtliche Besiedelung. Leipzig, 1920.

Arc 1163.14 Rademacher, M. Die Worttrennung in angelsächsischen Handschriften. Inaug. Diss. Münster, 1921.

Arc 66.2.85 Radet, G. Correspondance d'Emmanuel Roux. Bordeaux, 1898.

Arc 530.13 Radet, G. Cybébé. Paris, 1909.

Arc 66.2.80 Radet, G. L'histoire et l'oeuvre de l'école française d'Athènes. Paris, 1901.

Arc 66.1.63 Radet, Georges. La Lydie et le monde grec. Paris, 1893.

Arc 66.1.63.5 Radet, Georges. La Lydie et le monde grec au temps des Mesmnades, 687-546. Roma, 1967.

Arc 848.29.5 Radig, Werner. Germanischer Lebensraum. 4. Aufl. Stuttgart, 1934.

Arc 420.7 Radloff, W. Tpya...Atraer. St. Petersburg, 1892.

Arc 726.255 Radmilli, Antonio Mario. Abruzzo preistorico. Firenze, 1965.

Arc 936.155.5 Radnesrednevekovye goroda i pos. Chuiskoi doliny. (Kozhemiako, P.N.) Frunze, 1959.

Arc 1588.4.80 Radoměřský, Pavel. Nález přemyslovských denárů iz století v Hodkově u Kutné Hory. Kutná Hora, 1964.

Arc 889.33 Raepsuet, Georges. La céramique en terre sigillée de la ville belgo-romaine de Robelmont, campagnes 1968-1971. Bruxelles, 1974.

Arc 905.78 Rätsel um Carnuntum. (Kreuz, Trans.) Wien, 1939.

Arc 943.8 Rafn, K.C. Cabinet d'antiquités americaines. Copenhagen, 1858.

Arc 880.44 Raftery, J. Prehistoric Ireland. London, 1951.

Arc 815.27 Ragghianti, C.L. Pittori di Pompei. Milano, 1963.

Arc 726.73.5 Ragguagli di varii scavi. (Hadrawa, N.) Dresda, 1794.

Arc 726.73 Ragguagli di varii scavi. (Hadrawa, N.) Napoli, 1793.

Arc 1033.17.326 Ragguaglio...della arcangelo San Michele. Napoli, 1846.

Arc 1025.27 Ragguaglio critico dei monumenti delle arti cristiane. (Cavedoni, Celestino.) Modena, 1849.

Arc 1030.29 Ragguaglio critico del discorso sopra le iscrizioni cristiane. (Gazzera, C.) Modena, 1851.

Arc 1030.40 Ragguaglio critico delle iscrizioni cristiane. (Cavedoni, C.) Modena, 185-?

Arc 1020.17 Ragguaglio della univerzione...dei S.S. Martue. (Pannelli, D.) Pesaro, 1751.

Arc 1027.27.13 Ragguaglio di due antichi cimiteri. (Cavedoni, C.) Modena, 1853.

Arc 1033.12.38 Ragionamenti della sacra sindone. (Balliani, C.) Torino, 1610.

Arc 861.201 Rahtz, Philip. Beckery Chapel, Glastonbury, 1967-68. Glastonbury, 1974.

Arc 861.194 Rahtz, Philip. Excavations at King John's hunting lodge, Writtle, Essex, 1955-57. London, 1969.

Arc 838.36 Las raices de España. (Gómez Tabanera, José Manuel.) Madrid, 1967.

Arc 726.341.5 Rainey, Froelich G. The search for Sybaris, 1960-1965. Roma, 1967.

Arc 1148.37 Rainò, Beniamino. Giovanni Onorio da Maglie, trascrittore di codici greci. Bari, 1972.

Arc 505.10 Raint. Lettre sur un plan du Haram El-Khalil. Paris, 1886.

Arc 853.67 Raiser, J.N. von. Die römischen Alterthümer zu Augsburg. Augsburg, 1820.

Arc 430.2F Rájendralála Mitra. Antiquities of Orissa. Calcutta, 1875-80. 2v.

Arc 441.1F Rájendralála Mitra. Buddha Gayá. Calcutta, 1878.

Arc 936.14.10 Rajewski, Z. Biskupin. Varsovie, 1959.

Arc 936.14.345 Rajewski, Zolzisław. Biskupin. wyd. 1. Warszawa, 1970.

Arc 457.10 Rājgir. 4. ed. (Ķuraishi, M.M.Ḥ.) Delhi, 1956.

Arc 1480.50 Rajic, H.P. Ilustrovani katalog novaca rimskih i vizantiskih vladaoca. Beograd, 1939?

Arc 1590.9 Rajić, N.P. Illustr. katal. nov. srpekhikh tsareva, 700-1710 g. Beograd, 1940.

Arc 905.1 Rambles and studies in Bosnia. (Munro, Robert.) Edinburgh, 1895.

Arc 905.1.5 Rambles and studies in Bosnia-Herzegovina and Dalmatia, with an account of the proceedings of the congress of archaeologists and anthropologists. 2. ed. (Munro, Robert.) Edinburgh, 1900.

Arc 652.2 Rambles and studies in Greece. (Mahaffy, J.P.) London, 1876.

Arc 760.7 Rambles in Rome. (Forbes, S. Russell.) London, 1882.

Arc 843.2 Ramis y Ramis, J. Inscripciones romanas que existen en Menorca. Mahon, 1817.

Arc 1027.28 Rampolla, M. Catalogo cimiteriale romano. Roma, 1900.

Arc 1016.219 Rampolla, M. De cathedra romana B. Petri. Roma, 1868.

X Cg Arc 513.13 Ramsay, W.M. The historical geography of Asia Minor. v.1-2. London, 1890.

Arc 513.13 Ramsay, W.M. The historical geography of Asia Minor. v.1-2. Photoreproduction. London, 1890.

Arc 513.13.5 Ramsay, W.M. Studies in history and art...Eastern Provinces, Roman Empire. Aberdeen, 1906.

Arc 1413.25 Ramsden, H.A. Corean coin charms and amulets. Yokohama, 1910.

Arc 1680.15 Ramsden, H.A. Siamese porcelain and other tokens. Yokohama, 1911.

NEDL Arc 1353.4 Ramus, Christian. Catalogus numorum veterum graecorum et latinorum. pt. 1-2. Hafniae, 1816.

Arc 1033.17.90 Ranaldi, Giuseppe. Memorie storiche di S. Maria del Glorioso. Macerata, 1837.

Arc 705.205 To ranathēnaikon stadion. (Polites, N.G.) Athēnai, 1896.

Arc 1153.44.5F Rand, Edward K. The earliest book of Tours. Cambridge, Mass., 1934.

Arc 1153.44.25 Rand, Edward K. A preliminary study of Alcuin's Bible. Cambridge, 1931.

Arc 585.21 Randall-MacIver, D. Amrah and Abydos. 1899-1901. London, 1902.

Arc 743.11 Randall-MacIver, D. The Etruscans. Oxford, 1927.

Arc 606.1 Randall-MacIver, David. Areika. Oxford, 1909.

Arc 606.7 Randall-MacIver, David. Buhen. Philadelphia, 1911. 2v.

Arc 723.15.7 Randall-McIver, David. The iron age in Italy. Oxford, 1927.

Arc 723.15.15 Randall-McIver, David. Italy before the Romans. Oxford, 1928.

Arc 723.15F Randall-McIver, David. Villanovans and early Etruscans. Oxford, 1924.

Arc 893.30F Randsborg, Klavs. From period III to period IV. Copenhagen, 1972.

Arc 457.15 Rang Mahal. (Rydh, Hanna.) Lund, 1959.

Arc 700.2 Rangabé, A.R. Ausgrabung beim Tempel der Hera Unweit Argos. Halle, 1855.

Arc 670.1 Rangabé, A.R. Souvenirs d'une excursion d'Athènes en Arcadie. Paris, 1857.

Arc 435.20.45 Rangāchārya, V. A topographical list of the inscirptions of the Madras presidency (collected till 1915) with notes. Madras, 1919. 3v.

Arc 600.160F Ranke, Hermann. Koptische Friedhöfe bei Karâra und der Amontempel Schesehonks I bei El Hibe. Berlin, 1926.

Arc 853.18 Ranke, Johannes. Die akademische Kommission. München, 1900.

Arc 750.206.10 Die Ranken der Ara Pacis. (Kraus, Theodor.) Berlin, 1953.

Arc 925.50.265 Ranni slov'iany mizh Dnistrom i pnypiatkii. (Baran, Volodymyr D.) Kyïv, 1972.

Arc 925.323.5 Rannie bolgary na Volge. (Gening, Vladimir F.) Moskva, 1964.

Arc 925.50.60 Rannotrypil's'ke poselennia lenkivtsi seredn'omu Dnistri. (Chernysh, K.K.) Kyïv, 1959.

Arc 543.65.5 Ranov, V.A. Kamennye rek Tadzhikistana. Dushambe, 1965.

Arc 925.340 Ranshenbakh, Vera M. Novye nakhodki na chetyrekhstolbovom ostrove. Moskva, 1969.

Arc 451.5 Rao, Shikaripur R. Lothal and the Indus civilization. N.Y., 1973.

Arc 1468.10 Raoul-Rachette. Mémories de numismatique et d'antiquité. Paris, 1840.

Arc 1025.7.11 Raoul-Rochette, D. Le catacombe di Roma. Milano, 1841.

Arc 1025.7.5 Raoul-Rochette, D. Tabelau des catacombes de Rome. Paris, n.d.

Arc 1025.7.7 Raoul-Rochette, D. Tableau des catacombes de Rome. Paris, 1853.

Arc 1025.7 Raoul-Rochette, D. Troisième mémoire sur les antiquités chrétiennes des catacombes. Paris, 1838.

Arc 555.2 The rape of the Nile. (Fagan, Brian M.) N.Y., 1975.

Arc 1458.6 Raper, M. An inquiry into the value of the ancient Greek and Roman money. London, 1772.

Arc 1077.2.41 Rapp, Edward. Das Labarum und der Sonnen-Cultus. Bonn, 1865.

Arc 1510.36 Der Rappenmünzbund. (Cahn, Julius.) Heidelberg, 1901.

Arc 402.20 Rapport, S.B. Archaeology. N.Y., 1963.

Arc 1390.5 Rapport...concernant le trésor de Vallon. (Blancard, Louis.) Marseille, n.d.

Arc 530.6 Rapport...de la Cilicie et de la Petite-Arménie. (Langlois, Victor.) Paris, 1854.

Arc 416.4 Rapport...mission archéologique (Cambodge, Siam, presqu'île Malaise, Inde). (Lunet de Lajonquière, E.E.) Paris, 1907-08.

Arc 838.23 Rapport...sur une mission archéologique en Portugal et dans le sud de l'Espagne. (Boutroue, A.) Paris, 1893.

Arc 935.11 Rapport. (Mas Latrie.) Paris, 1846.

Arc 820.8F Rapport de la commission...sur les antiquaires gallo-romaines. (Société Nationale des Antiquaires de France.) Paris, 1830.

Arc 547.5.25 Rapport fait à l'Académie royale des sciences. (Geoffroy Saint Hillaire, E.) Paris, 1826.

Arc 488.14.10 Rapport résumé de quinze mai de voyage. (Karimi, B.M.) Teheran, 1950?

Arc 1077.3 Rapport sur la chape arabe de Chinon. (Reinaud, J.) Paris, 1856.

Arc 582.4F Rapport sur les fouilles d'Abou-Roarch. (Institut Français d'Archéologie Orientale du Caire.) Le Caire. 1922-1924

Arc 830.141F Rapport sur les fouilles d'antiquités. pts.1-3. (Aix. Commission d'Archéologie.) Aix, 1841-44.

Arc 582.5F Rapport sur les fouilles de Dair el Médineh. (Institut Français d'Archéologie Orientale du Caire.) Le Caire. 1922-1951 10v.

Arc 582.6F Rapport sur les fouilles de Médamoud. (Institut Français d'Archéologie Orientale du Caire.) Le Caire. 1925-1932 7v.

Arc 582.7F Rapport sur les fouilles de Tell Edfou. (Institut Français d'Archéologie Orientale du Caire.) La Caire. 1921-1933 2v.

Arc 386.10 Rapport sur les questions archéologiques...Congrès de Stockholm. (Bertrand, A.) Paris, 1875.

Arc 30.10 Rapport sur les travaux de fouilles et consalidations. (Algeria. Services des Monuments Historiques.) Algeria. 2v.

Arc 493.2.15 Rapport sur l'état actuel des ruines de Persépole. (Herzfeld, Ernst E.) Berlin, 1928.

Arc 1584.1.6 Rapport sur l'ouvrage intitulé. (Brosset, M.F.) St. Petersbourg, 1847.

Arc 543.8 Rapport sur une collection d'instrument en pierre. (Daubrée, Auguste.) Paris, 1868.

Arc 497.4 Rapport sur une mission scientifique. (Rey, E.G.) Paris, 1867.

Arc 1033.17.601 Rapporto cronistorico della formazione...del simolacro...Vergine Maria di Trapani. (Galizia, C.M.) Palermo, 1733.

Arc 642.3 Rapporto d'un viaggio fatto nella Grecia nel 1860. (Conze, A.) Roma, 1861.

Arc 726.59.35 Rapporto preliminare della campagna. (Missione archeologica italiana a Malta.) Roma. 1963+ 6v.

Arc 600.5.20 Rapporto preliminare delle campagine di Scavo 1966-1967. (Missione di Scavo a Medinet Madi.) Milano, 1968.

Arc 545.227.25 Rapports. (Maspero, Gaston.) Le Caire, 1909. 2v.

Arc 608.6.3 Rapports adressés à M. le ministre de l'instruction publique et des cultes. (Renier, Léon.) Paris, 1852.

Arc 66.2 Rapports de la commission des écoles d'Athènes et de Rome. (France. Institutes.) Paris. 1878-1889 2v.

Arc 923.106 Les rapports et les informations des archéologues de l'URSS. Moscou, 1962.

Arc 584.1 Rapports sur la Marche, 1899-1910. (Egypt. Antiquities Department.) Le Caire, 1912.

Arc 1027.72 Rapports sur les fouilles des catacombes d'Hadrumète. (Leynaud, A.F.) Paris, 1905.

Arc 720.214F Rappresentazione...edifizi...di Piza. (Grassi.) Piza, 1839.

Arc 1418.12 Rapson, E.J. Indian coins. Strassburg, 1897.

Arc 1335.39 Rare coins and medals of William S. Appleton. (Elder, Thomas L.) N.Y., 1913.

Arc 1613.19 The rare coins of America, England, Ireland, Scotland, France, Germany, and Spain. (Von Bergen, W.) Cambridge, Mass., 1899.

Arc 1468.25 Rare Greek coins. (Greenwell, W.) London, 1893.

Arc 1490.30 Rariora magnae Graeciae numismata...1592. (Parisio, Prospero.) n.p., 1683.

Arc 1033.24.5 Una rarita del secolo XIX...sacro tesoro del G.C. Rossi. (Vecchi, G. de.) Roma, 1896.

Arc 505.80 Ras-Shamra. (Saadé, Gabriel.) Beyrouth, 1954.

Arc 1340.1.2 Rasche, J.C. Lex. univ. rei numariae veterum. Supplement. Leipzig, 1802-05. 3v.

Arc 1340.1 Rasche, J.C. Lex. univ. rei nummariae. v.1-5, pt.1-2; v.6, pt.1. Leipzig, 1785-95. 11v.

Arc 1033.17.98.7 Rasgo histórico acerca de nuestra Señora de la antigua de Guadalajara. (García, Juan C.) Guadalajara, 1884.

Arc 510.215.5 Raskopki...1904 godu. (Marr, N.) Sankt Peterburg, 1906.

Arc 540.4 Raskopki goradishcha kiteia v 1928 g. (Marti, I.I.) Simferopol, 1929.

Arc 925.235F Raskopki kurganov Eniseiskoi gubernii. (Urusov, V.P.) Moskva, 1902.

Arc 925.173F Raskopki po chasti vodorazdela verkhnikh pritokov Dnepra i Volgi, 1903 g. (Bulychov, Nikolai I.) Moskva, 1903.

Arc 925.50.190F Raskopki severianskikh kurganov v Chernigove vo vremia XIV arkheologicheskago s"ezda. (Samokvasev, Dmitrii I.) Moskva, 1916.

Arc 543.153 Raskopki Tillia-tepe v Severnom Afganistane. (Sarianidi, Viktor I.) Moskva, 1972.

Arc 497.75 Raskopki v bibleiskikh stranakh. (Kryvelev, Iosif A.) Moskva, 1965.

Arc 530.82 Raskopki v golovino. (Martirosian, A.) Erevan, 1954.

Arc 1390.12 Rasmusson, Nils L. Commentationes de nummis saeculorum IX-XI in suecia repertis. Stockholm, 1961- 2v.

Arc 608.2.60 I rasoi punici. (Acquaro, Enrico.) Roma, 1971.

Arc 1016.222 Rasponi, C. De basilica et patriarchio Lateranensi. Roma, 1656.

Arc 1027.26.15 Rassegna archeologica. Iscrizioni cristiana dei catacombe di Siracusa. (Carini, I.) Palermo, 1876.

Arc 1317.4.12 Rassegna numismatica. Orbetello. 1-38,1904-1941 12v.

Arc 936.165.45 Ratalovich, Isak A. Slaviane VI-IX wkov v Moldavii. Kishinev, 1972.

Arc 380.203 Rathgeber, D.G. Archäologische Schriften. Gotha, 1851-57.

Arc 1470.8 Rathgeber, G. Neumundneunzig Silberne Münzen der Athenaier. Weissensee, 1858.

Arc 1512.2F Rathgeber, Georg. Aufbau der niederländischen Kunstgeschichte und Museologie...Niederländische Münzen und Medaillen dis Herzoglichen Museums zu Gotha. Weissensee, 1839.

Arc 543.70.5F Rathjens, Carl. Sabaeica. Hamburg, 1953.

Arc 543.79 Rathjens, Carl. Vorislamische Altertümer. Hamburg, 1932.

Arc 1033.3.5 Ratti, N. Sopra un sarcofago cristiano con travole. Roma, 1828.

Arc 925.50.5 Ratych, O.O. Drevnorus'ki arkheologii pam'iatky na teryt. Kyïv, 1957.

Arc 853.341 Rau, Hermann Gunther. Das urnenfelderzeitliche Gräberfeld von Aschaffenburg-Streitwald. Kallmünz, 1972.

Arc 1153.58 Rauh, Rudolf. Paläographie des mainfränkischen Monumentalinscriften. Inaug. Diss. München, 1935.

Arc 925.267 Raushenbakh, V.M. Srednee Zaural'e v epokhu neolita i bronzy. Moskva, 1956.

Arc 1076.4.10 Rausing, Gad. The bow; some notes on its origin and development. Bonn, 1967.

Arc 861.33.3 Rauthmell, R. Antiquitates Bremetonacenses, or Roman antiquitites of Overborough. Kirkby Lonsdale, 1824.

Arc 861.33 Rauthmell, R. Antiquitates Bremetonacenses. London, 1746.

Arc 82.1.10 Ravaisson-Mollien, F. Lettre à Mollien le directeur de la Revue archéologique. Paris, 1876.

Arc 1470.41 Ravel, O.E. Les "Poulains" de Corinthe; monographie des statères corinthiens. Bâle, 1936-48. 2v.

Arc 1076.3.31 Raven, J.J. The bells of England. London, 1906.

Arc 1076.3.55 Raven, John J. The church bells of Suffolk. London, 1890.

Arc 861.74 Ravenhill, T.H. The Rollright stones and the men who erected them. Birmingham, 1926.

Arc 1020.30 Ravennatische Studien. (Dütschke, H.) Leipzig, 1909.

Arc 1033.3.41 Die ravennatischen Sarkophage. (Goldmann, K.) Strassburg, 1906.

Arc 1020.30.5 Ravenne. (Diehl, Charles.) Paris, 1907.

Arc 785.13.27 Ravioli, Camillo. Regionamento del Foro Romano. Roma, 1859.

Arc 1348.21 Rawlings, G.B. Coins and how to know them. N.Y., n.d.

Arc 402.1 Rayet, O. Études d'archéologie et d'art. Paris, 1888.

Arc 510.7 Rayet, O. Milet et le golfe latmique. Paris, 1877-85.

Arc 830.114 Raymond, Paul. L'arrondissement d'Uzès avant l'histoire. Paris, 1900.

Arc 1625.3 Raymond, W. The coins of Mexico in silver and copper, 1536-1939. N.Y., 1940.

Arc 1645.2 Raymond, Wayte. The coins of South America; silver and copper. British Guiana, Dutch Guiana, French Guiana. N.Y., 1942.

Arc 1400.7.2 Raymond, Wayte. Coins of the world, twentieth century issues. 2. ed. N.Y., 1945.

Arc 3.1.28 Le rayonnement des civilizations grecque et romaine sur les cultures périphériques. (Congrès International d'Archéologie Classique, 8th, Paris, 1963.) Paris, 1965. 2v.

Arc 302.20 Razkopki i prochzvani. (Sofia. Naroden Arkheologicheski Muzei.) Sofiia. 1+

Arc 302.20F Razkopki i prochzvani. (Sofia. Naroden Arkheologicheski Muzei.) Sofiia. 3+

Arc 1163.3.70 Razvitie slaviano-russkoi paleografii v dosrevoluitsionnoi Rossii. (Zhukovskaia, L.P.) Moskva, 1963.

Arc 1033.141 Razy, E. Saint Jean-Baptiste, sa vie, son culte. Paris, 1880.

Arc 545.236.5F Das Re-Heiligtum des Ne-Woser-Re. (Bissing, F.W.) Berlin, 1905-23. 2v.

Arc 435.2.21F Rea, Alexander. Châlukyan architecture. Madras, 1898.

Arc 435.2.17F Rea, Alexander. List of architectural and archaeological remains in Coorg. Madras, 1894.

Arc 435.2.25F Rea, Alexander. Monumental remains of the Dutch East India Company in the presidency of Madras. Madras, 1897.

Arc 435.2.34F Rea, Alexander. Pallava architecture. Madras, 1909.

Arc 435.2.15F Rea, Alexander. South Indian Buddhist antiquities. Madras, 1894.

Arc 969.1 Read, M.C. Archaeology of Ohio. Cleveland, 1888.

Arc 1478.85 Reading and dating Roman imperial coins. 3. ed. (Klawans, Zander H.) Racine, Wis., 1963.

Arc 1018.05 Real-Encyclopädie der Christlichen Alterthümer. (Kraus, Franz X.) Freiburg, 1882-86. 2v.

Arc 793.11 Reale Accademia Ercolanese di Archeologia, Naples. Memorie. v.1-9. Napoli, 1822-62. 10v.

Arc 1020.9.64 La reale chiesa del SS. Sudario in Roma. (Iozzi, Oliviero.) Roma, 1910.

Arc 389.6.2 Realités et énigmes de l'archéologie. 2. éd. (Eydoux, Henri Paul.) Paris, 1964.

Arc 848.4 Reallexikon der germanischen Altertumskunde. (Hoops, J.) Strassburg, 1911. 4v.

Arc 848.4.2 Reallexikon der germanischen Altertumskunde. v.1-2, pt.1-5. 2. Aufl. Berlin, 1968-

Arc 375.6 Reallexikon der prähistorischen, klassischen...Altertümer. (Forrer, R.) Berlin, 1907.

Arc 375.8 Reallexikon der Vorgeschichte. v.1-15. (Ebert, Max.) Berlin, 1924-32. 16v.

Arc 1093.2.30 The realm of the great goddess; the story of the megalith builders. (Cles-Reden, Sibylle.) London, 1961.

Arc 1500.41 Réapparitions du type gaulois dans le coin du moyen age. (Lelewel, Joachim.) Bruxelles, 1841.

Arc 968.1.2 Reasons why the state should acquire the famous burial mound of the Seneca Indians. (Conover, G.S.) n.p., n.d.

Arc 772.1.2 Reber, F. von. Die Ruinen Roms. Leipzig, 1863.

Arc 772.1 Reber, F. von. Die Ruinen Roms. Leipzig, 1879.

Arc 682.3 Reber, F. von. Und die Verhältniss der mykenischen zur dorischen Baustiel. München, 1896.

Arc 1500.46 Recamier, E. Monnaies romaines. Paris, 1925.

Arc 1475.201 Recensio nummorum qui secusii. (Vernazza de Freney, J.) Augustae Taurinorum, 1812.

Arc 858.63 Recent archaeological excavations in Britain. (Bruce-Mitford, R.L.S.) London, 1956.

Arc 612.79 Recent archaeological excavations in Europe. London, 1975.

Arc 958.1 Recent archaeological explorations in the Valley of the Delaware. (Abbott, Charles C.) Boston, 1892.

Arc 936.195.140 Recent archaeological finds in Czechoslavakia. (Filip, Jan.) Prague, 1966.

Arc 1010.29F The recent archaeology of the Sydney district: excavations, 1964-1967. Canberra, 1974.

Arc 943.27 Recent discoveries attributed to early man in America. (Hudlicka, A.) Washington, 1918.

Arc 785.13.17.5 Recent discoveries in the Forum, 1898-1904. (Braddeley, S.C.) London, 1904.

Arc 785.13.17 Recent discoveries in the Forum. (Braddeley, S.C.) N.Y., 1904.

Arc 861.4 The recent discoveries of Roman remains found in the...City of Chester. (Earwaker, J.P.) Manchester, 1888.

Arc 505.5.81 Recent discoveries on the Temple Hill at Jerusalem. 2. ed. (King, J.) London, 1885.

Arc 590.15 The recent discovery of ancient Egyptian mummies at Thebes. (Wilson, E.) London, 1883.

Arc 543.3.55F Recent excavations at Khawazm. (Field, Henry.) Ann Arbor, 1948.

Arc 1025.9 Recent excavations in American Christian cemeteries. (Smyth, E.) Worcester, 1882.

Arc 785.13.11 Recent excavations in the Roman Forum. (Burton Brown, E.) N.Y., 1905.

Arc 785.13.9 Recent excavations in the Roman Forum. 1898-1904. (Burton Brown, E.) N.Y., 1904.

Arc 1027.40.5 La recente condroversia sul cimitero Ostriano. (Marucchi, O.) Roma, 1903.

Arc 785.31 Recenti scoperte dell'Iseo Compense. (Marucchi, O.) Roma, 1883.

Arc 726.33 Le recenti scoperte di antichita in Verona. (Milani, L.A.) Verona, 1891.

Arc 1020.29 Le recenti scoperte nel Duomo di Parinzo. (Marucchi, O.) Roma, 1896.

Arc 1027.15.9 Le recenti scoperte presso il cimitero di San Valentino. (Marucchi, O.) Roma, 1888.

Arc 887.1F Receueil d'antiquités romaines et gauloises trouvées dans la Flandre. (Bast, M.J. de.) Gand, 1808.

Arc 380.207 Recherche curieuse d'antiquité. (Chevalier, N.) Utrecht, n.d.

Arc 403.4 Recherche curieuse d'antiquité. (Spon, J.) Lyon, 1683.

Arc 785.50 Recherche des limites du Grand Arque. (Bigot, Paul.) Rome, 1909.

Arc 830.18.7 Recherche sur divers lieux du pays des Silvanectes. (Peigné-Delacourt, A.) Amiens, 1864.

Arc 1020.84.5 Recherches...emaux du trésor de la Cathedrale de Troyes. (Le Brun Dalbaune.) Troyes, 1862.

Arc 66.1.220 Recherches archéologique en territoire Volsinien. (Bloch, Raymond.) Paris, 1972.

Arc 608.1.55 Recherches archéologiques à Haïdra. (Baratte, François.) Paris, 1974.

Arc 608.35.5 Recherches archéologiques à la Qal'a des Banû Hammâd. (Golvin, Lucien.) Paris, 1965.

Arc 608.2.45 Recherches archéologiques à Marrakech. (Meunié, Jacques.) Paris, 1952.

Arc 822.1 Recherches archéologiques à Pareds. (Baudry, F.) La-Roche-sur-Yon, 1874. 21 pam.

Arc 689.3.15 Recherches archéologiques à Phères de Thessalie. (Béquignon, Y.) Paris, 1937.

Arc 689.3.17 Recherches archéologiques à Phères de Thessalie. Thèse. (Bequignon, Y.) Strasbourg, 1937.

Author and Title Listing

Arc 688.3F Recherches archéologiques à Stratos d'Acarnanie. (Courby, F.) Paris, 1924.
Arc 608.88.5 Recherches archéologiques à Tanger et dans sa région. (Ponsich, Michel.) Paris, 1970.
Arc 608.6.35 Recherches archéologiques en Algérie. (Gsell, Stéphane.) Paris, 1893.
Arc 416.8 Recherches archéologiques en Asie centrale (1931). (Hackin, J.) Paris, 1936.
Arc 936.7 Recherches archéologiques en Pologne? (Zawisza, Jan.) Warszawa, 1874.
Arc 608.22 Recherches archéologiques et ethnographiques au Tassili des Ajjers (Sahara Central). (Perret, Robert.) Paris, 1936.
Arc 830.100 Recherches archéologiques sur le térritoire de Mantoche. (Gasser, A.) Gray, 1901.
Arc 384.10 Recherches d'archéologie et d'histoire de l'art (antiquité). Louvain, 1970.
Arc 608.7.5 Recherches des antiquités dans le nord de l'Afrique. (Université de l'Instruction Publique.) Paris, 1890.
Arc 1478.36 Recherches des monnaies impériales romaines non décrites dans l'ouvrage de H. Cohen. (Belfort, A.) Macon, 1884.
Arc 985.210F Recherches historiques et archéologiques. (Hamy, M.E.T.) Paris, 1885.
Arc 1264.9 Recherches historiques sur le tabellionage royal. (Barabé, A.) Rouen, 1863.
Arc 915.4.5 Recherches historiques sur les antiquités d'Augst. (Jacob-Kolb, G.) Rheims, 1823.
Arc 1670.53 Recherches numismatiques...les médailles celtiberiennes. (Lorichs, G.D. de.) Paris, 1852.
Arc 561.2 Recherches pour servir à l'histoire de l'Égypte. (Letronne, J.A.) Paris, 1823.
Arc 608.66 Recherches préhistoriques dans l'Ahazzar nord-occidental. (Hugot, Henri J.) Paris, 1963.
Arc 47.3 Recherches suisses d'archéologie copte. Genève. 1,1967+ 2v.
Arc 1349.45 Recherches sur Bertrand Andrieu de Bordeau. (Fayolle, A. Evrard.) Chalon-sur-Saone, 1902.
Arc 673.3 Recherches sur Délos. (Lebègue, J.A.) Paris, 1876.
Arc 830.89.7 Recherches sur la géographie ancienne et les antiquités du département des Basses-Alpes. 2e éd. (Henry, Dominique M.J.) Digne, 1842.
Arc 608.7.15 Recherches sur la géographie comparée de la Maurétanie Tingitane. (Tissot.) Paris, 1877.
Arc 830.105 Recherches sur la nature et l'etendue d'un ancien ouvrage des Romains. (La Sauvagère, F.) Paris, 1740.
Arc 1490.15 Recherches sur la numismatique...des nomands de Sicile. (Engel, A.) Paris, 1882.
Arc 66.1.198 Recherches sur la statuaire en pierre étrusque archaique. (Hus, A.) Paris, 1961.
Arc 608.2.12 Recherches sur la topographie de Carthage. (Dureau de la Malle, Adolphe.) Paris, 1835.
Arc 66.1.174 Recherches sur l'agora grecque. (Martin, R.) Paris, 1951.
Arc 66.1.109 Recherches sur l'conographie de l'évangile aux XIV, XV et XVI siècles. (Millet, G.) Paris, 1916.
Arc 830.37 Recherches sur le lieu...bataille d'Attila en 451. (Peigné-Delacourt, A.) Paris, 1860. 2v.
Arc 505.18.7 Recherches sur l'emplacement...du tombeau d'Hélène. (Saulcy.) Paris, 1869.
Arc 66.1.25 Recherches sur l'entrée de Spagne. (Thomas, A.) Paris, 1882.
Arc 543.7.30 Recherches sur l'érosin des gres des monuments d'Angkor. (Delvert, Jean.) Paris, 1963.
Arc 785.76 Recherches sur les amphores romains. Rome, 1972.
Arc 1500.30 Recherches sur les anciennes monnaies du comté de Bourgogne. (Grappin, Pierre-Philippe.) Paris, 1782.
Arc 953.13 Recherches sur les antiquités de l'Amérique. (Warden, D.B.) Paris, 1827.
Arc 853.20.9 Recherches sur les antiquités romaines dans la vallée de la Moselle de Trèves. (Wyttenback, J.H.) Trèves, 1840.
Arc 830.44 Recherches sur les aqueducs et cloaques de la Gaule. (Blanchet, A.) Paris, 1908.
Arc 66.1.169 Recherches sur les armées hellénistiques. (Launey, Marcel.) Paris, 1949. 2v.
Arc 1663.10 Recherches sur les comtes de Looz et sur leurs monnaies. (Perreau, A.) Bruxelles, 1845.
Arc 66.1.217 Recherches sur les cultes de Délos à l'époque hellénistique et à l'époque impériale. (Bruneau, Philippe.) Paris, 1970.
X Cg Arc 1500.29F Recherches sur les empereurs qui ont régné dans les Gaules. (Witte, Jean.) n.p., 1920.
Arc 1480.29 Recherches sur les insignes de la questure et sur les récipients monétaires. (Longpérier, Adrien.) Paris, 1868.
Arc 823.55 Recherches sur les lingots de cuivre et de plomb d'époque romaine dans les régions de Languedoc-Roussillon et de Provence-Corse. (Laubenheimer-Leenhardt, F.) Paris, 1973.
Arc 1076.1 Recherches sur les lits antiques. (Heuzey, Léon.) Paris, 1873.
Arc 1495.2 Recherches sur les monnaies. (De Sauley, F.) Paris, 1843.
Arc 1500.51 Recherches sur les monnaies de Wallincourt en Cambrésis. (Chalon, Rénier.) Bruxelles, 1847.
Arc 1520.12 Recherches sur les monnaies des Comtes de Hainout. Supplement. (Chalon, Renier.) Bruxelles, 1848-54. 2v.
Arc 1500.68 Recherches sur les monnaies des ducs hereditaires de Lorraine. (Saulcy, Felicien de.) Metz, 1841.
Arc 1590.3 Recherches sur les monnaies frappées dans l'île de Rhodes. (Friedlaender, J.) Paris, 1855.
Arc 1500.35 Recherches sur les monnaiss qui ont en cours en Roussillon. (Colson, Achille.) Perpignan, 1853.
Arc 1093.2.2 Recherches sur les monuments cyclopéens. (Petit-Radel, L.C.F.) Paris, 1841.
Arc 600.6.30 Recherches sur les monuments thébains de la XXVe dynastie dite éthiopienne. (Leclant, Jean.) Le Caire, 1965. 2v.
Arc 562.3 Recherches sur les origines de l'Égypte. (Morgan, J.) Paris, 1896-97.
Arc 540.15 Recherches sur les pheniciens a Chypre. (Masson, Oliviér.) Genève, 1972.
Arc 925.9.9 Recherches sur les populations primitives. (Viviendekt-Martin, Louis.) Paris, 1847.
Arc 800.10 Recherches sur les ruines d'Herculanum. (Bondaroy, F. de.) Paris, 1770.
Arc 66.1.154 Recherches sur l'histoire, la religion et la civilisation. (Heurgon, J.) Paris, 1942.
Arc 612.60 Recherches sur l'origine et l'évolution des complexes leptolithiques. (Laplace, Georges.) Paris, 1966.
Arc 1020.92 Recherches sur precieuses reliques...dans la Sainte Eglise de Vienne. Vienne, 1876.
Arc 386.16 Das Recht an Denkmälern. Inaug. Diss. (Beyermann, Erich.) Halle, 1917.

Arc 1480.25.1 Die Rechtstitel und Regierungsprogramme auf römischen Kaisermünzen. (Schulz, Otto Theodor.) N.Y., 1968.
Arc 1020.73.17 Récit...sur les translations...1239 et 1241...reliques de la Passion. (Wailly, J.N. de.) Nogent-le-Rotrou, n.d.
Arc 1020.101 Récit de la fondation de l'Eglise de Notre Dame de Long-Pré. Abbéville, 1818.
Arc 785.49 I reclami del Foro Trajano esposti al pubblico e giustificati. (Fea, Carlo.) Roma, 1832.
Arc 935.12 Reconnaissance archéologique...cours de l'Érigon et des ruines de Stobi. (Heuzy, Leon.) Paris, 1873.
Arc 726.202 The reconstruction of two Apulian tomb groups. (Oliver, Andrew.) Bern, 1968.
Arc 967.1.2 Records of ancient races. (McAdams, William.) St. Louis, 1887.
Arc 1475.7.2 Records of Roman history. (Hobler, F.) n.p., n.d. 2v.
Arc 1475.7 Records of Roman history. (Hobler, F.) Westminster, 1860. 2v.
Arc 1535.8 Records of the coinage of Scotland. (Cochran-Patrick, R.W.) Edinburgh, 1876. 2v.
Arc 18.2 Records of the past. N.Y. 1-13,1902-1914 12v.
Arc 501.19 The recovery of Jerusalem. (Morrison, W.) London, 1871.
Arc 505.127 The recovery of Jerusalem. (Wilson, Charles.) London, 1871.
Arc 1020.49.1 Recueil...reliques...Nôtre Dame d'Aix la Chapelle. Aix, 1776?
Arc 387.1.2 Recueil d'antiquités. (Caylus, A.C.P.) Paris, 1761.
Arc 823.18 Recueil d'antiquités dans les Gaules. (La Sauvagère, F.) Paris, 1770.
Arc 920.2 Recueil d'antiquités de la Scythie. (Russia. Commission Impériale Archéologique.) St. Petersbourg, 1866. 2v.
Arc 915.6.2 Recueil d'antiquités de la Suisse. (Schmidt, F.S.) Francfort sur le Meyn, 1771.
Arc 387.1 Recueil d'antiquités égyptiennes. (Caylus, A.C.P.) Paris, 1752. 7v.
Htn Arc 915.6* Recueil d'antiquités trouvées à Avenches...de la Suisse. (Schmidt, F.S.) Berne, 1760.
VArc 416.2 Recueil d'archéologie orientale. (Clermont-Ganneau, Charles.) Paris, 1888-1924. 8v.
Arc 1223.3 Recueil de cachets sur la Montagne jeune. (Hsiang, Huai-shu.) Saigon, 1932?
Arc 1498.3 Recueil de documents...monnaies frappées par les rois de France depuis Philippe II jusqu'à François I. (Saulcy, L.F.J.C. de.) Paris, 1879-92. 4v.
Arc 1160.11 Recueil de fac-simile...paléographie moderne. (Kaulek, J.) Paris, 1889.
Arc 1135.202 Recueil de facsimiles d'écritures du XIIe au XVIIe siècle. (Prou, Maurice.) Paris, 1892.
Arc 1135.202.5 Recueil de facsimiles d'écritures du XIIe au XVIIe siècle. (Prou, Maurice.) Paris, 1896.
Htn Arc 1033.133* Recueil de la vie, mort, invention et miracles de S. Jean Baptiste. (Viseur, R.) Amyens, 1618.
Arc 800.3.5 Recueil de lettres de M. Winckelmann. (Winckelmann, J.) Paris, 1784.
Arc 1345.1.8 Recueil de médailles allemandes, XVIe et XVIIe siècles. Paris, 1858.
Arc 1370.4.2 Recueil de médailles de peuples. (Pellerin, J.) Paris, 1763. 3v.
Arc 1370.4 Recueil de médailles de rois. (Pellerin, J.) Paris, 1762.
Arc 1345.1.7 Recueil de médailles italiennes, XVe et XVIe siècles. Paris, 1858. 2v.
Arc 1500.63 Recueil de monnaies...de Douai. (Dancoisne, Louis.) Douai, 1836.
Arc 823.16 Recueil de monumens antiques. v.1-2. (Grivaud de la Vincelle, C.M.) Paris, 1817.
Arc 545.233 Recueil de monuments egyptiens. (Capart, J.) Bruxelles, 1902-05. 2v.
Arc 925.7 Recueil de quelques antiquités. (Wapel, Leon de.) Berlin, 1803.
Arc 830.83 Recueil des antiquités et monumens marseillos. (Grossen, J.B.B.) Marseille, 1773.
Arc 1030.48.5 Recueil des inscriptions de la Gaule antérieures à la Renaissance carolingienne. Paris, 1975-
Arc 545.227.13 Recueil des inscriptions grecques. (Lefebvre, G.) Le Caire, 1907.
Arc 66.1.91 Recueil des inscriptiosn chrétiennes du Mont Athos. (Millet, J.) Paris, 1904.
Arc 1215.1 Recueil des sceaux du Moyen Âge dits sceaux gothiques. (Migieu.) Paris, 1779.
Arc 66.1.142 Recueil Edmond Pottier. Paris, 1937.
Arc 1345.1.16 Recueil général de bas-reliefs et d'ornements. Paris, 1858. 2v.
Arc 848.14.35 Recueil général des bas-reliefs. (Espérandieu, Émile.) Paris, 1931.
Arc 1470.14 Recueil général des monnaies grecques d'Asie Mineure. (Waddington, W.H.) Paris, 1904. 4v.
Arc 1660.15F Recueil général des pieces obsidionales. (Duby, P.A.T.) Paris, 1786.
Arc 1033.12.75 Recueil historique...du...sang...Bruges. Bruges, 1761.
Arc 1663.33 Recueil illustré des ordres de chevalerie et decorations belges de 1830 à 1963. 5. éd. (Quinot, Henri.) Bruxelles, 1963.
Arc 1033.7 Recuerdos de un viaje a Santiago de Galicia. (Fita y Colomé, Fidel.) Madrid, 1880.
Arc 497.19 Redding, M.W. Antiquities of the Orient unveiled. N.Y., 1872.
Arc 710.7 Rede zum Winckelmann-Zage. (Milchhoefer, A.) Kiel, 1898.
Arc 1522.6 Reding, Lucien. Les monnaies gauloises du Tetelbierg. Luxembourg, 1972.
Arc 963.2.20 Rediscovering Illinois. (Cole, Fay C.) Chicago, 1937.
Arc 1185.10.15 Redlich, Oswald. Der Privaturkunden des Mittelalters. München, 1967.
Arc 384.16 Redman, Charles L. Research and theory in current archeology. N.Y., 1973.
Arc 1093.5 Redslob, E. Die fränkischen Epitaphen im 4. und 5. Jahrhundert. Inaug. Diss. Nürnberg, 1907.
Arc 1027.19.40F Reekmans, Louis. La tombe du Pape Corneille et su région cimetriale. Città del Vaticano, 1964.
Arc 505.5.8 Reeland, Adriaan. De spoliis templi Hierosolymitani. Utrecht, 1716.
Arc 497.3 Reeland, Adriaan. Palaestina. Utrecht, 1714. 2v.
Arc 1033.17.97.8 Reflecciones sobre la aparición de la santísima virgen de Guadalupe. (Sotomayor, José F.) México, 1870.
Arc 1494.50 La reforma monetaria de 1868; catalogo de monedas. (Fontecha y Sanchez, Ramon de.) Madrid, 1965.
Arc 1033.175 Refrigerium interim. (Stuiber, Alfred.) Bonn, 1957.
Arc 1033.35.37 Réfugié à Jérusalem au VIe siècle. (Kohler, C.) Nogent-le-Rotrou, n.d.

Author and Title Listing

Arc 537.3 Regaldi, G. Le antichita di Cipro. Roma, 1879.
Arc 1033.35 Regazzi, A. De sacrosancta...cruce...quae in S. Crucis osservantur. Roma, 1777.
Arc 225.10 Régészeti dolgozatok. (Budapest. Tudomany Egyetem-Régészeti Intézet.) 3,1959+ 4v.
Arc 225.35 Régészeti füzetek. Series 2. Budapest. 1-13,1958-1964 5v.
Arc 920.204F Régészeti tanulmányok az Oroszföldon. v.3-4. (Pósta, Béla.) Leipzig, 1905. 2v.
Arc 66.1.118 Le régime politique et les institutions de Rome au Moyen-Age, 1252-1347. (De Boüard, A.) Paris, 1920.
Arc 404.2 Reginald Cambell Thompson. (Driver, Godfrey Rolles.) London, 1944.
Arc 785.22.20 Regio urbis decima. (Lugli, G.) Roma, 1960.
Arc 830.345 La région montpelliévaine à l'époque préromaine (750-121 avant J.-C.). (Richard, Jean-Claude M.) Bruxelles, 1973.
Arc 673.1.40F La région nord du sanctuaire de l'épogue archaïque à la fin du sanctuaire. (Pouilloux, Jean.) Paris, 1960. 2v.
Arc 785.13.27 Regionamento del Foro Romano. (Ravioli, Camillo.) Roma, 1859.
Arc 770.3A Die Regionen der Stadt Rom. (Preller, L.) Jena, 1846.
Arc 1550.8.10 Regis Daniae. (Lauring, P.) København, 1961.
Arc 1318.3.6 Regiser zu Bulletin, v.1-11; Revue suisse de numismatique, v.1-24. (Société Suisse de Numismatique.) Bern, 1929.
Arc 1325.1.5 Register. (Sallet, A. von.) Berlin. 1-20,1884-1898
Arc 65.3.2 Register zu Mittheilungen. Athens. 1-5
Arc 65.3.3 Register zu Mittheilungen. Athens. 6-10
Arc 65.3.4 Register zu Mittheilungen. Athens. 11-15
Arc 65.3.5 Register zu Mittheilungen. Athens. 16-20
Arc 65.1.2 Register zur archaeologische Zeitung. Berlin. 1-43,1843-1885
Arc 1261.3.10 Registro general del sello. (Spain. Archivo General de Simancas.) Valladolid. 1,1950+ 12v.
Arc 1468.14 Regling, H. Griechischen Münzen der Sammlung Warren. Text and plates. Berlin, 1906. 2v.
Arc 1470.15 Regling, K. Terina. Berlin, 1906.
Arc 1372.3 Regling, Kurt. Die antike Münze als Kunstwerk. 1. Aufl. Berlin, 1924.
Htn Arc 1480.35F* Regum et imperatorum Romanorum numismata. (Croy, Charles.) Antverpiae, 1654.
Arc 1365.1 Regum veterum numismata. v.1-2. (Khevenhueller, F.A.) Vienna, 17- .
Arc 1510.132 Rehle, Q. Die Münzen der Stadt Kaufbeuren. Kaufbeuren, 1880.
Arc 497.101 Rehork, Joachim. Archäologie und biblisches Leben. Bergish Gladbach, 1972.
Arc 402.22 Rehork, Joachim. Faszinierende Funde; Archäologie heute. Bergisch Gladbach, 1971.
Arc 1018.33 Reichensperger. Bermischte Schriften über christliche Kunst. Leipzig, 1856.
Arc 1510.20 Der Reichsstadt Nürnberg. (Scholler, Ernst.) Nürnberg, 1916.
Arc 510.201.2 Reiden in Lykien, Milyas und Kibyratis. (Petersen, E.) Vienna, 1889.
Arc 497.49 Reifenberg, A. Ancient Hebrew arts. N.Y., 1950.
Arc 1423.18.5 Reifenberg, A. Ancient Hebrew seals. London, 1950.
Arc 1423.18.4 Reifenberg, A. Ancient Jewish coins. Jerusalem, 1965.
Arc 1423.18 Reifenberg, A. Ancient Jewish coins. 2. ed. Jerusalem, 1947.
Arc 1423.18.10 Reifenberg, A. Israel's history in coins from the Maccabees to the Roman conquest. London, 1953.
Arc 1138.19 The reign of the manuscript. (Sinks, Perry W.) Boston, 1917.
Arc 853.135F Die Reihengräber der karolingisch-ottonischen Zeit. (Stroh, Armin.) Kallmünz, 1954. 2 pam.
Arc 853.292 Reihengräberfriedhöfe. (Wegewitz, Willi.) Neumünster, 1968.
Arc 853.294 Ein Reihengräberfriedhof in Sontheim an der Brenz. (Neuffer-Müller, Christiane.) Stuttgart, 1966.
Arc 853.275F Reihengräberfriedhofe des 8. bis 11. Jahrhunderts. (Rempel, Heinrich.) Berlin, 1966.
Arc 830.86 Reims pendant la domination romaine. (Loriquet, Charles.) Reims, 1860.
Arc 407.30.15 Rein, Ulrike G.M. Winckelmanns Begriff der Schönheit. Bonn, 1972.
Arc 402.2.25 Reinach, S. Bibliographie de S. Reinach. Paris, 1936.
Arc 618.1 Reinach, S. Les celtes dans les vallées du Po et du Danube. Paris, 1894.
Arc 402.2 Reinach, S. Chroniques d'Orient. Paris, 1891. 2v.
Arc 785.15.13 Reinach, S. La colonne trajane au Musee de Saint-Germain. Paris, 1886.
Arc 657.1 Reinach, S. Conseils aux voyageurs archéologues en Grèce. Paris, 1886.
Arc 402.2.2 Reinach, S. Esquisses archéologiques. Paris, 1888.
Arc 402.2.9 Reinach, S. Le mirage oriental. Paris, 1893.
NEDL Arc 1372.1 Reinach, T. L'histoire par les monnaies. Paris, 1902.
Arc 1372.1.5 Pamphlet vol. Reinach, T. Numismatics. 7 pam.
Arc 1423.10.5 Reinach, Théodore. Jewish coins. London, 1903.
Arc 1423.10 Reinach, Théodore. Les monnaies juives. Paris, 1887.
Arc 402.10 Pamphlet vol. Reinach, Theodore. Pamphlets on art, archaeology and ancient history. 25 pam.
Arc 1033.35.39 Reinartz, J.L. Notice sur le reliquaire de la sainte croix...à Tongres. n.p., n.d.
Arc 1077.3 Reinaud, J. Rapport sur la chape arabe de Chinon. Paris, 1856.
Arc 1418.4 Reinaud, J.T. Explication de cinq médailles...du Bengale. Paris, 1823.
Arc 853.264F Reinbacker, E. Börnicke. Berlin, 1963.
Arc 383.75 Reinecke Festschrift zum 75. Geburtstag von Paul Reinecke. (Behrens, Gustav.) Mainz, 1950.
Arc 848.38 Reinerth, Hans. Vorgeschichte der deutschen Stämme. Leipzig, 1940. 3v.
Arc 1335.156 Reinfeld, Fred. Catalogue of the world's most popular coins. Garden City, 1965.
Arc 1494.5 Reis de Sanches Ferreira, M. Opataco apontamentos para a sua historia. Coimbra, 1911.
Arc 421.14 Reischauer, E.O. Japanese archaeological work on the Asiatic continent. Baltimore, 1940.
Arc 426.9 Reischauer, E.O. The thunder-weapon in ancient Japan. Baltimore, 1940.
Arc 681.1 Reise auf der Insel Lesbos. (Conze, A.) Hannover, 1865.
Arc 726.34.5 Reise auf der Insel Sardinien. (Waltzan, H.) Leipzig, 1869.
Arc 642.3.2 Reise auf Inseln des Thrak. Meeres. (Conze, A.) Hannover, 1860.
Arc 497.8 Reise in Syrien und Mesopotamien. (Sachau, E.) Leipzig, 1883.
Arc 600.2 Reise nach der grossen Oase El-Khargeh. (Brugsch-Bey, H.) Leipzig, 1878.
X Cg Arc 510.202 Reisen in Kleinasien und Nordsyrien. Text and atlas. (Humann, K.) Berlin, 1890. (Changed to XP 9867) 2v.
Arc 510.201 Reisen in Lykien und Karien. (Benndorf, O.) Vienna, 1884.
Arc 513.9 Reisen nach Kos, Halikarnassos, Rhodos. (Ross, L.) Halle, 1852.
Arc 657.2.3 Reisen und der griechischen Inseln. v.1-3. (Ross, L.) Stuttgart, 1840-45.
Arc 660.1 Reisen und Forschungen in Griechenland. pt.1-2. (Ulrichs, H.N.) Bremen, 1840.
Arc 657.2.2 Reisen und Reiseronten durch Griechenland. (Ross, L.) Berlin, 1841.
Arc 595.23.5F Reisner, G.A. A history of the Giza mecropolis. Cambridge, Mass., 1942- 2v.
Arc 595.23FA Reisner, G.A. Mycerinus; the temples of the third pyramid at Giza. Cambridge, 1931.
Arc 402.16 Pamphlet vol. Reisner, G.A. Miscellaneous papers. 10 pam.
Arc 402.15 Pamphlet vol. Reisner, G.A. Miscellaneous papers. 14 pam.
Arc 600.41FA Reisner, George A. The development of the Egyptian tomb down to the accession of Cheops. Cambridge, 1936.
Arc 495.13FA Reisner, George A. Harvard excavations at Samaria 1908-1910. Cambridge, 1924. 2v.
Arc 567.3 Pamphlet vol. Reisner, George Andrew. 13 pam.
Arc 567.3.5 Pamphlet vol. Reisner, George Andrew. 9 pam.
Arc 853.69.15 Reith, A. Vorgeschichte der Schwäbischen Alb. Leipzig, 1938.
Htn Arc 1020.120* Relaçam do solenne recebimento que se fez em Lisboa. (Campos, Manoel de.) Lisboa, 1588.
Arc 1033.17.202 Relación verdadera de la imagen...Alcay. Valencia, 1665.
Arc 605.1 Relation d'un voyage dans la Marmarique. Text, plates. (Pacho, J.R.) Paris, 1827. 2v.
Arc 608.1.39 Relation d'une mission archéologique en Tunisie. (Hérisson, M. d'.) Paris, 1881.
Arc 670.3 Relations between inscriptions and sculptured representations on Attica tombstones. (Hastings, H.R.) Madison, 1912.
Arc 66.1.151 Les relations des papes d'Avignon. (Renouard, Yves.) Paris, 1941.
Arc 853.330 Die relative Chronologie des Neolithikums in Südwestdeutschland und der Schweiz. Diss. (Mauser-Goller, Katharina.) Basel, 1969.
Arc 389.5 Relative chronologies in old world archaeology. (Ehrich, R.W.) Chicago, 1954.
Arc 843.45 Relatorio sobre o comiterio romano. (Teixeira de Aragão, A.C.) Lisboa, 1868.
Arc 1027.27.5 Relazione...cimitero di cristiani. (Pasquini, G.) Montepulciano, 1833.
Arc 726.62 Relazione. (Terra d'Otranto. Commissione Conservatrice dei Monumenti Storici e di Belle Arti.) Lecci.
Arc 1033.17.581 Relazione del principio, e cause della venerazione dell'immagine..vergine. Firenze, 1704.
Arc 1033.17.29 Relazione del prodigioso...aprimento di Occhi di una immagine di Maria...Ancona. Venezia, 1796.
Arc 1033.17.422 Relazione della...coronazione della miracolosa imagine dell Sma. Vergine di Monte Nero. Pistoia, 1694.
Arc 1027.68 Relazione della chiesa sotterranea di S. Lorenzo in Sanseverino. (Servanzi-Collis, S.) Macerata, 1838.
Arc 1033.17.153 Relazione della venta a Montevarchi del socrosanto latte. (Sigoni, I.) Firenze, 1653.
Arc 1020.58 Relazione delle Sante Relique...della città di Firenze. (Cionacci, T.) Bologna, 1685.
Arc 726.14 Relazione delli scari fatti in Luni. (Remedi, A.A.) Sarzana, 1860.
Arc 1033.105 Relazione dello scoprimento del corpo del...martire S. Eusanio. (Coppola, G.) Roma, 1749.
Htn Arc 1020.11* Relazione dello scuoprimento...in Ancona. Roma, 1756.
Arc 1033.150 Relazione dell'origine...Firenze...Bastone del S.P. Giuseppe. (Favilli, A.) Lucca, 1721.
Arc 726.25 Relazione di un viaggio ad Ostia. (Fea, Carlo.) Roma, 1802.
Arc 1015.208.13 Relazione generale degli scavi e scoperte...via Satina. (Garrucci, R.) Roma, 1859.
Arc 1027.1.17 Relazione severamente i vasi...sangue dei martiri. (Bartolini, D.) Roma, 1863.
Arc 730.206 Relazione sommaria intorno agli. (Salinas, A.) Roma, 1894.
Arc 726.78F Relazione sopra gli scavi eseguiti a Norba nell'estate dell'anno 1901. (Savignoni, L.) Roma, 1902.
Arc 672.1.31F Relazione sugli scavi...in Gortyna. (Halbherr, F.) Roma, 1889.
Arc 726.89 Relazione sulle antichita prehistoriche rinvenute nella contrado comino presso Guardeagrele. (Ferrare, F.) Guardeagrele, 1913.
Arc 858.15 Relics of antiquity in Great Britain. London, 1811.
Arc 66.1.183 Le relief culturel greco-romain. (Will, Ernest.) Paris, 1955.
Arc 87.1.63 Das Relief des Archelaos von Priene. (Watzinger, C.) Berlin, 1903.
Arc 87.1.26 Relief eines roemischen Kriegers. (Huebner, E.) Berlin, 1866.
Arc 705.200 Die Reliefs an der Balustrade der Athena Nike. (Kekulé, R.) Stuttgart, 1881.
Arc 750.1.5 Die Reliefs der Trajanssäule. v.1,2, plates. v.2,3, text. (Cichorius, C.) Berlin, 1896-1900. 4v.
Arc 740.202 I relievi delle urne etrusche. (Brunn, H.) Rome, 1870-1916. 3v.
Arc 838.3.5 Religiões da Lusitania. (Leite de Vasconcellos, J.) Lisboa, 1897. 3v.
Arc 600.241 Die religiöse Bedeutung der sogenannten Grabräuberschächte in den ägyptischen Königsgräbern der 18. bis 20. Dynastie. (Abitz, Friedrich.) Wiesbaden, 1974.
Arc 66.1.131 La religion domestique. (Bulard, M.) Paris, 1926.
Arc 66.1.178 La religion romaine de Venias depuis les origines jusqu'au temps d'Auguste. (Schilling, R.) Paris, 1954.
Arc 1033.115 The religious environment of early Christianity. (Emerton, E.) Cambridge, 1910.
Arc 861.21.25F Reliquae isurianae; remains of Roman Isurium. (Smith, Henry E.) London, 1852.
Arc 1033.35.161 Les reliquaires de la Vraie Croix. (Frolow, Anatole.) Paris, 1965.
Arc 1020.85 Un reliquare romano Byzantin (Auverogne). (Guélou, P.F.) Clermont-Ferrand, 1883.
NEDL Arc 142.2 The reliquary...archaeological journal. (Allen, J.R.) London. 1860-1909 49v.

Author and Title Listing

Arc 1033.35.160 La relique de la Vraie Croix. (Frolow, Anatole.) Paris, 1961.
Arc 1020.94 Reliques...données par St. Louis, roi de France, au couvent des Dominicains de Liége. (Helbig, Jules.) Bruxelles, 1881.
Arc 505.42 Les reliques de l'art syrien dans l'Égypte du nouvel empire. (Montet, Pierre.) Paris, 1937.
Arc 1020.69 Reliques de l'église de Moyenmoutier. (Deblaye, L.F.) Nancy, 1856.
Arc 1020.93 Reliques de trois tombeaux saints de Clairvoux...a Ville-sous-la-Ferté (Aubé). (Salore, Charles.) Troyes, 1877.
Arc 1033.35.155 Die Reliquiare des christlichen Kultes und ihre Entwicklung. (Braun, J.) Freiburg, 1940.
Arc 1020.79 Reliquiario armeno...convento...Alessandria in Piemonte. (Promis, V.) Torino, 1883.
Arc 1020.114 Die Reliquien des Klosters Allerheiligen. (Schenkel, I.I.) Schaffhausen, 1866.
Arc 1020.1.3 Der Reliquienschatz des Leibfrauen-Münsters zu Aachen in seinen Kunstreichen Behältern. (Bock, F.) Aachen, 1860.
Arc 1020.127 Les reliquies del Monastir de Sant Cugat del Vallès. (Más, Joseph.) Barcelona, 1908.
Arc 66.1.126 Relius Aristide. (Boulanger, André.) n.p., n.d.
Arc 767.4.2 The remains of ancient Rome. (Middleton, J.H.) London, 1892. 2v.
Arc 858.1 Remains of Pagan Saxondom. (Akerman, J.Y.) London, 1855.
Arc 861.26 Remains of Roman art Corinum. (Newmarch, C.H.) London, n.d.
Arc 858.9.5 Remains of the Prehistoric Age in England. (Windle, B.C.A.) London, 1904.
Arc 858.9.6 Remains of the Prehistoric Age in England. (Windle, B.C.A.) London, 1909.
Arc 875.40 Remarkable ruins and romantic prospects of North Britain. (Cordiner, Charles.) London, 1788-95.
Arc 1033.34.17 Remarks on...Saint Peter's chair. (Wiseman, N.) Rome, 1833. 2v.
Arc 723.4 Remarks on antiquities, arts and letters. (Forsyth, J.) Boston, 1818.
Arc 723.4.2 Remarks on antiquities, arts and letters. 3. ed. (Forsyth, J.) London, 1824. 2v.
Arc 723.4.4 Remarks on antiquities, arts and letters. 4. ed. (Forsyth, J.) London, 1835.
Arc 766.2 Remarks on the antiquities of Rome and its environs. (Lumisden, A.) London, 1797.
Arc 861.15.5 Remarks on the Garianorum...Romans. 2. ed. (Ives, J.) London, 1774.
Arc 861.15 Remarks on the Garianorum...Romans. 2. ed. (Ives, J.) Yarmouth, 1803.
Arc 684.4 Remarks on the topography of Oropia and Diacria. (Finlay, G.) Athens, 1838. 2 pam.
Arc 1470.7 Remarks upon a coin of Sicyon. (Phillips, H.) Philadelphia, 1882.
Arc 983.5 Remarks upon chipped stone implements. (Putnam, F.W.) Salem, 1885.
Arc 590.11 Remarks upon the cover of the granite sarcophagus of Rameses III in the Fitzwilliam Museum. (Birch, Samuel.) Cambridge, Eng., 1876.
Arc 530.53 Remarques stylistiques sur les reliefs de Malatya. (Akurgal, E.) Istanbul, 1946.
Arc 785.61 Remarques sur la pièce antique de bronze. (Chevalier, N.) Amsterdam, 1694.
Arc 726.14 Remedi, A.A. Relazione delli scari fatti in Luni. Sarzana, 1860.
Arc 1148.27 Rémondon, R. Papyrus grecs d'Apollônos anô. Le Caire, 1953.
Arc 853.275F Rempel, Heinrich. Reihengräberfriedhofe des 8. bis 11. Jahrhunderts. Berlin, 1966.
Arc 723.42 The Renaissance discovery of classical antiquity. (Weiss, Robert.) Oxford, 1969.
Arc 495.7 Renan, E. Mission de Phénicie. Paris, 1864. 2v.
Arc 383.34.10 Renard, M. Hommages à Albert Grenier. Bruxelles, 1962. 3v.
Arc 977.2 Renaud, E.B. Archaeological survey of eastern Wyoming, summer 1931. Denver, 1932.
Arc 953.25 Renaud, E.B. Classification and description of Indian stone artifacts. Gunnison, 1941.
Arc 605.204.5F Renault, Jules. Cahiers d'archéologie tunisienne. v.1-4. Tunis, 1908-11.
Arc 1.14.10 Rendiconti. (Accademia...Rome. Accademia Romana di Archeologia.) 1,1921+ 31v.
Arc 612.89 Renfrew, Colin. Before civilization; the radiocarbon revolution and prehistoric Europe. London, 1973.
Arc 1590.9.5 Rengjeo, Ivan. Corpus der mittelalterlichen Münzen von Kroatien, Slavozien, Dalmatien und Bosnien. Graz, 1959.
Arc 608.6.3 Renier, Léon. Rapports adressés à M. le ministre de l'instruction publique et des cultes. Paris, 1852.
Arc 522.7 Rennell, J. Observations on the topography of the plain of Troy. London, 1814.
Arc 1077.7.5 Der Rennwagen bei ben Italikern. (Nachod, H.) Leipzig, 1909.
Arc 1077.7 Der Rennwagen in Griechenland. (Mercklin, E. von.) Leipzig, 1909.
Arc 66.1.151 Renouard, Yves. Les relations des papes d'Avignon. Paris, 1941.
Arc 1668.5.3 Rentzmann, W. Numismatisches Legenden-Lexicon. Berlin, 1881.
Arc 1668.5 Rentzmann, W. Numismatisches Legenden-Lexicon. v.1-2. Berlin, 1865-66.
Arc 1665.3 Rentzmann, W. Numismatisches Wappen-Lexicon. Berlin, 1876.
Arc 1665.3.5 Rentzmann, W. Numismatisches Wappen-Lexicon. Index. Berlin, 1876.
Arc 955.2.13 The repair of Casa Grande ruin, Arizona, in 1891. (Mindeleff, C.) Washington, n.d. 2 pam.
Arc 1498.1 Répertoire...de la numismatique française. (Engel, A.) Paris, 1887-89. 2v.
Arc 1498.1.2 Répertoire...de la numismatique française. Supplément et table. (Engel, A.) Paris, 1889.
Arc 830.198 Répertoire archéologique du département de la Meuse. (Toussaint, M.) Bar-le-Duc, 1946.
Arc 830.196 Répertoire archéologique du département de la Moselle. (Toussaint, M.) Nancy, 1950.
Arc 823.4.7 Répertoire archéologique du département de la Niène. (Souttrait, J.H.) Paris, 1875.
Arc 830.185 Répertoire archéologique du département de la Seine. (Toussaint, M.) Paris, 1953.
Arc 830.190 Répertoire archéologique du département de la Seine-et-Marne. (Toussaint, M.) Paris, 1953.
Arc 823.4.6 Répertoire archéologique du département de la Seine-Inférieure. (Cochet, J.B.D.) Paris, 1871.
Arc 823.4 Répertoire archéologique du département de l'Aube. (D'Arbois de Jubainville.) Paris, 1861.
Arc 830.215 Répertoire archéologique du département de l'Aube. (Toussaint, M.) Paris, 1954.
Arc 823.4.2 Répertoire archéologique du département de l'Oise. (Woillez, E.) Paris, 1862.
Arc 823.4.5 Répertoire archéologique du département de l'Yonne. (Quantin, M.) Paris, 1868.
Arc 830.194 Répertoire archéologique du département de Meurthe-et-Moselle. (Toussaint, M.) Nancy, 1947.
Arc 830.26.20 Répertoire archéologique du département de Seine-et-Oise. (Toussaint, M.) Paris, 1951.
Arc 830.199 Répertoire archéologique du département des Ardennes. (Toussaint, M.) Paris, 1955.
Arc 823.4.8 Répertoire archéologique du département du Hautes-Alpes. (Roman, M.J.) Paris, 1887.
Arc 823.4.3 Répertoire archéologique du département du Morbihan. (Rosenzweig, L.) Paris, 1863.
Arc 823.4.4 Répertoire archéologique du département du Tarn. (Croyes, H.) Paris, 1865.
Arc 830.336 Répertoire bibliographique. (Prévost, R.) Arras, 1958.
Arc 830.320 Répertoire des dessins archéologiques. (Niort, France. Bibliothèque Municipale.) Niort, 1915.
Arc 545.227.19 Repertoire genealogique et onomastique. (Legrain, G.) Genève, 1908.
Arc 600.110F Répertoire onomastique de Deir et Médineh. (Černý, Jaroslav.) Le Caire, 1949.
Arc 1488.11F Repertoiro generale delle monete coniate in Italia. (Sambon, Giulio.) Parigi, 1912.
Arc 1488.27 Repertorio alfabetico di numismatica medioevale e moderna. (Ciferra, Raffaello.) Pavia, 1963. 2v.
Arc 843.5.30 Repertorio de bibliografía arqueológica. v.1-2, 4-6. (Fletcher y Valls, D.) Valencia, 1951. 4v.
Arc 726.242 Repertorio di antichità. (Cassani, Lino.) Novara, 1962.
Arc 1468.9 Repertorio numismatico. v.1-2. (Dominicis, F. de.) Naples, 1826.
Arc 73.5 Repertorio universale dell'opere dell'instituto. (Rome. Istituto.) Rome. 1834-1885 5v.
Arc 1360.1 Repertorium zur antiken Numismatik. (Friedlaender, J.) Berlin, 1885.
Arc 1510.11.5 Repertorium zur Münzkunde Bayerns und Forzetz. v.1-3. (Kull, J.V.) München, 1894. 2v.
Arc 1033.12.192 Réponse à la lettre du père Mabillon...prétendue sur larme. (Thiers, J.B.) Cologne, 1700.
Arc 1311.1.3 Report, proceedings. (Liverpool Numismatic Society.) Liverpool. 1,1871
Arc 1.5.11 Report. (American School of Classical Studies at Athens. Alumni Association.) 1942
Arc 589.5 Report. (British School of Archaeology in Egypt.) London. 13-20,1907-1914
Arc 967.1.11 Report. (Conference on Midwestern Archaeology, St. Louis.) Washington, 1929.
Arc 535.3 Report. (Cyprus. Department of Antiquities.) Nicosia. 1936+ 6v.
Arc 435.2 Report. (India. Archaeological Survey.) London. 1-5,1874-1883// 4v.
X Cg Arc 435.2 Report. (India. Archaeological Survey.) London. 3
Arc 435.57 Report. (India. Archaeological Survey. Punjab Circle.) Calcutta. 1888-1889
Arc 13.15 Report - Moated Site Research Group. (Moated Site Research Group.) Kirkleavington. 1,1973+
Arc 893.2 Report addressed by the Royal Society of Northern Antiquaries ot its British and American members. (Copenhagen. Kongelige Nordiske Oldskrift-Selskab.) Copenhagen, 1836.
Arc 875.50 Report and inventory of monuments and constructions. (Great Britain. Commissions. Ancient and Historical Monuments of Scotland.) Edinburgh. 1-13,1909-1957 11v.
Arc 136.4.5 Report for 1909. (Excavation Committee.) Oxford, 1910.
Arc 136.4 Report for 1909-1911. Old Sarum Excavation fund. (London Society of Antiquaries.) Oxford, 1912.
Arc 1138.108F Report in search of the condition of manuscripts in Egypt. (Awad, G.) n.p., 1957?
Arc 435.2.26F Report of a tour of exploration of the antiquities in the Tarai, Nepal. (Purna Chandra, Mukhopādhyāya.) Calcutta, 1901.
Arc 1.5.4.20 Report of excavations at Gözlü Kule. (American School of Classical Studies at Athens.)
Arc 1.13.3 Report of executive committee. (American Academy, Rome.) Rome? 1913
Arc 950.208 Report of mound explorations of Bureau of Ethnology. (Thomas, C.) Washington, 1894.
Arc 127.3.2 Report of proceedings. (Congress of Archaeological Societies in Union with the Society of Antiquaries.) London. 1901-1913
Arc 136.5 Report of research committee. (London Society of Antiquaries.) Oxford. 1-30 26v.
Arc 858.24.5F Report of the committee. (Great Britain. Ancient Monuments Advisory Committee.) London, n.d.
Arc 127.3 Report of the committee on ancient earthworks. (Congress of Archaeological Societies in Union with the Society of Antiquaries.) London? 1905-1920
Arc 136.9.6 Report of the council. (London and Middlesex Archaeological Society.)
Arc 127.3.4 Report of the earthworks committee. (Congress of Archaeological Societies in Union with the Society of Antiquaries.) 1921-1939
Arc 1.1.6 Report of the fellow in American archaeology. (Archaeological Institute of America.) N.Y., 1907.
Arc 435.51F Report of the superintendent. (Burma. Archaeological Survey.) Rangoon. 1901-1939 5v.
Arc 545.227.5 Report on antiquities of Lower Nubia. (Weigal, A.E.P.) Oxford, 1907.
Arc 861.75 Report on excavations at Grime's Graves, Weeting, Norfolk, March-May, 1914. (Prehistoric Society of East Anglia.) London, 1915.
Arc 861.118 Report on excavations at Wroxeter...1923-1927. (Atkinson, Donald.) Oxford, 1942.
X Cg Arc 861.6 Report on excavations made on the site of the Roman Castrum at Lymne. (Smith, C.R.) London, 1852.
Arc 450.30 Report on Humrahar excavations. (Altekar, Anant L.) Patna, 1959.
Arc 600.1.3 Report on prospects of research in Alexandria. (Hogarth, D.G.) London, 1895.
Arc 545.234 Report on some excavations...Theban necropolis. (Marius of Northampton.) London, 1908.

Arc 440.1 Report on the Amarāvati Tope. (Sewell, R.) London, 1880.

Arc 453.15 Report on the excavations at Nasik and Jorve. 1. ed. (Sankalia, Hasmukh Dhirajlal.) Poona, 1955.

Arc 455.1.5 Report on the excavations at Pātaliputra. (Waddell, L.A.) Calcutta, 1903.

Arc 545.210 Report on the island and temples of Philae. (Lyons, H.G.) Cairo, 1896.

Arc 726.51F Report on the Phoenician and Roman antiquities in the group of the islands of Malta. (Caruana, A.A.) Malta, 1882.

Arc 545.210.5 Report on the temples of Philae. (Lyons, H.G.) Cairo, 1908.

Arc 1.1.3 Report on the Wolfe Expedition to Babylonia, 1884-85. (Ward, W.H.) Boston, 1886.

Arc 983.2.7 Report to the Columbian historical exposition at Madrid. (United States. Commission.) Washington, 1895.

Arc 426.5 Report upon archaeological research. (Kyoto. University. Archaeological Institute.) Tokyo. 3-10,1919-1927 4v.

Arc 950.206 Report upon geographical surveys west of the one hundredth meridian. v.7. Archaeology. (United States.) Washington, 1879.

Arc 935.9.25 Report upon the excavations carried out in and near the hippodrome of Constantinople. (British Academy.) London. 1-2,1927-1928

Arc 1.5.17 Reports. (American School of Classical Studies in Rome. Chairman of Managing Committee.) Princeton, N.J.

Arc 320.2 Reports. (Harvard University. Peabody Museum.) Cambridge. 1-3 3v.

Arc 435.1.1 Reports. (India. Archaeological Survey.) Varanasi, 1966-72. 24v.

Arc 32.8F Reports and memoirs. (Centro Scavi e Ricerche Archeologiche in Asia dell'I.M.E.O. e di Torino.) Roma. 1,1962+ 13v.

Arc 1.3 Reports of annual meeting. (Archaeological Institute of America. Wisconsin Society.) Madison.

Arc 586.1 Reports of annual meetings. (Egypt Exploration Society.) London. 1884-1937 6v.

Arc 320.1 Reports of proceedings. (Numismatic and Antiquarian Society of Philadelphia.) Philadelphia. 1865-1935 5v.

Arc 537.10 Reports on excavations in Cyprus. (Sjoeqvist, Erik.) Stockholm, 1947. 2v.

Arc 66.1.172 Les représentations dans la céramique attique du IV siècle. (Metzger, H.) Paris, 1951. 3v.

Arc 30.12.3F Reprint [of the] American Institute. (American Institute for Iranian Art and Archaeology.) N.Y.

Arc 1494.25 Uma reproducão em cabre de moeda de retrato datado de 1630. (Costa Couvreur, Raul de.) Lisboa, 1956.

Arc 1281.1F Reproduction d'anciens cachets russes. (Russia. Commission d'Impression des Lettres Patentes et Traités.) Moscou, 1880.

Arc 1460.4 Les reproductions des statues. (Lacroix, L.) Liège, 1949.

Arc 1490.19 La repubblica di San Marino sue monete medaglie decorazioni. (Perini, L.) Roverto, 1900.

Arc 1490.27 La repubblica romana del 1849 e le sue monete. (Perini, Quintilio.) Rovereto, 1903.

Htn Arc 845.210F* Rerum Augustanar. Vindelicar. Libri octo. (Velser, Marcus.) Venetiis, 1594.

Arc 1590.25 Resch, Adolf. Siebenbürgishe Münzen und Medaillen von 1538 bis zur Gegenwart. Montreal, 1965.

Arc 823.75 Rescurrection de la Gaule. (Eydoux, Henri Paul.) Paris, 1961.

Arc 384.16 Research and theory in current archeology. (Redman, Charles L.) N.Y., 1973.

Arc 143.6 Research papers. (Surrey Archaeological Society.) Guildford. 5

Arc 128.5 Research report. (Derwent Archaeological Society.) Matlock, Derbyshire, Eng. 1,1973+

Arc 135.5 Research report. (Kent Archaeological Research Groups' Council.) Bromley. 1,1968+ 2v.

Arc 143.8 Research volume. (Surrey Archaeological Society.) Castle Arch. 1,1974+

Arc 513.5 Researches in Asia Minor, Pontus and Armenia. (Hamilton, W.J.) London, 1842. 2v.

Arc 505.27F Researches in prehistoric Galilee, 1925-1926. (Turville-Petre, F.) London, 1927.

Arc 505.12 Researches in Sinai. (Petrie, W.M.F.) London, 1906.

Arc 958.1.3 Researches upon antiquities of man, Delaware Valley. (Abbott, Charles C.) Boston, 1897.

Arc 307.3.9 Reseña de la segunda sesion del XVII Congresso...de Americanistes. (International Congress of Americanists, 17th, May 1910 (2d meeting, Mexico, Sept. 1910).) México, 1912.

Arc 830.72 Reser, François. Mémoires sur les ruines de Lillebonne. Evreux, 1821.

Arc 1588.6.15 Resimli Turk paralari. (Butak, Bekzad.) Istanbul, 1947.

Arc 935.33.5 Resit Mazhar Ertüzün. Kapidagi Yariniadasi ve Cevresindeki Adalar. Ankara, 1964.

Arc 1033.34.8 Resoconto...della disputa...fra sacerdoti e ministri...venuta di San Pietro. Roma, 1872.

Arc 1033.34.7 Resoconto...della disputa...fra sacerdoti e ministri...venuta di San Pietro. Roma, 1872.

Arc 1675.94 Respublička Izložba Hrvatskih Medalja i Plaketa. 1st, Zagreb, 1964-65. Medalja u hrvatskoj. Zagreb, 1964?

Arc 396.12 La restauration des monuments anciens. (Lemaire, Raymond.) Anvers, 1935.

Arc 761.6F Restauri della Roma imperiale. (Gatteschi, Giuseppe.) Roma, 1924.

Arc 391.8 Il restauro dei monumenti. (Giovannoni, G.) Roma, 1941?

Arc 785.45 Il restauro del tiempo della Fortuna Virile. (Munoz, A.) Roma, 1925.

Arc 761.3PF Restauro grafico del Monte Capitalino. Maps and text. Roma, 1897.

Arc 395.24 Restavratsiia arkheologicheskikh predmetov. (Kir'ianov, A.V.) Moskva, 1960.

Arc 726.93F A restoration of "Horace's Sabine Villa". (Price, F.) n.p., 1932.

Arc 630.13 Restorations of classical buildings. (Stevens, G.P.) Princeton, N.J., 1955.

Arc 505.7.5 Resultats...archéologies des fouilles entreprises à Jérusalem. (Clermont-Ganneau, Charles.) n.p., 1872.

Arc 1010.15 Results of an archaeological survey of the southern region of Moreten Bay and of Moreten Island, 1963-64. (Ponosov, V.V.) St. Lucian, Brisbane, 1967.

Arc 1493.17 Resumen historico. (Gracia de la Fuente, Arturo.) Madrid, 1934.

Arc 386.29 La résurrection des villes mortes. v.1-2. (Brion, Marcel.) Paris, 1948-49.

Arc 726.319 Le rete stradale romana fra Brescia, Bergamo e Milano. (Coradazzi, Giovanni.) Brescia, 1974.

Arc 1588.10.5 Rethy, Landislaus. Corpus nummorum Hungariae. Graz, 1958.

Arc 858.28 Retrospections, social and archaeological. (Smith, Charles R.) London, 1883-91. 3v.

Arc 1030.32 Reumont, A. Inscriptiones christianae urbis Romae. n.p., 1862.

Arc 853.125 Reusch, Wilhelm. Augusta Treverorum. Trier, 1958.

Arc 1018.4 Reusens, E. Eléments d'archéologie chrétienne. Louvain, 1871-75. 2v.

Arc 600.130 Reuterswaerd, Patrick. Studien zur Polychromie der Plaskik. Stockholm, 1958- 2v.

Arc 688.7F Reuther, Oskar. Der Heratempel von Samos. Berlin, 1957.

Arc 432.8 Revealing India's past. (Cumming, John.) London, 1939.

Arc 830.29.10 Pamphlet vol. Rever, F. Mémoires sur diverses antiquités de la Normandie. 6 pam.

Arc 830.85 Rever, Marie F. Mémoire sur les ruines du Vieil-Évreux. Évreux, 1827.

Arc 136.1.11 Review of Archaeologia. (London Society of Antiquaries.) London, 1881.

Arc 1443.2 Revillout, Eugène. Lettre à M.P. Charles Robert sur les monnaies égyptiennes. Macon, 1884.

Arc 1423.2 Révillout, Eugène. Note sur les plus anciennes monnaies hébraiques. Macon, 1884.

Arc 785.13.63 A revised history of the column of Phocas in the Roman Forum. (Nichols, Francis M.) Westminster, 1890.

Arc 441.3F Revised list of ancient monuments in Bengal, 1886. (Bengal. Public Works Department.) Calcutta, 1887.

Arc 435.2.16F Revised lists of antiquarian remains in the Bombay presidency. (Burgess, James.) Bombay, 1897.

Arc 94.10 Revista. (Asociación Artistico-Arqueológica Barcelona.) Barcelona. 1-5,1896-1908 5v.

Arc 1317.4 Revista italiana di numismatica. (Ambrosoli, S.) Milano. 1,1888+ 43v.

Arc 1317.4F Revista italiana di numismatica. (Ambrosoli, S.) Milano. 37,1924

Arc 1645.5 La revolución de Mayo en la medalla. (Ferrari, Jorge N.) Buenos Aires, 1960.

Arc 830.5 Revon, L. La Haute-Savoie avant les Romains. Paris, 1878.

Arc 18.1 Revue archéologique. Paris. 1844+ 185v.

Arc 18.1.3 Revue archéologique. Index, v.23, 1870-1890. 3d series. Paris, 1893.

Arc 18.1.2 Revue archéologique. Index, 1860-1869. Paris, n.d.

Arc 18.1.5 Revue archéologique. Tables des années, 1900-1955. Paris, 1949- 2v.

Arc 112.5 Revue archéologique de l'est et du centre-est. Dijon. 1,1950+ 13v.

Arc 112.5.5 Revue archéologique de l'est et du centre-est. Tables décennales, v.1-10, 1950-1959. Dijon, 1960.

Arc 101.13 Revue archéologique de Narbonnaise. Paris. 1,1968+ 2v.

Arc 142.10 Revue archeologique du centre. Vichy. 1,1962+ 6v.

Arc 273.2.25 Revue belge d'archéologie et d'histoire de l'art. Bruxelles. 1,1931+ 24v.

Arc 1317.3 Revue belge de numismatique. Bruxelles. 1842+ 91v.

Arc 1317.3.2 Revue belge de numismatique. Table alphabetique. 1842-1880 3v.

Arc 1317.2 Revue Charlemagne. Paris. 1911 2v.

Arc 1317.1 Revue de la numismatique françoise. Blois. 1,1836+ 94v.

Arc 112.3 Revue des musées et collections archéologiques. Dijon. 1-6,1925-1931 2v.

Arc 1318.3.5 Revue suisse de numismatique. (Société Suisse de Numismatique.) Genève. 1,1891+ 19v.

Arc 497.4 Rey, E.G. Rapport sur une mission scientifique. Paris, 1867.

Arc 682.25.25 Rey, Léon. Observations sur les premiers habitats de la Macédoine. Paris, 1921-22. 2v.

Arc 1190.86.10 Reychman, Jan. Handbook of Ottoman-Turkish diplomatics. The Hague, 1968.

Arc 1494.30 Los reyes de Taijas. (Prieto y Vives, Antonio.) Madrid, 1926.

Arc 608.32 Reyniers, F.L.M. Port à Utique. Alger, 1952.

Arc 885.22 Reynolds, P.K.B. Excavations on the site of the Roman fort of Kanovium at Caerhun. Cardiff, 1938.

Arc 66.1.189 Rhégion et Zanale. (Vallet, Georges.) Paris, 1958.

Arc 628.6 Rheinhard, H. Album des klassischen Alterthums. Stuttgart, 1882.

Arc 202.5 Rheinische Ausgrabungen. Düsseldorf. 3,1968+ 14v.

Arc 1269.35 Rheinisches Siegel- und Urkundenbuch. (Korn, Otto.) Brühl, 1952.

Arc 600.6A Rhind, A.H. Thebes. London, 1862.

Arc 609.1.25 Rhodesia (Southern). Bureau of Publicity. The great Zimbabwe ruins. Bulawayo, 1930.

Arc 638.4 Der Rhombus in der Orchestra des Dionysustheaters zu Athen. (Kirchhoff, C.) Altona, 1885. 3 pam.

Arc 1510.17 Rhon, G. Exercitatio historica de Joh. Uratislaviensibus. Uratslaviae, 1693.

Arc 1030.18 Riant, Paul de. Trois inscriptions...rapportées de Constantinople. Paris, 1880.

Arc 925.205 Riazanskaia zemlia. (Mongait, A.L.) Moskva, 1961.

Arc 1675.47 Ribagarza, Martin de Gurrea y Aragon. Discursos de medallas y antiguedades. Madrid, 1903.

Arc 843.220 Ribeiro, Fernando Nunes. O bronze meridional português. Beja, 1965.

Arc 1033.17.449 Ricci, A.M. Septenaire ou sept allégresses de Notre Dame de Mont Carmel. Paris, 1839.

Arc 785.60 Ricci, Corrado. Via dell'impero. Roma, 1933.

Arc 1488.10 Ricci, S. Storia della moneta in Italia. Padova, 1937.

Arc 1349.30 Ricci, Serafino. L'opera numismatica di Solone Ambrosoli. Milano, 1908.

Arc 1663.16 Ricciardi, E. Medaglie del Regno delle due Sicilie 1735-1861. Napoli, 1900.

Arc 1663.16.5F Ricciardi, E. Medaglie del Regno delle due Sicilie 1735-1861. 2. ed. Napoli, 1930.

Arc 1480.3 Riccio, G.G. Catalogo di antiche medaglie consolari e di famiglie romane. Naples, 1855.

Arc 1480.2 Riccio, G.G. Le monete delle antiche famiglie di Roma. 2. ed. Naples, 1843.

Arc 750.223F Riccy, G.A. Dell'antico pago Lemonio in oggi Roma Vecchia. Roma, 1802.

Arc 435.21.5F Rice, B.L. Epigraphia carnatica. Bangalore, 1923.

Arc 435.21 Rice, B.L. Epigraphia carnatica. v.1-2. Bangalore, 1889-15v.

Arc 435.2.39F Rice, B.S. Epigraphia caratica. Madras, 1914.

Arc 943.45 Rice University. Prehistoric man in the new world. Chicago, 1964.

Arc 1033.73 Ricerche...del sacro pallio ecclesiastico. (Cavedoni, C.) Modena, 1856.

Author and Title Listing

Arc 1033.81 Ricerche...SS. Eutichete ed Acuzio. (Stornaiuolo, C.) Napoli, 1874.
Arc 785.23 Ricerche archeologico e topografico nel monto Albano. (Rossi, G.B. de.) Roma, 1874.
Arc 1033.44.13 Ricerche critiche...medaglie di Constantino. (Cavedoni, C.) Modena, 1858.
Arc 736.3 Ricerche ed osservazioni. Fatte in Segesta. (Fraccia, G.) Palermo, 1855.
Arc 1153.61 Ricerche paleografiche intorno all'arcidiacono pacifico di Verona. (Venturini, T.) Verona, 1929.
Arc 726.320 Ricerche puniche nel Mediterraneo centrale. Roma, 1970.
Arc 726.342 Ricerche sulla topografia e i monumenti di Locri. (Franciscis, Alfonso.) Napoli, 1971-
Arc 726.49 Ricerche sull'antica città di Eclano. 2a ed. Appendice. (Guarini, R.) Napoli, 1814-15.
Arc 785.9 Ricerche sulle XIV regioni urbane. (Lanciani, R.) Roma, 1890.
Arc 1027.47 Ricersa...tomba S. Cecilia. (Bufalieri da Montécelio, P.) Roma, 1891.
Arc 1033.5.9 Rich, Anthony. The legend of Saint Peter's chair. London, 1851.
Arc 1020.62 Richard, J.M. Le trésor...de Notre Dame de Lens au XVe siècle. Arras, 1876.
Arc 830.345 Richard, Jean-Claude M. La région montpelliévaine à l'époque préromaine (750-121 avant J.-C.). Bruxelles, 1973.
Arc 561.1.10 Richard Lepsius. (Ebers, George.) N.Y., 1887.
Arc 861.53 Richardson, G.B. Pons Aelii; the site of the Roman station. Newcastle-upon-Tyne, 1852.
Arc 497.41 Richardson, George H. Biblical archaeology, its use and abuse. London, 1938.
Arc 1500.56 Richebé, C. Les monnaies féodales d'artois. Paris, 1963.
Arc 397.5 Richerche intorno...Grimaldi. (Müntz, Eugène.) Firenze, 1881. 8 pam.
Arc 772.16 Richmond, Ian A. The archaeology of the Roman empire. Oxford, 1957.
Arc 785.29.10 Richmond, Ian A. The city wall of imperial Rome. Oxford, 1930.
Arc 700.35 Richter, G.M.A. Archaic attic gravestones. Cambridge, 1944.
Arc 1016.210 Richter, J.P. The golden age of classic Christian art. London, 1904.
Arc 87.1.45 Richter, O. Antike Steinmetzzeichen. Berlin, 1885.
Arc 785.19 Richter, O. Beiträge zur römischen Topographie. v.1-2,3. Berlin, 1903. 2v.
Arc 772.5 Richter, O. Geographie und Geschichte des Römischen Altertums. Nordlingen, 1889.
Arc 772.5.5 Richter, O. Topographie der Stadt Rom. Nordlingen, 1889.
Arc 843.135 Rico García, Manuel. Memoria relativa a los nuevos descubrimientos de la antigua Lucantum, 1892. Aicante, 1958.
Arc 387.10.10 Ricordi Canavesani. Luigi Palma di Cesnola. (Roversi, Luigi.) N.Y., 1901.
Arc 1033.34.70 Ricordi di San Pietro sul lago di Tiberiade. (Corbo, Virgilio.) Jerusalem, 1969.
Arc 1025.42 Ricordi di viaggio ad catacumbas. (Emiliani, A.) Livorno, 1883.
Arc 793.3.8 Ricordi Vesuviani. (Miola, Alfonso.) n.p., 1879.
Arc 1598.15 Riddell, J.L. A monograph of the silver dollar, good and bad. New Orleans, 1845.
Arc 66.1.69 Ridder, A. de. Catalogue des bronzes de la société archeologique d'Athènes. Paris, 1894.
Arc 66.1.74 Ridder, A. de. Catalogue des bronzes trouvés sur l'Acropole. Paris, 1896. 2v.
Arc 858.54 The riddle of prehistoric Britain. (Beaumont, Comyns.) London, 1946.
Arc 595.69 The riddle of the pyramids. (Mendelssohn, Kurt.) London, 1974.
Arc 412.22.1 The riddles of three oceans. (Kondratov, Aleksandr M.) Moscow, 1974.
Arc 1372.2 Ridgeway, W. The origin of metallic currency and weight standards. Cambridge, 1892.
Arc 397.25 Riding a hobby in the classical lands. (McDaniel, Walton B.) Cambridge, 1971.
Arc 1329.3 Riechmann, A. and Co. Numismatische Literatur. Halle am der Saale, 1926.
Arc 66.1.11 Riemann, O. Études sur la langue de Yite-Live. Paris, 1879.
Arc 66.1.8 Riemann, O. Les îles ioniennes. Paris, 1879-80. 3v.
Arc 1033.17.501 Rienzo, G. de. Notizie storiche sulla...effigie di Maria...Paterno. Napoli, 1829.
Arc 905.126.1 Rieth, Adolf. Die Eisentechnik der Hallstattzeit. Photoreproduction. Leipzig, 1942.
Arc 412.12 Rieth, Adolf. Vorzeit gefälscht. Tübingen, 1967.
Arc 1185.11 Rietsch, K.F. Handbuch der Urkundwissen. Berlin, 1904.
Arc 1500.22 Rigollot, M.J. Monnaies inconnues des évêques des innocens. Paris, 1857.
Arc 746.27 Riis, Poul J. Tyrrhenika, an archaeological study of the Etruscan sculpture in the archaic and classical periods. Copenhagen, 1941.
Arc 1675.19.20 Rikhter, Vladimir G. Sobranie trudov po russkoi voennoi medalistike i istorii. v.1-2. Parizh, 1972.
Arc 936.165.12 Rikman, Emmanuil A. Khudozhestvennye sokrovishcha drevnei Moldavii. Kishinev, 1969.
Arc 936.165.40 Rikman, Emmanuil A. Ocherki istorii kul'tury Moldavii (II-XIV vv). Kishinev, 1971.
Arc 936.165.10 Rikman, Emmanuil A. Pamiatniki drevnego iskusstva Moldavii. Kishinev, 1961.
Arc 843.110 Rileas i Bertran, Marià. El poblament d'Ilduro. Barcelona, 1952.
Arc 726.205F I rilievi dell'anfiteatro Campano. (Pesce, Gennaro.) Roma, 1941.
Arc 746.50 Rilli, Nicola. Gli estruschi a Sesto Fiorentino. Firenze, 1964.
Arc 938.109 Rimantienė, Rimutė Jablonskytė. Pirmieji Lietuvos gyventojai. Vil'ius, 1972.
Arc 726.50 Rimini avanti il principio. v.1-2. (Tonini, Luigi.) Rimini, 1848.
Arc 936.221 Rimljani na kosovu i Metohiji. (Čerškov, Emil.) Beograd, 1969.
Arc 858.22 Rimmer, Alfred. Ancient stone crosses of England. London, 1875.
Arc 936.42F Rimska mozaika ot Ulpiia Eskus. (Ivanov, T.) Sofiia, 1954.
Arc 1020.140 Rimskaia katakomby i pamiatniki pervonachal'nago Khristianskago iskusstva. (Friken, A.) Moskva, 1872-
Arc 936.230 Rimske izkopanine v Šempetru. (Klemenc, J.) Ljubljana, 1961.
Arc 936.43 Rimskiiat grad Abritus pri Razgrad. (Litsov, Khristo.) Razgrad, 1959.
Arc 1490.96 Rinaldi, Alfio. Catalogo delle medaglie papali annuali da Pio VII a Paolo VI. Verona, 1967.
Arc 1018.16 Rinaldi, P. De falea veterum christianorum rituum. Romae, 1777.
Arc 1153.102. Rinascimento giuridico e scrittura carolina a Bologna nel secolo XII. (Orlandelli, Gainfranco.) Bologna, 1965.
Arc 853.54 Der Ringwälle in der früheren preusischen Provinz Posen. (Schumacher, P.) Leipzig, 1924.
Arc 925.344 Rinskie importnye izdeliia v Vostochnoi Evrope. (Kropotkin, Vladislav V.) Moskva, 1970.
Arc 1033.35.81 Rioja, F. de. Titulo de la cruz de Christi. n.p., n.d.
Arc 730.204 Riolo, G. La porta arabo-normanna. Palermo, 1871.
Arc 1335.51 Riordinamento del museo numismatico. v.1-2. (Bellissima, G.B.) Siena, 1914.
Arc 1025.1 Rip, W.I. The catacombs of Rome. N.Y., 1854.
Arc 785.20.5 Ripostelli, Giuseppe. La Via Appia en ruine et en reconstruction. Rome, 1904.
Arc 785.39.10 Ripostelli, Giuseppe. Les Thermes de Caracalla. 4. éd. Rome, 191- .
Arc 785.20.7 Ripostelli, Giuseppe. La Via Appia, à l'époque romaine et de nos jours. Rome, 1908.
Arc 630.9 Rise and progress of classical archaeology. (Cook, Arthur B.) Cambridge, Eng., 1931.
Arc 1163.4.25F The rise of the north Arabic script and its Kur'ānic development. (Abbott, N.) Chicago, 1939.
Arc 1033.12.163 Risposta...alla seconda replica del celebre autore delle letterarie di Firenze. (Serantoni, G.M.) Lucca, 1767.
Arc 743.5 Risposta. (Gori, A.F.) Firenze, 1739.
Arc 1033.24 Risposta al P. Grisar...contre il sacro tesoro. (Di Carlo.) Tivoli, 1896. 3 pam.
Arc 895.36.20 En ristning på lös skifferplatta. (Rydh, Hanna.) n.p., 1921. 2 pam.
Arc 925.39 Risunki na skalakh. (Savvateev, Iurii A.) Petrozavodsk, 1967.
Arc 875.132 Ritchie, James Neil Graham. Edinburgh and southeast Scotland. London, 1972.
Arc 1053.19F Il ritratto nell'arte antica. (Paribeni, R.) Milano, 1934.
Arc 726.210 I ritrovamenti dell'antro cosiddetto "di Tiberio" a Sperlongo. (Jacopi, Giulio.) Roma, 1958.
Arc 726.315 I ritrovamenti fenici e punici in Sardegna. (Cecchini, Serena Maria.) Roma, 1969.
Arc 726.295 Rittatore Vonwiller, Ferrante. La necropoli preromana della Ca'Morta, Scavi 1955-1965. Como, 1966.
Arc 1212.6 Rittel, Erich. Siegel. Braunschweig, 1970.
Arc 458.2.2 Ritter, C. Die Stupa's (Topes). Berlin, 1838.
Arc 458.2 Ritter, C. Die Stupa's (Topes). Berlin, 1838.
Arc 772.7 Riva, Giuseppe. Sito di Roma e la carta. 2. ed. Vicenza, 1846.
Arc 733.2 Rivela, A. The dead cities of Sicily. Palermo, 1905.
Arc 1675.3.9 Le rivendicazioni italiane del Trentino...nelle medaglie. (Johnson, Stephen C.) Milano, 1919-20.
Arc 983.15 River basin surveys papers. (United States. Inter-Agency Archaeological Salvage Program.) Washington, 1958.
Arc 870.34 Rivet, Albert L.F. The Roman villa in Britain. London, 1969.
Arc 93.28F Rivista. (Istituto di Archeologia e Storia dell'Arte.) Roma. 1,1929+ 22v.
Arc 93.24 Rivista archeologica della provincia e antica diocesi di Como. Como. 59,1910+ 19v.
Arc 93.24.3 Rivista archeologica della provincia e antica diocesi di Como. Indice generale, 85-139, 1923-1957. Como, 1934-1958. 2v.
Arc 66.4.4 Rivista di archeologia cristiana. Milano. 1923
Arc 66.4.6 Rivista di archeologia cristiana. Roma. 1,1924+ 25v.
Arc 925.4.50 Rizhskii, Mikhail I. Iz glubiny vekov. Irkutsk, 1965.
Arc 730.209F Rizzo, G.E. Il teatro greco di Siracusa. Milano, 1923.
Arc 1455.5 Rizzo, G.E. Vasi greci della Sicilia. Roma, 1904.
Arc 785.83 The roads that led to Rome. (Hagen, Victor Wolfgang von.) London, 1967.
Arc 772.14 Robathan, D. The monuments of ancient Rome. Rome, 1950.
Arc 87.1.50 Robert, C. Homerische Becher. Berlin, 1890.
Arc 87.1.39 Robert, C. Thanatos. Berlin, 1879.
Arc 1675.4 Robert, Charles. Les médailleurs de la Renaissance. Paris, 1882.
Arc 402.7 Robert, Charles. Mélanges d'archéologie. Paris, 1875.
Arc 1500.17 Robert, Charles. Monnaies gauloises. Paris, 1880.
Arc 66.1.147 Robert, Fernand. Thymélè. Paris, 1939.
Arc 513.22 Robert, L. Villes d'Asie Mineure. Paris, 1935.
Arc 513.22.2 Robert, L. Villes d'Asie Mineure. 2. éd. Paris, 1962.
Arc 1468.34 Robert, Louis. Études de numismatique grecque. Paris, 1951.
Arc 530.162 Robert, Louis. Nouvelles inscriptions de Sardes. Paris, 1964.
Arc 1500.34 Robert, M.P.C. Sur la prétendue restauration du pouvoir de Maurice Tibère. Paris, 1883.
Arc 1148.30 Roberts, C.H. Greek literary hands. Oxford, 1955.
Arc 957.1.25 Roberts, Frank H.H. Early pueblo in the Piedra district. Washington, 1930.
Arc 968.2.30 Roberts, Frank H.H. Shabik'eschee village. Washington, 1929.
Arc 968.2.35 Roberts, Frank H.H. A survey of southwestern archaeology. Washington, 1936.
Arc 968.2.32 Roberts, Frank H.H. The village of the great Kivas on the Zuñi reservation, New Mexico. Washington, 1932.
Arc 875.100 Robertson, Anne. An Antonine fort. Edinburgh, 1957.
Arc 875.100.5 Robertson, Anne. The Roman fort at Castledykes. Edinburgh, 1964.
Arc 875.13.10 Robertson, Anne S. Bar Will. Oxford, 1975.
Arc 855.207 Robertson, D.H. The sculptured stones of Leith. Leith, 1851.
Arc 1540.17 Robertson, John D. Handbook to coinage of Scotland. London, 1878.
Arc 1478.29 Robinson, A.E. False and imitation Roman coins. n.p., 1932.
Arc 497.28A Robinson, George L. The sarcophagus of an ancient civilization. N.Y., 1930.
Arc 1335.41.5 Robinson, John. Oriental numismatics - catalogue of collections of books related to coinage of the east presented to Essex Institute, Salem. Salem, 1913.
Arc 609.37 Robinson, Keith Radcliffe. The early Iron Age in Malawi: an appraisal. Zomba, 1969.
Arc 609.35 Robinson, Keith Radcliffe. The Iron Age of the southern lake area of Malawi. Zomba, 1970.
Arc 402.3 Robiou, F. Chefs-d'oeuvre de l'art antique. 1st ser., 1-3; 2d ser., 1-4. Paris, 1867. 7v.

Htn	Arc 1076.3.110*	Rocca, Angelo. De campanis commentarius. Romae, 1612.
	Arc 843.20	Rocha Peixoto, A.A. da. A pedra dos namorados. Porto, 1903. 4 pam.
	Arc 1033.12.194	Rochambeau, E.A. de. Voyage à la sainte-larme de Vendome. Vendome, 1874.
	Arc 830.112	Roche, J.J. Notices historiques sur les anciens cintrons. Moutiers, 1819.
	Arc 830.63.9	La Roche aux Feés. (Léon des Ormeaux, A.) Laval, 188-?
	Arc 387.1.25	Rocheblave, S. Essai sur le comte de Caylus. Paris, 1889.
	Arc 830.19	Rochebrune, R. de. Sépulture d'un légionnaire romain. Niort, 1878.
	Arc 830.178	Le Rocher aux pieds du mas d'île à Lessac. (Baudouin, M.) Paris, 1915.
	Arc 889.7	Les roches-polissoirs du "Bruzel" à Saint-Mard, province de Luxembourg. (Loë, Alfred de.) Bruxelles, 1896.
	Arc 830.18.15	Rochetin, L. Étude sur la viabilité romaine dans le département de Vauclus. Avignon, 1883.
	Arc 441.4	Rock-cut temples around Bombay. (Vakil, K.H.) Bombay, 1932.
	Arc 432.1.2	Rock-cut temples of India. (Fergusson, F.) London, 1864.
	Arc 432.1.3	Rock-cut temples of India. (Fergusson, J.) London, 1864.
	Arc 587.10.15	Rock drawings of southern upper Egypt. (Winkler, Hans A.) London, 1938-39. 2v.
	Arc 609.15	Rock painting of the southwest Cape. (Johnson, Townley.) Capetown, 1959.
	Arc 609.12F	Rock paintings and petroglyphs of south and central Africa. (Rosenkranz, Ingrid.) Capetown, 1958.
	Arc 584.4F	The rock-picutres of Lower Nubia. (Dunbar, J.H.) Cairo, 1941.
	Arc 444.1	Rock-temples of Elephanta. (Burgess, James.) Bombay, 1871.
	Arc 444.2.5	Rock temples of Elurâ or Verul. (Burgess, James.) Bombay, 1877.
	Arc 444.2	Rock temples of Elurâ or Verul. (Burgess, James.) Bombay, 1877.
	Arc 587.7	The rock tombs of Deir el Gebrâevi. (Davies, N. de Garis.) London, 1902. 2v.
	Arc 587.8	The rock tombs of El Amarna. (Davies, N. de Garis.) London, 1903. 6v.
	Arc 587.10F	The rock tombs of Meir. (Blackman, A.M.) London, 1914-24. 6v.
	Arc 587.6	The rock tombs of Sheikh Said. (Davies, N. de Garis.) London, 1901.
	Arc 1330.40	Roda y Delgada, Juan de Dios de la. Bibliografia numismatica española. Madrid, 1886.
	Arc 750.217F	Rodacanchi, E. Les monuments de Rome après la chute de l'empire. Paris, 1914.
	Arc 682.10F	Rodenwaldt, G. Der Fries des Megarons von Mykenai. Halle an der Saale, 1921.
	Arc 815.7	Rodenwaldt, G. Komposition der Pompejanischen Wandgewälde. Berlin, 1909.
	Arc 684.1.45F	Rodenwaldt, G. Olympia. Berlin, 1926.
	Arc 710.14.2	Rodenwaldt, Gerhart. The acropolis. 2. ed. Oxford, 1957.
	Arc 710.14F	Rodenwaldt, Gerhart. Die Akropolis. Berlin, 1930.
	Arc 87.1.76	Rodenwaldt, Gerhart. Griechische Porträts aus dem Ausgang der Antike. Berlin, 1919.
	Arc 905.10	Rodlow, O.W. von. Die Brennerstrasse im Alterthum und Mittelalter. Prag, 1900.
	Arc 905.11	Rodlow, O.W. von. Der Verkehr...Pass von Pontelba-Pontafel...Predil. Prag, 1898.
	Arc 723.40	Rodmilli, Antonio M. La preistoria d'Italia alla luce delle ultime scoperte. Firenze, 1963.
	Arc 750.207	Rodocanachi, E. Le capitole romain. Paris, 1904.
	Arc 785.14.5	Rodocanachi, E. The Roman capitol in ancient and modern times. N.Y., 1906.
	Arc 843.7.5	Rodriquez de Berlanga, M. Los bronces de Osuna. Malaga, 1873.
	Arc 843.7.7	Rodriquez de Berlanga, M. Los nuevos bronces de Osuna. Malaga, 1876.
	Arc 925.50.200	Rodynnyi al'bom. (Humenna, Dokiia.) Niu-Iork, 1971.
	Arc 545.227.31	Roeder, G. Debod bis Bal Kalabach. Le Caire, 1911. 3v.
	Arc 600.35.15	Roeder, Günther. Ein Jahrzehnt deutscher Ausgrabungen in einer ägyptischen Stadtruine. Hildesheim, 1951.
	Arc 600.35.5	Roeder, Günther. Vorläufiger Bericht über die Ausgrabungen in Hermopolis 1929-30. Augsburg, 1931 .
	Arc 600.35.10	Roeder, Günther. Vorläufiger Bericht über die detsche Hermopolis-Expedition, 1931-32. Augsburg, 1932.
	Arc 853.240	Röder, J. Toutonenstein und Heinesäulen bei Mildenburg. Kallmünz, 1960.
	Arc 853.283	Die Römer am Rein und Main. (Schmid, Armin.) Frankfurt, 1972.
	Arc 853.369	Die Römer am Rhein. (La Baume, Peter.) Bonn, 1973.
	Arc 905.148	Die Römer an der Donau. Wien, 1973.
	Arc 853.24.5	Die Römer in Bayern. (Wagner, F.) München, 1928.
	Arc 853.24.22	Die Römer in Bayern. 2. Aufl. (Kellner, Hans-Jörg.) München, 1972.
	Arc 848.5	Die Römer in Deutschland. (Koepp, F.) Bielefeld, 1912.
	Arc 853.13.25	Die Römer in Württemberg. pt.1-3. (Hertlein, F.) Stuttgart, 1928-32. 3v.
	Arc 853.11	Das Römerkastell Saalburg. Text und plates. (Jacobi, L.) Homburg vor der Höhe, 1897 2v.
	Arc 853.10.15	Das Römerkastell Saalburg. 4. Aufl. (Cohausen, August.) Homburg vor der Höhe, 1893.
	Arc 853.27.10F	Das Römerlager in Oberaden. (Albrecht, C.) Dortmund, 1938. 2v.
	Arc 853.74	Das Römerlager Vetera bei Hauten. (Lehner, Hans.) Bonn, 1926.
	Arc 905.17	Die Römerstadt Agunt. (Meyer.) Berlin, 1908.
	Arc 905.12.35	Römerstadt Carnuntum. (Obermayr, August.) Wien, 1967.
	Arc 853.29	Die Römerstadt Nida bei Heddernheim. (Wolff, G.) Frankfurt, 1908.
	Arc 853.366	Römerzeitliche Siedlungen in Nordhessen. (Mildenberger, Berhard.) Marburg, 1972.
	Arc 853.286	Das römisch-fränkische Gräberfeld vor Krefeld-Gellep. (Pirling, Renate.) Berlin, 1966. 2v.
	Arc 845.4	Das Römisch-Germanische Centralmuseum. (Mainz, Germany. Römisch-Germanische Centralmuseum.) Mainz, 1889.
	Arc 73.20.10F	Römisch-germanische Forschungen. Berlin. 1,1928+ 24v.
	Arc 608.7	Das römische Afrika. (Schulten, A.) Leipzig, 1899.
	Arc 762.3	Römische Altertümer. (Hula, E.) Leipzig, 1901.
	Arc 759.2	Römische Antike und frühes Christentum. (Egger, Rudolf.) Klagenfurt, 1962-63. 2v.
	Arc 761.2	Roemische Ausgrabungen. (Gsell-Fels, T.) Hildburghausen, 1870.
	Arc 853.24	Das römische Bayern, in antiquarischer Hinsicht. (Hefner, J. von.) München, 1842.
	Arc 900.208	Die römische Begräbnisstätte von Bugant. (Jenny, S.) Wien, 1898.
	Arc 1480.44	Das römische Bildnis in Meisterwerken der Münzkunst. (Lanckorónski, L.M.) Amsterdam, 1944.
	Arc 853.38.5	Das römische Bonn. (Sadie, Emil.) Bonn, 1925.
	Arc 853.234F	Das römische Brand- und Körpergräberfeld. (Nierhaus, Rolf.) Stuttgart, 1959.
	Arc 726.29	Römische Bronzeindustrie von Capua und von Niedergermanien. (Willers, H.) Hannover, 1907.
	Arc 1480.60	Der römische Denarfund von Vyşkovce aus der Frühkaiserzeit. (Ondrouch, V.) Bratislava, 1934.
	Arc 762.7	Römische Funde. (Huelsen, Hans von.) Göttingen, 1960.
	Arc 853.62	Römische Funde in Pommein. (Jungklaus, Ernst.) Greifswald, 1924.
	Arc 73.20.15F	Römische-germanische Kommission. (Archäologisches Institut des Deutschen Reichs. Funfundzwanzig Jahre Römisch-Germanische Kommission.) Berlin, 1930.
	Arc 785.34.20	Römische Götteraltaere. (Herman, Werner.) Kallmuerz, 1961.
	Arc 1086.2	Römische Grablampen. (Bachofen, J.J.) Basel, 1890.
	Arc 853.55F	Römische Grabmäler des Mosellandes. (Deutsches Archaeologisches Institut. Römisch-Germanische Kommission.) Trier. 1-2,1924-1932 3v.
	Arc 853.105	Der römische Grenzwald bei Hanau mit dem Kastellen zu Rückingen und Markäbel. (Wolff, G.) Hanau, 1885.
	Arc 853.7.1	Der römische Grenzwall in Deutschland. Text, atlas. Faksimile. (Cohausen, August.) Walluf bei Weisbaden, 1973 2v.
	Arc 853.101.5	Das römische Hans mit dem Dionysos-Mosaik vor dem Sudportal des Kölner Domes. (Fremersdorf, F.) Berlin, 1956.
	Arc 1053.3.1	Römische Ikonographie. v.1-2. (Bernoulli, J.J.) Hildesheim, 1969. 4v.
X Cg	Arc 1053.3	Römische Ikonographie. v.2, pt.1. (Bernoulli, J.J.) Stuttgart, 1882-94.
	Arc 1478.39	Römische Kaisermünzen. (Hirmer, Max.) Leipzig, 1941.
	Arc 1480.66	Römische Kaiserporträts in Münzbild. (Franke, Peter.) München, 1961.
	Arc 777.1	Die Roemische Kampagne. (Westphal, J.H.) Berlin, 1829.
	Arc 1027.90	Römische Katakombenbilder in Catania. (Achelis, H.) Berlin, 1932.
	Arc 87.2.85	Das roemische Koeln. (Veith, C.) Bonn, 1885.
	Arc 87.2.88	Roemische Lager in Bonn. Bonn, 1888.
	Arc 905.9	Römische Lampen aus Poetovio. (Fischbach, O.) Graz, 1896.
	Arc 853.170	Der römische Limes in Deutschland. (Schleiermacher, Wilhelm.) Berlin, 1959.
	Arc 900.209	Der römische Limes in Österreich. (Vienna. Akademie.) Wien, 1900- 20v.
	Arc 1025.62.15F	Römische Märtyrergrüfte. (Styger, Paul.) Berlin, 1935. 2v.
	Arc 853.4.15	Römische Militärgrabsteine der Donauländer. (Hofmann, H.) Wien, 1905.
	Arc 82.2	Römische Quartalschrift für...Kirch. Rom. 1,1887+ 52v.
	Arc 82.2.2	Römische Quartalschrift für...Kirch. Supplementheft. v.1-31. Rom, 1893. 14v.
	Arc 815.5.5	Die römische "Scenae Frons". (Cube, G. von.) Berlin, 1906.
	Arc 1027.8	Die römische Sebastianuskirche. (Grisar, H.) Rom, 1895.
	Arc 853.40.5	Die römische Staatsstrasse. (Maassen, F.) Bonn, 1881.
	Arc 900.206	Römische Strasen in Bosnien. (Ballif, P.) Wien, 1893.
NEDL	Arc 775.1	Roemische Topographie in Leipzig. (Urlichs, K.L.) Stuttgart, 1845.
	Arc 756.1	Die römische Topographie in Rom. (Becker, W.A.) Leipzig, 1844.
	Arc 853.20.7	Das römische Trier. (Krencher, D.) Berlin, 1923.
X Cg	Arc 545.216	Roemische und Byzantinische Seiden-Textilien aus.....Achmim-Panopolis. (Forrer, R.) Strassburg, 1891.
	Arc 87.2.51	Roemische Villa bei Weingarten. (Overbeck, J.A.) Bonn, 1851.
	Arc 830.210	Das römische Zabern. (Forrer, Robert.) Strassburg, 1918.
	Arc 853.67	Die römischen Alterthümer zu Augsburg. (Raiser, J.N. von.) Augsburg, 1820.
	Arc 845.1.5	Die Römischen Brandgräber. (Chlingesnsperg-Berg, M. von.) Braunsch, 1896.
	Arc 1480.42F	Die römischen Bronze- und Kupfermünzen mit schlagmarken um legionslager Vindonissa. (Grunwald, Michael.) Basel, 1946.
	Arc 853.3	Die römischen Denkmäler in und bei Mainz. (Klein, C.) Mainz, 1861.
	Arc 915.54F	Die römischen Fibeln in der Schweiz. (Ettlinger, Elisabeth.) Bern, 1973.
	Arc 845.205F	Die Römischen Fingerringe der Rheinlande. (Henkel, F.) Berlin, 1913. 2v.
	Arc 785.17	Die römischen Glasspiegel. (Steinmetz, G.) n.p., 1897.
	Arc 785.33	Die römischen Grabaltäre der Kaiserzeit. (Altmann, W.) Berlin, 1905.
	Arc 785.33.1	Die römischen Grabaltäre der Kaiserzeit. (Altmann, W.) N.Y., 1975.
	Arc 853.13	Die römischen Inschriften und Bildwerke Württembergs. v.1-2. (Hang, F.) Stuttgart, 1898-1900.
	Arc 853.13.2	Die römischen Inschriften und Bildwerke Württembergs. v.1-3. (Hang, F.) Stuttgart, 1913.
	Arc 853.13.3	Die römischen Inschriften und Bildwerke Württembergs. 2. Aufl. (Hang, F.) Stuttgart, 1914-15.
	Arc 1025.62.10F	Die römischen Katakomben. (Styger, Paul.) Berlin, 1933.
	Arc 1025.16	Die römischen Katakomben. (Wolter, M.) Frankfurt, 1866.
	Arc 1025.72	Die römischen Katakomben und ihre Martyrer. (Hertling, Ludwig.) Wien, 1950.
	Arc 1025.72.5	Die römischen Katakomben und ihre Martyrer. 2. Aufl. (Hertling, Ludwig.) Wien, 1950.
	Arc 900.213	Die römischen Meilensteine in Salzberg. (Klose, O.) Wien, 1902.
	Arc 853.376F	Die römischen Metallfunde von Augsburg-Oberhausen. (Huebener, Wolfgang.) Kallmünz, 1973.
	Arc 853.12	Die römischen Militarstrassen. (Naelier, J.) Strassburg, 1887.
	Arc 905.80	Die römischen Ruinen unter dem Hohen Markt. (Neumann, Alfred.) Wien, 1950.
	Arc 905.80.3	Die römischen Ruinen unter dem Hohen Markt. 2. Aufl. (Neumann, Alfred.) Wien, 1957.
	Arc 905.15.9	Die römischen Schutzbezirke an der Oberen Donau. (Gnirs, Anton.) Augsburg, 1929.
	Arc 848.2	Die römischen Steindenkmäler der Provinzialmuseum zu Trier. (Hettner, Felix.) Trier, 1893.
	Arc 900.212	Römischen Strassen und Befestigungen in Krain. (Premerstein, A.) Wien, 1899.
	Arc 1020.9.97	Die römischen Titelkirchen im Altertum. (Kirsch, Johann P.) Paderborn, 1918.

Author and Title Listing

Arc 530.110 Die römischen und byzantinischen Denkmäler von Iznik-Niçaea. (Schneider, A.M.) Berlin, 1943.
Arc 232.2 Römisches Österreich. Wien. 1,1973+
Arc 1568.6 Rønning, Bjørn R. Norges mynter. Oslo, 1971.
Arc 1570.5 Rønning, Bjørn R. Norges mynter i 150 år, 1816-1966. Oslo, 1967.
Arc 1568.7 Rønning, Bjørn R. Norges mynter og pengesedler etter 1874. Oslo, 1972.
Arc 895.35 Rogalands stenalder. (Gjessing, H.J.) Stavanger, 1920.
Arc 618.2 Roger, J.C. Celticism a myth. 2. ed. London, 1889.
Arc 402.8 Roger-Milès, L. Vingt siècles de travail. Paris, 1902.
Arc 1423.16 Rogers, Edgar. A handy guide to Jewish coins. London, 1914.
Arc 830.79 Roget de Belloguet, Dominique F.L. Origines dijonnaises. Dijon, 1851.
Arc 1033.12.53F Rohault de Fleury, C. Memoire sur les instruments de la Passion. Paris, 1870.
X Cg Arc 1016.207 Rohault de Fleury, C. La messe études archéologiques sur ses monuments. v.1-2,8. Paris, 1883- 3v.
Arc 1016.207 Rohault de Fleury, C. La messe études archéologiques sur ses monuments. v.3-7. Paris, 1883- 5v.
X Cg Arc 1016.207.5 Rohault de Fleury, C. La Sainte Vierge. Paris, 1878. 2v.
Arc 1020.104 Rohault de Fleury, G. Un tabernacle chrétien du Ve siècle. Arras, 1880.
Arc 520.35 Rohde, Elisabeth. Pergamon: Burgberg und Altar. 2. Aufl. Berlin, 1961.
Arc 1480.33 Rohde, T. Die Münzen des Kaisers Aurelianus. v.1-2. Miskoloz, 1881-82.
Arc 925.155.5 Rola Mirmekionu w zyciu gospoelarczym panśtwa bosforskiego. 1. wyd. (Sztetyƚƚo, Zofia.) Warszawa, 1972.
Arc 1093.2.17 Le rôle des phénomènes naturels dans l'éclatement. Thèse. (Pei Wen Chung.) Paris, 1936.
Arc 66.1.7 Role historique de Bertrand de Born. (Clédat, L.) Paris, 1879.
Arc 936.40.50 Roliata i kulturata na prabulgarite. (Féher, Géza.) Sofiia, 1940.
Arc 1580.40 Roll, Karl. Die Schaumünzen auf die Salzburger Emigration. Halle, 1925.
Arc 830.175.10 Rolland, Henri. Glanum. Paris, 1949.
Arc 830.315 Rolland, Henri. Glanum. Paris, 1960.
Arc 830.175.11 Rolland, Henri. Glanum. Saint-Remy-de-Provence, 1974.
Arc 1500.57 Rolland, Henri. Monnaies des comtés de Provence, XII-XV siècles. Paris, 1956.
Arc 66.1.71 Rolland, R. Histoire de l'Opera en Europe. Paris, 1895.
Arc 1015.204 Roller, T. Les catacombes di Rome. Paris, 1881. 2v.
Arc 769.1 Rolli, P. Degli avanzi dell'antica Roma. Londra, 1739.
Arc 1335.88F Rollin et Teuardent, firm, Paris. Monnaies d'or romaines et byzantines. Paris, 1887.
Arc 1335.88.25F Rollin et Teuardent, firm, Paris. Monnaies d'or romaines et byzantines vente aux enchères publiques 20-28 avril, 1896. Paris, 1896.
Arc 861.74 The Rollright stones and the men who erected them. (Ravenhill, T.H.) Birmingham, 1926.
Arc 397.18.10F Roloff Beny interprets in photographs Pleasure of ruins. (Macaulay, Rose.) London, 1964.
Arc 754.1 Pamphlet vol. Rom, 1880-1901. 14 pam.
Arc 754.2 Pamphlet vol. Rom. Provincial Kunst, 1890-1903. 22 pam.
Arc 756.13.5 Rom mit dem Triumphzuge Constantins im Jahre 312. 4. Aufl. (Bühlmann, J.) München, 1894.
Arc 765.5 Rom und seine Welt. (Kaehler, Heinz.) München, 1958.
Arc 1027.5.3 Roma; scavi nel cimitero de Domitilla. (Rossi, G.B. de.) Roma, 1877.
Arc 757.4 La Roma antica...desegnii inedite. (Cyriacus. Anconitanus.) Roma, 1907.
Arc 766.4.10 Roma antica. (Lugli, Giuseppe.) Roma, 1946.
Arc 768.1 Roma antica. (Nardini, F.) Roma, 1666.
Arc 768.1.25 Roma antica. 4. ed. (Nardini, F.) Roma, 1818-20. 4v.
Htn Arc 772.2* Roma antica e moderna. Roma, 1750. 3v.
Htn Arc 772.2.5* Roma antica e moderna. Roma, 1765. 3v.
Arc 1020.10.15 Roma christiana nei primi secoli. (Dandolo, C.J.) Asisi, 1865-67. 3v.
Htn Arc 761.5.2* Roma descritta ed illustrata. 2. ed. v.1-2. (Guattani, G.A.) Roma, 1805.
Arc 757.7 Roma imperiale nelle XIV regioni Agustee secondo. (Clementi, F.) Roma, 1935. 2v.
Arc 772.11 Roma medio republicana. Aspetti culturali di Roma e del Lazio. Roma, 1973.
Arc 768.2 Roma monumentale dinanzi all'umanita. (Nispi-Landi, Ciro.) Roma, 1892.
Arc 757.5 Roma nel III secolo - era volgare. (Carnevale, C.G.) Roma, 1896.
Arc 768.3.5 Roma nell'anno 1838. (Nibby, Antonio.) Roma, 1838-41. 4v.
Arc 1015.202.5 Roma scotterranea. (Bosio, A.) Paris, 1658.
Arc 1015.202 Roma scotterranea. (Bosio, A.) Roma, 1651. 2v.
Arc 1015.205 La Roma scotterranea christiana. (Rossi, G.B. de.) Roma, 1864-77. 4v.
Arc 1025.2 Roma Sotterranea, die römischen Katakomben. (Kraus, F.K.) Freiburg, 1879.
Arc 1015.206.5 Roma sotterranea; il cimitero di S. Castolo M. (Iozzi, Oliviero.) Roma, 1904.
Arc 1025.5 Roma sotterranea. pts.1-3. (Northcote, J.S.) London, 1879. 2v.
Arc 1025.29.21 La Roma sotterranea cristiana...dal G.B. de Rossi. (Tonini, P.) Firenze, 1879.
Arc 1015.205.5 Roma sotterranea cristiana. pt.1-2. Roma, 1909-14.
Arc 1025.35 Roma subterranea novissima. (Bosio, A.) Arnhemi, 1671.
Arc 671.10 Rōmaios, K.A. Ho Makedonikoi taros tēs Berginas. Athēnai, 1951.
Arc 402.19 Romaios, K.A. Mikra meletēmata. Thessalonikē, 1955.
Arc 843.195 Román, Carlos. Antigüedades ebusitanas. Barcelona, 1913.
Arc 1500.27 Roman, J. Classement des monnaies épiscopales. Paris, 1886.
Arc 1264.8A Roman, J. Manuel de sigillographie française. Paris, 1912.
Arc 823.4.8 Roman, M.J. Répertoire archéologique du département du Hautes-Alpes. Paris, 1887.
Arc 785.83.10 Roman Alpine routes (with map showing chief Roman passes). (Hyde, Walter Woodburn.) Philadelphia, 1935.
Arc 530.2.4F Roman and Christian sculpture. (Morey, Charles B.) Princeton, 1924.
Arc 848.27 Roman and pre-historic remains in central Germany. (Balch, E.S.) Philadelphia, 1903.
Arc 1478.40 Roman anniversary issues. (Grant, Michael.) Cambridge, Eng., 1950.
Arc 861.28 Roman antiquities at Lyndney Park. (Bathurst, W.H.) London, 1879.
Arc 855.210 Roman antiquities recently discovered. (Whichcord, J.) London, 1873.
Arc 754.4 Pamphlet vol. Roman Archaeology. 16 pam.
Arc 754.6 Roman archaeology in the city of Rome. Diss. (Piale, S.) Rome, 1832-33. 12 pam.
Arc 861.40.20 Roman Bath discovered. (Cunliffe, Barry W.) London, 1971.
Arc 861.40.10 The Roman baths of Bath. (Taylor, A.J.) Bath, 1923.
Arc 815.36 A Roman bridal drama at the Villa of the Mysteries. (Little, Alan.) Wheaton, Md., 1972.
Arc 858.45 Roman Britain, 1914-1928. (Macdonald, George.) London, 1931.
Arc 858.25 Roman Britain in 1913- v.1-2. (Haverfield, F.) Oxford, 1914- 5v.
Arc 755.3.2 The Roman campagna in classical times. (Ashby, Thomas.) London, 1970.
Arc 861.2.5 Roman Canterbury. London. 1-7
Arc 785.14.5 The Roman capitol in ancient and modern times. (Rodocanachi, E.) N.Y., 1906.
Arc 1025.45 The Roman catacombs. (Mommesen, T.) Londin, 1871.
Arc 1025.4 The Roman catacombs. (Northcote, J.S.) London, 1857.
Arc 1025.4.2 The Roman catacombs. (Northcote, J.S.) Philadelphia, 1857.
Arc 861.3.9 Roman Cheshire. (Watkin, W.T.) Liverpool, 1886.
Arc 861.3.10 Roman Cheshire. (Watkin, W.T.) Wakefield, Eng., 1974.
Arc 723.11 Roman cities in Italy and Dalmatia. (Frothingham, Arthur L.) N.Y., 1910.
Arc 723.11.5 Roman cities in Northern Italy and Dalmatia. (Frothingham, Arthur L.) London, 1910.
Arc 861.18.16.15 The Roman city of London. (Merrifield, Ralph.) London, 1965.
Arc 1478.15.5 Roman coins. (Gnecchi, F.) London, 1903.
Arc 1478.87 Roman coins. (Sutherland, Carol H.V.) London, 1974.
Arc 1478.24.7 Roman coins from the earliest times to the fall of the Western Empire. (Mattingly, Harold.) London, 1928.
Arc 1478.24.7.2 Roman coins from the earliest times to the fall of the Western Empire. 2. ed. (Mattingly, Harold.) London, 1960.
Arc 723.30.5 Roman construction in Italy from Nerva through the Antonines. (Blake, Marion E.) Philadelphia, 1973.
Arc 723.30 Roman construction in Italy from Tiberius through the Flavians. (Blake, Marion E.) Washington, 1959.
Arc 585.23.2 Roman Ehnasya. 1904. Supplement. (Petrie, W.M.F.) London, 1905.
Arc 1050.202 Roman emperors. (Portraits I.) n.p., n.d.
Arc 861.39.5 The Roman era in Britain. (Ward, John.) London, 1911.
Arc 861.16.2 Roman fen road in Cambridgeshire. (Little, W.C.) n.p., n.d.
Arc 861.65.15 Roman Folkestone. (Winbolt, S.E.) London, 1925.
Arc 875.10.7 The Roman fort at Balmuildy. (Miller, S.N.) Glasgow, 1922.
Arc 875.10.13 The Roman fort at Cadder near Glasgow. (Clarke, John.) Glasgow, 1933.
Arc 875.100.5 The Roman fort at Castledykes. (Robertson, Anne.) Edinburgh, 1964.
Arc 861.84 The Roman fort at Ribchester. 3. ed. (Hopkinson, J.H.) Manchester, 1928.
Arc 885.9 The Roman fort near Brecon. (Wheeler, R.E.M.) London, 1926.
Arc 885.6 Roman fort of Gelly Gaer in...Glamorgan. (Ward, John.) London, 1903.
Arc 861.70 The Roman forts of Templeborough near Rotherham. (May, Thomas.) Rotherham, 1922.
Arc 875.13 The Roman forts on the Bar Hill, Dumbartonshire. (Macdonald, G.) Glasgow, 1906.
Arc 785.13.57 The Roman Forum; the Palatine. (Bartoli, Alfonso.) Milan, 1924.
Arc 785.13.51 The Roman Forum. (Artioli, Romolo.) Rome, 19- .
Arc 785.13.95 The Roman Forum. (Grant, Michael.) London, 1970.
Arc 785.13.24 The Roman Forum. (Huelsen, Christian.) Rome, 1906.
Arc 785.13.23 The Roman Forum. (Huelsen, Christian.) Rome, 1906.
Arc 785.13.24.5 The Roman Forum. (Huelsen, Christian.) Rome, 1909.
Arc 785.13.53A The Roman forum. (Lansiani, Rodolfo.) Rome, 1910.
Arc 785.13.90 The Roman Forum. (Staderini, G.) Rome, 19- .
Arc 785.13.35.5 The Roman Forum and the Palatine. (Marucchi, O.) Rome, 1906.
Arc 830.362 Roman France. (MacKendrick, Paul Lachlan.) N.Y., 1972.
Arc 885.19.5 The Roman frontier in Wales. (Nash-Williams, Victor Erle.) Cardiff, 1954.
Arc 885.19.7 The Roman frontier in Wales. (Nash-Williams, Victor Erle.) Cardiff, 1969.
Arc 855.9 A Roman frontier post and its people. (Curle, James.) Glasgow, 1911.
Arc 861.125 Roman Gloucester. (Fullbrook-Leggatt, Lawrence Edward Wells Outen.) Gloucester, 1950.
Arc 861.126 Roman Gloucester. (Fullbrook-Leggatt, Lawrence Edward Wells Outen.) Lansdown, 1968.
Arc 861.35 Roman Hayling. (Ely, Talfourd.) London, 1914.
Arc 861.35.5 Roman Hayling. 2. ed. (Ely, Talfourd.) London, 1908.
Arc 1478.40.5 Roman history from coins. (Grant, Michael.) Cambridge, Eng., 1958.
Arc 1478.24 The Roman imperial coinage. v.1-9. (Mattingly, Harold.) London, 1923-38. 10v.
Arc 1478.40.2 Roman imperial money. (Grant, Michael.) London, 1954.
Arc 861.49 Roman Lancashire. (Watkin, W.J.) Liverpool, 1883.
Arc 861.18.16 Roman London. (Home, Gordon.) London, 1926.
Arc 861.18.16.10 Roman London. (Home, Gordon.) London, 1948.
Arc 861.18.16.5 Roman London. (Home, Gordon.) N.Y., 1926.
Arc 861.90 Roman Malton and district. Report. (Yorkshire Archaeolgical Society.) York. 2-7 6v.
Arc 858.93F The Roman milestones of Britain. (Sedgley, Jeffrey.) Oxford, 1975.
Arc 1478.24.15 Roman numismatics. (Mattingly, Harold.) London, 195-?
Arc 875.80 The Roman occupation of southwestern Scotland. (Miller, S.N.) Glasgow, 1952.
Arc 1478.3.10 Roman Republican coinage. (Crawford, Michael H.) N.Y., 1974. 2v.
Arc 870.15 Roman road from Rochester to low barrow bridge. (Ross, Percival.) Bradford, 1916.
Arc 870.15.11 The Roman road to Portslade. (Dunning, J.E.) London, 1925.
Arc 870.4 Roman roads in Britain. (Codrington, Thomas.) London, 1903.
Arc 870.4.21 Roman roads in Britain. (Margary, Ivan D.) London, 1955. 2v.
Arc 870.4.21.2 Roman roads in Britain. (Margary, Ivan D.) London, 1967.
Arc 870.4.2 Roman roads in Britain. 2. ed. (Codrington, Thomas.) London, 1905.
Arc 870.4.3 Roman roads in Britain. 3. ed. (Codrington, Thomas.) London, 1918.

Arc 870.4.4 Roman roads in Britain. 3. ed. (Codrington, Thomas.) N.Y., 1919.
Arc 870.4.21.3 Roman roads in Britain. 3. ed. (Margary, Ivan D.) London, 1973.
Arc 870.4.15 Roman roads in south-east Britain. (Hughes, G.M.) London, 1936.
Arc 870.23 The Roman roads of Cheshire. (O'Dwyer, Stanhope.) Newtown, 1935.
Arc 885.16 The Roman roads of Wales. (O'Dwyer, S.) Newtown, 1936.
Arc 785.34.14 Roman sacrificial altars. (Bowerman, H.C.) Lancaster, Pa., 1913.
Arc 861.11.10 Roman Silchester. (Boon, George Counsell.) London, 1957.
Arc 861.21.35 Roman sites in Yorkshire. (Garlick, Tom.) Lancaster, 1971.
Arc 838.35 Roman Spain. (Wiseman, F.J.) London, 1956.
Arc 785.92 Roman theater-temples. (Hanson, John A.) Princeton, 1959.
Arc 861.110 The Roman town and villa at Great Casterton. (Corder, Philip.) Nottingham, 1951.
Arc 853.304 Roman Trier and the Treveri. (Wightman, Edith Mary.) London, 1970.
Arc 861.41.9 The Roman villa at Bignor, Sussex. (Winbolt, S.E.) Oxford, 1925.
Arc 861.41.10 The Roman villa at Bignor, Sussex. (Winbolt, S.E.) Oxford, 1930.
Arc 870.34 The Roman villa in Britain. (Rivet, Albert L.F.) London, 1969.
Arc 870.14F The Roman wall. 3. ed. (Bruce, John C.) London, 1867.
Arc 875.13.5 The Roman wall in Scotland. (Macdonald, G.) Glasgow, 1911.
Arc 875.13.7 The Roman wall in Scotland. 2. ed. (Macdonald, G.) Oxford, 1934.
Arc 870.14.12 The Roman walls. 2. ed. (Mariette, E.) Paris, 1906.
Arc 870.4.20 Roman ways in the Weald. (Margary, Ivan D.) London, 1948.
Arc 870.4.22 Roman ways in the Weald. (Margary, Ivan D.) London, 1965.
Arc 861.21.15 Roman York. (Home, Gordon.) London, 1924.
Arc 861.199.1 Roman Yorkshire. 1. ed. (Pearson, Frederick Richard.) Wakefield, 1973.
Arc 82.4 Romana tellus. Roma. 1-2,1912-1913
Arc 397.12 Romance of archaeology. (Magoffin, Rolf V.D.) London, 1930.
Arc 875.31.7 The romance of Bewcastle cross. (Hewison, J.K.) Glasgow, 1923.
Arc 562.6 The romance of excavation. (Masters, D.) N.Y., 1923.
Arc 793.4 Romanelli, D. Viaggio a Pompei a Pesto e di ritorno ad Ercolano ed a Pozzuoli. Napoli, 1817.
Arc 793.4.5 Romanelli, D. Voyage à Pompéi. Paris, 1829.
Arc 608.18F Romanelli, P. Leptis Magna. Roma, 1925.
Arc 936.24 Romania. (Berciu, Dumitru.) N.Y., 1967.
Arc 936.24.5 Romania. (Condurachi, Emil.) London, 1971.
Arc 66.1.193 La Romanie vénitienne au Moyen Age. (Thiriet, Freddy.) Paris, 1959.
Arc 1016.245F Der romanische Speisekelch. (Weiss, Karl.) Wien, 1860.
Arc 1030.37 Romano, C.C. Dell'arte...le iscrizione lapidarie. Roma, 1846.
Arc 1033.55 Romano, G.B. Memorie sacre della cappella...e di...la Scola Santa. Roma, 1798.
Arc 861.40.15 The Romano-British baths at Well. (Gilyard-Beer, R.) Leeds, 1951.
Arc 861.39 Romano-British buildings and earthworks. (Ward, John.) London, 1911.
Arc 861.160.20 The Romano-British cemetery at Trentholm Drive. (Wenham, Leslie.) London, 1968.
Arc 861.11.5 The Romano-British city of Silchester. (Davis, F.) London, 1898.
Arc 861.97 A Romano-British industrial settlement near Tiddington, Stratford-upon-Avon. (Fieldhouse, William J.) Birmingham, 1931.
Arc 861.60 The Romano-British site on Lowbury Hill in Berkshire. (Atkinson, Donald.) Reading, 1916.
Arc 1423.17 Romanoff, P. Jewish symbols on ancient Jewish coins. Philadelphia, 1944.
Arc 936.14.475 Romanow, Jerzy. Tomice, pow. Wrocław, 1973.
Arc 861.72 The Romans in Cleveland. (Elgee, Frank.) Middlesbrough, 1923.
Arc 861.212 Romans in Lancashire. (Shotter, David Colin Arthur.) Yorkshire, 1973.
Arc 861.200 Romans in the Lake counties. (Garlick, Tom.) Clapham, 1970.
Arc 1018.10 Rome, Italy. Collections. Stromation archaiologikon. Rome, 1900.
Arc 82.1.3 Rome, Italy. École Française. Mélanges. Antiquité. Rome. 83,1971+
Arc 82.1 Rome, Italy. École Française. Mélanges d'archéologie et d'histoire. Paris. 1-82,1881-1970// 81v.
Arc 82.1.2 Rome, Italy. École Française. Mélanges d'archéologie et d'histoire. Tables des tomes 58-72, 1941-60. Paris, n.d.
Arc 726.339 Rome, Italy. Università. Istituto di Topografia Antica. Lavinium. Roma, 1972- 2v.
Arc 66.1.124 Rome, la Grèce, et les monarchies hellénistiques. (Holleaux, Maurice.) Paris, 1921.
Arc 756.11.2 Rome, l'antiquité. (Bertaux, Émile.) Paris, 1904.
Arc 756.11 Rome; l'antiquité. 2. éd. (Bertaux, Émile.) Paris, 1907.
Arc 756.11.3 Rome, l'antiquité. 3. éd. (Bertaux, Émile.) Paris, 1913.
Arc 756.11.4 Rome, l'antiquité. 4. éd. (Bertaux, Émile.) Paris, 1924.
Arc 770.7 Rome, notes d'histoire et d'art. 11. éd. (Paléologue, M.) Paris, 1921.
Arc 770.7.5 Rome, notes d'histoire et d'art. 22. éd. (Paléologue, M.) Paris, 1935.
Arc 755.6 Rome; restauration archéologique. (Aucler, Paul.) Paris, 1899.
Arc 1020.10.29 Rome. (Bertaux, E.) Paris, 1905.
Arc 78.3 Rome. Accademia dei Lincei. Notizie degli Scavi. Rome. 1876+ 99v.
Arc 78.3.2 Rome. Accademia dei Lincei. Notizie degli Scavi. Indici epigrafici. 1876-85. Rome, 1886.
Arc 78.3.3 Rome. Accademia dei Lincei. Notizie degli Scavi. Indici generali, 1876-1955. Milano, 1904-1961. 3v.
Arc 82.3 Rome. Escuela Espagnola de Arqueologia é Historia. Cuadernos de trabajos. Madrid. 3-11 6v.
Arc 73.7 Rome. Institut Archéologique. La Section Française. Nouvelles annales. Paris. 1-2,1836-1839 2v.
Arc 73.1 Rome. Istituto. Annali, bulletino, and tavole. Rome. 1829-1883 65v.
Arc 73.2 Rome. Istituto. Monumenti - annali - bulletini 1854-5 and Monumenti - annali 1856. Rome.
Arc 73.4 Rome. Istituto. Nuove memorie dell'instituto. Leipzig, 1865. 2v.
Arc 73.5 Rome. Istituto. Repertorio universale dell'opere dell'instituto. Rome. 1834-1885 5v.
Arc 720.211 Rome. Istituto di Archeologia. Instituto archeologica centrum semertria. Roma, 1879.
Arc 391.15 Rome. Istituto di Studi Romani. Giulio Quirino Giglioli. Roma, 1958.
Arc 1030.26 Rome. Italy. Santa Maria in Via Lata. Tabularium. pt.1-3; plates. Vienna, 1895. 4v.
Arc 1480.4 Rome. Museo Kircheriano. L'aes grave del Museo Kircheriano. Text and atlas. Roma, 1839. 2v.
Arc 505.63F Rome. Pontifico Istituto Biblico. Teleilát Ghassúl. Roma, 1934.
Arc 726.247 Rome. Università. Monte Sirai. Roma, 1964. 4v.
Arc 77.8 Rome. Università. Centro di Studi Micenei. Incunabula Graeca. 1,1961+ 56v.
Arc 82.6 Rome. Università. Seminario di Archeologica e Storia dell'Arte Greca e Romana. Studi miscellanei. 1-16 6v.
Arc 772.10 Rome (City). Istituto di studi romani. Campania romana. Napoli, 1938.
Arc 726.260 Rome (City). Università. Istituto di Topografia Antica. Saggio di fotointerpretazione archeologica. Roma, 1964.
Arc 505.124.5F Rome (City). Università. Missione Archeologica. Il colle de Rachele. Roma, 1960.
Arc 756.7.2A Rome and Pompeii. (Boissier, Gaston.) N.Y., 1896.
Arc 756.5 Rome and the campagna. (Burn, R.) Cambridge, 1871.
Arc 407.18 Rome beyond the imperial frontiers. (Wheeler, Robert Eric Mortimer.) London, 1954.
Arc 1020.10.5 Rome chrétienne. (La Gournerie, E. de.) Paris, 1843. 2v.
Arc 66.1.94 Rome et la Grèce de 200 a 146 avant Jésus-Christ. (Colin, G.) Paris, 1905.
Arc 66.1.105 Rome et la Renaissance de l'antiquite. Photoreproduction. (Hautecoeur, L.) Paris, 1912.
Arc 756.10 Rome imperiale. (Bigot, P.) Rome, 1911.
Arc 762.6 Rome of the kings. (Hill, Ida T.) N.Y., 1925.
Arc 758.5 Rome of to-day and yesterday. (Dennie, John.) Boston, 1894.
Arc 758.5.5 Rome of to-day and yesterday. 5. ed. (Dennie, John.) N.Y., 1910.
Arc 1025.75 Rome souterraine. (Denis-Boulet, Noële M.) Paris, 1965.
Arc 1025.6 Rome souterraine. 2. éd. (Northcote, J.S.) Paris, 1874.
Arc 1025.69 De romeinsche catacomben en haar frescos. (Bakhuitzen van den Brink, J.N.) 's-Gravenhage, 1933.
Arc 785.102 De Romeinsche fascas. (Kristensen, W.B.) Amsterdam, 1932.
Arc 889.4.10 De Romeinsche villa's in België. (Maeyer, R. de.) Antwerpen, 1937.
Arc 1480.62 De romeinse muntvondsten uit de drie noordelijke provincies. (Es, W.A. van.) Groningen, 1960.
Arc 1025.15 Romeke, K. Rom's christliche Katakomben. Leipzig, 1886.
Arc 1625.2 Romero de Terreros y Vinent, Manuel. Los tlacos coloniales. México, 1935.
Arc 1025.53 Rom's altchristliche Coemeterien. (Becker, T.) Düsseldorf, 1874.
Arc 1025.15 Rom's christliche Katakomben. (Romeke, K.) Leipzig, 1886.
Arc 936.28F Romstorfer, K.A. Cetalea Sucerii. București, 1913.
Arc 1663.28.10 Romussi, Carlo. Garibaldi nelle medaglie del Museo del Risorgimento in Milano. Milano, 1905.
Arc 746.47.5 Roncalli, Francesco. Le lastre dipinte da Cerveteri. Firenze, 1965.
Arc 712.3 Ronchaud, L. de. Au Parthénon. Paris, 1886.
Arc 1675.12 Rondot, N. Les médailleurs et l. graveurs de monnaies. Paris, 1904.
Arc 1033.17.242 Ronzini, D. Brevi notizie sul celebre santuario di Maria sma. nel Sacro Monte di Novi. Napoli, 1853.
Arc 1033.3.47 Roosval, J. Junius Bassus sarkofag och dess datering. Stockholm, 1932.
Arc 1033.3.46 Roosval, J. Petrus- och Moses-gruppen bland Roms sarkofagy. Stockholm, 1932.
Arc 1675.14 Rosa, A. Coleccion de leyes, decretos. Buenos Aires, 1891.
Arc 1660.12 Rosa, A. Estudios numismaticos. Buenos Aires, n.d.
Arc 1643.2 Rosa, A. Monetario americano. Buenos Aires, 1892.
Arc 1033.17.98.3 Rosa, Agustin de. Defensa de la aparición de Nuestra Señora de Guadalupe. Guadalajara, 1896.
Arc 1033.17.98 Rosa, Agustin de. Dissertatio historico-theologica de apparitione B.M.V. de Guadalupe. Guadalaxarae, 1887.
Arc 567.1.5 Rosellini, Ippolito. Ippolito Rosellini e il suo giornale della spedizione letteraria toscana in Egitto. Roma, 1925.
Arc 505.5.19 Rosen, G. Das Harom von Jerusalem und Tempelplatz des Maria. Gotha, 1866.
Arc 1423.32 Rosen, Josef. Münzen aus biblischer Zeit. Basel, 1968.
Arc 1423.32.1 Rosen, Josef. Münzen aus biblischer Zeit. n.p., 1969.
Arc 1675.11 Rosenberg, S. Medaillen auf Privat-Personen. Frankfurt, n.d.
Arc 905.13 Rosenegger, J. Tabellarisische Ubersicht der Alterthumer in Roseneggers Garten. Salzburg, 1824.
Arc 609.12F Rosenkranz, Ingrid. Rock paintings and petroglyphs of south and central Africa. Capetown, 1958.
Arc 1185.18 Rosenmund, R. Die Fortschritte der Diplomatik seit Mabillon. München, 1897.
Arc 823.4.3 Rosenzweig, L. Répertoire archéologique du département du Morbihan. Paris, 1863.
Arc 545.241F The Rosetta stone. (Budge, Ernest A.) London, 1913.
Arc 402.4 Ross, L. Archaeologische Aufsaetze. Leipzig, 1855. 2v.
Arc 513.9 Ross, L. Reisen nach Kos, Halikarnassos, Rhodos. Halle, 1852.
Arc 657.2.3 Ross, L. Reisen und der griechischen Inseln. v.1-3. Stuttgart, 1840-45.
Arc 657.2.2 Ross, L. Reisen und Reiseronten durch Griechenland. Berlin, 1841.
Arc 716.10 Ross, Ludwig. Das Theseion und der Tempel des Ares in Athen. Halle, 1852.
Arc 870.15 Ross, Percival. Roman road from Rochester to low barrow bridge. Bradford, 1916.
Arc 736.7 Rossbach, Otto. Castrogiovanni...nebst einer Untersuchung. Leipzig, 1912.
Arc 1033.12.67 Rossi, B. de. Teatro dell'umana rendenzione...relazione istorica del...sangue...Sarzana. Massa, 1708.
Arc 1030.5.50 Rossi, G.B. de. Adunanze solenne in commemorazione di Guglielmo Henzen. Roma, 1887.
Arc 1027.25.15 Rossi, G.B. de. Albo dei sottoscrittori pel busto marmoreo. Roma, 1892.
Arc 1033.67 Rossi, G.B. de. Antichi Mulini in Roma e nel Lazio. Roma, 1857.
Arc 1025.29.5 Rossi, G.B. de. Aperçu général sur les catacombes de Rome. Paris, 1867.

Arc 785.32 Rossi, G.B. de. L'ara massima ed il tempio d'Ercole. Roma, 1854.

Arc 1027.30.19 Rossi, G.B. de. Arcosolio dipinto del cimitero di Ciriaca. Roma, 1876.

Arc 1027.4.35 Rossi, G.B. de. La basilica di S. Silvestro nel cimitero di Priscilla. Roma, 1890.

Arc 1027.71 Rossi, G.B. de. Il cimitero di S. Ippolito presso la via Tiburtina. Roma, 1882.

Arc 1033.92 Rossi, G.B. de. Commemorazione del P. Luigi Bruzza. Roma, 1883.

Arc 1027.5.4 Rossi, G.B. de. Il cubicolo di Ampliato nel cimitero di Domitilla. Roma, 1900.

Arc 1027.63 Rossi, G.B. de. Decouvertes dans l'arenaire situé...sur la voie Salaria. Rome, 1873.

Arc 1020.28 Rossi, G.B. de. Découvertes de divers monuments chrétiens en Sardaigne. Rome, 1873.

Arc 1030.5.43 Rossi, G.B. de. Del arco fabiano nel foro. Roma, 1859.

Arc 1025.29 Rossi, G.B. de. Del luogo appellato ad Caprean. Roma, 1888.

Arc 1030.5.17 Rossi, G.B. de. Della praepositus della via flaminia. n.p., 1888.

Arc 1016.215 Rossi, G.B. de. Dell'antichissimo codice della Bibbia Graeca. Roma, 1860.

Arc 1030.5.25 Rossi, G.B. de. Delle sillogi epigrafiche di Smezio e di Panvinio. Roma, 1862.

Arc 1259.1 Rossi, G.B. de. Di una bolla plumbea papale. Roma, 1882.

Arc 1033.26 Rossi, G.B. de. Dissertazione postume del P. Luigi Bruzza. Roma, 1889.

Arc 1030.5.13 Rossi, G.B. de. D'una mutila epigrafe...nel torrione della porta flaminia. Roma, 1877.

Arc 1030.5.21 Rossi, G.B. de. L'elogio funebre di Turia...Q. Lucrezio Vespillone. Roma, 1880.

Arc 1027.69.5 Rossi, G.B. de. Epigrafi rinvenute nell'arenaria tra i cimiteri di Trasone e dei Giordani sulla via Salaria. Roma, 1873.

Arc 1033.68 Rossi, G.B. de. Esame...dell'Immagine di Urbano II. Roma, 1881.

Arc 1027.7.17 Rossi, G.B. de. Escavazioni nel cimitero dei SS. Pietro e Marcellino. Roma, 1882.

Arc 1027.15.19 Rossi, G.B. de. Fibula d'oro aquiliforme. Roma, 1894.

Arc 1030.5.9 Rossi, G.B. de. Frammenti di fasti di Ludi Capenati. Roma, 1884.

Arc 1033.1.5 Rossi, G.B. de. Frammento di Becchiere Vitreo. Roma, 1885.

Arc 1027.65 Rossi, G.B. de. Le horrea sotto l'aventino. Roma, 1885.

Arc 1027.5 Rossi, G.B. de. Importantes decouvertes...cimetiere de Domitille. Paris, 1875.

Arc 1030.5.31 Rossi, G.B. de. L'inscription du tombeau d'Hadrien I. Rome, 1888.

Arc 1033.1.4 Rossi, G.B. de. Insigne...Battesimo d'una fanciulla. Roma, 1872.

Arc 1030.5.59 Rossi, G.B. de. Iscrizione cristiana di Tropea in Calabria. Roma, 1857. 2v.

Arc 1030.5.40 Rossi, G.B. de. Iscrizione della statua...di Nicomaco Flaviano Seniore. Roma, 1849.

Arc 1016.215.5 Rossi, G.B. de. Iscrizione in scritta e lingua Nabatea...Madaba. Roma, 1893.

Arc 1030.5.35 Rossi, G.B. de. Iscrizione in un spillo d'oso, trovato a Bolsena. Roma, 1890.

Arc 1027.5.2 Rossi, G.B. de. Isigni scoperte nel cimitero di Domitilla. Roma, n.d.

Arc 1027.25.24 Rossi, G.B. de. Melanges G.B. Rossi. Paris, 1892.

Arc 1030.5.15 Rossi, G.B. de. Memorie degli apostoli Pietro e Paolo. Roma, 1877.

Arc 1015.205.13 Rossi, G.B. de. Il museo epigrafico cristiano pio-sateranense. Roma, 1877.

Arc 772.4.5 Rossi, G.B. de. Note di Ruderi e monumenti antico di Roma. Roma, 1883.

Arc 772.4 Rossi, G.B. de. Note di topographia romana. Roma, 1882.

Arc 1033.86 Rossi, G.B. de. Oratorio privato del secolo IV...nel Monte della Giustizia. Roma, 1876.

Arc 726.27 Rossi, G.B. de. Porticus triumphi. Roma, 1889.

Arc 785.23 Rossi, G.B. de. Ricerche archeologico e topografico nel monto Albano. Roma, 1874.

Arc 1027.5.3 Rossi, G.B. de. Roma; scavi nel cimitero de Domitilla. Roma, 1877.

Arc 1015.205 Rossi, G.B. de. La Roma scotterranea christiana. Roma, 1864-77. 4v.

Arc 1030.5.29 Rossi, G.B. de. Il sarcofago di S. Siro. Roma, 1876.

Arc 1030.5.55 Rossi, G.B. de. Scavi nell'orto di S. Sabina sull'Aventino. Roma, 1856.

Arc 1027.69 Rossi, G.B. de. Scoperte nell'arenaria tra i cimiteri di Trasone e dei Giordani sulla via Salaria. Roma, 1872.

Arc 1030.5.5 Rossi, G.B. de. Sepolcri del secolo ottavo...di S. Lorenzo in Lucina. Roma, 1872.

Arc 1020.27 Rossi, G.B. de. Spiciligio d'archeologia cristiana nell'Umbria. Roma, 1871.

Arc 1030.5.3 Rossi, G.B. de. Il tomo secondo delle conferenze di Chiusura. Roma, 1888.

Arc 1015.205.9 Rossi, G.B. de. Verre representant le temple de Jerusalem. Genes, 1883.

Arc 1033.1.7 Rossi, G.B. de. Vetro graffito con immagini di santi. Roma, 1878.

Arc 1020.9.80 Rossi, G.B. di. Incrementi del museo sacro della Biblioteca Vaticana di Leone XIII. Roma, n.d.

Arc 1020.9.45 Rossi, G.B. di. Miscellania...la topografia...dei monumenti de Roma. Roma, 1889.

Arc 1020.9.47 Rossi, G.B. di. Panorama circolari di Roma, deliniato nu 1534. Roma, 1892.

Arc 1016.6F Rossi, J. de. Inscriptionae christianae urbis Romae. Romae. 1-3 7v.

Arc 1016.6.3F Rossi, J. de. Inscriptionae christianae urbis Romae. Supplement. Romae. 1,1925

Arc 1027.25.9 Rossi, J.B. de. Albo dei sottoscrittori...medaglio d'oro. Roma, 1882.

Arc 1033.71 Rossi, J.B. de. La capsella d'argent africaine. Caen, 1890.

Arc 1027.22.5 Rossi, J.B. de. De christianis monumentes Ichthys. Paris, 1855.

Arc 505.5.9 Rossi, J.B. de. Verre colorie representant le temple de Jerusalem. Paris, 1882.

Arc 505.5.10 Rossi, J.B. de. Verre representant le temple de Jerusalem. Genes, 1883.

Arc 1027.29 Rossi, M.S. Dell'ampiezza. Romane catacombe macchina. Roma, 1860.

Arc 1015.205.15 Rossi, M.S. de. Analsi geologica ed archilettonica de Cemet de Callisto. Roma, 1867.

Arc 1015.205.2 Rossi, M.S. de. Appendice...al tomo terzo della Roma sotterranea. Roma, 1877.

Arc 785.23.5 Rossi, M.S. de. Collare di servo fuggitivo novo Scoperto. Roma, 1892.

Arc 1015.227 Rossi, M.S. de. Duale metodo tecnico per dirigere l'escavazione. Roma, 1880.

Arc 785.23.3 Rossi, M.S. de. Scavi e studi nel tempio di Giove Laziale. Roma, 1876.

Arc 402.5 Rossignol, J.P. Services de l'archéologie aux études classiques. Paris, 1878.

Arc 1500.25 Rossignol. Jetons des états de Bourgogne. Autun, 1851.

Arc 1317.5 Rossiiskaia Akademiia Istorii Material'noi Kul'tury. Trudy Numizmaticheskoi Kommissii. Sankt Peterburg. 1-6,1921-1927

Arc 923.11 Rossiiskii istoricheskii muzei. (Tolstoi, I.) Moskva, 1893.

Arc 726.36 Rosso, G. del. Saggio...sui monumenti della antica città di Fiesole. Firenze, 1814.

Arc 925.50.47 Rostov on the Don (Province). Muzei Kraevedeniia. Arkheologicheskie raskopki na Donu. v.2, photoreproduction. Rostov na Donu, 1962- 2v.

Arc 505.45.15 Rostovtsen, M.I. Dura-Europas and its art. Oxford, 1938.

Arc 936.55 Rostovtsev, M. Une tablette votive thraco-mithriaque du Louvre. Paris, 1923.

Arc 925.13.55 Rostovtsev, M.I. The animal style in south Russia and China. Princeton, 1929.

Arc 925.13 Rostovtsev, M.I. Ellinstvo i iranstvo na iuge Rossii. Petrograd, 1918.

Arc 925.13.5 Rostovtsev, M.I. Iranians and Greeks in south Russia. Oxford, 1922.

Arc 815.12 Rostovtsev, M.I. Mifologicheskii peizazh 3-go pompeiaiskago stilia. n.p., n.d.

Arc 925.13.10 Rostovtsev, M.I. Skifiia i Bospor". Leningrad, 1925.

Arc 925.13.12 Rostovtsev, M.I. Skythien und der Bosporus. Berlin, 1931.

Arc 750.37.1 Rostovtsev, Mikhail Ivanovich. Tesserarum urbis Romae et suburbi plumbearum sylloge. Supplement. St. Petersbourgh, 1905.

Arc 785.119.1F Rostovtsev, Milchail Ivanovich. Tesserarum urbis Romae et suburbi plumbearum sylloge. Text and atlas. Leipzig, 1975. 2v.

Arc 1033.12.68 Rota, S.A. Verita trionfante...della fede in...narrazione delle reliquie del Sangue...Venezia. Venezia, 1763.

Arc 853.267 Roth, H. Wetterauer Fundberichte, 1941-49. Friedberg, 1951

Arc 726.343 Roth, Helmut. Die Ornamentik der Langobarden in Italien. Bonn, 1973.

Arc 853.65.5 Rothert. Die mittlere Steinzeit in Schlesien. Leipzig, 1936.

Arc 1348.60 Roubier, Jean. Dauernder als Erz. Wien, 1958.

Arc 547.4 Rougé, E. de. Notice sommaire des monuments égyptiens du Musée du Louvre. Paris, 1855.

Arc 1443.1 Rougé, Jacques de. Description de quelques monnaies nouveaux des nomes d'Egypte. Paris, 1882.

Arc 1016.208 Roulin, E. L'ancien trésor de l'Abbaye de Silos. Paris, 1901.

Arc 861.10 Round about notes...Isle of Man. (Halliwell, J.O.) London, 1863.

Arc 880.11 Round towers of Ireland. (Doherty, W.J.) Dublin, 1881.

Arc 880.1 The round towers of Ireland. (O'Brien, H.) London, 1834.

Arc 820.222F Roussel, Jules. Atlas monumental de la France. Paris, 1922.

Arc 66.1.122 Roussel, Louis. Grammaire descriptive du Roméique littéraire. Paris, n.d.

Arc 66.1.111 Roussel, Pierre. Délos; colonie athénienne. Paris, 1916.

Arc 875.14.25 Roussell, Aage. Norse building customs in the Scottish isles. Copenhagen, 1934.

Arc 66.1.199 Roux, Georges. L'architecture de l'Argolide aux IV et IIIe siècles avant J.-C. Paris, 1961. 2v.

Arc 387.10.10 Roversi, Luigi. Ricordi Canavesani. Luigi Palma di Cesnola. N.Y., 1901.

Htn Arc 1675.6* Roville, G. Prima-seconda parte del prontuario de le medaglie de piu illustri et fulgenti huomini et donne. Lione, 1553.

Htn Arc 1675.6.5* Roville, G. Promtuarii iconum insigniorum a secule homenum. pt.1-2. 2. ed. Lugduni, 1581.

Arc 750.203 Le rovine di Roma. (Suardi, B.) Milano, 1875.

Arc 726.20.7PF Le rovine di Veleia misurate e disegnate. Pt.1-2. (Antolini, G.) Milano, 1819-22.

Arc 608.17.21 Rowe, Alan. Cyrenaican expedition of the University of Manchester. Manchester, Eng., 1956.

Arc 861.1.3 Rowlands, Henry. Mona antiqua restaurata. Dublin, 1723.

Arc 861.1.6 Rowlands, Henry. Mona antiqua restaurata. 2. ed. London, 1766.

Arc 450.38 Roy, Sita Ram. Karian excavations, 1955. Patna, 1965.

Arc 432.29 Roy, Sourindranath. The story of Indian archaeology, 1784-1947. New Delhi, 1961.

Arc 608.24F The Royal cemeteries of Kush. (Dunham, D.) Hambridge, 1950-63. 5v.

Arc 497.96 Royal cities of the Old Testament. (Kenyon, Kathleen Mary.) N.Y., 1971.

Arc 858.24.30F Royal Commission on Historical Monuments. (Royal Institute of British Architects, London. Library.) London, 1958.

Arc 1470.31.10 Royal Greek portrait coins. (Newell, E.T.) N.Y., 1937.

Arc 855.2 The Royal House of Stuart. (Skelton, J.) London, 1890.

Arc 858.24.30F Royal Institute of British Architects, London. Library. Royal Commission on Historical Monuments. London, 1958.

Arc 880.49 Royal Irish Academy, Dublin. Museum. A descriptive catalogue of the antiquities. Dublin, 1857.

Arc 1313.1 Royal Numismatic Society. Numismatic chronicle. London. 1,1894+ 105v.

Arc 1313.2 Royal Numismatic Society. Proceedings. London. 1836-1837

Arc 1313.1.10 Royal Numismatic Society. Special publications. 1-8 8v.

Arc 1313.2.25 Royal Numismatic Society. Transactions of the International Numismatic Congress. London, 1938.

Arc 1313.1.9 Pamphlet box. Royal Numismatic Society. Miscellaneous pamphlets.

Arc 590.14 Royal sarcophagi of the XVIII Dynasty. (Hayes, William C.) Princeton, 1935.

Arc 247.15 Pamphlet vol. Royal Society. Northern Antiquaries, Copenhagen.

Arc 587.8.5F The royal tomb at El-Amana. (Martin, Geoffrey Torndike.) London, 1974.

Arc 682.13F The royal tombs at Dendra near Midea. (Persson, A.W.) Lund, 1931.

Arc 585.18A The royal tombs of the First Dynasty. v.1; v.2, pt.1-2. (Petrie, W.M.F.) London, 1900. 3v.

Author and Title Listing

Arc 416.17F Rozanthal, A. Arts antiques de l'Asie occidentale. Nice, 1948.

Arc 925.50.1 Rozvitok radians'koi arkheolohii na Ukraini. (Shovkoplias, Ivan H.) Kyiv, 1969.

Arc 936.14.230 Rozwój archeologii województwa zielonogórskiego w dwudziestoleciu Polski Ludowej. (Kołodziejski, Adam.) Zielona Góra, 1965.

Arc 674.1 Rubensohn, O. Die Mysterienheiligtuemer in Eleusis und Samothrake. Berlin, 1892.

Arc 925.16.10 Rubinshtein, N.L. Arkheologicheskii sbornik. Moskva, 1947.

Arc 710.22 Rubió y Lluch, Antonio. La acrópolis de Atenas en la época catalana. Barcelona, 1908.

Arc 1033.12.100 Rubram Jesu Christi chlamydem...exponent...respondens. (Lindovius, J.) Jenae, 1772?

Arc 1190.40 Ruddiman, T. A introduction to James Anderson's Diplomata Scotiae. Edinburgh, 1773.

Arc 1093.2 Rude stone monuments. (Fergusson, J.) London, 1872.

Arc 925.13.8.10 Rudenko, S.I. Gornoaltaiskie nachadki iskify. Moskva, 1952.

Arc 925.13.8 Rudenko, S.I. Iskusstvo. Moskva, 1949.

Arc 543.52.1 Rudenko, Sergei I. Die Kultur der Hsiung-nu und die Hügelgräber von Noin Ula. Bonn, 1969.

Arc 543.52 Rudenko, Sergei I. Kul'tura khunnov i Noinulinskie kurzany. Moskva, 1962.

Arc 543.50 Rudenko, Sergei I. Der zweite Kurgen von Pasyryk. Berlin, 1951.

Arc 925.38.16 Rudenko, Sergei Ivanovich. Frozen tombs of Siberia. 1. English ed. Berkeley, 1970.

Arc 925.38.15 Rudenko, Sergei Ivanovich. Kul'tura naseleniia Gornogo Altaia v skifskoe vremiia. Moskva, 1953.

Arc 1018.45 Rudimentos de arqueología sagrada. (Villa Amil y Castro, J.) Lugo, 1867.

Arc 1535.4 Ruding, R. Annals of the coinage of Great Britain. London, 1817. 4v.

Arc 1535.4.2 Ruding, R. Annals of the coinage of Great Britain. 3. ed. London, 1840. 3v.

Arc 925.50 Rudins'kyi, M. Materialy...stantsiia. Bila Hira pid Poltavoiu. Kyïv, 1926.

Arc 1510.14.3 Rudolph, E. Ergänzungen und Berichtigungen. Dresden, 1908.

Arc 1510.14.5 Rudolph, E. Zusammenstellung der Taler. Dresden, 1904.

Arc 925.50.75 Rudyns'kyi, M.I. Kam'iana Mohyla. Kyïv, 1961.

Arc 545.233.5FA Une rue de tombeaux a Saqqarah. (Capart, J.) Bruxelles, 1907. 2v.

Arc 1081.1.5 Ein Rückblick auf die Gräberforschung. (Duhn, F. von.) Heidelberg, 1911.

Arc 1510.138 Rueppell, E. Beschreibung der Münzen und Medaillen. Frankfurt am Main, 1857.

Arc 1153.41 Ruess, F. Ueber die Tachygraphie der Römer. Inaug. Diss. München, 1879.

Arc 1020.21 Ruggieri, C. De portuensi S. Hippolyti. Romae, 1771.

Arc 1033.43.5 Ruggieri, E. Dell'antico Pellegrinaggio XVIII centenario Martirio Pietro e Paolo. Roma, 1867.

Arc 1033.17.245 Ruggieri, S. Istoria dell'immagine di S. Maria di Pozzano. Napoli, 1743.

Arc 785.13.48 Ruggiero, E. de. Il Foro Romano. Roma, 1913.

Arc 772.8 Ruggiero, E. de. Lo stato e le opere pubbliche in Roma antica. Torino, 1925.

Arc 790.210.5F Ruggiero, Michele. Discorso pronunziato in Pompei. Napoli, 1879.

Arc 790.210 Ruggiero, Michele. Storia degli scavi di Ercolano. Napoli, 1885.

Arc 815.1 Ruggiero, Michele. Studi sopra gli edifizi e le arti meccaniche dei Pompeiani. Napoli, 1872.

Arc 1347.1 Ruhe, C.F. Specimen philolgiae numismatico-latinae primum. Frankfort, 1708-29. 3 pam.

Arc 608.7.25 Ruhlmann, A. Les grottes préhistoriques d'"El Khenzira" (région de Mazagan). Thèse. Nogent-le-Rotrou, 1936.

Arc 843.115 Ruig y Cadafalch, José. Noves des cobertes a la catedral d'Egara. Barcelona, 1948.

Arc 843.105.5 Ruinas de Mirobriga dos Célticos. (Almeida, Fernando de.) Lisboa, 1964.

Arc 875.55 Ruined castles. (Spence, James.) Edinburgh, 1873.

Arc 543.1 The ruined cities of Ceylon. (Cave, H.W.) London, 1897.

Arc 543.1.4 The ruined cities of Ceylon. 4th ed. (Cave, H.W.) London, 1907.

Arc 609.1 The ruined cities of Mashonaland. (Bent, J.T.) London, 1892.

Arc 865.1.10 The ruined temple Stonehenge. (Barclay, E.) London, 1911.

Arc 772.1.2 Die Ruinen Roms. (Reber, F. von.) Leipzig, 1863.

Arc 772.1 Die Ruinen Roms. (Reber, F. von.) Leipzig, 1879.

Arc 772.6 Die Ruinen Roms. 2. Aufl. (Holtzinger, H.) Stuttgart, 1912.

Arc 756.3 Die Ruinen und Museen Roms. (Braun, Emil.) Braunschweig, 1854.

Arc 705.203 Ruinen und Überbleibsel von Athen. (Sayer, R.) Augsburg, 1764.

Arc 530.12.30 Die Ruinen von Boğazköy, der Hauptstadt des Hethiterreiches. (Bittel, Kurt.) Berlin, 1937.

Arc 530.14.25 Die Ruinen von Priene. (Schede, Martin.) Berlin, 1934.

Arc 530.14.26 Die Ruinen von Priene. 2. Aufl. (Schede, Martin.) Berlin, 1964.

Arc 47.5 Ruinenstaedte Nordafrikas. Basel. 1-4 3v.

Arc 543.7 Les ruines d'Angkor. (Carpeaux, C.) Paris, 1908.

Arc 510.215 Les ruines d'Ani, capitale de l'Arménie. Text and atlas. (Brosset.) St. Petersbourg, 1860. 2v.

Arc 673.1.3 Les ruines de Delphes. (Bourguet, E.) Paris, 1914.

Arc 608.36 Les ruines de Dougga. (Poinssot, Claude.) Tunis, 1958.

Htn Arc 720.7.5* Les ruines de Paestum. (Major, T.) Londres, 1769.

Arc 810.1 Les ruines de Poméi. (Aloe, Stanislas d'.) Naples, 1852.

Arc 810.1.3 Les ruines de Pompéi. (Aloe, Stanislas d'.) Naples, 1850-51. 3 pam.

Arc 810.1.2 Les ruines de Pompéi. (Aloe, Stanislas d'.) Naples, 1851.

Arc 830.82 Les ruines de Sanxay découvertes en 1882. (Vachon, Marius.) Paris, 1883.

Arc 608.6.5 Les ruines de Timgad. (Ballu, Albert.) Paris, 1897.

Arc 608.6.7 Les ruines de Timgad. (Ballu, Albert.) Paris, 1911.

Arc 608.6.9 Ruines romaines au nord de l'Aurès. Rome, 1894. 2 pam.

Arc 830.40.9 Les ruines romaines de Noyers-sur-Andelys (Eure); villa rustica et théatre. (Coutil, Léon.) Évreux, 1928. 2 pam.

Arc 830.104 Ruines romaines de Tintignac (Corrèze). (Lalande P.) Brive, 1885.

Arc 766.1.5A Ruins and excavations of ancient Rome. (Lanciani, R.) Boston, 1897.

Arc 766.1.10 The ruins and excavations of ancient Rome. (Lanciani, R.) Boston, 1900.

Arc 766.1.6 The ruins and excavations of ancient Rome. (Lanciani, R.) London, 1897.

Arc 756.3.4 The ruins and museums of Rome. (Braun, Emil.) Brunswick, 1854.

Arc 386.7 Ruins of ancient cities. (Bucke, C.) London, 1840. 2v.

Arc 543.3.8A Ruins of desert Cathay. (Stein, Mark Aurel.) London, 1912. 2v.

Arc 968.12A The ruins of Great Ireland in New England. (Goodwin, William B.) Boston, 1946.

Arc 402.6 Ruins of sacred and historic lands. London, 1853.

Arc 1163.3.17 Rukovět hlaholské paleografie. (Vajs, Josef.) Praha, 1932.

Arc 74.4.14 Rules and list of members. (Society for the Promotion of Hellenic Studies.) London, 1891. 2 pam.

Arc 1301.1.9 Rules of the British Numismatic Society. London, 1908.

Arc 395.18.5.5 Rumaki Lizypa i inne opowiadania. 2. wyd. (Kosidowski, Zenon.) Warszawa, 1974.

Arc 303.18.5 Rumania. Comisune Monumentelar Istoriće. Buletiuul. 1-38,1908-1945 13v.

Arc 402.18 Rumpf, A. Archäologie. Berlin, 1953-56. 2v.

Arc 708.2.3 Ein Rundgang durch die Ruinen Athens. (Baumgarten, Fritz.) Leipzig, 1888.

Arc 708.2 Ein Rundgang durch die Ruinen Athens. (Baumgarten, Fritz.) Wertheim, 1887.

Arc 861.10.5 Runic and other monumental remains...Isle of Man. (Cumming, J.G.) London, 1857.

Arc 875.31 Runic roods of Ruthwell and Bewcastle. (Hewison, J.K.) Glasgow, 1914.

Arc 1588.10.35 Rupp, Jakab. Magyarorszag ekkorig ismeretes pénzei. Budan, 1841.

Arc 853.5 Rupp, T. Aus der Verzeit Reuthingens. 2. Aufl. Stuttgart, 1869.

Arc 870.26 Rural settlement in Roman Britain. London, 1966.

Arc 482.204F Rusafa. (Spanner, H.) Berlin, 1926.

Arc 925.50.310 Rusanova, Irina P. Slavianskie drevnosti VI-IX vv. mezhdu Dneprom i Zapadnym Bugom. Moskva, 1973.

Arc 936.140.60 Ruskite ucheni i bulgarskite starini. (Vuzharova, Zhivka N.) Sofiia, 1960.

Arc 1190.7 Russi, M. Paleografia e diplomatica...province napolitane. Napoli, 1883.

Arc 292.30.2F Russia. Arkheologicheskaia Kommissiia. Al'oom risunkov...v otchetakh. Sankt Peterburg. 1882-1906

Arc 292.40PF Russia. Arkheologicheskaia Kommissiia. Compte rendu. St. Petersbourg, n.d.

Arc 292.40F Russia. Arkheologicheskaia Kommissiia. Compte rendu. St. Petersbourg. 1-21,1859-1888 9v.

NEDL Arc 292.10 Russia. Arkheologicheskaia Kommissiia. Izvestiia. Sankt Peterburg. 1-66,1901-1918 21v.

Arc 292.20F Russia. Arkheologicheskaia Kommissiia. Materialy po arkheologii Rossii. Petrograd. 3-37,1888-1918 24v.

Arc 292.30F Russia. Arkheologicheskaia Kommissiia. Otchet". Petrograd. 1889-1915 8v.

Arc 292.30.5 Russia. Arkheologicheskaia Kommissiia. Ukazateli k otchetame za 1882-98. Sankt Peterburg, 1903.

Arc 1281.1F Russia. Commission d'Impression des Lettres Patentes et Traités. Reproduction d'anciens cachets russes. Moscou, 1880.

Arc 920.2 Russia. Commission Impériale Archéologique. Recueil d'antiquités de la Scythie. St. Petersbourg, 1866. 2v.

Arc 1675.19 Russia. Monetnyi. Opisanie russkikh medalei. Sankt Peterburg, 1908.

Arc 922.1 Pamphlet vol. Russia - Antiquities. 6 pam.

Arc 290.1 Russische Alterthümer 1844. (Kruse, F.) Dorpat, 1844.

Arc 1584.30 Russische Münzstätten, Münzzeichen, Münzmeisterzeichen. (Kairn, Reinhold.) Braunschweig, 1971.

Arc 1583.28 Russische Numismatik. (Kaim, Reinhold.) Braunschweig, 1968.

Arc 1582.5F Russkaia dopetrovenaia numismatika. (Tolstoi, I.I.) Sankt Peterburg, 1884-86. 2v.

Arc 1163.3.45 Russkaia paleografiia. (Chaev, N.S.) Moskva, 1946.

Arc 1163.3.55 Russkaia paleografiia. (Cherepnin, L.V.) Moskva, 1956.

Arc 1163.3.4 Russkaia paleografiia. (Shchepkin, Viacheslav N.) Moskva, 1967.

Arc 1163.3.85 Russkaia paleografiia. (Tikhomlrov, Mikhail N.) Moskva, 1966.

Arc 923.30 Russkaia paleograiuiia. (Shliapkin, I.A.) Sankt Petersburg, 1913.

Arc 1282.10 Russkaia spagistika i geral'dika. (Kamentseva, Elena I.) Moskva, 1963.

Arc 923.20F Russkie klady. (Kondakov, N.) Sankt Petersburg, 1896.

Arc 923.111F Russkie klady IX-XIII vv. (Korzukhina, G.F.) Moskva, 1954.

Arc 920.207F Russkiia drebnosti b' pamiatnikakh iskusstva. v.1-3, 4-6. (Tolstoi, I.) Sankt Petersburg, 1889-99. 2v.

Arc 1584.12 Russkiia monety do 1547 g. (Opeshnikov, A.V.) Moskva, 1896.

Arc 292.120F Russkoe Arkheologicheskoe Obshchestov, Leningrad. Izvestiia. Sankt Peterburg. 1-10,1859-1881// 6v.

Arc 292.140 Russkoe Arkheologicheskoe Obshchestvo, Leningard. Zapiski Numizmaticheskago otdeleniia. Sankt Peterburg. 1-2,1906-1913

Arc 293.2 Russkoe Arkheologicheskoe Obshchestvo, Leningrad. Bulletin. St. Pétersbourg. 21-25

Arc 293.1 Russkoe Arkheologicheskoe Obshchestvo, Leningrad. Mémoires. St. Pétersbourg. 1-6,1847-1852 6v.

Arc 292.125 Russkoe Arkheologicheskoe Obshchestvo, Leningrad. Protokoly obshchikhe sobraniia. Petrograd. 1899-1908

Arc 292.127 Russkoe Arkheologicheskoe Obshchestvo, Leningrad. Protokoly zasedaniia. Sankt Peterburg. 1897-1898

Arc 292.160 Russkoe Arkheologicheskoe Obshchestvo, Leningrad. Trudy vostochnago otdeleniia. v.1-11,13-14,16; photoreproductions. Sankt Peterburg. 1-22,1855-1898// 20v.

Arc 923.95 Russkoe arkheologicheskoe obshchestvo, Leningrad. Zapiska dlia obozreniia russkikh drevnostei. Sankt Petersburg, 1851.

Arc 292.110 Russkoe Arkheologicheskoe Obshchestvo, Leningrad. Zapiski. Sankt Peterburg. 1-13,1851-1918// 10v.

Arc 292.90 Russkoe Arkheologicheskoe Obshchestvo, Leningrad. Zapiski. Sankt Peterburg. 1-14,1847-1858 8v.

Arc 292.100 Russkoe Arkheologicheskoe Obshchestvo, Leningrad. Zapiski. Nouviia seriia. Sankt Peterburg. 1-12,1886-1902 10v.

Arc 292.163 Russkoe Arkheologicheskoe Obshchestvo, Leningrad. Zapiski vostochnago otdeleniia. Sankt Peterburg. 1886-1921 12v.

Arc 292.145 Russkoe Arkheologicheskoe Obshchestvo v Korolevstve S.Kh.S., Belgrade. Sbornik. Belgrad. 1,1927

Arc 1453.9 Russkoe Arkheologischeskoe Obshchestvo, Leningrad. Muzei. Katalog evropeiskikh medalei i monet. Sankt Peterburg, 1864.

Arc 292.130 Russkoe Arkheologisheskoe Obshchestvo, Leningrad. Zapiski klassicheskago otdeleniia. Sankt Peterburg. 1-9 5v.

Arc 925.95.5 Russkoe kwznechmoe remeslo XVI-XVII vv. (Nikitin, Arkadii.) Moskva, 1971.

Arc 1033.17.135 Russo, M. dello. Storia della sma. Cintola de Prato. Napoli, 1858.

Arc 612.37 Rust, Alfred. Werkzeuge des Frühmenschen in Europa. Neumünster, 1971.

Arc 858.26 Rust, J. Druidism exhumed. Edinburgh, 1871.

Arc 875.30 The Ruthwell cross. (McFarlan, J.) Dumfries, 1896.

Arc 875.31.10 The Ruthwell cross and its story. (Dinwiddie, J.) Dumfries, 1927.

Arc 670.8 Rutkowski, Bogdan. Cult places in the Aegean world. Wrocław, 1972.

Arc 672.10 Rutkowski, Bogdan. Larnaksy egejskie. Wrocław, 1966.

Arc 861.38.5 Rutter, John. Delineations of the northwest division of the county of Somerset. London, 1829.

Arc 861.38.6 Rutter, John. Delineations of the northwest division of the county of Somerset. London, 1829.

Arc 885.7.5 Rutter, Joseph G. Prehistoric Gower; early archaeology of West Glamorgan. Swansea, 1948.

Arc 1500.52 Rybat, N.V.L. Armorican art. Jersey, 1952.

Arc 772.12 Ryberg, Inez. An archaeological record of Rome from the seventh to the second century B.C. v.1-2. Philadelphia, 1940.

Arc 895.38F Rydbeck, Otto. Den medeltida borgen i Skanör. Lund, 1935.

Arc 612.27 Rydh, H. Grott-människornas årtusenden. Stockholm, 1926.

Arc 895.39.5 Rydh, Hanna. Ett bidrag till frågan om suöroornamentiken på stenålders boplatsernas lerkärl. Lund, 1937.

Arc 895.39F Rydh, Hanna. Förhistoriska undersökningar på Adelso. Stockholm, 1936.

Arc 895.21.30 Rydh, Hanna. Hos stenåldersfolket. Stockholm, 1933.

Arc 457.15 Rydh, Hanna. Rang Mahal. Lund, 1959.

Arc 895.36.20 Rydh, Hanna. En ristning på lös skifferplatta. n.p., 1921. 2 pam.

Arc 890.207 Rygh, O. Norske oldsager. Christiania, 1885.

Arc 1584.15 Ryms'ka moneta naterytorii Ukraïny. (Braichevs'kyi, M.I.) Kyïv, 1959.

Arc 612.57.5 Ryndina, Nataliia Vadimovna. Drevneishee metalloobrabatyvainshchee proiznodstno Vostochnoi Evropy. Moskva, 1971.

Arc 936.14.297 Rzemiosło rogounicze na Pomorzu wczesnośredniowiecznym. (Cnotliwy, Eugeniusz.) Wrocław, 1973.

Arc 936.14.115 Rzeszow, Poland. Muzeum. Rzeszowskie w zaraniu dziejów. Rzeszów, 1961.

Arc 302.49 Rzeszowski Ośrodek Archeologiczny. Materiały i sprawozdania. Rzeszów. 1964+

Arc 936.14.115 Rzeszowskie w zaraniu dziejów. (Rzeszow, Poland. Muzeum.) Rzeszów, 1961.

Arc 1033.61 S. Agnese nella tradizione e nella leggenda. (Franchi de Cavalieri, P.) Roma, 1899.

Arc 1033.60 S. Beatrice vergine e martire. (Calo, Luigi.) Napoli, 1894.

Arc 1016.9.9 S. Bonifazio e S. Alessio sull'aventino. (Lugari, G.B.) Roma, 1894.

Arc 1027.51 S. Damaso poeta insigne di martiri. (Cascioli, C.G.) Roma, 1898.

Arc 1333.13F The S. Lockhart collection of Chinese copper coins. (Lockhart, J.H.S.) Shanghai, 1915.

Arc 1033.58 S. Sebastiano; memorie. (Lugari, G.B.) Roma, 1889.

Arc 1033.12.127 S. spina di Vicenza. (Bortolan, D.) Vicenza, 1887.

Arc 600.225 Saad, Zaki Yusef. The excavations at Helwan. 1st ed. Norman, 1969.

Arc 505.80 Saadé, Gabriel. Ras-Shamra. Beyrouth, 1954.

Arc 1077.2.49 Det saakaldte Hagekors's Anvendelse og Betydning i Aldtiden. (Müller, Ludvig.) København, 1877.

Arc 845.204 Saalburg Jahrbuch 1910-1913. (Saalburg Museum.) Frankfurt am Main. 1,1910+ 25v.

Arc 845.204 Saalburg Museum. Saalburg Jahrbuch 1910-1913. Frankfurt am Main. 1,1910+ 25v.

Arc 853.238 Saarland. Staatliches Konservatoramt. Bericht der Staatlichen Denkmalpflege im Saarland. Saarbrücken. 6,1953+ 5v.

Arc 543.70.5F Sabaeica. (Rathjens, Carl.) Hamburg, 1953.

Arc 510.212 Sabatier, J. Chronologie du Royaume de Bosphore. St. Petersbourg, 1849.

Arc 1478.4 Sabatier, J. Description générale des monnaies byzantines. Text and plates. Paris, 1862. 2v.

Arc 1254.2 Sabatier, J. Plombs, bulles et sceaux byzantins. Paris, 1858.

Arc 1373.1 Sabatier, P.J. Production de l'or, de l'argent et du cuivre. St. Petersbourg, 1850.

Arc 785.51 Sabatini, F. La torre delle milizie, erroneamente denominala torre di Nerone. Roma, 1914.

Arc 830.139 Sacaze, Julien. Histoire ancienne de Luchon. Saint-Gaudens, 1887.

Arc 726.18 Saccardo, G. I pilastri acritani. Venezia, 1887.

Arc 66.1.26 Sacerdoces anthéniens. (Martha, J.) Paris, 1882.

Arc 497.8 Sachau, E. Reise in Syrien und Mesopotamien. Leipzig, 1883.

Arc 1510.3.10 Sachens Münzen im Mittelalter. (Posern-Klett, Karl Friedrich von.) Leipzig, 1970.

Arc 773.1 Sachse, K. Geschichte und Beschreibung der alten Stadt Rom. Hannover, 1824.

Arc 900.214 Sacken, E. von. Das Grabfeld von Hallstatt. Wien, 1868.

Arc 612.9 Sacken, Eduard. Leitfaden zur Kunde des heidnischen Alterthümes. Wien, 1865.

Arc 750.201 Sacr. Vat. Basilicae. (Dionisi, F.L.) Roma, 1773.

Arc 1027.54.5 Sacra imagine della beata Virgine Maria. (Cavedoni, C.) Modena, 1855.

Arc 1020.51.10 Sacrarium Agrippinae...praecipuarum reliquarum. (Winheim, Erharde.) Coloniae Agrippinae, 1736. 2 pam.

Arc 1020.51.5 Sacrarium Agrippinae...praecipuarum reliquarum. (Winkeim, Erharde.) Coloniae, 1607. 2 pam.

Arc 1015.230 Sacrarum vaticanae...cryptarum. (Dionysius, P.L.) Romae, 1773.

Arc 1018.28 Sacred archaeology...dictionary. (Wolcott, M.E.C.) London, 1868.

Arc 600.100 The sacred beetle. (Ward, J.) London, 1902.

Arc 1033.12.167 Sacro chiodo del redentore. (Buonafede, G.) Siena, 1653.

Arc 1033.102 Sacro-historica disquisitio emblematibus in Cimelio. (Carpini, J.) Roma, 1691.

Arc 1033.12.134 Sacro pellegrinaggio al Monte Sano per adorar il volto...del Salutor. Genova, 1660.

Htn Arc 773.5F* Sadeler, Marco. Nestigi della antichita di Roma. Roma, 1660.

Arc 853.38.5 Sadie, Emil. Das römische Bonn. Bonn, 1925.

Arc 936.14.455 Sądowel we wczesnym średniowieczu. (Lodowski, Jerzy.) Wrocław, 1972.

Arc 493.6.45 Sadykhzade, S.G. Drevnie ukrashcheniia Azerbaidzhana. Baku, 1971.

Arc 785.29.15F Säflund, G. Le mura di Roma republicana. Uppsala, 1932.

Arc 726.125F Säflund, G. Le terremare delle provincie di Modena. Lund, 1939.

Arc 1030.8.12 Saeki, P.Y. The Nestorian monument in China. London, 1916.

Arc 1490.60 Särström, M. A study in the coinage of the Mamertines. Lund, 1940.

Arc 1493.7F Saez, Liciniano. Apendice á la crónica nuevamente impressa del señor rey don Juan el II. Madrid, 1786.

Arc 1492.203F Saez, Liciniano. Demonstración histórica del verdadero valor detodas las monedas que corrian en Castilla. Madrid, 1796.

Arc 1493.8 Saez, Liciniano. Demostración histórica del verdadero valor de todas las monedas que corrián en Castilla. Madrid, 1805.

Arc 1261.2F Sagarra, Ferran de. Sigillografía catalana. v.1-3. Barcelona, 1916-32. 5v.

Arc 93.15 Saggi di dissertazioni accademiche. (Accademia Etrusca, Cortona.) Roma. 1-9,1742-1791 9v.

Arc 396.15F Saggi di explorazione archeologica. (Lugli, Giuseppe.) Roma, 1939.

Arc 726.120 Saggi di varia antichità. (Maiuri, Amedeo.) Venezia, 1954.

Arc 726.36 Saggio...sui monumenti della antica città di Fiesole. (Rosso, G. del.) Firenze, 1814.

Arc 1478.32F Saggio cronologico, ossia storia della moneta romana. (Pizzamiglio, Luigi.) Roma, 1867.

Arc 1330.35 Saggio di bibliografia numismata medioevale italiana. (Ciferri, Raffaello.) Pavia, 1961.

Arc 726.260 Saggio di fotointerpretazione archeologica. (Rome (City). Università. Istituto di Topografia Antica.) Roma, 1964.

Arc 1033.17.548 Saggio di notizie istoriche relative ai tre sagri monumenti, che si portano in processione la Mallina del di 17. gennajo 1798. n.p., 1798? 2 pam.

Arc 1033.17.304 Saggio istorico e coroncina della taumalurga immagine di Maria Sma. (Spada, G.N.) Napoli, 1839.

Arc 1033.17.304.5 Saggio storico con coroncina di Maria Sma. l'aconavetere. (Spada, G.N.) Foggia, 1917.

Arc 1033.17.244 Saggio storico della portentosa immagine di S. Maria di Campiglione. Napoli, 1848.

Arc 1588.6.20 Saglani, O.F. Simdiye kadar görülmiyen Cimri Sikkesi. n.p., 1949.

Arc 1020.9.25 Sagrestica vaticana eretta...Pio Sesto. (Cancellieri, F.) Roma, 1784.

Arc 843.56.5 Sagunto. 1. ed. (Gomzalez Simancos, M.) Sagunto? n.d.

Arc 895.22.25 Sahlström, K.E. Om Västergötlands stenålders bebyggelse. Stockholm, 1915.

Arc 458.9 Sahni, Daya Ram. Guide to the Buddhist ruins of Sarnath. 5. ed. Delhi, 1933.

Arc 387.35 Said and done. (Crawford, Osbert Guy S.) London, 1955.

Arc 1390.3 Le saiga mérovingien dérive de la silique byzantine. v.1-2. (Blancard, Louis.) Marseille, 1883.

Arc 497.14 St. Aignan, L. de. Découvertes récentes en Terre-Sainte. n.p., 1874.

Arc 505.5.52 Saint-Aignan. Temple de Salomon; sa description d'après découvertes récentes. Paris, 1875.

Arc 830.76 Saint-Amans, J.F.B. Essai sur les antiquités du département de Lot-et-Garonne. Agen, 1859.

Arc 935.23F St. Andrews. University. The great palace of the Byzantine emperors. London, 1947-58. 2v.

Arc 66.1.145 Saint Augustin et la fin de la culture antique. v.1-2. (Marrou, Henri-Irénée.) Paris, 1958.

Arc 1033.20.25.2 Saint Clement, pope and martyr. 2. ed. (Mullooly, Joseph.) Rome, 1873.

Arc 1033.20.25 Saint Clement, pope and martyr and his Basilica in Rome. (Mullooly, Joseph.) Rome, 1869.

Arc 1033.12.166 Saint Clou à la cathédrale de Toul. (Barbier de Montault, X.) Nancy, 1885.

Arc 1033.12.166.15 Le Saint Clou de Toul. Nancy, 1888. 3 pam.

Arc 1020.31.25 Saint Étienne et ses sanctuaires à Jérusalem. (Mommert, Carl.) Jérusalem, 1912.

Arc 1020.31.23 Saint Étienne et son sanctuaire à Jérusalem. (Lagrange, Marie.) Paris, 1894.

Arc 1333.15F St. Florian, Austria. Die Münzsammlung. Wien, 1871.

Arc 830.18.11 Saint Gens, ermite et Boèce. Supplément. v.1-2. (Gilles, Isidore.) Avignon, 1885.

Arc 1033.141 Saint Jean-Baptiste, sa vie, son culte. (Razy, E.) Paris, 1880.

Arc 1033.53.20 Saint Maurice et le Légion Thébéenne. (Ducis, C.A.) Annecy, 1882.

Arc 1033.12.170 Saint mors de Carpentras et son reliquaire. (Terris, F.) Carpentras, 1874.

Arc 1033.12.171 Saint mors de Carpentras et son reliquaire. (Terris, F.) n.p., n.d.

Arc 66.1.167 Saint Paulin de Nole. (Fabre, P.) Paris, 1949.

Arc 1027.8.13 Saint-Sébastien hors les murs. (Chéramy, H.) Paris, 1925.

Arc 1033.12.8 Le Saint Suaire. (Gourgues, A. de.) Perigueux, 1868.

Arc 1033.31 Le Saint Suaire de Turin. (Mély, F. de.) Paris, 1902?

Arc 1033.12.9.5F Le Saint Suaire de Turin devant la science. 2. éd. (Vignon, P.) Paris, 1939.

Arc 1033.119 Sainte Anne de Jérusalem et Sainte Anne d'Auray. (Charles, archbishop of Alger.) Alger, 1879.

Arc 66.1.121 Sainte Catherine de Sienne. (Fawtier, Robert.) Paris, 1921.

Arc 66.1.135 Sainte Catherine de Sienne. (Fawtier, Robert.) Paris, 1930.

Arc 1020.4.5 La sainte-chapelle de Bourges. (Boissoudy, A. de.) n.p., 1884.

Arc 1020.73.14 Sainte-Chapelle de Paris. Notice historique, archéologique et descriptive. (Troche, N.M.) Paris, 1853.

Arc 1033.12.132 Sainte-face de la cathédrale de Laon. (Lecomte, A.) Laon, 1885.

Arc 1033.12.196 Sainte-larme de Selincourt. Notice historique et bibliographique. Amiens, 1876.

Arc 608.2 Sainte-Marie, E. de. Mission à Carthage. Paris, 1884.

Arc 969.15.10 Sainte-Marie among the Hurons. (Jury, Wilfrid.) Toronto, 1954.

Arc 1016.13.5 Sainte Marie antigue. (David, J.) Roma, 1911.

Arc 1033.12.113 Sainte tunique. Discours...Argeteuil...1865. (Davin, V.) Paris, n.d.
X Cg Arc 1016.207.5 La Sainte Vierge. (Rohault de Fleury, C.) Paris, 1878. 2v.
Arc 1033.35.51 La sainte vraie croix de Douchy. (Cellier.) Valenciennes, 1863.
Arc 1020.67 Les saintes reliques...chateau de Manosque. (Feraud, J.J.M.) Digne, 1885.
Arc 935.40 Sakir, M. Sinop ta candar ogullarizamanina. Istanbul, 1934.
Arc 600.115 Sakkarah. (Drioton, E.) Le Caire, 1939.
Arc 540.14.5F Salamine de Chypre. Paris. 1,1969+ 6v.
Arc 540.2 Salaminia. (Cesnola, L.P.) London, 1882.
Arc 540.14 Salamis; recent discoveries in Cyprus. (Karageōrgēs, Basos.) N.Y., 1969.
Arc 1494.4 Salat, Josef. Tratado de las monedas labradas...de Cataluña. v.1-2. Barcelona, 1818.
Arc 1645.6F Salazar Bondy, Sebastian. Lima, su moneda y su ceca. v.1-2. Lima, 1964.
Arc 1675.30 Salgado, Vicente. Conjecturas sobre huma medallia de bronze. Lisboa, 1784.
Arc 830.107 Salin, Édouard. Le cimetière barbare de Lezéville. Nancy, 1922.
Arc 830.107.5 Salin, Édouard. Manuel des fouilles archéologiques. 1e éd. Paris, 1946.
Arc 403.6 Salinas, A. Miscellanea di archaeologia, storia, e filologia. Palermo, 1907.
Arc 730.207 Salinas, A. Nuove metope arcaiche selinantine. Roma, 1892.
Arc 730.206 Salinas, A. Relazione sommaria intorno agli. Roma, 1894.
Arc 1490.98.5F Salinas Gargotta, Antonino. Le monete dell'antiche città di Sicilia. Palermo, 1867-72.
Arc 1490.98 Salinas Gargotta, Antonino. Su di alcune monete puniche di Mozia. Palermo, 1858.
Arc 520.12 Salis, A. von. Der Altar von Pergamon. Berlin, 1912.
Arc 522.5 Salisbury, S. Troy and Homer. Worcester, 1875.
Arc 1093.6.12 Salktis, Progenitor der Svastika. (Paegle, Eduard.) Würzburg, 1957.
Htn Arc 720.203* Sallengre, A. de. Novus thesaurus antiquitatum romanorum. The Hague, 1716. 3v.
Arc 1470.11 Sallet, A. von. Beiträge zur Geschichte und Numismatik...des Pontus. Berlin, 1866.
Arc 1470.5 Sallet, A. von. Die Künstlerinschriften auf Griechischen Münzen. Berlin, 1871.
Arc 1470.2 Sallet, A. von. Die Nachfolger Alexanders des Grossen. Berlin, 1879.
Arc 1325.1.5 Sallet, A. von. Register. Berlin. 1-20,1884-1898
Arc 1325.1 Sallet, A. von. Zeitschrift für Numismatik. Berlin. 1-42,1894-1935 37v.
Arc 1033.143 Salmon, C. Histoire du chef de S. J.-Baptiste...Amiens. Amiens, 1876.
Arc 925.136.10 Sal'nikov, Konstantin V. Drevnieshie pamiatniki istorii Urala. Sverdlovsk, 1952.
Arc 925.136.5 Sal'nikov, Konstantin V. Ocherki drevnei istorii Iuzhnogo Urala. Moskva, 1967.
Arc 1033.96 Salomoni, P. De Liminibus Apostolorum. Romae, 1775.
Arc 785.80 Salomonson, Jan Willem. Chair, sceptre and wreath. Amsterdam, 1956.
Arc 1020.84.13 Salore, Charles. Probationes cultus sanctorum Diocesis Trecensis. Troyes, 1869.
Arc 1020.93 Salore, Charles. Reliques de trois tombeaux saints de Clairvoux...a Ville-sous-la-Ferté (Aubé). Troyes, 1877.
Arc 1020.56 Salore, Charles. Le trésor de Clairvaux. Paris, 1875.
Arc 600.195 The salvation of the Nubian monuments. (United Arab Republic. Ministry of Culture and National Guidance.) Cairo, 196-
Arc 1027.30.9 Salvatore da Morrovalle, P. La basilica di S. Lorenzo fuor delle mura. Bologna, 1861.
Arc 510.1 Salzmann, A. Nécropole de Camiros. Paris, 1875.
Arc 505.39.12 Samaria. (Parrot, André.) N.Y., 1958.
Arc 505.39A Samaria in Ahab's time. (Jack, J.M.) Edinburgh, 1929.
Arc 505.39.5 Samaria-Sebaste; reports of the work of the joint expedition in 1931-1933. London, 1938-42. 3v.
Arc 505.39.10 Samarie. (Parrot, André.) Neuchatel, 1955.
Arc 66.1.96 Samarin, C.M.D. La fiscalité pontificale en France XIVe siècle. Paris, 1905.
Arc 750.208.5F Sambon, Arthur. Catalogue des fresques de Boscoreale. Macon, 1903.
Arc 750.208 Sambon, Arthur. Les fresques de Boscoreale. Paris, 1903.
Arc 1488.5 Sambon, Arthur. Les monnaies antiques. Paris, 1903.
Arc 1335.37 Sambon, G. Catalogo delle monete italiane...collezione A. Cantoni di Milano. Milano, 1887.
Arc 1675.52 Sambon, Giulio. Catalogo delle medaglie del rinascimento e moderne di uomini illustri. Roma, 1883.
Arc 1488.11F Sambon, Giulio. Repertoiro generale delle monete coniate in Italia. Parigi, 1912.
Arc 1478.16 Samer, K. Geschichte älteren römischen Münzwesens...200 B.C. Wien, 1883.
Arc 493.30 Sami, A. Pasargadae. Shiraz, 1956.
Arc 493.2.20 Sami, A. Persepolis. Shiraz, 1954.
Arc 493.2.5 Sami, A. Persepolis. 2. ed. Shiraz, 1955.
Arc 530.54 Samial. (Landsberger, Benno.) Ankara, 1948.
Arc 530.54.5 Samial. Photoreproduction. (Landsberger, Benno.) Ankara, 1948.
Arc 1675.54 Samlung merkwürdiger Medaillen. Nürnbueg. 1-8,1737-1744 8v.
Arc 402.14 Sammarco, Angelo. Alessandro Ricci e il suo giornale dei viaggi. v.2. Cairo, 1930.
Arc 535.201 Die Sammlung Cesnola. (Doell, J.) St. Petersburg, 1873.
Arc 1335.101.71 Sammlung Consul Eduard Friedrich Weber, Hamburg. (Hirsch, Jacob.) München, 1908-09. 2v.
Arc 905.98 Sammlung der bisher erschienenen Aufsätze. (Sausgruber, L.) Feldhirch, 1918.
Arc 1335.29 Sammlung des G.F. Ulex; Münzen und Medaillen von Nord-, Central-, und Süd-Amerika. (Ulex, G.F.) Frankfurt, 1908.
Arc 1508.20 Sammlung des Herrn Alexander Fiorino in Cassel. (Fiorino, Alexander.) Frankfurt am Main, 1917.
Arc 1335.49 Sammlung Gustav Philipsen. (Hirsch, J.) München, 1909.
Arc 1335.120F Sammlung Hollschek. v.1-3. (Hollschek, Karl.) Wien, 1956? 2v.
Arc 1335.120 Sammlung Hollschek. v.4-20. (Hollschek, Karl.) Wien, 1956? 4v.
Arc 1510.35 Sammlung Pfalzischer. (Hamburger, L.) Frankfurt am Main, 1929.
Arc 1478.88.1F Sammlung römischer Münzen der Republik und des West-Kaiserreichs. (Bahrfeldt, Max von.) Aalen, 1972.
Arc 1510.32F Sammlung schleswig-holsteinischer Münzen und Medaillen. (Lange, C.C.A.) Berlin, 1908-12. 2v.
Arc 1503.9 Sammlung Schweizer Münzen und Medaillen des Herrn Theodor Grossmann. (Grossmann, Theodor.) Frankfurt, 1926?
Arc 1675.51.15F Sammlung von Medaillen. (Tyszkiewicz, E.) Riga, 1871.
Arc 920.208F Samokbasov, D.Ia. Opisanie arkheologicheskich raskopok. Moskva, 1908.
Arc 925.326 Samokrasov, Dmitrii I. Severianskaia zumlia i severiane po gorodishcham i mogilam. Moskva, 1908.
Arc 925.35.5F Samoksavov, D.I. Atlas gochevskikh drevnostei. Moskva, 1915.
Arc 925.50.190F Samokvasev, Dmitrii I. Raskopki severianskikh kurganov v Chernigove vo vremia XIV arkheologicheskago s"ezda. Moskva, 1916.
Arc 925.27F Samokvasov, D. Sbornik topograffiia sved. o kurgana. St. Peterburg, 1888.
Arc 688.7.5F Samos. v.1,5-8,12,14. (Deutsches Archäologisches Institut.) Bonn, 1961- 7v.
Arc 1470.42 Samos and Samian coins. (Gardner, Percy.) London, 1882.
Arc 688.6 Samothrace. (Lehmann, Karl.) N.Y., 1955.
Arc 688.6.5F Samothrace. v.1-4,6. (Lehmann, Karl.) N.Y., 1959-64. 5v.
Arc 1588.6.2.10 San alti osmanli padişahi zamaninda Istanbulda basilan gümuç paralor. (Ölçer, Cüneyt.) Istanbul, 1966.
Arc 1033.147 San Giovanni Battista e i Genovesi. Genova, 1879.
Arc 726.340 San Giovenale. Results of excavations conducted by the Swedish Institute of Classical Studies. Stockholm, 1972-
Arc 1033.34.13 San Pietro a Roma. (Cornoldi, G.M.) Roma, 1872.
Arc 1033.34.60 San Pietro e sepolto in Vaticano? (Corte, Nicola.) Roma, 1957.
Arc 1033.34.25 San Pietro in Roma. Monumenti e testimoni. (Giovanni, V. di.) Palermo, 1895.
Arc 1033.34.65 San Pietro nei monumenti di Palestina. (Bagatti, Bellarmino.) Cairo, 1960.
Arc 488.16 Sanadi, H.A. Les découvertes fortuites. n.p., 1960.
Htn Arc 1033.17.97* Sánchez, Miguel. Imagen de la virgen Maria...de Guadalupe. México, 1648.
Arc 435.25.8F Sanchi, Bhopal State. Museum of Archaeology. Catalogue of the Museum of Archaeology at Sanchi, Bhopal State. Calcutta, 1922.
Arc 458.1 Sanchi and its remains. (Maisey, F.C.) London, 1892.
Arc 1033.12.235 Sanchis y Sivera, José. El santo cáliz de la cena (santo grial) venerado en Valencia. Valencia, 1914.
Arc 1510.21 Sancta colonia numis antiquissimis illustrata et monumentis historicis explicata. (Scholtz, Henrico.) Ploenae, 1738.
Arc 1033.23 Il sancta sanctorum...tesoro sacro. (Grisar, H.) Roma, 1907.
Arc 726.24.7 Sanctis, D. de. Dissertazioni...la villa d'Orazio, il mausoleo di Plauzj in Tivoli. Ravenna, 1784.
Arc 1033.21.5 Sanctorum septem dormientium...Musei Victorii. (Victorius Franciscus.) Roma, 1741.
Arc 689.5F Le sanctuaire d'Aléa Athéna à Tégée au IVe siècle. Text and atlas. (Dugas, C.) Paris, 1924. 2v.
Arc 505.2.20 Le sanctuaire de Baalshamin à Palmyre. (Mission Archeologique Suisse en Syrie.) Rome, 1969- 4v.
Arc 608.1.28 Le sanctuaire de Base-Saturne à Dougga. (Carton, Louis B.C.) Paris, 1896.
Arc 530.125 Le sanctuaire de Sinuri prés de Mylasa. Paris, 1945.
Arc 785.46.5 Le sanctuaire des dieux orientaux au Janicule. (Nicole, Georges.) Rome, 1909.
Arc 785.46 Le sanctuaire syrien du Janicule. (Gauckler, P.) Paris, 1912.
Arc 936.40.25F Le sanctuaire thrace prés du village de Batkoun. (Tsonchev, D.) Sofia, 1941.
Arc 673.11F Les sanctuaires et les cultes du Mont Cynthe a Délos. Thèse. (Plassart, A.) Paris, 1928.
Arc 1025.60 Les sanctuaires primitifs de Rome et des Gaules. (Davin, V.) Paris, 1873?
Arc 543.3A Sand-buried ruins of Khotan. (Stein, Mark Aurel.) London, 1903.
Arc 543.3.2 Sand-buried ruins of Khotan. (Stein, Mark Aurel.) London, 1904.
Arc 543.83 Sand über den Tempeln Arabiens. 2. Aufl. (Gerlach, Eva.) Leipzig, 1967.
Arc 861.192 Sandal Castle; a short account of the history of the site and the 1964 excavations. (Joint Excavation Committee of the Wakefield Corporation and the Wakefield Historical Society.) Wakefield, Eng., 1965.
Arc 861.192.5 Sandal Castle excavations, 1967. (Joint Excavation Committee of the Wakefield Corporation and the Wakefield Historical Society.) Wakefield, Eng., 1967?
Arc 823.50 Sandars, Nancy K. Bronze Age cultures in France. Cambridge, Eng., 1957.
Arc 1033.48 Sandellius, D. De Priscorum Christianorum Synaxibus. Venetiis, 1770.
Arc 609.38 Sandelowsky, B.H. Fingira; preliminary report. Zomba, 1968.
Arc 1603.3.5 Sandham, Alfred. Coins, tokens and medals of the Dominion of Canada. Montreal, 1869.
Arc 1603.3.6 Sandham, Alfred. Coins, tokens and medals of the Dominion of Canada. Montreal, 1962.
Arc 1663.5.5 Sandham, Alfred. Historic medals of Canada. Quebec, 1873.
Arc 1663.5 Sandham, Alfred. Medals commemorative of the visit of H.R.H. the Prince of Wales to Montreal. Montreal, 1871.
Arc 1603.3.7 Sandham, Alfred. Supplement to coins, tokens and medals. Montreal, 1872.
Arc 1033.17.626 Sangiovanni, V. Storia della Madre di Dio...del Monte Berico. Vicenza, 1776.
Arc 453.18 Sankalia, Hasmukh Dhirajlal. Chalcolithic Navdatoli; the excavations at Navdatoli, 1957-59. 1. ed. Poona, 1971.
Arc 440.11 Sankalia, Hasmukh Dhirajlal. Excavations at Ahar (Tambavati) [1961-62]. 1. ed. Poona, 1969.
Arc 450.5 Sankalia, Hasmukh Dhirajlal. Excavations at Brahmapuri, 1945-46. Poona, 1952.
Arc 451.3 Sankalia, Hasmukh Dhirajlal. Excavations at Langhnaj, 1944-63. 1. ed. v.1-2. Poona, 1965.
Arc 452.10 Sankalia, Hasmukh Dhirajlal. The excavations at Maheshwar and Navdatoli. Baroda, 1958.
Arc 453.16 Sankalia, Hasmukh Dhirajlal. From history to pre-history at Nevasa. Poona, 1960.
Arc 453.15 Sankalia, Hasmukh Dhirajlal. Report on the excavations at Nasik and Jorve. 1. ed. Poona, 1955.
Arc 1093.9 Sankalia, Hasmukh Dhirajlal. Stone age tools. 1. ed. Poona, 1964.
Arc 432.24 Sankalis, Hasmukh Dhirajlal. Prehistory and protohistory in India and Pakistan. Bombay, 1962.
Arc 1033.122 Sanna Solaro, G. Acquisito conservazione, ristaurato degli arredi sacri. Torino, 1886.
Arc 1033.40.9 Santa Cecilia et La Sua Basilica nel Trastevere. (Bianchi-Cagliesi.) Roma, 1902. 2 pam.

Arc 843.66 Santa Eulalia de Bóveda. (Lopez Martí, L.) Lugo, 1934.
Arc 1033.101 Santa Lucia di Siracusa. (Barreca, C.) Roma, 1902.
Arc 1020.124.5 Santa María la mayor de la catedral de Burgos y su culto. (Hergueta y Martin, Domingo.) Lérida, 1922.
Arc 1033.12.37 Santa sindone. Sermone. (Pietro, S. di.) Torino, 1884.
Arc 730.6.5 Santangelo, M. Selinunte. Roma, 1953.
Arc 1033.17.545 Santelamazza, M. Cenni intorno la chiesa di S. Salvatore alle Coppelle. Roma, 1863.
Arc 1190.55 Santifaller, Leo. Bozner Schreibschriften der Neuzeit. Jena, 1930.
Arc 1185.33.3 Santifaller, Leo. Urkundenforschung. 3. Aufl. Darmstadt, 1968.
Arc 1033.17.100 La santissima virgen de Guadalupe. (Cuevas, J. de J.) México, 1887.
Arc 1033.35.23 Santissime croci di Brescia. (Velentini, A.) Brescia, 1882.
Arc 1033.28.8 La santità del matrimonio. (Marucchi, O.) Roma, 1902.
Arc 1033.12.235 El santo cáliz de la cena (santo grial) venerado en Valencia. (Sanchis y Sivera, José.) Valencia, 1914.
Htn Arc 1020.90* Il santoario di Parma. (Farnese.) Parma, 1593.
Arc 1027.31 Santoni, M. La cripta di S. Angelo de Profoglio...Camerino. Camerino, 1892.
Arc 835.202F Santos Rocha, A. dos. Antiquidades prehistoricas do conselho da Figueira. v.1-4. Coimbra, 1888-1900. 2v.
Arc 843.27 Santos Rocha, A. dos. Estações pre-romanas da idade do ferre nas visinhanças da figueira. Porto, 1908.
Arc 403.23 Santos Rocha, Antonio dos. Memórias e exploraçoes arquelógicas. Coimbra, 1971-
Htn Arc 1020.32.5* Santuario della città e diocesi di Milano. (Morigi, P.) Milano, 1603.
Arc 1020.71 Il santuario delle relique...di Padova. (Gonzati, B.) Padova, 1851.
Arc 1033.17.249 Santuario di Maria Sma. di Gibilmanna. (Bronte, G. da.) Catania, 1856.
Arc 1033.17.107 Santuario Mariano e historia das imagẽs milagrosas de Nossa Senhora. (Agostinho de Santa Maria.) Lisboa, 1707-23. 10v.
Arc 1027.4.25 Santucci, S. Sulla lapide sepolcrale di S. Filomena. Roma, 1837.
Arc 302.37 Saopštenja. (Belgrade. Zavod za zoš title i naučno proučavanje e spomenika kulture NR Srbije.) 2+ 3v.
Arc 543.66.60 Sapallitepa. (Askarov, A.A.) Tashkent, 1973.
Arc 505.35.10 Sapir, Baruch. Capernaum (Kfar-Nochum). Tel Aviv, 1967.
Arc 588.15 Saqqara Mastabas. (Murray, M.) London, 1905-37. 2v.
Arc 726.195 Sarcafagi romani di Sardegna. (Pesce, Gennaro.) Roma, 1957.
Arc 590.20 I sarcofagi egizi dalle origini alla fine dell'antico regno. (Donadoni Roveri, Anna Maria.) Roma, 1969.
Arc 1020.137 Sarcofagi paleocristiani della Spagna. (Bovini, G.) Roma, 1954.
Arc 1033.3.23 Sarcofago cristiano nel templo di Fermo. (Cavedoni, C.) Roma, 1843.
Arc 1033.3.21 Sarcofago cristiano nel templo di Fermo. (Minicis, G. de.) Roma, 1848.
Arc 1030.5.29 Il sarcofago di S. Siro. (Rossi, G.B. de.) Roma, 1876.
Arc 1033.3.33 Le sarcophage chrétien de Luc de Biarn. Paris, 1880.
Arc 66.1.210 Les sarcophages romains à representations dionysiaques. (Turcan, Robert.) Paris, 1966.
Arc 497.28A The sarcophagus of an ancient civilization. (Robinson, George L.) N.Y., 1930.
Arc 726.246 Sardegna punica. (Pesce, Gennaro.) Cagliari, 1961.
Arc 396.11 Sardi, Jorge. Obras completas. San Salvador, 1960.
Arc 726.245 Sardinia. (Guido, M.) London, 1963.
Arc 1425.4F Sardis, coins. v.11. (Bell, H.W.) Leiden, 1916.
Arc 530.2.8 Sardis newsletter. Cambridge, Mass. 1958+
Htn Arc 969.1.9* Sargent, W. Papers relative to certain American antiquities. Philadelphia, 1796.
Arc 543.153 Sarianidi, Viktor I. Raskopki Tillia-tepe v Severnom Afganistane. Moskva, 1972.
Arc 543.146.5 Sarianidi, Viktor I. Tainy ischeznuvshego iskusstva Karakumov. Moskva, 1967.
Arc 543.146 Sarianidi, Viktor I. Za barkhanami, proshloe. Moskva, 1966.
Arc 443.3 Sarkar, Sasanka Sekhar. Ancient races of the Deccan. New Delhi, 1972.
Arc 590.9F Sarkofager, muniekister og muniehylstre i det gamle a Egypten. (Schmidt, Valdemar.) København, 1919.
Arc 1016.211.5F Der Sarkophag des Iunius Bassus. (Gerke, F.) Berlin, 1936.
Arc 1016.211 Sarkophag des Junius Bassus. (Waal, A. de.) Rom, 1900.
Arc 830.153 Pamphlet vol. Sarmarobriva. 4 pam.
Arc 925.13.170 The Sarmatians. (Sulimirski, Tadeusz.) London, 1970.
Arc 925.126 Sarmatskie znaki severnogo Prichernomor'ia. (Solomonik, E.I.) Kiev, 1959.
Arc 936.185 Sarmizegetusa. (Daicovicui, C.) București, 1960.
Arc 1033.20.9 Sarnelli, Pompeo. Antica basilicografia. Napoli, 1686.
Arc 936.14.335 Sarnowska, Wanda. Kultura unietycka w Polsce. Wrocław, 1969-1975. 2v.
Arc 1153.46 Sarpe, Gustav. Prolegomena ad tachygraphiam Romanam. Rostochii, 1829.
Arc 482.201F Sarre, Friedrich. Archäologische Reise im Euphrat. Berlin, 1911-20. 4v.
Arc 482.202.2F Sarre, Friedrich. Die Keramik von Samarra. Berlin, 1925.
Arc 1148.33 Sarros, D.M. Palaiographikos eranos. Konstantinoypolei, 1914.
Arc 726.280 Sarsina: la cita romana, il museo archeologico. Faenza, 1967.
Arc 513.18.5 Sartiaux, Félix. L'archéologie française en Asie Mineure et l'expansion allemande. Paris, 1918.
Arc 935.33 Sartiaux, Felix. Eski foca, foca taukin koker. Izmir, 1952.
Arc 530.17 Sartiaux, Felix. Les sculptures et la restauration du temple d'Assos. Paris, 1915.
Arc 522.17 Sartiaux, Felix. Troie, la guerre de Troie. Paris, 1915.
Arc 513.18 Sartiaux, Félix. Villes mortes d'Asie Mineure. Paris, 1911.
Arc 1455.6F Sartiges. Collection du vicomte de Sartiges. Paris, 19- ?
Arc 1433.60.5 Sasanian remains from Qasr-i Abu Nasr; seals, sealings, and coins. (Frye, Richard N.) Cambridge, 1973.
Arc 1208.15 Sasanidskie gemmy. (Borisov, Andrei Ivan Iakovlevich.) Leningrad, 1963.
Arc 936.225 Šašel, Jaro. Vodnik po Emoni. Ljubljana, 1955.
Arc 1433.38.10F Sassanian coins. (Paruck, F.D.J.) Bombay, 1924.
Arc 1033.17.582 Sassi, G.A. Notizie istoriche intorno alla miracolosa immagine...Maria. Milano, 1765.
Arc 448.1.30 Sastri, K.N. New light on the Indus civilization. Delhi, 1957-65. 2v.
Arc 1663.26 Saterical and controversial medals of the reformation. (Barnard, F.P.) Oxford, 1927.
Arc 505.86 Der Satrapen-Sarkophag aus Sidon. (Kleemann, Ilse.) Berlin, 1958.
Arc 726.337 Satrianum. (Holloway, Robert Ross.) Providence, 1970.
Arc 1663.22 Satterlee, Alfred H. An arrangement of medals and tokens struck in honor of the presidents of the United States. N.Y., 1862.
Arc 66.1.205 Saturne africain; histoire. (Leglay, Marcel.) Paris, 1966.
Arc 608.70 Saturne africain; monuments. (Leglay, Marcel.) Paris, 1961. 2v.
Arc 87.1.40 Der Satyr aus Pergamon. (Furtwaengler, A.) Berlin, 1880.
Arc 712.14 Sauer, B. Der...Kopf und die Giebelgruppen der Parthenon. Berlin, 1903.
Arc 705.204 Sauer, B. Das Sergenannte Theseion. Berlin, 1899.
Arc 746.12 Sauer, Hertha. Die archaischen etruskischen Terracottasarkophage aus Caere. Diss. Rendsburg, 1930.
Arc 1663.17 Saulcy, Félecien. Souvenirs numismatiques de la révolution de 1848. Paris, 1850.
Arc 1500.68 Saulcy, Felicien de. Recherches sur les monnaies des ducs hereditaires de Lorraine. Metz, 1841.
Arc 1433.19 Saulcy, L.F.J.C. de. Lettres sur quelques points de la numismatique arabe. Lettres 4,5, et 6. Paris, 1841.
Arc 1425.3 Saulcy, L.F.J.C. de. Numismatique de Croisades. Paris, 1847.
Arc 1423.5 Saulcy, L.F.J.C. de. Numismatique de la Terre-Sainte. Paris, 1877.
Arc 1498.3 Saulcy, L.F.J.C. de. Recueil de documents...monnaies frappées par les rois de France depuis Philippe II jusqu'à François I. Paris, 1879-92. 4v.
Arc 505.18 Saulcy. Memoire sur...maçonneril...du Haram-Ech-Cherif de Jerusalem. Paris, 1866.
Arc 505.18.7 Saulcy. Recherches sur l'emplacement...du tombeau d'Hélène. Paris, 1869.
Arc 501.2 Saunders, T. Brief geographical account of the survey of Western Palestine. London, 1882.
Arc 501.3 Saunders, T. Introduction to the survey of Western Palestine. London, 1881.
Arc 600.156F Sauneron, Serge. Catalogue des ostraca hiératiques littéraires de Deir el Médineh. Le Caire, 1959- 2v.
Arc 600.188.5 Sauneron, Serge. Les ermitages chrétiens du désert d'Esna. Le Caire, 1972.
Arc 600.188 Sauneron, Serge. Esna. Le Caire, 1959- 5v.
Arc 1500.50 Saunier, Charles. Augustin Dupré: ofèvre, médailleur et graveur général des monnaies. Paris, 1894.
Arc 830.160 Saurel, Ferdinand. Aeria. Recherches sur son emplacement. Paris, 1885.
Arc 1033.12.107 Sauren, J. Pilgerbuchlein zum heiligen Rock in Trier. Köln, 1891. 2 pam.
Arc 905.98 Sausgruber, L. Sammlung der bisher erschienenen Aufsätze. Feldhirch, 1918.
Arc 830.119 Sautel, Joseph. Vaison dans l'antiquité. Avignon, 1926-27. 2v.
Arc 830.119.7 Sautel, Joseph. Vaison dans l'antiquité. pts.1-3. Lyon, 1926.
Arc 830.119.5 Sautel, Joseph. Vaison dans l'antiquité. v.1-2. Avignon, 1926.
Arc 830.12 Sauvage, H.E. Notes d'archéologie gallo-romaine. Boulogne, n.d.
Arc 493.50 Sauvaget, J. Quatre décrets seldjoukides. Beyrouth, 1947.
Arc 938.101 Sauvateev, Iurii A. Zalavruga. Leningrad, 1970.
Arc 608.33.15 Savary, Jean Pierre. Monuments en pierres séches du Fadnoun, Tassili n'Ajjer. Paris, 1966.
Arc 1433.40 Savelbev', P. Monety dzhuchidov' dzhagataidov", I.D.R. Sankt Peterburg, 1858.
Arc 1433.40.5 Savelbev', P. Topografiia kladov' s' vosiochnymi monetami. Sankt Peterburg, 1846.
Arc 925.4.3F Savenkov, I.T. O drevnikh pamiatnikakh na Enisev. Moskva, 1910.
Arc 726.78F Savignoni, L. Relazione sopra gli scavi eseguiti a Norba nell'estate dell'anno 1901. Roma, 1902.
Arc 726.42.5 Savini, Gaetano. Per i monumenti e per la storia di Ravenna. Ravenna, 1914.
Arc 885.25.5 Savory, Hubert Newman. Excavations at Dinorben, 1965-69. Cardiff, 1971.
Htn Arc 1373.2* Savot, L. Discours sur les médailles antiques. Paris, 1627.
Arc 925.13.110 Savromaty. (Smirnov, K.F.) Moskva, 1964.
Arc 1163.3.6 Savva, archbishop of Tver. Paleograficheskie snimki. Moskva, 1863.
Arc 925.39 Savvateev, Iurii A. Risunki na skalakh. Petrozavodsk, 1967.
Arc 925.50.370 Savych, Volodymyr P. Pizn'opaleolitychne naselennia pivdenno-zakhidnoï Volyni. Kyïv, 1975.
Arc 830.120 Sawtell, R.O. Primitive hearths in the Pyrenees. N.Y., 1927.
Arc 861.87F Saxon obsequies illustrated by ornaments and weapons. (Neville, R.C.) London, 1851.
Arc 1510.2 Saxonia Numismatica, oder Medaillen-Cabinet von Bedächtnissmünzen. (Tentzel, W.E.) Dresden, 1705. 2v.
Arc 1510.3 Saxonia Numismatica, oder Medaillen-Cabinet von Münzen. (Tentzel, W.E.) Dresden, 1705. 2v.
Arc 392.3.25 Sayce, A.H. David George Hogarth, 1862-1927. London, 1928.
Arc 705.203 Sayer, R. Ruinen und Überbleibsel von Athen. Augsburg, 1764.
Arc 292.145 Sbornik. (Russkoe Arkheologicheskoe Obshchestvo v Korolevstve S.Kh.S., Belgrade.) Belgrad. 1,1927
Arc 923.13 Sbornik' arkheologicheskikh statei. Sankt Petersburg, 1911.
Arc 383.18 Sbornik Boris Liabovich. (Plovdiv, Bulgaria. Durzhavna biblioteka "Ivan Vazov".) Plovdiv, 1927.
Arc 923.124 Sbornik dokladov na IX i X vsesoiuznykh arkheologicheskikh studencheskikh konferentsiiakh. (Vsesoiuznaia Arkheologicheskaia Studencheskaia Konferentsiia, 9th, Moscow, 1963.) Moskva, 1968.
Arc 923.107 Sbornik dokladov na VI i VII vsesoiuznykh arkheologicheskikh studencheskikh konferentsiiakh. (Vsesoiuznaia Arkheologicheskaia Studencheskaia Konferentsiia, 6th, Moscw, 1960.) Moskva, 1963.
Arc 1030.50 Sbornik' grech. nadlisei Chrisi bre.-men'. (Latyshchev', B.B.) Sankt Peterburg, 1896.
Arc 925.295.5 Sbornik materialov po arkheologii adygei. (Maikop. Adygeiskogo Nauchno-Issledovatel'skogo Instituta Iazyka, Literatury, Istorii i Ekonomiki.) Maikop, 1961.

Author and Title Listing

Arc 1163.3.35 Sbornik paleograficheskikh snimkov. (Ivanov, P.I.) Moskva, 1844.
Arc 925.230 Sbornik po arkheologii Vologodskoi oblasti. (Vologda, Russia (City). Ablastnoi Kraevedcheskii Muzei.) Vologda, 1961.
Arc 1160.210F Sbornik snimkov s russkago pis'ma. (Moskovskii Arkheologicheskii Institut.) Moskva, 1913. 2v.
Arc 1160.210.5F Sbornik snimkov s russkago pis'ma XIII-XVIII vv. (Moskovskii Arkheologicheskii Institut.) Moskva, 1908.
Arc 1282.9F Sbornik' snimkov's' drevnikh' pechatei. (Ivanov, I.) Moskva, 1858.
Arc 923.40 Sbornik statei po arkheologii SSSR. Moskva, 1938. 2v.
Arc 925.27F Sbornik topograffiia sved. o kurgana. (Samokvasov, D.) St. Peterburg, 1888.
Arc 1583.6 Sbornik' ukazov' po monetnomu delu. (Demmeni, M.) Sankt Peterburg, 1887. 3v.
Arc 1348.30 Sbōronos, I.N. Articles on numismatics. Athenes, 1898-1903. 16 pam.
Arc 1440.200 Sborōnos, I.N. Ta nomiomata toy kratoys tōn ptolemaiōn. Athēnai, 1904. 2v.
Arc 1468.21.6 Sborōnos, Ioannēs N. Numismatique de la Crète ancienne. Bonn, 1972.
Arc 1468.21 Sborōnos, Ioannēs N. Synopsis de mille coins faux du faussaire C. Christopoulos. Athènes, 1922.
Arc 1018.31 Scaglia, P.S. Manuale di archeologia cristiana. Roma, 1911.
Arc 1018.31.3 Scaglia, P.S. Manuel d'archéologie chrétienne. Turin, 1916.
Arc 773.3 Scaglia, S. La promenade archéologique. Rome, 1911.
Arc 1033.23.5 Scaglia, Sisto. Nova circa thesaurum sacelli Palalini "sancta sanctorum". Roma, 1909
Arc 1027.87 Scaglia, Sisto. Osservazioni sopra i recenti studi intorne ai cimiteri di Marco e Marcelliano. Saronno, 1909. 3 pam.
Arc 893.21 Scandinavian archaeology. (Shetelig, H.) Oxford, 1937.
Arc 730.203 Scarabelli, Gommi. Stazione prehistorica sul monte del Castel. Imola, 1887.
Arc 600.12.5A Scarabs. (Newberry, P.E.) London, 1906.
X Cg Arc 545.235F Scarabs and cylinders with names. (Petrie, W.M.F.) London, 1917. (Changed to XP 9838 F)
Arc 726.330 Scarani, Renato. Civiltà preromane del territorio parmense. Parma, 1971.
Arc 861.40 Scarth, H.M. Aquae solis...Roman Bath. London, 1864.
Arc 93.32F Scavi de ostia. Roma. 1,1953+ 8v.
Arc 740.6 Gli scavi della Certosa in Bologna. (Zannoni, A.) Bologna, 1876-84. 2v.
Arc 905.35 Gli scavi di Aquileia. (Brusin, G.) Udine, 1934.
Arc 790.201 Gli scavi di Pompei dal 1861 al 1872. (Fiorelli, G.) Napoli, 1873.
Arc 746.9.25F Scavi di Spina. v.1, pt.1-2. Roma, 1960- 2v.
Arc 726.115 Gli scavi di Stabia a cura del Comitato per gli scavi di Stabia. (Orsi, Libero d'.) Napoli, 1954.
Arc 726.108 Scavi e scoperte di antichità il pontificato di Pio VI. 2. ed. (Pietrangeli, Carlo.) Roma, 1958.
Arc 785.23.3 Scavi e studi nel tempio di Giove Laziale. (Rossi, M.S. de.) Roma, 1876.
Arc 1027.39.9 Scavi eseguiti nell'antica Basilica di S. Agapito. (Marucchi, O.) Roma, 1899.
Arc 1027.5.25 Scavi nel cimitero di Domitilla. (Stevenson, H.) Roma, 1898.
Arc 1015.225.9 Scavi nella Platonia. (Marucchi, O.) Roma, 1892.
Arc 1025.28.30 Scavi nelle catacombe romane. (Marucchi, O.) Roma, 1899.
Arc 785.39.45 Scavi nelle terme di Novato ed in altri luoghi di Roma. (Pellegrini, A.) Roma, 1870.
Arc 1030.5.55 Scavi nell'orto di S. Sabina sull'Aventino. (Rossi, G.B. de.) Roma, 1856.
Arc 785.13.7 Gli scavi recenti nel Foro Romano. (Vaglieri, Dante.) Roma, 1903.
Arc 785.13.8 Gli scavi recenti nel Foro Romano. Supplemento. (Vaglieri, Dante.) Roma, 1903.
Arc 1261.1 Le sceau de Loja et la sigillographie pittoresque. (Travers, Émile.) Paris, 1885.
Arc 1264.2 Le sceau et les armoiries...Saint Pierre de Troyes. (Lalore, C.) Troyes, 1887.
Arc 1260.2 Sceau inédit de Boniface de Montferrat. (Schlumberger. G.) Paris, 1886.
Arc 1212.1 Les sceaux. (Lecoy de la Marche, A.) Paris, 1889.
Arc 1254.6 Sceaux byzantins; les églises, les couvents, les palais. (Schlumberger, G.) n.p., n.d.
Arc 1345.1.12 Sceaux des communes, communautés, évêques. Paris, 1858.
Htn Arc 1271.1.5* Les sceaux des comtes de Flandre. (Wree, Olivier de.) Bruge, 1641.
Arc 1345.1.11 Sceaux des grands feudataires de la couronne. Paris, 1858.
Arc 1345.1.10 Sceaux des rois et des reines de France. Paris, 1858.
Arc 1345.1.9 Sceaux des rois et reines d'Angleterre. Paris, 1858.
Arc 1254.8 Sceaux en plomb de chefs des Manglavites impériaux. (Schlumberger, G.) Paris, 1882.
Arc 1232.1 Sceaux et bulles de l'Orient Latin au Moyen Âge. (Schlumberger, G.) Paris, 1879.
Arc 1254.13 Sceaux et bulles des comnènes. (Sorlin-Dorigny, A.) Paris, 1876.
Arc 1027.2.19 Les scènes de banquets. (Lefort, L.) Paris, 1883.
Arc 87.1.75 Scenika 75. Programm zum Winckelmannsfeste der Achäologischen Gesellschaft zu Berlin. Berlin, 1915.
Arc 557.4.5 The scepter of Egypt. (Hayes, William Christopher.) Cambridge, 1960.
Arc 557.4 The scepter of Egypt. (Hayes, William Christopher.) N.Y., 1953. 2v.
Arc 726.25.30 Schaal, Hans. Ostia, der Welthafen Roms. Bremen, 1957.
Arc 853.340 Schach-Dörges, Helga. Das jungkaiserzeitliche Gräberfeld von Wilhelmsaue in Brandenburg. Berlin, 1969.
Arc 682.12F Die Schachtgräber von Mykenai. Text and plates. (Karo, Georg.) München, 1930-33. 2v.
Arc 407.30.5 Schadewaldt, Wolfgang. Winckelmann und Rilke: zwei Beschreibungen des Apollon. Pfullingen, 1968.
Arc 416.19 Schaeffer, C.F. Stratigraphie comparée. London, 1848-
Arc 540.7 Schaeffer, C.F.A. Enkomè-Alasia. Paris, 1952.
Arc 537.9 Schaeffer, C.F.A. Missions en Chypre, 1932-1935. Paris, 1936.
Arc 830.124.15 Schaeffer, F.A. Un dépôt d'outils et un trésor de bronzes...à Seltz. Haguenau, 1927.
Arc 1504.15 Schaffhausen Münz- und Geldgeschichte. (Wielandt, Friedrich.) Schaffhausen, 1959?
Arc 838.38F Die Schaftzfunde der Iberischen Halbinsel. (Raddatz, Klaus.) Berlin, 1969. 2v.
Arc 815.3 Scharf, G.J. The Pompeian court in the Crystal Palace. London, 1854.
Arc 1580.40 Die Schaumünzen auf die Salzburger Emigration. (Roll, Karl.) Halle, 1925.
Arc 1675.80 Die Schaumünzen der Universität Halle-Wittenberg. (Bahrfeldt, Max.) Halle, 1926.
Arc 1335.65 Die Schausammlung des Münzkabinetts im Kaiser Friedrich Museum. (Berlin. Staatliche Museum. Kaiser Friedrich Museum.) Berlin, 1919.
Arc 710.12.5 Schede, Martin. The acropolis of Athens. Berlin, 1924.
Arc 530.37 Schede, Martin. Ankara und Augustus. Berlin, 1937.
Arc 710.12 Schede, Martin. Die Burg von Athen. Berlin, 1922.
Arc 530.14.25 Schede, Martin. Die Ruinen von Priene. Berlin, 1934.
Arc 530.14.26 Schede, Martin. Die Ruinen von Priene. 2. Aufl. Berlin, 1964.
Arc 1510.13 Schediasma de nummis antiquis. (Schlegel, C.) Dresdae, 1518.
Arc 861.23.5 Schedule of antiquities in the county of Surrey. (Johnston, P.M.) London, 1913.
Arc 861.4.3 Schedule of the Roman remains of Chester. (Lawson, P.H.) Chester, 1928.
Arc 1500.66 Scheers, Simone. Les monnaies de la Gaule inspirées de celles de la republique romaine. Leuven, 1969.
Arc 1096.1 Scheffer, J. De re vehiculari veterum libri duo. Francofurti, 1671.
Arc 630.15 Schefold, Karl. Basler Antiken im Bild. Basel, 1958.
Arc 630.12 Schefold, Karl. Orient, Hellas und Rom in der archäologischen Forschungszeit 1939. Bern, 1949.
Arc 815.26.2 Schefold, Karl. La peinture pompéienne; essai sur l'évolution de sa signification. Bruxelles, 1972.
Arc 815.26 Schefold, Karl. Pompejanische Malerei. Basel, 1952.
Arc 815.26.10 Schefold, Karl. Vergessene Pompeji. Bern, 1962.
Arc 815.26.5 Schefold, Karl. Die Wände Pompejis. Berlin, 1957.
Arc 726.4 Scheletri cumani. (Jorio, A. de.) Napoli, 1810.
Arc 1335.40 Die Schellhass'sche Münzsammlung. (Erbstein, J.) Dresden, 1870.
Arc 1490.16 Schembri, H.C. Coins and medals of knights of Malta. London, 1908.
Arc 440.2F A scheme for the protection and conservation of antient buildings...city of Ahmedabad. (Crawley-Boevey, A.W.) Bombay, 1886.
Arc 1020.114 Schenkel, I.I. Die Reliquien des Klosters Allerheiligen. Schaffhausen, 1866.
Arc 568.2 Schenkel, W. Frühmittelägyptische Studien. Bonn, 1962.
Arc 600.4.9 Scherben aus Naukratis. Proefschrift. (Jong, E.F.P.) n.p., 1925.
Arc 773.7 Scherer, M.R. Marvels of ancient Rome. N.Y., 1955.
Arc 1027.24.13 Scherillo, G. Archeologia sacra: Catacombe napolitane. Napoli, 1875.
Arc 1025.21 Scherillo, G. Archeologia sacra. v.1-2. Napoli, 1875.
Arc 1093.6.18 Scheuermann, W. Woher kommt das Hakenkreuz? Berlin, 1933.
Arc 853.77 Scheuermayer. Auffindung eines römischen Bades in Augsburg. n.p., 1867?
Arc 830.106 Scheurer, F. Fouilles du cimetière barbare de Bourgogne. Paris, 1914.
Arc 595.30F Schiaparelli, E. Il significato simbolico delle piramidi egiziane. Roma, 1884.
Arc 1153.43.7 Schiaparelli, L. Avviamento allo studio delle abbreviature latine nel medievo. Firenze, 1926.
Arc 1200.28 Schiaparelli, Luigi. Raccolta di documenti latini. Torino, 1969.
Arc 726.170 Schiavo, Armando. Acquedotti romani e medioevali. Napoli, 1935.
Arc 1248.2 Schiffe auf Siegeln. 1. Aufl. (Ewe, Herbert.) Rostock, 1972.
Arc 670.2 Schildt, A. Die Giebelgruppen von Aegina. Leipzig, 1895.
Arc 87.1.37 Schillbach, D. Beitrag zur griechischen Gewichtskunde. Berlin, 1877.
Arc 66.1.178 Schilling, R. La religion romaine de Venias depuis les origines jusqu'au temps d'Auguste. Paris, 1954.
Arc 1200.8 Schillmann, F. Beiträge zum Urkundenwesen der ältern Bischöfe. Leipzig, 1908.
Arc 688.1 Schinas, D. Archaiologia tēs Nesou Sikinou. Athēnai, 1837.
Arc 853.165 Schindler, Reinhard. Ausgrabungen in alt Hamburg. Hamburg, 1958.
Arc 853.165.5 Schindler, Reinhard. Studien zum vorgeschichtlichen Siedlungs- und Befestigungswesen des Saarlandes. Trier, 1968.
Htn Arc 1020.6.15* Schioppalalba, I.B. In perantiquam sacram tabulam...S. Mariae Caritatis. Venetiis, 1767.
Arc 488.31 Schippmann, Klaus. Die iranischen Feuerheiligtümer. Habilitationsschrift. Berlin, 1971.
Arc 1570.2 Schive, C. Im et fund af norske mynter fraa Sando. Kjøbenhavn, 1866.
Arc 1565.2 Schive, C.I. Norges mynter i middetalderen. pt.1-6. Christiania, 1858-65.
Arc 1411.10F Schjöth, F. The currency of the Far East. London, 1929.
Arc 522.25 Das Schlachtfeld vor Troja, eine Untersuchung. (Mey, Oscar.) Berlin, 1926.
Arc 505.13 Schlaugenstein im Kidrontal bei Jerusalem. (Kittel, D.R.) Leipzig, 1907.
Arc 905.24 Schlechter, Max. Beiträge zur alten Geschichte des Obergailthales in Kärnten. Wien, 1885.
Arc 1510.13 Schlegel, C. Schediasma de nummis antiquis. Dresdae, 1518.
Arc 853.353 Schleier, Wilhelm. Cambodunum-Kempten. Bonn, 1972.
Arc 853.170 Schleiermacher, Wilhelm. Der römische Limes in Deutschland. Berlin, 1959.
Arc 375.5 Schlemm, J. Wörterbuch zur Vorgeschichte. Berlin, 1908.
Arc 853.65.10 Schlesiens Urgeschichte. (Seger, Hans.) Leipzig, 1913.
Arc 186.1 Schlesiens Vorzeit in Bild und Schrift. (Suchs, H.) Breslau. 1-6,1870-1912 13v.
Arc 1510.105F Die schlesischen Münzen des Mittelalters. (Friedensburg, F.) Breslau, 1931.
Arc 1285.27F Die schlesischen Siegel von 1250 bis 1300 beziehentlich 1324. (Pfotenhauer, P.) Breslau, 1849.
Arc 416.49 Schleuder und Bogen in Südwestasien; von der frühesten Belagen bis zum Beginn der historischen Stadtstaaten. (Korfmann, Manfred.) Bonn, 1972.
Arc 1033.17.55 Schlichter, C.L. Ecloga historia qua fabula pontificia de Luca Pictore exploditur. Halae, 1734.
Arc 1668.3 Schlickeysen, F.W.A. Erklärung der Abkürzungen auf Münzen der neueren Zeit. Berlin, 1882.
Arc 1668.3.2 Schlickeysen, F.W.A. Erklärung der Abkürzungen auf Münzen der neueren Zeit. Graz, 1961.
Arc 684.1.33 Schlief, Hans. Der Zeus-Altar in Olympia. Diss. Berlin, 1935.
X Cg Arc 510.10 Schliemann, H. Altas des antiquités troyennes. Leipzig, 1874.

Author and Title Listing

Arc 522.4.7 Schliemann, H. Bericht ueber der Ausgrabungen in Troja im Jahre 1890. Leipzig, 1891.
Arc 658.3.1 Schliemann, H. Briefe von Heinrich Schliemann. Berlin, 1936.
Arc 522.4.5 Schliemann, H. Ilios. Leipzig, 1881.
Arc 522.4.5.3 Schliemann, H. Ilios. London, 1880.
Arc 522.4.6 Schliemann, H. Ilios. N.Y., 1881.
Arc 658.3 Schliemann, H. Ithaka, der Peleponnes und Troja. Leipzig, 1869.
Arc 522.4 Schliemann, H. Troia und seine Ruinen. Rostock, 1875?
Arc 522.4.4A Schliemann, H. Troja. London, 1884.
Arc 522.4.4.2 Schliemann, H. Troja. London, 1884.
Arc 522.4.2 Schliemann, H. Trojanische Alterthuemer. Leipzig, 1874.
Arc 522.4.3A Schliemann, H. Troy and its remains. London, 1875.
Arc 658.3.7 Schliemann, Heinrich. Abenteuer meines Lebens. Leipzig, 1960.
Arc 403.16.20 Schliemann, Heinrich. Briefwechsel. Berlin, 1953. 2v.
Arc 682.1.16 Schliemann, Heinrich. Catalogue des trésors de Mycènes au Musée d'Athènes. Leipzig, 1882.
Arc 682.1.17 Schliemann, Heinrich. Catalogue des trésors de Mycènes au Musée d'Athènes. Leipzig, 1882.
Arc 403.16.15 Schliemann, Heinrich. Heinrich Schliemann. Selbstbiographie. 7. Aufl. Leipzig, 1949.
Arc 403.16.10 Schliemann, Heinrich. Heinrich Schliemann. 3. Aufl. Leipzig, 1939.
Arc 403.16.17 Schliemann, Heinrich. Heinrich Schliemann. 8. Aufl. Wiesbaden, 1955.
Arc 403.16.35 Schliemann, Heinrich. Kein Troja ohne Homer. Nürnberg, 1960.
Arc 682.1.3A Schliemann, Heinrich. Mycenae; a narrative. N.Y., 1878.
Arc 682.1.2 Schliemann, Heinrich. Mycenae; a narrative. N.Y., 1880.
Arc 682.1 Schliemann, Heinrich. Mycenae; a narrative of researches and discoveries at Mycenae and Tiryns. London, 1878.
Arc 682.1.5 Schliemann, Heinrich. Mykenae; Bericht über meine Forschungen und Entdeckungen in Mykenae und Tiryns. Faksimile. Darmstadt, 1964.
Htn Arc 684.2* Schliemann, Heinrich. Orchomenos. Athēnai, 1883.
Arc 684.3 Schliemann, Heinrich. Orchomenos. Leipzig, 1881.
Arc 658.3.8 Schliemann, Heinrich. Schliemann in Indianapolis. Indianapolis, 1961.
Arc 403.16.5 Schliemann, Heinrich. Selbstbiographie bis zu seinem Tod vervollständigt. 2. Aufl. Leipzig, 1936.
Arc 682.1.9 Schliemann, Heinrich. Tiryns; the prehistoric palace of the kings of Tiryns. London, 1886.
Arc 682.1.8 Schliemann, Heinrich. Tiryns; the prehistoric palace of the kings of Tiryns. N.Y., 1885.
Arc 658.3.14 Schliemann. (Ludwig, Emil.) Berlin, 1932.
Arc 658.3.16 Schliemann. (Ludwig, Emil.) Boston, 1931.
Arc 658.3.15A Schliemann. (Ludwig, Emil.) Boston, 1932.
Arc 658.3.8 Schliemann in Indianapolis. (Schliemann, Heinrich.) Indianapolis, 1961.
Arc 658.3.17 Schliemann of Troy. (Ludwig, Emil.) London, 1931.
NEDL Arc 658.3.4 Schliemanns Ausgrabungen. (Schuchhardt, K.) Leipzig, 1890.
Arc 658.3.5A Schliemanns Ausgrabungen. (Schuchhardt, K.) Leipzig, 1891.
Arc 658.3.3A Schliemann's excavations. (Schuchhardt, K.) London, 1891.
Arc 658.3.20 Schliemann's first visit to America, 1850-1851. (Weber, Shirley H.) Cambridge, 1942.
Arc 853.61F Schliz, A. Das steinzeitliche Dorf Grossgartach. Stuttgart, 1901.
Arc 543.130 Schlumberger, D. The excavations at Surkh Kotal and the problem of Hellenism in Bactria and India. London, 1961.
Arc 505.2.10 Schlumberger, D. La Palmyrène du Nord-Ouest. Thèse. Paris, 1951.
Arc 1254.9 Schlumberger, G. Cinq sceaux de l'époque byzantine. Paris, 1883.
Arc 1208.6 Schlumberger, G. Collections sigillographiques de G. Schlumberger. Paris, 1914.
Arc 1254.7 Schlumberger, G. Deux chefs normands des armées byzantines. Paris, 1881.
Arc 1254.12 Schlumberger, G. Deux epagia...sceau d'un capitaine arménien. Paris, 1884.
Arc 1590.4 Schlumberger, G. Deux plombs satiriques. Paris, 1878. 3 pam.
Arc 1254.10 Schlumberger, G. Documents pour servir à l'histoire des thémes byzantines. Paris, 1883.
Arc 1423.6 Schlumberger, G. Monnaie inédite des seigneurs du Toron, en Syrie. Paris, 1875.
Arc 1428.2 Schlumberger, G. Les monnaies à légendes grecques. Paris, 1880.
Arc 930.204 Schlumberger, G. Monuments byzantins inédits. Macon, 1884.
Arc 1473.3 Schlumberger, G. Monuments numismatiques et sphragistiques...byzantin. Paris, 1880.
Arc 1590.1 Schlumberger, G. Une nouvelle monnaie a legende grecque...de Cappadoce. Paris, 1887.
Arc 1425.2 Schlumberger, G. Numismatique de l'Orient Latin. Paris, 1878.
Arc 1425.2.2 Schlumberger, G. Numismatique de l'Orient Latin. Paris, 1882.
Arc 1428.6 Schlumberger, G. Les principautés Franques du Levant. Paris, 1877.
Arc 1254.6 Schlumberger, G. Sceaux byzantins; les églises, les couvents, les palais. n.p., n.d.
Arc 1254.8 Schlumberger, G. Sceaux en plomb de chefs des Manglavites impériaux. Paris, 1882.
Arc 1232.1 Schlumberger, G. Sceaux et bulles de l'Orient Latin au Moyen Âge. Paris, 1879.
Arc 1254.16F Schlumberger, G. Sigillographie de l'empire byzantin. Paris, 1884.
Arc 1430.1 Schlumberger, G. Le trésor de San'a. Paris, 1880.
Arc 1254.11 Schlumberger, G. La vierge, le Christ, les saints sur les sceaux byzantins. Paris, 1883.
Arc 1453.13 Schlumberger, Hans. Goldmünzen Europas seit 1800. 3. Aufl. München, 1973.
Arc 1468.38 Schlumberger, P. L'argent grec l'empire achémenide. Thèse. Paris, 1953.
Arc 1260.2 Schlumberger. G. Sceau inédit de Boniface de Montferrat. Paris, 1886.
Arc 1020.31.19 Schmaltz, Karl. Mater ecclesiarum. Strassburg, 1918.
Arc 726.27.3 Schmatz, Joseph. Baiae, das erste luxusbad der Römer. Regensburg, 1905-06.
Arc 853.283 Schmid, Armin. Die Römer am Rein und Main. Frankfurt, 1972.
Arc 1025.51 Schmid, G. Das unterirdische Rom. Brixen, 1908.
Arc 905.25 Schmid, Walter. Flavia Solva. 2. Aufl. Graz, 1917.
Arc 672.2 Schmidt, B. Korkyraeische Studien. Leipzig, 1890. 2v.
Arc 953.10 Schmidt, E. Vorgeschichte Nordamerikas im Gebiet der Vereinigten Staaten. Braunschweig, 1894.
Arc 488.17F Schmidt, E.F. Flights over ancient cities of Iran. Chicago, 1940.
Arc 493.2.10F Schmidt, E.F. Persepolis. Chicago, 1953-70. 3v.
Arc 915.6.2 Schmidt, F.S. Recueil d'antiquités de la Suisse. Francfort sur le Meyn, 1771.
Htn Arc 915.6* Schmidt, F.S. Recueil d'antiquités trouvées à Avenches...de la Suisse. Berne, 1760.
Arc 482.206 Schmidt, J.H. Friedrich Sarre Schriften. Berlin, 1935.
Arc 853.75F Schmidt, R.R. Jungsteinzeit-Siedlungen im Federseemoor. Augsburg, 1930-37.
Arc 547.16 Schmidt, V. Den aegyptiske samlung. Copenhagen, 1899.
Arc 590.9F Schmidt, Valdemar. Sarkofager, muniekister og muniehylstre i det gamle a Egypten. København, 1919.
Arc 520.9 Schmidt. Pergamon. Lübeck, 1899.
Arc 1077.2.42 Die Schmiedkreuze Westböhmens. (Bergmann, Alois.) Elbogen, 1926.
Arc 1470.34 Schmitz, Hermann. Ein Gesetz der Stadt Olbia zum Schulze ihres Silbergeldes. Freiburg, 1925.
Arc 1200.13 Schmitz, Karl. Ursprung und Geschichte der Devotionsformeln. Stuttgart, 1913.
Arc 1150.202 Schmitz, W. Commentarii notarum tironianarum. Lipsiae, 1893. 2v.
Arc 1150.203 Schmitz, W. Monumenta tachygraphica codicus parisienis Latini. Hannoverae, 1882.
Arc 915.2 Schnarrenberger. Die Pfahlbauten des Bodensees. Konstanz, 1891.
Arc 935.20 Schneider, A.M. Byzanz; Vorarbeiten zur Topographie und Archäologie der Stadt. Berlin, 1936.
Arc 936.85 Schneider, A.M. Die Grabung in Westhofler Sophienkirche zu Istanbul. Berlin, 1941.
Arc 530.110 Schneider, A.M. Die römischen und byzantinischen Denkmäler von Iznik-Nicaea. Berlin, 1943.
Arc 530.49 Schneider, A.M. Die Stadtmauer von Iznik. Berlin, 1938.
Arc 1030.61 Schneider, Fedor. Die Epitaphien der Päpste und andere stadtrömische Inschriften des Mittelalters. Rom, 1933.
Arc 625.13 Schneider, R. von. Album...Antike-Sammlung. Wien, 1895.
Arc 612.93 Schneider, Renate-Ursula. Zur Südabgrenzung des Bereichs der nordischen jüngeren Bronzezeit in Periode IV nach Montelius. Hamburg, 1971.
Arc 543.40.15 Schnitger, F.M. Forgotten kingdoms in Sumatra. Leiden, 1939.
Arc 895.19 Schnittger, Bror. Förhistoriska flintgrufvor och kulturlager vid kvarn. Stockholm, 1910.
Arc 1020.133 Schnyder, William. Acht Studien zur christlichen Altertumswissenschaft und zur Kirchengeschichte. Luzern, 1937.
Arc 520.20 Schober, A. Die Kunst von Pergamon. Wien, 1951.
Arc 700.70 Schoder, Raymond Victor. Ancient Greece from the air. London, 1974.
Arc 853.10.20 Schoeberger, H. Führer durch das Römerkastell Saalburg. Bad Homburg, 1957.
Arc 1508.5 Schönemann, C.P.C. Zur vaterländischen Münzkunde. Walfenbüttel, 1852.
Arc 196.2 Schoenenberg, J. Festschrift zum 50 Jährigen Jubiläum des Lahnsteiner Altertumsvereins. Oberlahnstein, 1930.
Arc 810.24 Schoener, R. Pompeii. Beschreibung der Stadt. Stuttgart, n.d.
Arc 1470.84 Schoenert-Geiss, E. Griechisches Münzwerk. Berlin, 1965. 2v.
Arc 1510.20 Scholler, Ernst. Der Reichsstadt Nürnberg. Nürnberg, 1916.
Arc 1530.10 Scholten, C. The coins of the Dutch overseas territories, 1601-1948. Amsterdam, 1953.
Arc 1510.21 Scholtz, Henrico. Sancta colonia numis antiquissimis illustrata et monumentis historicis explicata. Ploenae, 1738.
Arc 853.215 Schoppa, Helmut. Die fränkischen Friedhöfe von Weilbach Maintaunuskreis. Weisbaden, 1959.
Arc 600.184 Schott, Siegfried. Wall scenes from the mortuary chapel of the Mayor Poser at Medinet Habu. Chicago, 1957.
Arc 1433.24.5 Schott, W. W. Grigorjew's Beschreibung kufischer Münzen. n.p., n.d.
Arc 1550.11F Schou, Hans Henrich. Beskrivelse of danske og norske mønter. Kjøbenhavn, 1926.
Arc 87.1.60 Schrader, H. Sechziges Program zum Winckelmannsfeste. Berlin, 1900.
Arc 1033.12.126 Schreck, J.A. Jesu...coronam spineam. Lipsiae, n.d.
Arc 903.5 Schreiber, Georg. Den Funden nach zu Schliessen. Wien, 1960.
Arc 903.5.1 Schreiber, Georg. Den Funden nach zu schliessen. 2. Aufl. Wien, 1965.
Arc 386.31.5 Schreiber, Hermann. Vanished cities. N.Y., 1957.
Arc 386.31 Schreiber, Hermann. Versunkene Städte. Wien, 1955.
Arc 628.5 Schreiber, T. Atlas of classical antiquities. London, 1895.
Arc 547.14 Schreiber, T. Der Gallier. Leipzig, 1896.
Arc 1540.35 Schreier, Ulrich. Die Münzen der Kanal-Inseln. Dortmund, 1965?
Arc 853.22 Schreiner, P.W. Eining die Dortigen Römerausgrabungen. Landsbut, 1882. 2v.
Arc 853.344 Schrickel, Waldtraut. Die Funde vom Wartberg in Hessen. Marburg, 1969.
Arc 848.56 Schrickel, Waldtraut. Westeuropäische Elemente im neolithischen Grabbau Mitteldeutschlands und die Galeriegräber Westdeutschlands und ihre Inventare. Bonn, 1966. 2v.
Arc 1033.123.5 Schrift Mensa und Confessio und P. Emil Dorsch. (Wieland, F.) München, 1909.
Arc 905.14 Schriften. (Historischer Verein für Innerösterreich.) Graz, 1848.
Arc 1175.3 Schrifttafeln zum Gebrauch bei diplomatischen Vorlesungen. (Pertz, G.H.) Hannover, 1844.
Arc 1163.40.2 Schrifttafeln zur deutschen Paläographie. v.1-2. 2. Aulf. (Duelfer, Kurt.) Marburg, 1967.
Arc 1143.3.2 Schriftwesen im Mittelalter. 2. Aufl. (Wattenbach, W.) Leipzig, 1875.
Arc 1143.3.4 Das Schriftwesen in Mittelalter. 4. Aufl. (Wattenbach, W.) Graz, 1958.
Arc 1138.70 De schrijfkunst in de Bijbellanden. (Raalte, James van.) Baarn, 1955.
Arc 1433.52 Schroeder, Albert. Annam; études numismatiques. Text et atlas. Paris, 1905. 2v.
Arc 87.1.74 Schröder, Bruno. Griechische Bronzeeimer im berlinen Antiquarium. Berlin, 1914.

Arc 87.1.67 Schröder, Bruno. Die Victoria von Calvatone. Berlin, 1907.
Arc 1540.9 Schröder, J.H. De moneta Anglo-Saxonica. Upsaliae, 1849.
Arc 1540.9.5 Schröder, J.H. Numismata Angliae vetusta. pt.1. Upsaliae, 1833.
Arc 674.20 Schroeder, Johan. Epidauros en Kreta. Amsterdam, 1960.
Arc 1510.16 Schrötter, F.F. von. Die Münzen F. Wilhelms des Grossen Kurfürst und Friedrichs III von Brandenberg. Berlin, 1913.
Arc 1340.8 Schrotter, F. Wörterbuch der Münzkunde. Berlin, 1930.
Arc 1076.3.41 Schubart, F.W. Die Glocken in herzogtum Anhalt. Dessau, 1896.
Arc 853.27 Schuchhardt, C. Aliso...Ausgrabungen bei Haltern. Haltern, 1906.
Arc 848.15.10 Schuchhardt, C. Deutsche Vor- und Frühgeschichte in Bildern. München, 1936.
Arc 848.22 Schuchhardt, C. Nordwestdeutschland und die Frage des Germanenursprungs. n.p., 1928.
Arc 848.15 Schuchhardt, C. Vorgeschichte von Deutschland. München, 1928.
Arc 848.15.5 Schuchhardt, C. Vorgeschichte von Deutschland. 3. Aufl. München, 1935.
Arc 848.15.7 Schuchhardt, C. Vorgeschichte von Deutschland. 5. Aufl. München, 1943.
Arc 612.11.2 Schuchhardt, Carl. Alteruopa; eine Vorgeschichte unseres Erdteils. 2. Aufl. Leipzig, 1926.
Arc 612.11.4 Schuchhardt, Carl. Alteuropa. Berlin, 1941.
Arc 612.11 Schuchhardt, Carl. Alteuropa. Strassburg, 1919.
NEDL Arc 658.3.4 Schuchhardt, K. Schliemanns Ausgrabungen. Leipzig, 1890.
Arc 658.3.5A Schuchhardt, K. Schliemanns Ausgrabungen. Leipzig, 1891.
Arc 658.3.3A Schuchhardt, K. Schliemann's excavations. London, 1891.
Arc 520.14F Schuchhardt, W.H. Die Meister des grossen Frieses von Pergamon. Berlin, 1925.
Arc 403.18 Schuckhartt, C. Aus Leben und Arbeit. Berlin, 1944.
Arc 843.222 Schuele, Wilhelm. Die Meseta-Kulturen der iberischen Halbinsel. Berlin, 1969. 2v.
Arc 889.1 Schuermans, H. Objets étrusques découvertes en Belgique. pt.1-5. Bruxelles, 1872.
Arc 1200.20 Schütt, Otto. Die Geschichte der Schriftsprache im ehemaligen Amt und in der Stadt Heusburg bis 1650. Heusburg, 1919.
Arc 1200.19 Schütt, Otto. Heusburgen Akten- und Urkundensprache im 14., 15., und 16. Jahrhundert. Heusburg, 1919.
Arc 853.115 Schuldt, E. Pritzier. Berlin, 1955.
Arc 853.274 Schuldt, Ewald. Behren-Lübchin. Berlin, 1965.
Arc 853.246F Schuldt, Ewald. Hohen Viecheln. Berlin, 1961.
Arc 1027.23.17 Schulke, V. Die altchristlichen Bildwerke. Erlangen, 1889.
Arc 1027.50.5 Schulke, V. Theologische Etrag...Katakombenforschung. Leipzig, 1882.
Arc 1528.12.1 Schulman, Jacques. Handboek van de Nederlandsche munten van 1795 tot 1969. 4. druk. Amsterdam, 1969.
Arc 1528.12 Schulman, Jacques. Handboek van de Nederlandsche munten van 1795-1945. Amsterdam, 1946.
Arc 520.18.10 Schulte, Eduard. Carl Humann. Dortmund, 1971.
Arc 520.36 Schulte, Eduard. Chronik der Ausgrabung von Pergamon. Dortmund, 1963.
Arc 608.7 Schulten, A. Das römische Afrika. Leipzig, 1899.
Arc 843.50.10 Schulter, Adolf. Tarraco. Barcelona, 1948.
Arc 848.30.4 Schultz, W. Altgermanische Kultur in Wort und Bild. 3. Aufl. München, 1935.
Arc 848.30.5 Schultz, W. Altgermanische Kultur in Wort und Bild. 4. Aufl. München, 1937.
Arc 1025.56 Schultze, M.V. De christianorum viterum rebus sepulchralibus. Gothae, 1879.
Arc 1025.8 Schultze, V. Die Katakomben. Photoreproduction. Leipzig, 1882.
Arc 1027.21 Schultze, V. Die Katakomben von San Gennaro die Poveri. Jena, 1877.
Arc 1018.5 Schultze, Victor. Archäologie der altchristlichen Kunst. München, 1895.
Arc 1018.5.5 Schultze, Victor. Archäologische Studien über altchristliche Monumente. Wien, 1880.
Arc 1018.5.9 Schultze, Victor. Grundriss der christlichen Archäologie. München, 1919.
Arc 726.42 Schulz, Bruno. Das Grabmal des Theoderich zu Ravenna. Würzburg, 1911.
Arc 1480.25.1 Schulz, Otto Theodor. Die Rechtstitel und Regierungsprogramme auf römischen Kaisermünzen. N.Y., 1968.
Arc 848.20 Schulz, Walther. Die germanische Familie in der Vorzeit. Leipzig, 1925.
Arc 848.20.5 Schulz, Walther. Staat und Gesellschaft in germanischer Vorzeit. Leipzig, 1926.
Arc 682.1.15 Schulze, E. Mykenai - eine kritische Untersuchung der Schliemannschen Alterthümer. St. Petersburg, 1880.
Arc 1190.1.12 Schulze, H. Handbuch der Urkundenlehre für Deutschland und Italien. 2. und 3. Aufl. Berlin, 1960.
Arc 726.318 Schumacher, Erich. Die Protovillanova-Fundgruppe. Bonn, 1967.
Arc 501.15.4 Schumacher, G. Abila of the Decapolis. London, 1889. 3 pam.
Arc 501.15 Schumacher, G. Across the Jordan. London, 1886.
Arc 501.15.2 Schumacher, G. Across the Jordan. London, 1889.
Arc 501.15.8 Schumacher, G. The Jaulân. London, 1888.
Arc 501.15.5 Schumacher, G. Northern Ajlûn. London, 1890.
Arc 726.10 Schumacher, K. Eine Praenestinische Ciste. Heidelberg, 1891.
Arc 853.54 Schumacher, P. Der Ringwälle in der früheren preusischen Provinz Posen. Leipzig, 1924.
Arc 403.13F Schumacher-Festschrift. Mainz, 1930.
Arc 1510.141 Schurnkowski, Walter. Zur Münzgeschichte der chemaligen Wettinischen Lande um 1180-1230. Halle, 1936.
Arc 1053.8 Schuster, P. Über die erhaltenen Porträts der griechischen Philosophen. Leipzig, 1876.
Arc 635.224F Schwab, G.H. An archaeological cruise in the Levant. N.Y.? 1904.
Arc 915.52 Schwab, Hanni. Jungsteinzeitliche Fundstellen im Kanton Freiburg. Basel, 1971.
Arc 520.13 Schwabe, L. von. Pergamon und seine Kunst. Tubingen, 1882.
Arc 1510.166 Schwalbach, Carl. Die neueren deutschen Taler. Lübeck, 1962.
Arc 600.135 Schwaller de Lubicz, R.A. Le Temple de l'homme. Paris, 1957. 3v.
Arc 848.9.3 Schwantes, G. Aus Deutschlands Urgeschichts. 3. Aufl. Leipzig, 1921.
Arc 1468.55 Schwarz, Dietrich Wallo Horman. Aus einer Sammlung griechischer Münzen. Zürich, 1961.
Arc 383.42 Schwarz, K. Strana praehistorica...Martin John. Halle, 1948.
Arc 1190.85 Schwarz, Klaus. Osmanische Sultansurkunden des Sinai-Klosters in türkischer Sprache. Freiburg, 1970.
Arc 853.150F Schwarz, Klaus. Die vor- und frühgeschichtlichen Gebäudedenkmäler Oberfrankens. Kallmünz, 1955. 2v.
Htn Arc 1143.9.5* Schwarz, M.C.G. Ornamentis librorum. Lipsiae, 1756.
Arc 1143.9 Schwarz, M.C.G. Ornamentis librorum apud veteres usitatis. v.1-3. Lipsiae, 1705-
Arc 1510.122 Schwarzenau, J.L. Ansehnlichen Vorrath von Thalern und Schaustücken des langraflich-hessischen Gesamthauses. n.p., 1776.
Arc 684.5 Schwarzstein, A. Eine Gebäudegruppe in Olympia. Strassburg, 1909.
Arc 895.36.15F Schwedische Felsbilder von Göteborg zu Strömstad. Hagen, 1919.
Arc 853.24.15F Schweighauser, J.G. Antiquités de Rheinzabern. Strasbourg, 181-.
Arc 403.20 Schweitzer, B. Zur Kunst der Antike. Tübingen, 1963. 2v.
Arc 1590.7 Schweitzer, F. Brevi cenni storici...una medaglià di Ugone III. Trieste, 1846.
Arc 1490.4 Schweitzer, F. Indice delle Zecche d'Italia. Trieste, 1857.
Arc 1490.55F Schweitzer, F. Serie dei nummi aquilejesi. Trieste, 1848.
Arc 1485.3 Schweitzer, F. Serie delle monete e medaglie d'Aquilya e di Venezia. v.1-2. Trieste, 1848-52.
Arc 600.85F Schweitzer, U. Löwe und Sphinx im alten Ägypten. Glückstadt, 1948.
Arc 913.25 Die Schweiz zur Merowingerzeit. (Moosbrugger, Leu Rudolf.) Bern, 1971. 2v.
Arc 913.8 Die Schweiz zur Rentierzeit. (Bandi, Hans.) Frauenfeld, 1947.
Arc 173.5 Schweizer Beiträge zur Kulturgeschichte und Archäologie des Mittelalters. Olten. 1,1974+
Arc 1318.6 Schweizer Münzblätter. Basel. 1-14,1950-1964 7v.
Arc 173.1 Schweizerische Gesellschaft für Urgeschichte, Zürich. Jahresbericht. Zürich. 1,1909+ 23v.
Arc 1348.24 Schweizerische Münz- und Geldgeschichte. (Escher, A.) Bern, 1881.
Arc 1503.5 Schweizerische Münzkataloge. Bern. 1-3
Arc 1503.1 Schweizerisches Münz- und Medaillenkabinet. v.1-2. (Haller, G.E. von.) Bern, 1780-81.
Arc 87.2.48 Schwert des Giberins. (Lersch, J.H.L.) Bonn, 1849.
Arc 895.46 Schwertartbänder der Wikingerzeit. (Paulsen, P.) Stuttgart, 1953.
Arc 705.207 Schwerzek, Karl. Erläuterungen...Rekonstruktion des östlichen Parthenongiebels. Wien, 1904.
Arc 705.208 Schwerzek, Karl. Erläuterungen...Rekonstruktion Westgiebels des Parthenongiebels. Wien, 1896.
Arc 1510.26 Schwinkowski, Walter. Münz- und Geldgeschichte der Mark Meissen und Münzen. Frankfurt am Main, 1931.
Arc 505.5.48 Sciagraphia templi Hierosolymitano. (Sturm, L.C.) Lipsiae, 1694.
Arc 412.7 Science and archaeology. (Symposium on Archaeological Chemistry.) Cambridge, Mass., 1971.
Arc 1348.7 La science des médailles. (Jobert, L.) Paris, 1715.
Arc 403.24 Scientific methods in medieval archaeology. Berkeley, 1970.
Arc 400.26 The scientist and archaeology. (Pyddoke, E.) N.Y., 1964.
Arc 1348.7.1 La scienza delle medaglie. (Jobert, L.) Venezia, 1756. 2v.
Arc 936.14.235 Sciezki archeologów. (Nadolski, Andrzej.) Łódź, 1967.
Arc 936.14.320 Szkice z najdawniejszej przesstosci Mazausza. Wrocław, 1968.
Arc 387.15 Sclopis de Salerano, F. Notizie degli studi conte Giancarlo Conestabile della Staffa. Torino, 1877.
Arc 1020.9.125 Scognamiglio, A. Cripta di S. Gennaro nel cimeterio. Roma, 1863.
Arc 1027.25 Scognamiglio, A. De phiala cruenta...Christo martyrii. Paris, 1867.
Arc 1025.41 Scognamiglio, A. In Roma i cristianai...soterranei cimiteri. Roma, 1863.
Arc 1033.53.5 Scognamiglio, A. Ne' primi tre secoli di persecuzione cristiane. Napoli, 1869.
Arc 1015.212 Scognamiglio, A. Notice sur deux catacombs. Paris, 1863.
Arc 66.1.27 Scolies du ms. d'Aristophane à Ravenne. (Martin, A.) Paris, 1882.
Arc 1027.40 Scoperta...cripta S. Emerenziana...cimiteri Ostriano. (Armellini, M.) Roma, 1877.
Arc 540.1 Scoperta del tempio di Venere a Golgos. (Cesnola, L.P.) Turin, 1871.
Arc 1033.30 Scoperta della cripta di Santa Emerenziana e di una memoria relativa alla cattedra di San Pietro. (Armellini, Mariano.) Roma, 1877.
Arc 746.17 Scoperta di un bronzo etrusco. (Tononi, A.G.) Milano, 1879.
Arc 1027.39 Scoperta d'un graffito storico...cimiteri di Pretestato. (Armellini, M.) Roma, 1874.
Arc 1033.70 Scoperta d'una pittura nel Laterno. (Armellini, M.) Roma, 1880.
Arc 1033.21 Scoperta oratorio presso Via Appia. (Arnellini, M.) Roma, 1875.
Arc 1018.62 Le scoperte archeologiche sui giudeo-cristiani. (Mancini, Ignazio.) Assisi, 1968.
Arc 1027.69 Scoperte nell'arenaria tra i cimiteri di Trasone e dei Giordani sulla via Salaria. (Rossi, G.B. de.) Roma, 1872.
Arc 726.165 Scoperte paletnologiche e archeologiche nella provincia di Treviso. 1. ed. (Berti, Leo.) Firenze, 1956.
Arc 875.14.20 Scotland before the Scots. (Childe, V.G.) London, 1946.
Arc 875.3 Scotland in early Christian times. (Anderson, Joseph.) Edinburgh, 1881.
Arc 875.3.2 Scotland in early Christian times. 2. series. (Anderson, Joseph.) Edinburgh, 1881.
Arc 875.4.2 Scotland in Pagan times. The Bronze and Stone Ages. (Anderson, Joseph.) Edinburgh, 1886.
Arc 875.4 Scotland in Pagan times. The Iron Age. (Anderson, Joseph.) Edinburgh, 1883.
Arc 875.29.7 The Scots mercat "cross"; an inquiry as to its history and meaning. (Black, William G.) Glasgow, 1928.
Arc 1025.17 Scott, B. Contents...catacombs of Rome. London, 1873.
Arc 1347.3 Scott, W.H. On the Parthian coins. London, 1836-54. 28 pam.
Arc 1373.3 Scotti, V.N. Della rarità delle medaglie antiche. Florence, 1809.
Arc 1373.3.3 Scotti, V.N. Della rarità delle medaglie antiche. Roma, 1838.

	Arc 143.3	Scottish archaeological studies. Aberdeen. 1-2,1922-1936
	Arc 1540.17.15	The Scottish coinage. (Stewart, Ian Halley.) London, 1955.
	Arc 855.5	Scottish market crosses. (Small, J.W.) Stirling, 1900.
	Arc 700.19.5	Scranton, R.L. The chronology of Greek walls. Thesis. Chicago, 1941.
	Arc 700.19	Scranton, R.L. Greek walls. Cambridge, 1941.
	Arc 1125.10	Scriptorium; international review of manuscript studies. Bruxelles. 1,1946+ 35v.
	Arc 1153.106	Scriptorum opus: Schreiber-Mönche am Werk. Wiesbaden, 1971.
	Arc 1153.73	Scriptura latina libraria. (Kirchner, J.) Monachii, 1955.
	Arc 1163.2	Scripturae hispanae veteris. (Muñoz y Rivero, J.) Matriti, 1890.
	Arc 567.1.15F	Scritti dedicati alla memoria di Ippolito Rosellini. (Florence. Università.) Firenze, 1945.
	Arc 1185.34	Scritti di diplomatica e archivistica. (Vittani, Giovanni.) Milano, 1974-
	Arc 1153.104.2	Scritti di paleografia e diplomatica. 2. ed. (Lazzarini, Vittorio.) Padova, 1969.
	Arc 1138.40	Scritti di paleografia e diplomatica in onore de Vincenzo Federici. Firenze, 1944.
	Arc 398.4	Scritti in onore di Bartolomeo Nogara. Città del Vaticano, 1937.
	Arc 383.50	Scritti in onore di Guido Libertini. (Catania. Università.) Firenze, 1958.
	Arc 66.1.92	La sculpture attique avant Phidias. (Lechat, Henri.) Paris, 1904.
	Arc 716.3.5	The sculpture of the Nike temple parapet. (Carpenter, Rhys.) Cambridge, 1929.
	Arc 712.32	The sculpture of the Parthenon. (Corbett, Peter Edgar.) Harmondsworth, 1959.
	Arc 950.204	Sculptured anthropoid ape heads. (Terry, J.) N.Y., 1891.
	Arc 518.6	Sculptured columns...Temple of Diana at Ephesus. (Murray, A.S.) London, 1895-96.
	Arc 421.18	Sculptured stone tombs of the Lion dynasty. (Torü, P.) Peking, 1942.
	Arc 855.207	The sculptured stones of Leith. (Robertson, D.H.) Leith, 1851.
	Arc 855.4	Sculptured stones of Scotland. (Stuart, J.) Aberdeen, 1856. 2v.
	Arc 700.7	Sculptured tombs of Hellas. (Gardner, P.) London, 1896.
	Arc 505.2	Sculptures et inscriptions de Palmyre. (Simonsen, D.) Copenhagen, 1889.
	Arc 530.17	Les sculptures et la restauration du temple d'Assos. (Sartiaux, Felix.) Paris, 1915.
	Arc 520.4	Sculptures of the Great Pergamon Altar. (Mitchell, L.M. (Mrs.).) N.Y., 1882.
	Arc 712.12	Sculpures...Parthenon. (British Museum.) London, 1900.
	Arc 608.17.11	Lo scultore del grande bassorilievo. (Caputo, Giacomo.) Roma, 1948.
	Arc 1015.203	Sculture e pitture sagre estratte dai cimitery de Roma. (Bottari, G.G.) Roma, 1737-54. 3v.
	Arc 547.24.15	Sculture inedite del Museo Greco-Romano. (Breccia, E.) Alexandrie, 1931.
	Arc 925.13.50	Scythian art. (Borovka, Grigorii I.) London, 1927.
	Arc 925.13.52	Scythian art. (Borovka, Grigorii I.) London, 1928.
	Arc 925.13.186	Scythian rattles in the Carpathian Basin and their eastern connections. (Bakay, Kornél.) Amsterdam, 1971.
	Arc 925.12	Scythians and Greeks...ancient history and archaeology. (Minns, E.H.) Cambridge, 1913.
	Arc 925.12.20F	Scythians and Greeks. (Minns, Ellis Hovell.) N.Y., 1971.
	Arc 505.21	Scythische Denkmahlen in Palästina. (Cramer, F.) Kiel, 1777.
	Arc 672.1.19A	The sea-kings of Crete. (Baikie, James.) London, 1910.
	Arc 672.1.21	The sea-kings of Crete. 3. ed. (Baikie, James.) London, 1920.
	Arc 672.1.22	The sea-kings of Crete. 4. ed. (Baikie, James.) London, 1926.
	Arc 403.1	Seabird, H. Element of archaeology. n.p., 1878.
	Arc 1538.27.3	Seaby, Herbert Allen. The English silver coinage from 1649. 3. ed. London, 1968.
	Arc 1318.8	Seaby's coin and medal bulletin. London. 1958+ 16v.
	Arc 1538.28	Seaby's standard catalogue of British coins. pt.1-2. London. 14,1975+
	Arc 682.15A	Seager, R.B. Explorations in the island of Mochlos. Boston, 1912.
	Arc 1221.7	The seal cylinders of western Asia. (Ward, William Hayes.) Washington, 1910.
X Cg	Arc 1212.3	Seals. (Birch, William de Gray.) London, 1907?
	Arc 1212.5	Seals and documents. (Poole, Reginald Lane.) London, 1919?
Htn	Arc 1208.5.15*	Seals of Gianfrancesco Pico della Mirandola. n.p., n.d.
	Arc 1237.1	Seals of Siam. n.p., n.d.
	Arc 726.341.5	The search for Sybaris, 1960-1965. (Rainey, Froelich G.) Roma, 1967.
	Arc 608.39	The search for the Tassili frescoes. (Lhote, Henri.) London, 1959.
	Arc 961.1.25	Sears, William H. Excavations at Kolomoki. v.1-2. Athens, 1950?
	Arc 1033.3.42A	The season sarcophagus in Dumbarton Oakes. (Hanfmann, G.M.) Cambridge, 1951. 2v.
	Arc 1349.65	Sebastian Dadler. (Więcek, A.) Gdańsk, 1962.
	Arc 925.50.42	Sebastopol. Khersoneskii Gosudarstvennyi Istoriko-Arkheologicheskii Muzei. Khersones Tavricheskii. Simferopol', 1962.
	Arc 925.50.20	Sebastopol'. Khersoneskii Gosudarstvennyi Istoriko-Arkheologicheskii Muzei. Soobshcheniia. v.1-3. Simferopol', n.d. 2v.
	Arc 1488.20	Secchi, Alberto. Le monete decimali sabaude. Milano, 1955.
	Arc 1030.22	Secchi, G. Epigramma greco christiano...Autun. Roma, 1840.
	Arc 1016.237	Secchi, P.G. La cattedra Alessandrina di San Marco Evangelista e Martire. Venezia, 1853.
	Arc 87.1.60	Sechziges Program zum Winckelmannsfeste. (Schrader, H.) Berlin, 1900.
	Arc 608.24.5F	Second cataract forts. (Dunham, D.) Boston, 1960-67. 2v.
	Arc 672.1.146	The secret of Crete. (Wunderlich, Hans-Georg.) N.Y., 1974.
	Arc 530.12.35	The secret of the Hittites. (Marek, Kurt W.) N.Y., 1956.
	Arc 915.8.5	Secretan, Eugène. Aventicum. Lausanne, 1896.
	Arc 915.8	Secretan, Eugène. Aventicum. Lausanne, 1905.
	Arc 672.1.90	Secrets of Minos. 1. ed. (Honour, Alan.) N.Y., 1961.
	Arc 595.63	Secrets of the great pyramid. (Tompkins, Peter.) London, 1973.
	Arc 858.93F	Sedgley, Jeffrey. The Roman milestones of Britain. Oxford, 1975.
	Arc 588.34	Sedment I, II. (Petrie, W.M.F.) London, 1924. 2v.
	Arc 925.355	Sedov, Valentin V. Dlinnye kurgany krivichei. Moskva, 1974.
	Arc 925.348	Sedov, Valentin V. Novgorodskie sopki. Moskva, 1970.
	Arc 810.68	Seedorff Pedersen, Hans H.O. Pompeji. København, 1966.
	Arc 609.5	Seekirchner, A. Die geographischen und geopolitischen Grundlagen der sudafrikanischen Ruinenkultur. Memmingen, 1933.
	Arc 1033.12.121	Seelen, I.H. Memorabilium...specimen sive de festo lanceae et clavorum. Flensburgi, 1715.
	Arc 421.8	Ségalen, V. Mission archéologique en Chine (1914). Paris, 1935.
	Arc 420.8F	Segalen, V. Mission archéologique en Chine (1914 et 1917). Atlas. Paris, 1923-24. 2v.
	Arc 853.65.10	Seger, Hans. Schlesiens Urgeschichte. Leipzig, 1913.
	Arc 825.3.20	Segni, Emile. Le trésor de la Maison Carrée. Nîmes, 1937?
	Arc 885.12.5	Segontium and the Roman occupation of Wales. (Wheeler, R.E.M.) London, 1923.
	Arc 830.179	Segret, Gabriel. Une maison d'époque romaine à Blesle. Clermont-Ferrand, 1925.
	Arc 830.15.7	Seguin, J. Les antiquités d'Arles. Avignon, 1877.
	Arc 825.11	Seguin, J.F. L'ancienne inscription de la Maison Carrée. Paris, 1759. 4 pam.
	Arc 1373.4.2	Seguin, P. Sel. numismata antiqua. Paris, 1684.
Htn	Arc 1373.4*	Seguin, P. Sel. numismata antiqua. Paris, 1684.
	Arc 736.1	Sehnbring, J. Historische Topographie von Akragas in Sicilien. Leipzig, 1870.
	Arc 853.367	Seidel, Martin Fredrich. Thesaurus Orcivus Marchicus. Faksimile. Berlin, 1972.
	Arc 1390.18	Seifedolini, M.A. Monety il'khakov XIV veka. Baku, 1968.
	Arc 830.32.8	La Seine-Inférieure historique et archéologique. 2e éd. (Cochet, J.B.D.) Paris, 1866.
	Arc 595.7	Seiss, J.A. A miracle in stone, or The Great Pyramid of Egypt. Philadelphia, 1877?
	Arc 595.7.4	Seiss, J.A. A miracle in stone, or The Great Pyramid of Egypt. 4th ed. Philadelphia, 1877.
	Arc 853.346	Seitz, Hermann Josf. Die Steinzeit im Donaumoos. Augsburg, 1965.
	Arc 1588.4.70	Sejbal, Jiří. Moravská mince doby husitské. Brno, 1965.
Htn	Arc 1373.4*	Sel. numismata antiqua. (Seguin, P.) Paris, 1684.
	Arc 1373.4.2	Sel. numismata antiqua. (Seguin, P.) Paris, 1684.
	Arc 403.16.5	Selbstbiographie bis zu seinem Tod vervollständigt. 2. Aufl. (Schliemann, Heinrich.) Leipzig, 1936.
	Arc 1433.100	Selcuklulonn nadir paralarendon borilom. Istanbul, 1972.
	Arc 1468.13.5F	Select Greek coins. (Hill, G.F.) Paris, 1927.
	Arc 1675.20F	Select Italian medals of the Renaissance. (British Museum. Department of Coins and Medals.) London, 1915.
	Arc 1330.7	Select numismatic bibliography. (Clain-Stepanelli, Elvira Eliza.) N.Y., 1965.
	Arc 1027.19.35	Selecta ex coemeterio Si Callisti. (Trappists.) Roma, 189-?
	Arc 543.75.5	Selected studies in Indonesian archaeology. (Bosch, Frederick D.K.) The Hague, 1961.
	Arc 1478.6	Selectiorum numismatum, praecipue Romanorum expositiones. (Landi, C.) Leyden, 1695.
	Arc 1175.11	Selectus diplomatum et numismatum Scotiae Thesaurus. (Anderson, J.) Edinburgi, 1739.
	Arc 1423.11	The Seleucid mint of Antioch. (Newell, E.T.) N.Y., 1918.
	Arc 1423.11.5F	Seleucidarum imperium. (Foy-Vaillant, J.) Hagae-Comitum, 1732.
	Arc 412.27	Selhus, Wilhelm. Und sie waren doch da: wissenschaftliche Beweise für den Besuch aus dem All. München, 1975.
	Arc 493.6.30	Selimkhanov, I.S. Istoriko-khimicheskie i analiticheskie issledovaniia drevnikh predmetov iz mednykh splavov. Baku, 1960.
	Arc 730.6	Sélimonte. (Hulot, J.) Paris, 1910.
	Arc 730.6.5	Selinunte. (Santangelo, M.) Roma, 1953.
	Arc 938.95	Selirand, J. Läbi aastatuhandete. Tallinn, 1963.
	Arc 938.95.5	Selirand, Jüri. Estlaste matmiskombed varafeodaalsete suhete tärkamise perioodil (11.-13. sajand). Tallinn, 1974.
	Arc 543.3.57	Sel'skie poseleniia afriyid skogo Khorezma. (Nerazik, Elena E.) Moskva, 1966.
	Arc 1470.27	Seltman, C.J. The temple coins of Olympia. Cambridge, Eng., 1921. 2v.
	Arc 1468.29.10	Seltman, C.T. A book of Greek coins. London, 1952.
	Arc 1465.80F	Seltman, Charles Theodore. Athens, its history and coinage before the Persian invasion. Cambridge, 1924.
	Arc 1465.80.1	Seltman, Charles Theodore. Athens; its history and coinage before the Persian invasion. Chicago, 1974.
	Arc 1373.01	Pamphlet box. Seltman, E.J.
	Arc 1018.17	Selvaggio, J.L. Antiquitatum christianarum institutiones. Vercellis, 1778. 3v.
	Arc 925.9.30	Semenov, L.P. Arkheologicheskie i etnograficheskie razyskaniia v Ingushetii v 1925-32 gg. Groznyi, 1963.
	Arc 925.13.115	Semenov-Zuser, Semen A. Opyt istoriografii skifov. Khar'kov, 1947.
	Arc 925.13.60	Seminar Kondakovianum, Prague. Ekufika. Praha. 1-4,1929-1931 2v.
	Arc 432.32	Seminar on Indian Prehistory and Protohistory, Deccan College Post Graduate and Research Institute, 1964. Indian prehistory. 1. ed. Poona, 1965.
	Arc 323.4	Seminars in archaeology: 1955. (Society for American Archaeology.) Salt Lake City, 1956.
	Arc 495.204.4	Semitic inscriptions. (Littman, Enno.) N.Y., 1904.
	Arc 853.78	Die Semnonen im Havelland zur frühen Kaiserzeit. Diss. (Guthjahr, R.) Greifswald, 1934.
	Arc 435.2.53	Sen, B. Some historical aspects of the inscriptions of Bengal. Calcutta, 1942.
	Arc 383.29	Sen, D. Studies in prehistory; robert Bruce Foote memorial volume. Calcutta, 1966.
	Arc 66.1.52	Le Sénat Romain depuis Dioclétien. (Lécrivain, C.) Paris, 1888.
	Arc 938.17.5	Senatnes pédás. (Graudonis, J.) Riga, 1961.
Htn	Arc 800.3*	Sendschreiben von den Herculanischen Entdeckungen. (Winckelmann, J.) Dresden, 1762. 4 pam.
	Arc 188.2	Sendschriften. (Deutschen Orient Gesellschaft.) Leipzig. 1-6,1901-1938 7v.
	Arc 830.158.15F	Sénéchal, Robert. Contribution à l'étude de la céramique à reflects métalliques recueillie à Alésia. Dijon, 1972.
	Arc 1588.9	Sengbusch, R. von. Heinrich Jochumsen. Verzeichnis aller bisher nachweisbaren boltischen Münzen und der Desiderata der Sammlung Anton Buchholtz. Riga, 1928.
	Arc 925.16.65	Senigova, Taisiia N. Srednevekovyi taraz. Alma-Ata, 1972.
	Arc 830.92	Le sénonais préhistorique. (Hure, Auguste.) Sens, 1921.

Author and Title Listing

Arc 1588.11 Senoues lietuviu pinigai. (Karys, Jonas K.) Bridgeport, Conn., 1959.
Arc 936.241 Seoba naroda. (Zemun. Narodni Muzej.) Zemun, 1962.
Arc 726.44 Il sepolcreto de Remedello-Sotto. (Colini, Giuseppe A.) Parma, 1899-1902.
Arc 1030.5.5 Sepolcri del secolo ottavo...di S. Lorenzo in Lucina. (Rossi, G.B. de.) Roma, 1872.
Arc 1027.6 Sepolcro apostolico delle catacombe. (Marucchi, O.) Roma, 1892.
Arc 1015.210.5 Il sepolcro dei ss martiri Proto e Giacinta. (Marchi, Giuseppe.) Roma, 1845.
Arc 1015.225 Il sepolcro gentilizio di Sant'Ambrogio. (Marucchi, O.) Milano, 1897.
Arc 505.4.8 Sepp, J.N. Meerfahrt nach Tyrus zur Ausgrabung der Kathedrale mit Barbarossa's Grab. Leipzig, 1879.
Arc 497.16 Sepp, J.N. Neue architektonische Studien...Forschungen in Palästina. Würzburg, 1867.
Arc 1033.17.449 Septenaire ou sept allégresses de Notre Dame de Mont Carmel. (Ricci, A.M.) Paris, 1839.
Arc 113.10 Septentrion. Calais. 1,1969+
Arc 87.1.46 Septizonim des Septimius Severus. (Huelsen, C.) Berlin, 1886.
Arc 1016.200 Die sepulcralen Jenseits Denkmäler. (Kaufmann, C.I.) Mainz, 1900.
Arc 1087.3 Die Sepulkralmasken, ihre Gebrauch und Bedeutung. (Kugnezow, S.) Kasan, 1906.
Arc 830.19 Sépulture d'un légionnaire romain. (Rochebrune, R. de.) Niort, 1878.
Arc 726.21 Sepultures à l'incinération de Poggio Renzo. (Bertrand, A.) n.p., 1874.
Arc 913.15 Les sépultures du second âge. Thèse. (Viollier, David.) Genève, 1916.
Arc 830.29.5 Sépultures gauloises, romaines. (Cochet, J.B.D.) Paris, 1857.
Arc 1333.11 Serafini, C. Monete e bolle plumbee...del Medaghere Vaticano. Milano, 1910. 4v.
Arc 1033.12.158 Serantoni, G.M. Apologia del Volto santo di Lucca. Lucca, 1765.
Arc 1033.12.163 Serantoni, G.M. Risposta...alla seconda replica del celebre autore delle letterarie di Firenze. Lucca, 1767.
Arc 936.220.01 Pamphlet vol. Serbia. Antiquities. 5 pam.
Arc 302.2.14 Serdika; arkheologicheski materiali. (Bulgarska Akademiia na Naukite, Sofia. Arkheolgicheski Institut.) Sofiia, 1964.
Arc 925.50.210 Seredni viky na Ukraini. Kyïv, 1971.
Arc 925.50.290 Seredn'ostohivs'ka kul'tura epokhy midi. (Telehin, Dnytro I.) Kyïv, 1973.
Arc 608.38 Sérée de Roch. Tebessa. Alger, 1952.
Arc 705.204 Das Sergenannte Theseion. (Sauer, B.) Berlin, 1899.
Arc 723.17 Sergi, Giuseppi. Italia, le origini. Torino, 1919.
Arc 273.16 Série A: Répertoires archéologigues. (Centre National de Recherches Archéologiques en Belgique.) Brussel. 1,1960+ 4v.
Arc 273.16.3 Série B: Collections. (Centre National de Recherches Archéologiques en Belgique.) Bruxelles. 1,1965+
Arc 273.16.5 Série C: Répertoires divers. (Centre National de Recherches Archéologiques en Belgique.) Brussel. 1,1964+ 2v.
Arc 1675.7 Serie dei conj di medaglie pontificie da Martino V. Roma, 1824.
Arc 1490.55F Serie dei nummi aquilejesi. (Schweitzer, F.) Trieste, 1848.
Arc 1485.3 Serie delle monete e medaglie d'Aquilya e di Venezia. v.1-2. (Schweitzer, F.) Trieste, 1848-52.
Htn Arc 1053.6.9* Series Augustorum, Augustarum, Caesarum. (Patarolo, Lorenzo.) Venetiis, 1702.
Arc 1053.6.12 Series Augustorum, Augustarum, Caesarum. 3. ed. (Patarolo, Lorenzo.) Venetiis, 1740.
Arc 1053.7 Series Augustorum, Augustarum, Caesarum. 4. ed. (Patarolo, Lorenzo.) Venetiis, 1743.
Htn Arc 1540.13* Series of English medals. (Perry, Francis.) London, 1762.
Arc 542.207F Serindia. (Stein, Mark Aurel.) Oxford, 1921.
Arc 1033.12.36 Sermone sulla SS. Sindone di Torino. (Pellegrini, C.) Torino, 1844.
Arc 945.3 Serpent symbol and worship of nature in America. (Squier, E.G.) N.Y., 1851.
Arc 843.35 Serra-Vilaró, J. Escornalbou prehistòrich. Castell de Sant Miquel d'Escornalbou, 1925.
Arc 843.15.14 Serra-Vilars, J. De mental-lurgia prehistorica a Catalunya. Solsona, 1924.
Arc 843.15.12 Serra-Vilars, J. El vas companiforme a Catalunya i las caves sepulcrals eneolitequeis. Solsona, 1923.
Arc 730.201 Serradifalco. Le antichita della Sicilia. Palermo, 1834. 5v.
Arc 1088.1.17 Serre, Paul. Les marines de guerre. Paris, 1885.
Arc 1518.4 Serrure, Raymond. Dictionnaire géographique de l'histoire monétaire belge. Bruxelles, 1880.
Arc 1518.5 Serrure, Raymond. Elements de l'histoire monétaire de Flandre. Gand, 1879.
Arc 1027.68 Servanzi-Collis, S. Relazione della chiesa sotterranea di S. Lorenzo in Sanseverino. Macerata, 1838.
Arc 1208.7 Le service sigillographique et les collections d'empreintes de sceaux des archives. (France. Archives Nationales.) Paris, 1916.
Arc 402.5 Services de l'archéologie aux études classiques. (Rossignol, J.P.) Paris, 1878.
Arc 936.14.410 Sesja naukowa Zorzanizowana Zokazji 50- Lecia Katedry Archeologii Pradziejavej i Wczesnoś Redniowiecznej UAM, Poznań, 1969. Problemy badań archeologicznych Polski połnocnozachodniej. 1. wyd. Poznań, 1972.
Arc 1588.1.105 Sesja Numizmatyczna, 3rd, Nowa Sól, 1970. III Sesja Numizmatyczna w Nowej Soli poświęcona monecie i mennicom Wielkopolski, 10-11 listopada 1970 r. Nowa Sól, 1972.
Arc 1468.19 Sestini, D. Descrizione d'alcune medaglie greche. Firenze, 1821.
Arc 1470.9 Sestini, D. Descrizione degli stateri antichi. Florence, 1817.
Arc 1373.10 Sestini, Domenico. Classes generales seu moneta vetus urbium populorum et regum ordine. Florentiae, 1821.
Arc 66.1.162 Seston, William. Dioclétien et la tétrarchie. Paris, 1946. 2v.
Arc 635.221 Seta, A.D. La genesi dello Scorcio nell'arte greca. Roma, 1907.
Arc 723.19.2 Seta, Alessandro. Italia antica. 2a ed. Bergamo, 1928.
Arc 1033.20.17 Le sette basiliche di Roma. (Globočnik, G.N.) Venesia, 1877.
Arc 1015.211 Settele, G. Illustrazione di un antico monumento cristiano. Roma, 1829.
Arc 712.25 The setting of the Periclean Parthenon. (Stevens, G.P.) Baltimore, 1940.
Arc 875.129 Settlement types in post-Roman Scotland. (Laing, Lloyd Robert.) Oxford, 1975.
Arc 682.7 Seunig, Vingenz. Die kritisch-mykenische Kultur. Graz, 1921.
Arc 925.23 Sev. Prichernomor'e v antich. epolu. (Kallistov, D.P.) Moskva, 1952.
Arc 726.323 Seven Italic tomb-groups from Narce. (Davison, Jean M.) Firenze, 1972.
Arc 588.65F Seven Memphite tomb chapels. (Petrie, W.M.F.) London, 1952.
Arc 307.3.8 Seventeenth international congress of Americanists. (Currier, C.W.) Washington, 1910?
Arc 565.1.5 Seventy years in archaeology. (Petrie, W.M.F.) London, 1931.
Arc 565.1.6A Seventy years in archaeology. (Petrie, W.M.F.) N.Y., 1932.
Arc 1033.35.43 Sévérac, G. Notice sur la vraie croix de St. Guilhelm-du-Désert. Lodève, 1861.
Arc 1020.9.50 Severano, G. Memorie sacre delle sette chiese di Roma. Roma, 1630.
Arc 925.326 Severianskaia zumlia i severiane po gorodishcham i mogilam. (Samokrasov, Dmitrii I.) Moskva, 1908.
Arc 936.225.25F Severno emonsko grobišče. (Plesničar-Gec, Ljudmila.) Ljubljana, 1972.
Arc 925.8.45 Severnoe prichernomor. (Zhebelev, S.A.) Moskva, 1953.
Arc 925.115 Severnoe Prichernomor'e i Rim. (Golubtsova, E.S.) Moskva, 1951.
Arc 925.50.33 Severnoe prisivash'e v V-I tysiacheleliiakh do nashei ery. (Shchepinskii, Askold A.) Simferopol', 1969.
Arc 843.28 Severo, Ricardo. Os braceletes d'ouro de arnozella. Porto, 1905. 2 pam.
Arc 925.97 Severskii kurgan. (Smirnov, K.F.) Moskva, 1953.
Arc 936.140.25 Sevtopolis. (Chichikova, Mariia.) Sofiia, 1970.
Arc 440.1 Sewell, R. Report on the Amarāvati Tope. London, 1880.
Arc 435.2.8F Sewell, Robert. Lists of inscriptions and sketch...dynasties of southern India. Madras, 1884.
Arc 435.2.7F Sewell, Robert. Lists of the antiquarian remains in the presidency of Madras. Madras, 1882.
Arc 522.18 Seyk, V. Das Wahre und richtige Troja-Ilion. Prag, 1926.
Arc 853.14 Seyler, E. Die Drusenverschanzungen bei Deisenhofen. München, 1900.
Arc 1212.2 Seyler, Gustav A. Geschichte der Siegel. Leipzig, 1894.
Arc 743.9 Seymour, F. Up hill and down dale in ancient Etruria. London, 1910.
Arc 1077.2.5 Seymour, W.W. The cross. N.Y., 1898.
Arc 810.52 Seymour-Browne, C. Notes on Pompei. Naples, 1913.
Arc 406.2 Sforza, G. Ennio Quirion Visconti Giacobino. n.p., n.d. 2 pam.
Arc 1285.10.7 Sfragistyka. (Gumowski, M.) Warszawa, 1960.
Arc 968.2.30 Shabik'eschee village. (Roberts, Frank H.H.) Washington, 1929.
Arc 588.57F Shabtis. (Petrie, W.M.F.) London, 1935.
Arc 682.11 The shaft graves and bee-hive tombs of Mycenae and their interrelation. (Evans, Arthur.) London, 1929.
Arc 1540.2 Shafter, E.F. The copper coinage of the Earl of Stirling. Boston, 1874.
Arc 493.62 Shah Diz of Isma'ili fame. (Minasian, Caro Owen.) London, 1971.
Arc 925.50.240 Shaitan-Koba - mustievs'ka stoianka Knymii. (Kolosov, Iurii H.) Kyïv, 1972.
Arc 543.45A Shakur, M.A. A dash through the heart of Afghanistan. Peshawar, 1947.
Arc 432.16 Shakur, M.A. A handbook to the Inscription Gallery in the Peshhawar Museum. Peshawar, 1946.
Arc 925.9.80 Shamba, G.K. Akhachcharkhu-drevnii mogil'nik nagornoi Abkhazii. Sukhumi, 1970.
Arc 450.32 Sharma, G.R. The excavations at Kauśāmbī (1957-59). Allahabad, 1960.
Arc 590.4.2 Sharpe, S. Alabaster sarcophagus of Oimenepthah. London, 1864.
Arc 590.4 Sharpe, S. Triple mummy case of Aroeri-Ao. London, 1858.
Arc 435.2.11F The Sharqi architecture of Jaunpur. (Führer, A.A.) Calcutta, 1889.
Arc 1675.19.15 Shaten, Anatolii V. Sovetskaia memorial'naia medal', 1917-1967. Moskva, 1970.
Arc 925.180.15 Shavkunov, Ernst V. Gosudarstvo bokhai i pamiatniki ego kul'tury v Primor'e. Leningrad, 1968.
Arc 746.20 Shaw, C. Etruscan Perugia. Baltimore, 1939.
Arc 609.17.10 Shaw, Thurstan. A bibliography of Nigerian archaeology. Ibadan, 1969.
Arc 609.17F Shaw, Thurstan. Excavation at Dawu. Edinburgh, 1961.
Arc 925.50.33 Shchepinskii, Askold A. Severnoe prisivash'e v V-I tysiacheleliiakh do nashei ery. Simferopol', 1969.
Arc 1163.3.4 Shchepkin, Viacheslav N. Russkaia paleografiia. Moskva, 1967.
Arc 1163.3.5 Shchepkin, Viacheslav N. Uchebnik russkoi paleografii. Moskva, 1918.
Arc 443.6 Shchetenko, Anatolii I. Drevneishie zemledel'cheskie kul'tury Dekana. Leningrad, 1968.
Arc 925.11 Shchtern, E. von. K voproscho proiskhozhdenii gotskago stilia. Odessa, 1897.
Arc 923.11.5F Shchukinym, P.I. Kratkoe opisanie novago vladaniia imperatopskago rossiiskago istoricheskago muzeia. Moskva, 1906.
Arc 1077.1.9 Sheet-copper from the mounds. (Moore, C.B.) Washington, 1903.
Arc 1318.4 The shekel. N.Y. 1,1968+ 3v.
Arc 967.3.5 Sheldon, J.M.A. (Mrs.). Pitted stones. Deerfield, 1925.
Arc 1615.10 Sheldon, W.H. Early American cents, 1793-1814. 1. ed. N.Y., 1949.
Arc 925.125 Shelov, D.B. Antichnyi mir v severnom Prichernomor'e. Moskva, 1956.
Arc 925.120 Shelov, D.B. Monetnoe delo Bospora. Moskva, 1956.
Arc 925.20.5 Shelov, Dmitrii B. Tanais, poteriannyi i naidennyi gorod. Moskva, 1967.
Arc 925.20.10 Shelov, Dmitrii B. Tanais i Nizhnii Don v III-I vv. do n.e. Moskva, 1970.
Arc 925.20.15 Shelov, Dmitrii B. Tanais i Nizhnyi Don v peroye veka nashei erg. Moskva, 1972.
Arc 493.26 The Shemshāra tablets. (Laessøe, Jørgen.) København, 1959.
Arc 925.16.25 Sher, Iakov A. Kamennye iz vaianiia Semirech'ia. Leningrad, 1966.
Arc 925.4.29 Shestakovskie kurgany. (Martynov, Anatolii I.) Kemerovo, 1971.
Arc 893.21 Shetelig, H. Scandinavian archaeology. Oxford, 1937.

Arc 858.56 Shètelig, H. Viking antiquities in Great Britain and Ireland. pts.1-3, 4-6. Oslo, 1940. 2v.

Arc 895.17.12 Shetelig, Haakon. Préhistoire de la Norvège. Oslo, 1926.

Arc 895.17.9 Shetelig, Haakon. Primitive tider i Norge. Bergen, 1922.

Arc 925.12.6 Shevchenko, V. Sokrovishcha ischeznuvshikh gorodov. Moskva, 1948.

Arc 1680.10 Shiells, Robert. Story of the token. N.Y., 1891.

Arc 925.322.30 Shikhsaidov, Amri Rzaevich. Nadpisi rasskazyvaiut. Dagknigoizdat, 1969.

Arc 505.131 Shiloh; the Danish excavations at Tall Sailūn, Palestine, in 1926, 1929, 1932, and 1963. (Buhl, Marie Louise.) Copenhagen, 1969.

Arc 609.32 Shinnie, Peter L. The African Iron Age. Oxford, 1971.

Arc 773.6F Shipley, F.W. Chronology of the building operations in Rome from the death of Caesar. n.p., 1931.

Arc 943.13 Shipp, B. The Indian and antiquities of America. Philadelphia, 1897.

Arc 1088.1.11 Ships and seamanship in the ancient world. (Casson, Lionel.) Princeton, N.J., 1971.

Arc 412.16 Shipwrecks and archaeology: the unharvested sea. 1. ed. (Throckmorton, Peter.) Boston, 1970.

Arc 923.30 Shliapkin, I.A. Russkaia paleograiuiia. Sankt Petersburg, 1913.

Arc 530.29 Shober, Arnold. Der Fries des Hekateions von Lagina. Baden, 1933.

Arc 953.11 Short, J.F. The North Americans of antiquity. N.Y., 1879-80.

Arc 547.6.9 A short description of the objects from the tomb of Tutankhamun now exhibited in the Cairo Museum. Cairo, 1926.

Arc 875.35 Short essay on age and uses of brochs...Orkeney Islands. (Fergusson, James.) London, 1877.

Arc 861.160.10 A short guide to Roman York. (Yorkshire Architectural and Archaeological Society.) York, 1962.

Arc 785.22.15 A short guide to the Palatine. (Carettoni, G.) Bologna, 1948.

Arc 785.13.70 A short guide to the Roman Forum. (Carettoni, G.) Bologna, 1948.

Arc 870.13 Short history of sepulchral cross-slabs. (Styan, K.E.) London, 1902.

Arc 1148.20 Short manual of Greek palaeography. (Groningen, B.A.) Leiden, 1940.

Arc 1148.20.2 Short manual of Greek palaeography. 2. ed. (Groningen, B.A.) Leiden, 1955.

Arc 1148.20.3 Short manual of Greek palaeography. 3. ed. (Groningen, B.A.) Leyden, 1963.

Arc 861.19.5 Shortt, W.T.P. Collectanea curiosa antiqua Dunmonia. Londinium, n.d.

Arc 1480.17 Shortt, W.T.P. Sylva antiqua iscana. Londini, n.d.

Arc 861.212 Shotter, David Colin Arthur. Romans in Lancashire. Yorkshire, 1973.

Arc 925.50.25 Shovkoplias, Ivan H. Arkheolohichni doslidzheniia na Ukraini 1917-1957. Kyïv, 1957.

Arc 925.50.27 Shovkoplias, Ivan H. Mezinskaia stoianka. Kiev, 1965.

VArc 925.50.135 Shovkoplias, Ivan H. Osnovy arkheolohii. Kyïv, 1964.

Arc 925.50.137 Shovkoplias, Ivan H. Osnovy arkheolohii. 2. vyd. Kyïv, 1972.

Arc 925.50.1 Shovkoplias, Ivan H. Rozvitok radians'koi arkheolohii na Ukraini. Kyiv, 1969.

Arc 936.3.10F Shqiperia arkeologjike - Archaeological Albania. Tiranë, 1971.

Arc 925.280 Shramko, B.A. Drevnosti Severskogo Dontsa. Khar'kov, 1962.

Arc 1583.7 Shrapeznikov', A.N. Katalog' monet' chekannyk' v' Rossii. Sankt Peterburg, 1909.

Arc 585.5F The shrine of Saft el Henneh. (Naville, E.H.) Malagny, 1887.

Arc 785.77 The shrine of St. Peter. (Toynbee, J.M.) London, 1956.

Arc 587.13 The shrines and rock-inscriptions of Ibrim. (Caminos, Ricardo A.) London, 1968.

Arc 1020.15 Shrines of British saints. (Wall, J.C.) London, 1905.

Arc 1033.12.9.10 The shroud. (Walsh, J.E.) N.Y., 1963.

Arc 1033.12.9 The shroud of Christ. (Vignon, P.) Westminster, 1902.

Arc 925.13.145 Shtambok, Anatoii A. Iz tsarstva Ateia v Neapol' Skifskii. Moskva, 1968.

Arc 1582.7 Shubert, Fedor F. Monnayes russes, 1547-1855. Leipsic, 1857.

Arc 1582.7.2PF Shubert, Fedor F. Monnayes russes, 1547-1855. Atlas. Leipsic, 1857.

Arc 1583.1 Shubert, Fedor F. Opisanie Russkikh monet. Sankt Peterburg, 1843.

Arc 1490.92 Shuhaievs'kyi, Valentyn. Funde venezianischer Münzen des 13. Jahrhundert in der Ostukraine als geschichtliche Quelle. Berlin, 1944.

Arc 925.85 Shul'ts, P. Maveolei neapole skifskogo. Moskva, 1953.

Arc 1680.15 Siamese porcelain and other tokens. (Ramsden, H.A.) Yokohama, 1911.

Arc 733.3 Sicilia antiqua. Catania. 1-2,1925-1927 2v.

Arc 1490.98.10F Sicilia numismata. (Giesecke, Walther.) Leipzig, 1923.

Arc 1485.6 Sicilia numismatica. v.1-3. (Paruta, F.) Lugdunum Batavorum, 1723. 2v.

Arc 1490.8.10 Siciliae veteres nummi. (Pennisi, Agostino.) Acireale, 1940.

Arc 733.6 I Siciliani di 15 mila anni fa. (Belgiorno, Franco Libero.) Catania, 1965.

Arc 730.202 Sicula, guibus Sicilae veritis ruderd. (Orville, J.P. d'.) Amsterdam, 1764.

Arc 530.145F Side agorasi ve civarindaki binalar. (Mansel, A.M.) Ankara, 1956.

Arc 705.11 Sieben Karten zur Topographie von Athen. (Curtius, E.) Gotha, 1868.

Arc 705.11PF Sieben Karten zur Topographie von Athen. Atlas. (Curtius, E.) Gotha, 1868.

Arc 1580.20 Die Siebenbürgischen Münzen des furstlich Montenuoro'schen Münzcabinets. (Hess, A.) Frankfurt, 1880.

Arc 1590.25 Siebenbürgishe Münzen und Medaillen von 1538 bis zur Gegenwart. (Resch, Adolf.) Montreal, 1965.

Arc 936.8 Siedziba paleolityczna. (Czarnowski, S.J.) Warszawa, 1910-14. 4 pam.

Arc 1018.26 Siegel, C.C.F. Handbuch der christlich-kirchlichen Alterthümer. Leipzig, 1836-38. 4v.

Arc 1212.6 Siegel. (Rittel, Erich.) Braunschweig, 1970.

Arc 1269.22.3 Siegel. 2. Aufl. (Berchem, E.F. von.) Berlin, 1923.

Arc 1269.5 Die Siegel der Beschöfe von Freising. Inaug. Diss. (Siferlinger, C.) München, 1925.

Arc 1269.10F Die Siegel der deutschen Kaiser und Könige von 751 bis 1913. (Posse, Otto.) Dresden, 1909-13. 5v.

Arc 1269.45 Siegel des Mittelalters von Polen, Lithauen, Schiesien, Pommern und Preussen. (Vossberg, F.A.) Berlin, 1854.

Arc 1510.85 Siegel und Wappen in Sachsen. (Blaschke, Karlheinz.) Leipzig, 1960.

Arc 1212.4 Siegelkunde. (Ewald, W.) München, 1914.

Arc 1298.1.5 Das Siegelrecht des Mittelalters. (Guenther, M.) Stuttgart, 1870.

Arc 1335.150F Die Siegelsammlung des Mannheimer. (Gesellschaft der Freunde.) Manheim, 1897.

Arc 1223.2 Die Siegelschrift (Chuan-shu) in der Ch'ing-Zeit. (Ledderhose, Lothar.) Wiesbaden, 1970.

Arc 1269.5 Siferlinger, C. Die Siegel der Beschöfe von Freising. Inaug. Diss. München, 1925.

Arc 1274.7 Sigilla ecclesiae Hibernicae illustrata. pt.1-4. (Caulfield, R.) Dublin, 1853.

Arc 1255.1F Sigilli antichi romani raccolti e publicati da Vittorio Poggi. (Poggi, Vittorio.) Torino, 1876.

Arc 1259.3F I sigilli dell'archivio vaticano. v.1-3. (Vatican. Archivio Vaticano.) Città del Vaticano, 1937- 5v.

Arc 1261.2F Sigillografía catalana. v.1-3. (Sagarra, Ferran de.) Barcelona, 1916-32. 5v.

Arc 1264.11 Sigillographie de la Normandie. (Farcy, Paul de.) Caen, 1875.

Arc 1264.13 Sigillographie de la ville d'Arras. (Guesnon, A.) Arras, 1865.

Arc 1254.16F Sigillographie de l'empire byzantin. (Schlumberger, G.) Paris, 1884.

Arc 1264.15 Sigillographie des universités de France. (Gardilhon, R.) Paris, 1952.

Arc 1263.3 Sigillographie du Périgord. (Bosredon, P. de.) Perigneux, 1880.

Arc 1264.12 Sigillographie du Poitou jusqu'en 1515. (Eygun, F.) Poitiers, 1938.

Arc 1264.12.5 Sigillographie du Poitou jusqu'en 1515. Thèse. (Eygun, F.) Macon, 1938.

Arc 1264.7 Sigillographie française. (Blanchet, A.) Paris, 1902.

Arc 1261.4 Sigilografía española. (Escudero de la Penna, José Marie.) Madrid, 1875.

Arc 1153.45 Siglarium romanum. (Gerrard, John.) Londini, 1792.

Arc 1330.11 Sigler, Phares O. Numismatic bibliography. Dearborn, Mich., 1951.

Arc 1077.2.3 Le signe de la croix avant de Christianité. (Mortillet, G. de.) Paris, 1866.

Arc 612.34.5 La signification de l'art rupestre paléolithique. (Laming, A.) Paris, 1962.

Arc 595.30F Il significato simbolico delle piramidi egiziane. (Schiaparelli, E.) Roma, 1884.

Arc 1625.5 El signo de pesos. (Moreno, Alvaro.) México, 1965.

Arc 1335.115 Signorelli, A. Collezione del Prof. Angelo Signorelli. pt.1-2. Roma, 1951-52.

Arc 572.2 Signs and wonders upon Pharaoh. (Wilson, John Albert.) Chicago, 1964.

Arc 1033.17.153 Sigoni, I. Relazione della venta a Montevarchi del socrosanto latte. Firenze, 1653.

Arc 895.28 Sigtunna och Norrsunda. (Gihl, Gunnar.) Uppsala, 1925.

Arc 93.42 Sikelika. Palermo. 2-5 5v.

Arc 726.11 Der Silberschatz von Boscoreale. (Michaelis, A.) Berlin, 1896.

Arc 861.31.30 Silbury Hill: background information on the Silbury dig. (Atkinson, Richard J.C.) London, 1968.

Arc 861.11.11 Silchester, the Roman town of Calleva. (Boon, George Counsell.) Newton Abbot, 1974.

Arc 497.100 Silent cities, sacred stones: archaeological discovery in the land of the Bible. (Landay, Jerry M.) London, 1971.

Arc 1510.107 Silesia numismatica. (Dewerdeck, G.) Jauer, 1711.

Arc 1510.135 Silesii in nummis, oder Berühmte Schlesier in Müntzen. (Kundmann, J.C.) Bresslau, 1738.

Arc 1030.4.9 Silloge di alcune iscrizioni. (Marucchi, O.) Roma, 1881.

Arc 403.10 Silva, J.P.N. da. Noções elementares de archeologia. Lisboa, 1878.

Arc 1030.55PF Silvagni, Angelo. Monumenta epigraphica christiana saeculo XIII. v.1-2. Civitate Vaticana, 1943-

Arc 1470.26 The silver coinage of Crete. (MacDonald, George.) London, 1919?

Arc 1538.8 The silver coins of England. (Hawkins, E.) London, 1887.

Arc 403.21 Silverberg, R. Great adventures in archaeology. N.Y., 1964.

Arc 1138.7 Silvestre, J.B. Universal palaeography. London, 1850. 2v.

Arc 1033.100 Simbolismo dei primi secoli. (Carini, Isidoro.) Romae, 1890.

Arc 1588.6.20 Simdiye kadar görülmiyen Cimri Sikkesi. (Saglani, O.F.) n.p., 1949.

Arc 838.12 Simões, A.F. Escriptos diversos. Coimbra, 1888.

Arc 838.13 Simões, A.F. Introducção à archeologia da Peninsula Iberica. pt.1. Lisboa, 1878.

Arc 630.22 Simon, Erika. Die Geburt der Aphrodite. Berlin, 1959.

Arc 66.1.166 Simon, Marcel. Verus Israel. Paris, 1948.

Arc 1488.18 Simonetti, Luigi. Manuale di numismatica ialiana medioevale e moderna dalla caduta dell'impero romano alla rivoluzione francese. v.1, pt. 1. Firenze, 1965.

Arc 497.38 Simons, J.J. Opgravingen in Palestina. Roermond-Maaseik, 1935.

Arc 505.5.120 Simons, Jan Jozef. Jerusalem in the Old Testament; researches and theories. Leiden, 1952.

Arc 505.2 Simonsen, D. Sculptures et inscriptions de Palmyre. Copenhagen, 1889.

Arc 391.5 Simony, C. de. Un curieuse figure d'artiste, Girault de Prangey, 1802-1892. Dijon, 1937.

Arc 853.10 Simony, F. Die Alterthümer vovon Hallstätter Salzberg. Wien, 1851.

Arc 723.38 Simposia Internazionale di Protostoria Italiana. Atti. Roma, 1969.

Arc 861.21.12 Simpson, H.T. Archaeologia Adelensis...West Riding of Yorkshire. London, 1879.

Arc 403.8 Simpson, J.Y. Archaeological essays. Edinburgh, 1872. 2v.

Arc 870.7 Simpson, J.Y. Archaic sculpturings of cups, circles. Edinburgh, 1867.

Arc 1680.13 Simpson, Justin. List of the Lincolnshire series of tradesmen's tokens. London, 1880.

Arc 875.90 Simpson, William D. Dundarg Castle. Edinburgh, 1954.

Arc 875.44 Simpson, William D. The province of Mar. Aberdeen, 1943.

Arc 875.95 Simpson, William D. The Viking congress. Edinburgh, 1954.

Htn Arc 1033.12.32* Sindon evangelica. (Pingone, E.F.) Augustae Taurinorum, 1581.

Arc 1033.12.32.2 Sindon evangelica. (Pingone, E.F.) Augustae Taurinorum, 1777.

Arc 1020.9.28 Sindone, R. Altarium et reliquarum...basilicae vaticanae. Romae, 1744.

Arc 1027.12.11 Sindone. Della sacrosanta basilica di S. Pietro. Roma, 1750.

Arc 1033.12.41 Sindone evangelica, historica e theologica. (Solaro, A.) Torino, 1627.

Arc 1330.15 Singhal, C.R. Bibliography of Indian coins. v.1-2. Bombay, 1950-52.

Arc 1138.19 Sinks, Perry W. The reign of the manuscript. Boston, 1917.

Arc 1033.10 Sinnbildliches die koptische Kunst. (Ebers, G.) Leipzig, 1892.

Arc 935.40 Sinop ta candar ogullarizamanina. (Sakir, M,) Istanbul, 1934.

Arc 700.64 Sinos, Stefan. Die vorklassischen Hausformen in der Ägäis. Mainz, 1971.

Arc 1033.35.71 Sionnet, A. Lettre à...Piolin sur la legende hébraïque du titre de la viaie croix. n.p., n.d.

Arc 432.34 Sir Alexander Cunningham and...Indian archaeology. (Abu, Imam.) Dacca, 1966.

Arc 397.15 Sir George Macdonald, 1862-1940. (Curle, Alexander O.) London, 1941?

Arc 402.11 Sir Hercules Read. (Dalton, O.M.) London, 1936.

Arc 736.2.2 Siracusa pei Viaggiatori. (Politi, G.) Siracusa, 1835.

Arc 830.74 Sirand, Alexandre. Antiquités générales de l'Ain. Bourg-en-Bresse, 1855.

Arc 458.12 Sircar, Dineschandra. Indian epigraphical glossary. 1. ed. Delhi, 1966.

Arc 435.86 Sircar, Dineschandra. Indian epigraphy. 1. ed. Delhi, 1965.

Arc 835.5 Siret, H. Les premiers ages du métal dans le sud-est de l'Espagne. Antwerp, 1887. 2v.

Arc 1033.12.24 Siriiskaia chasha v Ushgule. (Chubinashvili, G.N.) n.p., 1941.

Arc 936.220.120 Sirmium. Beograd, 1971- 3v.

Htn Arc 1163.17.10* Sisson, C.J. Photographic slides of English manuscripts. n.p., n.d.

Arc 925.13.205 Sistemy znakov Severnogo Prichernomoria. (Drachuk, Viktor S.) Kiev, 1975.

Arc 505.51 Le site archéologique de Mishrifé-Qatna. Thèse. (Mesnil du Buisson, R. du.) Paris, 1935.

Arc 830.160.10 Le site d'Aeria. (Chevalier, Alexandre.) Valence, 1968.

Arc 830.337 Le site et les lampes votives du Chasterland de Lardiers. (Dupont, J.) Cavaillon, 1962?

Arc 889.30.5 Le site sacré de Fontaine-Valmont. (Faider-Feytmans, Germaine.) Morlanwelz? 196-.

Arc 455.5 Site urbain et sites funéraires des environs de Pondichéry. (Casal, Jean Marie.) Paris, 1956.

Htn Arc 726.55* Sito, et antichita della città di Pozzuolo e del sus amenissimo distretto. (Mazzella, S.) Napoli, 1606.

Arc 772.7 Sito di Roma e la carta. 2. ed. (Riva, Giuseppe.) Vicenza, 1846.

Arc 635.213 Sittl, C. Parerga zur alten Kunstgeschichte. Würzburg, 1893.

Arc 936.14.295 Siuchniński, Kazimierz. Klasyfikacja czasowo-przestrzenna kultur neolitycznych na Pomorzu zachodnim. wyd. 1. Szczecin, 1969.

Arc 543.25.15 Sivaramamenti, C. Le stupa du Barabudur. Paris? 1961.

Arc 1418.13 Sivaramamurti, C. Numismatic parallels of Kālidāsa. Madras, 1945.

Arc 432.15 Sivaramamurto, C. Indian epigraphy and south Indian scripts. Madra, 1952.

Arc 1480.54 The six main AES coinages of Augustus. (Grant, Michael.) Edinburgh, 1953.

Arc 1020.117 Six months in the Apennines. (Stokes, Margaret.) London, 1892.

Arc 588.6 Six temples at Thebes. 1896. (Petrie, W.M.F.) London, 1897.

Arc 505.65F A sixth century monastery at Beth-Shan (Scythopolis). (Fitzgerald, G.M.) Philadelphia, 1939.

Arc 1190.82 Siyakat yazisi. (Yazir, Mahmud.) Istanbul, 1941.

Arc 1190.80 Die Siyâquat-Schrift in der türkischen Finanzverwaltung. (Fekete, Lajos.) Budapest, 1955.

Arc 537.10 Sjoeqvist, Erik. Reports on excavations in Cyprus. Stockholm, 1947. 2v.

Arc 895.62 Sjoevold, T. The iron age settlement of Arctic Norway. v.1-2. Tromsö, 1962-74.

Arc 1568.5 Skaare, Kolbjørn. Moneta Norwei. Oslo, 1966.

Arc 1588.4 Skalsky, G. Denár knizete Vaclava Svatého a. Praha, 1929.

Arc 890.209 Skandinairens hällristningar. (Holmberg, A.E.) Stockholm, 1848.

Arc 893.8 Skandinaviska nordens ur-invånare. (Nilsson, S.) Stockholm, 1862-66. 2v.

Arc 875.14.10 Skara Brae. (Childe, V.G.) London, 1931.

Arc 1433.75 Skarb dirhemov arabskich z Czechowa. (Czapkicwicz, A.) Warszawa, 1957.

Arc 1588.1.50 Skarb monet arabskich z klukowicz powiat siemiatycze. (Polskiej Akademja Nauk. Instytut Historyjka Kultury Materialnej.) Wrocław, 1964.

Arc 1588.1.38 Skarb monet arabskich z okolic Drohiczyna nad Bugiem. (Czapkiewicz, Maria.) Kraków, 1960.

Arc 1588.1.40 Skarb srebrny z miejscowosci Ochle. (Kmietowicz, A.) Wrocław, 1962.

Arc 936.4 Skarby brązowe z epoki wspólnoty. (Szafrański, W.) Warszawa, 1955.

Arc 682.25.40 Skeat, T.C. The Dorians in archaeology. London, 1932?

Arc 1163.17 Skeat, W.W. Twelve facsimiles of old English manuscripts. Oxford, 1892.

Arc 609.23 The skeletal remains of Bambandyanalo. (Galloway, Alexander.) Johannesburg, 1959.

Arc 855.2 Skelton, J. The Royal House of Stuart. London, 1890.

Arc 87.1.20 Die Skene der Alten. (Lohde, L.) Berlin, 1860.

Arc 1625.1 Sketch of coinage of Mexican revolutionary General Morelos. (Low, Lyman H.) N.Y., 1886.

Arc 823.20 Sketla segobrani. v.1-3. Sant-Brieg, 1923-25.

Arc 925.13.160 Skifi. (Petrov, Viktor P.) Kyiv, 1968.

Arc 925.13.10 Skifiia i Bospor". (Rostovtsev, M.I.) Leningrad, 1925.

Arc 925.13.75 Skifiia VII-V vekov do nashei ery. (Iatsenko, I.V.) Moskva, 1959.

Arc 925.13.195 Skifskie drevnosti. Kiev, 1973.

Arc 925.13.155 Skifskii dospekh. (Chernenko, Evgenii V.) Kiev, 1968.

Arc 925.13.175 Skify. (Grakov, Boris N.) Moskva, 1971.

Arc 925.13.120 Skify. (Smirnov, Aleksei P.) Moskva, 1966.

Arc 925.13.140 Skify dneprovskogo lesostepnogo Levoberezh'ia. (Il'inskaia, Vervara A.) Kiev, 1968.

Arc 925.13.25 Skify i gunny. (Toll', N.R.) Praga, 1928.

Arc 925.50.315 Skify skhidnego Krymu v V-III st. do n.e. (Iakavenko, Ieleonora V.) Kyïv, 1974.

Arc 595.8 Skinner, J.R. The Great Pyramid of Jizeh. Cincinnati, 1871. 2 pam.

Arc 758.2.5F Das Skizzenbuch des G. Dosio im staatlichen Kupferstichkabinett zu Berlin. (Dosio, G.A.) Berlin, 1933.

Arc 530.15 Skizzierte Gedanken eines Kunst freundes. (Wedel, F.) Neustadt, 1905.

Arc 936.100.45 Škobalj, Ante. Obredne gomile. Sveti Križ na Čiovu, 1970.

Arc 302.36 Skopje, Yugoslavia. Arheoloski muzej zbornik. 1955+ 2v.

Arc 1588.1.96 Skorowidz monet polskich od 1506 do 1825. (Beyer, Karol.) Warszawa, 1973.

Arc 936.140.10 Škorpil, Hermeneyild. Mogili Ot. Kh. i K. Shkorpil. Plovdiv, 1898.

Arc 635.218 Skovgaard, N.K. Apollon - Gavlgruppen fra Zeustemp. Olympia. København, 1905.

Arc 83.3.5 Skrifter. (Svenska Institutet i Rom.) Lund. 2-10 6v.

Arc 925.12.15 Skul'ptura i zhivopis' Bospora. (Ivanova, A.P.) Kiev, 1961.

Arc 674.3.3 Die Skulpturen des Asklepiostempels von Epidauros. (Crome, J.F.) Berlin, 1951.

Arc 684.1.25 Die Skulpturen des Zeustempels zu Olympia. (Buschor, E.) Giessen, 1924. 2v.

Arc 936.195.175 Skutil, Josef. Pravěké nálezy na Kloboucku. Klobuka, 1939.

Arc 925.13.12 Skythien und der Bosporus. (Rostovtsev, M.I.) Berlin, 1931.

Arc 983.6 Slafter, E.F. Prehistoric copper implements. Boston, 1879.

Arc 1615.1 Slafter, E.F. The Vermont coinage. Montpelier, 1870.

Arc 600.65F The slain soldiers of Neb-hebek-Re' Mentu-hotpe. (Winlock, H.E.) N.Y., 1945.

Arc 853.200 Ślask starożytny a Imperium Rzymskie. (Konik, E.) Warszawa, 1959.

Arc 853.65.55 Śląsk w pradziejach Polski. Wrocław, 1970.

Arc 1675.51.25 Śląski medalier Jan Wysocki. (Wichura-Zajdel, E.) Katowia, 1961.

Arc 185.2.5 Slaskie sprawozdania archeologiczne. Wrocław. 6,1963+

Arc 925.50.390 Slaviane Dneprovskogo Levoberezh'ia. (Sukhobokov, Oleg V.) Kiev, 1975.

Arc 923.118 Slaviane i Rus'. Moskva, 1968.

Arc 936.165.45 Slaviane VI-IX wkov v Moldavii. (Ratalovich, Isak A.) Kishinev, 1972.

Arc 936.40.5 Slaviano-bulgarskato selishte brai selo Popina. (Vuzharova, Z.) Sofiia, 1956.

Arc 1163.3.60 Slaviano-russkaia paleografiia. (Sololevskii, A.I.) Sankt Peterburg, 1908.

Arc 1163.3.15 Slavianskaia kirillovskaia paleografiia. (Karskii, E.F.) Leningrad, 1928.

Arc 936.40.35 Slavianski i slavianobulgarski selishta v bulgarskite semi. (Vŭzharova, Zhivka N.) Sofiia, 1965.

Arc 925.150.45 Slavianskie drevnosti Belorussii. (Pobol', Leonid D.) Minsk, 1971.

Arc 925.150.46 Slavianskie drevnosti Belorussii. (Pobol', Leonid D.) Minsk, 1973.

Arc 925.150.47 Slavianskie drevnosti Belorussii. (Pobol', Leonid D.) Minsk, 1974.

Arc 925.50.310 Slavianskie drevnosti VI-IX vv. mezhdu Dneprom i Zapadnym Bugom. (Rusanova, Irina P.) Moskva, 1973.

Arc 1163.3 Slavjano-russkaja paleografija. (Sreznevski, T.T.) Sankt Peterburg, 1885.

Arc 936.195.290 Slavníkova Libice. (Turek, Rudolf.) Praha, 1946.

Arc 936.14.30 Sławianski rodowod. (Tasienica, P.) Warszawa, 1961.

Arc 936.195.215 Slawisch-awarisches Gräberfeld in Nové Zámky. (Čilinská, Zlata.) Bratislava, 1966.

Arc 936.195.160 Slawisch-awarisches Gräberfeld in Šturovo. 1. Aufl. (Točík, Anton.) Bratislava, 1968.

Arc 923.50 Slawische Altertumskunde das östlichen Mitteleuropa im 9. und 10. Jahrhundert. v.1-3. (Preidel, Helmut.) Grafeling bei München, 1961-

Arc 853.254F Die slawischen Funde aus dem hanoverschen Wendland. (Grenz, Rudolf.) Neumünster, 1961.

Arc 1276.15F Slesvigske kobstaeders og herreders segl indtil 1660. (Grandjean, P.B.) København, 1953.

Arc 936.220.115 Sliri i Grci, njihcvi kulturni odnosi u prošlosti naše zemlje na osnovu arheološkog materijala. (Mano-Zisi, Djordje.) Beograd, 1959.

Arc 287.2F Slisok izdanii. (Moskovskoe Arkheologicheskoe Obshchestvo.) Moskva, 1913.

Arc 936.195.100F Slovanská pohřebiště za střední doby hradištní na Moravě. (Dostál, Bořivoj.) Praha, 1966.

Arc 936.195.40F Slovanské mohyly v Skalici. (Budinsky-Krička, V.) Bratislava, 1959.

Arc 936.195.280 Slovansko-avarské pohrebisko pri Z'ahoiskej Bystrici. 1. vyd. (Kraskovská, L'udmila.) Bratislava, 1972.

Arc 936.195.105 Slovenská Akademia Vied. Archeologický Ústav, Nitra. Pravek Slovenska. Bratislava, 1965- 2v.

Arc 302.46 Slovenská Akadémia Vied. Archeologický Ústav, Nitra. Studijné zvesti. Nitra. 2,1957+ 6v.

Arc 1318.9 Slovenská numizmatika. Bratislava. 1,1970+ 2v.

Arc 936.15.20 Slovensko a rémske impérium. (Pelikan, 'Old.) Bratislava, 1960.

Arc 936.195.37.5 Slovensko na úsvite dejím. 1. vyd. (Chropovský, Bohuslav.) Bratislava, 1970.

Arc 936.195.65 Slovensko v mladšij dobe kaminej. (Novotný, B.) Bratislava, 1958.

Arc 925.50.180 Slov'iano-rus'ki starozhytnosti. Kyïv, 1969.

Arc 925.50.385 Slov'iany ta ïkh susidy v stepovomu Podniprov'ï II-XIII st. (Smilenko, Alla T.) Kyïv, 1975.

Arc 936.14.243 Słowianie w pradziejach siem polskich. (Nosek, Stefan.) Kraków, 1946.

Arc 875.2 Small, A. Interesting Roman antiquities recently discovered in Fife. Edinbrugh, 1823.

Arc 875.45 Small, Alan. Craig Phadrig; interim report on 1971 excavation. Dundee, 1972.

Arc 875.133 Small, Alan. St. Ninian's Isle and its treasure. London, 1973. 2v.

Arc 855.5 Small, J.W. Scottish market crosses. Stirling, 1900.

Arc 1033.12.234 A small brass cup...Rodil, Harris. (Murray, D.) Glasgow, 1898.

Arc 1480.32 A small bronze of Nero. (Mabbott, T.O.) Rome, 1936.

Arc 858.91 The small towns of Roman Britain. Oxford, 1975.

Arc 925.50.115F Smilenko, Alla T. Hlodos'ki skarby. Kyïv, 1965.

Arc 925.50.385 Smilenko, Alla T. Slov'iany ta ïkh susidy v stepovomu Podniprov'ï II-XIII st. Kyïv, 1975.

Arc 925.175 Smipnov, A.P. Arkheologicheskie pamiatniki na territorii Mariiskoi ASSR. Kozmodem'iansk, 1949-

Arc 925.50.50 Smirniv, A.P. Problemy istorii Sever. Prichernomor'ia. Moskva, 1959.

Arc 925.50.35 Smirnov, A.P. Istoriia ii arkheologiia srednevek. Kryma. Moskva, 1958.

Arc 925.135 Smirnov, A.P. Novaia nakhodka vostochnogo serebra v Priural'e. Moskva, 1957.

Arc 925.13.120 Smirnov, Aleksei P. Skify. Moskva, 1966.

Arc 925.13.110 Smirnov, K.F. Savromaty. Moskva, 1964.

Arc 925.97 Smirnov, K.F. Severskii kurgan. Moskva, 1953.

Arc 1433.91 Smirnova, O.I. Katalog monet s gorodischa Pendzhikent...1949-1956 gg. Moskva, 1963.

Arc 925.50.55 Smishko, M.I. Karpats'ki kurhany pershoi polov. I tysiacholettia nash. ery. Kyïv, 1960.

Arc 1030.42 Smit, E.L. De oud christelijke monumenten van Spanje. 's-Gravenhage, 1916.

X Cg Arc 855.8 Smith, A.C. Guide to British and Roman antiquities in north Wiltshire. n.p., 1884. 2v.

Arc 1613.12 Smith, A.M. Coins and coinage. The United States Mint, Philadelphia. Philadelphia, 1884.

Arc 861.31.15F Smith, Alfred Charles. Guide to the British and Roman antiquities of the North Wiltshire downs. 2. ed. Devizes, 1885.

Arc 1340.7 Smith, Alfred M. Illustrated encyclopedia of gold and silver coins of the world. Philadelphia, 1886.

Arc 861.8 Smith, C.R. The antiquities of Richborough, Reculver, and Lyme. London, 1850.

Arc 403.2 Smith, C.R. Collectanea antiqua. London, 1848-80. 7v.

Arc 858.7 Smith, C.R. Etchings of ancient remains. London, 1852.

Arc 861.18 Smith, C.R. Illustrations of Roman London. London, 1858.

X Cg Arc 861.6 Smith, C.R. Report on excavations made on the site of the Roman Castrum at Lymne. London, 1852.

Arc 973.10 Smith, Carl S. The two Teeth site [South Dakota]. Lincoln, 1968.

Arc 858.28 Smith, Charles R. Retrospections, social and archaeological. London, 1883-91. 3v.

Arc 600.4.13 Smith, E.M. Naukratis. Diss. Vienna, 1926.

Arc 975.10 Smith, E.R. The archaeology of Deadman Cave, Utah. Salt Lake City, 1941.

Arc 435.2.35F Smith, E.W. Akbar's tomb, Sikandarah, near Agra. Allahabad, 1909.

Arc 435.2.30F Smith, E.W. Moghul colour decoration of Agra. Allahabad, 1901.

Arc 861.16.7 Smith, F. Prehistoric man and the Cambridge gravels. Cambridge, Eng., 1926.

Arc 815.2 Smith, F.W. The Pompeia. Saratoga, 1890.

Arc 875.34 Smith, Frederick. Some investigations into palaeolithic remains in Scotland. Glasgow, 1898-99.

Arc 870.11 Smith, Frederick. The stone ages in northern Britain and Ireland. London, 1909.

Arc 590.8F Smith, G. Elliot. Mémoires présentés à l'Institut Égyptien. Le Caire, 1906.

Arc 861.41 Smith, H. Notes on prehistoric burial in Sussex. n.p., n.d.

Arc 953.19.5 Smith, Harlan I. An album of prehistoric Canadian art. Ottawa, 1923.

Arc 956.1 Smith, Harlan I. Archaeological collection from the southern interior of British Columbia. Museum of Geological Survey, Canada. Ottawa, 1913.

Arc 953.19 Pamphlet box. Smith, Harlan I. Archaeology. United States and Canada.

Arc 1333.9 Smith, Harlan P. Catalogue...coins of the U.S. Philadelphia, 1906.

Arc 861.21.25F Smith, Henry E. Reliquae isurianae; remains of Roman Isurium. London, 1852.

Arc 861.31.25 Smith, Isobel F. Windmill Hill and Avebury. Oxford, 1965.

Arc 865.13 Smith, John. Choir Gaur...Orrery of Druids...Stonehenge. 2. ed. Salisbury, 1771. 2 pam.

Arc 865.13.2 Smith, John. Choir Gaur...Orrery of Druids...Stonehenge. 2. ed. Salisbury, 1771.

Arc 605.201 Smith, R.M. History of the recent discovery at Cyrene. London, 1864.

X Cg Arc 435.2.20F Smith, V.A. The Jain stûpa and other antiquities of Mathûra. Allahabad, 1901.

Arc 1373.9 Smith, W. Literae de re nummaria. Newcastle-upon-Tyne, 1729.

Arc 547.28 Smith, W.S. Ancient Egypt as represented in the Museum of Fine Arts. Boston, 1942.

Arc 861.18.13 Smith, Washington G. On a palaeolithic floor at north east London. London, 1884.

Arc 403.9 Smolin, V.F. Opyt instruktsii po sostaleniiu arkheologicheskikh kart. Kazan', 1921.

Arc 69.2 Smyrna. Enaggelikēs Scholēs. Moyseion kai Bibliothēkē. Smyrna. 1873-1886 3v.

Arc 925.50.320 Smyrnov, Stanislav V. Paleolit Dniprovs'koho Nadporizhzhia. Kyïv, 1973.

Arc 595.9.5 Smyth, C.P. Life and work at the Great Pyramid. Edinburgh, 1867. 3v.

Arc 595.9.2 Smyth, C.P. Our inheritance in the Great Pyramid. London, 1864.

Arc 595.9 Smyth, C.P. Our inheritance in the Great Pyramid. London, 1877.

Arc 595.9.3 Smyth, C.P. Our inheritance in the Great Pyramid. 4. ed. London, 1880.

Arc 1025.9 Smyth, E. Recent excavations in American Christian cemeteries. Worcester, 1882.

Arc 923.130 Snariazhenie vsadnika i verkhovogo konia na Rusi IX-XIII vv. (Kirpicknikov, Anatolii N.) Leningrad, 1973.

Htn Arc 1535.1* Snelling, T. A view of the silver coin and coinage of England. London, 1762.

Arc 672.1.61 Snijder, G.A.S. Kretische Kunst. Berlin, 1936.

Arc 1148.16 Snimki ne" Kondakaria XII-XIII. (Amphilochii, A.) Moskva, 1869.

Arc 700.68A Snodgrass, Anthony M. The dark age of Greece: an archaeological survey of the eleventh to the eighth centuries B.C. Edinburgh, 1971.

Arc 1660.8 Snowden, J.R. A description of the medals of Washington. Philadelphia, 1861.

Arc 983.9.9 Snyder, J.F. A primitive urn-burial. Washington, 1891.

Arc 785.63 The so-called Altar of Calvinus on the Palatine hill, in Rome. (Broderick, B.F.) N.Y., 1930. 3 pam.

Arc 983.8 The so called "gorgets". (Peabody, Charles.) Andover, 1906.

Arc 936.12.5 Sobociński, M. Materiał kostny zwierzecy z wykopalisk wczesnośredniowiecznego grodziska w Bonikowie. Poznań, 1963.

Arc 1675.19.20 Sobranie trudov po russkoi voennoi medalistike i istorii. v.1-2. (Rikhter, Vladimir G.) Parizh, 1972.

Arc 1623.6 Sobrino, Jose Manuel. La moneda mexicana. Mexico, 1972.

Arc 405.3 Sochineniia. (Usov, S.A.) Moskva, 1892. 2v.

Arc 1018.30 Die socialen Verhältnisse. (Böhmer, W.) Breslau, 1836.

Arc 94.7 Sociedad Arqueologica de Carmona. Memorias de la sociedad arqueologica de Carmona. Carmona, 1887. 9v.

Arc 94.52 Sociedad Arqueológica Tarraconense. Premio "Cronista José Pujol". Tarragona. 2,1953

Arc 94.15 Sociedad Cordobesa de Arqueología y Excursiones. Boletín. Córdoba. 1928

Arc 838.16F Sociedad Española de Amigos del Arte. Exposición de arte prehistórico español. Madrid, 1921.

Arc 838.27 Sociedad Española de Antropología, Etnografía y Prehistoria. Corona de estudios. Madrid, 1941.

Arc 383.95 Società Archeologia Comense. Raccolta di scritti. Como, 1954.

Arc 93.37F Società di Storia Patria per la Sicilia Orientale, Catania. Monografie archeologiche della Sicilia. Series 3. 1,1956

Arc 1488.3 Società Numismatica Italiana. Bibliografia numismatica. Milano, 1918-20.

Arc 93.7 Società Piemontese di Archeologia e Belle Arti. Atti. Torino. 1875-1958 15v.

Arc 93.3 Societa Reale di Napoli. Memorie della Reale Academia. Napoli. 1-6,1911-1942 4v.

Arc 584.100.15 La Société archéologique d'Alexandrie à 80 ans. (Lackany, Rudames Sany.) Alexandrie, 1973.

Arc 830.78.100F Société Archéologique d'Eure-et-Loire. Dallas tumulaires et pierres tombales du département d'Eure-et-Loire. Chartres, 1895-1930. 2v.

Arc 113.3.20 Société Archéologique du Midi de la France. Bulletin. Toulouse. 1869-1945 19v.

Arc 584.2 Société d'Archéologie Copte, Cairo. Bulletin. 4,1938+ 10v.

Arc 584.2.2 Société d'Archéologie Copte, Cairo. Bulletin. Index, 1-10, 1935-44. Le Caire, n.d.

Arc 113.5 Société d'Archéologie de Saint-Jean-d'Angély et de sa Région. Bulletin. Saint-Jean-d'Angély. 2,1924+

Arc 396.4.20 Société des Antiquaires de l'Ouest, Poitiers. Monument érigé à la mémoire de R.P. de la Croix. Poitiers, 1912.

Arc 830.155 Société des Antiquaires du Centre, Bourges. Catalogue du Musée lapidaire de Bourges. Bourges, 1873.

Arc 101.11 Société d'Histoire, d'Archéologie et de Tradition Gauloises. Centre de documentation. Circulaire d'information. Paris. 1,1964+

Arc 101.10 Société d'Histoire, d'Archéologie et de Tradition Gauloises. Gaule. Paris. 2-24,1956-1963 2v.

Arc 830.167 Société d'Histoire et d'Archéologie de Châlon-sur-Saône. Musée Denon. Catalogue des collections lapidaires. Châlon-sur-Saône, 1936.

Arc 101.5 Société d'Histoire et d'Archéologie de Nimes et du Gard. Bulletin. Nimes. 1933-1939

Arc 830.16.5 Société Eduenne. Autun archéologique. Autun, 1848.

Arc 1315.1 Société Francaise de Numismatique. Annuaire. Paris. 1-20,1866-1896 20v.

Arc 1315.1.5 Société Francaise de Numismatique. Comptes rendu. Paris, 1869-75. 7v.

Arc 19.4 Société Française des Fouilles Archéologiques. Bulletin. Paris. 1-5,1904-1924 2v.

Arc 113.1 Société Française pour la Conservation des Monuments Historiques, Séances tennes en 1839. Caen, 1839.

Arc 830.50 Société Historique et Archéologique de Langres. Catalogue du Musée. Langres, 1902.

Arc 830.49 Société Historique et Archéologique du Périgord. Questionnaire. Périgueux, 1874.

Arc 100.1.10 Société Nationale des Antiquaires de France. Annuaire. Paris. 1848-1855 4v.

Arc 100.1.8 Société Nationale des Antiquaires de France. Bulletin. 1901+ 36v.

Arc 100.1.7 Société Nationale des Antiquaires de France. Centenaire (1804-1904). Compte-rendu de la journée du 11 avril 1904. Paris, 1904.

Arc 100.1.6 Société Nationale des Antiquaires de France. Centenaire 1804-1904. Recueil de mémoires. Paris, 1904.

Arc 383.53 Société Nationale des Antiquaires de France. Mélanges en hommage à la mémoire de Fr. Martroye. Paris, 1940.

Arc 100.1 Société Nationale des Antiquaires de France. Mémoires. Paris. 1-9 86v.

Arc 830.200 Société Nationale des Antiquaires de France. Mémorial d'un voyage d'études. Paris, 1953.

Arc 820.8F Société Nationale des Antiquaires de France. Rapport de la commission...sur les antiquaires gallo-romaines. Paris, 1830.

Arc 100.1.12 Pamphlet box. Société Nationale des Antiquaires de France.

Arc 403.12.2 Société Préhistorique de France. Manuel de recherches préhistoriques. 2. éd. Paris, 1929.

Arc 584.100 Société Royale d'Archéologie d'Alexandrie. Bulletin. Alexandrie. 1-41,1898-1956 11v.

Arc 584.100.3 Société Royale d'Archéologie d'Alexandrie. Bulletin. Index analytique, 1-41 (1898-1956). Alexandrie, 1937-63. 2v.

Arc 584.100.5 Société Royale d'Archéologie d'Alexandrie. Conférence. Alexandrie. 1,1964+

Arc 584.100.10 Société Royale d'Archéologie d'Alexandrie. Mémoires. Le Caire. 1-8,1922-1936 4v.

Arc 584.100.20F Société Royale d'Archéologie d'Alexandrie. Monuments de l'Egypte gréco-romaine. Bergamo. 1-2,1926-1934 3v.

Arc 273.10 Société Royale d'Archéologie de Bruxelles. Annales. Bruxelles. 1-50,1887-1961 38v.

Arc 273.10.5 Société Royale d'Archéologie de Bruxelles. Annuaire. Bruxelles. 16-26,1905-1925 5v.

Arc 273.10.12 Société Royale d'Archéologie de Bruxelles. Bulletin. Bruxelles.

Arc 273.10.8 Société Royale d'Archéologie de Bruxelles. Tables des publications. Bruxelles. 1887-1911

Arc 1518.10 Société Royale de Numismatique de Belgique. Exposition numismatique, Bruxelles, Bibliothèque Albert I., 30 avril-24 mai, 1966. Bruxelles, 1966.

Arc 1318.3.7 La Société Suisse...de 1879 à 1896, notices divers. (Société Suisse de Numismatique.) Genève, 1896.

Arc 1318.3 Société Suisse de Numismatique. Bulletin. Fribourg. 1-11,1882-1892 4v.

Arc 1318.3.6 Société Suisse de Numismatique. Regiser zu Bulletin, v.1-11; Revue suisse de numismatique, v.1-24. Bern, 1929.

Arc 1318.3.5 Société Suisse de Numismatique. Revue suisse de numismatique. Genève. 1,1891+ 19v.

Arc 1318.3.7 Société Suisse de Numismatique. La Société Suisse...de 1879 à 1896, notices divers. Genève, 1896.

Arc 323.4 Society for American Archaeology. Seminars in archaeology: 1955. Salt Lake City, 1956.

Author and Title Listing

Arc 48.10 Society for Libyan Studies. Annual report. London. 1,1969+
Arc 970.2 Society for Pennsylvania Archaeology. Publications. Athens. 1,1931
Arc 74.4.12 Pamphlet box. Society for Promotion of Hellenic Studies.
Arc 74.4.15 Society for the Promotion of Hellenic Studies. A classified catalogue of the books, pamphlets and maps in the library. London, 1924.
Arc 74.4.17 Society for the Promotion of Hellenic Studies. First supplementary catalogue of lantern slides. London, 1914.
Arc 74.4.1 Society for the Promotion of Hellenic Studies. Journal. Index. v.9-42. London, 1898-1923. 3v.
Arc 74.4.1.5 Society for the Promotion of Hellenic Studies. Journal. Numismatic index, 1880-1969. Cambridge, Eng., 1971.
Arc 74.4.2F Society for the Promotion of Hellenic Studies. Journal. Plates 1-83. v.1-8. London, 1888?
Arc 74.4 Society for the Promotion of Hellenic Studies. Journal of Hellenic studies. London. 1,1880+ 60v.
Arc 74.4.14 Society for the Promotion of Hellenic Studies. Rules and list of members. London, 1891. 2 pam.
Arc 74.4.16 Society for the Promotion of Hellenic Studies. Supplement to subject catalogue of joint library. London. 1-19 15v.
Arc 74.4.4F Society for the Promotion of Hellenic Studies. Supplementary papers. London. 1-2 2v.
Arc 74.4.4 Society for the Promotion of Hellenic Studies. Supplementary papers. London. 3,1900+ 5v.
Arc 143.2.5 Society of Antiquaries of Scotland. Account of the institution and progress of the society. Edinburgh. 2,1784
Arc 143.2 Society of Antiquaries of Scotland. Archaeologia Scotica. Edinburgh, 1792- 5v.
NEDL Arc 143.1 Society of Antiquaries of Scotland. Proceedings. Edinburgh. 1-63,1851-1929
Arc 143.1 Society of Antiquaries of Scotland. Proceedings. Edinburgh. 64,1929+ 32v.
Arc 143.1.5 Society of Antiquaries of Scotland. Proceedings. Index. v.25-81. Edinburgh, 1897-1968. 2v.
Arc 143.1.10 Pamphlet box. Society of Antiquaries of Scotland.
Arc 41.1 Society of Biblical Archaeology. Proceedings. London. 1-40 37v.
Arc 41.1.5 Society of Biblical Archaeology. Proceedings. Index, v.11-30. London, n.d. 2v.
Arc 41.2 Society of Biblical Archaeology. Transactions. London. 1-9 9v.
Arc 41.2.2 Society of Biblical Archaeology. Transactions. Index, v.1-9. London, n.d.
Arc 136.1.6 Society of Noviomagus. Momentores minutes of the meeting. London, 1845.
Arc 628.2 Socrate et Diotime. (Jahn, O.) Greifswald, 1846. 9 pam.
Arc 1033.44.15 Sodo, G. Il monogramma del nome ss. di Gesú. Napoli, 1885.
Arc 1153.32 Söldner, Georg. Die abgeleiteten Verba in den tironischen Noten. Inaug. Ddiss. Borna, 1916.
Arc 1550.5 Sølo-og guldmøntfod. (Wilcke, Julius.) Kjøbenhavn, 1930.
Arc 1548.5 Soemod, Jørgen. Danmarks og Norges mønter, 1448-1540. Kjøbenhavn, 1967.
Arc 936.40.30F Sofia. Naroden Arkheologicheski Muzei. Madara. Sofiia, 1934.
Arc 302.20 Sofia. Naroden Arkheologicheski Muzei. Razkopki i prochzvani. Sofiia. 1+
Arc 302.20F Sofia. Naroden Arkheologicheski Muzei. Razkopki i prochzvani. Sofiia. 3+
Arc 815.16F Sogliano, A. La Basilica di Pompei. Napoli, 1911. 6 pam.
Arc 790.214F Sogliano, A. Le pitture murali campane. Napoli, 1880.
Arc 810.51 Sogliano, A. Pompei nel suo sviluppo storico. Roma, 1937.
Arc 600.40 Soknopaiou Nesos. (Boak, A.E.R.) Ann Arbor, 1935.
Arc 925.12.6 Sokrovishcha ischeznuvshikh gorodov. (Shevchenko, V.) Moskva, 1948.
Arc 925.13.165 Sokrovishcha prichernomorskikh kurganov. (Tsvetaeva, Galina A.) Moskva, 1968.
Arc 936.165.65 Sokrovishcha pyrkolaba Gangura. (Ketraru, Nikolai A.) Kishinev, 1973.
Arc 925.13.130 Sokrovishcha skifskikh tsarei. (Brashinskii, I.) Moskva, 1967.
Arc 543.110 Solá Solé, J.M. Las dos grandes inscripciones sudarabigas del dique de Marib. Barcelona, 1960.
Arc 743.6 Solari, A. Topografia storica dell'Etruria. Pisa, 1914-18. 3v.
Arc 743.6.2 Solari, A. Topografia storica dell'Etruria. Appendix. Pisa, 1915.
Arc 1033.12.41 Solaro, A. Sindone evangelica, historica e theologica. Torino, 1627.
Arc 861.21.30 Soldier and civilian in Roman Yorkshire; essay to commemorate the nineteenth century of the foundation of York. (Butler, Ronald Morley.) Leicester, 1971.
Arc 608.90 Soleb. (Mission Michela Schiff Giorgini.) Firenze, 1965- 2v.
Arc 1027.25.27 Solenne festa in onore del Comm. G.B. de Rossi. (Marucchi, O.) Roma, 1883.
Arc 1033.74 Solenne Ricevimento della testa di S. Andrea Apostolo. (Fortini, E.) Roma, 1848.
Arc 1033.78 Le solenni feste della traslazione dei martiri di Atripalda. (Taglialatela, G.) Pompei, 1888.
Arc 608.94F Solignac, Marcel. Les pierres écrites de la Berbérie orientale. Tunis, 1928.
Arc 1163.3.60 Sololevskii, A.I. Slaviano-russkaia paleografiia. Sankt Peterburg, 1908.
Arc 505.70 Solomiac, Michel. Les tours royales de Josèphe Flavius. Jérusalem, 1936.
Arc 925.126 Solomonik, E.I. Sarmatskie znaki severnogo Prichernomor'ia. Kiev, 1959.
Arc 505.5.6 Solomon's temple. (Paine, T.O.) Boston, 1861.
Arc 495.203 Solomon's Temple. (Paine, T.O.) Boston, 1886.
Arc 925.9.151 Solov'ev, L.N. Pervobytnoe obshchestvo na territorii Abkhazii. Photoreproduction. Sukhumi, 1971.
Arc 1285.35 Solovjev, A.V. Istorija srpskog grba. Melburn, 1958.
Arc 1053.16 Solution d'un problème iconographique. (Barbier de Montault, X.) Poitiers, 1877.
Arc 595.1 The solution of the Pyramid problem. (Ballard, R.) N.Y., 1882.
Arc 1027.4.19 Soluzione di un problema...cimitero di Priscilla. (Bonavenia, G.) Roma, 1903.
Arc 950.202.35 Some aboriginal sites in Louisiana and Arkansas. (Moore, C.B.) Philadelphia, 1913.
Arc 950.202.33 Some aboriginal sites on Mississippi River. (Moore, C.B.) Philadelphia, 1911.
Arc 950.202.32 Some aboriginal sites on the Red River. (Moore, C.B.) Philadelphia, 1912.
Arc 861.13.15 Some accounts of the Bewcastle Cross. (Cook, A.S.) N.Y., 1914.
Arc 432.13 Some ancient cities of India. (Piggott, Stuart.) London, 1945.
Arc 885.12 Some ancient stone forts in Carnarvonshire. (Paget, Clara.) Cambridge, 1896.
Htn Arc 726.73.15* Some antiquarian notes. (Douglas, N.) Napoli, 1907.
Arc 1163.17.5 Some examples of English handwriting. (Essex, England. Record Office.) Chelmsford, 1949.
Arc 435.2.53 Some historical aspects of the inscriptions of Bengal. (Sen, B.) Calcutta, 1942.
Arc 875.34 Some investigations into palaeolithic remains in Scotland. (Smith, Frederick.) Glasgow, 1898-99.
Arc 858.97 Some Iron Age Mediterranean imports in England. (Harbison, Peter.) Oxford, 1974.
Arc 1480.54.5 Some new studies of the Roman republican coinage. (Mattingly, Harold.) London, 195-.
Arc 861.96 Some notes on recent archaeological discoveries at Broadstairs. (Hurd, Howard.) Broadstairs, 1913.
Htn Arc 1025.66* Some of the notes...on various subjects, especially the catacombs. (Englefield, T.B.) n.p., n.d.
Arc 1010.17 Some problems pertaining to the racial history of the Indonesian region. (Jacob, Teuku.) Utrecht, 1967.
Arc 483.7.2 Some works on the antiquities in the Abbasid Palace. 2. ed. (Iraq. Department of Antiquities.) Baghdad, 1956.
Arc 143.7 Somersetshire, England. Museum. Publication. 2v.
Arc 609.18 Something rich and strange. (Green, L.G.) Capetown, 1962.
Arc 726.300 Sommella, Paolo. Antichi campi di battaglia in Italia. Roma, 1967.
Htn Arc 861.2* Somner, W. The antiquities of Canterbury. London, 1640.
Arc 861.24 Somner, W. Treatise of Roman ports and forts. Oxford, 1693.
Arc 530.171 Son kari ve arasturmalann i syei altinda Penge tanhi. (Pekmon, A.) Ankara, 1973.
Arc 1353.15 Sonder Münzenouktion. v.1-2,3. (Zeno, Apostalo.) Wien, 1955. 2v.
Arc 1033.111 Les songes et les visions des martyrs. (Le Blant, E.) Rome, 1892.
Arc 1093.2.35 Der Sonnwendbogen. (Hirsch, Friedrich.) Lahr, 1965.
Arc 925.50.20 Soobshcheniia. v.1-3. (Sebastopol'. Khersoneskii Gosudarstvennyi Istoriko-Arkheologicheskii Muzei.) Simferopol', n.d. 2v.
Arc 1453.5 Soothe, J.C. von. Auserlesenes und hochstansehnliches Ducatenkabinett. Hamburg, 1784.
Arc 708.26 Sophoules, T. Peritou Archaioterou Attikou Ergastēriou. Athēnai, 1887.
Arc 936.100.50 Sopotsko-lendjelska kultura. (Dimitrijevic, Stojan.) Zagreb, 1968.
Arc 1260.3 Sopra alcuni piombi sardi. (Manno, Antonio.) Torino, 1878.
Arc 1033.35.31 Sopra la insigne reliquia della S. Croce. (Magrini, A.) Thiene, 1860.
Arc 1033.13.13 Sopra l'anno LXII dell'era...Pietro e Paolo. 2. ed. (Bartolini, D.) Roma, 1867.
Arc 1020.9.142 Sopra l'antichissimo altare di legno...Lateranense. (Bartolini, D.) Roma, 1852.
Arc 1027.60 Sopra l'antico oratorio...regione de Marsi. (Bartolini, D.) Roma, 1855.
Arc 1033.114 Sopra l'età di alcuni Bolli di figuline. (Lugari, G.B.) Roma, 1895.
Arc 1030.3.9 Sopra l'iscrizione sepolcrale di S. Gemello. (Cavedoni, C.) Modena, 1839.
Arc 726.83 Sopra un cista in bronzo con rapparesentanze a graffito. (Conestabile, Giancarlo.) Firenze, 1866.
Arc 1033.12.128 Sopra un patrio monumento di antica oreficeria. (Gonzati, L.) Vicenza, 1871.
Arc 1033.3.5 Sopra un sarcofago cristiano con travole. (Ratti, N.) Roma, 1828.
Arc 1016.233.5 Sopra una iscrizione cimiteriale. (Visconti, F.A.) Roma, 1831.
Arc 1033.35.19 Sopra un'antica croce nel duomo di Termini-Imerese. (Michele, I. de.) Palermo, 1859.
Arc 672.2.10 Sordinas, Augustus John. Stone implements from northwestern Corfu, Greece. Memphis, 1970.
Arc 1033.43.13 Soresinas, I.M. De capitibus S. apostolorum Petri et Pauli in Lateran. Roma, 1673.
Arc 1033.55.6 Soresini, G.M. Compendio istorico cronologico delle cose più cospicul concernenti la Scala Santa. Roma, 1674.
Arc 1033.55.5 Soresini, I.M. De scala sancta ante S. Sanctorum in Lateran. Roma, 1672.
Arc 1033.12.136 Soresinus, J.M. De imagine SS. Salvatoris...ad Sancta Sanctorum. Roma, 1675.
Arc 1473.5 Soret, Frédéric. Trois lettres sur des monnaies byzantines. Genève, 1837.
Arc 1033.35.121 Sorio, B. Sunto storica della croce e del crocefisso nel suo svolgimento. n.p., n.d.
Arc 1254.13 Sorlin-Dorigny, A. Sceaux et bulles des comnènes. Paris, 1876.
Arc 399.3.5 Sorok let sredi sibirskikh drevnostei. (Larichev, Vitalii E.) Novosibirsk, 1970.
Arc 925.50.10 Sorokina, N.P. Tuzlinskii nekropol'. Moskva, 1957.
Arc 1033.17.134 Sorte invidiabile di Prato...della sagra Cintola. (Gervasi, F.A.) Firenze, 1742.
Arc 689.3.20F Soteriou, G.A. Ai Christianikai Thebai tēs Thessalias kai at palaiochristianikai basilikai tēs Ellados. Athēnai, 1931.
Arc 1335.89 Sotheby, W. Catalogue of the collection of Greek coins in gold. London, 1894.
Arc 1033.17.97.8 Sotomayor, José F. Reflecciones sobre la aparición de la santísima virgen de Guadalupe. México, 1870.
Arc 1033.27.5 La sotterranea confessoni...di San Marco. (Bartolini, D.) Roma, 1844.
Arc 936.195.120 Soudský, Bohumil. Bylany. Praha, 1966.
Arc 9.5 Sources archeologiques de la civilisation européenne. International Association of South-East European Studies. Bucarest, 1970.
Arc 1433.70 Sourdel, D. Inventaire des monnaies musulmanes anciennes du musée de Caboul. Damas, 1953.
Arc 843.212 Sousa Gomes, A. A citânia de briteiros através dos séculos. Lisboa, 1967.
Arc 843.26 Sousa Maia. A necropole de condidello (Terrada-Maia). Porto, 1908.
Arc 1020.9.103 Les souterrains et le tresor...St. Pierre à Rome. (Barbier de Montault, X.) Rome, 1866.
Arc 875.124 The souterrains of southern Pictland. (Wainwright, Fredrick Threlfall.) London, 1963.

Arc 1330.25 South African numismatics, 1652-1965; a bibliography. (Noble, Fiona Virginia.) Capetown, 1967.

Arc 416.47 South Asian archaeology; papers. 1. U.S. ed. Park Ridge, N.Y., 1973.

Arc 861.198 South east England. (Jessup, Ronald-Ferederick.) London, 1970.

Arc 435.2.15F South Indian Buddhist antiquities. (Rea, Alexander.) Madras, 1894.

Arc 435.2.9F South-Indian inscriptions. (India. Department of Archaeology.) Madras. 1890-1949 16v.

Arc 858.74 South west England. (Fox, Aileen H.) London, 1964.

Arc 543.83.10 Southern Arabia. (Doe, Brian.) London, 1971.

Arc 953.29 Southwestern archaeology. 2. ed. (McGregor, John Charles.) Urbana, 1965.

Arc 323.3 Southwestern lore. Gunnison, Colo. 1,1935+ 8v.

Arc 823.4.7 Souttrait, J.H. Répertoire archéologique du département de la Niène. Paris, 1875.

Arc 1433.18 Souveniers numismatiques des croisades. Photoreproduction. (Dirks, J.) Bruxelles, 1861.

Arc 608.2.3 Souvenir de la Croisade de Saint-Louis trouvé à Carthage. (Delattre, A.L.) Lyon, 1888.

Arc 708.15.5 Souvenirs d'Athènes. Trieste, 186-?

Arc 925.9.10 Souvenirs de deux missions an Caucase. (Bapst, Y.) Paris, 1886.

Arc 1027.19.13 Souvenirs du cimetière de Saint Calliste. (Pillet, A.) Arras, 1881.

Arc 670.1 Souvenirs d'une excursion d'Athènes en Arcadie. (Rangabé, A.R.) Paris, 1857.

Arc 1663.17 Souvenirs numismatiques de la révolution de 1848. (Saulcy, Félecien.) Paris, 1850.

Arc 82.1.8 Souvenirs romains. (Carcopino, Jérome.) Paris, 1968.

Arc 746.13 Sovana, topografia ed arte. (Bianchi-Bandinelli, R.) Firenze, 1929.

Arc 1033.17.109 Soveral, Roque do. Historia do insigne aparecimento de N. Senhora da Luz. Lisboa, 1610.

Arc 925.4.40 Soveshchanie po Problemam Khronologii i Kul'turnoi Prinadlezhnosti Arkheologicheskikh Pamiatnikov Zapadnoi Sibiri. Tomsk, 1970. Problemy khronologii i kul'turnoi prinadlezhnosti arkheologicheskikh pamiatnikov Zapadnoi Sibiri. Tomsk, 1970.

Arc 340.25 Sovetskaia arkheologicheskaia literatura; bibliografiia. Leningrad. 1918+ 4v.

Arc 293.5 Sovetskaia arkheologiia. Moskva. 1958+ 23v.

Arc 1675.19.15 Sovetskaia memorial'naia medal', 1917-1967. (Shaten, Anatolii V.) Moskva, 1970.

Arc 543.3.1 Sovetskaiia arkheologiia frednei Azii i Kushanskaia problema. v.1-2. (International Conference on the History, Archaeology and Culture of Central Asia in the Kushan Period, Dushanbe, 1968.) Moskva, 1968.

Arc 925.180.10 The Soviet Far East in antiquity. (Okladnikov, Aleksei Pavlovich.) Toronto, 1965.

Arc 1030.25 Sovra un'antica lapida cristiana. (Pasini, P.) n.p., 1843.

Arc 1588.6.2 Sovyet Rusya Müzelerindeki, Moskova ve Leningrad, Nardir Osmanli raralon. (Ölçer, Cüneyt.) Istanbul, 1972.

Arc 682.20 Ta sōzomena Ithōmēs Messenes kai tōn Perix. (Olkonomlkes, S.) Athēnai, 1879.

Arc 895.67 Spår från tusentals år. (Moberg, Carl Axel.) Stockholm, 1966.

Arc 1033.17.304 Spada, G.N. Saggio istorico e coroncina della taumalurga immagine di Maria Sma. Napoli, 1839.

Arc 1033.17.304.5 Spada, G.N. Saggio storico con coroncina di Maria Sma. l'aconavetere. Foggia, 1917.

Arc 407.10.11 Spadework. (Woolley, Charles L.) London, 1953.

Arc 407.10.10 Spadework in archaeology. (Woolley, Charles L.) N.Y., 1953.

Arc 1027.52.5 Spadoni, O.L. Tombs and catacombs of the Appian Way. Rome, 1892.

Arc 785.52.5 Der spätantike Bildschmuch. (L'Orange, N.P.) Berlin, 1939.

Arc 1053.6.25 Spätantike Kaiserporträts. (Delbrück, R.) Berlin, 1933.

Arc 853.358 Spätkaiserzeitliche Funde in Westfalen. Münster, 1970.

Arc 853.269F Die spätneolithische Siedlung. (Müller-Karpe, H.) Kallmünz, 1961.

Arc 915.25 Die spätrömischen Wachthürme am Rhein von Basel bis zum Bodensee. (Stehlin, Karl.) Basel, 1957.

Arc 915.30 Spahni, Jean Christian. Les megálithes de la Suisse. Basel, 1950.

Arc 1490.80 Spahr, Rodolfo. Le monete siciliane dagli Aragonisi ai Borboni. Palermo, 1959.

Arc 1261.3.10 Spain. Archivo General de Simancas. Registro general del sello. Valladolid. 1,1950+ 12v.

Arc 1261.3.5 Spain. Archivo Historico Nacional, Madrid. Sección de Sigilografía. Catálogo. Madrid, 1918.

Arc 1261.3.15 Spain. Archivo Histórico Nacional, Madrid. Sección de Sigilografía. Catálogo de sellos de la Sección de Sigilografía del Archivo Histórico Nacional. Madrid, 1974- 3v.

Arc 1261.3 Spain. Archivo Historico Nacional, Madrid. Sección de Sigilografía. Catálogo i sellos españoles de la edad media por Juan Menéndez Pidal. Madrid, 1907.

Arc 843.32F Spain. Comisión ejecutiva de las excavaciones de Numancia. Excavaciones de Numancia. Madrid, 1912.

Arc 1318.7 Spain. Consejo Superior de Investigaciones Cientificas. Instituto Antonio Agustin de Numismatica. Numario hispánico. 1-10,1952-1961 5v.

Arc 94.5 Spain. Junta Superior de Excavaciones y Antiguedades. Memoria. Madrid, 1915-1926. 7v.

Arc 905.6 Spalato und die römischen Monumente Dalmatiens. (Hauser, A.) Wien, 1883.

Arc 1185.7 Spangenberg, E. Lehre von dem Urkundenbeweise. Heidelberg, 1827. 2v.

Htn Arc 1373.5* Spanheim, E. Diss. de praestantia et usu numismata antiqua. Rome, 1664.

Htn Arc 1350.1* Spanheim, E. Dissertation de praestantia et usu numismatum. Londoni, 1706-17. 2v.

Arc 482.204F Spanner, H. Rusafa. Berlin, 1926.

Arc 1138.127 Sparrow, John. Visible words. London, 1969.

Arc 925.2 Spasskii, Grigorii I. Bostor Kimmeriiskii sego drevnostiami i dostopamiasnostiami. Moskva, 1846.

Arc 925.5 Spasskii, Grigorii I. De antiquis quibusdam sculptures. Petropoli, 1822.

Arc 925.5.5 Spasskii, Grigorii I. Odastoporimiechatel'ineishikh pamatnikakh sibirskikh drevnatei. Sankt Petersburg, 1857.

Arc 1584.27 Spasskii, Ivan G. Denezhnoe khoziaistvo Russkogo gosudarstva. Leningrad, 1961.

Arc 1584.26 Spasskii, Ivan G. Po sledam odnoi redkoi monety. Leningrad, 1964.

Arc 1584.20 Spasskii, Ivan G. Talery v russkom denezhnom obrashchenii 1654-59 godov. Leningrad, 1960.

Arc 1478.80 Die spatrömische Kupferprägung. (Bruck, Guide.) Graz, 1961.

X Cg Arc 500.2 Special papers. (Wilson, C.) London, 1881.

Arc 1313.1.10 Special publications. (Royal Numismatic Society.) 1-8 8v.

Arc 1550.9 Specie. (Wilcke, Julius.) Kjøbenhavn, 1929.

Arc 895.36 Specimen historicum de monumento Kiwikensi. (Forssenius, A.C.) Londini Gothorum, 1780.

Arc 1347.1 Specimen philolgiae numismatico-latinae primum. (Ruhe, C.F.) Frankfort, 1708-29. 3 pam.

Arc 1367.1 Specimen universae rei nummariae antiquae. (Morel, Andre.) Paris, 1683.

Arc 1163.10A Specimena codicum orientalium. (Tisserant, E.) Bonnae, 1914.

Arc 861.5.9 Specimens of ancient Cornish crosses, fonts. (Hingston, F.C.) London, 1850.

Arc 1163.4.10 Specimens of Arabic and Persian palaeography. (India Office Library.) London, 1939.

Arc 1163.4.13F Specimens of calligraphy in the Delhi Museum of Archaeology. (Delhi. Museum of Archaeology.) Calcutta, 1926.

Arc 1163.17.20FA Specimens of sixteenth-century English handwriting. (Judge, C.B.) Cambridge, 1925.

Arc 1148.14.5 Specimina codicum graecorum vaticanorum. (Franchi de' Cavalieri, P.) Berolini, 1929.

Arc 1148.14 Specimina codicum graecorum vaticanorum. (Franchi de' Cavalieri, P.) Bonniae, 1910.

Arc 1153.24.2F Specimina codicum latinorum Vaticanorum. (Ehrle, Franz.) Berolini, 1932.

Arc 953.26 Speck, F.G. Eastern Algonkian block stamp decoration. Trenton, New Jersey, 1947.

Arc 136.1.63 A speech...23rd April 1784. (King, Edward.) London, 1784.

Arc 1163.15 Spehr, Harald. Der Ursprung der isländischen Schrift und ihre Weiterbildung bis zur Mitte des 13. Jahrhunderts. Inaug. Diss. Halle, 1929.

Arc 600.15.15 Speleers, L. Les figurines funéraires égyptiennes. Bruxelles, 1923.

Arc 557.3.5 The spell of Egypt. (Hichens, Robert.) Leipzig, 1910.

Arc 557.3.3 The spell of Egypt. (Hichens, Robert.) London, 1910.

Arc 875.55 Spence, James. Ruined castles. Edinburgh, 1873.

Arc 830.29 Spencer-Smith, I. Précis...monument arabe du moyen âge en Normandie. Caen, n.d.

Arc 726.60.5 Speranza, G. Il Piceno dalle origini alla fine d'ogni sua autonomia sotto Augusto. v.1-2. Ancona, 1934.

Arc 1510.24 Sperl, Karl. Die Münzgeschichte Regensburgs. Inaug. Diss. Kallmünz, 1928.

Arc 1668.6 Sperling, Otto. De nummorum bracteatorum et cavorum. Lubecae, 1700.

Arc 66.1.186 Le sphinx. (Dessenore, André.) Paris, 1957.

Arc 48.1 Sphinx. Revue critique. Upsala. 1-21 11v.

Arc 1510.75 Sphragistische Aphorismen. (Hohenlohe Waldenburg, Friedrich.) Heilbronn, 1882.

Htn Arc 1135.209* Spicilegium palimpsestorum. Bevronae, 1913.

Arc 1020.27 Spiciligio d'archeologia cristiana nell'Umbria. (Rossi, G.B. de.) Roma, 1871.

Htn Arc 380.208* Spiciligium antiquitates. (Beger, L.) Coloniae Brandenburgicae, 1692.

Htn Arc 1020.32* Spiegazione...sacri monumenti antichi di Milano. (Allegranza, G.) Milano, 1757.

Arc 726.41 Spiegazione di alcuni monumenti degli antichi Palasgi. (Bourguet, Louis.) Pesaro, 1735.

Arc 1675.50 Spigolando tra medaglie e date, 1848-71. (Mondini, R.) Livorno, 1913.

Arc 746.9.20F Spina. (Olfieri, Nereo.) München, 1958.

Arc 810.57F Spinazzola, Vittorio. Pompei alla luce degli scavi novi di Via dell'Abondanza (anni 1910-1923). Roma, 1953. 2v.

Arc 853.259 Spindler, Konrad. Magdalenenberg. Villingen, 1971. 3v.

Arc 1333.14F Spink and Son, Ltd. Numismatic circular. London. 1-72,1893-1964 36v.

Arc 1333.14.7 Spink and Son, Ltd. Numismatic circular of coins, medals, war medals, books, offered for sale. London. 1,1940+ 19v.

Arc 612.10 Spinn und Webewerkzeuge. (Kimakowicz-Winnicki, M.) Würzburg, 1910.

Arc 853.81 Spinnen und Weben. (Stofar, Walter.) Leipzig, 1938.

Arc 1076.23 Spiritza, Juraj. Spišské zvony. Vyd. 1. Bratislava, 1972.

Arc 1675.51.5 Spis medalów poliskich lub z dziejami krainy polskiej stycznych. (Bentkowski, F.) Warszawa, 1830.

Arc 1163.3.75 Spisok. russkim pamiatnikam, sluzhashchim k postavleniiu istorii khudozhestv i otechestvennoi paleografii. (Koppen, P.I.) Moskva, 1822.

Arc 1076.23 Spišské zvony. Vyd. 1. (Spiritza, Juraj.) Bratislava, 1972.

Arc 925.25 Spitsyn, A. Arkheologicheskii razvedki. St. Peterburg, 1908.

Arc 925.343F Spitsyn, Aleksandr A. Gdovskie kurgany v raskopkakh U.N. Glazova. Sankt Petersburg, 1903.

Arc 936.70 Spomenitse kulture. Beograd, 1951.

Arc 403.4 Spon, J. Recherche curieuse d'antiquité. Lyon, 1683.

Arc 628.10 Spon, J. Voyage d'Italie, de Dalmatie, de Grèce. La Haye, 1724. 2v.

Arc 630.7 Spoor, Henricus. Favissae utriusque antiqtam Romanae quam Graecae. Ultrajecti, 1707.

Arc 1016.233 Sposizione di alcune antiche iscrizione cristiane. (Visconti, P.E.) Roma, 1824.

Arc 936.9 Spostrzeżenia lat ostatnich w dziedzinie starozytnoşci krajowych. v.1-2. Warszawa, 1875-76.

Arc 513.30 Die Sprache der Ruinen. (Diez, E.) Wien, 1962.

Arc 853.260 Sprater, Friedrich. Die Pfalz unter den Römern. Speier, 1929-30. 2v.

Arc 853.258 Sprater, Friedrich. Die Urgeschichte der Pfalz. Speier, 1928.

NEDL Arc 513.10 Spratt, T.A.B. Travels in Lycia, Milyas, and the Cibyratis. London, 1847. 2v.

Arc 302.55 Sprawozdania z badań archeologicznych prawadzonych na terenie Województwa Koszalińskiego. Koszalin. 1966+

Arc 936.14.425 Sprawozdania z badań archeologicznych prowadzonych na terenie województwa koszolińskiego w Labach 1967-1968. Koszolin, 1969.

Arc 1190.4.15 Sprenger, G. Diplomatische und rechtsgeschichtliche Untersuchungen über Immunität und Königsschutz in Deutschland seit dem 12. Jahrhundert. Inaug. Diss. Breslau, 1936.

Arc 893.25 Sprockhoff, E. Und zeugen von einem stolzen Geschlecht. Oslo, 1945.

Arc 853.276F Sprockhoff, Ernst. Atlas der Megalithgräber Deutschlands. Text and atlas. Bonn, 1965-75. 4v.

Arc 853.357 Spuren römerzeitlicher Siedlungsvorgänger im Dorfund Stadtbild Süddeutschlands und seiner Nachbargebiete. (Findeisen, Jürgen.) Bonn, 1970.

Arc 968.1 Squier, E.G. Antiquities of the state of New York. Buffalo, 1851.

Arc 967.1 Squier, E.G. Observations on the aboriginal monuments of the Mississippi Valley. N.Y., 1847.

Arc 945.3 Squier, E.G. Serpent symbol and worship of nature in America. N.Y., 1851.

Arc 925.267 Srednee Zaural'e v epokhu neolita i bronzy. (Raushenbakh, V.M.) Moskva, 1956.

Arc 925.50.350 Srednes Podneprov's na rubezhe nashei ery. (Maksimov, Evgenii V.) Kiev, 1972.

Arc 925.10.5 Srednevekovye bashni i sklepy Balkarii i Karachaia (XIII-XVIII vv). (Miziev, Ismail M.) Nal'chik, 1970.

Arc 925.337.5 Srednevekovye poseleniia na Nizhnem Donu. (Artamonov, Mikhail I.) Leningrad, 1935.

Arc 543.138.5 Srednevekovyi gorod Srednei Azii. (Belenitskii, Aleksandr Markovich.) Leningrad, 1973.

Arc 925.50.105 Srednevekovyi Krym. (Iakobson, A.L.) Leningrad, 1964.

Arc 543.145 Srednevekovyi Shakhristan. (Negmatov, Numan.) Dushambe, 1966.

Arc 925.16.65 Srednevekovyi taraz. (Senigova, Taisiia N.) Alma-Ata, 1972.

Arc 416.28 Sredniaia Aziia i drevnii Vostok. (Masson, V.M.) Leningrad, 1964.

Arc 543.3.65 Sredniaia Aziia v epokhu Kamnia i bronzy. (Akademiia nauk SSSR. Institut Arkheologod.) Leningrad, 1966.

Arc 925.50.245 Srednii period bronzovogo veka v Severnoi Ukraine. (Bevezans'ka, Sofiia S.) Kiev, 1972.

Arc 936.220.5 Srednjevekovna nekropola w Mirijevu. (Bajalović-Biztašević, Marya.) Beograd, 1960.

Arc 925.9.120 Srednovekoraia Ingushetiia. (Krupnov, Evgenii I.) Moskva, 1971.

Arc 936.140.30 Srednovekovnoto selishte nad trakiiskiia grad Sevtopolis. (Changova, Iordanka.) Sofiia, 1972.

Arc 936.220.32 Srejović, Dragoslav. Lepenski vir. Beograd, 1969.

Arc 1148.17 Sreznevski, I.I. Paleograficheskiia navliudeniia. v.1-2. Sankt Peterburg, 1876.

Arc 1163.3 Sreznevski, T.T. Slavjano-russkaja paleografija. Sankt Peterburg, 1885.

Arc 936.105 Srpska Akademia Nauka Belgrade. Arkheol. Institut. Arkheologika slomenichi i malazishta u Srbiji. v.1-2. Beograd, 1953.

Arc 936.220.55 Srpska Akademija Nauka i Umetnosti, Belgrade, Galerije. Stare kul'ture u Djerdapu. Beograd, 1969.

Arc 936.220.95 Srpska Akademija Nauka i Umetnosti, Belgrade. Arheološki Institut. Caričin Grad, 1912-62. Beograd, 1962.

Htn Arc 1020.96* SS. episcoparum...antiqua monumenta. (Bagatas, R.) Venetiis, 1576.

Arc 861.104 St. John of Jerusalem, Clerkenwell. (Clapham, A.W.) London, 1912.

Arc 1033.17.60 St. Lukas als Maler der Maria. (Klein, Dorothee.) Berlin, 1933.

Arc 1033.17.650 St. Maria Culm das ist Bremdliche Historia. (Dörffel, F.) n.p., 1721.

Arc 875.133 St. Ninian's Isle and its treasure. (Small, Alan.) London, 1973. 2v.

Arc 875.115F St. Ninian's isle treasure. (O'Dell, Andrew.) Edinburgh, 1960.

Arc 1020.107 St. Paul's Cathedral...account of the treasures. (Payne, J.O.) London, 1893.

Arc 848.20.5 Staat und Gesellschaft in germanischer Vorzeit. (Schulz, Walther.) Leipzig, 1926.

Arc 746.56 Staccioli, Romolo Augusto. Modelli di edifici etrusco-italici. Firenze, 1968.

Htn Arc 858.13* Stackhouse, T. Two lectures on the remains of ancient pagan Britain. London, 1833.

Arc 612.49 Stacul, Giorgio. La grande madre. Roma, 1963.

Arc 785.13.90 Staderini, G. The Roman Forum. Rome, 19- .

Arc 716.9 Das Stadion von Athen. (Köster, A.) Berlin, n.d.

Arc 889.35 Stadskernonderzoek in Amsterdam (1954-1962). Groningen, 1966.

Arc 708.16 Die Stadt Athen im Alterthum. (Wachsmuth, C.) Leipzig, 1874- 2v.

Arc 518.12 Die Stadt des siebenten Weltwunders. (Alzinger, Wilhelm.) Wien, 1962.

Arc 736.2.4 Die Stadt Skyrakus im Alterthum. (Lupus, B.) Strassburg, 1887.

Arc 530.49 Die Stadtmauer von Iznik. (Schneider, A.M.) Berlin, 1938.

Arc 853.41 Städtischen historischen Sammlungen. (Baden-Baden.) Baden-Baden. 1908-1910

Arc 853.90 Städtischen Kulturamt Schriftenreihe. (Crefeld, Germany.) Krefeld. 1-2,1937-1938 2v.

Arc 936.1.8 Stählin, F. Pharsalos. Nürnberg, 1914.

Arc 1076.3.103 Staercke, Alphonse E. de. Cloches et carillons. Bruxelles, 1947.

Arc 1150.14 Staerk, Antonio. Monuments de l'abbaye celtique. Tournai, 1914.

Arc 688.8 Staés, B. To Eounion. Athēnai, 1920.

Arc 1027.57 Le stagione nell'antichità...arte christiano. (Colasanti, A.) Roma, 1901.

Arc 830.367 Stahl-Weber, Martine. Dix ans de recherches archéologiques région de Mulhouse. Mulhouse, 1972.

Arc 1088.1.15 Stahlecker, R. Über die verrchiedenen Versuche der Rekonstruktion. Ravensburg, 1897.

Arc 1076.3.13.5 Stahlschmidt, J.C.L. The church bells of Kent. London, 1887.

Arc 1076.3.13 Stahlschmidt, J.C.L. Surrey bells and London bell-founders. London, 1884.

Arc 1540.10 Stainer, C.L. Oxford silver pennies, 925-1272. Oxford, 1904.

Arc 1680.5 Stainsfield, C.W. Descriptive catalogue of Australian tradesmen's tokens. London, 1883.

Arc 672.4 Staïs,V. Ta ez antikythēren eyrēmata. Athēnai, 1905.

Arc 938.68 Stakliškių lobis. (Daugudis, V.) Vil'nius, 1968.

Arc 936.220.100 Stalio, Blaženka. Gradac. Beograd, 1972.

Arc 870.31F Stamp and roulette decorated pottery of the La Tème period in Eastern England. (Elsdon, Sheila M.) Oxford, 1975.

Arc 395.11.5 Stampfuss, Rudolf. Gustav Kossinna. Leipzig, 1935.

Arc 936.30 Stanchev, S. Neuropolüt do novi pazar. Sofiia, 1958.

Arc 905.3 Stancovick, P. Dello anfiteatro di Pola. Venice, 1822.

Arc 1603.5 Standard catalogue of Canadian coins, tokens, and paper money. Racine, Wis. 15,1967

Arc 1613.18 The standard catalogue of United States coins and tokens from 1652 to present day. N.Y. 1941

Arc 1335.86.5 Standard coin and medal catalogue of the world. (Stockvis, Albert.) Cleveland. 1940-1945 3v.

Arc 1033.182 Der Standort des Liturgen am christlichen Altar vor dem Jahre 1000. Diss. (Nussbaum, Otto.) Bonn, 1965.

Arc 885.13 Stanley, W.O. Memoirs on remains of ancient dwellings in Holyhead Island. London, 1871.

Htn Arc 861.69* Stapleton, A. A history of the public crosses of old Nottingham. Nottingham, 1893.

Arc 936.220.20 Stare kulture i narodi na tlu Beograd. (Todorović, Jovan.) Beograd, 1963.

Arc 936.220.55 Stare kul'ture u Djerdapu. (Srpska Akademija Nauka i Umetnosti, Belgrade, Galerije.) Beograd, 1969.

Arc 936.195.285 Staré Město-Velehrad. 1. vyd. (Hrubý, Vilém.) Praha, 1964.

Arc 936.195.285.5 Staré Město-Veligrad. (Hrubý, Vilém.) Gottwaldov, 1955.

Arc 936.195.35 Staří Moravané budiyí svůj stát. (Poulík, Josef.) Gottwaldov, 1960.

Arc 1285.35.5 Stari srpski pečati i grbovi. (Ivić, Aleksa.) Novi Sad, 1910.

Arc 936.180.15 Stariji neolit u Dalmaciji. (Batović, Šime.) Zadar, 1966.

Arc 302.18F Starinar; organ Arkheoloshkog Instituta. Beograd. 1,1950+ 12v.

Arc 302.19 Starine Crne Gore. Cetinje. 2

Arc 302.50 Starine Kosora i Metohije. Pristina. 4,1968+

Arc 403.3 Stark, K.B. Handbuch der Archäologie der Kunst. Leipzig, 1880.

Arc 968.2.65 Starkweather ruin: a Mogollon-Pueblo site in the Upper Gila area of New Mexico. Diss. (Nesbitt, Paul H.) Chicago, 1938.

Arc 1163.3.65F Starobulgarski glayolicheski i kirilski nadpisi ot IX i X v. (Goskev, Ivan.) Sofiia, 1961.

Arc 936.14.40 Starodawna kruszwica. (Hensel, Witold.) Wrocław, 1961.

Arc 1470.8.5 Starr, Chester. Athenian coinage, 480-449 B.C. Oxford, 1970.

Arc 925.50.220 Staryi Halych. (Pasternak, Iaroslav.) Krakiv, 1944.

Arc 502.1 Statements. (Palestine Exploration Society, New York.) N.Y. 1-4,1871-1877 4v.

Arc 905.130 La station du paléolithique moyen d'Erd-Hongrie. (Gábori-Csánk, V.) Budapest, 1968.

Arc 830.73 La station préhistorique de Panacelle. (Guillaume, Paul.) Gap, 1878.

Arc 543.66.45 Statisticheskoe izuchenie kul'tury grota Obi-Rakhmat. (Suleimanov, R.K.) Tashkent, 1972.

Arc 403.22 Statistiko-kombinatornye metody v arkheologii. Moskva, 1970.

Arc 830.338 Statistique archéologique du département du Nord. (Commission Historique du Département du Nord.) Lille, 1867. 2v.

Arc 772.8 Lo stato e le opere pubbliche in Roma antica. (Ruggiero, E. de.) Torino, 1925.

Arc 726.342.5 Stato e società in Loori. (Franciscis, Alfonso.) Napoli, 1972.

Arc 543.2.10 La statuaire khmère son évolution. (Boisselier, Jean.) Saigon, 1955. 2v.

Arc 600.1.17 Una statuetta del Buon Pastore da Marsa Matruh. (Breccia, E.) Alexandria, 1931.

Arc 726.248 Le statuette puniche di Bithia. (Pesce, Gennaro.) Roma, 1965.

Arc 400.18 Les statuettes feminines paléolithiques dites venus stéatophyges. Thèse. (Passemard, L. (Mme).) Nimes, 1938.

Arc 913.7 Staub, Johannes. Die Pfahlbauten in den Schweizerseen bei Fluntern. Zürich, 1864.

Arc 1033.35.33 Stauroteca di San Leonzio...Napoli. (Taglialatela, G.) Napoli, 1877.

Arc 543.3.80 Staviskii, Boris Ia. Arkheologicheskie raboty muzeia v Srednei Azii. Moskva, 1969.

Arc 543.3.60 Staviskii, Boris Ia. Mezhdu Pamirom i Kaspiem. Moskva, 1966.

Arc 628.21 La stazione della coorte VII dei vigili e i ricordi istorici. 2. ed. (Visconti, Pietro E.) Roma, 1867. 19 pam.

Arc 730.203 Stazione prehistorica sul monte del Castel. (Scarabelli, Gommi.) Imola, 1887.

Arc 1018.14 Ste. Agnès et son siècle. (Belloc, J.T. de.) Lille, 1893.

Arc 936.175 Stećci na Blidinju. (Bešlagić, Š.) Zagreb, 1959.

Arc 1082.5F Steensberg, Axel. Ancient harvesting implements. København, 1943.

Arc 895.29 Steenstrup, Japetus. Det store sølofund ved Gundestrup i Jylland 1891. Kjøbenhavn, 1895.

Arc 600.105F Stefanski, E. Coptic ostraca from Medinet Habu. Chicago, 1952.

Arc 1145.207 Steffens, Franz. Proben aus griechischen Handscriften und Urkunden. Trier, 1912.

Arc 853.11.15 Steger, Adrian. De vis militaribus romanorum in vetiri Germania. Lipsiae, 1738.

Arc 915.25 Stehlin, Karl. Die spätrömischen Wachthürme am Rhein von Basel bis zum Bodensee. Basel, 1957.

Arc 1318.5 Steigerwalt's coin journal. Lancaster, Pa. 1-2,1883-1884

Arc 853.359 Stein, Frauke. Adelsgräber des achten Jahrhunderts in Deutschland. Berlin, 1967. 2v.

Arc 416.15 Pamphlet box. Stein, Mark. Reprints.

Arc 416.13 Pamphlet vol. Stein, Mark. Reprints. 13 pam.

Arc 430.10F Stein, Mark A. Archaeological reconnaissances in north-western India and south-eastern Iran. London, 1937.

Arc 488.13 Stein, Mark A. Archaeological reconnaissances in southern Persia. London, 1934.

Arc 493.20 Stein, Mark A. An archaeological tour in the ancient Persis. Oxford, 1936.

Arc 441.5 Stein, Mark A. Detailed report of an archaeological tour with the Buner Field Force. Lahore, 1898.

Arc 488.14A Stein, Mark A. Old routes of western Iran. London, 1940.

Arc 458.8A Stein, Mark A. On Alexander's track to the Indus. London, 1929.

Arc 543.3.5A Stein, Mark Aurel. Ancient Khotan. Oxford, 1907. 2v.

Htn Arc 543.3.15F* Stein, Mark Aurel. Innermost Asia. Oxford, 1928. 4v.

Arc 543.3.17F Stein, Mark Aurel. Innermost Asia. Oxford, 1928. 4v.

Arc 543.3.20 Stein, Mark Aurel. On ancient Central-Asian tracks. N.Y., 1964.

Arc 543.3.19A Stein, Mark Aurel. On Central-Asian tracks. London, 1933.

Arc 543.3.3 Stein, Mark Aurel. Preliminary report on a journey of archaeological exploration...Turkestan. London, 1901.

Arc 543.3.8A Stein, Mark Aurel. Ruins of desert Cathay. London, 1912. 2v.

Arc 543.3A Stein, Mark Aurel. Sand-buried ruins of Khotan. London, 1903.

Arc 543.3.2 Stein, Mark Aurel. Sand-buried ruins of Khotan. London, 1904.

Arc 542.207F Stein, Mark Aurel. Serindia. Oxford, 1921.

Arc 543.3.10 Stein, Mark Aurel. A third journey of exploration in Central Asia, 1913-16. London, 1916.

Arc 853.308 Die Steinbeile und Steinarte im Gebiet der Niederrheins und der Maas. (Hoof, Dieter.) Bonn, 1970.

Arc 380.202 Steinbüchel, A. von. Antiquarischer Atlas. Wien, 1833.

Arc 853.20.19 Steinhausen, J. Archäologische Siedlungskunde des trierer Landes. Trier, 1936.

Arc 1077.12 Steinkreuze in Westfalen. (Brockpaehler,W.) Münster, 1963.

Arc 785.17 Steinmetz, G. Die römischen Glasspiegel. n.p., 1897.

Arc 853.110 Steinpockungsgräber von Köthen. (Brunn, W.A. von.) Berlin, 1954.

Arc 853.65 Die steinurnen Streitäxte und Keulen Schlesiens. Inaug. Diss. (Geschwendt, F.) Breslau, 1931.

Arc 853.92 Die Steinwerkzeuge der jüngeren Steinzeit. Inaug. Diss. (Nickel, E.) Würzburg, 1938.

Arc 853.346 Die Steinzeit im Donaumoos. (Seitz, Hermann Josf.) Augsburg, 1965.

Arc 853.155F Die Steinzeit im kieslische Katalog der steinzeitlichen Altertümer. (Dohn, Wolfgang.) Kallmünz, 1954.

Arc 888.1 Die Steinzeit in der Niederlanden. (Åberg, Nils.) Uppsala, 1916.

Arc 853.61F Das steinzeitliche Dorf Grossgartach. (Schliz, A.) Stuttgart, 1901.

Arc 612.26 Die steinzeitlichen Keulen Mitteleuropas. Inaug. Diss. (Fock, G.) Düsseldorf, 1937.

Arc 938.106 Die steinzeitlichen Kulturen des Baltikums. (Śturms, Edward.) Bonn, 1970.

Arc 848.37 Steinzeitseidlungen im Teutoburger Walde. (Diekmann, H.) Bielefeld, 1931.

Arc 1580.50 Steirische Münzfunde. (Luschin von Ebengreath, Arnold.) Graz, 1971.

Arc 497.39 Stekelis, M. Les monuments megalithiques de Palestine. Thèse. Paris, 1935.

Arc 505.133 Stékélis, Moshé. Archaeological excavations at Ubeidiya, 1964-1966. Jerusalem, 1969.

Arc 505.151 Stékélis, Moshé. The Yarmukian culture of the Neolithic period. Jerusalem, 1972.

Arc 726.296 Le stele di Monte Sirai. (Bondi, Sandro Filippo.) Roma, 1972.

Arc 830.172 La stèle du danseur d'Antibes et son decor végétal. (Cumont, Franz.) Paris, 1942.

Arc 726.246.5 Le stele puniche di Nora nel museo nazionale di Cagliari. (Moscati, Sabatino.) Roma, 1970.

Arc 830.121 Les stèles funéraires enforme de maison chez les médiomatriques et en Gaule. (Linckenheld, E.) Paris, 1927.

Arc 608.1.41F Stèles trouvées à Hadrumète. (Berger, P.) Paris, 1884.

Arc 848.26 Stemmermann, P.H. Die Anfänge der deutschen Vorgeschichtsforschung. Inaug. Diss. Quakenbrück, 1934

Arc 895.15.25 Stenåldersboplatserna vid Siretorp i Blekinge. (Bagge, A.) Stockholm, 1939.

Arc 895.25 Stenaldersbebyggeken på Arnst och Tjöm. (Enquist, Arvid.) Uppsala, 1922.

Arc 895.22.3 Stenberger, M. Das Grabfeld von Västerbjers auf Gotland. Stockholm, 1943.

Arc 895.34.5F Stenberger, Mårten. Öland under äldre järnaldern. Stockholm, 1933.

Arc 895.34F Stenberger, Mårten. Öland under äldre järnaldern. Stockholm, 1933.

Arc 895.61 Stenberger, Marten. Sweden. London, 1942?

Arc 203.5 Stendal, Germany. Altmarkisches Museum. Jahresgabe. 2v.

Arc 1053.11 Stenersen, L.B. De historia variisque generibus statuarum iconicarum. Christianiae, 1877.

Arc 1565.1 Stenersen, L.B. Myntfundet fra Graeslid i Thydalen. Christiania, 1881.

Arc 1033.17.104 Stengel, K. Hoedoporicum Mariana Benedictinum seu historia de imaginibus. Augsbourg, 1659.

Arc 1033.168 Stentrup, F. Die Translatio sancti viti. Münster, 1906.

Arc 545.227.10F The step pyramid. (Firth, C.M.) Le Caire, 1935-36. 2v.

Arc 936.195.110 Štěpánek, Miroslav. Opevněná sídliště 8.-12. století ve střední Ezvropě. Praha, 1965.

Arc 925.332.5 Stepanov, Pavel D. Osh Paudo. Saransk, 1967.

Arc 540.11F Stephania; a middle and late bronze-age cemetery in Cyprus. (Hennessy, J.B.) London, 1964.

Arc 1335.52 Stephanik, J.W. Cabinet de monnaies. Amsterdam, 1904.

Arc 390.6 Stephaniskos. Ernst Fabricius. Freiburg, 1927.

Arc 925.13.65 Steppenvölker und Germanen. (Domanovszky, G.) Budapest, 1939.

Arc 712.28 Ho stereobatēs toy Parthenonos. (Syriopoulos, K.T.) Athēnai, 1951.

Arc 513.1 Sterrett, J.R.S. Leaflets from the notebook of an archaeological traveller in Asia Minor. Austin, 1889.

Arc 513.1.5 Sterrett, J.R.S. A plea for research in Asia Minor. Ithaca, 1911.

Arc 1373.8 Steuer. Die Geschichte im Lichte der Münzen. Luckenwalde, 1911.

Arc 403.5 Stevens, E.T. Flint chips. A guide to pre-historical archaeology. London, 1870.

Arc 865.16 Stevens, E.T. Jottings on some of the objects of interest in the Stonehenge excursion. Salisbury, 1882.

Arc 865.15 Stevens, Frank. Stonehenge today and yesterday. London, 1916.

Arc 865.15.5 Stevens, Frank. Stonehenge today and yesterday. London, 1924.

Arc 710.19FA Stevens, G.P. The Periclean entrance court of the acropolis of Athens. Cambridge, 1936.

Arc 630.13 Stevens, G.P. Restorations of classical buildings. Princeton, N.J., 1955.

Arc 712.25 Stevens, G.P. The setting of the Periclean Parthenon. Baltimore, 1940.

Arc 870.1.9 Stevens, J. Descriptive lists of flint implements. St. Mary Bourne. London, 1867.

Arc 861.44 Stevens, J. On newly discovered Roman remains at Finkley near Andover. London, n.d.

Arc 1027.25.33 Stevensen, H. Giovanni Battista de Rossi. Roma, 1895.

Arc 1027.20 Stevenson, E. Il cimitero di Zotico. Dec miglio...Labicana. Modena, 1876.

Arc 1018.6.18 Stevenson, E. Lettera intorno...premessa all...Armellini. Roma, 1898.

Arc 1027.28.5 Stevenson, Enrico. Di un nuovo insigne esemplare...indice dei cimiteri cristiani di Roma. Roma, 1897.

Arc 1027.41.15 Stevenson, H. L'area di Lucina sulla via Ostiense. Roma, 1898.

Arc 1027.17 Stevenson, H. Das Coerneterium de H. Christina zu Bolsena. n.p., n.d.

Arc 1027.70 Stevenson, H. Escavazione di un antico diverticolo della via Tiburtina. Roma, 1878.

Arc 1015.229 Stevenson, H. Escavazioni in un ipogeo cristiano de Bolsena. Roma, 1881.

Arc 1027.41.9 Stevenson, H. Osservazione sulla topografia della via Ostiense. Roma, 1897.

Arc 1027.5.25 Stevenson, H. Scavi nel cimitero di Domitilla. Roma, 1898.

Arc 1340.2.2 Stevenson, Seth William. A dictionary of Roman coins, republican and imperial. London, 1964.

Arc 1340.2 Stevenson, Seth William. A dictionary of Roman coins. London, 1889.

Arc 889.10 The Stevensweert Kantharos. (Brom, Leo H.M.) The Hague, 1952.

Arc 983.13 Steward, J.H. Petroglyphs of the United States. Washington, 1937.

Arc 540.8F Stewart, E.M. Vounous 1937-38. Lund, 1950.

Arc 1540.17.15 Stewart, Ian Halley. The Scottish coinage. London, 1955.

Arc 672.1.112 Stibbe, C.M. Kreta en Mykene. Zeist, 1964.

Arc 1166.1.5 Stichometrische Untersuchungen. (Ohly, Kurt.) Leipzig, 1928.

Arc 1166.1 Stichometry. (Harris, J.R.) Baltimore, 1883.

Arc 1335.22 Stickel, J.G. Die grossherzogliche morgenländische Münzsammlung in Jena. Jena, 1846.

Arc 1138.36 Stieg, Lewis. An introduction to palaeography for librarians. Chicago, 1938.

Arc 1153.115 Stiennon, Jacques. Paléographie du Moyen Age. Paris, 1973.

Arc 520.15A Stier, Hans Erich. Aus der Welt des Pergamonaltars. Berlin, 1932.

Arc 1558.1 Stiernstedt, A.V. Description des monnaies de Cuivre...Suedois. Stockholm, 1871-72.

Arc 1138.30 Die Stilentwicklung der Schrift im christlichen Abendlande. (Coellen, Ludwig.) Darmstadt, 1922.

Arc 935.30 Les stiles funéraires de Byzance gréco-romaine. (Firatli, Nezih.) Paris, 1964.

Arc 407.17 Still digging. (Wheeler, Robert Eric Mortimer.) London, 1955.

Arc 705.7 Stillman, W.J. The acropolis of Athens. London, 1870.

Arc 635.214 Stillman, W.J. On the track of Ulysses. Boston, 1888.

Arc 726.67F La stipe tributata alle divinità delle acque Apollinari. (Marchi, G.) Roma, 1852.

Arc 1138.124 Stipišić, Jakov. Pomoćne povijesne znanosti u teoriji i praksi. Zagreb, 1972.

Arc 895.78 Stjernquist, Berta. Beiträge zum Studium von bronzeitlichen Siedlungen. Bonn, 1969.

Arc 1077.13 Stjernqvist, Berta. Cesta a cordoni (Rippenzisten); Produktion-Funktion-Diffusion. v.1-2. Bonn, 1967.

NEDL Arc 87.1.34 Stoa der Koenigs Attalos. (Adler, F.) Berlin, 1874.

Arc 936.180.35 Stobi; a guide to the excavations. (Wisaman, James.) Beograd, 1973.

Arc 1033.34.29 Stocchi, P. Viaggio ed episopato romano di San Pietro. Roma, 1867. 2 pam.

Arc 1077.2.30 Stockbauer, J. Kunstgeschichte des Kreuzes. Schaffhausen, 1870.

Arc 421.6 Stockholm. Astasiatiska bulletin. v.1-30,35-42. Stockholm, 1929-58.

Arc 1558.2 Stockholm. Statens Historiske Museum och Myntkabinett. Anglosachisiska mynt i svenska kongliga myntkabinette funna i sveriges jord. Stockholm, 1881.

Arc 890.210F Stockholm. Svenska Statens Historiska Museum. Techningar. v.1-3. Stockholm, 1873-83.

Arc 1390.15.5 Stockvis, Albert. Critical survey of mediaeval Teutonic and Spanish coinage. Cleveland, 1960.

Arc 1390.15 Stockvis, Albert. Effective research on unknown mediaeval coinage. 1. ed. Cleveland, 1955.

Arc 1335.86.5 Stockvis, Albert. Standard coin and medal catalogue of the world. Cleveland. 1940-1945 3v.

Arc 936.195.270 Stocký, Albin. La Bohême préhistorique. Prague, 1929.

Arc 853.81 Stofar, Walter. Spinnen und Weben. Leipzig, 1938.

Arc 923.132 Stogi i perspektivy razvitiia sovetskoi arkheologii. (Akademiia nauk SSSR. Institut Arkheologii.) Moskva, 1945.

Arc 936.115.10 Stoian, Iorgu. Etudes histriennes. Bruxelles, 1972.

Arc 855.221 Stokes, Margaret. Notes on the Cross of Cong. Dublin, 1895.

Arc 1020.117 Stokes, Margaret. Six months in the Apennines. London, 1892.

NEDL Arc 880.19 Stokes, William. The life and labors in art and archaeology of George Petrie. London, 1868.

Arc 925.136.15 Stokolos, Vladimir S. Kul'tura naseleniia bronzovogo veka Iuzhnogo Zaural'ia. Moskva, 1972.

Arc 853.373 Stolberg, Friedrich. Befastigungsanlagen im und am Harz von der Frühgeschichte bis zur Neuzeit. Ein Handbuch. Hildesheim, 1968.

Arc 925.50.335 Stolitsa feodoritov. (Dombrovskii, Oleg I.) Simferopol', 1973.

Arc 403.16.25 Stoll, Heinrich A. Die Traum von Troja. Berlin, 1957.

Arc 853.345.1 Stoll, Hermann. Die Alamannengräber von Hailfingen. Photoreproduction. Berlin, 1939.

Arc 895.20 Stolpe, H. Naturhistoriska och arkaeologiska undersökninger pa Björkö i Mälaren. Stockholm, 1872.

Arc 895.30F Stolpe, Hjalmar. Graffältet oid Vendel. Stockholm, 1912.

Arc 1053.25 Stommel, Edward. Beiträge zur Ikonographie der konstantinischen Sarkophagplastik. Bonn, 1954.

Arc 392.1 Stone, bronze and iron ages. (Hunter-Duvar, J.) London, 1892.

Arc 865.17 Stone, E.H. The stones of Stonehenge. London, 1924.

Arc 861.141 Stone, J.F.S. Wessex before the Celts. London, 1958.

Arc 861.63 The stone age and Lake Lothing. (Chambers, J.) Norwich, 1911.

Arc 446.10 Stone age and Pleistocene chronology in Gujarat. 1. ed. (Zluner, F.E.) Poona, 1950.

Arc 441.10 Stone age cultures of Bellary. 1. ed. (Subbarao, B.) Poona, 1948.

Arc 454.1.5 The stone age cultures of Orissa. 1. ed. (Mohapatra, Gopal Chandra.) Poona, 1962.

Arc 459.5 The stone age hill dwellers of Tekkalakota. (Nagaraja Rao, M.S.) Poona, 1965.

Arc 609.19 Stone age hunters of the Kafue. (Gabd, Creighton.) Boston, 1965.

Arc 432.6 The stone age in India. (Crinwasa Aiyangar, P.T.) Madras, 1926.

Arc 968.4.5 Stone age in New Jersey. (Abbott, Charles C.) Washington, 1877.

Arc 953.18 The stone age in North America. (Moorehead, W.K.) Boston, 1910. 2v.

Arc 875.85 The Stone Age in Scotland. (Lacaille, A.D.) London, 1954.

Arc 505.57 The stone age of Mount Carmel. (Joint Expedition of the British School of Archaeology in Jerusalem.) Oxford, 1937-1939. 2v.

Arc 608.42 The stone age of Northern Africa. (McBurney, Charles.) Harmondsworth, 1960.

Arc 1093.9 Stone age tools. 1. ed. (Sankalia, Hasmukh Dhirajlal.) Poona, 1964.

Arc 870.11 The stone ages in northern Britain and Ireland. (Smith, Frederick.) London, 1909.

Arc 723.10A Stone and bronze ages in Italy and Sicily. (Peet, T.E.) Oxford, 1909.

Arc 861.47.5 Stone crosses of county of Northampton. (Markham, C.A.) London, 1901.

Arc 1093.2.4 The stone hammer and its various uses. (McGuire, J.D.) Washington, 1891.

Arc 970.1 Stone implements; Potomac-Chesapeake Province. (Holmes, W.H.) Washington, 1893-94.

Arc 672.2.10 Stone implements from northwestern Corfu, Greece. (Sordinas, Augustus John.) Memphis, 1970.

Arc 416.3 Stone implements in Asia. (Fischer, H.) Worcester, 1884.

Arc 968.2.60 The stone lions of Cochite. (Prince, Le B.B.) Santa Fe, 1903.

Arc 615.5 Stone monuments...of remote ages. (Waring, J.B.) London, 1870.

Arc 963.1 Stone monuments in northwestern Iowa and southwestern Minnesota. (Lewis, T.H.) n.p., 1890?

Arc 865.27 Stonehenge; a new theory. (Peach, Wystan A.) Cardiff, 1961.

Arc 865.2 Stonehenge; plans, descriptions and theories. (Petrie, W.M.F.) London, 1880.

Arc 865.11 Stonehenge...by the light of ancient history. (Gidley, L.) London, 1873.

Arc 865.22 Stonehenge. (Atkinson, R.J.C.) London, 1956.

Arc 865.29 Stonehenge. (Bergström, Theo.) London, 1974.

Arc 865.23 Stonehenge. (Twist, Richard Marsden.) Truro, 1964.

Arc 865.28 Stonehenge: a classical interpretation. (Twist, Richard Marsden.) St. Anthony, 1971.

Arc 865.7 Stonehenge: story of its building and its legends. (Ireland, A.J.) London, 1903.

Arc 865.10 Stonehenge and its barrows. (Long, william.) Devizes, 1876.

Arc 865.21 Stonehenge and its date. (Cunnington, R.H.) London, 1935.

X Cg Arc 865.1 Stonehenge and its earth works. (Barclay, E.) London, 1895.

Arc 865.8 Stonehenge and other British stone monuments. (Lockyer, N.) London, 1906.

Arc 865.24 Stonehenge decoded. 1. ed. (Hawkins, Gerald Stanley.) Garden City, N.Y., 1965.

Arc 865.4 Stonehenge handbook. (Clapperton, W.) Salisbury, n.d.

Arc 865.26 Stonehenge of the kings: a people appear. (Crampton, Patrick.) London, 1967.

Arc 865.15 Stonehenge today and yesterday. (Stevens, Frank.) London, 1916.

Arc 865.15.5 Stonehenge today and yesterday. (Stevens, Frank.) London, 1924.

Arc 743.4 The stones of Etruria and marbles of ancient Rome. (Taylor, G.L.) London, 1859.

Arc 865.17 The stones of Stonehenge. (Stone, E.H.) London, 1924.

Arc 726.261 Stoop, Maria W. Floral figurines from south Italy. Assen, 1960.

Arc 585.1 The store-city of Pithom. 3. ed. (Naville, E.H.) London, 1888.

Arc 895.29 Det store sølofund ved Gundestrup i Jylland 1891. (Steenstrup, Japetus.) Kjøbenhavn, 1895.

Arc 1675.57 Storelli, A. Jean-Baptiste Nini. Tours, 1896.

Arc 1663.6 Storer, H.R. Les médailles de la Princesse Charlotte d'Angleterre. Bruxelles, 1888-91. 2 pam.

Arc 1675.17.5 Storer, H.R. Medals, jetons and tokens illustrative of obstetrics and gynaecology. Bridgeport, Conn., 1887.

Arc 1675.17 Storer, H.R. Medals and tokens of Rhode Island. Boston, 1895.

Arc 1675.17.10 Storer, H.R. Medicina in nummis. Boston, 1931.

Arc 720.9 Storia degli antichi popoli italiani. v.1-3; atlas. (Micali, G.) Firenze, 1832. 4v.

Arc 720.9.2 Storia degli antichi popoli italiani. 2. ed. (Micali, G.) Firenze, 1833.

Arc 720.9.7 Storia degli antichi popoli italiani. 3. ed. v.1-4. (Micali, G.) Firenze, 1849. 2v.

Arc 790.210 Storia degli scavi di Ercolano. (Ruggiero, Michele.) Napoli, 1885.

Arc 766.1.17A Storia degli scavi di Roma. v.1-4. (Lanciani, R.) Roma, 1902. 5v.

Arc 1020.31.15 La storia della Basilica di Santa Croce in Gerusalemma. (Besozzi, R.) Roma, 1750.

Arc 723.16PF Storia della cività latina dalle origini al secolo V avante Christo. (Pinza, Giovanni.) Roma, 1924.

Arc 1033.12.186 Storia della corona ferrea dei re d'Italia. (Bombelli, R.) Firenze, 1870.

Arc 1033.17.626 Storia della Madre di Dio...del Monte Berico. (Sangiovanni, V.) Vicenza, 1776.

Arc 1488.10 Storia della moneta in Italia. (Ricci, S.) Padova, 1937.

Arc 1490.8.20 Storia della moneta siciliana. (Holm, Adolf.) Bologna, 1965.

Arc 1033.17.135 Storia della sma. Cintola de Prato. (Russo, M. dello.) Napoli, 1858.

Arc 1033.17.34 Storia della translazione...immagine di Santa Maria di Constantinopoli. 2a ed. (Gregorio.) Napoli, 1813.

Arc 1033.17.35 Storia della translazione...immagine di Santa Maria di Constantinopoli. 2a ed. (Gregorio.) Napoli, 1824.

Arc 726.77F Storia della vite e del vino in Italia. (Marescalchi, A.) Milano, 1931-37. 3v.

Arc 1033.17.26 Storia dell'apparizione...di Nostra Signora di Misericordia di Savona. Genova, 1760.

Arc 1033.17.27 Storia dell'apparizione di Nostra Signora di Misericordia in Savona. Napoli, 1838.

Arc 385.20 Storia dell'archeologia. (Arias, Paolo Enrico.) Milano, 1967.

Arc 1033.17.22 Storia dell'imagine...Santa Maria in portico di Campitelli. (Erra, C.A.) Roma, 1750.

Arc 73.15.5 Storia dell'Instituto archeologico germanico, 1829-1879. (Michaelis, A.) Roma, 1879.

Arc 387.13.10 Storia dello spirito tedesco. (Pasquali, G.) Firenze, 1953.

Arc 800.15 Storia di Ercolano. (Catalano, V.) Napoli, 1953.

Arc 1033.34.39 Storia di San Pietro apostolo. (Mauro di Polvica, Francesco di.) Bologna, 1872.

Arc 723.25 Storia politica d'Italia. (Patroni, G.) Milano, 1937. 2v.

Arc 1027.21.9 Stornaiolo, C. Alcuni recenti scavi nelle catacombe di San Gennaro. Roma, 1879.

Arc 1033.81 Stornaiuolo, C. Ricerche...SS. Eutichete ed Acuzio. Napoli, 1874.

Htn Arc 1480.16* The story...of the Thorngrafton "Find". (Bruce, J.C.) n.p., 1871.

Arc 858.88 The story of archaeology in Britain. (Jessup, Ronald Frederick.) London, 1964.

Arc 432.29 The story of Indian archaeology, 1784-1947. (Roy, Sourindranath.) New Delhi, 1961.

Arc 505.66 The story of Jericho. (Garstang, John.) London, 1940.

Arc 1680.10 Story of the token. (Shiells, Robert.) N.Y., 1891.

Arc 936.14.340 Stosunki społeczno-gospodarcze i polityczne. (Kramarkowa, Irena.) Opole, 1969.

Arc 635.10 Strack, J.H. Das Altgriechisches Theatergebäude. Potsdam, 1843.

Arc 1480.28F Strack, Paul L. Untersuchungen zur Geschichte der Kaiser Nerva, Traian und Hadrian. Inaug. Diss. Stuttgart, 1930.

Arc 1478.28F Strack, Paul L. Untersuchungen zur römischen Reichsprägung des zweiten Jahrhunderts. Stuttgart, 1931-37. 3v.

Htn Arc 1373.7* Strada, J. de. Epitome du thresor des antiquitez. Lyon, 1553.

Arc 1490.31 Strada, M. La zecca di Milano e le sue monete. Milano, 1930.

Arc 383.42 Strana praehistorica...Martin John. (Schwarz, K.) Halle, 1948.

Arc 853.20.8 Stranger's guide to Roman antiquities of the city of Treves. (Wyttenback, J.H.) London, 1839.

Arc 830.166 Strasbourg-Argentorate. (Forrer, Robert.) Strausbourg, 1927. 2v.

Arc 830.205 Strasbourg au temps des Romaims. (Hatt, Jean J.) Strasbourg, 1953.

Arc 905.75 Die Strassen der Römer. (Jandaurek, H.) Wels, 1951.

Arc 66.1.41 Les stratèges athéniens. (Hauvette-Besnault, A.) Paris, 1885.

Arc 853.38 Die strategischen Rheinübergange der Römer bei Bonn. (Hauptmann, Carl.) Bonn, 1912.

Arc 66.1.113 Stratēgos Ypatos. (Holleaux, Maurice.) Paris, 1918.

Arc 1237.5.2 Stratified cylinder seals from the Diyala region. (Frankfort, Henri.) Chicago, 1964.

Arc 416.19 Stratigraphie comparée. (Schaeffer, C.F.) London, 1848-

Arc 830.123 Straub, A. Le cimetière gallo-romain de Strasbourg. Strasbourg, 1881.

Arc 1348.34 Stray leaves from the journal of a traveler. (Pfister, J.G.) London, 1857.

Arc 736.9F Strazzeri, Niccolo. Teatro di Taormina. n.p., n.d.

Arc 1025.26 Strazzula, V. Museum epigraphicum. Panormi, 1897.

Arc 1077.2.21 Strazzulla, V. Indagini archeologiche del "Signum Christi". Palermo, 1899.

Arc 1027.16 Strazzulla, V. Nouvi studi su alcuni elemente Pagani. Messina, 1900.

Arc 1030.20 Strazzulla, V. Studio critico sulle iscrizioni cristiane di Siracusa. Siracusa, 1895.

Arc 936.195.30F Stredoveká zaniknuta osada na Spiši. (Polla, B.) Bratislava, 1962.

Arc 588.62F A street in Petra. (Murray, M.A.) London, 1940.

Arc 1053.6.7F Strelkov, A. Faymskii portret. Moskva, 1936.

Arc 628.14 Strema Helbigiana. Leipzig, 1900.

Arc 386.19F Strena Buliciana; commentationes gratulatoriae F. Bulić. Zagrebiae, 1924.

Arc 1190.84 Strennon, Jacques. L'écriture diplomatique dans le diocèse de Liège. Paris, 1960.

Arc 853.91 Ströbel, R. Die Feuersteingeröte der Pfahlbaukultur. Leipzig, 1939.

Arc 1335.53 Stroehlin, P.C. Collections numismatiques. Genève, 1909.

Arc 895.74 Strömberg, Märta. Der Dolmen Trollasten in St. Köpinge, Schonen. Bonn, 1968.

Arc 895.56.6 Strömberg, Märta. Die Megalithgräber von Hagestad. Lund, 1971.

Arc 895.56 Strömberg, Märta. Untersuchungen zur jüngeren Eisenzeit in Schonen. Bonn, 1961.

Arc 853.130F Stroh, Armin. Katalog Günzburg. Kallmünz, 1952.

Arc 853.135F Stroh, Armin. Die Reihengräber der karolingisch-ottonischen Zeit. Kallmünz, 1954. 2 pam.

Arc 925.9.145 Stroitel'noe delo i arkhitektura poselenii Iuzhnogo Kavkaza. (Dzhavakhishvili, Aleksandr I.) Tbilisi, 1973.

Arc 1018.10 Stromation archaiologikon. (Rome, Italy. Collections.) Rome, 1900.

Arc 1033.12.55 Stromenti che servirono alla Passione...nostro signori. (Anguissola, G.B.) Piacenza, 1812.

Arc 1315.5 Strozzi, Carlo. Periodico di numismatica e sfragistica per la storia d'Italia. Firenze, 1868-74. 6v.

Arc 1348.41 Strozzi, Carlo. Quadro di geografia numismatica da servire. Firenze, 1836.

Arc 1458.16 Strozzi. Collection Strozzi. Médailles grecques et romaines aes grave. Paris, 1907.

Arc 1138.105F Strubbe, Egied I. Groudbegrippen van de paleografie. 3. druk. Gent, 1961. 2v.

Arc 674.1.6 Strube, Carl. Studien über den Bilderkreis von Eleusis. Leipzig, 1870.

Arc 936.14.535 Struktura i rozwój zasiedlenia południowowschedniej strefy nadbałtyckiej u sckyłku starożytności. 1. wyd. (Przewoźna, Krystyna.) Warszawa, 1974.

NEDL Arc 1033.17.3 Strumz, Franz. Unsere liebe Frau in Österreich. Zürich, 1921.

Arc 746.7 Stryk, F. von. Studien über etruskischen Kammagräber. Dorpat, 1910.

Arc 403.7.3 Strzygowski, J. Die Baukunst der Armenier und Europa. Wien, 1918. 2v.

Arc 600.1.9 Strzygowski, J. Hellenistische und koptische Kunst in Alexandria. Wien, 1902.

Arc 708.15 Stuart, J. Die Alterthuemer von Athen. Darmstadt, 1829-31. 2v.

Htn Arc 705.5* Stuart, J. Antiquities of Athens. London, 1762-1816. 4v.

Arc 855.4 Stuart, J. Sculptured stones of Scotland. Aberdeen, 1856. 2v.

Arc 875.26.2 Stuart, Robert. Caledonia Romana...Roman antiquities of Scotland. Edinburgh, 1852.

Arc 875.26 Stuart, Robert. Caledonia romana. Edinburgh, 1845.

X Cg Arc 568.1.2 Stuart, V. The funeral tent of an Egyptian queen. London, 1882.

Arc 568.1 Stuart, V. Nile gleanings. London, 1879.

Arc 658.15 Stubbings, Frank Henry. Prehistoric Greece. London, 1972.

Arc 785.15.20 Stucchi, S. Contributo alla conoscenza della topografia dell'arte e della storia nella Colonna Traiana. Udine, 1960.
Arc 785.13.85 Stucchi, S. I monumenti della parte meridionale del Foro Romano. Roma, 1958.
Arc 608.17.35 Stucchi, Sandro. L'Agorà di Cirene. Roma, 1965.
Arc 785.16 Stuck-Reliefs...Casa Farnesina in Rom. (Bayer, J.) Wien, 1897.
Arc 1348.15 Stuckelburg, E.A. Der Münzsammler. Zürich, 1899.
Arc 93.36F Studi d'archeologia e d'arte. Milano. 1,1939
Arc 83.2 Studi di antichita cristiana. Roma. 1,1929+ 30v.
Arc 1020.136 Gli studi di archeologia cristiana in Sicilia. (Agnello, G.) Catania, 1950.
Arc 1153.114 Studi di paleografia e diplomatica. (Costamagna, Giorgio.) Roma, 1972.
Arc 19.1 Studi e materiali di archeologia e numismatica. v.1-3. (Milani, L.A.) Firenze, 1899. 4v.
Arc 746.18.5 Studi e ricerche su Orvieto etrusca. (Puglisi, S.) Catania, 1934.
Arc 743.13 Studi etruschi. (Comitato Permanente per l'Etruria.) Firenze. 1,1927+ 41v.
Arc 743.13.5 Studi etruschi. Indici, v.1-40, 1927-1972. (Comitato Permanente per l'Etruria.) Firenze, 1968- 2v.
Arc 567.1.10 Studi in memoria di Ippolito Rosellini nel primo centerario della morte. (Pisa. Università.) Pisa, 1949. 2v.
Arc 766.4.20 Studi minori di topografia antica. (Lugli, Giuseppe.) Roma, 1965.
Arc 82.6 Studi miscellanei. (Rome. Università. Seminario di Archeologica e Storia dell'Arte Greca e Romana.) 1-16 6v.
Arc 815.1 Studi sopra gli edifizi e le arti meccaniche dei Pompeiani. (Ruggiero, Michele.) Napoli, 1872.
Arc 726.235F Studi storici; topografici ed archeologici sul Portus Augusti di Ravenna e sul territorio classicano. Firenze, 1961.
Arc 530.165 Studi sui rilie vi di Karatepe. (Matthiae, Paolo.) Roma, 1963.
Arc 726.145 Studi veleiati. (Convegno di Studi Plorici e Archeologici Veleiati, 1st, Piacenza.) Piacenza, 1955.
Arc 938.102 Studia archaelogica in memoriam Harri Moora. Tallinn, 1970.
Arc 225.15 Studia archaeologica. Budapest. 1,1963+ 5v.
Arc 19.8 Studia archaeologica. Roma. 1-13 5v.
Arc 383.39 Studia archaeologica Gerardo Van Hoorn Oblata. Leiden, 1951.
Arc 936.14.100 Studia i materialy do badań nad Neolitem Malopolski. (Polska Akademia Nauk. Oddzial w Krakowie. Prace Komisja Archeologicznej.) Wroclaw, 1964.
Arc 936.14.550 Studia nad archeologią średniewiecznego Mazowsza. Wyd. 1. (Gierlach, Boguslaw.) Warszawa, 1975.
Arc 1190.90.5 Studia nad dokumentem polskim. (Maleczyński, Karol.) Wroclaw, 1971.
Arc 936.14.225 Studia nad kulturą ceramiki sznurowej w Malopolsce. (Machnik, Jan.) Wroclaw, 1966.
Arc 1285.10 Studia nad legendą pieczęci miejskiej. (Haisig, Marian.) Wroclaw, 1953.
Arc 936.6.40 Studia nad poludniowym i poludniowowschodnim pograniczem kultury luzyckiej. (Bukowski, Zbigniew.) Wroclaw, 1969.
Arc 936.14.465 Studia osadnicze nad neolitem wyżym lessowych. (Kruk, Janusz.) Wroclaw, 1973.
Arc 83.3.2 Studia Palmyreńskie. Warszawa. 1,1966+
Arc 936.10 Studia wczesnośredniowieczne. Warszawa. 1-5,1952-1962 5v.
Arc 416.40 Studia z archeologii Azji Przedniej i Starożytnego Wschodu. Wyd. l. Kraków, 1970.
Arc 302.45.5 Studie. (Československá Akademie Věd. Archeologický Ústav. Pobočka v Brně.) Praha. 1,1972+
Arc 726.34 Studie recenti sopra i Nuraghi. (Centurione, P.A.M.) Prato, 1886.
Arc 383.79.12 Studie z antiky; Antonínu Salsčovi. (Československá Adademie věd. Sekoe Jazyka a Literatury.) Praha, 1955.
Arc 1269.27 Studien über Amtssiegel des 13. und 14. Jahrhunderts vornehmlich in Hessen. Inaug. Diss. (Kaufmann, E.) Marburg, 1937.
Arc 1018.9 Studien über christliche Denkmäler. (Ficker, J.) Leipzig. 1-24,1902-1937 19v.
Arc 767.3 Studien über das alte Rom. (Mayerhoefer, A.) München, 1887.
Arc 674.1.6 Studien über den Bilderkreis von Eleusis. (Strube, Carl.) Leipzig, 1870.
Arc 746.7.9F Studien über die etruskischen Gräber. (Åkerström, Åke.) Uppsala, 1934.
Arc 895.45F Studien über die schwedische Bootaxtkultur. (Oldeberg, A.) Stockholm, 1952.
Arc 853.96.10 Studien über elbgermanische Gräber felder im der ausgehenden Latènezeit und der alteren Kaiserzeit. Habilitationsschrift. (Capelle, Torsten.) Hildesheim, 1971.
Arc 746.7 Studien über etruskischen Kammagräber. (Stryk, F. von.) Dorpat, 1910.
Arc 853.356 Studien über steinerne Äxte und Beile der jüngeren Steinzeit und der Stein-Kupferzeit Nordwestdeutschlands. (Brandt, Karl Heinz.) Hildesheim, 1967.
Arc 386.6 Studien und Skizzen. (Braun, J.) Mannheim, 1854.
Arc 505.5.75 Studien zum Salomonischen Tempel. Inaug. Diss. (Möblenbrinck, K.) Stuttgart, 1931.
Arc 853.165.5 Studien zum vorgeschichtlichen Siedlungs- und Befestigungswesen des Saarlandes. (Schindler, Reinhard.) Trier, 1968.
Arc 888.55 Studien zur älteren und mittleren Steinzeit der Niederen Lande. Habilitationsschrift. (Narr, Karl J.) Bonn, 1968.
Arc 853.25 Studien zur ältesten Geschichte der Rheinlands. v.1-9. (Mehlis, C.) Leipzig, 1875-1886. 2v.
Arc 905.147 Studien zur Bükker Kultur. (Lichardus, Ján.) Bonn, 1974.
Arc 612.74 Studien zur europäischen Vor- und Frühgeschichte. Neumünster, 1968.
Arc 647.2 Studien zur Geschichte der griechischen Kunst. (Herzog, A.) Leipzig, 1888.
Arc 853.120 Studien zur Geschichte Mitteldeutschlands während der älteren Latènezeit. (Hachmann, Rolf.) Hamburg, 1950.
Arc 1143.12 Studien zur griechischen Paläographie. (Hanger, H.) Wien, 1954.
Arc 1148.12 Studien zur griechischen Tachygraphie. (Gitlbauer, M.) Berlin, 1903.
Arc 1185.22 Studien zur mittelterlicher Urkundenlehre. (Zatschek, Heinz.) Brünn, 1929.
Arc 600.130 Studien zur Polychromie der Plaskik. (Reuterswaerd, Patrick.) Stockholm, 1958- 2v.
Arc 785.13.75 Studien zur Topographie des Forum Romanum. (Welin, Erik.) Lund, 1953.
Arc 391.4 Studien zur vorgeschichtlichen Archäologie Alfred Götze. Leipzig, 1925.
Arc 19.3 Studien zur westeuropäischen Altertumskunde. Neuwied.
Arc 895.23 Studier i Upplands bebyggelse-historia. (Ekholm, Gunnar.) Uppsala, 1915.
Arc 612.21 Studjer öfver den yngre stenildern i Norden och Vosteuropa. (Åberg, Nils.) Norrköping, 1912.
Arc 895.47 Studier over den yngre Bronzealder Danmark. (Broholm, Hans Christian.) København, 1933.
Arc 895.17 Studier over Norges stenalder. (Brøgger, A.W.) Christiania, 1906.
Arc 895.41 Studier over Vestjyllands oldtidsbebyggelse. (Mathiassen, T.) København, 1948.
Arc 895.5.25 Studier tillägnade Oscar Montelius. (Montelius, Oscar.) Stockholm, 1903.
Arc 612.68 Studies in ancient Europe. Leicester, 1968.
Arc 83.4 Studies in classical archaeology. Stockholm. 3-5 3v.
Arc 421.12 Studies in early Chinese culture. (Creel, H.G.) London, 1938.
Arc 332.5 Studies in historical archeology. Sydney. 1,1973+
Arc 513.13.5 Studies in history and art...Eastern Provinces, Roman Empire. (Ramsay, W.M.) Aberdeen, 1906.
Arc 543.75 Studies in Indonesian archaeology. (Stutterheim, W.F.) The Hague, 1956.
Arc 83.5F Studies in Mediterranean archaeology. Lund. 1-20 4v.
Arc 48.8 Studies in Mediterranean archaeology. Pocket-book. Göteborg. 1,1974+
Arc 303.45F Studies in North-European archaeology. Stockholm. 1-3
Arc 303.46 Studies in North-European archaeology. Series B. Stockholm. 3,1971+
Arc 383.29 Studies in prehistory; robert Bruce Foote memorial volume. (Sen, D.) Calcutta, 1966.
Arc 448.1.15 Studies in proto-Indo-Mediterranean culture. (Heros, Henry.) Bombay, 1933.
Arc 936.180.36 Studies in the antiquities of Stobi. Beograd. 1,1973+
Arc 815.22F Studies in the archaeology of the forum at Pompeii. (Van Buren, A.W.) Bergamo, 1918.
Arc 505.148 Studies in the lithic industries of Israel and adjacent countries. (Prausnitz, Moshe W.) Jerusalem, 1970.
Arc 537.6 Studies on prehistoric Cyprus. Inaug. Diss. (Gjerstad, Einar.) Uppsala, 1926.
Arc 383.77 Studies presented to David Moore Robinson. (Mylonas, G.C.) St. Louis, 1951-53. 2v.
Arc 585.40F Studies presented to F.L. Griffith. (Egypt Exploration Society.) London, 1932.
Arc 303.35 Studii si cercetări de istorie veche. (Academia...Bucharest. Academia Republicii Socialiste România. Muzeul National de Antichitati.) Bucureşti. 5,1954+ 15v.
Arc 1300.5 Studii si certcetari de numismatica. (Academia...Bucharest. Academia Republicii Populare Romêne, Bucharest.) 1-5 5v.
Arc 936.251 Studije o kamenom i bakarnom dobu u sjeverozapadnom Balkanu. (Benae, Alojz.) Sarajevo, 1964.
Arc 302.46 Stuḍijné zvesti. (Slovenská Akadémia Vied. Archeologický Ústav, Nitra.) Nitra. 2,1957+ 6v.
Arc 1027.4.29 Studio archaeologico...iscrizione di Filomena. (Marucchi, O.) Roma, 1907.
Arc 1030.20 Studio critico sulle iscrizioni cristiane di Siracusa. (Strazzulla, V.) Siracusa, 1895.
Arc 1138.129 Studium novověkého písma. (Polák, Stanislav.) Příbram, 1973.
Arc 936.120.5 Studniozka, Franz. Tropaeum Traiani. Leipzig, 1904.
Arc 1490.60 A study in the coinage of the Mamertines. (Särström, M.) Lund, 1940.
Arc 1418.11 A study of ancient Indian numismatics. (Chakrabortty, S.K.) Calcutta, 1931.
Arc 556.1 The study of Egyptology. (Griffith, Francis L.) Oxford, 1901.
Arc 453.10 A study of Muslim inscriptions. (Bendrey, F.) Bombay, 1944?
Arc 407.6.5 Study of prehistoric anthropology. (Wilson, John Albert.) Washington, 1890.
Arc 1153.85 A study of the language of eighth century Lombardic documents. (Politzer, R.L.) N.Y., 1949.
Arc 726.10.11 Study of the topography of Preneste. (Dernan Mugoffin, R.) Baltimore, 1908.
Arc 1027.80 Stückelberg, E.A. Die Katakombenheiligen der Schweiz. Kempten, 1907.
Htn Arc 1510.3.7* Stürmer, Wolff. Vortzeichnus und Gedräge der groben und kleinen Müntzsorten. Leipzig, 1572.
Arc 1033.3.37 Stuhlfauth, G. Un frammento di sarcofago cristiano. Roma, 1897.
Arc 1033.175 Stuiber, Alfred. Refrigerium interim. Bonn, 1957.
Arc 1540.1 Stukeley, W. The medallic history of M.A.V. Carausins. London, 1757-89.
Arc 1538.15 Stukeley, W.M. Twenty-three plates of the coins of the ancient British kings. London, 17- .
Arc 855.214 Stukeley, William. Albury. Temple of the British Druids. London, 1743.
Arc 858.30 Stukely, William. Palaeographia brittanica. London, 1743. 2 pam.
Arc 543.25.15 Le stupa du Barabudur. (Sivaramamenti, C.) Paris? 1961.
Arc 441.6F The stûpa of Bharhut. (Cunningham, Alexander.) London, 1879.
Arc 458.2.2 Die Stupa's (Topes). (Ritter, C.) Berlin, 1838.
Arc 458.2 Die Stupa's (Topes). (Ritter, C.) Berlin, 1838.
Arc 625.9 Sturgis, R. Classical archaeology on the shores of the Mediterranean. Rochester, n.d.
Arc 785.5 Sturm, J. Das kaiserliches Stadium auf dem Palatin. Würzburg, 1888.
Arc 505.5.48 Sturm, L.C. Sciagraphia templi Hierosolymitano. Lipsiae, 1694.
Arc 938.106 Šturms, Edward. Die steinzeitlichen Kulturen des Baltikums. Bonn, 1970.
Arc 543.35.15 Stutterheim, W.F. Indian influences in old Balinese art. London, 1935.
Arc 543.35 Stutterheim, W.F. Oudheden van Bali I. Singaradja, 1930.
Arc 543.75 Stutterheim, W.F. Studies in Indonesian archaeology. The Hague, 1956.
Arc 870.13 Styan, K.E. Short history of sepulchral cross-slabs. London, 1902.
Arc 1033.58.15 Styger, Paolo. Il monumento apostolico a San Sebastiano sulla Via Appia. Roma, 1925.
Arc 1025.62 Styger, Paul. Die altchristliche Grabeskunst. München, 1927.

Arc 1025.62.15F Styger, Paul. Römische Märtyrergrüfte. Berlin, 1935. 2v.

Arc 1025.62.10F Styger, Paul. Die römischen Katakomben. Berlin, 1933.

Arc 658.10 Styrenius, Carl Gustaf. Submycenaean studies. Lund, 1967.

Arc 1490.98 Su di alcune monete puniche di Mozia. (Salinas Gargotta, Antonino.) Palermo, 1858.

Arc 1033.35.61 Su la vera forma delle croce di N. Signore. (Ceva Grimaldi, F.) Medina, n.d.

Arc 736.1.5 Su l'akropoli Akragantina. (Bonfiglio, S.) Girgenti, 1897.

Arc 1020.26 Su l'antica basilica di S. Nicola in Bari. (Bartolini, D.) Roma, 1882.

Arc 736.4 Su le origini di Erice. (Tummarello, F.) Trapini, 1898.

Arc 750.203 Suardi, B. Le rovine di Roma. Milano, 1875.

Arc 843.55 Suarez de Salazar, Juan B. Grandezas y antiguedades de la isla y ciudad de Cadiz. Cadiz, 1610.

Arc 726.155 Suasa senonum. (Giorgi, Gello.) Parma, 1953.

Arc 441.15 Subbarao, B. Baroda through the ages. Baroda, 1953.

Arc 441.10 Subbarao, B. Stone age cultures of Bellary. 1. ed. Poona, 1948.

Arc 658.10 Submycenaean studies. (Styrenius, Carl Gustaf.) Lund, 1967.

Arc 440.3 Subramanian, K. Buddhist remains in Andhra. Madras, 1932.

Arc 1510.19F Suchier, Reinhard. Die Münzen der Grafen von Hanau. Hanau, 1897.

Arc 1588.1.85 Suchodolski, Stanisław. Mennictwo polskie w XI-XII wieku. Wrocław, 1973.

Arc 1453.10 Suchodolski, Stanisław. Początki mennictwa w Europie Środkowej, Wschodniej i Połnocnej. Wrocław, 1971.

Arc 186.1 Suchs, H. Schlesiens Vorzeit in Bild und Schrift. Breslau. 1-6,1870-1912 13v.

Arc 936.20.40 Sucidara; une cité daco-romaine en Dacie. (Tudor, D.) Bruxelles, 1965.

Arc 48.6 Sudan. Antiquities Service. Museum pamphlet. Khartoum. 1,1953+

Arc 48.4 Sudan. Antiquities Service. Occasional papers. Khartoum. 1-5 3v.

Arc 853.270.10 Sudholz, Gisela. Die ältere Bronzezeit zwischen Niederrhein und Mittelwesen. Hildesheim, 1964.

Arc 895.5 La Suède préhistorique. (Montelius, Oscar.) Stockholm, n.d.

Arc 923.15.2 Südrussland im Altertum. (Ebert, Max.) Aalen, 1973.

Arc 1093.2.8 Südwesteuropäische Megalithkultur. (Wilke, Georg.) Würzburg, 1912.

Arc 853.6 Suettich, S. Der 'Puestrich' zu Sondershausen. Naumburg an der Saale, 1894.

Arc 750.222F Sugli antichi edifizj. (Canina, Luigi.) Roma, 1840.

Arc 785.22.8 Sugli edifizi palatini. (Gori, Fabio.) Roma, 1867.

Arc 740.6.5 Sugli scavi della Certosa. (Zannoni, A.) Bologna, 1871.

Arc 1508.11 Suhle, Arthur. Deutsche Münz- und Geldgeschichte von den Anfanger bis zum 15. Jahrhundert. Berlin, 1955.

Arc 1508.10 Suhle, Arthur. Die deutschen Renaissance-Medaille. Leipzig, 1950.

Arc 1348.84.2 Suhle, Arthur. Die Münze von der Anfängen bis zur europäischen Neuzeit. 2. Aufl. Leipzig, 1970.

Arc 785.37 Sui munimenti ed altre costruzione poligonie...provincia romana. (Fonteanive, R.) Roma, 1887.

Arc 830.108 Suite de recherches archéologiques relatives à la préhistoire du département de la Gironde. 7e série. (Augey, Edmond.) Bordeaux, 1910.

Arc 925.50.390 Sukhobokov, Oleg V. Slaviane Dneprovskogo Levoberezh'ia. Kiev, 1975.

Arc 403.17 Sukhov, P.A. Arkheologicheskie pamiatniki. Moskva, 1941.

Arc 1016.239 Sul dittico eburneo de santi martiri Teodoro ed Acacio. (Dragoni, A.) Parma, 1810.

Arc 1020.6.3 Sul frontale dell'altar maggiore in San Marco. (Passini, A.) Venezia, 1881.

Arc 1033.34.19 Sul ragguaglio...cattedra di San Pietro. (Wiseman, N.) Roma, 1832.

Arc 1033.17.323 Sul santuario di Polsi sito...Gerace memorie. (Fera di Plati, D.) Napoli, 1851.

Arc 1033.22 Sul tesoro di antiche suppellettili sacre. (Gori, F.) Spoleto, 1891.

Arc 1033.65 Sul valore storico del'atti S.S. Flavia Domitilla, Nereo, Achilleo. (Ferrari, L.F. dei.) Roma, 1880.

Arc 543.66.45 Suleimanov, R.K. Statisticheskoe izuchenie kul'tury grota Obi-Rakhmat. Tashkent, 1972.

Arc 923.120 Sulimirski, Tadeusz. Prehistoric Russia; an outline. N.Y., 1970.

Arc 925.13.170 Sulimirski, Tadeusz. The Sarmatians. London, 1970.

Arc 1020.95 Sulla Cattedra Alessandria di S. Marco. (Fabiani, G.) Modena, 1869.

Arc 736.1.15 Sulla collocazione dei Telamoni nel Tempio. (Griffo, Pietro.) Agrigento, 1952.

Arc 1033.4 Sulla comunione christiana nei primi secoli. (Bucci, P.) Roma, 1862.

Arc 750.38 Sulla fognatura della città di Roma. (Narducci, P.) Roma, 1889. 2v.

Arc 1016.218 Sulla grandezza della primitiva basilica ostiense. (Belloni, P.) Roma, 1853.

Arc 1027.4.25 Sulla lapide sepolcrale di S. Filomena. (Santucci, S.) Roma, 1837.

Arc 1160.204 Sulla questione...codice di Arborea. (Foerster, W.) Torino, 1905.

Arc 1025.29.18 Sulla Roma sotterranea dal G.B. de Rossi. (Odorici, F.) Milano, 1866.

Arc 1016.216.3 Sulla sedia pontificale della basilica di S. Paolo. (Moreschi, L.) n.p., n.d.

Arc 1016.216 Sulla sedia pontificale della basilica di S. Paolo. (Moreschi, L.) Roma, 1838.

Arc 736.1.10 Sulla topografia d'Agrigento del F.S. Cavallari. (Dara, G.) Girgenti, 1883.

Arc 733.1 Sulla topografia di Talune città greche. (Cavallari, F.S.) Palermo, 1879.

Arc 726.2.4 Sull'antico sito di Napoli e Palepoli dubbie e conghietture. (Capasso, B.) Napoli, 1855.

Arc 505.5.25 Sull'antico Tempio Salomone. (Bartolini, D.) Roma, 1868.

Arc 1033.38 Sull'autenticità del capo di S. Lorenzo. (Giorgi, Calisto.) Roma, 1864.

Arc 726.48 Sulle antiche città picene Falera e Tignio. (Colucci, G.) Fermo, 1777.

Arc 93.25F Sull'ordinamento del servizio archeologico. (Italy. Direzione generale della antichità e belle arti.) Roma, 1885.

Arc 1588.6.2.5 Sultan Mohmut II zamomuda darpedilen osmanli madeni porolori. (Ölçer, Cüneyt.) Istanbul, 1970.

Arc 835.200 Sumario de las antiqüedades Romanas que hay en España. (Cean-Bermudez, J.A.) Madrid, 1832.

Arc 307.3.4 Sumarios de la conferencias y memorias presentadas al congreso. (International Congress of Americanists, 17th, Buenos Aires, 1910.) Buenos Aires, 1910.

Arc 630.5 Sumbolae Leitt. im Honorem Julii de Petra. Neapoli, 1911.

Arc 48.3 Sumer; a journal of archaeology in Iraq. Baghdad. 1,1945+ 24v.

Arc 48.3.2 Sumer; a journal of archaeology in Iraq. Index, v.1-21, 1945-1965. Baghdad, 1960-1968.

Arc 861.55 Summer, H. Excavations on Rockbourne Downs, Hampshire. London, 1914.

Arc 609.34 Summers, Roger. Ancient ruins and vanished civilizations of southern Africa. Capetown, 1971.

Arc 609.1.45 Summers, Roger. Zimbabwe. Johannesburg, 1963.

Arc 861.66 Sumner, H. The ancient earthworks of New Forest. London, 1917.

Arc 858.44 Sumner, H. Local papers. London, 1931.

Arc 1080.5 Sundwall, J. Die älteren italischen Fibeln. Berlin, 1943.

Arc 1468.18 Sundwall, J. Attischen Münzen des neueren Stiles. Helsingfors, 1907.

Arc 885.23 Sunken cities. (North, F.J.) Cardiff, 1957.

Arc 1033.35.121 Sunto storica della croce e del crocefisso nel suo svolgimento. (Sorio, B.) n.p., n.d.

Arc 938.27 Suomalais-Ugrilaisen muinaistutkinnon alkeita. (Aspelin, Johan R.) Helsingissä, 1875.

Arc 938.27.5 Suomen asukkaat pakanuuden aikana. (Aspelin, Johan R.) Helsingissä, 1885.

Arc 938.85 Suomen esihistoria. (Kivikoski, Ella.) Helsinki, 1961.

Arc 938.85.10 Suomen kiinteät muinaisjäännökset. (Kivikoski, Ella.) Helsinki, 1966.

Arc 282.1 Suomen Muinaimuistoyhdestys, Helsinki. Finska fornminnesföreningens tidskrift. 16,1896+ 24v.

Arc 938.75F Suomen rantakauden kuoasto. (Kivikoski, Ella.) Helsinki, 1947-51. 2v.

Arc 825.2.4 Supplément à l'édition de 1829 de l'Histoire des antiquités de la ville de Nismes. (Ménard, L.) Nîmes, 1830.

Arc 95.3.10 Supplément commercial de la revue "Arethuse.". 2v.

Arc 1603.3.7 Supplement to coins, tokens and medals. (Sandham, Alfred.) Montreal, 1872.

Arc 74.4.16 Supplement to subject catalogue of joint library. (Society for the Promotion of Hellenic Studies.) London. 1-19 15v.

Arc 1015.206 Supplementa alla Roma sotterranea cristiana. (Iozzi, Oliviero.) Roma, 1898.

Arc 1274.2.3 Supplemental descriptive catalogue of ancient Scottish seals. (Laing, Henry.) Edinburgh, 1866.

Arc 1.5.15A Supplementary papers. (American School of Classical Studies in Rome.) N.Y. 1-2,1905-1908 2v.

Arc 31.7F Supplementary papers. (British School of Archaeology in Jerusalem.) London.

Arc 74.4.4F Supplementary papers. (Society for the Promotion of Hellenic Studies.) London. 1-2 2v.

Arc 74.4.4 Supplementary papers. (Society for the Promotion of Hellenic Studies.) London. 3,1900+ 5v.

Arc 1485.4.5F Supplemento alle monete dei papi. (Vitalini, O.) Camerino, 1892.

Arc 1490.24.2 Supplemento all'opera Le monete del reame de Due Sicilie. Napoli. 2-3,1912-1913

Arc 1370.4.4 Suppléments aux six volumes. (Pellerin, J.) Paris, 1767.

Arc 1033.5 La supremazia della sede romana considerata nei monumenti dei primi secoli. (Marucchi, O.) Roma, 1897.

Arc 895.36.9 Sur des rochers sculptés decouverts en Scanie. (Bruzelius, N.G.) Stockholm, 1875.

Arc 1093.2.3 Sur la construction des ralles dites des géants. (Frederik VII, king of Denmark.) Copenhague, 1857.

Arc 1500.34 Sur la prétendue restauration du pouvoir de Maurice Tibère. (Robert, M.P.C.) Paris, 1883.

Arc 1480.10 Sur les chiffres romaines ou grecs...des monnaies impériales. (Blancard, Louis.) Marseille, n.d.

Arc 895.37 Sur les différents types des haches en Silex suédoise. (Montelius, Oscar.) Stockholm, 1875. 5 pam.

Arc 830.158 Sur les mouvements stratégiques de César...avant le siége d'Alise. (Fallue, Léon.) n.p., 1856. 12 pam.

Arc 1254.4 Sur les sceaux et plombs byzantins. (Mordtmann, A.D.) Constantinople, 1873.

Arc 1433.16 Sur l'origine du monnayage musulman. (Blancard, Louis.) Paris, n.d.

Arc 1500.12 Sur quelques points obscurs de la numismatique de Charles VIII. (Blancard, Louis.) Paris, n.d.

Arc 1408.2 Sur un Dirhem Kakweïhide inédit. (Tornberg, E.J.) Bruxelles, 1858.

Arc 1020.81 Sur un reliquare...monastère de St. Évroult. (Galeron, F.) n.p., n.d.

Arc 823.19.120 Sur une inscription inédite. (Thédenat, H.) Paris, 1884.

Arc 1030.9.5 Sur une pierre tumulaire. (Le Blant, E.) Arras, 1877.

Arc 925.50.130 Surov, E.G. Khersones Tavricheskii. Sverdlovsk, 1961.

Arc 143.6 Surrey Archaeological Society. Research papers. Guildford. 5

Arc 143.8 Surrey Archaeological Society. Research volume. Castle Arch. 1,1974+

Arc 1076.3.13 Surrey bells and London bell-founders. (Stahlschmidt, J.C.L.) London, 1884.

Arc 880.15 A survey of antiquarian periods on...Inismurray. (Wakeman, W.F.) London, 1893.

Arc 530.6.5F A survey of coastal cities in Western Cilicia. (Alfoldi-Rosenbaum, Elizabeth.) Ankara, 1967.

Arc 1330.10 A survey of numismatic research 1960-1965. v.1-3. Copenhagen, 1967.

Arc 968.2.35 A survey of southwestern archaeology. (Roberts, Frank H.H.) Washington, 1936.

Arc 861.23.15 A survey of the prehistory of the Farnham district, Surrey. (Oakley, K.P.) Guildford, 1939.

Arc 500.5.5 The survey of Western Palestine. (Hull, E.) Adelphi, 1886.

Arc 726.251 Susini, Giancarlo. Fonti per la storia greca e romana del Salento. Bologna, 1962.

Arc 1478.19.2 Susomni, J.B. Numismata imperatorum romanorum. Supplementum. Vindobonae, 1767.

Arc 83.2.10 Sussidi allo studio della antichita cristiane. Roma. 1-4,1936-1954 3v.

Arc 1348.55 Sutherland, C.H.V. Art in coinage. London, 1955.

Arc 1348.55.2 Sutherland, C.H.V. Art in coinage. N.Y., 1956.

Arc 1478.42 Sutherland, C.H.V. Coinage in Roman imperial policy. London, 1951.

Arc 1373.11 Sutherland, Carol H.V. Ancient numismatics. N.Y., 1958.

Arc 1478.87 Sutherland, Carol H.V. Roman coins. London, 1974.

Arc 1538.21 Sutherland, Carol Humphrey Vivian. Anglo-Saxon gold coinage in the light of the Crondall hoard. London, 1948.

Arc 1540.23 Sutherland, Carol Humphrey Vivian. Coinage and currency in Roman Britain. London, 1937.
Arc 1538.21.5 Sutherland, Carol Humphrey Vivian. English coinage, 600-1900. London, 1973.
Arc 875.20 Sutherland, G. Outlines of Scottish archaeology. Edinburgh, 1870.
Arc 861.100.10 Sutton-Hoo. (Green, C.) London, 1963.
Arc 861.100.2 The Sutton-Hoo ship burial. (Bruce-Mitford, Rupert Leo.) London, 1951.
Arc 861.100.15 The Sutton-Hoo ship burial. (Bruce-Mitford, Rupert Leo.) London, 1968.
Arc 861.100.5 The Sutton-Hoo ship burial. (Magoren, F.P.) Cambridge, Mass., 1952.
Arc 861.100 The Sutton-Hoo ship burial. 1. ed. (British Museum. Department of British and Mediaeval Antiquities.) London, 1947.
Arc 600.35 Suys, Émile. Vie de Petasiris, grand prêtre di That à Hermopolis-la-Grande. Bruxelles, 1927.
Arc 925.6.10 Suzhdenskoe doietoricheskoe kladbishche. (Talko-Hryncewicz, J.) Moskva, 1899.
Arc 1558.8.2 Svensk numismatisk uppslagsbok. 2. upp. (Tingström, Bertel.) Stockholm, 1968.
Arc 383.43F Svenska arkeologiska samfundet. Arkeologiska forskningar och fynd. Stockholm, 1952.
Arc 340.6 Svenska Arkeologiska Samfundet. Swedish archaeological bibliography. Uppsala. 1939+
Arc 83.3.5 Svenska Institutet i Rom. Skrifter. Lund. 2-10 6v.
Arc 1318.2 Svenska Numismatika Föreningen. Numismatiska meddelanden. Stockholm. 1-29,1874-1943 7v.
Arc 503.8F Svenske Syrien expeditionem, 1952-1953. Lund, 1956.
Arc 1663.12 Sveriges konungahusets minnespenningar. (Hildebrand, B.E.) Stockholm, 1874. 2v.
Arc 1560.1 Sveriges mynt under medeltiden. (Hildebrand, H.) Stockholm, 1887.
Arc 1020.138 Sviatyni Egipta; zemlia egipet kak sad gospoden. (Gavrilova, A.) Buenos Aires, 1960.
Arc 925.50.345 Svieshnikov, Ihor K. Istoriia naselennia Peredkarpattia, Podillia i Volyni v kintsi III-na pochatku II tysiacholittia do nashoï ery. Kyïv, 1974.
Arc 340.9 Sviridova, I.N. Po sledam drevnikh kul'tur. Moskva, 1966.
Arc 936.195.305 Svoboda, Bedřich. Neuerworbene römische Metallgefässe aus Stáže bei Piešťany. 1. Aufl. Bratislava, 1972.
Arc 390.4 Swanton, J.R. Jesse Walter Fewkes. Washington, 1931.
Arc 858.95 Swanton, M.J. A corpus of pagan Anglo-Saxon spear-types. Oxford, 1974.
Arc 968.2.25 The Swarts ruin...New Mexico. (Cosgrove, H.S.) Cambridge, 1932.
Arc 450.1 Swarup, B. Konarka. Bengal, 1910.
Arc 1093.6 The swastika, the earliest known symbol. (Wilson, Thomas.) Washington, 1896.
Arc 1093.6.9 The swastika. (Doering, J.F.) Kitchner, Ontario, 1936.
Arc 1093.6.5 The swastika. (Murray-Aynsley, L.H.G.M.) Margate, 1891.
Arc 895.61 Sweden. (Stenberger, Marten.) London, 1942?
Arc 895.5.27F Swedish antiquities. (Montelius, Oscar.) Stockholm, 1922.
Arc 340.6 Swedish archaeological bibliography. (Svenska Arkeologiska Samfundet.) Uppsala. 1939+
Arc 537.7F The Swedish Cyprus expedition...1927-1931. v.1-4. (Gjerstad, Einar.) Stockholm, 1934-48. 8v.
Arc 670.7F The Swedish excavations at sea in Arcadia. (Holmberg, E.J.) Lund, 1944.
Arc 682.20.5F The Swedish Messenia expedition. (Valmin, M.N.) Lund, 1938.
Arc 895.40 Swenska Farnminnesföreningen. Arkeologiska studier tillägnade H.K.H. kronprins Gustaf Adrolf. Stockholm, 1932.
Htn Arc 1373.6* Swinton, J. Metilia: sive de quinario gentis metiliae. Oxford, 1750.
Arc 905.12.12 Swoboda, Erich. Carnuntum. Wien, 1949.
Arc 905.12.20 Swoboda, Erich. Carnuntum. Wien, 1953.
Arc 905.12.23 Swoboda, Erich. Carnuntum. 3. Aufl. Graz, 1958.
Arc 905.17.5 Swoboda, Erich. Führer durch Aguntum. Baden, 1935.
Arc 1033.112.5 Swoboda, Franz. Die liturgischen Kämme. Thesis. n.p., 1963?
Arc 530.39F Swoboda, H. Denkmäler aus Lykaonien, Pamphylien und Isaurien. Brunn, 1935.
Arc 1020.123 Swoboda, H. Neue Funde aus dem altchristlichen Österreich. Wien, 1909.
Arc 426.4 The sword book, in Honiko Gunkiko. (Arai, Hakuseki.) Reading, 1913. 2 pam.
VArc 543.152 Syallam tolmács küldetése Naagy Sändor folokog. (Bendefy, Lásylo.) Budapest, 1941.
Arc 1175.1 Sybel, H. von. Kaiserurkunden in Abbildungen. v.1-11 and atlas. Berlin, 1880-91. 12v.
Arc 1018.23 Sybel, L. von. Christliche Antike. Marburg, 1906. 2v.
Arc 1033.43.11 Sybel, L. von. Der Herr der Seligkeit. Archäologische Studie. Marburg, 1913.
Arc 708.24 Sybel, L. von. Katalog der Sculpturen zu Athen. Marburg, 1881.
Arc 630.4 Sybel, L. von. Die klassische Archäologie und die altchristliche Kunst. Marburg, 1906.
Arc 1480.26 Sydenham, E.A. Aes grave; a study of the cast coinage of Rome and Central Italy. London, 1926.
Arc 1428.23 Sydenham, E.A. The coinage of Caesarea in Cappadocia. London, 1933.
Arc 1480.19.10 Sydenham, E.A. The coinage of the Roman republic. London, 1952.
Arc 1480.19 Sydenham, E.A. Historical references on coins of the Roman empire. London, 1917.
Arc 1660.11 Sylloge numismatum elegantiorum. (Luckius, J.J.) Argentina, 1620.
Arc 1335.112PF Sylloge nummoium Graecorum. v.1, pt.2. (American Numismatic Society.) N.Y., 1961.
Arc 1578.1 Sylloge nummorum ex arg. uncialium. v.1-3. (Melle, Jakob von.) Lubeck, 1697-98.
Arc 1578.2 Sylloge nummorum ex arg. uncialium. v.1-3. (Melle, Jakob von.) Lubeck, 1698-99.
Arc 1468.67F Sylloge nummorum Graecorum, Sweden. Stockholm, 1974-
Arc 1468.28F Sylloge nummorum Graecorum. (British Academy.) London, 1931-51. 4v.
Arc 1468.28.5F Sylloge nummorum Graecorum. pt.1-18. Berlin, 1957- 13v.
Arc 1353.7F Sylloge nummorum Graecorum. v.1-30,41-42. (Copenhagen. National Museet.) Copenhagen, 1942- 20v.
Arc 1468.66F Sylloge nummorum Graecorum Grèce. Athènes, 1970- 2v.
Arc 1468.60F Sylloge numorum Graecorum. v.1-3. Berlin, 1968.
Arc 1538.23.6 Sylloge of coins of the British Isles. London, 1968.
Arc 1538.23 Sylloge of coins of the British Isles. Series A. London, 1958- 23v.
Arc 1538.23.2 Sylloge of coins of the British Isles. Series B. London, 1966.
Arc 1480.17 Sylva antiqua iscana. (Shortt, W.T.P.) Londini, n.d.
Arc 1027.22 Das Symbol des Fisches...Fischi der Römische Katakombe. (Achelis, H.) Marburg, 1888.
Arc 1077.2.35 Das Symbol des Kreuzes. (Bunsen, E. von.) Berlin, 1876.
Arc 1433.13 Symbolae ad rem numariam Muhammedan. (Tornberg, Carl Johan.) Upsaliae, 1846-62.
Arc 1082.15 Le symbole de la main. (Verbrugge, A.R.) Courauces, 1958.
Arc 391.3 Symbolia litterariae. Decas I. (Gori, A.F.) Florentiae, 1748-53. 10v.
Arc 391.3.5 Symbolia litterariae. Decas II. v.1-10. (Gori, A.F.) Romae, 1751-54. 5v.
Arc 518.13 Symbolica Dianae Ephesiae statua a Claudio Menetreio exposita. (Menestrier, C.F.) Romae, 1657. 3 pam.
Arc 1668.10 Die Symbolik der Mittlaltermünzen. v.1,2-3. (Friedensburg, F.) Berlin, 1913-22. 2v.
Arc 1470.24 Symbolism on Greek coins. (Baldwin, Agnes.) N.Y., 1916.
Arc 1077.2.47 Le symbolisme de la croix. (Guénon, René.) Paris, 1931.
Arc 1077.2.47.2 Le symbolisme de la croix. (Guénon, René.) Paris, 1970.
Arc 612.46 Symposium Consacre aux Problèmes du Neolithique Européen. L'Europe à la fin de l'âge de la pierre. Praha, 1961.
Arc 412.7 Symposium on Archaeological Chemistry. Science and archaeology. Cambridge, Mass., 1971.
Arc 612.92 Symposium über die Entstehung und Chronologie der Badener Kultur, Archäologisches Institut der Slowakischen Akademie der Wissenschaften, 1969. Symposium über die Entstehung und Chronologie der Badener Kultur. Bratislava, 1973.
Arc 612.92 Symposium über die Entstehung und Chronologie der Badener Kultur. (Symposium über die Entstehung und Chronologie der Badener Kultur, Archäologisches Institut der Slowakischen Akademie der Wissenschaften, 1969.) Bratislava, 1973.
Arc 936.253 Symposium zu Problemen der jüngeren Hallstattzeit. (Symposium zu Problemen der Jüngeren Hallstattzeit in Mitteleuropa, Smolenice, 1970.) Bratislava, 1974.
Arc 936.253 Symposium zu Problemen der Jüngeren Hallstattzeit in Mitteleuropa, Smolenice, 1970. Symposium zu Problemen der jüngeren Hallstattzeit. Bratislava, 1974.
Arc 612.69 Sympozjum Paleolityczne, 3d, Kraków, 1967. III. sympozjum paleolityczne, Kraków 30 XI-2 XII, 1967. v.1-2. Kraków, 1967.
Arc 1468.21 Synopsis de mille coins faux du faussaire C. Christopoulos. (Sborōnos, Ioannēs N.) Athènes, 1922.
Arc 1468.3 Synopsis numorum Graecorum. (Arneth, J.) Vienna, 1837.
Arc 1335.76.13F Synopsis numorum veterum. (Athens. Ethnikon Nomismatikon Mouseion.) Athenes, 1878.
Arc 1675.55 Synopsis of the contents of the British Museum. (British Museum. Department of Coins and Medals.) London, 1881.
Arc 1470.4.5F Syracusan dekadrachmas. (Gallatin, A.E.) Cambridge, 1930.
Arc 1470.4.15 Syracusan "medallions" and their engravers in the light of recent finds. (Evans, A.J.) London, 1892.
Arc 48.2 Syria; revue d'art oriental et d'archeologie. Paris. 1,1920+ 39v.
Arc 501.16.8 Syrian stone-lore. (Conder, C.R.) N.Y., 1887.
Arc 905.29.5 Les Syriens à Intercisa. (Fitz, Jeno.) Bruxelles, 1972.
Arc 685.5 Syriopoulos, K. Hē proistoria...Peloponnēsou. Athēnai, 1964.
Arc 712.28 Syriopoulos, K.T. Ho stereobatēs toy Parthenonos. Athēnai, 1951.
Arc 1423.13.5 Die Syrische Provinzialprägung von Augustus. (Wruck, W.) Stuttgart, 1931.
Arc 1423.13 Die Syrische Provinzialprägung von Augustus bis Klaudius. Inaug. Diss. (Wruck, W.) Stuttgart, 1931.
Arc 388.18 Systematics in prehistory. (Donnell, Robert C.) N.Y., 1971.
Arc 1478.34 Die Systeme des römischen Silbergeldes. (Mickwitz, G.) Helsingfors, 1933.
Arc 1018.36 Syxtus, P. Notiones archaeologiae christianae. v.1-2. Romae, 1909-10. 4v.
Arc 936.4 Szafrański, W. Skarby brązowe z epoki wspólnoty. Warszawa, 1955.
Arc 510.2.10F Szalay, Akos. Die hellenistischen Arsenale. Berlin, 1937.
Arc 520.37 Szczepański, Jan A. Ołtarz i miasto. Wyd. 1. Kraków, 1974.
Arc 590.5 Szedlo, G. Le grand sarcophage du Musée civique de Bologne. Bologne, 1876.
Arc 225.20 Szeged, Hungary. Móra Ferenc Múzeum. Kiadványok. 3v.
Arc 225.20F Szeged, Hungary. Móra Ferenc Múzeum. Kiadványok. 2
Arc 497.92 Szekrényi, Lajos. A bibliai régiségtudomány kézikönyve. Szeged, 1894.
Arc 905.27F Szekszár der Alterthümer. (Kubinyi, August von.) Pest, 1857.
Arc 936.14.250 Szeligi pod Płockiem na początku wczesnego średniowiecza. (Szymański, Wojciech.) Wrocław, 1967.
Arc 1190.70 Szentpetery, Imre. Magyar oklevéltan. Budapest, 1930.
Arc 905.95F Szilágyi, János. Aquencum. Budapest, 1956.
Arc 925.155.5 Sztetyłło, Zofia. Rola Mirmekionu w zyciu gospoelarczym państwa bosforskiego. 1. wyd. Warszawa, 1972.
Arc 936.7.10 Szymański, W. Kontakty handlowe Wielkopolski w IX-XI wieku. Poznań, 1958.
Arc 936.14.250 Szymański, Wojciech. Szeligi pod Płockiem na początku wczesnego średniowiecza. Wrocław, 1967.
Arc 612.73 Tabaczyński, Stanisław. Neolit środkowaeuropejski. Wrocław, 1970.
Arc 1025.7.5 Tabelau des catacombes de Rome. (Raoul-Rochette, D.) Paris, n.d.
Arc 1458.3 Tabellarische Übersicht der gewoehnlichsten Altrömische Münzen. (Hartmann, H.L.) Leipzig, 1828.
Arc 905.13 Tabellarisische Ubersicht der Alterthumer in Roseneggers Garten. (Rosenegger, J.) Salzburg, 1824.
Arc 1020.104 Un tabernacle chrétien du Ve siècle. (Rohault de Fleury, G.) Arras, 1880.
Arc 100.1.25 Table alphabétique...l'Académie Celtique...Antiquaires de France. (Prow, M.) Paris, 1894. 2v.
Arc 1317.1.5 Table de la revue numismatique. (Dieudonné, A.) Paris. 1836-1915 2v.
Arc 273.2.5 Table des publications de l'Académie Royale d'Archéologie de Belgique, 1843 à 1900. (Académie Royale d'Archéologie de Belgique.) Anvers? n.d.
Arc 820.202.2 Table générale de la Collection Caranda. (Pilloy, J.) Paris, 1908.
Arc 1033.12.50 Tableau de mortification...stigmates...Christ...S. Suaire. (Paleotti, A.) Paris, 1609.
Arc 1025.7.7 Tableau des catacombes de Rome. (Raoul-Rochette, D.) Paris, 1853.

Arc 1348.43 Tableau du titre. (Darier, Hugues.) Geneve, 1807.
Arc 1020.57 Les tableaux...appartenant aux églises...de Douai. (Dechristé, Louis.) Douai, 1877.
Arc 273.10.8 Tables des publications. (Société Royale d'Archéologie de Bruxelles.) Bruxelles. 1887-1911
Arc 18.1.10 Tables générales de l'année épigraphique. 1901-1950. Paris, 1912-1932.
Htn Arc 1350.4* Tables of ancient coins, weights and measures. (Arbuthnot, J.) London, 1727.
Htn Arc 1535.3* Tables of English silver and gold coins. (Folkes, M.) London, 1763. 2v.
Arc 1010.5 Une tablette de l'ile de Pâques. (Hirmenech, H.P.) Paris, 1912.
Arc 936.55 Une tablette votive thraco-mithriaque du Louvre. (Rostovtsev, M.) Paris, 1923.
Arc 1588.1.16 Tablice do dziela o monetach dawnej Polski. (Zagorski, I.) Warszawa, 1845.
Arc 1125.42 Tabulae palaeographicae. Amsterdam. 1,1968+
Arc 1030.26 Tabularium. pt.1-3; plates. (Rome. Italy. Santa Maria in Via Lata.) Vienna, 1895. 4v.
Arc 1018.22 Tacchi-Venturi, P. Correspondenza di L.A. Muratori. Roma, 1901.
Arc 1153.110 Tachigrafia notarile e scritture segrete medioevali in Italia. (Costamagna, Giorgio.) Roma, 1968.
Arc 1148.2 Die Tachygraphischen Abkürzungen der griechischen Handschriften. (Lehmann, O.) Leipzig, 1880.
Arc 421.16 Tadatel'nie kosti iz Khznani. (Bunakov, I.V.) Moskva, 1935.
Arc 1033.70.5 Taeggi, O.P. Avanzi di pitture del secolo IX in una cripta. n.p., 1885.
Arc 935.1 Tafel, G.L. Via militaris Romanorum Egnatia. Tubingae, 1841.
Arc 785.52.5PF Tafeln. (L'Orange, N.P. Der spätantike Bildschmuch.) Berlin. 10,1939
Arc 830.170 Taffanel, O. Le cayla de Mailhac, Aube. Carcassonne, 1938.
Arc 936.1.7 Tafrali, O. La cité pontique de Dionysopolis. Paris, 1927.
Arc 936.1 Tafrali, O. Mélanges d'archéologie et d'epigraphie byzantines. Paris, 1913.
Arc 936.1.5 Tafrali, O. Topographie de Thessalonique. Paris, 1912.
Arc 936.1.6 Tafrali, O. Topographie de Thessalonique. Paris, 1913.
Arc 395.7.5 Tagebücher. (Kraus, Franz Xaver.) Köln, 1957.
Arc 1033.25 Taglialatela, G. L'arte cristiana nello studio della storia della chiesa. Napoli, 1901.
Arc 1033.79 Taglialatela, G. Del primo vescovo di Napoli Sant'Aspreno. Napoli, 1879.
Arc 1027.53 Taglialatela, G. Dell'antica basilica e della catacomba di Prata. n.p., n.d.
Arc 1027.24.5 Taglialatela, G. Di una imagine de S. Protasio, nella catacombe severiana. Napoli, 1874.
Arc 1033.78 Taglialatela, G. Le solenni feste della traslazione dei martiri di Atripalda. Pompei, 1888.
Arc 1033.35.33 Taglialatela, G. Stauroteca di San Leonzio...Napoli. Napoli, 1877.
Arc 659.15 Tagung das Problem der Klassik im Alten Orient und in der Antike, Halle, 1966. Das Problem der klassik im Alten Orient und in der Antike. Berlin, 1967.
Arc 543.4.15 Tai, Tse tsan. The cradle of humanity. n.p., 1926.
Arc 830.49.15F Taillefer, W. Antiquités de Vésone. Périgneux, 1826. 2v.
Arc 925.180.25 Taina kamennoi cherepakhi. (Larichev, Vitalii E.) Novosibirsk, 1966.
Arc 543.146.5 Tainy ischeznuvshego iskusstva Karakumov. (Sarianidi, Viktor I.) Moskva, 1967.
Arc 925.50.325 Tainy stepnykh kurganov. (Pislarii, Ivan A.) Donetsk, 1972.
Arc 412.22 Tainy tsekh okeanov. (Kondratov, Aleksandr M.) Leningrad, 1971.
Arc 983.10 The Taki, the Swastika, and the Cross in America. (Brinton, D.G.) Philadelphia, 1889.
Arc 1033.12.42 Talamini, G. Della Santissima Sindone e la vanda dei piedi. Torino, n.d.
Arc 830.368 A tale of two caves. (Bordes, François.) N.Y., 1972.
Arc 1584.20 Talery v russkom denezhnom obrashchenii 1654-59 godov. (Spasskii, Ivan G.) Leningrad, 1960.
Arc 925.6.10 Talko-Hryncewicz, J. Suzhdenskoe doietoricheskoe kladbishche. Moskva, 1899.
Arc 493.15F Tall-i-Bakun A, season of 1932. (Langsdorff, A.) Chicago, 1942.
Arc 49.8 Taloha; publication hors série consacrée à l'archéologie des Annales de Université de Madagascar. Tananarive. 1,1965+
Arc 925.8.20 Tamaie. (Knipovick, T.N.) Moskva, 1949.
Arc 925.195 Tamanskii sarkofag. (Piatysheva, N.V.) Moskva, 1949.
Arc 600.220F Tamit, 1964. (Missione Archeologica in Egitto.) Roma, 1967.
Arc 925.20.5 Tanais, poteriannyi i naidennyi gorod. (Shelov, Dmitrii B.) Moskva, 1967.
Arc 925.20 Tanais. (Knipovich, Tatiana N.) Moskva, 1949.
Arc 925.20.10 Tanais i Nizhnii Don v III-I vv. do n.e. (Shelov, Dmitrii B.) Moskva, 1970.
Arc 925.20.15 Tanais i Nizhnyi Don v peroye veka nashei erg. (Shelov, Dmitrii B.) Moskva, 1972.
Arc 1020.9.163 Tani, A.D. Le chiese di Roma. Torino, 1922.
Arc 600.75 Tanis, douze années de fouilles. (Montet, Pierre.) Paris, 1942.
Arc 585.2.2F Tanis. Pt.1. 2. ed. (Petrie, W.M.F.) London, 1889.
Arc 1163.17.15A Tannenbaum, S.A. The handwriting of the Renaissance. N.Y., 1930.
Arc 585.2A Tannis. Pt.1-2. (Petrie, W.M.F.) London, 1885-88. 2v.
Arc 936.5 Tanusz, Bohdan. Kultura przedhistoryczne podola. Lwów, 1919.
Arc 905.23F Tappeiner, Franz. Zum Schluss der Majafrage. Muan, 1897.
Arc 1027.13 Tarantini, G. Di alcunce cripte nell'agro di Brindisi. Napoli, 1878.
Arc 938.50.5 Tarasenka, P. Priešistorine lieŀuwa. Kaunas, 1927.
Arc 820.218F Tardieu, A. La ville gallo-romaine de Beauclair. Clermont-Ferrand, 1882.
Arc 66.1.148 Tarente; des origines a la conquête romaine. (Wirilleumier, Pierre.) Paris, 1939. 2v.
Arc 726.76F Tarentiner Grabkunst. (Klumbach, H.) Reuttingen, 1937.
Arc 1485.7.5 Tariffa di monete medioevale e moderne italiane. (Dotti, E.) Milano, 1913.
Arc 522.40 Tarova harabesi. 2. basi. (Kandemir, Selâhattin.) Istanbul, 1938.
Arc 726.215.5 Tarquinia and Etruscan origins. (Hencken, Hugh O'Neill.) London, 1968.
Arc 843.50.10 Tarraco. (Schulter, Adolf.) Barcelona, 1948.
Arc 608.31 Tarradell, M. Guia arqueológica del Marruecos Español. Tetuán, 1953.
Arc 843.198 Tarradell, M. Les arrels de Catalunya. Barcelona, 1962.
Arc 843.50.5 Tarragona i els seus antics monuments. (Martorell, Jeroni.) Barcelona, 1920.
Arc 843.50 Tarragona prehistòrica i protohistòrica. (Gibert, Augusté M.) Barcelona, 1909.
Arc 936.180.20 Tasić, Nikola. Badenski i vučedolski kulturni kompleks u Jugoslaviji. Beograd, 1967.
Arc 936.180.25 Tasić, Nikola. Crnokalačka bara. Kruševac, 1969.
Arc 936.14.30 Tasienica, P. Sławianski rodowod. Warszawa, 1961.
Arc 936.195.185 Taskjňa Domica, najuznačnejšie sidlisko i udu bukovohorskej kultúry. 1. vyd. (Lichardus, Jan.) Bratislava, 1968.
Arc 935.60 Taslikliogiu, Zafer. Anadolu'da Apollon kültu ile ilgili kaynaklar. Istanbul, 1963.
Arc 935.50 Taslikliogiu, Zafer. Trokya'da epigrafya arastirmalari. Istanbul, 1961-71. 2v.
Arc 1185.1 Tassin, R.P. Nouveau traité de diplomatique. Paris, 1750-65. 6v.
Arc 861.71 Tate, George. The ancient British sculptured rocks of Northumberland. Alnwick, 1865.
Arc 1254.15 Taurent, Vitalieu. Les bulles métriques dans la sigillographie byzantine. Eetjia, 1932.
Arc 925.16.5 Tavadze, F. Bronzy drevnei Gruzii. Tbilisi, 1959.
Arc 830.55 La Tavola Bronzea di Narbona. (Zocco-Rosa, A.) Catania, 1912.
Arc 750.39PF Tavole...foro romano. Atlas. (Canina, Luigi.) Roma, 1845.
Arc 815.23F Le tavolette cerate di Pompei. (Petra, Giulio de.) Roma, 1876.
Arc 459.3.20 Taxila. (Marshall, John.) Cambridge, 1951. 3v.
Arc 861.40.10 Taylor, A.J. The Roman baths of Bath. Bath, 1923.
Arc 875.120 Taylor, B. Archaeology of Tayside. Dundee, 196-?
Arc 743.4 Taylor, G.L. The stones of Etruria and marbles of ancient Rome. London, 1859.
Arc 861.49.5 Taylor, H. Ancient crosses and holy wells of Lancashire. Manchester, 1906.
Arc 540.10F Taylor, Joan. Myrton-Pigadhes. Oxford, 1957.
Arc 412.2 Taylor, Joan du Plat. Marine archaeology. London, 1965.
Arc 1400.2 Taylor, S. Gold and silver coin examiner. N.Y., 1846-57. 3 pam.
Arc 875.134 Tayside before history. (Dundee, Scotland. Museum and Art Gallery.) Dundee, 1971.
Arc 386.22 Tea, Eva. Giacomo Boni nella vita del suo tempo. Milano, 1932. 2v.
Arc 843.74 El teatro de Mérida. (Mélida, José R.) Madrid, 1915.
Arc 1033.12.67 Teatro dell'umana rendenzione...relazione istorica del...sangue...Sarzana. (Rossi, B. de.) Massa, 1708.
Arc 608.30.5 Il teatro di Sabatha e l'architettura teatrale africana. (Caputa, Giacomo.) Roma, 1959.
Arc 736.9F Teatro di Taormina. (Strazzeri, Niccolo.) n.p., n.d.
Arc 730.209F Il teatro greco di Siracusa. (Rizzo, G.E.) Milano, 1923.
Arc 726.25.13 Il teatro romano di Ostia. (Calza, Guido.) Roma, 1927.
Arc 726.180 Il teatro romano di Verona. (Forno, Federico dal.) Verona, 1954.
Arc 608.38 Tebessa. (Sérée de Roch.) Alger, 1952.
Arc 890.210F Techningar. v.1-3. (Stockholm. Svenska Statens Historiska Museum.) Stockholm, 1873-83.
Arc 13.5 Technische Beiträge Archäologie. (Mainz. Römisch-Germanisches Zentralmuseum.) 1,1959+ 2v.
Arc 407.31 Technische und naturwissensachaftliche Beiträge zur Feldarchäologie. (Wilkinson, Edward M.) Köln, 1974.
Arc 412.5 The technology of industiral archaeology. (Pannell, John Percival Masterman.) Newton Abbot, 1966.
Arc 1468.40 Tecnica e cronologia delle monete greche. (Gabrici, E.) Roma, 1951.
Arc 588.7 Teh Rainesseum. 1896. (Quibell, J.E.) London, 1898.
Arc 556.3 Tehena. (Galassi, G.) Roma, 1942.
Arc 20.5 Teheraner Forschungen. Berlin. 1-2 3v.
Arc 843.45 Teixeira de Aragão, A.C. Relatorio sobre o comiterio romano. Lisboa, 1868.
Arc 1478.27 Teixeira de Aragão, Augusto. Descripção historica das moedas romanas existentes no gabinete numismatico de S.M. el Rei o Senhor Dom Luiz I. Lisboa, 1870.
Arc 843.5 Teixidor, J. Antiquedades de Valencia. Valencia, 1895. 2v.
Arc 925.95 Tekhnika obra botki metala v drev. ruhssi. (Kolchin, B.A.) Moskva, 1953.
Arc 925.9.35 Tekhov, Bagrat V. K istorii izucheniia pamiatnikov epokhi eneolita i bronzy v nizhnem. Tbilisi, 1963.
Arc 925.9.125 Tekhov, Bagrat V. Ocherki drevnei istorii i arkheologii Iugo-Osetri. Tbilisi, 1971.
Arc 925.50.170 Telehin, Dmytro I. Dnipro-donets'ka kul'tura. Kyïv, 1968.
Arc 925.50.290 Telehin, Dnytro I. Seredn'ostohivs'ka kul'tura epokhy midi. Kyïv, 1973.
Arc 505.63F Teleilát Ghassúl. (Rome. Pontifico Istituto Biblico.) Roma, 1934.
Arc 1020.120.15 Telfer, William. The treasure of São Roque. London, 1932.
Arc 501.16.11 The Tell Amarna tablets. (Conder, C.R.) London, 1893.
Arc 501.16.12 The Tell Amarna tablets. (Conder, C.R.) London, 1893.
Arc 501.16.13A The Tell Amarna tablets. 2. ed. (Conder, C.R.) London, 1894.
Arc 505.115 Tell Chuēra in Nordost-Syrien. (Moortgat, Anton.) Köln, 1960.
Arc 505.115.2 Tell Chuēra in Nordost-Syrien. (Moortgat, Anton.) Köln, 1962.
Arc 505.115.3 Tell Chuēra in Nordost-Syrien. (Moortgat, Anton.) Köln, 1965.
Arc 503.1 Tell El Mutesellim. Leipzig, 1908-1929. 3v.
Arc 510.2.9F Das Temenos für den Herrscher Kult. (Boehringer, C.) Berlin, 1937.
Arc 635.207.9 Der Tempel der Aphaia auf Aegena. (Fiechter, E.R.) München, 1906.
Arc 785.71 Die Tempel der Fortuna und der Mater Matuta am Forum Boarium in Rom. (Lyngby, H.) Berlin, 1939.
Arc 785.1 Tempel der Vesta und das Haus der Vestalinnen. (Jordan, Henri.) Berlin, 1886.
Arc 520.1 Tempel des Athena Polias zu Pergamon. (Bohn, R.) Berlin, 1881.
Arc 505.5.7 Der Tempel von Jerusalem. (Wolff, P.O.) Graz, 1887.
Arc 505.5.110 Der Tempel von Jerusalem von Salomo bis Herodes. (Busink, T.A.) Leiden, 1970.
Arc 726.85 Die Tempel von Paestum. (Lamb, Carl.) Leipzig, 1944.
Arc 726.24 Tempel zu Tivoli bei Rom. (Müller, G.A.) Leipzig, 1899.

Arc 853.20.25F Der Tempelbezirk im Altbachtale zu Trier. (Loeschcke, S.) Berlin, 1938-42.
Arc 726.10.17 Il tempio della fortuna prenestina. (Marucchi, Orazio.) Roma, 1908.
Arc 608.30F Il tempio d'Iside in Sabratha. (Pesce, G.) Roma, 1953.
Arc 608.17.19F Il tempio e l'altare di Apollo a Cirene. (Pernier, Luigi.) Bergamo, 1935.
Arc 830.164 Temple, P. La préhistoire du département de l'Avignon. Thèse. Nîmes, 1935.
Arc 457.20 Temple, Richard C. Notes on antiquities in Ramannadesa. Bombay, 1894.
Arc 458.4.5 Temple, Richard C. Notes on the seven pagodas. London, 1928-29.
Htn Arc 505.5.5* The temple. (Lightfoot, J.) London, 1650.
Arc 1470.27 The temple coins of Olympia. (Seltman, C.J.) Cambridge, Eng., 1921. 2v.
Arc 545.227.38 Le temple d'Amada. (Gauthier, H.) Le Caire, 1913.
Arc 600.55.5 Le temple d'Amon-Rê à Karnak. (Barguet, Paul.) Le Caire, 1962.
Arc 543.7.19F Le temple d'Angkor Vat. pt.2. (École Française d'Extrême-Orient, Hanoi, Indo-China.) Paris, 1930. 2v.
Arc 820.201 Le temple d'Auguste et la nationalité. (Bernard, A.) Lyon, 1863.
Arc 505.5.50 Temple de Jérusalem. (Herrmann, J.) Valenciennes, 1882.
Arc 505.5.35 Le Temple de Jérusalem. (Parrat, André.) Neuchâtel, 1954.
NEDL Arc 495.6PF Le temple de Jérusalem. (Vogue, M. de.) Paris, 1864.
Arc 545.227.29 Le temple de Kalabach. (Gauthier, M.H.) Le Caire, 1911. 2v.
Arc 600.135 Le Temple de l'homme. (Schwaller de Lubicz, R.A.) Paris, 1957. 3v.
Arc 545.227.36 Temple de Ouadi Es-Seboua. (Gauthier, H.) Le Caire, 1912.
Arc 505.5.52 Temple de Salomon; sa description d'après découvertes récentes. (Saint-Aignan.) Paris, 1875.
Arc 585.12.2 The temple of Deir el Bahari. (Naville, E.H.) London, 1894.
Htn Arc 585.14F* The temple of Deir el Bahari. (Naville, E.H.) London, 1895-1908. 7v.
Arc 545.227.33 Temple of Dendûr. (Blackman, A.M.) Le Caire, 1911.
Arc 545.227.40 The temple of Derr. (Blackman, A.M.) Le Caire, 1913.
Arc 518.4 The Temple of Diana at Ephesus. (Fergusson, J.) London, 1883.
Arc 600.30 The temple of Mut in Asher. (Benson, Margaret.) London, 1899.
Arc 889.15 The temple of Nehalennia at Domburg. (Hondius-Crone, Ada.) Amsterdam, 1955.
Arc 785.56 Temple of Quirinus. Thesis. (Pickett, Cora Aileen.) Philadelphia, 1930.
Arc 505.5.15 The Temple of Solomon. (Osgood, P.E.) Chicago, 1910.
Arc 588.13 Temple of the Kings at Abydos. (Caulfield, A.S.G.) London, 1902.
Arc 736.2 Les temples de Syracuse. (Beulé, C.E.) n.p., n.d.
Arc 585.47 Temples of Armant. (Mond, Robert.) London, 1940. 2v.
Arc 600.53F The temples of Kawa. v.1-2; plates. (MacAdam, M.F.L.) London, 1949- 4v.
Arc 1478.38 Temples of Rome as coin types. (Brown, D.F.) N.Y., 1940.
Arc 540.5F The temples of Soli. (Westholm, A.) Stockholm, 1936.
Arc 505.5 The temples of the Jews. (Fergusson, J.) London, 1878.
Arc 505.5.30 Templet i Jerusalem. (Lindberg, N.) Kolding, 1880.
Arc 505.5.32 Templet i Jerusalem. (Lindberg, N.) Stockholm, 1881.
Arc 785.67F I templi della Zona Argentina. (Munoz, A.) Roma, 1929.
Arc 889.4.2 Les temps préhistoriques en Belgique. 2. éd. (Dupont, Édouard.) Bruxelles, 1872.
Arc 895.5.3 Les temps préhistoriques en Suède. (Montelius, Oscar.) Paris, 1895.
Arc 861.130 Ten seasons digging, 1945-1954. (Lincoln Archaeological Research Committee.) Lincoln, 1955.
Arc 565.1 Ten years' digging in Egypt. (Petrie, W.M.F.) N.Y., 1892.
Arc 565.1.2 Ten years' digging in Egypt. 2. ed. (Petrie, W.M.F.) London, 1893.
Arc 858.11 Ten years' diggings in Celtic and Saxon grave hills. (Bateman, T.) London, 1861.
Arc 958.1.8 Ten years' diggings in Lenâpè Sand, Delaware. (Abbott, C.C.) Trenton, New Jersey, 1912.
Arc 1680.10.9 Tenney, M.M. Communion tokens. Grand Rapids, 1936.
Arc 501.16.5 Tent work in Palestine. (Conder, C.R.) London, 1878. 2v.
Arc 501.16.7 Tent work in Palestine. (Conder, C.R.) London, 1887.
Arc 1510.2 Tentzel, W.E. Saxonia Numismatica, oder Medaillen-Cabinet von Bedächtnissmünzen. Dresden, 1705. 2v.
Arc 1510.3 Tentzel, W.E. Saxonia Numismatica, oder Medaillen-Cabinet von Münzen. Dresden, 1705. 2v.
Arc 945.2 Teocalli e piramidi. (Grossi, V.) Torino, 1888.
Arc 1254.1 Teodora Ducaina Paleologhina. (Carrara, F.) Vienna, 1840.
Arc 1033.17.18 Teodoro di Santa Maria. Memorie...miracolosa immagine della Madonna Ssma detta della Vittoria. Roma, 1796.
Arc 925.50.90 Terenozhkin, A.I. Predskifskii period na Dneprovskom Pravoberezh'e. Kiev, 1961.
Arc 1510.171.1 Tergast, Pefrus. Die Münzen Ostfrieslands. Leer, 1974.
Arc 853.94 Tergast. Die beidniscken Alterthümer Ostfrieslands. Emden, 1879.
Arc 905.134 Tergolape. (Bamberger, Anton.) Linz, 1966.
Arc 1470.15 Terina. (Regling, K.) Berlin, 1906.
Arc 1588.1.32 Terlecki, W. The catalogue of Polish coins. Warsaw, 1960.
Arc 1588.1.33 Terlecki, W. Ilustrowany katalog monet polskich bitych w okresie 1916-1965. 2. wyd. Warszawa, 1965.
Arc 1588.1.34 Terlecki, W. Katalog monet polskich. Warszawa, 1960.
Arc 1588.1.70 Terlecki, W. Mennica warszawska 1765-1965. Wrocław, 1970.
Htn Arc 785.40.10* Le terme dei Romani disegnate. (Palladio, A.) Vicenza, 1797.
Arc 785.38.7 Le terme di Agrippa. (Maes, Constantino.) Roma, 1882.
Arc 608.18.5F Le terme di Lepcis (Leptis Magna). (Bartoccini, R.) Bergamo, 1929.
Arc 543.66.23 Termezskaia Arkheologicheskaia Kompleksnaia Ekspeditsiia, 1937, 1961-1962. Buddiiskie peshchery Kara-tepe v starom Termeze. Moskva, 1969.
Arc 543.66.24 Termezskaia Arkheologicheskaia Kompleksnaia Ekspeditsiia, 1937, 1961-1962. Buddiiskii kul'tovyi tsentr Kara-tepe v starom Termeze. Moskva, 1972.
Arc 543.66.20 Termezskaia Arkheologicheskaia Kompleksnaia Ekspeditsiia, 1937, 1961-1962. Kara-tepe. Moskva, 1964.
Arc 1033.17.203 Terninck, A. Notre-Dame du Joyel, ou Histoire légendaire et numismatique de la chandelle d'Arras. Arras, 1853.
Htn Arc 790.9* Ternite, W. Wandgemälde aus Pompeii und Herculanum. Berlin, 1858?
Arc 726.62 Terra d'Otranto. Commissione Conservatrice dei Monumenti Storici e di Belle Arti. Relazione. Lecci.
Arc 66.1.34 Terracine. (La Blanchere, M.R. de.) Paris, 1884.
Arc 925.13.190 Terrakotovye statuetki. v.3- Moskva, 1974- 2v.
Arc 726.125F Le terremare delle provincie di Modena. (Säflund, G.) Lund, 1939.
Htn Arc 1163.2.3* Terreros y Pando, E. Paleografía española. Madrid, 1758.
Arc 600.6.9 Terres mortes. (Chenillon, A.) Paris, 1897.
Arc 1411.8 Terrien de Lacouperie, A.E.J.B. Catalogue of Chinese coins from the 7th century B.C. to A.D. 621. London, 1892.
Arc 1033.12.170 Terris, F. Saint mors de Carpentras et son reliquaire. Carpentras, 1874.
Arc 1033.12.171 Terris, F. Saint mors de Carpentras et son reliquaire. n.p., n.d.
Arc 950.204 Terry, J. Sculptured anthropoid ape heads. N.Y., 1891.
Arc 659.10 Terzaghi, Nicola. Prometeo; scritti di archeologia e filologia. Torino, 1966.
Arc 635.219 Tés Ellados. (Mnémeia.) Athēnai, 1906.
Arc 93.35 Tesi dl laurear. (Milan. Università. Istituto di Archeologia.) Roma. 1-2
Arc 1588.6.35 Tesla-Zarić, Dobrila. Katalog novca Osmanske imperije sakupljenog- na području SFR Jugoslavije. Beograd, 1974.
Arc 1020.6.7 Il tesoro di San Marco in Venezia. (Passini, A.) Venezia, 1878.
Arc 1033.17.99.5 Tesoro guadalupano. (Vera, Fortino Hipólito.) Amecameca, 1887.
Arc 1033.17.463 Tesoro nascosto minifestato per la miracolosa invenzione di Santa Maria...Napoli. (Corvino, R.) Napoli, 1831.
Arc 726.225F Il tesoro romano barbarico di Reggio Emilia. (Degani, Mario.) Firenze, 1959.
Arc 1494.10 El tesoro visigotico de la Capilla. (Fernandez Lopez, M.) Sevilla, 1895.
Arc 750.37.1 Tesserarum urbis Romae et suburbi plumbearum sylloge. Supplement. (Rostovtsev, Mikhail Ivanovich.) St. Petersbourgh, 1905.
Arc 785.119.1F Tesserarum urbis Romae et suburbi plumbearum sylloge. Text and atlas. (Rostovtsev, Milchail Ivanovich.) Leipzig, 1975. 2v.
Arc 505.2.15F Les tessères et les monnaies de Palmyre, 1944. (Bibliothèque Nationale. Département des Médailles et Antiques.) Paris, 1962. 2v.
Arc 1185.30.2 Tessier, Georges. La diplomatique. 2. éd. Paris, 1962.
Arc 1190.87 Tessier, Georges. Diplomatique royale française. Paris, 1962.
Arc 785.115 Testaguzza, Otello. Portus. Roma, 1970.
Arc 388.14 Testaments of time. 1. ed. (Deuel, Leo.) N.Y., 1965.
Arc 550.10F Testimane in Egittto. (Angioletti, Giovanni B.) Firenze, 1958.
Arc 1020.142 Testimonianze archaeologiche della tradizione paolina a Malta. (Cagiano de Azevedo, Michelangelo.) Roma, 1966.
Arc 1025.12 Testimony of the catacombs. (Marriott, W.B.) London, 1870.
Arc 1018.55 Testini, P. Archeologia cristiana. Roma, 1958.
Arc 600.17 Les têtes de pierre...tombeaux égyptiens. (Naville, E.) Genève, 1909.
Arc 1053.15 Un tétraptique russe. (Martinov, Jean.) Arras, 1877.
Arc 1490.8.9 Die Tetrodrachmenprägung von Segesta. (Lederer, Philipp.) München, 1910.
Arc 848.17 Teudt, Wilhelm. Germanische Heiligtümer. Jena, 1929.
Arc 848.17.5 Teudt, Wilhelm. Germanische Heiligtümer. 4. Aufl. Jena, 1936.
Arc 905.24.5 Teurnia; die römischen und frühchristlichen Altertümer Oberkärntens. (Egger, Rudolf.) Wien, 1924.
Arc 905.24.6 Teurnia. 2. Aufl. (Egger, Rudolf.) Wien, 1926.
Arc 905.24.14 Teurnia. 4. Aufl. (Egger, Rudolf.) Klagenfurt, 1955.
Arc 324.5 Texas. University. Department of Anthropology. Archaeology series. Austin.
Arc 510.4 Texier, Charles. Description de l'Asie Mineure. Paris, 1839-1849. 3v.
Arc 510.9 Texier, Charles. Principal ruins of Asia Minor. London, 1865.
Arc 612.15 A text-book of European archaeology. (Macalister, R.A.S.) Cambridge, Eng., 1921.
Arc 395.1.5 Textbuch zu Th. Schreibers Kulturhistorischem Bilderatlas des klassischen Altertums. (Bernhardi, K.) Leipzig, 1888.
Arc 600.3.15 Textes biographiques du Sérapéum de Memphis. (Vercoutter, J.) Paris, 1962.
Arc 935.32 Tezcan, Burhan. 1962 iki 1963. Ankara, 1904.
Arc 935.32.10 Tezcan, Burhan. 1964 kaçumbeli kazese. Ankara, 1966.
Arc 935.32.5 Tezcan, Burhan. 1964 yalencak köyü çaleşmalare. Ankara, 1966.
Arc 923.114 Tezisy dokladov. (Vsesoiuznaia Sessiia, Posviashchennaia Itogam Arkheologicheskikh i Etnograficheskikh Issledovanii 1966 goda.) Kishinev, 1967.
Arc 853.96 Thärigen, Günter. Die Nordharzgruppe der Elbgermanen bis zur sächsischen Überlagerung. Berlin, 1939.
Arc 1237.10 Thailand. Ministry of Interior. Changwat seals. Bangkok, 1968.
Arc 608.73 Thamurida, fouilles du Service des antiquités du Maroc. v.1-2. Paris, 1965. 3v.
Arc 87.1.39 Thanatos. (Robert, C.) Berlin, 1879.
Arc 726.290 Tharros. (Pesce, Gennaro.) Cagliari, 1966.
Arc 689.9 Hē Thasos. (Lazarides, D.I.) Thessalonikē, 1958.
Arc 716.7.10F The Erechtheum. (Paton, James M.) Cambridge, 1927.
Arc 716.7.10PF The Erechtheum. Atlas. (Paton, James M.) Cambridge, 1927.
Arc 716.2.15 The theater of Dionysus in Athens. (Pickard-Cambridge, Arthur Wallace.) Oxford, 1946.
Arc 674.3.8F Das Theater von Epidauros. (Gerhan, Armen.) Stuttgart, 1961.
Arc 530.14.15F Das Theater von Priene. (Gerkan, Armin von.) München, 1921.
Arc 608.1.29 Le théâtre de Dougga. (Carton, Louis B.C.) Paris, 1902.
Arc 635.206 Le théâtre de Polyclète. (Dumon, K.) Paris, 1889.
Arc 830.21.5 Le théâtre de Vesontio. (Castan, Auguste.) Besançon, 1873.
Arc 830.13 Le Théâtre d'Orange. (Hermann, M.J.) Paris, 1897.
Arc 716.2.5 The theatre of Dionysus. (Wheeler, James R.) n.p., n.d.
Arc 600.20 Theban ostraca. Toronto, 1913.
Arc 586.15F The Theban tombs series. London. 1-5,1915-1933 5v.
Arc 600.6.15F Thèbes. (Capart, Jean.) Bruxelles, 1925.
Arc 600.6.20F Thèbes. (Carlier, A.) Paris, 1948.
Arc 600.6A Thebes. (Rhind, A.H.) London, 1862.
Arc 545.223 Thebes and its five greater temples. (Abney, W. de W.) London, 1876.
Arc 823.19.45 Thédenat, H. Antiquaires 1880. Paris, 1880.
Arc 823.19.60 Thédenat, H. Antiquaires 1881. Paris, 1881.
Arc 823.19.90 Thédenat, H. Antiquités romaines trouvées aux Lilas-Romainville. Paris, 1881.
Arc 823.19.10 Thédenat, H. Cachet d'oculiste. Paris, 1879.
Arc 823.19.40 Thédenat, H. Cachet du médecin Feror. Paris, 1880.
Arc 823.19.4F Thédenat, H. Cognitio cognitionibus. Parisiis, 1873.

Author and Title Listing

Arc 823.19.5F Thédenat, H. Commentariensis a commentarus commentarius. Parisiis, 1873.
Arc 823.19.95 Thédenat, H. Critique, 1881. Paris, 1881.
Arc 823.19.110 Thédenat, H. Critique, 1882. Paris, 1882.
Arc 823.19.25 Thédenat, H. Critique 1880. Paris, 1880.
Arc 823.19.85 Thédenat, H. De Villefosse. Inscription de Gordien. Vienne, 1881.
Arc 823.19.155 Thédenat, H. Deux masques d'enfants. Paris, 1886.
Arc 823.19.130 Thédenat, H. Diffusion du droit latin. Paris, 1885.
Arc 823.19.30 Thédenat, H. Droit latin de O. Hirschfeld. Paris, 1880.
Arc 823.19.15 Thédenat, H. L'epigraphie romaine en France. Paris, 1879.
Arc 823.19.125 Thédenat, H. Étude sur Lambèse par Wilmanns. Paris, 1884.
Arc 823.19.70 Thédenat, H. Etvi à collyre égyptien. Paris, 1881.
Arc 823.19.75 Thédenat, H. Exposition d'Utique. Paris, 1881.
Arc 823.19.100 Thédenat, H. Extrait des procès-verbaux. Nogent-le-Rotrou, 1881.
Arc 750.209 Thédenat, H. Le forum romain et la voie sacrée. Paris, 1905.
Arc 823.19.170 Thédenat, H. Inscription de la caserne des Vigiles à Ostie. Paris, 1904.
Arc 823.19.115 Thédenat, H. Inscriptions latines des fouilles d'Utique. Vienne, 1882.
Arc 823.19.80 Thédenat, H. Lettre a M. Ernest Desjardins. Paris, 1881.
Arc 823.19.168 Thédenat, H. M. Henri Thélier et Mlle Henriette Filhos. Paris, 1903.
Arc 823.19.50 Thédenat, H. Les médecins Magillius et D. Gallius Sextus. Paris, 1880.
Arc 823.19.150 Thédenat, H. Milliaires du Var. Paris, 1886.
Arc 823.19.20 Thédenat, H. Les noms des deux premiers Gordiens par Sallet. Paris, 1883.
Arc 823.19.35 Thédenat, H. Notes sur deux inscriptions fausses. Paris, 1880.
Arc 823.19.55 Thédenat, H. Observations sur l'èpigraphie des Alpes maritimes de M.E. Blanc. Paris, 1881.
Arc 810.22 Thédenat, H. Pompéi. Vie privée. Histoire. Paris, 1906.
Arc 810.22.2 Thédenat, H. Pompéi. Vie publique. Paris, 1906.
Arc 810.22.5 Thédenat, H. Pompéi. Vie publique. Paris, 1910.
Arc 823.19.120 Thédenat, H. Sur une inscription inédite. Paris, 1884.
Arc 823.19.145F Thédenat, H. Les trésors d'argenteuie trouvés en Gaule. Paris, 1885. 3v.
Arc 823.19.105 Thédenat, H. Zénobie vaballathus...Philippe le Jeune par Mommsen. Paris, 1882.
Arc 823.19.65 Thédenat, H. 14 juillet, 1881. Paris, 1881.
Arc 823.19.165 Pamphlet vol. Thédenat, H. 1888-1902. 9 pam.
Arc 785.13.5 Thédenat, Henry. Le Forum Romain et les Forum impériaux. Paris, 1900.
Arc 1027.23.20 Themes from St. John's gospel in early Roman catacomb painting. (Lamberton, C.D.) Princeton, 1905.
Arc 659.20F Theocharēs, Dēmētrios R. Neolithikē Hellas. Athēnai, 1973.
Arc 600.7 Die Theodor Graf'schen Funde in Aegypten. (Karabaček.) Wien, 1883.
Arc 407.14 Theodor Wiegand. (Watzinger, C.) München, 1944.
Arc 402.10.25 Theodore Reinach, (1860-1928). (Jamot, Paul.) Paris, 1928.
Arc 1027.50.5 Theologische Etrag...Katakombenforschung. (Schulke, V.) Leipzig, 1882.
Arc 635.20F Thera 1895-. (Hiller von Gärtringen.) Berlin, 1899- 4v.
Arc 785.38 Die Thermen des Agrippa. (Huelsen, C.) Rom, 1910.
Arc 608.2.65 Les thermes d'Antonin à Carthage. (Lézine, Alexandre.) Tunis, 1969.
Arc 785.39.10 Les Thermes de Caracalla. 4. éd. (Ripostelli, Giuseppe.) Rome, 191- .
Arc 785.40.15 Les thermes des Romains. v.5. (Bertotti Scamozzi, Ottavio.) Vicenza, 1797.
Arc 1353.5 Thesauro Caesarum...Numorun Gemmarumque. (Eckhel, J.) Budae, 1799.
Arc 720.205 Thesaurus antiquitatum beneventanarum. (Vila, G. de.) Romae, 1754.
NEDL Arc 720.200 Thesaurus antiquitatum et historiarum Italiae. (Graevuis, J.G.) Lugdunum Batavorum, 1704-23. 16v.
NEDL Arc 720.200.2 Thesaurus antiquitatum et historiarum Siciliae. v.1-15. (Graevius, J.G.) Lugdunum Batavorum, 1723-25. 8v.
Htn Arc 1455.1* Thesaurus Brandenburgicus. (Beger, L.) Colonia Marchica, 1696. 3v.
Arc 1018.40 Thesaurus commentationum...antiquiorum...illustrandis antiquitatibus christianis. (Volbeding, J.E.) Lipsiae, 1847. 2v.
Htn Arc 1475.3* Thesaurus Morellianus. (Morelli, A.) Amsterdam, 1734. 2v.
Arc 1370.1 Thesaurus numismatum. (Patin, C.) Amsterdam? 1672.
Arc 1335.15 Thesaurus numismatum. (Thott, O.) Copenhagen, 1789.
Htn Arc 1370.2* Thesaurus numismatum. v.1-2. (Patin, C.) Amsterdam? 1672.
Arc 1663.57 Thesaurus numismatum modernorum huius seculi, sive numismata mnemonica et iconica qui bus praecipui eventus et res gestae ab anno MDCC illustrantur. (Koernlein, Melchior.) Norimbergae, 1711-17?
Arc 853.367 Thesaurus Orcivus Marchicus. Faksimile. (Seidel, Martin Fredrich.) Berlin, 1972.
Arc 1369.1 Thesaurus sel. numismata antiqua. (Oesel, J.) Amsterdam, 1677.
Arc 716.10 Das Theseion und der Tempel des Ares in Athen. (Ross, Ludwig.) Halle, 1852.
Arc 87.1.38 Thesens und Minotauros. (Conze, Alexander.) Berlin, 1878.
Arc 689.3 Thessalika Mnēmeia. (Arvanitopoulas, A.S.) Athēnai, 1909.
Arc 85.3 Thessalonikā archaiologikon periodikon dēmosieuma. Bolos. 1-3,1958-1960
Arc 830.354 Thevenon, Urbain. La nécropole du monastier à Vagnas. Saint-Etienne, 1961.
Arc 830.201 Thévenot, Emile. Le Beaunois gallo-romain; ouvrage présenté et complété. Bruxelles, 1971.
Arc 710.16 Thibaudet, A. L'acropole. Paris, 1929.
Arc 1153.111 Thiel, Helmut van. Mittellateinische Texte: ein Handschriften-Lesebuch. Göttingen, 1972.
Arc 1070.206 Thiele, G. Antike Himmelsbilder. Berlin, 1898.
Arc 785.13.45 Thiele, Richard. Das Forum Romanum. 2. Aufl. Erfurt, 1906.
Arc 830.45 Thiellen, A. Hommage à Boucher de Perthes. Paris, 1904.
Arc 630.20 Thieman, Eugen. Hellenistische Vatergottheiten. Münster, 1959.
Arc 1033.12.191 Thiers, J.B. Dissertation sur la sainte larme de Vendome. Amsterdam, 1751.
Arc 1033.12.192 Thiers, J.B. Réponse à la lettre du père Mabillon...prétendue sur larme. Cologne, 1700.
Arc 1076.3.35 Thiers, J.B. Traitez des cloches. Paris, 1721.
Arc 510.204 Thiersch, F. Die Koenigsburg von Pergamon. Stuttgart, 1883.
Arc 915.1 Thioly, F. Epoques antéhistoriques an Mont Salève. Genève, 1867.
Arc 589.7 The third Egyptian dynasty. (Garstang, J.) Westminster, 1904.
Arc 543.3.10 A third journey of exploration in Central Asia, 1913-16. (Stein, Mark Aurel.) London, 1916.
Arc 66.1.193 Thiriet, Freddy. La Romanie vénitienne au Moyen Age. Paris, 1959.
Arc 1077.10 Thoby, Paul. Le crucifix. Nantes, 1959.
Arc 1077.10.2 Thoby, Paul. Le crucifix. Supplément. Nantes, 1963.
Arc 858.84 Thom, Alexander. Megalithic sites in Britain. Oxford, 1967.
Arc 66.1.35 Thomas, A. Francesco da Barberino. Paris, 1883.
Arc 66.1.25 Thomas, A. Recherches sur l'entrée de Spagne. Paris, 1882.
Arc 905.100F Thomas, Baja. Archäologische Funde in Ungarn. Budapest, 1956.
Arc 983.12 Thomas, C. Burial mounds of the northern sections of the United States. Washington? 1884?
Arc 943.9.5 Thomas, C. Introduction...study North American archaeology. Cincinnati, 1903.
Arc 950.208 Thomas, C. Report of mound explorations of Bureau of Ethnology. Washington, 1894.
Arc 983.12.5 Thomas, C. Work in mound exploration of the Bureau of Ethnology. Washington, 1887.
Arc 861.174 Thomas, Charles. Christian antiquities of Camborne. St. Austell, Cornwall, 1967.
Arc 858.105 Thomas, Charles. The early Christian archaeology of Northern Britain. London, 1971.
Arc 969.1.15 Thomas, Cyrus. The problem of the Ohio mounds. Washington, 1889.
Arc 497.86 Thomas, David Winton. Archaeology and Old Testament study. Oxford, 1967.
Arc 1405.1 Thomas, E. Marsden's Numismata orientalia. v.1. London, 1874.
Arc 1408.6 Thomas, E. On the coins of the kings of Ghazni. London, 1848.
Arc 830.16.7 Thomas, Edme. Histoire de l'antique cité d'Autun. Autun, 1846.
Arc 875.16 Thomas, F.L.W. Primitive dwellings and hypogea of the Outer Hebrides. Edinburgh, 1869.
Arc 830.116 Thomas, Henri. Une nouvelle page ajoutèe à l'histoire de Rosny-sur-Seine. Paris, 1893.
Arc 858.80 Thomas, Nicholas. A guide to prehistoric England. London, 1960.
Arc 858.96 Thomas, Stanley E. Pre-Roman Britain. London, 1965.
Arc 543.40F Thomassen à Thuessink van der Hoop, A.N.J. Megalithische oudheden in Zuid-Sumatra. Proefschrift. Zutphen, 1932.
Arc 404.1.30 Thompson, Alexander Hamilton. A bibliography of the published writings of Sir William St. John Hope. Leeds, 1929.
Arc 1166.6 Thompson, D.V. Medieval parchment-making. London, 1935.
Arc 1143.2.3 Thompson, Edward Maunde. Handbook of Greek and Latin palaeography. Ann Arbor, 1973.
Arc 1143.2 Thompson, Edward Maunde. Handbook of Greek and Latin palaeography. N.Y., 1893.
Arc 1143.2.11 Thompson, Edward Maunde. Hencheiridion Hellēnikēs. Athēnai, 1903.
Arc 1143.2.5A Thompson, Edward Maunde. Introduction to Greek and Latin palaeography. Oxford, 1912.
Arc 1143.2.7 Thompson, Edward Maunde. Paleografia greca e latina. Milano, 1899.
Arc 861.155 Thompson, F.D. Deva: Roman Chester. Chester, Eng., 1959.
Arc 588.36 Thompson, H. The gospel of St. John. London, 1924.
Arc 1468.64 Thompson, Margaret. An inventory of Greek coin hoards. N.Y., 1973.
Arc 925.329 Thompson, Michael W. Novgorod the Great. London, 1967.
Arc 392.9.80 Thompson, R.C. Harry R.H. Hall, 1873-1930. London, 1930.
Arc 1335.50 Thomsen, C.J. Catalogue de la collection de monnaies. v.1, pt.1-2; v.2, pt.1-3; v.3, pt.1-2. Copenhague, 1869-76. 7v.
Arc 497.43 Thomsen, P. Palästina und seine Kultur in fünf Jahrtausenden. 2. Aufl. Leipzig, 1917.
Arc 1478.65F Thomsen, Rudi. Early Roman coinage. København, 1957. 3v.
Arc 861.11.7F Thomson, James. A great free city; the book of Silchester. London, 1924. 2v.
Arc 1153.98F Thomson, Samuel Harrison. Latin bookhands of the later Middle Ages, 1110-1500. Cambridge, Eng., 1969.
Arc 785.22.10F Thon, C. Il palazzo de' Cesari sul monte Palatino. Roma, 1828.
Arc 689.10 Thorikos. Bruxelles. 1,1963+ 3v.
Arc 1335.15 Thott, O. Thesaurus numismatum. Copenhagen, 1789.
Arc 407.6.10 Thousands of years. (Wilson, John Albert.) N.Y., 1972.
Arc 608.28 Thouvenat, R. Volubilis. Paris, 1949.
Arc 66.1.149 Thouvenot, R. Essai sur le province romaine de Béteque. Paris, 1940.
Arc 1138.1 Thoyts, E.E. How to decipher and study old documents. London, 1893.
Arc 1470.21 Den thraciske konge Lysimachus's mynter. (Müller, L.) Kjøbenhavn, 1857.
Arc 936.195.115F Thrakisches Gräberfeld der Hallstattzeit in Chotín. (Dušek, Mikuláš.) Bratislava, 1966.
Arc 136.1.60 Three...tables...exhibiting a state of...Society of Antiquaries. (Fenn, John.) London, 1784. 2 pam.
Arc 861.10.22 Three Viking graves in the Isle of Man. (Bersu, Gerhard.) London, 1966.
Htn Arc 1348.38* Het thres oor aft schat van alle de specien. Gheprint Tautluerpen, 1580.
Arc 412.16 Throckmorton, Peter. Shipwrecks and archaeology: the unharvested sea. 1. ed. Boston, 1970.
Arc 974.1 Thruston, G.P. The antiquities of Tennessee. Cincinnati, 1890.
Arc 390.5.5 Thulin, Oskar. Johannes Ficker. Halle, 1936.
Arc 426.9 The thunder-weapon in ancient Japan. (Reischauer, E.O.) Baltimore, 1940.
Arc 853.320 Die thuringischen Brandgräber der spätrömischen Zeit. (Mildenberger, Gerhard.) Köln, 1970.
Arc 66.1.147 Thymélè. (Robert, Fernand.) Paris, 1939.
Arc 716.3 Die Thymele der Athena Nike. (Bötticher, Karl.) Berlin, 1880.
Arc 1083.2 Thymiateria. Inaug. Diss. (Wigand, Karl.) Bonn, 1912.
Arc 1540.20.1 Tickets and passes of Great Britain and Ireland. (Davis, William John.) N.Y., 1973.
Arc 1540.20 Tickets and passes of Great Britain and Ireland struck or engraved on metal, ivory. (Davis, William John.) Leamington Spa, 1922.
Arc 608.6.50 Tiddis. (Berthier, A.) Alger, 1951.

Author and Title Listing

Arc 1020.95.11 Tiepolo, G. Trattato delle sanctissime reliquie...San Marco. Venet, 1617.
X Cg Arc 1665.1 Tier- und Pflanzenbilder auf Münzen und Gemmen. (Imhoof-Blumer, F.) Leipzig, 1889.
Arc 1460.7.1 Tier- und Pflanzenbilder auf Münzen und Gemmen des klassischen Altertums. (Imhoof-Blumer, Friedrich.) Hildesheim, 1972.
Arc 530.160 Tiergefässe in Kopf- und Protomengestalt. (Tuchelt, Klaus Franz.) Berlin, 1962.
Arc 1319.1 Tijdschrift van het (Koninklyk) genootschap. (K. Nederlandsch Genootschap voor Munt en Penningkunde.) Amsterdam. 1-21,1893-1913 14v.
Arc 1319.1.5 Tijdschrift van het (Koninklyk) genootschap. Index, 1-20, 1893-1912. (K. Nederlandsch Genootschap voor Munt en Penningknude.) Amsterdam, 1903.
Arc 1163.3.85 Tikhomlrov, Mikhail N. Russkaia paleografiia. Moskva, 1966.
Arc 435.2.41F Tile-mosaics of the Lahore fort. (Vogel, J.P.) Calcutta, 1920.
Arc 1582.1 Tilesius von Tilenau, Adolf. Explication de la figure problématique. St. Petersbourg, 1864.
Arc 505.12.5 Till el Hesy (Lachish). (Petrie, W.M.F.) London, 1891.
Arc 1076.3.75 Tilley, H.T. The church bells of Warwickshire. Birmingham, 1910.
Arc 389.3 Time and chance; story of Arthur Evans and his forebears. (Evans, Joan.) London, 1943.
Arc 543.142 Time off to dig. (Matheson, S.) London, 1961.
Arc 400.11.30 Times and places. (Peake, Harold J.E.) Oxford, 1956.
Arc 605.205 Timgad, une cité africaine. (Boeswillwald, E.) Londres, 1892-
Arc 608.6.4 Timgad. (Courtois, C.) Alger, 1951.
Arc 605.205.5 Timgad und die römische Provinzial-Architektur. (Holtzinger, H.) Berlin, 1906.
Arc 853.31.15 Timpel, Wolfgang. Burgen, Gräber, alte Kreuze. Weimar, 1970.
Arc 936.195.55 Tinelka, Karel. Cezavy u Bluciny ve svetle archeologickych vyskumû a nalezû. Brno, 1957.
Arc 608.6.75 Tingad chrétien. (Monceaux, Paul.) Paris, 1911.
Arc 1558.8.2 Tingström, Bertel. Svensk numismatisk uppslagsbok. 2. upp. Stockholm, 1968.
Arc 608.16.15 Tipasa. (Baradez, J.L.) Alger, 1952.
Arc 1474.5 Tipi monetali etruschi. (Cesano, Secondina L.) Roma, 1926.
Arc 1480.27 Il tipo.di Roma dei denari consolari. (Pansa, Giovanni.) Milano, 1911.
Arc 672.1.114 Tiré, Claire. Guide des fouilles françaises en Crète. Athènes, 1966.
Arc 1580.46 Der Tiroler Taler. (Innsbruck, F.) Innsbruck, 1963.
Arc 459.20 Tirumalai-Tirupati Devasthanem epigraphical series. Madras. 1-6,1930-1938 8v.
Arc 682.1.9 Tiryns; the prehistoric palace of the kings of Tiryns. (Schliemann, Heinrich.) London, 1886.
Arc 682.1.8 Tiryns; the prehistoric palace of the kings of Tiryns. (Schliemann, Heinrich.) N.Y., 1885.
Arc 635.223F Tiryns. v.1-8. (Frickenhaus, A.) Athēnai, 1912- 9v.
Arc 923.4 Tishchenko, Andrei V. A.V. Tishchenko. Petrograd, 1916.
Arc 1588.4.45.5 Tisíc let české vládní mince (929-1929). (Katz, Viktor.) Praha, 1929.
Arc 1163.10A Tisserant, E. Specimena codicum orientalium. Bonnae, 1914.
Arc 608.7.15 Tissot. Recherches sur la géographie comparée de la Maurétanie Tingitane. Paris, 1877.
Arc 855.205 Tite, Will. Notes on Roman architectural remains. London, 1867. 2 pam.
Arc 861.17.9 Tite, William. Descriptive catalogue of antiquities...Roman London. London, 1848.
Arc 659.12 Titov, Valerii S. Neolit Gretsii. Moskva, 1969.
Arc 875.9 Tituli Hunteriani, an account of the Roman stones in the Hunterian Museum. (Macdonald, J.) Glasgow, 1897.
Arc 1033.35.81 Titulo de la cruz de Christi. (Rioja, F. de.) n.p., n.d.
Arc 1433.37 Titulos y nombres propios monedas arábigo-españolas. (Codera y Zaidin, F.) Madrid, 1878.
Arc 608.67 Tixier, Jacques. Typologie de l'épipaléolithique du Maghreb. Paris, 1963.
Arc 1433.42F Tizengauzen', V. Monety bostochnago khalifata. Sankt Peterburg, 1873.
Arc 1335.80 Tizengauzen', V. Novyia numizmaticheskiia priobreteniia N.P. Linevicha. Sankt Peterburg, 1896.
Arc 1033.50 Tizzani, V. La celebre contesa fra S. Stefano e S. Cipriano. Roma, 1862.
Arc 1027.10 Tizzani, V. Commissione de archeologia sagrada...Basilica di San Clemente. Roma, 1886.
Arc 530.95.5 Tkeshelashvili, G. Mtskheta; putevaditel'. Tbilisi, 1958.
Arc 1625.2 Los tlacos coloniales. (Romero de Terreros y Vinent, Manuel.) México, 1935.
Arc 543.10 Tobler, T. Golgatha, seine Kirchen und Kloster. St. Gallen, 1851.
Arc 1480.23 Tochon D'Annecy, J.F. Mémoire sur les médailles de Marinus. Paris, 1817.
Arc 936.195.155 Točík, Anton. Altmagyarische Gräberfelder in der Südwestslowakei. Bratislava, 1968.
Arc 936.195.160 Točík, Anton. Slawisch-awarisches Gräberfeld in Šturovo. 1. Aufl. Bratislava, 1968.
Arc 930.200.5F Tocilescou, G.G. Fouilles et recherches archéologiques en Roumanie. Bucarest, 1900.
Arc 930.200 Tocilescou, G.G. Das Monument von Adamklissi. Wien, 1895.
Arc 600.172 Tôd, 1934 à 1936. (Bisson de la Roque, Fernand.) Le Caire, 1937.
Arc 936.140 Todorov, Ianko. Antichna kultura v Bulgariia. Sofiia, 1942?
Arc 936.220.10 Todorović, Jovan. Banjica, naselje vinčanske kulture. Beograd, 1961.
Arc 936.220.22 Todorović, Jovan. Katalog praistorijskih metalmih predmeta. Beograd, 1971.
Arc 936.220.45 Todorović, Jovan. Kelti na tlu Beograda. Beograd, 1968.
Arc 618.11 Todorovic, Jovan. Kelti u jugoistočnoj Evropi. Beograd, 1968.
Arc 936.220.85 Todorović, Jovan. Praistorijska Karaburma. Beograd, 1972.
Arc 936.220.20 Todorović, Jovan. Stare kulture i narodi na tlu Beograd. Beograd, 1963.
Arc 1675.95 Todorović, Nada. Jugoslovenske i inostrane medalje. Beograd, 1964.
Arc 688.7.10 Tölle-Kastenbein, Renate. Die antike Stadt Samos. Mainz am Rhein, 1969.
Arc 1076.14 Tönendes Erz. (Weidenbaeck, A.) Graz, 1961.
Arc 938.107 Tönisson, Evald. Die Gauja-Liven und ihre materielle Kultur. Tallinn, 1974.
Arc 387.10.15 Toesca di Castellazzo, G. Commemoriazione del generale Luigi Palma di Cesnola. Torino, 1905.
Arc 925.255.10 Toettermann, A. Fünf Sulfekinschriften. Helsingfors, 1891.
Arc 1033.12.157 Tofanelli, S. Primo ritratto del crofifisso...historia della miracolosa şcultura. Napoli, 1644.
Arc 600.1.13 Togheb, A.M. de. Études sur l'ancienne Alexandrie. Paris, 1909.
Arc 674.3.5 Toieron toy asklēpioy. (Kabbaria.) Athēnai, 1900.
Arc 543.66.15 Tok-kala. (Gudkova, A.V.) Tashkend, 1964.
Htn Arc 1680.4.5* Token coinage of South London...eighteenth and nineteenth centuries. (Waters, A.W.) Leamington, 1904.
NEDL Arc 1680.6.5 The token coinage of Warwickshire. (Davis, William John.) Birmingham, 1895.
Arc 1680.9 Tokens issued in seventeenth century England...by corporations. (Boyne, William.) London, 1858.
Arc 1680.20 Tokens of South Africa. (Africana Museum, Johannesburg.) Johannesburg, 1966.
Arc 1680.12 Tokens of the eighteenth century connected with booksellers. (Longman, W.) London, 1916.
Arc 925.13.25 Toll', N.R. Skify i gunny. Praga, 1928.
Arc 522.16A Tolman, H.C. Mycenaean Troy. N.Y., 1903.
Arc 726.72 Tolomei, Antonio. La cappella degli Scrovigni e l'arena di Padova. Padova, 1881.
Arc 785.13.200F Tolonei, Arnaldo. La via Cavour e i fori imperiali. Roma, 1903.
Arc 923.11 Tolstoi, I. Rossiiskii istoricheskii muzei. Moskva, 1893.
Arc 920.207F Tolstoi, I. Russkiia drebnosti b' pamiatnikakh iskusstva. v.1-3, 4-6. Sankt Petersburg, 1889-99. 2v.
Arc 1582.9PF Tolstoi, I.I. Monety vel. kniazhestva Kievskago. Sankt Peterburg, 1882.
Arc 1582.5F Tolstoi, I.I. Russkaia dopetrovenaia numismatika. Sankt Peterburg, 1884-86. 2v.
Arc 1473.7 Tolstoi, Jean. Monnaies byzantines. v.1-4,8-9. St. Petersbourg, 1912-14. 4v.
Arc 1433.102 Tolunogullan ve povalan. Istanbul, 1972.
Arc 774.1 Tomassetti, G. La campagna romana. Roma, 1910. 4v.
Arc 774.3 Tomassetti, G. Della campagna romana. Roma, 1885.
Arc 774.3.5 Tomassetti, G. Della campagna romana. Roma, 1907.
Arc 590.10 The tomb of Alexander. (Clark, Edward.) Cambridge, 1805.
Arc 545.232 Tomb of Hâtshopsitu. Life and monuments of queen. (Naville, E.) London, 1906.
Arc 545.232.5 The tomb of Iouiya and Touiyou. (Davis, T.M.) London, 1907.
Arc 600.38 The tomb of Perneb. (New York (City). Metropolitan Museum of Art.) N.Y., 1916.
Arc 545.232.9 The tomb of Queen Tiyi. (Davis, T.M.) London, 1910.
Arc 1027.12.20 The tomb of Saint Peter. (Guarducci, Margherita.) N.Y., 1960.
Arc 545.232.13 The tomb of Siptah. (Davis, T.M.) London, 1908.
Arc 609.8.5 The tomb of the dated inscription at Gedi. (Kirkman, James Spedding.) London, 1960.
Arc 600.6.25F The tomb of Thoutmôsis. (Carter, H.) Westminster, 1904.
Arc 746.47 La tomba delle iscrizioni a Cerveteri. (Cristofani, Mauro.) Firenze, 1965.
Arc 590.10.5 La tomba di Alessandro Magno. (Breccia, E.) Alexandria, 1930.
Arc 1027.12.13 La tomba di San Pietro. (Mecchi, F.E.) Roma, 1893.
Arc 726.336 Le tombe a Tholos di Quinto nel comune di Sesto Fiorentino. (Chiostri, Frido.) n.p., 1969.
Arc 1015.224 Tombe apostoliche di Roma. (Grisar, H.) Roma, 1892.
Arc 1025.28.15 Le tombe dei martiri nelle catacombe romane. Roma, 1896.
Arc 815.19.5 Le tombe di Pompei a schola semicircolare. (Borrelli, L.) Napoli, 1937.
Arc 726.79 Tombe dipinte scoperte nel territorio Pestano. (Marzulla, A.) Salerno, 1935.
Arc 1027.19.40F La tombe du Pape Corneille et su région cimetriale. (Reekmans, Louis.) Città del Vaticano, 1964.
Arc 726.16 Tombe ed antichità galliche in Italia. (Monteluis, O.) Roma, 1877.
Arc 830.184 La tombe gallo-romaine. Thèse. (Hatt, Jean J.) Paris, 1951.
Arc 936.80F Le tombeau antique près de Kazanlak. (Mikov, Vasil.) Sofia, 1954.
Arc 830.32.5 Le tombeau de Childéric. (Cochet, J.B.D.) Paris, 1859.
Arc 505.17 Tombeau de Josué. Note sur le Khirbet-Tibneh. (Guérin, V.) Paris, 1865.
Arc 1027.76 Le tombeau de la chrétienne. (Berbrugger, M.) Alger, 1867.
Arc 600.193 Tombeau de Pannout à Aniba. (Haykal, Fa'iza.) Le Caire, 196-.
Arc 545.227.21F Le tombeau de Petosiris. v.1-3. (Lefebvre, G.) Le Caire, 1923-1924.
Arc 820.211F Tombeaux antiques. (Lacour, Pierre.) Bordeaux, 1806.
Arc 830.88.5 Les tombes à l'incinération du Musée de Clermont-Ferrand. (Audollent, A.) Paris, 1911. 3 pam.
Arc 1027.52.5 Tombs and catacombs of the Appian Way. (Spadoni, O.L.) Rome, 1892.
Arc 672.1.120 The tombs of Mesara; a study of funerary architecture and ritual in southern Crete, 2800-1700 B.C. (Branigan, Keith.) London, 1970.
Arc 421.11 Tombs of old Lo-yang. (White, W.C.) Shanghai, 1934.
Arc 1027.12.19 The tombs of Peter and Paul ad catacumbas. (La Piana, George.) Cambridge, 1920.
Arc 588.37 Tombs of the courtiers and oxyrhynkhos. (Petrie, W.M.F.) London, 1925.
Arc 1285.25.5 Tomczyk, Damian. Pieczęcie górnośląskich cechów rzemieslniczych z XV-XVIII wisku i ich znaczenie historyczne. Wyd. 1. Opolu, 1975.
Arc 936.14.475 Tomice, pow. (Romanow, Jerzy.) Wrocław, 1973.
Arc 1030.5.3 Il tomo secondo delle conferenze di Chiusura. (Rossi, G.B. de.) Roma, 1888.
Arc 1163.3.115F Tomović, Gordana. Morfologija ćiriličkih natpisa na Balkanu. Beograd, 1974.
Arc 595.63 Tompkins, Peter. Secrets of the great pyramid. London, 1973.
Arc 925.4.18 Tomsk, Siberia. Oblastnoi Kraevedcheskii Muzei. Nekotorye voprosy drevnei istorii Zapadnoi Sibiri. Tomsk, 1959.
Arc 936.20.10 Tonescu, G.M. Etiopienii in Dacia preistorica. București, 1926.
Arc 273.18 Tongres, Belgium. Musée Provincial Gallo-Romains. Publicaties. 1,1964+
Arc 726.50 Tonini, Luigi. Rimini avanti il principio. v.1-2. Rimini, 1848.
Arc 1025.29.21 Tonini, P. La Roma sotterranea cristiana...dal G.B. de Rossi. Firenze, 1879.
Arc 726.20 Tononi, A.G. Documenti inediti...scoperta di Velleia. Modena, 1881.

Arc 746.17 Tononi, A.G. Scoperta di un bronzo etrusco. Milano, 1879.

Arc 726.20.3 Tononi, A.G. Velleia studiata da un erudita francese. n.p., 1887.

Arc 588.30A Tools and weapons. (Petrie, W.M.F.) London, 1917.

Arc 942.4 Pamphlet vol. Topics in American archaeology. 9 pam.

Arc 1433.40.5 Topogafiia kladov' s' vosiochnymi monetami. (Savelbev', P.) Sankt Peterburg, 1846.

Arc 756.8 Topografia di Roma antica. (Borsari, L.) Milano, 1897.

Arc 766.1 Topografia di Roma antica. (Lanciani, R.) Roma, 1880.

Arc 1465.76 Topografia e numismatica dell'antica Imera, Sicily. (Gabrici, E.) Napoli, 1893.

Arc 905.4 Topografia e scavi di Salona. (Carrara, F.) Trieste, 1850.

Arc 93.52 Topografia e storia delle ricerche archeologiche in Orvieto e nel suo contado. Roma. 1,1972+

Arc 743.6 Topografia storica dell'Etruria. (Solari, A.) Pisa, 1914-18. 3v.

Arc 743.6.2 Topografia storica dell'Etruria. Appendix. (Solari, A.) Pisa, 1915.

Arc 756.12 Topografie starověkého Řima. (Brtnický, L.) Praha, 1925.

Htn Arc 756.2* Topographia Romae. pt.1-6. Frankfort, 1627 (Boissard, J.J.) 2v.

Arc 673.1.30 Topographia tōn Delphōn. (Keramopoullos, A.D.) Athēnai, 1917.

Arc 548.5 Topographical bibliography of ancient Egyptian hieroglyphic texts, reliefs. (Porter, Bertha.) Oxford, 1927-39. 7v.

Arc 548.5.10A Topographical bibliography of ancient Egyptian hieroglyphic texts. v.1, pt.1-2; v.2; v.3, pt.1. 2. ed. (Porter, Bertha.) Oxford, 1960- 4v.

Arc 770.4.10 A topographical dictionary of ancient Rome. (Platner, S.B.) London, 1929.

Arc 435.20.45 A topographical list of the inscirptions of the Madras presidency (collected till 1915) with notes. (Rangāchārya, V.) Madras, 1919. 3v.

Htn Arc 522.8* Topographie de la Troade. (Barker-Webb, P.) Paris, 1844.

Arc 936.1.5 Topographie de Thessalonique. (Tafrali, O.) Paris, 1912.

Arc 936.1.6 Topographie de Thessalonique. (Tafrali, O.) Paris, 1913.

Arc 505.4 La topographie de Tyr. (Berton, J. de.) Paris, 1881.

Arc 772.5.5 Topographie der Stadt Rom. (Richter, O.) Nordlingen, 1889.

Arc 764.1 Topographie der Stadt Rom in Alterthum. v.1-2. (Jordan, Henri.) Berlin, 1878. 4v.

Arc 936.20.71 Topographie des fortifications romaines en Dobroudja. (Gajewska, Halina.) Wrocław, 1974.

Arc 889.3 Topographie des voies romaines de la Belgique. (Dessel, Camille.) Bruxelles, 1877.

Arc 708.9 Topographie von Athen. (Leake, W.M.) Halle, 1829.

Arc 756.4 The topography and antiquities of Rome. (Burgess, R.) London, 1831. 2v.

Arc 495.204 Topography and itinerary (American archaeological exedition to Syria). (Garrett, Robert.) N.Y., 1914.

Arc 770.4A Topography and monuments of ancient Rome. (Platner, S.B.) Boston, 1904.

Arc 770.4.2 Topography and monuments of ancient Rome. 2. ed. (Platner, S.B.) Boston, 1911.

Arc 708.9.2 The topography of Athens. (Leake, W.M.) London, 1821.

Arc 708.9.3 The topography of Athens. (Leake, W.M.) London, 1841. 2v.

Arc 761.1.2 The topography of Rome and its vicinity. (Gell, W.) London, 1834. 3v.

Arc 761.1 The topography of RomeAnd its vicinity. (Gell, W.) London, 1846. 2v.

Arc 510.203 The topography of Troy. (Gell, W.) London, 1804.

Arc 905.115F Töräh, Gyula. Die Bewohner vor Halimbacseres noch. Leipzig, 1959.

Arc 853.24.7 Torbruegge, Walter. Bilder zur Vorgeschichte Bayerns. Konstanz, 1968.

Arc 853.225F Torbruegge, Walter. Die Bronzezeit in der Oberpfalz. Kallmünz, 1959.

Arc 853.136 Torbruegge, Walter. Die Hallstattzeit in der Oberpfalz. v.2. Kallmünz, 1965.

Arc 505.12.10F Torczyner, H. Lachish I (Tell Ed Durveir). v.1-4. London, 1938-1940. 6v.

Arc 1033.28.15 Tori, G. Dei riti nuziali degli antichi cristiani. Perugia, 1793.

Arc 1033.3.17 Torlonia, L. Di un sarcofago cristiano del palazzo torlonia. Roma, 1897.

Arc 1510.60F Tornau, Otto. Münzwesen und Münzen der Grafschaft Mansfeld von der Mitte. Prag, 1937.

Arc 1388.1 Tornberg, C.J. Fölhagen-fyndet. Stockholm, 1870.

Arc 1433.12.3 Tornberg, Carl Johan. Découvertes récentes de monnaies koufiques. Bruxelles, n.d.

Arc 1433.12 Tornberg, Carl Johan. Numi cufici regii numophylacii Holmiensis. Upsaliae, 1848.

Arc 1433.12.5 Tornberg, Carl Johan. Om de i Svensk jord funna Österländska mynt. Stockholm, 1857.

Arc 1433.13 Tornberg, Carl Johan. Symbolae ad rem numariam Muhammedan. Upsaliae, 1846-62.

Arc 1408.2 Tornberg, E.J. Sur un Dirhem Kakweïhide inédit. Bruxelles, 1858.

Arc 1088.1.8 Torr, Cecil. Ancient ships. Cambridge, 1894.

Arc 1088.1.9A Torr, Cecil. Ancient ships. Cambridge, 1895.

Arc 1088.1.7 Torr, Cecil. Ancient ships. Chicago, 1964.

Arc 785.53 La torre del Monzone presso il Ponte Ratto. (Gori, Fabio.) Roma, 1872.

Arc 785.51 La torre delle milizie, erroneamente denominala torre di Nerone. (Sabatini, F.) Roma, 1914.

Arc 1020.9.12 Torres, C.A. Cenni sulla forma primitiva del panteon di Roma. Roma, 1838.

Arc 387.13.15 Torso. (Curtius, Ludwig.) Stuttgart, 1958.

Arc 938.17.15 Tortianikovaia stoiankor Sarnate. (Vankina, Lutsiia V.) Riga, 1970.

Arc 421.18 Torü, P. Sculptured stone tombs of the Lion dynasty. Peking, 1942.

Arc 1163.2.9 Tos, Joaquin. Paleografía que para inteligencia de les manuscrites. Barcelona, 1820.

Arc 726.45.15 Toscanelli, N. Pisa nell'antichità dalle età preistoriche alla caduta dell'impero romano. Pisa, 1933. 2v.

Arc 723.18 Toscanelli, Nello. Le origini italiche. Milano, 1914.

Arc 843.214 Toscanos, die altpunische Faktorei an der Mündung des Rio de Vélez. (Niemeyer, Hans G.) Berlin, 1969.

Arc 1433.99 Tosun, Mebrure. Mejopotamya silindir muhurlerinder hurri mitanni usulü. Ankara, 1956.

Arc 905.86 Tot, Tibor A. Antropologicheskie dannye k voprosu o velikom peseselenii narodov. Leningrad, 1970.

Arc 612.25 Totenehre im alten Norden. (Hahne, Hans.) Jena, 1929.

Arc 726.175 Toti, Odoardo. La città medioevale di Centocelle. Allumicre, 1958.

Arc 595.10 Totten, C.A.L. The metrology of the Great Pyramid. N.Y., 1884.

Arc 404.4 Touchard, Michel C. L'archéologie mystérieuse. Paris, 1972.

Arc 830.61 Toulmoudre, Adolphe. Histoire archéologique de l'époque gallo-romaine de la ville de Rennes. Rennes, 1847.

Arc 66.1.212 Toulouse antique des origines à l'établissement des Wisigoths. (Labrousse, Michel.) Paris, 1968.

Arc 830.22.11 Toulouze, Eugène. Mes fouilles dans le sol du vieux Paris. Dunkerque, 1888.

Arc 543.4.25F Toumchoug. v.2. (Pelliot, Paul.) Paris, 1961-1964.

Arc 743.2 Tour to the sepulchres of Etruria. (Gray, H. (Mrs.).) London, 1840.

Arc 830.109 La Touraine préhistorique. (Dubreuil-Chambardel, Louis.) Paris, 1923.

Arc 889.12 Tourneur, V. Les Belges avant César. Bruxelles, 1944.

Arc 1518.3 Tourneur, Victor. Catalogue des medailles du Royaume de Belgique. Bruxelles, 1911.

Arc 1348.79 Tourneur, Victor. Initiation à la numismatique. Bruxelles, 1945.

Arc 1205.5 Tourneur-Nicodème, Mariette. Bibliographie générale de la sigillographie. Besançon, 1933.

Arc 505.70 Les tours royales de Josèphe Flavius. (Solomiac, Michel.) Jérusalem, 1936.

Arc 830.198 Toussaint, M. Répertoire archéologique du département de la Meuse. Bar-le-Duc, 1946.

Arc 830.196 Toussaint, M. Répertoire archéologique du département de la Moselle. Nancy, 1950.

Arc 830.185 Toussaint, M. Répertoire archéologique du département de la Seine. Paris, 1953.

Arc 830.190 Toussaint, M. Répertoire archéologique du département de la Seine-et-Marne. Paris, 1953.

Arc 830.215 Toussaint, M. Répertoire archéologique du département de l'Aube. Paris, 1954.

Arc 830.194 Toussaint, M. Répertoire archéologique du département de Meurthe-et-Moselle. Nancy, 1947.

Arc 830.26.20 Toussaint, M. Répertoire archéologique du département de Seine-et-Oise. Paris, 1951.

Arc 830.199 Toussaint, M. Répertoire archéologique du département des Ardennes. Paris, 1955.

Arc 830.158.5 Toutain, Jules. Les fouilles d'Alésia de 1909-10. Semur-en-Auxois, 1912.

Arc 853.240 Toutonenstein und Heinesäulen bei Mildenburg. (Röder, J.) Kallmünz, 1960.

Arc 386.18 Touzeskul, V. Otkrytyia XIX i nachala XX v. Sankt Peterburg, 1923.

Arc 1261.50 Tovar. Esfragistica medieval portuguesa. Lisboa, 1937.

Arc 543.131.5 Towards Angkor in the footsteps of the Indian invaders. (Wales, Horace Geoffrey Q.) London, 1937.

Arc 880.7 Towers and temples of ancient Ireland. (Keane, Marcus.) Dublin, 1867.

Arc 861.195 Town and country. (Branigan, Keith.) Bourne End, 1973.

Arc 1274.6 The town council seals. (Porteous, A.) Edinburgh, 1906.

Arc 858.34 The towns of Roman Britain. (Bevan, J.O.) London, 1917.

Arc 785.77 Toynbee, J.M. The shrine of St. Peter. London, 1956.

Arc 785.34.25 Toynbee, Jocelyn M.C. The Ara Pacia reconsidered and historical art in Roman Italy. London, 1954.

Arc 1588.10.25 Tözen, Ibrahim. Türkiye cumhuriyeti madeni ponohr. Istanbul, 1973.

Arc 420.7 Tpya...Atraer. (Radloff, W.) St. Petersburg, 1892.

Arc 608.92 Tra Cartagine e Roma. (Moscati, Sabatino.) Milano, 1971.

Arc 94.50 Trabalhos. (Associação dos Arqueologos Portugueses.) Lisboa. 1-6,1934-1942 6v.

Arc 426.1 Traces of an early race in Japan. (Morse, E.S.) N.Y., 1879.

Arc 861.10.13 Traces of the Norse mythology. (Kinnebrook, William.) London, 1904.

Arc 1476.5 Pamphlet vol. Tractatus tres de nummis antiquorum. 3 pam.

NEDL Arc 953.4 Tracts for archaeologists. First series, 1880-91. (Lewis, T.H.) St. Paul, 1892.

Arc 1680.16.5 Trade tokens; a social and economic history. (Whiting, John Roger Scott.) Newton Abbot, 1971.

Arc 1680.9.3 Trade tokens...seventeenth century...England, Wales and Ireland. (Boyne, William.) London, 1889. 2v.

Arc 1680.18 Tradesmen's tickets and private tokens: 1785-1819. (Bell, Robert Charles.) Newcastle-upon-Tyne, 1966.

Arc 1680.14 The tradesmen's tokens of the eighteenth century. (Atkins, James.) London, 1892.

Arc 953.9 Traditions of De-coo-dah and antiquarian researches. (Pidgeon, W.) N.Y., 1858.

Arc 936.14.170 Tradycje celtyckie w obrzędowości Protosłowian. (Przeworska, Janina.) Wrocław, 1964.

Arc 936.220.38 Tragam drevnih kultura Crme Gore. (Mijović, Pavle.) Titograd, 1970.

Arc 1663.15.5 Die tragbaren Ehrenzeichen des Deutschen Reiches. (Hesse, Waldemar E.) Berlin, 1940.

Arc 785.15.15 Die Traianssäule. (Bartoli, P.S.) Voorburg, 1941.

Arc 915.37 Traininas, Davidas. Beiträge zur Kenntnis der Haustiere der romischkeltischen Ansiedlung auf der Engehalbinsel bei Bern. Bern, 1933.

Arc 1390.8 Traite de numismatique en moyen age. (Engel, A.) Paris, 1891. 3v.

Arc 1033.63.9 Traité des instruments de martyre. (Gallonio, A.) Paris, 1904.

Arc 1348.33F Traité des monnaies d'or et d'argent qui circulent chez les différens peuples. (Bonneville, P.F.) Paris, 1806.

Arc 1500.21 Traité des monnaies gauloises. v.1-2. (Blanchet, A.) Paris, 1905.

Arc 1458.13 Traite des monnaies grecques et romaines. (Babelon, E.) Paris, 1901-33. 8v.

Arc 1498.2 Traité historique des monnayes de France. (Leblanc, F.) Amsterdam, 1692.

Arc 1498.2.5 Traité historique des monnayes de France. (Leblanc, F.) Paris, 1690.

Htn Arc 1033.131* Traite historique du chef de S. Jean Baptiste. (Du Cange, C. du F.) Paris, 1665.

Arc 1076.3.35 Traitez des cloches. (Thiers, J.B.) Paris, 1721.

Arc 785.15.9 Trajan's column. (The British Academy). (Boni, G.) London, n.d.

Arc 785.15.5 Trajans Dakische Kriege. (Petersen, E.) Leipzig, 1899.

Arc 726.70.10F Der Trajansbogen in Benevent. (Garger, E.) Berlin, 1943.

Arc 785.15.11FA Die Trajanssaule. Text and Atlas. (Lehmann-Hartleben, Karl.) Berlin, 1926. 2v.

Arc 936.65F Trakya-Kirklareli. (Mansel, A.M.) Ankara, 1943.

Arc 1093.2.9F Un tranche-tête. (Peigne-Delacourt, M.) Paris, 1866.

Arc 125.8.5 Transactions. (Ancient Monuments Society.) London. 1,1953+ 20v.

Arc 125.12 Transactions. (Architectural and Archaeological Society of Durham and Northumberland.) Gateshead on Tyne. 1-10,1862-1953 9v.

Arc 136.9 Transactions. (London and Middlesex Archaeological Society.) London. 1,1860+ 25v.

Arc 16.1 Transactions. (Pennsylvania. University. University Museum.) Paris. 1-2,1904-1907

Arc 41.2 Transactions. (Society of Biblical Archaeology.) London. 1-9 9v.

Arc 1324.1 Transactions. (Yorkshire Numismatic Society.) Hull. 1,1913

Arc 41.2.2 Transactions. Index, v.1-9. (Society of Biblical Archaeology.) London, n.d.

Arc 125.4.5 Transactions at its 2nd Congress, 1845. (British Archaeological Association.) London, 1846.

Arc 1313.2.25 Transactions of the International Numismatic Congress. (Royal Numismatic Society.) London, 1938.

Arc 537.3.3 Transformations and migrations of certain statues in the Cesnola collection. (Cook, C.) N.Y., 1882.

Arc 66.1.37 Transformations politiques de l'Italie. (Jullian, C.) Paris, 1884.

Arc 1033.62.40 Die Translatie S. Alexandri. (Wetzel, A.) Kiel, 1881.

Arc 1033.168 Die Translatio sancti viti. (Stentrup, F.) Münster, 1906.

Arc 530.25 Trapezunt', ego sviatyni i drevnosti. (Bezobrazov, P.V.) Petrograd, 1916.

Arc 1027.19.35 Trappists. Selecta ex coemeterio Si Callisti. Roma, 189-?

Arc 925.13.95 Trapsh, M.M. Pamiatniki kolkhidskoi i skifskoi kul'tur v sele kulanurkhva abkhazskoi ASSR. Sukhumi, 1962.

Arc 404.3 Trapsh, M.M. Trudy. v.2. Sukhumi, 1969.

Arc 1018.53 Tratado de arqueología eclesiástica. (Aragón Fernández, A.) Barcelona, 1935.

Arc 1494.45 Tratado de la moneda jaquesa y otras de oro. (Lastanosa, V.J. de.) Zaragozana, 1681.

Arc 1494.4 Tratado de las monedas labradas...de Cataluña. v.1-2. (Salat, Josef.) Barcelona, 1818.

Arc 1494.8 Tratado de numismática. (Codera y Zaiden, F.) Madrid, 1879.

Arc 1020.95.11 Trattato delle sanctissime reliquie...San Marco. (Tiepolo, G.) Venet, 1617.

Arc 723.8 Trattato di archeologia e storia dell'arte italiano. (Gentile, I.) Milano, 1901. 2v.

Arc 1033.84 Trattenimento...S. Igino Papa e Martire. (Pellino, G.) Napoli, 1831.

Arc 1153.4.7 Traube, L. Die Geschichte der tironischen Noten. Berlin, 1901.

Arc 403.16.25 Die Traum von Troja. (Stoll, Heinrich A.) Berlin, 1957.

Arc 1660.15.5F Trauté des monnaies des barons. (Duby, P.A.T.) Paris, 1790. 2v.

Arc 895.26 Le travail de l'or en Suède à l'époque mérovingienne. (Janse, Olov Robert.) Orléans, 1922.

Arc 459.2F Travancore. Archaeological Survey. Annual report for M.E. 1085 (1909-1910). n.p., 191-?

Arc 49.2 Travancore archaeological series. Madras. 1-7,1910-1931 4v.

Arc 1302.6 Travaux. (Cercle d'Études Numismatiques.) Bruxelles. 1,1964+

Arc 302.9.5 Trayaux. (Polska Akademia Nauk. Zaktad Archeologii Sródziemnomorskiej.) Warsaw. 1968+ 2v.

Arc 400.20 The traveller's journey is done. (Powell, D.) London, 1943.

Arc 513.7 Travels and discoveries in the Levant. (Newton, C.T.) London, 1865. 2v.

Arc 513.4.6 Travels and researches in Asia Minor. (Fellows, C.) Hildesheim, 1975.

Arc 513.4.5 Travels and researches in Asia Minor. (Fellows, C.) London, 1852.

Arc 32.2F Travels and studies in...nearer East. (Almstead, A.T.) Ithaca, N.Y., 1911.

Arc 672.1 Travels in Crete. (Pashley, R.) Cambridge, 1837. 2v.

Arc 572.5 Travels in Egypt. December 1880-May 1891. (Wilbour, Charles E.) Brooklyn, 1936.

Arc 400.3 Travels in Georgia, Persia. (Porter, R.K.) London, 1821-22. 2v.

NEDL Arc 513.10 Travels in Lycia, Milyas, and the Cibyratis. (Spratt, T.A.B.) London, 1847. 2v.

Arc 605.203 Travels in the footsteps of Bruce in Algeria and Tunis. (Playfair, R.L.) London, 1877.

Arc 1261.1 Travers, Emile. Le sceau de Loja et la sigillographie pittoresque. Paris, 1885.

Arc 830.28 Travers, Emile. Une voie Saxonne à Caen. Caen, 1875.

Arc 608.52F Traversari, Gustavo. L'altorilievo di Afrodite a Cirene. Roma, 1959.

Arc 936.220.70 Trbuhović, Vojislav B. Donja toponica. Prokuplje, 1970.

Arc 936.220.65 Trbuhović, Vojislav B. Problemi porekla i datovanja bronzanog doba u Srbiji. Beograd, 1968.

Arc 1015.208.8 Tre sepolcri con pitture ed iscrizione. (Garrucci, R.) Napoli, 1852.

Arc 1020.32.12 I tre sepolcri santambrisiani scoperti...1864. (Biraghi, L.) Milano, 1864.

Arc 943.32 Treasure in the dust. 1. ed. (Hibben, F.C.) Philadelphia, 1951.

Arc 1020.120.15 The treasure of São Roque. (Telfer, William.) London, 1932.

Arc 861.100.20 The treasure of Sutton-Hoo. 1. ed. (Grohskoph, Bernice.) N.Y., 1970.

Arc 628.20.5 Treasure of the Greeks and Romans. Thesis. (Couch, Herbert N.) Menasha, 1929.

Arc 853.26 The treasure-trove of Hildesheim. (Blume, T.) Hildesheim, n.d.

Arc 1033.12.89 The treasures of Syrian silverwar. (Bréhier, L.) Paris, 1921.

Arc 416.24 The treasures of time. 1. ed. (Deuel, Leo.) Cleveland, 1961.

Arc 628.20 The treasuries of the Greeks and Romans. (Couch, Herbert N.) Menasha, 1929.

Arc 572.1.15 The treasury of ancient Egypt. (Weigall, Arthur Edward Pearse Brome.) Chicago, 1912.

Arc 1025.50 Treat, J.H. The catacombs of Rome. Boston, 1907.

Arc 1025.33 Treat, J.H. The catacombs of Rome. n.p., n.d.

Arc 861.24 Treatise of Roman ports and forts. (Somner, W.) Oxford, 1693.

Arc 400.8 Treatise on the study of antiquities. (Pownall, T.) London, 1782.

Arc 87.1.35 Tren, G. Grosse Thongefaesse in Statuetten- und Buestenform. Berlin, 1875.

Arc 673.1.9 Trendelenburg, A. Die Anfangsstreke der heiligen Strasse in Delphi. Berlin, 1908.

Arc 87.1.36 Trendelenburg, A. Der Musenchor. Berlin, 1876.

Arc 87.1.70 Trendelenburg, A. Phantasiai. Berlin, 1910.

Arc 66.1.153 Les trépieds du Ptoion. (Guillon, P.) Paris, 1943.

Arc 1020.76 Le tresor, les corps saints...dans l'eglise royale de S. Denys. Paris, 1715.

Arc 1020.62 Le trésor...de Notre Dame de Lens au XVe siècle. (Richard, J.M.) Arras, 1876.

Arc 1020.49.3 Trésor d'Aix-la-Chapelle. 1.-3. éd. Aix, 1818-20? 3 pam.

Arc 820.6PF Le trésor d'argenterie de Berthouville, près Bernay. (Bibliotheque Nationale, Paris. Département des Médailles et Antiques.) Paris, 1916.

Arc 726.11.7 Le trésor d'argenterie de Boscoreale. (Héron de Villefosse, Antoine.) Paris, 189-.

Arc 1356.3 Le trésor d'Auriol et les dieux nègres de la Grèce. (Blancard, Louis.) Marseille, n.d.

Arc 1020.52 Le trésor de Chartres. (Mély, F. de.) Paris, 1886.

Arc 1020.56 Le trésor de Clairvaux. (Salore, Charles.) Paris, 1875.

Arc 673.1.20F Le trésor de Cyrène à Delphes. Thèse. (Bousquet, Jean.) Paris, 1952.

Arc 1433.92F Trésor de dirhems du IXe siècle. (Miles, George Carpenter.) Paris, 1960.

Arc 1500.69 Le trésor de Fécamp et la monnayage en Francie occidentale pendant la seconde moitié du Xe siècle. (Dumas-Dubourg, Françoise.) Paris, 1971.

Arc 1480.75 Le trésor de Guelma. Thèse. (Turcan, Robert.) Paris, 1963.

Arc 1020.50 Le trésor de la cathédrale de Bénévent. (Barbier de Montault, X.) Arras, 1879.

Arc 1016.1 Le trésor de la cathédrale de Coire. (Molinier, E.) Paris, 1895.

Arc 1020.59 Le trésor de la cathédrale de Gran. (Martinov, J.) Arras, 1881.

Arc 1020.68 Le trésor de la cathédrale de Moutiers. (Barbier de Montault, X.) Tours, n.d.

Arc 825.3.20 Le trésor de la Maison Carrée. (Segni, Emile.) Nîmes, 1937?

Arc 1020.108 Trésor de la ste. chapelle des ducs de Savoie. (Fabre, A.) Lyon, 1875.

Arc 1020.72.5 Le trésor de l'abbaye de Ste. Croix de Poitiers. (Barbier de Montault, X.) Poitiers, 1883.

Htn Arc 1020.2* Le trésor de l'Abbaye St. Bénique de Dijon. (Prost, B.) Dijon, 1894.

Arc 1020.61 Le trésor de l'église cathédrale de Lausanne. (Chavannes, E.) Lausanne, 1873.

Arc 1020.125 Trésor de l'église de conques. (Darcel, Alfred.) Paris, 1861.

Arc 1020.6 Trésor de l'église Saint-Marc à Venise. (Durand, J.) Paris, 1862.

Arc 1663.9 Un trésor de monnaies des comtes de la Marche. v.1-2. (Cessac.) Paris, 1882.

Arc 1020.112 Trésor de Notre-Dame-de-Liesse...de 1655 à 1790. (Fleury, E.) Paris, 1854.

Arc 1345.1 Trésor de numismatique et glyptique, numismatique des rois grecs. Paris, 1858.

Arc 1430.1 Le trésor de San'a. (Schlumberger, G.) Paris, 1880.

Arc 1020.84.9 Trésor de St. Etienne...collegiale de Troyes. (Coffinet, L'Abbé.) Paris, 1860.

Arc 1016.201 Le trésor de Trèves. (Palustre, L.) Paris, 1886.

Arc 830.346 Le trésor de Vix; histoire et portée d'une grande découverte. (Joffroy, René.) Paris, 1962.

Arc 493.25 Le trésor de Ziwiyè. (Godard, André.) Haarlem, 1950.

Arc 493.25.5 Le trésor de Ziwiyè. (Godard, André.) Teheran, 1949.

Arc 1020.49 Le trésor du dame d'Aix-La-Chapelle. (Barbier de Montault, X.) Tours, 1877.

Arc 1033.17.549F Le trésor du Sancta Sanctorum. (Lauer, Philippe.) Paris, 1906.

Arc 1016.246F La trésor liturgique de Cherves en Angoumois. (Barbier de Montault, X.) Angoulême, 1897.

Arc 1020.5 Le trésor sacré de la cathédrale d'Arras. (Van Drival, E.) Arras, 1860.

Arc 945.8 Trésors d'archéologie américaine et océanienne. (Nantes.) Nantes, 1958?

Arc 823.19.145F Les trésors d'argenteuie trouvés en Gaule. (Thédenat, H.) Paris, 1885. 3v.

Arc 1500.54 Les trésors de monnaies romaines découverts dans le département du Loiret. (Chevallier, Guy.) Gien, 1958.

Arc 1020.51 Les trésors sacrés de Cologne. (Bock, Franz.) Paris, 1862.

Arc 925.301 Tret'iakov, P.N. Drevnii gorodishcha Smolenshchiny. Leningrad, 1963.

Arc 925.351 Tret'iakov, Viktor P. Kul'tura iamochno-grebenchatoi keramiki v lesnoi polose evropeiskoi chasti SSSR. Leningrad, 1972.

Arc 493.6.20 Trever, K.V. Ocherki po istorii i kul'ture Kavkozskoi Albanii. Moskva, 1959.

Arc 530.80A Trever, K.V. Ocherki po istorii kultur' Erevnei Armenii. Moskva, 1953.

Arc 853.20.12 Treves. Rheinisches Landesmuseum. Aus der Schatzkammer des antiken Trier. Trier, 1951.

Arc 853.20.12.5 Treves. Rheinisches Landesmuseum. Aus der Schatzkammer des antiken Trier. 2. Aufl. Trier, 1959.

Arc 204.5 Treves. Rheinisches Landesmuseum. Führungsblätter.

Arc 392.11 A tribute to Sir George Hill on his 80th birthday. Oxford, 1948.

Arc 1500.60F Tricou, Jean. Médailles lyonnaises du XVe au XVIIIe siècle. Paris, 1958.

Arc 1500.61 Tricou, Jean. Numismatique des corporations. Paris, 1957.

Arc 1033.17.95.5 Triduo in ossequio di Maria santissima di Guadalupe. Roma, 1792.

Arc 1088.1.23 La trière antique et la guerre navale. (Boisacq, E.) Bruxelles, 1905.

Arc 66.1.20 La trière athénienne. (Cartault, A.) Paris, 1881.

Arc 853.20.15 Trierer Grabungen und Forschungen. Augsburg. 2,1955+ 12v.

Arc 905.5.5 Trieste. Il museo civico di antichita. Trieste, 1879.

Arc 943.42 Trimborn, Hermann. Das alte Amerika. Stuttgart, 1959.

Arc 1027.1.13 Trina comunicazione...vasello col sangui. (Gaetani, V.) Palermo, 1895.

Arc 830.60 Trion. (Allmer, Auguste.) Lyon, 1888.

Htn Arc 1033.35.21F* Trionfante e gloriosa croce trattato. (Bosio, I.) Roma, 1610.

Arc 1077.2.44 Il trionfo della croce. (Cecchelli, Carlo.) Roma, 1954.

Arc 1088.1.20.5 Trionfo navale ovvero prassima estrazione. (Maes, Constantino.) Roma, 1899.

Arc 590.4 Triple mummy case of Aroeri-Ao. (Sharpe, S.) London, 1858.

Arc 1.14.30 Triplice omaggio a sua santita Pio XII. (Accademia...Rome. Accademia Romana di S. Tommaso di Aquina.) Città de Vaticano, 1958. 2v.
Arc 497.6 Tristram, H.B. The land of Moab. London, 1873.
Arc 726.70F The triumphal arch of Trajan at Beneventum. (American School of Classical Studies in Rome.) Rome, 1896.
Arc 726.70.5 The triumphal arch of Trajan at Beneventum. (American School of Classical Studies in Rome.) Rome, 19- ?
Arc 1033.35.29 Triumphe van het heilig kruise Christi. Brugge, 1871.
Arc 110.1 Tro Nervia. Avesnes. 1-5,1923-1929
Arc 522.41 The Troad; an archaeological and topographical study. (Cook, John Manuel.) Oxford, 1973.
Arc 522.20 "Troad" da dört yerleş me yeri. (Kosay, Hamit.) Istanbul, 1936.
Arc 1020.73.14 Troche, N.M. Sainte-Chapelle de Paris. Notice historique, archéologique et descriptive. Paris, 1853.
Arc 935.18 Pamphlet vol. Troesmis, 1864-1868. 8 pam.
Arc 830.48 Les troglodytes en Anjou à travers les âges. (Fraysse, Jean.) Cholet, 1963.
Arc 522.10.3 Troia und Neu-Ilion. (Brentano, E.) Heilbronn, 1882.
Arc 522.4 Troia und seine Ruinen. (Schliemann, H.) Rostock, 1875?
Arc 522.17 Troie, la guerre de Troie. (Sartiaux, Felix.) Paris, 1915.
Arc 510.209 La Troie d'Homère. (Normand, Charles.) Paris, 1892.
Arc 600.90F Trois flottilles de la VIIème dynastie des pharaons. (Paujade, J.) Djibouti, 1948.
Arc 1030.18 Trois inscriptions...rapportées de Constantinople. (Riant, Paul de.) Paris, 1880.
Arc 1473.5 Trois lettres sur des monnaies byzantines. (Soret, Frédéric.) Genève, 1837.
Arc 1025.7 Troisième mémoire sur les antiquités chrétiennes des catacombes. (Raoul-Rochette, D.) Paris, 1838.
Arc 685.1.5 Troizen und Kalaureia. (Welter, Gabriel.) Berlin, 1941.
Arc 522.4.4A Troja. (Schliemann, H.) London, 1884.
Arc 522.4.4.2 Troja. (Schliemann, H.) London, 1884.
Arc 522.15 Troja und Ilion. (Dörpfeld, W.) Athen, 1902. 2v.
Arc 522.12 Troja 1893. (Dörpfeld, W.) Leipzig, 1894.
Arc 522.4.2 Trojanische Alterthuemer. (Schliemann, H.) Leipzig, 1874.
Arc 522.4.18 Der Trojanische Humbug. (Boetticher, E.) Berlin, 1911.
Arc 935.50 Trokya'da epigrafya arastirmalari. (Taslikliogłu, Zafer.) Istanbul, 1961-71. 2v.
Arc 936.120.5 Tropaeum Traiani. (Studniozka, Franz.) Leipzig, 1904.
Arc 936.120 Le trophée d'Adamclissi. (Antonescu, Teohari.) Jarsy, 1905.
Arc 830.161 Le trophée d'Auguste a la Turbie. (Casimir, Philippe.) Marseille, 1932.
Arc 66.1.187 Les trophées romains. (Picard, Gilbert.) Paris, 1957.
Arc 1033.25.7 Troppanneger, C. De lucernis veterum christianorum sepulcralibus. Vitembergae, 1710?
Arc 545.222 La trouvaille de Deir-el-Bahari. (Brugsch, E.) Cairo, 1881.
Arc 522.35.5F Troy. Supplementary monographs. Princeton, N.J. 1-3,1951-1963 3v.
Arc 522.35F Troy. v.1-4, pt.1-2. (Blegen, Carl William.) Princeton, N.J., 1950-51. 8v.
Arc 522.5 Troy and Homer. (Salisbury, S.) Worcester, 1875.
Arc 522.4.3A Troy and its remains. (Schliemann, H.) London, 1875.
Arc 522.36 Troy and the Trojans. (Blegen, Carl William.) London, 1963.
Arc 830.366 Truc, J.B. Osmin. Forum Voconii aux Arc sur Argens. Paris, 1864.
Arc 302.2.4 Trudove na sektsiata za slavianska arkheologiia. (Bulgarska Akademiia na Naukite, Sofia. Arkheologicheski institut.) Sofiia. 1-2,1947-1948
Arc 275.10F Trud'y. (Arkheologicheskii s"ezd.) 1869-1911 28v.
Arc 925.9.75 Trudy. (Kakhetskaia arkheologicheskaia ekspeditniia, 1965.) Tbilisi, 1969.
Arc 288.1 Trudy. (Nauchnoe Obshchestvo po Izucheniiu Votskogo Kraia.) Moskva. 4,1928
Arc 404.3 Trudy. v.2. (Trapsh, M.M.) Sukhumi, 1969.
Arc 1317.5 Trudy Numizmaticheskoi Kommissii. (Rossiiskaia Akademiia Istorii Material'noi Kul'tury.) Sankt Peterburg. 1-6,1921-1927
Arc 292.160 Trudy vostochnago otdeleniia. v.1-11,13-14,16; photoreproductions. (Russkoe Arkheologicheskoe Obshchestvo, Leningrad.) Sankt Peterburg. 1-22,1855-1898// 20v.
Arc 612.20 Die Trugspiegelung orientalischer Kultur in den vorgeschichtlichen Zeitaltern Nord- und Mitteleuropas. (Much, M.) Jena, 1907.
Arc 726.254 Trump, David H. Central and suthern Italy before Rome. London, 1966.
Arc 726.59.45 Trump, David H. Malta: an archaeological guide. London, 1972.
Arc 586.60 The truth about the Egypt Exploration Society. (Winslow, W.C.) Boston, 1903.
Arc 1311.2 Trutsy otts. numizmatiki. (Leningrad. Ermitazh.) Leningrad. 1,1945 4v.
Arc 936.40.45 Tsarevgrad Turnov. Dvoretsutna bulgarskite tsare prez Utorata bulgarska durzhava. Sofiia, 1973-74. 2v.
Arc 913.23 Tschumi, O. Einführung in die Vorgeschichte der Schweiz. 2. Aufl. Bern, 1918.
Arc 913.17 Tschumi, O. Urgeschichte der Schweiz. Frauenfeld, 1926.
Arc 913.17.10 Tschumi, O. Urgeschichte der Schweiz. Frauenfeld, 1949-
Arc 543.3.85 Tsentral'naia Aziia i karasukskaia problema. (Novgorodova, Eleonora A.) Moskva, 1970.
Arc 543.3.1.5 Tsentral'naia Aziia v kushanskuiu spokhu. (International Conference on the History, Archeology and Culture of Central Asia in the Kushan Period, Dushanbe, 1968.) Moskva, 1974- 2v.
Arc 925.9.130 Tsentral'nyi i severo-vostochnyi Kavkaz v skitskoe vremia. (Vinogradov, Vitalii B.) Groznyi, 1972.
Arc 936.40.16 Tsonchev, D. Contributions a l'histoire du stade antique de Philippopolis. Sofia, 1947.
Arc 936.40.15F Tsonchev, D. Prinosi kum "starata ist. na Ploadir". Sofiia, 1938.
Arc 936.40.25F Tsonchev, D. Le sanctuaire thrace prés du village de Batkoun. Sofia, 1941.
Arc 682.2 Tsountas, C. Mukyrai. Athēnai, 1893.
Arc 659.5 Tsountas, Chrēstos. Istoria tēs archaias Hellēnikēs technēs. Athēnai, 1928.
Arc 659.3 Tsountas, Chrēstos. The Mycenaean age. London, 1897.
Arc 635.220 Tsoynta, C. Ai Proistorikai...diménioy kaiseskloy. Athēnai, 1900.
Arc 1413.3 Tsukamoto, Toyojino. The old and new coins of Japan. Tokyo, 1930.
Arc 925.13.165 Tsvetaeva, Galina A. Sokrovishcha prichernomorskikh kurganov. Moskva, 1968.
Arc 925.130 Tsvetkova, I.K. Volosovskii klad. Moskva, 1957.
Arc 530.160 Tuchelt, Klaus Franz. Tiergefässe in Kopf- und Protomengestalt. Berlin, 1962.
Arc 936.195.50F Tučik, Añton. Opevnina osada z doby bronzovej vo Veselom. Bratislava, 1964.
Arc 936.65.10 Tudor, D. Oltenia română. Bucureşti, 1968.
Arc 936.20.40 Tudor, D. Sucidara; une cité daco-romaine en Dacie. Bruxelles, 1965.
Arc 820.213F Tudot, Edmond. Carte des voies romaines du départment de l'Allier. Paris, 1859.
Arc 383.34 Tübingen. Universität. Vor- und Frühgeschichtliches Institut. Festschrift für Peter Goessler. Stuttgart, 1954.
Arc 1033.34.55 La tumba de San Pedro y las catacumbas romanas. (Kioschbaum, Engelbert.) Madrid, 1954.
Arc 736.4 Tummarello, F. Su le origini di Erice. Trapini, 1898.
Arc 880.38.15 A tumulus at Carrowlesdooaun, County Mayo. (Hencken, H.O.) n.p., 1935. 2 pam.
Arc 830.2.15 Le tumulus de cote-er-garf, en elven et les sépulture de l'age du bronze dans le Morbihan. (Marsille, Louis.) Vannes, 1913.
Arc 510.211 Le Tumulus de Nemroud-Dagh. (Hamdy Bey, O.) Constantinople, 1883.
Arc 830.20 Le tumulus de Reuilly. (Boucher de Molandon.) Orléans, 1887.
Arc 830.138 Les tumulus du département de la Côte-d'Or. Thèse. (Henry, Françoise.) Paris, 1932.
Arc 830.137 Les tumulus du plateau de Ger. (Pathier, Edgard L.F.) Paris, 1900.
Arc 421.27 Tung, Tso-pin. Fifty years of studies in oracle inscriptions. Tokyo, 1964.
Arc 608.1.15 Tunis. Compte rendu de la marche du service. Tunis, 1898.
Arc 608.1.31 Tunis. Direction des Antiquités et Arts. Notes et documents. Paris. 1,1908+ 9v.
Arc 608.1.35 Tunisie. (Balut, Georges.) Tunis, 1903.
Arc 923.5 Turaeb, B.A. Drevnii mir' na Iug' Rossii. Moskva, 1918.
Arc 66.1.210 Turcan, Robert. Les sarcophages romains à representations dionysiaques. Paris, 1966.
Arc 1480.75 Turcan, Robert. Le trésor de Guelma. Thèse. Paris, 1963.
Arc 925.9.110 Turchaninov, Georgii F. Pamiatniki pis'nu i iazyka narodov Kavkaza i vostochnoi Evropy. Leningrad, 1971.
Arc 936.195.45 Turek, R. Čechy na úsvitě dějin. Praha, 1963.
Arc 936.195.290 Turek, Rudolf. Slavníkova Libice. Praha, 1946.
Arc 547.19 Turin. R. Museo di Antichità. Catalogo illustrato dei monumenti egizii. pt. 2. Torino, 1855.
Arc 530.135.10 Turk muzeciliéine bir bakis. (Arik, Remri Ogur.) Istanbul, 1953.
Arc 935.80 Türk Tarih Kurumu. Mansel'e armagan. Melanges mansel. Ankara, 1974. 3v.
Arc 935.26F Türk Tarih Kurumu tarafindan apilan Pazarli kafreyati raporu. (Kosay, Hâmit Z.) Ankara, 1941.
Arc 530.55F Türk Tarih kurumu tarafindan yapelan karakoyuk hafreyate raporu. (Özgüc, T.) Ankara, 1947.
Arc 530.75 Türk Tarih kurumu tarafindan yapelan Kültepe kazisi raporu, 1948. (Özgüc, T.) Ankara, 1950.
Arc 530.76F Türk Tarih kurumu tarafindan yapelan Kültepe kazisi raporu, 1949. (Özgüc, T.) Ankara, 1953.
Arc 935.24F Türk Tarih Kurumu tarafindan yapilan Alaca Höyük kafriyati. (Kosay, Hâmit Z.) Ankara, 1938.
Arc 935.24.10 Türk Tarih Kurumu tarafindan yapilan Alaca Höyük karisi. (Kosay, Hâmit Z.) Ankara, 1973.
Arc 530.178F Türk Tarih kurumu tarafindan yapilan Alaca noyük nafriyoti. (Arik, Remri Ogur.) Ankara, 1937.
Arc 935.28F Türk Tarih Kurumu tarafindan yapilan Etiyrkusu kafiryati raporu. (Kansu, S.) Ankara, 1940.
Arc 935.32.15 Turkey. Maarif Vekaleli Antikiteler ve Muzeler Direktorlügü. Aniflari Koruma Kurulu. Kilavuzlar. v.1,4,6. Ankara, 1935- 7v.
Arc 530.176 Turkey beyond the Maeander, an archaeological guide. (Bean, George Ewart.) London, 1971.
Arc 1588.10.25 Türkiye cumhuriyeti madeni ponohr. (Tözen, Ibrahim.) Istanbul, 1973.
Arc 530.135.5 Turkiye de 1936 yelendaki arkeoloji isleri. (Arik, Remri Ogur.) Istanbul, 1938.
Arc 340.38 Türkiyede 50 yilda yayimlanmiş Arkeoloji, sanat tarihi...bibliyografyasi. (Ödekan, Ayla.) Istanbul, 1974.
Arc 1588.8 Turkizenin ankils deviedeke meskukatina. (Bosch, E.) Ankara, 1949.
Arc 412.28 Türkuiye'de sualt, arkeolojisi. (Alpözen, Oğuz.) Istanbul, 1975.
Arc 1148.36 Turner, Eric Gardiner. Greek manuscripts of the ancient world. Oxford, 1971.
Arc 861.59 Turner, William. Ancient remains near Buxton. Buxton, 1899.
Arc 969.1.12 The Turner group of earthworks, Hamilton County, Ohio. (Willoughby, C.C.) Cambridge, 1922.
Arc 1588.4.20F Turnwald, K. Česki a Moravské denary a brakteaty. Praha, 1949.
Arc 522.40.5 Turova harabeleri ve skalor. (Kandemir, Selâhattin.) Izmir, 1933.
Arc 726.215 Turquinia. (Pallottino, Massimo.) Milano, 1959.
Arc 505.27F Turville-Petre, F. Researches in prehistoric Galilee, 1925-1926. London, 1927.
Arc 84.5 Tuscia antiqua. Roma. 1,1963+
Arc 572.1.10 Tutankhamen, and other essays. (Weigall, Arthur Edward Pearse Brome.) London, 1923.
Arc 785.14.9 Tutte le rovine, le memorie storiche. (Maes, Costantino.) Roma, 1900.
Arc 925.225.5 Tuva v skifskoe vremia. (Mannai-ool, Mongush.) Moskva, 1970.
Arc 925.50.10 Tuzlinskii nekropol'. (Sorokina, N.P.) Moskva, 1957.
Arc 1475.8 The twelve Caesars. (Morris, R.) La Grange, Ky., 1877.
Arc 1163.17 Twelve facsimiles of old English manuscripts. (Skeat, W.W.) Oxford, 1892.
Arc 810.35 Twelve photographs of Pompeii. n.p., n.d.
Htn Arc 1535.6* Twelve plates of English silver coins. London, 1756.
Arc 1.13.7F Twenty fifth anniversary. (American Academy, Rome.) N.Y.? 1920?
Arc 501.5A Twenty-one years' work in the Holy Land. (Besant, W.) London, 1886.
Arc 1538.15 Twenty-three plates of the coins of the ancient British kings. (Stukeley, W.M.) London, 17- .
Arc 861.31 Twining, T. Avebury in Wiltshire. London, 1723.
Arc 865.23 Twist, Richard Marsden. Stonehenge. Truro, 1964.
Arc 865.28 Twist, Richard Marsden. Stonehenge: a classical interpretation. St. Anthony, 1971.
Arc 861.196 Two Anglo-Saxon cemeteries at Winnall, Winchester, Hampshire. (Meany, Audrey.) London, 1970.

Author and Title Listing

Arc 421.4.10 Two bronze drums. (Ferguson, J.C.) Peking, 1932.

Arc 843.62.10 Two Celtic waves in Spain. (Bosch-Gimpera, P.) London, 1939.

Arc 1540.22 Two dissertations upon the mint and coins of Durham. (Noble, Mark.) Birmingham, 1780.

Arc 305.3.5 Two great gifts. The Lummies Library and collections; the Munk Library. (Archaeological Institute of America. Southwest Society, Los Angeles.) Los Angeles, 1910.

Arc 585.9 Two hieroglyphic papyri from Tanis. (Griffith, F.L.) London, 1889.

Htn Arc 858.13* Two lectures on the remains of ancient pagan Britain. (Stackhouse, T.) London, 1833.

Arc 493.2 Two Persepolitan casts in the U.S. National Museum. (Adler, C.) Washington, 1893.

Arc 1130.5 Two select bibliographies mediaeval historical study. (Moore, Margaret F.) London, 1912.

Arc 973.10 The two Teeth site [South Dakota]. (Smith, Carl S.) Lincoln, 1968.

Arc 600.6.5 Two Theben queens. (Campbell, C.) London, 1909.

Arc 1076.3.14 Tyack, G.S. A book about bells. London, 1898.

Arc 1077.2.33 Tyack, G.S. The cross in ritual architecture and art. 2. ed. London, 1900.

Arc 543.25 The Tyandi-Barabudur in Central Java. (Groneman, I.) Samarang, 1901.

Arc 543.25.5 The Tyandi-Barabudur in Central Java. 2. ed. (Groneman, I.) Samarang, 1906.

Arc 1433.3 Tychsen, O.G. Introductio in rem numariam Muhammedanorum. Rostock, 1794. 2 pam.

Arc 1335.25 Tychsen, T.C. De numis cuficis in biblio. regia Gottingense. n.p., n.d.

Arc 1423.4 Tychsen, T.C. De numis Hasmonaeorum paralipomena. n.p., 1792.

Arc 1075.5F Tyler, Alan. Neolithic flint axes from the Cotswold Hills. Oxford, 1976.

Arc 612.12A Tyler, John Mason. The new stone age in northern Europe. N.Y., 1921.

Arc 861.18.3 Tylor, Alfred. New points in the history of Roman Britain, as illustrated by discoveries at Warwick Square. Westminster, 1884.

Arc 853.266 Typen ostpreussischer Hügelgräber. (Engel, Carl.) Neumünster, 1962.

Arc 1510.11.20 Typenkatalog der Münzer der bayerischen Herzöge und Kurfürsten, 1506-1805. (Hahn, Wolfgang Reinhard Otto.) Braunschweig, 1971.

Arc 1490.23 Les types monétaires de la guerre sociale. (Bompois, H.F.) Paris, 1873.

Arc 1465.2 The types of Greek coins. (Gardner, P.) Cambridge, Eng., 1883.

Arc 608.67 Typologie de l'épipaléolithique du Maghreb. (Tixier, Jacques.) Paris, 1963.

Arc 895.37.5 Die Typologie der nordischen Streitäxte. (Åberg, Nils.) Würzburg, 1918.

Arc 716.14.2 The tyrant slayers of Kritios and Nesiotes: a critical study of the sources and restorations. 2. ed. (Brunnsaaker, Sture.) Stockholm, 1971.

Arc 746.27 Tyrrhenika, an archaeological study of the Etruscan sculpture in the archaic and classical periods. (Riis, Poul J.) Copenhagen, 1941.

Arc 1470.31.5 Tyrus rediviva. (Newell, E.T.) N.Y., 1923.

Arc 1588.1.60 Tysiąc lat monety na ziemiach poliskich. (Breslau. Zakład Narodowy im Ossalińskikh. Biblioteka.) Wrocław, 1966.

Arc 1588.1.44F Tysiac lat monety polskiej. (Kałkowski, Tadeusz.) Kraków, 1963.

Arc 1588.1.37 Tysiąc lat monety polskiej. (Lublin (City). Museum Lubelskie.) Lublin, 1966.

Arc 1588.1.44.2 Tysiac lat monety polskiej. Wyd. 2. (Kałkowski, Tadeusz.) Kraków, 1974.

Arc 404.1.5A Tyskiewicz, M. Memories of an old collector. London, 1898.

Arc 1076.3.60 Tyssen, A.D. The church bells of Sussex. Lewes, 1915.

Arc 1675.51.15F Tyszkiewicz, E. Sammlung von Medaillen. Riga, 1871.

Arc 1588.1.13 Tyszkiewicz, J. Guide de l'amateur de monnaies polonaises. Posen, 1890.

Arc 936.14.530 Tyszkiewicz, Jan. Mozowsze północno-wschodnie we wczesnym średniowieczu. 1. wyd. Warszawa, 1974.

Arc 700.60 U istokov evropeiskoi kul'tury. (Zlatkovskaia, Tat'iana D.) Moskva, 1961.

Arc 395.27 U źródeł archeologii. (Kramarkowa, Irena.) Wrocław, 1972.

Arc 915.32 Uber die Colonia Raurica und den Ursprung von Basel. 2. Aufl. (Laur-Belart, Rudolf.) Basel, 1959.

Arc 1033.109 Uccelli, P.A. Dei santi martiri Domno, Domnione ed Eusebia. Bergamo, 1874.

Arc 1153.18 Učebna kniha palaeografie latinské. (Friedrich, G.) Praha, 1898.

Arc 1088.7F Ucelli, Guido. Le navi di Nemi. 2. ed. Roma, 1950.

Arc 1163.3.5 Uchebnik russkoi paleografii. (Shchepkin, Viacheslav N.) Moskva, 1918.

Arc 925.6 Über alte süd-sibirische Gräberfunde. (Frähn, C.M.J.) St. Petersburg, 1837.

Arc 391.2.5 Über archäologische Sammlungen und Studien. (Gerhard, Eduard.) Berlin, 1860.

Arc 1018.32 Über Begriff...christlichen Archäologie. (Kraus, F.X.) Freiburg, 1879.

Arc 1298.2 Über Blei- und Goldbullen. (Eitel, Anton.) Freiburg, 1912.

Arc 1215.2 Ueber Blei- und Goldbullen im Mittelalter. (Eitel, Anton.) Freiburg, 1912.

Arc 1138.8 Ueber Buecher-Handschriften. (Pfeiffer, A.F.) Erlangen, 1810.

Arc 87.1.57 Ueber Copien einer Frauenstatue. (Kekule, R.) Berlin, 1897.

Arc 1478.9 Über das römische Münzwesen. (Mommsen, T.) Leipzig, 1850.

Arc 726.13 Über das römische System der Wege in alten Italien. (Voigt, M.) n.p., 1872.

Arc 395.10 Ueber das Studium des Alterthums. (Klotz, C.A.) Halle, 1766.

Arc 400.5 Ueber dea Verhaltniss des Broncealters. (Petersen, C.) Hamburg, 1868.

Arc 1053.5.3 Ueber den Antinous. (Levezow, R.) Berlin, 1808.

Arc 1093.2.3.7 Über den Bau des Riesenbetten der Vorzeit. (Frederik VII, king of Denmark.) Kopenhagen, 1863.

Arc 1027.1.5 Über den gegenwärtigenStand der Frage. (Kraus, F.X.) Freiburg, 1872.

Arc 710.4 Über den jetzigen Zustand der Akropolis von Athen. (Michaelis, A.) Frankfurt, 1861.

Arc 1027.24 Über die ältesten christlichen Begrabnisstätten. (Bellermann, C.F.) Hamburg, 1839.

Arc 710.7.5 Über die alten Burgheiligthümer in Athen. (Milchhoefer, A.) Kiliae, 1899.

Arc 746.1 Über die Ausgrabungen der Certosa von Bologna. (Brunn, H.) München, 1887.

Arc 712.10 Über die Composition der Giebelgruppen am Parthenon. (Michaelis, A.) Tübingen, 1870.

Arc 925.9.90 Über die culturgeschtliche Stellung des Kaukasus. (Virchow, Rudolf.) Berlin, 1895.

Arc 1053.8 Über die erhaltenen Porträts der griechischen Philosophen. (Schuster, P.) Leipzig, 1876.

Arc 505.45.10 Über die Fresken der Synagoge von Dura Europas. (Ehrenstein, Theodor.) Wien, 1937.

Arc 609.1.4 Über die geschichtlichen Ergebnisse der Th. Bent'schen Reisen in Ostafrica. (Dillmann, A.) Berlin, 1894.

Arc 1053.2 Über die griechische Porträtkunst. (Winter, F.) Berlin, 1894.

Arc 600.8 Über die in altägyptischen Texten erwähnten Bau- und Edelsteine. (Wendel, F.C.H.) Leipzig, 1888.

Arc 700.18 Über die Lade des Kypselos. (Overbeck, J.) Leipzig, 1865.

Arc 391.2 Über die Metallspiegel der Etrusker. (Gerhard, Eduard.) Berlin, 1836. 11 pam.

Arc 746.2 Über die Metallspriegel der Etrusker. (Gerhard, E.) Berlin, 1838.

Arc 1153.41 Ueber die Tachygraphie der Römer. Inaug. Diss. (Ruess, F.) München, 1879.

Arc 382.3 Über die Tempel und Gräber im alten Ägypten. (Dümichen, J.) Strassburg, 1872. 7 pam.

Arc 382.6 Ueber die typisch gewordenen Abbildungen menschlichen Kopfformen. (Carus, K.G.) Jena, 1863. 15 pam.

Arc 1088.1.15 Über die verrchiedenen Versuche der Rekonstruktion. (Stahlecker, R.) Ravensburg, 1897.

Arc 1433.27 Über die wissenschaftlichen Werth...Arabischen Münzen. (Bohlen, P. von.) n.p., 1835.

Arc 87.1.61 Über ein Bildnis des Perikles in den Königlichen Museum. (Kekule, R.) Berlin, 1901.

Arc 1148.4 Ueber eine bisher Unbekanntes griechisches Schriftsystem. (Gomperz, T.) Wien, 1884.

Arc 87.1.54 Ueber einen bisher Marcellus genannten Kopf. (Kekule, R.) Berlin, 1894.

Arc 853.45 Über Megalithgräber und sonstige Grabformen der Lüneburger Gegend. (Lienau, M.M.) Würzburg, 1914.

Arc 1470.12 Über mehrere im...Posen...griechische Münzen. (Levezow, J.A.K.) n.p., 1833.

Arc 796.2F Über Stilleben aus Pompeji und Herculaneum. (Beyen, Hendrik G.) 's-Gravenhage, 1928.

Arc 547.2 Uebersichtliche Erklaerung Aegyptischer Denkmaeler des Koenigliche Neuen Museum zu Berlin. (Brugsch, H.) Berlin, 1850.

Arc 547.11 Uebersichtung der Sammlung Aegyptischen Alterthuemer des Allerhöchsten Kaiserhauses. (Bergmann, E.) Vienna, 1880.

Arc 530.155 Ülgen, Ali Saim. Collection of cuttings from Turkish archeological periodicals. n.p., n.d.

Arc 936.3F Ugalini, L.U. Albania antica. Roma, 1927-42. 3v.

Arc 513.1.10 Ugarit-Bibliographie/Manfried Dietrich. Neukirchen, 1973. 4v.

Arc 726.59.15 Ugolini, L.M. Malta; origini della civiltà mediterranea. Roma, 1934.

Arc 570.1A Uhlemann, M. Handbuch der gesammten aegyptischen Alterthumskunde. v.1-4. Leipzig, 1857. 2v.

Arc 1478.84 Uhlich, Gottfried. Versuch einer Numismatik für Künstler. Lemberg, 1792.

Arc 861.208 Uhthoff-Kaufmann, Raymond R. The archaeology of Jodrell Hall (Terra Nova), Cheshire. Wilmslow, 1971.

Arc 396.20 Uit de school van de spade. (Leopold, Hendrik M.R.) Zutphen, 1928-34. 6v.

Arc 905.42 Ujabb tanulmányok a honfoglalasi kor emlékeiral. (Hampel, J.) Budapest, 1907.

Arc 302.2.7 Ukaz, kumuizv na bulgarekoto archeologichesko. (Gerasimov, T.) Sofiia, 1934.

Arc 936.140.50 Ukazatel na predmeti izobrazeni vurkhu antichni pametnitsi ot Bulgariia. (Krusteva-Nozharova, Gina.) Sofiia, 1958.

Arc 292.30.5 Ukazateli k otchetame za 1882-98. (Russia. Arkheologicheskaia Kommissiia.) Sankt Peterburg, 1903.

Arc 925.50.70 Ukraina davna i terazniejsza. (Grabowski, M.) Kijów, 1850.

Arc 1335.29 Ulex, G.F. Sammlung des G.F. Ulex; Münzen und Medaillen von Nord-, Central-, und Süd-Amerika. Frankfurt, 1908.

Arc 513.20.5 Ülgen, Ali Saim. Anitlaria koranmasi ve onarilmasi. Ankara, 1943.

Arc 746.9.15 Ulisse (pseud.). Figure mitologiche degli specchi "Etruschi". pt.1-7. Roma, 1929-37.

Arc 1153.53 Ullmann, B.L. Ancient writing and its influence. N.Y., 1932.

Arc 1153.53.5 Ullmann, B.L. The origin and development of humanistic script. Rome, 1960.

Arc 1510.40 Ulmer Münz- und Geldgeschichte des Mittelalters. (Haeberle, Adolf.) n.p., 1935.

Arc 1490.32 Ulrich-Bansa, O. Monete mediolanensis. Venezia, 1949.

Arc 660.1 Ulrichs, H.N. Reisen und Forschungen in Griechenland. pt.1-2. Bremen, 1840.

Arc 880.35 Ulster. (Lawlor, H.C.) Belfast, 1928.

Arc 810.42.10 L'ultima fase edilizia di Pompei. (Maiuri, Amedeo.) Roma, 1942.

Arc 1153.90F Umbrae codicum acidentalium. Amsterdam. 1,1961+ 10v.

Arc 853.76.5 Umbreit, Carl. Die Ausgrabung des steinzeitlichen Dorfes von Berlin-Britz. Inaug. Diss. Leipzig, 1936.

Arc 853.76 Umbreit, Carl. Neue Forschungen zur ostdeutschen Steinzeit und frühen Bronzezeit. Leipzig, 1937.

Arc 936.195.20 Umělecký řemeslo v pravěku. (Filip, Jan.) Praha, 1941.

Arc 682.3 Und die Verhältniss der mykenischen zur dorischen Baustiel. (Reber, F. von.) München, 1896.

Arc 412.27 Und sie waren doch da: wissenschaftliche Beweise für den Besuch aus dem All. (Selhus, Wilhelm.) München, 1975.

Arc 893.25 Und zeugen von einem stolzen Geschlecht. (Sprockhoff, E.) Oslo, 1945.

Arc 612.47 Under the Mediterranean. (Frost, H.) London, 1963.

Arc 412.26 Underwater archaeology. (Cleator, Philip.) London, 1973.

Arc 903.1 Undset, F. Etudes sur l'age de bronze...Hongrie. Christiana, 1880.

Arc 895.11 Undset, F. Fra Norges aeldre jernalder. Kjøbenhavn, 1880.

Arc 612.1 Undset, F. Jernalderens Begyndelse i nord Europa. Kristiania, 1881.

Arc 1083.1 Undset, I. Das erste Auftreten des Eisens in Nord-Europa. Hamburg, 1882.

Arc 893.4 Undset, I.M. Norske oldsager i fremmede museer. Christiania, 1878.

Arc 380.204 Unedirte antike Bildwerke. (Gaedechens, R.) Jena, 1873.

Author and Title Listing

Arc 1670.3 Unedited and rare Russian medals. (Iversen, J.) St. Petersburg, 1874.
Arc 405.2F UNESCO. Monuments et sites d'art. Paris, 1950.
Arc 1542.3F Unionstidens udmøntninger. (Galster, Georg.) København, 1972.
Arc 600.215 United Arab Republic. Centre of Documentation and Studies on Ancient Egypt. Kalabsha. Cairo, n.d.
Arc 595.64 United Arab Republic. Ministry of Culture and National Guidance. Nocturnal magic of the pyramids. Paris, 1961.
Arc 600.195 United Arab Republic. Ministry of Culture and National Guidance. The salvation of the Nubian monuments. Cairo, 196-
Arc 1613.29 United States. Domestic and foreign coins manufactured by mints of the United States, 1793-1973. Washington, 1974.
Arc 950.206 United States. Report upon geographical surveys west of the one hundredth meridian. v.7. Archaeology. Washington, 1879.
Arc 983.2.7 United States. Commission. Report to the Columbian historical exposition at Madrid. Washington, 1895.
Arc 953.22 United States. Department of the Interior. Annual report of department archaeologist. Washington. 1928-1931
Arc 983.15 United States. Inter-Agency Archaeological Salvage Program. River basin surveys papers. Washington, 1958.
Arc 976.8 United States. National Park Service. Excavations at Green Spring Plantation. Yorktown, 1955.
Arc 1615.2 United States coinage of 1793, cents and half cents. (Crosby, S.S.) Boston, 1897.
Arc 1615.9 United States commemorative coins, 1892-1939. (Mosher, S.) N.Y., 1940.
Arc 1615.6 The United States half cents. (Gilbert, Ebenezer.) N.Y., 1916.
Arc 1335.16 United States Mint, Philadelphia. A description of ancient and modern coins. Philadelphia, 1860.
Arc 1335.16.5 United States Mint, Philadelphia. Guide. Washington, 1913.
Arc 1615.4 United States Mint. Catalogue of coins, tokens, and medals. Washington, 1912.
Arc 1615.4.2 United States Mint. Catalogue of coins, tokens, and medals. 2. ed. Washington, 1913.
Arc 1615.4.3 United States Mint. Catalogue of coins, tokens, and medals. 3. ed. Washington, 1914.
Arc 1613.9 United States Mint. Catalogue of coins of the United States. Washington, 1928.
Arc 1615.4.10 United States Mint. Medals of the United States Mint. Washington, 1969.
Arc 1615.4.11 United States Mint. Medals of the United States Mint. Washington, 1972.
Arc 1613.7.5 United States pattern, trial, and experimental pieces. (Adams, E.H.) N.Y., 1913.
Arc 1613.24 United States pattern. (Judd, T. Hewitt.) Racine, 1959.
Arc 1613.25 United States war medals. (Belden, Bauman.) N.Y., 1916.
Arc 1138.7 Universal palaeography. (Silvestre, J.B.) London, 1850. 2v.
Arc 608.7.5 Université de l'Instruction Publique. Recherches des antiquités dans le nord de l'Afrique. Paris, 1890.
Arc 893.14 Universitetets oldsakamlings skrifter. (Brøgger, A.W.) Oslo, 1929.
Arc 545.229 University of California. Hearst Egyptian Expedition. Egyptian archaeology. Leipzig. 1-7 6v.
Arc 685.4 The unpublished objects from the Palaikastro excavations, 1902-06. (Bosanquet, Robert.) London, 1923.
Arc 861.29.5 Unriconium. (Wright, Thomas.) London, 1872.
Arc 1190.4 Unsere Kanzleisprache. (Müller, Karl.) Dresden, 1926.
NEDL Arc 1033.17.3 Unsere liebe Frau in Österreich. (Strumz, Franz.) Zürich, 1921.
Arc 793.14.5A Untergang und Auferstehung von Pompeji und Herculaneum. 3. Aufl. (Corti, Egon C.) München, 1941.
Arc 1025.51 Das unterirdische Rom. (Schmid, G.) Brixen, 1908.
Arc 726.32 Unteritalische Grabdenkmäler. (Pagenstecher, R.) Strassburg, 1912.
Arc 1348.18 Unterricht von dem Münzwesen. (Joachim, J.F.) Halle, 1754.
Arc 630.3 Untersuch über Silikat und Carbenatbiblung in antiken Morteln. (Jordt, H.) Leipzig, 1906.
Arc 1143.10 Untersuchungen...antiken Buchwesens. (Dziatzko, K.) Leipzig, 1900.
Arc 785.39.50 Untersuchungen an der Caracallathermen. (Broedner, Erika.) Berlin, 1951.
Arc 1285.25 Untersuchungen über die Besiegelung der schlesichen Herzogsurkunden im 13. Jahrhundert. Inaug. Diss. (Nehmiz, H.) Breslau, 1938.
Arc 796.1 Untersuchungen über die campanische Wandmalerei. (Helbig, W.) Leipzig, 1873.
Arc 497.34 Untersuchungen über die Steinzeit Palästina-Syriens. Inaug. Diss. (Köppel, Robert.) Rom, 1933.
Arc 785.27 Untersuchungen über Ziegelstempel des Geno Domitia. (Dressel, H.) Berlin, 1886.
Arc 1088.1.2 Untersuchungen und das Seewesen des Alterthums. (Graser, B.) Göttingen, 1867.
Arc 785.83.5 Untersuchungen zu den römischer Reichsstrassen. (Pekáry, Thomas.) Bonn, 1968.
Arc 936.242F Untersuchungen zu Grabkomplexam der älteren römischen Kaiserzeit in Böhmen unter Aspekten der religiösen und sozialen Gliederung. (Köhler, Ralf.) Neumünster, 1975.
Arc 848.33 Untersuchungen zur Geschichte der ältern Bronzezeit im Nordwestdeutschland. Inaug. Diss. (Dittmann, K.H.) Hamburg, 1938.
Arc 1480.28F Untersuchungen zur Geschichte der Kaiser Nerva, Traian und Hadrian. Inaug. Diss. (Strack, Paul L.) Stuttgart, 1930.
Arc 1480.65 Untersuchungen zur Geschichte Sullas. Inaug. Diss. (Wosnik, Bernhard.) Würzburg, 1963.
Arc 895.56 Untersuchungen zur jüngeren Eisenzeit in Schonen. (Strömberg, Märta.) Bonn, 1961.
Arc 1478.28F Untersuchungen zur römischen Reichsprägung des zweiten Jahrhunderts. (Strack, Paul L.) Stuttgart, 1931-37. 3v.
Arc 1433.62F Unvala, Jamshedji M. Coins of Tabaristān and some Sassenian coins from Susa. Paris, 1938.
Arc 386.40 Uomini e libri. (Breccia, E.) Pisa, 1959.
Arc 743.9 Up hill and down dale in ancient Etruria. (Seymour, F.) London, 1910.
Arc 858.38 The upper palaeolithic age in Britain. (Garrod, D.A.E.) Oxford, 1926.
Arc 265.1 Upsala. Universitet. Museum för Nordiska Fornsaker. Acta Musei antiquitatum septrionalium. Uppsala. 1-3,1942-1945 3v.
Arc 383.92A Ur- und Frühgeschichte als historische Wissenschaft. (Kirchner, H.) Heidelberg, 1950.
Arc 936.14.332 Ur- und Frühgeschichte Polens. (Hensel, Witold.) Berlin, 1974.
Arc 726.135.5 Ur- und Frühgeschichte Südtirols. (Lunz, Reimo.) Bozen, 1973.
Arc 1077.5 Ur-Engur. Treatise on canephorous statues. (Johns, C.H.W.) N.Y., 1908.
Arc 175.1 Ur-Schweiz. Basil. 10-33,1946-1969 7v.
Arc 925.265 Ural'skoe Arkheologicheskogo Soveshchanie. 2d, Sverdlovsk, 1961. Materialy. Sverdlovsk, 1961.
Arc 1423.27 Uranius Antoninius. (Baldus, Hans Roland.) Bonn, 1971.
Arc 530.22.11 Urartu. (Piotrovskii, Boris Borisovich.) London, 1969.
Arc 412.8 Urbanistica de las grandes ciudades del mundo antiguo. (García y Bellido, Antonio.) Madrid, 1966.
Arc 936.14.110 Urbańska, A. Wytwórczość włokiennicza predniowiecznego międzyrzeeza. Poznań, 1964.
Htn Arc 758.2* Urbis Romae aedificae illustrae quae supersunt reliquiae. (Dosio, G.A.) n.p., n.d.
Htn Arc 767.2.2* Urbis Romae topographia. (Marliani, B.) Colophon, 1544.
Arc 893.8.5 Die Ureinwohner des Scandinavischen Nordens. (Nilsson, S.) Hamburg, 1863-68. 2v.
Arc 893.8.6 Die Ureinwohner des Scandinavischen Nordens. pt.1-2. (Nilsson, S.) Hamburg, 1865-66.
Arc 612.2 Urgeschichte der bildenden Kunst in Europa. (Hoernes, M.) Wien, 1898.
Arc 612.2.2 Urgeschichte der bildenden Kunst in Europa. 2. Aufl. (Hoernes, M.) Wien, 1915.
Arc 398.5 Urgeschichte der Kultur. (Nau, Karl J.) Stuttgart, 1961.
Arc 853.258 Die Urgeschichte der Pfalz. (Sprater, Friedrich.) Speier, 1928.
Arc 913.19 Urgeschichte der Schweiz. (Heierli, J.) Zürich, 1901.
Arc 913.17 Urgeschichte der Schweiz. (Tschumi, O.) Frauenfeld, 1926.
Arc 913.17.10 Urgeschichte der Schweiz. (Tschumi, O.) Frauenfeld, 1949-
Arc 853.365 Die Urgeschichte des Kreises Kusel. (Bantelmann, Niels.) Speyer, 1972.
Arc 915.46 Urgeschichte des Thurgaus. (Keller-Tarnuzzer, Karl.) Frauenfeld, 1925.
Arc 612.4 Urgeschichte Europas. (Müller, S.) Strassburg, 1905.
Arc 925.9.12 Urgeschichte Kaukasuns. (Hancăr, Franz.) Wien, 1937.
Arc 612.31 Die urgeschichtlichen Grundlagen der europäischen Kultur. (Pittioni, Richard.) Wien, 1949.
Arc 853.8.10 Urholstein. (Hofmeister, H.) Glückstadt, 1932.
Arc 1190.35.5 Urkunden- und Aktenlehre der Neuzeit. (Meisner, H.O.) Leipzig, 1950.
Arc 1190.35.7 Urkunden- und Aktenlehre der Neuzeit. 2. Aufl. (Meisner, H.O.) Leipzig, 1952.
Arc 1185.16 Urkunden und Akten. (Brandi, Karl.) Leipzig, 1913.
Arc 205.2F Urkunden zur Vor- und Frühgeschichte aus Hohenzolleen. Stuttgart. 1-4 4v.
Arc 1185.33.3 Urkundenforschung. 3. Aufl. (Santifaller, Leo.) Darmstadt, 1968.
Arc 1185.3 Urkundenlehre. (Leist, F.) Leipzig, 1882.
Arc 1185.9 Urkundenlehre. v.1,3. (Erben, Wilhelm.) München, 1907. 2v.
Arc 1185.3.2 Urkundenlehre. 2. Aufl. (Leist, F.) Leipzig, 1893.
Arc 684.1.4 Urlichs, K.L. Bemerkungen über den olympischen Tempel und seine Bildwerke. Würzburg, 1877.
Arc 775.1.2 Urlichs, K.L. Codex urbis Romae topographicus. Wirceburg, 1871.
Arc 87.2.46 Urlichs, K.L. Dreizehn Gemmen. Bonn, 1846.
NEDL Arc 775.1 Urlichs, K.L. Roemische Topographie in Leipzig. Stuttgart, 1845.
Arc 87.2.67 Urlichs, L. Die Gruppe des Pasquino. Bonn, 1867.
Arc 520.5 Urlichs, L. Pergamon - Geschichte und Kunst. Leipzig, 1883.
Arc 628.11 Urlichs, L. von. Beiträge zur Kunstgeschichte. Leipzig, n.d.
Arc 395.13 Der Urmensch als Schöpfer. 2. Aufl. (Kraft, G.) Tübingen, 1948.
Arc 853.341 Das urnenfelderzeitliche Gräberfeld von Aschaffenburg-Streitwald. (Rau, Hermann Gunther.) Kallmünz, 1972.
Arc 853.60 Der Urnenfriedhof auf der Schanze bei Grossromstedt. (Eichhorn, G.) Leipzig, 1927.
Arc 638.1 Die Urspruenge der Stadt Pergamos in Kleinasien. (Hesselmeyer, E.) Tübingen, 1884-85. 7 pam.
Arc 1163.15 Der Ursprung der isländischen Schrift und ihre Weiterbildung bis zur Mitte des 13. Jahrhunderts. Inaug. Diss. (Spehr, Harald.) Halle, 1929.
Arc 1027.73 Ursprung und Entwickelung der Chorkrypta. (Hoferdt, E.) Breslau, 1905.
Arc 1200.13 Ursprung und Geschichte der Devotionsformeln. (Schmitz, Karl.) Stuttgart, 1913.
Arc 925.13.100F Ursprung und Herkunft der zentralrussischen Fatjanowo Kultur. (Ozols, Jekabs.) Berlin, 1962.
Arc 848.8.13 Ursprung und Verbreitung der Germanen in vor-und frühgeschichtlicher Zeit. (Kossinna, Gustaf.) Leipzig, 1928.
Arc 925.235F Urusov, V.P. Raskopki kurganov Eniseiskoi gubernii. Moskva, 1902.
Arc 726.275 Usai, Angelino. Il villaggio nuragico di Seleni, Lanusei. Cagliari, 1966.
Arc 1033.164 Usener, H.K. Acta martyris Anastasii Persae. Bonnae, 1894.
Arc 1033.171 Usener, H.K. Acta S. Timothei. Bonn, 1877.
Arc 848.35 Uslar, R. von. Westgermanische Bodenfunde. Berlin, 1938.
Arc 405.3 Usov, S.A. Sochineniia. Moskva, 1892. 2v.
Arc 923.65 Uspekhi sovetskoi arkheologii. (Obladnikov, A.P.) Leningrad, 1950.
Arc 50.5 Uspekhii sredneaziatskoi arkheologii. Leningrad. 1,1972+
Arc 923.100 Uspenskii, L.V.P. Za sem'iu pechatiami. Izd. 2. Moskva, 1962.
Arc 510.213 Ussing, J.L. Pergamos seine Geschichte und Monumente. Berlin, 1899
Arc 325.2 Utah. University. Archaeological number. 1,1910
Arc 1360.2 Utilitas rei numariae veteris. (Froelich, E.) Viennae, 1733.
Arc 608.32.5 Utique. (Lézine, Alexandre.) Tunis, 1970.
Arc 943.25 Utzinger, Rudolf. Indianer-Kunst. München, 1921.
Arc 923.25F Uvarob, A.S. Arkheologiia Rossii. Moskva, 1881. 2v.
Arc 405.1.30 Uvarov, Aleksei S. Katalog sobraniia drevnostei. v.1,3-11. Moskva, 1887- 10v.
Arc 936.6.20 Uwagi v gospodarce i strukturze społecznej ludności kultury łuzyckiej. (Gedl, Marek.) Kraków, 1961.
Arc 935.34 Uzuncaburç ve Ura kilavuzu. (Boysal, Yusuf.) Istanbul, 1962.
Arc 925.16.70 V glub' vekov. Alma-Ata, 1974.

Arc 936.14.138 V konferencja naukowa w Busknzdroju i w Wislicy, 19-20 maja, 1966. Vyd. 1. (Warsaw. Uniwersytet. Zespoł Badan nad Polskim Sredniowieczem.) Warszawa, 1968.
Arc 925.9.40 V kraiu zolotogo runa. (Pachulia, Vianor P.) Moskva, 1964.
Arc 925.9.41 V kraiu zolotogo runa. Izd. 2. (Pachulia, Vianor P.) Moskva, 1968.
Arc 385.9 V poiskakh ischeznuvshikh tsivilizatsii. (Amal'rikh, Aleksei S.) Moskva, 1959.
Arc 385.9.2 V poiskakh ischeznuvshikh tsivilizatsii. Izd. 2. (Amal'rikh, Aleksei S.) Moskva, 1966.
Arc 925.347 V strane srekh solnts. (Derevianko, Anatolii P.) Khabarovsk, 1970.
Arc 925.9.52 V strane vainakhor. (Markovin, Vladimir I.) Moskva, 1969.
Arc 925.9.50 V ushchel'iakh Arguna i Fortangi. (Markovin, Vladimir I.) Moskva, 1965.
Arc 1448.8 Vaccaro, Francesco. Le monete di Aksum. Casteldario, 1967.
Arc 830.82 Vachon, Marius. Les ruines de Sanxay découvertes en 1882. Paris, 1883.
Arc 1428.29 Vacquier, Polydore. Numismatique des Scythes et des Sarmates. Paris, 1881.
Arc 505.136 Vademecum der Grabung Kamid-el-Loz. (Hachmann, Rolf.) Bonn, 1969.
Arc 925.237 Vadetskaia, El'ga B. Drevnie idoly Eniseia. Leningrad, 1967.
Arc 726.25.7 Vagliere, Dante. Ostia; cenni storici e guida. Roma, 1914.
Arc 726.25.5 Vagliere, Dante. Piccola giuda di Ostia. Roma, 1914.
Arc 785.13.7 Vaglieri, Dante. Gli scavi recenti nel Foro Romano. Roma, 1903.
Arc 785.13.8 Vaglieri, Dante. Gli scavi recenti nel Foro Romano. Supplemento. Roma, 1903.
Arc 746.40.5F Vagnetti, Lucia. Il deposito votivo di Competti a Veio. Firenze, 1971.
Htn Arc 1475.6* Vaillant, J. Numi antiqui familiae romanarum. Amsterdam, 1703. 2v.
Htn Arc 1455.4* Vaillant, J. Numismata imperatorum. Amsterdam, 1700.
Arc 1180.2 Vaines, J. de. Dictionnaire raisonnè de diploéatique. Paris, 1774. 2v.
Arc 830.119 Vaison dans l'antiquité. (Sautel, Joseph.) Avignon, 1926-27. 2v.
Arc 830.119.7 Vaison dans l'antiquité. pts.1-3. (Sautel, Joseph.) Lyon, 1926.
Arc 830.119.5 Vaison dans l'antiquité. v.1-2. (Sautel, Joseph.) Avignon, 1926.
Arc 1163.4.20F Vajda, Georges. Album de paléographie arabe. Paris, 1958.
Arc 1163.3.17 Vajs, Josef. Rukovět hlaholské paleografie. Praha, 1932.
Arc 441.4 Vakil, K.H. Rock-cut temples around Bombay. Bombay, 1932.
Arc 925.13.7 Vaksel, H.C.L. Izobrazheniia raznykh' pamiashchnikov drevnosti. Sankt Petersburg, 1801.
Arc 785.42 Valadier, G. Narrazione artistica dell'operato finora nel ristauro dell'arco di Tito. Roma, 1822.
Arc 600.156.10F Valbelle, Dominique. Ouchebtis de Deir el-Médineh. Le Caire, 1972.
Arc 843.5.15 Valcarcel, A. Lucentum, oy La ciudad de Alicante. Valencia, 1780.
Arc 386.27 Vale, Giuseppe. Gian Domenico Bertoli. Aquileia, 1946.
Arc 1185.26 Valenti, Filippo. Il documento medioevale. Modena, 1961.
Arc 936.100.40 Valentic, Mirko. Kameni spomenici hrvatsko XIII-XIX stoljeća. Zagreb, 1969.
Arc 1433.36 Valentine, W.H. Modern copper coins of the Muhammadan states. London, 1911.
Arc 1025.35.20 Valeri, A. Cenni biografici di Antonio Bosio. Roma, 1900.
Arc 1020.10 Valeri, A. Monumenti cristiani del Foro Romano. Roma, 1900.
Arc 1015.217.5 Valeria; historische Erzahlung. (Waal, A. de.) Regensburg, 1884.
Arc 858.22.5 Vallance, A. Old crosses and lychgates. London, 1920.
Arc 66.1.144 La Vallée du spercheios. (Béquignon, Yves.) Paris, 1937.
Arc 688.5 La vallée du Spercheios des origines au IVe siècle. Thèse. (Béquignon, Y.) Paris, 1937.
Arc 1480.38 Vallemont, P. Nouvelle explication d'une médaille d'or du cabinet du roy. Paris, 1699.
Arc 736.22 Vallet, Georges. Megara Hyblaca. v.2,4. Text and atlas. Paris, 1964- 4v.
Arc 66.1.189 Vallet, Georges. Rhégion et Zanale. Paris, 1958.
Arc 1675.5 Vallet de Viriville, A. Notice historique sur la médaille...en souvenir de l'expulsion. Paris, n.d.
Arc 66.1.157 Vallois, René. L'architecture hellénique et hellenistique a Délos. Paris, 1944-53. 2v.
Arc 936.165 Le vallum de la Moldavie inférieure et le mur d'Athanaric. (Vulpe, Radu.) 's-Gravenhage, 1957.
Arc 861.12.9 Vallum Romanum...Cumberland and Northumberland. (Warburton, J.) London, 1753.
Arc 682.20.5F Valmin, M.N. The Swedish Messenia expedition. Lund, 1938.
Arc 1020.64.5 Valouse, V. de. Inventaires du trésor de l'église de Lyon. Lyon, 1877.
Arc 497.67 Van aartsvaders tot prafeten. (Franken, Hedricus J.) Amsterdam, 1967.
Arc 543.150 Van Beek, Gus Willard. Hajar Cin Humeid. Baltimore, 1969.
Arc 776.2A Van Buren, A.W. Ancient Rome as revealed by recent discoveries. London, 1936.
Arc 785.62F Van Buren, A.W. The Aqua Traiana and the mills on the Janiculum. Bergamo, 1917.
Arc 810.41 Van Buren, A.W. A companion to Pompeian studies. Rome, 1927.
Arc 815.22F Van Buren, A.W. Studies in the archaeology of the forum at Pompeii. Bergamo, 1918.
Arc 793.13 Van Buren, Albert W. A companion to the study of Pompeii and Herculaneum. Rome, 1933.
Arc 1033.17.49 Vandel, R.P. Les impressions d'un pelerinou l'ecole de Marie à Pontmain. Issoudun, 1872.
Arc 785.13.39 Van Deman, E.B. The Atrium Vestae. Washington, 1909.
Arc 785.6.17F Van Deman, E.B. The building of the Roman aqueducts. Washington, 1934.
Arc 1520.5 Vandenpeereboom, A. Essai de numismatique yproise. Bruxelles, 1877.
Arc 1020.54 Van de Putte, F. La Chapelle des Comtes de Flandre à Courtrai. Bruges, 1875.
Arc 1033.35.7F Van de Putte, F. Collégiale de S. Walburge à Furnes. Relique de la croix. Bruges, 1864. 3 pam.
Arc 571.5 Vandier, Jacques. Manuel d'archéologie égyptienne. v.1-5; atlases. Paris, 1952. 10v.
Arc 1020.5 Van Drival, E. Le trésor sacré de la cathédrale d'Arras. Arras, 1860.
Arc 1020.63 Van Drival. Catalogue de l'exposition d'objets d'art...à Lille en 1874. 2. éd. Lille, 1874.
Arc 386.31.5 Vanished cities. (Schreiber, Hermann.) N.Y., 1957.
Arc 938.17.15 Vankina, Lutsiia V. Tortianikovaia stoiankor Sarnate. Riga, 1970.
Arc 1020.9.85 Vannitelli, V. Memorie sacre Lateranensi. Roma, 1900.
Arc 530.22.10 Vanskoe tsarstvo (Urartu). 2. Izd. (Piotrovskii, Boris Borisovich.) Moskva, 1959.
Arc 608.23.10 Vantini, Giovanni. The exavations at Faras. Thesis. Bologna, 1970.
Arc 383.89F Varia archaeologica. (Grimm, Paul.) Berlin, 1964.
Arc 760.6 Varieta di notizie economiche fisiche antiquarie. (Fea, Carlo.) Rome, 1820.
Arc 1027.12.15 I varii seppellimenti...Pietro e Paolo. (Lugari, G.B.) Roma, 1898.
Arc 600.55F Varille, Alexandre. Karnak. v.1,3-4. Le Caire, 1943-51. 4v.
Arc 302.2.9.5 Varna, Bulgaria. Naroden Muzei. Izvestiia. 1,1965+ 4v.
Arc 302.2.9 Varnensko Arkheologichesko Druzhestvo, Stalin. Izvestiia. Stalin. 3-13 10v.
NEDL Arc 1088.1.10 Vars, J. L'art nautique dans l'antiquité. Paris, 1887.
Arc 302.39 Varstvo spomenikov. Ljubljana. 10,1965+
Arc 843.15.12 El vas companiforme a Catalunya i las caves sepulcrals eneolitequeis. (Serra-Vilars, J.) Solsona, 1923.
Htn Arc 402.13* Vasconcellos, Joaquim de. Conde de Raczynski (Athanasius). Porto, 1875.
Arc 66.1.125 Les vases grecs à reliefs. (Courby, Fernand.) n.p., n.d.
Arc 66.1.209 Les vases plastiques rhodiens. (Ducat, Jean.) Paris, 1966.
Arc 1455.5 Vasi greci della Sicilia. (Rizzo, G.E.) Roma, 1904.
Arc 936.220.110 Vasić, Rastko. Kulturne grupe starijeg grozdenog doba u Jugoslaviji. Beograd, 1973.
Arc 399.3.2 Vasilevskii, Ruslan S. Annotirovannaia bibliografiia nauchnykh trudov akademika A.P. Okladnikova (1968-1973 gg). Ulan-Ude, 1974.
Arc 1010.27 Vasil'evskii, Ruslan S. Drevnie kul'tury Tikhookeanskogo Severa. Novosibirsk, 1973.
Arc 936.140.55 Vasiliev, Asen. Ivanovskite stenopisi. Sofiia, 1953.
Arc 1033.12.40F Vassalli, M. Discorso sopra la sacra sindone...Torino. Parma, n.d.
Arc 820.219F Vasseur, G. L'origine de Marseille. Marseille, 1914.
Arc 1259.3F Vatican. Archivio Vaticano. I sigilli dell'archivio vaticano. v.1-3. Città del Vaticano, 1937- 5v.
Arc 1208.8 Vatican. Biblioteca Vaticana. Le bolle d'oro dell'archivio vaticano. Città del Vaticano, 1934.
Arc 447.6.5F Vats, Madho Sarup. Excavations at Harappa. Delhi, 1940. 2v.
Arc 1613.5 Vattemare, A. Collection de monnaies et médailles de l'Amérique. Paris, 1861.
Arc 600.155F Vaudier, Jacques. Catalogue des ostraca figurés de Deir el Médineh. Pt. 4. Le Caire, 1959.
Arc 785.58F Vaudoyer. Description du théâtre de Marcellus à Rome. Paris, 1812.
Arc 603.5 Vaufrey, Raymond. Prehistoire de l'Afrigue. Paris, 1955.
Arc 672.1.140 Vaughan, Agnes C. The house of the Double Axe; the palace at Knossos. Garden City, 1959.
Arc 672.1.35 The vaulted tombs of Mesará. (Xanthoudídes, S.) London, 1924.
Arc 505.58 Vaux, R. de. Fouilles à Qaryet el-'Enab Abu-Gôch. Paris, 1950.
Arc 406.4 Vayson de Pradenne, A. La préhistoire. Paris, 1938.
Arc 406.4.5 Vayson de Pradenne, A. Prehistory. London, 1940.
Arc 1494.60 Vaz, Joaquin Ferraro. Livro das moedas de Portugal. Book of the coins of Portugal. Braga, 1969-70. 2v.
Arc 1033.24.5 Vecchi, G. de. Una rarita del secolo XIX...sacro tesoro del G.C. Rossi. Roma, 1896.
Arc 406.1 Vecchi, M.M. Il Mediterraneo illustrato. Firenze, 1841.
Arc 890.208 Vedel, E. Bornholms oldtidsminder og oldsager. Kjøbenhavn, 1886.
Arc 890.208.2 Vedel, E. Efterskrift oldtidsminder og oldsager. Kjøbenhavn, 1897.
Arc 432.7 Vedic antiquities. (Jouveau-Dubreuil, D.) London, 1922.
Arc 387.10.5 Vedova, Giuseppe. Il conte L. Palma di Cesnola e il Museo metropolitano di Nuova York. Roma, 1899.
Arc 853.13.30F Veeck, Walther. Die Alamannen in Württemberg. Berlin, 1931. 2v.
Arc 830.130.30 Veelter, Daniel. Glozel, und die Einwanderung von Semiten im heutigen französischen Departement. Strassburg, 1929.
Arc 843.181 Vega de la Sella, Ricardo. Astucias. v.1-4. Madrid, 1916.
Arc 843.180 Vega de la Sella, Ricardo. El dolmen de la capilla de Santa Cruz. Madrid, 1919.
Arc 1027.38 Le veglie notturne al cimitero di Cimella. (Cassini da Perinaldo, F.) Genova, 1858.
Arc 393.1 Vegni, V. de. Notizie biografiche del cavaliere Francesco Inghirami. Volterra, 1849.
Arc 835.203FA Veiga, Estacio da. Antiquidades de Mafra. Lisboa, 1879.
Arc 830.369 Veillard, Jean Yves. Celtes et Armorique. Rennes, 1971.
Arc 87.2.85 Veith, C. Das roemische Koeln. Bonn, 1885.
Arc 1584.31 Veksler, Aleksandr G. Moskovskie klady. Moskva, 1973.
Arc 1033.35.53 Velasco, Alfonso A. Historia de la milagrosa renovación. México, 1845.
Arc 830.265 Le Velay gallo-grec. (Boudon-Fashermes, Albert.) Rodez, 1958.
Arc 1494.1 Velazquez, L.J. Congeturae sobre las medallos. Malaga, 1759.
Arc 1675.21 Velazquez, L.J. Congeturas sobre las medallas de los reyes godos y suevos de España. Malaga, 1759. 2 pam.
Arc 1138.90 Velazquez de Velasco, L.J. Ensayo sobre los alphabetos de las letras des conocidas. Madrid, 1952.
Arc 1033.35.23 Velentini, A. Santissime croci di Brescia. Brescia, 1882.
Arc 726.105 Velitrae. (Cressedi, G.) Roma, 1953.
Arc 936.195.125 Velkomoravské hradisko sv. Klimenta u Osvětiman. (Hrubý, Vilém.) Brno, 1961.
Arc 936.195.165.5 Velkomoravské hradiště Mikulčice. 1. vyd. (Poulík, Josef.) Gottwaldov, 1959.
Arc 936.140.5 Velkov, Ivan. Murtvi gradove. Sofiia, 1933.
Arc 936.65.5 Velkov, V.I. Gradŭt v Trakiia i Dakiia prez kŭsnata antichnost. Sofiia, 1959.
Arc 522.19.10 Vellay, Charles. Controverses autour de Troie. Paris, 1936.
Arc 522.19 Vellay, Charles. Les nouveaux aspects de la question de Troie. Paris, 1930.
Arc 522.19.2 Vellay, Charles. Les nouveaux aspects de la question de Troie. Paris, 1930.
Arc 522.19.5 Vellay, Charles. La question de Troie. Chartres, 1931. 4 pam.
Arc 726.20.3 Velleia studiata da un erudita francese. (Tononi, A.G.) n.p., 1887.

Htn Arc 845.210F* Velser, Marcus. Rerum Augustanar. Vindelicar. Libri octo. Venetiis, 1594.

Arc 1020.6.9 Veludo, G. Dichiarazione di un monumento sepolcrale cristiano. Venezia, 1877.

Arc 936.172F Venechikov, Ivan. The Panagynoishte gold treasure. Sofia, 1961.

Arc 936.40.41 Venedikov, Ivan. Nessebre. Sofia, 1971.

Arc 1020.9.63 La veneranda antica chiesa di S. Andrea e Gregoria. (Iozzi, Oliviero.) Roma, 1902.

Arc 726.305 Venetia. Padova, 1967- 2v.

Arc 1033.17.621 Venezia favorita da Maria. Relazione delle imagine...di Maria...in Venezia. Venezia, 1758.

Arc 726.135 La Venezia Tridentina nella preistoria. (Battisti, C.) Firenze, 1954.

Arc 1488.26F Venice. Museo. Catalogo della raccolta numismatiça Papadopoli-Aldobandino. Venezia, 1925. 2v.

Arc 1613.21 Venn, T.J. Large United States cents. Chicago, 1915.

Arc 1335.64 Vente aux enchères publiques de la collection de médailles grecques. (Jandolo et Lavazzi, Rome, auctioneers.) Roma, 1908.

Arc 1663.16.10 Ventitre medaglie borboniche napoletane. (Majorca Mortillaro, L.M.) Pitigliano, 1889.

Arc 1153.61.5 Venturini, M. Vita ed attività dello "Scriptorium" veronese nel secolo XI. Verona, 1930.

Arc 1153.61 Venturini, T. Ricerche paleografiche intorno all'arcidiacono pacifico di Verona. Verona, 1929.

Arc 1033.17.70 Venuta, et i progressi miracolosi della S. Madonna...S. Luca...1160-1617. (Malvasia, D.) Bononia, 1617.

Arc 1033.34.5 Venuta di San Pietro in Roma. (Caprara, C.) Roma, 1872.

Arc 1033.35.27 Venuti, F. De cruce cortonensi dissertatio. Florenzia, 1781.

Arc 800.5.10 Venuti, N.M. de. A description of the first discoveries of...ancient city of Heraclea. London, 1750.

Htn Arc 800.5* Venuti, N.M. de. Descrizione delle prime scoperte dell'antica città d'Ercolano. Venezia, 1749.

Arc 800.5.2 Venuti, N.M. de. Descrizione delle prime scoperte dell'antica città d'Ercolano. Roma, 1748.

Arc 830.81 Venuti, Niccolo M. Dissertations sur les anciens monumens de la ville de Bordeaux. Bordeaux, 1754.

Arc 776.1.3 Venuti, R. Accurata e succinta descrizione topografica delle antichità di Roma. Roma, 1824. 2v.

Htn Arc 776.1.2* Venuti, R. Accurata e succinta descrizione topografica delle antichità di Roma. 2. ed. Roma, 1803. 2v.

Arc 776.1.7 Venuti, R. Accurata e succinta descrizione topografica delle antichità di Roma moderna. Roma, 1767. 4v.

Arc 1333.1 Venuti, R. Antiqua numismata. v.1-2. Rome, 1739-44.

Arc 726.39 Venuti, R. Osservazioni sopra il fiume Clitunno. Roma, 1753.

Htn Arc 750.219* Venuti, Ridolfino. Veteris Latii antiqua vestigia urbis moenia. Romae, 1751.

Arc 1480.1 Venutis, P. de. Duodenorum nomismatum antehac ineditorum brevis expositio. Leghorn, 1760.

Arc 1033.17.99 Vera, Fortino Hipólito. Informaciones sobre la milagrosa aparición de la virgen de Guadalupe. Amecameca, 1889.

Arc 1033.17.99.5 Vera, Fortino Hipólito. Tesoro guadalupano. Amecameca, 1887.

Arc 1260.1 La vera arma della città di Crema. v.1-2. (Daugnon, F.F.) Fermo, 1874.

Arc 830.15.15 Véran, Auguste. Arles antique. Tours, 1876.

Arc 1076.3.47 Verband Deutscher Vereine für Volkskunde. Bericht über die Sammlung der Glockensprüche, Glockensagen und Glockenbräuche. Freiburg, 1918.

Arc 1082.15 Verbrugge, A.R. Le symbole de la main. Couraucès, 1958.

Arc 726.23 Vercelli, C. di. Per un ricordo al padre L. Bruzza. Vercelli, 1884.

Arc 600.3.15 Vercoutter, J. Textes biographiques du Sérapéum de Memphis. Paris, 1962.

Arc 273.8 Vereeniging tot Bevordering der Kennis van de Antieke Beschaving. Bulletin. 's Gravenhage. 1,1926+

Arc 273.9 Vereeniging tot Bevordering der Kennis van de Antieke Beschaving. Bulletin. Index, v.1-40, 1926-1965. Leiden, n.d.

Arc 1033.34.43 Die Verehrung des Heiligen Petrus bei den Franken und Angelsachsen. Inaug. Diss. (Zwölger, Theodor.) Stuttgart, 1929.

Arc 905.12.9 Verein Carnuntum, Wien. Carnuntum 1885-1910. Wien, 1911.

Arc 905.12.9.5 Verein Carnuntum, Wien. Carnuntum 1885-1910. Wien, 1935.

Arc 206.6 Verein für Geschichte und Altertumskunde Westfalens. Altertums-Kommission. Mitteilungen. Münster. 1-7,1899-1922// 4v.

Arc 1588.4.50 Vereine für Numismatik. Beschreibung. Prag, 1852-70.

Arc 1490.45 Vergare, Cesare A. Monete del regno di Napoli da Roggiero. Roma, 1715.

Arc 1033.12.69 Vergaro, G.C. Racconto dell'apparato...espositione del Sangue Venetia...1617. Venezia, 1617.

Arc 815.26.10 Vergessene Pompeji. (Schefold, Karl.) Bern, 1962.

Arc 716.2 Vergleichung der Überreste vom Theater des Dionysuszu Athen. (Kirchhoff, F.C.) Altona, 1882.

Arc 1033.12.68 Verita trionfante...della fede in...narrazione delle reliquie del Sangue...Venezia. (Rota, S.A.) Venezia, 1763.

Arc 905.11 Der Verkehr...Pass von Pontelba-Pontafel...Predil. (Rodlow, O.W. von.) Prag, 1898.

Arc 925.200 Verkhne-metliaevskii klad. (Maksimenkov, G.A.) Irkutsk, 1960.

Arc 925.322.20 Verkhneguninbskoe poselenie-pamiatnik epokhi bronzy gornogo Dagestana. (Kotovich, Valentina M.) Makhachkala, 1965.

Arc 630.11.5 Vermächtnis der antiken Kunst. (Herbig, R.) Heidelberg, 1950.

Arc 1613.30 Vermeule, Cornelius Clarkson. Numismatic art in America. Cambridge, 1971.

Arc 720.11.5 Vermiglioli, G.B. Dei monumenti di Perugia etrusca e romana. Pt.1. Perugia, 1855.

Arc 720.11 Vermiglioli, G.B. Dei monumenti di Perugia etrusca e romana. pts.1-4. Perugia, 1855-70. 2v.

Arc 720.11PF Vermiglioli, G.B. Dei monumenti di Perugia etrusca e romana. Table. Perugia, 1870.

Arc 1490.40F Vermiglioli, G.B. Della zecca e delle monete perugine. Perugia, 1816.

Arc 1490.20 Vermiglioli, G.B. Di un quadrante unico ed inedito. Perugia, 1825.

Arc 1615.1 The Vermont coinage. (Slafter, E.F.) Montpelier, 1870.

Arc 402.12 Vernadskii, G.V. M.I. Rostovtsev. Praga, 1951.

Arc 1475.201 Vernazza de Freney, J. Recensio nummorum qui secusii. Augustae Taurinorum, 1812.

Arc 830.43 Verneau, R. L'homme de la Barma-Grande. 2e éd. Baoussé-Roussé, 1908.

Arc 503.4 Veröffentlichung. (Gesellschaft für Palästina. Forschung.) Wien. 1,1910

Arc 589.75F Veröffentlichungen. (Ernst von Sieglin Expedition in Ägypten.) Leipzig. 1-6,1912-1936 6v.

Arc 191.2 Veröffentlichungen. (Gesellschaft für Österreichische Frühmittelalterforschung.) Linz.

Arc 726.140 Verona romana. (Marconi, Pirro.) Bergamo, 1937.

Htn Arc 1020.9.106* Veronesia fatris...de praecipius urbis. (Panvinus, Onuphrus.) Romae, 1570.

Arc 505.5.9 Verre colorie representant le temple de Jerusalem. (Rossi, J.B. de.) Paris, 1882.

Arc 1015.205.9 Verre representant le temple de Jerusalem. (Rossi, G.B. de.) Genes, 1883.

Arc 505.5.10 Verre representant le temple de Jerusalem. (Rossi, J.B. de.) Genes, 1883.

Arc 830.59 La verrerie en Gaule à l'époque romaine. (Morin-Jean.) Le Mans, 1913.

Arc 830.59.2 La verrerie en Gaule sous l'empire romain. (Morin-Jean.) Paris, 1913.

Arc 830.59.5 La verrerie en Gaule sous l'empire romain. (Morin-Jean.) Paris, 1923.

Arc 943.34 Verrill, A.H. America's ancient civilizations. N.Y., 1953.

Arc 630.1 Der Verschluss bei den Griechen und Römern. (Fink, J.) Regensburg, 1890.

Arc 1335.59 Versteigerungskatalog nr. 57. (Cahn, A.E.) Frankfurt, 1926.

Arc 1335.59.5 Versteigerungskatalog nr. 63. v.2. (Cahn, A.E.) Frankfurt am Main, 1929.

Arc 1335.59.10 Versteigerungskatalog nr. 71. v.2. (Cahn, A.E.) Frankfurt am Main, 1931.

Arc 1510.12 Versuch einer Abhandlung von den Nutzen der teutschen Münzwissenschaft. (Heusinger, F.) Nürnberg, 1750.

Arc 1510.147 Versuch einer chur-sächsischen Münzgeschichte von den Ältesten, bis auf jetzige Zeiten. v.1-2. (Klotzsch, Johann Friedrich.) Chemnitz, 1779-80.

Arc 1510.146 Versuch einer Münzgeschichte Augsburgs in dem Mittelalter. (Beyschlag, Daniel Eberhardt.) Stuttgart, 1835.

Arc 1510.22 Versuch einer Münzgeschichte des Elsasses. (Berstett, A.) Freiburg, 1840. 2 pam.

Arc 1478.84 Versuch einer Numismatik für Künstler. (Uhlich, Gottfried.) Lemberg, 1792.

Arc 895.36.7F Versuch einer Typologie der Felszeichnungen von Bohuslän. Inaug. Diss. (Lohse, E.) Dresden, 1934.

Arc 1510.37 Versuch über die Brakteaten. v.2. (Mader, Joseph.) Prag, 1808.

Arc 386.31 Versunkene Städte. (Schreiber, Hermann.) Wien, 1955.

Arc 743.20 Das versunkene Volk. (Cles-Reden, S.) Innsbruck, 1948.

Htn Arc 1273.2F* Vertue, G. Medals, coins, great seals, impressions from the elaborate works of Thomas Simon. London, 1753.

Arc 66.1.166 Verus Israel. (Simon, Marcel.) Paris, 1948.

Arc 87.1.41 Die Verwendung von Terrakotten. (Doerpfeld, W.) Berlin, 1881.

Arc 618.9 Verworm, M. Keltische Kunst. Berlin, 1919.

Arc 1510.20.5 Verzaichnus der Bösessmüntzsortens. n.p., 1571.

Arc 938.11 Verzeichnis archäologischer Fundorte in Liv-, Est- und Kurland. (Litzka, J.) Jurjew, 1896.

Arc 1478.60 Verzeichnis der römischen Reichsprägungen von Augustus bis Anastasius. 2. Aufl. (Elmer, Georg.) Graz, 1956.

Arc 1335.70 Verzeichniss einer grossen und sehr gewählten polnischen Münz- und Medaillen-Sammlung. (Mikocki, Leon.) Wien, 1850.

Arc 1580.10 Verzeichnung...wiennerischer...Müntzen. (Hanthaler, C.) Lintz, 1745.

Arc 600.222 Der verziete Löffel; seine Formgeschichte und Verwendung im alten Ägypten. (Gamer-Wallert, Ingrid.) Wiesbaden, 1967.

Arc 925.230.5 Ves' i Slaviane na Belom ozere X-XIII vv. (Golubeva, Leonilla A.) Moskva, 1973.

Arc 292.150 Veselovskii, H.I. Istorii. Sankt Peterburg, 1900.

Arc 925.17 Veselovskii, N.I. Pervobytnyia drevnosti. Tuapse, 1904.

Arc 785.1.8 Vesta e vestali. 2. ed. (Maes, C.) Roma, 1884.

Arc 87.1.25 Vesta und die Laren auf einem pompischen Wandgemälde. (Jordan, Henri.) Berlin, 1865.

Arc 785.1.3 Der Vestatempel und der Vestalenhof am römische Forum. (Meschler, M.) Freiburg, 1898.

Arc 861.27 Vestiges of the antiquities of Derbyshire. (Bateman, T.) London, 1848.

Htn Arc 750.31* I vestigi dell'antichità di Roma. (DuPerac, E.) Roma, 1575.

Arc 608.20 Vestigia di colonie agricole romane Gebel Nefusa. (Corò, Francesco.) Roma, 1928.

Htn Arc 760.2* Le vestigia e rarità di Roma antica. (Ficoroni, F. de.) Rome, 1744.

Arc 830.49.25 Vesunna Petrucoriorum. (Barrière, P.) Périgueux, 1930.

Htn Arc 750.25* Veteres Arcus Augustorum. (Bellori, G.A.) Roma, 1690.

Arc 1333.4 Veteres pop. et reg. numi. (British Museum.) London, 1814.

Htn Arc 750.219* Veteris Latii antiqua vestigia urbis moenia. (Venuti, Ridolfino.) Romae, 1751.

Arc 1086.2.9F Veterum lucernae sepulcrales. (Bartoli, Pietro.) Lugduni Batavorum, 1723. 2 pam.

Arc 1016.206 Vetri cimiteriali con figure in oro conservati nell Museo Britannico. (Iozzi, Oliviero.) Roma, 1900.

Arc 1016.206.3 Vetri cimiteriali con figure in oro conservati nell Museo Sacro Vaticano. (Iozzi, Oliviero.) Roma, 1900.

Arc 1015.216 Vetri cristiani della collezione di Campo-Santo. (Armellini, M.J.) n.p., n.d.

Arc 1015.208 Vetri ornati di figura in oro. (Garrucci, R.) Roma, 1858.

Arc 1015.208.2 Vetri ornati di figure in oro. (Garrucci, R.) Roma, 1864.

Arc 1033.1.7 Vetro graffito con immagini di santi. (Rossi, G.B. de.) Roma, 1878.

Arc 1490.10 Vettori, Francesco. Il fiorino d'oro antico illustrato. Firenze, 1738.

Arc 1030.30 Vettori, P. Dissertatio philologica qua nonnulla monimenta sacrae vetera ex museo Vict. Roma, 1751.

Arc 746.48F Vetulonia e la sua necropoli antichissima ed anastatica. (Falchi, Isidoro.) Roma, 1965.

Htn Arc 382.1* Vetustissimae tabulae aeneae. (Pignoria, L.) Venetiis, 1605.

Arc 1335.21 VI catalogo dei duplicati delle raccolte. (Morbio, Carlo.) Milano, 1876.

Arc 936.14.139 VI konferencja naukowa w Warszawie 10-11 stycznia 1969. (Warsaw. Uniwersytet. Zespol Badan nad Polskim Sredniowieczem.) Warszawa, 1970.

Arc 785.20.7 La Via Appia, à l'époque romaine et de nos jours. (Ripostelli, Giuseppe.) Rome, 1908.

Arc 785.55 Via Cassia. (Martinori, E.) Roma, 1930.

Author and Title Listing

Arc 785.13.200F La via Cavour e i fori imperiali. (Tolonei, Arnaldo.) Roma, 1903.
Arc 785.59F Via dei trionfi isolamento del Campidoglio. 2a ed. (Munoz, A.) Roma, 1933.
Arc 785.69.5F La via del Circo Massimo. 2. ed. (Munoz, A.) Roma, 1934.
Arc 785.60 Via dell'impero. (Ricci, Corrado.) Roma, 1933.
Arc 935.1 Via militaris Romanorum Egnatia. (Tafel, G.L.) Tubingae, 1841.
Arc 830.18.19 Viae, apud arvenos Romanae. Thesis. (Gobin, Léon.) Augustonemeti, 1896.
Arc 1020.97 Viage...para reconocer las reliquias de santos, sepulcros reales. (Morales, Ambrosio de.) Madrid, 1765.
Arc 793.4 Viaggio a Pompei a Pesto e di ritorno ad Ercolano ed a Pozzuoli. (Romanelli, D.) Napoli, 1817.
Arc 720.219F Viaggio antiquario ad Ostia. (Nibby, Antonio.) Roma, 1829.
Arc 726.3 Viaggio archeologico sulla Via Salaria. (Persichetti, N.) Roma, 1893.
Arc 1033.34.29 Viaggio ed episopato romano di San Pietro. (Stocchi, P.) Roma, 1867. 2 pam.
Arc 1025.36 Viaggio nelle catacombe di Roma. (Agincourt, G.B.L.G. d'.) Milano, 1835.
Arc 733.4.5 Viaggio per tutte le antichita della Sicilia. 3a ed. (Paterno, I.V.) Palermo, 1817.
Arc 406.6 Viana, Abel. Algumas noções elementares do arqueologia pratica. Beja, 1962.
Arc 1153.14 Vianini, G. Raccolta...abbreviazioni e frasi abbreviate. Roma, 1898.
Arc 925.13.85 Viaz'mitina, M.I. Zalsta balka. Kyiv, 1962.
Arc 925.50.280 Viaz'mitina, Mariia I. Zolotobalkovskii mogil'nik. Kiev, 1972.
Arc 1493.25 Vicenti, Jose A. España, 1869-1973: la peseta. 8. ed. Madrid, 1973.
Arc 830.230 Vichy gallo-romain. (Morlet, Antonin.) Macon, 1957.
Arc 726.63 Vicovaro e la villa di Q. Orazio Flacco. (Miceli, Salvatore.) Roma, 1929.
Arc 1675.38 Victoria and Albert Museum. Catalogue of Italian placquettes. London, 1924.
Arc 87.1.67 Die Victoria von Calvatone. (Schröder, Bruno.) Berlin, 1907.
Arc 1033.21.5 Victorius Franciscus. Sanctorum septem dormientium...Musei Victorii. Roma, 1741.
Arc 87.2.71 Vicus Aurelii. (Keller, O.) Bonn, 1871.
Arc 843.185 La vida de nuestros antecesores paleolíticos. (Hernández-Pacheco, E.) Madrid, 1923.
Arc 625.7 La vie...des Grecs et des Romains. (Fongères, G.) Paris, 1894.
Arc 600.35 Vie de Petasiris, grand prêtre di Thot à Hermopolis-la-Grande. (Suys, Émile.) Bruxelles, 1927.
Arc 66.1.184 Vie economique et sociale de Rome. (Delumeau, Jean.) Paris, 1957. 2v.
Arc 66.1.104 La vie municipale dans l'Égypte Romaine. (Jouguet, P.) Paris, 1911.
Arc 66.1.38 La vie municipale en Attique. (Haussoullier, B.) Paris, 1884.
Arc 635.217.10 La vie privée des Déliens. (Deonna, W.) Paris, 1948.
Arc 810.65 La vie quotidienne à Pompéi. (Etienne, Robert.) Paris, 1966.
Arc 736.5 Le vie romane in Sicilia. (Garafalo, F.B.) Napoli, 1901.
Arc 608.69 La vie rurale en Afrique romaine d'après les mosaiques. (Precleur-Canonge, Thérèse.) Paris, 1962.
Arc 1025.38 Vie sacre. 2a ed. (Partenio, G.M.) Roma, 1806-07. 2v.
Arc 830.1.9 Vieilles pierres bretonnes. (Waquet, H.) Quimper, 1920.
Arc 843.79 Vielva, M. De re arqueologica. Valencia, 1924.
Arc 86.1 Vienna. Abhandlungen des archaeologisches-epigrammisches Seminars. Wien. 1-15,1880-1913 5v.
Arc 900.209 Vienna. Akademie. Der römische Limes in Österreich. Wien, 1900- 20v.
Arc 518.7 Vienna. Kaiserhaus. Ausstellung von Fundstücken aus Ephesos im unteren Belvedere. Wien, 1905.
Arc 1020.1.5 Vienna. St. Stephansdom. Das Wiener Heiligthumbuch. Wien, 1882.
Arc 1333.17F Vienna. U.L.F. zu den Schotten. Benedictine Monastery. Die Münzensammlung des Stiftes Schotten in Wien. Wien, 1910-20. 2v.
Arc 1254.11 La vierge, le Christ, les saints sur les sceaux byzantins. (Schlumberger, G.) Paris, 1883.
Arc 66.1.101 La vierge de miséricorde. (Perdrizet, P.) Paris, 1908.
Arc 1033.17.56 Vierge de Saint Luc à S.-Marie Majeure. (Milochau, A.) Paris, 1862.
Arc 1490.11 Vierzig Münzen der Normannen Hohenstaufen. (Marks von Marksfeld, J.) Mailand, 1858.
Arc 302.7 Viestnik. (Hrvatsko Arheološko Društvo u Zagrebu.) Zagreb. 1-14 4v.
Arc 302.7.5 Viestnik. New series. (Hrvatsko Arheološko Društvo u Zagrebu.) Zagreb. 1-23,1895-1942 17v.
Arc 969.1.17 Vietzen, R.C. Ancient man in northern Ohio. Lorain, Ohio, 1941.
Arc 1540.16 View of coinage of Scotland, tables. (Lindsay, John.) Cork, 1845.
Arc 1538.6 View of the coinage of Ireland. (Lindsay, J.) Cork, 1839.
Htn Arc 1535.1* A view of the silver coin and coinage of England. (Snelling, T.) London, 1762.
Arc 497.77 Views of the Biblical world. Jerusalem, 1958- 4v.
Htn Arc 1033.12.58* Vigerius, M. Controversia de excellentia instrumentorum passionis. Roma, 1512.
Arc 1490.9 Vignoli, Giovanni. Antiquiores pontificum romanorum denarii. Romae, 1709.
Arc 1033.12.9.5F Vignon, P. Le Saint Suaire de Turin devant la science. 2. éd. Paris, 1939.
Arc 1033.12.9 Vignon, P. The shroud of Christ. Westminster, 1902.
Arc 1033.12.35 Vigo, G.B. Ad carolum...de Sindone Taurinensi. Augustae Taurinorum, 1768.
Arc 275.101 VIII Arkheologicheskii s"ezd v Moskve. (Miliukov, P.N.) Moskva, 1890.
Arc 384.15 VIIIe Congrès international d'archéologie classique. Photoreproduction. (Congrès International d'Archéologie Classique, 8th, Paris, 1963.) Paris, 1963.
Arc 858.56 Viking antiquities in Great Britain and Ireland. pts.1-3, 4-6. (Shetelig, H.) Oslo, 1940. 2v.
Arc 875.95 The Viking congress. (Simpson, William D.) Edinburgh, 1954.
Arc 720.205 Vila, G. de. Thesaurus antiquitatum beneventanarum. Romae, 1754.
Arc 726.24.11 La villa Adriana; guida e descrizione. (Lanciani, R.) Roma, 1906.
Arc 726.24.24F Villa Adriana. (Aurigemma, S.) Roma, 1961.
Arc 726.24.20 La villa Adriana. 2a ed. (Aurigemma, S.) Tivoli, 1953.
Arc 726.24.17 La villa Adriana presso Tivoli. (Aurigemma, S.) Tivoli, 1948.
Arc 1018.45 Villa Amil y Castro, J. Rudimentos de arqueología sagrada. Lugo, 1867.
Arc 726.334 La Villa Augustea in Somma Vesuviana. (Angrisani, Mario.) Aversa, 1936.
Htn Arc 362.1.20* Villa Borghese. (Manilli, Jacomo.) Roma, 1650.
Htn Arc 815.13.15F* La villa dei misteri. (Maiuri, Amedeo.) Roma, 1931.
Htn Arc 815.13.15PF* La villa dei misteri. Plates. (Maiuri, Amedeo.) Roma, 1931.
NEDL Arc 815.13 Die Villa des Mysterien in Pompei. (Macchiaro, V.) Neapel, 1926?
Arc 790.35 Villa ercolanese dei Pisoni i suoi monumenti. (Comparette, D.) Torino, 1888.
Arc 720.213 La villa imperiale de Tibur. (Gusmann, P.) Paris, 1904.
Arc 726.24.15 The villa of the emperor Hadrian at Tivoli. (Paribeni, R.) Milan, 1930?
Arc 790.208 La villa pompeiana. (Barnabei, F.) Roma, 1901.
Arc 726.326 La villa romana di Minori. (Franciosa, Nicola.) Minori, 1968.
Arc 968.2.32 The village of the great Kivas on the Zuñi reservation, New Mexico. (Roberts, Frank H.H.) Washington, 1932.
Arc 726.275 Il villaggio nuragico di Seleni, Lanusei. (Usai, Angelino.) Cagliari, 1966.
Arc 723.15F Villanovans and early Etruscans. (Randall-McIver, David.) Oxford, 1924.
Arc 66.1.195 Villard, Francois. La ceramique grecque de Marseilles. Paris, 1960.
Arc 505.25.5 La ville de David. (Meistermann, B.) Paris, 1905.
Arc 830.115 La ville de Rodez à l'époque romaine. (Lunet, B.) Rodez, 1888.
Arc 820.11PF La ville de Rouhling. Texte et atlas. (Huber, Émile.) Metz, 1905.
Arc 708.3 La ville et l'acropole d'Athènes. (Burnouf, E.) Paris, 1877.
Arc 820.218F La ville gallo-romaine de Beauclair. (Tardieu, A.) Clermont-Ferrand, 1882.
Arc 830.89 Villeneuve-Bargemon, Christophe. Fragment d'un voyage dans les Basses-Alpes. Agen, 1811. 3 pam.
Arc 830.6 Villes antiques - Vienne et Lyon gallo-romain. (Bazin, H.) Paris, 1891.
Arc 513.22 Villes d'Asie Mineure. (Robert, L.) Paris, 1935.
Arc 513.22.2 Villes d'Asie Mineure. 2. éd. (Robert, L.) Paris, 1962.
X Cg Arc 510.206 Les villes de la Pamphylie et de la Pisidie. (Niemann, S.) Paris, 1890-1893. 2v.
Arc 608.6.18 Villes d'or. (Algeria. Directoire de l'Intérieur et de Beaux-Arts.) Alger, 1951.
Arc 513.18 Villes mortes d'Asie Mineure. (Sartiaux, Félix.) Paris, 1911.
Arc 392.6 Les villes retrouvées. (Hanno, Georges.) Paris, 1881.
Arc 1033.17.425 Villette, E.N. Histoire de Notre-Dame de Liesse. Laon, 1708?
Arc 1460.6 Vimi nacijum. (Orlov, Georgije.) Beograd, 1970.
Arc 505.5.66 Vincent, Louis H. Jérusalem de l'Ancien Testament. Pt.1-3. Paris, 1954. 3v.
Arc 505.5.65F Vincent, Louis H. Jérusalem sous terre. Londres, 1911.
Arc 495.207F Vincent L.H. Hebron le haram el-Khalîl, sépulture des patriachs. Paris, 1923. 2v.
Arc 1033.51.5 Vincenti, D. de. Nitizie dei Sante Rufino e Cesidio Martire. Avezzano, 1885.
Arc 1540.21.5 A vindication of the Celtic inscription on Gaulish and British coins. (Poste, Beale.) London, 1862.
Arc 843.218 Vindius; el lado septentrional clasico de Hispania. (Martinez Hombre, Eduardo.) Madrid, 1964.
Arc 905.76 Vindobona. Die römische Vergangenheit Wiens. (Neumann, Alfred.) Wien, 1972.
Arc 402.8 Vingt siècles de travail. (Roger-Milès, L.) Paris, 1902.
Arc 936.100.35 Vinkovci. Gradski Muzej. 20 godina Muzeja Vinkovci 1946-66. Vinkovci, 1966.
Arc 925.9.100 Vinogradov, Vitalii B. Cherez khrebty vekov. Grozny, 1970.
Arc 925.9.130 Vinogradov, Vitalii B. Tsentral'nyi i severo-vostochnyi Kavkaz v skitskoe vremia. Groznyi, 1972.
Arc 785.8.5 Viola, Joseph. Das Kolosseum. Rom, 1913.
Arc 530.18 Viollet, H. Description du palais de al-Montasim. Paris, 1909.
Arc 915.9 Viollier, David. Carte archéologique du Canton de Vaud des origines à l'époque de Charlemagne. Lausanne, 1927.
Arc 913.16 Viollier, David. Essai sur les rites funéraires en Suisse des origines à la conquête romaine. Paris, 1911.
Arc 913.15 Viollier, David. Les sépultures du second âge. Thèse. Genève, 1916.
Arc 522.6 Virchow, R. Beitraege zur Landeskunde der Troas. Berlin, 1879.
Arc 920.7 Virchow, R. Das Gräberfeld von Koban. Text und Atlas. Berlin, 1883. 2v.
Arc 1050.203 Virchow, R. Porträt-Munzen und Grafs...Porträt Gallerie. Berlin, 1903.
Arc 925.9.90 Virchow, Rudolf. Über die culturgeschtliche Stellung des Kaukasus. Berlin, 1895.
Arc 600.235 Virey, Philippe. Quelques observations sur l'épisode d'Aristée; à propos d'un monument égyptien. Paris, 1889. Paris, 1889.
Arc 1033.17.45 La Virgen. 4. ed. (Orsini, Mathieu.) Barcelona, 1867. 2v.
Arc 1020.10.50F Le visage de Rome chrétienne. (Goyau, Georges.) Genève, 1926.
Arc 1016.226 Visconti, A. Dissertazione...cristianita di Costantino Magno. Roma, 1835.
Arc 726.22 Visconti, A. Lettera al signor Giuseppe Carnevali di Albano. Roma, 1817.
Arc 1033.63.5 Visconti, C.L. Dell'uso...dei monumenti cristiani cronologici. Roma, 1856.
Arc 785.13.25 Visconti, C.L. Deux actes de Domitien. Rome, 1873.
Arc 1033.3.27 Visconti, C.L. Dichiarazione di un sarcofago cristiano ostiense. Roma, 1859.
Arc 740.8 Visconti, C.P.E. Antichi monumenti sepolcrali nel ducato di Ceri. Roma, 1836.
Arc 726.7 Visconti, E.A. Monumenti gabini della Villa Pinciana. Milano, 1835.
Arc 726.7.5 Visconti, E.A. Monumenti gabini della Villa Pinciana. Roma, 1797.
Arc 1053.20 Visconti, E.Q. Iconografia greca. Milano, 1923-25. 3v.
Arc 712.5 Visconti, E.Q. Mémoires sur des ouvrages de sculpture du Parthénon. Paris, 1818.

Author and Title Listing

Arc 1016.233.5 Visconti, F.A. Sopra una iscrizione cimiteriale. Roma, 1831.

Arc 1027.7.5 Visconti, P.E. Di un nuovo tratto catacombe San Marcellino Pietro. Roma, 1839.

Arc 1016.227 Visconti, P.E. Dissertazione...iscrizione cristiana. Roma, 1833.

Arc 1016.233 Visconti, P.E. Sposizione di alcune antiche iscrizione cristiane. Roma, 1824.

Arc 628.21 Visconti, Pietro E. La stazione della coorte VII dei vigili e i ricordi istorici. 2. ed. Roma, 1867. 19 pam.

Htn Arc 1033.133* Viseur, R. Recueil de la vie, mort, invention et miracles de S. Jean Baptiste. Amyens, 1618.

Arc 1138.127 Visible words. (Sparrow, John.) London, 1969.

Arc 1053.21F Les visions apocalyptiques dans l'art byzantin. (Bréhier, L.) Bucarest, 1930?

Arc 858.31.5 Visions of the times of old. (Bigsley, R.) London, 1848. 3v.

Arc 505.35.5 A visit to Capharnaum. (Loffreda, Stanislao.) Jerusalem, 1972.

Arc 505.35.7 A visit to Capharnaum. 2d ed. (Loffreda, Stanislao.) Jerusalem, 1973.

Arc 1025.4.5 A visit to the Roman catacombs. (Northcote, J.S.) London, 1877.

Arc 1020.9.51 Visita...delle sette chiese. (Fioravanti, G.A.) Fermo, 1763.

Arc 505.5.54 Visite au temple de Jerusalem et à la Mosquée d'Omar. (Isambert, E.) Paris, 1860.

Arc 1025.4.7 Visite aux catacombes de Rome. (Northcote, J.S.) Paris, 1878.

Arc 1020.55 La visite de la Cathédrale St. Bertrand de Comminges. (Barbier de Montault, X.) Montpélier, 1877.

Arc 726.237 Visscher, Fernand de. Héraclès Epitrapezios. Paris, 1962.

Arc 1033.52 Vita, martiro e culto di S. Ambrogio. (Angelini, N.) Frascati, 1884.

Arc 1033.82 Vita...S. Pardi...de SS. Primiano, Firmiano et Casto. (Pollidoro, J.B.) Roma, 1741.

Arc 726.122 Vita d'archeologo. (Maiuri, Amedeo.) Napoli, 1959.

Arc 1033.49 Vita di S. Severino e di S. Vittorio. (Canallotti, G.B.) Pariso, 1643.

Arc 1153.61.5 Vita ed attività dello "Scriptorium" veronese nel secolo XI. (Venturini, M.) Verona, 1930.

Arc 1033.94 Vita SS. Apostoli Filippo e Giacono Minore. (Laurenti, V.) Roma, 1873.

Arc 608.17.15 Vitali, L. Fonti per la storia della religione cyrenaica. Padova, 1932.

Arc 1485.4.5F Vitalini, O. Supplemento alle monete dei papi. Camerino, 1892.

Arc 925.328 Vitkov, Z.A. Pervobytnye liudi na Kol'skom poluostrove. Murmansk, 1960.

Arc 1185.34 Vittani, Giovanni. Scritti di diplomatica e archivistica. Milano, 1974-

Arc 843.71 Vives, José. Inscripciones cristianas de la España romana y visigoda. Barcelona, 1942.

Arc 843.71.2 Vives, José. Inscripciones cristianas de la España romana y visigoda. 2. ed. Barcelona, 1969.

Arc 1433.37.10 Vives y Escudero, A. Monedas de las dinastiás arábigo-españolas. Madrid, 1893.

Arc 608.2.19 Vives y Escudero, Antonio. Estudio de arqueología cartaginesa. Madrid, 1917.

Arc 1493.13 Vives y Escudero, Antonio. La moneda hispánica. Madrid, 1926. 2v.

Arc 968.2.85 Vivian, G. Gran Quivira. Washington, 1964.

Arc 925.9.9 Viviendekt-Martin, Louis. Recherches sur les populations primitives. Paris, 1847.

Arc 302.7.6 Vjesnik. Series III. (Zagreb. Arheološki Muzej.) Zagreb. 1,1958+

Arc 936.195.260 Vladár, Josef. Pohrebiská zo staršej doby bronzovej v Branči. 1. vyd. Bratislava, 1973.

Arc 925.9.7 Vladimirova, N. Drevnosti chernomorskia poberezh'ia kavkaza. Sankt Petersburg, 1900.

Arc 1020.9.164F La voce delle chiese antichissime di Roma. (Hendrichs, F.) Roma, 1933.

Arc 936.195.295 Vocel, Jan E. Pravěk země české. Praha, 1866-68.

Arc 936.225 Vodnik po Emoni. (Šašel, Jaro.) Ljubljana, 1955.

Arc 600.44 Völker und Völkerbewegungen im vorgeschichtlichen Oberägypten im Lichte neuer Felshilderfunde. (Winkler, H.A.) Stuttgart, 1937.

Arc 435.2.36F Vogel, J.P. Antiquities of Chamba state. Calcutta, 1911.

Arc 458.7 Vogel, J.P. Indian serpent-lore. London, 1926.

Arc 435.2.41F Vogel, J.P. Tile-mosaics of the Lahore fort. Calcutta, 1920.

Arc 609.24.5 Vogel, Joseph O. Kamanejoza: an introduction to the Iron Age cultures of the Victoria Falls region. London, 1971.

Arc 635.225F Vogell, A. Griechische Alterthümer südrussischen Fundorts. Cassel, 1908.

Arc 600.43 Vogliano, A. Primo rapporto degli scavi condotti dalla Missione archeologica d'Egitto della R. Università di Milano. Milano, 1936-37. 2v.

Arc 915.11F Vogt, Emil. Der Lindenhof in Zürich. Zürich, 1948.

X Cg Arc 1470.29 Vogt, Joseph. Die alexandrinischen Münzen. v.1-2. Stuttgart, 1924. (Changed to XP 9970)

Arc 1428.7 Vogué, C.J. Monnaies inédites des Croisades. Paris, 1864.

Arc 497.7 Vogüé, M. de. Fragments d'un journal de voyage en Orient. Paris, 1855.

NEDL Arc 495.6PF Vogue, M. de. Le temple de Jérusalem. Paris, 1864.

Arc 505.5.23 Vogüé. Note sur le Temple de Jerusalem. n.p., n.d.

Arc 865.19 A voice from Stonehenge. pt.1. (Grover, Henry M.) London, 1847.

Arc 967.7 Voices from the rapids: an underwater search for fur trade artifacts, 1960-73 (Minnesota). St. Paul, 1975.

Arc 1138.75.5 Voices in stone. (Doblhofer, Ernst.) N.Y., 1961.

Arc 830.28 Une voie Saxonne à Caen. (Travers, Emile.) Caen, 1875.

Arc 820.214F Voies romaines...de la Côte-d'Or. (Côte-d'Or. Commission des Antiquités.) Dijon, 1872.

Arc 830.18.9 Les voies romaines après la table Théodosienne. (Lion, J.) Amiens, 1907.

Arc 830.18.27 Les voies romaines chez les Volkes-Arécomiques. (Charvet, G.) Alais, 1874.

Arc 830.22.13 Les voies romaines de l'antique Lutèce. (Nagne, Charles.) Paris, 189-?

Arc 830.18 Les voies romaines en Gaule. (Bertrand, Alexandre.) Paris, 1864.

Arc 830.18.10 Les voies romaines et massiliennes. (Gilles, Isidore.) Avignon, 1884.

Arc 1580.7 Voigt, A. Beschreibung der bisher bekaunten böhmischen Münzen. v.1-2,3-4. Prag, 1771-87. 2v.

Arc 1175.7 Voigt, Karl. Beiträge zur Diplomatik der langodardischen Fürsten. Göttingen, 1902.

Arc 726.13 Voigt, M. Über das römische System der Wege in alten Italien. n.p., 1872.

Arc 830.98 Voisin, F. Monuments gallo-romains du département de l'Jndre. Chateauroux, 1877.

Arc 1335.153 Die Voit von Salzburg'sche Münz. (Erlangen. Universität. Bibliothek.) München, 1933.

Arc 1018.46 La voix des monuments. (Jerphanion, G. de.) Paris, 1930.

Arc 1018.46.5 La voix des monuments. (Jerphanion, G. de.) Rome, 1938.

Arc 1285.30 Vojtišek, V. O pečetech a erbech měst pražskych a jinych českych. Praha, 1928.

Arc 1018.40 Volbeding, J.E. Thesaurus commentationum...antiquiorum...illustrandis antiquitatibus christianis. Lipsiae, 1847. 2v.

Arc 958.1.5 Volk, E. The archaeology of the Delaware Valley. Cambridge, 1911.

Arc 938.110 Volkaitė-Kulikauskienė, Regina. Lietuvio kario žirgas. Vil'nius, 1971.

Arc 938.65.5 Volkaitė-Kulikauskienė, Regina. Punios piliakalnis. Vilnius, 1974.

Arc 938.65 Volkerite-Kulikauskiené, R. Lietuvos archeologiniai pom̃inklai ir jų tyrinejimai. Vil'nius, 1958.

Arc 895.22.17F Die Volkerwanderungszeit Gotlands. (Newman, B.) Stockholm, 1935.

Arc 853.250 Vollrath, Friedrich. Die Hunbirg. Nürnberg, 1961.

Arc 925.230 Vologda, Russia (City). Ablastnoi Kraevedcheskii Muzei. Sbornik po arkheologii Vologodskoi oblasti. Vologda, 1961.

Arc 925.130 Volosovskii klad. (Tsvetkova, I.K.) Moskva, 1957.

Arc 936.195.93 Volovek, V. Pohřebiště a súdliště lidu popelnicóvych poh v Třebešově. Hradec Králové, 1966.

Arc 936.195.90 Volovek, V. Pravek vychodnich a severovychodnich Cech. Hradec Králové, 1962.

Arc 1027.36 Volpi, A.T. Dell'indentila dei S. Corpi dei S. Fermo Rustico, e Procolo. Milano, 1761.

Arc 726.99 Volterra nell'antichità. (Consortini, L.) Volterra, 1940.

Arc 608.28 Volubilis. (Thouvenat, R.) Paris, 1949.

Arc 936.14.03 Pamphlet vol. Volumes on archaeology and numismatics in Poland. 6 pam.

Arc 770.6.2 Vom alten Rom. 2. Aufl. (Petersen, Eugen.) Leipzig, 1900.

Arc 770.6.5 Vom alten Rom. 3. Aufl. (Petersen, Eugen.) Leipzig, 1904.

Arc 1093.6.20 Vom Hakenkreuz. (Lecher, Jörg.) Leipzig, 1921.

Arc 1093.6.22 Vom Hakenkreuz. 2. Aufl. (Lecher, Jörg.) Leipzig, 1934.

Arc 1076.3.89 Von den Glocken. pt.1-2. (Edel, Friederich W.) Strassburg, 1862-63.

Arc 1018.47 Von der Antike zum Christentum. Stettin, 1931.

Arc 905.126 Von frühen Eisen und reichen Salzherren die Hallstattkultur in Osterreich. (Kromer, Karl.) Wien, 1964.

Arc 497.51.5 Von Jerusalem nach Ugarit. (Jirku, Anton.) Graz, 1966.

Arc 628.16 Von Rom nach Sardes. (Lang, G.) Stuttgart, 1900.

Arc 416.38 Von Schanidar bis Akkad. 1. Aufl. (Brentjes, Burchard.) Leipzig, 1968.

Arc 1613.19 Von Bergen, W. The rare coins of America, England, Ireland, Scotland, France, Germany, and Spain. Cambridge, Mass., 1899.

Arc 1528.10.5 Voogt, W.J. de. Bijdragen tot de numismatiek van Gelderland. Arnhem, 1869.

Arc 407.12 De voor historische mens. (Wieringen, J.H. van.) Zutphen, 1938.

Arc 52.4 Vooraziatisch-Egyptische Gezelschap "Ex Oriente Lux". Jahresbericht. Leiden. 3,1935+ 10v.

Arc 52.2 Vooraziatisch-Egyptische Gezelschap "Ex Oriente Lux". Mededeelingen en verhandelingen. Leiden. 1,1934+ 4v.

Arc 888.45.5 De voorgeschiedenis der Lage Landen. (Laet, Siegfried J. de.) Groningen, 1959.

Arc 888.10 De voorgeschiedenis nou Nederland. (Byvonck, A.W.) Leiden, 1944.

Arc 889.26 Voorgeschiedenis van Zuid Limburg. (Beckers, H.J.) Maastricht, 1940.

Arc 296.5 Voprosy arkheologii Urala. Sverdlovsk. 1,1961+ 10v.

Arc 295.5 Voprosy istorii i arkheologii Mordovskoi ASSR. Saransk. 2,1973+

Arc 493.6.22 Voprosy istorii Kavkazskoi Albanii; sbornik statei. (Akademiia Nauk Azerbaidzhanskoi SSR, Baku. Institut Istorii.) Baku, 1962.

Arc 923.135 Voprosy okhrany, klassifikatsii i ispol'zovaniia arkheologicheskikh pamiatnikov. Moskva, 1974.

Arc 925.100 Voprosy skifo-sarmatskoi arkheologicheskoi. (Akademiia Nauk SSSR. Institut Istorii Materialy Kul'tury.) Moskva, 1954.

Arc 853.220 Vor- und Frühgeschichte Arnstadts und seiner weiteren Umgebung. (Cämmerer, Erich.) Jena, 1956.

Arc 853.364 Vor- und Frühgeschichte des Kreises Ahrweiler. (Kleemann, Otto.) Bonn, 1971.

Arc 612.29 Vor- und Frühgeschichte des Nordens und des Mittelmeerraumes. (Philipp, H.) Berlin, 1937.

Arc 853.24.25 Vor- und frühgeschichtliche Archäologie in Bayern: Beiträge. München, 1972.

Arc 853.363 Die vor- und frühgeschichtliche Besiedlung der Kreise. (Fehr, Horst.) Speyer, 1972.

Arc 853.66 Die vor- und frühgeschichtliche Besiedlung des Unterharzes und seines Vorlandes auf Grund der Bodenfunde. Inaug. Diss. (Grimm, Paul.) Halle an der Saale, 1931.

Arc 195.3F Vor- und frühgeschichtliche Untersuchungen. (Kiel. Universität. Schleswig-Holsteinisches Museum Vorgeschichtlicher Altertümer.) Neumünster. 1,1933+ 27v.

Arc 853.31 Die vor- und frühgeschichtlichen altertümer Thüringens. (Götze.) Würzburg, 1902.

Arc 853.71.5F Die vor- und frühgeschichtlichen Burgwälle der Bezirke Halle und Magdeburg. (Grimm, Paul.) Berlin, 1958. 2v.

Arc 206.4F Die vor- und frühgeschichtlichen Denkmäler und Funde im Gebiet der Deutschen Demokratischen Republik. Schwerin. 1-3 3v.

Arc 853.150F Die vor- und frühgeschichtlichen Gebäudedenkmäler Oberfrankens. (Schwarz, Klaus.) Kallmünz, 1955. 2v.

Arc 853.175 Vor- und Frühgeschichts des bayerischen Untermaingebietes. (Endrich, Peter.) Aschaffenburg, 1961.

X Cg Arc 893.1.5 Vor oldtisminder Danmarks. (Mueller, S.) Kjøbenhavn, 1897.

Arc 488.25 Vorderasiatische Archäologie. (Bittal, Kurt.) Berlin, 1964.

Arc 848.38 Vorgeschichte der deutschen Stämme. (Reinerth, Hans.) Leipzig, 1940. 3v.

Arc 853.69.15 Vorgeschichte der Schwäbischen Alb. (Reith, A.) Leipzig, 1938.

Arc 853.236 Die Vorgeschichte des magdeburger Landes. (Bogen, Alfred.) Magdeburg, 1937.

Arc 853.368 Vorgeschichte im Landkreis Lüneburg. (Körner, Gerhard.) Lüneburg, 1971.
Arc 953.10 Vorgeschichte Nordamerikas im Gebiet der Vereinigten Staaten. (Schmidt, E.) Braunschweig, 1894.
Arc 853.377 Vorgeschichte und römische Zeit zwischen Main und Lahn. Beiträge. Bonn, 1972.
Arc 848.15 Vorgeschichte von Deutschland. (Schuchhardt, C.) München, 1928.
Arc 848.15.5 Vorgeschichte von Deutschland. 3. Aufl. (Schuchhardt, C.) München, 1935.
Arc 848.15.7 Vorgeschichte von Deutschland. 5. Aufl. (Schuchhardt, C.) München, 1943.
Arc 609.3F Die Vorgeschichte von Süd- und Südwestafrica. (Lebzelter, Viktor.) Leipzig, 1930-34. 2v.
Arc 853.21.15 Vorgeschichte von Westpreussen in ihren Grundzügen allgemeinverstandlich dargestellt. (LaBaume, W.) Danzig, 1920.
Arc 853.1 Vorgeschichtliche Alterthuemer. (Mestorf, J.) Hamburg, 1885.
Arc 853.51 Die vorgeschichtliche Besiedelung. (Rademacher, C.) Leipzig, 1920.
Arc 853.84 Vorgeschichtliche Eisenbütten Deutschlands. (Weiershausen, P.) Leipzig, 1939.
Arc 612.6 Das vorgeschichtliche Europa. (Hahne, Hans.) Bielefeld, 1910.
Arc 22.5 Vorgeschichtliche Forschungen. Berlin. 1,1924+ 13v.
Arc 905.18.5 Das vorgeschichtliche Hallstatt. (Mahr, Adolf.) Wien, 1925.
Arc 482.202.5F Die vorgeschichtlichen Töpfereien von Samarra. (Herzfeld, Ernst E.) Berlin, 1930.
Arc 853.58.10 Vorgeschichtliches aus dem Lumdstale. (Kunkel, Otto.) Giessen, 1919.
Arc 22.3 Vorgeschichtliches Jahrbuch. Berlin. 1-4 4v.
Arc 913.21 Vorgeschichtliches Leben in den Alpen. (Franz, L.) Wien, 1929.
Arc 938.50 Vorgeschichtsforschung und Nationalbewusstsein in Litauen. Inaug. Diss. (Puzinas, Jonas.) Kaunas, 1935.
Arc 1033.123.9 Der vorirenäische Obferbegriff. (Wieland, F.) München, 1909.
Arc 543.79 Vorislamische Altertümer. (Rathjens, Carl.) Hamburg, 1932.
Arc 720.212.5 Die vorklassiche Chronologie Italiens. (Monteluis, O.) Stockholm, 1912. 2v.
Arc 700.64 Die vorklassischen Hausformen in der Ägäis. (Sinos, Stefan.) Mainz, 1971.
Arc 513.15 Vorläufiger Bericht...Expeditionen Kleinasien. (Jüthner, J.) Prag, 1903.
Arc 600.35.5 Vorläufiger Bericht über die Ausgrabungen in Hermopolis 1929-30. (Roeder, Günther.) Augsburg, 1931 .
Arc 600.35.10 Vorläufiger Bericht über die detsche Hermopolis-Expedition, 1931-32. (Roeder, Günther.) Augsburg, 1932.
Arc 3.1.26 Vorläufiges Programm. (Congrès International d'Archéologie Classique, 6th, Berlin, 1939.) Berlin? 1939?
Arc 86.2.2PF Vorlegeblätter für archaeologische Uebungen. (Benndorf, O.) Wien. 1888-1891 3v.
Arc 853.70 Vorneolithische Kulturen der südlichen Lüneburger Heide. Inaug. Diss. (Piesker, Hans.) Hildesheim, 1932.
Arc 426.15 Vorob'ev, M.V. Drevniaia Iaponiia. Moskva, 1958.
Arc 428.10 Vorob'ev, M.V. Drevniaia Korea. Moskva, 1961.
Arc 853.56 Die vorrömische Metallzeit im östlichen Westfalen. (Krebs, Albert.) Leipzig, 1925.
Htn Arc 1510.3.7* Vortzeichnus und Gedräge der groben und kleinen Müntzsorten. (Stürmer, Wolff.) Leipzig, 1572.
Arc 206.2 Vorzeit am Bodensee; Mitteilungen zur Vor- und Frühgeschichte und Heimatkunde des Bodenseeraumes. Überlingen. 1952-1963 2v.
Arc 412.12 Vorzeit gefälscht. (Rieth, Adolf.) Tübingen, 1967.
Arc 845.207F Vorzeitfunde aus Niedersachsen. (Hahne, Hans.) Hannover, 1915-25.
Arc 395.8 Vospominaniia i dumy. (Kondakov, N.P.) Praga, 1927.
Arc 925.12.5 Vosporskoe tsarstvo. (Ashik, Anton.) Odessa, 1848.
Arc 400.6 Voss, Albert. Merkbuch. 2. Aufl. Berlin, 1894.
Arc 1153.25 Voss, Ulrich. Lateinische Stenographie...Wilhelm Stolze. Berlin, 1907.
Arc 1269.45 Vossberg, F.A. Siegel des Mittelalters von Polen, Lithauen, Schiesien, Pommern und Preussen. Berlin, 1854.
Arc 1510.173F Vossberg, Friedrich August. Münzgeschichte der Stadt Berlin. Berlin, 1869.
Arc 513.40 Vostochnoe sredizemnamor'e v drevneishuiu epokhu. (Kink, Khilida A.) Moskva, 1970.
Arc 540.8F Vounous 1937-38. (Stewart, E.M.) Lund, 1950.
Arc 1033.12.194 Voyage à la sainte-larme de Vendome. (Rochambeau, E.A. de.) Vendome, 1874.
Arc 545.16 Voyage à l'Oasis de Thèbes. pt.1-2. (Cailliand, F.) Paris, 1821.
Arc 793.4.5 Voyage à Pompéi. (Romanelli, D.) Paris, 1829.
Arc 505.9 Voyage archéologique au Safâ. (Dussaud, René.) Paris, 1901.
X Cg Arc 651.1 Voyage archéologique en Grèce et en Asie Mineure. (Le Bas, P.) Paris, 1888.
Arc 635.17 Voyage archéologique en Grèce et en Asie Mineure. (Lebas, P.) Paris, 1847-77. 5v.
Arc 830.3 Voyage archéologique et historique dans l'ancien Comté de Comminges. (Cenac-Moncaut, J.E.M.) Tarbes, 1856.
Arc 642.4 Voyage dans la Macédoine. (Cousinéry, E.M.) Paris, 1831. 2v.
Arc 522.1.2.3 Voyage dans la Troade. 2. éd. (Lechevalier, Jean Baptiste.) Paris, 1799.
Arc 551.2 Voyage de la Haute Egypte. (Blanc, C.) Paris, 1876.
Arc 522.1.2 Voyage de la Troade. (Lechevalier, Jean Baptiste.) Paris, 1802. 3v.
Arc 608.21 Voyage d'étude dans une partie de la Maurétanie césarienne. (La Blanchère, R. du C.) Paris, 1883.
Arc 495.200 Voyage d'exploration à la Mer Morte. (Luynes, H.T.P.J. d'Albert de.) Paris, 1874. 3v.
Arc 628.10 Voyage d'Italie, de Dalmatie, de Grèce. (Spon, J.) La Haye, 1724. 2v.
Arc 1428.10 Voyage en Asie-Mineure au point du vie numismatique. (Waddington, W.H.) Paris, 1853.
Arc 635.211 Voyage en Grèce. (Cabrol, E.) Paris, 1890.
Arc 723.14 Voyage en Italie. (Barthélemy, J.J.) Paris, 1801.
Arc 513.24F Voyages archeologiques dans la Turquie orientale. (Gabriel, Albert.) Paris, 1940. 2v.
Arc 545.15F Voyages dans la Basse et la Haute Égypte. (Denon, V.) London, 1807.
Arc 545.15PF Voyages dans la Basse et la Haute Égypte. Atlas. (Denon, V.) London, 1807.
Arc 635.203 Voyages dans la Gréce. (Bröndsted, P.O.) Paris, 1826.
Arc 1025.59 Voyages dans les catacombes de Rome. (Artaud de Montor, A.F.) Paris, 1810.
Arc 510.3 Voyate de l'Asie Mineure. (Laborde, L. de.) Paris, 1838.
Arc 895.50F Vråkulturen. (Flarin, Sten.) Stockholm, 1958.
Arc 505.3.9 Le vraie forme primitive...du Saint Sépulcre. (Cyprien.) Paris, 1879.
Arc 1153.9 Vries, S.G. de. Boethii fragmentum notis Tironianis descript. Lugduni Batavorum, 1893.
Arc 1163.7 Vries, S.G. de. Middeleeuwsche handschriften kunde. Leiden, 1909.
Arc 510.220F Vroulia [Rhodes]. (Kinch, K.F.) Berlin, 1914.
Arc 923.108 Vsesoiuznaia Arkheologicheskaia Studencheskaia Konferentsiia, 8th, Leningrad, 1962. Arkheologicheskii sbornik trudy. Leningrad, 1964.
Arc 923.109 Vsesoiuznaia Arkheologicheskaia Studencheskaia Konferentsiia, 11th, Erevan, 1965. Doklady, prochitannye na XI Vesesoiuznoi studencheskoi arkheologicheskoi konferentsii 1965 g. v Erevane. Erevan, 1968.
Arc 923.124 Vsesoiuznaia Arkheologicheskaia Studencheskaia Konferentsiia, 9th, Moscow, 1963. Sbornik dokladov na IX i X vsesoiuznykh arkheologicheskikh studencheskikh konferentsiiakh. Moskva, 1968.
Arc 923.107 Vsesoiuznaia Arkheologicheskaia Studencheskaia Konferentsiia, 6th, Moscw, 1960. Sbornik dokladov na VI i VII vsesoiuznykh arkheologicheskikh studencheskikh konferentsiiakh. Moskva, 1963.
Arc 923.114 Vsesoiuznaia Sessiia, Posviashchennaia Itogam Arkheologicheskikh i Etnograficheskikh Issledovanii 1966 goda. Tezisy dokladov. Kishinev, 1967.
Arc 925.70 Vseukrains'kii arkheologichnii komitet. Zapiski. (Akademii Nauk URSR, Kyïv.) Kyïv, n.d.
Arc 925.65 Vseukrains'kii arkheologichnii komitet Tripil'ska kul'tura na Ukraini. (Akademii Nauk URSR, Kyïv.) Kyïv, n.d.
Arc 543.105 Vtoroi buddiiskii khram Ak-Beshimskogo gorodishcha. (Ziablin, L.L.) Frunze, 1961.
Arc 746.60 Vulci étrusque et étrusco-romaine. (Hus, Alain.) Paris, 1971.
Arc 861.7.5 Vulliamy, Colwyn E. The archaeology of Middlesex and London. London, 1930.
Arc 936.165 Vulpe, Radu. Le vallum de la Moldavie inférieure et le mur d'Athanaric. 's-Gravenhage, 1957.
Arc 936.40.5 Vuzharova, Z. Slaviano-bulgarskato selishte brai selo Popina. Sofiia, 1956.
Arc 936.140.40 Vuzharova, Zhivka N. O proiskhczhdenii bolgarskikh pakhotnykh orudii. Moskva, 1956.
Arc 936.140.60 Vuzharova, Zhivka N. Ruskite ucheni i bulgarskite starini. Sofiia, 1960.
Arc 936.40.35 Vŭzharova, Zhivka N. Slavianski i slavianobulgarski selishta v bulgarskite semi. Sofiia, 1965.
Arc 1365.5 Vvedenie v antichnaia numizmatiku. (Kazamanova, Liudmila N.) Moskva, 1969.
Arc 385.3.5 Vvedenie v arkheologiiu. 3. izd. (Artsikhovshii, A.V.) Moskva, 1947.
Arc 340.8 Výběrova bibliografie československé archeologie. Praha. 1958+
Arc 925.331 Vychegodskii krai. (Burov, Grigorii M.) Moskva, 1965.
Arc 302.13 Výhledy do pravěku evropsk lidstva. Praha. 3,1948+
Arc 925.50.250 Vynokur, Ion S. Istoriia da kul'tura cherniakhivs'kykh veemen dnistro-din'provs'koho mezhyrichchia. Kyïv, 1972.
Arc 925.9.5 Vyrubov, V. Predmety drevnosti. Tiflis, 1877.
Arc 595.11 Vyse, H. Operations carried on at the pyramids of Gizeh in 1837. London, 1840. 2v.
Arc 925.50.275 Vysotskaia, Tat'iana N. Pozdnie skify viugo-zapadnom Kryma. Kiev, 1972.
Arc 1588.4.90 Výváeňazi a medailí na Slovensku. (Hlinka, Jozef.) Bratislava, 1970.
Arc 1433.24.5 W. Grigorjew's Beschreibung kufischer Münzen. (Schott, W.) n.p., n.d.
Arc 961.1.15 W.P.A. excavations at Irene Mound, Savannah, Georgia, May 4, 1938. (Fewkes, J.W.) Savannah, 1938.
Arc 1015.217 Waal, A. de. La platonia ossia il sepolcro apostolico della via Appia. Roma, 1892.
Arc 1016.211 Waal, A. de. Sarkophag des Junius Bassus. Rom, 1900.
Arc 1015.217.5 Waal, A. de. Valeria; historische Erzahlung. Regensburg, 1884.
Arc 1097.5 Waals, Johannes D. van der. Prehistoric disc wheels in the Netherlands. Proefschrift. Groningen, 1964.
Arc 672.1.51F Wace, A.J.B. A Cretan statuette in the Fitzwilliam Museum. Cambridge, Eng., 1927.
Arc 635.222 Wace, A.J.B. Prehistoric Thessaly. Cambridge, 1912.
Arc 600.35.20F Wace, Alan John. Hermopolis Magna. Alexandria, 1959.
Arc 936.14.555 Wachowski, Krzysztof. Cmentarzyska doby wczesnopiastowskiej na Śląsku. Wrocław, 1975.
Arc 708.16 Wachsmuth, C. Die Stadt Athen im Alterthum. Leipzig, 1874- 2v.
Arc 455.1 Waddell, L.A. Discovery of Pātaliputra. Calcutta, 1892.
Arc 455.1.5 Waddell, L.A. Report on the excavations at Pātaliputra. Calcutta, 1903.
Arc 1470.14 Waddington, W.H. Recueil général des monnaies grecques d'Asie Mineure. Paris, 1904. 4v.
Arc 1428.10 Waddington, W.H. Voyage en Asie-Mineure au point du vie numismatique. Paris, 1853.
Arc 1590.30 Die Währung in der Ländern der böhmischen Krone. (Pošvář, Jaroslav.) Graz, 1970.
Arc 815.26.5 Die Wände Pompejis. (Schefold, Karl.) Berlin, 1957.
Arc 853.41.5F Wagner, E. Hügelgräber und Urnen-Friedhöfe. Karlsruhe, 1885.
Arc 853.24.5 Wagner, F. Die Römer in Bayern. München, 1928.
Arc 1153.93 Wagner, L. Proba centum scripturarum. Leipzig, 1963. 2v.
Arc 848.23 Wahle, Ernst. Deutsche Vorzeit. Leipzig, 1932.
Arc 848.23.3 Wahle, Ernst. Deutsche Vorzeit. 3. Aufl. Bad Homburg, 1962.
Arc 522.18 Das Wahre und richtige Troja-Illion. (Seyk, V.) Prag, 1926.
Arc 1588.4.15 Die Wahrheit übes den St. Wenzel-Denar. (Chaura, K.) Praha, 1929.
Arc 608.16.7 Waille, Victor. De Caesareae monumentis quae supersunt. Alger, 1891.
Arc 1020.73.17 Wailly, J.N. de. Récit...sur les translations...1239 et 1241...reliques de la Passion. Nogent-le-Rotrou, n.d.
Arc 875.122 Wainwright, Frederick Threlfall. The northern isles. Edinburgh, 1962.
Arc 875.124 Wainwright, Fredrick Threlfall. The souterrains of southern Pictland. London, 1963.
Arc 885.28 Wainwright, G. Coygan Camp; a prehistoric Romano-British and Dark Age settlemant in Carmarthenshire. Cwmgwyn, 1967.
Arc 585.29F Wainwright, G.A. Balabish. London, 1920.

Author and Title Listing

	Arc 595.70.1	Wake, Charles Staniland. The origin and significance of the great pyramid. Minneapolis, 1975.
	Arc 880.4.8	Wakeman, W.F. Archaeologia Hibernica. Dublin, 1848.
	Arc 880.15	Wakeman, W.F. A survey of antiquarian periods on...Inismurray. London, 1893.
	Arc 880.4	Wakeman, W.F. Wakeman's handbook of Irish antiquities. Dublin, 1903.
	Arc 880.4	Wakeman's handbook of Irish antiquities. (Wakeman, W.F.) Dublin, 1903.
	Arc 875.42.5	Waldie, G. Walks along the northern Roman wall. Linlithgow, 1913.
	Arc 800.6A	Waldstein, C. Herculaneum, past, present and future. London, 1908.
	Arc 543.131.5	Wales, Horace Geoffrey Q. Towards Angkor in the footsteps of the Indian invaders. London, 1937.
	Arc 885.8.5	Wales and archaeology. (Wheeler, R.E.M.) London, 1929.
	Arc 385.5	Walker, John. John Allen. London, 1956?
Htn	Arc 1460.2*	Walker, O. The Greek and Roman history illustrated by coins and medals. London, 1692.
	Arc 875.42.5	Walks along the northern Roman wall. (Waldie, G.) Linlithgow, 1913.
	Arc 762.1	Walks in Rome. (Hare, A.J.C.) London, 1871. 2v.
	Arc 762.1.4	Walks in Rome. (Hare, A.J.C.) London, 1878. 2v.
	Arc 762.1.3	Walks in Rome. (Hare, A.J.C.) N.Y., 1875.
	Arc 762.1.2.5	Walks in Rome. 4. American ed. (Hare, A.J.C.) N.Y., 1874.
	Arc 762.1.2	Walks in Rome. 4. ed. (Hare, A.J.C.) London, 1874. 2v.
	Arc 762.1.3.5	Walks in Rome. 6. American ed. (Hare, A.J.C.) N.Y., 1877.
	Arc 762.1.3.7	Walks in Rome. 7. American ed. (Hare, A.J.C.) N.Y., 187-.
	Arc 762.1.3.9	Walks in Rome. 8. American ed. (Hare, A.J.C.) N.Y., 1882.
	Arc 762.1.4.5	Walks in Rome. 13th ed. (Hare, A.J.C.) London, 1893. 2v.
	Arc 762.1.5	Walks in Rome. 14th ed. (Hare, A.J.C.) N.Y., 1899. 2v.
	Arc 762.1.5.5	Walks in Rome. 15th ed. (Hare, A.J.C.) N.Y., 190-?
	Arc 762.1.6	Walks in Rome. 16th ed. (Hare, A.J.C.) London, 1903. 2v.
	Arc 762.1.9	Walks in Rome. 20th ed. (Hare, A.J.C.) London, 1913.
	Arc 762.1.10	Walks in Rome. 21st ed. (Hare, A.J.C.) London, 1923.
	Arc 1020.15	Wall, J.C. Shrines of British saints. London, 1905.
	Arc 810.14	Wall, J.W. Naples and Pompeii. Burlington, 1856.
	Arc 861.18.9	The wall of Hadrian. (Bruce, J.C.) Newcastle-upon-Tyne, 1874.
	Arc 600.184	Wall scenes from the mortuary chapel of the Mayor Poser at Medinet Habu. (Schott, Siegfried.) Chicago, 1957.
	Arc 971.1	Wallbridge, T.C. On some ancient mounds upon the shores of the Bay of Quinte. Toronto, 1860.
	Arc 1675.91	Wallfahrts-, Bruderschafts- und Weihe. (Pachinger, A.M.) Wien, 1908.
	Arc 1335.75	Wallraf, F.F. Beschreibung der köllnischen Munzsammlung des domherrn und kurfürstlich-weltlichen Hofgerichts Präsidenten von Merle. Kölln am Rhein, 1792.
	Arc 407.1	Walpole, R. Memoirs relating to European and Asiatic Turkey. London, 1817-20. 2v.
	Arc 1033.12.9.10	Walsh, J.E. The shroud. N.Y., 1963.
	Arc 1377.1	Walsh, R. An essay on ancient coins, medals, and gems. 2. ed. London, 1828.
	Arc 670.4.5F	Walston, Charles. The Argive Heraeum. Boston, 1902-05. 2v.
	Arc 670.4F	Walston, Charles. Excavations at the Heraion of Argos. 1892. Boston, 1892.
	Arc 1076.3.18.15	Walter, Henry Beauchamp. The church bells of Shropshire. Oswestry, 1915.
	Arc 1076.3.115	Walter, Karl. Glockenkunde. Regensburg, 1913.
	Arc 710.15A	Walter, Otto. Athen, Akropolis. Wien, 1929.
	Arc 1076.3.17	Walters, Henry Beauchamp. Church bells. London, 1908.
	Arc 1076.3.18	Walters, Henry Beauchamp. Church bells of England. London, 1912.
	Arc 1076.3.18.10	Walters, Henry Beauchamp. Church bells of Wiltshire. Devizes, 1927-29.
	Arc 726.34.5	Waltzan, H. Reise auf der Insel Sardinien. Leipzig, 1869.
	Arc 1335.154	Wambolt, F. von. Katalog des grossen Freiherrlich von Wambolt'schen Münzkabinets in Heidelberg. v.1-2. Heidelberg, 1833.
	Arc 968.1.5.5	Wampum and shell articles used by the New York Indians. (Beauchamp, W.M.) Albany, 1901. 2 pam.
	Arc 790.205	Die Wanddekoration in Pompeji. (Presuhn, E.) Leipzig, 1877.
	Arc 915.42	Wandeler, Max. LuzernStadt und Land in römischer Zeit. Luzern, 1968.
	Arc 858.39	Wanderings in Roman Britain. (Weigall, A.E.P.B.) London, 1926.
	Arc 766.1.19	Wanderings in the Roman campagns. (Lanciani, R.) Boston, 1909.
	Arc 1020.9.147	Wanderings through ancient Roman churches. (Lanciani, R.) Boston, 1924.
	Arc 1025.18	Eine Wanderung...römischen Katakomben. (Wiegand, F.) Erlangen, 1893.
	Arc 608.5	Wanderungen...Kuestenlaender...Mittelmeeres. (Barth, H.) Berlin, 1849.
Htn	Arc 790.9*	Wandgemälde aus Pompeii und Herculanum. (Ternite, W.) Berlin, 1858?
	Arc 790.203	Wandgemaelde der...Staedte Campaniens. (Helbig, W.) Leipzig, 1868. 2v.
	Arc 815.15.2	Die Wandmalerei Pompejis. (Curtius, Ludwig.) Darmstadt, 1960.
	Arc 815.15	Die Wandmalerei Pompejis. (Curtius, Ludwig.) Leipzig, 1929.
	Arc 482.202F	Der Wandschmuck der Bauten. (Herzfeld, Ernst E.) Berlin, 1923.
	Arc 905.37	Wankel, Jindřich. Die prähistorische Jagd in Mähren. Olmütz, 1892.
	Arc 608.17.30F	Wanyanga. (Arkell, A.J.) London, 1964.
	Arc 925.7	Wapel, Leon de. Recueil de quelques antiquités. Berlin, 1803.
	Arc 830.1.9	Waquet, H. Vieilles pierres bretonnes. Quimper, 1920.
	Arc 861.12.9	Warburton, J. Vallum Romanum...Cumberland and Northumberland. London, 1753.
	Arc 1468.11	Ward, J. Greek coins and their parent cities. London, 1902.
	Arc 600.100	Ward, J. The sacred beetle. London, 1902.
	Arc 861.39.5	Ward, John. The Roman era in Britain. London, 1911.
	Arc 885.6	Ward, John. Roman fort of Gelly Gaer in...Glamorgan. London, 1903.
	Arc 861.39	Ward, John. Romano-British buildings and earthworks. London, 1911.
	Arc 1.1.3	Ward, W.H. Report on the Wolfe Expedition to Babylonia, 1884-85. Boston, 1886.
	Arc 1221.7	Ward, William Hayes. The seal cylinders of western Asia. Washington, 1910.
	Arc 861.62	Wardell, James. Antiquities of the borough of Leeds. London, 1853.
Htn	Arc 861.62.10*	Wardell, James. Historical notices of Ilkley, Rombald's Moor, Baildon Common. 2. ed. Leeds, 1881.
	Arc 953.13	Warden, D.B. Recherches sur les antiquités de l'Amérique. Paris, 1827.
	Arc 615.5	Waring, J.B. Stone monuments...of remote ages. London, 1870.
	Arc 855.216	Warne, C. The Celtic Tumuli of Dorset. London, 1866.
	Arc 855.218	Warne, Charles. Ancient Dorset. Bournemouth, 1872.
	Arc 662.6	Warner, R. Eternal Greece. N.Y., 1962.
	Arc 861.40.5	Warner, Richard. An illustration of the Roman antiquities discovered at Bath. Bath, 1797.
	Arc 500.1	Warren, C. Jerusalem. London, 1884.
	Arc 590.2	Warren, J.C. Description of an Egyptian mummy. Boston, n.d.
	Arc 1470.6	Warren, J.L. An essay on Greek federal coinage. London, 1863.
	Arc 672.1.118	Warren, Peter. Minoan stone vases. Cambridge, Eng., 1969.
	Arc 682.42	Warren, Peter. Myrtos: an early Bronze Age settlement in Crete. London, 1972.
	Arc 936.14.125	Warsaw. Uniwersytet. Zespoł Badan nad Polskim Sredniowieczem. Badania archeologiczne w okolicy wislicy. Warszawa, 1963-64.
	Arc 936.14.135	Warsaw. Uniwersytet. Zespoł Badan nad Polskim Sredniowieczem. II konferencja naukowa w Warszawie...1961. Warszawa, 1963.
	Arc 936.14.136	Warsaw. Uniwersytet. Zespoł Badan nad Polskim Sredniowieczem. III konferencja naukowa w Warszawie. Warszawa, 1964.
	Arc 936.14.137	Warsaw. Uniwersytet. Zespoł Badan nad Polskim Sredniowieczem. IV konferencja w kielcach, 5 kwietnia 1963. Warszawa, 1965.
	Arc 936.14.215	Warsaw. Uniwersytet. Zespół Badań nad Polskim Średniowieczem. Kolegiata wislicka. Kielce, 1965.
	Arc 936.14.120	Warsaw. Uniwersytet. Zespoł Badan nad Polskim Sredniowieczem. Odrycia w wiślecy. Warszawa, 1963-64.
	Arc 936.14.138	Warsaw. Uniwersytet. Zespoł Badan nad Polskim Sredniowieczem. V konferencja naukowa w Busknzdroju i w Wislicy, 19-20 maja, 1966. Vyd. 1. Warszawa, 1968.
	Arc 936.14.139	Warsaw. Uniwersytet. Zespoł Badan nad Polskim Sredniowieczem. VI konferencja naukowa w Warszawie 10-11 styczhia 1969. Warszawa, 1970.
	Arc 936.14.134	Warsaw. Uniwersytet. Zespoł Badan nad Polskim Srezniowieczem. I konferencja naukowa w Warszawie...1968. Warszawa, 1962.
	Arc 708.17	Warsberg, A. von. Die Kunstwerke Athens. Wien, 1892.
	Arc 810.39	Warscher, Tatiana. Pompeji; ein Führer durch die Ruinen. Berlin, 1925.
	Arc 810.45	Warsher, Tatiana. Pompeii in three hours. Rome, 1930.
	Arc 1423.1	Waserus, C. De antiquis numis. Zürich, 1605.
	Arc 700.59	Wąsowicz, Aleksandra. Obróbka drewna w Starożytnej Grecji. Wrocław, 1966.
	Arc 905.65	Die Wasserburg Neydharting. (Beninger, E.) Linz, 1959.
	Arc 520.2	Die Wasserleitungen von Pergamon. (Graeber, F.) Berlin, 1888.
	Arc 888.20	Wat aarde bewaarde. (Heemskerck Düker, W.F. van.) Den Haag, 1942?
	Arc 1660.7	The Waterloo medal. (Myer, I.) Philadelphia, 1885.
	Arc 505.53	Waterman, Leroy. Preliminary report of the University of Michigan excavations at Sepphoris, Palestine, in 1931. Ann Arbor, 1937.
	Arc 1680.4	Waters, A.W. Notes...eighteenth century tokens. Leamington, 1906.
Htn	Arc 1680.4.5*	Waters, A.W. Token coinage of South London...eighteenth and nineteenth centuries. Leamington, 1904.
	Arc 861.49	Watkin, W.J. Roman Lancashire. Liverpool, 1883.
	Arc 861.3.9	Watkin, W.T. Roman Cheshire. Liverpool, 1886.
	Arc 861.3.10	Watkin, W.T. Roman Cheshire. Wakefield, Eng., 1974.
	Arc 861.16.10	Watkins, A. Archaic tracks round Cambridge. London, 1932.
	Arc 858.40	Watkins, A. The old straight track. London, 1925.
	Arc 861.88	Watkins, Alfred. The old standing crosses of Herefordshire. London, 1930.
	Arc 501.7	Watson, C.M. Fifty years' work in the Holy Land, 1924-1948. London, 1915. 2v.
	Arc 1540.32	Watson, J.H. Ancient trial plates, a description of the ancient gold and silver. London, 1962.
	Arc 421.24	Watson, William. Archaeology in China. London, 1960.
	Arc 421.23	Watson, William. China before the Han dynasty. London, 1961.
	Arc 421.32	Watson, William. Cultural frontiers in ancient east Asia. Edinburgh, 1971.
	Arc 1153.7	Wattenbach, W. Anleitung zur lateinischen Palaeographie. Leipzig, 1869.
	Arc 1153.7.4	Wattenbach, W. Anleitung zur lateinischen Palaeographie. 4. Aufl. Leipzig, 1886.
	Arc 1143.3.2	Wattenbach, W. Schriftwesen im Mittelalter. 2. Aufl. Leipzig, 1875.
	Arc 1143.3.4	Wattenbach, W. Das Schriftwesen in Mittelalter. 4. Aufl. Graz, 1958.
	Arc 87.1.63	Watzinger, C. Das Relief des Archelaos von Priene. Berlin, 1903.
	Arc 407.14	Watzinger, C. Theodor Wiegand. München, 1944.
	Arc 497.36	Watzinger, Carl. Denkmäler Palästinas. v.1-2. Leipzig, 1933-35.
	Arc 442.10	Wauchope, Robert S. Buddhist cave temples of India. Calcutta, 1933.
	Arc 1027.23.5	Die Waud- und Decken-Gernälde Römischen Katakomben. (Becker, F.) Düsseldorf, 1874.
	Arc 861.193F	Wawcott II, a stratified Mesolithic succession. (Froom, F.R.) Oxford, 1976.
	Arc 858.29	Wa5derings of an antiquary. (Wright, Thomas.) London, 1854.
	Arc 936.14.205	Wczesnośredniowieczne cmentarzyska szkieletowe Małopolski. (Zoll-Adamikowa, Helena.) Wrocław, 1966-71. 2v.
	Arc 853.65.50	Wczesnośredniowieczne grodziska nyczyńskie na Śląsku. (Kramarek, Janusz.) Wrocław, 1969.
	Arc 936.12	Wczesnośredniowieczne grodziska w Bonikowie. (Hołowińska, Z.) Poznań, 1956.
	Arc 936.200	Wczesnosredniowieczne grodzisko w Daleszynie (st. 2) w pow. gostynskim. (Hilczerowna, Z.) Poznań, 1960.
	Arc 936.14.390	Wczesnósredniowieczne skarby srebrne z Wielkopolski. (Malinowska, Marie.) Poznań, 1970.
	Arc 1390.19	Wczesnośredniowieczny skarb srebrny z zalesia powiat słupca. (Kmietowicz, Anna.) Wrocław, 1969-74. 2v.

Author and Title Listing

Arc 1020.65 Weale, W.H.J. Catalogue des objets d'art religieux...à l'Hotel Liederkerke à Malines. 2. éd. Bruxelles, 1864.
Arc 1418.9 Webb, W.W. The currencies of Hindu states of Réjputána. Westminster, 1893.
Arc 974.1.5 Webb, William S. An archaeological survey of the Norris Basen in eastern Tennessee. Washington, 1938.
Arc 1468.23 Weber, Hermann. The Weber collection...Greek coins. v.1-3. London, 1922-29. 6v.
Arc 1088.1.5 Weber, L. Die Lösung der Frierenrätsels. Danzig, 1896.
Arc 658.3.20 Weber, Shirley H. Schliemann's first visit to America, 1850-1851. Cambridge, 1942.
Arc 1468.23 The Weber collection...Greek coins. v.1-3. (Weber, Hermann.) London, 1922-29. 6v.
Arc 400.25.5.2 Webster, Graham. Practical archaeology. 2. ed. London, 1974.
Arc 530.15 Wedel, F. Skizzierte Gedanken eines Kunst freundes. Neustadt, 1905.
Arc 861.38.10 Wedlake, William. Excavations at Camerton, Somerset. Camerton, 1958.
Arc 936.14.445 Wędrowki po wjkopaliskach. wyd. 1. (Węgzynowicz, Teresa.) Warszawa, 1972.
Arc 936.14.510 Wędrówki Sącza. (Żaki, Andrzej.) Kraków, 1974.
Arc 889.9 Weerd, H. van de. Inleiding tot de Gallo-Romeinsche archeologie der Nederlanden. Antwerpen, 1944.
Arc 87.2.61 Weerth, E. Bad der roemische Villa bei Allenz. Bonn, 1861-1870.
Arc 670.2.9 Weeter, G. Aigina. Berlin, 1938.
Arc 853.292 Wegewitz, Willi. Reihengräberfriedhöfe. Neumünster, 1968.
Arc 407.15 Wegner, Max. Altertumskunde. Freiburg, 1951.
Arc 207.5 Wegweiser zur Vor- und Frühgeschichte Niedersachsens. Hildesheim. 1,1971+
Arc 936.14.445 Węgzynowicz, Teresa. Wędrowki po wjkopaliskach. wyd. 1. Warszawa, 1972.
Arc 810.17.13 Weichardt, C. Pompei vor der Zerstoerung. 3. Aufl. München, 1909.
Arc 810.17 Weichardt, C. Pompeii before its destruction. Leipzig, n.d.
Arc 681.1.10 Weickert, Carl. Das lesbische Kymation. Leipzig, 1913.
Arc 1468.59 Weidauer, Liselotte. Probleme der frühen Elektronprägung. n.p., n.d.
Arc 1076.14 Weidenbaeck, A. Tönendes Erz. Graz, 1961.
Arc 1510.148 Weidhas, J.F. Die Brandenburger Denare von Heinrich König der Wenden bis auf Friedrich I. Kurfürst aus dem Hause Hohenzollern. Berlin, 1855.
Arc 853.84 Weiershausen, P. Vorgeschichtliche Eisenbütten Deutschlands. Leipzig, 1939.
Arc 545.227.5 Weigal, A.E.P. Report on antiquities of Lower Nubia. Oxford, 1907.
Arc 858.39 Weigall, A.E.P.B. Wanderings in Roman Britain. London, 1926.
Arc 572.1.20 Weigall, Arthur Edward Pearse Brome. Ancient Egyptian works of art. London, 1924.
Arc 572.1.5A Weigall, Arthur Edward Pearse Brome. The glory of the Pharaohs. N.Y., 1923.
Arc 572.1 Weigall, Arthur Edward Pearse Brome. Guide to the antiquities of upper Egypt. London, 1910.
Arc 572.1.2 Weigall, Arthur Edward Pearse Brome. A guide to the antiquities of upper Egypt from Abydos to the Sudan frontier. N.Y., 1910.
Arc 572.1.15 Weigall, Arthur Edward Pearse Brome. The treasury of ancient Egypt. Chicago, 1912.
Arc 572.1.10 Weigall, Arthur Edward Pearse Brome. Tutankhamen, and other essays. London, 1923.
Arc 87.1.44 Weil, R. Kuenstlerinschriften der sicilienischen Muenzen. Berlin, 1884.
Arc 505.25 Weill, Raymond. La cité de David. Plans and atlas. Paris, 1920. 2v.
Arc 1522.5 Weiller, Raymond. Monnaies antiques découvertes au Grand-Duché de Luxembourg. Berlin, 1972.
Arc 383.34.5 Weinberg, S.S. The Aegean and the Near East. N.Y., 1956.
Arc 830.125 Weise, Georg. Zwei fränkische Königspfalzen. Tübingen, 1923.
Arc 1016.245F Weiss, Karl. Der romanische Speisekelch. Wien, 1860.
Arc 723.42 Weiss, Robert. The Renaissance discovery of classical antiquity. Oxford, 1969.
Arc 1490.85 Weiss, Roberto. The medals of Pope Sixtus IV, 1471-1484. Rome, 1961.
Arc 1480.86 Weissgerber, Clemens. Der Fröndenberger Münzschatzfund römischer Denare. Dortmund, 1969?
Arc 662.4 Weissmann, K. Beiträge zur Erklärung...griechische Kunstwerke. Schweinfurt, 1903.
Arc 1660.14F Welch, Charles. Medals struck by the corporation of London. London, 1894.
Arc 628.8 Welcker, F.G. Alte Denkmäler. v.1-5. Göttingen, 1849-64. 4v.
Arc 716.1 Welcker, F.G. Der Felsaltar des Höchsten Zens oder das Pelasgikon zu Athen. Berlin, 1852.
Arc 410.1.18 Welcker, F.G. Zoega's Leben. Stuttgart, 1819. 2v.
Arc 1229.10 Welfen, Peter. Die Königs-Stempel. Wiesbaden, 1969.
Arc 1020.129F Der Welfenschatz. (Falke, Otto von.) Frankfurt, 1930.
Arc 785.13.75 Welin, Erik. Studien zur Topographie des Forum Romanum. Lund, 1953.
Arc 861.21 Wellbeloved, C. Eburacum, or York under the Romans. York, 1842.
Arc 708.27 Weller, C.H. Athens and its monuments. N.Y., 1913.
Arc 708.27.5 Weller, C.H. Athens and its monuments. N.Y., 1924.
Arc 691.2 Weller. The cave at Vari. n.p., n.d.
Arc 785.7 Wells, C.L. The amphitheatres of ancient Rome. Boston, 1884.
Arc 848.13 Wels, K.H. Die germanische Vorzeit. Leipzig, 1923.
Arc 1540.38 Welsh tokens of the seventeenth century. (Cardiff, Wales. National Museum of Wales.) Cardiff, 1973.
Arc 685.1.5 Welter, Gabriel. Troizen und Kalaureia. Berlin, 1941.
Arc 1510.164 Welter, Gerhard. Die Münzen der Welfen seit Heinrich dem Löwen. Braunschweig, 1971-73. 2v.
Arc 1093.2.15 Weltgeschichte der Steinzeit. (Menghin, O.) Wien, 1931.
Arc 600.8 Wendel, F.C.H. Über die in altägyptischen Texten erwähnten Bau- und Edelsteine. Leipzig, 1888.
Arc 609.20.5 Wendorf, Fred. A Middle Stone Age sequence from the Central Riff Valley, Ethiopia. Wrocław, 1974.
Arc 861.160.20 Wenham, Leslie. The Romano-British cemetery at Trentholm Drive. London, 1968.
Arc 1033.34.50 Wenzel, P. Die Ausgrabbungen unter der Peterskirche in Rom. Leipzig, 1953.
Arc 1675.35 Die Werke des Medailleur's Hans Frei in Basel, 1894-1906. (Meili, Julius.) Zürich, 1906.
Arc 612.37 Werkzeuge des Frühmenschen in Europa. (Rust, Alfred.) Neumünster, 1971.
Arc 830.192 Werner, J. Der Fund von Ittenheim. Strassburg, 1943.
Arc 853.160F Werner, Joachim. Das alamannische Gräberfeld von Mindelheim. Kallmünz, 1955.
Arc 684.1.12 Wernick, F. Olympia. Leipzig, 1877.
Arc 1335.20 Werveke, N. van. Catalogue descriptive des monnaies luxembourgeoises. Luxembourg, 1880.
Arc 407.7 Werveke, N. van. Mélanges archéologiques. Luxembourg, 1882.
Arc 1335.13 Wesener, F.J. Die Gotthard mimus'sche Thaler und Medaillensammlung. Wien, 1874.
Arc 958.1.15 Weslager, Clinton Alfred. Delaware's buried past. Philadelphia, 1944.
Arc 1030.51 Wessel, C. Inscriptiones graecae christianae veteres occidentes. Diss. inaug. Halae Saxonum, 1936.
Arc 861.141 Wessex before the Celts. (Stone, J.F.S.) London, 1958.
Arc 861.82F Wessex from the air. (Crawford, O.G.S.) Oxford, 1928.
Arc 1478.50 West, Louis. Gold and silver coin standards in the Roman empire. N.Y., 1941.
Arc 861.165 The west Kennet long barrow. (Piggot, Stuart.) London, 1962.
Arc 848.56 Westeuropäische Elemente im neolithischen Grabbau Mitteldeutschlands und die Galeriegräber Westdeutschlands und ihre Inventare. (Schrickel, Waldtraut.) Bonn, 1966. 2v.
Arc 848.35 Westgermanische Bodenfunde. (Uslar, R. von.) Berlin, 1938.
Arc 684.1.29 Der Westgiebel des olympischen Zeustempels. (Wolters, Paul.) München, 1908.
Arc 540.5F Westholm, A. The temples of Soli. Stockholm, 1936.
Arc 1468.17 Weston, S. Historic notices of coins in Greece. London, 1826.
Arc 777.1.5 Westphal, Enrico. Guida per la campagna di Roma. Roma, 1854.
Arc 777.1 Westphal, J.H. Die Roemische Kampagne. Berlin, 1829.
Arc 777.2 Westropp, H.M. Early and imperial Rome. London, 1884.
Arc 407.9.2 Westropp, Hodder Michael. Handbook of archaeology. 2. ed. London, 1878.
Arc 407.25 Westropp, Hodder Michael. Pre-historic phases. London, 1872.
Arc 855.208 Westwood, J.O. Lapidarium Walliae. Oxford, 1876-79.
Arc 746.61 Wetter, Erik. Med kungen på Acquarossa. Malmö, 1972.
Arc 853.267 Wetterauer Fundberichte, 1941-49. (Roth, H.) Friedberg, 1951
Arc 1033.62.40 Wetzel, A. Die Translatie S. Alexandri. Kiel, 1881.
Arc 853.354 Wetzel, Robert. Die Bocksteinschmiede im Lonetal (Markung Ramminger, Kreis Ulm). Stuttgart, 1969. 2v.
Arc 853.19 Weynand, R. De cipporum germaniae romanorum ornamentis. Bonnae, 1902.
Arc 30.12.5 What it is, etc. (American Institute of Persian Art and Archaeology.) N.Y., 1932.
Arc 497.47 What mean these stones? (Burrows, M.) New Haven, 1941.
Arc 875.37 What means these stones? (Maclagan, Christian.) Edinburgh, 1894.
Arc 785.35 What Rome was built with. (Porter, M.W.) London, 1907.
Arc 723.23A Whatmough, J. The foundations of Roman Italy. London, 1937.
Arc 662.5 Wheeler, J.R. Archaeology. N.Y., 1908.
Arc 716.2.5 Wheeler, James R. The theatre of Dionysus. n.p., n.d.
Arc 455.3 Wheeler, R.E. Five thousand years of Pakistan. London, 1950.
Arc 885.8 Wheeler, R.E.M. Prehistoric and Roman Wales. Oxford, 1925.
Arc 885.9 Wheeler, R.E.M. The Roman fort near Brecon. London, 1926.
Arc 885.12.5 Wheeler, R.E.M. Segontium and the Roman occupation of Wales. London, 1923.
Arc 885.8.5 Wheeler, R.E.M. Wales and archaeology. London, 1929.
Arc 442.2 Wheeler, Robert. Chārsada. London, 1962.
Arc 493.2.25 Wheeler, Robert E. Flames over Persepolis: turning point in history. London, 1962.
Arc 407.20 Wheeler, Robert Eric Mortimer. Alms for oblivion: an antiquary's scrapbook. London, 1966.
Arc 407.16 Wheeler, Robert Eric Mortimer. Archaeology from the earth. Oxford, 1954.
Arc 432.26 Wheeler, Robert Eric Mortimer. Civilizations of the Indus Valley and beyond. London, 1966.
Arc 407.18 Wheeler, Robert Eric Mortimer. Rome beyond the imperial frontiers. London, 1954.
Arc 407.17 Wheeler, Robert Eric Mortimer. Still digging. London, 1955.
Htn Arc 635.215* Wheler, G. A journey into Greece. London, 1682.
Arc 855.210 Whichcord, J. Roman antiquities recently discovered. London, 1873.
Arc 861.23.9 Whimster, D.C. The archaeology of Surrey. London, 1931.
Arc 843.8 Whishaw, B. Illustrated descriptive account of the museum of Andalucian pottery and lace. Seville, 1912.
Arc 736.6.5 Whitaker, J.I.S. Motya. London, 1921.
Arc 407.19 White, Anne Terry. Lost worlds; the romance of archaeology. N.Y., 1941.
Arc 730.208 White, J.W. Oeri tou pelaryikon epiperikleous. Athēnai, 1894.
Arc 716.5 White, J.W. The Opisthodomus on the Acropolis at Athens. n.p., 1894?
Arc 710.17 White, John W. The apisthodomus on the acropolis at Athens. Boston, 1895.
Arc 855.6 White, T.P. Architectural sketches in Scotland - Kintyre. Edinburgh, 1873.
Arc 855.6.2 White, T.P. Architectural sketches in Scotland - Knapdale. Edinburgh, 1875.
Arc 421.11 White, W.C. Tombs of old Lo-yang. Shanghai, 1934.
Arc 870.20 White horses. (Marples, M.) London, 1949.
Arc 870.2 The white horses of the west of England. (Plenderleath, W.C.) London, 1886.
Arc 965.1 Whiteford, Guy L. Indian archaeology in Saline County, Kansas. Salina, 1941.
Arc 600.5.3 Whitehouse, F.C. Lake Moeris and the pyramids. n.p., 1884?
Arc 1663.6.20 Whiting, John Roger Scott. Commemorative medals. Newton Abbot, 1972.
Arc 1680.16.5 Whiting, John Roger Scott. Trade tokens; a social and economic history. Newton Abbot, 1971.
Arc 1322.15 Whitman numismatic journal. Racine, Wis. 1,1964+ 2v.
Arc 1473.18 Whitting, Philip David. Byzantine coins. London, 1973.
Arc 1033.12.85 Who are the figures on the chalice of Antioch? (Filson, F.V.) n.p., 1942.
Arc 553.1 Who was who in Egyptology. (Dawson, W.R.) London, 1951.
Arc 1322.5 Wiadomości numizmatyczne. Warszawa. 1+ 6v.
Arc 1322.10F Wiadomości numizmatyczno-archeologiczne. Krakowie. 1-21,1889-1948 8v.

Arc 1510.18 Wibel, Ferdinand. Zur Münzgeschichte der Grafen von Wertheim. Hamburg, 1880.
Arc 1675.51.25 Wichura-Zajdel, E. Sląski medalier Jan Wysocki. Katowia, 1961.
Arc 1663.6.15 Widdington, M. Catalogue of Jacobite medals and touch pieces. Leeds, 1938.
Arc 685.1 Wide, S. Ausgrabungen auf Kalaureia. n.p., n.d.
Arc 1510.1 Widmer, M.J. von. Domus Wittelbachensis numismatica. Munich, 1784-85.
Arc 1510.1.2 Widmer, M.J. von. Dormus Wittelbachensis numismatica. Munich, 1784.
Arc 684.6 Wie sind die Figuren im Ostgiebel des Zeustempels zu Olympia anzuordnen. (Quaatz, H.) Berlin, 1908.
Arc 1349.65 Więcek, A. Sebastian Dadler. Gdańsk, 1962.
Arc 1663.15.10 Więcek, Adam. Medale Piastów Śląskich. Wyd. 1. Warszawa, 1958.
Arc 905.12 Der Wiederauflau von Carnuntum. (List, G.) Wien, 1900.
Arc 830.360 Wiederbelebung historischer Stadtviertel; die Lösing in Frankreich als mögliches Vorbild. (Foramitti, Hans.) Graz, 1965.
Arc 600.112 Die Wiedergewinnung von Medinet Habu im westlichen Theben. (Hoelsche, Uvo.) Tübingen, 1958.
Arc 1025.18 Wiegand, F. Eine Wanderung...römischen Katakomben. Erlangen, 1893.
Arc 505.2.5F Wiegand, T. Palmyra; Ergebnisse der Expeditionen von 1902 und 1917. Text and plates. Berlin, 1932. 2v.
Arc 495.5.5F Wiegand, Theodor. Baalbek. v.1-3; atlas. Berlin, 1921-25. 4v.
Arc 510.218F Wiegand, Theodor. Milet-Ergebnisse der Ausgrabungen. Berlin, 1906- 18v.
Arc 530.14 Wiegand, Theodor. Priene. Leipzig, 1910.
Arc 530.14.5F Wiegand, Theodor. Priene: Ergebnisse der Ausgrabungen. Berlin, 1904.
X Cg Arc 510.216 Wiegand, Theodor. Prierre. Berlin, 1904.
Arc 87.1.73 Wiegand, Theodore. Bronzefigur einer Spinnerin. Berlin, 1913.
Arc 380.214 Wieland, C.A. Der Denkmal und Heimatschutz...der Gegenwart. Basel, 1905.
Arc 1033.123 Wieland, F. Altar und Altargrab der christlichen Kirchen...Mensa und Confessio. v.1-2. München, 1906-12.
Arc 1033.123.5 Wieland, F. Schrift Mensa und Confessio und P. Emil Dorsch. München, 1909.
Arc 1033.123.9 Wieland, F. Der vorirenäische Obferbegriff. München, 1909.
Arc 1504.30 Wielandt, Friedrich. Münz- und Geldgeschichte des Standes Luzern. Luzern, 1969.
Arc 1504.25 Wielandt, Friedrich. Münz- und Geldgeschichte des Standes Schuyz. Schuyz, 1964.
Arc 1510.156 Wielandt, Friedrich. Münze und Geld in Pforzheim. Pforzheim, 1968.
Arc 1504.15 Wielandt, Friedrich. Schaffhausen Münz- und Geldgeschichte. Schaffhausen, 1959?
Arc 936.14.500 Wielkie grody dorzecza góinej Wisły. (Dąbrowska, Elżbieta.) Wrocław, 1973.
Arc 936.6 Wielkopolska w czasach. (Kostrzewski, Józef.) Poznań, 1914.
Arc 936.6.5 Wielkopolska w czasach. (Kostrzewski, Józef.) Poznań, 1923.
Arc 936.6.10 Wielkopolska w pradziejach. 3. wyd. (Kostrzewski, Józef.) Warszawa, 1955.
Arc 936.14.470 Wielkopolska wdobie Prasłowian. wyd. 1. (Malinowski, Tadeusz.) Poznań, 1973.
Arc 785.110 Wielowiejski, Jerzy. Kontakty Noricum i Pannonii z ludami połnochymi. Wrocław, 1970.
Arc 505.29 Wiener, H.M. The altars of the Old Testament. Leipzig, 1927.
Arc 1020.1.5 Das Wiener Heiligthumbuch. (Vienna. St. Stephansdom.) Wien, 1882.
Htn Arc 1660.4F* Wiener Medailleure, 1899. (Loehr, August.) Wien, 1899.
Arc 1660.4.2F Wiener Medailleure. Nachtrag, 1901. (Loehr, August.) Wien, 1902.
Arc 407.12 Wieringen, J.H. van. De voor historische mens. Zutphen, 1938.
Arc 777.4 Wiesel, Julius Maxim. Das alte Rom zur konstantinischen Zeit undHeute. Mainz, 1964.
Arc 1078.1 Wieseler, F. Das Diptychon Quirinianum zu Brescia. Göttingen, 1868.
Arc 87.2.68 Wieseler, F. Hildesheimer Silberfund. Bonn, 1868.
Arc 700.12.15 Wiesner, J. Grab und Jenseits. Berlin, 1938.
Arc 1083.2 Wigand, Karl. Thymiateria. Inaug. Diss. Bonn, 1912.
Arc 853.304 Wightman, Edith Mary. Roman Trier and the Treveri. London, 1970.
Arc 889.32 Wijster; a native village beyond the imperial frontier, 150-425 A.D. Text and atlas. (Es, William Albertus van.) Groningen, 1967. 2v.
Arc 1153.4.23 Wikenhauser, A. Der heilige Cassian. Berlin, 1906.
Arc 936.6.30 Wiklak, Henryk. Początki kultury łużyckiej w Polsce Środkowej. Łodź, 1963.
Arc 608.17.13 Wilamowitz-Moellendorff, U. Cirene. Bergamo, 1930.
Arc 493.2.30 Wilber, Donald Newton. Persepolis, the archaelogy of Parsa. N.Y., 1969.
Arc 572.5 Wilbour, Charles E. Travels in Egypt. December 1880-May 1891. Brooklyn, 1936.
Arc 1453.7 Wilcke, Julius. Daler. Kjøbenhavn, 1931.
Arc 1550.6 Wilcke, Julius. Kurantmønten. Kjøbenhavn, 1927.
Arc 1550.7 Wilcke, Julius. Montvaesenet under Christian IV og Frederik III i tidsrummet, 1625-70. Kjøbenhavn, 1924.
Arc 1550.5 Wilcke, Julius. Sølo-og guldmøntfod. Kjøbenhavn, 1930.
Arc 1550.9 Wilcke, Julius. Specie. Kjøbenhavn, 1929.
Arc 497.37 The wilderness of Zin. (Woolley, C.L.) London, 1936.
Arc 870.30 Wildman, Samuel Gerald. The black horsemen: English inns and King Arthur. London, 1971.
Arc 388.7 Wilhelm Dörpfeld. (Goessler, F.P.) Stuttgart, 1951.
Arc 853.23.5 Wilhelmi, K. Les anciens tombeaux germaniques. Heidelberg, 1831.
Arc 853.23 Wilhelmi, K. Beschreibung der 14alten deutschen Todtenhügel. Heidelberg, 1830.
Arc 672.5 Wilisch, E. Beiträge zur Geschichte des alten Korinth. Zittau, 1901.
Arc 1093.2.8 Wilke, Georg. Südwesteuropäische Megalithkultur. Würzburg, 1912.
Arc 708.18 Wilkins, W. Atheniensia, or Remarks on the topography and buildings of Athens. London, 1816.
Arc 407.31 Wilkinson, Edward M. Technische und naturwissenschaftliche Beiträge zur Feldarchäologie. Köln, 1974.
Arc 66.1.183 Will, Ernest. Le relief culturel greco-romain. Paris, 1955.
Arc 968.10 Will, G.F. The Mandans. [North Dakota]. Cambridge, 1906.
Arc 888.6 Willems, W.J.A. Een bijdrage tot de kennis der vóór-Romeinsche urnenvelden in Nederland. Proefschrift. Maastricht, 1935.
Arc 726.200 Willemsen, C.A. Apulia, imperial splendor in southern Italy. N.Y., 1959.
Arc 1480.14 Willers, H. Geschichte der römischen Kupferprägung. Leipzig, 1909.
Arc 726.29 Willers, H. Römische Bronzeindustrie von Capua und von Niedergermanien. Hannover, 1907.
Arc 609.28 Willett, Frank. Ife in the history of west African sculpture. N.Y., 1967.
Arc 384.17 Willey, Gordon Randolph. Archaeological researches in retrospect. Cambridge, Mass., 1974.
Arc 1200.26 William of Hoo, S. The letter-book of William of Hoo. Ipswich, 1963.
Arc 403.19 William Stukely. (Piggott, Stuart.) Oxford, 1950.
Arc 875.25 Williams, J. An account of some remarkable ancient ruins. Edinburgh, 1777.
Arc 382.2 Williams, John. On Carn Goch in Caermarthenshire. London, 1853. 17 pam.
Arc 497.74 Williams, Walter George. Archaeology in Biblical research. N.Y., 1965.
Arc 861.51 Williams-Freeman, J.P. Introduction to field archaeology...Hampshire. London, 1915.
Arc 1423.14.5 Williamson, G.C. The money of the Bible. N.Y., 18- ?
Arc 1423.14 Williamson, G.C. The money of the Bible illustrated by numerous woodcuts. London, 1894.
Arc 861.37.3 Williamson, W.C. Description of the Tumulus. 3. ed. Scarborough, 1872.
Arc 942.9 Pamphlet vol. Willoughby, C. Archaeological and ethnological papers. 22 pam.
Arc 969.1.12 Willoughby, C.C. The Turner group of earthworks, Hamilton County, Ohio. Cambridge, 1922.
Arc 609.1.5 Willoughby, J.C. A narrative of further excavations at Zimbabye (Mashonaland). London, 1893.
Arc 1335.26 Wilmersdörffer, M. von. Max Ritter von Wilmersdörfferische Münzen-Sammlung. Frankfurt am Main, 1905-07. 2v.
Arc 1033.12.105 Wilmowsky, J.N. von. Heilige Rock; eine archäologische Prüfung...Trier. Trier, 1876.
Arc 1027.3 Wilpert, G. La croce sui monumenti delle catacombe. Roma, 1902.
Arc 1033.70.23 Wilpert, G. Le pitture della Basilica primitiva di S. Clemente. Roma, 1906.
Arc 1015.213.12 Wilpert, J. La cripta dei Papi et la capella di Santa Cecilia. Roma, 1910.
Arc 1015.232F Wilpert, J. Ein Cyclus christologischer Gemälde. Freiburg, 1891.
Arc 1027.7.9 Wilpert, J. Di un cielo di rappresent cristianità...SS. Pietro ed Marcelino. Roma, 1892.
Arc 1015.213.9 Wilpert, J. Fractio Panis. Freiburg, 1895.
Arc 1033.112 Wilpert, J. Die Gewandung der Christen in den ersten Jahrhunderten. Köln, 1898.
Arc 1016.209 Wilpert, J. Die Gottgeweihten Jungfrauen. Freiburg, 1892.
Arc 1015.213 Wilpert, J. Die Katakombengemalde. Ihre alten Copiers. Freiburg, 1891.
Arc 1027.19.29 Wilpert, J. Die Malerein der Sacramentskapellen in der Katakombe des honorable Callistus. Freiburg, 1897.
Arc 1018.12.8 Wilpert, J. Nochmals Principienfragen. Rom, 1890.
Arc 1015.5.5 Wilpert, J. Die Papstgräber und di Cäciliengruf. Freiburg, 1909.
Arc 1018.12 Wilpert, J. Principienfragen der christliche Archäologie. Freiburg, 1889.
Arc 1025.65 Wilpert, Josef. Erlebnisse und Ergebnisse im Dienste der christlichen Archäologie. Freiburg, 1930.
Arc 1093.6.15 Wilser, L. Das Hakenkreuz nach Ursprung, Vorkommen und Bedeutung. 5. Aufl. Leipzig, 1922.
Arc 848.16.2 Wilser, Ludwig. Deutsche Vorzeit. 2. Aufl. Steglitz, 1918.
X Cg Arc 500.2 Wilson, C. Special papers. London, 1881.
Arc 505.127 Wilson, Charles. The recovery of Jerusalem. London, 1871.
Arc 875.6 Wilson, D. The archaeology and prehistoric annals of Scotland. Edinburgh, 1851.
Arc 858.70A Wilson, David McKenzie. The Anglo-Saxons. London, 1960.
Arc 593.5 Wilson, E. Cleopatra's needle. London, 1878.
Arc 590.15 Wilson, E. The recent discovery of ancient Egyptian mummies at Thebes. London, 1883.
Arc 1433.5 Wilson, H. A descriptive account of antiquity and coins of Afghanistan. London, 1841.
Arc 407.6 Wilson, John Albert. Prehistoric art. Washington, 1898.
Arc 572.2 Wilson, John Albert. Signs and wonders upon Pharaoh. Chicago, 1964.
Arc 407.6.5 Wilson, John Albert. Study of prehistoric anthropology. Washington, 1890.
Arc 407.6.10 Wilson, John Albert. Thousands of years. N.Y., 1972.
Arc 458.5 Wilson, Thomas. Minute stone implements from India. n.p., 1892.
Arc 1093.6 Wilson, Thomas. The swastika, the earliest known symbol. Washington, 1896.
Htn Arc 875.36* Wilson, Wilson D. Description of an ancient cross at Kilmory. Edinburgh, 1839.
Arc 1680.16 Wiltshire Archaeological and Natural History Society, Devizes. Museum. Catalogue of the collection of Wiltshire trade tokens. Devizes, 1893.
Arc 858.62 Winbolt, S.E. Britain B.C. Harmondsworth, Eng., 1945.
Arc 861.65.15 Winbolt, S.E. Roman Folkestone. London, 1925.
Arc 861.41.9 Winbolt, S.E. The Roman villa at Bignor, Sussex. Oxford, 1925.
Arc 861.41.10 Winbolt, S.E. The Roman villa at Bignor, Sussex. Oxford, 1930.
Arc 1433.14 Winbom, Jonas A. Dissertatio de recentioribus numis Arabicis. Upsaliae, 1815.
Arc 861.171 Winchester, England. Winchester excavations, 1949-1960. Winchester, Hants, 1964.
Arc 861.171 Winchester excavations, 1949-1960. (Winchester, England.) Winchester, Hants, 1964.
Arc 800.3.13 Winckelmann, J. Critical account of the situation and destruction by the first eruptions of Mount Vesuvius. London, 1771.
Arc 800.3.7 Winckelmann, J. Lettre à Monsieur le Comte de Brühl. Dresde, 1764.
Htn Arc 380.209* Winckelmann, J. Monumenti antichi inedite. v.1-2. Roma, 1767.
Arc 800.3.5 Winckelmann, J. Recueil de lettres de M. Winckelmann. Paris, 1784.
Htn Arc 800.3* Winckelmann, J. Sendschreiben von den Herculanischen Entdeckungen. Dresden, 1762. 4 pam.
Arc 407.30 Winckelmann. 1. ed. (Leppmann, Wolfgang.) N.Y., 1970.

Author and Title Listing

Arc 407.30.5 Winckelmann und Rilke: zwei Beschreibungen des Apollon. (Schadewaldt, Wolfgang.) Pfullingen, 1968.
Arc 407.30.15 Winckelmanns Begriff der Schönheit. (Rein, Ulrike G.M.) Bonn, 1972.
Arc 87.1.78 Winckelmannsprogramm. (Archäologische Gesellschaft zu Berlin.) Berlin. 77,1921+ 29v.
Arc 858.9 Windle, B.C.A. Life in early Britain. London, 1897.
Arc 858.9.3 Windle, B.C.A. Life in early Britain. N.Y., 1897.
Arc 858.9.5 Windle, B.C.A. Remains of the Prehistoric Age in England. London, 1904.
Arc 858.9.6 Windle, B.C.A. Remains of the Prehistoric Age in England. London, 1909.
Arc 857.5 Windle, Bertram. A collection of archaeological pamphlets on Roman remains...Great Britain. n.p., n.d. 12v.
Arc 861.31.25 Windmill Hill and Avebury. (Smith, Isobel F.) Oxford, 1965.
Arc 1540.15 Wingate, James. Illustrations of coinage of Scotland. Glasgow, 1868.
Arc 1020.51.10 Winheim, Erharde. Sacrarium Agrippinae...praecipuarum reliquarum. Coloniae Agrippinae, 1736. 2 pam.
Arc 870.15.15 Winholt, S.E. With a spade on Stane Street. London, 1936.
Arc 710.2.4 Winke für Akropolis-Pilger. (Buschor, Ernst.) München, 1960.
Arc 1020.51.5 Winkeim, Erharde. Sacrarium Agrippinae...praecipuarum reliquarum. Coloniae, 1607. 2 pam.
Arc 893.19 Winkel Horn, F. Kort udsigt over Nordens oldtidsminder. Kjøbenhavn, 1883.
Arc 600.44 Winkler, H.A. Völker und Völkerbewegungen im vorgeschichtlichen Oberägypten im Lichte neuer Felshilderfunde. Stuttgart, 1937.
Arc 587.10.15 Winkler, Hans A. Rock drawings of southern upper Egypt. London, 1938-39. 2v.
Arc 600.54 Winlock, H.E. Excavations at Deir el Bahri, 1911-1931. N.Y., 1942.
Arc 600.65F Winlock, H.E. The slain soldiers of Neb-hebek-Re' Mentu-hotpe. N.Y., 1945.
Arc 87.1.59 Winnefeld, H. Altgriechisches Bronzebecken aus Leontini. Berlin, 1899.
Arc 1213.1 Winnefeld, H. Hellenistische Silberreliefs. Berlin, 1908.
Arc 785.103 Winslow, E.M. A libation to the gods. London, 1963.
Arc 600.10 Winslow, W.C. Egyptian antiquities for our museums. n.p., 1900.
Arc 600.4 Winslow, W.C. Naukratis - a Greek city in Egypt. Boston, 1887.
Arc 586.60 Winslow, W.C. The truth about the Egypt Exploration Society. Boston, 1903.
Arc 554.1.15 Winslow, William C. The queen of Egyptology. n.p., 1892.
Arc 87.1.55 Winter, F. Eine attische Lekythos. Berlin, 1895.
Arc 1053.2 Winter, F. Über die griechische Porträtkunst. Berlin, 1894.
Arc 700.19.10 Winter, F.E. Greek fortifications. London, 1971.
Arc 700.19.11 Winter, F.E. Greek fortifications. Toronto, 1971.
Arc 1510.70 Wintz, Hermann. Erlangen in Spiegel der Münze. Erlangen, 1936.
Arc 66.1.148 Wirilleumier, Pierre. Tarente; des origines a la conquête romaine. Paris, 1939. 2v.
Arc 407.11 Wirth, Herman. Der Aufgang der Menschheit. Jena, 1928.
Arc 915.48.5 Wirtschaft und Gesellschaft in der Jungsteinzeit. (Wyss, René.) Bern, 1973.
Arc 936.180.35 Wisaman, James. Stobi; a guide to the excavations. Beograd, 1973.
Arc 588.63 Wisdom of the Egyptians. (Petrie, W.M.F.) London, 1940.
Htn Arc 407.2* Wise, F. Letter to Dr. Mead. Oxford, 1738-64. 4 pam.
Arc 1333.2 Wise, F. Numismata antiqua. Scriniis bodleianis rec. catalogus. Oxford, 1750.
Arc 838.35 Wiseman, F.J. Roman Spain. London, 1956.
Arc 1033.34.17 Wiseman, N. Remarks on...Saint Peter's chair. Rome, 1833. 2v.
Arc 1033.34.19 Wiseman, N. Sul ragguaglio...cattedra di San Pietro. Roma, 1832.
Arc 1232.5 Wisemar, D.J. Gotter und Menschen im Rollsiegel. Prague, 1958.
Arc 936.14.300 Wiślański, Tadeusz. Podstawy gospodarcze plemion neolitycznych w Polsce połnocno-zachodniej. Wrocław, 1969.
Arc 1348.65 Wissenschaftliche Abhandlunger des deutschen Numismatikertages. (Deutscher Numismatikertag, Göttingen.) Göttingen, 1959.
Arc 503.3F Wissenschaftliche Veröffentlichungen. v.1-6. (Deutsch-Turkischer Denkmalschutz-Kommando.) Berlin, 1920-
Arc 543.83.5 Wissmann, Hermann. Zur Archäologie und antiken Geographie von Südarabien. Istanbul, 1968.
Arc 777.3 Wissowa, G. Analecta Romana topographica. Halis, 1897.
Arc 870.15.15 With a spade on Stane Street. (Winholt, S.E.) London, 1936.
Arc 1025.11 Withrow, W.H. Catacombs of Rome. London, 1877.
Arc 391.2.15 Witte, J. Notice sur Edouard Gerhard. Bruxelles, 1871.
Arc 673.1.2 Witte, J. de Baron. Monumens de Delphes. Roma, 1842.
X Cg Arc 1500.29F Witte, Jean. Recherches sur les empereurs qui ont régné dans les Gaules. n.p., 1920.
Arc 1148.28F Wittek, Martin. Album de paléographie grecque. Gand, 1967.
Arc 853.79 Witter, W. Die älteste Erzgewinnung im nordischgermanischen Lehenskreis. Leipzig, 1938. 2v.
Arc 1016.12 Wittig, Joseph. Die altchristlichen Skulpturen...deutschen Nationalstiftung am Campo Santo. Rom, 1906.
Arc 1269.40 Wittmer, C. Inventaire des sceaux des archives de la ville de Strasbourg de 1050 à 1300. Strasbourg, 1946.
Arc 1588.1.25F Wittyg, W. Pieczecie miast dawnej Polski. Kraków, 1905.
Arc 905.2 Wo stand das "Flavium Solvense?" (Knabl, R.) n.p., n.d.
Arc 905.15 Wocel, J.E. Grundzüge der böhmischen Alterthumskunde. Prag, 1845.
Arc 785.118 Wodociągi rzymskie i wczesnobizantyjskie z obszaru Mezji Dolnej i Północnej Tracji. (Biernacka-Lukańska, Małgorzata.) Wrocław, 1973.
Arc 630.8 Woelcke, Karl. Beiträge zur Geschichte des Tropaions. Bonn, 1911.
Arc 1340.8 Wörterbuch der Münzkunde. (Schrotter, F.) Berlin, 1930.
Arc 375.5 Wörterbuch zur Vorgeschichte. (Schlemm, J.) Berlin, 1908.
Arc 1093.6.18 Woher kommt das Hakenkreuz? (Scheuermann, W.) Berlin, 1933.
Arc 672.1.150 Wohin der Stier Europa trug. (Wunderlich, Hans-Georg.) Reinbek bei Hamburg, 1972.
Arc 848.21 Der Wohnbau im jungsteinzeitlichen Deutschland. pt.1-2. Inaug. Diss. (Kadig, Werner.) Leipzig, 1930.
Arc 823.4.2 Woillez, E. Répertoire archéologique du département de l'Oise. Paris, 1862.
Arc 936.14.290 Wojtasik, Jerzy. Cmentarzysko wczesnośredniowieczne na wzgórzu "Młynówka" w Wolinie. Szczecin, 1968.
Arc 1588.1.36 Wojtulewicz, H. Moneta polska od X-XX wieku. Lublin, 1960.
Arc 1663.62 Wojtulewicz, Henryk. Medale polskie XVI-XX w. Lublin, 1968.
Arc 1018.28 Wolcott, M.E.C. Sacred archaeology...dictionary. London, 1868.
Arc 572.11 Wolf, Walther. Funde in Ägypten. Göttingen, 1966.
Arc 830.124 Wolff, F. Handbuch der staatlichen Denkmalpflege in Elsass-Lothringen. Strassburg, 1903.
Arc 853.29 Wolff, G. Die Römerstadt Nida bei Heddernheim. Frankfurt, 1908.
Arc 853.105 Wolff, G. Der römische Grenzwald bei Hanau mit dem Kastellen zu Rückingen und Markäbel. Hanau, 1885.
Arc 505.5.7 Wolff, P.O. Der Tempel von Jerusalem. Graz, 1887.
Arc 1020.9.95 Wolff. Geschichtsbilder aus alt christlicher Zeit. Roms. Berlin, 1907.
Arc 1025.16 Wolter, M. Die römischen Katakomben. Frankfurt, 1866.
Arc 1458.8.5 Woltereck, C. Electa rei numariae. Hamburgi, 1709.
Htn Arc 1458.8* Woltereck, C. Electa rei numariae. Hamburgi, 1709.
Arc 684.1.29 Wolters, Paul. Der Westgiebel des olympischen Zeustempels. München, 1908.
Arc 810.10.5 The wonders of Pompeii. (Monnier, Marc.) N.Y., 1870.
Arc 392.5 Wonders of the past; the romance of antiquity and its splendours. (Hammerton, J.A.) N.Y., 1925-26. 4v.
Arc 392.5.7 Wonders of the past. (Hammerton, J.A.) N.Y., 1937. 2v.
Arc 858.73 Wood, E.S. Collins field guide to archaeology. London, 1964.
Htn Arc 1605.1* Wood, H. Canadian blacksmith coppers. Philadelphia, 1910.
Arc 518.1.3 Wood, J.T. Discoveries at Ephesus. Boston, 1877.
Arc 518.1 Wood, J.T. Discoveries at Ephesus. London, 1877.
Arc 518.1.5 Wood, J.T. Modern discoveries on the site of ancient Ephesus. London, 1890.
Arc 865.18 Wood, John. Choir Gaure, vulgarly called Stonehenge. Oxford, 1747.
Arc 880.20A Wood-Martin, W.G. The lake-dwellings of Ireland. Dublin, 1886.
Arc 880.3 Wood-Martin, W.G. Pagan Ireland. An archaeological sketch. London, 1895.
Arc 861.86F Woodhenge. (Cunnington, M.E. (Mrs.)) Devizes, 1929.
Arc 609.22.5 Woodhouse, Herbert Charles. Archaelogy in southern Africa. Capetown, 1971.
Arc 861.191F Woodhouse, Jayne. Barrow Mead, Bath, 1964: excavation of a medieval peasant house. Oxford, 1976.
Arc 662.3 Woodhouse, W.J. Aetolia, its geography and antiquities. Oxford, 1897.
Htn Arc 861.18.17* Woodward, J. Account of some urns. London, 1713. 2 pam.
Arc 1613.6 Woodward, W.E. Catalogue of American and foreign coins, medals, tokens. Providence, 1866.
Arc 1613.6.2 Woodward, W.E. Catalogue of American and foreign coins, medals, tokens. Roxbury, 1867.
Arc 1335.6 Woodward, W.E. Catalogue of the numismatic collection of F.S. Hoffman. N.Y., 1866.
Arc 1084.5 The Woodward collection of jades and other hard stones. (Getz, John.) n.p., 1913.
Arc 861.57F Wookey Hole; its caves and cave dwellers. (Balch, H.E.) London, 1914.
Arc 861.205 Woolf, Charles William. An introduction to the archaeology of Cornwall. Truro, 1970.
Arc 530.70 Woolley, C.L. A forgotten kingdom. Baltimore, 1953.
Arc 606.3 Woolley, C.L. Karanòg, the Romano-Nubian cemetery. Philadelphia, 1910. 2v.
Arc 606.5 Woolley, C.L. Karanòg, the town. Philadelphia, 1911.
Arc 497.37 Woolley, C.L. The wilderness of Zin. London, 1936.
Arc 407.10.20 Woolley, Charles L. As I seem to remember. London, 1962.
Arc 407.10 Woolley, Charles L. Dead towns and living men. London, 1920.
Arc 407.10.5 Woolley, Charles L. Digging up the past. Harmondsworth, 1937.
Arc 407.10.7 Woolley, Charles L. Digging up the past. Harmondsworth, 1956.
Arc 407.10.15 Woolley, Charles L. History unearthed. London, 1958.
Arc 407.10.18 Woolley, Charles L. History unearthed. N.Y., 1962.
Arc 407.10.11 Woolley, Charles L. Spadework. London, 1953.
Arc 407.10.10 Woolley, Charles L. Spadework in archaeology. N.Y., 1953.
Arc 870.10 Woolls, C. Barrow diggers. London, 1839.
Arc 147.5 Worcestershire archaeology newsletter. Worcester. 1,1967+
Arc 662.2 Wordsworth, C. Athens and Attica. Journal of a residence there. London, 1837.
Arc 983.12.5 Work in mound exploration of the Bureau of Ethnology. (Thomas, C.) Washington, 1887.
Arc 861.172 Workers' Educational Association. Slough and Eton Branch. The Middle Thames in antiquity. Slough, Bucks, 1966.
Arc 23.5 World archaeology. London. 1,1969+ 4v.
Arc 384.2 The world of archaeology. (Marek, Kurt W.) London, 1966.
Arc 497.79 World of the Bible. (Palestine Exploration Fund.) South Kensington, 1965?
Arc 392.14 The world of the past. 1. ed. (Hawkes, Jacquetta.) N.Y., 1963. 2v.
Arc 855.209.2F Worlebury - an ancient stronghold. (Dymond, C.W.) Bristol, 1886.
Arc 855.209F Worlebury - an ancient stronghold. (Dymond, C.W.) Bristol, 1902.
Arc 895.15 Worsaae, J.J.A. Blekingske mindemaerker fra hedenold. Kjøbenhavn, 1846.
Arc 895.7.5 Worsaae, J.J.A. Danmarks oldtid oplyst ved oldsager og gravhøie. Kjøbenhavn, 1843.
Arc 895.7 Worsaae, J.J.A. The industrial arts of Denmark. London, 1882.
Arc 893.5.4 Worsaae, J.J.A. Nordene forhistorie. Kjøbenhavn, 1881.
Arc 895.7.9 Worsaae, J.J.A. Om jernålderen i Denmark. Kjøbenhavn, 1858.
Arc 895.29.15 Worsaae, J.J.A. Om Sleswigs eller Sønderjyllands oldtidsminder. Kjøbenhavn, 1865.
NEDL Arc 893.5.3 Worsaae, J.J.A. The pre-history of the North. London, 1886.
Arc 893.5.2A Worsaae, J.J.A. The primeval antiquities of Denmark. London, 1849.
Arc 572.10.5 Wortham, John David. British Egyptology, 1549-1906. Newton Abbot, 1971.
Arc 572.10 Wortham, John David. The genesis of British Egyptology, 1549-1906. 1st ed. Norman, 1971.
Arc 1163.14 Die Worttrennung in angelsächsischen Handschriften. Inaug. Diss. (Rademacher, M.) Münster, 1921.

Arc 905.7 Wosinsky, M. Das prähistorische Schanzwerk von Lengyel. Budapest, 1888.
Arc 1480.65 Wosnik, Bernhard. Untersuchungen zur Geschichte Sullas. Inaug. Diss. Würzburg, 1963.
Arc 936.14.325 Woyda, Stefan. Bibliografia archeologiczna Mazowsza. wyd. 1. Warszawa, 1970.
Arc 936.14.365 Woźniak, Zenon. Osadnictwo celtyckie w Pobie. Wrocław, 1970.
Arc 612.91 Woźniak, Zenon. Wschodnie pogranicze kultury lateńskiej. Wrocław, 1974.
Arc 936.14.25 Woźnicka, Z. Wyroby bednarskie i tokarskie średniowiécznego Medzurzecza. Poznań, 1961.
Arc 670.3.10 Wrede, W. Attika. Athens, 1934.
Htn Arc 1271.1.5* Wree, Olivier de. Les sceaux des comtes de Flandre. Bruge, 1641.
Arc 1458.17 Wren, C. Numismatum antiquorum sylloge populis Graecis. Londini, 1708.
Arc 545.240F Wreszinski, Walter. Atlas zur altaegyptischen Kulturgeschichte. Leipzig, 1914. 4v.
Arc 545.240PF Wreszinski, Walter. Atlas zur altaegyptischen Kulturgeschichte. v.2. Leipzig, 1939.
Arc 1190.3.6 Wright, Andrew. Court-hand restored, or The student's assistant in reading old deeds. London, 1974.
Arc 1190.3 Wright, Andrew. Court hand restored. 2. ed. London, 1778.
Arc 1190.3.2 Wright, Andrew. Court hand restored. 8. ed. London, 1867.
Arc 1190.3.3 Wright, Andrew. Court hand restored. 9. ed. London, 1879.
NEDL Arc 1190.3.5 Wright, Andrew. Court hand restored. 10. ed. London, 1912.
Arc 1163.17.25 Wright, Cyril Ernest. English vernacular hands from the twelfth to the fifteenth centuries. Oxford, 1960.
Arc 497.31.5 Wright, G.E. Biblical archaeology. Philadelphia, 1962.
Arc 407.3 Wright, G.F. Early man. Cleveland, 1883.
Arc 858.52 Wright, G.R. Archaeologic and historic fragments. London, 1887.
Arc 969.15 Wright, James V. The laurel tradition and the middle woodland period. Ottawa, 1967.
Arc 1540.26 Wright, L.V.W. Colonial and commonwealth coins. London, 1959.
Arc 858.12 Wright, T. The archaeological album; or Museum of National Antiquities. London, 1845.
Arc 407.4A Wright, T. Essays on archaeological subjects. v.1-2. London, 1861.
Arc 861.89.5 Wright, Thomas. A lecture on the antiquities of the Anglo-Saxon cemeteries of the ages of paganism. Liverpool, 1854.
Arc 880.12.2 Wright, Thomas. Louthiana, or Introduction to antiquities of Ireland. London, 1758.
Arc 861.29.5 Wright, Thomas. Unriconium. London, 1872.
Arc 858.29 Wright, Thomas. Wa5derings of an antiquary. London, 1854.
Arc 810.60 The writing on the wall. (Lindsay, J.) London, 1960.
Arc 400.14.25 Writings of A. Kingsley Porter. (Porter, Lucy W. Kingsley.) Cambridge, 1934.
Arc 1473.6A Wroth, W. Catalogue of imperial Byzantine coins in the British Museum. London, 1908. 2v.
Arc 1423.13.5 Wruck, W. Die Syrische Provinzialprägung von Augustus. Stuttgart, 1931.
Arc 1423.13 Wruck, W. Die Syrische Provinzialprägung von Augustus bis Klaudius. Inaug. Diss. Stuttgart, 1931.
Arc 612.91 Wschodnie pogranicze kultury lateńskiej. (Woźniak, Zenon.) Wrocław, 1974.
Arc 1349.73 Wspomnienia numizmatyka. (Gumowski, Marian.) Kraków, 1966.
Arc 1588.1.55 Wstęp do numizmatyki polskiej wieków średnich. (Kiersnowski, Ryszard.) Warszawa, 1964.
Arc 1084.15F Wu, Henry H. Ancient Chinese jade. n.p., 1933.
Arc 1510.55 Württembergische Münz- und Medaillen-Kunde. (Binder, C.) Stuttgart, 1846.
Arc 1269.30 Würzburger Zunftsiegel aus fünf Jahrhunderten. (Engel, W.) Würzburg, 1950.
Arc 830.70.10 Wuilleumier, P. L'eglise et la nécropole Saint-Laurent dans le quartier lyonnais de Chaueand. Lyon, 1949.
Arc 830.186 Wuilleumier, P. Les médaillons d'applique gallo-romain. Paris, 1952.
Arc 672.1.146 Wunderlich, Hans-Georg. The secret of Crete. N.Y., 1974.
Arc 672.1.150 Wunderlich, Hans-Georg. Wohin der Stier Europa trug. Reinbek bei Hamburg, 1972.
Arc 845.208F Wurttembergisches Landesamt für Denkmalpflege. Cannstatt zur Römerzeit. Stuttgart, 1921.
Arc 407.5.2 Wussow, A. von. Die Erhaltung der Denkmäler. Berlin, 1885.
Arc 407.5 Wussow, A. von. Der Erhaltung der Denkmäler. Berlin, 1885.
Arc 1663.1 Wyatt, T. A description of the national medals of America. N.Y., 1854. 2 pam.
Arc 905.8 Wycieczki archeologizne po...Wisly. (Przyborowski, J.) Warszawa, 1874.
Arc 1411.3 Wylie, A. Coins of the Ta-ts'ing dynasty. Shanghai, 1858.
Arc 861.34 Wylie, W.M. Fairford graves. Oxford, 1852.
Arc 960.2 Wyman, J. Fresh-water shell mounds...St. John's River, Florida. Salem, 1875.
Arc 1273.1 Wyon, A. The great seals of England. London, 1887.
Arc 936.14.25 Wyroby bednarskie i tokarskie średniowiécznego Medzurzecza. (Woźnicka, Z.) Poznań, 1961.
Arc 662.1 Wyse, T. An excursion in the Peloponnesus. London, 1865-2v.
Arc 915.48.2 Wyss, René. Die Egolzwiler Kultur. 2. Aufl. Bern, 1971.
Arc 915.48.5 Wyss, René. Wirtschaft und Gesellschaft in der Jungsteinzeit. Bern, 1973.
Arc 936.14.85 Wystawa Objazdowa Kielecczyzna w Swietle Wykopolisk. Przewodnik. Kielce, 1962.
Arc 853.20.2 Wyttenback, J.H. Forschungen über die römischen Alterthümer. 2. Aufl. Trier, 1844.
Arc 853.20 Wyttenback, J.H. Neue Forschungen über Römischen architektonisch Alterhümer. Trier, 1835.
Arc 853.20.9 Wyttenback, J.H. Recherches sur les antiquités romaines dans la vallée de la Moselle de Trèves. Trèves, 1840.
Arc 853.20.8 Wyttenback, J.H. Stranger's guide to Roman antiquities of the city of Treves. London, 1839.
Arc 936.14.110 Wytwórczość włokiennicza predniowiecznego międzyrzeeza. (Urbańska, A.) Poznań, 1964.
Arc 590.22 X-raying the pharaohs. (Harris, James E.) N.Y., 1973.
Arc 530.3 The Xanthian marbles. (Fellows, C.) London, 1843.
Arc 530.3.5 The Xanthian marbles. (Lloyd, W.W.) Londdon, 1845.
Arc 672.1.35 Xanthoudídes, S. The vaulted tombs of Mesará. London, 1924.
Arc 1251.2 Xenakē-Sakellariou, Agnē. Mykēnaike Zphragidoglyphia. Athēnai, 1966.
Arc 585.25 XI Dynasty temple at Deir El-Bahari. (Naville, E.H.) London, 1907-13. 3v.
Arc 513.19.5 Ximinez, S. Asia Minor in ruins. N.Y., 1925.
Arc 843.225 El yacimiento prehistórico de Pinedo, Toledo, y su industria triedrica. (Martín Aguado, Máximo.) Toledo, 1963.
Arc 505.84.5 Yadin, Yigael. Hazor; the head of all those kingdoms. London, 1972.
Arc 505.128 Yadin, Yigael. Masada; Herod's fortress and the Zealot's last stand. N.Y., 1966.
Arc 505.128.1 Yadin, Yigael. Masada: Herod's fortress and the Zealot's last stand. London, 1966.
Arc 1335.58 Yale College. Catalogue of the cabinet of coins belonging to Yale College. New Haven, 1863.
Arc 1458.2 Yale College. Catalogue of the Greek and Roman coins in the numismatic collection. New Haven, 1880.
Arc 505.45.20 Yale University. The excavations at Dura-Europas. New Haven, 1943-1949. 13v.
Arc 421.20 Yale University. Gallery of Fine Arts. An exhibition of Chinese antiquities from Ch'ang Sha. New Haven, 1939.
Arc 843.77.10 Yali Lassaletta, Aurelio. Historia de Italica. Sevilla, 1892.
Arc 505.151 The Yarmukian culture of the Neolithic period. (Stékélis, Moshé.) Jerusalem, 1972.
Arc 1335.17 Yates, J. Descriptive catalogue of a collection of current coins of all countries. London, 1862.
Arc 1190.82.5 Yazir, Mahmud. Eski yazilari okuma anahtari. Istanbul, 1942.
Arc 1190.82 Yazir, Mahmud. Siyakat yazisi. Istanbul, 1941.
Arc 830.173 Ydier, F. Découverte de trois sarcophages merovingiens du VIIe siècle aux Sables-d'Olonne. La Roche-sur-Yon, 1925.
Arc 125.8 Year book. (Ancient Monuments Society.) Manchester. 1926
Arc 497.52 Yeivin, Samuel. Archaeological activities in Israel. Jerusalem, 1955.
Arc 497.65 Yeivin, Samuel. A decade of archaeology in Israel, 1948-1958. Istanbul, 1960.
Arc 530.174 Yesaian, Stepan. Erevan. Erevan, 1969.
Arc 530.167 Yesaian, Stepan. Oruzhie i voennoe delo drevnei Armenii. Greoan, 1966.
Arc 1588.6.2.15 Yildivim Bayezid'in agullanu ait akçe ve mangirlav. (Ölçer, Cüneyt.) Istanbul, n.d.
Arc 861.90 Yorkshire Archaeolgical Society. Roman Malton and district. Report. York. 2-7 6v.
Arc 861.160.10 Yorkshire Architectural and Archaeological Society. A short guide to Roman York. York, 1962.
Arc 1324.2 Yorkshire Numismatic Fellowship. Annual report. Hull. 1,1909
Arc 1324.1 Yorkshire Numismatic Society. Transactions. Hull. 1,1913
Arc 1324.3 Pamphlet box. Yorkshire Numismatic Society.
Arc 1335.38 Young, Matthew. Catalogue of...coins and medals in gold, silver, and copper. pt.1. London, 1839.
Arc 1493.15 Yriarte, José de. Catalogo de los reales de a ocho espanoles. Madrid, 1955.
Arc 421.25 Yu. Inschrift des Yu. Halle, 1811.
Arc 936.220.25 Pamphlet vol. Yugoslavia. Antiquities. 6 pam.
Arc 936.220.91 Yugoslavia before the Roman conquest. (Alexander, John.) N.Y., 1972.
X Cg Arc 66.1.88 Yver, G. Le commerce et les marchands. Paris, 1903.
Arc 936.14.286 Z badań nad kulturą ceramiki nytej. Wyd. 1. Kraków, 1970.
Arc 936.14.285 Z badań nad kulturą ceramiki promienistej. Kraków, 1968.
Arc 936.14.02 Pamphlet vol. Z badań nad przeszlością Ziemi Lubuskiej. 6 pam.
Arc 936.14.01 Pamphlet vol. Z badań nad przeszlością Ziemi Lubuskiej. 5 pam.
Arc 853.205 Z badań nad rzemiostem we wczesnośredniowiecznym Kotobrzegu. (Łosiński, Władysław.) Poznań, 1959.
Arc 936.14.103 Z badnań nad neolotem i wczesną epoką brącu w Małopolsce. Wrocław, 1973.
Arc 936.6.3 Z dziejów badań archeologja w Wielkopolsce. (Kostrzewski, Józef.) Wrocław, 1958.
Arc 936.14.375 Z dziejów polskiej archeologii. wyd. 1. (Gąsgowski, Jerzy.) Warszawa, 1970.
Arc 936.14.145 Z dziejów prednowiecz sieradza. (Kaminska, Janina.) Wrocław, 1964.
Arc 936.14.350 Z dziejsw regionu koninskiego. Wrocław, 1970.
Arc 395.25 Z mego życia. (Kostrzewski, Józef.) Wrocław, 1970.
Arc 936.14.75 Z najdawniejszych dziejow Giecza. (Kostrzewski, B.) Wrocław, 1962.
Arc 26.5 Z otchłani wieków. Wrocław. 24,1958+ 7v.
Arc 384.13 Z polskich badań nad epokş kamienia. Wrocław, 1971.
Arc 853.65.65 Z pradzisjów zieme dolnosląskiej lod około. (Gardawski, Aleksander.) Wrocław, 1973.
Arc 936.14.65 Z przeszłosci międzyrzecza. (Kurnatowski, S.) Poznań, 1961.
Arc 936.14.130 Z przeszłósci Pomorza Wschodniego. (Polskie Towarzystwo Archeologiczne.) Wrocław, 1962.
Arc 853.65.20 Z przesztośći Sląska. (Polskie Towarzystwo Archeologiczne.) Wrocław, 1960.
Arc 543.146 Za barkhanami, proshloe. (Sarianidi, Viktor I.) Moskva, 1966.
Arc 923.100 Za sem'iu pechatiami. Izd. 2. (Uspenskii, L.V.P.) Moskva, 1962.
Arc 1335.32 Zabriskie, A.C. Catalogue of the collection of American coins and medals. N.Y., 1909.
Arc 936.6.45 Zabytki metalowe epoki brązu między dolną wisłą a Niemnem. (Dąbrowski, Jan.) Wrocław, 1968.
Arc 930.201 Zabytki przedhistoryczne Ziem Polskich. (Ossowski, G.) Krakow, 1879-88.
Arc 1030.19 Zaccheri, G. L'iscrizione di Abercio. Roma, 1898.
Arc 300.5 Zadneprovskii, I.A. Arkheologicheskie pamiatniki iuzhnykh raionov osnskoi oblasti. Frunze, 1960.
Arc 925.16.20 Zagadka zolotogo kurgana. (Chernikov, Sergei.) Moskva, 1965.
Arc 923.110 Zagadki drevnikh Kurganov. (Iskhizov, M.D.) Saratov, 1961.
Arc 1076.24 Zagadki zvuchashchego metalla. (Pukhnachev, Iurii V.) Moskva, 1974.
Arc 936.14.265 Zagadnienia okresu lateńskiego w Polsce. (Polska Akademia Nauk. Oddział w Krakowie. Prace Komisja Archeologicznej.) Wrocław, 1968.
Arc 936.14.5 Zagadnienie ciągłosci zaludnienia ziem polskich co pradziejach. (Kostrzewski, Józef.) Poznań, 1961.
Arc 925.80 Zagadnienie wpływów Bl. wschodnie. (Przeworski, S.) Warszawa, 1933.
Arc 695.2 Zagora I; excavation season 1967. Sydney, 1971.
Arc 1588.1.15 Zagorski, I. Monety fawney Polski jakotez prowincyj i nuast. Warszawa, 1845.

Author and Title Listing

Arc 1588.1.16 Zagorski, I. Tablice do dziela o monetach dawnej Polski. Warszawa, 1845.

Arc 1588.1.91 Zagórski, Ignacy. Monety dawnej Polski. Warszawa, 1969.

Arc 925.150.10 Zagorul'ski, Edward M. Arkheologiia Belorussii. Minsk, 1965.

Arc 302.7.6 Zagreb. Arheološki Muzej. Vjesnik. Series III. Zagreb. 1,1958+

Arc 302.34 Zagreb. Univerzitet. Filozofski Fakultet. Odsjek za Arheologiju. Opuscula archaeologia. 1-5,1956-1961

Arc 790.6 Zahn, W. New Entdeckte Wandgemälde in Pompeji. München, 1828.

Arc 1190.60 Zajączkowski, Anan. Zarys dyplomatyki osmánsko-tureckiej. Warszawa, 1955.

Arc 936.14.70 Zak, Jan. Importy skandynawskie na ziemiach zachodnioslowianskich. Poznań, 1963. 3v.

Arc 936.14.515 Żaki, Andrzej. Archeologia Małopolski wczesnośredniowiecznej. Wrocław, 1947.

Arc 936.14.510 Żaki, Andrzej. Wędrówki Sącza. Kraków, 1974.

Arc 936.195.60 Základy archeolog. vyskumu v teréne. (Janšak, Stefan.) Bratislava, 1955.

Arc 672.1.122 Zakros: the discovery of a lost places of ancient Crete. (Platon, Nikolaos Eleutheriou.) N.Y., 1971.

Arc 938.101 Zalavruga. (Sauvateev, Iurii A.) Leningrad, 1970.

Arc 925.13.85 Zalsta balka. (Viaz'mitina, M.I.) Kyiv, 1962.

Arc 1433.71F Zambaur, Edward K.M. von. Die Münzprägungen des Islams. Wiesbaden, 1968.

Arc 726.59 Zammit, Themistocles. Prehistoric Malta; the Tarxien temples. London, 1930.

Arc 726.97F Zancani Montuoro, P. Heraion. v.1-2, atlases. Roma, 1951. 4v.

Arc 1485.9F Zanetti, G.A. Nuova raccolta delle monete e zecche d'Italia. Bologna, 1775-89. 5v.

Arc 936.195.190 Zaniklá turz Semonice. (Huml, Václav.) Hradec Králové, 1967.

Arc 936.195.265 Zaniklé středověké vesnice v ČSSR ve svetle archeologických výzkumů. (Celostátní Seminář o Problematice Zaniklých Středověkých Vesnic, 3rd, Uherské Hradiště, Czechoslovak Republic, 1971.) Uherské Hradiště, 1972.

Arc 740.6 Zannoni, A. Gli scavi della Certosa in Bologna. Bologna, 1876-84. 2v.

Arc 740.6.5 Zannoni, A. Sugli scavi della Certosa. Bologna, 1871.

Arc 1584.1.10 Zapadno-gruzinskie monety XIII-XIV vv. (Abramishvili, T.I.) Tbilisi, 1959.

Arc 925.13.70 Zapadnopontiiskie gopoda. (Blavatskaia, T.V.) Moskva, 1952.

Arc 1163.3.120 Zapisi i letopisi. Skopje, 1975.

Arc 923.95 Zapiska dlia obozreniia russkikh drevnostei. (Russkoe arkheologicheskoe obshchestvo, Leningrad.) Sankt Petersburg, 1851.

Arc 920.8 Zapiski...knigai. (Berzhe, A.) Tiflis, 1875.

Arc 292.110 Zapiski. (Russkoe Arkheologicheskoe Obshchestvo, Leningrad.) Sankt Peterburg. 1-13,1851-1918// 10v.

Arc 292.90 Zapiski. (Russkoe Arkheologicheskoe Obshchestvo, Leningrad.) Sankt Peterburg. 1-14,1847-1858 8v.

Arc 292.100 Zapiski. Nouviia seriia. (Russkoe Arkheologicheskoe Obshchestvo, Leningrad.) Sankt Peterburg. 1-12,1886-1902 10v.

Arc 26.10 Zapiski archeologiczne. Warszawa. 3-12,1954-1959

Arc 292.130 Zapiski klassicheskago otdeleniia. (Russkoe Arkheologisheskoe Obshchestvo, Leningrad.) Sankt Peterburg. 1-9 5v.

Arc 292.140 Zapiski Numizmaticheskago otdeleniia. (Russkoe Arkheologicheskoe Obshchestvo, Leningard.) Sankt Peterburg. 1-2,1906-1913

Arc 292.163 Zapiski vostochnago otdeleniia. (Russkoe Arkheologicheskoe Obshchestvo, Leningrad.) Sankt Peterburg. 1886-1921 12v.

Arc 399.2 Zaratti-Bianco, Umberto. Paolo Orsi. n.p., n.d.

Arc 1033.36 Zardetti, C. Monumenti cristiani. Milano, 1843.

Arc 1675.98 Zaretti, Vincenzo. Della medaglie di Murano. Bologna, 1965.

Arc 1190.60 Zarys dyplomatyki osmánsko-tureckiej. (Zajączkowski, Anan.) Warszawa, 1955.

Arc 1076.22 Zarys dziejów lvdwisarstwa na ziemiach b. Wielkiego Księstwa Litewskiego. (Brensztejn, Michał E.) Wilno, 1924.

Arc 936.14.105 Zarys historii badań archeologicznych w Małopolsce. (Nosek, Stefan.) Wrocław, 1967.

Arc 1588.1.20 Zarys numizmatyki Polskiej. (Gumowski, Marian.) Łódź, 1952.

Arc 1185.22 Zatschek, Heinz. Studien zur mittelterlicher Urkundenlehre. Brünn, 1929.

Arc 612.32 Zatz, L.F. Altsteinzeitkunde Mitteleuropas. Stuttgart, 1951.

Arc 853.65.15 Zatz, Lothar. Die Altsteinzeit in Niederschlesien. Leipzig, 1939.

Arc 936.7 Zawisza, Jan. Recherches archéologiques en Pologne? Warszawa, 1874.

Arc 547.45 Zayid, Abd al-Hamid. Egyptian antiquities. Cairo, 1962.

Arc 1153.69 Zazo, Alfredo. Paleografia latina e diplomatica. 6. ed. Napoli, 1946.

Arc 936.14.220 Zé studiów nad grupą brzesko-kujawską kultury lendzielskiej. (Gabałówna, Lidia.) Łódź, 1966.

Arc 1490.31 La zecca di Milano e le sue monete. (Strada, M.) Milano, 1930.

Arc 726.216 Zecchini, Michelangelo. L'archeologia nell'Arcipelago toscano. Pisa, 1971.

Arc 543.116.1 Zehren, Erich. Die biblischen Hügel. Berlin, 1961.

Arc 543.116 Zehren, Erich. The cresent and the bull; a survey. N.Y., 1962.

Arc 1138.75 Zeichen und Wunder. (Doblhofer, Ernst.) Wien, 1957.

Arc 1093.7.2 Das Zeichenbuch. 2. Aufl. (Koch, Rudolf.) Offenbach am Main, 1926.

Arc 66.1.112 Zeiller, Jacques. Les origines chrétiennes...provinces danubiennes. Paris, 1918.

Arc 838.24F Zeiss, Hans. Die Grabfunde aus dem spanischen Westgotenreich. Berlin, 1934.

Arc 55.1 Zeitschrift der Deutschen Palaestina-Vereins. Leipzig. 1+ 47v.

Arc 55.1.3 Zeitschrift der Deutschen Palaestina-Vereins. Index, v.6-25. Leipzig, n.d. 2v.

Arc 26.15 Zeitschrift für Archäologie des Mittelalters. Köln. 1,1973+

Arc 1325.2 Zeitschrift für Münz, Siegel und Wappenkunde. (Kölme, B.) Berlin. 1-6 3v.

Arc 1325.1 Zeitschrift für Numismatik. (Sallet, A. von.) Berlin. 1-42,1894-1935 37v.

Arc 1125.40 Zeitschrift für Papyrologie und Epigraphik. Bonn. 1,1967+ 7v.

Arc 180.2F Zeitschrift für schweizerische Archaeologie und Kunstgeschichte. Basel. 1,1939+ 24v.

Arc 210.5 Zeitschrift zür Geschichte und Auslegung der alten Kunst. Göttingen. 1,1817

Htn Arc 1480.18* Zelada, F.X. de. De nummis aliquot...epistola. Romae, 1778.

Arc 910.1 Zeller-Werdmüller, H. Denkmäler aus der Feudalzeit im Lande Uri. Zürich, 1884.

Arc 925.90.5 Zemdsd v antichnikh gorodov severnogo Prichernomor'ia. (Blavatskii, V.D.) Moskva, 1953.

Arc 530.22.15 Zemledelic i skotovodstvo Urartu. (Arutiunian, Nikolai V.) Erevan, 1964.

Arc 543.85 Zemledelie i skotovodstvo u Azerbaidzhane v epokhu bronzy. (Zuniatov, T.A.) Baku, 1957.

Arc 1282.7 Zemskaia nechat' Moskovskago gosudarstva. (Likhachen, N.I.) Moskva, 1914.

Arc 936.241 Zemun. Narodni Muzej. Seoba naroda. Zemun, 1962.

Arc 403.25 Zenner, Klaus. Gang durch versunkene Städte; ein Ausflug ins Reich der Archäologie. Leipzig, 1974.

Arc 1353.15 Zeno, Apostalo. Sonder Münzenouktion. v.1-2,3. Wien, 1955. 2v.

Arc 823.19.105 Zénobie vaballathus...Philippe le Jeune par Mommsen. (Thédenat, H.) Paris, 1882.

Arc 94.47 Zephyrus. Salamanca. 1,1950+ 15v.

Arc 1033.12.187 Zerbi, L. Corona ferrea al funebri nazionali di Vittorio Emanuele. Monza, 1878.

Arc 830.285F Zervos, Christian. L'art de l'époque du Renne en France. Paris, 1959.

Arc 684.1.33 Der Zeus-Altar in Olympia. Diss. (Schlief, Hans.) Berlin, 1935.

Arc 925.8.45 Zhebelev, S.A. Severnoe prichernomor. Moskva, 1953.

Arc 925.50.18 Zheleznaia maska iz Khersonesa. (Piatysheva, Natalia V.) Moskva, 1964.

Arc 936.250 Zhelezoplavil'noe proizvodstvo v drevnei Gruzii. (Gzelishvili, Iosif.) Tbilisi, 1964.

Arc 925.50.225 Zhilye ansambli drevnei Ol'vii IV-II vv. do n.e. (Knyzhitskii, Sergei D.) Kiev, 1971.

Arc 543.55A Zhivopis drevnogo Piandzhikenta. (Akademiia nauk SSSR. Institut Istorii Materialii Kul'tura.) Moskva, 1954. 2v.

Arc 1349.70 Zhizn' i trudy P.S. Savel'eva. (Grigor'ev, V.V.) Sankt Peterburg, 1861.

Arc 1163.3.70 Zhukovskaia, L.P. Razvitie slaviano-russkoi paleografii v dosrevoluitsionnoi Rossii. Moskva, 1963.

Arc 925.173.5F Zhurnal raskopok po chasti vodorazdela verkhnikh pritokov Volgi i Dnepra. (Bulychov, Nikolai I.) Moskva, 1899.

Arc 543.105 Ziablin, L.L. Vtoroi buddiiskii khram Ak-Beshimskogo gorodishcha. Frunze, 1961.

Arc 665.1 Ziebarth, E. Kulturbilder aus griechischen Städten. Leipzig, 1907.

Arc 925.75 Ziebell, W. Olbia. Hamburg, 1937.

Arc 853.271F Ziegart, Helmut. Zur Chronologie und Gruppengliederung des westlichen Hügelgräberkultur. Berlin, 1963.

Arc 810.15 Ziegeler, E. Aus Pompeji. Guetersloh, 1895.

Arc 608.84 Ziegert, Helmut. Gebel Ben Ghnema und Nord-Tibesti; Habilitationsschrift. Wiesbaden, 1969.

Arc 780.1 Ziegler, C. Das alte Rom. Stuttgart, 1882.

Arc 1163.8.10 Ziemer, Meline. Datierung und Lokalisierung nach den Schreibformen von K und Z im Althochdeutschen. Inaug. Diss. Breslau, 1933.

Arc 936.14.95 Ziemia gnieźnieńska w okresie powstawania państwa polskiego. (Posen (City). Museum Archeologicznej Oddział w Gnieznie.) Poznań, 1961.

Arc 936.14.330 Ziemie polskie w pradziejach. wyd. 1. (Hensel, Witold.) Warszawa, 1969.

Arc 609.1.40 Zimbabwe; Rhodesia's ancient greatness. (Bruwer, Andries Johannes.) Johannesburg, 1965.

Arc 609.1.45 Zimbabwe. (Summers, Roger.) Johannesburg, 1963.

Arc 609.1.57 The Zimbabwe culture: ruins and reactions. 2. ed. (Caton-Thompson, Gertrude.) London, 1971.

Arc 895.14 Zinck, L. Nordisk archaelogi. Kjøbenhavn, 1890.

Arc 1185.15 Zinkernagel, K.F.B. Handbuch für angehende Archivare und Registratoren. Nördlingen, 1800.

Arc 545.227.42F Zippert, Erwin. Der Gedächtnistempel Sethos' Izu Abydos. Berlin, 1931.

Arc 936.100 Živa stariua. (Karaman, L.) Zagreb, 1943.

Arc 936.195.15 Zivot a umenie doby železnej na Slovensku. (Poulík, Josef.) Bratislava, 1962.

Arc 1470.60 Zkskursy v oblast' drevnsi numizmatiki cherno morskago pobereniia. (Oreshnikov, A.) Moskva, 1914.

Arc 700.60 Zlatkovskaia, Tat'iana D. U istokov evropeiskoi kul'tury. Moskva, 1961.

Arc 446.10 Zluner, F.E. Stone age and Pleistocene chronology in Gujarat. 1. ed. Poona, 1950.

Arc 612.78 Zmierzch epoki kamicnia. (Kowalczyk, Jan.) Wrocław, 1971.

Arc 936.14.380.5 Znaki i napisy na mieczach średniowiecznych w Polsce. (Głosek, Marian.) Wrocław, 1973.

Arc 1480.68 Znaleziska monet rzymskich na Śląsku. (Konik, Eugeniusz.) Wrocław, 1965.

Arc 938.98 Zo let. (Lietuvos BR Mokslų Akademije, Vilna. Istorijas Institutas.) Vil'nius, 1968.

Arc 1493.4 Zobel de Zangroniz, J. Estudio de la moneda antigua española. Madrid, 1878. 2v.

Arc 1033.17.25 Zocca, I.M. Apparitione della Madonna Santissima di Misericordia di Savona. Modena, 1632.

Arc 830.55 Zocco-Rosa, A. La Tavola Bronzea di Narbona. Catania, 1912.

Arc 1033.17.462 Zodiaco di Maria...Napoli. (Montorio, S.) Napoli, 1715.

Arc 1033.35.146 Zöckler, Otto. The cross of Christ. London, 1877.

Arc 1033.35.145 Zöckler, Otto. Das Kreuz Christi. Gütersloh, 1875.

Arc 545.20 Zoega, G. De origine et usu obeliscorum. Rome, 1797.

Arc 410.1.18 Zoega's Leben. (Welcker, F.G.) Stuttgart, 1819. 2v.

Arc 936.14.205 Zoll-Adamikowa, Helena. Wczesnośredniowieczne cmentarzyska szkieltowe Małopolski. Wrocław, 1966-71. 2v.

Arc 925.50.280 Zolotobalkovskii mogil'nik. (Viaz'mitina, Mariia I.) Kiev, 1972.

Arc 766.4 La zona archeologica di Roma. (Lugli, Giuseppe.) Roma, 1924.

Arc 785.75 La zona di piazza S. Sepolcro. (Calderini, A.) Milano, 1940.

Arc 755.4 La zona monumentale di Roma. (Associazione artistica fra i cultori di architecttura.) Roma, 1910.

Arc 772.9F La zona monumentale di Roma e l'opera commissione reale. (Italy. Commissione reale per la zona monumentale di Roma.) Roma, 1910.

Arc 750.224F — La zona monumentale di Roma e l'opera della Commissione reale. (Italy. Commissione reale per la zona monumentale di Roma.) Roma, 1914.

Arc 936.170 — Zontschew, Dimiter. Der Goldschatz von Panagjurischte. Berlin, 1959.

Arc 712.1 — Der Zophorus am Parthenon. (Boetticher, K.) Berlin, 1875.

Arc 936.220.125 — Zotovič, Ljubica. Mitraizam na thu Jugoslavije. Beograd, 1973.

Arc 853.375 — Zotz, Lothar F. Die mittelpaläolithische Geröllgeräteindustrie aus der Umgebung von Kronach in Oberfranken. Kallmünz, 1973.

Arc 936.14.180 — Zrodła archeologiczne do studiow nad wczesnosredniowiecznym osadnictwem grodowym na terenie wojewodztwa. (Olczak, Jerzy.) Poznań, 1966- 4v.

Arc 936.14.525 — Źródła archeologiczne zterenu zamku krzyżackiego w Towniu. 1. wyd. (Chudziakowa, Jadwiga.) Warszawa, 1974.

Arc 843.61 — Zuazo y Palacios, J. Meca. Madrid, 1916.

Arc 1033.12.182 — Zucchi, B. Historia della corona ferrea...Monza descritta. Milano, 1707.

NEDL Arc 180.1.2 — Zürich. Antiquarische Gesellschaft. Denkschrift zu fuenfzigjaehrigen Stiftungsfeier. Zürich, 1882?

Arc 180.1 — Zürich. Antiquarische Gesellschaft. Mittheilungen der Antiquarischen Gesellschaft. Zürich. 31-43 26v.

NEDL Arc 180.1 — Zürich. Antiquarische Gesellschaft. Mittheilungen der Antiquarischen Gesellschaft. Zürich. 1-30,1841-1931

Arc 853.13.35 — Zuern, Hartwig. Hallstattforschungen in Nordwürttemberg. Stuttgart, 1970.

Arc 853.290 — Zuern, Hartwig. Das jungsteinzeitliche Dorf Ehrenstein. Stuttgart, 1965. 3v.

Arc 925.5.10 — Zuikov, B.B. Pod volnami Issyk-Kuha. Moskva, 1962.

Arc 1480.12 — Zum corpus numorum aeris gravis. (Haeberlin, E.J.) Berlin, 1905.

Arc 712.6 — Zum Parthenonfries. (Flasch, A.) Wuerzburg, 1877.

Arc 905.23F — Zum Schluss der Majafrage. (Tappeiner, Franz.) Muan, 1897.

Arc 543.85 — Zuniatov, T.A. Zemledelie i skotovodstvo u Azerbaidzhane v epokhu bronzy. Baku, 1957.

Arc 543.83.5 — Zur Archäologie und antiken Geographie von Südarabien. (Wissmann, Hermann.) Istanbul, 1968.

Arc 853.271F — Zur Chronologie und Gruppengliederung des westlichen Hügelgräberkultur. (Ziegart, Helmut.) Berlin, 1963.

Arc 905.90 — Zur Cronologie der Bronzezeit des Karpatenbeckens. (Folteny, Stephan.) Bonn, 1955.

Arc 1138.50 — Zur Einführung in die Papyrusausstellung. (Berlin. Staatliche Museen.) Berlin, 1908.

Arc 87.1.13 — Zur Erklärung der Plinius. (Panofka, T.S.) Berlin, 1853.

Arc 936.14.8 — Zur Frage der Siedlungsstetigkeit in der Geschichte Polens. (Kostrzewski, Józef.) Wrocław, 1965.

Arc 635.216 — Zur Geschichte des Wegebaus bei den Griechen. (Curtius, E.) Berlin, 1855.

Arc 1480.22 — Zur Geschichte von Städten des römischen Kaiserreiches. (Kubitschek, Wilhelm.) Wien, 1916.

Arc 1076.3 — Zur Glockenkunde Thürigens. (Bergner, H.H.) Jena, 1896.

Arc 1458.14 — Zur griechischen und römischen Münzkunde. (Imhoof-Blumer, Friedrich.) Genf, 1908.

Arc 1138.17 — Zur Handschriftenkunde. v.1-2. (Ebert, F.A.) Leipzig, 1825.

Arc 1086.1 — Zur Hochächerfrage. (Hartmann, A.) München, 1876.

Arc 1020.99.15 — Zur Ikonographie des Menas-Ampullen. (Kaufmann, C.M.) Cairo, 1910.

Arc 403.20 — Zur Kunst der Antike. (Schweitzer, B.) Tübingen, 1963. 2v.

Arc 522.10 — Zur Loesung der Troianischen Frage. (Brentano, E.) Heilbronn, 1881.

Arc 1510.158 — Zur mittelalterlichen Münzgeschichte der Grafen von Mansfeld und der Edlen Hessen von Querfurt. (Erbstein, Julius.) Dresden, 1876.

Arc 1510.141 — Zur Münzgeschichte der chemaligen Wettinischen Lande um 1180-1230. (Schurnkowski, Walter.) Halle, 1936.

Arc 1510.18 — Zur Münzgeschichte der Grafen von Wertheim. (Wibel, Ferdinand.) Hamburg, 1880.

Arc 1470.3 — Zur Münzkunde Grossgriechenlands. (Imhoof-Blumer, Friedrich.) Wien, 1887.

Arc 1583.9 — Zur Münzkunde Russlands. (Krug, A.L.) St. Petersburg, 1805.

Arc 1433.23 — Zur Muhammedanischen Münzkunde. (Erdmann, F. von.) St. Petersburg, 1856.

Arc 845.206F — Zur Prähistorie Nordwest-Sachsens. (Jacob, Karl H.) Halle an der Saale, 1911.

Arc 756.1.2 — Zur römischen Topographie. (Becker, W.A.) Leipzig, 1845.

Arc 612.93 — Zur Südabgrenzung des Bereichs der nordischen jüngeren Bronzezeit in Periode IV nach Montelius. (Schneider, Renate-Ursula.) Hamburg, 1971.

Arc 708.6.2 — Zur Topographie Athens. (Forchhammer, P.) Göttingen, 1833. 2 pam.

Arc 600.1 — Zur Topographie des alten Alexandria. (Kiepert, H.) Berlin, n.d.

Arc 708.6 — Zur Topographie von Athen. (Forchhammer, P.) Göttingen, 1873.

Arc 383.42.5 — Zur Ur- und Frühgeschichte Nordwestdeutschlands. (Zylmann, Peter.) Hildesheim, 1956.

Arc 1508.5 — Zur vaterländischen Münzkunde. (Schönemann, C.P.C.) Walfenbüttel, 1852.

Arc 1510.14.5 — Zusammenstellung der Taler. (Rudolph, E.) Dresden, 1904.

Arc 705.202 — Der Zustand der Antiken Athenischen Bauwerke. (Durm, J.) Berlin, 1895.

Htn Arc 726.30* — Zuzzeri, G.L. D'una antica villa. Venezia, 1746.

Arc 1340.10 — Zvarych, Volodymyr V. Numizmatychnyi slovnyk. L'viv, 1972.

Arc 936.195.96 — Zvolen v období lužickej kultúry. (Balaša, Gejza.) Banská Bystrica, 1964.

Arc 1153.4.5 — Zwei Abhandlungen...tironischen Noten. (Breidenbach, H.) Darmstadt, 1900.

Arc 830.125 — Zwei fränkische Königspfalzen. (Weise, Georg.) Tübingen, 1923.

Arc 853.93F — Das zweischneidige Schwert der germanischen völkerwanderungszeit. (Behmer, E.) Stockholm, 1939.

Arc 905.12.15 — Das zweite Amphitheater von Carnuntum. (Miltner, F.) Wien, 1939.

Arc 1510.39 — Der zweite Brakteatenfund von Mödesse und die Kunst der Brakteaten zur Zeit Heinrichs des Löwen. (Jesse, Wilhelm.) Braunschweig, 1957.

Arc 543.50 — Der zweite Kurgen von Pasyryk. (Rudenko, Sergei I.) Berlin, 1951.

Arc 1033.34.43 — Zwölger, Theodor. Die Verehrung des Heiligen Petrus bei den Franken und Angelsachsen. Inaug. Diss. Stuttgart, 1929.

Arc 936.14.296 — Zycie codzienne na Pomorzu wczesnósredniowiecznym, wiek X-XII. (Kiersnowska, Teresa.) Warszawa, 1970.

Arc 695.1F — Zygouries. (Blegen, Carl W.) Cambridge, 1928.

Arc 1232.10 — Zylinder- und Stempelsiegel aus Karahöyük bei Konya. (Alp, Sedat.) Ankara, 1968.

Arc 383.42.5 — Zylmann, Peter. Zur Ur- und Frühgeschichte Nordwestdeutschlands. Hildesheim, 1956.

Arc 925.50.255 — Zymnivs'ke horodyshche-slov'ians'ka pam'iatka. (Aulikh, Vitold V.) Kyïv, 1972.

Arc 388.8.2 — 4,000 years under the sea. (Diolé, P.) N.Y., 1954.

Arc 823.19.65 — 14 juillet, 1881. (Thédenat, H.) Paris, 1881.

Arc 936.100.35 — 20 godina Muzeja Vinkovci 1946-66. (Vinkovci. Gradski Muzej.) Vinkovci, 1966.

Arc 612.6.5 — 25 Jahre Siedlungsarchäologie. (Hahne, Hans.) Leipzig, 1922.

Arc 936.14.385 — 25 lat archeologii na Dolnym Śląsku, 1945-70. Wrocław, 1971.

Arc 505.11 — 30 Ansichten der deutschen Ausgraben Baalbek. (Bechstein, O.) Berlin, 1905.

Arc 684.1.55 — 100 Jahre deutsche Ausgrabung in Olympia. München, 1972.

Arc 674.2.5 — 1600 years under the sea. (Falcon-Barker, T.) London, 1960.

Arc 935.45 — 1952 yilinda arkeolojik. (Duyaran, Rüstem.) Istanbul, 1953.

Arc 935.32 — 1962 iki 1963. (Tezcan, Burhan.) Ankara, 1904.

Arc 935.32.10 — 1964 kaçumbeli kazese. (Tezcan, Burhan.) Ankara, 1966.

Arc 935.32.5 — 1964 yalencak köyü çaleşmalare. (Tezcan, Burhan.) Ankara, 1966.

VArc 396.21 — 500 zagadek archeologicznych. (Lesicjewicz, Anna.) Warszawa, 1966.